HANDBOOK OF INFORMATION SECURITY

Key Concepts, Infrastructure, Standards, and Protocols

Volume 1

Hossein Bidgoli
Editor-in-Chief
California State University
Bakersfield, California

John Wiley & Sons, Inc.

This book is printed on acid-free paper. ♾

Published by John Wiley & Sons, Inc., Hoboken, New Jersey.
Published simultaneously in Canada.

For general information on our other products and services please contact our Customer Care Department within the U.S. at (800) 762-2974, outside the United States at (317) 572-3993 or fax (317) 572-4002.

Wiley also publishes its books in a variety of electronic formats. Some content that appears in print may not be available in electronic books. For more information about Wiley products, visit our web site at www.Wiley.com.

Library of Congress Cataloging-in-Publication Data:

The handbook of information security / edited by Hossein Bidgoli.
p. cm.
Includes bibliographical references and index.
ISBN-13: 978-0-471-64830-7, ISBN-10: 0-471-64830-2 (CLOTH VOL 1 : alk. paper)
ISBN-13: 978-0-471-64831-4, ISBN-10: 0-471-64831-0 (CLOTH VOL 2 : alk. paper)
ISBN-13: 978-0-471-64832-1, ISBN-10: 0-471-64832-9 (CLOTH VOL 3 : alk. paper)
ISBN-13: 978-0-471-22201-9, ISBN-10: 0-471-22201-1 (CLOTH SET : alk. paper)
1. Internet–Encyclopedias. I. Bidgoli, Hossein.
TK5105.875.I57I5466 2003
004.67′8′03–dc21

2002155552

Printed in the United States of America

10 9 8 7 6 5 4 3 2

To so many fine memories of my mother, Ashraf, my father, Mohammad, and my brother, Mohsen, for their uncompromising belief in the power of education.

About the Editor-in-Chief

Hossein Bidgoli, Ph.D., is professor of Management Information Systems at California State University. Dr. Bidgoli helped set up the first PC lab in the United States. He is the author of 43 textbooks, 27 manuals and over five dozen technical articles and papers on various aspects of computer applications, information systems and network security, e-commerce and decision support systems published and presented throughout the world. Dr. Bidgoli also serves as the editor-in-chief of *The Internet Encyclopedia* and the *Encyclopedia of Information Systems*.

The *Encyclopedia of Information Systems* was the recipient of one of the *Library Journal's* Best Reference Sources for 2002 and *The Internet Encyclopedia* was recipient of one of the PSP Awards (Professional and Scholarly Publishing), 2004. Dr. Bidgoli was selected as the California State University, Bakersfield's 2001–2002 Professor of the Year.

Editorial Board

Contents

Part 3: Standards and Protocols for Secure Information Transfer

Volume II: Information Warfare; Social, Legal, and International Issues; and Security Foundations

Part 1: Information Warfare

Volume III: Threats, Vulnerabilities, Prevention, Detection, and Management

Part 1: Threats and Vulnerabilities to Information and Computing Infrastructures

Part 2: Prevention: Keeping the Hackers and Crackers at Bay

Part 3: Detection, Recovery, Management, and Policy Considerations

Contributors

Tarek F. Abdelzhaer
University of Virginia
Security and Web Quality of Service
Dawn Alexander
University of Maryland
Protecting Web Sites
Edward Amoroso
AT&T Laboratories
Network Attacks
Michael R. Anderson
SCERC
Computer Forensics—Computer Media Reviews in Classified Government Agencies
Nadeem Ansari
Wayne State University
Home Area Networking
Amy W. Apon
University of Arkansas
Public Network Technologies and Security
Onur Ihsan Arsun
Isik University, Turkey
Security Insurance and Best Practices
Vijay Atluri
Rutgers University
Mobile Commerce
Pierre Balthazard
Arizona State University
Groupware: Risks, Threats, and Vulnerabilities in the Internet Age
William Bard
The University of Texas, Austin
Digital Communication
William C. Barker
National Institute of Standards and Technology
E-Government Security Issues and Measures
Kent Belasco
First Midwest Bank
Online Retail Banking: Security Concerns, Breaches, and Controls
István Zsolt Berta
Budapest University of Technology and Economics, Hungary
Standards for Product Security Assessment
Bhagyavati
Columbus State University
E-Mail and Instant Messaging
Hossein Bidgoli
California State University, Bakersfield
Guidelines for a Comprehensive Security System
Internet Basics
Gerald Bluhm
Tyco Fire & Security
Patent Law
Andrew Blyth
University of Glamorgan, Pontypridd, UK
Computer Network Operations (CNO)
Robert J. Boncella
Washburn University
Secure Sockets Layer (SSL)
Wireless Threats and Attacks
Charles Border
Rochester Institute of Technology
Client-Side Security
Nikita Borisov
University of California, Berkeley
WEP Security
Noureddine Boudriga
National Digital Certification Agency and University of Carthage, Tunisia
Forensic Computing
IPsec: AH and ESP
Security Policy Guidelines
Server-Side Security
Sviatoslav Braynov
University of Illinois, Springfield
E-Commerce Vulnerabilities
Susan W. Brenner
University of Dayton School of Law
Cybercrime and the U.S. Criminal Justice System
Roderic Broadhurst
Queensland University of Technology
Combating the Cybercrime Threat: Developments in Global Law Enforcement
Christopher L. T. Brown
Technology Pathways
Evidence Collection and Analysis Tools
Duncan A. Buell
University of South Carolina
Number Theory for Information Security
The Advanced Encryption Standard
Levente Buttyán
Budapest University of Technology and Economics, Hungary
Standards for Product Security Assessment
Jon Callas
PGP Corporation
E-Mail Security
L. Jean Camp
Harvard University
Peer-to-Peer Security
Randy Canis
Greensfelder, Hemker & Gale, P.C.
Copyright Law
Lillian N. Cassel
Villanova University
Security and the Wireless Application Protocol

Tom S. Chan
Southern New Hampshire University
Spyware
Steve J. Chapin
Syracuse University
Forensic Analysis of Windows Systems
Thomas M. Chen
Southern Methodist University
Electronic Attacks
Hamid Choukri
Gemplus & University of Bordeaux, France
Fault Attacks
Chao-Hsien Chu
Pennsylvania State University
Hacking Techniques in Wired Networks
Fred Cohen
University of New Haven
The Use of Deception Techniques: Honeypots and Decoys
J. Philip Craiger
University of Central Florida
Computer Forensics Procedures and Methods
Law Enforcement and Digital Evidence
Lorrie Faith Cranor
Carnegie Mellon University
P3P (Platform for Privacy Preferences Project)
Marco Cremonini
University of Milan, Italy
Contingency Planning Management
Network-Based Intrusion Detection Systems
Dipankar Dasgupta
University of Memphis
The Use of Agent Technology for Intrusion Detection
Magnus Daum
Ruhr University Bochum, Germany
Hashes and Message Digests
Jaime J. Davila
Hampshire College
Digital Divide
S. De Capitani di Vimercati
Università di Milano, Italy
Access Control: Principles And Solutions
Mathieu Deflem
University of South Carolina
Law Enforcement and Computer Security Threats and Measures
Lynn A. DeNoia
Rensselaer Polytechnic Institute
Wide Area and Metropolitan Area Networks
David Dittrich
University of Washington
Active Response to Computer Intrusions
Hackers, Crackers, and Computer Criminals
Hans Dobbertin
Ruhr University Bochum, Germany
Hashes and Message Digests
Hans-Peter Dommel
Santa Clara University
Routers and Switches
Matthew C. Elder
Symantec Corporation
Electronic Attacks
Mohamed Eltoweissy
Virginia Tech
Security in Wireless Sensor Networks
David Evans
University of Virginia
Hostile Java Applets
G. E. Evans
Queen Mary Intellectual Property Research Institute, UK
Online Contracts
Ray Everett-Church
PrivacyClue LLC
Privacy Law and the Internet
Trademark Law and the Internet
Seth Finkelstein
SethF.com
Electronic Speech
The Digital Millennium Copyright Act
Susanna Frederick Fischer
Columbus School of Law, The Catholic University of America
Internet Gambling
Dario V. Forte
University of Milan, Crema, Italy
Forensic Analysis of UNIX Systems
Allan Friedman
Harvard University
Peer-to-Peer Security
Song Fu
Wayne State University
Mobile Code and Security
G. David Garson
North Carolina State University
E-Government
Karin Geiselhart
University of Canberra and Australian National University, Canberra, Australia
International Security Issues of E-Government
Craig Gentry
DoCoMo USA Labs
IBE (Identity-Based Encryption)
Michael Gertz
University of California, Davis
Database Security
Robert Gezelter
Software Consultant
Internet E-Mail Architecture
OpenVMS Security
April Giles
Johns Hopkins University
Protecting Web Sites
Julia Alpert Gladstone
Bryant University
Global Aspects of Cyberlaw
James E. Goldman
Purdue University
Firewall Architectures
Firewall Basics

Nicole Graf
University of Cooperative Education, Germany
Security Architectures
Sven Graupner
Hewlett-Packard Laboratories
Web Services
Robert H. Greenfield
Computer Consulting
Security in Circuit, Message, and Packet Switching
Steven J. Greenwald
Independent Information Security Consultant
S/MIME (Secure MIME)
Qijun Gu
Pennsylvania State University
Hacking Techniques in Wired Networks
Mohsen Guizani
Western Michigan University
TCP over Wireless Links
Harald Haas
International University Bremen (IUB), Germany
Air Interface Requirements for Mobile Data Services
Mohamed Hamdi
National Digital Certification Agency, Tunisia
Forensic Computing
Security Policy Guidelines
David Harley
NHS Connecting for Health, UK
E-Mail Threats and Vulnerabilities
Jan Ll. Harris
University of Salford, UK
Hacktivism
Robert W. Heath Jr.
The University of Texas, Austin
Digital Communication
Peter L. Heinzmann
University of Applied Sciences, Eastern Switzerland
Security of Broadband Access Networks
Kenneth Einar Himma
Seattle Pacific University
Active Response to Computer Intrusions
Legal, Social, and Ethical Issues of the Internet
Hackers, Crackers, and Computer Criminals
Chengdu Huang
University of Virginia
Security and Web Quality of Service
Ali Hushyar
San Jose State University
Multilevel Security Models
Renato Iannella
National ICT, Australia (NICTA)
Digital Rights Management
Cynthia E. Irvine
Naval Postgraduate School
Quality of Security Service: Adaptive Security
Security Policy Enforcement
Gene Itkis
Boston University
Forward Security Adaptive Cryptography: Time Evolution

William K. Jackson
Southern Oregon University
E-Education and Information Privacy and Security
Charles Jaeger
Southern Oregon University
Cyberterrorism and Information Security
Spam and the Legal Counter Attacks
Sushil Jajodia
George Mason University
Intrusion Detection Systems Basics
Markus Jakobsson
Indiana University, Bloomington
Cryptographic Privacy Protection Techniques
Cryptographic Protocols
Abbas Jamalipour
University of Sydney, Australia
Wireless Internet: A Cellular Perspective
Jiwu Jing
Chinese Academy of Sciences, Beijing, China
Information Assurance
Ari Juels
RSA Laboratories
Encryption Basics
Jonathan Katz
University of Maryland
Symmetric Key Encryption
Charlie Kaufman
Microsoft Corporation
IPsec: IKE (Internet Key Exchange)
Doug Kaye
IT Conversations
Web Hosting
Rick Kazman
University of Hawaii, Manoa
Risk Management for IT Security
Wooyoung Kim
University of Illinois, Urbana-Champaign
Web Services
Nancy J. King
Oregon State University
E-Mail and Internet Use Policies
Jerry Kindall
Epok, Inc.
Digital Identity
Dominic Kneeshaw
Independent Consultant, Germany
Security Architectures
David Klappholz
Stevens Institute of Technology
Risk Management for IT Security
Graham Knight
University College, London, UK
Internet Architecture
Prashant Krishnamurthy
University of Pittsburgh
Wireless Network Standards and Protocol (802.11)
Christopher Kruegel
Technical University, Vienna, Austria
Host-Based Intrusion Detection
Priya Kubher
Wayne State University
Home Area Networking

Stan Kurkovsky
Central Connecticut State University
VPN Architecture
Selahattin Kuru
Isik University, Turkey
Security Insurance and Best Practices
Zenith Y. W. Law
JustSolve Consulting, Hong Kong
Fixed-Line Telephone System Vulnerabilities
Margarita Maria Lenk
Colorado State University
Asset–Security Goals Continuum: A Process for Security
Arjen K. Lenstra
Lucent Technologies Bell Laboratories and Technische Universiteit Eindhoven
Key Lengths
Albert Levi
Sabanci University, Turkey
Digital Certificates
Timothy E. Levin
Naval Postgraduate School
Quality of Security Service: Adaptive Security
John Linn
RSA Laboratories
Identity Management
Helger Lipmaa
Cybernetica AS and University of Tartu, Estonia
Secure Electronic Voting Protocols
Peng Liu
Pennsylvania State University
Hacking Techniques in Wired Networks
Information Assurance
David J. Loundy
Devon Bank University College of Commerce
Online Stalking
Michele Luglio
University of Rome Tor Vergata, Italy
Security of Satellite Networks
Chester J. Maciag
Air Force Research Laboratory
Forensic Analysis of Windows Systems
Normand M. Martel
Medical Technology Research Corp.
Medical Records Security
Prabhaker Mateti
Wright State University
Hacking Techniques in Wireless Networks
TCP/IP Suite
Cavan McCarthy
Louisiana State University
Digital Libraries: Security and Preservation Considerations
Patrick McDaniel
Pennsylvania State University
Computer and Network Authentication
J. McDermott
Center for High Assurance Computer System, Naval Research Laboratory
The Common Criteria
David E. McDysan
MCI Corporation
IP-Based VPN
Daniel J. McFarland
Rowan University
Client/Server Computing: Principles and Security Considerations
Matthew K. McGowan
Bradley University
EDI Security
John D. McLaren
Murray State University
Proxy Firewalls
A. Meddeb
National Digital Certification Agency and University of Carthage, Tunisia
IPsec: AH and ESP
Mark S. Merkow
University of Phoenix Online
E-Commerce Safeguards
M. Farooque Mesiya
Rensselaer Polytechnic Institute
Mobile IP
Pascal Meunier
Purdue University
Cracking WEP
Software Development and Quality Assurance
Mark Michael
Research in Motion Ltd., Canada
Physical Security Measures
Physical Security Threats
Pietro Michiardi
Institut Eurecom, France
Ad Hoc Network Security
Brent A. Miller
IBM Corporation
Bluetooth Technology
Refik Molva
Institut Eurecom, France
Ad Hoc Network Security
Robert K. Moniot
Fordham University
Software Piracy
Roy Morris
Capitol College
Voice-over Internet Protocol (VoIP)
Scott Nathan
Independent Consultant
Corporate Spying: The Legal Aspects
Randall K. Nichols
The George Washington University & University of Maryland University College
Wireless Information Warfare
Daryle P. Niedermayer
CGI Group Inc.
Security in Circuit, Message, and Packet Switching
Peng Ning
North Carolina State University
Intrusion Detection Systems Basics
M. S. Obaidat
Monmouth University
Digital Watermarking and Steganography
Forensic Computing
IPsec: AH and ESP
Security Policy Guidelines

Server-Side Security
Wireless Local Area Networks
VPN Basics

S. Obeidat
Arizona State University
Wireless Local Area Networks

Stephan Olariu
Old Dominion University
Security in Wireless Sensor Networks

G. Massimo Palma
Università degli Studi di Milano, Italy
Quantum Cryptography

Cynthia Pandolfo
Villanova University
Security and the Wireless Application Protocol

Raymond R. Panko
University of Hawaii, Manoa
Computer Security Incident Response Teams (CSIRTs)
Digital Signatures and Electronic Signatures
Internet Security Standards

G. I. Papadimitriou
Aristotle University, Greece
VPN Basics
Wireless Local Area Networks

C. Papazoglou
Aristotle University, Greece
VPN Basics

S. Paraboschi
Università di Bergamo, Italy
Access Control: Principles and Solutions

Radia Perlman
Sun Microsystems Laboratories
PKI (Public Key Infrastructure)

Sebastien Petit
Gemplus, France
Smart Card Security

Thomas L. Pigg
Jackson State Community College
Conducted Communications Media

Mark Pollitt
DigitalEvidencePro
Law Enforcement and Digital Evidence

A. S. Pomportsis
Aristotle University, Greece
VPN Basics

Daniel N. Port
University of Hawaii, Manoa
Risk Management for IT Security

Stephanie Porte
Gemplus, France
Smart Card Security

Dennis M. Powers
Southern Oregon University
Cyberlaw: The Major Areas, Development, and Information Security Aspects

Anupama Raju
Western Michigan University
TCP over Wireless Links

Jeremy L. Rasmussen
Sypris Electronics, LLC
Password Authentication

Indrajit Ray
Colorado State Univesity
Electronic Payment Systems

Julian J. Ray
University of Redlands
Business-to-Business Electronic Commerce

Drummond Reed
OneName Corporation
Digital Identity

Slim Rekhis
National Digital Certification Agency and University of Carthage, Tunisia
Server-Side Security

Jian Ren
Michigan State University, East Lansing
Managing A Network Environment

Vladimir V. Riabov
Rivier College
SMTP (Simple Mail Transfer Protocol)

Marcus K. Rogers
Purdue University
Internal Security Threats

Pankaj Rohatgi
IBM T. J Watson Research Center
Side-Channel Attacks

Arnon Rosenthal
The MITRE Corporation
Database Security

Emilia Rosti
Università degli Studi di Milano, Italy
IP Multicast and Its Security

Neil C. Rowe
U.S. Naval Postgraduate School
Electronic Protection

Bradley S. Rubin
University of St. Thomas
Public Key Algorithms

K. Rudolph
Native Intelligence, Inc.
Implementing a Security Awareness Program

B. Sadoun
Al-Balqa' Applied University, Jordan
Digital Watermarking and Steganography

Akhil Sahai
Hewlett-Packard Laboratories
Web Services

Antonio Saitto
Telespazio, Italy
Security of Satellite Networks

Atul A. Salvekar
Intel Corporation
Digital Communication

Pierangela Samarati
Università di Milano, Italy
Access Control: Principles and Solutions
Contingency Planning Management

Shannon Schelin
The University of North Carolina, Chapel Hill
E-Government

William T. Schiano
Bentley College
Intranets: Principals, Privacy, and Security Considerations
Matthew Schmid
Cigital, Inc.
Antivirus Technology
E. Eugene Schultz
University of California–Berkeley Lab
Windows 2000 Security
Denial of Service Attacks
Mark Shacklette
The University of Chicago
UNIX Security
P. M. Shankar
Drexel University
Wireless Channels
J. Eagle Shutt
University of South Carolina
Law Enforcement and Computer Security Threats and Measures
Nirvikar Singh
University of California, Santa Cruz
Digital Economy
Robert Slade
Vancouver Institute for Research into User Security, Canada
Computer Viruses and Worms
Digital Courts, the Law and Evidence
Hoax Viruses and Virus Alerts
Nigel Smart
University of Bristol, UK
Elliptic Curve Cryptography
Richard E. Smith
University of St. Thomas
Multilevel Security
Min Song
Old Dominion University
Mobile Devices and Protocols
Mike Speciner
Independent Consultant
Data Encryption Standard (DES)
Richard A. Spinello
Boston College
Internet Censorship
Lee Sproull
New York University
Online Communities
Evdoxia Spyropoulou
Technical Vocational Educational School of Computer Science of Halandri, Greece
Quality of Security Service: Adaptive Security
William Stallings
Independent Consultant
Kerberos
Operating System Security
Mark Stamp
San Jose State University
Multilevel Security Models
Philip Statham
CESG, Cheltenham, Gloucestershire, UK
Issues and Concerns in Biometric IT Security
Charles Steinfield
Michigan State University
Click-and-Brick Electronic Commerce
Electronic Commerce
Ivan Stojmenovic
University of Ottawa, Cananda
Cellular Networks
Robin C. Stuart
Digital Investigations Consultant
Digital Evidence
M. A. Suhail
University of Bradford, UK
Digital Watermarking and Steganography
Wayne C. Summers
Columbus State University
Local Area Networks
Jeff Swauger
University of Central Florida
Law Enforcement and Digital Evidence
Mak Ming Tak
Hong Kong University of Science and Technology, Hong Kong
Fixed-Line Telephone System Vulnerabilities
Thomas D. Tarman
Sandia National Laboratories
Security for ATM Networks
Paul A. Taylor
University of Leeds, UK
Hacktivism
Dale R. Thompson
University of Arkansas
Public Network Technologies and Security
Jimi Thompson
Southern Methodist University
Electronic Attacks
Stephen W. Thorpe
Neumann College
Extranets: Applications, Development, Security, and Privacy
Amandeep Thukral
Purdue University
Key Management
Michael Tunstall
Gemplus & Royal Holloway University, France
Fault Attacks
Smart Card Security
Okechukwu Ugweje
The University of Akron
Radio Frequency and Wireless Communications Security
István Vajda
Budapest University of Technology and Economics, Hungary
Standards for Product Security Assessment
S. Rao Vallabhaneni
SRV Professional Publications
Auditing Information Systems Security
Nicko van Someren
nCipher Plc., UK
Cryptographic Hardware Security Modules

Phil Venables
Institute of Electrical and Electronics Engineers
Information Leakage: Detection and Countermeasures
Giovanni Vigna
Reliable Software Group
Host-Based Intrusion Detection Systems
Linda Volonino
Canisius College
Security Middleware
Richard P. Volonino
Canisius College
Security Middleware
Ashraf Wadaa
Old Dominion University
Security in Wireless Sensor Networks
Blaze D. Waleski
Fulbright & Jaworski LLP
The Legal Implications of Information Security: Regulatory Compliance and Liability
Jonathan Wallace
DeCoMo USA Labs
Anonymity and Identity on the Internet
Siaw-Peng Wan
Elmhurst College
Online Retail Banking: Security Concerns, Breaches, and Controls
Yongge Wang
University of North Carolina, Charlotte
PKCS (Public-Key Cryptography Standards)
John Warren
University of Texas, San Antonio
Groupware: Risks, Threats, and Vulnerabilities in the Internet Age
James L. Wayman
San Jose State University
Biometric Basics and Biometric Authentication
Edgar R. Weippl
Vienna University of Technology, Austria
Security in E-Learning
Stephen A. Weis
MIT Computer Science and Artificial Intelligence Laboratory
PGP (Pretty Good Privacy)
RFID and Security
Susanne Wetzel
Stevens Institute of Technology
Bluetooth Security
A. Justin Wilder
Telos Corporation
Linux Security
Raymond Wisman
Indiana University Southeast
Search Engines: Security, Privacy, and Ethical Issues
Paul L. Witt
Texas Christian University
Internet Relay Chat
Avishai Wool
Tel Aviv University, Israel
Packet Filtering and Stateful Firewalls
Cheng-Zhong Xu
Wayne State University
Mobile Code and Security
Xu Yan
Hong Kong University of Science and Technology, Hong Kong
Fixed-Line Telephone System Vulnerabilities
Mustafa Yildiz
Isik University, Turkey
Security Insurance and Best Practices
Adam L. Young
Cigital, Inc.
Trojan Horse Programs
Meng Yu
Monmouth University
Information Assurance
Sherali Zeadally
Wayne State University
Home Area Networking
Jingyuan Zhang
University of Alabama
Cellular Networks
Xukai Zou
Purdue University
Key Management
Public Key Standards: Secure Shell
William A. Zucker
Gadsby Hannah LLP
Corporate Spying: The Legal Aspects

Preface

The Handbook of Information Security is the first comprehensive examination of the core topics in the security field. *The Handbook of Information Security*, a 3-volume reference work with 207 chapters and 3300+ pages, is a comprehensive coverage of information, computer, and network security.

The primary audience is the libraries of 2-year and 4-year colleges and universities with computer science, MIS, CIS, IT, IS, data processing, and business departments; public, private, and corporate libraries throughout the world; and reference material for educators and practitioners in the information and computer security fields.

The secondary audience is a variety of professionals and a diverse group of academic and professional course instructors.

Among the industries expected to become increasingly dependent upon information and computer security and active in understanding the many issues surrounding this important and fast-growing field are: government, military, education, library, health, medical, law enforcement, accounting, legal, justice, manufacturing, financial services, insurance, communications, transportation, aerospace, energy, biotechnology, retail, and utility.

Each volume incorporates state-of-the-art, core information, on computer security topics, practical applications and coverage of the emerging issues in the information security field.

This definitive 3-volume handbook offers coverage of both established and cutting-edge theories and developments in information, computer, and network security.

This handbook contains chapters by global academic and industry experts. This handbook offers the following features:

1) Each chapter follows a format including title and author, outline, introduction, body, conclusion, glossary, cross-references, and references. This format allows the reader to pick and choose various sections of a chapter. It also creates consistency throughout the entire series.
2) The handbook has been written by more than 240 experts and reviewed by more than 1,000 academics and practitioners from around the world. These experts have created a definitive compendium of both established and cutting-edge theories and applications.
3) Each chapter has been rigorously peer-reviewed. This review process assures accuracy and completeness.
4) Each chapter provides extensive online and off-line references for additional readings, which will enable the reader to learn more on topics of special interest.
5) The handbook contains more than 1,000 illustrations and tables that highlight complex topics for further understanding.
6) Each chapter provides extensive cross-references, leading the reader to other chapters related to a particular topic.
7) The handbook contains more than 2,700 glossary items. Many new terms and buzzwords are included to provide a better understanding of concepts and applications.
8) The handbook contains a complete and comprehensive table of contents and index.
9) The series emphasizes both technical as well as managerial, social, legal, and international issues in the field. This approach provides researchers, educators, students, and practitioners with a balanced perspective and background information that will be helpful when dealing with problems related to security issues and measures and the design of a sound security system.
10) The series has been developed based on the current core course materials in several leading universities around the world and current practices in leading computer, security, and networking corporations.

We chose to concentrate on fields and supporting technologies that have widespread applications in the academic and business worlds. To develop this handbook, we carefully reviewed current academic research in the security field from leading universities and research institutions around the world.

Computer and network security, information security and privacy, management information systems, network design and management, computer information systems (CIS), decision support systems (DSS), and electronic commence curriculums, recommended by the Association of Information Technology Professionals (AITP) and the Association for Computing Machinery (ACM) were carefully investigated. We also researched the current practices in the security field carried out by leading security and IT corporations. Our research helped us define the boundaries and contents of this project.

TOPIC CATEGORIES

Based on our research, we identified nine major topic categories for the handbook.

- Key Concepts and Applications Related to Information Security
- Infrastructure for the Internet, Computer Networks, and Secure Information Transfer
- Standards and Protocols for Secure Information Transfer
- Information Warfare
- Social, Legal, and International Issues

- Foundations of Information, Computer, and Network Security
- Threats and Vulnerabilities to Information and Computing Infrastructures
- Prevention: Keeping the Hackers and Crackers at Bay
- Detection, Recovery, Management, and Policy Considerations

Although these topics are related, each addresses a specific concern within information security. The chapters in each category are also interrelated and complementary, enabling readers to compare, contrast, and draw conclusions that might not otherwise be possible.

Though the entries have been arranged logically, the light they shed knows no bounds. The handbook provides unmatched coverage of fundamental topics and issues for successful design and implementation of a sound security program. Its chapters can serve as material for a wide spectrum of courses such as:

Information and Network Security
Information Privacy
Social Engineering
Secure Financial Transactions
Information Warfare
Infrastructure for Secure Information Transfer
Standards and Protocols for Secure Information Transfer
Network Design and Management
Client/Server Computing
E-commerce

Successful design and implementation of a sound security program requires a thorough knowledge of several technologies, theories, and supporting disciplines. Security researchers and practitioners have had to consult many resources to find answers. Some of these resources concentrate on technologies and infrastructures, some on social and legal issues, and some on managerial concerns. This handbook provides all of this information in a comprehensive, three-volume set with a lively format.

Key Concepts and Applications Related to Information Security

Chapters in this group examine a broad range of topics. Theories, concepts, technologies, and applications that expose either a user, manager, or an organization to security and privacy issues and/or create such security and privacy concerns are discussed. Careful attention is given to those concepts and technologies that have widespread applications in business and academic environments. These areas include e-banking, e-communities, e-commerce, e-education, and e-government.

Infrastructure for the Internet, Computer Networks, and Secure Information Transfer

Chapters in this group concentrate on the infrastructure, popular network types, key technologies, and principles for secure information transfer. Different types of communications media are discussed followed by a review of a variety of networks including LANs, MANs, WANs, mobile, and cellular networks. This group of chapters also discusses important architectures for secure information transfers including TCP/IP, the Internet, peer-to-peer, and client/server computing.

Standards and Protocols for Secure Information Transfer

Chapters in this group discuss major protocols and standards in the security field. This topic includes important protocols for online transactions, e-mail protocols, Internet protocols, IPsec, and standards and protocols for wireless networks emphasizing 802.11.

Information Warfare

This group of chapters examines the growing field of information warfare. Important laws within the United States criminal justice system, as they relate to cybercrime and cyberterrorism, are discussed. Other chapters in this group discuss cybercrime, cyberfraud, cyber stalking, wireless information warfare, electronic attacks and protection, and the fundamentals of information assurance.

Social, Legal, and International Issues

Chapters in this group explore social, legal, and international issues relating to information privacy and computer security. Digital identity, identity theft, censorship, and different types of computer criminals are also explored. The chapters in this group also explain patent, trademark, and copyright issues and offer guidelines for protecting intellectual properties.

Foundations of Information, Computer, and Network Security

These chapters cover four different but complementary areas including encryption, forensic computing, operating systems and the common criteria and the principles for improving the security assurance.

Threats and Vulnerabilities to Information and Computing Infrastructures

The chapters in this group investigate major threats to, and vulnerabilities of, information and computing infrastructures in wired and wireless environments. The chapters specifically discuss intentional, unintentional, controllable, partially controllable, uncontrollable, physical, software and hardware threats and vulnerabilities.

Prevention: Keeping the Hackers and Crackers at Bay

The chapters in this group present several concepts, tools, techniques, and technologies that help to protect information, keep networks secure, and keep the hackers and computer criminals at bay. Some of the topics discussed include physical security measures; measures for protecting client-side, server-side, database, and medical records; different types of authentication techniques; and preventing security threats to e-commerce and e-mail transactions.

Detection, Recovery, Management, and Policy Considerations

Chapters in this group discuss concepts, tools, and techniques for detection of security breaches, offer techniques and guidelines for recovery, and explain principles for managing a network environment. Some of the topics highlighted in this group include intrusion detection, contingency planning, risk management, auditing, and guidelines for effective security management and policy implementation.

Acknowledgments

Many specialists have helped to make the handbook a resource for experienced and not-so-experienced readers. It is to these contributors that I am especially grateful. This remarkable collection of scholars and practitioners has distilled their knowledge into a fascinating and enlightening one-stop knowledge base in information, computer, and network security that "talks" to readers. This has been a massive effort, as well as a most rewarding experience. So many people have played a role, it is difficult to know where to begin.

I would like to thank the members of the editorial board for participating in the project and for their expert advice on selection of topics, recommendations of authors, and review of the materials. Many thanks to the more than 1,000 reviewers who provided their advice on improving the coverage, accuracy, and comprehensiveness of these materials.

I thank my senior editor, Matt Holt, who initiated the idea of the handbook. Through a dozen drafts and many reviews, the project got off the ground and then was managed flawlessly by Matt and his professional team. Many thanks to Matt and his team for keeping the project focused and maintaining its lively coverage.

Tamara Hummel, editorial coordinator, assisted the contributing authors and me during the initial phases of development. I am grateful for all her support. When it came time for the production phase, the superb Wiley production team took over. Particularly, I want to thank Deborah Schindlar, senior production editor. I am grateful for all her hard work. I thank Michelle Patterson, our marketing manager, for her impressive marketing campaign launched on behalf of the handbook.

Last, but not least, I want to thank my wonderful wife, Nooshin, and my two children, Mohsen and Morvareed, for being so patient during this venture. They provided a pleasant environment that expedited the completion of this project. Mohsen and Morvareed assisted me in sending out thousands of e-mail messages to authors and reviewers. Nooshin was a great help in designing and maintaining the authors' and reviewers' databases. Their efforts are greatly appreciated. Also, my two sisters, Azam and Akram, provided moral support throughout my life. To this family, any expression of thanks is insufficient.

Hossein Bidgoli
California State University, Bakersfield

Guide to The Handbook of Information Security

The Handbook of Information Security is a comprehensive coverage of the relatively new and very important field of information, computer, and network security. This reference work consists of three separate volumes and 207 different chapters on various aspects of this field. Each chapter in the handbook provides a comprehensive overview of the selected topic, intended to inform a broad spectrum of readers, ranging from computer and security professionals and academicians to students to the general business community.

This guide is provided to help the reader easily locate information throughout *The Handbook of Information Security*. It explains how the information within it can be located.

Organization

This is organized for maximum ease of use, with the chapters arranged logically in three volumes. While one can read individual volumes (or articles) one will get the most out of the handbook by becoming conversant with all three volumes.

Table of Contents

A complete table of contents of the entire handbook appears in the front of each volume. This list of chapter titles represents topics that have been carefully selected by the editor-in-chief, Dr. Hossein Bidgoli, and his colleagues on the editorial board.

Index

A subject index for each individual volume is located at the end of each volume.

Chapters

The author's name and affiliation are displayed at the beginning of the chapter.

All chapters in the handbook are organized in the same format:

Title and author
Outline
Introduction
Body
Conclusion
Glossary
Cross-References
References

Outline

Each chapter begins with an outline that provides a brief overview of the chapter, as well as highlighting important subtopics. For example, the chapter "Internet Basics" includes sections for Information Superhighway and the World Wide Web, Domain Name Systems, Navigational Tools, Search Engines, and Directories. In addition, second-level and third- level headings will be found within the chapter.

Introduction

Each chapter begins with an introduction that defines the topic under discussion and summarized the chapter, in order to give the reader a general idea of what is to come.

Body

The body of the chapter fills out and expands upon items covered in the outline.

Conclusion

The conclusion provides a summary of the chapter, highlighting issues and concepts that are important for the reader to remember.

Glossary

The glossary contains terms that are important to an understanding of the chapter and that may be unfamiliar to the reader. Each term is defined in the context of the particular chapter in which it is used. Thus the same term may be defined in two or more chapters with the detail of the definition varying slightly from one chapter to another. The handbook includes approximately 2,700 glossary terms. For example, the chapter "Internet Basics" includes the following glossary entries:

Extranet A secure network that uses the Internet and Web technology to connect two or more intranets of trusted business partners, enabling business-to-business, business-to-consumer, consumer-to-consumer, and consumer-to-business communications.

Intranet A network within the organization that uses Web technologies (TCP/IP, HTTP, FTP, SMTP, HTML, XML, and its variations) for collecting, storing, and disseminating useful information throughout the organization.

Cross-References

All chapters have cross-references to other chapters that contain further information on the same topic. They appear at the end of the chapter, preceding the references. The cross-references indicate related chapters that can be consulted for further information on the same topic. The handbook contains more than 1,400 cross-references in all. For example, the chapter "Computer Viruses and Worms" has the following cross references:

Hackers, Crackers and Computer Criminals, Hoax Viruses and Virus Alerts, Hostile Java Applets, Spyware, Trojan Horse Programs.

References

The references in this handbook are for the benefit of the reader, to provide references for further research on the given topic. Review articles and research papers that are important to an understanding of the topic are also listed. The references typically consist of a dozen to two dozen entries, and do not include all material consulted by the author in preparing the chapter.

PART 1

Key Concepts and Applications Related to Information Security

Internet Basics

Hossein Bidgoli, *California State University, Bakersfield*

INTRODUCTION

This chapter provides a basic introduction to the Internet and Web technologies. It provides a brief history of the Internet and then explains domain name systems, navigational tools, and search engines. The chapter defines intranets and extranets and compares and contrasts them with the Internet. The chapter concludes with a brief survey of popular applications of the Internet in various industries and fields, including tourism and travel, publishing, higher education, real estate, employment, banking and brokerages, software distribution, healthcare, and politics. Other chapters throughout the *Handbook* discuss in more detail most of the topics presented here.

INFORMATION SUPERHIGHWAY AND THE WORLD WIDE WEB

The backbone of the information superhighway and electronic commerce (e-commerce) is the Internet. The Internet is a collection of millions of computers and networks of all sizes. Simply put, the Internet is the "network of networks." The information superhighway is also known as the Internet. No one actually owns or runs the Internet. Each network is locally administered and funded, in some cases by volunteers. It is estimated that, in 2005, more than 200 countries are directly or indirectly connected to the Internet. This number is increasing on a daily basis and makes global e-commerce a reality.

The initial phases of the Internet started in 1969 as a Defense Department project called ARPANET (Advanced Research Projects Agency Network). It served from 1969 through 1990 as the basis for early networking research and as a central backbone network during the development of the Internet. Since the Internet began, it has grown rapidly in size.

ARPANET evolved into the NSFNET (National Science Foundation Network) in 1987. NSFNET is considered the initial Internet backbone. The term "Internet" was derived from the term "internetworking," which signified the connecting of networks. NSFNET initially connected four supercomputers located in San Diego, California; Cornell University in Ithaca, New York; Pittsburgh, Pennsylvania; and Illinois to form the backbone. Other universities and government laboratories were subsequently added to the network. These backbones linked all existing networks in a three-level structure:

backbones;
regional networks; and
local area networks (LANs).

Backbones provide connectivity to other international backbones. The NAPs (network access points) are a key component of the Internet backbones. An NAP is a public network exchange facility where Internet service providers (ISPs) can connect with one another. The connections within NAPs determine how traffic is routed over the Internet and also are the focus of Internet congestion. LANs provide the standard user interface for computers to access the Internet. Phone lines (twisted pair), coaxial cables, microwaves, satellites, and other communications media are used to connect LANs to regional networks. TCP/IP (transmission control protocol/Internet protocol) is the common language of the Internet that allows the network systems to understand each other. TCP/IP divides network traffic into individually addressed packets that are routed along different paths. Protocols are conventions and rules that govern a data communications system. They cover error detection, message length, and transmission speed. Protocols provide compatibility among different manufacturers' devices.

The National Science Foundation (NSF) and state governments have subsidized regional networks. NSFNET's acceptable use policy initially restricted the Internet to research and educational institutions; commercial use was not allowed. Because of increasing demand, additional backbones were eventually allowed to connect to NSFNET and commercial applications began.

The World Wide Web (WWW or the Web) changed the Internet by introducing a true graphical environment. It has been around since 1989, when it was proposed by Tim Berners-Lee at CERN. The WWW is an Internet service that organizes information using hypermedia. Each document can include embedded references to audio, text, images, full-motion video, or other documents. The WWW constitutes a large portion of the Internet that contains hypermedia documents. Hypermedia is an extension of hypertext. Hypertext allows a user to follow a desired path by clicking on highlighted text to follow a particular "thread" or topic. This involves accessing files, applications, and computers in a nonsequential fashion. It allows for combinations of text, images, sounds, and full-motion video in the same document. It allows information retrieval with the click of a button. Hypertext is an approach to data management in which data are stored in a network of nodes connected by links. The nodes are designed to be accessed through an interactive browsing system. A hypertext document includes document links and supporting indexes for a particular topic. A hypertext document may include data, audio, and images. This type of document is called hypermedia. In hypertext documents, the physical and logical layouts are usually different. This is not the case in a paper document. In a paper document, the author of the paper establishes the order and readers follow this predetermined path.

A hypertext system provides users with nonsequential paths to access information. This means that information does not have to be accessed sequentially, as in a book. A hypertext system allows the user to make any request that the author or designer of the hypertext provides through links. These link choices are similar to lists of indexes and allow the reader to choose a "custom path."

Any computer that stores hypermedia documents and makes them available to other computers on the Internet is called a server or a Web server. The computers that request these documents are called clients. A client can be a personal computer at home or a node in a LAN at a university or an organization. The most exciting feature of the Internet and the WWW is that these hypermedia documents can be stored anywhere in the world. A user can easily jump from a site in the United States to a site in Paris, France, all in a few milliseconds.

DOMAIN NAME SYSTEMS

Before a user can begin to navigate the Internet and use it for personal use or e-commerce applications, an understanding of domain name systems (DNS) (also called domain name servers) is essential. Domain names are unique identifiers of computer or network addresses on the Internet. The following are examples of domain names:

Netscape.com
Microsoft.com
UN.org
Whitehouse.gov

Table 1 Organizational Domains (Generic Top-Level Domains, gTLD)

.com	Commercial organizations (e.g., Microsoft)
.edu	Education and academic organizations (e.g., California State University)
.int	International organizations (e.g., United Nations)
.mil	U.S. military organizations (e.g., U.S. Army)
.gov	U.S. government organizations (e.g., Internal Revenue Service)
.net	Backbone, regional, and commercial networks (e.g., the National Science Foundation's Internet Network Information Center)
.org	Other organizations such as research and nonprofit organizations (e.g., the Internet Town Hall)

They come in two forms: English-like names and numeric or IP (Internet protocol) addresses.

The Internet Corporation for Assigned Names and Numbers (ICANN) is the nonprofit corporation that assigns and keeps track of these addresses. This was previously performed under U.S. government contract by IANA (Internet Assigned Numbers Authority) and other entities.

IP addresses are less convenient because numbers are more difficult to remember. The English-like names are electronically converted to IP addresses for routing (transferring information from one network to another network). Domain names are used in URLs (uniform resource locator or universal resource locator) to identify a particular Web page. A URL is basically the address of a file or a site on the Internet. For example, in the URL http://www.csub.edu/~hbidgoli, the domain name is csub.edu. Every domain name has a suffix that indicates to which top-level domain (TLD) it belongs. In this example the suffix is edu, which stands for educational institutions. Combinations of the letters of the alphabet as well as the numerals 0 through 9 can be used in domain names. The hyphen is the only other character utilized; spaces are not allowed.

The TLD is the data that comes after "www." It denotes the type of organization or country the address specifies. TLDs are divided into organizational (generic) and geographic (country code) domains. (See Tables 1 through 3.)

This system makes it easy to identify the type or location of the organization by looking at the last section of the domain name. Organization, which is the second field from the right, refers to the name of the organization. A name for a small company is as easy as a company name. The two leftmost fields of the domain name refer to the computer. This is relevant for large organizations with several levels of subdomains. An example of a relatively complete Internet address is the address of a document in the Virtual Tourist Web site: http://www.vtourist.com/vt/usa.htm. A brief explanation from left to right follows:

http—Means of access, hypertext transfer protocol. This is how the majority of Web documents are transferred.

Table 2 Examples of Proposed New Domain Names

.aero	For the aviation industry
.arts	For entities emphasizing cultural and entertainment activities
.biz	For businesses
.coop	For cooperative or cooperative service organizations
.firm	For businesses or firms
.inc	Corporations
.info	For entities providing information services
.law	For those in the legal profession
.museum	For a museum or professionally affiliated personnel
.name	For a noncommercial site associated with a private individual
.nom	For individuals or family names
.pro	For a site associated with a certified professional or professional organization
.news	For news-related sites
.rec	For entities emphasizing recreation and entertainment activities
.shop	For businesses offering goods and commodities
.store	For electronic storefronts
.web	For entities emphasizing activities related to the WWW
.xxx	For adult content

www.vtourist.com—This is the address of the Web site. It is uniquely defined and differentiated from all other Web sites. WWW is an Internet service that organizes information using hypermedia.

vt—This is a path or directory. A server may be divided into a series of directories for better organization.

usa.htm—This is the document itself. The htm extension indicates that this is an HTML (hypertext markup language) document. It is the authoring language used to create documents on the Web. HTML defines the structure and layout of a Web document by using a variety of tags and attributes. Most hypermedia documents are written in HTML format. Servers that do not support long extensions display "htm," whereas other servers display "html."

Table 3 Sample Geographic Domains (Country Code Top-Level Domains, ccTLD)

.au	Australia
.br	Brazil
.ca	Canada
.fr	France
.de	Germany
.hk	Hong Kong
.il	Israel
.ir	Iran
.jp	Japan
.kr	Korea (Republic)
.ru	Russia
.es	Spain
.uk	United Kingdom
.us	United States
.va	Vatican City State
.zw	Zimbabwe

NAVIGATIONAL TOOLS, SEARCH ENGINES, AND DIRECTORIES

Navigational tools allow the user to surf the Internet and search engines provide access to various resources available on the Internet, such as those that provide library searches for writing a term paper or reservations for an airline ticket. Directories use indexes of information based on key words in the document. As will be discussed elsewhere in this chapter, Yahoo! is a popular directory on the Internet.

The original command language of the Internet was based on computer commands and was difficult to learn for most users. Character-based languages were used for tasks such as downloading files or sending e-mails. These languages are UNIX based, which meant the user was required to know the specific syntax of many commands. Everything was communicated in plain text, and graphics, sound, and animation data were not available. The introduction of graphical browsers such as Netscape Navigator changed all of this. Microsoft Internet Explorer and Netscape Navigator are the best-known graphical browsers available for navigating the Internet. Each of these browsers combine powerful graphics, audio, and video capabilities. Each Web server has a "homepage" or a Web site that publishes information about the location. Using character-based browsers such as Lynx, a user will find this information in text form, whereas graphical browsers such as Microsoft Internet Explorer support images and sound clips as well.

Navigational Tools

Microsoft Internet Explorer is the most popular graphical browser in the Internet world. With strong marketing support from Microsoft and improvement in its features, Internet Explorer (IE) has gained the lead in the browser market. Netscape Navigator is another graphical browser available for all major operating system platforms. Netscape, similar to IE, provides a true graphical environment that allows the user to surf the Internet using a mouse and the point-and-click technique. Similar to other Windows applications, both IE and Netscape Navigator feature a standard menu bar and toolbar buttons for frequently used commands.

Directories and Search Engines

There are several search engines and directories in use. Yahoo! is the most popular directory and Google, Excite, and Infoseek are three of the most popular search engines. These programs allow a user to scan the Internet and find information through the use of key words or phrases. A search could be for research for a term paper, finding an exotic antique for a personal collection, or anything in between. The following paragraphs briefly describe Yahoo!, Google, and Excite (Bidgoli, 2002).

Jerry Yang and Dave Filo founded Yahoo! in April 1994. Yahoo! is one of the best-known directories on the Internet. A directory is a search service that classifies Web sites into a hierarchical, subject-based structure. For example, Yahoo! includes categories such as art, business, and entertainment. These categories are organized by topic. The user can go to a category and then navigate for specific information. Yahoo! also includes an internal search engine that can expedite the search process. Yahoo! soon expanded to offer other services and became a portal on the Internet. A portal or gateway for the WWW is an application that serves as an information search organizer. Portals provide a single-point integration and navigation through the system. Portals create an information community that can be customized for an individual or a corporation. Portals serve as the major starting sites for many individuals who are connecting to the Internet. Some of the services offered by Yahoo! include Yahoo! Travel, Yahoo! Classifieds, Yahoo! Pager, and Yahoo! Autos.

Excite, Inc. was founded in June 1994. Its basic mission is to provide a gateway to the Internet and to organize, aggregate, and deliver information to meet users' needs. The Excite Network, including the Excite and WebCrawler brands, contain a suite of specialized information services that combine proprietary search technology, editorial Web reviews, aggregated content from third parties, and bulletin boards. The Excite Network serves as a central place for consumers to gather and interact during each Web experience. Excite PAL is an instant paging service. By entering the names and e-mail addresses of friends, family, and colleagues into Excite PAL, a user can find them online.

Larry Page and Sergey Brin, two Stanford Ph.D. candidates, founded Google in 1998. Google helps its users find the information they are looking for with high levels of ease, accuracy, and relevancy. The company delivers its services to individuals and corporations through its own public site, http://www.google.com, and through cobranding its Web search services. To reach the Google Web site, the user simply types www.google.com (its URL) into the location box of the Web browser and presses the Enter key. At the initial Google screen, the user enters the desired search item(s), for example "computer viruses," and then again presses the Enter key or clicks on the "Google Search" button. In a few seconds, the items that closely match the search items will be displayed. Although the Web site's default language is English, the user can choose a different language by clicking the down arrow to the right.

INTERNET SERVICES THAT SUPPORT ELECTRONIC COMMERCE

Electronic mail (e-mail), news and discussion groups, Internet Relay Chat (IRC), instant messaging, and the Internet phone are among the services offered by the Internet that could enhance a successful e-commerce program. Other chapters in the *Handbook* will provide a more in-depth discussion of these services. In this chapter a brief overview of these services is presented (Bidgoli, 2002).

E-mail is one of the most popular services available on the Internet. Using e-mail, a user can create a message electronically and send it via the communications media. New products and services can be announced to customers using e-mail. Confirmations can be sent using e-mail and also many business communications can be effectively performed using e-mail. When a user sends an e-mail, the message usually stays in the recipient's e-mail server until the recipient reads it. In most e-mail systems, the receiver is able to store the e-mail message in an electronic folder for future reference. E-mail is fast and will get to the recipient's computer in a matter of seconds or minutes. All that is needed to send an e-mail message is the e-mail address of a recipient. A user can also send a single e-mail message to a group of people at the same time. A user can apply all the word processing tasks such as spell-checking and grammar correction before sending the e-mail message. Document files and/or multimedia files can be attached to an e-mail message and a user could ask for delivery notification. With e-mail, a user can usually establish various folders with different contents and send a particular e-mail to a specific group. Using e-mail enables a user to establish an effective message-distribution system for advertising products and services. (For detailed information on this topic, consult the chapter on E-Mail and Instant Messaging.)

The Internet brings together people with diverse backgrounds and interests. Discussion groups to share opinions and ideas facilitate this. Each person in a discussion group can post messages or articles that can be accessed and read by others in the group. Newsgroups can be established for any topic or hobby and allow people to get together for fun and entertainment or for business purposes. For example, a user may join a newsgroup interested in ancient civilization, or a user may join a newsgroup that can help in writing and debugging a computer program in a specific programming language. Newsgroups can serve as an effective advertising medium in an e-commerce environment.) For detailed information on this topic, consult the chapter on Online Communities.)

Internet Relay Chat (IRC) enables a user to interactively communicate in written form with other users from all around the world. It is similar to a coffee shop where people sit around a table and start chatting. The three major differences between this electronic coffee shop and a real coffee shop are that there is no coffee, the user does not see the people that he/she is chatting with, and IRC leaves a "chat trail," which can be used later. However, a user is able to participate in many different discussions with people anywhere in the world who have the same interest. (For detailed information on this topic, consult the chapter on Internet Relay Chat.)

Instant messenger (IM) is a communication service that enables a user to create a private chat room with another user. Different instant messengers offer different capabilities. They typically alert a user whenever someone on the user's private list is online so that a user may initiate a chat session with that particular individual. (For detailed information on this topic consult the chapter on E-Mail and Instant Messaging.)

Internet telephony is the use of the Internet rather than the traditional telephone-company infrastructure to exchange spoken or other audible information. Because access to the Internet is available at local phone connection rates, an international or other long-distance call will be much less expensive than through the traditional calling arrangement. This could be a major cost savings for an e-commerce site that offers hotline, help desk, and other services. (For detailed information on this topic, consult the chapter on Voice over Internet Protocol [VoIP].)

Three new services are now or will soon be available on the Internet:

1. The ability to make a normal voice phone call (despite whether the person called is immediately available; that is, the phone will ring at the location of the person called). In most of the technologies currently available, a "phone meeting" must be arranged in advance, and then both parties log onto the Internet at the same time to conduct the conversation.
2. The ability to send fax transmissions at very low cost (at local call prices) through a gateway point on the Internet in major cities.
3. The ability to leave voice mail at a called number.

WHAT IS AN INTRANET?

The excitement created by the Internet has been transferred to another growing application called intranets. In simple terms, whatever a user can do with the Internet, a user should also be able to do with an organization's private network, or intranet.

An intranet provides users with easy-to-use access that can operate on any computer regardless of the operating system in use. Intranet technology helps companies disseminate information faster and more easily to both vendors and customers and can be of benefit to the internal operations of the organization. Although intranets are fairly new, they have attracted a lot of attention in a very short time (Bidgoli, 1999, 2002).

The intranet uses Internet and Web technologies to solve organizational problems traditionally solved by proprietary databases, groupware, and scheduling and workflow applications. An intranet is different from a LAN or wide area network (WAN), although it uses the same physical connections. An intranet is an application or service (or set of applications or services) that uses the computer networks (the LANs and WANs) of an organization, and that is how it is different from LANs and WANs. The intranet is only logically internal to the organization. Intranets can physically span the globe, as long as access is specifically defined and limited to the specific organization's community of users behind a firewall or a series of firewalls.

In a typical intranet configuration, all users in the organization can access all the Web servers. The system administrator must define the degree of access for each user. They can constantly communicate with one another and post information on their departmental Web servers. However, usually a firewall (or several firewalls) separates these internal networks from the Internet (the worldwide network).

Within these departmental Web servers, individual employees can have their own Web pages, divided by department. For example, the following departments each may include several Web pages as parts of the organization's intranet program:

finance,
human resources,
information services,
manufacturing,
marketing, and
sales.

So what is an intranet? In simple terms, an intranet is a network within the organization that uses Web technologies (TCP/IP, HTTP, FTP [file transfer protocol], SMTP [simple mail transfer protocol], HTML, and XML [extensible markup language]) for collecting, storing, and disseminating useful information throughout the organization. This information supports e-commerce activities such as sales, customer service, and marketing.

Employees can find internal information and they can bookmark important sites within the intranet. Furthermore, individual departments can create their own Web sites to educate or inform other employees about their departments by implementing intranet technology. For example, marketing can present the latest product information, and manufacturing can post shipping schedules and new product designs. The human resources department can post new jobs, benefit information, new promotions, and 401K plan information. The finance and accounting departments can post cost information and other financial reports on their sites. The president's office might post information about the next company picnic on its site. This information collectively supports a successful e-commerce program. (For detailed information on this topic, consult the chapter on Intranets: Principals, Privacy and Security Considerations.)

INTERNET VERSUS INTRANETS

The Internet is a public network. Any user can access the Internet, assuming the user has an account with an ISP. The Internet is a worldwide network, whereas intranets are private and are not necessarily connected to the Web. Intranets are connected to a specific company's network, and usually the users are the company's employees. An intranet is separated from the Internet through the installation and use of a firewall (or several firewalls). Intranets usually have higher throughput and performance than the Internet and are usually more secure than the Internet.

Apart from these differences, the two have a lot in common. They both use the same network technology, TCP/IP, and they both use browsers for accessing information. They both use documents in HTML and XML formats, and both are capable of carrying documents with multimedia formats. Also, they both may use the Java programming (or its derivatives) language for developing applications.

Table 4 Internet versus Intranet

Key Feature	Internet	Intranet
User	Anybody	Employees only
Geographical scope	Unlimited	Limited to unlimited
Speed	Lower than that of an intranet	Usually higher than that of the Internet
Security	Lower than that of an intranet	Usually higher than that of the Internet
Technology used	TCP/IP	TCP/IP
Document format	HTML	HTML
Multimedia capability	Could be lower than that of an intranet	Could be higher than that of the Internet

Intranets may or may not use any of the technologies beyond HTML, that is, Java programming, JavaScript or VBScript, Active X, Dynamic HTML, or XML. One of the advantages of an intranet is that because the organization can control the browser used, it can specify a browser that will support the technologies in use. Beyond Web documents, the organization can also specify the use of the Internet phone, e-mail, video conferencing, and other Web technologies supported by the chosen browser. Table 4 summarizes the similarities and differences of these two technologies.

SELECTED APPLICATIONS OF AN INTRANET

A properly designed intranet can make the type of information listed in Table 5 available to the entire organization in a timely manner. This information directly or indirectly can improve the efficiency and effectiveness of an organization (Bidgoli, 1999, 2002).

Many internal applications in use today can be easily converted to an intranet or can be supported using an intranet. Human resources applications, such as job information, name and phone number lists, and medical benefits, can be displayed on a human resources Web site. The finance Web site might present information on time cards, expense reports, or credit authorization. Employees can easily access the latest information on a server. With e-mail, e-mail distribution lists, and chat lines, employees can retrieve meeting minutes and much more.

The intranet also allows organizations to evolve from a "calendar-" or "schedule"-based publishing strategy to an "event-driven" or "needs-based" publishing strategy. In the past, companies published an employee handbook once a year. Traditionally, the handbooks would not be updated until the following year even though they may have been outdated as soon as they arrived on the users' desks. Some of these organizations sent a few loose pages as an update every so often. The employee is supposed to add these additional pages to the binder. After a while, these materials become difficult to go through to retrieve specific information.

With an intranet publishing strategy, information can be updated instantly. If the organization adds a new

Table 5 Possible Information Provided by an Intranet

Human Resources Management
401K plans
Calendar events
Company mission statement and policies
Contest results
Department information
Employee classifieds
Employee stock options
Job postings
Job descriptions
Leave of absence and sabbatical news
Maps
Medical benefits
New-hire orientation materials
Online training
Telephone listings
Time cards
Training manuals
Training schedules
Travel authorization
Organizational charts
Meeting minutes
Personnel policy
Press releases
Salary ranges
Software program tutorials
Suggestion box
Upcoming functions
Employment applications
Security policies and procedures
Web usage and e-mail policies

Sales and Marketing
Call tracking
Data regarding the latest actions taken by the competitors
Customer information
Order tracking and placement
Newscast on demand to desktop, custom filtered to client profile
Sales tips
Product information

Production and Operations
Equipment inventory
Facilities management
Industry news
New product offerings
Product catalog
Project information
Distribution of technical drawings

Accounting and Finance
Budget planning
Credit authorization
Expense report

mutual fund to the 401K programs, content on the benefits page can be updated immediately to reflect that change, and the company internal homepage can include a brief announcement about the change. Then, the employees have the new information at their desktops as soon as they look up the 401K programs.

Intranets dramatically reduce the costs and time of content development, duplication, distribution, and utilization. The traditional publication model includes a multistep process including:

creation of content,
production of the draft,
revision of the draft,
final draft preparation,
migration of the content to the desktop publishing environment,
duplication, and
distribution.

However, intranet technology reduces the number of steps to only two (it eliminates the duplication and distribution steps):

creation of content and
migration of content to the intranet environment.

However, content still needs review and approval regardless of the medium used for delivery.

WHAT IS AN EXTRANET?

Interorganizational systems (IOSs) facilitate information exchange among business partners. Some of these systems, such as electronic funds transfer (EFT) and e-mail, have been used in traditional businesses as well as in the e-commerce environment. Among the most popular IOSs are electronic data interchange (EDI) and extranets. Both EDI and extranets provide a secure connection among business partners. Their roles in business-to-business e-commerce are on the rise. These systems create a seamless environment that expedites the transfer of information in a timely matter.

Some organizations allow customers and business partners to access their intranets for specific business purposes. For example, a supplier may want to check the inventory status or a customer may want to check account balances. These networks are referred to as extranets. It should be noted that an organization usually makes only a portion of its intranet accessible to these external parties. Also, comprehensive security measures must ensure that access is given only to authorized users and trusted business partners. (For detailed information on this topic, consult the chapter on Extranets: Applications, Development, Security and Privacy.)

An extranet is defined as a secure network that uses Internet and Web technology to connect two or more intranets of business partners, enabling business-to-business, business-to-consumer, consumer-to-consumer, and consumer-to-business communications. Extranets are a network service that allows trusted business partners to secure access to useful information on another organization's intranet. Table 6 provides a comparison of the Internet, intranets, and extranets (Bidgoli, 2002; Fletcher, 1997).

There are numerous applications of extranets in the e-commerce world. Toshiba America Inc. is an example of a company that uses an extranet. Toshiba has designed an extranet for timely order-entry processing. Using this extranet, more than 300 dealers can place orders for parts until 5 p.m. for next-day delivery. Dealers can also check accounts receivable balances and pricing arrangements, read press releases, and much more. This secure system has resulted in significant cost savings and has improved customer service (Jones, 1998).

Another example of an extranet is the Federal Express Tracking System (http://www.fedex.com). Federal Express uses its extranet to collect information and make it available to its customers over the Internet. The FedEx Web site is one of the earliest and best-known examples of an extranet—an intranet that is opened to external users. The customer can access FedEx's public site, enter a package's tracking number, and locate any package still in the system. Using this system, a customer can enter all the information needed to prepare a shipping form, obtain a tracking number, print the form, and schedule a pickup.

Extranets provide very secure, temporary connections over public and private networks between an organization and a diverse group of business partners outside of the organization. These groups may include:

customers,
vendors,
suppliers,
Consultants,
distributors,
resellers, and
outsourcers, such as claim processors, or those with whom the company is doing research and development (R&D) or other collaborative work, such as product design.

Table 6 Comparison of the Internet, Intranets, and Extranets

	Internet	Intranet	Extranet
Access	Public	Private	Private
Information	Fragmented	Proprietary	Proprietary
Users	Everybody	Members of an organization	Groups of closely related companies, users, or organizations

Extranets not only allow companies to reduce internetworking costs, they also provide companies with a competitive advantage, which may lead to increased profit. A successful extranet program requires a comprehensive security system and management control. The security system should provide comprehensive access control, user-based authentication, encryption capability, and comprehensive auditing and reporting capabilities.

An extranet offers an organization the same benefits that an intranet offers while also delivering the benefits that derive from being linked to the outside world. Some of the specific advantages of an extranet include (Bidgoli, 2002):

Coordination—An extranet allows for improved coordination among participating partners. This usually includes suppliers, distributors, and customers. Critical information from one partner can be made available so that another partner can make a decision without delay. For example, it is possible for a manufacturer to coordinate its production by checking the inventory status of a customer.

Feedback—An extranet enables an organization to receive instant feedback from its customers and other business partners. It gives consumers an opportunity to express their views about products or services before those products or services are even introduced to the market.

Customer satisfaction—An extranet links the customer to an organization. This provides the customer with more information about products, services, and the organization in general. This also makes ordering products or services as easy as a click of the mouse. Expediting business-to-business e-commerce is definitely one of the greatest benefits of an extranet.

Cost reduction—An extranet can reduce the inventory costs by providing timely information to the participants of a supply network program. Mobil Corporation, based in Fairfax, Virginia, designed an extranet application that allows distributors throughout the world to submit purchase orders. By doing this, the company significantly increases the efficiency of the operation. It also expedites the delivery of goods and services (Maloff, 1997).

Expedite communication—Extranets increase the efficiency and effectiveness of communication among business partners by linking intranets for immediate access to critical information. A traveling salesperson can receive the latest product information remotely before going to a sales meeting. A car dealer can provide the latest information to a customer on a new model without making several phone calls and going through different brochures and sales manuals.

SELECTED INTERNET APPLICATIONS

Several segments of service industries have significantly benefited from the Internet and its supporting technologies. The Internet has enabled these businesses to offer their services and products to a broad range of customers with more competitive prices and convenience.

Table 7 Popular Internet Applications

Marketing and advertising
Distance learning
Electronic conferencing
Electronic mail (e-mail)
Electronic posting
Healthcare management
Home shopping
Interactive games
Inventory management
News groups and discussions
News on demand
Online banking
Online employment
Online software distribution
Online training
Online politics (voting, participating in political forums, chat groups, and using the Internet for political fund raising)
Remote login
Sale of products and services
Telecommuting
Transferring files with FTP
Video on demand
Videophones
Online demonstrations of products and services throughout the world
Virtual reality games
Online request for proposal (RFP), request for quotes (RFQ), and request for information (RFI)

The Internet offers numerous tools and advantages to these businesses to sell their products and services all over the world. Table 7 lists popular Internet applications.

In the following pages, some of the major beneficiaries of the Internet and e-commerce will be reviewed.

Tourism and Travel

Tourism and travel industries have significantly benefited from various Internet and e-commerce applications. As an example, the Tropical Island Vacation (http://www.tropicalislandvacation.com) homepage directs prospective vacationers to an appropriate online brochure after vacationers respond to a few brief questions about the type of vacation they would like to take. Customers simply point and click on appealing photographs or phrases to explore further. Another example is Zeus Tours (http://zeustours.com), which has been very effective at offering unique and exciting tours, cruises, and other travel packages online. Many Web sites allow customers to reserve tickets for planes, trains, buses, cruises, hotels, and resorts. Sites such as biztravel.com (http://biztravel.com) allow its business customers to plan a trip, book a vacation, gather information on many cities, gather weather information, and much more. Expedia.com, Travel.com, Travelocity.com, Priceline.com, hotels.com and Yahoo! Travel are other examples of sites that offer all types of travel and tourism services.

Publishing

Many major textbook publishers in the United States and Europe have homepages. An interested individual can read the major features of forthcoming books or books in print before ordering them. The Web sites of some publishers include a sample chapter from specific books, or entire books that can be read online for free for 90 days, whereas others allow online customers to purchase portions of a book rather than the entire book. The Web site of John Wiley & Sons (http://wiley.com), publisher of *The Handbook of Information Security*, allows a prospective buyer to search the online catalog based on the author's name, the title of the book, and so forth. When the desired book is found, it can be ordered online.

Higher Education

Major universities also have homepages. An interested individual can go on a tour of a university and read about different departments, programs, faculty, and academic resources. Many universities throughout the world are creating virtual divisions that offer entire degree programs on the Internet. Many professional certificate programs are also offered through the Internet. These programs and courses provide a real opportunity and convenience for individuals in remote areas and individuals who cannot attend regular classes to enroll in these courses. They also provide a source of revenue for many colleges and universities that are facing enrollment decline in their service areas. They also allow renowned experts to teach courses to broad geographic audiences. (For detailed information on this topic, consult the chapters on E-Education and Information Privacy and Security and Security in E-Learning.)

Real Estate

Numerous real estate Web sites provide millions of up-to-date listings of existing and new homes for sale throughout the world. These sites are devoted entirely to buying and selling real estate. The buyer or seller can review neighborhoods, schools, and local real estate prices. These sites allow the customer to find a realtor, find brokerage firms, and learn many home-buying tips. Some of these sites offer or will soon offer "virtual tours." These virtual tours enable a buyer to view a prospective property from distance. This is achieved by using virtual reality technologies. Some of the services offered by a typical real estate site are listed below:

appraisal services,
buying,
checking neighborhood profiles,
checking schools profiles,
financing,
home improvement advice,
obtaining credit reports,
posting a free listing,
renting services,
selling advice, and much more.

Table 8 lists examples of major real estate sites.

Table 8 Examples of Online Real Estate Sites

Prudential California (http://www.prudential.com) provides wireless listing services and property data for agents.
ERA (http://www.era.com) is an Internet-based application with listing information for agents.
Century 21 (http://www.century21.com) is an electronic system for tracking agent referrals worldwide and also offers home buying, home selling, financing, and property listings.
Re/Max (http://www.remax.com) is a contact management tool for agents that interfaces with personal digital assistant (PDA) devices.
Homestore.com (http://www.homestore.com) provides a listing of more than 1 million properties throughout the United Sates.
Mortgage Expo.com (http://www.mortgageexpo.com) provides a listing of more than 800 home lenders throughout the United States.

Employment

Employment service providers have established Web presences. Table 9 provides a listing of some of the popular sites to use for finding or recruiting for a job, especially if it involves information technology.

Banking and Brokerage Firms

Online banking is here. Many U.S. and Canadian banks and credit unions offer online banking services. Although online banking has not been fully accepted by customers, many banking-related resources are being utilized. For example, many banks use e-mail to communicate with their corporate customers. E-mail is a less expensive and more convenient alternative to a telephone call, especially for long distance communications. Financial reports for banks can be easily distributed via e-mail to mutual fund investors or customers.

The banking industry's ultimate goal is to carry out many of their transactions through the Internet. Consumer acceptance is the major factor that has kept this business from exploding. It is generally believed that a secure nationwide electronic banking system is almost in place. Soon people will be able to use their personal computers (PCs) and the Internet to do all types of banking activities.

As is discussed in another chapter in the *Handbook*, digital signatures are a key technology for the banking

Table 9 Some of the Popular Sites to Use for Finding or Recruiting for a Job

http://www.careermosaic.com
http://www.hotjobs.com
http://www.monster.com
http://www.webhire.com
http://www.dice.com
http://www.guru.com

Table 10 Some of the Services Available via the Internet for Banking Activities

24/7 customer service by e-mail
Accessing current and old transactions
Categorizing transactions and producing reports
Exporting banking data to popular money management software
Obtaining online funding for checking accounts
Obtaining online mortgage and certificate of deposit applications
Obtaining written guarantee against frauds and late payments
Obtaining instant approval for personal loans
Obtaining interactive guides to aid selection of a proper banking product or service
Obtaining interactive tools for designing a savings plan, choosing a mortgage, and/or obtaining online insurance quotes all tied to applications
Obtaining online application for both checking and savings accounts
Obtaining online forms for ordering checks and issuing a stop payment
Obtaining free checks and free foreign ATM use
Obtaining IRA and brokerage account information
Obtaining loan status and credit card account information online
Paying bills
Paying credit card accounts
Transferring funds
Viewing digital copies of checks

and brokerage industry because they provide an electronic means of guaranteeing the authenticity of the sending party and assurance that encrypted documents have not been changed during transmission. The current mergers and acquisitions taking place and the frequent downsizing within the financial industry are two reasons to support Internet banking. Table 10 lists some of the services available via the Internet for banking activities. (For detailed information on this topic, consult the chapter on Online Retail Banking: Security Concerns, Breaches, and Controls.)

Many brokerage firms offer stock and other security transactions online. They provide quotations for stocks, bonds, and other securities. To encourage more customers to use these services, they may offer discounts.

Software Distribution

Several major software vendors offer software on the Internet. Customers can view listings of available software, order, and designate an installation time. Nearly all hardware manufactures offer drivers and patches as updates on the Web. Microsoft and several other software companies already offer free software via the Internet. Routine downloading of the Netscape Navigator and Microsoft Internet Explorer browser applications are two good examples. Both are relatively small programs. In contrast is the Microsoft Office Suite, which would take significantly longer to download through an online application service provider. Given today's communications throughput and bandwidth limitations, program size definitely poses a challenge to online software distribution.

A successful application in this area is the distribution of antivirus programs over the Internet. Several of the vendors of this software application are already using the Internet to sell their software to prospective buyers. A major advantage of this method is the frequency of automatic updates that vendors provide for their customers. The Internet makes this process a cost-effective venture for both the vendors and the customers.

The development of online copyright-protection schemes continues to be a challenging problem. If users need an encryption code to "unlock" software, backups may not be possible. However, the odds are in favor of online software distribution because it provides an inexpensive, convenient, and speedy method of purchase and implementation (Cross, 1994; Hayes, 1995).

Healthcare

Electronic patient records on the Internet could provide complete medical information and allow physicians to order laboratory tests, admit patients to hospitals, refer patients to other physicians or specialists, and order prescriptions. Test and consultation results would be directed automatically to electronic patient records. The advantages of this approach include the fact that all patient information would be accessible from one central location. Another positive side of this application is that it would allow easy access to critical health information. Imagine a person who is far away from home and has a serious health problem because of injury or other causes. Any physician in any location will be able to download the complete medical history of this patient and prescribe a suitable treatment in a short period. However, these systems may offer disadvantages, such as potential problems with information privacy, accuracy, and currency.

Telemedicine (http://telemedtoday.com) may provide the medical profession with the ability to conduct remote consultation, diagnosis, and conferencing. This could result in major annual savings in travel costs and overhead for medical care professionals. As part of the information superhighway, a personal health information system (PHIS) could conceivably provide interactive medical tools to the public. Public kiosks located in shopping malls would be equipped with user-friendly computer equipment for Internet access. Patients would be prompted through the diagnosis procedure by a series of questions. Premature onset of disease could be minimized with this aggressive and proactive approach (Anonymous, 1994).

Virtual medicine on the Internet may allow specialists at major hospitals to operate on patients remotely. Telepresence surgery, as this is called, would allow surgeons to operate all over the world without physically traveling anywhere. A robot would perform the surgery based on the digitized information sent by the specialist via the Internet. Robots would have stereoscopic cameras to create three-dimensional images for the surgeon's virtual reality goggles. Physicians would operate in a virtual operating room. Tactile sensors on the robot would provide position information to the surgeon so that he/she can feel what the robot feels. Already, prescription drugs are sold online and there are several Web sites that offer medical services (Bazzolo, 2000). (For detailed information on this topic, consult the chapter on Security of Medical Records.)

Politics

In the United States in recent years, the Internet has become a major promotional tool for all major political contenders in races for the White House, the House of Representatives and Senate, and other races. Political candidates use the Internet to announce the platforms that they are running on, their major differences with their opponents, their leadership styles, forthcoming debates, political events, and so forth. They even use the Internet for fund-raising.

The Internet may facilitate empowering voters and revitalizing democracy. Twenty-first century citizens may vote using a computer connected to the Internet, resulting in increased participation. Part-time legislators may have remote access to Washington and they may be able to remain geographically close to their constituents. Of course, an identification system would have to be in place, which could very likely use voice identification, face scan, finger image, or some other biometric verification technology. If such a system becomes available, then the security of the voting application, security of voting results, and counting accuracy must be carefully analyzed. Currently, the U.S. House of Representatives is attempting to put all pending legislation online. Presidential documents can be found on the Internet. Full-text versions of speeches, proclamations, executive orders, press briefings, daily schedules, the proposed federal budget, health-care reform documents, and the Economic Report of the President are available. There are a number of repositories of this information that can be found using search engines. (For detailed information on this topic, consult the chapters on Legal, Social, and Ethical Issues of the Internet and Secure Electronic Voting Protocols.)

GLOSSARY

ARPANET (Advanced Research Projects Agency Network) Started in 1969 and continued through 1990 as the basis for early networking research and as a central backbone network during development of the Internet.

Directories An index of information based on key words in a document. Yahoo! is a popular directory on the Internet.

Domain Name Systems (or Domain Name Servers, DNS) Unique identifiers of computer or network addresses on the Internet. Whitehouse.gov and csub.edu are two examples. The first one uniquely identifies the White House and the second identifies California State University in Bakersfield.

Extranet A secure network that uses the Internet and Web technology to connect two or more intranets of trusted business partners, enabling business-to-business, business-to-consumer, consumer-to-consumer, and consumer-to-business communications.

Hypermedia This allows links for combinations of text, images, sounds, and full-motion video in the same document. It allows information retrieval with a click of a button.

Hypertext This provides users with nonsequential paths to access information whereby information does not have to be accessed sequentially, as in a book.

Internet A collection of millions of computers and networks of all sizes. Simply put, the Internet is the "network of networks."

Intranet A network within the organization that uses Web technologies (TCP/IP, HTTP, FTP, SMTP, HTML, XML, and its variations) for collecting, storing, and disseminating useful information throughout the organization.

Navigational Tools These allow the user to surf the Internet; Microsoft Internet Explorer and Netscape Navigator are two prime examples.

Search Engines These provide access to various resources available on the Internet, such as library searches for writing a term paper or resources for making a reservation for an airline ticket. Google.com is an example.

URL (Uniform/Universal Resource Locator) The address of a file or a site on the Internet used to identify a particular Web page.

CROSS REFERENCES

See *Digital Economy; Electronic Commerce; Extranets: Applications, Development, Security and Privacy; Intranets: Principals, Privacy and Security Considerations*.

REFERENCES

Anonymous (1994, August). Heath care on the information superhighway poses advantages and challenges. *Employee Benefit Review*, 24–29.

Bazzolo, F. (2000, May). Putting patient at the center. *Internet Health Care Magazine*, 42–51.

Bidgoli, H. (1999, Summer). An integrated model for introducing intranets. *Information Systems Management*, *16*(3), 78–87.

Bidgoli, H. (2002). *Electronic commerce: Principles and practice*. San Diego: Academic Press.

Cross, R. (1994, October). Internet: The missing marketing medium found. *Direct Marketing*, 20–23.

Fletcher, T. (1997, September 29). Intranet pays dividends in time and efficiency for investment giant. *InfoWorld*, 84.

Hayes, M. (1995, January 2). Online shopping for software. *Information Week*, 23–24.

Jones, K. (1998, February 8). Copier strategy as yet unduplicated. *Inter@ctive Week*, *5*(5), 41.

Maloff, J. (1997, August). Extranets: Stretching the Net to boost efficiency. *NetGuide*, 62.

FURTHER READING

Bayles Kalman, D. (2003a). Intranets. In H. Bidgoli (Ed.), *Encyclopedia of Information Systems:* (Vol. 2, pp. 683–692). San Diego: Academic Press.

Bayles Kalman, D. (2003b). Extranets. In H. Bidgoli (Ed.), *Encyclopedia of Information Systems:* (Vol. 2, pp. 301–312). San Diego: Academic Press.

Bidgoli, H. (2000). *Handbook of business data communications: A managerial perspective*. San Diego: Academic Press.

Bidgoli, H. (2003). Electronic commerce. In H. Bidgoli (Ed.), *Encyclopedia of Information Systems: Volume II* (pp. 15–28). San Diego: Academic Press.

Sullivan, D. (2001, December 18). *Search engine sizes*. Retrieved March 19, 2005, from http://searchenginewatch.com/reports/sizes.html

Sullivan, D. (2002, April 29). *Jupiter Media Metrix search engine ratings*. Retrieved March 19, 2005, from http://searchenginewatch.com/reports/mediametrix.html

Underdahl, B., & Underdahl, K. (2000, May). *Internet bible* (2nd ed.). Hoboken, NJ: Wiley

Digital Economy

Nirvikar Singh, *University of California, Santa Cruz*

INTRODUCTION

> "IT and the Internet amplify brain power in the same way that the technologies of the industrial revolution amplified muscle power."
>
> —Bradford DeLong, Professor of Economics, University of California, Berkeley, quoted in Woodall (2000)

The purpose of this chapter is to explain what the "digital economy" is and how it fits into broader economic trends that are shaping the economies of the United States and other countries. Essentially, the term "digital economy" can refer to the use of digital information technology in various forms of economic activity and its effects on economic activity. As such, the term includes more specific activities, such as e-commerce and e-business, and is closely related to terms such as knowledge economy and information economy.

All groups in the economy are affected by the pervasive use of information technology: this includes consumers, business firms, and governments. Activities that are not directly commercial, such as personal communications, are also affected. The fundamental driving force is the falling costs of processing, storing, and transmitting data or information that has been put in digital electronic form as a result of innovations in these areas. These declines in costs have made further innovations possible that permit easy and widespread communications via extensive networks, the existence of large and rich databases of information and knowledge that are freely or easily accessible, and the ability to conduct most or all stages of economic transactions over long distances, without relying on alternative methods of information exchange. These new applications have, at the same time, spurred innovation in the core technologies of storage, processing, and transmission, creating a "positive feedback loop."

The additional results of these expanded capabilities for accessing, using, and sharing information in digital form include new and more efficient ways of organizing markets; new and more efficient methods for businesses to communicate and transact with each other and with consumers, employees, and job seekers; dramatically lower costs for individuals in locating or gathering information of all kinds, including market and product-related information; changes in the organization of business firms and in their strategic behavior; and changes in the overall societal organization of work, leisure, and general communities of shared interest.

The chapter is organized as follows. In the section titled Information Technology, the Digital Economy, and E-Commerce, we discuss the definitions of the basic terms, including those we have used in this introduction. Size and Growth of the Digital Economy provides some data on the size and growth of the digital economy and e-commerce and discusses the measured effects of information technology on the economy as a whole, as well as some of the problems of measurement. Implications for Markets and Organizations describes changes in the nature, structure, and performance of firms and markets as digital technologies help make information more ubiquitous and as information increases in importance as an economic good. Security examines several aspects of security and how they interact with or affect the other developments in the digital economy. Government Policies examines several aspects of government policy with respect to the digital economy, including intellectual property law, privacy, antitrust and other regulation, and international trade. Work, Play, and Communities briefly discusses broader implications of the information revolution, examining how it changes the ways in which individuals work, play, and interact within organizations and communities.

INFORMATION TECHNOLOGY, THE DIGITAL ECONOMY, AND E-COMMERCE

Although there is no absolute agreement on what the digital economy is, this section provides a working definition, discusses how the term is related to e-commerce and e-business, and discusses the measurement of the digital economy and the effects on overall economic activity.

Defining the Digital Economy

A computer is essentially a machine for storing and processing data. Although one might count the abacus or mechanical, gear-based calculating machines as computers, the term typically refers to electronic machines that use on/off electrical signals to convey and process data. The two states, "on" and "off," based on whether an electric current is flowing or not, represent the digits 1 and 0. These are "binary digits" or "bits." Ultimately, all data that are input to a computer, and are processed by it, are translated into bits. "Information" refers to data organized in meaningful ways, although "information" is often used to subsume "data" and we follow this practice here. Information technology (IT) therefore refers to anything connected to the storage, processing, and transmission of information converted to digital form. The use of IT for purposes related to economic transactions gives us the term "digital economy." Here is one possible definition:

> The digital economy involves conducting or facilitating economic activities electronically, based on the electronic processing, storage, and communication of information, including activities that provide the enabling physical infrastructure and software.

Dramatic and rapid reductions in the costs of processing information, storing it, and transmitting it to others (see Table 1) have made the uses and benefits of IT potentially span the whole economy, spurring further innovation in core technologies and leading to an "information revolution." On the basis of these falling costs, innovations such as personal computers, color graphics, point-and-click interfaces, and other developments have made IT much easier to use. The Internet and the World Wide Web are the latest elements of the progress of IT over the past half-century, adding easy two-way communication of rich information (text, graphics, audio, video, etc.). The changes that the increased importance of IT brings about in people's daily lives are captured in the term "new economy." The term suggests that IT and the Internet shift the focus of economic activity to information and away from traditional activities such as manufacturing, although it must be recognized that the manufacturing industry has used IT to improve efficiency in various aspects of operations, such as scheduling, quality control, and assembly. Similar terms are possibly more descriptive: knowledge economy, information economy, and digital economy. The last of these, as noted, emphasizes the fundamental technology that drives everything: the conversion of information to digital form.

Table 1 Falling Costs of Computing (US $)

Costs of Computing	1970	1999	2004
1 MHz of processing power	7,600	0.17	<0.02
1 megabyte of storage	5,260	0.17	<0.01
1 trillion bits transmitted	150,000	0.12	<0.01

Note: For processing and storage, these are hardware and basic software costs and do not include ongoing costs of use and management of the hardware and software. For transmission, these are average costs based on full capacity use.
Source: 1970 and 1999, Woodall (2000), p. 6, Chart 1 (see also http://www.dallasfed.org/fed/annual/1999p/ar99.pdf, Exhibit 3); 2004, author's estimates from various sources and calculations, viz. processing power from Moore's Law and trends in prices of Intel chips, storage based on cost of desktop hard drives, and transmission from current costs of basic data transfer.

The terms "information economy" and "knowledge economy" focus on what is being digitized. Information and knowledge are related, but distinct concepts, even though the distinction is sometimes fuzzy (we postpone a discussion of information and knowledge as economic goods to the section Implications for Markets and Organizations). Information in this context is more general and basic, as it denotes anything that can be put into concrete form before digitization. For example, a popular song is information, from an IT perspective. The sounds can be reduced to a digital file that can be stored, transmitted, and processed by various kinds of computers. If a person internalizes information about the song (its title, tune, lyrics, etc.), then that constitutes knowledge, just as the ability to write computer programs that allow users all over the world to share songs (as digital files) is knowledge. To push these examples further, a particular song-sharing software program is also information. In this case, knowledge helps to produce and transmit information. People can also gather information, process it in some way, and gain knowledge, as when they study how to program in a particular computer language. Some of the same distinction comes up in the differences between copyright and patent law, which protect different kinds of intellectual property rights (see Government Policies): copyright law protects particular expressions of ideas, or information, whereas patent law protects inventions, or the ideas themselves, if they are useful knowledge. In all these cases, digitization (through the use of IT generally, and the Internet in particular) amplifies the benefits of knowledge and makes the spread of information easier.

E-Commerce

E-commerce (or electronic commerce) is a popular term that emphasizes the use of the Internet and associated aspects of IT for business purposes. While businesses previously adopted IT for many internal and back-end activities (see the next section), the Internet and World Wide Web have allowed business-to-consumer (B2C) commercial interactions to be more closely and comprehensively mediated by IT. Examples of e-commerce include buying retail items using a Web interface and paying for them by providing credit card information online; downloading a media player or other software (for a trial, free use, or through a purchase) via the Internet; checking the news, weather, and movie reviews on a portal, possibly "paying" for these services by giving attention to online advertisements; going to an auction Web site and bidding on collectibles or other items; and paying a monthly subscription for Internet access to chat online with friends or others one meets in cyberspace.

More formal definitions of e-commerce encompass all these examples and include commercial transactions among all kinds of organizations, not just B2C interactions. Here are two general definitions:

> Electronic commerce refers generally to all forms of transactions relating to commercial activities, including both organizations and individuals, that are based upon the processing and transmission of digitized data, including text, sound and visual images. (OECD, 1997)
>
> In ever greater numbers, people are shopping, looking for jobs, and researching medical problems online. Businesses are moving their supply networks online, participating in and developing online marketplaces, and expanding their use of networked systems to improve a host of business processes. And new products and services are being created and integrated into the networked world. (U.S. Department of Commerce, 2000, p. 7)

The scope of what constitutes commercial transactions is quite broad in these definitions. Information gathering or exchange that does not directly involve a direct monetary payment may still have an economic motivation. Even leisure-related activities typically require some measured economic activity. In the example of using the Internet for chatting, one pays for access to the infrastructure that enables the leisure activity. Activities that involve the government (e.g., filing one's individual tax return electronically over the Internet) are not commercial in the narrow sense but are clearly related to economic activity that is measured in the national accounts statistics.

Of course, not all IT-based activities qualify as e-commerce in the sense of involving the Internet. For example, many home activities involving personal computers (PCs) do not involve Internet use at all: record keeping, children's homework, creating (paper) greeting cards, typing holiday newsletters, and so on. Similarly, small retail stores may have computerized inventory systems that have no links to any other computer. However, this gap between computer use and Internet use is shrinking, and for many individuals and businesses, using computers or IT automatically means using the Internet.

E-Business

The encompassing definition of e-commerce presented earlier includes a broad range of online transactions and interactions that are connected to some economic motive. Therefore, this is broader than the term "e-business," defined here as the use of IT, including networked computing, by business firms. For example, if individuals transact directly online, so that no business firm is directly involved, then that would qualify as e-commerce but not e-business. Similarly, we include government/individual transactions in e-commerce but not in e-business.

E-business (and therefore e-commerce) includes not just transactions across firms but also activities that take place within the boundaries of a business but that do not cross them. Internal accounting, inventory control, and other forms of business record keeping and tracking have been electronically based in industrial countries for more than a decade, especially in larger businesses. These purely internal records and transactions, when handled electronically, are often to what e-business is taken to refer. The use of IT provides cost advantages over traditional means (i.e., paper) in terms of storage, manipulation, and retrieval of large amounts of information, provided that the scale of use is large enough to spread the substantial fixed costs initially associated with IT investments. In fact, until computers became affordable as household items as a result of falling costs and associated innovations, large organizations were the only purchasers of IT products and services.

In fact, the digital economy, in the form of business-to-business (B2B) transactions based on older electronic communication methods (electronic data interchange or EDI, using proprietary software and dedicated communication links), substantially predates the Internet and the World Wide Web. Electronic links between financial firms and between large retailers and their suppliers were two prominent examples of this form of e-business, or B2B e-commerce. The Internet and World Wide Web have extended the economic feasibility of such links to a much wider range of businesses through their use of shared networks and nonproprietary communication software and the resulting reduction in the costs of information exchange. Advances in ease of use and speed of transmission have also contributed to this trend by further increasing accessibility and flexibility. Another potential effect of these developments, which supports the use of broader definitions of terms such as e-commerce and e-business, is the blurring of the boundaries of the firm, as information flows more freely across firms as well as within them.

SIZE AND GROWTH OF THE DIGITAL ECONOMY

The size and growth of the digital economy can be gauged in several ways. Basic measures of numbers of Internet users, Web sites, and so forth are popular. Clearly, these do not directly measure the economic activity that takes place online, though the provision of Internet access is itself an economic activity. More direct and better measures are data on transactions that take place online, as well as the share of IT-related activities in the overall economy. This section examines in turn these different approaches to measuring the digital economy and its effects. None of the measures is perfect, which reflects the newness of the digital economy as a challenge for economic statisticians.

Internet Use

Three kinds of statistics that are often used to gauge the growth of the digital economy are the number of people with Internet access, the number of unique Web pages, and the number of Web sites, with the latter two being conceptually very close. The U.S. Department of Commerce, using data from the U.S. Census Bureau, reported that 143 million Americans, or 54 percent of the population were using the Internet in September 2001, up from 117 million thirteen months earlier (U.S. Department of Commerce, 2002. Nielsen NetRatings, 2001, estimated a higher number of Americans, 168 million, online in January, 2001). Furthermore, a broader cross section of Americans is using the Internet, reducing earlier fears of a "digital divide" between those with access to these new communication tools and those without (especially the poor). In fact, the growth in Internet use during the period 2000–2001 was fastest among Americans with household income less than $15,000 a year (U.S. Department of Commerce, 2002). By February 2004, according to another survey, 204 million Americans had Internet access from home, representing close to 75% of the population (Nielsen Net Ratings, 2004). Another important trend that has emerged recently in the United States is the acceleration in the proportion of Internet-connected households with broadband access, crossing 45% in February 2004 (Websiteoptimization, 2004, March).

The Internet is also increasingly global, with the worldwide number of users estimated at 729 million (Global Reach, 2004), of whom more than half used a language other than English. With the exception of the United States and a few European and Asian countries, the numbers of Internet users are still low relative to population sizes, which reflects generally lower levels of income in much of the world, but as costs continue to fall, even poor villagers in Asia, Africa, and Latin America are beginning to use the World Wide Web to get weather and crop price information or to check on village land-ownership records from government Web sites. This represents another aspect of overcoming the initial digital divide introduced by the Internet. Table 2 gives a sampling of Internet use by language, from Global Reach. In most cases, there is a close correspondence between countries and languages, with English, Arabic, Spanish, and Chinese being more dispersed.

Table 2 Global Internet Use, 2004

Language	Internet Users (millions)	Total Population (millions)
English	287.5	508
European languages (excluding English)	276.0	1,218
Arabic	10.5	300
Chinese	102.6	874
Japanese	69.7	125
Korean	29.9	78

Source: Global Reach (n.d.).

Rough measures of the Internet resources available to the growing number of users are given by counts of the number of Web pages and Web sites. The number of unique World Wide Web pages was reported to be more than 1 billion by January 2000, up from just 100 million in October 1997 (Inktomi, 2000; NUA, 1997). The number of Web sites in August 2004 was more than 53 million, well up from the 43 million estimated a year earlier and a different order of magnitude altogether from the 19,000 sites estimated in August 1995 (Netcraft, 2004a and 2004b). Of course, neither measure indicates how much time people actually spend online or how that time affects economic activity. In particular, they do not tell us how much money people spend directly or indirectly as a result of their Internet use. For that, one would use the approach of national income and product accounting, which estimates value added in market transactions. There are problems with this way of measuring economic activity, such as the failure to account for the value of time used in nonmarket transactions or in activities that affect market transactions,[1] but official methods of calculating economic activity are the best we have. In particular, they are designed to capture market-based economic activity relatively well and to avoid problems such as double counting, which occurs if the gross values of transactions at various stages of the value chain are added up.

Types and Measures of Online Transactions

The problem of double counting is avoided when one looks at final sales to consumers. B2C e-commerce seemed to hold out great potential in 1999 and the early part of 2000, resulting in a rather frenzied burst of entrepreneurial activity backed by eager venture capitalists. This fever has cooled, but the growth remains. The U.S. Bureau of the Census estimated electronic retail (e-tail) sales in 2001 to be $34.3 billion, $44.3 billion in 2002, and $56.0 billion in 2003. However, even after this impressive growth, online sales remained just under 2 percent of all U.S. retail sales.[2] In Europe, figures for online retail sales are less standardized, but one estimate for 2002 put them at about $30 billion, or comparable to the U.S. figures in magnitude.[3] A more recent survey by VISA estimated

[1] For example, time spent in gathering information that affects purchase decisions is not valued in national accounts. Shifts in this activity from traditional, physical methods (such as browsing print media, telephoning, and driving around to stores) to online search will not show up in the data, except as changes in business spending (from magazine ads to Web ads), or even *reductions* in economic activity (less spending on magazines by consumers).

[2] These statistics are reported at http://www.census.gov/mrts/www/data/html/04Q4.html (U.S. Census Bureau, 2004), which also gives historical data, calculation methods, and charts. Other surveys give somewhat higher figures. For example, AOL reported that its members alone spent $33 billion online in 2001 (CNET, 2002). However, this may include travel spending, which, if excluded reduces estimates considerably. The figures reported in the text exclude travel spending, which would add another 50% to those figures if included. See comScore, 2002.

[3] The estimate is from Forrester Research, as reported in the International Herald Tribune (2002). Gartner, another IT research firm, estimated somewhat higher numbers (GartnerG2, 2002), but they seem too high compared with U.S. figures, given somewhat lower Internet penetration in Europe. Higher numbers for Europe may include travel and financial services transactions. See OECD (2002a) for a discussion and detailed comparisons.

that e-tailing took off in the beginning of 2004 in several European countries, doubling in the first quarter as compared to a year earlier (European Online Sales up Across the Continent, 2004). Statistics for online retail sales in Asia are still less reliable, but one can estimate them to be about one quarter to one third of European figures, based on various Internet sources.

B2B transactions may involve products that are indistinguishable from consumer products (computers and office supplies, for example). The only difference is that they are sold to businesses rather than to households or consumers. However, a large segment of B2B transactions involve raw materials and intermediate products, as well as services that are specific to businesses (for example, accounting, human resource management, and, increasingly, IT services). Although estimates of B2B e-commerce vary widely, it is widely agreed that the numbers are much more substantial than for B2C e-commerce. The reasons have to do chiefly with the historical scale of IT, compounded by the cost-saving incentives of businesses in competitive markets. As noted in the previous discussion of e-business, Internet-based e-commerce represents the effect of cost reductions in expanding the size of the communications network, and hence the market, from just large firms to including small firms as well as households.

There is a conceptual problem with most estimates of B2B e-commerce, which simply add up revenues from a variety of firms. Because B2B transactions involve intermediate products and services, aggregating revenues across businesses will involve double counting, because revenues for intermediate products sold to other businesses are a cost for those businesses. Still, one can use the numbers, and changes in them, to get some idea of the importance of B2B e-commerce. Although the U.S. Census Bureau does not yet estimate B2B e-commerce, private forecasters do. Estimates for 2001 varied widely,[4] ranging in a sample of forecasters (based on a combination of surveys and guesswork) from US$ 474 billion to US$ 1,138 billion for worldwide B2B e-commerce, with 70–80% of this being in the United States (estimates are from surveys; eMarketer, 2002). The numbers vary greatly across sources, but they are all of similar orders of magnitude, and all project substantial growth. One can safely conclude that B2B e-commerce substantially exceeds B2C in size, and it may be growing somewhat faster on average. Finally, the cost advantages of using the Internet,[5] plus the benefits of being part of a larger network, are expected to cause a relative shift to the Internet from EDI. Small businesses, in particular, can use Internet-based e-commerce where EDI would not be economical for them. Furthermore, electronic marketplaces are potentially economically viable using the Internet, but not with traditional EDI, because the Internet permits more flexible and less costly access.

One final category of e-commerce is consumer-to-consumer (C2C). Although firms such as eBay—which is the dominant C2C marketplace, with more than 60% of market share (Rudl, 2003)—have entered the popular imagination through their electronic auctions for collectible or unique items, the value of C2C transactions is relatively small. However, eBay now handles B2C and B2B transactions as well. In 2003, eBay's net sales, from transaction fees on $15 billion in gross revenues, reached $1.2 billion (Hof, 2003). Again, one should caution that the total value of a transaction does not represent the economic value added of an activity. If a used item is bought and sold through a dealer, the dealer's profit is a better measure of the value created in the overall transaction, and this is what is measured in the national accounts. Thus eBay's own revenues, adjusted appropriately for its market share, may be a better indicator of the importance of C2C e-commerce than the value of goods transacted through eBay. A complication for this approach is the increasing use of eBay for B2C sales. Of course, a used item sold privately (say, in a flea market) will not show up at all in that official accounting.

Information Technology and GDP

E-commerce, measured as actual transactions conducted online, represents only a small fraction of the U.S. gross domestic product (GDP), which was 10.9 trillion dollars in 2003. However, overall spending on IT may be a better measure of the significance of the digital economy, because the use of IT has become pervasive in businesses of all kinds and sizes. A useful discussion and justification for this view is OECD (2002a). This includes the use of computers for managing transactions, inventory, and logistics, even without use of the Internet. At the same time, the boundaries between general IT use and e-commerce are increasingly blurred. Networks exist within corporate walls and simultaneously are part of the larger network of the Internet. Telecommunications infrastructure that carries telephone conversations is also used for World Wide Web data. Total IT spending in the United States (without any double counting) now makes up about 7% of GDP, or more than 700 billion dollars.[6] This includes hardware, software, services, and telecommunications spending. This means that there is still a substantial part of economic activity that is not directly related to information technology. However, it is a reasonable forecast that the 7% figure will increase over the next few decades. A slightly different measure, the percentage of ICT value added in business sector value added, yielded an average of close to 10% for 25 OECD countries in 2000, with the United States being somewhat above this average, and extremes ranged from more than 15% for Ireland and Finland to about 5% for Greece and Mexico.

---

[4] One area where differences in estimates can arise is with respect to EDI, which uses private networks and proprietary software, and has been restricted to larger firms. For example, the Boston Consulting Group estimated U.S. EDI for 1998 at $571 billion, dwarfing its estimate of Internet-based B2B e-commerce of $92 billion. At the same time, they projected EDI to grow only slowly, to $780 billion in 2003, while projecting US Internet-based B2B e-commerce to be $2 trillion in 2003.

[5] For example, retailer Sears Roebuck, one of the pioneers of EDI, has an EDI system that costs it about $150 per hour. Internet-based exchange with its suppliers could reduce this figure to as little as $1 an hour. See Guy (2000).

[6] See Jorgenson (2001) for detailed estimates. Figures from IT market research groups such as International Data Corporation (IDC) are a little higher.

(The "C" refers to "communication," which has become increasingly digitized, and is counted with IT in many statistical and conceptual exercises. The data are from OECD, 2002b.)

One factor working *against* an increase in IT as a proportion of GDP is the fall in the costs of IT. The empirical regularity observed by Intel cofounder Gordon Moore, and enshrined as "Moore's Law," says that the number of transistors per microprocessor doubles every 18 months. This ability to pack more and more circuitry on tiny wafers of silicon keeps reducing the cost of processing power. Similar factors are at work in storage and communication of information, resulting in enormous reductions in the overall cost of computing (recall Table 1). To the extent that only expenditures are measured when economic activity is calculated, some of the impact of the digital economy is being missed. For a simple example, a $2,000 home computer is many times faster than a $2,000 home computer available five years ago; it has much more storage capacity and it can communicate much faster with other computers than was possible half a decade earlier. Even neglecting adjustments for inflation (which would mean that the $2,000 computer now is cheaper in real terms), the same amount of money spent now allows one to work more quickly and effectively or to enjoy one's leisure more. Thus, the same spending on information technology today gives much more "bang for the buck" than five years ago.

The changes in computing go beyond having more capacity or saving time and encompass activities that were impossible in the past: online games, music listening and sharing, interactive distance learning, and so on. Again, these increased capabilities are not fully accounted for in the standard accounting of economic activity. Of course, these measurement problems have always existed. Innovation that introduces new products or improves the quality of old products has always been difficult to account for. One might argue, however, that IT has accelerated innovation and magnified the problem of underestimating the benefits of certain economic activities (Brynjolfsson & Hitt, 2000).

The problem of accounting for improvements in quality and variety goes beyond the IT sector. If IT can be used to more effectively design new products or improve the design of existing products, then its value will be greater than is simply reflected in spending on IT itself. In other words, better, cheaper, more versatile computers make it possible to have better, cheaper, more varied cars, houses, toys, and so on. This is partly what Brad DeLong (see Introduction) means when he says that IT amplifies brainpower. For example, in crash testing new cars, actually crashing a car could cost approximately $60,000 each time. This is how it used to be done, with the results analyzed partly by computer. Simulating the entire crash on a computer can now instead be done for close to $100 (Woodall, 2000, p. 5).

Despite these seemingly obvious benefits of IT, one paradox that proponents of the new economy have faced has been the lack of hard evidence for these benefits in the overall GDP data, which measure economic activity. Initially, increased investment in IT did not appear to be improving productivity in any measurable way. The conclusion of skeptics was that much of this IT spending had no real effect. We turn to this issue next.

Information Technology, Growth, and Productivity

Much of the attention to productivity growth has been with respect to the United States, which has spent the most on IT and which had a prolonged slowdown in productivity growth in the 1970s and 1980s. Early investments in IT seemed to have no countervailing effect to reverse or mitigate this slowdown. Analysis of the introduction of electric power a hundred years ago (David, 2000) suggests that the benefits of innovation can take decades to appear in quantifiable form. This seems to fit with what happened in the last five years of the twentieth century, when U.S. productivity growth did increase substantially, just as the penetration of PCs into homes approached 50% and as the Internet took off.

Some work on the recent U.S. experience (Gordon, 2000) suggests that the increase in productivity growth is confined to a small segment of the economy (computers and durable goods). Furthermore, the productivity boost may have been entirely the result of the prolonged economic expansion in the United States (productivity rises during economic booms). This skeptical view is supported by studies that find productivity gains have been low in sectors where IT investments have been high. For example, measured productivity in banking and education actually fell from 1987 to 1997, even though these were the sectors with the highest spending on IT as a proportion of output. Possible explanations for the failure of IT investments to show up as improved productivity include, on the benefit side, the inability to account for time savings, increased outputs of public knowledge, availability of greater variety, and general improvements in the quality of products and services. Thus, some of the most important benefits of the digital economy could also be the ones that slip through the cracks in measuring economic activity. Alternatively, the benefits may simply not be there, rather than being unmeasured. Explanations include lags in learning how to get the most from new technologies, the need for complementary investments required to boost output, and the presence of network effects, which limit gains unless there are many adopters. Baily (2004) and Gordon (2004) provide detailed reviews of these and other cautionary arguments with respect to the impact of IT on productivity growth.

Despite the caveats, two recent, comprehensive analyses, by Jorgenson (2001) and Stiroh (2002), suggest that IT has been an important contributor to productivity growth in the 1990s. (See also Oliner & Sichel, 2002.) Jorgenson directly traces this effect to the rapid fall in the prices of semiconductors and of IT products in general, especially after 1994. For 1995–1999, Jorgenson estimates that two thirds of the United States' productivity gains were the result of IT use. Stiroh goes even further, with a detailed, industry-level analysis of the United States. He finds that the U.S. productivity revival was indeed broad-based, that much of it took place in IT-producing industries, and that industries that are IT-use-intensive also had higher productivity gains. Thus Stiroh's work appears to tilt the scales in favor of a positive assessment of the effects of the digital economy, at least for the United States. Work by Triplett and Bosworth (2003) provides additional positive evidence, estimating that IT investments have been significant in contributing to productivity growth in the service sector.

Studies for other countries are also beginning to find significant impacts of IT on productivity growth. Daveri (2000) reaches positive conclusions with respect to the impact of IT on overall economic growth. His exercise includes 18 OECD countries, and his results for the United States are broadly similar to those of Jorgenson and Stiroh. For Canada, Japan, Australia, New Zealand, and 13 European countries, he obtains varied results, with Canada, Australia, New Zealand, the Netherlands, and the United Kingdom having relatively high contributions of ICTs to growth, with Italy and Spain at the other extreme. Daveri also argues why his results are more positive than those of another cross-country study (Colecchia & Schreyer, 2002), which uses a narrower definition of IT. These studies use data for 1991–1997, and therefore miss the end of the 1990s, when significant growth in IT, as well as overall growth, took place. Jorgenson (2004) examines data for the G7 countries (Canada, France, Germany, Italy, Japan, the United Kingdom, and the United States) for 1980–2001. He documents the importance of IT capital spending for the overall contribution of capital investment to growth, as well as the effect of IT production on overall productivity growth. The results across the G7 are not too dissimilar, indicating that the United States has not been an outlier in this respect.

IMPLICATIONS FOR MARKETS AND ORGANIZATIONS

This section discusses how the use of IT and the Internet affect the structure and outcomes of markets and the organization and strategies of firms, all from a microeconomic perspective. The consequences of the special nature of information as an economic product are also highlighted.

Information and Markets

The most basic way that the information revolution changes the economics of the marketplace is in making information about all kinds of products and services more widely available. Although basic models of the market system often take it for granted that information about products and about buyers and sellers is abundant, in practice, this is not the case. In fact, one of the virtues of the competitive market system is its ability to economize on the use of information. Textbook-style competitive markets cannot overcome some kinds of lack of information: for example, the quality of a product may be observable to sellers who provide it, but not to buyers. In practice, many kinds of institutions arise to overcome informational problems: brand names, warranties, consumer protection laws, and so on. Business firms and other organizations may themselves be viewed partly as a response to information problems that prevent the use of markets for all transactions (Coase, 1937), with such transactions being internalized within firms. With firms as major actors, the market economy can be viewed as a scene of constantly shifting attempts to create advantages over competitors by finding opportunities for greater efficiency or satisfying wants more effectively.

In this situation, the availability of greater information about products and services may upset existing institutions by changing the relative costs and benefits of current ways of doing things. How firms organize their own internal operations and transactions can change, and how they interact with consumers can also change. New kinds of firms may arise simply to manage the new possibilities for market interaction. For example, firms may specialize in providing price or quality comparisons to consumers, in ways that were not cost-effective before. Firms may find it easier to outsource manufacturing, because they can maintain closer links with suppliers through regular electronic information exchange. Other firms may provide combinations of services that were impossible or unlikely in the past, combining traditional media content (news, entertainment, and product information) with individual services such as auctions and communications.

From the perspective of consumers, or buyers more generally, the Internet lowers search costs by providing large amounts of product-related information anytime and anywhere. In addition to information from sellers, buyers can also more easily access information from intermediaries that rank products or make price comparisons or from other buyers. In consumer markets, this ability to gather information from dispersed buyers represents a major extension of word-of-mouth methods of information sharing.

Preliminary work on the functioning of markets online suggests that there are measurable effects of the greater availability of information. A survey by Smith, Bailey, & Brynjolfsson (2000) examines the evidence on four dimensions of price competition in B2C online markets, as compared to traditional transactions mediated through physical stores:

1. Price Levels: Are posted prices lower online?
2. Price Dispersion: Are prices of online sellers less spread out?
3. Price Adjustment: Do sellers adjust posted prices more finely or frequently online?
4. Price Sensitivity: Are buyers more responsive to price changes online?

Overall, the results of various empirical studies indicate that prices are lower online, there is less price dispersion, and prices are adjusted more often and in smaller increments. All of these conclusions are consistent with the general hypothesis that online markets are more competitive. The results on price sensitivity are mixed and may be related to factors that cannot be controlled for, such as differences in the characteristics of online consumers. The lack of evidence for perfect competition (persistence in price dispersion, for example) can be explained by the continued importance of factors such as trust and reputation, switching costs associated with search that is still costly (though less so), investments by consumers in seller-specific information, loyalty programs, and price discrimination—possibly supported by customization of offerings (e.g., with "dynamic packaging" of vacation packages at online travel sites) where resale or consumer-to-consumer information exchange is not effective.

These studies examined only posted price markets, in the context of a small number of products such as books and compact discs (CDs). Possible efficiency gains exist through the better matching of buyers and sellers in markets that otherwise relied on more costly methods of intermediation. In addition to online auctions of collectibles and other used items, job markets, personal-relationship matching markets, and many fragmented B2B markets appear to have taken off precisely because the Internet and Web allow buyers and sellers to match more efficiently, which creates higher-value matches as well as lower costs associated with agreeing on a price and completing a transaction. Three important consumer markets where the Internet also appears to have had an impact are those for automobiles, housing, and financial services. All these markets have been characterized by high search costs and the presence of intermediaries with significant market power (car dealers, real estate agents, stock brokers, insurance agents, and so forth). The use of the Internet for basic information search and price comparisons appears to be providing some degree of increased competition in all these cases. In some cases, particularly digital products such as financial assets, the entire transaction can be completed online. In others, the Internet provides a vehicle for a significant proportion of the information exchange that accompanies a transaction.

The Internet also expands markets across national boundaries and affects international trade through its ability to increase the quantity and richness of the information that is available. As in complex transactions within national boundaries, the kind of information that the Internet can provide does not remove the potential need for traditional face-to-face interactions, particularly when a relationship is being formed. However, it reduces the cost of much of the search process, in terms of where a potential buyer might want to invest more time and money in gathering the information necessary to decide whether to transact. Furthermore, once a relationship is established, the ongoing costs of routine information exchange and even transactions are reduced. In such cases, the products that are traded may well be traditional physical products: e-commerce does not involve transforming the products, but rather changing the nature of the search and transaction processes. Even in this case, the savings in terms of transaction costs may be substantial enough to significantly boost international trade. For small consumer items such as handicrafts, the Internet and Web provide a cost-effective way for even rural artisans in developing countries to advertise globally.

Information as an Economic Product

A basic effect of the information revolution is on information itself as an economic good. The best-known example of the magnitude of this impact is what happened to the *Encyclopedia Britannica*. The *Britannica* was the premier encyclopedia, with thousands of pages of articles by renowned experts. It sold for thousands of dollars, priced to recover the cost of a well-paid direct sales force as well as the high printing cost for its two dozen volumes. This business was destroyed by the ability to put a reasonably large amount of information on a single CD-ROM, sold for under a hundred dollars, or even bundled in "free" with a home computer system. CD-ROM encyclopedias were inferior in academic quality but were "good enough" for most people, and the price was right.

The ability to store, process (including copying), and transmit large quantities of digital information at lower and lower costs is now the central characteristic of information as an economic product. A world where the marginal costs of providing information approach zero is a world where businesses that deal in information have to find new ways to provide value to consumers, ways for which they can actually charge enough to recover the costs of producing the information in the first place. To do this, information may have to be bundled, personalized, or managed within a service that creates a long-term relationship with the buyer. To the extent that other products and services have also been bundled with information in the marketplace, and that this bundling changes, firms have to create new bundles of value. For example, online retailers try to provide their customers with suggestions and ideas, based on tracking the buying and browsing patterns of individual customers and those with similar interests. This is not dissimilar to the old personalized service in the local store but can be done at a scale that was earlier impossible. Bundling may also take place without personalization, the combination of hardware and software being the most obvious example.

The ability to process large quantities of information in increasingly sophisticated ways is at the heart of the information revolution, extending not only to the ability to make suggestions about existing products, but also to design products in collaboration with individual customers, and to do it at a large scale. Flexible mass customization, referring to the ability to quickly satisfy the diverse wants of large numbers of individual consumers, is one of the possible pillars of business strategy in the digital economy (see the next section). In all these cases, businesses also have to be able to capture the value that they create, which may require strategies including a combination of technology (e.g., software to control copying), law (e.g., enforcement of copyrights—see the next section), and economics (e.g., pricing).

In addition to the low marginal cost of providing information, there are several additional aspects of information or knowledge as an economic product that affect the working of markets and organizations. In particular, information is a shareable or nonrival good in consumption, where the terms refer to the ability of more than one person to consume the same thing. Low-cost copying, storage, and transmission enable this shareability to be implemented in new ways, such as peer-to-peer music-file swapping, which bypasses traditional commercial distribution channels. In many cases, the use value of the information is unaffected by its being shared, or it may even be increased. For example, news and entertainment can be conveyed to large numbers of people simultaneously or sequentially, and no single person's enjoyment of a TV program is diminished as a result and may even be higher if the program can subsequently be discussed with friends (a positive externality). In other cases, the value of information may be reduced if others have access to it (a negative externality). Information that affects the value of financial assets is a good example, where insider knowledge bestows an advantage in the marketplace. A seller's knowledge of a buyer's circumstances (or vice versa) is another example, in which one party may be better off without the other side knowing their valuation. In the examples of the previous subsection, where the effect of better information about the products and market opportunities was discussed, the market-related information could involve either type of externality. In cases where information is the final consumption good itself, such as entertainment, status considerations might create negative externalities, but the positive externality case seems more common.

The shareable nature of information and knowledge also raises concerns for the legal definition and enforcement of property rights, which are crucial for all market economies. In the digital economy, knowledge is increasingly important as a driver of economic activity and growth. To play this role, it must be part of the system of economic incentives. Knowledge or information is legally characterized as intellectual property (IP), but this is fundamentally different from physical property and requires its own system of legal definitions and rights. Thus, IT and the Internet amplify not only brainpower but also the importance of the legal system that governs the economic rewards to brainpower. Furthermore, technological advances that make copying and sharing of information of all kinds incredibly quick and inexpensive are having a major impact on legal issues relating to intellectual property, as in the case of music-file swapping. We give a flavor of the issues here.

Briefly, there are four areas of IP law: (a) trade secret law, which protects valuable information not generally known that has been kept secret by its owner; (b) trademark law, which protects words, names, and symbols used by manufacturers and businesses to identify their goods and services; (c) patent law, which protects new, useful, and "nonobvious" inventions and processes; and (d) copyright law, which protects original "works of authorship." All these concepts of intellectual property predate e-commerce by centuries, of course, developing along with capitalism and the industrial revolution. The information revolution provides some new challenges in this arena, especially in the area of copyright law, although patent law also has been stretched by the information revolution and the rise of e-commerce, and issues of trademarking have arisen with respect to basic online activities such as the use of hyperlinks on the World Wide Web.

Although patents are not granted for scientific truths or their mathematical expression (including computer programs as mathematical algorithms), an invention including software is patentable if the software controls real-world processes or numbers that represented real-world concepts. The commercial use of IT fits this description in ways that were unimaginable when the courts ruled in this way, and software patenting has exploded in the last few years. E-commerce software patents include broad (many argue, too broad) ideas such as one-click buying and reverse auctions. In addition, the increased use of IT to govern internal business processes such as inventory control and work flow has also generated numerous software patents. Although a strong system of granting and enforcing patents is consistent with the idea of providing incentives for innovation, it may reduce the social benefits that accrue from widespread adoption of innovations. Policy and legal debates are likely to continue, because there is no universal right answer to the issue of the nature and degree of optimal patent protection.

Copyright law differs from patent law in preventing the unauthorized copying of the expression of ideas but not ideas themselves. Therefore, copyright law does not protect against someone stealing an invention or someone else independently creating a similar expression. However, copyright does provide some protection against "nonliteral infringement," such as the near duplication of screen displays. The primacy of information products, or "content," in e-commerce, and the ease with which digital information can be copied and distributed, have made copyright law for the Internet a major area of concern. Again, there are arguments on both sides, with associations of copyright owners of content such as music and movies pushing for strict controls on digital copying and others supporting broader notions of fair use and free expression as limits on copyright law.

In addition to legal and technological strategies to enforce copyrights (see the section Intellectual Property), IP holders have also turned to innovations in business strategy to capture the potential value of their IP. Several initial attempts to create Web-based music download services foundered because of lack of breadth of offerings, mispricing, or poor marketing. More recently, Apple's iTunes service has been a substantial success, offering a wide range of songs for download at 99 cents each in the United States. In addition to pricing, marketing, and breadth of product offering, a key success factor in this case has been the availability of attractive portable hardware for playing the downloaded music. In fact, Apple's sole source of profits so far has been sales of its iPods, rather than song downloads. Attempts by competitors to offer compatibility across hardware and software platforms suggest that this market may not have reached long-run equilibrium. Nevertheless, there does seem to be evidence that viable business models of paid digital delivery of copyrighted material can be constructed. In fact, this observation extends to other forms of digital content, such as news and research material, although these markets are not as prominent as that for music and other entertainment.

Market Structure and Strategy

The nature of information, where marginal costs of delivery are small and fixed costs of production may still be large, is often alleged to favor winner-take-all outcomes, because a single firm serving the whole market has the lowest average costs. These supply-side economies are reinforced by economies of scale on the demand side, that is, the benefits of creating and controlling large networks. Consumers will presumably join the network that is already large to get the highest benefits of being able to select a transaction partner from a bigger pool or other advantages of interaction. Thus buyers will look on eBay, because it is the largest online auction site, whereas sellers will list there for the same reason. The size advantage associated with these positive network externalities (that joining a network increases the benefits to others as well as oneself) keeps reinforcing itself, because the marginal value of the network is an increasing function of the network's size. On the other hand, if individuals can simultaneously participate in more than one network, and if a smaller, competing network can offer a price break to attract them, then the advantage of the winner will be limited and taking all may not be feasible. Intellectual property rights may also create winner-take-all outcomes, if a single firm is able to establish a default technical standard for an entire market (e.g., desktop operating systems). All these factors may push firms to seek first-mover status, with competition being for the market itself rather than market share.

Even in cases where traditional competition for market share remains paramount, focusing on information leads to a different emphasis in terms of the economics of business strategy. Pure price competition has to be less important than competition along an array of different dimensions, because price competition over homogeneous goods in a world of high fixed costs and low marginal costs will lead to firms losing money. (For example, the Bertrand model of price competition suggests that firms with homogeneous products will be pushed toward pricing at marginal cost, making it impossible to recover their sunk fixed costs.) Pricing itself becomes more complex because the use of IT increases the possibilities for price discrimination, differentiating across consumers and over time. Pricing strategy must be combined with strategies for marketing, product differentiation, and raising the costs that customers incur in switching to competitors. All these dimensions of strategy exist independently of the Internet and e-commerce, but they become more salient in a world where information technology operates throughout the stages of production (what business strategists call the "value chain"), as well as in the interaction of buyers and sellers in the marketplace. The ability to gather information about buyers and sellers, to organize this information, and to analyze it creates the potential to integrate the different dimensions of strategy in ways that were not possible earlier. For example, travel packages offered online can be created, priced, and offered in real time as a potential customer searches and can take account of aspects of the individual's search pattern and even past purchase information.

One can distinguish between two separate aspects of firms' strategies and how they can change as a result of IT and the Internet. First, firms can create more value by meeting consumer wants more effectively. Thus, being able to elicit consumer preferences more directly and at lower cost potentially allows firms to design products and services that create greater consumer surplus. The design, manufacture, and delivery (the last particularly in the case of digital products such as content or software, although IT also improves the logistics of physical delivery) of these products can also be made more efficient through the use of IT within the firm and in its communications with its direct and indirect suppliers (its "supply chain"). (As discussed in the next subsection, these efficiencies may come about through changes in the organization of firms, with less need for vertical integration of the stages of production under common ownership.) Furthermore, consumer tastes not only can be better matched on average but also can be served through greater customization, in which products and services can be designed and manufactured to precisely meet individual tastes as specified by the customer online. This customization is particularly valuable for information products, such as content, and also for very personal items such as cosmetics and beauty products. The use of IT internally, and through the supply chain, allows for the more flexible approach to production required by mass customization. Where the products and services are digital, product differentiation can also include bundling in new ways. For example, online portals provide bundles of content and services that are not matched by traditional media companies or content aggregators such as newspapers and magazines.

The second aspect of business strategy is value capture. In this case, the greater ability to gather information about buyer preferences through tracking online behavior—including observational and information-gathering behavior as well as buying patterns—allows for pricing to be more finely tuned so that prices are closer to buyers' maximum willingness to pay. Thus, the ability to potentially use online interactions to gather and analyze buyer information allows for greater value capture through various kinds of price discrimination. In such cases, product differentiation may be an important supporting strategy for value capture, in addition to its role in value creation. Product differentiation can reduce the ability of competitors to undercut a price discrimination strategy. The ability to vary prices more easily and often in online markets may also be used as part of a price discrimination strategy, just as seasonal sales are used in traditional retailing. Bundling of products is another example of how firms may tailor products to capture greater value from buyers, although it is not always used for this purpose.

A slightly different way of analyzing business strategies in e-commerce is to think of online shopping as offering a bundle of three different categories of goods and services: the products themselves, the service of time in physically assembling the order and delivering it, and an information service that is made possible by the infrastructure of the Internet and the World Wide Web. The digital information processing and communication capability of this infrastructure is what makes the bundling of the other two services economical. In the case of many physical products, such as groceries, the service of assembling the order and delivering it would not be cost-effective without the information infrastructure and service. The nature of the information service is what particularly distinguishes catalog shopping for physical products from online shopping, because catalog shopping offers more limited information exchange. In the case of shopping in a store for physical products, the bundle offered to the buyer is further differentiated, because in store shopping the buyer bears the costs of "last-mile" fulfillment (bringing the product home). Interestingly, hybrid models of online search and transaction, with physical pickup by the buyer from a store, are also emerging. In the case of digital products and services, the differences are greatest compared with traditional methods, because the product itself can be delivered via the same infrastructure that is used for ordering. As one might expect, online transactions for digital products and services provide greater potential for changing ways of doing business.

Changes in Firm Organization

The use of digital technologies has several different possible implications for the organization of firms. A simple hypothesis is based on the transaction cost theory of the firm (Coase, 1937), which argues that firms exist to overcome transaction costs associated with market exchange. If using IT and the Internet reduces market transaction costs by increasing the speed and richness of information flows, then firms will be replaced by markets. Although this argument has merit, the use of IT within firms also improves, so the opposite case can be made—that firms are able to become larger as a result of IT. Certainly, the globalization of firms in areas such as sourcing inputs, or serving different geographic markets, appears to be aided by the use of IT, and the Internet in particular.

One reason that firms will not disappear is that the need to control complementary assets, especially different kinds of skilled labor or human capital, is a reason for the existence of firms that is not invalidated by improved information flows. In general, one can argue that efficient incentive provision—for current effort as well as investment-related activities—often requires the use of hierarchical organizational forms, rather than pure reliance on market transactions.

Nevertheless, two trends are evident, and both appear to be accelerated by the developments in IT and communications. First, the growth of markets, which has been driven by lower transportation costs and trade barriers, and by higher incomes, as well as dramatically improved communications, permits greater outsourcing and therefore some decrease in vertical integration of firms (Brynjolfsson & Hitt, 2000, p. 36). This is an example of Adam Smith's classic maxim that the division of labor is limited by the extent of the market. The economic logic is that serving a larger market allows specialized firms to emerge along portions of the value chain, because they are able to spread the fixed costs of a separate organization more effectively. Contract manufacturing is an important example of the phenomenon of outsourcing, where the supply chain becomes more geographically dispersed as well as being more divided among different firms. Business process outsourcing has, more recently, followed manufacturing along this path. These trends illustrate a broader concept, that of "virtualization," which emphasizes the use of IT to create changing networks of firms along a value chain. As we have argued, the need to control complementary assets in a coordinated manner places limits on virtualization to the extent that it involves separation of ownership.

Second, even when they do not outsource, firms themselves are becoming more decentralized as they incorporate IT in their internal business processes. For example, one study of large firms found that greater internal levels of IT use were associated with "increased delegation of authority to individuals and teams, greater levels of skill and education in the workforce, and greater emphasis on pre-employment screening for education and training" (Brynjolfsson & Hitt, 2000, p. 35). Other studies indicate that the IT investments of decentralized firms are more productive and that such firms have higher market values, which suggests that market pressures will favor greater decentralization in the long run. The use of IT within an organization can also be seen as a form of virtualization, because control and collaboration can be retained in essential ways without physical proximity.

From the perspective of economies of scale and scope (Chandler, 1990), the factors affecting firm organization pull in different directions. On one hand, firms can become more specialized because their ability to serve geographically dispersed markets is enhanced by the Internet. For example, niche retailers can potentially sell globally because their marginal costs of reaching new customers are substantially reduced. Trading scope for scale means that the overall impact on firm size is indeterminate. In general, however, the lower cost of entry in online business—a Web site is cheaper to set up and operate than a physical store—suggests that smaller firms will thrive. At the other extreme, large firms can expand their scale and scope more easily using online presence and interactions, and especially in the case of digital products and services, offer very large ranges of offerings. Therefore, one plausible prediction is that the size distribution of firms will become more spread out, with firms in the middle losing out to those at either end (e.g., *The Economist*, 2002).

Returning to globalization, an important consequence of digitization is the ability to deliver digital products and services across national boundaries using the Internet. A related issue is the effect of greater information availability, which expands market reach. In both cases, the ability to complete transactions online is an additional feature, although not an essential one. Skills provision and services provision are examples of electronic delivery across national boundaries, with examples of these broad categories including software development, business process outsourcing, retail transactions, and customer care. Small IT projects may be handled entirely online. In other cases, there is typically some face-to-face meeting (the "high bandwidth" information exchange) and agreement, followed by more routine exchanges or deliveries of services that take place online. The outsourcing of software development from the developed world to countries such as India and Israel represents an important example of such activities. In another example, retail financial services may be conducted entirely online across national boundaries. An investor in Europe trading in U.S. stocks can fill out the application forms, transfer money into a U.S. account, and trade without using paper or moving from her screen. Commissions earned by the online brokerage then represent a payment for services that are international.

A final aspect of changes in firm organization in the digital economy is related to the new kinds of products, services, and delivery methods that are possible. In many cases, new types of digital economy firms are essentially new intermediaries, which provide expertise or reputation, or economize on transaction costs. The following classification of firms is in terms of how they combine information, time services, and goods and services in new ways in their offerings to customers. It does not include traditional firms that merely include the Internet as another communication channel, nor does it classify firms by traditional sectors (e.g., finance) or functions (e.g., manufacturing).

1. Information request services provide general information on demand through search engine technology, a very basic aspect of the World Wide Web.
2. Content providers package particular sets of content, rather than just enable general searches for any kind of information, and can be considered a new kind of media firm.
3. E-tailers are a carryover from the world of physical retailing, including catalog sales, but offer a different bundle of products, time, and information services than traditional retailers.
4. Exchanges and brokers operate electronically without physically bringing together buyers and sellers or the objects being sold and act as "market-makers" or "market-expanders."
5. Community creators provide online mechanisms for communication, networking, and collaboration.
6. Infomediaries focus only on providing information pertaining to potential market opportunities and are potentially neutral with respect to buyers and sellers.
7. Portals are aggregators, or diversified firms, that combine the previous six types of firms.
8. Infrastructure providers make and sell the hardware, software, and services that allow other firms to process, store, and send the information that makes their businesses possible. These include communications equipment, Web-hosting equipment, connectivity services, hosting services, application services, and many kinds of software developers.

As the seventh category itself suggests, there are many overlaps and combinations possible in these functions within different digital economy firms.

SECURITY

The need for security in exchanging information is as old as history. The earliest measures to ensure messages from falling into the wrong hands involved hiding the message itself. A famous example of this is the story told by the Greek chronicler, Herodotus, writing more than 2,000 years ago. The sender shaved the messenger's head, wrote the message on his scalp, and waited for the hair to grow back before sending the messenger on his way. In more mundane instances, one simply seals communications in envelopes before mailing them and relies on legal penalties to deter would-be snoops. A different sort of concealment is obtained through writing a message in a code that only the recipient knows how to decipher. Julius Caesar, for example, commonly used ciphers for military missives. Concealment and encryption are independent and can be combined in many ways. Other security issues revolve around correctly identifying the sender and recipient of information, protecting information from tampering, and authenticating information.

Security Issues

One of the peculiarities of the Internet and the Web is their inherent openness. This openness is what has allowed them to grow so quickly and so fruitfully. As long as the information being exchanged can itself be made public without any loss, this is fine. The job seeker who posts her resume or the hobbyist who lists information about his favorite computer games may not mind if the whole world has access to that information. However, for electronic commerce to be successful, more and more commercially sensitive and private information, from business purchasing orders to individual credit card numbers, must be stored in electronic databases connected to the Internet and transmitted over it. Hence, security for electronic storage and communications is essential, otherwise those possessing unauthorized information (ranging from individual credit card numbers to complete identities, as in identity theft) can cause substantial financial harm.

There are several dimensions of security. First, we may want to prevent unauthorized people from accessing certain information. To accomplish this, the information may be encrypted, so that even if it falls into the wrong hands, it cannot be read. Also, barriers can be erected to prevent unauthorized access to information. In the case of postal mail, we simply use sealed paper envelopes, accompanied by heavy legal penalties for tampering with mail. Electronic barriers are more complex. An example of an electronic barrier is a firewall, which prevents unauthorized access. At the same time, security also must allow authorized recipients to have access to the information. When we receive an important legal document by courier, we typically have to sign for it. We provide private information that identifies us when we use an automated teller machine (ATM) or obtain bank balance information via the telephone. Similar kinds of authentication mechanisms are required for electronic transmission of information. One of the biggest problems emerging now on the Internet is the forging of corporate identities in e-mail to elicit personal financial information from unwary recipients (a practice known as "phishing"). Again, the problem can be seen as one of identity authentication.

Another kind of authentication involves authorization of transactions. A user of a credit card may not only have to establish identity, but also his or her credit status. The latter is done through a verification procedure, now purely electronic, but one that originally involved a telephone call to the card issuer. A related idea is nonrepudiation of transactions, which ensures that a purchaser does not subsequently claim that he was not responsible for a valid transaction.

A third aspect of security is preventing tampering with information. This problem may well be correlated with the issue of access. A hacker may just as well want to damage information to which he obtains unauthorized access as to use that access for personal benefit without tampering. On the other hand, tampering may occur without unauthorized access. Authorized users of information could alter it, or they could be unsuspecting carriers of

Table 3 Traditional Security Mechanisms

Security Service	Nonelectronic Mechanisms	Electronic Mechanisms
Authentication	Photo ID card Knowledge of mother's maiden name Check with trusted person or institution	Encryption Passwords/PINs Biometric scanning Digital signatures
Access control	Locks and keys Checkpoint guard Passwords	Passwords/PINs Firewalls
Confidentiality	Sealed letter Invisible ink	Encryption
Integrity	Indelible ink Hologram on credit card	Check-values
Nonrepudiation	Notarized signature Certified mail	Digital signatures
Fraud detection	Inspection of ledgers and other records	Electronic inspection Data mining

Source: Adapted from Ford & Baum (1997), Table 4.1. Note: most electronic security mechanisms incorporate some form of encryption.

viruses or worms that damage digitally stored information. Thus firewalls have to deal with such problems as well by weeding out harmful programs as well as preventing unauthorized access. Detection of tampering, or accidental alteration of information, is a related security tool.

Yet another aspect of security pertains to monitoring and auditing electronic databases. Much of this involves a carry-over of traditional financial auditing roles to electronic accounts. Issues here can involve internal as well as external fraud or theft. In the former case, access may be fully authorized, but the individual acts in an illegal manner. Effective detection of such actions is the security objective in this case, and this is accomplished through the use of data mining or other statistical analysis, for example, to identify unusual transactions. A related issue is the auditing for regulatory compliance with respect to record keeping in general, in areas such as financial and health care services.

Table 3 provides a summary classification of security issues and gives familiar nonelectronic examples of achieving security goals, as well as electronic substitutes or equivalents for digital information. We next briefly consider the various security techniques that are employed on electronic databases and communication networks.

Security Techniques

We summarize techniques of encryption, authentication, and screening, as well as how combinations of these techniques are implemented through firewalls or similar measures. Details on these techniques can be found elsewhere in this *Handbook*.

Encryption. The process of encryption involves using a rule to transform information, such as a text message, into something that is unintelligible without reversing the process. The rule used can be very simple (replace A with Z, B with Y, etc.) or can involve complicated mathematical transformations. Digitized text, which is represented as a sequence of bits, can be encrypted in this way, using computers to perform the transformation. The real conceptual difficulty is in developing an encryption system that can be applied practically. The most straightforward system of encryption involves both the sender and the receiver knowing a "key," which is a string of bits used in both the encryption transformation and its reverse. Only the sender and the receiver know the key, which is private. Because the same key is used at both ends, the system is symmetric. IBM developed the first widely used commercial symmetric encryption system in the 1970s, the Data Encryption Standard (DES), which was adopted as a standard by the U.S. government in 1977 and the financial industry in 1981. The practical difficulty with private key systems is how to securely and efficiently distribute the keys. This problem was conceptually solved in 1976, with the demonstration that public-key encryption systems were feasible. Later, the RSA encryption algorithm (named for creators Ron Rivest, Adi Shamir, and Len Adleman) solved the further problem of constructing a usable asymmetric cipher. Such systems use a pair of different but related keys, one for encryption and one for decryption. To protect message content, as when a customer is sending a credit card number over the Internet, the message can be encrypted using the public key. Only the merchant, who already knows the private key, is able to use it to decrypt the message. All customers of the merchant can use the same public key, unlike the case of private key encryption, where each communicating pair requires a different key. The different keys make the encryption system asymmetric, because the person who has only the public key can encrypt a message but cannot decrypt it.

Message Integrity. Suppose that confidentiality of a message is not an issue, but that the recipient needs to be sure that the message was not tampered with, or accidentally altered, along the way. For example, in traditional postal communications, the recipient might see that the envelope has been opened and resealed or the contents damaged. With digital communications over the Internet, the risk of tampering or accidental alteration could be relatively high, and detection methods are not obvious. The approach that is taken is to use a mathematical transformation that calculates a particular value based on all the bits in the message: a "check value." The method of generation of this check value must itself be encrypted. This can be done with a symmetric, private-key system. A public-key system can also be used for encrypting the transformation that computes the check value. In either case, the check value is transmitted along with the message. The financial industry uses a standard called MAC (Message Authentication Code), which was agreed upon in 1986.

Authentication. Another problem that can be tackled with encryption technologies is that of making sure that the sender of the message is genuine. In face-to-face communications and transactions, or via the telephone, we use special numbers, other private knowledge, or photographs to establish who we are. An asymmetric encryption system can be used to achieve authentication in electronic communications. The sender uses her private key to encrypt her message. Recipients use the corresponding public key to decrypt it. Note that this does not achieve confidentiality, because anyone can get and use the public key to view the message. The roles of the private and public key are reversed from the case where message confidentiality is desired. However, anyone who decrypts the message knows who the sender is, because the public key only works with the sender's corresponding private key. One proposed approach to controlling spoof e-mails (those using false originating addresses) is authentication through encrypted digital signatures. Another uses a version of "caller ID," where the authenticity of incoming e-mail is verified by checking it against the domain name system (DNS) database. There are several other methods of authentication on the Internet. Passwords and personal identification numbers (PINs)—familiar from using ATMs and telephone bank enquiries—are the most common ones in use on the World Wide Web. Third-party authentication is also possible: for example, a trusted firm may perform the initial authentication and then vouch for the identity of an individual thereafter. The identity of computers on a network may also be authenticated, using encryption or other checking methods, as in the case of dealing with spam e-mails. These tools also play a role in electronic authentication of transactions. In non-Internet situations, information technology is often used to enable biometric authentication methods, where computer software analyzes facial features or physical characteristics to verify identity. This approach is now being extended to long-distance authentication, using specially equipped computer mice to read fingerprints.

Digital Signatures. A digital signature typically combines authentication with message-integrity checking. Again, it uses basic encryption technologies to achieve this. For example, the sender "signs" the electronic document using a private key and the receiver verifies the signature using a public key. Digital signatures must also be able to support nonrepudiation. This means that the sender cannot later deny that the signature is hers. Obviously, the recipient or anyone else should not be able to forge the digital signature. One way to implement digital signatures is to use RSA-type technology in the authentication mode by encrypting the message with the private key and sending it along with the unencrypted message. Decrypting the encrypted version and comparing it with the plaintext message provides a check on the contents and the sender. This can be costly in terms of computing resources and bandwidth, so an additional step is introduced in practice. A one-way mathematical transformation (i.e., one that cannot be reversed) is applied to the message. The transformation is called a hash function, and its output is a message digest. Tampering with the message will alter the digest. The digest is encrypted with a private key, and this acts as the digital signature. Different mathematical transformations provide alternatives to RSA-based digital signatures.

Access Control. Passwords provide a standard form of individual access control. A different sort of control prevents access from certain machines. Finally, certain forms of content and applications may be prohibited or screened. A firewall typically acts as a screen for controlling access and the entry of content and applications. Firewalls typically exist between internal corporate networks and the public part of the Internet. They can control incoming traffic and only allow authenticated users access from outside, and limit how internal users connect to the external network. Firewalls can also screen for malicious programs, such as viruses, which can cause damage to the internal network. Antivirus programs themselves exist independently of firewalls and are now a standard part of every computer's armory. Firewalls include special hardware and software, such as screening routers to filter incoming data, proxy servers to screen requests for Internet services such as access to Web sites, and perimeter networks that act as buffers between internal networks and everything outside. Firewalls may also perform encryption tasks in linking two physically separate networks securely over the Internet to create what is called a virtual private network (VPN).

Web Security. Tampering with information on Web sites and electronic eavesdropping to steal valuable information such as credit card numbers are two of the greatest potential security problems on the Web. The most common general-security software is the secure sockets layer (SSL) protocol developed by Netscape. SSL works on top of the transmission control protocol (TCP) used for Internet communications and can be used to achieve security for hypertext transfer protocol (HTTP) and file transfer protocol (FTP) communications. It performs several functions, including authenticating the Web server (through a private key mechanism) so that a fake site is not gathering sensitive information from unsuspecting customers, checking integrity check values for message content, and encrypting for confidentiality. SSL is not specifically for preventing hacking into Web sites: to stop that, firewalls must be employed. Other security methods are also available for the Web. In particular, Visa and MasterCard combined to develop the secure electronic transaction (SET) protocol for bankcard payments made during online shopping transactions. SET is based on a public key infrastructure that provides encryption, authentication of different participants in the transactions (cardholders, merchants, transaction processors), and integrity checking.

Legal and Market Approaches

Traditional commercial transactions are governed by well-defined laws and legal precedents. In particular, there is a clear concept of what constitutes a legally binding contract. Paper documents with signatures are the norm for contracts. Sometimes, notarization to authenticate the signatures is required. There are also disclosure requirements and escape clauses, particularly for consumers transacting with businesses. The legal issues in e-commerce contracting revolve around how identities can be verified, signatures can be authenticated, and content can be protected, when information is stored, processed, and transmitted electronically. Such techniques were discussed in the previous subsection.

Another category of problems arises in communications. We accept the U.S. mail and private courier services as reliable, secure methods of delivering physical documents. Tampering in such cases is difficult and costly to accomplish on a large scale, possible to detect, and subject to severe penalties. On the other hand, large-scale electronic eavesdropping or tampering with communications is not as difficult or costly. Scanning large volumes of electronic communications is quite different from opening hundreds or thousands of envelopes to check what is inside. As a result, ordinary e-mail via the Internet is much less secure than first-class mail via the U.S. Postal Service. Furthermore, tampering with the U.S. mail is a well-defined and serious legal offense. The same kind of legal protections and standards are still evolving for Internet communications.

Certification Authorities. In traditional transactions, where assuring identity is extremely important (large financial transactions in particular), signatures are often required to be authenticated by being done in the presence of a notary public, who acts as a trusted third party. Certification authorities in e-commerce are intermediaries that address verification problems relating to identity but without the physical proximity that traditional methods require (you have to be physically present to sign in front of the notary). A certification authority (CA), therefore, is a public or private entity that issues digital certificates to authenticate identities and messages or to attest that an action has occurred. CAs can provide verification or assurance of identity, verification of message content, and verification of events or actions. Private CAs in e-commerce have stepped in to fulfill roles traditionally played by trusted government agencies such as the U.S. Postal Service. How do private CAs themselves establish trust? They may need to be certified themselves or they can build a reputation in the marketplace. In the long run, as e-commerce grows in scope and complexity, transactional certificates and time stamping may be more significant functions of CAs than simple identification, which will become more standardized over the Internet.

Contracts. The growth of e-commerce itself will depend on the ability of two parties to complete a contract, sign it in a legally binding manner, and transmit it, all purely electronically. The technology is not the stumbling block to this goal. The issue is one of clear, generally agreed on legal standards. For example, in the United States in June 2000, the president signed (electronically as well as with the traditional pen) a bill that sets these standards and will make it possible for businesses to close deals with electronic contracts and digital signatures. Similar legislation has been passed in other industrial countries. Electronic contracts are especially attractive for B2B transactions. However, the possibility of electronic contracting will probably require some updating of rules that protect consumers. Because a large percentage of households are not online, presumably consumers should still have the right to have all contract details and subsequent pertinent notices on paper without financial penalty. This makes the cost saving that electronic dealings offer to businesses harder to achieve, but presumably these will come with time, as electronic communications become cheaper and more ubiquitous. The technology of digital certification will also have to become more widespread and widely understood for it to serve the everyday needs of B2C transactions.

Communications. The problem of electronic communications is more widespread and basic than that of electronic contracts, because many communications are not directly relevant to transactions. One area where electronic distribution of information is very attractive, because of its speed, flexibility, and capacity, is in financial services. The Securities and Exchange Commission, which regulates financial services related to securities markets and transactions, noted in 1995 the "promise of electronic distribution of information in enhancing investors' ability to access, research, and analyze information, and in facilitating the provision of information by issuers and others" (SEC, 1995). The SEC went on to state that "given the numerous benefits of electronic distribution of information and the fact that in many respects it may be more useful to investors than paper, its use should not be disfavored." The SEC's approach used the analogy of traditional paper-based communications to define the parameters of what would be acceptable for electronic communications from financial services firms to investors. In 1997, the New York Stock Exchange handed down guidelines to its member firms, essentially following the SEC's lead. Prospectuses, stock trade confirmations, and statements are examples of documents that are required to be sent to investors and that may be delivered electronically once there is a sufficient level of trust and acceptance of the technology and the providers of the service. Content integrity, authentication, time stamping, and overall security and reliability are important for such financial communications. Private startups, as well as the U.S. Postal Service, are developing products and services that meet these needs in ways that ordinary e-mail does not.

GOVERNMENT POLICIES

Any market economy relies on government regulation to maintain a framework of laws and property rights that allow production and exchange activities to occur in a stable environment. The rise of the digital economy has several effects on government management of the economy. We briefly examine several of these effects in this section.

Intellectual Property

Phenomena such as the widespread copying of digital music, using file-sharing software available from many different commercial and noncommercial providers, have heightened concerns about enforcement of copyrights on the Internet. Some have called for more stringent copyright laws, and, in the United States, the Digital Millennium Copyright Act (DMCA) of 1998 did introduce some additional protections in the guise of updating previous law to cover new technologies. The DMCA, combined with previously existing laws, provides quite strong protection, as indicated by court rulings against Napster and other providers of file-sharing software as well as successful recording industry lawsuits against individual file sharers. At the same time, the courts, in recent rulings, have placed some limits on the extent to which Internet infrastructure providers can be held responsible for illegal file sharing.

The DMCA included penalties for cracking protections designed to protect unauthorized copying. However, the legal application of the DMCA has had an effect on free speech, as demonstrated by examples such as a professor of computer science who forwent the presentation of a research paper that outlined methods of overcoming copy protection, when the professor was threatened with a lawsuit. Lobbying by industry groups that have ownership interests in copyright has also motivated potential U.S. legislation that requires copy protection be hardwired into consumer electronics items. In such cases, the doctrine of "fair use" in copyright law also appears to come under attack. In the United States, the DMCA was complemented by another law, which resulted in extending copyright protections by 20 years. Although European copyright laws have not tilted so much against users, the United States is a global leader in the production of copyrighted material such as music and films.

In the arena of patents, it has been court interpretations, as noted in Information as an Economic Product, rather than new legislation that has increased the scope of patent law, with hundreds of relatively broad software patents being granted in recent years. It has been suggested that a new category of patents, with a shorter lifetime, be granted for software, but this is likely to create further problems for assessing patent applications. It also misses the real problem, which is that of inadequate resources in the U.S. Patent and Trademark Office. Again, the United States is the largest market for intellectual property, and U.S. patent rules are disproportionately significant in the global context. In general, the apparent broadening of both copyright and patent protection can be seen as a response to a situation where intellectual property is increasingly important for creating economic value but also easier to copy or imitate. Thus, these legal trends are a symptom of the digital information/knowledge economy.

Privacy

The digital economy, with its greater flows and tracking of information, raises serious concerns about privacy. Information about consumers allows firms to increase profits through various kinds of price discrimination. At the same time, some consumer information can help firms to tailor their products more effectively to consumer preferences. Privacy concerns often center on how the information is collected: do consumers realize that their behavior online is being tracked or that cookie files are being deposited on their computers?

Further issues arise with respect to who else may properly see the information collected. A customer may not mind a seller tracking the consumer's buying habits to serve her better, but she may not want the firm to sell that information to other firms. A related issue is the use of such information for mass marketing e-mails, commonly known as "spam." Employees, too, may find that their electronic communications and Internet browsing from work can be monitored by employers with great precision and intrusiveness. Finally, there are all kinds of information that various public agencies collect. Often such agencies are required to make that information available in response to requests from members of the public. However, making that information available online makes access much easier and broader than other forms of availability, with possible negative consequences.

The U.S. legislative branch was actively considering Internet privacy legislation after a report from the Federal Trade Commission in mid-2000 indicated that self-regulation was not working uniformly and some Web sites were proving resistant to privacy concerns. One stumbling block for legislative agreement was the simple issue of whether businesses should be required to explicitly get consumers to "opt in" to allow their personal data to be used beyond the specific transaction or relationship, or whether the burden should be on consumers to explicitly "opt out." Businesses naturally favored the latter approach, which gives them much more leeway. Business-supported groups have tried to argue that privacy legislation would be inordinately costly and also that consumers do not care enough for it to be worthwhile. On the other side are groups such as the American Civil Liberties Union and Consumers Union, which want stronger safeguards against data-collection practices that do not involve explicit consent. The aftermath of 9/11 has tilted the scales against strengthening privacy, because security has become a much greater concern. Therefore, it seems unlikely that any meaningful Internet privacy legislation will be passed any time soon in the United States, which leaves its online privacy laws some way behind those of the European Union, which protect consumer privacy more stringently.

Antitrust Policy and Regulation

Antitrust laws are designed to prevent monopolization of industries and anticompetitive practices such as price fixing. Does the digital economy require modifications in the government's enforcement of antitrust policy or even a change in the antitrust laws themselves? There are three key areas in which the proponents of a modified approach to antitrust policy make their points. First, there is the argument that antitrust enforcement must account for the effects on future innovation. The second argument is that network externalities and the economies of scale associated with information goods make monopolies more likely or more natural (winner takes all) and hence they must be tolerated—otherwise there will be no market or unnecessarily high costs. The third argument is that complementarities in information goods require firms to cooperate in ways that might seem collusive by more traditional measures.

The first of these, the increased importance of technological innovation and of patenting, certainly makes these variables more important in a firm's business strategy, but it does not, by itself, imply that antitrust law has to change. Firms can innovate profitably, using patent law, without having to run afoul of antitrust law. Second, network effects are demand-side economies of scale, which can interact with the usual cost-side economies of scale to promote market dominance. If information goods are subject to both kinds of economies of scale, one might have to be resigned to more cases of "natural" monopoly, driven purely by the structural characteristics of the market rather than by any illegal behavior. However, the importance of such natural monopolies is probably overstated, and their persistence is unlikely if the protection for patents is not too stringent.[7] Finally, technology goods have to work in systems and are characterized by strong complementarities. This often requires firms to collaborate in research and development, as well as in production and installation. However, as long as single firms, or firms acting together, do not engage in behavior that reduces competition or harms competitors, there is no violation of antitrust laws. What is needed is not a reform of the laws, but simply enforcement by government officials who understand technology well enough to sort out different kinds of cooperative behavior among technology-oriented firms. Clearly, this is more difficult when markets are interrelated and technology evolves very rapidly.

Laws to manage privacy issues and antitrust laws can both be considered major examples of regulation by the government of private economic activity. They are not the only ones. There are specialized regulations for different sectors of the economy, such as financial services and telecommunications. There are also regulations meant to protect certain groups or to control certain types of activity. For example, pornography and hate materials are controlled, and gambling is a heavily regulated activity. All these forms of regulation are affected by the Internet. Much of the problem is simply in the freedom with which information can be disseminated and shared on the Internet. The location of activities is also a problem: for example, online gambling can escape controls that are designed to operate within geographic jurisdictions. Controls on forms of payment, for instance, by using the major credit card companies, can be a way to solve the jurisdictional problem. The credit card companies cannot afford to be partners in crime. Here the law needs to change to deal with ability of digital activities to escape the requirement of meeting in a particular place.

In the case of financial services, the issues have to do with the quantity and the veracity of information that is made available. The Internet makes scams easier to implement in some ways, but the basic laws do not need to adjust. In the case of telecommunication companies, regulatory issues are centered on the technological changes that digitization has introduced, which make more effective competition possible. The U.S. Telecom Act of 1996 began the process of moving regulation into the modern era. Some regulation is still needed because parts of the network are still potential monopolies. Local telephone companies—the so-called Baby Bells—in particular have maintained their strongholds. Regulations to allow interconnection to parts of the Baby Bell networks by competing carriers have not really enabled the latter to gain significant market shares. While protecting their traditional markets in voice communications, the Baby Bells have been lobbying for the ability to compete more freely in markets for data communications, that is, the underpinnings of the Internet. The convergence of communications technologies that have been governed by different regulatory frameworks also creates regulatory challenges. For example, in 2003, a U.S. court ruled that the Federal Communications Commission (FCC) incorrectly classified cable networks as "information services" rather than "telecommunications services," where only the latter are required to share their broadband access lines.

International Trade

Countries often have customs duties or tariffs on imports, and these clearly affect international trade. They may also use quantitative restrictions on the entry of certain goods and services. An extreme case of this would be a total ban. Various reasons for restricting international trade do exist: to raise government revenue, to control undesirable materials, to protect some domestic groups, and so forth. Individual country choices made without coordination may lead to outcomes that are worse for all countries. Therefore, to try to achieve some measure of cooperation that can improve outcomes, trading nations use the World Trade Organization (WTO) to frame and enforce rules for international trade. Having such an organization does not remove conflicts, but it provides a mechanism for more orderly handling of disputes, as well as a clear set of "rules of the game."

The current provisional WTO agreement is that trade restrictions should not apply to electronic transmissions via the Internet. This leads to a symmetric treatment of

[7] Arguments relating to network externalities as well as to innovation have been made in the Microsoft antitrust investigations, both of which concluded with out-of-court settlements. One can argue that any monopoly that Microsoft might have is related more to traditional anticompetitive practices such as the nature of its contracts with distributors, rather than any special features of the digital economy. In the European Union, there is an ongoing antitrust investigation of Microsoft.

online and offline transactions, as in the example of a European purchasing U.S. stocks or a U.S. hotel room while on vacation. In other cases, however, there is a difference. Thus, purchasing a large number of music CDs from another country might be subject to a customs duty (small purchases from abroad are exempt in the U.S., though not in many countries), but obtaining the same quantity of music as electronic files would escape the import tariff. This is superficially similar to the issue of sales taxation within the United States, but here we are looking across national borders, whereas in the U.S. sales tax case, the tax must be paid if the transaction is in-state rather than across states. Hence, the two cases are somewhat different although broadly related in spirit.

The WTO also includes provisions for trade-related intellectual property rights (TRIPS). The TRIPS agreement came about in the 1990s and sets minimum standards for copyright and patent law for member countries. In addition, these laws cannot discriminate between local citizens and citizens of other TRIPS signatories. The TRIPS agreement was substantially predated by the World Intellectual Property Organization (WIPO), which is a United Nations agency and has a substantially different governance structure. Global intellectual property rights (IPR) issues end up being debated in the WTO as well as in the WIPO, with the former providing more stringent protections and enforcement mechanisms in theory. However, there are substantial difficulties in enforcing IPRs across national borders, and worldwide low-cost digital copying of copyrighted material such as music, movies, and software is a substantial concern for copyright holders in countries such as the United States.

A further issue with respect to information products in particular is the blurred line between goods and services. For example, software development is a service that is now offered across national boundaries. Also, software is typically licensed rather than sold, and leasing software is common. Because traditional services, such as those in the financial sector, have been treated under a separate set of rules (the General Agreement on Trade in Services, or GATS), which is newer and more restrictive than the rules for goods or products, there is disagreement as to which set of rules should govern software. Countries such as the United States that are producers and net exporters of information and related services argue for the application of the rules for conventional trade, rather than the GATS.

WORK, PLAY, AND COMMUNITIES

Work is a large fraction of our lives. It is useful to recognize how drastically work was altered by the industrial revolution, the introduction of factories, and the rise of large corporations. Cottage or home production became relatively insignificant, as mechanization and economies of scale caused work to be concentrated in factories and offices. Now IT has loosened the bonds of location, making work once again more flexible for many.

Location of Work

Several trends have driven the changes in work. First, the increase in the importance of services relative to manufacturing and of the information economy in general reduced the proportion of factory jobs. Next, the falling cost of computing power allowed many tasks to potentially be performed at home rather than in the office. Most important, the Internet has removed the isolation of the home worker. Communication and collaboration can take place among workers in different locations. Physical proximity for many jobs becomes only a part-time requirement. Clearly, this is most pronounced for jobs that involve "knowledge work," where collaboration involves exchanges of information: software development is a prime example of this kind of job. In other cases, remoteness is no longer a barrier to carrying out some functions. A technical support person may guide a computer user through steps to repair a problem. Many software fixes can be done from a remote location. Even some surgery can now be performed by a doctor at a remote site who manipulates instruments through long-distance communications and control. Although these changes are just in freedom of location, there are also changes in the nature of the firm itself, sometimes reducing the bonds that define a firm, as was discussed in Implications for Markets and Organizations. Employees in such cases can become independent contractors, with their own capital (human and physical), almost harking back to the preindustrial era of home production.

Freedom of location has begun to affect the global distribution of work. The customer in the United States may have a telephone query answered by someone in Ireland, India, or the Philippines. Computer programming or program testing assignments may be sent via the Internet to wherever people with those skills are available, to be completed and sent back the same way. The supply of some kinds of skills becomes global rather than local or national. There is also a time dimension to this geographical dispersion of work. Time differences across the globe allow 24-hour customer service to be more cost-effective. In areas such as software development, they also allow global shift work. For example, two project teams in the United States and India can collaborate to achieve an almost continuous workflow by utilizing the night-and-day time difference between the two countries. However, the ubiquity of digital communication devices means that the notion of times and places where work does not intrude is severely eroded. A knowledge worker may find she is expected to access her e-mail via a wireless handheld computer at home, on vacation, and in general outside the normal place and time of work.

Finally, there are concerns that the efficiency gains of the digital economy come at the expense of jobs and workers. This is an old concern, which reflects the continued substitution of capital for labor that has occurred since the Industrial Revolution. In the United States in the early 21st century, this concern is arising because of the slow pace of job creation as the economy recovers from a recession. Although there has been some shifting of service jobs, such as call centers and business processes, to developing countries, this currently represents only a small fraction of the jobs that would normally be created. The alternative explanation is that the use of IT reduces the need for workers. Although such concerns may be valid in the short run, it is clear that in the long run new kinds of jobs are created as productivity gains allow firms to develop new products and services or to expand existing markets. Perhaps a more significant issue is that of potential effects on income distribution: will a knowledge economy reward people more unequally? Clearly, access to education and training will be an important determinant of how this issue plays out in the future.

Leisure Activities

Leisure activities in the industrial age have been shaped by scale and specialization, just as happened in the case of work. Sports and the performing arts have become large-scale spectator or audience events. Radio and television introduced broadcasting, which created mass markets for entertainment while removing locational barriers. Recording technologies expanded the scope for listening to music or watching movies while introducing greater choice into consumer decisions. All these developments in people's leisure activities are enhanced and broadened by the Internet. Inexpensive digital recording and transmission of music and video provide a range of options unimaginable in the past.

Perhaps the greatest effect of the substitution of bandwidth for being in the same place has been in game playing. One can play traditional games, such as bridge and chess, via the Internet, with opponents and partners who may be anywhere in the world. More widespread is the enormous expansion of online game playing. Computer games become virtual worlds where individuals act out their fantasies and try out strategies. Game characters take on lives of their own, becoming valuable commodities themselves for game players who want to win any way they can. At one level, the interaction is no different from that of board games that have been played for hundreds or thousands of years, that of stylized competition. However, the complexity of such games has increased exponentially, and the Internet has demolished distance in creating the communities of game players.

Just as IT has allowed work to intrude into leisure spaces, it has also allowed the reverse phenomenon to take place. Workers who sit at a computer may play solitary games. If they have Internet access, they may engage in all kinds of leisure activities, including browsing news and entertainment content, shopping, and chatting as well as game playing. Hence, employers may respond with new kinds of monitoring and restrictions, as was discussed earlier in the context of privacy. However, the breaking down of barriers between work and play may be inevitable, to the extent that it represents a more natural existence for human beings. In this respect, the digital economy may provide the kind of interconnection that existed before the factory system came to dominate production methods.

Online Communities

From online game players to members of a project team designing a software program, people at work and play form communities based on shared goals or interests. IT allows these communities to be freed from the need to share a physical space. Interactions take place on computer screens instead of face-to-face, but the interactions that are possible in cyberspace are getting richer and richer, which allows more and more communities to form. In particular, work collaborations of increasing complexity are becoming possible on the Internet, with simultaneous or asynchronous participation in activities involving product research, design, and development.

Work and play are not the only glue that binds communities. Any kind of shared interest can provide the impetus. Those suffering from a particular disease, fans of a rock star, or collectors of sports memorabilia can join together to exchange information, ideas, and experiences over the Internet. These communities may provide commercial opportunities, because they provide access to that ever-scarcer commodity, "attention," but they may also lead to more profound social changes. Political organization, in particular, takes on a new dimension, perhaps expanding the scope of democracy, while definitely changing its nature. Possibilities exist for Internet-based comment, feedback, and even voting by citizens in communication with their governments. Many of these possibilities are now lumped together under the concept of "social networking," where the Internet is used as a tool to create and maintain general or special purpose communities, based on shared interest, mutual help, or other common features.

Perhaps the most remarkable change of all is how, in just a few short years, the majority of people in the industrialized world have come to take for granted so many possibilities that alter their lives and may reshape the social fabric. The Internet, at its core, is a very human-centered development. This may seem somewhat paradoxical. The underlying IT is complex and abstract. But the Internet and its associated technologies allow people to be creative, to express their individuality, and to communicate and connect with other individuals in new ways and with new freedom. This extension of basic human capabilities, amplifying humanity and not just brainpower, is why the Internet excites so many and inspires sometimes-overstated rhetoric.

CONCLUSION

The digital economy is much more than simply online shopping. It involves a fundamental transition that has been taking place for more than two decades and which is based on the rapidly falling costs of processing, storing, and transmitting information in digital electronic form. Some of this transition was obscured by the dot-com mania, which often focused on using the Internet as a marketing and retailing channel. In fact, the digital economy includes this as just a small part. The internal organization of firms is changing, their nature is changing, the kinds of interactions that are possible between different economic agents are changing, and the location of different activities is changing. Social relations, governance, and leisure activities are all affected by the pervasiveness of digital technology. Measures of the digital economy can understate or overstate the current effects, but they do emerge in recent academic work, and they appear to be increasing.

GLOSSARY

Bandwidth Technically, the difference between the lowest and highest frequencies in a transmission channel, but more often informally used to refer to the speed with which digital data can be transferred via a specific connection (telephone wire, cable, optical fiber, or wireless), for example, 10 Mbps, or 10 megabits per second.

Cyberspace All electronic interactions and data, especially those that are mediated by the Internet. The term was coined by William Gibson in his science-fiction novel *Neuromancer*.

Digital Divide A situation where particular socioeconomic groups have access to the Internet and information technology at levels that are substantially higher than other groups.

Digital Economy A term that emphasizes the importance for the overall economy of information that is stored, processed, and exchanged in digital electronic or optical formats.

E-Business A subset of e-commerce, including all electronically aided transactions and activities of businesses, including internal accounting, inventory control, and communications.

E-Commerce Short form of electronic commerce that refers to doing business electronically, based on the electronic processing, storage, and communication of information, including activities that provide the enabling physical infrastructure and software.

E-Commerce Interaction Types: B2B, B2C, C2G, C2C, B2E Acronyms for different interactions, implicitly but not necessarily electronic, among businesses, consumers, governments, and employees (e.g., B2B means business-to-business).

EDI (Electronic Data Interchange) A term that refers to the use of proprietary software and leased telecommunications lines for communications among firms, typically at different points of the value chain

E-Tailing Short for electronic retailing, which is the use of the Internet and World Wide Web for offering consumer products and services for sale and for completing transactions.

Flexible Mass Customization The ability to quickly satisfy the diverse wants of large numbers of individual consumers.

Information Economy A term that emphasizes the importance for the overall economy of all kinds of information, including entertainment, news, market and business information, research, and personal communications.

Information Revolution A term that emphasizes the dramatic effects of the steep fall in the costs of processing, storing, and communicating information as a result of advances in information technology.

Information Technology Any aspect of technology, including hardware, software, and services, that involves data in digital electronic or optical formats, including technologies for processing, storing, and transmitting such data.

Intellectual Property Useful inventions, original expressions of ideas, and names or symbols used in business the ownership of which is protected by various categories of law (trade secret, patent, copyright, and trademark).

Knowledge Economy A term that emphasizes the importance for the overall economy of all kinds of knowledge, including various types of expertise, skills, and understanding of particular markets, with an implicit emphasis on science, mathematics, and technology.

Moore's Law An empirical regularity, described by Intel cofounder Gordon Moore, that the processing power of microprocessors (measure by the number of transistors per square inch on integrated circuits) doubles every 18 months; therefore, an indicator of the rapid pace of innovation in the digital economy.

Network Externalities A situation where the value of being part of a network depends on the number of other members of a network. Typically, this value is positive. For example, if the value of a network with n members to an individual depends on the number of possible connections in the network, then this value is proportional to $n(n-1)/2$ (roughly, the square of the number of users, which is known as "Metcalfe's Law"), and the marginal value of an additional member is proportional to n, the network size.

New Economy A term that encompasses the ideas behind the terms "digital," "information," and "knowledge" economy, but also sometimes connotes that the workings of the economy are changed, either because information is a good with high fixed and low marginal costs, so competition is less stable, or because faster information flows reduce adjustment times and hence reduce swings in the economy.

Online Being actively connected to or being a user of the Internet (and possibly other electronic networks).

Supply Chain From the perspective of a firm, this is the portion of its value chain that involves its direct and indirect suppliers. From the perspective of the industry, it coincides with the value chain, with the emphasis being more on the physical processes and logistics as opposed to value added.

Value Chain A schematic representation of a firm's (or industry's) stages of production, possibly including activities that take place upstream or downstream of the firm's own activities. Examples of value chain stages include inbound logistics, production operations, outbound logistics, marketing and sales, and after-sales support. The emphasis is on the value added at each stage.

Winner-Take-All A market situation where the leader dominates because the high fixed costs and low marginal costs of producing information favor one or a few large firms, or because users of a network get much higher benefits when the network is larger.

CROSS REFERENCES

See *Click-and-Brick Electronic Commerce; Digital Divide; Electronic Commerce; Internet Basics; Legal, Social, and Ethical Issues of the Internet.*

REFERENCES

Baily, M. N. (2004, April). Recent productivity growth: The role of information technology and other innovations.

Federal Reserve Bank of San Francisco Economic Review, 35–41.

Brynjolfsson, E., & Hitt, L. M. (2000, Fall). Beyond computation: Information technology, organizational transformation and business performance. *Journal of Economic Perspectives, 14*(4), 23–48.

Chandler, A. (1990). *Scale and scope: The dynamics of industrial capitalism.* Cambridge, MA: Belknap Press.

CNET. (2002). AOL members set shopping record. Retrieved August 2, 2004, from http://news.com.com/2100-1017-800049.html

Coase, R. (1937). The nature of the firm. *Economica, 4,* 386–392.

Colecchia, A., & Schreyer, P. (2002, April). ICT investment and economic growth in the 1990s: Is the United States a unique case? A comparative study of nine OECD countries. *Review of Economic Dynamics, 5*(2), 408–442.

ComScore. (2002). U.S. online consumer sales surge. Retrieved May 28, 2003, from http://www.comscore.com/news/ecommerce_2001_review.htm

Daveri, F. (2000, September). *Is growth an information technology story in Europe too?* (Working Paper). University di Parma and IGIIER, Parma, Italy.

David, P. A. (2000). Understanding digital technology's evolution and the path of measured productivity growth: Present and future in the mirror of the past. In E. Brynjolfsson & B. Kahin (Eds.), *Understanding the digital economy* (pp. 49–98), Cambridge, MA: MIT Press.

The Economist. (2002, February 2–8). The real-time economy: Re-engineering in real time.

EMarketer. (2002). E-commerce trade and B2B exchanges. Retrieved May 28, 2003, from http://www.emarketer.com/products/report.php?2000091

European online sales up across the continent. (2004, June 24). Retrieved August 2, 2004, from http://www.emarketer.com/Article.aspx?1002885

Ford, W., & Baum, M. (1997). *Secure electronic commerce.* Upper Saddle River, NJ: Prentice Hall, p. 99.

GartnerG2. (2002). GartnerG2 Says European Online Shopping Market Will Reach 97.8bn in 2002—2.3 Percent of Total Retail Sales Retrieved March 18, 2005 from http://www.gartnerg2.com/press/pr2002-03-19b.asp

Global Reach. (2004, August). Global Internet Usage Statistics Retrieved August 2, 2004, from http://www.glreach.com/globstats/

Gordon, R. J. (2000, Fall). Does the 'new economy' measure up to the great inventions of the past? *Journal of Economic Perspectives, 14*(4), 49–74.

Guy, S. (2000, February 29). Sears, French giant in online venture. *Chicago Sun-Times,* p. 45.

Hof, R. D. (2003, August 25). The eBay economy. Business Week. Retrieved August 2, 2004, from http://www.businessweek.com:/print/magazine/content/03_34/b3846650.htm?mz

Inktomi. (2000, January). Inktomi WebMap (Press Release). Quoted at http://www.onlinemag.net/OL2000/engine5.html. Retrieved May 28, 2003

International Herald Tribune. (2002). E-tailers are primed for happier holidays. Retrieved August 2, 2004, from http://www.iht.com/articles/78016.html

Jorgenson, D. W. (2001, March). Information technology and the U.S. economy. *American Economic Review, 91*(1), 1–32.

Jorgenson, D. W. (2004, August). Information technology and the G7 economies (Draft). Retrieved September 27, 2004, from http://post.economics.harvard.edu/faculty/jorgenson/papers/handbook.extract.2001update08052004dwj.pdf

Netcraft. (2004a). Netcraft Web Server Survey Archive. Retrieved August 2, 2004, from http://www.netcraft.com/Survey/archive.html

Netcraft (2004b), January 2004 Web Server Survey. Retrieved August 2, 2004, from http://news.netcraft.com/archives/web_server_survey.html

Nielsen NetRatings. (2001, February 15). Sixty percent of Americans are online. Retrieved March 18, 2005 from http://www.nua.ie/surveys/index.cgi?f=VS&art_id=905356461&rel=true

Nielsen NetRatings. (2004, March 18). Three out of four Americans have access to the Internet (Press Release). Retrieved August 2, 2004, from http://www.netratings.com/pr/pr_040318.pdf

NUA. (1997, October 3). Internet volume is doubling every 90 days. October 3 news story quoting David Peterschmidt, President of Inktomi, reproduced at http://www.nua.com/surveys/index.cgi?f=VS&art_id=875893545&rel=true, Retrieved May 28, 2003

Organisation for Economic Co-operation and Development (OECD). (2002a, April 17). *Reviewing the ICT sector definition: Issues for discussion, directorate for science, technology and industry committee for information, computer and communications policy, working party on indicators for the information society.* Retrieved August 4, 2004, from http://www.oecd.org/dataoecd/3/8/20627293.pdf

Organisation for Economic Co-operation and Development (OCED). (2002b). *The ICT sector.* Retrieved August 4, 2004, from http://www.oecd.org/document/11/0,2340,en_2825_495656_2766475_1_1_1_1,00.html

Rudl, C. (2003, October 6). Profiting from online auction sites. Retrieved August 2, 2004, from http://www.entrepreneur.com/article/0,4621,311268,00.html

Securities and Exchange Commission (SEC). (1995, October 13). Use of electronic media for delivery purposes. Securities Act Release No. 33-7233. Retrieved March 18, 2005. http://www.sec.gov/rules/concept/33-7233.txt.

Smith, M. D., Bailey, J. P., & Brynjolfsson, E. (2000). Understanding digital markets: Review and assessment. In E. Brynjolfsson & B. Kahin (Eds.), *Understanding the digital economy: Data, tools, and research.* Cambridge, MA: MIT Press, pp. 99–136.

Stiroh, K. J. (2002, December). Information technology and the U.S. productivity revival: What do the industry data say? *American Economic Review, 92*(5), 1559–1576.

Triplett, J. E., & Bosworth, B. P. (2003, September). Productivity measurement issues in services industries: "Baumol's disease" has been cured. *Federal*

Reserve Bank of New York Economic Policy Review, 23–33.

U.S. Census Bureau. (2004). Quarterly Retail E-Commerce Sales. Retrieved March 18, 2005, from http://www.census.gov/mrts/www/data/html/04Q4.html

U.S. Department of Commerce, Economics And Statistics Administration and National Telecommunications and Information Administration. (2002, February). *A nation online: How Americans are expanding their use of the Internet*. Retrieved March 18, 2005. http://www.ntia.doc.gov/ntiahome/dn/html/anationonline2.htm

U.S. Department of Commerce. (2000). *Digital Economy 2000*. Retrieved April 30, 2003, from http://www.stat-usa.gov/pub.nsf/vwNoteIDLookup/NT00002282/$File/digital2000.pdf

Websiteoptimization. (2004, March) U.S. broadband penetration jumps to 45.2%. Retrieved August 2, 2004, from http://www.Websiteoptimization.com/bw/0403/

Woodall, P. (2000, September 21). The New Economy. *The Economist*, 6.

FURTHER READING

Committee for Information, Computer and Communications Policy, Organisation for Economic Co-operation and Development. (1997). *Measuring electronic commerce*.

ComScore: An Internet marketing and audience measurement company. Retrieved April 30, 2003, from http://www.comscore.com/

Emarketer.com: E-business research source. Retrieved April 30, 2003, from http://www.emarketer.com/

Gordon, R. J. (n.d.). Five puzzles in the behavior of productivity, investment, and innovation. Retrieved August 4, 2004, from http://faculty-Web.at.nwu.edu/economics/gordon/FivePuzzles.pdf

Jupiter Research: An Internet marketing and audience measurement company. Retrieved April 30, 2003, from http://www.jupiterresearch.com/

Netcraft: An Internet services company that provides data on the number of Internet servers. Retrieved April 30, 2003, from http://www.netcraft.com/

Nielsen NetRatings: An Internet audience measurement company. Retrieved April 30, 2003, from http://www.nielsen-netratings.com/

NUA Surveys: Resource for Internet trends and statistics. Retrieved April 30, 2003, http://www.nua.com/surveys/

Oliner, S. D., & Sichel, D. E. (2002, Fall). Information technology and productivity: Where are we now and where are ee going? *Atlanta Federal Reserve Bank Review, 87*, 15–44.

Organisation for Economic Co-operation and Development (OECD). (2002). *Measuring the information economy*. Retrieved January 23, 2004, from http://www.oecd.org/dataoecd/16/14/1835738.pdf

STAT-USA/Internet: A service of the U.S. Department of Commerce is a site for the U.S. business, economic and trade community, providing authoritative information from the Federal government. Retrieved April 30, 2003, from http://www.stat-usa.gov/

U.S. Department of Commerce. (2002). *Digital economy 2002*. Retrieved March 18, 2005, from https://www.esa.doc.gov/reports/DE2002_AUTH.pdf

Wyckoff, A. (1999). *The economic and social impact of electronic commerce: Preliminary findings and research agenda*. Paris, France: Organisation for Economic Co-operation and Development, 1999.

Online Retail Banking: Security Concerns, Breaches, and Controls

Kent Belasco, *First Midwest Bank*
Siaw-Peng Wan, *Elmhurst College*

INTRODUCTION

When the Internet backbone was privatized in the mid-1990s, it transformed the way many individuals conduct their day-to-day activities. It established a new and more efficient way for individuals to purchase plane tickets, order the latest best-sellers, or research a particular product of interest.

Bank-related activities are also among the growing activities that individuals perform online on a daily basis. According to a 2003 report from Jupiter Research, approximately 29.6 million households in the United States banked online in 2003, and this number is expected to reach 56 million households by 2008 (Greenspan, 2003). This will represent an average annual growth rate of about 14% in the 5-year period.

One of the driving factors for the increasing number of online banking activities is the customers' ease and convenience of accessing these services. Bank customers are no longer limited by the business hours of a bank to carry out their bank-related activities. They can now access a number of banking services via the Internet at anytime and from any location. Because the Internet has become a viable channel for them to serve their customers, banks are increasing their online offerings. Banks also realized that customers who conduct their banking activities online are more satisfied compared with customers who conduct their banking activities offline. They found that more-satisfied customers tend to have greater loyalty to their banks, which means that they are more likely to go to their banks to take out mortgages, loans, and equity lines. Not only are these products traditionally more profitable for the banks, they deepen the relationship with the customers and, hence, their share of wallet (Miles, 2002).

Despite the number of benefits associated with online banking, it has created a number of challenges for banks, specifically in the area of risk management. Although risk management has historically been a concern for banks, the advent of online banking is creating a more complex environment for risk management because it has changed the way banks control their risk.

Prior to online banking, banks had full control over the risks they encountered. However, once customers order online banking services, some of these controls are relinquished. With online banking services, banks are offering their customers the convenience of accessing their accounts on demand via the Internet. Allowing the customers to access their accounts on demand means that a bank's customers will interact directly with a bank's internal system, thus permitting access to customers' accounts via the Internet. This means that a bank's internal system is now connected and accessible via the Internet, which is a public network. In addition, many of the increasingly sophisticated online banking services offered by banks involve new and evolving technologies, which are often beyond the capabilities of many banks and therefore require reliance upon third-party vendors to provide the online banking applications and platforms.

TYPES OF ONLINE RETAIL BANKING SERVICES

Online banking was first introduced in the mid-1980s, when a select number of bank customers were offered the opportunity to conduct a limited number of activities using their personal computers. Unfortunately, this delivery channel did not grow in popularity because of the need for proprietary software and the fact that networks, at the time, were not very user friendly (Sorkin, 2002). It was not until the mid-1990s that online banking found a new lease on life. The privatization of the Internet provided banks an opportunity to offer banking services over a public network that customers could access simply with a browser.

Wells Fargo bank, in 1994, was the first bank to establish a Web site to offer their customers information (Hall, 2003) and Security First Network bank, in 1995, was the first bank to offer online banking services (Hoffman & Kim, 1995).

Online offerings from many banks initially were limited to providing information related to their offline products and services. Many banks were skeptical of the Internet's potential as a channel to offer banking services and products to their customers. However, as online competition from entities other than banks, such as brokerage firms and financial Web sites, intensified, many banks began to step up their online banking offerings to individual customers (i.e., online retail banking services, Wan, 2004).

Today, banks offer a variety of banking-related (and non-banking-related) services to their individual customers via bank Web sites. These online retail banking services can be grouped into three categories: sources of information, customer services, and account-related activities (Wan, 2004).

Sources of Information

Banks are taking advantage of the Internet's qualities to deliver a variety of information to various target audiences and to provide interactive and unique experiences to those accessing these information sources. Customers accessing the banks' Web sites can retrieve a wealth of information regarding the variety of banking products and services offered. With their Web sites, banks are able to provide information that is more detailed than what is available in print and can update the information in a much more timely manner.

Many banks also understand that an educated customer is a good customer. It is no longer sufficient for banks to simply provide information about their products and services. They need to help their customers understand why they need these products and services. An increasing number of banks are offering an extensive collection of educational materials on a wide range of financial topics, such as planning for college and retirements, to help their customers better understand how various banking products can assist them in achieving their financial goals.

Customer Services

The Internet enables many banks the opportunity to reduce many of the costs associated with customer service by allowing them to offer, via their Web sites, many of the services they provide. A large number of banks have established Frequently Asked Questions (FAQ) sections to offer answers to many of the questions traditionally fielded by their call centers. An increasing number of banks are offering their customers e-mail notifications with their accounts. For example, an e-mail will automatically be generated when a customer's account balance falls below a specified level. In addition, many banks have now set up online automated services that enable their customers to perform certain functions so that they no longer have to go to the banks or call a customer service representative. Customers can now perform online a number of account-related activities such as reordering checks, ordering paper copies of cancelled checks and bank statements, or requesting a stop payment on a check. Furthermore, customers can also change certain personal information, such as their addresses and PINs (personal identification numbers), easily online without having to fill out a number of forms at a local branch.

Account-Related Activities

A majority of the online bank offerings concentrate on providing customers with a wide range of account-related activities. The three most common online offerings available at most banks' Web sites include opening bank accounts, accessing account information, and initiating transactions.

Opening an account: Most banks allow their customers to initiate the account application process online by filling out an application. Some banks provide the account application forms on their Web sites, and require their customers to download and print the forms, fill them out, and either drop them off at a local branch or mail (or fax) them to the banks. On the other hand, some banks expand on this capability by allowing their customers to complete and submit their applications fully online.

Accessing account information: Once bank customers activate online banking services with their banks, they can access a variety of information related to their accounts via the banks' Web sites. They can view the account balances of their checking, savings, certificate of deposits, and other accounts. Some banks also offer their customers the opportunity to view their bank statements online. Customers can also easily determine when a particular check has cleared by simply clicking on the link associated with that particular check. Some banks' Web sites even allow their customers to view images of their cleared checks.

Initiating transactions: When bank customers sign up for online banking services with their banks, they can choose which accounts they would like to be linked online. Once the linkages have been established, customers can easily transfer payments among these accounts. In addition, many banks are now offering their customers the ability to pay their bills online. Once this feature has been activated, bank customers can schedule future payments for up to a year in advance or even set up recurring payments, such as their mortgage payments. Some banks are also bundling online bill-presentment service with their online bill-payment service. If bank customers choose to activate the online bill-presentment feature, they will be able to receive electronic bills rather than paper bills from selected billers. The bank customers can then pay these bills using the banks' online bill-payment features, which will transfer the funds from the customers' accounts to the billers' accounts.

ONLINE BANKING SECURITY CONCERNS

As the variety and complexity of online banking offerings increase, many offerings are also fast becoming targets for unauthorized activities, which exploit the nature of online banking services and the flaws in the systems that host the applications and platforms used to offer these services.

Each of the three areas of online banking offerings can be vulnerable to tampering. For example, a bank's Web site can be hacked and contents on the Web sites modified, which means that the integrity of the Web sites as sources of information has been compromised. Fraudulent e-mails can be sent to bank customers, notifying them that their accounts have been compromised, which undermines a bank's use of e-mail as a communications channel with its customers. Furthermore, many of these fake e-mails often provide links to spurious Web sites that look strikingly similar to the bank's Web site. The intention of the phony Web site is to extract information from the bank's customers so that the information can be used later to access their accounts or to commit other acts of identity theft.

A number of security breaches related to online banking have occurred since the late 1990s, when an increasing number of bank customers began to take advantage of such offerings from their banks. The most common security breach is associated with an e-mail fraud in which customers are requested to reactivate their online accounts and thus reveal sensitive personal and financial information. Cases of e-mail-related fraud have been on the rise. In 2003 alone, customers of Citibank, Wachovia bank, Bank of America, and Commonwealth Bank of Australia were targeted by e-mail scams (Hall, 2003; Secure Science Corporation, 2003). However, some of the online banking security breaches are the result of banks offering their services without fully testing their systems. For example, in 1999, X.com Bank, which is a division of First Western National Bank, unintentionally allowed its customers to transfer funds from any person's account in the country into their accounts as long as they had that person's account number and routing number (Markoff, 2000).

These security breaches are undermining the confidence of many bank customers in online banking services. According to a June 2003 report from Tower Group, concern about security is the number one factor that kept many bank customers offline (Hall, 2003). In addition, banks are also more concerned about security breaches as online banking transactions have become more complex and involve increasingly higher account values. Although bank customers have always been concerned with confidentiality, even in the pre-electronic era, the advent of automated teller machines (ATMs), voice response units, and other self-activated technologies have perpetuated an increasing concern about the loss of financial wealth and the loss of identity. Of foremost notoriety and concern is the loss of identity, or "identity theft." Until recently this threat, or rather its urgency, was seldom emphasized. However, with the proliferation of e-commerce and the expansive electronic access and transmission of data prevalent today, the opportunity for theft of critical customer information (i.e., social security numbers) has become of paramount concern to customers. In addition, other sensitive information, such as account information, has also become a major concern, especially in light of the amount of online shopping and online business transactions occurring today. The final, and maybe the most obvious, events that have heightened customer concern over the protection of their information are the Y2K scare and, of course, 9/11. These two independent events alone have raised the attention level to its present state.

Banks, on the other hand, while sharing the concerns of customers, have a more expansive set of issues and focuses. As financial institutions, banks are considered fiduciaries with respect to their customers. As such, they are not only privy to a wide range of sensitive customer information, but also to information that is important to the functioning of the bank. In addition to expanding legal liability on the part of the board of directors for the protection of such information, banks also have an obligation to their shareholders to establish the controls and mechanisms which will protect client information. In this regard, banks' information security concerns are far-ranging, encompassing a large volume of both internal and external threats that have the potential to compromise their ability to protect customer information, and are an ongoing concern.

Internal threats are those risks that emanate from within the bank or within the network of the bank that could compromise systems or information. External threats, on the other hand, are those originating outside of the bank and attempt to access, maliciously, the systems to manipulate, destroy, or render systems and information unusable. Banks are predominantly concerned with mitigating risks and therefore must perform risk assessments to understand and identify all of the risks that might affect the bank and its functioning. In general, the risks that affect a bank are those specific concerns that would impair the bank's ability to deliver on their objectives or function as an ongoing concern. Among the variety of specific adverse risks affecting banks are loss of corporate image, financial loss, loss of customer trust (which could cause a run on the bank), loss of shareholder trust (resulting in a sell-off of stock), inaccurate customer or bank information, and legal liability. As part of the risk assessment process, banks must be concerned with the risks and the controls relative to three risk attributes: assets, threats, and impacts.

Assets

Assets represent the myriad of tangible and intangible items of value that a bank possesses that could be adversely affected by a threat to its utility. Assets range from a variety of things including, but not limited to, information, physical technical devices, brick-and-mortar buildings, and equipment.

Threats

Threats are potential sources of harm, which could cause an impact to one or more of the bank's assets. Major threat categories include the following:

Technical. Technical threats are those sources of harm that are precipitated by the utilization of some form of technology. The most prevalent of these are computer viruses. Computer attacks and "hacking" are among the major concerns of any bank that has an Internet presence and conducts business or presents information about the bank through a Web interface. These threats are voluminous and occur with a high degree of frequency. As a result, it is imperative that safeguards be instituted to prevent penetration and preclude an effect on bank assets.

Human. Human threats generally emanate from four predominant sources: outsiders (terrorists), customers, partners, and insiders. These threats can vary in type; however, their common feature is direct human involvement that affects a bank's assets in some way. This could be through sabotage and espionage (both internal and external), as well as through partners who may be privy to information and other assets, which could constitute a risk. Terrorist activities, similar to the events involving the World Trade Center, are the most obvious of the human threats. With this recent example, the risk from human threats has grown tremendously in importance and focus for banks and other organizations alike. Customers, as well, can impact a bank's assets through physical access and exposure to information and other assets.

Natural. The final category of threats affecting banks is composed of those that occur naturally. Tornados, storms, fires, snow, and ice all constitute likely threats to bank assets. Although these events can and do occur randomly in the environment, they nevertheless must be addressed to avoid affecting key bank assets.

Impacts

Impacts represent the outcomes or the consequences of a particular threat. Because a threat (any of those identified) will affect a bank's assets in some way, one or more of the following will occur as a result:

Unauthorized disclosure of information. Banks are always concerned with the disclosure of sensitive bank or client information to other parties not authorized to view it and who could be in a position to use that information in ways to cause harm. This can occur through negligence or outright attempts at obtaining information.

Unauthorized modification of information. Once information is accessed by unauthorized sources, the information may be subject to modification in some way, which could result in negative consequences to the customer or bank. Examples of modification include manipulation of monetary amounts or displayed information to cause harm, to create advantage, or simply to disrupt.

Unauthorized destruction of information. In some cases information is accessed by unauthorized sources with the sole intent of destroying it or rendering it unavailable to authorized individuals. This impact is severe, greatly exposes the bank to legal liability, and can threaten the bank's existence.

Unauthorized use of information or systems. This impact is more subtle but equally as dangerous, if not more so, than the others. In this case, information that is accessed by unauthorized sources is used in ways to create advantage where none existed, to discredit, or simply for the purposes of theft, such as in the case of identity theft. The use of the information, in this regard, would appear to be appropriate and normal on the surface; however, the user of the information is not.

Improper use of information or systems. This refers to gaining unauthorized control of information and/or systems in such a way as to use them for unintended purposes. Taking control of a Web site and displaying information or messages not intended by the bank is a good example of this.

Unavailable systems. Natural threats and human threats (terrorist activities) are probably the most obvious sources that could render systems unavailable. Tornados and fires, for example, could destroy servers or central computers, which could cause the loss of data, affecting customers and the bank. Terrorist activities could be as blatant as the destruction of a physical site or as subtle as a computer virus that renders the computer unusable. In any situation, the net result is the inability to use a system that was previously relied upon.

All of these relate to the broad categories of integrity, confidentiality, and availability of information previously discussed. The purpose of risk assessment is to understand where threats may come from (sources), the effect on the bank (unauthorized disclosure, modification, or destruction of information), and to determine the appropriate controls necessary to mitigate these risks (authentication controls, password controls, etc.).

DEFINITION OF SECURITY

According to *Webster's Dictionary*, security is "freedom from risk or danger; safety." In the context of this chapter, this definition is expounded upon with an emphasis on "information security," in contrast to physical security. Physical security relates to protecting or securing the physical branch or location and access to sensitive material and/or negotiable instruments, such as bearer bonds, CDs, and endorsed checks. Information security, on the other hand, is the "process by which an organization protects and secures systems, media, and facilities that process and maintain information vital to its operations" (Federal Financial Institutions Examinations Council, 2002). As a discipline, information security has grown in importance, particularly with the proliferation of the Internet and applications for banking. At the turn of the 21st century, bank regulators were intensely focused on the issues attendant to transitioning and recovering information that possibly could have been impaired because of outdated code. Since that time, the focus has shifted from merely recovering data to a more comprehensive focus centering on information and protecting the integrity, confidentiality, and availability of customer information.

In 1999, the Gramm-Leach-Bliley Act was passed, which documented requirements for protecting the privacy of customer information. This laid the foundation for the development of a much more sophisticated means of defining and mitigating information security risks on the part of banks. More specifically, section 501(b) of the act outlines detailed requirements of what member financial institutions must do to protect client information. This section further requires regular communication and oversight responsibility on the part of the board of directors and mandates compliance.

Information Security Objectives

In 1999, the Office of the Comptroller of the Currency developed very specific guidelines for bank information systems departments to follow. The development of these standards resulted in URSIT, the Uniform Rating System for Information Technology (Office of the Comptroller of the Currency, 1999). URSIT not only standardizes the basis by which financial institutions' information technology (IT) departments are evaluated, but also provides effective guidelines for understanding the objectives of information security. URSIT, as a rating system, comprises four areas of focus (Office of the Comptroller of the Currency, 1999):

1. The adequacy of the bank's risk management practices.
2. Management of IT resources.
3. The integrity, confidentiality, and availability of automated information.
4. The degree of supervisory concern posed by the institution.

Although all four areas are a focus of the bank exam, the third item most specifically outlines the objectives for sound information-security practices and represents the key areas of focus as it relates to "customer" information.

Data integrity. This objective refers to both data and systems and attempts to define policies and procedures to ensure that neither have been altered or manipulated by unauthorized individuals, which could comprise the information or systems themselves. Data integrity is concerned with ensuring that systems and information have not been comprised by unauthorized individuals or access. Controls to mitigate risks in this area include separation of duties, balancing and reconcilement activities to check input and output, master file controls, changing management controls for system changes, access levels consistent with job functions, and strong authentication and password management (Office of the Comptroller of the Currency, 1999).

Data confidentiality. Data and system confidentiality refers to protecting sensitive information from unauthorized access and/or use while in transit or otherwise. This objective is at the heart of the Gramm-Leach-Bliley Act with regard to privacy of information. The goal of this objective is to avoid the disclosure of client data unintentionally, which could compromise the system and/or customer. Controls include intrusion detection systems, encryption of data, and monitoring mechanisms to detect and prevent unauthorized access (Office of the Comptroller of the Currency, 1999).

Data availability. Data and system availability ensures that systems and data are accessible to customers and other authorized users. Data availability is the closest to recovering data and therefore is concerned with backup procedures, redundancy, and other mechanisms that prevent the loss of access to data when needed. Controls include business resumption contingency policies and plans, event management procedures (including incident response), physical access to information and sensitive areas, virus protection, and backup and recovery procedures (Office of the Comptroller of the Currency, 1999).

The defined security objectives, in conjunction with URSIT, established the structure for information security and risk management for financial institutions. Banks are regularly reviewed, during their "safety and soundness" audits, to ensure adherence to these guidelines with the overall objective of protecting the privacy of the customer.

SOURCES AND CONTROLS OF EXTERNAL INFORMATION SECURITY BREACHES

Definition and Problem Statement

External threats can occur at any time. As outlined previously, threats fall into three categories: technical, human, and natural. Each of these threats represents a concern for the bank with regard to protecting client and sensitive bank information, as well as the uninterrupted functioning of the bank. In today's environment, external threats are a way of life and will continue to be perpetrated against banks intentionally and/or through natural occurrence. Regardless of the threat, banks must be prepared and establish the appropriate controls to avoid the effects on the bank and customer information.

From a customer's perspective, with the expanded use of the Internet, external threats against the bank are not merely concerns of the bank but equally concerns of the customer because of the potential for loss or unauthorized use of the customer's own information. As a result, the bank must enact a wide array of controls to protect against these threats.

Sources and Controls of External Threats

Threats, as previously outlined, emanate from technical, natural, and human sources. The actual occurrence of a threat, resulting in an impact to the bank, is manifested as an "event." Events are noticeable changes affecting systems. Externally, any and all of these are possible and therefore must be considered when protecting the bank's information. Table 1 summarizes the sources, controls, and effects of external threats, although a more detailed explanation of each is outlined below.

Technical threats. For the most part, technical threats affecting banks represent attacks on the bank's Web site and/or network with the purpose of performing specific functions on behalf of the perpetrator. These originate from the outside and consist of the following types:

1. *Malicious code:* These are programs developed and perpetrated by hackers and crackers to actually capture information, determine passwords, modify information, or even to "mask" the occurrence of the virus and prevent its detection from audit logs or other monitoring techniques. The most common types of malicious code are computer viruses and worms.
2. *Unauthorized access:* Unauthorized access events permit the hacker access to a wide range of information. These events could be direct access to a customer's account (both a customer and bank concern) or to other parts of the bank's network to access and read network packets as well as other subversive access that may not easily be detected and/or lie dormant awaiting use. Of major concern, obviously, is the access to critical bank and customer information that would permit

Table 1 External Information Security Breaches

Sources	Effects	Controls
1. Technical threats		
• Malicious code • Unauthorized access • Information probing • Disruption of service • Misuse • Espionage • Hoaxes	• Unauthorized modification, destruction, and/or use of information • Improper use of information	• Firewall • Intrusion detection • Server hardening • Antivirus software • Virus patches • External penetration testing
2. Human threats		
• Unauthorized access • Inadvertent viewing of sensitive information • Sabotage • Theft of information • Terrorism	• Unauthorized disclosure, modification, destruction, and/or use of information • Improper use of information • Unavailable systems	• Awareness/education • Key/card access security systems • Automatic "time-out" features • Oversight management of third parties/partners • Social engineering testing • Strong authentication
3. Natural threats		
• Ice • Fire • Earthquake • Tornado • Storms	• Unavailable systems	• Identification of critical systems • Risk assessment and impact to the bank • Hot sites • Redundant systems • Recovery procedures and testing

the hacker to review and modify information for profit or pleasure.

3. *Information probing:* Probes are less obtrusive but nevertheless constitute an invasive action on the part of the perpetrator. Probes can be technical or nontechnical. In the technical world, the program sent is designed to be similar to "bug" or monitoring devices, which gather information that can be used at the convenience of the hacker. Probes are designed to be silent and undetected but nevertheless constantly gathering information. Nontechnical probing, on the other hand, is a human threat and is discussed under that category.
4. *Disruption of service:* Another name for these types of threats are "denial of service" (DOS) events. Denial or disruption of service is exactly what the name implies, an attack designed simply to disrupt. DOS events literally can preclude the bank, or customer, from accessing information or services. Some DOS attacks flood networks with spurious information, which indirectly prevent legitimate information from getting through to the server or to the database to conduct business. Essentially, depending upon the success of the DOS attack, this threat can virtually render a bank inoperable.
5. *Misuse:* This threat can be both internal and external. Misuse occurs when the perpetrator (either outside or inside of the bank) accesses the bank's systems for the purpose of conducting personal or other business unrelated to the bank. This could involve utilizing the bank's database or Web site to conduct business, without authorization.
6. *Espionage:* This threat relates more to terrorist activities than others, although it is not limited to this source. Espionage relates directly to theft and the theft of information for the purpose of causing harm to the bank or to a customer; in other words, direct intent to cause harm to the enterprise.
7. *Hoaxes:* A hoax is a fraudulent or false reporting of viruses or other attacks that actually do not exist. The purpose of a hoax is to disrupt, even though the presence of the actual threat is not real. This type of event is more common and much easier to perpetrate because the technical development of an actual program to do what it is alleged to do is not required. Nevertheless, the harm and disruption they can cause are quite real.

Controls to monitor and prevent the external threats that may occur against the bank can take a variety of forms. The Federal Financial Institutions Examination Council provides, if not mandates, the development and implementation of specific controls to protect information from attack. The objective of the controls, used in this vernacular, is designed to provide layers of techniques to filter, detect, prevent, and ultimately stop attacks from affecting sensitive servers (Federal Financial Institutions Examination Council, 2002) Unfortunately, there is no one technique or control that can guarantee success. As a result, controls occur at various levels so that if one does not stop the attack, the next may, and so on. Among the more common techniques used to protect against external threats are these:

1. *Firewall:* First and foremost, if a bank has an externally available Web site, whether through an outsourced provider or not, the Web site and other devices on the network must be protected from attack from the outside. Firewalls are devices designed specifically to monitor and restrict (or stop) various types of attacks and information flows that are not defined within the rule sets established for the firewall itself. Firewalls actually stop information, programs, viruses, and other attacks from hitting the Web server or others. Unfortunately, the firewall cannot be engineered to prevent all types of attacks and still permit the flow of normal business. For this reason other techniques are necessary to prevent compromise.
2. *Intrusion detection:* Intrusion detection systems are "appliances" that reside on the network of the bank. Their purpose is to monitor and report on the presence of attacks, but not to prevent attacks. This is a monitoring device that can detect defined attack profiles and report that they have occurred and have penetrated the firewall. Because they do not stop the attack, alert processes are normally established along with these devices so that appropriate bank personnel can be alerted to immediately assess the impact of such attacks. Intrusion detection is based upon an in-depth analysis of prevalent attack profiles in the environment that would trigger an alert. Because new attack profiles continue to evolve in the environment that have not been defined, constant updates to profiles are critical. Unfortunately, new attack profiles are constantly occurring; therefore, other controls are also important to mitigate the risk of attack.
3. *Intrusion prevention:* Because of the shortcomings of intrusion detection, another, more direct control mechanism (and relatively new) is intrusion "prevention" software. These systems are designed to stop or prevent attacks from entering the bank environment in contrast to merely monitoring and reporting. Systems of this nature are designed to assess the characteristics of the traffic patterns and to detect aberrant type behavior and stop or prevent it from accessing the sensitive systems.
4. *Server hardening:* File servers are the predominant technical devices that house the systems, programs, and information that attacks are directed against. If an attack is able to get through the firewall undetected by intrusion detection devices and is not stopped by the intrusion prevention software, then the file server is vulnerable and exposed. At this point, the only protection against compromise would be the "hardening" of the server itself. Hardening generally refers to ensuring that the appropriate patches and other protection means are completely up-to-date and are at the ready for stopping attacks and preventing compromise. This generally involves antivirus software, among other controls.
5. *Antivirus software:* Antivirus software is installed locally at the personal computer or file server level. The software protects the computer from viruses that may enter the system via diskette, network, or other means. Although the bank may have a firewall, intrusion detection, or even intrusion prevention systems, antivirus software is still needed because viruses do get through. The reason for this is that hackers are prolific; that is, new viruses are constantly being developed that may pass undetected through a firewall or intrusion protection system. When this occurs, the last defense is antivirus protection that is designed to protect the device from compromise. Unfortunately once the software is installed, it is already out of date. Therefore, a mechanism to automatically update the software with the latest virus signatures must be a part of this control to protect systems from the very latest virus.
6. *Virus patches:* The final step in the process is patching. Patches are "fixes" for a particular virus that may be prevalent in the environment. It is not enough to simply have antivirus software installed and even to have the latest update; patches must still be distributed and installed. Patches protect against a particular virus from reoccurring and reinfecting the device, without which the risk of reinfection is high even though the virus may have been previously eradicated.
7. *External penetration testing:* Although not in itself a control, external penetration testing is typically conducted periodically by a third party of the bank. This testing is designed to attempt to electronically gain access, technically, to the bank's Web site, files, or other devices on an unauthorized basis. The results from these tests will highlight vulnerabilities and guide the bank in establishing the appropriate controls.

Human threats. Banks are very much concerned with human threats that may affect the client and/or bank information. These threats emanate from outsiders, partners, and customers. The difficulty with human threats, unlike technical threats, is that the bank can protect the perimeter through the myriad of controls previously mentioned but it is difficult to protect against the human interaction and traffic that is necessary to conduct business. Banks typically partner with many organizations to supply them with equipment, forms, electronics, and even money. Human threats involve unauthorized access or inadvertent viewing of sensitive information, sabotage of physical devices, theft of information or documents, and so forth. These threats occur because banks have branches that are open to outsiders, customers, and partners and therefore create some level of exposure to the bank and the systems the bank manages.

Controls of human threat over and above those in place to protect against external technical threats consist of the following:

1. *Awareness/education:* Security awareness programs can be very useful and important for bank customers. These programs outline the threats and define what

customers can and should do to protect themselves as well as their information from external threats and the theft of information. Banks can accomplish this through periodic seminars, Web site updates, or other brochures.

2. *Key/card access security systems:* Areas that are sensitive or contain devices that house critical bank or client information must be secured and protected from casual access. This relates specifically to central computers, servers, or mainframes that contain customer data files and/or the Web server. By restricting access to only authorized personnel using this mechanism, exposure and personnel access to these critical systems are limited and therefore the risk is mitigated.
3. *Automatic "time-out" features:* Because banks are public places, and because bankers have computers on their desks, the opportunity for inadvertent disclosure of information that may be left on a computer screen while the banker is away from his or her desk is high. Therefore, a control to prevent this type of disclosure is a program that automatically "logs off" the banker after a short period without activity. Presumably, if a banker steps away and leaves a client's account information on the screen, a security risk occurs. To guard against this threat, after time intervals of 10–15 minutes of inactivity the system will automatically log the banker off, thereby reducing the risk of unauthorized access to information.
4. *Oversight management of third parties/partners:* Bank partners generally have access to banks and bankers for a variety of reasons. As a result, the risk is not only while they are on the bank premises but also through the information or service they provide. Banks must manage partners to ensure that they have appropriate security controls in place to protect them from the same risks and threats banks face. The reason for this is that it may indirectly (or directly) affect the bank if the partner has unknowingly been compromised. Because the bank may rely on the services of the partner, compromised information or systems may be spread to the bank inadvertently. As a result, the only control is to closely and periodically review the partner and their respective security controls to gain comfort or assurance that they have done all they can to prevent compromise. Covenants can also be included in the contract to ensure that the partner adheres to certain parameters; otherwise, the bank will cease to continue doing business with that partner.
5. *Social engineering testing:* Although not a control per se, social engineering testing is conducted by a third party on behalf of the bank to test against outsiders calling or attempting to obtain information that they are not privy to. This can occur through the phone or through e-mail scams that attempt to entice the recipient to disclose information, such as a social security number or other sensitive information, about a customer or other bank data. This relates also to internal controls, in that internal awareness training (discussed later) is a reasonably effective means for controlling this.
6. *Strong authentication:* A bank's requirement of complex and not easily cracked customer passwords is another method of controlling unauthorized access to data. Bank customers, themselves, represent a threat in that they are users of the bank's systems. As such, they too can be enticed to take advantage of the access they have by attempting to gain access to other information. By establishing strong authentication controls for system access, this risk can be mitigated. Strong authentication involves methods to access sensitive information using various techniques that cannot easily be "cracked" or guessed. Passwords are merely one means of authentication; many more exist today. Because most users tend to develop passwords that make it easier for them to remember (e.g., birth dates and anniversaries), it is relatively easy to guess someone's password, even by a complete outsider. Strong authentication for passwords consists of incorporating symbols, alpha and numeric characters, and upper and lower case letters. In this way, passwords would be virtually impossible to crack. Because complex passwords are also difficult to remember, other devices such as tokens are used to eliminate this concern and enhance authentication. Tokens such as SecurID cards have PINs that change every ten seconds. Other more advanced techniques for strong authentication include fingerprints, voice imaging, digital certificates, and electronic signatures, all designed to strengthen authentication and prevent casual determination.

Natural Threats. Natural threats, which occur in the environment, include fires, storms, tornados, and other physical threats to the bank and the bank's information. Because these cannot be predicted, they expose the bank to a loss of both information and services to the customer. Among the predominant services that customers may lose are Internet banking, ATMs, and voice response systems.

Controls for these threats pertain more to protecting "data availability" than the other concerns outlined previously. Because one cannot entirely control the threat of fires, storms, and tornados, all that can be accomplished is to establish a mechanism for the protection and recovery of information. Most banks have, or should have, well-organized disaster recovery plans. The purpose for these plans is to outline how data can be recovered quickly and how services can be restored to the customer to ensure continued and uninterrupted banking. Specific controls include the following:

1. *Identification of critical systems, locations, and functions:* The first step that banks would follow includes the identification of the most critical systems within the bank that house client and other sensitive information. In addition, bank locations that house critical systems and functions must also be included and/or identified in the event that they become completely inoperable because of a natural disaster.
2. *Risk assessment and impact to the bank:* The second control is to understand the relative financial risk the critical system, function, or location represents to the bank and whether its loss or impairment would or would not have a negative impact on the bank. Once determined, specific recovery and action plans can take place based upon the criticality of the system.

3. *Hot sites:* Hot sites can be established for specific enterprise-related critical functions or systems in the event the location becomes inoperable. These sites are established to back up critical functions such as call centers or other functions that require physical setup to be used on short notice.
4. *Redundant systems:* Particularly in the case of Internet banking, redundant Web servers or other database servers can be deployed at alternate sites to be activated in the event a server is destroyed, impaired, or even compromised.
5. *Recovery procedures and testing:* Recovery procedures and testing are the final steps and actions to be taken in the event that the location, device, or function is impaired in any way. These procedures typically would be tested once or twice per year to ensure that they are effective in the event of a disaster.

SOURCES AND CONTROLS OF INTERNAL INFORMATION SECURITY BREACHES

Definition

Internal sources of security breaches may fall within the broad categories of technical, human, and natural threats, as with external sources. Because these have been outlined in some detail in the External Sources section, they will not be repeated here. In lieu of those, other internal sources that may be more obvious to the bank will be discussed. Internal sources of security breaches affecting the bank involve, predominantly, the employees of the bank and the functions they perform. Because bank employees have a wide variety of access to systems, the potential for security breach emanating from this source can be relatively high. In addition, the threat that employees of the bank may inadvertently disclose information that may have been coaxed from them through fraud or deception is also present. Nevertheless, internal sources of security breach are those that emanate from within the bank or the bank's systems. Table 2 provides a synopsis of the sources, controls, and impacts of internal threats, with more detailed explanations of each contained in subsequent sections.

Sources of Security Breaches

1. *Negligence:* Security breaches can and do occur through employee negligence. Employees, while performing their jobs, may inadvertently leave sensitive documentation out and available for casual observation by customers, outsiders, or other unauthorized individuals. Another form of negligence is discarding information, in paper form, that could be easily retrieved in the trash by unauthorized individuals. The last form of negligence on the part of employees is not adhering to internally derived end-user policies that protect the bank regarding Internet use, e-mail policies, and strong authentication of passwords.
2. *Sabotage:* Internal sabotage can occur by disgruntled employees that potentially have some access to servers. Another form of sabotage is making available sensitive customer information to outsiders, competitors, or others who can gain value from the information. This could consist of client lists and other types of information.
3. *Deception:* Deception occurs when calls are placed or e-mails are sent to internal staff requesting information fraudulently. This can occur in many forms but most often would be through the telephone or e-mail.

Controls

Controls should be enacted internally to ward against the threats and/or risks that can occur from within the bank. Unfortunately, these threats are equally as lethal as those that occur externally but often do not get as high a priority as those emanating from external sources. Nevertheless specific controls are available, and recommended, to mitigate the risks the bank faces. Among these are

1. *Employee awareness programs:* Employee awareness is paramount to the success of risk mitigation. Employees often are not adept at the nuances of hackers, viruses, or the subtleties of a sensitive document left available on the desktop. The purpose of awareness is not so much education as it is sensitization. Employees do not generally, in a busy workday, consider logging off and onto their systems, as this is construed to be nonproductive or is simply not considered. Employees, as a rule, tend to open e-mail attachments when reading mail. The objective of awareness is to cause employees to consider or rethink routine functions in the course of completing or executing their jobs, so as to prevent the aforementioned effects of unauthorized disclosure, modification, use, or availability of information or systems.
2. *Separation of duties:* As part of URSIT, separation of duties creates an "arm's length" distance in functional

Table 2 Internal Information Security Breaches

Sources	Impact	Control
• Negligence • Sabotage • Deception	• Unauthorized disclosure, modification, destruction, and/or use of information • Improper use of information • Unavailable systems	• Employee awareness • Separation of duties • Rapid disablement of security access for terminated employees • End-user policies • Internal penetration testing

areas that have authority for monetary and other sensitive transactions affecting clients and the bank. One means of mitigating this risk is taking care to analyze functions to ensure that an independent staff member has review capability to check the work of another. In this way, the opportunity for internal misuse of information or systems can be thwarted.

3. *Rapid disablement of security access for terminated employees:* Employee resignations and terminations occur relatively frequently in large organizations. It is imperative that the bank have a process to immediately terminate passwords and user identification numbers quickly to prevent the possibility of unauthorized access or use of information during this transition.
4. *End-user policies:* Security breaches can easily occur through infected diskettes and other devices brought into the bank from the outside. The bank can protect itself by establishing strict policies that define what can and cannot be used from the outside. Policies are not absolute assurance, however. This requires that the bank consider having an annual review and sign-off of these policies to ensure awareness and compliance; a zero-tolerance approach may also be considered to enforce the policies.
5. *Internal penetration testing:* Although not a control itself, internal penetration testing is used to test the internal controls the bank has established. Similar to external penetration testing, a bank typically engages a third party to periodically perform these tests to provide the bank with guidance and areas where vulnerabilities exist.

CONCLUSION

Overall, external and internal sources of security breach are common in the banking world today and are growing. Bank regulators are very focused on the risks to the financial industry and therefore have incorporated very specific guidelines into their ongoing examinations of banks to uncover and mitigate these risks. However, even with intensified regulatory examinations, the business of risk management is a dynamic one. As new technologies evolve, so too will new avenues of breach and therefore the need for expanded controls. With the proliferation of file servers and databases housing a myriad of sensitive client and bank data, banks must be focused on not only protecting the perimeter but also ensuring that every data reservoir in the bank is completely hardened against attack. In the long run, customers will demand this to do business with the bank.

Need for Customer Assurance

When ATMs arrived on the scene, it took some time before customers became comfortable with using them as an alternative to a live teller. Even today, many bank clients are reluctant to deposit funds in an ATM for fear of loss of deposits, yet most will withdraw funds. The Internet and online banking is progressing in a similar direction. The lessons learned from ATMs can be helpful to banks in helping customers to gain comfort with this evolving delivery channel. In many ways, the reason bank branches have not gone away, and in fact have grown in demand, is due primarily to the need for face-to-face contact or, possibly, security of transactions. Monetary transactions are very sensitive and few people are willing to expose hard-earned savings to risk of loss or theft resulting from insecure channels of delivery. Because of these concerns, banks must focus on addressing customer needs through both education and possibly guarantees.

Education. Similar to the steps banks are taking internally to educate employees, the same is necessary for bank clients. Training ATMs can be found in bank branches that educate customers on the usage of ATMs, while at the same time alleviating the fear of loss of funds through use of these devices. Kiosks are now growing at branch locations with the sole intent of breaking down fears of Internet banking and helping clients to become more comfortable with this evolving avenue. Unfortunately, client education is challenging. A means of communicating to clients that will be used by clients is necessary to educate them. This can be done through the Web site itself; however, with the amount of information already contained on the Web site, this may not accomplish its purpose unless done properly.

A possible approach to client education may have to originate from the federal government rather than banks. The preparation for Y2K (at the turn of the century) was well communicated and adopted by the federal government, through bank regulators, to prevent customers' adverse actions, resulting from lack of education. The national communications helped to prevent bank runs and other negative actions that would have dramatically affected the banking industry and thus our economy. Similarly, it may become necessary for bank regulators to do the same thing to guarantee security. This is all part of client education, which will become completely necessary as the Internet becomes no longer an interesting new technology but rather a commodity.

Guarantees. Another option to increase customers' comfort is to provide some level of guarantee of transactions, particularly transactions that might be compromised. The credit card industry, through the Fair Credit Lending Act, provides customers with avenues to address fraudulent purchases that may occur, without loss to the cardholder. The same will likely be required for Internet banking. This could be manifested in association with organizations that become recognized, that guarantee "secure" transactions, and that provide insurance that the customer will be protected from financial loss should it occur.

The future is left to be seen. As banks have come to alter their view of Internet banking, from a unique product to now another delivery channel, Internet banking will become a necessity for banking. Similar to ATMs, Internet banking will become, and is, a necessity for customers to do business with a bank. Banks that do not offer ATMs, debit cards, or now Internet banking will not attract and maintain their client base. In this regard, information security, risk management, and the controls banks develop will play a major role in the growth of online banking in the years to come.

GLOSSARY

Authentication The process of permitting access to a particular system or information via means of a password, a secure device, and so forth, which is constrained to the individual using it. Authentication is the process that compares the method used to access the data with the "accepted" access defined for the user.

FFIEC (Federal Financial Institutions Examination Council) It is a "formal interagency body empowered to prescribe uniform principles, standards, and report forms for the federal examination of financial institutions by the Board of Governors of the Federal Reserve System (FRB), the Federal Deposit Insurance Corporation (FDIC), the National Credit Union Administration (NCUA), the Office of the Comptroller of the Currency (OCC), and the Office of Thrift Supervision (OTS) and to make recommendations to promote uniformity in the supervision of financial institutions" (Federal Financial Institutions Examination Council, 2003). The agency provides guidance, in terms of policies and procedures, to member banks to develop and maintain internal controls on a uniform basis. Not all financial institutions are examined by the same examiners indicated here. However, the FFIEC, through their Web site and the aforementioned policies and procedures, provides a uniform set of materials that are adopted by all of the examining bodies and incorporated into their procedures. In this way a reasonably uniform method of controls is established for commercial banks, savings institutions, and credit unions. The FFIEC, within this context, has provided very detailed explanations of risks and controls for the management of information security, among others, within these financial institutions.

Firewall Electronic devices (appliances) that sit in front of a bank's network and Web server. They are designed to filter incoming Internet traffic and stop unwanted traffic and/or viruses from compromising bank systems.

Intrusion Detection An electronic "appliance" placed on the bank's network, behind the firewall, to monitor viruses and other types of attacks that are perpetrated against the bank's Web site. Intrusion detection does not stop attacks, but merely monitors their existence and reports them.

Intrusion Prevention Software installed on file servers that relies on specific defined patterns to monitor and assess traffic and actually stop it in the event that the pattern of behavior is not considered "normal" or is not following a predefined pattern.

Retail Banking Bank sales are generally divided between "commercial" and "retail" sales. Commercial refers to business banking, which includes small business, large businesses, and even cash management services, in some cases. Commercial sales are focused on providing seasonal and other lending services to the business community. Retail, on the other hand, is centered on providing bank products (e.g., checking accounts, savings accounts, money markets, installment loans, etc.) to individual consumers (customers). This group of clients uses, in many cases, individual products based upon need and does not have any corporate or business affiliation.

URSIT (Uniform Rating System for Information Technology) A rating system used by bank regulators to evaluate the effectiveness of banking information technology practices.

CROSS REFERENCES

See *EDI Security; Electronic Commerce; Electronic Payment Systems; Internet Basics.*

REFERENCES

Federal Financial Institutions Examinations Council (FFIEC). (2002, December). *Information Security, IT Examination Handbook*. Retrieved October 1, 2003, from http://www.ffiec.gov/ffiecinfobase/booklets/information_secruity/information_security.pdf

Federal Financial Institutions Examinations Council (FFIEC). (2003). *About the FFIEC—Mission*. Retrieved October 1, 2003, from http://www.ffiec.gov/about.htm

Greenspan, R. (2003, November 21). *E-banking, online bill paying growth ahead*. Retrieved March 1, 2004, from http://www.clickz.com/stats/markets/finance/article.php/3112511

Hall, P. (2003, August 21). Still green; online banking, though 21 years old, hasn't really caught on yet. *Hartford Courant*, D3.

Hoffman, T., & Kim, N. (1995, October 23). In 'net we trust. *Computerworld*, vol. 29 issue 43, 14.

Markoff, J. (2000, January 28). Security flaw discovered at online bank. *New York Times*, C1.

Miles, S. (2002, October 21). What's a check? After years of false starts, online banking is finally catching on. *Wall Street Journal*, R5.

Office of the Comptroller of the Currency (OCC). (1999, January 29). *Uniform rating system for information technology* (OCC 99-3).

Secure Science Corporation. (2003, November 13). *Banking scam revealed*. Retrieved December 22, 2003, from http://www.securityfocus.com/infocus/1745

Sorkin, A. R. (2002, May 30). Your money where your modem is. *Wall Street Journal*, G1.

Wan, S. (2004). Online banking and beyond: Internet-related offerings from U.S. banks. In H. Bidgoli (Ed.), *The Internet Encyclopedia* (Vol. 2, pp. 720–732). Hoboken, NJ: John Wiley & Sons.

FURTHER READING

Barker, C. (2002, December 26). *Ghosts in the machine: The who, why, and how of attacks on information security* (SANS Institute White Paper). Retrieved March 15, 2004, from http://www.sans.org/rr/papers/47/914.pdf

Bonnette, C. (2003, July 9). *Assessing threats to information security in financial institutions* (SANS Institute White Paper). Retrieved March 15, 2004, from http://www.sans.org/rr/papers/60/1267.pdf

Boyce, R. (2001, July 12). *Vulnerability assessment: The pro-active steps to secure your organization* (SANS Institute White Paper). Retrieved March 15, 2004, from http://www.sans.org/rr/papers/60/453.pdf

Brackin, C. (2002, August 29). *Vulnerability management: Tools, challenges, and best practices* (SANS Institute White Paper). Retrieved March 15, 2004, from http://www.sans.org/rr/papers/60/1267.pdf

Garg, A., Curtis, J., & Halper, H. (2003). The financial impact of IT security breaches: What do investors think? *Information System Security*, 22–33.

Office of the Comptroller of the Currency (OCC). (2001). *Information Technology, Community Bank Supervision* (draft) (OCC 2001-35, Attachment B).

Ridgway, L. (2003, October 27). *Disaster recovery: Survivability and security*. (SANS Institute White Paper). Retrieved March 15, 2004, from http://www.sans.org/rr/papers/index.php?id=1274

Digital Libraries: Security and Preservation Considerations

Cavan McCarthy, *Louisiana State University*

INTRODUCTION

Defining Digital Libraries

A digital library (DL) combines the advantages of digital access with the services and quality information traditionally found in a library. Digital libraries can be characterized as the "high end" of the Internet: that sector of the Internet that maintains a tradition of shared resources and easy access while offering quality content from authoritative sources, such as libraries and universities.

The author has developed the following definition of a digital library: a system that permits, via the Internet and the World Wide Web (WWW), easy access to a collection of high-value, quality digital content, which has been selected and organized to facilitate use, and is supported by appropriate services. The digital content may reflect the traditional textual orientation of many libraries or take advantage of the WWW's facilities to deliver graphics and multimedia.

Texts for the field offer the following definitions of digital libraries:

> Digital libraries are organized collections of digital information. They combine the structuring and gathering of information, which libraries and archives have always done, with the digital representation that computers have made possible.... [T]he digital library must have content; it can either be new material, prepared digitally, or old material, converted to digital form. (Lesk, 1997, pp. xix, 2)
>
> An informal definition of a digital library is a managed collection of information, with associated services, where the information is stored in digital formats and accessible over a network. A crucial part of this definition is that the information is managed.... Digital libraries contain diverse collections of information for use by many different users. Digital libraries range in size from tiny to huge. They can use any type of computing equipment and any suitable software. The unifying theme is that information is organized on computers and available over a network, with procedures to select the materials in the collections, to organize it, to make it available to users, and to archive it. (Arms, 2000, p. 2)

The common feature of these definitions is that a digital library must contain content. A site which simply points toward informational resources, a Yahoo!-style system, cannot be considered a true digital library. Three parallel terms exist: digital, electronic, and virtual libraries. These are normally used interchangeably (Saffady, 1995). In practice, digital library is the general term in North America whereas electronic library is preferred in Europe. Schwartz (2000) analyzed no fewer than 64 different formal and informal definitions of "digital library." Chowdhury and Chowdhury (2003) devote an entire chapter of their *Introduction to Digital Libraries* to definitions and characteristics of the field.

Categories of Digital Libraries

Despite their short history, digital libraries already demonstrate remarkable diversity. This overview is abbreviated; for a more detailed discussion, see this author's recent article in *The Internet Encyclopedia* (McCarthy, 2004).

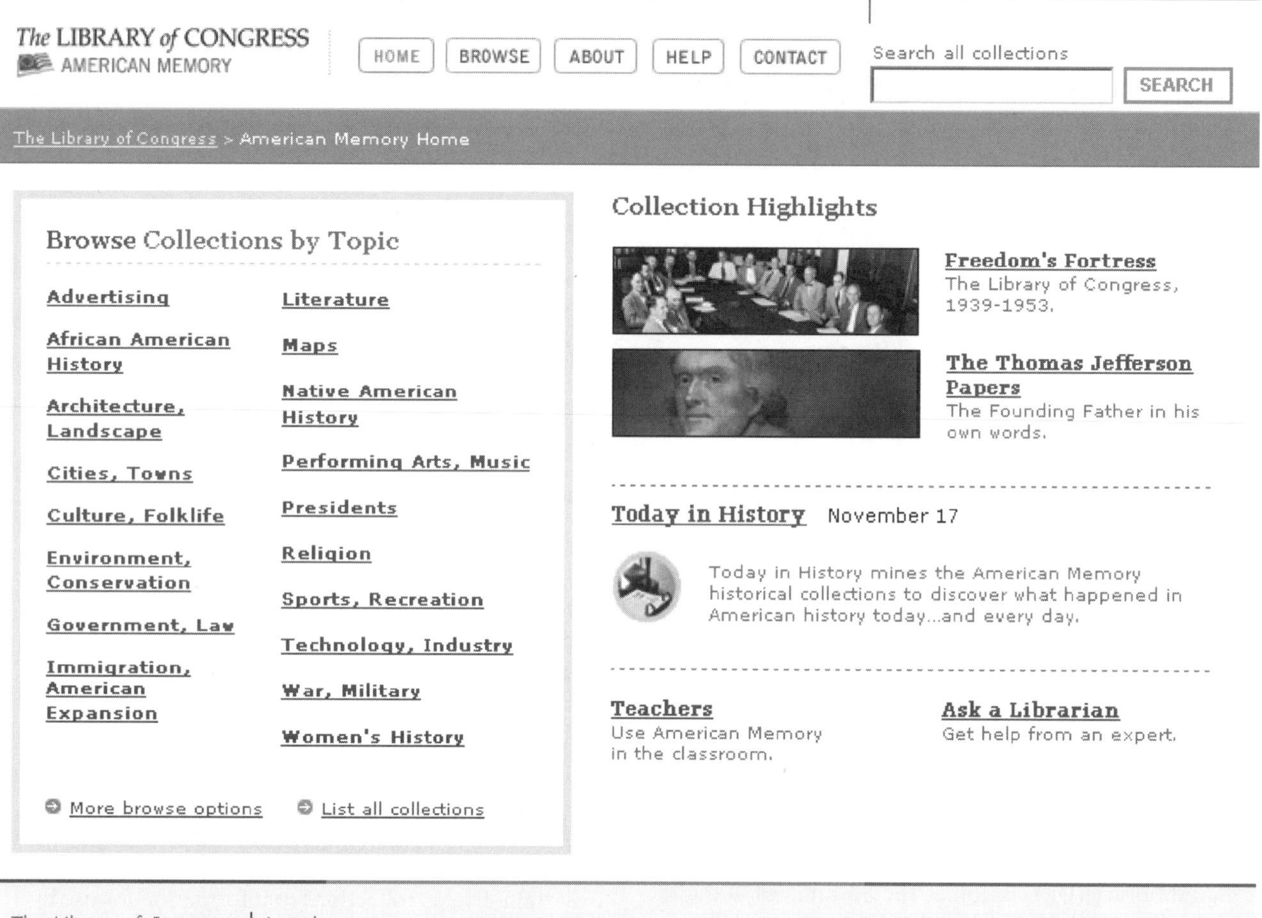

Figure 1: Opening screen, American Memory, Library of Congress.

Multimedia Collections

As digital libraries use computers as their interface, they can present a variety of materials, such as books, photographs, film, audio, and other media, with equal facility. A major multimedia collection, and one of the world's most important digital libraries, is the American Memory project, the Historical Collections of the National Digital Library, maintained by the Library of Congress (Figure 1; http://memory.loc.gov/). This now includes more than 100 collections, a total of 7 million digital items, including photographs, manuscripts, rare books, maps, sound recordings, and moving pictures.

Another source of multimedia content in a digital library is the Berkeley Digital Library SunSITE (http://sunsite.berkeley.edu/), by the Library of the University of California at Berkeley in collaboration with Sun Microsystems. Their Jack London collection, for instance, offers multiple approaches, such as the full text of many of London's books, reproductions of letters and documents, photographs, and audio (http://sunsite.berkeley.edu/London/). The objective of ibiblio (http://ibiblio.org/index.html) is to make information freely available for the public domain. It is a collaboration of the Center for the Public Domain and the University of North Carolina at Chapel Hill and includes software, music, literature, art, history, science, politics, and cultural studies. Apart from written texts, it also includes music and poetry archives, sports statistics, large text database projects, and software archives.

Book-Oriented Collections

Project Gutenberg, a book-oriented collection, is often considered the first significant digital library (http://www.gutenberg.net/). It was founded in 1971 at the University of Illinois and has always concentrated on simple presentations, originally file transfer protocol (FTP) downloads of "plain vanilla" ASCII texts, readable on almost any platform. Many of Project Gutenberg's 10,000 free texts are now available in HTML, and the volunteer-supported project has numerous mirror sites. The University of Michigan is responsible for several significant book-oriented projects, notably the Making of America (Figure 2; http://www.hti.umich.edu/m/moagrp/). This contains 8,500 books and 50,000 journal articles on 19th-century American social history from the antebellum period through Reconstruction. Sophisticated software offers a choice of image, text, or PDF (portable document format) files, in normal, large, and small sizes.

The University of Virginia Electronic Text Center (http://etext.lib.virginia.edu), founded in 1992, now offers

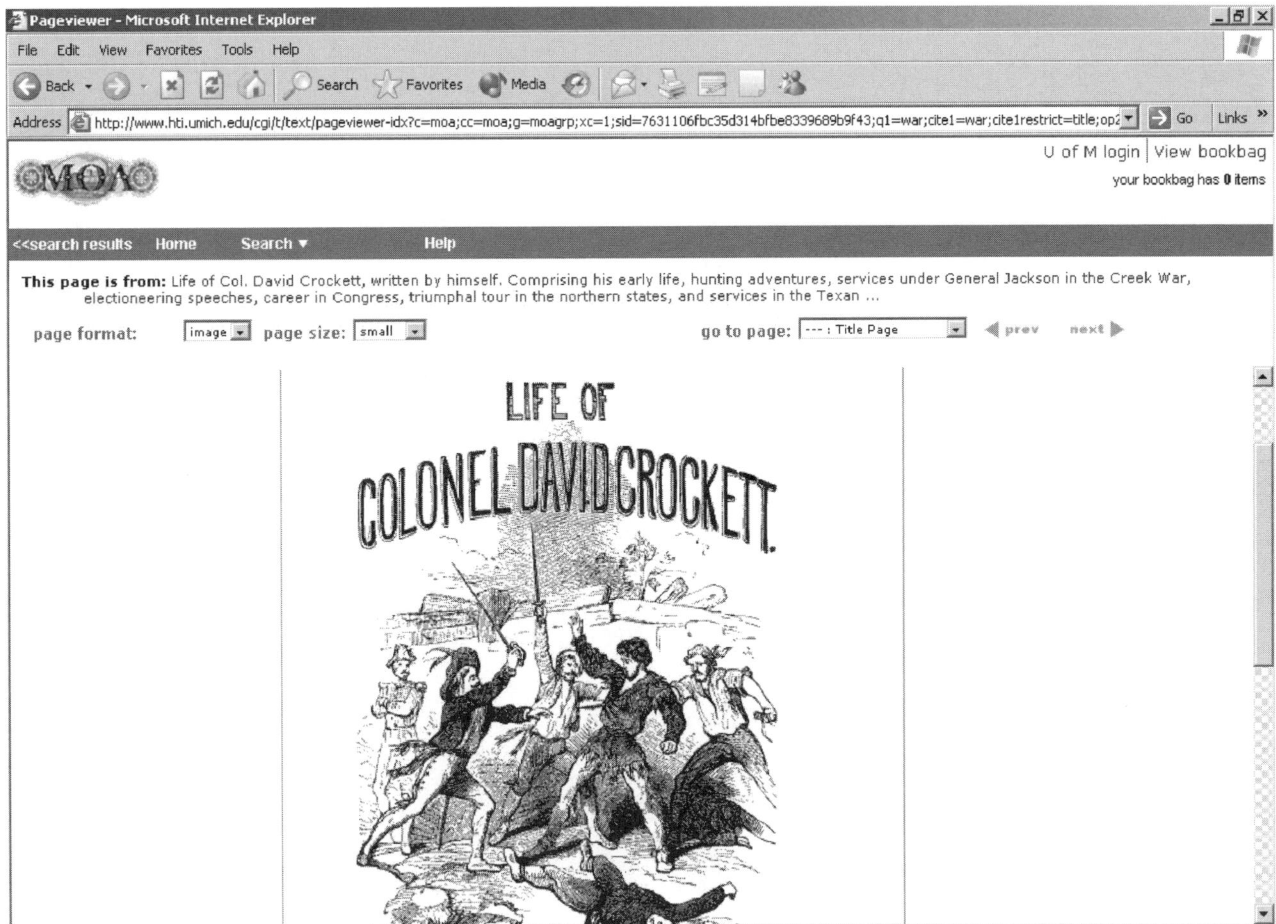

Figure 2: Screen from the Making of America Collection, the University of Michigan. Note bibliographic data at head of page, "page format" settings (image, text, PDF), "page size" settings (small, large, normal), and controls to move from page to page.

70,000 humanities texts, which have been downloaded more than 6 million times. The Center also offers much valuable information on digitization, and links to other English-language, full-text Web resources (http://etext.lib.virginia.edu/eng-oth.html). It is necessary to point out, however, that at the moment digital libraries exclude most modern commercially published books and most copyright-protected resources (i.e., exactly the texts that are generally in high demand). The Online Books Page (http://digital.library.upenn.edu/books/), a wide-ranging catalog of online books, covers more than 20,000 titles. The Digital Book Index (http://www.digitalbookindex.com/) claims to list more than 90,000 English-language book texts, of which more than 50,000 are said to be free, but many texts are available in multiple versions.

Image-Oriented Collections

A significant portion of the digital library field is dedicated to photographs and still images. The Library of Congress maintains a collection of 160,000 black-and-white Farm Security Administration photographs, focusing on American rural life during the Depression (Figure 3; http://memory.loc.gov/ammem/fsowhome.html). Keyword, subject, creator, and geographic indexes are available.

The Bancroft Library at the University of California, Berkeley, offers the California Heritage Collection, 30,000 images illustrating California's history and culture (http://sunsite.berkeley.edu/CalHeritage/).

Manuscripts

Digital libraries have blurred the line between archives and libraries. The Library of Congress offers the papers of George Washington (http://memory.loc.gov/ammem/gwhtml/gwhome.html), 60,000 items; and the papers of Abraham Lincoln (http://memory.loc.gov/ammem/alhtml/malhome.html), 61,000 images and 10,000 transcriptions. The papers of Wilbur and Orville Wright were added in 2003 (http://memory.loc.gov/ammem/wrighthtml/wrighthome.html).

Ephemeral Materials

The Internet is an excellent medium for ephemeral materials, so it is no surprise that digital libraries frequently preserve and disseminate ephemera. A well-organized example is the Broadside Ballads collection of one of Britain's oldest libraries, the Bodleian Library of Oxford University (http://www.bodley.ox.ac.uk/ballads/). Three thousand items of historic American sheet music from the collections of Duke University can be found at http://

fsa2004000020/PP - Microsoft Internet Explorer

File Edit View Favorites Tools Help

Address http://lcweb2.loc.gov/cgi-bin/query/D?fsaall:24:./temp/~ammem_B941::

AMERICAN MEMORY | PREVIOUS | NEXT | ITEM LIST | NEW SEARCH

America from the Great Depression to World War II: Black-and-White Photographs from the FSA-OWI, 1935-1945

Photograph 24 of 26

Click on picture for larger image, full item, or more versions. [Rights and Reproductions]

Destitute pea pickers in California. Mother of seven children. Age thirty-two. Nipomo, California.

Lange, Dorothea, photographer.

OTHER TITLES
Migrant mother.

CREATED/PUBLISHED
1936 Feb.

SUMMARY
Portrait of Florence Thompson with her children.

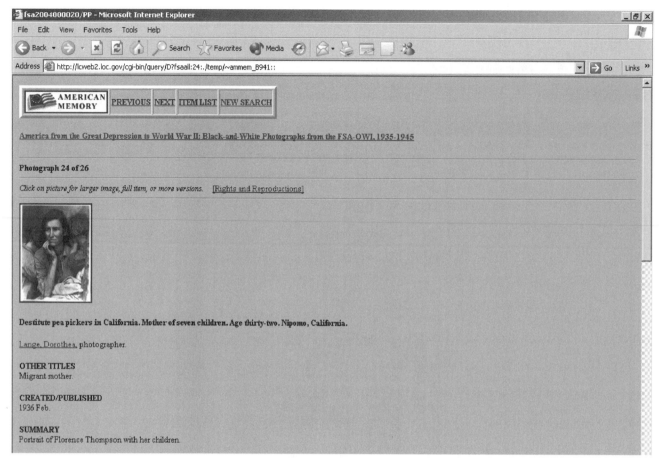

Figure 3: Photograph from the Farm Security Administration collection at the Library of Congress. Taken by Dorothea Lang, this photograph is usually referred to as the "Migrant Mother."

memory.loc.gov/ammem/award97/ncdhtml/hasmhome.html. Spanish Civil War posters were digitized at the University of California at San Diego (Figure 4; http://orpheus.ucsd.edu/speccoll/visfront/).

Audio and Motion Picture Files

The previous section on multimedia digital libraries gave several examples of systems that offer partial audiovisual content. For instance, fascinating content from the dawn of the cinema can be found in the Early Motion Pictures collection of the American Memory collection: (http://memory.loc.gov/ammem/vshtml/vsfilm.html). The Prelinger Archives of Ephemeral Films, a series of nearly 2,000 short films, mostly illustrating various aspects of American life in the 20th century, is freely available from the Internet Archive (http://www.archive.org/movies/prelinger.php). A major site dedicated to audio files is History and Politics Out Loud (http://www.hpol.org/), with speeches of Roosevelt, Churchill, and many others.

Commercially Oriented Digital Libraries

NetLibrary (Figure 5; http://www.netlibrary.com), which offers 60,000 titles, has always concentrated on selling through libraries. An unusual feature is that it only

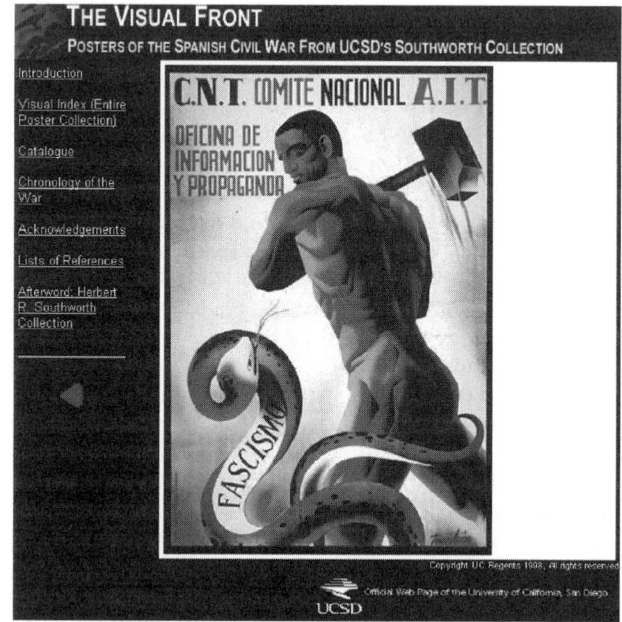

Figure 4: Spanish Civil War poster, digitized at the University of California, San Diego.

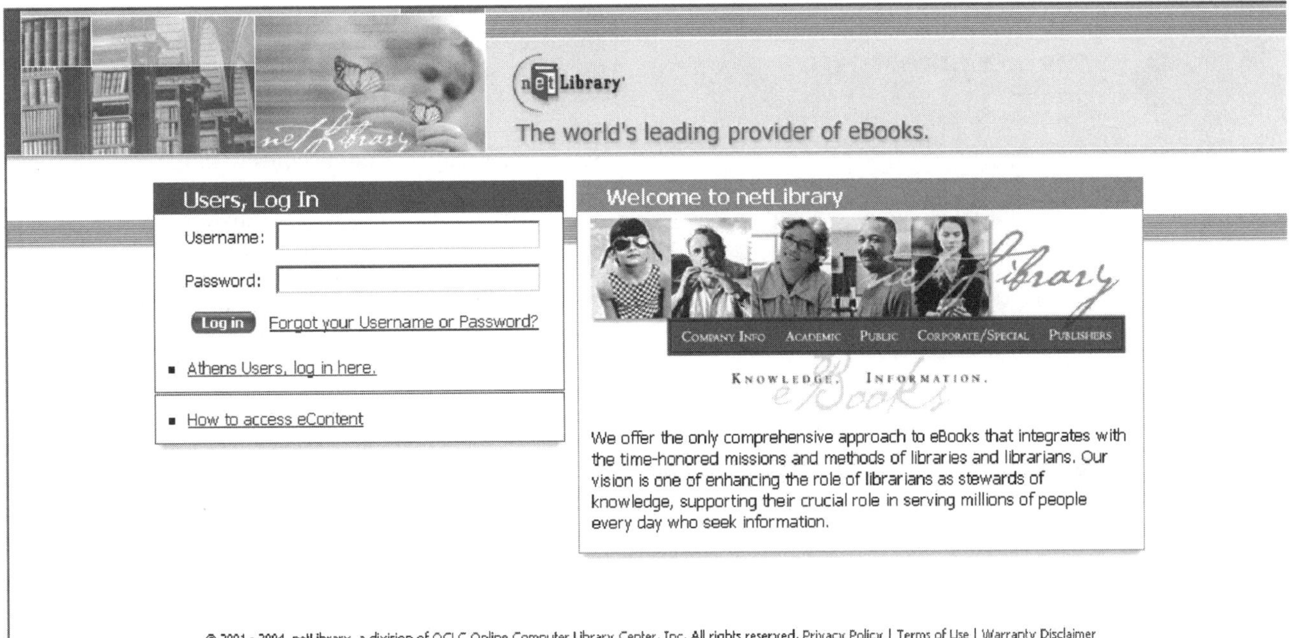

Figure 5: Opening screen of netLibrary.

permits access to a limited number of copies of each book at any one time. This appears strange in view of the Internet's capability of generating an unlimited number of copies of a digital text, but this restriction encourages publishers to join the system. Rapid printing of multiple pages is also inhibited. NetLibrary is part of OCLC (Online Computer Library Center; http://www.oclc.org/), a cooperative system that supplies automated cataloging data to more than 40,000 libraries.

Houston-based Questia (http://www.questia.com/) digitized a core collection in the humanities and social sciences and offers nearly 50,000 books and nearly 400,000 articles. There is an excellent advanced software interface and full access costs $19.95 a month as of this writing. O'Reilly Network, a major publisher of computer related books, offers digital versions of 2,000 texts on information technology and programming to libraries through the Safari Bookshelf (http://safari.oreilly.com/). The Association for Computing Machinery is an outstanding example of a professional association that has been able to successfully implement a paid-access digital library, the ACM Digital Library (http://portal.acm.org/portal.cfm/); it has the advantage of an audience with a high level of computer literacy. Consumers in traditional bookstores have always had the right to flip through a few pages of the text. Amazon.com now permits this in an electronic environment via a digital archive of more than 120,000 books (Wolf, 2003). The entire digital text is searchable, but it is not possible to print out text and only a few pages can be viewed at a time. Usage of "Search Inside the Book" is limited to people whose credit card numbers are on file with Amazon.com.

Electronic Journals (E-Journals)

This is an area where digital penetration has been intense and often both commercially driven and controversial. The field can be divided into three major categories: commercial, semicommercial, and free e-journals.

The commercial e-journal situation has its roots in the second half of the 20th century, when the publishing of scientific journals came to be dominated by a handful of specialized companies. They gained a reputation for constantly increasing prices, but as faculty and researchers considered journals essential for research, libraries were under pressure to keep subscribing to ever more expensive periodicals. The introduction of e-journals offered no relief: major publishers now offer both paper and electronic versions of their journals; there is often little cost advantage in subscribing to electronic versions alone. Libraries end up subscribing to bundles of e-journals, including titles in which they have little interest; prices for the bundles increase constantly and cancellation of individual titles brings little relief. Journals published by Elsevier (http://www.elsevier.com/) are frequently cited in this context (Knight, 2003, Carnevale, 2003a). The 121 members of the Association of Research Libraries spend about $480 million per year on journals, an average of $4 million each (http://www.arl.org/create/home.html). Elsevier maintains Science Direct (http://www.sciencedirect.com/), which offers controlled electronic access to 1,800 titles and 4 million articles. Other agents for e-journal subscriptions include Ebsco, long established as an agent fulfilling library journal subscriptions, which now permits libraries to access more than 8,000 e-journals and 4 million articles (http://www.ebsco.com/home/ejournals/default.asp), and also Blackwell's Synergy system, which permits nonsubscribers to purchase single items (http://www.blackwell-synergy.com/).

Semicommercial approaches are seen as a solution. SPARC, the Scholarly Publishing and Academic Resources Coalition (http://www.arl.org/sparc/index.html), has set up a collaborative system for academic e-journal

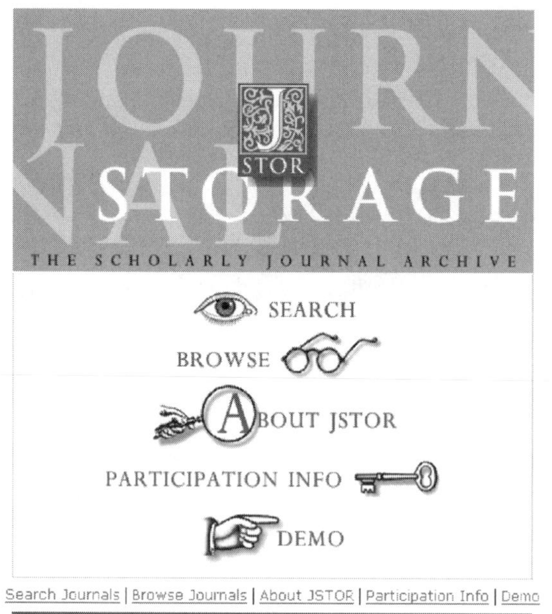

Figure 6: Opening screen of JSTOR, the Scholarly Journal Archive, from the University of Michigan.

production. Two important university initiatives offer reasonably priced access to members of participating academic institutions. Project Muse, of Johns Hopkins University Press (http://muse.jhu.edu/), has more than 200 titles. JSTOR, the scholarly journal archive (Figure 6; http://www.jstor.org/), organized by the University of Michigan, has 360 titles.

The Public Library of Science (PLoS) is a nonprofit organization of scientists and physicians, which treats the costs of publication as the final step of the research funding process (http://www.publiclibraryofscience.org/). The International Consortium for the Advancement of Academic Publication, based at Athabasca University, Canada (http://www.icaap.org/), offers a collaborative system for publishing specialized e-journals. Another solution to the e-journal problem is offered by preprint archive systems such as arXiv (http://arxiv.org/), which permits rapid access to preprints in physics, mathematics, and science.

Free e-journals have also expanded rapidly. Three thousand titles are listed at the Internet Public Library (http://www.ipl.org/div/serials/). An additional list of e-journals can be found at the World Wide Web Virtual Library (http://www.e-journals.org/). The Internet Library of Early Journals offers free access to six 18th- and 19th-century journals (http://www.bodley.ox.ac.uk/ilej/).

Digital Newspaper Collections

NewspaperArchive is a commercial undertaking from Cedar Rapids, which has 20 million indexed pages available online; full access costs $12.95 per month (http://www.newspaperarchive.com/DesktopDefault.aspx). The Missouri Historical Newspapers Collection (http://newspapers.umsystem.edu/archive/Skins/Missouri/navigator.asp) offers advanced access to local newspapers; readers are able to click on any article, photograph, or advertisement, which is then enlarged and presented in a separate window. This uses Olive ActivePaper Archive software (http://www.olivesoftware.com/home.html). Several newspaper-clipping collections are now available. An indexed collection of clippings from newspapers published in the Pacific Northwest of the United States is available at http://content.wsulibs.wsu.edu/pncc/pncc.htm. For World War II, a collection of more than 144,000 newspaper articles compiled by a Canadian newspaper has been digitized and indexed at http://www.warmuseum.ca/cwm/newspapers/index.html.

Electronic Theses and Dissertations

A general reference point for this field is the Networked Digital Library of Theses and Dissertations (NDLTD; http://www.ndltd.org/). A founding member was Virginia Tech, which now offers unrestricted access to more than 5,000 digital theses (http://scholar.lib.vt.edu/theses/). Experience suggests that digital availability stimulates use and promotes the author's reputation. West Virginia University reports more than 1.4 million hits on its digital theses collection (http://www.wvu.edu/~thesis/News/WVU_ETDS_Over_1_Million_Served.htm). MIT (http://thesis.mit.edu/) permits online reading of theses in a presentation that inhibits printing; users can buy PDF versions online or have printed copies sent by mail. ProQuest, formerly UMI, which disseminates 55,000 graduate theses each year, now accepts electronic submission of theses (Olsen, 2003a).

E-Books for Specialized Distribution Media

Systems cited in the previous sections distribute digital information via Internet browser, but some important related areas need to be mentioned. Commercially produced e-books downloaded to users' devices have had considerable effect since 2000, when half a million people downloaded Stephen King's e-book, *Riding the Bullet*. Common formats include MS Reader (Microsoft's downloadable e-book software), the well-known Adobe Acrobat PDF format, and the Palm and Mobipocket formats for mobile devices. Rosetta Books (Figure 7; http://www.rosettabooks.com) offers e-books in all four of these formats. Rosetta Books received considerable publicity in 2001 when Random House tried to stop them from distributing electronic versions of works by Kurt Vonnegut, William Styron, and Robert B. Parker. The judge ruled in favor of Rosetta Books, determining that e-books are a separate medium from the original product because they offer full-text searching, hyperlinking, and other electronic advantages (Stein, 2001). Older contracts in which authors had assigned rights to publish "books" would not therefore automatically cover electronic versions.

Palm Digital Media (http://www.palmdigitalmedia.com/) offers 11,000 titles for sale. PDABooks.org links to 2,600 texts, all of which are freely available (http://www.pdabooks.org/). Manybooks (http://www.manybooks.net/) contains more than 10,000 public domain e-books, formatted for reading on Palm, PocketPC, or other devices. The University of Virginia Electronic Text Center offers 1,800 downloadable books for Palm Pilots or

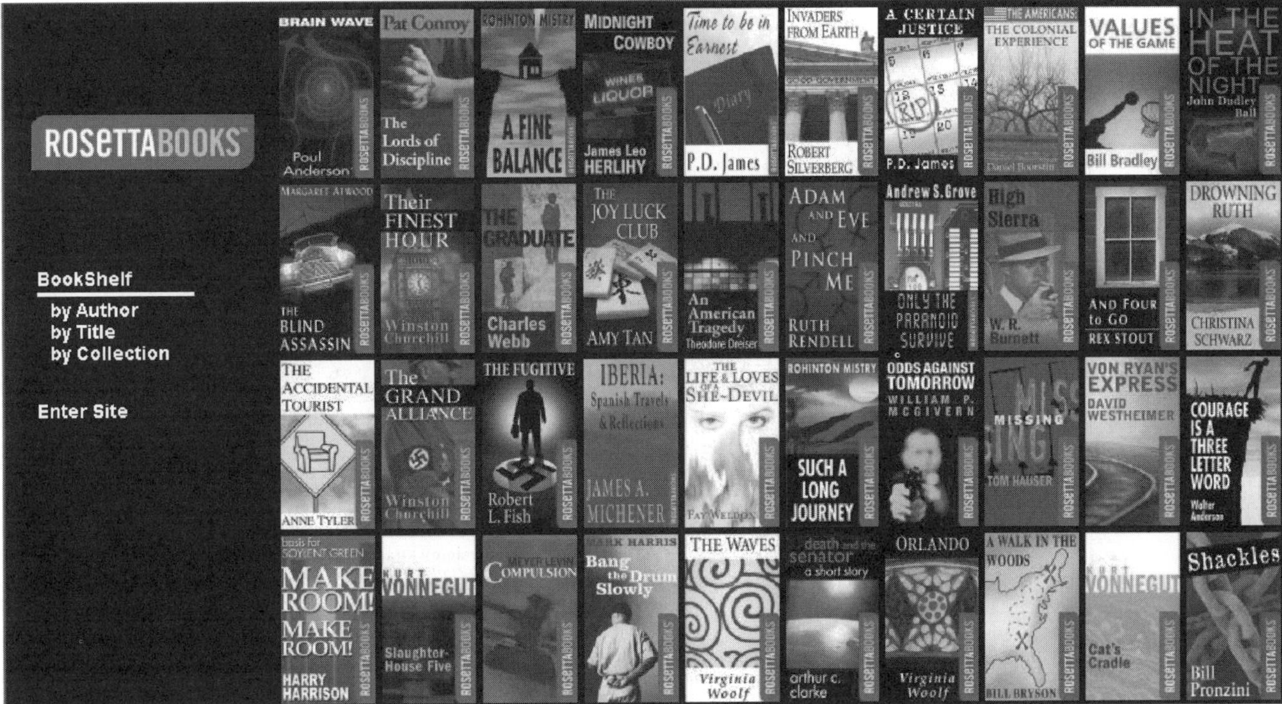

Figure 7: Opening screen of Rosetta Books, a major e-book publisher.

MS Reader (http://etext.lib.virginia.edu/ebooks/ebooklist.html). The variety of formats available is not an indication of the health of the e-book field. In fact, it has been a major factor in deterring readers from spending money on equipment and texts (Crawford, 2000). Consumers have demonstrated almost total lack of interest in specially designed e-book readers. In a major shakeout in late 2003, Barnes&Noble.com (http://www.barnesandnoble.com/) announced it was shuttering its e-books store (Albanese, 2003). Publishers say that Barnes&Noble.com's decision will not affect their e-book programs, which they maintain are still showing rapid growth. Amazon (http://www.amazon.com/) maintains its e-books division. Readers have to download special software to use ebrary (http://www.ebrary.com/) and can only view one page at a time. Major publishers, including Random House and McGraw-Hill, finance ebrary, which, like NetLibrary, seeks to sell subscriptions to libraries. The National Yiddish Book Center (http://www.yiddishbookcenter.org/) in Amherst, Massachusetts, maintains the Steven Spielberg Digital Yiddish Library, which has processed 14,000 texts. Digital versions are not disseminated, but paper copies are produced via a print-on-demand system for $48 per hardcover, library-bound volume. As a result, Yiddish is the language that has the highest proportion of its literature immediately available.

Institutional and Informational Resources in the Digital Library Field

The Digital Library Federation (http://www.diglib.org) is a consortium of 32 major institutions, based in Washington, D.C. It maintains a guide to public access collections at http://www.hti.umich.edu/cgi/b/bib/bib-idx?c=dlfcoll. This offers simple searching, advanced searching, a list of more than 370 digital libraries whose descriptions can be searched, and a list of the participating institutions. An additional 460 digital library initiatives were cataloged by the Association of Research Libraries (ARL) Digital Initiatives Database, a collaboration between the University of Illinois at Chicago and ARL (http://www.arl.org/did/index.html).

Important general information sources for the digital library field include Berkeley's SunSITE (http://sunsite.berkeley.edu/). Resource pages are maintained by Ben Gross at Illinois (http://bengross.com/dl/), Candy Schwartz at Simmons (http://web.simmons.edu/~schwartz/dl.html), and Tom Kochtanek and Rafee Kassim at Missouri (http://www.coe.missouri.edu/~rafee/iDLR/index.php). Chowdhury and Chowdhury (2000) compares the information retrieval features of 20 important digital libraries. Major textbooks for the field have been authored by Lesk (1997), Arms (2000), and Chowdhury and Chowdhury (2003). For recent printed overviews of the field, see Fox and Urs (2002) or McCarthy (2004). Greenstein and Thorin (2002) prepared a biography of the digital library based on six case studies.

The digital library field is often financed by special government grants. Of vital importance to digital library development in the United States was the National Science Foundation's Digital Libraries Initiative. Phase 1 projects, 1994–1998, are at http://www.dli2.nsf.gov/dlione/ and were discussed by Fox (1999). Phase 2 projects can be seen at http://www.dli2.nsf.gov/ and were summarized by Lesk (1999). An important current source of financing for digitization projects in the United States is the Institute of Museum and Library Services (IMLS;

Search | Back Issues | Author Index | Title Index | Mirrors

D-Lib® Magazine

Vol. 10 No. 11
ISSN: 1082-9873

doi:10.1045/dlib.magazine

November 2004

EDITORIAL

Digital Records Management and Preservation
by Bonita Wilson
doi:10.1045/november2004-editorial

Letters
doi:10.1045/november2004-letters

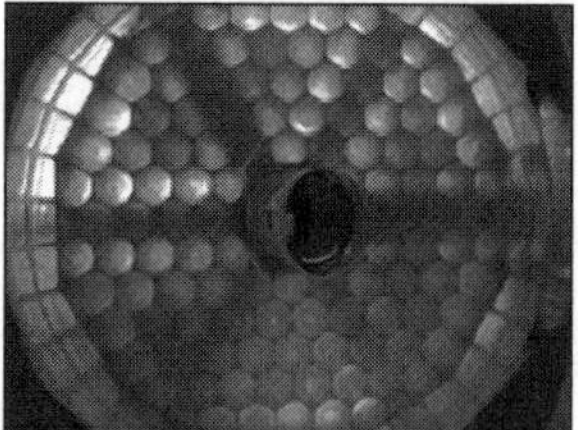

SOFIA's Mirror (An astronomical mirror). Astronomy picture of the day for October 22, 2004. Image Credit: Ron Strong (ARC / NASA). Courtesy of Astronomy Picture of the Day.

Astronomy Picture of the Day is *D-Lib Magazine's* featured collection this month.

ARTICLES

Archiving and Accessing Web Pages: The Goddard Library Web Capture Process
Alessandro Senserini and Robert B. Allen, University of Maryland; and Gail Hodge, Nikkia Anderson, and Daniel Smith, Jr., Information International Associates, Inc.
doi:10.1045/november2004-hodge

Toward a Metadata Generation Framework: A Case Study at Johns Hopkins University
Mark Patton, David Reynolds, G. Sayeed Choudhury, and Tim DiLauro, Johns Hopkins University
doi:10.1045/november2004-choudhury

A Web Service Interface for Creating Concept Browsing Interfaces
Tamara Sumner, Faisal Ahmad, and Qianyi Gu, Universtiy of Colorado, Boulder; Francis Molina and Stedman Willard, American Association for the Advancement of Science; Michael Wright, Lynne Davis, and Sonal Bhushan, University Corporation for Atmospheric Research, and Greg Janée, University of California, Santa Barbara
doi:10.1045/november2004-sumner

Figure 8: Recent issue of *D-Lib Magazine,* a leading electronic journal for the digital library field.

http://www.imls.gov/index.htm). For examples of IMLS support, see http://www.imls.gov/closer/cls_po.asp.

The Canadian Inventory of Digital Initiatives provides descriptions of Canadian information resources created for the Web (http://www.collectionscanada.ca/initiatives/erella.htm). Nicholson and MacGregor (2003) describe a major digitization program aimed at improving online access to U.K. cultural resources from the United Kingdom's museums, libraries, and galleries. The EnrichUK program (http://www.enrichuk.net/) is supported by lottery funding of $50 million and provides free access to the country's cultural, artistic, and community resources. Digital library development in Brazil was discussed by McCarthy and Cunha (2003).

Research in the digital library field has been reviewed by Chowdhury and Chowdhury (1999). As might be expected, the digital library field is well served by e-journals. The principal U.S. e-journal is *D-Lib Magazine*, published by the D-Lib Forum (Figure 8; http://www.dlib.org/).

From Britain come *Ariadne* (http://www.ariadne.ac.uk/) and the *Journal of Digital Information* (JoDI; http://jodi.ecs.soton.ac.uk/). The major U.S. conference in this area is the Joint Conference on Digital Libraries (JCDL; http://www.jcdl.org/), sponsored by the Association for Computing Machinery and the Institute of Electrical and Electronics Engineers (IEEE). The European equivalent is the European Conference on Research and Advanced Technology for Digital Libraries (ECDL), and Asia has the International Conference on Asian Digital Libraries (ICADL).

CONSTRUCTING DIGITAL LIBRARIES

Digital libraries are complex systems that require careful planning and design; their construction involves a series of interlocking considerations of a technical and intellectual, legal, and even esthetic nature.

Copyright and Digital Libraries

Copyright laws were written to control the sale and distribution of physical objects; they adapt poorly to digital environments and represent a major constraint to digital libraries. Lesk presents the history of copyright law from the point of view of digital libraries (1997, pp. 224–229). According to the U.S. Constitution, copyright is granted for "limited times," but terms have been continually extended, largely in response to pressures from film studios. The Sonny Bono Copyright Act, 1998, fixed copyright in the United States at the life of the author plus 70 years. Pre-1978 works in copyright are protected for 95 years from the date copyright was first secured. Most materials produced in 1923 or after are protected by copyright. Consult the "Public Domain and Copyright" page of Project Gutenberg (http://promo.net/pg/vol/pd.html) or "When works pass into the public domain" (http://www.unc.edu/~unclng/public-d.htm). Note that all works are protected—books, films, photographs, ephemera, newspapers, computer files—anything fixed in tangible form, regardless of whether anybody is interested in protecting their rights in these materials. In 1930, about 10,000 books were published in the United States; today fewer than 200 are still available from publishers (*Brief of Amici Curiae: The Internet Archive*, 2002). The other 9,800 may well include texts that might usefully be made available to the public in digital form, but they continue to enjoy full copyright protection until 2019. No institution could risk digitizing them, for fear that rights-holders might suddenly appear. Most book publishing contracts signed in the United States in the 20th century state that rights return to the author a few years after the book goes out of print (Lynch, 2001). When the authors die, these rights pass to their descendents. This has created a huge class of "orphan books," items for which no rights-holder can be traced. The situation is even less clear for photographs, ephemera, and sheet music. Eric Eldred, whose Eldritch Press (http://www.ibiblio.org/eldritch/) freely disseminates public domain texts, recently challenged the extension of copyright laws. The Supreme Court, however, found against him; CNN reported: "Decision seen as victory for movie, recording industry" (Mears, 2003).

In many cases, digital libraries find it simpler to limit themselves to pre-1923 materials, to avoid the troublesome process of identifying rights-holders. Even if a rights-holder can be identified, the digital library has to go through a lengthy, expensive, and often fruitless process of negotiating rights. One possible solution is to operate within the "fair use" provisions of current U.S. copyright law. The legal situation is complex, but fair use might be invoked when a nonprofit library or archive makes materials available for research and private study. It should be made clear that the institution does not condone further distribution or usage, such as commercial exploitation or print publication. Many digital library sites have relevant disclaimers; for example, the Library of Congress (http://www.loc.gov/homepage/legal.html) and Duke University's Rare Book, Manuscript, and Special Collections Library (http://scriptorium.lib.duke.edu/copyright.html).

Until recently, freelance authors who wrote for newspapers or magazines did not formally surrender rights to put articles into databases, because this market was small or nonexistent. Under the 2001 Tasini decision (New York Times, 2001), the Supreme Court agreed they had rights when their materials were published in this way. Dissemination of materials via a database, in which they could be consulted individually, was considered a separate usage from print or microfilm. The *New York Times* was said to be purging from its database 115,000 articles by 27,000 different freelance writers (Stern, 2001). The decision has only retrospective effects because since the mid-1990s publishers routinely retain all digital rights for freelance articles.

If copyright materials are posted to the Internet, there must be a mechanism whereby they can be taken down, as a result of either an informal request or a formal demand made under the Digital Millennium Copyright Act. Because of their historical and academic bias, digital libraries are rarely the target of "takedown" or "cease and desist" orders. There is little interest from authors, who are, in effect, asking to be taken out of the historical record. This situation arises more frequently with search engines, which have to devote considerable effort to meeting takedown demands. The Chilling Effects Clearinghouse (http://www.chillingeffects.org) maintains coverage of such requests.

One solution for copyright problems is to work with copyright-free niche collections. The Government Publications from World War II digital library at Southern Methodist University (http://worldwar2.smu.edu) is perfectly legal, because U.S. government publications are not copyrighted. The University of Iowa maintains medical documentation on its Virtual Hospital and Virtual Children's Hospital sites (Figure 9; http://www.vh.org or http://www.vh.org/pediatric/index.html/); these are based

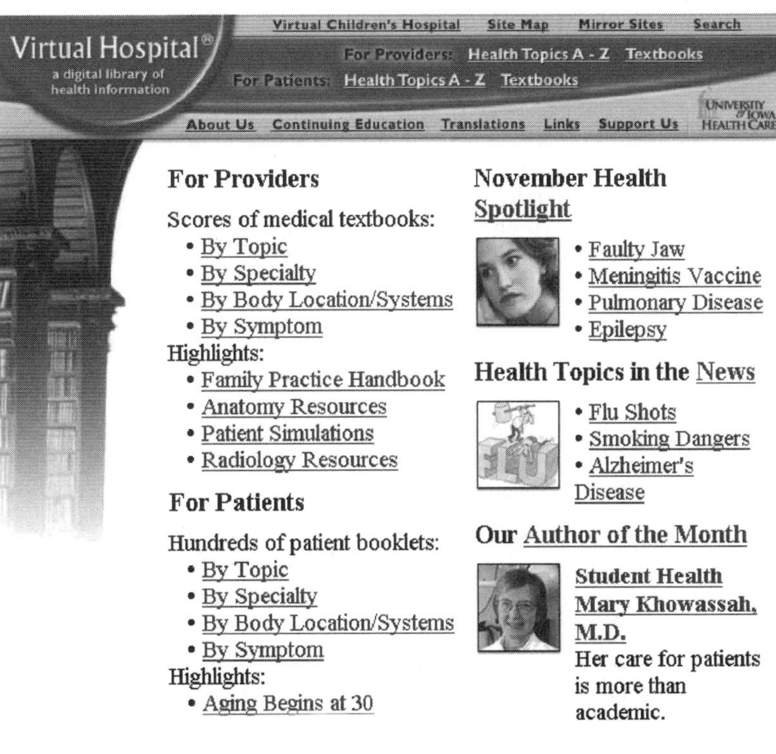

Figure 9: Opening screen of the Virtual Hospital, a health-oriented digital library from the University of Iowa.

on noncopyrighted government publications and texts contributed by faculty of the University of Iowa.

PubMed, set up by the National Library of Medicine, facilitates public awareness of 11 million items of medical literature (http://www.ncbi.nlm.nih.gov/entrez/query.fcgi); there are no copyright problems because abstracts, rather than full text, are offered. Further possibilities are opened up by licensing systems, such as Creative Commons (http://creativecommons.org/), which does for publications what Open Source licensing does for software. Creative Commons work can be made freely available, but attribution can be required, commercial use can be prohibited, and the original creator can demand that derivative works must also be made publicly available. The license relieves authors of liability or implication of warranty. Ashling (2003) discusses a variety of models for open access and the public domain.

Selection of Materials for Digital Libraries

Hazen and colleagues devote a short monograph to the selection of research collections for digitization (1998). The first criterion they present is, predictably, copyright. They then propose a careful analysis of the intellectual nature of the materials to be digitized, together with an estimate of current and potential users. The actual and anticipated nature of the use of the materials must be considered, as must the format and nature of the digital product. It will be essential to describe and deliver the digital product, while retaining archival copies. The relationship to other digital efforts must be considered, and, last but not least, costs and benefits need to be carefully analyzed. Collections that score well on all or most of these considerations will be given priority in the digitization process.

Digitization of Materials for Digital Libraries

Image access is used for individual visual resources, such as photographs, posters, drawings, and so forth. The classic method of offering access to these materials is by a series of three types of image. Scanning produces a high-quality archive image, which is then used to generate an access image for general public use. Finally, a small thumbnail image is produced, for quick reference (Boss, 2001; Lee, 2001). The list that follows describes these terms in more detail.

Archive image: A high-quality image, scanned directly from the original material, and destined for long-term preservation. Normally an uncompressed TIFF (tagged image file format) image is used for this; TIFFs can preserve high-quality images and a resolution of 600 dpi (dots per inch) is standard. As scanning is an expensive operation, which exposes original materials to possible damage, the archive image has considerable value and will be carefully preserved. Archive images must always exist at system level but may not always be made available to the end user. TIF files occupy significant server space and imply lengthy download times. Another factor is that some DLs will want to sell their own hard-copy prints of quality images. Frey (1997) discusses technical standards for digital imaging of photographic collections.

Access image or working image: A quality image, adequate for consultation and serious study by digital library users. This is normally a high-quality JPG (Joint Photographic Experts Group) image, generated from the archival TIFF. JPG files are widely used on the Internet and offer quality spatial and color reproduction, together with a high compression ratio. For DL purposes, JPG images will often be generated at a resolution of 300 dpi; a size of 640 × 480 pixels is also common.

Thumbnail image: A small reference image, which gives the user an immediate general idea of the access image before it is downloaded. It is typically a medium- to low-quality JPG, generated from the access image, but about one-tenth of its size, and is commonly produced at a resolution of 72 dpi. GIF format (graphic interchange format) can also be used for thumbnails.

Detailed information by practitioners in the area is available from *Digitization Guidelines* from Arizona State Library, Archives and Public Records (http://www.lib.az.us/digital/dg_a4.html), the *Western States Digital Imaging Best Practices* from the Colorado Digitization Program (http://www.cdpheritage.org/resource/scanning/documents/WSDIBP_v1.pdf), Washington State Library's *Digital Best Practices* (http://digitalwa.statelib.wa.gov/newsite/best.htm), and *Moving Theory into Practice: Digital Imaging Tutorial* from Cornell University Library (http://www.library.cornell.edu/preservation/tutorial/index.html). The Digital Library Federation offers a *Benchmark for the Faithful Reproduction of Monographs and Serials* (http://www.diglib.org/standards/bmarkfin.htm). Further standardization and development can be expected in this field; notably, there is increasing interest in a major upgrade of the original JPG format, known as JPEG 2000 (http://www.jpeg.org/jpeg2000/index.html). JPEG 2000 images offer high quality and excellent compression; they could possibly displace TIFFs in archival roles.

Books available in multiple copies may be disbound for sheet by sheet digitization. Fragile and older materials require careful handling. Automated digitizers, which can turn the pages of books and even newspaper volumes, are beginning to emerge. An early model, by 4DigitalBooks (Figure 10; http://www.4digitalbooks.com/), is about the size of a sports utility vehicle and can process more than 1,000 pages an hour (Markoff, 2003). This Swiss-designed robot is considered cost-effective only for projects that involve more than 5.5 million pages.

A smaller automated digitizer, based on technology developed by Xerox, is being offered by Kirtas Technologies (http://www.kirtas-tech.com/).

Digital libraries that offer textual content also need to convert page images to text that can be manipulated. This would now normally be HTML text, although early systems used plain ASCII text files. Conversion to text is undertaken using quality OCR (optical character recognition) software, such as OmniPage Pro (University of Virginia Electronic Text Center, 1998) or the Russian ABBYY software (http://www.abbyy.com/). Even first-class scanning software can confuse certain words, for example clean/dean and modern/modem. Careful proofreading is therefore essential. The problem is especially acute in digital libraries that pride themselves on offering quality content but that process a large proportion of older and specialized texts, with rarely used terms, unusual spellings, unusual fonts, and so forth. Highly qualified personnel are required to proofread such texts.

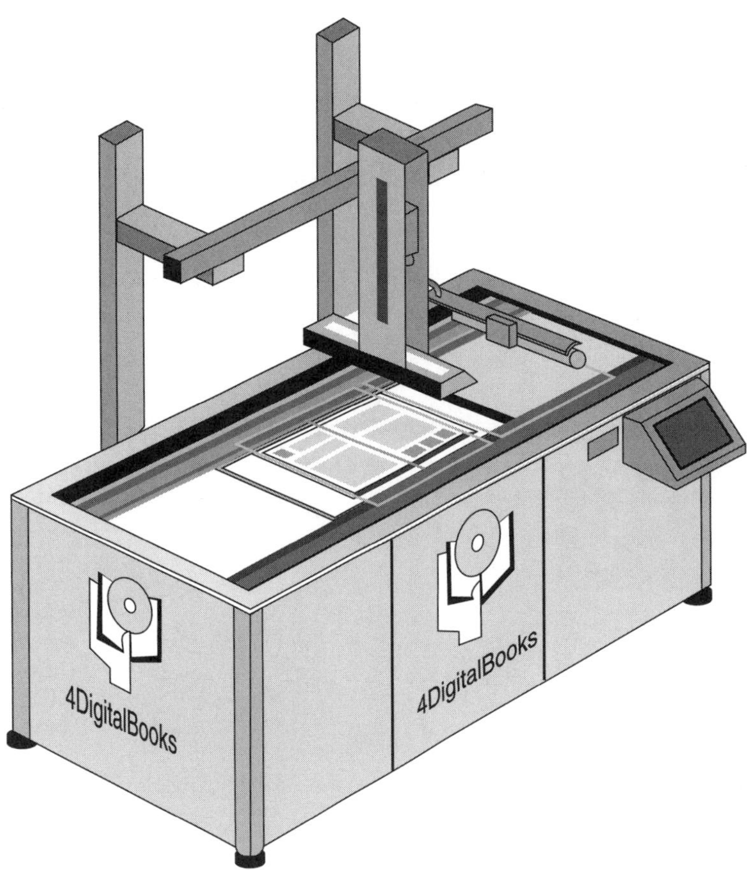

Figure 10: Automated digitizer, developed by 4DigitalBooks.

An obvious way to guarantee delivery of correct text is to offer both an HTML version and a page image. The page image can be a JPEG image; medium quality is often adequate for plain text, without illustrations. It is also possible to use Adobe's Portable Document Format (PDF) for text. Results are generally satisfactory, images correctly represent the originals, certain security parameters can be easily set (e.g., to inhibit printing), and most serious Internet users have already downloaded the free Adobe reader. Several U.S. federal agencies are collaborating on the development of an archiving version of the portable document format; a standard should be defined by the end of 2005 (Jackson, 2004). For a major project that offers books in both text and page-image form, see the University of Michigan's Making of America (http://www.hti.umich.edu/m/moagrp/). Here, sophisticated software offers a choice of image, text, or PDF files, in normal, large, and small size. The Digital Quaker Collection (http://esr.earlham.edu/dqc/) contains full text and page images of more than 500 individual Quaker works from the 17th and 18th centuries.

Software for Digital Libraries

It is possible to create small-scale digital collections by hand, using standard HTML editing software. However, because of the complexity and variety of the field, software designed for this purpose is now in common use. In alphabetical order, principal options are as follows.

CONTENTdm Digital Media Management Software Suite: A high-performance storage and retrieval software for multimedia collections, which is rapidly gaining acceptance (http://contentdm.com/index.html). It was developed at the University of Washington and is offered to libraries, museums, and nonprofit archives by OCLC, the major supplier of bibliographic data to libraries (http://www.oclc.org/contentdm/default.htm). Collections using CONTENTdm include the Louisiana Digital Library (http://louisdl.louislibraries.org/) and Early Las Vegas from the University of Nevada, Las Vegas (http://www.library.unlv.edu/early_las_vegas/index.html).

DLXS: DLXS is offered by the University of Michigan Digital Library eXtension Service; it is a comprehensive suite of software especially suited to indexing and presenting multipage documents (http://www.dlxs.org/). It has already been mentioned as being used for the University of Michigan's the Making of America collection, which has approximately 8,500 books and 50,000 journal articles from the antebellum period through Reconstruction (http://www.hti.umich.edu/cgi/t/text/text-idx?tpl=browse.tpl&c=moa&cc=moa). An additional 3,000 books can be found in the Wright American Fiction collection, 1851–1875 (http://www.letrs.indiana.edu/web/w/wright2/).

Dspace: A "Durable Digital Depository," designed to capture, distribute, and preserve the intellectual output of universities and similar institutions (http://dspace.org/). It is a joint project between MIT Libraries and the Hewlett-Packard Company; the original DSpace can be searched at https://dspace.mit.edu/index.jsp; full-text documents are presented in PDF. An open-source software,

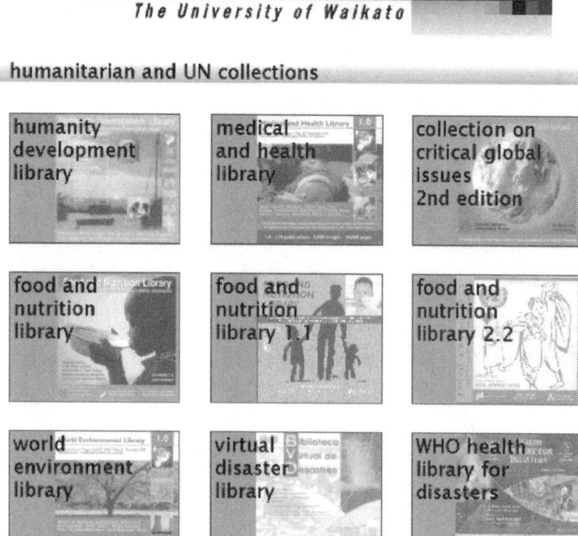

Figure 11: Opening screen of the New Zealand Digital Library.

DSpace can be freely downloaded from http://sourceforge.net/projects/dspace/ (Atwood, 2002; Carnevale, 2003b).

EXist: An open-source XML database created in Germany (http://exist.sourceforge.net or http://exist-db.org/). It was used for an ambitious project, The Proceedings of the Old Bailey, 1674 to 1834 (http://www.oldbaileyonline.org/). This is considered the largest body of texts detailing the lives of nonelite people ever published and covers more than 100,000 criminal trials held at London's central criminal court.

Greenstone Digital Library Software: An open-source suite, developed in New Zealand at the University of Waikato (http://www.greenstone.org/). It automatically creates organized collections of digitized documents with a standardized interface, creates automatic full-text indexes, lists titles, and so forth (Witten & Bainbridge, 2002). It handles large collections of documents in a variety of formats and works on server or desktop; it even exports to CD-ROM. It was used for the New Zealand Digital Library (Figure 11; http://www.nzdl.org/), notable for humanitarian and United Nations collections in a variety of languages and scripts, including Arabic and Chinese.

Greenstone is distributed free of charge under the GNU Public License and can be downloaded from http://www.greenstone.org/cgi-bin/library?a=p&p=download. All texts in Project Gutenberg can be searched via Greenstone at http://public.ibiblio.org/gsdl/cgi-bin/library?a=p&p=about&c=gberg.

Hyperion Digital Media Archive: This archive organizes and offers full-text indexing, storing, and accessing of nonbook holdings in a digital format (http://www.sirsi.com/Sirsiproducts/hyperion.html). It was produced by Sirsi, an Alabama company that supplies automated cataloging and circulation systems to all types of libraries. An important application is the Civil Rights in Mississippi Digital Archive of materials on race relations, created by the University of Southern Mississippi (http://www.lib.usm.edu/~spcol/crda/).

Insight image management and delivery system: A system that was produced by Luna Imaging, a joint enterprise between the J. Paul Getty Trust, California, and Eastman Kodak (http://www.luna-imaging.com/). It is high-quality imaging software, noted for its powerful zoom capability, and is used for works of art, photographs, and maps. For an example, see the David Rumsey Historical Map Collection (http://www.davidrumsey.com/), which features more than 8,000 maps and won a Webby Award in 2002.

Olive ActivePaper Archive software: This software permits historical newspapers to be scanned from the originals or from microfilm, creating fully searchable digital collections. Readers can click on any article, photograph, or advertisement, which is then enlarged in a separate window. For an operational system, see the Missouri Historical Newspapers Collection (http://newspapers.umsystem.edu/archive/Skins/Missouri/navigator.asp). Olive Software is located in Denver (http://www.olivesoftware.com/home.html).

Open-source software is widely used for server software and in academic environments. It is therefore natural that it is often used for digital library database construction. Zhang and Gourley (2003) review a range of open-source software options for the management and presentation of digital collections. The best known standardized language for databases is SQL (structured query language). In the digital library field, it is normally applied via open-source, server-side database software, of which PostgreSQL and MySQL are frequently cited as powerful alternatives. A combination of MySQL with PHP has drawn much attention recently. PHP (http://www.php.net) is a server-side, Web-scripting language whose predefined function set easily interfaces with MySQL. The Digital Library Toolkit (Noerr, 2000) contains a useful overview of software. ColdFusion is an additional alternative; its current version is Macromedia ColdFusion MX 6.1 (http://www.macromedia.com/software/coldfusion/?promoid=home_prod_cf_082403). If the project involves querying traditional library catalogs and bibliographic databases, it will be necessary to adopt software compliant with the Z39.50 standard, which permits advanced searches using Boolean, truncation, and similar procedures (Z39.50, 2001).

Metadata

The addition of metadata, or subject terms and descriptive elements characterizing the digital object, adds significant value to digital records. The use of metadata is clearly demonstrated in Figures 12 and 13, from the LOUISiana Digital Library (http://louisdl.louislibraries.org/).

The value of this photograph of a famous building in the French Quarter of New Orleans is greatly enhanced by the metadata elements added to it:

Note that the metadata terms are hyperlinked; for example, by clicking on "Wrought-iron" the user is taken to other images of wrought iron.

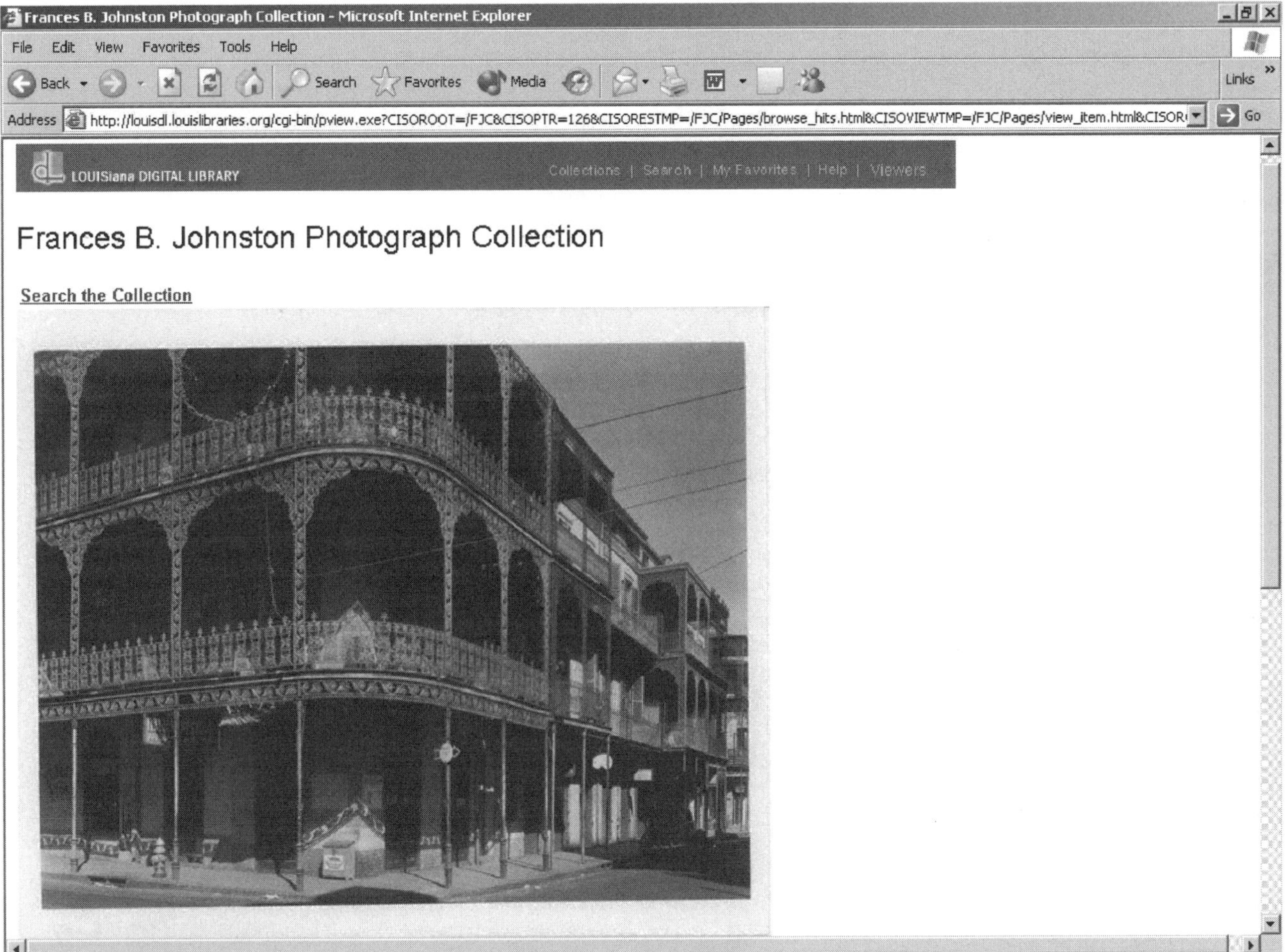

Figure 12: Photograph of a building in the French Quarter of New Orleans, taken by Frances B. Johnston, digitized by the LOUISiana Digital Library.

There are various types of metadata; typical categories include the following:

Descriptive metadata: Used for the indexing, discovery, and identification of a digital resource, such as author, title, abstract, subject headings, and so forth.

Structural metadata: The information used to display and navigate digital resources; also includes information on the internal organization of the digital resource. Structural metadata might include the structural divisions of a resource (i.e., the chapters in a book) or sub-object relationships (such as individual diary entries in a diary section).

Administrative metadata: Management information for the object, which may include technical information, such as the hardware and software used in producing the image, the resolution the image was scanned at, compression information, pixel dimensions, and so forth (*What Is Metadata?*, 2003). Technical metadata must be recorded accurately and consistently to ensure that the image files remain useable well into the future; standards are currently being developed (http://www.niso.org/committees/committee_au.html). Digital rights management information, such as contact information and rules for appropriate use of the data, is another important element of administrative metadata (*What Is Metadata?*, 2003). Correct legal language must be employed to specify digital rights.

Metadata can be:

1. **embedded** within the resource to which it relates; for example, as HTML metatags;
2. **stored** in a data management database separate from but linked to the resource;
3. **included** in a resource discovery service, such as a library catalog, with a link to the resource (National Library of Australia, 2002).

For an in-depth discussion of metadata, see Vellucci's 1998 paper in the *Annual Review of Information Science and Technology*. Traditional library or archive systems can include entire collections of photographs on a single catalog or container record; digital presentation requires detailed metadata. The best known metadata system, specifically developed for a digital environment, is the Dublin Core, first developed at a meeting in Dublin, Ohio, in 1995. The Dublin Core Metadata Element Set (http://dublincore.org/documents/dces/) specifies metadata elements such as title, creator, subject, and rights (for digital

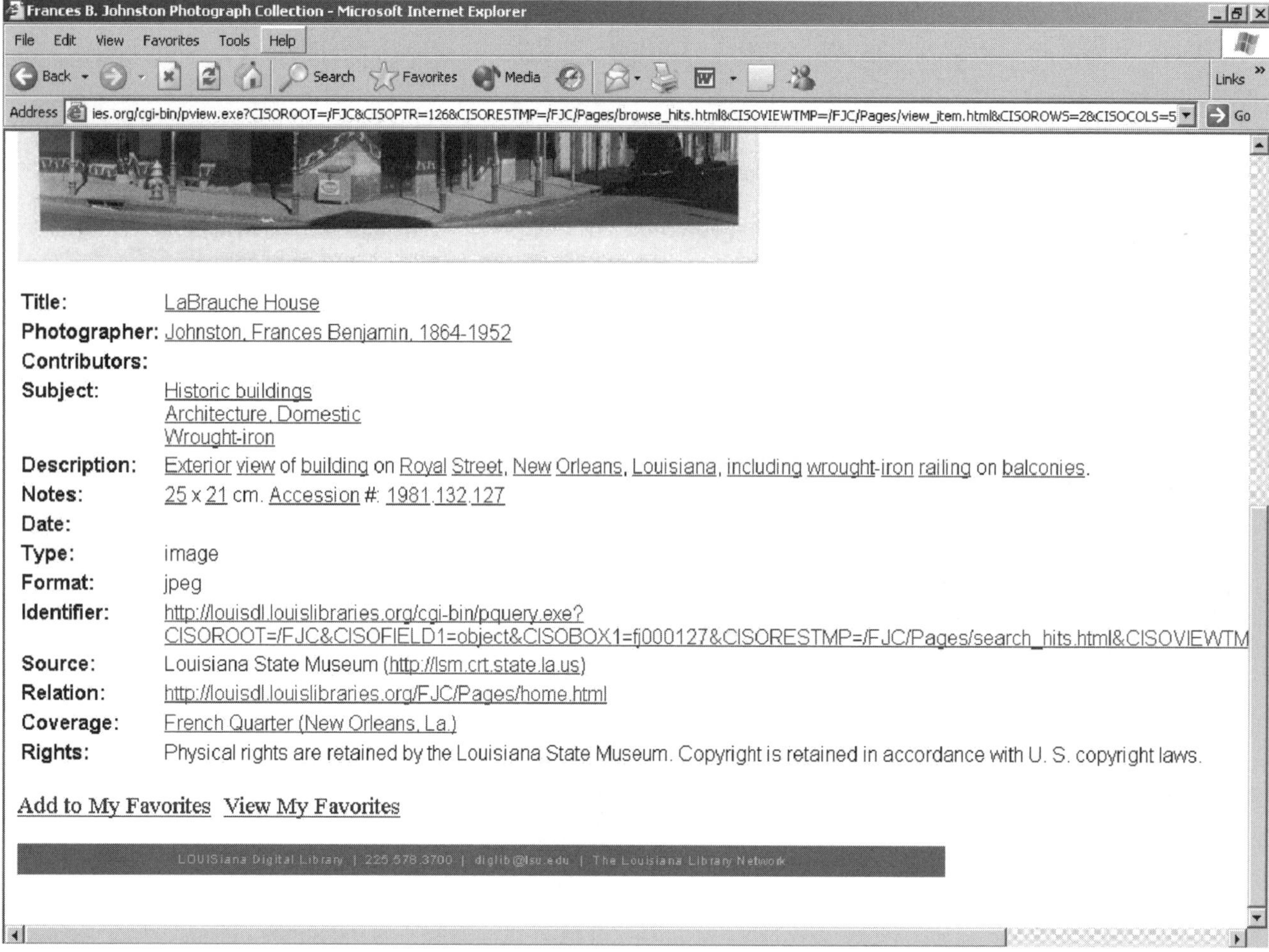

Figure 13: Metadata for a photograph of a building in the French Quarter of New Orleans; metadata generated by the LOUISiana Digital Library.

rights management information). Metadata analysts normally work with a list of acceptable terms, such as the Art and Architecture Thesaurus of the Getty Museum (http://www.getty.edu/research/conducting_research/vocabularies/aat/) or the Thesaurus for Graphic Materials, from the Library of Congress (http://www.loc.gov/rr/print/tgm1/). The long-established Library of Congress Subject Headings are widely used, notably in the American Memory collections. Inconsistent or locally created terms will not provide accurate retrieval, but metadata creation adds significantly to both the value and the cost of systems. Good metadata can represent half or more of project costs.

Metadata is widely available through the Open Archives Initiative (OAI; http://www.openarchives.org/), which is based on harvester/server architecture. Participating data stores make simple metadata available in standardized format. Information systems harvest the metadata, which is then used to power subject gateways. The metadata in thousands of systems worldwide can be collected centrally (Digital Library Federation, 2001). Lagoze and Van de Sompel (2001) outline the origins and development of the Open Archives Initiative. Nelson and colleagues (2003) describe OAI harvesting from the NASA Technical Reports Server (http://ntrs.nasa.gov). OAIster, from the University of Michigan, offers a sophisticated search interface to a wide variety of freely available, academically oriented digital resources (http://oaister.umdl.umich.edu/o/oaister). The Experimental OAI Registry at Grainger Engineering Library, University of Illinois at Urbana-Champaign, has collected sample records from numerous OAI compliant repositories, input them to a database, indexed them, and made them searchable (http://gita.grainger.uiuc.edu/registry/searchform.asp).

Text Indexing

Complete, word-by-word text indexing is a valuable feature of most digital libraries. Specialized software for this area includes the XPAT search engine, part of the University of Michigan Digital Library eXtension Service (DLXS) software suite (http://www.dlxs.org/). This powers the Legacy National Tobacco Documents Library (LNTDL), a collection of more than 6 million documents, which were obtained through the legal discovery process for a lawsuit and relate to scientific research, manufacturing, marketing, advertising, and sales of cigarettes (Figure 14; http://legacy.library.ucsf.edu/index.html).

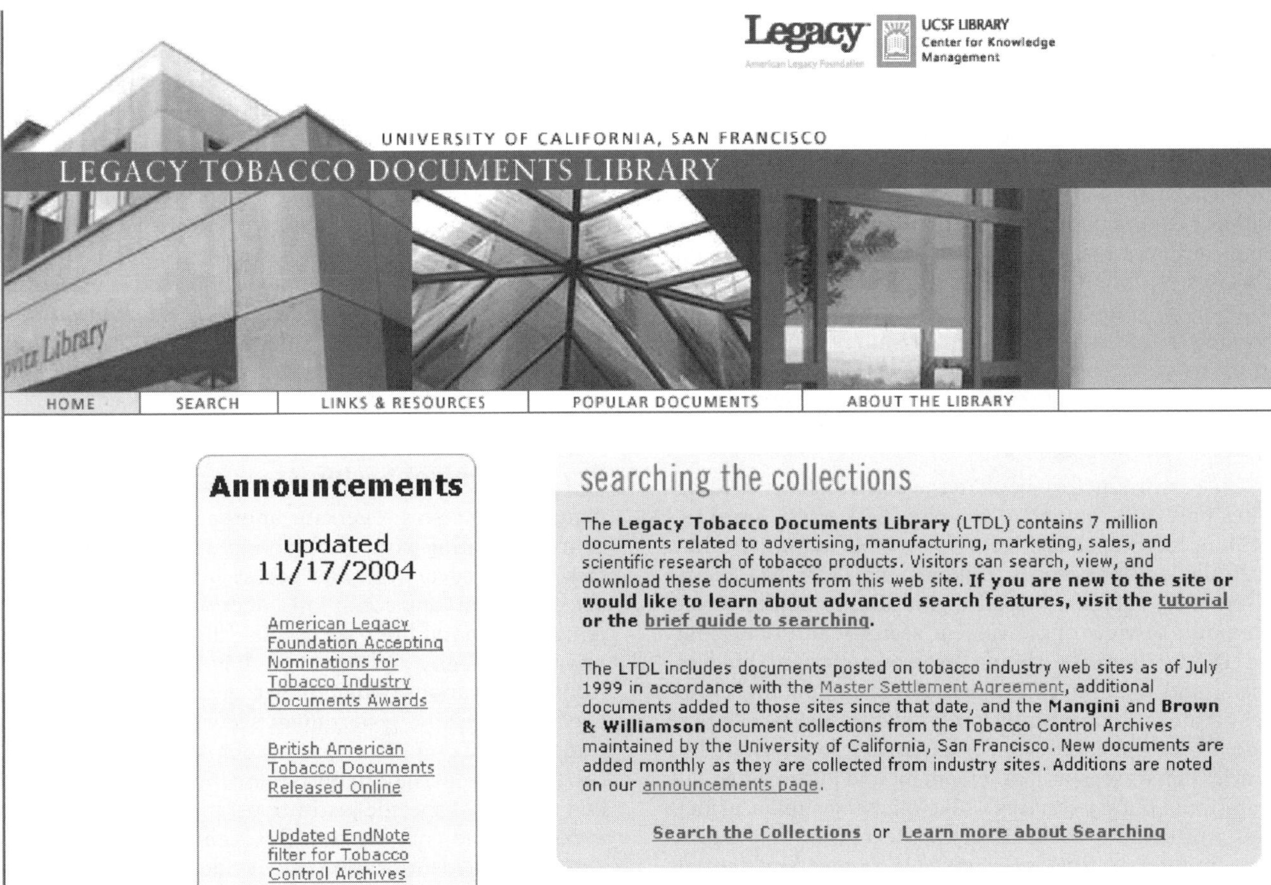

Figure 14: Opening screen of the Legacy Tobacco Documents Library, from the University of California, San Francisco.

Another specialized example is the Simple Web Indexing System for Humans—Enhanced (SWISH-E; http://swish-e.org/). This open-source software enables full-text indexing in many locations, including the Berkeley Digital Library SunSITE (http://sunsite.berkeley.edu/cgi-bin/search.pl) and even the Apache Web Server site (http://search.apache.org/). Another option is WebGlimpse (http://webglimpse.net/) from the University of Arizona. It is free to educational users and is widely used, for instance for the papers of President George Bush, Senior (http://bushlibrary.tamu.edu/research/paper.html/; test index with "saddam"). Fluid Dynamics Software (http://www.xav.com/scripts/search/) is used for the Encyclopedia Titanica (http://www.encyclopedia-titanica.org/index.php), a well-presented collection of documents and information relating to the sinking of the Titanic. Indexing software from Master.com (http://www.master.com/texis/master/app/home.html) offers advanced Boolean search (AND, OR, NOT) capacity; for a digital library example, see the documents of the Chicago Women's Liberation Union (http://cwluherstory.master.com/texis/master/search/?q=CWLU&s=SS&cmd=Options).

SECURITY AND DIGITAL LIBRARIES

In the digital library area, security can be defined as "techniques and practices that preserve the integrity of computer systems, and digital library systems and collections" (Arms, 2000, p. 281). At the most basic level, digital libraries contribute significantly toward document security because they permit the rapid dissemination of multiple copies. History has shown that documents available in a large number of copies have a much better chance of survival.

Security of Original Materials During the Digitization Process

Security problems during the digitization process are very similar to those encountered during microfilming. Old and fragile documents need to be handled carefully. Valuable materials will be digitized on-site to avoid any risks during the transportation process. The team responsible for the digitization process will carefully count and number all items before they are digitized. Digitization today may involve outsourcing, notably to countries such as India and the Philippines. This is only viable for materials that can be replaced if lost in transit. Offshore digitization has also been combined with XML markup; this, of course, requires that offshore staff be trained in XML.

Security of Online Resources

Even digital libraries that make their materials freely available to the public need to take normal firewall precautions against hackers, crackers, and individuals who attempt to download large proportions of their content. For general overviews of IT security in higher education in the United States, see the *Effective Security Practices Guide* produced by the EDUCAUSE/Internet2 Computer and Security Task Force (http://www.educause.edu/security/guide/) or the IT Security in Higher Education site maintained by Syllabus (http://www.syllabus.com/campussecurity/index.asp). Materials within digital libraries represent the best of an institution's collection, whereas older materials may be out of copyright and could possibly be redistributed. There are many considerations in terms of potential abuse of images; if users can steal an image, the institution may lose possible use and publication fees, an important source of revenue for cultural heritage repositories.

Lesk's introductory book to the digital library field devotes part of a chapter to security (Lesk, 1997, pp. 139–142); he suggests basic security, sensible administration, firewalls, and passwords. Gladney and Lotspiech (1997) discuss the safeguarding of digital library content from the point of view of convenient security and data quality. Digital libraries should protect copyright holders, users, and themselves against misuse of content, either deliberate or inadvertent. Unobtrusive programs can provide protection without inconveniencing users. Digital libraries can be seen as a development and improvement of traditional library services while following similar principles. Authenticity in the library context becomes integrity for computer professionals; privacy becomes confidentiality and intellectual property rights are guaranteed by security systems. Collectively they ensure quality services. In a later paper (Gladney & Lotspiech, 1998), they offer specific solutions, via the use of cryptographic envelopment of document packets. This should provide end-to-end protection while demanding a lower network infrastructure and administration. Protocols can enforce information owners' rules governing how users might select, request, possibly pay for, and eventually gain access to digital materials. It is also important to note that Gladney (1998b) recognizes that technology can contribute toward digital libraries only within a framework of administrative, legal, and social practices. Technical considerations are secondary to issues of public policy, law, and ethics. Gladney (1998b) stated that computer professionals were able to design systems with sufficient flexibility to work within these constraints.

A paper by Kohl and colleagues (1997) considers that there are major advantages to retaining the library as an intermediary between publisher and customer in a digital environment. Under these circumstances, digital library services must protect transactions between publishers and users. Content must be secured, via guarantees of payment and copy and usage rights; user privacy must also be protected. This can be done using either secure connections or secure packages; the latter are considered more appropriate to a digital library environment. A further consideration might be whether the library should shoulder the cost of protection and security in these transactions. The authenticity of digital resources is discussed by Bearman and Trant (1998); this is an important aspect of security in a digital library context, because it is not impossible to find resources apparently representing the same document at different sites. It is essential to be able to establish the relative authenticity of different representations by analyzing the methods used to transform the original into digital form. It is also essential to be able to determine the integrity of a specific digital copy. Cox (2001) discusses the user's participation in computer security from a digital library point of view. An organization such as a university computing services center should not reveal too much information about protective measures. However, users should be told about the extent of external attacks; this would give them a stronger appreciation of the value of computing services' activities and a greater understanding of the value of stable networks.

Access Control Systems

Arms (1998) offers a general approach to the problems of implementing policies for access management. Policies should cover who can access information and under what terms and conditions. Access management is required for digital libraries because of donor restrictions, privacy, obscenity, and copyright. It is also needed for electronic publications, which may require payment for use, needed because of government security, and needed for trade secrets. Commercial or academic digital library access, where copyright materials are involved, is often limited to users of specific institutions. In these cases, access is restricted to computers with specific addresses (Internet protocol identification, or IP identification) and to users with passwords. Arms also devotes a chapter of his textbook on digital libraries to access management and security (Arms, 2000, pp. 123–142). Access management procedures begin when users identify themselves; authentication procedures then validate the users, verifying that they are really who they claim to be; after validation, users can be allocated to specific categories. Digital materials also have to be identified and authenticated, whereas materials in specific subcollections or subject to varying licensing arrangements may be treated in different ways. Operations management policies may restrict extent of use (e.g., stopping downloads of large quantities of material) or inhibit subsequent use of downloaded items. Policies must be carefully drawn up, be viable and appropriate to the environment, and be clearly communicated to the end users. Trusted digital repositories are essential. Security techniques discussed by Arms include encryption, private key encryption, dual key encryption, digital signatures, and public key encryption.

In the only significant case of violation of an institutional digital library to come to public attention, 50,000 scholarly journal articles were downloaded from JSTOR (http://www.jstor.org/), the University of Michigan's scholarly journal archive (Olsen, 2003b). The hacker took advantage of IP authentication. The owners of JSTOR have recently posted a strong statement concerning unauthorized access (http://www.jstor.org/about/unauthorized.html). JSTOR is experimenting with new open-source software, Shibboleth (http://shibboleth.internet2.edu/index.html), which prevents such incidents by improving online authentication. Shibboleth was developed by Internet2 researchers with National

Science Foundation support; it supports interinstitutional sharing of Web resources subject to access controls.

Lesk (1997, pp. 140–142) suggests access control systems that use constantly updated passwords, or "one-time passwords," such as the SecurID system, in which users carry a matchbox-sized token that generates a new six-digit number every 60 sec. Each user also has a personal identification number (PIN), which is entered in conjunction with the six-digit number. An alternative technology is the S/Key system invented by Bellcore. Gladney (1997) presents a document access control system developed for digital library environments by IBM. This follows established organizational practices in respect to privilege controls and makes access control information a part of ordinary objects. The resulting document access control method (DACM) scales efficiently, is functionally flexible, and can be either embedded into a library or be implemented externally. A library can establish varying policies for different document classes, for example, distinguishing between defense documents and other documents. A security key based on a credit card number was recently adopted as the basis of security at Palm Digital Media (http://www.palmdigitalmedia.com/). This system gives wide latitude to the buyer, who can, for instance, purchase an e-book, accidentally delete it, and then download a second copy. At the same time, illegal copying is effectively inhibited (Becker, 2004).

Intellectual property management problems at Case Western Reserve University were examined by Alrashid and colleagues (1998), who describe a series of small-scale projects that deliver supplemental instructional resources directly to student dorm rooms. Rumsey (1999) describes a smart card application called TOLIMAC (total library management concept), which is designed to control access to electronic library services; it was developed by a Belgian, French, and British consortium. Networked digital system security and firewalls are discussed from a digital library perspective by Peacock (1999). He suggests running applications in a restricted environment that the client would visualize as a "full" machine. Any attacker would only be able to damage the restricted environment. Guenther (2001) examines ways for librarians to authenticate users of their digital collections, emphasizes the importance of authentication, and discusses methods of authentication, including user name and password, cookie files, smart cards, and biometrics. Saeednia (2000) presents a brief overview of two main network security problems related to digital libraries, privacy and authentication, and proposes practical solutions that are applicable to digital libraries of any type and size, such as a key exchange protocol and an identification scheme whose security is based on the difficulty of computing discrete logarithms and factoring large integers.

Distributed access control and secure content distribution in the context of digital libraries are examined by Yagüe and colleagues (2002). They present a system that combines the use of an external authorization infrastructure, together with a software protection mechanism and a modular language, to control access to content. Solbakk (2003) describes basic architectural choices for the access to and preservation of digital objects at the National Library of Norway. A digital repository is the core element for the handling of both access to and preservation of the digital objects. Strategies for giving access to the complete holdings include the use of a powerful search engine and the OAI protocol to harvest metadata from conventional catalog systems to make textual or structured indexes. Access management for the subject portals set up to provide the United Kingdom higher education community with access to distributed resources in the areas of biomedicine, engineering, humanities, physical sciences, and social sciences are examined by Pinto (2003). Each hub is able to customize a portal for its specific needs, while offering common functions, such as access management, user profiling, and cross searching. Users will have streamlined access to subject-specific datasets and personalized services, while being able to obtain authorization to access protected remote resources.

Sturges and colleagues (2003) discuss the other side of digital library security, the privacy of users. With digital technology, libraries can archive detailed information about users; this information is generally considered confidential but could be of interest for law enforcement, security, and commercial organizations. Their project at Loughborough University, England, during 2000–2002 found that users were not concerned about privacy when using libraries because they expected that libraries would not pass on personal information. Librarians respected user privacy but did not rank it as a primary consideration. A significant minority of libraries needed better data protection; the project developed guidelines for privacy policy.

Commercial Digital Library Systems

Herzberg (1998) discusses charging for content by digital libraries and other providers of online content and offers an overview of a variety of different charging mechanisms, both existing and proposed. Charge card payments involve minimal fees, as well as delay, which makes them inappropriate for very small purchases. It is possible to provide free content and finance it via advertising revenues, but these tend to be limited in the digital library area. It is also possible to package content and sell access, for instance, in the form of subscriptions. In practice, relatively few users are willing to subscribe, and fees often have to be shared with intermediaries. There has been considerable interest in the use of micropayments, or payments whose value is too small to justify the cost and delay of a charge card transaction (roughly speaking, under one dollar). They are an attractive option in theory, but their widespread adoption depends on the creation of mechanisms capable of rapid transfer of small amounts of money at a low cost per transaction. Herzberg also examines the requirements for successful charging mechanisms. Credit card charging mechanisms using the SSL protocol were the most common at that time; the SET (secure electronic transaction) standard for charge card payments was also outlined. The MiniPay micropayment mechanism for charging small amounts "per click" is compared to other micropayment mechanisms. Herzberg helped develop both SET and MiniPay, which are IBM systems. A content management system that detects users who attempt to make illegal copies of materials in fee-charging digital libraries was created by Mun and colleagues (2002); they define a set of rules that permit the identification of abnormal access behavior patterns.

A recent development is that commercial digital library systems are forced to adopt a series of precautions to protect themselves when they offer access via credit card, even when they are only selling technical or academic documents. Should a commercial system accept a stolen credit card number, it will make an inappropriate charge against the cardholder. This can be easily annulled, but if this occurs frequently, the credit card company may charge the digital library heavily. Another problem may arise when commercial digital libraries offer trial access to collections to credit card holders. Credit card preauthorization is not normally a problem, because it only costs the digital library a few cents per card. However, if foreign scammers use automated systems to generate credit card numbers and submit several thousand numbers to verify their validity, significant charges may be incurred. To protect themselves against these problems, commercial digital libraries may automatically refuse requests from IP addresses located in foreign countries known for "scams" of this type. An alternative would be to insist on address verification for credit card transactions, which will limit their sales to North America.

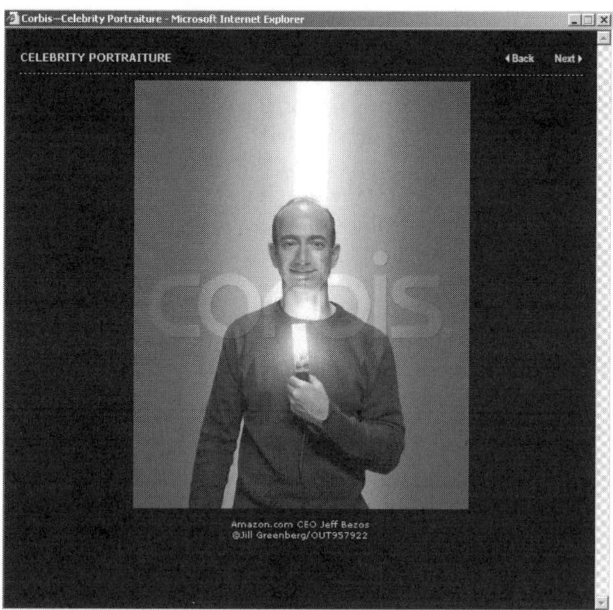

Figure 15: This sample image, from the Corbis image agency, has been protected by a clearly visible watermark.

Watermarking

Watermarks are a security technique familiar to all users of paper currency, but they can be easily transposed to the digital environment. A classic watermark would be a visible subsidiary image inserted in a protected image. In the digital field, watermarks may be coded so as to be invisible to the end user. Visible watermarks are routinely used to mark the sample images that can be examined free of charge in commercial photograph collections, such as that at the New York Times (http://www.nytimes.com/nytstore/photos/index.html) or Corbis (Figure 15; http://pro.corbis.com/).

Mintzer, Lotspiech, and Morimoto (1997) are responsible for a seminal paper on watermarking in a digital library environment. They define "digital watermarks" as imperceptible, or barely perceptible, transformations of digital data. They are mostly applied to digital images but can be applied to other forms of digital data, for example, videos and music. The term "invisible watermarks" can be used to describe digital watermarks that are imperceptible but that can be extracted by a computer. When the imperceptible watermarks themselves contain data, the term "data hiding" is used. A password may be needed to extract the digital watermark; this is called a "watermark key." Mintzer and colleagues do not consider watermarking to be a total solution for digital library security; better security can be achieved by combining it with encryption and digital signatures. The paper describes a variety of technologies, including some that were relatively unproven at that time. Mintzer also collaborated on a major paper describing the application of watermarks to images of priceless materials in the Vatican Library (Gladney, Mintzer & Schiattarella, 1997). IBM collaborated with the Vatican in an early experiment to explore the technical, financial, and practical challenges of making illustrated medieval manuscripts accessible via the Internet. Gladney and colleagues note that making images and text available via WWW or CD-ROM is quite easy; the challenge is to do so in a way that enhances and preserves the value of the materials. The situation is especially difficult when libraries need to make new services pay for themselves. Safeguards are nearly always imperfect, but digital watermarks can make misuse economically unattractive.

Komatsu and Tominaga (1990) suggest embedding a digital watermark in each document image sold; it would therefore be possible to track illegal copying. Video steganography, or how to secretly embed a signature in a picture, is discussed by Matsui and Tanaka (1994). Zhang and colleagues (2002) propose a novel watermarking scheme for still images in digital libraries. The image is decomposed, and a logo watermark is embedded into the low-frequency band. They provide a detailed technical description of the method, which they consider more robust than conventional approaches. Sasaki and Kiyoki (2003) propose to systematically protect digital library materials, especially images, by using patentable content-based retrieval processes.

Audio watermarking is less common but was discussed in a digital library context in two papers relating to the National Gallery of the Spoken Word (NGSW; http://www.ngsw.org/). Seadle and colleagues (2002) approach the problem from the general point of view. The development of audio watermarking technologies is an important research consideration for the NGSW, which considers audio watermarking a particularly desirable method of intellectual property protection. Even the courts accept watermarks as legitimate means of copyright protection. Watermarking facilitates redress, while representing a protective technology that can be used by universities without prejudice to their mission to disseminate knowledge. Intellectual property techniques adopted by the NGSW are described by Deller and colleagues

(2001); their discussion centers around an audio watermarking algorithm called \textit (transform encryption coding; TEC), which offers several advantages.

PRESERVATION AND DIGITAL LIBRARIES

Although their major objective is to increase access to materials, digital libraries serve an important preservation function by reducing the need to handle the original every time somebody wants to view it or read it. All digital library policy and design should be influenced by considerations of preservation, both of the original materials and of the digital surrogates. For instance, even when the public will have access only to working JPEG images, provision should be made for the long-term storage of high-quality archival images.

Preservation of Original Materials

Originals of photographs and broadsides will normally be retained, even after digitization. Books, which may be printed on brittle paper and may have been unbound to facilitate digitization, can be more difficult to preserve. Microfilm has been the standard answer, but libraries have recently been criticized for failing to retain the originals of microfilmed newspapers (Baker, 2001). In the future, there will, no doubt, be strong pressure on libraries to preserve originals after digitization, especially when they are the last available copies. A series of difficult decisions will have to be made. Will minor restoration work, such as mending tears, be undertaken before digitization? The cost of restoration work can rarely be included in digital library projects. Should images be processed to restore original color? The aim of digitization will normally be to faithfully represent the original as it is now.

Preservation of Digital Materials

Protection of digital resources is essential to preservation activities. Libraries have traditionally thought in terms of centuries, whereas computer software only lasts a few years before being replaced by new, and often incompatible, systems. All types of digital information are at risk. Software and hardware quickly become obsolete, and file formats and versions constantly change, rendering important data unusable. Even simple data formats are in danger because of the degradation and obsolescence of computer media. As a result, high-quality information resources, such as databases and e-journals, can become entirely or partially unreadable. By the time the problem is detected, it may be too late to save them (Ray et al., 2002).

Arms devotes a chapter of his textbook on digital libraries to repositories and archives (Arms, 2000, pp. 245–262). He offers criteria for the evaluation of repositories, storage of metadata, and interoperability. Digital archival operations are seen in terms of refreshing and migrating data; he also discusses digital archeology, or the process of recovering data from superseded systems. Arms is careful to distinguish between migration and emulation:

Migration: The "preservation of digital content, where the underlying information is retained but older formats and internal structures are replaced by newer."

Emulation: "[T]he replication of a computing system to process programs and data from an early system that is no longer available" (Arms, 2000, p. 276–279).

Chowdhury and Chowdhury's textbook also devotes a chapter to digital library archiving and preservation (2003, pp. 214–226). They discuss problems and strategies for digital preservation and outline principal projects in the area. A general overview of the preservation landscape is offered by Abby Smith (2004) of the Council on Library and Information Resources (CLIR). She points out that the fundamental questions of stewardship (what is to be collected and preserved, for whom, for how long, and by whom) have changed significantly. Key questions include these: is it possible, or even desirable, to select or preserve rapidly growing Web resources? Is it possible for institutions to collaborate in collection development, metadata creation, or preservation services? How can institutions such as libraries preserve digital informational resources that are owned by commercial rights-holders and simply licensed for use by the library? Who is going to pay for preservation in the digital age? Is it possible to envision a rights regime that provides an incentive for good stewardship?

Gould and Ebdon (1999) conducted a survey for the International Federation of Library Associations (IFLA) and United Nations Educational, Scientific and Cultural Organization (UNESCO) on the digitization and preservation policies of major libraries worldwide. Sixty-four percent of the libraries or archives that digitized materials had a preservation policy for digitized documents. A large majority, 83%, continued to allow access to the original document after digitization. Sixty-seven percent of the libraries and archives surveyed stored the originals in special conditions. Slightly more than half of the respondents had a policy for migrating data to more recent platforms. In all cases, when data were migrated, all data were processed. Data migration was always an internal procedure; it was never contracted out.

Digital files must be carefully refreshed at regular intervals. Simple steps that any webmaster can take to safeguard digital resources are outlined by the National Library of Australia in *Safeguarding Australia's Web Resources: Guidelines for Creators and Publishers* (2002). For a British initiative in digital preservation by CURL (Consortium of University Research Libraries), see CEDARS (CURL Exemplars in Digital ARchiveS). This project lasted from 1968 to 2002 and generated numerous papers and the prototype of a distributed digital archive. Documentation is still available via the University of Leeds (http://www.leeds.ac.uk/cedars/index.html).

The Digital Library SunSITE at Berkeley suggests four levels of collecting; each level implies a different commitment to preservation:

Archived: The material is hosted here, and the library intends to keep the intellectual content of the material available on a permanent basis.

Served: The material resides here, but the library has not (yet) made the level of commitment to keeping it available that it has for "archived" materials.

Mirrored: A copy of material residing elsewhere is hosted here, and the library makes no commitment to archiving. Also, an institution other than the library has primary responsibility for the content and its maintenance.

Linked: The material is hosted elsewhere and the library points to it at that location. Therefore the library has no control over the information.

Material in any category except Archived may be re-designated from one level to another as required to meet changing information needs, remote server accessibility or responsiveness, local resource demands, etc. Material that receives the Archived designation cannot be downgraded to a lower status. (http://sunsite.berkeley.edu/Admin/collection.html) The Digital Library SunSITE at Berkeley offers additional resources on preservation at http://sunsite.berkeley.edu/Preservation.

Lorie (2001) discusses the technical, social, and organizational challenges that have to be overcome to guarantee the long-term preservation of digital data. Technical challenges involve ensuring that today's information can survive changes in storage media, data formats, and devices. He suggests distinguishing between the archiving of data files and the archiving of programs. Program behavior would be reenacted in the future, because the original executable object code would be saved alongside the specification of the processing required for each original machine instruction. Data files would be preserved, together with a specification of the processing that needs to be performed on the data so as to return the information to a future client. Processing would be based on a universal virtual computer model that would be general in nature and sufficiently basic to remain relevant in the future. A logical view of the data would also be archived. In a follow-up paper to a later digital library conference, Lorie (2002) continued his discussion of long-term archiving of digital data using a universal virtual computer (UVC). To render archived data comprehensible to a future client, a certain amount of information must be preserved indefinitely to guarantee that the client will be able to recover the information. Lorie calls this a "Convention" and presents the first version of one in his paper, together with the architecture of the UVC.

Rothenberg (2000) discusses emulation as an option for a major European library. His report was issued as part of the NEDLIB (Networked European Deposit Library) project (http://www.kb.nl/coop/nedlib/index.html), which had as its objective the long-term storage of European digital publications. Holdsworth and Wheatley (2001) discuss emulation as a preservation technique. They describe the CAMiLEON project, a joint undertaking between the Universities of Michigan (U.S.) and Leeds (U.K.) to develop and evaluate a range of technical strategies for the long-term preservation of digital materials (http://www.si.umich.edu/CAMILEON/index.html). Its best known achievement was the rescue of the data in the BBC Domesday Project (http://www.atsf.co.uk/dottext/domesday.html). A mass of information on life in Britain in the 1980s was recorded on large videodiscs, using an unusual format that could only be read by an obsolete computer (http://www.si.umich.edu/CAMILEON/domesday/what.html). There was great relief when the data were finally recovered (*Digital domesday book unlocked*, 2002).

A distributed, object-based design for digital library repositories is described by Lagoze (1995). He proposes inter-operable secure object stores (ISOS) and defines interfaces to secure repositories that permit interoperability with other repositories, with clients, and with other infrastructure services. The interfaces to ISOS are defined as classes in a distributed object system, using network interoperability protocols such as CORBA (common object request broker architecture) or OLE (object linking and embedding). Lagoze also defines an extension to CORBA security that can be used by repositories to secure access to themselves and to their digital objects.

Tennant (2001) discusses disaster protection in the digital library context. He recommends RAID (redundant array of inexpensive [or independent] disks) technology. RAID level one involves mirroring data or making one complete copy. RAID level five distributes data across several physical disks. Uninterruptible power supplies and fire and alarm systems constitute necessary disaster infrastructure. Data also need to be backed up at a distant location.

The preservation of digital content at one of the world's major digital libraries, the National Digital Library Program (NDLP) of the Library of Congress, is discussed by Arms (2000). All files offered by the Library's servers are currently on magnetic disk, with built-in mirroring capability. Full backups of the entire system are made to magnetic tape cartridges in a robotic "library" on a 2-week cycle; backups of files that have been modified or created are made nightly. Two new features were planned: snapshot archives of digital collections and an off-site location for an additional robotic backup facility; this would be accessible via the storage network. In December 2002, the U.S. Congress approved NDIIPP's Preserving Our Digital Heritage: Plan for the National Digital Information Infrastructure and Preservation Program, making it possible for the Library to proceed with the work of developing an infrastructure for the collection and preservation of digital materials (National Digital, 2002). Another national library, the National Library of Australia, maintains an important Web site for digital preservation. PADI: Preserving Access to Digital Information (http://www.nla.gov.au/padi/) covers strategies, data documentation and standards, sources of information, and a series of other topics. In the United States, the Online Computer Library Center (OCLC) offers practical support to libraries and maintains a digital archive that permits members to store their digital assets either item by item or as entire collections (http://www.oclc.org/digitalarchive/default.htm).

The Internet Archive and the Wayback Machine (Figure 16; http://www.archive.org/) permit nostalgic surfing through the Web of several years ago and access to special collections recording specific events.

In view of their role, it is interesting to note their archival procedures. Their hardware consists of PCs with clusters of IDE (integrated device electronics) hard drives. Data is stored on DLT (digital linear tape) and hard drives in various formats (http://www.archive.org/about/about.php). Although DLT is rated to last 30 years, the industry rule of thumb is to migrate data every 10 years;

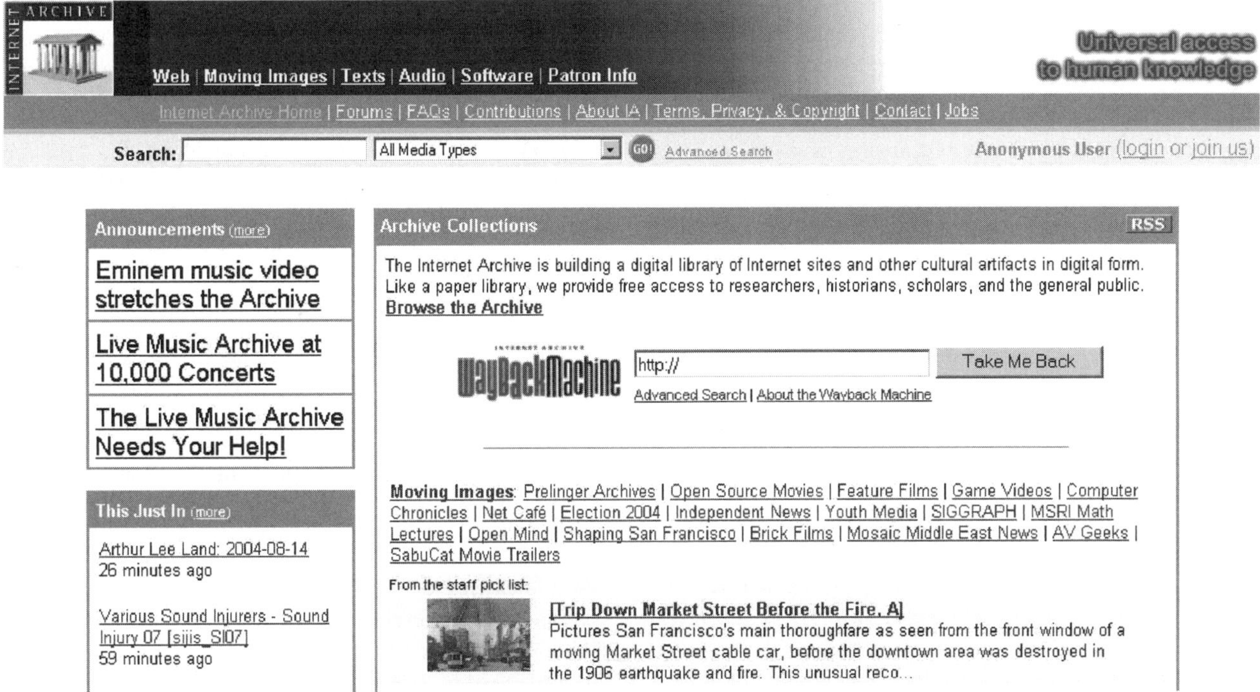

Figure 16: The Internet Archive and the Wayback Machine.

the Internet Archive expects to migrate more frequently. Web data are stored in 100-MB WWW archive (ARC) files designed to meet the specific demands of the system (http://pages.alexa.com/company/arcformat.html). Each archive file contains many individual files and multiple copies are stored in different locations. The Internet Archive also collects software and emulators that will aid future researchers, historians, and scholars in researching the history of the Internet and social communication patterns.

For a unique, open-source approach to archiving digital materials at a library level, see Lots of Copies Keep Stuff Safe or LOCKSS, implemented at Stanford University (http://lockss.stanford.edu/index.html). This permits libraries to maintain local archive copies of the Web journals to which they subscribe; the system polls the Web journals regularly and downloads new material to a local cache. These are the procedures libraries have always adopted with periodicals, now updated to a digital format. Lavoie (2000) discusses the preservation process for electronic scholarly journals from the point of view of a major intermediary, the Online Computer Library Center (OCLC).

Cooper and Garcia-Molina (2001) discuss the creation of cooperative trading networks, which could protect digital archives against failure by maintaining copies at remote sites. Simulations assist in calculating space requirements and the optimum number of partner sites. A paper at the same conference by Crespo and Garcia-Molina (2001) points out that it is difficult to design an archival repository because there are many possible alternatives, all with different levels of reliability and cost. They analyze the cost of these repositories and suggest evaluation criteria that permit the selection of the most reliable and cost-effective procedures. They have developed a simulation tool that aids in the decision process. Chapman (2003) discusses the cost of digital preservation and compares the centralized repositories of Harvard University Library and the Online Computer Library Center (OCLC). Both organizations recover operational expenses by charging owners; Harvard Depository assesses rates for analog storage per billable square foot; OCLC assesses rates per gigabyte for storage of digital objects. Formats are significant factors in deciding preservation costs; the definition of content integrity and tolerance for risk are important variables that can change over time.

Preservation of CDs and DVDs

The archival TIFF files produced directly from original materials are of great value and must be carefully preserved. It is common practice for digital libraries today to save these on a series of CD-Rs (compact disc, readable). Even relatively small systems may have more than 1,000 CD-Rs. Byers (2003) produced a comprehensive guide to the care and handling of CDs and DVDs for librarians and archivists that covered topics such as the types of media in use, how they are made and how they work, the care of optical media, their longevity, and conditions that affect their life expectancy. The "write-once" CD-Rs used to record digital data in DLs should have a life of at least a hundred years, if well looked after. More serious problems arise with mass-produced audio CDs, which may have a life of only 20 years, even when carefully stored. The Library of Congress' Preservation Research & Testing Division recently examined preservation problems of CDs (Library of Congress, 2003). Program objectives included developing storage guidelines and using an accelerated aging procedure to estimate the lifetime of CDs. If the rate at which optical and physical changes occur can be determined, it is possible to anticipate when discs will need to be reformatted. Samples of the CD collections of the Library of Congress are monitored periodically. These problems recently came to wide public attention when a music enthusiast noted that 15–20% of his audio CDs suffered from "CD rot" and would no longer play (Baig, 2004).

An additional problem with handling thousands of CD-Rs is that information has to be carefully organized so that specific images can be quickly retrieved when necessary. This requires careful planning, especially with simplified systems where file names may be limited to eight characters.

Legal Deposit of Digital Materials

Legal deposit of books with national libraries has long been the cornerstone of bibliographic preservation. The concept is now being extended to digital works. The International Federation of Library Associations (IFLA) and the International Publishers Association (IPA) recently made a joint statement on the archiving and preserving of digital information (International Federation of Library Associations, 2002). They pointed out that an increasing amount of the information published only in electronic form has enduring cultural and documentary significance. It is just as important as more traditional information, and action must be taken to guarantee its long-term availability. Both organizations would work to add long-term archiving and preservation to international agendas. Industry standards, systems, and research for digital archiving and preservation are essential for the success of this program. Libraries are in a good position to take responsibility for long-term archiving, working with publishers. National libraries are experimenting with the acquisition of digital publications and should take the lead in long-term archiving of digital publications.

UNESCO recently promulgated the important *Charter on the Preservation of the Digital Heritage* (UNESCO, 2003). This states that member nations need to secure and protect their digital heritage via appropriate legal and institutional frameworks. Archives legislation and legal or voluntary deposit in libraries, archives, and other repositories are key elements of national preservation policy and should embrace national digital heritage. Adequate access should be assured to legally deposited digital heritage materials. It is essential that appropriate legal and technical frameworks be created to guarantee authenticity and prevent manipulation or intentional alteration of digital materials. For archival work, it is essential that electronic materials should be verifiable.

The British Library has begun a project that may eventually lead to the archiving of all U.K. Web sites (Marson, 2004). A trial project to preserve 6,000 U.K. Web sites was announced by the U.K. Web Archiving Consortium, led by the British Library and including the National Archives and the Scottish and Welsh national libraries. All types of Web content, from government documents to blogs, will be covered. The British Library will not censor the material and ultimately would like to archive all U.K. Web sites. Because of U.K. copyright laws, permission is needed to archive a site, but the British Library is asking the government to extend the law to permit preservation of the U.K. Web. A British Library Web site (http://www.bl.uk/news/webcase.html) somberly predicted that "Without new legislation to ensure non-print materials are saved for future generations, the 21st century will be seen as a cultural Dark Age which failed to archive a substantial and vital part of the nation's published heritage." It is interesting to compare digital and audio materials in this context: the United States only introduced legal deposit for sound recordings in the 1970s; as a result, many early recordings are not in the Library of Congress (Lesk, 1997, p. 179).

PANDORA (Preserving and Accessing Networked Documentary Resources of Australia) is Australia's Web archive, created by the National Library of Australia in 1996 (http://pandora.nla.gov.au/index.html). Because of the lack of legal deposit provisions covering online publications in Australia, PANDORA seeks permission from publishers before including materials in the archive (http://pandora.nla.gov.au/legaldeposit.html). An assistant director-general of the National Library of Australia has given an interesting account of archiving the Web in Scandinavian countries (Cathro, 2001). Progress has been made in Finland, Norway, Sweden, and Iceland, but serious legal obstacles still need to be overcome. The first efforts of the French National Library to archive the French Web are described by Abiteboul and colleagues (2002). Specific problems included the exact definition of the perimeter of the French Web and the specification of appropriate intervals for the production of successive archive copies of regularly updated Web pages.

CONTINUITY OF DIGITAL LIBRARIES

Continuity of Resource Identifiers

The problem of "dead links" is a familiar source of annoyance to all Internet users. Digital libraries, which offer quality materials, should make special efforts to maintain their URLs over time. Many digital libraries contain links to outside resources. These links have to be checked regularly, biweekly, weekly, or even daily. Dead links have to be removed or updated, often a laborious process. Simple approaches include organizing Web sites so that it is unnecessary to move resources, or even maintaining older materials on the Web site (National Digital Information Infrastructure and Preservation Program, 2002).

One solution is to use persistent identifiers, such as PURLs (persistent URLs; http://purl.oclc.org/). To the end user, a PURL looks and functions like a URL. However, instead of pointing at an Internet resource, a PURL points to an intermediate resolution service. The PURL resolution service associates the PURL with the current URL and returns that URL to the client, who is switched seamlessly via a standard HTTP redirect.

Gladney (1998a) discusses methods of unambiguously identifying each digital library item needing protection. The best-known operational system uses digital object identifiers or DOIs (http://www.doi.org/index.html). DOIs consistently identify content objects in a digital environment, permitting persistent identification, management of intellectual content, and links between users and content suppliers. Information about a digital content object may change and its location on the network may be altered, but the DOI will remain the same. DOIs are presented in the form "DOI:Directory.Registrant/Suffix." In the example "DOI:10.1234/999ABC," "10" represents the directory of DOIs for a specific geographic region or industry, "1234" is the registrant's prefix, which identifies the company or institution supplying the content, and "999ABC" is the suffix, a unique identifier supplied by the company. The suffix can be an existing product number or code. The director of the International DOI Foundation, writing in *D-Lib Magazine* in June 2003, stated that 10 million DOIs have been distributed, mostly for textual content objects (Paskin, 2003). Articles in *D-Lib Magazine* (http://www.dlib.org/) receive DOIs that commence with "DOI:10.1045"; the DOI of Paskin's article is "DOI:10.1045/june2003-paskin"; this can be used to retrieve the paper via a search engine, such as Google.

Continuity of Digital Libraries as Institutions

Digital libraries are relatively new and are often created by institutions with solid foundations, such as universities. As a result, almost all the systems implanted appear to be still operational. It is easy to find a listing of dead search engines: Notess (2004) lists about 20. However, there is no listing of dead digital libraries. The few closures that have occurred are related to changes in government policy. The U.S. Department of Energy used to maintain PubSci (formerly at http://pubsci.osti.gov), a site that permitted researchers to examine more than 1,000 peer-reviewed journals free of charge through a single interface, instead of searching multiple Web sites. This was closed on the grounds that it duplicated commercial services (Foster, 2002). The ERIC database (http://www.eric.ed.gov/) of 1.2 million documents and journal articles on education research and practice, founded in 1966, is one of the world's best known information resources. In 2003–2004, it underwent major transformations; notably contracts with its 16 clearinghouses were not renewed (ERIC, 2004). ERIC users expressed concern about the changes (Potter, 2003).

McArthur and colleagues (2003) review work on sustainability of digital libraries within the NSF-supported National Science Digital Library (NSDL) program. In the digital library environment, sustainability can be visualized as covering a wide range of topics, from technical issues relating to digital preservation to social questions concerning long-term accessibility of resources. The Institute of Museum and Library Services (IMLS) continually stresses the importance of sustainability. Its *Framework of Guidance for Building Good Digital Collections* presents as the third principle of successful collection building the following statement: "A collection should be sustainable over time. In particular, digital collections built with special funding should have a plan for their continued usability beyond the funded period" (http://www.imls.gov/pubs/forumframework.htm). IMLS proposals normally include a section on sustainability; for an easily viewed example, see *Connecticut History Online* (http://www.cthistoryonline.org/project/IMLSproposal.htm#sustainability).

CONCLUSION

An important paper by Lynch (2001) points out that the new technologies have a potentially steep social price, because they provide new levels of control, monitoring, and usage restrictions for digital books. The paradox is that unless publishers are able to establish what they consider adequate levels of control, in-print books may not move to digital form. They certainly will not migrate quickly or in large numbers. It is likely that publishers will favor appliance book readers, but it is also possible that print-on-demand publishing (POD) will occupy a significant niche in the future. As this chapter went to press, there were encouraging signs of growth in e-book sales (Becker, 2004). Adoption is expected to continue to be gradual, because the book publishing business is traditional and decentralized. Current growth in e-books has been fueled by users reading them on devices they already have: PCs, laptops, and handheld computers, or personal digital assistants (PDAs). As equipment of this type becomes ever more common, the demand for digital materials can be expected to grow. The long-term potential for digital libraries seems excellent. Kurzweil (1999) published a seminal book, *The Age of Spiritual Machines,* in which he forecast that paper books and documents would rarely be used by the year 2019; all documents and multimedia would be digitized by the year 2029. Libraries will, no doubt, continue to make quality and older materials available. As demonstrated in this chapter, much in the digitization of cultural materials by institutions such as libraries and archives has already been achieved in a few years. This is an important beginning, because, over the next few decades, a major aim of humanity will be the digitization of our cultural heritage. There will, of course, be significant costs, not only in creating, but also in maintaining, digital archives of this scope. If publishers are able to develop secure business models that guarantee significant commercial returns from digital information, they will, no doubt, migrate in force to the digital environment and contribute significantly to this process.

Digital publications are still in their earliest stages, equivalent to print books at the time of Gutenberg. They have little more than a decade of life and will doubtless develop rapidly in the near future. At the moment, the digital library field is unequally developed and characterized by a bewildering variety of systems. Standards are urgently required and will doubtless evolve rapidly. The same is true of security and preservation measures in the digital library field.

GLOSSARY

Access Controls Procedures to control access to digital libraries, based on use of passwords, recognition of IP addresses, and similar features.

American Memory The Historical Collections of the National Digital Library, maintained by the Library of Congress (http://memory.loc.gov/); one of the world's largest digital libraries, with more than 100 collections and a total of 7 million digital items, including photographs, manuscripts, rare books, maps, sound recordings, and moving pictures.

Digital Library A system that permits, via the Internet and the WWW, easy access to a collection of high-value, quality digital content, which has been selected and organized to facilitate use and is supported by appropriate services. The digital content may reflect the traditional textual orientation of many libraries or take advantage of the WWW's facilities to deliver graphics and multimedia.

Digital Preservation Process of guaranteeing the long-term preservation of digital objects by storage of files in secure repositories, migration to other platforms, and other means.

Digital Rights Management Procedures that ensure that holders of digital rights are clearly identified and receive the stipulated payment for their materials; they may also impose further restrictions on use of digital objects, for example, inhibiting printing or prohibiting further distribution.

Digitization Process of converting analog documents (e.g., paper, film, maps) to digital form.

Electronic Journals (E-Journals) Journals, such as scientific and professional journals, available in digital form.

Electronic Theses and Dissertations (ETDs) Theses and dissertations available in digital form.

Emulation The replication of a computing system to permit the processing of programs and data from an earlier system that is obsolete or no longer available.

Indexing The process of systematically generating pointers or keys to the content of texts to permit readers to go directly to pages that contain specific words or deal with specific topics.

Metadata Data about data. Keys, guides, or indications of the content of a document or dataset and stipulations of appropriate use.

Migration Transfer of digital data from one format or platform to another; normally, digital data are migrated from an older format or platform to a newer format or platform to guarantee preservation.

Multimedia Digital Library Digital library that delivers content in a variety of formats: text, photographic images, audio, short films, and so forth.

Project Gutenberg One of the longest running digital libraries (http://promo.net/pg/or http://gutenberg.net/), founded in 1971. It has always concentrated on simple, copyright-free texts that can be read on almost any computing platform. Now offers more than 10,000 texts and is supported by a network of mirror sites.

Sustainability The capacity of a digital system to continue operating for the foreseeable future. Sustainability depends on factors such as organizational or governmental commitment, a secure financial model, adequate protection from external attack, use of appropriate formats and platforms, and collections that are of lasting interest or capable of being updated.

CROSS REFERENCES

See *Database Security; E-Education and Information Privacy and Security; Internet Basics; Security in E-Learning.*

REFERENCES

Abiteboul, S., Cobéna, G.; Masanes, J., & Sedrati, G. (2002). A first experience in archiving the French Web. In *Research and Advanced Technology for Digital Libraries: Proceedings of the 6th European Conference on Research and Advanced Technology for Digital Libraries (ECDL 2002): Lecture Notes in Computer Science, 2458,* (pp. 1–5). Heidelberg: Springer-Verlag.

Albanese, A. (2003). Barnes & Noble drops ebooks citing sales, unwieldy devices. *Library Hotline: The Weekly Newsletter from Library Journal and School Library Journal, 32*(38), 1.

Alrashid, T. M., Barker, J. A., Christian, B. S., Cox, S. C., Rabne, M. W., Slotta, E. A., & Upthegrove, L. R. (1998). Safeguarding copyrighted contents: Digital libraries and intellectual property management: CWRU's rights management system. *D-Lib Magazine, 4*(4). Retrieved November 19, 2004, from http://www.dlib.org/dlib/april98/04barker.html

Arms, W. Y. (1998). Implementing policies for access management. *D-Lib Magazine, 4*(2). Retrieved November 19, 2004, from http://www.dlib.org/dlib/february98/arms/02arms.html

Arms, W. Y. (2000). *Digital libraries. (digital libraries and electronic publishing)*. Cambridge, MA: MIT Press.

Ashling, J. (2003). Open access and the public domain. *Information Today, 20*(5), 27–29.

Atwood, S. (2002). MIT's superarchive: A digital repository will revolutionize the way research is shared and preserved. *Technology Review, 104*(12). Retrieved November 19, 2004, from http://www.technologyreview.com/articles/atwood1202.asp

Baig, E. C. (2004, July 7). Life has gotten even shorter in digital age. *USA Today [Digital Edition]* Retrieved November 19, 2004, from http://www.usatoday.com/tech/news/2004-07-26-longevity_x.htm?POE=click-refer

Baker, N. (2001). *Double fold: Libraries and the assault on paper*. New York: Random House.

Bearman, D., & Trant, J. (1998). Authenticity of digital resources: Towards a statement of requirements in the research process. *D-Lib Magazine, 4*(6). Retrieved November 19, 2004, from http://www.dlib.org/dlib/june98/06bearman.html

Becker, D. (2004, August 17). Have e-books turned a page? *CNET News.com*. Retrieved November 19, 2004, from http://zdnet.com.com/2100-1104_2-5326015.html?tag=zdfd.newsfeed

Boss, R. W. (2001). Imaging for libraries and information centers. *Library Technology Reports. 37*(1), 1–59.

Brief of Amici Curiae: The Internet Archive: Filed on behalf of petitioners. (2002). Retrieved November 19, 2004, from http://www.arl.org/info/frn/copy/ia_brief.html

Byers, F. R. (2003). *Care and handling of CDs and DVDs: A guide for librarians and archivists*. Washington, DC: Council on Library and Information Resources (CLIR). Retrieved November 19, 2004, from http://www.clir.org/pubs/abstract/pub121abst.html

Carnevale, D. (2003a). Libraries with tight budgets renew complaints about Elsevier's online pricing. *The Chronicle of Higher Education, 50*(17), A33.

Carnevale, D. (2003b). Six institutions will help fine-tune a popular new archiving program. *The Chronicle of Higher Education, 49*(23), 36. Retrieved November 19, 2004, from http://chronicle.com/free/2003/01/2003013001t.htm

Cathro, W. (2001). Archiving the Web. *Gateways [National Library of Australia]*, 52. Retrieved November 19, 2004, from http://www.nla.gov.au/ntwkpubs/gw/52/p11a01.html

Chapman, S. (2003). Counting the costs of digital preservation: Is repository storage affordable? *Journal of Digital Information, 4*(2). Retrieved November 19, 2004, from http://jodi.ecs.soton.ac.uk/Articles/v04/i02/Chapman/

Chowdhury, G. G., & Chowdhury, S. (1999). Digital library research: Major issues and trends. *Journal of Documentation, 55*(4), 409–448.

Chowdhury, G. G., & Chowdhury, S. (2000). An overview of the information retrieval features of twenty digital libraries. *Program, 34*(4), 341–373.

Chowdhury, G. G., & Chowdhury, S. (2003). *Introduction to digital libraries*. London: Facet Publishing.

Cooper, B., & Garcia-Molina, H. (2001). Creating trading networks of digital archives. In: *Proceedings of the First ACM/IEEE-CS Joint Conference on Digital Libraries (JCDL 2001)* (pp. 353–362). New York: Association for Computing Machinery (ACM).

Cox, A. (2001). Do they need to know? Computer security. *Ariadne, 30*. Retrieved November 19, 2004, from http://www.ariadne.ac.uk/issue30/web-security/

Crawford, W. (2000). Nine models, one name: Untangling the e-book muddle. *American Libraries, 31*(8), 56–59.

Crespo, A., & Garcia-Molina, H. (2001). Cost-driven design for archival repositories. In *Proceedings of the First ACM/IEEE-CS Joint Conference on Digital Libraries (JCDL 2001)* (pp. 363–372). New York: Association for Computing Machinery (ACM).

Deller Jr., J. R., Gurijala, A., & Seadle, M. S. (2001). Audio watermarking techniques for the National Gallery of the Spoken Word. In *Proceedings of the First ACM/IEEE-CS Joint Conference on Digital Libraries (JCDL 2001)* (pp. 237–238). New York: Association for Computing Machinery (ACM).

Digital Domesday book unlocked. (2002). BBC News/Technology. Retrieved November 19, 2004, from http://news.bbc.co.uk/1/hi/technology/2534391.stm

Digital Library Federation. (2001). *A new approach to finding research materials on the Web.* Retrieved November 19, 2004, from http://www.diglib.org/architectures/vision.htm

ERIC reauthorization news. (2004). Retrieved November 19, 2004, from http://www.lib.msu.edu/corby/education/doe.htm

Foster, A. L. (2002). Energy Department seeks to close Web site that searches scientific journals. *The Chronicle of Higher Education, 49*(2), A46.

Fox, E. (1999). Digital Libraries Initiative (DLI) projects 1994–1999. *Bulletin of the American Society for Information Science, 26*(1), 7–11. Retrieved November 19, 2004, from http://www.asis.org/Bulletin/Oct-99/fox.html

Fox, E., & Urs, S. (2002). Digital libraries. *Annual Review of Information Science and Technology, 36*, 503–589.

Frey, F. (1997). Digital imaging for photographic collections: Foundations for technical standards. *RLG DigiNews, 1*(3). Retrieved November 19, 2004, from http://www.rlg.org/preserv/diginews/diginews3.html#com

Gladney, H. M. (1997). Safeguarding digital library contents and users: Document access control. *D-Lib Magazine, 4*(6). Retrieved November 19, 2004, from http://www.dlib.org/dlib/june97/ibm/06gladney.html

Gladney, H. M. (1998a). Safeguarding digital library contents and users: A note on universal unique identifiers. *D-Lib Magazine, 5*(4). Retrieved November 19, 2004, from http://www.dlib.org/dlib/april98/04gladney.html

Gladney, H. M. (1998b). Safeguarding digital library contents and users: Interim retrospect and prospects. *D-Lib Magazine, 5*(7–8). Retrieved November 19, 2004, from http://www.dlib.org/dlib/july98/gladney/07gladney.html

Gladney, H. M., & Lotspiech, J. B. (1997). Safeguarding digital library contents and users: Assuring convenient security and data quality. *D-Lib Magazine, 4*(5). Retrieved November 19, 2004, from http://www.dlib.org/dlib/may97/ibm/05gladney.html

Gladney, H. M., & Lotspiech, J. B. (1998). Safeguarding digital library contents and users: Storing, sending, showing, and honoring usage terms and conditions. *D-Lib Magazine, 5*(5). Retrieved November 19, 2004, from http://www.dlib.org/dlib/may98/gladney/05gladney.html

Gladney, H. M., Mintzer, F., & Schiattarella, F. (1997). Safeguarding digital library contents and users: Digital images of treasured antiquities. *D-Lib Magazine, 4*(7–8). Retrieved November 19, 2004, from http://www.dlib.org/dlib/july97/vatican/07gladney.html

Gould, S., & Ebdon, R. (1999). *IFLA/UNESCO survey on digitisation and preservation.* Wetherby, West Yorkshire, U.K.: IFLA Offices for UAP and International Lending. Retrieved November 19, 2004, from http://www.unesco.org/webworld/mdm/survey_index_en.html

Greenstein, D., & Thorin, S. E. (2002). *The digital library: A biography*. Washington, D.C.: Digital Library Federation, Council on Library and Information Resources. Retrieved November 19, 2004, from http://www.clir.org/pubs/reports/pub109/pub109.pdf

Guenther, K. (2001). Knock, knock, who's there? Authenticating users. *Computers in Libraries, 21*(3), 54–57.

Hazen, D., Horrell, J., & Merrill-Oldham, J. (1998). *Selecting research collections for digitization.* Washington, D.C.: Council on Library and Information Resources. Retrieved November 19, 2004, from http://www.clir.org/pubs/reports/hazen/pub74.html

Herzberg, A. (1998). Safeguarding digital library contents: Charging for online content. *D-Lib Magazine, 5*(1). Retrieved November 19, 2004, from http://www.dlib.org/dlib/january98/ibm/01herzberg.html

Holdsworth, D., & Wheatley, P. (2001). Emulation, preservation, and abstraction. *RLG DigiNews, 5*(4). Retrieved November 19, 2004, from http://www.rlg.org/preserv/diginews/diginews5-4.html#feature2

International Federation of Library Associations (IFLA) & International Publishers Association (IPA). (2002).

Preserving the memory of the world in perpetuity: A joint statement on the archiving and preserving of digital information. Retrieved November 19, 2004, from http://www.ifla.org/V/press/ifla-ipa02.htm

Jackson, J. (2004). Feds help create PDF archiving standard. *Government Computer News, 1*(1). Retrieved November 19, 2004, from http://gcn.com/vol1_no1/daily-updates/25986-1.html

Knight, J. (2003). Cornell axes Elsevier journals as prices rise. *Nature, 426*(6964), 217.

Kohl, U., Lotspiech, J., & Kaplan, M. A. (1997). Safeguarding digital library contents and users: Protecting documents rather than channels. *D-Lib Magazine, 3*(9). Retrieved November 19, 2004, from http://www.dlib.org/dlib/september97/ibm/09lotspiech.html

Komatsu, N., & Tominaga, H. (1990). A proposal on digital watermarks in document image communication and its application to realizing a signature. *Electronics and Communications in Japan, Part 1 (Communications), 73*(5), 22–23.

Kurzweil, R. (1999). *The age of spiritual machines: When computers exceed human intelligence*. New York: Penguin.

Lagoze, C. (1995). A secure repository design for digital libraries. *D-Lib Magazine, 1*(12). Retrieved November 19, 2004, from http://www.dlib.org/dlib/december95/12lagoze.html

Lagoze, C., & Van de Sompel, H. (2001). The Open Archives Initiative: Building a low-barrier interoperability framework. In *Proceedings of the First ACM/IEEE-CS Joint Conference on Digital Libraries (JCDL 2001)* (pp. 54–62). New York: Association for Computing Machinery (ACM).

Lavoie, B. (2000). *Benchmarking the preservation process for electronic scholarly journals*. Dublin, OH: Office of Research, OCLC Online Computer Library Center. Retrieved November 19, 2004, from http://www.oclc.org/research/staff/lavoie/dlf_1100.ppt

Lee, S. D. (2001). *Digital imaging: A practical handbook*. New York: Neal-Schuman Publishers.

Lesk, M. (1997). *Practical digital libraries: Books, bytes, and bucks*. (*The Morgan Kaufmann series in multimedia information and systems*). San Francisco: Morgan Kaufmann Publishers.

Lesk, M. (1999). Perspectives on DLI-2—Growing the field. *D-Lib Magazine, 5*(7–8). Retrieved November 19, 2004, from http://www.dlib.org/dlib/july99/07lesk.html

Library of Congress. Preservation Research & Testing Division. (2003). *Compact disc preservation*. Retrieved November 19, 2004, from http://www.loc.gov/preserv/resear.html#cd

Lorie, R. A. (2001). Long term preservation of digital information. In *Proceedings of the First ACM/IEEE-CS Joint Conference on Digital Libraries (JCDL 2001)*(pp. 346–352). New York: Association for Computing Machinery (ACM).

Lorie, R. A. (2002). A methodology and system for preserving digital data. In *Proceedings of the Second ACM/IEEE-CS Joint Conference on Digital Libraries (JCDL 2002)* (pp. 312–319). New York: Association for Computing Machinery (ACM).

Lynch, C. (2001). The battle to define the future of the book in the digital world. *First Monday, 6*(6). Retrieved November 19, 2004, from http://www.firstmonday.org/issues/issue6_6/lynch/index.html

Markoff, J. (2003, May 12). The Evelyn Wood of digitized book scanners. *New York Times on the Web*. Retrieved November 19, 2004, from http://www.nytimes.com/2003/05/12/technology/12TURN.html

Marson, I. (2004, June 24). British Library plans to archive whole UK Web. *ZDNet UK*. Retrieved November 19, 2004, from http://news.zdnet.co.uk/internet/0,39020369,39158517,00.htm

Matsui, K., & Tanaka, K. (1994). Video-steganography: how to secretly embed a signature in a picture. *Technological Strategies for Protecting Intellectual Property in the Networked Multimedia Environment, 1*(1), 187–206.

McArthur, D. J., Giersch, S., & Burrows, H. (2003). Sustainability issues and activities for the NSDL. In *Proceedings of the Third ACM/IEEE-CS Joint Conference on Digital Libraries (JCDL 2003)* (p. 395). New York: Association for Computing Machinery (ACM).

McCarthy, C. (2004). Digital libraries. In H. Bidgoli (Ed.), *The internet encyclopedia*, (Vol. 1, pp. 505–525). New York: John Wiley & Sons.

McCarthy, C., & Cunha, M. B. (2003). Digital library development in Brazil. *OCLC Systems and Services Journal, 19*(3), 114–119.

Mears, W. (2003, January 15). Supreme Court upholds copyright extensions: Decision seen as victory for movie, recording industry. *CNN.com*. Retrieved November 19, 2004, from http://www.cnn.com/2003/LAW/01/15/scotus.copyrights/index.html

Mintzer, F., Lotspiech, J., & Morimoto, N. (1997). Safeguarding digital library contents and users: Digital watermarking. *D-Lib Magazine, 4*(12). Retrieved November 19, 2004, from http://www.dlib.org/dlib/december97/ibm/12lotspiech.html

Mun, H., Ok, S., & Woo, Y. (2002). A digital content management model for making profits in digital content sites. In *Digital libraries: People, knowledge, and technology: Proceedings of the 5th International Conference on Asian Digital Libraries (ICADL 2002): Lecture Notes in Computer Science*, 2555 (pp. 516–517). Heidelberg: Springer-Verlag.

National Digital Information Infrastructure and Preservation Program (NDIIPP). (2002). *Program announcement*. Retrieved November 19, 2004, from http://www.digitalpreservation.gov/index.php?nav=4

National Library of Australia. (2002). *Safeguarding Australia's Web resources: Guidelines for creators and publishers*. Retrieved November 19, 2004, from http://www.nla.gov.au/guidelines/webresources.html

Nelson, M. L., Rocker, J., & Harrison, T. L. (2003). OAI and NASA's scientific and technical information. *Library Hi Tech, 21*(2), 140–150. Retrieved November 19, 2004, from http://techreports.larc.nasa.gov/ltrs/PDF/2003/jp/NASA-2003-lht-mln.pdf

New York Times Co. Inc., et al. v. Tasini et al. (2001, June 25). *Certiorari to the United States Court of Appeals for the Second Circuit*. Retrieved November 19, 2004, from http://a257.g.akamaitech.net/7/257/2422/

28jun20011200/www.supremecourtus.gov/opinions/00pdf/00-201.pdf

Nicholson, D., & MacGregor, G. (2003). Distributed digital libraries; "NOF-Digi": Putting UK culture online. *OCLC Systems and Services, 19*(3), 96–99.

Noerr, P. (2000). *The digital library toolkit* (2nd ed.). Retrieved November 19, 2004, from http://www.sun.com/products-n-solutions/edu/whitepapers/pdf/digital_library_toolkit.pdf

Notess, G. (2004). *Search engine showdown reviews*. Retrieved November 19, 2004, from http://searchengineshowdown.com/reviews/

Olsen, F. (2003a). Archiving company creates online-submission process for dissertations and theses. *The Chronicle of Higher Education, 49*(18). Retrieved November 19, 2004, from http://chronicle.com/free/2003/01/2003011001t.htm

Olsen, F. (2003b). Seeking additional security after a big theft, JSTOR tests Internet2's Shibboleth. *The Chronicle of Higher Education, 49*(30), A35.

Paskin, N. (2003). DOI: A 2003 Progress Report. *D-Lib Magazine, 9*(6). Retrieved November 19, 2004, from http://www.dlib.org/dlib/june03/paskin/06paskin.html

Peacock, I. (1999). Sandboxes using chroot: Using the change root function to protect files in a networked environment. *Ariadne, 20*. Retrieved November 19, 2004, from http://www.ariadne.ac.uk/issue20/unix/

Pinto, F. (2003). Access management, the key to a portal. *Ariadne, 35*. Retrieved November 19, 2004, from http://www.ariadne.ac.uk/issue35/SPP/

Potter, W. (2003). Education Dept. seeks to end clearinghouses. *The Chronicle of Higher Education, 49*(34), A31.

President's Information Technology Advisory Council. Panel on Digital Libraries. (2001). *Digital libraries: Universal access to human knowledge: Report to the President*. Washington: PITAC.

Ray, J., Reich, V., Dale, R., Underwood, W., Moore, R., & McCray, A. T. (2002). Panel on digital preservation. In *Proceedings of the Second ACM/IEEE-CS Joint Conference on Digital Libraries (JCDL 2002)* (pp. 365–367). New York: Association for Computing Machinery (ACM).

Rothenberg, J. (2000). *An experiment in using emulation to preserve digital publications*. Den Haag: Koninklijke Bibliotheek. Retrieved November 19, 2004, from http://www.kb.nl/coop/nedlib/results/emulationpreservationreport.pdf

Rumsey, S. (1999). Smart card people are happy people: TOLIMAC project for information system user authentication. *Ariadne, 20*. Retrieved November 19, 2004, from http://www.ariadne.ac.uk/issue20/tolimac/

Saeednia, S. (2000). How to maintain both privacy and authentication in digital libraries. *International Journal on Digital Libraries, 2*, 251–258.

Saffady, W. (1995). Digital library concepts and technologies for the management of library collections: An analysis of methods and costs. *Library Technology Reports, 31*, 221–380.

Sasaki, H., & Kiyoki, Y. (2003). A proposal for digital library protection. In *Proceedings of the Third ACM/IEEE-CS Joint Conference on Digital Libraries (JCDL 2003)* (p. 392). New York: Association for Computing Machinery (ACM).

Schwartz, C. S. (2000). Digital libraries: An overview. *Journal of Academic Librarianship, 26*(6), 385–393.

Seadle, M., Deller Jr., J. R., & Gurijala, A. (2002). Why watermark? The copyright need for an engineering solution. In *Proceedings of the Second ACM/IEEE-CS Joint Conference on Digital Libraries (JCDL 2002)* (pp. 324–325). New York: Association for Computing Machinery (ACM).

Smith, A. (2004). *Access in the future tense*. Washington, DC: Council on Library and Information Resources (CLIR). Retrieved November 19, 2004, from http://www.clir.org/pubs/abstract/pub126abst.html

Solbakk, S. A. (2003). Critical technological and architectural choices for access and preservation in a digital library environment. *Library Review, 52*(6), 251–256.

Stein, S. H. (U.S. District Judge) (2001). *Random House, Inc. v. Rosetta Books LLC; F. Supp. 2d, 2001 U.S. Dist. Lexis 9456* (S.D.N.Y. 2001). Retrieved November 19, 2004, from http://www.law.cornell.edu/copyright/cases/ebooks.htm

Stern, C. (2001, June 26). Freelancers win fight over reuse of works; Justices say databases require permission. *Washington Post*. p. E1.

Sturges, P., Davies, E., Dearnley, J., Iliffe, U., Oppenheim, C., & Hardy, R. (2003). User privacy in the digital library environment: An investigation of policies and preparedness. *Library Management, 24*(1–2), 44–50.

Tennant, R. (2001). Coping with disasters. *Library Journal, 126*(19), 26.

UNESCO. (2003). *Charter on the preservation of the digital heritage* (Document 32 C/28). Retrieved November 19, 2004, from http://portal.unesco.org/ci/ev.php?URL_ID=8967&URL_DO=DO_TOPIC&URL_SECTION=201

University of Virginia Electronic Text Center. (1998). *Text scanning: A basic helpsheet*. Retrieved November 19, 2004, from http://etext.lib.virginia.edu/helpsheets/scantext.html

Vellucci, S. L. (1998). Metadata. *Annual Review of Information Science and Technology, 33*, 187–222.

What is Metadata? Western States digital imaging best practices, Version 1.2. (2003). Denver: Western States Digital Standards Group; University of Denver; Colorado Digitization Program. Retrieved November 19, 2004, from http://www.cdpheritage.org/resource/metadata/wsdcmbp/whatismetadata.html

Witten, I. H., & Bainbridge, D. (2002). *How to build a digital library.* San Francisco: Morgan Kaufmann Publishers.

Wolf, G. (2003). The great library of Amazonia. *Wired, 11*(12). Retrieved November 19, 2004, from http://www.wired.com/news/print/0,1294,60948,00.html

Yagüe, M. I., Maña, A., López, J., Pimentel, E., & Troya, J. M. (2002). Secure content distribution for digital libraries. In *Digital libraries: People, knowledge, and technology: Proceedings of the 5th International Conference on Asian Digital Libraries (ICADL 2002): Lecture Notes in Computer Science, 2555* (pp. 516–517). Heidelberg: Springer-Verlag.

Z39.50, part 1: An overview. (2001). Biblio Tech Review, Tech Briefings. Retrieved November 19, 2004, from http://www.biblio-tech.com/html/z39_50.html

Zhang, A., & Gourley, D. (2003). A digital collections management system based on open source software. In *Proceedings of the Third ACM/IEEE-CS Joint Conference on Digital Libraries (JCDL 2003)* (p. 381). New York: Association for Computing Machinery (ACM).

Zhang, J., Xiong, F., & Wang, N. (2002). Hiding a logo watermark in an image for its copyright protection. In *Digital libraries: People, knowledge, and technology: Proceedings of the 5th International Conference on Asian Digital Libraries (ICADL 2002): Lecture Notes in Computer Science, 2555* (p. 527). Heidelberg: Springer-Verlag.

E-Mail and Instant Messaging

Bhagyavati, *Columbus State University*

INTRODUCTION

E-mail and IM systems are the two main categories of software described in this chapter, and emphasis is placed on security issues and solutions. After a brief introduction to electronic mail and instant messaging, a more detailed look at each system is presented. In today's world of increasing cybercrime, security in e-mail and IM environments is an important concern. Security issues and possible solutions are examined in depth for both e-mail and IM. Following this discussion, e-mail and IM usage policies are suggested. The conclusion is followed by a glossary of key terms and a list of references.

ELECTRONIC MAIL

Electronic mail is ubiquitous in communication today. Before the usefulness of e-mail was perceived, the Internet was widely employed initially for military and academic use. The growth in popularity of the Internet was due, in part, to e-mail. Compared to other modes of communication such as postal mail, e-mail is cheaper, faster, and more convenient. The ability to forward communication to many people and to address more than one recipient, as well as the asynchronous nature of the communication, makes e-mail popular. The advent of mailing lists and address books added convenience and ease of use, leading to an upsurge in the use of e-mail.

Definition of E-Mail

Per the popular usage of the term, e-mail can be defined as mail sent via electronic means. According to Lombardi (2003), e-mail messages use standard conventions for addressing and delivering content across the public Internet. An e-mail has two mandatory parts: a header and a message. Other components, including attachments, are optional. In the beginning of e-mail history, all e-mails were in text format. As e-mail systems evolved, different formatting styles other than plain text began to be used. The e-mail header contains information on where the e-mail originated, the route it has traveled, and to whom it is addressed. Although most e-mail users may dismiss the header as irrelevant to their communication, technical staff needs to know the source, destination, and route of the e-mail in case of problems.

Brief History of E-Mail

Ray Tomlinson adapted an existing internal e-mail program to the ARPAnet file transfer technology and sent the first e-mail message from one computer to another in 1971 (Griffiths, 2002). After the first message, "Testing 1-2-3," was successfully sent and received by two different computers, Tomlinson sent a message to all ARPAnet users and gave them instructions for sending and receiving electronic mail. The convention username@hostname, which is the basis for e-mail today, dates from this time.

Initially, e-mail was cumbersome and user-unfriendly. However, most of the modern e-mail features were implemented within a year of the first e-mail transmission (Griffiths, 2002). The ability to delete, forward, and save messages, together with a standard protocol to transfer messages between programs, was established by 1972. Thus, e-mail evolved along with the network now known as the Internet. In 1977, a standard specification of e-mail was published in a document called RFC 733, which was revised in 1982 to describe domain name syntax explicitly for the first time (Crocker, 2003).

Eric Allman developed the sendmail program in the 1980s, which was derived from e-mail relaying on the UNIX operating system at the University of California at Berkeley. In 1988, Vinton Cerf sent the first commercial e-mail by connecting MCI Mail to the NSFnet (National Science Foundation network). This event marked a milestone in the history of e-mail because it paved the way for network service providers America Online and Delphi to connect their proprietary e-mail systems to the Internet. The exponential growth in e-mail use can be traced to this moment when the benefits of e-mail were globally recognized.

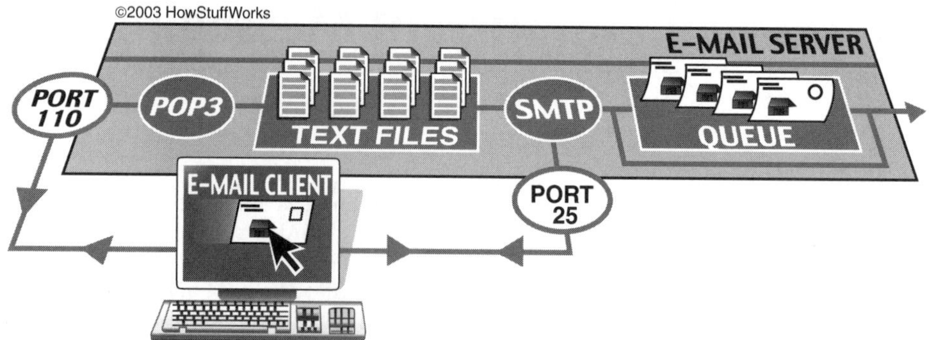

Figure 1: How e-mail works.

Advantages and Features of E-Mail

Some people consider one of the advantages of e-mail to be its informal style of communication. Although people expect typed letters to be formal and perfect, no such expectations exist for e-mail. E-mail became more popular because of its relatively low cost, high reliability, and almost instantaneous delivery as compared with regular mail (Living Internet, 2003). E-mail provides a high level of informality, a sense of community and sharing, wide tolerance of spelling and typographical errors, and brevity of expression. It has been theorized that the style of e-mail communication was a factor in its early and continued success. Also, e-mail does not demand an immediate response, unlike the telephone (Griffiths, 2002).

Scientists and researchers working in the ARPAnet (precursor to the Internet) community started to recognize the immense promise of e-mail to change the way people communicate in all sectors of society, including the academic, business, and cultural sectors (Myer & Dodds, 1976). Productivity gains were realized by businesses through the use of e-mail. Today, e-mail has become indispensable in academic, governmental, and business organizations around the world because of ease of use, convenience, low cost, asynchronous nature, range of features, and communication efficiency.

Current E-Mail Systems

An e-mail system has three components: the transport agent and the delivery agent on the server, and the user agent or client (Preetham, 2002). Popular graphical-user-interface-(GUI-) based e-mail clients such as Eudora, Mozilla, Microsoft's Outlook and Outlook Express, and Pegasus incorporate features such as e-mail forwarding, read receipts, e-mail filtering, and spam blocking. Besides the GUI-based e-mail clients mentioned previously, popular text-based e-mail clients include elm and pine. An e-mail client can use either the post office protocol (POP) or the Internet mail access protocol (IMAP). Whereas POP copies e-mails from the server to the computer on which the client resides, IMAP works by copying e-mail headers to the client computer—actual e-mail messages are not copied unless selected (Nevis, 2004).

On Outlook for Microsoft Exchange server, messaging application programming interface (MAPI) can be used for retrieving e-mail. For sending e-mail, simple mail transfer protocol (SMTP) is the de facto standard for transmission, whereas multipurpose Internet mail extensions (MIME) is another popular protocol available for e-mail clients (Wikipedia, 2004). For server software, Exchange and sendmail protocols are popularly used. On Linux, qmail is a widely used protocol on the e-mail server. Other chapters in this *Handbook* present more information on these e-mail protocols (MIME and SMTP). Howstuffworks.com has simple diagrams (reproduced in Figures 1 and 2) that provide a clearer understanding of the e-mail transfer process and SMTP protocol. Figure 1, How E-mail Works, and Figure 2, How SMTP Works, are both available at howstuffworks.com.

E-mail addresses can be grouped together into mailing lists. A manager program automates the tedious maintenance of the list by adding, modifying, and deleting users and their e-mail addresses. Most corporations use standard naming procedures to make e-mail administration and management easier (Tittel, 2002). Popular e-mail server software can be categorized into proprietary intranet solutions such as Microsoft's Exchange program and the Internet-based sendmail program. Web-based e-mail software abounds and providers make these clients available to users for free. For instance, Yahoo! and Hotmail provide free e-mail quotas of 100 MB and 250 MB to each user.

Disadvantages and Vulnerabilities of E-Mail

Although more detail can be found in the chapter "E-Mail Threats and Vulnerabilities," this chapter provides a high-level perspective on e-mail vulnerabilities and disadvantages. The very advantages of e-mail can be construed as disadvantages under certain circumstances. The asynchronous nature of e-mail results in disadvantages such as the lack of face-to-face presence that is vital to effective communication. Terse messages can mislead the recipient, especially if previous threads to an e-mail conversation are not attached. E-mail is hampered by the lack of visual cues that are sometimes necessary to understand what the sender really means (Counseling, 2003). Some people find it ineffective to communicate solely via e-mail because its asynchronous nature means there is an absence of immediate, real-time responses.

Today's e-mail systems are more vulnerable to attacks than earlier ones because of the many additions made to the basic model. Advanced formatting such as hypertext markup language (HTML) and the sending of attachments

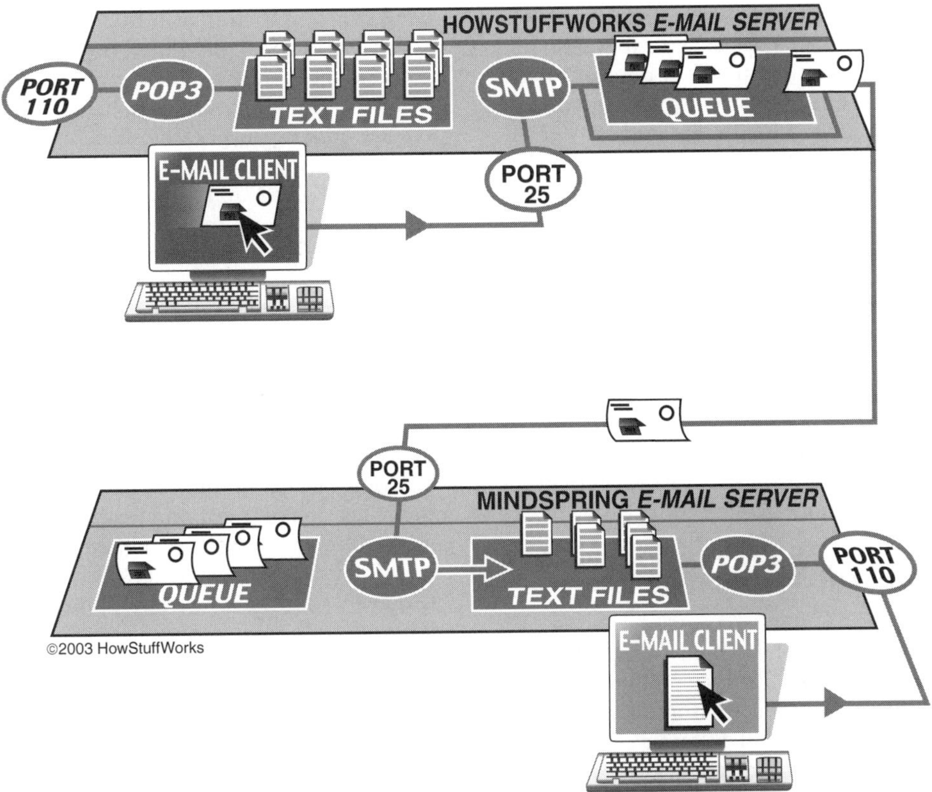

Figure 2: E-mail transfer and communication.

via e-mail contribute to the propagation of viruses and spam. It is also easy to impersonate others via e-mail. Recipients may be led to believe that the e-mail is from someone they know, but the sender's name and e-mail address could have been impersonated by a crook.

Standard procedures and default configurations are vulnerabilities in e-mail systems. For example, standard naming procedures that ease e-mail management are predictable and thus exploited by hackers. Malicious users hide their identity by using anonymous addresses of publicly available Web-based e-mail providers such as Yahoo! and Hotmail (Kruse & Heiser, 2002). Source addresses can be spoofed. Even if the sender's Internet protocol (IP) address is logged, the hacker might be using a computer in a public place, such as a library or an airport.

Other threats to e-mail include interception and modification of messages and distortion of message headers and content to hide the source and route of traversal (Pfleeger, 1997). Sophisticated protection systems exist today to resolve these threats. E-mail filters work in conjunction with firewalls and intrusion protection systems to create layers of blocking measures for potential malicious software. Sender identity and e-mail privacy are resolved by security measures such as public/private key encryption and digital signatures.

The chapters in this *Handbook* titled "Encryption Basics," "Secret Key Cryptography," "Data Encryption Standard (DES)," "Advanced Encryption Standard (AES)," "Hashes and Message Digests," "Number Theory," "Public Key Algorithms," "Elliptic Curve Cryptography," "IBE (Identity Based Encryption)s," "Cryptographic Protocols," "Quantum Cryptography" and "Digital Signatures and Electronic Signatures" have detailed information about encryption and digital signatures.

Spam, or unsolicited e-mail (often undesirable), is an ever-growing problem and has surpassed legitimate e-mail in volume. In July 2004, spam constituted 65% of all e-mail messages (Greenspan, 2004). Because of this record increase, spam filters for e-mail have grown in popularity. Employee productivity and network bandwidth are adversely affected if spam is not blocked. Commercial implementations of spam filters include SpamAssasin and BrightMail. Spam filters use many techniques for preventing false positives, that is, legitimate e-mails flagged as spam. Bayesian learning techniques, bouncing spam back to the sender, Turing test filters, and e-mail stamps have been used successfully against spam.

The Bayesian spam filter has an initial time period to "learn" user preferences about spam e-mails and legitimate e-mails (Graham, 2002). Spam filters also exist that can send a fake bounce message to the spammer after simulating an e-mail delivery failure. The Turing test filter requests a human response for a potential spam e-mail before placing it in the inbox (Knight, 2003). With e-mail stamps, a charge can be imposed before allowing the spam messages to go through to the sender.

Malicious people such as virus writers usually exploit the features of e-mails to spread their destructive payload. An e-mail virus usually spreads from computer to computer by automatically mailing itself to all the e-mail addresses in the victim's address book. The Melissa virus of 1999 spread through Microsoft Word documents attached via e-mails (Brain, 2004). Social engineering attacks are also common via e-mail. The "I Love You" virus that spread in 2000 was an example. Another example is the recent spate of "phishing" attacks that exploit e-mail's ubiquity in order to harvest confidential data of unsuspecting users who click on an apparently genuine URL in an e-mail purportedly from a legitimate authority (FTC, 2003).

A key concern is the confidentiality of e-mail communication. Because an e-mail can pass through many servers from source to destination, it can be stored and/or retrieved at any point along its route. Network administrators and high-level managers have the right to read all e-mail passing through their networks. Employees may not be aware that e-mail communication is neither private nor confidential. Law enforcement officials can confiscate e-mail on servers and backups for investigative purposes. Later in this chapter, e-mail use policies are described that elaborate on the procedures necessary to alert employees about e-mail communication.

Safeguards for E-Mail: Filters and Usage Policies

Several vulnerabilities posed by e-mail communication make the presence of monitoring systems inevitable today, especially in large corporate environments. According to Lyris, a provider of e-mail filtering services, the process of monitoring e-mail and taking certain actions based on predefined criteria is referred to as e-mail filtering (Lyris Solutions, 2003). E-mail that is monitored can be incoming or outgoing; messages need to match predefined criteria, which can be changed at any time. E-mail filters can help sort, forward, and delete incoming and outgoing e-mail. On an organization-wide level, e-mail filters might be installed:

1) to disinfect viruses from attachments,
2) to block unsolicited e-mail (spam),
3) to block confidential information from going outside the company,
4) to block incoming and outgoing offensive content, and
5) to prevent unauthorized usage of corporate e-mail systems (Bhagyavati, 2004).

E-mail filtering software is currently available from Lyris, SurfControl, and MailWasher. Although e-mail filters are necessary to monitor spam and offensive e-mail, their implementation can have unintended consequences, such as blocking legitimate e-mail or blacklisting naïve users accused of sending unsolicited e-mail. Cross-compatibility issues among e-mail filters and antivirus software may cause unintentional propagation of viruses. Monitoring and matching measures add extra time to the delivery of e-mail. These security measures also inhibit the free flow of communication that is vital for research and creativity in organizations. The unintended effect of these filters could cause a shift away from e-mail by annoyed employees (Koprowski, 2003). The Chapter "Spam and the Legal Counter Attacks" provides more details about spam and legal countermeasures.

Because e-mail is frequently used to communicate with colleagues, peers, and superiors, a lack of usage guidelines can lead to confusion over appropriate content and message form. Lack of an e-mail use policy can have serious consequences in cases of inappropriate communication. If corporations do not have policies on e-mail use, employees can misuse corporate-owned e-mail systems without fear of consequences. In creating a written e-mail policy, all "do's and don'ts" need to be included. The chapter on "E-Mail and Internet Use Policies" can be perused for more information regarding e-mail and Internet use policies.

Employees must also be trained fully to understand why policies are important. Implementation of the rules can be monitored by management tools (EmailReplies.com, 2001). Professionalism, efficiency, and liability protection are the primary reasons for an organization to implement etiquette rules and train its employees on them. Sending e-mails in uppercase letters, attaching unnecessary files, making grammatical and spelling errors, and requesting read receipts frequently are all etiquette policy violations. Consequences for policy violations vary widely by state and by demographic segment. Sample policy guidelines follow (SANS, 2004).

1) Office e-mail may not be used for commercial purposes or for personal gain. Distribution of spam or flame e-mails is not tolerated from office computers.
2) Confidential and sensitive information should not be sent via e-mail, unless it is encrypted. Because e-mail communication is free and open, anyone can obtain such sensitive information. Encryption makes the message impossible to read if the deciphering key is not available.
3) E-mail communications on office systems will be monitored for appropriateness of use.
4) Due diligence needs to be practiced while communicating via e-mail; although an e-mail has been deleted by the recipient, it can be retrieved and used against the sender or the workplace.
5) Inappropriate and offensive material, which is not suitable for distribution otherwise, should not be transmitted through e-mail. For example, off-color remarks, racist comments, pornographic material, and other unsuitable material should not be sent through office e-mail.
6) E-mail communication needs to be concise and work-related. Incidental personal use is only permitted if it does not interfere with office operations.
7) E-mail recipients should be limited to only those with a need to know the contents of the communication. Forwarding and copying to everyone in the workplace should be avoided.
8) If copyrighted information or trademarks are sent via e-mail, the recipient must have a need to know the information and should be able to securely receive the e-mail.
9) Use of office e-mail implies that the sender acts as an agent on behalf of the employer. Appropriateness of tone, style, content, and form of e-mail will ensure that high standards of work and professionalism are maintained.

INSTANT MESSAGING

Instant messaging systems extended the chat service available on time-shared computers to the Internet. IM client programs on users' computers connect to specialized servers that monitor all IM users and maintain buddy lists for each user. America Online (AOL) popularized the IM service with its AIM (AOL Instant Messenger), which is freely available for download from its Web site. IM can be thought of as an online, real-time version of e-mail (Day, Rosenberg, & Sugano, 2000). In today's fast-paced corporate environment, employees do not wish to wait for recipients to check e-mails and then respond; instead, real-time and interactive responses are expected. The use of instant messaging grew exponentially in the late 1990s (Ralston, Reilly, & Hemmendinger, 2003).

Definition of IM

Instant messaging is a type of real-time communication via the Internet that enables a user to create a private chat room with another user (Webopedia, 2004). Whereas e-mail can be compared to postal mail, IM can be compared to a telephone conversation. However, a telephone conversation is voice-based, whereas an IM conversation is largely text-based. The IM system allows a user to create and maintain a buddy list of other users; the system alerts the user when any of the buddies is online. The user is then free to initiate an IM session with the buddy. For IM to work, both users must download and install an IM client, and both users must be logged on to the Internet at the same time.

Brief History of IM

Internet Relay Chat (IRC) was a messaging program invented in 1988 that was IM-like in its functionality. More about IRC can be found in the chapter titled "IRC (Internet Relay Chat)." In November 1996, four Israeli programmers introduced ICQ ("I seek you"), which was a free instant-messaging utility that anyone could use by downloading a client capable of real-time communication (Tyson, 2004). Because of the sense of community it created, online services were popular even before the growth in popularity of the Internet.

America Online, long considered the pioneer of the online community, had provided chat rooms for its users before it introduced AIM, its version of IM services. Although AIM uses proprietary protocols to enable users to IM each other, non-AOL users can talk to AOL users; this explains the dominance of AIM in the IM marketplace. The development of standards and protocol specifications by the Internet Engineering Task Force popularized the use of IM and pushed the technology to the mainstream (Day, Rosenberg, & Sugano, 2000).

The future of instant messaging appears promising because of heightened interest among the business and common user community. Predictions by Gartner that IM use is anticipated to be 60% of all real-time communication in 2004 has resulted in several organizations trying to develop security solutions for IM's loopholes, such as file sharing and transfer vulnerabilities (FaceTime, 2004). Companies have recognized the promise of IM and are planning to deploy the next generation of secure IM products for internal and external communications in the workplace.

Advantages and Features of IM

IM appears attractive to people on projects that require more real-time interaction than e-mail can provide. Employees on team projects need not check their e-mails frequently; instant messaging provides interactive and real-time contact among them (Deutschle, 2003). Synergies of work and a boost in productivity are usually reported when an organization deploys IM. Communicating in real-time streamlines interactions saves time and money. In addition, free IM client software implies reduced licensing and contractual fees for communication. Employee frustration can also be minimized because IM facilitates immediate access to colleagues.

Long-distance telephone bills can be reduced by using IM. Spam can be reduced because the sender and recipient communicate in real time. IM provides an opportunity for employees to hold conferences and chats (IM-Age, 2002). It also speeds up internal and external communications and provides network-independent access to communication. However, several corporations are hesitant to deploy IM because of inadequate security. Corporate policy sometimes may not deter employees from using public domain IM clients without IT approval. This activity may result in inadvertent disclosure of confidential corporate information.

Current IM Systems

Although AIM and ICQ are the leaders in the IM race, other popular IM systems include Microsoft's MSN Messenger and Yahoo! Messenger (YM). Utilities such as Odigo and Omni allow the user to combine multiple IM services in one application (Tyson, 2004). MSN Messenger and YM allow users to talk via IM just like via the telephone, provided both parties have the necessary equipment, such as microphone and speakers, to access the voice feature. Today's IM programs also incorporate file sharing and file transfer capabilities. Mobile devices such as handhelds, tablet personal computers (PCs), and Internet-enabled cellular telephones are capable of communicating via instant messaging systems.

There are two main categories of second-generation secure IM products: (a) IM clients with security features built in and (b) IM management software that can monitor any of the products currently popular among users. Zone Labs' product "Integrity" and IM-Age's "Policy Manager" management solution belong to the latter category. These products do more than secure IM; they handle policy management and provide centralized security (Zone Labs, 2004; IM-Age, 2002). For example, Zonelabs' IM Policy Manager authenticates internal IM users, blocks file transfers, and monitors employee communications. Niksun's "NetDetector" can detect anomalies, reconstruct IM sessions, and archive IM for long-term storage (Niksun, 2002). The diagram in Figure 3, How IM Works, appears in Learnthenet.com and shows an IM system.

Figure 3: How IM works.

Disadvantages and Vulnerabilities of IM

Basic IM is not a secure way to communicate. The content of instant messages and information about user (network) connections are maintained on servers controlled by the IM provider. Although most of the large IM providers offer encryption, user logs have been captured by malicious hackers in the past (Deutschle, 2003). The perception among employers is that IM is uncontrollable; therefore the whole network becomes compromised. Buffer overflow vulnerabilities in IM clients can lead to attacks that result in denial of service and/or execution of arbitrary code. Open ports can be found by hackers via file transfer on IM. Malware can be spread using file sharing and transfer.

Proprietary client software, word limits on messages and sessions, potential for employee misuse, and security concerns have managed to restrain the popularity of IM in the business environment. Because IM does not leave an audit trail, the corporation cannot monitor the conversation. Proprietary consumer products such as MSN Messenger and ICQ are unsuited for enterprises because they allow unencrypted data and bypass the virus protection at the corporate network's gateway servers. The file transfer capability of IM is especially insecure in this regard. Service providers such as AOL and Sprint have developed separate enterprise versions of their proprietary IM solutions that address corporate security concerns.

Safeguards for IM and Usage Policies

Buffer overflow vulnerabilities found in popular instant messaging applications such as Yahoo! Messenger and AIM serve as a reminder that hackers can take control over other machines for coordinated attacks at a later time (Weber, 2004). Because consumer-level IM programs do not use encryption, these programs cannot be used in corporate environments without modification. IM also allows hackers to become aware of user presence, that is, whether the user is online or offline. Social engineering, which can lead to identity theft, is also common because of poor authentication practices. Security concerns are, therefore, paramount in presence-aware IM environments.

According to security experts, insecure IM is the new target for hackers who seek to steal sensitive corporate information. Firewalls and intrusion detection systems are not useful unless they are integrated with IM-security software (Gaudin, 2002). Employees sending non-corporate information on IM can waste network bandwidth. IM can also cause easy distraction and loss in productivity. Offensive jokes propagated through IM can led to harassment suits. Because of legal and ethical ramifications of IM use, an enterprise needs to structure IM use policies and train employees before deploying the IM solution. Sample policies include the following:

1) Confidential and sensitive information should not be sent via IM unless it is encrypted. Because IM communication is insecure, anyone can obtain such sensitive information.
2) IM communications on office systems will be monitored for appropriateness of use.
3) Inappropriate and offensive material, which is not suitable for distribution otherwise, should not be transmitted through IM. For example, off-color remarks, racist comments, pornographic material, and other unsuitable material should not be sent through office IM.
4) IM communication needs to be concise and work-related. Incidental personal use is only permitted if it does not interfere with office operations.
5) Use of office IM implies that the sender acts as an agent on behalf of the employer. Appropriateness of tone, style, content, and form of IM will ensure that high standards of work and professionalism are maintained.

SECURITY IN E-MAIL AND IM ENVIRONMENTS

Security is a significant area of concern in an e-mail environment because e-mail is the most crucial form of communication medium available on the Internet (Preetham, 2002). To ensure the integrity of e-mail communication, various measures have been implemented. Not caring about e-mail security could result in the sender's identity being compromised, the recipient's identity being compromised, or leakage of sensitive information. If the transfer agent and client of an e-mail system can be secured on the network, the service provider can secure the delivery agent. Encryption software can ensure security on the communication channel. Security measures can also guard against address spoofing and anonymous e-mail.

Features of secure environments include confidentiality of message content, authentication of sender and recipient, and assurance of message integrity (Kurose & Ross, 2003). Public key cryptography (more detail in later chapters, e.g., chapter 67), symmetric key cryptography, digital signatures (chapter 179), message digests (chapter 112), message integrity checks, trusted key distribution, and certificate validating authority are essential to secure all e-mail communication within the environment. Because IM clients are used on mobile handheld devices such as PDAs and cellular telephones in addition to desktop and laptop computers, the security risks are higher because of the inherent vulnerabilities of wireless transmission. The lack of secure environments exacts a productivity and monetary toll.

More detail on public key cryptography can be found in the chapters "Public Key Standards: PKCS (Public-Key Cryptography Standards)," " Public Key Algorithms," "Elliptic Curve Cryptography," "Cryptographic Protocols," "Quantum Cryptography" and "Public Key Standards: SSH (Secure Shell)." Digital signatures can be studied in greater depth in "Digital Signatures and Electronic Signatures" and "Encrypting E-mail." Message digests can be explored in the chapter on "Hashes and Message Digests."

E-Mail Security: Issues and Practices

User awareness and training are probably the most important tools to secure e-mail. Deleting unsolicited messages, not opening suspicious attachments, encrypting sensitive information sent via e-mail, and using spam filters are effective practices for ensuring the security of e-mail communications (Weber, 2004). Corporate policies will not amount to much if users are not trained on implementing the policies and made aware of the consequences of violations. Security-savvy users can thwart social engineering attacks that try to obtain login and password information from them.

Other security measures to follow in an e-mail environment include using proxy servers to forward e-mail to the clients and employing an updated antivirus program to check all incoming and outgoing e-mail. Modern antivirus programs are capable of heuristic analysis of viruses by safely monitoring their behavior under controlled conditions (Sandhu, 2002). Installation of antivirus software must be augmented by prompt updating of virus definitions and patterns; otherwise, the antivirus software will not be effective against newly generated viruses and other malware, such as Trojan horses and worms, which may infect application software.

IM Security: Issues and Practices

Patch management and avoidance of spying software are the first steps in securing IM systems. Antivirus software and intrusion detection and protection programs will limit the security vulnerabilities of IM systems. However, corporate entities can ensure IM security by not allowing their employees to use public domain IM systems such as AIM and YM. Proprietary solutions combined with end-to-end security provide a better defense than freeware.

Solutions such as the Enterprise IM Management Suite from FaceTime Communications, Inc., have managed to allay the fears of some corporate IT departments regarding the use of IM among employees. These providers claim that viruses sent through IM will be detected, unintentional transmission of sensitive information will be controlled, and the IM security solution will be integrated with preexisting antispam, content scanning, and encryption programs (FaceTime, 2004). For example, if unauthorized IM or P2P (peer-to-peer) connections are detected, they are blocked and logged.

Realizing that the corporate environment was not ready to accept insecure IM systems, service providers such as AOL and Sprint developed enterprise versions of their IM clients, specifically tightening or adding security features. AOL's Enterprise AIM service allows system administrators to manage IM use from behind the corporate firewall (Deutschle, 2003). Although the security features come at a steeper price than the virtually free consumer-end versions, companies are expected to invest in IM's long-term advantages. Other security-hardened IM products include IBM's Lotus Sametime and Bantu's Presence Platform. An encrypted version of Sametime is used by the U.S. military and some academic institutions.

Security providers such as Zone Labs have developed management platforms for securing IM in the enterprise. Zone Labs' product, IMsecure Pro, is advertised as ensuring privacy for IM communications (Zone Labs, 2004). This program is independent of the IM client and can execute equally well on AIM, MSN Messenger, and YM. According to Zone Labs, this product is compatible with its firewall product, so both can be integrated to form an end-to-end solution. Featuring IM encryption, spam blocking, password protection, and security logging, this product is geared toward the security-conscious corporate marketplace. Other vendors such as IM-Age and Niksun have also developed secure IM products or IM management software.

CONCLUSION

E-mail has become one of the primary means of communication for people today (Tyson, 2004). E-mail clients that allow users to send, receive, and manage their messages evolved from different formats and storage systems. E-mail clients differ in how they track e-mail and where they store archived data (Nelson, Phillips, Enginger, Steuat, 2004). Hence, no single security solution can be provided for their varying vulnerabilities and differing reactions to threats.

Because of its ubiquitous nature, several viruses now use e-mail as a distribution and reproduction mechanism because of its potential for rapid, worldwide spread. Security concerns must be weighed critically before sending confidential data through the system. Behavior-based monitoring of virus activity, integrity checks, detection of changes in content and sources and destinations of e-mail, signature-based searches, and heuristic, real-time scanning can mitigate security risks (Slade, 2004).

The Gartner Group, in October 2001, opined that IM, like e-mail, could cause a company to operate as a real-time enterprise if it is properly managed and integrated into the underlying infrastructure. Today, IM is being used by more than 210 million people; 10% are using IM at workplaces (Goldsborough, 2004). Although IM is perceived to be ephemeral, every message can be stored by the service provider or the organization. These archives can be monitored and even used in evidence. Hence, it is prudent to exercise care in sending e-mail and IM messages.

GLOSSARY

Antivirus Software Software programs that detect and eliminate viruses, worms, Trojan horses, and other malware.

Authentication The process of ensuring that the individual is who she says she is.

Confidentiality The act of keeping sensitive information secretive.

Demilitarized Zone (DMZ) A computer or a subnetwork that is installed between a trusted internal network and an untrusted external network.

Digital Certificate An attachment to an e-mail used for security purposes such as verifying the sender's identity to the receiver.

E-mail An asynchronous communication tool analogous to postal mail; it is used to transmit messages via the Internet.

Encryption The process of translating data into a secret code; it is the most effective way to achieve data confidentiality.

Filter Software or hardware that monitors and blocks incoming and outgoing e-mail traffic.

Firewall Hardware and/or software designed to prevent unauthorized access to or from a private network.

Instant Messaging An interactive, synchronous tool for engaging in real-time communication via the Internet.

Intrusion Detection System A system that inspects all inbound and outbound network activity to identify suspicious patterns that may indicate an attack.

Malware and Spyware Malicious software designed to damage a system. Spyware is software that gathers user information through the Internet connection without his or her knowledge, usually for advertising purposes.

Message Integrity This refers to the validity of e-mail transmissions.

Nonrepudiation When the recipient of a communication has the ability to ensure that the sender is unable to deny the sending of the message or the authenticity of its signature on the communication.

Patch Management Process of updating and managing patches and temporary fixes on a frequent and regular basis so as to remain current on the latest updates of the software.

Proxy Server A server that sits between a client application and another server; it intercepts all requests to the actual server. Proxy servers improve efficiency and filter harmful traffic.

Spam Electronic junk mail or unsolicited, targeted advertisement via e-mail.

Use Policies Policies regarding employee use of organization-owned computers for e-mail and IM.

Virtual Private Networks A private network developed by using public wires to connect nodes. A virtual private network employs encryption and other security mechanisms, thus ensuring that corporate data is safe traveling on the public Internet.

Viruses, Worms, and Trojan Horses Malicious software that infect a host computer, then replicate and spread to other computers via the network to cause more damage.

Vulnerabilities and Threat Assessment A process of proactively identifying vulnerabilities (weaknesses) in computers of a network to determine if and where a system can be exploited and/or threatened (attacked).

CROSS REFERENCES

See *Internet E-Mail Architecture; Local Area Networks; Passwords; PGP (Pretty Good Privacy); S/MIME (Secure MIME); SMTP (Simple Mail Transfer Protocol).*

REFERENCES

Bhagyavati, Rogers, N., & Yang, M. (2004, January 5). *Email filters can adversely affect free and open flow of communication*. Paper presented at the Winter International Symposium on Information and Communication Technologies, WISICT 2004, Cancun, Mexico.

Brain, M. (2004). *How computer viruses work*. Retrieved April 3, 2005, from http://computer.howstuffworks.com/virus.htm/printable

Counseling. (2003). *Disadvantages of counselling by email*. Retrieved April 3, 2005, from http://counsellingresource.com/counselling-service/online-disadvantages.html

Crocker, D. (2003). *Email history: Living Internet*. Retrieved April 3, 2005, from http://livinginternet.com/e/ei.htm

Day, M., Rosenberg, J., & Sugano, H. (2000, February). *A model for presence and instant messaging* (RFC 2778). Internet Engineering Task Force. Retrieved April 3, 2005, from http://www.ietf.org/rfc/rfc2778.txt?number=2778

Deutschle, S. (2003, August 8). *Security issues keep instant messaging out of workplace*. In Depth: Tech & Telecom. Retrieved April 3, 2005, from http://www.bizjournals.com/columbus/stories/2003/08/11/focus3.html

EmailReplies.com. (2001). *Email etiquette*. Retrieved April 3, 2005, from http://www.emailreplies.com

FaceTime (2004). *FaceTime Enterprise IM Management Suite of solutions: Secure, manage and extend IM in the enterprise*. Retrieved April 3, 2005, from http://www.facetime.com/solutions/solutions.aspx

FTC. (2003, July). *FTC consumer alert: How not to get hooked by a 'phishing' scam*. Retrieved April 3, 2005, from http://www.ftc.gov/bcp/conline/pubs/alerts/phishingalrt.htm

Gaudin, S. (2002, September 6). *IM security risks spark workplace monitoring debate*. Retrieved April 3, 2005, from http://itmanagement.earthweb.com/secu/article.php/1458241

Goldsborough, R. (2004, August 1). *Instant messaging: Managing the risks and rewards*. Retrieved April 3, 2005, from http://www.infotoday.com/linkup/lud080104-goldsborough.shtml

Graham, P. (2002, August). *A plan for spam*. Retrieved April 3, 2005, from http://www.paulgraham.com/spam.html

Greenspan, R. (2004, July 12). *The deadly duo: Spam and viruses, June 2004*. Retrieved April 3, 2005, from http://www.clickz.com/stats/big_picture/applications/article.php/3379701

Griffiths, R. T. (2002, October 11). *Chapter three: History of electronic mail*. Retrieved April 3, 2005, from http://www.let.leidenuniv.nl/history/ivh/chap3.htm

IM-Age. (2002). *IM-Policy Manager v4.0*. Retrieved April 3, 2005, from http://www.im-age.com/_product/policy.html

Knight, W. (2003, January 3). *Turing tests filter spam email*. Retrieved April 3, 2005, from http://www.newscientist.com/news/news.jsp?id=ns99993227

Koprowski, G. J. (2003, September 30). *Spam filtering and the plague of false positives*. Retrieved April 3, 2005, from http://www.technewsworld.com/perl/story/31703.html

Kruse II, W. G., & Heiser, J. G. (2002). *Computer forensics: Incident response essentials*. Addison-Wesley, New York, NY.

Kurose, J. F., & Ross, K. W. (2003). *Computer networking: A top-down approach featuring the Internet*. Pearson Education, Boston, MA.

Living Internet. (2003). *Electronic mail*. Retrieved April 3, 2005, from http://livinginternet.com/ttoc_e.htm

Lombardi, J. V. (2003). *Managing universities: The Internet and glossary*. Retrieved April 3, 2005, from http://courses.umass.edu/lombardi/edu03/gloss.html#Email

Lyris Solutions. (2003, September 7). *Lyris email basics: Email filtering*. Retrieved April 3, 2005, from http://www.lyris.com/solutions/email_filtering.html

Myer, T. H., & Dodds, D. W. (1976). *Notes on the development of message technology*. Paper presented at the Berkeley Workshop on Distributed Data Management and Computer Networks (LBL-5315). Lawrence Berkeley Laboratories, Berkeley, CA.

Nelson, B., Phillips, A., Enfinger, F., & Steuat, C. (2004). *Guide to computer forensics and investigations*. Course Technology, Thomson Learning, Hoboken, NJ.

Nevis. (2004). *Nevis POP versus IMAP guide*. Retrieved April 3, 2005, from http://www.nevis.columbia.edu/mail/pop-vs-imap.html

Niksun. (2002). *Is Instant messaging a threat to your network?*. (White paper). Retrieved April 3, 2005, from http://www.niksun.com/Instant_Messaging.htm

Pfleeger, C. P. (1997). *Security in computing*. Prentice Hall PTR, Upper Saddle River, NJ.

Preetham, V. V. (2002). *Internet security and firewalls*. Premier Press, Cincinnati, OH.

Ralston, A., Reilly, E. D., & Hemmendinger, D. (2003). *Encyclopedia of computer science* (4th ed., 1284). New York, NY: Wiley.

Sandhu, R. J. (2002). *Disaster recovery planning*. Premier Press, Cincinnati, OH.

SANS. (2004). *Email use policy*. SANS Institute. Retrieved April 3, 2005, from http://www.sans.org/resources/policies/Email_Policy.pdf

Slade, R. (2004). *Software forensics: Collecting evidence from the scene of a digital crime*. Columbus, OH: McGraw-Hill.

Tittel, E. (2002). *Schaum's outlines: Computer networking*. McGraw-Hill, Columbus, OH.

Tyson, J. (2004). *How instant messaging works*. Retrieved April 3, 2005, from http://computer.howstuffworks.com/instant-messaging.htm

Weber, M. J. (2004). *Invasion of privacy: Big brother and the company hackers*. Premier Press, Cincinnati, OH.

Webopedia. (2004). *What is instant messaging?* Retrieved April 3, 2005, from http://www.webopedia.com/TERM/I/instant_messaging.html

Wikipedia. (2004). *The free encyclopedia*. Retrieved April 3, 2005, from http://en.wikipedia.org/wiki/Main_Page

Zone Labs. (2004). *Zone Labs integrity: Check point integrity*. Retrieved April 3, 2005, from http://www.zonelabs.com/store/content/company/corpsales/intOverview.jsp

FURTHER READING

Babu, M. (2000). *Instant messaging: The future of communication?* Retrieved April 3, 2005, from http://www.expressitpeople.com/20021007/abroad1.shtml

Brightmail. (2004). *Spam statistics: Spam percentages*. Retrieved April 3, 2005, from http://enterprisesecurity.symantec.com/products/products.cfm?ProductID=642%20

Burkhardt, J., Henn, H., Hepper, S., Rintdorff, K., & Schack, T. (2002). *Pervasive computing: Technology and architecture of mobile Internet applications*. Pearson Education Limited, Boston, MA.

Hardy, I. R. (1996). *The evolution of ARPANET email.* Retrieved April 3, 2005, from http://www.ifla.org/documents/internet/hari1.txt

Holden, G. (2003). *Guide to network defense and countermeasures*. Course Technology, Thomson Learning, Hoboken, NJ.

Licklider, J. C. R., & Vezza, A. (1978, November). Applications of information networks. *Proceedings of the IEEE, 66*(11), p. 1330–1346.

Russell, D., & Gangemi Sr., G. T. (1991). *Computer security basics*. O'Reilly and Associates, Sebastopol, CA.

Sullivan, B. (2003, September 10). *Spam wars: How unwanted email is burying the Internet.* MSNBC News. Retrieved April 3, 2005, from http://msnbc.com/news/941040.asp?0cb=-115171549

Internet Relay Chat

Paul L. Witt, *Texas Christian University*

SECURE COMMUNICATION USING INTERNET RELAY CHAT

Defining Statement

Internet Relay Chat (IRC) is a worldwide system of synchronous, text-based conferencing on the Internet. IRC was the first online chat system to achieve widespread adoption, and despite the increasing popularity of Web-based chat rooms and instant messaging systems, it continues to be the synchronous medium of choice for many Internet users. Numerous sites on the World Wide Web contain IRC tutorials, network information, and software downloads. Because IRC is based on a client–server networking model, users simply install client software on their local computer and access the Internet to create a new channel (chat group) or join an existing channel. Using established network protocols, messages travel from an individual's computer to an IRC server, and then are relayed through other servers if necessary before being delivered to the designated recipient(s). IRC supports private, one-on-one conversations (analogous to real-time e-mail) as well as the simultaneous distribution of messages to all users in the channel (analogous to a real-time Listserv or newsgroup). Interactions on IRC channels involve users from all over the world, take place in many different languages, and focus on a wide range of topics. Most interactions on IRC are casual and "chatty" in nature, but sometimes they involve specific personal, academic, or organizational communication objectives. At any given moment, tens of thousands of IRC users are conversing about sports, science, technology, academics, news, recreation, and entertainment, as well as engaging in spontaneous personal and social interaction.

Historical Development

After the earliest experiments in real-time chat systems in the 1960s and 1970s, IRC was created in 1988 by Jarkko Oikarinen, an engineering student at the University of Oulu, Finland. By extending the features of an early UNIX-based function called Talk, Oikarinen's innovative technology allowed multiple users at different geographical locations to enter designated channels and engage in synchronous, online discussion. By 1990, the system had expanded to include 38 IRC servers located at universities in Scandinavia and the United States (Hamman, 1999). IRC gained notoriety as a strategic global communication system in 1991, when real-time messages were received from IRC users inside Kuwait during Iraqi occupation. In 1993, IRC enabled computer users in Moscow to communicate with outsiders during the uprising against President Yeltsin. Following the terrorist attacks in New York and Washington, D.C., in September 2001, IRC networks became extremely active, initially to support communication with survivors and rescue workers, and later to allow users from around the globe to vent their feelings, rally support for victims, and engage in political and ideological debate. When other communication systems failed or became congested during these international crises, computer users with access to the Internet used IRC for up-to-the-minute interaction with external parties.

In recent years, rapid growth in the number of individuals with Internet access has contributed to rapid growth in the use of IRC. At the beginning of the 21st century, hundreds of thousands of users were communicating via IRC networks. Charalabidis (2000) reported that the total number of IRC users was increasing as much as 30% annually, and that the largest IRC networks had tens of thousands of channels and sometimes experienced more than 50,000 simultaneous connections. Although many Web users gravitate to popular, easy-to-use messaging systems such as ICQ ("I Seek You") and Instant Messenger, IRC continues to appeal to the more technology-oriented specialist. In fact, "newbies" (newcomers) may find the IRC communication climate to be unfriendly or hard to understand at first. IRC commands and interfaces are not especially complicated, but casual Web users are often more accustomed to the very simple interfaces of browser-based Web chat systems. Furthermore, experienced users on some networks adopt an exclusivist attitude by refusing to communicate with newbies, or by using vague or highly specialized jargon that is unintelligible to outsiders. On these networks, newcomers are more likely to obtain advice and direction from channels devoted to IRC help.

STRUCTURE AND OPERATION

Infrastructure

Because IRC works on the client–server networking model, the IRC server is the central point of communication through which all messages pass en route to individual client computers. In the simplest IRC network structure, the computer of each user runs a client program to connect to a common server. The server runs an application called an IRC daemon (ircd), which allows connections from individual users and relays messages from one client to another by passing them through the server. Some IRC chat systems consist of a simple network in which a single server manages connections and communications among all its clients. However, most IRC servers are connected to other IRC servers, thus opening the IRC system to potential communication among all users with connections to all the servers on the network. Originally, there was only one IRC network, consisting of a few servers, but as IRC grew in popularity and complexity, it splintered into multiple networks. Today, there are hundreds of IRC networks that are constantly evolving through expansion and redefinition. They range in size from very small, family-oriented chat networks to global networks such as EFnet or the expansive IRCnet, which links more than 100 servers and supports thousands of chat groups, or channels (see Table 1). Channel names are fairly stable, but channel topics change regularly, and the announced topic frequently bears no relation to the conversation actually occurring on the channel.

To engage in IRC, users select an IRC network and connect to one of the available servers, using a nickname (e.g., *SuperTig*) rather than their real name. Using the */list* command, users can consult a list of public channels currently available on that server. The channels listed as *#channelname* are global and can be accessed through any server on the network; channels listed as *&channelname* are available through that server alone. Some channels are designated "secret" and not open to others. By entering the command */join #channelname*, users join a channel and usually receive the MOTD (message of the day) containing some basic information from the server's database about current activity on the channel (topic, nicknames of current users, etc.). The new user is then ready to communicate with others by sending a message that will appear more-or-less synchronously on the screens of all channel participants (see Figure 1). Newbies can usually find help on the channel *#irchelp*, and other help channels may be listed in the MOTD. The command */leave* or */part* will terminate the connection to the channel, and the command */quit* will terminate the connection to the network. In reality, connecting to an IRC server is not always simple, especially for newcomers. Connection may be prevented if the user enters an incorrect server name, chooses an unacceptable nickname, or has been *K-lined* (specifically banned from the server for some reason). Users who connect to the Internet through large, popular ISPs (Internet service providers) may find some channels closed to them, based on the stereotype that such subscribers are probably newbies and therefore unwelcome on certain channels.

Table 1 Some of the Largest IRC Networks

	Number of Servers	Help Site and Server List
Efnet	40	http://efnet.org
IRCnet	>120	http://www.ircnet.com
DALnet	30	http://www.dal.net
Undernet	40	http://www.undernet.org
GalaxyNet	30	http://www.galaxynet.org
WebNet	15	http://www.webchat.org
NewNet	15	http://www.newnet.net
ChatNet	15	http://www.chatnet.com

When using text-based IRC client software such as ircII, users manually enter commands in the typical command-line format familiar to UNIX users. When using graphical interface client software such as mIRC and Ircle, users click the mouse on an icon to generate the same result. Because the original IRC source code was not copyrighted, some networks have developed proprietary functions and features unique to their IRC system. The result is that all commands are not standardized across all IRC networks. Most of the basic commands are recognized by all IRC servers, however, and users who frequent a network typically learn specialized commands quickly through observation and by inquiring on a channel devoted to IRC help.

Although most users connect through IRC servers, the major IRC client programs also allow a direct client connection (DCC). Two clients who are connected to the same IRC network can initiate a direct connection between themselves. IP (Internet protocol) addresses are typically used to establish the DCC connection, and messages or shared files pass directly from one client to the other without being relayed by the IRC server. Many of the more experienced users prefer to use DCC for their one-on-one interactions and file transfers, because DCC frequently results in faster message exchange, a higher degree of privacy, and avoidance of network problems such as lags and netsplits. Netsplits occur when one or more servers are disconnected from the network.

IRC networks are not immune to problems of congestion or breakdown. As with all other packet-switching Internet communication systems, users sometimes experience delays in the transmission of electronic messages. This delay (known to IRC users as "lag") is irritating to all Internet users, but it is especially problematic in synchronous communication systems characterized by real-time interaction. A 10-second lag can dramatically change the timing and effectiveness of some types of online interaction, as threads of conversation become entangled and users appear to be "talking over" one another. The jumble

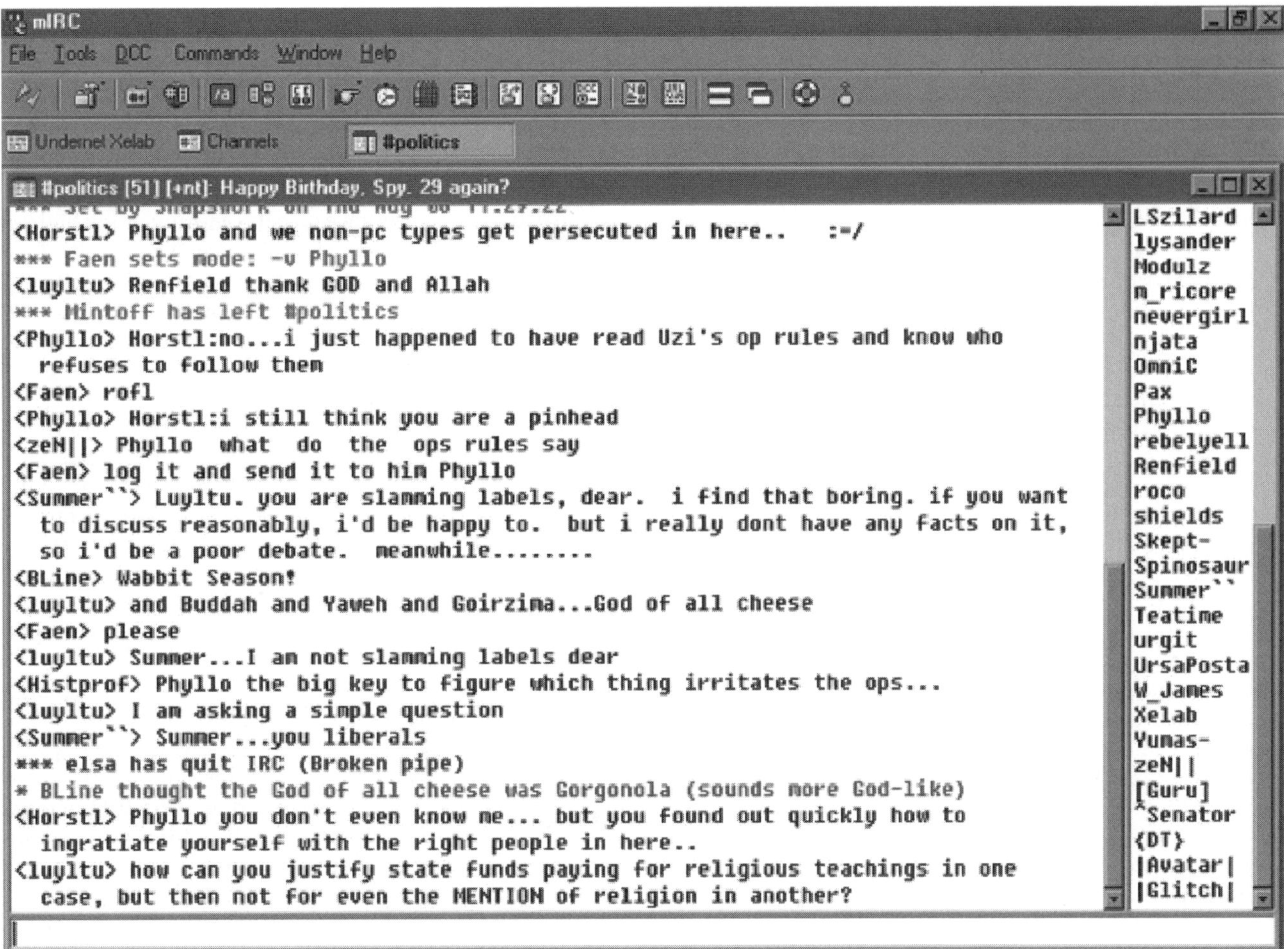

Figure 1: Screenshot of online interaction using mIRC.

of multiple conversations is a common characteristic of interaction on public IRC channels (Herring, 1999a), and lag serves to exacerbate the problem. Increased lag may be caused by heavy traffic on the Internet or IRC network, a malfunctioning server, flooding, or a denial of service attack (see following sections). Lag is sometimes related to a netsplit, which occurs when one or more IRC servers lose their connection to the network. Netsplits fracture the network and effectively create separate network fragments that may or may not continue to operate separately. Netsplits often result in a buildup of packets queued for delivery to servers that are no longer available. After a netsplit, servers sometimes reconnect to the network and are able to update the server with activity that occurred during the netsplit. Sometimes a netsplit results when an IRC operator revises the network connection to other servers to achieve a more efficient or more desirable network configuration.

Software

To engage in online communication using IRC, users need access to the Internet through an ISP or direct network connection. They must also install a communications software program called an IRC client. The client software serves as the interface between the individual computer (the client) and the IRC server (serving the needs of multiple clients). The IRC client processes the commands that are typed or clicked by the user and then employs network protocols, such as TCP/IP (transfer control protocol/Internet protocol) to transmit them to the server.

IRC supports communication across different operating platforms, enabling the flow of messages between PC and Macintosh computers, as well as UNIX-based computing systems. IRC clients for these and other operating systems are readily available, and free downloads or demonstration copies can be found on most of the major FTP (file transfer protocol) sites on the Internet. Some IRC clients are available as shareware, meaning that if users wish to continue using it after a free trial period, they are asked to purchase the software or pay a modest registration fee. Generally, the cost of IRC client software is quite reasonable.

Text-Based IRC Clients. Early IRC users were almost exclusively UNIX-based, and the majority of today's IRC servers are UNIX servers. Individual computer users who use a terminal emulation program to establish a dial-in connection to an organization for Internet access effectively turn their computer into a terminal by use of a shell account on the UNIX system. The most common IRC client for UNIX and related systems (such as shell accounts and Linux) is ircII. This full-featured, text-based client was the first widely used IRC client and still serves as a reference standard for essential commands and functions. More advanced users sometimes use ircII's scripting language to create scripts that streamline complex processes, generate customized output, or perform certain functions automatically when prescribed conditions occur.

Graphical Interface IRC Clients. The majority of online communicators connect to the Internet through Windows-based PCs or Macintosh computers. IRC clients have been developed for both platforms, offering the point-and-click ease of use characteristic of graphical user interfaces (GUIs). The major GUI clients receive ongoing attention from their developers, and excellent support is available for learners. The client of choice for many PC users employing Windows operating systems is mIRC, a powerful, intuitive, and reliable application. Because PC users outnumber those on UNIX and Macintosh platforms, mIRC is probably the most widely used IRC client on the Internet today. Easy-to-use menus and buttons, customizable functions, and extensive user support contribute to the popularity of mIRC (see Figure 1). The most widely used IRC client for Macintosh computers is Ircle. A stable, full-featured IRC client, Ircle provides buttons, menus, and icons to facilitate common IRC functions. Ircle users may also employ AppleScript to modify the client to their custom specifications. Good user support and innovative features place IRC interactions within easy reach even for beginning Ircle users.

Users

The IRC system hierarchy of networks, servers, channels, and clients is reflected in an administrative hierarchy of people who oversee each level of the system. End users who direct their IRC client to connect to a network should be aware of the scope of authority and control exerted by IRC operators and channel operators. Newbies sometimes embarrass themselves and irritate others by inappropriately posing questions or filing complaints with the person they perceive to be in charge of a channel or server.

IRCops. IRC operators generally oversee the operation of an IRC server, maintain routing functions in relation to other servers on the network, modify server settings, and monitor general activity on the server. Sometimes the original server administrator fulfills the role of IRCop, and sometimes the administrator selects one or more experienced and qualified users to serve as IRCop. Servers typically have more than one operator, to ensure constant observation of activity on the server. In the event of a server failure or network fault, IRCops work to restore network connections. They also enforce the policies and procedures of the server they oversee. If a user violates policy or misbehaves in some way, the IRCop usually issues a warning. Users who are reprimanded by an IRCop are sometimes unaware of the power the operator has to control activity on the server. For example, an IRCop can issue a */kill* command that effectively bans the offending user from further access to the server and, in some cases, the entire network. Determining the identity of a server's IRCops is not always easy. When they are listed in the MOTD (message of the day) or active user lists, their "user mask" (nickname plus host name) is usually marked with an asterisk *(*Stinkbug!skb220@rhl.net)*. The command */stats o* may be used to identify active operators, and some IRC clients support the command */who -oper*. Many IRC users never have direct communication with an IRC operator unless their activity on the server violates accepted practice and attracts the operator's attention. IRC operators do not exert control over channel activities; they leave those functions to the channel operators.

Chanops. Each IRC channel (chat group) is initiated or overseen by a channel operator, or chanop. Channel operators exert management and control over the channel's topic, mode, and settings, and they regulate how many users and specifically which users are allowed to interact on the channel. If users misbehave, become obnoxious, or irritate the channel operator, most chanops do not hesitate to ban them from the channel. Any user may become a chanop by creating a new channel or by being given operator status by a chanop on an existing channel, so it is not uncommon for chanops to misbehave as well (Herring, 1999b). Chanop status is valid only for the duration of the current IRC session, and when chanops leave the channel, they ordinarily lose their operator status. However, if operators are registered as super-ops with an IRC channel service, they can effectively maintain control over a channel even during their absence. Many IRC channels have several operators active at any given time, but occasionally a channel may function without an operator at all. Channel operators are usually identified with an @ sign before their nickname (*@SuperTig*). Most IRC clients support the command */who -chops* as a means of identifying channel operators.

Chanops can remove users from a channel and ban them from future access. On password-protected channels, they can invite users to join and can issue them the key to enter. On moderated channels, chanops can give selected users a voice that allows them to post messages to the channel while other users can only receive messages. Channel operators can grant chanop status to other users, and they can remove chanop status from other operators. Any IRC user who creates a new channel with the */join #channelname* command automatically becomes the operator for that channel. When a new channel is created, some basic channel modes and settings should immediately be set to establish guidelines for the activity allowed by users and operators on the channel.

Users. Users get to choose their nicknames and can use them as long as they are the first to log into a channel with that nickname. If someone else is using it, then users can either choose another nickname or ask the incumbent user to give it up. If the incumbent user refuses, then the user is best advised to choose another nickname. This same etiquette applied when there was a universal nickname registry for IRC called "NickServ," a service operated in Germany until it discontinued in 1994. There is no evidence that NickServ will resume IRC nickname registration operations.

Table 2 Basic User Commands

Command	Description
/join #channelname	Joins the user to a global channel on the network, unless the user is banned or the channel is restricted (invite-only, secret, etc.)
/join #channel1,#channel2	Allows the user to simultaneously participate in both of the channels listed
/mode MyNickname + i	Sets the mode of the user "MyNickname" to invisible, enhancing privacy and security
/list	Produces a list of channels on the server; often used with various flags and parameters
/set hold_mode on	Prevents a long list from scrolling beyond the monitor's limits
/names	Shows a list of nicknames of users currently on the network (potentially a huge listing, so always use parameters)
/names #channelname	Shows a list of nicknames of users currently on the channel (also very large on some channels, so use parameters)
/who #channelname	Lists nicknames, usermasks, and other information about current users on a channel
/whois NewName	Produces basic information from the server's database about the user "NewName"
/msg NewName	Sends a private message to the user NewName; messages to all users are entered without the */msg* command
/dcc chat NewName	Requests Direct Client Connection with the user "NewName"; if NewName accepts, a direct private chat will bypass the IRC server (may be more private, less lag)
/nick othername	Changes a user's nickname to the one specified
/ignore badguy	Blocks or ignores messages from user called "badguy"
/part or */leave*	Signs a user off of a channel, may be followed by a parting comment
/quit	Terminates connection to the network, may include a brief comment

Commands

Table 2 contains a sampling of user commands commonly employed across different IRC clients and servers. Users of text-based clients enter these commands manually, whereas users of GUI clients usually click on icons or drop-down menus to engage the function, and the client automatically generates the command. Some commands contain specific parameters or are qualified by "flags" that set the limits of the command output. Table 3 contains the most common commands used by channel operators.

SOCIAL FACTORS

IRC and Online Community

As with all online communication systems, IRC is more than a network of computers relaying electronic files among themselves. Fundamentally, IRC systems are composed of humans who utilize the computer network to exchange information or conversation with others. As a somewhat specialized online community, IRC has drawn those who are more technically proficient, whose computer skills enable them to easily perform such tasks

Table 3 Basic Channel Operator Commands

Command	Description
/join #NewChannel	Creates a new channel with the specified name
/mode #NewChannel +o|l|m|v|t	Sets the channel modes to Operator (chanop status can be assigned or removed), Limit (limits the number of users allowed at one time), Moderated (all users receive, but only some can post messages), Voice (grants selected users the ability to post messages), and Topic (set by operators only); several other modes are available
/mode #NewChannel	Reveals all the current mode settings for the channel
/mode #NewChannel +o mybuddy	Gives the user "mybuddy" operator status
/mode #NewChannel −o mybuddy	Removes chanop status from the user "mybuddy"
/mode #NewChannel +l 20	Limits the number of users on NewChannel to 20
/mode #NewChannel −l	Removes the limit on number of users
/mode #NewChannel +v angelbaby	Allows the user "angelbaby" to post messages to NewChannel
/topic #NewChannel IRC clients	Changes channel topic to "IRC clients"
/kick #NewChannel satanson	Kicks the user "satanson" off the channel
/invite mybuddy #NewChannel	Invites the user "mybuddy" to join NewChannel

as the following: downloading and installing software from an FTP site; learning intuitively the features and functions of new software applications; using line commands, scripting, or hand coding to accomplish tasks; adapting to the specific styles and conventions of online communication forums; and maintaining sufficient safeguards to protect their personal privacy and system security.

Many individuals "meet" regularly on IRC channels where, in much the same way as with instant messaging and Web chat, they develop close relationships and a true sense of community. On some channels, the basis for commonality is the agreed-upon topic (such as advanced applications of certain software), and participants willingly share techniques and resources in mutual support of one another. Other channels are predominantly social in nature, marked by spontaneous, casual conversation. In both types of IRC communities, casual, online acquaintances are the norm, but significant one-on-one relationships sometimes develop. There are reports of IRC users who decided to move their relationships offline and meet face to face, and some have become business partners or marriage partners (e.g., Hoff & Hoff, n.d.) Of course, the majority of IRC relationships are restricted to the online context, but they constitute legitimate relationships that fill meaningful social roles for many users. Friends made on IRC are not only "virtual" friends but also "real" friends.

Communication researchers study the social, relational, and communicative dynamics of online communication forums such as IRC. Overall, these studies indicate that computer-mediated communication systems do support the development of meaningful relationships, effective decision-making groups, and a legitimate sense of community (Finholt, Sproull, & Kiesler, 1990; Reid, 1991; Walther, 1996, 1997; Wood & Smith, 2001). Nevertheless, research has also identified some important differences between face-to-face and online communication. For example, in face-to-face interactions, people normally communicate interpersonal liking through such nonverbal cues as eye contact, smiles, proximity, touch, open body positioning, and vocal expressiveness (Richmond & McCroskey, 1999). Because the usual nonverbal behaviors are absent in the online context, a greater responsibility is placed on verbal messages for feedback, affect, and nuances of meaning. Typically, IRC users attempt to replace nonverbal messages through various means (Werry, 1996), such as using acronyms like IMHO ("in my humble opinion") and LOL ("laughing out loud"), or by inserting affect cues <grin>, demonstrative punctuation (no!!!!!!!!!), or emoticons such as the smiley face :-) and its many variant forms. The absence of nonverbal communication cues led some early researchers to judge online communication as incapable of conveying subtle relational messages and therefore an unsatisfactory medium for meaningful interpersonal exchange (Kiesler, Siegel, & McGuire, 1984). However, in the intervening years, online skills have improved and online communication norms have evolved, with the result that modern communicators routinely use IRC and other computer-mediated communication systems to engage in effective and meaningful interaction of all types.

IRC and Relationship Development

As IRC users employ new communication strategies, they sometimes find relationship opportunities in the online community that do not exist for them in face-to-face contexts. For example, research has shown that the decision to initiate face-to-face interaction with someone may be directly or indirectly affected by the other person's physical appearance, nonverbal behaviors, vocal attributes, age, gender, or ethnicity (Berscheid & Walster, 1978). It may seem unkind or unfair, but people often choose whether or not to interact with others on the basis of these traits. When people go online to engage in conversation on IRC or Web chat, however, these physical characteristics are obviously not visible. Many users choose a nickname that is not gender-specific and avoid revealing details of personal identity when queried for their "ASL" (age, sex, location). Because physical attraction is a less influential factor in computer-mediated communication than in face-to-face interaction, unattractive people can relate as equals with the beautiful and handsome; those with vocal or speech problems can engage in fluent expression; those who painfully experience bias or discrimination in face-to-face encounters may confidently enter chat groups as social equals, perhaps for the first time in their lives.

Therefore, computer-mediated communication systems may actually enhance the potential for long-term relationship development by expanding the ways interpersonal relationships develop. An example is seen in the "matching hypothesis" (Walster, Walster, & Berscheid, 1978), which theorizes that people usually date and marry someone with approximately the same physical attributes as themselves (e.g., both are attractive or both are plain in appearance). By contrast, couples who first met on IRC may vary considerably in physical attractiveness. Online relationships can deepen over time through self-disclosure, empathic "listening," and progressively more intimate communication. When existing online relationships are moved offline for face-to-face meetings, differences in physical appearance may seem relatively unimportant in comparison with the many points of commonality already discovered. In such cases, IRC may provide a more just and balanced communication context than traditional meeting places.

Anonymity and Virtual Identity

The relative anonymity that enhances relationship development on IRC might also introduce an element of deception. Obviously, users may project a virtual identity very different from their true identity. Their intent in doing so might be harmless and recreational, or it might be deceptive and dangerous (Donath, 1999). IRC, like all online communication systems, occasionally draws users who are malicious, misleading, or mentally unstable. For example, pedophiles frequently pose as youngsters in forums frequented by children, hoping that a child will trust them with information or engage in conversation with them. According to accounts in the popular press, some long-term relationships that seemed healthy and secure online turned out to be dangerous when the couple met face to face, because one of the parties had been projecting a virtual identity to conceal unwholesome motives.

SECURITY AND LEGAL ISSUES

Hate and Harassment on IRC

The anonymous nature of online communication systems such as IRC may contribute to the use of aggressive or inflammatory verbal abuse in the form of harassment or hate speech. Most IRC interactions involve the use of nicknames only, and users rarely reveal their true identities. This anonymity may contribute to a perception of low accountability, with the result that some IRC users may verbally lash out against individuals or groups in ways that are offensive and illegal. For example, Herring (2002, 2003) documented instances of flagrant sexual harassment on IRC and posited that male-dominated online environments are often hostile to participants whom they perceive to be female.

For American citizens, First Amendment (free speech) privileges extend to IRC interactions, but so do criminal laws preventing hate speech, inciting violence, and stalking. U.S. federal laws expressly forbid cyberstalking and online harassment (Executive Order 13133, Unlawful Conduct Using the Internet), which occur when a user annoys, abuses, threatens, or repeatedly initiates unwanted communication with another. Responsible channel operators seek to eliminate such activity on IRC by banning the offending user and, if necessary, reporting them to legal authorities. Occasionally, however, chanops themselves engage in unethical communication behaviors (Herring, 1999b). IRC communications are subject to surveillance by law enforcement authorities acting pursuant to lawful court orders. IRC service providers, including operators, are required by law to cooperate with law enforcement authorities to effectuate the surveillance. Of course, many IRC participants are not U.S. citizens and not constrained by American laws, which points to the ethical and legal complexities of global communication networks.

Children and IRC

Although a significant percentage of overall Internet users are under the age of 18, the percentage of minors on IRC may be relatively smaller. In truth, IRC is not especially suited to the needs and concerns of children. The more widely known Web-based chat systems maintain terms of service that restrict certain activities and topics of discussion. Offenders in these chat rooms can be quickly and effectively removed by administrators. IRC channels, on the other hand, are generally not restricted, and people may talk about anything they choose. It is not infrequent to encounter adult conversations and offensive language on IRC that would be unsuitable for children. On moderated channels, chanops can always remove a user's "voice" and disable the offender's ability to contribute to further discourse, but such censorial functions are not characteristic of most IRC channels. IRC is perceived by many to be spontaneous, free-wheeling, unrestricted, and unpredictable—a kind of "wild West" communication context.

In carefully controlled and appropriate IRC channels, children may benefit from online conversation with other children from around the world, with teachers and classmates, and with extended family members or parents who are traveling. Unsupervised, however, children on IRC may encounter such risks as cyberstalking, which could possibly lead to physical stalking if the child reveals personal information; offensive and harmful conversations with unwholesome characters such as pedophiles; and exposure to sexual content, viruses, or other harmful material if the child accepts a file transfer from an unknown IRC user. Numerous laws and regulations exist to protect minors on the Internet, and responsible IRC users should immediately report any suspicious activity involving a minor on IRC. Since 1997, the FBI has vigorously investigated and prosecuted online pedophiles and stalkers of children through its "Innocent Images" program. Agents go online and pose as children to attract the attention of these criminals. Once these criminals make their moves on what they think are vulnerable children, they are arrested and brought to justice. The program has already produced several hundred convictions.

Scripts and Viruses

Informed IRC users are aware of the many risks involved with file transfers, through both hard media and the Internet. When users install new software, download Web pages, or receive files from external sources through either networking or hard media such as disks or compact discs (CDs), some degree of security risk is introduced. It is a rare occurrence, but even respected commercial software has been distributed with inadvertent flaws that damage systems. More common is the intentional or unintentional passing of a virus or harmful script from user to user through various Internet connections, including IRC. Responsible users minimize these risks by maintaining awareness of current security threats, practicing discretion when networking, and taking steps to keep applications and operating systems up to date.

Most viruses are in .exe or .ini files, but they can also be concealed in zipped files or embedded in completely unrelated files such as .jpg or .gif files. When launched by an unsuspecting user, viruses can cause irreparable harm to individual computers and potentially spread throughout entire systems. Some viruses are not destructive but merely irritating, such as those with pop-up messages of a humorous or salacious nature. Others may disable or destroy hard drives, data files, operating systems, and peripheral components or create havoc throughout entire networks.

People who share word processing files, script files, graphics, or other types of files on IRC may potentially be spreading viruses, Trojans, or worms. Trojans (or Trojan horses) are spread by users who transfer seemingly benign files that contain harmful concealed code. Worms are viruses that propagate themselves and migrate from one application to another within a computer, and from one computer to another within a network.

Scripts represent another source of external control and increased security risk. Scripts are files containing macros (or mini-programs) that enable an application to combine or automate various functions. IRC users have created scripts for such tasks as completing nicknames from typed initials, automatically performing ping operations, generating automated "away" responses, and customizing the output of IRC interactions. Some early IRC users enhanced the function of their IRC clients by writing scripts that have subsequently been incorporated into more recent versions of the software. Within the IRC community, techniques of scriptwriting constitute a frequent topic of conversation, and the sharing of scripts among users is relatively common. A number of Web sites or FTP download sites serve as archives or clearing houses for the open sharing of scripts and script paks (sets of coordinated scripts) for various IRC clients. When an IRC user downloads a script file from an archive or another user, however, there is always risk that the file may contain concealed or deceptive code that may launch unexpected or harmful functions in the receiver's system.

Most IRC clients include options to limit or disable the automatic or unintentional running of scripts, just as the major Web browsers include settings to control scripting functions encountered on the World Wide Web. Because harmful functions can be inserted into otherwise legitimate scripts, cautious IRC users run scripts only after proofreading every line of the code. Safe practice also calls for the careful screening of IRC users before accepting from them any files of any type. Common practice states that files should never be accepted from an unknown person, and file transfers from known parties should always be scanned for viruses before being opened.

Mischief and Sabotage on IRC

Many people use IRC safely and never experience viruses, takeovers, or threats to their security. It is not uncommon, however, to encounter less serious offenses allegedly launched by mischievous youngsters known as "script kiddies." (For a more serious perspective on "script kiddies," see Gilboa, 1996.) Anyone who has been on IRC very long has probably observed attempts by an aggressive user to take charge of a channel or disrupt the flow of messages on a channel or network. "Channel taking" may be accomplished if a user is granted chanop status or deceptively uses an operator's nickname, then "de-ops" the other operators and indiscriminately bans users, kicks them off the channel, or silences their voices by turning the channel into a moderated one. Sometimes malicious users simultaneously send multiple files to another user, a practice known as "flooding." If practiced on a large scale, flooding can significantly increase lag on a channel or entire network. Most IRC clients include optional settings that limit flooding to that client.

A more serious form of sabotage exists in denial of service (DoS) attacks, which involve harmful data packets that sneak through loopholes in an operating system's security and launch erroneous messages from or to the client. DoS attacks, sometimes called "nukes," are against the law and can cause the host to disconnect from the Internet, freeze, or crash entirely. IRC can be exploited to facilitate a DoS attack by sending scripts called "bots" to unsuspecting users. Bots use vulnerabilities in the operating system to initiate the attack simultaneously from multiple computers. Engaging in such destructive practices violates federal law, specifically the Computer Fraud and Abuse Act (18 U.S.C. § 1030), as well as many state statutes. As a result of these laws, even first-time offenders can get jail time and stiff fines.

Because internal security is especially critical to certain types of organizations, some companies or institutions have restricted the use of IRC and other Internet functions through the use of firewalls that prohibit any computer in their network from connecting to an IRC server. For any IRC user, whether institutional or private, the best defense against mischief and sabotage is to refuse to accept file transfers or DCC chat requests from unknown individuals, to carefully peruse every line of script code before launching it, and to maintain updated security files for operating systems, IRC clients, and virus protection software.

Ensuring Privacy and Security

All Internet users should take three basic steps to maximize privacy and security when connecting to IRC, the World Wide Web, or any other online communication network. First, the user's operating system should be kept current by logging onto the publisher's Web site (e.g., http://www.windowsupdate.com), scanning for updates, and downloading and installing modifications as advised by the publisher. Such updates are usually free and consist of security patches (minor adjustments that close potential breaches) or more substantial service packs that modify file architecture or essential processes. Failure to keep the operating system current could expose the host computer to intrusion, including unauthorized access to the data it contains or the takeover of the computer to launch denial of service attacks.

Second, users should install and continuously run a firewall to protect the host computer from unauthorized intrusion while connected to IRC or other parts of the Internet. A firewall is software that provides an intrusion detection system to manage and monitor the ports or connection points between the host computer and the Internet. Although some firewalls can be found on the Internet and downloaded for free, many users prefer to purchase full-featured programs from well-known software publishers, thus entrusting their system's security to major players in the Internet security marketplace. The routine use of a firewall is important for all users but absolutely essential for those who maintain continuous connection to the Internet (e.g., through cable or DSL connections). A continuous Internet presence provides potential hackers with uninterrupted access to probe the host computer's ports in hopes of gaining a point of entry. Users who spend time communicating with others on IRC channels but who do not continually run a firewall to monitor the connection place themselves at greater risk of a security breach.

A third important security component is the installation and maintenance of virus detection software, which scans incoming and outgoing data transfers such as IRC messages, e-mail, Web pages, graphics, and attachments. If a known or potential virus is found during these file transfers, the virus detection program isolates the file before it damages the computer, alerts the user to the presence of a suspected virus, and offers tools to clean both the file and the user's system, should it become infected.

Fortunately, virus protection software is inexpensive and readily available on all operating platforms. Major publishers market these programs and maintain them on an ongoing basis with newly developed virus definition files. After installing the program, registered users are encouraged to log onto the publisher's site frequently and download the latest data files to combat new viruses as they emerge. This update service is usually free or available at minimal cost, and the crucial nature of maintaining up-to-date virus protection justifies the time and expense required. It is frequently reported that as many as half of all Internet users do not run virus detection software at all, and many of those who have installed the software do not conscientiously update the virus definition files. In summary, IRC users can minimize the likelihood of privacy or security breaches by routinely updating their operating systems, running reputable firewalls, and using up-to-date virus detection software continually during online interactions.

FUTURE OF IRC

Organizational Applications

In some organizations, real-time, online communication systems such as IRC are viewed as little more than a novelty. In fact, use of the word "chat" in serious organizational contexts may cause some institutional leaders or educators to grimace and assume that the medium only promotes idle chit-chat. As a generic communication medium, however, synchronous communication systems such as IRC, instant messaging, and Web chat can assist modern communicators in reaching important organizational and personal communication goals. For example, these systems are used in many organizations to support real-time collaboration among employees at different geographic locations, thereby contributing to productivity while keeping down long-distance communication costs. Probably the most common computer-mediated communication (CMC) mode selected for these purposes is instant messaging, which most people find easier to use and generally more secure and private than IRC. In fact, security concerns have prompted some organizations to install firewalls that prevent the use of IRC and other external file-sharing applications on their networks. Of course, an organization could choose to maintain an internal IRC server with no connections to outside networks, or to use moderated or secret channels on existing networks.

Individual Applications

IRC was the first synchronous text-based conferencing system to gain widespread use by individual Internet users, and the number of IRC users continues to grow at a rapid pace (Charalabidis, 2000). Nevertheless, in recent years, the use of IRC for interpersonal interaction has been largely supplanted by instant messaging systems that provide easy access or quick integration with Web browsers. Not only are command-line systems such as IRC less familiar to Internet users today, but there is a growing perception that IRC is frequented by those who engage in pirating or illicit file sharing, and that the medium has become quite risky. In the years ahead, as new communication technologies emerge to support increasing demands for private and secure communication networks, IRC will face the challenge of evolving into a medium capable of serving the legitimate needs of 21st-century communicators. Otherwise, it may be relegated to the Internet history books or lose its place of respectability as a safe and effective network available to the entire Internet community.

GLOSSARY

Ban Status of a user forbidden by a chanop to enter a channel.

Channel A virtual chat group in which users interact, discussing specific topics or engaging in general conversation.

Chanops Channel operators; they monitor and maintain a channel by setting the parameters and inviting or expelling users.

Client Software run by the local computer of an IRC participant, which converts the user's actions into commands recognized by an IRC server.

Daemon (IRC daemon, or ircd) Software run by a server connected to the Internet, accepting connection requests from clients and relaying messages among users.

Direct Client Connection (DCC) Connection established between two users that allows them to bypass the network for increased privacy and faster connection.

Flooding Simultaneously sending many messages to a single user, thus "flooding" a channel or an entire network with unwanted messages and probably increasing lag.

Internet Relay Chat (IRC) Real-time, text-based communication medium that employs a network of servers to connect geographically separated users.

IRCops IRC operators who monitor and maintain IRC servers; they generally have very little to do with the operation of channels.

Lag A delay in the transmission of messages among users or between a user and a server.

MOTD (Message of the Day) An automated confirmation message containing certain information about practices relating to a channel, its activities, and its current participants.

Netsplit Disruption in the connection among servers that results in the fracturing of the network into subdivided parts and the disconnection of some users.

Newbie A newcomer to IRC or other online contexts.

Nickname An invented name that uniquely identifies the user on the network.

Scripts Files containing code that enables an application to combine or automate various functions.

CROSS REFERENCES

See *Anonymity and Identity on the Internet; E-Education and Information Privacy and Security; Legal, Social, and Ethical Issues of the Internet; Online Communities; Privacy Law and the Internet.*

REFERENCES

Berscheid, E., & Walster, E. H. (1978). *Interpersonal attraction*. Reading, MA: Addison-Wesley Publishing Company.

Charalabidis, A. (2000). *The book of IRC*. San Francisco: No Starch Press.

Donath, J. (1999). Identity and deception in the virtual community. In M. A. Smith & P. Kollock (Eds.), *Communities in Cyberspace* (pp. 29–59). New York: Routledge.

Finholt, T., Sproull, L., & Kiesler, S. (1990). Communication and performance in ad hoc task groups. In J. Galagher, R. E. Kraut, & C. Edigo (Eds.), *Intellectual teamwork: Social and technological foundations of cooperative work* (pp. 291–325). Hillsdale, NJ: Erlbaum.

Gilboa, N. (1996). Elites, lamers, narcs and whores: Exploring the computer underground. In L. Cherny & E. R. Weise (Eds.), *Wired_Women: Gender and New Realities in Cyberspace* (pp. 98–113). Seattle: Seal Press.

Hamman, R. (1999). *History of the Internet*. Retrieved March 29, 2002. from http://www.socio.demon.co.uk/history.html

Herring, S. C. (1999a). Interactional coherence in CMC. *Journal of Computer-Mediated Communication, 4*(4). Retrieved March 16, 2005, from http://www.ascusc.org/jcmc/vol4/issue4/herring.html

Herring, S. C. (1999b). The rhetorical dynamics of gender harassment on-line. *The Information Society, 15*(3), 151–167.

Herring, S. C. (2002). Cyber violence: Recognizing and resisting abuse in online environments. *Asian Women, 14*, 187–212.

Herring, S. C. (2003). Gender and power in online communication. In J. Holmes & M. Meyerhoff (Eds.), *The Handbook of Language and Gender* (pp. 202–228). Oxford: Blackwell Publishers.

Hoff, M., & Hoff, J. *Chatting on the Net*. Retrieved January 16, 2004, from http://www.newircusers.com

Kiesler, S., Siegel, J., & McGuire, T. W. (1984). Social psychological aspects of computer-mediated communication. *American Psychologist, 39*, 1123–1134.

Reid, E. M. (1991). Electropolis: Communication and community on Internet Relay Chat. Retrieved March 15, 2005, from http://eserver.org/cyber/reid.txt

Richmond, V. P., & McCroskey, J. C. (1999). *Nonverbal behavior in interpersonal relations* (4th ed.). Boston: Allyn and Bacon.

Walster, E., Walster, G. W., & Berscheid, E. (1978). *Equity: Theory and research*. Boston: Allyn & Bacon.

Walther, J. B. (1996). Computer-mediated communication: Impersonal, interpersonal, and hyperpersonal interaction. *Communication Research, 23*, 3–43.

Walther, J. B. (1997). Group and interpersonal effects in international computer-mediated collaboration. *Human Communication Research, 23*, 342–369.

Werry, C. (1996). Linguistic and interactional features of Internet Relay Chat. In S. C. Herring (Ed.), *Computer-mediated communication: Linguistic, social and cross-cultural perspectives* (pp. 47–64). Amsterdam: John Benjamins.

Wood, A. F., & Smith, M. J. (2001). *Online communication: Linking technology, identity, and culture*. Mahwah, NJ: Lawrence Erlbaum Associates.

FURTHER READING

Caraballo, D., & Lo, J. (2000). *The IRC prelude*. Retrieved March 15, 2005, from http://www.irchelp.org/irchelp/new2irc.html

Internet Relay Chat. Retrieved March 15, 2005, from http://www.livinginternet.com/r/r.htm

Lo, J. (Ed.) (1994). *Internet Relay Chat help archive*. Retrieved March 15, 2005, from http://www.irchelp.org

Reed, D., & Oikarinen, J. (1993). *Internet Relay Chat protocol*. Retrieved March 15, 2005, from ftp://nic.merit.edu/documents/rfc/rfc1459.txt

Rodino, M. (1997). Breaking out of binaries: Reconceptualizing gender and its relationship to language in computer-mediated communication. *Journal of Computer-Mediated Communication, 3*(3). Retrieved March 15, 2005, from http://www.ascusc.org/jcmc/vol3/issue3/rodino.html

Online Communities

Lee Sproull, *New York University*

INTRODUCTION

The Internet was not invented as a social technology, but it has turned out to be one. From the earliest days of the ARPAnet (a network of communicating computers established in the late 1960s with U.S. government funding), people have shaped and used the technology for social purposes. Today, millions of people use the Net as a means of making and maintaining connections with other people who share a common experience, interest, or concern. The Net-based social contexts range from family e-mail to fantasy games with hundreds of thousands of players. This chapter focuses on a subset of Net-based social contexts, which in recent years have come to be called "online communities." These are large voluntary online groups, composed primarily of people who have no preexisting ties with one another and who may never meet face-to-face. Their members interact with one another primarily, if not exclusively, via the Net. Online communities range in technical sophistication from Usenet discussion groups to complex multiplayer fantasy games supported by proprietary software. They range in purpose from entertainment to developing free software to political dissent. They range in accessibility from totally open to completely hidden behind corporate firewalls. Some express no concern for security and privacy. Some, particularly those whose focus is on medical or psychological conditions, are concerned about member privacy. A few have as their common interest the topic of Internet security or Internet fraud.

This chapter describes how technical and social factors mutually interact to produce and sustain online communities. It also begins to offer a differentiated view of online communities. Online communities share some underlying attributes and processes, but they differ in member interests, goals, processes, and consequences for their members, sponsors, and society. A more differentiated view will make possible more productive theorizing, research, and design.

DEFINITION AND ATTRIBUTES

Definition

Communities in the physical world are defined as collectivities based on members' shared experience, interest, or conviction, and their voluntary interaction in the service of member welfare and collective welfare (Bender, 1978; Etzioni & Etzioni, 1999; Knoke, 1986). Examples include neighborhood communities; religious communities; civic and social communities, such as youth scouting or service clubs; and collections of like-minded enthusiasts, such as sports fans. Communities in the physical world can be described by structural attributes such as rules, roles, and resources that exist independent of any member (e.g., Lin, 2001). Thus, one can talk about the size of a community, membership requirements and obligations, resources and amenities, member characteristics, and interaction patterns. Communities can also be described by psychological attributes internal to their members, such as feelings of trust, alienation, identification, and commitment. Both structural and psychological attributes exist along a continuum, so one can find more or less well-structured communities with more or less committed members. In casual usage, the term "community" usually suggests positive feelings, prosocial behavior, and choice. (People rarely talk about a prison community even though its inmates interact and have experiences in common.) Analytically, however, the term is a neutral one. Communities can do physical and economic damage to their members, neighbors, and enemies, just as they may produce beneficial outcomes.

The definition of online community is also based on shared experience, interest, or conviction, and voluntary interaction among members in the service of member welfare and collective welfare. An online community is defined as a large, voluntary collectivity whose primary goal is member or collective welfare; whose members share a common interest, experience, or conviction; and whose members interact with one another primarily via the Net. Online communities can have more or less structure and more or less committed members. They may yield positive or negative consequences for their members, sponsors, and society. This definition excludes electronic work groups and virtual teams, whose primary goal is economic gain, whose members are paid, and whose size is relatively small. It excludes ad hoc friendship groups and buddy lists, which are relatively small and unstructured and whose members interact primarily in the offline world. These two exclusions highlight our focus on common-interest groups of large size with voluntary members. It also excludes nominal groups such as "all –the –people –who –use –Google" (who neither share a common interest nor interact with one another), "all –the –people –who –donate –cycles –to Seti@home," and "all –the people who read a particular Web log" (who may share a common interest but do not interact with one another). This exclusion highlights our focus on social interaction around a common interest. It is difficult to tightly bind the concept of community because human interaction occurs in a continuum of social organization—from the dyad to the nation state. Nevertheless, the definition of electronic community used in this chapter excludes some forms of electronic social interaction for reasons of focus and because they are deserving of consideration in their own right. Others who have offered definitions of electronic communities include Figallo (1998), Kim (2000), Powazek (2002), Preece (2000), Rheingold (2000), and Werry and Mowbray (2002).

Until the mid-1990s, almost no one used the term "online community." Instead, these groups were named after the technology that supported them and were called "newsgroups," "listservs," "mailing lists," "bulletin board systems," or "freenets." In some ways, the online communities that are the focus of this chapter bear little resemblance to communities in the physical world. They own few tangible resources; they require no visible or tangible commitment from members (such as taxes, dues, or attendance at meetings); members may never see or meet one another face –to face. Yet, some online communities have resources that may be economically valuable: their domain name, the wisdom accumulated in their FAQs (frequently asked questions), or the intellectual property created by their members. Fantasy game characters and properties have yielded nontrivial sums for their creators on eBay auctions. The members of one voluntary online community collected enough money in member donations to buy a new server to host the community (Boczkowski, 1999). Nevertheless, calling any electronic site where people may gather an "online community" does not make it one. As in the physical world, the term carries positive connotations, and some who have used it are merely guilty of wishful thinking. This wishful thinking characterizes those who, in the late 1990s, aspired to create online communities for profit (e.g., Bressler & Grantham, 2000; Hagel & Armstrong, 1997).

Supporting Technologies

In addition to the packet-switching technology of networked communication, many online communities rely on message-based group communication applications to support member interaction. These applications generally support either asynchronous or synchronous discussion and interaction. In asynchronous interaction, people do not have to be logged on at the same time because messages are saved for later reading. In synchronous discussion, people must be logged on at the same time because messages are not stored. Asynchronous discussion is often supported via mailing lists or bulletin board applications. Mailing lists, a push technology, send group messages to a person's e-mail inbox where they intermingle with the person's other e-mail and are saved until the recipient logs on to read them. With bulletin boards, a pull technology, a person reads group messages organized by topic in a file exclusively devoted to that group. (Some people establish filters to move all mailing list messages into separate folders, thereby making distribution lists function somewhat more like bulletin boards.) Synchronous discussion may be supported via talk programs such as IRC (Internet Relay Chat), Instant Messenger, or text-based virtual reality (VR) environments. MUDs (multiuser dungeon, domain, or dimension) and MOOs (MUD object oriented) began as text-based virtual reality games, computer-based versions of fantasy games such as Dungeons and Dragons. Today, some are still organized as fantasy games; others are organized for professional or social purposes. Their spatial metaphors and programmable objects and characters are the precursors of today's graphically based fantasy games.

With the spread of the Web and graphical browsers in the late 1990s, online communities could support more varied forms of interaction on their Web sites. Some use real-time chat for discussions that are scheduled and announced in advance. Some use special file formats to share image, sound, or video files. Wikis support community discussion through collaborative authoring of Web pages. Blogs (Web logs) support community discussion through comments on blog pages. Online game communities are supported by more or less elaborate software that supports play in board games such as chess or supports character creation and interaction in fantasy worlds. Most discussion among members on online community Web sites still occurs in message-based discussions, however. Even the fantasy games have discussion boards.

General Attributes and Processes

In synchronous online communities, people can participate from any place that has the appropriate technology available. In asynchronous online communities, people can also participate at any time as well as from any place. Common interest and enabling technology become the only two requirements for community participation. The enabling technology for online community, which is largely a keyboard-supported message-based technology, leads to some general behavioral implications.

Social Psychology of Message-Based Communication

Electronic discussion communities are characterized by reduced social context cues relative to the social context cues available in face-to-face discussions. Weak social context cues mean that messages carry few explicit reminders of the size of the group or members' physical appearance, social status, or nonverbal reactions as compared with face-to-face or telephone communication. (In virtual reality communities, people can create entirely new personas.) Social context cues help to regulate communication in face-to-face and telephonic interaction. They provide feedback as to whom is receiving communications and how those communications are being received and interpreted. People adjust the style and substance of their communications as a function of these cues. When those cues are attenuated, communication tends to be relatively frank and open (Kendall, 2002;

Reid, 1999; Sproull & Kiesler, 1991). Weak social context cues can lead to different effects, even for people within the same community. They can increase affiliation and commitment among members because objective differences among them are obscured and subjective similarities, based on their common interest, are magnified (Galegher, Sproull, & Kiesler, 1998; Mackenna & Bargh, 1998; Sproull & Faraj, 1995). Alternatively, they can increase disaffection and dropout because it may be more difficult to establish common ground or consensus and manage conflict (Carnevale & Probst, 1997; Cramton, 2001; Dibbell, 1998; Herring, 1994; Kollack & Smith, 1996). Asynchrony and weak social context cues condition communication in many online communities. They allow for a potentially greater geographic and social diversity of participants than many physical communities do. At the same time, they offer few cues to that social diversity in interaction, except those revealed through linguistic cues (e.g., Herring, 2001).

Microcontributions

Many of the tools for electronic community discussion are based on a relatively fine granularity of time and attention—the text message. Although messages can be any length, ones sent to asynchronous discussion communities typically range between 10 to 30 lines or one to two screens of text. For example, Winzelberg (1997) reported a mean of 131 words; Galegher et al. (1998) reported a mean of 8 to 20 lines of new text; Wasko and Faraj (1999) reported a mean of 25 to 30 lines of text; Sproull and Faraj (1995) reported a mean of 22 to 42 lines of new text. Individual contributions in a synchronous chat room or VR environment are usually even shorter. In asynchronous communities, people can read one or more messages and post or send one or more messages at their convenience. The message can be thought of as a microcontribution to the community. When people are online much of the day as a part of their work, voluntary microcontributions can be interspersed throughout the workday. Even in synchronous communities, some members report that they keep a community window open on their screen while they are working. Every once and a while they "check in" on the community (Kendall, 2002). Participation can also be interspersed with other activities at home in the evenings. Some people may devote hours a week to an online community, but they can do so in small units of time at their own convenience.

Communities based on microcontributions have relatively low barriers to entry. It is fairly easy to read enough microcontributions to know if a particular community is relevant or appropriate. If so, that same reading readily demonstrates the appropriate form that a newcomer's own microcontributions should take. The production and posting of initial microcontributions is relatively low effort. Then, if all goes well, the newcomer receives positive reinforcement in the form of (easy to produce) responding microcontributions from other community members. Whereas microcontributions create low barriers to entry, they may also create high barriers to commitment. It can be difficult to develop complex arguments or achieve nuanced understanding through microcontributions. Communities that are easy to join are often just as easy to leave (Butler, 2001).

Aggregation Mechanisms

Although people can make ad hoc contributions to online communities at random, microcontributions must be organized into larger units for efficiency and social effectiveness. Both technical and social mechanisms are employed to organize the smallest unit of contribution into larger units that are useful to participants. Software for asynchronous discussion lets people indicate that their contribution is a response to a previous one. All contributions so designated can be aggregated by the software and displayed as "threads"—a seed message and all reactions to it. Forms of threads common from the earliest days of the Net include a question with replies and a proposal or statement with comments. Threads organize microcontributions so that everyone can see their constituent parts, making it easy for potential contributors and beneficiaries to see what has already been said. (Software also allows readers to mark threads they have already read or to display only unread messages.)

Asynchronous discussion communities may have tens or hundreds of threads active at the same time, necessitating a level of organization beyond the self-organizing thread. In these cases, a human designer may suggest or impose a topic map or architecture to group threads into more general topic categories. (In some older bulletin board systems, people would vote to create a new top-level topic, which would get its own separate bulletin board.) Web-based software can display these maps graphically so that users may click on a topic that interests them and see all threads related to that topic. The shared interest of a group usually suggests the type of topical map that may be created. For example, medical concern communities may have topics for symptoms, medications and their side effects, negotiating the health care system, and managing relationships with family and friends. Movie or television fan communities may have topics for major and minor characters, actors who play those characters, and past and future episodes. Communities that build software may have categories for different types of code, bug reports, patches, and documentation.

Threads and topic maps may be insufficient to structure extremely large numbers of messages. Another form of microcontribution, the rating message, adds a quality dimension to message structuring. Some Web sites now give members the opportunity to rate the contribution of others' messages. Software then aggregates and displays these ratings in an overall quality index for contributions (e.g., Slashdot) or contributors (e.g., MotleyFool). Overt ratings of contribution quality surely increase economic trust within an electronic market such as eBay buyer and seller ratings (Kollock, 1999). It is an open question whether they increase or inhibit emotional trust and cohesiveness within an electronic community setting.

Software for synchronous interaction may organize contributions in channels or use a spatial metaphor to organize contributions in "rooms." Online communities associated with a geographic locality may organize contributions around civic functions such as the garden club or public library (e.g., Sproull & Patterson, 2004). As these communities increase in size, the organizers or members themselves construct new rooms, buildings, and territories to organize interaction. Some also offer rating and review functions to rate characters, contestants, and properties.

Norms and Motivations

Some norms of community behavior, which were visible from the early days of the ARPAnet, prevail across many types of online communities. One is peer review of content (Benkler, 2002). In most electronic discussion communities and collaborative work communities, there are no "authorities" to certify the accuracy of message content. Instead, it is expected that members themselves will comment on the quality, accuracy, completeness, and so on of one another's contributions. Similarly, peer review of behavior is also expected: it is normative for members to chastise or complain about inappropriate behavior and praise helpful behavior. Most important is the norm of altruism. Online community members freely offer information, advice, and emotional support to one another with no expectation of direct reciprocity or financial reward.

The fundamental dynamic supporting discussion communities is that someone asks a question or makes a proposal or statement and other people provide answers or comments. Utilitarian self-interest may be all that motivates the askers—a personal need for information. However, pure self-interest does not explain the behavior of people who reply. By definition, volunteer members are not paid for their replies. Because they are unlikely to have a personal relationship with the person they help, neither friendship obligation nor the expectation of direct reciprocity is likely to impel their behavior. Indeed, an early influential paper (Thorn & Connolly, 1987) predicted that computer-based information exchange systems that relied on volunteers would be doomed to failure. The authors argued that people who could give the best replies would have no incentive to participate because they would receive few benefits for doing so. It was unlikely that anyone could answer their questions; their time would be unrewarded. (In social dilemmas, helping in these situations is known as the "sucker's choice.") Over time, therefore, the quality of help would decline until people no longer even bothered to ask questions. The fallacy in this argument is the assumption that rewards to people who reply must come in the same form as the help they give. Yet, motivations for helping behavior can be quite complex. In studies of volunteers in the physical world, motivations include commitment to the cause or interest associated with the community, the desire to help others, benefits from displaying expertise, and the personal satisfaction and self-esteem derived from helping others (e.g., Clary et al., 1998; Omoto & Snyder, 1995). Studies of electronic discussion communities document a similar combination of motivations for people who answer questions and otherwise support their online community (e.g., Butler et al., 2004; Kollock, 1998; Lakhani & von Hippel, 2003; Wasko & Faraj, 2000).

In virtual reality (VR) communities, the environment indexes participants' motives (Reid, 1999). In VR game communities, the motives are tied to the rules of the game: amass property, kill enemies, design an award-winning room, and so on. In VR professional communities, the motives are tied to the profession: contribute to shared databases, review articles, participate in policy discussions, and so forth. In VR social communities, the motives are tied to exploring social worlds.

HISTORY OF ONLINE COMMUNITIES

Both the technical and social trajectories of electronic communities began with the design and early deployment of networked computing in the late 1960s and early 1970s. (See Table 1 for timeline.) Whereas computer networking was initially conceived as a way to share scarce computing resources located in one place with researchers at other places via remote access, it soon became a convenient way for people to gain remote access to other people as well as to computers (Licklider & Veza, 1978; Sproull & Kiesler, 1991). During the 1970s and 1980s, people created additional networks and wrote e-mail and bulletin board software, which represented technical innovations and improvements that made networked computing more useful for supporting human communication. During the 1990s, the technical innovations of the Web and the graphical browser supported the broad diffusion of electronic communication to millions of U.S. households and hundreds of millions of people worldwide.

The social trajectory of electronic discussion communities had its beginnings in the same technical community that invented the ARPAnet. By the mid-1970s, ARPA program officers and researchers around the country had begun using group e-mail to share results, discuss plans, and organize meetings. Some researchers also began using group e-mail for purposes unrelated to work: for example, to share opinions on cheap Chinese restaurants in Boston and Palo Alto, favorite science fiction books, inexpensive wine, and new movies. This research community invented both the technology (group communication tools) and the new form of social organization (the voluntary electronic group). They appropriated technologies that were created for utilitarian purposes to create self-organizing forums for the voluntary discussion of common interests. The social trajectory of VR communities began in 1979–1980 with an effort to program a game that would be like the fantasy game Dungeons and Dragons that was played in the physical world. The first multiuser VR game was accessible on the ARPAnet in 1980.

By the 25th anniversary of the ARPAnet in 1994, electronic group communication had become a taken-for-granted process and voluntary electronic discussion communities had become a taken-for-granted organizational form in universities, technical communities and scientific disciplines, and some corporations (e.g., Finholt & Sproull, 1990; Kiesler & Sproull, 1987; Orlikowski & Yates, 1994; Walsh & Bayma, 1996). Multiplayer games were also becoming popular on university campuses. Despite their growth, at this point both discussion groups and games were still in large measure the province of young, technically adept men. The final years of the 20th century saw Net-based communication enter the mainstream of U.S. life because of a combination of technical and economic developments. The technical

Table 1 Timeline for Community-Oriented Group Communication on the Net

Date	Name	Technical Developments	Social Developments
1965–68	ARPA projects	Research on networking to share scarce computing resources	Networking research community forms across small number of laboratories
1969	ARPAnet	First four ARPA sites connected	
1972	RD	First ARPAnet e-mail management program	
1973			75% of ARPAnet traffic is e-mail
1975	MsgGroup	First ARPAnet mailing list	
1978	BBS	First bulletin board system	
1979	Usenet	Free software to share bulletin board discussions	
1979	MUD	First multiuser VR game	
1979	CompuServe	Began offering e-mail to customers	
1980	MUD	MUD first played over ARPAnet	
1981	Bitnet	Computer network for non-ARPAnet universities	University computer center directors band together to support this
1981	Sendmail	Free software to send mail across networks	
1984–85	Delphi, Prodigy, AOL	Commercial information services founded that offered e-mail	
1985	Listserv	Free software to manage e-mail lists	
1986	IETF		Volunteers focused on technical operation and evolution of Internet
1988			>1,000 public listservs
1990			>1,000 Usenet groups; >4,000 posts per day
1990	World Wide Web	Invented by Tim Berners-Lee	
1990	LambdaMOO	VR environment created at Xerox PARC	
1991	Linux	Free computer operating system	First message about Linux posted to Usenet group
1992	AOL	Connects to Internet	
1994	Netscape	Introduced graphical Web browser	
1994			>10,000 Usenet groups; >78,000 posts per day; estimated 3.8 million subscribers to commercial online services
2000			34 million AOL subscribers; 44 million U.S. households online
2001			90,000 Usenet groups; 54,000 public Listserv groups
2004			65% of U.S. citizens are online 600 million people worldwide are online

IETF = Internet Engineering Task Force; MUD = multiuser dungeon, domain, or dimension; VR = virtual reality.

developments were the Web and the graphical browser, which made it much easier for ordinary people to find and access information and groups on the Net. The economic developments were the commercialization of the Net and AOL's business model. Once the Net began to be commercialized, corporations began to see potential economic value in electronic communities and so endeavored to support them and, indeed, to "monetize" them (e.g., Hagel & Armstrong, 1997). The online game industry began to grow. AOL's business model emphasized e-mail and member discussion forums in contrast with other commercial services that were still emphasizing access to databases. By 2000, AOL had 34 million members—more than all the other commercial services combined—and many of them were participating in electronic forums and communities of interest. That year, 44 million U.S. households were on the Net. (In 2004, nearly two thirds of Americans were online [Fallows, 2004].) Despite the enormous influx of people very different from the ARPAnet pioneers, four themes evident from the earliest days of the ARPAnet continued to characterize electronic communication at the beginning of the 21st century: access to people as much as to databases, group communication as well as dyadic communication, personal interest topics as well as utilitarian ones, and self-organizing, voluntary electronic communities.

TYPES OF ONLINE COMMUNITIES

Until the early 1990s, most electronic communities used similar technology and their members had similar attributes. Highly educated, young, technically adept people congregated electronically with similar others who shared similar interests. These congregations were relatively homogeneous in structure, process, and membership. At the beginning of the 21st century, however, the diversity of Internet users and group goals and processes is so great that it is helpful to differentiate types of communities to understand their costs and benefits in more detail. This section categorizes and describes types of online communities based on the interest that members or sponsors have in common. (See Table 2 for examples.) It is neither an exhaustive nor a mutually exclusive characterization, but it does represent some prevalent types. Despite the differences across types of shared interest, all of these communities are characterized by anytime, anyplace communication with weak social context cues, aggregated microcontributions, and norms of interaction. The boundaries across types can be fuzzy; the descriptions indicate central tendencies within types.

Types by Member Interest

Consumer Communities: Brands and Fans

Consumer communities are composed of people who share a common interest in and are loyal to a particular brand, team, entertainer, or media property. Although people organized fan clubs prior to the Net, it was difficult for them to arrange activities on a large scale and frequent basis. Online customer communities have a much broader reach. People voluntarily share their information and passion with thousands or hundreds of thousands of others who share their interests in a particular product, entertainer, or media property. AudiFans, for example, is composed of more than 1,000 Audi enthusiasts who exchange information about parts suppliers and mechanics, post photos of their cars, and share the joys and sorrows of Audi ownership. The Britney Spears portal contains pictures, MP3 files, news, and forums where thousands of people comment (positively or negatively) on all things having to do with Britney. For most members of consumer communities, the shared interest may be an intense one, but it typically represents a fairly small and often short-lived portion of members' lives.

(A)vocation Communities

Experts and enthusiasts form and join voluntary (a)vocation communities to increase their pleasure and proficiency in their hobbies or work. Whereas a particular product may be a means to advancing a common interest in an (a)vocation community, it is not the primary focus of attention as it is in a consumer community. From bicycling to computer programming, dog training to quilting, karate to the Civil War, there are online communities for people who share these interests. "How-to" information prevails in (a)vocation community discussions and people who share their expertise are greatly appreciated. Network and Internet security are topics for some (a)vocation communities. Usenet, for example, supports more than 25 groups on the topics of cracking, hacking, and network security where people discuss how to make or break secure systems. BikeForums, for example, has more than 3,500 members who discuss and debate bicycle commuting, mountain biking, tandem biking, racing, training, and so on. TappedIn is a professional VR community for K–12 educators whose 14,000 members discuss curriculum, share lesson plans, and so on. The Internet Chess Club has more than 25,000 members who play chess with other members, take lessons, play in tournaments, watch grandmaster competitions, and so on. Everquest and Ultima are large online communities for people who delight in fantasy games. The shared community interest in (a)vocation communities may represent a relatively enduring part of members' lives.

Place-Based Communities

These online communities are organized by and for people who live in a particular locale. Their genesis in the early 1980s had a political agenda—to give residents a (electronic) voice in the local political process (e.g., Schuler, 1996; Schuler & Day, 2004). More recent versions have had the broader goal of building social capital by increasing the density of electronic social connections among residents of physical communities (Hampton & Wellman, 1999; Kavanaugh, 2003; Sproull & Patterson, 2004). In principle, the shared interest should last at least as long as people reside in the community. (Recent developments like MeetUp.com let people use the Internet to find others in their geographic area who share a common interest for the purpose of scheduling face-to-face meetings. These applications are not included in this discussion because they focus primarily on arranging face-to-face meetings, not on sustaining broader electronic discussion without regard to geography.)

Table 2 Examples of Online Communities

Consumer Communities	
http://www.audifans.com	Fans of the Audi marque
http://www.lugnet.com	Adult fans of Lego
http://www.Britney-Spears-portal.com	Fans of Britney Spears
http://Rec.arts.tv.soaps	Soap opera fans
(A)vocation Communities	
http://www.mastersrowing.org	For masters rowers and scullers
http://www.bikeforums.net	For the avid cyclist
http://www.Everquest.com	For Everquest players
http://www.chessclub.com	For chess fans
http://www.tappedin.sri.com	For K–12 teachers
http://www.LambdaMoo.info/	Virtual reality environment for social interaction
Place-Based Communities	
www.bev.net	Blacksburg Electronic Village
http://web.mit.edu/knh/www/downloads/khampton01.pdf	Wired suburb of Toronto, Canada
Condition Communities	
http://www.seniornet.org	For people over age 50
http://www.systers.org	For female computer scientists
http://www.deja.com/group/alt.support.depression	Usenet group for sufferers of depression
http://www.geocities.com/heartland/prairie/4727/bhnew.htm	Mailing list for people with hearing loss
http://www.deja.com/group/rec.soc.argentina	Mailing list for Argentinian expatriates
Concern Communities	
http://www.clearwisdom.net	For practitioners of Falun Gong
http://www.419legal.org	For Internet antifraud activitists
http://www.moveon.org	For online political activists
http://www.deja.com/group/talk.guns	Usenet group for handgun advocates
http://www.deja.com/group/soc.religion.mormon	Usenet group for believers in Mormonism
Collaborative Work Communities	
http://vger.kernel.org/	Mailing list for developing the Linux kernel
http://www.wikipedia.com	Collaborative project to produce an encyclopedia
http://www.ietf.org	For maintaining and improving the Internet
http://www.rhizome.org	For creating and discussing new media art
http://www.pgdp.net	For digitizing public domain books

Common Condition Communities

In these communities, people share the experience and interest of a common condition. The condition may be based on a demographic characteristic such as race, age, or ethnic background; a medical or psychological condition such as arthritis or depression; or being an alumnus/a of a particular organization such as a college or branch of the military. People join condition communities to learn how others experience or are coping with their condition and to share their own experiences. Along with practical information and advice, a "you are not alone" sentiment prevails in many discussions. BeyondHearing, for example, has more than 1,000 members who have a hearing loss or who have a loved one with a hearing loss. Topics range from cochlear implants to the best audiologists to funny stories about lip reading mistakes. Systers' membership is more than 3,500 female computer scientists and engineers who discuss female-friendly graduate schools and employers, how to manage male subordinates in the workplace, and so on. The shared community interest is often a long-term or lifetime one for members.

Concern Communities

In these communities, members share an interest in a common political, social, or ideological concern. Because members often wish to influence the state of affairs in the physical world, these communities usually have multifaceted ties to that world. They may announce and comment on real-world events and organize letter-writing campaigns, rallies, fundraisers, and so forth. They may use click-and-donate applications to raise money or pledges of volunteer time. MoveOn, for example, began as an online petition drive to censure, but not impeach, former U.S. President Bill Clinton and has grown to include many online advocacy groups that organize volunteer campaigns. The Howard Dean presidential candidacy used the Net for organizing in 2003–2004. More than 1,000 members of soc.religion.mormon discuss and debate Mormon doctrine and practices. The shared interest of concern communities is likely to be a deep and abiding one for their members.

Collaborative Work Communities

Unlike other community types whose primary output is talk or amusement, members of collaborative work communities use the Net to voluntarily produce real products, be they software, literary works, or other creations. Much open source software is produced in voluntary communities today despite the growing interest of the corporate sector (e.g., Raymond, 1999). Indeed, much of the design and engineering of the Internet itself is accomplished by a voluntary community that conducts much of its business electronically: the Internet Engineering Task Force (n.d.). Poets participate in writers' communities whose members thoroughly critique one another's work. A more pragmatic writing community is creating a new encyclopedia. The community project has produced more than 346,000 entries as of August 2004 (http://www.wikipedia.org/wiki/Main_Page). The distributed proofreaders' project has digitized, proofread, and posted more than 5,000 public domain books. The shared interest of collaborative work communities is likely to be deeply involving for members, although it need not be as enduring as the shared interest in concern communities.

Types by Sponsor Interest

Only within the past 10 years have online communities been sponsored or organized by anyone other than members themselves (with a few exceptions such as the Well and geographically based bulletin board systems called freenets). Many recent third-party sponsors or organizers have been motivated by the profit potential of online communities with revenue models based on either sales (of advertising, membership lists, products, etc.) or subscriptions. During the dot-com boom, third-party sponsors of some customer and demographic condition communities used sales-based revenue models. Profit-oriented community sites were created for L'eggs panty hose, Kraft food products, women (iVillage), Asian Americans (Asia Street), and African Americans (NetNoir), for example. Some third-party-sponsored communities based on subscriptions are relatively healthy; arguably a substantial (but unknown) fraction of AOL's customer base is a function of online community memberships. Within the game industry, subscription-based revenue models have been successful. Several multiplayer game communities have thousands or hundreds of thousands of members. Members of one game, EverQuest, report spending an average of more than 22 hours a week playing it (Yee, 2001).

Some corporations have avoided revenue-based models and instead have supported online communities to build market share or increase customer satisfaction and loyalty. Sun Microsystems sponsors the Java Developer Connection, an (a)vocation community designed to support and expand the Java software developer community worldwide. The Lego Corporation supports several "adult –fans–of Lego" sites, in addition to sponsoring its own site, to support loyal customers. Various software companies support voluntary technical discussion and support communities in the interest of increasing high-quality, inexpensive tech support. Harley-Davidson uses H.O.G., its online members-only group, to reinforce the brand loyalty of Harley owners worldwide.

In the not-for-profit sector, foundations and service organizations have sponsored communities for their target populations with the goal of improving their welfare. Thus, for example, The Markle Foundation sponsored the creation of Seniornet, a not-for-profit online community for people over age 50, which currently has 39,000 members. The National Science Foundation sponsored TappedIn, a not-for-profit online community for K–12 schoolteachers and curriculum developers, which currently has more than 14,000 members.

ONLINE COMMUNITY CONSEQUENCES

Positive Consequences

Benefits to Members

Not surprisingly, most studies of online community members report that information benefits are important to them (e.g., Baym, 1999; Lakhani & von Hippel, 2003; Wasko & Faraj, 2002). What is noteworthy is the form that the information takes. It is not the disembodied, depersonalized information that can be found in databases or official documents, which are themselves easily accessible on the Web. Instead, it is often profoundly *personalized* information. Its form and content are personal—personal experiences and thoughts. Likewise, its audience is personal. Questions or requests for comment do not look like database queries: They are framed for human understanding and response. (A discourse analysis of Usenet groups found that almost all questions included a specific reference to readers; the few that did not were much less likely to receive replies; Galegher et al., 1998.) Replies typically address the person or situation engendering the request and are based on the replier's own situation or experience. In consumer communities, personalized information can increase members' pleasure in using or experiencing the product or property. Personalized information can increase members' pleasure or competence in practicing their (a)vocation. It can also challenge one's assumptions and beliefs (e.g., Kendall, 2002).

Members derive more than information benefits from online communities, however. Some also derive the social benefits that can come from interacting with other people: getting to know them, building relationships, making friends, having fun (e.g., Baym, 1999; Butler et al., 2004; Cummings, Sproull, & Kiesler, 2002; Kendall, 2002; Quan y Hasse, Wellman, Witte, & Hampton, 2002; Rheingold, 2002). Occasionally these social benefits are strong enough that they lead some members to organize ancillary face-to-face group activities, such as parties, rallies, show and tell, reunions, or meetings at conferences or shows.

Members of medical and emotional condition communities may derive actual health benefits from their participation in addition to information and social benefits. The evidentiary base for these benefits is small but comes from carefully designed studies that use either random assignment or statistical procedures to control for other factors that could influence health status. Benefits for active participants include shorter hospital stays (Gray et al., 2000), decrease in pain and disability (Lorig et al., 2002), greater support seeking (Mickelson, 1997), decrease in social isolation (Galegher, Sproull & Kiesler, 1998), increase in self-efficacy and psychological well-being (Cummings, Sproull & Kiesler, 2002; Mackenna & Bargh, 1998).

Membership benefits do not accrue equally to all members of online communities. Passive members, those who only read messages, as a class may benefit least. This speculation is consonant with research on groups and communities in the offline world that finds that the most active participants derive the most benefit and satisfaction from their participation (e.g., Callero, Howard, & Piliavin, 1987; Omoto & Snyder, 1995). Most studies of online communities investigate only active participants because they use the e-mail addresses of posters to identify their research population; they have no way of identifying or systematically studying people who never post but only read. Research that has studied passive members systematically finds that they report mostly information benefits; their total level of benefits is lower than that for more active participants; they are more likely to drop out (Butler, Kiesler, Kraut & Sproull, 2004; Cummings, Sproull, & Kiesler, 2002; Nonnecke & Preece, 2000).

Among active participants, people who participate more extensively report having a greater sense of online community (Kavanaugh, 2003; Quan y Hasse, Wellman, Witte, & Hampton, 2002). More frequent seekers of information report receiving more helpful replies than less frequent seekers (Lakhani & von Hippel, 2003). More frequent providers of information report greater social benefits, pleasure in helping others, and pleasure in advancing the cause of the community (Butler, Kiesler, Kraut, & Sproull, 2004).

Benefits to Third Parties

Many attempts to directly "monetize" online communities through sales revenue from advertising or commerce have been relatively disappointing (Cothrel, 2001; Figallo, 1998; Sacharow, 2000). Although the potential customer base could be quite large for brand or demographic communities, attracting and retaining customer/members is difficult. By contrast, subscription revenues—in the online game industry at least—have been relatively robust. Specific figures are hard to get from privately held companies. However, estimates are that revenues from online games were more than $200 million in 2000 and will grow to more than $1 billion in 2004 (Zito, quoted in Castronova, 2001).

In consumer communities and (a)vocation communities, substantial nonrevenue benefits may accrue to corporations through reinforcing customer brand loyalty and increasing customer satisfaction. Voluntary personal testimonials about a product or experience in the context of giving help can be quite persuasive, both to the person who asked for help or comment and to others reading the exchange. Motivational theories of attitude formation (e.g., Festinger, Schachter, & Back, 1950) and information processing theories of decision making (e.g., Nisbett & Ross, 1980) both point to the influential nature of voluntary personal testimonials. The process can be so powerful that there have been unsubstantiated reports of paid shills masquerading as community members in consumer communities (Mayzlin, 2001).

Much of the help offered in consumer communities and (a)vocational communities is personalized customer support—and potentially quite high-quality support at that. In the software industry, online communities have been recognized as the Best Technical Support Organization of the Year for 1997 and 1999 (Foster, 1999). Information that solves customers' problems or enhances their product experience is likely to increase their satisfaction and loyalty. When it is provided by self-organized volunteers, the corporate cost is minimal and the benefits are substantial.

Some online communities offer potential product development benefits. Most remarked are probably open source software communities that have generated product revenues for companies like Red Hat and product enhancements for companies like IBM and Sun Microsystems. Some game and hobby communities offer extensive product testing before widespread product release (e.g., Wallich, 2001). Some actively propose, design, and discuss new product features (von Hippel & Krogh, 2003).

The strategic question for corporations today centers on what type of corporate involvement in online communities is likely to bring the greatest benefit. With few, but important, exceptions, direct corporate ownership and control of online communities is unlikely to be the answer. (This is not to say that corporations will not benefit from Web-based sales and customer support; e-commerce can be profitable even if online community revenue models are not likely to be.) Forging positive and productive relationships with independent online communities can be challenging, however.

Benefits to Society

Rigorous empirical evidence is almost nonexistent for online community benefits to society. If members of condition communities achieve improved health status, the cost of their medical care to themselves and society could decrease. Alternatively, better-informed members may seek out additional tests or treatments, thereby increasing the cost of their care. If members of targeted populations such as K–12 schoolteachers or senior citizens derive cognitive, social, and emotional benefits from participating in online communities, then the larger society may benefit as well. Data from Blacksburg Electronic Village suggests that participation in online community activities can increase civic involvement (Kavanaugh, 1999). If members of online concern communities can more effectively mobilize, then the causes served by their advocacy are likely to benefit (e.g., Gurak, 1997; Quan y Hasse et al., 2002). Note, however, that online communities can advocate for harmful causes just as easily as they can for helpful ones.

Negative Consequences

Although anecdotes are widespread, systematic evidence on the negative consequences of online communities is sparse. Members can be harmed by erroneous, malicious, or destructive information. The norm of peer review of content in discussion communities acts as a damper on this kind of harm but cannot prevent it entirely. More seriously but less likely, individual members can be harmed by unhealthy, dangerous relationships that can form via online communities. Unscrupulous or criminal intent can be masked by an online persona that inspires trust and friendship within the community context. If a relationship moves away from community scrutiny and into private e-mail, it can lead to emotional harm, economic damage, or even physical danger. This is a particular concern when predators use online communities to identify children. Within VR communities, there have been a small number of widely publicized "attacks" that caused emotional harm to their members (Dibbell, 1998; Schwartz, 2001). A group itself can harm its members: cults can exist in cyberspace as well as in the offline world. One such, Pro-Ana, extols the joys and personal freedom of anorexia. Its members share tips on how to hide weight loss from family and friends, discuss the importance of personal choice, and praise members' announcements of their weight loss.

Although participating in an online community may not be directly harmful to its members, involved members may withdraw from their relationships and responsibilities in the offline world. People who spend a great deal of time online must be spending less time doing something else. The research thus far has only examined the effects of aggregate number of hours spent online. One study found it was associated with a small decrease in social involvement and psychological well-being for a particular group of new users (Kraut et al., 1998), but that effect was erased with continued use (Kraut et al., 2002). Some studies have found it to be associated with an expanded social circle (Katz & Apsden, 1997; Quan y Hasse et al., 2002; Kraut et al., 2002).

Just as members may be harmed by erroneous or malicious information, so too may be corporations. Corporate security weaknesses may be described and disseminated through cracker communities. Network attacks may be organized in the same way. Companies may fear liability if advice promulgated in an online community leads to product failure or product-related damages. Customer complaints can be shared very rapidly with large numbers of people and can snowball into widespread mobilization. The Intel Corporation had to manage a wave of Internet protest, much of it organized through Usenet groups, as it learned about and took steps to correct a flaw in its Pentium processor. Ultimately, of course, fixing the error benefited Intel and its customers (Uzumeri & Snyder, 1996). In a different case, members of a number of Internet groups mobilized to protest the introduction of a new household database product created by the Lotus Development Corporation. That protest led to the withdrawal of the planned product (Culnan, 1991). Online communities are not the only means of mobilizing discontent on the Net (e.g., Gurak, 1997), but because they are characterized by member commitment, they can be particularly potent.

Intellectual property infringement is another area of potential harm for corporations. Trademark infringement is easy to spot in many consumer communities. Copyright infringement can be particularly troublesome for media property companies. Fan community members create and discuss fan fiction, that is, new story lines or alternate plot endings for their favorite shows, movies, or characters. Corporations routinely issue cease and desist orders against these groups, fearing loss of copyright control (Jenkins, 2002; Silberman, 1996). As with mobilizing discontent, online communities are not the only mechanism on the Net for intellectual property infringement. Unauthorized media file sharing represents a larger area of intellectual property harm for media companies at the moment, but the social reinforcement that is generated when community members praise or critique one another's (arguably intellectual property infringing) creative work can be potent.

RESEARCH METHODS AND ISSUES

Two broad research traditions encompass much of the research on online communities. In caricature, these can be labeled "insider studies" and "outsider studies." Participant observation studies began with Howard Rheingold's (2000) description of the Well, a Northern California online community begun in 1983. Examples of scholarly ethnographies include those of a soap opera discussion community (Baym, 1999), a social MUD (Kendall, 2002), a lesbian café (Correll, 1995), and an IRC arts community (Danet, 2001). In each case, the writer/analyst was a member of the community for an extended period of time. The ethnography evokes the language, personalities, beliefs, interpretations, and daily lives of people inhabiting these worlds.

"Outsider studies" typically extract records of online behavior or attitudes for study outside the community context. Linguists may extract text records for linguistic analysis of online talk (e.g., Herring, 1996; Herring, 2001). Sociologists may analyze text records for norm development and strength (Sassenberg, 2002; Moon, 2004). Social psychologists may use questionnaires to survey community members about their social support systems in the online world and the offline world (e.g., Cummings et al., 2002; Mackenna & Bargh, 1998). Sociologists and political scientists may use questionnaires to survey members about their social and civic activities and attitudes (Kavanaugh, 1999; Wellman & Hayathornthwaite, in press).

Online communities are appealing subjects for researchers. New or newly visible social phenomena are intrinsically interesting to the social scientist. Moreover, online access to one's subjects of study offers beguiling efficiencies. Ethnographers can do ethnographic work without leaving the office. Survey researchers can administer questionnaires to multinational samples of respondents without buying a single postage stamp. Linguists have access to entire cultural corpora in digital form. The efficiencies are not problem-free, however. Ethnographers have an incomplete picture of their community members' offline lives. Survey researchers often have no access to members who never post (e.g., Nonnecke & Preece, 2000). Linguists do not see private or back channel communication. Still, despite the drawbacks, the past 10 years have seen a substantial growth in social scientists and social science methods oriented toward understanding online communities.

Whereas general principles of ethical research are widely shared within the academic social science community (and are governed by federal regulation), procedures for implementing those principles in research on online communities are under debate. Consider just the principles of informed consent and subject anonymity. If a person's words in a community discussion are considered private, consent should be obtained before analyzing them. If they are considered public, consent should be obtained before quoting them (except for fair use). If a researcher plans a participant observation study, she or he should seek permission from community members before beginning the study. Because most communities are open, members who join after the study has begun do not have the same opportunity to give or revoke permission, however. When publishing results, the researcher must honor promises of anonymity by disguising participant identity. Yet powerful full-text search engines can use verbatim text, even with no identifier, to find the original (identified) source. Bruckman (2002) pointed out that norms in the humanities encourage attribution and reproduction. Several scholarly and professional associations are currently grappling with the ethics of online research (Frankel & Siang, 1996; Thomas, 1996).

CONCLUSION

The Internet has been a home for self-organizing voluntary groups since its inception. As the Net grew, so did the pace of people and technology mutually adapting to form and support new online communities of interest (e.g., Boczkowski, 1999). Despite the large number of online communities and online community members today, the social form has been widespread for less than a decade. The nature of the Net means that experimentation and evolution into new variants of the social form can occur rapidly. The next 10 years should see more new community types, new ways of aggregating microcontributions, and new community processes.

The social form is also immature in terms of effect on members and on the offline world, but with a more differentiated view of community types, we should be able to better specify which types of online communities should or could have which kinds of effects on which types of members. Nevertheless, people also live in the offline world. The biggest online community design payoffs may come from supporting online extensions of the places where people live, work, send their kids to school, recreate, vote, and worship (e.g., Hampton, 2001). Television has had an enormous effect on family communication patterns, teen culture, political activity, and consumer behavior. Most of the decisions that led to those effects were made by an extremely small number of wealthy and influential individuals. In online communities, by contrast, everyone has the opportunity to shape the processes that will make a difference.

GLOSSARY

Dot-com Internet sites or businesses designed to make money during the late 1990s.

Internet Relay Chat (IRC) A program for simultaneous text communication among two or more users.

Listserv A program for managing a distribution list of e-mail addresses.

Multi-user Dungeon/Domain/Dimension (MUD) A text-based virtual reality environment, initially used for fantasy games, now also used for social and professional purposes.

MUD Object Oriented (MOO) Text-based virtual reality environment in which users can program objects that have persistence.

Seti@home An activity organized over the Net in which people donate idle central processor unit (CPU) cycles to process data looking for radio signals.

Usenet A system of electronic bulletin boards.

Virtual Reality (VR) A text-based or graphics-based environment that evokes a self-contained world.

Wiki A specific type of editable, Web-based document collection.

CROSS REFERENCES

See *Anonymity and Identity on the Internet; Internet Basics; Legal, Social and Ethical Issues of the Internet; Privacy Law and the Internet.*

REFERENCES

Baym, N. (1999). *Tune in, log on: Soaps, fandom, and online community (new media cultures)*. Thousand Oaks, CA: Corwin Press.

Bender, T. (1978). *Community and social change in America*. New Jersey: Rutgers University Press.

Benkler, Y. (2002). Coase's penguin, or, Linux and the nature of the firm. *The Yale Law Journal, 112*, 369–446.

Bidgoli, Hossein (ed.) (2004). *The Internet Encyclopedia*. Hoboken, NJ: John Wiley & Sons.

Boczkowski, P. J. (1999, Spring). Mutual shaping of users and technologies in a national virtual community. *Journal of Communication*, 86–108.

Bressler, S. E., & Grantham, C. E. (2000). *Communities of commerce*. New York: McGraw-Hill.

Bruckman, A. (2002). Studying the amateur artist: A perspective on disguising data collected in human subjects research on the Internet. *Ethics and Information Technology, 4*, 217–231.

Butler, B. S. (2001). Membership size, communication activity, and sustainability: The internal dynamics of networked social structures. *Information Systems Research, 12*(4), 346–362.

Butler, B. S., Kiesler, S., Kraut, R. E., & Sproull, L. (2004). Community effort in online groups: Who does the work and why? In S. Weisband & L. Atwater (Eds.), *Leadership at a Distance*. Lawrence, KA: Erlbaum. Retrieved

April 9, 2003, from http://opensource.mit.edu/papers/butler.pdf

Callero, P. L., Howard, J. A., & Piliavin, J. A. (1987). Helping behavior as a role behavior: Disclosing social structure and history on the analysis of prosocial action. *Social Psychology Quarterly, 50,* 247–256.

Carnevale, P. J., & Probst, T. M. (1997). Conflict on the Internet. In S. Kiesler (Ed.), *Culture of the Internet* (pp. 233–255). Mahwah, NJ: Erlbaum.

Castronova, E. (2001). *Virtual worlds: A first-hand account of market and society on the cyberian frontier.* Retrieved January 4, 2003, from http://papers.ssrn.com/abstract=294828

Clary, E. G., Snyder, M., Ridge, R. D., Copeland, J., Stukas, A. A., Haugen, J., et al. (1998). Understanding and assessing the motivations of volunteers: A functional approach. *Journal of Personality and Social Psychology, 74,* 1516–1530.

Correll, S. (1995). The ethnography of an electronic bar: The lesbian café. *Journal of Contemporary Ethnography, 24,* 270–298.

Cothrel, J. (2001). *Measuring the success of online communities.* Retrieved October 27, 2002, from http://www.participate.com/research/art-measuresuccess.asp

Cramton, C. (2001). The mutual knowledge problem and its consequences for dispersed collaboration. *Organization Science, 12,* 346–371.

Culnan, M. J. (1991). *The lessons of Lotus Marketplace: Implications for consumer privacy in the 1990s.* Presented at the First Conference on Computers, Freedom and Privacy. Retrieved October 27, 2002, from http://www.cpsr.org/conferences/cfp91/culnan.html

Cummings, J., Sproull, L., & Kiesler, S. (2002). Beyond hearing: Where real world and online support meet. *Group Dynamics: Theory, Research, and Practice, 6,* 78–88.

Danet, B. (2001). *Cyberpl@y: Communicating online.* Oxford, UK: Berg; distributed in the United States by NYU Press.

Dibbell, J. (1998). *My tiny life: Crime and passion in a virtual world.* New York: Holt.

Etzioni, A., & Etzioni, O. (1999). Fact-to-face and computer-mediated communities, a comparative analysis. *The Information Society, 15,* 241–248.

Fallows, D. (2004). *The Internet and daily life.* Washington, DC: Pew Internet and American Life Project.

Festinger, L., Schachter, S., & Back, K. (1950). *Social pressures in informal groups.* New York: Harper.

Figallo, C. (1998). *Hosting Web communities: building relationships, increasing customer loyalty, and maintaining a competitive edge.* New York: Wiley.

Finholt, T., & Sproull, L. (1990). Electronic groups at work. *Organization Science, 1,* 41–64.

Foster, E. (1999). Best technical support: It may not be the guy on the telephones any more. *InfoWorld.* Retrieved from http://www.infoworld.com/articles/op/xml/99/11/29/991129opfoster.xml

Frankel, M. S., & Siang, S. (1999). Ethical and legal aspects of human subjects research on the Internet: A report of a workshop. Retrieved from http://www.aaas.org/spp/dspp/sfrl/projects/intres/main.htm

Galegher, J., Sproull, L., & Kiesler, S. (1998). Legitimacy, authority, and community in electronic support groups. *Written Communication, 15,* 493–530.

Gray, J. E., Safran, C., Davis, R. B., Pompilio-Wietzner, G., Stewart, J. E., Zacagnini. L., et al. (2000). Baby CareLink: Using the Internet and telemedicine to improve care for high-risk infants. *Pediatrics, 106,* 1318–1324.

Gurak, L. J. (1997). *Persuasion and privacy in cyberspace: The online protests over Lotus Marketplace and the clipper chip.* New Haven, CT: Yale University Press.

Hagel, J., & Armstrong, A. G. (1997). *Net gain: Expanding markets through virtual communities.* Cambridge, MA: Harvard Business School Press.

Hampton, K. N. (2001). Living the wired life in the wired suburb. Unpublished doctoral dissertation, University of Toronto.

Hampton, K. N., & Wellman, B. (1999). Netville online and offline: Observing and surveying a wired suburb. *American Behavioral Scientist, 43,* 475–492.

Herring, S. (2001). Computer-mediated discourse. In D. Schriffin, D. Tannen, & H. E. Hamilton (Eds.), *Handbook of discourse analysis* (pp. 612–634). Oxford: Blackwell Publishing Ltd.

Herring, S. (1994). Politeness in computer culture: Why women thank and men flame. In M. Bucholtz, A. C. Liang, L. A. Sutton, & C. Hines. (Eds.), *Cultural Performances: Proceedings of the Third Berkeley Women and Language Conference* (pp. 278–294). Berkeley: Berkeley Women and Language Group, University of California.

Herring, S. (Ed.). (1996). *Computer-mediated communication: Linguistic, social and cross-cultural perspectives.* Amsterdam: John Benjamins.

Internet Engineering Task Force. (n.d.). A novice's guide to the Internet Engineering Task Force. Retrieved September 22, 2002, from http://www.ietf.org/tao.html

Jenkins, H. (2002, July). Treating viewers as criminals. *Technology Review.*

Katz, J. E., & Aspden, P. (1997). A nation of strangers? *Communications of the ACM, 40,* 81–86.

Kavanaugh, A. (2003). When everyone is wired. In J. Turow & A. Kavenaugh (Eds.), *The Wired Homestead.* Cambridge: The MIT Press.

Kendall, L. (2002). *Hanging out in the virtual pub: Masculinities and relationships online.* Berkeley, CA: University of California Press.

Kiesler, S., & Sproull, L. (1987). *Computing and change on campus.* New York: Cambridge University Press.

Kim, A. J. (2000). *Community building on the Web: Secret strategies for successful online communities.* Berkeley, CA: Peachpit Press.

Knoke, D. (1986). Associations and interest groups. *Annual Review of Sociology, 12,* 1–21.

Kollock, P. (1999). The production of trust in online markets. *Advances in Group Processes, 16,* 99–123.

Kollock, P. (1998). The economics of on-line communication. In M. A. Smith & P. Kollack (Eds.), *Communities in cyberspace.* London: Routledge.

Kollock, P., & Smith, M. (1996). Managing the virtual commons: Cooperation and conflict in computer communities. In S. C. Herring (Ed.), *Computer mediated communication: Linguistic, social, and cross-cultural perspectives* (pp. 226–242). Philadelphia: Benjamins.

Kraut, R., Patterson, M., Lundmark, V., Kiesler, S., Mukophadhyay, T., & Scherlis, W. (1998). Internet paradox: A social technology that reduces social involvement and psychological well-being? *American Psychologist, 53,* 1017–1031.

Kraut, R., Kiesler, S., Boneva, B., Cummings, J., Helgeson, V., & Crawford, A. (2002). Internet paradox revisited. *Journal of Social Issues, 58,* 49–74.

Lakhani, K. R., & von Hippel, E. (2003). How open source software works: Free user to user assistance. *Research Policy, 32*(6): 923–943.

Licklider, J. C. R., & Veza, A. (1978). Applications of information networks. *IEEE Proceedings, 66,* 1330–1346.

Lorig, K. R., Lorca, K. R., Laurent, D. D., Deyo, R. A., Marnell, M. E., Minor, M. A., et al. (2002). Can a back pain e-mail discussion group improve health status and lower health care costs? *Archives of Internal Medicine, 162,* 792–796.

Mackenna, K. Y. A., & Bargh, J. A. (1998). Coming out in the age of the Internet: Identity 'de-marginalization' from virtual group participation. *Journal of Personality and Social Psychology, 75,* 681–694.

Mayzlin, D. (2001). *Promotional chat on the Internet.* Unpublished manuscript, Yale University.

Mickelson, K. D. (1997). Seeking social support: Parents in electronic support groups. In S. Kiesler (Ed.), *Culture of the Internet* (pp. 157–178). Mahwah, NJ: Erlbaum.

Moon, J. (2004). Identification processes in distributed electronic groups: A study of voluntary technical support groups on the Net. Unpublished doctoral dissertation, New York University.

Nisbett, R., & Ross, L. (1980). *Human inference: Strategies and shortcomings of social judgment.* Englewood Cliffs, NJ: Prentice-Hall.

Nonnecke, B., & Preece, J. (2000). Lurker demographics: Counting the silent. In *Computer-Human Interaction 2000* (pp. 73–80). New York: ACM Press.

Omoto, A., & Snyder, M. (1995). Sustained helping without obligation: Motivation, longevity of service, and perceived attitude change among AIDS volunteers. *Journal of Personality and Social Psychology, 68,* 671–687.

Orlikowski, W., & Yates, J. (1994). Genre repertoire: The structuring of communicative practices in organizations. *Administrative Science Quarterly, 39,* 541–574.

Powazek, D. (2002). *Design for community: The art of connecting real people in virtual places.* Indianapolis, IN: New Riders.

Preece, J. (2000). *Online communities: Designing usability, supporting sociability.* New York: Wiley.

Quan y Hasse, A., Wellman, B., Witte, J. & Hampton, K. (2002). Capitalizing on the Internet: Social contact, civic engagement, and sense of community. In B. Wellman & C. Haythornthwaite (Eds.), *The Internet in Everyday Life,* pp. 291–394. Oxford: Blackwell.

Raymond, E. (1999). *The cathedral & the bazaar: Musings on Linux and Open Source by an accidental revolutionary.* Cambridge, MA: O'Reilly.

Reid, E. (1999). *Hierarchy and power: Social control in cyberspace.* In M. A. Smith & P. Kollock (Eds.), *Communities in cyberspace* (pp. 107–133). London: Routledge.

Rheingold, H. (2000). *The virtual community* (rev. ed.). Cambridge: MIT Press.

Sacharow, A. (2000). *Consumer-created content: Creating and valuing user-generated programming. Vision Report.* New York: Jupiter Media Metrix.

Sassenberg, K. (2002). Common bond and common identity groups on the Internet; Attachment and normative behavior in on-topic and off-topic chats. *Group Dynamics, 6,* 27–37.

Schuler, D. (1996). *New community networks: Wired for change.* Reading MA: Addison-Wesley.

Schuler, D. and Day, P. (eds.) (2004). *Shaping the Network Society: The Future of the Public Sphere in Cyberspace.* Cambridge: MIT Press.

Schwartz, J. (2001, January 4). Virtual mayhem arouses real anger at hackers' attack. *New York Times.* Retrieved January 4, 2003, from http://www.nytimes.com/2001/01/04/technology/04HACK.html.

Silberman, S. (1996). Paramount locks phasers on Trek fan sites. *Wired News.* Retrieved February 12, 2001, from http://www.wired.com/news/culture/0,1284,1076,00.html

Sproull, L., & Faraj, S. (1995). Atheism, sex and databases: The net as a social technology. In B. Kahin & J. Keller (Eds.), *Public access to the Internet* (pp. 62–81). Cambridge, MA: MIT Press.

Sproull, L., & Kiesler, S. (1991). *Connections: New ways of working in the networked organization.* Cambridge, MA: MIT Press.

Sproull, L., & Patterson, J. (2004). Making information cities livable. *Communications of the ACM, 47*(2), 33–37.

Thomas, J. (Ed.). (1996). *The Information Society, 12* [Special issue].

Thorn, B. K., & Connolly, T. (1987). Discretionary data bases; a theory and some experimental findings. *Communication Research, 14,* 512–528.

Uzumeri, M. V., & Snyder, C. A. (1996). Information technology and accelerated science: The case of the Pentium™ Flaw. *California Management Review, 38,* 44–63.

VonHippel, E., and Krogh, V. (2003). Opensource software and the "Private-Collective" innovation model: Issues for organization Science. *Organization Science, 14,* 209–223.

Wallich, P. (2001, September). Mindstorms: Not just a kid's toy. *IEEE Spectrum,* 52–57.

Walsh, J. P., & Bayma, T. (1996). The virtual college: Computer-mediated communication and scientific work. *The Information Society, 12,* 343–363.

Wasko, M. M., & Faraj, S. (2000). "It is what one does": Why people participate and help others in electronic communities of practice. *Journal of Strategic Information Systems, 9,* 155–173.

Wellman, B., & Haythornthwaite, C. (Eds.). (2002). *The Internet in everyday life.* Oxford, UK: Blackwell.

Werry, C., & Mowbray, M. (2000). *Online communities: Commerce, community action, and the virtual university.* New York: Prentice-Hall.

Winzelberg, A. (1997). The analysis of an electronic support group for individuals with eating disorders. *Computers in Human Behavior, 13,* 393–407.

Yee, N. (2001). *The Norrathian scrolls: A study of Ever Quest.* Retrieved from http://www.nickyee.com/eqt/report.html

Groupware: Risks, Threats, and Vulnerabilities in the Internet Age

Pierre Balthazard, *Arizona State University*
John Warren, *University of Texas, San Antonio*

INTRODUCTION

Groupware refers to computer- and network-based technologies that help people accomplish a group's objective. Some forms provide greater support for real-time collaboration (such as electronic meeting support systems, chat rooms, shared whiteboards, and real-time videoconferencing) than others, some can support the individual's work, as well as work that can only be accomplished collaboratively (collective writing, for example). Helping people who are in the same place at the same time (meetings, for example) is the forte of some types of groupware, whereas other forms excel at connecting group members who might be continents and time zones away (such as e-mail and shared database access). Some are geared to support specific group subtasks (e.g., shared calendaring and scheduling, e-mail), whereas some forms are designed for a wider array of integrated support functions (such as dispersed project management). To make this more complicated, the Internet has driven both the amazing popularity and adoption of these tools, but has also driven the creation of new classes of tools that are proving important (shared databases, for example). In this chapter, we first remark on the reason for groupware and then present some defining concepts and classifications for these myriad of tools. We then explore some generic and common functionalities of groupware tools, turn to detailed descriptions of some popular modern examples, and show how these examples map to our classifying scheme. We then adopt a management perspective and present a theory-based framework for mapping these functionalities to the varying circumstances of individual and group work. The final part of the chapter addresses issues of human productivity and groupware as well as issues surrounding the changes in organizational and human processes that often accompany the proliferation of groupware-supported work.

WHY GROUPWARE?

There has been more than five centuries of research devoted to group and team processes in an effort to understand why the desired synergy of group work is often elusive and why the group work is instead often difficult and inefficient. Figure 1 lists the more common positive (+) and negative (−) influences on collaborative work.

Many things can go wrong with group work. Participants may fail to understand their goals, may lack focus, or may have hidden agendas. Some people may be afraid to speak up, whereas others may dominate the discussion. Misunderstandings occur through different interpretations of language, gesture, or expression. Besides being difficult, teamwork is expensive. A meeting of several managers or executives may cost several thousands of dollars per hour in salary costs alone. In *Fortune 500* companies, there are more than 12 million formal meetings per day in the United States. That is more than three billion meetings per year. American managers typically spend about 20% of their time in formal meetings and up to 85% of their time communicating. For all its difficulties, though, group work is still essential. People must still collaborate to solve tough problems. And, as business becomes more global in scope and computers become more ubiquitous in the workplace, the need for collaboration–and the means to achieve it–has surely continued to increase. Enter groupware, with functionalities that, when appropriately selected, applied, and managed, can bring users tremendous support for their group's tasks (Collaborative Strategies, 2002).

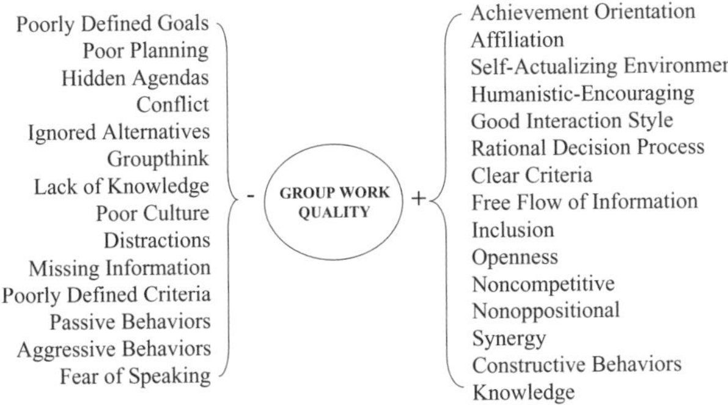

Figure 1: Influences on the quality of group work.

GROUPWARE AND SECURITY

Groupware systems, including group support systems (GSS), group decision support systems (GDSS), and electronic meeting systems (EMS), all have one thing in common. They use computer technology to facilitate the exchange of information and ideas between individuals and teams. Often, teams use these technologies to facilitate teamwork in distributed environments where the members are often separated by spatial distance and time.

Every organization in today's global, wired environment should be concerned about information systems security. Of particular importance should be the goal of keeping systems and data that are used by teams working in distributed environments secure from unauthorized access. However, as indicated by recent hacker attacks (e.g., "slammer worm"), companies are still experiencing problems keeping their information safe. Teams that work in distributed environments using groupware must be very careful about what kind of information they are exchanging and via what means. The security of the network and software is very important. The risk of exchanging valuable and proprietary information through insecure media can lead to considerable financial losses.

Slammer: The First Flash Attack Worm

On Saturday, January 25, 2002, at 05:30 UCT, a worm began to spread throughout the Internet. This worm was called by several names, including Sapphire and Slammer. The worm spread with astonishing speed. Slammer reached its peak packet-attack traffic in an amazing 3 min. Within 10 min, it had infested about 90% of all vulnerable hosts on the Internet. Although Slammer was brought under control within hours, it had achieved its aim of infesting nearly all vulnerable servers before the world even realized what was happening.

Many articles described Slammer as a minor attack that did not do widespread damage. However, although Slammer did not delete files or do other deliberate damage, it took many critical database servers out of service, resulting in extensive damage worldwide. Most of Bank of America's 13,000 automated teller machines (ATMs) became unavailable. Continental Airlines experienced some flight delays because of the need to revert to paper transaction handling. A Boston medical center experienced slowdowns for about 6 hr, during which the center had to revert to paper-based processing for patient orders and other processes. Police and fire dispatchers outside Seattle also had to revert to slow paper processing at a 911 call center serving two suburban police departments and at least 14 fire departments. Other companies hit by the worm included Countrywide Financial Corporation, American Express, and several U.S. and Canadian banks (Panko, 2003).

Defining the Problem

A survey conducted by the CSI/FBI indicated that 75% of surveyed firms and agencies detected computer security breaches and acknowledged financial losses as a result of computer breaches (Power, 2002). Through the continual monitoring of hundreds of *Fortune 500* companies, Symantec found that general Internet attack trends are showing a 64% annual rate of growth (Anderson & Shane, 2002). Information systems are not necessarily risky. However, when humans interact with computer systems, it is the behavior of humans that is risky. Thus, the analysis of threats/risk in groupware should start with the analysis of the behavior of individuals, and technological improvements in system security should be based on an analysis of human behavior.

In a study investigating areas of risk in groupware (Gallegos, 1999), the authors indicated that one of the greatest risks is the possibility of information leaks that would permit outsiders to assess the present state and characteristics of an organization. Controls should be provided for the security of sensitive information wherever a user has contact with data. Methods should focus on controlling access to the organizational databases and controlling the use of data. Controls must also exist to detect and report possible security violations.

Beyond common sense, there are now "enhanced regulatory compliance" provisions from the federal government that affect the implementation and use of groupware systems in organizations. We will introduce here the HIPAA and Sarbanes–Oxley Act.

- **HIPAA.** HIPAA is an acronym for the Health Insurance Portability and Accountability Act of 1997. This is a federal law that protects the privacy of a patient's personal and health information and provides for electronic and physical security of personal and health information. It affects companies that store and transmit protected health information in electronic form, which includes health plans, health care clearinghouses, and health care providers. HIPAA is not legislation that sets standards for computer applications' functional capabilities. It sets standards of behavior and requires the use of best practice.

  All health care organizations and related entities must implement complete and effective security solutions that will protect their valuable information assets. The portion of HIPAA that is security related can be found in Title II, which includes a section, known as "administrative simplification," that requires improved efficiency in healthcare delivery by standardizing electronic data interchange, protection of confidentiality, and security of health data through setting and enforcing standards.

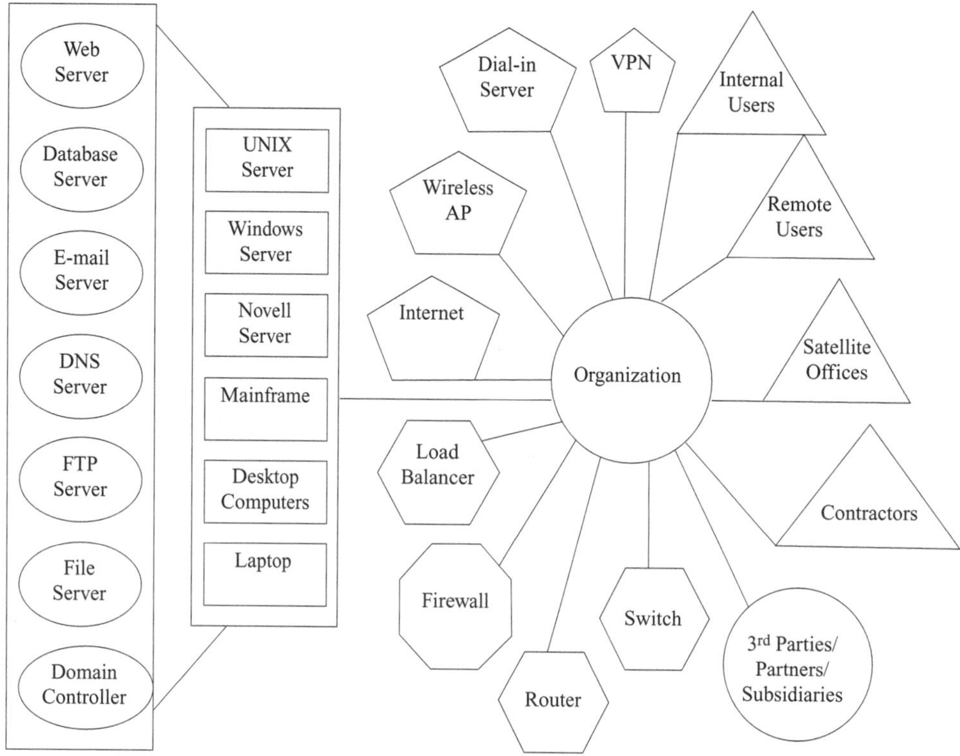

Figure 2: Common network security target model.

At the time of this writing, there was no HIPAA compliant software, HIPAA providers, HIPAA firewall, or any other HIPAA security term for which you could put the characters "HIPAA" in front of. The issue is applying adequate security to your processes and treating patient data according to HIPAA privacy regulation. Two ways to ensure compliance are by (a) deploying digital signature technology and (b) using public key infrastructure (PKI) to protect information integrity (Articsoft, 2003).

- **Sarbanes—Oxley Act.** The Sarbanes–Oxley Act of 2002 includes provisions addressing audits, financial reporting and disclosure, conflicts of interest, and corporate governance at public companies. It holds executives personally liable for many operational aspects of a company, including computer security, by making them pledge that the company's internal controls are adequate.

Under this legislation, the Securities and Exchange Commission holds executives accountable for reliable internal controls, record retention, and fraud detection. As a result, executives are looking to information systems (IS) and to IS auditors for help (Volonino, Gessner, & Kermis 2004). They state that

> while the act stops short of mandating detailed security provisions, the requirements for companies to produce audit reports is driving a recognition that IT security policies and procedures are an essential part of the process.... 'Enhanced Regulatory Compliance' regulations, such as Gramm–Leach–Bliley, SARBOX, and HIPAA, require organizations to ensure that unauthorized users cannot access systems that contain sensitive data.

Groupware Risks, Threats, and Vulnerabilities

Risks, threats, and vulnerabilities are constantly changing as the technologies used by different organizations change and new technologies are created, and as threats adapt and evolve with the technology. Figure 2 (Horton and Mugge, 2003) depicts a model that indicates different areas of an information system network that should be considered for protection. In the model, it identifies the key services and applications present, such as the organization's firewall, users, contractors, and so forth. Next, the operating systems exposed should be inventoried and, finally back-end organization should be defined, keeping in mind reliance on people, process, and technology.

E-mail has traditionally been considered to be a separate application from groupware. In a true groupware implementation, for security reasons, there should be minimal or no content exchanged via e-mail. However, e-mail is increasingly being integrated with groupware (e.g., Lotus Notes, Groove, Kubi, and Microsoft Outlook). For example, Kubi Software's groupware product "enables business users to collaborate spontaneously without having to leave Email—the application in which they 'live' for most of the business day" (Kubi Software, 2004). Today, we have access to increasingly rich graphic interfaces that provides workspaces in a familiar e-mail environment.

Many distributed teams communicate via e-mail because it is fast, very familiar to users, inexpensive, and convenient. However, it can also expose private messages to "snoopers" and "hackers" if not encrypted. Users of e-mail must be careful about messages that have files attached that may be suspicious. These files can carry viruses, worms, or other malicious computer code. A virus can be damaging to distributed computer systems because it spreads by executing infected programs. Worms are self-propagating malicious pieces of computer codes that are highly automated.

Parasites refer to unsolicited commercial software that often gets installed on computers, unbeknown to the user. Antivirus software programs or firewalls often do not detect these programs. These programs can cause unwanted pop-up advertising, capture information about the user's activities on the Web, and sometimes alter browser settings.

Deception

The visual anonymity inherent in most computer-mediated communication (CMC) systems results in a lack of certainty regarding an individual's identity. This provides opportunities for users to engage in different types of deception practices. Deception is an area in computer-mediated communications that has only recently begun to receive attention. It is defined by Buller and Burgoon as "a message knowingly transmitted by a sender to foster a false belief or conclusion by the receiver" (Buller & Burgoon, 1994).

It should come as no surprise that information technology (IT) is being used to transmit deceptive information, given that deceptive communication is common during traditional face-to-face interactions and given that CMC is widely used in organizations and individual homes (e.g., instant messaging, e-mail, discussion groups, usernets, etc.). Some of the ways in which humans deceive others in CMC generally include identity play, impersonations, lies, fabrications, concealments, misdirection, bluffs, trolling, fakery, deflections, evasions, exaggerations, and the like. More specific and increasingly troublesome forms of deception are e-mail hoaxes, social engineering, and gender bending.

Examples of e-mail hoaxes include claims offering recipients money for forwarding messages to others and messages warning recipients to delete virus files on their computers that are really system files. Social engineering occurs when a person poses as someone else to obtain access to off-limits information or to persuade the deceived to comply with some other type of request. It has been described as "hacker-speak" for tricking a person into revealing a password. A classic social engineering trick is for a hacker to send e-mail claiming to be a system administrator. The hacker will claim to need your password for some important system administration work and ask you to e-mail it to him/her. Often the hacker will send this message to every user on a system, hoping that one or two users will fall for the trick. Similarly, "phishing" is an increasingly common practice where cyberthieves fish for information among thousands of potential victims, using cleverly disguised e-mails to trick recipients into volunteering personal and financial information. The e-mails claim to be from a legitimate source, such as a bank or government entity, and usually ask recipients to update their account or personal information.

Gender bending involves experimenting with gender identities in CMC. This phenomenon is more commonly observed in multiple user dialogues (MUDs) and in chat rooms. It often involves men posing as women, women posing as men, or either posing as nongendered or "neutral" characters.

The problem is that people are not very good at detecting deception, especially in CMC, where there is often the absence of certain verbal and nonverbal cues. George and Marett suggest that one possible remedy for improving detection accuracy is to educate people about various indications of deception and then train them to spot these indicators when they are used in normal communication (George & Marett, 2004).

Denial of Service

DoS and DDoS (denial-of-service and distributed denial-of-service) attacks have been a growing concern as more and more businesses do business via the Internet. DoS attacks are deliberate attempts by intruders to prevent legitimate users from accessing and using a site or a particular service. In DDoS attacks, the Internet is often used to break into computers, thereby using the compromised computers to attack a network. As a result, several computers across the Internet can be used to attack other systems. Such attacks can be directed at an operating system or at the network. Routers can also be used as attack platforms. Some examples of DoS and DDoS attacks include

- attempts to "flood" a network, thereby preventing legitimate traffic;
- attempts to disrupt connections between two machines, thereby preventing access to a service;
- attempts to prevent a particular individual from accessing a service;
- attempts to disrupt service to a specific system or person; and
- consumption of scarce resources (Cert Coordination Center, 2001).

Bandwidth consumption is a kind of DoS attack where an intruder uses up all of the victim's bandwidth or uses all of a system's resources on a server. Intruders can also shut down a system by generating an excessive number of e-mail messages, thus flooding the network.

DoS Attack

In February 2000, a number of popular Web sites were slowed or shut down by distributed denial of service attacks. Amazon.com, buy.com, CNN.com, eBay, E*Trade, and ZDNet were all victims of these attacks. Analysts estimated that Yahoo! lost $500,000 in e-commerce and advertising revenue when it was knocked offline for 3 hr (Dunne, 2001).

Solutions for Security Problems

Tackling the information security problem for individuals using groupware can be achieved in much the same way as with computer systems in general. This can be achieved by the organization's creation of a team responsible for evaluating the various internal and external risks and their potential effects on the organization, and then developing and practicing a detailed, comprehensive, and easy-to-follow plan. The goal should be to avoid unauthorized access, prevent intrusion, and stop secret information disclosure.

Risk Analysis

An analysis of risk should include both internal and external risks. Internal risks include human error and physical computer security threats. External risks include the potential for unauthorized users to gain access to computer systems.

Cryptography software is used to protect companies from hackers. This software encrypts and decrypts messages. Encryption transforms (scrambles) data into unreadable forms, and decryption restores data to the original forms. Secure socket layer protocol (SSL) provides a method that encrypts information passed between a server and a browser (on the client machine) to prevent others from accessing user information.

Access Controls

To gain access to the system, users should be required to authenticate their identities via the use of password codes (e.g., personal identification numbers), magnetically coded badges, voice print analysis, or other biometric authentication devices. Procedures should exist to authenticate which users will have read-only, write-only, or read-and-write access.

Other measures include third-party certification, firewalls, and intrusion detection systems. Third-party certification refers to a neutral third party who has verified the authenticity of a Web site and has issued the owners of that Web site a unique certificate (e.g., VeriSign, Inc. is a certificate provider). Firewalls are software or hardware that is placed between the company's network and the Internet to provide ongoing protection by denying suspicious traffic. An intrusion detection system informs companies when they are under attack.

Horton and Mugge (Horton & Mugge, 2003) give the following as effective security defense measures:

- Protect user accounts.
- Protect administrative accounts and remote management interfaces.
- Protect against Trojan applications, viruses, and other malicious scripts.
- Protect against software architecture design flaws.
- Protect against system and application configuration errors.
- Protect against software programming errors.
- Protect against user naiveté, carelessness, or stupidity.
- Protect against eavesdropping (from network sniffing to shoulder surfing).
- Protect against user impersonation (electronically or by phone).
- Protect against physical theft (office, datacenter, traveling, and remote locations).
- Protect against inappropriate use of resources.

Symantec provides the following 10 steps to protect your enterprise from denial of service attacks (http://enterprisesecurity.symantec.com):

1. Adopt a security policy and educate, educate, educate.
2. Use multiple internet service providers (ISPs, i.e., use different providers who use different pipes).
3. Practice good load balancing. Distribute your site's load across multiple servers—even multiple sites, if possible.
4. Insure redundancy (or "fail over") in all network devices, servers, and power sources.
   Develop recovery plans covering each potential failure point for your site.
5. Protect your critical systems with a hardened firewall. Although any firewall can control access by using Internet protocol (IP) addresses and allowing "only port 80" to the Web server, be sure your firewall also can analyze the incoming Web access data stream to filter out sophisticated attacks embedded within the protocol and hypertext markup language (HTML).
6. Auto-check your Web site.
7. Keep the system simple. Minimize the number of services running on the systems by turning off the options you don't need.
8. Stay current on upgrades, updates, vendor advisories, and security bulletins.
9. Stay vigilant through testing and monitoring.
10. Be ready to respond.

DEFINING AND CLASSIFYING GROUPWARE IN THE INTERNET AGE

Groupware is technology—typically software and networks—designed to support people working in groups. Under this broad definition, any technology that is used to communicate, cooperate, coordinate, solve problems, compete, or negotiate is classified as groupware. This definition can apply to some of the newest forms such as informational Web pages and multiuser database applications, as well as to more established and familiar forms such as e-mail, newsgroups, videophones, or chat. The simplicity and breadth of this definition is intentional because definitions of groupware tend to evolve as rapidly as the technologies themselves, often becoming outdated because new technologies support group work in ways that were not represented. For example, an early definition for groupware was "intentional group processes plus software to support them." At the time, this definition placed more emphasis on the activities of the group and much less on the technologies, which were quite limited. As we will see, although much of that early definition is valid, the reality that it does not address is that much group work contains a great deal of individual work. Many modern forms of groupware, as we explain, support not only the actual group work, but also much of the individual group members' work that may precede, be contemporaneous with, or follow that actual interactive group processes.

Table 1 Traditional Dimensions of Groupware

	Same time (synchronous)	Different time (asynchronous)
Same place (collocated)	GSS, GDSS, presentation support	shared workspaces
Different place (dispersed)	videophones, whiteboards, chat, virtual rooms	e-mail, threaded discussion, workflow

A later definition of groupware by Robert Johansen (1988) is "specialized computer aids that are designed for the use of collaborative work groups." Again, this definition rightly focused on the actual group collaborative processes but does not mirror the current reality of how the tools extend to support the individual work processes that underpin group work. A major contribution by Johansen and others, however, was to provide a categorization scheme for groupware technologies that is still valuable today. As shown in Table 1, groupware technologies can largely be categorized along two primary dimensions:

1. whether users of the groupware are working together at the same time (real-time or synchronous groupware) or different times (asynchronous groupware), and
2. whether users are working together in the same place (collocated or face-to-face) or in different places (distributed or dispersed).

Another way to understand groupware is by the generic group processes that it supports: communication (pushing or pulling information), collaboration (sharing information and building shared understanding), and coordination (delegating task, group technique, sequential sign-offs, etc.). Some definitions of groupware call erroneously for the added dimension of a common goal. Although all systems require some agreement among participants (at minimum that they should agree to participate in the process), groupware can readily support negotiation-type interactions. Management of conflict is often a crucial feature of a groupware system (a voting tool is a good example of this incorporated in groupware designed to support meetings). However, this classification scheme also does not pay much attention to individual work processes that can be supported by groupware and are a component of group work, and it does not emphasize geographic location or temporality.

To build on these earlier perspectives and integrate them with the realities of individual work processes, as well as to reflect the ubiquity of access afforded by the Internet (and, commonly, proprietary organizational networks and intranets), we offer a new model of groupware. Table 2 illustrates an emerging model for groupware as represented by a 3 × 3 matrix of the nine discrete yet interrelated software groups. From a user's perspective, the horizontal axis represents a spectrum between synchronous and asynchronous functionality (in typical usage) but now includes "any time/any place" to connote the accessibility to information or functionality that the tool can provide. As we discuss, many modern forms of groupware, although primarily synchronous or asynchronous, have features that are accessible any time and any place if one has an Internet or intranet connection and a browser (Coleman, 1997). The vertical axis represents the group size targeted by the technology. In this representation, the "place" dimension of Table 1 has disappeared—networks have so increased in speed and computers have become so ubiquitous and powerful that geographical dispersion has

Table 2 Categorization of Groupware Systems by Time and Targeted User Audience

	Asynchronous groupware	Any time/Any place groupware	Synchronous groupware
Large	Database-oriented Portals Collaborative portals E-community Newsgroup/Usenet List servers	E-learning/virtual classrooms	Web real-time communication (RTC) Audio/video conferencing
Limited	Telework virtual workplaces Workflow systems Personal portals Group calendars	Distributed project management Collaborative writing Threaded discussion	Group decision support systems (GDSS) Meeting support Chat Shared whiteboard
Individual/dyad	Electronic mail	Mobile/wireless messaging	Collaborative customer relationship management (CRM)

lost its categorization power. For instance, any computer-supported meeting can be attended in face-to-face mode or by cyberspace connection.

GROUPWARE FUNCTIONALITIES IN THE INTERNET AGE

Common Groupware Functionalities

Although stand-alone groupware components such as e-mail can still be purchased separately, many modern products offer a number of common functionalities (e.g., e-mail) integrated in one suite. These common functionalities (or characteristics) might include the following:

- **Graphical user interfaces (GUIs).** Most groupware programs today can take advantage of the color graphics and sound capabilities of multimedia computers. They are often made available via the Internet as either a client/server application or an application that uses a common browser interface.
- **WYSIWIS.** This stands for What You See Is What I See. It is analogous to two people each at their own homes watching the same television show at the same time. Computer technology extends this concept in groupware products and allows users to interact and communicate in a WYSIWIS environment.
- **Integration.** Most groupware products integrate components of different applications into a standard interface so the product feels like a multifaceted tool.
- **Online communication.** Discussions can be held in real time, with active interaction between participants. Several products allow for textual and video exchanges in real time.
- **Replication/synchronization.** Replication is the process of duplicating and updating data in multiple computers on a network, some of which are permanently connected to the networks. Others, such as laptops, may only be connected at intermittent times. Synchronization is the goal of having all computers in a distributed network providing the same information at the same time. The replication/synchronization concept has two components: (a) everyone should have access to the same information in the database and be able to replicate the data locally; (b) several users can make changes to the same document, and somehow the system synchronizes all those changes into one master copy of the database. If the replication manager has multiple update requests to the same record, the system sends messages out asking for clarification as to what the correct entry should be. An example of this function is the use of a shared database of product inventory by a distributed sales force. When each person sells some units, the database would update itself so that there is an accurate count of inventory available to all users.
- **Remote access.** Using database replication/synchronization, remote users can access and update information held in a groupware database (see previous example).
- **Workflow.** Workflow is a typical groupware subsystem that manages a task through the steps required for its completion. It results in the automation of standard procedures (such as records management in personnel operations) by imposing a set of agreed-upon business rules on the procedure. Each task (or set of tasks), when finished, automatically initiates the next step in the process, until the entire procedure is completed. Although some users implement self-contained work flow systems, the technology often appears in more recent groupware and image management systems. Lotus Notes for Domino, for example, provides work flow applications that can be customized to an organization's particular needs.
- **Time management.** These groupware products offer group calendar diaries and group project schedules to help managers and subordinates better coordinate their time. Microsoft Outlook, among other products, offers these and related functionalities.
- **Secretarial functions.** These are background processes that perform "clean up" or "overhead" services for users. For example, the secretary would manage the real-time messaging system to manage the receipt of messages by accepting high-priority interactions but blocking unnecessary interruptions and redirecting (and prioritizing) those less important messages to the users' electronic mail platform. These filtering functions are common in many e-mail groupware products.
- **Project management.** Groupware's increasing adoption is due to its ability to easily support project management endeavors. As personal computers and networks have become more powerful, they provide the necessary performance for today's groupware, imaging, and document management applications. These technologies, originally distinct, have become more integrated in many organizations with the aim of supporting project management. This type of system improves distributed project management through controlling management of documents, schedules, and personnel; and allowing project personnel to be geographically dispersed without regard to location or time; providing communication among project personnel through a variety of means, including e-mail and discussion forums. Because project personnel and project information are linked, project information remains current and accessible. The right information gets to the right people at the right time.

Cutting-Edge Groupware Functionalities

As we noted in previous sections, it is still useful to categorize groupware tools on the basis of whether they support synchronous or asynchronous work, although some modern groupware tools support processes that do not fit neatly into these two forms. For simplicity's sake, we divide our discussion of modern Internet-age groupware into these two categories and comment on how the technologies fit in our classification scheme (Table 2).

Asynchronous Groupware

Asynchronous groupware can take a variety of forms from the early and simple (but very useful and enduring), such as electronic mail, to the most modern and complex, such as Lotus Notes for Domino. Although some forms such as e-mail have been free-standing organizational communication support systems often run on a firm's local area network, all of the forms we describe can and typically do run on the Internet (as well as on private portions of the Internet such as corporate intranets and extranets). Below are functional descriptions of some of these systems.

System Profile: Lotus Notes/Domino—A Database-Oriented Portal

Lotus Notes is a sophisticated asynchronous groupware system from the Lotus Corporation, a subsidiary of IBM. It enables users to quickly and easily build secure and reliable messaging, calendaring and scheduling, and collaborative application solutions. Notes provides traditional group support functions that are tightly integrated to provide a virtual "workspace," library, and secretary for its users. Group members are able to communicate via e-mail, store all digitized information related to a project in a dedicated and secure database, and the scheduling and calendaring support functions aid in project management. These functions let an organization and its workers interact so that users at different geographic locations can share information with each other; exchange comment publicly or privately; and keep track of project schedules, guidelines and procedures, plans, white papers, and so forth. Notes keeps track of changes and makes updates to replications of all databases in use at any site.

Notes runs on a special server called the Lotus Domino Server. The servers and workstations use a client/server processing model and replicated databases are updated using special programs called remote procedure call (RPC) requests. Notes can be coordinated with Web servers and applications on a company's intranets.

In addition, Notes has strong workflow structuring capabilities and provides the basis for a document management system that is well integrated with its database functions. Although it ships with these and a number of other customizable application "shells," Notes also provides simple facilities so that custom end-user applications can be developed. Given the product's inherent complexity, new users, as well as application developers, face a steep learning curve.

Some aspects of Notes (e.g., the database functions) can be used by individuals as well as small and large groups. The database, for example, also would fit into our "any time/any place" dimension by virtue of its Internet or intranet accessibility. Other aspects such as e-mail fit more neatly into our "asynchronous" dimension and our individual/dyad dimension, although the latter could extend to large groups when used to support list server functions.

It should be noted that Notes is not a relational database and that the organization of a Notes database is different from that of a relational database (Moignard, 2004). A relational database contains tables of same-type "records," or sets of fields, and is optimized for rapid access by table-oriented operations. In contrast, Notes has no schema, does not implement referential integrity, and keeps application code and data in the one database. Its database can contain any number of notes, and a note can contain any number and type of field.

- **Collaborative portals.** Found on the Internet or intranets, collaborative portals are a single point of useful, comprehensive, ubiquitous, and integrated access. There are corporate, community (e-community), and personal portals that cater to specific communities of interest by providing tailored content. Groupware has recently been developed to automate the technical aspects of deploying a Web–browser–based portal so that end users are freed from the rigid limitations of traditional portal technology (Web page development) and end users can conduct business by the terms of their own communities, interests, tasks, and job responsibilities. Portals are increasingly becoming collaborative tools: they can manage personal data, create spontaneous collaborative work spaces, have real-time chat capabilities, and increase communication effectiveness by keeping track of who is online within the community (with pertinent information about users, such as topics of interest and job functions). These tools are also "any time/any place" and can support small groups. They may be asynchronous, serving more as passive postings of information, or when enabled with the appropriate technology, support near-synchronous interaction (e.g., a chat room).

Blackboard 6—Community Portal System features a highly customizable community portal environment that unifies academics, commerce, communities, and administrative services online through one integrated interface. This advanced functionality is backed by a sophisticated product architecture that runs on relational databases and can be scaled to support tens of thousands of users utilizing a multiserver configuration.

First Class 8.0 is a highly scalable, feature-rich messaging and communications solution for enterprises, learning organizations, governments, and service providers. Their collaborative groupware provides users with the ability to build online communities and provide unified communications.

Microsoft 2003 Microsoft's newest office suite, focuses on getting users to work together faster and smarter. The program's expanded XML (extensible markup language) lets a company tie data from a back-end server database (e.g., SQL Server or Oracle) to the Microsoft Office documents its employees use day in and day out. Using XML in Office applications can give users who share documents more accurate data automatically.

Microsoft Office 2003's SharePoint Portal Server gives users quick access to business-critical information throughout an organization. It integrates basic document management functions such as check-in, check-out, document profiles, and document publishing with Microsoft Office products used every day. In addition, users can create SharePoint Portal Server workspaces that could improve a team's efficiency. Some examples of the team collaboration and team management features include the following:

- Share information with enhanced security and work together with employees and customers from any location.

- Document alerts—automatic e-mail notifications alert your team to content changes.
- Online discussions—document discussions, facilitate collaboration and team review.
- Assign users different levels of access using flexible, role-based security.
- Simple Web hosting and document file sharing.

- **Newsgroups/Usenet.** Usenet is a collection of user-submitted notes or messages on various subjects that are posted to servers on a worldwide network. Each subject collection of posted notes is known as a newsgroup. There are thousands of newsgroups and it is possible for users to form new ones. Newsgroups are similar in spirit to e-mail systems except that they are intended for messages among large groups of people instead of one-to-one communication. In practice, the main difference between newsgroups and mailing lists is that newsgroups only show messages to a user when they are explicitly requested, whereas mailing lists deliver messages as they become available. Most browsers, such as those from Netscape and Microsoft, provide Usenet support and access to any newsgroups that users select. On the Web, Google and other sites provide a subject-oriented directory as well as a search approach to newsgroups and help users register to participate in them. In addition, there are other newsgroup readers that run as separate programs. This technology is typically asynchronous with any time/any place access via the network and supports large and small groups.
- **Listserv.** Listserv is a small program that automatically redistributes electronic mail to names on a mailing list. Users can subscribe to a mailing list by sending an e-mail note to a mailing list they learn about; Listserv will automatically add the name and distribute future e-mail postings to every subscriber. (Requests to subscribe and unsubscribe are sent to a special address so that all subscribers do not see these requests.) This technology is typically asynchronous with any time/any place access via the network and supports large and small groups.
- **Work Flow Systems.** These allow digital versions of documents to be routed through organizations through a relatively fixed process. A simple example of a work flow application is an expense report in an organization: an employee enters an expense report and submits it; a copy is archived then routed to the employee's manager for approval; the manager receives the document, electronically approves it, and sends it on; and the expense is registered to the group's account and forwarded to the accounting department for payment. Work flow systems may provide features such as routing, development of forms, and support for differing roles and privileges.

  Work flow systems can be described according to the type of process they are designed to deal with. Thus we define three types of work flow systems:

  - *Image-based work flow systems* are designed to automate the flow of paper through an organization by transforming the paper into digital "images." These were the first work flow systems that gained wide acceptance. These systems are closely associated with "imaging" technology and emphasize the routing and processing of digitized images. Lotus Notes, for example, supports both document management (via scanning or "imaging") and work flow by directing the digitized material via user-defined routes.
  - *Form-based work flow systems* are designed to intelligently route forms throughout an organization. These forms, unlike images, are text based and consist of editable fields. Forms are automatically routed according to the information entered on the form. In addition, these form-based systems can notify or remind people when action is due. This can provide a higher level of capability than image-based workflow systems. Notes can also provide customizable forms (invoices, for example).
  - *Coordination-based work flow systems* are designed to facilitate the completion of work by providing a framework for coordination of action. The framework is aimed to address the domain of human concerns (business processes), rather than the optimization of information or material processes. Such systems have the potential to improve organizational productivity by addressing the issues necessary for customer satisfaction, rather than automating procedures that are not closely related to customer satisfaction. Customer relationship management systems, for example, can be set up to route customer problems to specialists.

  Work flow systems can support individual and dyadic functions but are typically used to support larger groups. They are typically asynchronous and may permit any time/any place access.
- **Group Calendars.** These allow scheduling, project management, and coordination among many people and may provide support for scheduling equipment as well. Typical features detect when schedules conflict or find meeting times that will work for everyone. Group calendars also help to locate people. Typical concerns are privacy (users may feel that certain activities are not public matters), completeness, and accuracy (users may feel that the time it takes to enter schedule information is not justified by the benefits of the calendar). Calendars are also typically asynchronous with any time/any place access.
- **E-Mail.** E-mail is by far the most common groupware application. Although the basic technology is designed to pass simple messages between two people, even relatively basic e-mail systems today typically include interesting features for forwarding messages, filing messages, creating mailing groups, and attaching files with a message. Other features that have been explored include automatic sorting and processing of messages, automatic routing, and structured communication (messages requiring certain information). E-mail, although typically asynchronous, can appear to become "near synchronous" with a fast-enough network.
- **Handheld Computers.** These are also referred to as palmtops and personal digital assistants (PDAs) and are changing the way people use and interact with information (e.g., PDAs featuring Palm OS and Windows CE). Because of their small size, users can take their most important information with them. The highest level of PDA use is in the area of teamwork and collaboration.

"Palmtop computers can be synchronized with programs such as Lotus Notes and Novell Groupwise for team scheduling and project management. Databases and documents can be shared to monitor organizational goals. Communications such as e-mail and Web-based discussions take on new meaning. Wireless networks allow instant messaging and communication anywhere in the network" (Pownell & Bailey, 2000). Microsoft Outlook is another program that can exchange information such as e-mail, schedules, and contacts with a variety of handheld devices.

Synchronous Groupware

Synchronous groupware systems are interactive computer-based environments (physical and virtual) that support individuals (collocated or dispersed) working together at the same time. This emerging generation of groupware is also incorporating new technologies, such as Internet telephony, videoconferencing, speech recognition, and simplified yet secure connections, with corporate databases. However, the key point of collaborative software remains connecting the "islands of knowledge" represented by each employee for the organization's greater good.

Featured Systems: GroupSystems, Groove Virtual Office, and Kubi Client

GroupSystems is a meeting support system that offers a comprehensive suite of tools that can shorten the cycle time for business processes such as strategic planning, product development, and decision making. There are three main features that apply to all tools in the GroupSystems suite:

- Simultaneous contribution—everyone is "speaking" at once, which saves time and increases productivity.
- Anonymity—the identity of each contributor is unknown, so participants tend to feel freer to express their opinions, and ideas are evaluated more objectively.
- Complete records—at the end of a meeting, you can easily produce a complete and accurate report of all ideas, comments, and vote results, in .doc or .rtf format.

There are seven different tools in the GroupSystems suite. Each focuses on a specific aspect of a group effort, including idea generation, evaluation, organization, and exploration. For example, their electronic brainstorming module (EBS), a tool that supports simultaneous and anonymous idea sharing, is commonly used for team building, broad or focused brainstorming, and visioning or strategic planning sessions. Their group-voting module supports eight voting methods, including a customizable point scale, and makes the decision process efficient, flexible, and powerful. Organizations use the voting module to evaluate, make decisions, and build consensus.

Early forms of the GroupSystems tool set were designed to run on local area networks, often in dedicated meeting rooms with networked personal computers (PCs), electronic whiteboards, and audiovisual support. More recent forms are now Web-enabled and provide similar functionality to distributed meetings. In addition, these systems are among the oldest and best researched types of groupware (e.g., Nunamaker, Briggs, Mittleman, Vogel, & Balthazard, 1997).

Groove Virtual Office 3.0 was designed to help users share documents, track issues, hold ad hoc meetings, and access legacy system data. Users can work securely over the Internet as if they and their team are in the same physical location. Beyond being able to share files, Groove's work space includes a discussion board, work flow, a chat window, and common tasks such as setting alerts.

Kubi Client's collaborative e-mail is a new class of collaboration software that tightly couples the power of collaborative functionality and ease of use of e-mail. Kubi makes it easy for e-mail users to spontaneously share documents, discussions, contacts, events, and tasks in organized team spaces without leaving e-mail. Team members can join Kubi Spaces, begin collaborating immediately, and share knowledge, documents, and ideas with others. It can be integrated to work with other software products such as Microsoft Outlook and Lotus Notes.

Typical synchronous groupware includes the following types.

- **Chat Systems.** They permit many people to write messages in real time in a public space. As each person submits a message, it appears at the bottom of a scrolling screen. Chat groups are usually formed by listing chat rooms in a directory by name, location, number of people, topic of discussion, and so forth. Chat systems, like their cousin e-mail, may be accessed any time/any place when hosted on an Internet server or may be available only at certain times or via certain connections if run on a proprietary intranet.
- **Shared Whiteboards.** An electronic whiteboard is one of several kinds of writeable presentation display systems that can be used in a classroom or videoconference. These whiteboards generally fall into one of three categories: standalone *copy boards*, where the content of the whiteboard can be scanned and printed out; *peripheral boards*, which transfer information in the form of digital files to an attached computer; and *interactive boards*, which are like large touchscreen monitors that can be synchronized to an attached computer (users can interact with the display, visit Web sites, and access databases directly from the board). Some peripheral boards can accommodate a projector that can be calibrated to the display, making them interactive. There are a number of add-on *whiteboard digitizer* products available that can also be used to make traditional dry-erase whiteboards interactive.

  In cyberspace, a whiteboard is a space on the display screen in which one or more participants write or draw, using a mouse, keyboard, or other input device. It allows users to view and draw on a shared drawing surface even from different locations. This can be used, for instance, during a phone call, where each person can jot down notes (e.g., a name, phone number, or map) or to work collaboratively on a visual problem. Most shared whiteboards are designed for informal conversation, but they may also serve structured communications or more sophisticated drawing tasks, such as collaborative graphic design, publishing, or engineering applications. Microsoft's NetMeeting allows collaborative real-time use of its PowerPoint application via the Web. Users can pass control of the cursor to each other while sharing a single view of a common screen, thus collaborating on the development of a slide or graphic. Although whiteboards themselves might be real physical devices or may be virtual representations, the information they capture can be accessed any time/any place when they are connected to a network.

- **Collaborative Customer Relationship Management (CRM) Systems.** Collaborative customer relationship management (CRM) systems are groupware that support the communication and coordination across the customer life cycle between channels and customer touch points. They are aimed at providing an enhanced understanding and management of the customer relationship—increasing knowledge of customer behavior, building switching costs, and increasing customer satisfaction and retention—especially relationship-centric, process-centric, and productivity-centric collaboration. Collaborative CRM addresses the problems of traditional CRM solutions that are inwardly focused on an enterprise, not on the customer. By understanding the heterogeneous environment of most enterprise application portfolios, collaborative CRM provides a framework where sales, service, marketing, and product development organizations can work together but still maintain their unique way of doing business. Some CRM functions are very similar to work flow and are asynchronous, but other functions support the synchronous interaction that organizational teams utilize to provide customer support.
- **Videoconference.** A videoconference is a live connection between people in separate locations for the purpose of communication, usually involving audio and often text as well as video. At its simplest, videoconferencing provides transmission of static images and text between two locations. At its most sophisticated, it provides transmission of full-motion video images and high-quality audio between multiple locations.

  Videoconferencing software is quickly becoming standard computer equipment. For example, Microsoft's NetMeeting is included in Windows 2000 and is also available for free download from the NetMeeting homepage. For personal use, free or inexpensive videoconference software and a digital camera afford the user easy and inexpensive live connections to distant friends and family. Although the audio and video quality of such a minimal setup is not high, the combined benefits of a video link and long-distance savings may be quite persuasive.

  The tangible benefits for businesses using videoconferencing include lower travel costs and profits gained from offering videoconferencing as an aspect of customer service. The intangible benefits include the facilitation of group work among geographically distant teammates and a stronger sense of community among business contacts, both within and between companies. In terms of group work, users can chat, transfer files, share programs, send and receive graphic data, and operate computers from remote locations. On a more personal level, the face-to-face connection adds nonverbal communication to the exchange and allows participants to develop a stronger sense of familiarity with individuals they may never actually meet in the same place.

  A videoconference can be thought of as a phone call with pictures—Microsoft refers to that aspect of its NetMeeting package as a "Web phone"—and indications suggest that videoconferencing will some day become the primary mode of distance communication. Web-enabled videoconferencing is accessible any time/any place, although bandwith considerations can limit the quality of transmission and reception.
- **Audio/Video Communications (RTC).** Real-time communication (RTC) systems allow two-way or multiway calling with live video, which is essentially a telephone system with an additional visual component. Cost and compatibility issues limited early use of video systems to scheduled videoconference meeting rooms. Video is advantageous when visual information is being discussed but may not provide substantial benefit in most cases where conventional audio telephones are adequate. In addition to supporting conversations, video may also be used in less direct collaborative situations, such as by providing a view of activities at a remote location.

  Many RTC systems allow for rooms with controlled access or with moderators to lead the discussions, but most of the topics of interest to researchers involve issues related to unmoderated, real-time communication, including anonymity, following the stream of conversation, scalability with number of users, and abusive users. Although chat-like systems are possible using nontext media, the text version of chat allows a direct transcript of the conversation, which not only has long-term value but also allows for backward reference during conversation, which makes it easier for people to drop into a conversation and still pick up on the ongoing discussion.
- **Threaded-Discussion Systems.** Threaded-discussions systems are systems where messages can be posted for public display. The groupware tool allows participants to communicate with each other asynchronously. Communication takes place by having participants create a continuous chain of posted messages on a single topic. This chain is known as a "thread" or a "threaded discussion." Several parallel threads can make up a full conversation. The threads can then be used to build a hierarchy with the content. In some instances, a threaded discussion may also be called a bulletin board or a forum. A discussion can be used to discuss general issues, discuss the specifics of an issue, or organize related content. With a threaded-discussion tool, users can read posted messages, compose new messages, attach documents to posted messages, and search and compile posted messages. Similar to its relatives, e-mail and its variants, these systems are any-time/any-place accessible with the right connection and hardware.
- **Rich Internet Applications.** Rich Internet applications (RIAs) are new technologies that offer the benefits of distributed, server-based Internet applications with the rich

interface and interaction capabilities of desktop applications. RIAs possess the functionality to interact with and manipulate data rather than simply visualize or present it.

This technology was developed as a response to the limitations inherent in HTML-based applications. Although the cost of HTML deployment is low, and it is easy to learn, certain applications are not a good fit with HTML. Some complex applications may require several page redraws to complete a transaction, resulting in unacceptable slow interaction. In contrast, RIAs utilize relatively robust client-side rendering engines that can present very dense, responsive, and graphically rich user interfaces. Also, data can be cached in the client, which allows a significantly more responsive user interface.

- **Decision Support Systems.** Decision support systems (DSSs) are designed to facilitate decision-making. They provide tools for brainstorming, critiquing ideas, putting weights and probabilities on events and alternatives, and voting. Such systems enable presumably more rational and even-handed decisions. Primarily designed to facilitate meetings, they encourage equal participation by, for instance, providing anonymity or enforcing process structure (such as a nominal group technique or a Delphi technique). Although in the past some forms were primarily designed for same-place/same-time situations, many individual tools can be installed on a network for any-time/any-place access. Some integrated suites such as GroupSystems (profiled previously) are now Web-enabled.
- **Virtual Workplace.** The virtual workplace concept seeks to create an electronic facsimile of an office workplace where coworkers would meet and work. This is typically manifest as a Web site that has pictures of team members, links to instant messaging, a link to asynchronous discussion boards, and access to all the documents and database links needed. The goal is to enhance also the sense of being on a team by giving dispersed team members a "place" to go, where they can all "meet" (i.e., communicate textually and possibly telephonically and/or visually in real time). Lotus Notes/Domino features a number of functionalities that support this goal.
- **Collaborative Writing Systems.** These may provide both real-time support and offline support. Word processors may provide asynchronous support by showing authorship and by allowing users to track changes and make annotations to documents. Authors collaborating on a document may also be given tools to help plan and coordinate the authoring process, such as methods for locking parts of the document or linking separately authored documents. Synchronous support allows authors to see each other's changes as they make them and usually needs to provide an additional communication channel to the authors as they work (via videophones or chat). Microsoft's NetMeeting provides this synchronous functionality with their Word application, and similar functionality with their spreadsheet (Excel), database (Access), and graphics programs (PowerPoint, as noted previously).
- **Mobile/Wireless Messaging.** Messaging is the ability to easily see whether a chosen friend or coworker is connected to a network and, if they are, to exchange relatively short messages with them. Messaging differs from electronic mail in the immediacy of the message exchange and also makes a continued exchange simpler than sending e-mail back and forth. Most exchanges are text only. However, some services now allow voice and attachments.

  For messaging to work, the sender and receiver must both subscribe to a network service and be online at the same time, and the intended recipient must be willing to accept instant messages. Under most conditions, messaging is truly "instant." Even during peak Internet usage periods, the delay is rarely more than a second or two. It is possible for two people to have a real-time online "conversation" by messaging each other back and forth.

Mapping Groupware Functionality to Work Processes

The broad (and expanding) range of modern groupware functionality means that those who adopt the technology would benefit from some guidance. To this end, the "groupware grid" (Figure 3) can serve as a theory-based, heuristic model for mapping the functionalities of groupware technology to organizational work. The groupware grid is useful for managers to understand the dimensions of individual and group work that can be supported by the different general functionalities. It is consistent with our technology-oriented classification scheme presented earlier but places its emphasis on the type of work that would be supported.

Team Theory and the Groupware Grid

The horizontal axis of the groupware grid derives from the team theory of group productivity (adapted from Briggs, 1994). *Webster's Dictionary* defines a team as a collection of people working together for some specific purpose. Team theory is a causal model for the productivity of a team. It asserts that team members divide their limited attention resources among three cognitive

	Communications support	Deliberation support	Information access support
Concerted work level			
Coordinated work level			
Individual work level			

Figure 3: Groupware grid.

processes: communication, deliberation, and information access. Team theory posits that these processes interfere with one another, which limits group productivity.

Team theory's communication construct posits that people devote attention to choosing words, behaviors, images, and artifacts and presenting them through a medium to other team members. Team theory's deliberation construct asserts that people devote cognitive effort to forming intentions toward accomplishing the goal-solving activities: Make sense of the problem, develop and evaluate alternatives, select and plan a course of action, monitor results, and so on. The information-access construct addresses the attention demands of finding, storing, processing, and retrieving the information the group members need to support their deliberation. Team theory posits that a key function of information is to increase the likelihood that the outcome one expects will be obtained by choosing one course of action over another. Information has value to the extent that it is available when a choice must be made, to the extent that it is accurate and to the extent that it is complete. However, the value of information is offset by the cost of acquiring, storing, processing, and retrieving it.

Team theory also posits that the cognitive effort required for communication, deliberation, and information access is motivated by goal congruence—the degree to which the vested interests of individual team members are compatible with the group goal. Team members whose interests are aligned with those of the group will exert more effort to achieve the goal than those whose interests are not served by the group goal. The groupware grid does not address goal congruence because goal congruence may have more to do with the way a team wields the technology than with the technology's inherent nature. Therefore, the horizontal axis of the grid addresses the potential for technology to reduce the cognitive costs of joint effort. Groups may become less productive if the attention demands for communication, deliberation, or information access become too high. Groupware may improve productivity to the degree that it reduces the attention costs of these three processes.

Three Levels of Group Work and the Groupware Grid

The vertical axis of the groupware grid consists of three levels of group effort (Figure 4). Sometimes a team may operate at the individual work level, with members making individual efforts that require no coordination. At other times, team members may interact at the coordinated work level. At this level, as with a technical sales team, the work requires careful coordination between otherwise independent individual efforts. Sometimes a team may operate at the concerted work level. That is, several parts of an organization must support the sales team to ensure future results. Teams working at this level must make a continuous concerted effort beyond short-lived coordination. For example, the sales department of an industrial manufacturer must routinely interact with its engineering department to help determine customer specifications on a new product. Today, there are even interorganizational cross-functional teams that provide concerted efforts to support increasingly complex value chains for products and services.

Figure 4: Three levels of group work.

The demands placed on the team vary depending on the level of work in which they are engaged. There is groupware technology to support teams working at all three levels. The groupware grid can thus be used to map the contributions of a single groupware tool or an entire groupware environment (Figure 5). A given technology will probably provide support in more than one cell. The potential for groups' productivity in different environments can be compared by examining their respective grids. For example, the shared database aspect of a product such as Lotus Notes is often used asynchronously and offers little support at the concerted work level but offers strong support for communication and information access at the coordination level. Furthermore, a team database offers only indirect support for deliberations at the coordination level, but a project management and work flow automation system offers strong support for deliberations at that level.

Synchronous groupware that supports meetings, for instance, offers a great deal of support for communication, deliberation, and information access at the concerted work level. For example, the parallel input and anonymous interventions can improve communication during a concerted effort. Other groupware tools affect deliberation in different ways. For instance, a brainstorming tool prevents a group from thinking deeply while encouraging them to diverge from familiar thinking patterns. An idea organizer, on the other hand, encourages a divergent group to focus quickly on a narrow set of key issues. With ubiquitous access to the Internet and client/server access to corporate databases, emerging synchronous groupware tools can support information access at the concerted work level by providing rapid access to the information in the minds of teammates, by providing permanent transcripts of past electronic interactions, or by providing an information search engine.

GROUPWARE MANAGEMENT ISSUES: PRODUCTIVITY AND ORGANIZATIONAL EFFECTS

Perhaps the most important management issues surrounding Web-based collaboration tools are how to use them to enhance productivity and how to manage their

	Communications support	**Deliberation support**	**Information access support**
Concerted work level	Anonymity Parallel contributions Virtual presence Synchronous communication	Structured processes Distributed participation Alternative analysis Process focus	Database access Online search engines Organizational memory Concept classification
Coordinated work level	Asynchronous communication Sequential contributions	Distributed project management Scheduling Automated workflow	Shared data Coordinated filtering
Individual work level	Message preparation Communication structure	Modeling support Simulation support Hypothesis testing Logic analysis	Individual data Filtering Categorizing

Figure 5: Potential contributions of groupware to support productivity processes, as viewed in the groupware grid.

organizational effects. Not all organizations that adopt groupware reap the potential benefits, and this is often due to the same factors that can plague the adoption of any information technology. Companies may try to implement a product that is not designed for its intended use, companies may not think through exactly what benefits they wish to accrue with the technology, companies may not invest sufficient efforts in training and support, and companies may not understand that some of its processes are amenable to team and group work (technologically supported or not) but others are not. Adoption of Web-based collaboration support systems is often tantamount to a large and often ill-defined management initiative such as TQM or business process reengineering. That is, success or failure of the adoption is often difficult to measure, benefits will emerge at different and often unpredictable rates, and human issues such as culture, politics, power, incentive, and personality either facilitate success or bring the project to its knees. We cannot pursue systems planning and development here but instead devote some discussion first to groupware issues that derive from individual users and their interaction with groupware-supported team members and second to issues that derive from an organization's larger culture.

Groupware and Productivity

Organizations may not realize that some group or team members may not have the personality, motivation, or teamwork and communication skills to be effective in their roles. These issues are now beginning to receive attention from researchers examining the performance of groupware-supported workers and teams (e.g., Potter & Balthazard, 2002). Findings suggest that first, people collaborating via groupware do not leave their personalities at the virtual door simply because their new communication mode is textual and possibly asynchronous (e.g., Hiltz & Turoff, 1993). People's personalities drive how they interact with one another in both the face-to-face world and the virtual world, and in both modes, people are similarly affected by each other's individual style of interacting. These effects can determine whether a group enjoys enhanced or diminished information sharing, enhanced or diminished task performance (e.g., decision making), and positive or negative sentiments such as buy in to the team's solution or product, satisfaction with the team's processes, and the team's cohesion. The important implication is that groupware means group work, and not all people are equally skilled in group communication and work processes or otherwise predisposed to work best in a team situation. Interventions such as training are needed to help some groupware-supported people adopt more appropriate interaction skills before they tackle a task. Alternatively, future groupware could incorporate interfaces, communication aids, protocols, and intelligent agents designed to promote participation, constructive interaction, and team building, for example.

Organizational Effects of Groupware

For several years, researchers have compiled evidence that information technology such as groupware or other forms of computer-mediated communication can alter a number of relationships and processes in the workplace (e.g., DeSanctis & Fulk, 2002). An organizational hierarchy that has traditionally exhibited mostly top-down dispersion of information may find that the communication support capacities of a collaborative information system create new lateral and bottom-up flows of information. In more radical manifestations, command-and-control structures in the organization can be circumvented as employees reinvent information-intensive processes based on expertise, interest, and resources, rather than restrictive operating procedures, protocols, or customs. Some researchers suggest that once in place, collaborative systems become the vehicle for organizational redesign, and as such, their more profound effects are largely emergent. In many cases, not all purposes or uses of the systems can be identified beforehand. As such, their management should reflect a "wait and see" attitude and accept that they may give rise to a number of benefits that were not anticipated (e.g., Orlikowski, 1992).

Another common finding is the spontaneous creation of online communities of interest and/or professional practice. These can be the gateways into larger organizational strategic concerns such as knowledge management. Effectively managed collaborative technologies can and often do provide the venue for knowledge sharing—an important input into the knowledge management process, particularly when derived from communities of professional practice or interest (Pickering & King, 1999; Constant, Sproull, & Kiesler, 1999).

The national cultures of groupware users can also become a management issue for transnational organizations. Different traditions, social mores, and internal and national political realities can drive preferences for certain technologies and interaction modes (e.g., text, video, threaded discussion, and e-mail) (Potter & Balthazard, 1999). In addition, preference of various groupware technologies can also differ by gender (Potter, Balthazard, & Elder, 2000).

This more expansive "sociological" view of the management of these systems is informed by knowing the politics and culture of the organization, on one level, and the personalities of system users, on another level. These—as much as the technology's functionality—will ultimately drive the use and potential benefits of the system. As noted previously, some suspension of "standard operating procedure" or organizational status quo is a very common result of these systems, and leaders often have to deal with relatively rapid changes in how things are done and, perhaps more important, how they are thought of in their organization. Many aspects of an organization's culture are "genies in a bottle" that are released when a new communication and collaboration system allows transcendence of predetermined, traditional communication paths. The good news is that installing the collaborative communication technology found in many groupware products into healthy organizations will likely spur new organizational knowledge, improved practices, and synergistic relationships to emerge.

CONCLUSION

Modern Internet-based groupware offers a plethora of useful functionality that is driving sizeable gains in organizational productivity by streamlining collaborative work that was traditionally encumbered by distance and time. It is also driving the reinvention of business processes, spontaneously altering the nature and connection of communication-driven relationships and enabling an unprecedented growth in organizational and professional knowledge. At the same time, these effects can represent important management challenges that need to receive increased attention from managers and researchers alike as the proliferation of Internet-based groupware continues. Thoughtful assessment of groupware functionalities matched with a true understanding of the human side as well as the work process side of the organizational context will ensure the creative and effective adoption of these revolutionary technologies in the foreseeable future.

GLOSSARY

Any Time/Any Where Groupware components and resources such as databases and threaded discussions that can be accessed via the Internet from any location at any time.

Asynchronous Groupware Groupware that does not allow users to interact in real time.

Groupware Technology—typically software and networks—designed to support people working in groups.

Groupware Grid A theory-based, heuristic model for mapping the functionalities of groupware technology to organizational work.

Organizational Effects Effects on work processes, social and authority hierarchies, and communication pathways and processes that can occur with groupware adoption.

Synchronous Groupware Groupware designed to allow two or more users to interact in real time.

Team Theory A causal model for the productivity of a team developed by Briggs (1994). It asserts that team members divide their limited attention resources among three cognitive processes: communication, deliberation, and information access.

CROSS REFERENCES

See *E-mail and Instant Messaging; Intranets: Principals, Privacy and Security Considerations; Local Area Networks; Online Communities*.

REFERENCES

Articsoft. (2003). Retrieved from http://www.articsoft.com

Anderson, F. F., & Shane, H. M. (2002). The impact of Netcentricity on virtual teams: The new performance challenge. *Team Performance Management, 8*(1–2): 5–12.

Briggs, R. O. (1994). *The focus theory of group productivity and its application to the design, development, and testing of electronic group support technology*. Unpublished doctoral dissertation, The University of Arizona, Tucson.

Buller, D., & Burgoon, J. (1994). Deception: Strategic and non-strategic communication. In J. A. Daly & J. M. Wiemann (Eds.), Strategic Interpersonal Communication (pp. 191–223). Hillsdale, NJ: Erlbaum.

Cert Coordination Center. (2001). Retrieved from http://www.cert.org

Coleman, D. (1997). *Groupware: Collaborative strategies for corporate LANs and intranets*. Upper Saddle River, NJ: Prentice-Hall PTR.

Collaborative Strategies. (2002). Retrieved from http://www.collaborate.com

Constant, D., Sproull, L., & Kiesler, S. (1999). The kindness of strangers: The usefulness of electronic weak ties for technical advice. In G. DeSanctis & J. Fulk (Eds.), *Shaping organization form: Communication, connection, and communicty*. Thousand Oaks, CA: Sage.

DeSanctis, G., & J. Fulk (Eds.) (1999). *Shaping organization form: Communication, connection, and community*. Thousand Oaks, CA: Sage.

Dunne, D. (2001). *What is a denial of service attack?* Retrieved from http://www.darwinmag.com

Gallegos, F. (1999). Decision support systems: Areas of risk. *Information Strategy: The Executive's Journal, 15*(5): 46–48.

George, J. F., & K. Marett (2004). *Training to detect deception: An experimental investigation*. Paper presented at the 37th Hawaii International Conference on System Sciences, Hawaii.

Hiltz, S. R., & Turoff, M. (1993). *The network nation: Human communication via computer*. Cambridge, MA: MIT Press.

Horton, M., & Mugge, C. (2003). *Hacknotes: Network security portable reference*. New York: McGraw-Hill/Osborne.

Johansen, R. (1988). *Groupware*. New York: Free Press.

Kubi Software. (2004). Retrieved from http://www.kubisoftware.com

Moignard, M. (2004). *Notes is not a relational database*. Retrieved from http://www.dominopower.com/issues/issue200406/00001307001.html

Nunamaker, J. F., Briggs, R., Mittleman, D. D., Vogel, D. R., & Balthazard, P. (1997, Winter). Lessons from a dozen years of group support systems research: A discussion of lab and field findings. *Journal of Management Information Systems, 13*(3).

Orlikowski, W. (1992). Learning from NOTES: Organizational issues in groupware implementation. In *Proceedings of the ACM conference on computer-supported cooperative work* (pp. 362–369). Toronto: ACM Press.

Panko, R. R. (2003). *Slammer: The rirst flash attack worm*. Retrieved from http://pankosecurity.com/slammer.doc

Pickering, J. M., & King, J. L. (1999). Hardwiring weak ties: Interorganizational computer-mediated communication, occupational communities, and organizational change. In G. DeSanctis and J. Fulk (Eds.), *Shaping organization form: Communication, connection, and communicty*. Thousand Oaks, CA: Sage.

Potter, R. E., & Balthazard, P. A. (2002). Understanding human interaction and performance in the virtual team. *The Journal of Information Technology Theory & Application*. Retrieved from http://www.jitta.org

Potter, R. E., & Balthazard, P. A. (1999). Supporting integrative negotiation via computer-mediated communication technologies: An empirical example with geographically dispersed Chinese and American negotiators. *Journal of International Consumer Marketing, 12*(4).

Potter, R. E., Balthazard, P. A, & Elder, K. L. (2000). Toward inclusive dialogue in the classroom: Participation and interaction in face-to-face and computer-mediated discussions. *Journal of Information Systems Education, 11*(2).

Power, R. (2002). CSI/FBI computer crime and security survey. *Computer Security Issues and Trends, 8*(1): 1–22.

Pownell, D., & Bailey, G. D. (2000). *The next small thing—Handheld computing for educational leaders*. Retrieved from http://www.intel.com

Volonino, L., Gessner, G. H., & Kermis, G. F. (2004). Holistic compliance with Sarbanes–Oxley. *Communications of the Association for Information Systems, 14*: 219–233.

FURTHER READING

Groupsystems. Retrieved from http://www.groupsystems.com

Groove Virtual Office. Retrieved from http://www.groove.net

Lotus Notes/Domino. Retrieved from http://www.lotus.com

Microsoft Office 2003. Retrieved from http://www.microsoft.com

Symantec. (2001). *Ten steps to protect your enterprise from DoS attacks*. Retrieved from http://enterprisesecurity.symantec.com

Search Engines: Security, Privacy, and Ethical Issues

Raymond Wisman, *Indiana University Southeast*

INTRODUCTION

Serious discussion of security for any system must confront two central issues: what is at risk and defenses that can reduce risk. Understanding the value of a thing to an attacker is necessary to understanding the risk. Risk never can be eliminated but, when the degree of risk is understood, risk can be managed by a balanced defense against attacks. The key is to prevent a ruinous failure, often by providing multiple layers of defense and risk management. Willie Sutton, though wrongly attributed the quote on robbing banks "Because that's where the money is," understood the reason to attack a bank (Sutton and Linn, 1976). Banks knowingly create risk by accumulating large amounts of cash in one location both for customer convenience and to manage risk economically through several defensive layers such as safes, guards, and the legal threat of incarceration. Despite these defenses, robbers still launch successful attacks, but banks still remain open and operate at a profit. Banks and bank robbers will be with us as long as banks hold the money and banks continue to manage the risk of attack economically.

Entities such as banks, or other well-known focal points for things of value, invite attack. Security measures attempt to discourage the predictable attacks but are typically designed as defense against past successful attacks; such security measures obviously cannot completely prevent the unexpected attack. If complete security against attack is not possible, security failure must be expected and managed. Complete trust in the security of a system such as the Web, exposed to attacks from the entire planet, is naive at best. Since security can fail, determining the risk and the cost of failure is critical. Retailers understand that it makes no sense to expend more to secure something than the something is worth; risk reduction usually comes at some cost. Stores suffer shoplifting and would be made more secure by frisking customers before they leave the store. However, storeowners have found it more cost-effective to hire guards and buy security technology to manage the risk and raise prices to cover added costs; owners know that lost sales due to unhappy customers represent a greater risk to their existence than shoplifting costs.

Is search risky? In the connected Web, the common, apparently free, and seemingly anonymous act of search exposes risks to security and privacy. Anything of value is at risk and Web search has great value. Consider the Web without search; with no means to navigate, there could be no Web as we know it. Web search is relatively new, valuable, primarily shaped by private industry and individual effort, with few enforceable standards of behavior, mostly unregulated and little enforcement; something as America's Wild West must have been.

This chapter examines some of the most egregious risks surrounding Web search and suggests a number of defenses. The chapter organizes search risks along the lines of the three main parties involved: the searcher, the search engine, and the sites searched to provide focus for those readers whose interest lies primarily with one or more of the three. There are inherent problems with this approach. Because the purpose of search technology is to interconnect the three parties of search, the chapter must often fail in a complete separation of the security and privacy issues of one party from that of another. A further complication is that, although all parties need and naturally benefit from the others, one party can, and often does, overtly attempt to place another at some risk to their own advantage. The chapter ends with a limited examination of ethical issues surrounding search as it intersects with the three parties.

The technologies that make Web search possible are discussed along the way to reveal the technical sources of risk and some insight into reasonable defenses by each of the parties. However, the full details of the underlying technology are well beyond the scope of this chapter, which gives only the rudimentary level necessary to recognize the security threats and the worth of defenses. Readings from other chapters of this text will be especially valuable for a more detailed understanding of the related technologies and threats referenced within the chapter.

Why Search

Why is searching the Web necessary and worth doing for even a small amount of risk? A simple answer is that the Web is too large and unorganized to find much useful information. Search engines represent a single point where the information of the Web is concentrated, organized, and can be scrutinized as a whole. The original Web design purpose was simply to interconnect bits and pieces of scattered information with no plan to find information other than by a searcher manually moving from one piece of information to another by following hyperlinks connecting one page to another. In some sense, the search engine merely automates the process, following a vast number of hyperlinks while collecting information along the way for later retrieval. Although any published number about the Web immediately falls short of current counts, some sense of scale is suggested by the announcement that the Google search engine surpassed 6 billion items indexed by February 17, 2004 (Google press release, 2004).

Search engines play a key role in the discovery of information on the Web. One analysis (OCLC, 2002) indicated that college students use search engines 96% of the time when seeking information for assignments. Much of the information sought is for profit in some way; search engines are the top way consumers find new Web sites online, used by over 73% of those surveyed (Van Boskirk, Li, Parr, & Gerson, 2001). Commerce drives Web growth, shopping for everything from individuals buying shoes to businesses searching for a community in which to locate a new factory.

Risk

Security implies safety; privacy implies secrecy; search creates risk for both. Search has value, and things of value are nearly always at some risk. Who is at risk, what are the threats surrounding search, and what are reasonable defenses against those threats? Before those questions can be considered in detail, one needs a foundation for discussing risk in the context of Web search based upon some knowledge of how the tools of search, the search engine and browser, operate and of the Web infrastructure that makes search possible yet vulnerable.

Web search has risk in part because the Internet encourages communication at a distance, allowing us to do things at a faraway place without the physical journey. Although the communicating parties can be distant, we still need and expect at least the relative level of security provided through face-to-face communication, regardless of the communication form. The Internet carries Web communication, and by design depends upon many cooperating intermediaries for passing communication between any two parties. In search, not only are all three of the communicating parties separated by distance, only one, at most, is human.

For our discussion of search engine security and risk, the definitions of three, interdependent security services, authentication, encryption, and verification, will be useful:

- *Authentication* is the proof of one's identity. We need to know that the search engine claiming to be www.search.com actually is www.search.com. Generally, we require some trusted third-party authority that can not only authenticate an identity but also ensure that the authentication is trustworthy.
- *Encryption* transforms an easily read message into a form that, without knowledge of the transformation details, is much more difficult to read. Decryption transforms the encrypted message back to a readable form. Ideally, only the authenticated sender can encrypt the message and only the intended receiver can decrypt and read the message, keeping the message contents secret and private from all others.
- *Verification* determines whether the message received was the message sent; no tampering has occurred.

Each of these services depends upon the others; proof of the sender's identity is of reduced value if the message sent cannot be verified or an encrypted message from an unauthenticated sender could be a replay of an earlier message. A failure of any one of these services can precipitate the failure of the others. Any communication, whether electronic or not, using these services correctly can greatly reduce the degree of risk to the communicating parties.

Security and privacy are issues that most affect the searcher. Since we generally agree security and privacy to be important, the reader should now reasonably expect a discussion on using the Web for secure search engine communications based on authentication, encryption, and verification. Unfortunately, the discussion must focus on managing risk due to the lack of security and privacy as there is little or no attempt to provide either for search. As necessary background for our discussion, the following sections provide a brief overview of the Internet, browser, and search engine operation useful in understanding the specific threats and defenses detailed in the later sections on the searcher, search engine, and searched Web site.

Internet Fundamentals

The Internet infrastructure carries the communications and consists of a large and growing conglomeration of machines, communication channels, and software that abide by an interdependent assortment of communication protocols. The fundamental element of the Internet is the routable protocol, which defines the datagram passed from one point of the Internet to another, also known as the Internet protocol (IP); the current predominant version is Internet protocol version 4 (IPv4). Other protocols, such as the transport control protocol (TCP) used by Web servers and browsers, depend upon IP for routing messages across the Internet so a weakness in IP affects virtually all Internet communications. Developed before security was a concern, IPv4 protocol does not address authentication, verification, or encryption, obviously a serious security vulnerability for all communications built upon the protocol. Figure 1 provides details of interest for security concerns of the IPv4 format.

Web search not only explicitly involves three parties: the searcher, search engine, and Web site searched, but also requires extensive use of the Internet infrastructure and protocols for the three to communicate. A simplified network configuration necessary for search or other

Version	…	Protocol	…	Checksum	…	Source Address	Destination Address	…	Data

Figure 1: The header fields defined within an IPv4 datagram that are the most important to security and privacy.

1. *Version* defines the protocol version used for the header; important for the eventual transition to the more secure IPv6.
2. *Protocol* defines the protocol specification for the *Data* field; commonly used protocols are TCP by Web services such as search engines and UDP by the domain name system.
3. *Checksum* is the computed header checksum used for transmission error checking.
4. *Source address* specifies the four-octet IP address belonging to the data sender. The dotted decimal notation address, 123.45.67.89 for example, is the common representation. IPv4 provides no authentication of this field, allowing use of a bogus address or a different source address to replace the original sender's address undetected by the protocol. Without authentication, the true sender cannot be determined and one sender can masquerade as another.
5. *Destination address* specifies the four-octet IP address of the intended data receiver. Intermediate routers examine the address to determine where to deliver the data; by changing the address, one changes the data delivery location.
6. *Data* contains the message carried within the datagram. When the *Protocol* field specifies TCP, the *Data* field content is treated as a TCP message. Without strong encryption implemented outside of IP, the data can be read easily; without verification, the data can be changed undetected.

Web use (Figure 2) consists of the searcher machine that connects to the Internet through an Internet service provider (ISP) and includes a domain name system (DNS) server. The ISP is the usual searcher's connection point to the Internet; all datagrams between the Internet and the searcher must pass through the ISP. The ISP is one point at which the real identity of an individual is known for billing purposes or can be traced back to an individual machine. The DNS server is necessary to translate site names such as www.search.com used in Web pages into the IP addresses used by Internet routers. When given a name a DNS server returns the corresponding address; for example, given www.search.com the DNS server responds with the corresponding 167.89.12.34 address.

Although the interaction between parties and use of the Internet infrastructure necessary for search or other Web application is too extensive and detailed for all but a superficial scrutiny, a coarse observation is useful to our later examination of risk to security and privacy. The following lists the basic steps necessary for a searcher to receive the search engine's home page:

1. Searcher enters *www.search.com* in browser address.
2. Browser requests DNS server (145.89.67.23) to translate *www.search.com* into an IP address.
3. DNS server responds to browser with 167.89.12.34 address.
4. Browser requests that 167.89.12.34 send its default page.
5. *www.search.com* responds to browser with the search engine's default page.
6. Browser displays search engine's default page; searcher can now enter query, sending a search request that would repeat the process again.

The searcher may query the search engine a number of times; each time the above steps repeat; each time the datagrams between the searcher and www.search.com pass over the Internet and through the ISP. Eventually the searcher might find something of interest and follow a link to www.BigU.edu, where the basic steps listed above remain essentially the same. Given the number of cooperating machines, software, and communication complexity, the reliability of the Internet is remarkable.

However, the lack of intrinsic Internet security using IPv4 becomes an issue when communication passes openly across a public network. Recall that each datagram must contain a destination address for Internet router delivery and a source address to identify where to send a response, the data field that holds the actual message. With no security, as the datagram traverses the Internet from source to destination, these and other fields are open for reading and writing along the path where communication can be monitored, stolen, or changed.

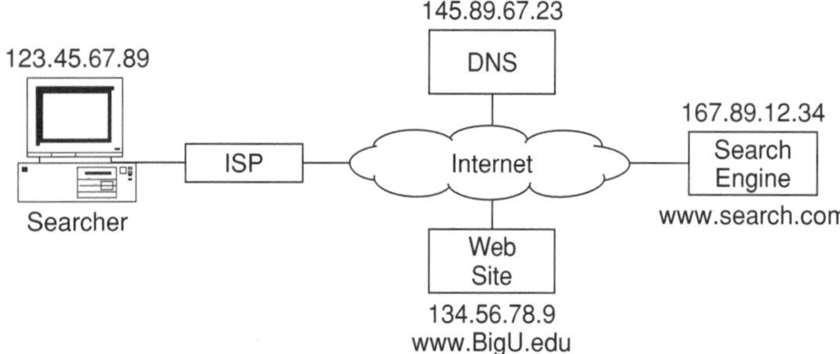

Figure 2: A typical network for Web search. The Internet cloud holds the communication channels and routers for passing datagrams between sending and receiving points of the network.

```
GET /search?hl=en&lr=&ie=UTF-8&oe=UTF-8&q=babble HTTP/1.1
Accept: image/gif, image/x-xbitmap, image/jpeg, image/pjpeg, */*
Accept-Language: en-us
Accept-Encoding: gzip, deflate
User-Agent: Mozilla/4.0 (compatible; MSIE 6.0; Windows NT 5.1; .NET CLR 1.0.3705)
Host: www.google.com
Connection: Keep-Alive
Cookie: PREF=ID=6badbe492bad4u60:TM=1055825476:LM=1055825476:S=PY-bEWHY-ONOTSPY
```

Figure 3: Browser communication sending query "babble" to www.google.com search engine.

Browser Fundamentals

The browser and search engine communicate via the hypertext transfer protocol (HTTP), a standard that specifies valid interactions between a client such as a browser and a server such as a search engine (RFC 2616). HTTP is a stateless protocol, meaning that each connection is independent of previous ones; there is no state information contained within the protocol. In search practice, this means that each query appears independent to the search engine, providing some measure of privacy. An example browser message presented in Figure 3 sent the query "babble" to the Google search engine. The browser sends instructions that include the query string "babble" and automatically volunteers useful data to the search engine server such as the type of images the browser might render. The search engine prefaces its reply by instructions to the browser, followed by search results written in hypertext markup language (HTML) for rendering by the browser.

Of special interest to privacy is the cookie, data stored on the searcher's machine, sent by the browser with the query to the search engine. The search engine server placed the cookie on the searcher's computer during a previous query, the browser returns the cookie automatically whenever contacting a server whose host domain name and cookie match. The browser can be set to accept or reject cookies: if accepted the cookie contents are under the control of the server; otherwise, rejecting cookies often comes at the cost of reduced service to the user. A common use of cookies is to identify each browser machine uniquely to track visits, something generally not possible with a stateless protocol. The ID field of this cookie would presumably give information to the search engine for associating this browser's current actions with past and future queries, allowing search personalization and possibly sharpening the future search results. Although normally there is no browser information that explicitly identifies an individual, giving personal information such as an e-mail address would allow cookie, queries, and an identity to be directly connected.

Cookies obviously then present some risk to privacy, and several defensive options exist. The most obvious is to recognize that manually disabling cookies does not seriously affect results on major search engines. Another option is to locate the cookie directory and delete the file holding the cookie; Internet Explorer stores cookies in the directory "C:\Documents and Settings\username\Cookies", and the Google cookie would be under the filename "username@google[1].txt".

The search engine reply in Figure 4 to the query in Figure 3 begins with a HTTP header followed by the text in HTML listing the search results. The search engine has sent another cookie; if accepted the browser will return the cookie data on the next visit to the search engine. Notice that the cookie contains what appears to be encoded data (i.e. S=X60DAR7nmCtEjlxa) retrievable on the next visit to the search engine. Cookies have expiration dates after which the browser will discard; this cookie expires in 2038, allowing tracking of the browser activity on the search engine for a long time.

In addition to the obvious risk to privacy, using cookies for authentication, such as logging in to a banking account, presents a security risk. The risk is primarily due to the lack of any consideration for security in the cookie design; with no standards, any cookie security must be implemented by individual Web sites (Sit & Fu, 2001), producing uneven results. Many sites do encrypt cookies. Still, attackers can obtain a cookie by masquerading as the original site that stored the cookie; the browser automatically gives up the cookie if contacted by what it believes to be the owner of the cookie. In addition, an eavesdropper can capture the cookie during transmission between the browser and server. Once captured, merely storing the cookie file on another computer and contacting the same server could replay the login automatically.

Search Engine Fundamentals

Although Web search is commonplace, much of the chapter's discussion depends upon a rudimentary knowledge of the interplay between search engines, the searcher, and Web site searched. The following brief section is intended for those readers who may appreciate such a basic explanation; those with some knowledge of search engines can safely skip this section.

```
HTTP/1.1 200 OK
Cache-control: private
Content-Type: text/html
Set-Cookie: PREF=ID=6badbe492bad4u60:TM=1073216819:LM=1073216819:S=X60DAR7nmCtEjlxa;
        expires=Sun, 17-Jan-2038 19:14:07 GMT; path=/; domain=.google.com
Server: GWS/2.1
Transfer-Encoding: chunkedDate: Mon, 19 Jan 2004 16:40:19 GMT
```

Figure 4: Preface of the reply to query "babble" from www.google.com search engine.

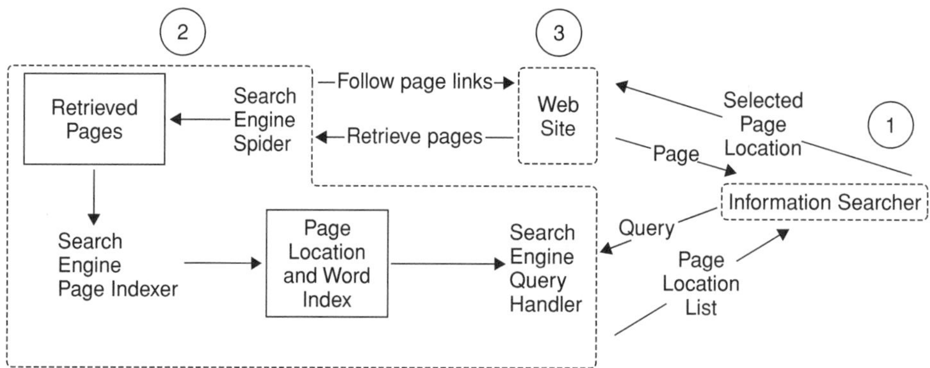

Figure 5: An overview of a search engine and its relation to Web sites and information searchers. The basic steps to Web search are as follows: a search engine spider visits a Web site to retrieve and index pages for later searches; the searcher sends queries to the search engine and receives a list of page locations; the searcher selects and retrieves pages from the Web site.

Search engines are merely specialized Web servers; the obvious work of a search engine is communicating with the searcher's browser, either receiving or answering queries; less obvious is the mostly unnoticed but protracted work of gathering information from Web sites. Figure 5 illustrates the characteristic interaction between the three partners in search: 1) the searcher, 2) the search engine, and 3) the Web site searched. The first key step occurs when a Web site creates pages with information and sends the main Web site page location to a search engine. Next, in the typical search engine architecture (Arasu, Cho, Garcia-Molina, Paepcke, & Raghavan, 2001), one search engine component called a spider (or crawler, robot, etc.) visits the Web site to retrieve pages linked from the main page much as a person using a browser would follow links to new pages. The spider follows links, indexing meaningful words of the retrieved pages to be stored along with the page's Web site location in a specialized database on the search engine for later searches and retrievals. As the searcher sends queries to the search engine, the engine consults the database for pages containing similar words and phrases. After ranking the pages for relevancy to the query, the engine returns the ranked list of Web site page locations. The searcher selects location entries from the list and retrieves pages directly from the Web site. Closing the information gap between the searcher and sought-after Web site pages is the primary purpose of the search engine.

The remainder of the chapter, forming its core, focuses on the threats and defensive measures for the three parties to search. The first section considers how the act of searching exposes one to threats. The second section examines the search engine in more detail, how search engines operate and their known vulnerabilities. The third section examines how search exposes the Web site to threat and how sites attempt to manipulate search engines and searchers to their own benefit.

SEARCHER

The searcher is the reason search engines exist. Does search have risk? First, we must determine what is of value to determine what is at risk. The user of a search engine is searching for information, which the search engine gives freely. As the information is free, it would seem there is nothing of value, so nothing is at risk. However, most of us value our privacy and expect our communication to be private and free from surveillance. We also place value on the results we receive from a search engine and assume the results are from an honest attempt by the search engine to respond to our query.

As we will see, the searcher has little guarantee of privacy and high likelihood of exposure to varying degrees of pretense, particularly by Web sites. Unfortunately, there are many places and methods for attacking privacy or conducting fraud against the searcher. To maintain a focus on the searcher, this section deals primarily with privacy and fraud attacks waged directly against an individual searcher by an agent other than the search engine or a searched Web site; specific sections will cover those issues.

Privacy

Privacy implies secrecy. To ensure secret communication the message transfer must occur privately, through no intermediaries or pass through intermediaries who are unable to either read the message or determine who is communicating. Is search communication secret? Internet communication, passing between the searcher and search engine through many public intermediaries, is not private. Search engine messages fail secrecy in at least two ways. Messages are generally in plaintext, readable by anyone able to intercept the message, and Internet messages list in the plaintext source who is communicating and destination addresses. Search communication is not currently secret. Although useful measures exist, such as encrypting messages between the searcher and engine, the search engine site must implement those measures and most do not.

Nevertheless, even with secret communication between the searcher and search engine, search has privacy risks. Search seems anonymous and free, and there is usually no authentication required for search. Search engines can and commonly do collect privileged data that can connect the searcher's real identity with search behavior. The cookie placed by the search engine on your computer

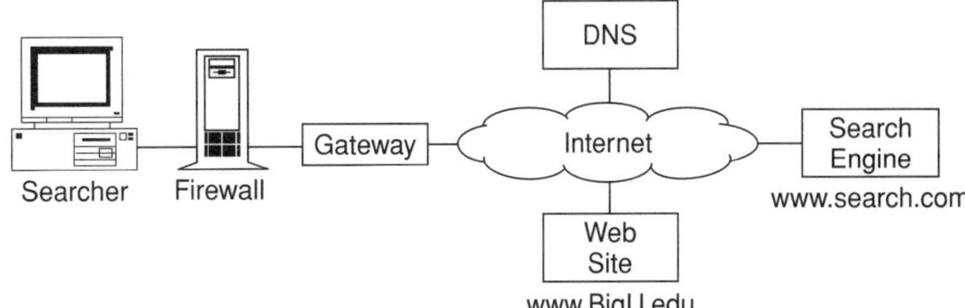

Figure 6a: All communications physically pass through one machine, such as a firewall, allowing that machine to read, change, or delete any communication.

uniquely identifies the searcher, making it a simple matter for the engine to store the search details in a database. In theory, future searches can factor in those past and produce results tailored to your search behavior; no personal data required. Connecting the cookie with an e-mail address or other personal information, the same search data can produce such minor intrusions as targeted marketing to serious invasions of privacy such as monitoring your Web site preferences. No perfect solution exists although measures discussed earlier on deleting cookie files, avoiding the use of personal identification, and using a public computer for sensitive searches can help.

Eavesdropping

Eavesdropping or secret monitoring of the conversation between the searcher and search engine is an attack on privacy. The search conversation consists of sending query terms to the search engine from a browser and receiving a list of ranked results in return. The searcher's first vulnerability is due to the transmitting of the query and response in plaintext. To make matters worse, the browser generates and transmits information that can identify the searcher. Sending communication in plaintext is the standard for the HTTP protocol used for communication between the browser and search engine. The open conversation between the searcher and search engine can be covertly monitored at many points on the communication path, allowing a third party to easily determine the search terms and at least the host machine, if not the identity, of the searcher.

Surveillance

Eavesdropping differs from surveillance only by being conducted in secret. Many employers regularly monitor Internet communication to limit employee access to presumably non-work-related sites. Surveillance is relatively easy for the network administration given the unlimited access to traffic at communication concentration points, see Figure 6a, such as firewalls, content filters, gateways, and routers. For the searcher, the risk to privacy continues to exist wherever communication is in plaintext. The institution that operates the network represents a more formidable risk to privacy than the average eavesdropper primarily due to superior opportunity, resources, and incentive to monitor Web use in general. The surveillance software needed is widely available, often marketed explicitly to track or limit employees' use of the Web. The software is tunable to capture all communication between the host of a specific searcher and a particular search engine, making it possible to capture the complete search session.

Monitoring communication between the searcher and search engine occurs in many ways; the two discussed here are merely among the most widely accessible. Casual eavesdropping is particularly a problem on broadcast networks such as Ethernet where there is no native security and any host computer physically connected to the same network wire can generally read all messages transmitted over the network. Using widely available packet sniffing software such as Ethereal or Dsniff (http://www.monkey.org/~dugsong/dsniff), the technically unsophisticated eavesdropper can listen in from the comfort of their office down the hall. Figure 6b illustrates how communication over a hub between searcher and gateway to the Internet automatically broadcasts to the eavesdropper on the same hub. When communication between the browser and search engine transmits as plaintext, the eavesdropper can easily read each bit passed through the hub. Wireless base stations (802.11b) can extend the network range several hundred meters beyond the end of the Ethernet wire or your home cable modem, which is great for eavesdropping attacks by someone in a car parked down the street. Although enforcing restrictions on joining a wireless network are relatively simple, many networks automatically configure to operate with no restrictions, opening the wireless network to the same eavesdropping attacks possible through Ethernet hubs.

Law enforcement and security agencies in many countries have extended their surveillance to the Internet. The FBI developed a packet-sniffing system named DCS1000 (previously named Carnivore) that passively captures and records specified packets from network traffic. Within the United States, the Electronics Communications Privacy Act restricts domestic surveillance by law enforcement agencies. Under authorization by a federal district court judge, the statute allows the capture of all communication, such as content between a searcher and a search engine, and obliges the cooperation of service providers (Graham, 2004). Strongly encrypted communications

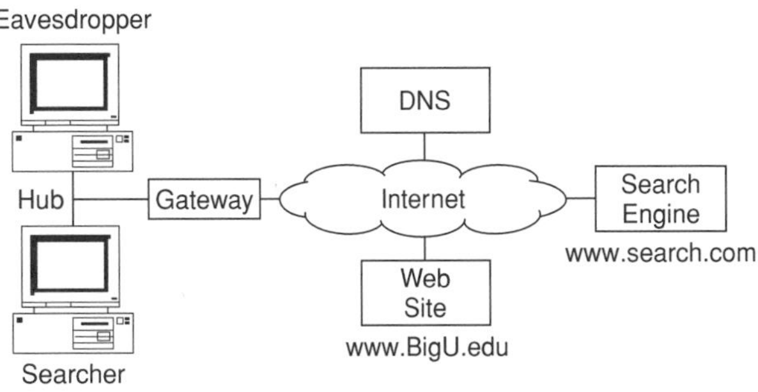

Figure 6b: A hub broadcasts all communications to others on a local area network; eavesdropping is easy.

that are easily copied cannot necessarily be read; however, individuals can be compelled by law to provide the decryption key. For U.S. citizens, intelligence agencies are required by the Foreign Intelligence Surveillance Act (FISA) to obtain a court order from the Foreign Intelligence Surveillance Court to conduct domestic surveillance. Order (E.O.) 12333 requires approval by the attorney general for surveillance of citizens in foreign countries (Legal Standards for the Intelligence Community in Conducting Electronic Surveillance report required by FY 2000 Intelligence Authorization Act, 2004).

However, the September 11, 2001, terrorist attacks raised significantly the tolerance for domestic surveillance, precipitating the rapid passage of the USA PATRIOT Act (Uniting and Strengthening America by Providing Appropriate Tools Required to Intercept and Obstruct Terrorism, USAPA), H.R. 3162, on October 26, 2001 (U.S. 107th Congress, 2001). Although the act contained many provisions not related to privacy, the act generally widened government authority to conduct surveillance while weakening judicial oversight. Although many of the act's provisions expire December 31, 2005, additional legislation of the "Domestic Security Enhancement Act of 2003," also known as "PATRIOT Act II," includes further and permanent changes to domestic surveillance. According to the American Civil Liberties Union, much of the act is aimed at proving greater government access to electronic communication such as the Internet (Edgar, 2003).

Considerable confusion and debate surrounds details on the interpretation and application of current law and in particular on the effectiveness of privacy safeguards. However, the broad purpose of the USAPA was to remove a number of restrictions from the CIA and FBI on monitoring individuals, including domestic electronic communications. Previously, law enforcement could obtain a "'trap and trace" order, which allowed access to numbers dialed and received by a specific telephone; under USAPA the scope of accessible information has been extended to "dialing, routing, and signaling." Routing refers specifically to Internet use and recording source and destination address. Although the PATRIOT Act states that trap and trace orders may not be used to obtain communication "contents," the term is not defined. In addition, the routing and contents of Internet communication are parts of a single message and not easily separated for capture. The order giving access to routing also gives access to content, entrusting government agents to view only the routing information. Technologies used to gather routing information, such as Carnivore, must be trusted not to gather information about coincidental users of the same ISP or law enforcement agencies must be trusted to filter out information on other users. This raises privacy issues for not only legitimate targets of investigation but also those who happen to be customers of the same ISP.

Privacy and Security

Privacy and security are under threat from many directions, inside and outside the ISP, legal and illegal. Eliminating all threats is not practical but defensive actions can manage most threats. In the United States, a common defense against burglary is the security alarm system and the security company sign in front of the house; other countries use high walls topped with broken glass to discourage attacks. The purpose is the same: to present a more difficult target for attack than others; to send the less-than-determined attacker somewhere else.

Search Computer

Search depends upon connection to the Internet, automatically exposing your computer and communication to outside attack. Attacks against networked personal computers are too numerous and varied to even begin a limited enumeration; but reasonable defenses do exist. Basic protection includes disabling any services, protocols, and ports not necessary, operating a firewall to restrict access to those that are necessary, and installing security patches regularly.

Local Infrastructure

Certain threats are beyond the control of the average searcher, sometimes occurring far out on the Internet infrastructure. For example, your ISP has, by necessity, extraordinary access to network equipment and communications and is the sole agent who can maintain certain defenses on your behalf. Nevertheless, the ISP presents a serious threat for actively monitoring communications and passively by failing to secure the network infrastructure from attack. The following describes the more common threats when an attacker has access to the local infrastructure and suggests some defense, none of which is foolproof.

As discussed earlier, communication surveillance is easier when one has physical access to the communication infrastructure; perhaps as simple as running free packet-sniffing software on your local area network (LAN). The majority of LANs use the Ethernet protocol, which broadcasts all communications over the wire to all stations connected by hubs. All stations connected to the network can monitor each other's full communications. A simple defense that requires more work of an attacker uses switches rather than hubs as connection points to the network, isolating each station's communication from others connected to that switch. In Figure 6c, communication between the searcher and gateway is isolated from a casual eavesdropper, requiring at least some effort to conduct a monitoring attack.

However, a more determined attacker with access to a connected station can trick the switch to gain control

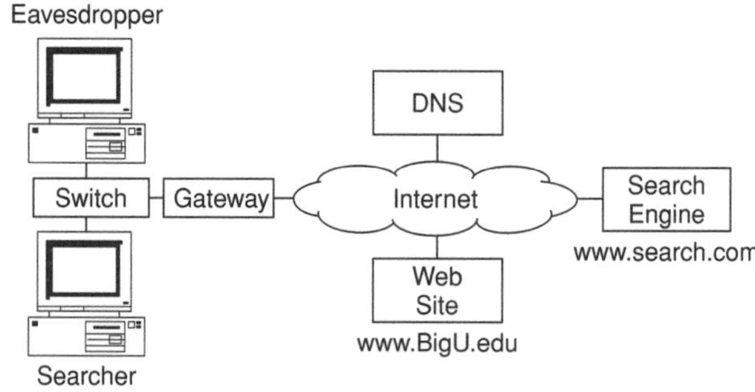

Figure 6c: A switch separates communications from others on a local area network; eavesdropping is more difficult. All communication between Internet and LAN must pass through the gateway.

of communications. A medium access control (MAC) address on a LAN such as Ethernet uniquely identifies each station network connection. A switch stores source MAC addresses when a station sends a message; by storing the source address of the message the switch knows on which port to send later messages destined for that station. To trick the switch, the attacker sends a message with the source MAC address of the searcher's station; the switch will then send messages destined to the searcher instead to the attacker. LANs connect to the Internet through a gateway that has a MAC address on the LAN side of the network. By tricking the switch to store the attacker's port for both the searcher and gateway addresses, the attacker can in theory capture communications destined for both. This is not the perfect or simple attack for several reasons. Ideally, for the attacker, they monitor and change communications in both directions, placing themselves in the middle of the searcher and the gateway to the Internet search engine. However, when the searcher sends messages, the switch updates the source address to the searcher's port connection; the attacker is now in a race to change the switch back to the attacker address. The same is true for the gateway. One defense is to define the MAC addresses and connections stored by the switch statically and not allow them to change; attempting to do so could also signal a warning that an attack was in progress. The downside to this defense, as with many others, is the inconvenience of updating the switch each time a computer physically changes its connected port on the switch.

With physical access to a LAN connection, a moderately determined attacker can attempt another, potentially more successful attack: address resolution protocol (ARP) spoofing. ARP spoofing tricks the searcher's machine into treating the attacker as the gateway to the search engine, placing the attacker between the searcher and the gateway, able to not only monitor but also change communications. The purpose of ARP is to bind IP addresses used by the Internet to MAC addresses used on a LAN such as Ethernet. As noted earlier, computers on the LAN communicate to the Internet through a gateway attached to the LAN and Internet. Normally, when the searcher's machine first contacts the search engine, it knows the IP address of the gateway needed for Internet connections but not the gateway MAC address needed for communicating over Ethernet. To discover the gateway's MAC address, the searcher's computer broadcasts the IP address of the gateway and receives a reply matching the gateway IP with its MAC addresses. Spoofing subverts ARP by the attacker sending a reply to the searcher's machine that instead matches the gateway IP with the attacker's MAC address. Believing the attacker to be the gateway, the searcher now sends all communication to the attacker who can examine and change the communications before forwarding to the real gateway. The gateway returns any search engine replies back to the attacker who again can examine and change the message before returning it to the searcher. The attacker has effectively placed herself between the searcher and search engine; ARP spoofing is another of the man-in-the-middle attacks. The problem for the attacker is that, because the searcher broadcasts an ARP request for the gateway, the gateway will also respond; the attack is not reliable. A related, more reliable attack known as cache poisoning, sends the targeted station directly the bogus ARP request using the target's MAC address; the target now matches the gateway IP with the attacker's MAC address in a cache of addresses without any conflicting response from the gateway. By directly sending the gateway the searcher's IP and the attacker's MAC address, the attack is complete, all that remains is to monitor the communications.

Wireless LANs are open to most of the same threats as wired LANs with the added problem that a physical connection is not necessary, only in reasonably close proximity of a few hundred meters to a wireless access point. In an attempt to make wireless installation simple, the default mode of the wireless network often is to broadcast in clear text; anyone within range can then easily connect and attack the network. The IEEE 802.11 standard describes a wired equivalent privacy (WEP) for encrypting communication in which each station shares a key with the wireless base station. Although WEP is far from perfect, having several known flaws such as community keys for stations and access points, enabling WEP can make an attacker's work somewhat more difficult. One reasonable defense is to require individual authentication for each station to connect, such as afforded by using a virtual private network (VPN) (Miller, 2001).

Message Encryption

As noted earlier, a key source of privacy risk in search is search engines that use HTTP for plaintext communication over the Internet. Encrypting the end-to-end communication between the searcher and search engine using a protocol such as HTTPS (Secure HTTP) makes eavesdropping, surveillance, and man-in-the-middle attacks considerably more difficult. HTTPS is HTTP in conjunction with SSL (secure sockets layer) and is widely used for securing financial transactions over the Internet. SSL acts as a new protocol layer between HTTP and transport control protocol responsible for data encryption and compression. The browser vendor Netscape Communication Corporation introduced SSL in 1995; since then most browsers and servers have incorporated SSL.

The basic purpose of HTTPS is to secure communication between the two communicating ends; it requires both the searcher's browser and the search engine to use HTTPS. Where normally HTTP relies upon TCP to carry plaintext between client and server Web applications, HTTPS uses SSL to determine a common key and encrypt plaintext messages before passing to TCP for delivery. Unfortunately, although SSL is widely available on browsers and servers, none of the major search engines supports HTTPS (i.e., SSL) so most search communications remain in plaintext.

The searcher is generally interested in ensuring they are communicating with the authentic search engine, the communication is private, and communication is unaltered. HTTPS using SSL attempts to accomplish these by the following means:

1. Two-party negotiation of parameters to agree upon SSL version, cryptographic algorithms, key size, compression, and other options. The searcher's browser sends preferences and a random number for later encryption use to the search engine. The search engine responds

with preferences, a random number, and an authentication certificate containing its public key.

2. Authentication through certificates issued by trusted certification authorities (CAs) allows the browser to confirm the search engine's identity. The CA certifies proof of identity and digitally signs a publicly available certificate that contains the search engine's public key. Browsers are preloaded with a list of well-known, trusted CAs, allowing the browser to authenticate the search engine's certificate and public key. Normally the browser end has no need to be authenticated.
3. SSL uses public-key cryptography for secret communication to determine a common session key. After authenticating the search engine certificate, the browser responds with a random premaster key encrypted using the search engine's public key, allowing decryption of the premaster key only by using the search engine's private key. The common session key used for encryption can only be computed from the premaster key and the random numbers exchanged between the search engine and the browser. At this point, we have two important results. The searcher can be confident that all subsequent communications will be with the search engine and not some other site masquerading as the search engine. Secondly, all communications can now be encrypted using the common session key, allowing only the searcher and search engine to write and read subsequent messages. Some other site masquerading as the search engine could attempt but, without the common session key to write or read messages, would be unsuccessful. Without the common session key, an eavesdropper would be unable to read messages.
4. Data integrity protection ensures that messages have not been altered during transit. Each message and the session key is hashed using an agreed upon algorithm such as MD5; the resulting hash is appended to the message, encrypted using the session key and transmitted. The receiving end decrypts the message and recomputes the hash to verify the message integrity. The need of the session key to decrypt the message thwarts attacks that intercept and modify messages between the searcher and search engine. Because constructing a different message with the same hash value is computationally unfeasible, verifying the hash ensures that the message is genuine.

Although the majority of e-commerce applications use SSL to secure financial transactions SSL is not used more generally to protect privacy and ensure no one has tampered with communications. The major search engines do not use SSL but communicate in plaintext. One reason is the added burden and delay placed on the search engine to negotiate a SSL connection; rather than sending a single message with search results back to the searcher, several are required. There is also the overhead to perform the necessary encryption, decryption, compression, and hash computations on messages. However, the major reason is that search engines and most other Web servers operate as stateless applications, meaning they keep no memory of the searcher's visits from one to the next, other than by a cookie. Being stateless allows the search engine implementation to be much simpler, makes it possible to distribute new queries among a group of search engines independent of previous queries, generally requiring less resources of a search engine when responding (we will see later that search engines do log query information but typically not for answering queries). Because each query is independent of those made previously, the search engine response only depends upon the current query. For large search engine sites consisting of multiple identically functioning systems, the independence of queries implies that any system can answer any query, a critical point for load balancing. From the search engine's point of view, there is little benefit to remembering the history of each searcher, only to answer their immediate query. For a major search engine with millions of daily searches, the additional time required for SSL is significant.

Proxies and Anonymous Search

Anonymity on the Internet results in privacy, anonymization proxies attempt to cloak one's identity by acting as intermediaries between the searcher and search engine. In their simplest form, a proxy merely passes data between the searcher and search engine. Proxies are useful to searcher privacy in two important ways: one is to maintain searcher anonymity with the search engine; the other is to provide the searcher encryption of communication. Placing an internal proxy (see Figure 7) physically between the searcher and the Internet gateway gives the proxy complete control of all communication; the proxy is able to examine and modify messages, such as changing addresses. A proxy may also be located on the Internet, handling only communication the searcher explicitly routes through it. In either case, using proxies improves the possibility but, unfortunately, does not guarantee privacy.

In theory, the searcher can remain anonymous by relaying communications through an intermediate proxy connection to the search engine or other Web sites, hiding the searcher's identity, at least from the search engine

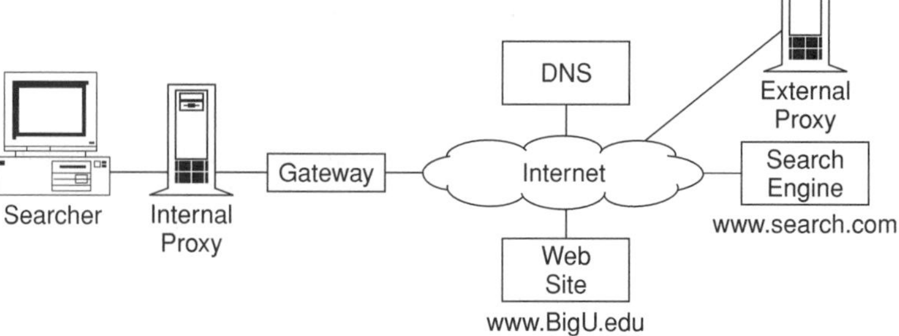

Figure 7: Two types of proxies: the internal proxy passes all Internet communication through it whereas the external proxy passes only communication explicitly routed through it by the searcher.

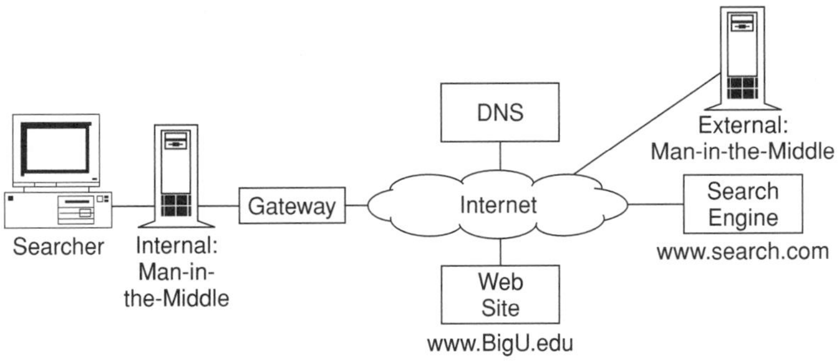

Figure 8: Two forms of the man-in-the-middle attack. The conceptually simpler internal network attack depicted requires physically arranging communications to pass directly through the attacker, giving the attacker access to all communication regardless of the destination address. The more technically sophisticated external attack requires tricking the searcher into addressing communication to the attacker rather than the search engine.

if not the proxy. The proxy performs the anonymization service by receiving a searcher's request and forwarding it with the proxy's identification IP source address. The proxy then receives and returns the search engine results to the searcher (Berghel & Womack, 2003). In practice, simple measures taken against the searcher's browser by search engine or other Web site can render anonymization services ineffective. A browser allowed to execute JavaScript can return identifying data that the proxy leaves intact, although some anonymization services filter or at least comment out all JavaScript destined to the browser. The browser can quietly be redirected by HTML tags (such as the meta-tag REFRESH property) on the page received from an external proxy to another location, bypassing the proxy and exposing the identification of the searcher. Filtering page redirections out is possible but is not necessarily an attempt to bypass proxies, for example, as it is often innocently used on Web sites that have moved to a different location.

As noted, search engines generally communicate only in plaintext, rendering the searcher open to unsophisticated eavesdropping, particularly on a LAN. For encrypted communication, the searcher establishes a SSL connection with the proxy that in turn communicates in plaintext with the search engine; the proxy serves to encrypt and decrypt communication between the searcher and search engine. Although communication between the searcher and proxy over a SSL connection is secure, the proxy can still be bypassed using many of the same methods already discussed.

The anonymization service itself may present the greatest danger to privacy. Enlisted as a trusted intermediary, the service occupies the coveted man-in-the-middle position with access to communications between the searcher, the search engine, and other Web sites. The service may also require a registration based on your real identity, now directly associated to any communications.

Fraud

Fraud is defined as deceit, trickery, or cheating. Whereas listening to communications is a passive attack on privacy, fraud is an active and more nefarious attack. For our discussion, fraud results in the searcher receiving false or misleading information from an agent other than the search engine, such as being directed to a bogus Web site. Fraud is the usual purpose of the man-in-the-middle attack, where all communication between the searcher and the search engine is intercepted, giving the attacker total control over the communication between the searcher and search engine. Privacy is lost if the attacker can decipher the communication and fraud can be conducted if the communication is changed and forwarded clandestinely. There are two essentially different approaches to implementing this attack, depending upon whether the attack is physical to the searcher's own internal network or external through the Internet infrastructure.

Internal

Physically attacking the local network, although effective, requires the attacker to be present and places the attacker in some personal danger; it is not the method of choice when remote attacks are possible. However, the physical model is useful for understanding remote attacks. In both cases, the attacker seeks to be in a position where all communication passes through the attacker. Figure 8 illustrates a physical but unrealistic case of man-in-the-middle; the attacker needs two network connections, one to the searcher network and the other leading eventually to the search engine. All communication between the searcher and search engine then physically flows through the attacker. The attack is unrealistic because the effort needed to get access to the network is unnecessary when much easier and safer methods are available. As discussed earlier, ARP spoofing places the attacker where needed without rearranging network cabling.

After establishing the man-in-the-middle attack, all communication between the searcher and search engine is completely open to attack. With HTTP using plaintext communication, the attacker can easily modify any part of the communication in either direction or covertly act as the searcher or the search engine. For example, the attacker can read the search engine result, make changes, and forward on to the searcher to whom the changes are opaque. Using HTTPS to encrypt the communication can still allow the attacker to read and change the communication after exchanging keys with both the searcher and the search engine. The attack depends upon the searcher accepting a certificate not signed by a trusted certification authority when warned by the browser. After the searcher accepts the certificate, the attacker completes the SSL setup with the searcher's browser and completes a separate SSL setup with the search engine. The attacker can now decrypt communication in any direction, make changes to the plaintext, and encrypt and forward without detection.

External

The external attack requires more sophistication to implement because the attacking agent must be in control

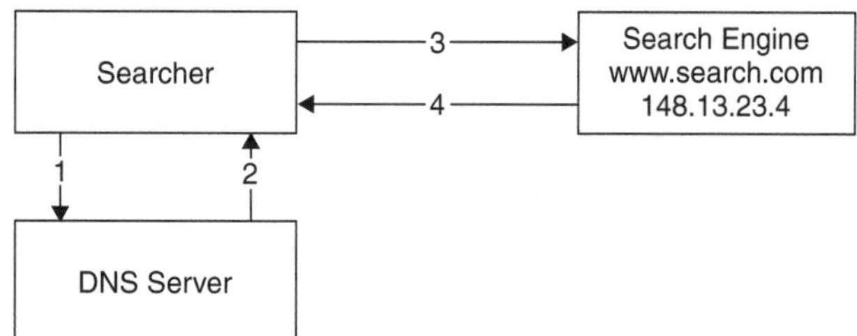

Figure 9a: Normal DNS operation.

1. Searcher's browser contacts DNS server for IP of www.search.com.
2. DNS server replies with IP 148.13.23.4 of www.search.com.
3. Browser sends search query to search engine at IP 148.13.23.4.
4. Search engine returns results.

of the communication without being physically near the searcher, but now the attack can come from anywhere on the Internet. The basic approach again deceives the searcher into addressing packets directly to the attacker rather than the search engine; the attack is similar to the ARP spoofing but using an Internet protocol rather than a LAN protocol. With the searcher fooled, the attack can then proceed much as before as the attacker places their own address as the source and forwards messages to the search engine; the search engine addresses replies to the attacker who places the searcher address as the destination and forwards to the searcher. Again, with plaintext HTTP the attacker can easily monitor or modify any part of the communication in either direction.

Tricking the searcher into addressing packets to the attacker rather than the search engine is itself the key trick. One deception is through DNS spoofing (Tannenbaum, 2002). Normally DNS servers supply IP addresses that correspond to some search engine name on the Internet; the searcher client machine sends the name such as www.search.com to a DNS server and receives back the IP address as in Figure 9a. The client then caches the IP address for a limited time for future references to the search engine name. DNS servers are organized into a hierarchy of servers where each has authority for resolving names to IP addresses for a specific domain. When a client requests a name unknown to the DNS server, that server requests another designated server in the hierarchy to resolve the name; the process of passing the request to other servers in the hierarchy continues until the name is resolved or not. Iterative queries pass the response directly to the client from the resolving DNS server while recursive queries pass the response back to the local DNS server to respond to the client. The distinction is important as recursive queries have the advantage of informing the local DNS server of the IP address for resolving the name again later but also open the door for DNS spoofing.

DNS spoofing is possible in a number of ways but each with the result of the searcher using an attacker's IP address instead of that of the search engine. The goal of DNS spoofing is again to place the attacker in the middle of communications between the searcher and search engine site name such as www.search.com. DNS servers maintain a database of paired (DNS name, IP address) from which they answer requests for DNS name with IP address. When the DNS server cannot answer a request from the searcher, the request is sent to a higher authority server. DNS servers can request that the higher authority return the response directly to the searcher, an iterative request, or return the response to itself, a recursive request, caching the response in the database and returning to the searcher. Configuring DNS servers for recursive requests assumes future requests can be answered from the cache without the overhead and delay of contacting a higher authority. The fundamental trick of the spoof places the record (www.search.com, attacker IP address) on the DNS server used by the searcher; DNS servers configured for recursive requests are open to attack because the cached record is not permanent. In Figure 9b, the attacker first sends a request to the searcher's DNS server for the IP address of www.search.com counting on that DNS server to consult a higher DNS server to locate the IP address. The attacker then follows the request with a forged response from a higher authority DNS server that contains the attacker's IP address. The searcher's DNS server now caches the forgery pair (www.search.com, attacker IP address) in its database. In Figure 9c, when our searcher tries to contact www.search.com they receive the attacker IP address instead and the man-in-the-middle attack can begin.

DNS spoofing is amenable to brute force attacks where the attacker requests the victim DNS server to resolve a search engine name requiring a higher authority (Sacramento, 2002) and fakes multiple higher authority responses until one is accepted. Responses are discarded by the DNS server when the transaction identification (TID), used to connect a response with a request, received does not agree with the TID expected. The attack blindly sends many responses until the DNS server eventually

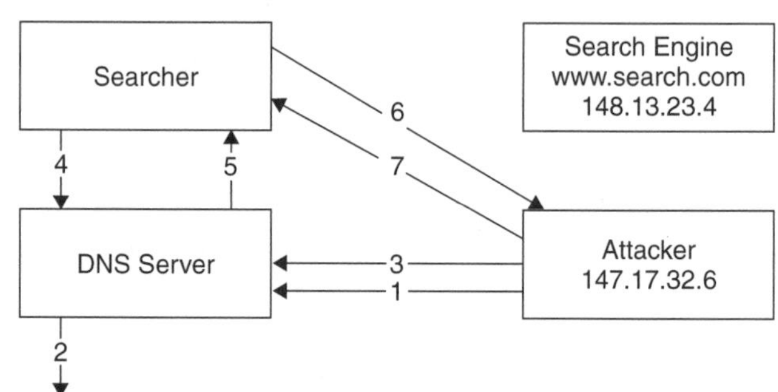

Figure 9b: Attacker masquerading as a search engine.

1. Attacker contacts DNS server for IP of www.search.com.
2. DNS server requests IP of www.search.com from higher authority DNS server.
3. DNS server receives attacker's IP 147.17.32.6 response to www.search.com.
4. Searcher's browser contacts DNS server for IP of www.search.com.
5. DNS server replies with attacker's IP 147.17.32.6 of www.search.com.
6. Browser sends search query to attacker at IP 147.17.32.6.
7. Attacker returns results.

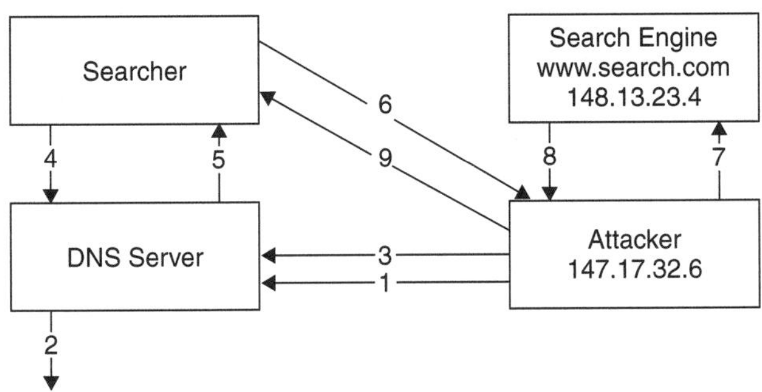

Figure 9c: Attacker intercepting communication between searcher and search engine.

1. Attacker contacts DNS server for IP of www.search.com.
2. DNS server requests IP of www.search.com from higher authority DNS server.
3. DNS server receives attacker's IP 147.17.32.6 response to www.search.com.
4. Searcher's browser contacts DNS server for IP of www.search.com.
5. DNS server replies with attacker's IP 147.17.32.6 of www.search.com.
6. Browser sends search query to attacker at IP 147.17.32.6.
7. Attacker forwards query to search engine.
8. Search engine sends response to attacker.
9. Attacker forwards response to searcher.

accepts one, which can easily be determined when the victim DNS server responds with the attacker's IP number for the search engine name. On older DNS servers, the TID is incremented for each request allowing the attack to be more efficient by discovering a recent TID used in the victim DNS server request and sending higher numbered responses. Launching the attack begins by sending the victim DNS server a request that requires contacting a valid DNS server under the control of the attacker. The TID of the request is noted, a new request for the search engine IP is then sent to the victim DNS server, followed by multiple fake higher-authority responses with the attacker IP and incremented TIDs to ensure acceptance by the victim DNS server.

Fraud Defense

Whether message interception is local or by spoofing the result is the same: the attacker can completely monitor and control communication. Defense is often beyond the control of the average searcher who must rely upon network administrators to secure the network infrastructure.

DNS spoofing is fundamentally a problem of the DNS protocol (Schuba, 1993). An attack is more difficult by using random TIDs but analysis (http://www.kb.cert.org/vuls/id/457875) has shown DNS is still susceptible to spoofing. Among the best protections is for DNS administrators to upgrade BIND, the Berkeley Internet Name Domain software used by nearly all DNS servers on the Internet, which addresses problems with the TID random number generator, and to limit forwarding to only one of multiple requests for the same name to a higher authority.

The best personal defense is to practice safe computing: keep antivirus and operating system software updated and signatures current. Always confirm SSL certificates when making secure online transactions and never accept a certificate not signed by a trusted authority. If you suspect spoofing, contact the ARIN WHOIS records at http://www.ARIN.net/whois to determine whether an IP address pairs with an assigned name. Eventually DNSSec, secure DNS, will allow domain servers to have cryptographically signed records, but it is not widely implemented at this time.

SEARCH ENGINE

Search engines have value to the searcher due to the access it gives to an otherwise opaque Web, to the site searched through the wide public exposure, and to the search engine owners through advertising revenue. As with anything of value, Web search engines are under threat of attack, a curious circumstance as the product, access to the accumulated public data of the Web, is freely available and willingly yielded upon request. Unlike traditional targets of theft such as cash or property, search engine attacks are frequently subtle, often through manipulation by the very Web sites that search benefits. Major search engines are high-profile sites and prime targets for malicious attack, such as denial of service, which if successful serves to advertise the attacker's power and the vulnerability of the technology. Search engines can also assist attackers by providing a source of information on Web sites or individuals and for methods of attack. This section examines how search engines work, common threats, and some of the standard defenses.

Although search engines are careful to distinguish themselves by the algorithmic details of how they determine responses to queries, they share general operational principles with major search engines that search the Web and local engines that search a single Web site, the key difference being the scale of information searched. To a searcher, a search engine purpose is to match their query words with words on Web pages and list those pages containing the matching words. Entering the query word "zucchini" returns a list of pages containing the word "zucchini." In practice, Web search engines examine vast numbers of pages to calculate the page ranking to reduce quantity and improve relevance or quality of the information. Accurately determining page rank based on a few query words is challenging and can produce completely irrelevant results. Entering the single word "zucchini" will find any page mentioning "zucchini," from gardening to cooking to diet; which "zucchini" page is important is ultimately in the mind of the searcher. Determining how to rank one document against thousands of others is a key point of competition between search engines, the identical search on any two will often produce different results; searchers may need to consult several to have confidence in the results. Meta-search engines automate searching on multiple sites by sending the search query to a number of search engines and creating a fusion of the results.

Web search engines have two main tasks: placing keywords from each page into a searchable index and answering search queries from that index. Web-based search engines are only recent versions of traditional full-text systems, such as the SMART and SIRE systems (Salton & McGill, 1983). Rather than employing human editors to manually extract and index subject information from pages, such systems perform automatic indexing of complete pages into a database, creating lists of words and the page locations that contain each word. Answering queries from the index compares query words to page words, retrieving those pages that have some high, calculated relationship value to the query.

Indexing

A Web site creates pages with information and a search engine spider (or crawler, robot, etc.) visits the Web site to retrieve pages for indexing. The spider begins at a root page on the site and follows links to other pages on the site, indexing meaningful words of the retrieved pages along with the page's Web site location on the search engine for later searches and retrievals. The automatic indexing of a page first removes most common or stop words such as "a," "the," and "it"; because almost all pages contain those words they are nearly useless in discriminating between pages. Each remaining word then has a weight factor calculated based in part on word frequency. Weight measures also may give greater or lesser importance to words in different parts of the page; for example, title words generally receive more weight than regular text words. A word that occurs in few pages also has a higher weight, based on the proportion of times that the word occurs in a single page relative to all other pages indexed. A word that occurs on only one page would then have relatively high weight whereas a word occurring on all pages would have low weight, the rationale being that a rare word is more useful in finding a page than a word common to many pages. The same rationale applies to the removal of stop words. Conceptually, the resulting index contains all words from all pages, excluding stop words. Included with each word is a list of all the pages that contain the word; for each page in the list, the frequency the word occurs in the page is stored for weight calculation along with the location of the page for retrieval.

Web search engines differ significantly from traditional search engines in that pages are scattered across many thousands of Web sites and each page can have connections to many other pages. To find pages and build the index, the indexing spider program must then visit Web sites as one would with a browser, starting at a page, visiting connected pages on the site, indexing each page as it goes.

Because spiders visit Web sites and pages much as someone browsing the Web, they are subject to many of the same attacks (e.g., man-in-the-middle). More common are Web sites that play bait-and-switch on a spider by hosting two different sets of pages, one for normal visitors, and special pages presented to visiting spiders. Spiders follow specific rules when indexing a Web site; the rules define which pages on the site are indexed, which parts and how much of the page is selected, and how links to other pages are treated. Visiting spiders are shown the bait pages designed specifically for the spider's indexing rules; a searcher visit is switched to the real page. Not only can the site content be switched on the spider, the Web site can also manipulate the spider through the indexing rules; exactly how is examined in the section "What Search Engines Search."

Retrieval

The traditional retrieval process produces a ranking of all pages that contain one or more query words entered by the searcher. The retrieval operation consists of converting the query words to the same representation as the pages, calculating a similarity measure between the query and each page in the collection, and retrieving pages from the collection ranked in order of high to low similarity.

A common similarity measure is the cosine of the angle between the words of the query and the words from individual pages. Determining the cosine similarity measure requires representing the words of the query and pages as vectors in a multidimensional word space where each axis corresponds to a different word drawn from the indexed pages. Roughly described, if a page matches the query, the angle between the query and the page vector is zero; having fewer words in common produce a greater angle or smaller similarity. Figure 10 illustrates the indexing of pages p1 and p2 containing the words "weight" and "diet loss," respectively, where each axis corresponds to one of the three words. Representing the pages and query as vectors in three-dimensional space, the query vector for "diet" has a smaller angle with respect to the "diet loss" page p2 than with respect to the "weight" page p1. Intuitively, the "diet" query is somewhat similar to the "diet loss" page and not similar to the "weight" page. Based strictly on similarity to the query "diet," the search engine would return a high ranking for the p2 page and a low ranking for the p1 page.

Retrieval, particularly the calculation of page rank from the search query words, is vulnerable to manipulation, creating a service industry devoted to increasing the rank of a client's Web site pages. The purpose of manipulating search engine rank is to promote traffic to the Web site holding that page. The manipulation depends upon constructing pages that exploit known characteristics of

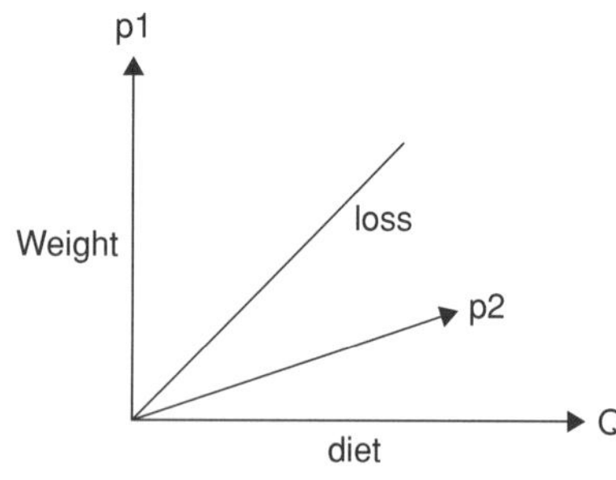

Figure 10: Two pages indexed on the words "weight," "loss," and "diet," where page p1 contains the word "weight" and p2 contains the words "loss" and "diet." Measuring similarity is as the cosine of the angle between a page and query vectors; the smaller angle corresponds to greater similarity. A query of "diet" would have some similarity to page p2 but no similarity to the "weight" page p1.

the spider and the ranking algorithm to produce a higher rank for specific queries. For example, a search engine might use a similarity measure that ranks pages highest that contain the greatest number of matches with query words. Pages can achieve a higher ranking for a given query by adding gratuitous but frequently used query words, a practice known in the trade as "spamdexing" where pages contain hidden words from a list of those most commonly used in actual queries. Standard candidates include "thong," "jobs," and "maps," with "santa" making the list near Christmas. Such words may have nothing to do with the Web page's apparent purpose and seldom appear when viewing the page in a browser. Other, crude manipulations include repeating the same word many times to increase the page rank; more manipulation details are in the following sections.

People continue to search because they trust search engine results to some degree; although the results may not always be useful, we expect a best effort on the part of the search engine. Manipulation places that trust of a search engine in jeopardy; as a defense, manipulation attempts generally deemed excessive can lead to the banning of a Web site by a search engine. Manipulation must exist to some degree, as Web pages are, of course, designed to attract an audience. The problem is the degree of manipulation; deciding between excessive and reasonable attempts at manipulation is up to the search engine site. Indexing and retrieval algorithms follow predictable patterns that attempt to produce highly relevant search results. A Web site aids the search engine and itself with pages crafted to match those characteristics, that is, manipulation; the ethical dividing line lies somewhere between truthful content with no attempt at manipulation and overt manipulation practices such as "spamdexing."

Web search engines attempt to exploit the special features of Web pages to improve retrieval quality beyond those possible using traditional text retrieval methods alone. Assigning specific elements of a page, such as title words or links to other pages, special weight can improve the results over a strict similarity measure ranking. Page popularity and importance measures utilize the natural links between Web pages to refine rank calculated on word matches alone. Popularity assigns a higher rank to pages having more references from other pages under the assumption that a frequently referenced page is more relevant than a page with fewer references. Figure 11 illustrates the popularity of page A to be greater than that of either B or C, as more links or references are to A than to either B or C.

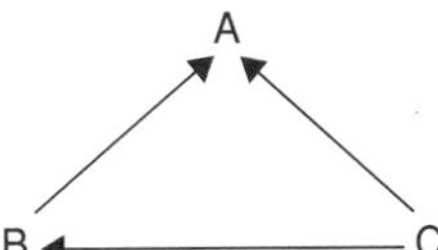

Figure 11: The number of links to a page measures its popularity. Two links confer on page A the greatest popularity, B the next, and C the least popularity. The ranking based on popularity would be ABC.

However, a popular page is not automatically important. One definition of page importance is in terms of the number of links to the page and the importance of the linking sites. For example, a link from an Internal Revenue Service page to a page on taxes is intuitively more important and adds greater rank than a link from a random individual to the same page. This global ranking scheme is the basis of PageRank (Page, Brin, Motwani, & Winograd, 1998), used by the search engine Google.

Although a discussion of the full PageRank algorithm is beyond the scope of this chapter, the basic concepts (Arasu et al., 2001) are relatively clear when limited to a Web where every page is reachable by every other page. For that assumption, let $1, 2, 3, \ldots, m$ be pages on the Web; let $N(i)$ be the number of links from page i; let $B(i)$ be the set of pages linking to page i. Then $r(i)$, the simple PageRank of page i, is

$$r(i) = \sum_{j \in B(i)} \frac{r(j)}{N(j)}.$$

Note that dividing by $N(j)$, the number of pages linked from a page, reduces the ranking contribution of a page as the number of pages linked to increases. This fits one's intuition that a page with links to many, possibly loosely related pages should not contribute as much rank as a page that links to only a few, likely more closely related pages.

In practice, the algorithm ranks a page higher than an otherwise identical one if a large enough set of pages link to that same page. This characteristic of the algorithm has proven sensitive to manipulation by a relatively few cooperating Web sites. Called "Google bombing," pages on multiple Web sites are constructed to hold essentially the same phrase and links to the target page. As more Web sites add the manipulation page, the rank of the target page increases to the point where a matching search query returns a high ranking of the target page. After a successful bombing, the algorithm ranks the targeted page higher than the referring pages that contain the actual query words. A manipulation page could consist of only the HTML tag <a href='http://www.bomb.com'>bomb phrase</a>; after indexing enough sites containing the bomb page, Google will respond to the query "bomb phrase" by returning a highly ranked link to the target site www.bomb.com. This particular manipulation method appears to have been first recognized by an individual (Mathes, 2001) when searching for "internet rockstar" using Google.

WEB SITE

Web sites provide the fodder, the reason to search; though the site is dependent on search to attract visitors, the exposure naturally places the site at greater risk to external attack. Web sites are also threats to the other parties of search, having the most to gain by deceiving and manipulating the search engine and by intrusion upon the searcher's privacy; some manipulation practices can result in banishment from a search engine or legal action. Web sites are also vulnerable; attacks against searchers (discussed in the section "Searcher") can redirect them to bogus Web sites and search can expose sensitive data, threatening privacy and security. This section examines only the special facets of Web site security, privacy, and threats that are most directly a result of search while necessarily ignoring the important but more general issues surrounding Web server and site security.

Web Site Discovery

Most Web sites have the goal of attracting visitors who most often find a new site via a search engine; building an easily found and searchable site is critical. A study of search success (Users Don't Learn to Search Better, 2001) illustrates the difficulties and necessity of designing a Web site for search. After watching 30 searchers search different sites for content that was on the sites, the study concluded, "The more times the users searched, the less likely they were to find what they wanted." Single searches found the content 55% of the time, those searching twice found the content only 38% of the time, and those searching more than twice never found the content. Nearly 23% of the searchers received a "no results" response on their first searches, causing most to give up immediately. For those who continued to search, results only grew worse. Further compounding search problems is the prevalence of invalid links to pages no longer accessible; one study (Lawrence et al., 2000) gives the percentage of invalid links ranging from 23% of 1999 pages to 53% of 1993 pages.

How does a search engine discover a Web site? Given that any search engine indexes only a small fraction of the Web (Lawrence & Giles, 1999), the answer is of critical importance to the Web site designer hoping to attract visitors. Most search engines accept free submissions for indexing all or part of the Web site and paid submission to multiple search engines is available through service companies. Complementary links with other sites will also widen visibility and speed the discovery of a Web site; sites with few links have a lower probability of indexing. The most certain and direct approach is to purchase key words on a search engine; a query with a site's key word is guaranteed to return the site, though normally distinguished from those listed by the merit of rank. Once a Web site is discovered by search engines, the methods to influence automated search become important, though often the best strategy is to develop and maintain high-quality content to attract and cultivate loyal visitors. Where content quality or time is in shorter supply than money, the paid listing can guarantee that a site is highly ranked for specific query words.

What Search Engines Search

Since Web sites compete against one another for a high page rank and search engines sell placement at the top, the searcher has reason to question the accuracy and veracity of the ranking results. Driving the competition for visitors are searchers who are more likely to visit the higher ranked sites first; given that search engines bring in the majority of first-time visitors, high placement in the ranking means money to the commercial Web site. The search engine positioning industry has sprung up to evaluate and manipulate search engine bias in order to raise the ranking of their client's Web site. Pages can be crafted to match the spider indexing and search engine ranking algorithms in an attempt to indirectly manipulate the query results. Indexing and ranking algorithm rules are often sensible but sometimes appear fickle. Some rules are based on apparently common sense approaches such as assigning the page title a higher weight than other text; other rules look for patterns considered abusive that when discovered can theoretically lead to banning of the site. Arbitrarily changing the rules as defense against too successful manipulations such as the "Google bomb" noted earlier is common among search engines. The following Content and Tag Sections details those parts of the Web page most commonly used for indexing and ranking.

Web pages can be richer sources of search and ranking information than traditional documents such as books and journals due to the natural connections formed to related pages and the characteristics of the HTML used for writing Web pages. Web search engines generally seek to improve upon traditional retrieval systems by extracting added information from the title, description, and key word HTML tags and by analyzing the connecting links to and from a page.

Recognizing the parts of a Web page that attract the attention of indexing spiders is critical to Web site designers attempting to raise the visibility of the Web site. Ideally, a Web site designer could give instructions to visiting spiders on precisely how best to index the page to produce high-quality search results. Unfortunately, self-promoting Web sites generally have a history of hijacking spider indexing rules for their own benefit. In response to blatant self-promotion, few spiders observe a published protocol as to which page to index or which parts of the page are considered important. However, most observe published guidelines to Web site promotion (Sonnenreich & Macinta, 1998).

Risks of Search

Web sites by nature expect global exposure and increased risk over operating in a closed environment; search tends to exacerbate any existing risks to privacy and security. Public exposure of personal information, either accidental or purposely, is a serious risk to individual privacy. For example, many individuals place personal e-mail addresses on pages for specific reasons; an instructor might include their e-mail address on a course syllabus for students. Privacy can suffer by using public information for unintended purposes, such as when e-mail spammers automate address collection by seining for pages containing the "mailto" tag.

There are some privacy defenses for personal information exposed on the Web. The most common and effective protection places sensitive information, such as an e-mail address, in an image. Spiders do not index images, only text, foiling direct harvesting through a search engine; requiring a human to read the information, a prohibitive inconvenience and expense for e-mail spammers. A different approach effectively hides the mailing information in JavaScript code since spiders generally do not index JavaScript source or execute the source and examine the results; the browser can execute the JavaScript to display the address for normal use. The simple JavaScript

```
<script language="JavaScript">
    document.write('<a href="mailto:Me@');
    document.write('mail.com">');
    document.write('Me@');
    document.write('mail.com</a>');
</script>
```

Figure 12: Hiding sensitive information in program code from spiders.

in Figure 12 displays clickable text and "mailto" attribute of Me@mail.com in a browser but forces the spider to execute JavaScript for indexing. Camouflaging, such as in JavaScript or images, makes visible to humans information that should be hidden from spiders.

A form of piracy, copying images, content, pages, or even the entire site, is made easy and potentially undetected; stealing from a top-ranked site is one way to mimic their success. In most cases, the HTML, script, and images of pages viewed in the browser can also be saved and published in a few seconds on another Web site; robots that copy each page while traversing each site link can automate stealing the entire site. One defense makes public only encrypted pages that the browser can automatically decrypt for viewing. The page is encrypted and delivered with a program script to decrypt the page; the browser must execute the script in order to render the page for viewing. Although copying the page is still possible, the encrypted portion cannot easily be decrypted into plaintext without executing the script outside the browser; probably more effort than the page is worth to the average pirate. However, encrypting the page makes it unreadable to nondecrypting spiders also and therefore not searchable.

Content

The end result of search leads to a Web site and some page content that the searcher sees and reads. The readable text, as displayed by a browser in Figure 13, provides the bulk of the words indexed by the spider. As noted in the section on search engine implementation, the spider ignores stop words, which are worthless in distinguishing one page from another. Less common words increase the page rank but are valuable only if a searcher uses that word in a query. Using many different words in a page improves search breadth but the words again must be used by the searcher. Including important key words in the title, increasing the frequency of a key word in the text, and placing key words near the beginning of the page content can improve page rank on most search engines. Be aware that repeating a key word multiple times in the title may gain a higher ranking but many search engines ban blatantly bogus attempts at manipulation and may reject the page or site entirely. The challenge to the page author is to find the right key words rare enough to stand out, descriptive of the content subject and familiar to the searcher. Bear in mind that most indexing spiders only examine the first few hundred words of content so it is important to provide descriptive key words early in the content text.

Web sites that present deceptive content threaten the trust of searchers and, by implication; the search engine reputation is jeopardized. But Web site authors intentionally follow practices in writing page content with the purpose of achieving a higher ranking by search engines, much as any author attempts to attract readers. However, most search engines consider manipulating content to achieve an artificially high rank abusive and, in theory, can result in banning of the site by the search engine. This raises some important questions—where is the line drawn between good writing to attract searchers and abusive practices? Who decides when the line is crossed? What is appropriate punishment? For a commercial Web site, banishment from a major search engine can be devastating to attracting new business. Search engines, due to lack of any formal regulations, are for now the de facto Web police, with the motivation and power to control at least some aspects of site content and promotion.

Search engines also face a conundrum. The search engine manipulation policy, if enforced and a site is banished, has potentially serious consequences that could affect the conscientious Web site; but if Web sites face no serious threat to their abuse, search engines face a race to the bottom in deceptive practices to achieve a higher ranking. At least one search engine (Ask Jeeves, 2004) posted a policy outlining abusive practices as part of the agreement for submitting a Web site. The policy is concise but leaves considerable room for interpretation by the search engine and Web site writer. The policy defines abuse in terms of spamming techniques designed to return a result unrelated to a user's query or that is ranked artificially high. Examples given of manipulation include Web pages that contain:

1. deceptive text
2. intentionally misleading links
3. deceptive self linking referencing patterns among others in a group
4. off-topic or excessive keywords
5. duplicate content
6. different content than the spidered pages
7. material designed to lead users to other web pages
8. metadata that do not accurately describe the content of a Web page

Crafting the metrics of such a policy is obviously difficult, given that simply stating some fixed number of keywords above which is excessive, is arbitrary and invites other abuse. The approach apparently taken by search

Automated Search Engines
Automated Web search engines have two main tasks; one of indexing the Web information, the second of answering search queries from the index. First, an indexing program visits a Web site much as you would with a browser, normally starting at the default home page, visiting connected pages, and indexing the site information (see Figure 14).

Figure 13: How the HTML of Figure 14 would appear in a browser.

```
<html>
<head>
<meta name = "description" content = "Human lists and automated search engines.">
<meta name = "key words" content = "search engine, indexing">
<title>How Search Engines Work</title>
</head>
<body>
<h1>Automated Search Engines</h1>
Automated Web search engines have two main tasks; one of indexing the Web information, the second of
answering search queries from the index. First, an indexing program visits a Web site much as you would
with a browser, normally starting at the default home page, visiting connected pages, and indexing the site
information (<a href = "Figure14.html">see Figure 14</a>).
</body>
</html>
```

Figure 14: An HTML page contains visible parts displayed by the browser and hidden parts that can help spiders index the page more accurately, provide descriptive information to the searcher, and link to other HTML pages.

engines has been to offer threats more strongly than action in specific cases and to modify indexing and ranking parameters as a more general response to disruptive practices.

Tags

HTML tags are not generally visible to the reader but do contain information important to the spider and are one source of abuse cited by search engine policies. Along with content key words, spiders also extract the page location and may examine HTML tags when indexing a page. The Web site designer can influence the page rank and provide more descriptive search results through the tags. Figure 14 gives the source for a HTML page to illustrate the page content and use the following tags.

Key word: The HTML key word meta-tag contains human-defined key words to augment the automated indexing of the page content. One use of the tag is to provide alternative words or phases for those in the content, for example, using "PDA" in the content and "personal digital assistant" as key words. Unfortunately, promoters have so often abused the key word tag that Web search engines probably ignore it. As noted in the Ask Jeeves (2004) spam policy, the search engine policy forbids excessive key words, indicating that the key word tag will be spidered but not what number constitutes "excessive."

Description: The description meta-tag provides a short content summary for display when the search engine retrieves the page. Figure 15 illustrates how a search engine would display the description tag with other page information.

How Search Engines Work Human lists and automated search engines. http://www.insearchof.org/how.htm

Figure 15: An example of how a search engine might respond to a query. The word "indexing" is part of the key word meta-tag and embedded in the text content. The title is "How Search Engines Work" and the description meta-tag is "Human lists and automated search engines." The document URL "http://www.insearchof.org/how.htm" and the title provide links to the complete document.

Title: Indexing the title tag independently allows explicit searches on the title; the search engine can also display the title as part of the page information, as in Figure 15. As previously mentioned, key words placed in the title are intended to define the page purpose and improve page rank.

Heading: The large print of headings catches the attention of the reader and is important to an indexing spider. The influence of headings on rank generally follows the scale of the heading number, so that weight of the words of a level 1 heading is greater than the weight of the words of a level 2 heading.

Links: The spider follows link connections to other documents through the attribute and hypertext reference tag; for example, "<a href = 'Figure15.html'>" directs the spider to follow the link to the index page "Figure15.html." The popularity ranking method would generally rank a page with many links from other pages relatively high. A cross-listing agreement with other sites serves to increase the rank of each site involved. One could, of course, take the low road and maintain a number of complementary linked sites specifically to manipulate search engine ratings. Despite the apparent advantage to a site connected by links from others, legal challenges have been mounted to stop what is known as "deep linking" (Rosencrance, 2000). The complaint is that unauthorized direct links to deep pages rather than the home page take control of the visitor experience away from the site owners, allowing different visitors to visit different pages, possibly avoiding revenue-generating advertising. Because search engines are effective precisely because they find and link directly to pages, such litigation could have a chilling effect on search.

What Search Engines Ignore

Most spiders purposely ignore or cannot see large parts of a page that human readers might see and use, effectively hiding that part from search engines. Page designers normally expect the spider to index the full page and follow links to other pages but some sensitive material should be excluded from search. By accident or design, spiders can be excluded from indexing some or all pages of a Web site.

Frames: Visibly dividing a browser screen into several parts is the purpose of frames, but unfortunately, frames can stop an indexing spider and create confusion for visitors arriving from a search engine. Frames require at least three separate pages: a hidden frameset page that defines the frames and links visible pages into the frames, a second page for visible content, and a third often for navigation. A spider normally arrives at the hidden frameset page but must understand how to handle frames in order to follow links to the other, visible pages. Spiders that do not understand frames simply stop and never index further. For those spiders and browsers that do not understand frames, the remaining site pages are unreachable unless alternative links exist.

HTTPS: Spiders generally use only HTTP for communications with Web servers and do not normally index a server requiring HTTPS.

Scripts: Most spiders ignore script programs written in JavaScript or other scripting languages; others simply index the script program text. Spiders ignore scripts for two main reasons: the spider must be able to execute the script, which requires an interpreter for the script language; and the spider must simulate any required human interactions such as button clicks. Both are doable but currently not considered worth the effort by spider developers. As a result, scripts can hide sensitive information; see Figure 12 for an example.

Java applets and plug-ins: To a spider, a Java applet, plug-in, or other browser-executed program is invisible since no text is given, other than that needed to execute the program. Unless the spider is willing and able to execute the program, there is nothing to index; if executed by the spider, the program output is likely to be graphical and unreadable by the spider.

Server-generated pages: Spiders may ignore any unusual link references, such as ones that do not end in "HTM" or "HTML." For example, a spider will follow the connecting link "<a href = 'mainpage.HTML'>" but may not follow the link to the Web server program of "<a href = 'mainpage.ASP'>" due to the ending "ASP." Generating the Web site main page with a server program can mean that some spiders ignore the complete site.

Forms: Collecting visitor information is one of the most important functions of many Web sites, but spiders do not know how to fill out forms. Spiders that do index the content and links of the page containing the form create potential problems by leading visitors directly to the form page from a search engine rather than through the pages intended to precede the form.

Robot exclusion: Forms represent one good reason to exclude spiders from indexing certain pages; sensitive information is another. Two standards exist that instruct well-behaved spiders on excluding specified pages. The recognized standard is the "robots.txt" file that lists acceptable and unacceptable directories, pages, and robots (i.e., spiders). A single robot.txt file exists for the entire Web site, which only the site administrator can access, creating a maintenance bottleneck as multiple designers make changes to the site. A distributed but less accepted solution defines a special "robots" meta-tag to specify how to index each individual page. Options are that every spider or no spider should index the page, the page should be indexed or not, or the page links should be followed or not. Neither of the standards prevents a badly behaved spider, such as an e-mail address harvester, from ignoring the exclusion instructions.

Images: Spiders may index the image location, image title, and alternate text but that is probably all due to the effort required to analyze an image.

Meta-tags: The purpose of meta-tags is to provide specific information, such as the character set to browsers or key words to spiders. Most spiders now ignore meta-tags due to past attempts by Web sites to manipulate rank.

Deeply linked pages: Most spiders index only small sites completely, generally indexing only a limited number of pages on each site. Spiders limit indexing to several connecting deep links, ignoring pages linked beyond that depth.

Measuring Success and Tracking Visits

A site can determine whether efforts to attract search engine attention have been a success; the site can also determine information about visitors and their point of arrival. Search engines offer one of the most obvious and direct means for checking whether and to what extent a specific search engine has indexed a site by limiting search to that Web site. These same controls used by searchers can also provide feedback to point out search problems with the Web site. Although tests with individual search engines will determine whether and how a Web site has been indexed, it will not tell if, why, or how anyone visits.

A site can perform visitor tracking by logging and analyzing the details of each visit. Logging by itself is useful for the site administrator to locate problems but also to track a searcher's behavior and discover elements of their identity. The site server holds visitor information in the server access log file with details about every attempted or successful visit. Table 1 lists the information retained in the Web server access log following the Common Logfile Format. Free and commercial analysis software can produce detailed summaries and graphs of the log; the most telling information about search success is contained in the following three fields:

Client request line: This field contains the page on the server the visitor requested. For visitors arriving from a search engine, this contains the link to the page indexed by the spider.

Table 1 Server Access Log Fields in Common Logfile Format

Access Log Field	Example
Client IP address	24.10.2.3
Client identity—unreliable	—
Authenticated client userid	—
Time request completed	[01/May/2002:17:57:03 -0400]
Client request line	"GET/mainpage.htm HTTP/1.1"
Server status code	404
Referring site	"http://www.food.com/ search.html"
Client browser	"Mozilla/4.08 [en] (WinNT; I;Nav)"

Server status code: Status codes starting with a 2 indicate success; those starting with 4 indicate that the visitor probably encountered a mistake. In Table 1, the "mainpage.htm" page does not exist, earning the visitor a "404 Not Found" response from the Web site.

Referring site: Search engines respond to queries by supplying pages that link or refer back to the original page found by the spider. When the browser follows a link from the search engine page, it reports the search engine address that supplied the page or referred them. In Table 1, the visitor arrived via a reference to "mainpage.htm" made by the "www.food.com" search engine.

The log has many legitimate functions in maintaining the Web site but also represents risks to the privacy of visitors. The client IP address and request line alone are sufficient to track visitor behavior on the site, providing information on who (the IP) and what pages (the request line) were visited. Simple analysis of behavior is possible; merely sorting each IP address by the time field yields the page order visited by each client. The search engine used can be determined from the referrer field, which contains the referrer link the visitor followed to the site. Deeper analysis requires additional data; to determine what search brought the visitor to the site requires the query from the search engine; to determine the real identity of the visitor requires connecting the client address to personal data. Such connections intrude upon one's privacy but such inferences are possible by combining cookies or other sources of personal data with the data in the site log.

The log's main utility goes beyond tracking visitors. Examination of the log entries can point out the Web site errors and successes. Counting the number of visitor requests (i.e., client request line) to each page immediately grades pages on success in attracting visitors and, by their absence, identifies those pages that failed. Investigating the referrer list will show how visitors arrive at a Web site; search engines missing from the list have not indexed the Web site or rank its pages below others. A table of visitor page requests with the referring site will clearly show which search engines successfully found specific pages and can flag pages that create indexing problems for particular search engines. As discussed earlier, some spiders are stopped by frames, only index the first few content lines, or crawl a limited number of links on each site. Pages never accessed can indicate indexing problems for the spider or navigation problems for the visitor. Examining the access log file is a good starting point for finding these and other potential search engine and link problems.

Self-Search

Many sites maintain their own local search engine but why does a site need its own search? Are there any special benefits or risks involved in operating a search engine? One can easily provide visitors with search by placing a link on site pages to a Web search engine. Spiders are far from perfect at indexing Web sites, ignoring some pages that are important, and Web search results focus not on the one site alone but must compete with results from other sites. Moreover, spiders ignore changes to sites because of long periods between their visits; Web search would be unsatisfactory for a news site. Web search engines, which bring most new visitors to a Web site, are poorly suited for searching a site exclusively. However visitors arrive, one authority (Neilsen, 2000) has found that many visitors immediately use search on arrival as the preferred means of locating information and ignore site navigation aides; those visitors need a search engine tailored to the Web site.

Operating the search engine and the Web site allows deeper analysis of search behavior and possibly to connect that behavior with personal information. The Web server site log contains visitor IP address, pages viewed, and referrer page data; the search engine can log searcher IP address and query; combined with cookies to track multiple visits, the site can build a profile of an individual. Shopping sites make use of these techniques in determining purchasing patterns to suggest purchases similar to those others have made. One can imagine the site monitoring failed searches to determine new stock to carry, a smart business strategy. One can also imagine abuse of the same information.

What should a site designer look for in a search engine? A search engine for a site is comparable in function to a Web search engine but can limit search to the given site. Beyond the raw power required to index a complete Web site, a key capability is to create and search specified branches of the Web site. Indexing every word of the entire site is easy to do but ignores the different reasons visitors search the site and the principle that search works best when the information searched is narrow and homogenous. For example, search of a university Web site should give visitors the choice of whether to search the business and science separately or all school categories combined.

Separating business from science capitalizes upon natural and recognized differences to create a narrower, homogenous, and recognizable information area to search. Another issue is the sophistication and flexibility of the search engine. Does it support automatic or manual word stemming, common misspellings, indexing of the HTML tags, synonyms, inclusion and exclusion query operators, and phrase and proximity search?

Two basic options exist for search dedicated to a site: site operated or retained by an off-site search service. Having someone else handle search is the easier solution but does not necessarily match the owner's needs; handling search oneself can be more flexible but involves more work and expense.

Search Service

Search service companies will index a few pages or an entire Web site, will operate the search engine on their computer, and are in some cases free. The free services generally index a limited number of pages; in return the service places advertising on each search result page. A good service should index pages located on any Web site, index with reasonable promptness whenever the owner chooses, and provide regular summaries of search activity for the site. The main advantage is that someone else maintains the search engine and bears the responsibility for security.

Operational concerns of a search service are the continued cost, the possible limit on pages indexed, scheduling the occasional reindexing, the lack of control over the search results or the result page appearance, and the advertising banners that may not impress your site visitors. Analysis of search behavior may not be possible since access to the search engine log may not be allowed. However, the most serious problem occurs should the service company drastically change policies or technology or go out of business, forcing the Web site search to change.

Security issues include those normal to Web search engines such as denial of service attacks combined with the additional concern over the impact of a search service failure; search is critical to certain site operations such as an automobile parts business. Susceptibility of the search service to attacks and overall security management can be difficult to determine.

Privacy concerns are similar to those for Web search, an issue for both searchers and the site. Searchers are at risk because the search engine service can use cookies or other means and the search query log to track search behavior of an individual. The search engine is in a position to gather detailed search data on a complete site, data that would be useful for refining the site for search and to other competitive sites for the same purpose. Privacy policies of search services vary widely; not to sell spammers your e-mail address is the only stated policy of at least one search engine.

Reasons for a Private Search Engine

The only compelling reason to operate a private search engine is to benefit site visitors, at least under the theory that what is good for the visitors is good for the site. For private search, operating a basic search engine can be relatively easy and many Web server systems include a search engine. Commercially packaged Linux systems come with the ht://Dig engine installed and ready to index the entire server; the owner need only type the "./rundig" command and add a search form link to the site pages.

The main advantages of a private search engine are control of parameters such as indexing depth and access to the information of the logs produced by the search engine during indexing and visitor queries. The obvious disadvantages relate to maintaining the infrastructure necessary to support search, likely an additional computer and software for searching, and the exposure to additional security risks. In addition to the usual concerns of operating a Web server, most search engine software has proven open to attack in some way; ht://Dig has been reported vulnerable to a denial of service attack (SecurityFocus, 2001).

The following examines common search engine parameters that provide some control over search and much of the motivation to operate a search engine:

Excerpts: Search results can include text excerpted from a page to help place query key words in context. Because the excerpting generally takes place during indexing, the searcher needs a little luck for the excerpt to include at least some of his or her query terms. Controlling the size of the excerpt improves the likelihood that the excerpt will contain some query key words or possibly an entire page.

Indexing: It is important to control the number of words indexed and how often indexing of the site occurs. Although most pages contain fewer than 2000 words or about 7 pages of typed text, indexing spiders with the word limit too low can routinely miss indexing important parts of large pages. Also important to sites with news, pricing, and other frequently updated information is how often indexing occurs and whether it occurs whenever information changes.

Stop Words: Stop words often include numbers and common words such as "the," "computer," "system," and "HTML" and should not be indexed. Words that occur often on many Web site pages should also be included in the stop word list. For example, on a bread Web site, the word "baking" would possess little value in discriminating one page from another.

Measuring Success: Successful searches mean that the visitor follows or "clicks through" to a suggested page. The Web server access log will list the page the visitor follows but only the search engine can log the query words entered to find the page; connecting the query words with the referred page measures the effectiveness of search on a Web site. Other measures of search success are whether visitors actually sought the information they received or immediately searched again, and whether they followed the referred page further to accomplish some task such as buying a car or registering for a class. Failed queries are also valuable for determining words to add to pages as indicated by the key words searchers used, expecting to find information, but failing.

Measuring Failure: Failed searches are valuable in identifying what visitors actually want and expect to find on the site. Visitors are sending a clear message if a Web site for programmers sells nothing except Java programming tools but 75% of the searches are for FORTRAN. Search engines that log failed searches give insight into possible improvements. For example, queries containing predictable misspellings of FORTRAN can succeed after adding misspellings such as FOTRAN to the engine's synonym list.

SEARCH ETHICS

On the surface, particularly to the average user, search appears safe, anonymous, free, and very useful; an unusual bargain. Why is a discussion of ethical issues relevant to search? As we have seen, search has value and poses hazards to security and privacy; and, on many issues that matter is unregulated. While such a discussion will not by itself reduce potential danger or damage, it can play a role in the process of marking the boundaries of acceptable behavior. There are some actions that are clearly improper, such as reading another's communications, and have been examined in previous sections from a technical perspective; actions of an individual will be examined in this section from an ethical perspective.

Ethical behavior by an individual conforms to the standards of right and wrong for their member group. Web search intersects the behavior of at least three groups, the searcher, search engine, and Web site, in addition to deliberate attackers. While not to discount the reasoned ethics of attackers, the discussion focus will continue on members of the first three groups. Membership in the search engine and the Web site group is sharply defined, by nature being public knowledge and exposure, reasonably long term presence, and each having a financial investment in search. Membership in the searcher group is transitory and usually anonymous, with individuals having no knowledge of other searchers, nothing obviously in common other than search, and essentially no financial investment in search. Laws and the threat and cost of exposure provide some of the motivation for ethical behavior, particularly on the part of search engines and Web sites. Search engines are motivated to follow ethical practices to maintain public trust. Web sites may be guided by legal codes or professional organizations, such as the Web site promotion industry, which publish a code to their membership on the ethical issues of the profession and appropriate behavior. Individual searchers bring with them their own ethical standards.

What are the ethical issues in Web search?

Search engines have an interest in maintaining a public appearance of ethical behavior given that the public trust in search results form the foundation of their continued existence. Two key ethical issues for which search engines are directly responsible are bias in site indexing and ranking of search results. Bias in site indexing is spider behavior idiosyncrasies that result in ignoring some legitimate pages and sites, or through deliberate policy decisions by the search engine owners. Spider bias is in part a practical requirement that limits what and how much of a page or site the spider indexes due to technical limitations such as the search engine storage capacity, communication demands, and the relationship of indexing to the retrieval algorithm performance. In theory, bias is then a result of technical decisions to improve search results. In practice, search engines also apply policies that restrict search to approved parts of the Web. The stated target of these policies is spammers, those Web sites who use tactics the search engine finds abusive. Search engines publish spamming polices but do not publish indexing rules and occasionally change those rules as Web site promoters (termed search engine optimization or SEO) eventually infer enough indexing patterns to increase a site's ranking artificially. Such behavior is a defense against attempts at Web site manipulation by SEOs but can reduce traffic and income of conscientious sites when indexing rules seemingly arbitrarily change; a number of search engines warn against specific manipulation practices (Google, 2004). Related to intentional manipulation attempts by a Web site to improve search ranking is the selling of rank placement by search engines. Web sites can pay to have their site prominently displayed on the search response to specific query words; responsible search engines clearly identify these sponsored links as essentially paid advertising.

There is obvious competition between the search engine and an SEO in the selling of visibility to Web sites and a financial interest in each manipulating search to their advantage. The search engine holds the key levers of control; it owns the search service, controls the indexing and ranking rules, sets and enforces the spamming policy, and can decide to make changes to any of these arbitrarily. The search engine by default plays a shadow role of enforcing standards on Web sites, at least those submitting agreements to be searched. One concern here is that financial issues rather than technical performance may influence decisions directly affecting the search engine behavior and the ultimate ranking of a Web site.

Should search engines prevent search of objectionable sites? Spamming policies are evidence that search engines possess at least some technical means to enforce standards by restricting the sites searched and therefore what is generally visible on the Web. Given the cost of operating a large search engine, only a handful exists, creating one of the few central points where access to the Web can be influenced. Currently search is restricted only to those sites deemed abusive for purposes of the search engine.

Should search engines prevent objectionable searches? The automated search engine indexes words from across the Web and responds to queries that contain a subset of those words, generally with no recognition of the semantic value of the search or the intent of the searcher. A search for "build a nuclear weapon" is currently handled the same as a search for "build a swing set" with no attempt or real ability to understand either search. The "build a nuclear weapon" search returns sites on constructing the weapon but also news of efforts to restrict nuclear weapon proliferation; current search engines do not understand the search query beyond simply matching words and calculating a corresponding rank. Network attackers use search engines to locate victims, by marketers trolling for e-mail addresses to harvest, by shoppers hoping to spend less money, and by young children who stumble upon adult material. Most would agree that the attacker, shopper, and child occupy starkly different poles of the ethical spectrum covering search engine use and shades of ethical behavior exist somewhere in between. By the apparent absence of legal implication of search engines in criminal or civil cases, one can infer that current standards have not yet connected responsibility for the use by the searcher of search engine results back to the search engine.

What harm can a search engine cause an individual? Search engines certainly make locating any personal data that happen to be published on the Web much easier. One can reasonably argue that is not the fault or concern of the search engine but the Web site to avoid exposing sensitive data to search. The Web search engine service is usually free to the searcher. The search engine only has access to information posted on a public Web page. The information is freely, if not always consciously or intentionally, available and exposed to the world. What are the standards for use of the search engine and retrieved information? Does placing your e-mail address on a Web page imply an invitation for e-mail spamming? Most would agree that spammers violate no U.S. law, as of yet, but also consider spam an annoyance at best and occasionally causing harm. Although spammers use their own engines to automate e-mail address harvesting, search engines make it possible for individuals to locate personal information from Web pages. Obviously the difference is in how the information is used, whether to contact an old friend or to send thousands of e-mails.

However, search engines often store cookies on the client machine for holding information, perhaps of a personal nature, used in tracking individual behavior if not an individual. A searcher can choose to disable cookies on their browser. Whereas sites that require authentication generally require enabled cookies, major search engines have no authentication and no required need, so cookie use is up to the individual. However, cookies allow the search engine to construct a history of searches identified by a specific machine if not the individual. The search engine generally does not monitor the sites visited or pages viewed through the search, although with site cooperation, that can be performed also. Given that a site may have data that connect to an individual's identity, such cooperation can connect identity to search behavior. Such possible exposure is not expected by most searchers. Collecting data imparts responsibility for its safeguarding and proper use, requiring technical competency to secure the data and motives to protect the individual from harm.

What are the Web site concerns? Web sites far outnumber search engines and span a broader range of behavior; unlike search engines that need long-term trust of the public, Web sites can benefit from disingenuous behavior. Web sites that attempt to gain ranking and traffic by presenting one site to a spider and another to a browser misrepresents the site, seemingly a clear violation of ethics; one that harms the accuracy of the search engine and misleads the searcher. Because spider and search engine manipulation ranges over a continuum, one usually measured by degrees rather than discrete events, objectively categorizing actions is difficult. However, the business of a SEO involves methods that benefit their client's Web site; though the methods are not necessarily manipulative, they do target known search engine behavior to gain some advantage for their client. Whereas the SEO industry is not unethical, the methods often employed characterize the excesses of some Web sites; hence a natural tension exists between search engines and SEOs. It is instructive to examine some of the industries' own ethical standards; one company's ethical code (Search Engine Ethics, 2002) states that "Any SEO should not use any methodology which may result in having a client removed from a search engine index or directories, or rendered inoperative." It goes on to say that published search engine rules should not be violated, copyrights must be respected, and confidential information is not to be disclosed; a concise statement of ethical behavior. Web sites as a group have no representative body and no published standards of conduct other than that enforced by search engines and regulatory agencies such as the Federal Trade Commission. The global nature of the Web search brings into question the standards applicable to a Web site.

Are the interests of society being served? What behavior serves the long-term interests of the search community and the larger interests of society? Are new laws and regulations needed to protect and promote the future development of the Web and search? Search engines have democratized information retrieval much as the Web has democratized authorship; it is now easy for a large number of the privileged people in the world, from students to hobbyists, to publish and be discovered electronically. Society benefits from the wide and rapid exchange of ideas, Web search occupies a potentially historic position in the communication of knowledge. Does placing work on the Web place the work in the public domain? Most would agree that the act of publishing does not yield one's rights to benefit from the work. However, a work published on the Web often garners different treatment than one published and printed in the traditional manner. The sharpest distinction is on cost; traditional publishing is financially risky, in large part due to the inventory and distribution of the physical product. Publishing electronically, requiring no inventory, has a much lower risk, being able to generate the product on demand for each sale.

Society gains when ideas are exchanged. The printing industry gains from copyright laws that serve to protect the financial investment in producing the means of expression. Society trades gains in the sharing of ideas for some restrictions by offering protection through these same laws. However, some argue that on the Web, plagiarism matters more than copyright piracy to society (Snapper, 1999). Copyright piracy causes harm to the copyright owner; plagiarism fails to give due credit. For example, including copyrighted work without permission in a published collection may deprive the copyright owner the opportunity of future sales. Failure to credit the creator of the work is plagiarism. Society has laws against copyright piracy but not against plagiarism, implying that protection of the means of expression is important to society but not credit for the idea. Failure to credit the author is not a punishable offense, except for good reasons, among academics. Injury to society results because plagiarism breaks the intellectual trail established by citations, when prior work is not cited the trail is broken.

Plagiarism is an old problem encouraged by the modern Web and search engine technologies. By definition, a plagiarist passes off another's ideas as his or her own.

One can define degrees of plagiarism that ranges from the modest, perhaps unintentional, parroting of a well-turned phrase to the lifting of complete passages or programs to the blatant copying of complete Web sites. The search engine technology only locates and exposes the Web page to the searcher; the searcher must intentionally copy the page to their computer. Although the same ethical issues of recognizing ownership apply to Web pages as to traditional work, search has made locating intellectual property and the Web has made copying almost effortless.

Society's interest lies at the new intersection between piracy and plagiarism formed by Web search. Can copying a published Web page be any more or less ethical than copying from a published book? Is society better served by a loosening of copyright laws and a strengthening of plagiarism prohibition on the Web? The dynamics of the Web are different from traditional printed publications. Whereas printed work cannot easily be revised after publication, Web published works can be changed without evidence of the revision. Whereas there are many printed copies distributed after publication, Web published works may exist as a single copy. The conundrum of the Web is that citations may reference a work that has changed, moved or no longer exists; breaking the intellectual trail valuable to future work. Where in the past, citing a work was sufficient to establish the trail; certainty of the work's existence in the form cited can only be ensured by archival of the work. This practice is already common among academic journals but not on the Web generally. Loosening copyright protection to allow archival copying by individuals and strengthening prohibitions on plagiarism may benefit the future development and growth of Web-based work.

One small irony; the search engine both promotes and exposes plagiarism of Web page information as many student authors of term papers have discovered. Surprisingly, many fail to recognize that phrases copied from a Web page originally found by a search engine serve as the perfect query to produce an unambiguous target back to the source. Evidence of copying entire pages is clear from many queries that return identical pages from several different sites that fail to credit the author. Sadly, pages on computer ethics have appeared nearly verbatim on other Web sites with no acknowledgements.

CONCLUSION

Web search is critical to navigating the Web but is still in its infancy, with many remaining details to sort out; accuracy will improve as efforts to make Web content more searchable progress and the new models needed for sharing and maintaining legacy information will develop. The chapter paints a somewhat gloomy picture of the current security and privacy when searching the Web, a Web that depends upon an infrastructure designed and implemented with little thought for risk management. Although there are measures that individuals, ISPs, and Web sites can take to manage risk, all require extra effort and continued diligence. Technology exists and efforts are underway that eventually will result in Internet communications and Web search designed with security in mind, so the future does hold out the promise that successful attacks will become technically more difficult. However, many non-technical issues affecting privacy, such as identification and monitoring of search behavior by search engines, government agencies, and employers will remain and almost certainly grow with the importance of Web search as a source of information.

GLOSSARY

ARP (Address Resolution Protocol) A protocol for associating IP addresses to local area network addresses.

Common Logfile Format A standard format for logging and analyzing Web server messages.

Cookie Information stored and retrieved through the browser on the client computer.

DNS (Domain Name System) The Internet service that translates mnemonic site names to IP site addresses.

HTTP (Hypertext Transfer Protocol) Protocol used by Web servers and browsers for communications.

Index List of words extracted from pages and the location of each page where the word was extracted, used for matching query words and locating the pages containing the matches.

Meta-search The fusion of the results from multiple search engines simultaneously searching on the same query.

Page A Web document containing plaintext and hypertext markup language for formatting and linking to other pages.

PageRank A system of ranking Web pages where a link from page A to page B increases the rank of page B.

Phrase search A search for documents containing an exact sentence or phrase specified by a user.

Precision The degree to which a search engine matches pages with a query; when all pages are relevant to the query, precision is 100%.

Query Words given to search engine in order to locate pages containing the same words.

Recall The degree in which a search engine matches relevant pages; when all relevant pages are matched, recall is 100%.

Relevancy The degree to which a page provides the desired information, as measured by the searcher.

Search engine The software that searches an index of page words for query words and returns matches.

SEO (Search Engine Optimizer) A business that attempts to match a client's Web site design with those features likely to produce a high ranking by a search engine.

Spider The software that locates pages for indexing by following links from one page to another.

SSL (Secure Socket Layer) A communications software layer for secure end-to-end communications between two parties.

Web site A Web location holding and providing access to pages via the World Wide Web.

CROSS REFERENCES

See *Anonymity and Identity on the Internet; Internet Basics; Legal, Social, and Ethical Issues of the Internet; Privacy Law and the Internet.*

REFERENCES

Arasu, A., Cho, J., Garcia-Molina, H., Paepcke, A., & Raghavan, S. (2001). Searching the Web. *ACM Transactions on Internet Technology, 1*(1), 2–43.

Ask Jeeves. (2004). *Site submit service terms and conditions*. Retrieved January 28, 2004, from http://ask.ineedhits.com/programterms.asp?n=u.

Berghel, H., & Womack, K. (2003). Digital village: Anonymizing the net. *Communications of the ACM 46*(4), 15—20.

Dsniff. Retrieved January 14, 2004, from http://www.monkey.org/~dugsong/dsniff.

Edgar, T. (2003). Interested Persons Memo: Section-by-Section Analysis of Justice Department draft "Domestic Security Enhancement Act of 2003," also known as "PATRIOT Act II," American Civil Liberties Union Legislative Update, February 14, 2003. Retrieved September 12, 2004, from http://www.aclu.org/SafeandFree.

Google Information for Webmasters. (2004). Retrieved September 11, 2004, from http://www.google.com/webmasters/seo.html.

Google Press Release. (2004). *Google achieves search milestone with immediate access to more than 6 billion items*, February 17, 2004. Retrieved September 11, 2004, from http://www.google.com/press/pressrel/ 6billion.html.

Graham, R. (2004). *Carnivore*. Retrieved April 7, 2005, from http://www.totse.com/en/privacy/privacy/161818.html.

Hock, R. (2001). *The extreme searcher's guide to Web search engines* (2nd ed.). Medford, NJ: CyberAge Books, Information Today.

Lawrence, S., Coetzee, F., Glover, E., Flake, G., Pennock, D., Krovetz, B., et al. (2000). Persistence of information on the Web: Analyzing citations contained in research articles. In *Proceedings of the Ninth International Conference on Information and Knowledge Management* (pp. 235–242). New York: ACM Press.

Legal Standards for the Intelligence Community in Conducting Electronic Surveillance report required by FY 2000 Intelligence Authorization Act. Retrieved January 18, 2004, from http://www.fas.org/irp/nsa/standards.html#2.

Mathes, A. (2001). *Filler Friday: Google bombing*. Retrieved January 15, 2004, http://www.uber.nu/2001/ 04/06/.

Miller, S. (2001). Facing the challenge of wireless security. *Computer*, IEEE Computer Society Press, July 2001.

Mowshowitz, A., & Kawaguchi, A. (2002). Bias on the Web. *Communications of the ACM, 45*(9), 56–60.

Neilsen, J. (2000). Is navigation useful? The Alertbox: Current issues in Web usability. Retrieved May 2002 from http://www.useit.com/alertbox/20000109.html.

OCLC (2002). How Academic Librarians Can Influence Students' Web-Based Information Choices. *White Paper on the Information Habits of College Students*. June 2002. Retrieved April 7, 2005, from http://www. mnstate.edu/schwartz/informationhabits.pdf

Page, L., Brin, S., Motwani, R., & Winograd, T. (1998). The PageRank citation ranking: Bringing order to the Web (Technical report). Stanford University, Stanford, CA.

Rosencrance, L. (2000). Ticketmaster accuses Tickets.com of misrepresenting judge's 'deep-linking' ruling. *Computerworld*, March 31, 2000.

Sacramento, V. (2002). *Vulnerability in the sending requests control of Bind versions 4 and 8 allows DNS spoofing*. Alertas do CAIS ALR-19112002a, Brazilian Research Network CSIRT, November 19, 2002. Retrieved September 20, 2004, from http://www.rnp.br/cais/alertas/2002/cais-ALR-19112002a.html.

Salton, G., & McGill, M. (1983). *Introduction to modern information retrieval*. New York: McGraw–Hill.

Schuba, C. (1993). *Addressing weaknesses in the domain name system protocol*. Masters Thesis, Purdue University. Retrieved September 20, 2004, from http://ftp.cerias.purdue.edu/pub/papers/christoph-schuba/schuba-DNS-msthesis.pdf.

Search Engine Ethics. (2002). SEO code of ethics. Retrieved September 20, 2004, from http://www.searchengineethics.com/seoethics.htm.

SecurityFocus. (2001). CLA-2001:429: ht://Dig DoS and remote exposure. Oct 10, 2001. Retrieved February 7, 2004, from http://www.securityfocus.com/advisories/3590.

Sit, E., & Fu, K. (2001). Inside risks: Web cookies: not just a privacy risk. *Communications of the ACM, 44*(9), 120.

Snapper, J. (1999). On the Web, Plagiarism Matters More than Copyright Piracy. *Ethics and Information Technology, 1*, 127–136.

Sonnenreich, W., & Macinta, T. (1998). *Guide to search engines*. New York: Wiley.

Sutton, W., & Linn, E. (1976). *Where the money was*. New York: Viking Press.

Tannenbaum, A. (2002). *Computer networks* (4th ed). Upper Saddle River, NJ: Prentice Hall.

United States 107th Congress. (2001). *USA PATRIOT Act (Uniting and Strengthening America by Providing Appropriate Tools Required to Intercept and Obstruct Terrorism, USAPA)*, H.R. 3162. Retrieved September 20, 2004, from http://frwebgate.access.gpo.gov/cgi-bin/getdoc.cgi?dbname=107_cong_public_laws&docid=f:publ056.107.

Users Don't Learn to Search Better (November 27, 2001). *UIEtips*. Retrieved May 2002 from http://world.std.com/~uieweb/Articles/not_learn_search.htm.

Van Boskirk, S., Li, C., Parr, J., & Gerson, M. (2001). *Driving customers, not just site traffic*. Retrieved May 2002 from Forrester Web site: http://www.forrester.com/ER/Research/Brief/0,1317,12053,00.html.

FURTHER READING

Belew, R. (2000). *Finding out about*. New York: Cambridge University Press.

Berghel, H. (2001). Caustic cookies. *Communications of the ACM 44*(5), 19–22.

Dreilinger, D., & Howe, A. (1997). Experiences with selecting search engines using metasearch. *ACM Transactions on Information Systems, 15*(3), 195–222.

Kleinberg, J. (1999). Authoritative sources in a hyperlinked environment. *Journal of the Association for Computing Machinery, 46*(5), 604–632.

Mowshowitz, A., & Kawaguchi, A. (2002). Bias on the Web. *Communications of the ACM, 45*(9), 56–60.

Powell, T. (2000). *The complete reference: Web design.* Berkeley, CA: Osborne/McGraw-Hill.

Rosenfield, L., & Morville, P. (1998). *Information architecture for the World Wide Web.* Sebastopol, CA: O'Reilly and Associates.

Spinello, R., & Tavani, H. (2004). *Readings in CyberEthics.* Boston: Jones and Bartlett Publishers.

Sullivan, D. (2001). *Search features chart.* Retrieved May 2002 from Search Engine Watch Web site: http://searchenginewatch.com/facts/ataglance.html.

Web Services

Akhil Sahai and Sven Graupner, *Hewlett-Packard Laboratories*
Wooyoung Kim, *University of Illinois, Urbana-Champaign*

INTRODUCTION

There were two predominant trends in computing over the past decade—(i) a movement from monolithic software to objects and distributed components and (ii) an increasing focus on software for the Internet. Web services (or e-services) are a result of these two trends.

Web services are described as distributed services that are identified by URI's, whose interfaces and binding can be defined, described, and discovered by XML artifacts, and that support direct XML message-based interactions with other software applications via Internet-based protocols. Web services that perform useful tasks would often exhibit the following properties:

- *Discoverable:* One of the foremost requirements for a Web-service to be useful in a commercial scenario is that it can be discovered by consumers (humans or other Web services).
- *Communicable:* Web services follow a message-driven operational model exchanging messages in XML syntax. The operational model is thus also referred to as document object model. Various communication patterns are used between Web services: synchronous, and asynchronous as well as transactional communication.
- *Conversational:* Sending a document or invoking a method and getting a reply are the basic communication primitives. However, complex interactions between Web services involve multiple steps of communication that are related to each other.
- *Secure and manageable:* Properties such as security, manageability, availability, and fault tolerance, as well as transactions, quality of service, and reliability, are critical for a commercial Web-service.

A gradual paradigm shift from object-oriented (monolithic) software to software available as a service via the Internet is taking place.

THE GENESIS OF WEB SERVICES

Contrary to public perception, the development of Web services has followed a rather modest evolutionary path. The underpinning technologies of Web services borrow heavily from object-based distributed computing and the development of the World Wide Web (Berners-Lee, 1996). In this chapter, we review related technologies that help shape the notion of Web services.

Tightly Coupled Distributed Software Architecture

The study of various aspects of distributed computing can be dated back as early as the invention of time-shared multiprocessing. Despite the early start, distributed computing remained impractical until the introduction of object management group (OMG) common object request broker architecture (CORBA) and Microsoft's distributed component object model (DCOM), a distributed extension to component object model (COM). Both CORBA and DCOM create an illusion of a single machine over a network of (heterogeneous) computers and allow objects to invoke remote objects as if they are on the same machine, thereby vastly simplifying object sharing among applications. They do so by building their abstractions on more or less OS- and platform-independent middleware layers. In these software architectures, objects define a number of interfaces and advertise their services by registering the interfaces. Discovery of interfaces and objects implementing them is done by using unique identifiers assigned to them when they are created. In addition, CORBA supports discovery of objects using descriptions of the services they provide. Sun Microsystems' Java remote method invocation (RMI) provides a similar functionality, where a network of platform-neutral Java virtual machines provides the illusion of a single machine. Java RMI is a language-dependent solution though Java native interface (JNI) provides language independence to some extent.

The software architectures supported by CORBA and DCOM are said to be tightly coupled because they define their own binary message encoding and thus objects are interoperable only with objects defined in the same software architecture; for example, CORBA objects cannot invoke methods on DCOM objects. Also, it is worth noting that security was a secondary concern, although some form of access control is highly desirable, partly because method-level/object-level access control is too fine-grained and incurs too much overhead, and partly because these software architectures were developed for use within the boundary of a single administrative control, typically a small local area network.

Loosely Coupled Distributed Software Architectures

As computing becomes more pervasive, more intelligent and autonomous devices with powerful computing capabilities have sprung up in the market. The fundamental changes in computing landscape make it rather microscopic to reason about utilization of these devices in terms of object invocation. For instance, viewing document printing as a printing service provided by a printer is more intuitive than viewing it as a method invocation on a proxy object of a printer. Thus, the notion of a service-centric view of computing has emerged.

These services tend to be dispersed over a wider area, often crossing administrative boundaries for better resource utilization through load balancing and exploitation of locality. Such physical distribution has called for more loosely coupled software architectures where scalable advertising and discovery are a must and low-latency, high-bandwidth interprocessor communication is highly desired. Specifying and enforcing security policies as well as protecting data themselves at every corner of a system can no longer be put off.

A slew of service-centric middleware developments has came to light. We note three distinctive systems from the computer industry's research laboratories, namely, HP's client utility, Sun Microsystems' Jini, and IBM's TSpaces (here listed in the alphabetic order). These have been implemented in Java for platform independence.

Client Utility Systems

HP's client utility is a somewhat underpublicized system that became the launching pad for HP's e-Speak. Its architecture represents one of the earlier forms of the peer-to-peer system suitable for Web service registration, discovery, and invocation (Kim, Graupner, & Sahai, 2002). The fundamental idea is to abstract every element in computing as a uniform representation called "service" (or "resource"). Using the abstraction as a building block, it provides three facilities, namely, advertising and discovery service, dynamic service composition, and fine-grain capability-based security. What distinguishes client utility from the other systems is the fact that it makes advertisement and discovery visible to clients. Clients can describe their services using vocabularies and can state specifically what services they want to discover.

Jini

Jini technology at Sun Microsystems is a set of protocol specifications that allows services to announce their presence and discover other services in their vicinity. It prevails a network-centric view of computing. However, it relies on the availability of multicast capability, practically limiting its applicability to services/devices connected with a local area network (such as a home network). Jini's Unicast overcomes this limitation by providing a discovery mechanism in which a service user can find services that reside beyond the local network. Jini exploits Java's code mobility and allows a service to export stub code, implementing a communication protocol using Java RMI. Joining, advertisement, and discovery are done transparently from other services. It has been developed mainly for collaboration within a small, trusted workgroup and offers limited security and scalability supports.

TSpaces

IBM's TSpaces (TSpaces, 1999) is network middleware that aims to enable communication between applications and devices in a network of heterogeneous computers and operating systems. It is a network communication buffer with database capabilities, which extends Linda's Tuple space communication model with asynchrony. TSpaces supports hierarchical access control on the Tuple space level. Advertisement and discovery are implicit in TSpaces and provided indirectly through shared Tuple spaces.

Convergence of the Two Trends

Web services are defined at the cross point of the evolutionary paths of service-centric computing and the World Wide Web, where the idea is to provide service-centric computing via the Internet. Services are delivered over the Internet (or intranet), whereas the World Wide Web has strived to become a distributed, decentralized, all-pervasive infrastructure where information is put out for other users to retrieve. It is this distributed, decentralized paradigm of information dissemination that upon meeting the concept of service-centric computing has led to the germination of the concept of Web services.

The Web services paradigm has caught the fancy of the research and development community. A large number of efforts in industry and universities are actively defining standards, platforms, and concepts that will determine how Web services are created, deployed, registered, discovered, and composed as well as how Web services will interact with each other.

WEB SERVICES TODAY

Web services are appearing on the Internet in the form of e-business and portal sites. For example, Priceline.com

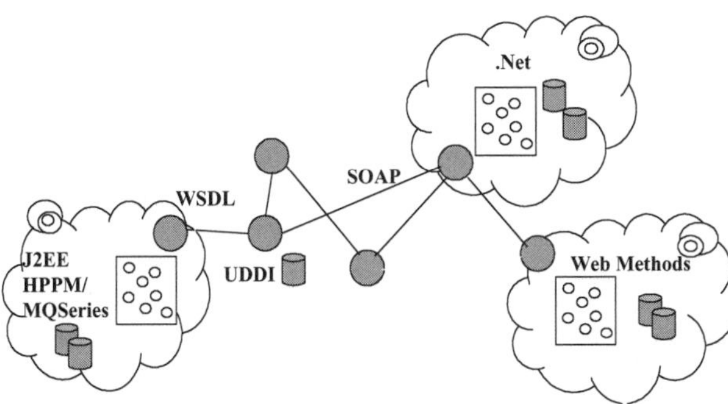

Figure 1: Web services.

and Expedia.com act as the broker for airline, hotel, and rental car bookings. They are statically composed Web services that have a prenegotiated understanding with certain airlines and hotels and broker their services through their portal sites. These are mostly a business-to-consumer (B2C) kind of Web services. A large number of technologies and platforms are emerging and are being standardized so as to enable the paradigm of Web services for satisfying business-to-business (B2B) and B2C scenarios alike in a uniform manner. These standards and platforms enable creation and deployment, description, discovery, and communication amongst them. Web services description language (WSDL) is used to describe service interfaces and to publish them together with the services' access points (i.e., bindings) and supported interfaces, both of which are described in an extensible markup language (XML)-based description language (see Figure 1). The universal description, discovery, and integration (UDDI) technology is used to discover described and registered Web services. After having discovered its partners, Web-services use the document model to exchange documents, and simple object access protocol (SOAP) to invoke service (which is an incarnation of remote procedure call (RPC) in XML) over hypertext transfer protocol (HTTP). Most services are implemented using platform-independent languages such as Java and C# on platforms such as J2EE and .Net. The primary means for enforcing security are digital signature and strong encryption with public/private key pairs. Standards such as SAML, XKMS, and XACML are appearing in this area. A large number of payment mechanisms are being defined, too.

Web Services Description

In traditional software development environment, software component interfaces are defined through interface definition languages (IDL). The interfaces describe the operations the software component supports, their inputs, and the expected outputs. This enables the interfaces to be decoupled from the actual implementation. As Web services are envisaged as software available on the Web that other services or users will use, they need to be described so that other components can easily use them without coupling the interfaces with the implementations. Web services description language is thus an attempt to describe the interfaces.

WSDL enables creation of flexible and generic interaction models for Web services, and enables description of the services irrespective of the message formats and network protocols used. For example, in WSDL a service is described through a set of end points. An end point is in turn a set of operations. An operation is defined in terms of messages received or sent out by the Web service:

- Binding: a concrete protocol and data format specification for a particular port type.
- Message: an abstract definition of data being communicated consisting of message parts.
- Operation: an abstract definition of an action supported by the service. Operations are of the following types, namely, one way, request–response, solicit–response, notification.
- Port: a single end point defined as a combination of a binding and a network address.
- Port type: an abstract set of operations supported by one or more end points.
- Service: a collection of related end-points.

As the implementation of the service changes or evolves in time, the WSDL definitions must be continually updated, and versioning of the descriptions must be tracked.

Web Services Discovery

When the Web is browsed for information, search-engines are used to find relevant Web sites based on key words. However, this leads to a lot of unnecessary links that need to be sifted through, before the relevant sites can be found. Similarly, before Web services can interact to undertake business, they need to discover whether they are compatible with each other. The registration and discovery of Web services necessitates other entities to act as intermediaries, such as universal description discovery integration. UDDI is supported by IBM, Microsoft, and HP, and is a group of Web-based registries (operator sites) maintained by these organizations to expose information about a business and its technical interfaces and APIs. The core component of UDDI is its business registration, an XML file used to define businesses and the Web services they provide. There are three parts to the business registration, namely, *white pages* for name, address, contact, and other identifiers; *yellow pages* for classification of business under standardized taxonomies; and *green pages* for technical information about the Web services that are exposed. It also exposes a set of APIs for inquiry and publication of information related to Web services. The inquiry APIs enable browsing of the information in the repository site (e.g., find_business) and also drilling down (e.g., get_businessDetail). The publication APIs enable publishers to place their information on these repositories.

Marketplaces have been proposed as virtual meeting places managed by an intermediary to supply a series of benefits to participating Web services in addition to the basic registration and discovery functionality, namely:

- Enabling inter-Web service interaction with or without the direct participation of the e-marketplace in the actual interaction after the discovery;
- Enabling supply-and-demand mechanisms like traditional catalogue purchasing, RFP, or the more dynamic auctions and exchanges;

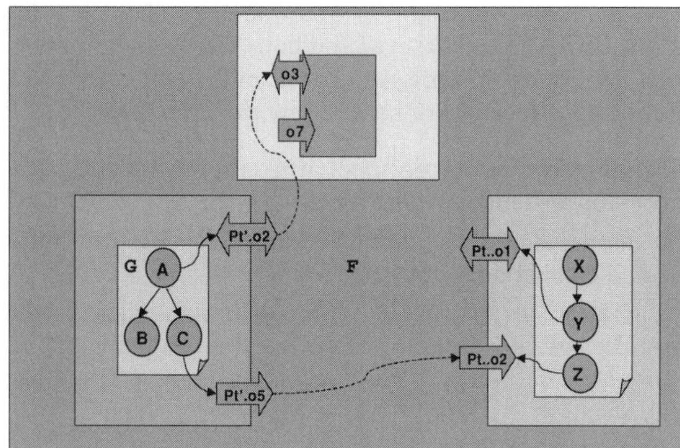

Figure 2: Intra- and inter-Web service modeling and interaction.

- Providing value-added services, such as rating, secured payment, financial handling, and certification and notification services; and
- Managing supply chains through collaborative planning and inventory handling.

Marketplaces could thus be developed as entities that use UDDI operator sites and provide value-added services on top of the basic functionality of registration and discovery. Vertical and horizontal marketplaces have been steadily coming up. VerticalNet, GlobalNetXchange, and Retailers Market Exchange are examples of the former targeting a specific section of the industry with key players performing B2B transactions. Other examples, such as Chemdex, E-Steel, and DirectAg.com, have been successful in their respective industries. Horizontal exchanges in turn are directed at a broad range of players, such as e-Bay targeting a wide range of clients and businesses.

Web Services Orchestration

Web services usually expose a subset of enterprise business processes and activities to the external world through a set of operations defined in their WSDL. The enterprise business processes must be defined, and some of their activities must be linked to the WSDL operations. This requires modeling of the Web service's back-end business processes, which necessitates intra-Web service modeling and interaction (see Figure 2). In addition, Web services need to interact with other Web services, which happens through a sequence of message exchanges, termed a *conversation*. The conversations can be described independently of the internal flows of the Web services and can be described simply by sequencing the exposed operations and messages of the Web services (as mentioned in their WSDLs). However, such an inter-Web service interaction automatically leads to coupling of the internal processes of the Web services to form what is called a *global process*. The participating Web services may or may not be aware of the whole global process, depending on their understanding with each other and the internal information they are willing to expose.

Intra-Web Service Modeling and Interaction

Modeling of processes is usually done through languages like XLANG/WSFL. The Web services flow language (WSFL) introduces the notion of activities and flows, which are useful for describing both local business process flows and the global flow of messages between multiple Web services. XLANG is another standard, from Microsoft, that provides a mechanism for process definition and global flow coordination.

WSFL (Leymann, 2001) models business processes as a set of activities and links. An activity is a unit of useful work. The links could be control links where decisions are made to follow one activity or another, or data links where data are fed into one activity from another. These activities could be exposed through one or more operations grouped through end points (as defined in WSDL). A service is composed of a set of end points, and a service provider can provide multiple services. Just like internal flows, global flows can be defined, specifically as consisting of plug links that link up operations of two service providers, which helps in the creation of complex services that can be recursively defined.

XLANG defines services by extending WSDL. The extension elements describe the behavioral aspects. A behavior spans multiple operations, and has a header and a body. An action is an atomic component of a behavior, and could be an *operation*, a *delay* element, or a *raise* element. A delay element could be of types delayFor and delayUntil. The delayFor and delayUntil introduce delays in the execution of the process either to wait for something to happen (for example, a time-out) or to wait till an absolute date-time has been reached, respectively. Exceptions are flagged through raise constructs. A raise element handles the exceptions by calling the handlers registered with the raise definition. Processes combine actions in useful ways, and could be a sequence, switch, while, All, Pick, Context, Compensate, or Empty.

Inter-Web Service Modeling and Interaction

Web service to Web service interactions need to follow certain business protocols to actually undertake business on the Web. X-EDI, ebXML, BTP, TPA-ML, cXML, and CBL are some of the B2B technologies that have been proposed to enable this paradigm with Web services.

In ebXML (ebXML, 2001; see Figure 3) parties that engage in business have collaboration protocol profiles (CPP) that they register at ebXML registries. Each CPP is assigned a GUID by the ebXML registry. Once a party discovers another party's CPP they negotiate a collaboration protocol agreement (CPA). The intent of the CPA is not to expose the parties' business process internals

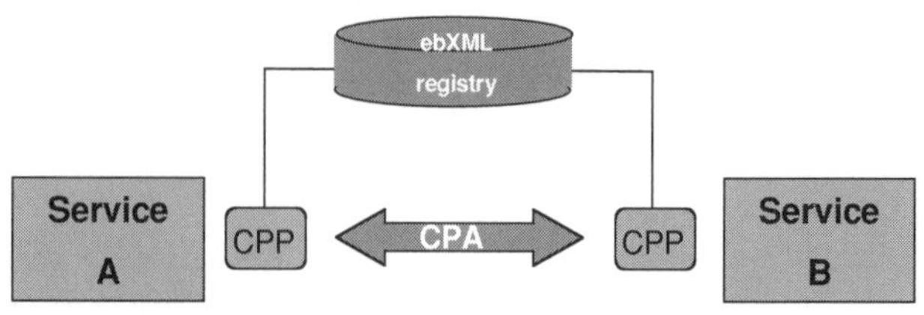

Figure 3: ebXML service-to-service interaction.

but to expose the visible process that involves interactions between the parties. The messages exchanged between the involved parties or business partners may utilize ebXML messaging service (ebMS). The CPA and the business process specification document it references define a *conversation* between the parties. This conversation involves multiple *business transactions*. A business transaction may involve an exchange of messages as request and replies. The CPA may refer to multiple business process specification documents. Any one conversation will involve only a single process specification document, however. Conceptually, the B2B server between the parties is responsible for managing the CPAs and for keeping track of the conversations. It also interfaces the functions defined in the CPA with the internal business processes. The CPP contains the following:

- *Process specification layer,* which details the business transactions that form the collaboration, and also specifies the order of business transactions;
- *Delivery channels,* which describes a party's message receiving and sending characteristics, and can specify more than one delivery channel;
- *Document exchange layer,* which deals with the processing of business documents such as digital signatures, encryption, and reliable delivery; and
- *Transport layer,* which identifies the transport protocols to be used (e.g., SMTP, HTTP, and FTP) and the end point addresses.

Web Services Platforms

Web services platforms are the technologies, means, and methods available to build and operate Web services. Platforms have changed and developed over the course of time. A classification into five generations of platform technology should help to structure the space:

- *First generation* (HTML/CGI): Web servers, static HTML pages, HTML FORMS for simple dialogs, and the CGI (common gateway interface) to connect Web servers to application programs, mostly Perl or Shell scripts.
- *Second generation* (Java): server-side dynamic generation of HTML pages, user session support; the Java servlet interface became popular to connect to application programs.
- *Third generation* (richer development and run-time environments): J2EE as foundation for application servers that later evolved toward the fourth generation.
- *Fourth generation* (XML Web services platforms): the introduction of XML and WSDL interfaces for Web services with SOAP-based messaging, and the emergence of a global service infrastructure for service registration and discovery (UDDI).
- *Fifth generation* (dynamic Web services aggregation): flow systems, business negotiations, agent technology, etc.

Technically, Web services have been built according to a pattern of an *n*-tier architecture (see Figure 4) that consists of: a front-end tier (firewall (FW) and load balancer

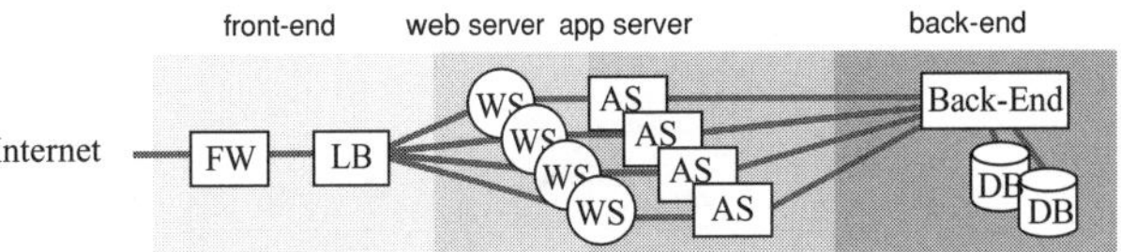

Figure 4: Basic four-tier architecture for Web services.

(LB)), a Web-server (WS) tier, an application (server) (AS) tier, and a back-end tier for persistent data, or the database tier (DB).

First Generation: CGI and Perl

The emergence of the World Wide Web facilitated the easy access and decent appearance of linked HTML markup pages in a user's browsers. In the early days, it was mostly static HTML content. Passive information services that provided users with the only capability of navigating though static pages could be built. However, HTML supported from the very beginning FORMS that allowed users to enter text or to select from multiple-choice menus. FORMS were treated specially by the Web server. They were passed onto an interface, CGI, behind which small applications, mostly Perl or Shell scripts, could read the user's input, perform respective actions, and return an HTML page according to the user's input that could then be displayed in the browser. This primitive mechanism enabled a first generation of services in the Web beyond pure navigation through static content.

Second Generation: Java

With the growth of the Web and the desire for richer services such as online shopping or booking, the initial means to build Web services quickly became too primitive. Java applets brought graphical interactiveness to the browser side, and Java became the language of choice for Web services. Servlets provided a better interface between the Web server and the application. Technology to support the dynamic generation of HTML pages at the server side was introduced: JSP (Java Server Pages) by Sun Microsystems, ASP (Active Server Pages) by Microsoft, and PHP pages in the Linux world enabled the separation of presentation, the appearance of pages in browsers, from content data. Templates and content were then merged on the fly at the server in order to generate the final page returned to the browser. Since user identification was critical for business services, user login and user sessions were introduced. Applications were becoming more complex, and it turned out that there was a significant overlap in common functions needed for many services such as session support, connectivity to persistent databases, and security functions.

Third Generation: Richer Development and Run-Time Environments

The observation that many functions were shared and common between Web services drove the development toward richer development environments based on the Java language and Java libraries. A cornerstone of these environments became J2EE (Java 2 Platform, Enterprise Edition), which is designed for enterprise-scale computing

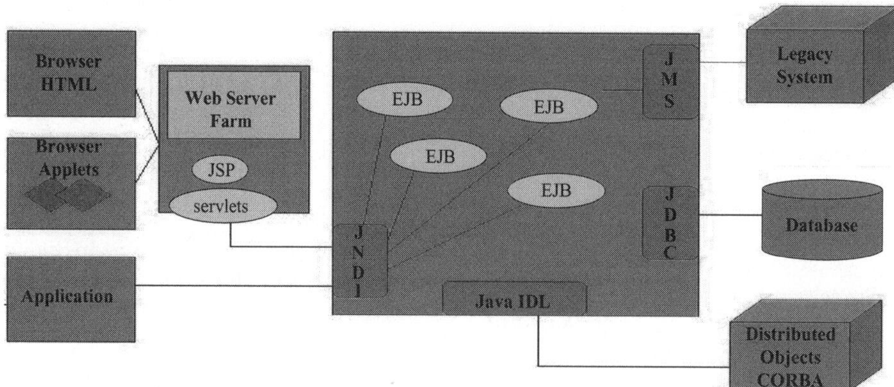

Figure 5: The J2EE platform.

(see Figure 5). Sun Microsystems (together with industry partners such as IBM) designed J2EE to simplify application development for Web services by decreasing the need for programming through reusable modular components and by providing standard functions such as session support and database connectivity.

Application Server. J2EE primarily manifests in a set of libraries used by application programs performing the various functions. Web service developers still had to assemble all the pieces, link them together, connect them to the Web server, and manage the various configurations, etc. This led to the emergence of software packages that could be easily deployed on a variety of machines. These packages later became application servers. They significantly reduced the amount of configuration work during service deployment such that service developers could spend more time on business logic and the actual function of the service. Most application server are based on J2EE technology. Examples are IBM's WebSphere suite, BEA's WebLogic environment, the Sun ONE Application Framework, and Oracle's 9*i* application server.

Fourth Generation: Web Services Platforms

Prior generations of Web services mostly focused on end users, people accessing services from Web browsers. However, accessing services from other services and not browsers turned out to be difficult. This circumstance has prevented the occurrence of Web service aggregation for a long time. Web service aggregation means that a user only has to contact one Web service, and this service then resolves the user's requests into further requests to other Web services.

HTML is a language defined for rendering and presenting content in Web browsers. It does not allow per se separating content from presentation information. With the occurrence of XML with its clean syntax and the capability to describe syntax in its own language as XML Schema, XML became the language of choice for Web services for providing interfaces that not only could be accessed by users through Web browsers but also by other services. XML is now pervasively being used in Web services messaging (mainly using SOAP) and for Web service interface descriptions (WSDL). In regard to platforms, XML enhancements were added to J2EE and application servers. The introduction of XML is the major differentiator between Web services platforms of the third and the fourth generations in this classification.

A major step toward service-to-service integration was the introduction of UDDI, a global, XML-based registry infrastructure for businesses offering Web services. Its goal is to enable companies and individuals to find one another on the Web in a much more structured and classified manner than is possible through search engines. Microsoft, IBM, and Ariba spearheaded UDDI.

Two major platforms that explicitly aim for further Web services interaction and integration are currently offered: Sun Microsystems' Sun ONE (Open Net Environment) and Microsoft's .NET.

Sun ONE. Sun ONE is Sun's standards-based software architecture and platform for building and deploying services on demand. Sun ONE's architecture is built around existing business assets: data, applications, reports, and transactions, referred to as the DART model. Major standards are supported: XML, SOAP, J2EE, UDDI, LDAP, and ebXML. The architecture comprises several product lines: the iPlanet Application Framework (JATO), Sun's J2EE application framework for enterprise Web services development, application server, portal server, integration server, directory server, e-commerce components, the Solaris Operating Environment, and development tools.

IBM WebSphere. IBM WebSphere is IBM's platform to build, deploy, and integrate one's e-business, including components such as foundation and tools, reach and user experience, business integration and transaction servers, and tools.

Microsoft. NET. Microsoft's .NET platform aims to provide lead technology for future distributed applications inherently seen as Web services. With Microsoft .NET, Web services' application code is built in discrete units, XML Web services, that handle a specified set of tasks. Because standard interfaces based on XML simplify communication among software, XML Web services can be linked into highly specific applications and experiences. The vision is that the best XML Web services from any provider from around the globe can be used to quickly and easily create a needed solution. Microsoft will provide a core set of XML Web services, called Microsoft .NET My Services, to provide functions such as user identification and calendar access.

Security and Web Services

Due to their public nature, security is vital for Web services. Security attacks can be classified as threats of information disclosure, unauthorized alteration of data, denial of use, misuse or abuse of services, and, more rarely considered, repudiation of access. Since Web services link networks with businesses, further attacks such as masquerading, stealing, or duplicating identity and conducting business under false identity, or accessing or transferring funds from or to unauthorized accounts need to be considered.

Security is vital for establishing the legal basis for businesses done over networks. Identification and authentication of business partners is the basic requirement. Integrity and authenticity of electronic documents is another. Electronic contracts must have the same binding legal status as conventional contracts. Refuse and repudiation of electronic contracts must be provable in order to be legally valid. Finally, payment and transferring funds between accounts must be safe and secure.

Security architectures in networks typically comprise several layers:

- *Secure data communication:* IPsec (Internet protocol security), SSL (secure socket layer), and TLS (transport layer security);
- *Secured networks:* VPN (virtual private networks);
- *Authenticity of electronic documents and issuing individuals:* digital signatures;
- *Secure and authenticated access:* digital certificates;
- *Secure authentication and certification:* PKI (public key infrastructure); and
- *Single sign-on and digital passports.*

Single Sign-On and Digital Passports

Digital passports emerged from the desire to provide an individual's identity information from a trusted and secure centralized place rather then repeatedly establish this information with each collaborating partner and maintain separate access credentials for each pair of collaborations. Individuals only need one such credential, the passport, in order to provide collaborating partners with certain parts of an individual's identity information. This consolidates the need to maintain separate identities with different partners into one single identification mechanism. Digital passports provide authenticated access to a centralized place where individuals have registered their identity information, such as phone numbers, social security numbers, addresses, credit records, and payment information. Participating individuals, both people and businesses, will access the same authenticated information, assuming trust in the authority providing the passport service. Two initiatives have emerged: Microsoft's .NET Passport and the Liberty Alliance Project, initiated by Sun Microsystems.

Microsoft .NET Passport (Microsoft .NET, 2002) is a single sign-on mechanism for users in the Internet. Instead of creating separate accounts and passwords with every e-commerce site, users, using an e-mail address and a single password, only need to authenticate with a single passport server. Then, through a series of authentications and encrypted cookie certificates, the user is able to purchase items at any participating e-commerce site without reverifying their identity.

Microsoft .NET Passport was initially planned for signing into Microsoft's own services. Expanding it toward broader use in the Web has been seen as critical and has given rise to the Liberty Alliance Project initiative, which is now widely supported by industry and public. The Liberty Alliance Project (Liberty Alliance Project, 2002), formed to create an open, federated, single sign-on identity solution for the digital economy via any device connected to the Internet, has three main objectives:

- To enable consumers and businesses to maintain personal information securely;
- To provide a universal, open standard for single sign-on with decentralized authentication and open authorization from multiple providers; and
- To provide an open standard for network identity spanning all network-connected devices.

Membership is open to all commercial and noncommercial organizations.

With the emergence of Web services, specific security technology has been emerging, the two major classes of which are:

- Java-based security technology, and
- XML-based security technology.

Both classes provide mappings of security technologies, such as authentication and authorization, encryption, and signatures as described in the following section, into their respective environments.

Java-Based Security Technology for Web Services

Java-based security technology is primarily available through the Java 2 SDK and J2EE environments in the form of sets of libraries:

- *Encryption:* JSSE (Java secure socket extension), the JCE (Java cryptography extension) provides a framework and implementations for encryption, key generation and key agreement, and message authentication code (MAC) algorithms. Support for encryption includes symmetric, asymmetric, block, and stream ciphers. The software also supports secure streams and sealed objects.
- *Secure messaging:* Java GSS-API (Generic Security Services Application Program Interface) is used for securely exchanging messages between communicating applications, and contains the Java bindings defined in RFC 2853. GSS-API offers application programmers uniform access to security services atop a variety of underlying security mechanisms, including Kerberos (Kohl & Neuman, 1993).

- *Single sign-on using Kerberos.*
- *Authentication and authorization:* JAAS (Java authentication and authorization service) for authentication of users, to reliably and securely determine who is currently executing Java code, and for authorization of users to ensure they have the access control rights (permissions) required to do security-sensitive operations.
- *Certification:* Java certification path API.
- *X.509 certificates and certificate revocation lists (CRLs) and security managers.*
- These libraries are available for use when Web services are built using Java. They are usually used when building individual Web services with application servers.

For Web services interaction, XML technology eliminates the tied binding to Java. Consequently, a similar set of XML-based security technologies that enables cross-services interactions is emerging.

XML-Based Security Technology for Web Services (Hallam-Baker & Maler, 2002)

The Organization for the Advancement of Structured Information Standards (OASIS) drives the idea of merging security into Web services at a level higher than that of the common Internet security mechanisms and practices described earlier. Proposals are primarily directed toward providing XML specifications for documents and protocols suitable for cross-organizational Web services interactions. XML-based security technology can be classified into the following:

- *XML document-level security:* encryption and digitally signing XML documents;
- *Protocol-level security for XML document exchanges:* exchanging XML documents for authentication and authorization of peers; and
- *XML-based security frameworks:* infrastructures for establishing secure relationships among parties.

XML Document-Level Security: Encryption and Signature. The (preliminary) *XML encryption specification* (Reagle, 2000) specifies how to digitally encrypt a Web resource in general, and an XML document in particular. XML encryption can be applied to a part or complete XML document. The granularity of encryption can be reduced to an element, attributes, or text content. Encryption can be recursive. The specification does not address confidence or trust relationships and key establishment, but does address both key-encrypting-keys and data keys. The specification will not address the expression of access control policies associated with portions of the XML document, which will be addressed by XACML.

XML signature defines the XML schema and processing rules for creating and representing digital signatures in any digital content (data object), including XML. An XML signature may be applied to the content of one or more documents. Enveloped or enveloping signatures are over data within the same XML document; detached signatures are over data external to the signature element. More specifically, this specification defines an XML signature element type and an XML signature application; conformance requirements for each are specified by way of schema definitions and prose respectively. This specification also includes other useful types that identify methods for referencing collections of resources, algorithms, and keying and management information.

The XML signature (Bartel, Boyer, Fox, LaMacchia, & Simon, 2002) is a method of associating a key with referenced data (octets); it does not normatively specify how keys are associated with persons or institutions, nor the meaning of the data being referenced and signed. Consequently, although this specification is an important component of secure XML applications, it itself is not sufficient to address all application security/trust concerns, particularly with respect to using signed XML (or other data formats) as a basis for human-to-human communication and agreement. Such an application must specify additional key, algorithm, processing, and rendering requirements.

The *SOAP digital signature extensions* define how specifically SOAP messages can be digitally signed. The following fragment shows how message digest information, obtained from algorithms such as MD5 applied on a certain region in a document, can be included in the document according to the specification.

Protocol-Level Security for XML Document Exchanges. Protocol-level security defines document exchanges with the purpose of establishing secure relationships among parties, typically providing well-defined interfaces and XML bindings to an existing public key infrastructure. Protocol-level security can be built upon document-level security.

The *XML key management specification* (Ford et al., 2001) defines protocols for validating and registering public keys, suitable for use in conjunction with the proposed standard for XML signature developed by the World Wide Web Consortium (W3C) and the Internet Engineering Task Force (IETF) and an anticipated companion standard for XML encryption. The XML key management specification (XKMS) comprises two parts: the XML key information service specification (X-KISS) and the XML key registration service specification (X-KRSS).

The X-KISS specification defines a protocol for a trust service that resolves public key information contained in XML-SIG document elements. The X-KISS protocol allows a client of such a service to delegate part or all of the tasks required to process <ds:KeyInfo> elements embedded in a document. A key objective of the protocol design is to minimize the complexity of application implementations by allowing them to become clients and thereby shielded from the complexity and syntax of an underlying public key infrastructure (PKI Forum, 2002) used to establish trust relationships-based specifications such as X.509/PKIX, or SPKI (Simple Public Key Infrastructure, 1999).

The X-KRSS specification defines a protocol for a Web service that accepts registration of public key information. Once registered, the public key may be used in conjunction with other Web services including X-KISS.

XML-Based Security Frameworks. XML-based security frameworks go one step further than those discussed earlier.

The *security assertion markup language* (SAML), developed under the guidance of OASIS (OASIS, 2002), is an XML-based framework for exchanging security information with established, SAML-compliant security services. This security information is expressed in the form of assertions about subjects, where a subject is an entity (either human or program) that has an identity in some security domain. A typical example of a subject is a person, identified by his or her e-mail address in a particular Internet DNS domain.

Assertions can convey information about authentication acts performed by subjects, attributes of subjects, and authorization decisions about whether subjects are allowed to access certain resources. Assertions are represented as XML constructs and have a nested structure, whereby a single assertion might contain several different internal statements about authentication, authorization, and attributes. Assertions containing authentication statements merely describe acts of authentication that happened previously.

Assertions are issued by SAML authorities, namely, authentication authorities, attribute authorities, and policy decision points. SAML defines a protocol by which relying parties can request assertions from SAML authorities and get a response from them. This protocol, consisting of XML-based request and response message formats, can be bound to many different underlying communications and transport protocols; currently it defines one binding: SOAP over HTTP.

SAML authorities can use various sources of information, such as external policy stores and assertions received as input in requests, in creating their responses. Thus, whereas clients always consume assertions, SAML authorities can be both producers and consumers of assertions

Web Services Security Standards

The WS security standard (Atkinson et al., 2002) was initially defined by an industry consortium centered around IBM, Microsoft, and Verisign in 2002. In 2004, WS security standards were adopted by the middleware standard of Grid Web Services, called the Web Services Resource Framework (WSRF, 2004).

The WS security standards, known as WS-Security, define enhancements to SOAP messaging by providing quality of protection through message integrity, message confidentiality, and single message authentication. WS-Security also provides a general-purpose mechanism for associating security tokens with messages. No specific type of security token is required by WS-Security. It is designed to be extensible (e.g., supporting multiple security token formats). For example, a client might provide proof of identity and proof that they have a particular business certification.

Additionally, WS-Security describes how to encode binary security tokens. Specifically, the specification describes how to encode X.509 certificates (Santesson et al., 1999) and Kerberos (Kohl & Neuman, 1993) tickets as well as how to include opaque encrypted keys. It also includes extensibility mechanisms that can be used to further describe the characteristics of the credentials included with a message. These mechanisms can be used independently (e.g., to pass a security token) or in a tightly integrated manner (e.g., by signing and encrypting a message and providing a security token hierarchy associated with the keys used for signing and encryption).

By using the SOAP extensibility model, SOAP-based specifications are designed to be composed with each other to provide a rich messaging environment. By itself, WS-Security does not ensure security nor does it provide a complete security solution. WS-Security is a building block used in conjunction with other Web service- and application-specific protocols to accommodate a wide variety of security models and encryption technologies. Although implementing WS-Security does not mean that an application cannot be attacked or that the security cannot be compromised, the goal is to ensure that security protocols constructed using WS-Security are not vulnerable to a wide range of attacks.

The Web services security language must support a wide variety of security models. The following list identifies the key driving requirements for WS-security:

- Multiple security tokens for authentication or authorization;
- Multiple trust domains;
- Multiple encryption technologies; and
- End-to-end message-level security and not just transport-level security.

WS-security defines the following terminology:

- *Attachment:* additional data that travel with a SOAP message, but are not part of the SOAP envelope.
- *Claim:* a statement made by a client (e.g., name, identity, key, group, privilege, or capability).
- *Confidentiality:* the process by which data are protected such that only authorized actors or security token owners can view the data.
- *Digest:* a cryptographic checksum of an octet stream.
- *Integrity:* the process by which it is guaranteed that information is not modified in transit.
- *Proof-of-possession:* data used in a proof process to demonstrate the sender's knowledge of information that should only be known by the claiming sender of a security token.
- *Security token:* a collection of claims.
- *Signature:* a cryptographic binding of a proof-of-possession and a digest, which covers both symmetric key- and public key-based signatures. Consequently, nonrepudiation is not always achieved.
- *Signed security token:* a security token that is asserted and cryptographically endorsed by a specific authority (e.g., an X.509 certificate or a Kerberos ticket).

WS-Security defines a message security model in terms of security tokens combined with digital signatures as proof of possession of the security token (key). Security tokens assert claims and signatures provide a mechanism for proving the sender's knowledge of the key. As well, the signature can be used to "bind" or "associate" the signature with the claims in the security token (assuming the token is trusted). Such a binding is limited to those elements covered by the signature. Furthermore WS-Security does not specify a particular method for authentication; it simply indicates that security tokens may be bound to messages.

A claim can be either endorsed or unendorsed by a trusted authority. A set of endorsed claims is usually represented as a signed security token digitally signed or encrypted by the authority. An X.509 certificate, claiming the binding between one's identity and public key, is an example of a signed security token. An endorsed claim can also be represented as a reference to an authority so that the receiver can pull the claim from the referenced authority. An unendorsed claim can be trusted if there is a trust relationship between the sender and the receiver. For example, the unendorsed claim that the sender is Bob is sufficient for a certain receiver to believe that the sender is in fact Bob, if the sender and the receiver use a trusted connection and there is an out-of-band trust relationship between them.

One special type of unendorsed claim is proof-of-possession, which proves that the sender has a particular piece of knowledge verifiable by appropriate actors. For example, a username/password is a security token with this type of claim. A proof-of-possession claim is sometimes combined with other security tokens to prove the claims of the sender. A digital integrity used for message integrity can also be used as a proof-of-possession claim, although such a digital signature is not considered as a type of a security token. This security model, by itself, is subject to multiple security attacks.

Message protection is an essential part of WS-Security. Protecting the message content from being intercepted (confidentiality) or illegally modified (integrity) are primary security concerns. The WS-Security specification provides a means to protect a message by encrypting or digitally signing a body, a header, an attachment, or any combination of them (or parts of them).

Message integrity is provided by using XML signature in conjunction with security tokens to ensure that messages are transmitted without modifications. The integrity mechanisms are designed to support multiple signatures, potentially by multiple actors, and to be extensible to support additional signature formats.

Message confidentiality uses XML encryption in conjunction with security tokens to keep portions of a SOAP message confidential. The encryption mechanisms are designed to support additional encryption processes and operations by multiple actors.

The message receiver should reject a message with invalid signature or missing or inappropriate claims as it is an unauthorized (or malformed) message. The WS-Security specification provides a flexible way for the message sender to claim the security properties by associating zero or more security tokens with the message. An example of a security claim is the identity of the sender; the sender can claim that he is Bob, known as an employee of some company, and therefore he has the right to send the message.

The WS-Security specification allows for multiple signatures to be attached to a message, each referencing different, even overlapping, parts of the message. This is important for many distributed applications where messages flow through multiple processing stages. For example, a sender may submit an order that contains an orderID header. The sender signs the orderID header and the body of the request (the contents of the order). When this is received by the order processing subsystem, it may insert a shippingID into the header. The order subsystem would then sign, at a minimum, the orderID and the shippingID, and possibly the body as well. Then when this order is processed and shipped by the shipping department, a shippedInfo header might be appended. The shipping department would sign, at a minimum, the shippedInfo and the shippingID and possibly the body and forward the message to the billing department for processing. The billing department can verify the signatures and determine a valid chain of trust for the order, as well as who has taken what action.

The <Security> header block in a WS-Security SOAP message is used to carry a signature for the purpose of signing one or more elements in the SOAP envelope. Multiple signature entries may be added into a single SOAP envelope. Senders should take care to sign all elements of the message, but care must be taken in creating a policy that will not to sign parts of the message that might legitimately be altered in transit.

THE FUTURE OF WEB SERVICES

In the future we will see the unleashing of a Web services phenomenon that will involve the fulfillment of dynamic Web service composition and orchestration vision, the appearance of personalized Web services, concepts of Web service management, and the development of Web service infrastructure as a reusable, reconfigurable, self-healing, self-managing, large-scale system.

Dynamic Web Services Composition and Orchestration

The vision of Web services intelligently interacting with one another and performing useful tasks automatically and seamlessly remains to become reality. Major milestones have been achieved: XML as syntactic framework and data representation language for interacting Web services, the Web infrastructure itself providing ubiquitous access to Web services, the emergence of global registration and discovery services, the technology to support the creation and maintenance of Web services, just to name a few. However, major pieces such as the formalization and description of service semantic are still missing. The effort of creating a semantic Web (Semantic Web, 2001) is an extension of the current Web in which information is given well-defined meaning, better enabling computers and people to work in cooperation. Ontologies define the structure, relationships, and meaning of terms appearing in service descriptions. The semantic Web vision is that these ontologies can be registered, discovered, and used for reasoning about Web service selection before undertaking business. Languages like DAML + OIL (DAML, 2001) have been developed in this context.

In addition, sending a document or invoking a method and getting a reply are the basic communication primitives. However, complex interactions between Web-services will involve multiple steps of communication that are related to each other. A conversation definition is a sequencing of document exchanges (method invocations in the network object model) that together accomplish some business functionality. In addition to agreeing upon vocabularies and document formats, conversational Web-services also agree upon conversation definitions before communicating with each other. A conversation definition consists of descriptions of interactions and transitions. Interactions define the atomic units of information interchange between Web services. Essentially, each service describes each interaction in terms of the documents that it will accept as input, or will produce as output. The interactions are the building blocks of the conversation definition. Transitions specify the ordering amongst the interactions. Web-services need to introspect other Web services and obtain each other's descriptions before they start communicating and collaborating (Banerji et al., 2002).

RosettaNet (RosettaNet, 2002) is a nonprofit consortium of major information technology, electronic components, and semiconductor manufacturing companies working to create and implement industry-wide, open e-business process standards, particularly targeting business-to-business marketplaces, and workflow and supply-chain management solutions. These standards form a common e-business language, aligning processes between supply chain partners on a global basis. Several examples exist. The centerpiece of the RosettaNet model is the partner interface process (PIP). The PIP defines the activities, decisions, and interactions that each e-business trading participant is responsible for. Although the RosettaNet model has been in development recently, it will be a while before Web services can start using them to undertake business on the Web.

Once these hurdles are overcome, the basis and platform for true Web services that would enable agent technologies to merge into Web services and provide the envisioned dynamic Web service aggregation on demand according to a user's specifications will exist.

Personalized Web Services

As Web service technology evolves, we anticipate that they will become increasingly sophisticated, and that the challenges the Web service community will face will also evolve to meet their new capabilities. One of the most important of these challenges will be the question of what it means to personalize Web services. Personalization can be achieved by using user (other Web services or humans) profiles to monitor user behavior, devices, and context to customize Web services (Kuno & Sahai, 2002) to achieve metrics like quality of experience (QoE) (van Moorsel, 2001). This would involve providing and meeting guarantees of service performance on the user's side. Personalization could also result in creation of third-party rating agencies that will register user experiences and could be instructive for other first-time users. These rating mechanisms already exist in an ad-hoc manner, e.g., e-bay and Amazon allow users to rate sellers and commodities (books), respectively. Salcentral.com and bizrate.com are third-party rating agencies that rate businesses. These services could be also developed as extended UDDI services. These mechanisms will also render Web services more "customer-friendly."

End-to-End Web Service Interactions

Web services are federated in nature as they interact across management domains and enterprise networks. Their implementations can be vastly different in nature. When two Web services connect to each other, they must agree on a document exchange protocol and the appropriate document formats. From then on, they can interoperate with each other by exchanging documents. SOAP defines a common layer for document exchange. Services can define their own service-specific content on the top of SOAP. Often, these Web service transactions will span multiple Web services. A request originating at a particular Web service can lead to transactions on a set of Web services. For example, a purchase order transaction that begins when an employee orders supplies and ends when he or she receives a confirmation could result in ten messages being exchanged between various services as shown in Figure 6.

The exchange of messages between Web services could be asynchronous. Services sending a request message need not be blocked waiting for a response message. In some cases, all the participating services are like peers; in which case there is no notion of a request or a response. Some of the message flow patterns that result from this asynchrony are shown in Figure 7. The first example in Figure 7 shows a single request resulting in multiple responses. The second example shows a broker scenario, in which a request is sent to a broker but responses are received directly from a set of suppliers.

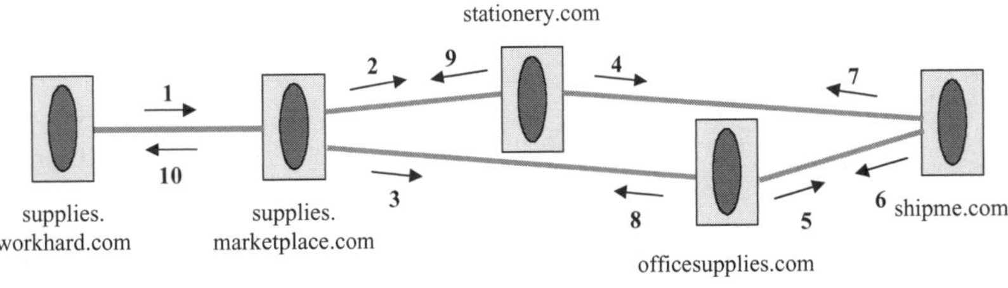

Figure 6: SOAP messages exchanged between Web services.

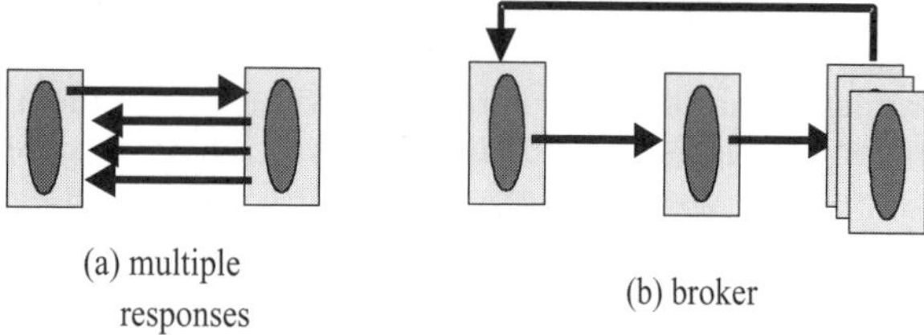

Figure 7: Asynchronous message patterns between Web services.

These Web services also interact with a complex Web of business processes at their back-ends. Some of these business processes are exposed as Web service operations. A business process comprises a sequence of activities and links as defined by WSFL and XLANG. These business processes must be managed so as to manage Web service interactions. Management of Web services thus is a challenging task because of their heterogeneity, asynchrony, and federation. Managing Web services involves managing business transactions by correlation of messages across enterprises (Sahai, Machiraju, & Wurster, 2001), and managing the business processes.

Also, in order to conduct real business on the Web, they will need to specify, agree, and monitor service level agreements with each other. As Web services will invariably have a large number of contracts and as little human intervention as desirable, it would necessitate automating the process as much as possible (Sahai et al., 2002b).

Web service to Web service interaction management can also be done through mediation. Web service networks vision is to mediate Web service interactions, so as to make it secure, manageable, and reliable. Such networks enable versioning management, reliable messaging, and monitoring of message flows (Flamenco Networks, GrandCentral, Transact Plus, and Talking Blocks).

Future Web Services Infrastructures

Deployment and operational costs are determinants in the balance sheets for Web service providers. Web service providers are optimizing their IT infrastructures to allow faster provisioning of new services and more reliable operation. Platforms and management solutions that reduce Web services' deployment and operational costs are emerging. Those platforms support the deployment of Web service (installation and configuration of software and content data), the virtual wiring of machines into application environments independently of the physical wiring in a data center. They allow rearrangements of Web services' applications among machines, the dynamic sizing of service capacities according to fluctuations in demands, and the isolation of service environments hosted in the same data center. Utility computing environments, like grid and data center environments, are good examples of such future Web service infrastructures.

CONCLUSION

The Web services paradigm has evolved substantially because of concerted efforts by the software community. Although the genesis of Web services can be traced to projects like e-speak, Jini, and TSpaces, it has received a boost recently because of standardization of technologies for description (WSDL) and discovery (UDDI). Platforms like J2EE compatible application servers and .Net have appeared for the creation and deployment of these Web services. Standards for security and payment are being agreed upon. The full potential of Web services, however, remains unrealized. The future will see the realization of Web services as a means of doing business on the Web, the vision of dynamic composition of Web services, personalized Web services, end-to-end management of Web service interactions, and having dynamically reusable service infrastructure that will adapt to variations in resource consumption.

GLOSSARY

BPEL4WS (Business Process Execution Language for Web Services) Language used to describe workflows/business processes.

Client Utility The architecture that led to HP's e-speak technology, one of the technologies considered as a precursor to Web services

Composition Two or more Web services working together to fulfill a bigger task.

Conversation Exchange of messages between Web services in a particular context.

J2EE The architecture for a Java-based application server middleware developed by SUN with varied implementations.

.Net Microsoft's technology that is actually a set of tools for creating Windows-based middleware.

SOAP (Simple Object Access Protocol) The standard format and exchange protocol for messages exchanged between web services.

UDDI (Universal Description and Discovery Interface) A global registry for Web services that has not taken off as expected.

Web service Distributed services that are accessible via the Web through uniform resource locators (URLs).

WSDL (Web Services Description Language) Language used to describe Web service interfaces.

WS-Security A standard for Web services security that provides a general-purpose mechanism for associating security tokens with messages

XML (Extended Markup Language) Language used to describe the documents exchanged by Web services.

CROSS REFERENCES

See *Client/Server Computing: Principles and Security Considerations; Internet Architecture; Peer-to-Peer Security; Security Middleware.*

REFERENCES

Atkinson, B., Della-Libera, G., Satoshi, H., Hondo, M., Hallam-Baker, P., Klein, J., et al. (April 2002). *Specification: Web services security (WS-Security).* Retrieved from http://www-106.ibm.com/developerworks/webservices/library/ws-secure.

Banerji, A., Bartolini, C., Beringer, D., Choplella, V., Govindarajan, K., Karp, A., et al. (2002). *Web services conversation language (WSCL) 1.0*. Retrieved from http://www.w3.org/TR/wscl10.

Bartel, M., Boyer, J., Fox, B., LaMacchia, B., & Simon, E. (2002). XML Signature Syntax and Processing, http://www.w3.org/TR/2002/REC-xmldsig-core-20020212.

Berners-Lee, T. (1996). The World Wide Web: Past, present and future. Retrieved from http://www.w3.org/People/Berners-Lee/1996/ppf.html.

The DARPA agent markup language + ontology interface layer (DAML + OIL). (2001). Retrieved from http://www.daml.org.

ebXML. (2001). Retrieved from http://www.ebxml.org.

Ford, W., Hallam-Baker, P., Fox, B., Dillaway, B., LaMacchia, B., Epstein, J., et. al. (March 2001). *XML key management specification (XKMS)*. Retrieved from http://www.w3.org/TR/xkms.

Hallam-Baker, P., & Maler, E. (Eds.). (2002). *Assertions and protocol for the OASIS security assertion markup language (SAML)*. Retrieved from http://www.oasis-open.org/committees/security/docs/draft-sstc-core-29.pdf.

Kim, W., Graupner, S., & Sahai, A. (2002). *A secure platform for peer-to-peer computing in the Internet*. 35th Hawaii International Conference on System Science (HICSS-35), Island of Hawaii, January 7–10, 2002.

Kohl, J., & Neuman, C. (September 1993). *The Kerberos network authentication service (V5)* (RFC 1510).

Kuno, H., & Sahai, A. (2002). *My agent wants to talk to your service: Personalizing Web services through agents* (HPL-2002-114).

Leymann, F. (Ed.). (May 2001). *Web services flow language (WSFL 1.0)*. IBM.

Liberty Alliance Project. (2002). Retrieved from http://www.projectliberty.org/.

Microsoft .NET Passport. (2002). Retrieved from http://www.passport.com/.

Organization for the Advancement of Structured Information Standards (OASIS). (2002). Retrieved from http://www.oasis-open.org.

PKI Forum. (2002). Retrieved from http://www. pkiforum.org/.

Reagle, D. (Ed.). (December 2000). *XML encryption requirements*. Retrieved from http://lists.w3.org/Archives/Public/xml-encryption/2000Oct/att-0003/01-06-xml-encryption-req.html.

RosettaNet. (2002). Retrieved from http://www.rosettanet.org.

Sahai, A., Machiraju, V., Ouyang, J., & Wurster, K. (2002a). *Message tracking in SOAP-based Web services*. IEEE/IFIP Network Operations and Management Symposium (NOMS 2002), April 2002, Florence, Italy. (Also as HP Technical Report HPL-2001-199.)

Sahai, A., et al. (2002b). *Automated SLA monitoring for Web services* (HPL-2002-191).

Santesson, S., et al. (1999). Internet X.509 public key infrastructure qualified certificates profile. Retrieved from http://www.ietf.org/html.charters/pkix-charter.html.

Semantic Web. (2001). Retrieved from http://www.w3.org/2001/sw/

Simple Public Key Infrastructure (SPKI). (1999). *SPKI certificate theory* (RFC 2693).

T-Spaces: Intelligent Connectionware. (1999). Retrieved from http://www.almaden.ibm.com/cs/TSpaces/.

Van Moorsel, A. (2001). *Metrics for the Internet age—Quality of experience and quality of business* (HPL-2001-179). Retrieved from http://www.hpl.hp.com/techreports/2001/HPL-2001-179.html.

WS-Resource Framework (WSRF). (January 2004). Retrieved from http://www.globus.org/wsrf.

FURTHER READING

Andrzejak, A., Graupner, S., Kotov, V., & Trinks, H. (2002). *Self-organizing control in planetary-scale computing*, IEEE International Symposium on Cluster Computing and the Grid (CCGrid), 2nd Workshop on Agent-Based Cluster and Grid Computing (ACGC), May 21–24, 2002, Berlin.

Austin, D., Barbir, A., & Garg, S. (29 April 2002). *Web services architecture requirements*. W3C Working Draft. Http://www.w3.org/TR/2002/WD-wsa-reqs-20020429.

Chaum, D. (1985). Security without identification: Transaction systems to make big brother obsolete. *Communications of the ACM*, 28.

Cryptologic eCash FAQ. (2002). Http://www.cryptologic.com/faq/faq-ecash.html.

Digital certificates, CCITT. (1988). Recommendation X.509: The Directory—authentication framework.

Graupner, S., Kotov, V., & Trinks, H. (2002). Resource-sharing and service deployment in virtual data centers. IEEE Workshop on Resource Sharing in Massively Distributed Systems (RESH'02), Vienna, Austria, July 2002.

HP Utility Data Center (UDC). (November 2001). Http://www.hp.com/go/hpudc.

IBM Autonomic Computing. Http://www.research.ibm.com/autonomic/.

Michel, T. (2002). *Micropayments overview*. Retrieved from http://www.w3.org/ECommerce/Micropayments/.

Millicent. (2002). Http://www.millicent.com/home.html.

Sahai, A., Ouyang, J., & Machiraju, V. (2000). *End-to-end transaction management for Web-based services*. Third International Workshop on Advanced Issues of E-Commerce and Web-based Information Systems (WECWIS), June 21–22, 2000, San Jose, California. (Also as HP Technical Report HPL-2000-168.)

Sahai, A., Machiraju, V., & Wurster, K. (2001). *Monitoring and controlling Internet-based services*. Second IEEE Workshop on Internet Applications (WIAPP'01), July 2001, San Jose, California. (Also as HP Technical Report HPL-2000-120.)

Secure Electronic Transactions LLC. (2002). Retrieved from http://www.setco.org/

Weber, R. (1998). Chablis—Market analysis of digital payment systems. Retrieved from University of Munich Web site: http://chablis.informatik.tu-muenchen.de/MStudy/x-a-marketpay.html

Electronic Commerce[1]

Charles Steinfield, *Michigan State University*

INTRODUCTION

The term *electronic commerce* came into widespread usage after the first graphical Web browser, Mosaic, was developed in 1993 and freely distributed around the world. Drawn by the browser's ease of use, millions of home consumers, businesses, and educators connected to the Internet, creating the conditions for Internet-based commerce. Indeed, Nielsen//Netratings estimates that there were over 200 million Americans, and more than 450 million people worldwide, who had access to the Internet from home in August 2004 (this number rises if we also include those who access the Internet from work or other public settings; see http://www.nielsen-netratings.com for the latest monthly estimates). Businesses, often backed by venture capital from investors enamored with the new opportunities created by Internet-based business, flocked to the Internet attracted by the ease of setting up electronic storefronts and the potential access to a global market of Internet subscribers. For example, Laudon and Traver (2003) estimate that more $120 billion was invested in 12,450 Internet start-up companies between 1998 and 2000, a period of significant growth in e-commerce. Impressively, despite the highly publicized dot-com failures in 2000 and 2001, total Internet sales of goods and services to consumers (i.e., business-to-consumer, or B2C, e-commerce) have grown steadily, exceeding $100 billion in 2003 (U.S. Department of Commerce, 2005). Even more dramatic has been the extent to which businesses have adopted the Internet for use to support exchanges with other firms such as suppliers and business customers. In the United States, business-to-business (B2B) e-commerce is predicted to grow to over $5 trillion, or 36% of total business trade, by 2006 (Laudon & Traver, 2003).

With the rapid growth of the Internet-using population in general, and the use of e-commerce in particular, have come increasing concerns about the security of online transactions. There has been a dramatic rise in the frequency and severity of all forms of Internet security incidents as reported by the Computer Emergency Response Team Coordination Center Coordination Center (CERT/CC) at Carnegie Mellon University (http://www.cert.org). CERT began tracking reports of Internet security incidents, such as attempted intrusions by hackers, in 1988 with six reported incidents. In 2003, the last year for which they collected these data, 137,529 incidents were reported (CERT/CC, 2004). Indeed, automated attacks against computers connected to the Internet have become so widespread and constant that it no longer makes sense to report individual incidents, and CERT has stopped publishing this number. A 2004 survey of U.S. firms found that 70% reported being a victim of at least one electronic crime or intrusion, resulting in approximately $666 million in costs. Moreover, the Federal Trade Commission (FTC) also reports dramatic increases in Internet-related security problems and most notably complaints of identity theft—stealing an individual's personal information such as a credit card number and using this information illegitimately—as well as online fraud. The FTC's Consumer Sentinel (a consumer complaint database) received over a half million complaints about consumer fraud and identify theft in 2003, resulting in reported losses of over $400 million. Total identify theft complaints rose from only 1,380 in 1999 to 214,905 in 2003 (Federal Trade Commission, 2004). The majority of fraud complaints were Internet related (55%), resulting in losses of $200 million, and in 58% of the cases, consumers indicated they were contacted through the Internet. This dramatic growth in Internet-related security problems has the potential to derail consumers' trust in e-commerce and inhibit future growth. Hence, in addition to a broad overview of e-commerce history and research, this chapter includes an introduction to the types of security approaches in use in e-commerce.

[1] Adapted from Steinfield, C. (2004). Electronic commerce and electronic business. In H. Bidgoli (Ed.), *The Internet encyclopedia* (vol. 1, pp. 601–612). New York: Wiley.

Chapter Overview and Themes

This chapter examines the development of e-commerce and its influences on the way that companies work with their suppliers, market their products to customers, and compete with old and new rivals. The historical development of e-commerce suggests that it only emerged as a powerful force once a truly open and standard data network—the Internet—was coupled with easy-to-use software—the graphical Web browser. Many innovative business models evolved in an attempt to take advantage of this new platform, coupled with a host of clever new marketing strategies. E-commerce opened up new avenues for consumers as well, creating new consumer-centric markets in which their bargaining power has been enhanced. Given the inherently open environment of the Internet, however, significant efforts to ensure the security of online transactions are required if e-commerce is to continue to flourish.

Despite these developments, many expected impacts have not yet occurred. A review of research on several anticipated impacts highlights the need to critically assess the early hype about the effect of e-commerce on competitive strategy, market structures, business-to-business relationships, and prices of goods and services.

The chapter concludes with a brief summary and a look toward what the future might hold now that the dot-com era has evolved into e-commerce as a mainstream business activity.

Defining E-Commerce

Today the term electronic (or e-) commerce most commonly refers to the process of buying and selling goods—both information and tangible products—and services over the Internet. Earlier definitions (e.g. Clarke, 1999, para. 1) emphasized the "conduct of commerce in goods and services using telecommunications-based tools." More recent definitions (e.g., Laudon & Traver, 2003, p. 10) emphasize the "use of the Internet and the Web to transact business" in what they call "digitally enabled commercial transactions," where there is some "exchange of value across organizational or individual boundaries in return for products and services." Narrower definitions require that complete transactions, including ordering and payment, occur entirely via the Internet, whereas broader definitions include information exchange in support of transactions, even if the actual payment occurs outside the Internet (often called an offline payment). More recently, the term *e-business* has become popular, which refers more broadly to the conduct of business over computer networks. E-business includes activities that are not purely commercial transactions, such as when two firms use the Internet to collaborate on product development or research or a firm provides customer service online. Some (e.g., Laudon & Traver, 2003) consider e-business to include only internal applications of a firm's computer network and not transactions that span across to other firms. However, today, the terms *e-commerce* and *e-business* are often used interchangeably, and we follow this practice in this chapter.

A BRIEF HISTORY OF E-COMMERCE

Long before the World Wide Web, electronic networks were used to support transactions between businesses and their various external constituents (e.g., suppliers or customers). In the 1970s, forward-thinking manufacturers and wholesalers deployed proprietary data networks and simple terminal-based remote ordering systems out to the premises of business customers. The value of computer networks to link business buyers and sellers was soon well established, and efforts to create standard electronic documents to support trade were occurring across many industries. These latter standards were collectively called electronic document interchange (EDI). In some industries, such as automobile manufacturing and chemical production, EDI transactions proliferated because their use was mandated by large dominant manufacturers. However, because EDI standards were complex and costly to implement, especially for small businesses, the extent of its diffusion was limited (Steinfield, Wigand, Markus, & Minton, forthcoming).

There were precursors to consumer-based e-commerce as well. The Home Shopping Network on cable television and the many 1980s era electronic information services collectively known as videotex in Europe and the United States resembled Web-based electronic retailing. The most successful of these systems in Europe was the French system popularly known as Minitel, named after the small terminal that initially was freely distributed to telephone subscribers. Beginning in 1983, French telephone subscribers could use their Minitels to look up a wealth of information, engage in home banking, and order a wide range of goods and services such as tickets, groceries, and other consumer products. Like the Internet, these services were offered over a public network to which anyone could connect, used a single standard, and relied extensively on graphical content. Unlike the Internet, a clear payment model was implemented, with France Telecom (at the time, the public administration responsible for the provision of all telecommunications networks and services in France) providing a billing and collection service for all companies that wished to sell via the Minitel. Consumers received the bill for their Minitel use on their regular phone bill, and France Telecom in turn paid the various service providers (Steinfield, Kraut, & Plumer, 1995).

In contrast, American electronic information services of the 1980s were still based on closed, rather than open systems, using what has been called a walled-garden approach. That is, services such as CompuServe and America Online (which are now merged) used their own proprietary networks, and their content and services were only available to their own subscribers. It was not until commercial traffic was permitted on the Internet that e-commerce as we know it today was born.

The early years of e-commerce had all the characteristics of a gold rush, as companies flocked to the Web to set up their electronic storefronts. Lured by the rapid growth of first movers such as Amazon.com, more than $125 billion in investment capital was poured into Internet initial public offerings (IPOs) between 1996 and 2000

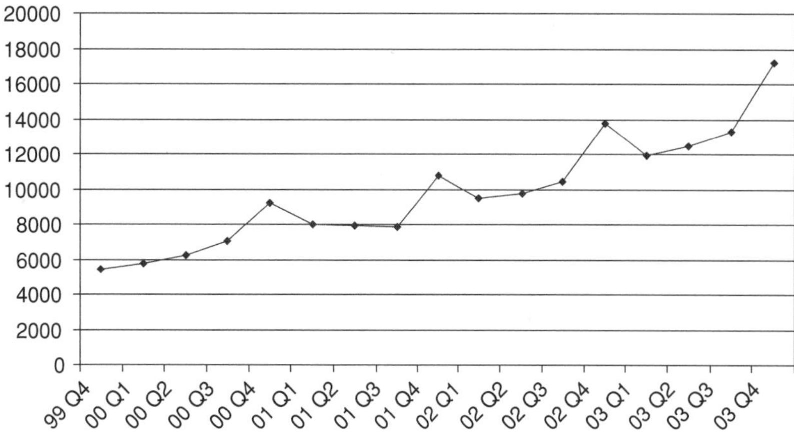

Figure 1: Quarterly U.S. Retail e-commerce sales, 4th quarter 1999–4th quarter 2003, in US$ billions. Source: U.S. Census Bureau, 2004.

(Laudon & Traver 2003). The birth of a new digital economy was proclaimed, characterized by a seemingly unending growth in productivity rooted in the supposedly frictionless commerce afforded by the Internet. The new Web-based businesses theoretically offered such benefits as access to a larger potential market, lower inventory and building costs, more flexibility in sourcing inputs, improved transaction automation and data mining capabilities, an ability to bypass intermediaries that added costs but little value, lower costs for adjusting prices (known as a menu costs) enabling more rapid response to market changes, increased ease of bundling complementary products, 24/7 access, and no limitation on depth of information provided to potential customers (Steinfield, Mahler, & Bauer, 1999). With all these advantages, and the reduced search costs faced by consumers, prices were expected to be lower, while at the same time the Internet firms would prosper.

Despite the rosy projections for e-commerce, in late 2000 and early 2001 many of the dot-com companies began to fail. Few ever made any profits, as their business approach revolved around scaling up to increase market share (Hawkins, 2004). This approach was based on the belief that Internet businesses would enjoy positive network externalities—implying that the more people who used a site, the more value it would have for each user. The dot-coms that could attract the most users the fastest would thus have an insurmountable competitive edge. In search of the required scale, Internet firms kept prices too low and quickly burned through the cash raised from venture capitalists. At the same time, the U.S. economy began to slip into a recession, and venture capitalists began to lose faith in the viability of start-ups that failed to return any profits. Stock prices, which were far too high by normal investment standards, dropped precipitously, and the venture capital community lost interest in dot-com businesses. By the end of 2001, the dot-com era was over, and by one estimate only about 10% of the dot-coms created since 1995 still survived (Laudon & Traver, 2003).

Business-to-business (B2B) oriented dot-coms experienced much the same fate. Large numbers of B2B electronic marketplaces were created to help match buyers and sellers in many industries, and by early 2000, more than 750 B2B e-markets were operating worldwide (U.S Department of Commerce, 2000). Yet most of the new dot-coms in this arena failed as well.

Despite the problems of the dot-coms, statistics on e-commerce use do show steady gains, particularly as traditional companies have moved to enhance their offerings with Internet-based sales channels. According to U.S. Census figures, even as the dot-coms were failing and the economy went through a recession, retail e-commerce sales in the United States grew at a brisk pace (see Figure 1). Annual U.S. retail e-commerce sales nearly doubled between 2000, the first full year that the government tracked this statistic, and 2003, rising from approximately $28.3 billion to more than $54 billion (U.S. Census Bureau, 2004). In the all-important fourth quarter, when holiday shopping occurs, online sales exceeded $17 billion in 2003, more than three times the total in the fourth quarter of 1999. Moreover, these figures are a low estimate, because they do not include sales from online travel, financial brokers, and online ticket sales. U.S. B2B online trade has also grown, rising to an estimated $466 billion in 2001 and projected to be as high $5.4 trillion in 2006 (Laudon & Traver, 2003).

INTERNET BUSINESS MODELS

Many innovative methods of doing business were created in the early years of e-commerce, which collectively came to be called Internet business models. Exactly what constituted a business model was the subject of much debate, as was the issue of which models were successful. Rappa (2004, para. 2), for example, defines a business model as the "method of doing business by which a company can sustain itself—that is, generate revenue. The business model spells-out how a company makes money by specifying where it is positioned in the value chain." Timmer (1998) considers a business model to include three basic components: (1) the architecture for the product, service, and information flows, (2) the potential benefits for the various business actors, and (3) the sources of revenues. Weill and Vitale (2001) characterize models as the roles and relationships among a firm's major stakeholders that result in flows of products, information, and money, leading to benefits for the participants. Other scholars offer what might be called an *ingredients* perspective on

Table 1 Taxonomies of Internet Business Models

Author(s)	Internet Business Models	Comments
Timmer, 1998	E-Shop E-Auction E-Mall Third-Party Marketplace E-Procurement Virtual Communities Value Chain Integrators Collaboration Platforms Value Chain Service Provider Information Brokerage Trust Services	In this early typology, Timmer organized observed models along two dimensions: (1) the degree of innovation (i.e., difference from traditional business models) and (2) the degree of functional integration. E-shops are simple translations from offline models, with low innovation and low integration of functions. Third party marketplaces provide a number of functions for both buyers and sellers and are seen as relatively more innovative.
Rappa, 2004	Brokerage Advertising Infomediaries Merchant Manufacturer Affiliate Community Subscription Utility	These models are largely organized by the primary source of revenue. For example, brokerage models such as eBay rely on fees or commissions. Infomediaries give discounted or free goods or services while they collect consumer information and sell to marketers. Affiliates derive revenue by referring customers to other e-commerce firms, who then provide a sales commission. Utility models refer to firms that charge customers on a metered, or pay-per-use, basis. In some cases, the models refer to a primary way in which value for customers is created—e.g., community models rely on users with common interests to provide content, so that they can charge for advertising. Also, within each model, Rappa defines many subtypes, such as the click-and-mortar versus virtual merchant business models in the merchant category.
Laudon and Traver, 2003	B2C Portal E-Tailer Content Provider Transaction Broker Market Creator Service Provider Community Provider B2B E-Distributor E-Procurement Exchange Industry Consortia Private Industrial Networks	These authors divide models by their consumer versus business focus. Within model types they describe the value proposition, as well as the many subtypes. For example, portals offer an integrated package of content and services and can be horizontal (targeting all users) or vertical (focused on a specific subject matter or market segment). Moreover, they illustrate that many Internet business models combine a number of sources of revenue, including advertising, subscription fees, transaction fees, margins on sales, and affiliate fees. In the B2B arena, they further illustrate the importance of private networks and industry consortia—models that suggest that existing business relationships are essential, even for Internet-based transactions.

Internet business models, suggesting that they each contain many facets such as a value proposition, sources of revenue, a market opportunity, a competitive landscape, a competitive advantage, a strategy for promotion in the market, an organizational development plan, and a management team (Afuah & Tucci, 2001; Laudon & Traver, 2003).

Along with the numerous definitions of business models can be found many taxonomies of models that are commonly seen on the Internet. Three well-known taxonomies are summarized in Table 1. These lists provide an illustration of the many complex business models that have appeared. Despite some superficial similarities, direct comparisons of models are difficult given the varying perspectives the authors have used in forming categories (Wang & Chan, 2003).

After the dot-com crash, attempts to list the many observed Internet business models gave way to analyses focusing on what was wrong with the models. For example, early in the e-commerce boom years, many felt that revenue from advertising would sustain e-commerce. This made some sense for content firms, such as online newspapers, magazines, radio stations, and other media-oriented companies that were accustomed to reliance on sponsors to bring down the costs for their viewers, listeners, and readers. However, one failed Internet business model, pursued somewhat by Buy.com, involved the use of advertising revenue to subsidize product sales, so that consumers could buy products at heavily discounted prices. Another problematic business model in the B2C arena involved manufacturers of products selling directly to end consumers and bypassing wholesale and traditional retail channels. Levi's, for example, attempted to sell its blue jeans directly to online shoppers. Existing retailers, however, threatened retaliation. Given the relatively small percentage of sales generated by the Internet, Levi's soon gave up on the direct-sale model and now uses its Web site mainly to promote sales of Levi's at traditional retail outlets or to sell online through its retailers' Web sites.

Hawkins (2004) criticizes the notion that the Internet required altogether new business models, arguing instead that it simply enabled some firms to apply models that heretofore had not been used by them in their particular market, but that had been common in markets for other types of goods and services. Moreover, he argued that a model does not convey competitive advantage in and of itself, but only if there were reasons to expect that a firm could prevent others from easily imitating it.

Critics of the early business model literature also point out that the dominant focus on revenue streams can encourage firms to ignore other benefits that e-commerce offers, such as cost reductions, improved customer relations, or enhanced performance of traditional channels (Steinfield, Bouwman, & Adelaar, 2002). For example, a virtual merchant (also sometimes called a digital pure-play) may be able to offer goods at lower prices due to its lower inventory holding costs and lower selling costs. However, a click-and-brick firm may use its Web site to help generate more traffic in its physical stores by offering coupons or searches of in-store inventory.

Despite the critiques, it is clear that the development of online commerce has enabled the application of many innovative strategies. One way to view the dot-com crash was simply as an inevitable shakeout that always follows the rapid entry of firms into a new area of business. In this perspective, those models that survived represent the winning approaches, promising significant opportunity for the firms that have successfully adopted them.

MARKETING STRATEGIES FOUND IN E-COMMERCE

Electronic commerce offers many new opportunities for firms to interact with customers. It enhances firms' abilities to offer many customer services in a cost-effective manner. Moreover, e-commerce companies have experimented with a wide range of innovative marketing strategies made possible through software, data mining, and other information technology (IT) capabilities. Several of the more popular e-commerce marketing techniques are briefly highlighted below.

- **Personalization.** An e-commerce vendor can personalize its interaction with customers, creating what some call a one-to-one marketing relationship. Personalization generally requires that the online shopper provide some information about his or her interests or preferences to the vendor. This information is then used to tailor the Web site so that it reflects these interests. Cookies are often used rather than requiring a login to identify particular customers, and each customer then receives his or her own dynamically constructed page. Yahoo! and other search engines and portals were among the first to develop these techniques. More elaborate techniques use purchase histories, clickstream information, and other data to personalize e-commerce services.
- **Customization.** Many e-commerce vendors offer customers a build-to-order option that allows some degree of customization of the products to suit buyer tastes. This is common for computer vendors, but other types of e-commerce companies have also used e-commerce to offer this value-added service to customers. Lands' End, for example, offers hem-to-order pants. Even Levi's, in their initial foray into e-commerce, attempted a made-to-measure blue jean product.
- **Upselling and Cross-selling.** Using simple automated rules as well as more sophisticated data-mining techniques, merchants can enhance their ability to both upsell and cross-sell to customers. Upselling involves convincing customers to trade up to a more expensive option or to add a complementary product to an order. Cross-selling involves suggesting other products that customers might like that are similar to the ones in an existing order.
- **Recommender Systems and Collaborative Filtering.** Many e-commerce sites use a variety of data-mining techniques to provide better product recommendations to customers and enable even more powerful cross-selling (Schafer, Konstan, & Riedl, 2001). Purchase histories and various association rules are often used to refine such product recommendations. In collaborative filtering, the purchases of other customers who have similar profiles are used as a source of recommendations. Amazon.com was one of the first to implement such a service. Whenever a customer selects a particular book, he or she is presented with a list of related books to consider. These recommended books were purchased by other shoppers who had also bought the initial book selected by the customer.
- **Affiliate Programs.** Vendors can use the wider Web community to help sell products. This involves more than simple reciprocal linking and can include payments to Web affiliates that refer a customer who purchases a product. Amazon.com was a pioneer in this area as well, allowing virtually anyone with a Web site to become an Amazon.com affiliate. For example, an author might provide a link from his or her personal Web site to the book's purchase page on Amazon.com. The link is coded to identify the referrer, who then earns a slight commission on any purchase originating from the referring site.
- **Incentive Programs.** In an effort to inspire greater customer loyalty, many e-commerce sites followed the lead of airlines and offered various types of incentive marketing programs. Frequent shoppers could build up points that entitled them to discounts and other benefits. Because all transactions are automated and it is so easy to collect information via the Web, these types of programs became much more accessible to all online merchants. As with airline frequent flyer programs, these techniques create switching costs, because customers who do not return know they will lose accumulated benefits.

- **Direct E-mail.** E-mail, the most popular application of the Internet, is a valuable e-commerce marketing tool. Companies obtain e-mail addresses of visitors and customers and regularly send targeted letters with new product information, announcements of sales, and other promotional content. Although diminished in usefulness today due to the overwhelming presence of spam, customers may still opt-in to receive information on product updates via e-mail.
- **Viral Marketing.** Increasingly, companies rely on customers to help spread the word about their products and services. Such a strategy is known as viral marketing, because the marketing material is carried by customers and spread throughout a target population. Often, dissemination is accomplished by giving users access to free services or games that require the participation of others. PayPal, for example, lets its customer send payments to others for free. Recipients must open an account with PayPal to transfer the funds into their regular bank account. This strategy has helped grow the number of PayPal account holders, which in turn entices more merchants to accept PayPal payments. Merchants, however, do pay a fee to receive funds.
- **Multichannel Marketing.** Brick-and-click firms and catalog companies capitalize on the synergies that arise from the integration of traditional and online channels (Steinfield et al., 2002). Traditional retailers, for example, can provide detailed product information online, immediate pickup in a store, and extensive support after the purchase online. Traditional catalog companies can refer to their Web site in every printed catalog mailed to customers. In this way, they can gain the benefit of a regular reminder to look at their merchandise, with the cost-savings that accrue when customers fill out online forms instead of calling a call center.

The various marketing strategies mentioned above are by no means an exhaustive list, but they do illustrate a number of possibilities to extend and enrich relationships with customers using network-based, computer-mediated transactions.

CONSUMERS IN E-COMMERCE

Up to now, the discussion has focused mainly on e-commerce companies. However, e-commerce also has implications for the way in which consumers interact with each other and with businesses. One of the most successful, and profitable, e-commerce businesses is eBay, which began as an auction broker for consumer-to-consumer transactions, providing the equivalent of a nationwide online garage sale. However, unlike real garage sales, buyers could not physically inspect merchandise, and there was no equivalent process to handing over the item in return for cash. eBay's innovative solution to this problem was to develop a feedback mechanism whereby buyers and sellers rate each other after each transaction. Buyers rate the promptness with which sellers actually delivered the purchased items, the quality of the items, how well they were packaged, the accuracy of the online description, and anything else that might help future buyers decide whether to do business with this particular seller. Sellers also rate buyers, scoring them well if they pay promptly and deal honestly. Privacy is protected because people use pseudonyms. There is an incentive to behave properly, because buyers and sellers develop a reputation (hence, these are often called reputation systems—see Resnick, Kuwabara, Zeckhauser, & Friedman, 2000). If someone develops a bad reputation, then he or she can only return to the system under a new pseudonym, and others may be less willing to deal with someone with no reputation.

eBay relies on an auction pricing format (although buyers now have the option to click on a Buy It Now button and forego the bidding process). Unfortunately, even with the elaborate reputation system, there remains some potential for fraud. Some unscrupulous sellers, for example, may fake numerous transactions with others to build a reputation. Others may have others make false bids on an item to artificially raise prices—this practice is known as shilling. Bidders can also cheat—for example, by using a confederate who makes a high bid to discourage other bidders. The fake bid is then retracted near the bidding deadline, so that the item can be acquired at a lower price. Even with a certain degree of fraud, however, eBay remains highly successful, perhaps in part due to the entertainment value associated with bidding on items.

Consumers play an important role in another well-known e-commerce service run by Priceline.com. Priceline also uses a form of electronic brokerage, in which they match consumers' bids for various goods and services with vendors willing to accept the bid. Priceline mainly deals with travel-related services, and especially airline tickets, although they attempted to expand this model to other sectors. In this way, airlines and others with perishable products have another outlet for goods and services that would otherwise go unsold. This business approach is called a reverse auction broker model and is sometimes referred to as consumer-to-business (C2B) e-commerce since the consumer initiates the transaction.

INFORMATION SECURITY AND ONLINE PAYMENT IN E-COMMERCE

Ensuring the security of online transactions is a fundamental requirement for e-commerce. Lack of trust in an online store, fear of financial loss through theft of a credit card or other banking information, and other concerns over the privacy of information transmitted to and stored by an online store are just some of the concerns faced by consumers in e-commerce transactions. In the earliest years of e-commerce, fears that credit card information would be intercepted while in transit over the Internet prompted most online stores to implement secure servers relying on Secure Socket Layer (SSL) transmission. However, e-commerce security involves much more than secure transmissions. Among the many requirements are needs to authenticate both consumers and online stores, preserve the confidentiality of information related to online transactions, and ensure the integrity of transaction-related information. Public and symmetric key encryption systems are the main methods for accomplishing these needs. The following sections provide a brief introduction to these topics, which are all described in more detail in other chapters in this Handbook.

Encryption Methods in E-Commerce

There are two basic approaches to encryption that form the foundation for secure transactions in e-commerce: secret or symmetric key encryption and public or asymmetric key encryption. Many of today's more sophisticated e-commerce vendors use a combination of both approaches (Juels, 2004).

Secret or Symmetric Key In a symmetric key system, the same code is used to encrypt a message (i.e., the credit card number or the order for a product) as to decrypt it. Hence, the sender and receiver must both possess the secret key needed to decode the encrypted text (also called ciphertext, as opposed to a plaintext message). One of the early and well-known symmetric systems was the Data Encryption Standard (DES), although today a common symmetric standard in wide use in e-commerce is called RC4 by RSA Laboratories (http://www.rsasecurity.com) (Juels, 2004). The main problem with symmetric key approaches is that it is difficult to distribute the secret key safely. Among a small trusted group, for example employees in a common work team, secret keys might be safely passed in person to each other, but this is not viable for an online store and all of its unknown potential customers. Simply sending the key in plain text gives eavesdroppers the chance to capture the key and decode all future encrypted transmissions. Nonetheless, symmetric key encryption is more efficient and rapid than the asymmetric approaches described below.

Public or Asymmetric Key In public key encryption systems, a pair of codes is needed to encrypt a plaintext message into ciphertext and then decrypt it to plaintext again. Essentially, the code pairs are numbers that have a special mathematical relationship—the second one is the only number that can possibly decrypt plaintext that has been encrypted with the first, and vice versa (Juels, 2004). Moreover, knowing one number in the pair does not enable potential thieves to determine the other—depending upon the size of the numbers (1024-bit keys are now common), it can take enormous processing power to uncover the matching key. In a public key system, a person or a store is assigned both a public key that is published and available to anyone (often called a certificate) and the matching private key that only its holder possesses. In this way, public key encryption systems are able to accomplish the needs for authentication and confidentiality noted above, without suffering from the problem of how to send secret keys over the insecure Internet. Suppose a buyer sends an order to an online store and encrypts it with his or her private key. Then, the only way that the store can read the order is to use the buyer's public key to decode it. If the buyer's public key does indeed work, it proves that the order did come from that buyer—demonstrating the authenticity of that buyer. In the same way, an online store may have a public key (its certificate) that the buyer can use to verify that the store is authentic. Note, though, that in both situations, confidentiality is not ensured, since anyone should be able to access public keys, as these should be published. To ensure confidentiality, the buyer would use the online store's public key to encrypt the message. Then, only the store would possess the matching private key, ensuring that only it would be able to decrypt the order. The combination of these two situations—the buyer encrypting with his or her private key and the store's public key—authenticates the buyer, since the store needs the buyer's public key, and ensures confidentiality, since only the store has its own private key.

Public Key Infrastructure To enable such systems in practice requires a trusted system to assign the keys in the first place and make sure that only the rightful owners obtain them. In addition, keys may need to be revoked in the event they are abused or appropriated by the wrong entities. Such a trusted party is often called a certificate authority, and the system to accomplish this is called a public key infrastructure (PKI; Housely, 2004). More on the PKI can be found in other chapters in this Handbook.

Combined Approaches and Digital Signatures In practice, public key encryption is processing intensive and is therefore impractical for large transmissions. The solution is to use a combination of symmetric and asymmetric systems, which can together enable the transmission of digital signatures. In this process, the buyer's computer uses an algorithm on his or message called a hash function to create an extract of it called a message digest. The idea behind such a function is that if there are any changes to the message, then the same algorithm would produce a different digest, revealing possible evidence of tampering with the contents. Then, the buyer encrypts this digest with his or her private key to create a digital signature guaranteeing that he or she sent the message. The full message, plus the digest/signature, could further be encrypted with a symmetric key. Now, the symmetric key must by encrypted with the store's public key, forming what is called a digital envelope. These envelopes, plus the encrypted message + digest/signature are then sent to the receiver. The receiving firm must use its private key to first obtain the symmetric key. Then it can decrypt the message and use the buyer's public key (which may have been also sent to the store in the symmetric key encrypted package, since we do not yet have published directories of public keys) to verify the signature. Finally, it can apply the same hash function to the unencrypted message and match the results to the digest to verify that no tampering occurred.

The above examples illustrate how encryption technology is evolving to help establish a more secure line of communication between online vendors and their buyers. However, some of the most well-known breaches of security have occurred outside the buyer–seller transaction link. In particular, one critical issue is the need to secure buyer information such as a credit card number once the vendor receives it. Servers storing thousands of credit card numbers are more desirable targets for hackers than an individual transaction. In fact, the most widely publicized e-commerce security breach to date occurred when a hacker compromised CD Universe's database, reportedly stealing 350,000 credit card numbers (Wolverton, 2000). The hacker attempted to extort $100,000 from CD Universe and, when that failed, posted thousands of stolen card numbers on a public Web site. This illustrates that e-commerce security encompasses more than secure transactions and must include a broad range of security practices that protect customers' information even after purchases take place.

E-Commerce Payment Methods

As alluded to above, to support complete transactions online, the e-commerce infrastructure must be capable of handling the financial settlement. Since the dawn of e-commerce, many financial and technology companies have worked to establish secure methods of electronic payment. In this section we group most forms of electronic payments into three broad categories: (1) closed user group systems, (2) systems that use secure transmissions of traditional payment methods, and (3) token-based systems for digital money. Each of these is briefly described below.

Closed User Groups A closed user group approach relies on payment occurring outside of the Internet. In general, this approach is used when online shoppers have an account and then are billed on some periodic basis for their usage or purchases. For example, an America Online (AOL) subscriber has made arrangements to pay AOL via a check each month or via his or her credit card. Any online purchases can then be appended to this regular bill. Likewise, a customer may have a private account with a vendor that offers products online. The customer then logs in with his or her account ID and password, purchases items, and receives a bill at the end of the month for all activity on the account. These are both closed groups—only members are able to make purchases, and a billing relationship is already established so that payment happens offline.

B2B exchanges often take place within a closed user group. For example, it is common for suppliers to have long-term contracts with their buyers with prenegotiated prices. Supply chain management systems can permit online ordering of needed supplies, while payment occurs through the normal offline billing and account management process.

Secure Transmission of an Existing Payment Method Many e-commerce vendors sell products to new customers who do not have accounts, and hence a closed user group approach would not work. Rather, the most common method of payment in e-commerce is to set up a secure transmission link to accept an existing form of payment, such as a credit card or an electronic check. One elaborate standard, known as the Secure Electronic Transaction (SET), was developed and supported by the credit card firms, including Visa and MasterCard. However, the system so far has proved to be too costly and cumbersome, and most sites simply use some variation of the original SSL approach to enable shoppers' browsers and e-commerce servers to set up a secure link. Credit card information is encrypted to prevent interception and theft as it travels over the Internet. Merchants must verify the credit card, and consumers, of course, must pay their credit card bill through normal offline means each month.

B2B payments may also occur using secure transmissions, even when the companies are not in a closed user group as described above. Secure transmission of electronic checks, such as offered by eCheck, have been promoted as a safe means of transferring funds between businesses. Consumers may also use echecks for their payment needs.

Token or Digital Money Systems One problem with credit cards is that the fees charged by credit card companies makes them less viable for inexpensive purchases. Content-oriented e-commerce companies are particularly interested in better methods of low-value payment. Some music sites, for example, might find it viable to charge just a few pennies to play a song, counting on generating millions of transactions so that the total translates into real money. In these cases, one solution is to have users set up accounts and then provide a periodic bill that aggregated usage. However, such an approach sets up a barrier to spontaneous usage. Instead, researchers have attempted to develop digital money that could reside in an electronic wallet on a hard drive or in a mobile device. The basic idea is to have the consumer download some funds into his or her computer. This electronic cash could then be spent online, with appropriate controls so that once handed over to a vendor, it is properly debited from the shopper. Ideally, digital money could support micropayments (even fractions of a penny), enable anonymous transactions, and prevent anyone from using the same tokens to pay more than one recipient. A famous example of an electronic cash system is the now defunct eCash from a company known as Digicash. Most of the digital money systems have not met with much success in the market (McCullagh, 2001).

One of the most successful e-commerce payment systems actually combines some elements from the above types of systems. PayPal, a payment service provider used on such services as eBay, *operates somewhat* like a closed user group, a credit card system, and digital money. *It also operates somewhat* like an online bank account, from which customers can make purchases from vendors who use it. They can put funds into their accounts using a credit card or through funds transfer from their regular bank account. But PayPal is more open than other closed systems and relies on more than simple secure transmissions of card numbers. As noted earlier, account holders can send money to anyone with an e-mail address. This is an excellent example of what is called a viral marketing strategy, because anyone receiving payment by PayPal has to open up an account to actually obtain the money.

EMERGING TECHNOLOGIES

The technologies that support e-commerce are constantly evolving, creating new capabilities and opportunities. Here we mention a few of the many technological developments that are shaping the future of e-commerce, including some that are now in widespread use and others just beginning to emerge. We briefly highlight six areas: 3D and virtual environments, software agents, mobile commerce, location-based services, extensible markup language (XML), and Web services.

There is a continuing focus on enhancing the richness and vividness of the e-commerce experience, in an attempt to make it as compelling as shopping in real life (Daugherty, Li, & Biocca, 2005). Work on virtual and 3D environments is ongoing, in anticipation of the day when consumers will have computers with fast processors and 3D video cards coupled with broadband Internet access. Early approaches have been used by clothing catalog companies such as Lands' End, which allows shoppers to create their own 3D model that can try on clothes. Each shopper can modify the shape and appearance of his or her model and then get some idea how particular articles of clothing might look without personally trying them on. Virtual reality approaches go one step further, placing the online shopper into a synthetic environment. This is ideal for tourism, real estate walkthroughs, museum visits, and other types of products or services requiring a more experiential selling approach.

Another set of technologies influencing e-commerce involves software agents that act on behalf of an online shopper or vendor. One early type of agent was known as a shopping bot (short for robot), which could search out items and provide price comparisons (Brynjolfsson & Smith, 2000). Agents can be programmed to perform such tasks as tracking and placing bids at auctions, finding and negotiating prices on desired items, and buying and selling stocks. Research today explores how agents behave, especially when interacting with other agents in multiagent systems.

One exciting new e-commerce development to watch is the extension of online shopping into the mobile arena. Mobile handset manufacturers such as Nokia are building cellular phones with Web browsing capability. Next-generation cellular networks support packet switching and Internet protocol traffic. Protocols such as the wireless application protocol, wireless mark-up language, and compact hypertext markup language (CHTML) were developed to enable the quick translation of Web pages into a format readable on small cellular phone and personal digital assistant screens. As next generation cellular infrastructures speed up access times, and this user and network infrastructure is in place, people will no longer be tied to a desktop computer to surf the Internet and shop online. They are free to engage in e-commerce anytime and anyplace. Surprisingly, even before Web-enabled phones have achieved widespread adoption, early forms of mobile commerce have occurred with simple text messaging (e.g., via short message service or SMS). With hybrid models, cell phone users can make requests or respond to advertisements by sending SMS messages. Clearly, mobile or m-commerce is generating much interest, and not the least because the global number of cellular subscribers is more than a billion, which exceeds the number of people who have computers connected to the Internet (International Telecommunication Union [ITU], 2004).

Many m-commerce services will be based upon the particular location of shoppers, allowing someone in a car, for example, to find the nearest vendor of a particular product (Steinfield, 2004). These types of services are collectively known as location-based services. In the United States, the Federal Communications Commission has mandated that all cellular operators be capable of determining the location of cell phone users to support emergency 911 services. However, there are numerous e-commerce uses of location data, and we are likely to see a wide range of services appear. Users may use their mobile device to search for available vendors in an area, receive directions from their current location to a vendor, make payments at the point-of-sale device, and receive advertisements based upon their interests when they are near particular locations. Location-based services thus blend e-commerce and physical commerce in new ways, blurring the traditional online/offline distinctions of the past.

XML has had a significant impact on e-commerce, helping to move it from a basic presentation focus to a transactional focus. Like HTML, XML relies on tags to mark up text files. However, the emphasis is not on tags that define how information is to be formatted and presented, but on tags to describe data (see Dorfman, 2004, for a detailed description of how XML works). Moreover, users can define their own tags (hence, the notion of extensiblility) based on the data they are providing. XML makes databases portable over the Internet and has been the basis for a growing family of transaction standards. As more firms use XML-based standards, particularly for B2B transactions, a new opportunity has arisen to develop industry-wide data standards. Essentially, XML has become an enabler for EDI over the Internet. Steinfield and colleagues (forthcoming) have documented the growth of vertical industry standards using XML, illustrating the many challenges that industries face in agreeing on such factors as data definitions and transaction formats.

Building upon XML, the last development to highlight here is the growth in what has come to be called Web services. Web services are self-contained, modular e-commerce applications built on standardized protocols, made available over the Internet to e-commerce users and vendors through standardized XML messaging (Ritsko & Davis, 2002). They are helping to complete the transformation of the Web from a presentational medium into a transactional medium (Gottshalk, Graham, Kreger, & Snell, 2002). For example, a shopping cart function is a common Web service that a merchant may use to support its e-commerce site, rather than writing its own cart software. To enable Web services, standards for making XML-based requests (e.g., simple object access protocol, SOAP), describing the services that are available (e.g., Web Services Description Language, WSDL), and publishing service descriptions in online directories in a manner that permits requesters to search for needed services (e.g., universal description, discovery, and integration, UDDI) are required (Gottshalk et al., 2002). Some of the most famous Web vendors now enable business partners to link to their service via a Web services architecture (e.g., see Amazon.com's Web services offerings at http://www.amazon.com/gp/aws/landing.html). As the notion of Web services continues to expand, so too are efforts by major software vendors to provide development platforms to speed up service deployment. Microsoft's .NET platform and Sun's J2EE are the two most well known today (Sahai, Graupner, & Kim, 2004).

BARRIERS TO E-COMMERCE DEVELOPMENT

E-commerce has grown rapidly, but still accounts for only a small fraction of purchases due to a number of critical barriers. Three mentioned here include lack of infrastructure access in some parts of the world, problems associated with online trust, and consumers' needs for immediate fulfillment for some types of products.

Economic and technological barriers can explain low e-commerce usage in many parts of the world. Obviously, e-commerce, especially when directed at consumers, has little relevance in places where there is limited computer penetration and most households do not have phone lines. Yet even in countries such as the United States, where 94% of households have telephone service, two thirds have computers, and more than half of the population now uses the Internet, less than 2% of retail trade occurs online. Among the more frequent explanations for low take-up of e-commerce are lack of trust in online vendors, security concerns, and incompatible consumer needs and desires.

How to establish trust in online commerce is one of the most heavily researched e-commerce areas, which became an issue when thousands of new and unfamiliar dot-com companies flooded the Internet (Grabner-Kräuter & Kaluscha, 2003; Koufaris & Hampton-Sosa, 2004; Tan & Thoen, 2002). Consumers are reluctant to shop at unfamiliar online stores for fear that their orders may not be fulfilled or they may not be able to return defective merchandise. The same problem prevents businesses from buying from unfamiliar suppliers, who have not proved that they are both trustworthy and competent to handle the business. Much of the research has attempted to identify factors that influence the formation of trust, such as Web site quality, presence of Web assurance seals (verification from trusted third parties—firms like Verisign or Trust-E that vouch for the legitimacy of an online vendor), use of secure servers for transactions, and specification of privacy policies (Kim, Sivasailam, & Rao, 2004). To some extent, the growing familiarity of e-commerce brands and movement of established firms into e-commerce has helped. However, consumers have new concerns about how e-commerce companies will use the information they collect. This is a privacy issue on its face, but also reflects a lack of trust that online vendors will behave responsibly.

A related issue is the fear that many online users have over the security of online transactions. Theft of credit card numbers and personal information are chief concerns, and the statistics reported earlier on online fraud by the Federal Trade Commission suggest that trust and security remain a significant problem (Federal Trade Commission, 2004). Clearly, the continued use of strong encryption measures, such as those outlined in the section on information security and online payment, will help bridge the trust gap. Secure transactions are not enough—they must be accompanied by sound information security practices in all aspects of a firm's infrastructure. The cases of hackers breaking into corporate networks and stealing entire databases of credit card numbers stored on servers reminds us of the importance of an overall information security policy (Laudon & Traver, 2003). Other measures for establishing trust, however, are also needed for consumer-to-consumer markets such as eBay, as noted above. Reputation and feedback systems, as well as escrow systems, are some of the measures used to generate trust among strangers in such auction markets (Resnick et al., 2000).

Finally, for many purchases, e-commerce may not be the best approach given consumers' needs, desires, or home situations (Steinfield et al., 1999). For example, when people need a product immediately, they are much more likely to pick it up at a local store than wait one or more days for delivery. Click-and-mortar firms such as Best Buy recognize this need and now offer in-store inventory search and pick-up options for online shoppers. Other consumers see shopping as a social and entertainment activity, and a visit to the mall with friends is hardly replaceable by e-commerce. Finally, some services simply require too much of consumers to be viable. For example, to buy groceries including perishable items online, someone needs to be home at the time of delivery. This scheduling may be difficult, and to get around it, some companies attempted to use refrigerators in garages to which the deliverers had access. Yet this also requires consumers to open up their private space to strangers, and the costs of installing appliances at customer premises proved to be impractical. Moreover, not everyone had a garage, which limits the market. These are just a sampling of shopping situations for which e-commerce might not be the best option.

THE ECONOMIC AND COMPETITIVE IMPACTS OF E-COMMERCE

E-commerce represents both a threat and an opportunity for most companies. It can be expensive to implement, and firms must carefully evaluate the competitive benefits they might achieve. In this section, we examine some of the competitive and economic issues raised by the advent of e-commerce.

Competitive Advantage and E-Business

Information systems researchers have long recognized that information technologies are important competitive weapons (Porter & Millar, 1985). Innovative IT applications and networks help firms to lower costs and allow them to offer new value-added services that serve to differentiate a company from its competitors, which are the two basic competitive strategies discussed by Porter (1985). Information technologies and networks can be deployed throughout every firm's value chain, which is the set of activities through which any company converts inputs such as raw materials and labor into products that can be sold to customers. E-commerce can permeate the value chain, reducing the costs of acquiring supplies, enabling firms to reach into new markets via the Internet, and supporting such value-added services as product customization and the personalization of the information made available to customers.

By enabling access to distant markets without requiring expensive brick-and-mortar investments, e-commerce lowers important barriers to enter new markets. Moreover, because it is so easy to bundle new products over the Web, e-commerce can introduce new competitors into existing industries. Hence, one effect of e-commerce is that incumbent firms in any industry have faced new competitors that were formerly kept out by virtue of geography or other high cost factors. New technologies may also substitute for existing ones, such as when consumers use new music formats in place of purchasing compact discs at stores or online.

Yet, e-commerce has another effect due to its ability to help companies pursue a differentiation strategy. Companies that gather information from customers and then use this to help offer highly personalized services, or that provide incentives to keep customers returning to their Web site, create what has been called sticky e-commerce (Shapiro & Varian, 1999). In this way, e-commerce raises customers' switching costs (the costs to move to a different supplier of a good or service), raising a new barrier that can help prevent other firms from successfully attacking a particular market. Network externalities, which create positive feedback loops so that the larger the service is, the more attractive it is, also work to make it difficult for new firms to attack established players. For example, eBay is so attractive because its large user base increases the likelihood that people can always find the specific product they are seeking. This in turn draws more sellers, which attracts more buyers, and so on. Smaller systems have trouble competing with this dynamic. Such differentiation effects demonstrate that e-commerce does not make exchanges frictionless, and this result would not, in any case, be in the interest of merchants.

Alternative perspectives point out other reasons new entrants may find it difficult to dislodge incumbents in any industry. Afuah and Tucci (2001) point out that incumbent firms normally possess crucial resources that new entrants may not have. These are often called complementary assets and include such factors as established relationships with suppliers, experience, access to retailers, powerful information systems, and strong distribution networks. Indeed, the rise of click-and-brick e-commerce shows forcefully how incumbent retailers can better capitalize on e-commerce than the new dot-coms that do not possess the required complementary assets.

There are many other potential impacts of e-commerce on the competitive dynamics of industries. In addition to the rivalry among competitors in an industry, and the potential threat from new entrants and substitute products noted above, Porter (1980) directs our attention to threats arising from elsewhere in the value chain, including suppliers and buyers. A good example of e-commerce enhancing the bargaining power of suppliers occurs when manufacturers threaten to bypass retailers to sell directly to customers. To the extent this threat is credible, it may reduce the ability of retailers to capture more of the value when they resell products and services to end consumers. The threat of disintermediation is discussed in more detail below. Good examples of the ways that e-commerce can enhance buyer power are noted in the section on consumers in e-commerce. Reverse auctions such as Priceline illustrate how a market can become more buyer-centric. Other enhancements to buyer power through e-commerce occur when individual consumers band together to obtain the types of volume discounts normally only offered to larger business buyers. Third parties that organize this co-buying capability are known as buyer aggregators.

E-Commerce and Transaction Costs

The primary way that e-commerce helps companies reduce costs and enter new markets enable the entry into new markets is by reducing what economists call transaction costs (Williamson, 1975). Every commercial exchange, including those between consumers and businesses and business-to-business exchanges, is a transaction that can be broken into a number of discernible stages, each with its own set of costs to the participants. At the simplest level, we can consider any purchase to require an information or prepurchase phase, a purchase phase, and an after-sales or postpurchase phase. During the information phase, for example, buyers face search costs and sellers have costs to supply purchase information to buyers. During the purchase phase, other costs are associated with negotiation, monitoring contracts, and actual financial settlement. Postpurchase costs include repairs, returns, and other types of customer services. When transaction costs get too high, markets become inefficient, and prices can be higher than they should be. For example, imagine a small town with one seller of some product. Without the Internet, customers in this town face high search costs (e.g., driving to another city to look in stores there) with uncertain payoff. So they pay the higher prices charged by the local monopoly provider. With the Internet, customers' search costs for finding lower-priced suppliers are dramatically reduced, forcing the local monopoly seller to lower its prices. Because of this effect, many economists believe that the Internet will help reduce prices across all industries (Bakos, 1997). Indeed, it became popular to talk about the *death of distance* as a barrier to commerce due to the reduced transaction costs afforded by e-commerce. However, such an analysis overlooks many important influences on the price of any product, including the fact that online products differ in many ways from their counterparts in a store. Online products are not immediately available; cannot be touched, smelled, or otherwise physically examined; and perceived risks—e.g., ease of returns—may be higher. It further ignores the importance of established relations between buyers and sellers, a notion discussed next. Transaction cost frameworks must be extended to deal with these issues.

Market Structure and Buyer–Seller Relations

The reduction in transaction costs afforded by e-commerce is proposed to have another big economic effect, primarily at the B2B level. If transaction costs can be reduced, then market mechanisms may be used where they were not feasible beforehand, based on an early theoretical argument proposed by Malone and colleagues (Malone, Yates, & Benjamin, 1987). For example, suppose a company needed a very specific type of input, only available from one particular supplier in its area. In the past, this company was at a disadvantage. Due to information asymmetries (the supplier knew what it cost to make the goods, but the buying company did not) and lack of alternative providers, the supplier could charge higher prices. However, the reduced search costs and greater information available on the Internet reduce these asymmetries and increase choice. Hence, firms can avoid being locked into long-term relationships and use more spot-market buying behavior to source the inputs they need. The theoretical prediction was that such uses of e-commerce would give rise to large electronic marketplaces in which businesses could buy inputs based purely on the best available offers.

Although e-commerce did result in the formation of large B2B electronic marketplaces that offered both manufacturing (vertical) inputs and commodities (horizontal) supplies, the above prediction has not been entirely supported. First, most of the third-party-developed B2B markets have failed (Laudon & Traver, 2003). Substantial empirical evidence suggests that firms are more likely to use e-commerce to increase the efficiency of transactions with trusted suppliers than to enable spot transactions with new suppliers (Steinfield et al., 1995). Hence they were less likely to allow new third-party firms to position themselves as profit-making intermediaries in these well-established relationships. Instead, the bulk of B2B e-commerce occurs over private industrial networks typically organized by larger buyers or sellers. Often a large company will function as the leader in a value network that encompasses firms up and down the value chain. These value networks compete with other value networks as an extension to simple firm to firm competition. The B2B e-commerce links permit more than just simple buy-and-sell transactions—they enable collaborative e-commerce among networks of firms, allowing such activities as co-design of components and joint marketing efforts.

Intermediation and E-Commerce

As noted above, e-commerce can enable producers of goods and services to bypass intermediary firms such as wholesalers and retailers and sell directly to end customers. This effect has come to be called disintermediation and is often anticipated because of the belief that the Internet reduces producers' transaction costs for accessing end customers. Many producers were swayed by this logic and began to sell products directly from their Web sites. For some companies, such as Dell and Cisco, the direct-sale business model made a great deal of sense, and the Internet provided a cost-effective way to manage it. Most of their customers were businesses already connected to the Internet and accustomed to doing business in this way. For others, especially those selling to consumers, this approach made less sense. Sarkar and colleagues showed early on that, in fact, the Internet provided as much or more opportunity for new forms of intermediation and also helped to strengthen the role of existing intermediary firms (Sarkar, Butler, & Steinfield, 1995). They argued that intermediaries' transaction costs were also reduced, and the gains they get from e-commerce may negate any advantages producers might gain. They also note that intermediaries provide many functions to both buyers and sellers, such as needs assessment and evaluation, market information, and risk reduction, which are critical for many purchases. Many subsequent analyses demonstrated the fallacy of the disintermediation hypothesis (e.g., Schmitz, 2000). Marketing theorists caution that although any particular intermediary might be eliminated, their functions cannot be, suggesting that a role remains for intermediaries even in the age of e-commerce (Stern, El-Ansary, & Coughlan, 1996).

Pricing and E-Commerce

Because of the reduction in transaction costs, and access to information about prices of alternative vendors, a primary effect of e-commerce was supposed to be lower and more homogenous prices relative to traditional channels. Up to now, the evidence for lower prices is rather mixed, especially when the added costs for shipping are taken into account. Moreover, price dispersion remains high, contrary to the expectations of economists (Smith, Bailey, & Brynjolfsson, 2000). It appears that because it is so easy to change prices (referred to as menu costs), Internet companies make more changes in smaller increments to respond to the market.

Another reason there is variability in prices is that e-commerce makes it easier to engage in price discrimination, whereby vendors sell the same product to different customers at different prices. The goal, of course, is to learn what each customer's willingness to pay is and then charge him or her that price. One way that this can happen is through auction pricing, which allows customers to submit their willingness to pay in the form of bids. Another popular price discrimination approach is to charge different prices for different versions of the same product or service (e.g., a student version of software versus a professional version) (Shapiro & Varian, 1999). Sometimes e-commerce companies have tried to estimate willingness to pay based upon some aspect of online behavior. Amazon.com, for example, once angered its customers when it was revealed that the online vendor had attempted to charge higher prices to returning customers, based on the assumption that these loyal customers would be less likely to switch to other online sellers. They soon stopped this practice. Another method of price discrimination is to make assumptions about willingness to pay based upon the referring site. Thus, if a shopper arrives at an online retail site by way of a comparison shopping agent or a discount shopping site, he or she may be presented with a lower price than a shopper who had clicked on an ad in an upscale investment journal.

Collectively, the research in this area shows that e-commerce effects are not so straightforward as was once believed. Many popular notions about e-commerce effects, such as the rise of disintermediation, the death of distance, and the emergence of frictionless commerce are now viewed as myths.

CONCLUSIONS

In this chapter, we have defined and provided a broad overview of e-commerce and showed how the creation of a ubiquitous, easy-to-use, and open data network helped e-commerce emerge as a powerful force from the many precursor systems and technologies. We discussed the development of innovative business models, but noted the problems that dot-coms faced when they attempted to delay profits in exchange for market share. Many powerful marketing strategies were introduced, as well as the rise of consumer-centric markets. Ancillary technologies needed to enable e-commerce, such as encryption and payment systems and emerging technologies such as mobile commerce, XML, and Web services that will extend e-commerce were also discussed.

A critical theme of the chapter is that e-commerce impacts are not straightforward, and claims of revolutionary changes must be carefully scrutinized. Important barriers to its development remain. Research on the competitive and economic impacts yields many findings that run counter to early expectations.

Despite these barriers and unanticipated impacts, we expect that e-commerce will become increasingly pervasive, even without the headlines that tracked every new dot-com in the early years. There are a number of reasons for this expectation. First, as noted earlier, e-commerce usage is continuing to grow, even in what many consider to be a sluggish economy. Moreover, even though IT spending is down and telecommunications firms have recently struggled to stay profitable, the high pace of investment throughout the 1990s means that the infrastructure is now in place to support e-commerce. The Internet backbone networks are fully capable of supporting more traffic and can accommodate the growth in broadband access. It is hoped this will improve the responsiveness of e-commerce sites, encouraging more use. New technologies, such as the extension of e-commerce to mobile devices and increasing availability of Web services, will increase the pervasiveness of e-commerce. The dot-com bust may have caused some to be pessimistic, but it can also be viewed as a normal evolutionary process at the start of any new industry. Poor business models have failed, but viable ones have survived and are now prospering. Moreover, the entry of established companies into e-commerce is lending more legitimacy to the sector and is helping to overcome trust problems, as is the increasing use of powerful public key encryption systems to protect transaction data. These firms also have the resources and alternative sources of income to enable their e-commerce channels to develop appropriately, without reckless moves aimed at capturing market share at the expense of profits. Finally, continued B2B e-commerce development is enhancing efficiency in the supply chain, which can also carry over to B2C e-commerce. In summary, e-commerce will continue to spread throughout the economies of the world and will certainly require careful managerial attention given the complex outcomes uncovered in the research to date.

GLOSSARY

B2B Electronic Hub Electronic marketplaces where business buyers can acquire goods from suppliers. Vertical hubs focus on the provision of manufacturing inputs bringing together firms operating at various stages inside a particular industry value chain. Horizontal hubs focus across industries, bringing buyers and sellers of a wide range of maintenance, repair, and operation goods to the market.

Buyer Aggregation The process of organizing small buyers into a cooperative buying group to obtain volume discounts.

Collaborative E-Commerce A form of B2B e-commerce among cooperating networks of firms that involves more than just purchases, but also such activities as the co-design of components and joint marketing efforts.

Complementary Assets Resources possessed by a firm that enable it to take better advantage of innovations like e-commerce. These resources include established relationships, product know-how, existing business processes and systems, and distribution systems.

Disintermediation An effect of e-commerce whereby producing firms bypass traditional intermediaries to sell directly to end consumers. Hence, intermediaries such as wholesalers or retailers find their position in the market, and thus their very survival, threatened.

Dot-com A name given to Internet companies because their network name ended in ".com."

Electronic Document Interchange (EDI) A standard for transmitting business documents over computer networks.

Intermediary An entity that facilitates trade between buyers and sellers in markets. Wholesalers and retailers are considered to be intermediaries that help manufacturers sell their products to the end consumers. Real estate agents are intermediaries who bring together home buyers and sellers.

Internet Business Model A generic term referring to a variety of specific methods of doing business and generating revenue on the Internet.

Network Externalities A term describing the changes in benefit that an agent receives from a good or service due to changes in the number of other people using that good or service. The word externality implies that these benefits are not internalizedby the seller (i.e., captured in the price). They may be negative (e.g., congestion effects) or positive (e.g., more potential contacts). Often the term *network effect* is used to refer to the increasing benefits to customers associated with a larger user base in an online business.

Price Discrimination A pricing strategy whereby vendors sell the same product to different customers at different prices in an attempt to maximize overall revenue by matching prices to customers' willingness to pay.

Public Key Encryption An asymmetric method of encryption that requires two separate keys, one public and one private. Data encrypted with a public key can only be decrypted by the corresponding private key and vice versa. Asymmetric systems are in contrast to symmetric, or private, key systems that use the same key at either end to decrypt transmissions. Public key systems solve the problem of how to avoid the need to send keys over an insecure network and are often used in concert with symmetric systems—encrypting the symmetric key prior to sending it to the other party.

Switching Costs In e-commerce, such costs are the additional costs a user (or buyer) faces when changing to a different supplier of a good or service, caused by such factors as learning costs, loss of accumulated benefits, or contract requirements.

Transaction Costs Costs incurred by buyers and sellers as they complete a commercial exchange, including search and information gathering costs, monitoring and settlement costs, and after-sales and service costs.

CROSS REFERENCES

See *Business-to-Business Electronic Commerce; Click-and-Brick Electronic Commerce; EDI Security; Electronic Payment Systems; Internet Basics; Mobile Commerce.*

REFERENCES

Afuah, A., & Tucci, C. (2001). *Internet business models and strategies: Text and cases*. New York: McGraw-Hill Irwin.

Bakos, J. Y. (1997). Reducing buyer search costs: Implications for electronic marketplaces. *Management Science, 43*, 1676–1692.

Brynjolfsson, E., & Smith, M. D. (2000). Frictionless commerce? A comparison of Internet and conventional retailers. *Management Science, 46*, 563–585.

CERT/CC. (2004). *CERT/CC statistics: 1988-2004*. Retrieved October 6, 2004, from http://www.cert.org/stats/cert_stats.html.

Choi, S. Y., Stahl, D., & Whinston, A. (1997). *The economics of electronic commerce*. Indianapolis, IN: Macmillan Technical.

Clarke, R. (1999). Electronic commerce definitions. Retrieved October 6, 2004, from http://www.anu.edu.au/people/Roger.Clarke/EC/ECDefns.html#EC.

Daugherty, T., Li, H., & Biocca, F. (2005). Experiential ecommerce: A summary of research investigating the impact of virtual experience on consumer learning. In C. Haugtvedt, K. Machleit, & R. Yalch (Eds.), *Online consumer psychology: Understanding and influencing consumer behavior in the virtual world* (pp. 457–490). Mahwah, NJ: Lawrence Erlbaum.

Dorfman, R. (2004). Extensible markup language (XML). In H. Bidgoli (Ed.), *The Internet encyclopedia* (Vol. 1, pp. 732–754). New York: Wiley.

Federal Trade Commission. (2004). National and state trends in fraud and identity theft: January–December 2003. Retrieved October 6, 2004, from http://www.consumer.gov/idtheft/stats.html

Gottshalk, K., Graham, S., Kreger, H., & Snell, J. (2002). Introduction to Web services architecture. *IBM Systems Journal, 41*, 170–177. Retrieved October 6, 2004, from http://www.research.ibm.com/journal/sj41-2.html

Grabner-Kräuter, S., & Kaluscha, E. (2003). Empirical research in on-line trust: A review and critical assessment. *International Journal of Human-Computer Studies, 58*, 783–812.

Hawkins, R. (2004). Looking beyond the dot-com bubble: Exploring the form and function of business models in the electronic marketplace. In B. Priessl, H. Bouwman, & C. Steinfield (Eds.), *E-life after the dot-com bust* (pp. 65–81). Heidelberg: Physica-Verlag.

International Telecommunication Union. (2004). ICT statistics. Retrieved October 6, 2004, from http://www.itu.int/ITU-D/ict/statistics/

Juels, A. (2004). Encryption. In H. Bidgoli (Ed.), *The Internet encyclopedia* (Vol. 1, pp. 686–694). New York: Wiley.

Kim, D. J., Sivasailam, N., & Rao, H. R. (2004). Information Assurance in B2C Websites for Information Goods/Services. *Electronic Markets, 14*, 344–359.

Koufaris, M., & Hampton-Sosa, W. (2004). The development of initial trust in an online company by new customers. *Information and Management, 41*, 377–397.

Laudon, K., & Traver, C. (2003). *E-commerce: Business, technology, society* (2nd ed.). Boston: Addison-Wesley.

Malone, T., Yates, J., & Benjamin, R. (1987). Electronic markets and electronic hierarchies: Effects of information technology on market structure and corporate strategies. *Communications of the ACM, 30*, 484–497.

McCullagh, D. (2001, June 14). Digging those digicash blues. *Wired*. Retrieved October 6, 2002, from http://www.wired.com/news/exec/0,1370,44507,00.html

Porter, M. E. (1980). *Competitive strategy: Techniques for analyzing industries and competitors*. New York: Free Press.

Porter, M. E. (1985). *Competitive advantage*. New York: Free Press.

Porter, M. E., & Millar, V. E. (1985, July–August). How information gives you competitive advantage. *Harvard Business Review*, pp. 149–160.

Rappa, M. (2004). *Business models on the Web*. Retrieved October 6, 2004, from http://digitalenterprise.org/models/models.html

Resnick, P., Kuwabara, K., Zeckhauser, R., & Friedman, E. (2000). Reputation systems. *Communications of the ACM, 43*(12), 45–48.

Ritsko, J., & Davis, A. (2002). Preface to special issue on new developments in Web services and e-commerce. *IBM Systems Journal, 41*(2), 168–169. Retrieved October 6, 2004, from http://www.research.ibm.com/journal/sj41-2.html

Sahai, A., Graupner, S., & Kim, W. (2004). Web services. In H. Bidgoli (Ed.), *The Internet encyclopedia* (Vol. 3, pp. 754–766). New York: Wiley.

Sarkar, M., Butler, B., & Steinfield, C. (1995). Intermediaries and cybermediaries: A continuing role for mediating players in the electronic marketplace. *Journal of Computer Mediated Communication, 1*(3). Retrieved October 6, 2002, from http://www.ascusc.org/jcmc/vol1/issue3/vol1no3.html

Schafer, B., Konstan, J., & Reidl, J. (2001). Electronic commerce recommender systems. *Journal of Data Mining and Knowledge Discovery, 5*(1), 115–152.

Schmitz, S. (2000). The effects of electronic commerce on the structure of intermediation. *Journal of Computer Mediated Communication, 5*(3). Retrieved October 6, 2002, from http://www.ascusc.org/jcmc/vol5/issue3/

Shapiro, M., & Varian, H. (1999). *Information rules: A strategic guide to the network economy*. Boston: Harvard Business School Press.

Smith, M., Bailey, J., & Brynjolfsson, E. (2000). Understanding digital markets: Review and assessment. In E. Brynjolfsson and B. Kahin (Eds.), *Understanding the digital economy* (pp. 99–136). Cambridge, MA: MIT Press.

Steinfield, C. (2004). The development of location based services in mobile commerce. In B. Priessl, H. Bouwman, and C. Steinfield (Eds.), *E-life after the dot-com bust* (pp. 177–197). Heidelberg: Physica-Verlag.

Steinfield, C., Bouwman, H., & Adelaar, T. (2002). The dynamics of click-and-mortar e-commerce: Opportunities and management strategies. *International Journal of Electronic Commerce, 7*, 93–120.

Steinfield, C., Kraut, R., & Plummer, A. (1995). The effect of networks on buyer-seller relations. *Journal of Computer Mediated Communication, 1*(3). Retrieved October 6, 2002, from http://www.ascusc.org/jcmc/vol1/issue3/vol1no3.html

Steinfield, C., Mahler, A., & Bauer, J. (1999). Electronic commerce and the local merchant: Opportunities for synergy between physical and Web presence. *Electronic Markets, 9*, 51–57.

Steinfield, C., Wigand, R., Markus, M. L., & Minton, G. (forthcoming). Promoting e-business through vertical information systems standards: Lessons from the US home mortgage industry. In S. Greenstein & V. Stango (Eds.), *Standards and public policy*. Cambridge, England: Cambridge University Press.

Stern, L. W., El-Ansary, A. I., & Coughlan, A. T. (1996). *Marketing channels*. Upper Saddle River, NJ: Prentice-Hall International.

Tan, Y., & Thoen, W. (2002). Formal aspects of a generic model of trust for electronic commerce. *Decision Support Systems, 33*, 233–246.

Timmer, P. (1998). Business models for electronic markets. *Electronic Markets, 8*(2), 3–8. Retrieved November 1, 2002, from http://www.electronicmarkets.org/modules/pub/view.php/electronicmarkets-183

U.S. Census Bureau. (2004). *Service sector statistics*. Retrieved October 6, 2004, from http://www.census.gov/mrts/www/current.html

U.S. Department of Commerce. (2000). *Digital economy 2000*. Washington, DC: Author. Retrieved October 6, 2002, from https://www.esa.doc.gov/2000.cfm.

U.S. Department of Commerce. (2005). *E-Stats E-Commerce 2003 Highlights*. Washington, DC: Author. Retrieved May 16, 2005, from http://www.census.gov/eos/www/papers/2003/2003finaltext.pdf.

Wang, C. P., & Chan, K. C. (2003). Analyzing the taxonomy of Internet business models using graphs. *First Monday, 8*(6). Retrieved October 6, 2004, from http://www.firstmonday.dk/issues/issue8_6/wang/

Weill, P., & Vitale, M. (2001). *Place to space: Migrating to e-business models*. Boston: Harvard Business School Press.

Williamson, O. (1975). *Markets and hierarchies: Analysis and antitrust implications*. New York: Free Press.

Wolverton, T. (2000, January 10). FBI probes extortion case at CD store. *CNET News.com*. Retrieved March 1, 2004, from http://news.com.com/2100-1017-235418.html

EDI Security

Matthew K. McGowan, *Bradley University*

INTRODUCTION

Electronic data interchange (EDI) is the computer-to-computer exchange of business transactions in standardized formats. It is used for business-to-business (B2B) electronic commerce, the largest and fastest growing type of electronic commerce. EDI involves electronic links from one organization to another, classifying it as a type of interorganizational information system (IOIS). EDI includes support for a variety of business transactions. For example, Bell Helicopter (2002) uses EDI for invoices, payments, shipping schedules, and requests for quotes in conducting business with its suppliers. EDI uses standard formats for the electronic exchange of business transactions.

There are over 100,000 companies using EDI in the United States today (Cooke, 2002) and 200,000 users worldwide (Angeles, Corritore, Basu, & Nath, 2001). The viability of secure EDI over the Internet will increase the number of EDI users significantly (Cullinane, 1998). Security of EDI is one of the factors contributing to its successful implementation by U.S. firms for domestic and international EDI (Angeles et al., 2001).

The use of EDI includes administrative components such as the establishment of business relationships, modifications to business processes, and the execution of business transactions. Various technologies for implementing EDI, including file transfer protocol (FTP), electronic mail, Web services, and private service providers, are available. The general security mechanisms for EDI transactions are the same regardless of the technology used to implement EDI. The specific steps an organization takes to secure its EDI process will depend in part on the technologies it employs in its deployment of EDI. This chapter concerns the EDI security but the reader may wish to examine other chapters in this *Handbook* for more detailed information on particular technologies. Other relevant chapters in this *Handbook* are "Business-to-Business Electronic Commerce," "Electronic Commerce and Electronic Business," and "E-Commerce Safeguards."

THE BUSINESS ROLE OF EDI

The use of EDI to exchange business transactions does not occur until after two organizations have established a business relationship with each other. This characteristic is markedly different from business-to-consumer (B2C) electronic commerce. In B2C electronic commerce, the relationship often begins with an online transaction. The two organizations develop a trading partner agreement that specifies the terms and conditions for using EDI with each other before implementing EDI. Briefly, the process involved in conducting a transaction via EDI is for an organization to translate a business transaction into the agreed-upon EDI standard format, transmit the transaction electronically to the trading partner, and for the trading partner to translate the EDI format transaction into the format required by its information system. Refer to a later section of this chapter for a detailed discussion of the EDI process.

Traditionally, organizations have used communication service providers to act as intermediaries in communication exchanges with trading partners. The communication service provider would act as an electronic post office, directing messages to the appropriate electronic mail box, and allowing organizations to receive their messages. The introduction of the Internet has created other alternatives for sending and receiving EDI transactions: electronic mail, file transfer, and Web-based alternatives.

Often, these alternatives cost less than traditional EDI. Because the Internet is a public network, these EDI alternatives also introduce security risks for EDI transactions.

The following is a brief description of how a company might use EDI. The company's inventory management system detects that the quantity on hand of an item has fallen below the reorder point and generates an order for the item. The order moves electronically to an EDI software system that converts the order to the standard EDI format and sends it to the company's supplier. The supplier receives the order via its EDI system, converts it to the format required for its order processing system, and sends it to the order processing system for processing.

The fact that EDI uses standard formats permits businesses to convert the electronic documents to formats that their business systems use. The business systems can then process them in the same way other transactions are processed. Similarly, an information system could generate a transaction. When companies fully integrate EDI systems with their information systems, there is no need for human involvement in processing paperwork. EDI software can convert the transaction to the format needed by the application and send it to that system.

Companies have realized many benefits from the use of EDI. Lower transaction costs are frequently mentioned, and other benefits include increased accuracy, lower inventory costs, reduced labor costs, more timely information, and reduced cycle times (Copeland & Hwang, 1997; Raghunathan & Yeh, 2001; Waksmunski, 1996). EDI can improve accuracy by eliminating the rekeying of data. Because EDI transactions move electronically, it can eliminate paper costs and reduce communications costs.

Smaller organizations may adopt EDI to satisfy the requirements of a larger trading partner and may not reap similar benefits (Lee, Clark, & Tam, 1999). Implementing EDI involves both administrative and technical adjustments, and the technical expertise required to implement EDI may challenge small companies (Iacovou, Benbasat, & Dexter, 1995; McGowan & Madey, 1998). Larger trading partners should consider providing technical help to smaller organizations to ensure the process is secure at both ends.

THE EDI PROCESS

The first step for two trading partners to use EDI to exchange business documents is for them to establish an agreement specifying the terms and conditions for the use of EDI. Oftentimes the company initiating the EDI process has a standard agreement. Refer to the chapter on "Security Obligations in Vendor Contracts" for additional information.

EDI uses a standard format for exchanging business documents. Most company information systems do not directly support standard EDI formats, necessitating a translation to or from the formats used by the information system. Figure 1 illustrates the EDI process for an invoice from a supplier to a buyer. In this scenario, the supplier creates an invoice within its billing system, then extracts and formats the invoice information before sending it to EDI translation software. The EDI translation software takes the invoice information, formats it in the

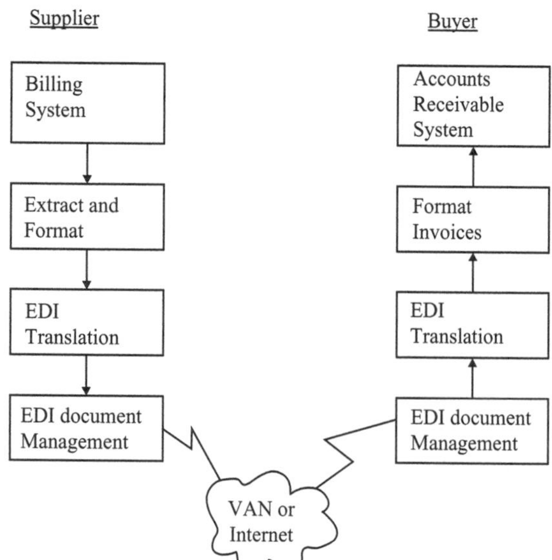

Figure 1: The EDI process for a supplier invoice.

EDI standard format, and sends it to the EDI document management software. The EDI document management system prepares the addressing information and transmits the EDI formatted electronic documents to the buyer via a communications network. On the buyer side, the buyer's EDI document management software receives the invoice and forwards it to EDI translation software. The EDI translation software formats the EDI transactions into the format required for the buyer's accounts receivable system for processing. The following section discusses the threats to EDI systems.

EDI VULNERABILITIES

The primary threats to EDI systems include interception (unauthorized access to data), interruption (prevention of transaction completion), modification (intentional or unintentional loss or destruction of data), and fabrication (fraudulent transactions). This section identifies threats to EDI data. Subsequent sections of this chapter identify countermeasures. Figure 1 provides a frame of reference for the discussion of EDI vulnerabilities.

Interception

EDI data are subject to interception at any point in the EDI process. The greatest threats occur when the data are in transit, particularly if the EDI process uses the Internet as the communications network. The originating system (billing system in Figure 1) and destination system (accounts receivable system in Figure 1) also provide opportunities for interception. Data interception is also possible if the data reside on a computer accessible to the Internet during the EDI process, for example, a server connected to the Internet.

Interruption

The EDI process often involves several software systems and multiple hardware platforms. If any one of these components is unreliable, it could lead to an interruption of the EDI process. For example, a denial of service attack on the computer used to send or receive EDI documents could lead to an interruption of the EDI process. Companies that initiate EDI with smaller trading partners may need to provide technical assistance to ensure the EDI process does not suffer interruption.

Modification

Modification to EDI data can be intentional or unintentional. The largest unintentional threats come from problems in the systems used for EDI. For example (refer to Figure 1), incorrect information might enter the originating system (billing), the system might not extract and format the data properly, the translation to the correct format may be improperly specified, or data may not be properly loaded to the destination system (accounts receivable). Using EDI can actually help reduce error rates in these business processes because data exchanges are electronic and do not involve rekeying. The most likely threats of intentional modification are from people who work with the source (billing) and destination (accounts receivable) systems.

Fabrication

Fraudulent transactions are one of the greatest threats associated with EDI. The threat is not due to the use of EDI. Proper administrative controls and system controls can reduce this threat significantly. One example of fraudulent transactions is a supplier who intentionally creates an invoice with one number and then creates a second invoice using a different invoice number for a shipment. Another form of fraud is to place a transaction and then deny that the transaction occurred.

The following section includes a discussion of security mechanisms that can help reduce the threats to the EDI process.

EDI SECURITY MECHANISMS

There are five general types of security mechanisms for reducing the security risks for EDI systems: access control, authentication (originator and receiver), nonrepudiation (originator and receiver), data integrity (content and sequence), and auditable history/paper trail. The EDI security mechanisms are summarized in Table 1 and discussed in detail in the following paragraphs. Later parts of the chapter include discussion of mechanisms related to particular EDI technologies.

Access Control

Access control concerns the issue of who is able to obtain and view the transaction and in what circumstances. Access controls must be in place for transaction origination, the duration of the transaction transmission, and transaction receipt. Transaction origination and receipt should be restricted to authorized users or applications. Organizations frequently employ controls requiring user identification and a password to gain access to such systems. This type of control can help prevent fabrication or modification of transactions.

Transactions in transit can be secured by using encryption. Although encryption does not prevent unauthorized access to the transactions, it limits the impact of such a compromise. This type of mechanism can reduce modification or interception. The threat of interception of transactions will vary according to the technologies used to implement EDI. The reader may wish to reference the chapter on "Access Control: Principles and Solutions" for additional information.

Authentication

Authentication is the process that verifies that the transaction is genuine and is authorized by the trading partner. Authentication of the transaction origination protects both the sender and receiver (Waksmunski, 1996). For example, the receiver of a purchase order does not want to send an unauthorized shipment. Similarly, an organization would not want to pay an invoice for a product that was never shipped. Authentication can help deter fabrication, and some authentication techniques allow detection of modifications.

Organizations use several techniques to authenticate transactions. One approach is to include a digital signature in the transmission of the transaction. A second approach is to present a certificate that the trading partner may validate with a trusted party. The authorization process may be a part of the authentication process. For example, an organization may require user identification and a password to originate a transaction online. Trading partners should also use acknowledgments for transactions. This provides feedback that the trading partner received the transaction. If an organization were to receive an acknowledgment for an unauthorized transaction, it could notify its trading partner. Organizations can achieve greater levels of security by using multifactor authentication, which is becoming more common today. For example, a file transfer of documents might require a user id and password to submit the documents, and the

Table 1 EDI Security Mechanisms

Mechanism	Description
Access control	Limit who is able to obtain and view the transaction and in what circumstances.
Authentication	Verify that the transaction is genuine and authorized by the trading partner.
Nonrepudiation	Validate through undeniable proof that the partner participated in the transaction.
Data integrity	Ensure the content and sequence of the transaction is valid, accurate, and complete.
Auditable history	Maintain a complete record of the transaction process.

documents themselves could contain a different identifier and password. Refer to the following *Handbook* chapters for additional information: "Digital Certificates" and "Digital Signatures and Electronic Signatures."

Nonrepudiation

Nonrepudiation (of origination) provides the recipient of the message with proof that a message has been sent and the proof should withstand any attempt by the originator to deny sending the message (Humphreys, 1995). Similarly, there is a need for authentication on the receiver side of the exchange so that the receiver cannot deny that it received the transaction.

To ensure nonrepudiation, an organization should keep a record of transactions received and sent, including any digital signatures or other authentication codes. Trading partners can use acknowledgments (and save these) as proof of transactions. These measures can assist in detecting fabrication or modification. If a company does not receive an acknowledgment, it could be an indicator of interruption.

Data Integrity

Data integrity refers to whether the content and sequence of the message is valid, accurate, and complete. Since EDI transactions are sent electronically, there is the possibility of transmission errors. EDI transactions may also be subject to tampering. The EDI transaction process needs to include a mechanism for ensuring data integrity.

EDI requires transactions to be in a structured, predetermined format. One check of data integrity is to validate that the transactions meet these requirements. A second technique for ensuring data integrity is for the originator to use hash totals (Sterling Commerce, 2003; Waksmunski, 1996). The transaction originator calculates a hash total based on summing certain fields, and then sends the total to the recipient. Upon receipt of the transactions, the recipient independently calculates the hash total and compares it to that sent by the originator. If the totals do not match, then there is an error (intentional or accidental) in the transmission. These techniques can detect modification.

Auditable History

Auditable history relates to the extent to which one can verify the entire transaction process. An audit trail is frequently necessary for accounting purposes. An audit history may be useful in detecting or recovering from fabricated or modified transactions. Traditional business transactions often leave a paper trail. By its very nature, EDI offers little in the way of a paper trail. EDI transactions should be stored for nonrepudiation, but audit needs often require organizations to keep records for longer periods. Another issue for electronic audit trails is ensuring that the auditors can access the electronic records. As new systems replace old systems, an organization may need to migrate audit records.

The following section explains the details of EDI and discusses several technological approaches to EDI.

COMMUNICATIONS NETWORK ALTERNATIVES

There are several alternatives for the communications network implemented for EDI. A company needs to choose which communications transmission technique to use and whether to use a value-added network (VAN) service provider. The exact configuration will depend on the specific arrangement the trading partners have agreed to implement, and many companies use more than one approach to accommodate different trading partners.

The security issues would be the same regardless of the communications network used. However, different types of communications networks would present different threats. For example, the public Internet offers less security than a private network. Security considerations for various EDI configurations are discussed in this section. The reader is encouraged to examine other chapters of this *Handbook* for more complete security information on various technologies.

The three most common transmission methods are the public Internet, a private line connection, and a public switched line (dial-up). The Internet is an unsecured, public network, so it poses various security risks, particularly related to access control. Alternative approaches to using the Internet for EDI are discussed in a later section. Private lines and dial-up connections are difficult for unauthorized users to penetrate, and thus provide a greater inherent degree of access control. However, EDI is moving toward the Internet because of the cost and connectivity benefits.

Value-Added Network Services (VANs)

Traditionally, most companies have opted to use VAN service providers to implement EDI. Among the services VANs provide are connectivity, electronic mailboxes, translation services, security features, and an audit trail (Copeland & Hwang, 1997). The VAN can act as a postal service by accepting EDI transactions from a company and storing them in its trading partners' mailboxes or forwarding them to the trading partners' VAN service providers. The electronic mailbox allows the company to retrieve its EDI documents as needed. A VAN service provider can also provide translation services. This would mean a company could send information from its business systems to the VAN and the VAN would translate the documents into EDI formats, an approach slightly different from that shown in Figure 1.

VAN service providers can assist with security. VAN services can include access control, authentication, and encryption (Copeland & Hwang, 1997). VANs normally restrict access by requiring a user identification and password to access a mailbox. Encryption services help limit the threat of information compromise. A VAN may provide secure connectivity options, including private line connections, dial-up connections (avoiding the Internet), or a virtual private network (VPN) connection for secured access via the Internet.

The VAN can assist with authentication by checking that only authorized trading partners sent transactions. VANs can also help with authentication and nonrepudiation by acting as a certification authority (Humphreys, 1995). The VAN can help ensure data integrity by examining transactions to see that they are complete and in valid formats. The VAN can assist with nonrepudiation and auditable history by providing and storing tracking information for documents.

Internet-Based EDI

The widespread availability of the Internet combined with its low cost as a communications network has led many companies to use EDI over the Internet. Some researchers believe that the use of the Internet will eliminate the need for VAN service providers (Threlkel & Kavan, 1999). VAN service providers have had to adjust their strategies to concentrate on other services besides communication services, including Internet-based services. Companies can use the Internet for EDI either with or without a VAN service provider.

Companies that use the Internet as a communications network for EDI can choose among several approaches: exchanging files of transactions using the file transfer protocol (FTP) (dmx.com, 2002; Threlkel & Kavan, 1999); exchanging transactions via e-mail using multipurpose internet mail extensions (MIME) (Chan, 2002); using VPNs (Threlkel & Kavan, 1999); or simply using the Web as a means of entering transactions via HTML (Bell Helicopter, 2002) or through extended markup language (XML) (Karpinski, 2001). The following chapters in the *Handbook* may provide additional information: "Internet Security Standards," "TCP/IP (Transmission Control Protocol/Internet Protocol) Suite," "Internet E-mail Architecture," "S/MIME (Secure MIME)," VPN Basics," and "Firewall Architectures."

XML Exchanges

XML is becoming a popular way to use the Internet for exchanging business documents and may permit smaller businesses to participate (Cooke, 2002; Witte, Grunhagen, & Clarke, 2003). Some XML configurations permit entry of business documents via a Web browser. Many companies have delayed implementing XML because of a lack of standards for business documents in XML format (Cooke, 2002). Vendors of EDI software are adding translation functions into their software packages that allow conversion between EDI and XML formats (Witte et al., 2003). The lack of standards, including standards for data content and security, has been a barrier to widespread implementation of XML for document exchange (Witte et al., 2003). The Organization for Advancement of Structured Information Standards (OASIS; see http://www.oasis-open.org) is one organization involved with the development of such standards.

OASIS and the United Nations Center for Trade Facilitation and Electronic Business jointly developed the electronic business XML (ebXML; see http://www.ebxml.org) standard. The ebXML standard is a standard for conducting secure, reliable data exchange over the Internet (Sullivan, 2004). Tony Scott, chief technology officer at General Motors, believes that ebXML will become the de facto method by which companies do business (Sullivan, 2004). The automotive industry is one of the early adopters of ebXML, and the Automotive Industry Action Group formed a working group to figure out how to use ebXML and other Web-services standards for the automotive industry (Sullivan, 2004). Refer to the chapter on "Web Services" for additional information.

Security Threats of Internet-Based EDI

Security is one of the largest concerns about using the Internet for business communications, including transmission of business documents (Witte et al., 2003). The Internet is a public network, so companies must not only try to prevent interception, but work to ensure that if interception does occur, the interceptor cannot interpret the message. Businesses need to implement firewalls for any computer involved with Internet-based EDI to prevent unauthorized access to the information stored there. An organization could configure its firewall to block traffic that does not come from a valid IP (Internet protocol) address of a trading partner.

Various types of encryption mechanisms can help protect documents in transit (reference the "Encryption Basics" chapter elsewhere in the *Handbook*). A VPN uses encryption to provide a secure, "private" link over the Internet. None of the other Internet-based EDI approaches include encryption, but an encryption mechanism could be used with any of them to provide message confidentiality should an EDI document be intercepted on the Internet. Organizations can use secure socket layer (SSL) or secure electronic transaction (SET) to provide security for Web-based EDI. Companies that use Internet-based EDI also need to be concerned about threats to their systems because of connections to the public network. Internet threats can include hackers attempting to access systems, worms or viruses penetrating the system, and denial of service attacks.

XML Security

XML uses tags to describe data elements in a document and to define the structure of a document. The tags make it easy to locate information in the document, a beneficial feature of XML that also makes it a potential security hole (Kay, 2002). XML documents can be secured in transit via SSL or through the use of VPN, but that does not eliminate the threat of hackers accessing data stored in XML formats on a server (Kay, 2002; Witte et al., 2003). There is commercial software available to encrypt data directly from an application (Kay, 2002) so that it is not stored in a vulnerable format.

EDI STANDARDS

EDI uses standard formats for the exchange of business documents. Early users of EDI such as Wal-Mart and K-Mart used proprietary formats for EDI (Choudhury, 1997). Using proprietary formats for EDI creates a problem for some trading partners because it means that they need to convert transactions into a variety of formats (Chan, 2002). Using a common standard means that a company needs only one translation process for each type of business transaction done via EDI instead of using different formats for different trading partners.

Common standards also ensure that trading partners have a common understanding and are more likely to result in correct use. The transportation industry was one group that saw the benefit of using common standards and used industry associations to develop industry standards. This consequently led to national and international standards.

There are two principal sets of standards for EDI, the United Nations Electronic Data Interchange for Administration, Commerce, and Transport (EDIFACT) standard, and the American National Standards Institute Accredited Standards Committee X12 (ANSI ASC X12, or more usually, X12) standard. Organizations in the United States more commonly use the X12 standard.

The ANSI X12 Standard

ANSI developed the X12 standard to help facilitate EDI in the United States. The X12 standard defines the data structure, syntax, content, and sequencing for business documents. The standard defines transaction sets for more than 275 different types of documents such as invoice, purchase order, and payment/remittance advice.

The X12 standard defines the following components for each transaction set: data dictionary, data segment, data segment directory, and data elements. The data dictionary defines the content and format of data elements that make up the transaction sets. For example, the data dictionary could define a data element representing the customer name as an alphanumeric field of up to 120 characters. A data segment is a collection of related data elements. For example, one data segment might include the data elements related to the customer's shipping address, and another data segment might include data elements related to the customer's billing address.

The segment directory defines the formats and contents of the data segments in transaction sets. For example, the purchase order transaction set may specify a purchase order identifier of 6 to 30 alphanumeric characters. A loop is a repeating group of segments or segment groups that belong to a transaction. For example, a purchase order transaction segment may contain loops consisting of line items for that purchase order.

The X12 standard specifies transmission control standards for the transmission format (interchange envelope) required to exchange data. A single interchange envelope may contain several types of transaction groups destined for the same recipient. Figure 2 illustrates the X12 interchange format. In this example, a single interchange envelope includes two purchase orders and one payment advice for transmission to a single customer. There is only one functional header for the purchase order documents. Each purchase order has its own transaction set header and transaction set trailer.

The X12 standard transaction sets provide users with a large number of possible data elements to include for a transaction. The purchase order transaction set specifies more than 160 possible data segments, with each segment having up to 6 data elements (dmx.com, 2002). Because of this overwhelming flexibility, many industries have developed conventions to specify the segments and data elements they will use. The airline industry has a set

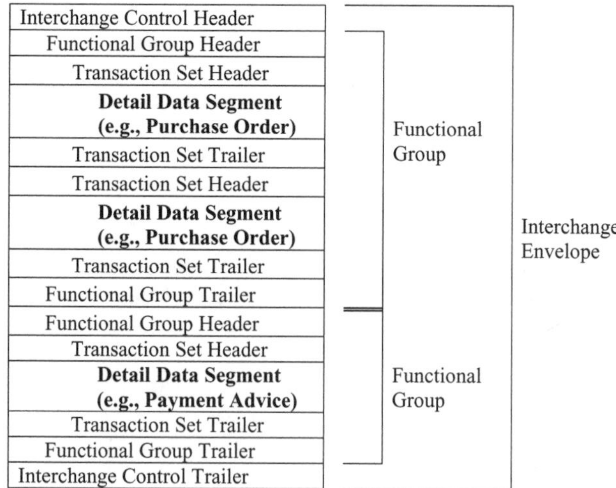

Figure 2: X12 EDI interchange format.

of conventions to specify the standards of use for industry transactions.

The X12 standard continues to evolve, with new transaction sets being added to those already defined. In the United States, the organization responsible for managing EDI standards is the Data Interchange Standards Association (http://www.disa.org). The organization is also responsible for managing EDIFACT standards for the United States (Houser, Griffin, & Hage, 1996).

EDIFACT

The United Nations developed EDIFACT as an international standard to help facilitate EDI for international commerce. The International Standards Organization (ISO) and the United Nations Economic Commission for Europe are jointly responsible for development and maintenance of the EDIFACT standard (Chan, 2002). The EDIFACT standard combines the trade data interchange (TDI) standard developed in the United Kingdom with the X12 standard from the United States (Chan, 2002). The EDIFACT standard is similar to the X12 standard. EDIFACT uses a different syntax and its design allows reuse of components. It has fewer and shorter segments than the X12 standard. Some users have criticized EDIFACT as being less robust than the X12 standard, but it is widely accepted and used extensively for international commerce (Witte et al., 2003).

Security Features of EDI Standards

The complexity of EDI standards provides some measure of security for EDI transmissions. For example, if someone intercepted an EDI transmission, it would still be necessary to interpret the contents. That would mean being able to translate the information from the EDI format into a format more readily accessible by people. Since that is readily accomplished by commercially available software, one could compromise the transmission by using such software to "decode" the information.

EDI standards provide some degree of protection against tampering. The EDI translation software can ensure that the EDI documents are in strict compliance with the EDI standards during the process of assembly and disassembly (Waksmunski, 1996). This will not eliminate someone from tampering with an EDI document and keeping its structure sound. However, it can help detect tampering when the standards are violated or the transmission compromises the integrity of the documents.

The X12 standard allows for inclusion of references for information such as user identification and passwords and sender/receiver authentication (Waksmunski, 1996). This control might prove ineffective unless trading partners employ it in conjunction with encryption or secure communications.

SECURE EDI APPLICATION EXAMPLES

Organizations are reluctant to share information about security because it can lead to a breach of security. The following examples provide some insights into steps organizations take to protect EDI transactions.

Navy Exchange Service Command (NEXCOM)

The description of the NEXCOM EDI implementation is a summary of information presented in Dennis Waksmunski's (1996) paper on EDI security at NEXCOM. NEXCOM manages a retail operation with over 400 selling locations worldwide. The retail outlets include small, medium, and large general merchandise stores, auto service centers, mini-marts, gas stations, and other retail outlets that together have sales over $2 billion. Nearly 200 suppliers receive purchase orders daily via EDI. In the early stages of EDI implementation NEXCOM was already realizing over $250,000 in annual savings from reduced document handling costs and improved order cycle times, and anticipated annual savings in the millions of dollars when its EDI system became fully operational.

The NEXCOM implementation plan calls for the automatic movement of data between internal business application systems and the software that translates data to and from EDI formats. NEXCOM uses a trusted VAN service provider for its communications services and data repository services. The VAN helps provide technical assistance to NEXCOM's trading partners and ensures that data sent by EDI maintains its integrity.

Its trading partners must agree in writing to terms and conditions that include a statement of responsibility, accountability, and liability. The agreement specifies that suppliers

1. must retrieve purchase orders from the VAN;
2. transmit functional acknowledgments within 48 hours of NEXCOM's transmission date;
3. not put merchandise on backorder;
4. not substitute other merchandise; and
5. not deviate from the purchase order.

NEXCOM designates one system as the primary computer for interfacing with the automated business systems. The system is fully redundant, and automatically switches to a mirror backup system if it fails. NEXCOM still supports a facsimile system for trading partners who are not EDI-capable, and trading partners can use that system as a backup to the EDI system. NEXCOM believes that it has implemented appropriate security measures to protect its EDI data.

Mayo Clinic

Threlkel and Kavan (1999) describe the EDI experiences of the Minnesota-based Mayo Clinic. The Mayo Clinic uses Internet-based EDI for ANSI X12 claim and payment transaction sets, and submits about 85% of patient claims via EDI to its trading partners who are responsible for payment. Mayo Clinic uses FTP in conjunction with Pretty Good Privacy (PGP) software to encrypt the data and uses several communications mechanisms to support EDI: the public Internet, a private healthcare network, and VPNs.

The electronic commerce specialist for the Mayo Clinic indicated that the implementation addressed four security objectives: privacy (access control), authentication, nonrepudiation, and data integrity. The encryption scheme helps limit the consequences of transmission interceptions so data remain private. The transmissions include digital signatures for authentication. The Clinic's EDI process uses hash totals to address data integrity. Trading partners respond to the Clinic's transmissions with acknowledgment transactions, closing the loop for the transaction process, and providing nonrepudiation.

Mayo Clinic decided not to use Web-based EDI because there are a high number of payers (over 5000) and each Web site has a different look and feel and different user identification and passwords. Using the Web-based EDI approach, Mayo Clinic employees would have had to become familiar with the Web interface offered by its many payers. The electronic commerce specialist for the Clinic believes that Internet-based EDI has reduced communication costs and the security measures implemented protect the data appropriately. The Health Insurance Portability and Accountability Act requires healthcare organizations to protect patients' privacy and specifies organizations must meet security requirements by April 2005.

Bank of America (BA)

Lankford and Johnson (2000) provide the following account of Bank of America's Internet-based EDI system with Lawrence Livermore National Labs (LLNL). LLNL sends payment information to BA via the Internet, and BA executes the payments to LLNL's vendors. The secure payment process takes minutes.

The process begins with LLNL extracting accounts payable information and translating it into payment orders that use the X12 standard 820 format. The EDI-formatted payment orders are routed through the secure Internet server where they are encoded in MIME format and encrypted using privacy-enhanced mail (PEM). LLNL sends the encrypted messages to the BA server. The firewall software on the BA server authenticates the access privileges contained in the messages, and then the secure Internet EDI server decrypts the messages and authenticates the digital signatures applied by LLNL. The secure Internet EDI server checks authenticated messages to ensure that they are consistent with the X12 standard.

The system creates an acknowledgment for validated messages, then encrypts the acknowledgment and sends it to LLNL using PEM/MIME. The BA Electronic Commerce System translator translates valid messages into BA-readable payment orders. The BA system performs additional edits to ensure that payment orders have the required data to execute a payment instruction. BA debits LLNL's account and credits the trading vendors' accounts. This system includes authentication mechanisms to prevent fabrication. The use of acknowledgments helps ensure nonrepudiation and can help detect interruption. The system reduces the risk of interception or modification by encrypting data.

GUIDELINES FOR MANAGING EDI SYSTEMS RISKS

Organizations may not realize the benefits of EDI if someone compromises their data or systems. By its very nature, EDI involves movement of data past organizational boundaries. Organizations need to ensure that their data remain secure throughout the EDI process. Electronic transactions create an opportunity for fraud because there is little or no human intervention in processing some transactions. Waksmunski (1996) mentions a supplier that intentionally submitted multiple electronic invoices for the same shipment using different invoice numbers each time. Systems risk concerns the extent to which systems have protection against loss or damage (Straub & Welke, 1998). All computer systems have some risks, but there are several risks common to EDI systems. Security experts recommend four sequential activities in security programs to decrease systems risk: deterrence, prevention, detection, and remedy (Straub & Welke, 1998).

Organizations can take actions to deter potential systems abusers by developing guidelines for proper use, educating users and managers of security benefits, and punishing abusers for their actions (Straub & Welke, 1998). For EDI systems, this might include the development of policies that limit access to EDI systems, and educating users about the security mechanisms (discussed previously in this chapter) for EDI systems.

The second activity in reducing systems risk is prevention. Organizations should establish good business relationships with trusted trading partners before they implement EDI systems. A written agreement should spell out the responsibility, accountability, and liability of each party. VAN service providers can help provide EDI security, but there should also be agreements with VANs and other vendors specifying their roles in securing EDI. Companies can employ EDI security mechanisms (access control, authentication, nonrepudiation, and data integrity) to prevent improper use of EDI systems. The use of hashing techniques, digital signatures, or certificates can prevent modified or fabricated transactions from being completed.

The third step in reducing EDI systems risks is to establish procedures for detecting misuses. Maintaining an auditable history of EDI transactions provides a tool to assist in detection. A company could use an audit trail reactively to document a security breach, or proactively as part of a system audit or for generating a suspicious activity report (Straub & Welke, 1998).

The final component of effective EDI system security is to remedy the effects of a misuse and to penalize the offender (Straub & Welke, 1998). Since EDI involves business-to-business transactions, one possible punishment would be to reduce the amount of business with that trading partner. That might also serve as an effective deterrent for other trading partners. Two planning tools that organizations can use to develop appropriate EDI security programs are to establish security requirements by data class and to assess system risks.

Establish Security Requirements by Data Class

Not all data have the same security requirements. Organizations need to implement security measures appropriate for the value of the data (Humphreys, 1995). The security program should identify classes of data and develop security requirements based on those classes (Cullinane, 1998). In developing classes of data, organizations need to consider the potential consequences if data are compromised (Cullinane, 1998). The amount of information someone could learn from a single transaction could be very small if the transaction were merely an acknowledgment of another transaction, or could be somewhat greater if the transaction were a shipping schedule. Even if someone were to access and translate the transaction, one might not be able to use the information obtained from such a transaction. If the transaction involved a shipping schedule for weapons, there could be more severe consequences if someone were to use the information to intercept the shipment. The risks may vary by industry and type of transaction (Cullinane, 1998), and there may be industry-wide controls available for these risks (Straub & Welke, 1998).

Assess Risks

The security program should also assess the potential risks and vulnerabilities in deciding on the appropriate EDI approach (Cullinane, 1998). Potential risk factors include the nature of the company, the type of technology used for EDI, and employees. Certain organizations may be popular targets because of their size, the nature of the business, political reasons, or other reasons.

Companies must consider the risks inherent in the various technologies used for EDI. Internet-based EDI (or XML) systems need to use firewalls to prevent hackers and denial of service attacks on the server. They should also use some form of encryption or secure protocol to protect the data in transit. For example, a company could use secure HTTP in conjunction with XML exchanges.

Organizations should not overlook the potential for risks internally. Appropriate administrative controls should limit users based on individual responsibilities (Wakmunski, 1996). Audit trails can help identify the culprit if there is fraud. Refer to the following chapters for additional information on risks and security policy: "Risk Assessment and Risk Management" and "Security Policy Guidelines."

CONCLUSIONS AND RECOMMENDATIONS

EDI is one of the oldest forms of electronic commerce. Companies have realized many benefits from EDI including reduced transaction costs and support for various business strategies. The use of the Internet reduces the cost of EDI further and makes it affordable even for small companies. The availability and use of affordable and effective security features will result in the long-term success of EDI (Humphreys, 1995).

Internet-based EDI introduces new threats to EDI, but solutions are available to organizations that address security in their implementation of EDI. Organizations need to consider the value of the data sent via EDI and assess the risks of data compromise. EDI security mechanisms include access control, authentication, nonrepudiation, data integrity, and auditable history. It is possible to achieve the business benefits of EDI using cost-effective, secure solutions.

GLOSSARY

DISA (Data Interchange Standards Association) The organization responsible for the development of EDI standards in the United States.

ebXML (Electronic Business XML) An extension to XML designed to accommodate electronic business.

EDI (Electronic Data Interchange) The computer-to-computer exchange of business transactions in standardized formats.

EDIFACT A set of standard formats for EDI transactions developed by a committee from the United Nations.

Internet-Based EDI The use of the Internet as the communications mechanism for electronic data interchange.

IOIS (Interorganizational Information System) An automated information system that involves information sharing between two organizations.

VAN (Value-Added Network) A company that provides a network and various other services for EDI.

X12 A set of standard formats for EDI transactions developed by the American National Standards Institute (ANSI).

XML (Extensible Markup Language) A Web data language designed for representing data structures and data values.

CROSS REFERENCES

See *Business-to-Business Electronic Commerce; Electronic Payment Systems; Extranets: Applications, Development, Security, and Privacy; Public Network Technologies and Security.*

REFERENCES

Angeles, R., Corritore, C. L., Basu, S. C., & Nath, R. (2001). Success factors for domestic and international electronic data interchange (EDI) implementation for US firms. *International Journal of Information Management, 21*, 329–347.

Bell Helicopter. (2002). *Bell Helicopter's Web-based EDI plan*. Retrieved April 17, 2002, from http://www.bellhelicopter.textron.com/content/eCommerce/edi/webplan.html.

Chan, S. C. (2002). *Introduction to electronic data interchange (EDI)*. Retrieved May 15, 2002, from http://home.hkstar.com/~alanchan/papers/edi.

Choudhury, V. (1997). Strategic choices in the development of interorganizational information systems. *Information Systems Research, 8*(1), 1–24.

Cooke, J. A. (2002). Is XML the next big thing? (Maybe not for a while). *Logistics Management & Distribution Report, 41*(5), 53, 55–56.

Copeland, K. W., & Hwang, C. J. (1997). *Electronic data interchange: Concepts and effects*. INET 97 Proceedings. Retrieved May 22, 2002, from http://www.isoc.org/inet97/proceedings/C5/C5_1.HTM.

Cullinane, D. (1998). Electronic commerce security. *Information Systems Security, 7*(3), 54–65.

dmx.com. (2002). *Chapter 10: The basics of electronic commerce and electronic data interchange*. Retrieved May 17, 2002, from http://www.dmx.com/edibasic.html.

Houser, W., Griffin, J., & Hage, C. (1996). EDI meets the Internet: Frequently asked questions about electronic data interchange (EDI) on the Internet (Network Working Group RFC 1865). Retrieved May 23, 2002, from http://www.doclib.org/rfc/rfc1865.html.

Humphreys, T. (1995). Electronic data interchange (EDI) messaging security. In M. D. Abrams, S. Jajodia, and H. J. Podell (Eds.), *Information security: An integrated collection of essays* (pp. 423–438). Los Alamitos, CA: IEEE Computer Society Press. Also available at http://www.acsac.org/secshelf/book001/18.pdf.

Iacovou, C. L., Benbasat, I., & Dexter, A. S. (1995). Electronic data interchange and small organizations: Adoption and impact of technology. *MIS Quarterly, 19*(4), 465–485.

Karpinski, R. (2001). J. B. Hunt's EDI swap-out. *Internet Week.com*, August 15. Retrieved May 31, 2002, from http://www.internetweek.com/transtoday01/ttoday081501.htm.

Kay, R. (2002) XML's dirty secret. *ComputerWorld*, May 27. Retrieved May 28, 2004, from http://www.computerworld.com/printthis/2002/0,4814,71436,00.html.

Lankford, W. M., & Johnson, J. E. (2000). EDI via the Internet. *Information Management and Computer Security, 8*(1), 27–30.

Lee, H. G., Clark, T., & Tam, K. Y. (1999). Research report: Can EDI benefit adopters? *Information Systems Research, 10*(2), 186–195.

McGowan, M. K., & Madey, G. R. (1998). The influence of organization structure and organizational learning factors on the extent of edi implementation in U. S. firms. *Information Resources Management Journal, 11*(3), 17–27.

Raghunathan, S., & Yeh, A. B. (2001). Beyond EDI: Impact of continuous replenishment program (CRP) between a manufacturer and its retailers. *Information Systems Research, 12*(4), 406–419.

Sterling Commerce (2003). E-business data exchange: Surviving the security audit. Retrieved September 9,

2003, from http://www.sterlingcommerce.com/apps/WhitePapers/DownloadPaper.asp?ID=6.

Straub, D. W., & Welke, R. J. (1998). Coping with systems risk: Security planning models for management decision making. *MIS Quarterly, 22*(4), 441–469.

Sullivan, L. (2004). Driving standards: The auto industry is moving to a new standard for data exchange in an effort to cut costs and simplify processes. *InformationWeek*, March 1. Retrieved June 2, 2004, from http://www.informationweek.com/shared/printableArticle.jhtml?articleID=18201098.

Threlkel, M. S., & Kavan, B. (1999). From traditional EDI to Internet-based EDI: Managerial considerations. *Journal of Information Technology, 14*, 347–360.

Waksmunski, D. (1996). Electronic data interchange security and information assurance. In *Government Information Technologies 1996: A View to the Future*, 75–84. Retrieved September 9, 2003, from http://www.gitec.org/pubs/view96.pdf.

Witte, C. L., Grunhagen, M., & Clarke, R. L. (2003). The integration of EDI and the Internet. *Information Systems Management, 20*(4), 58–65.

Electronic Payment Systems

Indrajit Ray, *Colorado State Univesity*

INTRODUCTION

Throughout the ages, from ancient times to the present day, money has played a very important role in the ordinary business of the life of different people. Money can be best defined as "anything that is widely used for making payment and accounting for debts and credits" (Davies, 2002). All sorts of things have been used as money at different times in the history of mankind including amber, beads, cowries, drums, eggs, feathers, gongs, hoes, ivory, jade, kettles, leather, mats, nails, oxen, pigs, quartz, rice, salt, thimbles, umiacs, vodka, wampum, yarns, and zappozats (decorated axes) (Davies, 2002). In recent times, we are witnessing the emergence of more intangible form of money, namely, electronic money. In fact, although much of the money used by individuals in their day-to-day transactions is still in the form of notes and coins, its quantity is miniscule compared to the intangible electronic money that exists only as records in the books of financial institutions. With the progression of technology we can envision a society, in the not too distant future, where physical money in the form of notes and coins will become as obsolete as amber and beads and cowry shells.

In this chapter, we will look at electronic payment systems. These systems enable the payment for goods and services over a computer network using some form of electronic money. We begin by identifying the requirements for such systems. We observe that the major technical challenge for developing such a system is ensuring its security. We discuss the different types of electronic payment schemes available to us, identifying, in the process, any special security requirement of each system. However, we do not cover the different technologies used to provide security services. These are covered elsewhere in this book. Interested readers are directed to Volume I, Parts 1 (Key Concepts and Applications Related to Information Security) and 3 (Standards and Protocols for Secure Information Transfer), and to Volume II, Part 3 (Foundations of Information, Computer and Network Security). We discuss some of the more important commercial products available today. Finally, we conclude by providing pointers to some of the resources available today to learn more about electronic payment systems.

REQUIREMENTS FOR ELECTRONIC PAYMENT SYSTEMS

Electronic payment systems have more or less the same set of requirements as traditional paper-based systems. The difference is that owing to the unique nature of electronic payment transactions, these requirements impose different types of challenges on the payment system design. Security is of paramount importance in electronic payment systems, more so probably than in traditional paper-based system. The reasons for this are numerous. First, a major portion of these transactions is carried out over open networks, which are rather easy to eavesdrop on even with a limited amount of resources. Thus, confidential financial information may no longer remain confidential if adequate protection mechanisms are not implemented. Second, since the transacting parties can remain faceless, it is quite easy to forge identities of end users and systems in the Internet. Anybody can masquerade as somebody else and continue on a transaction with impunity. Gathering evidence of a crime is also more difficult. Third, electronic payments are often carried out over an inherently unreliable medium. This implies that messages exchanged for execution of the transaction can be corrupted or altered during transit, resulting in unforeseen results. Last, but not the least, electronic payment transactions can span both geographical and judicial boundaries. Whereas this is also possible for traditional payment transactions, the implications for electronic payments are different. It is more difficult to identify a felon in an electronic payment crime and bring her/him to justice.

We begin by summarizing the requirements (from computer security perspective) for electronic payment systems in general and identifying the differences in challenges they impose for the design of the system. Later, as we discuss different types of payment systems, we identify the specific challenges for each system.

Need to Ensure Integrity for Payer, Payee, and Payment System

This is the first major rule of thumb in designing any payment systems. There is need to ensure that (i) nothing happens without authorization, and (ii) nothing happens without generating sufficient pieces of evidence. Moreover, technical and legal procedures for dispute handling should be made part of the system.

Ensuring proper authorization by itself is not a very large challenge. All that is needed is a provision for signatures, maybe notarized, at the right place for the authorization to be recorded. This needs to be accompanied by proper identification of the signatory and correct association of the signature to the signatory. Techniques for authentication and authorization are discussed in more details in Volume III, Part 2 of this book (Prevention: Keeping the Hackers and Crackers at Bay). However, in the context of electronic payment systems, authentication and authorization are more easily said than done. To begin with, although a digital counterpart of traditional signatures has been available for some time, some with nonforgeability properties even stronger than those of traditional signatures, the technology and infrastructure for these are not yet widely available. Many communities have yet to establish laws that recognize the validity of such digital signatures. Compounding the problem is the technical difficulty associated with identifying and authenticating the signatory. Users of computer systems remain faceless throughout a transaction. Thus, although it is easy to authenticate the process employed in the transaction, it is extremely difficult to associate the process with a real-life entity. This implies that it is quite easy for the digital signatory of a document to refute a signature later.

Generating sufficient pieces of evidence for electronic payments is also considerably difficult. This requires a proper audit trail of a transaction to be maintained at all times during the entire transaction life cycle and until such time as it is no longer needed. In addition, we must ensure that such audit trails are not tampered with after generation. This is quite difficult to ensure specially if we impose the requirement that such audit trails and other associated information may often need to be transmitted over open, unreliable networks. With currently available technology, it is not possible to prevent the tampering of audit trails completely. We must accept that there will be times when such tampering occurs. Obviously, this creates a number of technical challenges when disputes need to be handled based on audit trail data. Thus, in the event of audit trail tampering, we should be able to detect and prove the tampering. Further, we should have proper contingency plans for such eventuality. Although the technology for performing these individually has been available for many years, an integrated mechanism that incorporates the individual technologies into a cohesive framework that is also supported by proper legal and procedural methodologies is still not widely available.

Privacy for Payer and Payee

The requirement for ensuring payer and payee privacy arises in much the same way in electronic payment systems as in traditional payment systems. Users of the electronic payment system need the assurance that their financial information remains confidential throughout the transaction, that only such information that the user deems needed to be revealed is actually revealed. Further, the user needs the assurance that the piece of confidential information revealed is not misused by the recipient. Each of these requirements is extremely difficult to ensure in the electronic world.

To begin with, many electronic payment transactions are carried over open networks like the Internet. Such networks are susceptible to eavesdropping. Thus, if appropriate precautions are not adopted, any transmitted financial information is available to whoever is eavesdropping. The solution to this problem is to encrypt the information in an appropriate manner before transmission. Many people believe that proper encryption is the panacea of all confidentiality problems. This, however, is not really the case. To begin with, we need to remember that a brute force approach can always, in principle, break the strongest of currently available encryption technology. This is assuming that there is no hidden trapdoor in the encryption algorithm that makes the technique vulnerable. We can take some solace from the fact that such brute force approach is beyond the technical and physical capabilities of even the most powerful, however, we should realize that it is extremely difficult to prove formally that an encryption algorithm is strong. In fact, there is no theory that guarantees the strength for any conventional cryptographic system. Traditionally, encryption systems have been considered strong when they have been used and tested for a reasonably long period of time without anybody knowing how to break them efficiently, in a practical and practicable manner. Such testing can prove weakness of a particular scheme for a given level of effort; this cannot prove that there is no simpler approach to breaking the scheme. In addition, encryption technology is sometimes implemented incorrectly just like buggy software. Thus, there can be loopholes in the software that performs the encryption operation that can be exploited to breach confidentiality. Ensuring that encryption software is foolproof is not an easy task.

Assuming that we can protect confidential information from prying eyes while in transit, we note that it is very difficult to ensure that confidential information is treated in a confidential manner by the recipient. For example, many of us use credit cards for purchasing services. The merchant stores such credit card numbers electronically in its computer system. However, there is no guarantee that the merchant's computer systems are adequately protected. Although this is also the case for traditional financial transactions, we at least know to whom we are revealing confidential information. In the electronic world, the end parties are faceless. We may easily be led to believe that we are revealing information to trusted parties when we are not. In addition, we do not know whether the recipient handles the information in the appropriate manner.

A related problem is how to ensure the anonymity of the user of the electronic payment system. A user may want that not only its financial information remain confidential but also that it remain anonymous in the transaction. If a user is using traditional cash in a transaction, the user remains anonymous. It is not possible to link a transaction that has been paid for by traditional cash to a particular customer. It is also not possible to derive any personal information about the customer from this transaction. In the electronic world, this is more difficult to achieve. Part of the reason is that every message used in the transaction can be traced to a source address. Complex cryptographic protocols for achieving such anonymity or unlinkability are needed. At the same time allowing anonymity creates additional problems, namely in the way of ensuring authenticity, proper authorization, and *fair exchange*.

Fair Exchange

In the classical business environment, a transaction essentially involves fulfillment of some obligation by two parties; a contract describes the penalties if either party fails to meet its obligation. Since each transacting party has an identifiable place of doing business, if any party behaves unfairly, that party can be physically approached and held accountable for its unfair behavior. In the electronic world, on the other hand, a party does not always have a physically identifiable place of doing business. After behaving unfairly in the electronic transaction, a party can simply vanish without a trace. In such cases, it may be next to impossible to enforce the penalties of the contract, leading to losses for the other party. For example, let a customer buy a product from a merchant. The customer pays for the product in some electronic manner. However, once the merchant receives the payment the merchant never delivers the product. This causes financial loss for the customer. Thus, any electronic payment scheme must ensure that at the end of the protocol execution, each transacting party receives the other's product or none does. This is often referred to as the problem of fair exchange and is quite difficult to achieve particularly if this needs to be accompanied by anonymity for the payer or the payee.

In summary, it is fair to say that though electronic payment systems make it easier to perform commercial transactions over the Internet, there are a number of challenges remaining to make the scheme successful. In the following, we discuss some of the different types of electronic payment systems available today. We discuss some of the unique challenges to each scheme.

TYPES OF ELECTRONIC PAYMENT SYSTEMS

Electronic payment systems broadly use one of three different forms of electronic money: (i) token money, (ii) notational money, or (iii) hybrid money.

Token money is similar to real cash. It is used in a token-based or cash-like system. Transactions that have a certain value are performed with token money, and must be brought to a central authority before consumers are able to make any transaction. These systems do not support the notion of debt. Electronic cash and electronic purse are the two major types of token money systems. Notational money is used in credit/debit systems. The system consists of having an account and a central authority keeping a record of the amount in that account. Consumers exchange documents that are equivalent to value transfers. These exchanges consist of debiting the consumer's account and crediting the merchant's account. Systems using notational money can support the concept of fiscal debt. Electronic payment orders over the Internet and credit card billing over the Internet are the two most well-known systems that use notational money. Hybrid money combines the features of both token money and notational money. Automated clearing house and electronic checks form the major system using hybrid money. In the following, we discuss each of these systems in more detail.

Electronic Cash

Electronic cash (or e-cash) (Weber, 1998) is a payment method in which a unique number or identifier is associated with a given amount of money at a financial institution. It is often suggested as an alternative method to credit cards for purchases made over the Internet. Some definitions of electronic cash are much broader, describing it as any form of "prepaid, stored value that can be used for electronic purchases" (van Slyke & Belanger, 2003). However, these systems are better categorized as electronic purse systems. The use of electronic cash requires the customer to open an account in a bank and then deposit money into this account. The bank provides the customer with a unique digital coin (essentially a unique identifier) that is used for all electronic payments.

Any electronic cash system needs to possess five characteristic if it is to be usable and universally accepted. First, it must be ensured that the electronic cash is spendable only once; that is, double spending should be prevented at all costs. This is needed to ensure that both parties involved in the transaction know that the e-cash currency being received is not counterfeit or being used in two different transactions. Second, the e-cash system must be independent of any particular proprietary storage or transmission mechanism. Third, electronic cash must be portable; it should be able to pass transparently across international borders and be automatically converted to the recipient country's currency in all forms of peer-to-peer transactions. Fourth, electronic cash must be divisible. Divisibility determines the size of payment units. Both the number of different electronic cash units and their values can be defined independently of real currency. The denominations are up to the definers and are not limited to the typical breakdowns of a traditional cash system. Fifth and last, e-cash system should be anonymous, very much like their paper world counterpart. The consumer (and sometimes the seller) should be able to use e-cash without revealing her or his identity. However, as explained later, ensuring the last property also makes the prevention of double spending rather difficult.

Double spending can neither be detected nor prevented with truly anonymous electronic cash. Anonymous electronic cash is electronic cash that, like bills and coins, cannot be traced back to the person who spent it. To ensure anonymity or unlinkability of the customer, the payment protocol cannot associate any form of the customer's identification mark with the cash system—much in the same way as traditional cash systems. This implies that the bit string that represents electronic cash is not traceable to the customer who spends it. Since it is rather trivial to make multiple copies of the bit string representing cash, anybody can make counterfeit electronic cash, without fear of being caught and prosecuted. One way to be able to trace electronic cash (to prevent money laundering) is to attach a serial number to each electronic cash transaction. That way, cash can be positively associated with a particular consumer. This does not, however, solve the double spending problem completely. Although a single issuing bank can detect when two deposits of the same electronic cash are about to occur, it is impossible to ascertain who is at fault—the consumer or the merchant. If the duplicate electronic coins are presented to two different banks, the problem is exacerbated. Further, it is not easy to develop an electronic cash system where the cash can be traced back to its origin. Complex cryptographic algorithms are needed to create tamperproof electronic cash that can also be traced back. Electronic cash containing serial numbers additionally raises a number of privacy issues, because merchants could use the serial number to track spending habits of consumers. The whole purpose of electronic cash systems—namely the ability of a customer to remain anonymous—is lost. It is important that a procedure is available both to protect the anonymity of electronic cash users and to provide built-in safeguards to prevent double spending.

Electronic Purse or Stored-Value Card

Electronic purse, as defined by the United Kingdom Banking Code, is "any card or function of a card which contains real value in the form of electronic money which someone has paid for in advance, and which can be reloaded with further funds and which can be used for a range of purposes." These are essentially prepaid stored-value cards. As with electronic cash systems, the consumer needs to deposit real money with the issuer of the purse. The amount of money deposited is then encoded into the card. As purchases are made using the electronic purse, the value in the card is reduced and the amount is credited to the merchant's account. The development of electronic purses has been driven almost wholly by commercial and technological organizations rather than by demand from consumers. The organizations operating electronic purse systems gain from the use of the money stored on the cards. For banks, there are advantages in reducing the handling of cash and checks, which must be transported securely and are labor intensive to handle. For the retailer, the advantages are the reduction in handling of currency and checks. This includes reducing the delay in money being credited to the retailer's bank account. Another advantage is reducing the risk of theft.

A stored-value card can be as elaborate as a smart card or as simple as a plastic card with a magnetic strip. One of the most common stored-value cards is a prepaid phone, copy, subway, or bus card. These cards can be recharged with more value by inserting them into special machines, inserting currency into the machine, and withdrawing the card. Unlike smart cards, magnetic strip cards are passive. That is, they cannot send information such as a customer's digital certificate, nor can they receive and automatically increment or decrement the value of cash stored on the card. Smart card evolved from magnetic strip cards. Instead of encoding and storing data using magnetic strip, a computer microchip is embedded on the card itself containing information about the owner such as financial facts, private encryption keys, account information, credit card numbers, and so on. Like magnetic strip cards, smart cards can be used online and offline. Smart cards are better suited for Internet payment transactions because they have more processing capability than the magnetic stripe cards.

Electronic purses have gradually become one of the most widely used electronic payment systems for consumers. The advantages include ease of use, ability to pay the exact amount without fiddling for change, no authorization requirement, and the possibility of depositing additional value as and when required. However, a major disadvantage from the consumer's point of view is that the purse is as good as real money. If it is lost or stolen, the consumer loses. To protect against such losses, smart card technology that allows units of credit to be reloaded is now being more widely used.

Electronic Wallets

Today's online shoppers have begun to tire of repeatedly entering details about shipping and payment information each time they make an online purchase. Research has shown that filing out forms rank high on online customer's list of grievances about online shopping. Electronic wallet technology is intended to solve this problem. At the same time, an electronic wallet provides a secure storage place for credit card data and electronic cash. In short, an electronic wallet (or e-wallet) serves a function similar to a physical wallet; it holds credit cards, electronic cash, owner identification, and owner contact information and provides that information at an electronic commerce site's checkout counter. Occasionally, an e-wallet may contain an address book. Some wallets also hold an encrypted digital certificate, which securely identifies the wallet's owner. E-wallets make shopping more efficient. An e-wallet simplifies the online checkout process. A simple click inserts the e-wallet information into the payment forms on the merchant's site. E-wallets can also provide many additional services. They can keep track of the owner's purchases by saving receipts. An enhanced digital wallet can even suggest where a consumer may find the best price on an item that he or she purchases on a regular basis.

E-wallets are of two types based on where they are stored. A client-side e-wallet stores a consumer's information on the consumer's own computer. This shifts the

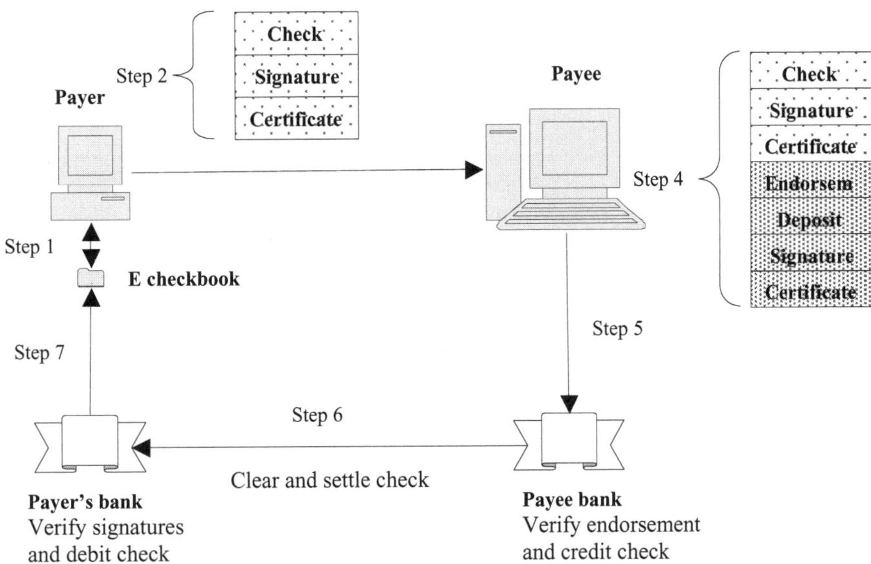

Figure 1: Payment using electronic check.

responsibility for ensuring the e-wallet's security to the end user. This can be regarded as both an advantage and a disadvantage. It is an advantage because the user has more control in keeping the e-wallet securely; it is a disadvantage because users may not always take appropriate measures. Many of early e-wallets were client-side wallets and required lengthy downloads, which was one of their chief disadvantages. Another disadvantage of client-side e-wallet is that they are not portable. They are not available when the owner is making a purchase at a location other than the computer on which the wallet resides. A server-side electronic wallet alleviates this problem; it stores a customer's information on a remote server belonging to a particular merchant or belonging to the wallet's publisher. The main weakness of server-side e-wallet is that a server-side security breach could reveal personal information for thousands of users. Server-side e-wallet systems typically employ strong security measures that minimize or eliminate the possibility of unauthorized disclosure.

For a wallet to be useful at many online sites, it should be able to populate the data fields in any merchant's form at any site that the customer visits. This accessibility means that the e-wallet manufacturer and merchants from many sites must coordinate their efforts so that a wallet can recognize what consumer information goes into each of a given merchant's form.

Electronic Check

Electronic checks are a comparatively new and still emerging technology that combines high security, speed, convenience, and processing efficiencies for online transactions. They are based on the premise that electronic documents can be substituted for paper, and public-key cryptography-based digital signatures can replace handwritten signatures. Thus, the attraction is that electronic checks can replace paper checks without the need to create a new payment instrument together with the implied legal, regulatory, and commercial practice changes. The technology promises several advantages. It leverages the time-tested paper-based check payment system and uses the same legal and business protocols. It works like a paper check but in a pure electronic form with all the associated efficiency. It can be used by all bank customers who have check-signing privileges. Last but not the least it includes enhanced security features that allow automatic verification of content and validity, thereby helping to reduce check fraud.

Electronic checks work the same way as a traditional paper check does (see Figure 1). The steps involved in an electronic check processing can be summarized as follows:

1. The payer retrieves an electronic check from an "electronic checkbook" and fills in the check just as he/she would fill in a paper check.
2. The payer digitally signs the check and includes any necessary certificates with the check.
3. The payer then gives the electronic check to the payee using one of several secure electronic means (for example, through secure e-mail or over secure Web connections).
4. The payee endorses the electronic check by putting its digital signature on the check.
5. The payee then electronically deposits the endorsed check in the payee's bank and receives credit.
6. The payee's bank submits the electronic check to the paying bank for clearing.
7. The paying bank validates the electronic check and then charges the payer's account for the check.

Automated Clearing House

The automated clearing house (ACH) system was developed in the United States in the 1970s by the banking industry in an effort to allow automatic fund transfer by

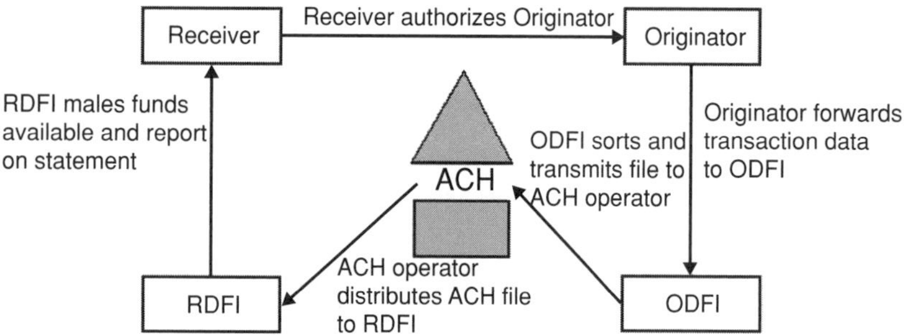

Figure 2: Automated clearing house operations. The ACH operations figure is courtesy of NACHA, the Electronic Payments Association, available from the NACHA Web site (http://www.nacha.org/About/what_is_ach_.htm).

replacing the paper check. The ACH system supports both debit and credit transactions. ACH payments include direct deposit of payroll, social security, and other government benefits tax refunds; direct payment of consumer bills such as mortgages, loans, utility bills, and insurance premiums; business-to-business payments, e-checks, and e-commerce payments.

The ACH system is a batch processing store-and-forward system. Transactions received by the financial institution during the day are stored and processed later in batch mode. ACH transactions are accumulated and sorted by destination for transmission. Typically, five participants are involved in an automated clearing house transaction (see Figure 2):

1. The originating company or individual (originator) initiates a fund transfer from its account.
2. The originating depository financial institution (ODFI) receives a payment instruction from an originator and forwards it to the ACH operator.
3. The receiving depository financial institution (RDFI) receives ACH entries from the ACH operator and posts the entries to the accounts of receivers.
4. The receiving company, employee, or customer (receiver) authorizes an originator to initiate an ACH entry into the receiver's account with the RDFI.
5. The ACH operator is the central clearing facility to or from which participating depository financial institutions transmit or receive ACH entries.

Electronic Bill Presentment and Payment Systems

These systems allow companies to bill customers for their services and in turn receive payments from them electronically over the Internet. There are two types of presentment models:

1. *Direct model*: A company (that is, a seller of a service) delivers the bill to customers (buyers of services) via either the company's own site (seller-direct model) or the customer's site (buyer-direct model).
2. *Consolidator model*: Bills from multiple issuers are delivered to a single site to be presented later in aggregate to the consumer for payment. A consolidator acts as an intermediary, collecting or aggregating invoices from multiple sellers for multiple consumers. Consolidators are generally third parties who may additionally provide a variety of financial services such as escrow, insurance, and credit ratings.

The following steps are involved in systems based on the direct model:

1. *Enrollment*: For seller-direct model the consumer enrolls in the company's bill-processing system using a standard Web interface. For buyer-direct model, the seller enrolls in the customer's Web site that has been set up for this purpose. The site at which bill information is exchanged is henceforth called the bill processor.
2. *Presentment*: This occurs in the following steps:
   a. The seller generates and/or transfers the invoice information to the bill processor.
   b. The consumer is informed that a bill is ready.
   c. The consumer accesses the bill-processing site to review and analyze the invoice information.
3. *Dispute handling*: The consumer may optionally dispute a bill. To do this the consumer contacts the seller for review of the bill.
4. *Payment*: This occurs in the following steps:
   a. The consumer authorizes either full or partial payment for the bill.
   b. If it is the seller-direct model, then the seller's financial institution processes the payment transaction; otherwise, the buyer's financial institution processes the transaction.
   c. The appropriate financial institution confirms payment execution—credit to account for seller-direct model and debit from account for buyer-direct model.
   d. The respective financial institution reports payment return or rejection information.

The consolidator model is very similar to the direct models. The differences are as follows:

1. *Enrollment*: Both the seller and the buyer must register at the consolidator's bill-processing system.
2. *Presentment and dispute handling*: These steps are done using the consolidator as the intermediary.
3. *Payment*: The following steps are performed:
   a. The consolidator initiates the payment and reports the activity to the buyer and the seller.
   b. The payment transaction is processed by either the buyer's or the seller's financial institution. Sometime the consolidator assumes the role of a financial institution.
   c. The financial institutions confirm execution of the payment.

d. Payment return or rejection information may be reported to both buyer and seller by their respective financial institution.

Electronic bill or invoice presentment and payment systems are gaining considerable popularity between both buyers and sellers. The major reason is that these are much faster and efficient than traditional systems. The advantage of the consolidator model over the direct model is that in this model both the seller and the buyer reduce the number of bill-processing sites each must interact with. The disadvantage is that each may have to pay a fee to the consolidator to avail of its services.

Credit Card-Based Systems

Credit cards are by far the most popular form of online payments for consumers. Credit cards are widely accepted by merchants around the world. Credit cards offer a number of benefits for both the consumer and the merchant. A consumer is protected by a grace period in which he or she can dispute a credit card purchase. A merchant has a high degree of confidence that a credit card can be safely accepted from an unknown and not trusted purchaser. Paying for online purchases with a credit card is just as easy as in a conventional purchase from a store. Merchants who already accept credit cards in an offline store can accept them immediately for online payment because they already have a merchant credit card account. Online purchases require an extra degree of security. This is because a credit card holder is not present and cannot be identified as easily as he or she can be when standing at the cash register. Online credit card services must somehow authenticate the purchaser as well as protect sensitive information as it is transmitted on the Internet.

A credit card, such as that offered by Visa or MasterCard, has a preset spending limit based on the user's credit limit; the credit limit is determined by the customer's credit history, income level, and total wealth. The limit ranges from few hundred dollars to several thousand dollars. The user uses these cards to purchase goods and services or obtain cash from the participating financial institutions. The user is required to pay his or her debt during the payment period. He or she can pay off the entire credit balance or pay a minimum amount each billing period. Credit card issuers change interest on any unpaid balance. A *charge card*, such as one from American Express, is similar to a credit card except that it does not carry preset spending limit, and the entire amount charged to the card is due at the end of the billing period. Charge cards do not involve lines of credit and do not accumulate interest charges. The distinction between credit cards and charge cards is unimportant in the discussion of processing credit and charge cards for electronic payment; the collective term *credit card* is used here to refer to both types.

Payment using credit cards generally involves one or more financial institutions for the processing of payment information. For some credit card systems, banks and other financial institutions serve as a broker between card users and the merchants accepting the cards. These types of arrangements are called closed loop systems because no other institution (local bank, national bank, or other clearinghouse) is involved in the transaction. American Express[1] and Discover Card are examples of closed loop systems because there is exactly one franchise for each of those systems. Open loop systems can involve three or more parties. Besides the customer's and the merchant's banks, a third party, called an acquiring bank, is involved. The acquiring bank passes authorization requests from merchant's bank to the customer's bank to obtain authorization for the credit purchase from the customer's bank. A response is sent back to the acquiring bank and onto the merchant. Similarly, the acquiring bank is responsible for contacting the merchant's bank and the many customers' banks to process sales drafts. The merchant's bank usually plays the role of the acquiring bank. Systems using Visa or MasterCard are the most visible examples of open loop systems because many banks issue both cards. Unlike American Express or Discover, neither Visa nor MasterCard issue cards directly to consumers. Member banks are responsible for handling all the details of establishing customer credit limits. For this discussion, we will assume that there are four players involved in a payment-card transaction: the customer that uses a credit card, the merchant that accepts a credit card toward a payment, the acquiring bank, and the issuing bank.

The following steps are involved in credit card processing:

1. The customer provides the credit card information to the merchant using a secure online communication channel. The communication channel needs to be previously established between the customer and the merchant and needs to provide such security services as authentication, confidentiality, and integrity.
2. The merchant processes the credit card using software provided by the acquiring bank. The software enables the merchant to submit electronically the credit card information to the acquiring bank. Usually the merchant submits the information via a dedicated communication channel to the acquiring bank.
3. The acquiring bank sends an authorizing request to the issuing bank authorizing payment for the particular charge incurred by the customer. This request is typically sent over a protected financial services network.
4. The issuing bank either approves or declines the charge. If the charge is approved, the issuing bank puts a hold on the customer's account for the funds needed to satisfy the current charge and forwards an approval code to the acquiring bank. If it is declined the acquiring bank is notified as such.
5. The acquiring bank sends the transaction (either the approval code or the decline information) back to the merchant.
6. The merchant completes the payment transaction.

Credit cards have several features that make them an attractive and popular choice with both consumers and merchants in online and offline transactions. For merchants, credit cards provide fraud protection. When a

[1] As of the time of this article going to the press. American Express in no longer considered an example of a closed loop system.

merchant accepts credit cards for online payment, he or she can authenticate and authorize purchases using a credit card-processing network. For consumers, credit cards are advantageous because various consumer credit protection acts limit the cardholder's liability to small amounts if a card is used fraudulently.

The largest advantage of using credit cards is their worldwide acceptance. A user can pay for goods with credit cards anywhere in the world, and the currency conversion, if needed, is handled by the card issuer. For online transactions, credit cards are particularly advantageous. When a consumer reaches the electronic checkout, he or she enters the credit card's number and his or her shipping and billing information in the appropriate fields to complete the transaction. The consumer does not need any special hardware or software to complete the transaction.

Credit cards have very few disadvantages; they do have one when compared to cash. Credit card service companies charge merchants per-transaction fees and monthly processing fees. For example, MasterCard charges $0.29 plus 2% of transaction value for each transaction. This is besides any fee that the acquiring bank may charge the merchant. Thus, credit card transactions are quite expensive. However, online (and offline) merchants view them as a cost of doing business. Any merchant who does not accept credit cards for purchases is probably losing significant sales because of it. In addition, credit cards typically provide a built-in safety net for merchants as merchants have a higher degree assurance that they will be paid through companies that issue credit cards. This makes credit cards generally lucrative to merchants for online payments. The consumer often does not pay any direct fees for using credit cards, but the price of goods and services are slightly higher than they would be in an environment free of credit cards altogether.

Debit Card-Based Systems

Debit cards are another form of electronic payment system that falls somewhere between credit cards and personal checks. Although they look very much like credit cards, they operate differently. Unlike credit cards, which make funds available through a financial institution, debit cards are a way to pay now and to subtract money automatically from the cardholder's bank account. There are two types of debit cards—PIN-based or online debit cards and signature-based or offline debit cards. They differ in the ways debit payments are processed.

PIN-based debit transactions are fast, convenient, and secure. It calls for customers to endorse payments by submitting a personal identification number (PIN) at the point of sale. The transaction is authorized in real time. Funds in the customer's account are set aside immediately to pay for the transaction. The money is transferred into the merchant's account in two to three business days. Merchants pay a nominal transaction fee, much lower than that for a typical credit card transaction. The fact that customers authorize charges with PINs, which are known only to them, virtually eliminates the risk to merchants of chargebacks. However, this type of debit transaction is currently available only in the physical world. This is because customers need access to a physical, discrete PIN-entry device (the PIN pad) that must be integrated with the payment system. A number of financial institutions are introducing technologies that attempt to mimic the functionality of PIN pads. However, widely accepted operating standards have yet to be established.

Signature-based debit cards do not involve PINs. These are typically offered by credit card companies and may be used everywhere that credit cards are accepted. Merchants complete the debit sale much in the same way as credit sales. The transaction is processed through a credit card-processing network for authorization. The customer signs the sales draft that authorizes the merchant to charge the customer's account. Transactions normally settle in two to three business days. Because these transactions are processed through the same networks as credit cards, they often incur the same transaction fees for the merchant.

Electronic Fund Transfer Systems

The discussion on different types of electronic payment systems would remain incomplete without discussing electronic fund transfer (EFT) systems. An EFT transaction provides for electronic payment and collection. It transfers funds initiated through an electronic terminal, telephone, computer, or magnetic tape that instructs a financial institution to either credit or debit a consumer's asset account. The term EFT itself does not refer to a specific product. Rather, it is a descriptor that defines payment vehicles that use electronic networks to conduct a transaction. Historically the core of consumer EFT networks has been the automated teller machine (ATM) and associated access cards. Currently, an EFT transaction involves payment processing through one or more of the electronic payment systems discussed earlier. The following are the most common EFT systems:

1. *Automated teller machines or 24-hour tellers*: These electronic terminals let a customer perform banking almost any time. Services offered through these computer systems, though limited, are quite comprehensive. Customers can withdraw cash, make deposits, query account balances, or transfer funds between accounts at the same bank. The customer initiates the transaction by inserting an ATM card and entering a PIN. The ATM card is encoded with the customer's account information on a magnetic strip. This information is transmitted to the bank's central computer by modem. After proper authentication, the bank's central computer allows the ATM to complete the transaction. Banks have formed global networks so that a customer of one bank can use an ATM of another. Often ATM networks are also connected to credit card- and debit card-processing networks. In these cases, the ATM machine allows a customer to use a credit or debit card; however, the customer is limited to withdrawing cash only. Such transactions are processed as typical credit card or debit card transactions.
2. *Direct deposit*: This lets the customer authorize specific deposits such as paychecks, stock dividends, and pensions to the customer's bank account either on a regular basis or on an ad hoc basis. It also allows the customer

to preauthorize direct withdrawals so that recurring bills such as insurance premiums, mortgages, and utility bills are paid automatically. By completing a standard enrollment form, a customer authorizes a company or organization to make a credit payment to or a debit payment from one or more of his accounts. The actual transaction is then processed over the ACH system as an ACH transaction.

3. *Pay-by-phone systems*: These systems let a customer call his or her financial institution with instructions to pay certain bills or to transfer funds between accounts. The customer must have a previous agreement with the bank for such transactions. Usually these transactions are limited to within the customer's bank only. That is, the customer cannot use a pay-by-phone system to transfer money to a different bank's accounts. For services such as bill-pay, the bank uses a system such as ACH to complete the transaction. To use pay-by-phone, the customer dials a special phone number on a touch-tone phone to access the central computer of the bank. After proper authentication of the customer, usually through a PIN, the computer allows the customer to proceed with the rest of the transaction. Pay-by-phone systems typically offer a limited number of services. Moreover, these systems are not very secure, which is due to the inherent vulnerability of the public telephone network. The popularity of these systems is gradually waning and being replaced by personal computer banking.
4. *Personal computer banking*: This allows the customer to handle many banking transactions over the Internet via a remote computer. The system works very much like pay-by-phone systems. The customer uses a computer to connect to the central computer of his or her bank. After proper authentication, the customer is allowed to view account balances, request transfer between accounts, and pay bills electronically. Bill payment is processed offline as ACH transactions. The ability to use strong cryptographic techniques makes these systems more secure than pay-by-phone systems.
5. *Electronic check conversion*: This system converts a paper check into an electronic payment at the point of sale or elsewhere, such as when a company receives the customer's check in the mail. Electronic check conversion links two existing technologies—a magnetic ink character recognition (MICR) scanner and the ACH network. The paper check is processed through a MICR scanner to capture the check number, the number that identifies the customer's bank, and the customer's account number. The information is used to make a one-time electronic payment from the customer's account. The check itself is not the method of payment. This means that the canceled check is not returned to the customer with his or her account statement.

REPRESENTATIVE TECHNOLOGIES

Electronic Cash Systems

CAFE

The European Union project CAFE (Conditional Access for Europe) (European Community's ESPRIT Program, 1995) began as an offline direct cash-like scheme that guaranteed customer anonymity. The CAFE project ended in mid-1997, but continued in the follow-up project OPERA. The partners in OPERA, i.e., banks that support CAFE, are continuing the trial of and improving the CAFE system. About 13 partners from several European countries are involved, Digicash and Siemens among them. The system is designed for use in shops rather than over the Internet. In a way it is the offline, portable version of the DigiCash eCash system, and is based on the system proposed by the brand's cash. The protocol has been disclosed for public review. The important feature of CAFE is the multiparty security. No mutual trust between parties of conflicting interest is assumed.

CAFE is an open secure system. It supports multiple issuers of electronic value and multiple currencies, including currency exchange during a payment. It provides the customer with a history log of their payments. The system uses public key signature and encryption and allows for offline purchase transactions. The basic purchase transaction mode is anonymous and untraceable for the customer and is performed offline; there is no need to connect to a third party online. Withdrawals and deposits are identified, traceable, and online. If payments exceeding a certain level must be confirmed, then some online interaction becomes necessary.

CAFE provides recovery of lost, stolen, and damaged cards. Although prepaid, it is loss tolerant and allows customers to recover their money if they lose their wallet. For this, an encrypted version of all tokens issued to the customer is held in a saved place. The customer must surrender its anonymity and untraceability, then the issued token backup can be decrypted and matched against the redeemed token database. To provide some loss tolerance for stolen wallets, the customer must authenticate itself to the wallet via a pass phrase (PIN) prior to a purchase.

The device receives coins by withdrawing them from the issuer account via an ATM using the blind signature method known from eCash. CAFE is prepaid and the tokens on the device do not exist as currency anywhere else. When the customer spends money the device transmits one or more tokens to the merchant and marks them as spent on the device. Transmissions are performed contactless via infrared channels. The merchant then owns the value of those tokens, which need to be deposited with an acquirer and accepted by the issuer for that value to be realized for the merchant. Thus, the primary flow of value in CAFE is that of withdraw, pay, and deposit; i.e., the payment model is the typical direct cash-like approach.

The basic Hardware device is a pocket calculator like electronic wallet, to be used for customer payments, access to information services and also identification. It aims to be non-proprietary. The electronic wallets and smart cards, i.e. the hardware, should become standardized and be available in shops just like other electronic consumer goods. The wallet contains a so-called guardian, a smartcard with a dedicated cryptographic processor. The wallet protects the interests of the customer, the guardian protects the interests of the money issuer, and both are holding part of each token withdrawn. No transactions are possible without the cooperation of the guardian; the guardian maintains a record of all the tokens spent to avoid double spending. The guardian chip authorizes each payment by signing it. CAFE tokens do not remain in circulation like real cash tokens do. Respendability is broken explicitly, the wallet signs to whom it pays a token and so only that payee can deposit the token.

As fallback—when the guardian is compromised—CAFE uses so-called offline digital coins that provide a once-concealed, twice-revealed feature. The money is encrypted and the identity of the customer signed by that customer is encoded into the token number. This is done in a way that the identity of the customer can only be recovered if the customer double spends. This feature works as follows: When the customer uses a token in payment, it is challenged by the merchant to reveal a certain part of the encoded customer identity. One part on its own, however, does not reveal anything useful. If, however, the customer tries to respend the same token a part of the customer identity is revealed again to the merchant, and now with a high probability the identity of the customer can be traced. For this, the issuer must hold a database of all reimbursed tokens that it already needs for the fault tolerance feature.

As a fixed denomination token system that distinguishes between customers and merchants, CAFE needs to address the making change problem. It allows the construction of coins that can be split into smaller coins if need be and of coins that—being more expensive than their denomination—may be spent more than once. These measurements reduce the unlinkability of the payments but not their integrity. For repeated very small payments to the same merchant, so-called phone ticks, CAFE provides a special way of surrendering a token in installments.

In CAFE transactions appear atomic to the user but not to the merchant. The tokens a merchant accepts in payment must be deposited with an acquirer and accepted by the issuer before their monetary value can be realized by the merchant. The value leaves the customer, but does not immediately arrive at the merchant.

PayPal

PayPal (eBay Inc., 2002) is a very popular electronic cash payment system for consumers to pay for online purchases. Owned by eBay Inc. and touted as the world's first e-mail payment service, PayPal.com is a free service that earns a profit on the float, which is money deposited in PayPal accounts. It is currently the number one electronic cash system used by eBay auction customers. PayPal eliminates the need to pay for online purchases by writing and mailing checks or using credit cards by allowing consumers to send money instantly and securely to anyone with an e-mail address, including an online merchant. It is a convenient way for auction bidders to pay for their purchases, and sellers like it because it eliminates the risks of accepting other types of online payments. When the transaction occurs, the sender's and receiver's accounts are instantly reduced and credited, respectively. Anyone with a PayPal account—online merchants and eBay auction participants alike—can withdraw cash from his or her account at any time.

To use PayPal, merchants and consumers first must register for a PayPal account. There is no minimum amount that a PayPal account must contain. Customers add money to their PayPal accounts by sending a check or using a credit card. Once members' payments are approved and deposited into their PayPal accounts, they can use their PayPal money to pay for purchases. Merchants must have a PayPal account to accept PayPal payments, but consumer-to-consumer markets such as eBay are more flexible. A consumer can use PayPal to pay a seller for purchases even if the seller does not have a PayPal account. When one uses PayPal to pay for purchases from a seller or merchant who does not have a PayPal account, the PayPal service sends the seller or merchant an e-mail message indicating that a payment is waiting at the PayPal Web site. To collect PayPal cash, the seller or merchant who received the e-mail message must register and provide PayPal with payment instructions.

Stored-Value Card Systems

Mondex

The most well-known example of an electronic purse or stored-value card system is the Mondex smart card (MasterCard International, 2004), a service of MasterCard International. It was introduced in the early 1990s, and had the largest pilot program of an electronic purse product to date. The Mondex smart card contains a microcomputer chip, and thus can accept electronic cash directly from a user's bank account. Cardholders can spend their electronic cash with any merchant who has a Mondex card reader. Two cardholders can even transfer cash between their cards over a telephone line. A single card works in both the online world of the Internet and the offline world of ordinary merchant stores. Another advantage of Mondex is that the cardholder always has the correct change for vending machines of various types. Mondex electronic cash supports micropayments as small as 3 cents, and Mondex has per-transaction costs lower than those of credit or debit cards since value transfer takes place locally just like cash. Thus it is a good choice for mini/micropayments. Finally, Mondex has the ability to provide user anonymity. This is because, just like cash systems, Mondex does not maintain any audit record. Mondex has some disadvantages too. The card carries real cash in electronic form, and the risk of theft of the card may deter users from loading it with a significant amount of money. Moreover, Mondex cannot compare with credit cards in the area of deferred payment. One can defer paying his/her charge or credit card bill for almost a month without incurring any interest. Mondex cards dispense their cash immediately. Last but not the least, a Mondex card requires special equipment; merchants who accept it must have a specific card reader at their checkout counter. A Mondex card must also be in physical contact with a special card reading-and-writing device during a merchant or recharge transaction. Internet users can transfer cash over the Internet using Mondex, but they must attach a Mondex reader with their PC in order to use the card. These requirements have proven to be barriers to the widespread use and success of Mondex.

A Mondex transaction consists of several steps that ensure that the transferred cash reaches the correct destination in a safe and secure manner. The following are the steps to transfer electronic cash from the buyer to the seller:

1. The card user inserts the Mondex card into a reader. The merchant and the card user are both validated to ensure that both the user and the merchant are still authorized to make transactions.
2. The merchant's terminal requests payment while simultaneously transmitting the merchant's digital signature.
3. The customer's card checks the merchant's digital signature. If the signature is valid, then the transaction amount is deducted from the cardholder's card.
4. The merchant's terminal checks the customer's just-sent customer digital signature for authenticity. If the cardholder's signature is validated, the merchant's terminal acknowledges the cardholder's signature by again sending back to the cardholder's card the merchant's signature.
5. Once the electronic cash is deducted form the cardholder's card, the same amount is credited to the merchant's electronic cash account. Serializing the debit and credit events before completing a transaction eliminates the creation or loss of cash if the system malfunctions in the middle of the process.

Currently only a few cities in United States accept Mondex. Worldwide, Mondex is available in several countries on the North and South American continents, Europe, Africa, the Middle East, Asia, Australia, and New Zealand. As a whole, stored-value cards are not yet very popular in the United States. People there still prefer credit cards rather than smart cards.

Electronic Check Systems

ECheck

The most well-known among the electronic check systems is eCheck (Financial Services Technology Consortium, 2002). It combines "the security, speed and processing efficiencies of all-electronic transactions with the familiar and well-developed legal infrastructures and business processes associated with paper checks" (from http://www.echeck.org/overview/what.html). An eCheck is the electronic version of a standard paper check. It contains the same information as paper checks, and is based on the financial services markup language (FSML). It provides strong authentication, strong encryption, and duplicate detection features. It can be used with existing checking accounts, has unlimited but controlled information carrying capability, and has some enhanced capabilities, such as effective dating, that are not provided in traditional checks. In addition, eCheck is often considered more secure than traditional paper checks. In eCheck, each electronic checkbook is assigned a unique eCheck account number that only the bank can map into the actual underlying account number. This account number is part of the distinguished name in the bank-issued account certificate, so it cannot be modified but is easily verified by anyone who receives an eCheck. Thus, compromise of an eCheck does not lead to possible compromise of the underlying account. Revoking an eCheck account number has no impact on the underlying account.

ECheck is the first and only electronic payment mechanism chosen by the U.S. Treasury to make high-value payments over the Internet. It is currently under enhancement in Singapore and is being considered for many online systems.

Electronic Bill Presentment and Payment Systems

CheckFree

CheckFree (CheckFree Corporation, 2004) is the largest online bill processor, and provides online payment processing service to both large corporations and individual Internet users. CheckFree Corporation provides a wide range of electronic commerce solutions, including online share portfolio management (in conjunction with the PAWWS system (http://www.pawws.com) and general online bill payment systems. CheckFree provides the infrastructure and software to permit users to pay all their bills with online electronic checks. It offers an electronic check payment service as replacement for traditional paper checks. This payment system results in a service similar to that of money orders. Their software is compatible to the wallet software from Cybercash. For bill processing, the customer receives a bill from a service provider and sends the payment information to CheckFree. The customer creates an account with CheckFree linked by direct debit to the customer's bank account. CheckFree pays the bill on the customer's behalf in the form of electronic checks. If required, CheckFree can also pay the bill in the form of a traditional paper check.

Electronic Wallet Systems

Many electronic wallet systems are commercially available for pocket, palm-sized, handheld, and desktop PCs. The current technology trend is to produce electronic wallets in the smart cards. In the electronic payment system developed in the CAFE project, the electronic wallet can be either in the form of a small portable computer with an internal power source or in the form of a smart card. Electronic money can be loaded into the wallets online and used for payments at point of sale (POS) terminals. Example of e-wallet applications include Microsoft's .NET Passport (Microsoft Corporation, 2004) (the system is used mainly as a form of single sign-on framework rather than as an electronic payment system), Ilium Software's eWallet (Ilium Software, 2004), VeriFone's Vwallet (http://www.verifone.com—now integrated into its integrated payment solutions payment software), and Qwallet.com's Q*Wallet (Qwallet.com, 2004). Numerous banks and companies have now developed their own e-wallets, such as AT&T's e-wallet or MasterCard's e-wallet.

Credit Card Payment Systems

Secure Electronic Transaction (SET) Protocol

Secure electronic transaction (SET) is a secure protocol jointly developed in 1996 by MasterCard and Visa with the backing of Microsoft, Netscape, IBM, GTE, SAIC, and other companies to facilitate credit card transactions over the Internet (Schneider & Perry, 2001). SET specifications were published in 1997 as an open standard, which allows all companies developing related applications to use this protocol and make their products work together successfully.

The objective of SET is to provide security for credit card payments as they traverse the Internet from the customer to the merchant sites and onto the processing banks. SET has been developed to secure the entire credit card payment process, including verifying that the consumer is indeed the owner of the credit card. Although Visa and MasterCard have publicly stated that the goal of proposing the SET protocol is to establish a single method for consumers and merchants to conduct payment card transactions on the Internet, acceptance of the standard has been slow. SET Co. is the consortium that manages and promotes the SET standard, which assumes an already established public key infrastructure. The SET specification uses public key cryptography and digital certificates for validating all participants in the transaction. In contrast to the SSL protocol, which only provides confidentiality and integrity of credit card information while in transit, the SET protocol provides confidentiality of information, payment data integrity, user and merchant authentication, consumer nonrepudiation, and payment clearinghouses (certificates).

The major components of SET are as follows:

1. The *issuer* (or customer's bank) is a financial institution that issues bankcards (credit cards or debit cards).
2. The *customer* (or cardholder) is an authorized user of the bankcard who is registered with SET. The customer participates in the SET transaction by use of an electronic wallet. SET calls this the cardholder wallet. This is where the customer/consumer's credit card information is stored in an encrypted manner. The wallet software is able to communicate and interoperate with other SET components.
3. The *merchant* is the seller of goods and services. The merchant uses the merchant server software to automatically process credit card authorizations and payments.
4. The *payment gateway* processes merchant authorization requests and payment messages including payment instructions from cardholders. It is operated by either an acquirer or some other party that supports acquirers (for example, the merchant's bank). It interfaces with financial networks to support the capture of SET transactions.
5. One or more *certification authorities* issue and verify digital certificates related to public keys of customers, merchants, and/or the acquirers or their gateways. The SET public key infrastructure proposes a top-down hierarchy of certification authorities comprising the following types:
   - *Root certification authority*: All certification paths start with this authority's public key. It is operated by an organization that the entire industry agrees to trust. The initial root key is built into the SET software with provision for replacing it in the future. It issues certificates to brand certification authorities.
   - *Brand certification authority*: These authorities are operated by different credit card brand owners like Visa and MasterCard. Each brand has considerable autonomy as to how it manages the certificate subtree rooted at it.
   - *Geo-political certification authority*: This is an optional level of certification authority. It allows a brand to distribute responsibility for managing lower level certificates across different geographic or political regions. This is to account for variations in how financial systems operate in different regions.
   - *Cardholder certification authority*: These authorities generate and distribute cardholder certificates to cardholders. Depending on brand rules, the certification authority maybe operated by an issuer or other party.
   - *Merchant certification authority*: These authorities issue certificates to merchants based on approval by an acquirer.

The SET infrastructure is deliberately planned not to interoperate with any other payment infrastructure other than the bankcard system. Although this maybe considered a restriction of SET, it ensures that the operating organizations are not subjected to any unknown risks. The main steps of SET are described in Figure 3. The sequence can be summarized as follows:

1. *Customer and merchant registration*: In this step (messages 0 in Figure 3), the customer and the merchant acquire relevant certificates from the corresponding authorities that will allow them to participate in the transaction. This needs to be done once before any SET transaction and needs to be re-executed if the certificates expire or are revoked.
2. *Browse and negotiate purchase*: This step (message 1) proceeds in an offline manner; it allows the customer to select the product and negotiate on a price. SET is not involved in this phase.
3. *Purchase request*: Once the customer has completed the product selection process, it invokes the cardholder wallet software on its machine. This is where the main SET protocol starts (message 2). The cardholder wallet initiates a SET session with the merchant server; it sends its certificate to the merchant and requests a copy of the merchant's certificate and the payment gateway's certificate. On receipt of these, the cardholder wallet creates a payment information (PI) and an order information (OI). The PI includes the cardholder's credit card account information and public key certificate, among others. The OI includes necessary information about the order. Two digests are computed, one each for PI and OI. They are concatenated and signed by the customer's private key. The PI is encrypted with the payment gateway's public key. Next, the OI and encrypted PI are together encrypted with the merchant's public key. Finally, the entire message is signed and sent to the merchant server. The merchant server verifies the cardholder's certificate. It verifies the signature on the PI and OI. If it agrees to OI, it forwards the encrypted PI to the payment gateway for authorization (message 3). While waiting for authorization, the

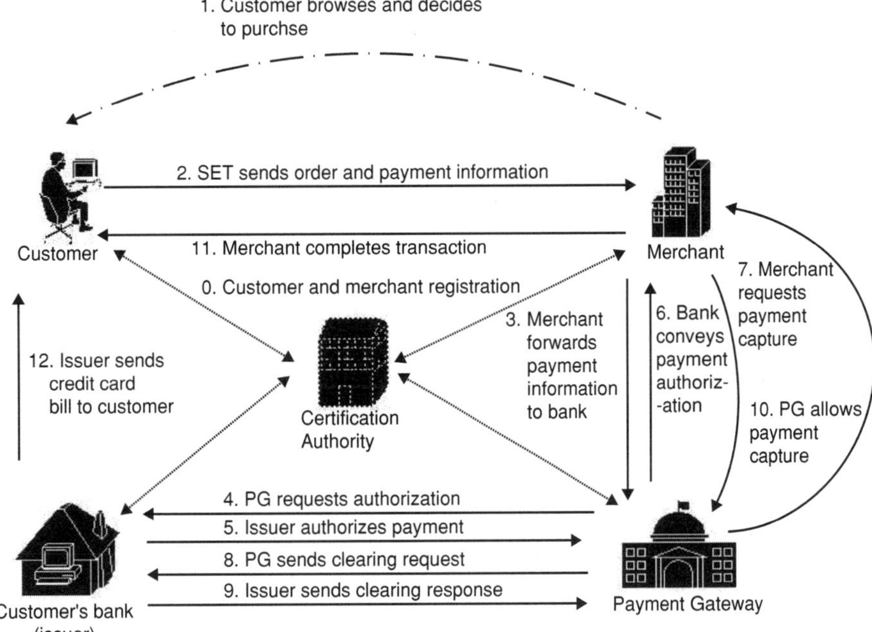

Figure 3: SET steps.

merchant prepares an order confirmation (OC), signs it with its private key, and sends it encrypted with the customer's public key.

4. *Payment authorization*: To request payment authorization, the merchant sends the encrypted PI (received in step 3) signed with its private key (message labeled 3) to the payment gateway. The payment gateway verifies the merchant's signature on the message, decrypts the PI with its private key, and retrieves the customer's certificate. It then verifies the relevant signature, and performs an authorization at the issuer (message 4). When the issuer authorizes payment (message 5), the payment gateway generates an authorization response (AR) and a capture token (CT). Both are signed by the payment gateway's private key and sent to the merchant encrypted with the latter's public key. The merchant, on receipt, stores the payment authorization response and capture token for later use.
5. *Payment capture*: The merchant prepares a payment capture request with the transaction identifier from the original OI and the CT obtained earlier. It signs the capture request (CR) and sends it encrypted with the payment gateway's (PG) public key (message 7). The payment gateway verifies the capture request message and sends a clearing request message to the issuer (CLR) (message 8). When the issuer clears the payment (message 9), the payment gateway generates a capture response (CR) and sends it encrypted with the merchant's public key. The merchant stores the CR and completes the transaction with the customer.

A major advantage of using SET over the SSL protocol for electronic credit card payment is that SET does not allow the merchant to view the customer's complete credit card information, which provides an additional degree of protection. In addition, SET prevents the payment gateway and/or the issuer bank from being able to view the terms of the transaction established between the merchant and the customer. This way the privacy of the customer is also enhanced. However, SET has received a lukewarm reception in the United States and, so far, has not attracted a large number of merchants and consumers, though it seems to be the "best" protocol for securing payment over the otherwise unsecured Internet. The major SET activities are in Asian and European nations. Part of the problem with the acceptance of SET is that apparently it is not as easy to implement nor as inexpensive as most banks and merchants had expected. The typical reaction of many banks has been that SET is clumsy and not tried and tested. The future might prove brighter for SET, though. After a few years of testing and trials, SET's supporters believe it is ready for widespread deployment.

Micropayment Systems

MilliCent

Micropayment fundamentally creates a new billing model, under which the individual items downloaded can be billed separately and individually. With micropayment methods, consumers can download a song or a chapter of a book and be billed as little as 50 cents or a dollar, with that small amount being charged to their Internet service provider (ISP) or phone bill. Security issues with micropayments are primarily centered on the premise that a small charge would not require extensive use of encryption technology or other means of fraud prevention. The widespread use of micropayments is a potential breeding ground for fraud that today is not apparent. The lack of an authoritative infrastructure standard, coupled with strong network externalities, has limited micropayments from becoming a dominant means of value transfer.

Micropayment models are not static in nature. Fundamentally, they will provide a means of transferring value for incremental items. The 900-telephone number system is considered the first successful micropayment method, but more online models will need to develop to feed the demand for quick and instant payment for performance. Technology will have to evolve to allow for things like a clear identification when a person is at the office, using a corporate ISP, and when that person is at home. Technology infrastructure is thus the first micropayment enabler. Merchants willing to provide content over a micropayment system for a large number of users are the second fundamental enabler for micropayments. Beyond path dependencies, external factors must be in place for the platform to be adopted. Content providers must have viral growth of their product through micropayments; this is the last enabler. Once these are achieved, the micropayment model will be ensured a key part of online success.

MilliCent (Glassman, Jones, & Manasse, 1997) is the most the widely known micropayment scheme. MilliCent is a proprietary voucher-based digital microcommerce system from the erstwhile Digital Equipment Corporation (acquired by Compaq and now part of HP Invent). It aims at the micropayment segment of electronic commerce and supports transactions with values of fractions of a cent. MilliCent considers that coins are treated differently than paper money, in the same manner that small denomination notes are treated differently from large denomination notes. As MilliCent represents very small coins, it uses lightweight security measures. A public trial of the MilliCent system involving toy money started in December 1997.

The system uses merchant-specific vouchers, the so-called scrip, a form of token only valid with a particular merchant for a limited period of time. Brokers act as intermediaries between merchant and customers. The fact that any type of scrip is only valid at a particular merchant means the merchant does not need to connect to a central issuer to validate the token. This reduces network traffic and the validation cost. To avoid customers having to maintain separate accounts with the individual merchants for mostly short-term relationships, brokers act as intermediaries. The long-term relationships are between brokers and customers, and brokers and merchants. A consumer registers with one broker and buys broker scrip in bulk—generic scrip. Brokers receive payment from consumers in a variety of ways, but the most common way the consumers pay brokers is with a credit card. When a consumer locates a product on a merchant's Web site that he or she would like to purchase, the consumer converts the broker scrip into vendor-specific scrip. Vendor-specific scrip is scrip that a particular merchant will accept. The consumer's new scrip is stored in an electronic wallet on the consumer's computer. Paying for an item involves simply transferring a merchant's scrip, which is in a consumer's wallet, to the merchant in exchange for a purchased item. Merchants can then send a broker their own scrip and obtain a check. The basic sequence of interactions is as follows:

1. The customer obtains a quantity of broker scrip at the outset.
2. The customer requests some specific vendor scrip that they will pay for later with the broker scrip.
3. The broker obtains the required vendor scrip from the vendor.
4. The broker sells the vendor scrip to the customer.
5. The customer buys the service with the vendor scrip.
6. The vendor gives change in vendor scrip.

Steps 1 to 4 are not required for every transaction; the customer can buy sufficient scrip from the broker for a period. Likewise, the broker can store enough vendor scrip to serve many customer requests or it can have a license from the vendor to create that vendor scrip directly. Although at first glance a lot of message passing seems to be required, there is no bottleneck from one single currency issuer being contacted during each transaction, especially once steps 1 to 4 are completed. Experiments at Digital indicate that MilliCent is efficient enough for transactions as low as 1/10 of a cent. A broker is required in the protocol for two reasons. First, the system of very small payments works because transactions can be aggregated so they are significant. That is, when a consumer buys a few dollars worth of scrip, there is little profit in the deal. However, when several consumers purchase scrip, the aggregate amount—even discounted so that the broker can make money—does make economic sense. The second reason for a broker is that it makes the entire system easier to use. A consumer must deal with only one broker to satisfy his or her scrip needs for many merchants. The broker buys the scrip in bulk and does all the hard work of organizing the retail selling to customers.

A significant feature of the MilliCent protocol is the trade-offs attempted at different points in the design. For example, MilliCent offers three different protocol versions—"private and secure," "secure without encryption," and "scrip in the clear." The least secure is "scrip in the clear," where the scrip is transferred between customer and vendor without any encryption or protection; thus the protocol is the most efficient and cheapest to implement. However, this allows any observer to change the scrip or replay it and spend it itself. Thus the customer can potentially suffer financial loss. Although amounts stolen this way will be quite small, it can be rather annoying to the customer to find their small changes to be invalid. The next level of security is provided by "secure without encryption," where personal information about the customer carried by a field in the scrip is available to the player involved in the scrip system. However, the scrip itself is protected from replays that allow an observer to spend the scrip itself. The most secure version of the protocol is the "private and secure." However, it too uses lightweight encryption technology, which is probably not too difficult to break. The philosophy is that the cost of breaking the protocol should be greater than the value of the scrip itself. Scrips can be minted at very low value. Thus, loss of scrip due to confidentiality or integrity breaches does not cause significant financial loss to the end user.

CONCLUSION AND FURTHER READING

In this chapter, we attempted to present an overview of electronic payment systems. One of our objectives has been to identify the technical challenges, mostly security related, that hinder the widespread deployment of such systems. We also surveyed some of the more well-known instances of electronic payment systems. Our survey is by no means complete. Many systems are regularly proposed. The majority of them do not survive the market forces. Those who do frequently are acquired by the larger players and their initial business focus gets lost.

A good source of information for electronic payment systems is Dr. Phillip M. Hallam-Baker's Web page on electronic payment schemes (Hallam-Baker, 2004) on the W3 Consortium Web site. This page categorizes electronic payment schemes along two dimensions—the level of abstraction for the payment scheme (namely *policy*, the semantics of the payment scheme; *data flow*, the requirements for storage of data and communication between parties; and *mechanism*, the security methods used) and the payment model for the protocol (namely cash, check, or card). The Web page contains a comprehensive list of Internet payment schemes and protocols. The author makes an earnest effort to keep the list as up-to-date as possible; however, this may not be the case always. The CAFÉ project of the European Community's ESPRIT program (European Community's ESPRIT Program, 1995) and the SEMPER project (European Commission's ACTS Program, 2000) of the European Commission's ACTS program are two important European projects that provide valuable information on electronic payment systems. The list (SIRENE, 2004) maintained by the SIRENE group is also a valuable resource for electronic payment systems. Leo van Hove's database on e-purse (van Hove, 2004) provides a collection of links and references on electronic purses (and related issues). The e-money mini-FAQ page (Miller, 2004), written by Jim Miller and maintained by Roy Davies, provides answers to some frequently asked questions about electronic money and digital cash. Roy Davies also maintains a comprehensive information resource for electronic money and digital cash (Davies, 2004). The Financial Services Technology Consortium (FSTC) has several projects (both past and present) aimed at developing technologies that facilitate electronic payment systems. Information about these projects can be found from the FSTC Projects Web page at http://www.fstc.org/projects/. Finally, some useful reference book for electronic commerce and electronic payment systems are the books by Hossein Bidgoli (2002), Gary Schneider and James Perry (2001), and Craig van Slyke and France Belanger (2003).

GLOSSARY

Acquirer The entity or entities that hold(s) deposit accounts for card acceptors (merchants) and to which the card acceptor transmits the data relating to the transaction; the acquirer is responsible for the collection of transaction information and settlement with acceptors.

Audit Trail A sequential record of events that have occurred in a system.

Automated Clearing House (ACH) An electronic rendezvous for financial institutions where payment orders are exchanged among the financial institutions primarily via magnetic media or communications network.

Automated Teller Machine (ATM) An electromechanical device that permits authorized users to use machine readable plastic cards to withdraw cash from their accounts at a particular financial institution and/or access other services, such as account balance enquiries, transfer funds between accounts, or deposit money into accounts.

Batch Processing The transmission or processing of a group of payment orders as a set at discrete intervals of time.

Card A general term used to describe several types of payment systems including ATM card or cash card, check guarantee card, chip card (or smart card), credit card, charge card, debit card, delayed debit card, prepaid card, retailer card, and stored-value card.

Cash Card Card for use only in ATMs or cash dispensers.

Certificate A document (physical or electronic) that evidences the undertakings of an issuer.

Charge Card Card issued by nonbanks indicating that the holder has been granted a line of credit. It enables the holder to make purchases but does not offer extended credit, the full amount of the debt incurred having to be settled at the end of a specified period. Typical issued by the travel and entertainment industry to their customers.

Check A written order from one party (the drawer) to another (the drawee, normally a bank) requiring the drawee to pay a specified sum on demand to the drawer or a third party of the drawer's choosing. Checks may be used for settling debts and withdrawing money from banks.

Check Card A card issued as part of a check guarantee system.

Check Guarantee System A system to guarantee checks, typically up to a specified amount by the issuer of the guarantee card.

Chip Card See smart card.

Clearing/Clearance The process of transmitting, reconciling, and, in some cases, confirming payment orders or security transfer instructions prior to settlement.

Credit Card A card indicating that the holder has been granted a line of credit. It enables the holder to make purchases and/or withdraw cash up to a prearranged ceiling; the credit granted can be settled in full by end of a specified period or can be settled in part, with the balance taken as extended credit.

Credit Card Company A company that owns the trademark of a particular credit card, and may also provide a number of marketing, processing, or other services to its members using the card services.

Debit Card A card that enables the holder to have his/her purchases directly charged to funds available in his/her account at a deposit-taking financial institution.

Delayed Debit Card A card issued by banks indicating that the holder may charge his/her account up to an authorized limit. It enables the holder to make purchases but does not offer extended credit; the full amount of the debt incurred needs to be settled at the end of the specified period.

Electronic Fund Transfer System A formal arrangement based on private contract or statute law with multiple membership, common rules, and standardized arrangements, for the electronic transmission and settlement of monetary obligations.

Electronic Payment System An electronic system consisting of a set of instruments, banking procedures, and typically interbank fund transfer systems that ensure the circulation of money.

Electronic Purse A reloadable multipurpose prepaid card that may be used for small retail or other payments instead of coins.

Electronic Wallet A computer device used in some electronic payment systems to store information needed to undertake a financial transaction.

Magnetic Ink Character Recognition (MICR) A technique using machine readable characters imprinted on a document using an ink with magnetic properties by which information on the document is interpreted by machines for electronic processing.

Payment The process of the payer's transfer of a monetary claim on a party acceptable to the payee.

PIN A numeric code that a cardholder may need to quote for verification of identity. It is often seen as the equivalent of a signature.

Prepaid Card A card on which value is stored and for which the holder has paid the issuer in advance; also known as stored-value card.

Provider The operator who establishes the hardware and software conditions for the conduct of transactions with electronic money without necessarily being the issuer of the electronic money units.

Settlement The act of discharging obligations in respect of fund transfers between two or more parties.

Smart Card A card with a built-in microprocessor and memory capable of performing calculations and storing information.

Stored-Value Card See prepaid card.

CROSS REFERENCES

See *Business-to-Business Electronic Commerce; EDI Security; Electronic Commerce; Extranets: Applications, Development, Security and Privacy*

REFERENCES

Bidgoli, H. (2002). *Electronic commerce: Principles and practice*. San Diego, CA: Academic Press.

CheckFree Corporation. (2004). *CheckFree*. Retrieved from http://www.checkfree.com/

Davies, G. (2002). *A history of money from ancient times to the present day* (3rd ed.). Cardiff: University of Wales Press.

Davies, R. (2004). *Electronic money, or e-money, and digital cash*. Retrieved from http://www.ex.ac.uk/~RDavies/arian/emoney.html

eBay Inc. (2002). *PayPal*. Retrieved from http://www.paypal.com/cgi-bin/webscr?cmd=p/gen/about-outside

European Commission's ACTS Program. (2000). *SEMPER—Secure electronic marketplace for Europe*. Retrieved from http://www.semper.org/index.html

European Community's ESPRIT Program. (1995). *CAFE—Conditional access for Europe*. Retrieved from http://www.semper.org/sirene/projects/cafe/index.html

Financial Services Technology Consortium. (2002). *eCheck*. Retrieved from http://www.echeck.org

Glassman, S., Jones, R., & Manasse, M. (1997). *Microcommerce on the horizon*. Retrieved from http://research.compaq.com/SRC/articles/199705/Millicent.html

Hallam-Baker, P. M. (2004). *Electronic payment schemes*. Retrieved from http://www.w3.org/ECommerce/roadmap.html

Ilium Software. (2004). *eWallet*. Retrieved from http://iliumsoft.com/site/ew/ewallet.htm

MasterCard International. (2004). *Mondex USA*. Retrieved from http://www.mondexusa.com

Microsoft Corporation. (2004). *Microsoft.NET passport*. Retrieved from http://www.passport.net/Consumer/default.asp?lc=1033

Miller, J. (2004). *E-money mini-FAQ (release 2.0)*. Retrieved from http://www.ex.ac.uk/~RDavies/arian/emoneyfaq.html

Qwallet.com. (2004). *Q*Wallet home*. Retrieved from http:// qwallet.com/index.shtml

Schneider, G. P., & Perry, J. T. (2001). *Electronic commerce* (2nd ed.). Course Technology.

SIRENE. (2004). *Electronic commerce, payment systems, and security*. Retrieved from http://www.semper.org/sirene/outsideworld/ecommerce.html

van Hove, L. (2004). *Leo Van Hove's DB on E-purse @ IPTS/JRC European Commission*. Retrieved from http://www.jrc.es/cfapp/leodb/recent.cfm

van Slyke, C., & Belanger, F. (2003). *E-business technologies: Supporting the Net-enhanced organization*. New York: Wiley.

Weber, R. (1998). *Chablis—Market analysis of digital payment systems* (Report TUM-I9819). Technische Universität München).

Intranets: Principals, Privacy, and Security Considerations

William T. Schiano, *Bentley College*

INTRODUCTION

An intranet is defined by the use of Internet technologies (HTTP, TCP/IP, FTP, SMTP) within an organization. By contrast, the Internet is a global network of networks connecting myriad organizations. The line becomes blurred when an internal system is opened to remote access, and parts of the system are made available to customers and suppliers. This extension of an intranet to selected outsiders is often called an extranet. Many of the applications accessed over intranets are run on ERP systems such as Oracle, Peoplesoft, and SAP that also service external users.

As wired and wireless connectivity continue to develop, distinctions among types of systems will become increasingly artificial and contrived, just as the once clear distinctions among hardware such as personal computers, servers, and minicomputers have lost meaning. When reading this chapter, concentrate on how the issues described may affect Internet technology-based systems within your organization, rather than on the specific definition of any one system.

Because they are based on open Internet standards, intranets are easy to implement technologically. This can be a blessing and a curse. Although they can offer robust functionality with little investment, they are often rolled out with little forethought and therefore may fail to make a significant contribution to the organization or may present security vulnerabilities.

Much of the research and background information applicable to intranets is now being published in other areas. The technological issues overlap with the broader Internet, and many of the internal applications offered on intranets are now encompassed by enterprise applications and knowledge management. Some authors even refer to business-to-employee (B2E) applications (Hansen & Deimler, 2001), emphasizing the importance of focusing on the access to systems by those within the organization. This chapter draws on these and other literatures to offer a broad perspective on intranets and their application. The chapter outlines what intranets are, how they are used, the technologies for constructing and running them, and how to manage them securely and efficiently.

FEATURES OF AN INTRANET

Few organizations question the value of having an intranet in some form. Indeed, over 90% of major U.S. corporations have intranets (Baker, 2000). The benefits can range from a reduction of paper and headcount, always having the current version of any data or document available, to a central interface, or portal, and repository for all corporate systems and data. Intranets may encompass many different types of content and features. Other benefits include the use of Internet-standard network protocols that facilitate connections to the broader Internet.

Portal

> A door or gate; hence, a way of entrance or exit, especially one that is grand and imposing.
>
> —*Webster's Revised Unabridged Dictionary*, 1913

Intranets are often designed to be "portals," serving as the central point of access to all information resources within an organization. The implication of grandiosity is deliberate and helpful, as good design can be a crucial determining factor in the success of an intranet. A portal also needs to be available regularly to a wide community, with access to multiple sources of data, both internal and external, with a useful search mechanism. The term portal often evokes third-party commercial portals such as Yahoo.com (http://www.yahoo.com) and vertical portals, also called vortals, such as plasticsnet (http://www.plasticsnet.com). These portals have struggled to establish successful business models, especially after the dot-com collapse. Portals inside organizations, in contrast, have thrived, often with the support of the information systems (IS) department and the business users.

One of the greatest frustrations for information technology users inside organizations is the necessity of multiple systems with varied interfaces, including command-line-based interfaces. With a portal, users have the ability to go to a single location; use a common, intuitive, and well-established graphical interface; and find their information. Such ease of use makes it more likely the systems will be used to their full potential, generating the efficiencies envisioned when they were designed. Types of information and services found on intranets are outlined in the following sections.

Human Resource Management

Human resource materials are an obvious and common type of content for intranets. Manuals on policies and procedures and frequently asked questions (FAQs) can be kept online, providing employees easy access, facilitating updates, and saving paper.

Benefits management is a significant cost for organizations; tax withholding, health care election choices in the United States, and retirement and pension accounting all involve substantial processing costs. These processing costs include printing, distributing, completing, collecting, and entering data from paper forms; providing support to fill out the forms; and managing subsequent changes. With a well-designed intranet, employees can process their own benefits, saving substantial overhead and time and reducing the need for HR staff. The forms tend to be highly structured, with well-defined fields, and the application can be scaled to all employees, reducing the cost of development per employee. These forms can also change regularly. Changing the online versions is much less expensive, and eliminates the possibility of employees filling out the wrong version of a form.

Human resources is also an excellent choice for intranet applications, particularly early in an intranet rollout, because every employee uses its services. Beginning with a common set of applications with which all or most employees interact may lead users to become familiar with other services located on the intranet as well. Self-service benefits also allow the human resource department to train less computer literate employees on an application that human resources knows intimately and that all employees must use (Meuse, 1999). This makes it an excellent introduction to the intranet. Unfortunately, most users only need to visit the employee benefits site once or twice a year, so it cannot be counted on to drive traffic throughout the year. However, newsletters can be published on the intranet, with notifications sent out via e-mail that may bring some traffic regularly.

Purchasing

For many organizations, especially larger ones, purchasing is a major cost that can be difficult to control. Managing the purchasing function and its information requirements is an inconvenience, and much of the cost is incurred in the overhead of processing purchases. The story of Ford's and Mazda's accounts payable departments has been retold many times and is famously cited by Hammer as an example of reengineering. Ford, with 500 people working in accounts payable, decided to compare itself to Mazda as a benchmark for its efficiency. Ford found that Mazda had only five people working in a similar department (Hammer & Champy, 1993). Although Mazda's efforts predated the Web, information processing was a crucial part of their efforts. This underscores the complexity and overhead often involved in purchasing. Intranets can greatly reduce purchasing overhead by simplifying the process and centralizing the collection of order data. Approval processes can be automated or at least facilitated, reducing paperwork and related clerical work.

Many office and maintenance, repair, and operations suppliers offer customizable versions of their product catalogs to be put onto client company intranets. This customization, which automates the process of billing and shipping, allows employees to order products directly without intervention from corporate purchasing departments. The order data are captured once, at the point of origin, stored in the appropriate database, and reused as needed without reentry, reducing mistakes and clerical staffing needs.

Operations

The intranet can be at the center of all operations for the company, serving in essence as an interface to all enterprise systems. This can include logistics, inventory, project management, and operational systems. With the increasing focus on customer responsiveness, time to market, and value chain integration, such operational transparency is becoming increasingly valued. These systems provide crucial links to extranets. For more on extranets, see chapter 15.

Directories

One simple, useful application is an electronic directory of employees. The directory can easily be kept current, and is regularly used by most employees, particularly if paper directories are no longer published.

Menus

Something as simple as cafeteria menus and catering information can be a useful tool to drive traffic to the site.

Calendar Systems

Centralized calendar systems are an excellent intranet application for many reasons. First, it is an extremely valuable service to all users who schedule meetings or other appointments. It is also something most people are likely to use on a daily basis. Benefits include the reduction of time spent in arranging meetings or other events, the elimination of "double booking," and the increased efficiency of all involved staff.

The system may be used to schedule meetings and conference rooms and to coordinate individual schedules. Such technologies can also synchronize personal digital assistants (PDAs), allowing employees to keep their calendars with them and also have them stored centrally. Organizations may also enable the PDAs to access the intranet remotely via wireless technologies including WiFi and Bluetooth. Convergence of standards, advances in security, and decreasing hardware cost make such wireless access relatively inexpensive and viable.

Intranets may also include time clocks. As organizations move closer to activity-based costing, they require additional data on employee productivity. In particular, as more employees become knowledge workers, time tracking becomes an increasingly valuable tool and intranet applications make the input and analysis of these data easier, with widely accessible, familiar, intuitive graphical interfaces.

Group Collaboration

An increasing amount of work in organizations is being done by multiple people working collaboratively in disparate geographic locations, often at different times. Many intranet- and Internet-based applications are available to support such work. These systems include those for group authoring, document management, change control, moderated and threaded message boards, shared whiteboards, and workflow management software. Benefits of these applications can be realized by employees working on-site and remotely, making the intranet a necessary component of any organization's attempts to expand remote work arrangements such as telecommuting, hoteling, and accommodating those employees who are frequently on the road.

Hewlett–Packard found that such traditional group collaboration tools were not sufficient because they lacked the "causal proximity" necessary for productive group work. They implemented passive cameras to indicate whether someone was at or near their desk, and included an intercom-enabled telephone system and instant messaging, to foster regular, brief conversations (Sieloff, 1999). Such richer media helped emulate the benefits of working in the same physical location.

Syndicated Data

Many organizations make regular use of purchased external data feeds for strategic and operational work. Stock prices, weather, and news streams may all be purchased and made available through the intranet, customized for users based on their needs. Coordinating these streams requires careful management to balance easy access to current data with security.

Knowledge Management

Knowledge management has received a great deal of attention in the business and popular press. As organizations move away from manufacturing toward services, more knowledge is in the minds of workers than embedded in physical systems, or even documentation. This increases the cost of employee turnover and can impede growth.

Part of the challenge of knowledge management is uncovering, storing, and retrieving tacit knowledge. Although many organizations struggle with simply managing explicit knowledge that can be readily articulated and documented, the greatest benefits often come from capturing tacit knowledge. The regular use of an intranet may encourage employees to store routinely information and knowledge and make explicit previously tacit knowledge.

Given the volume of information created in organizations, not only is indexing and retrieval important, but forgetting is also crucial. Archiving functions can move information out of the main databases to improve the relevancy of searches.

Implementing an intranet can fundamentally change the nature of the organization by reorganizing its business processes. By doing so, intranets can be a powerful lever of control (Simons, 1995), serving as a catalyst for change. General Motors credits its intranet, which links GM's 14 engineering centers with computer-aided design software and 3-D simulators, with an increase in creativity and even now recruits from the motion picture industry rather than just fine arts and automotive design programs (Rifkin, 2002) to take advantage of the Web-based skills. Such intranet-driven changes are so common that Pitt et al. have developed I-CAT, an instrument for measuring the effectiveness of an intranet as a catalyst for change (Pitt, Murgolog-Poore, & Dix, 2001).

TECHNOLOGY

The technology for intranets is straightforward and similar to any other Web-based system. With nearly all corporate networks running on TCP/IP, starting an intranet site is as simple as placing a machine on the network, or finding one already connected, and installing or enabling a Web server. Current versions of Microsoft Windows desktop and server software come with Web servers installed and can be easily configured by anyone comfortable with personal computers. Once the server is up and running, the server may operate in the background on an employee's ordinary PC workstation. Other employees may access the server by entering the IP address of the machine. Obviously, most users would prefer to type in a text domain name rather than a series of numbers. Such a text name would require either registration on the company's domain name server, which maps IP addresses to text names, or the use of Windows Internet Name Service (WINS), which serves the same purpose as DNS, but on Windows networks.

Content may be added to the Intranet in the form of HTML pages, which may be coded by hand, saved as HTML from word processors such as Microsoft Word, or written in HTML editors such as FrontPage and DreamWeaver. Simple programs for generating content in response to requests on the intranet may also be written in such languages as Cold Fusion, UltraDev, JSP, ASP, and Perl. HTML editors can generate simple scripts automatically for novice users. Such dynamic Web pages allow greater flexibility in the design of intranet Web pages.

Establishing the corporate portal/intranet as the access point for all information services is an appealing architecture for the IS department. Assuming the workstations are Windows-based, then all that needs to be installed on each machine is Microsoft Office with the Internet Explorer Web browser. This simplicity is one overarching benefit of an intranet over legacy network systems, since the need for individual computing support is significantly reduced by the common hardware and software, and user access is enabled through graphical, largely intuitive, interfaces.

All major software vendors have addressed the intranet market. Microsoft is working aggressively to integrate its desktop productivity software in Office with Web-based intranet tools, including video, Exchange server, SharePoint services, and Microsoft Project (Microsoft, 2004). Microsoft even ships wizards for the creation of intranets. Server software vendors such as Sun, IBM, and open-source Apache all offer intranet configuration suggestions and options for network and systems administrators familiar with those companies' products.

Enterprise system vendors have also focused heavily on Web-based access in the past several years. In that time, SAP, PeopleSoft, Baan, Oracle, and JD Edwards have all launched enterprise portal products to integrate their systems with a Web interface and other corporate intranet applications. Customer relationship management products such as Applix and Siebel have also launched portal interfaces in response to demands from the corporate market. The intranet/Web browser has become a common and accepted interface for corporate applications.

Extensible markup language (XML) is rapidly gaining support as a standard for Web documents. This is good news for intranets for several reasons. First, XML, with its focus on metadata, supports the complex, structured documents that populate most intranets. Second, as XML becomes a standard format for word processors, saving files to the intranet will become even easier. This approach has gained attention since Microsoft announced it intends to base its Office applications on XML. Finally, XML documents can be readily stored in databases and searched and retrieved quickly and easily, improving performance for large intranets.

Dot-coms were a major market for many of the software vendors who also compete in the intranet software market. With the collapse of the dot-coms, prices for Internet, and therefore intranet, software have dropped considerably. In addition, open-source software is becoming more robust, offering much less expensive alternatives to the major software vendors. Many companies use the open-source Apache suite to develop and manage their corporate intranets, and most major software vendors have started to support interface with Apache and other common open-source products.

As intranets grow, and increasing amounts of data are available, there must be a way to find information effectively. Information anxiety (Wurtman, 1989) is an inevitable challenge for intranets, given the volume of data likely to proliferate. Hewlett-Packard, for instance, found that within two years of launching its intranet, there were over two million documents stored on thousands of servers throughout the organization, and fewer than 5% of them were traditional official communications (Sieloff, 1999). Such volumes make information architecture (Rosenfeld & Morville, 2002) essential. Information architecture is a crucial component of successful intranets, and the hierarchical structure and navigation themes must be well thought out and implemented. An efficient and effective search engine available for the entire intranet is also required. Many organizations license third-party search engines to reduce the problems inherent in searching the wide variety and amount of information stored in an intranet.

Unless entries are key worded with metadata, users' searches are reduced to full-text searches, which are likely to return massive numbers of hits even with the best search engines. Proper metadata coding requires an appropriate taxonomy. Such a taxonomy may be available within the industry, or extant in the organization. If not, a thorough metadata taxonomy must be developed and implemented. Without a pre-hoc taxonomy, it is unlikely the metadata will be very useful. One survey found that only 31% of companies with enterprise portals had implemented a taxonomy (Answerthink, 2002), emphasizing the need for corporate information metadata management.

Establishing a taxonomy is only the first step; it must be used correctly and consistently to be effective. This requires all of those entrusted with entering data to use the taxonomy properly. This can be accomplished by simplifying the taxonomy so that there is no ambiguity in the interpretation, and there must be documentation and/or training to ensure consistency of the taxonomy's application at all data entry points. It is also likely that the taxonomy will need to evolve over time, requiring a plan for maintenance and continued training.

It may be possible to post much of the content on the intranet with limited metadata coding because most users would find the content via browsing, or the search engine would likely find it and rate it as highly relevant.

Personalization

For users, having the most applicable material readily accessible can be extremely powerful and empowering. Customization strategies for intranet access can be individualized or group based. For example, a different interface can be developed for selective categories of employees, offering some customization at low cost, or personalization software can be installed to generate pages based on an individual's expressed or inferred preferences or behaviors. Most Web servers, including Microsoft IIS, iPlanet, and Apache, now come with basic personalization functionality.

However, Web developers have found that personalization is not a silver bullet. Indeed, Yahoo!, one of the largest personalizable sites on the Web, learned that most users, if given the choice, do not customize their interfaces (Manber, 2000). This makes designing the default pages and customizations more important than extensive customization options. Yahoo! also discovered that any customizations applied in one section of the site should apply to all areas, or users will become frustrated because they expect to need to set up customization only once. Yahoo! did find that a cadre of power users customized their interfaces beyond all expectations of the developers. Lessons learned from these power users can be applied to other users through redesign of the default or group-customized pages, underscoring the power of an information architecture steering group with input from all user groups.

Content Management

The Yankee Group outlines a three-stage content delivery cycle: creation, management, and presentation (Perry, 2001). Content management systems such as Vignette and Interwoven's TeamSite manage all three of these stages by storing all Web site data in a database. They facilitate content management by accepting external and internal automated data streams through syndicated, operational, and financial data and receive input from publishers throughout the organization in word-processing, spreadsheet, presentation, XML, and HTML formats. These systems manage the data with change control, security, and workflow tools. Content management systems handle presentation by working with application servers such as BEA's WebLogic and IBM's WebSphere to create pages based on templates created by designers.

For large intranets, content management can be a worthwhile solution. Much of the data on the intranet change regularly, and updating a database is more efficient than making changes to all Web pages that contain it. Content management systems facilitate the distribution of intranet content over multiple channels, including multiple Web sites, possibly including externally accessible sites, high- and low-bandwidth versions, wireless/mobile, syndication, and even hard copy. Document management systems such as Documentum and Hummingbird and even document imaging software serve a similar purpose. In general, all of these products are evolving toward enterprise content management.

Ease of Use

The importance of usability is well established for all Web sites. In addition, usability has been linked to effective knowledge management (Begbie & Chudry, 2002). For intranets to be effective, they need a wide array of users across the organization. Providing extensive training and technical support to all users is not likely to be possible for reasons of cost and logistics. As employee turnover rises, reducing the learning curve for using the intranet becomes more important. Therefore the intranet must be well designed and simple to use.

BUILDING AND MAINTAINING SECURE INTRANETS

Although intranets may be developed easily within departments with little support from IS, if the intranet is to scale and to function well, there are several areas the IS department must address. As more crucial data are stored and accessed on the intranet, security becomes increasingly important. In addition, intranets are likely to fundamentally change the nature of systems analysis and design, as users become more intimately involved in the process (Perry, 1998).

Standards versus Flexibility

The question of how much to constrain users in the interest of promoting standards for efficiency has plagued information systems professionals for decades. With intranets, the implications are substantially greater as many people in the organization become, essentially, systems developers.

Controlling the use of spreadsheets and other personal productivity software was hard enough, but at least those systems were only accessed by one user, or perhaps disseminated over an informal "sneaker net." With intranet data, potentially the entire organization has access to what is developed, and the developers have no formal training in systems analysis, design, or security. Substantial duplication may arise, adding to costs and confusion. Poorly designed applications or content may lead to user rejection of the intranet, despite realizing other benefits, and data may be left unprotected from unauthorized access and without audit trails.

The power of such distributed systems lies in the empowerment of employees with access to the data, and the ability to enter and manipulate it online. This empowerment is consistent with the principles of reengineering, "just in time," customer relationship management, supply chain management, and other management trends of the past several decades: enter data only once, at the source.

Intranet standards can be set for data storage, color schemes, templates, navigation, file naming, graphics formats, file formats, file sizes, and narrative voice. Content management systems can automate much of this standardization, and also establish approval processes for implementation.

Intranets have the benefit of limited or no access by those outside the organization, and this insulation offers many a false sense of security about the lack of need to protect it. It is likely that much of the data on the intranet will make its way to suppliers and customers, whether indirectly or directly, because a successful intranet will be the primary source of information throughout the organization.

Training and Support

As applications and services are moved onto the intranet, and traditional physical channels are closed down, there will be a significant need for training and support. Often the systems are brought live by departments without thought of the need for training personnel, but the support demands are made to the IS department. A training program can obviate many of the support calls, but requires a coordinated effort and a willingness on the part of departments to support in principle, if not financially, such training programs. Given the expense of lost productivity, such programs are often politically unpopular, but necessary for a successful implementation of any internal system.

Support for the systems is also a challenge because these applications may change frequently and the IS department may not have been involved in their construction. It is unrealistic, however, to believe that the call center, or its equivalent in smaller companies, will not be the main source of intranet support, whether de facto or de jure. Successful, sustainable intranets involve the IS department, especially for support.

Access and Control

> If a Sun employee attaches a modem inside our network without going through the firewall, he's fired.
>
> —Geoffrey Baebr, Sun Microsystems chief network officer, *Information Week*, 1997

Intranet security is similar to security for any Web-based system, but potentially more complex because of the larger number of people with authorized access. When the Navy began implementing its Navy/Marine Corps Intranet (NMCI), it quickly found that the U.S. Department of Defense Information Technology Security Certification and Accreditation Process (DITSCAP) was difficult to apply. The Department of Defense needed to adapt the process to fit the needs of intranet development (Gerstmar, 2002).

Given that the vast majority of security lapses are from authorized users within the organization, intranets create numerous potential breaches. Access controls for data and process may be set at the operating system, directory, application server, and Web server levels. Authorization can be done through passwords, or even biometrics, depending on the value of the information.

Firewalls can be established not only at the border with the Internet to keep those outside the organization out, but also inside the organization to limit access to authorized employees. For more on firewalls, see chapters "Antivirus Technology" and "Biometric Basics and Biometric Authentication."

Access controls are more likely to be successful if the organization has implemented a single sign-on process, where users have only one username and password and are authorized through a centralized system. This allows centralized control of access levels and facilitates terminated access when employees leave the organization.

For the intranet to achieve its potential, it must displace other channels such as paper, phone, in person, and even e-mail. As these other channels are shut down, many employees who did not previously need access to a computer now need it to manage their benefits, enter a request for a repair with physical plant, look up a phone number, etc. This means providing access to all employees, many of whom have never needed computers previously. Custodial staff, warehouse employees, and others may not need individual workstations, but do need convenient access to a computer connected to the intranet. This may mean extending the network to areas of buildings previously left unwired. Although modern construction and wireless technologies make this less of an issue than previously, there may still be significant expense and effort to ensure intranet access to all. Access must also be established to legacy software systems that may not be Web-enabled.

Network Availability and Security

Intranets are easier to secure and keep reliable than the external Internet because companies have control over the network and servers on which they run. This greater control should not be used to excuse lower vigilance. Intranet access may substantially increase the need for bandwidth on the network. Bandwidth demands can easily grow exponentially when an intranet is introduced, especially as the cost of multimedia hardware continues to drop. Although the cost of bandwidth is also dropping, the complexity of network management increases substantially as more bandwidth is used. Also, as demand for the services increases, the need for network reliability also rises. Good networks are more than bandwidth. As more work is intranet-based and dependent on the corporate network, availability, reliability, service, support, and scalability of the network all become crucial.

With most companies distributed geographically, thought should also be given to the security of intranet transmissions. Even if access controls are well implemented, unauthorized access could be achieved by intercepting packets. Secure socket layer (SSL) can be easily enabled for any intranet pages that contain sensitive information. With increasingly powerful client machines and servers, the overhead involved in the encryption is no longer prohibitive. Many organizations should consider using SSL as the default on all intranet pages, relaxing security only when the content does not need to be protected.

Once an intranet site is established, IS will be held responsible for ensuring that the site is available whenever needed. This may mean 24/7 in some instances. For a traditional system, with a limited number of professional developers operating in a staged development environment with source control on systems running in a data center, this is a well-solved problem, depending on resource constraints. However, for systems often hosted within departments outside IS control, and developed by untrained personnel, keeping the systems running can be a challenge. One poorly constructed script can bring a system to its knees and make diagnosis difficult. These systems are often not backed up, and nearly all lack any form of source control. However, such carelessness is not inevitable, and traditional IS methodologies may be applied to ensure the reliability of intranets.

Implementation

It is well established that top management support is a crucial factor in the success of all information systems implementations. However, it is not always sufficient. Many intranets are small, bootstrapped applications implemented with little fanfare. For an intranet to be successful, the goals for the initiative must be articulated. This involves determining the audiences for the system, the services to be offered, and the extent to which they are to be used. Once the goals are known, then metrics can be established for measuring success. With metrics in place, a plan for implementing the system can be created. This is another reason to have a corporate information systems architecture that covers the development, implementation, and maintenance of all intranets.

Importance of Pilot Studies

Because intranet systems are Web-based, prototypes are easy and generally inexpensive to build. This makes pilot testing an effective tool for determining the relevance of this technology in relation to a company's needs. However, it is important to keep in mind the goal of the pilot study. Many people incorrectly view pilot studies as always determining definitively whether a given system will work within the target community. Rather, most initial pilot studies should be tests for proof of concept, and should be repeated several times in different areas of the organization to ensure the generalizability of the concept test.

If the pilot is testing for proof of concept, then the population chosen for the test should be the one likely to adopt it. The initial pilot will be closely watched by many in the organization, and a failure could set the project back significantly. Participation in the pilot study is also an opportunity for potential users of the production system to invest psychologically in it. Potential users may be coopted into adopting the technology by being brought into the development process as well as testing. IS research has shown that involvement in the design process makes people more likely to support and use the intranet system when implemented, and with intranet technologies, these people can be involved not only in the abstract design but in the actual construction, increasing their actual and perceived investment in the system, and therefore the likelihood of their support.

Successful intranets require momentum to achieve critical mass. Gladwell (2000) refers to a tipping point, where phenomena, including technology adoptions, either succeed or fail. Gladwell notes three factors that determine the tipping point of a technology: the law of the few, stickiness, and context.

The law of the few reflects the fact that not all users or decision-makers are equally influential. Gladwell identifies three types of people that are particularly influential: connectors, who know and interact with a large number of people; mavens, who are considered experts in a given area; and salespeople, who will advocate for a position in which they believe. When implementing an intranet, identifying and engaging people from each of these groups is crucial to the project's success.

Stickiness reflects the extent to which something is memorable. The term stickiness is often used in reference to Web pages to describe how long visitors stay. Time spent by visitors is an easily gathered measure of user interest in a page or site.

Finally, context refers to the way in which information about the innovation or technology is disseminated. For instance, something advocated by members of the business units is likely to be more successful than something promoted by an e-mail from the IS department.

When the concept has been firmly established as viable, and there is support within the organization, then a representative group that will be more likely to predict success in the organization as a whole may be chosen.

Once the system is implemented, it is essential to eliminate other sources of the same information or service. This can be done drastically or gradually. For instance, callers to the help desk or human resources could be asked whether the employee has gone through the Web site. If she/he has not accessed the intranet before calling for support, IS or HR staff could offer to guide the caller through the site for resolution before providing an answer directly.

Maintenance and Management

A major component of a successful intranet is a plan for its control. The first obvious question is who should control it. Four common configurations have emerged: IS, corporate, human resources, and distributed. Any one of the models may work, depending on the goals of the intranet and the structure of the organization.

With the IS department in control of the intranet, the technology is likely to be well aligned with the existing systems and architecture, making it more reliable. It is also likely to have the most robust security. However, in terms of prioritization, the IS department is likely to be the worst choice for deciding what needs to be updated first. At a minimum, putting IS in charge adds an additional layer of control beyond the creators of the content. Technologies such as content management can make it more viable for business units to control the system.

In a corporate structure, there is a decision-maker within the organization who oversees the business units involved in the intranet. This person makes strategic decisions about the intranet. Tactical decisions may be delegated farther down the organization. The systems themselves may be built by the business units or the IS department, and secured by IS.

Although human resources applications are among the most common and heavily used functions of intranets, as more operational information is added, most human resource departments are ill equipped to manage the systems.

The distributed model is appealing because the subject matter experts can be put in control of the data. With content management systems supported by the IS department, this model can be viable as the business users are relieved of responsibility for design and security, but retain control of content.

A plan for maintenance of the system is crucial. At a minimum, such a plan should address how often the information should be updated, who is responsible for removing out-of-date information, how information will be archived, and how often the design should be revisited. Redesigns should have a formal structure and budget process (Fichter, 2001). Regular updates should also be made to access lists.

There should also be a disaster recovery plan commensurate with the importance of the intranet. Depending on the organizational value of the intranet, the plan for business continuity in the event of a disaster may range from periodic backups with a restoration plan, to off-site mirrored servers.

An acceptable use policy is an integral part of any intranet plan. Such a plan makes clear what is appropriate for the intranet, and may also include guidelines for Internet access as well. Although filters can be helpful in reducing inappropriate content, they are not a substitute for a well-articulated policy. For guidelines on creating an acceptable use policy, see Lichtenstein and Swatman (1997).

Cost/Benefit Calculations

Calculating the value of information technology has been the subject of extensive research over the past decade. The term productivity paradox is often used to describe the argument that despite rapid increases in spending on information technology, there is not a concurrent increase in productivity.

Measuring the return on intranet investments poses the same complexities as other information systems: calculating all of the costs involved is difficult and attributing benefits to them is even more challenging. However, such calculations are feasible, and there is reason to believe that a well-planned intranet can be profitable (Healey, 2001).

Among the obvious and easily calculated costs of an intranet are the hardware and software required for the servers, including any support contracts, and development software purchased. The costs of development may be relatively easy to measure for IS personnel involved in the system construction if they are contracted, or if the internal IS shop tracks costs on a project basis. However, much of the construction will involve the time of those outside IS, and there may be no extant tools for tracking their time, nor easy access to data on the cost of their time. Network costs for running the intranet may not be easy to track, because both utilization and marginal cost would need to be calculated. A methodological change in how such costs are calculated could make the difference in positive or negative ROI. Training costs must be included, both for the trainers' time in development and delivery and for lost productivity for trainees.

Application service providers can provide all of the infrastructure and functionality of an intranet for an organization with only an Internet connection. Infostreet.com (http://www.infostreet.com), Intranets.com (http://www.intranets.com), and others offer a broad array of cost-effective intranet services to companies of all sizes.

The decision to outsource intranet development is much like the "make or buy" decision for types of information technology. Organizations must decide what, if any, aspects of the intranet should be produced or maintained outside the organization.

Whereas cost calculation is difficult, benefit calculation is even more difficult. Benefit calculation should include obvious direct cost reductions such as headcount, paper, and software licenses. One commonly used metric for efficiency is to credit the system for the prorated salary saved by using the intranet rather than the previous methods. However, this makes the assumption that all of the difference is saved. In many cases, the previous methods were not a complete loss; for instance, workers were doing other work while on the phone, or filled out forms during their commute. Not all of the recovered time will be used productively. Potentially more important than such bottom-line cost reductions are top-line enhancements in revenue. However, such improvements are harder to measure. Specifically, has the intranet contributed to better service, higher quality products, or improved time to market? If so, how much is that worth to the organization?

One excellent source of metrics for evaluating an intranet is the server access logs. All page accesses are automatically logged, along with the time and date of access, IP address of the user, which can be mapped to the specific intranet user, and the referring page, if any. These data may be analyzed to determine how employees are using the intranet and to identify potential enhancements. Estimates of the most and least popular pages, typical paths through the site, most used search terms, performance data, and other metrics are easily generated with simple analysis tools. This can be supplemented with direct surveys of users, online and through other channels.

Many surveys show intranet initiative failure rates of over 50%. Of course, it is important to keep this number in perspective, as surveys show similar percentages of all IS projects fail. These rates of failure may reflect unrealistic goals in some organizations, but often there are fundamental causes for failure. Table 1 outlines common

Table 1 Why Intranets Fail

Reasons for Failure	**Measures to Ensure Success**
Other channels are not shut down Electronic systems only save paper if the paper versions are eliminated. If an employee handbook is still printed, then the intranet version is simply an added cost, and confusion arises about which version is correct.	Commit to eliminating paper when intranet functionality is launched.
Intranet is not used Many intranet systems languish after expensive and extensive construction.	Monitor usage and identify issues early in the process.
Lack of maintenance Many intranets fall victim to good intentions. Intranets are often implemented, but are not made anyone's primary responsibility. There is often an initial burst of energy, but then no information is updated.	Make someone responsible for intranet content and management.
Poor planning	
Inadequate content	
Poor performance	Specify hardware to meet peak demand and optimize databases when appropriate.
Poor interface design	Involve people with formal training in systems design throughout intranet development.

reasons for failures of intranets and ways to prevent such failures.

Privacy

Intranets may contain a great deal of sensitive personal and organizational data. These clearly need to be protected. The fact that intranets are for internal use only offers some a false sense of security. This laxity can lead to greater risks if there is any exposure to external access.

Because the intranet is company property and all of the users are employees, companies have the right to gather and use any information they choose. Although this absolves companies of any legal obligation to reveal privacy policies, it is still advisable to publish a privacy statement modeled on those standard for externally accessible sites. For more on privacy policies, see chapter "Privacy Law and the Internet".

CONCLUSION

Intranets can be useful for organizations of any size to improve communication and information dissemination, and to lower costs. Powerful tools can be installed and configured quickly with relatively low investment. The technologies have standardized and are reliable and reasonably priced. Qualified, experienced personnel are readily available to build and maintain intranets. Success in intranet development and management simply requires the application of traditional business and information systems skills for establishing goals, planning, employing the proper architecture and technologies in response to business needs, and measuring outcomes.

GLOSSARY

Acceptable Use Policies How users may employ a system.

Content Management Systems Systems that use databases to store text, graphics, and other material to be displayed on a Web site, and then dynamically build pages based on previously designed templates.

Extensible Markup Language (XML) A language for describing the content and format of documents containing structured information.

Extranets Corporate systems containing sensitive data made accessible over the Internet to selected customers, suppliers, and business partners.

Hoteling An office configuration that allocates space temporarily on a first-come, first-served basis, similar to a hotel stay rather than assigning permanent space to workers who may not spend all of their time in the office.

Information Architecture The modeling of the structure of a Web site, including functionality and data, based on articulated goals.

Intranets Systems that use Web technologies such as HTTP, TCP/IP, FTP, and SMTP within organizations to facilitate communication and the distribution of information.

Knowledge Management The process of making explicit and codifying the knowledge in an organization.

Metadata The structure and content of data to facilitate future use of the data, particularly for searching.

Portals Web pages or sites that aggregate access to information and to other systems, serving as a starting point for users.

Reengineering The process of redesigning business processes to achieve radical improvements.

Self-Service Benefits The online management by employees of their human resource benefits administration without intervention by support staff.

Scripting Languages Programming tools for handling simple processing needs, two popular Web ones being Perl and JavaScript.

Syndicated Data Feeds that may be purchased to provide consistent or streaming updates such as weather, news, and stock prices.

CROSS REFERENCES

See *Extranets: Applications, Development, Security, and Privacy; Groupware: Risks, Threats, and Vulnerabilities in the Internet Age; Internet Basics.*

REFERENCES

Answerthink. (2002). Despite widespread portal technology adoption, business benefits remain elusive. *PR Newswire*.

Baker, S. (2000). Getting the most from your intranet and extranet strategies. *Journal of Business Strategy, 21*(4), 40–43.

Begbie, R., & Chudry, F. (2002). The intranet chaos matrix: A conceptual framework for designing an effective knowledge management intranet. *Journal of Database Marketing, 9*(4), 325–338.

Fichter, D. (2001). The intranet of your dreams and nightmares: Redesign issues. *Online, 25*(5), 74–76.

Gerstmar, T. (2002). Legacy systems, applications, challenge intranet rollout. *Signal, 57*(4), 29–31.

Gladwell, M. (2000). *The tipping point: How little things can make a big difference*. Boston: Little, Brown.

Hammer, M., & Champy, J. (1993). *Reengineering the corporation*. New York: Harper Business.

Hansen, M. T., & Deimler, M. S. (2001). Cutting costs while improving morale with B2E management. *Sloan Management Review, 43*(1), 96–100.

Healey, A. (2001). Using ROI to champion workplace portals. *Workspan, 44*(3), 22–30.

InformationWeek. (1997, June 2, 1997). *InformationWeek*, 10.

Lichtenstein, S., & Swatman, P. M. C. (1997). Internet acceptable usage policy for organizations. *Information Management and Computer Security, 5*(5), 182–190.

Manber, U. (2000, August). Experience with personalization on Yahoo! *Communications of the ACM*, 35–39.

Meuse, D. (1999). Making employee self-service work for employees and your company. *Benefits Quarterly, 15*(3), 18–23.

Microsoft. (2004). *Connect customers, partners, and employees with portals*. Retrieved September 13, 2004, from http://www.microsoft.com/business/productivity/processes/selectportal/default.mspx.

Perry, R. (2001). *Managing the content explosion into content-rich applications (Internet computing strategies)*. Boston: The Yankee Group.

Perry, W. G. (1998). What is an intranet, and how is it going to change systems analysis and design? *Journal of Computer Information Systems, 39*(1), 55–59.

Pitt, L., Murgolog-Poore, M., & Dix, S. (2001). Changing change management: The intranet as catalyst. *Journal of Change Management, 2*(2), 106–114.

Rifkin, G. (2002). GM's Internet overhaul. *Technology Review, 105*(8), 62–67.

Rosenfeld, L., & Morville, P. (2002). *Information architecture for the World Wide Web* (2nd ed.). Cambridge, MA: O'Reilly.

Sieloff, C. G. (1999). If only HP knew what HP knows: The roots of knowledge management at Hewlett-Packard. *Journal of Knowledge Management, 3*(1), 47–53.

Simons, R. (1995). *Levers of control: How managers use innovative control systems to drive strategic renewal*. Boston: Harvard Business School Press.

Webster's Revised Unabridged Dictionary. (1913). Springfield, MA: C. & G. Merriam Co.

Wurtman, R. (1989). *Information anxiety*. New York: Doubleday.

Extranets: Applications, Development, Security, and Privacy

Stephen W. Thorpe, *Neumann College*

INTRODUCTION

The Internet is a wide-area network that consists of thousands of organizational networks worldwide. The Internet became popular in the 1990s with the advent of the "World Wide Web." The Web provides information stored on servers connected to the Internet. Web browsers, such as Netscape Navigator and Microsoft's Internet Explorer, provide interfaces to interpret and display the Web pages. Documents accessible on the Web contain hyperlinks to move from one document to another. The benefits of the Internet include the ability to discover information more quickly and in larger volumes as well as increased opportunities for communication with individuals and groups. It is hard to imagine an organization today that does not have access to the Internet or does not maintain its own organizational Web site. In the early days of the Internet, an organizational presence on the Web provided a competitive advantage. Today, an organization's presence on the Web is an essential part of doing business.

The benefits of Internet technology and Web browsing led to the creation of organizational networks that provide restricted access for internal employees. The internal networks became known as "intranets," private enterprise networks that use the Internet and Web technologies for information gathering and distribution within the organization. By converting old applications or writing new applications for use on an intranet, organizations can eliminate dependence on a particular operating system/platform. The intranet has also become an effective communication vehicle for sharing information within the organization. The intranet provides easy access to internal information that can be published by departments within the organization. Other applications supported by the intranet include employee access to legacy systems, Web sites for human resources, payroll information, and even training programs. Intranets support collaborative processes between departments, such as scheduling, messaging, and discussion groups (Lloyd & Boyle, 1998). Intranets can also empower customer support center staff with intranet knowledge management systems that result in improved customer satisfaction (Phaltankar, 2000). Through the use of intranets, organizations have reduced costs while also increasing employee productivity.

The intranet is typically protected from the public Internet by a firewall, a device that acts as a gatekeeper between the organizational intranet and the outside Internet. The firewall permits internal employees to access the public Internet, but it prevents outside users (the public) from accessing the internal resources of the organization.

A natural extension of the intranet would allow selected external entities to access internal organizational resources. An "extranet" provides a collaborative network that uses Internet technologies to extend intranet applications and services to selected external organizations, thereby creating a community of interest beyond the walls of the organization. In addition, providing remote access to the intranet permits employees who are off-site to access intranet services; for example, employees working from home could access intranet resources through the deployment of an extranet. The extranet is typically not available to the general public but rather it is limited to "strategic partners." These strategic partners may include suppliers, vendors, customers, or other organizations involved in collaborative research and development. Bringing suppliers, partners, and even customers into the information loop is critical to developing a company's quick response and strategic movement as it adapts to an evolving market environment (Baker, 2000). Figure 1 depicts an organizational extranet.

STRATEGIC USES OF EXTRANETS

The role and importance of extranets appear to be increasing. In a 1999 study by Forrester Research of 50 large manufacturers who had implemented extranets, 80% of the interviewees said they expected to extend extranet access to all of their business partners within two years (Orlov, 1999). Whereas over two-thirds of those surveyed were

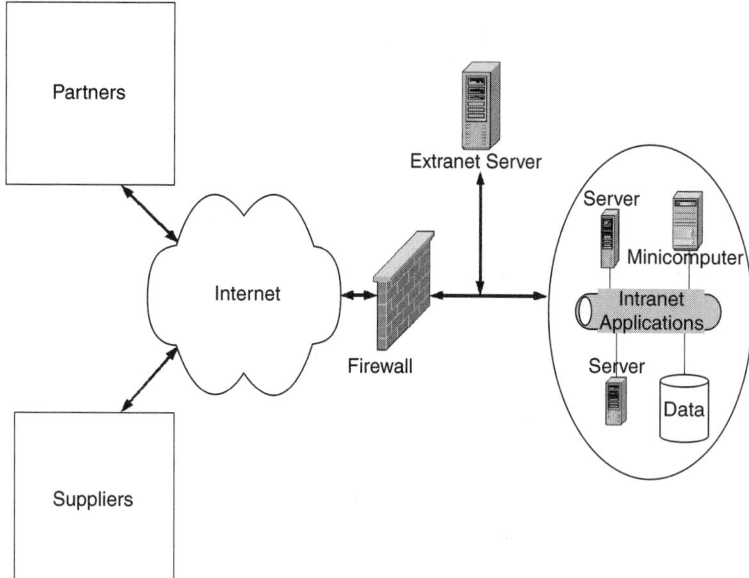

Figure 1: Organizational extranet.

already providing marketing and product specifications through their extranets, virtually all of the executives interviewed expected to expand their extranets to include online sales and sharing of inventory information. The manufacturers also anticipated a 32% reduction in support costs and a 17% increase in sales from their extranet applications.

Extranets provide several strategic advantages for organizations to extend their intranet applications to their business partners: business-to-business e-commerce, collaboration for research and development, and internal efficiency. Throughout the following section, several examples of extranets will be described to illustrate the application of extranets. The illustrations are intentionally drawn from a variety of industries to demonstrate the ubiquity of extranet deployment in business.

Business-to-Business E-Commerce

Business-to-business (B2B) e-commerce has taken off in recent years through the maturity of the Internet and the Web. Extranets provide a means for sharing existing intranet content for real-time communication between business partners. The extranet also provides external organizations with access to internal databases and legacy systems without necessarily connecting to the full intranet of the organization. Among the advantages of e-commerce, the extranet can be an effective tool in customer relationship management, supply chain management, and the electronic exchange of business transactions.

Customer Relationship Management (CRM)

Customer relationship management (CRM) involves integrating the customer service processes with a business, such as sales, marketing, customer service, and support. The idea behind CRM is to adapt business processes to a "customer-centric" business strategy. The deployment of an extranet achieves CRM strategies by providing customers with 24-hours-a-day, seven-days-a-week access to internal information without the involvement of business personnel. For example, extranets can support business-to-business transactions, such as sales, while also providing information resources for products and services. Several customer service components of an organization could potentially be deployed through an extranet. Through improved customer relations, organizations can increase customer loyalty, improve their image, and even increase customer recognition for improved service (Ling & Yen, 2001).

In the health care industry, Humana has developed an extranet application for physicians, consumers, employers, and brokers that may well transform the company and establish it as a technology leader in health care (Lewis, 2001). The extranet site, Emphesys.com, provides a customer-centric approach toward delivering information in real time for various organizational constituencies. The extranet offers Web portals for doctors, patients, and others to share real-time data as well as to access information from a medical database. The extranet includes links for doctors to access the National Institutes of Health and other research resources. In addition, physician offices will have online access to patient data ranging from claims status to prescription histories. For health care plan members, the extranet application provides information regarding Humana's various health plans and allows individuals to review their medical records and prescription data. The extranet application will permit members to enroll in the health care plan of their choice and provide expedited plan authorization. Efficiencies are gained through the extranet, which will provide a member's enrollment eligibility information to doctors within four hours, compared to two or more weeks that had been necessary before the extranet.

Supply Chain Management

Supply chain management involves the integration of business processes and technology to optimize information and product flows among the business partners within the supply chain, from suppliers to internal logistics, distribution, and customers. By providing suppliers with access to organization inventory systems through an extranet, the organization can implement "just-in-time" inventory replenishment policies. This provides a cost savings since the inventory is not maintained by the organization, but rather by the supplier. Extranets also provide the possibility of outsourcing the function of inventory management to suppliers.

Cisco Systems, a networking equipment maker, has deployed an extranet that links their component suppliers, distributors, and manufacturers to form a virtual, just-in-time supply chain (Koch, 2000). When a customer order arrives, typically through Cisco's Web site, a series of electronic messages are sent through the extranet to their business partners to produce the requested equipment. Contract manufacturers are able to access the supply chain process through Cisco's extranet that links to their manufacturing execution systems. On the other hand, Cisco has access to the contractor's assembly line and, when the equipment is ready, a connection is established for Cisco to complete product testing through their automated testing software. When testing is completed satisfactorily, Cisco releases the customer name and shipping address so the contractor can complete distribution to the customer. Through this innovative use of extranet applications, Cisco reduces or eliminates entirely the need for inventory space and paper invoices.

Electronic Data Interchange (EDI)

Extranets provide an economical method for the exchange of business transactions between organizations. To gain efficiencies in business-to-business transactions, large organizations adopted strategies for electronic data interchange to conduct business transactions through private, long-distance networks. Electronic data interchange is a computer-to-computer exchange of business information in a standard electronic format between business partners. These networks, however, required propriety protocols and were expensive to implement. The high cost of investing in private networks and the hardware and software for EDI was prohibitive for smaller organizations that could not realize the benefits of this technology.

Unlike traditional EDI systems that required private networking solutions, the extranet uses the public Internet to exchange transactional data. By eliminating the costs of private networking technologies, an extranet provides an economical alternative for medium and smaller companies to exchange transactional data with other businesses (Pfaffenberger, 1998; Salamone, 2000). Because the extranet uses the public Internet and TCP/IP protocols, it provides an open platform that is not limited to only participants who use the same protocols, Internet service providers, or operating systems.

Collaboration with Business Partners

Communication up and down the supply chain with business partners is typically handled by telephone, fax, or e-mail. The extranet, however, provides the ability to get all parts of the business community working together and communicating in a way that is more timely and effective (Meyer, 2000). By putting employees, customers, and strategic partners in closer contact, extranets promote real-time collaborative efforts and expedite the time to market for products. Because everyone involved in a project can see proposed changes in real time, the extranet can also support many more iterations of the design process than that possible with traditional techniques (Pfaffenberger, 1998).

The McCann Worldgroup is a marketing communications agency that uses collaboration software for internal and external communications to provide employees and clients with more effective ways to share work in progress (Maddox, 2001). The portal product, McWisdom, is both an intranet for internal communications and an extranet for client collaboration. By logging onto the secure area of the McCann Web site, employees as well as clients can review media plans, status reports on ad campaigns, and reports on campaign performance. The portal also provides clients with personalized views of projects in development.

Internal Efficiencies

The use of an extranet can simplify workflow and create internal efficiencies. By allowing authorized employees to access supplier extranets, for example, organizations can simplify processes for ordering supplies and products (Ling & Yen, 2001).

The implementation of an extranet for the Brunswick Corporation Boat Group, called Compass, has dramatically changed the way vendors, suppliers, and partners communicate. The extranet has reduced the time it takes to process boat warranty documents from 90 days to as little as 7 days (Chen, 2003). Moreover, the extranet facilitates processing warranty claims online, which can also reduce costs and enhance customer service. Prior to the extranet, processing warranty claims at Brunswick would take several weeks. With Compass, the processing time has been reduced to fewer than 10 days.

The Ketchum extranet speeds up interoffice communications and provides an efficient method for helping employees learn about new client businesses (Clark, 2001). Ketchum, a public relations firm, introduced MyKGN in March 2000, which allows employees to do research and work with customers online. In the past, research was done on a piecemeal basis. With the extranet, employees are able to research subject databases quickly and efficiently, while also working with clients in real time on such things as press releases and company logos. Ketchum has deployed over 400 collaborative client sites that are using MyKGN and estimates that its extranet application saves 90 minutes a week per employee. By 2003, Ketchum was to realize up to \$5.6 million in cash flow and productivity benefits (Clark, 2001).

Organizations can realize internal efficiencies by enabling customers or suppliers to search internal business databases to find and order products, check pricing and availability, and find product documentation without the intervention of employees within the organization. Beyond the benefits of providing faster access to information for customers, extranet applications relieve some of the demands on customer support service personnel

(Pfaffenberger, 1998). SunLife Financial, for example, recently deployed an extranet to attract insurance brokers to do business with them rather than their competitors. They hope the extranet will provide a competitive advantage while also holding down costs by allowing insurance brokers to obtain information without having to contact SunLife's call center. By making information available through the extranet, SunLife expects to be able to expand their business without having to increase call center resources (Messmer, 2000).

PLANNING AND IMPLEMENTING AN ORGANIZATIONAL EXTRANET

Planning and implementing an extranet require careful coordination between the organization and its business partners to identify the best business opportunities for an extranet, as well as an assessment of the potential risks to the organization once an extranet is implemented (Szuprowicz, 1998). Important issues to consider in building an extranet include defining the purpose and intended audience of the extranet and developing a content management approach, information privacy policies, and security strategies. Of these issues, clearly security of internal information that will be shared over the public Internet is a critical concern. However, defining the purpose and applications for the extranet is also critical if the extranet is to provide the organization with a competitive advantage. In addition, outsourcing the development of the extranet is a possibility for those organizations that do not have the time or expertise to invest in design, implementation, and management of an extranet.

Defining the Purpose for an Extranet

Developing an extranet involves a shift in management philosophy since traditionally internal corporate information was intended to remain internal. Changing the management philosophy will likely meet with cultural barriers among employees who may not be eager to share internal data with outside organizations (Harreld, 2000). People who controlled information in the past may feel threatened by an extranet approach that eliminates information silos and potentially the power bases of some individuals. It is a management imperative to anticipate and resolve internal opposition in order for the development and implementation of an extranet to be successful; in fact, failing to recognize and address resistance is one reason for extranet failure (Pfaffenberger, 1998; Szuprowicz, 1998).

In deciding to implement an extranet, the organization must have a clear purpose in mind, which in part requires a determination of the target audience. With extranet applications, the target audience is typically an established business partner with whom the organization is looking to make doing business easier, faster, and more economical. Without a clear understanding of the purpose and audience for the extranet, content developers will be unable to create a satisfactory site.

Although extranet design will be specific to the organization and its business opportunities, extranets tend to fall into three general categories: publishing, collaboration, and transactional (Pfaffenberger, 1998; Szuprowicz, 1998). Publishing extranets are intended to make internal documents available to external users. These documents might include technical documentation, training materials, specifications, and research data. Publishing extranets rely on servers and scripts to database applications for document retrieval. The primary focus of a publishing extranet is cost reduction by eliminating paper, mailing and faxing expenses, and even reducing customer service center expenses (Szuprowicz, 1998).

The easiest to implement, publishing extranets do not typically demand extensive privacy or security considerations. In many cases, the organization controls the content of what is published on the extranet and can therefore consider the issue of privacy of information when posting content. The security of the extranet can be as simple as a login procedure where authorization to view content is controlled by the identification of the user.

Collaboration extranets are designed to provide interaction between internal employees and external partners. The focus of collaboration extranets is to reduce the time to market of products by accelerating the product design cycle. The extranet examples cited earlier from the McCann Worldgroup and Ketchum facilitate communication between employees and clients in planning, designing, and reviewing marketing strategies in real time (Clark, 2001; Maddox, 2001). These extranets are more complex than publishing extranets since they must enable two-way interaction with outside users in addition to document sharing.

Issues of security and privacy become more complicated with collaboration extranets. From a privacy standpoint, the organization must ensure through privacy policies the ownership and protection of intellectual property. In addition, added efforts must be taken in extranet development to ensure that outside clients and partners can only access what the organization intends. Beyond standard security and password access for authorization, the content of the extranet should be partitioned to avoid outside access to sensitive information (White, 2003).

The most advanced extranets are transactional in nature and facilitate electronic commerce. These extranets are designed to support online transaction processing (for example, sales) and typically provide EDI services through the public Internet. Transactional extranets are complex to design and implement and require more extensive security, as discussed later in this chapter.

Inasmuch as the design of an extranet includes both an analysis of the business processes and the technical logistics, individuals who possess an understanding of the business as well as technical experts will need to work together to define the extranet applications, who will be invited to participate from the outside, and how the extranet will be deployed. Failure of extranet projects is often attributed to insufficient involvement of both business and technical people working together on the extranet project design (Covill, 1998).

Content Management Strategy

Once the purpose for an extranet is established, developing and managing content on the extranet become priorities. Unlike intranets where content is often developed in a distributed fashion for internal use, content on an extranet is shared with strategic partners and customers outside of the organization. In fact, simply providing access to the intranet, although expedient for implementation, may be inappropriate for extranet content and client access (White, 2003). A successful extranet will require a clear corporate identity, look, and feel (Baker, 2000). Because of this outside access, the content must be presented in a useable form, and links to resources must be operable. If information on an extranet site is incomplete, outdated, or missing, the organization's credibility and possibly sales will be lost (Reimers, 2001).

The importance of content management cannot be overemphasized. Failures of extranet sites can often be traced to insufficient content management and extranet site development. Successful extranets ensure that their sites offer valuable content and functionality so the users can find what they are looking for quickly. In addition, the extranet site must be fast and reliable.

Selecting products and services for developing and managing the content of an extranet site is a real challenge because of the evolving state of technology. Software tools, such as those for database integration, auditing, and performance evaluation, will be required for Web authoring and content management of the extranet site. Forrester Research, in their rankings of content management vendors in March 2001, suggested three key players should be identified when selecting content management software (Wilkoff, 2001). First, the dominant content source should be identified since this source will require high integration with the content management application. Second, content managers should be determined. Identifying the right content management software will depend on whether the content is going to be managed by a centralized information technology department or delegated to nontechnical business users. Finally, the audience of the content should be identified. If the target audience consists of consumers, then they will require greater performance than typical extranet users will. If the target audience of the extranet is buyers, on the other hand, then they will likely require personalization of content.

In developing extranet applications, consideration should be given to how much of the intranet content will be mirrored on the extranet site. Duplication of extensive databases and applications on an extranet can create problems with synchronizing the data stored on the intranet behind the firewall with the data provided on the extranet. For this reason, organizations may consider providing trusted partners with direct access to selected intranet servers, although this is more often the exception than the rule because of obvious security concerns.

From a security and privacy of information perspective, careful attention must be given to the types of information that will be provided to strategic partners. Related to privacy concerns, the organization must assess how its information will be used and by whom. Agreements with external partners should carefully outline the acceptable uses of extranet information and privacy of use expectations (Hallawell, 2001).

Beyond privacy policies, extranet developers must take care to ensure that sensitive information cannot be inadvertently accessed from documents freely provided through the extranet. An inadvertent hyperlink in a public document, for example, might provide outside clients with sensitive information not intended for distribution (White, 2003). To avoid these possibilities, intranet content may need to be rewritten for publication on the extranet. From a security perspective, developers may consider maintaining extranet content on a separate server that prohibits access to intranet documents and applications.

Outsourcing the Extranet

For organizations that do not have the internal expertise, the time, or the interest to develop and manage an extranet application, extranet service providers may provide a solution (Harreld, 2000). Outsourcing the extranet design, implementation, and management provides the organization with the expertise needed to deploy an extranet while freeing the organization to focus on content management concerns.

Several organizations provide outsourcing resources and technology for deployment of organizational extranets (see, for example, Szuprowicz, 1998). These services typically include extranet development, integration of existing intranets, facilities management, and security. Larger Internet service providers now provide extranet hosting services.

In evaluating outsourcing vendors, management should give serious consideration to security provisions and capabilities utilized by the application service provider. These precautions not only include security of data, but also security precautions to prevent other organizations who utilize these extranet services from accessing organizational resources (Pipping, 2002). Organizations considering outsourcing to extranet service providers would be well advised to ensure that all organizational data maintained by the service provider are proprietary and confidential to the organization. In addition to evaluating security precautions, organizations should also review and evaluate the corporate privacy policy of the potential service provider (Hallawell, 2001).

SECURITY AND INFORMATION PRIVACY

Security of the extranet and use of information are critical aspects of extranet development, which extends to both the organization and its partners (Phaltankar, 2000). Security issues must be considered through the design, implementation, and management of any extranet applications.

Developing a security plan for an extranet application should begin with a risk assessment to identify the potential sources of threat to the network, how likely these threats are to occur, and the investment (cost) in security that will be required. The level of security investment will vary depending on the nature of the extranet application, the threats of intrusion, and the sensitivity of the information content that will be shared through the extranet application.

Risk Assessment

The deployment of an extranet, as described earlier, can provide organizations with competitive and strategic advantages through business-to-business e-commerce, collaboration for research and development, and internal efficiencies. However, extending internal resources beyond the intranet walls introduces risk to information assets. Organizations must consider the risks associated with extending internal information to external business partners. Stated simply, additional levels of risk or network vulnerability will be introduced by extending access to corporate partners via an extranet application (Maier, 2000; Marcinkowski, 2001). As part of the risk assessment, the organization should consider the levels of security already in place for internal systems. Whereas intranets are typically protected behind firewalls, extranet applications will expose intranet applications to the public Internet. Therefore, internal security policies will most likely require some updating to extend authorized access for outside partners to the organizational intranet.

Through risk assessment, the organization must weigh the potential costs it is willing to accept in terms of economic loss of revenues, loss of reputation with customers, or even the costs of criminal prosecution from the compromise of information protected by federal privacy laws (Marcinkowski, 2001). As the value of the information asset rises, the level of risk aversion will increase, which will increase the level and cost of information security.

Another trade-off in risk assessment is security precautions versus performance of the extranet application. As a general rule of thumb, as security requirements are increased, the level of extranet performance will be decreased. Thus, risk aversion and performance issues will become trade-offs in designing security policies and procedures (Campbell, Calvert, & Boswell, 2004). Maier (2000) suggests that organizations consider the value of data and their location within the network, the method of data transmission that will define the degree of exposure between the organization and the external sites (for example, Internet, private network, wireless transmission, virtual private networks), along with the number of users and growth rate of the extranet that will provide guidance for performance expectations.

In considering risk assessment, the organization must also consider the partners for whom the extranet will be provided. Beyond the security of using the public Internet for business transactions, establishing business partnerships involves careful planning as well. Information technology professionals can design security systems to protect intranet resources from hackers on the public Internet. However, with extranets, the greater security threat may well be from within—disgruntled employees or business partners who have access to internal information (Marcinkowski, 2001). An organization's extranet partners may come and go, and therefore consideration must be given to guarding against potential misuse of internal information. Moreover, the security of the extranet may be compromised by insufficient security at the partner's site; that is, a security breach at a partner's site also exposes the organization's internal resources made available on the extranet (Schwartz, 2000). Weiler (2001) suggests several steps to safeguarding internal resources:

- Verify the security of internal systems before exposing them to extranet partners;
- Develop contracts between business partners that address expectations, process, hiring background checks, and security administration;
- Develop human resources notification systems for events such as employee termination;
- Examine security administration systems;
- Increase funding for security-awareness programs that will also be shared with business partners; and
- Plan strategies based on risk management and emerging business requirements rather than on technology.

Information Use and Privacy

In addition to the protection of information assets, organizations considering extranet partnerships must be concerned with how partners will use corporate information accessed through the extranet. Corporate partnerships can be dynamic and will likely change over time. Moreover, there is little control that can be exercised over the flow of information from one partner to another. Organizations need to consider the type of information that will be shared with partners, and these partnerships should be defined carefully. It seems reasonable, for example, that different partners might receive different information through extranet applications based on the type and value of the partnership. Stated another way, the organization should grant information that is important and necessary for the success of the partnership, but nothing more.

Extranet planners should also incorporate organizational privacy policies. Hallawell (2001) suggests that corporate privacy policies should be defined more broadly to describe how corporate information will be used and gathered within the extranet framework. Questions that should be addressed include how much data should be shared with corporate partners and how competitive and proprietary data that an organization does not want to share can be separated from information necessary for the partnership systems to operate. Security policies and procedures should include provisions for the protection of content and information provided through the extranet applications. Such policies and procedures should be endorsed by corporate partners as a necessary condition for access to extranet applications.

Goals of an Extranet Security Plan

The goals of a security plan will include access control, authentication, confidentiality, and data integrity (Meyer, 2000; Pfaffenberger, 1998). These goals, such as access control and authentication, become critically important for extranet deployment where access to the extranet is absolutely limited to specific individuals and/or organizations; thus, security procedures must eliminate the anonymous nature of the Internet. Moreover, extranet security steps must limit outside users to just that portion of the intranet that is necessary to conduct business over the extranet. The following sections discuss the goals of a security plan.

Access Control

Access control provides or denies access to the network and is usually implemented through deployment of a firewall. A firewall alone, however, is not a sufficient security strategy. Providing confidentiality of information while it is in transit over the public Internet can occur through encryption strategies. User authentication can take place in part at the firewall, but it is usually handled by the application service. User control, however, is almost always handled by the application service (Meyer, 2000).

Authentication

Authentication defines the external population that is permitted to access the extranet and ensures that the external interaction with the extranet is coming from an authorized course. The protection of extranet resources can be described by the model of authentication, authorization, and accounting (AAA). This model first and foremost requires the positive identification of the outside client or partner (authentication). Through authentication, the individual is granted access to resources (authorization), which is then monitored through an accounting process that records activity of the individual for later review if necessary. Although all three steps in the model are important, clearly the model will break down if authentication is not handled correctly. Authentication requires sufficient safeguards proportionate to the information assets that the organization seeks to protect (Campbell et al., 2004).

Assigning account names and passwords to extranet users is the typical method for implementing authentication. The identity of an extranet user is then confirmed when she presents both the account name and password to the host application. Some extranet applications have incorporated a single sign-on option that allows users, once authenticated, to move from one application to another without requiring additional usernames and passwords. Eliminating multiple usernames and passwords for different applications can reduce the potential security risk of users writing down their passwords as well as the potential for users to forget passwords.

Static passwords are not only the simplest way to control access, but also the least secure (Covill, 1998; Szuprowicz, 1998). Moreover, the password if transmitted over the Internet in text (versus encrypted) can be compromised by a password "sniffing" application. A security policy can resolve this potential security breach by using one-time-only passwords that expire once a user has been authenticated or encrypting the password before transmission over the Internet (Phaltankar, 2000).

The challenge handshake authentication protocol (CHAP) provides added security by encrypting the logon information. It has the added benefits of first establishing a trusted relationship between the authenticating server and the peer through a challenge-and-response sequence. Moreover, once the connection is successfully established, the authenticating server will continue to send new challenges to the peer at random intervals to ensure that it is still communicating with the same trusted peer (Campbell et al., 2004).

Additional options for authentication are available depending on the level of security required for the extranet. Source address authentication, for example, would authenticate an extranet user based on the IP address of their Internet connection (Maier, 2000; Phaltankar, 2000; Wack, Cutler, & Pole, 2001). This technique is typically used on intranets to restrict access based on those IP addresses that are internal to an organization. This method of authentication could be sufficient for small-scale extranets with few external organizations where the static IP addresses are known. This technique would not be ideal for global access to an extranet where the IP address of the user is unknown in advance.

Other forms of authentication include tokens, digital signatures, and smartcards to establish the identity of users (Pfaffenberger, 1998; Phaltankar, 2000). Token authentication schemes typically involve two levels of authentication. The first requirement is a personal identification number (PIN), whereas the second form of authentication is a number displayed on the token card. For example, the SecurID card from Security Dynamics displays a unique number every 60 seconds, which in combination with the user's PIN forms a unique password. The advantage of using tokens or other authentication schemes is that authentication requires two pieces of information: something from the card and something from the user. Without both the card and the valid PIN, authentication will not occur. Of course these additional techniques require additional investments in hardware and software to manage user accounts and for password synchronization between the extranet server and the user's token card (Phaltankar, 2000).

Confidentiality

The security goal of confidentiality requires strategies to protect information from unauthorized disclosure to third parties. Corporate privacy policies, discussed earlier, provide one means of ensuring that partners are aware of their obligation to protect information maintained on the extranet. However, from a networking standpoint, extranet developers must also consider the protection of data in transit over the public Internet.

Privacy of communication with the extranet and exchange of data are typically implemented through an encryption technique. Encryption is the process of scrambling data before transmission over the public Internet. Several techniques, such as the public and private-key cryptography systems developed by RSA (see http://www.rsasecurity.com), are available.

Exchanging information over the public Internet encounters the risk of alteration during transmission. Although encryption is an effective strategy for protecting the confidentiality of information during transmission, it does not prevent interception and alteration or guarantee that the data packets are received intact.

Data Integrity

Data integrity provides the assurance that the data transmitted over the public Internet are not modified in any way. Data integrity can be implemented by cryptographic checksums and hashing (Phaltankar, 2000). Hash functions create a fixed-size hash value that is a compressed, nonreadable form of a variable-length data message. One-way hash functions are preferred because the hash value cannot be reversed to reconstruct the original message (Covill, 1998). If the same hash value is not generated by the receiver when the data are received, the integrity of the data packet becomes questionable.

For most applications requiring privacy, encryption techniques such as a secure sockets layer (SSL) connection will provide sufficient data privacy and integrity. Virtually all Web browsers recognize the SSL protocol, among others, for data encryption. An organization can provide its business partners with access to an internal application via SSL and password authentication, similar to the way e-commerce Web sites currently interact with consumers (Wilson, 2001).

For sensitive applications or the exchange of strategic data, organizations may require additional security precautions, such as the creation of virtual private networks.

Virtual Private Networks (VPNs)

A virtual private network is a technique of implementing secure connections over the public Internet through encryption and authentication schemes. VPNs can also be used to provide secure access to organizational networks for employees who are remote from the organization or perhaps telecommuting. The creation of private networks is also possible through leased lines, X.25 packet-oriented public data networks, or other private IP networks available from major service providers. The use of VPNs is becoming increasingly popular because of the cost savings over implementing private networks or remote access facilities, such as modem pools (Pfaffenberger, 1998; Salamone, 2000).

VPNs require firewalls that support VPN technologies. The VPN adds additional protection for the confidentiality and integrity of data transmitted over the Internet by using additional protocols and encryption. The VPN creates a "tunnel" through the Internet that establishes a secured connection from the user site to the extranet (see Figure 2). Different protocols are available for implementing a VPN. One popular set of protocols is known as IPSec, the Internet security protocol (Wack et al., 2001). Other current VPN protocols include point-to-point tunneling protocol, which is a Microsoft standard, and the layer 2 tunneling protocol.

The state of VPN technology and standards for communication protocols are still evolving. The disadvantage of implementing a VPN solution is that it almost always requires the same vendor hardware and software product on both ends of the connection, from the organization hosting the extranet and its business partners. It may not be possible, therefore, to require an organization's partners to use one particular vendor's VPN application (Wilson, 2001).

Protocols such as IPSec and point-to-point tunneling VPNs present some problems in managing network access translation (NAT) traversals, access control for traffic within the secured tunnel, and client management (Fratto, 2003). Although site-to-site networking has been effectively implemented through IPSec VPNs, the same degree of success has not been achieved when deploying remote access VPNs to support end-user access. One potential solution is to deploy SSL VPNs since the SSL encryption protocol is available today within virtually all Web browsers. Thus, users can connect to the extranet with their Web browser as the client. The SSL VPN provides connectivity to a growing mobile workforce and may prove more cost-effective in terms of managing remote access authentication (Piscitello and Phifer, 2003).

Demilitarized Zones (DMZs)

In addition to these security mechanisms, the placement of the extranet within the organizational network can affect security. Early implementations of extranets provided direct access to intranet servers to select outside parties. More recently, a "middle ground" between the public Internet and the internal intranet has become the home of the extranet. This middle ground, called the demilitarized zone (DMZ), is a physical space between the public Internet and the firewall of the intranet (Wack et al., 2001). By placing the extranet in the DMZ, the intranet is protected from potential security breaches by outside parties, from both business partners and potential hackers. Figure 3 depicts an organizational extranet within the DMZ. The DMZ is also used for public access servers, and

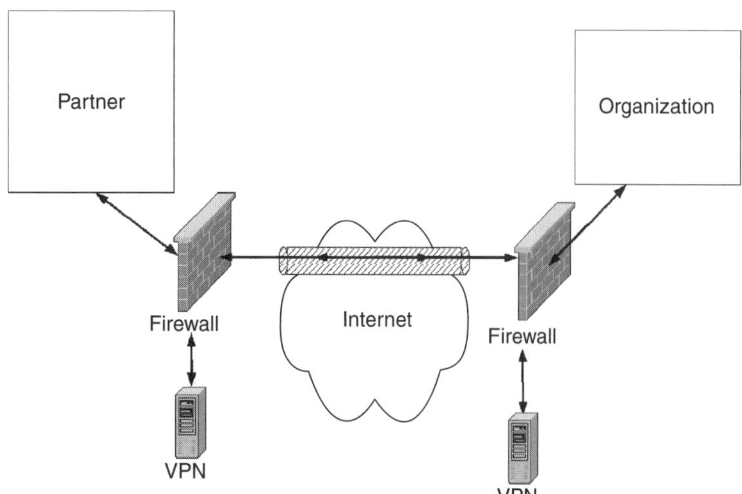

Figure 2: Virtual private network.

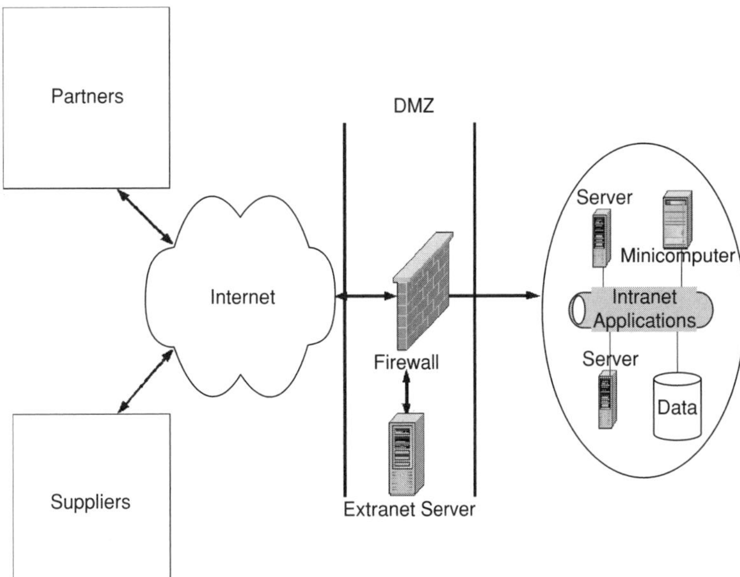

Figure 3: Organizational extranet within DMZ.

again restricts the intranet to internal access. In the single firewall example shown in Figure 3, the firewall provides security protection for both the intranet and the extranet. This configuration will support access from the intranet to update information on the extranet server. In this DMZ design, inbound traffic from the Internet to the extranet is allowed through the firewall and can be rejected if destined for the intranet. Because of the placement of the extranet behind the firewall, two-way traffic is permitted between the intranet and the extranet. This design would allow for updating of a Web server on the extranet, for example, from the internal network.

The dual firewall DMZ design would be better for larger operations that require the capability to offer multiple types of Web access and services to both internal and external networks. Figure 4 depicts a dual firewall organizational extranet within a DMZ. In this design, a true DMZ has been established as a "middle ground" separate from both the internal and external networks. This design is best used when multiple servers or hosts are required to provide more than one type of service and at multiple levels to internal and external networks, such as e-mail and Web servers.

Compared to the single firewall DMZ, the dual firewall design in Figure 4 requires more hardware and software for implementation, as well as greater effort in configuration and monitoring. However, this design provides the organization with greatest ability to control traffic between the external network, the extranet, and the internal network (Shimonski, et al., 2003).

CONCLUSION

Extranets can fundamentally change how organizations share internal resources and interact with outside suppliers, customers, and strategic business partners.

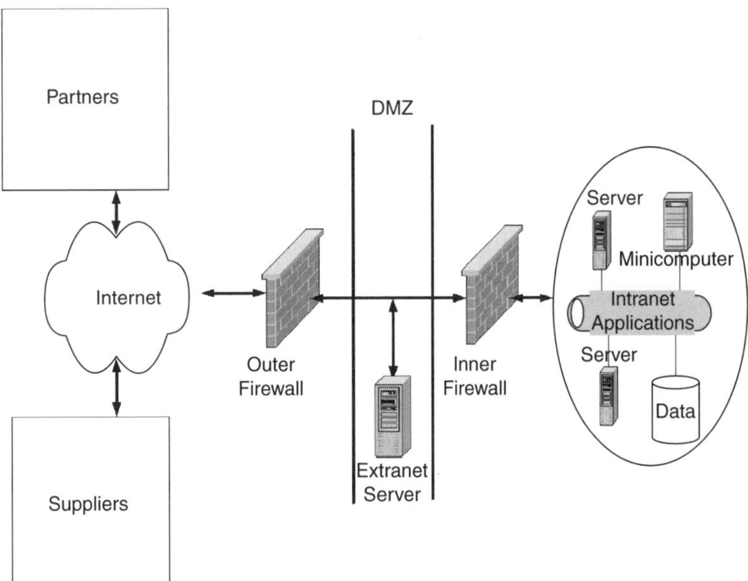

Figure 4: Dual firewall organizational extranet within DMZ.

The implementation of an extranet can be effective in developing tighter linkages in supply chain management and customer relationship management. The current trends suggest an increasing movement toward developing these linkages through extranet applications. Extranets provide a cost-effective means to improve collaboration and decrease the time to market for new products. Moreover, extranets can increase internal efficiencies within the organization. As the extranet examples have shown, applications for extranet deployment are not isolated to one type of industry. Extranets can be effective in seizing a competitive advantage in virtually any type of industry.

The implementation of an extranet solution for any business requires careful planning and a shift in business and management philosophy. Moreover, opening the corporate intranet requires careful assessment of security and privacy precautions, defining the external audiences who should have access, and establishing policies for content management and organizational access.

GLOSSARY

Demilitarized Zone (DMZ) A computer host or small network placed in a "neutral zone" between a public network (such as the Internet) and a company's private network.

Electronic Data Interchange A computer-to-computer exchange of business information in a standard electronic format between business partners.

Extranet A collaborative network that uses Internet technology to extend intranet application and services to selected entities external to an organization, such as suppliers, customers, or other businesses that share common goals.

Firewall A device that protects internal networks from unauthorized access from external sources, typically the Internet.

Internet A global network of interconnected networks, providing connection for private and public networks in one cohesive unit.

Intranet A private enterprise network that uses the Internet and Web technologies for information gathering and distribution within an organization.

Virtual Private Network A technique of implementing secure connections over the public Internet through encryption and authentication schemes.

CROSS REFERENCES

See *Business-to-Business Electronic Commerce; EDI Security; Intranets: Principals, Privacy, and Security Considerations; VPN Basics.*

REFERENCES

Baker, S. (2000). Getting the most from your intranet and extranet strategies. *Journal of Business Strategy, 21*(4), 40–43.

Campbelll, P., Calvert, B., & Boswell, S. (2004). *Security + in depth*. Boston, MA: Cisco Learning Institute.

Chen, A. (2003). Boating extranet sets sail. *eWeek, 20*(17), 54–55.

Clark, P. (2001). Extranet pays off in savings for Ketchum. *B to B, 86*(14), 6.

Covill, J. (1998). *Implementing extranets: The Internet as a virtual private network*. Boston, MA: Digital Press.

Fratto, M. (2003). The SSL alternative. *Network Computing, 14*(23), 75.

Hallawell, A. (2001). Understanding and managing new corporate privacy risks. *Gartner Research* (October).

Harreld, H. (2000). Inside extranets. *Federal Computer Week* (May 22).

Koch, C. (2000). Supply chain management: The big payoff. *CIO Magazine* (October 1).

Lewis, D. (2001). Managed-care firm takes lead with diverse extranet. *Internetweek, 50* (May 21).

Ling, R., & Yen, D. (2001). Extranet: A new wave of Internet. *S.A.M. Advanced Management Journal, 66*(2), 39–44.

Lloyd, P., & Boyle, P. (1998). *Web-weaving: Intranets, extranets, and strategic alliances*. Oxford: Butterworth-Heinemann.

Maddox, K. (2001). Shop turns to collaboration tool. *B to B, 86*(13), 10.

Maier, P. (2000). Ensuring extranet security and performance. *Information Systems Management, 17*(2), 33–41.

Marcinkowski, S. (2001). Extranets: The weakest link and security. *SANS Institute*. Retrieved January 8, 2002, from http://rr.sans.org/securitybasics/extranets.php.

Messmer, E. (2000). SunLife extranet to woo insurance brokers. *Network World* (November 13), 48–50.

Meyer, K. (2000). Building extranet communities. *Telecommunications, 34*(6), 77–78.

Orlov, L. (1999). Surviving the extranet shakeout. *The Forrester Report* (August).

Pfaffenberger, B. (1998). *Building a strategic extranet*. Foster City, CA: IDG.

Phaltankar, K. (2000). *Practical guide for implementing secure intranets and extranets*. Boston, MA: Artech House.

Pipping, J. (2002). Securing extranet applications. SANS Institute. Retrieved December 12, 2003, from http://www.sans.org/rr/papers/21/816.pdf.

Piscitello, D., & Phifer, L. (2003). Simplifying secure remote access: SSL VPNs. *Business Communications Review, 33*(4), 47.

Reimers, B. (2001). Content management: Integrate to dominate. *Internetweek* (August 13), 29–30.

Salamone, S. (2000). VPNs enter the extranet realm—IT managers planning to link business partners can't resist the cost benefits and security VPNs offer. *Internetweek* (May 8).

Schwartz, M. (2000). Good fences, good neighbors. *Computerworld* (October 2).

Shimonski, R., Schmied, W., Shinder, T., Chang, V., Simonis, D., & Imperatore, D. (2003). *Building DMZs for enterprise networks*. Rockland, MA: Syngress Publishing.

Szuprowicz, B. (1998). *Extranets and intranets: E-commerce business strategies for the future*. Charleston, SC: Computer Technology Research Corp.

Wack, J., Cutler, K., & Pole, J. (2001). *Guidelines on firewalls and firewall policy*. Washington, DC: National Institute of Standards and Technology, U.S. Department of Commerce.

Weiler, R. (2001). Integrating partners carries risk. *InformationWeek, 108* (May 14).

White, M. (2003). Passing through. *EContent, 26*(4), 31.

Wilkoff, N. (2001). Content management tech rankings: One size doesn't fit all. *Forrester TechRankings Tech Insight* (March 1).

Wilson, T. (2001). VPNs don't fly outside firewalls. *Internetweek* (May 28).

Business-to-Business Electronic Commerce

Julian J. Ray, *University of Redlands*

INTRODUCTION

The focus of business-to-business e-commerce (e-B2B) is on the coordination and automation of interorganizational processes via electronic means. E-B2B is conducted among business organizations and is a subset of all e-commerce activity including, among others, business-to-consumer (B2C), business-to-government (B2G), and consumer-to-consumer (C2C) activities. Many authors today identify e-commerce as one component of a more general form of electronic business termed e-business. The term e-business is generally used to identify the wider context of process automation that occurs between businesses, including automating provision and exchange of services, support, knowledge transfer, and other aspects of business interaction that do not necessarily result in the execution of a buy or sell transaction. Within this chapter the terms e-commerce and e-business are used interchangeably and refer in either case to the wider context previously defined.

With a reported value of $873 billion in 2002 and an estimated growth rate of 75% over the preceding years (Schifrin, 2003), e-B2B continues to be an integral component of the Internet economy. Today, organizations are investing heavily in e-B2B initiatives where they account for more than 20% of information technology (IT) budgets (Kearney, 2003). With these sustained rates of growth, e-B2B is likely to remain a significant driving force in the global economy for the foreseeable future. This growth, however, is not without risk. As businesses move to electronic forms of business interaction, cybercriminals are taking advantage of unsophisticated organizations and unsecured machines to perform low-overhead, high-profit crimes (Gartner Group, 2003). The level of activity and pervasiveness of cybercriminal activity is astounding. The Computer Security Institute, an FBI watchdog for computer-related criminal activity, reports that 56% of all U.S. companies surveyed in 2003 experienced some sort of financial loss resulting from cybercriminal activity. These losses occur across all sectors and sizes of organizations and result from a variety of criminal activities including theft of intellectual property, denial of service attacks, virus attacks, and financial fraud as the most widespread criminal activities (CSI, 2003). Evidence suggests, however, that financial losses are much higher and more widespread than actually reported as organizations are reticent to reveal the true extent of criminal activity, fearing a general loss of confidence in their systems and business processes. Indeed, of those organizations surveyed, fewer than 30% of incidents occurring in 2003 were reported to law enforcement (CSI, 2003).

FOUNDATIONS OF B2B E-COMMERCE

Although commonly regarded as a new business development, electronic commerce has been practiced in one form or another for over a century. The first identifiable forms of electronic commerce used early telecommunication systems, allowing organizations to conduct business deals by telephone, telegraph, and telex (Li, 2003). Achieving current levels of e-business participation, however, required several key developments including innovative application of information technologies, high-speed communication mediums suitable for transmitting e-B2B-related information, business and regulatory environments suitable for sustaining electronic business processes, and last but not least, a set of motivating forces driving organizations to consider forms of e-business as a means of achieving competitive advantage.

Innovations in Technology

The technological foundations of modern e-B2B have been developing over the past 30 years and reflect innovations in telecommunications and computer communications protocols and methods. During the 1970s, electronic funds transfer (EFT) and electronic data interchange (EDI) were communication standards designed to enable business exchanges over private computer networks. The costs of participating in these initial systems were high. Early EDI systems, for example, required expensive specialized data-processing equipment and dedicated telecommunications facilities, prohibiting participation by all but the largest businesses. Organizations that could afford to adopt these early electronic B2B systems could realize several benefits including greatly reduced labor costs and processing time for recording business transactions as well as vast increases in data quality and accuracy.

Private computer networks requiring dedicated telecommunications facilities, initially the only option for e-business, are still in use today and provide a secure medium for exchanging electronic data. Innovations in telecommunications, information security, and data encryption methods have made other technologies available for organizations, often at a lower cost. Value-added networks (VANs), for example, are semiprivate communication networks usually managed by a third-party provider. VANs enable companies to share business information using commonly agreed-upon data transmission and formatting standards such as EDI. E-business has also been quick to adopt the public Internet as a general purpose communication medium. The Internet provides high data transfer rates and significantly lower operational costs relative to other electronic communication systems, making it an affordable and viable alternative for organizations of all sizes. The Internet, however, is generally considered insecure as data moving over the system can be intercepted and read by anyone with access to it unless the data have been previously encrypted.

Virtual private networks (VPNs) are a form of secure communication using a combination of data encryption and specialized data transmission methods designed to protect proprietary business data as they move between business systems over the public Internet. This protection allows companies to use the public Internet as if it were a secure private communications system, facilitating development of low-cost extended private networks (extranets) that can connect businesses and business partners irregardless of their geographic separation.

Adopting the Internet as a communications platform to support e-business processes first requires developing commonly agreed-upon methods for transferring business data between organizations and for managing interoperability of business systems. Today, there are hundreds of protocols and standards governing almost every aspect of using the Internet to transmit and translate business data. Some of these protocols and standards are proprietary and associated with vendor-specific systems whereas others, such as extensible markup language (XML), are designed to be interoperable, allowing them to be understood and processed by a wide variety of heterogeneous computer systems. Some of these new and emerging standards build on earlier protocols such as EFT and EDI. When coupled with system-independent data communication protocols such as the Internet's TCP/IP, these early data translation protocols enable data to literally transcend organizational and technological boundaries. For example, although EDI documents can still be sent over private lines, it is also possible to complete the same transactions using the Internet and XML at a fraction of the cost of traditional EDI. This provides several benefits for companies. Those companies that invested heavily in early technologies such as EDI can maintain their original investment and are still able to participate in modern e-business initiatives. On the other hand, companies that could not afford such early technologies are now able to engage in intraorganizational data exchange with greatly reduced initial investments in technology.

Innovations in Business Processes

Greenstein, O'Leary, Ray, and Vasarhelyi (2005) identify the recent surge of e-B2B activity as a progression of an evolving process that has been evident throughout the industrial revolution. The authors attribute the rise of e-business as a response to dramatic improvements in both information processing and telecommunications systems that have facilitated revolutionary change in organizational business processes. Centered on the Internet, this latest technological revolution enables businesses to automatically place orders, send quotes, share product designs, communicate sales projections, and collect payment using electronic means, providing the potential for reducing operating costs, shortening time-to-market for new products, and receiving payment faster than ever. Modern computers, able to process thousands of transactions per second, can significantly reduce the time necessary to process business data, allowing organizations to share business information almost instantaneously. Moreover, businesses willing to commit to this digital economy can partner with other similarly focused businesses, creating tightly integrated supply chains and developing networks of loyal customers and trading partners who, research shows, collectively outperform their competitors.

Norris, Hurley, Hartley, Dunleavy, and Balls (2000) identify three stages that established companies go through as they evolve from a traditional organization to a mature e-business. Early e-B2B activities focus on increasing efficiencies of sales and/or purchasing processes while minimizing disruption to existing organizational culture and business processes. The second stage of adoption focuses on using electronic information technologies to integrate supply chain activities and streamline business processes. This stage is often aimed at reducing operating costs and increasing effectiveness of operations beyond sales and purchasing. The last stage involves developing strategic, tightly coupled relationships between companies in order to realize mutual benefits and joint rewards afforded by an optimized supply chain.

E-business strategies are not, however, limited to existing organizations. The Internet has engendered a number of new and innovative businesses dependent on the Internet as a primary means for generating revenue. The dot-com boom of the late 1990s, so visible in the B2C sector with companies such as Pets.Com and WebVan, carried over into the B2B sector. During this time, large numbers of highly innovative, technology-savvy, Internet-focused companies became immersed in all areas of e-B2B activity. These new economy companies relied on digital processes and often purely digital products and services. Online B2B exchanges, for example, emerged as a multibillion dollar industry virtually overnight, filling a need for increased speed and expediency of interorganizational electronic business transactions. By the year 2000, an estimated 2,500 online B2B exchanges, serving a wide variety of industries such as electronics, health care, chemicals, machinery, food, agriculture, construction, metals, printing, and medical lab equipment, were available (Wichmann, 2002). Like their B2C counterparts, however, many of these B2B dot-com companies failed because of weak business models and misguided, overzealous venture capital. Today, fewer than 150 of these exchanges remain.

Supply chain integration is another area that has engendered significant e-B2B activity. Companies acting as intermediaries provide technology and services necessary to support electronic supply chain management. Manugistics (http://www.manugistics.com), for example, successfully adapted its more traditional technologies and services to operate within the emerging e-business environment and now facilitates electronic supply chain operations across a broad array of industries. Elogex (http://www.elogex.com), on the other hand, is an example of a brand new, technology-savvy company developing supply chain management technology and services specifically for a narrow industry focus: consumer goods, food and groceries, in this case.

Benefits of B2B Electronic Commerce

Greenstein et al. (2005) identify four specific, measurable benefits directly related to investments in e-B2B systems integration initiatives:

- Improvements in data accuracy;
- Reduced cost per transaction;
- Increased speed of access to important information; and
- Enhanced management decision-making effectiveness.

Additional benefits including reduced risk, better planning and inventory management, strengthened relationships with business partners, and an increased ability to integrate with new business partners in a variety of interesting and innovative ways are also realizable by organizations willing to invest in e-business technologies.

Recent changes in the banking industry provide an example for understanding the potential benefits that can be achieved using electronic automation. The U.S. Federal Reserve along with six other central banks and sixty-six major financial firms implemented the Continuous Link Settlement System. This system automates trading, and settlement of foreign currency exchanges amounts to approximately $300 trillion each day. Traditionally, as a trade is being conducted, two banks agree on an exchange rate and wire the money to each other, a process that can take two to three days to complete. During the time between a trade being agreed upon and completed, interest is lost and events can change the value of a country's currency, ultimately affecting the final exchange rate. In extreme cases banks have gone bankrupt (Colkin, 2002). Accordingly, the risk associated with transaction latency justifies the $300 million technology investment made by the banking industry.

Small to mid-sized organizations, in particular, have significantly benefited from the Internet revolution as many of the barriers to participating in e-business have been removed. The financial overhead associated with implementing early e-business systems such as EDI was significant and out of reach of all but the largest corporations. Today, a combination of the Internet and reduced real costs of computer systems and software over the past decade has enabled companies of all sizes to develop e-business strategies. In fact, the inverse relationship between size and agility provides small to mid-sized firms some competitive advantages in e-business.

B2B STRATEGIES

E-business strategies are often classified by the nature of the interaction taking place between business partners. Four strategies that may be identified using this approach are e-selling, e-procurement, e-collaboration, and e-markets. Within each of these strategies we can further identify the vertical or horizontal industry focus of the participation and whether intermediaries are involved. Companies with a vertical focus usually operate within a single industry such as the automotive, chemical, energy, or food-retailing industries. In contrast, companies with horizontal focus provide products and/or services across a wide range of industries. Office supplies and computers are examples of products often regarded as horizontally focused. Intermediaries in e-B2B are most often associated with e-markets and electronic auctions where one company, the intermediary, operates as a broker allowing other companies to buy and sell products and services using technological infrastructure provided by the intermediary.

E-Selling

E-selling is concerned with the direct sale of products and services to other businesses using automated means. The business model is similar to the B2C direct-sale model but differs in that B2B interaction often requires prenegotiation of prices, catalog items, and identification of authorized users.

Two major methods for e-selling are in common use: electronic catalogs and electronic auctions (Turban, King, Lee, Warkentin, & Chung, 2002). Electronic catalogs can be customized in both content and price for specific businesses and can be coupled with customer relationship management software such as SAP's Internet Sales Solution (http://www.sap.com) to provide personalized, business-specific content delivery. Dell Computers (http://www.dell.com) and Staples (http://www.staples.com) are examples of companies providing direct sales to other businesses over the Web, allowing businesses to set up accounts and customize the content available for online purchase. Cisco (http://www.cisco.com) is another example of a company that has a very successful direct-sale approach using the Internet. Cisco reportedly receives 98% of their orders online, reducing operating costs by 17.5% and lead times by at least 50% over previous order-handling methods (Turban et al., 2002).

Electronic auctions are sites on the World Wide Web where organizations can quickly and efficiently dispose of surplus inventory. These auctions allow companies to save time and reduce costs of disposing with surplus inventory, often allowing companies to obtain better prices for items over traditional disposal methods. Ingram Micro, for example, receives 60% of an item's retail cost, on average, by selling surplus inventory through an online auction. This compares to an average 10 to 25% price recovery using traditional liquidation brokers (Schneider, 2002). Some companies create and manage their own auction sites. CompUSA's Auction Site (http://www.compusaauctions.com), for example, is designed to allow small and mid-sized companies to bid on their surplus inventory. Alternatively, companies can use existing general purpose or industry-specialized auction sites such as eBay (http://www.ebay.com) or ChemConnect (http://www.chemconnect.com). Both Sun Microsystems and IBM have successfully adopted eBay as an auction site for surplus computer hardware, software, training courses, and refurbished equipment. EBay, in this case, operates as a horizontally aligned intermediary between Sun Microsystems and the companies or individuals bidding on Sun's products. ChemConnect is an example of a specialized third-party auction site designed to manage the selling and buying of chemicals and plastic products using an auction format. Unlike eBay, which is horizontally focused, ChemConnect has vertical focus and concentrates on selling specifically to the chemical industry.

E-Procurement

E-procurement is concerned with automating the purchasing of goods and services from suppliers. These applications facilitate the exchange of electronic information between trading partners by integrating a buyer's purchasing processes with sellers' order entry processes (Davis & Benamati, 2002). E-procurement systems can be either buy- or sell-side applications. Buy-side applications reside on a buyer's system, controlling access to the ordering process, the authorization of orders, and possibly the list of trading partners allowed to receive orders. Sell-side applications reside on a supplier's system and allow authorized buyers to access and place orders directly on the supplier's system. Sell-side systems are often implemented as extranets where access to electronic catalogs and pricing information can be carefully controlled.

Early e-procurement implementations relied on fax, e-mail delivery, EDI, or real-time system processing to transfer data among trading partners. Newer e-procurement systems use Internet technologies to manage ordering processes. Recent surveys indicate that most commercial solutions now use XML and the Internet to share procurement data and provide access to online market places as part of the offering (Aberdeen Group, 2001b).

E-procurement systems can benefit companies in a variety of ways. In 1999 Federal Express identified e-procurement as a key strategy for reducing costs and saving time in the purchase order process. FedEx purchased a B2B e-commerce platform from Ariba Inc. (http://www.ariba.com), which was implemented within a month and returned a positive return on investment (ROI) within three months. The new purchasing system manages approximately 20% of FedEx's 25,000 annual requisitions and reduces purchasing cycle times from 20 to 70%, depending on the type of items purchased. The purchase of new PCs, for example, now takes 2 days rather than the 17 to 19 days it took using a traditional paper-based approach. FedEx also managed to reduce the purchasing department staff by half, allowing these extraneous staff to be reassigned (Aberdeen Group, 2001a). Microsoft reports similar success with MS Market, a desktop e-procurement system designed to run from a Web browser over the company's corporate intranet. MS Market is deployed to 55 Microsoft locations in 48 counties and saves the company an estimated $7.5 million annually (Microsoft, 2000). In the United States, Microsoft uses MS Market to order almost 100% of the company's requisitions at an average cost of $5 per requisition.

E-procurement is one of the main areas of e-B2B that is "delivering rapid and quantifiable results" (Aberdeen Group, 2001b). The type of products purchased by e-procurement systems, however, are generally limited and of relatively low value. Strategis (http://www.strategis.gc.ca), an online branch of Industry Canada, reports that 42% of e-procurement purchases by businesses in Canada in 2001 were for office supplies, furniture, and office equipment, followed by IT hardware and software (29% of total) and travel services (15% of total). Similarly, Microsoft Corp. reports that 70% of it annual 400,000 procurement purchases are for requisitions less than $1,000 in value (Microsoft, 2000).

E-Collaboration

E-collaboration is a term broadly used to describe any form of shared e-business activity in which companies collaborate with the common goal of providing a mutually more efficient business environment. E-collaboration can take many forms including supply chain integration, joint design and development of products, joint demand forecasting, and joint planning. General Motors, for example, shares specialized engineering software and data files with its suppliers as a means of reducing product development time. As part of this joint-product design strategy, General Motors partially or fully underwrites the costs of software licenses for some of its suppliers in order to standardize product design platforms across the supply chain. By standardizing and sharing design tools General Motors successfully reduced design-to-production cycles for new products by 50% (Slater, 2002).

Collaborative planning forecasting and replenishment (CPFR) is another form of collaboration allowing suppliers and sellers to jointly forecast demand for products in an attempt to better coordinate value chain processes such as restocking, managing exceptions, and monitoring effectiveness. The motivation underlying CPFR is that better forecasting between trading partners results in improved business processes, which in turn reduces costs while improving customer service and inventories. Wal-Mart's RetailLink is an example of a CPFR system operating over the Internet using EDI documents to share information. RetailLink enables Wal-Mart's suppliers to receive detailed information about store sales, inventory, effects of markdowns, and other operational information.

Access to this information allows Wal-Mart's suppliers to manage their inventory more effectively at each individual Wal-Mart store.

Collaborative approaches such as CPFR and supply chain integration can result in numerous benefits for companies. Following a recent study involving 81 companies, Deloitte and Touche report that companies that "collaborate extensively" with their supply chain partners while focusing heavily on customer loyalty and retention are almost twice as profitable as companies that are "below average" in the areas of supply chain collaboration (Rich, 2001).

E-Markets

E-markets provide third-party integration services by supplying online applications, allowing organizations to exchange goods and services using a common technology platform. In essence these electronic marketplaces bring suppliers and buyers together in a common forum with a common technology platform. E-markets are often vertically aligned, serving specific industries such as the energy or automotive industries. However, horizontally aligned e-markets servicing broad industries such as office supplies and information technology also are available.

Many e-markets are independent exchanges managed by intermediaries that are neither buyers nor sellers in the marketplace but, instead, provide specialized third-party services, enabling other businesses to collaborate through them. Alternatively, e-markets can be created and managed by a company or consortia of companies that are leaders in the industry being served. Covisint (http://www.covisint.com) is an example of a global marketplace sponsored by a consortium of industry leaders including DailmerChrysler, Ford, and General Motors among others. Covisint was jointly funded in 2000 to provide a global solution for the automotive industry with the mandate to "improve the effectiveness of mission critical processes such as collaborative product development, procurement and supply chain management. . .through implementation and use of a secure and comprehensive online marketplace" (Covisint, 2002). Covisint's mission is to "connect the automotive industry in a virtual environment to bring speed to decision making, eliminate waste and reduce costs while supporting common business processes between manufactures and their supply chain." This mission is achieved through a number of collaborative processes including online auctions and direct sales via online catalogs.

The total value of transactions managed by Covisint is very large, reportedly exceeding $129 billion in 2001. During 2001, General Motors purchased $96 billion worth of raw materials and parts through the exchange. The largest online bidding event to date was also recorded by Covisint in 2001 as DaimlerChrysler used the exchange to procure $3 billion worth of automobile parts. The exchange also helps reduce costs of purchases and transactions. Ford Motor Co. reported $70 million in savings in 2001, exceeding its $50 million initial investment in the exchange in a single year (Konicki, 2001). Recent research, however, has questioned the validity of savings claims made by e-exchanges in general as they often reflect maximum theoretical savings that could be achieved at the close of auctions, whereas actual savings are likely to be less (Emiliani & Stec, 2002).

METHODS FOR IMPLEMENTING B2B

Integrating business processes in one company with business processes in another requires that both companies provide a technology framework that enables the flow of electronic business information between their respective information systems. This integration could be as simple as establishing a system for sharing electronic information and files via e-mail, magnetic tape, or other digital media. More sophisticated integration techniques involve providing business partners access to real-time information stores such as database systems or applications performing supply chain management, procurement, and enterprise resource planning activities.

Point-to-Point Transfer Methods

By the 1950s companies had started to use computers to manage business transactions. At this time, paper forms were used to move business information between companies that had to be re-entered into recipient computer systems using manual methods: a process that was unreliable, expensive, and redundant (Schneider, 2002). In the 1960s, magnetic tape and punch cards replaced paper forms for recording and transferring business information. These encoded tapes or card decks could be transferred to a recipient computer system and automatically processed using card or tape readers, negating the need for expensive and error-prone redigitizing processes (Figure 1).

Tape and card decks have since been replaced by network-based file-transfer applications such as Tymnet, UUCP, and Kermit and more recently by applications implementing the Internet's file transfer protocol (FTP). File transfer applications allow one computer system to export business data from an application to an electronic data file. The file is then transferred to a recipient computer system in digital form over a phone line, computer network, or the Internet where it is subsequently loaded into the recipient application using specialized software.

These point-to-point file transfer methods are perhaps the simplest integration approaches to design and implement as the only factors in common between collaborating systems are a prenegotiated file format and common communication method. Such methods work well in situations where there is little change over time in the applications at either end of the process and where there is a high degree of collaboration between the business entities. Several disadvantages of the point-to-point approach, however, can be identified. With respect to the format of the data being shared, the sending and receiving applications must agree on a fixed file format, export and import logic is often restricted by the applications, and lastly the overall system is brittle and can fail if either system changes the data format. From a data management perspective: data transfer is conducted in batch mode rather than real time, which introduces latency into the system; there are also no methods for data recovery or guaranteed delivery of

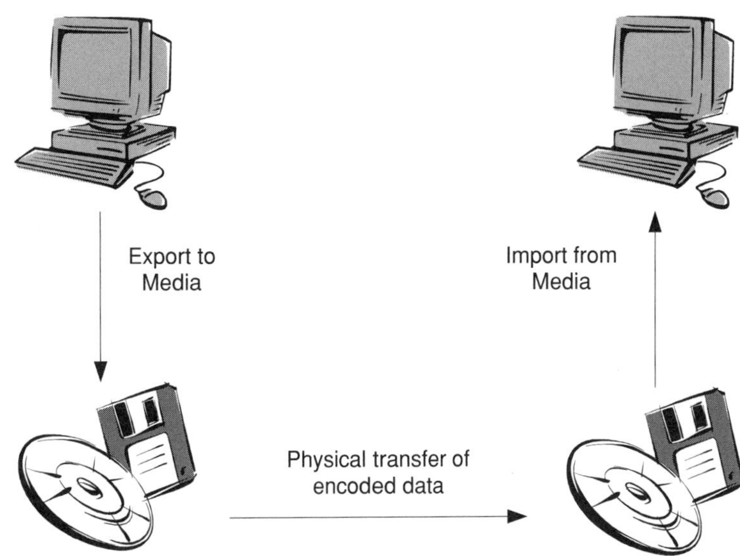

Figure 1: Point-to-point data transfer.

the data (Yee & Apte, 2001). Moreover, sharing data with multiple business partners becomes difficult to manage as the impact of these disadvantages becomes multiplied as each additional business partner is added.

Database Integration Methods

Allowing a business partner direct access to business information stored in a database can overcome many of the technical issues associated with point-to-point integration methods. Providing direct access to data stores can be relatively straightforward to implement using modern relational database management systems (RDBMSs) and given the correct set of business and technical conditions.

Relational database management systems such as Oracle's Enterprise Database, Microsoft's SQL Server, and IBM's DB2 can be thought of as layered applications consisting of many individual procedures that together provide a complete data management system. The lowest layer consists of actual data storage facilities and procedures that efficiently organize stored data on a host computer system. The top layer consists of a user interface providing capabilities for generating reports and managing stored data. Between the data and user interface layers are a suite of applications implementing the data management and query capabilities of the database system. This application layer typically uses a specialized computer language called structured query language (SQL) to manage all aspects of the database and to provide an interface between users and stored data (Figure 2).

In an e-business context, it is more likely that a business partner's application or software agent will initiate a data interaction than an actual person. When applications access a database they often use database connectivity middleware such as JDBC, ODBC, or ADO and bypass a database's user interface layers. Database connectivity middleware enables programmatic access to the data management and query services of a database by generating SQL commands directly from a remote application, enabling systems designers to create points of integration between business systems over a telecommunications system such as the Internet. Database connectivity middleware provides an abstraction layer for applications, shielding them from actual data storage mechanisms. This approach allows systems designers to overcome differences in storage formats and storage methods that can occur between disparate databases and computer systems. Applications sharing business information through a database need only understand how data are organized in a partner's database and have the ability and necessary permissions to access the database resources over a computer network.

Newer business systems tend to separate application logic from actual data storage methods and often use

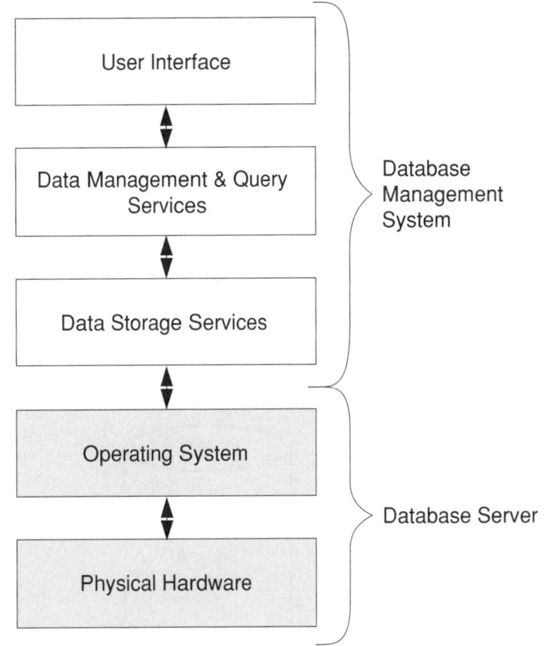

Figure 2: Database management system components.

commercial RDBMSs to manage and protect stored business data. This "two-tier system" design facilitates data integration between business partners, as business data stored in one database can, in theory, be accessed directly by any number of remote systems. Older business systems, however, tend to tightly couple business logic and business data, often using proprietary data storage formats. This approach makes integration at the data level problematic. Linthicum (2001) suggests that integration with these older closed systems is best managed at an application level as it is often impossible to deal with the database without also dealing with the application logic.

Many companies today deploy a number of databases within their organization, often of different vendor types. In these cases, database integration approaches can be more complicated as business partners might need to share data from two or more database systems simultaneously. Federated databases, also called database gateways, are middleware technologies that can be used to overcome these types of integration issues where there are multiple data sources. Database gateways are middleware providing proxy services. The database proxy accepts incoming requests for data from client systems, translating each client request into a form that can be executed against one or more underlying connected databases, then formats and returns the results (Figure 3).In essence, database gateway middleware systems create virtual databases for client applications by conjoining selected elements of underlying physical databases and managing interactions between the virtual and physical systems. IBM's Distributed Relational Database Architecture (DRDA) is an example of a database gateway delivered as part of IBM's DB2 enterprise database systems facilitating interoperation of multiple databases within heterogeneous computing environments.

Although proficient at providing read-only access to business data for remote applications, database gateways have limitations for e-business systems. Database gateways tend to be inefficient as queries against the virtual database must be recast to query underlying physical data sources and results from queries merged by the middleware to form reports that can be returned to client applications. The database approach to integration also bypasses any business rules that might be implemented in an application, resulting in redundant business logic that must be both developed and maintained at some cost (Yee & Apte, 2001).

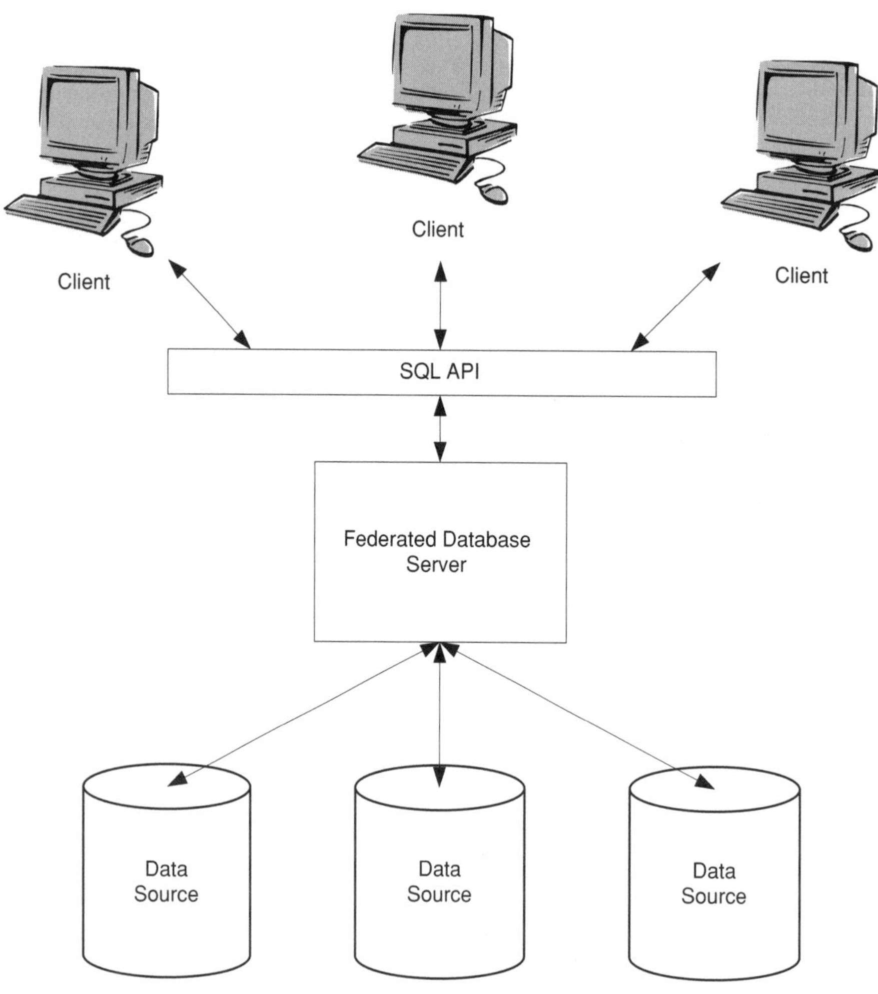

Figure 3: Database gateways.

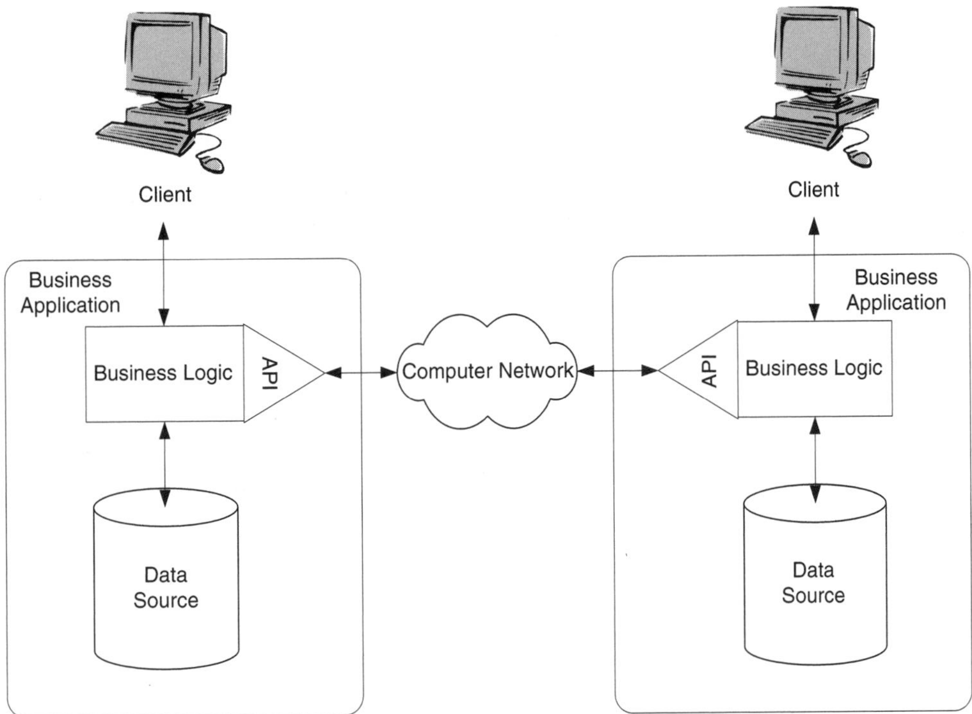

Figure 4: Data integration via application programming interfaces.

API Integration

An alternative to integrating business applications through direct access to business data is to enable applications to share information directly. This can be achieved by developing programmatic interfaces that are built into an application and specifically designed to be accessed by other applications. Application programming interfaces (APIs) allow external applications (clients) to share data and business logic with host applications (servers) over a computer network (Figure 4).Using this approach, applications can share computer data composed of text and numbers and even complex structured data objects representing atomic information components such as customers or purchase orders. Some APIs allow client systems to execute business logic on a server such as removing an element of data or performing some business interaction.

B2B integration via APIs is often more difficult in a heterogeneous computing environment as differences in computer systems affect how data and business logic can be accessed, how client systems can be authenticated, and how data components such as strings, numbers, dates, and complex higher-order objects are represented. These well-known system compatibility issues can often be overcome by middleware applications designed to broker the flow of information between different systems. Remote procedure calls (RPCs), initially developed for UNIX systems, are one such middleware technology providing a framework for translating system-specific data to and from a common data format. Once business data have been encoded into a common format, they can be transferred without loss of representation between client and server systems over a computer network. RPC frameworks are available for most computer systems used by businesses today and use a computer language called interface definition language (IDL) to represent business data in a system-independent form suitable for transmission between systems over a computer network. Other API middleware technologies are in common use. Microsoft (http://www.microsoft.com) have extended their component object model (COM) to allow computers to share data and methods between systems running different versions of Windows software over a network. This distributed COM (DCOM), also known as COM+, is available on all second-generation Microsoft Server products. The common object request broker architecture (CORBA) provides a processing model similar to Microsoft's DCOM and was developed as an open specification by the Object Management Group (http://www.omg.org), consisting of over 800 independent software developers. The initial CORBA specification was developed in 1991 and is still in use today, especially in the banking industry, which has adopted it as their standard method of systems integration.

Message-oriented middleware (MOM) addresses some of the issues associated with tightly coupled API solutions such as RPCs and DCOM. MOM applications transfer data between systems in the form of application-defined units of data called messages. Most message-driven applications use an asynchronous processing model rather than the synchronous model used by most tightly coupled systems. Unlike RPCs, which deliver data from a client to a server immediately, messages sent from one application to another using MOM are usually placed into a specialized piece of middleware responsible for storing and querying messages called a message queue (Figure 5).When a recipient application is ready to process messages it accesses the message queue and extracts those messages that have been sent to it by one or more client applications. This

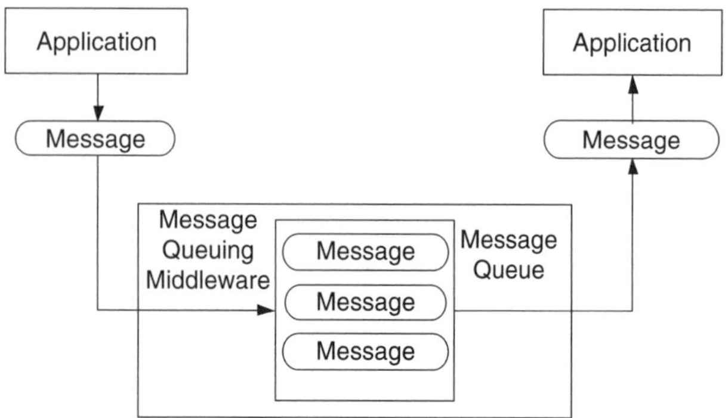

Figure 5: Message-oriented middleware.

processing model allows a system to send messages to possibly several recipient systems at the same time without having to wait for each recipient application to process the data, thereby allowing different systems to process data at different speeds. Newer MOM implementations guarantee message delivery even though a recipient application might not be available at the time a message was sent. Today, messaging middleware is a standard component of several systems development platforms including Microsoft's DCOM (MSMQ), Microsoft's .NET platform, and the Enterprise Java platform (JMS).

Java is a computer language developed by Sun Microsystems in the 1990s specifically for use on the Internet. Unlike traditional computer languages, Java uses a data format common to all Java implementations that is independent of any specific hardware/software environment, thereby allowing Java applications to be executed on any platform for which Java is available. This "write-once-run-anywhere" approach negates the need for intermediate data format languages such as IDL to represent data transmitted between applications over a computer network, greatly decreasing system development and maintenance costs for networks applications. The Java language has continued to grow from its initial form in the 1990s to meet the evolving needs of business communities. Today, versions of the Java language are available to meet the specific needs and challenges of enterprise and mobile applications. Java 2 Enterprise Edition (J2EE) provides a programmatic framework for developing robust distributed applications using specialized software platforms called application servers. J2EE application servers, such as BEA Systems Web Logic (http://www.bea.com), IBM's Web Sphere (http://www.ibm.com), and JBoss's open-source application server (http://www.jboss.org) provide all the middleware technology necessary for efficiently accessing remote databases, managing distributed transactions, creating message-driven applications, and developing Web-based user and application interfaces. In contrast, Java 2 Mobile Edition (J2ME) is a restricted version of the Java language specifically designed and optimized for use on mobile devices such as personal digital assistants and in-vehicle systems.

The recent adoption and proliferation of XML and XML-oriented middleware provides an alternative means for sharing data between systems and forms the basis of a new generation of interapplication data-sharing methods called Web services. Web services are similar to RPCs in that middleware responsible for formatting and transferring business data between systems exists on both client and server systems. Web services typically use a XML document format based on the simple object access protocol (SOAP) specification, developed jointly by Microsoft, IBM, and others to share data using commonly available Internet network protocols such as HTTP and TCP/IP for communication. Web services implement a service-oriented architecture (SOA), facilitating dynamic discovery and centralized service registries. These features allow client applications to automatically locate server applications provided by a business partner on the Internet and simultaneously discover all system interfaces and data formats necessary to enable a client application to couple to and interact with those services. This SOA model significantly reduces the complexity, cost, and time necessary to integrate disparate business systems.

Process-Oriented Integration

Process-oriented integration focuses on the logical sequencing of events and the processing of business information as it moves within and between business organizations. This form of e-B2B integration relies on business processes rather than technological foundations to increase competitive advantage. Process-oriented integration tends to be more strategic than tactical as results are often hard to measure in terms of traditional investments as they often involve developing trust relationships with business partners and involve sharing private and often confidential information in order to realize intangible benefits such as better products, increased customer satisfaction, and supply chain efficiencies. Sharing production forecasts and schedules with suppliers, for example, allows business partners to better plan their own production activities, which in turn can lead to lower costs overall as the guess work involved in anticipating demand can be removed and the likelihood of stock-outs diminished. Changes in production schedules can similarly be communicated, allowing suppliers to automatically adjust their own production schedules to match, thereby reducing waste and uncertainty and lowering inventories.

In its simplest form process-oriented integration can be implemented between a group of business partners by agreeing on a common technology platform to use for their internal systems and then deciding which processes they are willing to externalize as integration points. Establishing a common technology platform for business systems also establishes a common framework for sharing business information as data moving between businesses are guaranteed to be compatible and interchangeable. Many enterprise resource planning (ERP) systems such as SAP/R3 (http://www.sap.com) and Oracle's E-Business Applications Suite (http://www.oracle.com) are specifically engineered to facilitate this type of interoperability and provide integration points as part of the solution.

Evaluating and Selecting Integration Approaches

The wide variety of methods available for B2B system integration provides organizations in the planning phase of a B2B initiative with a number of alternatives. There are, however, several key issues that should be considered, including the level of effort necessary to integrate with new business partners and issues associated with security and privacy of both business systems and business information.

One of the key decisions to be made is determining the level of effort necessary for trading partners to couple and decouple from the trading environment. Facilitating integration by standardizing on internal systems such as SAP/R3, which requires specialized hardware, software, and connectivity environments, can be expensive and difficult to implement. Hershey Foods, for example, spent three years and $115 million implementing a software system from SAP. The new system was designed to replace a number of older systems and tie into supply chain management software from Manugistics and customer relationship management products from Siebel. Glitches in the ordering and shipping systems, however, resulted in a 12.4% drop in sales during the company's busiest quarter (Osterland, 2000).

A new generation of Internet-centric ERP software specifically designed to address implementation issues associated with sharing information across a supply chain is now available. ERP II enables companies that have already invested in ERP systems to leverage their existing investments and implement collaborative planning by upgrading their existing ERP systems (Bond et al., 2002). Other lightweight technologies like XML/SOAP-based Web services have been specifically engineered to provide points of integration between business systems and facilitate the flow of business information between organizations with relatively low costs of entry. A possible disbenefit of this relatively low cost of entry and ease-of-implementation is that trading partners can also couple to competitor systems with relative ease, thereby undermining trust relationships that might exist between companies.

When selecting technologies organizations should consider both the security of data as they move between their systems and those of their business partners, as well as the security of their own information systems. Organizations that expose internal systems to others over a computer network typically experience types of risk that do not affect more traditional organizations (Etteridge & Richardson, 2001), including theft of data and intellectual property, unauthorized access, and compromised customer privacy.

B2B E-COMMERCE CHALLENGES

Several types of challenges exist for companies planning an e-B2B strategy, including managing and valuing e-B2B projects and working within the many regulatory environments controlling e-B2B, as well as technical challenges associated with selecting, implementing, managing, and securing e-B2B technologies.

Management Challenges

Several significant management challenges that do not affect more traditional firms are associated with creating a successful and sustainable e-business. These challenges include accounting challenges associated with measuring true economic benefits of e-B2B activity, managing elevated levels of trust necessary between business partners, managing critical information technology infrastructures, and providing realistic expectations with respect to the benefits and costs of e-business implementations.

Measuring the tangible and intangible benefits of e-B2B investments is difficult for organizations and regulating bodies as many of the benefits arising from e-B2B activities are hard to isolate and quantify using purely economic measures but can affect how an investment is perceived by a company and its shareholders. Tangible benefits arising from e-B2B activities such as increased sales, decreased production time, and reduced waste can be estimated fairly accurately using traditional accounting methods. Other benefits such as increased customer satisfaction, heightened brand visibility, and stronger relationships with business partners, for example, are intangible benefits that are highly sought but difficult to measure. Similarly, benefits arising from increased global visibility through an electronic presence on the Internet might provide better hiring opportunities or more favorable investment opportunities for a company. Again, such benefits are extremely difficult to quantify but can significantly affect how a company is perceived and valued.

Coupling business processes through technological frameworks requires that participants trust each other with valuable and often confidential business information such as new product specifications, purchasing patterns, and production forecasts. As businesses move towards a pattern of sharing information in real time, a bond of trust must be established and proactively managed to ensure continued and mutual benefits for all companies involved. These trust relationships involve guaranteeing the security and confidentiality of data being shared, as well as guaranteeing and maintaining predefined levels of system performance and systems stability. Also important are agreements to apportion responsibility, establish procedures to manage routine maintenance, and upgrade cycles and determine minimum system availability.

IT groups in traditional companies are responsible for managing internal processes and providing support for other business functions within the organizations. These IT groups are often treated as overhead and run as cost centers, thereby reinforcing their supporting role with organizations. In contrast, IT organizations in successful e-businesses are often revenue generators and should be treated as competitive assets, allowing innovation within IT organizations to derive competitive advantage and help reduce costs. Information technology infrastructures within an e-business are foundations of business success and should be carefully managed to support the business goals of a company. The Hurwitz Report (Hurwitz Group, 2001) identifies several ways by which management solutions can maximize e-business success:

- Measuring the business impact of the infrastructure;
- Managing the infrastructure proactively;
- Ensuring availability and reliability of data;

- Securing transactions and data; and
- Deploying applications and services rapidly and reliably.

As e-businesses increasingly rely on electronic processes, potential consequences to a company and its business partners resulting from loss of service can be devastating. A survey of companies in 2001, for example, reports that 46% of companies surveyed would experience losses of up to $50,000 per hour, 28% would incur a loss of up to $250,000 per hour, and 26% would lose up to or over $1 million per hour through loss of e-business services (Contingency Planning Research, 2001).

Managing expectations of an e-business and effectively communicating potential benefits to business partners is another key factor in e-business success. After more than $1 billion had already been invested by the Boards of Grocery Manufacturers of America and Food Marketing Institute Trading Partners Alliance (TPA) in a variety of exchanges and electronic collaboration platforms, A.T. Kearney (2002) recommended several factors necessary to proactively encourage trading partners to join the alliance. Among these recommendations were:

- A need for better communication among partners to address common concerns over data synchronization;
- Education about the benefits of collaboration and implementating best practices; and
- Regular feedback through surveys and progress-tracking initiatives.

The need for individual companies, especially market leaders, to proactively encourage trading partners to join the trading partnership through training and sharing of best practices was also identified as a key success factor.

Monitoring and Regulation Challenges

Monitoring and regulating online businesses provides many challenges. These challenges associated with taxation, security, and privacy of e-business are more difficult to manage when applied in a global context where laws and ethics governing business are often conflicting rather than complementary. Standardizing accounting mechanisms for digital businesses and processes presents additional issues as traditional accounting principles must adapt to a digital business environment. Lastly, the global nature of the Internet creates issues for prosecuting those who attempt to disrupt or steal digital information, providing significant challenges for national and international legal organizations.

FASB, the U.S. Federal Accounting Standards Board, identifies several challenges to the accounting industry associated with the transition from a traditional paper-driven economy to one where business is transacted using digital documents. From an accounting perspective, there is no standard measure for determining the short- or long-term value of technology, knowledge capital, and intellectual property associated with implementing and managing e-business infrastructure. Companies, however, are investing huge amounts of resources in these activities that must be accounted for fairly. Valuing these intangible assets requires the accounting profession extend its province to nonfinancial areas of business operations and generate standard frameworks and metrics for reporting and tracking nonfinancial information (FASB, 2001).

E-B2B poses an even more complicated set of issues for those organizations charged with monitoring and regulating international business. The Internet compresses the natural geographic separation of businesses and related movement of products and money between these businesses, allowing business operations to easily span geopolitical borders. The Internet, however, is largely uncontrolled and business on the Internet follows suit. Governments of individual countries participating in online activities are responsible for regulating e-businesses within their borders and determining the degree of regulation, identifying legal bodies responsible for regulation, and determining the level to which they should accommodate rules and regulations established by other countries. There are, however, opposing forces at work within any country. Governments attempt to regulate the Internet in a way that stimulates their economies and encourages adoption and use. At the same time governments are responsible for protecting the rights of their citizens and existing businesses. It is not surprising that few Internet regulatory laws have been passed to date, even though e-B2B has been in place for many years. To further complicate the regulatory issue, the ubiquity of the Internet has resulted in a rapid expansion of businesses interoperating across international borders. Traditionally only large, well-financed companies could perform international commerce; today there are no limits to how small a multinational company can be.

As businesses and industries in general move toward higher degrees of digital collaboration issues with security and privacy of digital information being collected, stored, and transmitted as part of normal e-business operations become increasingly more important. Many of the regulatory laws that do exist are designed to protect personal and confidential business data. The United States has enacted legislation designed to protect personal finances and health care records from accidental or malicious exposure. The Health Insurance Portability and Accountability Act (HIPAA, 1996), for example, is an attempt to regulate movement, storage, and access to health care-related personal information through enforcement of privacy standards. HIPAA is a direct regulatory response within the United States to several well-publicized breaches of doctor–patient trust. Similarly, the Gramm–Leach–Bailey Act, promulgated by the Securities and Exchange Commission and Federal Trade Commission, outlines responsibilities of financial institutions for protecting the privacy of consumers' information and assessing liability for negligence (Personick & Patterson, 2003).

Regulating criminal activity associated with the Internet and e-business systems provides several problems for organizations and regulatory bodies. Different countries treat different types of computer attacks in different ways with little consensus as to the degree of criminality and severity of punishment. Turban et al. (2001) provide a comparison of computer crime legislation in several countries and note that attempting to hack a system, although legal in the United States, is illegal in the United Kingdom. However, successfully hacking a system and causing financial loss is criminal in both countries but punished far more severely in the United States where the crime carries a maximum penalty of 20 years in prison. With its global accessibility, the Internet presents a significant challenge to regulating hacking and other cybercrimes, as attacks levied against systems can be launched from countries with less-stringent regulations and lower rates of enforcement. In general, governmental intervention is primarily limited to identifying cybercriminals after an attack and attempting to prosecute perpetrators if they are in a country that has extradition treaties. The United States, for example, has caused international concern by successfully detaining and convicting foreign nationals accused of crimes against systems in the United States when the attacks were known to be launched from non-U.S.-based systems (U.S. Department of Justice, 2002). Not all cyberattacks, however, are malicious. So-called "white-hat" hackers often attack business systems as a means to draw public attention to issues of vulnerability with the intent of eliciting a general hardening of systems by the systems developers (Hulme, 2002).

Technological Challenges

Some of the most extreme information technology requirements found in the commercial business world are associated with designing and implementing large-scale e-business systems. Issues with the design and deployment of such systems include localizing applications for international users, managing quality of service, and protecting access to data and applications.

E-B2B is increasingly multinational, and differences in language and culture affect the usability and accuracy of these systems. Information shared across national and cultural borders must be both syntactically correct and unambiguous for all systems involved. Of particular importance to cross-cultural e-business systems is designing data storage and data processing systems that can accommodate locale-specific data and translate data between supported locales when necessary. Business data containing names, dates and times, addresses, telephone numbers, and currency present particular issues across locales as there are a large number of conventions and translations that might need to be accommodated. Microsoft's latest Windows platform, for example, supports over 130 separate locales (Microsoft, 2003).

Information services supporting e-B2B need to provide sufficient system functionality, capacity, and availability to meet planned demand. System demand translates loosely into estimating the number of transactions that will be processed by an information system in a given time period. Estimating this number requires understanding the demand on a system during normal operations and determining how demand might vary over the course of a single day, a week, a month, or year. System designers also need to plan sufficient capacity to accommodate special events, which can cause short-term increases in system use. Lastly, when designing e-B2B systems, system designers should understand how e-B2B interactions will translate into workload against other information systems in an organization. Internal ERP systems, for example, can be affected by increased activity resulting from external e-B2B systems. IT organizations should plan to match the capacity of internal systems with that of external e-B2B systems being designed so that the internal systems do not become the weak link in the processing chain.

Potentially sensitive information shared between businesses is at risk not only during transmission of information from one system to another, but also as it is stored on file servers and in databases accessible through computer networks. The general trend toward open systems poses transmission security issues as open systems often rely on text-based data formats such as EDI and XML. If intercepted, these documents can be read and understood by a variety of software publicly available on the Internet. Standards for encrypting XML documents are being developed but have yet to be universally adopted. Encryption technologies for securing data moving over the Internet between business partners, such as VPNs, are commonly available but rely on coordinating privacy schemes among businesses, including sharing encryption keys and developing effective implementation policies. To remain effective, such policies must be constantly revised and tuned to adapt to changing events.

Security and Privacy Challenges

There are many types of criminal activity associated with the Internet, ranging from petty acts of vandalism and copyright violations to organized systematic attacks with malicious intent to cause damage, financial loss, or in extreme cases, wholesale disruption of critical infrastructure. Additional threats to e-businesses arise internally from employees and ex-employees with access to systems containing proprietary and/or sensitive information and potential loss of critical systems due to hardware and software failures or widespread infrastructure failure such as a catastrophic loss of telecommunications systems or electrical grid. The first line of defense for any online organization must then be a well-planned and executed security policy that considers internal and external security threats as well as protection against exogenous events with potential to cause data loss and service disruption.

E-business security concerns generally fall into four main categories: loss of data integrity, loss of data privacy, loss of service, and loss of control (Otuteye, 2001). Creating an effective information security policy requires addressing these concerns through a number of major objectives: managing privacy and confidentiality, ensuring data integrity, maintaining systems availability, and non-repudiation (Proctor & Byrnes, 2002). Achieving the first objective requires identifying information within an organization that should be protected and, secondly, identifying those people or systems requiring access to it. As e-business often involves transferring proprietary information between business partners and/or customers, maintaining privacy and confidentiality of information necessitates providing protection for information as it is stored on computer systems and archive devices and also as the information is transferred between computer systems over a network.

Ensuring data integrity provides assurances that critical information is never damaged or changed in an inappropriate way. Managing this objective requires organizations protect access to information from unauthorized users and systems as well as protecting access to internal and external systems that could be used to change or corrupt data. Effectively achieving this objective requires organizations also consider broader issues of data recovery and disaster planning to prevent loss or corruption of information through human error, systems failure, or massive loss of critical infrastructure.

Managing systems availability requires ensuring that all systems and information are available to those who need it when it is needed. Achieving this objective requires planning against common causes of loss of availability such as denial of service (DoS) attacks and computer viruses that can affect the reliability and responsiveness of systems. Following the tragic events of 9/11/2001 in New York City, organizations are now considering holistic approaches to protecting access to business operations by also protecting access to critical applications such as e-mail and telecommunication systems, which their businesses and those of their business partners depend on (Garvy & McGee, 2002).

The last major objective, nonrepudiation, is a new approach to security management that can be used to verify claims and apportion responsibility in the case of liability (Otuteye, 2001). This objective is necessary to ensure that both parties in a business transaction are confident that they are dealing with the appropriate other party. Achieving nonrepudiation requires enabling an originator or recipient of a transaction to prove to a third party that their counterpart did take an action in question. For example, if one party orders a product from another party then later decides it was not needed and attempts to claim that the product was not, indeed, ordered by them, nonrepudiation would allow the claim to be validated or disapproved in a court of law. Today, nonrepudiation can be obtained through the use of digital signatures, confirmation services issuing digital receipts and timestamps, which can be used to prove that a document existed at a certain time (webopedia.com, 2003).

It is generally agreed that managing security of information for e-businesses requires proactively engaging in security practices rather than attempting to engineer security measures after systems have already been deployed. When designing appropriate security policies, e-business should consider several key factors:

- Security is expensive;
- Security is only as strong as its weakest link;
- Security can often get in the way of doing business;
- Security needs change as organizations and their systems evolve; and
- Security must be always on.

Further, as new technologies such as wireless wide- and local-area networks, Web services, and instant messaging enter the mainstream of enterprise information systems, new security threats arise that must be dealt with, requiring that organizations constantly re-evaluate their security needs.

B2B E-COMMERCE IN PERSPECTIVE

It is generally agreed that current rates of adoption and continuing pervasiveness of e-B2B activity across all business sectors and all types of industry indicate that e-B2B is and will remain a major driving force within the global economy. At the same time, however, e-B2B should be regarded as a nascent activity that is rapidly emerging and consequently exhibiting growing pains. Based on a survey of 134 companies around the world, the Cutter Consortium provides some interesting insight into e-B2B implementation experience to date (Cutter Consortium, 2000):

- Asked to rank the obstacles to e-business, respondents chose "benefits not demonstrated" as the number one obstacle, followed by financial cost and technological immaturity.
- Success with electronic supply chain management is mixed with half of those using it enjoying success rates of 76 to 100% and about a third experiencing success rates of 0 to 10%.

Similarly, Deloitte and Touche examining data from 300 U.S.- and U.K.-based companies in a wide variety of industries identifies a highly conservative trend toward e-business. Less than half the companies examined expect their e-business strategy to involve transforming business processes while the majority of companies expect their e-business strategy to be limited to simple Internet-based buying and selling. More telling is that only 28% of companies had developed a formal e-business strategy, the majority being in some stage of investigation (Rich, 2001).

E-business success stories, however, are highly compelling. Examples from General Motors, Federal Express, and Cisco clearly demonstrate the types of returns possible when e-business is implemented successfully. The bottom line is that performing business electronically is cheaper, more efficient, and more accurate than traditional means, providing a compelling set of factors for businesses to consider. These benefits, however, should be measured against the risks associated with increasing reliance on information technology and exposure of critical systems to unregulated telecommunication networks such as the Internet. Loss of access to business systems through systematic attacks such the DoS attacks experienced by several major Internet firms in February 2000, or simple system failures such as those experienced by eBay in June 1999, can result in interruptions of service and lead to significant short-term loss of revenues as well as long-term loss of investor confidence, which has shown not to reverse over time (Etteridge & Richardson, 2001).

Clearly, implementing an e-business strategy is highly technical, involving many facets of information technology new to most companies and indeed new to the information technology industry. Lack of knowledge about e-B2B technologies and its risks and rewards combine to make businesses cautious as they plan ahead for a connected future. These issues, however, can be overcome with time as the global corporate knowledge base grows, as more case studies illustrating successful and profitable implementations are available, and as e-enabling technology frameworks mature. A prerequisite for sustaining e-business, however, requires transforming the Internet into a system capable of promoting safe communication through regulation, monitoring, and prosecution of those who choose to maliciously interrupt the flow of e-business information. This goal must be planned and implemented in a global forum as the Internet and e-business necessarily exist in a global economy. The ultimate responsibility for information security, however, must start within each connected organization as effective security should be regarded as a competitive advantage with potentially significant fiscal and legal liabilities resulting from negligent and ineffective security practices.

ACKNOWLEDGMENTS

An earlier version of this chapter appears in *The Internet Encyclopedia* edited by Dr. Hossein Bigdoli and published by Wiley and Sons. The author is grateful for the comments and suggestions provided by the editor and reviewers on this and the earlier paper.

GLOSSARY

ActiveX Data Objects (ADO) Middleware developed by Microsoft Corp. for accessing local and remote databases from computers running a Windows-based operating system.

Application Programming Interface (API) Components of an application that allow other applications to connect to and interact with its data and services. APIs are usually published by the application developer as a formal library of functions.

Digital Signature A digital code that can be attached to an electronically transmitted message that can be used to uniquely identify the sender.

Dot-Com Companies that emerged during the Internet boom of the late 1990s with a focus on building applications for or selling products on the World Wide Web. Dot-coms were usually funded by large amounts of venture and private equity capital.

E-Business All types of business activity performed using electronic means; has a wider context than e-commerce and includes business exchanges that involve interorganizational support, knowledge sharing, and collaboration at all levels.

E-Commerce A form of e-business that results in a business transaction being performed using electronic means such as a buy or sell event.

Electronic Data Interchange (EDI) One of the first forms of e-business used to pass transactions in the form of electronic documents between computer systems often over private telecommunication lines or value-added networks; still used by many businesses today.

Electronic Funds Transfer (EFT) An early form of e-commerce used to transfer money electronically between banks.

Enterprise Resource Planning (ERP) A collection of applications designed to manage all aspects of a business. ERP systems are designed to integrate sales, manufacturing, human resources, logistics, accounting, and other enterprise functions within an organization.

Intermediary A company that adds value or assists other companies in performing supply chain activities such as connecting suppliers with buyers.

Java Database Connectivity (JDBC) Middleware used for accessing remote databases from an application written using the Java programming language.

Message-Oriented Middleware (MOM) Middleware used to integrate applications using a system of messages and message queues; allows systems to share data using an asynchronous processing model.

Middleware Software that enables the access and transport of business data between different information systems often over a computer network.

Open Database Connectivity (ODBC) Middleware originally designed by Microsoft Corp. to access remote databases from Windows platforms using a standard API. ODBC has since been ported to other platforms including UNIX and Linux.

Protocol A standard for the format and content of data passed between computers over a computer network. Protocols are often maintained by independent organizations such as the World Wide Web Consortium.

Remote Procedure Call (RPC) Middleware technology originally developed for UNIX systems for sharing data and methods between applications over a network.

Structured Query Language (SQL) A computer language developed by IBM in the 1970s for manipulating data stored in relational database systems; became the standard language of databases in the 1980s.

Supply Chain The end-to-end movement of goods and services from one company to another during a manufacturing process.

Transaction A record of a business exchange such as a sell or a buy event.

Transmission Control Protocol/Internet Protocol (TCP/IP) Communication protocols originally developed as part of ARPAnet that today form the basic communication protocols of the Internet.

Tymnet An early value-added network developed by Tymshare Inc. used by companies for transferring computer files between computer systems; the largest commercial computer network in the United States, but was later sold to MCI.

UNIX-to-UNIX-Copy (UUCP) A utility and protocol available on UNIX systems allowing two computers to share files using a serial connection or telephone network.

Value-Added Network (VAN) A form of computer network connection often between two companies to perform e-business managed by a third party; initially used to transfer EDI documents; modern VANs operate over the Internet.

Virtual Private Network (VPN) A form of network connection between two sites over the public Internet that uses encrypted data transmission to provide a private exchange of data.

CROSS REFERENCES

See *Click-and-Brick Electronic Commerce; EDI Security; Electronic Commerce; Electronic Payment Systems; Extranets: Applications, Development, Security, and Privacy; Internet Basics.*

REFERENCES

Aberdeen Group. (2001a). *FedEx taps e-procurement to keep operations soaring, cost grounded*. Retrieved November 16, 2002, from http://www.ariba.com/request_info/request_information.cfm?form=white_paper.

Aberdeen Group. (2001b). E-procurement: Finally ready for prime time. Retrieved November 16, 2002, from http://www.ariba.com/request_info/request_information.cfm?form=white_paper.

Bond, B., Genovese, Y., Miklovic, D., Wood, N., Zrimsek, B., & Rayner, N. (2002). ERP is dead—Long liveERP II. Retrieved January 18, 2003, from http://www.gartner.com/DisplayDocument?id=314701

Colkin, E. (2002, September 16). Hastening settlements reduces trading risk. *Information Week, 24*.

Computer Security Institute (2003). *CSI/FBI computer crime and security survey.* Retrieved November 16, 2003, from http://www.gocsi.com.

Contingency Planning Research. (2001). *2001 Cost of downtime survey.* Retrieved January 18, 2003, from http://www.contingencyplanningresearch.com.

Covisint. (2002). *Covisint Corporate Backgrounder*. White Paper, Retrieved January 18, 2003, from http://www.covisint.com.

Cutter Consortium. (2000). *E-business: Trends, strategies and technologies.* Retrieved November 16, 2002, from http://www.cutter.com/itreports/ebustrend.html.

Davis, W. S., & Benamati, J. (2002). *E-commerce basics: Technology foundations and e-business applications.* Boston: Addison–Wesley.

Emiliani, M. L., & Stec, D. J. (2002). *Aerospace parts suppliers' reaction to online reverse auctions*. Retrieved January 18, 2003, from http://www.theclbm.com/research.html.

Etteridge, M., & Richardson, V. J. (2001). Assessing the risk in e-commerce. In *Proceedings of the 35th Annual Hawaii International Conference on System Sciences*.

Financial Accounting Standards Board (FASB). (2001). *Business and financial reporting, challenges from the new economy* (Financial Accounting Series Special Report 219-A). Norwalk, CT: Financial Accounting Foundation.

Gartner Group. (2003). Retrieved November 9, 2003, from http://www4.gartner.com/press_releases/pr7aug2003b.html.

Garvy, M. J., & McGee, M. K. (2002, September 9). New priorities. *Information Week,* 36–40.

Greenstein, M., O'Leary, D., Ray, A. W., & Vasarhelyi, M. (forthcoming, 2005). *Information systems and business processes for accountants.* New York: McGraw Hill.

HIPAA. (1996, August 21). *Health Insurance Portability and Accountability Act of 1996, Public Law 104-191.* Retrieved November 16, 2002, from http://aspe.hhs.gov/admnsimp/pl104191.htm.

Hulme, G. (2002). With friends like these. *Information Week.* Retrieved November 16, 2002, from http://www.informationweek.com/story/IWK20020705S0017.

Hurwitz Group (2001). *E-business infrastructure management: The key to business success.* Framingham, MA: Hurwitz Group.

Kearney, A. T. (2002). *GMA-FMI Trading Partner Alliance: Action plan to accelerate trading partner electronic collaboration.* Retrieved November 16, 2002, from http://www.gmabrands.com/publications/docs/ecollexec.pdf.

Kearney, A. T. (2003). *E-Business Investment Benchmarking Study: August 2003.* Retrieved November 9, 2003, from http://www.line56.com/research/download/L56_ATKearney_Benchmarking_Research_0703.pdf.

Konicki, S. (2001, August 27). Great sites: Covisint. *Information Week.* Retrieved November 16, 2002, from http://www.informationweek.com/story/IWK20010824S0026.

Li, E. (2003). From e-commerce to e-business. *International Journal of Electronic Business, 1*(1), 1–2.

Linthicum, D. S. (2001). *B2B application integration: E-business enable your enterprise.* Boston: Addison-Wesley.

Microsoft. (2000). *MS market—Intranet-based procurement.* Retrieved March 22, 2005, from http://www. microsoft.com/downloads/details.aspx?FamilyID=00B0C78C-6B12-4E2D-ABC7-D9EDCB839128&displaylang=en.

Microsoft. (2003). *Global development and computing portal: Configurable language and culture settings*. Retrieved November 8, 2003, from http://www.microsoft.com/globaldev/reference/localetable.mspx.

Norris, G., Hurley, J., Hartley, K., Dunleavy, J., & Balls, J. (2000). *E-business and ERP: Transforming the enterprise.* New York: John Wiley & Sons.

Osterland, A. (2000, January 1). Blaming ERP. *CFO Magazine.* Retrieved November 16, 2002, from http://www.cfo.com/article/1,5309,1684,00.html.

Otuteye, E. (2001). *Framework for E-Business Information Security Management*. Retrieved November 6, 2003, from http://ebusinessroundtable.ca/documents/Framework_for_e-business_security.pdf.

Personick, S. D., & Patterson, C. A. (Eds.). (2003) *Critical information infrastructure protection and the law*. National Academy Press: Washington, DC.

Proctor, P. E., & Byrnes, F. C. (2002). *The secured enterprise: Protecting your information assets*. Englewood Cliffs, NJ: Prentice Hall.

Rich, N. (2001). *e-business: The organisational implications.* Retrieved March 22, 2005, from http://www.deloitte.com/dtt/research/0,1015,sid%253D3220%2526cid%253D6585,00.html

Schifrin, M. (2003). *B2Bs new pace*. Retrieved October 8, 2003, from http://www.forbes.com/best/2003/1002/003.html.

Schneider, G. P. (2002). *Electronic commerce* (3rd ed.). Canada: Thomson Course Technology.

Slater, D. (2002, April 1). GM shifts gears. *CIO Magazine.* Retrieved November 16, 2002, from http://www.cio.com/archive/040102/matters.html.

Strategis. (2002). *Electronic commerce in Canada.* Retrieved November 16, 2002, from http://ecom.ic.gc.ca/english/research/b2b/index.html.

Turban, E., King, D., Lee, J., Warkentin, M., & Chung, H. M. (2002). *Electronic commerce: A managerial perspective* (2nd ed.). Englewood Cliffs, NJ: Prentice Hall.

U.S. Department of Justice. (2002). *Russian computer hacker sentenced to three years in prison.* Retrieved January 19, 2003, from http://www.cybercrime.gov/gorshkovSent.htm.

webopedia.com. (2003). Retrieved November 11, 2003, from http://www.webopedia.com/TERM/N/nonrepudiation.html.

Wichmann, T. (2002). *Business-to-business marketplaces in Germany—Status quo, opportunities and challenges.* Retrieved March 22, 2005, from http://www.bbriefings.com/pdf/967/48.pdf.

Yee, A., & Apte, A. (2001). *Integrating your e-business enterprise.* Indianapolis, IN: Sams.

FURTHER READING

Small Business Administration (SBA) (2000). *Small business expansions in electronic commerce: A look at how small firms are helping shape the fastest growing segments of e-commerce.* Washington, DC: U.S. Small Business Administration Office of Advocacy.

Stewart, T. R. (1998). *The e-business tidal wave: Perspectives on business in cyberspace.* Deloitte Touche & Tohmatsu.

Click-and-Brick Electronic Commerce

Charles Steinfield, *Michigan State University*

INTRODUCTION

Despite the early fascination with dot-com companies, there is a growing recognition that the Internet is unlikely to displace traditional channels anytime soon, at least in the world of business-to-consumer (B2C) commerce. Rather, many traditional enterprises have moved to integrate e-commerce into their channel mix, using the Internet to supplement existing brick-and-mortar retail channels (Steinfield, Bouwman, & Adelaar, 2002). Electronic commerce researchers now consider the combination of physical and Web channels to be a distinct electronic commerce business model, most commonly referring to it as a "click-and-brick" or "click-and-mortar" approach (Laudon & Traver, 2004).

In this chapter, a broad overview of the click-and-brick approach to e-commerce is provided, with some attention to the information security implications of this form of e-commerce. The focus is on the use of the click-and-brick approach by firms selling consumer products and services via a combination of physical and Internet retail channels, given the relative prevalence of this situation in the e-commerce arena. Much of the discussion is also relevant to other types of organizations that rely on both Internet and physical channels, such as those involved in education and health care. In the first section, a brief look at the current e-commerce situation highlights the overall importance of taking an integrated brick-and-click approach to e-commerce development. In the second section, a detailed examination of the sources of synergy between traditional and Internet-based channels is provided. The third section introduces the dangers of product and channel conflict and points out possible management strategies to improve channel integration. The fourth section highlights the potential benefits that firms may reap when pursuing a more integrated approach to e-commerce. The fifth section introduces four brief cases that give concrete examples of click-and-brick strategies. The sixth section discusses several critical factors that may inhibit firms' attempts to more tightly integrate physical and Internet sales channels and introduces some recent evidence that illustrates the degree to which many retailers find it difficult to do so. The seventh section discusses information security issues in the click-and-brick model. Finally, the chapter closes with several conclusions regarding the importance of the click-and-brick approach in electronic commerce research and practice.

CLICK-AND-BRICK E-COMMERCE OVERVIEW

Many types of companies can be considered click-and-brick firms, including retailers of tangible products, sellers of financial and other services, health care providers, and educational organizations extending learning services via the Internet. Even nonprofit organizations have employed a click-and-brick approach as they seek new ways of reaching and extending service to their constituents. Essentially, all click-and-brick firms have both Internet and physical outlets and seek synergies between them to reduce costs, differentiate products and services, and find new sources of revenue. In the B2C area, electronic commerce can be considered a marketing channel, which can be defined as a means to interact with end consumers. Many firms rely on a mix of different channels such as physical stores, catalog sales, and e-commerce. Firms pursuing channel integration attempt to tightly coordinate the use of channels, even within a single sales activity, to improve their profitability (Friedman

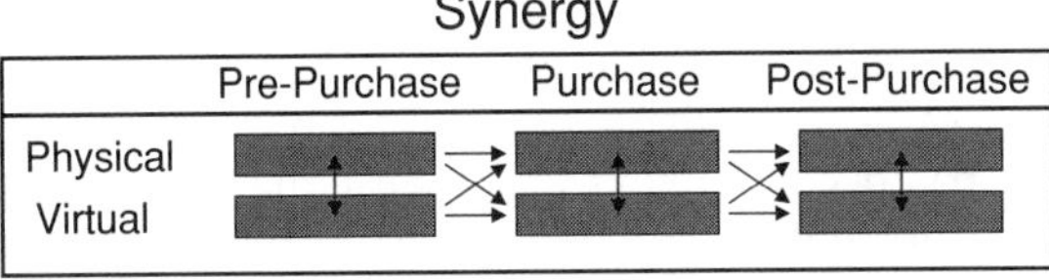

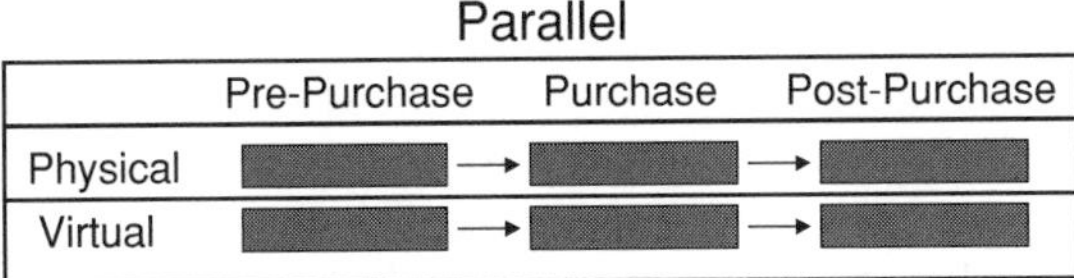

Figure 1: Contrasting Synergy with Parallel Approaches with Click-and-Brick E-Commerce.

& Furey, 1999). It is therefore helpful to distinguish the truly integrated click-and-brick approaches from those that treat electronic commerce more as a separate and parallel channel. The difference is illustrated in Figure 1. In the parallel case, customers are not able to move easily between electronic commerce and traditional channels. For example, many firms require that goods ordered online be returned directly to the e-commerce subsidiary, rather than through physical retail outlets. In the integrated, or synergy approach, customers are able to move seamlessly between channels as they interact with a firm. For example, a customer may do product research and initiate an order online but pick up the merchandise and obtain after-sales service in a physical outlet.

In the early years of electronic commerce, many in the industry felt that pure Internet firms (the dot-coms) had significant economic advantages over traditional firms. As a result, many traditional firms chose a parallel approach to the Internet in an attempt to avoid saddling e-commerce divisions with the burdens of higher costs and reduced innovativeness that they felt characterized their traditional physical channels. The widespread failure of dot-com firms, however, forced traditional retailers to rethink this approach and seek out synergies. Laudon and Traver (2004) noted that traditional retailers are replacing all but the most established dot-coms (e.g., Amazon) on the lists of top e-commerce sites. The electronic commerce activities of traditional retailers have helped to maintain a steady growth in online sales during the period in which large numbers of dot-com enterprises have failed. The U.S. Commerce Department estimated that the number of people who had purchased a product or engaged in banking online more than doubled between 2000 and 2001, growing from 13.3% of the U.S. population in August 2000 to more than 29% in September 2001 (National Telecommunications and Information Administration [NTIA], 2002). Additionally, the NTIA (2002) reported that more than a third of Americans, and fully two-thirds of the Internet users, now use the Internet to obtain product information. Meanwhile, the U.S. Census Bureau continues to measure strong growth in online sales relative to total retail sales, based on a panel of more than 11,000 retailers (U.S. Census Bureau, 2004). Online purchases for the first quarter of 2004 grew by over 28% from the first quarter of 2003, compared to 8.8% for total retail sales. Although still only about 2% of total retail sales in the United States, the proportion has increased steadily since measurement began in 1999. It is important to note as well that these figures underestimate total consumer-oriented e-commerce activity, because the census does not include online travel, financial services, and ticket agencies in their retail sample. Figures in other developed parts of the world such as Europe reveal similar growth of e-commerce activity (see, for example, the eBusiness Watch web site at http://www.ebusiness-watch.org). In essence, the steady growth of online sales suggests that e-commerce has become a mainstream activity, with an increasing number of major retailers now integrating it into their channel mix to supplement brick-and-mortar assets (Otto & Chung, 2000; Rosen & Howard, 2000; Steinfield, Adelaar, & Lai, 2002). Clearly all retailers should be carefully assessing their e-commerce strategy. Surprisingly, the evidence described in the later section "Click-and-Brick E-Commerce in Practice" suggests that a majority of retailers, however, are still reluctant to do so.

SOURCES OF SYNERGY BETWEEN TRADITIONAL AND E-COMMERCE CHANNELS

Click-and-brick firms have many potential sources of synergy not necessarily available to pure Internet firms or traditional firms without an e-commerce channel. Borrowing from classic competitive advantage theory (see Porter, 1985), such sources of synergy include common infrastructures, common operations, common marketing, common customers, and other complementary assets that can be shared between e-commerce and physical outlets.

Common Infrastructures

E-commerce channels can make use of a variety of existing infrastructures such as logistics or information technology (IT) systems to reduce costs or offer capabilities that would be difficult for dot-com firms to match. An example of the use of a common logistics infrastructure would be when a firm relies on the same warehouses and trucks for handling the distribution of goods for e-commerce activities as it does for delivery to its own retail outlets. Likewise, if a firm has a capable IT infrastructure, including product and customer databases, inventory systems, and a high-speed Internet protocol network with high bandwidth connections to the Internet, the adoption and use of Internet-based commerce can be enhanced. Firms can even use their Internet access to offer e-commerce services to customers who are actually in a store or branch—for example, via kiosks.

Common Operations

Existing retail operations can also be put to good use in support of e-commerce, permitting integrated applications to emerge. For example, an order processing system shared between e-commerce and physical channels may enable improved tracking of customers' movements between channels, in addition to potential cost savings.

Common Marketing

E-commerce and physical channels may also share common marketing and sales assets, such as a common product catalog, a sales force that understands the products and customer needs and directs potential buyers to each channel, or advertisements and promotions that draw attention to both channels.

Common Buyers

Instead of competing with each other, or pursuing different target markets, e-commerce channels and physical outlets in click-and-brick firms often target the same potential buyers. This enables a click-and-brick firm to be able to meet customers' needs for both convenience and immediacy, enhancing customer service and improving retention.

Other Complementary Assets

There are many other types of complementary assets that click-and-brick firms possess that purely Internet firms may not. The management literature, for example, notes such additional complementary assets as existing supplier and distributor relationships and experience in the market. As with the other sources of synergy, to the extent firms are able to share these assets across channels, they will be better able to take advantage of an innovation such as e-commerce (Afuah & Tucci, 2001; Teece, 1986).

Of course, click-and-brick firms also obtain many of the same benefits from the use of the Internet channel as other Internet companies. Certainly the Internet channel affords the possibility for 24-hours-a-day, seven-days-a-week customer access; lower cost access to many new markets; the opportunity to develop and maintain a community of customers; and an efficient communication channel for customer input.

MANAGING CHANNEL CONFLICT IN MULTICHANNEL FIRMS

The integration of e-commerce with existing physical channels is a challenging undertaking that can create problems for management. More specifically, firms with multiple channels may fall prey to a variety of channel conflicts. Channel conflicts can occur when the alternative means of reaching customers (e.g., a Web-based store) implicitly or explicitly competes with or bypasses existing physical channels and are nothing new to e-commerce (Stern, El-Ansary, & Coughlan, 1996). One danger is that these conflicts result in one channel simply cannibalizing sales from the other. This is particularly a problem when there are clear cost, convenience, or other advantages for customers using e-commerce, causing them to substitute Internet channels for traditional ones. Such cannibalization of sales becomes a strong threat to company viability if it is difficult to capture larger revenues online. Media companies such as newspaper companies, although not exactly brick-and-mortar firms in a traditional sense, have experienced such product-channel conflicts. This is exacerbated by customers' unwillingness to pay for online information or entertainment, necessitating free online versions that steal subscriptions from physically distributed media products. Some of the loss is made up by increased advertising revenue from online channels, but it has become increasingly clear that such business models are not sustainable in the current environment (Laudon & Traver, 2004). Additional, and potentially even more damaging, problems for the content industries that sell music and other nonperishable content (i.e., not news) arise from piracy and the massive and unlawful distribution of copyrighted content among Internet users. The rise of online music stores such as Apple's iTunes Music Store demonstrates that the Internet can be a powerful distribution channel for digitized content, threatening established physical channels. Clearly, the product–channel conflicts experienced by companies in the content industry represent a significant challenge. The review in this chapter focuses on a narrower definition of click-and-brick firms, however, in which actual click-and-brick outlets exist to support transactions with customers. Hence, this chapter does not deal directly with issues of copyright and piracy.

Cannibalization of sales is not only a problem for content firms. Price conflicts may arise for any click-and-brick firm when pressures to offer lower prices online surface and impact the attractiveness of goods in the traditional retail outlets (Turban, King, Lee, & Viehland, 2004). Perceived threats caused by competition and conflict across channels can have other harmful effects, including limited cooperation across the channels caused by staff conflicts, brand confusion caused by conflicting advertising and promotion strategies, problems when customers attempt to engage in transactions using the two uncoordinated channels, and even sabotage of one channel by the other (Friedman & Furey, 1999; Turban et al., 2004). Management must act to diffuse conflicts and ensure the necessary alignment of goals, coordination and control, and development of capabilities to achieve synergy benefits (Steinfield et al., 2002).

Goal Alignment

One of the first tasks for managers of click-and-brick firms is to ensure that all employees agree that an e-commerce channel is needed and that they will support it. This represents a process of goal alignment. Aligning goals across physical and virtual channels implies that all employees involved realize that the parent firm benefits from sales originating in either channel. One problem faced by click-and-brick firms is that the contributions made by the Internet channel may be intangible and difficult to measure. Managers must be open to such intangible benefits and not, for example, evaluate e-commerce divisions purely on the basis of online-only sales and profitability. For example, the improved communication with customers offered by Internet channels may enable firms to better understand customer satisfaction and needs, yielding better products and services and long-run customer retention. Such benefits may not show up in pure Internet sales figures, however. Moreover, there must be agreement as to what types of customers (e.g., existing versus new) are to be targeted by the new e-commerce channel. In essence, to avoid channel conflict, management must be proactive in obtaining the support of all employees, building consensus about the goals, methods of evaluating success, and targets for e-commerce. If management simply puts an e-commerce division into place without this goal alignment step, existing employees may feel threatened and may be uncooperative.

Coordination and Control Measures

In addition to obtaining consensus on goals, explicit coordination and control mechanisms are needed to move a click-and-brick firm more in the direction of integrated, rather than parallel channels. First, it is important for click-and-brick firms to design for interoperability across channels, so that customers may move freely between online and physical retail outlets. For example, customers may want to search a particular store's inventory from their own home computer to see whether a specific item is in stock. They may want the store to hold the item for them to pick up on their way home, rather than have it delivered. This implies that the online system connects and interoperates with the store system.

Another example of explicit coordination is the use of each channel to promote the other. For example, an online visitor may be informed about various in-store special sales, just as an in-store customer may be told about particular complementary services found on the click-and-brick firm's Web site. The use of kiosks in stores, for example, can directly enable customers on premises to access additional information, services, or promotions at precisely the moment they are considering a specific purchase. Cross-promotions enhance the perception that all the arms of the click-and-brick business are working together to add value for customers. They also create payoffs from e-commerce that can reduce resistance, such as when online promotions generate greater in-store traffic.

One of the most critical management issues for click-and-brick firms is to provide real incentives to employees to encourage cross-channel cooperation. Imagine a situation where store managers know that any time a customer buys something online instead of in the store, it represents lost revenue and lower compensation. Store personnel will invariably encourage customers to buy in the store, because this provides employees with real income. E-commerce sales may help improve customer relations, but no rational salesperson will knowingly direct customers to a sales channel that only ends up reducing his or her income. In many successful click-and-brick firms, efforts have been made to allocate online sales to particular establishments, so that e-commerce does not succeed at the expense of physical outlets. This often is possible when customers have accounts tied to a particular establishment, and online sales from specific accounts are credited to the home establishment. Another way of allocating online sales to a physical outlet is to use the address of the customer.

Finally, click-and-brick firms often find that they are able to capitalize on the unique strengths of each sales channel, affording the possibility for some degree of channel specialization (Steinfield et al., 2002). For example, costs for certain types of transactions may indeed be less in an online environment, suggesting that companies should encourage customers to use more efficient channels when possible. Banks, for example, have long attempted to persuade customers to use ATMs for routine cash transactions, rather than coming to a branch and occupying the services of a teller. On the other hand, many financial transactions require expert advice and counseling and are best done in-person at a branch. Hence, click-and-brick banks following a channel specialization strategy might offer customers incentives such as better interest rates or lower fees in return for the use of more efficient online channels for routine transactions like money transfers or bill payments. When more "advice-sensitive" transactions are sought, customers would be directed to their local physical bank branch (Steinfield et al., 2002).

When there is potential for severe product–channel conflicts, such as when customers decide to forego a newspaper or magazine subscription to read free content online, a channel specialization strategy may offer a viable alternative. For example, some newspaper and magazine companies derive additional revenue from their online versions using the unique search and archive advantages of the Web-based channel. A specific niche segment of their market may willingly pay for the ability to research back issues and articles on certain topics. This approach to adding value to an online version to encourage payment has been tried by such publications as the *Wall Street Journal* (Laudon & Traver, 2004).

Capability Development

In many situations, traditional firms may lack important competencies needed to achieve synergy benefits with e-commerce. For example, traditional firms may lack Web development skills or logistics skills needed to serve distant markets. Indeed, the ability to serve remote customers is an important prerequisite to successful Web-based commerce, which explains why catalog companies such as Lands' End have experienced so much success with e-commerce. It fits well with their existing capabilities and adds value in the form of enhanced transaction efficiencies and lower costs. When lacking such capabilities, alliances may be more useful than attempting to develop a virtual channel in-house. Managers must recognize whether the requisite competencies are present in the existing traditional company and, if a partner is needed, must carefully construct an alliance that ensures that their e-commerce partner is not simply siphoning business from physical retail outlets.

POTENTIAL BENEFITS OF AN INTEGRATED CHANNEL APPROACH

Once click-and-brick companies recognize the various sources of synergy across channels and develop management strategies to avoid conflicts and encourage cooperation across channels, numerous benefits may result. Four broad areas of benefit include (a) lower costs, (b) increased differentiation through value-added services, (c) improved trust, and (d) geographic and product market extension. The potential benefits from physical and virtual integration are discussed in this section.

Lower Costs

Cost savings may occur in a number of areas, including labor, inventory, marketing and promotion, and distribution. Labor savings result when costs are switched to consumers for such activities as looking up product information, filling out forms, and relying on online technical assistance for after-sales service. Inventory savings arise when firms find that they can avoid having to stock infrequently purchased goods at local outlets, while still offering the full range of choices to consumers via the Internet. Marketing and promotion efficiencies are garnered when each channel is used to inform consumers about services and products available in the other. Delivery savings may result from using the physical outlet as the pickup location for online purchases or as the initiation point for local deliveries.

Differentiation through Value-Added Services

Physical and virtual channel synergies can be exploited at various stages in a transaction to help differentiate products and add value. Examples of prepurchase services include various online information aids to help assess needs and select appropriate targets, or, conversely, opportunities in the physical environment to test products. Examples of purchase services include ordering, customization, and reservation services, as well as easy access to complementary products and services. Post-purchase services include online account management, social community support, loyalty programs, and various after-sales activities that may be provided either online or in the physical store. Typical opportunities are in the areas of installation, repair, service reminders, and training. Although many of these value-added services are potentially available to single-channel vendors, combined deployment of such services (e.g., online purchase of computer with in-store repair or training) can enhance differentiation and lock-in effects (Shapiro & Varian, 1999).

Across all transaction stages, the improved communications from the Internet channel (assuming a well-developed and fully functional site) can yield better insights into customer needs and wants. Such customer relationship management can ultimately add value for both parties over the lifetime of a customer's interaction with a click-and-brick firm, offering benefits in excess of the actual online sales by enhancing loyalty and retention.

Improved Trust

Three reasons for improved trust, relative to pure Internet firms, derive from the physical presence of click-and-brick firms, including reduced consumer risk, affiliation with and embeddedness in recognized local social and business networks, and the ability to leverage brand awareness. Lower perceived risk results from the fact that there is an accessible location to which goods can be returned or complaints can be registered. Affiliation and embeddedness in a variety of social networks may facilitate the substitution of social and reputational governance for expensive contracts or legal fees (Granovetter, 1985). For example, an online customer may be more prone to trust the Web site of a business when the store manager is a member of his or her church or when the customer's business and the online vendor are both members of the same chamber of commerce. Such ties are more likely to exist between geographically proximate buyers and sellers, suggesting that there may indeed be a preference for doing business with firms already physically present in the local market. Finally, marketing theorists have long recognized the power of branding as a means of building consumer confidence and trust in a product (Kotler, 1999). Established firms are able to leverage their familiar name to make it easier for consumers to find and trust their affiliated online services.

Geographic and Product Market Extension

Adding a virtual channel can help extend the reach of a firm beyond its traditional physical outlets, addressing new geographic markets, new product markets, and new types of buyers. Those in other geographic markets may be new or former customers who have moved away. Virtual channels can also extend the product scope and product depth of physical channels by enabling firms to offer new products that they do not have to stock locally. Moreover, firms may add new revenue-generating information services online that would not be feasible to offer in physical outlets. Finally, the Internet may help reach customers within an existing market who may not have visited the physical outlet but are otherwise attracted to the virtual channel due to its special characteristics.

SUMMARY OF THE CLICK-AND-BRICK FRAMEWORK

The click-and-brick framework elements can be assembled into the summary framework portrayed in Figure 2. The framework directs our attention to the sources of synergy, the need for management strategies to capitalize on click-and-brick applications, and the potential benefits that can result.

EXPLORING THE FRAMEWORK WITH SEVERAL CLICK-AND-BRICK CASES

The framework is best illustrated by describing several cases of click-and-brick firms. These examples were selected and adapted from a series of click-and-brick cases developed by Steinfield et al. (2002). Among their cases (the actual firm names were not reported based on the wishes of the interviewed companies) were a specialty retailer, a business-to-business (B2B) building materials supplier, an automobile manufacturer selling through dealerships, and a financial services firm. Each represents a different basic business arrangement—a multichannel retailer operating in the B2C arena, a B2B wholesaler, a manufacturer promoting sales to consumers through an affiliated, but independently owned, network of dealerships, and a firm selling information and services rather than tangible products. They nicely illustrate the robustness of the click-and-brick approach.

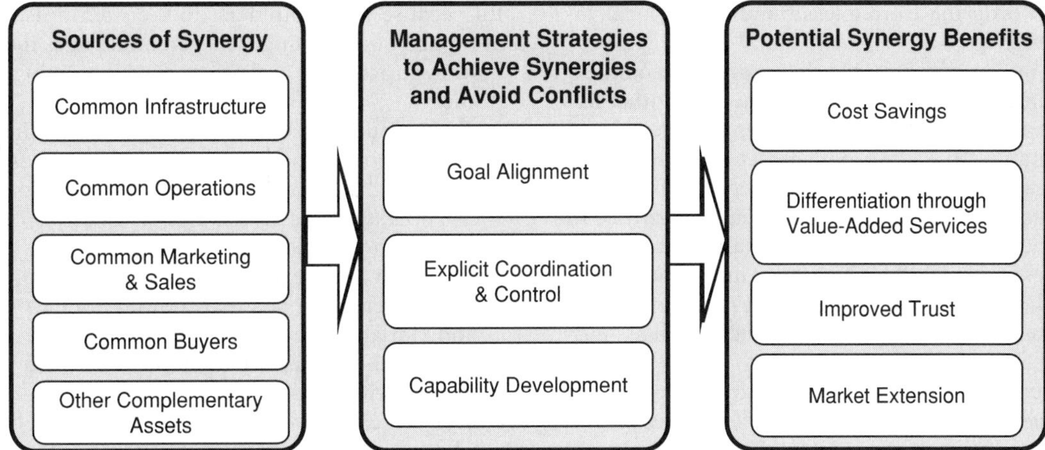

Figure 2: A Comprehensive Click-and-Brick Model (Adapted from Steinfield, Adelaar, & Lai, 2002).

An Electronics Retailer

This company is one of the largest specialty retailers of consumer electronics, personal computers, entertainment software, and appliances with more than 400 stores. The firm recently rolled out a new e-commerce site that featured both a deeper selection of products and a tighter integration with its traditional physical stores. The click-and-brick design strategy enables the firm to benefit from a range of synergies between their virtual and physical channels. The goal is to be "channel agnostic," letting customers choose whichever channel or combination of channels best suits their needs.

A number of sources of synergy are available to the firm. One key source is the firm's exploitation of a common IT infrastructure between their e-commerce and store channels. It accomplished this by tightly integrating the Internet operations with existing databases and other legacy systems. The firm also consciously capitalized on common operations, especially in terms of purchasing, inventory management, and order processing. That common marketing and common buyers were a source of synergy is evident in their emphasis on replicating and leveraging the store brand in their online services.

One of the services enabled by the tight IT integration allows online customers to check out the inventory of individual stores, so that they might order merchandise for immediate pickup in the nearest store. To achieve this value-added service and derive the differentiation benefit from it, the service had to be supported by a change in business processes that ensured interoperability across the two channels. For example, if only one or two items that an online purchaser desires are in stock, in-store customers might claim them by the time the Web customer arrives for pickup. To avoid this situation, store personnel must be notified that an online customer has requested an item for pickup. Then employees remove the item from the shelf and send an e-mail confirmation to the online customer. To ensure that stores cooperated with this new capability, management incentives were also considered to avoid or diffuse potential channel conflicts. In particular, the company included performance in fulfilling online orders as one of the parameters influencing store manager compensation.

This seemingly simple service thus reflects the main components of the framework. Several sources of synergy come into play. First, the firm built the service by tying the Internet to a common, integrated IT infrastructure. Second, it supports the service by using existing store inventory that was warehoused and delivered using common logistics infrastructure. Third, the shoppers can provide payment that is credited to the store, using existing operational systems such as credit card verification and approval systems already in place. Finally, the service targets common buyers, that is, people living near existing physical stores.

Management initiatives to achieve synergy and avoid conflict are also evident in this simple example. The online service depended on the cooperation of store personnel, reflecting a need for goal alignment. This was achieved by developing a service that brought traffic into the store, rather than simply bypassing it altogether. Moreover, management recognized that the Internet could assist in prepurchase activities, even if the eventual sale was consummated in the store. It did not require the e-commerce channel to generate its own profits. Additionally, it attended to the need for explicit coordination and control by developing a business process that ensured cross-channel interoperability. Finally, it created an incentive system that rewarded store personnel for their cooperation with the e-commerce channel.

Finally, the benefits of this one service are also captured well by the framework. Consider the cost savings in labor that stores accrue when customers search for products online, conduct research, order the product, and even make payment ahead of time, all without needing the assistance of a single employee. In terms of differentiation, this represents a prepurchase and purchase service that would be difficult for a non–click-and-brick firm to offer. It caters to the different needs and wants of store and online customers, improving satisfaction. Because of the tie-in to the local store, which is also part of a well-known national chain, customers perceive much lower risk than they would if ordering from a less familiar, nonlocal Internet business.

The tight integration between the e-commerce and existing retail infrastructure offers this firm many other advantages derived from the same sources of synergy and enabled by many of the same management strategies. For example, because of their integrated approach, customers who order products online with home delivery are able to return products to their local store, enhancing trust and reducing perceived risk. Moreover, the integration of IT systems enabled store employees to access customer and order data to improve customer assistance, such as finding complementary goods.

Channel cooperation extends in both directions. In-store customers who are unable to find a product on the shelf can search the firm's online site through kiosks available in the store. Because of the integrated approach to marketing, the firm is also able to undertake promotional campaigns, such as sales and contests that customers can access in the store and on the Web. In addition, the Web channel also enabled value-added services geared toward improving customer relationship management. In particular, the Web site allowed customers to store items under consideration in a "Think About" folder. This provides useful marketing information to the firm, because it can provide more targeted promotions related to desired products.

A Building Material Supplier

The building materials supply company has a double-pronged approach to e-commerce. First, it maintains its own Web site, offering rich information services to its primary customer base—the professional builder. Second, it has an alliance with a building supply portal that allows it to offer e-commerce transactions to its existing client base as well as to new customer segments.

Professional builders are provided with an account that allows them to use the e-commerce site. They can log in directly from the builder supply firm's home page. A local lumberyard where the builder has an account fulfills the orders. Essentially, each lumberyard caters to the market located within a radius of 100 miles. Prices are individualized, encouraging builders to consolidate their purchases for volume discounts.

The building supply portal works with other suppliers but is tightly coupled with the case study firm because both firms have the same principal stockholder. In addition to providing online supply ordering services to builders, it also enables the firm to offer value-added services, extend into the consumer home improvement market, and provide customers goods that the local lumberyard does not carry. Among the value-added services are a variety of accounting and management options that builders can use. These include maintaining an online ledger for a project—for example, a house—that can be used as a template for the next project, saving builders time on order entry. Each builder can have his or her own personal Web page, including a personal product usage and construction plan folder. Builders can also check the status of their orders on a daily basis and order material outside the regular store hours. This is helpful because many builders do their administrative tasks at home in the evening. The personal pages include information on activities and promotions occurring at the local branch.

By outsourcing consumer e-commerce transactions to the online portal, the company now has a presence in the growing home-improvement market now dominated by such superstores as Home Depot. Because of the other partners who participate in the portal, the company is able to offer their existing customers one-stop shopping services, even for goods that they do not carry.

Individual stores receive electronically all orders placed on the portal for their products and fulfill them through their normal supply chain and existing fleet of delivery trucks. New professional clients are first encouraged to set up an account at a local branch, where local employees negotiate individual pricing arrangements.

The Web-based service supports standard orders. The company still maintains outside sales representatives (OSRs), however, who visit with builders on job sites to maintain good customer relations. The increased use of online ordering by builders allows OSRs to pay less attention to administrative tasks and to focus on selling value-added services, giving advice, educating the client about the online channels, and strengthening customer relationships.

Through its online partner, the firm also completed a successful mobile service pilot using Palm Pilots. Builders were able to make on-site purchases for critical materials needed immediately. Materials were then brought out to the job by the local delivery truck. One interesting impact of this service is that it encouraged builders to wait until the last minute for some orders and to make orders in smaller quantities than they would through normal channels. This is, of course, less efficient for the supply firm, creating some challenges for their delivery system. It is, however, a new value-added service that strengthens their relationship with core clients.

An Automobile Manufacturer/Dealer Network

All automobile manufacturers realize that car shoppers are able to conduct extensive research online before buying a car. Carmakers have well-developed Web sites providing rich information about their models, but for a variety of reasons they are not able to sell cars directly to end customers through the Web. Hence, they must work with traditional dealers to offer a click-and-brick experience. In one carmaker's e-commerce service, customers can configure their desired car online, obtain a fixed price quote, and choose a local dealer from whom they wish to take delivery. The application locates the matching car from dealer inventories, and if in stock at a different dealer from that chosen by the customer, the dealers will swap cars with each other. The chosen dealer then gets full credit for the sale of the online-configured car, as well as the continuing service relationship to the customer. At the Web site, customers can also research cars and check the inventory of local dealers online. In addition, customers can apply online for credit and insurance, which is also submitted to the local dealer.

This approach helps the manufacturer sell more cars without alienating its existing dealer network. The company realizes that in the car market, because of the logistics of delivery and the need for a physical presence for service and warranty work, bypassing dealers will not work. In fact, in many states, it is illegal for car manufacturers to sell directly to end consumers. To secure support from dealers for the initiative, an e-dealer advisory board was created. The manufacturer has also introduced features such as online scheduling for maintenance and repair and an ownership Web site where customers can find accessories that go with their car and receive maintenance service reminders.

Other electronic services initiatives include the introduction of mobile in-car services for safety, security, and information. They are utilizing the combination of Global Positioning System with wireless technology to deliver emergency roadside assistance, stolen vehicle tracking, navigation aids, and other travel-related services. The selling dealer will activate these in-car wireless services and provide training to customers.

A Financial Services Provider

The final case described here is a large national bank offering a traditional range of banking and financial services. The company focuses on the consumer and small business segment and has more than 8 million households as customers. It took a somewhat different path from the other cases to arrive at a click-and-brick strategy. In fact, this bank, through acquisitions and mergers, had both a typical online banking service available to its account holders and an entirely separate Internet brand that solely targeted new customers over the Web. In the description of this case that follows, the former is referred to as the internal online banking service, whereas the latter is referred to as the Internet pureplay bank.

Their Internet pureplay bank was not successful, largely because of the high costs of customer acquisition and the lack of necessary synergies with the parent bank. One particularly troublesome problem faced by all Internet-only banks results from the difficulties and costs of transferring money into and out of the Internet bank. Because of customers' reluctance to deposit cash or checks in ATMs, Internet-only bank users first must deposit funds in a traditional banking account and then transfer money (e.g., via a check or bank transfer) to their Internet account. This implies that the Internet pureplay bank would always be a supplementary rather than a primary bank. Moreover, in this bank's earlier parallel approach, the Internet pureplay bank had to rely on other banks' ATM networks to allow customers to make cash withdrawals, resulting in relatively high surcharges.

On the other hand, the internal online banking channel service was closely tied to the brick-and-mortar branches, had much lower customer acquisition costs, and offered many customer retention services. Existing account holders were freely offered the opportunity to sign up for online access to their bank accounts and other banking services, allowing online customer acquisition at a fraction of the cost of finding entirely new bank account clients. Customer retention was enhanced by providing such services as online bill payment. Services such as this increase retention by raising switching costs, because customers need to reenter extensive billing information if they change to a new bank. Another synergy benefit the bank experienced with its internal online banking channel stemmed from cost savings at brick-and-mortar branches due to the ability to offload routine transactions to the cheaper and more convenient Web channel. In keeping with the channel specialization management strategy described earlier, price incentives were also introduced to stimulate the use of the online services.

The parent bank took advantage of IT infrastructure synergies between its branches and its integrated online banking service by designing financial applications once and implementing them across the virtual and physical channels. For example, an application to speed up the approval of home equity loans was "mirrored" between the Web and the physical branches. The bank effectively developed coordination and control measures to be able to offer seamless customer support, so that customers would not have to repeat any transactions on multiple channels. For example, if customers changed their address using one channel, all systems would be updated at the same time. To achieve this, the bank had to integrate systems so that Web services were integrated into the day-to-day operations of branches.

As a result of these experiences, the formerly separate Internet pureplay bank was reintegrated into the parent bank, tying it more closely to the click-and-brick branches. Networked kiosks in bank branch offices introduced the Internet brand more directly to existing bank clients. The parent bank now supplies many of the core services, including deposits and withdrawals, and its connection to the Internet brand creates the trust that had been lacking. The benefit for customers is that they have the choice of a more differentiated set of banking services, with more differentiated prices that reflect the costs of transactions.

CLICK-AND-BRICK E-COMMERCE IN PRACTICE

Most research on click-and-brick e-commerce has used a case study approach, yielding many of the insights discussed earlier. However, cases do not necessarily reveal trends in the broader population of retailers and cannot tell us whether the kinds of click-and-brick approaches described here are really all that widely used. Therefore, in the spring of 2002, an analysis of the use of the Web by approximately 3100 retailers was conducted (Steinfield, Adelaar, and Liu, 2005). The sample comprised companies drawn from nine different retail sectors according to the North American Industrial Classification System (NAICS), focusing on retail sectors where e-commerce sales have been reported to be higher. Despite more than a decade of e-commerce via the Internet, only slightly more than half (54%) had a Web presence, with less than a third (31.5%) having sites considered to be working and active. Those with working sites (note that to be working simply meant that the links functioned appropriately—it did not mean that the site supported full online transactions) numbered 979 and were included for further analysis.

Table 1 Summary of Firms Included in the Web Site Content Analysis[a]

Retail Sector	NAICS Code	Number of Firms	Avg. Annual Sales (in millions)	Avg. Number of Employees
Motor vehicle and parts dealers	441	200	361.5	593
Furniture and home furnishings	442	138	64.7	495
Electronics and appliances	443	144	359.2	1,715
Building material, garden equipment, and supplies dealers	444	121	737.0	4,186
Health and personal care	446	58	1,114.5	5,937
Clothing and clothing accessories	448	97	833.2	8,465
Sporting goods, hobby, book and music	451	141	120.0	1,135
General merchandise	452	55	6,591.9	47,451
Miscellaneous store retailers	453	29	674.1	4,196

[a]Adapted from Steinfield et al. (2005).

Table 1 provides a summary of the companies that were included in the content analysis.

Despite the expectations from the click-and-brick cases, a content analysis of retailer Web sites revealed a surprisingly low incidence of real integration between e-commerce and physical channels. Trained coders analyzed all of the company Web sites for the presence or absence of 16 different characteristics grouped into three categories:

1. features that are universal (i.e., they are found in nearly all firms' Web sites);
2. features that reflect an integrated, click-and-brick emphasis (i.e., they explicitly involve a retail outlet in some way); and
3. other features that reflect some degree of online expertise, but do not necessarily imply a click-and-brick orientation.

As shown in Table 2, nearly all firms included the telephone number (96%) and address of retail outlets (95.5%), and so these were considered universal features. Common click-and-brick features included providing a map or driving directions to retail outlets (71.4%), giving

Table 2 Relative Frequency of Selected Web Site Characteristics in Click-and-Brick Firms[a]

Web Site Characteristics	Number (%) of Sites with Feature
Universal features	
Phone number of retail outlets	946 (96%)
Mail address of retail outlets	941 (95.5%)
Features reflecting a click-and-brick orientation	
Map to retail outlets or driving directions	702 (71.4%)
Company background or history	565 (57.4%)
Hours of operation of retail outlets	516 (52.4%)
Information on retail outlet events or specials	443 (45%)
Coupons or gift certificates redeemable in retail outlets	248 (25.2%)
Ability to search the inventory of a retail outlet	189 (19.2%)
Ability to make an appointment or reservation for a service in the retail outlet	148 (15%)
Allow customers to return items purchased online to retail outlets	80 (8.1%)
Links to other businesses in the community where retail outlets are located	69 (7%)
Allow online orders to be picked up at retail outlet	61 (6.2%)
Other features reflecting online expertise, but not necessarily a click-and-brick orientation	
Ability to complete a full transaction online	330 (33.5%)
Allow customers to set up and manage accounts	266 (27%)
Allow checking on the status of an online order	206 (20.9%)
Allow customers to place items in a gift registry	64 (6.5%)

[a] Adapted from Steinfield et al. (2005).

historical background on the company (57.4%), listing store hours (52.4%), and providing information about in-store events or specials (45%). These all reflect informational strategies rather than transaction-oriented click-and-brick services or services illustrating interoperability between stores and Web sites. Few sites offered coupons or gift certificates redeemable in stores (25.2%), allowed users to search in-store inventories (19.2%), let customers make appointments (15%), let online buyers return goods to physical stores (8.1%), linked to other local businesses (7%), or allowed online orders to be picked up at a physical store (6.2%). In general, the results demonstrate the relative lack of sophistication of retailers vis-à-vis online sales, let alone click-and-brick integration. Indeed, in only a third of the sampled firms could customers even complete a full transaction online.

These results show that, despite the apparent benefits arising from the integration of online and offline channels, in practice most firms fail to pursue a click-and-brick strategy. Further analysis of the 2002 data show that mainly larger firms, and those selling large products (e.g., cars), are more likely to pursue a click-and-brick strategy. Larger firms have the IT resources to develop a credible e-commerce capability and are more likely to possess an established brand identity from which their e-commerce channel can establish trust. For firms selling large products like cars, the logistical issues involved with product shipping compel retailers such as automobile dealers to use the Web mainly to bring customers to their lots.

Click-and-brick integration may thus be used less widely than expected, mainly because of the need for significant IT and financial resources that smaller retailers lack.

INFORMATION SECURITY AND CLICK-AND-BRICK RETAILERS

In general, click-and-brick retailers face many of the same information security threats and must rely on the same techniques to protect customers as any Internet-based retailer. As in all other e-commerce, click-and-brick e-commerce requires the authentication of both consumers and the online store channel, the preservation of the confidentiality of information related to online transactions, and the guarantee of the integrity of transaction-related information (see chapter "Electronic Commerce", this volume). Click-and-brick customers who buy from the online channel must provide personal and financial information, and can suffer financial loss and fall prey to identify theft. Indeed, since click-and-brick businesses, by definition, have a physical outlet that, by and large, was in existence prior to the Internet, attention to information security issues in the online business is critical. Otherwise, such companies may end up alienating an established customer base should they suffer losses as a result of inadequate attention to information security. Click-and-brick firms must support secure transmissions using encryption techniques such as secure sockets layer (SSL; see chapter "Public Key Cryptography Standards", this volume) and both symmetric and public key encryption systems (see chapters "Internet E-Mail Architecture", "S/MIME (Secure MIME)", and "Secure Shell (SSH)", this volume).

There are, however, a number of important distinctions that can be mentioned when comparing information security issues in a click-and brick environment with general e-commerce security. One set of distinctions stems from the various ways that the physical outlet can augment customers' perceived security when engaging in transactions with the online channel. As noted earlier in the chapter, click-and-brick firms can benefit from an existing reputation and higher initial trust because they have physical outlets. Research has shown that this factor enhances trust because customers have a sense that there is a place to go to complain if transactions are not satisfactory, and if they want to return products. Moreover, highly integrated click-and-brick stores possess another critical advantage vis-à-vis payment for online purchases. Since they do have a physical outlet, the option of allowing offline payment in the store can help provide an additional layer of perceived security for those customers who fear inputting private financial information onto a Web form. Such customers can defer payment until they pick up purchased items at the store, limiting their online exposure.

On the other hand, the goal of integrating online and offline operations introduces new security challenges for click-and-brick firms. Highly integrated click-and-brick firms will want to allow more access to company information (e.g., store inventory), necessitating more sophisticated authentication and authorization, so that customers cannot access private company data. Moreover, the focus on existing customers who live near physical outlets will further necessitate the establishment of customer accounts, placing pressure on retailers to establish sound practices vis-à-vis computer account management, password management, and the like. Truly creative hybrid stores may also run into problems when their attempts at online and offline integration are developed on an insecure infrastructure. For example, firms that integrate wireless LAN technology into their physical sales infrastructure face challenges raised by the early problems with the security of the transmissions. Early encryption approaches in 802.11b wireless LANs (also known as wireless fidelity or Wi-Fi networks) such as the wireless equivalent privacy (WEP) protocol were quickly compromised by hackers (see chapters "Fault Attacks" and "Physical Security Measures", Volume III, this *Handbook*). In one well-known case, the large electronics retailer Best Buy found that it was possible to intercept transmissions of credit card numbers being sent via wireless LAN in the store to cash registers (Stone, 2002). This illustrates that despite the integration with physical outlets, click-and-brick retailers are not immune to the information and network security threats raised by e-commerce. Finally, as noted earlier, a large number of retailers seem to have difficulty establishing even the most basic online transaction capability. The research suggests that smaller and medium-sized enterprises lack the resources and IT sophistication to build e-commerce channels highly integrated with offline businesses. Hence, it seems likely that such firms would also face challenges in attending to the development of sound information security practices in their computer and network infrastructures. Lack of meaningful information security will thus remain a significant challenge to the growth of click-and-brick electronic commerce.

CONCLUSION

This chapter has provided a broad overview of the click-and-brick business approach, noting both the potential benefits as well as the challenges that firms face because of channel conflicts. A framework to help understand the dynamics of managing a click-and-brick enterprise was introduced. The framework begins by identifying potential sources of synergy available to firms that choose to integrate e-commerce with traditional forms of business. It further emphasizes the many actions that firms can take to minimize channel conflicts and help achieve the benefits of synergy, and it describes four categories of synergy-related benefits from the integration of e-commerce with traditional businesses, including potential cost savings, gains due to enhanced differentiation, improved trust, and potential extensions into new markets. Four case studies were described to provide a concrete illustration of the approaches taken by click-and-brick firms. The chapter acknowledges, however, that despite the potential benefits, truly integrated click-and-brick retailing remains the exception rather than the rule, largely due to a lack of IT and financial resources among retailers. The chapter addresses the theme of the *Handbook* by pointing out that click-and-brick retailers must be as attentive to information security as any e-commerce firm. Although they have some advantages, such as the ability to fall back on in-store payment and pickup for online orders, click-and-brick businesses also have their own unique security challenges. As such firms attempt to gain real synergies through online/offline systems integration, threats from inadequate security increase significantly. Finally, the lack of IT and financial resources does imply that many click-and-brick firms will be unable to support sound computer and network security practices necessary for comprehensive e-commerce information security.

ACKNOWLEDGMENT

I am grateful to the reviewers and editor for the thoughtful comments on an earlier version of this chapter.

GLOSSARY

Channel A means by which a seller interacts with end consumers. Many firms rely on a mix of different channels, such as physical stores, catalog sales, and e-commerce. Firms pursuing channel integration attempt to coordinate the use of channels tightly, even within a single sales activity, to improve their profitability.

Channel Conflict The conflict that occurs when an alternative means of reaching customers (e.g., a Web-based store) implicitly or explicitly competes with or bypasses existing physical channels. Perceived threats caused by competition and conflict across channels can have other harmful effects, including limited cooperation across the channels, confusion when customers attempt to engage in transactions using the two uncoordinated channels, and even sabotage of one channel by the other.

Channel Specialization The directing of customers by click-and-brick firms to the most appropriate channel (e.g., one that is the lowest cost or one that offers the requisite capabilities). It allows firms to capitalize on the unique strengths of each sales channel.

Complementary Assets Assets possessed by a firm, such as existing supplier and distributor relationships and experience in the market, that help it take advantage of innovations such as e-commerce.

Differentiation A competitive approach used by companies to set themselves apart from competitors through higher quality products and better customer services. Click-and-brick firms hope that they can use their combined channels to differentiate themselves from competitors.

Kiosks Self-service computer stations, often with a touch-screen display, located in malls, stores, and other places where customers can use them to locate products or information and access services electronically. Click-and-brick firms may offer networked kiosks on store premises to allow in-store customers access to the firms' e-commerce channel.

Synergy The combined effect of two actions that is greater than the sum of the individual effects. Click-and-brick firms hope that by combining traditional and online services, they can offer an experience to customers greater than that possible through each channel by itself.

CROSS REFERENCES

See *Business-to-Business Electronic Commerce; EDI Security; Electronic Commerce; Electronic Payment Systems; Internet Basics.*

REFERENCES

Afuah, A., & Tucci, C. (2001). *Internet business models and strategies: Text and cases*. New York: McGraw-Hill Irwin.

Friedman, L. G., & Furey, T. R. (1999). *The channel advantage: Going to market with multiple sales channels to reach more customers, sell more products, make more profit*. Boston: Butterworth Heinemann.

Granovetter, M. (1985). Economic action and social structure: The problem of embeddedness. *American Journal of Sociology, 91*, 481–510.

Kotler, P. (1999). *Marketing management* (10th ed.). Upper Saddle River, NJ: Prentice Hall.

Laudon, K., & Traver, C. (2004). *E-commerce: Business, technology, society* (2nd ed.). Boston: Addison-Wesley.

National Telecommunications and Information Administration. (2002). *A nation online: How Americans are expanding their use of the Internet*. Retrieved November 1, 2002, from http://www.ntia.doc.gov/ntiahome/dn.

Otto, J., & Chung, Q. (2000). A framework for cyber-enhanced retailing: Integrating e-commerce retailing with brick and mortar retailing. *Electronic Markets, 10*(4), 185–191.

Porter, M. E. (1985). *Competitive advantage: Creating and sustaining superior performance*. New York: Free Press.

Rosen, K. T., & Howard, A. L. (2000). E-retail: Gold rush or fool's gold? *California Management Review, 42*(3), 72–100.

Shapiro, C., & Varian, H. (1999). *Information rules: A strategic guide to the network economy*. Boston: Harvard Business School Press.

Steinfield, C., Adelaar, T., & Lai, Y. (2002). Integrating brick and mortar locations with e-commerce: Understanding synergy opportunities. *Proceedings of the Hawaii International Conference on Systems Sciences*, Big Island, Hawaii, January 7–10.

Steinfield, C., Adelaar, T., & Liu, F. (2005). Click and mortar strategies viewed from the Web: A content analysis of features illustrating integration between retailers online and offline presence. *Electronic Market, 15*(3), forthcoming.

Steinfield, C., Bouwman, H., & Adelaar, T. (2002). The dynamics of click and mortar e-commerce: Opportunities and management strategies. *International Journal of Electronic Commerce, 7*, 93–119.

Stern, L. W., El-Ansary, A. I., & Coughlan, A. T. (1996). *Marketing channels*. Upper Saddle River, NJ: Prentice Hall.

Stone, A. (2002). Learning from Best Buy. *Wi-Fi Planet*. Retrieved June 1, 2004, from http://www.wi-fiplanet.com/columns/article.php/1142171.

Teece, D. J. (1986). Profiting from technological innovation: Implications for integration, collaboration, licensing and public policy. *Research Policy, 15*, 285–306.

Turban, E., King, D, Lee, J., & Viehland, D. (2004). *Electronic commerce 2004: A managerial perspective*. Upper Saddle River, NJ: Prentice Hall.

U.S. Census Bureau. (2004). *Service sector statistics*. Retrieved June 1, 2004, from http://www.census.gov/mrts/www/current.html.

Mobile Commerce

Vijay Atluri, *Rutgers University*

INTRODUCTION

Mobile commerce (m-commerce) is the buying and selling of goods and services, or the exchange of information in the support of commercial activities through wireless handheld devices such as cellular telephones and personal digital assistants (PDAs). Mobile commerce enables users to access the Internet and conduct transactions with monetary value from anywhere, anytime. For mobile commerce to take off, it needs to build on the established habits and practices of the consumers, and on the infrastructure, and then should add specific benefits due to mobility. For instance, the added benefits may include instantaneous access and delivery, flexibility, convenience, personalization, location awareness, and better customer service. In addition, the ease-of-use, convenience, and ensuring of security and privacy should be the salient features of mobile commerce.

The increase in the demand for applications dealing with moving objects can be seen in the past decade. Furthermore, mobile phones and/or wireless PDAs are expected to evolve into wireless terminals that are global positioning system (GPS)-enabled. In addition to wireless computing devices, tracking of other moving objects such as boats, trucks, automobiles, airplanes, and soldiers has become a growing interest. With the great demand on mobile devices, mobile commerce has emerged as a gigantic market opportunity. The mobile customer base has grown to 1.52 billion, among which U.S. mobile users number 140 million (Wireless World Forum, 2004). A Yankee Group survey (Yankee Group Research, 2004.) suggests that U.S. consumers are not convinced they want or need mobile services and many think it is simply too complicated. This is in contrast to other global markets in Asia and Europe where "going online" means reaching for a mobile handset, but not turning on a PC. In Japan and Korea, for example, reports suggest that one-third of all mobile phone subscribers use their handsets for m-commerce activities (InStat/MDR, 2002).

Worldwide, mobile commerce revenues are expected to exceed $25 billion by 2006 (NUA Internet Surveys, 2002). According to Juniper Research, it is expected that retailers will make up to $40 billion in sales from customers who will use mobile phones to spend cash on everything from cinema tickets to hourly car parking (Ambassna-Jones, 2004). This excludes already popular m-commerce products like mobile phone ringtones, Java games, wallpaper, and screen savers. According to an IDC study, mobile entertainment will be worth $8 billion in Western Europe in 2008. The purchases consumers will make will mainly consist of low-priced items, or what the industry calls micropayments. It is also expected that radio frequency identification (RFID) and infrared technologies will have a major influence on the future development of devices that allow for payments. DoCoMo's i-mode mobile service has attracted over 41 million subscribers since its introduction in February 1999. The revenues from mobile services reached $2 billion by the end of 2002 and are expected to reach $18 billion by the end of 2006. These revenues are divided as follows: 31% in Western Europe, 22% in the United States, and 47% in Japan and the rest of the world. As such, the market for location-aware mobile applications such as mobile shopping, mobile advertising, mobile retailing, mobile entertainment, and mobile online banking is very promising. Figure 1 provides an overview of different mobile commerce components. We will review each of them in this chapter, with the exception of the standards and policies.

MOBILE COMMERCE APPLICATIONS

As content delivery over wireless devices becomes faster, more secure, and scalable, it is believed that mobile commerce may exceed the traditional e-commerce. Mobile commerce applications can be categorized into the following classes: business-to-business (B2B), business-to-consumer (B2C), consumer-to-consumer (C2C), business-to-employee (B2E) (Lehmann & Lehner, 2004), and government-to-citizen (G2C). Whereas security is not important in some information service applications, it is significant in certain transaction-oriented applications. For example, a cellular phone can be used as a personal trusted device (PTD). In such cases, mobile customers may use it to pay for goods and services that may typically include gas, soft drink, or a ticket to a football game, or check their bank balances. In such scenarios, the mobile service calls for confidentiality, integrity, identification, and authentication requirements.

Many aspects of the mobile communications industry, including the importance of mobile communications and mobile applications, and the competitive landscape of a mobile phone market based on competing protocols or standards, airtime carriers, and handset providers have been explored (Kumar, 2004). Table 1 summarizes different types of applications (not an exhaustive list) and their category. We describe these applications in detail in the following.

Mobile Financial Services

These services will encompass:

1. Mobile banking through which customers access their bank accounts and pay their bills using handheld devices, and
2. Mobile brokerage through which customers obtain stock quotes displayed on their handheld devices and conduct trading using these devices.

In both cases, the mobile customer uses his/her PTD to set up a secure session with the bank.

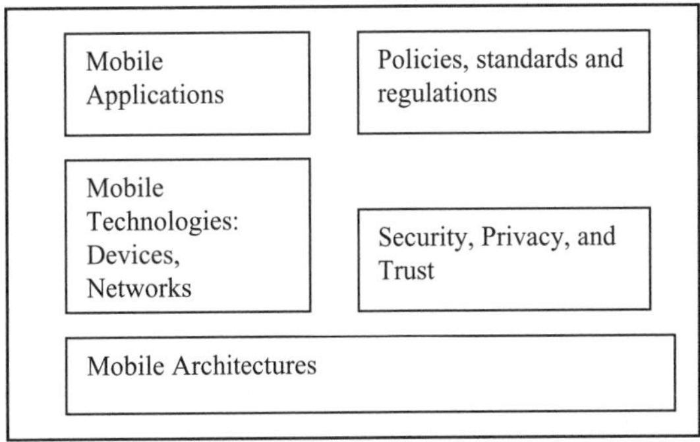

Figure 1: Mobile commerce: the big picture.

Mobile Telecommunications Services

These include services provided by telecommunication companies where a customers uses his/her handheld device for the purposes of service changes, bill payment, and account reviews.

Mobile Information Provisioning

These services include the delivery of financial and sports news and traffic updates to mobile customers. Other information service provisioning applications include integrated information services, such as tourist services, traffic coordination and management, way-finding, weather reports and forecasts, stock quotes, travel itineraries and nearby restaurants, news updates, business and technology news, local town information, telephone directory, restaurant guide, dictionary service, and cooking recipes, among others.

Mobile Security Services

Many public safety and security-related services can be provided through mobile devices as one can track and pinpoint the location of the device. These safety-related services include:

1. Tracking and locating stolen cars as well as automatically notifying the owner;
2. Remotely controlling a car, for example, disabling or starting the car engine, or honking the horn;
3. Tracking groups of vehicles and sending an alert when a vehicle crosses a predefined boundary;
4. Transmitting an alert when a laptop moves beyond a predefined area;

Table 1 Mobile commerce categories and their applications

Category	Application
B2B	Advertising, location-based services (e.g., supply chain management)
B2C	Financial services, telecommunications services, information provisioning, security services, remote shopping, on-site shopping, ticketing, advertising, entertainment, location-based services
C2C	User-to-user applications, wireless video conferencing
B2E	Wireless video conferencing, reporting, claim processing
G2C	Security services

5. Tracking children, people with Alzheimer's disease, or those mentally disabled, as well as pets, and transmitting an automatic notification to their parents or carers;
6. Sending remote control commands via phone or Web to let someone into the house, to turn down the thermostat, or to start an appliance;
7. Transmitting messages via a reverse 911 service to individuals in emergency situations; and
8. Helping to dispatch 911 services, including real-time delivery of information on crime mapping, and providing of access to federal and state databases and mug shots.

Mobile Remote Shopping

The mobile phone user browses in a wireless application protocol (WAP)-enabled shop, selects the desired goods, and pays for them with funds from his bank or credit card account. These include services or retail purchases as consumers are given the ability to place and pay for orders on-the-fly.

Mobile On-Site Shopping

A mobile user may select the desired goods in a retail store and use his/her PTD to pay by logging onto the department store's Bluetooth wireless LAN.

Mobile Ticketing

The user browses a WAP ticketer's site, selecting and purchasing a ticket for a movie, show, or game. All ticket information is stored in the PTD's transaction database. At the venue, the user goes up to one of the wireless access nodes on the premises (similar to an ATM), calls up the ticket information from the PTD's database, and sends it via Bluetooth to this access node, which then prints out the user's ticket.

Mobile Advertising

Mobile advertising includes personalized, location-aware, and context-sensitive advertising, as mobile devices are ideal for marketing channels for impulse buying. For example, mobile users can be pushed with information related to nearby hotels when they are not in their home location, nearby movies during evenings and weekends, or nearby restaurants based on their preferences.

Mobile Entertainment

Mobile entertainment may include location-based games, character download, horoscope and fortune telling, karaoke information, hit songs, downloadable ringtones, club event information, etc.

Wireless Video Conferencing

Wireless video conferencing can be enabled using voice over Internet protocol (VoIP) and full-motion video communication over both wireless fidelity (Wi-Fi) and universal mobile telecommunications system (UMTS)-based networks.

Mobile User-to-User Applications

Mobile user-to-user applications include mobile games, pictures, cartoons, or personal files shared between users and their friends and colleagues via the handset; user-to-user content provision; conversational applications (which provide the means for bidirectional communication with real-time end-to-end information transfer), such as video conferencing; groupware (collaborative work); and messaging applications (which offer user-to-user or user-to-user group communication), such as messaging of photographs and video.

Location-Based Services

The demand for location based services (LBS) can be categorized into the following types (Rao & Minakakis, 2003):

1. *Location and navigation service*: Maps, driving directions, directory and yellow page listings, and business descriptions in a given geographical radius all serve this purpose. These types of LBS have become popular in Japan, whereas they are a more recent phenomenon in the United States. GPS capabilities may allow customers to find their way to their destinations and alert friends and colleagues to their whereabouts. If a person gets relocated, they can use mobile location-based services to familiarize themselves with their new surroundings. Examples also include getting detailed maps and directions, real-time alerts on traffic conditions, and information about highway services like gas, food, and lodging. Although auto manufacturers are investing in making mobile platforms available in cars, currently relatively inexpensive handheld devices are serving this purpose. These include devices like golfing assistants mounted on golf carts that provide everything from course maps to teeing tips, fish finders that combine sonar and GPS capabilities to allow anglers to pinpoint locations of schools of fish, and people locators, which enable parents to locate children in urban areas and shopping environments (Spagat, 2002).
2. *Point-of-need information delivery*: This service is for requesting usable, personalized information to be delivered at the point of need, which can include automatic updates of travel reservations as well as information about new or interesting products and services, promotions, and targeting of customers based on more advanced knowledge of customer profiles and preferences. For example, a wireless shopping site can be designed to present users with targeted content such as clothing items on sale, based on prior knowledge of their preferences and/or knowledge of their current location, such as proximity to a shopping mall (Venkatesh, Ramesh, & Massey, 2003). To deliver such LBS, service providers require access to customers' preference profiles either through a proprietary database or through an arrangement with an LBS provider, who matches customer profiles to vendor offerings. In order to implement such services, customization and personalization based on the location information, customer needs, and vendor offerings are required.

3. *Industrial and corporate applications*: This type of LBS finds its way into a number of applications including tracking material through the supply chain and inventory, and tracking physicians, patients, and equipment in a hospital. This relies on the deployment of RFID technologies, which is becoming inexpensive and will likely be used by a number of retail businesses such as Wal-Mart.

BUSINESS MODELS IN THE M-COMMERCE ENVIRONMENT

A number of business models are being practiced by the vendors of mobile commerce. Notable ones among these include:

1. User fee business model;
2. Shopping business model;
3. Marketing business model;
4. Improved efficiency business model;
5. Advertising business model; and
6. Revenue sharing business model (Sadeh, 2002).

These are described briefly in the following.

User Fee Business Model

Under this model, payment can be based on a subscription fee, or based on usage. This model is best suited for regularly updated content such as customized news, location-sensitive weather, and traffic conditions. In reality, the content provider may rely on the mobile service provider to implement it and collect the appropriate fee. The obvious advantages of adopting a subscription fee-based model over the usage fee model are that it is easier to collect the fees and the income is relatively better predictable. However, the usage fee model would be more attractive to one-time or infrequent users.

Shopping Business Model

Under this model, the traditional Internet companies sell their goods and services through the new mobile medium to reach their customers to offer better services and convenience, and moreover to capture additional customers. Essentially, the traditional Internet companies seek a mobile presence. The payment is done with the mobile device, but typically involves a third party such as a credit card company or a bank.

Improved Efficiency Business Model

Whereas the shopping business model is adopted by traditional Internet companies for expanding their customer base, the improved efficiency business model offers mobile services, such as mobile banking and mobile ticketing, to those companies hoping to reduce their operating costs.

Marketing Business Model

The traditional brick-and-mortar companies push the information about their products and services directly to customers through mobile channels. However, the customers make payments using traditional methods, not mobile devices.

Advertising Business Model

The advertising business model involves the gathering of profiles and preferences of mobile customers and targeting advertising based on a customer's location, time, and preferences. Typically, the advertiser passes on the information to the content provider, who would deliver the advertisements relevant to the user's queries. The advertiser pays for the content provider by a flat fee, or based on traffic (number of ad impressions) or on performance (number of click-throughs or call-throughs).

Revenue-Sharing Business Model

Under the revenue-sharing business model, the mobile content owner utilizes the services of a mobile content provider, which is suitable in cases where the content provided by a single owner is not sufficient to attract the attention of mobile customers or is not valuable as standalone information. In such cases, the mobile content provider combines the content from different owners and may enhance it with value-added information before delivering it to the mobile customer. For example, local weather reports, local traffic conditions, stock quotes, and news updates can all be combined appropriately by the content provider. Typically the content provider collects the customer's payment and shares it with the content owners.

ENABLING TECHNOLOGIES

Mobile commerce has emerged as a result of the developments in several technologies. In this section, we review the advances in these different technologies that have propelled the growth of mobile commerce.

Mobile Devices

Mobile devices such as smart phones and personal digital assistants have reached new levels of usability, performance, and computing power. Increasingly, these devices are equipped with wireless communications capabilities and location technologies. In order to exploit the m-commerce market potential, a number of industry initiatives to enable secure and reliable mobile commerce transactions have taken place. Handset manufacturers such as Nokia, Ericsson, Motorola, and Qualcomm have been working with carriers such as AT&T Wireless and Sprint to develop WAP-enabled smart phones to transform a mobile phone into a PTD. In addition, IBM and other companies have been developing speech recognition software to ensure security in mobile commerce transactions. Using Bluetooth technology, smart phones offer fax, e-mail, and phone capabilities all in one, paving the way for m-commerce to be accepted by an increasingly mobile workforce. Although, the current speeds are limited, the new generations of wireless networks such as UTMS will provide much faster speeds. In addition, these technologies will provide always-on connectivity.

Wireless Networks

The enabling technologies for m-commerce include wide-area and short-range wireless communication technologies such as Wi-Fi, Bluetooth, and RFID technologies. In the following, we review their evolution over different generations—1G through 4G. Based on the technology use, the market growth in global GSM (global system for mobile communication) users has increased to 1.25 billion, global CDMA (code-division multiple-access) users to 202 million, global TDMA (time-division multiple-access) users to 120 million, and total 3G users to 130 million (http://www.cellular.co.za/stats/stats-main.htm). According to Pyramid Research (2004), Wi-Fi users will surpass 3G users, and it is expected that by the year 2008 the number of Wi-Fi users will reach 180 million, whereas that of 3G will be less than 100 million.

1G

The first generation of wireless technologies used analog transmission, which operates in the 800-MHz band and uses 30-kHz channels using frequency division multiple access (FDMA). It was introduced in North America in 1985 (advanced mobile phone service). Because of the limited bandwidth, this soon exhausted the available channels, thereby limiting the number of subscribers. Since digital signals can be compressed, enabling more effective use of the frequency spectrum, it was natural to employ digital technology.

2G

The second-generation systems, which digitized not only the control link but also the voice signal and used TDMA and CDMA, appeared in the early 1990s. Unlike 1G, which primarily supports voice signals, 2G networks are capable of supporting voice, data, paging, and fax services. Moreover, they provide better quality and higher capacity at lower cost to consumers. GSM was the first commercially operated digital cellular system based on TDMA.

2.5G

One of the major enhancements of 2.5G over 2G is the use of packet-switching technology. The general packet radio service (GPRS) is based on packet-switching technology, which sends packets of data over a radio wave (on the GSM network). GPRS was standardized by the European Telecommunications Standards Institute (ETSI), but today is standardized by the Third Generation Partnership Program (3GPP).

With GPRS, a maximum speed of up to 171.2 kbps, which is almost ten times faster than that of the current circuit-switched data services on GSM networks, can be achieved. However, realistically they currently only have a maximum downstream speed of 50 kbps and an upstream speed of 10–28 kbps. Speeds will also depend on which GPRS version an operator uses, as well as how busy the network is at a particular time. In addition to achieving higher transmission speeds, unlike the users served by circuit-switching networks, GPRS users are "always connected." GPRS data transmission technology is optimized for "bursty" communication services such as wireless Internet/intranet and multimedia services. It is also known as GSM-IP (Internet protocol) because it connects users directly to Internet service providers, allowing Web browsing, chat, e-mail, telnet and FTP, multimedia services, and instant messaging to be supported over the mobile network. GPRS therefore offers a smooth add-on to integrate into existing networks and supplements today's circuit-switched data and short message service. Future applications may have the ability to remotely access and control in-house appliances and machines. Voice calls can be made simultaneously over GSM-IP while a data connection is operating—depending on the phone class and type. Although users are always connected and always online, they may still be charged for the amount of data transported.

3G

Telecommunications companies around the world have been working toward the commercialization of third-generation (3G) mobile phone technology. It enables the transmission of high-quality video images in the 2-GHz frequency band and realizes new mobile multimedia communications services. NTT DoCoMo was one of the firsts in the world to begin research and development on W-CDMA, a key foundation for 3G mobile phone technology. The UMTS is a 3G mobile communications technology that provides wideband CDMA radio technology. With data rates up to 2 Mbps, UMTS provides increased capacity and data capability and a far greater range of services. A variation of CDMA, called the time-division synchronous CDMA (TD-SCDMA) was proposed by China Wireless Telecommunication Standards group (CWTS), which uses the time-division duplex (TDD) mode. The CDMA technology offers higher throughput, real-time services, and end-to-end quality of service (QoS), and is capable of delivering pictures, graphics, customized infotainment, streaming video, video messaging to locational services, and other multimedia information as well as voice and data to mobile wireless subscribers. UMTS is standardized by the 3GPP.

4G

The 4G mobile services are the advanced version of the 3G mobile communication services. The 4G mobile communication services are expected to provide broadband, large-capacity, high-speed data transmission, providing users with high-quality interactive multimedia services including teleconferencing, color video images, 3D graphic animation games, and audio services. In addition, 4G networks are expected to offer global mobility, service portability, and scalability at lower cost. They are expected to be based on orthogonal frequency division multiplexing (OFDM), which is capable of having hundreds of parallel channels. The data transmission rates are planned to be up to 20 Mbps. This next-next generation technology is expected to allow seamless merging between different wireless standards, making it possible for one mobile device to move from indoor networks such as wireless LANs and Bluetooth to cellular, radio, and TV broadcasting or to satellite communications. NewLogic claims that by the end of 2007 4G digital IP-based high-speed cellular systems will account for 14% of total mobile wireless data revenues, 50 million subscribers, and $5.3 billion in 4G infrastructure sales (*Electronic News*, 2003).

Wireless LANs

Similar to the use of 3G as a wide-area mobile networking technology, wireless LANs (WLANs) are also widely used for mobile commerce. IEEE 802.11 or Wi-Fi is a family of networking protocols developed by the working group 11 of IEEE 802. Wi-Fi is a trade term promulgated by the Wireless Ethernet Compatibility Alliance (WECA) and is used in place of 802.11b. Products certified as Wi-Fi by WECA are interoperable with each other even if they are from different manufacturers. A user with a Wi-Fi product can use any brand of access point with any other brand of client hardware built to the Wi-Fi standard. WLANs are cheaper than 3G to install, maintain, and use. Moreover, they are relatively mature technologies compared to the 3G.

The 802.11 family currently includes three separate protocols, 802.11a, 802.11b, and 802.11g. 802.11b was the first widely accepted wireless networking standard, which was later followed by 802.11a and 802.11g (http://grouper.ieee.org/groups/802/11/).

802.11b

802.11b has a range of about 50 m and has a maximum throughput of 11 Mbps. 802.11 runs in the 2.4-GHz spectrum and uses carrier sense multiple access with collision avoidance (CSMA/CA) as its media access method. Extensions have been made to the 802.11b protocol to increase speed to 22, 33, and 44 Mbps, but the extensions are proprietary and have not been endorsed by the IEEE.

802.11a

The 802.11a standard uses the 5-GHz band, and operates at a raw speed of 54 Mbps. 802.11a has not seen wide adoption because of the high adoption rate of 802.11b, and because of concerns about range: at 5 GHz, 802.11a cannot reach as far as 802.11b.

802.11g

In June 2003, a third standard, 802.11g, for encoding was ratified. This works in the 2.4-GHz band (like 802.11b), but operates at 54 Mbps raw, or about 24.7 Mbps net, throughput like 802.11a. It is fully backward compatible with 11-Mbps 802.11b. It uses orthogonal frequency division multiplexing (OFDM) technology, and enables streaming media, video downloads, and a greater concentration of users without interference.

802.11n

In January 2004 IEEE announced that it will develop a new standard for wide-area wireless networks. The real speed will be 100 Mbps, so up to four to five times faster than 802.11g, and perhaps fifty times faster than 802.11b. As projected, 802.11n will also offer a better operating distance than current networks. The standardization progress is expected to be completed by the end of 2006.

802.11i

This is an amendment to the 802.11 standard specifying security mechanisms for wireless networks. The draft standard was ratified on 24 June 2004, and supercedes the previous security specification, wired equivalent privacy (WEP), which was shown to have severe security weaknesses. Wi-Fi protected access (WPA) had previously been introduced by the Wi-Fi Alliance. It implemented a subset of 802.11i and makes use of the advanced encryption standard (AES) block cipher; WEP and WPA use only the RC4 stream cipher. In addition to improved encryption, it includes improvements in key management, user authentication through 802.1x, and data integrity of headers and contents using counter-mode/CBC-Mac protocol (CCMP).

Bluetooth

Other wireless technologies include short-range technologies such as Bluetooth, which can play an important role in some applications such as mobile payments. It is an industrial specification for wireless personal area networks (PANs). Bluetooth provides a way to connect and exchange information between devices like PDAs, mobile phones, laptops, PCs, printers, and digital cameras via a secure, low-cost, globally available short-range radio frequency. Bluetooth lets these devices talk to each other when they come in range, as long as they are within 32 feet of each other. Every device can be configured to constantly announce its presence to nearby devices in order to establish a connection. The protocol operates at 2.45 GHz and can reach speeds of 723.1 kbps. In order to avoid interfering with other protocols that use the 2.45-GHz band, the Bluetooth protocol divides the band into 79 channels and changes channels up to 1600 times per second.

Bluetooth should not be compared to Wi-Fi, which is a faster protocol requiring more expensive hardware that covers greater distances and uses the same frequency range. Whereas Bluetooth is a cable replacement creating personal area networking between different devices, Wi-Fi is a cable replacement for local area network access. The Bluetooth SIG works on versions 1.2 and 2.0. Bluetooth enhanced data rate (EDR), which will have a data rate of 2.1 Mbps, is expected to be finalized in the fourth quarter of 2004.

One of the ways Bluetooth technology may become useful is in VoIP. Bluetooth may be used for communication between a cordless phone and a computer listening for VoIP with an infrared peripheral component interconnect card acting as a base for the cordless phone. Cars can also install hands-free Bluetooth technology, which allows users with Bluetooth-equipped cell phones to make use of some of the phone's features.

RFID

Another emerging wireless technology is the radio frequency identification. RFID is a method of remotely storing and retrieving data using devices called RFID tags. An RFID tag can be either attached to or incorporated into a product. RFID tags can be either active or passive. Passive RFID tags do not have their own power supply, but can respond to incoming radio-frequency signals. The range of passive tags can vary from 10 mm to 5 m. As of 2004, these tags cost from $0.25. The aim to produce tags for less than $0.05 may make widespread RFID tagging commercially viable. Active RFID tags have a power source and have longer ranges and contain larger memory than their passive counterparts. Active tags may have ranges on the order of tens of meters, and a battery life of up to several years.

There are four different kinds of tags commonly in use, their differences being based on the level of their radio frequency: low-frequency tags (between 125 and 134 kHz), high-frequency tags (13.56 MHz), UHF tags (868 to 956 MHz), and microwave tags (2.45 GHz). Low-frequency tags are primarily used for identification and tracking of objects such as children and animals, anti-theft systems, etc. High-frequency RFID tags can be used to track library books, pallets, airline baggage, and retail goods as well as to control building access. UHF tags can be typically used in shipping yards to track pallets and containers as well as trucks and trailers. Microwave tags can be used in long-range access control of vehicles. Some tollbooths use RFID tags for electronic toll collection (e.g., the EZ-Pass system).

Using RFID tags in place of bar-code technology may have a number of advantages. Unlike bar codes, which are the same for the same type of product, RFID codes are unique for each product. As a result, a product may be individually tracked as it moves from location to location, from manufacturers to wholesalers, to retailers, and finally to consumers. This may help companies to combat theft and other forms of product loss, and can be used for point-of-sale automatic checkout with the option of removing the tag at checkout. Moreover, cards embedded with RFID chips are widely used as electronic cash, for example, to pay fares in mass transit systems and/or retails. EPCglobal is working on an international standard for the use of RFID and the electronic product code (EPC) to be used in tracking goods along the supply chain. It includes members from EAN International, Uniform Code Council, Gillette, Procter and Gamble, Wal-Mart, Hewlett–Packard, Johnson and Johnson, and Auto-ID Labs. Futuristic uses include monitoring the expiration dates of the food in the refrigerator, etc. In summary, RFID technology can be used for collecting information from moving objects, and can also be utilized in applications such as supply chain management, advanced product tracking, inventory control, warehouse management, the checking of compliance regulations, recall, enhancement, accountability, and documentation.

However, RFID technology may raise a number of privacy concerns as the tags affixed to products remain functional even after the products have been purchased and taken home, thus, capable of being read from a distance without the knowledge of the purchaser. This information can be potentially used for surveillance and other purposes not related to the supply chain inventory functions. Another privacy concern is due to RFID's support for anti-collision, in which a reader enumerates all the tags responding to it without them mutually interfering. As a result, all but the last bit of each tag's serial number can be deduced by passively eavesdropping on the RFID reader. Juels, Rivest, and Szydlo (2003) have proposed a selective blocking approach using a blocker tag as a way of protecting consumers from unwanted scanning of RFID tags attached to items they may be carrying or wearing. A blocker tag is a cheap passive RFID device that can simulate many ordinary RFID tags simultaneously and thus block RFID readers from reading the actual RFID tag. It can do so universally by simulating all possible RFID tags. Also a blocker tag can block selectively by simulating only selected subsets of ID codes, such as those of a particular manufacturer, or those in a designated privacy zone. Later, Juels & Brainard (2004) extended the blocker tag approach to enforce flexible privacy policies in which partial or scrubbed data are revealed about private tags, in lieu of the all-or-nothing policy enforced by a blocker tag. Privacy-related guidelines proposed by EPCglobal include the requirement to give consumers clear notice of the presence of EPC and to inform them of the choice that they have to discard, disable, or remove EPC tags (http://www.epcglobalinc.org/public_policy/public_policy_guidelines.html). Table 2 (partially from Umar (2003)) summarizes the bandwidth and range of different wireless technologies.

Other Technologies

Location Technologies

Although location technologies have been around for a number of years, they have evolved rapidly in recent years because of the increasing use of mobile applications. They can be broadly classified into outdoor and indoor technologies. Outdoor technologies include GPS, network-assisted GPS (A-GPS), time of arrival (TOA), up-link time of arrival (UL-TOA), enhanced observed time difference (E-OTD), and cell of origin (COO) (Andersson 2001, Durl 2001). Indoor technologies include Active Badge system developed by Olivetti Research Ltd. (ORL), PARC by Xerox, Shopping Assistant by AT&T Bell Laboratories, and Cyberguide by Georgia Institute of Technology, among others. Because most mobile applications rely on outdoor technologies, indoor technologies have

Table 2 Bandwidths and Ranges of Wireless Technologies

	Data Rate	Range
Bluetooth	1 Mbps	10 m
IEEE 802.11a	Up to 54 Mbps	<50 m
IEEE 802.11b	11 Mbps	100 m
IEEE 802.11g	Up to 54 Mbps	100 m
3G cellular	Up to 2 Mbps	Cell sizes 5 to 10 km
RFID	Up to 2.45 Gbps	Up to 10s of meters
Satellites	64 kbps	Thousands of miles

limited applications such as computerized visitor guides in museums. Wireless networks can provide approximate information about the location of a customer; this information exists as part of the routing information in the wireless network. GPS provides a more accurate location but requires some add-in to the mobile device. This technology is typically used for driver assistance systems and in military applications such as guided missiles. For indoor applications, other technologies such as the smart badge developed by Xerox Labs in the UK are used.

Application Protocols

The emerging technology behind m-commerce is the set of protocols called the wireless application protocols, which provide a functionality similar to that of the traditional Internet protocols such as TCP/IP, secure socket layer (SSL), and hypertext transfer protocol (HTTP). Typically the translation between the two sets of protocols is performed by some middleware at the mobile support station (MSS), which is part of the infrastructure of the wireless provider. (More details on WAP are provided in the next section.) WAP also includes a markup language based on XML, called the wireless markup language (WML). IMode-enabled Web sites utilize cHTML, a subset of the familiar HTML 4.0 (Barnes & Huff, 2003) that has been developed with the restrictions of the wireless infrastructure in mind, such as the limited bandwidth and high latencies of the networks, and small screens and limited functionality of the devices. Essentially, it removes certain features of conventional HTML, such as tables and frames. Mobile services equipped with WAP have been widely accepted, and the mobile devices equipped with Web-ready microbrowsers are much more common in Europe than in the United States. This growth is partly driven by the GPRS, WAP, and Bluetooth technologies and their use in mobile commerce applications.

Semantic Web Technologies

M-commerce is benefiting from emerging technologies such as Web services, .Net technologies, and ontologies. Several new technologies and standards are affecting the design of m-commerce applications. These include semantic Web technologies, such as RDF, DAML, DAML-S, DAML+OIL, and OWL, and service interaction technologies such as the universal description, discovery, and integration (UDDI) specifications. The .NET framework is the programming model for developing, deploying, and running Web services and applications. Web services are units of code that allow programs written in different programming languages and on different platforms to communicate and share data through standard Internet protocols such as, XML, SOAP, Web services description language (WSDL), and UDDI. They allow easy building of Web-based applications, including ERP, CRM, e-commerce, messaging and calendaring functionality, workflow services, and the like.

Languages

Another driving force to mobile commerce is the standardization of programming language for mobile devices. Languages such as Java 2 Mobile Edition (J2ME) makes it possible to write powerful applications that can leverage and integrate the different capabilities of the device including voice, telephony, security, communications, and location capabilities. These standards are geared for devices with small memory, and are therefore suitable for mobile devices.

ARCHITECTURAL COMPONENTS

A mobile communication network protocol should deliver functionalities similar to those provided by the different layers of the OSI model for enabling communication in the mobile Internet. Because destination nodes are mobile, traditional IP protocols are no longer applicable for the mobile communication environment. In the wired network, the convention is that the IP addresses are organized such that nodes in the same location have the same prefixes. This no longer holds well as the nodes themselves are moving and do not have a fixed location. To overcome this problem, the mobile IP uses the concept of a care-of-address, and employs tunneling. Essentially, under the mobile IP, each mobile node sends its location by sending its care-of-address to its home agent. The home agent then tunnels the packets destined to the mobile node by forwarding them to the care-of-address, which are then delivered to the mobile node. Several standards are in place today; however, they differ in the way in which they have adapted the standard transport and the network layer protocols of the TCP/IP. For example, the mobile IP is now part of the 3G standard; however, other standards such as the GPRS support only a simplified version of the mobile IP.

Whereas the IP layers are responsible for delivery of packets to the destination node, the TCP layers are responsible for reliably delivering the packets, assembling the packets in the right order, and finally handing them over to the target application. The TCP protocol is also responsible for congestion control to ensure graceful performance degradation. With respect to the mobile communication version of the TCP protocol, it must address specific problems due to the fact that connections are often lost and transmission errors are more common in the mobile communication environment, and, therefore, roundtrip times are harder to predict.

In addition to adapting the TCP/IP to the mobile communication environment, the mobile Internet needs to take into consideration the limited power, memory, computing capacity, and the screen size of the mobile devices. Moreover, because of the unreliable network connections, even the most common protocols such as HTTP do not work well. Furthermore, the Web languages responsible for displaying the Web content, such as HTML, must be modified.

The wireless application protocol has been proposed as a standard for addressing these challenges. The WAP Forum (http://www.wapforum.org) was founded in the summer of 1997 by Ericsson, Nokia, Motorola, and Unwired Planet for the purpose of defining an industry-wide specification for developing applications over wireless communications networks. Forum members represent over 90% of the global handset market, as well as leading infrastructure providers, software developers, and other organizations. The WAP Forum with Open Mobile Architecture

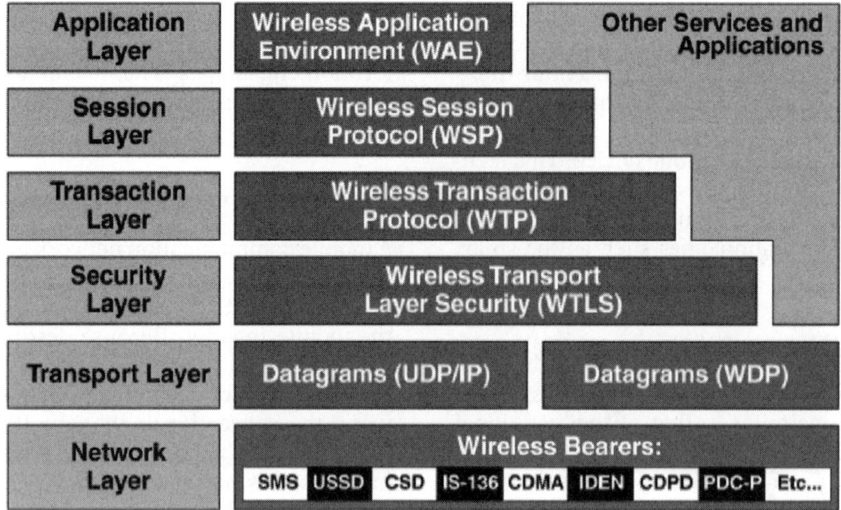

Figure 2: A comparison of WAP and Internet technologies. Source: WAP Forum.

formed, and has now become part of, the Open Mobile Alliance (OMA), which consists of several working groups, one of which is on mobile commerce. A comparison of the Internet and WAP technologies is provided in Figure 2. WAP architecture, as published by the WAP Forum, is shown in Figure 3. More details of the WAP are in the following.

- *WAP*: The wireless application protocol is the de facto standard for information services on wireless terminals. It is an intelligent messaging service for handheld mobile devices such as mobile phones. WAP is an application communication protocol, and is used to access services and information. It is an application environment and a set of communication protocols for wireless devices designed to enable mobile users technology-independent access to the Internet and advanced telephony services. In particular, WAP specifications define a set of protocols in application, session, and transport layers of the communication protocol, as well as provide transactional and security services.
- *WAE*: WAP also defines a wireless application environment (WAE) composed of a microbrowser, scripting facilities, e-mail, Web-to-mobile-handset messaging, and mobile-to-telefax access. It allows digital content to be displayed on special WAP-enabled GSM mobile phones in a standard text format. It uses WML (not HTML) to create Web applications for mobile devices so that they can be displayed in a WAP browser. As such, WAP is a protocol designed for microbrowsers. The WAP standard is based on Internet standards (HTML, XML, and TCP/IP). WML is defined as an XML application. It consists of a WML language specification, a WMLScript specification, and a wireless telephony application interface (WTAI) specification.

The functions of the different layers of the WAP are as follows: The WAP datagram protocol (WDP) is the transport layer that sends and receives messages via any available bearer network, including SMS, USSD, CSD, CDPD, IS–136 packet data, and GPRS. The wireless transport layer security (WTLS), an optional security layer, has encryption facilities that provide the secure transport service required by many applications, such as e-commerce. The WAP transaction protocol (WTP) layer provides transaction support, adding reliability to the datagram service provided by WDP. The WAP session protocol (WSP) layer provides a lightweight session layer to allow efficient exchange of data between applications. The HTTP interface serves to retrieve WAP content from the Internet requested by the mobile device. Wireless markup language is used to create pages that can be displayed in a WAP browser.

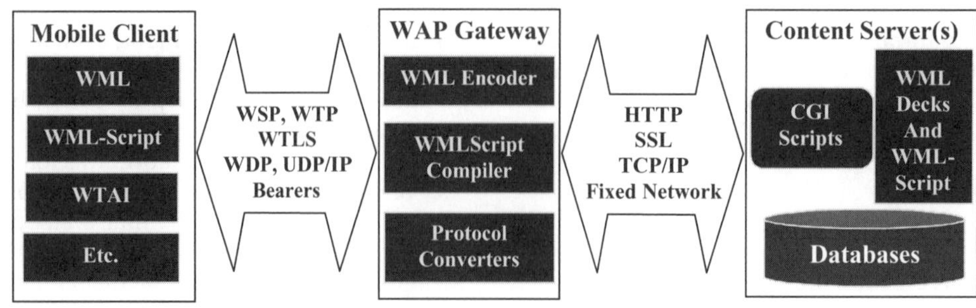

Figure 3: Architecture of the WAP gateway. Source: WAP Forum.

The WMLScript is a restricted JavaScript language used by WML to run simple code on the client machines. WML pages do not embed WML scripts, but only contain references to script URLs. Similar to the Java script, the WML scripts also need to be compiled into byte code on a server before they can run in a WAP browser. WAP uses a microbrowser to accommodate the small screens of the wireless devices. The microbrowser is a lightweight piece of software to display information written in WML and to interpret WMLScript.

SECURITY ISSUES

Similar to the traditional electronic commerce in the wired world, mobile commerce is also vulnerable to a range of security threats. However, since mobile commerce is a radio frequency-operated system, it is easier to perpetrate some types of attacks compared to those in wired systems. The security requirements include the following:

1. *Confidentiality*: requires the messages be kept secret from unauthorized recipients;
2. *Integrity*: requires that messages are unaltered during transit from sender to receiver;
3. *Authentication*: requires ensuring each party is who it claims to be;
4. *Nonrepudiation*: guarantees that neither the sender nor the recipient can deny that the message exchange took place; and
5. *Replay attack prevention*: ensures that any unauthorized resending of messages is detected and rejected.

Several standards have been established in WAP to provide security at the application, transport, and management levels, which are described in the following.

WTLS

The basis of WAP security is in the wireless transport layer security protocol, which is analogous to the Internet's transport layer security (TLS) accomplished using the standard SSL protocol. WTLS is similar to the TLS with a few differences. However, WAP 2.0 uses TLS instead of WTLS to overcome the WAP gap vulnerability (discussed in the next section), and to provide end-to-end security at the transport level. WTLS provides security services including authentication and digital signatures, confidentiality by encrypting data, integrity by employing hashing for detecting data modifications, and denial of service protection that detects and rejects data that have been replayed or not successfully verified. The WML script enables a user to digitally sign a message using the public key infrastructure.

Elliptic curve cryptography (ECC) is emerging as an attractive public key cryptosystem for mobile and wireless environments. Compared to traditional cryptosystems like RSA, ECC offers equivalent security with smaller key sizes, which results in faster computations, lower power consumption, and memory and bandwidth savings. As such, this is a more suitable choice for mobile devices since mobile devices typically have limited CPU, power, and network connectivity. In fact, traditional signature schemes are viewed as impractical to implement in the wireless environment, as they require much more processing, memory, and storage resources than those with ECC. The keys for elliptic curve are typically on the order of six times smaller than equivalent keys in other signature schemes, for example, 164 bits versus 1024 bits. This creates great efficiencies in key storage, certificate size, memory usage, and digital signature processing. ECC is fully supported by the WAP security standards and has been widely accepted by WAP device manufacturers.

The WAP identity module (WIM) is a tamper-resistant computer chip that resides in the WAP enabled device, e.g., a mobile phone or PTD. It is used to store the user's private key, the root public key of the PKI, etc. Mostly, WIMs are implemented using smart cards that typically have a CPU and some memory and storage for data and programs. WML Script Crypto API (WMLSCrypt) is an application programming interface that allows access to basic security functions in the WML Script Crypto Library (WMLSCLib), such as key pair generation, encryption and decryption of data, generation and verification of digital signatures, storage of keys and other personal data, and controlled access to stored keys and data. WMLSCrypt also allows WAP applications to access and use the security objects and basic security services managed by other WAP security standards. WML script may optionally employ WIM to provide the crypto functionality. Wireless profiled TCP (WP-TCP) provides connection-oriented services. It is optimized for wireless environments and is fully interoperable with standard TCP implementations in the Internet.

Wireless application PKI (WPKI) is not an entirely new set of standards for PKI, but it is an optimized extension of traditional PKI for the wireless environment. WPKI is concerned primarily with the policies used to manage the mobile business and security environment by WTLS/TLS and WMLSCrypt in the wireless application environment. WAP Forum provides the standards for WPKI (discussed in detail in the section Trust Issues).

The WAP Gap

One of the major security breaches in mobile commerce is due to the mobile network infrastructure employed. When the user information is transmitted from one mobile network to another, all the encrypted data need to be decrypted in order to send them to another network. When mobile devices make requests to the Web pages of a network server, these requests originating from the WTSL protocol need to be translated at the originating WAP gateway. They are then encrypted, typically using SSL, and sent to the destination network. This is then processed by the HTTP protocol in the destination network. During the translation process from one protocol to another, the data must be decrypted and then re-encrypted. Because those data are in cleartext, they are vulnerable to attacks if an intruder gains access to the mobile network. This vulnerability is commonly known as the WAP gap. To alleviate this problem of WAP gap, Juul (2002) proposes three alternative solutions: putting the WAP gateway inside the server, application layer, and mobile Internet.

PRIVACY ISSUES

The privacy of mobile users can be compromised either:

(1) by disclosing the location and movement (location privacy) or
(2) by revealing the sensitive profile information (user information privacy) of the mobile users to unintended users.

Location Privacy

Identifying the location of a mobile customer is required because of two reasons. First, to effectively function, location-based services require information about the location of the communication device. As described under Mobile Commerce Applications, the location-based services present a major new market for the mobile industry. Second, in places like the United States, Europe, and Japan, laws require that mobile telephones be able to provide location data with a fairly detailed accuracy for the purposes of emergency situations.

Unlike the Internet, location information has the potential to allow an adversary to physically locate a person, and therefore most wireless subscribers have legitimate concerns about their personal safety, if such information should fall into the wrong hands. The 1996 Telecommunications Act included location information as customer proprietary network information (CPNI), along with time, date, and duration of a call, and the number dialed. Because of the sensitive nature of location information, legal and regulatory approaches for controlling access to location information should be different from other CPNI. Specifically, consumers must be comfortable that they have control over who can obtain location information and when such information can be obtained in order that they will be willing to buy location-based services. Laws and rules of varying clarity, offering different degrees of protection, have been or are in the process of being enacted in the United States, the European Union, and Japan (Ackerman, Kempf, & Miki, 2003).

Beresford and Stajano (2003, 2004) have proposed techniques that let users benefit from location-based applications, while preserving their location privacy. Mobile users, in general, do not permit the information being shared among different location-based services. Primarily, the approach relies on hiding the true identity of a customer from the applications receiving the user's location, by frequently changing pseudonyms so that users avoid being identified by the locations they visit.

User Information Privacy

The needs of mobile commerce applications go beyond tracking users' locations; for example, they may additionally need to track user profiles and preferences in order to achieve mass personalization. This is because, to be effective, targeted advertising should not overwhelm the mobile consumers and must push information only to a certain segment of mobile consumers based on their preferences and profiles, and based on certain marketing criteria. Obviously, these consumers should be targeted only if they are in the location where the advertisement is applicable at the time of the offer. It is important to note here that user profile information may include both sensitive and nonsensitive attributes, such as name, address, linguistic preference, age group, income level, marital status, and education level.

Although mobile consumers like to benefit from personalization, they usually are not willing to share their sensitive profile information with all merchants. To ensure the privacy of mobile users, it is important that sensitive profile information is revealed to the respective merchants only on a need-to-know basis. Therefore, it is essential that the profile information be maintained by a third-party service, rather than by the merchant's system, to ensure the privacy of the mobile users. Typically, the tracking of mobile objects (consumers), i.e., maintaining the moving object database and responding to queries, is performed by the location service (LS). Obviously, this third-party service can be carried out by the LS. This is because it is prudent and economical to use the same service to maintain the profiles, instead of using another service just for this purpose. To ensure privacy of the mobile customers, a fine-grained access control mechanism that could be placed at the LS so that the customer profile information is disclosed to the merchants based on the choice of the customers has been proposed (Atluri, Adam & Youssef, 2003). A system for delivering permission-based location-aware mobile advertisements to mobile phones using Bluetooth positioning and wireless WAP push has also been developed (Aalto, Göthlin, Korhonen, & Ojala, 2004).

TRUST ISSUES

The public key infrastructure is considered wireless when the client devices used to communicate with other parties are wireless although the server could still be on a wired network. The fundamental concepts of PKI in wireless environments are not totally different from those of the wired network environment, and therefore the same concepts that have already been successfully employed in the traditional network environment can be directly applied to the wireless environment. However, access to the PTD over the mobile network environment poses some unique challenges. When compared to the traditional PKI, WPKI applications have to work with a diverse set of PTDs that typically have limited memory, processing, and battery power and smaller displays. Despite these limitations, the PTDs must be able to generate and register keys, manage end-user mobile identities, encrypt and decrypt messages, and receive, verify, store, and send certificates/digitally signed data. In many cases, PTDs are not able to fulfill all these requirements. The PTDs must at least be able to perform a digital signature function to permit the establishment of a WPKI. Typically external agents are responsible for performing certificate validation, archiving, and delivering certificates.

As noted earlier, the private keys are stored in tamper-resistant modules such as WIM/SWIM of PTDs or on a proxy server. However, the WIM/SWIM solutions are not mature enough, particularly in the area of key pairs generation by end users. Establishing trust is crucial for the success of applications that will exploit the opportunities created by PTDs. This trust is not only based on the technology itself, but also on the implementation of laws, policies, standards, and procedures, which includes the management of certificates by trusted certificate authorities. Unfortunately, currently there are no standards for the WPKI, which could be a major obstacle for the success of mobile commerce. However, the situation is similar to that of the wired environment. The issues of anonymity, privacy, and other policies and standards present challenges that must be addressed to enhance the level of trust.

WPKI requires the same components used in traditional PKI. However, the mobile device's applications and registration are implemented differently, and a new component referred to as the PKI portal is also required. The mobile device application in WPKI is implemented such that it runs in the WAP device. It relies on the WMLSCrypt API for key services and cryptographic operations as well as the traditional PKI functionalities.

WPKI is an optimization of the traditional IETF PKIX standards for the wireless environment. More specifically, it comprises optimized PKI protocols, certificate format, and cryptographic algorithms and keys. As opposed to using the traditional basic encoding rules (BER) and distinguished encoding rules (DER) to handle PKI service requests, WPKI protocols are implemented using WML and WMLSCrypt. Similarly, the WPKI certificate format specification is a new certificate format for server side certificates, which significantly reduces the size when compared to the standard X.509 certificate. Another significant reduction in the WPKI certificate can be attributed to ECC, with the savings in size being typically more than 100 bytes because of the smaller keys needed for ECC. WPKI has also limited the size of some of the data fields of the IETF PKIX certificate format. Since the WPKI certificate format is a subset of the PKIX certificate format, it is possible to maintain interoperability between standard PKIs.

RESOURCES

The various resources for this chapter include the Web pages of mobile technology vendors, conferences, and journals in the area of mobile networks, mobile commerce, and electronic commerce. Examples include the following:

The ACM International Conference on Mobile Computing and Networking: http://www.sigmobile.org/mobicom/

M-Business—The Second International Conference on Mobile Business: http://www.mbusiness2003.org/

International Journal of Mobile Communications: https://www.inderscience.com/browse/index.php?journalID=40

Wireless Communications & Mobile Computing: http://www.wileyeurope.com/WileyCDA/WileyTitle/productCd-WCM.html

Mobile Networks and Applications: http://www.kluweronline.com/issn/1383-469X

http://www.umtsworld.com/

http://en.wikipedia.org/wiki/Main_Page

http://www.nttdocomo.com/

http://www.links2mobile.com/ListSubs.asp?cid=52&hd=Mobile+Commerce&ban=4

http://www.bus.iastate.edu/mennecke/server/Mcommerce.htm

http://cms.syr.edu/connecting/wireless/glossary.html

GLOSSARY

802.11b (also 802.11) High rate or Wi-Fi applies to wireless LANs and provides 11-Mbps transmission (with a fallback to 5.5, 2, and 1 Mbps depending on range and signal strength) in the 2.4-GHz band. 802.11b uses only DSSS (direct-sequence spread spectrum), which is one of two types of spread spectrum radio. 802.11b was a 1999 IEEE ratification to the original 802.11 standard, allowing wireless functionality comparable to Ethernet.

3G (Third-Generation Wireless) A development in mobile communications that included increased bandwidth from 128 Kbps while moving at high speeds up to 2 Mbps for fixed stations, enabling multimedia applications and advanced roaming features.

AP Access point.

CCMP (The Counter-Mode/CBC-Mac Protocol) An IEEE 802.11i encryption algorithm. In the 802.11i standard, unlike WPA, key management and message integrity is handled by a single component CCMP built around an advanced encryption standard (AES).

CDMA (Code-Division Multiple Access) A digital method for simultaneously transmitting signals over a shared portion of the spectrum by encoding each distinct signal with a code chip. Terminals receive the aggregated signal from the tower and use specific codes to unbundle the signals. CDMA devices are noted for their excellent connection quality and long battery life.

DSSS (Direct-Sequence Spread Spectrum) A transmission technology used in wireless LAN (WLAN) transmissions where a data signal at the sending station is combined with a higher data rate bit sequence, or chipping code, that divides the user data according to a spreading ratio. The chipping code is a redundant bit pattern for each bit that is transmitted, which increases the signal's resistance to interference. If one or more bits in the pattern are damaged during transmission, the original data can be recovered because of the redundancy of the transmission.

GPS (Global Positioning System) Satellite-based radio-positioning system capable of providing specific location information to suitably equipped users anywhere.

GPRS (General Packet Radio Service) An enhancement to the GSM mobile communications system that supports data packets. GPRS enables continuous flows of IP data packets over the system for such applications as Web browsing and file transfer. GPRS differs from GSM's short messaging service (GSM-SMS), which is limited to messages of 160 bytes in length.

GSM (Global System for Mobile Communications) A digital cellular phone technology based on TDMA that is the predominant system in Europe, but is also used widely around the world. Developed in the 1980s, GSM was first deployed in seven European countries in 1992. Operating in the 900-MHz and 1.8-GHz bands in Europe and the 1.9-GHz PCS band in the United States, GSM defines the entire cellular system, not just the air interface.

QoS (Quality of Service) The ability to define a level of performance in a data communications system. A high QoS would ensure that the packets of data all arrive in time for undetectable reassembly.

UMTS (Universal Mobile Telecommunications System) The ITU standard for 3G wireless phone systems. UMTS, which is part of IMT-2000, provides service in the 2-GHz band and offers global roaming and personalized features. Designed as an evolutionary system for GSM network operators that will marry the benefits of CDMA with the interoperability benefits of GSM, multimedia data rates up to 2 Mbps are expected. There are three branches of the UMTS standard: TD-SCDMA, UMTS TDD, and W-CDMA. CDMA2000 is not UMTS.

WAP (Wireless Access Protocol) A set of standards that allows Web access on mobile devices, and is supported by most wireless networks and operating systems. It supports HTML and XML but is designed for WML.

Wi-Fi (Wireless Fidelity) Another name for IEEE 802.11b. It is a trade term promulgated by the Wireless Ethernet Compatibility Alliance (WECA). Wi-Fi is used in place of 802.11b in the same way that "Ethernet" is used in place of IEEE 802.3. Products certified as Wi-Fi by WECA are interoperable with each other even if they are from different manufacturers. A user with a Wi-Fi product can use any brand of access point with any brand of client hardware built to the Wi-Fi standard.

WLAN (Wireless LAN) A type of LAN that uses high-frequency radio waves rather than wires to communicate between nodes.

WML (Wireless Markup Language) A language developed to control the presentation of Web pages on mobile phones and PDAs in the same way that HTML does for PCs. Part of the wireless access protocol (WAP), WML is an open standard and is supported by most mobile phones.

XHTML A reworking of HTML 4.0 designed to work as an application of XML. It allows anyone to create sets of markup tags for new purposes.

CROSS REFERENCES

See *Bluetooth Security; Bluetooth Technology; Mobile Devices and Protocols; Radio Frequency and Wireless Communications Security; Security and the Wireless Application Protocol (WAP); Wireless Channels; Wireless Internet: A Cellular Perspective.*

REFERENCES

Aalto, L., Göthlin, N., Korhonen, J., & Ojala, T. (2004). Bluetooth and WAP Push based location-aware mobile advertising system. MobiSys.

Ackerman, L., Kempf, J., & Miki, T. (2003). Wireless location privacy: Law and policy in the U.S., EU and Japan. *Internet Society*, November.

Ambassna-Jones, M. (2004). *Mobile commerce (m-commerce) & micropayment strategies.*

Andersson, C. (2001). *GPRS and 3G wireless applications: The ultimate guide to maximizing mobile internet technologies.* New York: Wiley.

Atluri, V., Adam, N. R., & Youssef, M. (2003, October). Towards a unified index scheme for mobile data and customer profiles in a location-based service environment. Paper presented at the *Workshop on Next Generation Geospatial Information (NG2I'03).*

Barnes, S., & Huff, S. (2003). Rising sun: i-mode and the wireless Internet. *Communications of the ACM, 46*(11), 78–84.

Beresford, A. R., & Stajano, F. (2003). Location privacy in pervasive computing. *Pervasive Computing,* January–March.

Beresford, A. R., & Stajano, F. (2004). Mix zones: User privacy in location-aware services. Paper presented at the *IEEE Workshop on Pervasive Computing and Communication Security (PerSec) 2004,* a workshop in PerCom 2004.

Electronic News. (2003, Marcy 13). NewLogic invests in 4G mobile technology.

InStat/MDR. (2002). Worldwide wireless data/internet market: Bright spots in a dark industry.

Juels, A., & Brainard, J. (2004). Soft blocking: Flexible blocker tags on the cheap. In S. De Capitani di Vimercati & P. Syverson (Eds.), *Workshop on Privacy in the Electronic Society (WPES).*

Juels, A., Rivest, R. L., & Szydlo, M. (2003). The blocker tag: selective blocking of RFID tags for consumer privacy. Paper presented at the *Proceedings of the 10th ACM Conference on Computer and Communication Security.*

Juul, N. C. (2002). Security issues in mobile commerce using WAP. Paper presented at the *15th Bled Electronic Commerce Conference, E-Reality: Constructing the E-Economy, Bled, Slovenia, June 17–19, 2002.*

Kumar, S. (2004). Mobile communications: global trends in the 21st century. *International Journal of Mobile Communications (IJMC)*, 2(1).

Lehmann, H., & Lehner, F. (2004). *Is there a "killer application" in mobile technology? A tailored research approach* (working paper). University of Regensburg.

Nua Internet Surveys. (2002, March 21). *Frost & Sullivan: M-commerce transactions to hit USD25 billion.*

Pyramid Research. (2004, April). *Is Wi-Fi wagging the 3G dog?*

Rao, B., & Minakakis, L. (2003). Evolution of mobile location-based services. *Communications of the ACM, 46*(12).

Sadeh, N. (2002). *M-commerce: Technologies, services and business models*. New York: Wiley.

Spagat, E. (2002, September 11). Handheld homing devices: GPS hits household gadgets. *Wall Street Journal.*

Umar, A. (2004). *Mobile computing and wireless communications applications, networks, platforms, architectures, and security.*

Venkatesh, V., Ramesh, V., & Massey, A. P. (2003). Understanding usability in mobile commerce. *Communications of the ACM, 46*(12).

Wireless World Forum. (2004).

Yankee Group Research. (2004). *Mobile user survey results*.

FURTHER READING

Dornan, A. (2001). *The essential guide to wireless communications applications: From cellular systems to WAP and m-commerce.* Englewood Cliffs, NJ: Prentice Hall.

Gururajan, R. (2002). New financial transaction security concerns in mobile commerce. *Information & Security, 8*(1), 71–86.

Lehner, F., & Watson, R. (2001). *From e-commerce to m-commerce: Research directions* (working paper). University of Regensburg, 2001. NTT DoCoMo Backgrounder: Technologies and strategies.

Stafford, T. F., & Gillenson, M. L. (2003). Mobile commerce: What it is and what it could be. *Communications of the ACM, 46*(12).

E-Education and Information Privacy and Security

William K. Jackson, *Southern Oregon University*

INTRODUCTION

Early efforts in correspondence courses and self-learning through programmed instruction methodologies were ventures in alternatives to the traditional face-to-face, in the classroom modality of delivering and receiving education. Subsequent technologies have provided new and improved ways of delivering these self-paced course materials. Wrapped in today's technology and incorporating revised educational models e-education has evolved. In this chapter, e-education refers to the replacement or supplement of traditional face-to-face delivery of learning components with electronically based elements. Further, primary focus is on e-education where there is:

- Mediation, i.e., an instructor to evaluate the progress of the student;
- An acknowledgement of completion i.e., a degree, a certificate, or a grade; and
- Some form of measuring the student's progress or evaluation of accomplishment.

E-education is also referred to as online learning, virtual learning, and Web-based learning.

Societal needs for education in vocations and professions that are new or that now require more training or skills than in the past have increased the demand for knowledge and learning. At the same time the ability of many individuals to fit into the rigid schedules of traditional education because of work or family constraints has declined.

In a report addressing its internal computing plan, the University of Indiana noted that "The same array of teaching and learning technologies should be available for local or remote learners—in campus classrooms or residence halls, at students' homes, or in the workplace—to be chosen as appropriate to the instructional needs, and not constrained by location" (Indiana University, 1998). Although there are significant differences between virtual and traditional learning, there are also many characteristics that they have in common. Common elements include:

- Delivery of content;
- Discussions of topics;
- Questions and answers;
- Personal consultation;
- Research;
- Testing and assessment;
- Writing exercises; and
- Problem solving.

Two characteristics of e-education that set it apart from traditional education are that virtual education usually:

- Can be asynchronous in nature; and
- Is electronically based.

The issue of privacy associated with offering a course online takes on its own unique characteristics. While teaching a recent virtual learning class Lisa Neal made the following observation: "In the virtual classroom, keyed-in responses, virtual hand-raising, and feedback indicators provide information to the instructor—information that has traditionally remained private. All of this idiosyncratic, subjective and contextual data is captured and recorded" (Neal, 2003).

E-EDUCATION EXAMINED

Winograd and Moore (2003) paint an interesting picture of the e-education student in contrast to the traditional student struggling to get to class: "an estimated 2.23 million didn't [struggle]. Instead they stayed home, studied, listened to and spoke to or wrote to their teachers, chatted, . . . , did research . . . , took exams . . . and turned in assignments—without ever entering a classroom." Describing the extent of institutional participation in virtual learning Winograd and Moore reported that 85% of two-year colleges and 84% of four-year institutions were expected to offer distance education course by 2002 and most of the growth would utilize the Internet.

In an article examining e-education in higher education, Ralph Gomory of the Sloan Consortium states:

> They are continuing to provide the basic elements that are associated with classroom teaching, but

> they are providing them in a different way. Those basic elements of classroom teaching are, first, the professors. Then, second, there is the course material. A third important element is classmates. They help both in and out of class. They provide an element of shared experience, and they are people with whom both the course content and what the professor meant can be discussed between classes. They also provide important emotional support. (Gomory, 2001)

Gomory further suggests "using asynchronous learning networks provides a form of these elements electronically, without a campus, without a classroom, and without the necessity for either the learner or the professor to be at some fixed place or time when a lecture is being given."

There exists on ongoing debate concerning the quality and value of online learning and the online degree. There are both skeptics and proponents. Although the jury has not provided a final verdict, there is much evidence that the quality of online learning is not different from the quality of a brick-and-mortar counterpart (Winograd and Moore, 2003).

In a 2003 study of higher education academic leaders it was found that when asked to compare the quality of online courses with face-to-face instruction:

- 57% believed learning outcomes for online education are equal to or are superior; and
- Nearly one-third expected outcomes for online courses will be superior in three years.

The study further suggests that rather than examining the question of "Is it as good as?", one should perhaps ask "How is it better?" (Sloan Consortium, 2003). Although the Sloan study addresses institutions of higher education, there is no reason to believe that similar trends do not exist for other instances of e-education.

A framework for understanding important aspects of e-education that define its current state includes the following:

- E-education is driven by technology.
- Societal changes and pressures have altered the way many students view the whole educational process.
- There are many levels of participants in e-education including K–12, post-secondary two- and four-year and graduate degree programs, vocational education, and continuing education programs. This participation includes traditional educational institutions both public and private, professional organizations, and new educational ventures.
- E-education stakeholders include students, educators, course and media designers, providers of technology platforms, and consortiums of interested groups.

The Enabling Technologies of E-Education

Several technologies working together have created a reliable platform for e-education efforts. These technologies include the Internet, data communication systems, and personal computer hardware and software systems.

The Internet

The Internet has become almost a natural part of life for a great number of people. A report on Internet connectivity in the public school system revealed that at the end of 2001 99% of all public schools were connected (NCES, 2003). Efforts to improve connectivity can now focus on the availability and speed of these connections.

Data Communication Systems

One of the highly publicized and acknowledged constraints that the Internet faces is capacity or bandwidth. Increased availability of high-speed connections to the Internet will be a key factor in the success and acceptance of e-education efforts. Increased bandwidth will not only afford opportunities for increased use of valuable graphics, video, and audio within course content, but will also enable more synchronous connections among course participants using technologies supporting group activities such as net meetings and video conferencing. Several solutions to the problem of access and transfer at high speed are available today and the trend is to make broadband connections available at increasingly more affordable rates. Many support the notion that one of the keys to successful e-education is growth in high-speed connections.

Bringing connections and bandwidth in particular to schools and libraries has been a top priority in expanding the capabilities of the Internet. Much of the effort directed toward the well-publicized "information super highway" efforts of President Clinton's administration addressed the infrastructure. Concurrent with establishing connections, there has been an attempt to upgrade dial-up connections in homes to broadband. President G. W. Bush proposed an increase in broadband access in part to "be accessible in every corner of our country by the year 2007 to enhance educational and health-care services, particularly in rural areas. Ubiquitous broadband would let colleges offer education to students in their homes" (Primedia, 2004). About one U.S. household in five now pays up to $50 a month for high-speed Internet service delivered via DSL phone lines or cable TV modem connections (Bray, 2004). America Online (AOL) illustrates the challenge of shifting to broadband in two trends it recently noted with its customers as they shifted to higher speed connections: AOL lost 399,000 dial-up subscribers in the fourth quarter ending 2003, whereas they added nearly 400,000 broadband customers in the same time period (Yang, 2004).

Computer Hardware and Software

Ongoing developments in Internet browser capabilities are creating products that are more robust and feature rich. Many of these new features support the interactive, dynamic capabilities needed in e-education. Competition and ongoing improvements and upgrades in multimedia software are enabling more educators to become developers of course content and the standards and quality of the content to increase. The ability to use and create CD and DVD media with their large capacities reduces the cost of distributing large amounts of learning content.

Societal Changes

Societal changes are impacting the extent and format of the demand for education. Included in these changes are:

- The increase in degree requirements for many jobs;
- The need for continuing education and knowledge updates;
- Individuals reentering the job market after life-changing events;
- Mobility and job-related travel;
- Increased user familiarity and computer skills; and
- The increase in home schooling.

Societal changes and the impact they have on educational endeavors of individuals contribute to the growth of e-education. There are more potential students/learners. Family and work obligations are making traditional brick-and-mortar offerings not a viable solution for many. Increased demand for education comes from both new learners and additional needs of existing learners. Societal changes with respect to gender equity increases the demand for education. "One of the most notable changes since the 1960s resulting from social change and education reform is undoubtedly the large-scale enrollment of women at post-secondary institutions, especially universities" (Corbeil, 2003).

The financial value of education is widely known and accepted. The financial incentives associated with the successful pursuit of additional education are high. According to recent findings, "male graduates pocket 58 percent more and women 92 percent more than their peers with a high school diploma." In addition, the same study found "college graduates also enjoy a much lower rate of unemployment throughout the business cycle" (Farrell, 2003).

An Edventures study reveals that "despite the increasing premium placed by employers on having an undergraduate degree, almost three-quarters of Americans under 25 lack one." As fewer students go directly from high school to post-secondary education, larger numbers of nontraditional students seek alternatives to the traditional classroom setting to complete their degrees. Another avenue of education experiencing an increase in demand is certification. "We are moving to a certification-based society—there's great demand for getting a degree in addition to training" (Phillips, 2003).

Where E-Education Occurs

E-education is a delivery strategy present at all levels of education and training including preschool, K–12, post-secondary 2- and 4-year and graduate schools, and professional, adult, community, military, government, and industrial efforts.

Formal Education

E-education has a large presence in formal education including K–12, undergraduate, and graduate schools where diplomas and degrees are granted for completing an approved, accredited program of studies. Application of e-education technologies is widespread and pervasive in this traditional sector of education.

A Sloan Institute-sponsored study of institutions of higher education concluded the following:

- Students are willing to take online courses;
- Institutions of higher education are willing to embrace online courses;
- Some, but not all, faculty have embraced online education; and
- The quality of online education is as good as that of traditional education.

The study also noted that in 2002 more than 1.6 million students (11%) took at least one online course, 81% of all higher education institutions offer at least one online course, and 34% of institutions offer complete online degree programs. In addition, 57% of academic leaders believe learning outcomes for online courses are equal to or superior to traditional face-to-face instruction (Allen & Seaman, 2003).

According to a study of remedial education in post-secondary institutions in the fall of 2000, 64% of post-secondary institutions responding indicated that the Internet was the primary delivery method for remedial instruction (NCES, 2001).

Traditional Institutions and New Institutions

Traditional educational institutions are those that were in existence prior to the existence of e-education: the public and private K–12, trade schools, and institutions of higher education.

New organizations have been formed to take advantage of the explosion in e-education. Some of these organizations are completely new, whereas others have evolved into a new form to grow with the opportunities that participating in e-education offers. An interesting example of old institutions participating in the virtual learning world is the MIT OpenCourseWare initiative model, which offers the content of over 500 of its courses online (MIT, 2003). Additional examples of institutions that either are new or have incorporated online delivery of coursework as a significant part of their mission include:

- University of Phoenix;
- Nova Southeastern University;
- Devry Institute Online;
- American Intercontinental University Online;
- Capella University;
- Colorado Technical University;
- Regis University Online;
- Jones International University; and
- Western Governors University.

Professional and Continuing Education

Companies and professional organizations utilize e-education to provide continuing education and certification courses. An example of a company-sponsored venture into e-education can be found at Motorola, which has a developed number of courses to keep their employees current in their areas of employment. Many of these courses are online and can be found on the Motorola Web site (Motorola, 2003). A U.S. Congressional Commission study found in part that "Motorola, long the standard for industry, provides every employee with at least 40 hours of training each year" (Fulton, 2001).

The Public Broadcasting System (PBS) makes available a broad range of courses for various levels of credit to the general public through associated institutions. The offerings available through the PBS associates can be found on their Web site (PBS, 2003).

In professional fields such as medicine, continuing education is available from many sources in e-education format. The Harvard Medical School's Department of Continuing Education Web site is a representative example of professional continuing education credits being provided online (HMS-CME, 2004). Many other professional fields including accounting, nursing, architecture, project management, and law enforcement have similar providers of e-education-based continuing education.

Commercial and Other Support Organizations

There exists an industry of organizations providing support services and products for e-education. The mission and objectives of these companies are often focused on being third-party providers of solutions to the technical aspects of e-education.

Blackboard, Inc. (http://www.blackboard.com) and eCollege.com (http://www.ecollege.com) are examples of this type of organization. Both provide software products and services used by many institutions and organizations involved in e-education. Estimates of the size of this market sector suggest it reached a revenue level of $6 to $7 billion in 2002, and there are forecasts that revenues of $50 billion will be reached by 2010 (BizReport, 2003). *Business Week* recently reported that more than 2000 schools were using the software from Blackboard when schools opened in the fall of 2004 and that Blackboard is gaining presence in K–12 and foreign universities (*Business Week*, 2004). Organizations that are part of this group are often referred to as dot-coms, or they have a significant component that includes Web-related technology capabilities.

The Participants in E-Education

To understand the interrelationships present in e-education, a valuable perspective comes from examining the participants. Stakeholders in e-education include students, educators, providers, developers, sponsors, and consortiums. The following sections discuss each of these participants. In many implementations of e-education a single organization may provide multiple or even all of the components.

Students

Students are the recipients of the e-education product. The student group can be classified as K–12, post-secondary 2- and 4-year schools, graduate schools, training, and continuing education. Students participate in e-education from remedial to doctoral levels.

Educators

In all cases course content and delivery strategies need to be developed and implemented. The individual or group that puts the course together and is responsible for the evaluation of the success of the student in completing the course is considered to be the primary educator for a course. It is important to distinguish between course content and course management. In some instances content and management may be integrated; in others they may be separate. A computer science professor might use the BlackBoard system to manage the course and present course information while utilizing a series of CD-based MS PowerPoint presentations to present topic content on database design.

Providers

Providers supply the technical platform, the software, and the computer servers that students connect to and where educators store their courses. For institutions or organizations that do not have the ability to supply the technical platform needed to deliver courses themselves, they can subscribe to a wide range of services from a third party. An example of an organization that provides a wide range of services supporting virtual learning is eCollege. In their own words: "eCollege provides all of the necessary technology and services in an integrated approach to power the profitable growth of online distance programs" (eCollege, 2004).

Developers

In a report to President Clinton on the use of technology to strengthen K–12 education in the United States the Web-Based Education Commission pointedly observes that "There is widespread agreement that one of the principal factors now limiting the extensive and effective use of technology within American schools is the relative dearth of high-quality computer software and digital content designed specifically for that purpose" (Fulton, 2001). Although this comment was aimed at the K–12 area, especially the secondary schools, it probably applies equally to all forms of e-education. Third-party companies have formed and grown to fill the needs of educational institutions who do not have the internal resources to develop their own online course materials. An example of an organization that has been developing materials for online learning since 1971 is Bisk Education, Inc., which works with nationally known organizations and accredited universities to assist in creating course content (Bisk, 2003).

Sponsors

In e-education the sponsor is represented by the institution granting credit or certification for the successful completion of the course. The sponsor is the institution that the student interfaces with, often a school or professional organization. The standard practice for most sponsors is to be involved in all aspects of course development, delivery, and management, although some components may come from third parties.

Consortiums

To leverage and take advantage of the efforts being put into e-education and to be cost effective in implementing the results, several consortiums have developed to assist in the delivery of e-education. In many instances these consortiums serve as evaluators of life experiences and brokers of course completion work provided by members of the consortium. A good model for this approach is Western Governors University, founded by the governors of 19 western states and the only university to be accredited by four regional commissions (WGU, 2003). The consortium model varies greatly. Examples of other consortiums include:

- *Edlearn Consortium*: Member colleges have combined their course and program offerings on the consortium's Web site. Students can apply, register, and access student services from any of the member colleges with a single Web-based transaction. Students can take courses from across the consortium in completing their degree or program requirements (Edlearn, 2003).
- *Electronic Campus of the Southern Regional Education Board*: A consortium of several southern states that has the objective to "improve every aspect of education—from early childhood education to doctoral degrees and beyond" (SREB, 2003).
- *Keystone University Network*: Keystone University Network offers multiple degree and certificate programs through the 14 Pennsylvania state system universities (Keystone University, 2003).
- *Ohio Learning Network*: Currently there are more than 60 degrees and certificates listed in OhioLearns (Ohio Learning Network, 2003).
- *SUNY Learning Network*: Students can study, take classes, and complete entire degree programs at any time and from any place from more than 3,000 online courses with more than 50,000 statewide, national, and international student enrollments (SUNY Learning Network, 2003).
- *The Connecticut Distance Learning Consortium (CT-DLC)*: The Consortium was created in October 1996 when over 30 colleges and universities met and agreed that Connecticut needed to systematically mount distance deliverable education (CTDLC, 2003).
- *Cardean University*: Cardean University is an academic consortium with five elite institutions: Columbia School of Business, Stanford, University of Chicago, Carnegie Mellon, and the London School of Economics, collaborating with Cardean course designers and technology experts to create effective Internet learning (Cardean, 2003).

There can be little doubt in the presence of all of the enabling technologies, the societal pressures, and the wide and extensive participation that e-education has become a permanent part of the educational mix.

LEGAL FOUNDATIONS AND SECURITY AND PRIVACY ISSUES

The legal foundation controlling the establishment of policies and procedures for the participants in e-education comes from several directions as they apply to various aspects of privacy and security.

The Buckley Amendment, the Family Education Rights and Privacy Act (FERPA), in 1974 was the original enabling legislation providing guidelines for the proper handling and treatment of student information (NCES, 2002). This legislation preceded the advent and widespread usage of the Internet and e-education and the widespread electronic transmission of student data. Implementing compliance with FERPA since its initial passage has had to evolve to incorporate electronic data. One of the specific areas covered by FERPA is the definition of education records as they relate to the classroom. A definition of education records includes the statement "(1) contain information directly related to a student; and (2) are maintained by an educational agency or institution or by a person acting for such an agency or institution." This has been interpreted to include the collection of data from students while participating in a course (Bauer & Decman, 2002). FERPA and subsequent updates provide strong legislation that protects the privacy of student records. Institutions and agencies need policies and procedures that comply with these laws.

More recently the Uniting and Strengthening America by Providing Appropriate Tools Required to Intercept and Obstruct Terrorism (USA PATRIOT) Act has added an additional layer of legal requirements governing the correct collection and in particular the dissemination of data collected by institutions about their students. In effect the USA PATRIOT Act overrides and in some cases contradicts the FERPA rulings. FERPA protected the privacy of student information and restricted the release of student data without notice to and permission from the students. The USA PATRIOT Act requires immediate access to student data for identified law officials in tightly defined circumstances and prohibits notification that this access has been made (NCES, 2002).

Special privacy considerations are present when young users are considered. When there is e-education activity in the K–12 years, the legal ramifications of COPPA need to be understood and translated into policies and procedures that create compliance (TRUSTe, 2003b). Under COPPA requirements, a Web site directed toward children less than 13 years of age must comply with strict rules relating to data gathering and use (Gale Group, 2003).

Signed into law in 2002, the TEACH Act defines the terms and conditions that accredited, nonprofit educational institutions throughout the United States must follow when using copyright protected materials in distance education. Although this Act makes usage of copyright materials in distance education easier, it also requires strict institutional adherence to rigorous requirements of the law (American Library Association 2004).

An issue that needs to be understood and addressed in a balanced way is noted by the American Library Association: "the right of anonymity and privacy while people retrieve and communicate information must be protected as an essential element of intellectual freedom" (American Library Association, 2003).

In an article that addresses balancing security and privacy, Steve Worona notes that "And then came 9/11 and the need to find ways to protect the public against further terrorist attacks. Inevitably the balance between security and privacy shifted" (Worona, 2003). When the USA

PATRIOT Act is applied to educational settings it alters many of the aspects of student information guardianship. As Worona further notes, authentication has become an important issue. The creation of complete audit trails of all digital traffic with the ability to identify the originator has been proposed by some. It is not surprising that the proponents of anonymity oppose a push toward extreme implementation of authentication procedures.

Identity theft and other improper and illegal information misappropriations are related to authentication in education as digital requests for information are processed. In an article addressing identity and privacy issues, Joe F. Thompson writes:

> Businesses and institutions, such as colleges and universities, must recognize their role as inadvertent enablers of identity theft and must exercise due diligence in the confirmation of proffered identity, the quality control of marketed credit history information, and the adaptation of business practices to the speed and range of IT. (Thompson, 2002)

SECURITY AND PRIVACY IN E-EDUCATION

Industry Best Practices

There are many strategies employed by organizations developed to reduce risks related to security and privacy. General practices particularly relevant to e-education include the use or implementation of:

- Passwords and other access controls;
- Firewalls;
- Virus control;
- Backup and recovery plans;
- Hacker protection;
- E-mail attachment handling; and
- Retention and disposition of course-related materials.

Most institutions are aware of the issues and the strategies available to address these potential vulnerabilities, and they implement actions to guard against the obvious and known threats. Technical security should be implemented at the provider level and be end-to-end in nature. Explanatory statements of security and privacy policies are present on almost all Web sites for organizations involved in e-education. The educational environment is not one that generally welcomes controls. Long-held notions of academic and intellectual freedom may be at odds with controls that may not protect the privacy of activities engaged in by learners.

Issues

In a recent study addressing the issue of privacy and online learning, it was found that "Today students expect colleges and universities to protect these rights throughout the campus intranet and the Internet, that is, throughout the virtual learning environment." Students additionally expect protection to apply to information about personal activities such as card key access to buildings, purchases, access to online library resources, and login activity to campus networks and the Internet (Educause, 1998). There appear to be three areas receiving attention as organizations attempt to ensure both security and privacy in e-education activities:

- Selection and use of proper technology;
- Establishment and communication of policies; and
- Usage and updating of proper procedures.

Selection and Use of Proper Technology

Much has been written about the development and usage of computer protection models (Caruso, 2003; Kuavik, 2004). Proper security measures that generally apply to user and server security apply to e-education applications as well. All of the warnings and aptly described consequences resulting from improper Internet procedures are well documented (Educause, 2004).

Establishment and Communication of Policies

Most organizations involved in e-education appear to be aware of the need for policy statements regarding their position on security and privacy. Likewise, most Internet sites provide a link to policy statements concerning security and privacy. These policies typically address FERPA-related personal data, data collected from queries to the site, and data provided to register and gain access to the site. It is unusual for a privacy statement to address data collected by educators while a student is completing coursework. At a minimum, how the institution will implement adherence to the existing body of law including FERPA, the USA PATRIOT act, and appropriate state laws needs to be articulated and communicated. Most policies appear to focus on administrative tasks and related data and are not directed toward academic tasks and data related to academic activities. Although there is a legal basis for the custodianship of personal data, it is less clear how the guidelines for course-generated data should be treated. At a minimum, applicable legal dictates need to be followed.

Many educators do not keep current with the legal foundations controlling the privacy of data. This suggests that educators who are involved in e-education need to keep current regarding the consequences and legal implications of existing law. As a general guide for the creation of a policy statement, Dr. Armand Prieditis offers a 14-point question outline (Prieditis, 2001). These questions include asking whether the policy:

- Is prominent;
- Is explicit;
- Is clear;
- Is short;
- Defines what data are collected;
- States what the user gets;
- Explains how the organization uses the data;
- Identifies who else receives the data;
- Explains how often the data are distributed;

- Defines how permanent the data are;
- Describes how to correct/update/delete data;
- Has an opt-out feature;
- Includes special handling for children; and
- Includes contact information.

The content of privacy and security policies can be framed in an eight-point set of issues and recommendations from the Educause study on policy formulation (Educause, 1998):

- *Notification*: Students are informed concerning the what, who, and why data are being collected and what steps are being taken to guarantee the security of the data.
- *Minimization*: No more data are gathered than is necessary and the data are retained no longer than necessary, then they are properly disposed of.
- *Secondary use*: In most cases data are only used for the purpose for which they were collected or an academically sound related purpose.
- *Non disclosure and consent*: Student information should not be distributed to parties external to the institution. With online courses and a presence on the Internet, new questions arise because of the inherent availability associated with Internet access.
- *Need to know*: An individual within the virtual learning environment should be granted access to data only if they have a legitimate educational interest in the data.
- *Data accuracy, inspection, and review*: Data maintained by an educational institution must be correct, and students should have the right to examine and audit the information stored about them.
- *Information security, integrity, and accountability*: Security refers to the protection of information, integrity ensures the data will not be inappropriately altered, and accountability ensures an audit trail for the data exists.
- *Education*: A basic responsibility to ensure that faculty, staff, and administrators are educated about the privacy rights of students and the potential implications of misuse of the information exists.

If these eight issues are addressed in an ongoing effort, a comprehensive framework for establishing a broad and strong policy base will be in place.

To enhance the understanding of privacy issues relating to e-education perhaps something may be learned by examining the history and experience the medical field has had addressing concerns of privacy as it has gone online. Some experiences with the privacy issue in the health care field include the following (Goldman & Hudson, 2000):

- GlobalHealthtrax, which sells health products online, inadvertently revealed names, home phone numbers, and bank account and credit card information of thousands of customers on its Web site;
- Kaiser Permanente mistakenly sent an e-mail containing sensitive information to the wrong recipients; and
- Thousands of patient records were accidentally made available to the public on the University of Michigan Medical Center's Web site.

In a fairly comprehensive study examining the privacy policies and their implementation, Goldman and Hudson concluded that "On the whole, it appears that while web sites are generally more attentive to the need for privacy policies—as evidenced by the growing number of sites with privacy policies—these policies still fall short of a comprehensive privacy scheme" (Goldman, Hudson, & Smith, 2000). One of the results of this research is a fairly comprehensive set of guidelines for developing a Web site privacy policy.

In addition to the presence of a privacy policy, trust appears to play a large part in the acceptance of any privacy statement. Anything can be stated in a privacy policy. The question remains regarding what assurance does a visitor to a Web site have that the site will actually comply with its posted policy? A number of online privacy seals have been established in an attempt to reassure consumers about often confusing privacy policy provisions. These seals include TRUSTe, CPA WebTrust, BBBOnline, and SecureAssure. All of these seals set standards that participating sites must meet (TRUSTe, 2003a). A good outline for both students and teachers that focuses on the guidelines, specifically in educational settings, for trust development in creating privacy policies has been created (TRUSTe, 2003b).

Collection and Custodianship of Classroom Data

Supplemental to the legal issues about the custodianship of personal information there also are concerns regarding the collection of information generated during the conduct of a class. These concerns may be in at least three areas:

- Collection;
- Access and usage; and
- Disposition.

While sharing her recent experiences in teaching an online course, Lisa Neal stated "we need explicit policies clearly setting forth what data can be collected, for what purposes, who has access, and how long the data will be retained" (Neal, 2003). The issue of privacy in e-education is no different than that in traditional education. Even though the contact and conduct of the class is online rather than face-to-face, the elements of a course are approximately the same. The traditional elements and some of their online counterparts include the following, all of which may create a digital audit trail of data that can be associated with a particular student:

- *Presentation of content*: audio, video, and multimedia presentations;
- *Classroom discussions*: chat rooms, threaded discussion groups, and peer reviews;
- *Critical thinking*: research and assignments;

- *Testing and assessment*: online testing with immediate feedback and portfolio assessments;
- *Submission and grading of assignments*: e-mail with attachments;
- *Feedback*: e-mail, online discussions; and
- *Research*: online library access, Web search engines, and Internet databases.

Because of the virtual nature of e-education, communications that would have taken place in the classroom are now recorded digitally using a permanent storage media. This content is available for later retrieval and use by whoever has access. Information that in traditional settings would disappear immediately may now be permanently recorded.

What is not usually addressed in most formal policy statements is how information transmitted during the conduct of classroom activities such as discussion groups, assessment activities, and e-mail is to be treated. Policies often do not discuss the ownership, availability, and disposition of this level of information generated by participating in an e-course.

Whatever the answers to these questions are, it is only correct that they should be known to the students. In an editorial, Lisa Neal, editor of *eLearn Magazine*, shares a concern that came up in a class she was teaching online:

> When taking a course, students implicitly agree to the instructor's rules. Instructors have a certain amount of power over students through grades and other information they provide to the institution offering the course. However, most institutions deploy technology without providing adequate—if any—information about what data is captured and how it can be used. I first became aware of this when, years ago, I ran strategic planning sessions using anonymous brainstorming and voting tools. My client never asked me how the data was stored, but I could easily see who contributed which idea and how everyone voted. I'm glad no manager ever asked me to divulge this data because there was nothing in writing that would have protected my refusal on ethical grounds. (Neal, 2003)

One of the potential advantages of collecting data during the normal conduct of the course is in its potential to study and analyze patterns of success and failure that may exist. As is further stated in her editorial, "we need explicit policies clearly setting forth what data can be collected for what purposes, who has access, and how long the data is retained" (Neal, 2003). This common oversight in privacy policies needs to be addressed.

CONCLUSION

Often a birth date is used as an initial, temporary password, presumably a piece of information known to few people. This is likely not to be true. Visiting the Web site anybirthday.com allows you to discover the birth date of almost anyone. This ability should not surprise very many people, although it probably does. This ready access to personal data serves as an example of the type of information available on the Internet information that is often used for security purposes.

Several things seem apparent regarding e-education and issues relating to privacy and security. It is important that policies addressing privacy and security issues be developed and communicated at all levels. These policies should directly address the gathering, storage, usage, and disposal of both personal data and data collected during the conduct of a class. There is a consensus among professionals that these policies need to be complete and honest, follow industry standards, and be communicated to the user. To make these policies an important component of the course, trust in their usage must be established.

Specific focus on the importance of privacy and security in part depends on where in the educational delivery supply chain an individual resides. In a broader context that would include privacy and security, Professor Sarah Redfield suggests that "Since the liability will lie only where there is 'deliberate indifference' a reasonable, preventive, pre-existing system for review and response... can put the administrator in a position to avoid liability." Professor Redfield argues that educators need to know more law. They need to have a good knowledge of legal frameworks and to utilize a system to be kept current (Redfield, 2003).

If you are a student, you want assurances that personal information about you is kept private, is available for you to review, and is properly guarded from improper release. You want assurances that information generated by you and about you while taking a class is treated properly and is not used in ways other than intended and that you have been made aware of. You want to be sure you can pursue relevant research without fear of retribution. As the American Library Association has noted, "The rights of anonymity and privacy while people retrieve and communicate information must be protected as an essential element of intellectual freedom." This freedom received a fresh look after the events of September 11 and the subsequent passage of the USA PATRIOT Act, which may have caused the existing balance between security and privacy to shift in favor of the former (American Library Association, 2003). As a student you also want to be sure that services you subscribe to will not cause you any harm.

If you are an educator you need to understand the laws that govern data privacy issues and that the practical implications of these laws in the conduct of your classes. You also want to be sure that policies are in place to protect the privacy of instructor and student interactions and that these policies are communicated.

Sponsors need to be aware of all of the federal and state regulations appropriate to their business venture. A sponsor needs to make sure a written policy regarding security and privacy is created and that the policy is communicated, understood, and followed by the administration, the educators, and the students.

If you are a provider you need to be sure you understand the laws and liabilities that govern your interaction with your subscribers. Since the provider is the repository and source of content and connections to the participants, they need to be up-to-date on all of the current secure site technologies. Proper technology tools that ensure security and privacy need to be utilized.

Developers need to be aware of legal frameworks that govern appropriate content for the audience their products are intended and any controlling regulations that might determine how they can conform to regulations. The Americans with Disabilities Act might influence design and implementation strategies as products are developed.

Often consortiums and brokers are representing the products and services of others. They need to know the legal framework of the relationship between student and administration and that the true relationship between the student and sponsors, especially regarding privacy and security, is communicated and followed. This may be a source of liability concerns.

It is evident that e-education in its many forms is here to stay, and likely will increase in both size and quality. As the e-education industry matures, it will be interesting to observe how this new mode of education seeks its appropriate level.

GLOSSARY

ALN Asynchronous learning networks.

Asynchronous An activity that can occur without coordination with other similar events. In e-education it refers to the timing of course events and the fact that the student works on their schedule rather than a fixed schedule that everyone adheres to.

Bandwidth A measurement of how much data can be transmitted over a communications line; often used to describe the data communications capacity on an Internet connection.

Brick and Mortar Traditional classroom setting that takes place in a room where a teacher and students meet together.

Broadband A high-speed, high-capacity data communications connection.

Buckley Amendment Legislation passed in 1974 that provided rights and privacy protection. See the Family Education Rights and Privacy Act (FERPA).

Certification A formal recognition of achievement or knowledge in a specific area.

Chat An online tool for communicating in an asynchronous discussion group mode.

COPPA The Children's Online Privacy Protection Act applies to the online collection of personal information from children under 13. The new rules spell out what a Web site operator must include in a privacy policy, when and how to seek verifiable consent from a parent, and what responsibilities an operator has to protect the privacy and safety of children who are online.

Dial-up A data communications connection that utilizes the existing voice grade telephone system; a slow, low-capacity connection.

Digital Signature Encrypted transmission including the message plus the sender's key information.

Distance Learning Interaction at a distance between instructor and learners, enabling timely instructor reaction to learners. Simply posting or broadcasting learning materials to learners is not distance learning. Instructors must be involved in receiving feedback from learners.

E-Course An offering of an electronically based course; an instance of an e-education offering with content, completion, and assessment.

E-Education Education that utilizes electronic media, including the Internet, as the primary mode for interacting with students.

Face-to-Face The traditional educational setting where students and teachers are physically present together.

The Family Education Rights and Privacy Act (FERPA) Legislation passed in 1974 that provided rights and privacy protection; see also Buckley Amendment.

Life-Long Learners The trend that recognizes that learning will take place over a lifetime and does not end when a student "graduates."

Online Class A course where the content and communications take place over the Internet.

Online Learning Learning that is associated with content readily accessible on the Internet. Course content may be on the Internet, or simply installed on a CD-ROM or a computer hard disk.

Synchronous Events that adhere to a schedule. Traditional classes that meet at a certain time and cover specific topics at those specified times refer to synchronous learning. All students are approximately at the same point in the course at any given time.

TEACH Act Federal legislation that defines the rules for copyright usage in distance education and the requirements for qualifying institutions.

Uniting and Strengthening America by Providing Appropriate Tools Required to Intercept and Obstruct Terrorism (USA PATRIOT) Act Legislation that reduces the level of privacy of information in situations that have been deemed important to the security of the nation.

Virtual Learning A term often used to mean the e-education process.

Web-Based Learning Learning that is associated with materials delivered in a Web browser, including when the materials are packaged on CD-ROM or other media.

CROSS REFERENCES

See *Access Control: Principles and Solutions; Anonymity and Identity on the Internet; Internet Basics; Legal, Social and Ethical Issues of the Internet; Privacy Law and the Internet; Risk Management for IT Security; Security in E-Learning.*

REFERENCES

Allen, I. E., & Seaman, J. (2003). *Sizing the opportunity: The quality and extent of online education in the United States, 2002 and 2003.* Sloan Consortium: Needham, MA.

American Library Association. (2003). *Principles for the networked world.* Retrieved January 2, 2004, from http://www.ala.org/ala/washoff/washpubs/principles.pdf

American Library Association. (2004). *Distance education and the TEACH Act*. Retrieved October 4, 2004, from http://www.ala.org/Template.cfm?Section=Distance_Education_and_the_TEACH_Act&Template=/ContentManagement/ContentDisplay.cfm&ContentID=25939

Bauer, C., & Decman, J. (2002). *FERPA, IDE and Student Discipline: Navigating the "shark-infested waters."* Education Law Association Winter Seminar, Lake Tahoe, Nevada, March 21–24, 2002.

Bisk Education, Inc. (2003). Retrieved December 3, 2003, from http://www.bisk.com/

BizReport. (2003, July 17). *E-learning gains momentum, research*. Retrieved December 12, 2003, from http://www.bizreport.com//print.php?art_id=4635

Bray, H. (2004, January 26). *The Boston Globe*, p. C1.

Bruhn, M., and Petersen, R. (2003). Planning for improved security. *EDUCAUSE Review, 38*(6), 98–99. Retrieved December 18, 2003, from http://www.educause.edu/pub/er/erm03/erm03610.asp

Business Week. (2004, September 20). Big program on campus, 96–98.

Cardean University. (2003). Retrieved December 17, 2003, from http://www.cardean.edu

Caruso, J. B. (2003). *Information technology security policy: Keys to success*. Retrieved September 11, 2004, from http://www.educause.edu/LibraryDetailPage/666?ID=ERB0323

Connecticut Distance Learning Consortium (CTDLC). (2003). Retrieved January 3, 2004, from http://www.ctdlc.org/About/mission.html

Corbeil, J.-P. (2003). 30 years of education: Canada's language groups. *Canadian Social Trends, 71*, 8–12. Retrieved January 3, 2003, from LEXIS-NEXIS.

eCollege. (2004). eCollege Website. Retrieved January 5, 2004, from http://www.ecollege.com/indexflash.learn

Edlearn Consortium. (2003). Retrieved December 12, 2003, from http://www.edlearn.org

Educause. (1998). Privacy issues in a virtual learning environment. Retrieved December 18, 2003, from http://www.educause.edu/ir/library/html/cem9812.html

Educause. (2004, January). *Effective practices and solutions in security*. Retrieved February 1, 2004, from http://www.educause.edu/security/guide/

Farrell, C. (2003, September). *Remembering the value of education*. Scripps Howard, Inc. Retrieved December 18 from LEXIS-NEXIS.

Fulton, K. (2001, March/April). *From promise to practice: Enhancing student Internet learning*. Retrieved December 15, 2003, from http://www.infotoday.com/MMSchools/mar01/fulton.htm

Gale Group. (2003, March). *Privacy online*. Retrieved December 17 from LEXIS-NEXIS.

Goldman, J., & Hudson, Z. (2000). Virtually exposed: Privacy and e-health. *Health Affairs, 19* (November 6), 141. Retrieved December 12, 2003, from http://www.chcf.org/topics/view.cfm?itemID=12562

Goldman, J., Hudson, Z., & Smith, R. M. (2000). *Privacy report on the privacy and practices of health Web sites*. Retrieved December 18, 2003, from http://www.chcf.org/topics/view.cfm?itemID=12497

Gomory, R. E. (2001, December). Internet learning in the United States: Where it is and where it is going. *Higher Education in Europe, 26*(5). Retrieved December 15, 2003, from http://80-search.epnet.com.glacier.sou.edu/direct.asp?an=6885870&db=afh

Harvard Medical School, Department of Continuing Education. (2004). Retrieved from http://cme.med.harvard.edu/

Indiana University. (1998). *Information technology strategic plan, E.4 Teaching and learning: Content, access, distributed education*. Retrieved December 6, 2003, from http://www.indiana.edu/~ovpit/strategic/e_.html#d

Keystone University. (2003). Retrieved December 18, 2003, from http://www.keystoneu.net/

Kvavik, R. B. (2004). *Information technology, security: governance, strategy, and practice in higher education roadmap*. Retrieved September 4, 2004, from http://www.educause.edu/LibraryDetailPage/666&ID=ECM0305

MIT. (2003). *OpenCourseWare (OCW)*. Retrieved December 18, 2003, from http://ocw.mit.edu/index.html

Motorola. (2003). Retrieved January 4, 2004, from http://e-ww.motorola.com/webapp/sps/site/homepage.jsp?nodeId=05M0yzT167s

National Center for Education Statistics (NCES). (2001). *Post secondary education quick information system: Use of advance technology in remedial instruction*. Retrieved January 4, 2002, from http://nces.ed.gov/surveys/peqis/publications/2004010/6.asp

National Center for Education Statistics (NCES). (2002). *Chapter 1, Laws*. Retrieved January 4, 2004, from http://nces.ed.gov/statprog/rudman/chapter1.asp

National Center for Education Statistics (NCES). (2003). *Fast facts*. Retrieved November 19, 2003, from http://nces.ed.gov/fastfacts/display.asp?id=46

Neal, L. (2003, October 30). *Expectations of privacy*. Retrieved November 4, 2003, from http://www.elearnmag.org/index.cfm

Ohio Learning Network. (2003). Retrieved December 18, 2003, from http://www.oln.org/

PBS. (2003). *Adult learning service*. Retrieved January 4, 2004, from http://www.pbs.org/als/courses/courselistings/index.html

Phillips, S. (2003, November 28). The startling rise of 'pseudo universities'. *Times Higher Educaton Supplement*. Retrieved December 19, 2003, from NEXIS-LEXIS.

Prieditis, A. (2001). *Personalization vs. privacy Web agents*. Retrieved December 15, 2003, from http://www.infonortics.com/searchengines/sh00/prieditis%5ffiles/frame.htm

Primedia Insight Telephony. (2004, April). *Bush: Broadband key to health care, education advances*.

Redfield, S. E. (2003). The convergence of education and law: A new class of educators and lawyers. *Indiana Law Review, 36*, 609.

Sloan Consortium. (2003). *Sizing the opportunity: The quality and extent of online education in the United States, 2002 and 2003*. Retrieved January 4, 2004, from http://www.sloan-c.org/resources/overview.asp

Southern Regional Educational Board (SREB). (2003). Retrieved December 12, 2003, from http://www.sreb.org/

SUNY Learning Network. (2003). Retrieved December 18, 2003, from http://sln.suny.edu/

Thompson, J. F. (2002, November/December). Identity, privacy, and information technology. *EDUCAUSE*

Review, 64–65. Retrieved November 19, 2003, from http://www.educause.edu/ir/library/pdf/ERM0267.pdf

TRUSTe. (2003a). TRUSTe program principles. Retrieved November 19, 2003, from http://www.truste.com/programs/pub_principles.html

TRUSTe. (2003b). *Parents' and teachers' guide to online privacy*. Retrieved November 19, 2003, from http://www.truste.org/pdf/parents_teachers_online_privacy_guide.pdf

Western Governors University (WGU). (2003). Retrieved from http://www.wgu.edu/wgu/index.html

Winograd, K., & Moore, G. S. (2003). *You can learn online*. New York: McGraw-Hill Higher Education.

Worona, S. (2003, May/June). Privacy, security and anonymity: An evolving balance. *EDUCAUSE Review*, 62–63. Retrieved November 19, 2003, from http://www.educause.edu/ir/library/pdf/ERM0336.pdf

Yang, C. (2004, January 20). A hard corner for AOL to turn. *Business Week online*. Retrieved from http://www.businessweek.com/technology/content/jan2004/tc20040120_3250_tc055.htm

FURTHER READING

Baskin, J., & Surratt, J. (2001). Student privacy rights and wrongs on the Web. Retrieved November 19, 2003, from *The School Administrator* Web site: http://www.aasa.org/publications/sa/2001_09/focus_baskin.htm

Davenport, T. H. (2002, Summer). *eLearning and the attention economy: Here, there, and everywhere*. Retrieved December 12, 2003, from http://www.linezine.com/5.2/articles/tdeatae.htm

Draper, L. (2003). *Executive insights: Industry success depends on an educated workforce* (p. 4). PennWell Publishing.

Ferencz, S. K., & Goldsmith, C. W. (1998). Privacy issues in a virtual learning environment. CAUSE/EFFECT. Retrieved December 18, 2003, from http://www.educause.edu/ir/library/html/cem9812.html

Haley, C. C. (2004, January 28). *AOL to rally around broadband, ads*. Retrieved January 28, 2004, from http://www.internetnews.com/IAR/article.php/3305051

Interactive Data Corporation (IDC). (2003, January 21). Press Release: Worldwide corporate eLearning market continues to offer significant opportunities, IDC Says. Retrieved December 3, 2003, from http://www.idc.com/getdoc.jhtml?containerId=pr2003_01_14_145111

Spafford, G. (2001, May). *Protecting personal information in academia*. Retrieved November 18, 2003, from http://www.cra.org/CRN/articles/may01/spafford.html

University of North Texas (UNT). (2003). *Information security handbook for faculty, staff, and students*. Retrieved January 2, 2004, from http://www.unt.edu/ccadmin/security/security%20manual

Security in E-Learning

Edgar R. Weippl, *Vienna University of Technology, Austria*

INTRODUCTION

This brief introductory section begins by defining the term *e-learning.* I then provide a brief overview of security issues relevant to understanding the subsequent sections. The last subsection explains how the rest of this chapter is organized.

E-Learning

E-learning has been a buzzword for quite some time and is recently gaining even more importance. In this chapter, the term *e-learning* encompasses both Web-based *distance education* and Web-sites supplementing *in-class* teaching. Such course sites typically offer downloads of additional reading, online forums, journals, quizzes, and so on. The chapter does not explicitly cover non-Web-based forms of e-learning such as computer-based training (CBT) on CD-ROMs.

Research in e-learning is multidisciplinary, combining very different research areas. Some publications focus on the teaching process and pedagogical issues; others address mainly technical issues such as multimedia transmission, storage, indexing, and networking infrastructure; finally, research on project management in (public) universities, educational policies, and syllabus design contribute to the area of e-learning as well.

As e-learning increases in popularity and reach, more people run online courses and thus need to understand security issues relevant to this topic. Similar to all IT-projects, e-learning projects should commence with a thorough security risk analysis. The following sections therefore discuss typical threats to e-learning projects and show how these issues have been and should be addressed. This knowledge is essential to conduct a security risk analysis efficiently and effectively because participants need to be aware of common threats, protection mechanisms, and effort and cost issues.

As Neal (2004) pointed out, using electronic systems in an area leads to new security and privacy issues. For example, wireless transponders used for toll collection on roads also create electronic traces of the drivers. Similarly, participation rates and reaction times of students are recorded by e-learning systems.

Chadwick, Olivier, Samarati, Sharpston, and Thuraisingham (2003) presented opposing views on privacy and defined related terms such as pseudonyms, aliases, nicknames, anonymity, privacy, and confidentiality.

> Anonymity ensures that others cannot determine your true identity. An anonymous person effectively does not have an identity. A pseudonym on the other hand is an alternative (fictitious or assumed) identity for a person. Aliases are identical to pseudonyms, but the two are used with different connotations in different contexts.... Pseudonyms and aliases will usually not prevent the true identity of a person from being determined, although it may be difficult and may require law enforcement to enable it. Anonymity on the other hand should ensure that the true identity of a person is never found out, nor is capable of being found out. A nickname is also an alternative name for a person, and is often chosen as a friendlier variant of the person's formal name. Nicknames are not chosen so that the person's identity can be hidden (p. 332).

The importance of privacy considerations is reflected by recent laws such as the USA Patriot Act (2001) in the United States or the Rip Bill (2000) in Great Britain. The Patriot Act allows "a much broader category of cases to use information developed under the Foreign Intelligence Surveillance Act, where those subject to wiretaps are not informed of the surveillance even after the fact" (Swire and Steinfeld, 2002). In Great Britain, a comparable law, the Rip Act has been passed. Some provisions require that systems must allow law enforcement agencies to access to the data and that keys can be provided to decrypt encrypted content. Nonetheless, there seems to be no legal requirement to keep all data in long-term archives. Thus, the privacy of individuals can be increased in the long term by regularly reusing backup tapes so that old content is replaced.

Security

The term *security* cannot be defined without knowing specific requirements or potential threats. If defined formally, a system is secure if it is in an initial state that is secure and if from this state only transitions to secure states exist. A breach of security occurs when a system enters an unauthorized state (Bishop, 2002, p. 96). Whether a state is considered secure cannot be defined without requirements.

In more practical terms, there are four basic security requirements to which all real-world (composite) requirements can be traced:

1. Secrecy
2. Integrity
3. Availability
4. Nonrepudiation

The perhaps best known security requirement is *secrecy*. Users may obtain access only to those objects for which they have received authorization. They never get access to information they must not see.

Privacy can technically be seen as a form of secrecy, in which only an individual should have access to private information, whereas the public should be denied access. According to Palen and Dourish (2003), privacy is not a static concept but it changes dynamically. Clearly, individuals usually do not want to keep all personal information secret. Instead, they choose to disclose parts to participate in social processes. The teacher, for instance, needs to know name, student ID, and other information from students to be able to grade them.

Just as important but frequently neglected in daily life is the *integrity* of the data and programs. Integrity means that only authorized users or processes are permitted to modify data (or programs). *Secrecy of data* is closely connected to the *integrity of programs and operating systems*. If the integrity of the operating system is violated, then the reference monitor may no longer work. The reference monitor is a mechanism ensuring that only authorized users or processes are able to access data. Once this mechanism is compromised, the secrecy of information cannot be guaranteed. For this reason, it is important to protect the integrity of operating systems in order to guarantee secrecy of information.

Many users have become aware only through the Internet that *availability* is one of the major security requirements for computer systems. Productivity decreases dramatically if network-based applications are not available or are too slow because of denial-of-service attacks. If, for example, a Web-based authoring tool is too slow, then not only do users require more time to complete their tasks, they also might become frustrated, impairing productivity even more.

The fourth important security requirement, *nonrepudiation,* is that users are not able to deny (plausibly) to have carried out operations. This requirement is important when e-learning systems are used for exams and grading.

Organization of This Chapter

The second section explains how a security risk analysis works in the context of e-learning and briefly presents a standard method for conducting it. In addition, the perceptions of threats relevant to e-learning given by unprepared participants of a risk analysis are summarized.

Section 3 commences by analyzing typical threats to common activities in e-learning such as *creating content* or *teaching online*. Subsequently, we show how two major security requirements (secrecy of data, privacy) can be addressed in theory.

The fourth section elaborates how these theoretical results have been implemented in a modified version of Moodle, an open-source learning platform. Details on the implementation and data structures will help readers as a technical guideline when implementing similar features in other systems.

The fifth section points out additional security threats that implementers of e-learning programs will need to address once mobile e-learning (m-learning) is used in larger production environments. Although m-learning is still in its infancy and most current m-learning projects are mainly research prototypes, typical mobile services in e-learning can already be identified along with their corresponding threats to security and privacy. The final section offers a brief conclusion.

SECURITY RISK ANALYSIS

Before dealing with risk analysis, it is necessary to define the terms *risk* and *threat,* which are closely related and often wrongly used as synonyms. *A threat is a bad thing that can happen; a risk is the relative likelihood that a bad thing will happen* (Schneier, 2003, p. 20). Not every threat develops into a problem. A risk can also be considered to be a measure of financial loss for an organization. Clearly, threats lead to risks. Whether the risk is relevant depends not only on the threat but also on the environment and the nature of an organization.

With the help of a standard method, the basic procedure of a risk analysis is presented in this section. Peltier (2001) contained a detailed introduction to this topic that is recommended as a reference when conducting a security risk analysis for the first time.

Scope and Importance

Information is an important asset—not only for companies, but also for universities. Universities, in particular, depend on the transmission (aka *teaching*) and creation of information (aka *research*). To limit the maximum expenditure on security measures, it is necessary to estimate the value of the created assets accurately.

The following ways of evaluation are possible:

- Costs of (first) compilation of information
- Costs of restoration of information after destruction
- Damage caused if the information cannot be used

- Advantage another university or another researcher would have if he or she could use, modify, or destroy the information
- Sales revenue if information is sold
- Costs if secret information is published, modified, or destroyed
- Damage through decline in student numbers and loss of credibility in the academic arena

According to these estimates, one can decide which assets are worth protecting and which effort seems justified. Furthermore, one should bear in mind that too much security is just as unfavorable as too little security, especially in research and education. Apart from high costs, a system that is too prohibitive is inflexible and constricts users in their daily routines. Therefore, certain risks have to be accepted in e-learning in order not to prevent students from learning. For instance, in computer science, students should be able to so set up and maintain their own servers.

Standard Method

The following subsection takes a look at the most important steps of a risk analysis:

1. Identification of assets
2. Estimation or calculation of threats and risks
3. Setting priorities
4. Implementation of controls and countermeasures
5. Monitoring of risks and of the effectiveness of countermeasures

Identification of Assets

For a *qualitative risk analysis,* the exact asset values need not be known. Assets that may be worth protecting include networks and hardware, software, buildings, equipment, people, and operational procedures. For most e-learning projects, a qualitative risk analysis is the method of choice because it requires little effort and the results are sufficiently precise for small and medium-sized projects—the typical e-learning initiative at universities. With the help of a table (Table 1), value classes instead of the actual values can be determined. The values have to be chosen depending on the project to separate the assets clearly into different classes. The advantage of this method is that it is extremely fast. If e-learning is the focus of a business, however, more precise methods are required.

All the aforementioned items are related to the protection of information—the core of all large e-learning courses. In addition, hardware, buildings, and software are also obviously necessary to process data electronically.

Table 1 Example of Value Classes to Calculate the *Financial Loss Valuation Score*

Loss in EUR	Evaluation Score
<2000	1
2–15K	2
15–40K	3

Furthermore, the protection of people is essential because they affect the real value of the data. It is the people who turn data to information.

At first, it is important to define the scale of the security risk analysis. Usually, the risks for buildings, people, and so on are not covered within the framework of an e-learning project. In large-scale e-learning programs, however, in which larger parts of buildings are used exclusively for the planning, administration, and implementation of e-learning classes, these risks should be taken into consideration. However trivial the risk of fire may sound, it can threaten one's existence if the only e-learning lab is destroyed.

Estimation of Threats and Risks

Two basic forms of threats can be distinguished: *deliberate threats* such as attacking a system and *accidental threats* such as forgetting to create backup copies or a flood. For each asset, a list of threats needs to be compiled; a matrix (Table 2) can be used to organize this process. This list is not a complete taxonomy of threats; it serves as a template and needs to be adapted to the specific requirements. Some threats, such as power outage could also be classified as a "deliberate act." Whether such a threat needs to be considered in the security risk analysis for a specific e-learning project depends on the project's scope. Deliberate power outages (e.g., by cutting wires leading to the university) might already be covered in the security risk analysis of the campus and do not need to be considered in the security risk analysis of the project.

Setting Priorities

The vulnerability of an organization depends on various factors such as confidentiality of the data, training of staff, and staff members' familiarity with emergency procedures, protective mechanisms and monitoring, morale, and attitudes toward the university, economic environment, backup plans, etc.

To set priorities correctly, the *expected annual damage* can be calculated.

Expected annual damage
*= Value of assets * Probability of occurrence*

The disadvantage of this simple formula is that extremely rare events might not be taken into consideration at all, although their damage can be enormous. This is reinforced by the fact that the probability of rare events cannot be estimated very accurately. How likely, for example, is a war in Western Europe?

Many countermeasures reduce a risk but do not eliminate it completely. With regard to the estimate of costs, four types of costs have to be considered.

- Damage without countermeasure,
- Damage with countermeasure (usually smaller than damage without countermeasure, although additional threats may be introduced by a countermeasure. Consider, for instance, the threat of a hard disk failure. This interferes with the requirement 'availability.' However, the countermeasure 'backup tapes' creates new threats: Tapes can be stolen more easily than hard disks. Since

Table 2 An Example of Threats Relevant to Specific Assets

Type	Threats	Asset 1 Server	Asset 2 HTML Content
Natural	Fire	X	
	Storm		
	Volcanic eruption		
	Earthquake	X	
	Floods	X	
	Avalanches		
Deliberate act	Fraud		X
	Fire	X	
	Blackmail		
	Theft		X
	Bomb threat		
	Riots, war		
	Vandalism	X	
Unintended	Computer bug	X	
	Power outage	X	
	Handling error	X	
	Spilling of drinks	X	

all data are stored on these tapes, the new threat interferes with the requirements 'secrecy/confidentiality'),

- Costs of the countermeasure, and
- Costs of plan B.

Plan B is an alternative plan that can be implemented when the threat is about to turn into a problem. In some cases it may be advantageous not to implement a countermeasure, but merely to provide an alternative plan that is used when required.

Implementation of Controls and CounterMeasures

During implementation, the costs of countermeasures should be recorded. This is useful for subsequent projects and improves the accuracy of future estimates.

The point of documentation is not just to fulfill the requirements of an audit; the real purpose should be clear to everyone involved: By being able to compare the costs and the benefits, the importance of risk management can be demonstrated. Moreover, staff, faculty, and students become aware of the real costs of security threats.

Case Study: Tutorial and E-learning Module

Before performing a security risk analysis as previously described, it is advantageous to learn about the specific risks encountered by other academic staff in e-learning situations. Questionnaires used in tutorials at several conferences (Edmedia 2003, 2004; IIWAS 2003; ViewDet 2003) and a case study have provided insight into the current level of awareness of unprepared participants.

Most (72%) teachers and content authors had previous experience with two or three e-learning platforms. When using electronic bulletin boards, the three concerns mentioned most often were the following:

1. *Abusive language* (in open discussion boards)
2. *Stealing of e-mail addresses* by Web spiders (A search engine uses *robots* to index the Web. These robots are also referred to as *spiders* because they *crawl* through the Web. While visiting pages, spiders extract information such as key words or e-mail addresses. Franklin (2003) described Web spiders in more detail.)
3. Posting and downloading of *illegal content* or *viruses*

Concerning security issues, participants saw no significant difference between online and in-class discussions; the main difference they identified was *social incentive* to (or the fear of having to) participate in in-class discussions. The implicit archiving of discussions was perceived as an advantage of bulletin boards, not as a threat to privacy.

Denial of service attacks by students during exams were not seen as a major issue whereas unauthorized copying of digital content was considered a huge threat. This is probably caused by the media hype about peer2peer file sharing. Faculty acknowledged that they use resources retrieved from the Internet in their classes (readers, handouts) without considering copyright issues.

The central computing services of universities *backs up* data in many cases, but most people hardly ever test whether the procedure to restore data works reliably.

Sharing of passwords is still common, even though technical and science faculty seem to protect their passwords better than others.

Faculty does not feel uncomfortable discussing sensitive topics via e-mail. They *trust* that the *e-mail* servers are well secured. Teachers indicated some interest in logs showing which pages are viewed how often by students, but they also realized the impact this has on students' privacy.

Based on these experiences, an e-learning module on *security in e-learning* (Planet-ET, 2003) was designed. This course instructs teachers how to improve security in their online courses.

FROM REQUIREMENTS TO DESIGNING AND IMPLEMENTING SOLUTIONS

This section elaborates the most important security requirements in the context of e-learning and provides insight into how they have been and should be addressed in various projects.

General Discussion

Usually, there are three main processes in e-learning scenarios.

1. Creating Content
2. Teaching and Learning
3. Organization

Creating Content

Too often, security is considered a technology of hindrance. Things that work smoothly without security measures seem to become more complicated and complex by installing security mechanisms. Security, however, is an *enabling technology*.

Only if an adequate security standard has been implemented can people make use of the services offered. For example, distrust of e-banking was initially profound. It was not until confidence in the secure transfer of data had been established and transaction numbers (TANs) were used that e-banking gained acceptance.

The situation is similar when writing academic teaching material. Thanks to today's networking it would be easily possible for authors to provide access to teaching materials to a wide audience—colleagues and students. The reason many authors refrain from doing so is the fear that their compiled material might be passed on and processed without their knowledge.

When discussing security in e-learning, it is important to distinguish between the knowledge as such and the type of knowledge transfer. The knowledge imparted at universities can normally be acquired in self-study from books and other sources. The information (e.g., how to multiply matrices) is not a secret. It is the teaching style that makes a course worth protecting.

An example proving this distinction is provided by the Open Courseware initiative of the Massachusetts Institute of Technology. Although a variety of teaching contents are offered to the students on the Internet, this initiative does not endanger the existence of MIT. Not the teaching material but the interaction with fellow students and professors is why a course is worth its tuition fee.

The problem of controlling who is doing what with teaching materials is analogous to the music industry's problem with digital copies in MP3 format available on the Internet. In addition to the authors' intuitive need for copy protection, however, there are numerous other aspects of security.

The essential security requirements in e-learning are (Weippl, Essmayer, Gruber, Stockner, & Trenker, 2004):

- Readers must be able to rely on the correctness of the content.
- Readers want to read unobserved.
- There must be protection against unauthorized use.
- There must be protection against unauthorized modifications and reuse.
- There must be protection against destruction and loss of data.

In this context trust is essential. Even though undergraduate students tend to accept everything they read as true (Graham and Metaxas, 2003), they soon learn to value the trustworthiness of a source. Therefore, integrity of content including the author's identity is of paramount importance.

Teaching and Learning

Even though continuous evaluation has gained popularity over the last few years, the distinction between teaching and examining is still frequently drawn. Because there are different threats and security requirements in these two areas, a distinction between teaching and examining seems reasonable when discussing security.

Particularly in arts subjects and the social sciences, *discussions* are an essential component of the courses. Newsgroup discussions can complement in-class discussions or substitute them in distance teaching. A major difference between oral discussions in a classroom and online forum discussions is that all messages can be stored electronically.

Students legitimately have concerns that their contributions to a discussion might be stored and quotations might be published out of context. The implementation of security mechanisms and a policy that clearly states what will be stored for how long can minimize this risk for students. Privacy expectations are, however, dependent on the cultural environment and may differ significantly, for example, between the United States and Austria. In Austria, for instance, grades along with student names are normally published on printed lists at the university so that anyone who enters the building can read them.

In principle, an interaction in teaching is valuable (King, 2004), and only sound security mechanisms enable such interaction. For example, only course participants should have access to the corresponding forums and annotations, and they should be allowed to use pseudonyms. In this context, different forms of pseudonyms and anonymity can be distinguished: Students' identities may remain hidden (a) for teachers only, (b) for all course participants, or (c) entirely, even for system administrators.

The first option can be useful for surveys if teachers want to receive feedback on their courses but also allow students to know who posted which feedback. Using this approach, however, a student's anonymity can easily be disclosed either by fellow students or by the teacher who can register him- or herself as a student. It is common practice for teachers to create "student users" for themselves to preview and test courses from the students' perspective. The second option—remaining anonymous to all course participants—is the most common approach to surveys. The implementation is fairly easy, and privacy expectations of students are met. Because system administrators can still identify users, discussions on politically sensitive topics may be impaired. The third option is to guarantee anonymity at all levels. As discussed in a subsequent section (Privacy of Usage), there are still several locations where information is (temporarily) stored so that the users' privacy expectations might be compromised.

Exams

Thinking of "security" in connection with *examinations,* one frequently thinks of the prevention of cheating. When using new media and e-learning, new concepts of knowledge transfer and learning are frequently employed. Even though the mode of assessment is likely to change, traditional exams will certainly continue to be used for some time. Apart from students' cheating attempts, other security requirements such as availability and nonrepudiation of assessments are major factors that influence the success of an electronic examination system.

The first step of exams is the *identification* of students. In traditional paper-based exams, they simply fill in their names; electronic examination systems usually require a login name. *Authentication* of students (i.e., the process of verifying a claimed identity) is done during paper-based exams by checking the students' IDs. Taking the exam at home without supervision is not feasible because a student might collaborate with another person providing illegal support. As Weippl (2002) pointed out, the only way to know that a student does not receive outside help is a trusted examination center that checks students' IDs (or biometric features) and restricts access to exam rooms. The alternative is to grade on a continuous basis throughout the whole term. Although this does not render cheating impossible, it substantially increases the required effort. Another option is to enforce strict time constraints on multiple choice exams. Hamlin and Ryan (2003) stated that "if an exam consists of 10 multiple choice questions and a student has nine minutes to complete the exam, the chances of the student looking up each answer is slim because of the time restriction." Recording the completion time of exams can provide additional hints as to whether a student has cheated. The Associated Press (Weller, 2004) reported that 70 freshmen at the U.S. Air Force Academy were accused of cheating at an online test. The cheating was detected because cadets worked too quickly, answering 25 questions in 3 minutes.

The risk of cheating by helping other students also depends on the environment and the cultural setting. In Europe, for instance, schools usually grade on an individual level so that all students may fail a difficult exam, or a class of excellent students may receive above average grades. Such a setting makes mutual assistance (i.e., cheating) of students more likely. If however, only the top 10% receive an A grade—independent of the objective level they reach—the competitive situation dramatically reduces the risks of cheating and collusion.

Apart from collusion, there are other security threats to examinations. For example, a student might try to crash the testing application to avoid getting graded—an attack on system *availability*. He or she might also later deny having given the recorded answers. In a system that guarantees *nonrepudiation*, the student's claim can easily be refuted. The users' (i.e., students') confidence in the availability, nonrepudiation, and security of an e-learning system is a precondition for user acceptance and thus a condition sine qua non for the use of the system.

Organization

Even in classical in-class teaching at universities, new media are frequently used to amplify and enrich teaching. The security issues arising are similar to those in pure distance teaching. In this context, security is not so much a technical issue but more an organizational one. Using simple procedures for security can increase compliance of users and thus security much more effectively than the implementation of complex and theoretically more secure solutions. For instance, implementing a public-key infrastructure (PKI) system ensuring that only authorized people correctly transmit grades via e-mail may sound secure, but confirming unsigned e-mails via telephone might be a much better and simpler way of guaranteeing the authenticity of grades.

Security is an aspect that is often regarded as an additional supplement. It is the managers' responsibility to demonstrate the benefits of security to anyone involved in teaching, so that an appropriate concept of security can be developed and successfully implemented.

Secrecy of Uploaded Data (Preventing Unauthorized Views)

E-learning platforms are commonly used for both distance learning and to support in-class teaching. The widespread use of platforms such as Blackboard (2004), Web-CT (2004), or Moodle (2004a) makes it easy for faculty to publish supporting material and to share material (e.g., exam questions) with colleagues. When sharing teaching materials, however, many people accidentally also share content that should remain private, because, as Good and Krekelberg (2002) pointed out, many users do not exactly know which files they share with whom.

This subsection provides some examples that highlight why *mandatory access control* (MAC) and the Bell and La-Padula (BLP; 1975) model in particular make sense for e-learning systems. The BLP model is easy to understand and provides sufficient granularity of basic access control. In most cases, the BLP model is implemented using role-based access control (RBAC) as shown by Osborn et al. (2000), because RBAC is readily available in most operating systems and database management systems. The rationale for explaining the access control based on the BLP model and RBAC is BLP's straightforwardness. The no-read-up property is intuitive, and the no-write-down property is easy to understand for teachers and students. Explaining the underlying RBAC definitions, as shown in Figures 1–5, would be too confusing for the average user. Another option would be to use object-oriented access control (OOAC) as proposed by Essmayr, Pernul, and Tjoa (1997), which would rely on an object-oriented database as storage system.

Alice and Bob are users of a system. Alice is a student (s) in course *C1* and a teacher (t) in *C2*. Bob is teacher (t) of *C1* and student (s) in *C2*.

$$\text{Alice} = (\text{c1-s}), (\text{c2-t})$$

$$\text{Bob} = (\text{c1-t}), (\text{c2-s})$$

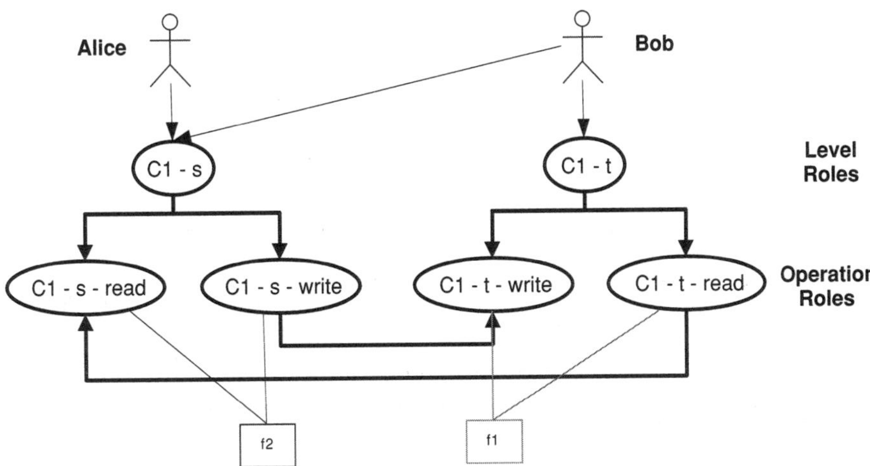

Figure 1: Two new files are created. f1: c1-t, f2: c1-s

Creating (Private) Files

In the first step, Bob creates a new file f1 as c1-t. Alice creates a file f2 as c1-s.

Bob can read files f1 and f2; he can write to f1 and not to f2—that is, the *no-write-down* property prevents the reading of f2. The *no-write-down* property protects data from being accidentally written to a lower level. Neither the user nor Trojans on his behalf can *downgrade* data, for example, from the teacher level to the student level. In our example, this means that Bob cannot create a file c1-s as long as he is logged in as teacher of C1. Only if he logs in as a student, he can create a c1-s-file. Alice can read and write f2 but cannot access f1.

Commenting Files

Bob reads f2 and wants to add comments in f3 as feedback to Alice. Due to the *no-write-down* property he first has to login as c1-s. Clearly, Alice can read f3.

Creating Exams

Bob wants to create an exam from a template that is stored at level c1-t. Obviously, he has to login as c1-t to read it. Based on this template, he creates the exam f4. As mentioned earlier, he cannot create files at a lower level.

Making Exams Available

Bob wants Alice to take the exam and therefore needs to provide her with read access. Because not only Alice but all students in the course c1 should be able to see the exam, he needs to *downgrade* it from c1-t to c1-s. This operation violates the no-write-down property. To avoid compromising overall system security, we propose allowing downgrading only with a special *system call* (Weippl & Essmayr, 2003).

Completing Exams

Alice writes answers to the exam f4 into a file f5. She chooses to write this file at level c1-t so that only Bob can read this file. Alice still sees her answers in the graphical user interface (GUI) but cannot access the file for reading. The rationale is that Alice can be sure that no fellow students can read her answers and use them to cheat.

This operation is permitted because the BLP model allows *write-up* operations since they do not compromise confidentiality (but integrity).

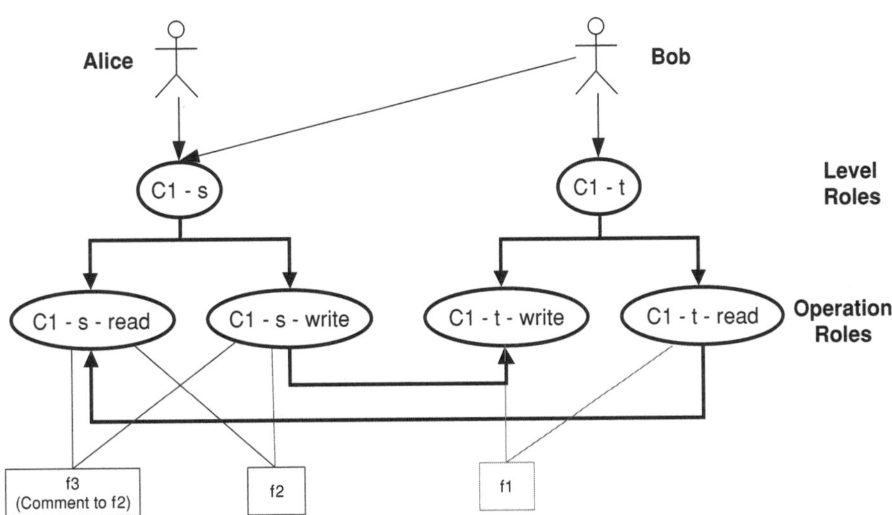

Figure 2: A third file is added. f3: c1-s

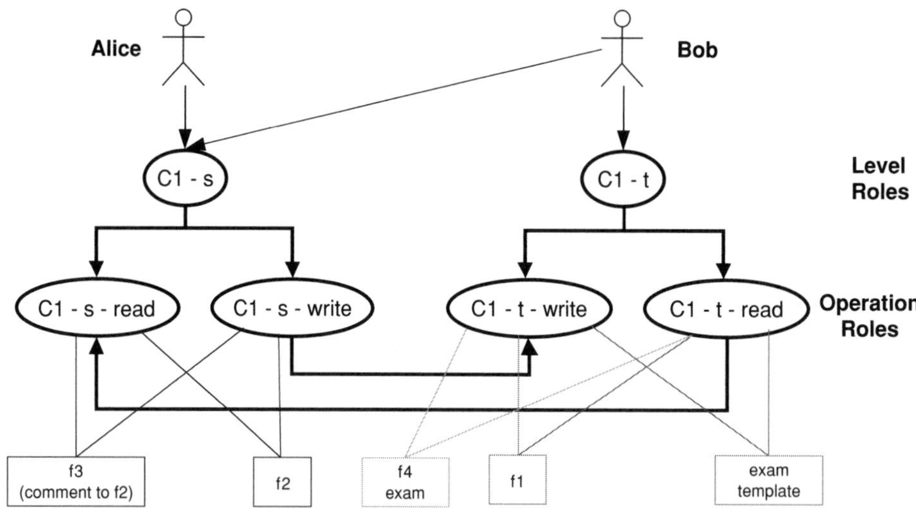

Figure 3: An exam is created based on an existing template. f4: c1-t

Implementing MAC With RBAC

The level role c1-t (Figure 5) comprises two operation roles, c1-t-write and c1-t-read. File f1, for instance, can be written by anyone who has role c1-t-write. c1-s-write contains c1-t-write as hierarchical subrole. Thus, Alice (c1-s) can write to file f1 ("write-up" via c1-s, c1-s-write and c1-t-write), but she cannot read it.

Bob can choose whether to use the level role c1-t or c1-s. To create f3—the comments to f2 that Alice should be able to read—he needs to use role c1-s. To create the exam (f4) based on the exam template, he has to change to c1-t again.

The dotted line in Figure 5 connecting f4 with c1-s-read indicates that this connection has not been generated by the default rules, but that system calls were used to *downgrade* levels.

Privacy of Usage (Tracing Users)

Users are becoming increasingly aware that all their actions in Web applications can be logged. Regarding e-learning applications, several locations can be identified where users leave traces (Figure 6).

Local Computers

If users share computers (e.g., in labs), browser caches, histories, and temporary files may reveal their actions. In addition, malicious software such as keystroke loggers could be installed to intercept passwords and other sensitive information. At university labs this threat should be taken seriously.

Internet Service Providers

The computer is connected via an Internet service provider (ISP) to the Internet. Most ISPs keep a record of which IP address was assigned to whom. Furthermore, all visited Web pages and interactions with e-learning platforms *could* be logged. Of course, storage of this information is illegal in most cases. It is simply because of the volume of data that ISPs will most likely not store this information.

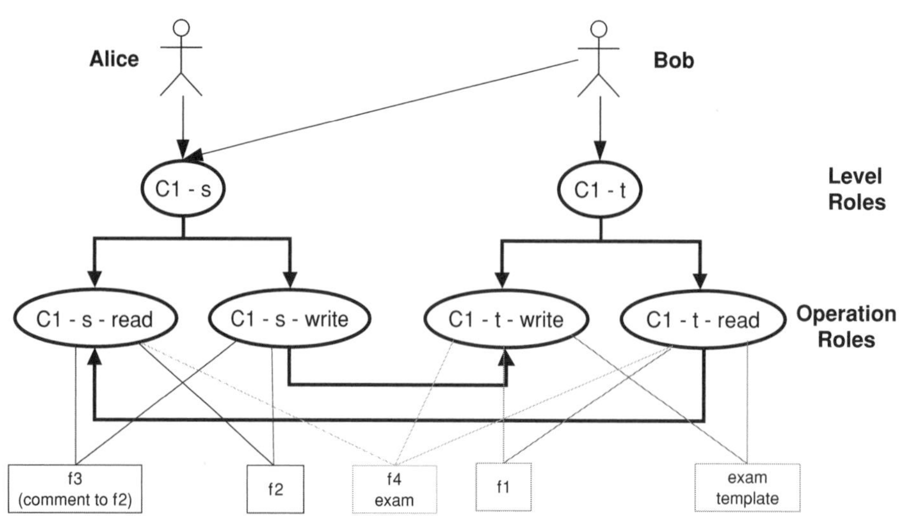

Figure 4: Alice, the student, is permitted access to the exam. f4: c1-s

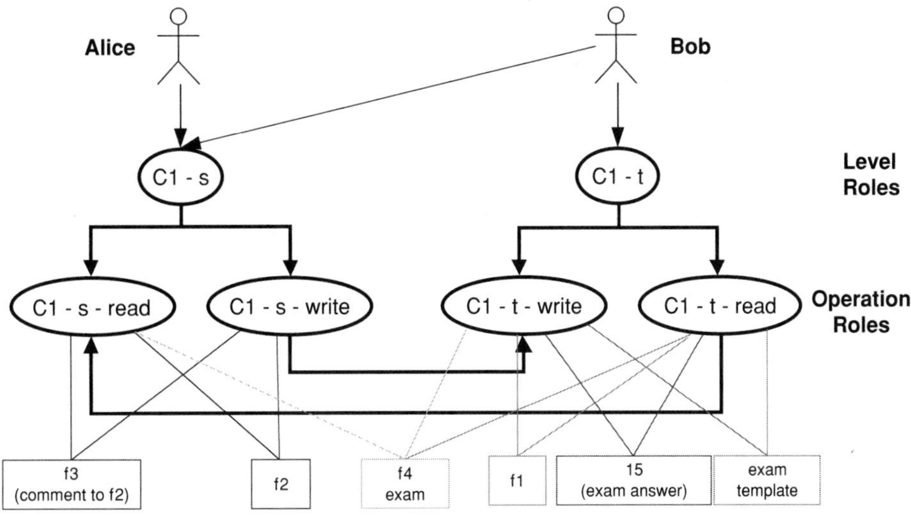

Figure 5: The answers given by Alice are only accessible for the teacher. f5: c1-t

Internet

Traffic routed through the Internet is subject to all known threats such as eavesdropping, spoofing, and so on. Well-targeted attacks against a specific user's privacy are improbable. Usually, high-profile companies such as Microsoft are victims of attacks (generally distributed denial of service attacks).

Web Server

An e-learning platform is hosted on a Web server. Most Web servers create log files that identify and store the IP addresses of each inbound connection along with the URL visited. These logs are usually discarded on a regular basis to limit their size.

E-Learning Application

Unlike in the aforementioned layers, the application layer can create much more specific and thus useful logging data because the user is known with her login, and the application knows which clicks are important and which are not.

Many e-learning systems are not only used as learning managements systems (LMS) but also as content management systems (CMS) to allow students to read course-related material. What used to be put on reserve at the college library is now accessible online. Although this may be more convenient for students, teachers can check who reads which material—information that according to Gorman (2000) a library would never provide to teachers. Privacy rights are affected by the Patriot Act (2001) and any information retained may have to be disclosed to the FBI. The American Library Association (2002) recommends that libraries establish clear policies with the help of legal counsels as to which information needs to be stored. Because CMSs may be used in a similar way as libraries, universities should create corresponding policies in cooperation with libraries.

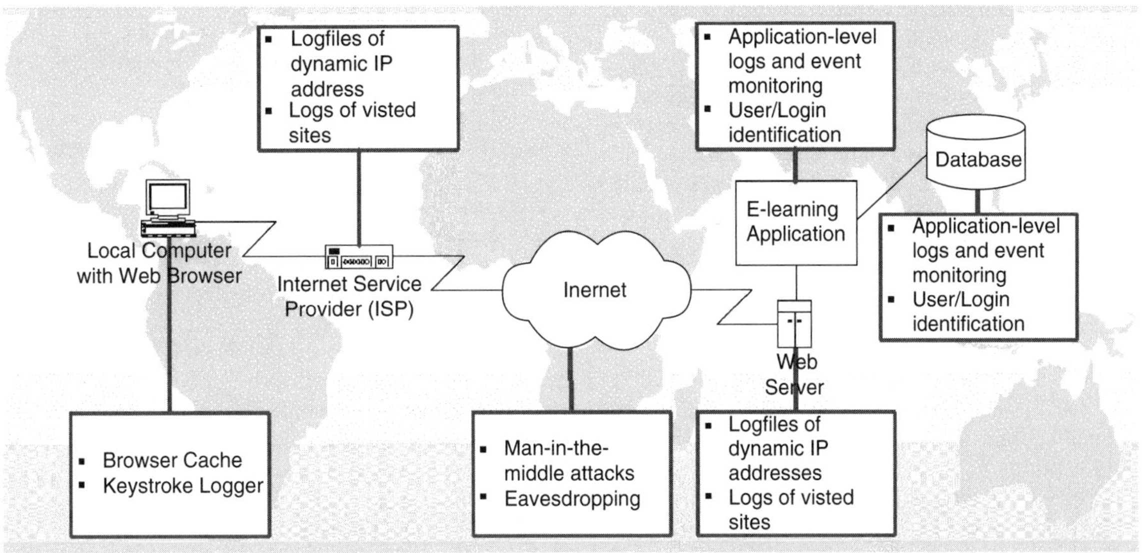

Figure 6: Each user's request is passed through several interfaces leaving traces.

Database

Most e-learning applications use a database to store data. DBMSs offer sophisticated tracing and login facilities. In many cases, however, the e-learning application connects to the database with a single user. Thus, user-specific traces are not as easy as on the database level.

Possible Solutions: Open Source Systems and anonymizers

As mentioned earlier, the functions that are most critical to privacy are based on the application layer. Open source software offers (experienced) users the option to check the code for any hidden functions or bugs by themselves (Cowan, 2003). Students cannot be absolutely sure that the university did indeed install the unmodified source code and that no Trojan compilers (Spinellis, 2003; Thompson, 1984) were used. These threats are usually very small, however, and mostly of academic interest. According to Hinman (2002), students usually trust faculty. Thus, clearly stating a privacy policy as suggested by Neal (2004) or Educause (1998) is an easy and effective step to align privacy expectations with the reality of employed e-learning systems. The platform for privacy preferences (P3P; Hochheiser, 2002; Reagle & Cranor, 1999) is a protocol to exchange a privacy policy between a Web browser and a Web server. The privacy policy is specified using XML (extensible markup language) so that the user's Web browser can automatically decide whether the user is willing to accept the policy based on his or her preferences. P3P, however, offers no way of guaranteeing that the server really honors the policy. Users simply have to trust that the policy is implemented as stated.

Anonymizers based on Chaum mixes (Chaum, 1981) or Dingledine, Mathewson, and Syverson's (2004) Tor system can be used to obfuscate traces at ISPs and Web servers. Chaum's system implements anonymity so that eavesdroppers do not know who is communicating with whom at what time. Tor is an improvement of the original Onion Routing system that routes each request encapsulated in encrypted packages via several nodes to make traffic analysis impossible. At the client side, however, privacy expectations can still be violated by locally installed software such as keystroke loggers.

Dourish and Redmiles (2002) clearly distinguished between *theoretical* and *effective* security. Theoretical security refers to the maximum level of security that can be achieved using a given technology. The level of security that is effectively achieved in daily routine tasks is usually much lower, however. Because many people are unable to determine the security implications of their decisions, easy-to-understand gouges can be used to visualize relevant parameters.

Case Study: Moodle

Moodle (2004b) is a course management system that is based on social constructionist pedagogy. The online help thoroughly explains to teachers not only how to use certain functions from a technical perspective but also illustrates pedagogical concepts. The explanations are brief and concise addressing also technical and science faculty that usually dislike "soft education mumbo jumbo." Moodle's design is centered on *communicating* with students. It offers different styles of forums, chats, journals, and workshops.

Privacy Concerns

We found that several teachers expressed concerns about their students' privacy even before conducting a systematic security risk analysis when using Moodle. As mentioned in subsection "Teaching and Learning," students might refrain from openly expressing their thoughts on controversial political and societal issues if electronic copies of their discussions are stored.

Moodle logs each user action and stores it in a database. For teachers, this feature is quite useful to analyze which pages are visited how often, and which students spend a lot of time in the system or who never logs on (Figures 7 and 8).

Anonymity in Moodle

Moodle logs all user actions in one central place. To avoid that the users' actions are written to the log file, we modified the logging function to log a dummy user ("anonymous user"). This approach is better than not making any log entries at all because anonymized usage statistics are still available.

Anonymous posting, however, does not imply that everyone can post a message. Access to the course's discussion site is still protected with a login requiring user name and password. Nonetheless, the notion of trust is weakened because the identity of the author is unknown. On the other hand, this can be used as a pedagogical advantage: Students often trust postings from the faculty as true without critically challenging them. In anonymous discussions, readers need to decide whether to trust the content based on the cited references.

Making the user anonymous in the forum is a little trickier, because the user has to remain identified to be able to edit his or her own entry. Moodle allows editing entries for a limited time after which they can no longer be modified. The first approach we implemented was to set the user to anonymous only after this initial period of time in the database. To avoid displaying the user name during this period, we introduced a flag that prevents the name from being displayed even though it is stored in the database.

Although users thought they posted anonymously, their contributions could be identified during the first 30 minutes after the posting by looking directly into the database. Because during this time frame backups can be made, we decided that this approach was dangerous because *users thought they acted anonymously even though they did not*. Therefore, we eventually decided to allow completely anonymous posts. As a trade-off, these postings cannot be edited or deleted by the author. If authors cannot be identified, it might be more difficult to follow the discussion as to who said what. The easiest approach to reduce this problem is to encourage the use of quotations and the treelike organization of discussion threads.

Known Limitations

As mentioned earlier, it is on the application layer that the most detailed logs are available. We modified the

Activity report: Outline Complete Today's logs All logs

Displaying 15 records

Tue 25 November 2003, 05:40 PM	[illegible].105.134	**Nikolaus**	forum view discussion	Windows XP Treibersignierung Nirtl, Roth, Wichtl, Stadler
Tue 25 November 2003, 05:40 PM	[illegible].105.134	**Nikolaus**	forum view forum	Abgabeforum Assignment 3
Tue 25 November 2003, 05:38 PM	[illegible].105.134	**Nikolaus**	forum view discussion	Windows 2000: Access Control und a bissl Auditing
Tue 25 November 2003, 05:38 PM	[illegible].105.134	**Nikolaus**	forum view forum	Abgabeforum Assignment 3
Tue 25 November 2003, 05:38 PM	[illegible].105.134	**Nikolaus**	course view	Security in E-Commerce
Tue 25 November 2003, 05:36 PM	[illegible].105.134	**Nikolaus**	forum view discussion	Assignment 3 - Termine
Tue 25 November 2003, 05:36 PM	[illegible].105.134	**Nikolaus**	forum add post	Re: Assignment 3 - Termine
Tue 25 November 2003, 05:34 PM	[illegible].105.134	**Nikolaus**	forum view discussion	Assignment 3 - Termine
Tue 25 November 2003, 05:34 PM	[illegible].105.134	**Nikolaus**	forum view forum	News forum
Tue 25 November 2003, 05:34 PM	[illegible].105.134	**Nikolaus**	forum view discussion	Assignment 3 - Termine
Tue 25 November 2003, 05:34 PM	[illegible].105.134	**Nikolaus**	user view	Martin Schwaiger
Tue 25 November 2003, 05:34 PM	[illegible].105.134	**Nikolaus**	forum view discussion	Assignment 3 - Termine
Tue 25 November 2003, 05:31 PM	[illegible].105.134	**Nikolaus**	forum view discussion	Assignment 3 - Termine

Figure 7: Each action by every user is stored in a database.

application so that users can switch to an anonymous mode. Nonetheless, our approach has some limitations. Because we mainly addressed privacy-related functions on an application level, there are still usage traces in other layers, for example, the Web server's log. Because these logs are usually only stored for a couple of weeks or months, there is little risk that the data will be available in the distant future. The main privacy concern in teaching is not so much the near future but long-term archiving. With in-class teaching, for example, the attending students remember discussions anyway, so that short-term archives of discussions introduce little additional threat to privacy. In contrast, out-of-context quotations decades later can be a threat. Just imagine that a candidate running for president in the United States is reported to have argued pro-communist when he was in college. Belotti and Sellen (1993) proposed a framework for designing feedback and control mechanisms in computing environments. The main idea is that users can *control* which information is captured, what it is used for, and

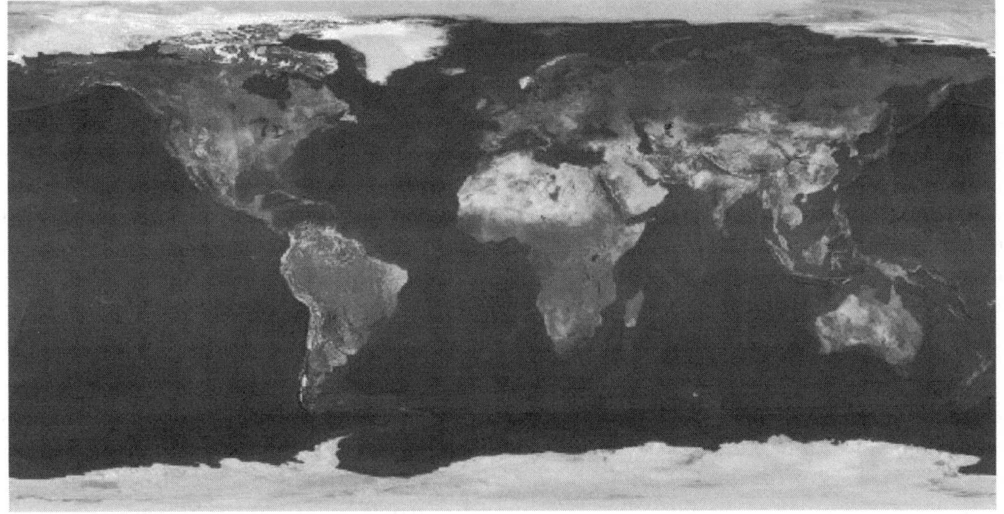

Jacob [Vienna, AT] : (**XX . XX .35.77**) is located in Vienna, Austria. (48.22, 16.37)

IP/Hostname: XX.XX.35.77 Submit [**preferences**] [**locate me**]

Figure 8: Each Internet Provider address can be traced to a geographic location.

who has access to it. In addition to control, users receive *feedback* on who uses which data for which purpose.

OUTLOOK: SECURITY IN M-LEARNING

Before analyzing security requirements of mobile users in a teaching–learning environment, this section briefly looks at the way mobile devices are used in an educational setting. Walker, Rockman, and Chessler (2000) provided an overview of how mobile technology influences education. Weippl (2004) provided additional details on how some of the related security issues might be addressed. Throughout this section, when referring to mobile devices or mobile computing, it means devices such as personal digital assistants (PDAs) or cell phones.

In-Class Teaching

Mobile devices are used to support the traditional in-class learning process by providing supporting information such as lecture schedules and venues. Both pull and push technologies are used: *pull* refers to information that students actively seek, whereas *push* means that students automatically receive it, such as cancellation of classes.

Sharples, Corlett, and Westmancott (2002) suggested that PDAs will improve learning outside of class (contextual learning) because they are easier to carry along and can thus be used in different situations compared with PCs. They describe a prototype system of a mobile learning device that is targeted at children aged 9 to 11 years. Being able to use the devices anytime leads to a deeper learning experience that can be considered a form of lifelong learning. Sharples et al. (2002) based their idea on Walker et al. (2000), who noted that students use laptop computers more efficiently to learn than desktop PCs because of their mobility.

The eClass project (formerly Classroom 2000; Abowd et al., 1998) supports in-class learning with mobile devices. During class time, the lecture is recorded electronically, including notes, and captured onto digital media. This makes the creation of e-learning content easier. Instead of creating a digital course on the author's desk, the course is created while a teacher gives a lecture—something that takes place in every university and requires no additional effort. Pimentel, Ishiguro, Abowd, Kerimbaev, and Guzdial (2001) connected in-class activity, in the form of captured lectures that are later made available on the Web, with collaborative discussion spaces. Based on the collaboration of students and teachers during lectures, digital content can easily be created.

We now briefly look at the most common risks to m-learning identified at security risk analyses. When mobile services support in-class teaching, this normally includes the publication of sensitive information such as grades and time-relevant notification services for changes of venue. Because potentially large groups of students could receive wrong information, message integrity and nonrepudiation are essential.

Notification Services

Notification services are useful to reduce time lags of asynchronous communication such as e-mail and news groups. Students frequently use bulletin boards to discuss class assignments and solutions. Just before the hand-in deadline, students often nervously await answers to their open questions. Mobile devices are used to send short message service SMS notifications to a user's cell phone as soon as an answer to her posting has been received.

Notification services depend on availability by their very nature. Students expect to be notified within minutes once an answer to an important question has arrived. Secrecy of data is relevant because recipients may want to remain anonymous. Natural language messages contain redundancy so that unintentional changes can be detected easily. Intentional modifications could point to a wrong event (i.e., posting) that caused the message to be sent. As soon as the message arrives (availability), the user simply has to check all his or her newsgroup postings that might have triggered the message. Thus, integrity and nonrepudiation are generally not considered important in this application context.

Registration Service

Students need to register for courses on a regular basis. Before registration, they often attend information sessions offered by teachers or want to talk to their lecturer personally. During this period of time, registration (or pre-registration) and de-registration via mobile devices may be a useful application. Using mobile devices to register for courses only makes sense at large universities and for large courses. In this case, teachers do not know students personally and rely on electronic records generated by the application used for registration. Registrations should be binding for students. In addition, students need to be certain that their registration was correctly received and that no one else can unregister them—for instance, a fellow student who was not able to register because the course was fully booked.

Field Data

In science classes, students occasionally need to collect data outside of labs. Mobile devices have been used a lot for this application scenario. Okoada, Tarumi, Yoshimura, and Moriya (2001), for instance, used mobile devices to incorporate learning of theoretical knowledge into field learning. Courses on environmental education allowed users to access background information while outside.

Gathering data in the field requires that data are stored correctly and that their integrity is preserved. The protection should focus mainly on unintentional modification. Availability is essential as well, because numerous measurements might be taken resulting in a high volume of data. In overload situations, measurements might be stored incorrectly (integrity) or not at all (availability).

Solutions for Authentication

Research in computer science offers a plethora of solutions for the aforementioned security requirements. Nonetheless, it has been established (Sharples et al., 2002) that the human factor is the weakest link in most application environments.

The first step for all mobile security issues is to establish securely the identity of a user and to verify his claimed identity. This process is called authentication (Sandhu & Samarati, 1996). In this context, we focus on the user's authentication via his or her device to other services and not how he or she may authenticate to the device itself. Depending on the application scenario, different forms of mobile authentication can be distinguished (Weippl et al., 2002).

Mobile identification is a service that implements identification without authentication. This is useful for services with low security requirements. It is useful, for example, to automatically sign in on class attendance lists; the equivalent "traditional" paper-based lists are also used without proper ID check. *Mobile authentication* requires the correct identity of the accessing person, for instance, when a student registers for a course. *Mobile pseudonymous authentication* is used to identify oneself with a fake name. This fake name should be reused every time when the user logs onto the same service. For different services, different identities can be claimed to prohibit profiling across services. Nonetheless, other people should not be able to claim the (fake) identity. Thus, some form of authentication is required.

Using mobile *anonymous authentication,* users may remain anonymous even if the service requires authentication. For example, a newsgroup server may require identification such as a unique user name and a password. To make it easier for users to protect their privacy, they will want to generate anonymous accounts automatically.

CONCLUSION

This chapter showed how to conduct a security risk analysis for e-learning projects and presented typical threats that people perceived before and after such a workshop. Focusing on two security requirements, the third section analyzed typical threats for common activities such as creating content or teaching online. Subsequently, it was shown how two major security requirements (secrecy of data, privacy) can and have been addressed in theory.

Based on these findings, the implementation described here illustrates that the required changes to existing platforms such as Moodle are not extensive. Picking up our approach other researchers and commercial e-learning providers can implement similar function in other platforms.

In the future, e-learning will most likely be enriched by m-learning features. However, new technology almost always introduces new threats. The main security threats identified here as relevant for m-learning were summarized.

GLOSSARY

Computer-Based Training (CBT) A term that encompasses the use of computers in both instruction (computer-assisted instruction; CAI) and management (computer-managed instruction; CMI) of the teaching and learning process (Learning Circuits Glossary, 2003). Training where a computer program provides motivation and feedback in place of a live instructor is considered to be computer-based training regardless of how the content is delivered (ELearners Glossary, 2003).

E-learning Dating back to the hype of the term e-commerce, e-learning is widely used in different ways; for instance, LineZine (2003) understands e-learning as ranging from the convergence of the Internet and learning, or Internet-enabled learning, to the use of network technologies to create, foster, deliver, and facilitate learning, anytime and anywhere, or the delivery of individualized, comprehensive, dynamic learning content in real time, aiding the development of communities of knowledge, linking learners and practitioners with experts. *ELearners Glossary* (2003) defines e-learning as any form of learning that utilizes a network for delivery, interaction, or facilitation. According to *ELearners Glossary* (2003), e-learning covers a wide set of applications and processes, such as Web-based learning, computer-based learning, virtual classrooms, and digital collaboration. It includes the delivery of content via Internet, intranet–extranet (LAN/WAN), audio- and videotape, satellite broadcast, interactive TV, and CD-ROM. I prefer the last definition because of its broadness. The "e" in e-learning stands for electronic and thus all forms of learning that involve electronic components should be considered to be e-learning in the broadest sense; obviously e-commerce mainly refers to commerce conducted via electronic networks, and e-learning therefore has strong ties with communication networks. Because computers no longer exist without networks, however, these stand-alone learning applications will eventually cease to exist. For instance, today, even the simplest CD-ROM courses contain links to the Web.

Instructor-Led Training (ILT) This term often refers to traditional classroom training, in which an instructor teaches a class to a room of students (Learning Circuits Glossary, 2003). With the rise of virtual classes, ILT can also be conducted using WBT or e-learning platforms. Teleconferencing software, for instance, can be adapted to support ILT.

Web-Based Training (WBT) The delivery of educational content via networks such as the Internet, intranets, or extranets. Web-based training is characterized by links to other learning resources including references and supporting material. Moreover, communication facilities such as e-mail, bulletin boards, and discussion groups are also often included. WBT may also be instructor-led, that is, a facilitator provides course guidelines, manages discussion boards, delivers lectures, and so on. Nonetheless, WBT also retains the benefits of computer-based training. Web-based training is considered a synonym of Web-based learning (Learning Circuits Glossary 2003).

According to ELearners Glossary (2003), WBT learning content is delivered over a network and may either be instructor-led or computer-based. The term WBT is often used as a synonym for e-Learning, but the term *training* implies that unlike education, this type of learning takes place on a professional or corporate level.

CROSS REFERENCES

See *Access Control: Principles and Solutions; Anonymity and Identity on the Internet; E-education and Information Privacy and Security; Legal, Social, and Ethical Issues of the Internet; Privacy Law and the Internet; Risk Management for IT Security.*

REFERENCES

Abowd, G. D., Atkeson, C. G. , Brotherton, J., Enqvist, T., Gulley, P., & LeMon, J. (1998). Investigating the capture, integration and access problem of ubiquitous computing in an educational setting. In *Proceedings of the SIGCHI conference on Human factors in computing systems* (pp. 440–447). Los Angeles, California, ACM Press/Addison-Wesley. Retrieved March 15, 2005, from http://doi.acm.org/10.1145/274644.274704.

American Library Association. (2002). Washington Office, Guidelines for Librarians on the USA PATRIOT Act: What to do before, during and after a "knock at the door?" Retrieved March 15, 2005, from http://www.ala.org/ala/washoff/WOissues/civillliberties/theusapatriotact/patstep.pdf

Bell, D., & La Padula, L. (1975). Secure computer system: Unified exposition and multics interpretation (Esd-tr-75-306, Technical Report mtr-2997). Bedford, MA: MITRE Corporation.

Bellotti, V., & Sellen, A. (1993). Design for privacy in ubiquitous computing environments. Proceedings of the Third European Conference of Computer-Supported Cooperative Work (ECSCW'93), Milano, Italy (pp. 77–92). Dordrecht: Kluwer Academic.

Bishop, M. (2002). *Computer security: Art and science*. Boston, MA: Addison-Wesley-Longman.

Blackboard. (2003). Retrieved March 15, 2005, from http://www.blackboard.com

Chadwick, D., Olivier M. S., Samarati, P., Sharpston, E., & Thuraisingham, B. (2003). Privacy and civil liberties. In E. Gudes & S. Shenoi (Eds.)., *Research directions in database and application security* (pp. 331–346). Cambridge, UK: Kluwer.

Chaum, D. L. (1981). Untraceable electronic mail, return addresses, and digital pseudonyms. *Communications of the ACM, 24*:84–90.

Cowan, C. (2003). Software security for open-source systems. *IEEE Security & Privacy, 1*:38–45.

Dingledine, R., Mathewson, N., & Syverson, P. (2004). Tor: The second-generation Onion Router. In *Proceedings of the 13th USENIX Security Symposium.* Retrieved March 15, 2005, from http://www.onion-router.net/Publications.html.

Dourish, P., & Redmiles, D. (2002). An approach to usable security based on event monitoring and visualization. In *Proceedings of the 2002 workshop on New security paradigms* (pp. 75–81). Virginia Beach, Virginia ACM Press. Retrieved March 15, 2005, from http://doi.acm.org/10.1145/844102.844116.

Educause. (1998). Privacy issues in a virtual learning environment. Retrieved March 15, 2005, from http://www.educause.edu/ir/library/html/cem/cem98/cem9812.html.

ELearners Glossary. (2003). Retrieved March 15, 2005, from http://www.elearners.com/resources/glossary.asp.

Essmayr, W., Pernul, G., & Tjoa, A. M. (1997, August). Access control by object-oriented concepts. In *Proceedings of the IFIP WG 11.3 Annual Working Conference on Database Security*, Lake Tahoe, California. Chapman & Hall.

Franklin, C. (2003). [Web page on web spiders]. Retrieved March 15, 2005, from http://computer.howstuffworks.com/search-engine1.htm.

Good, N. S., & Krekelberg, A. (2002). Usability and privacy: A study of kazaa p2p file-sharing (Technical report, HP Laboratories). Retrieved March 15, 2005, from http://www.hpl.hp.com/shl/papers/kazaa/KazaaUsability.pdf.

Gorman, M. (2000). Privacy (chapter 10). In *Our enduring values: Librarianship in the 21st century*, American Library Association, ALA, Chicago, 2000.

Graham, L., & Metaxas, P. T. (2003). Of course it's true; I saw it on the Internet!: Critical thinking in the Internet era. *Communications of the ACM, 46*, 70–75, Retrieved March 15, 2005, from http://doi.acm.org/10.1145/769800.769804.

Hamlin, L. S., & Ryan, W. T. (2003, May 1). Probing for plagiarism in the virtual classroom (syllabus). Retrieved March 15, 2005, from http://www.colin.cc.ms.us/vcclib/cheat.htm

Hinman, L. M. (2002). Academic integrity and the World Wide Web *SIGCAS Computers and Society, 32*, 33–42, Retrieved March 15, 2005, from http://doi.acm.org/10.1145/511134.511139

Hochheiser, H. (2002). The platform for privacy preference as a social protocol: An examination within the U.S. policy context. *ACM Transactions on Internet Technology, 2*, 276–306.

King, J. W. (2004). Seven principles of good teaching practice. Retrieved March 15, 2005, from http://www.agron.iastate.edu/nciss/kingsat2.html.

Learning Circuits Glossary. (2003). Retrieved March 15, 2005, from http://www.learningcircuits.org/glossary.html.

LineZine. (2003). Retrieved March 15, 2005, from http://www.linezine.com/elearning.htm.

Moodle. (2004a). Retrieved March 15, 2005, from http://www.moodle.org.

Moodle. (2004b). Retrieved March 15, 2005, from http://moodle.org/doc/?frame=philosophy.html.

Neal, L. (2004). Expectations of privacy. *eLearn Magazine*. Retrieved March 15, 2005, from http://www.elearnmag.org/subpage/sub_page.cfm?article_pk=9344&page_number_nb=1&title=COLUMN.

Okada, M., Tarumi, H., Yoshimura, T., & Moriya, K. (2001). Collaborative environmental education using distributed virtual environment accessible from real and virtual worlds. *ACM SIGAPP Applied Computing Review, 9*, 15–21, Retrieved March 15, 2005, from http://doi.acm.org/10.1145/570142.570147.

Osborn, S., Sandhu, R. S., & Munawer, Q. (2000). Configuring role-based access control to enforce mandatory and discretionary access control policies. *ACM Transaction on Information and System Security, 3*, 85–206.

Palen, L., & Dourish, P. (2003). Unpacking privacy for a networked world. In *Proceedings of the Conference on Human Factors in Computing Systems* (pp. 129–136). Ft. Lauderdale: FL: ACM Press.

Peltier, T. R. (2001). *Information security risk analysis*. Boca Raton, FL: Auerbach.

Pimentel, M. G., Ishiguro, Y., Abowd, G. D., Kerimbaev, B., & Guzdial, M. (2001). Supporting educational activities through dynamic Web interfaces. In *Interacting with Computers* (Special issue), *13*, 353–374.

Planet-ET. (2003). Retrieved 2004 Page: 1 from http://www.planet-et.at

Reagle, J., & Cranor, J. F. (1999). The platform for privacy preferences. *Communications of the ACM, 42*, 48–55.

Rip Bill. (2000). Regulation of Investigatory Powers Bill. Retrieved March 15, 2005, from http://www.parliament.the-stationery-office.co.uk/pa/ld199900/ldbills/061/2000061.htm or http://www.hmso.gov.uk/acts/acts2000/20000023.htm

Sandhu, R. S., & Samarati, P. (1996). Authentication, access control, and audit. *ACM Computing Surveys, 28*.

Schneier, B. (2003). *Beyond fear: Thinking sensibly about security in an uncertain world*. New York: Springer-Verlag.

Sharples, M., Corlett, D., & Westmancott, O. (2002). The design and implementation of a mobile learning resource. *Personal and Ubiquitous Computing, 6*, 220–234, Retrieved March 15, 2005, from http://dx.doi.org/10.1007/s007790200021.

Spinellis, D. (2003). Reflections on trusting trust revisited. *Communications of the ACM, 46*, 112.

Swire, P., & Steinfeld, F. (2002). Security and privacy after September 11: The health care example, In *Proceedings of the 12th Annual Conference on Computers, Freedom and Privacy* (pp. 1–13), San Francisco, CA: ACM Press.

Thompson, K. (1984). Reflections on trusting trust. *Communications of the ACM, 27*, 761–763. Retrieved March 15, 2005, from http://doi.acm.org/10.1145/358198.358210.

USA Patriot Act of 2001. H.R.03162 (2001). Retrieved March 15, 2005, from http://thomas.loc.gov/cgi-bin/bdquery/z?d107:h.r.03162.

Walker, L., Rockman, S., & Chessler, M. (2000). A more complex picture: Laptop use and impact in the context of changing home and school access. Research studies on Microsoft's Anytime Anywhere Learning program. Rockman.

WebCT. (2004). Retrieved March 15, 2005, from http://www.webct.com.

Weippl, E. (2002, June). The transition from computer-based training to e-education. In *Proceedings of ED-MEDIA 2002* (pp. 2034–2039), Denver, CO:. AACE.

Weippl, E. (2004, June). Improving security in mobile e-learning. In *Proceedings of EDMEDIA 2004* (pp. 2034–2039), Lugano, Switzerland: AACE.

Weippl, E., & Essmayr, W. (2003). Personal trusted devices for ebusiness: Revisiting multilevel security. *Mobile Networks and Applications, 8*, 151–157.

Weippl, E., Essmayr, W., Gruber, F., Stockner, W., & Trenker, T. (2002, September). Towards authentication using mobile devices: An investigation of the prerequisites. In B. Jerman-Blazic & T. Klobucar (Eds.), *Proceedings of the Sixth IFIP Communications and Multimedia Security Conference (CMS): Advanced Communications and Multimedia Security* (pp. 91–105), Portoroz, Slovenia: Kluwer Academic.

Weller, R. (2004). Cheating: Academy head takes the blame. Retrieved March 15, 2005, from http://www.signonsandiego.com/uniontrib/20040516/news_1n16academy.html, http://166.70.44.66/2004/May/05162004/nation_w/166985.asp, and http://www.wtopnews.com/index.php?nid=316&sid=202387.

E-Government

Shannon Schelin, *The University of North Carolina, Chapel Hill*
G. David Garson, *North Carolina State University*

INTRODUCTION

Although there is widespread interest in the topic, e-government lacks a common definition. The American Society for Public Administration (ASPA) and United Nations (UN) Division for Public Economics and Public Administration have defined e-government as "utilizing the Internet and the World Wide Web for delivering government information and services to citizens" (UN/ASPA, 2001, p. 1). Marche and McNiven (2003, p. 75) define e-government as "the provision of routine government information and transactions using electronic means, most notably those using Internet technologies." The U.S. General Accounting Office (2003, p. 1) has also operationalized e-government as referring to "the use of information technology (IT), particularly Web-based Internet applications, to enhance the access to and delivery of government information and services to citizens, to business partners, to employees, and among agencies at all levels of government." Finally, e-government is often summarized as a process revolutionizing the business of government through the use of information technology (IT), particularly Web-based technologies, which improve internal and external processes, efficiencies, and service delivery.

WHAT E-GOVERNMENT IS AND HOW IT IS USED

E-government has evolved from the IT revolution, particularly the proliferation of the World Wide Web. Information technology in government has long been acknowledged as a method for improving efficiency and communication (Kraemer & King 1977; Norris & Kraemer, 1996). The advent of the Internet has led to developments such as electronic mail (e-mail) that have had profound organizational consequences through the perceived erosion of limitations such as time and geography (Rahm, 1999). The main concerns of e-government move beyond the benefits of automating processes and employing new public information technologies and concentrate more on reinventing processes to exploit fully the potential of information technology. E-government involves government to citizen (G2C), government to government (G2G), government to business (G2B), and government to employee (G2E) interactions.

According to some proponents of e-government, it is more than just a shift in communication patterns or mediums. Theoretically, e-government involves a transformation of the organizational culture of the government. According to Fountain (2002), the cultural transformation that can be achieved through e-government resides in the elimination of redundancy and duplicity of service provision. These shifts in culture are not without difficulty, however. To reorient government culture successfully away from the stovepipes and limited integration and interoperability, data must be shared both vertically and horizontally. By creating a distributed data environment, the system will create winners and losers in terms of control over data. This battle, both political and bureaucratic, will hinder the cultural shifts associated with the promises of e-government.

Despite the issues associated with cultural reorientation, recent authors argue that information technology facilitates new governmental structures and parameters as demanded by citizens and businesses (Heeks, 1999; Ho, 2002; Osborne & Gaebler, 1992). These demands require services that cut across traditional departmental and agency lines, which in turn require government to improve communication and interaction (Alexander & Grubbs, 1998). These new requirements, which fundamentally alter the nature of government, are made possible through the strategic use of information technology. As Fountain (2001) noted, the reinvention process requires overcoming the rigidities and limits of traditional bureaucracy. Specific objectives may include the centralization of public data and the improvement of internal processes and communications (Alexander & Grubbs, 1998). This delivery of services and information also involves the integration of government networks and databases to allow for cross-agency communication and interaction (Moon, 2002). Again, the turf issues associated with the cultural context of government may preclude some of these efforts from reaching maturation. However, the impact of the information era in government can be witnessed in the increasing governmental movement to Web-based information, services, and transactions, as evidenced by recent national surveys (ICMA, 2002; West, 2000). Before looking at specific data about the expansion of e-government in the United States, we examine the history of federal legislation regarding public information technology and e-government.

HISTORY OF E-GOVERNMENT AT THE U.S. FEDERAL LEVEL

The U.S. groundwork for e-government at the federal level was laid in the 1980s. The Paperwork Reduction Act of 1980 (PRA) mandated an information resources management (IRM) approach to federal data, thereby for the first time establishing a single policy framework for information resource management at the federal level. The director of the Office of Management and Budget (OMB) was given responsibility for developing an IRM policy and for overseeing its implementation. A major revision of the PRA in 1995 mandated strategic planning for IRM.

At the same time this administrative structure was created, the infrastructure for the Internet was being developed. ARPAnet, a network project of the Department of Defense, had been implemented in 1969, uniting some 23 defense-related military, university, and research laboratory sites by 1973. It was the funding of NSFNet by the National Science Foundation in 1986, however, that really marked the beginnings of the modern Internet. This long-haul backbone network was placed under a cooperative agreement with IBM, MCI, and Merit Network, Inc., the following year and by the end of 1987, there were 10,000 Internet hosts. By 1989, there were 100,000. By the time Tim Berners-Lee developed the World Wide Web in 1992 and Mosaic software was released to surf the Web, the number of Internet hosts exceeded 1 million. One of these was the server, which housed the first White House home page, launched on the Web in 1992.

Up to 1992, access to the Internet backbone was limited by the NSF's Acceptable Use Policy, which prohibited commercial traffic on the Internet. With the support of Congressman Rick Boucher (D-VA), chairman of the Science Subcommittee of the House Committee on Science, Space, and Technology, legislation was passed, and in November 1992, President George H. W. Bush signed new legislation that repealed the Acceptable Use Policy, replacing it with language that permitted commercial traffic on the Internet backbone. In 1993, federal funding of the Internet ended and the Internet became a private sector entity.

With the full advent of the "Internet Age" in the early 1990s, early efforts that might be seen as part of building e-government centered on educational functions. The Information and Technology Act of 1992 sought to ensure technology development in public education, health care, and industry. It called on NSF to fund efforts to connect K-12 classrooms to the Internet. In 1993, the National Information Infrastructure Act was passed, targeting federal research and development funding to the accelerated development of high-performance computing and high-speed networking services at the university and research laboratory level.

An important part of the administrative background of e-government in the early to mid-1990s was the National Performance Review (NPR) created March 3, 1993, under the leadership of Vice President Al Gore, himself a strong technology advocate. NPR reflected the Clinton administration's emphasis on information technology as a tool to reform government. Its report, *Creating a Government That Works Better and Costs Less: Reengineering Through Information Technology,* was an important document of the "reinventing government" mandate. This administrative movement originated with a focus on traditional forms of decentralization, devolution, and privatization. "Reinvention" advocates quickly came to see, however, that e-government was a major reform thrust facilitating and implementing their own goals of a results-oriented, client-centered, market-reliant approach to government. In 1993, the Government Information Technology Services Board was created to help implement NPR in information technology areas.

As the momentum for e-government grew, so did awareness of a major impediment: the skew of access to the Internet toward the well-to-do, and lack of access for America's "have-nots." The Commerce Department's 1994 report, *Falling Through the Net*, brought public attention to the issue of the "digital divide." In response, the Telecommunications Act of 1996 provided for a Universal Service Fund fee (a telephone tax, also known as the "e-rate" fund or fee), part of which the Clinton administration used to provide modem-based Internet access to schools, libraries, Indian reservations, and other "digital divide" target groups. By the end of the decade, however, the digital divide problem had receded due to falling hardware and software prices, making Internet access affordable to the great majority of citizens.

Some credit must also be given to another Clinton administration initiative, openness in government. The Electronic Freedom of Information Act Amendment of 1996 (EFOIA) extended the right of citizens to view executive agency records to include access to electronic formats and online opportunities for access information.

Also in 1996 came a piece of legislation that provided the basis for centralizing in the OMB the authority to enforce implementation of e-government (as well as other IT practices) across the federal government. The Clinger-Cohen Act of 1996 (originally named the Information Technology Management Reform Act of 1996, an amendment to the Paperwork Reduction Act of 1980) established a chief information officer (CIO) in every agency, making agencies responsible for developing a plan that relates IT planning with agency missions and goals. The oversight role of the director of the OMB was strengthened, and later, when e-government became a priority, the existence of the CIO strategic planning structure was an important element facilitating e-government implementation at the federal level.

A variety of agency-centric developments extended e-government in the late 1990s. In 1997, the U.S. Department of Agriculture became the first agency to engage in e-rulemaking, soliciting Web-based comments on rules for organic foods. This initiative won the 1998 Government Technology Leadership Award and became the basis for one of the major projects of the e-government efforts of the current Bush administration (see the President's E-Government Strategy, available at http://www.whitehouse.gov/omb/inforeg/egovstrategy.pdf). The 1998

Amendments to the Rehabilitation Act required federal agencies to make their information technology and electronic information available to people with disabilities. The IRS Restructuring and Reform Act of 1998 promoted electronic filing of tax returns, requiring the IRS to establish that all forms, instructions, publications, and other guidance are available via the Internet. It also provided for taxpayer electronic access to their accounts by 2006.

In some ways, the official "start" of federal e-government might be traced to the Government Paperwork Elimination Act of 1998 (GPEA), which authorized the OMB to acquire alternative information technologies for use by executive agencies; support for electronic signatures; electronic filing of employment forms, with a deadline set for most forms to be in place by October 21, 2003. The GPEA was the legal framework for accepting electronic records and electronic signatures as legally valid and enforceable and also represented congressional endorsement of the e-government strategy (Fletcher, 2002).

In a Presidential Memo of December 17, 1999, titled Electronic Government, President Clinton endorsed the concept of a federal government–wide portal (later to be FirstGov.gov). In 2000, the President's Management Council adopted digital government as one of its top three priorities. On June 24, 2000, President Clinton made the first presidential Internet address to the nation, again calling for establishment of the FirstGov.gov portal. FirstGov.gov was launched September 22, 2000, as a Clinton management initiative. It is the official U.S. government portal, designed to be a trusted one-stop gateway to federal services for citizens, businesses, and agencies. At launch, it was a gateway to 47 million federal government Web pages. FirstGov.gov also links to state, local, District of Columbia, and tribal government pages in an attempt to provide integrated service information in particular areas, such as travel. The Office of Citizen Services and Communications, within the General Services Administration, manages FirstGov.

In Election 2000, both candidates (Gore and Bush) advocated digital government concepts. After the election, President Bush made e-government one of his central management reform themes (although opposing most "digital divide" funding advocated by Clinton and Gore). The President's Management Agenda, issued in August 2001, committed the Bush administration to five major management objectives, one of which was electronic government.

In June 2001, the OMB created the position of associate director for Information Technology and E-Government. This gave the OMB a key point of contact to force higher priority to IT initiatives, particularly the goal of creating a citizen-centric government. In essence, this position had a mandate to provide leadership to all federal IT implementation, including a special emphasis on e-government. The first incumbent was Mark Forman, who quickly took strong actions to implement e-government throughout federal agencies. On July 25, 2002, the first chief technology officer (CTO) for the federal government was appointed, responsible for overseeing implementation of e-government policies. The first incumbent was Casey Coleman, heading up the General Services Administration's Office of Citizen Affairs.

Table 1 Overview of U.S. Federal E-Government "Quicksilver" Projects

Government to Citizen (G2C)
- USA Service (GSA)
- EZ Tax Filing (Treasury)
- Online Access for Loans (DoEd)
- Recreation One Stop (Interior)
- Eligibility Assistance Online (Labor)

Government to Business (G2B)
- Federal Asset Sales (GSA)
- Online Rulemaking Management (DOT)
- Simplified and Unified Tax and Wage Reporting (Treasury)
- Consolidated Health Information (HHS)
- Business Compliance One Stop (SBA)
- International Trade Process Streamlining (Commerce)

Government to Government (G2G)
- E-Vital (SSA)
- E-Grants (HHS)
- Disaster Assistance and Crisis Response (FEMA)
- Geospatial One Stop (Interior)
- Wireless Networks (Justice)

Internal Effectiveness/Efficiency (Government to Employee [G2E])
- E-Training (OPM)
- Recruitment One Stop (OPM)
- Enterprise HR Integration (OPM)
- Integrated Acquisition (GSA)
- E-Records Management (NARA)
- Enterprise Case Management (Justice)

The OMB issued the cornerstone document, *E-Government Strategy,* on February 17, 2002. This document set forth Bush administration e-government principles: citizen-centric, results oriented, and market based. It also called for increased cross-agency data sharing. Some 34 specific projects were identified for funding, including those in the "Quicksilver Initiative" announced in October 2001, as noted inTable 1.

Among other recent developments in e-government at the federal level has been the implementation of e-procurement. The GSA and OFPP (Office of Federal Procurement Policy), with involvement from the Department of Defense, National Aeronautics and Space Administration, and National Institutes of Health, advanced e-procurement by establishing Past Performance Information Retrieval System (PPIRS) to give online access to past vendor performance records in 2002. Another development is the Dot Kids Implementation and Efficiency Act of 2002, passed in December 2002. This act created a new domain, like .com and .edu. Every site designated .kids will be a safe zone for children and will be monitored for content, for safety, and all objectionable material will be removed.[1]

The Electronic Government Act (EGA) of 2002 was passed by Congress November 15, 2002, and signed by

[1] Many civil liberties proponents have criticized this act as allowing government censorship, thereby reducing transparency.

the president on December 16, 2002. The act was sponsored by Senator Joe Lieberman (D-CT). It is intended to promote e-government in all federal agencies. The EGA establishes an Office of Electronic Government within the OMB. The head of this office is to be appointed by the president and is to report to the OMB director. In essence, this formalizes the administrative setup established by the OMB in 2001 under Mark Forman. It requires regulatory agencies to publish all proposed rules on the Internet and to accept public comments via e-mail as part of "e-rulemaking." All information published in the Federal Register must also be published on the Web. The federal courts must publish rulings and other information on the Web, and there are numerous other provisions. The EGA makes $45 million available for e-government projects in the current fiscal year 2003 and $345 million over 5 years. (This compares with $5 million for Forman in fiscal year 2002.)

Clearly, the legislation and mandates of the U.S. federal government indicate the importance of e-government. Other countries have even more sophisticated laws and procedures to guide e-government adoption. For example, Singapore has developed long-range strategic plans for e-government, incorporating the eCitizen Center as the one-stop shop for all G2C interactions. The United Kingdom also demonstrates one of the highest levels of executive commitment to e-government. The Office of the E-Envoy has been created to oversee the transition to e-government for all services by 2005. Many other examples from around the globe further demonstrate the shift toward e-government.

E-GOVERNMENT ADOPTION IN THE UNITED STATES

Following the detailed review of U.S. federal commitment to e-government, it is important to assess the levels of e-government adoption at the local government level, as well as to illustrate usage by citizens. This description focuses on the United States; however, other sources provide more international coverage (Demchak, Friis, & La Porte, 2001; UN/ASPA, 2002). By analyzing data obtained from the 2002 E-Government Survey conducted by the International City/County Management Association (ICMA), the adoption rates of e-government at the local level can be assessed. The survey was conducted to evaluate the involvement of local governments in e-government activities, including Web site development, electronic services, geographic information systems, changes associated with e-government adoption, and barriers preventing such adoption. The survey was sent to 7,844 municipal and county governments with populations over 2,500; 4,123 surveys were completed and returned, a response rate of 52.6%.

For the purposes of this analysis, the municipalities and counties have been divided into three population categories. Small jurisdictions contain less than 50,000 inhabitants. Medium jurisdictions contain 50,000 to 249,999 inhabitants, and large jurisdictions contain 250,000 or more. The responding jurisdictions represent all four geographic regions, Northeast, North-Central, South, and West, as defined by the ICMA.

The presence of local government Web sites, as gathered during the ICMA survey, is significant, with 74.2% of responding counties and municipalities having an official Web site. In terms of the municipalities, 71.1% of small jurisdictions, 97.9% of medium jurisdictions, and 100% of large jurisdictions have official Web sites. Furthermore, 58.8% of small counties, 92.8% of medium counties, and 98.4% of large counties have an official Web presence. The high rate of Web presence demonstrates the movement of local governments to the e-government model; however, static Web presence is not sufficient for true e-government.

To assess more effectively the required interactive component of e-government, the presence of Web-enabled transactional processes via governmental Web sites was analyzed. The ICMA survey queried respondents about several categories of transactions, including online payments of taxes, utility bills, fines and fees, form completion and submission, business license application and renewal completion and submission, online requests for records, online delivery of records, online requests for services, online registration for facility usage, online voter registration, online property registration, downloadable forms, and online communication with elected and appointed government officials. In the aggregate, few local governments are using Web-based transactions.Table 2 demonstrates the offering of transactions by municipalities, based on the population categories previously denoted.

The positive effect of size on the rate of transaction offerings is important to note. For example, only 1.8% of small municipalities offer online payment of taxes, whereas 5.3% of medium and 24.0% of large municipalities offer the same online service.

A similar trend regarding the increased offering of Web-based transactions based on population size is found in the counties.Table 3 highlights the percentage of counties offering specific transactions, by population grouping.

Although electronic transaction offerings are limited in local governments, there is increasing citizen and business demand for such Web-based services. A national survey conducted by the Pew Research Center during September 2001 demonstrates the widespread usage of governmental Web sites and their interactive services. The 2002 Pew Internet and American Life Project indicates that 58% (68 million people) of U.S. Internet users have accessed at least one governmental Web site (Larson & Rainie, 2002). Furthermore, 68% of Internet users indicate that government Web sites improve their interaction with at least one level of government. Approximately 63% of those surveyed have downloaded government forms, 16% have filed taxes online, and 12% have renewed automobile registrations online. The 2002 Pew Internet and American Life Project highlights the citizen interest in and use of the Internet to enhance standard interactions with government.

Although governments' use of the Internet is increasing, there is still a significant lag time compared with private sector adoption of new technologies. Both structural inertia and risk aversion, commonplace in the public sector, foster governments that are slow to adopt and

Table 2 Percentage of Transactional Offerings by Municipalities, by Population Grouping

Service	Small Municipalities (%)	Medium Municipalities (%)	Large Municipalities (%)
Online payment of taxes	1.8	5.3	24.0
Online payment of utility bills	3.0	13.5	15.4
Online payment of fines and fees	2.1	12.4	23.1
Form completion and submission	7.7	16.1	33.3
Business license application/renewal completion and submission	4.4	8.0	14.8
Online requests for records	26.4	31.9	38.5
Online delivery of records	16.2	21.4	25.9
Online requests for services	31.3	41.0	44.4
Online registration for facility usage	12.1	20.3	36.0
Online voter registration	1.5	1.7	9.5
Online property registration	2.1	5.0	5.3
Downloadable forms	50.2	75.3	92.0
Online communication with elected and appointed officials	68.7	84.2	96.0

implement new technologies. The inherent tension between the need for reliability and accountability contrasted with reliance on maintaining organizational status quo leads to the increased adoption lag time in governmental organizations. For government information technology adoption and implementation, the inertia that exists within the public sector means that organizations are often less willing and able to engage new technologies (Bretschneider, 1990). This inability to adapt to the rapidity of the information age creates a disconnect between the movement toward e-government and the need to consider all citizen requirements and needs. The most common example of this problem is demonstrated by the creation of governmental Web sites that are organized by administrative structure rather than by service orientation, which is more intuitive to constituents. To understand more fully the issues associated with e-government adoption, including challenges and benefits, it is crucial to understand the theory and typology associated with e-government.

THEORY AND TYPOLOGY OF E-GOVERNMENT

Using the theoretical frameworks of e-government of decentralization–democratization and normative–dystopian, as outlined by Garson (1999), one can begin to assess the benefits and challenges associated with e-government. The decentralization–democratization

Table 3 Percentage of Transactional Offerings by Counties, by Population Grouping

Service	Small Counties (%)	Medium Counties (%)	Large Counties (%)
Online payment of taxes	9.2	25.0	40.0
Online payment of utility bills	1.0	8.2	9.4
Online payment of fines/fees	1.9	9.2	11.1
Form completion and submission	5.6	13.6	21.1
Business license application/renewal completion and submission	1.9	5.2	16.1
Online requests for records	23.1	43.2	65.0
Online delivery of records	12.0	35.9	53.6
Online requests for services	7.6	17.9	25.9
Online registration for facility usage	6.7	10.6	21.4
Online voter registration	4.7	7.0	7.4
Online property registration	1.2	2.7	8.3
Downloadable forms	42.1	72.6	87.7
Online communication with elected and appointed officials	63.6	77.1	82.1

framework of e-government revolves around the progressive nature of technology and highlights governmental advances resulting from e-government. Essentially, decentralization–democratization highlights the fundamental restructuring of government interactions with its constituents through the strategic use of information technology, that is, greater efficiency, effectiveness, and increased participation. On the other hand, the normative–dystopian framework uses the high rates of conflict and failure associated with information technology applications and offers a pragmatic, even skeptical view of e-government. The normative–dystopian framework is associated with the notion that e-government is another medium for communication between constituents and the government; however, it does not support the concepts of reinvention of government often associated e-government. Although neither framework can be considered fully descriptive, taken together they provide a useful delineation of the theoretical literature on e-government.

Decentralization–democratization theory is the traditional view of e-government, beginning with Bozeman and Bretschneider's seminal article in 1986, which highlights the transformational, progressive nature of technology adoption in the government sector. Furthermore, Reschenthaler and Thompson (1996) contended that the power of public information technology, a prerequisite for e-government, lies in its ability to level the playing field for all sizes and types of governments. They viewed the basis for reengineering the business of government, refocusing its work on the needs of the citizens, and returning government to its core functions residing under the technology umbrella.

Another decentralization–democratization approach for examining the e-government model involves comparing and contrasting traditional bureaucratic design with the evolved e-government design. The traditional bureaucratic model of public service delivery (the Weberian model) focuses on specialization, departmentalization, and standardization (Ho, 2002). This traditional model has created departmental "silos" that resist functioning across agency boundaries, in the name of equitable and efficient governmental interactions. In the 1990s, however, the reinventing government movement sought to shift the core focus of government, moving from departmentalization and centralization to citizen-centric decentralization (Osborne & Gaebler, 1992).

The e-government paradigm, which emphasizes coordinated network building, external collaboration, and customer services, is slowly replacing the traditional bureaucratic paradigm and its focus on standardization, hierarchy, departmentalization, and operational cost-efficiency (Ho, 2002). In this view, the development and deployment of technology networks, shared databases, and Web-based interactions are the necessities that will facilitate seamless integration of government services. Although this shift to the e-government paradigm has not been fully realized, the Internet is a key enabler to this transformation because it provides government with the ability to use technology to impact customers directly, instead of simply reengineering internal processes (Scavo & Shi, 1999).

Decentralization–democratization proponents use e-government adoption rates as proxies for gauging the success of e-government. As the adoption and implementation rates increase, e-government technologies will enjoy increased legitimacy (Fletcher, 1999). Increasing citizen and business demand for e-government applications, which have permeated to the local government level, are central to greater adoption across all levels of government (Norris, Fletcher, & Holden, 2001). Response to the changing environment with improved service delivery, increased efficiency and reduced costs is key to e-government success (West, 2000). Beyond the optimistic prospects of the democratization–decentralization theorists, there is a concrete reality of governmental technology and e-government failures, which are explained in the normative–dystopian framework.

Issues of privacy, security, and the digital divide fall under the normative–dystopian model, which offers a critical approach to evaluating e-government. This view entertains concepts of dehumanization and isolation, resulting from the proliferation of information technology. The normative–dystopian theory addresses ethical issues that surround e-government. Recent concerns about the "digital divide," the technology gap that exists between distinct groups in the United States, highlight the issues associated with the move to e-government as a mode of service delivery because of the potential consequences for unconnected or underserved populations. Several studies note racial, regional, educational, gender, and age disparities among Internet users and technology owners (e.g., Norris, 2001; Novotny, 1998). These gaps are of great concern for public administrators, who must serve efficiently, effectively, and equitably to fulfill their public charge.

Using the normative–dystopian framework, Bovens and Zouridis (2002) examined the inherent problems associated with the shift toward an e-government paradigm. The emerging emphasis on information technologies as the medium for citizen interaction with government fundamentally alters the role of the bureaucrat. The traditional Weberian model uses street-level bureaucrats to interact with citizens and to determine the proper services and service levels to assist these citizens (Lipsky, 1980). This method allows for expertise, judgment, and practicality to be engaged in the decision-making process. In the e-government model, computer programs are used to interface with clients, assess eligibilities, and decide on proper levels of service (Boven & Zouridis, 2002). This model suggests that the street-level bureaucrats are losing their discretionary power, which can have deleterious effects on the clients. Bovens and Zouridis (2002) use the normative/dystopian framework to highlight the potential arbitrariness and threats to the legitimacy of governmental actions at the street level in the e-government model. Both frameworks for assessing e-government are valuable and valid; however, the rising citizen demand and increasing governmental use of e-government components indicate that e-government will only progress.

Stages 1–5 of E-Government

Several models have been developed to explain the progression of e-government (Layne & Lee, 2001; Moon, 2002). Nonetheless, the stages or iterations of e-government do not follow a linear progression. Often, e-government applications are developed for utility, an ad hoc approach, instead of according to a master project plan, a systematic approach. For example, one local government may offer the ability to pay property taxes online through an application service provider but still have a basic informational Web site without interactive enhancements. Furthermore, the various models to be described offer a broad categorization of each stage or iteration. These are arranged in a continuum in which governments can be within the same stage while having diverse service capacities or functionalities.

According to the UN and ASPA (2001), there are five main stages of e-government, which are precipitated by the recognition that some form of presence exists for the given locality. Stage 1, the emerging Web presence, presents static information and is often considered to be "brochure-ware" (UN/ASPA, 2001, p. 16). The main goal of this stage is to provide an online dissemination of general information about the government. Often, a Stage 1 Web site visually represents the "stovepipes" that exist within agencies and does not allow for continuity across various departmental pages.

The association of the Web site denotes enhanced Web presence, Stage 2, with information on services; however, it is still organized by departments. This stage often offers e-mail as a method of two-way communication. It offers limited communication and greater information about the services of the government but is not consistent with the citizen-centric approach that has been advocated for e-government (UN/ASPA, 2001, p. 17; Layne & Lee, 2001; Moon, 2002).

Stage 3, interactive Web presence, does offer some of the citizen-centric methods as advocated by e-government proponents (UN/ASPA, 2001, p. 18). Information is presented in intuitive groupings, rather than by departmental or agency association. Often, portals are used as a single point of entry into various departments and service areas. Major groupings in the portal design might include business, new resident, seniors, children, or other standard groups. Subsequently, end users would control their Web destination based on the grouping they select. Each sublevel under the group headings offers commonly requested services, information, and assorted items of interest to the particular group. Again, a specific agency or department does not designate the services and information contained within each group; they are offered as a bundle of interests to the target population. Stage 3 sites also have downloadable forms with online submissions, e-mail contact for various governmental employees, and links to other governmental Web sites.

Stage Four, transactional Web presence, allows secure online transactions (UN/ASPA, 2001, p. 19). User needs dominate the organization of this Web presence and the information presented is dynamic. Potential transaction offerings include online payments of taxes, utility bills, fines and fees, form completion and submission, business license application and renewal completion and submission, online registration for facility usage, online voter registration, and online property registration. As evidenced by the ICMA 2002 E-Government Survey, less than 15% of responding counties and municipalities offer these services. Furthermore, only 4.6% of the respondents offer online payments.

The final stage, Stage 5, involves seamless government. This stage represents an ideal, and no real example of its application is available. Stage 5 ideally involves a cross-agency, intergovernmental approach that only displays one front, regardless of service area (UN/ASPA, 2001, p. 20). For example, a portal may offer a compendium of local, state, and federal government services without user recognition of what level of government provides the service. A Stage 5 site would offer vertical and horizontal integration and would require true organizational transformation with respect to administrative boundaries (UN/ASPA, 2001, p. 20).

Drawing on the UN and ASPA typology, current literature indicates that the majority of local governments are in Stage 2, with enhanced Web presence. Moon's (2002) analysis of 2000 ICMA E-Government Survey indicates that a majority of municipalities with populations over 10,000 are not offering transactional Web sites. Furthermore, based on the 2002 ICMA E-Government Survey, only 62 (1.7%) municipalities offer online payment of taxes, 113 (3.1%) offer online payment of utility bills, and 91 (2.5%) offer online payment of fines and fees. The percentages for counties are only slightly higher, with 69 (16.3%) offering online payment of taxes, 17 (4.0%) offering online payment of utility bills, and 21 (5.0%) offering online payment of fines and fees. More robust transactional services can be found at the state and federal levels of government, as would be expected.

Using Ho's (2002) methodology for assessing municipal Web sites, a different dimension of e-government typology can be discerned. He centers on three primary orientations designed to demonstrate the shift from the Weberian bureaucratic model to the e-government paradigm. The first orientation is administrative-oriented Web sites, organized along departmental lines, which represents the traditional bureaucratic paradigm (p. 437). The second orientation is information-oriented, crossing departmental lines to provide a one-stop shopping experience to the user (p. 437). The final orientation is user-oriented, which categorizes information in intuitive groupings that offer end user control and rapid access to predetermined information (p. 437). This orientation also crosses traditional departmental lines in an attempt to provide an all-encompassing experience to the end user. Ho's analysis of the 55 largest municipalities' Web sites indicates that a majority has moved toward varying degrees of user-orientation (p. 438).

Further alternative approaches to defining the e-government typology use various levels of communication, applications of technology, and citizen participation in democratic forums to define its stages. One example of this approach is found in Moon's typology (2002), as adopted from Hiller and Bélanger. This framework also uses five stages, but its focus is on the communications between various stakeholders, including government to government (G2G), government to employee (G2E), and government to citizen (G2C). Stage 1 involves information dissemination and uses basic Web authoring tools and bulletin boards as methods of communication (p. 426). Two-way communication, utilizing e-mail and electronic data exchange (EDI), is found in Stage 2. Stage 3 highlights service and financial transactions, along with technologies such as EDI, electronic filing systems, digital signature, and public key infrastructure. Stage 4 centers on the concepts of vertical and horizontal integration of the technologies found in Stages 1, 2, and 3. It is similar to Stage 5 of the UN/ASPA model in its seamless outward appearance. Political participation is the mainstay of Stage 5 in moon's typology. It involves online voting, e-democracy, and e-participation. Few local governments have evolved to Stage 5, evidenced by the fact that only 2.1% of respondents to the 2002 ICMA E-Government Survey are using online voter registration. This alternative approach to the typology of e-government still acknowledges the importance of the user's view of e-government but extends the model to include digital civic engagement and enhanced electronic democracy.

The various models of e-government allow for broad comparisons across the various governmental Web sites, using similar benchmarking criteria. Such comparisons are useful to the extent that they can highlight the critical success factors associated with individual experiences, which can be generalized to the general population. One of these critical success factors is training for e-government. Issues of training are directly related to the need to move along the e-government continuum because training fosters greater understanding of the processes and applications and provides a method of eliciting user support. By examining the current training practices of governments with regard to e-government, one can begin to understand the need to bridge e-government expansion and training in order to create a holistic, enterprise approach.

SECURITY AND PRIVACY

Issues of security and privacy in the post-9/11 era are of grave concern to the majority of government constituents. Yet only a small minority of governments are actively addressing security and privacy issues. According to the 2002 ICMA E-Government Survey indicates that 15% of the survey respondents have or will make significant changes to their existing security practices as a result of 9/11. Additionally, over 10% indicate that they have removed information from their Web site for security reasons. Clearly, the issues of security and privacy are more salient than ever and governments must address constituent concerns if e-government is to achieve high levels of adoption and usage.

Security

Although security is important to citizens, the majority of security literature for the public sector revolves around intraorganizational security. In terms of the complexity of security, the issue is really one of trade-offs. For example, higher levels of security required increased costs, lower levels of privacy, and decreased functionality. Despite the trade-offs that must be made, attention to security for public sector technology is at an all-time high. In fact, leading technology think-tanks, such as the Harvard Policy Group, and federal agencies have produced major reports outlining the critical components of public sector IT security. Based on the work of these organizations, this article offers a high-level overview of security policy best practices.

Given the increasing numbers of computers, networks, hardware, and software in the public sector, it is critical for a security policy to be developed to protect the organizational investments. As such, the security policy should state that information resources are essential organizational assets and should be protected. Furthermore, top management must be involved in the security process to ensure adequate support and funding (see GAO, 1998; Harvard Policy Group, 2001).

The security policy should mandate that the team adopt standards for availability, confidentiality, authentication, integrity, and repudiation. These standards will be employed enterprisewide. It should recommend practical risk assessment procedures that create goal alignment between security concerns and organizational needs. Additionally, the security policy should security training mandate for all employees and should hold program and business managers accountable for breaches in security.

The policy should mandate that risk be managed on a continual basis via various security methods. One of the methods is physical security. The policy will include standard security measures such as locked doors and use of identification badges for staff and visitors. The policy should also mandate simple computer policies, such as locked terminals with password-protected screensavers, mandatory password rotation, consent to monitoring, and installation of antiviral software on all department computers. For example, one password policy may be that each password must be eight characters long and include one special character. The passwords must be changed every 90 days. At no time should passwords be written down or shared among employees, one of the most common security lapses.

The security policy should establish a central group to carry out departmental security training and enforcement. This group should be designated funding and staff sufficient to cover its needs. Another strategy for inclusion in the policy is enhancement of staff skills, both generic security measures and technical security advancements. All security policies established by the central group will be codified and included on the employee Intranet. Beyond placement on the Intranet, the security policies will be reviewed individually at group meetings to ensure that users understand risks and methods for combating them.

Finally, the policy should indicate that the central group responsible for security should use constant monitoring and frequent attack methods to ensure that security is being upheld. By monitoring the factors that contribute to security breaches, the team can create alternative policies to mitigate problems within the organization. Finally, the team should employ current security monitoring devices to prevent undetected intrusion. These devices must be proven before purchase, but there should not be a lag in technology between the public sector and private sector counterparts. It is evident that security is one of the highest priorities of the public sector. As such, a given security policy should lay the foundation for the establishment of a security team, as well as articulate guidelines for achieving high levels of security.

Privacy

Moving into the privacy arena, there is significant citizen concern about establishing and maintaining privacy rights. In the 1950s, the Freedom of Information movement, spurred on by McCarthyism, mobilized people to protect their right to know about governmental affairs, in particular, information collected by the government about the individual. The Freedom of Information Act was passed in 1966, but it had little impact because of lack of compliance regulations and lack of punitive structures. During the mid-1970s, the Freedom of Information Act was amended to address some of the grievances, such as limiting costs for access to information, and attaching penalties for noncompliance. By 1996, the act had been amended again to encompass electronic information and transmission. This amendment requires the agencies to offer electronic copies of traditional paper-based documents. The lack of real resources to complete the tasks required in the legislation has significantly reduced the value of the amendment, however. The Freedom of Information Act and Electronic Freedom of Information Act created a venue for obtaining information about government operations, but they also brought to light issues of personal privacy rights, which are the common context of today's privacy conversations.

Attention to privacy in terms of public sector information technology often involves Web site privacy and its relationship to website visitors. As such, high-level guidelines for Web site privacy policies are offered, based on a survey of best practices literature (see Berman & Bruening, 2001; Kent & Millett, 2002; O'Neil & Dempsey, 2000). First, the policy should state that the public sector organization is open to the public and its Web site is a vehicle for providing the desired openness and transparency as sought by citizens. It also should note that the organization only uses collected personal information for the purposes stated prior to collection. The policy should also indicate that information collected will not be disclosed, unless mandated by law.

The policy must define "personal information" such as name, address, e-mail, and so on. In terms of collection of personal information, the policy should indicate that information collection is limited to the requirements of the law and will not be collected for superfluous reasons. Furthermore, the individuals will be apprised as to how their information will be used prior to collection. As previously noted, personal information will not be shared or disclosed unless authorized by law. Individuals will also be allowed to access their personal information to ensure its correctness. The organizational policy must also state that security measures are strictly enforced in order to ensure the security of personal information. Finally, the privacy policy should note that electronic and nonelectronic information are afforded the same levels of privacy protection.

In terms of Web site collection of information, the privacy policy should note the types of information collected, as well as the manner of collection and storage. For example, if the Web site automatically tracks incoming Internet domains, browsers, operating systems, pages visited, or other such items, the users of the Web site should be informed about this collection via a link to the privacy policy. In addition, if the Web site collects "cookies," the user should be informed. Cookies are text files stored on a user computer to enable user recognition by the Web site. The Web user should be informed that their Web browser can be configured to refuse cookies or to notify the user when a site attempts to send a cookie.

Finally, the privacy policy developed by the subcommittee should mandate the use of privacy impact assessments (PIAs) for all technology projects. PIAs are designed to help the department determine whether new technology projects or initiatives meet set privacy requirements. PIAs also help to mitigate risks to privacy by identifying alternative solutions. PIAs involve four basic steps:

1. Project initiation—During this stage, the goal is to determine the scope of the PIA and to adapt the tools provided in the guidelines to the context.
2. Data flow analysis—This involves describing and analyzing the business processes and data flows to identify personal information transmission.
3. Privacy analysis—This step examines the data flows compared with accepted privacy policies and legislation.
4. Privacy impact analysis report completed—This is a written evaluation of privacy risks, implications, and alternative solutions for risk mitigation.

This model, although time-consuming, allows for standardized decision making about distribution of personal and, potentially, sensitive information.

Clearly, security and privacy are important concerns in the public sector technology arena. They create many challenges for public sector organizations and require significant attention and regulation to appropriately manage them. Regardless of the trade-offs, security and privacy are critical to maintaining citizen trust in government and efforts should be institutionalized in order to address these issues.

CONCLUSION: THE FUTURE OF E-GOVERNMENT

The march toward e-government has not been without setbacks, notably in the areas of universal access and governmental openness. Presidents Bush's 2003 budget proposed to eliminate two critically important community technology programs related to diminishing the "digital divide": the Technology Opportunities Program (TOP) and the Community Technology Center (CTC) initiative. A study by Brown University's Center for Public Policy studied 1,265 federal and state Web sites and found only six% had restricted areas requiring a password to enter. Likewise, the Environmental Protection Agency has removed risk management plans and other information pertaining to hazardous waste sites from its Web site, citing risk of terrorism outweighing the right of citizens to know hazardous waste risks near their homes, workplaces, and schools.

Nonetheless, the setbacks are far overshadowed by the remarkably rapid expansion of e-government. The Pew Internet and American Life Project, in the Larsen and Rainie (2001) report cited earlier, stated, "The rise of e-government has been one of the most striking developments on the Web" (p. 5). Because of citizen demand for things such as e-access to building permits, dog licenses, and birth certificates, the bandwagon effect for implementing e-government is strong (Moulder, 2001). There is now considerable momentum for government change along the e-government model. Governments are competing to be seen as being on the leading edge, not laggard adopters (Sprecher, 2001).

Many cities are moving away from traditional bureaucratic emphasis on standardization, departmentalization, and operational cost-efficiency, toward the "e-government" paradigm, which emphasizes coordinated network building, external collaboration, and customer services (Ho, 2002). In this way the reinventing government movement is tied to the e-government movement.

Many municipal governments have adopted e-government, but it is still at an early stage and has not obtained many of expected outcomes (cost savings, downsizing, etc.) that the rhetoric of e-government has promised[2] (Moon, 2002). There has been general progress in online services, privacy policy statements, and standardized navigational features but much less progress in disability and foreign language access. Most agencies used Web for one-way communication with no provision for two-way interaction with citizens (West, 2001). The desire to transcend limited progress is one motivation behind the push for public–private partnerships in support of e-government initiatives (Holmes, 2001).

It is still too early to assess e-government in terms of effect on democracy. Clearly, there are great hopes that e-government will provide new opportunities for widening civic engagement and participation (Milward & Snyder, 1996). In principle e-government increases the reliability and accountability of public organizations, but in Santa Monica, California, home to PEN, one of the first major community computing experiments, whereas city officials were eager to participate in a community computing experiment in its first year, by the sixth year most had ceased participation, citing lack of substance if e-forums and too much "flaming" and personal attacks by a minority of network participants (Docter & Dutton, 1998). The Electronic Government Act of 2002 has now mandated e-rulemaking, a critical aspect of e-democracy, and there are other e-democracy experiments, such as the fact that all hearings and committee sessions of the Michigan legislature are now broadcast in streaming video, live over nine channels. Although e-government may have a much less profound effect on e-democracy than it is already having in the provision of governmental e-services, at the very least new channels of two-way communication between citizens and their government are being enabled.

[2] This "rhetoric of e-government" promises cost savings and other benefits, which arguably are not realistic outcomes of e-government.

GLOSSARY

Citizen-Centric A new approach to organization of government information and dissemination of government services that focuses on citizen needs and desires instead of traditional bureaucratic functions. For example, a citizen-centric Web site may combine various services, provided by different departments or agencies, under a common heading based on life events.

E (electronic)-Democracy A new method of engaging citizens in political participation, including e-rulemaking, e-voting, and various means of communication with elected and appointed government officials.

E (electronic)-government A strategy for revolutionizing the business of government through the use of information technology (IT), particularly Web-based technologies, which improve internal and external processes, efficiencies, and service delivery.

E (electronic)-Procurement The online provision of goods and services by government agencies. E-procurement includes online requests for proposal (RFPs), online request for bids (RFB), online bid acceptance, and online monitoring of contracts.

E (electronic)-Services The provision of government services via the Internet, including online information, online forms, online transactions, and online referral processes.

Portal A one-stop, cross-department/business unit, and cross-jurisdictional Web site that serves as aggregation of government services in a given functional area or based on user needs.

"Stovepipe" The traditional orientation of government departments or business units, in which each department or business unit acts independently and autonomously. Lack of integration and interoperability and issues of duplication of efforts characterize "stovepipe" organizations.

CROSS REFERENCES

See *Digital Economy; E-government Security Issues and Measures; International Security Issues of E-Government; Internet Basics; Legal, Social and Ethical Issues of the Internet.*

REFERENCES

Alexander, J. H., & Grubbs, J. W. (1998). Wired government: Information technology, external public organizations, and cyberdemocracy. *Public Administration and Management: An Interactive Journal 3*(1). Retrieved from http://www.pamij.com/

Bovens, M., & Zouridis, S. (2002). From street-level to system-level bureaucracies: How information and communication technology is transforming administrative discretion and constitutional control. *Public Administration Review, 62*(2): 174–185.

Bozeman, B., & Bretschneider, S. (1986). Public management information systems: Theory and prescription. *Public Administration Review, 46*(Special edition): 475–487.

Bretschneider, S. (1990). Management information systems in public and private organizations: An empirical test. *Public Administration Review, 50*(5): 536–545.

Brown, M. M., & Brudney, J. L. (1998). Public sector information technology initiatives. *Administration and Society, 30*(4): 421–443.

Demchak, C. C., Friis, C. S., & La Porte, T. M. (1999). Webbing governance: National differences in constructing the face of public organizations. In G. D. Garson (Ed.)., *Handbook of public information systems* (179–196). New York: Marcel Dekker.

Docter, S., & Dutton, W. H. (1998). The First Amendment online: Santa Monica's public electronic network. In R. Tsagarousianou, D. Tambini, & C. Bryan (Eds.), *Cyberdemocracy: Technology, cities, and civic networks* (pp. 125–151). New York: Routledge.

Fletcher, P. D. (2002). Government Paperwork Elimination Act: Operating instructions for an electronic government. *International Journal of Public Administration, 25*(5): 723–736.

Fletcher, P. D. (1999). Strategic planning for information technology management in state governments. In D. G. Garson (Ed.), *Information technology and computer applications in public administration: Issues and trends* (pp. 81–97). Hershey, PA: Idea Group.

Fountain, J. (2001). *Building the virtual state: Information technology and institutional change.* Washington, DC: Brookings Institution.

Garson, G. D. (1999). Information systems, politics, and government: Leading theoretical perspectives. In D. G. Garson (Ed.), *Handbook of public information systems* (pp. 591–605). New York: Marcel Dekker.

Heeks, R. (1999). Reinventing government in the information age. In R. Heeks (Ed.), *Reinventing government in the information age* (pp. 9–21). New York: Routledge.

Ho, A.T-K. (2002). Reinventing local government and the e-government initiative. *Public Administration Review, 62*(4): 434–444.

Holmes, D. (2001). *Egov: Ebusiness strategies for government.* London: Nicholas Brealey.

Kraemer, K. L., and J. L. King, eds. 1977. *Computers and local government.* New York: Praeger.

Larsen, E., & Rainie, L. (2002). The rise of the e-citizen: How people use government agencies' Web sites. Pew Internet and American Life Project. Retrieved from http://www.pewinternet.org/reports/pdfs/PIP_Govt_Website_Rpt.pdf

Layne, K., & Lee, J. (2001). Developing fully functional e-government: A four stage model. *Government Information Quarterly, 18*(2): 122–136.

Lipsky, M. (1980). Street-level bureaucracy: Dilemmas of the individual in public services. New York: Russell Sage Foundation.

Marche, S., & McNiven, J. D. (2003). E-government and e-governmance: The future isn't what it used to be. *Canadian Journal of Administrative Sciences, 20*(1): 74–86.

Milward, H. B. & Snyder, L. O. (1996). Electronic government: Linking citizens to public organizations through technology. *Journal of Public Administration Research and Theory, 6*(2): 261–276.

Moon, M. J. (2002). The evolution of e-government among municipalities: Rhetoric or reality? *Public Administration Review, 62*(4): 424–433.

Moulder, E. (2001). E-government—if you build it, will they come? *Public Management, 83*(8): 10–14.

Norris, D. F., Fletcher, P. D., & Holden, S. H. (2001). Is your local government plugged in? Highlights of the 2000 electronic government survey. Prepared for International City and County Managers Association and Public Technologies, Incorporated. Retrieved from http://icma.org/download/catIS/grp120/cgp224/E-Gov2000.pdf

Norris, D., & Kraemer, K. (1996). Mainframe and PC Computing in American cities: Myths and realities. *Public Administration Review, 56*(6): 568–576.

Norris, P. (2001). *Digital divide: Civic engagement, information poverty, and the Internet worldwide.* Cambridge: Cambridge University Press.

Novotny, P. (1998). The World Wide Web and multimedia in the 1996 presidential election. *Social Science Computer Review, 16*(2): 169–184.

Osborne, D., & Gaebler, T. (1992). Reinventing government: How entrepreneurial spirit is transforming the public sector. Reading, MA: Addison-Wesley.

Rahm, D. (1999). The role of information technology in building public administration theory. *Knowledge, Technology, and Policy, 12*(1): 74–83.

Reschenthaler, G. B., & Thompson, F. (1996). The information revolution and the new public management. *Public Administration Research Theory, 6*(1): 125–143.

Scavo, C., & Shi, Y. (1999). World Wide Web site design and use in public management. In D. G. Garson (Ed.), *Information technology and computer applications in public administration: Issues and trends* (pp. 246–266). Hershey, PA: Idea Group.

Sprecher, M. H. (2000). Racing to e-government: Using the Internet for citizen service delivery. *Government Finance Review, 16*(5): 21–22.

United Nations and American Society for Public Administration. (2001). *Benchmarking E-Government: A Global Perspective-e-Assessing the UN Member States.* Retrieved from http://www.unpan.org/egovernment2.asp

West, D. M. (2000). *Assessing e-government: The Internet, democracy, and service delivery by state and federal government.* Taubman Center for Public Policy at Brown University. Retrieved from http://www.brown.edu/Departments/Taubman_Center/polreports/egovtreport00.html

FURTHER READING

Kim, S., & Layne, K. (2001). Making the connection: E-government and public administration education. *Journal of Public Affairs Education, 7*(4): 229–240.

Norris, D. F. (1999). Leading edge information technologies and their adoption: Lessons from US cities. In D. G. Garson (Ed.), *Information technology and computer applications in public administration: Issues and trends* (pp. 137–156). Hershey, PA: Idea Group.

Northrop, A. (2003). Information technology and public administration: The view from the profession. In D. G. Garson (Ed.), *Public information technology.* Hershey, PA: Idea Group.

Perry, J. L., & Kraemer, K. L. (1993). The implications of changing information technology. In F. J. Thompson (Ed.), *Revitalizing state and local public service: Strengthening performance, accountability, and citizen confidence* (pp. 225–245). San Francisco: Jossey-Bass.

West, D. M. (2003). *State and federal e-government in the United States.* Brown University. Retrieved from http://www.insidepolitics.org/egovt01us.html

E-Government Security Issues and Measures

William C. Barker, *National Institute of Standards and Technology*

E-GOVERNMENT INITIATIVES

Definitions of E-Government

E-government, a contraction of "electronic government," refers to the use by government agencies of information technologies (such as the Internet) to conduct interactions with citizens, with businesses, and with other arms of the government. E-government initiatives seek to improve delivery of government services to citizens, improve interactions with business and industry, empower citizens through access to information, and improve government management efficiency. E-government can potentially result in less corruption, more transparency, greater convenience, revenue growth, and cost reductions (World Bank Group, n.d.).

General

Traditionally, the interaction between a citizen or business and a government agency took place in a government office. With emerging information and communication technologies, it is possible to locate service centers closer to the clients. Such centers may consist of an unattended kiosk in the government agency, a service kiosk located close to the client, or the use of a personal computer in the home or office.

E-government is analogous to e-commerce, which allows businesses to transact with each other more efficiently and brings customers closer to businesses. E-government aims to make the interaction between government and citizens, government and business enterprises, and interagency relationships more friendly, convenient, transparent, and inexpensive.

U.S. Government–Specific

Within the United States, under the "e-gov" initiatives, e-government is to use improved Internet-based technology to make it easy for citizens and businesses to interact with the government, save taxpayer dollars, and streamline citizen-to-government communications. A major motivator for e-government within the U.S. government was the Government Paperwork Elimination Act (GPEA) of October 21, 1998, which required federal agencies, by October 21, 2003, to provide for the options of (a) electronic maintenance, submission, or disclosure of information, when practicable as a substitute for paper, and (b) use and acceptance of electronic signatures, when practicable. Implementation of the GPEA provides the management framework for electronic government. Office of Management and Budget (OMB) Memorandum M-00-10, dated April 25, 2000, provides procedures and guidance on implementing the GPEA. OMB's guidance, in addition to procedural guidance for Paperwork Reduction Act reporting, requires that an agency's implementation plan relate to strategic information technology planning in the budget process. If an agency needs additional resources to implement the plan, its budget request under OMB Circular A-11 should reflect that need, and agency GPEA reports should address progress in implementing the act and e-government initiatives. The E-Government Act of 2002 builds on the U.S. government's expanding e-government initiative with a comprehensive framework for information security standards and programs and uniform safeguards to protect the confidentiality of information provided by the public for statistical purposes. The act also assists in expanding the use of the Internet and computer resources to deliver government services, consistent with the principles of a citizen-centered, results-oriented, and market-based government.

The goal of these initiatives is to eliminate redundant systems and improve the government's quality of customer service for citizens and businesses. E-government does not just mean putting scores of government forms on the Internet. It aims to use technology to its fullest to provide services and information that are centered around citizen groups (E-Gov Web Site: http://www.whitehouse.gov/omb/egov/about_backgrnd.htm).

Examples of E-Government Program Types

There are a number of taxonomies of e-government service types. Some are based on functional relationships (e.g., government to citizen, government to business, government to government, and internal effectiveness and efficiency). Others focus on functional processes content and degree of interaction inherent in the services provided. For purposes of this security discussion, the services provided by e-government program are categorized with respect to functional processes as (a) publishing, (b) interactive processing, (c) transaction processing, and (d) service delivery.

Publishing

Publishing involves simply posting information on a publicly accessible Web site. The primary automated interaction of the public with e-government publishing services is limited to navigation around the Web site. The public should have no ability to modify government Web content.

The major challenge associated with e-government publishing is content management: the process of creating, updating, distributing, and publishing information on a Web site. Content management involves creating a central storage area for files, templates, images, and other material used to build a Web site. Content management templates support conformance of government Web pages to government standards. Content management systems also support review and approval of Web page content being published. Content management processes are also vehicles for periodic review and update of agencies' online information. Content work flow includes the following elements:

- Contribution—Content is written and placed in the Web page.
- Approval—Content is reviewed and approved or rejected.
- Publishing—Content is sent to the live site.

At each step in the work flow, someone must sign off. These sign-offs help to ensure accountability for content. No unauthorized modification of Web site content should be permitted.

To date, most e-government activity has centered on publishing.

Interactive Processing

E-government interactive processing involves private citizens or other user entities reading instructions published on agency Web sites and following those instructions to submit reports, applications, or other service requests (e.g., submit tax returns, apply for licenses or other services, renew licenses, order products or services, or provide notification of address or other status changes). Here, citizens or other private entities need to be able to write and modify some data files with which they are associated on the government Web site. No user entity, however, should be able to read or modify data files associated with another user entity, be able to read or modify data files restricted to agency use, or modify any Web page content (other than that entity's own data) or underlying program. In addition to dealing with content management issues associated with Web-based publication, agencies that host interactive Web sites need to be able to provide citizens and other customers with assurance that privacy, integrity, and binding to the originator will be preserved for information that is submitted to interactive government Web sites. Furthermore, the effective management of an interactive Web site also requires some mechanism for identifying the originator of Web-based reports, applications, and other requests with the information provided by the originator. Inputs to interactive e-government sites should not be permitted without prior completion of the following process:

- Application—The user identifies himself to the agency and requests an interactive account.
- Approval—The application is approved or rejected.
- Credentialing—The agency provides the user with an electronic credential (e.g., personal identification number, password, public key certificate) that can be used to associate information with the possessor of the credential.

Once in possession of the appropriate access credential, a user is able to access an e-government Web site, navigate to the appropriate form, enter the requested information, and submit the form. The Web site should be capable of invoking processes that receipt for the submission, including notification that the submission complied with rules regarding information format and completeness.

Interactive government Web sites are less numerous than sites limited to publication but are becoming more common.

Transaction Processing

Transaction processing includes processing of information submitted via interactive e-government Web sites, providing notification of approval for actions to be taken on the basis of that information, and activation of implementation processes (e.g., billing, payment, licensing, permit issuance, contract awards, invoice approvals, etc.). Transaction processing generally involves distributing data received from users to multiple databases and multiple processes and includes interactions with third parties. This characteristic multiplies the distribution of privacy and integrity mechanisms. It also requires a process for dissemination of the decision notification and any associated authorization information in a manner that binds the content of the notification to identity credentials associated with both the e-government originator and the user recipient. Government-issued interactive access credentials need to include some information that can be used to verify the origin and content integrity of information allegedly received from an e-government source. Cryptographic mechanisms are usually employed for this purpose.

Service Delivery

Service delivery goes beyond the transaction approval component to transaction processing, including the actual execution of actions approved on the basis of e-government interactions. Examples of such actions include acceptance of credit card payments or electronic funds transfers, execution of government payments (e.g., benefits, grants, refunds, or payments for services or products) by electronic fund transfers, and delivery of licenses or permits. Because service delivery can be difficult, expensive, or even impossible to repudiate, assured invocation and effectiveness of source authentication, destination authentication, authentication of any third-party authorization, and verification of the integrity and correctness of the information contained in the service delivery communication are essential.

SECURITY ISSUES ASSOCIATED WITH E-GOVERNMENT

Taxonomies of security issues associated with e-government usually include three to five major elements. Examples of major security categories include confidentiality, privacy, integrity, authentication, authorization, and nonrepudiation. For purposes of this discussion, the taxonomy employed by the E-Government Act of 2002 will be used. The E-Government Act of 2002, Section 3542(B), defines integrity, confidentiality, and availability attributes of security.

Threats to the security of information in an e-government environment can include natural and accidental events (e.g., flooding, fire, storms, human error, environmental problems) and deliberate threats (e.g., sabotage, fraud, information theft, Trojan horses, hacking, viruses, logic bombs). Deliberate attacks may come from criminals, hackers, terrorists, disenchanted employees, curious or mischievous users, journalists, state-sponsored or industrial spies, or state-sponsored or industrial saboteurs. The primary focus of this chapter is on threats and countermeasures affecting remote connections to e-government resources rather than on insider and other threats involving physical access to servers and other storage and processing facilities. It focuses also on the potential for denial, unauthorized alteration, and unauthorized disclosure of information rather than on some of the purposes for which successful compromise of information security can be employed. For example, the focus might be on *potential* for unauthorized access to information regarding an individual (e.g., Social Security numbers and mother's maiden name) rather than the use of that information to commit a crime such as identity fraud.

Availability

The E-Government Act of 2002 defines availability as "ensuring timely and reliable access to and use of information." Availability concerns affect publishing, interactive processing, transaction processing, and service delivery e-government activities. Availability concerns include those resulting from system faults, those intrinsic to the technologies employed to provide e-government services, and malicious activities intended to prevent access to or use of information (denial of service attacks). Although fault-related availability and intrinsic availability concerns are not usually treated as security issues, they can significantly affect access to and use of e-government services, and countermeasures that are employed against denial of service and integrity threats can often mitigate system fault and intrinsic availability concerns.

Fault-Related Availability Concerns

System faults that can affect availability of services include hardware faults, changes in program or data structures due to transients or design errors, and failures in other system facilities that are not computer based. An extensive literature addresses fault concerns (e.g., National Institute of Standards and Technology's [NIST, 1995] *A Conceptual Framework for Systems Fault Tolerance*, references listed in the *Selected Bibliography of Fault-Tolerant Computing at Hopkins* [Sullivan, 1996], and references listed in the *Bibliography on Byzantine Fault Independence* [Martin, 2004]).

Intrinsic Availability Concerns

Intrinsic availability concerns include obsolescence of storage and recovery mechanisms, deterioration of magnetic media, ephemeral continuity of access channels such as addresses and protocols, and loss of facilities due to physical damage or support infrastructure problems. Continued availability may require not only maintenance of backups and archives, but also migration to new media and formats for the backups and archives. Service availability concerns include reduced responsiveness of processes where provision is not made for, e-approval by alternate authorities (e.g., deputies, acting managers or functionaries) in the temporary actual or virtual (non-functioning automation component) absence of an approving authority resultant processing delays cannot be mitigated by "hand carrying" or other expediting mechanisms available for paper-based processes.

Obsolescence of storage and recovery mechanisms is a concern that is likely to become more acute as paperless records and transactions begin to predominate. The media (e.g., punched cards, magnetic tapes, floppy disks, CDs, DVDs, memory sticks) and formats (e.g., CP/M-, DOS-, Unix-, and Windows-) on which and in which information and information retrieval programs are stored are constantly evolving. New generations of data retrieval hardware and software tend to be incompatible with those of only a few years before. Organizations that stored volumes of information on 5¼-inch floppy disks often have failed to copy the information onto 3½-inch disks or more modern media and no longer possess either the hardware or software applications necessary to read or interpret the stored information. Where large databases are concerned, the recurring need to copy the data onto current storage media in currently accessible formats can be expensive and time-consuming. Failure to copy the information can result in loss of availability of the information.

Magnetic storage media can deteriorate over time due to oxidation, compression of plastic or metal housing components, or other causes. Again, copying the information may be necessary to maintain availability.[1]

E-government information access often involves links to related sites. Web sites are constantly changing, coming into existence, and being disestablished. If the links are not adequately maintained (e.g., maintaining currency and awareness of the status of linked sites and databases), information on which advertised e-government services are dependent may become unavailable.

In the case of cryptographically protected databases, the loss or corruption of keying material can result in loss of availability of information on which e-government services are dependent.

[1] For further information, see National Archives of Australia, Archives Advice 5, "Protecting and handling magnetic media," revised June 2002. Retrieved from http://www.aa.gov.au/recordkeeping/rkpubs/advices/advice5.html

Denial of Service Concerns

Government sites are attractive targets for malicious activities intended to prevent access to, or use of, information (denial of service attacks). These can range from relatively unsophisticated assaults that result in temporary degradation of service response times to crippling attacks that corrupt or destroy system resources. Denial of service attacks can be launched from a variety of sources and can take a number of forms.

Sources

The source of a denial of service attack can affect (a) the scale of the attack (available resources); (b) the efficiency with which large-scale attacking resources are employed; (c) timing of attacks in the context of maximizing impact on system resources and maximizing the number of e-government clients affected or criticality of services affected; (d) the intelligence information available to facilitate an attack and focus it on specific e-government services, the denial of which will cause maximum harm; (e) the degree to which the source of the attack can be obscured or otherwise shielded from countermeasures and retaliation; and (f) scale of compensation that can be extracted from or retaliation that can be invoked against an attacker.

Individual or Informally Organized Hackers

Most denial of service attacks against e-government services have been launched by individuals or informally organized groups of hackers. Some of these have resulted in significant disruption and expense to the taxpayer. Individuals have penetrated and "captured" large numbers of computers, without the knowledge or consent of their owners and used these captured computers to launch Internet-based attacks against government sites or against service providers on which e-government services are dependent. The "captured" computers employed by some individuals number in the thousands, or even tens of thousands. The computers employed often are not even in the same country as the individuals who launch the attacks.

In some cases, groups of individuals who share a common cause (e.g., religiously or politically motivated grievances against the government) cooperatively launch attacks against resources on which e-government resources are dependent. The degree to which the attacks can be coordinated tends to be limited when such groups are informally organized and their constituent individuals employ clandestine methods to avoid being identified and arrested.

Individual hackers do tend to share information. Whether they operate independently or cooperatively, they may share information regarding techniques, successes, and failures. Some of the hackers are extremely sophisticated and often are more technically capable than the government and government-sponsored personnel who are charged with defending against them. The most sophisticated designers of attacks are often not the individuals who launch them. They often simply share the attacks with other, much less sophisticated and less prudent individuals, who then launch the attacks. Historically, there is a delay between the posting of a potential attack by a designer and its launching by an attacker. This delay has often permitted detection by defenders and deployment of countermeasures in time to mitigate the effects of attacks (e.g., through distribution and implementation of software patches). However, the delays experienced between posting of potential attacks and launching of attacks has been decreasing.

Efficient allocation of defensive and law enforcement assets is relatively difficult in the case of individuals and informally organized groups. The target environment is excessively diffuse.

Nonstate Organizations

Attacks by formally organized groups can pose a much more serious threat than attacks by individuals and informally organized groups. This can result in increased efficiency with which large-scale attacking resources are employed and improved timing of attacks to maximize impact on system resources and the number of e-government clients or criticality of services affected; likewise, it can lead to improved availability and efficiency in exploiting intelligence information available to facilitate an attack and focus it on e-government services, the denial of which will cause maximum harm. On the other hand, many of the brightest hackers are individualists who have, so far, not tended to become subordinate to institutional management. Also, concentration of hacking resources into a formal organization permits more efficient employment of law enforcement and other resources charged with defending e-government systems. Although an organization may have resources to shield perpetrators of denial of service attacks, it presents an identifiable and resource-rich target against which defensive, law enforcement, and compensation assets may be employed.

State-Sponsored Attacks

State-sponsored denial of service attacks have long been a major concern for e-government activities. Very large sets of resources can be brought to bear on design and execution of attacks, and the state can (to some extent) shield the actual perpetrators from individual identification, capture, and retaliation. On the other hand, so far, many of the most effective hackers are individualists who have not tended to subordinate themselves voluntarily to government oversight. Also, if an attack can be demonstrated to be state sponsored, a range of remedies is available to discourage future attacks and extract compensation (e.g., economic sanctions, retaliation in kind, military action). State-sponsored denial of service attacks remains a largely unrealized concern.

Classes of Attacks

Denial of service attacks against e-government resources has been extensively defined and discussed in security literature. Examples include *Distributed Denial of Service (DDoS) Attacks/Tools* (Dittrich, 2004), *Denial of Service Attacks* (CERT Coordination Center, n.d.), and the Denial of Service Database. Denial of service attacks can take physical or logical forms.

Physical

Although physical attacks on e-government resources can have catastrophic and relatively enduring consequences, they usually involve significant risk exposure for the perpetrators and have a relatively uncertain prognosis. For example, the 2001 attack on the World Trade Center affected some e-government services, but some potentially catastrophic outages were avoided by chance. Some important service provider hardware remained in service in a heavily damaged building. In most cases to date, impacts on e-government services have been by-products rather than primary objectives of physical attacks.

It is possible for an individual or small organization to carry out significant attacks on e-government resources. The bombing of the Murrah Federal Building in Oklahoma City is an example of a large-scale attack on federal assets. However, the larger physical threat may still be posed by nation-states, state-sponsored organizations, and large nonstate organizations.

Logical

The simplest and so far most common denial of service attacks, logical attacks keep e-government servers so busy with fake data traffic that they can't employ their resources to provide services to their legitimate users. Most of the more common attacks take advantage of network protocol characteristics and are termed "flooding" attacks. Some flooding attack scenarios follow:

- An Internet control message protocol (ICMP) message to a server (also known as a "ping" on a server) produces an echo response to confirm the server's presence. When enough pings are sent, the target server can do nothing but respond to the requests.
- User datagram protocol (UDP) diagnostic services generate characters that are echoed back from the receiving end to the host, swamping the network with useless data.
- Multiple spoofed requests for transmission control protocol (TCP) connections force the server to keep ports open, waiting for responses.
- Some attacks (i.e., "Smurf" attacks) appear to originate from the target server's own Internet protocol address or somewhere else on the target's network. Targeted correctly, the attack can flood the network with pings and multiple responses.

Distributed denial-of-service attacks employ multiple computers across the Internet against a single target server. Most serious attacks today orchestrate the use of hundreds of machines and take the target server out of commission for the duration of the attack.

Integrity

The E-Government Act of 2002 states that the term integrity "means guarding against improper information modification or destruction, and includes ensuring information nonrepudiation and authenticity." Integrity concerns affect publishing, interactive processing, transaction processing, and service delivery of e-government activities. If published information, requests for information received from users, or authorizations or payments issued to users are improperly modified or destroyed, routed, or ascribed, then damage to confidence in the government, to user or customers, or to government assets can result.

Data Content Integrity Issues

Data content integrity issues are associated with unauthorized modification or destruction of e-government information content. This can involve modification or destruction of

- information electronically published by the government;
- information associated with reports, applications, or other service requests provided by private citizens or other user entities (e.g., submit tax returns, apply for licenses or other services, renew licenses, order products or services, or provide notification of address change or other status changes);
- notification to private citizens or other user entities of approval actions or activation of implementation processes (e.g., billing, payment, licensing, permit issuance, contract awards, invoice approvals, etc.); and
- information executing actions approved on the basis of e-government interactions (e.g., credit card payment information or electronic funds transfer information, electronic fund transfer information, and licenses or permits).

Loss of data content integrity can result from error-based integrity faults or from intentional modification or destruction of data. The consequences of loss of integrity from either cause can range from inconvenience or financial loss to users to unintentional violation of public laws or regulations by users. Impaired confidence in e-government systems is a likely consequence in any case.

Error-Based Integrity Faults

Although most error-based integrity faults (i.e., accidental losses of integrity) are not, strictly speaking, security concerns, they can have consequences similar to those of maliciously induced faults, and a number of the countermeasures to intentional modification of data are effective in mitigating the consequences of error-based faults. Note also that many fault-tolerance measures are also effective in mitigating the consequences of error-based integrity faults.

Intentional Modification of Data

Data may be modified or destroyed within e-government processors (e.g., Web servers) or in transit. In the case of the former, an attacker must gain write-access to the processor and to the desired data file or process within the processor. Penetration may be accomplished by defeating identification and authentication mechanisms or by inserting malicious code into a legitimate transaction. In some cases, information transits more than one government processor in the course of interactive or transaction processing or service delivery processes. In such cases, it may be sufficient to penetrate only one processor in the path between the originating process or database and the connection to external communications. Information transiting an intermediate processor can be modified or destroyed in that processor. In some systems, Web servers outside the security perimeter (e.g., outside the firewall) make attractive penetration targets. If the configuration of their access control mechanisms is inadequate, it may be possible for attackers to destroy, forge, or modify e-government information in these external processors (e.g., maliciously modifying Web pages).

Modification of information in transit can mean dynamic modification of information on a communications path, but it can also mean modification of information in an intermediate processor (e.g., a server belonging to an Internet service provider). It may be possible using either approach to forge or intercept and change legitimate e-government publications or transactions.

Connection Integrity Issues

Successful implementation of e-government services requires some degree of confidence on the part of private citizens or other user entities that information being read originated only with the assumed government source and that information being provided goes only to the appropriate government destination(s). Similarly, it is important to government electronic service providers that reports, service requests, and applications actually originate with the user entity claiming to make the submission and that service delivery transmissions and private or proprietary information go only to authorized destinations. Modification of header or routing information (see previous section, Intentional Modification of Data) can potentially result in distribution of information or service delivery instruments to unauthorized parties. The consequences can include simple violation of laws and regulations regarding privacy or proprietary information, identity theft with financial or legal consequences, erroneous or fraudulent issuance of permits or licenses, and diversion of services or funds.

Nonrepudiation Issues

Nonrepudiation involves proof of the origin and content integrity of data (including the property of not having been forged) in a form that can be verified at any time by a third party. Nonrepudiation most commonly applies to requests and reports from private citizens and other user entities, but there are cases in which user entities expect protection from repudiation of government-originated information or responses to requests. The following properties need to be satisfied to support nonrepudiation of e-government services:

- Publications and transaction information must be tightly bound to their claimed sources.
- Transactions must be difficult to forge without the forgery being detected.
- Transactions must be difficult to alter without the alteration being detected.
- Transactions must be verifiable.

Particularly in the case of reports required by law or regulation, it is important to the government that there be nonrepudiation with respect to both originator and content. Particularly with respect to approval actions and publication of regulations and requirements, it is important to user entities that there be nonrepudiation with respect to both originator and content. Neither the originator nor the recipient of information or a transaction request must be able to claim falsely and convincingly that the information or transaction request actually originated from a different source, was posted at a time different from when it was actually posted, or had different total content from that which was received. Particularly in the case of service delivery, the recipient must not be able to claim falsely and convincingly that information or transactions received were misdirected or not received for other reasons.

As the level of e-government service progresses from publication through interactivity and transaction processing to service delivery, the importance of nonrepudiation increases.

Confidentiality and Privacy

The E-Government Act of 2002 states that the term *confidentiality* "means preserving authorized restrictions on access and disclosure, including means for protecting personal privacy and proprietary information." E-government publication services involve primarily dissemination of information authorized to be in the public domain. Interactive e-government services may include communication to government facilities of information that is subject to laws or regulations restricting dissemination of private or proprietary information. The volume and frequency of occurrence of privacy and proprietary information increase in the cases of e-government transaction services and services delivery. In all cases, it is necessary to protect against use of e-government portals for unauthorized access to government information that has not been released into the public domain.

Distinguishing Confidentiality and Privacy Issues

The terms *privacy* and *confidentiality* are often used interchangeably. The U.S. Congress Office of Technology Assessment (OTA) has observed that "neither term possesses a single clear definition, and theorists argue variously that privacy and confidentiality (and the counterpart to confidentiality, secrecy) may be concepts that are the same, completely distinct, or in some cases overlapping" (U.S. Congress, Office of Technology Assessment, 1993). For purposes of this e-government discussion, confidentiality protection is protection against disclosure of information without the implicit or explicit consent of an entity that legitimately possesses the information, whereas privacy protection also includes protection against dissemination of information by an entity that legitimately possesses the information in violation of laws and regulations restricting the dissemination of that information.

Threats to Confidentiality and E-Government Vulnerabilities

Although intercept of transmissions between e-government facilities and user entities can be employed to achieve unauthorized disclosure of information, adversaries more commonly employ legitimate access facilities to gain unauthorized access to information (e.g., Internet connections, electronic mail, self-service kiosks and terminals, simputers[2] and other wireless devices). The adversaries can employ a variety of means to defeat system identification, authentication, filtering, and authorization mechanisms (e.g., legitimate messages that contain malicious code enclosures, password dictionary attacks, transmission of protocol messages or other control function sequences) to access information stored in government devices or alter (change or add to) address information and misdirect information transfers. The more flexible and user-friendly the e-government service, the more opportunities are usually presented to adversaries. For example, use of connectionless protocols (e.g., UDP) eliminates most effective firewall configuration options. Penetration of an e-government security perimeter often gives adversaries extensive opportunities to browse confidential, private, or proprietary files.

Impacts or Consequences of Unauthorized Exposure

The consequences of unauthorized exposure of information via e-government resources depend in large part on the specific information that is exposed.

Loss of Confidence in Institutions and Service Delivery Mechanisms

Public disclosure of e-government confidentiality breaches can result in loss of public confidence in e-government mechanisms and in the institutions that they serve. The future of e-government will be determined in large part by public acceptance of e-government mechanisms as a dependable approach to doing business with governments.

Impacts on Operations

Impacts of confidentiality breaches on government operations can include disruption of ongoing plans and operations, legal actions against government organizations, financial impacts on the public, or even public safety consequences. The U.S. National Institute for Standards and Technology's *Guide for Mapping Types of Information and Information Systems to Security Categories* (Barker & Lee, 2004) describes the impacts or consequences of unauthorized disclosure of 145 types of U.S. government information. It also identifies Executive Orders, Executive Directives, and federal laws mandating protection for various confidential, private, and proprietary information types. Probably the most damaging breach of confidentiality is unauthorized access to cryptographic variable information that would permit an adversary to pose as a legitimate user who is authorized access to sensitive or critical information (including transaction data).

Legal Issues

Government institutions are bound by law to protect confidential, private, and proprietary information from unauthorized disclosure. Consequences for government personnel can range from reprimand to fine and imprisonment, depending on the nature of the information that is disclosed and the degree to which the compromise is willful or negligent. Particularly, in the case of e-government transactions and service delivery, the legal consequences for government institutions can include breaches of contract and other bases for recovery from the government of compensatory and punitive damages.

SECURITY MEASURES FOR E-GOVERNMENT

Mechanisms and Techniques

Security mechanisms and techniques for countering availability, integrity, and confidentiality threats are described in detail in Parts 2 and 3 of this volume. The countermeasures information provided in this chapter focuses on e-government-specific considerations for application of security mechanisms and techniques.

Availability

Availability assurance features can include design characteristics (e.g., component or path redundancy, survivable design, isolation of resources), policy and procedural characteristics (e.g., access control policies, system certification and acceptance plans and procedures, recovery and continuity plans, data and program back-ups), and access mechanisms (e.g., reliable communications protocols, identification and authentication mechanisms). E-government mission requirements limit the application of some of these assurance features. For example, because public access is central to the purpose of e-government systems, physical isolation (e.g., of kiosk or terminal devices) and logical isolation of e-government assets must necessarily be limited. Use of surveillance devices and physical hardening and alarming of terminal logic components may be possible to raise the levels of difficulty and risk associated with unauthorized installation of mechanisms to capture key strokes or information in electromagnetic form within the terminal. However, significant residual risk is probably unavoidable. Terminal penetration can permit an adversary to bring down a system to which it connects and even use that system's interfaces to launch denial of service attacks against other systems. Similarly, ease of use is a major consideration for e-government applications. This includes ease of sign-on, user-friendly interfaces (graphical user interfaces), and support for a broad range of Web page development and support and mission-support applications. In the world of Web-based network services, the same properties that support user-friendly interfaces and a multiplicity of applications tend to offer more opportunities for penetration of the system and complicate security analysis beyond the point at which reasonable assurance can be achieved. As an example, network protocols necessary to support some widely used database management applications must be connectionless, thus preventing secure configuration of firewalls (see earlier section, Protocol and Operating System Mechanisms).

Integrity

Integrity mechanisms can include operating system-based (see chapter of this *Handbook*, "Operating System Security"), protocol based (see chapter of this *Handbook*, "Firewall Basics"), or cryptographically based mechanisms.

[2] The simputer is a low-cost personal computer with multiple connectivity options; see dmoz.org/Computers/Systems/Handhelds/Open_Source/Simputer/

Protocol and Operating System Mechanisms

Firewalls are front-end processors that employ primarily protocol-based screening mechanisms to protect internal systems and networks that may contain sensitive or critical information from exploitation from external sources (e.g., from Web servers accessible by the public). A primer on firewalls is provided by chapter of this *Handbook*, "Firewall Basics."

Operating system–based access control mechanisms are employed to protect e-government components outside the firewall(s) from modifications that alter either their content or their functionality. They are also used to protect the firewalls themselves from exploitation and components on internal networks from insider threats (including from unauthorized "back-end" connections to external networks or the public switched telephone network). Too often, security configuration of components outside the firewall is given insufficient attention. A number of highly embarrassing, and even damaging, unauthorized modifications to e-government publications and processes have resulted.

Ideally, processors employed to provide e-government services should have been evaluated as conforming to at least the EAL-4 level of the *Common Criteria* (CC).[3] However, most government agencies are required to employ commercial off-the-shelf (COTS) computer and communications components. It is commercial practice to modify systems regularly and replace current systems with new "improved" versions. Patches to software are constantly being made available to correct flaws or enhance capabilities. In this COTS environment, it is proving extremely difficult to maintain security configuration control. An initial CC rating (e.g., EAL-4) can mean little once the system has been patched or upgraded. Regression testing to ensure that critical security properties of systems have not been impaired can mitigate this problem.

Cryptographic Mechanisms

Digital signature (see chapter of this *Handbook*, "Digital Signatures and Electronic Signatures") and message authentication are the most commonly employed cryptographic integrity protection mechanisms. Time stamping and establishing a reliable chain of trust for the public key certificates used in digital signatures are also critical elements for providing nonrepudiation services. Public key systems rely on a chain of trust for source authentication of PKI (public key infrastructure) certificates that are used to distribute public keys (Federal Public Key Infrastructure Steering Committee, 2000). Although a PKI[4] has been developed by and is becoming standardized within the federal government, many government agencies currently contract public key management for nonnational security systems from the private sector. In this case, federal certificates that are used to transport the public keys employed to check the validity of digital signatures are generated and signed by a certification authority that is a private company. In addition, the private keys that are used to sign information (to provide source authentication and data content integrity) are also generated by, known by, and distributed by the private sector. In some cases, agencies generate the private keys and public key certificates employed within their own agencies. There is currently no common public key management system in use within the Federal government and no common chain of trust for e-government.

A complicating factor for e-government is maintenance and use of certificate revocation lists (CRLs). A CRL is a list of revoked public key certificates created and digitally signed by a certification authority. Policies and procedures regarding high-integrity distribution of notices listing revoked certificates in e-government applications are needed to achieve the level of assurance necessary to support high-value and mission-critical transactions and services delivery functions.

Currently, quantum computing (West, 2000) is in the early stages of research and development. However, if large-scale quantum computing becomes available, public key methods in current use are likely to become obsolete. Message authentication encoding based on symmetric key (secret key) cryptography will remain viable. However, distribution and management of secret keys for authenticating information is problematic, and message authentication alone does not provide the full range of digital signature services. Furthermore, there is no current infrastructure to support key notarization and other measures that would be necessary to replace public key cryptography-based digital signature. Also, there is no symmetric key infrastructure for unclassified government operations. Integrity of e-government transactions is likely to remain dependent on the security of PKI for the foreseeable future.

A final issue affecting employment of cryptographic integrity mechanisms in U.S. E-government is availability, use, and interoperability of mechanisms that meet federal standards. Federal agencies are legally bound to employ only government-approved cryptography. In the cases of unclassified systems, approved algorithms are the digital signature algorithm (DSA), the Rivest, Shamir, and Adelman (RSA) algorithm (American National Standards Institute [ANSI], 1998a), and elliptic curve DSA (ECDSA; ANSI, 1998b) as specified in the *Digital Signature Standard (DSS)*.[5] Minimum key sizes approved through the year 2010 are 1024-bit DSA, 1024-bit RSA, and 160-bit ECDSA. After 2010, 2048-bit RSA and DSA and 224-bit ECDSA will be the minima. Hash functions used in e-government digital signature processes must conform to the NIST *Secure Hash Standard* (NIST, 2002). After 2010, the 160-bit secure hash algorithm 1 (SHA-1) hash function may no longer be used in digital signatures to protect U.S. government information. It is incumbent on e-government service providers to ensure that digital signature mechanisms conform to these standards and that plans accommodate transition to the higher assurance requirements that will be in force after 2010.[6] In the case of message authentication encoding, either the triple data encryption algorithm (TDEA; Barker 2004) or the advanced encryption standard (AES) may be used, and encoding schemes employed in U.S. e-government

[3] *Common Criteria for IT Security Evaluation (CC)*. Retrieved from http://csrc.nist.gov/cc/

[4] See chapter of this handbook, "PKI (Public Key Infrastructure)."

[5] Soon to be superceded by FIPS 186-3, same title.

[6] Note that SP 800-57 will require still larger key sizes after the year 2030.

operations must conform to NIST's *Recommendation for Block Cipher Modes of Operation* (Gasser, 2004).

Confidentiality and Privacy

Access to e-government information and processes is dependent primarily on the identification and authentication processes that support e-government access control mechanisms (see Availability earlier in this section). If e-government information is intercepted in transit, or accessed in storage (e.g., following penetration of system access control mechanisms), it can still be protected by encryption. (See Volume II, Part 3: "Foundations of Information, Computer, and Network Security.")

Encryption is necessary to protect confidential information that is subject to intercept or access while stored or being processed in e-government systems.

Protocol and Operating System Mechanisms

Because e-government facilities generally need to be accessible by the general public to fulfill their missions, they are subject to a broad range of hacking and other penetration attacks. Front-end security processors (e.g., firewalls, screening routers as described in chapters "Digital Signatures and Electronic Signatures", "E-mail Security", "Security for ATM Networks", and "VPN Basics", of this *Handbook*) can be used to isolate those elements of e-government facilities that are publicly accessible from those that contain confidential, private, or proprietary information. These mechanisms separate internal government networks from publicly accessible e-government facilities. They can provide identification and authentication functions, access control functions, limit the protocols that are accepted (thus limiting adversaries' opportunities to tunnel into system compartments that contain confidential information). As noted in earlier, (see Availability), there tends to be an inverse relationship between flexibility and ease of use on one hand and strength of security mechanism on the other. U.S. e-government systems should conform to *Guidelines on Firewalls and Firewall Policy* (Wack, Cutler, & Pole, 2002).

Operating system-based access control mechanisms are employed to protect e-government components outside the firewall(s) from disclosure of configuration information or other information that can assist an adversary in making modifications that alter either the content or functionality of these components. Similarly, operating system–based access control mechanisms are employed to protect the confidentiality of government systems inside the firewall (as discussed earlier; see Protocol and Operating System Mechanisms).

Cryptographic Mechanisms

Several factors complicate encryption of e-government information. First, public key (asymmetric) cryptography is sufficiently computation-intensive that encryption of large volumes of data, or of data where high throughput is required, is undesirable. Second, because of threats of exposure over time and limitations on the volume of data that should be encrypted under a single key, encrypted information needs to be decrypted, then reencrypted under a different key. This is excessively expensive for large databases. Third, protection of secret keying material in a publicly accessible system is technically challenging. Finally, there is no common government symmetric key management infrastructure for unclassified systems.

As in the case of digital signatures, the encryption algorithms employed in e-government must be government-approved. Currently, only TDEA and AES are approved for encryption of U.S. government information. Encryption schemes employed in U.S. e-government operations must conform to NIST's *Recommendation for Block Cipher Modes of Operation*.[23] Through the year 2010, either two-key TDEA or three-key TDEA may be used (see NIST's *Recommendation for the Triple Data Encryption Algorithm (TDEA) Block Cipher*, Special Publication 800-67). After 2010, only three-key TDEA may be used; and after 2030, TDEA may no longer be used for protection of U.S. e-government information.[18] To avoid transition problems, use of AES rather than TDEA may be prudent.

Database Design

Some e-government services include provision of data that are derived from aggregation or analysis of information that is subject by law to privacy protection, are proprietary, or for which confidentiality must otherwise be maintained (e.g., provision of statistical information based on Privacy Act–protected data). A number of database design and management approaches have been developed to address this problem (e.g., *A Near-Term Design for the SeaView Multilevel Database System* (Lunt, 1998). This continues to be an active research topic.[7]

Implementation and Management

Interdependency of Measures/Mechanisms

Significant interdependency exists among the various countermeasures that may be employed to mitigate e-government security concerns. At the level of individual security mechanisms, computer security mechanisms (e.g., firewall and operating system[8] access control mechanisms) may play a role in protecting secret or private keys. At the same time, cryptographic processes used by authentication elements of access control mechanisms may employ one or more of the secret or private keys. At a "system of systems" level, source and data content integrity may depend on the aggregate performance and security of a private sector PKI certificate authority, an Internet service provider, the configuration of the e-government server that manages interactions with the public, the design and configuration of the firewall between the e-government server and the government processors inside the security perimeter, and the design and configuration of those internal government processors that process confidential or private information. Security of e-government systems is a total systems problem, and managers responsible for system security must address the adequacy of security

[7] See archive.infopeace.de/msg02567.html

[8] See the discussions of operating system security found in chapters "The Common Criteria", "Internal Security Threats", "Physical Security Threats", "Fixed-Line Telephone System Vulnerabilities", "E-Mail Threats and Vulnerabilities", "E-Commerce Vulnerabilities", "Hacking Techniques in Wired Networks", and "Hacking Techniques in Wireless Networks".

features and assurances associated with each subsystem and component mechanism.

Program Requirements

The Federal Information Security Management Act of 2002, the Paperwork Reduction Act of 1995, and the Information Technology Management Reform Act of 1996 (Clinger–Cohen Act), explicitly emphasize a risk-based policy for cost-effective security. In support of and reinforcing this legislation, the OMB through Circular A-130, Appendix III, *Security of Federal Automated Information Resources*, requires executive agencies[9] within the federal government to

- *plan* for security;
- *ensure* that appropriate officials are assigned security responsibility;
- *review* the security controls in their information systems; and
- *authorize* system processing prior to operations and periodically thereafter.

These management responsibilities presume that responsible government officials understand the risks and other factors that could adversely affect their missions. Moreover, these officials must understand the current status of their security programs and the security controls planned or in place to protect their information and information systems to make informed judgments and investments that appropriately mitigate risk to an acceptable level. The ultimate objective is to conduct the day-to-day operations of the agency and to accomplish the agency's stated missions with what OMB Circular A-130, Appendix III, defines as *adequate security*, or security commensurate with risk, including the magnitude of harm resulting from the unauthorized access, use, disclosure, disruption, modification, or destruction of information.

Policies, Procedures, and Infrastructures

E-government systems must establish security policies and procedures that address the access rights of the public, requirements for protection of the privacy of its users, requirements for protection of the confidentiality of government information contained in e-government systems and government systems connected to those systems, necessary service assurances, integrity and nonrepudiation requirements, and the laws and federal regulations on which these requirements are based. Systems managers must also establish operating procedures that permit compliance with these policies while satisfying e-government mission requirements. Finally, e-government managers must identify or establish the necessary processing, communications, and security (e.g., key management) infrastructures necessary to implement system policies and procedures.

Certification and Accreditation

As stated in the *Guide for the Security Certification and Accreditation of Federal Information Systems* (Johnson, Katzke, Ross, Stoneburner, & Swanson, 2004), the E-Government Act requires each federal agency to develop, document, and implement an agencywide information security program to provide information security for the information and information systems that support the operations and assets of the agency. An e-government information security program must include

- periodic assessments of risk, including the magnitude of harm that could result from the unauthorized access, use, disclosure, disruption, modification, or destruction of information and information systems that support the operations and assets of the agency;
- policies and procedures that are based on risk assessments, cost-effectively reduce information security risks to an acceptable level, and ensure that information security is addressed throughout the life cycle of each agency information system;
- subordinate plans for providing adequate information security for networks, facilities, information systems, or groups of information systems, as appropriate;
- security awareness training to inform personnel (including contractors and other users of information systems that support the operations and assets of the agency) of the information security risks associated with their activities and their responsibilities in complying with agency policies and procedures designed to reduce these risks;
- periodic testing and evaluation of the effectiveness of information security policies, procedures, practices, and security controls[10] to be performed with a frequency depending on risk, but no less than annually;
- a process for planning, implementing, evaluating, and documenting remedial actions to address any deficiencies in the information security policies, procedures, and practices of the agency;
- procedures for detecting, reporting, and responding to security incidents; and
- plans and procedures to ensure continuity of operations for information systems that support the operations and assets of the agency.

It is essential that e-government officials have the most complete, accurate, and trustworthy information possible on the security status of their information systems to make timely, credible, risk-based decisions on whether to authorize operation of those systems. The information and supporting evidence needed for security accreditation is developed during a detailed security review of an information system, typically referred to as security *certification*. The results of a security certification are used to reassess the risks and update the system security plan, thus providing the factual basis for an authorizing official

[9] An executive agency is (a) an Executive Department specified in 5 U.S.C., Section 101; (b) a Military Department specified in 5 U.S.C., Section 102; (c) an independent establishment as defined in 5 U.S.C., Section 104(1); and (d) a wholly owned government corporation fully subject to the provisions of 31 U.S.C., Chapter 91.

[10] Security controls are the management, operational, and technical controls (i.e., safeguards or countermeasures) prescribed for an information system to protect the confidentiality, integrity, and availability of the system and its information.

to render a security accreditation decision. Security accreditation is the official management decision given by a senior agency official to authorize operation of an information system and to accept explicitly the risk to agency operations, agency assets, or individuals based on the implementation of an agreed-on set of security controls.[29]

SUMMARY

E-government shows great promise for use of improved Internet-based technology to make it easier for citizens and businesses to interact with the government, save taxpayer dollars, and streamline citizen-to-government communications. With these potential benefits come real risks to the privacy of information provided by citizens and businesses, to the confidentiality of government information contained in e-government systems and systems connected to e-government systems, to the long-term availability of records stored only in electronic form by the government, and to the integrity of citizen-to-government transactions and government-to-citizen delivery of services. These risks are based on intrinsic technical characteristics of storage and processing systems, on the potential for accidents or system faults, and on the attractiveness of e-government systems as a target for malicious activity. A variety of countermeasures are available to mitigate these risks (e.g., fault-tolerant design, disaster recovery procedures, information backups, access control logic in front-end processors and e-government service systems, digital signature for transactions, encryption of sensitive information, and database design and management that permit use of privacy-protected data without divulging the privacy-protected elements to unauthorized sources. Law requires that the security mechanisms conform to federal standards and be evaluated in accordance with a federally mandated certification and accreditation process prior to the e-government systems being placed into operation. These policy requirements, together with the projected consequences of loss of public confidence in both e-government and government institutions in general, suggest that the process of converting paper-based services to e-government services cannot be accomplished without careful planning and systems-based oversight.

GLOSSARY

Asymmetric In the context of cryptography, a type of cryptographic system in which a participant publishes an encryption key and keeps private a separate decryption key. These keys are respectively referred to as public and private. RSA and D–H are examples of asymmetric systems. *Asymmetric* is synonymous with *public key*.

Authentication A process that establishes the origin of information or determines an entity's identity.

Availability The property of ensuring timely and reliable access to and use of information.

Confidentiality Preservation of authorized restrictions on access and disclosure, including means for protecting personal privacy and proprietary information.

Cryptography The discipline that embodies principles, means, and methods for the transformation of data to hide its information content, prevent its undetected modification, or prevent its unauthorized use.

Digital Signature The results of a cryptographic transformation of data that, when properly implemented, provides the services of origin, authentication, data integrity, and signer nonrepudiation.

Encryption The process of rendering a message (a *plaintext*) into a data string (a *ciphertext*) with the aim of transmitting it privately in a potentially hostile environment.

Integrity Guarding against improper information modification or destruction, which includes ensuring information nonrepudiation and authenticity.

Interactive Processing Service that permits private citizens or other user entities to read instructions published on agency Web sites and to follow those instructions to submit reports, applications, or other service requests.

Nonrepudiation A service that is used to provide assurance of the integrity and origin of data in such a way that the integrity and origin can be verified by a third party as having originated from a specific entity in possession of the private key of the claimed signatory.

Privacy Protection against disclosure of personal information in violation of laws and regulations restricting the dissemination of information.

Private Key In an asymmetric or public-key cryptosystem, the key that a communicating party holds privately and uses for decryption or completion of a key exchange.

Public Key In an asymmetric or public-key cryptosystem, the key that a communicating party disseminates publicly.

Publishing As used in this chapter, posting information on a publicly accessible Web site.

Secret Key A cryptographic key that is used with a symmetric cryptographic algorithm that is uniquely associated with one or more entities and is not made public.

Service Delivery Actual execution of actions approved on the basis of e-government interactions (e.g., acceptance of credit card payments or electronic funds transfers, execution of government payments by electronic fund transfers, and delivery of licenses or permits).

Symmetric In the context of cryptography, a cryptographic algorithm that uses one shared key, a secret key.

Transaction Processing Processing of information submitted via interactive e-government Web sites, providing notification of approval for actions to be taken on the basis of that information and activation of implementation processes. Transaction processing generally involves distributing data received from users to multiple databases and multiple processes and includes interactions with third parties.

CROSS REFERENCES

See *Computer and Network Authentication; Digital Signatures and Electronic Signatures; E-Government; Encryption Basics; International Security Issues of E-Government; Internet Basics; Legal, Social, and Ethical Issues of the*

Internet; Password Authentication; Privacy Law and the Internet.

REFERENCES

American National Standards Institute. (1998a). *Digital signatures using reversible public key cryptography for the financial services industry* (ANSI X9.31-1998).

American National Standards Institute. (1998b). *Public key cryptography for the financial services industry: The elliptic curve digital signature algorithm (ECDSA)* (ANSI X9.62-1998).

Barker, E., Barker, W., Burr, W., Polk, W., Smid, M., & Zeigler, L. (2004). *Recommendation for key management* [draft] (Special Publication 800-57). National Institute of Standards and Technology. Retrieved from http://csrc.nist.gov/CryptoToolkit/tkkeymgmt.html July 2004.

Barker, W. (2004). *Recommendation for the triple data encryption algorithm (TDEA) block cipher*. National Institute of Standards and Technology. Retrieved from http://csrc.nist.gov/publications/nistpubs/800-67/SP800-67.pdf July 2004.

Barker, W., & Lee, A. (2004). *Guide for mapping types of information and information systems to security categories* (Special Publication 800-60). National Institute of Standards and Technology.

CERT Coordination Center. (n.d.). *Denial of service attacks*. Retrieved from http://www.cert.org/tech_tips/denial_of_service.html July 2004.

Common Criteria Project. (2004). *Common criteria for information technology security evaluation*, version 2.2. Retrieved from http://www.commoncriteriaportal.org/public/files/ccpart1v2.2.pdf July 2004.

Denial of Service Database. Retrieved from http://www.attrition.org/security/denial/ July 2004.

Dittrich, D. (2004). *Distributed denial of service (DDoS) attacks/tools*. University of Washington. Retrieved from http://staff.washington.edu/dittrich/misc/ddos/ July 2004.

E-Government Act of 2002. Title III, Federal Information Security Management Act (FISMA), Pub. L. No. 107-347 (2002). Retrieved from http://thomas.loc.gov/bss/d107/d107laws.html July 2004.

Federal Public Key Infrastructure Steering Committee, Federal Chief Information Officers Council. (2000). *The evolving federal public key infrastructure*. Retrieved from http://www.cio.gov/fpkisc/library/pkireport053100.doc July 2004.

Gasser, M. (2004). *Recommendation for block cipher modes of operation* (Special Publication 800-38). National Institute of Standards and Technology. Retrieved from http://csrc.nist.gov/publications/ August 2004.

Government Paperwork Elimination Act. Title XVII, Pub. L. No. 105-277 (1998).

Information Technology Management Reform Act (Clinger–Cohen), Title LI. Pub. L. No. 104-106 (1996).

Johnson, A., Katzke, S., Ross, R., Stoneburner, G., & Swanson, M. (2004, May). *Guide for the security certification and accreditation of federal information systems* (Special Publication 800-37). National Institute of Standards and Technology. Retrieved from http://csrc.nist.gov/publications/nistpubs/800-37/SP800-37-final.pdf July 2004.

Lunt, T. (1988, May). *A near-term design for the SeaView multilevel database system*. Presented at the Institute for Electrical and Electronic Engineers Symposium on Security and Privacy, Oakland, CA.

Martin, J.-P. (2004). *Bibliography on Byzantine fault independence*. Austin: University of Texas. Retrieved from http://www.cs.utexas.edu/users/jpmartin/bib/bibReliability.html July 2004.

National Institute of Standards and Technology, Center for High Integrity Software systems Assurance. (1995). *A conceptual framework for systems fault tolerance*. Retrieved from http://hissa.ncsl.nist.gov/chissa/SEI_Framework/framework_1.html July 2004.

National Institute of Standards and Technology. (2000, January 27). *Digital signature standard (DSS)* (FIPS 186-2). Retrieved from http://csrc.nist.gov/publications/fips/fips186-2/fips186-2-change1.pdf July 2004.

National Institute of Standards and Technology. (2001, November 26). *The advanced encryption standard* (FIPS 197). Retrieved from http://csrc.nist.gov/publications/fips/fips197/fips-197.pdf July 2004.

National Institute of Standards and Technology. (2002, August). *Secure hash standard* (FIPS 180-2). Retrieved from http://csrc.nist.gov/publications/fips/fips180-2/fips180-2withchangenotice.pdf July 2004.

Sullivan, G. F. (1996). *Selected bibliography of fault-tolerant computing at Hopkins*. Baltimore, MD: Johns Hopkins University. Retrieved from http://www.cs.jhu.edu/~sullivan/ftbiblio.html September 2004.

U.S. Congress, Office of Technology Assessment. (1993). *Protecting privacy in computerized medical information* (OTA-TCT-576). Washington, DC: U.S. Government Printing Office.

Wack, J., Cutler, K., & Pole, J. (2002, January). *Guidelines on firewalls and firewall policy* (Special Publication 800-41). National Institute of Standards and Technology. Retrieved from http://csrc.nist.gov/publications/nistpubs/ 800-41/sp800-41.pdf July 2004.

West, J. (2000). *The quantum computer.* Pasadena: Computer Sciences at California Institute of Technology. Retrieved from http://www.cs.caltech.edu/~westside/quantum-intro.html September 2004.

World Bank Group. (n.d.). A definition of e*government. Retrieved from http://www1.worldbank.org/publicsector/egov/definition.htm July 2004.

International Security Issues of E-Government

Karin Geiselhart, *University of Canberra* and *Australian National University Canberra, Australia*

INTRODUCTION

The previous chapter in this *Handbook* documents the rise of e-government and its transformative effects. The digital representation of government activities leads to a wider spread of information and decision making, both vertically and laterally. This challenges hierarchical bureaucratic procedures and established agency roles. Responses include requirements to make key documents available electronically and the development of standards for electronic consultation, or e-rule making. This effect is apparent at every level of government, from the smallest local council to the largest nation state. At the same time, the issues governments deal with are also outgrowing traditional boundaries. Sometimes the issue expands outward, as when a regional government builds a dam that decreases the water flow to neighbors. Other times issues are imposed inward, for example if decisions made in another country affect the price of a local product.

E-government is evolving to deal with transborder issues. Government responses to these supranational issues become an element in emerging forms of global governance, but it cannot be assumed that the emerging systems will serve democratic goals. It is not even clear what global forms of democracy might mean or what they might 'look like' for citizens. It is, however, certain that patterns of digital representation and decision making will impact on the overall security of peoples in today's very insecure climate. Increasingly, the security and accuracy of the information being shared globally underpins the effectiveness of governmental response, and thus affects citizen safety. This applies to a myriad of socio-political-scientific issues, from climate change to terrorism to new disease vectors.

This chapter considers the overall context in which e-government is evolving and the importance of both administrative and democratic accountabilities. It then considers some issues for which information management and security cannot be contained within national borders. These include the global information infrastructure itself, which may be thought of as a global information "commons." Global e-governance is the complex of administrative, technical, and policy arrangements that collectively form a default pattern of governance on a particular international issue. The electronic representation is embedded in the human systems that give rise to them. Transborder issues are generally subject to different constraints than are localized issues and information. The role of nongovernment players in international information arenas is outlined, along with their influence on both physical and informational security with illustrative examples from particular areas of concern. Lastly, suggestions are offered for research and modeling global e-governance as a complex adaptive system. This issue is inherently transdisciplinary and is informed by a large body of work on complex adaptive systems in human behavior.

E-GOVERNMENT EVOLUTION

From local councils through state legislatures and national programs, electronic efficiencies are altering the pace and processes of government. Typically, electronic government addresses services, administrative procedures, and transactions. A current analysis of digital government (Pavlichev & Garson, 2004) documents the issues and current state of play of digital government at the national level and some of the aspects that overflow into international dimensions. The previous chapter in this *Handbook* describes the stages of digital government from information presentation through seamless access across agencies. Much of the literature on e-government focuses on the United States or may only consider local, state, and national governments. Writers on international relations, technology, and global governance, on the other hand, may not concern themselves with the digital representation of these issues. The extension of e-government to the international sphere is, however, the subject of much speculation, and the focus of this chapter. Both the administrative and democratic dimensions of emerging forms of international e-government are relevant to global information management and security.

Technology and the State

It is common to view information technology in government as an advanced expression of technocratic efficiency. However, information system design, management, and funding are also an expression of their socio-political-economic context. In a study of U.S. government information policies, Hernon and McClure (1993) found there was inadequate public involvement in this area, although it often involved fundamental issues about how society operates and the role of government. Not surprisingly, they found overlapping impacts, fragmentation, and difficulties of categorization in complex areas. There is a gulf between the theory of wide public involvement as a democratic ideal and the practice of e-government development.

Inevitably, information systems serve the political, economic, and social systems that fund them. Beniger (1986) showed the importance of information in all forms of evolution and control, including biological evolution. Feenberg (1991) provided a critical theory of technology and revealed how the democratizing potential of information technology makes it a site for ongoing power struggles. Sclove (1995) considered the need to embed democratic assumptions in technology design. Zuboff's (1988) concept of "informating" within organizations provided an adaptive learning element, which leads to complexity theory and the developmental role of democracy and policy. A key assertion of this chapter is that information and communication systems need to be considered as manifestations of governance. The implications compound when comparing information systems across national boundaries.

Current Dimensions and Limitations of E-Government

This section considers the dominant focus of digital government at the national level as a basis for extrapolation to the international level. From local councils to national agencies, governments have focused their technology efforts on service delivery and information provision. There has been less emphasis on citizen communications with government, input into policy making, or citizen-to-citizen communications. This trend has been identified in a survey of member nations of the Organisation of Economic Cooperation and Development (OECD; Gualtieri, 1998), at local government level in the United States (Musso, Weare, & Hale, 2000), and within agencies of the Australian government (Geiselhart, 1999). Because these patterns are observable at different scales, they may be seen as fractal. If supported by data and modeling, this insight from the field of complex adaptive systems could assist in the analysis of global technology systems and patterns. The possibility of modeling governance from a normative democratic perspective suggests how the linkages between local and global activities might be integrated. While commonplace for physical data such as climate, this has not yet been fully explored in the human sciences.

The study of information technology in government has tended to focus on developed democratic states, partly because they have been the trend setters that other nations emulate as they implement digital procedures. The United Nations provides a statistical index of e-government for member states based on infrastructure and access (see http://www.unpan.org/egovernment2.asp) but does not go into qualitative detail of information on governance in relation to transparency or online citizen engagement. Most analyses have an implicit understanding that electronic applications will support democracy as the more privileged nations understand that term. This assumption is questionable, however, as specific examples throughout this chapter illustrate. The World Bank, among others, is exploring the potential of new communication technologies to assist in democratic reform. One hypothesis of this chapter is that global information and physical security will be supported most effectively by emerging forms of global e-governance that facilitate digital equity and minimize democratic deficits within and between nations. A second hypothesis is that the patterns of technology use are determined by the values of the stakeholders, and these may not always favor wider social stability or equity. In a system driven by the values of the actors and the rules for their interaction, the patterns will reflect the overall democratic information 'value chain,' and highlight the weak links as gaps in transparency and accountability. The value chain, as in business applications, consists of the linkages and transferrals of goods and data between intermediaries. For democratic information purposes, this chain contains data but not goods, although it might also consist of services, such as monitoring and evaluation. It is truly a value chain, as every link gives actors options for passing along or withholding information. The degree to which all stakeholders are included also forms part of the pattern. For example, Clover (2004) argues that in most nations fishing policy caters to a relatively small industry, without mechanisms for including the public interest.

Branscomb (1994) identified at least four types of information needed by governments and their citizens: to fulfill voting obligations; to comply with legislative and judicial decisions; to be informed about environmental, welfare, medical, and other developments; and to manage government tasks effectively, for example, census and economic data. She noted that in meeting these requirements, governments must juggle their accountabilities to operate cost-effectively, maintain maximum access, and also encourage private sector development. A report by Accenture (2004) identifies five trends in e-government, including tangible savings, improved take-up by citizens, a continuing challenge of integration, and gradual personalization of online services. Neither of these catalogues adequately capture the need for democratic accountabilities in information management.

Information technology has been an important focus for public sector reform, both for the instrumental collection and processing of information and for the government's developmental obligations to promote participation by an informed citizenry. A client focus together with web technologies have vastly increased the amount of information available to the public. The pursuit of cost-effectiveness has also encouraged electronic access. Pressures for the cost recovery of information create inevitable trade-offs between equity and efficiency. At every stage of the policy process—agenda setting, planning, implementation, and evaluation—information is a key ingredient. International standards for electronic data interchange have, with some struggle, gradually evolved for greater interoperability. But similar standards for democratic transparency of data and information access remain a battleground both within and across jurisdictions. Political globalization increases the pressures for harmonization of data flows on matters of democratic interest and public concern.

Localized Accountabilities of E-Government

Not all aspects of e-government have international ramifications. Some issues for governments can be understood and managed with reference primarily to their own jurisdiction. At the most local level, this includes rates, services such as schools and garbage collection, planning, and development. Fully responsive local governments also promote cultural activities, heritage awareness and protection, responsible business growth, and environmental sustainability. When local e-government works well, these matters are represented transparently on a web site, with provision for citizens to engage with each other and their government. This helps to complete the loop by providing ongoing feedback. It can also provide a higher level accountability by ensuring that policies are effective. Early steam engines had a "governor" that kept the engine from exploding by keeping its function within the norms needed to run efficiently. E-rule making can avoid the worst of bad policy decisions by offering a normative and iterative "governor" to stabilize government activities. A carefully planned approach to citizen consultation, supported by appropriate use of digital communications, can help manage the democratic obligations of government. This pluralistic alternative to hierarchical decision making is described by Richard (2000). She elaborates on the ways a network model, actively enabled through appropriate digital techniques, can help achieve the transformative promise of e-government.

At a local or even regional level, achieving awareness and engagement is facilitated by geographic proximity to the issues. The site for a proposed toxic dump may be visited, and community discussion can take place casually. Corruption or nepotism may be difficult to conceal. These direct and analog sources of evidence provide a form of accountability for the information that is publicly presented. If people are getting sick or the roads are in bad repair, then those who provide data to the contrary can be questioned. The checks and balances can be immediate and provide a level of information security that is probably unsurpassable.

Problems of Scale for Information Accuracy and Security

Once the systems for information collection and display exceed what can be verified by the senses, a level of abstraction is necessary. Zuboff (1988) provided a powerful description of the changes technology brings to tasks that were previously capable of being physically monitored. Workers in a factory who could once go directly to a vat to see, hear, and smell its processes become dependent on gauges and displays to tell them what is happening. The abstractions of analog gauges are compounded by even purer digital representations.

For e-government, distance from both the sources of information and decisions about how it is represented become concerns for its verification. As the scope of government covers more territory, either encompassing more issues or over a wider area, the accuracy and integrity of the information can become attenuated, and therefore less secure.

Because government process is, virtually everywhere, underpinned by information, these issues of information security and integrity grow apace with the size of the government jurisdiction. The problems that scale poses for democracy as a particular form of government were raised by Dahl (1989), along with the possibilies of telecommunications in addressing these problems. The importance of democratic protocols to drive fractal patterns of technology governance was discussed in Geiselhart (1999). Figure 1 illustrates how fractal patterns can provide alternative systems of behavior. In the case of the famous Lorenz attractor, it is the weather system, but similar analyses have been provided for human systems of government (for example, Kiel, 1994).

For a complex adaptive system such as the weather, an attractor is a pattern that recurs with minor variations, such as wet winters. In human systems, all kinds of behaviours can settle into attractor patterns. From individual investment choices to mass movements of stock dumping, human behaviour can also display fractal patterns that repeat at several scales. Democratic attractors may be thought of as those that use negative or normative feedback loops to keep the system from spinning out of control, like a runaway thermostat. Sensitivity to the direction of change is a critical monitoring activity. A reasonable assumption for democratic process is that a dynamic of increasing inequality indicates a system moving further from democratic norms. This is because, given a level playing field of information and a fair voting process, most people would presumably not vote for benefits to flow from themselves. Managed and relatively stable inequality is assumed to be the "basin of attraction" for democratic systems.

Information management, in a broad sense that encompasses verification and communication, is analogous to the problem of infrastructure in a very large building. Bigger buildings, particularly very tall ones, require increasing amounts of resources and space devoted to

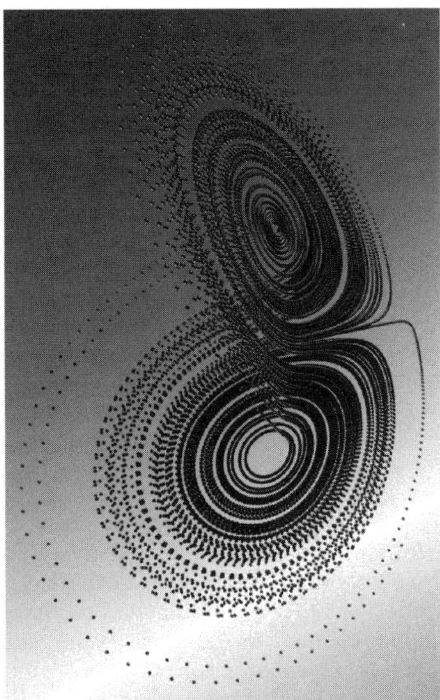

Figure 1: Lorenz Attractor, courtesy Paul Bourke, Centre for Astrophysics and Supercomputing, Swinburne University.

moving water, waste, energy, and people efficiently around the building. Likewise, as the size, scope, and scale of government expands, a proportionately large amount of resources are needed to ensure that the information necessary for good government is secure, accurate, useful, available, and democratically accountable. Of course, a dictatorship or a corrupt regime will not need to verify its information in the same way. For the purposes of this chapter, however, it is assumed that, at least theoretically, the goals of e-government aim to support democratic process. The next section outlines some of the factors affecting the management of the global information commons.

E-GOVERNMENT BEYOND NATIONAL BORDERS

Whether it involves buildings or information, efficient management has implications for both infrastructure and administration, which we may think of as a superstructure. For the global information infrastructure, it might be preferable for these to be determined on a practical basis, independent of political concerns. The realities of our globalized world mean, however, that inevitably, there will always be friction between the practical and the political. This leads to considerations of governance as a broad system of management, rather than government as a process of political control. This broader perspective also allows comparison and possibly modeling between government, nonprofit, and corporate systems.

The processes, possibilities, and problems accompanying e-government, as outlined in the previous section, do not recognize borders. Information has become central to exchanges between governments, as well as the currency of international commerce and communications. Global dynamics influence both the development of information technology and the evolution of e-government. Security in the broadest sense is now a key issue for all governments and is intimately entwined with the ways information is created, presented, distributed, and evaluated. It has become commonplace to think of the global information and communications infrastructure as a virtual neural system. This metaphor encourages consideration of the locus of control for this system. Unlike human neural networks, the networks of e-government do not access a centralized "brain."

Current manifestations of the overlap between international forms of governance and information security and management are the systems for protecting the information infrastructure. Groups such as the Communications-Electronics Security Group (http://www.cesg.gov.uk) in the United Kingdom, AusCERT in Australia, and the OECD Working Party on Information Security and Privacy (WPISP) represent high-level networks that bring together governments for collaboration and information sharing on key infrastructure security issues. Each national level group links to subnational groups and non-government players who communicate, negotiate, liaise, diffuse, and take responsibility for various aspects of information infrastructure security.

In Australia, the subnetwork is the Trusted Information Sharing Network for Critical Infrastructure Protection (TISN is at http://www.tisn.gov.au). TISN is a forum in which the owners and operators of critical infrastructure work together to share information on security issues which affect critical infrastructure. There are advisory groups for key industry sectors, such as banking, communications, emergency services, food chain, water services, etc. They share information on shared threats and vulnerabilities and appropriate measures and strategies to mitigate risk.

It is, in effect, a diffuse form of governance and management of the critical infrastructure. This infrastructure includes, but is not limited to, information. There is implicit acknowledgment that the wide range of security threats listed are linked through the information infrastructure and that defense of these assets and supplies is dependent on the quality of the information exchanges that monitor them.

Futher on this chapter outlines other international issues that are subject to similarly diffuse forms of management. In each case, their effective management is dependent on the governance arrangements for their information networks. Thus, management and security of information necessary for global citizenship is emerging as a form of governance in its own right, but without a unified or democratically accountable locus of control.

Taxation and Representation

One of the triggers of the American Revolution was colonists protesting against taxation without representation. In the 21st century, the protests come from both former colonies and nations who feel that their interests are not represented in international decision making and revenue gathering. Much consumer, citizen, and corporate activism is spurred by the lack of adequate participatory mechanisms. This presents an enormous challenge for all aspect of global e-governance. Clearly, the ability to amass revenue underpins the legitimacy and therefore also the sovereignty of governments everywhere. Perhaps less widely acknowledged is the way profit aggregation functions as a de facto form of taxation, particularly in trans-national contexts. Systems that allow information relevant to revenue collection to operate securely are as essential for international forms of governance as for existing governments. Corporations that amass and move enormous resources and revenues are increasingly subject to challenges to their legitimacy and calls for greater participation by those subject to their actions. Other dimensions of these twin issues of taxation and representation are discussed later in relation to information equity and the democratic deficit. The requirement for both resources and legitimacy is a key issue for all forms of information management, but particularly for those information security measures that are necessarily global in scope. Challenges of information governance are critical at all scales but are relatively uncharted waters for global issues.

E-Governance of Global Information Commons

At a global level, the telephone system and the Internet can only be managed through collaborative international effort. Short of a global empire or dictatorship, all nations are dependent on each other's good will to enable global communications. Global governance has been defined as "political management at the global level of a given area of human existence in the absence of global government" (Meyer & Stefanova, 2001).

This *Handbook* discusses the security aspects of these issues in depth. The routers and switches of the Internet are linked through an elaborate system of physical and administrative infrastructure. The human networks that manage the Internet include the Internet Engineering Task Force (IETF), but that is just the tip of the iceberg of organizations and agencies that develop and support the protocols that allow information to be transmitted securely. The domain name system of Internet addresses is managed by an international nonprofit corporation with appointed and elected members, the Internet Corporation for Assigned Names and Numbers (http://www.icann.org). Attempts to manage the global information commons multilaterally, for the good of all peoples, can be seen in the process for the World Summit for the Information Society, the WSIS (http://www.itu.int/wsis/).

In each of these examples, a set of players maps out agendas and actions. Even highly technical areas, such as mobile devices and protocols, have advocates of alternative approaches, standards, reporting mechanisms, and so on. The totality of infrastructure and networks for the establishment, maintenance, and accountability of a particular area constitute its governance. These may overlap, intersect, interfere, or conflict. Ultimately, however, all the pieces form a system, and it may be possible to map the overall patterns as an attractor. It may be functional in some ways and erratic in others, but the system altogether, changing and amorphous, makes up the global information commons. For democratic governance systems, the direction of change is as critical as the current state of the system. Identifying the patterns or attractors could aid predictability. It might be possible to see the outcomes of information systems with greater or less transparency and participation, by adjusting the number of nodes and rules for interaction between nodes.

The mutable networks that govern the global information commons have some resemblance to biological actors. For example, lawyers arguing about piracy may not be concerned about TCP, and the IETF may have little interest in intellectual property issues when they are developing wireless transmission protocols. Nonetheless, these separate groups might find themselves suddenly involved in negotiation over a common issue that involves all their expertise, such as identify theft. In such a case, a new network can appear, have a role, and fade away again. Although only some of the agencies or individuals might have a formal role, the cluster of actors becomes, at least for a time, an element in the global governance of the Internet. A recurrent theme is that governments are not always the key players in these patterns of global information management. As has been done for biological agents (see Kauffman, 2000), it should be possible to step back from these specifics to model the wider patterns through a normative democratic lens, and determine what outcomes result from existing rules and players.

Management of the collective set of infrastructure, resources and rules that comprises the global information systems is subject to the "tragedy of the commons." First described in relation to overgrazing of herding lands, this term refers to any resource in danger of being destroyed by undisciplined overuse and exploitation. Clover (2004) describes the impending collapse in many areas of fish stocks due to overfishing and the role of actors and governance structures (or rules) at many levels and globally. This issue dramatically illustrates how the failure of governance safeguards for the accuracy of the information, the integrity of the reporting systems and their transparency and accountability are major factors in tilting the system into unsustainability. The pattern formed by the not particularly democratic information value chain for this issue shows a sad but predictable tragedy of the commons in the making. Clover's solution includes the ultimate information-driven transparency: satellite monitoring over the Internet, live and public, of fishing boats. Transparency is a sine qua non of accountability, but cannot ensure it without other elements in the democratic information value chain.

Spam is a another example of a failure to manage part of the global information commons. The uncontrolled use of this marketing tool, most of it originating from the United States, illustrates the danger when information resources are not managed in the best interest of the widest group. This imposes costs on everyone, but particularly in a country such as Australia, which has volume-based Internet pricing. Intergovernmental arrangements for controlling this abuse are clearly inadequate, and individual businesses and consumers have little direct ability to influence their governments to enact stronger laws or interventions. Rather, a wide array of antispam activists, organizations, software solutions and networks at various levels and with varying degrees of formality have been set up to place control in the hands of users. Responses to spam show how power can seep into the gaps to create forms of management, action, and de facto governance where governments have proved inadequate.

Many information security issues are caught up in similar internationalized governance concerns. Legal matters such as identify theft, money laundering, and digital rights management (DRM) are dependent on the wide support of governments. Other aspects, such as standards and protocols for security architecture and products, require the cooperation of corporate players at least as much as governments. In the case of DRM, strong corporate lobbying on governments is countered by assertive activism by individuals and groups. Some elements, such as password protection and antivirus technology, cannot achieve widespread effectiveness unless individuals are adequately informed and motivated to take necessary precautions. The roles of nongovernment players in information security and management is expanded below.

Responsiveness, Monitoring, and Adaptation of Global Information

In addition to the difficulties of authenticating information, timeliness and quality of response also give rise to risk in a globalized world. These inadequacies have the potential to provide dysfunctional feedback patterns because power structures "circle the wagons" to deny or undermine attempts to learn from error. This deliberate political blindness to scientific information is a recurring theme in Clover's book on overfishing. A recent report from a coalition of nonprofit groups revealed that the U.S. government spent $6.5 billion in 2003 on preventing new documents from reaching the public domain. The report found that government secrecy is increasing and that secrecy between security agencies is stovepiping information, hindering the war on terrorism (Epstein, 2004).

A dynamic of diminishing access to information also makes it more difficult for the public to get the information people need to make their families safe from environmental hazards, such as the impact of toxic chemicals in the food chain. This is a direct example of information as security. Over the longer term, governance of information affects the capacity for reflectiveness and learning. If the ability to adapt is dampened, information can become not just less reliable, but dangerous. Governments that disguise risk from citizens soon find their legitimacy called into question, and these calls can come from both within and outside jurisdictional borders.

Skolnikoff (2001) outlined some of the pressures accompanying globalization that relate to technology and governance. He noted that domestic and international affairs are two parts of a whole. Governments have become ever more dependent on technology for their information, while the time for response has shrunk. Officials suffer from time scarcity, while the issues they must deal with have grown in scope and complexity. In this framework, they must make decisions which require urgent action, but whose consequences will be felt far into the future. Often the risks are high, and there may be multiple and perhaps disastrous unintended outcomes. Technical complexity of issues makes officials more dependent on specialists and experts and less able to communicate with their publics. Domestic agencies are drawn into international arenas, often inadequately prepared. Responses are caught up in bureaucratic entanglements with diplomatic offices, and cooperation with other states must be filtered through similar constraints within those nations. Skolnikoff predicted that greater autonomy may eventually be conceded to international organizations, driven by crises and system breakdowns.

Some of those who have been most successful in bypassing or undermining global security systems are the groups that are most able to mutate quickly and adapt to changed circumstances. These survival skills are as essential for legitimate regimes and industries as they are for biological viruses. For governments to survive, they need to adopt principles for information structuring, sharing, and security that mimic the most adept life forms. These approaches have been outlined in some detail for the corporate sector in relation to innovation (Tuomi, 2003) and also governmental and organizational adaptation (Kiel, 1994; Pascale, Millemann, & Gioja, 2000). These sources draw strongly on complex adaptive systems and nonlinearity as a new paradigm.

Consistency and Coordination of Global Information

The lack of uniform systems is one of the key features of information flows for international issues. Governments vary so greatly in their capacity to implement secure systems that consistency across nations is difficult to achieve. Coordination of systems suffers from not just technical discrepancies but human resource differences. Coordination is not easily outsourced to an international agency, for both practical and political reasons. A few high level institutions such as the World Bank, International Monetary Fund, and the United Nations have coordination roles, defined by their charter. Such institutions are limited by their bureaucratic distance from the individuals affected by the issues. Only a small subset of international agreements are truly enforceable, and these tend to be those relating to trade. Enforcement of the Kyoto Agreement on greenhouse emissions is limited, whereas the World Trade Organization and the World Intellectual Property Organization seem to have more potent enforcement mechanisms because strong stakeholders support them. As a result, WTO and WIPO agreements are more likely to have procedures for secure information documentation and storage and retrieval.

For most issues, there is no single global authority to direct or manage global information flows. Moreover, there is no direct representation of individuals' interests. Instead a plethora of amorphous and mutable institutions representing governments, corporations, clusters of organizations, and international entities all act on particular issues, often without coordination between them. Their lack of formal legitimacy and resources hampers their effectiveness. An example of great concern worldwide is cyber crime. Although many groups and levels of government have a strong interest in both defining and addressing cyber crime, a fully effective coordinated response is inhibited by the wide range of jurisdictions involved and the reticent cooperation of companies such as banks and Internet service providers (ISPs) to divulge commercial information or voluntarily bear associated costs. Furthermore, a government or jurisdiction that secures cooperation from its relevant industry sectors cannot guarantee that local solutions will be effective, as cyber crime, in its many manifestations described in this *Handbook,* is clearly an internationalized issue. As well as being a fundamental issue for information security and management, this problem overlaps with related areas, such as privacy, copyright protection, and electronic commerce. The tangle of approaches to this hydra-headed problem becomes, in effect, another imperfect governance system.

Citizens as well as governments incur blockages when dealing with issues that may affect them profoundly but lie beyond their legal entitlements. Hypothetically, how might a Malaysian obtain information about Indonesian plans to dump nuclear waste in common waters? There is no international provision for freedom of information, for example, to other countries. Citizens often have very limited rights to find out what is being planned, either by corporations or sometimes their own governments. This is one of many information black holes for issues that transcend national boundaries. Professor Alasdair Roberts's Web pages offer a starting point for international freedom of information issues, but there is a long way to go before freedom of information becomes a secure aspect of human rights in cyberspace. Pursuit of information generally has to go through often weaker international bodies with little enforcement capacity. There is little redress for nations, much less individual citizens. Nations can opt out of international agreements and treaties or simply not honor them. Enforcement depends on the cooperation of individual states, whereas within one country, standards for information, services, and reporting can be legislated on a national basis. Digital representation and interactivity also vary enormously among nations, reflecting an international digital divide based on another suite of infrastructure, skills, and attitudinal differences.

Under current arrangements for representation, the institutions for global governance are several links removed from citizen participation. Many countries also lack the democratic institutions and practices that foster effective participation. This has been observed in Asia, where lack of civil society structures delimits participation in the organization that manages the global Internet addressing system (Kang, 2003). However, even countries that rank well on Transparency International's assessments of corruption are subject to a democratic deficit, often in the form of more subtle undermining of democratic process. This is discussed in relation to Australia by Hindess (2004).

At a local or even a national level, it is possible to set priorities that lead to programs and systems to collect and manage the information that underpins government performance. These typically include policing and defense, health and education, but also social and economic goals. The accepted role for government leads to the services and transactions that are the bread and butter of e-government. Roads and hospitals, schools, and resource management all form part of the commons that governments exist to develop and protect. On an international level, the public goods are not so easy to reach agreement on or to quantify. One country may see its strategic goals in exactly the areas of resource development that may lead to environmental and social upheaval in another country. Even when there is accord on a universal right or a standard, there is contention over the who and how of enforcement. The involvement of non-government agents further complicates the ability of governments to negotiate equitable outcomes. World Bank studies have shown the link between good governance and economic development (Kaufman, Kraay, & Zoido-Lobaton, 1999, 2000). A corollary of this is that when government mechanisms for accountability shrivel, economic implosion may not be far behind.

Many international issues do not have clearly defined stakeholders. By their nature, they lack both geographic grounding and structures for distributed representation. Therefore, questions about the type and presentation of information, services, transactions, forms of communication, and so on tend to be answered according to importance placed on them by those with influence or resources. In the absence of uniform protocols for participation, transparency, and accountability, the establishment and monitoring of best practice in digital representation is difficult to determine and is often more driven by the relevant community of practice and influence than either public need or information technology enthusiasts.

Deterrents to Global E-Governance

The digital and democratic divides that separate nations and organizations present a huge hurdle for both global governance and managing the information commons. Highly developed countries will have organizations that are capable of advanced communications and information management. Countries and regions with few resources or minimal infrastructure will be unable to match these standards. Both their citizenry and their public institutions will be at a disadvantage in negotiating or implementing good information systems. To the extent that monitoring or evaluating a range of agreements or situations depends on information handling, these countries will be unable to exercise effective responses. If non-government players become the primary determiners of information security and control, national sovereignty is correspondingly compromised.

The gap between the "info rich" and "info poor" has long been a concern for many observers of the information society (Lyon, 1988). On a global level, this may be thought of as a scaling up of the digital divide that exists within communities. Areas at greatest disadvantage are likely to be Africa and remote areas of Asia and Latin America. Countries without adequate information infrastructure will not be able to compete economically, and this will further inhibit their ability to participate in shaping the information infrastructure to their advantage. This is also true of rural and remote areas of developed countries. In Australia, the ongoing drive to privatize fully the telecommunications carrier is being held up by the continuing inadequacy of rural infrastructure. This could become an information-as-security issue, given the vast and vulnerable northern coastline and repeated attempts at illegal landings by people smugglers. Research by the author found that remote electronic points of presence already provide a valuable service in providing information essential for the preparedness, management, response, and evaluation of natural disasters in outback Australia (Geiselhart, 2004b).

In keeping with the concept of a global information commons, the less developed countries may also be the ones whose information is critical for the well-being of the rest of the world. The challenge is to provide them with both the incentives and the ability to participate fully in information management and sharing. Countries are unlikely to be receptive to plans for globalized control of information or its infrastructure while they remain economically disadvantaged. Muslim nations might not be enthusiastic about systems for biometric identification of travelers, for example, if they thought this would place their citizens at risk of intrusive searches and delays. Some organizations claim that a global registration and surveillance infrastructure is being assembled to assist the US in anti-terrorism activities, but with profound implications for privacy and individual security (ICAMS, 2005). This could have implications for cooperation on other information issues, such as health and environment, discussed below.

The democratic deficit that exists even in the most highly developed nations offers a substantial obstacle to effective management of both the local and the global information commons. This, too, may be seen as a pattern that can be modelled and that repeats at several scales. Failures of democratic information process have much greater potential to undermine global security than inadequacies of technical standards and protocols. The democratic deficit embraces at least three interrelated aspects of governance: low voter turnout that reflects public disengagement in and cynicism about the political process; a lack of accountability in government; and the need for international governance in a globalized economy (Axworthy, 2003, 2004).

These problems with democracy that Axworthy described with reference to Canada can directly affect the security of information, as with the U.S. example on increasing government secrecy cited earlier. The democratic deficit can take many forms. A recent report indicates Australian politics is not free from corruption (McLennan, 2004). Sins of both omission and commission via information manipulation, together with the politicization of the public service, have led to debate but not much action. Endorsement of overseas intelligence claims about weapons of mass destruction, leading to commitment of Australian troops against popular opinion, and the subsequent reelection of the government that made those claims, indicates that democratic process is a complex beast indeed. Of course, the public is also part of the value chain of democratic accountability.

The democratic deficit highlights the relationship between security of information and the processes for its verification and transparency. This is particularly pertinent to global aspects of scientific decision making. Thousands of scientists in the United States, including 48 Nobel Prize winners, have signed a letter claiming political interference in scientific issues. These claims, even if only partly true, indicate how fragile knowledge can be, and the importance of checks and balances for its verification. There may not be much point in sharing information if the authentication and interpretation of that information is compromised. As with electronic financial data exchanges, scientific information needs to be free from both political and technical tampering en route, as it proceeds through policy channels. Climate scientists claim that vital information about global warming is not finding its way into government documents. This indicates the population's right to know is compromised, further weakening the entire chain of decision making. The governance dimensions of information can overtake scientific bias or error as sources of insecurity.

Another dimension to the democratic accountability of public information is the role of the media. It is only possible here to refer to the extensive literature on the role of the mass media in managing public opinion and determining what information is publicly available. A starting point for this research is McChesney (1999). This somewhat vague relationship to information security comes into sharper focus when linked to government procedures for freedom of information. Neither the "free" media nor interested individuals and organizations can easily leap the hurdles that accessing information can pose in even the most open societies. This encourages the informal networks that bypass government channels. The next section expands on the types and roles of nongovernment actors in relation to managing the information infrastructure and networks.

NONGOVERNMENT ACTORS AND GOVERNMENT INFORMATION

Actors outside governments are important influences on the overall flow of information. They are also critical players in the management of the information infrastructure and in the emerging forms of e-governance on specific issues. Networks of varying density and intensity connect nongovernment actors and stakeholders with each other and with governments. Like governments, these actors are also subject to the globalizing pressures of complexity, urgency, unquantifiable risk, time scarcity, and dependence on technological sources of information described by Skolnikoff (2001).

Each of the following sets of actors has the capacity to act and interact with the others and with governments, to form new and unexpected alliances, networks, and patterns of behavior. These can become the seeds of new regimes that support or undermine existing governments. They can also provide de facto forms of transnational e-governance through communities of practice and affiliation. The following perspective draws on Rosenau's "spheres of authority" analysis (including Rosenau, 1997) and Earnest's (2001) discussion of international relations and the changing role of the nation state. The underlying theory is a complex adaptive systems approach applied to governance, described in titles listed in the Further Reading section at the end of this chapter and in Geiselhart (1999, 2004a).

Corporate Sector

The global corporate sector has a double influence on both national and international aspects of e-governance. As systems and software contractors, they are both the subjects and the providers of digital information. They are strong lobbyists for information policy—for example, stronger IP and patent laws in areas such as biotechnology, entertainment, pharmaceuticals, and genetics. Consistent with the view presented earlier that technology design reflects its sociopolitical context, the systems design and architecture available for e-government are likely to support corporate interests and limitations.

The larger groups are relatively well resourced and often linked to global media systems. As a result, their voices tend to be clearly heard. Their role is to maximize profits, and this can lead to negative externalities. Good governance helps to manage their externalities and avoid tragedies of the commons. Their voice, like that of the public, is not homogeneous, but varies depending on the issue and where their interest lies. Some companies may be less than forthcoming when dealing with privacy invasion, pornography, software security issues, and so on if they are profiting from it. Others will be lobbyists for stronger protections and government intervention on issues that negatively affect them. All stakeholders (except perhaps cyber terrorists) seek stability, consistency, and appropriate forms of coordination.

On many issues, global corporations may band together to solve common problems of e-governance. For example, the development of electronic commerce is taking place through representation by industry bodies as well as intergovernmental panels. The International Telecommunications Union (http://www.itu.int), founded on the principle of cooperation between governments and the private sector, is active as part of a set of organizations involved with electronic commerce standards through a number of working groups, memoranda or understanding, and subprojects. Membership across the broad field of telecommunications generally includes policymakers and regulators, network operators, equipment manufacturers, hardware and software developers, regional standards-making organizations, and financing institutions. The ITU overtly states that its "activities, policies and strategic direction are determined and shaped by the industry it serves." (http://www.itu.int/aboutitu/overview/role-work.html, accessed May 13, 2005). Thus, although not formally structured to provide democratic accountabilities of representation or public good provision, the overall direction is nonetheless part of a sphere of authority that includes governments and their regulatory agencies as partners. It is a mutable, fast-evolving area, and like many organizations, the ITU aims for responsiveness and adaptation as their norm. The ITU has also been running the World Summit on the Information Society, as yet another aspect of their role that overlaps with many other dimensions of e-governance, digital divide and equitable development, and the engagement of civil society.

Another cooperative corporate project relating to e-governance is the Global Reporting Initiative (GRI). Although not directly related to information infrastructure or security, the GRI, like many global projects, makes good use of the Web's universal interface for its activities. The GRI (http://www.globalreporting.org/) is a set of consistent accounting standards used to track social, economic, and environmental outcomes. This is known as triple bottom-line accountability and illustrates how global information management of a particular form of data can occur without formal government or legal obligation. As compliance with these standards spreads, the GRI may become a valuable resource for nations as well as corporations. The impact may flow into the government sector, rather than governments attempting to impose it on the private sector. Accountabilities of the corporate sector extend beyond the nations where they have headquarters or pay taxes. Even small companies can have global reach, with global responsibilities that are often incompletely defined or enforceable.

Local Nongovernment Agencies

Many local government issues are informed by events elsewhere. Water management, urban design, drugs and crime as social concerns, best practice in early childhood development—the list is extensive. Local government authorities often need assistance in keeping up with this information. Community interest groups are often the best placed to capture and interpret additional information needed by governments. When suitably informed, they can lobby more effectively. Sometimes they can enlist the assistance of wider groups to their cause. A visiting expert with pertinent insights can cause a local welfare group to change direction abruptly in its approaches to a local government. Both success and failure can now be instantly conveyed, leading to reverberations in other localities.

This is not to underestimate the difficulties of transmitting information and gaining the benefits of local experience from around the globe, or even across the district. This is why many projects aim to facilitate networks for learning and sharing across geographic areas or communities of interest. The information networks and patterns of distribution are structural elements along with the actors that access and feed them.

International Nongovernment Agencies

These are an increasingly influential aspect of de facto global e-governance. The number of nongovernment agencies has mushroomed in recent decades. These organizations have the potential to achieve levels of trust that are often no longer available to the nation state, and thus they can speak quasi-independently to the media and over the Internet.

The larger international agencies, such as the Red Cross, Greenpeace, Human Rights Watch, Amnesty International, and Transparency International become respected players on the global relations circuit. Their reports, actions, and spokespersons often have high status at international conferences. They are supported by dispersed publics, their allegiances all the more valuable for being voluntarily given (Ernest, 2001). As part of their activities, they often contribute to, comment on, and distribute government information and reports. For example, groups such as those involved in antispam activism are players and stakeholders on issues with a direct input to information security. Thus, RIPE (http://www.ripe.net) is the regional internet registry for Europe. This independent, not-for-profit membership organisation supports the infrastructure of the Internet through technical coordination in its service region. It looks at issues of wide area IP networks but has formed an antispam working group to assist Europeans and others in combating this Internet plague. Its members, mainly Internet Service Providers (ISPs), telecommunication organisations and large corporations located in Europe and the Middle East, are part of the invisible web of cooperation that helps manage the Internet as a network of networks.

Some groups do not have a formal Web presence. For example, Al Qaeda's information is presented via other fundamentalist Web sites, including video footage of beheadings that has reverberated around the globe. The Chechen resistance is represented through the Web site http://www.kavkazcenter.com, which offers news and information about this Islamic uprising in three languages. They have designed the site so that media and others can easily keep up-to-date on their activities and relay this information to wider audiences.

Actors of all persuasions use networked strategies to assert their values and gain dominance. These include social activists as well as criminal and tax evasion syndicates. Extensive networks of information exchange and planning have underpinned, for example, the antiglobalization rallies that have become a feature at high-level international meetings. Indymedia (http://www.indymedia.org/) is just one prominent site for alternative news. Another activist group has been involved in the Civil Society gatherings of the WSIS process (http://www.wsis-cs.org/).

Political groups that embrace violence will have no compunctions about attacking information resources online to meet their ends. As a form of warfare, their skills are sophisticated and highly committed (Ronfeldt & Arquilla, 2001). Again, these tactics can be difficult for formal government processes to address, partly because they are more flexible, decentralized, and adaptive than bureaucratic structures. Even though they may be part of terrorism and be linked to cyber crime, money laundering, and attacks on infrastructure, their activities can be inadvertently protected by measures to protect identity and privacy online. Their very unaccountability to formal governance processes leaves them free to act and undermine information security globally.

Citizens Without Borders

Less ominously, citizens have responded to globalization with their own transborder activities. One of the best known features of electronic commerce is the ability to reach out to markets internationally. Likewise, activism now is more possible and more effective beyond national limits. Not all of this is mediated through organizations. Some is simple consumer choice that operates on the marketplace, often without political intent. Other dimensions, however, are overtly about creating a voice or change as diverse members of a diffuse public. One example is birdwatchers flocking together to count birds and incidentally become part of a global scientific project (Garreau, 2001).

Another area of individual (and group) activism concerns the maintenance of predigital rights. As noted earlier, digital rights management, or DRM, has become polarized between strong, almost coercive intellectual property protection versus those who want to protect "fair use" and the open exchange of ideas, information, and artistic expression. The Creative Commons project (http://creativecommons.org/) offers an alternative approach to the intense and expensive legalism of copyright law. Piracy and appropriate free use of digital material is one of the most contested areas of global e-governance.

On a formal political level, groups reach out to find the likeminded, regardless of where they might be. Parties set up convenient Web sites so expatriates can enroll to vote. The diaspora of many communities use electronic communications to inform and seek support. When disaster hits (such as a cyclone) or victory arrives (such as being awarded the privilege of staging the next Olympics) the international phone and Web links run hot for days, with congratulations, enquiries, and, if necessary, financial support. Some resource flows become semipermanent, as those in more economically advanced countries feed the organizations and movements of their choice. Inside repressive regimes dissidents continually change Web hosts and utilize all the tricks of online anonymity to get information and stories out.

Individuals need the protection of their identity, money, information, privacy, and so on when dealing within their own borders. This is usually provided by governments through legislation, policing, and so on. These protections are much less available for citizens roaming internationally, either as activists or consumers. This is where globalization gets personal, not just for nuisances such as spam and the notorious Nigerian e-mail fraud, but also for extensions of criminal behavior that endanger lives and livelihoods. Emerging forms of e-governance will need to respond to these concerns.

In enterprises such as Amazon.com, eBay, and myriad others, the inputs from many participants provide the data to shape the system. In advanced forms, the participants actually patrol and regulate the system. For example "eBay vigilantes" help flush out dishonest traders (Cronaca, 2004). Central to this approach is the ability for leaderless action, driven by intent and individual initiative. In human systems, the rules of interaction are generated by the values of the actors (Kiel, 1994; Pascale et al., 2000; Theys, 1998). Conflict between the values of various sets of actors inhibits harmonization of the global democratic information value chain and systems.

The outline just provided highlights the nature of today's globalized information interdependence. It is dispersed, mutable, and often uncontrollable and unpredictable. The following section of this chapter discusses some specific areas of high information security risk where governments are trending toward greater integration of global information systems. These reinforce earlier claims in the chapter about the critical role of information systems and their governance in wider security and sustainability concerns. In nearly all of the areas where

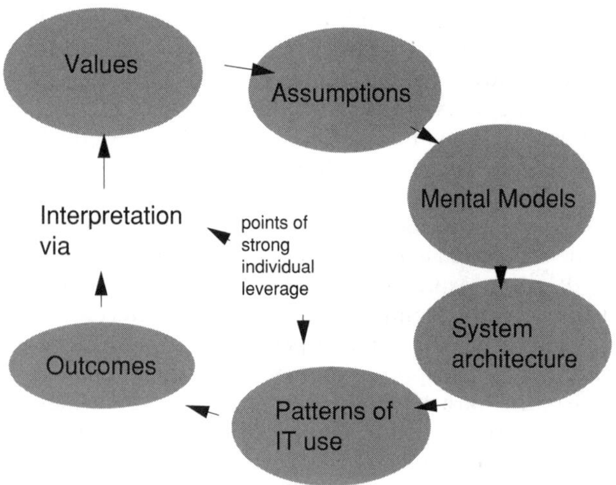

Figure 2: The IT system design value chain (Geiselhart, 1999).

formal governments operate, the processes that manage and integrate transnational information flows have a direct impact on personal, public, and national security. Figure 2 illustrates the cycle of information systems development and the role played by values in shaping these systems. At no point are patterns of governance independent of the values and mental models of the actors who shape them. This highlights the need to articulate and embed democratic values in systems of e-governance.

GLOBAL INFORMATION—AREAS OF HIGH RISK

These areas are indicative of the overlap between national and international information systems and the links between these and global security. For each of these, a long list of actors contribute to the information creating a dynamic sphere of authority, with smaller similar (fractal) patterns at national and local levels, frequently with implications for individuals. Each sphere also overlaps and is interdependent on the others, as illustrated in this section. For each, the key to information as a dimension of security lies in the patterns being created at all levels and how they interact, along with the information flows and their checks and balances. Each sphere of authority contributes to global e-governance on that issue.

International Information: Economic and Financial

The world economy is perhaps the most obvious manifestation of globalization, and the area where global e-governance is most highly coordinated. It consists of industries, flows of goods and services, resource manipulation, advertising and marketing, and consumption by governments, organizations, and individuals. Trade laws and sanctions of various kinds, unilateral, multilateral, and global, enforce and reinforce alliances or enmities. The largest industries, such as energy and agriculture, are subject to fluctuations and crises. These issues affect the ability of less well-developed nations, regions, and individuals to participate in the global economy because knowledge about innovation is also manipulated through legal and administrative controls, pricing regimes, and so on.

Where representation issues have been resolved, e-governance can be effective. For example, SWIFT (Society for Worldwide Interbank Financial Telecommunication, http://www.swift.com) is an industry-owned cooperative that provides the information infrastructure for much of global banking and finance. The banking industry is a "virtual community," with the capacity to design and manage their information systems to the mutual advantage of stakeholders. As a cooperative, its governance structures have commonalities with democratic representation. International financial and commercial transactions have rigorous requirements for digital documentation. The forms of information security include nonrepudiation, verification, and authentication. The governance role of many hybrid government and industry organizations in setting standards and norms is a theme of this paper. Similar patterns or attractors of representation, negotiation, and collaboration are repeated for many other aspects of the information superstructure.

For many forms of communication between sovereign nations, clarity about information structure, content, transparency, and security is much more elusive. Diplomatic communications, for example, are not likely to travel on public networks without strong encryption. Likewise, documents relating to the negotiation of treaties cannot be entrusted to public systems. Many reports and much research commissioned with public money will be provided to other governments for purposes of negotiation without being made available to citizens of either country. Further, the procedures by which such information might be made public are continually subject to contestability by relevant stakeholders, often on a subject by subject basis. The potential for a unified framework for disclosure, even within one country or jurisdiction, is restricted by political pressures and the bureaucratic artifacts of fragmentation and compartmentalization.

Legal and Administrative Information

Legal matters include taxation, treaties, and intellectual property, along with judicial and criminal issues relating to extremes of behavior from innovation to terrorism. Collecting tax becomes more difficult when individual and corporate actors can move and conceal their money and transactions. Some nations actively provide tax havens, and others seek global sanctions to eliminate them. Some corporate players position themselves to aid and abet tax avoidance as a market opportunity. Individuals as well as companies seek gaps in taxation monitoring and take advantage of the limited cooperation on reporting to shield their income from governments (Geiselhart & Singh, 2001). Addressing these taxation issues is a major concern for nations and relates closely to information security issues relating to support for terrorism. Transparency is the other side of the representation coin for e-governance. As global integration increases, questions of who will guard the guardians of information will intensify.

Again, there are national and nonstate actors, public organizations, and underground groups that seek influence in each of these spheres. The issues are notoriously entwined. One legal–economic example is the superannuation industry. Individual citizens have accounts and accumulate funds from various employers, in addition to their own contributions. This has a government element because the government agency sets the rules by which citizens can enter or withdraw as well as taxation limits and a whole range of administrative and legal issues. There is also a powerful corporate element because there are companies, both for profit and not for profit, that manage and administer the investments of these funds. Finally, there is also a substantial international dimension because the funds regularly invest both on- and offshore, thus bringing the superannuation fund into communication and perhaps negotiation with international governments, other legal systems, concerns about possible human rights or environmental practices, corruption, and so on.

A random sampler of other legal aspects of global e-governance includes the use of biometrics at national borders; the regulation of radio frequency identification tags on consumer goods; and spim, or the next generation of spam, which is unwanted text messages sent over mobile phones. In addition to their legal and regulatory aspects, each of these has a consumer dimension and a set of privacy concerns, in addition to the purely technical dimensions of standards and transmission. It is not clear where the representation of global citizens' interests falls in each of these. This is one function of modelling, to develop maps of how the parameters interact and identify their sources.

Environmental Information

A growing area is disaster planning, response, recovery, and evaluation. Natural and human events can disrupt the global communication system, precisely when and where coordination of information and response is most needed.

The broader field of secure information relating to environmental communications encompasses details of climate variation and communications about short-term events and medium and longer term dynamics, along with species identification, documentation and preservation, water resource allotment and management, air quality monitoring, and many other issues. Information on these matters is important not only for the ability to preview and model scenarios, but also to adopt precautions and preventive strategies where possible. Information sharing in response to catastrophe, both human and natural, as well as recovery and evaluation to promote learning, are other dimensions of global environmental management. There is an increasing risk of rogue states endangering the planet with chemical or nuclear weapons. One approach to minimizing these risks is international standards for reporting, documentation, and information sharing and enforcement on the total life cycle of materials with the potential to become weapons of mass murder. Many current systems for reporting do not include the full value chain of information to include democratic stakeholders.

The outstanding global example of the environmental dimensions of information as security is climate change. Information on this topic is highly debated. The overlaps with economic, legal, and also health and transport are self-evident. Alliances are forged along interest lines, and each faction produces copious information to support its stand. The level of risk is extreme, and potential for harmonization is limited by the relative power of key actors. This information cascades to every level of global structure because there is virtually no place on earth that is outside this sphere. Here, too, individual actors have to make risk assessment decisions based on the information available to them locally and their level of confidence in wider sources of information. Many writers are documenting the potential for a global form of 'open source politics' (Sifry, 2004) that compels the kinds of ultimate transparency and citizen monitoring that Clover (2004) has described for fisheries and that he sees on a smaller scale in Iceland.

Other aspects of environmental information reveal why some writers suggest environmental degradation will be the main security risk in this century (Kaplan, 1994). These issues are intimately entwined with the other spheres of authority. Thus concerns about security and quality of water are coupled with globalizing pressures to privatize supply, and increasing dependence on fossil fuels is coupled with uncertainty about reserves. According to Thomas (2001), the greatest undermining factor to security in a globalized system of trade, finance, and ecology is poverty. This may be seen as the weakest link in the democratic information value chain, creating vulnerabilities where disease or terror can fester.

Health Information

Health is a critical integrating area, where forms of information are inextricably caught up in their political context. Health crises are by nature complex and often defy state-centric approaches (Lee & Dodgson, 2000). Nations seeking to go it alone during an outbreak of a new disease, for example, can endanger multiple other populations beyond their borders.

Clearly, this is closely related to environment, but health issues are associated with additional information components that require global information sharing: epidemiological patterns and patterns of antibiotic resistance, new disease vectors, promulgation of best practice, and economically viable approaches.

Lee and Dodgson (2000) have documented the ways in which the patterns of cholera have reflected those of globalization. They maintain that the systemic ills of globalization itself are reflected in health challenges. They observe an erosion of spatial, temporal, and cognitive boundaries. They also note a failure of the rationalist thinking that says these problems can be solved by simply adding more information, when it is the patterns of interconnection that need to be addressed. This is another way of stating the importance of management and governance procedures for existing information.

Health and administrative–legal matters are closely related because the intellectual property arrangements for pharmaceuticals are a key focus for trade liberalization. Bilateralism can dampen plurality and transparency and result in essentially "a covert form of private governance" (Drahos & Henry, 2004). In such cases the information systems are likely to reflect the degree of covertness.

Consider a situation of a biological infestation in an exporting country's wheat crop. This can diminish food supply in one country and national income in another, as well as create hunger and stress at both end points. These large-scale dynamics are mediated at both ends by relevant national bureaus, industry groups, farmer organizations, welfare agencies, and unions. Every point of possible action is a node in a complex array of actors and rules for information transmission. There may be little or no direct communication between the end points of producer and consumer in the two countries. These groups will be more or less dependent on the quantity, quality, and timing of the information made available to them. The security of their livelihood or sustenance may, in the extreme case of famine, be as tenuous as the weakest link in these global flows. Equally important is the chain of accountability for the information that determines whether they will know that information has been withheld or distorted. This chain is only as strong as the civil and political institutions and values that generate the democratic information value chain.

This scenario of interdependence is repeated for other spheres of the global economy. The steel industry would have parallel sets of government, industry, and local worker and consumer groups. These spheres intersect through groups that have an overall role of coordinating economic development, or trade, or occupational health and safety, or biological safety, in the case of wheat. The information systems servicing these diverse actors and agencies can be secure, but closed to scrutiny, or they may be porous and open to review to a greater or lesser extent to those with an interest in holding them accountable. The urgency of each economic strand will depend on its role in the national and global economy and the current dynamics of its production. There is probably little current interest in, for example, the international paper clip industry, except as a very minor product in global steel production and exports.

Transport Information

Our last issue is transport, again connected with the others. The carriage and smuggling of dangerous materials is one aspect, including radioactive substances, chemicals, machines, and equipment of warfare and weapons of mass destruction. Legal and administrative matters overlap, for example, in the insurance arrangements that affect oil tankers and the consequences for spills.

The transport of people is also now a large international trade, both legal and illegal. These people bring not just disease vectors, but challenges to cultural, welfare, political, religious, and legal situations. Tourism is not an unmixed blessing for the host nations, particularly if it encourages terrorist attacks, as in Bali when Australians and Balinese met a common fate. There were claims that the Australian government had knowledge of the impending threat but did not provide warnings. Around the world, more travelers are paying closer attention to whatever information sources they think can provide a margin of safety through information about such matters.

CONCLUSIONS

This chapter has argued that democratic governance processes sit at the centre of information security issues, rather than on the periphery as a desirable but distant goal. It has shown that e-government is now more diffuse, particularly for the many issues that overlap national boundaries. In examining the drivers of e-government that flow beyond the nation state, many examples have demonstrated the other side of the information security coin: information as security. The author suggests that a democratic information value chain enhances transparency and participation and therefore accountability. In this scenario, government information becomes a tool to identify, manage, and defuse risk. The alternative is information as weapon and control, ultimately destabilizing when governments are unable to harness the new integrating dynamic. Yet another possibility is information out of control, where lies, misinformation, and hatred can infect both computers and minds. More optimistically, new forms of organization are emerging that provide "citizens sans frontiers" with the information tools to help shape and manage the global information commons. All these scenarios are the subject of intense debate and speculation. Figure 3 illustrates how actors at various levels or scales of influence might combine to determine the processes of information exchange. This figure is part of important work now being done on the role of open standards and social networks in developing trust relationships for Internet governance (see Reed, Le Maitre, Barnhill, David, & Labalme, 2004).

Given the paradigm shift toward a complex adaptive systems approach in recent years, it is likely that this perspective will inform modeling the protocols for a democratic management of the global commons. It is hoped

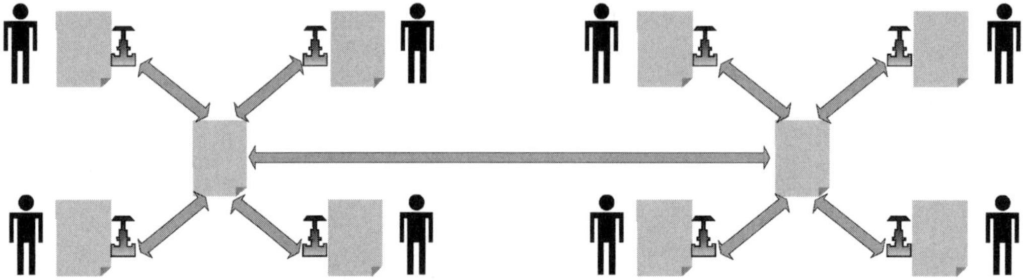

Figure 3: Representation of the ways groups can form membership in other groups in fractal patterns at many levels of complexity (from Reed et al., 2004).

that international e-governance and democratic information systems may eventually converge as part of a triple bottom line to address current environmental and political crises.

For all the issues discussed in this global context, the security of information is only as good as its distribution, management and governance. This chapter has provided a brief overview of the international dimensions of government information, and the implications for security. Information security and measures for transparency and accountability are an integral part of the risks associated with each issue. Issues with greatest acceleration are subject to the greatest risk, as these have the potential for sudden bifurcations. The compression of time makes pattern recognition more urgent, as does the interaction between issues and regimes to manage them. Government collection, creation, and dissemination of information is always and intensely a matter of national security. It is likely that modeling and simulations of governance, based on patterns for information creation, verification, transmission and access will become as common as economic and climate modeling is today.

Future research on international dimensions of e-government is needed to determine the forms of information sharing and management that will be most productive of protecting the global information commons. These may eventually take the form of protocols, growing out of such processes as the WSIS. There have been many attempts to codify the design features of democratic information systems, including Sclove (1995) and Geiselhart (1999). These principles for electronic democracy are based on a report from the OECD (2003) and may suggest the following avenues for research into specific information projects with global dimensions:

- create new public spaces for political interaction and deliberation
- provide for multidirectional, interactive communication flow
- integrate e-democratic processes within broader constitutional structures and developments
- facilitate and summarize public inputs
- ensure information is of high quality and trustworthy
- recruit the widest range of public voices
- provide equal access to the democratic process.

Another possibility is the development of an international charter of rights relating to the global information commons. Preliminary work on this has been done by Cameron and Geiselhart (1997). Work on the effects of information transparency and availability should help to establish which patterns are most productive of both information security and democratic process.

GLOSSARY

Attractor A state, condition or pattern that a system tends to stabilise in

Complex Adaptive System A system based on agents and rules for interaction, typified by evolution and unpredictability.

Democratic Deficit The gaps between formal democratic processes and government functioning and accountability.

Digital Divide The gap in communications technology knowledge, skills, and use between different groups.

Global E-Governance The electronic dimensions of emerging mechanisms for managing transnational issues and resources.

Global Information Commons The total human and physical infrastructure that supports the flow of information globally.

Globalization The process of increasing interdependency among countries, accompanied by convergent patterns of economic development and technology use.

Fractal Patterns that repeat at different scales, such as a coastline, or behaviors and institutions.

Triple Bottom Line Accounting procedures that include economic, environmental, and social elements.

CROSS REFERENCES

See *E-Government; E-government Security Issues and Measures.*

REFERENCES

Accenture. (2004). EGovernment leadership: High performance, maximum value. Fifth Annual Accenture eGovernment Study. Retrieved May 2005 from http://www.accenture.com/xd/xd.asp?it=enweb&xd=industries\government\gove_egov_value.xml

Axworthy, T. (2003–2004, December–January). The democratic deficit: Should this be Paul Martin's next Big Idea? *Policy Options,* pp. 15–19.

Beniger, J. R. (1986). *The control revolution—Technological and economic origins of the information society.* Cambridge, MA: Harvard University Press.

Branscomb, A. W. (1994). Who owns information? New York: Basic Books.

Cameron, J., & Geiselhart, K. (1998). A charter for citizens of the global information society. In J. Berleur & D. Whitehouse (Eds.), *The ethical global information society,* London: Chapman and Hall. Retrieved September 2004 from http://doctordemocracy.net/html/charter.htm

Clover, C. (2004). *The End of the Line: how overfishing is changing the world and what we eat.* Ebury Press: London.

Cronaca. eBay Vigilantes. (2004, March 22). No author provided. Retrieved June 2004 from http://www.cronaca.com/archives/002201.html

Dahl, R. A. (1989). Democracy and its critics. New Haven and London: Yale University Press.

Drahos, P., & Henry, D. (2004, May 29). The free trade agreement between Australia and the United States [Editorial]. *British Journal of Medicine, 328,* 1271–1272. Retrieved July 2004 from http://bmj.bmjjournals.com/cgi/content/full/328/7451/1271?etoc

Earnest, D. (2001, February). Will no one rid me of this meddlesome state? Social inequality and the new social contract. Author's draft of paper prepared for delivery at the 42nd Annual Convention of the International Studies Association, Chicago.

Epstein, E. (2004, August 27). White House takes secrecy to new levels, coalition reports. *San Francisco Chronicle,* August 27, 2004. Retrieved September 2004 from http://www.fas.org/sgp/news/2004/08/sfc082704.html

Feenberg, A. (1991). *Critical theory of technology.* New York and Oxford: Oxford University Press.

Garreau, J. (2001, May 9). Flocking together through the Web: Bird watchers may be a harbinger of a true global consciousness. *The Washington Post*. Pg C01 Retrieved May 2005 from http://www.changemakers.net/library/temp/wpost050901.cfm

Geiselhart, K. (1999). Does democracy scale? A fractal model for the role of interactive technologies in democratic policy processes. Doctoral dissertation, University of Canberra. Retrieved September 2004 from http://www.doctordemocracy.net/thesis

Geiselhart, K., & Singh, M. (2001). Tax issues for e-commerce, in e-commerce diffusion: Strategies and challenges (edited by M. Singh & T. Teo). Melbourne: Heidelberg.

Geiselhart, K. (2004a). Digital government and citizen participation in international context. In A. Pavlichev & D. Garson (Eds.), *Digital government: Principles and best practices*. Hershey: Idea Books.

Geiselhart, K. (2004b). The electronic canary: Sustainability solutions for Australian teleservice centres. Community TeleServices Australia, Inc. A report commissioned by the Networking the Nation Board, Department of Communications, Information Technology and the Arts, March 2004. Retrieved May 2005 from http://www.teleservices.net.au/

Global Reporting Initiative. Retrieved April 2004 from http://www.globalreporting.org/

Gualtieri, R. (1998). *Impact of the emerging information society on the policy development process and democratic quality.* OECD Public Management Service. (No longer available online).

Hernon, P., & McClure, C. R. (1993). Electronic US government information: Policy issues and directions. *Annual Review of Information Science and Technology (ARIST)*, 28, 45–110.

Hindess, B. (2004). Corruption and Democracy in Australia. Part of the Democratic Audit of Australia. Retrieved May 2005 from http://democratic.audit.anu.edu.au/focussedaudits.htm

ICAMS (International Campaign Against Mass Surveillance). (2005). The Emergence of a Global Infrastructure For Mass Registration and Surveillance: 10 Signposts. Retrieved May 2005 from http://www.i-cams.org/Surveillance_intro.html

International Telecommunications Union. http://www.itu.int. Accessed May 13, 2005.

Kang, M. (2001). Beyond underdevelopment of the public sphere: democratizing Internet governance in Asia. *Info—The Journal of Policy, Regulation and Strategy for Telecommunications, 3,* 348–358.

Kaplan, R. (1994, February). The coming anarchy. *Atlantic Monthly*. Retrieved May 2004 from http://www.theatlantic.com/politics/foreign/anarchy.htm (Now requires subscription). Also retrieved May 2005 from http://dieoff.org/page67.htm

Kauffman, S. (2000). Investigations. Oxford: New York.

Kaufman, D., Kraay, A., & Zoido-Lobaton, P. (1999). Aggregating governance indicators. World Bank Policy Research Working Papers (no. 2195). Retrieved July 2004 from http://www.worldbank.org/wbi/gac

Kaufman, D., Kraay, A., & Zoido-Lobaton, P. (2000). Governance matters. World Bank Policy Research Working Papers (no. 2196). Retrieved July 2004 from http://www.worldbank.org/wbi/gac

Kiel, D. (1994). *Managing chaos and complexity in government*. San Francisco: Jossey-Bass.

Lee, K., & Dodgson, R. (2000). Globalization and cholera: Implications for global governance. *Global Governance, 6*, 213–236.

Lyon, D. (1988). *The Information Society - Issues and Illusions.* Cambridge, England: Polity Press.

McChesney, R. (1999). Rich media, poor democracy: Communication politics in dubious times. Champaign: University of Illinois Press.

McLennan, D. (2004, August 17). Corruption rife in politics: Study. *Canberra Times*, p. 2.

Musso, J., Weare, C., & Hale, M. (2000). Designing Web technologies for local governance reform: Good management or good democracy? *Political Communication, 17,* 1–19.

Meyer, W. H., & Stefanova, B. (2001). Human rights, the UN Global Compact, and global governance. *International Law Journal, 34,* 501–522.

Organisation for Economic Co-operation and Development. (2003). *Promise and Problems of E-Democracy: Challenges of online citizen engagement.* Paris: Author.

Pascale, R., Millemann, M., & Gioja, L. (2000). *Surfing the edge of chaos: The laws of nature and the new laws of business.* New York: Crown Business.

Pavlichev, A., & Garson, D. (2004). *Digital government: Principles and best practices*. Hershey: Idea Books.

Reed, D., Le Maitre, M., Barnhill, B., Davis, O., & Labalme, F. The social Web: Creating an open social network with XDI. *Planetwork Journal.* Retrieved September 2004 from http://journal.planetwork.net/article.php?lab=reed0704&page=1

Richard, E. (2000). Lessons from the network model of Online Engagement of Citizens. Paper presented to LENTIC colloquium, Brussels. Retrieved August 2004 from the Canadian Policy Research Networks Web site: http://www.cprn.org

Roberts, A. (n.d.). Freedom of information resources. Retrieved September 2004 from http://www.foi.net

Ronfeldt, D., & Arquilla, J. (2001). Networks, netwars, and the fight for the future. *First Monday, 6.* Retrieved May 2004 from http://www.firstmonday.dk/issues/issue6_10/ronfeldt/index.html

Rosenau, J. (1997). *Along the domestic-foreign frontier: Exploring governance in a turbulent world.* Cambridge, England: Cambridge University Press.

Sclove, R. E. (1995). *Democracy and Technology.* New York: Guilford Press.

Sifry, M. (2004). The rise of open source politics. *The Nation*. Retrieved May 2005 from http://www.thenation.com/doc.mhtml?i=20041122&s=sifry

Skolnikoff, E. (2001). International governance in a technological age, in knowledge, politics and governance. In De la Mothe, J. (Ed.), *Science, 9*. London: Continuum.

Theys, M. (1998). The new challenges of management in a wired world. *European Journal of Operational Research, 109*, 248–263.

Thomas, C. (2001). Global governance, development and human security: Exploring the links. *Third World Quarterly, 22*, 159–175.

Trusted Information Sharing Network for Critical Infrastructure Protection (TISN). Retrieved May 2005 from http://www.tisn.gov.au/

Tuomi, I. (2003). *Networks of innovation: Change and meaning in the age of the Internet*. London: Oxford.

Zuboff, S. (1988). *In the age of the smart machine—the future of work and power.* Oxford: Heinemann Professional.

FURTHER READING

Bossomaier, T., & Green, D. (1998). *Patterns in the Sand: Computers, Complexity and Life.* Sydney: Allen Unwin.

Bourke, P. Web pages on fractals. Retrieved July 2004 from http://astronomy.swin.edu.au/~pbourke/fractals/ (Accessed September 2004.)

CALResCo Complexity Writings. Retrieved May 2005 from http://www.calresco.org/themes.htm

Holland. J. (1997). *Emergence: From chaos to order*. Boston: Addison-Wesley.

Organisation for Economic Co-operation and Development. (2003). http://hermia.sourceoecd.org/vl=12883288/cl=86/nw=1/rpsv/~6674/v2003n4/s1/p1l

Suarez, P. (n.d.) Urbanization, climate change and flood risk: Addressing the fractal nature of differential vulnerability. Retrieved July 2004 from http://www.iiasa.ac.at/Research/RMS/dpri2002/Papers/suarez.pdf

PART 2

Infrastructure for the Internet, Computer Networks, and Secure Information Transfer

Conducted Communications Media

Thomas L. Pigg, *Jackson State Community College*

INTRODUCTION

The Internet consists of millions of digital passages that carry signals all over the world. These conduits, which connect us to the World Wide Web, come in many shapes, sizes, and modes. The bewildering assortment and seemingly endless conduits, more commonly referred to as communication media, that are used to connect computers together can be boiled down to two types: conductive cable and wireless. Conductive media is simply a hard-wired connection, which requires someone to physically join network devices with some type of cable. The three major types of cable are coaxial, twisted pair, and fiber optic. The focus of this chapter is on conducted communications media. Wireless communication is the alternative to conducted communications media. This is accomplished using a variety of broadcast transmission technologies, including radio, terrestrial microwave, and satellite communications.

To aid in understanding conductive communications media, a short explanation of network transmission basics is discussed, followed by a detailed exploration of the three major types of media, mentioned earlier. In addition, a presentation of the similarities and contrasts between these media is provided. Finally, the suitability and application of each type of conducted media along with security concerns are discussed.

OVERVIEW OF NETWORK TRANSMISSION BASICS

Network Transmission Basics

When computers communicate over the Internet or on private networks, they must follow certain communication protocols. In short, each computer that connects to a network must follow rules that govern the type of hardware and software that is used for access to the network. These protocols consist of signal types and speeds, cable layouts, and communications access schemes.

Baseband and Broadband

Bandwidth is the range of frequencies that a particular network transmission media can carry. It also reveals the maximum amount of data that can be carried on the medium. A baseband transmission is a single, fixed signal that uses the entire available bandwidth. Baseband signals use a single channel to communicate with devices on a network, which allows computers to transmit and receive data on one cable (Tittel & Johnson, 2001). Baseband communications are typically used for local area networks (LANs). When LANs expand into a metropolitan area network (MAN) or a wide area network (WAN), baseband systems do not provide the bandwidths that are adequate for these larger networks.

Network connections that attach several LANs together, such as MANs or WANs, or that allow remote access from external users or networks to local servers often require multichannel bandwidths because of increased traffic flow. Broadband transmissions help to meet these needs. In contrast to the discrete digital signals produced in baseband communications, broadband transmission generates an analog carrier frequency, which carries multiple digital signals or multiple channels. This concept is much like cable television systems that carry many channels on one cable.

The decision to use baseband or broadband is determined by the application. If the network consists of a single LAN, baseband would be the best choice. If an organization has computer networks that spread over several geographic areas, multiple channels of communications between locations may be needed, which can be achieved only through broadband applications. Note that it is the network type and the particular network device that determines whether a signal is baseband or broadband, not the transmission media.

Cable Access Methods

A cable access method is how data are placed on the transmission media. Data are formatted into small pieces called packets. A packet contains header and trailer information about the contents, destination, error checking, and the actual data. A packet typically contains a specific amount of information, normally 1 to 2 Kbytes that is defined by the particular network protocol being used. It is a lot like an envelope used to hold a letter to be mailed. The outside of the envelope contains a destination address along with

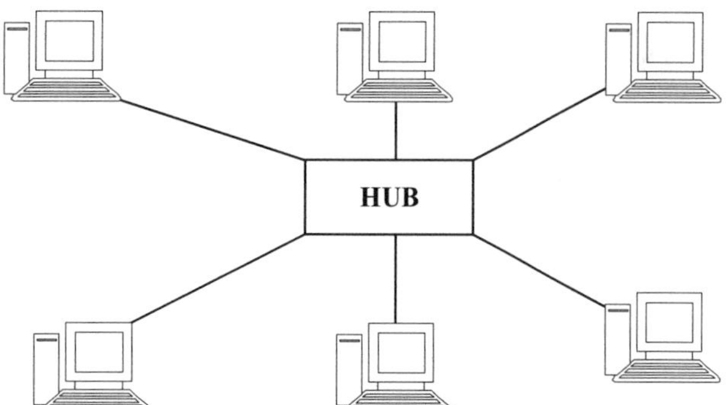

Figure 1: Star topology.

sender information. This information is used by the postal service to deliver the mail to its destination. When a wrong destination address is used, the postal service can notify the sender by means of the return address. Network packets are handled in a similar way (Tittel & Johnson, 2001).

Packets are placed on the communications line in several ways. Typically, the communication media used in a LAN will be shared by all network devices. In most cases, only one device can transmit information on the communication media at a time. This will often be in the form of a broadcast. A broadcast by a computer will be received by all of the devices connected to the particular network segment. For example, Ethernet, a widely used LAN protocol, uses a cable access method called carrier sense multiple access with collision detection (CSMA-CD). This method is a lot like a two-way radio broadcast, which allows only one person to talk at one time. CSMA-CD requires each participating network workstation to first listen to the communication line to determine whether it is clear before attempting to broadcast a packet of information, because it is possible that two or more workstations will begin broadcasting their packets at almost the same time. If this occurs, the collision detection (CD) feature of CSMA-CD will instruct the conflicting workstations to cease transmissions and assign a random delay before they are allowed to attempt to send another packet of data. Without a random delay, the colliding workstations would continue to rebroadcast at the same time, causing more collisions. Occasionally, a defective network interface card (NIC) may cause excessive collisions by constantly broadcasting packets. This is called a broadcast storm (Tittel & Johnson, 2001).

A similar access method, used by AppleTalk networks, is called carrier sense multiple access with collision avoidance (CSMA-CA). This scheme is similar to CSMA-CD except that CSMA-CA attempts to avoid collisions altogether. Network devices accomplish this by sending a short broadcast requesting control of the network segment before sending a packet. This helps prevent collisions of

Figure 3: T-connector.

complete packets, thus reducing network traffic due to rebroadcasting packets (Tittel & Johnson, 2001).

Another type of access method is called token passing, used by token ring protocol. Token passing eliminates network collisions altogether by passing a token from node to node on the network in one direction. A token is similar to a packet. When a network device receives a token, it examines it to determine whether its contents are for that particular node. If not, the network node rebroadcasts the token to the next device on the network. When the token finds its destination, it unloads the data and rebroadcasts an empty token to the next device. The empty token will ask each passing node whether it has any data to send. The empty token is passed on down the line until a device generates information to place in the empty token (Tittel & Johnson, 2001).

Network Topologies

A network topology is the physical cable layout or configuration. There are three basic types: star, bus, and ring. Each network protocol (i.e., Ethernet, token ring) will specify the cable type and topology supported. The star topology, as illustrated inFigure 1, requires a central wiring point for all network devices on a particular network segment. A device called a hub or concentrator is used to serve this purpose. A hub is a multiport repeater that regenerates signals received. In some applications a device called a switch is used. A switch is more intelligent than a hub because it can learn which devices are connected to its ports and send packets directly to the destination port only, thus reducing network traffic.

Figure 2: Bus topology.

Figure 4: Terminator.

The bus topology (seeFigure 2) requires no special external device for computers to connect to. It consists of network nodes connected to the communications media via a special T-connector that connects the computer's NIC to the bus (seeFigure 3). You will notice in Figure 2 that a small box is shown at both ends of the bus. This represents a terminator that is required for this cable layout (seeFigure 4). Its purpose is to prevent signal bounce, which occurs when a cable is not terminated. Signal bounce is the result of a broadcast signal that continues to oscillate. The terminator is used to absorb the signal once it has reached the end of the cable, thus eliminating signal bounce.

The ring topology (seeFigure 5) is similar to bus topology in that each computer is connected directly to its neighbor without the need for a hub or other special device. The big difference between the two is that ring topology provides a closed-loop design, which does not require termination.

In some applications more than one topology may be used. For example, the token ring protocol uses a topology called a star-wired ring, as shown inFigure 6. In this example, multistation access units (MAU) or concentrators are used to connect the network devices. The MAUs are then connected to each other in a physical ring configuration. The physical connection to the MAU represents the star portion of the topology; however, a logical continuous ring is actually created when using MAUs and the token ring cabling system. Figure 6 shows only the physical connections even though a token is passed into and back out of each MAU port that has a device connected to it in a continuous loop, which forms the logical ring.

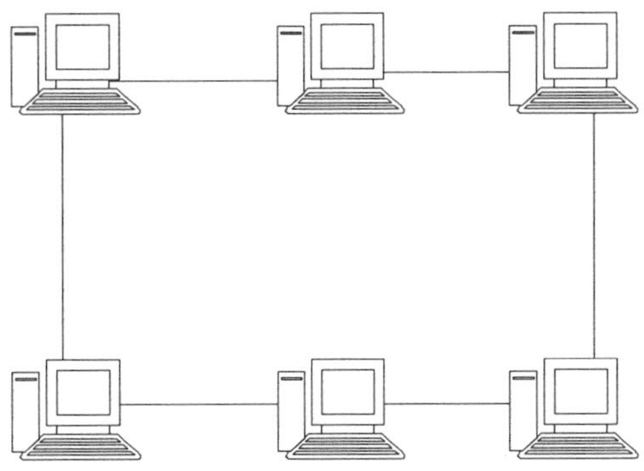

Figure 5: Ring topology.

Each topology has its advantages and disadvantages. For example, the bus topology has the advantage of low cost because it does not require any special devices to connect computers. A disadvantage, however, is that if there is a break in any of the cables, the entire network segment will go down because of a loss of termination. On the other hand, computers connected to a star topology would most likely remain operating on the network if one of the cables malfunctioned between a device and a hub. Star topology requires more wire than a bus topology, and it also requires hubs or switches, which is more costly. Ring topology has an advantage over bus and star topologies because it typically provides an alternate path for data transmission in case of a cable break. For instance, a star-wired ring topology provides a logical continuous ring that provides a redundant path if a cable was cut.

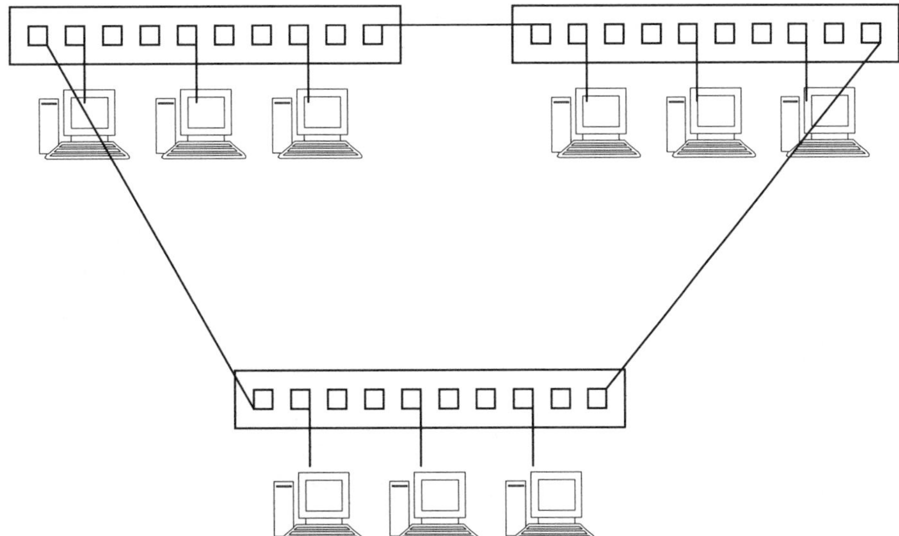

Figure 6: Star-wired ring.

The purpose of this section on network transmission basics is to help you understand the concepts and characteristics related to conducted transmission cable. Each media type differs in physical and electrical–optical characteristics, as well as in application. The following section discusses the three major types of conducted transmission cable: coaxial, twisted-pair, and fiber optic.

COAXIAL CABLE

Coaxial (coax) cable is used in a wide range of applications, including television, radio, and computer network communications. This section looks at the physical makeup of coaxial cable and the specific characteristics that distinguish the different types of coax.

Components

Coaxial cable consists of an inner and outer conductor that share the same axis, which is how it got its name, coaxial (Carr, 1999). The inner conductor, sometimes called the conducting core, is typically made of a copper alloy. Most applications use a solid core, except where flexibility is required, and then a stranded core may be used. The outer conductor is either braided metal or foil, which acts as a conductor and a shield to reduce interference. An insulator, or, more accurately, a dielectric, is between the two conductors. Depending on the type of coax, this material is made out of Teflon or an inert gas. Finally, for protection, there is an outer sheath that surrounds the inner components. This is made from PVC (polyvinyl chloride), or special fire-retardant material, for installations where wire must be run in the plenum areas above the false ceilings in a building (Carr, 1999; Tittle & Johnson, 2001).

Coaxial cables come in a variety of forms: flexible, helical line, and hard line. Flexible coax is made of flexible material in the outer conductor, typically braid or foil. This cable is mostly found in LANs and home television-to-antenna connections. Helical line coax is a semiflexible cable that consists of a slightly more rigid, spiral-wound outer conductor. Normally, this type of cable is used for network backbones or interconnections between networks that require long cable runs. This type of cable is able to carry a signal over longer distances at higher frequencies than can flexible cable types. Hard-line coaxial cable is used to connect equipment that transmits in the microwave frequency range. This form of coax uses a thin-walled pipe as an outer conductor, which is rigid and difficult to work with. As the frequency of a transmitted signal increases, there is a greater chance of the signal radiating beyond the outer conductor, which also acts as a shield, thus resulting in signal loss, or in the case of external electromagnetic interference, the type of outer conductor will determine which frequencies will be rejected from the transmitted signal (Carr, 1999).

Another characteristic of coaxial cable is its impedance. Impedance is the resistance of a cable to the transmitted signal, which is measured in ohms (Tittle & Johnson, 2001). Carr (1999) stated that the lowest loss of signal occurs at higher impedances; however, more power can be achieved when the impedance is low. Cable television uses coaxial cable rated at 75-ohm impedance because of its lower signal attenuation with long cable runs. Most network and radio applications use 50-ohm impedance as a middle ground between low signal loss and more power.

Cable manufacturers use a radio government (RG) specification for the coaxial cables they produce. Cable television uses RG-6, RG-11, or RG-59 spec cable. All of these are rated at 75 ohms. RG-6 and RG-11 are larger diameter cables used for major trunk lines. RG-59 is employed between the trunk lines and the customer's television.

RG-58 and RG-8 are 50-ohm cables used for computer network communications. As does cable television, computer networks use trunk lines to connect network segments together. RG-8 is the cable used for trunk lines or network backbones and is often referred to as thick-wire Ethernet, or thicknet for short. RG-58 is used with thin-wire Ethernet, or thinnet, to interconnect smaller segments of the network (Tittel & Johnson, 2001).

Coaxial Cable Network Applications

Thick-Wire Ethernet

Thicknet (RG-8) is typically used as an Ethernet backbone to connect various network segments together. Thicknet can be used to directly interconnect devices on the network, but usually thinnet is used for this purpose. Thicknet uses the bus topology with the CSMA-CD cable access method. Normally it is used as a network backbone, which consists of a length of RG-8 cable with network devices, such as hubs, connected to it. Each device connected to the backbone requires a special device called a transceiver. The transceiver is connected to the coax by use of a vampire tap (seeFigure 7). A special cable then attaches the transceiver to the device through its AUI (attachment unit interface) port (seeFigure 8).

Each conducted transmission cable exhibits certain standardized characteristics that describe its advantages and disadvantages within network applications.Table 1 describes thick-wire Ethernet characteristics. Each cable type reviewed contains similar specifications. The reason there is a maximum length is because of attenuation, which is the reduction in signal strength that occurs as cable lengths increase. At some point, the signal loss becomes excessive and causes the network to stop functioning. As with this and other wire specifications,

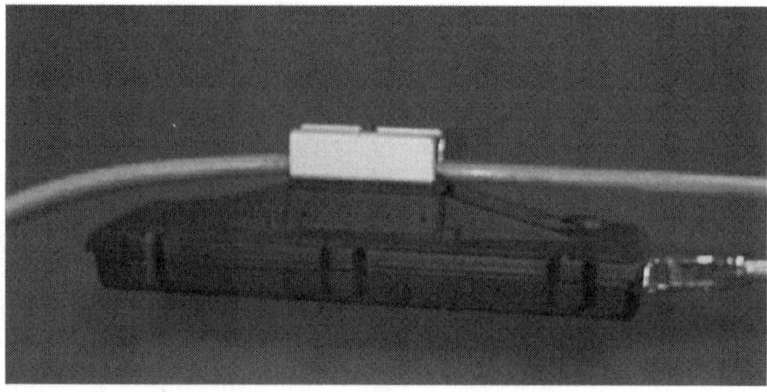

Figure 7: Thick-wire coax attached to transceiver via vampire tap.

Figure 8: AUX (attachment unit interface) cable connected to a transceiver.

cable manufacturers rely on IEEE (Institute of Electrical and Electronics Engineers) standards when producing their products. The Ethernet standards for thicknet and thinnet are covered in the IEEE 802.3 specification (Tittel & Johnson, 2001).

Table 1 shows a total network cable length of 2,500 m, which is based on the 5-4-3 rule. This rule states that each network cannot exceed a total of five cable segments connected by four repeaters, with not more than three of the segments populated by nodes (seeFigure 9).

Figure 9 shows five complete cable segments. Each segment is connected to a device called a repeater. A repeater is used to compensate for the attenuation caused by cable lengths that exceed 500 m for thicknet. Its function is to amplify and repeat what it receives so that its signal will be strong enough to reach another repeater or the end of the next cable segment. Note that two segments do not have any network devices connected to them. This implies that only three of the five segments may have network devices attached. Tittel and Johnson (2001) stated that in reality what this means is that any two network devices cannot be separated by more than four repeaters (five segments) with three populated segments. So the 5-4-3 rule does not say a network is limited to only five segments. It states only that network devices cannot communicate with each other if they are separated by more than five segments.

The AUX or drop cable length refers to the cable that attaches to the transceiver unit connected via the vampire tap to the thick-wire Ethernet backbone. This type of connection is used to connect such devices as repeaters or hubs to the Ethernet backbone. The AUX cable must be fewer than 50 m long.

Table 1 shows a maximum of 100 devices per segment for thick-wire Ethernet. Every time a device is attached to an Ethernet backbone, there will be some signal loss. Any device attached beyond the limit is not guaranteed to function properly. When designing a network, these limits should not be pushed. If a segment is fully populated, there is no room for expanding your network without adding another segment, assuming that the network is not already comprised of the maximum allowable five segments.

Some IEEE specifications, such as bandwidth, are preset and cannot be altered. If the network bandwidth will not support the needs of the network, a different protocol or standard will need to be used. The bandwidth specification of 10 Mbps for thick-wire Ethernet describes how much data can be transmitted, which ultimately determines the speed of communications. As with all bus topologies using coax, a terminator is required at both ends of the bus to eliminate signal bounce. Because thicknet coaxial cable is designed for 50-ohm impedance, a 50-ohm terminator is required. A terminator is simply a connector that has been retrofitted with a 50-ohm resistor between the inner and outer conductors.

Table 1 Thick-Wire Ethernet Specifications

Characteristic	Specification
Maximum cable segment length	500 m
Maximum total network length	2,500 m
AUX (drop cable length)	50 m
Maximum number of devices per segment	100
Maximum number of segments	Five connected by four repeaters, with not more than three populated segments
Bandwidth	10 Mbps (megabits per second)
Termination	50 Ohms
Cable Access Method	CSMA-CD

AUI = attachment unit interface.

Thinwire Ethernet

Networks can be quickly set up using little more than RG-58 cable and a few connectors. Thin-wire cable is commonly used to interconnect computers or other network devices on a network segment using the bus topology. In the past, thinnet was one of the most popular transmission cables for Ethernet networks because of its low cost and ease of setup.

Thinnet cable uses a special connector, called a BNC (British naval connector or bayonet nut connector) connector (seeFigure 10). Computers and other network devices are connected to the bus topology by way of a BNC T-connector (see Figure 3), which connects to the NIC. The NIC is a transceiver that provides the physical connection between the network device and the transmission media. In addition, the NIC is responsible for packaging the data coming from the network device into a form acceptable to the network cable.

As with thicknet, thinnet follows the IEEE 802.3 standard with regard to the use of RG-58 coaxial cable. Table 2 summarizesthese cable specifications. You will notice that thinnet characteristics are similar to thicknet except in cable lengths and number of devices per segment. Also, there is no specification for a drop cable for thin-wire Ethernet because the NIC card serves the same function as the external transceiver used by thicknet (Tittel & Johnson, 2001).

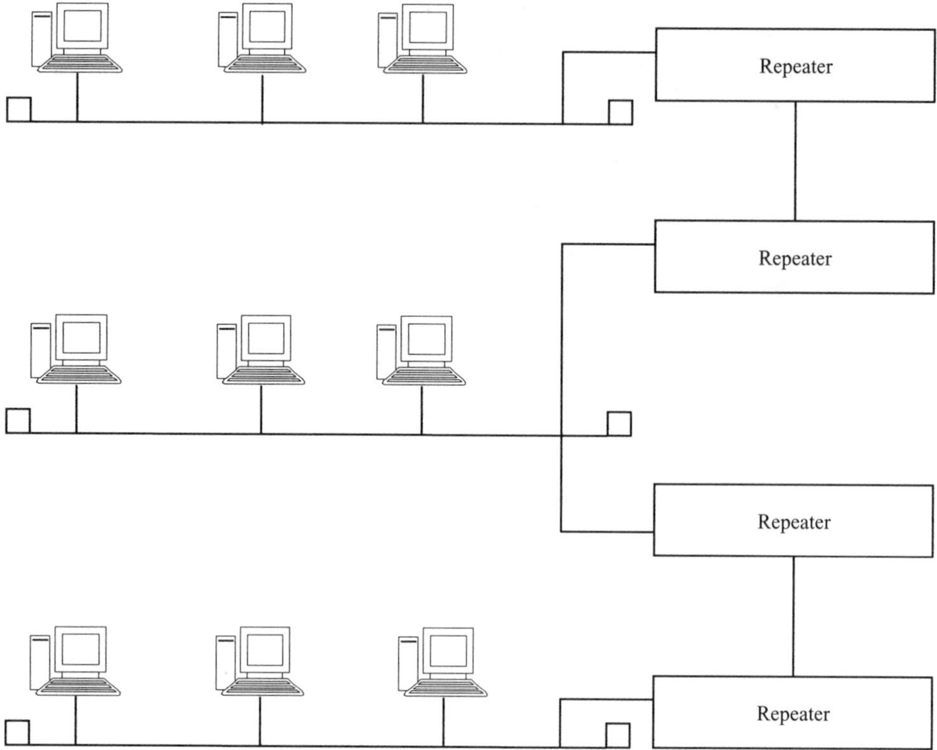

Figure 9: 5-4-3 rule diagram.

The physical characteristics of thin-wire coax attenuate signals over shorter distances than does thick wire. This is typically not an issue because thinnet is normally used to interconnect computers within a relatively small area. In situations where computers need to be separated by more than 185 m, a repeater can be used to accommodate these devices. The low cost of this wire often outweighs the distance limitations.

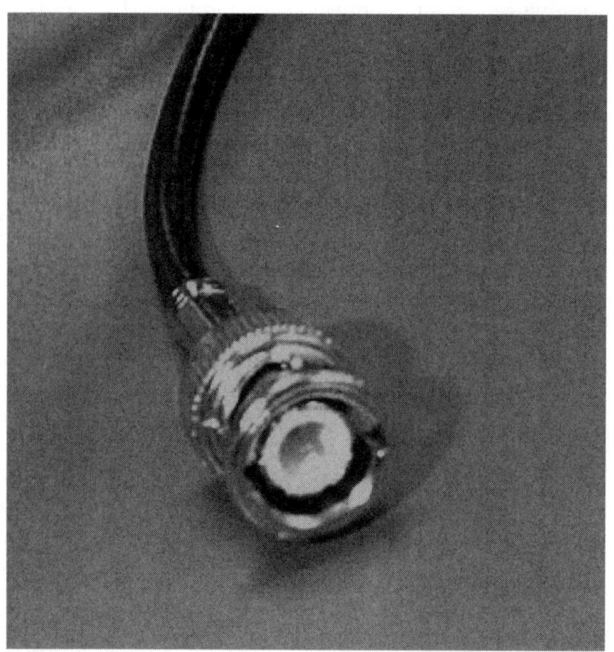

Figure 10: British naval or bayonet nut connector (BNC).

The number of devices that can be attached to a thinnet bus topology is 30. This is fewer than can be attached to thicknet because of the reasons noted in the previous paragraph for cable length. Be aware that a network can have more than one segment. With repeaters, thin-wire Ethernet can support multiple populated segments. The 802.3 standard specifies a maximum of 1,024 devices per network as long as the 5-4-3 rule is followed (Tittel & Johnson, 2001).

In addition to network protocol standards for Ethernet and token ring, IEEE references cable-type standards such as 10Base5 and 10Base2 for thick wire and thin wire,

Table 2 Thin-Wire Ethernet Specifications

Characteristic	Specification
Maximum cable segment length	185 m
Maximum total network length	925 m
Maximum number of devices per segment	30
Maximum number of segments	Five connected by four repeaters, with three populated segments
Bandwidth	10 Mbps (megabits per second)
Termination	50 ohms
Cable access method	CSMA-CD

CSMA-CD = carrier sense multiple access with collision detection.

respectively. The number 10 represents the bandwidth of the cable specification. Base refers to a baseband (single-channel) signal type and the last number represents the maximum length of a network segment in meters rounded to the nearest hundred. For example, 10Base5 refers to a coaxial cable that carries a baseband signal transmitted at 10 Mbps with a maximum segment length of 500 m (thicknet). Thinnet is referenced by 10Base2, meaning a baseband signal with a 10-Mbps bandwidth at 200 m, approximately. In reality, thin-wire Ethernet can only support 185-m segments. Twisted-pair and fiber optic cables carry 10BaseT and 10BaseF IEEE cable standards. These are discussed in more detail later.

There are several advantages to using coaxial cables for computer networks. For LANs, RG-58 uses the bus topology, which offers lower cost options and ease of installation. Also, the outer shielding of coax provides moderate protection from interference. 10Base2 applications allow for fairly long cable runs compared with other cables, such as twisted pair. The major drawback of coax is its narrow bandwidth compared with contemporary applications using twisted-pair and fiber optic cable. Plus, thicknet installations can be somewhat difficult and expensive because of the rigidity of the cable, the rather difficult task of installing network connections, and the overall cost of the interface devices.

TWISTED-PAIR CABLE

Twisted-pair cable consists of one or more pairs of twisted wire. Twisted pair has a longer history than coaxial cable, but its usage was restricted to voice only until the 1980s. Omninet or 10Net began to use twisted pair in the early 1980s for PC-based LANs. One of the first PC applications using twisted-pair cable was in 1984, when IBM introduced the token ring network protocol. By the end of the 1980s, Ethernet technology began using twisted pair. Some advantages of twisted-pair over coaxial cable include its light weight and flexibility, and in some cases, existing twisted-pair cables within buildings can be used without having to install new wiring ("Cabling," 1999).

Components

Twisted-pair media come in one of two forms: STP (shielded twisted pair) or UTP (unshielded twisted pair). STP consists of several pairs of twisted wires that are surrounded by a foil shielding and an outer jacket or sheath. The number of wire pairs can vary from either two or four for basic telephone and network applications, to hundreds of pairs for major communication trunk lines. Each wire within the pair consists of a solid or stranded copper center core surrounded by an insulating cover. Stranded wire is typically used where greater flexibility is required.

The reason for the twist in each pair of wire is to reduce crosstalk. When a signal travels down the wire, it produces a magnetic field. If not controlled in some way, this can produce unwanted interference with other pairs of wire within the same cable (crosstalk). The twist in the pairs works to reduce the effects of crosstalk. It also helps to reduce the magnetic field's effect on other pairs. Cables with more twists per foot offer the best performance and are normally more expensive. The foil shielding that surrounds the twisted pairs blocks sources of interference from electronic noise outside of the cable in addition to keeping stray noise from escaping to the outside world. STP is often the choice of transmission media when heavy electrical or electronic equipment exists near cable runs.

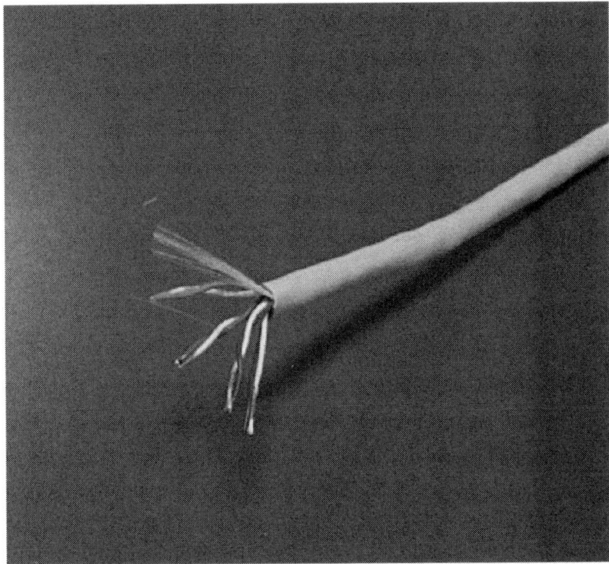

Figure 11: Unshielded twisted pair (UTP) cable.

The outer sheath exists to protect the inner components of the cable. Like many cables, twisted-pair jackets are made of some form of PVC or special plenum sheaths that are used in applications that require nontoxic and fire-resistant cable.

UTP is basically the same as STP except that it does not have a foil shield (seeFigure 11). Without the shield, it is more prone to crosstalk and other forms of interference, although some crosstalk is reduced because of the twists in the pairs of wire.

UTP is probably the most popular cable type for networks today. The Electronic Industries Alliance (EIA) and the Telecommunications Industries Association (TIA), with the endorsement of the American National Standards Institute (ANSI) have defined several categories of UTP cable for different applications ("Cabling," 1999; Fogle, 1995; Tittel & Johnson, 2001). Category 1 is traditionally used for telephone and voice transmissions. Category 2 is capable of data transmissions of up to 4 Mbps. Category 3 is certified for up to 10 Mbps for 10BaseT Ethernet and suitable for 4-Mbps token ring. New technology applications, including 100BaseT4 and 100Base-VG AnyLAN, can utilize this lower rated cable for 100-Mbps bandwidth. Category 4 can handle up to 16 Mbps, which includes token ring 16 Mbps and 10-Mbps Ethernet applications. Category 5 cable type supports bandwidths of up to 100 Mbps. Category 5E cable has been tested up to 400 MHz and supports 1,000 Mbps under the 1000BaseT (gigabit Ethernet) standard. The Category 5E cable is the cable of choice today because of its enhanced features and has taken the lead in twisted pair applications. Categories 6 and 7 are newly developed or in the development stage. These cables will basically support

Figure 12: RJ-45 connector.

higher bandwidths, further reductions in crosstalk, and increase stability at frequencies above 500 MHz (Global Technologies, 2002).

Twisted-Pair Cable Network Applications

Twisted-pair cable uses a special modular connector. Standard telephone wire uses a four-connection plug called an RJ-11. For network applications, an eight-connector RJ-45 is used (seeFigure 12). UTP cables often consist of a solid core with a thin layer of insulation. The installation of RJ-45 connectors, called insulation displacement connectors (IDCs), requires a special tool that pushes the insulated wire into the connector. When each wire is pushed into the connector, the insulation is sliced just enough to make contact with the center core of the wire (Spurgeon, 2000).

Twisted-pair cable is typically used for point-to-point wiring, such as with star topology configurations. UTP is connected to a network device via a NIC card's RJ-45 jack (seeFigure 13), with the other end connected to a hub, switch, or router. In some cases, a patch panel or punch-down block may be used to better organize cabling before it is attached to the devices.

There are several IEEE Ethernet standards for twisted-pair media. The most documented are the 10BaseT, 100BaseT, and 1000BaseT standards (seeTable 3). All twisted-pair Ethernet standards require a maximum cable length of 100 m and use star topology, which allows only one network connection for each cable segment. You

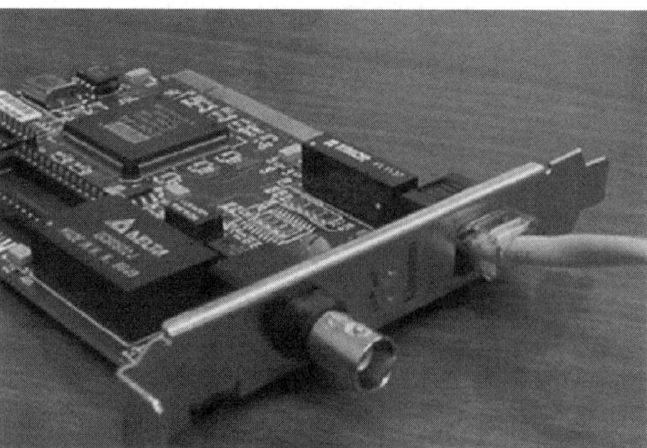

Figure 13: RJ-45 connection to a network interface card.

Table 3 Ethernet Twisted-Pair Cable Specifications

Characteristic	Specification
Maximum cable segment length	100 m
Maximum number of devices per segment	1
Bandwidth	
10BaseT	10 Mbps
100BaseT4, 100BaseTX	100 Mbps
1000BaseT	1,000 Mbps
Topology	Star
Cable access method	CSMA-CD

CSMA-CD = carrier sense multiple access with collision detection.

may note that this is considerably less than the coaxial cable specifications. It is much more difficult to control high-frequency signals over twisted pair; thus, shorter cable runs are used to cut down on the effects of a harsher electrical environment (Spurgeon, 2000). The major differences between 10BaseT, 100BaseT, and 1000BaseT are their bandwidths: 10, 100, and 1,000 Mbps, respectively.

Each IEEE specification describes which wire type is most suitable for a particular application. Category 3 cable is adequate for 10BaseT applications. In fact, only two of the four pairs of wire are actually used. The 100BaseT standard is a bit more complicated. There are three cable configurations for the 100BaseT standard: 100BaseT4, 100BaseTX, and 100BaseFX. 100BaseT4 can produce 100-Mbps bandwidth using all four pairs of category 3, 4, and 5 cables. With 100BaseTX, only two pairs of category 5 or 5E cable are used to transmit and receive at 100 Mbps. 100BaseFX is the fiber optic extension for 100BaseT. 100BaseT is often referred to as fast Ethernet.

One of the newest technologies, gigabit Ethernet, transmits 250 Mbps over each of the four pairs of category 5E wire simultaneously for a total bandwidth of 1 Gbps. Gigabit Ethernet is ideal for network backbones that connect network switches and hubs together. Many are now talking about 10 Gigabit Ethernet, which is in its early stages development and implementation. Currently the IEEE specification for 10-Gigabit Ethernet is for the use of fiber optic cable, but development for a copper based standard is underway and predicted to be completed within the next few years. Once a twisted pair specification comes for fruition, the cost for this super high speed Ethernet standard will be greatly reduced (10 Gigabit Ethernet Alliance, 1999, 2002; Tittel & Johnson, 2001; Violino, 2003).

Ethernet standards for UTP follow TIA/EIA 568 standards. Wire pairs within a particular category of cable are color coded. The preferred 568 standard dictates that wire pairs will consist of a green wire paired with a white wire with a green stripe, an orange wire paired with a white wire with an orange stripe, a blue wire paired with a white wire with a blue stripe, and a brown wire paired with a white wire with a brown stripe. Each pair will be attached to a specific connection on the RJ-45 connector (seeFigure 14). Tip and ring are used to identify the connections made by each pair. These terms come from the old telephone systems, which required a patch cable to connect one telephone line to another. The connector on the patch

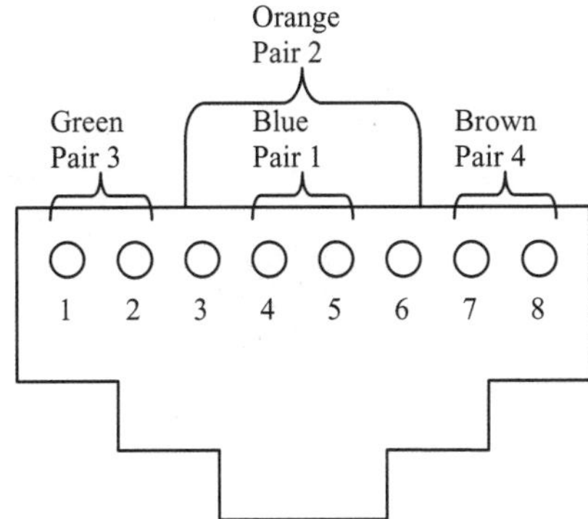

Figure 14: T568A wiring scheme.

cable consisted of a tip at the end and a ring separated by an insulator that separated the two conductors. These two conductors provided the path for transmitting or receiving communications. Traditional analog telephone lines require only one pair for operation. Network transmissions typically require two or four pairs. Note the earlier discussion regarding the required pairs for each of the Ethernet standards 10BaseT, 100BaseT, and 1000BaseT (Spurgeon, 2000).

The majority of network device connections using UTP use straight-through wiring, which means that both ends of the RJ-45 connector are wired exactly the same way. Each pair of cables either transmits or receives data. Likewise, each NIC card transmits data through certain connections and receives through others via its RJ-45 port. If a straight cable was connected to two NIC ports, the result would be that the transmit connections of both ports would be connected to each other, as would the receive links. It should be apparent that when one NIC card transmitted, the other would not receive it because of the direct connections between the ports. Therefore, there must be some kind of crossover that makes a connection between the transmit and the receive pairs. In reality, most network connections between devices are made via hubs or switches. These devices provide the crossover for the transmit and receive pairs.

For some applications, a special cable called a crossover cable is required. A crossover cable is made by crossing pairs two and three on the opposite end of the connecting cable. This allows you to connect two network devices together independently without using a hub or other central wiring point. For example, if you had a small office with two computers that you wanted to network, you could build or buy a crossover cable and connect the NICs from both computers together to form a small network without the expense of a hub. Crossover cables are also used to connect hubs or switches together if they are not supplied with an uplink port. Uplink ports are optional ports that take care of uncrossing the links between these centralized wiring points.

In comparison, there are several advantages and disadvantages to twisted-pair and coaxial cabling. Coax appears to have the distance contest won; however, it is waning with regard to the bandwidth race. During the mid-to-late 1980s, coax was the wire of choice, but now twisted-pair seems to be the predominate cable used for most LAN interconnections. Twisted-pair cable offers great flexibility within network design and layout. Even though maximum cable runs are shorter than coax, 100 m is still a significant distance for most network connections. With applications being developed to use the newest categories of UTP, Categories 6 and 7, the potential advances for twisted-pair cable are encouraging with regard to increased bandwidth and expanded connection options.

Token Ring Cabling

In the mid-1980s, IBM developed the token ring architecture that used a special type of twisted-pair wiring. IBM engineered a cabling system that included nine cable types, numbered from one to nine. These cable types included STP, UTP, and fiber optic mediums. For token ring networks, types 1 (STP) and 3 (UTP) were the most prevalent. Type 1 cable allowed for lengths of up to 101 m, with a maximum bandwidth of 16 Mbps. Because of its lack of shielding, type 3 cable runs were limited to 45 m and a bandwidth of 4 Mbps (Tittel & Johnson, 2001). Today, most token ring applications use UTP category 3 or 5 cable with RJ-45 connectors. As noted inTable 4, there have been some improvements in cable lengths with the use of this media (Feit, 2000).

The IEEE specification for token ring is 802.5, which describes the bandwidth of 4 or 16 Mbps using the token passing cable access method. In 1999, High-Speed Token Ring (HSTR) introduced an improved bandwidth of 100 Mbps with twisted-pair or fiber optic cable. Token ring uses a star-wired ring topology (see Figure 6). Fault tolerance is probably the biggest advantage the token ring architecture has to offer because of the logical continuous ring that is created when using the IBM cabling system along with the star-wired ring topology that provides a dual path for data transmission. Theoretically, if a cable is cut, the token ring network can continue to operate because of the redundant path. Another plus is the use of the token passing access method, which eliminates collisions (Dean, 2003; Feit, 2000; Tittel & Johnson, 2001).

FIBER OPTIC CABLE

The bandwidth capacities of coax and twisted pair are dwarfed by that of fiber optic cable. Consider that the capacity of a simple telephone line to carry data is equivalent to the flow of liquid through a drinking straw. It would

Table 4 Token Ring Cable Specifications

Characteristic	Specification
Maximum cable segment length	101 m (type 1) 45 m (type 3) 100 m (Cat 3) 225 m (Cat 5) 400 m (STP)
IEEE specification	802.5
Bandwidth	4, 16, or 100 Mbps
Topology	Star-wired ring
Cable access method	Token passing

IEEE = Institute of Electrical and Electronics Engineers.

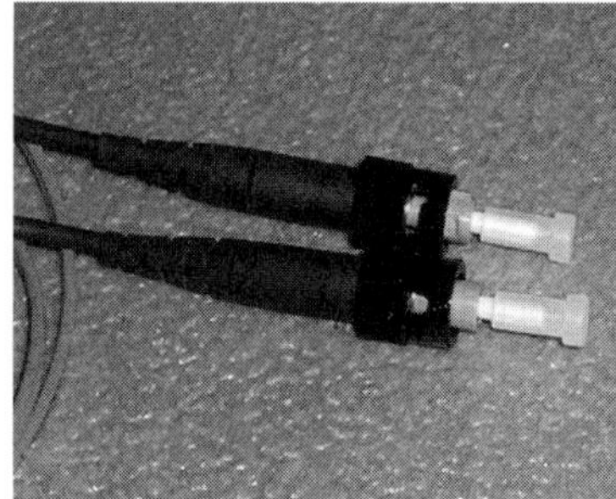
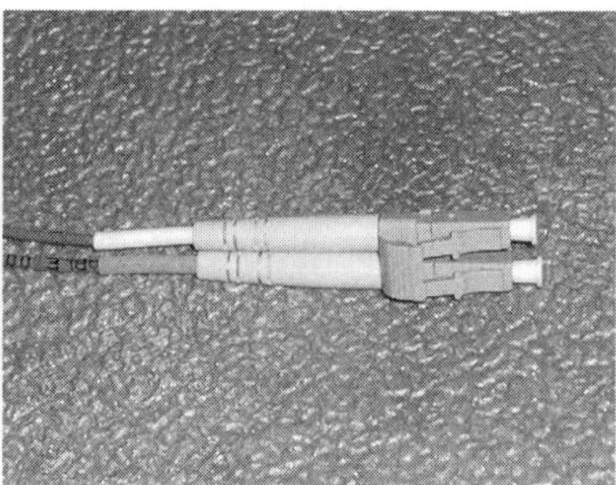
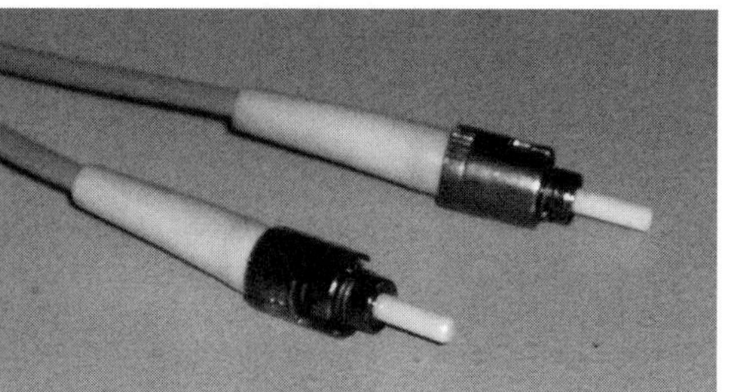

Figure 15: Fiber optic cable with connectors.

take a tunnel large enough to drive a bus through to equal the bandwidth of a single fiber optic strand using today's technologies. Furthermore, if technology existed to fully utilize fiber optic capabilities, it would take a tunnel the diameter of the moon to handle the flow of liquid equal to its potential bandwidth (Jamison, 2001).

Fiber optic cable carries optical pulses rather than electrical signals, which eliminates any possible electrical interference. All types of conducted communication media are vulnerable to electronic eavesdropping to some degree, but fiber optic cable is less prone to eavesdropping because its signal does not radiate outside of the media like copper-based wire. Therefore, the only way to intercept data from fiber optic cable would be to tap into it, which would require a great deal of effort and skill.

Fiber optic cable lengths are measured in kilometers rather than meters, which greatly reduces the number of signal repeating devices required for long-distance cable runs. One of the most impressive characteristics is the high volumes of data that can be pumped through optical fibers. All this makes fiber optic cable the medium of choice for many WAN applications, where network traffic can cause major bottlenecks (Tittel & Johnson, 2001). In addition, many people believe that fiber optic cables may become the norm rather than the exception for interconnecting network devices on a LAN (Kostal, 2001; Sinks & Balch, 2001; Vickers, 2001).

Components

Fiber optic cable consists of three components: a fiber core, cladding, and a protective outer sheath. The inner core is either glass or plastic fiber. Plastic is used when a flexible cable is needed; however, plastic cable is more susceptible to attenuation than glass, which limits the length of the cable. Cladding provides a coating that keeps the light waves within the fiber. The outer protective jacket is used to protect the fiber inside (Tittel & Johnson, 2001).

Fiber Modes

Fiber optic cable comes in two forms, single and multiple mode. Single-mode fiber is best for applications that require great distances. This fiber is very narrow and requires an extremely focused source of data transmission that can keep the light waves on a straight, continuous path. The narrow internal core makes room for one-way traffic only. This reduces obstacles (stray light) that might interfere with the delivery of packets, resulting in more reliable transmissions over longer distances. A laser is normally used as the generating source for single-mode transmissions because it can produce the narrow band of light needed (Jamison, 2001).

Multimode fiber (MMF) is less expensive than single-mode because its transmission devices consist of LEDs (light emitting diodes), which are not as costly as laser sources. MMF fibers also have a larger core than single mode. A wider core helps to compensate for information loss due to light dispersion when using less precise light-emitting sources. A larger core allows the light wave to bounce around, which results in shorter transmission distances. The connections to the fiber are easier to make to the larger core, however. MMF is ideal for shorter cable runs within single buildings for LAN backbones (Jamison, 2001).

Fiber Optic Cable Network Applications

There are four major types of fiber connectors: straight (ST), straight connection (SC), medium interface connector (MIC), and subminiature type A (SMA) (seeFigure 15). ST is often used for interconnections between individual fibers and optical devices. When joining optical fibers, an SC connector may be used. This connector consists of connections for two fibers: one for receiving and the other for sending. MIC connectors are one-piece connectors similar to the SC used to connect both the transmit and the receive fibers. It is primarily used with the fiber distributed data interface (FDDI) protocol. As with the ST connector, SMA uses individual connectors for each fiber. The major difference is that SMA uses either a straight or a stepped ferrule to ensure a precise fit, whereas the ST connector uses a bayonet twist-lock connection (Tittel & Johnson, 2001).

The major differences between fiber optic and other cable types are fiber optics' long-distance cable runs and high bandwidth. For example, the maximum fiber length for the 100BaseFX Ethernet standard is 2,000 m and the bandwidth for 1000baseSX tops out at 2,000 Mbps. These specifications easily exceed other cable specifications. The potential of fiber optic cable is limited by the technology that exists today. As the cost of fiber declines and the advances in transmission devices continue to improve, the use and performance of fiber will continue to grow.

In some applications, fiber optic is not needed for its high bandwidth, but to facilitate long cable lengths or to block unwanted electrical interference. For example, the 100BaseFX specification supports the use of fiber optic cable. With the exception of distance, the other

Table 5 Fiber Optic Cable Specifications

Characteristic	Specification
Maximum cable segment length	2,000 m
IEEE specification	802.3
Bandwidth	100 Mbps
Topology	Star
Cable access method	CSMA/CD

CSMA-CD = carrier sense multiple access with collision detection; IEEE = Institute of Electrical and Electronics Engineers.

specifications for 100BaseFX are essentially the same as that described for UTP cabling (seeTable 5). Token ring also has a cable specification for the use of fiber optic for connecting its MAUs. Again, this does not fully utilize fiber optic's full bandwidth potential, but it allows for longer cable runs.

Fiber optic applications do not stop at 100 Mbps. Gigabit Ethernet, 1000BaseLX and 1000BaseSX, each sport bandwidths of 1,000 Mbps. The major difference in these two standards is the type of laser used. 1000BaseLX uses a long-wavelength laser that can transmit a signal over 5,000 m of fiber in full-duplex mode. A short-wavelength laser is used in 1000BaseSX applications, which support a maximum cable length of 550 m and 2,000 Mbps bandwidth in full-duplex mode. Still in its early stages, 10-gigabit Ethernet is sure to accelerate the use of fiber optic cable into the future (10 Gigabit Ethernet Alliance, 2002; Tittel & Johnson, 2001).

The only thing holding fiber optic transmission rates at bay is the devices used to drive the signals through the fibers. As noted at the beginning of this section, the potential of fiber optic media is truly enormous. Currently, the primary application for fiber optic cabling is for long connections and network backbones. There are some limited applications of direct connections between individual computers and hubs, but many people feel that this will increase over time as equipment and installation costs continue to decrease.

COMPARISONS AND CONTRASTS

When comparing and contrasting the advantages and disadvantages of the various types of cables, you must look at the particular application. It may be true that fiber-optic cable has the potential to transmit data at much faster rates than UTP; however, if bandwidth is not an issue, the added complexity involved in installing fiber optic where it is not needed would make it a bad choice. One must look at all the characteristics of the transmission medium before choices are made. In some cases, a network may require a mixture of cables to meet specific needs for data transmission.Table 6 compares and contrasts each cable type discussed in this article, showing more clearly how a particular cable may be applied (Tittel & Johnson, 2001).

MEDIA SECURITY

When designing a network infrastructure, the security of conductive communications media should be a strong consideration in the overall network design. Most common security breaches are the result of someone hacking into an organization's network through security holes in user authentication policies or vulnerabilities in network operating systems from far distances. Security flaws of this order seem to upstage the potential risks associated with the physical security of network devices and cabling, but these risks are not inexistent. For example, a network's infrastructure could be at risk if the physical cable routes are not carefully thought out. The physical path of a cable must be secure to prevent someone from tapping into the network, which would result in an unauthorized connection. Also, connecting devices, such as hubs or switches, placed on the floor or up in a crawl space in a common area of a building may pose a security risk.

As noted earlier, the physical location of the network cabling has the potential of creating a security risk if not protected. Copper cabling, such as coax and twisted-pair, are probably the most vulnerable because of the simplicity of splicing into an exposed cable. Areas of special concern would be the cable routes that run through or above common areas of a building, along with cables that are run outside of the building or underground. In many ways, tapping into a computer network by an unauthorized cable tap may make a network more vulnerable to attacks than from external security threats. If access is gained via a wire tap to the internal network infrastructure, external security measures, such as firewalls, would provide no protection. Also with direct access to the LAN, a person might be able to use eavesdropping or sniffing utilities to access security devices and reconfigure them to allow external access. Once a security device has be reconfigured, sensitive company data, such as loss of product design secrets, customer information, or financial data, might be lost or stolen (Campbell, Calvert, & Boswell, 2003).

Another risk involving communications media security is electronic eavesdropping. Cable that uses a copper-type conductor can be vulnerable because of the electromagnetic emissions that it produces. With the right type of equipment, sensitive network traffic could be intercepted. Twisted-pair cables used in Ethernet applications

Table 6 Comparison of Cable Types

Cable	Bandwidth	Length	Interference	Installation	Cost
Thinwire coax	10 Mbps	185 m	Moderate	Easy	Low
Thickwire coax	10 Mbps	500 m	Low	Hard	High
UTP	100 Mbps	100 m	High	Easy	Low
STP	1,000 Mbps	100 m	Moderate	Moderate	Moderate
Fiber optic	10 Gbps	100 km	None	Hard	Expensive

are most likely targets for electronic eavesdropping because most of these cables are not shielded. This type of threat is often hard to combat if a network is constructed using nonshielded wire.

Once the potential physical security threats have been identified, it is fairly simple to eliminate many of these concerns. With regard to wiretaps, network designs should make sure that all cable runs are not exposed to unsecured areas or in the case where cables have to be routed in public areas or outside of buildings, copper-based media should be replaced with fiber optic cable, which is difficult to tap. Several options of protection are available for electronic eavesdropping. One is to reduce electromagnetic emissions by using a shielded twisted-pair cable. Another, expensive, option would be to replace copper-type transmission media with fiber optic cables, which would eliminate any possible electronic emissions. Of course it would be very expensive to use fiber throughout an entire network. A final alternative, which is orthogonal to transmission media decisions, would be to encrypt any sensitive company information before it is transmitted over the communication lines (Campbell et al., 2003).

Threats to a network's physical transmission media is real and needs to be considered in all infrastructure designs. In most cases, it is not expensive for an organization to protect its network from wiretaps and eavesdropping. Business and industry need to consider the possible holes in physical security and plan cable runs and use cable types that will reduce or eliminate the possible risks to the internal network. In addition, using encryption for sensitive data transmissions should protect against any breach of security with regards to electronic eavesdropping.

CONCLUSION

Conductive transmission cables provide the highway for data communications. This chapter has discussed the most popular types of cable in use today. As times change, the applications and uses for these various cable types will change. Some limiting factors for conductive transmission media are cable attenuation and the devices that drive the information through them such as NICs, hubs, and switches. We saw that bandwidths for twisted-pair cable have increased from around 1 to 1,000 Mbps. Transmission speeds over fiber optic cable are only now being realized. What are the limits? What does the future hold for conductive transmission cables? How do wireless technologies fit into network communications? No one knows the answers to these questions, but at least the questions are being asked, so researchers can continue to experiment and produce new applications for all transmission options.

GLOSSARY

Bandwidth The maximum range of frequencies a communications medium can carry.

Baseband A digital transmission signal that uses a single channel to communicate with devices on a network.

Broadband An analog transmission that carries multiple digital signals over multiple channels.

Crosstalk An electromagnetic field surrounding certain types of cable that may interfere with adjacent wires.

Hub A central wiring point for network devices configured in a star topology. Its purpose is to repeat the broadcast packets to all connected nodes.

Impedance The resistance of conducted communications media to a transmitted signal.

Insertion Loss The loss or attenuation of a signal that occurs each time a device is inserted into a network using conductive communications media.

Local Area Network (LAN) A collection of computers connected to a network within a single floor, or building.

Network Interface Card (NIC) An electronic device that is installed in a network node that provides a link to the network media.

Node Any device connected directly to a network.

Packet An entity that contains data plus other information, such as destination, origination, and error-checking bits and is transmitted over a network.

Protocol A set of rules that specify how communicating entities will format data and process events.

Signal Attenuation The loss of signal strength as data travel the length of the cable that is caused by the cable, connectors, or other devices on the conducted communication media.

Terminator A device attached to a cable configured with a bus topology that eliminates signal bounce.

Topology The physical cabling configuration of a network.

CROSS REFERENCES

See *Local Area Networks; Public Network Technologies and Security; Radio Frequency and Wireless Communications Security; Security in Circuit, Message, and Packet Switching; TCP/IP Suite; Wide Area and Metropolitan Area Networks; Wireless Channels*.

REFERENCES

Cabling. (1999). *Network Magazine.* Retrieved April 2, 2002, from http://www.networkmagazine.com/article/NMG20000724s0010.

Campbell, P., Calvert, B., & Boswell, S. (2003). *Security+ Guide to network security fundamentals.* Toronto: Course Technology.

Carr, J. J. (1999). Coax 'n' stuff. *Popular Electronics, 16* (9), 77–79.

Dean, T. (2003). *Enhanced networking+ guide to networks.* Toronto: Course Technology.

Feit, S. (2000). *Local area high speed networks.* Upper Saddle River, NJ: New Riders.

Fogle, D. (1995). Lay of the LAN—Cabling Basics

Global Technologies. (2002). Retrieved April 15, 2002, from http://www.globaltec.com/catext100.html

Jamison, E. (2001). Finding out about fiber. *Poptronics, 2*(11), 21–23.

Kostal, H. (2001). Switching to all-optical networks. *Lightwave, 18*(13), 106–108.

Network Magazine. April 1, 1995. Retrieved March 21, 2005, from http://www.networkmagazine.com/showArticle.jhtml?articleID=8702649

Sinks, C., & Balch, J. (2001). Fiber snakes its way closer to the desk. *Lightwave, 18*(11), 86–88.

Spurgeon, C. E. (2000). *Ethernet: The definitive guide*. Cambridge, MA: O'Reilly.

10 Gigabit Ethernet Alliance. (1999). Gigabit Ethernet: Accelerating the standard for speed. Gigabit Ethernet Alliance white paper.

10 Gigabit Ethernet Alliance. (2002). 10 Gigabit Ethernet technology overview white paper. http://www.intel.com/network/connectivity/resources/doc_library/white_papers/pro10gbe_lr_sa_wp. pdf (Date of access: April 6, 2005).

Tittel, E., & Johnson, D. (2001). *Guide to networking essentials*. Toronto: Course Technology.

Vickers, L. (2001). Emerging technology: Is fiber optic destined for the desktop. In *Network Magazine*. Retrieved April 2, 2002, from http://www. networkmagazine.com/article/NMG20010103S0004

Violino, B. (2003). Cutting 10G costs with copper. *Network World Fusion*. Retrieved from January 28, 2004, from http://www.nwfusion.com/research/2003/092210gcopper.html

Routers and Switches

Hans-Peter Dommel, *Santa Clara University*

INTRODUCTION

Communication networks are systems in hardware and software to facilitate information exchange in a broader arrangement than a single point-to-point link. The telephone network is the most familiar and ubiquitous communication network, designed primarily for voice transmission. A computer network is a communication infrastructure between computing devices in different locations to enable digital information exchange and sharing of resources such as messages, software, compute time, storage space, or peripherals. Finding efficient ways to share communication links is one of the main problems in designing networks. Network design traditionally seeks to optimize several criteria at the same time: minimizing the cost of deployment; maximizing the aggregate bandwidth between two end-points; avoiding "hot spots" where a small number of network nodes and links handle a large percentage of the total traffic; minimizing the latency between any sender and receiver, and maximizing scalability, that is, performance should scale with the number of nodes in the network.

Routers and switches are the key devices in meeting these demands and are traditionally attributed to Layer 2 and 3 in the 7-layer OSI model and the 5-layer TCP/IP protocol stack, with the latter shown in Figure 1 together with respective processing units. Routers process packets, whereas Layer-2 switches operate with frames. Layers indicate which device uses specific header information pieces to decide how to process and forward a message with the goal to cooperatively move frames and packets from one network segment to another to ultimately reach the designated receiver.

Today's routing and switching technology is a legacy from the early packet switching networks created for the ARPANET in the 1970s. With increasing Internet population and complexity of service provision, infrastructure security for more dependable communication is a major concern. A plethora of new services creates new loopholes for compromising the security of a computer network and requires steady countermeasure investigation and innovation. This article describes the working principles of routers and switches, their prominent security vulnerabilities, and suggests some best practices for router and switch security.

Principles of Routing and Switching

Although the various types of digital communication networks differ in how they are used and transmit information, they have routers and switches as architectural components in common. Routing is provided in a layer above switching and concerned with establishing an optimal communication path. Routing may also take quality-of-service concerns into account (Shenker, 1995). In the Internet, many protocols work together to accomplish this goal to establish end-to-end connectivity. For interior routing within administratively autonomous domains, protocols such as the routing information protocol (RIP) and open shortest path first (OSPF) are predominant. RIP is used in small to medium-sized networks and is simple to configure but slow in responding to network failures, which in itself can be a threat to network security. OSPF scales well in mid-size to very large networks, but incurs greater messaging and computation overhead. For inter-domain, policy-based routing the exterior path-finding protocol BGP (Border Gateway Protocol) is used as a standard in large routers (Huitema, 2000).

On the other hand, switching is mainly concerned with data relay and the associated policing and output scheduling. Switching is the mechanics of creating a connecting path between input and output in a switching device, with the goal to effectively relay a message from an incoming link to a chosen destination designated by an output port. It has played a vital role in telecommunication networks since first-generation telephone exchanges were installed. Switching technology seeks to maximize capacity for a given cost and reliability, and to minimize blocking and packet loss. With switching, data can be forwarded across dynamically created communication paths, whose sections are multiplexed among various senders and receivers. Switching is performed by telephone circuit switches for voice calls in the public switched telephone network (PSTN), "virtual circuit" switches in asynchronous transfer mode (ATM) networks with fixed-sized cells, or packet switches with variable-sized messages.

Circuit-switching, based on telecommunication services, pre-establishes a path from one end-system to another via a sequence of switches, where device resources are reserved to guarantee a dedicated circuit for the

#	LAYER	DEVICE
5	Application	Application Gateway
4	Transport	Transport Gateway
3	Network	Router, Packet Switch
2	Link	Bridge, Switch
1	Physical	Repeater, Hub

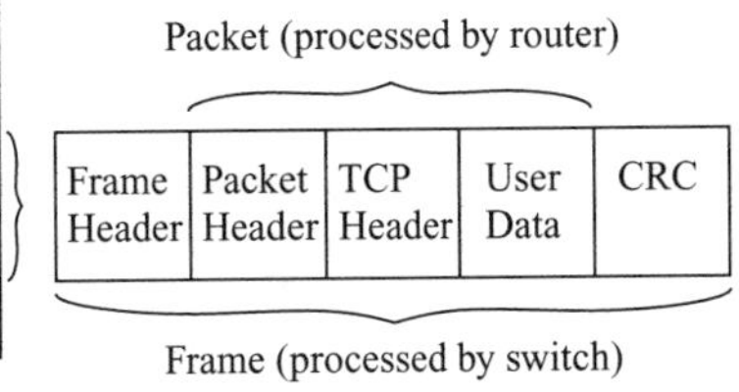

Packet (processed by router)

Frame Header	Packet Header	TCP Header	User Data	CRC

Frame (processed by switch)

Figure 1: Routers and switches in the TCP/IP protocol stack and processing units.

duration of the transmission. A circuit switch must reject a call if it cannot reserve a path from input to output, which is referred to as call blocking. Circuit switching is implemented as connection-oriented service in the public switched telephone network (PSTN), where voice samples are switched from a source to a receiver, or with virtual circuit-switching in ATM networks. Recent progress in peer-to-peer telephony has shown that it is also possible to establish connection-oriented communication in a self-organizing peer-based logical network.

In contrast, device resources are not reserved in packet-switched networks, but shared and utilized on demand by using statistical multiplexing among data packets, which are composed of a header with control information and the payload. Packet switching can be implemented connectionless using the Internet protocol (IP), or in connection-oriented mode using for example ATM. Routers performing connectionless packet switching are also called datagram or packet switches. In connectionless switching, packets are self-contained and independently routed towards a destination, whereas connection-oriented switching associates data to a specific, fixed forwarding path. Table 1 shows networking vs. switching modes with their prototypical implementation (Keshav, 1997). Besides ATM there are other connection-oriented packet switching technologies such as frame relay or X.25.

ROUTERS AND SWITCHES IN A NUTSHELL

How Routers Work

Routers are Layer 3+ devices (the + means that these devices may perform higher-layer routing functions.) A router forwards packets based on IP addresses and routing tables. Routers are available for small and large scale networks, for wired and wireless networks, and for non-optical and optical communication networks. Home networks typically are equipped with DSL or cable modems connected to access network routers. At the network edge we find enterprise wide-area-network (WAN) access switches and edge routers. Backbones use carrier class routers besides ATM switches or frame relay switches. Unlike switches, routers always require some configuration.

Routers pass traffic between two different IP networks which may be either LANs or WANs, forwarding packets on the best-possible path towards a destination, in terms of the number of hops, the cumulative delay, or some other optimization criterion. When a packet arrives at a router, the frame header and trailer are stripped off and the packet contained in the payload field of the frame becomes input for the routing software, which uses the packet header to choose an output line. Packets may be queued in a router until they can be switched through to the appropriate port based on a routing table lookup to find the best-possible path. An IP packet processed by a router will contain a 32-bit (IPv4) or 128-bit (IPv6) address. The routing software is oblivious of the frame address and whether the packet arrived from a LAN or point-to-point link. A router examines the destination IP address of each incoming packet and sends data through an egress port based upon a routing table entry. Routing tables can be manually configured or incrementally learned using discovery procedures in routing protocols. Such routing algorithms are either static or dynamic. Static routing is applicable when network topologies do not change significantly and route calculations can be performed offline. Typically, however, the dynamics of networks (Paxson, 1997) necessitates more sophisticated algorithms to allow routers to adapt to rapidly changing network conditions, where nodes and links can be congested, go down, or come up at any instant. Routers hence store and forward packets with the goal to adaptively optimize path-finding between sources and destinations in dynamic networks. While Internet routers until recently serviced packets in a first-come-first-served "best-effort" manner, differentiated service qualities are now required to cater to application

Table 1 Switching vs. Networking Modes

	Networking Modes	Connectionless	Connection-oriented
Switching modes	Packet Switching	IP	ATM
	Circuit Switching	—	PSTN

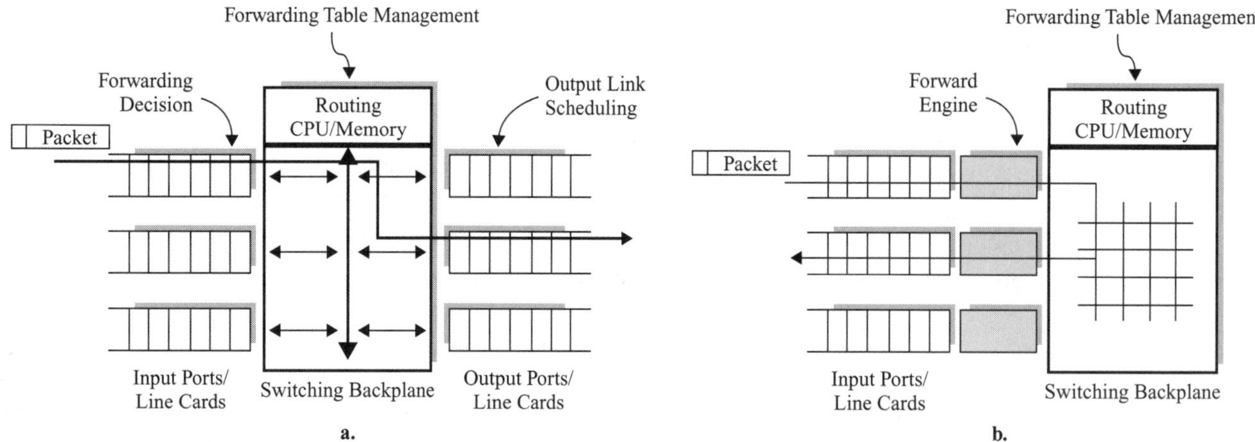

Figure 2: Traditional and Modern Router Design.

specifics, which necessitates that routers support new mechanisms such as admission control, per-flow queuing, resource reservation, and fair scheduling. These mechanisms require routers to use packet classification algorithms to distinguish and isolate traffic in different flows for suitable processing (Gupta and McKeown, 2001).

Router Architecture and Performance

Routers incorporate a hierarchical packet forwarding logic in hardware plus computational capabilities to maintain routing tables. A router consists of a set of input ports, a backplane, and a set of output ports, including a CPU and memory to maintain a routing table for shortest path calculations. In a black box view, a router is a device that switches data packets arriving at an input port to an output port according to a routing criterion and after some queuing delay. From an inside view, data are shifted in traditional design from input ports ideally collision-free through an internal fabric to an output port, as shown in Figure 2a.

In high-performance systems, datapath functions such as forwarding decision making, backplane switching, and output link scheduling are typically implemented in special purpose hardware, while control functions such as routing table exchanges with neighbors or management are software-based. Instead of shared, congested backplanes, modern router design now incorporates switched backplanes, which results in a compact, parallel design with extremely high throughput for both unicast and multicast traffic. Figure 2b depicts the use of more complex hardware on the main datapath and a crossbar design in the backplane to achieve more parallelism for high-speed routers (McKeown, 1997).

The main performance characteristics of a router are the number of ports or links, the throughput possible at each link, the maximum rate of packets that can be switched through, and the delay across the switch. Crucial for the performance of a router are fast table lookups and calculations of routes based on available network topology information (Keshav and Sharma, 1998). A current bare-bones router operates in software only without routing protocols and is simple to configure with built-in NAT. Low-end routers support around 200 Mbps full-duplex with Fast Ethernet and offer simple hardware-based operation, built-in NAT and firewall functionality, but lack fault tolerance. With an increasing number of channels transmitted on a single fiber, routers must scale port densities to handle these channels. Midrange routers add support for virtual LANs (VLANs) and virtual private networks (VPNs) with a broader range of WAN connectivity. High-end routers add component redundancy and resilience, scaling from 2.5 Gbps to 40 Gbps per slot with multi-terabit switching capabilities and several OC-192/STM-64 interfaces. A top-end ISP carrier router offers a theoretical capacity up to 92 Tbps with support for up to over 1000 OC-768c interfaces on the data plane and multimillion packet-per-second performance.

The advent of broadband access for end-users has raised expectations in IP reliability and performance. While earlier switches and routers offered single-purpose functionality, more recent products are convergence devices incorporating several functions in one box. Examples are combined firewall and VPN appliances (Cisco, 2004), wireless broadband routers with print server functionality, routers supporting VoIP and multimedia, or Layer 4+ content routers relaying packets based on URL semantics rather than IP-based semantics. As a result, there is great demand for rich-featured convergence devices used in SOHO and small business networks, and for Gigabit and Terabit (Singhal and Jain, 2002) electronic and optical routers used in backbones. These routers not only forward packets at a rate of billions of packets per second, but also must provide quality guarantees for differentiated services with data, voice, or video; work with a wide variety of interface types; offer scalability in terms of port density and capacity; and offer backward compatibility with various packet formats and routing protocols.

How Switches Work

A switch can be compared to a train station or airport dynamically interconnecting different travel pathways. Switches essentially interlink physical segments of a network and allow data to be exchanged between these segments. On a microscopic scale, the intrinsic design of a switch determines how effective this interlinking of communication paths is performed within each switch stage. On a macroscopic scale, the interlinking of switches in the overall network topology determines the aggregate performance of the network.

Switching functions vary depending on the operational needs of applications and may include higher layer switching functions. A typical switch operates at Layer 2 in the OSI model and TCP/IP stack. It checks address information in link and interface-level headers in hardware, and directs frames to the next hop on the path to some destination host based on data link layer addresses, for example Ethernet MAC addresses. Layer 2 switches are adequate for high-volume traffic generated between local devices, such as workstations and servers. A flat address space in broadcast domains, the possibility of broadcast storms, and the limited number of links supported by a Layer-2 switch led to the development of Layer-3 devices able to optimally route traffic in a hierarchy of nodes. Layer 3 switching is functionally identical to routing and typically added in large switches. Layer 4-7 switches deliver intelligent traffic and bandwidth management based on the application content of a session, not only based on network connections (Srinivasan et al., 1998) and can provide load balancing, denial-of-service attack protection, intelligent application scanning and virtual local area network (VLAN) configuration.

Switches are usually "plug-and-play", which simplifies installation. Switches operate either in store-and-forward or in cut-through mode. A store-and-forward switch accepts a frame on an input line, buffers it briefly in the input port, the fabric or output port, before forwarding it to the next processing stage ready to handle the entire frame. When frames arrive faster than they can be forwarded, buffers overflow and packet loss occurs. In contrast, cut-through switching is based on the idea to start forwarding a frame as soon as its destination header field has arrived, which is usually handled entirely in hardware. It boosts throughput at the possibility of forwarding bad frames, since the cyclic redundancy check (CRC) cannot be checked before transmission. The switching process is executed in hardware at wire-speed with effectively zero latency.

Switches originally linked segments with multiple devices but with dropping switch prices it became normal to attach a single device to each port, which is known as "switched" Ethernet. No packet collisions are possible with only one device per port, which improves network performance by allowing devices to run in full-duplex to achieve maximum throughput.

Depending on the layout of the physical space, multiple smaller switches or a few very large switches may be chosen in the design of a network, which is a matter of manageability, cost, traffic characteristics, and reliability, among other reasons. Figure 3 shows an unsecured sandbox network with switches connecting Ethernet cluster, which are again connected via the root switch R together to access a server farm and linked to a router connecting the intranet with the Internet. By using switches A, B, and C, traffic in leaf subnetworks is localized and degradation in one subnet does not affect the other parts of the network.

In the context of Ethernet LANs, switches are often called bridges, if used to connect multiple Ethernets, and run a spanning tree protocol to form a loop-free forwarding topology to relay traffic between LAN segments. Looping occurs when devices are linked in a way that creates a loop in the topology, for example by linking switches B and C directly (dashed link.) This means that packets could circulate between switch B and C, which can be avoided by forming a spanning tree if bridges are being used instead for B and C. The terms switch and bridge are often used

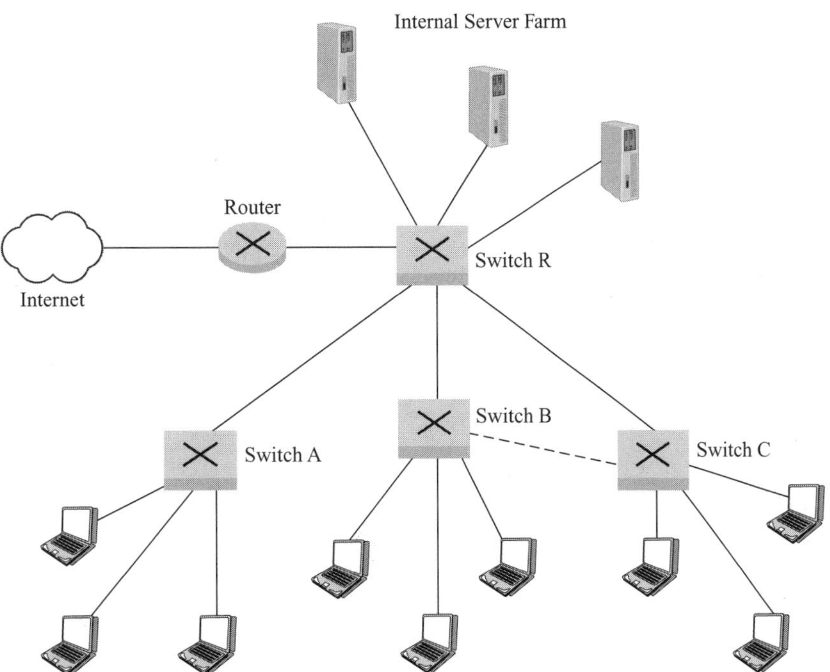

Figure 3: Switching in a LAN environment.

synonymously, because both devices route on frame addresses at Layer 2. While bridges are used to interconnect two or more LANs and perform frame forwarding in software, switches are typically used to connect individual computers, which requires many more line cards with buffer space for frames arriving on switch ports.

Instead of a bridge or switch in a switched Ethernet, devices could also be interlinked via a hub in a "shared Ethernet" architecture. A hub repeats any incoming transmission on all of its other ports, regardless of packet content and addressing information. If two or more packets arrive at the hub at the same time, packets from different network sections ("domains") collide. Unlike switches, which are capable of transmitting multiple packets full-duplex via different ports by examining source and destination addresses, hubs do not separate collision domains. The more transmissions are placed between disjoint senders and receivers, the larger the throughput advantage using a switch, which makes a hub an inefficient and outdated choice.

State-of-the-art switches come with a small number of ports in desktop form for small office/home office (SOHO) environments, or in modular, stackable form with hundreds of ports for wiring closets and enterprise deployment. They include support for the IEEE 802.3af standard for end devices, and Ethernet support for in-line power devices beyond IP phones and wireless LAN access points to connect more power-hungry devices such as IP-powered video surveillance cameras, security systems, or fire protection and motion detection devices.

Switch Architecture and Performance

Switches are essentially the distributor nodes, across which various communication lines fan in from different sources and fan out to different locations. First generation switching networks were purely electromechanical and blocking, i.e., an existing connection prevents links between other input and output ports. They were invented to automate the interlinking of segments in communication exchange due to the fact that building networks by laying out point-to-point links between each pair of users would be cost prohibitive and an enormous waste of resources. Over decades switch technology has evolved from electromechanical through electronic to optical or photonic switching (Veeraraghavan et al., 2001), and from using space-division switching in first-generation systems, through time-division circuit switching and multi-channel and multi-rate switching, to wavelength-division switching in photonic networks. The predominant relay mechanics in switches are consequently called time-division multiplexing (TDM), frequency-division multiplexing (FDM), and wavelength-division multiplexing (WDM).

The three prevalent implementation paradigms for switches are based on shared memory, time-division, or space-division fabrics. Shared-memory switches can be built simply from off-the-shelf components, and access shared memory space to carry out forwarding of packets from input port to output port. Time-division switches rearrange the order of incoming data on a multiplexed line according to a time schedule, whereas space-division switches, as common building blocks in high-performance networks, forward packets across a spatial fabric layout in a single stage or in multiple stages.

Crossbar switches are the most prominent example of a single-stage switch, where every input link is directly connected to every output port in a matrix with cross points that can be selectively enabled. With this simple principle of connectivity, such switches have no internal blocking and low latency due to the minimal number of connecting points between arbitrary input and output links, and can be easily implemented in VLSI. However, the number of cross points required grows quadratically with the number of input and output ports, which increases the capacitive loading and signal distribution time, and hence slows transmission. In addition, crossbars have no fault tolerance and are difficult to expand and too costly. Small crossbar switches are often used to as components in more complex switch designs.

Multistage switches are composed of networks of smaller switches, which works well if each stage in the pipeline takes the same time. The interlinking of low-complexity switches in intermediate stages increases reliability, because input and output can still be connected in case of failure of a component switch. An example is the knockout switch, which is a crossbar with concentrators modeled on a knockout tournament to reduce space complexity. Multistage switching can be more effectively implemented by recirculation or with spatially separate switches. This class is represented by Clos networks, Banyan networks, and Batcher sorting networks (Jajszczyk, 2003). In Clos networks, a strictly non-blocking switching network can be constructed with fewer cross points than a crossbar of the same capacity. Each switch of one stage has an output feeding into each switch of the next stage. With a minimum number of cross points, a Clos switch becomes strictly non-blocking, otherwise it is blocking. While Clos networks have been primarily of theoretical interest, they are considered again today as a promising architecture for optical cross-connect systems and for high-capacity and high-performance backbone IP routers. Banyan switches are self-routing using a binary representation of output ports. The direction at each stage is specified by a bit corresponding to that stage. Half of the traffic is blocked in the worst case, and multiple planes of latter stages are used to buffer blocked traffic. Batcher networks are based on the idea that sorting and switching are essentially the same, except that outputs need to be spread after sorting to account for idle ports (Ahmadi and Denzel, 1989). Buffer placement and scheduling turn out to be a greater challenge in switch design than creating the fabric.

Switching throughput is measured either in bits-per-second (bps) or packets-per-second (pps), which is correlated with link speeds, support for half or full-duplex connections, support for jumbo frames, and non-blocking behavior. The goal is to achieve an overall throughput equal to the sum of the full theoretical bandwidth of each switch port. Current low-end switches offer connectivity to a small user base, typically with 5 to 16 ports at 10 to 100 Mbps, and lack spanning tree protocol support, VLAN support, or remote management. A current typical midrange switch offers support for 16 to 250 users with a bandwidth of 10 Gbps (non-blocking), a packet forwarding throughput of 2 Mpps, and a packet buffer memory of

1 GB. Top-end midrange switches may include redundant power supply and forwarding engines to greater availability, a greater number of Ethernet ports, remote access and configuration, and support for VLANs, spanning trees and Layer 3 switching. These switches are either unmanaged Layer-2 devices with auto-sensing, or managed Layer 2 or 3 devices, which can be used to inexpensively off-load routers segmenting a network to lay the groundwork for innovative IP-based services such as IP telephony or video conferencing.

High performance switches (Newman et al., 1997) offer the same features as mid-tier switches, plus Layer 4-7 switching, security features, modular gigabit connectivity for several hundred full-duplex ports, integrated IP address lookup (Waldvogel et al., 1997), multicast support, an address database size of several thousand media access control (MAC) addresses per system, and a bandwidth of at least 10 Gbps. Multicast support inherently impacts blocking properties and the routing strategy to set up multicast connections via a switching network. At a packet size of 240 bytes, a router with a T1 line rate of 1.5 Mbps requires a lookup performance of 0.78 Kpps, or 5.21 Mpps at an OC-192 line rate of 10 Gbps. Current carrier-class switches can be scaled to 100 terabit per second (Tbps) capacity, processing hundreds of millions of packets per second (pps) depending on the switch fabric, the line cards and their performance, and port speeds ranging from OC-48 to OC-192.

ROUTER AND SWITCH SECURITY

Various taxonomies on Internet infrastructure security have been proposed to categorize vulnerabilities and propose remedies. Generally, threats can be aimed at the devices themselves, or attack the services provided. At more detail, four major areas of protection can be considered to secure routers and switches from external intrusions, as well as violations from within a network: physical access, administrative control over a switch or router, intrusions against a switch or router, or intrusions through a switch or router (Microsoft, 2004). Alternatively, Pfleeger and Pfleeger (2003) classify threats to computing systems into four kinds: interceptions, interruptions, modifications, or fabrications. Interception allows an attacker to read traffic and threatens confidentiality, interruption leads to lack of availability through service degradation or denial, modification threatens data integrity, and fabrication may cause traffic or service alteration and enable future attacks.

However, the majority of successful remote attacks on switches and routers can be traced to exploitation of a small number of security flaws. Chakrabarti and Manimaran (2000) identify four main categories of concrete concern for Internet infrastructure security: Domain name system (DNS) hacking, routing table poisoning, packet mistreatment, and denial-of-service attacks.

The implications of these attacks are as diverse as the nature of their approach. IP packets are misrouted, confidential information is disclosed, deceptive or incorrect information is injected into the network through message modification, wrong address-name translations corrupt the routing process, network activities are disrupted through denial of service attacks, and network partitions or congestion can occur. Countermeasures can be preventive or reactive, and may be implemented at the network edge or core, with the latter generally being more costly due to deployment issues.

Best Practices in Securing Routers and Switches

Router and switch security concerns device treatment aspects such as physical access, administrative access and access control, availability and reliability, and traffic treatment aspects such as authentication among routers, confidential exchange of control and regular messages, as well as the integrity of messages transferred. Device mistreatment can be divided into physical and network intrusions. Entry-level switches, such as plug-and-play devices, are relatively immune to network born violations, while mid-range switches and routers are typically most vulnerable. High-end routers and switches need various measures such as access control to hold off intrusion. Physical intrusions can be trivially prevented by limiting access to device, for example with a locked wiring closet. Network-based intrusions may be curtailed by adding firewalls to the network perimeter or to routers themselves and employing intrusion detection intelligence. Availability and reliability can be boosted through full duplication of equipment, but this solution adds considerable cost and necessitates automatic switchover. Traffic mistreatment is more complex due to the large spectrum of possible attacks. The next sections discuss notorious vulnerabilities (ISS, 2004) of routers and switches and suggest best practices for keeping attacks in reign.

Router Vulnerabilities and Attacks

Routing protocols to date have largely remained unprotected and open to attacks. Routing attacks can be targeted at the intra-domain and inter-domain level to disrupt correct routing in terms of the ability to reach the destination in compliance with a given forwarding policy. Generally, threats to routing protocols can be external or internal. External threats come from outside attackers who are non-participants in the protocol. Internal threats come from compromised protocol participants, which are referred to as Byzantine due their unpredictable nature. These attackers may corrupt, forge, or delay messages, or send conflicting messages (Puig et al., 2004).

These threats can be exerted in various ways. Deliberate exposure occurs when routing information is revealed to unauthorized parties, for example by taking control over a router. By sniffing on control exchanges, an attacker can observe or record routing information. Traffic analysis is a more systematic method to detect patterns and vulnerabilities in router exchanges. Spoofing is an identify change problem. Falsification includes misadvertising network resources, tampering with protocol header fields, and misstating route attributes. Finally, attackers can interfere with exchanges between legitimate routers, or place excess burden on such routers.

Threat actions may result in usurpation, deception, disruption, or disclosure, listed with decreasing impact. Usurpation lets an attacker gain control over legitimate

Table 2 Summary of threats to routers and their implications

Threat Source	Concerns	Threat Actions	Outcomes	Consequences	
				Infrastructure:	Hosts:
• Outside • Byzantine	• Access Control • Authentication • Availability • Confidentiality • Data Integrity • Physical Access • Reliability	• Deliberate Exposure • Sniffing • Traffic Analysis • Spoofing • Falsification • Interference • Overload	• Usurpation • Deception • Disruption • Disclosure	• Blackholing • Churning • Clog • Congestion • Instability • Looping • Overcontrol • Partition	• Cut • Delay • Eavesdrop • Looping • Starvation

router functions. Deception happens when a forged routing message is accepted as authentic by a legitimate router and results in similar damages as usurpation. Disruption, as in a denial-of-service attack, causes temporary service outage and becomes more pressing when its frequency, duration, or range increases. Disclosure allows attackers to monitor a link due to lack of confidentiality in routing exchanges. Table 2 summarizes this taxonomy (cf. Babir et al., 2005).

The consequences are varied, and may damage the infrastructure of the whole network, or damage communication for a particular host or network. Blackholing occurs when one router is overburdened with redirected traffic. Churning happens when network forwarding patterns change rapidly and cause large variation in data delivery. Clogging describes the situation, when a router runs out of resources to handle excessive load, as caused by blackholing or congestion. Congestion is caused by overburdening a network portion with traffic. When routing becomes unstable, a global forwarding state is not reached. Looping may result in data never delivered. Overcontrol happens when protocol control overhead dominates actual message exchanges, and partitioning designates artificial breaks in the network topology such that routers do not communicate with each other when they could. Consequences of attacks on particular routers include cuts, delays, eavesdropping, looping, and starvation. When routers are cut off, they do not communicate when in fact they could. Through eavesdropping, rogue routers receive and see traffic when they should not.

Frequent exchanges of routing updates among neighboring routers in distance vector routing, and flooding of updates in link state protocols make intra-domain routing protocols vulnerable to attacks. Various strategies have been proposed to protect routing updates, including adding sequence and predecessor information to updates, or introducing authentication and cryptographic measures for router exchanges such as digitally signing updates. Implied drawbacks are increased traffic volume and more processing overhead at routers. Although BGP is the de facto standard for inter-domain routing, it does not ensure the integrity, freshness and authentication of messages or the authenticity of path attributes and permits forging of path vectors, with the consequences that packets often get misrouted and BGP operation can be compromised. Butler et al., (2004) present a comprehensive overview on the various approaches to secure BGP, which include encryption of session information and message attributes, introduction of a public key mechanism into the routing infrastructure, route validation, using certificates for authenticating and authorizing network entities, and using a routing registry and building various forms of cryptography into BGP communication.

From a more concrete and practical perspective, at the administrative level a remote attacker could bypass *access control lists (ACLs)* in a router due to configuration errors. In an otherwise properly configured ACL, this problem could allow a remote attacker to connect through the switch onto the 'protected' side. Edge routers with an integrated DHCP server can be susceptible to a *BOOTP denial of service attack*. When a specially crafted BOOTP packet is sent to the router, a remote attacker could obtain sensitive information using a DHCP reply or cause the device to crash. An ADSL router integrated switch can also be vulnerable to *cross-site scripting*, when a remote attacker creates a malicious URL link containing embedded code, which would be executed in the victim's Web browser within the security context of the hosting site, once the link is clicked. Since any device in a network could send address resolution protocol (ARP) messages, an attacker on a LAN can easily spoof the gateway in a *gratuitous ARP attack*. Using *TCP sequence prediction*, an attacker could hijack another user's session or perform an IP spoofing attack to manipulate connections to the TCP services or modify the configuration of the router.

Router Configuration and Deployment Practices

Router security includes firmware and software patches and updates, administrative access, auditing and logging, intrusion detection, routing protocol configuration, and additional services. The National Security Agency (NSA, 2003) makes various recommendations to secure routers against intrusions.

First and foremost, most devices have back-door access and should therefore be physically locked up. A written router security policy should be maintained to define management and logging practices, in particular, who can access, configure, and update a router. Updates should always be tested before deploying them in a production environment. Administrative access must be restricted to specific locations and interfaces and use encryption to prevent hijacking, which entails strong password policies, using an administration access control system, controlling physical access, shutting down

Web-based configuration, and disabling unused interfaces. Passwords should be encrypted and configured securely for console and virtual terminal lines, and SSH should be adopted for remote administration. Consistent deployment of the same services across large scale networks can be provided by including the ability to rapidly configure routers for specific services with macro configuration templates comprising series of command line configuration commands, however, these templates and master versions of configuration files should be well commented, stored offline, and kept in sync with running configurations to diagnose attacks and enable fast recovery. Router security should be audited regularly, especially after any reconfiguration.

Protocol-level vulnerabilities are often the target of denial-of-service attacks, for example by flooding the network, and can be countered, among other measures (SANS, 2004) by using ingress and egress filtering, screening ICMP traffic, and limiting broadcast traffic or other unnecessary traffic. Unneeded services in the router such as BOOTP, Finger, SNMP, source routing, trace route, or protocols such as the Cisco discovery protocol (CDP) should be disabled. If SNMP is required for a network, it should be configured with ACLs and hard-to-guess community strings.

Loop-back addresses, source addresses from any internal network, and packets having the same source and destination address should be blocked in order to prevent TCP sequence number guessing of packets with obviously fake or reserved addresses from untrusted networks. Blocking illegal addresses not only prevents attackers from hijacking a router but also helps to diagnose poorly configured internal networks and hosts. ICMP echo and redirect may be used by remote attackers to scan a network and manipulate routing behavior, and should also be blocked. Broadcast packets, as generated by DHCP and BOOTP, should not be used on external interfaces or cross border routers and should be blocked. On border routers, only internal addresses should be allowed to enter the router from internal interfaces, and only traffic headed to internal addresses should be permitted from external interfaces. Multicast packets should only be allowed in networks supporting IP multicast.

Access control lists prevent certain traffic to enter or exit a network and should be implemented to allow only those protocols, ports, and IP addresses required by users and services and explicitly disallow any others. Previous access lists should be cleared out when implementing a new list and traffic address restrictions should be enforced at all times. Logging should be enabled for all denied traffic, and unusual traffic patterns should be audited, with logs being centrally stored and secured. Errors and blocked packets should be logged to an internal, trusted SYSLOG host, and SYSLOG traffic from untrusted networks should be blocked. Logs should include event timing and at least two network time protocol (NTP) servers should be configured to ensure availability and accuracy of timing information to enable precise tracking of network attacks.

Standard routers typically perform little filtering of data and therefore inherently may allow forwarding of compromised traffic. Stateful packet inspection (SPI) is a network layer mechanism to examine packet contents up through the application layer rather than merely looking at packet header information, and compiling connection state information in a table. Filtering decisions are hence established based on a context of prior packets having passed through the router and allow to establish dynamic filtering criteria beyond static administrator-defined rules. SPI also thwarts port scanning by closing off ports until a connection to a specific port is requested. Packet filtering is fairly effective and transparent to users, but difficult to configure and susceptible to IP spoofing.

Routers become application gateways when applying security policies to specific applications. Although a firewall is only a first line of defense against network intrusion, modern routers incorporate firewall features and contain numerous mechanisms in hardware and software to strengthen their lines of defense against attacks, with the idea to provide plug-and-play security. A variety of router security features handle denial-of-service attacks via detection and logging, dropped packet logging, time-based usage control, URL filtering, deep packet filtering, and trusted user identity management.

Router manufactures have therefore integrated such services increasingly in their hardware as a more efficient layer of defense for the network infrastructure. If a router acts as circuit-level gateway by applying security mechanisms to a transport level connection, packets could flow between hosts without further checking. For greater security, information exchanges should be encrypted. Current routers typically offer 56-bit to 168-bit encryption with DES, Triple DES, RC4, MD5, or SHA-1 encryption algorithms (Stallings, 2000).

As edge devices in local networks, routers can also shield private networks from outside access by mapping external, global addresses to internal addresses. Routers hence often include support for NAT, PPTP and L2TP, DHCP, DMZ, IPsec, and VRRP.

NAT (network address translation) is a popular but also controversial (Phifer, 2000) mechanism to counter IP address depletion, and makes a network appear to the outside world with a single IP address by hiding its internals. NAT serves the three main purposes of providing a type of firewall by hiding internal IP addresses, enabling a company to use more internal IP addresses, and combining multiple broadband connections into a single Internet connection. A translation table is maintained to map application-specific outside requests to internal IP addresses and associated port numbers. In static NAT, a private IP address is mapped to a public IP address, where the public address is always the same. This allows an internal host, such as a Web server, to have an unregistered, private IP address and still be reachable over the Internet. With dynamic NAT, a private IP address is mapped to a public IP address drawing from a pool of registered, public IP addresses. Dynamic NAT helps to secure a network as it masks the internal configuration of a private network and makes it difficult for someone outside the network to monitor individual usage patterns. A router using the point-to-point tunneling protocol (PPTP) or the Layer 2 tunneling protocol (L2TP) is able to establish secure, tunneled connections through an open network as a baseline service to establish VPN connections.

The dynamic host configuration protocol (DHCP, RFC 2131) enables routers to automatically obtain a different IP address when reconnecting mobile hosts with intermittent connectivity. It typically operates in conjunction with NAT and supports hybrid use of static and dynamic IP addresses. Due to the dynamic nature of the address assignment, attackers will regularly have to rescan a network to obtain current addresses.

A DMZ (demilitarized zone) inserts a neutral zone between a private network and public networks. Routers supporting setup of a DMZ allow users from the public network to access only the DMZ host. This "exposed host" provides limited access to company data, and can operate as proxy server for inside hosts to request data from the public network, but is not able to initiate sessions back into the private network.

IPsec operates with two different encryption modes, transport and tunnel, to introduce tighter security at the network layer. Transport mode encrypts only the data portion (payload) of each packet, but leaves the header untouched. In the more secure tunnel mode a router encrypts both the header and the payload. On the receiving side, an IPsec-compliant device is needed to decrypt each packet. For IPsec to work, the sending and receiving devices must share a public key through the Internet Security Association and key management protocol/Oakley (ISAKMP/Oakley) protocol, which allows the receiver to obtain a public key and authenticate the sender using digital certificates.

Finally, the virtual router redundancy protocol (VRRP) runs on a link in a fault-tolerant arrangement between one device operating as master and another device operating in standby mode, so each router knows whether the "alter ego" is alive and is able to react in failover mode if necessary.

Securing ad hoc routing presents difficulties not existent in traditional networks. Neither centrally administrated secure routers nor strict policies exist in ad hoc networks, where nodes communicate without regulation through centralized access points. If routers go mobile, a new class of security mechanisms needs to be introduced. So far, security provisions for wireless networks entail support for Wi-Fi protected access (WPA), preshared key (PSK), MAC authentication, SSID hiding, and wired equivalent privacy (WEP) (Miller, 2001). However, software-only defense solutions are not sufficient in the face of distributed denial-of-service attacks, spoofing, and other attacks bogging down the network. For example, while the WEP protocol was designed to provide confidentiality, access control, and data integrity, it fails to fulfill these goals due to keystream reuse and message authentication flaws (Borisov et al., 2001).

Greater service complexities in routers, such as differentiated quality or voice telephony support, create new loopholes and necessitate constant updating of security measures. Mechanisms such as IP traceback, while still a topic of research (Savage et al., 2000), could be useful in the future in pinpointing attackers. Newer development in security information management (SIM) tools and intrusion detection systems (IDS) may help to correlate feeds from various audits and logs to recognize and diagnose attacks, using database and visualization tools with "dashboard" functionality for more effective monitoring and securing of networks.

Switch Vulnerabilities and Attacks

Switch operation can be compromised at various service layers. An attacker, who gains administrative access to a vulnerable switch in *a password attack*, could take complete administrative control of the device. Proper password management, in particular the avoidance of default passwords, and restricted network and console access to these devices is therefore critical. In a *MAC address sniffing attack*, an attacker connected to a vulnerable switch could use a packet sniffing tool to obtain the MAC addresses of connected systems and can cause traffic to be broadcast to all systems connected to the switch. In a *frame injecting attack*, an attacker could inject 802.1q frames into a VLAN and transfer data to unauthorized network segments. In a *spanning tree protocol (STP) attack*, an attacker connected to two different switches could send bridge protocol data unit (BPDU) messages to gain root switch privileges over the tree and intercept transmissions among subtrees. In a *frame forwarding attack*, a switch receiving an 802.1x packet frame on a spanning tree protocol (STP) blocked port does not drop the packet but instead forwards it in the VLAN. This can cause an 802.1x frames network storm, which slows the performance of the network. By sending a malformed Internet control message protocol (ICMP) packet to a switch or to a computer behind it, a remote attacker can cause the switch to crash in a *denial-of-service attack*.

A remote attacker can also cause a denial of service by sending a flood of TCP SYN packets to the vulnerable device. In both cases, the power to the switch must be completely shut off and restored for the switch to regain normal functionality. A content switch can be vulnerable to a *denial of service attack* of *hypertext transfer protocol (HTTP) requests* to the Web management interface. A remote attacker could send a malformed HTTP POST request or extended markup language (XML) data to the Web management interface to cause the device to reboot, and hence deny services to legitimate users. A content service switch can also be vulnerable to a *UDP denial-of-service attack* when malformed UDP packets are sent to the management port (e.g., UDP port 5002) and a remote attacker can cause the device to reload. Finally, in a *Web-based switch management vulnerability* a remote attacker could access a switch via its administrative Web interface, and gain access to sensitive information without authentication by bookmarking the Web management URL.

Switch Configuration and Deployment Practices

The National Security Agency (NSA, 2004) recommends for threat defense that switches should be covered in an institution's network security policy, including operating systems, port management, passwords, network services, spanning tree protocol, logging and debugging, access control lists, authentication, authorization, and accounting. First and foremost, physical access to a switch must be restricted, and switches should be securely configured so that sessions automatically time out and only necessary network services are enabled. The switch configuration

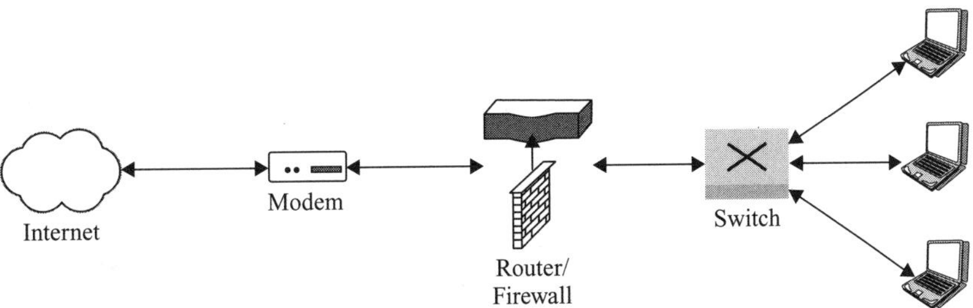

Figure 4: Simple secure SOHO Network.

file should be well commented and kept offline with limited access permissions. Software on switches should be regularly patched to run the latest stable release. Password access could be configured at different privilege levels, and SSH should be used instead of TELNET to administer a switch.

Securing a switch configuration entails various aspects, including the proper configuration of services and VLANs; the disabling of unused ports, the use of an access control system, and employing encryption, in particular on wireless links. Traditionally encryption is not implemented in a switch, but it ensures that intercepted packets are useless when an intruder sniffs on the same switched segment or where the switch is compromised. Switch management should be either "out-of-band" or on a separate VLAN for in-band management. Access control lists (ACLs) allow controlling of inter-VLAN traffic between IP subnets by restricting the flow of traffic between different segments of the network, and must be configured correctly. Typically, a simple static packet filter is used, in contrast to functions such as stateful packet inspection or application-layer proxying performed by dedicated firewall devices.

Port security should disable unused ports and limit access based on MAC addresses. The spanning tree protocol and auto-trunking should be disabled in loop-free topologies. A static VLAN configuration should be used when possible, the number of VLANs that can be transported over a trunk should be limited and trunk ports should be assigned to an otherwise unused native VLAN number. In addition, 802.1x and the extensible authentication protocol (EAP) can be used to leverage edge-security by authenticating a machine before it is allowed to access the network. Finally, logging should be enabled and logs should be sent to a dedicated, secure log server. Logs should be reviewed for incidents and archived in accordance with the general security policy. While these NSA recommendations are based on Cisco IOS products, they apply to switches in general.

Current software-based enhancement services of high-end switches include the ability to prevent MAC address flooding attacks by locking down ports, prevent attacks from false DHCP servers, and limit network access through port-level ACLs. Current switches also include authentication capabilities in standard IEEE 802.1x to be able to attribute authenticated traffic to a specific virtual LAN or add quality of service features as well as prevent denial-of-service attacks by dynamically inspecting address resolution protocol traffic and binding MAC and IP addresses to specific ports. Layer 2 and 3 switches also typically support standards such as IEEE 802.1Q (static VLAN groups), port-based VLAN (any one port can belong to different VLAN groups), IEEE 802.1p class of service (CoS), IEEE 802.1D spanning tree protocol, and manual port trunking as per IEEE802.3ad. In addition, IGMP snooping, port mirroring, RFC 1157 (SNMP), RFC 2819 (RMON), RFC 1213 MIB II, RFC 1643 (Ethernet managed objects), RFC 1493 (bridge managed objects), RFC 951 (BOOTP), RFC 2998 (differentiated services), and RFC 2865 (RADIUS) are often supported.

Case Studies

Deploying a switched network entails choosing which class of routers or switches is needed, what functionality is required, and where those devices should be placed in relation to each other. Decisions on current connectivity and future growth, communication between devices, the required bandwidth and acceptable latency, and what VLAN architecture may be required are all interdependent parameters affecting overall security. Among the many possible organizational structures, SOHO and multilevel switching architectures are most common. A simple, secured SOHO setup, shown in Figure 4, may include a modem, usually a cable or DSL modem, a router, and a switch, which are often combined in a low-cost broadband router acting as an Ethernet switch with a firewall function.

In an example for a basic secure multilevel design in Figure 5, routers separate the public Internet from an intranet through a perimeter network. The first segment uses a border router facing the Internet with initial firewall capability, switched to a perimeter firewall that in turn connects to a Web server cluster in the perimeter network via a switch. Another switch connects the server farm to an internal firewall, which is switched to backend PCs and internal servers. Aside from the border switch, which is located in a more vulnerable zone, all other switches could be separate VLANs on the same switch, which could be one larger unit or consist of multiple smaller devices. Scenarios far more complex than presented are conceivable, but composition and the idea of isolation of critical components are principally the same.

CONCLUSION

The phenomenal growth in digital communication traffic has transformed the Internet from a research testbed into

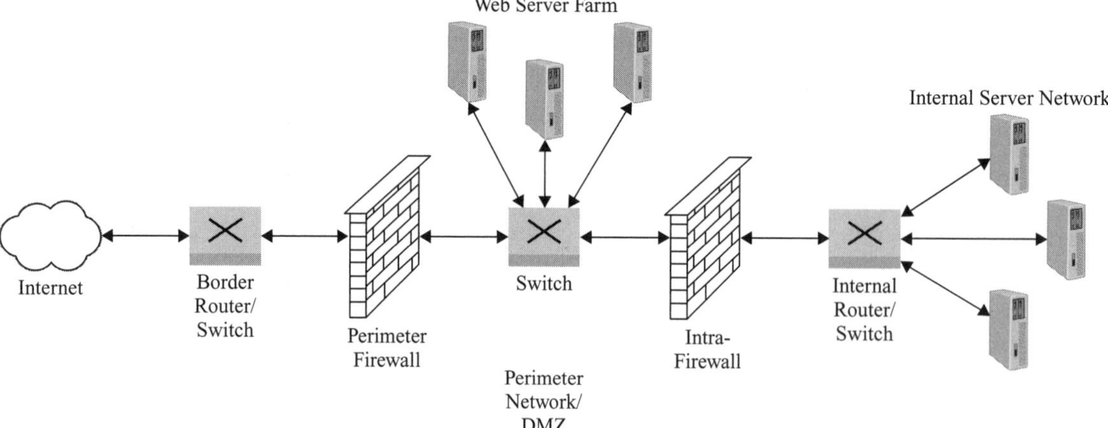

Figure 5: Secure multi-level switched network.

both a daily convenience and a mission-critical service. As critical network infrastructure components, routers and switches are key devices in controlling network traffic and linking together computer networks at greater scale. Routers, from small to very large scale, perform primarily path finding optimization based on interior routing protocols such as RIP and OSPF, or exterior policy-centric protocols such as BGP. In security terms, routers can be used to segregate intranets from Internetworks through packet filtering and address translation. While attacks on access network routers may only compromise the local network, vulnerabilities in backbone routers could create large-scale damage to a communication infrastructure. Switches can radically improve network throughput by reducing packet collisions in the forwarding process. Switches segment networks according to the operational and security policies of an organization. Physical and administrative loopholes can make switches vulnerable to attacks that may impact the greater network around the switch. Tight physical, administrative, and protocol-centric security measures hence need to be enacted upon routers and switches alike to minimize network downtime and to fend off attacks on the integrity of distributed communication.

At the dawn of the next generation of massively ubiquitous communication tools and interactive applications exchanging high-volume traffic, such as video conferencing, video-on-demand, multiplayer simulations, and distance learning, switching and routing technologies may once again have to change to adapt to the next wave of innovation in communication, and the implied greater needs in security. In this section we discussed the essentials of router and switch mechanics, their vulnerabilities, and some current best practices in securing these devices, with main focus on wired networks. Issues such as content switching and routing, quality-of-service provision in its interplay with security, or wireless security need to be addressed separately. The ultimate vision is to equip routers and switches with the inherent adaptive intelligence to make networks self-organizing, self-defending, and self-healing against any conceivable attack at the hardware or software level, while offering uninterrupted high-performance service.

GLOSSARY

ACL Access Control List, a predefined set of rules that configure router packet filtering capabilities for routed network protocols based on an organization's security policy.

ARP Address resolution protocol, a distributed protocol to convert an IP address into a physical (data link control) address such as an Ethernet address. A host broadcasts an ARP request with an IP address to a TCP/IP network and the host with this IP address replies with its physical address. With the reverse ARP protocol (RARP) a host broadcasts its physical address to receive an RARP reply with the host's IP address.

Autotrunking Multiple ports are configured to be one and the same trunk for data transferring from one network switch to another network switch with the same trunking features and settings, in order to increase bandwidth.

Crossbar Simple non-blocking switch with inputs and outputs arranged as rows and columns in a matrix, where data are switched by activating cross points in the matrix.

DHCP Dynamic host configuration protocol, a protocol for assigning IP addresses dynamically from a preconfigured pool of IP addresses to devices on a network. With dynamic addressing, a device can have a different IP address every time it connects to the network. Dynamic addressing simplifies network administration because the software keeps track of IP addresses rather than requiring an administrator to manage the task.

DMZ Demilitarized zone, a computer or small subnetwork placed between a trusted internal network, such as a corporate private LAN, and an untrusted external network, such as the public Internet.

DoS Denial-of-service, a type of attack on a network to bring the network to its knees by transmission of useless traffic. Many DoS attacks, such as the ping of death and teardrop attacks, exploit limitations in the TCP/IP protocols.

Firewall A system, implemented in both hardware and/or software, and designed to prevent unauthorized access to or from a private network as a first line of defense. A firewall examines each incoming or leaving message and blocks those that do not meet specific preconfigured rules.

Gateway Node on a network serving as entrance to another network. This term is often associated with both a router and a switch but modern uses of the term indicate higher-layer functionality. For example, an application-specific type of firewall is also called an application-level gateway.

Ingress Filtering Examination of packets going through a router from the outside network to the inside. The opposite is **egress filtering.**

IPsec IP security, a set of protocols developed by the IETF to support secure exchange of packets at the IP layer and implement VPNs.

L2TP Layer 2 tunneling protocol, an extension to the PPP protocol that enables ISPs to operate VPNs.

Line Card Contains physical layer components to interface external data link to the switch fabric.

NAT Network address translation, an Internet protocol standard that enables a local-area network (LAN) to use one set of IP addresses for internal traffic and a second set of addresses for external traffic. A NAT box located where the LAN meets the Internet makes all necessary IP address translations.

Network Processor Runs the routing protocol, computes the routing tables that are copied into each forwarding engine, handles network management, and processes special handling for unusual packets.

OC Optical carrier, a frame format and speed metric in the SONET multiplexing hierarchy used to assess high-performance network throughput. OC-1 offers a data rate 51.84 Mbps.

OSI Model The open systems interconnection reference model defines a 7-layer architecture of communication functions for cooperating network devices.

Pps Packets per second, a metric to measure switch and router performance.

PPTP Point-to-point tunneling protocol, used to ensure that messages transmitted from one VPN node to another are secure. With PPTP, users can dial in to their corporate network via the Internet.

Router An Internetworking Layer 3 device connecting two or more networks running the same routing protocol. It uses the Internet protocol to address devices and maintains routing tables to determine the next hop on the optimal path to forward packets based on header information and routing policies.

Spanning Tree Protocol Link management protocol in the IEEE 802.1 standard for bridges, which provides path redundancy in a network with several possible paths between hosts while preventing undesirable loops.

SPI Stateful packet inspection is a firewall architecture that works at the network layer. Unlike static packet filtering, which examines a packet based on the information in its header, stateful inspection tracks each connection traversing all interfaces of the firewall and makes sure they are valid. Also referred to as dynamic packet filtering.

Spoofing A variety of ways in which hardware and software can be fooled. In IP spoofing a message is altered in its header to appear as if it came from the authorized IP address of a trusted host.

Switch Fabric Interconnects the various components of router and offers higher aggregate capacity than the more conventional backplane bus.

Tunneling Encapsulation of packets to enable one network to send its data via another network's connections. Packets from one network protocol are embedded within TCP/IP packets carried through public Internet.

VLAN Virtual LAN technology is used to create logically separate LANs on the same physical switch and apply access control based on security rules to devices in logical network segments. A VLAN is a software-configured network of computers which behave as if they are connected to the same wire even though they may actually be physically located on different segments of a LAN.

VPN Virtual private network, a logical topology of computers across the public Internet.

CROSS REFERENCES

See *Access Control: Principles and Solutions; Denial of Service Attacks; Firewall Basics; Internet Architecture; Packet Filtering and Stateful Firewalls.*

REFERENCES

Ahmadi, H., & Denzel, W. E. (1989). A survey of modern high-performance switching techniques, *IEEE Journal of Selected Areas in Communications, 7*(7), 1091–103.

Barbir, A., Murphy, S., & Yang, Y. (2004). Generic threats to routing protocols, Internet-Draft draft-ietf-rpsec-routing-threats-07, Available at www.ietf.org/internet-drafts/draft-ietf-rpsec-routing-threats-07.txt, Date of access (DOA): March 30, 2005.

Borisov, N., Goldberg, I., & Wagner, D. (2001). Intercepting mobile communications: The insecurity of 802.11. Proc. MOBICOM, Rome, Italy.

Butler, K., Farley, T., & McDaniel, P. (2004). A Survey of BGP Security Issues and Solutions, Tech. Report TD-5UGJ33, *AT&T Labs - Research*, Florham Park, NJ: June 2004.

Chakrabarti, A., & Manimaran, G. (2000). Internet Infrastructure Security – A Taxonomy. *IEEE Network, 16*(6) 13–21.

Cisco Systems (2004). Security and VPN. Available at www.cisco.com/pcgi-bin/Support/browse/index.pl?i=Products&f=753&viewall=true, DOA: November 27, 2004.

Gupta, P., & McKeown, N. (2001). Algorithms for packet classification, *IEEE Network, 15*(2) 24–32.

Huitema, C. (2000). Routing in the Internet. Prentice Hall.

Internet Security Systems (2004). Security Alerts and Advisories. Available at xforce.iss.net, DOA: November 27, 2004.

Jajszczyk, A. (2003). Nonblocking, repackable, and rearrangeable Clos networks: fifty years of the theory evolution. *IEEE Communications Magazine, 41*(10) 28–33.

Keshav, S. (1997). *An engineering approach to computer networking,* Addison-Wesley.

Keshav, S., & Sharma, R. (1998). Issues and trends in router design. *IEEE Communications Magazine, 36*(5) 144–51.

McKeown, N. (1997). A fast switched backplane for a gigabit switched router, *Business Communications Review,* December 1997.

Microsoft Technet (2004). Router and switch design. Available at www.microsoft.com/technet/security/guidance/secmod40.mspx, DOA: December 10, 2004.

Miller, S. K. (2001). Facing the challenge of wireless security. *IEEE Computer 34*(7) 16–8.

National Security Agency (2003). Router security configuration guide. Available at www.nsa.gov/snac/downloads_cisco.cfm?MenuID=scg10.3.1, DOA: November 27, 2004.

National Security Agency (2004). Switch security configuration guide. Available at www.nsa.gov/snac/downloads_switches.cfm?MenuID=scg10.3.1, DOA: November 27, 2004.

Newman, P., Minshall, G., Lyon, T., & Huston, L. (1997). IP switching and gigabit routers, *IEEE Communications Magazine, 35*(1) 64–9.

Paxson, V. (1997). End-to-end routing behavior in the Internet. *IEEE/ACM Transactions on Networking, 5*(5) 601–15.

Perlman, R. (1992). *Interconnections: Bridges and routers.* Addison-Wesley.

Pfleeger C. P., & Pfleeger, S. L. (2003). Security in computing, 3rd ed. Prentice-Hall.

Phifer, L. (2000). The trouble with NAT. *The Internet Protocol Journal,* Available at www.cisco.com/warp/public/759/ipj_3-4/ipj_3-4_nat.html, DOA: November 30, 2004.

Puig, J. J., Achemlal, M., Jones, E., & McPherson, D. (2005). Generic security requirements for routing protocols, Internet-draft dr0ft-ietf-rpsec-generic-requirements-01, January 2005, Available at www.ietf.org/internet- drafts/draft-ietf-rpsec-generic-requirements-01.txt, DOA: March 30, 2005.

SANS Institute (2004). The twenty most critical Internet security vulnerabilities. Available at www.sans.org/top20/, DOA: December 10, 2004.

Savage, S., Wetherall, D., Karlin, A., & Anderson, T. (2000). Practical network support for IP traceback. *Proc. ACM SIGCOMM,* Stockholm, Sweden, pp. 295–306.

Shenker, S. (1995). Fundamental design issues for the future Internet. *IEEE Journal of Selected Areas in Communication, 13*(7) 1176–88.

Singhal, A., & Jain, R. (2002). Terabit switching: A survey of techniques and current products. *Computer Communications, 25*(6) 547–556.

Srinivasan, V., Varghese, G., Suri, S., & Waldvogel, M. (1998). Fast and scalable layer four switching. *Proc. ACM SIGCOMM,* pp. 191–202.

Stallings W., (2000). *Network security essentials – Application and standards.* Prentice Hall.

Veeraraghavan, M., Karol, M., Grobler, R., Karri, R., & Moors, T. (2001). Architectures and protocols that enable new applications on optical networks. *IEEE Communications Magazine, 39*(3) 118–27.

Waldvogel, M., Varghese, G., Turner, J., & Plattner, B. (1997). Scalable high speed IP routing lookups, *Proc. ACM SIGCOMM,* Cannes, France, pp. 25–36.

Radio Frequency and Wireless Communications Security

Okechukwu Ugweje, *The University of Akron*

INTRODUCTION

Radio-frequency (RF) wireless communication systems have been around for many years with applications ranging from garage-door openers to satellite communication. The technologies cover a broad range of capabilities oriented toward different uses and needs. These technologies have been advancing at an unprecedented rate, and their impact is evident in our daily lives. Less wiring means greater flexibility and efficiency and reduced wiring costs. In many parts of the world, wireless communication is the fastest growing area of the communication industry, providing a valuable supplement and alternative to existing wired networks ("Cellular communications services," n.d.). Based on the number of users of wireless communication products and subscribers to services, it is now the preferred method of communication ("Wireless Communications, Market & Opportunities,"2000). Many systems formerly carried over the wire are now carried over wireless media.

The remarkable success of cellular mobile radio and other wireless technology has fundamentally changed the way people communicate and conduct business. The wireless revolution has led to a new multi-billion-dollar wireless communications industry. Linking service areas, wireless communication has altered the way business is conducted. For example, with a laptop computer, a wireless modem, and a cellular phone, a business consultant can contact his or her office and clients and conduct business while traveling. Field service and sales personnel can access corporate databases to check inventory status, prepare up-to-the-minute price and delivery quotes, modify schedule activities, and fulfill orders directly to the factory while traveling. Company personnel can use two-way paging services to stay in close contact, even when traditional wired communication services are available. Handheld hybrid phone-computer-fax machines feed information to wireless communication networks, allowing an executive to make decisions while on a leisure outing.

For instance, wireless local area network (WLAN) devices allow users to move their laptops from place to place within their office environment without the need for wires and without losing network connectivity. Ad hoc networks, such as those enabled by Bluetooth, allow data synchronization with network systems and applications sharing between devices. Bluetooth can also eliminate cables for printer and other peripheral device connections. Handheld devices, such as personal digital assistants (PDA) and cell phones, allow remote users to synchronize personal databases, and they provide access to network services such as wireless e-mail, Web browsing, and Internet access. Moreover, these technologies offer dramatic cost savings and added capabilities to diverse applications ranging from the retail setting to the manufacturing shop floor to first responders.

Risk is typically associated with wireless communications technology, because the airwaves can be accessed by intruders. Potential risks include loss of confidentiality, loss of integrity, loss of resource availability, and loss of proprietary information, to mention only a few. Malicious users may gain access to the network and intentionally corrupt the data by spreading viruses, or they may simply launch attacks that prevent authorized users from accessing the network. Even if data confidentiality or integrity is not compromised, unauthorized users may steal bandwidth and cause a decrease in network performance or use a vulnerable wireless network as a platform for launching a network attack on a third party. These risks are not peculiar to wireless systems, but the risks are exacerbated by the nature of wireless connectivity.

This chapter presents a concise summary of the subject of radio frequency (RF) and wireless communications and introduces the concept of security for wireless communications. This includes a discussion of the general concepts and definitions of RF-based wireless communication, various forms and applications of RF wireless communication, synopsis of radio wave propagation, the cellular communication systems, and a general introduction of the security issues in wireless communications in general and WLAN in particular. Also presented is a summary of current and emerging wireless communication technologies. Of particular interest is the cellular mobile radio system, which has become the most widespread RF wireless communication system.

RF WIRELESS COMMUNICATION

RF wireless communication began at the turn of the 20th century, more than 100 years ago, when Marconi established the first successful and practical radio system. His experiment in 1895 demonstrated the transmission of radio signals a distance of 2 kilometers (Proakis & Salehi, 2002). He conducted additional experiments leading to 1901 when his radiotelegraph system transmitted radio signals across the Atlantic Ocean, from England to Newfoundland, about 1,700 miles away ("Mobile Telephone History," n.d.). Only telegraphic codes were transmitted, however. On December 24, 1906, Reginald Fessenden accomplished the first radio communication of human speech over a distance of 11 miles from Brant Rock, Massachusetts, to ships in the Atlantic Ocean ("Mobile Telephone History," n.d.). Radio was no longer limited to telegraph codes; it was no longer just a wireless telegraph. This was a remarkable milestone highlighting the beginning of the voice-transmitted age.

In the early years of RF wireless communication, radio broadcasting was the most deployed wireless communication technology. The invention of the vacuum tube and vacuum triode hastened the advancement in radio transmission of voice signals. Radio broadcast by way of amplitude modulation (AM) and, later by frequency modulation (FM), was made possible. Amplitude modulation of the radio frequency was used to carry information until FM was introduced in the late 1930s (Mark & Zhuang, 2003). After FM was introduced by Edwin H. Armstrong (Lathi, 1998), many other RF wireless systems such as television, one- and two-way radio, and radar, were introduced between the late 1920s and the mid-1950s. Another milestone was witnessed in the late 1970s, which marked the beginning of the growth in cellular mobile radios and personal communication services. The first successful commercial analog cellular mobile telephone was demonstrated in 1979 (Durgin, 2003). Currently, wireless communication of all kinds abounds in our society.

System Architecture

In RF wireless communication systems, radio waves are used to transfer information between a transmitter (Tx) and a receiver (Rx). RF systems can be classified as either terrestrial-based or space-based systems. Terrestrial-based systems include microwave point-to-point, WLANs, and cellular mobile radio, to mention only a few. Terrestrial microwave systems are limited in distance and line-of-sight (LOS) propagation is the limiting factor. Relay towers with carefully aligned directional antennas are often used to provide an unobstructed path over an extended distance. The data signal is processed, up- or down-converted, modulated or demodulated, filtered, and amplified at the transceivers. The transmitted signal propagates through the air and is attenuated by several propagation mechanisms (discussed later in the chapter).

Space-based systems (e.g., satellites) are similar to terrestrial microwave systems except that signals travel from earth-based ground stations to a satellite (uplink), and a signal is sent back from the satellite to another earth-based ground station (downlink). This achieves a far wider coverage area than the earth-based systems. The satellite system could be in geostationary earth orbit, medium earth orbit, or low earth orbit.

A typical wireless communication system is shown in Figure 1. It consists of a source of information, a hardware subsystem called the transmitter, the channel or means by which the signal travels, another hardware subsystem called the receiver, and a destination of the information (the sink).

The source supplies the information to the transmitter in the form of audio, video, data, or combination of the three. The Tx and Rx combination is used to convert the signal into a form suitable for transmission and then to convert the signal back to its original form. This is achieved through the process of modulation (or encoding) at the Tx side and demodulation (or decoding) at the Rx side. The channel is the medium by which the signal propagates, such as free space, unshielded twisted pair, coaxial cable, or fiber-optic cable. In wireless communication the channel is the free space. Noise and interference are added to the signal in the channel, which increases attenuation, distortion, and eventually error in the received signal.

The transmitter and receiver are complex systems consisting of many internal components. A block diagram representation of some of the components is shown in Figure 1. Components are denoted as transmitter processes, receiver processes, amplifiers, mixers, local oscillators (LO), filters, and antennas. The transmitter processes represent functions of the transmitter such as modulation, encoding, analog-to-digital conversion, multiplexing, addressing, and routing information. The receiver processes, on the other hand, denote the inverse functions such as demodulation, decoding, digital-to-analog conversion, and demultiplexing, as well as addressing and routing information. Effective transmission and reception of radio waves involve processes such as amplification and filtering of the signal at various internal stages, mixing of

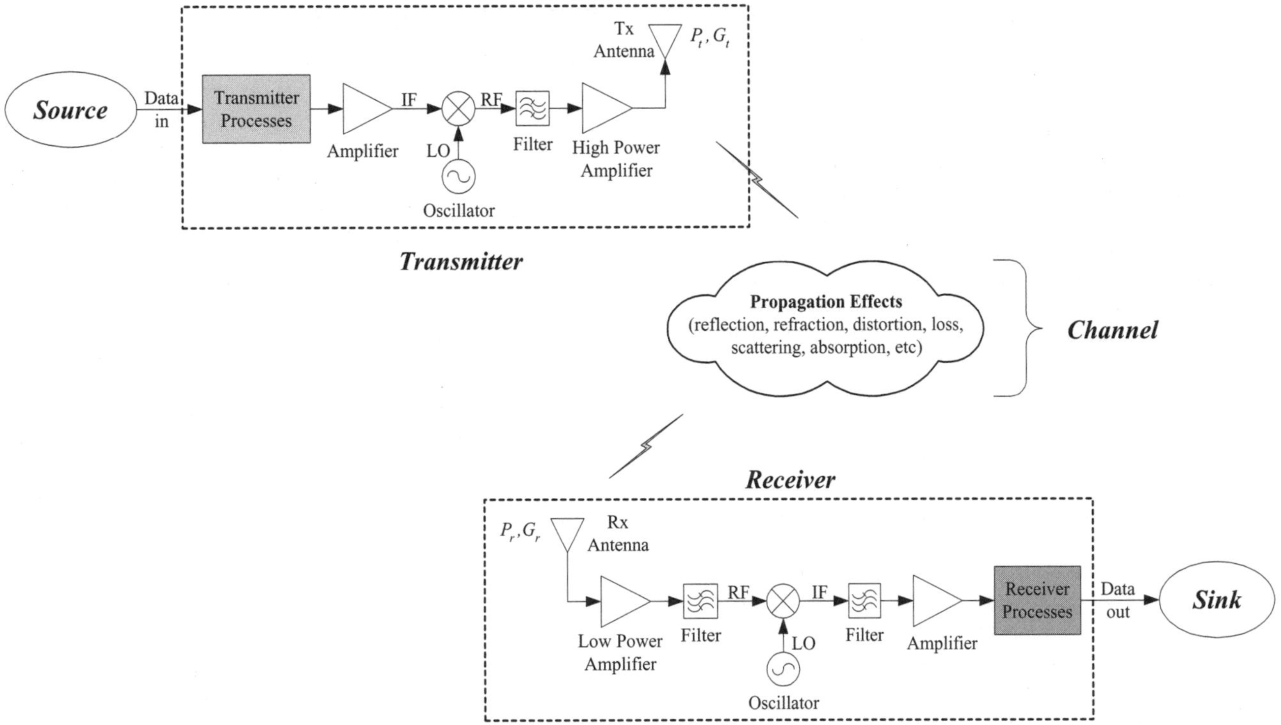

Figure 1: Simplified model of terrestrial-based RF wireless communication systems.

the desired signal with a local oscillator signal, translating the signal from one frequency to another, and transmission or reception of the RF energy through the antenna. The amplifier is characterized by its gain, noise figure (or output power), and linearity (Weisman, 2003). The gain (in dB) of the amplifier is a measure of how much bigger the output signal is than the input signal. The noise figure (or noise ratio) is a measure of the quality of the receiver system. Mixers are commonly found in the Tx and Rx subsystems and are used to create new frequencies or translate existing frequencies to new ones. They are sometimes called up or down converters. The most common translation of frequency is from intermediate frequency (IF) to RF and vice versa. The mixer performs this function by effectively multiplying two signals at two frequencies. A signal source that provides one of the inputs to the mixer is the LO. A common type of LO is a voltage-controlled oscillator. A function of the filter is frequency selectivity. Filters select signals based on their frequency components. Regardless of the construction, all filters can be classified as low pass, high pass, band pass, or band stop). These names are descriptive of the function of the filter. For example, a low pass filter will select signals with low frequency and reject signals with high frequency. A special type of filter commonly used in RF systems is the duplexer, a frequency-dependent device that may be used as a separator or a combiner of signals. The duplexer facilitates the use of one antenna for both transmission and reception. The sink or destination (receiver) can vary as much as the source (transmitter) insofar as the type of information processed.

In the RF propagation channel, external noise in the form of manmade noise (generated by electrical manmade objects), atmospheric noise, and extraterrestrial noise is introduced. Atmospheric noise is produced by electrical activities of the atmosphere. This type of noise is predominant in the range 0–30 MHz and is inversely proportional to its frequency. Extraterrestrial noise is produced by activities of the cosmos, including the sun. The RF propagation channel is time variant, hence the effectiveness of any system may vary because of the effects of atmospheric electrical activities (mostly solar ionization), weather, and random human-made noise sources. This time-variant channel requires careful consideration in the design of any wireless communications system.

In wireless communication, radio waves are used to transfer information, and because radio waves propagate in space, they are susceptible to some security risks. An intruder can intercept the signal or gain access to network services, without being an authorized user. The specific risk associated with wireless communication is presented later.

Radio Spectrum Classification

Radio frequencies or radio waves constitute the portion of the electromagnetic spectrum extending from 3 kHz to 300 GHz. The entire RF spectrum is classified into different bands and ranges, based on propagation properties. Baseband signals or source signals (e.g., audio signals) are in the low-frequency range below 30 kHz. This range of frequencies is classified as very low frequency (VLF), which must be translated into RF before transmission.

Radio waves are also described by their wavelength, as belonging to a particular wavelength range such as shortwave, medium-wave, or millimeter-wave. The higher the frequency, the lower the wavelength, because $\lambda = c/f_c$, where $c = 3.0 \times 10^8$ m/s is the speed of light, and f_c is the carrier frequency. The wavelength is related to the realizable antenna length, L, system bandwidth, B, and other practical system parameters. In general, higher frequency radio waves produce smaller λ, require shorter L, have lower bandwidth efficiency, ρ (assuming high bandwidth; Haykin, 2000, p. 347), are more susceptible to fading, are less susceptible to atmospheric electrical activity, and suffer from atmospheric thermal and weather distortion. Bandwidth efficiency is the number of information bits transmitted per second per unit of bandwidth (Hz) or the ratio of the bit rate to channel bandwidth expressed in bit per second per hertz (b/s/Hz). Considering that

$$\rho = \frac{R_b}{B} = \frac{\log_2 M}{BT_s} = \frac{1}{BT_b}\text{bits/s/Hz}, \tag{1}$$

it can be seen that as ρ increases, the required bandwidth decreases, if the bit rate R_b is constant. M is the symbol level and T is the period. Any digital system will become less bandwidth efficient if its BT_b value is increased. The capacity (C) of a digital communication system is directly related to bandwidth efficiency because $\rho_{\max} = C/B = \log_{10}(1 + S/N)$ bits/s/Hz, where S is the signal power and N is the noise power. Bandwidth efficient systems transmit more information bits per bandwidth.

The characteristics and applications of radio frequencies are summarized in Table 1. Within each frequency range, several bands of frequencies can be designated for communication. These bands are commonly identified by either f_c or a letter symbol, as illustrated in Figure 2 (Acosta, 1999; Federal Communications Commission [FCC], 1997). For example, in practical applications, one could describe an RF system as operating in the C, X, K, or K_A band instead of using the actual frequency numbers. A complete list of the radio-frequency allocation can be found at http://www.rfm.com/corp/new868dat/fccchart.pdf.

Because of the congestion or unavailability of usable spectrum at the lower frequency bands (below 20 GHz) and the recent demand for multimedia communication at high data-rate capabilities, system designers have directed their attention toward the use of SHF and EHF for communication (Acosta, 1999). Currently, there is a great deal of research on developing RF systems operating at frequencies above 20 GHz (K_A band and above; National Aeronautics and Space Administration, 1998).

This interest in the EHF band is justified because of its potential benefits, such as the availability of usable spectrum, high data-rate capability, reduced interference, and high achievable gain with narrow beam widths of small antennas (Ippolito, 1989). The drawback, however, is that at these frequencies atmospheric distortion, especially rain attenuation (absorption of the RF signal), is severe (Acosta & Horton, 1998; Xu, Rappaport, Boyle, & Schaffner, 2000). The severity of the meteorological effects increases with increasing frequency. At some frequency bands, the meteorological effects can cause a reduction in received signal amplitude, depolarization of the radio wave, and increase in thermal noise (Ippolito, 1989).

Radio Wave Characteristics

When electrical energy in the form of high-frequency voltage or current is applied to an antenna, it is converted to electromagnetic (EM) waves or radio-frequency energy. At the Tx, the antenna converts a time-varying voltage or current into a time-varying propagating EM wave. The resulting EM wave propagates in space away from the source (the antenna) at the speed of light with the succeeding wave front changing in amplitude as the voltage or current changes in amplitude. Radio waves propagate through space as traveling EM fields proportional to the time-varying voltage or current. The propagating RF energy is composed of an electric field and a magnetic field component. The two fields exist together because a change in the electric field generates a corresponding change in the magnetic field, and vice versa. At the Rx, the antenna performs an inverse operation of converting a time-varying propagating EM wave to a time-varying voltage or current.

Polarization of the radio wave is important and is given by the direction of the electric field component. Usually the construction and orientation of the antenna determine the electric field component. Many antennas are linearly polarized, either horizontally or vertically. The magnitude of the power radiated in the direction of propagation can be calculated as the effective isotropic (independent of direction) radiated power (EIRP) or effective radiated power (ERP). This is the maximum radiated power available from a Tx in the direction of maximum gain for isotropic or directional antennas, respectively. It is a measure of the effectiveness of an antenna in directing the transmitter power in a particular direction (Rappaport, 2002).

Forms of Radio Waves

Radio waves propagate in space in various forms. The characteristics of the propagating waves are of interest in many wireless communication systems designs. Propagating radio waves can be classified as direct (or free space), ground (or surface), tropospheric, and ionospheric. These types of waves are illustrated in Figure 3.

Direct waves, in which propagation is in free space without any obstruction, are the simplest kind of radio waves. They are projected in a straight LOS between the Tx and Rx. The two-way radio, cellular mobile telephone, and personal communication system seldom have this type of radio wave.

Ground waves are confined to the lower atmosphere or the surface of the earth. A ground wave includes that portion of the radio wave directly affected by terrain and objects on the terrain. It is guided along the surface of the earth, reflecting and scattering off buildings, vegetation, hills, mountains, and other irregularities on the earth's surface. These waves propagate outward from the antenna but undergo refraction due to variation in the density of the atmosphere (Garg & Wilkes, 1996). The signal strength decreases as the distance between the Tx and the Rx increases. This wave affects all frequencies in the MF, HF, and VHF ranges, and it is the dominant wave in cellular mobile radio systems. Vertical polarization, the direction of the electric-field component, is best for this type of

Table 1 Radio-Frequency Band Classifications and Characteristics

Frequency Band	Frequency Range	Propagation Characteristics	λ	ρ	L	Typical Use
Very low frequency (VLF)	<30 kHz	Low attenuation day and night; high atmospheric noise level	Long ↑	High ↓	Long ↑	Baseband signals; powerlines; home control systems; navigation and submarine communication
Low frequency (LF)	30–300 kHz	Slightly less reliable than VLF; absorption in daytime				Long-range navigation; marine communication; radio beacons
Medium frequency (MF)	0.3–3 MHz	Attenuation low at night, high in day; atmospheric noise				Maritime radio; direction finding; AM broadcasting
High frequency (HF)	3.0–30 MHz	Omni-directional energy radiation; quality varies with time of day, season, frequency, and solar activity				International broadcasting, military communication; long-distance aircraft and ship communication
Very high frequency (VHF)	30–300 MHz	Direct and ground waves; cosmic noise; antenna design is critical	Short	Low	Short	VHF TV; FM broadcast; two-way radio, AM aircraft communication and navigational aids
Ultra high frequency (UHF)	0.3–3 GHz	Line-of-sight (LOS); repeaters are used to cover greater distances; cosmic noise				UHF TV; cellular phone; radar; microwave links; personal communications services
Super high frequency (SHF)	3.0–30 GHz	LOS; atmospheric attenuation due to rain (>10 GHz), oxygen and water vapor				Satellite and radar communication; terrestrial microwave; wireless local loop
Extremely high frequency (EHF)	30–300 GHz	LOS; millimeter wave; atmospheric attenuation due to rain, oxygen and water vapor				Experimental; wireless local loop

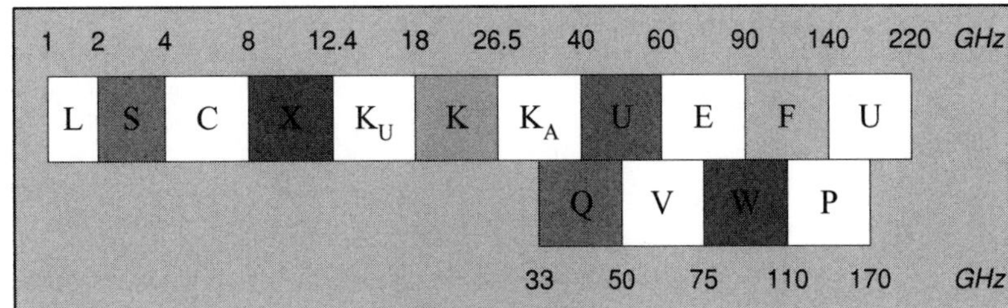

Figure 2: Typical symbol assignment for radio frequency bands.

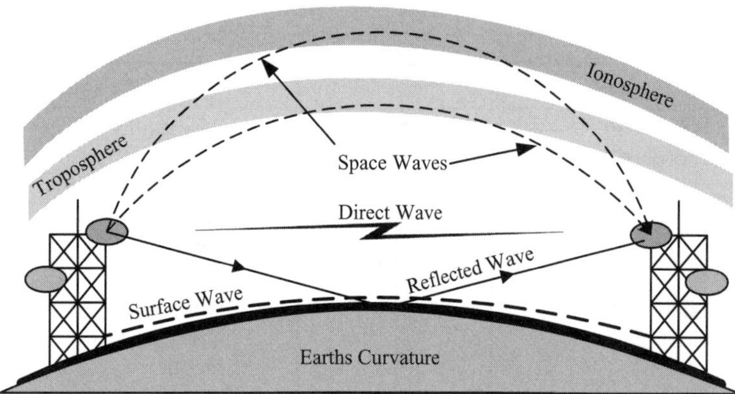

Figure 3: Common types of radio waves in wireless communication systems.

wave. The polarization is determined by the construction and orientation of the antenna.

Tropospheric and ionospheric waves are commonly referred to as sky waves. They propagate in outer space but can return to earth by reflection or scattering either in the troposphere or in the ionosphere. The tropospheric wave is that portion of the radio wave close to the earth's surface as a result of gradual bending in the lower atmosphere (Garg & Wilkes, 1996). The bending action is due to the changing effective dielectric constant of the atmosphere through which the wave is passing. Its reflective index gradually decreases with height, resulting in a bending path taken by the wave. The troposphere extends about 10 miles above the surface of the earth and applies to waves with wavelength shorter than 10 m (i.e., $\lambda < 10$ m). The ionospheric wave is similar to the tropospheric wave except that it travels farther and the reflection occurs in the ionosphere, 40–400 miles above the earth. Ionospheric propagation in the 3–30 MHz range is highly dependent on the state of solar activity and the subsequent levels of atmospheric ionization. This wave can be highly reliable for telemetry, tracking, weather forecasting, and tactical military applications. It is also used for global maritime, military, and aeronautical communications and shortwave broadcasting. Note that different wavelengths are reflected to dissimilar extents in the troposphere and ionosphere.

Radio-Frequency-Based Systems

Figure 4 shows the various forms of RF-based wireless communication systems, which is classified into six groups: microwave RF systems, fixed and mobile satellite systems, wireless networks and protocols, personal communication systems, remote sensing systems, and emerging wireless technologies. No distinction is made between the communication layers and protocols in this classification. These systems transmit and receive radio waves tuned to specific bands of frequencies. Microwave is loosely used to describe all radio frequencies between 1 and 40 GHz. This includes the UHF, SHF, and EHF systems. The lower microwave frequencies (i.e., UHF) are most often used for terrestrial-based RF systems, whereas the higher microwave frequencies (i.e., SHF and EHF) are used for satellite communications. A terrestrial microwave system transmits carefully focused beams of radio waves from a transmitting antenna to a receiving antenna. A terrestrial microwave system uses LOS propagation to communicate between the Tx and the Rx with a typical distance of 30 miles between relay towers.

Personal communications services (PCS) are a new generation of wireless-telephone technologies that introduce a wide range of features and services greater than those available in analog and digital cellular phone systems (International Engineering Consortium [IEC],

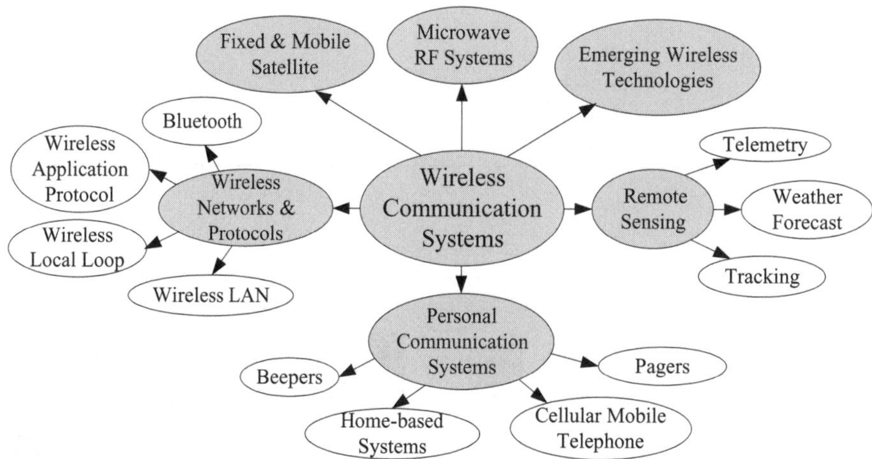

Figure 4: Different forms of radio-frequency (RF)-based wireless communication systems. LAN = local area network.

n.d., a). It includes any system that provides people with access to information services, such as cellular telephones, home-based systems (cordless telephones, remote control, short-range two-way radio), beepers, pagers, and much more (Goodman, 1997; Rappaport, 2002). PCS provides the user with an all-in-one wireless phone, paging, messaging, and data services. The most significant segment of this technology is the cellular mobile radio. It is the fastest growing segment of the telecommunications industry. Based on the number of new subscribers worldwide and the number of services, the cellular mobile radio system has evolved as the dominant wireless communication system. Its history dates back many decades, but the modern-day mobile radio became widespread in the 1980s (Rappaport, 2002). The cellular mobile radio system is discussed in more detail later. Wireless networks and protocols include systems such as WLAN, wireless local loops (WLL), wireless application protocol (WAP), and Bluetooth. These systems are used mainly to provide data communication. WLAN is an extension to or an alternative for a wired local area network (LAN). WLAN provides the functionality of wired LAN, without the physical constraints of the wire, combining data connectivity with user mobility (Bing, 2000; Geier, 1999; Wenig, 1996). WLANs have the potential to support user mobility and constant and unlimited access to information by linking several wireless devices to the wired infrastructure network. With WLAN, packets of data are converted into radio waves that are sent to other wireless devices or to a wireless access point (AP)–client connection from the wired LAN to the mobile user. The AP can reside at any node on the wired network and acts as a gateway for wireless users' data routed to the wired network. WLANs require special medium access control (MAC) layer protocols because of the broadcast nature of radio communication (Chen, 1994). A detailed discussion of WLAN is beyond the scope of this chapter. WLANs have gained strong popularity lately and are used widely in health care, industry, commerce, warehousing, and academia. An important feature of the WLAN is that it can be used independent of a wired network. That is, it can be used as a stand-alone network anywhere to link multiple computers together without extending a wired network. WLAN uses one of the three basic transmission protocols, namely, direct sequence spread spectrum (DSSS), frequency hopping spread spectrum (FHSS), or low-power narrowband. The majority of RF-based WLANs operate in the industrial, scientific, and medical (ISM) frequency bands, which are located at 902 to 928 MHz, 2.4 to 2.483 GHz, and 5.725 to 5.85 GHz, respectively. The different architectures of WLAN based on Agrawal and Zeng (2003) are summarized in Table 2, with symbols defined in the Glossary.

WLL is a system that connects telephone subscribers to the public switched telephone network using radio waves (IEC, n.d., b). With WLL, the traditional copper wire providing a link between the subscriber and the local exchange is replaced by a wireless RF network. WLL is advantageous for remote areas where the cost of wire would be prohibitive (i.e., adverse terrain or widely dispersed subscriber areas). With WLL, new service providers can quickly deploy wireless networks to meet customers' telephony needs rapidly. Existing landline operators can extend their networks using WLL. Cellular telephone companies can deliver residential service using WLL without going through the local telephone company.

WAP is an application environment and set of communication protocols (application, session, transaction, security, and transport layers) that allow wireless devices easy access to the Internet and advanced telephony services (WAP Forum, 2000; Stallings, 2002). WAP offers the ability to deliver unlimited range of mobile services to subscribers, independent of their network, manufacturer, vendor, or terminal. With WAP, mobile subscribers can access information and services from wireless handheld devices. WAP is based on existing Internet standards such as the Internet protocol (IP), extensible markup language (XML), hypertext markup language (HTML), and the hypertext transfer protocol (HTTP) and is designed to work with all wireless network technology. More information can be obtained from the WAP Forum (2000) and in the chapter on WAP in this encyclopedia.

Bluetooth is a wireless technology that makes possible connectivity to the Internet from mobile computers, mobile phones, and portable handheld devices without the need for cable connection. It facilitates fast and secure transmission of both voice and data, without LOS propagation. Some characteristics of Bluetooth technology are summarized in Table 2. Detailed information on Bluetooth can be found in another chapter in this encyclopedia.

Satellite communication is one of the traditional RF wireless communication systems. Signals can be transmitted directly from a ground station (GS) or gateway on earth to a satellite, and back to another GS. Sometimes the signal can be routed through another satellite (intersatellite) before it is transmitted back to the GS. We can identify a satellite system by how far the satellite is from the earth. The closer the satellite is to the earth, the shorter the time it takes to send signals to the satellite. There are three satellite orbits: low earth orbit (LEO), medium earth orbit (MEO), and geosynchronous earth orbit (GEO). A geosynchronous satellite completes one orbit around the earth in the same time it takes the earth to make one complete rotation. A geostationary satellite is in an orbit located directly above the equator.

LEO satellites are closest to the earth, beginning about 100 miles above the surface, and only take a couple of hours to circle the earth. Because LEO systems are orbiting so quickly, multiple satellites are required to provide constant coverage in one location. LEO systems have the capability to receive calls from the earth and pass them to an earth-based switching system in much shorter time than other satellites. However, because of the speed of the satellite, it is frequently necessary to hand off a particular call to a second satellite just rising over the horizon. This is similar to a cellular mobile radio system (discussed later), except that in this case it is the cell site (the satellite) that is moving rather than the user. The lower orbit has the advantage of allowing access to very low-power devices (Printchard et al., 1993). LEO satellites are used mainly for wireless transfer of electronic mail, pager systems, worldwide mobile telephony, spying, remote sensing, and video conferencing.

Table 2 Examples of Wireless Local Area Networks

Properties	IEEE 802.11	HiperLAN	Ricochet	HomeRF	Bluetooth
Spectrum (GHz)	2.400–2.48; 5.15–5.35, 5.525–5.825	5.15, 17.1	0.902–0.928	2.404–2.478	2.402–2.480
Range	150 feet	150 feet	1,000 feet	<150 feet	10 cm to 100 m
Power consumption	Not specified	Not specified	Not specified	100 mW	1 mW, 10 mW, and 100 mW
Energy conservation	Directory based	Yes	Unknown	Directory based	Yes
Physical layer	DSSS/FHSS/IR	DFS with BPSK/ QPSK/QAM	FHSS 162 hops/s	FHSS 50 hops/s	FHSS 1600 hops/s
Channel access	CSMA/CA	TDMA/TDD	TDMA	Hybrid TDMA and CSMA/CA	FHSS, Master slave TDMA
Mobility support	Not specified	Yes	Yes	No	No
Raw data rate	2, 11, 6–54 Mbps	23.5, 54 Mbps	288 kbps	1 and 2 Mbps	1 Mbps
Traffic	Data (DCF)	Data	Data	Voice + Data	Voice or Data
Speech coding	Unknown	OFDM	Not available	ADPCM, 32 bps	64 kbps with CSVD/log PCM
Security	40 bit RC-4	DES, Triple DES	RSA/RC-4	Blowfish	Minimal (in PHY)
Communication technology	Peer-to-peer, MS-BS	Peer-to-peer, MS-BS	Peer-to-peer	Peer-to-peer, MS-BS	Master/slave

Note. ADPCM = adaptive pulse code modulation; BPSK = binary phase shift keying; CDMA = code division multiple access; CSMA/CA = carrier sense multiple access with collision avoidance; CSVD = continuous variable slope delta; DES = data encryption standard; DFS = dynamic frequency selection; DSSS = direct sequence spread spectrum; FHSS = frequency hopping spread spectrum; IEEE = Institute of Electrical and Electronics Engineers; IR = infrared; MS-BS = mobile station–base station; OFDM = orthogonal frequency division multiplexing; PHY = physical layer; QAM = quadrature amplitude modulation; QPSK = quadrature phase shift keying; RC4 = Rivest cipher 4; RSA = Ron Rivest, Adi Shamir, and Len Adleman, inventors of the RSA code; TDD = time division duplexing; TMDA = time division multiple access.

GEO satellites circle the earth at a height of 22,300 miles, orbiting at the same rate as the earth rotates so that they appear stationary from the earth's perspective. Most GEO satellites rely on passive bent-pipe architecture so that they receive signals from transceivers on earth, amplify them, and send them back to specific regions on earth. GEO systems are used for a wide array of services including television broadcasts, long-distance telecommunications, and various scientific and military applications. GEO satellites are well suited to transmitting data but may be undesirable for voice communications because of the long propagation delay. It takes about one fourth of a second for a signal to travel from a terrestrial GS to the satellite and back. If the receiver GS replies, it takes another one fourth of a second, resulting in a total of half a second (Printchard, 1993). This is an unacceptably long delay for voice communication. Hence, voice communications are seldom carried via GEO satellites.

MEO satellites can be found between 1,000 and 22,300 miles and are mainly used for global positioning and navigation systems. MEO satellites are not as popular as the LEO or GEO for reasons beyond the scope of this chapter.

RADIO WAVE PROPAGATION

Propagation is the process of wave motion, which is important in the design and operation of RF systems. Because the received signal is always different from the transmitted signal, due to various propagation impairments, and because of the nature of the propagation itself, it is necessary to understand the properties of radio wave propagation. This is most important in telecommunication applications in predicting the transmission characteristics of the channel. When radio waves are radiated from an antenna, propagation is governed by the following mechanisms.

Free Space Propagation

This is the ideal propagation mechanism when the Tx and the Rx have direct LOS and are separated by a distance d between the Tx and the Rx. If P_t is the transmitted power, the received power P_r, a function of distance d, is given by (Rappaport, 2002)

$$P_r(d) = G_t G_r P_t \frac{\lambda^2}{(4\pi d)^2 L} = P_t \frac{A_{et} A_{et}}{(\pi d)^2 L}, \qquad (2)$$

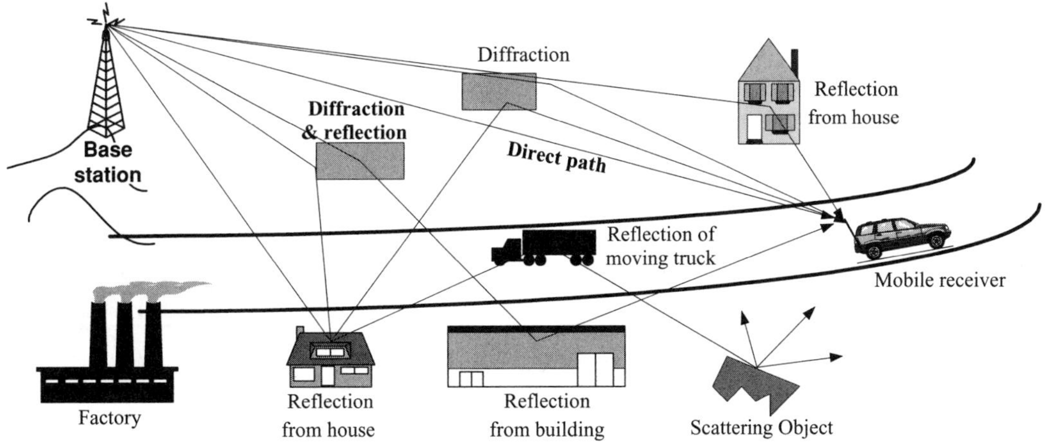

Figure 5: Illustration of reflection, diffraction, scattering, and absorption.

where A_e, G, and L are the effective area, antenna gain, and system loss factor, respectively. The subscripts t and r refer to the transmitter and receiver, respectively. From this relationship, we observe that the received power diminishes at the rate of 20 dB/decade as the distance increases. The product $P_t G_t$ is defined as EIRP, introduced earlier (i.e., $EIRP = P_t G_t$).

Reflection and Refraction

When a radio wave strikes an object with dimensions very large compared with its wavelength, reflection occurs. All radio waves will undergo reflection if the propagation medium undergoes abrupt changes in its physical properties. This is illustrated in Figure 5. The more abrupt the discontinuity, the more pronounced the reflection. Depending on the type of object, the RF energy can be partially reflected, fully reflected, or absorbed. It is possible to compute the amount of reflection from the properties of the two media. If the incident object is a good conductor, the wave is totally reflected and the angle of incidence is the same as the angle of reflection.

Refraction (see Figure 5) occurs at the boundary between two dielectrics, when the incident wave propagates into another medium at an angle. When radio waves propagate from a medium of one density to a medium of another density, the speed of the wave changes. This change in speed will cause the wave to bend at the boundary between the two media. The wave will always bend toward the denser medium.

Diffraction

Diffraction of radio waves occurs when the waves encounter some obstruction along their path and tend to propagate around the edges and corners and behind the obstruction. This is illustrated in Figure 5. The height or dimension of the obstruction has to be comparable to the wavelength of the transmission. The same obstruction height may produce lower diffraction loss at higher λ than at lower λ. The result of this effect is that the object shadows the radio wave. The field strength of the wave decreases as the receiver moves deeper into a shadowed region.

Scattering

Scattering is also illustrated in Figure 5. It is due to small objects and irregularities in the channel, rough incident surfaces, or particles in the atmosphere. When the radio wave encounters objects or particles with dimensions smaller than the wavelength of the wave, scattering occurs, which causes the signal to spread in all directions.

Interference

Interference can occur when the transmitted radio wave arrives at the same location via two or more paths (multipath). One of the ways this can happen is illustrated in Figure 6. This figure shows three waves arriving at a mobile receiver (the car) after traveling slightly different paths. Because of their phase differences, the radio waves can add either constructively or destructively at the receiver. If the phase shift experienced by the propagating waves is time-varying, then it can cause a rapid variation in the received signal, resulting in fading.

Absorption

Absorption describes the process where radio energy penetrates a material or substance and gets converted to heat. Two cases of absorption of radio waves are prevalent. One occurs when radio waves are incident upon a lossy medium and the other is due to atmospheric effects. When the radio wave strikes an object, the incident wave (perpendicular wave) propagates into the lossy medium and the radio energy experiences exponential decay with distance as it travels into the material. The wave either is totally dissipated or will reemerge from the material with smaller amplitude and continue the propagation. The skin depth is the distance for the field strength to be reduced to 37% of its original value—the energy of the wave is reduced by 0.37. Particles in the atmosphere absorb RF energy. Absorption through the atmosphere also depends on the weather conditions—fair and dry, drizzle, heavy rain, fog, snow, hail, and so on. Usually, the absorption of RF energy is ignored below 10 GHz.

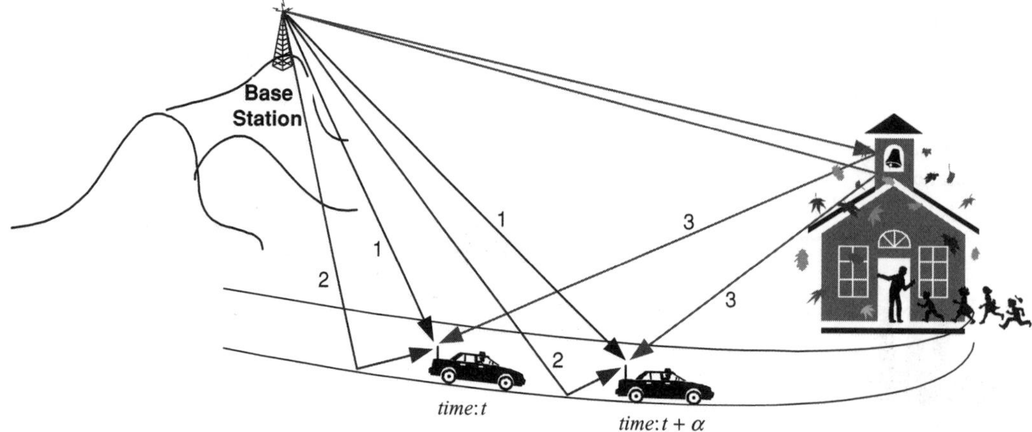

Figure 6: Interference of radio wave.

Doppler Effect

Doppler shift is the change in frequency due to the difference in speed between two points in space. It is observed whenever there is relative motion between the Tx and the Rx. For a mobile moving with a constant velocity v, the received carrier frequency f_c will be shifted by the amount

$$f_d = f_m \cos\theta = \frac{v\cos\theta}{\lambda} = \frac{v_{eff}}{\lambda} = \frac{v_{eff} f_c}{c}, \tag{3}$$

where θ is the path angle, $f_m = v/\lambda$ is the maximum Doppler frequency f_d, at $\theta = 0^o$; and v_{eff} is the effective velocity of the mobile (Garg & Wilkes, 1996). The Doppler shift, bounded by $\pm f_m$, is related to the phase change $\Delta\theta$ caused by the change in path length. Because each component of the received multipath signal arrives from a different direction, each contributes a different value to the Doppler spreading. This effectively increases the bandwidth of the received signal. Depending on the direction of motion and the source, the frequency can be shifted up or down (i.e., $\pm f_m$). The result of this shift is a random phase and frequency modulation of the received RF carrier, which may necessitate the use of differential phase and frequency detection techniques.

The propagation mechanisms just described strongly influence system design parameters such as the choice of transmitting and receiving antennas, Tx powers, modulation techniques, and much more. Each of these propagation mechanisms contributes to losses in the RF energy and hence limits system performance. In wireless mobile communications, propagation losses are commonly classified into path loss, shadowing, and multipath fading. These losses are described next.

Path Loss

Path loss (PL) refers to the large-scale envelope fluctuation in the radio propagation environment, which varies with the distance between the Tx and Rx. Because the Rx is located at some distance d from the Tx, a loss factor is used to relate the transmitted power to the received power. For amplitude fading, an increase in d normally results in an increase in PL. Different models have been used to model path loss, but each model obeys the distance propagation law. In free space, PL is expressed as the ratio of the radiated power P_t, to the received power P_r and is given by

$$PL(dB) = 10\log_{10}\frac{P_t}{P_r} = -10\log_{10}\left[\frac{G_t G_r \lambda^2}{(4\pi)^2 d^2}\right] \tag{4}$$

Shadowing

Because of topographical variations along the transmission path, the signal is diffracted and the average power of the received signal is not constant. Shadowing or large-scale fading refers to slow variations in the local mean of the received signal strength. This variation causes shadowing. The signal is shadowed by obstructions such as buildings and natural terrain, which leads to gradual variations in the mean power of the received signal. The effect is a very slow change in the local mean signal, say P_s. Shadowing is generally modeled by a lognormal distribution, meaning that $s_d = 10\log_{10} P_s$ is normally distributed, with s_d given in dB (Yacoub, 1993). Shadowing is the dominant factor determining signal fading.

Multipath Fading

The collective effect of reflection, refraction, diffraction, and scattering leads to multipath propagation. Because of reflection, refraction, and scattering of radio waves along the channel by manmade structures and natural objects along the path of propagation, the transmitted signal often reaches the receiver by more than one path. This results in the phenomenon known as multipath fading. The signal components arriving from indirect paths and a direct path (if it exists) combine at the receiver to give a distorted version of the transmitted signal. These radio waves are attenuated differently, and they arrive with different path gains, time delays, and phases. The resultant signal may vary widely in amplitude and phase depending on the distribution of intensity and relative propagation in time of wave and bandwidth of the transmitted signal. The number of paths may change drastically when the mobile unit changes its position depending on the increase or decrease in the number of intervening obstacles. Unlike shadowing, multipath fading is usually used to describe small-scale fading or rapid fluctuation in the amplitude of a radio signal over a short period of time or over short distances. It is affected by rapid changes in the signal strength over short distances or time intervals and random frequency variations due to varying Doppler shifts on different multipath signals (Rappaport, 2002).

The loss factor associated with multipath fading is usually modeled in the channel impulse response. A transmitted impulse will arrive at the Rx as the sum of several impulses with different magnitudes, delays, and phases. For M multipath, the composite impulse response $h(t, \tau)$ for any given locations of the Tx and Rx is given by

$$h(t,\tau) = \sum_{k=1}^{M} \alpha_k(t)\delta\left(t - \tau_k(t)\right)e^{-j\phi_k(t)}, \tag{5}$$

where $\alpha_k, (t), \tau_k(t)$, and $\phi_k(t)$ represent the time-varying amplitude, delay, and phase of the kth path signal, and $\delta(\cdot)$ is the Dirac delta function. This shows that, in general, the received signal is a series of time-delayed, phase-shifted, attenuated versions of the transmitted signal. The variables $h(t, \tau)$, $\alpha_k(t)$, $\phi_k(t)$, and $\tau_k(t)$ are random.

WIRELESS COMMUNICATION TECHNIQUES

Because the wireless channel is not a reliable propagation medium, techniques to achieve reliable and efficient communication are necessary. In mobile channels, for example, the Rx has to constantly track changes in the propagation environment to ensure optimal extraction of the signal of interest. As the receiver moves, the surrounding environment changes affecting the received signal's amplitude, phase, and delay. The multipath received signals are combined at the antenna either constructively or destructively. During destructive combining, the received signal may not be strong enough to produce reliable communication because of the degradation in the signal-to-noise ratio (SNR). It is not uncommon in shadowed signals for the amplitude of the received signal to drop by 30 dB or more within a distance of a fraction of a wavelength (Eng et al., 1996). Hence, achieving reliable communication over a wireless channel is a daunting task.

To counter this problem, techniques have been developed for efficient wireless communication. These include spread spectrum, multiple access, diversity, equalization, coding, and related techniques such as multicarrier modulation, orthogonal frequency division multiplexing, multicode and multirate techniques, and multiple input multiple output system, to mention only a few. All these techniques are aimed at increasing the reliability of the channel and the performance of the system. Discussion of some of these techniques is beyond the scope of this chapter. However, a summary of the major wireless communication techniques follows.

Spread Spectrum

Spread spectrum (SS) is a modulation technique in which the transmitted bandwidth B_{ss} is much greater than the data bandwidth B_s. The idea is to transform a signal with bandwidth B_s into a noise-like signal of much larger bandwidth B_{ss}. Spreading is usually achieved by modulating the data with a pseudo-random noise (PN) sequence called the "chip" at a rate that is much higher than the data rate. The significance of SS is evident from the capacity equation, given by

$$C = B\log_2(1 + SNR), \tag{6}$$

where C is the channel capacity in bits and B is the bandwidth in hertz. Observe that by increasing the bandwidth B, we may decrease the SNR without decreasing the capacity and, hence, the performance.

The main parameter in SS systems is the processing gain, G_p, defined as

$$G_p = \frac{\textit{Spread Bandwidth}}{\textit{Information Bandwidth}} = \frac{B_{ss}}{B_s} = \frac{T_b}{T_c}, \tag{7}$$

where T_b and T_c are the bit period and the chip period, respectively. G_p is sometimes known as the "spreading factor" (Rappaport, 2002). From a system viewpoint, G_p is the performance increase achieved by spreading. It determines the number of users that can be allowed in a system, and hence the amount of multipath reduction effect. It is used to describe the signal fidelity gained at the cost of bandwidth. It is through G_p that increased system performance is achieved without requiring a higher SNR. For SS systems, it is advantageous to have G_p as high as possible, because the greater the G_p, the greater the system's ability to suppress interference. SS techniques are used in cellular mobile telephones, global positioning satellites (GPS), and very small aperture satellite terminals. The strength of this system is that when G_p is large, the system offers great immunity to interference.

There are two major methods of SS modulation: direct sequence spread spectrum and frequency hopping spread spectrum. In DSSS, the frequency of the given signal is spread across a band of frequencies, as described earlier. The spreading algorithm changes in a random fashion that appears to make the spread signal a random noise source. FHSS is the repeated switching of f_c from one band to another during transmission. Radio signals hop from one f_c to another at a specific hopping rate and the sequence appears to be random. In this case, the instantaneous frequency output of the Tx jumps from one value to another based on the pseudo-random input from the code generator. The overall bandwidth required for FHSS is much wider than that required to transmit the same information using only one carrier. However, each f_c and its associated sidebands must stay within a defined bandwidth.

Diversity

Diversity is one of the techniques widely used to increase system performance in wireless communication systems. Diversity combining refers to the system in which two or more closely similar copies of some desired signal are available and experience independent fading. In diversity systems, the received signals from several transmission paths, all carrying the same information with individual statistics, are combined with the hope of improving the SNR of the decision variables used in the detection process. Diversity-combining techniques could be based on space (antenna), frequency, angle of arrival, polarization, and time of reception (Eng, 1996; Yacoub, 1993). For example, in space diversity, the transmitted signal is received via N different antennas with each multipath received through a particular antenna. This can be regarded as communication over N parallel fading channels. Diversity reception is known to improve the reliability of the systems without increasing either the transmitter power or the channel bandwidth. Regardless of the type of diversity used, the signals must be combined and detected at the receiver. A proper combination of the signal from various branches results in improved performance. The method of diversity combining chosen will affect the receiver performance and complexity. The common combining techniques in wireless communication are maximal ratio combining (MRC), equal gain combining (EGC), and selection diversity (SD). In MRC, the received signals from individual paths are weighted and added so as to emphasize more credible signals and suppress less credible ones (Yacoub, 1993). In EGC, the received signals are equally weighted and then combined without regard to the individual signal strength. In SD, the branch with the best or most desirable signal is selected and the weaker ones are ignored.

Multiple Access

Because the RF spectrum is finite and a limited resource, it is necessary to share the available resources between users. Multiple access techniques are the primary means of sharing the resources in wireless systems. These techniques are multiplexing protocols that allow more than a pair of transceivers to share a common medium, which can be achieved through frequency, time, or code, giving rise to three popular techniques known as frequency division multiple access (FDMA), time division multiple access (TDMA), and code division multiple access (CDMA). In FDMA, the whole spectrum is divided into subbands, and the subbands are assigned to individual users on demand. The users use the entire channel for the duration of their transmissions. If the transmission path deteriorates, the user is switched to another channel. This access technique is widely used in wireless multiuser systems. Instead of dividing the available frequency as in FDMA, the available time is divided into frames of equal duration in the case of TDMA. Only one user is allowed to either transmit or receive in each time frame. The transmissions from various users are interlaced into cyclic time structure. Instead of using frequencies or time slots, CDMA techniques distinguish between multiple users using digital codes. Each user is assigned a unique PN code sequence, which is uncorrelated with the data. Because the signals are distinguished by codes, many users can share the same bandwidth simultaneously (i.e., signals are transmitted in the same frequency at the same time).

CELLULAR COMMUNICATIONS

Currently, cellular mobile communication is undoubtedly the most popular RF wireless communication system. In cellular systems, instead of using a single large coverage area with one high-power transceiver (used in traditional mobile systems), the coverage area is divided into small, localized coverage areas called cells. Figure 7 compares the traditional mobile telephone with the cellular telephone structures. Each cell has a base station (BS) or cell site, which in comparison uses much less power. The BS can communicate with mobiles as long as they are within range. To prevent interference, adjacent cells are assigned different portions of the available frequencies.

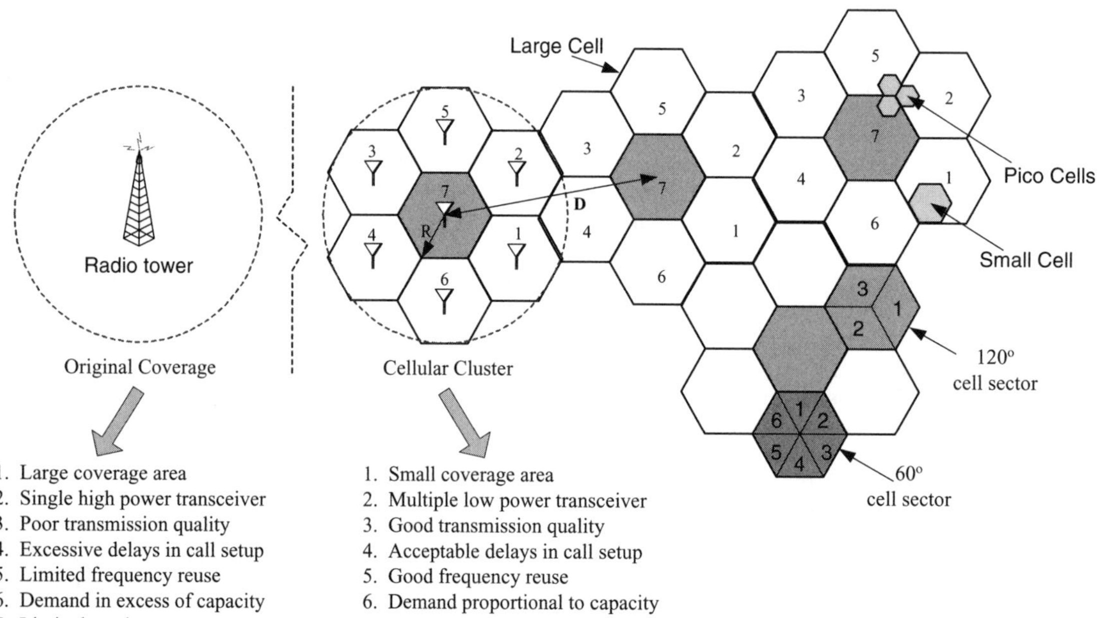

Figure 7: Traditional and cellular mobile radio structure showing frequency reuse, cell splitting, and cell sectoring (R = cell radius, D = frequency reuse distance).

With a certain distance between two cells, the assigned spectrum of a given cell can be reused. To explain the concept of cellular mobile communication, a summary of the major concepts and techniques is now presented.

Cells and Clusters

A cell is the basic geographic unit of a cellular system, commonly represented as a hexagon. The term *cellular* comes from this hexagonal or honeycomb shape of the coverage area. Each cell has a BS transmitting over a cell. Because of constraints imposed by natural terrain and manmade structures, the true shapes of cells are not hexagons. The coverage area of cells is called the footprint. The BS simultaneously communicates with many mobiles using one channel (pair of frequencies) per mobile. One frequency is for the forward link (BS to the mobile), and the other frequency is for the reverse link (mobile to the BS). Each cell size varies depending on the landscape, subscriber density, and demand within a particular region. Cells can be added to accommodate growth, for example, creating new cells by overlaying, splitting, or sectoring existing cells. These techniques increase the capacity of the system. Sectoring existing cells and then using directional antennas can also increase capacity.

A cluster is a group of cells. No frequencies are reused within a cluster. Figure 7 illustrates a 7-cell cluster, indicated by the dotted circle. Frequency can be reused for all cells numbered 7. Frequencies used in one cell cluster can be reused in another cluster of cells. A larger number of cells per cluster arrangement reduce interference to the system.

Frequency Reuse

Frequency reuse is a technique of allocating channels to cellular systems. Because of the unavailability of spectrum at the cellular band, channel frequencies must be reused. Cells are assigned groups of channels that are completely different from those of neighboring cells. Cells with the same number have the same set of frequencies. If the number of available frequencies is 7, the frequency reuse factor is 1/7, which implies that each cell is using one seventh of available frequencies (Rappaport, 2002). Frequency reuse introduces interference into the system.

Interference

In cellular mobile communications, there are two types of intrinsic interference: co-channel interference (CCI) and adjacent channel interference (ACI). These interferences are a result of frequency reuse. CCI is the interference between signals having the same frequency (i.e., the reuse frequencies), whereas ACI is the interference between signals having frequencies close together. For example suppose channel 1 has frequencies 825.030 MHz (mobile) and 870.030 MHz (BS), and channel 2 has frequencies 825.060 MHz and 870.060 MHz. Channels 1 and 2 have frequencies close to one another, which will result in ACI. Any other signals having the frequencies of channel 1, 825.030 (mobile) and 870.030 MHz (BS), are co-channel signals and will suffer from co-channel interference. Note that the interference effect is related to the ratio of the reuse distance D and the cell radius R. This is known as the Q-factor ($Q = D/R$) and is used to measure the level of CCI. A higher Q value improves transmission quality due to smaller CCI. That is, increasing D improves isolation of RF energy between cells and hence minimizes interference. The ACI is mainly due to imperfect filtering allowing nearby frequencies to leak into the passband of the desired signal (out-of-band interference).

Cell Splitting and Sectoring

Cell splitting is the process of subdividing a congested cell into smaller cells, each with its base station. As the traffic load carried by a large cell reaches capacity, cell splitting is used to increase system capacity. In this way, heavy-traffic regions can be split into as many smaller areas as necessary to provide acceptable service levels. Cell splitting decreases R, while leaving Q relatively unchanged. Notice that more cells imply that more cell boundaries will be crossed more often, increasing trunking and handoff. Only those cells that have traffic overloads are candidates for splitting. However, if cells are split in only a part of a system, serious channel assignment problems may result. The difficulty encountered when all the cell sites are not split can be resolved by implementing cell overlay.

Cell sectoring is the process of dividing cells into sectors and replacing a single omni-directional antenna with a directional antenna. Common sectors sizes are 120°, 90°, 60°, and 30°. Cell sectors of 60° and 120° are illustrated in Figure 7. When cells are sectored, R is unchanged, D is reduced, the amount of frequency reuse is increased, and hence capacity is increased. It is observed that the spectral efficiency of the system is enhanced because the frequency can be reused more often.

Handoff

Handoff is the process used to maintain a call in progress when the mobile user moves between cells. Handoff is generally needed when a mobile is at a cell boundary or reaches a gap in signal strength. Because adjacent cells do not use the same frequency, a call must either be dropped or transferred from one radio channel to another when a mobile user crosses the line between adjacent cells. Because dropping the call is unacceptable, the process of handoff is necessary. As the user moves between cells, the transmission is "handed off" between cells to maintain seamless service.

ELEMENTS OF WIRELESS COMMUNICATION SECURITY

In all communication systems, whether wireless or not, it is extremely important to ensure the authenticity of all messages. Also, because a wireless system consists of both wireless and wired components, system security involves the security of both components. In a wireless system, communication through an open-air medium makes the information more vulnerable to additional security risk. Given that RF signals propagate beyond walls and buildings, the task of securing wireless RF transmissions has become more complex. This situation is compounded by additional difficulties of a wireless system such as limited bandwidth, high latency, and unstable connections. In all cases, however, the objective is to authenticate the user, secure the data, and ensure that the traffic is not altered during communication.

Security Methods and Practices

One of the important ingredients in the security or integrity of information transmission is secrecy. The need for secure communications particularly over the airways is more profound than ever, given that the conduct of much of our commerce, business, and personal matters is being carried out by computer and communication systems. The main components of the security processes for communication systems cryptographic techniques, security protocols, access control methods.

Cryptography. Cryptography is the transformation of a message into coded form by encryption and the recovery of the original message by decryption. Encryption and decryption are the primary tools used to ensure secure communication, which makes the message indecipherable to anyone other than the intended user. Encryption of a message could be as simple as permuting the message bits in a prespecified manner before transmission or as complex as source and channel coding and decoding (Agrawal & Zeng, 2003). Cryptographic systems offer three important services: (a) *secrecy*—the denial of access to information by unauthorized users; (b) *authenticity*—the validation of the source and use of a message; and (c) *integrity*—the assurance that a message in transit is not modified by accidental or deliberate means.

Conventional cryptography, commonly referred to as *single-key cryptography* or *secret-key or shared-key cryptography,* uses a single piece of private and secret information known as *key*. This form of cryptography operates on the assumption that the key is known to the transmitter and the receiver only, and that once the message is encrypted, it is not possible to be deciphered without knowledge of the key. Another type of cryptography is the *public-key cryptography* or *two-key cryptography,* in which each user is provided with the key consisting of a public portion generating the public transformation, and a private portion (secret), generating the private transformation (Computer Security Resource Center [CSRC], 2001). Finally, because of the limited bandwidth and processing power of wireless systems (e.g., mobile device), robust encryption schemes may be difficult to attend.

Security Protocol. *Protocol* is a set of rules that govern the communication between the transmitter and the receiver. In wireless systems, wired equivalent privacy (WEP) and the wireless transport layer security (WTLS) are the two main *security protocols.* WEP is the standard for encryption in the IEEE 802.11 wireless LAN standard. One weakness of WEP is that a single key is shared between all the users (mobile stations) and access points (APs). This is not very reliable and also cumbersome to manage as security problems have been reported with the WEP (CSRC 2002a, 2002b). However, the Wi-Fi protected access (WPA) provided better security features compared with the WEP. Yet no matter how messy the birthing process, WPA seems to be a improvement over the present state of WLAN security by providing improved encryption and simple but robust user authentication that can be used in home wireless networks.

The WTLS is the security layer in the WAP that adds security to mobile devices with little computing power by making the encryption process efficient. At the WAP gateway, the wireless data must be unencrypted from WTLS and reencrypted into a wired encryption protocol like the secure socket layer (SSL).

Access Control. Illegal intrusions into a network are controlled by *access-control* methods or devices such as firewalls, RADIUS (remote authentication dial-in user service), and authentication servers. A firewall provides preliminary filtering of unauthorized traffic to specific resources or network segments, and a typical firewall classifies traffic on the basis of predefined addresses (IP addresses).

Authentication and authorization mechanisms restrict access to the network and its resources, enabling usage only when provided with a legal identification and password. With authentication the genuineness of the user, or lack of it, is determined. Unfortunately, this is not very reliable, because user identifications and passwords can be obtained or guessed, and therefore a user connecting to a network or service may not necessarily be the authorized user.

A secure wireless system must be capable of protecting the confidentiality, integrity, and nonrepudiation of the message (Bhargarva & Agrawal, 2001; Venkataraman & Agrawal, 2000). Threats on security can be viewed as potential violations of security. Hence, a wireless communication system requires secure medium access control (MAC) protocols. MAC protocols must be able to have various mechanisms to handle the diverse traffic demands of different services as securely as possible. Figure 8

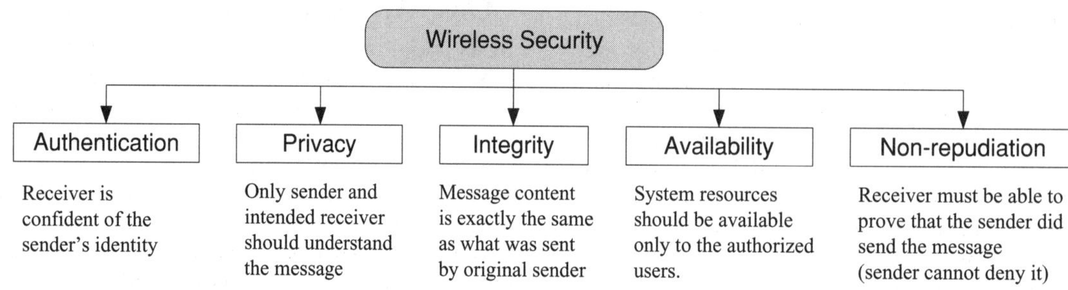

Figure 8: Wireless security services.

Table 3 List of Security Mechanisms

Security Mechanism	Remark
Security prevention	Enforces security during the operation of a system by preventing security violations. It is implemented to counter security attacks.
Security detection	Detects both attempts to violate security and to address successful security violations. An intrusion detection system (IDS) comes under this category
Recovery	Used to restore the system to a presecurity violation start after a security violation has been detected

summarizes the various categories of attacks that could be brought on wireless.

Security maintenance services enhance the security of all information transfers in the wireless system, by implementing countermeasures to the various possible attacks. Security requirements of wireless systems depend on the amount of investment and the characteristics of applications running on the system. For example, electronic funds transfer, reservation systems, and typical control systems have different levels of security demands and expectations. For most systems, the cost for security increases exponentially with increased level of security needed. Hence, there is a tradeoff between the level of increasing system security and the potential cost incurred. The wireless security services are summarized in Figure 8. To provide efficient security, the system must address the five cardinal security services depicted in Figure 8. Some of the mechanisms used for preventing or mitigating the effect of attacks in wireless systems are summarized in Table 3.

Wireless Security Risk and Threats

According the National Institute for Standards and Technology (NIST), security threats in general can be classified into one of the following categories (NIST, 2003): (a) fraud and theft, (b) malicious hackers, (c) malicious code, (d) threats to personal privacy, (e) employee sabotage, (f) loss of physical and infrastructure support, (g) industrial espionage, (h) errors and omissions, and (i) foreign government espionage. All of these represent potential threats in wireless systems as well. These threats, if successful, place information at risk. Security services (e.g., confidentiality, integrity, and availability) of wireless systems are the prime objectives of all security methods and practices.

Risks in wireless networks include the risks of wired networks in addition to the new risks introduced by the wireless nature of the system. Threats can be accidental or intentional. Accidental threats result due to operational mistakes of system and hardware or software failure. Intentional threats (attacks) are actions performed by an entity with an intention to violate security. Specific threats and vulnerabilities to wireless systems in general are summarized in Table 4.

Security attacks can be broadly divided into two groups: active and passive attacks. These two broad classes are then subdivided into other types of attacks as illustrated in Figure 9. An attack is said to be *passive* when an unauthorized user simply gains access to a network without modifying its content such as in eavesdropping and traffic flow analysis. In *eavesdropping,* the attacker simply monitors transmissions for message content. An example of this attack is a person listening in on transmissions on a local area network between two workstations, or tuning into transmissions between a wireless handset and a base station.

In *traffic analysis,* the attacker, in a more subtle way, gains intelligence by monitoring the transmissions patterns for messages between communicating units, which can yield significant amounts of information through the flow of information.

An attack is said to be *active* when an unauthorized user makes modifications to a message, data stream, or file. It is possible to detect this type of attack, but it may not be preventable. Active attacks may be in the form of one or more of the following: *masquerading, replay, message modification,* and *denial-of-service (DoS)*. In *masquerading,* the attacker impersonates an authorized user and thereby gains certain unauthorized privileges. In *replay,* the attacker monitors transmissions (passive attack) and, using the obtained information, retransmits messages as the legitimate user. *Message modification* involves an attacker who alters a legitimate message by deleting, adding to, changing, or reordering the message. In DoS, the attacker prevents or prohibits the normal use or management of communications facilities. DoS involves hijacking of the resources, thereby preventing authorized user from utilizing network resources.

In general, it is harder to detect passive attacks because they do not disturb the system. Encrypting messages can partly solve the problem. The consequences of passive or active attacks include loss of privacy, loss of proprietary information, legal and recovery costs, tarnished image, and loss of network service (Agrawal & Zeng, 2003).

SECURITY OF WLAN

The technology of a wireless network, which enables one or more devices to communicate without physical connection, ranges from complex systems such as cellular phones and WLAN to simple devices such as wireless headphones, microphones, and other devices that do not process or store information. All these technologies use radio waves for transmitting and receiving information. Based on the coverage area, wireless networks can be classified into wireless wide area network (WWAN), WLAN, and wireless personal area network (WPAN). WWAN technologies include mobile cellular network, cellular digital packet data (CDPD), global system for mobile communications (GSM), and Mobitex. WLAN includes systems such as IEEE 802.11a (54 Mbps @ 5 GHz), IEEE 802.11b (11 Mbps @ 2.4 GHz), IEEE 802.11g (54 Mbps @ 2.4 GHz), and HiperLAN (54 Mbps @ 5 GHz, used in Europe). WPAN are network technologies such as Bluetooth and HomeRF. Although their coverage areas are different, their communication techniques are similar because they transmit and

Table 4 Threats and Vulnerabilities to Wireless Systems in General

Security Risk and Threats	Remark
Wired system risks	These include all the vulnerabilities that exist in a conventional wired network.
Unauthorized access	This includes unauthorized access to a network through wireless connections, bypassing any firewall protections.
Fraud and theft	1. Due to the portability of wireless devices, theft is more likely to be committed by authorized and unauthorized users of the system. Hence, the information contained in the device can be compromised. 2. Stolen wireless devices can reveal sensitive or private information.
Malicious hackers	1. Malicious hackers or crackers can break into a system without authorization, usually for personal gain or to do harm. Such hackers may gain access to the wireless network access point by eavesdropping. 2. Sensitive information may be intercepted and disclosed and perhaps maliciously used. 3. Malicious entities may steal the identity of legitimate users and masquerade on the networks. 4. Malicious entities may be able to violate the privacy of legitimate users and be able to track their actual movements. 5. Data may be extracted without detection from improperly configured devices.
Malicious code	1. Denial of service attacks may be directed at wireless connections or devices. 2. Malicious code such as viruses, worms, Trojan horses, logic bombs, or other unwanted software, designed to damage files or bring down a system, can easily be introduced into a wireless system. 3. Sensitive data may be corrupted during improper synchronization. 4. Through wireless connections, malicious entities may connect to the wired network for the purposes of launching attacks and concealing their activity. 5. Interlopers may be able to gain connectivity to network controls and thereby disable or disrupt operations.
Industrial and foreign espionage	1. Industrial and foreign espionage involves gathering proprietary data from corporations or intelligence information from governments through eavesdropping. In wireless networks, the espionage threat stems from the relative ease with which eavesdropping can occur on radio transmissions. 2. Spying for military applications also falls under this category.

receive information using radio waves. Because wireless network and technology are so diverse, I limit our discussion on the security issues related to the IEEE 802.11 WLAN technology as an example.

Security Methods in Wireless LAN

WLAN is a flexible data communication system implemented as an extension to or as an alternative for, a wired LAN (CSRC, 2002). Using RF technology, WLAN transmits and receives data over the air, minimizing the need for wired connections. It combines data connectivity with user mobility. A WLAN has wireless client stations that use radio waves to communicate to an access point (AP). The client stations are generally equipped with a wireless network interface card (NIC) consisting of the radio modem and the necessary logic and software to interact with the access point. An AP, a stationary device that is part of the wired infrastructure, comprises essentially a radio modem on one side and a bridge to the wired network on the other. The AP is analogous to a cell-site (base station) in cellular communications. All communications between the client stations and the wired network go through the AP. Having gained strong

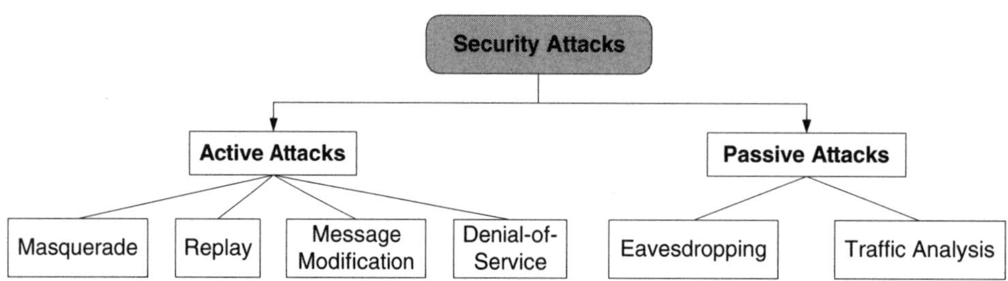

Figure 9: Different types of security attacks.

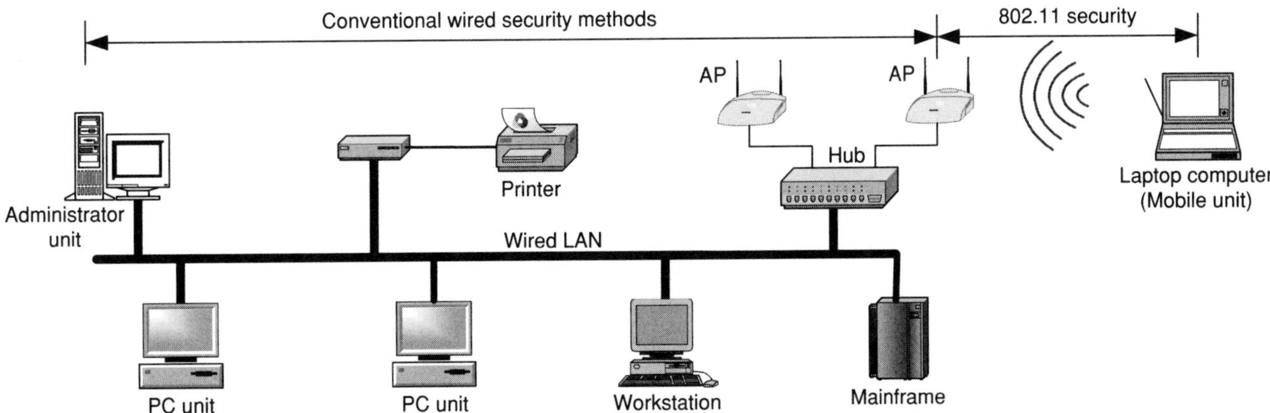

Figure 10: Security infrastructure in IEEE 802.11 wireless networks.

popularity lately, WLAN is used in health care, retail, manufacturing, warehousing, and academia.

The preferred protocol for WLAN is the IEEE 802.11 standard (The IEEE Working Group for WLAN Standards, n.d.). Without authentication and encryption, WLANs are extremely vulnerable. The security services are provided largely by the WEP security protocol. WEP has two main design goals: to protect against eavesdropping and to prevent unauthorized access. WEP uses RC4 encryption on a 40- or 128-bit shared key. Encrypts of payload is undertaken while frame is "in the air."

IEEE 802.11 defines mechanism for encrypting frames using WEP as follows:

1. A key is shared between all members of network.
2. The encryption algorithm for WEP is RC4. It is used to generate the key stream, which is added to the plaintext code using modulo-2 addition (exclusive-ORed) against plaintext to produce ciphertext.
3. The decryption algorithm for WEP is also RC4 which is exclusive-ORed with the ciphertext to reproduce plaintext.
4. WEP appends 24-bit initialization vector (IV) to the shared key and using this combined key + IV, it generates RC4 key schedule. WEP selects new IV for every packet.
5. Encapsulation transports the IV and ciphertext from sender (encryptor) to receiver (decryptor).
6. WEP uses a cyclic redundancy check (CRC) code of length 32 for integrity check of the frame. The CRC is computed over data payload and appended to the frame before encryption. WEP encrypts CRC with rest of data payload.
7. Authentication process is only a one-way client medium; access control protocol address only.

WEP does not provide end-to-end security, but only for the wireless portion of the connection, as shown in Figure 10.

Security Services for IEEE 802.11 Standards

The 802.11 standard addresses three basic security services—authentication, confidentiality, and integrity. These three basic security services are summarized as follows:

Authentication—WEP authentication process is used to provide access control to the network through denying access to client stations that cannot be authenticated properly. Authentication can be achieved through cryptography or noncryptographic means. The authentication process is illustrated in Figure 11. Please note that

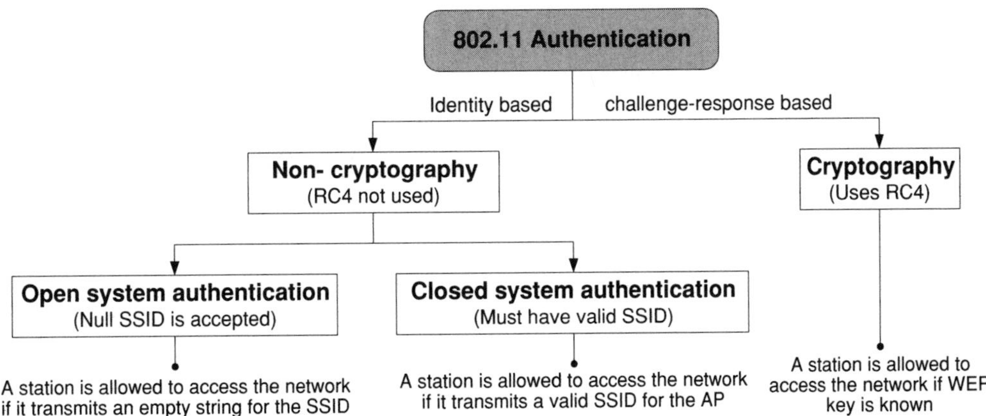

Figure 11: Authentication processes in 802.11 WLAN standards. AP = access point; SSID = service set identifier; WEP = wired equivalent privacy.

Table 5 Security Problems With Current 802.11 WLAN

Security Issues and Vulnerability	Remarks
Cryptography	1. Cryptographic keys are short. Standard 40-bit keys are inadequate and vulnerable to attacks. The longer the key, the less likely the key can be recomputed from a brute-force attack. It has been shown that 80-bit or more key size is more secure. 2. Keys are shared. If keys are shared, confidentiality could be compromised. 3. Keys not updated automatically and frequently. Cryptographic keys should be changed often to prevent brute-force attacks.
Authentication	1. No user authentication. In 802.11, only the device is authenticated. A stolen device can be used to access the network. 2. Device authentication is based on challenge-response. One-way challenge-response authentication is subject to attacks. Mutual authentication is required to provide verification that users and the network are legitimate. 3. Authentication not automatically enabled. Identity-based systems are highly vulnerable particularly in a wireless system because only simple service set identifier; identification occurs. 4. Authentications by MAC address lookup.
Wired equivalent privacy (WEP)	1. RC4 used in WEP has a weak key schedule. The IV in WEP uses a 24-bit key sent in the clear text portion. It has been shown that using this key combined with a weakness in the initial few bytes of the RC4 keystream, it is possible to attack the system successfully
Packet integrity	1. Packet integrity is poor. Cyclic redundancy check (CRC)-32 and other linear block codes are inadequate for cryptographic integrity. Message modification is possible. 2. Cryptographic protection is required to prevent deliberate attacks. 3. Use of noncryptographic protocols often facilitates attacks against the network.
Security hardware	1. Security features in hardware, although poor in some cases, are often not enabled when shipped, and users do not enable them when installed. Hence, many systems operate without security. 2. Bad security is generally better than no security.

the noncryptographic techniques are highly vulnerable to attacks

Confidentiality—In the 802.11 protocol, confidentiality or privacy is implemented through the use of cryptographic techniques with the RC4 symmetric-key encoding. Before transmission, the data stream is added to the "key stream" using modulo 2 additions. Key sizes ranging from 40 bits to 104 bits can be used. In practice, however, most WLANs use 40-bit keys, which is not reliable. In general, increasing the key size increases the security of a cryptographic technique. It has been shown that the WEP confidentiality approach is vulnerable to attacks (CSRC, 2002).

Integrity—Data integrity is achieved by using a simple encrypted CRC encoding and decoding technique. A CRC-32 code or a frame check sequence is computed on each packet prior to transmission. The integrity-sealed packet is then encrypted using the RC4 key stream to provide the encrypted message. On the receiving end, decryption is performed, and the CRC is recomputed on the message received. The CRC computed at the receiving end is compared with the one computed with the original message. Any discrepancy signifies a violation of integrity.

These three techniques are the only security services provided by the IEEE 802.11 WLAN protocol. Security services provided by the IEEE 802.11 WLAN protocol did not address other security services such as audit, authorization, and nonrepudiation.

Security Vulnerability in IEEE 802.11 Standards

The WEP protocol used in 802.11-based WLANs is perceived to have some security problems. The use of 40-bit key in the WEP cryptography has been found to be vulnerable to both passive and active attacks (CSRC, 2002; Ewalt, 2001). Because significant attention is now being focused on the security of 802.11, more vulnerability is likely to be discovered. To present a concise discussion on the issue of security for WLAN, some of the problems associated with WEP security techniques in the IEEE 802.11 WLAN standard are summarized in Table 5.

EMERGING TECHNOLOGIES AND SECURITY STANDARDS

The first-generation (1G) and second-generation (2G) of cellular mobile telephony were intended primarily for voice transmission. This will not be adequate for the new generation of users. The need for multimedia communications over wireless channels, the rapid growth of wireless voice subscribers, the continued popularity of the Internet, and the increasing use of portable computing devices suggest that high-speed, high-capacity, and high-quality wireless communication systems will become a major focus in the telecommunication industry. In today's technology era, emerging personal communication systems

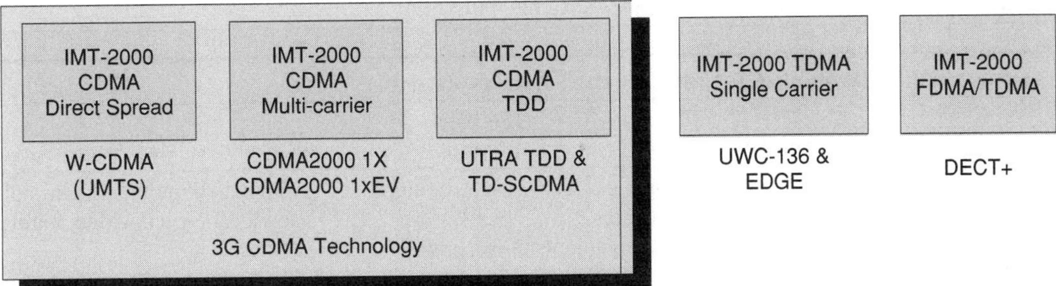

Figure 12: IMT-2000 terrestrial radio interfaces.

are expected to provide a wide range of services that require high data rates—not only for voice, but also in data, images, video, and multimedia information transmission over wireless channels. With the continued growth of the Internet and World Wide Web, mobile users are continually looking for high-performance wireless Internet technology to enhance their communication capabilities. The third-generation (3G) systems were intended to provide high data rates (between 384 kbps for low mobility users to 2 Mbps for stationary users; The Shoesteck Group, 2001), significantly expands the range of options available to users and allows multimedia communication via wireless terminals. Unfortunately, these objectives have not been fully realized.

One of the challenges of realizing these objectives is the effects of the wireless channel, which includes fading, delay spread, and co-channel interference. To achieve high-speed, high-quality, and high-capacity communications over wireless channels, countermeasures should be employed to combat these impairments.

New wireless or cellular mobile radio technologies, services, and applications are constantly under investigation. Some of the technologies are currently under research and development, and some are experiencing limited field tests. These technologies include the 3G technologies and the fourth-generation (4G) technologies. The goal of these technologies is to integrate seamlessly a wide variety of communication services such as high-speed data, video, and multimedia traffic as well as voice signals. Some of these technologies can be realized by combining existing technologies. For example, one of the most promising approaches to 3G is to combine a wideband code division multiple access air interface with the fixed network of a global system for mobile communications (GSM). It is expected that these new technologies will increase the performance of the existing wireless systems. These technologies will provide multimedia capability at much higher rates with Internet connectivity.

Although 3G technologies have been deployed, they have not experienced market success compared with the 2G systems. The 3G standard was created by the International Telecommunication Union (ITU) and is more widely known as International Mobile Telecommunications—2000 (IMT-2000). The aim of IMT-2000 is to harmonize worldwide 3G systems to provide global roaming. Harmonizing so many standards proved extremely difficult. Furthermore, the definition of what is and what is not "3G" is murky. Figure 12 shows the various terrestrial radio interfaces referred to as 3G standards and is based on the IMT-2000 standardization. Of many variants, only three dominant standards (wideband code division multiple access **(W-CDMA),** CDMA2000, and TD-SCDMA) allow full network coverage over macro cells, micro cells, and pico cells and can thus be considered as full 3G solutions. As shown in Figure 12, other non-CDMA technologies such as UWC-136 and DECT+ are also considered 3G technologies. In W-CDMA technology, data are transferred over wireless networks in digital format over a range of frequencies, which makes the data move faster but also uses more bandwidth than digital voice services. The competing 3G CDMA technologies differ technically but provide comparable services. Although there are five terrestrial standards, most of the attention in the industry has been focused on the CDMA standards. As technology improves, the functionality of handheld devices is becoming more feature-rich and portable. For example, mobile phones have increased functionality that now allows them to serve as PDAs and digital cameras in addition to phones. Smart phones can now provide voice services, e-mail, text messaging, paging, Web access, voice recognition, and digital camera capability. Next-generation mobile phones, already on the market, are quickly incorporating PDA, infrared (IR), wireless Internet, e-mail, and global positioning system capabilities. More significantly, manufacturers are combining standards as well, with the goal to provide a device capable of delivering multiple services. Table 6 summarizes the services and applications of the various generations of wireless services.

Another emerging application in wireless communication is the use of ultra wideband (UWB) systems for local area network. UWB is defined as any radio technology with a spectrum that occupies a bandwidth greater than 20% of the center frequency, or a bandwidth of at least 500 MHz (FCC, 2000; Intel, n.d.). UWB systems transmit signals across a much wider frequency than conventional systems. The amount of spectrum occupied by a UWB signal, that is, the bandwidth of the UWB signal, is at least 25% of the center frequency. In the United States, the FCC has mandated that UWB radio transmissions can legally operate in the range from 3.1 to 10.6 GHz, at a limited transmit power of –41 dBm/MHz. Consequently, UWB provides dramatic channel capacity at short range that limits interference. UWB communication systems offer several potential advantages. Because of the potentially large processing gain, many of the characteristics and advantages of spread spectrum communication carry over to UWB systems. For instance, a UWB system is capable of supporting multiple users; is robust against jamming,

Table 6 Service Differentiation by Wireless Communication Generations

2G	2.5G (Evolved 2G)	3G	3.5G (Evolved 3G)	4G
9.6–14.4 kbps	64–144 kbps	384 kbps– 2 Mbps	384 kbps– 20 Mbps	100 Mbps
1. Circuit switched 2. Voice 3. Simple message/SMS 4. Event notification 5. Fax	1. Packet services 2. Interactive 3. Web browsing, 4. E-mail and attachments 5. File transfers, transactions/e-commerce 6. Instant messaging	1. Seamless services over multiple accesses 2. Improvements of existing air-interfaces (including new spectrum) 3. Multimedia 4. High interactivity, real-time road maps 5. Medical imaging 6. Audio streaming 7. Video streaming 8. Video telephony		1. Interactive multimedia broadband services—voice, video, wireless Internet 2. High speed, high capacity, and low cost per bit 3. Global mobility, service portability, scalable mobile networks 4. Seamless switching, variety of services based on quality-of-service requirements 5. Better scheduling and call admission control techniques. 6. Ad hoc networks and multihop networks and high capacity optical networking 7. Advanced antenna systems and multihop systems 8. Multicarrier—CDMA or OFDM
	Fair QoS	**End-to-end QoS**		**End-to-end QoS**
• TDMA • GSM • PCD • PDC • CDMAone	• GPRS • EDGE	• 3GPP (EDGE, UMTS) • W-CDMA • CDMA2000 • TD-CDMA/TD-SCDMA • DECT and UWC-136		New air interface and protocols

Note. 3GPP = 3rd Generation Partnership Project—a joint venture of several Standards Development Organizations; CDMA = code division multiple access; CDMA2000 = a family of CDMA technologies that includes CDMA2000 1X and CDMA2000 1xEV; DECT = Digital European Cordless Telecommunications; DSSS = direct sequence spread spectrum; EDGE = Enhanced Data GSM Environment; FHSS = frequency hopping spread spectrum; GPRS = General Packet Radio Service; GSM = Global System for Mobile communications; OFDM = orthogonal frequency division multiplexing; PDC = Pacific Digital Cellular; PDC = Personal Digital Communication; QoS = Quality of Service; SMS = Short Message Service; TDMA = time division multiple access; TD-CDMA = Time Division Code Division Multiple Access; TD-SCDMA = Time Division – Synchronous Code Division Multiple Access; UMTS = Universal Mobile Telecommunications System IMT-2000 standard; UWC-136 = Universal Wireless Communications 136; W-CDMA = Wideband Code Division Multiple Access.

interference, and multipath fading; and is suitable for applications requiring low probabilities of interception and low probability of detection by unintended user. It follows that their wide bandwidth makes them more robust to multipath interference with multiuser access capability. UWB provides the highest bandwidths with the lowest vulnerability to multipath interference. It also offers potentially high bit rate transmission with capacity increasing almost linearly with power. The fine time resolution makes it a good candidate in applications such as ranging, remote sensing, search and rescue missions, and measurement applications under extremely harsh weather conditions.

Unfortunately, before UWB systems can become fully implemented and commercially viable, many challenging problems need to be resolved. Some of these include wideband antenna design, timing acquisition and synchronization, channel modeling, and interference from or to other systems. For example, the performance of UWB systems under a realistic channel model is being investigated. In addition, with low transmission power and a highly spread bandwidth, acquisition of a UWB signal is difficult (Fleming, Kushner, Roberts, & Nandiwada, 2002). For instance, if packets are transmitted, a long preamble is needed to ensure acquisition of each packet at the receiver, reducing throughput and increasing overhead. This problem is amplified when multiple hops are traversed in a network from the source to the destination. Also, because UWB systems are overlaid on existing wireless systems, issues of interference become critical (Fontana, 2002; Siwiak, 2001). Interference suppression algorithms are needed to minimize interference from or to other users. Other research interests include the implementation of UWB systems in a dense network environment.

Another wireless communication application is local multipoint distribution services (LMDS), a fixed wireless technology that operates in the Ka band and offers LOS coverage over distances up to 3–5 kilometers (Wireless Communications Association International, n.d.). It can be used to provide digital two-way voice, data, Internet, and video services to numerous customers from a single node. LMDS is a broadband wireless point-to-multipoint communication system operating in the Ka band and above. LMDS is one solution for bringing high-bandwidth services to homes and offices within the "last mile" of connectivity, an area where cable or optical fiber may not be convenient or economical. The technology is similar to the cellular systems in that network architecture of microwave radios placed at the client's location and at the company's base station to deliver fixed services—mainly telephony, video, and Internet access. With LDMS, customers can receive data rates between 64 kbps and 155 Mbps. Advantages of LMDS include low deployment costs, fast deployment capability, scalable system architecture, and variable component cost because no large capital investment is required. The system requires LOS between the base station hub and the customer premises, however, and LDMS signals are affected by weather conditions.

There are emerging security standards and technologies that should be mentioned. The security industry, standards organizations, and IEEE are all working to improve the security of wireless systems. For example, the Internet Engineering Task Force (IETF; Cox, 2003) and the IEEE 802.11 Task Working Group I (TGI; IEEE Working Group, 2003) are currently working on initiatives for improving WLAN security. The TGI is defining a second version of WEP, based on the newly released advanced encryption standard (AES). The AES-based solution will provide a highly robust solution for the future but will require new hardware and protocol changes.

In the meantime, a short-term solution to address the problems of WEP, using the temporal key integrity protocol (TKIP) has been proposed. The primary goal of TKIP is to remove all known vulnerabilities of WEP and allow operation on existing wireless-fidelity (Wi-Fi)-certified hardware. This will address the problems without requiring hardware changes (only changes to firmware and software drivers required).

CONCLUDING REMARKS

In this chapter, RF and wireless communication and the related security issues have been discussed. The concept and general definitions are presented. Within these topics, we have discussed the concept of radio waves as propagating electromagnetic waves, including their characteristics and behavior. For wireless and mobile radio systems, it is important to understand distinguishing features of the channel, the properties of the radio wave, and several techniques to enhance the reliability of the channel and increase the performance of the system. RF and wireless communication systems are being used in diverse arenas such as in the home; by the military; and for travel, education, stock trading, package delivery, disaster recovery, and medical emergencies. For example, with wireless technology, field employees can connect a portable computer via a wireless network to the area office. Sales professionals can stay in touch with customers about products and services and orders and contact the home office for status updates to home offices and inventory. Airline staff can gather information about ticketing, flight scheduling, and luggage using wireless devices. Public welfare agencies such as police, fire safety, and ambulance services can use wireless devices to relay information. Package delivery companies such as Federal Express, UPS, and DHL have adopted wireless and mobile computing technology for parcel tracking, as well as emergency shipment drops or pickups. Also, a summary of the various forms of wireless communication systems was presented, emphasizing cellular mobile radio, currently the most prevalent wireless communication system. Finally, emerging wireless technologies were briefly introduced.

Although wireless systems are commonplace in our society, the future of the industry is filled with both promise and challenge. Future wireless technologies under consideration include the full realization of 3G technologies and the development of 4G technologies. 4G wireless technology based on ultra-wideband communications could enable the use of low-power, high-bandwidth (100–500 Mbps) networks, supporting devices with sense and radar capabilities. Multimedia messaging will allow pictures and sound to be transmitted along with text message over the mobile phone in a seamless manner. Mobile handsets will support full-color display screens, some with embedded Java capabilities, others with built-in digital cameras. It is expected that Bluetooth technology will move from theory and hype to practicality, and issues regarding the security of mobile commerce and information security in general will dissipate.

GLOSSARY

1G, 2G, 3G, 4G First-, second, third-, and fourth-generation wireless systems.

Access Point A specially configured node that acts as a central transmitter and receiver for on a wireless local area network radio signals.

Ad Hoc Network A "spontaneous" network is a wireless LAN, in which some of the network devices are part of the network only for the duration of a communications session or while in some close proximity to the rest of the network.

Amplifier An electronic device used to boost the strength of a signal along a communications channel.

Antenna A device used for receiving or transmitting signals.

Authentication The process of determining the true identity of a user. Basic authentication is simply using a password to verify that you are who you say you are.

Bandwidth The capacity of a transmission channel.

Base station Central radio transmitter or receiver (or both) that maintains communications with a mobile radio user.

Bluetooth Short-range wireless protocol allowing mobile devices to share information and applications.

Broadband A classification of the information capacity or bandwidth of a communication channel.

Cellular Wireless communication technique used in mobile phones.

Channel A radio-frequency assignment made according to the frequency band used.

Cipher Transformations that convert plaintext to ciphertext using the Cipher key.

Ciphertext Data output from the cipher or input to the inverse cipher.

Cryptography The science of information security usually involving scrambling of plain text into encrypted text at the transmitter, and decrypting the encrypted text back into plain text at the receiver. The encrypted information cannot be understood by anyone for whom it is not intended or altered in storage or transmission without the alteration being detected.

Cyclic Redundancy Check (CRC) A method of encryption used by WEP to provide integrity protection for WLAN.

Data encryption standard (DES) Widely used method for data encryption using a private key that is difficult to break. It uses a 56-bit key for each 64-bit block of data. There are 72 quadrillion or more possible combinations of keys.

Decipher Inverse transformations that converts ciphertext to plaintext using the Cipher Key.

Decryption Decryption is the process of converting encrypted data back into its original form so that it can be understood.

DoS Denial-of-service. An attack that floods a network with an overwhelming amount of traffic, slowing its response time for legitimate traffic or grinding it to a halt completely.

Downlink Data transmission from a network to a subscriber.

Duplexer Device for isolating transmitter and receiver signals while permitting a shared channel.

Effective Isotropic Radiated Power (EIRP) Product of power supplied to an antenna and its gain.

Encryption The conversion of data into a form called a ciphertext that cannot be easily understood by unauthorized users.

Enhanced Data GSM Environment (EDGE) A faster version of the GSM wireless service designed to deliver data at rates up to 384 Kbps and enable the delivery of multimedia and other broadband applications to mobile phone and computer users.

Firewall A set of related programs located at a network gateway server that protects the resources of a private network from users from other networks.

Frequency Rate of signal oscillation in hertz (1 hertz is one cycle per second); the number of times a waveform repeats itself in a second.

Global Positioning System (GPS) A worldwide radio-navigation system.

Ground Station The ground equipment needed to receive or transmit satellite telecommunications signals, including a dish and other electronics components.

GSM Global system for mobile communications; the mobile phone platform used in Europe and many parts of the world.

Handoff Transfer of wireless call in progress from one site to another without disconnection.

HiperLAN HiperLAN is a set of WLAN communication standards primarily used in Europe, adopted by the European Telecommunications Standards Institute (ETSI).

HomeRF Home radio frequency (HomeRF) is a home networking standard that combines the 802.11b and digital enhanced cordless telecommunication portable phone standards into a single system. HomeRF uses a frequency-hopping technique to deliver speeds of up to 1.6 Mbps over distances of up to 150 feet.

IEEE 802.11 The IEEE's proposed standard for wireless LANs that places specifications on the parameters of both the physical and medium access control layers of the network.

Infrared (IR) An invisible band of radiation at the lower end of the electromagnetic spectrum.

Initialization vector (IV) A random data used encryption to make a message unique.

Institute of Electrical and Electronics Engineers (IEEE) A worldwide professional association for electrical and electronics engineers that sets standards for telecommunications and computing applications.

Isotropic Refers to a theoretical reference antenna that radiates equally well in all directions.

Local Area Network (LAN) A network that connects computers in close proximity via cable, usually in the same building.

Malicious Code A term used to refer to various types of software that can cause problems or damage to the network. The more common types of malicious code are viruses, worms, Trojan horses, macro viruses, and backdoors.

Modulation Process of varying a characteristic of a carrier with an information-bearing signal.

Personal Communications Services (PCS) Any of several types of wireless voice or data communications systems, typically incorporating digital technology.

Personal Digital Assistant (PDA) A handheld computer that serves as an organizer for personal information.

Propagation Radiation of electromagnetic waves.

Protocol A protocol is a set of rules or agreed-on guidelines for communication.

Public Switched Telephone Network (PSTN) A formal name for the landline telephone network.

Pulse Code Modulation (PCM) A basic form of digital modulation in which an analog signal is sampled, the sample is quantized independently of other samples, and is then converted to a digital signal.

Quadrature Phase Shift Keying (QPSK) A modulation method for digital satellite transmission.

Radio Frequency (RF) A radio signal.

Receiver A device on a transmission line that converts a signal to whatever type of signal is needed to complete the transmission.

Remote Authentication Dial-In User Service (RADIUS) Originally developed to manage dial-in access to Internet; now being used to manage access control for other systems including WLANs.

Rivest Cipher 4 (RC4) A common encryption algorithm used by the WEP protocol and TKIP.

Secure Sockets Layer (SSL) A protocol for managing the security of message transmission over the Internet.

Service Set Identifier (SSID) A sequence of characters that uniquely names a wireless local area network. This name allows stations to connect to the desired network when multiple independent networks operate in the same physical area.

Spectrum Range of electromagnetic radio frequencies used in signal transmission.

Spread Spectrum (SS) A communications technology in which a signal is transmitted over a broad range of frequencies and then reassembled when received.

Subscriber A cellular telephone user.

Temporal Key Integrity Protocol (TKIP) A wireless encryption protocol that fixes the known problems in the WEP protocol for existing 802.11b products.

Time Division Multiple Access (TDMA) A digital communication technology used by some carriers to provide service.

Transmitter The source or generator of any signal on a transmission medium.

Transport Layer Security (TLS) An authentication and encryption protocol for private transmission over the Internet. It provides mutual authentication with nonrepudiation, encryption, algorithm negotiation, secure key derivation, and message integrity checking.

Uplink Data transmission in the direction from the subscriber to the network (back to the provider or Internet provider).

Wavelength Distance between points of corresponding phase in two consecutive cycles of a wave.

Wideband Code Division Multiple Access (W-CDMA). A 3G mobile standard under the IMT-2000 banner, first deployed in Japan.

Wired Equivalent Privacy (WEP) A security protocol, specified in the IEEE 802.11 standard, that attempts to provide a WLAN with a minimal level of security and privacy comparable to a typical wired LAN.

Wireless Application Protocol (WAP) A technology designed to provide users of mobile terminals with limited access to the Internet. A standard for providing cellular telephones, pagers, and other handheld devices with secure access to e-mail and text-based Web pages.

Wireless Fidelity (Wi-Fi) The industry name for WLAN communication technology related to the IEEE 802.11 family of wireless networking standards.

Wireless Local Area Network (WLAN) Wireless network communication over short distances using radio signals instead of traditional network cabling.

Wireless Local Loop (WLL) A wireless system meant to bypass a local landline telephone system.

Wireless Transport Layer Security (WTLS) The security level for WAP applications that was developed to address the problematic issues surrounding mobile network devices—such as limited processing power and memory capacity and low bandwidth—and to provide adequate authentication, data integrity, and privacy protection mechanisms.

CROSS REFERENCES

See *Bluetooth Security; Bluetooth Technology; Digital Communication; Security and the Wireless Application Protocol (WAP); Wireless Channels.*

REFERENCES

Acosta, R. (1999). *Rain fade compensation alternatives for Ka-band communication satellites (NASA Technical Memo, 107534).* Cleveland, OH: National Aeronautics and Space Administration Glenn Research Center.

Acosta, R., & Horton, N. (1998). *V-band and W-band propagation campaign at NASA Lewis (white chapter).* Cleveland, OH: National Aeronautics and Space Administration Glenn Research Center.

Agrawal, D., & Zeng, Q. (2003). *Introduction to wireless and mobile systems.* Pacific Grove, CA: Brooks/Cole.

Bhargava, S., & Agrawal, D. P. (2001, October). Security enhancements in AODV protocol for wireless ad hoc networks. *Proceedings of the IEEE Vehicular Technology Conference* (pp. 2143–2147).

Bing, B. (2000). *High-speed wireless ATM and LANs.* Boston: Artech House.

Cellular communications services in the USA by Euromonitor International June 1, 2003. Retrieved December 29, 2003, from http://worldofinformation.safeshopper.com/40/778.htm?539

Chen, K. (1994). Medium access control of wireless LANs for mobile computing. *IEEE Network, 8*(5), 50–63.

Computer Security Resource Center, National Institute of Standards and Technology. (2001, January). *Cryptographic Toolkit.* Retrieved December 21, 2003, from http://www.csrc.nist.gov/CryptoToolkit/.

Computer Security Resource Center, National Institute of Standards and Technology. (2002a, August). *Security for telecommuting and broadband communications* (NIST Special Publication 800-46). Retrieved December 18, 2003, from http://csrc.nist.gov/publications/nistpubs/

Computer Security Resource Center, National Institute of Standards and Technology. (2002b, November). *Wireless network security: 802.11, Bluetooth, and handheld devices* (NIST Special Publication 800 48). Retrieved December 18, 2003, from http://csrc.nist.gov/publications/nistpubs/

Cox, J. (2003, November 10). WLAN protocol hits standards trail, LWAPP is on its way. Retrieved December 21, 2003, from http://www.techworld.com/news/index.cfm?fuseaction=displaynews&NewsID=636

Durgin, G. (2003). *Space–time wireless channels.* Upper Saddle River, NJ: Prentice Hall.

Eng, T., Kong, N., & Milstein, L. (1996). Comparison of diversity combining techniques for Rayleigh fading channels. *IEEE Transactions on Communication, 44,* 1117–1129.

Ewalt, D. M. (2001, December). RSA patches hold in wireless LANs: The fix addresses problems with the wireless equivalent privacy protocol, which encrypts communication over 802.11b wireless networks. *InformationWeek.* Retrieved November 15, 2003, from http://www.informationweek.com/shared/printableArticle.jhtml?articleID=6508201

Federal Communications Commission. (1997). Millimeter wave propagation: Spectrum management implications (FCC Bulletin No. 70).Washington, DC: Author. Retrieved November 25, 2003, from http://www.fcc.gov/oet/info/documents/bulletins/#70)

Federal Communications Commission. (2000, April). Revision of part 15 regarding ultra wideband transmission (FCC 02-48), ET Docket 98-153, first report and order. Retrieved October 15, 2004, from http://hraunfoss.fcc.gov/edocs_public/attachmatch/FCC-02-48A1.pdf

Fleming, R., Kushner, C., Roberts, G., & Nandiwada, U. (2002, May). Rapid acquisition for ultra-wideband localizers. *Proceedings of the IEEE Conference on Ultra-Wideband System and Technologies* (pp. 245–250), Baltimore Maryland.

Fontana, R. J. (2002, May). An insight into UWB interference from a shot noise perspective. *Proceedings of the IEEE Conference on Ultra-Wideband System and Technologies* (pp. 309–313), Baltimore, Maryland.

Garg, V., & Wilkes, J. (1996). *Wireless and personal communications systems*. Englewood Cliffs, NJ: Prentice Hall.

Geier, J. (1999). *Wireless LANs: Implementing interpretable networks*. Indianapolis, IN: Macmillan Technical.

Goodman, D. (1997). *Wireless personal communications systems*. Reading, MA: Addison Wesley.

Haykin, S. (2001). *Communications systems* (4th ed.). New York: John Wiley & Sons.

IEEE Working Group for WLAN Standards. (n.d.). IEEE 802.11™ wireless local area networks. Retrieved December 23, 2003, from http://grouper.ieee.org/groups/802/11/

Intel. (n.d.). Ultra-wideband (UBA) technology. Retrieved July 25, 2004, from http://www.intel.com/technology/ultrawideband/

International Engineering Consortium. (n.d., a). Personal communications service (PCS). Retrieved January 29, 2003, from http://www.iec.org/online/tutorials/pcs/index.html

International Engineering Consortium. (n.d., b). Wireless local loop (WLL). Retrieved January 10, 2003, from http://www.iec.org/online/tutorials/wll/

Ippolito, L. (1989). *Propagation effects handbook for satellite systems design* (NASA Reference Publication 1082[04]). Cleveland, OH: National Aeronautics and Space Administration, Glenn Research Center.

Lathi, B. P. (1998). *Modern Digital and Analog Communication Systems*, (3rd ed.). Oxford: Oxford University Press.

Mark, J., & Zhuang W. (2003). *Wireless communications and networking*. Upper Saddle River, NJ: Prentice Hall.

Mobile Telephone History. (n.d.). Retrieved December 12, 2002, from http://www.privateline.com/PCS/history4.htm

National Aeronautics and Space Administration. (1998). *Systems handbook—advanced communications technology satellite*. Technical Report TM-101490. Cleveland, OH: National Aeronautics and Space Administration, Glenn Research Center.

National Institute of Standards and Technology. (2001). *NIST handbook. An Introduction to Computer Security* (Special Publication 800-12). Retrieved from http://www.csrc.nist.gov/publications/nistpubs/800-12/handbook.pdf

Printchard, W., Suyderhoud, H., & Nelson, R. (1993). *Satellite communication systems engineering* (2nd ed.). Englewood Cliffs, NJ: Prentice-Hall.

Proakis, J. G., & Salehi, M. (2002). *Communications systems engineering* (2nd ed.). Upper Saddle River, NJ: Prentice Hall.

Rappaport, T. (2002). *Wireless communications: Principles and practice* (2nd ed.). Upper Saddle River, NJ: Prentice Hall.

The Shoesteck Group, CDMA Development Group. (2001, June). GSM or CDMA: The commercial and technology challenges for TDMA operators. Retrieved October 14, 2004, from http://www.cdg.org/technology/cdma_technology/shosteck/overview.asp

Siwiak, K. (2001, May). Impact of ultra wide band transmissions on a generic receiver. *Proceedings of the 53rd IEEE Vehicular Technology Conference* (Vol. 2, pp. 1181–1183).

Stallings, W. (2002). *Wireless communications and networks*. Upper Saddle River, NJ: Prentice Hall.

Venkataraman, L., & Agrawal, D. P. (2000, September). Authentication in ad hoc networks. *Proceedings of the 2nd IEEE Wireless Communications and Networking Conference* Chicago.

WAP Forum. (2000, June). Wireless application protocol (white chapter). Retrieved December 6, 2002, from http://www.wapforum.org/what/WAP_white_pages.pdf

Weisman, C. (2003). *The essential guide to RF and wireless* (2nd ed.). Upper Saddle River, NJ: Prentice Hall.

Wenig, R. (1996). *Wireless LANs*. Boston. Academic Press.

Wireless Communications Association International. (n.d.). LMDS overview. Retrieved July 25, 2004, from http://www.wcai.com/lmds.htm

Wireless communications, market & opportunities. (n.d.). Retrieved January 29, 2003, from http://www.igigroup.com/st/pages/chinav4.html

Xu, H., Rappaport, T., Boyle, B., & Schaffner, J. (2000). Measurements and models for 38-GHz point-to-multipoint radiowave propagation. *IEEE Journal on Selected Areas in Communications, 18*, 310–321.

Yacoub, M. (1993). *Foundations of mobile radio engineering*. Boca Raton, FL: CRC Press.

Wireless Channels

P. M. Shankar, *Drexel University*

INTRODUCTION

Wireless systems have become part of everyday life. In addition to their use in cell phones, they are used inside the homes for networking computers and peripherals, cordless phones, baby monitors, and so on. They are used in factories to ferry information between locations without the use of wires. Medical informatics commonly use wireless systems to exchange vital information between practitioners. These systems have unique operating frequency bands. The choice of the frequencies is often determined by the range of operation (a few meters for a cordless phone to thousands of kilometers for satellite communication systems), the medium through which the signal traverses (from urban areas with tall structures, vast empty spaces in rural areas, and multilevel–multistructure environments in factories and malls), the amount of data to be transmitted (low volume of data in maritime mobile systems to Gbits/s in satellite systems). Other factors that are equally important are the sizes of the transmitting and receiving antennas and the cost and maintenance of installations. Table 1 shows a classification of various frequencies used in wireless communications along with information on antenna sizes and achievable information rates.

Two important considerations of communication systems must be kept in mind:

1. The physical dimensions of an antenna are inversely proportional to its operating frequency. Thus, at low frequencies, the size of the antenna may be too large for these frequencies to be used in practical systems unless under specified conditions. For example, at 30 kHz, the wavelength is 10,000 m,

$$\left[\text{wavelength} = \frac{\text{velocity}}{\text{frequency}} = \frac{3 \times 10^8}{30 \times 10^3} = 10^4\, m\right].$$

   Note that under the assumption of a dipole antenna, the required size of the antennas will be on the order of a half wavelength. This means that for transmission at 30 kHz, we would require an antenna of length 5,000 m.
2. The amount of data that can be transmitted is directly proportional to the operating frequency. The data rates at 30 kHz will be less than 30 kbps, whereas the data rates at 1 GHz can be on the order of 1 Gbps. The actual data rates will be determined by a number of factors, such as the transmission distance, the characteristics of the intervening medium, the modulation–demodulation schemes and the performance bounds (error rates) set, and so on.

Once we take these considerations into account, it is clear that the very low frequencies can be eliminated from the range of operation of the practical wireless systems that demand transmission at very high data rates, portability (i.e., mobile systems), and compactness. The large size of antennas and low data rates associated with low frequencies eliminate them from considerations in modern wireless systems. Even though the frequencies on the higher end of the spectrum (Table 1) appear to offer smaller size antennae and higher data rates, their use in wireless systems is limited due to other factors. The primary reason for their unsuitability is the fact that these frequencies are severely attenuated by obstructions in their path. A case of a direct path (line of sight [LOS]) between the transmitter and a receiver is shown in Figure 1.

In a typical urban environment with several tall structures, the signals may not reach the receiver via an LOS path. Signals may have to reach the receiver through other physical mechanisms such as reflection, scattering, transmission, and diffraction. The presence of the various objects in the path of the signal as it travels from the transmitter to the receiver not only leads to loss of signal power, but also results in random fluctuations in signal power. The attenuation and fluctuations in signal power are two major detriments to the ability to provide the necessary capacity for the wireless operators. The third major detriment is the interference in wireless systems, a direct consequence of the reuse of the frequency bands in a given geographic location. These three major aspects of wireless systems—power loss, fading, and interference—are reviewed in the following sections, starting with the propagation related effects.

PROPAGATION OF SIGNALS

Power Loss

The mode of signal propagation depicted in Figure 1 is an ideal one. A typical example of the signal propagation in practical wireless systems is shown in Figure 2.

Table 1 Various Frequency Bands Used in Wireless Systems, Their Identification and Characteristics

Frequency Band	Frequency Range	Antenna Size	Data Rate
VLF (Very Low Frequency)	3–30 Kilohertz (kHz)	Large	Low
Low Frequency (LF)	30–300 kHz	↑	↓
Medium Frequency (MF)	300 kHz–30 MHz		
High Frequency (HF)	3–30 MHz		
Very High Frequency (VHF)	30–300 MHz		
Ultra High Frequency (UHF)	300-MHz–3 GHz		
Super High Frequency (SHF)	3–30 GHz		
Extra High Frequency (EHF)	30–300 GHz	Small	High

As the electromagnetic wave travels from the transmitter to the receiver, it encounters various objects in its path. In typical urban environments, it may not be possible to have a LOS path between the transmitter and the receiver. The signal leaving the transmitter reaches the receiver through a number of different mechanisms such as reflection, diffraction, and scattering (Institute of Electrical and Electronics Engineers [IEEE], 1988a; Rappaport, 2002; Shankar, 2001). Reflection occurs when the signal encounters objects that are much larger than the wavelength. Along with reflection, refraction of the wave may also take place, in which case the signal will penetrate the object, which may be a wall or a partition. The signal may also undergo diffraction (i.e., bending over obstacles) when the signal encounters sharp boundaries such as the ridges of buildings or rooftops. Scattering occurs when the surface of the object is rough and is on the order of the wavelength. The signal may scatter from buildings, trees, or other human-made or natural structures. Indoors, in places such as malls, factories, and office buildings, the signal will reach the receiver after penetrating floors, walls, ceilings, and so forth while undergoing effects of reflection, scattering, and diffraction. These multiple mechanisms may result in additional power loss suffered by the signal as it reaches the receiver relative to the signal power that would be observed in free space transmission. Signals may also penetrate structures undergoing further loss of signal strength. Environmental factors such as foliage, smog, raindrops (approaching the size of wavelength corresponding to the carrier frequency), and so forth may also influence the attenuation of the signal.

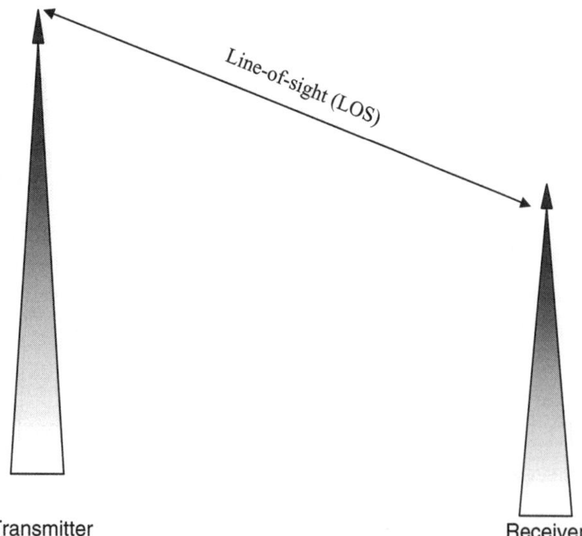

Figure 1: A line-of-sight propagation path is shown.

A typical signal received in urban wireless systems is shown in Figure 3a. It is seen that the received power decreases as the distance increases. The power is plotted in dBm (the relationship between power in watts and dBm is given in the Appendix). If we look at a short segment of this curve as shown in Figure 3b, we can see that the power is not monotonic. Fluctuations in power can be seen. They are referred to as long-term fading or shadowing (Parsons, 1996). If we zoom in further into the power-versus-distance curve, we see that the power fluctuates around a mean value. These fluctuations are of very short duration compared with those seen in Figure 3b. These short-term fluctuations, shown in Figure 3c, are referred to as short-term fading. They are also known as Rayleigh fading, based on the statistical fluctuations in the received envelope of the signal (Rappaport, 2002; Shankar, 2001; Steele and Hanzo, 1999; Stein, 1987). Nakagami fading and Rician fading are also used to describe short-term fading.

Thus, the signal propagation from the transmitter to the receiver is subject to several physical phenomena producing attenuation and fading of the signal. We now look at ways to model power loss and fading.

Modeling of Power loss

Several models are available to predict the median or mean value of the received power (Har, Xia, & Bertoni, 1999; Hata, 1980; Lee, 1986; Oda, Tsunkewa, & Hata, 2000; Okumura, Ohmori, & Fukuda, 1968; Vogel and Hong, 1988). These are available for both indoor and outdoor propagation (Bultitude et al., 1989; Harley, 1989; Rappaport & Sandhu 1994; Durgin et al., 1998; Lott & Forkel, 2001). They are also available for different frequency bands of interest in wireless communications. Instead of concentrating on these various models, we initially look at one of the simple ways of predicting loss based on the concept of *path loss exponent*. To understand the concept of the path loss exponent, consider the case of a LOS propagation in free space as shown in Figure 1. If P_t is the transmitted power in W (*Watts*), the received power P_d (W) at a distance d from the transmitter is given

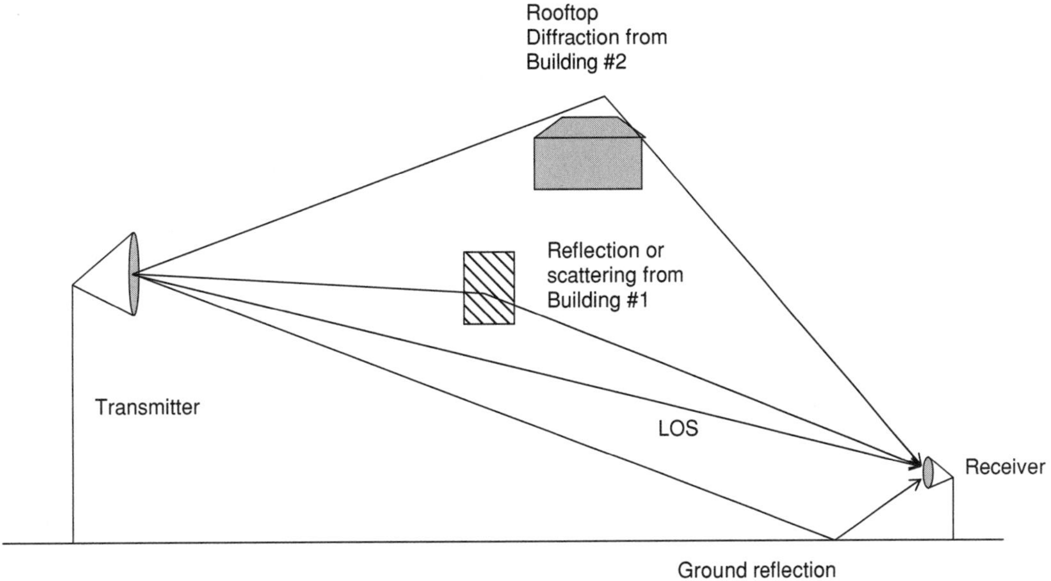

Figure 2: The signal reaches the receiver via reflection and scattering from buildings, diffraction from rooftops, reflection from the ground, and line-of-sight (LOS) transmission.

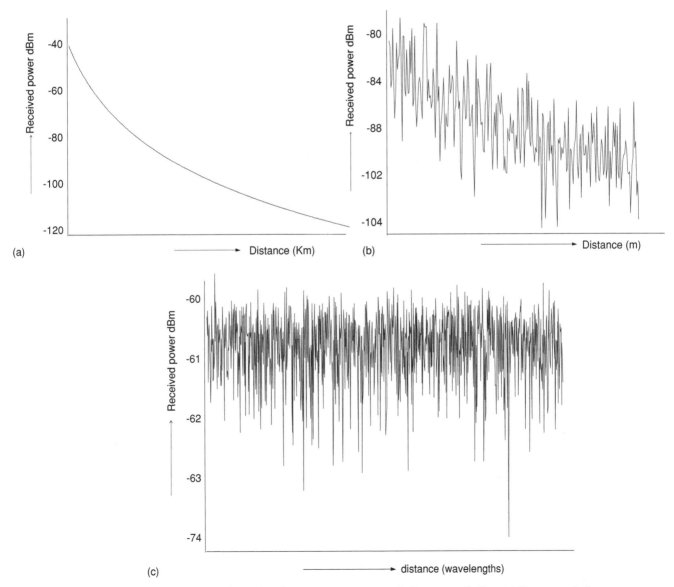

Figure 3: The plot of the received signal is shown. (a) Attenuation. (b) Long-term fading. (c) Short-term fading.

by the Friis formula (IEEE, 1988a, 1988b],

$$P_d = P_t G_t G_r \left(\frac{\lambda}{4\pi d}\right)^2 W, \tag{1}$$

where

G_t = gain of the transmitting antenna
G_r = gain of the receving antenna ,
λ = free space wavelength = $\frac{c}{f_0}$

c being the velocity of light and f_0 the signal frequency. Note that G_t, and G_r, are dimensionless (i.e., scale factors) and d and λ must have the same units (centimeters, meters, or kilometers). Assuming equal gain antennas ($G_t = G_r$), the received power can be expressed as inversely proportional to the square of the distance,

$$P_d \propto \frac{1}{d^2}. \tag{2}$$

Conversely, we can say that the loss experienced by the signal is directly proportional to the square of the distance. The path loss exponent or the path loss coefficient determines the decay of the power as distance increases and is denoted by n. In free space under LOS conditions, the path loss exponent n is 2. Because we have no obstacles in the path of the signal in LOS propagation in free space, no reflection, diffraction, or scattering takes place, and thus, $n = 2$ will be the best case scenario we can expect in signal transmission. In a general case, where propagation takes place in a region containing obstacles, we expect higher losses than those observed in free space, and n must be greater than 2. The loss experienced by the signal increases as n increases. The excess loss over $n = 2$ is plotted in Figure 4 as a function of the distance. Note that the path loss exponent n is also sometimes referred to as power decay index, distance power gradient, or slope factor.

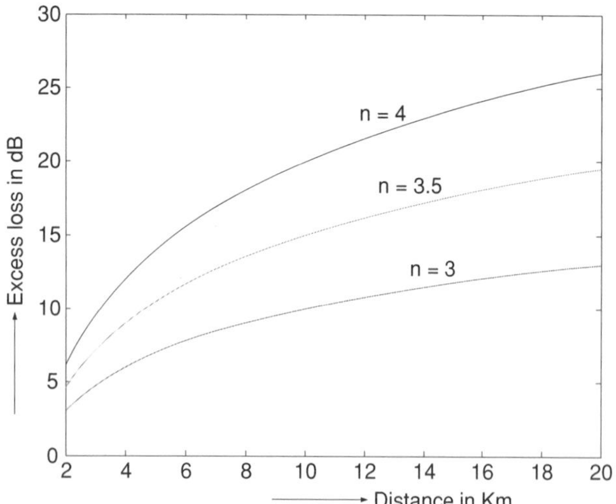

Figure 4: The losses at $n = 3$, 3.5, and 4 are compared with the free space loss ($n = 2$).

It must be noted that the low values of n also increase co-channel interference (see the section on interference later in this chapter), such as the interference coming from other cells using the same channel in a frequency reuse situation. As the value of n increases, the interference goes down, leading to an improvement in the capacity of the cellular communication systems.

Calculation of the Received Power

We have seen that the power received at any distance d is inversely proportional to the nth power of the distance,

$$P_d \propto \frac{1}{d^n}. \tag{3}$$

Equation 3 cannot be applied directly because we need to evaluate the proportionality factor. This is done by applying the Friis equation (Rappaport, 2002; Shankar, 2001) at a very short distance d_0 from the transmitter where it can be assumed that the conditions of free space or LOS exist. If P_{d_0} is the power at a distance of d_0 from the transmitter,

$$P_{d_0} = P_t \left(\frac{\lambda}{4\pi d_0}\right)^2. \tag{4}$$

Using Equation 3, we can now write Equation 4 as,

$$\frac{P_d}{P_{d_0}} = \frac{d_0^n}{d^n}. \tag{5}$$

Taking the logarithm, we get the expression for the received power at a distance d ($d > d_0$) from the transmitter to be

$$P_d(dBm) = P_{d_0}(dBm) - 10n\log_{10}\left(\frac{d}{d_0}\right), \tag{6}$$

where

$$P_{d_0}(dBm) = P_t(dBm) + 20\log_{10}\left(\frac{\lambda}{4\pi d_0}\right). \tag{7}$$

Note that in Equations 5 and 7, the power is expressed in decibel units, dBm. The question is now what value of d_0 is appropriate. Typically, this value, known as the *reference distance* ($\lambda < d_0$), is chosen to be 100 m in outdoor environments and 1 m in indoor environments (Rappaport, 2002; Shankar, 2001).

The models described so far can be applied for calculating the received power at various operating frequencies indoors and outdoors. A few points are in order. The received power according to the Friis equation as seen in Equation 1 decreases as the wavelength decreases. This means that as we move from the 900-MHz band to the personal communication systems (PCS) band operating at 1800–2000 MHz, the received power decreases. The loss is higher when one goes to the unlicensed frequency band used in homes, cordless phones, Bluetooth systems (Har, 2000), in the 2.4-GHz and 5.8-GHz systems (Durgin et al., 1998). Another factor that becomes critical as the frequencies go up is the inability of the signal to penetrate buildings. For example, in contrast with 900-MHz signals, 2-GHz signals will not travel far from the transmitter. Signals may even be blocked by a single building between the transmitter and receiver. Thus, the line-of-sight propagation becomes the predominant means by which the signal reaches the receiver. In the case of a microwave signal, a truck obstructing the path can bring down the received signal to extremely small levels (IEEE 1988a, 1988b). This issue is discussed later when we look at interference factors in wireless systems.

The approaches based on the path loss exponent are not the only ones available to estimate the attenuation suffered by the signal as it reaches the receiver. The disadvantage of the path-loss-based approach is that it does not directly take into account a number of system dependent factors such the heights of the transmitting and receiving antennas and their locations. Models such as the Lee model, the Hata model, the Walfish and Bertoni model (Har et al., 1999, Hata, 1980; Ikegami, Tekeuchi, & Yoshida, 1991; Lee, 1986; Oda et al., 2000; Okumura et al., 1968; Vogel & Hong, 1988) are also available to calculate the received power. These models take the antenna heights and other factors into account. Yet another approach is to use a two exponent model, where two values n_1 and n_2 are used. The loss increases slowly (i.e., the loss occurs as if we have propagation in free space with $n = n_1 = 2$) until a break point is reached. Beyond that point, the attenuation increases with distance at a higher rate, with n taking value of n_2 in the range 3 to 9 (Bertoni, Honcharenko, Maciel, & Xia, 1994; Rappaport & Sandhu, 1994).

The power loss L_p in decibels (dB) suffered by the signal is

$$L_p = P_t(dBm) - P_d(dBm), \quad (8)$$

where the transmitted power P_t and the received power P_d are once again expressed in decibel units.

The loss calculation in indoor wireless systems is less straightforward than for outdoor systems. It is possible to use Equations 6 and 7 to calculate the received power or predict the loss. Based on empirical measurements conducted indoors and outdoors, the range of values of n has been proposed by several researchers. Note that these values depend on the environments in which the wireless signal is propagating. The values of n are strongly influenced by the type of building materials used, floor arrangement, location of the transmitting antenna (inside the building or outside the building), height of the transmitting antenna, frequency used, and so on. The values of n range from 2 to 4 as one moves from an open space where free space LOS propagation is possible to urban areas with tall buildings and other structures. In indoor environments, the value of n less than 2 has been observed in grocery stores and open-plan factories (Dersch & Zollinger, 1994; Durgin et al., 1998; Rappaport & Sandhu, 1994). This low value (lower than $n = 2$ in free space) has been attributed to the strong reflections contributed to the received signal by the metallic structures in those places, resulting in higher power levels compared to a completely open space ($n = 2$). Thus, inside the buildings, n can take values in the range of 1.5 to 4 depending on the following:

1. The number of floors
2. Location of the transmitter
3. Type of partition (hard vs. soft) used

In indoor wireless systems, the base station (BS) can be outside the building. It is also possible to have the base station inside the building, depending on the building complex. The signal may have to travel through multiple floors and multiple walls, each of which may be of a different type, to reach the receiver. The loss calculations are therefore complex, and the wireless systems would have to be designed specifically for a given building complex. It is still possible to write a general equation for the calculation of the loss. The loss at a distance d, L_p can be expressed as

$$L_p(d)\,dB = L_p(d_0)\,dB + 10n_{eff}\log_{10}\left(\frac{d}{d_0}\right) + \sum_{k=1}^{K} P_k, \quad (9)$$

where n_{eff} is the effective loss exponent taking into account the multiple floors and walls in the building through which the signal traverses (Durgin et al., 1998; Rappaport & Sandhu, 1994). The loss at a distance of $d_0 = 1$ m is given by $L_p(d_0)$. The other factor in Equation 9 is the specific material attenuation in dB suffered by the signal as it traverses through K floors/walls.

Signal Variability and Fading

We will now briefly review the origins of signal variability seen in wireless propagation (Figure 3). The signal variability may be caused by short-term fading, long-term fading, or both. The short-term fading may result from multipath fading and Doppler fading. This section explores these fading mechanisms and diversity techniques used to mitigate the problems caused by fading.

Multipath Fading

The signal variability is the lack of predictability of the loss or received power (Hashemi, 1993; Kennedy, 1969; Rappaport, 2002). Recall that Figure 3 shows that power loss varies as the distance increases, with the mean or median fluctuations obeying the nth power of the distance. This random nature of the wireless signals is termed fading. This can lead to occasional loss of signal and network breakdown. This is because the systems require a minimum amount of power (threshold) to perform satisfactorily and power fluctuations may bring the power below this threshold. This can be taken into consideration by providing a power margin.

Even though the obvious effect of fading is the random fluctuations of the received power, fading is also responsible for limiting the bandwidth capability of the wireless systems. This section first discusses reasons for the fluctuation in power and the effects of fluctuations on

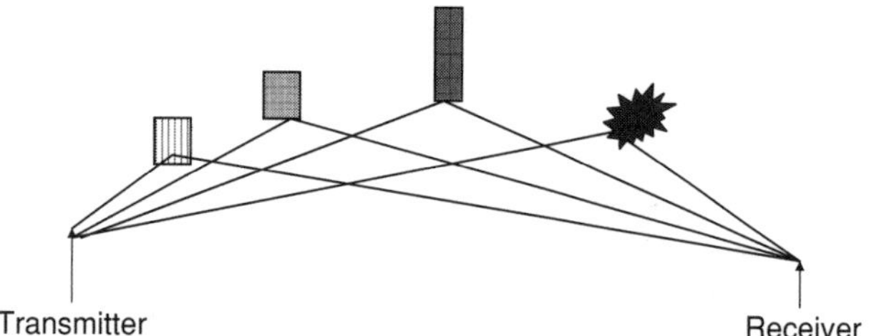

Figure 5: The existence of multiple paths between the transmitter and receiver.

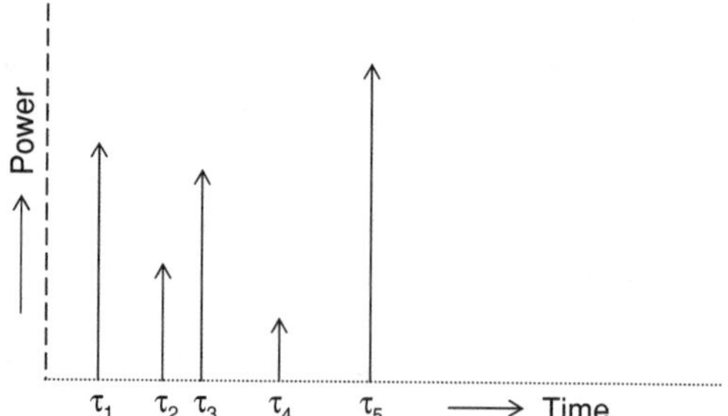

Figure 7: The impulse response of the wireless channel.

data transmission and then explains why fading limits the bandwidth.

In a typical wireless environment, the signal reaches the receiver after being reflected, scattered, diffracted, or refracted from a number of objects in its path (Jakes, 1974; Shankar, 2001). Thus, the signal does not follow only a single path to reach the receiver. Instead, the signal reaches the receiver over multiple paths, as shown in Figure 5.

These signals with different amplitudes and phases combine at the receiver. This multipath phenomenon is responsible for the fluctuations in the signal power observed in Figure 3c. This fluctuation in power or fading is termed as *short-term fading*, for which there are two major consequences. First, the random nature of these fluctuations (some times termed *Rayleigh fading*) increases the uncertainty in the received signal power, making it necessary to develop methods to mitigate fading through diversity. Second, the paths shown in Figure 5 take different times, leading to a broadening of the received pulse as shown in Figure 6. Figure 6a shows a transmitted pulse $h_p(t)$. This pulse takes multiple paths and the received pulse $r(t)$ can be expressed as

$$r(t) = \sum_{m=1}^{M} a_m h_p(t - \tau_m), \tag{10}$$

where a_m is the strength of the pulse and τ_m the time taken by the mth pulse. The number of paths is M. These delayed pulses of different strengths overlap, broadening the pulse at the receiver as seen in Figure 6b. Note that the data rate is inversely proportional to the pulse duration, and any broadening of the pulse will lead to overlapping of adjoining pulses resulting in intersymbol interference (ISI). ISI increases the bit error rate (BER). To prevent distortion, it is necessary to operate at a lower data rate when fading is present. If pulse broadening leads to a reduction in data rate or makes it necessary to put in place additional signal processing methods (typically adaptive equalization) to mitigate the effects of pulse broadening, the medium or channel in which this takes place is referred to as a *frequency selective fading channel*. On the other hand, if the pulse broadening is negligible, the medium is referred to as a *flat fading channel*. The relationship between the input and output pulses seen in Figure 6 can be expressed in terms of the impulse response $h(t)$ of the wireless channel as

$$h(t) = \sum_{m=1}^{M} p_m \delta(t - \tau_m), \tag{11}$$

where τ_m is the time taken by the mth path and p_m is the power in that component, as shown in Figure 7.

The multipath components arise from scattering, reflection, diffraction, or other phenomena described

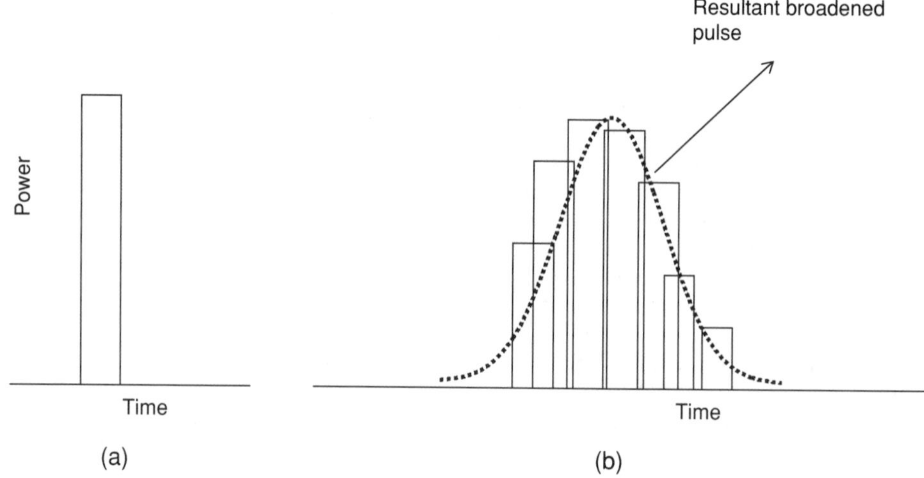

Figure 6: Transmitted pulse (a) and the received pulse (b) are shown.

earlier. The mean delay τ_{av} can obtained as

$$\tau_{av} = \frac{\sum_{m=1}^{M} p_m \tau_m}{\sum_{m=1}^{M} p_m}, \tag{12}$$

where p_m is the power in Watts and τ_m is in seconds. The root mean square (rms) delay σ_τ can be obtained as

$$\sigma_\tau = \sqrt{\frac{\sum_{m=1}^{M} p_m \tau_m^2}{\sum_{m=1}^{M} p_m} - \tau_{av}^2}. \tag{13}$$

The coherence bandwidth B_c of the wireless channel is expressed as

$$B_c = \frac{1}{5\sigma_\tau}. \tag{14}$$

If the information being transmitted through the channel has a bandwidth B, the channel is considered to be *flat* if

$$B < B_c \tag{15}$$

and *frequency selective* if

$$B > B_c. \tag{16}$$

Regardless of whether the channel is flat or frequency selective, the power fluctuations are associated with fading. They cause an increase in the bit error rates making it necessary to operate at higher powers. This case is illustrated in Figure 8, which shows the BER (also known as the probability of error) when no fading is present and also when Rayleigh fading (flat) is present. To maintain a bit error rate of 10^{-3}, we would require an increase in signal-to-noise (SNR) ratio of approximately 17 dB when fading is present, demonstrating the problems associated with fading.

Now consider a SNR of 10 dB. The results shown in Figure 8 indicate that in the presence of fading a SNR of 10 dB is not sufficient (Shankar, 2001) to have an acceptable level of performance (say, 10^{-3}). This leads to *outage*.

It is possible to have a direct path (LOS) between the transmitter and the receiver in addition to the multiple paths. This condition is more ideal than a pure multipath scenario because the LOS path provides a specular or steady component to the signal. As the strength of the specular component increases (over the multipath components) the deleterious effects of fading decrease. The presence of the specular component leads to a Rician distribution for the envelope of the backscattered signal (Stuber, 1996; Shankar, 2001). The fading channel having a specular component is known as the Rician channel. It can be shown that as the strength of the LOS component increases, the Rician channel starts approaching the ideal Gaussian channel, thus reducing the severity of fading.

The discussion of multipath fading would be incomplete without a few words about the effects of frequency selective fading. The ISI caused by the frequency selective fading not only increases the BER, it also starts to level off the BER to a "floor level." When ISI is present, the adjacent bits leak into the bit under consideration. If now the signal power continues to increase, so does the leakage and interference, effectively negating any improvement that will be expected from increasing signal levels leading to an error floor (Feher, 1995; Vaughn & Andersen, 2003). The effect leads to an "irreducible BER" in communication systems, shown in Figure 9. For a generic digital modulation, the BER is plotted against SNR for the cases of no fading, flat fading, and frequency-selective fading (three levels). As the value of σ_c increases from σ_{c1} to σ_{c3}, the error floor continues to increase.

Use of advanced signal processing techniques, such as adaptive equalization, can overcome the problems of fast fading (Feher, 1995; Vaughn & Andersen 2003).

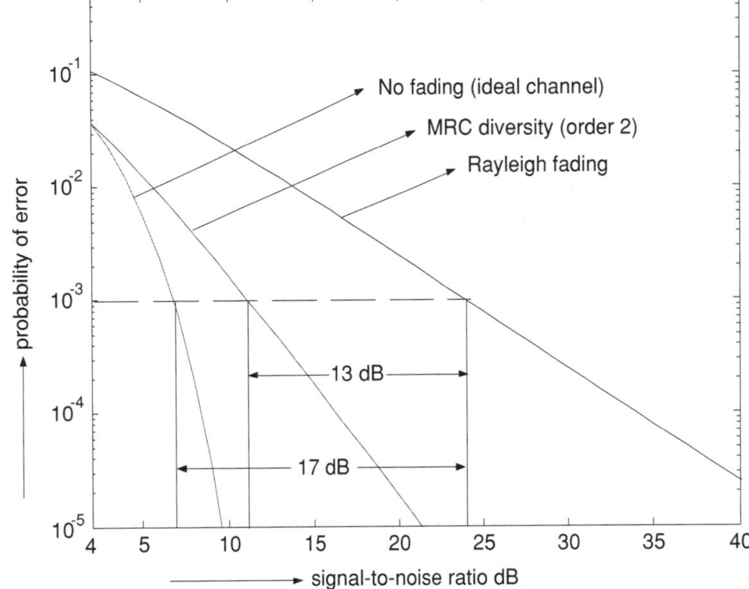

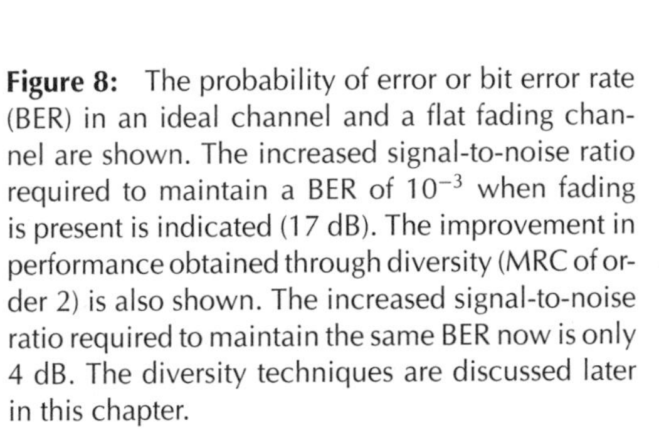
Figure 8: The probability of error or bit error rate (BER) in an ideal channel and a flat fading channel are shown. The increased signal-to-noise ratio required to maintain a BER of 10^{-3} when fading is present is indicated (17 dB). The improvement in performance obtained through diversity (MRC of order 2) is also shown. The increased signal-to-noise ratio required to maintain the same BER now is only 4 dB. The diversity techniques are discussed later in this chapter.

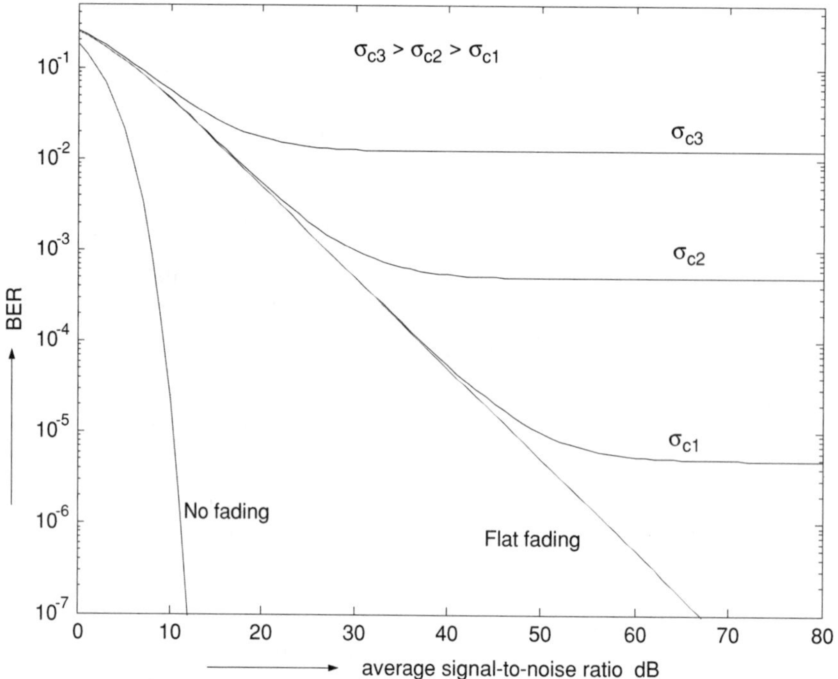

Figure 9: The concept of irreducible bit error rate (BER). BER does not come down as the signal-to-noise ratio (SNR) increases after a certain SNR is reached. This is a consequence of intersymbol interference.

Doppler Fading

The multipath fading mentioned earlier does not take into account any relative motion of the transmitter and receiver. If the wireless receiver (or transmitter) is mounted on a moving vehicle, the motion introduces Doppler broadening. Motion induced fading is referred to as *Doppler fading* and is responsible for further degradation in the performance of the wireless systems. If a pure tone of frequency f_0 is transmitted, the received signal spectrum will broaden (Doppler broadening) and contain spectral components ranging from $f_0 - f_d$ and $f_0 + f_d$, where f_d is the Doppler shift. If the bandwidth occupied by the information is much greater than the spectral broadening, Doppler spread ($B_D \sim f_d$) does not lead to any significant problems in transmission and reception. The channel in this case is referred to as a *slow-fading channel*. If the bandwidth is smaller than the Doppler spread, motion leads to the channel varying rapidly within the duration of the pulse. In this case, the channel is referred to as a *fast-fading channel*.

Thus, multipath fading decides whether the channel is flat or frequency selective, Doppler fading decides whether the channel is slow or fast (Jakes, 1974; Parsons, 1996). Whereas multipath fading leads to pulse spreading (time), Doppler fading leads to frequency spreading.

$$\left.\begin{array}{ll} B > B_c & \text{Frequency selective} \\ B < B_c & \text{Flat} \end{array}\right\} \text{multipath fading}$$
$$\left.\begin{array}{ll} B > B_D & \text{Slow} \\ B < B_D & \text{Fast} \end{array}\right\} \text{Doppler fading} \tag{17}$$

The various types of fading described in the preceding paragraphs are summarized in Figure 10.

Long-Term Fading

Figure 3 showed that the power fluctuations have a longer period in Figure 3b than those in Figure 3c. These fluctuations with larger periods are statistically described in terms of lognormal fading. Whereas short-term fading is caused by the existence of multipath, long-term fading is

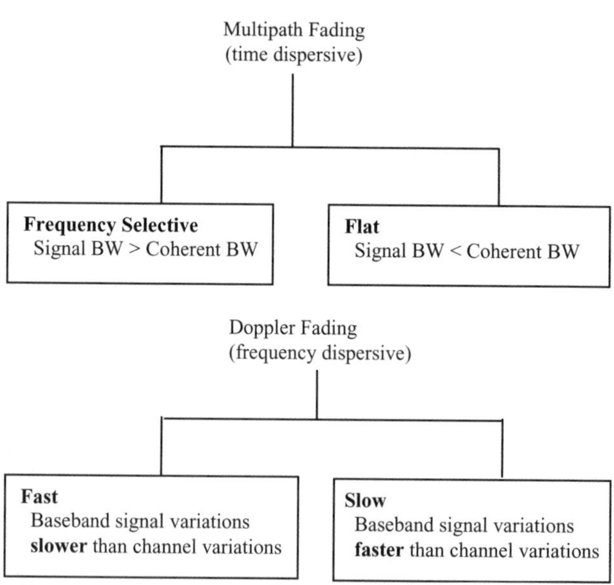

Figure 10: Overview of short-term fading. Pulse broadening (time dispersive) taking place in a frequency-selective channel can be described in terms of the relationship between the message bandwidth and coherence bandwidth. Doppler fading (frequency dispersive) can be described in terms of the variations in the channel relative to the signal.

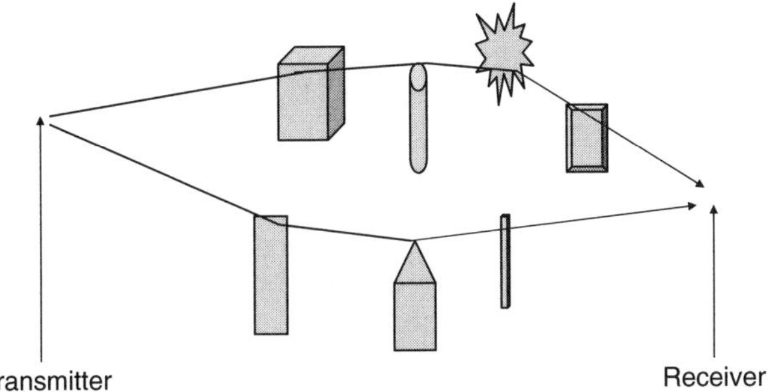

Figure 11: The signal from the transmitter reaches the receiver after multiple reflections, scatterings, and diffractions from human-made objects and foliage or transmission through them in its path. Two such paths are shown. Many such paths are encountered, each path a result of multiple reflections, scatterings, transmissions, and diffractions. This is different from the case shown in Figure 5 in which each path from the transmitter to the receiver undergoes only a single reflection, scattering, or diffraction.

caused by the existence of several objects in each of the paths. This scenario is depicted in Figure 11. Whereas in the case of a multipath fading, each path to the receiver is the result of a single scattering, reflection, diffraction from each of the objects, in the case of long-term fading each path arriving at the receiver is the result of multiple interactions with the objects. Thus, both multipath and multiple reflections coexist, leading to fluctuations in the average power. Thus, each path will be a result of a multiplicative process, the received signal in each path having a power determined by the number of objects in that path and the relative strengths of the components from each of these objects in that particular path. Because of this, the average power at any given location will be random.

The power expressed in decibels in this case can be shown to be normally distributed and the power in watts will therefore be lognormally distributed (Jakes, 1974; Rappaport, 2002; Steele & Hanzo, 1999). This statistical fluctuation in power caused by multiple structures is also sometimes referred to as *shadowing*. Such situations arise even in indoor channels. The reason for use of the term shadowing is that signal power fluctuation may be caused by the signal being blocked from the receiver by the buildings in outdoor areas or by walls inside the buildings (indoor). To account for the lognormal fading or shadowing, the loss terms in Equation 8 are modified by introducing a term X to the equation for the loss. X is a zero mean normal random variable with a standard deviation of σ_{dB} to take lognormal fading into consideration.

$$Loss = L_p(d) + X \tag{18}$$

The loss calculated now becomes the average of a normally distributed random variable with a standard deviation determined by the severity of the lognormal fading. The long-term fading will also cause outage if the variation in loss is not taken into account during the design of the wireless links. This situation is handled by including a *power margin* in the *link budget* calculations.

Diversity Techniques

Effects of short-term fading can be mitigated through diversity techniques that exploit the randomness existing in the channel. Consider a scenario where it is possible to create N ($N > 1$) multiple (diverse) independent (at least uncorrelated) versions of the signal. If the probability that the signal goes below a threshold is p, the probability that all these multiple versions of the signals will go below that threshold *simultaneously* is p^N. In other words, if we were to choose the strongest signal from this set, the probability that this chosen signal is above the threshold is $(1 - p^N)$, leading to fading mitigation, lessening the chances of outage. The signal processing technique of choosing the strongest signal is known as selection diversity. Other forms of diversity processing, such as maximal ratio combining (MRC), equal gain combining (EGC), and so on are also available to combine the signals from diverse branches (Stein, 1987). In MRC, the signals are combined with appropriate weights using an optimal algorithm resulting in the best performance. In EGC, the weights are equal. The selection diversity is the simplest of these. The improvement in performance through diversity is shown in Figure 8. The BER for the MRC diversity ($N = 2$) plotted along with Rayleigh faded and ideal channel cases show that the additional SNR required to maintain BER of 10^{-3} is brought down to 4 dB (from 17 dB in the absence of any diversity).

Diversity can be implemented either in the spatial domain (spatial diversity) or in the frequency domain (frequency diversity). In spatial diversity, multiple receivers operating at the same frequency band are used. In frequency diversity, the same information is transmitted over multiple carrier frequencies. Other forms of diversity, such as angle diversity, polarization diversity, time diversity, and rake receiver, are also available (Shankar, 2001; Stein, 1987).

Whereas the techniques just described constitute examples of microscopic diversity to mitigate effects of short-term fading, long-term fading or shadowing can be mitigated through macroscopic diversity techniques. Choosing the best base station with the strongest signal to serve a subscriber is a form of macroscopic diversity. It is also possible to combine the signals from different base stations to reduce the effects of long-term fading further.

INTERFERENCE IN CELLULAR ARCHITECTURE

The spectrum available for wireless systems is limited. One of the ways in which the available spectrum can be used to provide coverage to several users is through the repeated use of the same spectrum or frequency channels using the concept known as *frequency reuse*. This concept is shown in Figure 12. A small geographic region, otherwise known as a cell, uses a certain band of frequencies. As noted in the discussion on transmission loss, the power transmitted from the base station drops off as the distance increases. Thus, it is possible to use the same frequency band (A) in Cell 1 in another cell (Cell N) a certain distance away from it as long as the power from the transmitter in Cell 1 at the location of Cell N is less than a certain value

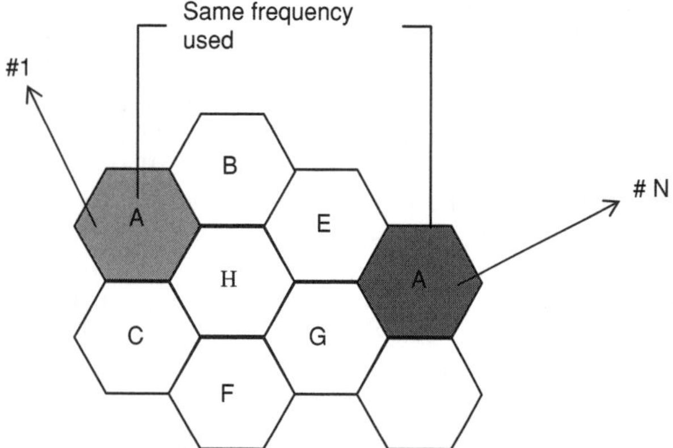

Figure 12: The cellular concept. Cells 1 and N use the same frequency band.

and vice versa. This process can be repeated by reusing the same frequency bands in other cells separated by a minimum distance, allowing the ability to provide service to more users. Several cells are grouped into what is known as a *cluster*. The cells in the cluster use the entire frequency spectrum available to the provider, with each cell using a portion of the spectrum. In the seven-cell cluster shown in Figure 12, frequency bands A through H are used in the seven cells as shown. For example, in Figure 12 frequency band A in Cell 1 is used in Cell N of the adjoining seven-cell cluster.

Interference

Cellular architectures present interference problems that affect the performance of the wireless systems. One is the co-channel interference (CCI), the result of signals from the distant cells in other clusters operating at the same frequency band (called co-channels) as the desired cell in the desired cluster. The second interference arises from within a cluster itself from channels at the adjoining frequency bands. The reason for this interference is the inadequate amount of filtering leading to some overlap between signals from adjoining frequency bands. Nonlinear effects (such as nonlinear amplifiers leading to harmonics) also lead to adjacent channel interference (ACI). Of these two interference factors, CCI is the most serious of the interference phenomena in cellular networks. The performance of the wireless can be measured in terms of signal-to-CCI ratio $\frac{S}{I}$ defined as

$$\frac{S}{I} = \frac{P_{desired}}{\sum_{k=1} P_{Ik}}, \tag{19}$$

where $P_{desired}$ is the signal strength (power) in the desired cell in the desired cluster and P_{Ik} is the power from the kth interfering cell. The summation is carried over all the cells operating at the same frequency band as the desired one. Given a specific geographic region (indoors or outdoors), the power at the receiver decreases as determined by the path loss exponent. If the path loss exponent is n, the received signal power (desired) will be proportional to $P_t d_s^{-n}$, where P_t is the transmitted power and d_s is the distance from its base station. If we assume that all the base station transmitters operate at the same power, the interference signal power from the kth co-channel will be proportional to $P_t d_k^{-n}$, where d_k is the distance of the receiver from the transmitter of the kth interfering channel (Base Station). The signal-to-CCI ratio in Equation 19 now becomes

$$\frac{S}{I} = \frac{P_t d_s^{-n}}{P_t \sum_{k=1} d_k^{-n}} = \frac{d_s^{-n}}{\sum_{k=1} d_k^{-n}}. \tag{20}$$

Consider a simple case of a single interferer ($k = 1$). The S/I ratio now becomes

$$\frac{S}{I} = \left[\frac{d_k}{d_s}\right]^n. \tag{21}$$

Thus, the signal-to-CCI ratio improves if d_k is large as seen in Figure 13. The signal-to CCI ratio also improves with n. Such an improvement comes at the cost of higher losses in the channel. This was stated earlier in the section on 'Modeling of Power Loss'.

If R is the radius of the hexagonal cell and D is the distance to the cell where the same frequency band is used, it is possible to define the frequency reuse factor q is defined as

$$q = \frac{D}{R}. \tag{22}$$

The number of cells, N_c, in a cluster can be shown to be related to q as

$$q = \sqrt{3N_c}. \tag{23}$$

This would mean that we must have more and more cells in a cluster, putting the interfering cells farther and farther from the desired cell. Such a step reduces interference and consequently increases the signal-to-CCI ratio. This increase in signal-to-CCI ratio comes at a price. If the frequency bands are reused farther and farther, it reduces the capacity of the overall network to provide coverage to more and more users.

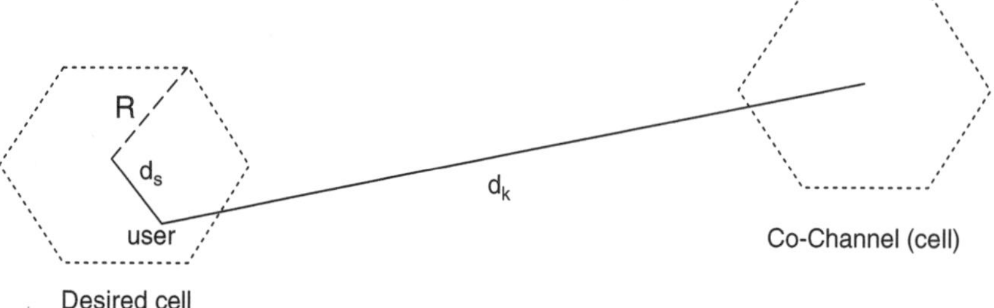

Figure 13: The desired cell and the co-channel. R is the radius of the cell.

Note that the frequency reuse depicted in Figure 12 applies to wireless systems employing frequency division multiple access (FDMA) and time division multiple access (TDMA). The frequency reuse factor in code division multiple access (CDMA) systems is unity because the same frequency is used in every cell. In TDMA and FDMA, the reuse factor is larger than unity.

Cell Splitting

While the need to maintain an acceptable value of signal-to-CCI ratio is paramount, the inherent limitation of reduced capacity arising out of larger separation (high values d_k) can be overcome by reducing the size of the cell. The reduction in the cell size is undertaken, maintaining the number of cells in the cluster to be the same. In this technique, known as *cell splitting,* the sizes of the cells are reduced keeping the signal-to-CCI ratio the same as in the case of the larger cells through a reduction in the transmit power. The power received at the boundary of an unsplit cell P_{ur} can be expressed as

$$P_{ur} \propto P_{ut} R^{-n}, \tag{24}$$

where P_{ut} is the transmitted power and R is the radius of the cell (maximum value of d_s). The received power P_{sr} at the boundary of a cell half the size will be

$$P_{sr} \propto P_{st} \left(\frac{R}{2}\right)^{-n}, \tag{25}$$

where P_{st} is the transmitted power. To keep the signal-to-CCI ratio the same in the original cell and the reduced size cell,

$$P_{ur} = P_{sr}. \tag{26}$$

This would mean that the transmitted power in the reduced cell must be reduced as well. If we use $n = 4$, we can obtain

$$P_{st} = \frac{P_{ut}}{16}. \tag{27}$$

Thus, if the size of the cell is reduced to half of the original cell size, the transmit power must be reduced to one sixteenth of the transmitted power in the original cell size to maintain an identical signal-to-CCI ratio. This leads to a larger number of cells in a given area providing increased capacity to accommodate more users without compromising the performance in terms of an acceptable level of signal-to-CCI ratio.

The sizes of the cells vary significantly depending on the traffic fluctuations and the number of users. They will be smaller in size in urban areas and larger in rural areas. A common way to separate these various cell sizes is to classify them as follows:

Mega Cells The cell sizes may be several hundred kilometers in radii. These are mainly used in satellite communication systems.

Macro cells These cells are typically used in traditional wireless systems, both large metropolitan and rural areas. The radii of these cells may be several kilometers—smaller in metropolitan areas and larger in urban areas.

Micro cells These cells are of several hundred meters in size and are used in urban areas. They are also necessary at higher frequencies of operation (1800 MHz and above) because of the higher levels of attenuation experienced.

Pico cells These are a few tens of meters in range and may be used to increase the capacity in heavy traffic areas. They are also used in wireless systems operating indoors.

Femto cells These cells have a range of a few meters and are typically used in a room to link several computers, printers, fax machines, personal digital assistants (PDAs), and cell phones. Such cells are also used in Bluetooth systems.

CONCLUDING REMARKS

This chapter presented an overview of the propagation characteristics of the wireless channel. Power loss, fading, and interference issues were discussed.

GLOSSARY

Base station (BS) A fixed station in a cellular system that communicates with mobile units within a cell and may be located at the center (or the edge of the cell). It has transmitting and receiving antennas mounted on a tower and is the link between a mobile unit and a mobile switching center.

Bit Error Rate (BER) The ratio of the number of bits received in error to the total number of bits received. It is also referred to as the *probability of error.*

Cell A geographic region served by a base station.

Doppler Shift The upshift or downshift in frequency resulting from the motion of the transmitter with respect to the receiver or vice versa. If the relative speed is v, the Doppler shift is $f_d = \frac{v\cos(\theta)}{c} f_0$, where c is the speed of the electromagnetic wave (3×10^8 m/s), f_0 is the carrier frequency, and θ is the angle between the directions of the transmitter and receiver.

Intersymbol Interference (ISI) The interference caused by the overlapping of adjoining symbols or pulses resulting in signal distortion. Viewed in the frequency domain, existence of ISI implies that the channel cannot carry all frequencies with equal gain, with gain decreasing as the frequencies go up.

Link Budget The process of computing the maximum transmission distance taking into account the transmitted power, loss or attenuation, and power margin.

Mobile Unit (MU), Mobile Station (MS), or Handset A mobile unit is carried by the subscriber. It may be handheld or vehicle mounted.

Outage Whenever the performance of the wireless system does not reach the minimum acceptable levels, the system goes into outage. For example, if a minimum power of P_{th} is required to have an acceptable performance, any time the received power goes below P_{th}, the system goes into outage. The rate at which this happens is the outage probability.

Power Margin The excess power budgeted to account for any effects other than the attenuation or the loss of the signal. For example, if a threshold power of P_{th} (dBm) is required to maintain acceptable performance and *MdB* is the power margin to account for fading, the minimum acceptable power $P_{\min}$ (dBm) at the receiver is required to be set to $P_{\min} = P_{th} + M$. This has the effect of reducing the separation between the transmitter and receiver.

APPENDIX (POWER UNITS)

Power is normally expressed in decibel units. Power (P_0) in milliWatts (mW) can be expressed in terms of decibel units, dBm as

$$P_0\,(dBm) = 10\log_{10}\left[\frac{P_0\,(mW)}{1\;mW}\right]. \tag{17}$$

Thus, the power in dBm is an absolute measure of power in mW. 10 mW of power is 10 dBm, 1 W is 30 dBm, and 1 μW is −30 dBm. The unit, dB, on the other hand, is the ratio of two powers in identical units. For example, if the average signal power is P_0 (mW) and the average noise power is P_n (mW), the signal-to-noise ratio (SNR) can be expressed as

$$(S/N)\,dB = 10\log_{10}\left[\frac{P_0\,(mW)}{P_n\,(mW)}\right]. \tag{A.1}$$

Thus, SNR expressed in dB carries information on the strength of the signal relative to the noise. If the SNR is 0 dB, the signal power and noise power are equal. If the SNR is 20 dB, the signal is 100 times stronger than the noise. If the SNR is −3 dB, the signal is only 50% of the noise. Loss or attenuation can be expressed in dB units as

$$Loss\,(dB) = Transmit\ power\ (dBm) - Receive\ power\ (dBm). \tag{19}$$

If the transmitted power is 10 mW and the received power is 1 μW, we can calculate the transmission loss as $10\log_{10}(10mW) - 10\log_{10}(1\mu W) = 10 - (-30) = 40dB$.

CROSS REFERENCES

See *Cellular Networks; Radio Frequency and Wireless Communications Security; Security and the Wireless Application Protocol (WAP).*

REFERENCES

Bertoni, H. L., Honcharenko, W., Maciel, L. R., & Xia, H. H. (1994). UHF propagation prediction for wireless personal communications. *Proceedings of the IEEE, 82,* 1333–1359.

Bultitude, R. J. C., Mahmoud, S. A., & Sullivan, W. A. (1989). A comparison of indoor radio propagation characteristics at 910 MHz and 1.75 GHz. *IEEE Transactions on Selected Areas in Communications, 7,* 20–30.

Dersch, U., & Zollinger, E. (1994). Propagation mechanisms in microcell and indoor environments. *IEEE Transactions on Vehicular Technology, 43,* 1058–1066.

Durgin, G., Rappaport, T. S., & Xu, H. (1998). Measurements and models for radio path loss and penetration loss in and around homes and trees at 5.85 GHz. *IEEE Transactions on Communications, 46,* 1484–1496.

Feher, K. (1995) *Wireless digital communications: Modulation and spread spectrum applications.* New York: Prentice Hall.

Har, D., Xia, H. H., & Bertoni, H. (1999). Path-loss prediction model for microcells. *IEEE Transactions on Vehicular Technology, 48,* 1453–1461.

Harley, P. (1989). Short distance attenuation measurements at 900 MHz and at 1.8 GHz using low antenna heights for microcells. *IEEE Journal of Selected Areas in Communications, 7,* 5–11.

Hashemi, H. (1993). The indoor radio propagation channel. *Proceedings of the IEEE, 81,* 943–968.

Hata, M. (1980). Empirical formulae for propagation loss in land mobile radio services. *IEEE Transactions on Vehicular Technology, 29,* 317–325.

Ikegami, F., Tekeuchi, T., & Yoshida, S. (1991). Theoretical prediction of mean field strength for urban mobile radio. *IEEE Transactions on Antennas and Propagation, 39,* 299–302.

Institute of Electrical and Electronics Engineers (IEEE Vehicular Technology Society Committee on radio propagation). (1988a). Coverage prediction for mobile radio systems operating in the 800/900 MHz frequency range, *IEEE Transactions on Vehicular Technology, 37,* 3–44.

Institute of Electrical and Electronics Engineers. (1988b, December). *IEEE Communications Magazine.*

Jakes, W. C. (Ed.). (1974). *Microwave Mobile Communications.* Piscataway, New Jersey: IEEE Press.

Kennedy, R. S. (1969). *Fading dispersive communication channels.* New York: Wiley.

Lee, W. C. Y. (1986). Elements of cellular mobile radio systems. *IEEE Transactions on Vehicular Technology, 35,* 48–56.

Lott, M., & Forkel, I. (2001). A multi-wall and floor model for indoor radio propagation. *IEEE Conference on Vehicular Technology, 35,* 464–468.

Oda, Y., Tsunkewa, K., & Hata, M. (2000). Advanced LOS path-loss model in microcelleular mobile communications. *IEEE Conference on Vehicular Technology, 49,* 2121–2125.

Okumura, T., Ohmori, E., & Fukuda, K. (1968). Field strength and variability in VHF and UHF land mobile service. *Review of Electrical Communication Laboratory, 16,* 825–873.

Parsons, D. (1996). *The mobile radio propagation channel.* West Sussex, England: Wiley.

Rappaport, T. S. (2002). *Wireless communications: Principles and practice* (2nd ed.). New Jersey: Prentice Hall.

Rappaport, T. S., & Sandhu, S. (1994). Radio wave propagation for emerging wireless communication systems. *IEEE Antennas and Propagation Magazine, 36,* 14–23.

Shankar, P. M. (2001). *Introduction to wireless systems.* New York: Wiley.

Steele, R., & Hanzo, L. (Eds.). (1999). *Mobile radio communications,* (2nd ed.). Piscataway, New Jersey: IEEE Press.

Stein, S. (1987). Fading channel issues in systems engineering. *IEEE Journal of Selected Areas in Communications, 5,* 68–89.

Stuber, S. (1996). *Principles of mobile communication.* Boston: Kluwer Academic.

Vaughn, R., & Andersen, J. B. (2003). *Channels, propagation and antennas for mobile communications.* Herts, United Kingdom: IEE Press.

Vogel, W. J., & Hong, U-S. (1988). Measurement and modeling of land mobile satellite propagation at UHF and L-Band. *IEEE Transactions on Antennas and Propagation, 36,* 707–719.

FURTHER READING

Additional reading material may be found in *IEEE Transactions on Wireless Communications, IEEE Transactions on Vehicular Technology, IEEE Communications Magazine, Wireless and Personal Communications,* and other sources. An excellent source of information on some of the topics presented in this chapter is http://www.antd.nist.gov/wahn_home.shtml (retrieved, May 14, 2005).

See also the following:

Haartsen, J. C., & Mattisson, S. (2000). Bluetooth: A new low power radio interface providing short range connectivity. *Proceedings of the IEEE, 88,* 1651–1661.

Padgett, J. E., Gunther, C. G., & Hattori, T. (1995). Overview of wireless personal communications. *IEEE Communications Magazine, 33,* 28–41.

Pahlavan, K., & Levesque, A. H. (1995). *Wireless information networks.* New York: Wiley.

Saunders, S. R. (1999). *Antennas and propagation for wireless communication systems.* West Sussex, England: Wiley.

Security in Circuit, Message, and Packet Switching

Robert H. Greenfield, *Computer Consulting*
Daryle P. Niedermayer, *CGI Group Inc.*

INTRODUCTION

Circuit, message, and packet switching are techniques for transferring information. These concepts are not unique to electronic networking. They have common, everyday models and historical prototypes. A ubiquitous example of circuit switching is a voice telephone conversation between two people. Message switching is seen every day in the paper-based postal system.

Visualizing packet switching takes more imagination. Let's move a complete business including staff, furniture, files, business machines, and so forth from an old location to a new one. We assume that the business is sufficiently large that it needs several automobiles and buses to move the people and a number of trucks to move the nonhuman assets. All these vehicles, each containing a portion of the company, move over a system of roads. Each vehicle travels independently, yet as an aggregate, the company is the sum of the payloads of all the vehicles.

We look at security aspects of circuit, message, and packet switching for digital communications networks and their more historical paper and electronic prototypes. Some of the security concerns are common no matter which technique is used, for example, we can communicate using a secret language. In the convoy example, we can keep the route secret until the last moment. Perhaps we can use a private, secret road, or even an underground tunnel, instead of the public highways.

We can take this "company moving" example a little further to illustrate datagrams and virtual circuits. If we allow all the cars, trucks, and buses to select their own routes from the source to the destination, we have a datagram example. Each vehicle arrives on its own schedule. However, if we dictate a specific route and mandate a convoy, or a parade, by assigning a placard—A, B, C, and so on—to all the vehicles and require them to stay in sequence, behind their predecessor, we illustrate a virtual circuit. Note that pedestrians in crosswalks, red lights, and cross traffic can interrupt and delay portions of the convoy. Nonetheless, all vehicles arrive at the destination in their scheduled sequence, albeit with varying delays.

Notice that the convoy model and the free-choice model, in which each vehicle is independently routed, have different security risks and needs. In the datagram mode, it is more difficult for an observer to watch all the vehicles.

We use the terms "switching" or "routing" because the circuits, messages, or packets traverse a mesh of links and nodes. Links connect nodes. Nodes are also called switches. We "route" or "switch" the entities from one node to another, using the links, from the source ultimate destination. The entire mass of links and nodes is a point-to-point network. Typically, wide area networks are point-to-point networks. Another kind of network is a broadcast network. Local area networks (LANs) are typically broadcast packet networks.

What do we own and control—the links, the nodes, everything, nothing? Can we encase our electronic systems so that no electromagnetic signals whatsoever escape into free space where they may possibly be monitored? If our communications employ optical fibers, then there is no electromagnetic leakage. If we employ broadcast radio techniques, with omnidirectional antennae, then everyone can monitor our signals. If we employ directional antennae, our signals are still "public," but more difficult to monitor. If we employ wired electronic communications, our signals are more protected than radio, but far less protected than optical signals in fibers.

In Figure 1, several nodes are shown with links connecting them. Not all nodes are directly connected to every other node. There may or may not be any loops in the network. Some nodes may be connected to only one other node. There are, however, a sufficient number of links so that, directly or indirectly, all nodes are connected to each other and form one complete network. At the same time, some nodes have more access to communications that do not belong to them. In particular, node D is advantageously situated to intercept communications from A, B, or C destined to E or F. The control and security of node D must either be well trusted or communications flowing through D should be encrypted so that information transmission is secure. The same holds true for other nodes: B can monitor traffic to and from A, and, depending on the routing protocols in use, C, E, and F can all intercept traffic destined for other nodes.

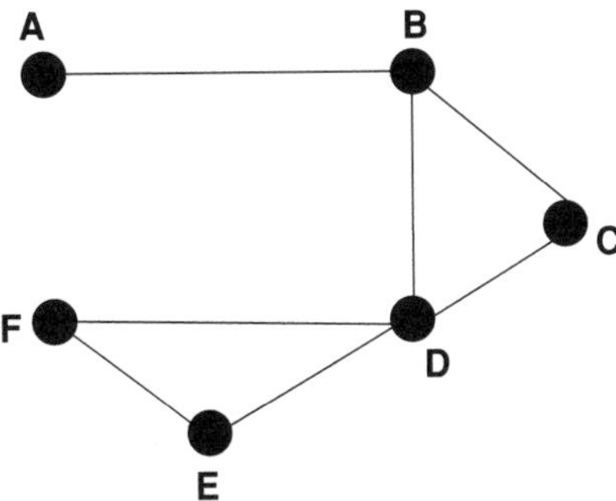

Figure 1: A point-to-point network.

The Internet is largely constructed using links and nodes. Consider a connection between station X in Canada and station Y the United States, just to select two nations. All nodes used to connect X and Y are likely located in the United States and in Canada, not in a third nation. Several designated "gateways" connect U.S. nodes to Canadian nodes. These gateways, like border-crossing stations, are excellent places to monitor communications between the nations. It is highly unlikely that nodes and links in a third nation—say, Mexico—are employed. Why? National security. The Internet has a traceroute diagnostic tool. Use it to examine routing between your location and a computer in another country. For both security and economic reasons, the route probably does not take you through a third nation.

Several nodes are shown in Figure 2. All nodes are contained within a cloud and share a common medium or ether. A pretty, puffy cloud artistically depicts the network's edges. What is important is that each node is inside the cloud. Each node can, via the common medium, communicate directly with every other node. There is no privacy. Everyone can listen to everything. Information security in such a network usually relies on a trust relationship among all nodes and barriers or firewalls to control gateways to external networks (cf. chapter 30, Local Area Networks), or on some form of asymmetric encryption (cf. chapter 65, Public Key Infrastructure).

LAYERING MODELS

We build and discuss networks using layers, just like houses are built on foundations, usually resting on earth.

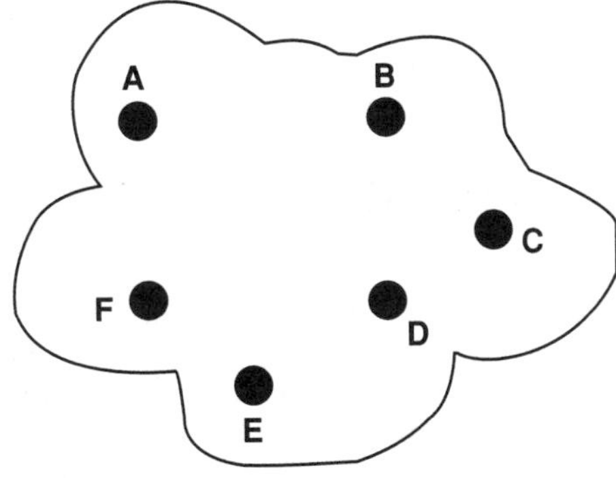

Figure 2: A broadcast network.

A house's frame rests on the foundation, the interior and exterior walls hang on the frame, and the roof sits on top.

Layering allows us to look at only a portion of the communications process at any one time. This simplifies our examination of something complex. For example, on the data link or network layers, we may use an assortment of protocols, one on each layer or sublayer, as appropriate to the specific network. On the Internet layer, we use IP (Internet protocol), a datagram protocol. On the transport layer, we use TCP (transmission control protocol), a virtual circuit protocol. On the application layer, we might employ SMTP (simple mail transport protocol), a message switching technique, ultimately to transport our electronic mail messages.

If we use a wired (or optical fiber) Ethernet on our own private property, complete with armed patrols and big dogs, we may be satisfied with the security of our communications. On the other hand, when we replace or augment the wired network with IEEE (Institute of Electrical and Electronics Engineers) 802.11 radio communications, we likely want, at a minimum, to employ WEP (wired equivalent privacy), a data link layer encryption scheme. Likely we want to do even more with higher layer encryption—to compensate for WEP, a weak technique that also provides no protection for a LAN user from other LAN users.

Just as a real network is constructed using several layers, each layer has its own set of addresses—for example, hardware addresses, IP addresses, and port numbers—to specify the location of devices and services. In the case of the Internet, addresses don't always neatly map into layers.

OSI Reference Model

One of the initial models for these layers or "stacks" is the seven-level open system interconnection (OSI) protocol developed by the International Standards Organization (ISO). The OSI standard is a protocol that has never been fully implemented in a production environment. Today it is used primarily for pedagogical purposes. TCP/IP, another, much more informal model, is the backbone of the modern-day Internet. TCP/IP includes many protocols including the two that give it its overall name (transmission control protocol–Internet protocol).

Table 1 outlines the OSI reference model and several variations of the TCP/IP model. Diverse TCP/IP model versions exist because TCP/IP is an informal, loosely defined protocol suite—that is, different authors prefer different models. For our purposes, we employ the three-layer version and discuss the supporting networks, Ethernet, IEEE 802.11, and so forth separately. The two models, OSI and TCP/IP, evolved independently. Exact equivalences cannot be made, and only loosely defined comparisons should be inferred.

TCP/IP Model

The layers of the TCP/IP model include application, transport, and internet layers, and sometimes a data link layer and a physical layer (see Table 1). An internet has no network layer because it is a network built on top of other (likely heterogeneous) networks. (Whatever we say about

Table 1 The OSI Reference Model and Versions of the TCP/IP Model

OSI layer	TCP/IP 5-layer	TCP/IP 4-layer A	TCP/IP 4-layer B	TCP/IP 3-layer
Application		Application		
Presentation	Application			Application
Session			Application	
Transport	Transport	Transport	Transport	Transport
	Internet	Internet		Internet
Network			Internet	
Data link	Network access			
Physical	Physical	Supporting networks	Supporting networks	

OSI = open system interconnection; TCP/IP = transmission control protocol–Internet protocol.

an internet in this section, also applies to the Internet and to intranets.) The strength of an internet is that it allows heterogeneous network layers to seamlessly interconnect. This is done using routers. For example a WAN component of a TCP/IP internet might use frame relay or ATM connections, whereas LAN components of the same internet might use Ethernet, switched Ethernet, or token ring as their physical network layers. Wireless portions might use the IEEE 802.11 protocols. For the nodes, however, the specific physical, data link, and network layers used by any other node is of no consequence. The routing tables and requisite repeaters, bridges, and routers are able to translate the TCP/IP traffic from all the nodes to the appropriate physical networks.

The data link, network, internet, transport, and application layers and security concerns and tools for each layer are discussed here. The physical layer is of interest to us, although it is not a part of the TCP/IP model, because the physical, data link, and network layers of the supporting networks raise security questions. In today's world, the OSI presentation layer as its own entity is pretty much ignored. The session layer is almost always considered a part of the transport layer. This leaves us the physical, data link, network, internet, transport, and application layers from the original OSI and TCP/IP models to examine for circuit, message, and packet switching techniques and their security issues.

Broadcast Model

The OSI reference model was constructed with point-to-point (wide area networks) in mind. It ignores broadcast networks which are not constructed with links joining nodes (Figure 1) but by a set of nodes all sharing the same medium (Figure 2). The OSI model can be adapted for broadcast networks by splitting the data link layer into two sublayers, the MAC (medium access control) and the LLC (logical link control).

MAC sublayer protocols determine how a node or station gains access to the broadcast medium needed to transmit packets into the network. LLC sublayer protocols define a language that stations can use to decode the packets. It also provides a common layer, or glue, for interfacing to upper layers. The LLC protocol defined by IEEE 802.2 defines a common protocol used by several MAC schemes such as Ethernet (802.3), token ring (802.5), and wireless (802.11). There are many IEEE 802 standards. Some, for example, 802.11, are rapidly evolving today. A fuller discussion is beyond our scope.

The older LLC (802.2), Ethernet (802.3), and token ring (802.5) protocols do not significantly address any security concerns. The newer wireless (802.11) protocol has a weak data link layer encryption scheme: wired equivalent privacy (WEP). There is currently much interest in developing wireless security standards because manufacturers are addressing security concerns with their own ad hoc proprietary extensions.

Broadcast networks can do some things more easily than point-to-point networks. One of these is to "broadcast" to all stations in the network. A special address designated as addressing all stations can exist. Packets with this address are copied by all stations in the network because all share the same medium, the same environment. In a point-to-point network, pains are taken that such broadcast packets are routed and repeated to all stations. This involves many copies of the packet in the point-to-point network compared with only one in the broadcast network.

Multicasting extends the idea of broadcasting. Groups of stations are defined to share a designated multicast address. Many such groups and many such addresses can be created. Packets destined to a multicast address are received by all stations. Those stations recognizing the address as significant should copy the information. Other stations should ignore the message.

Packets directed to a designated destination are read by all stations. The addressed station acts on the information, whereas other stations are expected to ignore it. Note the words "expected to ignore it." It is easy to spy and to copy everything. This is one of the motivations for using encryption on the higher layer protocols—to keep private information private.

CIRCUIT, MESSAGE, AND PACKET SWITCHING

If two people are in the same room and want to talk, the process of communication is relatively simple and straight forward: "Hey Jane, I've been meaning to ask you about. . . . " In the same way, data transmission between two nodes is relatively straightforward when both nodes are on the same network.

A more difficult problem emerges when the two people do not share physical proximity. They could use megaphones, but this becomes problematic if the other six thousand million people in the world want to talk at the same time and have equally powerful megaphones. Clearly, they need some way to transmit data that satisfies the following conditions:

- It is shared only between the sender and the recipient and no one else.
- The data must be transmitted over and through disparate networks. If one party uses a particular brand of telephone, computer, or application software, there should not be an implicit requirement that the other party use the same brand or product.

The connection may also need to be "reliable." Reliability refers to the quality that the sender can confirm that the outgoing communication is or is not received by the intended recipient. With a reliable connection, there is no ambiguity as to whether the message is received. It is analogous to sending a registered letter via traditional post: You know that the letter was received by its intended recipient or that it was lost en route.

This ability to transmit data between physically remote nodes requires some sort of network switching capability. Historically, three switching models have been employed: circuit, message, and packet switching. Before tackling the prime topic of packet switching, it is worthwhile to discuss circuit and message switching. This provides a context to understand why packets were invented and remain useful.

Circuit Switching

Circuit switching is easy to understand because its most common example, the voice telephone call, is so pervasive. Each call consists of three phases, establishment or setup, data transfer (i.e., the voice conversation), and termination. Establishment allocates resources to make the telephone call possible. Is the other telephone available? The called telephone could already be busy, or perhaps the line is cut or is otherwise unavailable. Is the desired person available? Are there sufficient resources within the telephone network to construct a route, or circuit, from the caller to the called station? Perhaps a natural disaster, such as a tornado or other usual weather, has caused many other people to attempt phone calls, thus leaving the switches and trunks (the links between the switches) devoid of capacity because they are fully used by others.

The data transfer phase, that is, the actual conversation, is the reason for making the call. The conversation usually has its own (application layer) protocol. Both people say "hello," engage in some kind of chit-chat, and eventually say "good-bye." The phones are replaced on their "hooks." Bills may be prepared, and the electronic facilities, switches, links, and so forth are freed for other calls.

Phone calls are usually metered and billed by measuring their duration in time and sometimes the distance between the stations. The number of phonemes, words, sentences, paragraphs, and information transferred are not measured. Long periods of silence (i.e., no information transfer) is handled in the same way as intensive information transfer.

We can use the same voice telephone calls to transfer "computer data" instead of analog voice information by using "modems." The basic paradigm remains: establishment, data transfer, circuit termination, breakdown, and the dedication of facilities by time duration, not information transfer.

Circuit switching is unique in terms of security implications. Although emulated circuit switching networks are becoming increasingly popular (one example is voice-over-IP, or VoIP), true circuit switches are dedicated resources usually supplied by a public telephone company. The supplier tightly controls and secures hardware used for the transmission and switching. A guarantee of secure communication is either explicit or implicit in the contractual arrangement between the vendor and supplier. Vulnerabilities are much more likely near either end of the circuit than in the switching regimes managed by the provider.

Except for an analog portion at each end of the call, today's (circa 2004) wired telephone communications are almost entirely digital between the central office of the telephone company and the subscriber. The voice conversations are digitized, transferred, and switched as digital signals and then converted back to analog voice just in time to deliver to the receiving party. Broadcast television is now making the conversion to digital transmission. Broadcast radio is also slowly making this same transition. The analog links can be monitored using simple technology and physical access. The digital portions of the circuit require more sophisticated equipment, and the physical access is also more difficult.

Old style, analog mobile telephone systems are extremely easy to monitor because they are simple FM radio systems. A listener, knowing the correct frequencies of the nearby cell phone towers, only has to listen. During their advent, one could simply buy a monitoring receiver and legally listen. Regulations in various countries have attempted to control or criminalize such interceptions.

More important than regulatory changes is the move from analog to digital spread spectrum technology. This makes it far more difficult (but not impossible) to monitor mobile telephone conversations. Digital mobile telephony also opens the door to the employment of encryption technologies, although government agencies in many countries limit the approved encryption algorithms or key lengths so they can reserve the right to wiretap or monitor telephony communications.

Message Switching

The great model for message switching is the paper-based postal system that delivers cards, letters, and packages (which can contain files, books, and even electronic media). At any selected time, the information is in one location, in a vehicle or in a carrier's bag (moving or not) or in one of the postal stations (being sorted, waiting to be sorted, or waiting to be loaded into a vehicle for transportation). The application layer SMTP (simple mail transport protocol, e-mail) is an old example of electronic message switching that survives into the present.

Let's look at how mail delivery using SMTP works. In addition to the two people sending and receiving the e-mail message, (at least) two kinds of software are involved. Typically the sender employs a UA (user agent) program to compose and address the message and typically sends the message to the sender's local MTA (mail transfer agent) using SMTP. The MTA accepts the message from the UA and promises to try to deliver the message to the recipient. Usually the MTA searches for another MTA, on a distant host, willing to accept the message for the recipient. The two MTAs try to create a connection and negotiate message delivery using SMTP. This can fail for a number of reasons. The sending MTA, which still holds the message, either looks for an alternate, intermediate MTA willing to accept the message, or holds onto it and tries again at a later time. The MTA holding the message is responsible for it until it passes it on to another MTA or until it returns it to the sender as being undeliverable. If the MTA passes a message on to another MTA, its responsibility for the message ends. Final delivery to the recipient's UA is not done by SMTP, but by other techniques (including POP and IMAP, other email-related protocols). This is why we added the parenthetical "at least" at the start of this paragraph.

What's important here? The message travels as a complete unit. At any one time, it exists completely in one place. Of course, we are only speaking about the application layer. What happens on the other layers is entirely another tale.

What can we do with security for this application layer? A message delivered by SMTP contains headers and text. Although headers usually must be transmitted in the clear without encryption, the text portion can be encrypted by the sender and decoded by the recipient.

Table 2 lists some possible protocols used on each layer to transfer an e-mail message using SMTP, using TCP/IP, over a telephone connection. This same TCP/IP connection, at another physical location might be supported by, say, an Ethernet LAN, because the Internet sits on top of heterogeneous networks.

Table 2 can be rewritten to employ a LAN and a privately owned network instead of a dial-up modem and telephone link. In this case, we might select an optical fiber Ethernet over an electrical Ethernet, over a wireless LAN. If we use an electrical network (i.e., metallic wires), we would attempt to shield the cables effectively. We would keep intruders far away from our equipment (to take advantage of the inverse square diminution of electromagnetic field strength). Ownership and control of a privately owned network, as you expect, is expensive and perhaps not justified. Each of the security-related techniques has monetary and ease-of-usage costs.

Packet Switching

Circuit switching can be inefficient. For example, the circuit switch model we know as the voice telephone conversation is always "on." Signals are always being transmitted even when both parties to the conversation are silent. This is a large waste of dedicated resources.

Think about online computer interactions such as reading e-mail from a server using IMAP (or POP), or obtaining files using file transfer protocol (FTP), or browsing the Web. A user initiates a connection to the Internet. Using IMAP, the user agent (UA) asks the mail server about received messages and gets a list. While the user stares at this list, the Internet connection is normally idle. A particularly interesting message catches the user's eye, and he asks to read it. Now the message is copied in a burst from the server to the UA (i.e., an e-mail program) and can be examined. Typically nothing happens while the recipient peruses the message, which may contain a huge attachment. The reader decides that he wants the attachment, and then, all of a sudden, a long burst of line activity occurs to bring the attachment from the server to the client.

As we can see, computer communications is characterized by short bursts of data transmissions between long periods of idleness. We want a fast link because we don't want to wait. However, most of the time a dedicated, fast, expensive line (or circuit) is idle because we are not using it. Packet switching cost-effectively shares the fast, expensive, high-speed lines with many users. In other words, packets provide something called "multiplexing."

With multiplexing, we chop our messages into units, cells, frames, packets, segments, PDUs (protocol data units). All these words are pretty much interchangeable in general usage. Mostly our packets are of varying size, but there are usually minimum and maximum sizes, that is, the packet cannot be too small or too big.

Along with the advantages of packet switched networks are disadvantages. Because each packet can have an independent path from source to destination, it must contain a header with enough information for the network to route it properly and for the destination to put the message

Table 2 Example of Techniques Used on Different Layers

Layer	Technique	Security Possibilities
Application	SMTP, message switching	Signing, encryption, SSL/TLS
Transport	TCP, virtual circuit	IPSec, IPv6 encryption, encrypted tunnels
Internet	IP, datagram PPP, virtual circuit	IPSec, IPv6 encryption
Data link	Digitization of the analog signal within the telephone plant Modulation of an analog signal using digital data	PPP link encryption
Physical	Modem, telephone circuits, circuit switching	Physical control of circuits, physical layer encryption

PPP = ; SMTP = simple mail transport protocol; SSL/TLS = ; TCP = transmission control protocol.

Table 3 Advantages and Disadvantages of Circuit Switched and Packet Switched Networks

Circuit Switched Network	Packet Switched Network
Dedicated	Shared
Constant, predictable transmission rates	Varying and sometimes unacceptable delays
No overhead, higher maximum throughput	Packet overhead reduces effective throughput
Expensive	Efficient, economical
Often idle	Minimal idle time

back together in sequence. This header information is not part of the message proper and so constitutes "overhead" that reduces the effective transmission rate of the message when compared with dedicated circuits. Additional steps need to be taken to ensure that no malefactor on the network substitutes a bogus packet for a legitimate one.

Finally, there is a statistical risk that all users want to download a large file or use a network simultaneously. Such instances reduce the effective transmission rate far below the nominal rate of the network and may result in unacceptable delays in data transmission. This problem of delays caused by network congestion is a genuine problem in VoIP communication and constitutes a major technical challenge before VoIP becomes widely adopted.

A brief comparison of the relative advantages of circuit switching vis-à-vis packet switching is provided in Table 3.

Two packet switching techniques are commonly employed: datagrams and virtual circuits.

Datagram Networks

Datagrams have no guarantee of delivery: If source A sends out a bunch of datagrams a, b, and c, to destination B, there is no guarantee that any or all the datagrams arrive at their destination. Furthermore, datagrams have no guarantee as to the sequence in which a, b, or c arrive. This is like the Kentucky Derby. If the horses leave the starting gate at approximately the same time, we have no knowledge as to the sequence in which they arrive at the finish line. In fact, with a small probability, one or more of the horses may never cross the finish line. Unlike a horse, should a datagram fail to reach the finish line, we will never know. There is no mechanism to confirm if a datagram ever reached its destination or if it was even expected in the first place.

The Internet protocol employs datagrams, which makes it resilient. One of its original design specifications in the late 1960s, by the U.S. Department of Defense, is nuclear survivability. Although the Internet has not been tested against a nuclear attack, all sorts of other things have been tossed against it. It keeps on working.

Recall that the IP is the layer that connects and sits above the constituent networks. Above the internet layer is the transport layer. There are two Internet protocols on the transport layer, UDP (user datagram protocol), a datagram protocol, and TCP, a connection-oriented protocol. We can select the most appropriate protocol, TCP or UDP, for our application.

Network survivability was tested to a limited degree at the World Trade Center, in New York City, on September 11, 2001. There was significant damage to fiber-optic links under the towers, the local telephony infrastructure, as well as electrical blackouts and failure of backup power systems. There were serious problems throughout New York City. Most Internet traffic was automatically rerouted and caused little notice. Secondary to the physical damage was the change of Internet traffic patterns caused by users flooding particular Web sites and Internet service providers seeking news about the tragedy that might not be broadcast on radio and television. In addition to general news, people sought information about relatives, friends, and colleagues via the Internet in addition to attempting to reach them via telephone (see Barrett & Silverman, 2001).

Datagrams provide simplicity by avoiding the creation of a circuit. Often, we simply want to send a small amount of information from the sender to the recipient and perhaps receive a reply. We gain by omitting the overhead of circuit establishment, maintenance, and breakdown for only a very short exchange. If we really do want a reply, when we don't get one, we simply retry the exchange de novo.

There are two disadvantages to using datagrams. Each datagram must find its own way through the network; the experience of previous datagrams, for example, how they found a good route, is ignored. It is also possible for a datagram to wander about, to never reach its destination, and to be destroyed. For this reason, datagrams are unreliable. There is no confirmation that they were delivered and no validation that they came from their alleged source.

Datagrams are used for short, noncritical communications such as traceroutes to determine the current optimal route between two network nodes or DNS lookups of a single host or IP address. (If a reply isn't received from the first DNS server, a secondary DNS server is consulted.) DNS, discussed later, refers to the domain naming system, the method used on the Internet to map domains and URLs (uniform resource locators) to IP addresses.

UDP, transport layer datagrams, rely on IP, internet layer datagrams. The connection-oriented TCP segments also rely on IP datagrams. In the Internet scheme, the internet layer is constructed using datagrams. On the transport layer, there is a choice of using either TCP (virtual circuit connections) or UDP (a datagram, connectionless service).

Another important application suitable for UDP is NTP (network time protocol), which seeks to keep the computer's clock correct. An intruder who can successfully manipulate a computer's timekeeping can create all sorts of mischief. Examples can range from improper time stamps on stock market trading or time-critical messages to compressing or expanding the amount of time a

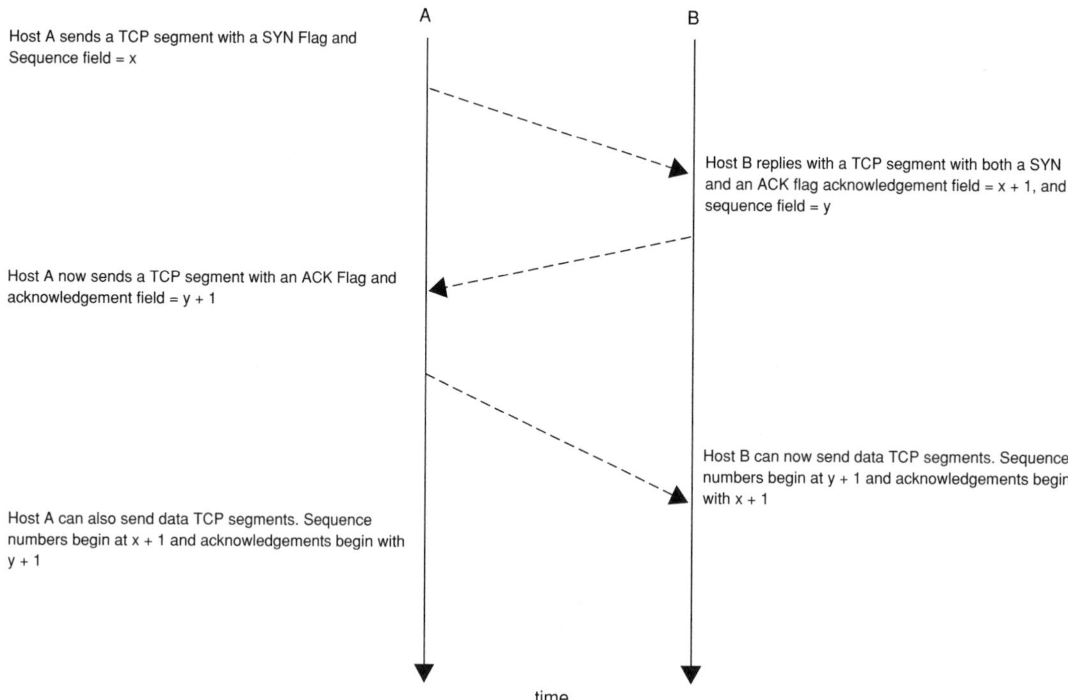

Figure 3: The transmission control protocol three-way handshake protocol.

computer process takes and adjusting billing for the computer's services (McNamara, 2003).

We see that datagrams have advantages and disadvantages. There are times when it is better to use a connection-oriented protocol.

Virtual Circuit Networks

TCP is the connection-oriented protocol on the Internet transport layer, resting on the (datagram) internet or IP layer. Just as in circuit switching, we establish a route (calling it a virtual circuit), we transfer data through it, back and forth, and then we disassemble the circuit and return the resources for reuse. Unlike circuit switching, the physical resources the virtual circuit uses are concurrently available to other virtual circuits as well.

We do the work of allocating, maintaining, and disassembling resources with the expectation that we will make sufficient use of the virtual circuit to pay us back for our effort. What kind of payback can we expect? Because we have constructed a tube, like a garden hose, through the network, when the source sends segments, that is, packets, a, b, and c, into the pipe, we can expect them to arrive, in order, a, b, and c, at the destination. This guaranteed sequencing is an important property. As well, we no longer need the complete source and destination addresses in each packet because this information is managed by the underlying virtual circuit that we initially constructed. Each packet still needs identification, however, saying which virtual circuit it belongs to and what its sequence is in the parade in case it is destroyed in transit.

Packets in a virtual circuit scheme usually employ sequence numbers of some kind because they are part of a parade, with each packet having its own place. Packets are often numbered using three bits, 0, 1, 2, 3, 4, 5, 6, 7; seven bits, 0, 1, 2, ..., 126, 127; or even larger sequences such as the 32-bit TCP sequence number. These sequence numbers are more overhead but are needed to identify damaged or missing segments so that the receiver can ask for them again using a "negative" acknowledgment. The sequence numbers are also used for flow control, to moderate or slow the sender when the network or the receiver cannot handle the packets as quickly as they are sent.

For reliability and security, establishing a connection uses a technique, the three-step handshake (see Figure 3). First, the initiating host, A, sends a TCP packet to the recipient host, B, containing an arbitrary and random sequence number, x, and a flag, the SYN (for synchronize) flag. On receipt of this first packet, B responds back to A with a second TCP segment containing another arbitrary and random sequence number, y, an acknowledgment field of $x + 1$, and both a SYN and an ACK (for acknowledgment) flag. The last step of the connection setup has A replying to B with a TCP packet containing an acknowledgment field with value $y + 1$ and only an ACK flag. At this point, B can now send data packets to A. The next packet from B to A includes sequence numbers beginning with $y + 1$ and acknowledgments beginning with $x + 1$. The next packet from A to B includes sequence numbers beginning with $x + 1$ and acknowledgments beginning with $y + 1$.

Note that after the first three segments are exchanged, each host knows the initial sequence number of the other host and, by way of the acknowledgment field, has told the other host what number it is expecting in return. Subsequent packets contain increasing sequence numbers where the increase is equal to the number of data bytes in the previous packet.

SECURITY CONSIDERATIONS

Packet switching has provided a fast, efficient, and reliable means of data communication. This efficiency comes with a cost. Packet-switched communications have security risks not encountered in circuit or message switching. We first discuss how packets are addressed so that they are reliably delivered from a source host to a destination application on the intended recipient host. Only then are we in a position to understand some of the historical attacks and ongoing security concerns inherent in packet-switched environment.

Packet Addressing

Packet addressing is a multifaceted and complex topic. Simplifying the issues for our purposes, we look at four types of addressing: hardware addressing is used to reference machines and hardware on the same physical network. We use TCP/IP addressing to address devices located on other networks or in locations around the world. Machines use IP addresses (numbers), but people prefer a more mnemonic method of naming machines; DNS allows IP addresses to be mapped to the more humane URLs with which we are all familiar. (Some people correctly say that URLs are *not* user-friendly. They may be correct, but alphameric domain names are much nicer than numeric IP addresses!) Finally, we look at port numbering as a convenient way to flag the kind of data contained within a packet and thus what application they should be delivered to on the destination host.

Hardware Addresses

00:05:02:d6:eb:7e, a 48-bit Ethernet address, written using 12 hexadecimal digits, is an example of a hardware address. This unique number is manufactured into each interface card; the first six digits are assigned to the card manufacturer (prefix 00:05:02 is assigned to Apple Computers: cf. http://www.coe.uky.edu/~stu/nic/nic.cfm, retrieved May 2004), and the last six digits are a serial number assigned to the card by the manufacturer. Each interface card is made with a unique Ethernet address. The hardware or MAC (media access control) address only identifies the card and not its location or routing paths; therefore, the MAC address is only useful at the local network level. The other computers on this machine's local network as well as its local router know both its IP address and its MAC address. Unless this machine is on our local network, however, we have no idea where the Apple computer with this MAC address is located. Although using MAC addresses is much faster and more efficient than using numeric IP addresses when communicating within the local physical network, communicating with machines outside the local network requires IP addresses. For most of us, we never need to see the MAC address unless there is a problem to solve.

The discussion about hardware Ethernet addresses also applies to wireless IEEE 802.11 addresses. Both sets of addresses are identical in format and are taken from the same pool. Both Ethernet and 802.11 interface cards are manufactured with hardware addresses. Both also have the ability to employ a specified address, supplied by computer software. Thus, an interface card can assume the identity of another card. In a wired network, an intruder need only to learn a valid MAC address, set that address into his or her card, ensure that the real device with this address is powered off and not active, and then physically connect his or her machine to the network. (Two cards with identical MAC addresses on the same network cause all sorts of problems, thus exposing the stealth attack.) The wireless intruder employs the same steps, except that a physical attachment is not needed. The interloper only needs to be nearby for network access. For this reason, the WEP is provided to offer some limited measure of encryption for wireless networks.

TCP/IP and Other Addresses

Internet, IP version 4 (written as IPv4) addresses are 32-bit numbers specifying a host. A host can have several IP addresses (i.e., one for each interface), but every networked host must have at least one unique IP address. IP addresses are commonly written using dotted decimal format, four decimal numbers in the range 0–255, separated with periods (e.g., 198.169.198.4). Each group of four numbers in an IP address is commonly referred to as an "octet" (because it can be written as a sequence of eight bits).

Numeric IP addresses are grouped into networks. For example, all IP addresses of the form 198.169.198.nnn belong to an organization known as GPFN. When a packet is sent anywhere with these first three octets, it is routed to the GPFN network. The GPFN router's job is to deliver traffic to the correct machine based on the last octet.

For these reasons, IP addresses cannot be arbitrarily acquired. Addresses from the available pool of numbers must be registered with an appropriate agency so that Internet routing is properly able to switch to the correct destinations.

IPv4 addresses are 32 bit numbers, a shortage of addresses was anticipated because of the meteoric growth of the Internet. For this reason and for others, IPv6 was adopted as a replacement scheme. The IPv6 address space is 128 bits in size, a huge increase over today's limits. As well, IPv6 permits a number of other security and other performance enhancements over the IPv4 system employed today.

Domain Naming System

Addressing using IP addresses has two problems: people have difficulty remembering long numeric sequences and the roles of a particular node within a network can change over time. For these reasons the domain naming system was created. The DNS maps numeric IP addresses to domain and host names and vice versa. An example of such a domain name is "gpfn.ca." These mnemonic names are good for people to recognize and remember. They are not at all like the 32-bit IP addresses that they represent. IP addresses are great—for computers! The DNS is an important scheme implemented through sophisticated Internet applications running on many computers. Additionally significant, the DNS allows us to easily change IP addresses and maintain permanence by retaining the DNS name. The computers are told about the new association, and soon the change is complete.

Three common security attacks subvert DNS employment of datagrams for IP lookups:

- Because DNS heavily relies on UDP datagram packets and because datagrams are unreliable, a rogue DNS server can be positioned to intercept a DNS request for a domain and then respond with a bogus reply, thus redirecting a user to a fake host.

- Because each datagram is an independent packet with no concept of a request–response session, bogus nameserver cache loading relies on the fact that a legitimate DNS server might be fooled into caching a DNS response even if there was no matching DNS request. Thus a legitimate server is loaded with false information using a process known as "DNS spoofing."
- Finally, an attacker can use UDP flooding to overwhelm a legitimate DNS server with invalid responses, crippling the server's ability to respond to valid queries from its users. A client requesting a DNS lookup might then accept a response from the attacker as if it came from the legitimate DNS server. A remedy to these problems could use Secure DNS. Secure DNS uses SSL (Secure Socket Layers, which we discuss later) to sign a DNS query with the server's private key; the client can verify the accuracy of the response by matching the response with the server's known public key. Secure DNS is available in software such as BIND version 9.

Cybersquatting, purchasing a domain name in bad faith, is another DNS-related issue. The practice is not uncommon. By registering a domain in another jurisdiction or top-level domain, the victim can be cajoled into doing "business" with an unknown entity.

Using the previous example, a user may mistakenly go to www.gpfn.com instead of www.gpfn.ca (an honest and easy mistake)—especially if a spam e-mail assumed they were a gpfn.ca customer and asked them to visit their account and update their profile–a practice known as "phishing". If the owner of the gpfn.com domain is clever enough to mirror the visual identity of gpfn.ca, the visitor might be persuaded to divulge credit card information or other personal data from the regular and trusting clients of gpfn.ca. Legal redress and diligent protection of a firm's branding and domain registrations are the most useful remedies for cybersquatting.

Port Numbers

Port numbers in the Internet model are 16-bit numbers specifying communications to a specific process on a host. The host is selected using an IP address (or more commonly, a DNS name that is translated into an IP address). Thus, this combination of two IP addresses (the source and destination IP addresses) and their corresponding two port numbers (again, the source and destination port numbers) uniquely identify any connection. By convention, port numbers less than 1024 are reserved as "privileged" ports and generally used by the system for server-side connections such as Web servers, mail servers, or other services, that is, they are "well-known" ports that are supposed to provide access to an expected application on any host. Ports numbered above 1023 and below the 16 bit limit of 65,535 can be used by servers or clients to initiate or accept connections.

Applications bind themselves to specific ports to request service in the case of client software, or to provide service in the case of server programs. Some "well-known" ports have mnemonic names, for example, FTP (port 21), HTTP (hypertext transfer protocol; port 80), SMTP (port 25), IMAP (port 143), and POP3 (port 110); the latter two are used for receiving mail from a mail server. The port numbers provide a glue between the Internet transport layer and application processes on the hosts. Firewalls are configured to manage the type of connections permitted by blocking or permitting access by examining combinations of IP and port numbers (i.e., two IP addresses and two port numbers).

For example, a corporate firewall might block internal users from connecting to port 80 on external servers but permit connections to port 80 within the corporate LAN. The result is that employees of that company are not able to surf the Web directly from work but are allowed to view the corporate intranet site. A corporate proxy server might allow internal users to view only those external sites approved by corporate policy. The proxy server is an intermediate computer programmed to accept requests (in this case, from inside the corporate LAN) and perhaps to fetch those Web documents from the outside. The proxy server likely collects statistics on which internal computer accesses which external Web documents.

Encrypted Packet Transmissions

Because packet communications are so pervasive yet easy to intercept, much effort is spent trying to encrypt packet streams so that they are decipherable only to the sender and the recipient. Encryption combines a unique sequence of binary digits called a digital "key" with the data to be encrypted. An encryption algorithm is shared and used by all parties to the communication.

If the same key is used by all parties to encipher and decipher the data, then the encryption protocol is said to be a "symmetric" encryption protocol. Although symmetric algorithms are computationally efficient, they are only as secure as the digital key that all parties must share.

For this reason, another class of cryptographic algorithms known as "asymmetric" protocols are used. Asymmetric protocols have every party to a communication owning two complementary parts of a key: One part is a public key that is shared with the rest of the community, and the second is a private key that is tightly guarded. A data source enciphered with a party's private key can only be deciphered with that party's public key, and vice versa. Because each party tightly guards its private key, there is less chance that a single security breach can compromise the entire community than with a symmetric system. Because each party to the system has its own key pair, symmetric encryption also allows for digitally "signing" a message (by encrypting it with the author's private key), or allowing only one person to view the message (by encrypting it with the recipient's public key), or both (by encrypting a signed message a second time with the recipient's public key). Asymmetric protocols require much larger keys for the same level of security, however, and thus much more computational overhead to encipher and decipher messages.

Hybrid cryptosystems were established to address these respective strengths and weaknesses. Using an asymmetric protocol, two parties establish a trusted connection and use it to share a symmetric "session" key used

Table 4 Unsecured Internet Services and Their Corresponding Secure Socket Layer Secure Services

Service	Port	Secure Service	Port
telnet	23	telnets	992
smtp	25	smtps	465
http	80	https	443
pop3	110	pop3s	995
ntp	123	Secure ntp	123
imap	143	imaps	993
BSD rlogin	513	ssh	22

only for the duration of the session. Once the connection is ended, the session key is discarded. On the next connection, a new session key is negotiated in the same manner.

Two of the most common packet encryption schemes are SSL and tunnels, more commonly called virtual private networks (VPNs). One common tunnel protocol is called IPSec and is part of the IPv6 protocol.

SSL Encryption

SSL, an application-level encryption protocol, is a hybrid cryptosystem developed by Netscape Communications. It is only used to encrypt certain types of TCP traffic, such as web (HTTP), e-mail (SMTP), or log-in connections. Because each type of TCP traffic connects to a "well-known" port on the server, many of these ports are duplicated and used for SSL-encrypted TCP sessions through which the same information can pass. In this way, even if someone is able to intercept the data transmission, the encryption shields the meaning of the transmitted information.

For example, whereas HTTP (Web traffic) uses the well-known port 80, port 443 is used for encrypted Web traffic (also known as HTTPS, hypertext transfer protocol secure); similarly, unencrypted traffic over telnet (port 23) can be encrypted and transferred using SSH (secure shell) over port 22. Other examples include SMTP over SSL/TLS (port 465), IMAPS (secure IMAP) on port 993, and POP3S (secure pop3) on port 995. See Table 4 for examples of services and their well-known ports.

If you view the security information with your Web browser when visiting a secure Web site, you see that the key used by the Web server is generated by some trusted vendor of digital certificates such as Thawte™, http://www.thawte.com/ (retrieved May 2004) or Verisign™, http://www.verisign.com/ (retrieved May 2004) and matched to the owner of the Web site. This certificate generates browser warnings if it is used by another Web site or if it is not signed by a trusted vendor. Although a site administrator can use an unsigned SSL key on their site, most commercial sites pay an annual fee to a certificate vendor to ensure that these warnings do not appear to the user. Certificate vendors, for their part, exercise due diligence to ensure that the certificate buyer has a legal right to use the name, address, and other details of the certificate and do not misrepresent themselves or their Web sites.

When secure communications is a requirement and packets travel over a hostile or unsecured network, using SSL-encrypted channels is often the only available means to ensure security.

Virtual Private Networks and Encrypted Tunnels

Another way to enhance security is to create an encrypted tunnel. Although IP header information must be sent in the clear (for the Internet to be able to route it to its destination), any payload data sent into this tunnel is enciphered at its source and deciphered at its destination. Because all data through the tunnel is encrypted, this process uses more computational and network overhead. The benefit, however, is the security of all the information sent through the tunnel. A number of key management systems, both symmetric and hybrid, can be used to create the tunnel; because of the computational overhead of encrypting data streams through the tunnel, pure asymmetric encryption is not used.

Because the tunnel is constructed at the transport layer, any application—even those that do not have any encryption functionality—can use the tunnel and have its data secured in transit. In fact, any application using the tunnel necessarily has its transmission encrypted. Because these encrypted tunnels simulate a secure private network within the hostile public Internet space, they are often called VPNs.

Security Concerns with TCP Packets

Historically, there have been a number of security issues with TCP packets. We discuss six of these because they are, to some measure, still relevant today. The first relates to blocking incoming connections, which is commonly managed by firewalls. The TCP sequence prediction attack relies on the predictability of the acknowledgment numbers used in the TCP three-way handshake protocol. Blind spoofing exploits a common weakness in the random number generator used to generate the initial value in the three-way handshake's acknowledgment number.

Firewalls and Connection Blocking

Many home and business networks support internal users opening connections to some external Internet services, but they eschew outsiders initiating connections into their internal machines. Firewalls can block incoming connections by scanning the TCP headers. If an incoming TCP header contains a SYN flag but not an acknowledgment number, then the firewall recognizes the first step of the three-step handshake to initiate a connection and discards the packet.

Firewalls can also block outgoing connections to a particular port number regardless of the destination IP. In this way, internal users are prevented from accessing a particular Internet service such as FTP or streaming media sites.

TCP Sequence Prediction Attack

The TCP sequence prediction attack was made famous by Kevin Mitnick's attack on Tsutomu Shimomura's computers (Tsutomu Shimomura, n.d.):

- The attacker monitors the communication between two systems, one of which is the target system.

- Next, the attacker ensures that he or she can communicate with the target before the other trusted system responds, usually by overloading the trusted system with a flood of network packets or launching some other form of denial-of-service attack.
- Finally, the attacker issues packets to the target system with the source IP address of the trusted system that is communicating with the target system.

Because the packets issued by the attacker have the sequence numbers that the target system is expecting, the target continues to communicate, unaware that an attacker has now replaced the trusted host (Comer, 1997).

SYN Flooding

Using the three-way handshake protocol, a denial-of-service attack (DoS) is attempted by having one or more rogue hosts attack a target by sending a flood of TCP packets containing only SYN packets to the target, thus initiating a TCP connection, but refusing to respond to the target's attempt to consummate the second leg of the connection. Because the target has finite resources to manage incomplete connections, all of its available connection ports are consumed with "hung" connections, preventing legitimate connections from other users.

Remedies for this type of attack include:

- shortening the time that a host waits for the initiator to respond with an ACK packet;
- simulating the third leg of the handshake to force the connection open and release blocked resources;
- using a proxy server to manage the connection handshake until the connection is consummated, then handing the connection off to the intended host for the data transmission;
- returning connection information to the client in a data packet attached to the SYN response, known as a SYN cookie; and
- restricting the number of simultaneous connections from a single remote host.

Blind Spoofing Attack

The third security issue involves predicting the initial sequence number (ISN) of a target computer. If the ISN can be predicted, an attacker can spoof both the source IP address of a trusted host and the ISN returned by the target machine in the acknowledgment packet. This way, the attacker can force a one-way connection. For this reason, the TCP standard calls for a 32-bit ISN and relies on a strong pseudo-random number generator to ensure that the ISN cannot be easily anticipated. Not all operating system vendors use strong pseudo-random number generators, making the "blind spoofing attack" a topic of ongoing research (Forouzan, 2001).

CONCLUSION

Modern data networks utilize a layered approach to manage data transmissions efficiently and flexibly. The most commonly used layered model, TCP/IP, is the technique used on the Internet.

Data transmission uses switching technology so that information can be correctly and reliably routed between a source and destination. Three such switching models include circuit, message, and packet switching. Although circuit switching, analogous to traditional telephone conversations, is the most secure and robust, it is also the most expensive in that an entire set of resources are allocated for the duration of the communication regardless of how much or how little data are actually being transmitted. Message switching, comparable to traditional postal systems, introduces cost efficiencies compared with circuit switching but also loses some of the inherent security of circuit switching.

In modern networks, packet switching is the most commonly employed switching paradigm. In fact, it is so pervasive that circuit switching and message switching are now emulated by packet switching networks. Packet switching networks come in two flavors: Datagram networks do not promise reliability in that the sender has no guarantee or confirmation as to whether a message is or is not successfully delivered, whereas virtual circuit networks do afford this reliability.

Packet switching relies on addressing to ensure that a packet is correctly routed from its source to its destination. The dominant addressing model employed by the Internet is TCP/IP. The IP address supports a resilient and robust packet delivery paradigm throughout the world. The process of mapping this IP address to the domains and URLs we are all familiar with when accessing the Internet is managed by a system called "Domain Naming System" or DNS.

In addition to IP and hardware addresses, the Internet also uses port numbers. Port numbers allow two nodes to support multiple simultaneous communications. It also supports the concept of "well-known" ports whereby each service provided by the Internet is addressed using a unique port number.

By default, most TCP/IP connections are not encrypted or secured in any way. As such, any interloper can intercept mail, Web, or other data transmissions and use the contents for malicious purposes. Two solutions to this problem are commonly employed: SSL is an encryption scheme employed at the application layer. SSL-enabled servers and browsers work in tandem to encrypt their communication in a way that foils the designs of any interloper. Tunneling technology such as VPNs can also be employed at the transport layer to encrypt all communication between two nodes so that even if the applications using the connection between the two nodes are incapable of encrypting their communications, an interloper is not able to decipher the data stream.

Finally, a number of security considerations exist when using TCP packet switching. These considerations include how to block incoming connection attempts using firewalls and how to ensure that an attacker does not incapacitate a trusted node and then masquerade as that node to intercept communications.

GLOSSARY

Address Something that specifies a location or a unique instance. A person's name, an apartment number, a house number and street name, and a telephone number are common examples.

Address, Hardware An unchangeable address that is built into a device. An Ethernet address, manufactured into a network adapter, is an example.

Address, IP The Internet Protocol address (version IV) is a 32-bit number assigned to a host computer on the Internet. (A host can have more than one address.) The address is used to specify a particular machine. An example is 198.169.198.4, using dotted decimal notation. Four decimal numbers, 0-255, written with dots separating them, is commonly used to write an IP address. IP addresses are used in selecting routes through the Internet from a source to a destination.

Address, Port A 16-bit number. Each IP address has two complete pools of these numbers, one for TCP and one for UDP. Thus, at any one time, each IP address can sustain 65,535 TCP connections and 65,535 UDP transactions. The port numbers connect specific application instances, or processes, to the Internet. Each set of two IP addresses and two port numbers, at any specific time, are completely unique and specify one TCP connection.

Asymmetric Encryption An encryption scheme in which each party has a private and a public key. Messages enciphered with a private key need the corresponding public key to be deciphered and vice versa. The private key is closely guarded by its owner, whereas the public key is broadly disseminated. If the originator enciphers the message with the recipient's public key, only the recipient can decipher the message. If the originator enciphers the message with his private key, we have a digitally signed message (cf. chapter 184). Popular asymmetric encryption protocols include PGP and RSA.

Blowfish A symmetric encryption algorithm designed by Bruce Shneier. It is designed for 32-bit microprocessors, uses as little as 5 kB of memory, uses simple hardware operations, is very fast, and uses keys up to 448 bits. For these reasons, it has become popular for many personal computer applications and utilities. The source code is publicly available.

Circuit A route or path through a network. A circuit can exist in a circuit switching network or in a packet switching network. We habitually choose slightly different, and more specific, terms, such as virtual circuit or route depending on what kind of network we are discussing.

Circuit Switching The technique of establishing a route through a network that completely dedicates facilities of the links used to create the "circuit" entirely for one connection. The capacity of the circuit can be completely used, completely unused, or anything between. The circuit is dedicated, for example, a telephone call.

Data Encryption Standard, (DES) One of the first and most thoroughly tested symmetric encryption algorithms. It was adopted by the U.S. government as a federal standard in November 1976.

Datagram An unconnected UDP packet on the transport layer of the TCP/IP model. An unconnected IP packet on the internet layer of the TCP/IP model. A generic term for a packet that travels through a network independently, from source to destination.

Digital Certificate A unique series of bits used by an encryption algorithm to encipher, decipher, or sign a block or stream of data. The uniqueness of the certificate is important to verify that the data was indeed issued by the alleged sender. A certificate is often issued by a certification authority that signs the digital certificate with its own trusted certificate, thus creating a chain of trusted certificates, known as a "certificate chain."

Digital Signature Algorithm (DSA) or Digital Signature Standard (DSS) The DSS specifies a DSA appropriate for applications requiring a digital rather than a written signature. The DSA digital signature is a pair of large numbers represented in a computer as bit strings. It is computed using a set of rules (i.e., the DSA) and parameters that identify the signer and the integrity of the data. The DSA provides the capability to generate and verify signatures. Signature generation makes use of a private key, whereas signature verification requires the use of a corresponding public key (cf. private key, public key). See Beyda (2000).

Encryption A formula or algorithm that combines a "key" and a unit of information so that only those knowing the key can discern meaning from the information. See also symmetric and asymmetric encryption.

Hybrid Cryptosystem A technique combining the advantages of both asymmetric and symmetric encryption schemes. Asymmetric systems effectively transfer information so that it can only be deciphered by the intended recipients, can be verified to be authentically generated by its alleged composer, or both. Asymmetric systems are computationally intensive, requiring keys many magnitudes of bytes larger than symmetric keys to offer the same level of cryptographic security. Symmetric systems are much less demanding in terms of computational power to encipher and decipher messages but lack efficient key management systems; should any malefactor gain access to the cipher key, all communications between any party using that key including archived communications are vulnerable. For this reason, many systems use asymmetric encryption to exchange securely a symmetric session key that is then used to encipher and decipher large data blocks transmitted between the two parties for the duration of that session.

Internet The worldwide network of networks employing TCP/IP. The underlying foundation networks are not homogeneous. Note the upper case "I." The Internet is a very public place and thereby has more need of effective security tools than does a physically secured network.

internet A network of networks usually employing TCP/IP. The underlying foundation networks need not be homogeneous. Note the lower case "i." A physically secured internet is called an "intranet."

intranet See internet.

Layer Computer code, hardware, protocols (i.e., rules) that constitute an entity designed to perform a specific job. The layer is supported by lower level layers. In turn, it supports higher level layers. Ideally (OSI reference model), a layer is totally independent of its higher and lower neighbors, that is, the layer can be entirely replaced without its peers being aware of the swap. Realistically (TCP/IP model), this is not always true: TCP and UDP are useless without IP supporting it. IP has little use without TCP or UDP above it.

Layer, Application The highest layer, associated with human beings and application programs.

Layer, Data Link The layer immediately above the physical layer, concerned with communications on links between nodes (hosts, routers, switches) of a network. This layer exists only between two nodes.

Layer, Internet The layer above supporting networks that creates a uniform internet on top of (likely heterogeneous) networks. This is the IP layer.

Layer, Network The layer above the data link layer. It encompasses the entire network.

Layer, Physical The lowest layer consisting of hardware and its mechanical, electrical, functional, and procedural specifications.

Layer, Transport The layer above the network or the internet layer, depending on context, concerned with the end-to-end delivery of packets (UDP datagrams and TCP segments for an internet).

Local Area Network (LAN) A network in a limited geography, that is, a room, a building, or a campus. Usually LANs are broadcast networks.

Message A complete entity. Examples include the contents of a book between its covers, the contents of an envelope in the paper-based postal system, a computer file, an e-mail (message).

Message Switching The transport of a message through a network as a complete unit. The message is not broken into smaller units (i.e., packets, e.g., a letter in the postal system).

Metropolitan Area Network (MAN) A network typically covering an area the size of a metropolis. The common example of a point-to-point MAN is the local cable TV distribution system. An example of a broadcast MAN is an FM transmitter sending information to the city. MANs are typically constructed as point-to-point networks but can be broadcast networks.

Multiplexing Various techniques for transparently sharing a transmission resource among disparate users. These include frequency and time division multiplexing for electronic signals and wave division multiplexing (WDM) for optical signals. Using packets is a form of multiplexing.

Network, Broadcast A network employing a common medium or "ether." It consists of nodes and a medium accessible to all the nodes. An example is all CB radio operators tuned to a particular channel in a restricted geographic area. A network can be broadcast on one layer and point-to-point on another layer.

Network, Datagram A network organization that has packets traveling as independent units, that is, uses datagrams. There are no circuits nor connections.

Network, Point-to-Point A collection of nodes or switches, connected with links. The telephone system is a good example. A network can be point-to-point on one layer and broadcast on another layer.

Network, Unconnected see Network, Datagram.

Network, Virtual Circuit A network organization that has the packets in a "connection" follow an established path through the network, in sequence, one after another.

Octet A grouping or unit of eight bits. Those in the field of communications prefer this more specific term over the less specific "byte."

OSI Reference Model A seven-layer (physical, data link, network, transport, session, presentation, application) pedagogic model for networks developed by the International Standards Organization (ISO). It is an old model that represents no modern network but is useful in categorization.

Packet A "bunch" of data, usually with delimiting headers and trailers, typically tens to tens of thousands of octets, transmitted as a unit.

Packet Switching The technique of breaking information into discrete "packets" and routing them through a network. The routing of the individual packets can be unconnected or connected.

PGP, Pretty Good Privacy A company specializing in asymmetric encryption software products. In addition to its commercial products, it has freeware versions available for private, noncommercial use. For more information, visit http://www.pgp.com/, retrieved May 2004.

Port Number See Address, Port.

Private Key A secret key used in asymmetric encryption schemes. It is not shared and is used to sign or decipher electronic documents digitally. By signing a document with one's private key, the signature can be verified at a later date using the alleged signatory's public key. By enciphering a document with the intended recipient's (or recipients') private key(s), the document can only be deciphered by the recipient using the private key.

Proxy Server A router used to break an Internet connection into two legs. Instead of opening a TCP connection to a remote host, a client opens a connection with the proxy server, supplying the connection details for the remote host. The proxy server then opens this second connection on the client's behalf and passes the contents from the remote host back to the client. Proxy servers can provide an effective way to filter virus, certain types of files and file extensions, specified port numbers, or content deemed "inappropriate" to the user, or block access to certain hosts or domains.

Public Key A widely disseminated key used in asymmetric encryption schemes. It is used by other parties to validate or authenticate a person's identity. It should be shared broadly provided that it is distributed or received through a trusted source. A public key corresponds to, but is not the same as, the private key. In this way, anyone can verify a digital signature by employing the alleged sender's public key. Similarly, anyone can encrypt a message that can only be deciphered by enciphering it with the recipient's public key. In this case, the recipient would use the private key to decipher the message.

Route See Circuit.

Routing The process of discovering and constructing a path, circuit, or route through the network from the source to the destination.

RSA The first robust algorithmic implementation of a public-key encryption algorithm. The acronym RSA references its three inventors: Ron Rivest, Adi Shamir, and Leonard Adleman. RSA is also the name of a company making commercial encryption software products based on the RSA algorithm (cf. http://www.rsasecurity.com/, retrieved May 2004).

Secure Socket Layer (SSL) A hybrid cryptosystem developed by Netscape Communications. It provides an encrypted pathway between two hosts to exchange a session key. These keys are typically 128-bits in length. Anything less is not considered secure. SSL can be used to encrypt any type of Internet traffic. SSL is most commonly used for secure Web sites (given the URL prefix https), secure shell sessions, and secure e-mail gateways (using TLS/SSL) and mail servers (imaps, and pop3s).

Security The process of protecting information so that it is only meaningful to the originator and intended recipient(s) of the information.

Segment A connected, TCP packet on the transport layer of the TCP/IP model.

Symmetric Encryption An encryption scheme in which recipients and originators share the same key, that is, the key used to encipher the information is the same key used to decipher the information. Popular examples include DES, Triple DES, and Blowfish (cf. hybrid cryptosystems, asymmetric encryption).

TCP/IP Model A three-layer (internet, transport, application) model for the Internet. This ad hoc model, developed to create a practical working network, sits on top of a foundation provided by other networks or LANs. Because there is no true standard for this model, it is variously defined as a three-, four-, or five-layer model by including one or more of the lower layers on which the TCP/IP layers rest. TCP/IP is something practical that works and has become popular and widely disseminated.

Triple DES A variation of the DES symmetric encryption scheme which churns the data through the DES algorithm three times, resulting in a much higher level of security. Whereas an exhaustive search for a DES key takes 2^{56} attempts, the same search for a triple DES key requires 2^{112} attempts.

Tunnel A networking construct in which an encrypted channel is formed between two nodes. The encryption is provided by a lower level of the network stack and sometimes by hardware. Applications communicating between these nodes have their data enciphered by the sending station and deciphered by the receiving station without having to incorporate encryption algorithms at the application level.

Voice-over-Internet Protocol (VoIP) A method for transporting voice using the Internet. Whereas traditional telephony environments rely on circuit switching, a growing phenomenon is voice communications using packet switching over IP networks. It reduces costs and allows for new features and options in voice communication. The use of packet switching exposes voice communications to many of the same security risks inherent in other packet switching environments, however.

Wide Area Network (WAN) A network covering a large region. Usually larger than a metropolitan area. Typically, it is a point-to-point network.

Wired Equivalent Privacy An encryption protocol for use on IEEE 802.11 networks. As the name implies, the protocol is only intended to give 802.11 wireless networks the same level of privacy as hardwired networks; It is not meant to offer any assurance that a wireless transmission is not intercepted and deciphered by a malefactor.

CROSS REFERENCES

See *Client/Server Computing: Principles and Security Considerations; Local Area Networks; Public Network Technologies and Security; TCP/IP Suite; VPN Basics; Wide Area and Metropolitan Area Networks.*

REFERENCES

Barrett, D. J., & Silverman, R. E. (2001). *SSH, the secure shell: The definitive guide.* O'Reilly.

Beyda, W. J. (2000). *Data communications: From basics to broadband* (3rd ed.). Prentice Hall.

Comer, D. E. (1997). *The Internet book* (2nd ed.). Prentice Hall.

Forouzan, B. A. (2001). *Introduction to data communications and networking* (2nd ed.). McGraw-Hill Higher Education.

McNamara, J. (2003). *Secrets of computer espionage: Tactics and countermeasures*. Wiley.

Tsutomu Shimomura. (n.d.). *How Mitnick hacked Tsutomu Shimomura with an IP sequence attack*. Retrieved May 2004 from http://www.totse.com/en/hack/hack_attack/hacker03.html

FURTHER READING

Ateniese, G., & Danilov, C. (n.d.). *Integrating openSSH with secure DNS*. Retrieved May 2004 from http://www.cs.jhu.edu/~claudiu/projects/dnssecssh.html

Committee on the Internet Under Crisis Conditions, Computer Science and Telecommunications Board, [U.S.] National Research Council of the National Academies. (2003). The Internet under crisis conditions: Learning from September 11. *ACM SIGCOMM Computer Communications Review, 33*(2):1–8.

Forouzan, B. A. (2000). *TCP/IP protocol suite.* McGraw-Hill Higher Education.

Garfinkel, S., & Spafford, G. (1996). *Practical Unix and Internet security.* O'Reilly

Greenfield, R. (2003). Circuit, message, and packet switching. In H. Bidgoli (Ed.), *The Internet encyclopedia.* Wiley.

Internet Software Consortium. (2000, 2001). *BIND 9 administrator reference manual*. See http://www.isc.org (retrieved May 2004)

Keogh, J. (2001). *The essential guide to networking.* Prentice Hall.

Kurose, J. F., & Ross, K. W. (2001). *Computer networking.* Addison Wesley Longman.

Mills, D. L. (2003). NTP retrospective. *ACM SIGCOMM Computer Communications Review, 33*(2): 9–21.

National Institute of Standards and Technology. (1994, May). *Digital signature standard* (Federal Information Processing Standards Publication 186). Retrieved May 2004 from http://www.itl.nist.gov/fipspubs/fip186.htm

Schneier, B. (1996). *Applied cryptography* (2nd ed.). New York: John Wiley & Sons Inc.

Shay, W. (1995). *Understanding data communications and networks*. PWS publising.

Stallings, W. (2000). *Data & computer communications* (6th ed.). Upper Saddle River, NJ: Prentice Hall.

Tanenbaum, A. S. (1996). *Computer networks* (3rd ed.). Upper Saddle River, NJ: Prentice Hall.

Voice Scrambling and Encryption. (n.d.). Retrieved May 2004 from http://seussbeta.tripod.com/crypt.html

Zalewski, M. (2001). *Strange attractors and TCP/IP sequence number analysis*. Bindview Corporation. Retrieved May 2004 from http://razor.bindview.com/publish/papers/tcpseq/print.html

Digital Communication

Robert W. Heath Jr. and William Bard, *The University of Texas, Austin*
Atul A. Salvekar, *Intel, Inc.*

INTRODUCTION

Digital communication is the process of conveying digital information from a transmitter to a receiver across an analog channel. The origin of the binary data is known as a *source*; the destination of the binary data is known as a *sink*. Although binary data may be derived from an analog source such as music or a digital source such as a Web page, the means by which the binary data was created has little influence on the operation of the digital communication system. Digital communication could also be defined for nonbinary sources, but this is not standard for current transmission systems.

The principles of digital communication have been recognized and rediscovered many times during the past few thousand years. Early forms of digital communication used technology such as smoke signals, torch signals, signal flares, or drums. Most of these systems were visual meaning that the message was conveyed based on sight by signaling according to some prearranged code. One of the more successful signaling systems is the heliograph, discovered in ancient times and still in use today, which uses reflections from the sun on a small mirror to convey digital signals. Digital communication using electrical signals is more recent and dates back to the invention of the telegraph by Samuel Morse in the 1830s. The telegraph used Morse code, essentially a mapping from letters to quaternary sequences (long pulses, short pulses, letter spaces, and word spaces), to convey digital information over long distances via cable. Marconi patented a wireless telegraph in 1896—this is the origin of wireless digital communication. The facsimile (fax) machine is a sometimes-surprising example of early digital communication. First patented in 1843 by Alexander Bain, the fax machine both then and now scans documents line by line and digitally encodes and conveys the presence or absence of ink.

Digital communication systems offer a number of advantages over comparable analog systems. Of course, a significant advantage is that they are fundamentally suitable for transmitting digital data. Digital communication systems, however, offer other advantages including higher quality compared with analog systems, increased security, better robustness to noise, reductions in power, and easy integration of different types of sources, for example, voice, text, and video. Because the majority of the components of a digital communication system are implemented digitally using digital signal processing, digital communication devices take advantage of the reductions in cost and size enjoyed by digital signal processing technology. In fact, the majority of the public switched telephone network, except the connection from the local exchange to the home, is digital.

All aspects of the Internet are enabled by digital communication technology. Digital communication technology is a mix of analog and digital components. The backbone of the Internet uses digital communication over optical fibers. All last-mile access technologies, despite the different transmission media, are fundamentally digital including broadband wireless, voice-band modems, cable modems, and digital subscriber lines. Local area networks use different digital communication technologies such as Institute of Electrical and Electronics Engineers (IEEE) 802.3 (Ethernet) for wired access or IEEE 802.11.16 for wireless access. Digital communication allows remote access to the Internet via cellular systems through CDPD in first-generation systems and Genral Packet Ratio Servise (GPRS), High Data Ratio Servise (HDR), or Enhanced Data Rate for Globolize Evolution (EDGE) in second-generation systems such as wamax. Third-generation cellular systems harmonize voice and data access because they have been designed with Internet access in mind.

This chapter presents the fundamentals of digital communication. Many topics of relevance to digital communication are treated elsewhere in this encyclopedia. A more thorough description of wireline communication media and wireless media are available in (2002–2004). Radio frequency communication is treated in more detail in (2002–2004). Readers who are interested in only a cursory overview can read the next section. Those who want a more thorough treatment beyond this article should read "Fundamentals of Design Communication" and "Important Concepts in Digital Communication sections 2–3 as well as consult select references in "Further Reading."

FUNDAMENTALS OF DIGITAL COMMUNICATION

Digital Communication System Overview

Over what is known as the physical layer, a typical digital communication system is illustrated in Figure 1. The physical layer is one of a number of layers of abstraction of a communication network and deals with the transmission and reception of waveforms. There are several steps in the transmission and reception process, some of which involve digital signal processing (DSP) and some of which involve analog processing. So although digital communication involves the transmission of digital information, the transmission and reception process involves both digital and analog processing. In this chapter, we focus on the DSP aspects of digital communication, in particular, the aspects at the physical layer where the analog waveforms are generated and processed.

The block diagram for a typical digital communication system in Figure 1 is divided into three parts: the transmitter, the channel, and the receiver. The transmitter processes a bit stream of data for transmission over a physical medium. The channel is the physical medium that adds noise and distorts to the transmitted signal. It accounts for the propagation medium as well as any analog effects in the transmitter and receiver. The receiver attempts to extract the transmitted bit stream from the received signal.

The first basic transmitter block is devoted to source encoding. The purpose of source encoding is to compress the data by removing inherent redundancies. The input to the source encoder is called $s[n]$, the source sequence. The output of the source encoder is called $i[n]$, the information sequence. Source encoding includes both lossy and lossless compression. In lossy compression, some degradation is allowed to reduce the amount of data that needs to be transmitted. In lossless compression, redundancy is removed, but upon inverting the encoding algorithm, the signal is exactly the same. That is, if f and g are the source encoding and decoding processes, then $\hat{s}[n] = g(i[n]) = g(f(s[n]))$, for lossy compression $s[n] \cong \hat{s}[n]$ and for lossless compression $s[n] = \hat{s}[n]$. Data compression is treated in more detail in (2002–2004). So, from the source encoder $s[n]$ is transformed into $i[n]$, both of which are in bits. The bit rate R_b is the rate at which information bits are transmitted through the channel.

Following source encoding is encryption. The purpose of encryption is to scramble data to make it difficult for an unintended receiver to interpret. Generally encryption involves applying a lossless transformation to the information sequence $i[n]$ to produce an encrypted sequence $e[n] = p(i[n])$. Decryption reverses this process by applying an inverse transform $p^{-1}(\cdot)$ to produce $i[n] = p^{-1}(p(i[n]))$. Unlike source coding, encryption does not compress the data; rather, it makes the data appear random to an uniformed receiver. Methods of encryption and security more generally are discussed briefly in the last section of this chapter and in more detail in Part 3 of Volume II.

The next block is the channel coder. Channel coding adds redundancy to the encrypted sequence $e[n]$ in a controlled way to provide resilience to channel distortions and to improve overall throughput. Using common coding notation, for every k input bits, or information bits, there is an additional redundancy of r bits. The total number of bits is $n = k + r$; the coding rate is defined as k/n. Two types of channel codes are prevalent: forward error correction codes and error detection codes. Forward error correction codes are used to provided redundancy that enables errors to be corrected at the receiver. They come in varieties such as trellis codes, convolutional codes, or block codes (Bossert, 1999). Error detection codes, CRC (cyclic redundancy check) codes being the most common, provide redundancy that allows the receiver to determine whether an error occurred during transmission. The receiver can use this information either to discard the data in error or request a retransmission.

Following channel coding, the bits are mapped to *waveforms* by the modulator. Typically, groups of bits are mapped to *symbols*. Following the symbol mapping, the modulator converts the digital symbols into

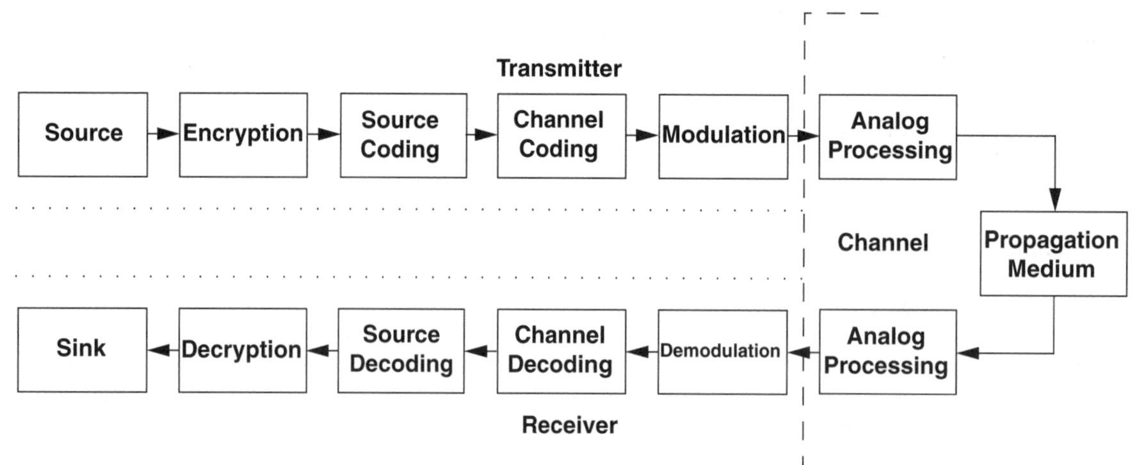

Figure 1: The components of a typical digital communication system.

corresponding analog waveforms for transmission over the physical link. This can be accomplished by sending the digital signal through a digital to analog (D/A) converter into a shaping filter and, if needed, mixed onto a higher frequency carrier. Symbols are sent at a rate of R_s symbols per second, also known as the baud rate; the symbol period $T_s = 1/R_s$ is the time difference between successive symbols. This is the demarcation point at which basic transmitter-side digital signal processing for communications ends. The signal generated by the transmitter travels through a propagation medium, which could be a radio wave through a wireless environment, a current through a telephone wire, or an optical signal through a fiber, to the receiver.

The first block at the receiver is the analog front end (AFE), which, consists at least of filters to remove unwanted noise, oscillators for timing, and analog to digital (A/D) converters to convert the data into the digital regime. There may be additional analog components such as analog gain control and automatic frequency control. This is the demarcation point for the beginning of the receiver-side digital signal processing for digital communication.

The channel, as illustrated in Figure 1, is the component of the communication system that accounts for all the noise, distortion and intersymbol interference introduced by the analog processing blocks and the propagation medium. Noise is a random disturbance that degrades the received signal. Sources of noise include the thermal noise that results from the material properties of the receiver, the quantization noise caused by the D/A and the A/D, and the external interference from other communication channels. Intersymbol interference is a form of signal distortion that causes the transmitted signal to interfere with itself. Sources of intersymbol interference include the distortion introduced by the analog filters as well as the propagation medium. Sources of distortion include clippned non their amplirfiction is the analog elements.

The first digital communication block at the receiver is the demodulator. The demodulator uses a sampled version of the received waveform, and perhaps knowledge of the channel, to infer the transmitted symbol. The process of demodulation may include equalization, sequence detection, or other advanced algorithms to help in combatting channel distortions.

Following the demodulator is the decoder. Essentially, the decoder uses the redundancy introduced by the channel coder to remove errors generated by the demodulation block. The decoder may work jointly with the demodulator to improve performance or may simply operate on the output of the demodulator. Overall, the effect of the demodulator and the decoder is to produce the closest possible $\hat{e}[n]$ given the observations at the receiver.

After demodulation, decryption is applied to the output of the demodulator. The objective is to descramble the data to make it intelligible to the receiver. Generally, decryption applies the inverse transformation $p^{-1}(\cdot)$ corresponding to the encryption process to produce an estimate of the transmitted information $\hat{i}[n] = p^{-1}(\hat{e}[n])$.

The final block in the diagram is the source decoder that essentially reinflates the data back to the form it was sent: $\hat{s}[n] = g(\hat{i}[n])$. This is basically the inverse operation of the source encoder. After source decoding, the digital data is delivered to higher level communication protocols that are beyond the scope of the chapter.

For Internet traffic, common transmitter–receiver pairs include digital subscriber line (DSL) modems, fiber optic transceivers, local area networks, or even storage devices like a disk drive. Although their physical media are diverse and the speeds at which they transmit may be significantly different, the fundamental model for each of these digital communication systems is the same.

Processing in the Digital Domain

There are three basic classes of signals in digital communication. They are *continuous-time*, *discrete-time*, and *digital*. Continuous-time signals are those whose value at time t is $x(t)$, where t and $x(t)$ can take values on a continuum, for instance the real number line or the complex plane. Discrete-time signals take values only at integer times n, but the signal $x[n]$ takes values on a continuum. Finally, digital signals are those that have value at integer times and take on values on some finite (perhaps countably infinite) set.

The link between the analog and the digital domains is through the D/A and the A/D, as illustrated in Figure 2. At the transmitter, the D/A converts a digital signal $x[n]$ to an analog signal $x(t)$ essentially by letting $x(nT_s) = x[n]$ and interpolating the remaining values. At the receiver, the A/D samples the received signal $y(t)$ at some period T (typically a fraction of T_s) to produce $y[n] \cong y(nT)$, where this is approximate equality because $y[n]$ is quantized to some set of values. This new signal is called $y_d[n]$ and is

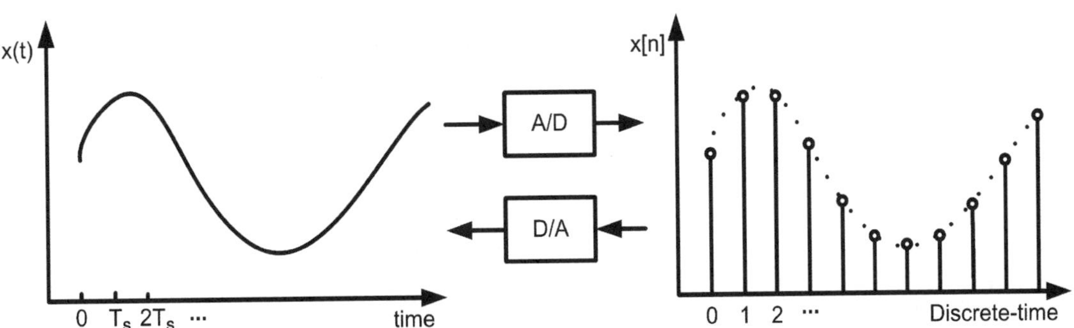

Figure 2: The relationship between a continuous-time signal and a discrete-time signal.

the digital waveform derived from the continuous-time waveform $y(t)$.

The Nyquist sampling theorem gives flexibility in the choice of whether to process $y(t)$ or $y[n]$. Ignoring quantization noise, the Nyquist sampling theorem states that if the inverse of the sample rate is greater than twice the maximum frequency in $y(t)$ (or equivalently the bandwidth), then there is no loss in the sampling process. This implies that any processing done on the continuous-time waveform can be done equally well on the sampled waveform given that the conditions stated in the Nyquist sampling theorem are satisfied. Several practical considerations, however, make digital the domain of choice.

The biggest advantage of doing as much processing as possible in the digital domain is that it allows full exploitation of the benefits of digital technology. Many digital platforms exist that are highly customizable and easy to alter, for instance, field programmable gate arrays (FPGAs) and digital signal processors. This hardware has been designed to have very good tolerances and reproducibility. Because the DSP machinery is easy to change, it is also well suited to adaptation if parameters may need to be adjusted over time. Analog circuitry, on the other hand, can be extremely bulky and expensive to produce. Moreover, if a change has to be made to the design, analog equipment may need to be redesigned as well. For these reasons, doing processing in the digital domain has become very relevant to digital communication. This is not to say that all analog processing can be obviated. For instance, the fundamental noise limits for a modem may be the noise produced by the analog components or the A/D converter. Another advantage of processing in the digital domain is a byproduct of the shrinking transistor size. The shrinking of transistor size offers both dramatic increases in processing power as well as significant reductions in overall cost. Thus, doing the majority of the processing in the digital domain improves cost, performance, and flexibility.

Key Resources: Power and Bandwidth

The two primary resources in any communication system, both digital and analog, are power and bandwidth. Systems whose performance is limited by the available power are power-limited, whereas those that are limited by bandwidth are bandwidth-limited. Most practical systems are to some extent both power and bandwidth limited.

The power of a signal is roughly defined as the average energy over time. Mathematically, this is often written as $P = \lim_{T\to\infty}(1/T)\int_{-T/2}^{T/2}|x(t)|^2 dt$. Power may be measured in watts but is more often measured in decibels relative to 1 watt (dB) or 1 milliwatt (dBm). The decibel is a relative measure that is defined as $(P/Q)_{dB} = 10\log_{10}(P/Q)$. When used to measure the power of P in dB, Q is assumed to be 1 watt, whereas to measure the power of P in dBm, Q is assumed to be 1 milliwatt.

There are two different but related notions of power in a communication system: transmit power and the received power. Naturally, the transmit power is the average energy over time of the transmitted signal, and the receive power is the average energy over time of the received signal.

The transmitted power in a communication system is limited by the maximum power available to transmit a signal. Generally system performance will be better if there is high transmitted power (and thus received power). Practical constraints on cost, properties of the transmission medium, battery life (in mobile systems), or regulatory constraints, generally imply low transmitted power.

Because propagation media are lossy and dispersive, the received power is a function of the transmit power and the channel. In all media, the loss due to the channel increases as some function of the distance between the transmitter and receiver. Thus, the larger the distance, the smaller the received power.

The minimum received power required at the receiver, known as the *receiver sensitivity*, is determined by the parameters of the system, the quality of the hardware, and the desired operating characteristics. The range of the system can be inferred from the ratio of the maximum transmit power to the minimum received power. Generally, increased data rate in a given *bandwidth* or lower bit error rates increase the required minimum received power requirments.

Besides power, bandwidth is the other design constraint in a communication system. Unfortunately, there are many definitions of bandwidth, and different notions are used in different systems. The most generic definition of the bandwidth of a signal $x(t)$ is the portion of the frequency spectrum $X(f) = \int_{-\infty}^{\infty} x(t)e^{-j2\pi ft}dt$, for which $X(f)$ is nonzero. Because the true bandwidth of a finite duration signal is infinite, systems often use the "3-dB bandwidth," which is the contiguous range of frequencies over which the power spectrum is at least 50% of the maximum value. Other definitions of bandwidth are also possible; see Couch (2001) for details.

The definition of bandwidth differs depending on whether the communication system is *baseband* or *bandpass*. Baseband communication systems operate at DC, and bandpass communication systems convey information at some carrier frequency f_c. Figure 3 illustrates the different bandwidth notions of absolute and 3-dB bandwidth in these types of systems.

The bandwidth available in a communication system depends on the transmission medium. In wireless systems, bandwidth is a precious and expensive commodity that is regulated by the government. Thus, although in wireline systems, the bandwidth is determined by the type and quality of the cable and the interconnects. Generally, the larger the bandwidth, the larger the potential data rate that can be supported. Exploiting larger bandwidths, however, typically requires more sophisticated receiver processing algorithms and more expensive analog components.

Bandwidth and power are related through the concept of the power spectral density (PSD). The PSD is a measure of the power in a signal as a function of frequency. The integral of the PSD is hence the power of the signal.

Measures of Performance

A number of potential measures are used to evaluate the performance of a digital communication system. The choice of a performance measure depends significantly

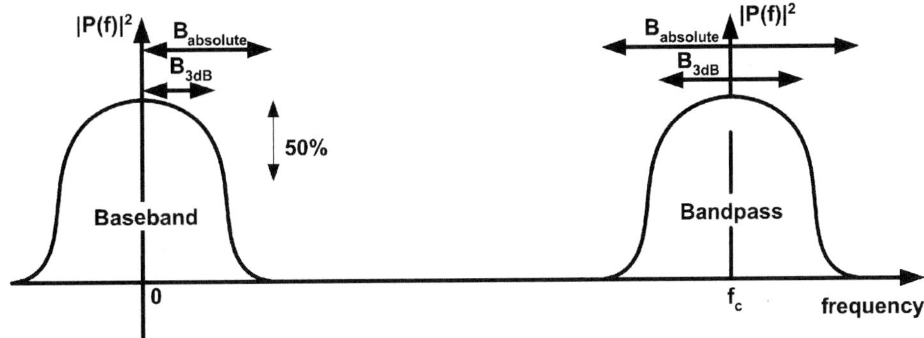

Figure 3: Illustration of two notions of bandwidth in baseband and bandpass signals.

on the application and other aspects of the system. Broad classes of performance measures include the probability of error, the outage probability, and the capacity. In this chapter, we discuss the probability of error and the capacity. The probability of error is a measure of the rate at which errors occur, and the capacity is a measure of the maximum data rate that can be supported by a channel with a given *signal to noise ratio* (SNR) and an arbitrarily small probability of error.

Of the two measures, the probability of error is the more pragmatic indicator of system performance. There are various types of the probability of error, including the probability of bit error, probability of symbol error, and the probability of frame error. Equivalently, these measures are known as the bit error rate (BER), the symbol error rate (SER), and the frame error rate (FER).

The BER provides the average number of bit errors. For example, a BER of 10^{-2} means that on average about 1 bit out of every 100 will be in error. The BER can be measured at various places in the receiver but is typically most meaningful after demodulation (the uncoded BER) and after error correction (the coded BER).

The performance needs of the application determine the required BER. For example, voice communication in cellular systems might require a coded BER of 10^{-2}, whereas data communication in the same system might require a coded BER of 10^{-5}. In most communication systems, the uncoded BER is a function of the data rate and the modulation scheme and can be readily related to the SNR. The SNR is essentially the ratio of the received signal power to the noise power in the signal bandwidth. Thus, the BER is a function of both the received power and the bandwidth of the signal, although more generally the channel model will also play a role.

The fundamental limit to data communications can be most simply described by the so-called capacity of a channel, C, which is the maximum average number of bits that can be supported by a channel with a given SNR at an arbitrarily small probability of error. The capacity is measured in units of bits per second and is essentially a bound on the achievable data rate. Often, the capacity is normalized by the bandwidth. The normalized capacity C/B measures the bits per channel use in units of bits per second per Hértz. Unlike the BER, the capacity provides an upperbound (instead of the actual performance) of a communication system because it is optimized over all possible modulation and coding schemes. Like the BER, the capacity is typically a function of the SNR, the bandwidth, and the channel.

The capacity is a measure for determining the fundamental limit on the data rate imposed by the given communication channel. The BER is more useful for evaluating the performance of an actual coding and modulation scheme. Typically, a target BER will be defined, and a coding and modulation scheme will be proposed to achieve the largest data rate possible R. Naturally, it should be the case that $R < C$. Spectrally efficient digital communication systems have a rate R that closely approaches the capacity C for the desired operating point.

IMPORTANT CONCEPTS IN DIGITAL COMMUNICATION

Modulation

The modulator in a digital communication system maps binary data onto waveforms for transmission over the physical channel. The modulator maps a group of bits (or symbols) onto a finite number of waveforms each symbol period. Binary modulations map each bit to one of two possible waveforms, whereas M-ary modulations map each group of $\log_2 M$ bits to one of M possible waveforms. The analog waveforms are designed with the constraints of the channel such as the bandwidth or the carrier frequency in mind.

There are two basic forms of modulation known as linear and nonlinear modulation. Linear modulation schemes are typically more spectrally efficient, that is, they are able to come closer to the capacity. Nonlinear modulations typically have other properties, such as constant envelope, that make them easier to implement and less susceptible to various impairments in the channel. The choice of a modulation scheme depends on the desired throughput, the target bit error rate, the spectral efficiency of the modulation scheme, the power efficiency of the modulation scheme, robustness to impairments, and the implementation cost and complexity.

Modulations may also have memory or they may be memoryless. When a symbol is only a function of the bits from the current symbol period, it is said to be memoryless. When a symbol is a function of the bits from previous symbols periods, the modulation is said to have memory. Having memory in the modulation scheme may have some practical advantages such as reducing the peak-to-average ratio of the transmitted signal or simplifying noncoherent detection at the receiver. Modulations with memory can also provide some additional resilience to errors, and thus they are sometimes called coded modulation schemes.

To illustrate the concept of modulation—in particular, linear modulation—let us first define the concept of signal space and then relate that to common modulation formats found in practice. A vector space is defined to be a set of vectors (in this case continuous signals), $\{\phi_i(t)\}$ with two operations: (a) addition of those vectors (i.e., $\phi_i(t) + \phi_j(t)$ is defined and is an element of the vector space) and (b) multiplications of those vectors by a scalar (i.e., $k\phi_i(t)$ is defined and an element of the vector space). Other technical rules for being a vector space can be found in Anton and Rorres (1991). In communications, typically these vectors are orthogonal, that is

$$\int_{-\infty}^{\infty} \phi_i(t)\phi_j(t)dt = \delta_{ij}, \tag{1}$$

where δ_{ij} is 1 for $i = j$ and 0 otherwise. Because these waveform vectors are orthogonal, they are also a basis for the vector space and are sometimes referred to as basis functions.

A digital communication system may be baseband or bandpass depending on whether the symbols are conveyed at baseband (DC) or at some carrier frequency (see Figure 3). ADSL (asymmetric DSL) is an example of a baseband communication system. Most digital communication systems are bandpass, including all narrowband wireless systems, optical systems, and cable modems. Although bandpass systems convey information at a carrier frequency, the modulator and demodulator do not need to generate signals at that carrier frequency. Instead, the modulator and demodulator work with the *baseband equivalent* waveform. At the transmitter, the *upconverter* in the analog processing block converts the baseband equivalent signal to the bandpass signal by shifting it to the desired carrier frequency. At the receiver, the *downconverter* in the analog processing block shifts the bandpass signal down to zero frequency. The advantage of the baseband equivalent notion is that it makes the digital operations of the communication system independent of the actual carrier frequency.

Let us first consider baseband pulse amplitude modulation (PAM). PAM transmission is used in HDSL (high bit-rate DSL), HDSL-II, and optical transmission. It is a linear and memoryless modulation. An M-PAM system is a form of M-ary modulation in which $m = \log_2 M$ bits at a time are mapped to an element of the set of M possible amplitudes $\mathcal{C}_{PAM}$ which is the constellation. For 4-PAM, a set of possible amplitudes is $\mathcal{C}_{PAM} = \{-3, -1, 1, 3\}$, which are equally spaced apart. A pulse-shaping filter $\phi(t)$ with a bandwidth B is modulated to produce the transmitted waveform $x(t) = \sum_n x[n]\ \phi(t - nT_s)$, where $x[n] \in \mathcal{C}_{PAM}$. So the set $\mathcal{C}_{PAM}$ is the constellation, $x[n]$ is the symbol transmitted starting at time nT_s, and $\phi(t)$ is the basis waveform. The spectrum of the PAM waveforms is determined by the pulse-shaping filter $\phi(t)$. The choice of pulse-shaping filter is a complicated one involving several competing requirements including resistance to timing jitter, minimized spectral bandwidth, and noise immunity.

A nice generalization of PAM that is preferable for bandpass systems is known as quadrature amplitude modulation (QAM). As with PAM, QAM is a linear and memoryless modulation. An M-QAM modulation is defined for M that are a power of four. Let $m = 1/2 \log_2 M$ and consider the same set of 2^m possible amplitudes $\mathcal{C}_{PAM}$ and pulse-shaping waveform $\phi(t)$. For M-QAM, at some carrier frequency f_c, the transmitted waveform is

$$\begin{aligned} x(t) &= \left(\sum_n i[n]\ \phi(t - nT_s)\right)\cos(2\pi f_c t) \\ &\quad - \left(\sum_n q[n]\ \phi(t - nT_s)\right)\sin(2\pi f_c t), \end{aligned} \tag{2}$$

where $i[n] \in \mathcal{C}_{PAM}$ corresponds to the symbol transmitted on the inphase component $\cos(2\pi f_c t)$ and $q[n] \in \mathcal{C}_{PAM}$ corresponds to the symbol transmitted on the quadrature component $\sin(2\pi f_c t)$. Assuming that f_c is much greater than $1/B$, the modulated inphase and quadrature components are orthogonal; thus, QAM has double the data rate of a PAM system, which would use only the inphase or quadrature component. Of course, recalling the discussion about Figure 3, note that a bandpass QAM system also uses twice the bandwidth of a baseband PAM system thus the spectral efficiency of QAM at bandpass and PAM at baseband is the same. The ordered pair $(i[n], q[n])$ is the symbol transmitted starting at time nT_s, and $\phi(t)\cos(2\pi f_c t)$ and $\phi(t)\sin(2\pi f_c t)$ are the basis waveforms. For M-QAM, the constellation $\mathcal{C}_{QAM}$ is composed of all possible ordered pairs that can be generated from choosing the $2^m - PAM$ points for the inphase and quadrature components. Thus, the M-QAM constellation has two dimensions. The baseband equivalent of the QAM signal in Equation 2 is a complex function and is given by

$$\sum_n (i[n] + jq[n])\ \phi(t - nT_s),$$

where $j = \sqrt{-1}$. Quadrature modulation schemes have complex baseband equivalents to account for both the inphase and quadrature components. The spectrum of the QAM waveform is determined by the pulse-shaping filter $\phi(t)$ and is shifted in frequency by f_c. PAM and QAM modulation are illustrated in Figure 4.

Not all bandpass systems are capable of using QAM modulation. For example, in optical transmission phase information is not available, so the constellations are defined for positive amplitudes only. If the constellations values are 0 and A, this is known as On–Off Keying (OOK).

Another common form of modulation is multicarrier modulation in which several carriers are modulated by QAM modulation simultaneously. These carriers can be thought of as a basis waveform modulated by sinusoids of differing frequencies. This is not easy to accomplish, so an IFFT (inverse fast Fourier transform) is used to approximate this operation. The inverse fast Fourier transform

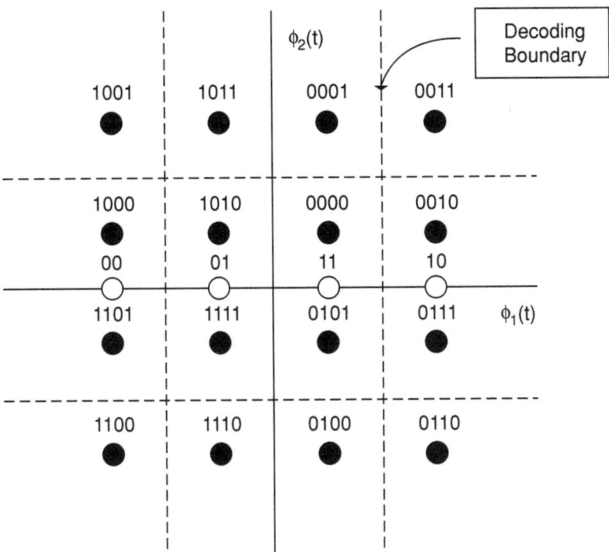

Figure 4: Signal space illustration of pulse amplitude modulation (white circles) and quadrature amplitude modulation (black circles) signalling. The numbers represent the mapping of bits to the constellation points.

of a set of constellation points is in fact the sum of a set of sampled sinusoids multiplied by the constellation points. In IFFT the digital domain, each of these waveforms can be independently demodulated. These samples are sent through a single pulse shaping filter (basis waveform) and transmitted through the channel. The receiver samples the waveform and performs the inverse operations, an FFT. Multicarrier modulation has become important because of its robustness to impulsive noise, ease of equalization, and its ability to do spectral shaping by independently controlling the carriers. Discrete multitone (DMT) is the most common baseband version of multicarrier modulation, and orthogonal frequency division multiplexing (OFDM) is the most common bandpass version.

Intersymbol Interference Channels

After modulation, the analog waveform $x(t)$ corresponding to an input sequence of bits is transmitted over the communication medium. Communication media, whether fiber optic cable, coax cable, telephone cable, or free space, generally have a dispersive effect on the transmitted signal. The effect of the medium on $x(t)$ is often modeled using a concept from signal processing known as a linear and time-invariant (LTI) system. The linearity implies that if $y_k(t)$ is the response to $x_k(t)$, then $\alpha y_1(t) + \beta y_2(t)$ is the response to the input signal $\alpha x_1(t) + \beta x_2(t)$. Time invariance means that the response to $x(t+\tau)$ is $y(t+\tau)$, that is, the behavior of the channel is not a function of time. Practically all physical channels are time varying (because of changes in environmental factors), especially wireless channels; however, over short periods of time, they can be modeled as time invariant. Optical channels can also exhibit nonlinear behavior, and thus other models may sometimes be appropriate.

The LTI assumption about the communication medium allows the distortion to the input signal to be modeled using the convolution operation

$$y(t) = \int_{-\infty}^{\infty} h(\tau)x(t-\tau)d\tau.$$

The function $h(\tau)$ is known as the impulse response of the channel and includes all the analog effects such as filtering at the transmitter and receiver in addition to the distortion in the medium. From basic Fourier transform theory, LTI systems have the nice property that in the frequency domain $Y(f) = H(f)X(f)$ where $Y(f)$ is the Fourier transform of $y(t)$, $H(f)$ is the Fourier transform of $h(t)$, and $X(f)$ is the Fourier transform of $x(t)$. Essentially, the channel acts as a frequency-selective filter that operates on the input signal. LTI systems induce distortion that is multiplicative in the frequency domain.

In an ideal channel, $|H(f)| = 1$, and there is no distortion (only a delay) of the input signal. Equivalently, in the time domain an ideal channel produces $y(t) = x(t-\tau)$, where τ is an arbitrary delay. When the channel is not ideal, a more serious problem is encountered known as intersymbol interference. To illustrate this concept, suppose that $x(t)$ is generated at baseband using PAM as described in the previous section.

In the absence of a channel, ideal sampling of $x(t)$ at the receiver at time mT_s (more details on this in the next section), results in $\sum_n x[n]\,\phi(mT_s - nT_s)$. The pulse-shaping filter $\phi(t)$, however, is often a Nyquist pulseshape, which means that $\phi(0) = 1$ and $\phi(nT_s) = 0$ for $n \neq 0$. Thus sampling at time mT_s yields symbol $x[m]$. Now consider a nonideal channel. Let $\tilde{\phi}(t)$ be the convolution of $\phi(t)$ and $h(t)$. For a nontrivial channel, it will generally be the case that $\tilde{\phi}(t)$ is no longer a Nyquist pulseshape, and thus $y[m] = \sum_n x[n]\tilde{\phi}((m-n)T_s)$. In this case, there are multiple superpositions of symbols at each sampling instant—thus, the notion of intersymbol interference. Compensating for intersymbol interference is known as equalization and is an important part of the receiver processing when intersymbol interference is present.

Noise and Interference

Noise and interference are the most ubiquitous forms of degradation in any communication system. Essentially, both can be modeled as random disturbances that are unrelated to the desired signal. Intersymbol interference also results in degradation; however, the effect is different because it causes the signal to interfere with itself. Noise usually refers to the disturbances generated in the receiver as a result of the analog components, analog to digital conversion, and material properties of the receiver. Generally, noise can be reduced, but never eliminated, by using higher quality materials. Interference generally refers to disturbances generated by external signals. Typically, interference has more signal structure than noise, and thus it can be mitigated by more complex processing at the expense of higher cost.

There are various sources of noise in communication systems. Common examples include thermal noise, shot noise, and quantization noise. Thermal noise is a result of the Brownian random motion of thermally excited electrons. It is generated by resistors and the resistive parts of other devices such as transistors. Shot noise is more impulsive and may be more related to the signal, for example the random arrival rates of photons in optical systems. Quantization noise is a result of digitizing the amplitude of the discrete-time signal. Because thermal noise limits the performance in most systems (with the exception of optical system), we focus our explanation there.

Because noise is fundamentally not deterministic, it is often modeled as a random process. For thermal noise, the Gaussian random process has been found to be adequate for the job. When applied to model thermal noise, the process is assumed to be zero mean, uncorrelated from sample to sample, and have a variance σ^2 that is generally proportional to kBT_e, where k is Boltzman's constant $(1.23 \times 10^{-23}\ J/K)$, B is the signal bandwidth, and T_e is the effective noise temperature of the device. The latter, T_e, is a parameter determined by the analog portion of the receiver. Essentially for thermal noise the variance increases linearly as a function of the bandwidth. Thus signals with larger bandwidths incur an additional noise penalty while enjoying a higher signaling rate.

The effect of thermal noise is additive; therefore, the received signal can be written $z(t) = y(t) + v(t)$, where $v(t)$ is a realization of the noise process. Because $v(t)$ is unknown to the receiver, its presence degrades the performance of subsequent processing blocks. The severity of thermal noise is quantified by the SNR.

The origin of interference is usually an undesired communication signal. Examples include adjacent channel interference, crosstalk, and cochannel interference. Adjacent channel interference refers to the interference caused by signals operating in adjacent frequency bands. Because practical signals cannot have a finite absolute bandwidth, when the carrier frequencies of two signals are close together, there is often leakage from one signal to the other. Crosstalk is a form of interference in wireline systems. It results from the electromagnetic coupling among the multiple twisted pairs making up a phone cable. Cochannel interference is the wireless equivalent of crosstalk. Because of the limited availability of frequencies, wireless cellular systems reuse each carrier frequency. Essentially, cochannel interference is the interference among users sharing the same communication frequency.

Like thermal noise, interference is also additive. Thus a signal with interference may be written $z(t) = y(t) + \sum_k y_k(t)$, where $y_k(t)$ refers to the distorted interfering signals. Performance degrades because $y_k(t)$ is both random and unknown at the receiver. More generally, noise is also present, and thus

$$z(t) = y(t) + \sum_k y_k(t) + v(t).$$

In some cases, the interference is modeled as another Gaussian noise source. Then performance is characterized by the signal to interference plus noise (SINR) ratio, which is essentially $P_y/(P_i + P_v)$, where P_y is the power in the desired signal, P_i is the power in the sum of the interfering signals, and P_v is the power in the noise. Systems for which $P_i \ll P_v$ are called noise limited, and those for which $P_v \ll P_i$ are called interference limited. If the source of the interference is crosstalk or cochannel interference, then the interfering signals $\{y_k(t)\}$ all have a structure (modulation, coding, etc.) similar to the desired signal. In this case, advanced signal processing algorithms can be used to mitigate the impact of the interference. Examples of algorithms include joint demodulation in which all the signals are demodulated simultaneously, interference cancellation in which the interference is partially cancelled, and optimum filtering in which filters are constructed that partially eliminate the interference. Removing or mitigating interference improves performance by reducing the required transmit power to achieve a given BER for a given data rate or by allowing the data rate at a given BER to be increased for a given transmit power.

Timing and Synchronization

Prior to demodulation and symbol recovery at the receiver, a number of timing and synchronization tasks need to be performed, including phase synchronization, frequency synchronization, symbol timing, and frame synchronization. Synchronization is performed to ensure that the transmitter and receiver operate in a synchronous manner. The process of synchronization typically consists of first estimating the synchronization error then correcting this error. Typically the processing required for synchronization is done in a mixture of the analog and digital domains.

In bandpass systems, information is modulated onto sinusoids as illustrated in the QAM example in Equation 2. To demodulate this signal at the receiver, these sinusoids must be exactly reproduced. The problem of ensuring the phases are accurate is known as phase synchronization. The problem of estimating the transmitted carrier frequency is known as frequency synchronization. Estimating and tracking the phase of the sinusoid is typically more difficult than the frequency; however, phase differences can sometimes be included as part of the channel and removed during equalization.

At the receiver, the A/D samples the analog waveform for subsequent digital processing. Optimal processing requires two aspects of symbol synchronization: symbol timing and sampling clock recovery. Symbol timing is the problem of knowing exactly where to sample the received signal. Even in systems with ideal channels, symbol timing errors can lead to intersymbol interference because of timing errors. Often the symbol timing problem is solved by oversampling the received signal and choosing the best subsample. Sampling clock recovery refers to the problem of ensuring that the sampling period T_s at the receiver is identical to that at the transmitter. Sampling clock recovery is typically more important in baseband systems because in bandpass systems the sampling clock can be derived from the carrier.

In systems where the fundamental unit of information is a frame and not a symbol, an additional synchronization step is required. This process, known as frame synchronization, is required to determine where the beginning of the frame is located. Frame synchronization is often assisted by the presence of synchronization sequences that mark the beginning of the frame.

Demodulation

The goal of the demodulator is to convert the sampled received waveform back into a sequence of bits. Of course, demodulation is highly dependent on the modulation and the channel therefore this section provides only a cursory overview.

The first step in the demodulation process is to sample the waveform. Typically, this is done via a frontend filter that removes unwanted noise, followed by a sampler. The sampled data comes from an A/D converter, so the data is in the digital domain. The sampled signal includes residual noise left after filtering, the noise from the sampling device, and the signal of interest. For example, assuming perfect timing, synchronization, and no interference, in the presence of an ideal channel the sampled PAM signal at the receiver $y(nT_s)$ is

$$y[n] = x[n] + v[n],$$

where $x[n]$ is the transmitted PAM symbol and $v[n]$ represents the sampled thermal noise and the quantization noise. The samples $y[n]$ are sent through a decision device that processes the data to make a decision. Typically, the decision device determines the most likely symbol from the given constellation that was transmitted. An inverse symbol mapping operation then converts the symbols to bit form.

Because the noise is unknown to the receiver, the role of the decision device is to produce its best guess about the transmitted data. One common criterion is to find the symbol that is the most likely input given the observations. If X and Y are vectors representing the input $x[k]$ and the output $y[k]$ respectively, then

$$\hat{X} = \arg\max_{X} P(X\,|Y),$$

where $P(X|Y)$ is the probability that $x[k] = X$ given that observation of $Y = y[k]$. The maximization is taken over all possible points in the constellation to find the point with the maximum conditional probability and is called the maximum a posteriori decision. When the source data are equally likely, it turns out that this is equivalent to the maximum likelihood detection rule which is given by:

$$\hat{X} = \arg\max_{X} P(Y\,|X).$$

In this case the decision rule determines the symbol that was most likely to have produced the observation. For the additive white Gaussian noise channel (AWGN), the conditional probabilities we have described have a known form.[1] For instance, when the input symbols are equally likely, it turns out that the detection principle is simply to minimize the Euclidean distance between the observation and the set of possible inputs

$$\hat{X}[k] = \arg\min_{x[k]\in C} ||y[k] - x[k]||^2. \tag{3}$$

[1] In the AWGN channel, there is no intersymbol interference and the only source of degradation is uncorrelated Gaussian noise.

In this case, the detector is known as a slicer. The operation of the slicer can be described by Figure 4. For a QAM/PAM waveform, if a received sample is within a decoding boundary of a point, it is mapped to that point. Because of the simple decoding boundaries, the test is essentially a series of threshold tests, and hence the name slicer.

In the absence of an ideal channel, even with perfect timing and synchronization, there will be intersymbol interference and thus the sampled PAM signal may have the form

$$y[n] = \sum_{l=0}^{L} h[l]x[n-l] + v[n],$$

where $h[l]$ is the sampled equivalent channel impulse response. Optimum decoding requires considering the channel response in the decision device. Because of the memory in the channel, it is no longer possible to make a decision on a symbol by symbol basis. Instead, sequences must be decoded. Thus, given a sequence of observations $\{y[p]\}_{p=0}^{P-1}$, we must determine the sequence $\{x[n]\}_{n=0}^{N-1}$, that was most likely to have been transmitted. We allow for $P \geq N$ at the receiver to account for multiple observations of the received signal via oversampling or multiple antennas, for example. Clearly, the complexity of the search grows with both N and P. Using the fact that memory of the channel is finite, however, allows lower complexity approaches such as the Bahl, Cocke, Jelenick, and Raviv (BCJR) algorithm to help in maximum a posteriori decoding and the Viterbi algorithm for maximum likelihood decoding (see, e.g., Wicker & Kim, 2002).

Alternatively, to correct for intersymbol interference, many transmission systems use equalizers that attempt to remove the effect of the channel before the slicing operation. Some common equalizers are zero-forcing equalizers (ZFE), which invert the channel; minimum mean square error (MMSE) equalizers, which include the effects of noise; and decision feedback equalizers (DFE), which use the detected symbols to remove some portion of the trailing intersymbol interference. Equalization generally gives inferior performance relative to sequence decoding but offers much lower complexity.

A PERFORMANCE EXAMPLE

The AWGN channel provides an analytically tractable baseline case by which performance in other channels can be compared. First consider the capacity of the AWGN channel. It can be shown in this case that the capacity expression is remarkably simple

$$C = B\log_2(1 + SNR)\,, \tag{4}$$

where B is the channel bandwidth. The theoretical spectral efficiency that can be achieved in this channel is thus C/B bits per second per Hertz. The normalized capacity as a function of SNR is illustrated in Figure 5.

The capacity expression in Equation 4 provides an interesting means for evaluating system performance. For instance, if a coded system provides 3 dB increased immunity to noise, the SNR will increase by a multiple of

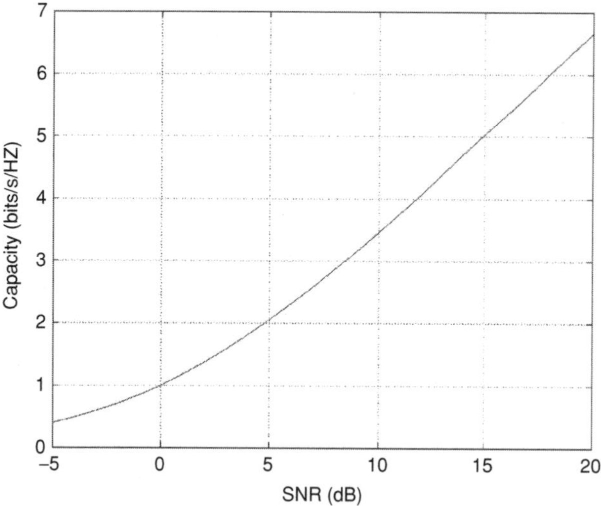

Figure 5: The normalized capacity of an additive white Gavssian noise channel as a function of the sound to noise ratio (SNR).

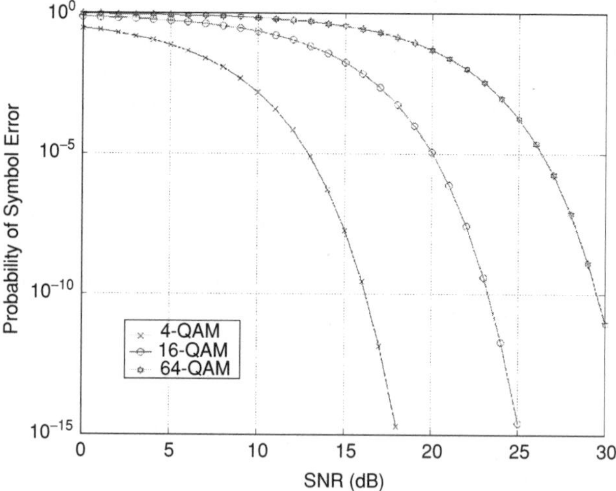

Figure 6: The symbol error rate for quadrature amplitude modulation (QAM) transmission in an additive white Gaussian noise channel as a function of sound to noise ratio (SNR).

two ($10\log_{10} 2 \cong 3dB$). Hence, the amount of information that can be transmitted will increase by about 1 bit per transmission for high SNR because $\log_2(1 + 2 \cdot SNR) \cong \log_2(2 \cdot SNR) \cong \log_2(SNR) + 1$.

Unlike the capacity, the symbol error rate in an AWGN channel is a function of the modulation scheme that is employed. For uncoded M-PAM or M-QAM transmission, the probability of symbol error is given by

$$P_e = 2\left(1 - \frac{1}{M}\right) Q\left(\sqrt{\frac{3\ SNR}{M^2 - 1}}\right) \text{ for PAM} \tag{5}$$

and

$$= 4\left(1 - \frac{1}{\sqrt{M}}\right) Q\left(\sqrt{\frac{3\ SNR}{M - 1}}\right) - 4\left(1 - \frac{1}{\sqrt{M}}\right)^2 \times \left(Q\left(\sqrt{\frac{3\ SNR}{M - 1}}\right)\right)^2 \text{ for QAM,} \tag{6}$$

where $Q(x) = 1/\sqrt{2\pi}\int_x^\infty e^{-t^2/2}dt$ for $x \geq 0$ is the area under the tail of the Gaussian probability distribution function. The probability of symbol error for QAM transmission is illustrated in Figure 6 as a function of SNR. Notice how the error rate is exponentially decreasing as the SNR increases. For a given probability of error (at high SNR), observe that there is approximately a 6 dB difference between the SNR required for 4 QAM and 16 QAM or between 16-QAM and 64-QAM.

By inverting the formulas in Equations 5 and 6, for a target probability of error, a useful expression for the maximum spectral efficiency obtained is

$$R = \log_2\left(1 + \frac{SNR}{\Gamma}\right), \tag{7}$$

where the gap, Γ, can be calculated as a function of M and the target probability of error. Conveniently, Equation 7 allows direct comparison with the capacity in Equation 4. The gap, Γ, effectively determines the loss in capacity, that is, the gap between the actual spectral efficiency and the maximum spectral efficiency. Coded modulation schemes generally reduce the gap (toward the ultimate limit of $\Gamma = 1$). The effect of coding is most often expressed in dB as the coding gain, ϕ_{dB}, making the effective gap smaller, so that $\Gamma_{db}^{new} = \Gamma_{dB} - \phi_{dB}$.

CONNECTIONS WITH SECURITY

Owing to their versatility and efficiency, today's digital communication systems are the targets for various threats, malevolent actions, and attacks. Security, the general subject of this *Handbook*, is an essential component of any digital communication system.

The provision of security services for digital communication systems can be accomplished at various levels of the communicating entity. In this chapter, we consider security implemented at the physical layer, as illustrated in Figure 1. In this figure, the *encryption* block follows the source coding block of the transmitter and the *decryption* block preceeds the source decoding block of the receiver. These functional blocks permit encryption and decryption of the source. This processing, in turn, provides a confidentiality service and, if appropriate management of encryption keys are implemented, it also provides authentication. An example of this type of processing, offering both confidentiality and authentication, is the Wired Equivalent Privacy feature of IEEE 802.11b wireless communication (, 2004).

The actual primitives that implement the encryption and decryption functions can be divided into two general classes:

1. **Symmetric (secret) key encryption.** This encryption scheme employs the same encryption key at both the transmitter and receiver. The scheme is characterized by its efficiency. It provides large data rates in converting *plaintext* to *ciphertext* while requiring minimal

memory resources. Examples of symmetric ciphers include the Data Encryption Standard (, 2004) and the Advanced Encryption Standard (, 2004). Symmetric ciphers are implemented algorithmically, employing sequences of permutations and substitutions based on the key. Although efficient, symmetric methods require that the secret key be available at both transmitter and receiver. After generation by one party, the secure communication of the key to the other party represents a significant logistical problem; in other words, the key sharing assumes a secure means of communication to establish a secure means of communication. In a mesh network of N duplex entities, $N(N-1)/2$ secret keys are required to implement secure communication and each of these keys must be securely communicated between the entities that share it. From a security perspective, such a network employs $O(N2)$ *shared* secrets.

2. **Asymmetric (public) key encryption.** This encryption scheme employs two encryption keys, a *public key* and a *private key*. Either can accomplish a transformation from plaintext to ciphertext (encryption), with the other key being required to accomplish the inverse transformation (decryption). In other words, if a message is encrypted with one of the keys, for example, the *private* key, then the message can only be decrypted with the corresponding *public* key. In operation, one of the keys, the *private* key, is known only to the entity the generates it. A second key, the *public* key, is universally advertised as being associated with the generating entity.

If Party A wishes to communicate a message confidentially to Party B, then A obtains B's public key, encrypts the message, and sends it to B. Because only B's private key can decrypt the message, and B alone possesses that key, B can be assured that the contents of the message are not available to any third party.

Because the private key remains in the exclusive possession of its owner, if a message is encrypted with this key, the resulting ciphertext requires that the owner of the private key perform the encryption, and therefore this operation is called signing the message and the ciphertext can be considered the digital signature. If A encrypts a message with its private key and sends it to B, then when B decrypts the message with A's public key, then B is assured that the message originated with A. Note that because A's public key is available to anyone, encryption with the private key only provides proof of origin (authentication) and not confidentiality.

Asymmetric key schemes are significantly less efficient than symmetric key methods. They are implemented via mathematical functions as opposed to algorithms. Examples include RSA, named for its inventors, Ron Rivest, Adi Shamir, and Ken Adleman (, 2004) and elliptic curve (, 2004). Unlike symmetric key methods, an N node mesh network only requires $O(N)$ asymmetric keys to secure communication and no shared secrets are necessary.

In addition to symmetric and asymmetric cryptographic operations, another tool is frequently employed in cryptographic processing. This tool, the message digest function, associates a number having a fixed maximum magnitude with a message of arbitrary length. The association between a message and its digest is assumed to be unique. Therefore, the digest can be employed as an abbreviated form of the message. For example, the message digest of a message, encrypted with the originator's private key, represents one form of digital signature for the message. Today's message digest functions typically are 128 or 160 bits in length, for example, message digest version 5 (MD5) or secure hash algorithm (SHA-1; , 2004).

The taxonomy of communication system attacks is hierarchical: Passive attacks monitor communications. In the most subtle instance, traffic analysis, the eavesdropper simply learns that two parties are communicating. A more aggressive passive attack, message disclosure, causes the communication between two parties to be disclosed to other, unauthorized, parties.

Active attacks modify or deny communications. Modification involves changing the content of a communication, whereas masquerading involves fraudulently changing the origin of the communication. Replay causes a valid communication to be sent, one or more times, after the original communication was received. Denial of service simply prevents communication.

Communication security is responsible for providing a systematic countermeasure for each type of threat or attack against the communication system. These countermeasures are articulated by the International Telecommunication Union in their Recommendation X.800—Security Architecture for OSI. The countermeasures are considered security services that are provided by the communication system. Each service is intended to address one or more threats:

Access Control. This service guarantees that resources can only be accessed by appropriately authorized parties.

Authentication. This service makes it possible to prove the identity of a communicating party.

Availability. This service ensures that communication is possible between appropriately authorized parties.

Confidentiality. This service ensures that information will not be disclosed to unauthorized entities.

Integrity. This service guarantees that information will not be altered in transit.

Nonrepudiation. This service prevents a participant in a communication from denying participation in the communication.

In general, each service may employ a combination of cryptographic primitives and the implementation of one service may automatically provide another. For example, the nonrepudiation service employs both asymmetric key cryptography and message digest functions as noted earlier. Consider a transmitter with a large message, for example, several gigabytes, that must be communicated in such a manner that its origin can not be repudiated. The transmitter would first compute the message digest function of the message. This relatively small value is uniquely associated with the larger message, and it can be encrypted using the transmitter's private key far more efficiently than the message it represents. The transmitter then transmits the message and its encrypted message digest to the receiver. At the receiver, the message is again processed through a message digest function, and the result is compared with the decryption, using the transmitter's public key, of the appended encrypted message digest. Upon equality, the receiver is assured that the message was sent by sender (nonrepudiation) and that it was not altered in transit (integrity).

Frequently, the implementation of the communication security service is accomplished beyond the actual digital communication system. In the earlier example, the message and its encrypted message digest could easily be regarded as source input to the digital communication system. Similarly, the secure socket layer (SSL) or transport layer security (TLS) used to provide authentication, confidentiality, and integrity security services for Web-based digital content is implemented as part of an application that would provide source input to a digital communication system.

SSL is noteworthy both because of its broad usage in securing Web-based financial and purchasing transactions and because it effectively makes use of a combination of cryptographic primitives to provide its security services. As an example, when a Web browser initiates an SSL session with a server, a unique session key is initially generated via asymmetric methods. This key is then employed with a symmetric algorithm and message digests to achieve processing efficiency.

As one might expect, communication security services implemented at different levels of a system may duplicate services. For example, a Web session employing SSL may be served by an operating system that provides Internet Protocol security (IPsec) services, which, in turn, may employ a WEP enabled wireless communication interface. In this example, the confidentiality service may be redundantly provided by all three components of the system.

The security of digital communications may also be provided incidentally to communication function itself. For example, code division multiple access (CDMA) wireless communications rely on the transmitter and receiver possessing a common sequence of bits, or pseudo-noise (PN). The PN is necessary to separate a specific signal from other similar signals sharing the same frequency band. However, because the PN is effectively a shared secret between the transmitter and receiver, it is capable of being employed to provide both confidentiality and authentication services.

CONCLUSION: FURTHER READING

Digital communications is a broad area that draws on many different but related aspects of electrical engineering. Perhaps the standard academic references for digital communication are *Digital Communications* by John G. Proakis (2000) and *Digital Communication* by Edward Lee and David Messerschmitt (1994). The text *Digital Communications* by Bernard Sklar (2000) provides an intuitive presentation of the concepts of digital communications. A good online manuscript by John Cioffi (n.d.-a, n.d.-b, n.d.-c) is available online. A good technical discussion of digital communication in wireless systems is found in *Principles of Mobile Communication* by Gordon L. Stuber (2001). The *Coding Theory and Cryptography—The Essentials* reference edited by Darrel Hankerson (2000) provides a good introduction to cryptography, which is perhaps the most relevant aspect of security for digital communications. The standard reference for digital signal processing is *Discrete-Time Signal Processing* by Alan V. Oppenheim and Ronald W. Schafer (1999). For a basic reference on vector spaces, *Elementary Linear Algebra: Applications Version* by Howard Anton and Chris Rorres (1991) is a good text.

There are many advanced concepts in digital communication that were just barely covered. For example, *Elements of Information Theory* by Thomas M. Cover and Joy A. Thomas (1991), provides a more thorough introduction to information theory. The book *Synchronization Techniques for Digital Receivers* by Umberto Mengali and Aldo N. D'Andrea (1997) provides a current treatment of synchronization in digital communication systems. Forward error correction is a topic that was only briefly mentioned yet is of significant importance. A classic reference is *Error Control Coding: Fundamentals and Applications* by Shu Lin and Dan J. Costello (1982). A text that treats some current topics is *Fundamentals of Codes, Graphs, and Iterative Decoding* by Stephen B. Wicker and Saejoon Kim (2002).

Current research in digital communication appears in a variety of journals including the *IEEE Transactions on Communications* (http://www.comsoc.org/pubs/jrnal/transcom.html), the *IEEE Transactions on Signal Processing* (http://www.itsoc.org), the *IEEE Transactions on Information Theory* (http://www.ieee.org/organizations/society/sp/), among others. Research in the areas of security and digital communication appears in these journals as well as the *ACM Transactions on Information and System Security*.

GLOSSARY

A/D Analog to digital converter.

Asymmetric Key Encryption An encryption process that employs one key for the encryption process and a separate key for the decryption process.

Bandpass A type of communication signal that has information modulated onto a carrier.

Baseband A type of communication signal that does not have information modulated onto a carrier.

Capacity The maximum data rate for which nearly errorless transmission can occur.

Carrier A high frequency sinusoid that shifts the spectrum of a baseband signal to higher frequencies, making it bandpass.

Channel Coding The process of adding redundancy to the transmitted data stream for the purpose of improving resilience to errors caused by the channel.

Ciphertext The information produced by the process of encryption.

D/A Digital to analog converter.

Decryption The process of transforming encrypted data to its original unencrypted form.

Demodulation The process of extracting the transmitted digital data from the continuous waveform observed at the receiver.

Digital Signature An encryption-based authentication method employing secret information used to affirm the origin of electronic documents.

Downconversion Process of converting a bandpass signal to a baseband signal by removing the carrier frequency.

Encryption The process of encoding data to prevent unauthorized access during transmission.

IP (Internet Protocol) Security An Internet network layer security protocol providing authentication, confidentiality, and message integrity services.

Message Digest Function An assumed one-way function, for which the domain is all positive integers and the range is a set of fixed length integers.

Modulation The process of converting digital data to continuous waveforms for transmission on a communication medium.

Plaintext Information before the process of encryption.

Private Key A key employed in asymmetric cryptography that is available only to its owner in the protocol.

Public Key A key employed in asymmetric cryptography that is shared with all participants in the protocol.

Receiver Sensitivity The minimum required signal level for a receiver to be able to demodulate the received signal.

Secure Socket Layer (SSL) An Internet application layer security protocol providing authentication, confidentiality, and message integrity services.

Signal to Noise Ratio (SNR) Essentially the ratio of the received signal power to the noise power.

Source Generic name for the component that generates the information stream that is the input to the transmitter.

Source Encoding The process of removing redundancy from the information stream provided by the source.

Symbol A representation of a set of bits in the digital or analog domain.

Symmetric Key Encryption An encryption process that employs the same key for both encryption and decryption.

Synchronization The process of ensuring that the transmitter and receiver operate in a synchronous manner.

Upconversion Process of converting a baseband signal to a bandpass signal by increasing the carrier frequency.

CROSS REFERENCES

See *Conducted Communications Media; Radio Frequency and Wireless Communications Security; Routers and Switches; Wireless Channels.*

REFERENCES

Borisov, N. (2006) *WEP security*. In H. Bidgoli (Ed.), *The Handbook of Information Security* (Vol. 3). Hoboken, NJ: John Wiley & Sons.

Bossert, M. (1999). *Channel coding for telecommunications*. Wiley.

Buell, Duncan A. (2006). *The advanced encryption standard (AES)*. In H. Bidgoli (Ed.), *The Handbook of Information Security* (Vol. 2). Hoboken, NJ: John Wiley & Sons.

Cioffi, J. M. (n.d.-a). EE 379A—Digital communication: Signal processing. Retrieved from http://www. stanford.edu/class/ee379a/

Cioffi, J. M. (n.d.-b). EE379B—Digital communication II: Coding. Retrieved from http://www.stanford.edu/class/ee379b/

Cioffi, J. M. (n.d.-c). EE 379C—Advanced digital communication. Retrieved from http://www.stanford.edu/class/ee379c/

Costello, D. J., & Lin, S. (1982). *Error control coding*. Prentice Hall.

Couch, L. W. II. (2001). *Digital and analog communication systems* (6th ed.). Prentice Hall.

Cover, T. M., & Thomas, J. A. (1991). *Elements of information theory*. Wiley-Interscience.

Daum, M., & Dobbertin, H. (2006) *Hashes and message digests*. In H. Bidgoli (Ed.), *The Handbook of Information Security* (Vol. 2). Hoboken, NJ: John Wiley & Sons.

Guizani, M. (2004) *Wireless communications and applications*. In H. Bidgoli (Ed.), *The Internet Encyclopedia* (Vol. 3). Hoboken, NJ: John Wiley & Sons.

Hankerson, D. (Ed.). (2000). *Coding theory and cryptography—The essentials* (2nd ed.). Marcel Dekker.

Howard, A., & Rorres, C. (1991). *Elementary linear algebra: Applications version* (6th ed.). Wiley.

Kim, C.-S, & Jay Kuo, C.-C. (2004) *Data compression*. In H. Bidgoli (Ed.), *The Internet Encyclopedia* (Vol. 1). Hoboken, NJ: John Wiley & Sons.

Lee, E., & Messerschmitt, D. (1994). *Digital communication* (2nd ed.). Kluwer Academic.

Mengali, U., & D'Andrea, A. N. (1997). *Synchronization techniques for digital receivers*. Plenum.

Oppenheim, A. V., Schafer, R. W., & Buck, J. R. (1999). *Discrete-time signal processing* (2nd ed.). Prentice Hall.

Pigg, T. L. (2004) *Conducted communications media*. In H. Bidgoli (Ed.), *The Internet Encyclopedia* (Vol. 1). Hoboken, NJ: John Wiley & Sons.

Proakis, J. G. (2000). *Digital communications* (4th ed.). McGraw-Hill.

Rubin, Bradley S. (2006) *Public key alogrithms*. In H. Bidgoli (Ed.), *The Handbook of Information Security* (Vol. 2). Hoboken, NJ: John Wiley & Sons.

Smart, N.P. (2006) *Elliptic curve cryptography*. In H. Bidgoli (Ed.), *The Handbook of Information Security* (Vol. 2). Hoboken, NJ: John Wiley & Sons.

Speciner, M. (2006) *Data encryption standard (DES)*. In H. Bidgoli (Ed.), *The Handbook of Information Security* (Vol. 2). Hoboken, NJ: John Wiley & Sons.

Sklar, B. (2000). *Digital communications* (2nd ed.). Prentice Hall.

Stuber, G. L. (2001). *Principles of mobile communication* (2nd ed.). Kluwer Academic.

Ugweje, O. C. (2004) Radio frequency and wireless communications. In H. Bidgoli (Eds.), *The Internet Encyclopedia* (Vol. 3). Hoboken, NJ: John Wiley & Sons

Wicker, S. B., & Kim, S. (2002). *Fundamentals of codes, graphs, and iterative decoding*. Kluwer Academic.

Local Area Networks

Wayne C. Summers, *Columbus State University*

INTRODUCTION TO LOCAL AREA NETWORKS

A network is a collection of two or more devices linked together. Typically the connection is a physical connection using wires or cables, although wireless connections are also possible for networks. In addition to the hardware required for this connection, there is communication software necessary to allow the communications to occur. Networks facilitate the sharing of resources, including hardware, software, and data, as well as providing a mechanism for enhancing communications between computers and users of computers.

Networks can be primarily classified as local area networks and wide area networks (WANs). The main distinction between these classifications of networks is the radius of the network. A Local Area Network is a network where the computers are physically close together. This may mean that the computers are in the same room, the same building, or even at the same site. Computers in a Wide Area Network are often distributed beyond metropolitan areas. The Internet is an example of a WAN. Other classifications of networks may include metro area networks (MANs) and storage area networks (SANs).

Why Do We Want to Network Computers?

In the early days of computing, there were a small number of computers, which could be used by only one person at a time. With the emergence of time-sharing in the 1960s, individual computers were able to be used by more than one user simultaneously. This significantly expanded the functionality of computers but had several limitations. Chief among the limitations was that as more users connected to the shared computer, the amount of resources available to each user's transaction became less. In the late 1970s and early 1980s, the personal computer (PC) resulted in the return of one computer/one user (Figure 1). Finally in the 1990s, hardware and software became available to network multiple PCs (Figure 2). Before LANs, copies of data needed to be kept by every user of the data on each computer, copies of software or application programs used by each user had to be installed on each computer, and every computer needed its own printer. Networking computers alleviates some of this need for redundancy, although there will also be some redundancy needed for backup purposes.

Data in a networked environment can be shared. Each user can access the data from other computers via the network. This feature of networks helped speed the transition from mainframe computing to networked computing. Networked computers allow important information to be shared among different computer users. Rather than keeping copies of data on each computer, one copy of the data can be kept on a server and accessed remotely via the network. Changes to the data can be made once and then accessed by all.

Rather than installing software on every computer, software can be shared in a network environment. Application programs can be stored on one computer and run remotely from another computer. In an office configured with multiple nonnetworked computers, each computer must have installed a copy of each application program that is used. In addition to the need to purchase copies of the software for each computer, the software must be

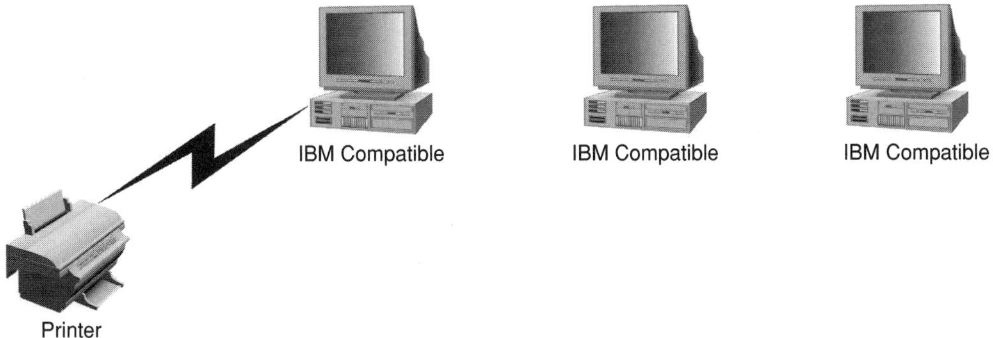

Figure 1: Before networks.

installed and maintained on each computer. Network versions of many application programs can be purchased. A networked version of software is typically much cheaper than purchasing large numbers of a particular piece of software. Network software needs to be installed only once on a server, allowing users on the other computers to access the software. When it is time to upgrade the software, it needs to be done only once on the server, instead of on all of the computers. Installing software on multiple computers simultaneously can be facilitated using a computer network.

Networks facilitate the sharing of hardware. Hardware can be installed in one location and accessed over the network from other computers. Printers can be networked so that multiple users can share the same printer or other hardware device. Other peripheral devices, including modems, CD and DVD ROMs, and networking devices, such as routers, can all be shared using a LAN.

Before LANs, computer users who needed to communicate with others had to use traditional methods, such as physically visiting another user, calling on the telephone, or have a letter delivered to the other person. Communications has been enhanced tremendously with e-mail and instant messaging (IM). E-mail and IM are facilitated by the use of a LAN.

TYPES OF LANs

A computer that can access a network are often referred to as a computer workstation or host. Any device (workstation, printer, modem, etc.) that connects to a network is called a node.

Many of the early networks allowed simply the sharing of resources among PCs. These types of networks are called peer-to-peer networks. Each computer has the same potential for sharing files and hardware devices. A peer-to-peer network is easy to design and maintain but is limited in its capabilities.

Most networks today are classified as client/server networks. In a client/server network, one or more of the computers function as servers, whereas the remainder of the computers functions as clients. A server is a computer that provides a service, whereas a client computer makes use of the service provided. Examples of servers include print servers, file servers, mail servers, and Web servers. A print server (Figure 3) is a computer or peripheral device that provides access to one or more printers across the network. Print servers were among the earliest type of servers. A file server provides a repository for files that can be accessed by other computers over the network. A mail or communication server manages the flow of incoming and outgoing electronic mail for users accessing the server from client workstations. A Web server runs software that provides access to World Wide Web documents.

Computers on a network can run more than one type of server software and can function as multiple types of servers. For example, a computer can have both Web server and e-mail server software installed and function as both a Web server and a communications server. A workstation can be both one type of server and a client for another type of server. For example, a computer can be running Web server software but print through the network using another computer that functions as a print server. It is generally not recommended that one computer

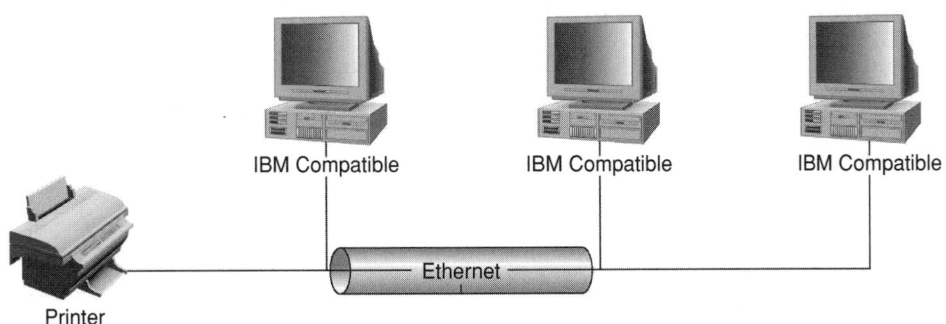

Figure 2: After networks.

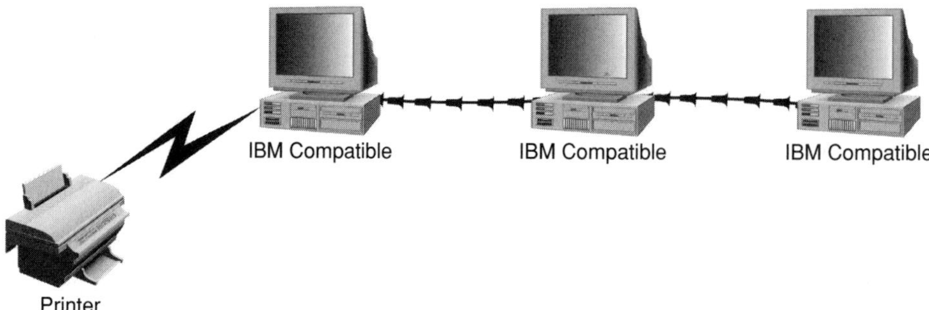

Figure 3: Print server.

function as more than one server. Doing so increases the likelihood of one point of attack on the network. However, using a separate computer for each server results in more potentially vulnerable computers. This increases the points of attack and needs to be taken into consideration. Running only one main service (e.g., e-mail) can significantly increase the reliability of the network as instability and maintenance associated with that service will typically not affect other services running on separate servers.

Similarly, it is recommended that servers not function as clients. Using a server as a client increases the opportunity for introducing security vulnerabilities that might compromise the security of the server.

Difference between LANs and WANs

As mentioned under Introduction to Local Area Networks, the main distinction between LANs and WANs is the radius of the network. A LAN is a network where the nodes are physically close together. In most cases, the nodes are in the same room, although they may be in the same building or in nearby buildings. Historically, networks with a radius greater than a kilometer or two are typically classified as WANs. Other ways of distinguishing between LANs and WANs include transmission speed and ownership. LANs are typically faster networks with speeds of at least 10–1000 megabits per second (Mbps). WANs are generally significantly slower, with most connections to WANs at around 1.5 Mbps, although there exist very high-speed WANs. LANs are owned by the organization where the network is used. WANs generally use hardware that is owned and operated by a network provider, although there are public agencies that do own and operate their own WANs. A final distinction is with the difference in protocols used by LANs and WANs. The next section describes two of the protocols (Ethernet and token ring) used by LANs. WANs typically use different protocols, including frame relay, ATM, and X.25. Recently Ethernet has started to be deployed in WANs as Metro Ethernet. These distinctions continue to blur significantly over the last several years as WANs get faster and LANs get larger.

LAN Topology

LANs can be organized in a variety of ways. One way to classify networks is by their electrical configuration or **logical topology**. This is often called the signal topology and is determined by how the nodes communicate with each other. This is basically the way that the data is transmitted between nodes. The main two logical topologies are **bus** and **ring**.

In a bus network, the data is broadcast from one node to all other nodes in the LAN even though the data may be intended for only one node. Each of the nodes receives the data but they are "read" only by the node where the data is intended. The data include an address for the destination node or nodes. Ethernet is the primary protocol that supports the bus logical topology.

In a ring network, the data are sent from one node to the next in sequential order in a circular fashion. Each node inspects the destination address of the data packet to determine if the data are meant for it. If the data are not meant for the node, the data packet is passed along to the next node in the logical ring.

LANs can also be classified by the physical layout of the network. The way that the nodes are physically connected to the network is known as the **physical topology**. The physical topology of the network can have a significant influence on a LAN's performance and reliability. The three main physical topologies are **bus, ring,** and **star**. There are also hybrid networks, including star-bus and star-ring, which incorporate parts of both types of networks.

In a bus topology (Figure 4), the nodes are arranged in a linear fashion, with terminators (Figure 5) on each end. The nodes are connected to the "bus" with connectors. Bus networks are easy to install but not very reliable. Any break in the connection, or a loose connection, will bring down a portion of the network and possibly the entire network.

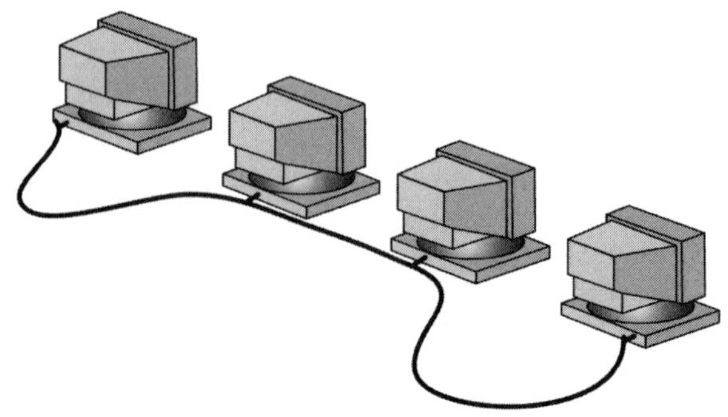

Figure 4: Bus network.

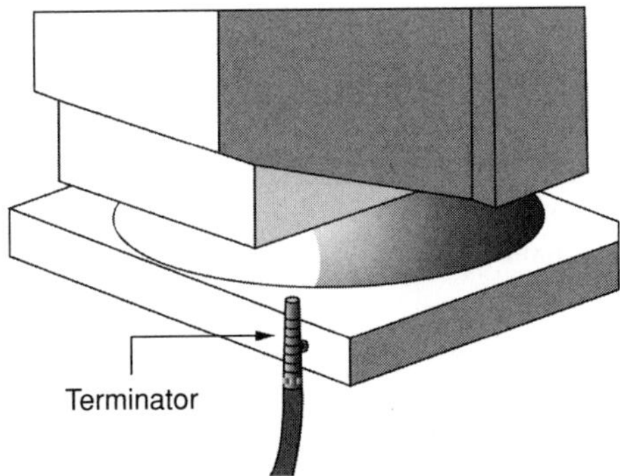

Figure 5: Terminator and BNC T-connector.

In a ring topology (Figure 6), each connected node is an active participant in the ring network. Each data packet is received by a node, and, if it is not intended for the node, it is passed along the ring to the next node. If one of the nodes or its network card malfunctions, a portion of the network stops functioning.

In a star network (Figure 7) each connected node is attached to a central device. Typically this device is a hub or a switched hub, but it could also be other devices, including a multistation access unit (MAU). Star networks are more economical and easier to troubleshoot. Star networks do require an additional hardware device, such as a hub or switch, and additional cable. Because each node is independently connected to the central device, a failure affects only the single node. Of course, if the central device fails, the entire network fails.

A network's physical and logical topologies are not necessarily the same. For example, a twisted-pair Ethernet network is physically arranged with a star topology although the data are transmitted via a bus topology.

LAN Architecture

The most popular network architecture for LANs today is Ethernet. Ethernet was developed by Robert Metcalfe and others at the Palo Alto Research Center (PARC) around 1973. Ethernet uses the carrier sense multiple access with collision detection (CSMA/CD) access method. Carrier sense refers to each node being able to "listen" for other users using the network, only attempting to use the network if it is not being used. Multiple access means that any node on the network may use the network without requiring further permission. Collision detection lets the node know if a message was not delivered and controls the mechanism for retransmitting the data packet. CSMA/CD is most efficient when there are a limited number of nodes requesting access to the network.

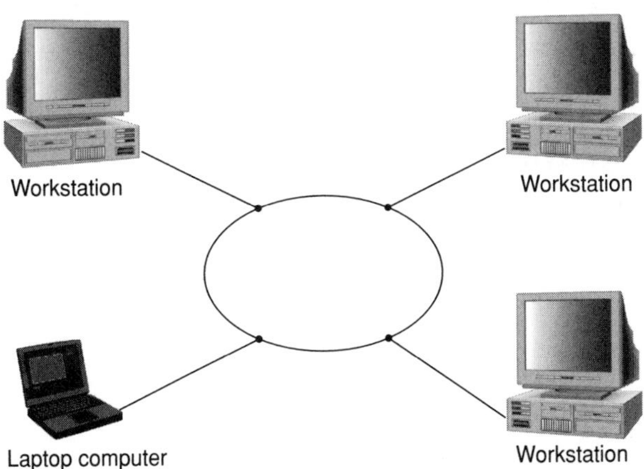

Figure 6: Ring network.

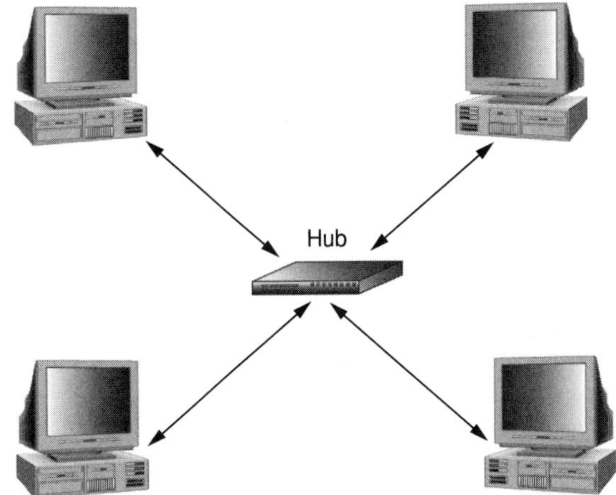

Figure 7: Star physical network.

In 1981, the first Ethernet standard was developed by a consortium composed of Digital, Intel, and Xerox. This was followed by a second Ethernet standard in 1982, called Ethernet II. Ethernet II (Figure 8) had the following characteristics:

- Bus topology
- Coaxial cable using baseband signaling
- 10 Mbps data rate
- Maximum station separation of 2.8 kilometers
- 1024 maximum number of stations

In addition, the IEEE developed a standard, also often referred to as Ethernet, called the IEEE 802.3 standard (Figure 9). The two standards are very similar and have similar frame layouts as shown.

Ethernet can run over a variety of media types, including several types of coax cable, twisted pair cable, and fiber optic cable, as well as wireless formats, including radio signals and infrared. Table 1 lists several of these media types. The first number indicates the speed in megabits

Destination MAC Address 6 octets	Source MAC Address 6 octets	Type 2 octets	Data Unit 46-1500 bytes	Frame Check Sequence 4 octets

Figure 8: Ethernet II frame layout.

Destination MAC Address 6 octets	Source MAC Address 6 octets	Length 2 octets	Logical Link Control IEEE 802.2 Data 46-1500 bytes	Frame Check Sequence 4 octets

Figure 9: IEEE 802.3 frame layout.

Table 1 Types of Network Media

Standard	Popular Name	Speed (Mbps)	Media	Maximum Segment Length (Meters)
10Base2	Thinnet; cheapnet	10	Thin coaxial cable RG-58	185
10Base5	Thicknet, yellow hose	10	Thick coaxial cable RG-8 or RG-11	500
10BaseT	10BaseT twisted pair Ethernet UTP	10	Unshielded twisted pair CAT3, CAT5	100
100BaseT4	Fast Ethernet	100	4 pair telephone grade cable	100
100BaseTX	Fast Ethernet	100	2 pair data grade cable	100
10BaseFL	Fiber Ethernet FOIRL	10	Multimode fiber optic cable	1000
100BaseFX	Fast Ethernet	100	2 strands fiber cable	412
1000BaseT	Gigabit Ethernet	1,000	Cat5e	100
10GBase	10 Gigabit Ethernet	10,000	Fiber	300

per second; the *base* refers to **baseband transmission,** meaning that the entire bandwidth is dedicated to just one data channel; and the last number or letter indicates the approximate maximum segment length or the media type.

A second network architecture, token ring (Figure 10), was developed in early 1970s by IBM. A token ring is often preferred for time-sensitive and mission-critical applications. Token ring uses the token passing access method. Only the computer that has the 24 bit packet of data called the token may use the network. This token is generated by a designated computer, called the active monitor, and passed around the ring until one of the computers wishes to use the network. When a computer wants to use the network, it seizes the token, changes the status of the token to busy, inserts its data frame onto the network and releases the token only when it receives a confirmation that the data packet has been received. A token ring network uses a sequential logical topology, which was traditionally a ring physical topology but now is typically a star topology. IBM specified two architectures that operated at 4 and 16 Mbps. Ethernet and token ring standards are typically associated with the Data Link Layer of the OSI model.

LAN HARDWARE AND MEDIA

There are a variety of media choices for connecting computers to a local area network. Early networks used copper wires, either coaxial or twisted pair. The standards detailing the LAN hardware and media are associated with the physical layer of the OSI model.

Copper Wire

Coaxial cable consists of a center wire surrounded by insulation and then a grounded shield of braided wire. The shield minimizes electrical and radio-frequency interference. Coaxial cable was typically either **thinnet** or **thicknet**. Thicknet (Figure 11) was the original standard for Ethernet and is defined by the IEEE 10Base-5 standard and uses 50-ohm coaxial cable (RG-8 or RG-11 A/U) with maximum lengths of 500 meters. Thinnet (Figure 12) is defined by the IEEE 10Base-2 standard and uses 50-ohm coaxial cable (RG-58 A/U) with maximum lengths of 185 meters. RG-58 is similar to the coaxial cable used with cable TVs. Cables in the 10Base-2 system connect to other devices with BNC connectors (Figure 13).

Twisted pair networking cable also has two different forms: **UTP** (unshielded twisted pair) and **STP** (shielded twisted pair). Both types of cable consist of either two or four pairs of wire. Each pair is twisted together. Shielded twisted-pair cable has an additional layer of conducting material surrounding the twisted pairs of wires. Unshielded twisted pair cable has no additional layer. Telephone companies use UTP cable with two twisted pairs of wires. UTP is the most common and least expensive method for networking computers (Figure 14). There are six categories of unshielded twisted pair cabling ranging from **Category 1** (**CAT1**), which is ordinary telephone cable used to carry voice, to **Category 6** (**CAT6**) (Figure 15), which is designed for high-speed networks. CAT6 uses 23 AWG copper as opposed to the 24 AWG used in Cat5e and lower, therefore the signal attenuates less with speed and distance. Cat6 also uses a tighter twist ratio that cuts down on internal crosstalk. UTP uses RJ45 connectors (Figure 16) to plug into the different networking devices.

Fiber Wire

Fiber-optic cable (Figure 17) is becoming more common as demand increases for higher transmission speeds. Fiber optic cable transmits data using pulsating laser light

Starting delimiter 1 octet	Access Control 1 octet	Frame control 1 octet	Destination address 6 octets	Source address 6 octets	Optional Routing Information Field up to 18 octets	Optional LLC Fields 3 or 4 octets	DATA Unlimited size	Frame Check Sequence 4 octets	Ending delimiter 1 octet	Frame status 1 octet

Figure 10: IEEE 802.5 token frame layout.

Figure 11: RG-58 coaxial cable.

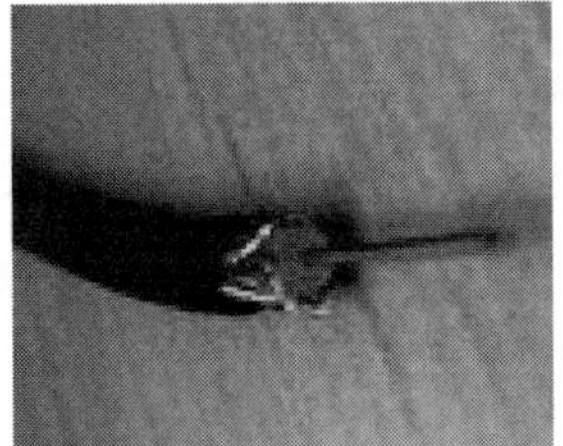

Figure 12: RG-8 coaxial cable.

Figure 13: BNC connector.

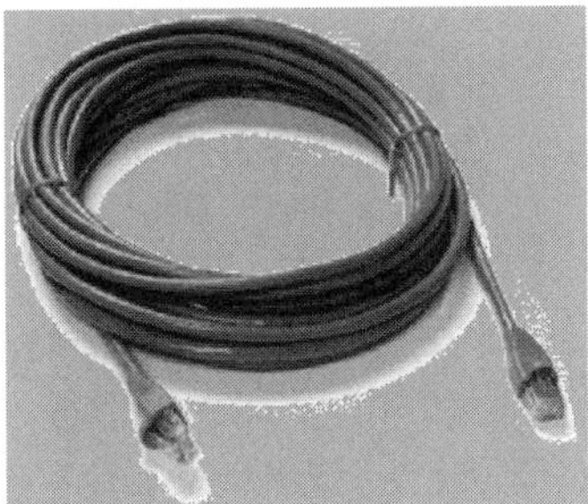

Figure 14: CAT5 patch cable.

Figure 15: CAT6 twisted pairs of wires.

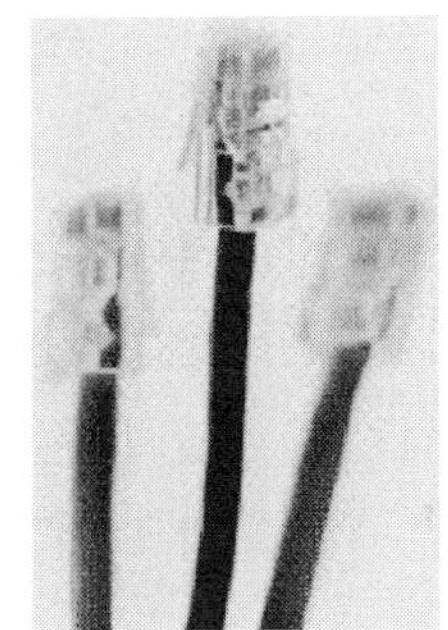

Figure 16: RJ45 connector.

instead of electricity. Fiber optic cable consists of a thin glass or plastic filament protected by thick plastic padding and an external plastic sheath. A light signal travels faster, farther, more reliably, and more securely than electricity. Fiber cable can send reliable signals at speeds of 100 GB/s as far as 10 kilometers. Unfortunately, fiber-optic cable is expensive to buy, install, and maintain. Although not impossible, it is more difficult to intercept data carried by fiber optic cable.

Wireless

Wireless LANs are rapidly becoming commonplace in businesses and homes. Early wireless LANs were light based using infrared light to transmit the data. Wireless LANs that are light based require line of sight for all devices on the network. Because of this limitation and the slow data speed, there are few light-based infrared wireless LANs.

Most wireless LANs use radio waves to transmit the data. Each device in a wireless network requires an antenna to receive and transmit the radio signals. Wireless LANs can be peer-to-peer or ad hoc networks (Figure 18) that require only that each device be equipped with a wireless network card that contains the antenna or a more complete network called an infrastructure network that requires an **access point** (Figure 19). The access point contains an antenna, a radio transmitter, and a wired network interface, typically an RJ45 port. The access point acts as a base station (similar to a hub) for the wireless network and also as a bridge between the wireless and wired networks.

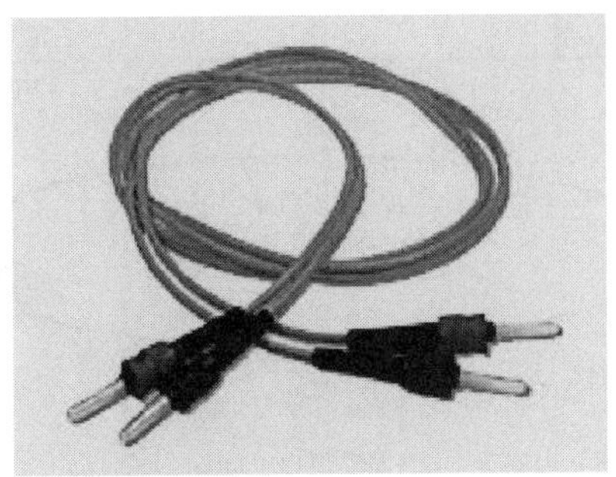

Figure 17: Fiber optic cable.

Figure 18: Peer-to-peer wireless network.

Regardless of whether the network is wired or wireless, every device on the network must be connected to the network with a network adapter or network interface card (NIC) (Figures 20–22). The card must be physically connected to the device, either installed directly into a slot in the computer or connected via a port, such as a USB port. The network card provides the interface between the node on the network and the network media. Because communication in a wireless network occurs through the air, it is easier for the signal to be intercepted. As wireless becomes more pervasive, security has become a significant issue.

Hardware Devices

Several factors limit the radius of a local area network. The farther a signal travels along a twisted pair or coaxial cable, the more likely it is to be degraded by noise. As the signal travels, it loses energy and becomes weaker, thus becoming difficult to read. As the network cable comes longer, it becomes more likely that two or more machines will transmit at the same time, causing a "collision." It will take longer for the machines to detect the collision. There are several ways to increase the radius of a network.

The simplest is to use a repeater. A repeater (Figure 23) is an electronic device used to extend the distance of a network by amplifying the signal and reducing the electrical interference within the network. The repeater relays the data from one segment of the network to another without inspecting or modifying the data. Repeaters can also be used to connect segments of the network that use different cable media. Repeaters operate at the physical layer of the network.

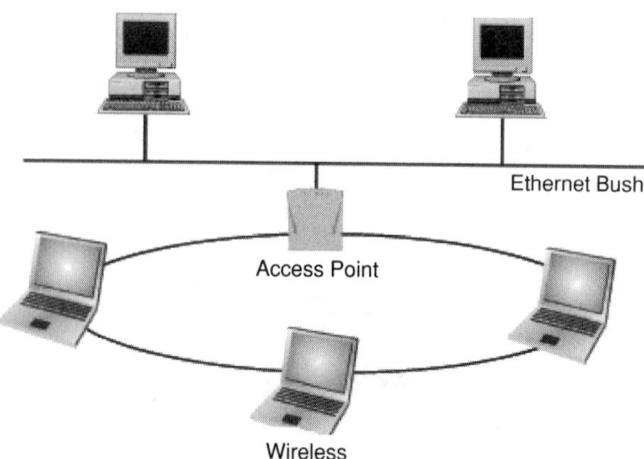

Figure 19: Wireless network with access point.

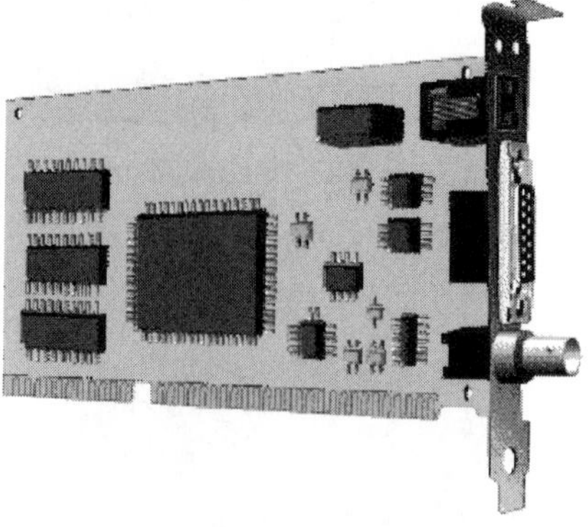

Figure 20: Network interface card with RJ45, BNC, and AUI connections.

Figure 21: Network interface card with RJ45 connection.

Figure 22: PCMCIA wireless NIC.

Figure 23: Repeater.

Figure 24: Four-port hub.

A hub (Figure 24) is a multiport repeater that allows the distance of the network to be extended as well as allowing multiple devices to connect to the LAN. A hub is a device that brings all of the connections together (Figure 25). Like a repeater, the hub does not inspect or modify the data. Ethernet networks with only hubs and repeaters are constrained by the 5-4-3 rule, which limits the connections between two nodes to no more than five segments with no more than four repeaters where no more than three of the repeaters connect additional nodes.

Repeaters and hubs boost the signals on a network but do not solve problems involving collisions. Other devices, however, alleviate this problem by limiting traffic on the network. A bridge (Figure 26) is an electronic device that connects two or more networks typically running the same network protocols. It allows the isolation of the different networks. The different networks may have different topologies. Bridges are used to increase the efficiency of a network by limiting the collision domain to "one side" of the bridge. By doing this, networks can be expanded with no significant increase of traffic. Bridges operate at the physical and data link layers and make use of the physical addresses associated with the network cards.

A switch (Figure 27) is a multiport bridge. Switches are often referred to as switching hubs. A switch combines the appearance and functionality of a hub with the additional functionality of a bridge. Switches provide full duplex transmission between nodes eliminating collisions and enhancing the performance of the networks. Switches have typically replaced hubs in most local area network installations. A specialized type of bridge or switch called a *translating bridge* can be used to connect two of more networks using different protocols (i.e. Ethernet and token ring).

Although typically not part of a LAN, routers provide the interface between a LAN and WAN or between different LANs. Routers route the traffic between different networks by maintaining tables of networks and their addresses. Routers forward Layer 3 IP datagrams between different Layer 2 broadcast domains. Routers are more sophisticated than switches and bridges and work at a higher level of the network.

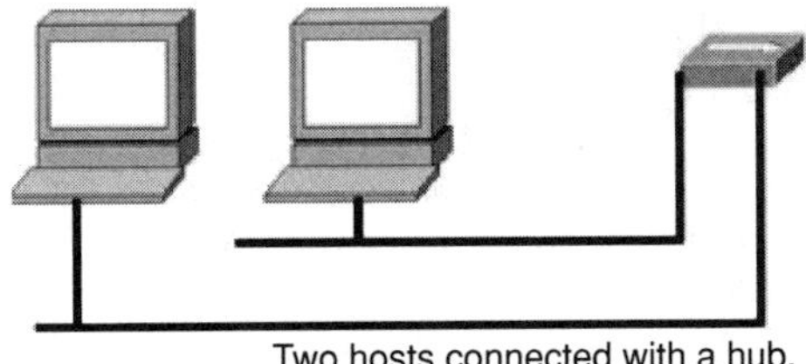

Figure 25: Hub connecting two hosts.

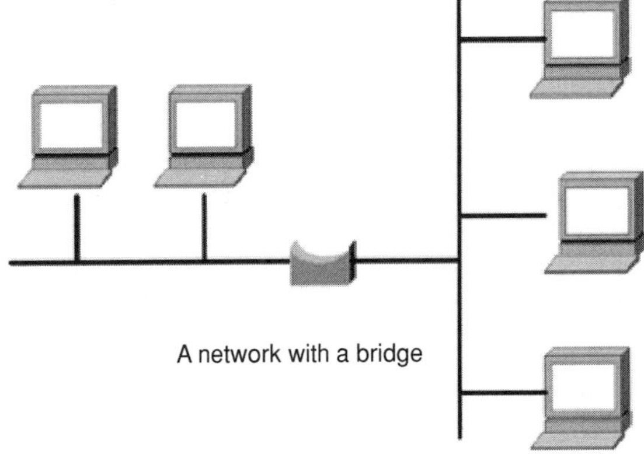

Figure 26: Bridges.

LAN SOFTWARE

Local area network software can be classified into three categories: network operating systems, network utilities, and network applications. Not too long ago, operating systems and network operating systems were distinct. Today almost all operating systems have the functionality of a network operating system built in. In other words, you do not need to add any additional software to the operating system to get the computer to function on a network. All of today's popular operating systems, including all recent versions of Microsoft Windows, all versions of Linux and UNIX, and all versions of the Macintosh OS, will support the connection of a computer to a network right out of the box. In addition to the usual computing tasks performed by an operating system, a network operating system also

- Manages the network connection
- Directs data traffic onto and off of the network
- Manages the flow of data between the different devices
- Manages communication and messages between the network users
- Provides for security of the data and other resources available the network

8-port switch

Figure 27: Switches.

The network operating system provides the interface between the LAN hardware and the applications running on the host.

Included with most of the network operating systems are specific network utilities, such as ping, ARP, and traceroute, which provide network functions. Ping sends an Internet control message protocol (ICMP). ECHO_REQUEST and ECHO_REPLY packet data to another device to indicate the time it takes to reach a target machine. Ping is a useful utility for troubleshooting networking problems. Address resolution protocol (ARP) is used to map the physical address of a networked device to the corresponding network IP address that has been assigned to the device. Traceroute uses the ping utility to map the route packets of data taken from a source to a destination machine. Network operating systems typically include drivers for most network adapters so the adapter can be plugged into the computer and the computer can be functioning on the network without too much additional configuration.

Network application software includes client front-end software that is specific for use by client computers. This would include programs such as Web browsers and e-mail software clients that would be run when needed. Hosts functioning as servers would have server software that would be constantly running, waiting for connections from clients (e.g., Web servers and e-mail servers). Other types of network application software include database client and server software as well as groupware software.

ROLE AND APPLICATIONS OF LANs IN THE INTERNET, INTRANET, EXTRANET, AND E-COMMERCE WORLDS

One of the major uses of local area networks is to facilitate connections by users to the Internet. This requires the connection of the LAN to the Internet via a dial-up telephone connection, a broadband connection, or a leased line. A dial-up connection requires a modem that converts the network's serial digital signal to the phone line's analog signal. A broadband connection typically requires a digital subscriber line (DSL), integrated digital services network (ISDN) or cable modem and a router and hub. A leased line connection requires a router that is then connected to another hardware device called a CSU/DSU (channel service unit/data service unit). The CSU/DSU in turn connects the network's router to the end of the leased line (e.g., T1) and converts the network's serial data signal to and from the leased line's digital signal. The leased line provides a high-speed Internet connection for the organization owning the LAN. The leased line is typically leased from a telecom provider through an Internet service provider (ISP). The ISP maintains the actual connection to the Internet using its own router.

Connecting a LAN to the Internet requires that the devices on the LAN support the TCP/IP suite of protocols that provide the foundation of the Internet. These protocols are necessary for computers on the LAN to be able to communicate with devices in other parts of the Internet. The TCP/IP suite of protocols include the following:

- Transmission control protocol (TCP) establishes and maintains the Internet connection
- Internet protocol (IP) handles the routing of packets of data across the Internet
- Simple mail transfer protocol (SMTP) receives and delivers e-mail messages
- Hypertext transfer protocol (HTTP) facilitates the delivery of Web documents
- File transfer protocol (FTP) transfers files
- Telnet allows users to remotely connect to other computers over the Internet

Many organizations have set up their own internal Internet called an intranet. An intranet is a private network that uses many of the same protocols as the Internet. An intranet appears to the user like the Internet, but it is typically not open to anyone outside the organization. An intranet is not a replacement for a LAN but rather runs within a LAN and supports many of the same applications as the Internet, typically Web servers and browsers, and e-mail servers and clients, as well as additional groupware software. The core of most intranets is the Web site, which typically contains most of the internal documents that need to be disseminated among the organization's members. Setting up an intranet site on an organization's LAN requires a lot of organization and planning in selecting the hardware, software, and data needed to create a functional intranet.

Some organizations have taken the intranet concept one step further and linked distributed parts of the organization together through the Internet via an extranet. An extranet is basically an intranet that may include access by customers, suppliers, and trusted partners.

WIRELESS LOCAL AREA NETWORKS

Wireless local area networks (WLANs) are rapidly becoming commonplace in offices and homes. WLANs provide the freedom to access data without being tethered to the network with wires. WLANs enable users to take laptops and handheld computers anywhere, anytime, and still be able to access the network. This is becoming more important in today's world of information.

Wireless networks are easier and less expensive to install. Wireless networks require spending less money on cable and not needing to spend additional money and time installing the cable. Wireless access points and NICs have become much cheaper in the past year. Installing a wireless network involves turning on the access points, installing the software for the access points and NICs, and identifying the access points for the NICs to connect to. Modifying a wireless network is easier but does have its issues. There is no need to remove and/or relocate cable. There is no longer a concern for network cable failure.

Companies are using WLANs for keeping track of inventory in warehouses. Workers who need to be constantly in contact with their network are more frequently using WLANs. WLAN devices have become commonplace among workers in the health care industry. One area where WLANs are beginning to have a great impact is in education. Students and faculty no longer need to find wired computer labs to communicate and work. With wireless devices, students and faculty can access the networks in any buildings where wireless access points have been installed.

Wireless networks still have some drawbacks. Chief among them are the limitations on distance and bandwidth. The radius of a WLAN can be extended by adding additional access points and RF repeaters to the network. Adding additional access points on the same channel can also help increase the bandwidth of the WLAN. There are also new standards and associated wireless devices emerging that support increased bandwidth. 802.11b and 802.11g use the unlicensed 2.4-GHz ISM band and support transmission speeds up to 11 and 54 Mbps respectively. A third standard, 802.11a, uses the 5-GHz UNII band and supports transmission speeds up to 54 Mbps.

The other major drawback for WLANs is security. A WLAN transmits radio signals over a broad area. This allows an intruder to lurk anywhere and intercept the signals from the wireless network. One way of inhibiting access to wireless network is to turn on wired equivalent privacy (WEP). WEP relies on a secret key that is shared between a mobile station and the access point. The secret key is used to encrypt packets before they are transmitted, and an integrity check is used to ensure that packets are not modified in transit. Even though WEP is easily compromised, it is still useful for home-based LANs as a first line of defense. Additional levels of security are now being developed and implemented to protect the transmission of data.

LAN INSTALLATION

Before a LAN is installed, a lot of planning needs to take place. The process can typically be broken down into seven steps as follows:

1. Needs analysis
2. Site analysis
3. Equipment selection
4. Site design
5. Server configuration
6. Installation schedule
7. Installation

Needs Analysis

The first aspect of installing a local area network is determining the needs of the organization and the users. Is a local area network needed? What aspects of the network are needed? Who will be using the network? What will they be using the network for? Will a local area network help the bottom line of the organization?

Reasons for installing a local area network might include the following:

- Need for improved communication
- Need for centralizing data
- Need for sharing hardware
- Need for application sharing
- Need for automating work flow
- Need for enhanced security of data

Site Analysis

Once a need has been established, it is necessary to determine where the LAN will be installed. What parts of the organization's site will be networked? Where will the servers be located? A site plan will need to be drawn. If a fire escape plan is available, it can be used as a template for the building and location of rooms and doors. It is best if the architectural plans can be found. The site plan (Figure 28) is a map of the location where the network is installed and should include the following:

- The dimensions of the site, including the location of each employee

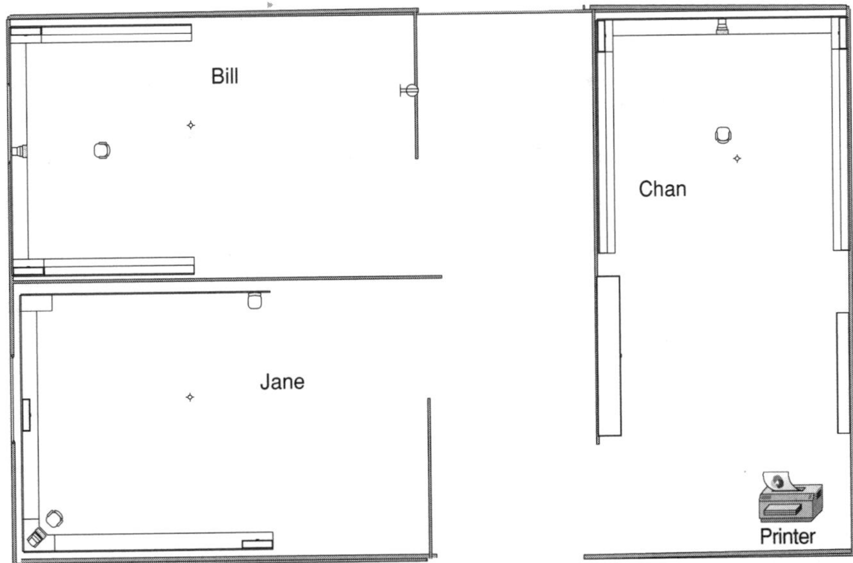

Figure 28: Sample site plan.

Table 2 Equipment Inventory Form

Serial Number	xxxxxxxxxxx
Processor	Intel Pentium 4—1.8 GHz
RAM size and configuration	256 MB; 2 × 128 MB DIMM
Hard disk	20 Connor GB
Other drives	One 3.5″, 1.44 MB
CD-ROM	Toshiba 24X
Monitor	17″ Toshiba XVGA
Warranty information	Expires Jan. 2003

- The location of all immovable objects, including doors and windows
- The current location of all moveable objects
- The location of heating, ventilation, and air conditioning systems and ducts
- The location of electrical outlets and the current wiring scheme
- The current location of all computer equipment and the planned location for any additional devices

Equipment Selection

As the site plan is developed, an inventory of available equipment needs to be conducted. An inventory of equipment will identify the capabilities of the equipment incorporated into the proposed network. This will identify which equipment will be obsolete once the network is installed and which equipment will require modification. Older workstations may still be useful as print servers. Table 2 shows the features to be noted in the equipment survey.

Once the current equipment has been inventoried, it is now time to identify new equipment that will need to be purchased. This list should be correlated with the user needs identified earlier. Once this list is prepared, vendors can be contacted, soliciting their recommendations for meeting the hardware and software needs. Be sure to consider any infrastructure constraints including electrical power and distances. Table 3 is an example of a form that could be used to compare different vendor proposals.

Site Design

Once the site plan from the site analysis has been completed and the equipment lists have been completed, it is time to create a working site design (Figure 29). This design will include details of where all devices including networking devices will be located. The location for all network connections must be indicated. The location of all network cable, patch panels, and riser backbone must be delineated.

Server Configuration

Once the computers arrive that will be installed as servers, they need to be configured. Server software needs to be installed and the directory structure of the server needs to be organized. The directory structure begins with the root directory with all other directories within it and the files and subdirectories within those. Typically, you will have directories for the network operating system, separate directories for each server application, and directories for the clients who will be connecting to the server. Network information, including MAC and IP addresses for all devices, needs to be recorded.

Installation Schedule

Networks take a considerable amount of time to install. It is important to have an installation schedule. There will be times when employees' computers will need to be turned off and possibly moved. Disruption needs to be minimized wherever possible. Be sure to include in the installation schedule the possibility for shipping delays on the equipment that has been ordered. Be sure to read the manuals before the installation begins so that there will be no surprises once the installation starts. Also, prepare the site before the installation begins. This may

Table 3 Vendor Worksheet

	Vendor 1			**Vendor 2**			**Vendor 3**		
	Model	**Quan.**	**Price**	**Model**	**Quan.**	**Price**	**Model**	**Quan.**	**Price**
Server									
H'ware									
S'ware									
Workstations									
H'ware									
S'ware									
NIC									
Switches/hubs									
bridges									
Access points									
Routers									
Cabling									
Other									
TOTAL COST:									

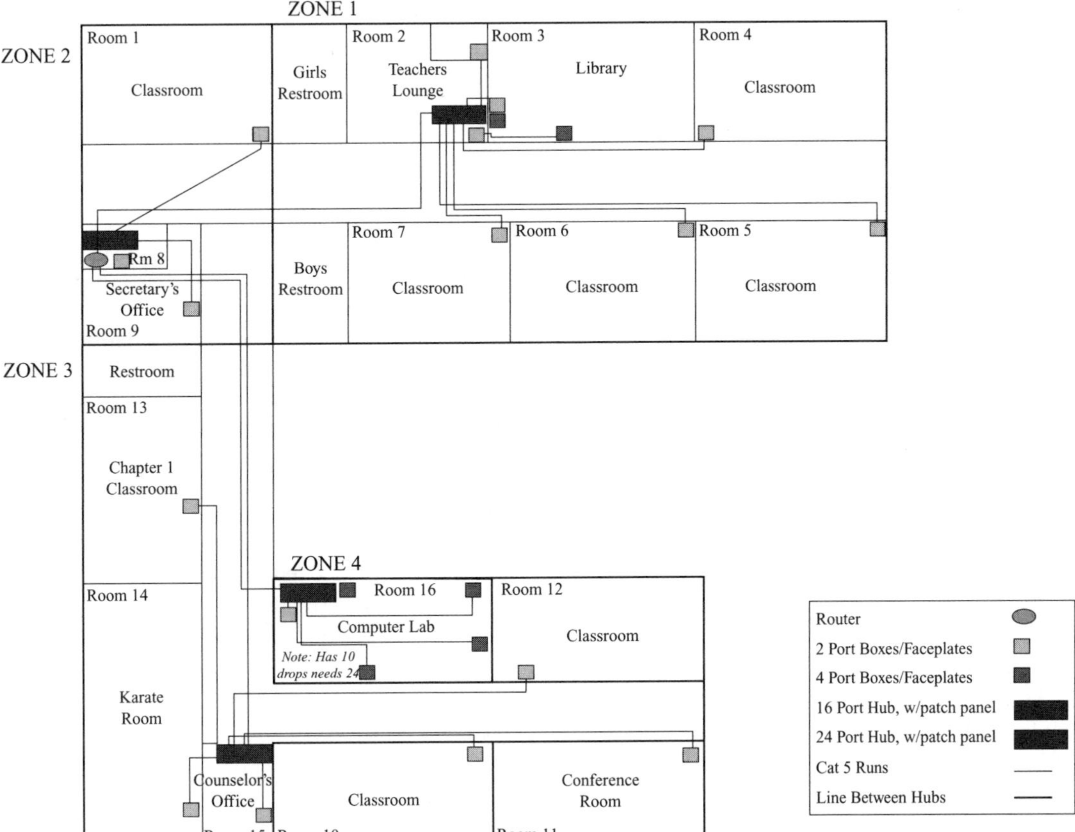

Figure 29: Sample site design.

involve moving furniture, installing new outlets, and removing equipment that will no longer be used. Do not forget to back up any data on systems that will be affected by the move.

Installation

Before the installation begins, it is best to discuss everything with someone who has been through a LAN installation before. Have this person look over the designs, schedules, and forms to ensure that nothing has been forgotten. Depending on the size of the installation, it may take anywhere from a couple hours to a couple of days. Be prepared for delays. If this is a wired network, conduit needs to be installed and the cable media will need to be pulled. This is the part that typically takes the longest time. While the cable media are being pulled or shortly thereafter, the remaining components will need to be installed. This would typically include the patch panels in the communications rooms and the wall outlets for each device that will be networked. Once this is completed, the electronic devices (hubs, switches, etc.) will need to be installed. If network cards need to be installed in the older computers, this will be done next. Finally, the software for the network cards will need to be installed on each workstation and server if it hasn't already been done. Be sure to install the appropriate network software.

The final two stages of the installation are the testing and training. Every device will need to be tested to ensure that its network connection works. This should be done before any of the users access the network. Be sure to test all of the network devices and the networked printers. Applications, service, and end-to-end testing must be performed. The final phase is training. Users will need to be trained in the procedures they will need to follow to use the network.

LAN ADMINISTRATION

Once the LAN has been installed, there are several key aspects of administering the network.

Configuration List

Using the equipment inventory forms developed during the installation along with similar documentation for the new devices, a set of configuration lists needs to be developed. These would include a list of all computers similar to the equipment inventory form, directory lists for each server that is installed, a list of all server users, a list of all printers and other shared devices. It is also very important to keep copies of the network plans developed for the installation of the network.

System Log

The system log is documentation for the network. It provides a detailed history of the network's hardware, software, and configuration features. As changes are made to the network, these changes need to be documented in the system log. As problems arise with the network, these also need to be documented in the system log. This log needs to be maintained from the beginning. The system log should include all hardware and software warranties, hardware and software information, current setup structure, backup and recovery plan, backup logs, and error/downtime logs.

Training

Training does not end after the network has been installed. The network is a dynamic part of an organization's computing system. As changes are made, employees will need additional training.

Backup

As more and more data are kept on networked servers and shared by more than one user, it becomes critical that a procedure be established for backing up critical data. This may be the most important task for a network administrator. Hardware and software can be replaced. New employees can be hired. But it is difficult to recreate large amounts of data. The network administrator must establish a schedule for backing up all critical data. Separate SANs or NASs may be needed to provide added storage protection. Critical software may not necessarily be replaced and should be backed up as well. Configuration files should be backed up also.

Security

Once computers become accessible to other individuals, security issues need to be considered. In a networked environment, users will need user ids and passwords. If security is extremely important, then encryption of data might also need to be implemented. If the local area network is attached to another network, then a firewall may be necessary to control access to critical data between the two networks.

LAN SECURITY

In today's world of ubiquitous local area networks, security is of the utmost importance. This is true whether the LAN is a peer-to-peer or client/server network. Security is all about confidentiality, integrity, and availability. Where necessary, information should be confidential. The information should be only available to those who are authorized to access it. The integrity of the information must be maintained. We need to be assured that the information has not been altered. The availability of the information must be preserved. Authorized users need to be able to access the information and computing resources when needed.

Securing a LAN requires a multilayered approach. One of the main themes in security is "defense in depth," where multiple layers of technology and multiple procedures need to be implemented to minimize the threats to the local area network.

Physical Security

"I touch it, I own it!" Without physical security, there is no security. Having physical access to the devices and computers on a network is the greatest vulnerability in network security. No matter how strong other facets of security, if an attacker can physically access computers and other devices, the LAN can be easily compromised.

All LAN servers must be locked in a physically secure area. Network devices and cable need to be protected from intentional and unintentional disruption. To avoid inadvertent compromises, servers should not be used as client workstations. It is too easy for client-based vulnerabilities to be compromised and affect the server software running on the same computer. Securing a LAN includes more than preventing attacks. An inadvertent loss of power to the computers and network devices can be catastrophic. All devices should be protected by surge protectors. Power to servers and other critical hardware needs to be stabilized using uninterruptible power supplies (UPS). The UPS battery needs to be checked regularly. An alternate power supply, such as a generator or second utility grid, should be available, especially for mission-critical LANs.

Access Security

The first line of defense is access control. Access to servers and data needs to be controlled. This can be implemented by instituting controls at the network level as well as individual controls at the directory and file levels. Connections to all servers and the network should be controlled through authentication procedures. All users must be registered and authenticated. There should be no guest accounts. Minimally the use of user ids and passwords should be required for all connections to the network. All users need to use nontrivial passwords that are difficult to "guess." These passwords should be frequently changed and checked. Unfortunately, too many passwords can create operational issues. Often, users will forget their passwords. A mechanism needs to be in place to address this problem. All default passwords for servers, operating systems, and applications must be changed immediately. All obsolete user accounts need to be terminated immediately. It may also be necessary to restrict user access to certain days and times to better control access to sensitive data.

There should be several levels of access to directories and files. These typically would include read, write, and execute. Users need to be given the minimum privileges to access all their files and directories. All data must be protected from access by unauthorized users. It is important that authorization is carefully planned. Audit logs of successful and unsuccessful access to systems and files may need to be kept to allow for tracking of problems that have arisen.

Data Security

Where necessary, critical data need to be protected. In addition to those mechanisms discussed above, additional layers of security may be necessary. In the case of databases, views need to be provided to permit users to access only the minimum that is necessary.

Data confidentiality is especially important. Where necessary, encryption software needs to be used to protect confidential and sensitive data. Controls need to be implemented to protect all confidential and sensitive data stored and/or processed on the LAN. These controls should include any removable media associated with the LAN. It is important that all confidential and sensitive data be removed before disposing of the media on which the data reside. Remember that simply deleting a file that contains the data may not be enough. Be sure to delete any copies of the files stored on backup media.

Backup procedures need to be implemented. All files servers need to be automatically backed up on a regularly scheduled basis. The backup media need to be kept on-site for immediate recovery. Copies of the backup media need to be kept off-site in case the on-site backups are compromised. Both sets of backups need to be tested and audited to ensure recovery.

Network Security

There are two major approaches to securing a local area network: host-based security and network-based security. Typically, both approaches are combined to provide multiple levels of security.

In host-based security, selected hosts are separately protected. This could range from installing antivirus software or personal firewalls on each computer in the network to installing a host-based intrusion detection system on each server. Minimally, every server should be protected with antivirus software and a personal firewall. If possible, the important servers should also be shielded by a host-based intrusion detection system.

Network-based security is equally important. Hardware-based security devices such as firewalls and intrusion detection devices can be placed at the perimeter of the network, typically inside the router, where they can monitor all traffic coming in and out of the local area network. Intrusion detection and intrusion protection devices can also be set up with agents installed on those hosts needing the most protection. These agents can then be monitored and managed from a central location. In more secure environments, there may be layers of network-based security both at the perimeter of the LAN as well as internal to the network. One layer of security is the placement of a firewall device (Figure 30) between the LAN (trusted network) and the outside (untrusted networks).

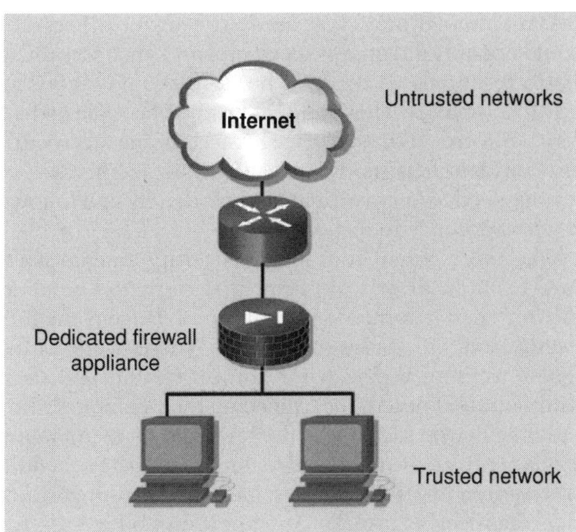

Figure 30: Placement of a firewall.

The network should be audited for illicit use of inappropriate software (e.g., sniffers and traffic monitors.) No unauthorized connections to the network should be permitted. This would include rogue wireless access points and modems connections.

Malware

Malware includes programs such as viruses and worms. To protect against most malware attacks, antivirus software needs to be installed on all servers and clients. It is imperative that this software be kept up to date on all computers. Most antivirus software vendors have procedures for automatically updating the software. The auto-update feature should be configured to the shortest time that is tolerable by the users. All foreign media and all files downloaded from the Internet must be scanned for malware. The antivirus software needs to be running continuously. In addition to updating the antivirus software, it is mandatory that all operating systems and applications running on all computers in the network be patched. "Patching host software is probably the single most important thing companies can do to improve their security" [Panko, 2004]. Users should be trained in how to disconnect their device from the network in the event of a virus attack to isolate their host. One vulnerability in an operating system or application can destroy the entire network of computers.

Policy, Procedures, and Awareness

"Security is not a product, it's a process" [Schneier, 1999]. Using any security product without understanding what it does, and what it does not protect against, is a recipe for disaster. Keep in mind that added security features tend to increase the complexity of the system and may decrease the degree of usability of the systems. Usability needs to be balanced with the increased need for security.

Any organization implementing or using a LAN must have a well-documented security policy. The policy should incorporate physical security procedures, e-mail, Internet acceptable usage, and network usage procedures. The policy should include procedures for incident response and a LAN risk analysis. The policy should include a focus on software use to ensure compliance with license agreements. All unauthorized copies of software should be removed from workstations and servers. The policy needs to outline what additional response is necessary when unauthorized software is discovered.

The policy must include procedures for ensuring that all software is patched on a regular basis. This is especially important for all security software, including antivirus software and any intrusion detection and prevention software protecting the LAN and its resources.

As mentioned, audit logs need to be invoked. These logs should not only document successful and unsuccessful access to resources on the LAN but also should record any and all anomalies. These audit logs must be reviewed regularly with procedures in place for addressing any security alerts or identified anomalies. All attacks and breaches of security need to be investigated immediately and followed up with appropriate responses.

"The most potent tool in any security arsenal isn't a powerful firewall or a sophisticated intrusion detection system. When it comes to security, knowledge is the most effective tool . . ." [Schweizer, 2003]. There needs to be a regular training program for administration and users. Administrators need to be trained on their responsibilities in managing the security of the LAN and its components. Regular security awareness sessions need to be scheduled and required for all employees, including training against social engineering attacks. An important policy is to train before deploying any component in the network.

CONCLUSION

Local area networks have played a very important role in providing computer access to large numbers of users. They have allowed users to share hardware, software, and, most importantly, data. They now also provide access to the Internet as well as organizations' intranets and extranets. With the emergence of wireless local area networks, the applications of local area networks will continue to expand. It is imperative that we secure the local area networks to ensure confidentiality, integrity, and availability of the data stored and processed by the LAN.

GLOSSARY

Access Point A hardware device consisting of one or more antennae, a radio transmitter, and a wired network interface. Used as a bridge between a wireless network and a wired network.

Bridge A network device for connecting two or more local area networks that typically use different media but the same network protocol.

Bus Network A network where the nodes are connected to the same wire. Data are broadcast from one node to all other nodes in the LAN even though the data may be intended for only one node.

Ethernet A common data link layer protocol for networking computers in a LAN.

Extranet A private portion of the Internet treated as an extension of an organization's intranet and allowing access to the organization's data by the organization's partners, customers, and so on.

Hub The central device in a star network for connecting multiple nodes to a network. It functions as a multiple-point repeater.

Internet A worldwide collection of networks linked together and built around the TCP/IP suite of protocols. It was originally conceived in 1969 by the Advanced Research Projects Agency (ARPA) of the U.S. government.

Intranet An organization's private internal network based on the TCP/IP suite of protocols.

Local Area Network (LAN) A data communication network of computers, peripheral devices and other network devices allowing data to be communicated at high speeds over short distances.

Logical Topology Based on how the devices of the network are electrically configured; also called electrical topology.

Network An interconnection of two or more computers or devices.

Network Interface Card (NIC) An adapter for connecting a computer or device to the network media.

Physical Topology Based on the way the nodes are physically configuration in the network.

Repeater A network device that retransmits the communication signal and is used for extending the radius of a network. It operates at the OSI physical layer.

Ring Network A network where the nodes are arranged in a closed loop where each device is connected directly to two adjacent devices.

Router A special-purpose network device that connects two or more networks at the OSI network layer.

Star Network The nodes are arranged so that each device is connected to a central device, typically a hub or a switch.

Switch A network device operating at the OSI data link layer that connects multiple network segments. It functions as a multiport bridge, allowing two devices to communicate only with each other at that moment.

Wide Area Network (WAN) A data communication network spanning geographically dispersed areas.

CROSS REFERENCES

See *Conducted Communications Media; Extranets: Applications, Development, Security and Privacy; Groupware: Risks, Threats, and Vulnerabilities in the Internet Age; Intranets: Principals, Privacy and Security Considerations; Wide Area and Metropolitan Area Networks; Wireless Local Area Networks.*

REFERENCES

Bishop, M. (2003). *Computer security: Art and science*. Boston, MA: Addison Wesley Professional.

Ciama, M. (2001). *Guide to designing and implementing wireless LANs*. Boston, MA: Course Technology.

Comer, D. (2001). *Computer networks and internets with internet applications, 3rd Edition*. Upper Saddle River, NJ: Prentice Hall.

Ethernet Codes master page. Available: http://www.cavebear.com/CaveBear/Ethernet/ (Date of access: September 8, 2004).

Goldman, J. (1997). *Local area networks: A client/server approach*. New York: John Wiley & Sons.

Goldman, J. (1998). *Applied data communications: A business-oriented approach, 2nd edition*. New York: John Wiley & Sons.

IEEE 802.3 CSMA/CD (ETHERNET). Available: http://grouper.ieee.org/groups/802/3/index.html (Date of access: September 8, 2004).

Link-layer technologies. Available: http://www.cs.columbia.edu/~hgs/internet/ethernet.html (Date of access: September 8, 2004).

Official Internet Protocol Standards. Available: http://www.rfc-editor.org/rfcxx00.html (Date of access: September 8, 2004).

Panko, R. (2001). *Business data communications and networking, 3rd edition*. Upper Saddle River, NJ: Prentice Hall.

Panko, R. (2004). *Corporate computer and network security*. Upper Saddle River, NJ: Prentice Hall.

Pfleeger, C. (2003). *Security in computing*. Upper Saddle River, NJ: Prentice Hall.

Schneier, B. (1999). Crypto-gram newsletter. Available: http://www.schneier.com/crypto-gram-9912.html

Schweizer, D. (2003). The state of network security. Available: http://processor.com (Date of access: August 22, 2004).

Spurgeon, C. Ethernet Web site. Available: http://www.ethermanage.com/ethernet/ethernet.html (Date of access: October 7, 2002).

Stallings, W. (2000). *Data & computer communications, 6th edition*. Upper Saddle River, NJ: Prentice Hall.

Subramanian, M. (2000). *Network management: Principles and practice*. Boston, MA: Addison Wesley.

Summers, W. (2004). Local area networks. In *The internet encyclopedia* (Vol. 2, pp. 515–526). New York: John Wiley & Sons,.

Taylor, E (2000). *Networking handbook*. New York: McGraw-Hill.

Thomas, R. (1989). *Introduction to local area networks, 2nd edition*. San Francisco: Sybex Network Press.

Webopedia. Available: http://www.pcwebopaedia.com/TERM/l/local_area_network_LAN.html (Date of access: September 8, 2004).

Wide Area and Metropolitan Area Networks

Lynn A. DeNoia, *Rensselaer Polytechnic Institute*

INTRODUCTION

In today's social, political, and economic environment, individuals and organizations communicate and operate over ever-increasing geographic distances. This means that access to and sharing of information and resources must extend beyond the "local" office, building, or campus out across cities, states, regions, nations, continents, and even beyond the planet. Bridging this diversity of distances in ways that satisfy application requirements for speed, capacity, quality, timeliness, and so on at reasonable cost is no simple task from either a technical or a business perspective. Additionally, increasing use of shared, public resources such as the Internet raises levels of concern over security. In this chapter we concentrate on the main elements required to meet such challenges in wide area and metropolitan area networks.

HISTORY AND CONTEXT

Definitions

The public networking arena has typically been divided into two segments with the following characteristics:

- Metropolitan area networks (MANs) are built and operated by service providers (SPs) who offer network services to subscribers for a fee, covering distances up to tens of miles, often within or surrounding a major city. MANs are often built by telecommunication companies, utility companies, or municipal agencies.
- Wide area networks (WANs) are built and operated by SPs who offer network services to subscribers for a fee, covering distances up to hundreds or thousands of miles, such as between cities, across or between countries, across oceans, and so on. WANs designed for voice are usually built by telecommunication companies. WANs for data are also called public data networks (PDNs).

Enterprises may choose to build private MANs and WANs instead of subscribing to public services. If it does not own its own cable or transmission facilities to all network locations, the enterprise can lease cable or transmission capacity from an SP but provides and operates all its own network equipment at the ends of each transmission link. Private networks may provide a higher degree of security when the traffic travels over dedicated cable or connections rather than through shared links or switching equipment.

Local area networks (LANs) are usually built and operated as private networks by individuals or enterprises for their own use. In addition, landlords may offer LAN services to tenants. In either case, the geographic scope of a LAN is typically limited to a building or campus environment, where all rights of way for cabling purposes belong to the individual/enterprise/landlord. The boundaries among LANs, MANs, and WANs began to blur as geographic limitations of networking technologies were extended with increasingly capable implementations over fiber optic cabling. Even the distinctions between private and public networks became more difficult to draw with the advent of "virtual private network" equipment and services.

Challenges

The number of options available to network designers in both the enterprise and SP communities continues to grow for both MANs and WANs. Multiple technologies and standards, increasing numbers and types of applications, higher expectations for MAN and WAN performance comparable to (or at least approaching) that found in a LAN environment, and pressure to keep unit costs low all combine to create enormous challenges for MAN and WAN builders. Infrastructure choices must last long enough, not just for cost recovery but also to achieve return on the investment. Designers must marry new

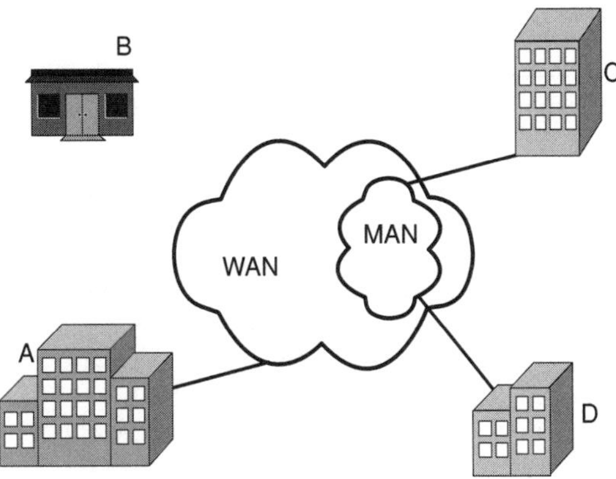

Figure 1: Connectivity.

technologies to their existing installed base, create smooth transitions (e.g., for network upgrades and new service rollouts) with minimal disruption to customer services, and add or enhance services to meet advancing customer expectations, all in an environment of economic and competitive pressure. Many SPs have begun to recognize that their long-term survival depends on a strategy of reducing the complexity (e.g., fewer technologies, fewer equipment vendors, fewer equipment types, and fewer management systems) of their infrastructure while maintaining the flexibility to adapt to changing application, user, and competitive requirements.

Functional Requirements

The basic function that subscribers seek from MAN and WAN providers is the ability to deliver traffic from one place to another (point-to-point) or to multiple others (multipoint). This begins with *connectivity*. For the network in Figure 1, traffic can flow from A to C and/or D but not to B. Once connectivity is established, the network must have sufficient *capacity* in bandwidth, switching, and routing to get the traffic from the source to its intended destination. Subscribers want services that are reliable, as measured by the percentage of time network resources are available when needed and by the amount of traffic (preferably none) that gets lost. Subscribers also want services that perform well enough so that their traffic gets delivered in a timely fashion, with minimal delay (low latency is particularly important for delay-sensitive traffic such as voice or video). Providers, conversely, want an infrastructure that is cost-effective, manageable, and capable of supporting revenue generation and profits. This especially includes adaptability to support a variety of new services as markets and technology develop.

Another characteristic of particular interest for subscriber traffic traversing shared resources in a public MAN/WAN (e.g., switches, transmission links, and storage) is security. Subscribers wishing to ensure data integrity and privacy can take responsibility for security by themselves implementing appropriate mechanisms (such as encryption) at their end points, or can contract with providers for security services.

Evolution and Coexistence

The first WANs were built from circuit-switched connections in the telephone system because that is what was available to cover the distances involved. Circuit switching continues to be useful, particularly when the computer devices being connected need to exchange messages in real time or with guaranteed delivery. For occasional traffic, dial-up connections similar to an individual telephone call are used. For continuous traffic or when applications cannot tolerate the delay involved in call setup, circuits are leased from a telephone company and "nailed up" into permanent connections that effectively become private as well as dedicated. For two connected locations the leased line is called a *point-to-point* connection (Figure 2a). More than two locations can be connected with a *multipoint* link (Figure 2b) if a sharing discipline is imposed to prevent traffic from one source interfering with traffic sent from another at the same time. With leased lines being dedicated to a particular subscriber, security is improved because traffic does not traverse any shared facilities among the SP's public network resources.

Two devices connected by a leased line may or may not send traffic continuously, wasting capacity when the line is idle. If there are multiple devices in one location to be connected to one or more devices in a destination location, a single leased line may be shared using a device at each end of the line called a multiplexer. Statistical multiplexing allows more devices to be connected than the capacity of the line could support in real time if all were to transmit simultaneously. This is called oversubscription. On average, it is quite likely that only some devices will be active, and the line is shared effectively with little traffic delay and less wasted capacity. However, when many devices are active, performance can be degraded. The sending multiplexer adds a label to each unit of traffic transmitted; the receiver reads (and removes) the label to figure out which device is the intended recipient and switches the traffic onto the appropriate output link. Packet switching is a form of statistical multiplexing, sharing network resources as packets are forwarded to their destinations. Each shared element is a potential point of security risk where eavesdropping could occur or where packets could be misdirected to an unauthorized or unintended destination.

Originally, circuit switching was designed to carry analog voice traffic and packet switching was designed for digital data. Today, however, public networks convert all types

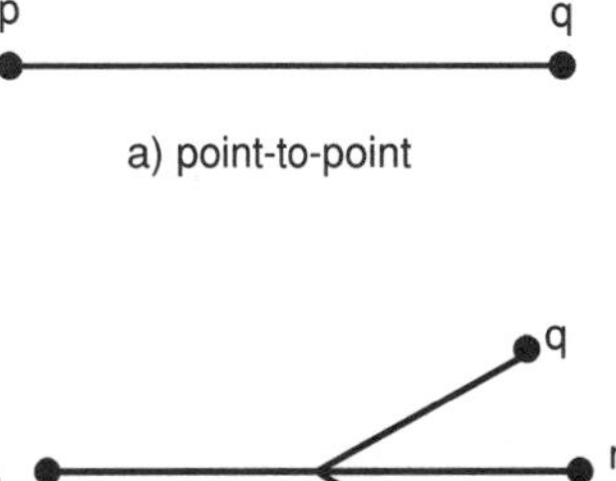

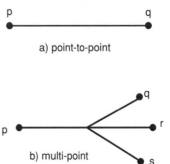

Figure 2: Connections.

of traffic into digital form for cost-effective transport. We could say that "bits are bits," whether they belong to voice, data, video, or some other application (an oversimplification, as we shall see later). The same network might well be used to deliver multiple types of bits, instead of having distinct networks dedicated for voice, data, and so on. This is the concept of *convergence*, where a single network carries various types of traffic. In the context of convergence, the important question shifts from whether circuit or packet switching is better to what support a network must provide so that traffic delivery meets user expectations and application requirements. The concept of convergence is certainly not new. Early WANs transformed digital data into analog signals and used time-division multiplexing (TDM) to carry it over public networks that had been designed for voice. Today, convergence is based on statistical multiplexing and offers many more options for what traffic to combine and how to do it.

FACILITIES AND INFRASTRUCTURE

Digital Transmission

The heritage of digital WANs dates from the early 1960s, when the Bell System first introduced the T-carrier system of physical components to support transport of digital signals in the United States. The accompanying TDM digital signal scheme, called a digital hierarchy, was based on a standard 64-kilobits per second (Kbps) signal designed to carry one analog voice signal transformed by pulse-code modulation (PCM) into digital form. This basic unit is known as *DS0*. The International Telecommunication Union (ITU) now supports an entire set of digital signaling standards (Table 1), incorporating elements from the North American (United States/Canada), European, and Japanese standard hierarchies.

The traditional U.S. multiplexing hierarchy began with combining 24 DS0-level signals into one DS1. It is commonly called a *T1* stream and consists of a sequence of 24 channels combined to create 1 frame. Each channel is filled with 8 bits (an octet or byte) representing one PCM sample. A particular challenge of the time was to ensure synchronization between transmitter and receiver, which can be accomplished in several ways. For example, each frame could be introduced by a unique starting sequence of 12 bits to allow receiver synchronization to be renewed on a frame-by-frame basis. The U.S. designers decided instead to distribute the 12 bits over 12 frames, reducing transmission overhead at the expense of receiver complexity. The 12-frame sequence was called a superframe. With improved hardware, synchronization is more easily maintained over longer periods, and an extended superframe (ESF) has replaced the superframe. ESF comprises 24 frames but needs only 6 bits for synchronization, freeing up 4 Kbps that have been used to improve management and control.

In the European scheme (also used by many other countries around the world), the basic *E1* stream aggregates 32 PCM channels. Rather than adding synchronization bits, E1 dedicates the first PCM channel for synchronization and the seventeenth for management and control signaling.

Table 1 Digital Signal Hierarchy

Designation	Capacity (Mbps)	Number of DS0s
DS1	1.544	24
E1	2.048	32
DS2	6.312	96
E2	8.448	128
J3	32.064	
E3	34.368	512
DS3	44.736	672
J4	97.728	
E4	139.264	2,048
DS4	274.176	4,032

Note: Abbreviations: DS, North America; E, Europe; J, Japan.

Table 2 Basic SONET Levels

Designation	Line Rate[a]	SDH Equivalent
OC-1	51.840 Mbps	
OC-3	155.250 Mbps	STM-1
OC-9	466.560 Mbps	STM-3
OC-12	622.080 Mbps	STM-4
OC-18	933.120 Mbps	STM-6
OC-24	1.24416 Gbps	STM-8
OC-36	1.86624 Gbps	STM-12
OC-48	2.48832 Gbps	STM-16
OC-96	4.97664 Gbps	STM-32
OC-192	9.95328 Gbps	STM-64

[a] 1Gbps = 1,000 Mbps; 1 Mbps = 10^6 bits per second.

Optical Fiber Systems

Service providers first used digital multiplexing within their own networks (e.g., trunking between central offices) to improve the return on and extend the life of their copper cable infrastructure investments. By the 1980s, however, interest had shifted to fiber optics for longer distance, higher speed communications. Standards were defined for the Synchronous Optical NETwork (SONET in the United States, equivalent to the Synchronous Digital Hierarchy, SDH, in Europe and elsewhere) to carry TDM traffic cost-effectively and reliably over metropolitan and wide area distances. Today SONET specifies both a standard optical interface signal and a digital signaling hierarchy tailored to the fiber transmission environment. The hierarchy is based on an 810-octet frame transmitted every 125 microseconds (μs) to create synchronous transport signal-level 1 (STS-1) for electrical signals. Each octet is equivalent to a 64-Kbps PCM channel. For fiber transmission, the STS-1 equivalent is optical carrier-level 1 (OC-1). Higher level signals are formed from specific multiples of OC-1 (Table 2). Each SONET frame is structured into transport overhead and a synchronous payload envelope (SPE), which consists of both path overhead and payload. It is only the payload portion that carries subscriber traffic to be routed and delivered through the SONET network.

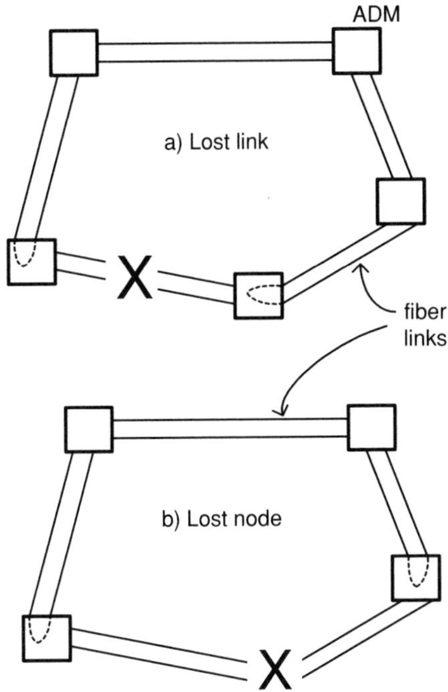

Figure 3: SONET Ring Survivability.

The major building blocks for SONET networks are the point-to-point multiplexer and, for point-to-multipoint configurations, the add–drop multiplexer (ADM). In particular, the ADM allows traffic to be dropped off and the resultant free capacity to be reused to carry traffic entering the network at that point. SONET ADMs can also be employed to create highly survivable networks that maximize availability using diverse routing and self-healing, survivable ring structures. Figure 3a shows a dual-ring structure where the network accommodates loss of a link by looping traffic back on each side of the break, and Figure 3b shows how loss of a network node can be handled similarly. SONET has been deployed extensively by service providers in metropolitan areas to create highly reliable and scalable transport capabilities. Once the fiber and switching equipment are in place, transport capacity can be increased by installing higher speed signaling interfaces.

Another approach to increasing the capacity of fiber systems has become available with advances in optical component technology. Rather than using the entire range of wavelengths that can be carried over fiber as a single transmission channel, newer equipment allows us to divide the range into multiple channels for simultaneous transmission using wavelength-division multiplexing (WDM). This is quite similar to sending multiple television channels over a coaxial cable. Channels must be spaced far enough apart to limit the interference between adjacent signals that would degrade signal quality. In *coarse* WDM (CWDM) the channels are widely spaced; for *dense* WDM (DWDM), they are very close together (spacing $\leq$25–50 GHz). By combining WDM and high-speed signaling, transmission capacities of OC-192, OC-768, and greater become possible, limited primarily by the quality of existing fiber installations.

Access Technologies

To get traffic in and out of a MAN or WAN, subscribers must have physical connections, or *access*, to the appropriate SPs or enterprise network resources. In the regulated telecommunications environment of the United States, this typically means acquiring connectivity from a local exchange carrier (LEC) to tie the subscriber's physical premises to a WAN service provider's (i.e., interexchange carrier, IXC) equipment as physically located in a point of presence (POP). In a metropolitan area, a single company may be allowed to provide both local exchange connections and MAN services. The primary means of accessing MAN and WAN service provider networks are described below.

Dial-up access is appropriate for occasional connections of limited duration, as for making a telephone call. Where the physical facilities used for dial-up were designed and installed to support analog voice traffic, two characteristics are particularly important for data networking:

- Digital data must be converted to analog using a modem at the subscriber end and reconverted to digital by a modem at the provider end of the connection.
- Data rates are limited by the analog frequency range accepted at provider receiving equipment and by the signal modulation techniques of the modem devices. The most widely accepted standards today support maximum data rates of 56 Kbps.

Leased-line access is more appropriate for connections that need to be continuous and/or of better quality for higher speed transmission. Such facilities are dedicated to the use of a specific subscriber. For example, a business may lease a T1 access line as its basic unit of connection capacity (1.544 Mbps), particularly for access to Internet service providers. Fractional-T1 and multiple-T1 lines are also available in some areas. A newer technology designed to be digital from end to end over copper cabling, called digital subscriber line (DSL), is becoming more popular and prevalent as a lower cost alternative to the traditional T-carrier. Leased-line access requires matching equipment at each end of the line (subscriber and service provider) to ensure transmission quality suitable to the desired data rates.

Wireless access is growing in popularity, both for mobile individuals who do not work from a fixed location (e.g., salespeople, customer service representatives, and travelers) and for business connections to MAN or WAN resources (e.g., "first-mile/last-mile" alternative to cabled connections). From a data perspective, the IEEE has two groups focused on wireless access: the 802.16 working group published its WirelessMAN standard for broadband wireless access (BWA) to wireless MANs in April 2002 and the 802.20 mobile broadband wireless access (MBWA) working group, chartered in December 2002, is developing a packet interface optimized for transport of IP-based services.

The cellular industry is also working to improve wireless access beyond the low-speed data transport capabilities of second-generation (2G) technologies (e.g., cellular modems or data cables connecting computers to cellular phones) with packet-switched, third-generation (3G) capabilities that grew out of an early effort by the ITU for international mobile telecommunications called IMT-2000. Unfortunately the international representatives were unable to agree on a single approach to creating such a standard and multiple technologies or modes of operation developed. IMT-2000 thus includes five different radio interfaces, some based on code-division multiple access (CDMA) and some on time-division multiple access (TDMA). These are taking hold in different areas of the world according to support by various telecommunication companies. For example, wideband CDMA (W-CDMA or universal mobile telecommunications system, UTMS) is popular for its ability to interoperate with the 2G standard called GSM (global system for mobile communications). However, in the United States the designated frequency spectrum has already been used for other services, so support for CDMA-2000 is more prevalent. Typical wireless access speeds are up to 144 Kbps for mobile users and 2 Mbps for fixed connections.

Wireless access methods depend on broadcasting signals through an open, shared medium, making user authentication and privacy of data major concerns. The IEEE has addressed these security issues through its 802.1× standard, based on the extensible authentication protocol (EAP) for both user authentication and encryption key exchange. Once a user is authenticated (e.g., by password, token, or digital certificate), keys are generated and exchanged for encrypting data transfers.

Cable modem access is typically provided by cable television companies who have expanded their business into data networking. A modem designed to transmit data signals over coaxial, broadband television cable is connected, usually via Ethernet technology, to the subscriber's internal network or computer equipment. In residential applications, subscribers in a neighborhood typically share data networking capacity on the aggregate cable that carries traffic back to their provider's central service location. This is different from a leased-line approach, where access capacity is dedicated from each subscriber location all the way to the provider's POP. Enterprise use of cable modem access is often supplemented by virtual private networking (VPN) technology to counteract the security risk of shared transport.

Cable modems in the Americas are predominantly based on the DOCSIS (data over cable service interface specification) standard from CableLabs, whereas in Europe DVB/DAVIC (digital video broadcasting/Digital Audio-Video Council) competes with a European version of DOCSIS (EuroDOCSIS). An important characteristic that distinguishes cable modems from most other access methods is the difference in bandwidth for traffic *from* the subscriber (typically 3 Mbps shared by all on the same cable leg) and *to* the subscriber (27–52 Mbps, again, shared).

Management

Management for MANs and WANs typically began with proprietary systems sold to service providers by each manufacturer of telecommunications switching equipment. Networks composed of equipment from multiple vendors thus contained multiple management systems. Equipment management and service management functions are often tied together by an *operations support system* (OSS) to automate *o*perations (e.g., performance monitoring), *a*dministration (e.g., ordering and billing), *m*aintenance (e.g., diagnostics, fault detection, and isolation), and *p*rovisioning (OAM&P) functions. Many SPs tailored what they could acquire as a basic OSS to accommodate their own specific sets of equipment and services, making it difficult to share information, provide consistent management data in a multiprovider environment, and keep up to date with new functional requirements. This often leaves customers who need services from multiple providers without a single, coherent view of their enterprise WAN resources.

Beginning in 1988, the Telecommunication Standardization sector of the International Telecommunication Union (ITU-T, formerly the Consultative Committee on International Telephony and Telegraphy, CCITT) set about establishing the precepts for a standard *telecommunications management network* (TMN). Although the concept of a TMN encompasses the entire set of OAM&P applications in the network, what they do, and how they communicate, ITU-T standards focus on the information required and how it should be communicated rather than how it is processed (M.3000 recommendation series). Two types of telecommunications resources are encompassed: managed systems (such as a switch), which are called network elements (NE), and management systems, usually implemented as operations systems (OS). TMN standards are organized into interface specifications that define the interconnection relationships possible between resources. Figure 4 shows the relationship between the TMN and the telecommunication network for which it is responsible.

TMN is based on the open systems interconnection (OSI) management framework, using object-oriented

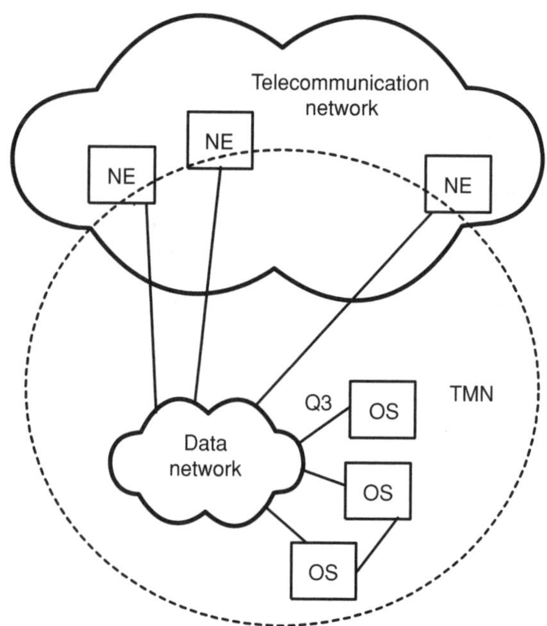

Figure 4: TMN and the Network It Manages.

Table 3 TMN Architecture

Logical Layer	Functional Responsibilities
Business management	Provides an enterprise view that incorporates high-level business planning and supports setting goals, establishing budgets, tracking financial metrics, and managing resources such as products and people.
Service management	Provides the basic contact point for customers (provisioning, billing and accounting, troubleshooting, quality monitoring, etc.) as well as for service providers and other administrative domains.
Network management	Provides an overall view of the network resources, end to end, based on the information from below about network elements and links. Coordinates activities at the network level and supports the functional requirements of service management.
Element management	Provides a view of individual network elements or groupings into subnetworks. Element managers (OSs) are responsible for subsets of all network elements, from the perspective of TMN-manageable information such as element data, event logs, activity, and so on. Mediation devices belong in this layer, communicating with OSs via the Q3 interface.
Network elements	Presents the TMN-manageable information of individual network resources (e.g., switches, routers, and Q-adapters).

principles and standard interfaces to define communication for purposes of managing the network. The primary interface specification, Q3, allows direct communication with an OS. Any network component that does not implement Q3 may not access an OS directly, but must go through a mediation device (MD) instead. Legacy equipment and systems that rely on proprietary ASCII messages for communication are accommodated by means of a Q-adapter (QA) that can translate between messages representing the legacy information model and the object-oriented representation expected in today's TMN.

TMN defines a layered architecture (ITU-T standard M.3010) as a logical model for the functions involved in managing a telecommunication network effectively (Table 3). The object is to create a framework for interoperability across heterogeneous operation systems and telecommunication networks that is flexible, scalable, reliable, easy to enhance, and, ultimately, inexpensive to operate. Standard management services have been defined for alarm surveillance (Q.821), performance management (Q.822), traffic management (Q.823), ISDN Service Profile Management (Q.824), call detail recording (Q.825), and routing management (Q.826).

Despite the standards for TMN, an organization using multiple SPs cannot necessarily get a single, coherent view of their entire network because not all carriers implement all of the required network interfaces. Worse yet, if the network/network interface (NNI) specifically is not in place, data cannot even be transferred from one carrier's network to another.

Differences around the World

Creating and operating WANs or MANs in different countries may present challenges well beyond identifying a service provider and getting connections established. A particular type of service may not be available in the desired location, a single provider may not offer services in every location, or the capacity required may not be available. Such differences may be because of telecommunication infrastructure of varying ages and technologies or different regulations on service offerings in various countries. For example, T1 service is readily available in most U.S. cities. Mexico, however, employs the European standard hierarchy and would thus offer E1 service. To communicate across such boundaries, a lower common-denominator service might need to be selected and the differences in capacity and framing would have to be handled appropriately by the network equipment at each end of the link.

In most countries, telecommunication is a regulated industry subject to many government-imposed rules, and there may be no or a limited choice of carriers. Some countries have begun to deregulate, resulting in multiple carriers competing for subscriber business, often creating more choices in technology and services, as well as better pricing. In either case, service availability may differ from one location to another: DSL access might be easily obtained in greater Boston but not available in a rural area; T1 service might be acquired readily in Singapore but perhaps not everywhere in New York City.

Do not make the mistake, however, of assuming that more highly developed areas or countries always have better service options than developing ones. An established metropolitan area experiencing rapid growth in demand for telecommunications may be less able to adapt or expand existing cable and switching capacity to meet new orders than a new suburban business park where there is plenty of room to install new cables and switches to provide higher speed services. Similarly, developing countries that have very little investment in old infrastructure may be able to skip generations of technology, installing the latest where there was previously none. Economics tend to dictate that this does not happen uniformly, but rather emphasizes locations more likely to provide rapid payback for the particular technology investment (e.g., urban rather than rural, business rather than residential, and high-density population areas). Often it is the access infrastructure that lags behind, because the upgrade costs cannot be amortized across multiple subscribers the way backbone investments can. This is especially true where the end points are individuals with more limited budgets than business or organizational enterprises.

SWITCHING, ROUTING, AND SIGNALING

Network Architecture

MANs and WANs are usually divided into three logical segments (Figure 5). *Access* typically includes the customer premises equipment (CPE) located in a subscriber's building or office area and the link that physically connects from there to the SP's point of presence. This link is connected to a device at the *edge* of the SP's network, and the edge device is connected to devices that compose the *core* (also called the backbone) of the SP's network. Different technologies are often used in the access and core portions, with the edge required to translate between the two. The ratio of the aggregate input capacity from all subscriber connections to an edge device to the output capacity from the edge into the core describes the degree of oversubscription. For example, if the sum of all access links is 200 Mbps and the core link is 100 Mbps, then the oversubscription ratio is 2:1. A ratio less than or equal to 1 is called nonblocking; the network performance for values greater than 1 depends on the bursty nature of data traffic to minimize the probability that traffic will be delayed excessively (by buffering) or discarded (when buffers become full).

Some form of packet switching is employed in most core data networks today. Various techniques are used to meet customer expectations for reliable, timely, and effective delivery of traffic to its intended destination. For example, a *virtual circuit* can be established to approximate the service characteristics available in a circuit-switching environment, such as guaranteed delivery of packets in the same order as they were transmitted. However, virtual circuits do not dedicate resources along the path from source to destination, so the network must have sufficient intelligence to keep traffic moving well enough to meet subscriber expectations.

Choosing the best place to put network intelligence (at the edge or in the core) has been a subject of ongoing discussion among SPs for many years. For enterprises, however, the question becomes what intelligence performing which functions resides in their own equipment as opposed to what happens within the SP network. In particular, where security functions such as access control, encryption, or other firewall capabilities are handled may be important both to network performance and the user's degree of confidence in data protection.

Switching Technologies

In the OSI reference model, layer 2, the data link layer, is responsible for switching traffic point-to-point based on the layer 2 destination address (see the Routing Technologies section for layer 3 switching). However, much of the WAN switching technology for data networking was developed from experience with X.25, an ITU-T packet-switching protocol standard developed in the 1970s to support public data networking that is still in use today. X.25 creates a connection-oriented network out of packet-switching resources by employing virtual circuits to handle packet flow, keeping the data link layer simpler but requiring circuits to be established before packets can be sent. Circuits that are prebuilt from a source to a particular destination and then left in place are *permanent* virtual circuits (PVCs), whereas *switched* virtual circuits (SVCs) are established only on demand. SVCs are like dial-up connections, requiring circuit establishment to the specified destination for each call before traffic can flow, an end-to-end function beyond the capabilities of layer 2.

X.25 is a three-layer protocol suite (Figure 6). The OSI network layer equivalent is the Packet-Layer Protocol (PLP), which has operational modes for call establishment, data transfer, and call termination, plus idle and restarting operations. These functions are implemented through the services of a data link protocol called the Link Access Procedure, Balanced (LAPB), which is responsible for framing data and control commands and for basic

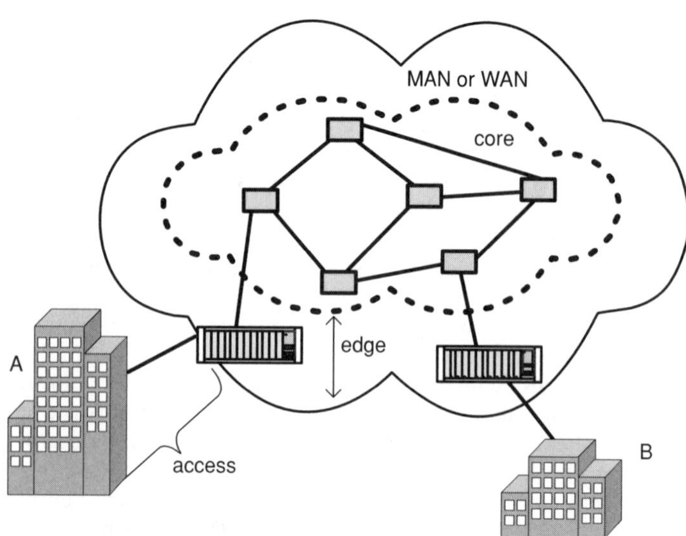

Figure 5: WAN/MAN Architecture.

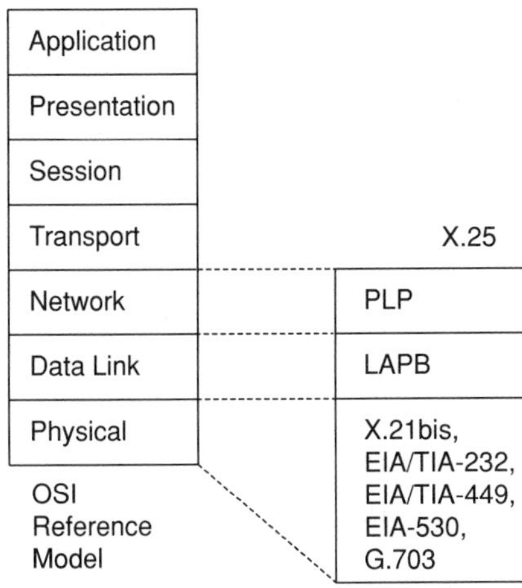

Figure 6: X.25 Protocol Suite.

error checking through use of a frame-check sequence (Figure 7). During call establishment, the PLP sets up SVCs using X.121 standard addresses. These include the international data number (IDN), made up of a four-digit data network identification code (DNIC, to specify the packet-switching network containing the destination device) and a national terminal number (NTN) consisting of as many as 10 digits. The NTN specifies the exact destination device to which packets will be forwarded.

Frame relay is the most widely used packet-switching WAN technology. As WAN facilities became more reliable during the 1980s, interest rose in streamlining X.25 to improve performance and efficiency. The CCITT thus began work on frame relay (FR) in 1984. However, it was not until 1991, when several major telecommunication equipment manufacturers formed a consortium called the Frame Relay Forum (FRF) to work out interoperability issues and foster acceptance, that frame relay began to be more widely deployed. In particular, FRF defined extensions to the CCITT work called the local management interface (LMI) to improve SPs' abilities to provision and manage FR services.

Frame relay networks (Figure 8) are based on the concepts of data-terminal equipment (DTE) and data circuit-terminating equipment (DCE) first defined by X.25. Subscriber hosts, servers, workstations, personal computers, and terminals connected to an FR network are all considered to be DTE. The DCE is usually built as an interface into the SP's packet-switching equipment (PSE) rather than just being a modem at the edge of an X.25 network. Frame relay also uses virtual circuits to create a bidirectional communication path between a pair of DTE devices. FR virtual circuits are distinguished by data link connection identifiers (DLCIs), which may have local

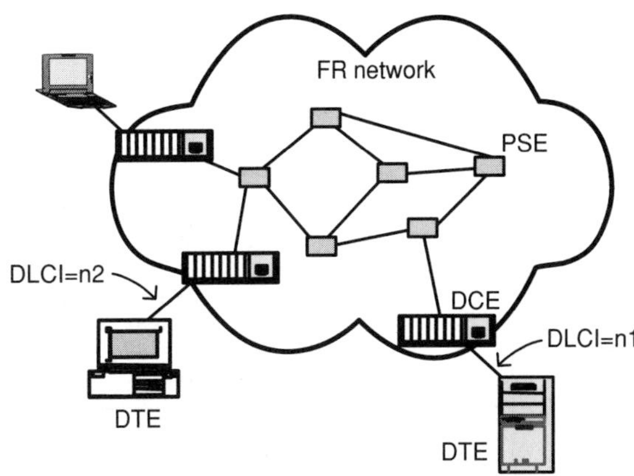

Figure 8: Frame Relay Network Elements.

significance only, meaning that each end of a single virtual circuit could have a different DLCI assigned by the FR service provider.

The format for FR data combines LAPB's address and control fields into one 16-bit address field that contains the 10-bit DLCI, an extended addressing indicator bit (for future use), a command/response bit that is not used, and congestion control information. To minimize network overhead, the congestion control mechanisms are quite simple:

- One forward-explicit congestion notification (FECN) bit that tells a DTE that congestion occurred along the path in the direction *from* the source *to* the destination
- One backward-explicit congestion notification (BECN) bit that tells a DTE that congestion occurred along the path in the direction *opposite* to the transmission from the source to the destination
- One discard-eligibility (DE) bit to indicate whether this is a lower priority frame that may be discarded before others (those not marked DE) in a congested situation.

As a packet-switching technology, FR also depends on the bursty nature of data traffic to make efficient use of its transmission facilities for larger numbers of subscribers than could be served with physically dedicated connections. The ability to overbook resources is fundamental to a SP's business model, as well as being a benefit to subscribers, who may be able to insert traffic occasionally at a higher rate than nominal for their access link (called bursting). For enterprises that build private FR networks by leasing private lines and installing their own FR equipment at each end, bursty traffic means more users can be served with less capacity (as in statistical multiplexing).

Flag (frame delimiter)	Address (command or response indicator)	Control (frame type, sequence #, function)	DATA	FCS (frame check sequence)	Flag (frame delimiter)
1 byte	1 byte	1 byte	variable	2 bytes	1 byte

Figure 7: LAPB Frame Format.

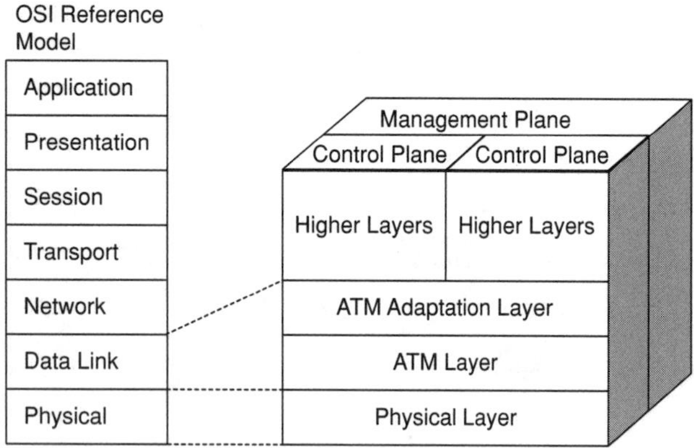

Figure 9: ATM Reference Model.

Integrated Services Digital Network (ISDN) is a set of telecommunication standards first developed from the perspective of telephony networks to accommodate multiple types of traffic such as voice, fax, data, alarm systems, video, and so on, all in digital format, over a single network. The goal was to develop standard interfaces, both for access and within the network, that would allow all types of digital traffic to be transported end to end, reliably, and in a timely fashion according to the needs of its application. The best known elements of ISDN are the user interface definitions for connecting subscriber equipment to the network: the primary rate interface (PRI), intended to replace T1 and E1 services, and the basic rate interface (BRI), designed with multiple channels for voice or data traffic from an individual subscriber.

Asynchronous Transfer Mode (ATM) was selected as the OSI layer 2 transport technology for broadband ISDN (B-ISDN) in 1988. It was designed to be useful across WAN, MAN, and LAN communications, as well as to accommodate multiple types of traffic in a single network (voice, data, video, etc.) and scale for very large networks. Other design goals included support a variety of media types (e.g., fiber and copper), leverage signaling standards already developed for other technologies, promote low-cost switching implementations (potentially one-tenth the cost of routing), adapt readily to future requirements, and enable new, large-scale applications. The challenges inherent in such a diverse set of goals brought together designers from many different backgrounds and resulted in a rather complex architecture (Figure 9).

Basically, ATM is a connection-oriented technology that switches fixed-length packets called *cells*. The 53-byte cell size (5 bytes of header information and 48 bytes for the payload) was chosen as a compromise between the optimal size for voice traffic and the larger size preferred for data applications. The fixed size and format mean that very fast cell switches can be built across a broad range of transmission rates, from megabits to gigabits per second and beyond. ATM interfaces are often characterized by their equivalent optical-carrier levels whether they employ fiber or copper media. The most popular interfaces tend to be OC-3, OC-12, and OC-48 (Table 2), according to their application in WANs, MANs, or LANs.

An important feature of ATM is the definition of service categories for traffic management:

- *Constant Bit Rate* (CBR) was designed to emulate traditional circuit-switched connections. It is characterized by minimum and maximum cell rates specified at the same, constant value. Typical CBR applications include uncompressed voice and video or television, all sensitive to both delay and delay variation.
- *Variable Bit Rate* real-time (VBR-rt) and non-real-time (VBR-nrt) are characterized by specified minimum and maximum cell rates, much like frame relay. Typical applications include compressed voice or video and multimedia e-mail. VBR-rt handles applications sensitive to delay variation, whereas VBR-nrt is suitable for bursty traffic.
- *Unspecified Bit Rate* (UBR) handles traffic on a best-effort basis, without guaranteeing delivery or any particular rate. This is used to carry data (such as store-and-forward e-mail) that is not sensitive to delay. In a highly congested network situation, UBR cells may be discarded so that the network can meet its traffic contracts for the other types.
- *Available Bit Rate* (ABR) is characterized by a guaranteed minimum cell rate but may offer additional bandwidth when network resources are available. Rate-based flow control provides the adjustment mechanism. When it is offered, ABR is often preferred for data traffic.

ATM's service categories are crucial to meeting user demands for *quality of service* (QoS), which generally means guaranteed, timely delivery of traffic to match the needs of particular applications. An ATM end system will request a particular level of service for traffic entering the network, forming a traffic contract with the network. The ATM switches throughout the network are responsible for meeting the terms of the contract by traffic shaping (using queues to smooth out traffic flow) and by traffic policing to enforce the limits of the contract. The capabilities of ATM to provide QoS end to end across a network for multiple types of traffic simultaneously are the most sophisticated to date and distinguish ATM from other packet-switching technologies. Its suitability by design for LAN, MAN, and WAN applications made ATM especially popular with SPs, because they could use one technology throughout to manage their own infrastructure and to support a large variety of service offerings to their customers. For enterprise LANs, however, ATM has been superseded by higher speed versions of Ethernet.

Ethernet became the dominant LAN technology in the latter 1990s, as extensions from the original 10 Mbps were defined for 100 Mbps and then 1,000 Mbps (= 1 Gbps) and 10 Gbps, and shared media gave way to switched networks. As physical layer definitions for Ethernet over copper were supplemented by fiber standards, Ethernet became practical over longer distances. New communication companies with no telephony heritage began laying optical fiber and leasing capacity for short-haul (i.e., MAN) or long-haul (i.e., WAN) connections rather than selling services, as was typical in public networks. This meant that customers could specify the technology used to put bits on the medium rather than subscribing only to specific services offered by providers. As advances in optics and use of switching allowed Ethernet to cover

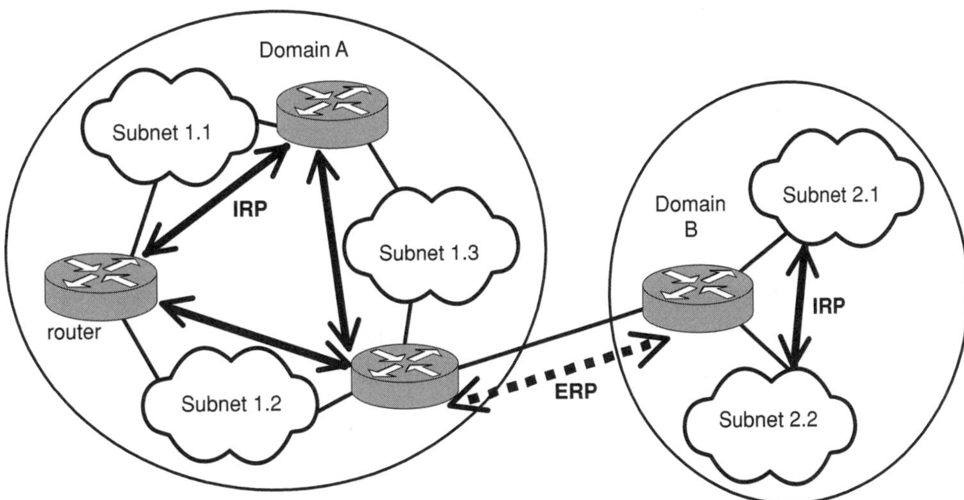

Figure 10: Routing within and between Autonomous Domains.

even greater distances, the geographic limits that distinguished LAN from MAN technologies began to disappear. In fact, new providers sprang up offering Ethernet connectivity from the business doorstep to other locations across town or beyond, taking Ethernet from the access layer right into the network core. The great competitive question was whether Ethernet MANs could be made as reliable and fault-tolerant as more traditional MAN/WAN technologies built over SONET.

Resilient Packet Ring (RPR) is an effort begun by the IEEE 802.17 working group in late 2000 to design a high-speed access protocol combining familiar Ethernet interfaces with the fault-tolerance and rapid restoration capability of ring-based MAN technologies like SONET. RPR defines a new medium access control (MAC sublayer of OSI layer 2) protocol that extends Ethernet framing from the LAN into the MAN/WAN environment. As seen by the RPR Alliance (an industry consortium designed to promote adoption of RPR), this approach combines the cost-effective scalability of Ethernet access interfaces with a MAN that can be optimized for rapidly increasing volumes of data traffic. Because it focuses on the MAC sublayer, RPR is independent of the underlying layer 1 technology, making it suitable to run over much of the MAN infrastructure already in place.

Routing Technologies

In the OSI reference model, routing takes place at layer 3, the network layer. Essentially routing consists of three major functions: maintaining information about the network environment, finding a path through the network from particular sources to destinations, and forwarding packets at each relay point. Layer 3 switching is a shortcut through the traditional OSI protocol stack that allows packets to be switched on the basis of their (layer 3) network destination address. The Internet protocol (IP) is the dominant method of interconnecting packet-switched networks (i.e., for internetworking) at layer 3. It provides connectionless network services (CLNS), with no guarantee of delivery or packet ordering, and is widely used today for private and public LANs, MANs, and WANs, including the Internet. The IP is primarily concerned with the format for packets (also called datagrams), the definition and structure of addresses, a packet-forwarding algorithm, and the mechanisms for exchanging information about conditions in and control of the network.

Routing responsibility in an internetwork is divided between intradomain or interior routing protocols (IRPs) and interdomain or exterior routing protocols (ERPs) as shown in Figure 10. IRPs are used for internetworks that belong to a single administrative authority, such as an enterprise LAN, a single service provider's MAN, or a private WAN. ERPs are used when routers tie together networks belonging to multiple independent authorities, as in the Internet. These protocols differ in how much information is kept about the state of the network and how routing updates are performed using the mechanisms defined by IP.

IP version 4 (IPv4) was defined by the Internet Engineering Task Force (IETF) for the original ARPAnet and published as (Request for Comments) RFC 791 in 1981. It specifies that each interface capable of originating or receiving internetwork traffic be identified by a unique 32-bit address consisting of an ordered pair containing a network identifier (net_ID) and a host/interface identifier (host_ID). Three primary classes of network addresses (A, B, and C) were designed to promote efficient routing, with additional classes defined for special or future uses (Figure 11). Although the Internet is not centrally managed, it was necessary to establish a single authority to assign addresses so that there would be no duplicates or conflicts.

As the Internet grew through the 1980s, a number of limitations in the design of IPv4 became apparent. The allocation of addresses, especially classes A and B, tended to be wasteful. For example, a single class B address assigned to one organization accommodates one network with over 64,000 IP interfaces—much larger than is practical or needed for most, meaning that a lot of address space can be wasted. Conversely, a single class C address accommodates only 255 interfaces, which is too small for most organizations, requiring them to have more than

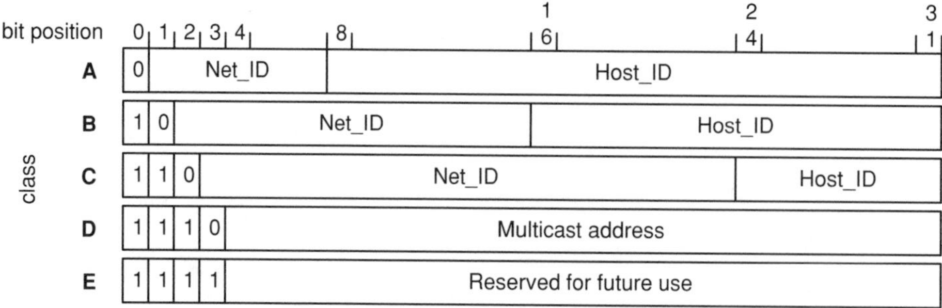

Figure 11: IPv4 Addressing Format.

one. From a routing perspective, the two-level hierarchical address structure means that routers need to keep track of over 16 million net_IDs just for class C networks, as well as calculate paths through the Internet to each one. A number of schemes were developed to solve some of the addressing and router problems (subnet masking, classless interdomain routing or CIDR), but those were not the only issues. Rising interest in using the Internet to carry voice, video, multimedia application, and commercial transaction traffic increased the demand for security and quality of service support, neither of which were built into IPv4. Consequently, the IETF began work on a new version, IP-ng, to handle the next generation.

IP version 6 (IPv6) represents that next generation of network layer services. It extends the addressing space from 32 to 128 bits, simplifies the packet header and allows for future expansion, and adds new capabilities to label flows of packets (same source to a single destination), to assign packets priority in support of QoS handling, and to provide authentication and security. Several of these features (CIDR, DiffServ, and IPsec) were designed so they could be added onto IPv4. In fact, such retrofitting solved IPv4 problems well enough in the late 1990s that people began to question whether a move to IPv6 was necessary. Upgrading the large numbers of routers involved with Internet traffic would be expensive, time consuming, and require careful coordination. Transition strategies and mechanisms would likely be needed over a considerable period of time. Unfortunately, retrofits cannot do much about the size of IPv4 addresses. Sufficient growth in the numbers and types of devices people want to connect to or through the Internet (e.g., handheld devices, household appliances, and automobile systems) and international pressure from countries without enough addresses will eventually make IPv4 addressing inadequate. The only question seems to be when.

Border Gateway Protocol (BGP) is the exterior routing protocol used by independent or autonomous systems (ASs) to exchange routing information throughout the Internet. Published in 1995 as RFC 1771, it defines procedures to establish *neighbor* relationships and to test the *reachability* of neighbors and other networks. A router at the edge of an AS uses BGP to work with adjacent (i.e., directly connected) routers in other ASs. Only after two routers (one in each AS) have agreed to become neighbors can they exchange routing information or relay traffic for each other's AS. Unlike IRPs, which use the services of IP to accomplish their communication, BGP uses the reliable transport services of TCP (transmission control protocol, running over IP). In this way, BGP can be simpler because it depends on the error control functions of TCP and its messages are not limited in size by the constraints of an IP datagram.

BGP is purposefully designed to allow an AS to control what detail of internal information is made visible outside the AS (aggregating routes using CIDR, for example). Typically each BGP router screens potential routing updates or reachability advertisements against a configuration file that specifies what type of information it is allowed to send to each particular neighbor. This approach promotes policy-based routing, but at the expense of needing to calculate paths from incomplete detail about the network topology. Thus BGP will not always choose the optimal path across an internetwork to reach a particular destination. It does, however, allow a country or company constituting an AS to make appropriate political or business decisions about when and where to route its traffic.

Questions about the scalability of BGP have been raised in light of predictions for continued substantial growth in Internet traffic, and particularly as more organizations consider deploying delay-sensitive applications over the Internet (e.g., voice, video, and conferencing). Intelligent route control, virtual routing, and new approaches to traffic engineering are among the options being explored to solve performance problems before they become serious impediments to effective use of the Internet.

Multiprotocol Label Switching (MPLS) has been designed by the IETF to improve the performance of routed networks by layering a connection-oriented framework over an IP-based internetwork. MPLS requires edge routers to assign labels to traffic entering the network so that intermediate routers (called label switched routers, LSRs) can make forwarding decisions quickly, choosing the appropriate output port according to the packet's label and rewriting that label (which is intended to have local significance only) as necessary (Figure 12). MPLS represents a significant shortcut from the usual IP approach, where every relay node must look deeply into the packet header, search a routing table for the best match, and then select the best next hop toward the packet's destination. All packets with the same MPLS label will follow the same route through the network. In fact, MPLS is designed so that it can explicitly and flexibly allocate network resources to meet particular objectives such as

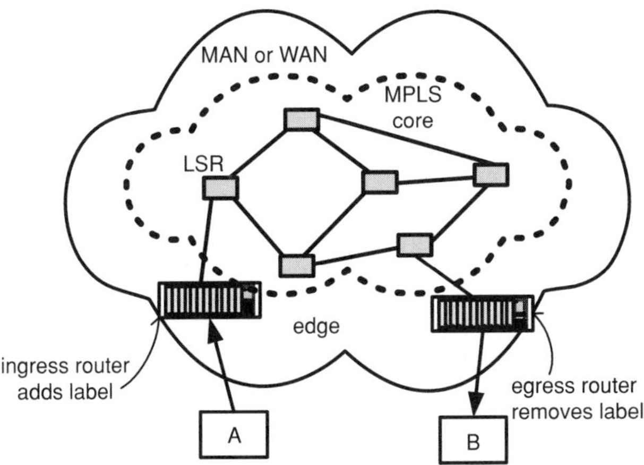

Figure 12: MPLS Architecture.

assigning fastest routes for delay-sensitive packet flows, underutilized routes to balance traffic better, or multiple routes between the same end points for flows with different requirements. This is called *traffic engineering* and serves as the foundation for both optimizing performance and supporting QoS guarantees.

Nothing about the MPLS design limits its use to the IP environment; it can work with suitably equipped ATM and frame relay routers as well. In fact, it can coexist with legacy routers not yet updated with MPLS capabilities, and it can be used in an internetwork that contains a mix of IP, ATM, and FR. Another powerful feature is the ability to stack labels on a last-in/first-out basis, with labels added or removed from the stack by each LSR as appropriate. This allows multiple label-switched paths to be aggregated into a tunnel over the common portion of their route for optimal switching and transport. MPLS is also a convenient mechanism to support virtual private networks, especially when multiple Internet SPs are involved along the path from one end to the other.

Signaling and Interworking

Connection-oriented networks require specific mechanisms for establishing a circuit (physical or virtual "connection" through which all traffic subsequently travels) prior to traffic flow and for terminating the circuit afterwards. In the circuit-switched telephony environment, call setup and termination are part of a well-developed set of telecommunication system control functions referred to as *signaling*. MANs and WANs that were built for voice included signaling as an integral part of their designs, because resources were dedicated to each call as it was established and needed to be released after call completion.

The ITU-T began developing standards for digital telecommunication signaling in the mid-1960s; these have evolved into common channel interoffice signaling system 7 (CCIS7, known in the United States as Signaling System 7, or just *SS7* for short), currently in use around the world. SS7 is an out-of-band mechanism, meaning that its messages do not travel across the same network resources as the conversations it was designed to establish and control. In fact, SS7 uses packet switching to deliver control messages and exchange data, not just for call setup, but also for special features such as looking up a toll-free number in a database to find out its real destination address, call tracing, and credit card approvals. Out-of-band delivery of the messages allows SS7 to be very fast in setting up calls, to avoid any congestion in the transport network, and also to provide signaling any time during a call.

In packet-switched MANs and WANs, signaling had been associated primarily with establishing and tearing down switched virtual circuits (SVCs) that required no further control during the data transfer phase. With a rising interest in multimedia communications (e.g., video and especially voice over IP, VoIP), however, the ITU-T quickly recognized a need for additional capabilities. Their *H.323* recommendations encompass an entire suite of protocols that cover all aspects of getting real-time audio and video signals into packet form, signaling for call control, and negotiation to ensure compatibility among sources, destinations, and the network. H.323 takes advantage of prior ITU work (such as ISDN's Q.931 signaling protocol) and defines four major elements (Figure 13):

1. *Terminals* are the end-user devices that originate and receive multimedia traffic.
2. *Gateways* primarily handle protocol conversions for participating non-H.323 terminals, as would be found in the public switched telephone network (PSTN).
3. *Gatekeepers* are responsible for address translation, call control services, and bandwidth management.

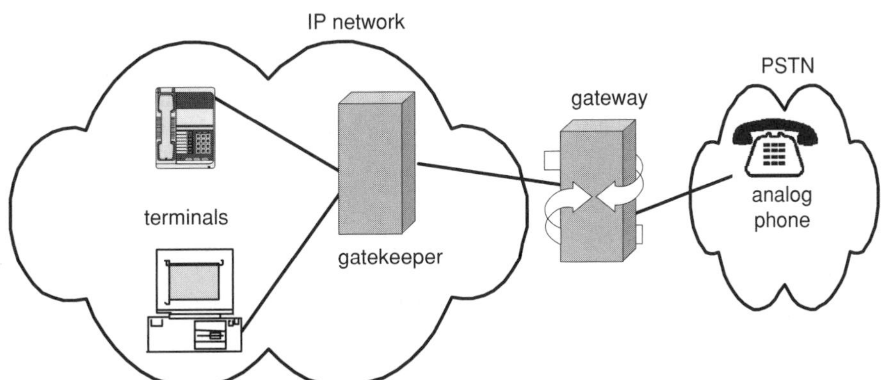

Figure 13: H.323 Network Elements.

4. *Multipoint Control Units* (MCUs) provide multiconferencing among three or more terminals and gateways.

The IETF took a simpler approach to signaling with the *session initiation protocol* (SIP), which was designed as a lightweight protocol simply to initiate sessions between users. SIP borrows a great deal from the hypertext transfer protocol (HTTP), using many of the same header fields, encoding rules, error codes, and authentication methods to exchange text messages. Like H.323, SIP assumes that the end-point devices (i.e., terminals) are intelligent, running software known as the user agent. The agent has two components: the *User Agent Client*, which is responsible for initiating all outgoing calls, and the *User Agent Server*, which answers incoming calls. In the network itself, SIP provides support with three types of servers:

1. *Registration* servers keep track of where all users are located.
2. *Proxy* servers receive requests and forward them along to the next appropriate hop in the network.
3. *Redirect* servers also receive requests and determine the next hop, but rather than forwarding the request, they return the next-hop server address to the requester.

An alternative approach to multimedia communication control developed by the IETF is called the media gateway control protocol (MGCP). It is quite different from H.323 and SIP because it assumes that the end-user devices are not very intelligent. Consequently MGCP takes a central server approach to communication coordination and control. Two elements are defined: the *Media Gateway Controller* (also known as the call agent), which provides the central intelligence and controls all of the *Media Gateways*, which perform a variety of interface functions such as with the PSTN, residential devices, business private branch exchanges (PBXs), and so on. MGCP defines the communication that takes place between the call agent and the Gateways that execute its commands.

In practice H.323, SIP, and MGCP will likely coexist to support multimedia communication in the Internet environment because each has advantages for specific applications or coverage. MGCP is particularly useful to MAN/WAN service providers with large installed bases of unintelligent end-point devices, and its gateway approach allows for tailored interfaces to each different underlying technology. The simplicity of SIP is more attractive to enterprise networks designed primarily for data traffic with smaller requirements for supporting voice and video. Finally, H.323 is the most mature and most comprehensive. As usual in the telecommunication industry, vendor support and suitability to customer business models are likely to determine which, if any, one approach becomes dominant.

PROVIDERS AND SERVICES

Carriers and Service Providers

The public provision of telecommunication services to subscribers for a fee has a history of being government regulated in most parts of the world (the term *common carrier*, for example, dates back to public transportation for people, first by stagecoach, then by trains, buses, etc.). Regulation was required because access to telecommunication services depended on cabling that was run from subscriber premises (residential or business) across public property (e.g., along roads) to a provider's central office as a service point. Governments could also impose standards to ensure that services offered by providers in different locations would be compatible enough to interoperate. In some countries, infrastructure was built and services operated by the government itself (e.g., PTTs that provided postal, telegraph, and telephone services nationwide). In the United States, telephone industry regulation was divided between LECs, whose cabling and local services go to individual premises, and IXCs, who provided the interconnection (i.e., long-distance services) between LECs.

The Internet as a means of public data communication has grown up rather differently, driven largely by the U.S. regulatory environment, where telecommunication companies were prohibited from providing unregulated data services (e.g., participation in the Internet). Consequently, a new type of company called an Internet service provider (ISP) was born. Data would move from a subscriber's premises across cables belonging to an LEC to ISP equipment in a point of presence, where it was transferred onto Internet resources. The subscriber thus had to be a customer of both the LEC and the ISP unless a private (non-LEC) link could be installed directly to the ISP's POP. The Internet connections from one ISP location to another are most often lines leased from an IXC. As telecommunication services have been increasingly deregulated worldwide, the distinctions among voice and data service providers have become blurred.

It is important to remember that "the Internet" is not really a single entity but rather an interconnected set of autonomous networks whose owners have agreed to cooperate and use a common set of standards to ensure interoperability. *Peering* is a form of interconnection where ISPs agree to exchange traffic for their respective customers, based on a specific set of business terms. Peering points are where the networks actually connect to effect this exchange. The number and location of peering points and partners is decided by each ISP according to customer demand and its own business criteria. Subscribers may need to be aware of these agreements to understand fully the performance they can expect end to end across the Internet. Multiple providers may also influence a subscriber's choice of security mechanisms.

Just as the background and emphasis of traditional voice and traditional data SPs differ, so do their business models and their choices of technology. Some offer only transport for traffic, either between subscriber sites or to the Internet. Others offer access to applications or management services. Local telecommunication carriers tend to offer MAN services over an ATM and SONET infrastructure, whereas data providers would be more likely to offer IP services or simply Ethernet access and transport. Cable television and wireless SPs also offer access services according to the characteristics of their infrastructure technologies. The options available will likely continue to grow as technology progresses.

Class of Service, Quality of Service

As interest in carrying multimedia or multiple-service traffic (i.e., voice, data, video) over MANs and WANs has grown, managing the traffic to provide performance appropriate to each application has become more important. Quality-of-service techniques are expected to guarantee performance and delivery, usually in terms of bandwidth allocation, timeliness of delivery, and minimal variation in delay (e.g., ATM service categories). Class-of-service (CoS) techniques do not make such guarantees, but rather attempt to meet user requests on a best-effort basis. Typically CoS works by grouping together traffic with similar requirements (e.g., voice or streaming video) and using a priority queuing system so that switches and routers forward the traffic accordingly. Connectionless network services such as IP offer CoS traffic management, whereas connection-oriented services such as ATM provide QoS.

QoS cannot really be guaranteed unless it is available all the way from end to end of the connection. This creates a challenge for MAN and WAN environments where multiple technologies from one or more SPs may be involved in delivering user traffic and especially when the traffic originates or terminates in a LAN of yet another different technology. Several groups are involved in developing standard techniques for CoS and QoS. The problem is making sure that appropriate translation mechanisms can carry user application requirements across network and SP boundaries:

- IEEE 802.1p is a layer 2 tagging mechanism to specify priority using three bits in the layer 2 frame header.
- IETF's differentiated services (DiffServ) indicates how packets are to be forwarded using per-hop behavior (PHB) queuing or discarding if there is not sufficient bandwidth to meet performance requirements.
- ATM traffic management defines service categories and traffic classes.

Data flows may need to be mapped across mechanisms multiple times as they travel from edge to core to edge.

Virtual Private Networks

A virtual private network (VPN) is a special service that amounts to establishing a closed user group capability over a shared or public network infrastructure. This means that access is restricted to authorized users only; traffic belonging within the VPN does not get out or become visible to unauthorized users, and outside traffic does not get in. Additional mechanisms may be needed to assure data privacy, such as use of IP security (IPsec) or secure sockets layer (SSL). VPNs are becoming a very attractive way for organizations to reduce the cost of private WANs while improving the security for traffic that travels over public networks. Where high-speed MAN and WAN services are available, long-distance performance can even be kept reasonably close to what the remote users would experience if they were directly connected to the LAN. VPNs may also be built to send traffic across the Internet, with one or more SPs providing the access links between the Internet and various geographically dispersed customer sites. Internet VPNs can be significantly less expensive than the private lines or networks they replace.

Management and Security

The OSI model for network management encompasses five functional areas: configuration management, performance management, fault management, accounting management, and security management. A MAN or WAN service provider must cover these both from the perspective of operating the entire network effectively and balancing the needs and expectations of paying customers who could always choose to take their business elsewhere. Operation must be reliable, there must be sufficient capacity to meet traffic needs and performance expectations, and privacy must be maintained not only for the content of the traffic carried but also for data about the customers. At the same time, subscribers typically want the ability to manage the performance and flow of their own traffic through their allotment of SP resources. SP operation systems must be capable and sophisticated to meet all these requirements.

A primary mechanism used to establish and manage expectations between customers and providers is the *service level agreement* (SLA). SLAs are the defining documents (contracts) that spell out what services and levels of support will be provided to the customer at a specified price. Successful SLAs are built on a solid, shared understanding of business priorities and service impact for both the service user and the service provider. Detail about roles and responsibilities, metrics and reporting, added cost for incremental services or enhancements, escalation procedures, and change management are just some of what should be covered in an SLA. Many customers also build in penalties in case the SP fails to deliver services at the level specified in the SLA. This may be necessary legally to protect the service user's interests, but it is important to remember that failure of the provider to deliver service typically means that the user has failed to meet a business requirement as well. Consequently it is in both the customer's and SP's best interests if the penalty clause is never invoked.

CONCLUSION

The boundaries among local area, metropolitan area, and wide area networks have become less clear over time, because of the increasing variety of implementation choices available to network designers. For MANs and WANs in particular, classifying equipment, services, and management responsibilities by architectural category (access, edge, and core) may help to distinguish among options so that choices can be made in alignment with the business priorities of each designer's organization. Flexibility to accommodate change and growth, reliable service delivery, and optimal cost/performance ratios are the major characteristics typically desired for every network design. The tension between network users wishing to maximize cost-effectiveness and service providers trying to maximize profit continues to work with technological developments to create opportunity for new business approaches. The primary challenge always seems to lie in balancing expensive, long-term infrastructure investments with new technologies and services that meet changing application requirements.

GLOSSARY

Circuit A complete connection between a source and destination for the purposes of transferring information (i.e., for communication).

Circuit Switching A *connection-oriented* approach to networking where the entire path from source to destination is determined and sufficient resources are allocated along the path to carry the traffic before any traffic can flow.

Local Area Network (LAN) A network covering a single office, building, or campus that is built and operated as a private network, by an individual or organization, for his/her/its own use.

Metropolitan Area Network (MAN) A network covering distances up to tens of miles, often within or surrounding a major city. Public MANs are built and operated by service providers who offer network services to subscribers for a fee.

Packet A portion of a message to be carried from a source to a destination.

Packet Switching A *connectionless* networking approach where each packet is routed through the network independently.

Private Network A network built, owned, and operated by a single individual or organization for his/her/its own use.

Public Network A network built to offer resources or services to a set of subscribers who are typically independent from each other and from the owner of the network. Most people think of the Internet as the only truly "public" network.

Routing Determining where a packet should go next to get it closer to its intended destination (i.e., deciding what is the next hop along the path).

Service Provider (SP) Builds and/or operates a network for the purpose of selling capacity or services to subscribers for a fee.

Service User Subscriber to the offerings of a public network.

Switching Placing a packet on the appropriate transport mechanism to get it to the network device representing the next hop.

Wide Area Network (WAN) A network covering distances up to hundreds or thousands of miles, such as between cities, across or between countries, across oceans, and so on. Public WAN facilities are built and operated by service providers who offer network capacity or services to subscribers for a fee. Private WANs are built by organizations for their own use.

CROSS REFERENCES

See *Circuit, Message, and Packet Switching; Conducted Communications Media; Local Area Networks; Public Network Technologies and Security; Wireless Channels*.

FURTHER READING

ATM Forum. (2002). *ATM service categories: The benefits to the user.* Retrieved April 14, 2004, from http://www.atmforum.com/aboutatm/6.html

Cisco Systems, Inc. (2001, August 19). *Fundamentals of DWDM technology*. Retrieved April 14, 2004, from http://www.cisco.com/univercd/cc/td/doc/product/mels/cm1500/dwdm/dwdm_ovr.htm

DSL Life. (2004). *DSL tutorial*. Retrieved April 14, 2004, from http://www.dsllife.com/dsltut.htm

Frame Relay Forum. (2002). Retrieved April 14, 2004, from http://www.mplsforum.org/frame/

H.323 Forum. (2004). Retrieved April 14, 2004, from http://www.h323forum.org

Horak, R. (2001, July 30). *T-carrier basics*. Retrieved April 14, 2004, from http://www.commweb.com/8705550

International Engineering Consortium. (2003). *Cable modems*. Retrieved April 14, 2004, from http://www.iec.org/online/tutorials/cable_mod

International Engineering Consortium. (2003). Various other tutorials. Retrieved April 14, 2004, from http://www.iec.org/online/tutorials

International Telecommunication Union, Telecommunication Standardization Sector. (2004). Retrieved April 14, 2004, from http://www.itu.int/ITU-T/

Internet Engineering Task Force. (n.d.). Retrieved April 14, 2004, from http://www.ietf.org

Internet Engineering Task Force. (2003, February 3). *Differentiated services (diffserv)*. Retrieved April 14, 2004, from http://www.ietf.org/html.charters/OLD/diffserv-charter.html

IPv6.org. (2003). *IPv6*. Retrieved April 14, 2004, from http://www.ipv6.org

MPLS Forum. (2003). Retrieved April 14, 2004, from http://www.mplsforum.org

OpenH323.org. (2003). *H.323 standards*. Retrieved April 14, 2004, from http://www.openh323.org/standards.html

Pacific Bell Internet. (1999). *Classless Inter-Domain Routing (CIDR) overview*. Retrieved April 14, 2004, from http://public.pacbell.net/dedicated/cidr.html

Performance Technologies. (2004). *SS7 tutorial*. Retrieved April 14, 2004, from http://www.pt.com/tutorials/ss7

Protocols.com. (n.d.). *ISDN*. Retrieved April 14, 2004, from http://www.protocols.com/pbook/isdn.htm

Resilient Packet Ring Alliance. (2003, May 19). *A summary and overview of the IEEE 802.17 Resilient Packet Ring standard*. Retrieved April 14, 2004, from http://www.rpralliance.org/articles/overview_of_draft_22.pdf

RFC Editor. (2002, August 12). Retrieved April 14, 2004, from http://www.rfc-editor.org/

RSA Security. (2003). *Making sense of WLAN security.* Retrieved April 14, 2004, from http://www.rsasecurity.com/products/securid/whitepapers/MSWLAN_WP_0803.pdf

Rybczynski, T. (1999). *IP: Getting some class*. Retrieved April 14, 2004, from http://www.nortelnetworks.com/solutions/financial/collateral/nov98_ipcos_v1.pdf

Sangoma Technologies. (2004). *X.25 packet switching*. Retrieved April 14, 2004, from http://www.sangoma.com/x25.htm

Simple Web. (1999). *Introduction to TMN*. Retrieved April 14, 2004, from http://www.simpleweb.org/tutorials/tmn/

SIP Forum. (2002). Retrieved April 14, 2004, from http://www.sipforum.org

SONET.com. (2000, April 26). *Educational information*. Retrieved April 14, 2004, from http://www.sonet.com/edu/edu.htm

Spurgeon, C. (2002, August 24). *Charles Spurgeon's Ethernet Web site*. Retrieved April 14, 2004, from http://www.ethermanage.com/ethernet/ethernet.html

Web Host Industry Review, Inc. (2003). (VPN) Virtual Private Network News. Retrieved April 14, 2004, from http://findvpn.com/news/

Welcome to get IEEE 802. (2003). Retrieved April 14, 2004, from http://standards.ieee.org/getieee802/

Home Area Networking

Sherali Zeadally, Priya Kubher, and Nadeem Ansari, *Wayne State University*

INTRODUCTION

Home area networks (HANs) facilitate communication among appliances, home systems, entertainment products, and information devices in a home so that they can work cooperatively and share information. A device connected to an HAN gains the capabilities of other networked devices, and as a result the device can provide a service or function that it would have otherwise been incapable of providing alone (CEA, 2004). Several factors are pushing for the development and adoption of HANs. These include the advancement in telecommunications technologies, the wide proliferation of personal computers, the decreasing costs of smart devices that allow users to control and monitor events in consumer-based appliances, and consumer demand for content rich applications.

HANs enable users to get information about the home's condition, to remotely control home systems and appliances, and to gain access to information and entertainment resources both from inside (such as a computer hard drive) and outside the home (for instance, from the Internet) (Bose, 2001). To provide these benefits to home consumers, different devices of the home network must be able to communicate with each other to provide services despite their implementation differences. This requires the management and coordination of discovery methods that work across heterogeneous device technologies and complex home networking architectures. To achieve this management and coordination transparently without user intervention is a complex task that until now has been the major factor responsible for impeding the wide acceptance and delivery of advanced services into the home. A common solution is to exploit a central connection point often referred to as a residential gateway. The residential gateway acts as a "bridge" between the wide area network (e.g., Internet) and the home network as illustrated in Figure 1. The gateway provides users access to home devices and control over the contents and leverages two technological trends, namely the ubiquity of broadband connectivity and Internet access in homes, offices, vehicles, and mobile/portable devices and the emergence of new applications and services. As Figure 1 illustrates, the residential gateway provides a central coordination connection point for different heterogeneous communication technologies such as Jini and UPnP using physical Ethernet or IEEE 802.11 network connectivity (Marples & Kriens, 2001).

In this chapter, we discuss the design and implementation of such a residential gateway based on the Open Services Gateway Initiative (OSGi) (Gong, 2001; OSGi Forum, 2004). We place special emphasis on the development of an architecture that enables seamless interoperability among different device technologies by exploiting the OSGi architecture.

RELATED WORK AND NOVELTY OF CONTRIBUTION

Related Work

The OSGi expert group (OSGi Forum, 2004) is currently focusing on the development of drivers for all possible and probable protocols to be used in home networks. Saif, Gordon, and Greaves (2001) discussed the design and implementation of a residential gateway in the context of the AutoHan project. Dobrev et al. (2002) proposed a framework to extend the OSGi framework to enable redefining gateway services and to provide a smart querying technique for users and devices to look up services with particular attributes. The authors also addressed the interoperability feature and proposed implementing it through the extension of OSGi services. Wils et al. (2002) discussed the integration of Universal Plug and Play (UPnP) (UPnP Forum, 2004) and Jini (Sun Microsystems 2004 a, 2004b) with the OSGi framework.

Novelty of Contribution

As mentioned previously, one of the main goals of this work is to investigate the *interoperability* feature of OSGi by design and implementation. In doing so, our proposed

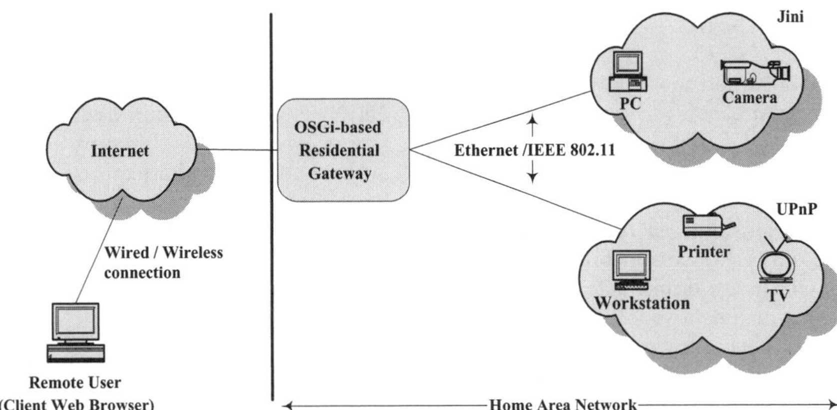

Figure 1: Remote Internet access to a heterogeneous home area network via an OSGi-based residential gateway.

design architecture enables different devices using different technologies (e.g., UPnP and Jini) to seamlessly operate with each other to provide services to home network users. In this work, we focus on OSGi to provide this capability and in this context this work differs from Saif and colleagues who do not use OSGi in their architectural design. In contrast to Wils and colleagues' work that merely proposed support for OSGi-Jini services and OSGi-UPnP services, our work *unifies* Jini and UPnP, and we demonstrate the seamless communication between Jini and UPnP via actual implementations of Jini and UPnP drivers within the OSGi framework. In contrast to other previous works, our implementation also deals with the security issues involved during remote Internet access to an HAN.

SECURITY IN HOME AREA NETWORKS

One of the main concerns for HAN users is the need to create and maintain a secure working environment. Two distinct approaches in addressing the security issues include *security prevention* and *security detection*. An example of *security prevention* would be a firewall device that restricts specific traffic/ports to or from specific hosts. Although this provides protection against unauthorized traffic, it has no means to determine if an attack is being attempted via some authorized port. An example of *security detection* could be an intrusion detection system (IDS) device that contains a signature to identify a specific attack via authorized or unauthorized ports. Different security services (authentication, confidentiality, integrity, access control, and possibly nonrepudiation) need to be provided to different players (e.g., end user, operator, and service provider). Furthermore, the nature of the network infrastructure technology has an impact on the security of the entire system. Certain network infrastructure technologies are inherently more secure than others. Similarly, the security mechanisms incorporated within certain communication protocols are more sophisticated than those in others. The two network infrastructure categories include infrastructure technologies and communication protocols used to interconnect the various *devices within the home network* and infrastructure technologies and communication protocols used to *interconnect a home area network to a wide area network* (WAN).

Securing Networked Devices within the HAN

Session Initiation Protocol Security Applied to Networked Appliances

The session initiation protocol (SIP) (Handley, Schulzrinne, Schooler, & Rosenberg, 1999) provides simple application layer signalling for setting up, maintaining, and terminating multimedia sessions such as voice calls, videoconferences, and instant messaging sessions. SIP can also be used between the external access device and the residential gateway and can be used for naming, addressing, routing of messages, and for secure access to HAN-based networked appliances. SIP leverages the standard SIP capabilities to communicate directly with appliances even when they are behind firewalls, as compared to NATs or other entities that prevent direct end-to-end communication. The primary advantage of using SIP for networked appliances is its ability to provide connectivity across a WAN. For general SIP security some form of public key (Galvin & Murphy, 1995) technology must be employed to provide security. In the case of remote access to devices and appliances within the home, however, shared secrets (Algesheimer, Camenisch, & Shoup, 2002) can be used to provide privacy and authentication. In this case, a one-to-one (or few-to-one) correspondence exists between authorized users and the home area network devices with which they will be communicating. Users will have the opportunity to designate a shared secret (Handley, Schulzrinne, Schooler, & Rosenberg, 1999) for use in their communication with the HAN devices. The secret may be shared either with the home residential gateway or firewall in the case where the user directly communicates with the home devices. In general, secret key methods are preferable to public key because of their higher level of security and increased efficiency. SIP describes two methods of achieving privacy: by encrypting either *end-to-end* or on a *hop-by-hop* basis. In the case of remote access to an HAN, end-to-end encryption is more efficient when the home user and the home residential gateway/firewall (or service provider proxy) share a secret key.

Securing HAN Devices

An HAN typically has many devices on the network, some belonging to the entire household and others belonging to individuals within the home. The security domain for HANs can be defined as a set of objects (a user can also be an object) that are allowed to interact with each other. However, a security policy is the specification of how objects in a security domain are allowed to interact. The security policy and domain taken together can be used to control and administer privileges to the various HAN devices. For example, a networked home alarm system might be in a security domain with one particular control application on the family personal computer that can only be accessed by one user (such as the head of the family). Other family members or other applications on that computer would not be allowed access to it.

To ensure that actions and access to devices residing on the home network have the proper authorizations, we can support device authentication using various key distribution mechanisms (Ellison, 2004; Strategis, 2001):

- **Passwords**: Since passwords are used for authentication, similar to keys, they are considered as part of the key distribution mechanism. Most often passwords are converted by algorithms to cryptographic keys. The disadvantage of password is that, if it is too simple, then it is easy to crack the password. But if the password is complex people tend to have a tendency to write it down and therefore it is subject to being leaked.
- **DES, AES, or WEP keys**: There are symmetric encryption algorithms, such as Data Encryption Standard (DES) and Advanced Encryption Standard (AES), and protocols using symmetric algorithms, such as wired equivalent privacy (WEP). The keys for these algorithms and protocols are similar to passwords in that both ends of a communication need to know the key. These are typically expressed in hexadecimal digits and have the advantage that they can carry more entropy (information) than a typical password but have the disadvantage that they are not memorable. They must therefore be written down, which makes them potentially available to someone other than the user although not to attackers on the Internet.
- **Public Keys**: Public key (PK) cryptography differs from symmetric key cryptography in that one encrypts with a different key from the one used to decrypt. It is also a characteristic of PK systems that one key, called the private key, can easily be used to generate the other key, called the PK, but the reverse is not true. As only the PK is made available, this is a more secure method.
- **PKI**: A traditional public key infrastructure (PKI) is a mapping from names to PKs and the mapping being created by some trusted third party (usually called a certification authority or CA).

Once a user or device has been authenticated the next step is to identify the privileges that the device or user has been granted (Bergstrom, Driscoll, & Kimball, 2001). This is important as different users may have different privileges for different devices. Some of the main authorization mechanisms (Ellison, 2004) include the following:

- **Access Control List (ACL)**: An ACL (one per device) is a protected table residing in memory in the same device as the resource whose access is being protected. Access to a device can be controlled by using just the ACL. It is an array of entries, and each entry contains the following: subject (an identifier of the entity being granted access), authorization (an indicator of the rights being granted that subject), delegation (a flag, indicating whether the subject may further delegate these rights), and validity (optional conditions on validity of the entry, such as a "not-after" date and time). The disadvantages are that ACL need time and space because of editing if the number of ACLs or subjects is large. ACLs also require persistent storage as they must survive a power failure.
- **Authorization Server (Strategis, 2001)**: In the case of a large number of devices, all of which need the same ACL, if that ACL is large because of many entries, and if network costs are low, then it might make sense to move the ACL from each local machine to a server, often called an authorization server. This does not eliminate the need for an ACL in each device. The device needs an ACL listing the authorization server. That ACL, in effect, grants all access rights to the server and allows it to delegate rights to others. Even though each device needs an ACL, there might still be advantages to using a server because the ACL in each device is very small (one entry) and should rarely have to change. But this system is unlikely to find acceptance in HANs, as it is very complex implement. We can delete this section as it does not seem very viable for HANs and is in more line with the corporate environment.
- **Authorization Certificate**: This is a digitally signed ACL used to administer authorization. A subject listed in the device ACL might be given the right to delegate some set of permissions.

Securing the Interconnection between the HAN and the WAN Using Addressing and Firewall

Private Addressing

Private addressing can be used to secure devices and communication protocols within the HAN. Private IPv4 addresses may be assigned to devices within an HAN to cope with limited IPv4 address space. Because assignment of private IP addresses comes with no extra cost to the user, it is attractive from a pricing perspective as well. A clear division of public and private hosts and the resulting need to renumber makes uncontrolled outside connectivity difficult.

When a device within the HAN needs to communicate with a device that is outside the HAN, we can adopt one of following two possible approaches for addressing:

1. **Network Address Translators** (NATs) (Sengodan & Ziegler, 2001): NATs residing at the boundary of the home area network replace the private IP address with a public address when the packet leaves the home network and vice versa.
2. **Realm-Specific IP** (RSIP) (Borella, 1999): A realm-specific IP implementation involves the creation of servers and clients running the realm-specific IP (RSIP) protocol. RSIP is a new protocol developed (as an alternative to the NAT), with the additional requirement to preserve end-to-end packet integrity. RSIP enables an enterprise to keep many private Internet addresses behind a single public Internet address. RSIP functions by leasing public IP addresses and ports to RSIP hosts located in private addressing domains. The RSIP client requests registration with an RSIP server or gateway. The server in turn delivers either a unique public IP address or a shared public IP address and a unique set of transfer control protocol/user datagram protocol (TCP/UDP) ports and attach the RSIP host's private address to this public address. The RSIP host uses this public address to send packets to public destinations. The packets contain both the public and private addresses, and the RSIP server strips off the private address header and sends the packet on with a public IP header.

Firewall

A firewall for a HAN requires access to all traffic into and out of the HAN. The firewall monitors the flow of data, regulating traffic between the HAN and the Internet. It uses a set of packet filtering rules that specify traffic that should be permitted or denied. But a firewall cannot protect devices that bypass the firewall's protection. Devices on the HAN that access the external world (using a modem, wireless adapter, Ethernet over power line, or broadband connector) all require the protection of a firewall and should not set up connections to the Internet that bypass the firewall. Typically, firewalls can be classified in the following categories:

- ***Packet Filters*** (Pike, 2002; Sengodan & Ziegler, 2001): There are of two kinds – *static* packet filters (Cheswick & Bellovin, 1996) and *stateful* packet filters (Bosworth & Kabay, 2002). Static packet filters have a static configuration based on which packets are either granted or denied access. They do not maintain any state about the session and handle packets on a per-packet basis. Stateful packet filters maintain information on session state, and based on this information, packets may dynamically be granted or denied access. The nondynamic nature of static packet filters makes them unsuitable for home networks because of the typical dynamic nature of port assignment for several home network sessions. Stateful packet filters are neither adequate nor economically feasible, and the performance requirements are too high for a low-end single-point-of-access gateway. Unfortunately, it is difficult for the average consumer to correctly administer policies at the packet level. Firewall configuration requires detailed information about the communication characteristics of applications—information that is not apparent to most consumers. In addition, new applications may be installed that change the communication characteristics of the home and require an update to the packet-filtering rules. Some home PC firewalls address the packet-filtering configuration problem by generating an alarm that asks the user for approval to allow the communication. This works well for a single machine, but when there is a central firewall on the home gateway, there is no standard way to reflect the firewall activity back to the application initiating the activity.
- ***Circuit Gateways*** (Cheswick & Bellovin, 1994): The most common circuit gateway is SOCKS. SOCKS is a networking proxy protocol that enables hosts on one side of a SOCKS server to gain full access to hosts on the other side of the SOCKS server without requiring direct IP reachability. SOCKS are often used as a network firewall, redirecting connection requests from hosts on opposite sides of a SOCKS server. The SOCKS server authenticates and authorizes requests, establishes a proxy connection, and relays data between hosts. A SOCKS server normally resides at the edge of the HAN. The SOCKS server establishes a TCP connection (or circuit) to each of the communicating endpoints and relays the session data. The SOCKS client within the HAN authenticates the establishment of such a virtual circuit. However, the complexity associated with this mechanism, and its dependence on TCP (and therefore not possible for UDP traffic), make it unsuitable for home networking solutions.
- ***Application-Level Gateways*** (Oppliger, 2002): Application-level gateways (also known as proxies) operate by being aware of the application. Although this approach can be very secure, it is not scalable because such a solution would require that each application require a proxy at the edge of the home network. In addition, this is an expensive solution.

Based on the previous observations, it can be seen that traditional firewall solutions are unsuitable for home networks, and novel security solutions are needed for HANs. One such new technique that shows great promise is based on the concept of a firewall control interface (Mercer, Molitor, & Hurry, 1999) between a device within the home network and the firewall. This interface provides the gateway the ability to manage the firewall, opening specific TCP permissions for well-known or registered ports, in support of VoIP services and applications, and opening only the negotiated TCP and UDP port permissions necessary to allow relevant applications. A firewall control interface opens a single "pinhole" in the firewall implemented by a filtering device. The application logic remains in the end systems and requests are made over a secure channel to the firewall to open and close pinholes and to manipulate or read NAT table entries. This allows the use of both encrypted signaling traffic and address translated endpoints.

A combination of the authorization mechanisms along with firewall solutions can be used to guard against malicious attacks.

DESIGN AND IMPLEMENTATION OF AN OSGI-BASED RESIDENTIAL GATEWAY

The complex diversity of home networking architectures and device technologies need to be coordinated to enable home users to fully exploit and reap their benefits. As mentioned earlier, management of these network architectures and services frequently burden most homeowners and is one of the main reasons impeding the proliferation and acceptance of sophisticated networking services into the home (Dobrev et al., 2002). The advent of OSGi simplifies management of home networks composed of multiple heterogeneous communication technologies. It is worthwhile noting that OSGi specification provides only the application programming interface (API) rather than the underlying implementation making OSGi-based gateways both platform and application independent. This independence gives considerable freedom and flexibility to application developers and designers in their service offerings. The OSGi service platform benefits also include security, service collaboration, and multiple network support (OSGi Forum, 2004). In this work, we focus on the capability of OSGi to provide *multiple network support*. OSGi specifies a framework (similar in functionality to an application server) where it is possible to dynamically load and manage software components also known as ***service bundles*** (Marples & Kriens, 2001). These bundles can be instantiated by OSGi to implement specific services required.

Integration of Discovery Technologies in OSGi

In recent years, several architectures such as UPnP, Jini, and Salutation (Salutation Consortium, 2004) have emerged to provide plug and play capabilities requiring little planning and minimal human intervention. A fundamental component common to all of these architectures is the *service discovery concept* exploited by each. Other technologies that provide service discovery include service location protocol (SLP) (Guttman, Perkins, Veizades, & Day, 1999) and Bluetooth (Bluetooth SIG, 2004). The device access specification (DAS) of OSGi allows multiple devices to be discovered and their services advertised thereby making these services available to other devices, services, and applications. Integration of discovery technologies with OSGi is based on an import/export model. Briefly, registered OSGi devices and services are exported out of the OSGi framework. For instance, an OSGi printing service can be exported to a Jini network to appear as a Jini printer. Similarly, devices and services found by native discovery techniques can also be imported into the OSGi framework to appear as valid OSGi entities and accessible to other OSGi entities. It is this importing/exporting feature that allows cross-technology discovery and promotes interoperability among multiple device types (Dobrev et al., 2002).

Our main goals in this chapter are threefold:

1. First, we demonstrate how the implemented residential gateway provides remote access to an Internet user.
2. Second, we also illustrate, by design and implementation interoperability between Jini and UPnP devices by exploiting OSGi capabilities. To achieve this, we exploit APIs of OSGi, which provide access from the OSGi framework to UPnP or Jini devices and services in the network. The APIs also make OSGi services available to members of UPnP or Jini networks. Consequently, the APIs provide bidirectional service discovery between UPnP or Jini devices and OSGi services: UPnP-OSGi or Jini-OSGi (*importing* UPnP or Jini device services into OSGi) and OSGi-UPnP or OSGi-Jini (*exporting* OSGi services to UPnP or Jini networks) (Dobrev et al., 2002). The software that we have designed and implemented to achieve these functionalities is called a driver bundle: the driver bundle responsible for interacting with the UPnP network will be henceforth referred as the ***UPnP driver bundle*** or ***UPnP base driver***. The driver responsible for interacting with the Jini network will be henceforth referred to as the ***Jini driver bundle or Jini base driver***.
3. Third, we describe the security features we have incorporated in our residential gateway design to provide secure access to the OSGi services offered by the different device technologies that constitute the HAN.

Internet Access to HAN Devices Residing on the UPnP and Jini Networks

By enabling the hypertext transfer protocol (HTTP) service (as shown in Figure 2) in the OSGi framework of the residential gateway, a remote user can use a username/password combination to gain access and perform operations on the bundles and services from anywhere on the Internet. This access allows users to remotely retrieve information from, and send control to, services supported by the residential OSGi-based gateway using a standard Web browser. Communication to and from the residential gateway is done using encryption through Secured Sockets Layer (SSL) to provide security and privacy to the user. The information from the browser is coded by using an encryption algorithm and at the residential gateway the information is decoded by using the corresponding decryption algorithm. We used *javax.crypto.** library to encrypt data using a secret key.

Bundle developers typically need to develop communication and user interface solutions using standard technologies such as HTTP, hypertext markup language, extensible markup language (XML), and servlets to enable users to access the OSGi resources via the HTTP service of the OSGi gateway. The HTTP service in the Java Embedded Server executes as a lightweight HTTP server. By exploiting the HTTP server, we can register OSGi services as HTTP services. In our gateway implementation, we exploit servlets to deliver OSGi services remotely via Web browsers to clients. A uniform resource identifier (URI) is used to remotely access the residential gateway.

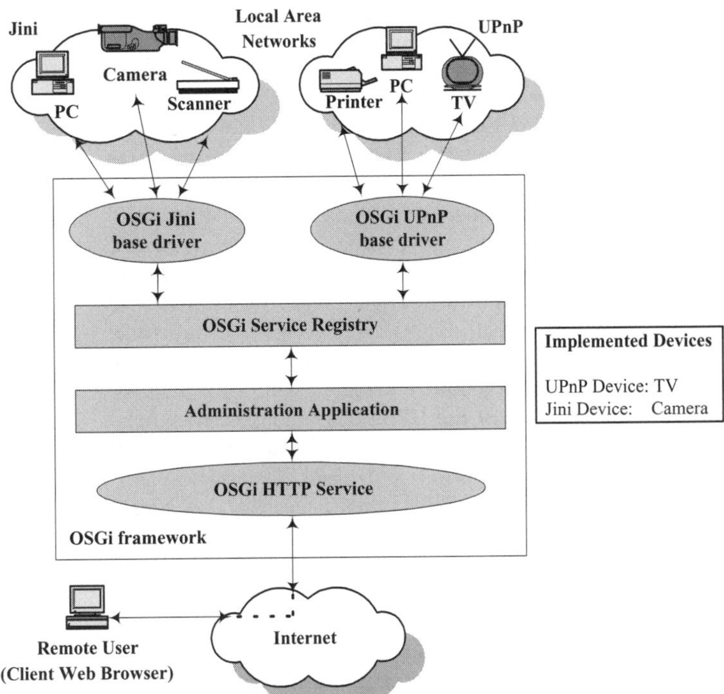

Figure 2: Design of OSGi-based residential gateway enabling Internet access to UPnP and Jini devices.

Once access is granted, OSGi services become available to the remote user. These services have been previously registered with the OSGi registry by using the registerResources() method of HttpContext object.

UPnP Device as an OSGi Service

The UPnP device architecture specification provides the protocols for a peer-to-peer network. It specifies how to join a network and how devices can be controlled using XML messages sent over HTTP. The UPnP specifications leverage Internet protocols (IP, TCP, HTTP, and XML).

This section describes our implementation of an OSGi bundle that interoperates with UPnP devices and UPnP control points. The implementation is based on the UPnP device architecture specification (UPnP, 2004) and the OSGi Service-Platform Release 3 (OSGi Forum, 2004). However, we had to make some changes where necessary to test it on a *Release 2* framework as implemented by Sun on the Java Embedded Server (JES2.0). Our implementation does not support exporting of OSGi services to a UPnP network.

To provide a comprehensive service for a UPnP device in an OSGi framework, we designed and implemented a UPnP base driver. This base driver enables the OSGi platform to offer UPnP services to its users by means of an interface registered with the service registry. This interface is made available through the implementation of the *org.osgi.service.upnp* service package that includes core components such as *UPnPDevice* (represents an imported UPnP device on a local network), *UPnPService* (representing services provided by the device), and *UPnPAction* (providing device controlling mechanisms).

There were some software development kits (SDKs) available to implement UPnP devices and control points in Java, but most of them were not open source, making it difficult to incorporate into the OSGi framework. The only open source SDK available (and which we chose in our implementation) is from CyberLink for Java (Konno, 2004). The implemented base driver listens on the UPnP network for device announcements. As soon as the UPnP base driver detects a new device, it extracts the information about that device according to the UPnP specification for further processing. Using this extracted (advertised) information, the UPnP base driver creates a `UPnPDevice` object and registers it in the OSGi Service Registry with a property of `DEVICE-CATEGORY="UPnP,"` along with other properties, such as a unique device name called `UDN`, similar to a unique resource locator (URL) for device matching purposes. This `UPnPDevice` object is an instance of a class that represents an interface in the package *"org.osgi.service.upnp."* This package has been implemented according to the OSGi's specifications and provides an interface for a UPnP device in an OSGi framework. The UPnP device interface exposed by this package contains the `UPnPDevice` Java interface and other Java interfaces, which together with the UPnP base driver, constitute a UPnP Device Service in an OSGi framework.

Any bundle (*ServiceListener*) listening at the OSGi's service registry for a service with a *DEVICE-CATEGORY="UPnP,"* will be informed about the UPnP device. The listener bundle can query the interface about the properties offered by this `UPnPDevice` service and if interested can accept the service (control the device) according to the OSGi's UPnP device service specification. However, in most cases, a "refined" service is easier to use, if provided by the vendor. This refined service can provide a direct access to the functionalities of the registered devices, instead of dynamically finding the services and functionalities of a UPnP device. For UPnP devices in OSGi, a refined service is an OSGi service that knows about a specific device and its functionalities in detail. Such a service provides targeted functionalities of the device it is serving, through its interface in the OSGi service registry. This refined service does not communicate directly to a UPnP device on a UPnP network; instead it utilizes already registered generic `UPnPDevice` (as mentioned previously). The difference between a generic `UPnPDevice` Service and a refined service is that a generic device service exposes the device's functionalities dynamically and a user does not know a priori these functionalities, whereas a refined service is static and the consumer knows in advance the functionalities available. For example, a `UPnPDevice` service interface provides a service for getting and invoking an action name, its arguments, and possible values associated with a state variable of the UPnP device on the network. Thus, to utilize a generic `UPnPDevice` service, a user input using menu options and their description for achieving particular goals becomes necessary. However, in the case of a refined service for the same device, the exposed functionalities such as *setPower* on or off or *getPowerStatus* to know whether TV is on or off, may be offered.

The unique device name (*UDN*) for this device is *edu.wayne.upnp.tv001* (in our implementation). As mentioned earlier, this UDN is a unique URL. However, the given format is our choice and is not specified by the UPnP forum. The UPnP base driver in the OSGi's framework detects this device, communicates with it, and after some information exchange, the base driver finally registers a `UPnPDevice` service in the OSGi's service registry. Based on the device matching criteria using properties such as UDN registered with the device service, or exposed by registered service interface, a refined service named *edu_wayne_upnp_tv001* (can be provided by some device vendor but in this case is our implementation) associates itself to this `UPnPDevice`. This refined service exports its interface so that other bundles in the OSGi framework know the functionalities this service offers. Some of the functionalities we have implemented include operations such as turning on and turning off the TV, or getting the current status of the TV.

Some functionality of a TV may involve video playback from some video source. This video stream may be provided by a Jini camera service in the OSGi framework. Our OSGi implementation can be further extended to monitor activities of these services. For instance, based on some stored correlation of functionalities in a database, an automated control command may be sent to the other device if one device starts an activity. For example, if a correlation is set such that whenever a camera playback is turned on, its video stream output is used as an input video stream for playback by the TV after the TV is switched on. As soon as the camera status changes to stop or record, a signal is sent to turn the TV off. Monitoring the two services and then invoking appropriate interface methods based on correlation stored in a database achieve the interoperability.

Security in UPnP

UPnP Security has defined a combination device and control point called the security console (SC). The SC takes security ownership of devices and authorizes control points (or other security consoles) to have access to devices over which the SC has control. An SC can own a device, meaning that it has the right to edit that device's access control list, or it can be given some subset of rights to the device and have the privilege to grant all or some of those rights to another SC or CP (by way of an authorization certificate). The SC also defines the names of individual or groups of control points.

Vulnerabilities in UPnP Security

UPnP was originally designed for the relatively benign security environment of a typical home—specifically, one that was not continuously connected to the global Internet. UPnP is susceptible to various security threats. Several countermeasures may be employed to address security threats, including encryption, authentication (requiring users or devices to prove who they are), access control and authorization (granting permission to only particular users to do certain operations), digital signatures (which ensure a message was actually sent by whoever claims to have sent it), message integrity checking (ensuring a message is not altered in transit), and others.

UPnP does not directly implement these countermeasures. Instead, it assumes that measures such as network isolation (gateways, firewalls, and proxies), MAC layer encryption (provided by the network adapters), and physical access control will be employed to protect not only UPnP traffic, but also the rest of the HAN. Some security concerns associated with UPnP include the following:

- Allowing the use of UPnP-enabled equipment in public facilities, such as printer kiosks in airports, protecting the service providers from fraudulent use, and protecting sensitive information on the UPnP equipment.
- Preventing unauthorized users from using home wireless power line or telephone networks to discover devices present in an HAN and misusing these devices.
- Enabling homeowners to remotely access, control, and monitor their home equipment securely over the Internet.
- Enabling service providers such as electric utilities to securely access, control, and configure equipment, such as power meters, in the home over the Internet.
- Allowing UPnP-enabled equipment, such as digital cameras, from the home to be taken to the office and used with computers there, without interfering with enterprise security or becoming visible to others on the network.

The eEye Digital Security advisory (eEye, 2001) identified a few vulnerabilities within Microsoft's UPnP implementation: a *remotely exploitable buffer overflow* to gain system-level access to any default installation of Windows XP and *Denial of Service (DoS)/Distributed Denial of Service (DDoS)* attacks (Lough, 2001).

The system remote exploit: This vulnerability within the Microsoft's implementation of the UPnP protocol can result in an attacker gaining remote system-level access (highest level of access) to any default installation of Windows XP. During testing of the UPnP service, it was discovered that by sending malformed advertisements at various speeds one could cause access violations on the target machine. Most of these violations were because of pointers being overwritten. Authors found instances of stack and heap overflows, both of which were exploitable. In the case of the heap overflow authors discovered pointers being overwritten for both buffers and functions. The Simple Service Discovery Protocol (SSDP) service also listens on multicast and broadcast addresses. Therefore gaining system access to an entire network of Windows XP-based machines is possible with only one anonymous UDP SSDP attack session.

DoS and DDoS: When a UPnP-enabled device is installed on a UPnP-based network, the device sends out an advertisement to notify control points of its existence. On a default Windows XP installation, no support is added for device control because the installation of UPnP would take place from the "Network Services" configuration. Microsoft added default support for an "Internet gateway device" to enable leading hardware manufacturers to make UPnP-enabled "gateway devices." However, if an application is set up to "sniff" a network with Windows XP, then Windows XP can be observed searching for this device as Windows XP loads. By sending a malicious spoofed UDP packet containing an SSDP advertisement, an attacker can force a Windows XP client to connect back to a specified IP address and passes on a specified HTTP/HTTPS request. When the XP machine receives this request, it will interpret the URL following the location header entity. Without any checking, the URL is passed to the Windows Internet services API functions and a new session is created. A malicious attacker could specify a service on a remote machine causing the Windows XP client to connect and get caught in a tight read/malloc loop. This loop will throw the machine into an unstable state with maximum CPU utilization, and memory is allocated to the point where it is totally exhausted. As a result, the remote Windows XP system becomes completely unusable and requires a physical power-off shutdown. Attackers could also use this exploit to control other Windows XP-based machines, forcing such machines to perform unicode attacks, double decode, or random CGI exploiting. Because of the insecure nature of UDP, an attacker can also exploit security holes on a Web server using UPnP with almost total anonymity. A more serious problem arises when such attack becomes a DDoS attack, because a SSDP announcement can be sent to broadcast addresses and multicast. It is therefore possible to send one UDP packet causing all Windows XP machines on the target network to be navigated to the URL of choice, performing an attack of choice. Moreover, because parts of the UPnP service are implemented using UDP, this makes these attacks completely untraceable.

Jini Device as an OSGi Service

Jini (Sun Microsystems 2004) is a framework based on the idea of federating groups of users and the resources required by those users. The focus of the framework is to make the network a more dynamic entity that better reflects the dynamic nature of the workgroup by enabling the ability to add and delete services flexibly. Jini systems provide mechanisms for service construction, lookup, communication, and use in a distributed system. Jini technology uses a *lookup service* with which devices and services register. When a device joins a Jini network, it goes through a phase called discovery and join-in. The device first locates the *lookup service* (discovery) and then uploads an object that implements all of its services' interfaces (join in). To use a service, a user or a program locates it using the *lookup service*. The service's object is copied from the *lookup service* to the requesting device where it will be used. Integrating Jini Services with OSGi would mean registering the services in the OSGi framework as OSGi services. This will make the registered Jini services accessible to any service or bundle in OSGi.

The OSGi specification works with various device access standards and is compatible with and can enhance a Jini environment. As mentioned previously, an OSGi implementation can also provide bridging capability between the Jini environment and non-Jini devices, such as UPnP, HAVi, and others.

Registering Jini Services as OSGi Services

To register Jini services in the OSGi framework, we designed and implemented a Jini base driver in the OSGi environment. The Jini driver is a bundle in the OSGi framework that imports Jini services into OSGi services. To import services, the Jini driver service transforms any Jini services discovered on the network to OSGi services thereby defining a bridge between a Jini network and an OSGi service platform. The importing of Jini services enables applications in the OSGi framework to interact with Jini services. Thus, OSGi bundles need not include extra components to use Jini Services and furthermore they do not even have to be aware of the fact that the service platform is Jini enabled. Figure 3 illustrates the steps

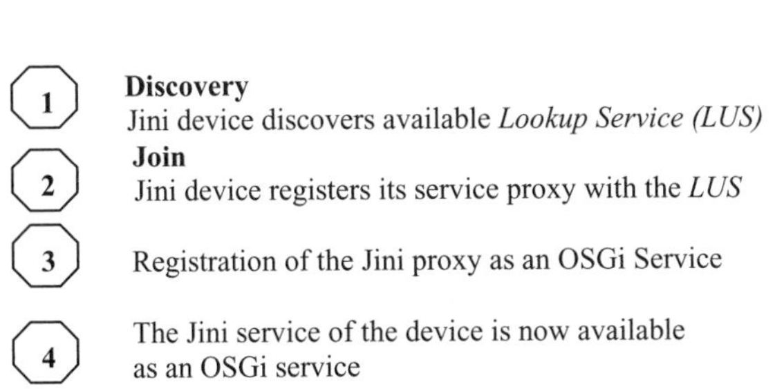

1
Discovery
Jini device discovers available Lookup Service (LUS)
Join
2
Jini device registers its service proxy with the LUS
3
Registration of the Jini proxy as an OSGi Service
4
The Jini service of the device is now available
as an OSGi service

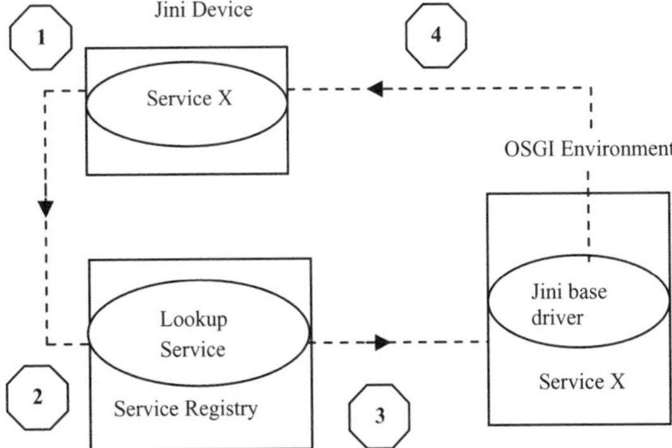

Figure 3: A device joins a Jini network and registers its services with OSGi.

involved when a device is introduced into the Jini network and registering its services as OSGi services in the OSGi platform.

After the Jini base driver (bundle) has been started in the OSGi framework, it waits for a Jini device to join the network. When the *JiniCamera* (a Jini device) is introduced into the network, the Jini base driver detects that a Jini device has joined the network and imports all the information needed to register that service as an OSGi service. The registration of the discovered Jini services is only possible if the interfaces under which they are registered are available to the OSGi framework. When the *JiniCamera service* is registered as an OSGi service using a `BundleContext` objects that provides a reference to a `ServiceRegistration` object. If the registration is successful, the following properties are set:

- `DEVICECATEGORY:` The property that must be used to participate in the OSGi device access mechanisms. The Jini base driver sets the value of this property to Jini when it imports a Jini service.
- `SERVICEID:` A unique Jini service identifier. Each service is required to have a unique service identifier. The Jini base driver sets this property to the identifier of the service in the service registry.

After registration, any application that is running on the OSGi framework can access and use the Jini services that are registered as the OSGi services. Applications that use these services do not and need not be aware that these are Jini and not OSGi devices.

When a Jini device (in this case the *JiniCamera)* is started, it registers its services with the LUS. The implemented *JiniCamera* service allows the following operations: `start, stop, record,` and `playback`.

The *JiniCamera* service provides an importable service that can be used by any other applications in the Jini network. The *JiniDriver,* a bundle in OSGi, gets access to this service and registers a proxy of this importable Jini service with the OSGi service registry.

Security in Jini

The design of the security model for Jini is built on the notions of a *principal* and an *access control list*. Jini services are accessed on behalf of some entity—the principal—which generally traces back to a particular user of the system. Services themselves may request access to other services based on the identity of the object that implements the service. Whether access to a service is allowed depends on the contents of an access control list associated with the object. The central difference between Jini and the other service location protocols such as Salutation, service location protocol, and UPnP is protocol independence. That is, Jini does not mandate any specific communication protocol between the clients and the services (except for bootstrapping the system), but relies on dynamic Java class loading instead (Eronen & Nikander, 2001). Because the proxies are written in Java, the system also claims operating system independence; this is in contrast with the other service location protocols that usually use nonportable device drivers. The protocol independence of Jini presents new security challenges. The Jini architecture does not include any security other than the normal Java security facilities (for protecting the client Java virtual machine (VM) from malicious proxy code), and (jvm) the security aspects of remote method invocation, which by themselves do not provide adequate security. Because all communication goes through downloaded proxy objects, security methods used in environments with fixed protocols cannot usually be used without some adaptation. Haselmeyer, Kehr, and Vob (2000) and Eronen and Nikander (2001) have identified the following security requirements for Jini:

- *Principal authentication:* The Jini client should be able to verify that it is communicating to the right service and through the right proxy. Likewise, the service should be able to verify the identity of the requester of the service. It is important to note that authentication is impossible several situations. For example, in a pure ad hoc network there may be no prior information about the communicating peers.
- *Secure principal attributes:* In many circumstances, human readable and recognizable names are required for authentication. Services might also have other attributes such as security level (for example, a printer for printing classified documents) or the "owner" of the service. Users might have other attributes such as memberships in groups or roles. Not all clients or services necessarily have names with any uniqueness beyond one client or server.
- *Service access control:* Based on the result of principal authentication and/or capabilities presented by the client and/or other circumstances, the service should allow some operations and deny others.
- *Protection from applications:* The client JVM may run multiple applications, some of which are not fully trusted, such as applets and games. Untrusted applications should not be able to access services with the user's privileges.
- *Protection from proxies:* The downloaded proxy code needs some special permissions (for example, to make network connections) while running inside the client JVM. Some proxies may need more permissions than others and these proxies need to be controlled. Although Java does provide some security facilities, they are inadequate for many applications.
- *Mobile code security issues:* One of the main differences between the Jini architecture and the "traditional" client/server systems such as CORBA or the World Wide Web is that in all these systems the client permanently contains the code for communicating with a server. The protocol code is part of the client and therefore part of the client's trusted computing base. If a client needs some form of security (e.g., authentication or integrity), it can use any protocol that provides the required security properties (e.g., SSL). In contrast, the Jini approach is fundamentally different. Jini clients do not implement any network protocol. Instead, the clients rely on the service's proxy object to perform the communication with the server. Proxy objects usually originate from some (usually untrusted) source on the network. This includes the downloading and execution of code from that source. A Jini client does not and cannot

know what a proxy object does with the supplied data. A security approach that is different from those of traditional client/server systems is therefore required. Because the proxy is supplied by its associated service it should know the appropriate level of security for its application domain. This approach relies on trusting the proxy to enforce the required security constraints. To establish trust in a proxy object, we need to ensure its integrity. The proxy object should not be changed on its way from the service (via the lookup service) to the Jini client. Digitally signing the object's code as well as the use of encrypted connections between the lookup service and the Jini clients are required to provide secure in-transit service descriptions.

- *Lookup service interaction:* Even with encrypted communication and authenticated objects, we still need Jini clients to trust the lookup service they are communicating with. This trust can be achieved by requiring the lookup service to authenticate itself to the Jini clients.

Integrating UPnP and Jini Services in OSGi

One of the main goals of this chapter is to demonstrate, by design and implementation, the seamless interoperability between Jini and UPnP devices and services by exploiting the OSGi framework. To achieve this we implemented an integration bundle we called the *UPnP–Jini bundle*. The UPnP–Jini bundle obtains a reference to both the *JiniCamera* and the *UPnPTv* by searching the service registry using `DEVICECATEGORY` as the search keyword and the value Jini or UPnP device. Once objects to *JiniCamera* and *UPnPTv* are obtained, the UPnP–Jini bundle uses methods for both devices to pass information and images between the *JiniCamera* and *UPnPTv*. Thus in our implementation, the UPnP-Jini bundle acts as a bridge for the Jini and UPnP devices. In this way, both the *JiniCamera* and *UPnPTv* have access to the services offered by each other and seamlessly interoperable and communicate with each other via OSGi as depicted in Figure 4.

The major task in our design was the implementation of the base drivers, which conforms to OSGi specifications, and handles the registration of UPnP or Jini services in the OSGi's registry. To test the driver and service implemented, a UPnP and Jini device were implemented. In our prototype implementation, we have the UPnP device (simulating a TV) and the Jini (simulating a camera) each executing separately on a workstation. The OSGi bundles (UPnP, Jini, UPnP-Jini bundles) were all executed on a third workstation running JES 2.0. All workstations resided on a 100 Mbits/s Ethernet local area network. The implementation was tested as follows: the JiniCamera was used to pass images to the UPnPTv, which then displayed them on its screen. When the "record" of the JiniCamera was activated, the camera sent a series of JPEG images to the residential gateway (OSGi framework), which passed the images to the UPnPTv (another workstation in our prototype). The UPnP device captured the images and displayed them on the screen. In this way, our design and implementation demonstrate how an event in one device (for instance, switching on the "record" function on the JiniCamera) triggers an event in another device (display images on the UPnPTv), thereby enabling devices in two different networks (Jini and UPnP) to interoperate through OSGi.

OSGi Security Implementation Issues for Secure Internet Access to the HAN

Security is an essential requirement for residential gateways and often involves many different aspects. Security in the OSGi framework is based on the Java 2 security architecture (Gong, 2001). Many methods defined by the OSGi API require the caller to have certain permissions. *Permission* is the authority to access some resource or to perform some operation. The bearer of certain permission is allowed to access a resource or to perform an operation specified in the permission, and the lack of it denies the caller an access or operation. For any service gateway, such as the residential gateway we have designed and implemented, the issue of security is of paramount importance because the gateway will be accessed by service providers and homeowners. In our residential gateway design, we address, by implementation, the following

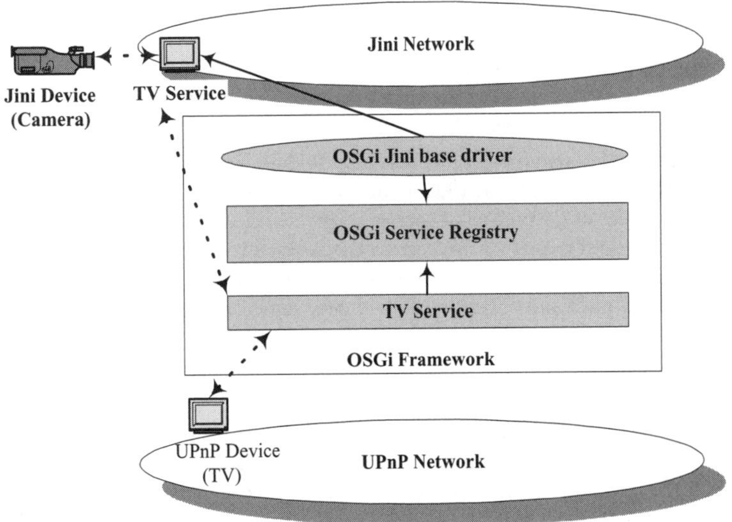

Figure 4: Integrating Jini and UPnP services through OSGi.

security issues during remote access to OSGi-based services:

- ***Dispatch the right service to the right person:*** When enabling Internet access to an HAN, security and authentication become an important concern. A basic authentication that is used to verify a user identity can also be used as a means to identify the services to which the user is authorized. An encrypted username/password is used to map to the services to which the user has access rights. Our implementation exploits OSGi-based HTTP authentication. The Java Embedded Server's HTTPService provides the necessary operations (via the handleSecurity method) to implement any HTTP-related authentication schemes. The handleSecurity method uses the BasicSchemeHandler (service of the JES framework), which performs the necessary authentication by checking the user's username/password combination.
- ***Maintain the integrity of the services:*** The integrity of the services is guaranteed by exploiting the three-level security model of the OSGi framework: service (level 1)-, package (level 2)-, and admin (level 3)- level privileges defined by the ServicePermission, PackagePermission, AdminPermission classes of OSGi (subclasses of *java.security.BasicPermission*), respectively. The service privilege is the very first or basic protection as it permits authentication on a per service level. This privilege permits a user to "register" a service or to "get" a service from the service registry. The package privilege represents a permission to import or to export a package. A package name and an action must be specified. This kind of permission grants a user access to all the resources that are contained in that package whether it is a service or a bundle. Similarly, a user can also export a package. The admin privilege is the highest permission level and users with this kind of privilege can perform administrative operations in the OSGi-based residential gateway. However, the admin privilege can be subject to abuse in that a bundle with such privilege has full control over the OSGi service platform.

  We have implemented all the three types of permissions mentioned previously. In our implementation, we exploit the *java.security.Policy* to grant permission to classes loaded using the Java security manager, which enforces the permissions that have been granted. It does so by examining the set of permissions owned by a calling class against the required permission. If a class has the needed permission then the execution proceeds; otherwise, access is denied.
- ***Protect the services from intruders:*** The services and their implementation details are protected from malicious attacks by means of secure sockets and authentication. Even if a user has access to the service it is not possible to modify the service implementation (i.e., code) because package- or admin-level privileges will still be required.

By implementing the three-level security permission in the OSGi framework we have protected the service and bundles that reside in the OSGI-based residential gateway. Security and authentication for remote access is provided by the HTTP basic authentication scheme. By combining these security features, we are able to provide secure, Internet access to the HAN via the OSGi-based residential gateway.

CONCLUSION

In this chapter, we describe the design and implementation of an OSGi-based residential gateway that provides seamless communication and interoperability between heterogeneous Jini and UPnP devices. We achieve this by designing and implementing Jini and UPnP base drivers. Our proposed solution enables the capability to bridge disparate discovery technologies and allows a richer device interaction and service delivery. In addition, our OSGi-based gateway also provides secure, remote access to the HAN devices and services. We are currently working on automation of device actions based on a one-time initialization by the user. This feature will make it possible to trigger several devices automatically to achieve the desired actions of several devices that the user may want to activate based on certain set criteria or home user preferences.

Although tremendous progress has been made within the home networking industry in recent years, several challenges remain. Particularly, making such a system secure from an end-to-end perspective is a critical area that needs greater investigation. For instance, one may have a scenario where Jini is used to discover available services within a community, following which an OSGi bundle is installed within the residential gateway and HAVi is used to actually deliver the service itself. In such a case, the interworkings of different technologies require greater investigation into the security implications.

GLOSSARY

Access Control List A set of data that informs a computer's operating system which permissions, or access rights, that each user or group has to a specific system object, such as a directory or file.

Advanced Encryption Standard A symmetric 128-bit block data encryption technique.

Certification Authority A certificate authority (CA) is an authority in a network that issues and manages security credentials and public keys for message encryption.

Data Encryption Standard Data Encryption Standard (DES) is a widely used method of data encryption using a private (secret) key.

Denial of Service Denial of service (DoS) attack is an incident in which a user or organization is deprived of the services of a resource they would normally expect to have.

Home Area Network Home area networks (HANs) facilitate communication among appliances, home systems, entertainment products, and information devices in a home so that they can work cooperatively and share information.

Home Audio/Video Interoperability A standard, developed by several leading electronics and computer manufacturers, that allows a number of different home entertainment and communication devices to operate from a single controller device such as your TV set.

HyperText Markup Language The authoring language used to create World Wide Web documents.

HyperText Transfer Protocol The underlying protocol used by the World Wide Web. HTTP defines how messages are formatted and transmitted and what actions Web servers and browsers should take in response to various commands.

Jini Software from Sun Microsystems that seeks to simplify the connection and sharing of devices, such as printers and disk drives, on a network.

Mobile Information Device Profile A set of Java 2 Micro Edition (J2ME) APIs that define how software applications interface with cellular phones and two-way pagers.

Network Address Translator An IETF standard that enables a local area network to use one set of IP addresses for internal traffic and a second set of addresses for external traffic.

Open Services Gateway Initiative An industry plan for a standard way to connect devices such as home appliances and security systems to the Internet.

Public Key Infrastructure A system of digital certificates, certificate authorities, and other registration authorities that verify and authenticate the validity of each party involved in an Internet transaction.

Realm Specific Internet Protocol An IP address translation technique that is an alternative to NAT.

Remote Method Invocation A set of protocols being developed by Sun's JavaSoft division that enables Java objects to communicate remotely with other Java objects.

Service Location Protocol A protocol or method of organizing and locating the resources (such as printers, disk drives, databases, e-mail directories, and schedulers) in a network.

Session Initiation Protocol An Internet Engineering Task Force (IETF) standard protocol for initiating an interactive user session that involves multimedia elements such as video, voice, chat, gaming, and virtual reality.

Simple Service Discovery Protocol The service discovery protocol provides a mechanism for client applications to discover the existence of services provided by server applications as well as the attributes of those services.

Transmission Control Protocol A set of rules (protocol) used along with the Internet protocol (IP) to send data in the form of message units between computers over the Internet.

Universal Plug and Play A standard that uses Internet and Web protocols to enable devices such as PCs, peripherals, intelligent appliances, and wireless devices to be plugged into a network and automatically know about each other.

Wide Area Network A network that spans over large distances; usually connects many other networks together.

Wired Equivalent Privacy A security protocol for wireless local area networks defined by the IEEE 802.11b standard.

Wireless Application Protocol A specification that allows users to access information instantly via handheld wireless devices such as mobile phones, pagers, two-way radios, smart phones, and communicators.

Wireless Markup Language An XML language used to specify content and user interface for WAP devices.

Extensible Hypertext Markup Language Hybrid between HTML and XML specifically designed for networked device displays.

Extensible Markup Language A specification (designed especially for Web documents) developed by the World Wide Web Consortium (W3C).

Extensible Stylesheet Language Transformation The language used in XSL style sheets to transform XML documents into other XML documents.

ACKNOWLEDGMENTS

We thank Aruna Banda for her security contributions and ideas on Jini and UPnP, and Mohammad Saklay for his help on a home area networking survey. We express our gratitude to all the anonymous reviewers who made excellent suggestions and comments that led to improvements of the chapter. We also thank Hossein Bidgoli and his excellent editorial board team for their kind encouragements and support during the preparation of this chapter. We are grateful to Farhan Siddiqui for her remarks, which helped to improve the presentation of this chapter. This work was supported by grants from Sun Microsystems (Palo Alto), Microsoft Corporation (Seattle), OPNET (Maryland), and Ixia Corporation (Calabasas).

CROSS REFERENCES

See *Firewall Basics; Internet Basics; Local Area Networks; Wide Area and Metropolitan Area Networks*.

REFERENCES

Algesheimer, J., Camenisch, J., & Shoup, V. (2002). Efficient computation modulo a shared secret with application to the generation of shared safe-prime products. In *Proceedings of Crypo'02, LNCS 2442*, Santa Barbara, CA.

Bergstrom, P., Driscoll, K., & Kimball, J. (2001). *Making home automation communication secure*. Retrieved August 18, 2004, from http://ranger.uta.edu/~huber/cse4392_SmartHome/bergstrom01.pdf

Bluetooth SIG, Inc. (2004). *Specification of the Bluetooth system*. Retrieved August 18, 2004, from http://www.bluetooth.org/

Borella, M. (1999). Realm specific IP. In *Proceedings of the 44th Internet Engineering Task Force (IETF)*, Minneapolis, March 1999. Retrieved August 18, 2004, from http://www.ietf.org/proceedings/99mar/slides/nat-realm-99mar/sld004.htm

Bosworth, S., & Kabay, M. (2002). Firewalls and proxy servers. In *Computer security handbook* (4th ed.). New York: John Wiley & Son.

Consumer Electronics Association. (2004). Retrieved August 18, 2004, from http://www.ce.org/publications/books_references/techhome/home/default.asp

Cheswick, W., & Bellovin, S. (1994). *Firewalls and Internet security*. Reading, MA: Addison-Wesley.

Cheswick, W., & Bellovin, S. (1996). A DNS filter and switch for packet-filtering gateways. In *Proceedings of The Sixth USENIX Security Symposium*, San Jose, CA, July.

Dobrev, P., et al. (2002). Device and service discovery in home networks with OSGi. *IEEE Communications Magazine, 40*(8), 86–92.

eEye Digital Security. (2001). *UPNP—Multiple remote Windows XP/ME/98 vulnerabilities*. Retrieved August 18, 2004, from http://www.eeye.com/html/Research/Advisories/AD20011220.html

Ellison, C. (2002). Home network security. *Intel Technology Journal, 6*(4). Retrieved August 18, 2004, from http://developer.intel.com/technology/itj/2002/volume-06 issue04/

Eronen, P., & Nikander, P. (2001). Decentralized Jini security. In *Proceedings of the Network and Distributed System Security Symposium* (NDSS 2001).

Galvin, J., & Murphy, S. (1995). Using public key technology: Issues of binding and protection. In *Proceedings of INET 95*, Honolulu, Hawaii, June.

Gong, L. (2001). A software architecture for open service gateways. *IEEE Internet Computing, 5*(1), 64–70.

Guttman, E., Perkins, C., Veizades, J., & Day, M. (1999). *Service location protocol, version 2*. RFC 2608, IETF, June.

Handley, M., Schulzrinne, H., Schooler, E., & Rosenberg, J. (1999). *SIP: Session initiation protocol*. RFC 2543, Internet Engineering Task Force, March.

Haselmeyer, P., Kehr, R., & Vob, M. (2000). *Tradeoffs in a secure Jini architecture*. Munich: Springer-Verlag.

Konno, S. (2004). *CyberLink for Java*. Retrieved August 18, 2004, from http://www.cybergarage.org/net/upnp/java/

Lough, D. (2001). *A taxonomy of computer attacks with applications to wireless networks*. Ph.D. dissertation, Virginia Polytechnic Institute and State University, Blacksburg, VA, April.

Marples, D., & Kriens, P. (2001). The open services gateway initiative: An introductory overview. *IEEE Communications, 39*(12), 110–114.

Mercer, S., Molitor, A., & Hurry, M. (1999). Network area Internet draft, IETF. Retrieved August 18, 2004, from http://www.iptel.org/info/players/ietf/firewall/oldmidcom/draft-rfced-info-mercer-00.txt

Merrick, C., Dunstan, R., & Jeronimo, M. (2001). Extending the PC in the home. *Intel Technology Journal, May*, 2001.

Oppliger, R. (2002). *Internet and intranet security* (2nd ed.). New York: Artech House.

OSGi Forum. (2004). *OSGi service-platform, release 3*. Retrieved August 18, 2004, from http://www.osgi.org

Pike, J. (2002). Firewalls. In *Cisco network security*. Upper Saddle River, NJ: Prentice Hall.

Rose, B. (2001). Home networks: A standards perspective. *IEEE Communications Magazine, 39*(12), 78–85.

Saif, U., Gordon, D., & Greaves, D. (2001). Internet access to a home area network. *IEEE Internet Computing, January/February*.

Salutation Consortium. (2004). *Salutation architecture specification, version 20.c—Part 1*. Retrieved August 18, 2004, from http://www.salutation.org

Sengodan, S., & Ziegler, R. (2001). On securing home networks. Nokia Research Center Ericsson Telecom AB, Proceedings of INET 2001, Stockholm, Sweden, June.

The Strategis Group, Inc. (2001). *Residential high-speed Internet: Cable modems, DSL, and fixed wireless*. Internal Report, January.

Sun Microsystems. (2004a). *Jini connection technology*. Retrieved August 18, 2004, from http://wwws.sun.com/software/jini/

Sun Microsystems. (2004b). *Service location protocol*. Retrieved August 18, 2004, from http://www.srvloc.org/

UPnP. (2004). *UPnP device architecture*. Retrieved August 18, 2004, from http://www.upnp.org/download/UPnPDA10_20000613.htm

UPnP Forum. (2004). *Universal plug and play device architecture*. Retrieved August 18, 2004, from http://www.upnp.org/

Wacks, K. (2002). Standards for network appliances. In *Proceedings of the 4th IEEE's international workshop on networked appliances*, Gaithersburg, MD, January. Retrieved August 18, 2004, from http://www.caba.org/search/index.cfm?action=getfile&i=238&dc=ER

Wils, A., et al. (2002). Device discovery via residential gateways. *IEEE Transactions on Consumer Electronics, 48*(3), 478–483.

Public Network Technologies and Security

Dale R. Thompson and Amy W. Apon, *University of Arkansas*

INTRODUCTION

Networks for the transfer of data between computers, both public and private, are ubiquitous in today's business world. A public network is one that is publicly available to subscribers (Stallings, 2001). It provides service to multiple subscribers and is built and maintained by a public network provider. Internationally, the term *public network* is often applied to networks that are under government control or are a national monopoly. However, a network can also be a privately owned network whose services are sold to the public. Whether the network is under government control or is a privately owned network whose services are sold to the public, businesses access the network by installing an access device at each site and using an access line to the nearest point of presence (POP) of the public network provider (Panko, 2001).

This chapter gives an overview of the secure use of public networks. It begins by describing public network concepts and services and the structure of the public switched telephone network (PSTN) system. The technologies used both for access to a public network and within the public network itself, issues related to choosing a public or a private network, the secure use of public networks, and public networks in the Internet and e-commerce environments are covered.

OVERVIEW OF PUBLIC NETWORK CONCEPTS, SERVICES, AND STRUCTURE

Traditionally, companies desiring to connect business computers in different geographic locations have used private networks. That is, they have used point-to-point leased lines between business sites to create their own circuit-switching or packet-switching networks for their data communication requirements (Panko, 2001). Unlike telephone calls, which set up the required capacity as needed, leased lines provide dedicated transmission capacity between sites. These networks are called private networks (Stallings, 2001). By using leased lines, companies have a dedicated, guaranteed network capacity. In many cases, volume discounts are offered for the bandwidth available on the leased line. An example of a private network is shown in Figure 1.

There are several disadvantages to private networks. Private networks require higher initial costs. The leased line connections must be planned and installed. The switching devices must be provided. In addition, once a network is operational there are ongoing management and maintenance costs of the networks (Panko, 2001). A public network is an alternative to a private network.

A public network provides connectivity to other locations as a service. There are advantages to using a public network. A public network requires no complex network of leased lines and switching devices that the business must plan and install. There is commonly one access line installed per site. Even if a leased line is used to connect to the nearest POP, there are usually fewer leased lines required. For example, if there are 10 sites using the public network, then there are 10 leased lines. Compare this to a fully meshed private network that requires 45 leased lines. For N locations, $N(N-1)/2$ leased lines are required for a connection to and from each site. Even if not every site is connected to every other site in the private network, but sites are connected through intermediate sites, the number of leased lines for a public versus a private network is generally smaller. Finally, because of competitive pricing, public networks are less expensive than private networks (Stallings, 2001). Figure 2 illustrates an example of a public network.

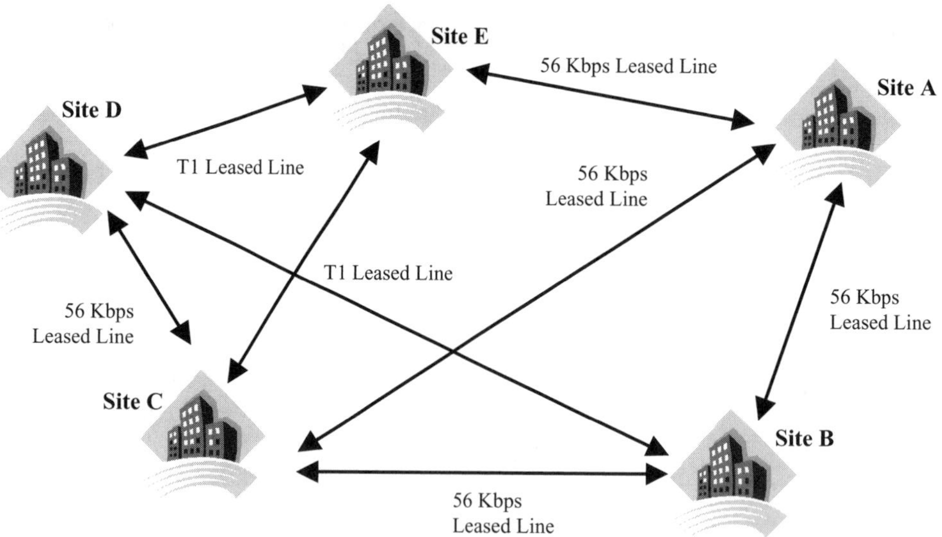

Figure 1: A private switched data network.

The global Internet is a network that is publicly accessible worldwide. The Internet is not one single network but is composed of several networks connected together and communicating with standard Internet technologies (Moody, 2001). Access to the Internet is achieved via an Internet service provider (ISP). The Internet allows a business to have a worldwide presence, and purchases can be made automatically using e-commerce software.

A network that transfers data and information only within a single business is called an intranet (Moody, 2001). Intranets are used to carry corporate information that can range from being routine, such as e-mail, manuals, and directories, to sensitive information such as that of project management and internal purchasing. Intranets use the same technologies as the Internet but access is restricted to employees. A private network that uses Internet technologies is naturally an intranet. A public network can be used by a business as an intranet by asking that the data be restricted to go only to other locations of the same business. Of course, the bandwidth is still shared with other businesses that use the same public network.

An extranet is a hybrid between the public Internet and the private intranet (Moody, 2001). A portion of the intranet is extended to business partners in a controlled and restricted way. The extranet can be used for project management of projects between partners. Another common and practical use of the extranet is to allow partners access to stock levels and shipping status, for example direct online purchasing of supplies and other applications are made possible through the use of an extranet. A public network provider has a value-added network if it owns the packet-switching nodes and leases transmission capacity from an interexchange carrier such as AT&T (Stallings, 2001). It is called a value-added network because the leased lines add value to the packet switching nodes. A network provider that provides a value-added network is

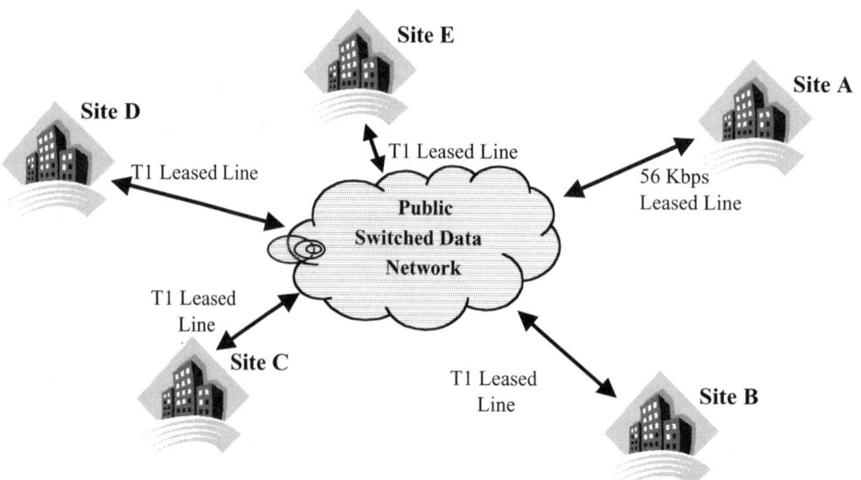

Figure 2: A public switched data network.

sometimes called a value-added carrier. In many cases, a public network provider will partner with companies that provide services that require network connectivity such as Web hosting and give discounts to them for using their network. A business that bundles a service with a particular public network provider is called a value-added reseller.

Public network providers often offer services such as Web hosting to subscribers in addition to connectivity between sites. These additional services are called value-added services. These services include asset management, configuration control, fault management, monitoring, Web-based reporting, Web hosting, e-mail services, and content delivery networks.

Asset management is keeping inventory of devices that are connected to the network. As devices are added or taken off the network, the asset management system will keep an up-to-date log of the assets. Configuration control is about maintaining and keeping records of the configuration of networked devices. The network provider typically maintains the configuration of the packet switching node that connects each of the subscriber locations to the network. A provider will also monitor devices to detect faults and either fix them or notify the appropriate on-site personnel. This is called fault management. A provider can invest in large network operation centers for monitoring their subscribers' network devices. This includes maintaining a firewall to prevent unwanted users into the network and intrusion detection systems for detecting activity that is consistent with common hacker techniques. With Web-based reporting, the provider gives the subscriber reports about the status of their network and a history of its downtime and performance.

One of the most popular value-added services is Web hosting. The provider maintains one or more servers and allocates space on them for the subscriber's Web site. The provider maintains the server and performs backups. Subscribers are given access to their portions of the server to post their Web sites and control their content. An advantage to using this value-added service is that it is likely that the subscriber has other sites that are connected to the same public network. If the server is connected to the same public network, it provides faster response times to the end users.

Medium to large users who have high volumes of content serving a distributed set of users may consider a value-added service called a content delivery network (CDN). A CDN intelligently distributes the content to multiple locations and closer to the end user. By moving the customized content closer to the end user, faster response times are achieved (Allen, 2001). Queries to the main server or group of servers are routed to the location that can best respond to the query. Content is cached at each of the locations and future requests are serviced more quickly because the information traverses fewer links in the network. There are three main advantages to a CDN. First, end users receive faster response times. Second, it relieves congestion on the original server that maintains the master copy of the content. Finally, it reduces the amount of data transmission capacity required on the network because the content is distributed to multiple locations and does not have to come from the original server. Some of the popular CDN providers are Akamai (http://www.akamai.com) and Mirror Image (http://www.mirror-image.com).

Structure of the Public Switched Telephone Network System

The PSTN system is often used to provide the technology that a business uses to access a public network or is the technology of the public or private lines. The structure of the PSTN in the United States has evolved from one that was almost entirely controlled by a single company to one that allows competition in a free market. Before January 1, 1984, AT&T (also known as the Bell System) controlled 80% of the PSTN in the U.S. (Bellamy, 2000). A Justice Department antitrust suit filed in 1974 and a private antitrust case by MCI resulted in a breakup of AT&T (Noam, 2001). The suit argued that AT&T used its control of the local operation as an unfair advantage against competing long-distance carriers.

On January 1, 1984, AT&T was divided into smaller companies. The breakup involved the divestiture of seven Bell operating companies (BOCs) from AT&T. The seven regional BOCs, known as "baby Bells" or regional BOCs (RBOCs), initially carried only regional telephone and mobile service. The network was partitioned into two levels (Bellamy, 2000), and the remaining part of AT&T retained the transport of long-distance telephone service.

The United States was divided into local access and transport areas (LATAs), which are controlled by local exchange carriers (LECs). LECs can transport telephone calls within a LATA (called intra-LATA traffic) but are not permitted to transport traffic between different LATAs (called inter-LATA traffic), even though the same BOC may control both LATAs. The inter-LATA traffic is transported by interexchange carriers (IXCs), commonly known as long-distance carriers. Each IXC interfaces at a single point in the LATA called a point of presence. At divestiture, AT&T became an IXC and it opened the door to competition for other companies' long-distance service. The major IXCs in the United States include AT&T, MCI–WorldCom, and Sprint.

The divestiture decree was supervised by District Judge Harold Greene and known as the modified final judgment (Noam, 2001). LECs had to grant equal access to all IXCs. The service offered by the LECs to the IXCs had to be equal in type, quality, and price (Bellamy, 2000). In addition, users could specify their "primary" IXC to transport their long-distance and international calls (Noam, 2001). Alternatively, users could use other IXCs on a call-by-call basis by dialing a prefix.

Another major change in the U.S. PSTN occurred with the 1996 Telecommunications Act that amended the Communications Act of 1934 (Noam, 2001). RBOCs had to comply with a list of tasks before they were permitted to provide long-distance service within their regions. The list permitted competition in the RBOCs regions. It was argued that it was necessary to induce competition in these local markets. RBOCs were required to provide interconnection to new market competitors, unbundle their network, permit competitors to resell their service, and provide users with number portability.

The new local service providers became known as competitive local exchange companies (CLECs) (pronounced "see-lecks") (Noam, 2001). The incumbent LECs became known as ILECs. For a CLEC to be competitive with the ILEC requires that it is able to interconnect with the users cost-effectively. Therefore, there came a great struggle between CLECs and ILECs on the issue of collocation because the ILEC had a significant advantage with the existing network. In *physical collocation* a CLEC places its cables and equipment inside the ILEC's central office (CO) to hand off traffic. In another arrangement called *virtual collocation* the physical handoff of the traffic occurs inside or outside the CO, but uses ILEC-owned equipment and must be the economic equivalent of physical collocation.

It may appear from the previous discussion that the breaking up of the U.S. PSTN is relevant only to the United States but the trend is happening in other parts of the world as well (Noam, 2001). Japan opened its markets to competition. In addition, the Europeans have privatized their service. Noam argues that at first a network is not feasible unless supported by outside sources such as governments. As the network grows the average costs decline initially and then rise as a few high-cost users are added. Without regulation, the network would not grow beyond a certain point because of the high cost of adding these high-cost users. From a political and societal point of view the network becomes a necessity instead of a convenience and should be offered to everyone. Therefore, the monopolistic breakdown of the network is caused by its own success.

Data Public Networks and the Internet Protocol

The volume of *data* traffic carried by networks exceeded the volume of *voice* traffic in the late 1990s and continues to grow at a rate of about 100% per year (Autorité de Regulation des Telecommunications, 2003). Also, many businesses are now carrying their long-distance and international voice traffic that was previously carried over circuit-switched voice networks over packet-switched data networks. Unlike the circuit-switched networks that carry voice traffic, packet-switched data traffic is divided into pieces called packets that vary in size from 100 to 1000 bytes (Panko, 2001). Each packet has a header that contains the source address and destination address to route the data to the correct destination. The most widely used protocol for carrying data in packets is the Internet protocol (IP) used in the Internet. An IP address is like a telephone number for a packet-switched network and uniquely identifies a computer.

PUBLIC NETWORK TECHNOLOGIES

To use a public network for data services, a user must access the public network through some network service from the user's computing equipment to the nearest public network node. Factors in selecting a particular service include the cost of the service that is provided and the features, including the transmission speed, that are provided by the technology. Generally, the higher the transmission speed that a technology can support, the more costly the service becomes. Transmission speeds for networks are described in bits per second. Unlike when memory size is described, 1 Kbps is exactly equal to 10^3 bits per second, 1 Mbps is exactly equal to 10^6 bits per second, and 1 Gbps is exactly equal to 10^9 bits per second.

Many technologies are available for access to a public network and for use within the public network. The most inexpensive network access is through a voice-grade modem. A modem is used to convert a digital computer signal to an analog signal that can be sent across ordinary telephone lines. Voice-grade modems can receive data at up to 56 Kbps. In contrast, digital lines that are used to access the network range in transmission speed from 56 Kbps to 10 Gbps. Within the public network a few technologies, including X.25, frame relay, asynchronous transfer mode (ATM), and synchronous optical network (SONET), have become the most commonly used technologies. Table 1 lists the most common technologies along with a comment about usage. Table 1 also compares the transmission speed and the time to download a 10-Mb (1.2 Megabyte) file.

Voice-Grade Modems

A modem is the most inexpensive and easiest to use access technology. The use of modems for data transmission will be substantial for many years to come (Stallings, 2001). Voice-grade modems use a 4-kHz bandwidth on an ordinary telephone line, the same bandwidth that is used for voice signals. Modems can be packaged inside an information product, such as a personal computer. Companies often have modem banks that allow employees to dial in directly to the company intranet or to access a large computer system.

On March 1, 1993, the International Telecommunications Union (ITU) Telecommunications Standardization Sector (ITU-T) was created as a permanent organ of the ITU, an agency of the United Nations. The charter of the ITU-T is to standardize techniques and operations in telecommunications. Several standard specifications for voice-grade modems have been designated by the ITU-T. Two of the most significant modem specifications are V.32, which is a dial-up modem that transmits at 9600 bps, and V.90, also a dial-up modem. V.90 sends at 33.6 Kbps and receives at 56 Kbps, the highest rates available for voice-grade modems (Stallings, 2001).

Digital Subscriber Lines

A faster service than voice-grade modems that is being offered by telephone companies is the digital subscriber line (DSL). A widely publicized version of this is asymmetric digital subscriber line (ADSL). ADSL offers high-speed downstream access to the customer site and a lower speed upstream access from the customer. The ITU-T has developed a standard for low-speed ADSL called G.992.2, or G.Lite. G.Lite specifies downstream speeds of 1.5 Mbps, but sometimes lower downstream speeds are used. Most users find asymmetric speeds to be acceptable, because upstream traffic frequently consists of keystrokes or the transmission of short e-mail messages, whereas downstream traffic may include Web pages or large amounts of data. In addition to data speed, an advantage of DSL over voice-grade modems is that DSL modems allow voice

Table 1 Common Network Technologies

Service	Usage Comments	Transmission Speed	Download
Voice-Grade Modem	Modems are inexpensive, telephone rates reasonable for modest connect times	Upload: up to 33.6 Kbps Download: up to 56 Kbps	3 min or more
Digital Subscriber Line	More expensive than voice-grade modems, downlink rates higher than uplink	Upload: from 16 to 640 Kbps Download: from 786 Kbps to 9 Mbps	1.1–13 s
Cable Modems	Download rates depend on the number of simultaneous customers and configuration	Upload: from 64 to 256 Kbps Download: from 10 Mbps to 30 Mbps	0.3–1 s
Satellite	A cost-effective choice in remote locations	Upload: from 56 to 256 Kbps Download: from 150 Kbps to 1 Mbps	10–67 s
Fixed Wireless WiFi	Rates depend on distance from access point and on the number of customers	Upload: from 1 to 11 Mbps Download: from 1 to 11 Mbps	1–10 s
Integrated Services Digital Network	Charges generally based on duration of call	Basic rate: 128 Kbps, higher rates available	1.3 min
Digital leased lines: 56 Kbps (DS0), T1 (DS1), T3 (DS3), . . .	Most common leased line for high-traffic voice and data; fixed price for a specific capacity	DS0: 56 Kbps T1, DS1: 1.54 Mbps T3, DS3: 44.7 Mbps	56 Kbps: 3 min T1: 6.5 s T3: 0.22 s
SONET	Specification for optical links, highest speed	From 155.52 Mbps to 2.488 Gbps leased	0.004–0.06 s
X.25	Older technology, still in use in public networks	56 Kbps, but can be slower or faster	3 min or more
Frame Relay	Fixed price per month for a specific capacity, widely installed and used	From 16 Kbps to 44.736 Mbps	0.22–625 s
ATM	Universal technology for wide area networking	From 1.544 Mbps to 2.488 Gbps for access	0.004–6.5 s
Ethernet Passive Optical Network	Future passive technology based on Ethernet	From 100 Mbps to 10 Gbps	0.001–0.1 s

traffic to be multiplexed onto the telephone wires coming into the customer site. A customer can talk on the telephone at the same time that data are being transferred.

The telephone company does not have to install any special equipment to use voice-grade modems. However, when the telephone company offers DSL service it has to install digital subscriber line access multiplexers at the end offices. Because special equipment has to be installed, DSL service is not available in all areas. One factor that determines the availability of ADSL is the distance to the central office. In general, if the distance is greater than 18,000 feet ADSL service is not available. Also, the prices are fluctuating as DSL becomes available in more and more areas.

Cable Modems

Cable modems are a service offered by cable television companies. Often, the cable television company or the telephone company operate as both a transmission carrier and a network provider. As with ADSL, the downstream speed of cable modem is much faster than the upstream speed. The upstream speeds are similar to ADSL, but the downstream speeds can be several times faster. However, multiple customers on the same cable line share the capacity. When many customers are accessing the network at the same time the real downstream transmission speed can be much lower. If network traffic is bursty, though, the chances are unlikely that all customers are downloading at exactly the same moment so that sharing does not become as issue until about 100 customers share the same cable service (Panko, 2001).

Satellite

An often cost-effective alternative for network access is the use of satellite technology. This may be particularly true in areas where other wire-based technologies are not yet available. For example, many rural areas do not have the density of potential users that can justify the cost of installation of wire-based technologies such as DSL or cable modems.

Satellites are characterized by the type of orbit they use. The most common type of satellite is the geostationary satellite. These satellites orbit the Earth at about 22,300 miles directly above the equator at exactly the same speed as the Earth's rotation. Because of this, the satellite always appears to be in the same position in the sky and tracking of the satellite by stations on Earth is simplified (Stallings, 2001). The disadvantage of this type of satellite is that the propagation time it takes for the signal to be sent from a transmission station on the Earth to the satellite, and then to be received back on the Earth is about 0.24 s. For large data downloads this is not noticeable because the time overlaps with the time to receive the entire message. However, for interactive computer use or for applications such as telephone calls the time is noticeable and can be annoying. In addition, geostationary satellite signals are not received well in very far northern or southern regions of the Earth.

Two other types of orbits include low and medium Earth-orbiting satellites. This technology is being proposed for use with mobile terminals and remote locations that need stronger signals and less propagation time. Successful businesses that use this technology are rare. One company currently operating under bankruptcy regulations, Iridium, provides global, mobile satellite voice and data solutions with complete coverage of the Earth through a constellation of 66 low Earth-orbiting satellites (Iridium Satellite, 2002).

At least one company offers packages with two-way, always-on, high-speed Internet access via satellite that is specifically designed to meet the needs of small businesses (StarBand Communications, 2002). StarBand uses a 24 × 36 inch dish and a special modem at the customer's site to connect the user's site to the network. StarBand also serves as a network provider. Fees include an initial equipment fee and a monthly fee for access. Value-added services such as domain registration and networking support for setting up small office networks can be a part of the package.

Fixed Wireless

Fixed wireless access to public networks is available in some public places such as airports and coffee shops, called hotspots, to provide Internet access for customers. It is also popular for private individuals and businesses to provide access to the wired public Internet. The preferred wireless access technology is known as Wireless Fidelity (WiFi) and is defined in the IEEE 802.11b standard (Henry & Luo, 2002). The IEEE 802.11 is a family of specifications for wireless technology (Webopedia, 802.11, 2003). The 802.11b specification provides up to 11-Mbps transmission in the 2.4-GHz band, the 802.11g specification provides 20+ Mbps in the 2.4-GHz band, and the 802.11a specification provides 54 Mbps in the 5-GHz band.

Wired equivalent privacy (WEP) is the standard for securing WiFi networks, but it is often not enabled because of its complexity (Henry & Luo, 2002). When WEP is not enabled, a hacker can sit in a car in the parking lot outside of a business and read the network traffic, which may include information such as credit card numbers. Even if WEP is enabled, the encryption key can be recovered with a small amount of effort to read the traffic. The best way to provide secure access over WiFi is to run a virtual private network (VPN) with encryption such as IPSec to provide a secure end-to-end channel. But this is also a complex configuration to support.

Although the IEEE 802.11 standards such as WiFi are very popular, they have performance limitations when supporting more than just a few users. A new standard is being developed to provide broadband wireless access for longer distances and broader coverage called IEEE 802.16 (Geier, 2003). The IEEE 802.16 standard was published in April 2002 and is meant to provide network access to homes, small businesses, and commercial buildings. The IEEE 802.16 standard supports point-to-multipoint connections, with data rates as high as 120 Mbps in the 2 to 66 GHz band. At these frequencies only line-of-sight transmission is possible. A version called IEEE 802.16a, published in January 2003, operates between 2 and 11 GHz to provide non-line-of-sight access.

Integrated Services Digital Network

Many telephone companies offer integrated services digital network (ISDN), a digital service that runs over ordinary telephone lines. As with voice-grade modems the ITU-T has set standards for ISDN. ISDN can be used as an access technology and within a public network. Basic ISDN service includes two "B" channels, each at 64 Kbps, and a "D" channel that is used for signaling. It is possible to use one "B" channel for voice and one for data, but most service providers bond the two "B" channels together to provide a 128 Kbps data rate. Standards for higher rates also exist. Like ADSL, ISDN requires that the telephone company install special equipment at the end office before an ISDN service can be offered. A special ISDN "modem" is used at the customer site.

ISDN is the result of efforts in the early 1980s by the world's telephone companies to design and build a fully digital, circuit-switched telephone system (Tanenbaum, 1996). Because ISDN is circuit-switched, there is never any congestion on the line from the customer to the network service provider. However, because data traffic is generally bursty, the user pays for bandwidth that may not be used. ISDN is expensive compared to the modest gain in transmission speed. The customer generally has to pay for the ISDN line to the telephone company and then has to pay an additional fee to a network service provider. The use of ISDN is likely to decline as other technologies that have higher speed and are more economical become available.

Digital Leased Lines

In terms of number of circuits, the most common leased lines are 56 Kbps (Panko, 2001). The transmission capacity of a 56 Kbps is actually 64 Kbps but 1 bit of 8 is used for signaling, leaving the user with 56 Kbps. A 56 Kbps line is the same as digital signal zero (DS0). The next higher transmission speed is a T1 (DS1), which provides

1.544 Mbps. Although a 56-Kbps leased line is relatively inexpensive, the difference in cost and performance between a 56 Kbps and a T1 line is large. Therefore, fractional T1's are also available at 128 Kbps, 256 Kbps, 384 Kbps, and so on. In Europe and other parts of the world a different digital hierarchy of transmission capacities is used. The standards are defined in the Council of European Postal and Telecommunications authorities (CEPT). The E1 standard operates at 2.048 Mbps and is analogous to the T1 standard. The next step is a T3 (DS3) at 44.7 Mbps and the corresponding CEPT E3 standard operating at 34.4 Mbps. Higher transmission capacities are available using synchronous optical network (SONET) and the synchronous digital hierarchy (SDH) and range from 155.52 Mbps to 10 Gbps.

Digital leased lines can be used to build a company's leased line private network, as shown in Figure 1, or can be used in combination with a public network, as shown in Figure 2. When leased lines are used to access a public network the traffic between several sites must be multiplexed over the single access line. Therefore, it is important to be sure that the leased line is fast enough to support this traffic. For example, if a site has fifteen 56 Kbps leased lines connected point-to-point with other sites and wants to convert this to a single access line to a public network, then the access line would require at least 840 Kbps of capacity. From Table 1, this would require a T1 line (Panko, 2001).

Synchronous Optical Network

SONET defines a hierarchy of standardized digital data rates. A compatible synchronous digital hierarchy version has been published by the ITU-T. SONET is intended to provide a specification for high-speed digital transmission over optical fiber.

SONET, or SDH, is the highest speed and most costly digital leased lines. SONET/SDH operates in multiples of 51.84 Mbps. Standards are specified as OCx for SONET and STMx for the SDH specification. A common SONET/SDH speed is OC3/STM1 at 156 Mbps. Other common rates include 622 Mbps, 2.5 Gbps, and 10 Gbps. SONET technology can be used for access both to the public network and within the public network. It is installed in a ring for a fault tolerant network (Dunsmore, Skandier, Martin, McKelvey, & Woods, 2003).

X.25

X.25 was developed during the 1970s for use in public packet-switching networks, and this standard was later ratified by the ITU-T (Tanenbaum, 1996). X.25 is very slow, often running at only 9600 bps, but it is fast enough for the text-based transmissions of early networks. Its use is declining, but it is still popular in the United States for low-speed applications such as a department store's point-of-sale transaction network. Also, there are many X.25 legacy connections, particularly in Europe and in countries where the telecommunications infrastructure is lagging. X.25 is one of a few standards that have been set by the ITU-T for public switched data networks. Other standards set by the ITU-T for public networks include ISDN, frame relay, and ATM.

Frame Relay

Frame relay is the most popular technology choice within public switched data networks today (Panko, 2001). Its speed range matches the needs of the greatest corporate demand, and it has very competitive pricing. Frame relay can also be used instead of leased lines as an access technology or to connect company private networks. Its low overhead even makes it suitable for interconnecting LANs and high-speed stand-alone systems (Stallings, 2001). Current commercial offerings of frame relay include MCI–WorldCom, which offers frame relay service access speeds from 28.8 Kbps to 45 Mbps (MCI–WorldCom, 2002), and Qwest, which offers frame relay service access speeds from 64 Kbps to 45 Mbps (Qwest, 2002).

Typically, a company accesses a public frame relay network through a leased line. Several frame relay virtual circuits are multiplexed over a single access line to the public network. A virtual circuit is a connection from source to destination and represents an end-to-end path that all packets from the same source to the same destination go through. Virtual circuits simplify forwarding decisions and make the costs of the switches cheaper. A permanent virtual circuit (PVC) is one that is set up manually when a company first subscribes to a public network and changes only when the site changes. For a large company network, a PVC is established for every pair of sites that would get a leased line in a private leased line network as seen in Figure 3.

The frame relay protocol includes functions for detection of transmission errors and congestion control functions. The frame relay protocol allows users to negotiate a committed information rate (CIR) when a connection is set up. The CIR is the network's commitment to deliver data in the absence of errors and represents the user's estimate of its "normal" traffic during a busy period. Any traffic sent above the CIR is not guaranteed to arrive but may arrive if the network has the capacity to deliver it. In addition, a maximum allowable rate is defined, and all traffic above this level is discarded (Frame Relay Forum, 2002).

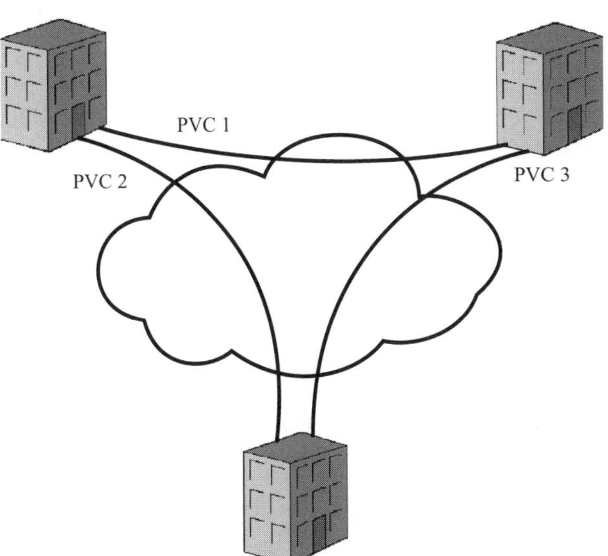

Figure 3: Permanent virtual circuits.

Pricing for frame relay is usually divided into several different components. First, the company needs a frame relay access device. This is a router that has been modified to allow it to communicate with the frame relay's first switch. Second, the company must lease an access line to the nearest POP of the public network. If the POP is a long distance away, then the customer must use expensive, long-distance access lines. The leased line must be fast enough to handle the available bit rate on the line.

At the POP, the leased access line connects to a port on the frame relay switch of the public network. The fee for the port is usually the largest single element in frame relay pricing. To prevent wasting port capacity, the speed of the leased line should be at least as fast as the port speed. There is usually a monthly fee for each PVC and this fee depends on the speed of the PVC. Finally, some vendors build in other fees, such as per-bit traffic charges or fees to set up and tear down switched virtual circuits that are established on a call-by-call basis. Frequently there are substantial initial charges to install the access device, leased line, port connection, and PVC.

Asynchronous Transfer Mode

Asynchronous transfer mode is sometimes viewed to be the universal technology for networking and may replace many other current offerings (Stallings, 2001). ATM is not as popular as when it was first introduced but still is used in many networks. Just as frame relay allows messages to be divided into many frames that can be sent across a switched network, ATM uses cell relay. Like frame relay, ATM multiplexes many logical connections over the same physical interface, sending information in fixed size 53-byte cells. ATM can support data, video, voice, and Internet traffic on a single access line.

The use of cells in ATM allows many important features to be defined for a virtual channel. For example, users can negotiate the ratio of cells lost to cells transmitted, cell delay variation and parameters such as the average rate, peak rate, burstiness, and peak duration for a virtual channel (ATM Forum, 2002). The ATM service can use permanent virtual channels for static connections. ATM also allows switched virtual channels to be set up dynamically on a call-by-call basis.

Four classes of ATM service have been defined as follows (Stallings, 2001):

1. **Constant bit rate:** The network provider ensures that this rate is available, and the customer is monitored to be sure the rate is not exceeded.
2. **Variable bit rate (VBR):** A sustained rate for normal use is defined, and a faster burst rate for occasional use is also defined. The faster rate is guaranteed, but not continuously. The ATM Forum divides VBR into real-time VBR (rt-VBR) and non-real-time VBR (nrt-VBR) (ATM Forum, 2002). With rt-VBR the application has tight constraints on delay and delay variation, but the rate is allowed to vary according to parameters specified by the user. The nrt-VBR is for applications that are bursty but do not have tight constraints on delay and delay variation.
3. **Available bit rate (ABR):** The user has a guaranteed minimum capacity. When additional capacity is available on the network, the user may burst above this without risk of cell loss.
4. **Unspecified bit rate (UBR):** Cells are delivered with best effort, meaning that any cell may be lost. The main difference between UBR and ABR is that ABR provides feedback to the user so that the user can control the amount of data being sent and reduce the risk of loss.

ATM is a high-performance service and is expensive. In the range of speeds where ATM speeds overlap with frame relay, frame relay is more attractive because it is cheaper. However, as customer needs increase, ATM becomes a more attractive option. ATM is widely used within high-speed public networks and by companies that need higher speed private networks. Most ATM public switched data network providers currently offer speeds from 1 to 156 Mbps, with higher speeds on the way. These public networks require access lines ranging from T1 to a SONET OC-3 line. MCI–WorldCom offers ATM access speeds from 1.544 to 622 Mbps (MCI–WorldCom, 2002). Qwest offers ATM access speeds from 1.544 to 155 Mbps (Qwest, 2002).

Passive Optical Networks

The telecommunication backbone networks capacity has grown much faster than the access networks (Kramer & Pesavento, 2002). The access network, sometimes called the *last mile*, between the backbone networks and business local area networks is still the bottleneck. Today, cable modems and digital subscriber lines are the most widely deployed solutions. The capacity that they provide will be too small for future applications and they require placing electronic devices near the users that are too far away from the CO. One of the highest costs is providing and maintaining electrical power for these devices (Kramer, 2002). Fiber optical cables can provide the needed capacity. One configuration for the last mile problem is to run a separate fiber optical cable from the CO to every business and home, but the expense of multiple point-to-point links is too great. Another possible solution is for multiple users to share a fiber optical cable as in passive optical networks (PON). A PON uses a point-to-multipoint architecture as seen in Figure 4, where the internal components are passive optical components such as splitters that require no power (Kramer, 2002).

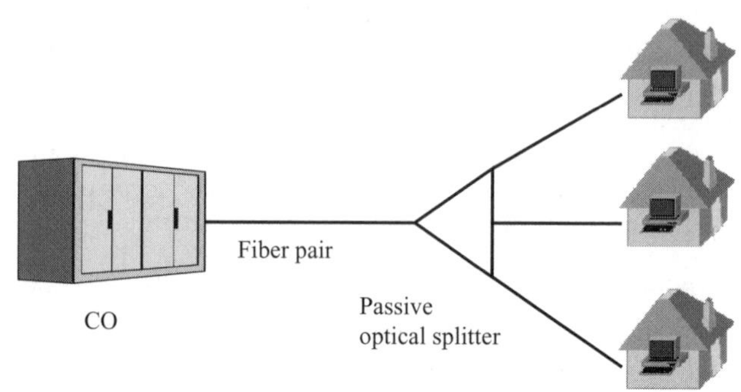

Figure 4: Passive optical network.

Originally, it was assumed that a PON would use ATM as its data link layer protocol (Kramer, 2002). The use of ATM is described in the ITU-T standard G.983.1 (Effenberger, 2001). But ATM has not kept up with the popularity of Ethernet in the LAN (Kramer, 2002). Ethernet is widely available and an accepted standard so may be the protocol of choice for a PON and is sometimes called an Ethernet PON (EPON). In the downstream direction from the CO to the user, Ethernet packets pass through a passive optical splitter and are delivered to 4 to 64 users. The users extract only the packets that are directed to their media access control (MAC) address. In the upstream direction from the user to the CO, Ethernet packets reach only the CO, not other users. However, the packets may interfere with each other because they share the link from the splitter to the CO. Because packets destined for a single user are broadcast to multiple users encryption should be used to provide privacy (Kramer, 2002).

Choosing a Private Network or a Public Network Provider

There are several categories to consider when one decides whether to use a private network or a public network. If a public network is chosen, then these same categories can help in choosing a network provider. A survey of ISPs conducted in 2001 found that the top three areas that differentiated the best ISPs from the rest were reliability, performance, and low cost (Greenfield, 2001). Subscribers to ISPs in the survey also considered support to be important. In addition, network control is a factor in deciding, whether to choose a private network or a public network. Other factors mentioned in the survey include breadth of service, security, installation, repairs, and remote access.

Reliability is defined as the amount of time the network service is available. Reliability can be difficult to evaluate because several different things can cause downtime. For example, if a user is trying to transfer data from a server that is down then from the user's point of view the network is down. When a packet switching node or dedicated leased line in a large complex network does fail it affects a large amount of transmission capacity and therefore a large number of users. For example, MCI–WorldCom's frame relay outage in August 1999 lasted 8 days and affected 30% of MCI's frame relay customers, perhaps as many as 70,000 users (Orenstein & Ohlson, 1999).

An advantage to using a private network is that the redundancy of the network can be designed according to the business requirements. The major disadvantage is that it requires investment in redundant packet switching nodes and leased lines for fault tolerance, personnel training, disaster recover planning, and testing. These expenses are often overlooked or have less priority when a private network is designed (Snow, 2001). Or, once the private network is operational, these expenses are considered low priority. Therefore, when there is an outage the business is not prepared for it, and its effects are worse than if a disaster recovery plan had been written.

The reliability of a public network has advantages and disadvantages. The advantage of using a public network is that because the cost is spread out over several subscribers added investment in reliability can be cost-effective. The disadvantage is that a subscriber is completely dependent on the provider for reliable service. Service level agreements have to be negotiated with clear and strict penalties if the provider does not meet the negotiated reliability. If reliability is of high importance to a business, then they may subscribe to two or more public network providers for added reliability.

The choice between a public and private network includes determining the trade-offs between the cost and performance of the network. The performance of the network is defined by throughput and delay. The throughput is the actual data speed seen by the user in bits per second. The delay is the maximum end-to-end delay that a packet will incur in the network.

The costs of the network may vary depending on the type and volume of traffic that the network will carry. The type of traffic on a network is classified as either stream or bursty (Stallings, 2001). Stream traffic is long and relatively constant and therefore more predictable than bursty traffic. An example of stream traffic would be voice traffic or uncompressed video. Bursty traffic is short and sporadic such as computer-to-computer communication in the Internet. Although sporadic, bursty traffic often requires a large transmission capacity for brief periods of time. Many Internet applications such as the Web and e-mail create such bursty traffic. If there are several bursty traffic sources that share a communications link and the volume of the combined traffic is high then the aggregate traffic on the link may be considered stream traffic.

Bursty traffic requires a different type of network than stream traffic. For example, if one file is required to be transferred from an office to a central site once a day, then a dial-up connection may be the most feasible. Conversely, if there is bursty traffic to be transferred among a small number of sites and the aggregate of the bursty sources has a high volume, then a private packet-switching network would be more efficient. Leased lines are not dependent on volume but have a constant fixed rate for a given transmission capacity and distance. If the percentage of use of the leased line is high enough then the volume discount given by the constant fixed rate can be cost-effective. For example, large nationwide contracts can negotiate T1 access lines for $200 a month, whereas users in metropolitan areas can get T1 access for approximately $900 per month (The Yankee Group, 2001). Compare this to $50 per phone times 24 channels; this is $1,200 per month for an equivalent amount of bandwidth.

If there is a moderate volume of bursty traffic to be transferred among a medium to large number of sites, then a public network may be a better choice. Because the public network provider has several subscribers, the aggregate volume of traffic is great enough to have high use and therefore is cost-effective for the provider. These savings are passed on to subscribers who do not have enough volume of traffic to justify a private network.

The costs for some network technologies can be negotiated with the expected performance in mind. For example, with frame relay, the user chooses the committed information rate in bits per second and committed burst size (Frame Relay Forum, 2002). A frame relay network provider will also specify a maximum end-to-end delay for a frame in their network. These parameters are a part of the pricing for frame relay service.

The price of a network is usually divided into a fixed cost and a variable cost. The fixed access cost depends on the type of access technology that a user connects to the POP with and the distance the user is from the POP. There may not be a variable cost, but if there is, the price is dependent on the volume of traffic. A user may subscribe to a certain data rate from the network for a fixed cost and if the user exceeds the limit, the user is charged for the additional usage.

Support is defined as the quality of a provider's technical and logistical help. In one survey the complaint most cited was the lack of support (Greenfield, 2001). Networks do break and fail. A good network provider should be fast to respond and correct problems. A business should consider where the nearest technician would be coming from to service their sites. Service-level agreements will define minor and major problems and the type of responses that the network provider will provide.

An organization relies on its network to operate its business (Stallings, 2001). Management requires control of the network to provide efficient and effective service to the organization. There are trade-offs between a private and public network when considering control. Three areas of control need to be considered, including strategic control, growth control, and day-to-day operations.

Strategic control of a network is designing and implementing a network to satisfy the organization's unique requirements. If the organization operates its own private network then it can determine the configuration of the network. But, if the organization uses a public network the organization does not have strategic control over the configuration of the network. The public network provider designs the network for the average subscriber.

Growth control of the network is the ability to expand and make modifications to meet the changing requirements of the organization. It includes adding switching nodes and leased lines, modifying the capacities of the leased lines, and changing the network technology. A private network provides the maximum flexibility for growth control because the organization has complete control over the network. If an organization is a subscriber to a public network it has almost no growth control. All requirements are constrained by the capabilities of the public network.

The other type of control is the day-to-day operation of the network. This includes the ability to handle traffic during peak times, to diagnose problems, and to repair problems quickly. In a private network the organization sets the priorities of the day-to-day operation to fit their business. But, with a private network, they also have to hire or develop in-house expertise to maintain the often complex network. In addition, the organization has to address the reliability of the network by determining where to install redundant packet-switching nodes and dedicated leased lines. If an organization is a subscriber to a public network then it is dependent on the public network provider. There are peak traffic times and the public network provider may focus its efforts on the overall health of the network and not on an individual user. Conversely, the provider can afford more redundancy and hire or develop more in-house expertise because these costs are spread out over several subscribers.

Other factors that are important in choosing a network solution include breadth of service, installation, repairs, and remote access. Many network providers offer a wide breadth of value-added services, as previously described. A provider that can provide value-added services such as Web hosting bundled with its network service can have a big advantage. If the server is on the same network that other customers are connected to then performance is better.

The installation and repairs category includes the timeliness and quality of an installation. Networks are complex and often require coordination among multiple organizations. For example, in the United States if a leased line crosses two different LATAs, then at least one local provider and at least one IXC will be required. Also, realistic time schedules are important because a rushed installation usually results in a poor-quality installation and long-term problems.

For many businesses remote access is important to be competitive. Remote access permits users in a business to communicate often with e-mail and to access corporate data. Remote access is dependent on the number and location of the network provider's in-dial modem pools. If this is an important part of the business model, then a business should look for a provider that has multiple access points in the areas that their employees travel.

PUBLIC NETWORK SECURITY

When data from multiple sources is shared on the same public network, such as the Internet, there are several security concerns about the data. For example, it is possible that the data can arrive at a destination that did not originate from the expected location. Authentication is a mechanism for ensuring that a message was sent by the user identified as the sender in the message and that the original message content has not been modified. A second security concern is that the data may have been maliciously altered. Verifying that the data has not been modified is called maintaining integrity. In addition, the data may be monitored by a third party. Confidentiality prevents users other than the two communicating users from reading the exchanged messages by scrambling the content of the message in such a way that only the receiving user can unscramble the message. Protecting the confidentiality of the data may be important.

The global Internet can be used to provide an intranet or an extranet by creating a virtual private network (VPN). A VPN is a private network that is deployed over public facilities but provides the additional levels of security, confidentiality, quality of service, and manageability over public networks (Cisco, 2001). A VPN can be created when all sites are already connected to the Internet. With a VPN, hosts at different sites communicate across the Internet using either a tunnel mode between local networks or by using a direct transport communication.

Security issues still exist with VPNs because the company no longer has control over the entire data network. One problem is the confidentially of the data, because the Internet was not designed to support confidential transmission. This problem can be solved using encryption and by using tunnel mode for communication. A second problem is congestion on the Internet. Congestion is a security issue as well as a performance issue. Congestion can cause data to be lost or delayed. Additionally, a malicious user or group of users can perform a denial-of-service attack. In a denial-of-service attack, the network is flooded with malicious data and useful data is prevented from using the network.

Security can be implemented in the individual applications. For example, electronic mail can use S/MIME or PGP to secure the message or the Web can use SET to secure credit card transactions (Stallings, 2003). Authentication services such as Kerberos or X.509 restrict access to authorized users and authenticate requests for service. Security can be implemented between the application layer and the transport layer that transfers information between hosts as in SSL or TLS. One of the most successful security protocols SSL is typically integrated into Web browsers but can be used by other applications. Finally, security can be implemented at the network layer securing all information that is transmitted on the public network even though the application may not be aware of it as in IPSec. This provides security for all applications, including those that have no inherent security built in. At a minimum, a firewall should be installed to protect internal applications and hosts from being accessed by external unauthorized users. Many times these security mechanisms are applied at the application, transport, and network layers providing multiple layers of security.

Authentication Services

An authentication service is one that verifies the identity of the party who sent the data and the integrity of the data. A principal is the party whose identity is verified, and the verifier is the party who demands assurance of the principal's identity. Data integrity is the assurance that the data that is received is the same as the data that was sent. An authentication service verifies a principal on behalf of a third party that is the target of the communication. Two of the most commonly used authentication services are X.509 and Kerberos.

X.509 and several secure network protocols, including S/MIME, IPSec, SSL/TLS, and SET, use public key cryptography in some manner (Stallings, 2003). With public key cryptography there are two keys, a private key that is only known to the owner of the private key and a public key. The private key/public key pair can be used to encrypt and decrypt messages. For example, if Alice wants to send an encrypted message to Bob, Alice can encrypt the message, called plaintext, using Bob's public key and send the encrypted message, called ciphertext, to Bob. After receiving the ciphertext, Bob can use his private key to decrypt the message. The idea behind this encryption is that, given the public key, the amount of computing time that it would take to calculate the private key (and then to decrypt the message) is much longer than the usefulness of the encrypted message.

Public key encryption also works using the keys in the other direction. Alice can use her private key to encrypt the message and send the encrypted message to Bob. Once Bob receives the message, he can decrypt the message using Alice's public key. A message that is encrypted by a sending party using the sender's private key is said to have a digital signature. A receiver can decrypt the message with the sender's public key and be assured that only the sender could have sent it. To be secure, however, a user must be assured that the public key is in fact the public key of the identified user and not an imposter. If authentication and confidentiality is required, Alice can sign the message using her private key and then encrypt the result with Bob's public key.

The X.509 authentication service maintains a repository of public keys that are signed by a certificate authority. A certificate is a public key of a user that is signed (i.e., encrypted) with the private key of a trusted certificate authority (CA). The certificate is stored in a directory server so that other users can obtain a copy. Any user that has a copy of the certificate authority's public key can then verify a registered user's certificate by obtaining a copy of the certificate and then checking the digital signature of the certificate. The process to communicate securely using the X.509 authentication service is as follows. First, Bob registers his public key with the CA. The CA signs Bob's public key with the CA's private key. Alice wants to communicate with Bob and has a trusted copy of the CA's public key but does not have Bob's public key. Alice requests a certificate for Bob, which is Bob's public key signed by the CA's private key. Alice verifies the signature by decrypting the CA's encrypted copy of Bob's public key using the CA's public key and comparing it to the copy provided by Bob. If the two keys are the same, then Alice is sure that it is Bob's public key and then uses it to securely communicate with Bob.

An alternative to public key cryptography is secret key cryptography. With secret key cryptography there is a single key that is shared between parties that want to exchange messages. If Alice wants to send an encrypted message to Bob she encrypts the message with the shared secret key and sends the ciphertext to Bob. Bob uses the same secret key to decrypt the message. Secret key cryptography is preferred to public key cryptography because the time to encrypt and decrypt, for the same length key, is much faster. In addition, secret key cryptography is considered more secure than public key cryptography because none of the key information is made public. With public key cryptography there is a very small probability, depending on the length of the key, that the private key could be calculated quickly enough to be able to decrypt the message while it is still useful. However, the difficulty with secret-key cryptography is how to exchange the shared secret key between a client and a server without a third party discovering it.

Secret key cryptography is faster than public key cryptography, but requires exchange of a shared secret key. A hybrid system that solves the key distribution problem, but is faster, uses both secret key and public key cryptography. Public key cryptography is used to exchange a secret session key. This session key is used as input into a secret key algorithm for encrypting and decrypting messages during a session. The session key could be used for a single session or may last for a limited amount of time.

Kerberos is a distributed authentication service that allows a process (a client) running on behalf of a principal (a user) to prove its identity to a verifier (an application server, or just server) without sending any shared secret key across the network (Neuman & Ts'o, 1994). Kerberos uses secret key cryptography to create a new shared secret key and exchange it between two parties who want to have a secure communication. Because a shared secret key can be regenerated at any time, Kerberos uses a timeout to cause the shared secret key to expire in a time period that is much shorter than the computing time that it would take an attacker to calculate the shared key by seeing only the ciphertext.

With Kerberos the client and the application server do not initially share a secret key. The basic Kerberos authentication protocol allows the client to obtain a shared secret key, called a session key, with the application server. In the basic protocol, the client shares a secret key (i.e., a password) with a special authentication server. Similarly, each application server shares a secret key with special server called a ticket-granting server. When the client contacts the authentication server, the authentication server generates a special key, called a Kerberos ticket, which authenticates the client to the ticket-granting server. The Kerberos ticket is encrypted using the client's secret key, along with a timestamp, and sent back to the client. The client then uses the client secret key to decrypt the message and retrieve the Kerberos ticket, and timestamp. With this technique no passwords are ever sent over the network. The client then uses the Kerberos ticket in a series of messages with the ticket-granting server to obtain the shared secret session key with the application server.

Kerberos is not effective against password attacks. If a user selects a poor password then an attacker can impersonate the user. Also, if the computer in which the password is being entered has been compromised then the password may be able to be obtained by an attacker. To be useful, Kerberos must be integrated with all parts of the system so that all application servers require the Kerberos protocol to be observed (i.e., the servers must be "Kerberized") before granting access to a client. Since it was first developed in the mid-1980s, Kerberos has gone through several enhancements to improve the level of security that it provides. A free implementation of the Kerberos protocol is available from the Massachusetts Institute of Technology and in several commercial products (Kerberos, 2003).

Application-Layer Security

PGP (Pretty Good Privacy) is a general-purpose application providing confidentiality and authentication service (PGP, 2003). The first version of PGP was released in 1991 and was one of the first widely available packages to offer confidentiality and authentication service to the public. PGP packages several algorithms for public key encryption and symmetric key encryption into an easy to use package that runs on many platforms such as Windows, UNIX, and Macintosh. It is used for providing secure and authenticated communication, e-mail, and file storage. It was not developed by the government, nor does the government control it. A freeware version is available for individual, noncommercial use. PGP is popular and OpenPGP is on the standards track for the Internet community (RFC 3156, 2001).

S/MIME (Secure/Multipurpose Internet Mail Extension) is a standard way to provide confidentiality and authentication service for the MIME Internet e-mail format originally developed by RSA Data Security, Inc. (Internet Mail Consortium, 2003). It is defined in several RFCs and an overview can be found in (Internet Mail Consortium, 2003). It is an industry standard for commercial and organizational use. S/MIME uses public key certificates in the X.509 version 3 format. S/MIME and PGP/MIME are the two proposed methods for providing secure e-mail and provide the same type of services to users, but the formats are very different.

SET (Secure Electronic Transactions) is an open technical standard developed by Visa and MasterCard for secure payment card transactions over the Internet (Webopedia, "SET," 2003). SET uses digital signatures for authentication to allow merchants to verify that buyers are who they claim to be. In addition, SET provides a mechanism for a buyer to transfer a credit card number directly to the credit card issuer for billing and verification without requiring that the merchant have access to the credit card number (Webopedia, SET, 2003). SET operates by using a hierarchy of Certificate Authorities and a method of entity authentication called trust chaining. The trust chain begins with the card holder and them moves up to the merchant CA and on to a Payment Gateway CA and up the hierarchy to the CA at the top of the hierarchy, which is referred to as SET Root CA. Each CA is validated by the CA above it in the hierarchy. SET Root CA is owned and operated by SET Secure Electronic Transaction LLC and is the only CA that can issue digital certificates to a Brand or a financial institution that has its own distinct logo and issues and accepts payment cards or accounts. Current SET Brands are Maestro, MasterCard International, PBS International A/S/Dankort, and Visa International (SET Brands, 2003).

PayPal enables online transactions between buyers and sellers who do not have the resources to process credit cards (PayPal, 2004). Sellers establish accounts with PayPal. Then, buyers go to PayPal's Web site and pay by credit card or bank account. PayPal pays the seller minus a fee based on the amount and a static transaction fee. The service is free for the buyer. PayPal is not an escrow service. Escrow services take money from potential buyers and hold the funds until the buyer receives and inspects the merchandise. There are escrow services such as escrow.com available.

Socket-Layer Security

The secure socket layer (SSL) was originally developed by Netscape and came bundled with their Web browser to secure credit card transactions across the Internet (Stallings, 2003). It prevents an adversary from intercepting an online order with the credit card number. It also authenticates the server to the client so that an adversary cannot set up a Web site that appears to be a legitimate business, but just gathers credit card numbers and makes fraudulent charges. It is an interface between an application layer protocol and the TCP transport layer. The original and most common use of SSL is by the application layer protocol hypertext transfer protocol (HTTP) for Web transactions. SSL is embedded in specific applications such as Netscape and Microsoft Internet Explorer. The use of SSL over HTTP is set by using "https" instead of "http" in the Uniform Resource Locator. SSL can also be used for other application layer protocols. Transport layer security (TLS) is based on SSL and is defined in RFC 2246 (RFC 2246, 1999). There are two differences between TLS and SSL. First, TLS uses the HMAC authentication method described in RFC 2104 (RFC 2104, 1997), which is slightly different than the one defined for SSL. Second, the authentication covers more fields in TLS than in SSL.

At the beginning of a SSL session the client and server negotiate an encryption algorithm, the session keys, and authenticate the server to the client. As an option, the client can be authenticated to the server although this is not common. After setup, SSL encrypts all the data using the session key providing a secure channel for exchange of information such as credit card numbers, online banking, and stock trading. At the sender, SSL/TLS receives the data from the application such as HTTP, encrypts it, and then sends it over the transport layer protocol TCP. At the receiver, TCP hands the data to SSL/TLS, which decrypts it and passes on to the application.

Network-Layer Security

Security implemented at the network layer secures all information that is received or transmitted over a public network. This provides security for all applications, including those that have no inherent security built in. A business that connects to a public network such as the Internet should have a firewall that restricts and controls access to internal information resources from external users. This provides one level of security for applications and operating systems that have no inherent security or have security vulnerabilities. In addition, the Internet has developed an architecture for the Internet protocol that operates at the network level and is called IP security or, more commonly, IPSec for securing received and transmitted information (RFC 2401, 1998). IPSec defines an architecture for providing security at the network layer in which there are several options. The individual components of IPSec are defined in several RFCs and a list of these RFCs are listed in RFC 2411 (RFC 2411, 1998). A high-level overview of IPSec is presented in (Stallings, 2003).

It is essential for businesses to have Internet connectivity. However, the connection to this public network permits the outside world to have access to the assets of the business. Because it is impractical to secure all systems in many businesses, a firewall is placed between the private network and the public Internet to protect the business from external attacks on their internal systems (Stallings, 2003). All traffic between the private and public network is directed to the firewall providing a single choke point to enforce defined security policies. The firewall is configured to only pass authorized traffic. A single choke point simplifies management and gives the business an ability to monitor and audit events. It also provides a platform for IPSec.

There are several ways to configure and operate a firewall. A packet-filtering firewall filters traffic based on IP addresses and TCP port numbers. Systems are addressed by IP addresses on the Internet and individual applications on a system are referenced by TCP port numbers. E-mail and web server applications operate on particular TCP port numbers. Therefore, a packet-filtering firewall restricts services by restricting the access to certain hosts based on the IP address and restricts access to services based on TCP port numbers. Stateful inspection firewalls creates a directory of output TCP connections and matches their profiles with incoming connections to control access. Application-level firewalls have a proxy server that relays application-level traffic. If the application-level firewall does not support an application, then no communication is possible between the private and public networks. In addition, certain specific features of an application can be restricted. This can be more secure than the other types of firewalls, but requires a system that can support the processing needs of all users. In other words, it does not scale well to a large community of users.

IPSec is used for secure office connectivity over public networks, secure remote access, extranet and intranet connectivity, and to enhance electronic commerce (Stallings, 2003). A remote office can use IPSec to connect to the main office network over a public or private network to provide connectivity and make it appear that the remote office is directly connected to the main network. IPSec can also be used by mobile users such as salesmen to provide a secure remote access to the main office network. The user can connect to a local ISP and with IPSec software connect to the main office network. It can also be used to provide secure communications to a partner in an extranet, providing limited access to internal resources. Finally, it can be used to secure electronic commerce for financial transactions.

Two protocols are used to provide security in IPSec. The authentication protocol adds an authentication header (AH) to the packet to authenticate the data. The second protocol combines encryption and authentication to provide confidentiality and authentication by adding an encapsulating security payload (ESP) header. ESP can be used with or without authentication.

There are two modes of operation in IPSec: transport mode and tunnel model. In transport mode the data being transferred is kept confidential and/or authenticated, but the source and destination addresses are known. Therefore, an adversary can determine the two parties that are communicating and could infer something from it. For example, a large amount of traffic between an individual and a bank is most likely financial transactions. This is called traffic analysis in the security community. Transport mode is used for remote, host-to-host, or host-to-intermediate connectivity.

Tunnel mode is commonly used to create an intranet over a public network. The data being transferred and the source and destination addresses are kept confidential and/or authenticated. This information is carried in a packet that has a new source and destination address. These new addresses are the addresses of an intermediate device, often a firewall, which connects between the internal business network and the public network.

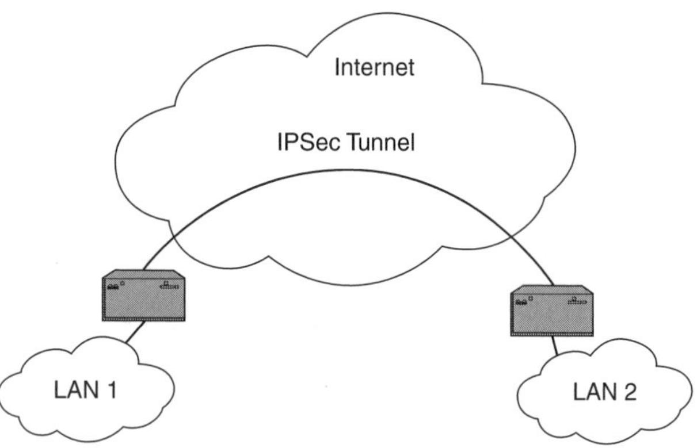

Figure 5: IPSec tunnel mode.

Figure 5 shows using tunnel mode in IPSec. Using tunnel mode hides the original source and final destination addresses preventing traffic analysis.

To provide authentication and confidentiality in IPSec requires that secret keys be exchanged between the communicating parties. IPSec supports either manual or automated exchange of secret keys. In manual mode an administrator manually configures the devices with the secret keys. This is practical only for relatively small networks. For automated exchange of keys, IPSec has defined a protocol called the Internet Security Association and Key Management Protocol (ISAKMP). ISAKMP provides a framework to negotiate a specific key exchange algorithm, but specifies no specific algorithm. The default specific key exchange algorithm is the Oakley key determination protocol.

Remote users that need access to a corporate network can establish an encrypted virtual private network (VPN) connection (Poptop, 2004). A popular protocol called point-to-point tunneling protocol (PPTP) uses a client/server model for establishing VPN connections. It was developed by a consortium, including Microsoft. Server software called Poptop is available to connect PPTP clients to Linux servers.

PUBLIC NETWORKS IN THE INTERNET AND E-COMMERCE ENVIRONMENTS

Public networks provide a cost-effective solution for small businesses to connect to the Internet and participate in e-commerce because they provide connections to the public Internet through one or more locations. Access to the Internet is restructuring the marketing, sales, management, production, accounting, and personnel management in businesses (Moody, 2001). The Internet provides online up-to-the-minute reports for marketing. Marketing can easily monitor their competitors by accessing the online information and competitors can easily monitor a business. The Internet has had two effects on sales. First, a business can have a worldwide presence. Second, customers are demanding the correct information for deciding which business to buy from. The online purchase is now being handled automatically by software (e-commerce). Members of the sales department can access corporate information over the network while on the road. Management can now have access to more of the organization. They can access information from marketing, sales, production, accounting, and personnel, including previous years' sales and regional performance of a product. They can have online meetings and stay in contact with e-mail. Production can receive quicker feedback from the field and have feedback from suppliers about their stock levels. Accounting can pay online and receive up-to-the-minute information. Personnel information such as directories can be provided online and manuals and training material can be placed online.

CONCLUSIONS

Public networks are an increasingly popular solution for businesses to link multiple sites together to exchange information and to connect to the Internet. Public networks offer several advantages over private networks composed of leased lines, including lower cost for a given performance, value-added services, and fewer requirements of maintaining in-house expertise for network maintenance, support, and similar administrative and management tasks. Public networks do have some disadvantages, including potential variation in performance because of congestion on the public network, lack of control over day-to-day operations, upgrades, and long-range planning for capacity changes and concerns for security. However, public networks that combine connectivity with extra services for secure communication are a good choice for many businesses.

Security concerns about public networks can be addressed with a variety of services and protocols, including the installation of VPNs, firewalls, authentication services and enhancements to the application, socket, and network layers. In the future, only organizations with special requirements in the areas of performance, control, and security will continue to maintain and install private networks. Even organizations that continue to have private networks will have at least one connection to the one global public network called the Internet to participate in activities such as e-mail and e-commerce.

GLOSSARY

Asynchronous Digital Subscriber Line A digital service that uses ordinary telephone lines to connect a customer to a public network. Asynchronous DSL has download speeds that are much faster than the upload speeds.

Asynchronous Transfer Mode A network technology characterized by sending data in fixed-size 53-byte cells and offering various levels of service.

Authentication Verifying the identity of the party; that is, being assured that that party is who he says he is.

Authorization Verifying that an authenticated party has permission to access a service or data.

Certificate A public key of a user that is signed (i.e., encrypted) with the private key of a trusted certificate authority (CA).

Certificate Authority A trusted service that maintains a database of public keys. The certificate authority guarantees that the keys in the database are legitimate by signing (i.e., encrypting) them with its own private key.

Ciphertext In cryptography, this is the result of encoding a plaintext message.
Confidentiality Ensuring that the data is only viewed by authorized parties.
Content Delivery Network (CDN) A value-added service that distributes the content to multiple locations and closer to the end user. By sophisticated caching schemes a CDN reduces response times.
Data Integrity The assurance that the data that was received is the same as the data that was sent.
Digital Signature The encryption of a document with a user's private key.
Firewall A gateway router, often between an internal business network and the public network, that has special functionality to filter out unwanted traffic or to redirect traffic to addresses that are hidden from the outside world.
Frame Relay The most popular technology choice within public switched data networks. Data are divided into frames that are sent on switched networks.
Interexchange Carrier A long-distance carrier in the public switched telephone network system.
Internet Service Provider An organization that provides access to the Internet by providing an Internet address and support of Internet protocols to the subscriber.
Leased Line A digital line that provides dedicated transmission capacity between sites.
Local Exchange Carrier A carrier that controls traffic within a single local access and transport area.
Plaintext In cryptography, this is the original message before it has been encoded.
Private Key One of the pair of keys used in public key encryption.
Private Network A business network composed of point-to-point leased lines between sites.
Public Key One of the pair of keys used in public key encryption.
Public Key Cryptography An encryption technique that uses two different keys, a public key and a private key.
Public Network A network that is publicly available to subscribers. A public network can be under government control, operate as a national monopoly, or can be a privately owned network whose services are sold to the public.
Public Switched Telephone Network The network that makes up the public telephone system.
Secret Key The key that is shared between two parties in secret key encryption.
Secret Key Cryptography An encryption technique that uses a single key for both encryption and decryption.
Secure Channel A communication channel or network that connects authenticated senders and receivers and provides encryption to maintain the confidentiality of the data.
Session Key A secret key that is valid only during a session, that is, between the time that a user logs in and the user logs out, or until a certain time period has elapsed.
Value-Added Carrier A network provider that provides a value-added network.
Value-Added Network A network constructed by a network provider that owns the packet-switching nodes and leases transmission capacity to add value to the network.
Value-Added Reseller A business that provides a service (e.g., Web hosting) that requires network connectivity and sells it for use with a particular public network provider. The network provider often gives discounts to the business for using the network.
Virtual Private Network A network that uses a collection of technologies applied to the public network to provide the same levels of privacy, security, quality of service, and manageability as private networks.

CROSS REFERENCES

See *Home Area Networking; VPN Basics; Wide Area and Metropolitan Area Networks.*

REFERENCES

Allen, D. (2001, December 5). Content delivery networks come home. *Network Magazine*. Retrieved May 9, 2002, from http://www.networkmagazine.com/article/NMG20011203S0017

ATM Forum. (2002). Retrieved July 17, 2002, from http://www.atmforum.com

Autorité de Regulation des Telecommunications. (January 2003). Retrieved October 15, 2003, from http://www.art.telecom.fr

Bellamy, J. C. (2000). *Digital telephony* (3rd ed.). New York: John Wiley & Sons.

Cisco. (2001). Secure business communications over public networks. Retrieved April 4, 2002, from http://www.cisco.com/warp/public/cc/pd/rt/800/prodlit/sbcp_wp.htm

Dunsmore, B., Skandier, T., Martin, C., McKelvey, & Woods, T. (2003). *Telecommunications technologies reference.* Indianapolis, IN: Cisco Press.

Effenberger, F. J., Ichibangase, H., & Yamashita, H. (2001, December). Advances in broadband passive optical networking technologies. *IEEE Communications Magazine*, 39(12), 118–124.

Frame Relay Forum. (2002). Retrieved May 7, 2002, from http://www.frforum.com

Geier, J. (2003). IEEE 802.11 and 802.16: a tale of two standards. Retrieved December 16, 2003, from http://www.spectrum.ieee.org/WEBONLY/publicfeature/sep03/wiresb2.html

Greenfield, D. (2001, September 5). Slugfest results. *Network Magazine*. Retrieved May 7, 2002, from http://www.networkmagazine.com/article/NMG20010823S0012

Henry, P. S., & Luo, H. (2002, December). WiFi: What's next? *IEEE Communications Magazine, 40*(12), 66–72.

Internet Mail Consortium. (2003). S/MIME and OpenPGP. Retrieved December 15, 2003, from http://www.imc.org/smime-pgpmime.html

Iridium Satellite. (2002). Retrieved May 7, 2002, from http://www.iridium.com

Kerberos. (2003). MIT Kerberos home page; Kerberos: The network authentication protocol. Retrieved December 14, 2003, from http://web.mit.edu/kerberos/

Kramer, G., & Pesavento, G. (2002, February). Ethernet passive optical network (EPON): Building a next-generation optical access network. *IEEE Communications Magazine, 40*(2), 66–73.

MCI–WorldCom. (2002). Retrieved May 7, 2002, from http://www.worldcom.com

Moody, G. (2001). The business potential of the Internet. Retrieved December 12, 2001, from http://www.worldcom.com/generation_d/whitepapers/

Neuman, B. C., & Ts'o, T. (1994). Kerberos: An Authentication Service for Computer Networks. *IEEE Communications Magazine, 32*(9), 33–38. Retrieved September 1994 from http://www.isi.edu/gost/publications/kerberos-neuman-tso.html

Noam, E.M. (2001). *Interconnecting the network of networks.* Cambridge, MA: The MIT Press.

Orenstein, C. S., & Ohlson, K. (1999, August 13). MCI network outage hits Chicago trading board hard. *Computerworld.*

Panko, R. R. (2001). *Business data communications and networking.* Upper Saddle River, NJ: Prentice Hall.

PayPal. (2004). Retrieved March 31, 2004, from http://www.paypal.com

PGP Corporation. (2003). Retrieved December 15, 2003, from http://www.pgp.com

Poptop. (2004). Retrieved March 31, 2004, from http://www.poptop.org

Qwest. (2002). Retrieved May 7, 2002, from http://www.qwest.com

RFC 2104. Krawczyk, H., Bellare, M., & Canetti, R. (February 1997). HMAC: keyed-hashing for message authentication. *IETF RFC 2104.* Retrieved December 16, 2003, from http://www.rfc-editor.org/rfc/rfc2104.txt

RFC 2246. Dierks, T., & Allen, C. (January 1999). The TLS Protocol version 1.0. *IETF RFC 2246.* Retrieved December 16, 2003, from http://www.rfc-editor.org/rfc/rfc2246.txt

RFC 2401. Kent, S., & Atkinson, R. (November 1998). Security architecture for the Internet protocol. *IETF RFC 2401.* Retrieved December 16, 2003, from http://www. rfc-editor.org/rfc/rfc2401.txt

RFC 2411. Thayer, R., Doraswamy, N., & Glenn, R. (November 1998). IP security document roadmap. *IETF RFC 2411.* Retrieved December 16, 2003, from http://www.rfc-editor.org/rfc/rfc2411.txt

RFC 3156. Elkins, M., Del Torto, D., Levien, R., & Roessler, T. (August 2001). MIME security with OpenPGP. IETF RFC 3156. Retrieved December 16, 2003, from http://www.rfc-editor.org/rfc/rfc3156.txt

SET (2003). Retrieved December 14, 2003, from http://www.setco.org/set.html

SET Brands (2003). Retrieved December 14, 2003, from http://www.setco.org/brand_ca.html

Snow, A.P. (2001). Network reliability: the concurrent challenges of innovation, competition, and complexity. *IEEE Transactions on Reliability, 50*(1), 38–40.

Stallings, W. (2001). *Business data communications.* Upper Saddle River, NJ: Prentice Hall.

Stallings, W. (2003). *Cryptography and network security: Principles and practice* (3rd ed.). Upper Saddle River, NJ: Prentice Hall.

StarBand Communications. (2002). Retrieved May 7, 2002, from http://www.starband.com

Tanenbaum, A. S. (1996). *Computer networks.* Upper Saddle River, NJ: Prentice Hall.

Webopedia, "SET" (2003). Retrieved December 14, 2003, from http://networking.webopedia.com/TERM/S/SET.html

Webopedia, "802.11" (2003). Retrieved December 16, 2003, from http://www.webopedia.com/TERM/8/802_11.html

The Yankee Group. (2001, December 31). Endless pressure—Price and availability review for private lines and dedicated access services. Retrieved April 23, 2002, from http://www.yankeegroup.com

Client/Server Computing: Principles and Security Considerations

Daniel J. McFarland, *Rowan University*

INTRODUCTION

The name of an information system often describes the utility it provides. The functionality of a transaction processing system, a decision support system, and an executive information system are self-evident. However, client/server computing is broadly defined; rather than describing system utility, client/server describes the system's architectural configuration. As a result, a client/server system may incorporate a broad range of technologies and address a variety of business situations.

Client/server computing is a form of cooperative processing. Specifically, a client/server system includes at least two software processes working together to provide application functionality. At the most basic level, a client software process requests services from a server software process. In turn, the server process supplies services to the client process. The service request may provide access to an organizational resource, such as a database, a printer, or e-mail.

Client/server computing involves the coordination of assorted computing/networking devices and the coordination of various software processes. The client/server *system* architecture describes the physical configuration of the computing and networking devices and the client/server *software* architecture describes the partitioning of an application into software processes.

The system architecture focuses on the physical architecture of the system. In this context, clients and servers are seen as computers rather than software processes. Simple client/server system architectures include a client (e.g., a personal computer) that links to a server (e.g., a mid-range computer) using a network (e.g., a local area network). Each computer provides processing and memory resources to the client/server application. The system architectural perspective views a client/server application as a network of computers sharing resources to solve a problem.

The client/server *software* architecture describes the partitioning of an application into software processes. In this context, clients and servers are seen as software processes rather than computers. These processes may reside on the same computer or they may be distributed across a network of computers. The software architectural perspective views a client/server application as a set of programming modules sharing resources to solve a problem. This chapter focuses on the client/server *software* architectural perspective; consequently, a client shall refer to a software process that requests services from other software processes and a server shall refer to a software process that provides services to other software processes.

The resulting architectural complexity and physical separations within a client/server application introduce many security weaknesses. A typical client/server application consists of a set of software processes spread across several computers using exposed interprocess communications over a network. Beyond managing the overall configuration and increase exposure, each individual component (e.g., process, computer, and network) has its own set of security threats.

An effective security analysis consists of several activities, including an examination of the attractiveness of an attack to an adversary, a detailed list of security vulnerabilities, the likelihood and potential damage of each violation, and a list of existing and potential countermeasures (CCPS, 2002). The attractiveness of an attack to an adversary is influenced by many factors such as disgruntled employees, contractors, and trading partners; symbolism of the system assets, the system itself, and the organization; the number of and fundamentalism of activists; interests from foreign governments and terrorists; industry competitiveness; intellectual challenge; potential for adversary notoriety; potential adversary benefits; and the degree of impact to the organization, local/regional/national governments, and the community. Because the threat environment is constantly evolving, vulnerability analysis is exceedingly difficult. Within this chapter, we will identify several of the hardware, software, and data security vulnerabilities associated with client/server systems.

The damage from an information security violation may include a loss of system integrity, availability, and/or confidentiality. Integrity strives to maintain data and process precision, accuracy, consistency, and usability. An available system provides authorized parties making an appropriate request with timely, complete responses. Confidentiality encompasses both privacy and access control. Privacy maintains the secrecy of data and user identities. For instance, an online shopper does not want others to learn his or her identity, credit card information, contact information, or buying behaviors. Access controls inhibit nonauthorized people from using a system and from knowing what system assets exist. Access controls may target systems, applications, particular functions, and/or specific data elements. Password protections are commonly used to control access.

This chapter begins with a review of three common client/server classification methodologies. The first methodology classifies a client/server application based on the computational role of the constituent processes. In particular, how an application distributes its presentation, application processing, and data services determines how the application is classified. The second methodology classifies an application based on the number of constituent processes; this is known as the tier-based classification. Finally, a server-based classification methodology is presented; it describes a client/server application in terms of the server process utility.

The subsequent section describes three broad categories of enabling technologies. The first set of enabling technologies, middleware, provides a client/server application the ability to integrate client processes with server processes. The second set of enabling technologies, component software, provides self-contained, self-describing software modules that may be combined to form applications. The third set of enabling technologies, networking technologies, bridges the gap among the computing and networking devices.

The final part of this chapter reviews intranets, extranets, and the Internet, three popular client/server implementations.

CLIENT/SERVER CLASSIFICATION

A client/server classification provides information about the particular system architectural configuration. Three client/server classifications are reviewed below. The first classification employs the PAD architecture, which describes the computational role of the client process. The second classification describes the number of separate processes in a client/server application, otherwise known as the number of tiers. The final classification describes the functional role of the server process.

Presentation/Application/Data Architecture

Client/server computing divides an application into two or more separate processes. The PAD architecture describes the computational role of both the client and server processes. In particular, the PAD architecture defines the computational requirements of an application in terms of presentation services, application services, and data services. The presentation services layer details the interaction between the user and the application. The application services layer includes the embedded programming and business logic. The data services layer describes the connectivity to organizational resources such as data, printers, and e-mail (Goldman, Rawles, & Mariga, 1999).

Presentation Services

Presentation services represent the interactions an application has with the external environment. At the most basic level, these interactions involve user input and application output. User input represents the portion of the user's knowledge submitted to an application. Input provides application boundaries, operating parameters, and/or data. Application output strives to provide the user/process/application with new knowledge. Output includes printed reports, audio signals, screen displays, and data. In many cases, a client/server application receives input from and provides output to multiple sources, such as users, other software processes, and/or other applications.

Presentation services can also influence the degree to which a person will use an application. A complex, synergistic relationship exists among the user, the business problem/context, and the application (Dix, Finlay, Abowd, & Beale, 1998). Several areas of study explore how people and technology interact, such as cybernetics, human–computer interaction, ergonomics, human factors analysis, technology acceptance, and industrial engineering.

Security vulnerabilities for presentation services include impersonation, interception, modification, and interruption. Impersonation describes when a person or program disguises itself as someone or something else. Interception is when a person or program intentionally receives a message addressed for another party. Modification attacks involve altering the content of a message. A presentation service interruption would involve an intentional blockage of communications.

Application Services

Application services describe how input is transformed into output. The application services layer represents the procedural knowledge (i.e., business logic) embedded in the application. These services include statistical, mathematical, graphical, and/or data transformations.

Application services suffer from malicious code attacks and inadvertent programming errors. Malicious code attacks include viruses, worms, Trojan horses, and information leaks. A virus is malicious software that alters and propagates itself to other files. A worm is similar to a virus; however, a worm propagates itself throughout a network. A Trojan horse is a program that disguises itself as another program, satisfies the functions of the original software, and performs additional malicious acts. An information leak describes a process that secretly collects and transmits sensitive information to others.

Although malicious code receives most of the media attention, inadvertent programming errors cause much more damage (Pfleeger & Pfleeger, 2003). Inadvertent programming errors result from insufficient software debugging, sloppy coding practices, misinterpretation of requirements, and/or unforeseen application longevity/utility. Commonly exploited errors include validation errors, buffer overflows, inadequate authentication, and serialization errors. Exposed interprocess

Table 1 PAD Architectural Classification of Client/Server Applications

Computational Service	Distributed Presentation	Local Presentation	Distributed Application Logic	Local Application Logic	Distributed Data
Data services	Server	Server	Server	Server	*Shared*
Application services	Server	Server	*Shared*	Client	Client
Presentation services	*Shared*	Client	Client	Client	Client

communications make application services vulnerable to receiving intentionally altered messages. Unfortunately, because data validation is typically handled by the presentation services, application services often neglect to further validate requests. A buffer overflow describes when a process writes data into an area of memory that is owned by another process or the operating system. Overwriting data can have potentially crippling effects on a system. Inadequate authentication procedures provide an opportunity for an adversary to assume another's identity. Serialization errors result in the delay experienced in sequencing requests and responses. Serialization errors might allow an individual to execute commands as a different user by exploiting the time between authorization and request transmission.

Data Services

Data services provide access to organizational resources including information-based resources (e.g., databases), hardware-based resources (e.g., printers), and communication-based resources (e.g., e-mail). The data services layer provides utility to the application services layer and/or the presentation services layer.

Organizational resources are often difficult to access as a result of security, budgetary, and/or technical constraints. Security rules restrict access to sensitive data such as payroll information. Budgetary constraints restrict accessibility to consumable resources such as printers. Additionally, technology-based resources, such as databases, often require special and/or proprietary interfaces. As a result, data services often attempt to hide the implementation difficulties associated with accessing and using organizational resources.

Security vulnerabilities include data theft, physical damage, data value integrity, data structure integrity, availability, auditability, accessibility, authentication, and confidentiality. Data theft includes eavesdropping, unauthorized replication, and unauthorized removal of resources. Data values integrity is compromised when data are maliciously or inadvertently altered, deleted, inserted, or moved. Data structure integrity involves the validity, consistency, and accuracy of the relationships shared among the data elements. Data structures allow data to be located, retrieved, combined, and understood. As a result, the data structures are as important as the data values themselves. Availability means that appropriate and timely responses are provided to authorized parties during prescribed operating hours. Auditability allows administrators to track and retrace the actions of users and processes. Accessibility defines which parties have access to which system resources at what times and under what circumstances. Although controlling direct accessibility is relatively straightforward, adversaries may access nonsensitive data in several ways to indirectly infer or derive sensitive data. Controlling indirect data access is particularly challenging. Authentication ensures that each party is specifically and accurately identified for accessibility and audit purposes. Confidentiality describes when the content of a message and identities of the parties are kept private.

PAD Architecture-Based Client/Server Classification

The PAD architecture classifies client/server applications based on the distribution of computational services between the client process and the server process. As seen in Table 1, the PAD architectural framework includes five client/server classification levels. Each level is defined by the client-side PAD functionality.

In the first level, *distributed presentation*, the client shares the presentation processing with the server and the server handles all application and data services. In the second level, *local presentation*, the client handles the presentation services and the server handles the application and data services. In the third level, *distributed application logic*, the client addresses the presentation services and a portion of the application services; the server handles the data services and shares the application services with the client. In the fourth level, *local application logic*, the client handles the presentation and application services and the server handles the data services. In the last level, *distributed data services*, the client handles all presentation and application services and the data services are shared by the client and the server.

Tier-Based Client/Server Classification

Client/server computing partitions an application into two or more separate processes. The tier-based classification methodology views each software process as a computational component/layer/tier within the overall application.

A two-tier system is the simplest and oldest client/server architecture. In a two-tier system a client communicates with a server directly. This architecture often strives to provide reusable, robust links to organizational resources, such as printers and data.

In a three-tier system, a client communicates to a server through an intermediary process. This intermediary process provides functionality as well as connectivity. Middle-tier functionality may include message queuing, application execution, and database staging. The middle tier also provides encapsulation for the data source and abstraction for the presentation services. As a result, changes to the data structure and/or user interface are less disruptive and more transparent. Furthermore, data encapsulation improves connectivity with legacy and/or mainframe systems. A three-tier system may support a large number of concurrent users and is able to handle very complex processing (Carnegie Mellon Software Engineering Institute, 1997e).

The *n*-tier client/server architecture is a natural extension of the three-tier architecture. An *n*-tier system has an undetermined number of intermediary processes and server processes. A client process might call upon a middle-tier process, which in turn might call upon another middle-tier process. In combining narrowly focused processes together, the *n*-tier architecture strives to provide application flexibility and software reusability.

Server Functionality Client/Server Classification

Many client/server applications strive to reuse server process functionality. Because a server process often embeds and hides complicated implementation details, reusing a process significantly reduces system development time and effort. Furthermore, reusing successful, robust server processes improves overall system reliability (Weiss, 2001).

To promote reusability and clarity, the functional role of a server process often describes the server. The following list describes a few server types. Table 2 provides a summary of the servers listed below.

Web Server

A Web server creates a standardized way for objects to communicate with each other over the Internet. A Web server provides session connectivity to clients running Web browsers. Early Web servers fetched files for clients without processing or interpreting the content. However, technologies such as common gateway interface (CGI), active server pages (ASP), JavaServer Pages (JSP), Java Applets, ColdFusion, extensible markup language (XML), and Web services have dramatically expanded the processing and interactivity capabilities of Web servers.

Application Server

Application servers provide interactivity and processing functionality to clients. An application server may execute programming logic, store and process information, and/or manage user interactivity. Centrally storing programming logic allows developers to reuse existing, proven application functionality as well as simplifying software version control and software deployment.

Wireless Server

A wireless server provides network and Internet connectivity for wireless devices. Two popular wireless servers are *wireless enablers* and *wireless gateways*. A wireless enabling server stores information specifically designed for wireless devices, such as wireless markup language (WML). WML is a wireless-friendly version of hypertext markup language (HTML). A wireless client accessing a wireless enabling server would be provided with a WML file rather than an HTML file. Unlike a wireless enabler, a wireless gateway typically does not store content. It accepts requests from wireless and traditional devices and routes each request to an appropriate server based on the request and device type. Some wireless gateway servers also translate wireless and traditionally formatted messages to/from WML and HTML. These translations allow wireless devices to access both traditional and wireless content.

Transaction Processing Monitoring Server

A transaction processing (TP) monitoring server introduces performance efficiencies when serving a large number of users. These servers accept client requests, merge requests together by type, and then transmit the resulting consolidated messages to appropriate servers. In addition, a TP monitor might monitor, prioritize, schedule, process, balance, and/or rollback service requests.

Message Server

A message server accepts and routes messages. A message is a service request that is packaged with destination information. An e-mail request is a message; it has embedded intelligence regarding the specific message destination. As a result, an e-mail server is a message server.

Table 2 Functional Descriptions for Several Server Types

Server Type	Functional Description
Web server	Connectivity and interactivity to clients running Web browsers
Application server	Interactivity and processing functionality
Wireless server	Wireless content locating services and/or wireless-friendly content
Transaction processing (TP) server	User responsiveness, processing prioritization, scheduling, and balancing
Message server	Message routing and delivery
E-mail server	Electronic-mail storage, routing, and delivery
Fax server	Fax storage, routing, and delivery
Proxy server	Intermediary content and processing functionality
Firewall	Access restriction based on a predetermined set of security criteria
Dynamic host configuration protocol (DHCP) server	Dynamic reuse of network addresses
File transfer protocol (FTP) server	File transfer capabilities

E-mail Server

An e-mail server accepts, routes, stores, and delivers electronic mail (e-mail) messages; it handles incoming and outgoing e-mail messages. Several e-mail standards exist, such as messaging application programming interface (MAPI), X.400, and the Internet e-mail standard. Any compliant software product, regardless of the authoring product, may read standardized messages.

Fax Server

A fax server is similar to an e-mail server. It accepts, routes, stores, and delivers faxes; it handles incoming and outgoing faxes. Most fax servers provide additional features such as a direct-to-print option (i.e., allowing a fax to be sent to a printer rather than an electronic inbox).

Proxy Server

A proxy server is an intermediary process. It intercepts client requests and attempts to satisfy each request itself. If a request cannot be satisfied, the proxy server routes the request to an appropriate server.

A proxy server may control and manage Internet usage. Because all client requests go through the proxy server, an organization is able to monitor and/or limit Internet usage. A proxy server that filters Internet requests and/or logs Internet usage is acting as a firewall.

Firewall

A firewall reduces the risks associated with unauthorized access to a network and inappropriate use of networking resources. All requests entering or leaving a network must pass through a firewall. The firewall rejects those requests failing to satisfy the predetermined security criteria. A firewall might also record request and network activities. Firewalls are highly configurable based on organizational security and auditing concerns.

Dynamic Host Configuration Protocol Server

Like a postal address for a brick-and-mortar building, each computer on a network must possess a unique address. Traditionally, these addresses were fixed, meaning (1) each computer required individual configuration, (2) potential conflicts were inevitable, and (3) organizations were required to manage large blocks of addresses.

A dynamic host configuration protocol (DHCP) server dynamically assigns Internet addresses to computers on the network. This permits an organization to standardize computer configurations, to reduce network address contention, and to continually recycle a smaller number of network addresses.

File Transfer Protocol Server

A file transfer protocol (FTP) server transfers files from one computer to another using a network. An FTP server accepts file uploads (i.e., copying files to a server) and file downloads (i.e., copying files from a server). Although many FTP servers provide unrestricted access, others provide access to authorized users only.

Targeted Malicious Code

The reusable nature and global availability of server functionality provides many benefits; however, these circumstances also provide adversaries with fixed targets. Although generic and script-based malicious code indiscriminately infects any system (e.g., viruses and worms), targeted malicious code infects only specific types of applications. Examples of targeted malicious code include SQL injection attacks, trapdoors, covert channels, and salami attacks. SQL is a standardized, simple to use, powerful, and very popular language used to interact with databases. An SQL injection attack describes when an adversary uses the exposed interprocess communications to alter the SQL code being sent to the server. Successful SQL injection attacks can allow adversaries to read, insert, delete, and/or alter organizational data. A trapdoor is undocumented access point into a system; they are often intentionally created to provide support and/or future enhancements. A covert channel surreptitiously sends data to others in plain sight. A covert channel will encode a message in a standard report or in a seemingly benign message. A salami attack introduces subtle modifications to data. Consider an adversary who shaves 10 cents off of every $1000.00 transaction. Even if this inaccuracy is noticed, the organization might tolerate it as within acceptable margins of error. Furthermore, the organization may feel it would be too costly to fix such a seemingly insignificant error. However, over time or with large enough transactions an adversary may be able to redirect large sums of money.

ENABLING TECHNOLOGIES

Enabling technologies allow heterogeneous software processes, computing devices, and networking devices to interoperate. Enabling technologies include technological standards, organizing frameworks, and product implementations. Three enabling technologies are discussed: middleware, component software, and networking technologies.

Middleware

Middleware is a primary enabler of client/server computing. Middleware acts like glue holding together the separate software processes. Middleware products simplify the design, development, and implementation of complex applications by hiding server location issues, networking protocol details, and operating system differences (Carnegie Mellon Software Engineering Institute, 1997a). Middleware is broadly defined; it may be a type of program-to-program interface, a set of standards, or a product. Table 3 provides a summary of the middleware categories listed below.

Transactional Middleware

Transactional middleware supports transaction-processing functionality; it strives to provide responsiveness and data integrity while supporting a large number of users. It often includes load balancing, replication, and/or two-phase commits. The Customer Information Control System (CICS) from IBM is a transactional

Table 3 Middleware Categories and Implementation Examples

Middleware Category	Implementation Examples
Transactional middleware	CICS—IBM
	DTP—Open Group
	BEA Tuxedo—BEA Systems Systems
Procedural middleware	ONC RPC—IETF
	DCE RPC—Open Group
Message-oriented middleware	WebSphere MQ—IBM
	JMQ—Sun Microsystems

middleware product. CICS is common on IBM mainframes and on several other IBM platforms, including OS/2, AS/400, and RS/6000. The distribute transaction processing (DTP) protocol from the Open Group is another transactional middleware standard. Many relational and object-oriented database management systems support DTP. BEA Tuxedo, from BEA Systems, is another popular transactional middleware product.

Message-Oriented Middleware

Message-oriented middleware (MOM) supports client/server processes using asynchronous, peer-to-peer messages. A MOM does not require continuous, active communication between the client and the server. A client sends a message and does not wait for a response. If a server is busy or unavailable, received messages wait in a queue until they are satisfied. MOM solutions are well suited for event-driven and object-oriented applications. However, many MOM implementations are proprietary. As a result, they tend to be inflexible, difficult to maintain, and lack interoperability and portability (Carnegie Mellon Software Engineering Institute, 1997b). MOM middleware products include WebSphere MQ (formerly MQSeries) from IBM and Java Message Queue (JMQ) from Sun Microsystems. WebSphere MQ is a mature product supporting over 35 platforms (http://www.ibm.com). JMQ is based on Java Message Service (JMS), which is a Java application programming interface (API) included in the Java 2 Platform, Enterprise Edition (J2EE). JMS is one of the many standards included in J2EE, which is a platform for developing distributed applications using the Java programming language. J2EE, using the CORBA/IIOP communications infrastructure, specifies many services including asynchronous communications using JMS, naming services using Java Naming, Directory Interface (JNDI), transaction services using Java Transaction API (JTA), and database access services using Java Database Connectivity (JDBC). J2EE implementations are developed and provided by a variety of vendors (Sun, J2EE, n.d.a; Alur, Crupi, & Malks, 2001).

Procedural Middleware

A remote procedure call (RPC) supports synchronous, call/wait process-to-process communications. When using an RPC, a client requests a service then waits for a response. As a result, an RPC requires continuous, active participation from the client and the server. Each RPC request is a synchronous interaction between exactly one client and one server (Carnegie Mellon Software Engineering Institute, 1997d). Open Network Computing Remote Procedure Call (ONC RPC), developed by Sun Microsystems and now supported by the Internet Engineering Task Force (IETF), was one of the first RPC protocols and is widely deployed to a variety of platforms (IETF, n.d.). The Distributed Computing Environment (DCE), developed and maintained by the Open Group (formerly known as the Open Systems Foundation), is a set of integrated services supporting the development of distributed computing environments. DCE provides distributed services and data-sharing services, including RPC, directory services (i.e., the ability to identify and locate system resources), time services, security services, and thread services (i.e., the ability to build concurrent applications). DCE data-sharing services include diskless support and distributed file system services (Open Group, 1996). DCE RPC is the protocol used by several object and component middleware solutions, such as Microsoft's Distributed COM (DCOM) and COM+ and it is also an optional protocol in the Object Management Group's Common Object Request Broker Architecture (CORBA).

Component Software

Component software strives to improve software development productivity through the reuse of self-describing, self-contained software modules called components. Each component provides specific functionality. An application calls upon components at run time.

Component software exists within a component model, which defines the way components are constructed and the environment in which a component will run. The component model consists of an interface definition language, a component environment, services, utilities, and specifications. An interface definition language (IDL) defines how a component interacts with other components to form applications. The components exist within a component environment. A component environment is a computing environment providing the ability to locate and communicate with components. Popular component models include Microsoft's Component Object Model (COM), the Object Management Group's CORBA, Sun Microsystems's Enterprise Java Beans (EJB), and Web services.

Component Object Model (COM)

Microsoft's COM is a way for multivendor software components to communicate with each other. It provides a software architecture that allows applications to be built from binary components supplied by different software vendors. COM provides the foundation for many technologies, including object linking and embedding (OLE), ActiveX, and Microsoft transaction server (MTS). Distributed COM extends COM by allowing remote component interactions. COM+ further expands the COM by encapsulating DCOM, MTS, and a host of other services, including a dynamic load-balancing service, an in-memory database, a publish-and-subscribe events service, and a queued-components service. COM components require the COM application server, available on the Windows operating system platforms (Microsoft COM Technologies, 1998).

Common Object Request Broker Architecture

CORBA is an open, vendor-independent architecture describing object-oriented process interactions over a network. CORBA, supported by the Object Management Group (OMG), utilizes a standard communication protocol IIOP (Internet inter-ORB protocol). IIOP allows a CORBA process running on one computer to interact with a CORBA process running on another computer without regard to network, vendor, programming language, or platform heterogeneity. CORBA supports a variety of services, including asynchronous and synchronous, stateless and persistent, and flat and nested transactions (OMG, n.d.).

Enterprise Java Beans

Similar to CORBA, Sun Microsystems's EJB is a specification. An EJB must be programmed using Java and must be hosted on a J2EE application server. EJBs interact with each other using Java remote method invocation (RMI). An RMI is a set of APIs used to create distributed applications using Java; it is also an implementation that operates in a homogeneous environment using Java virtual machine (JVM). RMI allows Java objects to communicate remotely with other Java objects. Alternatively, an EJB built with EJB 2.0 specification, or higher, may communicate using the message-oriented-middleware, JMS (Marinescu & Roman, 2002).

An EJB system consists of three parts, the EJB component, the EJB container, and the EJB object. An EJB component exists within an EJB container running on an EJB server. The EJB object provides access to the EJB components. An EJB component is a software module that provides specific functionality; it may be discovered and manipulated dynamically at run time. The EJB container provides the execution environment for the EJB components; it handles the communication and interface details. An EJB container may support more than one EJB component. Although an EJB component runs on a server, an EJB object runs on a client. An EJB object remotely controls the EJB component (Sun, n.d.c).

Web Services

Web services are an extremely promising set of technologies; they may represent the first successful cross-platform component architecture. A Web service is a self-contained program providing a specific function that is packaged in such a way that it may be called upon remotely. A Web service is a platform-independent module that utilizes existing Internet standards, primarily XML, to provide, validate, and interpret data; hypertext transfer protocol (HTTP) to provide synchronous communications; and simple mail transfer protocol (SMTP) to provide asynchronous communications.

Web services provide Internet-accessible, building block functionality to developers; they allow for incremental development and deployment. Web services support new application development and promise to provide access to existing applications. By wrapping traditional processes in Web service protocols, an existing computing infrastructure can improve interoperability and utilization without having to reprogram existing applications. Furthermore, an existing application may enhance functionality by integrating with new Web services.

Web services are distinctive in several ways. Although a traditional server process is designed to provide function to a particular client, a Web service strives to provide global access to a very specific function. A Web service is not duplicated or moved; it is simply called upon as required at run time by applications. Furthermore, unlike other distributed application environments, such as CORBA, J2EE, and COM+, Web services do not dictate the underlying communications framework (Singh et al., 2002).

Open, standardized interfaces are the heart of Web services. Standards define how a Web service communicates, how it exchanges data, and how it is located. Simple object access protocol (SOAP) is an XML-based protocol for exchanging information in a distributed environment. SOAP is platform independent; it consists of an envelope, a set of encoding rules, and a convention describing procedure calls. A SOAP envelope describes what is inside the message and how the message should be processed. The encoding rules describe the application-specific data types. The conventions describe remote procedure calls and responses. Other standards include the Web services description language (WSDL), which defines the Web service interfaces, and the universal description, discovery, and integration (UDDI), which allows developers to list/post new Web services and to locate existing Web services (Ewald, 2002).

Networking

The Internet consists of host computers, client computers, routers, applications, protocols, and other hardware and software. As an organizing framework, these technologies may be categorized using three broadly defined functional areas, namely network access, network core, and network edge.

As seen in Table 4, network access describes how devices connect to the Internet. The network core describes the intercommunications among the computing

Table 4 Internet Networking Categories and Components

Internet Networking Category	Components
Network access	Internet access providers Internet connectivity: Dial-up, ISDN, ADSL, HFC, wireless, T1/T3
Network core	Routers and bridges Data routing: circuit-switching, packet-switching
Network edge	Computers, users, applications Internet protocol stack

Table 5 Comparison of the OSI Model and the Internet Protocol Stack

OSI Model	Internet Protocol Stack	Layer Description	Protocols
Application Presentation Session	Application	Specifies how applications and processes will communicate with each other	HTTP, SMTP, MIME, DNS, NFS. Middleware products: RPC, MOM, CORBA/IIOP, CICS, DTP
Transport	Transport	Specifies how information is transmitted	TCP, UDP
Network	Network	Specifies host and application addressing	IP
Link	Link	Specifies how the media are shared	PPP, SLIP, ATM, Ethernet
Physical	Physical	Specifies the physical characteristics of the media	100BaseT, IEEE802.5, IEEE802.11, Token Passing, TCS, PDM

and networking devices. The network edge describes those objects using the Internet such as clients, servers, and applications (Kurose & Ross, 2001; Peterson & Davie, 1999).

Network Access

An Internet access provider (IAP) provides Internet access. The structure of an IAP is roughly hierarchical. At the lowest level, a local Internet service provider (ISP) provides connectivity for residential customers and small businesses. The local ISP connects to a regional ISP. The regional ISP connects to a national/international backbone provider (NBP). The various NBPs interconnect using private connections and/or public network access points (NAP) to form the backbone of the Internet.

To communicate with an IAP, a connection must be established and maintained. Several connection alternatives exist, including dial-up, integrated services digital network (ISDN), asymmetric digital subscriber line (ADSL), hybrid fiber coax (HFC, via a cable modem), radio wireless, cellular wireless, satellite wireless, microwave wireless, T1, and T3.

The Network Core

The network core describes how networking devices interconnect with each other. The backbone of the Internet is an extremely large mesh. Data are sent through this mesh using either circuit-switching or packet-switching channels. A circuit-switching network establishes and maintains a circuit (i.e., a specific network path) for the entire duration of an interaction. A circuit-switching network knows where to look for messages and the data are received in the order in which they are sent. A packet-switching network divides each transmission into a series of individually addressed packets. Because each packet is addressed, the network path need not be determined and packets may be sent using whatever bandwidth exists at the time the message is transmitted. As a result, each packet might take a different network path. The receiver of the message is responsible for unpackaging and sequencing the packets.

The Network Edge

The network edge consists of those objects using the Internet such as clients, servers, and applications. To communicate, objects must adhere to the same networking protocol. A protocol is an agreed-on set of rules governing a data transmission. The Internet supports a variety of protocols. Some protocols are competing, meaning they serve the same purpose; others are complementary, meaning they serve different purposes.

Internet Protocol Stack

A protocol stack is a framework used to organize and describe networking protocols. Each layer in a protocol stack serves a particular networking need. Furthermore, the lower layers of the stack provide a foundation for the upper layers (Kurose & Ross, 2001; Peterson & Davie, 1999). As seen in Table 5, the Internet protocol stack is a variation of the widely accepted OSI model. The OSI model has the following seven layers: physical, link, network, transport, session, presentation, and application. The Internet protocol stack has the following five layers: physical, link, network, transport, and application. The application layer on the Internet protocol stack envelops the application, presentation, and session layers of the OSI model. A description of each layer of the Internet protocol stack follows.

Physical Layer. The physical layer of the Internet protocol stack describes the physical characteristics of the networking media. Media can be broadly categorized as guided or unguided. Guided media includes copper and fiber optics. Unguided media include radio, microwave, and satellite. The media type influences bandwidth, security, interference, expandability, contention, and costs. Examples of physical layer protocols include 10BaseT, 100BaseT, Gbit Ethernet, IEEE802.5 Token Passing, IEEE802.11 Wireless, transmission convergence sublayer (TCS) and physical medium dependent (PMD) for asynchronous transfer mode (ATM), and transmission frame structures T1/T3.

Link Layer. The link layer of the Internet protocol stack describes how devices share the physical media. These protocols define host/host connections, host/router connections, and router/router connections. The primary role of link layer protocols is to define flow control (i.e., how to share the media), error detection, and error correction. Link layer protocols include point-to-point (PPP) and serial line Internet protocol (SLIP), which allow clients to establish Internet connections with Web servers. Ethernet and ATM are also popular link layer protocols.

Network Layer. The network layer of the Internet protocol stack defines host and application addressing. The Internet protocol (IP) assigns a unique number, called the IP address, to devices connected to the Internet. The IP address uniquely identifies every computer connected to the Internet.

Transport Layer. The transport layer of the Internet protocol stack defines how information is shared among applications. The Internet transport protocols include transmission control protocol (TCP) and user datagram protocol (UDP). TCP is a connection-oriented protocol. A TCP-based application establishes and maintains a connection for the entire duration of each transaction. This connection provides reliability and congestion control. Applications using TCP include e-mail, file transfers, and Web browsing. UDP is a connectionless protocol. An UDP-based application communicates by sending individual datagram packets. Datagrams support applications requiring large bandwidth and those tolerating some degree of data loss. Applications using UDP include telephony, streaming video, and interactive games.

Application Layer. The application layer of the Internet protocol stack defines application/application communications. For example, the HTTP allows Web clients to locate, retrieve, and interpret HTML objects and other Web-based objects (e.g., VBScript, Java Applets, JPG files). SMTP sends and stores Internet e-mail messages. Multipurpose Internet mail extension (MIME) supports e-mail attachments. Post office protocol (POP3) and Internet mail access protocol (IMAP) allow clients to download e-mail messages from e-mail servers. FTP allows file transfers between computers. The domain name system (DNS) resolves IP addresses and universal resource locator (URL) names. Telnet allows for remote terminal access over the Internet. The network file system (NFS) protocol allows for remote storage of files.

Networking Security Vulnerabilities

Networks suffer from many security vulnerabilities including accessibility or altering of programs or data; intercepting, creating, or modifying data in transit; and blocking traffic. These attacks may involve social engineering, performing reconnaissance, launching denial of service attacks, impersonating users, or spoofing systems. A social engineering attack strives to manipulate or trick users and/or support staff into divulging sensitive information. These attacks may be direct such as asking for a password reset or they may be indirect whereby an adversary may infer or derive sensitive information from the responses of several "individually nonsensitive" questions. Reconnaissance is an information finding activity. Adversaries may engage in reconnaissance activities ranging from searching through physical and virtual recycle bins to analyzing design diagrams and configuration information. A port scan is a common reconnaissance activity. A port is a virtual communications channel used by specific applications. A port scan is a program that systematically searches hosts to determine available ports and what applications are using the ports. A denial of service attack inundates a server with requests with the intent of overwhelming and significantly reducing the performance of the system. Impersonation describes when a party assumes the identity of another person or process. Spoofing occurs when an adversary acts on behalf of another party. Spoofing includes masquerading and session hijacking. Masquerading involves pretending to be someone else. Session hijacking involves intercepting a connection that has been established by another party.

CLIENT/SERVER IMPLEMENTATIONS

Internet

The Internet is a network of networks. Hundreds of millions of computers, users, and applications utilize the Internet. The Internet utilizes a variety of protocols, including TCP/IP, HTTP, and FTP. The Internet supports Web browsing, online chatting, multiuser gaming, e-mail delivery, fax delivery, and telephony.

The size, heterogeneity, complexity, globalization, and varied utility of the Internet make it extremely vulnerable to security attacks. Because the Internet supports hundreds of millions of client/server applications, it suffers from and is the breeding ground for practically every maliciously program designed to inflict harm on a client, a server, or a network. In addition, the World Wide Web (WWW) introduces several new threats, including Web site defacement, relative addressing issues, cookies, and Web bugs. Web site defacement describes when a Web page is vandalized with graffiti or unauthorized information. Because the WWW often passes parameters and data in an exposed, human readable form, adversaries can easily alter interprocess messages. Relative addressing attacks describe when the directory path and/or filename shown in a browser's address window are intentionally altered. A cookie is a data object copied to a user's computer that stores information about the user. The author of the cookie is able to use this information to specifically identify and recall prior transactions of a visitor. By retrieving or intercepting a cookie an adversary may be able to impersonate another user and/or gain accessible to sensitive information. Furthermore, because cookies are typically encrypted, a user is unable to read the information that a server is collecting and transmitting about himself/ herself. A Web bug is a hidden image placed on a Web site in an e-mail message. When a Web page or e-mail message is opened, the Web bug is automatically activated. This bug, in cooperation with cookies, might send information about you to someone on the Internet and/or it might copy an executable file to your hard disk. These executable files are able to secretly collect and transmit information from your personal documents. Furthermore, executable Web bugs are able to secretly send copies of your files to someone over the Internet.

Intranet

An intranet is a private network using the same technologies as the Internet. Because the foundation, protocols, and toolsets are the same, an intranet looks, feels, and behaves like the Internet. The difference between an intranet and the Internet is scope. An intranet user is limited to visiting only those Web sites owned and maintained by the company hosting the intranet, whereas an Internet user may visit any publicly accessible Web site. Because intranets are private, individuals outside the organization are unable to access intranet resources. As a result, organizations may publish internal and/or confidential information such as organizational directories, company policies, promotion procedures, and benefits information. A firewall protects an intranet from the nonsecure, public Internet.

Extranet

An extranet is an intranet that provides limited connectivity with the Internet. Specifically, an extranet allows authorized Internet users to access a portion of the company's intranet. This access is granted through a firewall. An Internet visitor submits a username and password to the firewall. If authenticated, the visitor is permitted limited access to the company's internal intranet. Similarly, an extranet may provide authorized internal users limited access to the Internet.

Extranets often support field personnel and employees working from home. In addition, extranets are designed to interconnect suppliers, customers, and other business partners. The exposure of the extranet is based on the relationships a company has with its partners and the sensitivity of the content stored on the extranet. In the most relaxed scenario, individuals gain access to common business materials by completing a brief survey. In more restrictive scenarios, an organization may sign a contract detailing acceptable use of the extranet or consumers may be required to pay subscription fees.

CONCLUSION

Client/server computing is so broadly defined, that it says little about a particular system. A client/server application may provide national security services to a government or it may provide publicly available editorials and commentaries. Additionally, client/sever computing encompasses several architectural interpretations. The client/server *system* architecture describes the physical configuration of the computing and networking devices. In this context, clients and servers are seen as computers. The client/server *software* architecture describes the configuration of the software processes. In this context, clients and servers are seen as software processes. Furthermore, client/server computing utilizes an enormous array of heterogeneous technologies, protocols, platforms, and development environments. Although some client/server applications are relatively simple, involving only a few technologies, others are extremely complex, involving a large variety of technologies.

Common to all client/server systems is the partitioning of an application into separate processes. Two general categories of processes exist, those that request services (i.e., clients) and those that provide services (i.e., servers). A client process works together with a server process to provide application functionality.

A client/server classification provides information that describes a particular system. A classification may describe the computational role of the processes, the physical partitioning of an application into tiers, or the functional role of the processes. Although these classification methodologies help describe systems, they also highlight the variety and complexity among client/server implementations. The computational and functional role of the processes varies from system to system. Furthermore, a client may interconnect with many servers and a server may interconnect with many clients.

Enabling technologies strive to provide seamless integration of hardware and software in complex environments. Specifically, middleware governs the interactions among the constituent software processes, component software provides the ability to create applications using existing, self-contained software modules, and networking technologies bridge the gap among the computing and networking devices.

Early distributed computing consisted of vendor- and platform-specific implementations. However, the trend in client/server computing is to provide standardized connectivity solutions. Web services represent one of the most promising new client/server developments. Web services strive to utilize the communication infrastructure of the Internet to deploy client/server applications. Although it is too early to know whether Web services will fulfill their potential, they promise to change the way application programs are developed and deployed. As the excitement and investments in such technologies continue to grow, the standardization and globalization of client/server computing will likely become a reality in the near future.

The ever-increasing flexibility, power, standardization, and globalization of client/server computing provide unprecedented capabilities; however, these same characteristics make the technology extremely vulnerable to undesirable, illegal, and malicious acts. Although the vast majority of people use client/server computing in productive and meaningful ways, there are underground communities that support, educate, and encourage malicious acts. Ironically, these communities exist within the environment in which they intend to damage and destroy. Even unsophisticated users (called script kiddies) can access these communities to download and execute malicious scripts capable of causing significant damage. A script kiddy may not even be aware of the damage he or she is causing.

Security is established and enforced through management practices rather than technological innovations (Panko, 2004). Security management involves defining, maintaining, and enacting security policies and security training programs. Security policies articulate the security rules (e.g., conduct a daily search for software patches), the violation reporting procedures, and the resulting sanctions (i.e., punishments). Enforcement is essential to a security policy; a security policy is only as strong as its enforcement. Furthermore, effective training is a prerequisite for just and impartial enforcement. Training programs engender awareness, appreciation, and understanding of the security policies for users, developers, and support personnel.

The security rules detail the countermeasures used to protect organizational assets from adversaries. Security countermeasures strive to prevent, detect, and respond to security violations. Prevention involves deterring, blocking, and isolating security abuses. Deterrence begins with well-publicized security policies, procedures, standards, and guidelines (Volonino & Robinson, 2004). Blocking entails firewalls, encrypting data and messages (e.g., AES, DES, and RSA), establishing secure communication channels (e.g., IPsec, SSL, S-HTTP, PPTP, and WTLS), disabling unused communication ports, and access controls. Isolation efforts include hardware, software, and data redundancy, physically separating sensitive and public data, providing a staging area for newly developed hardware/software solutions, and physical security. Detection includes monitoring, auditing, and verifying system and user activities. Monitoring products seek out malicious code and system malfunctions. Monitoring also involves continually searching for unauthorized user and host access, frequent reviews of audit logs, surveillance equipment, observation windows, and security personnel rounds. Auditing entails maintaining a detailed, time-oriented, permanent record of all system, user, and security activities. Verification procedures strive to validate system and user activities. Organizations should implement security countermeasures in a redundant manner, providing several layers of protection. In an adequately protected environment, several countermeasures must fail for a violation to occur.

Once a security violation is detected reaction measures strive to minimize the impacts and to recover the systems and/or data. Reaction measures include system and data recovery, disaster planning, emergency response planning, the ability to quarantine data and software, notification procedures, debugging, and cleansing. Finally, after the violation is contained and the recovery efforts are complete, a forensic analysis is employed to learn from the adversaries who successfully violated the system. Analyzing adversary practices goes beyond identifying exploited weaknesses, it provide insights into the strategies and motivations of adversaries. These insights help organizations anticipate and prepare for future attacks.

GLOSSARY

Client Process A software program that requests services from one or more server processes.

Client System A computer that supports a client process and requests services from one or more server systems.

Client/Server Software Architecture The logical and physical partitioning of an application into software processes.

Client/Server System Architecture The architectural configuration of computing and networking devices supporting a client/server application.

Client/Server Tier A well-defined, separate process representing a portion of a client/server application.

Component A self-contained, self-describing software module that provides specific functionality, where several can be combined to build larger applications.

Component Environment A computing environment providing the ability to locate and communicate with components.

Component Model The way components are constructed and the environment in which a component will run, consisting of an interface definition language, a component environment, services, utilities, and specifications.

Enabling Technology Provide a client/server application with the ability to locate, communicate with, and/or integrate the constituent processes.

Extranet An intranet that provides limited access to/from the Internet using firewall technology.

Interface Definition Language (IDL) Defines how a program may communicate with a component.

Internet Protocol Stack A subset of the OSI model, and a framework that organizes and describes Internet networking protocols.

Internet A global network of networks supporting hundreds of millions of computers, networking devices, applications, and users.

Intranet A private network based on Internet protocols and technologies.

Middleware The software governing the interaction among the client and server processes.

***n*-Tier System** An application that is partitioned into an unspecified number of separate processes that work together to provide system functionality.

OSI Model A general framework that organizes and describes networking protocols.

PAD Architecture Defines an application in terms of the following three computational services: presentation services, application services, and data services.

Process An executing program.

Server Process A software program that provides services to one or more client processes.

Server System A computer that supports a server process and provides services to one or more client systems.

Three-Tier An application that is partitioned into three separate processes that work together to provide system functionality.

Two-Tier An application that is partitioned into two separate processes that work together to provide system functionality.

CROSS REFERENCES

See *Extranets: Applications, Development, Security and Privacy; Intranets: Principals, Privacy and Security Considerations; Local Area Networks; Security Middleware; TCP/IP Suite.*

REFERENCES

Alur, D., Crupi, J., & Malks, D. (2001). *Core J2EE patterns*. Upper Saddle River, NJ: Prentice Hall.

Box, D., Ehnebuske, D., Kakivaya, G., et al. (2000, May 8). Simple object access protocol (SOAP) 1.1. Retrieved August 1, 2002, from http://www.w3.org/TR/SOAP/

Carnegie Mellon Software Engineering Institute. (1997a). Software technology review: Middleware. Retrieved

March 14, 2002 from http://www.sei.cmu.edu/str/descriptions/middleware_body.html

Carnegie Mellon Software Engineering Institute. (1997b). Software technology review: Message-oriented middleware. Retrieved March 25, 2002 from http://www.sei.cmu.edu/str/descriptions/momt_body.html

Carnegie Mellon Software Engineering Institute. (1997d). Software technology review: Remote procedure call. Retrieved March 25, 2002 from http://www.sei.cmu.edu/str/descriptions/rpc_body.html

Carnegie Mellon Software Engineering Institute. (1997e). Client/server software architectures—An overview. Retrieved March 25, 2002 from http://www.sei.cmu.edu/str/descriptions/clientserver_body.html

CCPS. (2002, August). *Guidelines for analyzing and managing the security vulnerabilities of fixed chemical sites*. New York: Center for Chemical Process Safety (CCPS), American Institute of Chemical Engineers.

Common Criteria. (n.d.). International Common Criteria Support Environment (CCSE). Retrieved November 12, 2003 from http://www.commoncriteria.org/index.html

Dix, A., Finlay, J., Abowd, G., & Beale, R. (1998). *Human-computer interaction* (2nd ed.). New York: Prentice Hall.

Ewald, T. (2002). Understanding XML Web wervices: The Web services idea, Microsoft Corporation. Retrieved March 22, 2003 from http://msdn.microsoft.com/webservices/understanding/readme/default.aspx

Goldman, J. E., Rawles, P. T., & Mariga, J. R. (1999). *Client/server information systems: A business-oriented approach*. New York: John Wiley & Sons.

IETF. (n.d.). The Internet Engineering Task Force (IETF) Security Area. Retrieved November 12, 2003 from http://sec.ietf.org/

Kaufman, C., Perlman, R., & Speciner, M. (2002). *Network security: Private communication in a public world* (2nd ed.). Upper Saddle River, NJ: Prentice Hall.

Kurose, J. F., & Ross, K. W. (2001). *Computer networking: A top-down approach featuring the Internet*. New York: Addison Wesley.

Marinescu, F., & Roman, E. (2002). *EJB design patterns: Advanced patterns, processes, and idioms*. New York: Wiley.

Microsoft COM Technologies. (1998). DCOM. Retrieved February 12, 2002 from http://www.microsoft.com/com/tech/dcom.asp

NIST. (n.d.). National Institute of Standards and Technology Computer Security Resource Center. Retrieved November 12, 2003 from http://csrc.nist.gov/

OMG. (n.d.). CORBA. Retrieved February 12, 2002 from http://www.corba.org/

Open Group. (1996). What is distributed computing and DCE? Retrieved March 3, 2002 from http://www.osf.org/dce/

Panko, R. R. (2004). *Corporate computer and network security*. Upper Saddle River, NJ: Prentice Hall.

Peterson, L. L., & Davie, B. S. (1999). *Computer networks: A systems approach* (2nd ed.). San Francisco: Morgan Kaufmann.

Pfleeger, C. P. & Pfleeger, S. L. (2003). *Security in computing* (3rd ed.). Upper Saddle River, NJ: Prentice Hall.

Singh, I., Stearns, B., Johnson, M., et al. (2002). *Designing enterprise applications with the J2EETM platform* (2nd ed.). Boston: Addison Wesley.

Stallings, W. (2003). *Network security essentials: Applications and standards* (2nd ed.). Upper Saddle River, NJ: Prentice Hall.

Sun. (n.d.a). Java 2 Platform, Enterprise Edition (J2EE). Retrieved August 1, 2002 from http://java.sun.com/j2ee/

Sun. (n.d.c). Java remote method invocation (RMI). Retrieved August 1, 2002 from http://java.sun.com/j2se/1.4.1/docs/guide/rmi/

Volonino, L., & Robinson, S. R. (2004). *Principles and practice of information security: Protecting computers from hackers and lawyers*. Upper Saddle River, NJ: Prentice Hall.

Weiss, A. (2001, January 29). The truth about servers. Retrieved April 25, 2002 from http://www.serverwatch.com/tutorials/article.php/1354991

Peer-to-Peer Security

Allan Friedman and L. Jean Camp, *Harvard University*

INTRODUCTION

Peer-to-peer systems (P2P) have grown in importance over the past 5 years as an attractive way to mobilize the resources of Internet users. As more and more users have powerful processors, large storage spaces, and fast network connections, more actors seek to coordinate these resources for common goals. Because of their unique decentralized nature, security in these systems is both critical and an interesting problem. How do you secure a dynamic system without central coordination? Good security on P2P systems must reflect the design goals of the system itself. In this chapter, we introduce some basic concepts for P2P systems and their security demands and then discuss several case studies to highlight issues of robustness, privacy, and trust. We analyze systems that offer secure distributed routing, privacy-enhancing and censorship-resistance publishing, shared storage, and decentralized collaborative work spaces. We conclude by examining how accountability and trust mechanisms must be built into a secure system.

ABOUT PEER-TO-PEER SYSTEMS

What Is Peer-to-Peer?

Peer-to-peer systems have two dominant features that distinguish them from a more standard client/server model of information distribution: they are overlay networks that have unique namespaces. P2P systems link different, possibly heterogeneous, systems as "peers" and allow them to interact on top of existing network configurations. It does this by defining relationships unique to that system, usually in the form of a topology by which systems are linked. Occasionally a system will piggyback atop an existing namespace, such as the IP/port labeling, but still treats these separately from the Internet-layer protocols. The combined effect of independent systems interacting through a unique namespace is *decentralization*. Not every system generally considered a P2P system is strictly decentralized in management—the infamous Napster actually ran through a centralized server—but the matter of decentralization brings out important concerns for system security.

Although they have won the most attention for their roles as (often illicit) file-swapping networks, peer-to-peer systems can serve many functions, and design considerations must reflect these. One proposed use of a P2P system was that of shared expertise. A Gnutella pioneer has suggested that the system could be used to propagate queries of any sort through a network until a peer felt that it could respond to the query, anything from a lexical lookup to a specialized calculation (Kan, 2000). In a network with varied resource availability, P2P systems have been used to distribute those resources to those who need or want them the most. The shared resources in question are usually computation or storage. This can create efficient resource usage, given a low marginal cost of using a resource not otherwise needed. Beyond sharing computation power for enormous tasks, P2P networks have been proposed as an escrow system for digital rights management, or for distributing searches across a wide range of other peers. A new class of business software systems known as groupware uses many P2P principles. Groupware networks are closed networks that support collaborative work, such as the Groove network discussed below. Finally, the decentralized nature of peer systems offers many positive features for publishing and distribution systems, not least of which is their resilience to legal and physical attacks and censorship. P2P architectures have many different functions, and different functions lead to different design conclusions with respect to overall system structure and specifically to security issues.

A Sample Architecture: Gnutella

Gnutella can illustrate the role of security in the design of a P2P system. Developed in 2000, this system was one of the first widely deployed truly decentralized P2P networks and was used largely for file swapping. Nodes keep a list of other nearby nodes in the network. When they have a query, a node will send the message to all neighbors, with a time-to-live counter measured in hops. Nodes will pass the query along until the counter runs to zero; any node that can positively respond to the query will contact the original node directly, using network location information embedded in the original query. Nodes discover each other through IP/port announcements, which are unauthenticated, opening the way for flooding or denial of service attacks. Peers are not required to authenticate either the query or the response. An attacker can return an erroneous response, directing the querying node to download files from the target node: if enough seekers are duped, the target node cannot identify or defend itself against the denial of service attack. Moreover, because a node, its query, and its target are not secured with information-hiding techniques, information about all can be exposed. This has been exploited by vigilantes to publicly expose the machines of those who sought child pornography and by the recording industry to identify holders of illegally obtained music files. Concerns about security for P2P systems have very real ramifications.

Before we can examine security in a P2P system, it pays to have a brief look at the components of a P2P system for construction. Like all complex systems, designing peer-to-peer networks is a matter of trade-offs. Because they are defined by their heterogeneous environment, it is impossible to optimize for everything. Once distributed, implementing additional control structures is much more difficult, so the original design must at least consider the following issues. The system consists of clients running on hosts. Hosts must be made aware of each other and have a means to communicate, forming nodes in a network. Nodes that wish to communicate to other nodes without a direct connection need a routing mechanism to go through the network. A routing mechanism may or may not need special consideration for the return path. Routing is distinct from the default network-level routing used by the host and rides above that layer. Instead, the namespace of the P2P system is used to find appropriate peers. Routing for specific queries can take different forms, including a broadcast to all known nodes, a multicast through neighbors with a search horizon, or an interconnection through well-placed "superpeers" at key junctions in the network. If attention is not paid to how nodes are distributed throughout the network, there can be load-balancing issues resulting in traffic problems. If we assume a dynamic Internet, then nodes need to know how to enter the network and how to leave gracefully. The existing network must be able to integrate new nodes, and recover after a node failure. As more nodes join, the network must scale well to maintain functionality. Many standard design trade-offs, such as redundancy versus efficiency, are made all the more salient by the heterogeneous environment we assume in P2P.

Peer-to-Peer and Security

Security expert Bruce Schneier is often quoted as claiming that "security is a process." As such, it matters very much whether security administration is centralized or decentralized. The basic model of the commercial Internet is the client/server relationship. As the network user base grew, less and less responsibility for administration was placed on the edges of the network and more was concentrated in smart "servers." This model is most evident on the World Wide Web, but file servers, mail servers, and centralized security administration mechanisms such as virtual private networks have all grown apace. In a centralized system, security policy can be dictated from a single location, and a "that which is not permitted is forbidden" policy can be enforced with firewalls, monitoring, and intervention.

Conversely, centralization offers a single point of failure. Both direct malicious attacks and lax or negligent administration at the heart of a centralized network can undermine security for an entire system. With a single breach, outgoing or incoming content can be corrupted or intercepted or the system can be rendered inoperable with a denial of service attack. Critical infrastructure systems such as the domain name system (DNS) have redundant implementation exactly because a single point of control is vulnerability in and of itself. In a decentralized P2P system, bad behavior has a locality impediment. Malicious attacks need to occur at or near every part of the system it wishes to affect.

P2P systems lack the tools available to a centralized administrator, so it can be much more difficult to implement security protections on a deployed P2P system. Moreover, the absence of a defensible border of a system means that it is hard to know friend from foe. Malicious users can actively play the role of insiders—that is, they can run peers themselves and often a great number of them. Douceur (2002) notes that this is incredibly hard for any open system to defend itself against this sort of attack, known as a Sybil attack (named after a famous Multiple-Personality Disorder case study). Several solutions are discussed below. As such, many systems are designed with strong security considerations in mind, depending on their function, from cover traffic to prevent monitoring of file transfer to a reputation system that can discourage single actors from controlling too many trusted nodes. As above, the wide range of security issues makes optimizing for all a nonfeasible option. This will become evident in our discussions of actual P2P systems below, but first we present some of the more common security demands.

One way to think about P2P is whether it applies at the network level, the application level, or the user level. At the network level, an adversary may try to break the routing system, block access to information by impeding queries, or partition the network. At the application level, an adversary can attempt to corrupt or delete data stored in the system or in transit. Finally, the users themselves can be the subject of attack if an adversary goes after anonymity and privacy protections.

Camp (2003) offers an operational definition of trust based on the risk that a system will fail to perform as specified. This is a broader view of security, but one that suits our purposes. In a P2P system, we are interested in not only how one aspect of the system behavior withstands attack but also how the entire system is defended. Because policy is not set dynamically, but is the sum of all behavior in the network, security also includes the expected behavior of other peers and what their incentives are. Layers of protection interact. These levels translate into more specific security goals for system to operate reliably.

In the examples that follow, we highlight security features of these systems, and the design choices made to offer optimal security for a given task. Discussions of cryptanalysis and other field-specific security issues employed by P2P systems are outside the scope of this chapter, as are more complete descriptions of these systems and their performance. Instead, these descriptions are intended to illustrate security mechanisms rather than fully describe all nuances of any P2P system.

The case studies below highlight some of these goals. Secure distributed transport mechanisms such as Tarzan ensure that the identity of the user and the content of the message remain a secret, whereas secure overlay mechanisms are designed to ensure that the message gets through and gets there efficiently. Freenet and Free Haven ensure adequate file maintenance, so that users can reliably access any file they want or any file that has been published, respectively. Groove allows networks of peers to manage themselves. Distributed storage mechanisms can create conditions for cooperative behavior and coordinated dependencies. Finally, we discuss how accountability devices protect against free riding and nodes that are known to misbehave.

IMPLEMENTING SECURE PEER-TO-PEER SYSTEMS

Anonymous Transport: Tarzan

Peer-to-peer systems can serve disparate functions, and although many of them primarily act as applications or services, they can also serve as transport-layer anonymizers. The Tarzan system is a decentralized, distributed Chaumian mix system that enables client applications to seamlessly direct traffic through an anonymous network at the transport layer. Unlike a centralized server-based anonymous traffic system such as Anonymizer, Tarzan's P2P nature ensures that no one actor needs to be trusted for anonymous communication at the IP level. Users can direct their traffic into a tunnel through the network of peers, so the packets exiting the tunnel cannot be traced back to the original sender, even in the face of substantial networkwide traffic analysis.

Tarzan, as described by Freedman and Morris (2002), works as follows. Each node selects, from what it can see of the network, a set of peers to act as mimics. Initial node discovery and subsequent network maintenance is based on a gossip model, where nodes share their view of the network. Mimics are selected randomly from the available nodes for security and balance, in some verifiable manner. Each node exchanges a constant rate of cover traffic of fixed-size packets with its mimics using symmetric encryption. Symmetric keys are distributed using the relays' public keys. Actual data can now be interwoven into the cover traffic without an observer detecting where a message originates.

To build a path, the sending node randomly selects a given number of mimics and wraps the message in an "onion" of symmetric keys (Syverson, Goldschlag, & Reed, 1997) from each node on the path. The sender passes the packet—outwardly indistinguishable from cover traffic—to the first node in the chain, which removes the outermost wrapper with its private key, and then sends it along to the next node. With the exception of the last node, each node in the chain is aware of the node before and after it in the chain, but has no way of telling where it is in the chain itself. That is, the node cannot tell if it is the first hop or the penultimate hop. The final node in the chain of mimics acts as the network address translator for the transport layer and sends the packet to its final destination through the Internet. This final node must know the content and destination but has no information about the sender.

Nodes store a record for the return path, so a reply from the Web host contacted can be received by the final node in the chain, rewrapped with its private key, and sent back to the penultimate hop. The message is then passed back through the chain, with each node adding another layer of encryption. The originating node can use the public keys of each node to unwrap the layers and read the message. Because it is the only node to know the public keys of each hop along the path, the content is secure.

The P2P nature of this system makes a network decentralized and thus highly scalable. The presence of cover traffic and the fact that all nodes are peers means that no actor inside or outside the system can readily identify the originator of the message. Unlike onion routing, the sender does not have to trust the first hop, and the list of available nodes can be dynamically maintained for participant flexibility. Moreover, the majority of cryptographic work is performed by the original sender, which must decrypt n public keys to read the reply through and n-node chain. Each node in the chain only performs one encryption or decryption, and implementation results have shown that the computational time is dominated by the expected latency of the underlying Internet.

Efficient Robust Routing: Secure Overlays

Like Tarzan, routing overlays also seek to provide a secure layer of communication, but they differ in their security objectives. Rather than protecting the anonymity and content of communications, routing overlays such as Chord, CAN, and Pastry try to provide mechanisms for nodes to access objects in a fashion resistant to malicious interference. Overlays use their namespace structure to build robust routing mechanisms so that an adversary with a significant number of nodes in the system could not cripple communication and access throughout the system. How the nodes and objects manifest themselves at the application layer is not directly relevant to the overlay design: these systems can be used for storage, publication, or even multicasting.

The salient feature of all routing overlay models is a large ID space, from which node identifiers and object keys are defined, forming a large, distributed hash table. Each object key is mapped through the overlay to a unique participating node, called the object's *root*. The protocol routes messages with a given object's key to the object's root. An object is replicated throughout the system to ensure greater robustness; each protocol uses a replica function to map an object's key to its replica's key, which can then be used to find the copy of the object stored at the replica's root. Like any hash tables, lookup can be very efficient, but distributed hash tables pose unique security questions.

Each overlay system is somewhat different, of course, but most follow a given structure. The generic system here is based on the discussion in Castro, Druschel, Ganesh, Rowstron, and Wallach (2002) and the Pastry system (Rowstron & Druschel, 2001). Nodes maintain two lists of other nodes, a routing table of other nodes throughout the ID space and a list of "neighbors" or nodes that are in close proximity inside the number space. Each entry in the table consists of an identifier in the namespace and the IP address of the node belonging to that identifier. To route a message, a node consults these tables, and attempts to forward the message closer to the identifier keyed in the message. Routing tables are organized by key prefix, such that a host will try to find the node with an identifier closer in the namespace to the query key. Failing that, it will pass the message along to its neighbors in an attempt to find the proper location in the namespace. If the key is not found in the routing table or the neighborhood, the query is dropped.

This system is effective, but is not in and of itself secure, because there is no guarantee that an object will be placed on legitimate, trusted replica nodes. Nodes must regularly maintain their routing tables for arrivals and departures of other nodes. Such operations are difficult, especially in the face of high node churn, but are generally feasible in well-behaved networks. More importantly, malicious nodes or collections of nodes can seek to undermine routing efforts or even censor documents. For instance, an attacker could surround an object's root with collaborating neighbors and pass on no message to that object's root. To prevent this, secure overlay systems implement secure routing primitives.

First, node identifiers must be guaranteed to be randomly assigned to every node. If this is not the case, nodes under malicious control can simply choose their IDs to ensure that all the keys of a given object will point to hostile nodes. This randomization is not difficult if there is a centralized server solely responsible for handing out identifiers on joining the network; proof-of-work techniques or micropayments can be used to prevent Sybil attacks or pseudospoofing. Of course, P2P systems are often designed to explicitly avoid a centralized server of any sort, even one used only to assign names. Wallach (2002) acknowledges that, without a central authority, current means of assigning random identifiers can impose additional security risks. Routing table maintenance must also be secure against attack so that the chances of having a corrupt node in ones routing table will not be greater than the percentage of corrupt nodes in the system.

Secure overlay models can provide for message delivery to as many noncorrupt nodes as possible. Much of this is predicated on the fact that one's ID space neighbors are very likely to be geographically disparate and thus less likely to be under the control of a single adversary. If we to sacrifice some performance by filling the routing table based on diversity rather than low latency, security increases. In Pastry, when less than 30% of nodes are not trustworthy, there is a 99.9% probability that at least one valid replica will receive the message (Castro et al., 2002). This particular defense may decline in utility if the attack is coordinated through a large set of geographically dispersed peers, such as an array of PCs under the control of Trojan horse malware.

One criticism of routing through the overlay model, rather than a higher application level, is that it is harder to eject a misbehaving node. Although nodes may recognize that other nodes are not behaving as they should, proving systematic misbehavior is difficult at the routing layer. Apparently malicious behavior could be ascribed to the underlying network and vice versa. Thus, any accusation mechanism could be used to attack legitimate nodes and the system itself.

Secure overlay mechanisms and Tarzan both focus on message delivery but with different security objectives. Tarzan focuses on protecting the end parties, their identities, and the content of the message. A secure overlay such as Pastry is designed to protect the traffic flow itself. Both can be implemented in such a fashion to aid in the others goal. Tarzan, for instance, can add on control mechanisms to guarantee flow control, and Pastry can add layers of encryption and even use a multihop system to replicate a mix-net. Neither of these solutions, however, would be as secure in their objective as the other system. Security objectives of P2P systems need to be designed in from the beginning.

Censorship-Resistant Anonymous Publishing: Freenet and Free Haven

P2P systems can also be application specific. One of the more common applications of P2P systems is publication and storage of documents. Again, the security design of these systems is based largely on the purposes of the system and the security goals of the designers. Several systems have been designed for the express purpose of censorship-resistant publishing to make real the rhetoric of the freedom of ideas that the Internet was supposed to enable. However, a single server can be blocked for an entire nation (Zittrain & Edelman, 2003) and open documents can be identified and blocked. Secure P2P systems can be much harder to block, because they lack a single point of attack to block or destroy documents. We present, for comparison, two such systems, Freenet (Clarke, Sandberg, Wiley, & Hong, 2000) and Free Haven (Dingledine, Freedman, & Molnar, 2000b).

Freenet is designed to acknowledge that censorship can take the form of eliminating sought-after documents or punishing those who can be observed reading those documents. It consists of a network of peers that host encrypted documents. Peers use keys to request documents. Its two unique features are the structure of its storage space and the system of using keys to access content.

The storage mechanism of Freenet can be thought of as a nested caching structure in that data is stored as it is used. A peer request propagates through the network, with each node knowing only the node that passed the request along. A node that can positively respond to the request will pass the document back through the chain, one node at a time. Each node may keep a local copy of the document, in addition to sending it along toward its destination, so that it can respond to future requests itself, rather than passing the query to network neighbors again. This means that copies of the document will be duplicated as they are requested. It also prevents a single hosting node from being overwhelmed by requests for a popular file. Finally, this local caching policy causes a locality of resources, where documents tend to be hosted close to regions of the network where the document is heavily demanded. As nodes fill their storage space with documents that they pass along to others, they will replace older and larger documents first. This leads to a more efficient use of network space, where peers host documents that are highly demanded and small enough not to be a burden on network resources, as well as creating an incentive to minimize file size of documents stored on the network.

As mentioned above, peers use keys to locate and access the encrypted documents on the network, and there are four key styles that can be used. Keys are used to identify the document sought and decrypt it once it is obtained. The simplest is just a key derived from a hash of the document itself. This insures that the key is unique and the document is tamperproof. However, they can be difficult to remember, and how does one obtain the key of a document one doesn't know about ahead of time? Moreover, the fact that the documents are tamperproof with respect to the key means that they cannot be edited (capabilities that allow you to trust the integrity of an editable document require an infrastructure like that of Groove, described below). For easier searching, Freenet allows keys to be derived from keyword strings. A one-way function is used to convert the keywords into a key, which is also used to access the document as above. This method has two flaws, however. First, popular key words can be vulnerable to dictionary attacks, where malicious nodes will attempt to use the client's transformation function to find the key value of specific search strings. With this, they can censor specific search strings while still appearing, to an outside observer, to be a fairly well-behaved node. Moreover, there is no guarantee that multiple separate documents will not be signed with the same keyword-generated keys. Imagine, for example, the number of distinct documents that could be "The Bible." These two flaws make false replies fairly simple.

To allow for document editing, Freenet offers signature verification keys, where document keys are generated along with a public/private key pair. This allows the author of the document to resign the key with every edit, enabling a persistent pseudonym in the form of a public key. Users can now better trust the authenticity of a document as associated with a specific online identity. Finally, redirects allow queries for specific key words to return the content hash key, rather than the document itself, and the hash key can obtain a verifiable copy of the original document.

All documents in the system are encrypted with some type of key, so the host node may not know what documents it is serving at any point. This also allows plausible deniability should any one legally or physically attack the owner of a node. The creators of Freenet acknowledge that if a document is notorious enough, its digital signature will be recognized, and hosts can purge it from their system and refuse to process requests. However, should some one wish to have it in the system, it is a simple matter to extract it, change a single bit to generate a completely new digital signature, and reinsert the document into the network. Actively trying to remove a document from inside the system is difficult.

Freenet's P2P structure ensures that documents spread in a "sticky" fashion to resist attempts to stamp out popular information while still protecting those who would either access or host that information.

Free Haven, like Freenet, is designed to be a censorship-resistant publishing network but places its design priorities on highly robust anonymity and document durability. Free Haven uses cryptographic techniques to protect the identity of the reader, the server, the author, the document, and the query, preventing any party other than that which is explicitly authorized to read or link information. Unlike some of the other P2P systems described in this chapter, its routing structure is relatively simple but uses very sophisticated techniques to protect anonymity and robust storage in a hostile environment.

As usual, content is kept on some number of machines in the network. The user, either a server in the network or an outside machine, broadcasts a request to as many servers as possible, who then reply directly to the querying machine. The initiator sends a request to a server that consists of the following: the initiator's public key (which can be temporary), a hash of the public key of the document sought, and a reply block. A reply block consists of an encrypted nested chain of addresses, so that a party can use it to pass a message to a destination through several intermediary parties that do know either the originator or destination of the message nor the content. If any recipient server has a document whose hash matches the hash of the given key, they encrypt that document with the requester's public key and send it back using the reply block. Thus, although the client must know of the existence of a server, it has no information about which server offered the document, nor does the server know anything of the client.

Free Haven's strength as a P2P publisher lies not just with its robust anonymity but also with its document management, which maintains the files in the system against strong attacks. Before inserting a document into the system, it is encrypted and broken up into a large number of shares, only some fraction of which are necessary to recreate the document. That is, a client can rebuild the document without finding every share. The parameters of the number of shares generated and the number required for regeneration are chosen to minimize not only the number of shares necessary for reassembly but also the size of each file that must be acquired. Each share has a duplicate "buddy" share, and the two contain location and storage information about each other for system robustness. Shares also have expiration dates, before which servers make an effort to keep shares alive.

Once on a server, the document shares do not necessarily rest on the same server but rather are traded between servers. Trading provides cover traffic to hide actual information queries, as well as allowing servers to find a home for their shares before exiting the system. The constant movement also makes it more difficult to locate and attack all the shares of a document. The buddy system creates some degree of accountability, as a share will notice if its buddy is no longer available from the server on which it was last residing. Each trade involves updating the buddies of the shares traded. Servers hosting machines with lost buddies can communicate to other servers their knowledge of the unreliability of the negligent (or malicious) nodes. We discuss how the system uses reputation to track good behavior below.

Free Haven was designed to be robust in the face of many different attacks. Reader and server anonymity are protected with the reply-block mechanism but can always be subverted with embedded malicious code in the documents or very extensive traffic analysis across the network. To attack the publishing system, an adversary would have to acquire many shares. Simply destroying servers will not help if the number of required shares for reassembly is small enough. Conversely, increasing the number of shares in the entire network minimizes the chances of deleting both a share and its buddy to attack the accountability mechanism.

Neither Freenet nor Free Haven can be said to be truly superior, or even more secure, because they have different design objectives and, thus, different security demands. The designers of Freenet did not worry about a networkwide traffic analysis attack, because they assumed any adversary with that many resources could mount a more direct legal or physical attack on users (Langley, 2000). The designers of Free Haven chose to take advantage of recent cryptographic developments to build a system that could stand up to a powerful cryptanalytic attack. At the same time, Free Haven was concerned with protecting *all* documents in the system, whereas Freenet was more concerned with guaranteeing access to those highly demanded at any given time. Dingledine et al. (2000b) suggest that their system might be used to protect a phone book from a war zone, whereas Freenet designers envisioned spreading a current issue of a dissident newspaper. P2P systems must be built for specific goals, and their security should reflect this.

Secure Groupware: Groove

Groupware is a designed forum and set of tools for sharing information and communication channels to enable collaborative work. Designing a secure P2P workspace is every bit as challenging as the systems described above for two reasons. First, a workspace has multiple internal applications, and the system must securely provide them all. Second, businesses that design workspaces must make them accessible to the average corporate computer user; user intervention as complex as assembling a reply block, or even verifying a digital signature, can be too complex for a product to be widely attractive. Ray Ozzie's Groove Network is a collaborative digital space that is built to be secure but designed to have as much security as possible completely transparent to the user (Groove Networks, 2003). At the same time, security mechanisms need to be self-organizing from the client level rather than dictated by a policy administrator. The proprietary system was built to be used in a business environment, which means addressing not only the potential presence of a highly motivated adversary but also the likelihood of a highly heterogeneous environment. Groove is designed to ensure a robust collaborative work environment even with some parties behind firewalls, others on low-bandwidth channels, and still more with intermittent connections. Moreover, everyone in the group may not expressly trust the other actors *inside* the system. Protection is offered at a finer level than that of the enterprise. The system employs fairly established cryptographic techniques but uses them in innovative ways.

Groupware requires the negotiation of trust between appropriate parties while excluding those who do not belong. Each user in Groove has an account resident on each machine and one or more identities associated with each account. This enables users to use the same identity from multiple devices, as well as allowing a single user to have multiple identities in different contexts. A software engineer can use Groove to collaborate with his firm's research group, as well as work with several friends to develop a startup business without having to worry about information leaking between the two projects or even allowing either project to know about the other. Identities are manifested in shared spaces, which can allow for either mutual trust or mutual suspicion. In the former, users are presumed to trust each other's identities, so verifiability of authorship is relaxed in favor of efficiency. In a mutually suspicious space, Groove enables tools to verify authorship of statements. We describe how this works next.

Whoever decides to initiate a shared space decides whether to declare it a trusted or suspicious space and can specify several security parameters if desired. All data are encrypted, both on the wire and on disk. Messages are reliable, and even in a trusting mode, Groove can offer confidentiality and integrity of messages. Privileges can also be revoked.

All applications running on the Groove network use "delta" messages, or document updates, that communicate changes of state to other members of the network, whether in a collaborative file or in a chat session. Each delta is encrypted using the group's symmetric key for fast encryption and decryption. The group has a separate shared key for authentication, which is used to sign the digest to ensure message integrity; both keys are reestablished every time some one leaves the group. Local files log all changes initiated by any actor.

When users might have reason to be suspicious, however, shared keys are not sufficient to instill trust in the integrity of authorship. After the author signs the delta message with the group encryption key, he signs a separate hash of the message body using his private key and the public key of the recipient. As implemented, Groove actually precomputes distinct pairwise keys from the Diffie–Hellman public keys of each group member and the sender's private key, which results in a smaller key and a less expensive verification procedure. Thus, appended to each message there will be a signed hash for all recipients in the group, who can use their own pairwise key of the sender and their private key to verify authenticity. The sender can even sign the message with her own key to verify its integrity on another device.

Messages do not have to broadcast to all nodes but can use their local knowledge of the network structure to pass the delta messages to key central nodes. Moreover, messages are sequenced, so if a recipient misses a message for some reason, such as being offline, he or she can fetch another copy from the sender or from any other member of the group. Other members of the group leave the pairwise keys intact, allowing the node to be confident of the authenticity of the message and its sender.

Of course, all this depends on entry into the group-space, trusted or untrusted. Untrusted here does not mean a purely malicious actor, because all members of any group will have the ability to read messages sent through the group. Rather, it refers to a competitive situation, where users may need to know for certain who sent which message. If this is not the case, significant encryption overhead can be saved. Still, how does a user join a trusted group?

Suppose Alice wants to invite Bob into a Groove shared space. Bob must have a copy of the client software, of course. The most important aspect is for both Alice and Bob to trust that the identities "Alice" and "Bob" in the system match their belief of who the individuals actually are. This requires some out-of-band communication. That is, Bob must verify that the information being sent actually belongs to Alice and vice versa. This process can be as simple as a phone call, where both trust that the phone number leads to the other person and they can recognize the other's voice. Using some trusted non-Groove channel, they can verify the authenticators supplied by Groove (a public key) are valid, and Bob can join the group. There is no need to change the existing group keys because Bob may need access to existing files. Should the existing group want to deny Bob access to certain information in the group, they must form a new shared space for Bob's involvement that does not involve the protected documents.

Groove has a fairly rigid set of security policies, but the P2P nature of the system protects system security and increases system usability. Lacking a central point of failure, or a nexus where permissions can be negligently or maliciously opened, Groove's decentralization improves robustness. Anyone can start a group, but little active administration is required: all encryption after the initial trust phase described above is transparent to the user. This openness means that the parties do not need to rely on a third party to negotiate trust among group members.

Secure Distributed Storage

Using a P2P system for simple storage, rather than interactive or static publishing, poses a different set of security requirements. The encryption used for document security and integrity does not have to be as complex, because only the original owner need access the document itself: a strong symmetric cipher is completely adequate. Storage is a problem of coordination. A user may seek to store files on a network to as a standard data backup measure or to hide a document for later retrieval. Keeping data on a range of nodes offers strong fault tolerance and survivability compared to the single point of failure in a solitary remote storage site. The security problem to be solved by a P2P storage system is instead a coordination problem.

It is obvious that the amount of storage consumed by a given node must be in proportion to the amount of storage space they will give the network. Otherwise, free riding will result in too much data for the storage space available. There are a number of fairly straightforward ways for a centralized administrator to coordinate storage. A third party can give each client a quota and refuse access to the system for any part breaking their quota. This third party must be trusted and reliable, however. Some sort of currency can be used for storing clients to pay warehousing clients, but this requires a trusted currency and clearing mechanism. Alternatively, the trust can be placed in hardware, with a smart card containing a secure internal counter and an endorsement of the right to store information on the network. Of course, this removes only the need for centralization by one degree, because a trusted party must issue the cards, sign attestations about a right to store, and verify that storage has been reclaimed before certifying a new counter value.

Centralized authority is not necessary if storage is distributed symmetrically. For ephemeral resources, such as downloading a single file, a tit-for-tat mechanism works well. The BitTorrent file distribution system lets peers download segments of large files from other clients also trying to access the same file. Clients essentially swap the segments that they have not yet downloaded. Each client uploads to others based on how much they have downloaded from those clients. Thus, every client has an incentive to upload what it has to other machines, so it can continue to download. This works well but is not designed for long-term storage. A reduction in demand for a file will limit the number of BitTorrent clients that will swap segments to complete the download.

Long-term storage necessitates accountability. Of course, a symmetric configuration constrains how storage arrangements work out, if each actor must trace through a network of obligations before finding someone who is owed storage space. If we use a simple barter system for the entire network, where a given actor can simply claim they have a right to store data on any computer in the network based on their own local storage, some certification is still needed for that claim. A trusted group of quota managers can prevent free riding by verifying those claims, but there is no real incentive for these nodes to take responsibility for auditing an entire network.

The storage system presented here by Ngan, Wallach, and Druschel (2003) offers a mechanism for the publication and auditing of storage records for an entire network without relying on a single trusted party. Each node publishes a record of their storage activities, and a series of random, self-interested auditing is enough to encourage honesty.

Each node in the network advertises its total local storage capacity, the list of others' files stored locally, and its own files stored remotely. The first list can be thought of as the "credits" to each node and the second as "debits" to the system. Each record in this usage file contains an identifier and size information for the file, as well as an identifier and location information for the node. When node A seeks to store a file on another machine, the potential host examines the balance sheet of the would-be storer. If A is not consuming more storage than its capacity, the remote machine accepts storage if it has room itself. Each agent that is storing a file for node A finds that it is in its self-interest to check on A to confirm that A does indeed have the hosted file in its debit file. Otherwise, the node in question can delete A's stored file and free up disk space for others to acquire most system "capital." As long as A does not know when any node will audit its published file, it will keep its debit file accurate for fear of losing stored data. This auditing mechanism prevents a node from hiding its own use of the storage network to store more than its share. It is important to note that the auditing communication must be anonymous and randomly timed, so that A cannot detect which creditor is auditing it and coordinate its response accordingly.

This standard auditing does not prevent a greedy node from claiming that it is storing files it actually is not. That is, A could claim a huge capacity but then falsely assert that it is being used by some other node. Thus, A would not have to share capacity but could use the capacity of the network. Fully auditing all outgoing obligations would be very expensive. The file I claim I store should be on some node's debit list, but a chain of obligations could go on for some time. Eventually, there must be an "anchor" that claims it is storing a file that is on no node's debit list. Finding this anchor, however, involves searching through deep trees of dependency. If all nodes are honest, there is no effective way to bound this search. The system requires that all nodes occasionally pick a node at random and examines its outgoing list. Although this is not as effective as a full recursive audit, Ngan et al. show that it is much cheaper and shows that perpetrators can still be caught with high probability even in the face of infrequent audits. Moreover, because the usage file has been digitally signed, it provides hard evidence of malfeasance, and the node can be ejected.

This model of a P2P storage architecture focuses on security against node collusion to free-ride on the system. Nodes can encrypt data for storage to protect it, and knowledge of some identifying information about the other node is necessary to coordinate storage. Like other P2P systems, it could be further enhanced by a reputation mechanism. If nothing else, an incentive to acquire a good reputation serves as a disincentive to get thrown out of the system once a good reputation is obtained. This is further discussed in the next session. Distributed storage can be an effective way to securely backup data, but attention must be paid to a secure alignment of incentives.

REPUTATION AND ACCOUNTABILITY

Peer-to-peer systems require the effective cooperation of disparate parties. Unlike a centralized client/server model, where system satisfaction rests only with the successful performance of one party, many different peers must all work together within the confines of the system. Yet systems must reflect the fact that there may well be actors who are not eager to cooperate and who may seek to free ride on the resources of others or actively subvert the system. Fortunately, the initial solution is trivial—avoid interactions with nodes that do not behave. Unfortunately, this is much more complex in practice. A simple list of who not to trust requires good information collection and distribution and does not scale well. Use of reputation can make this easier.

A full discussion of reputation—or even an attempt at a formal definition—is outside the scope of this chapter. However, reputation presents several interesting security issues as a solution and a new problem. For our purposes, reputation can be thought of as information about an actor that can aid in the prediction of future behavior. It serves two complementary purposes. First, the reputation of other actors can guide a decision maker's choice in selecting transaction partners. Second, it can act as an incentive for good behavior for those who fear acquiring bad reputations. A bad reputation often involves some sort of punishment or reduced privileges, so a good reputation can be a motivating factor for good behavior.

Reputation systems have been a popular topic in recent information technology literature, and they have blossomed in practice as well. The Search for Extraterrestrial Intelligence (SETI) is a P2P system that uses spare processing power on users' PCs to examine radio telescope data for patterns that might lead to the discovery of life beyond our solar system. It uses an advertised positive reputation system with group identities to encourage people to share computer resources. The desire to acquire a good reputation for social reasons grew so strong that people began to cheat, undermining the entire signal processing project. SETI was forced to implement an accountability mechanism that replicates all computations for quality control. This security control reduced the effectiveness of the system by half.

In general, reputation requires an enduring identifier of some sort and the ability to map information about past transactions to that user. If a user wishes to base his or her opinion on anything other than his or her own experiences, he or she can solicit reputation information from others but now must have some metric to trust the information of others. This need for credibility adds an additional layer of complexity to the system. There are several ways to apply reputation to a P2P system.

First, one can ignore reputation within the system and rely on users or applications to obtain and use the information they need. The P2P system can make this easier with good security. For instance, a Groove workspace offers no aid to a participant in evaluating the quality or trustworthiness of a document or fellow participant. Groove can, however, use cryptographic techniques to enable the user to know exactly who sent what information, so that an out-of-band reputation system based on external identities can be mapped into a Groove-supported work environment. It is also possible to imagine a reputation system layered on top of a P2P system, where users can define their own parameters of trust and simply rely on the underlying P2P layer to provide information, which is evaluated at the reputation layer. This information can then be passed back to the P2P layer for a decision about storage, transmission, or whatever function the P2P system provides. By layering them in this fashion, the reputation system can be adjusted independently of the P2P system, following good security procedures of separating functionality whenever possible.

Dingledine, Mathewson, and Syverson (2003) take the opposite approach, arguing that bolting security into an existing system is the incorrect solution. Their Free Haven system uses published reputations to encourage servers to keep shares they have promised other servers they will keep. Recall that documents are kept alive by servers trading them. Any server finding its trading contract broken can broadcast proof malfeasance with the signed contract and certified proof of failure to deliver. Verifying disputed claims grow to be complex very quickly, however, especially if the document in question was traded to another party. Free Haven uses credibility metrics to evaluate contested claims, which are in turn built from reputation records over time. The additional computation required for secure attestations places a fair bit of overhead on the system, without full incentives for any one node to follow through on the veracity of others' claims. The authors acknowledge that "designing the original system without a clear idea of the reputation and verifiability requirements made Free Haven's design complex and brittle."

The proprietary file-swapping software Kazaa also built in some degree of reputation to prevent free riding. If more than one user requests a given document from a server, the requesters are queued, and order in the queue is determined by reputation rather than order of arrival. Positive reputation is accrued by sharing files with others. This mechanism was designed with no security protections, however, so when the source code was reverse engineered, competing vendors distributed a client that could set its own reputation. Because all reputation information is kept locally by the client itself, there is no structural way to prevent this. Where the reputation mechanism is integral to the design of a P2P system, the reputation mechanism must itself be secure. Otherwise, it becomes the weakest link in a system that might otherwise be secure.

A final aspect of the reputation mechanism is the cost of acquiring a new identity. If a fresh reputation is easily acquired, then anyone with a bad reputation will handily jettison their bad name for a new one. This creates a world where bad reputations simply will not exist. Unfortunately, an actor choosing by reputation must now assume the strong possibility that anyone with a new (neutral) reputation is untrustworthy. This puts honest newcomers at a disadvantage. One way around this is to require some form of payment to obtain a new identity in the system. Of course, this also imposes a penalty on newcomers. Friedman and Resnick (2001) have shown that any identity-bound reputation system with nonpermanent identities must impose some cost on newcomers, either as an outright entry fee or with a below-neutral reputation.

A final way to enforce good behavior is through a transitive reputation tokens or a microcurrency. Rather than fixing reputation to an identity, microcurrency can be thought of as signaling information that can be passed from one person to another. There are many security issues with micropayment and electronic currency schemes that have been discussed elsewhere (see, e.g., Camp, 2000). One system that implemented a successful micropayment scheme is Mojo Nation, a P2P file-sharing system that used tokens known as "mojo" to encourage good behavior (Wilcox-O'Hearn, 2002). Every transaction required an exchange of mojo, so the more altruistic actor received something for giving up something of value. Thus, each actor had an incentive to offer files to the network in the form of the ability to barter for more files from others. Mojo Nation avoided some of the cryptographic hurdles of a distributed system by relying on a centralized token server for market clearing. However, the market was structured in such a way that trading could continue even if the token server was temporarily unavailable.

One definition of a secure system is one in which a user can have confidence of appropriate functionality. Peer-to-peer systems need security to defend proper operation of the underlying mechanism but may also need additional layers of security to encourage proper operation of other peers. Some of the systems described in this chapter, such as the secure overlay, are designed to require as little reputation information as possible. Others, such as the secure storage system, are predicated on their ability to overcome the free rider problem without a centralized coordinator. Reputation and accountability mechanisms can play a key role in the security and functionality of P2P systems, but they must be designed and implemented as an integral part of the system.

CONCLUSION

Peer-to-Peer systems are incredibly flexible and can be used for a wide range of functions, often more effectively than their client/server analogs. They can be used to anonymously or robustly route through a network of peers, protect content from censorship, enhance and protect collaborative processes, and coordinate use of diverse services. Security could be a concern to any of these functions and should be treated accordingly. In the systems discussed in this chapter, the security is always on: no administrator can accidentally or maliciously turn it off. This constant presence and absence of centralized support means that good security practices must be built into the protocols of the system. Each system has different design goals, and just as the security should reflect the purposes of the system, system design should reflect security exigencies.

GLOSSARY

Anonymity Not associated with a personal identifier. In the context of information networks, it is the ability to keep identifying information about the user from being known. There are different degrees of anonymity based on the set of possible identities and the strength of the attacker determined to ascertain a given identity.

Censorship Attack An attempt to keep the content from being accessible. It can manifest itself as an attempt to prevent content distribution, to prevent the content from being located, to pollute the content beyond use, or to expunge the content completely from the system.

Centralized Describes a system with a single point of control, with policy emanating from that one source. Such systems can be easier to directly administer, are useful for coordinating different tasks that need common information, such as sequential ID assignment, and can offer great economies of scale. However, the users must trust the centralized server; they are also particularly vulnerable to targeted attacks such as distributed denial of service attacks.

Decentralized Describes a system designed and implemented without a single administrative point of control. Decentralized systems can be more fault tolerant if properly designed, but it can be harder to coordinate behavior within the system.

Delta Message A message in groupware that contains only the changes to a given document. Delta messages often contain auditable information to create a history of the document and security information to maintain document integrity.

Distributed Hash Table (DHT) A hash lookup system that routes queries through nodes, where the local routing table of each node is used to forward the query to the node that is ultimately responsible for the key.

Groupware Software that enables shared, closed environments for an identified set of users, particularly for collaborative work. It can allow users in different environments to share common tools and documents.

Locality A node's place in the network topology, either in the overlay network or the underlying internet architecture. Systems can be designed to capitalize on locality, such as Freenet's ability to "push" content closest to where has been recently demanded, or ignore locality, such as a secure overlay's tendency to map close internet addresses to random parts of the namespace.

Namespace A context formed by a set of unique identifiers that allows each object referenced to have a mapping from identifier to object such that there is no ambiguity to which object a name points to. The domain naming system (DNS) is an example of a namespace where every internet object is referenced by at least one URL and every URL references at most one object.

Node A point on a network that is capable of sending or receiving information either for itself or to relay a message to or from others.

Onion Routing A system for anonymous network communication designed to be resistant to both eavesdropping and traffic analysis from threats inside and outside the system. Messages are passed wrapped in layers (like an onion) of encryption, each corresponding to the key of one of the routing nodes, so that only the destination node can decrypt the message or even determine the route of the message.

Out-of-Band A message that is not passed across the network in question but through some other channel. Out-of-band messages can be used to help secure the identity of a party where different channels can reinforce beliefs the end parties have about their respective identities. Out-of-band messages can be passed on the same physical network but using a secure overlay network, as with signaling the telephone network.

Overlay Network A communication network that functions above the transport layer. A virtual network that is built on top of the basic Internet architecture and that provides additional functionality such as searching, routing, encryption, and so on.

Peer-to-Peer (P2P) A style of network in which nodes communicate to other nodes via ordinary intermediate network nodes rather than a centralized server with full knowledge of the network so that each node performs client and server operations. Most P2P systems are overlay networks with unique namespaces.

Reply Block A list of anonymous remailers with the recipients address at the end, used to direct a message to the final account without disclosing the address to the sender or any intermediary. Reply blocks are used to allow anonymous communication between two parties, where the sender might want to receive a reply from the recipient but not disclose his or her identity.

Reputation Information about a actor's past action that is believed to be is correlated future behavior.

Shared Space In a groupware environment, the shared space is the common namespace of specific set of nodes in a single zone of administrative control. Common tools and documents can be available to all users while the groupspace exists.

Signature Verification Key The public half of a public/private key pair, used to verify that a document was signed by the private key. In the Freenet P2P system, a signature verification keys allow a document to be tracked by a pseudonymous author's signature verification key rather than a key based on a hash of the document or specific key words.

Survivability The ability to survive while under attack by exhibiting gradual degradation rather than failing entirely. Characterized by graceful degradation rather than catastrophic failure.

Sybil Attack Also known as pseudospoofing, an attacker acquires multiple identifiers in the system to undermine some function of the system, such as attempting to control a large portion of the key space in a distributed hash table. These attacks have proven hard to defend against in open, anonymous systems and often inspire the use of reputation or cost-driven overlays.

CROSS REFERENCES

See *Client/Server Computing: Principles and Security Considerations; Internet Architecture; Security Middleware; Web Services.*

REFERENCES

Camp, L. J. (2000). *Trust and risk in Internet commerce.* Cambridge MA: MIT Press.

Camp, L. J. (2003). Design for trust. In R. Falcone (Ed.), *Trust, reputation and security: Theories and practice* (pp. 15–29). Berlin: Springer-Verlag.

Castro, M., Druschel, P., Ganesh, A., Rowstron, A., & Wallach, D. S. (2002). *Security for peer-to-peer routing overlays.* Fifth Symposium on Operating Systems Design and Implementation (OSDI '02), Boston, MA.

Clarke, I., Sandberg, O., Wiley, B., & Hong, T. W. (2000). *Freenet: A distributed anonymous information storage and retrieval system.* Workshop on Design Issues in Anonymity and Unobservability (PET2000), Berkely, CA.

Dingledine, R., Freedman, M. J., & Molnar, D. (2000a). Accountability measures for peer-to-peer systems. In A. Oram (Ed.), *Peer-to-peer: Harnessing the power of disruptive technologies*. Sebastopol, CA: O'Reilly.

Dingledine, R., Freedman, M. J., & Molnar, D. (2000b). *The Free Haven Project: Distributed anonymous storage service*. Workshop on Design Issues in Anonymity and Unobservability (PET2000), Berkeley, CA.

Dingledine, R., Mathewson, N., & Syverson, P. (2003). *Reputation in P2P anonymity systems*. Workshop on Economics of P2P Systems, Berkeley, CA.

Douceur, J. R. (2002) *The Sybil attack*. First International Workshop on Peer-to-Peer Systems (IPTPS '02). Cambridge, MA.

Freedman M. J., & Morris R. (2002) *Tarzan: A peer-to-peer anonymizing network layer.* ACM Conference on Computer and Communications Security (CCS 9), Washington, DC.

Friedman, E., & Resnick, P. (2001). The social cost of cheap pseudonyms. *Journal of Economics and Management Strategy, 10*(2), 173–199.

Groove Networks. (2003). Groove security architecture. Retrieved February 25 2004, from http://www.Groove.net/pdf/security.pdf

Kan, G. (2000). Gnutella. In A. Oram (Ed.), *Peer-to-peer: Harnessing the power of disruptive technologies*. Sebastopol, CA: O'Reilly.

Langley, A. (2000). Freenet. In A. Oram (Ed.), *Peer-to-peer: Harnessing the power of disruptive technologies*. Sebastopol, CA: O'Reilly.

Ngan, T. W., Wallach, D. S., & Druschel, P. (2003). *Enforcing fair sharing of peer-to-peer resources.* 2nd International Workshop on Peer-to-Peer Systems (IPTPS '03), Berkeley, CA.

Rowstron, A., & Druschel, P. (2001). *Pastry: Scalable, distributed object location and routing for large-scale peer-to-peer systems.* IFIP/ACM International Conference on Distributed Systems Platforms, Heidelberg, Germany.

Syverson, P. F., Goldschlag, D. M., & Reed, M. G. (1997). *Anonymous connections and onion routing.* IEEE Symposium on Security and Privacy, Oakland, CA.

Wallach, D. S. (2002). *A survey of peer-to-peer security issues.* International Symposium on Software Security, Tokyo, Japan.

Wilcox-O'Hearn, B. (2002). *Experiences deploying a large-scale emergent network.* First International Workshop on Peer-to-Peer Systems (IPTPS '02), Cambridge, MA.

Zittrain, J., & Edelman, B. (2003). Internet filtering in China. *IEEE Internet Computing, 7*(2), 70–77.

Security Middleware

Linda Volonino and Richard P. Volonino, *Canisius College*

INTRODUCTION

Security Middleware Architecture

Middleware refers to a broad range of software that enables communication or data exchange between network-based applications across networks. This type of software is often described as "glue" because it connects or integrates business-critical software applications to other applications. With today's networked-based applications—especially enterprise resource planning (ERP), supply chain management (SCM), customer relationship management (CRM), and business-to-business (B2B) and business-to-consumer (B2C) electronic commerce (e-commerce)—business operations depend on secured data transfers between these applications. Figure 1 shows a generic security middleware infrastructure. This diagram shows security middleware acting as an integrator of applications and data and as a provider of secure connectivity and interoperability.

In a simplest description of how it functions, middleware sits between two or more applications to accept requests for access to information or network services and then responds to those requests. For example, when a user requests information from a Web site's database, middleware provides the services and security necessary for that exchange. As such, it is also considered the "plumbing" or utility layer in networks. By promoting standardization and interoperability, middleware makes advanced network applications easier to use securely. Middleware provides security, identity, and the ability to access information regardless of location in addition to authentication, authorization, directories, and encryption.

Because it is a general term for any programming that serves to "glue together" or mediate between two separate and typically already-existing programs, middleware is used to refer to either software or infrastructure. As software, it is the layer between a network and the applications that use it. In addition, middleware is an infrastructure that manages security, access, and information exchange on behalf of applications to make it easier and more secure for people to communicate and collaborate. It can be used to find people or objects (e.g., directory services) or to keep them confidential (e.g., security services).

Middleware programs are also used to provide messaging services so different applications can communicate. This systematic tying together of disparate applications is known as enterprise application integration (EAI). A common middleware application is to enable programs written for access to a specific database to access other databases.

For end users, middleware makes sharing of network resources transparent and much easier. Moreover, it increases security by protecting against unauthorized or inappropriate use. The problem of security in a distributed environment is too difficult to be solved properly by each individual application. Without middleware, applications would have to provide these services themselves, which could result in competing and incompatible standards—and increase the risk of unauthorized access. Therefore, having the middleware assume this responsibility leads to more robust and consistent solutions. This is done primarily through single sign-on (SSO) technologies. SSO makes it possible for a user to enter his or her credentials only once and remain authorized within the network until logging off. A widely used SSO technology is Kerberos. SSO and Kerberos are discussed in detail in the following sections.

For company networks or e-commerce operations, middleware plays a pivotal role in connecting enterprise information technology (IT) environments to the Internet. Secure connections are achieved using middleware to control access; that is, it allows only authenticated users, applications, or network end points to connect to an organization's services, applications, and data.

The CIA Triad and Access Control

There are three main principles of information security, which are referred to as the *CIA triad*. These three principles are as follows:

1. Confidentiality: Sensitive information is protected against disclosure.

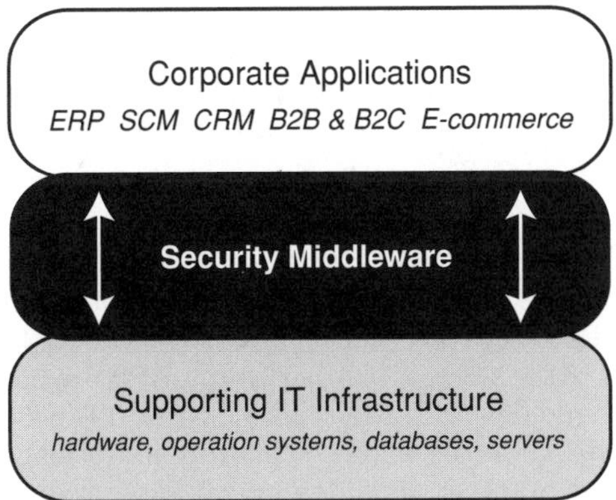

Figure 1: Generic architecture of security middleware operating between the supporting information technology (IT) infrastructure and corporate applications.

2. Integrity: Information and systems are protected against unauthorized modification.
3. Availability: Information and systems are protected against disruption.

To achieve these three goals, access to applications must be controlled. Without access control, there is no security. Access control means that only authorized (or intended) users can gain access to a network or application and that those users have only the level of access needed to accomplish authorized tasks. This concept is known as *least privilege.* Examples of tasks are reading data, writing data, or downloading files. The problematic part is that access controls must be incorporated in a layered approach; each layer needs to be understood, and the relationship of each layer with other layers needs to be understood (Harris, 2002). When implementing middleware to enforce access control, these technical issues must be addressed so that vulnerabilities are not overlooked and controls do not conflict with each other.

The essential access control services provided by security middleware include identity management (or identification), authentication, authorization, directory services (or directories), application program interfaces (API), and abstraction.

It is helpful to define the terms *subject*, *object*, *principal*, *access*, and *open* because they are used often when discussing access control:

- A *subject* is a person (user) or application that requests access to data, a service, application, and so on.
- An *object* is the data, service, or application that is being accessed by a subject.
- A *principal* refers to either a subject or object whose identity can be verified (e.g., a workstation user or a network server).
- *Access* refers to the tasks carried out on an object, such as read, write, modify, delete, and so on.
- *Open* means unprotected, such as an open network.

SECURITY MIDDLEWARE PROCESSES AND SERVICES

Before a subject can be authenticated, it has to be identified with an identifier. An identifier is a unique way of naming something. A social security number or personal e-mail address is an identifier because they uniquely name an individual—that is, unless two or more people share an account. In middleware, identifiers can name anything, including abstract concepts such as certain applications or a certain security clearance. The entity named by the identifier is known as its subject.

The key security middleware defense services providing access control are authentication, authorization, directories, application program interfaces (API), and abstraction.

Authentication

Authentication is the process of providing a private piece of information or physical token to establish whether a subject is who or what its identifier (e.g., username) claims it is. During authentication, a user or object proves it is the subject of an identifier. This service is generally performed by the middleware layer so that applications above it do not need to have their own authentication mechanism.

Identity is authenticated by the presentation of digital credentials. As explained previously, a user must present credentials to a network to gain access to it. In the case of people, the most common credentials used for confirming identity include the following:

- Something the subject knows, such as a password
- Something the subject has, such as a USB token, digital ID (certified public/private key), smartcards, or challenge-response mechanisms
- Something the subject is, such as photo identification, fingerprints, or biometrics

As such, authentication is the validation of a user's electronic identity based on proof provided by that user, typically a unique user id/password pair. If a user cannot be authenticated, then he or she would not be granted access to nonpublic network services.

Authentication is most frequently done by asking a user to enter a username and password. Although there are more secure approaches, passwords are often transmitted through open communication channels, which compromise security. The quality of the authentication depends on the guarantee that can be given that the authentication process was not fraudulent or compromised by a hacker attack, such as correctly guessing a password.

The primary issues to be considered about any authentication system pertain to how secure or strong the authentication process is. The security of any authentication process depends on several variables, primarily the number of factors used to authenticate a subject. Single-factor authentication such as using only a password is much less secure than using a USB token activated by a password, which would be a two-factor authentication.

Figure 2 illustrates and describes the steps involved in authentication in a distributed environment, such as secure Web pages. Several of the concepts illustrated in this figure (e.g., Kerberos) are described in subsequent sections.

Authorization and Directories

Once authentication has been performed, more credentials or attributes about a subject are needed before that subject can be given access permissions. Authorization is process of determining whether to allow a subject access to a specific resource or service or other subject. It is also the process of assigning authenticated subjects the rights to carry out specific operations.

Only having one valid identifier does not provide enough information about a subject. Although an authenticated identity may be sufficient for some purposes, it is often important to acquire more information, such as preferences, e-mail aliases, electronic credentials, and so on. Identifiers become far more powerful when they are combined with a technology known as directories. Along with its many other uses, a directory links an identifier with other attributes about a common subject.

A directory stores permissions and regulates permissions, such as viewing files. Directories are, in effect, databases composed of many sets of information with a similar format. A set of information is generally called an entry, and a piece of information within an entity is called an attribute. A primary function of a directory is to look up a given attribute from a given entry, such as a user's read or write privileges for a specific object (e.g., a payroll file). Because directories make information available, access to them must also be adequately protected. Access controls can be set to regulate who can read or update specific directory fields.

There is a one-to-many relationship between authentication and authorization. For example, once a subject has been authenticated during a session, then many authorizations for that subject can occur with a single cached authentication. During a Web browsing session, a user would need to authenticate only once to access many pages for which the user needs authorization. In this way, different applications can use the same authentication, but have different authorization permissions. Usually, authorization checks do not involve any input from the authenticated user because the system already knows that the user is authenticated and the permissions of that user. Of course, authentication may also be required for every new application, requiring multiple sign-ons in a single session. Single sign-on (SSO) is discussed under Application-Based Authentication.

The two major technical components of a middleware implementation are client software and enterprise middleware servers that provide authentication and directories. The client side does not require much work because most middleware functions can be performed by existing programs, such as Web browsers and e-mail clients. In contrast, the server side needs to perform many new services. The middleware system must provide an effective and secure layer for communication between client and server. The major client-side technological challenge is establishing the authentication system. Although these systems can be built around passwords, public keys, smart cards, or other schemes, it must be available on every machine that a user will want to use to authenticate to the middleware server.

Application Programming Interfaces

APIs exist for (almost) all middleware products and establish the interface with which clients (applications) request services of the servers. In other words, APIs are part of all types of middleware, not a separate type. APIs provide for data sharing across different platforms. Specifically, an API is a set of standards and protocols by which a software application can be accessed by other software, or for communication between application programs. APIs enable the exchanging messages or data between two or more different software applications. The API must exist before a program can be called by an external program and before it can send a response to an external program.

There are several types of APIs that enable data sharing between different software applications on single or distributed platforms. Those APIs include the following:

- Remote procedure calls (RPCs): These are protocols that provide high-level communications. An RPC implements a logical client-to-server communications system specifically for network applications
- Standard query language (SQL): SQL is an ANSI standard computer language for accessing and manipulating databases
- File transfer: Transporting or sharing files between remote machines
- Message delivery: Reliable message delivery ensures that Web services architecture, protocols, and interfaces deliver secure, interoperable, transactional, and robust solutions (IBM, 2003)

Common Object Request Broker Architecture

Common object request broker architecture (CORBA) is an architecture and specification for creating, distributing, and managing distributed program objects in a client/server network. Distributed objects are also known as components or programs. CORBA enables programs at remote locations, which were developed by different vendors, to communicate in a network through an "interface broker." CORBA 3 is the latest version of this specification.

CORBA was developed by a consortium of vendors through the Object Management Group (OMG), consisting of over 500 member companies. Both International Organization for Standardization (ISO) and X/Open have sanctioned CORBA as the standard architecture for distributed objects. However, Microsoft has not adhered to CORBA and has its own distributed object architecture called the distributed component object model (DCOM). CORBA and Microsoft have agreed on a gateway approach so that a client object developed with the DCOM and COBRA servers can communicate with each other.

CORBA is based on the object request broker (ORB). ORB support in a multivendor client/server network

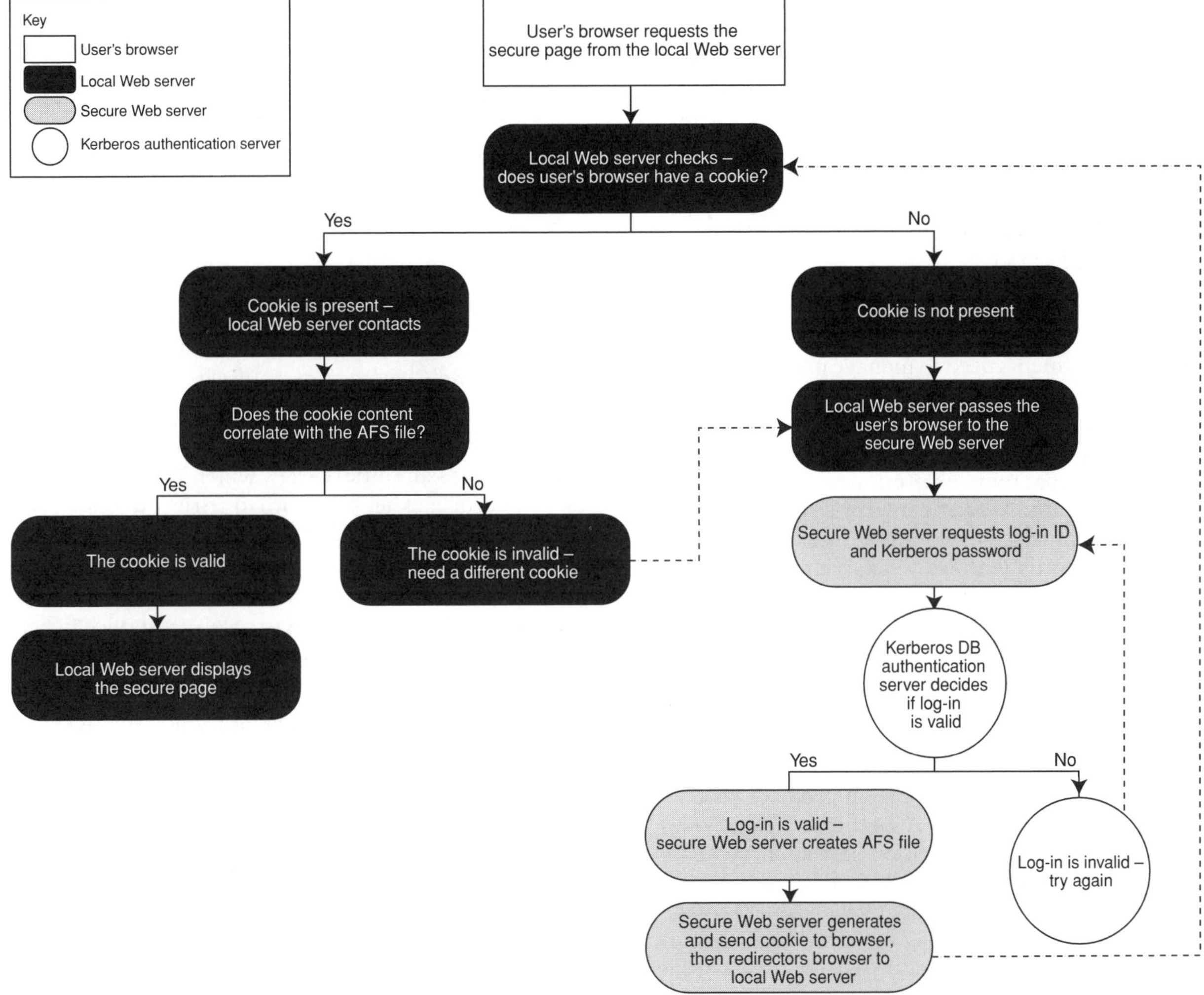

STEPS:

1. User's browser requests the secure page from the local web server (Go to 2)
2. Local web server checks: Does user's browser have a cookie? (Go to either 2A or 2B)
   - **A. Yes** (Go to 2Ai)
     - i. Cookie is present. Local web server contacts AFS server (Go to 2Aii)
     - ii. Does the cookie content correlate with the AFS file? (Go to 2Aiia or 2Aiib)
       - **a. Yes**
         - The cookie is valid
         - Local web server displays the secure page.
       - **b. No**
         - The cookie is invalid. Need a different cookie. (Go to 2Bii)
   - **B. No** (Go to 2Bi)
     - i. Cookie is not present (Go to 2Bii)
     - ii. Local web server passes the user's browser to the secure web server (Go to 2Biii)
     - iii. Secure web server requests login ID and Kerberos password (Go to 2Biv)
     - iv. Kerberos DB authentication server decides if login is valid (Go to 2Biva or 2Bivb)
       - **a. Yes**
         - Login is valid. Secure web server creates AFS file
         - Secure web server generates and sends cookie to browser, then redirects browser to local web server. (Go to 2)
         - Local web server displays the secure page.
       - **b. No**
         - Login is invalid. Try again. (Go to 2Biii)

Figure 2: Flowchart model of distributed authentication for secure Web pages.
Source: http://distauth.ucdavis.edu/docs/dachart.html

means that any object (e.g., a client program) can request services from a server object without knowing the server's location is in a distributed network or its interface. To request or reply between ORBs, programs use the general inter-ORB protocol (GIOP); for the Internet, programs use the Internet inter-ORB protocol (IIOP). IIOP maps GIOP requests and replies to the Internet's transmission control protocol (TCP) layer in each computer.

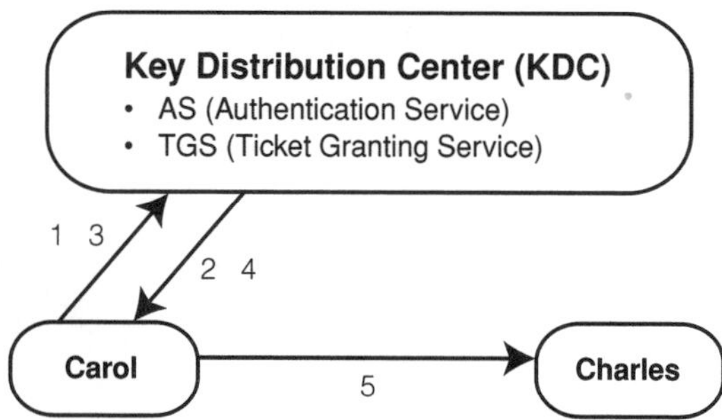

Figure 3: KDC ticket authentication process.

APPLICATION-BASED AUTHENTICATION

As discussed, authentication is a method for confirming a user's identify to control access to enterprise information assets. IT departments need to manage user identities and system access across the enterprise and keep them simple and convenient to use. Users cannot be expected to securely remember multiple log-in (sign-on) routines. Authorized users cannot remember numerous usernames and passwords to be able to access enterprise information assets many times during the workday. So users tend to create simple passwords that are weak, which increases the risk of compromising the network and sensitive data.

To control access to enterprise information assets and services by authorized users (e.g., employees, customers, and partners), single sign-on technology is used.

Single Sign-On and Kerberos

Kerberos is a ticket-based authentication protocol based on symmetric-key cryptography. A Kerberos ticket is a certificate issued by an authentication server, encrypted using the server key. It allows principals communicating over networks to prove their identity to each other while preventing eavesdropping or replay attacks. The components used in Kerberos are as follows:

- Key distribution center (KDC): The KDC holds the user and service secret keys, provides authentication, and creates and distributes session keys
- Authentication service (AS): The AS is the component of the KDC that performs the authentication
- Ticket-granting service (TGS): The TGS is the component of the KDC that creates and distributes tickets to the principals (users, applications, resources, or services). Those tickets contain the session keys
- Ticket-granting ticket (TGT): The TGT is the initial ticket sent from the AS to the principal

The steps taken by Kerberos to authenticate users and other principals are necessary because the principals do not directly trust each other, but they do trust the KDC (Harris, 2002). Kerberos provides a means of verifying the identities of principals on an open network. This is accomplished without basing trust on host operating systems or addresses and without requiring physical security of all the hosts on the network. It is assumed that packets traveling along the network can be read, modified, and inserted without authorization or detection. Figure 3 illustrates the steps in the KDC ticket authentication process.

The process is accomplished as follows, using the names Carol and Charles as examples:

1. At login, Carol authenticates to the AS.
2. Carol receives an initial ticket, which is the TGT from the AS. Carol uses her password to retrieve a session key encrypted in the reply. The TGT allows Carol to obtain tickets from a TGS for other Kerberized services.
3. Carol requests to access Charles. For this request, *Carol* presents her TGT to the TGS to receive a service ticket.
4. The TGS creates a new service ticket with session keys for Carol.
5. Carol extracts one session key and sends the ticket to Charles. To authenticate to *Charles*, *Carol* constructs a timestamp (to prevent reply attacks), proving to *Charles* that she knows the session key inside of the service ticket.

The basic Kerberos authentication process proceeds as follows (Neuman, Yu, Harman, & Raeburn, 2004):

- A client sends a request to the authentication server (AS) requesting "credentials" for a given server
- The AS responds with these credentials, encrypted in the client's key. The credentials consist of a "ticket" for the server and a temporary encryption key (often called a "session key")
- The client transmits the ticket (which contains the client's identity and a copy of the session key, all encrypted in the server's key) to the server
- The session key (now shared by the client and server) is used to authenticate the client and may optionally be used to authenticate the server. It may also be used to encrypt further communication between the two parties or to exchange a separate subsession key to be used to encrypt further communication

Many applications use Kerberos's functions only at the initiation of a data stream network connection. Therefore, unless an application performs encryption or integrity protection for the data stream, the identity verification applies only to the initiation of the connection and does not guarantee that subsequent messages on the connection originate from the same principal.

Version 5 of the Kerberos protocol (released in 2004) has evolved from Version 4 based on new requirements and desires for features not available in Version 4. The design of Version 5 of the Kerberos protocol was led by Clifford Neuman and John Kohl with contributions from the community. Reference implementations of both version 4 (V4) and version 5 (V5) of Kerberos are publicly available and commercial implementations have been developed and are widely used. Details on the differences between Kerberos Versions 4 and 5 can be found at http://www.isi.edu/people/bcn/krb-revisions/krbclar/krbclar-draft-07.nroff. Although V4 still runs at many sites, V5 is considered to be standard Kerberos.

Kerberos has significant limitations and needs to be integrated with other security measures. In particular, Kerberos is vulnerable to dictionary or password guessing attacks. If a user selects a weak password, then an attacker who has guessed that password can impersonate the user, in effect gaining all of the user's access privileges. Those privileges can be used to gain even greater unauthorized access to the network or databases.

Another limitation of Kerberos is that it requires a trusted path through which passwords are entered. If the user enters a password to a program that has already been compromised by an attacker or a Trojan horse, or if the path between the user and the initial authentication program is being sniffed or monitored, then an attacker may obtain sufficient information to impersonate the user. As such, Kerberos should be used with other access control defenses.

Secure Socket Layer

Secure Socket Layer (SSL) is a commonly used protocol for managing the security of a message transmission on the Internet. It transmits communications over the Internet in an encrypted form. SSL is used to ensure that the information is sent unchanged and only to the intended server. Most e-commerce and online shopping sites use SSL technology to safeguard transmission of credit card information.

SSL operates at the application/session layer. There are two strengths of SSL depending on the length of the session key generated by the encrypted transmission—40 and 128 bit. The 128 bit is exponentially more difficult to break than the 40 bit. Most browsers support 40-bit SSL sessions. Netscape Communicator 4.0 and higher allows 128-bit SSL sessions.

TLS (transport layer security) is replacing Netscape's earlier SSL protocol. The TLS layer resides between the transport and session layers of the TCP/IP stack. Many protocols use TLS to establish secure connections, including HTTP, IMAP, POP3, and SMTP. As with SSL, all of these protocols protect communications privacy over a public network with cryptography. It should be noted that HTTP, POP3, and so on are clear-text protocols by design. That is why they have to use other things such as SSL for confidentiality. They allow client/server applications to communicate in a way that is designed to prevent eavesdropping, tampering, or message forgery. From a security and identity perspective TLS provide a tremendous value to Internet commerce. The ease of monitoring Internet traffic, spoofing Internet domains, and tricking individuals into providing sensitive information makes identifying the server side of an Internet transaction important.

Public Key Infrastructure and Message-Oriented Middleware

Public Key Infrastructure (PKI) technology is widely used on the Internet with SSL communication. The basis for PKI is a certificate that is generated by an authorized certificate authority (CA). Digital certificates are discussed in Digital Certificates. However, SSL by itself is not enough protection so PKI and SSL are used together to provide for message-oriented middleware (MOM) authentication (Lingel, 2004). In an SSL handshake, the MOM manager first verifies that the certificate has been generated by a trusted CA and not been altered. The manager then creates a unique session key for this conversation, encrypts it with the subject's public key, and sends it back to the subject. The originator has the private key, so it will be the only process that can decrypt the session key. From that point, the session key is used. This guards against replay attacks. The private key equivalent to a password never goes out over the network. Certificates provide user names, who/what issued the certificate, the issue's digital signature, and activation and expiration dates

NETWORK-BASED AUTHENTICATION

As with application-based authentication, processes and procedures are needed to authenticate or verify users on a wired or wireless network. Examples of middleware for network based authentication are as follows:

- Lightweight directory access protocol (LDAP)
- Wired equivalent privacy (WEP)
- Virtual private networking (VPN)
- Internet protocol security (IPSec)
- Web services security (WS Security)

These protocols and services make use of many of the techniques already discussed, including digital certificates, CAs, smart cards, secure tokens, biometrics, or a combination of efforts that verify and authenticate the validity of each party involved in a transaction.

Lightweight Directory Access Protocol

The LDAP specification was developed at the University of Michigan in the early 1990s as middleware between PCs and X.500 directories. X.500 directories were based on global standards but were complex and overhead intensive. LDAP emerged as a standard to bridge the gap between end users and the complex X.500 directories. In the most basic of terms, LDAP provides a locator service for a person who may be listed in multiple locations on a network in different formats.

Altough LDAP's original role was to interface with X.500 directories, it can interface with any directory that follows the X.500 standards. User access to network resources can be controlled by an LDAP accessible directory. The directory can be hosted by any number of database servers on the market today.

Recent advances in the LDAP specification have allowed the service to remain viable from a security perspective. The LDAP specification allows for encryption communication among multiple LDAP servers via SSL. In addition, extensions are available to allow for non-ASCII and non-English characters.

There are three main components to an LDAP environment; they are as follows:

1. LDAP client: The client portion can be hardware or software that can request information from an LDAP server. The standards based nature of LDAP allows for many vendors to create software to connect to LDAP servers. The LDAP client would be considered a *subject* as it is attempting to access data from the LDAP server. In addition, the LDAP client could be attempting to verify the identity of a user and, therefore, can also be considered a *principal*.
2. LDAP server: The LDAP server "listens" for LDAP requests on a network and translates the client requests into requests to the X.500 directory. The results from the X.500 directory query are then sent back to the requesting LDAP client to complete the lookup. The LDAP server can be considered an *object* as it a service being accessed by a *subject*, the LDAP client.
3. X.500 directory: The X.500 directory can be any database that adheres to the X.500 standard. The database can house many thousands, if not millions, of records. As the databases are optimized for read transactions they perform exceptionally well. The X.500 directory houses *access* information for a particular *subject*.

The openness and standard based architecture of LDAP ensures the standard will be a viable mechanism to access large amounts of information using standard access methods. Microsoft's Active Directory and Novell's Novell Directory Services are both based on LDAP standards to provide security control for computer and user accounts in the enterprise.

Wired Equivalent Privacy

One of the fastest growing technology areas is wireless local area networks based on the Wi-Fi or wireless fidelity standards. These networks can be established quickly without the cost of a wired infrastructure with little of no technology knowledge. There are, however, drawbacks to the initial convenience of a Wi-Fi network. Early Wi-Fi networks lacked the availability of encryption. WEP was established to add encryption to Wi-Fi networks. However, the initial version was based on a 40-bit key and was easily compromised. More recent WEP standards based on a key length of 104 bits are less vulnerable to compromise and provide more security. Actually, 104-bit WEP is just as vulnerable, but it takes longer to attack. Refer to chapter 150 for an explanation of WEP.

WEP is a protocol used to encrypt information sent between access points and stations. Access points receive and transmit wireless signals, convert them into their wired counterparts, and send them to their destinations on the network. Stations are equipped with wireless transceivers that allow access to network resources by converting network requests into radio signals that are passed to access points. WEP technology uses 40- or 104-bit secret keys on both access points and authentication stations and to encrypt information transmitted over the radio waves.

The station or PC is considered the subject and the principal. The access point is considered an object because it is being accessed by the station. For example, if a new station or PC attempts to connect via Wi-Fi to an access point where WEP is required, the following steps are necessary to authenticate the station:

1. The station or *subject* requests authentication to an access point or *object*.
2. The access point or *object* creates a random 128-byte message and forwards it to the *subject*.
3. The *subject* accepts the message, encrypts it with its WEP key, and sends the encrypted message back to the access point.
4. The access point decrypts the message with its WEP key and compares it to the original message.
5. If the original unencrypted message matches the unencrypted message from the *subject*, the *subject* is associated or authenticated with the access point.

After successful authentication, all wireless traffic between the subject and access point are encrypted with the same WEP key that is used for authentication.

There are several caveats to the above process. First, it is considered poor practice to use the same key for authentication and data encryption. Second, the WEP keys must be preshared and manually installed on every access point and potential subject. It should be noted that newer 802.11 protocols are fixing this requirement. The second step creates an administration problem when the keys are updated. As is true with Kerberos, when used alone, WEP security can be very insecure. However, when layered with multiple methods of authentication and encryption, wireless communication can be moderately secure.

Virtual Private Networking

VPN is replacing traditional dial-up modem pools. With a VPN, remote users typically connect to an Internet service provider (ISP) or a private IP-based network. Then they establish a secure connection with network servers via an encrypted tunnel. VPNs can also be used for secure communication across a LAN or WAN.

Hardware or software can be used to create and maintain the encrypted tunnels on public networks. In many organizations, a hardware solution is used to create "always-on" VPN tunnels with remote offices or trading partners. VPN tunnels based on software are often used to connect home offices or individuals who travel.

VPN tunnels require two connections. First, a common network connection is required. Usually the Internet is used, but any common network can be used. Second, an encrypted connection between the two parties is established, commonly called a tunnel. In both the hardware and software configurations, the tunnel provides access to all applications and services located on the destination network. Of course, additional layers of security may be installed to protect sensitive data. Because of the many ways a VPN connection could be established and maintained, most VPN products are not compatible from one vendor to another.

The remote VPN client is considered the *subject* as well as the *principal*. It is considered the *subject* because it is attempting to access data or services from the destination network and the *principal* because the destination VPN service must verify the identity of the remote VPN client. The *object* could be any number of applications, network services or data the remote VPN client is attempting to access.

Establishing VPN tunnels is a cost-effective way for an organization to extend network services without the cost of expensive leased lines or slow modem pools.

Internet Protocol Security

The Internet protocol security (IPSec) is widely used to establish secure virtual private network communications over IP networks. IPSec allows for preshared or dynamically created keys to create an encrypted tunnel on an open or unsecured IP network. IPSec secures and authenticates network traffic on both public and private IP networks such as the Internet, preestablished VPN connections, or company-to-company extranets. IPSec is unique because it functions at the network layer of the OSI model. Encapsulation of data is supported through the Internet key rxchange (IKE) protocol. Operating at the network or IP layer, IPSec offers companies a large amount of flexibility in supporting configurations and applications.

In a typical configuration, software is installed on a remote user's computer, preshared keys are exchanged and communication software is configured. Within minutes the end user can have full access to all network services and applications.

Internet key exchange (IKE) is a key-sharing protocol that follows the public/private key pair used to mutually authenticate both parties of an IP conversation. See the chapter titled Public Key Infrastructure for details. Before data can be securely shared, a security agreement (SA) must be established. The SA defines all the security parameters and keys the session will use. To ensure data are securely transmitted, IKE uses a two-phase approach to communication. During the first phase, also called the main mode, a secure authenticated channel is established. This phase includes policy negotiation, exchange of public keys, and authentication. Typical Phase I communications include the following:

1. Negotiation details of the encryption and integrity algorithms and authentication methods.
2. Key public key exchange of base information for the Diffie–Hellman key determination algorithm.
3. Authentication via a Diffie–Hellman key exchange. Without successful authentication, communication will not proceed. The master key is used, in conjunction with the negotiation algorithms and methods, to authenticate identities.

Phase 2 of the communication requires an established SA from phase 1 to operate. The first step of Phase 2 is for both of the IKE participants to negotiate a mutually acceptable IPsec policy. These polices are locally established and if there is no common policy this phase will fail. After the peers agree, the keying material is agreed on and the IPSec SAs are established. Future communication in this tunnel is encrypted and keys for the encryption are changed based on the mutually acceptable policy.

Web Services Security

First, it is helpful to understand Web services before describing WS-Security. Web services create a layer of middleware as part of a service-oriented architecture (SOA) to enforce policies for services, such as security, routing, and workflow. Web services are also referred to as SOA middleware. Applications based on Web services plug into the middleware layer to support application reuse of components and service and to make it easier to compile Web services into composite applications (Fontana, 2004). The SOA includes shared services, control, and a common security model and interface language. Current interest in SOA is not indicative of a new technology but rather another iteration of existing concepts (Bednarz, 2004). Earlier attempts at popularizing SOA, which included CORBA, were hindered by a lack of standard middleware and APIs. Web services can be the link that makes SOAs mainstream.

Some key aspects of Web services are that Web services are based on top of prevalent Internet-related standards (http, XML, etc.) rather than on particular, less prevalent, architectures or implementations. The problem with CORBA, which is also an architecture for distributed objects and services, is that both the client and the server need to use CORBA. DCOM components can interact only with other DCOM components (without some bridging technology). Web services, however, have no such architecture or implementation dependencies and work better in highly heterogeneous environments.

WS-Security provides a mechanism for associating security tokens with messages, but no specific type of security token is required by WS-Security. It is designed to be extensible and support multiple security token formats. WS-Security improves protection through message integrity, message confidentiality, and single message authentication. These mechanisms work with numerous different security models and encryption technologies.

Additionally, WS-Security describes how to encode binary security tokens. The specification describes how to encode X.509 certificates and Kerberos tickets as well as how to include opaque encrypted keys. It also includes extensibility mechanisms that can be used to further describe the characteristics of the credentials that are included with a message (Atkinson et al., 2002). See the chapter entitled Digital Certificates for more information.

GLOSSARY

Access Refers to the tasks carried out on an object, such as read, write, modify, delete, and so on.

Access Control Only authorized (or intended) users can gain access to a network or application. Users have only the level of access, or least privilege, needed to accomplish authorized tasks.

API A set of standards and protocols by which a software application can be accessed by other software or for communication between application programs.

Application Communication Middleware Middleware used to communicate among applications, software services, and components.

Application Communication Middleware Architecture Facilitates and simplifies the communication between diverse, distributed applications.

Authentication The process of providing a private piece of information or token to establish whether a subject is who or what its identifier (e.g., username) claims it is.

Authorization The process of determining whether to allow a subject access to a specific resource service or other subject.

Availability User access to data files or applications that are stored on networked computers. Information and systems are protected against disruption.

Certificate Authority (CA) An entity that issues digital certificates and vouches for the binding between the data items in a certificate, such as X.509 certificates.

CIA triad Refers to confidentiality, integrity, and availability of information and computing resources.

Common Object Request Broker Architecture (CORBA) An architecture for creating, distributing, and managing distributed program objects in a network.

Confidentiality Sensitive information is protected against disclosure.

Distributed Component Object Model (DCOM) Microsoft's proprietary distributed object architecture, which it developed instead of adhering to CORBA.

Encryption The process of changing a message (a *plaintext*) into meaningless data (a *ciphertext*).

Enterprise Application Integration The systematic tying together of disparate enterprise applications.

Integrity Information and systems are protected against unauthorized modification.

Kerberos A ticket-based authentication protocol based on symmetric-key cryptography.

Kerberos Ticket A certificate issued by an authentication server, encrypted using the server key.

Message Oriented Middleware (MOM) Application communication middleware that sends messages among software components. Applications using MOM can be deployed on multiple platforms using multiple programming languages.

Middleware Software and APIs that act as intermediaries among application programs and services, such as gateway software between LAN-based database servers and mainframe databases. This software layer provides application, component, and data access communication.

Object The data, service, or application that is being accessed by a subject.

Object Request Broker (ORB) In a network of clients/servers on different computers, a client program (an object) can request services from a server program or object without having to understand where the server is in a distributed network or what the interface to the server program looks like.

Open Unprotected, such as an open network.

Packet A collection of data that is transmitted as a bundle across a network connection.

Packet Switching The process of routing and transferring packets of data via a network.

Plaintext A message in human-readable form.

Platform A combination of computer hardware and operating system software.

Portability The capability to move software across different platforms.

Principal Either a subject or object whose identity can be verified (e.g., a workstation user or a network server).

Private Key The key that a communicating party holds privately and uses for decryption or completion of a key exchange.

Protocol A set of rules for communication or rules for managing the network, transferring data, and synchronizing the states of network components. Protocols enable independent technology components to communicate with each other.

Public Key The key that a communicating party sends publicly.

Server A computer that provides shared services to computer workstations over a network (e.g., file server, print server, and mail server). In TCP/IP, a server accepts and responds to the requests of a remote system, called a client.

Single Sign-On (SSO) Technology Makes it possible for a user to enter his/her credentials only once and remain authorized within the network until logging off.

Subject A person (user) or application that requests access to data, a service, application, and so on.

Web Services Security (WS-Security) Provides a mechanism for associating security tokens with messages, thus improving protection through message integrity, message confidentiality, and single message authentication.

CROSS REFERENCES

See *Access Control: Principles and Solutions; Client/Server Computing: Principles and Security Considerations; Computer and Network Authentication; Secure Sockets Layer (SSL); VPN Basics; Web Services.*

REFERENCES

Atkinson, B. et al. (2002). Web Services Security (WS-Security) Version 1.0 05 April 2002. Retrieved January 1, 2003, from http://www-106.ibm.com/developerworks/webservices/library/ws-secure/

Bednarz, A. (2004). Taking applications to the next step. *Network World*, Feb. 16, p. 22.

Corporation for Research and Educational Networking. (CREN) (2002). Middleware: authentication, authorization, and directory issues. Retrieved January 2, 2003, from http://www.cren.net/crenca/pkirscpages/middleware_1.html

Dzubeck, F. (2004, January 26). Key network issues for 2004. *Network World*, p. 49.

Fontana, J. (2004, February 23). Web Services Components Coming. *Network World*, p. 29.

Franklin, C. (2004, April 15). GNOME Attack Puts Penguin on Guard. *Network Computing*, p. 23.

Harris, S. (2002). *All-in-one CISSP certification guide.* New York: Osborne/McGraw-Hill.

IBM. (2003). Reliable message delivery in a Web services world: a proposed architecture and roadmap. Retrieved March 15, 2003, from http://www-106.ibm.com/developerworks/library/ws-rmdev/

Internet2 Middleware Initiative http://middleware.internet2.edu/docs/draft-nklingenstein-k12-primer-00.html

Internet2 Security http://security.internet2.edu/

Kerberos Network Authentication Service, http://www.kerberos.isi.edu/

Levin, C. (2004, July 13). The service-oriented nation: middleware rides the next wave of corporate computing. *PC Magazine*, p. M12.

Lingel, K. (2001). Security requirements for message-oriented middleware. *EAI Journal*, June: 61–63. Retrieved January 2, 2003, from: http://www.eaijournal.com/PDF/MomSecure.pdf

Linux and TLS http://www.linuxsecurity.com/docs/Hack-FAQ/cryptology/tls-transport-layer-security.shtml

Mearian, L. (2004, February 9). IBM aims middleware at financial firms. *Computerworld*, p. 17.

Middleware Architecture Committee for Education. (MACE). http://middleware.internet2.edu/MACE/

Neuman, B. C., Yu, T. Hartman, S., & Raeburn, K. (2004). The Kerberos Network Authentication Service (V5), USC-ISI, MIT. Retrieved August 11, 2004, from http://www.isi.edu/people/bcn/krb-revisions/krbclar/krbclar-draft-07.nroff and http://www.isi.edu/gost/publications/kerberos-neuman-tso.html

Roiter, N. (2003, March). Single sign-on. *Information Security*, p. 79.

FURTHER READING

The importance of security middleware is increasing. Security middleware are ever-evolving layers of network and data services. These services reside between the network and more traditional applications. Their role is to manage security, access and information exchange, and the sharing of distributed resources, such as computers, data, and networks. Despite its security features, middleware has become the target of attack. A case in point—intruders penetrated servers hosting GNOME, an open-source project offering interfaces and development tools to Linux users. This attack has demonstrated that intruders depend not only on vulnerabilities within operating systems but also increasingly on applications, databases, Web servers, and middleware (Franklin, 2004).

For information on the most widely publicized middleware initiatives, review the following:

- Open Software Foundation's Distributed Computing Environment (DCE) http://www.sei.cmu.edu/str/descriptions/dce.html
- Object Management Group's Common Object Request Broker Architecture (CORBA) http://www.sei.cmu.edu/str/descriptions/corba.html
- Microsoft's COM/DCOM (Component Object Model/Distributed COM) http://www.sei.cmu.edu/str/descriptions/com.html
- Cookie Eaters (MIT) http://pdos.lcs.mit.edu/cookies/
- Gettes, M. R. (2000) A Recipe for Configuring and Operating LDAP Directories http://www.duke.edu/~gettes/giia/ldap-recipe/
- Kerberos Papers and Documentation http://www.kerberos.isi.edu/
- Kornievskaia, O., Honeyman, P. Doster, B., and Coffman, K. (2001). "Kerberized Credential Translation: A Solution to Web Access Control." http://www.usenix.org/events/sec01/full_papers/kornievskaia/kornievskaia_html/index.html
- Middleware http://www.sei.cmu.edu/str/descriptions/middleware.html
- NSF Middleware Initiative http://www.nsf-middleware.org/
- Object request broker (ORB) http://www.sei.cmu.edu/str/descriptions/orb.html
- Open Group Messaging Forum http://www.opengroup.org/messaging/
- Remote Procedure Calls http://www.cs.cf.ac.uk/Dave/C/node33.html
- Securities Industry Middleware Council (SIMC), Inc. http://www.simc-inc.org/
- SSH Communications Security, http://www.ssh.com
- TLS http://www.fact-index.com/t/tr/transport_layer_security.html

Internet Architecture

Graham Knight, *University College, London, United Kingdom*

INTRODUCTION

The Internet is a rather loose assemblage of individual networks; there is little in the way of overall administration. The individual networks are owned by a huge number of independent operators. Some of these are major corporations with large, high-capacity networks; others are private individuals operating tiny networks of two or three computers their homes. Between them these networks employ just about every networking technology yet invented. The great strength of the Internet is that it allows these diverse networks to act together to provide a single global network service.

The interactions between a network and its neighbors are, in essence, both simple and robust. This makes for easy extendibility and fueled the early growth of the Internet. New participants needed only to come to an agreement with an existing operator and set up some fairly simple equipment to become full players. This was in great contrast to the situation within the world of telephone networks, where operators were mostly large and bureaucratic and where adding new interconnections required complex negotiation and configuration and, possibly, international treaties.

This chapter is organized into four main sections. I begin with a discussion of network interconnection and how a new service, the IP service, enables it to be achieved. In the second section, I look at how useful applications can be built on the IP service. Next I take a more detailed look at how the IP service is provided in practice. Finally I take a brief look at how the Internet is developing into a "multiservice" network capable of carrying many types of traffic.

NETWORK INTERCONNECTION—THE IP SERVICE

The Internet story began in the early 1960s with the invention of the idea of sending data through computer networks in discrete lumps (called "packets") rather than as continuous streams of bits. In general, large objects such as computer files would need to be chopped up into several packets and reassembled at the destination. A major early experiment in packet-switching was the ARPANET, instigated by Leonard Kleinrock, Lawrence G. Roberts, and others, and sponsored by the U.S. Department of Defense. By the end of 1969, the ARPANET was up and running, with four computers connected. The network grew over the next few years and began to support applications such as file transfer and electronic mail. In 1972, Bob Kahn, who had been influential in ARPANET design, began to turn his attention to network interconnection or "internetting." One of Kahn's key insights was that there would, in the future, be many independent networks, each based on a different technology. He recognized that it would be impossible to require all these networks to be compatible with the ARPANET way of doing things. Instead he designed an open "internetworking architecture." Essentially, networks could do what they wanted internally, but if they wanted to interwork with other networks they would need to implement the interworking architecture as well. Kahn, in collaboration with Vint Cerf, went on to flesh out these basic ideas. They devised a set of rules called the *transmission control protocol* (TCP), which specified how two computers should cooperate to provide reliable delivery of data across the internetwork. Shortly after, it was recognized that not all applications would want the same levels of reliability guarantees, so TCP was split into two parts: one part provided reliability and retained the name TCP, whereas the other part dealt with the delivery of packets and was called the *Internet protocol* (IP). TCP and IP have survived, unaltered in most important respects and continue today—a tribute to their designers in the early 1970s.

The ideas of Kahn and Cerf were soon put into practice in a three network "internet" consisting of the ARPANET itself, a packet radio network, and a packet satellite network. The latter gave the internetwork an international reach with a node run by Peter Kirstein at University College London in the United Kingdom. Originally it was thought that one day there might be perhaps 100 participating networks. The invention of local area networks (LANs) in the 1980s changed all that and brought an explosive growth in the number of participating networks that, today, are numbered in hundreds of thousands. In 1986 the U.S. National Science Foundation funded a backbone network linking five supercomputing centers. This network (NSFNET) grew into the first real Internet backbone with connections to many countries around the world. By 1995 it was clear that the Internet, for many years a research and academic network, had a major commercial future, and NSFNET's backbone role was handed on to a set of linked commercial network providers.

Network Technologies and the Services They Provide

The fundamental components of the Internet are *packet networks* (called simply *networks* for the remainder of this chapter). This term indicates any technology that is capable of transferring data packets from one computer to another; Figure 1 shows an abstract view of such a network. Usually many computers are attached to the network, which consequently provides them with *addresses* that can be used to specify the source and destination of packets. Most of the computers connected to networks are classified as hosts. These are computers that run programs; desktop PCs and servers come into this category. A few computers provide functions related solely to network operation. For example, *gateways*, *routers*, or *bridges* relay packets between networks.

There is a huge variety of technologies that fit into this general model. For example, local area networks (LANs) such as Ethernet (Metcalfe & Boggs, 1976) use so-called medium access control (MAC) addresses. These are 48-bit addresses allocated by the manufacturers of the interface cards that are plugged into the hosts. The "network service" provided by a LAN is simple: a computer constructs a packet, including a destination MAC address, and asks the network to deliver it—exactly like posting a letter. This is termed a *connectionless* (CL) service. A rather different style of service is provided by, for example, asynchronous transfer mode (ATM) (Vetter, 1995) networks. In these networks, there is an initial negotiation phase during which the computer tells the network what kind of data it wants to send and the address of the destination. This gives the computer the opportunity to specify the quality of service (QoS) it requires (bounds on throughput, transit delay, etc.). The network must decide whether it can meet the request. If it can, it tells the computer that a "connection" has been established to the destination and that data transfer can begin. This is similar to making a telephone call in which one dials a number and establishes a call before speech can begin and is termed a *connection-oriented* (CO) service. Addresses in CO networks are used only during the connection setup phase.

Interconnection via "Convergence"

Virtually all networking technologies provide services similar to those just described, even though the mechanisms they use to implement the service may be radically different. Within these broad categories, however, there are many awkward differences: each technology imposes its own limit to the size of packet that may be sent, each has its own idiosyncratic addressing scheme, some technologies allow subtle control of QoS, whereas others do not and so on. These differences pose difficulties for network interconnection. We cannot simply take a packet from one network and forward it onto the next; all sorts of subtle transformations would be needed. The solution is "convergence." We invent an abstract network service and, for each networking technology, we provide "convergence functions" to implement the abstract service. Through these means we make all networks look the same and the interconnection problem becomes manageable.

The Internet Protocol—A Convergence Protocol

The IP provides a convergence function. Version 4 of the protocol (still the most widely deployed) and the abstract network service it implements are specified in RFC 791 (Postel, 1981a) published in 1981. (Many Internet RFCs,

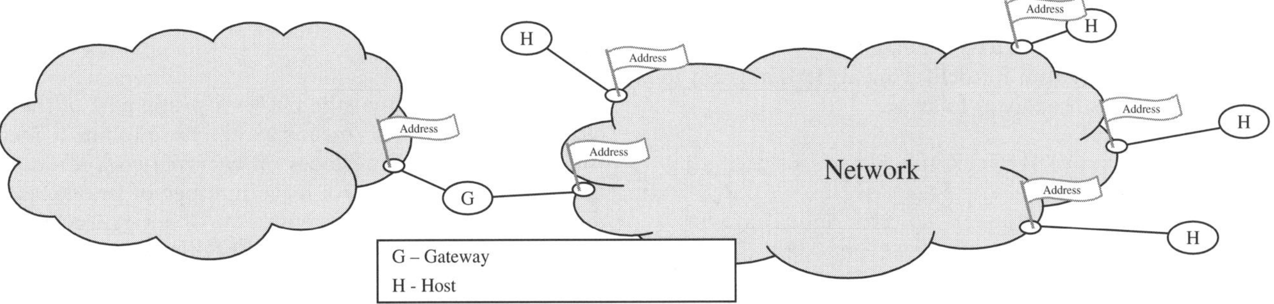

Figure 1: An abstract view of a network. Computers, termed *hosts* have physical interfaces to the network. These interfaces have addresses. The network is capable of delivering packets to hosts identified by their addresses.

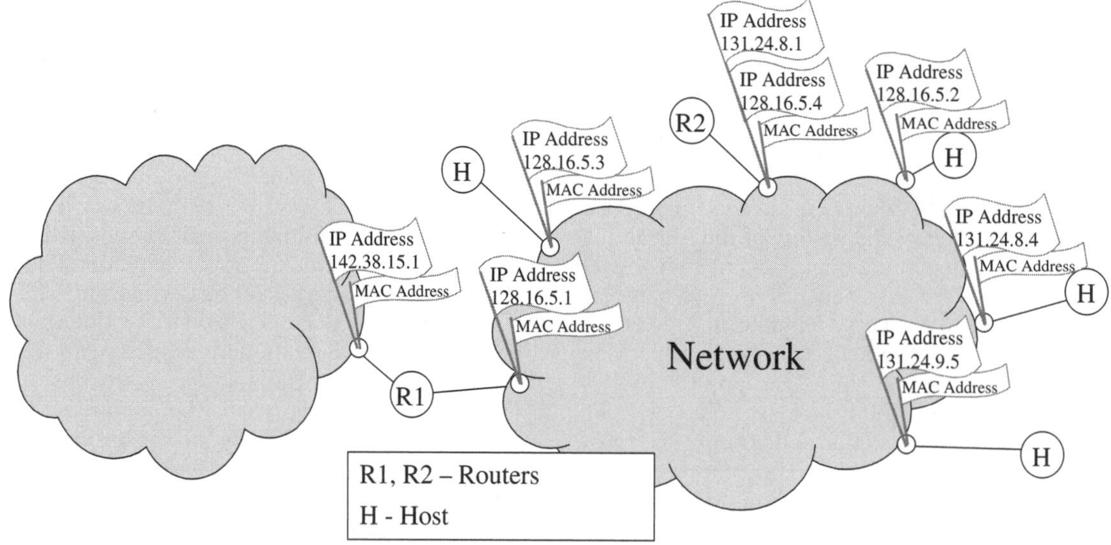

Figure 2: Internet Protocol addresses allocated to network interfaces. In this case, the first 16 bits of the IP address identify the IP network. Thus there are three IP networks: 142.38, 128.16, and 131.24.

or requests for comment, are cited in this article. All are available online on the Web site of the Internet Engineering Task Force: http://www.ietf.org/rfc.html) The service is a simple CL one that allows single packets (called IP datagrams) to be sent to destinations identified by "IP addresses." An IP address is a 32-bit quantity that is divided into two portions. The first portion, the "network prefix," identifies an "IP network" (sometimes now called an "IP subnetwork"). The second portion identifies an interface on that network. The 32 bits are normally written as four decimal bytes separated by dots (e.g., 128.16.5.2).

Hosts, IP Networks, and Routers

Figure 2 shows the network from Figure 1 set up to implement the IP service. Each interface has now acquired an IP address in addition to its original "technology-based" address. To make things a little more concrete, we will assume the networks are LANs, in which case the "technology-based" addresses will be MAC addresses. An important point is illustrated here: An IP network is an abstract thing and does not necessarily correspond one-to-one with a physical network. In Figure 2 we see one physical network partitioned into two IP networks (128.16 and 131.24). The reverse is also possible with several physical networks operating as a single IP network. Traffic is relayed between one IP network and the next by devices called *routers* (the term *gateway* was used in early Internet documents and survives to some extent).

The basic algorithm for delivering an IP datagram to its destination is broadly as follows:

```
If (destination network prefix = = "my"
   network prefix),
   send datagram direct to its destination
   across the local physical network
else
   choose a suitable router
   send datagram to router across the local
   physical network
```

This algorithm is executed by the source host and, if necessary, by a succession of routers along the path to the destination. Thus a datagram sent from host 128.16.5.2 in Figure 2 to host 128.16.5.3 would be sent directly, whereas one to host 150.23.4.1 would be sent to router interface 128.16.5.1. Note that this router interface belongs to the same IP network as the source host, a requirement of classical IP operation. To make the configuration in Figure 2 complete we have had to add a second router (R2) so that the hosts in the 131.24 IP network can communicate with the rest of the world. This router is mandated solely by the Internet routing architecture; it provides no additional physical connectivity.

The step in the algorithm "choose a suitable router" is easily stated but less easily implemented. Sometimes there will be several possible routers, and hosts and routers must maintain "routing tables" indicating which router is the best one to use as the "next hop" on the path to a particular IP network. Because there are hundreds of thousands of IP networks in the world, maintaining such tables can be a problem. In practice, most tables contain entries for just a few "local" IP networks. Datagrams for all other networks are sent to a single "default" router that, it is hoped, will know what to do with them. (Routing is discussed in more detail under Making the IP Layer Work.)

IP Addresses

We have assumed that the network prefix part of the IP address is 16 bits. This means we can have 16 bits to identify the individual interfaces on each network a total of 2^{16}(= 65,536), which is a large number of interfaces to have on one network. Therefore, the IP designers decided there should be three classes of IP address to suit the requirements of small, medium, and large networks. For small networks, the network prefix was 24 bits and the host part 8 bits, allowing 256 hosts (in fact, it is 254 because one was used for "this host" and another for local

<-- 32 bits -->

Version	IHL	Type of Service	Total Length		
Identification			Flags	Fragment Offset	
Time to Live		Protocol	Header Checksum		
Source Address					
Destination Address					
Options					Padding
Data		Data	Data		Data
Data		Data	Data		Data
...		...	...		...

Figure 3: Internet protocol datagram header format. Note the 32-bit source and destination IP addresses. The remaining fields are discussed briefly in the text.

broadcast). Obviously routers needed to know how many bits there were in the network prefix because these are the bits they look up in their routing tables. This information was encoded in the first few bits of the address according to the following scheme, where N indicates the network prefix and H the host part:

Class A	0NNNNNNN	HHHHHHHH	HHHHHHHH	HHHHHHHH
Class B	10NNNNNN	NNNNNNNN	HHHHHHHH	HHHHHHHH
Class C	110NNNNN	NNNNNNNN	NNNNNNNN	HHHHHHHH

As the Internet grew, and more organizations requested IP network addresses, this scheme proved problematic. Class B networks were in short supply and many were inefficiently used because few organizations approached 65,536 hosts. Class C networks, though in abundant supply, were too small for many organizations. Multiple class C networks could be issued but this meant that the organization would need multiple entries in Internet routers instead of the single one that would have sufficed had a class B network been available. Potentially this would lead to much larger tables in routers and consequent inefficient operation. Consequently, the class-based scheme has been abandoned in favor of one that allows the network prefix to be of arbitrary length. This scheme is discussed under Making the IP Layer Work. (Note that Class D addresses also exist. These relate to multicast transmission and are discussed in a later section.)

The Internet Assigned Numbers Authority (IANA) is the top-level authority for allocating IP addresses. IANA delegates authority over blocks of addresses to regional authorities who, in turn, allocate blocks to Internet service providers (ISP). Finally ISPs assign IP addresses to end users.

The IP Datagram and the Service It Offers

The basic IP service is simple; a host constructs a packet of data and gives this to the IP service along with the IP address of the destination. The IP service then makes its "best effort" to deliver the datagram. The service offers no guarantees of success, however. It may lose the datagram without informing either the source or the intended destination, delivery may be subject to arbitrary delay, two datagrams dispatched to the same destination may be misordered on arrival—it may even deliver two copies of one datagram. If an application running in a host finds this rather cavalier attitude toward service unacceptable, it is up to the application to do something about it. For example, many applications exploit the TCP (Postel, 1981b), which keeps track of wayward datagrams, retransmits missing ones, and ensures sequenced delivery. (More details on TCP are provided under Building on the IP Service.)

In fact, simplicity is the IP service's greatest strength and one of the main reasons for its considerable success. A simple convergence protocol is easy to implement, which encourages its deployment on as wide a range of technologies as possible. Having only minimal features in the network service maximizes flexibility for applications running in hosts. For example, some applications may happily tolerate the occasional lost datagram, especially if this avoids problematic costs and delays imposed by retransmission. If the network service itself took on the responsibility for retransmission these applications would suffer. Thus the design exemplifies the end-to-end argument as propounded in Saltzer, Reed, and Clark (1984).

IP datagrams themselves have a simple structure consisting of a header (typically 20 bytes) plus a "payload," the data the datagram is carrying across the Internet. The header format is shown in Figure 3. The fields are interpreted as shown in Table 1.

Implementing the IP Service

The IP datagram delivery algorithm given earlier includes the phrase "send datagram direct to its destination across the local physical network." We must specify how this is to be done for each network technology. The three main issues involved in this are discussed next.

Encapsulation in "Native" Formats

Each network technology specifies its own packet format. Usually this consists of a header, which often contains addresses, followed by the data payload, perhaps followed by a checksum used to detect errors. In essence, encapsulation means we construct our IP datagram and make this the payload of the packet. Figure 4 shows this in the case of Ethernet (note that it is common to refer to Ethernet "frames" rather than "packets"). Encapsulation would be similar for the other LAN technologies that have been standardized by the IEEE. CRC (cyclic redundancy check) is a checksum intended to discover transmission errors.

It is important to remember the strict division of labor here. The Ethernet technology pays no regard to the payload; it is interested only in the Ethernet header and the CRC. Likewise, Internet technology—routers and so on—is interested only in the IP datagram and its header.

In practice things may be slightly more complex than Figure 4 suggests. An Ethernet may be carrying other protocols in addition to IP datagrams. Systems processing incoming Ethernet frames need to be able to determine what protocol the frame is carrying. This entails the insertion

Table 1 Meanings of the IP Header Fields

Internet protocol (IP) version	4 for IPv4, 6 for IPv6
IHL	The length of the IP header (normally 5 32 bit words)
Type of service	This is discussed in the section on quality of service
Total length	Total length in bytes (including the header)
Identification, fragment offset	Used to implement fragmentation
Flags	Bits used to mark special status of a datagram
Time to live	A counter that is reduced by one by each router through which the datagram passes; when it reaches zero, the datagram is discarded (normally an error message is returned to the source), ensuring misrouted datagrams do not circulate forever
Protocol	A number to identify the protocol that this datagram is carrying (Transmission Control Protocol, User Datagram Protocol, etc.)
Header checksum	Used to pick up transmission errors that might corrupt header fields.
Source/destination addresses	Discussed earlier
Options	Rarely used (space precludes discussion here)

of another header between the MAC and IP headers. This header will include a "protocol identifier," a "well-known" number indicating "this is an IP datagram."

Some technologies require special treatment. ATM, for example, uses small packets, called cells, each of which carries 48 bytes. An associated standard, ATM adaptation layer 5 (AAL5), explains how a larger packet, an IP datagram, for example, can be fragmented into cells and reassembled at the destination.

Address Resolution

Each network technology has its own addresses; in this chapter, these are termed *physical addresses*. Obviously a technology understands its own physical addresses; no networking technology understands IP addresses, however. These are processed exclusively by the convergence function. Once the IP delivery algorithm has determined whether an IP datagram can be delivered direct or whether it must be sent to a router, we are left with the problem of determining the correct physical address to use. The business of mapping from an IP address to the corresponding physical address is called *address resolution*. Two techniques are used to achieve this:

1. Most LANs have a "broadcast service." All systems attached to the LAN will receive and process a frame sent to the MAC broadcast address. For address resolution a frame is sent to the broadcast address containing an address resolution protocol (ARP) (Plummer, 1982) request for the desired IP address. The host that recognizes the specified IP address as its own replies with an ARP response containing its own MAC (physical) address.
2. For nonbroadcast network technologies it is normal to deploy an ARP server that maintains a table of mappings. Attached systems register their mappings with the ARP server at boot time. Systems that need to resolve IP addresses send ARP requests to the server and receive ARP responses.

   In both cases, mappings are cached by the requesting system for future use.

Fragmentation

Each network technology imposes its own limit on the number of data bytes that may be carried in a frame, referred to as the maximum transfer unit (MTU). These limits pose problems for IP because the path to a destination may traverse dozens of networks and the system that originates the IP datagram knows only the first hop of the route. Consequently, it cannot know the smallest MTU on the complete path (the "path MTU"). In IP version 4 (IPv4), this is solved by allowing hosts and routers to fragment datagrams. An IP datagram that is too large will be split into two or more smaller IP datagrams (each complete with its IP header). The destination host will reassemble the original IP datagram from the various fragments.

Unfortunately fragmentation is not an efficient procedure. Suppose the originating system generates a series of

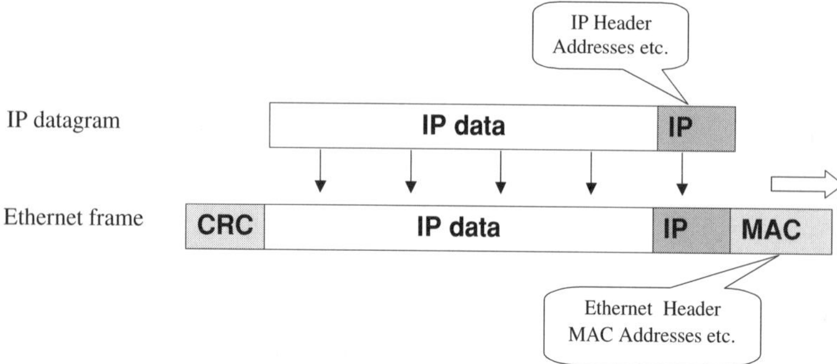

Figure 4: Simple encapsulation of an Internet protocol datagram in an Ethernet frame; the datagram simply becomes the payload of the frame.

IP datagrams of length 1600 bytes and somewhere along the path there is a network with an MTU of 1500 bytes. Every IP datagram will be split into two fragments, doubling the work for the remaining routers along the path. If the originating host knew the path MTU in advance, it could have divided its data into 1500-byte pieces, avoiding fragmentation and causing less work for the routers. A second problem arises if one fragment of a datagram is lost. Reassembly will not now be possible so all the work done by the networks and routers in delivering the other fragments will have been wasted.

The modern approach is to avoid fragmentation in routers by probing the network to discover the path MTU. This can be done by sending IP datagrams with a flag set that means "do not fragment." A router that is unable to forward such an IP datagram because it exceeds the MTU for the next hop network must discard it. When it does so, it sends an Internet control message protocol (ICMP) message (discussed under Management in the IP Layer) back to the originating host explaining what has happened. The originator can then try again with a somewhat smaller IP datagram. This is the approach favored in the latest version of IP, IP version 6 (IPv6), which actually prohibits fragmentation in routers.

BUILDING ON THE IP SERVICE

It is clear that the service provided by IP is inadequate for some applications. Several IP datagrams may be needed to carry one Web page. We care that all these datagrams are delivered exactly once and in the right order. There are many applications that have similar requirements. Rather than each of them inventing its own mechanisms to meet them a common protocol—TCP—is used.

TCP—The Transmission Control Protocol

TCP is an automatic repeat request (ARQ) protocol; such protocols send packets of data that each include a sequence number. It is up to the receiver to check the sequence numbers, ensure that all packets have arrived, and reorder them if necessary. The receiver sends "acknowledgment" packets back to the transmitter. The transmitter retransmits packets that are not acknowledged sufficiently promptly. In the TCP case, the packets are termed *segments*, each of which is carried in an IP datagram. Each segment consists of a TCP "header" (containing the sequence and acknowledgment numbers) that may be followed by a block of data (see Figure 5). At any instant there are likely to be data bytes that have been sent but not yet acknowledged. A limit, termed a *window*, is set on the number of these bytes. This window is specified by the receiver in the acknowledgments it sends. By reducing this window the receiver may slow down or even stop the flow of data. This flow control mechanism is essential in preventing a slow receiver from being overwhelmed by a fast transmitter.

The TCP protocol, although it uses the IP service, is independent of it. The components that implement the IP service, including all the routers, are interested only in the IP header—the fact that a particular IP datagram is carrying a TCP segment is of no importance whatsoever to these components. The components that are interested in TCP are the pieces of software that implement the logic of the TCP protocol. These exist in the end systems or hosts; typically such software is supplied as part of an operating system such as Linux or Windows.

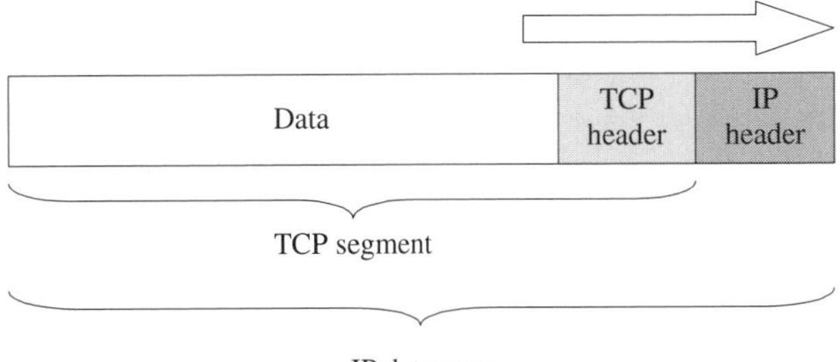

Figure 5: A transmission control protocol (TCP) segment carried in an Internet protocol (IP) datagram. Coincidentally, both the TCP and IP headers are normally 20 bytes long. The data part may be any length subject to a limit imposed by the IP protocol and the network technology in use. See also Figure 4.

This independence between the TCP "layer" and the IP "layer" is illustrated in Figure 6. TCP is just one possible "transport protocol" and will be used for most applications that require reliable, sequenced delivery. Logically we can think of the two TCP modules in the hosts as exchanging segments and acknowledgments directly with each other (represented by the broken, horizontal arrow). Physically, however, a TCP module must pass its segments down to the local IP module (also a piece of software within the operating system) that will wrap it in an IP datagram and send it on its way. The IP module at the receiver will unwrap the IP datagram, retrieve the TCP segment, and pass this up to the local TCP module. This is represented by the vertical arrows.

TCP's Role in Congestion Control

A weakness in the Internet architecture is the limited control over congestion it affords. Just as in road transport networks, congestion occurs when too much traffic attempts to pass through a particular point. Were the IP layer CO, there would be an opportunity to refuse new connections if these seemed likely to overload some router along the path. The Internet's basic CL service has to accept all the traffic that is thrown at it, however, and do the best it can. TCP can help alleviate this problem. As part of its normal operation a TCP module becomes aware of dropped or delayed IP datagrams because these manifest themselves as missing or delayed TCP acknowledgments. When these occur, TCP concludes (usually correctly) that congestion is occurring and employs a "congestion control" algorithm attributable to Jacobsen (1988). This algorithm results in TCP temporarily slowing its data transmission rate. If all the TCP connections passing through the congested router behave in this way, the congestion should be relieved.

This mechanism has been observed to work well in practice. Unfortunately there has been a recent growth in real-time multimedia applications that, typically, use user

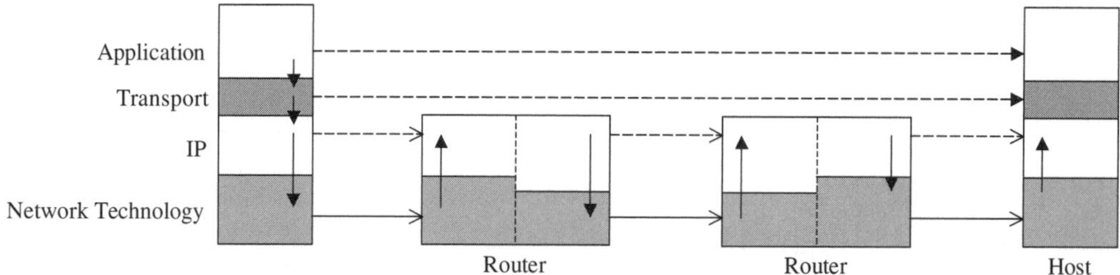

Figure 6: The fundamentals of the Internet architecture. The Internet protocol (IP) layer provides convergence, allowing many network technologies to take part. It also provides the relaying operation from router to router toward the destination host. Above IP comes the transport layer, which is where TCP fits. This layer is entirely the responsibility of the hosts.

datagram protocol (UDP; Postel, 1980) rather than TCP. UDP is almost a null protocol and lacks all of TCP's reliability and congestion control mechanisms, leaving such issues to the applications themselves. Efforts are being made to endow such applications with "TCP-like" behavior, but it seems unlikely that this alone will suffice to deal with the congestion problem. Some kind of resource management inside the Internet seems essential; approaches to this are outlined in the final section of this chapter.

Ports—Identifying Applications and Processes

Hosts are identified by IP addresses. Assuming we know the IP address of our intended recipient, the IP layer will (usually) deliver our IP datagram successfully. We need also to identify a particular application, service or process present on the host, however. This is the role of transport layer ports. Here one can draw a close analogy with telephone extensions; the telephone number (IP address) identifies the building, the extension number (port) identifies an individual within the building. All Internet transport protocols include source and destination ports in their headers; these are simply 16-bit integers.

A client/server model of communication is assumed; the client is the piece of software that initiates requests, and the server software waits and responds to client requests as these arrive. Public services usually use "well-known" ports (see Table 2). Thus, when a browser (client) requests a page from a Web server, the TCP segments it sends will have the destination port set to 80 in the TCP header. The operating system on the server host will have a table that tells it that port 80 is the WWW server. It will ensure that the WWW server software receives the incoming data and processes it. The client system chooses a source port. It should choose a value that is not currently in use for any other purpose. This source port will be used as the destination port in any replies from the server.

Table 2 Some "Well-Known" Transport Ports and Associated Protocols

Service	Protocol	"Well-Known" Port
HTTP (Web server)	TCP	80
FTP (FTP server)	TCP	21
Telnet (remote rlogin)	TCP	23
SMTP (e-mail)	TCP	25
DNS (name and address mappings)	UDP	53

Note. A client wishing to contact one of these services will use these as the "destination port" in the messages it sends. DNS = domain name service; FTP = file transfer protocol; HTTP = hypertext transfer protocol; SMTP = simple mail transfer protocol.

Other Internet Transport Protocols

Some applications do not need the reliable sequenced delivery provided by TCP, especially because TCP buys this reliability at the cost of delays when retransmissions occur. A great strength of the Internet architecture is that such applications can select a different transport protocol. The simplest is the UDP, which adds nothing to the basic IP service; however, its simple header does include the ports necessary for application selection. UDP is a popular choice for delay-sensitive, loss-tolerant applications and also for applications that just need to send one message and get one reply. It is sometimes favored by applications that work mostly within a LAN; for example, the SUN Network File System (NFS) can use UDP instead of TCP.

Several other protocols are in widespread use, including the real time protocol (RTP; Schulzrinne, Casner, Frederick, & Jacobson, 1996), which provides sequence numbering and time stamping for applications such as streamed audio and video. Sometimes two transport protocols are used in tandem: RTP is often carried inside UDP datagrams; transport layer security (TLS; Dierks & Allen, 1999), which provides authentication and confidentiality, may be used in conjunction with TCP.

Naming Internet Objects

We have seen that IP addresses provide globally unique labels for the interfaces between computers and the Internet. Such numeric labels, such as telephone numbers, are efficient for computers but not especially memorable for humans. They are also liable to change according to technological diktat—for example, when a computer is moved to a new IP network. Furthermore, the Internet makes many other sorts of object accessible—networks, e-mail accounts, files, and so on—and we need globally unique labels for these. Internet domain names (DN; Mockapetris,

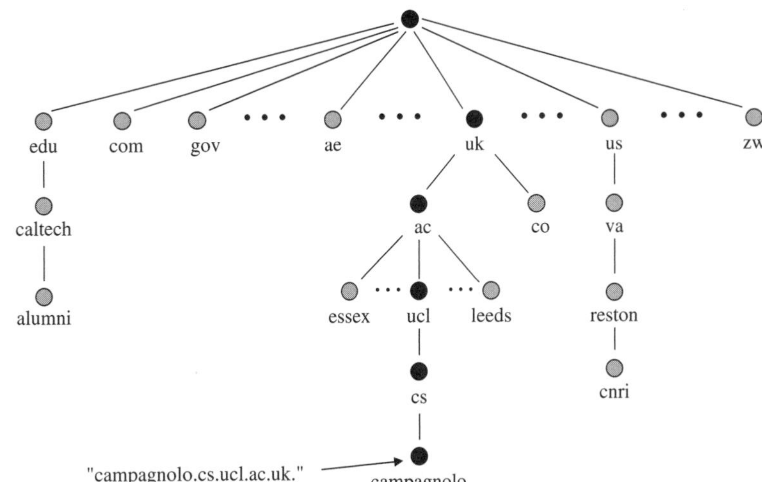

Figure 7: A portion of the domain name tree.

1987a) solve these problems by providing a systematic way of generating globally unique and reasonably user-friendly names. Like other schemes with similar objectives the DN scheme relies on a recursive devolution of authority over the namespace.

Figure 7 shows a portion of the domain namespace. Each node (leaf or nonleaf) represents a domain that consists of itself and all the nodes in the subtree beneath it. A fully qualified domain name is a concatenation of the labels on the path from a node all the way back to the root (e.g., *campagnolo.cs.ucl.ac.uk*). The authority for a zone is responsible for ensuring that no two sibling nodes have the same name. The top-level domains include the worldwide generic domains (*com*, *org*, *net*, *edu*, etc.), two United States-only generic domains (*mil* and *gov*), and country code domains (e.g., *us* for the United States and *uk* for the United Kingdom). Each authority has its own rules for name allocation and each may delegate authority over subdomains. For example, in the United Kingdom, the Department of Trade and Industry, which administers the "uk" domain, has allocated an "ac" subdomain and has delegated authority over it to a joint board of UK universities. This board has allocated domains, and delegated authority, to individual universities.

Although the principal use of DNs is the naming of computers and interfaces, they can be used for any purpose. Furthermore, there are no inherent relationships between domains and IP networks. It happens that the computer named "*campagnolo*" with address 128.16.23.3 belongs to the Computer Science department of University College London, an academic institution in the UK and its DN, *campagnolo.cs.ucl.ac.uk*, reflects this closely. There is nothing to stop the department from allocating the name to a computer on some other network in some other country, however; the name is theirs to use as they like.

The Domain Name System

The domain name system (DNS; Mockapetris, 1987b) is a distributed directory service that supports, among other things, the automatic mapping of DNs to IP addresses. Generally speaking, each domain must provide a computer on which runs a DNS nameserver that maintains a table of mappings for the names in its domain. This is termed the primary nameserver for the domain. The DNS protocol allows hosts to query these mappings and so to map names onto addresses. Local DNS servers hold mappings for local machines and answer queries for these directly. Nonlocal names are passed on to other DNS servers. Figure 8 illustrates this when a local nameserver cannot resolve the DN *www.ibm.com*. Steps 2 through 5 show the iterative mode; the query is passed to the *root* nameserver for the *com* domain which refers its questioner to a different nameserver. The local nameserver will cache the result of the query so that, next time around, we will see, at most, steps 1 and 6. As with all caching strategies, there is a danger that the cached information will become out of date, so a time-out is used. In addition to this, nameserver responses always contain a flag to indicate whether they are *authoritative*, that is, whether they come direct from a primary nameserver.

The DNS can answer a number of other queries. Especially important are "MX" mappings. These map a DN used in an e-mail address to the name of a host willing to accept mail for the domain. Thus an e-mail client wishing to deliver a message to *bloggs@cs.ucl.ac.uk* can discover the mapping *cs.ucl.ac.uk* ⇒ *smtp.cs.ucl.ac.uk*.

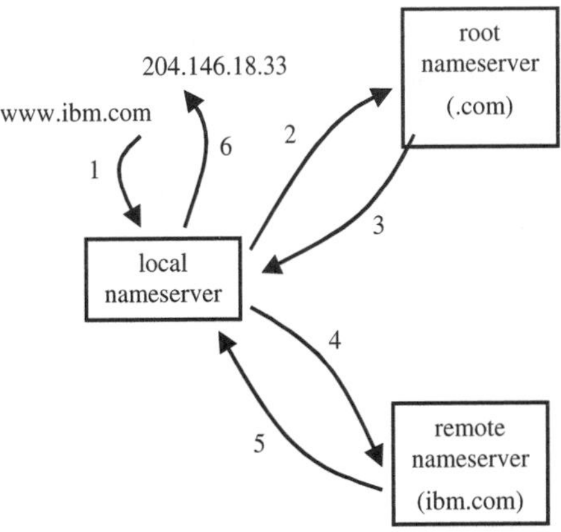

Figure 8: Distributed operations in the domain name system. The name cannot be resolved by the local nameserver, which passes the query to the nameserver for the top-level (com) domain and so on.

Universal Resource Locators

Universal resource locators (Berners-Lee, Fielding, & Masinter, 1998) are the familiar URLs used on the World Wide Web. The URL format is flexible; however, most URLs that users encounter have the following format:

```
<protocol>://<domain name>/<local name>
```

The domain name is a DN as described in the previous section. It identifies a host on which runs a Web server program that has access to the resource (a file, for example) identified by local name. Although it is common for hosts used for this purpose to be given a DN starting "WWW," there is no particular need for this, and any name will do. The protocol indicates the application protocol to be used when contacting the WWW server. These days this is usually the hypertext transfer protocol (HTTP; Fielding et al., 1999), described in a later section. It is still quite common, however, to see FTP, the original Internet file transfer protocol (Postel & Reynolds, 1985).

Internet Applications

Like transport protocol modules, applications are implemented by software residing in hosts. Application software exchanges messages across the Internet. In the most widely used applications, these messages are formatted using structured ASCII text. For example, a browser application (Internet Explorer, Netscape, etc.) uses HTTP to retrieve information from a Web server. An example of an HTTP "GET" request message is the following:

```
GET http://www.cs.ucl.ac.uk/research/index.htmlHTTP/1.0
Authorization: Basic QWxhZGRpbjpvcGVuIHNlc2FtZQ==
```

HTTP employs TCP in the transport layer. Therefore HTTP messages like the one above (encoded into binary using ASCII codes) will form the data part of a TCP segment. If all goes well, the HTTP response will include the file "index.html". Typically this is likely to be too big to fit into a single TCP segment, so several will need to be sent. Other familiar applications (e.g., FTP for file transfer and SMTP for e-mail; Klensin, 2001) use similar protocols. Designing such protocols is a matter of deciding what messages need to be sent, under what circumstances each needs to be sent, and specifying the format to be used.

Some application protocols provide generic services on which specific applications can be built. Among this group are the remote procedure call and remote invocation protocols such as CORBA and Java RMI. These adopt an object oriented model with one part of the application invoking operations on objects on a remote host. Each operation requires parameters to be sent and results to be returned. CORBA and Java RMI provide general mechanisms for handling these aspects.

In most operating system environments applications exist in user (rather than kernel) space. To operate they need to interact with the transport layer modules that usually reside in the kernel. The operating system will provide a set of system calls to support basic operations such as opening a TCP connection, sending or receiving a block of data, and so on. The so-called socket system calls, which originated with Berkeley Unix, are a widely adopted standard.

MAKING THE IP LAYER WORK

The previous sections established the basic components of the Internet architecture:

- An Internet layer, which allows IP datagrams to be sent to destinations identified by IP addresses
- A transport layer, which enhances the Internet layer service to provide a service satisfying an application's requirements; a variety of transport protocols exist, each of which resides exclusively in hosts and operates end to end
- An application layer, which includes multiple applications, each of which employs a suitable transport layer

This section considers the operation of the Internet layer in more detail.

IP Routers

The basic algorithm for IP delivery has already been described. Every IP router implements this algorithm and applies it to each IP datagram it receives. The router must make such a "forwarding decision" for every IP datagram it receives. The router must look at the destination IP address, extract the network prefix, and look this up in its routing table. As a result of this lookup, the router will know the IP address of the "best" next-hop router (or host). Once this has been accomplished, all necessary fragmentation, encapsulation, and address resolution can be performed and the IP datagram dispatched. This style of operation is called "incremental routing" because each router concerns itself only with the next hop of the route and not with the complete route.

In this section a second look at network prefixes is taken and how routing tables can be maintained is considered.

IP Networks, Subnets, and Supernets

Recall that an IP network is a logical entity—a collection of interfaces in which all IP addresses share a common network prefix. As mentioned above, the three principal IP address classes defined in the original architecture proved insufficiently flexible. Consequently, today, the length of the prefix is specified explicitly. Two notations are in use:

1. The length is appended to the address, for example, 128.16.0.0/20 indicates a 20 bit prefix.
2. A "subnet mask" is used. This is an IP address with 1s in place of all the network prefix bits and 0s otherwise. The mask for the scheme above would be 255.255.240.0 (11111111.11111111.11110000.00000000 in binary).

To accommodate this scheme, modifications were needed to the operation routers so that each routing table entry included a prefix length as well as the network address. When routers communicate routing information to other routers they must now include the prefix lengths.

This scheme offers plenty of flexibility. For example, an ISP might be allocated a block of addresses 128.16.0.0/16 (a class B address under the old scheme). The ISP can then partition these addresses into portions of sizes suitable for its customers. Thus they might derive sixteen 20-bit networks as follows:

128.16.0.0/20 (10000000.00010000.00000000.00000000)
128.16.16.0/20 (10000000.00010000.00010000.00000000)
128.16.32.0/20 (10000000.00010000.00100000.00000000)
...
128.16.240.0/20 (10000000.00010000.11110000.00000000)

Smaller partitions are then possible. For example, the final 20-bit network could be split into four 22 bit networks as follows:

128.16.240.0/22 (10000000.00010000.11110000.00000000)
128.16.244.0/22 (10000000.00010000.11110100.00000000)
128.16.248.0/22 (10000000.00010000.11111000.00000000)
128.16.252.0/22 (10000000.00010000.11111100.00000000)

Allocating addresses in this hierarchical way may have a further benefit—that of address aggregation. It may well be that all traffic for the ISP's customers is routed through a single router owned by the ISP. If such is the case, Internet routers need have just one routing table entry for the ISP (128.16.0.0/16 in the example above) and this will serve for all the ISP's customers.

Subnets

Partitioning is not solely an issue for ISPs. An organization that has been allocated a single address block may, nevertheless, want to install internal routers. These may be needed to allow interconnection between two dissimilar network technologies such as Ethernet and ATM. Another motivation might be the desire to partition a large LAN into several smaller LANs; large LANs can suffer from many "collisions" as multiple hosts compete to send traffic. The classical IP delivery algorithm requires that distinct network prefixes must be used on either side of such routers. This can be achieved by the organization partitioning the allocated space into several smaller IP subnets. For example, if the organization has been allocated the block 128.16.252.0/22, which allows about $2^{10} = 1024$ hosts, they may decide to partition this into four 24-bit subnets each with up to $2^8 = 256$ hosts. Of course, none of this will be effective unless all the routers and hosts involved know that 24-bit network prefixes are in use. They must be told this explicitly—an extra piece of configuration information for each participating system.

Note that these subnets are an internal matter. To the outside world the network just described still appears as a single 22-bit IP network. Thus the advantages of address aggregation are preserved.

Supernets

In the example above, the ISP began its partitioning with the block 128.16.0.0/16—effectively an old class B address. However, with care, it is also possible to make similar use of the old class C addresses. Table 3 shows 16 class C IP network addresses chosen so that they share the same first 20 bits.

In the literature, this is referred to as an IP supernet, with address 210.50.160.0/20. Once allocated, supernets can be further partitioned or subnetted exactly as other

Table 3 16 Class C IP Network Addresses Sharing the Same First 20 Bits

11010010	00110010	10100000	210.50.160
11010010	00110010	10100001	210.50.161
11010010	00110010	10100010	210.50.162
11010010	00110010	10100011	210.50.163
...	...	...	...
11010010	00110010	10101111	210.50.175

networks. Once more the address aggregation benefit can be seen as we now need just one routing table entry for the supernet rather than 16 entries for the individual class C networks.

Supernets, subnets, and explicit network prefix lengths are all part of a scheme termed classless interdomain routing (CIDR; Fuller, Li, Yu, & Varadhan, 1993).

Routing Tables

Figure 9 shows a configuration of networks and subnets that we can use to illustrate the use of routing tables. (In reality, there would be many more hosts; most have been omitted for clarity). We assume this configuration is operated by a single administration that has decided to partition the network 128.16.0.0/16 into several subnets. The main partition is into three 20-bit subnets, two on the main site and one for a set of remote machines that are accessible via ISDN (integrated services digital network). (Note that ISDN is not an IP network; it merely provides links between a router on the main site and those at the remote sites.) The "remote" subnet is further partitioned. This kind of sub-subnetting assists with routing.

Consider the transmission of an IP datagram from host *darhu* on the main site to host *mavic* on remote site B. The routing table on *darhu* can be very simple (Table 4). Our datagram for *mavic* (128.16.23.2) matches the default entry and so will be forwarded to *router1*. *Router1* is the main router giving access to the rest of the Internet. Its routing table could be large but must include at least the entries shown in Table 5. These include entries for the two local subnets and the entire remote subnet; notice that there is no need to have separate entries for each individual remote site. Our datagram matches the third entry and so will be sent to *router2*. *Router2* does need to distinguish between the various remote sites (Table 6). Here ISDN1 and ISDN2 represent the two ISDN calls. These are dial-up calls and would be managed so that they were only set up when data needed to be transferred. Our datagram matches the third entry and so will be sent to the router called *dawes*.

Suppose now that *mavic* is important so that we wish to have a permanent connection to it rather than relying on ISDN; we might lease a line to provide a permanent point-to-point link between *mavic* and *router2*. We would now need to modify *router2*'s table as follows (Table 7):

In Table 7 we now have a special entry for *mavic* (note that there is no need to put anything in the "next hop" column because there is only one possible destination at the other end of the leased line). Our datagram now matches two entries; there is a 24-bit match for the third entry and

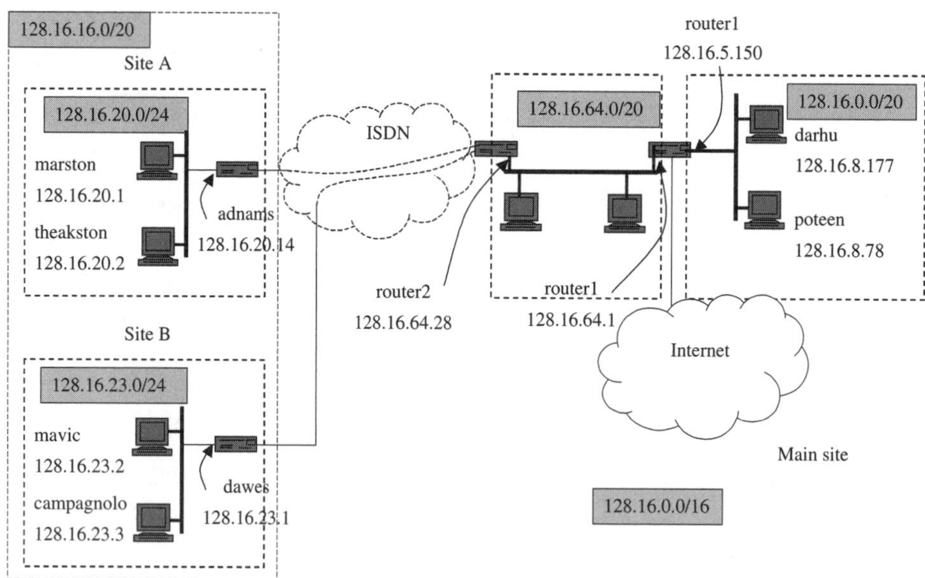

Figure 9: An IP network (128.16.0.0/16) partitioned into two subnets for the main site (128.16.0.0/20 and 128.16.64.0/20) and one for remote sites (128.16.16.0/20). The remote site subnet is further partitioned into two 24-bit subnets.

Table 4 Internet Protocol Routing Table for Host *darhu*

Network	Interface	Next Hop
128.16.0.0/20	Ethernet	Direct
Default	Ethernet	128.16.5.150

a 32-bit match for the fourth entry. This is a common situation and the tie-break rule is "choose the longest prefix match."

In some cases another factor is included in the forwarding decision, a metric signifying the cost of a particular route. This can be used to choose between two otherwise equivalent routes to a destination. Many metrics can be used. The simplest is a hop count, an estimate of the number of routers along the route to the destination. Other possibilities are estimates of delay, error rate, or throughput along a particular route. Some systems maintain multiple metrics and choose which one to use according to the QoS to be given to the datagram (this is discussed in more detail in the section on Traffic Management in the Internet). If we are using a dynamic routing protocol (see Routing Information), the metrics may vary with time to reflect changing network conditions.

It is clear from this discussion that the forwarding decision can be complex. Because this decision must be made for every datagram passing through a router, its efficiency is crucial to router performance. Router manufacturers expend a great deal of effort in devising clever ways of speeding up the forwarding decision and so increasing the throughput of their systems.

Table 5 Internet Protocol Routing Table for Router 1

Network	Interface	Next Hop
128.16.16.0/20	Ethernet2	128.16.64.28
128.16.0.0/20	Ethernet1	Direct
128.16.64.0/20	Ethernet2	Direct

Routing Information

It is crucial to Internet operation that information in routing tables is both timely and accurate. If routers have inconsistent information, it is possible for a datagram to circulate among a group of routers without ever reaching its destination—a "routing loop." The problem is compounded by the fact that the Internet is controlled by thousands of independent and autonomous administrations. A section of the Internet run by a single administration is called an autonomous system (AS). An AS is free to decide for itself how to manage routing internally. It may employ "static routing," whereby routes are worked out by hand and the corresponding routing tables are installed in all the administration's routers. Alternatively, the administration may decide to adopt a "dynamic routing protocol" that enables routers to exchange information on the current state of the network and so derive routing tables according to some algorithm. Most routers within an AS have detailed knowledge only of networks and subnets

Table 6 Internet Protocol Routing Table for Router 2

Network	Interface	Next Hop
128.16.64.0/20	Ethernet	Direct
128.16.20.0/24	ISDN1	128.16.20.14
128.16.23.0/24	ISDN2	128.16.23.1
Default	Ethernet	128.16.64.1
...	...	...

Table 7 Modified Internet Protocol Routing Table for Router 2

Network	Interface	Next Hop
128.16.64.0/20	Ethernet	Direct
128.16.20.0/24	ISDN1	128.16.20.14
128.16.23.0/24	ISDN2	128.16.23.1
128.16.23.2/32	Leased	—
Default	Ethernet	128.16.64.1
...	...	...

belonging to the home AS. Traffic for a network in a "foreign" AS will be sent, by default, to a router that acts as an "exterior gateway," that is, one that has a link to an exterior gateway belonging to a neighboring AS. These exterior gateways exchange information on which networks they can reach. These exchanges enable exterior gateways to learn plausible routes for reaching any network on the entire Internet.

Dynamic Routing and Routing Protocols

The original Internet architects were keen to ensure that, as far as possible, the Internet would be self-managing. For example, if some Internet component failed or its performance was degraded, the network should automatically reconfigure so as to direct traffic away from the problematic component. Dynamic routing protocols can help to achieve this. Early work on the ARPANET adopted a routing protocol of a class called "distance vector." These work as follows.

Periodically each router receives reports from its neighbors containing estimates of the neighbors' "distances" from other networks. The information in these reports is combined with information about local links so as to derive a new routing table. For example, if a router measures its current distance to neighbor X as 10 and X reports its distance as 100 from network Y, this means that Y is reachable via X at a distance of 110. Various measures of distance have been tried. The original ARPANET algorithm used queue length—the number of datagrams awaiting transmission on a link. The routing information protocol (RIP; Malkin, 1998), which is still in widespread use, uses a simple hop count. Changes occurring in network state are reflected in local measurements made by routers. These, in turn, are reflected in the information sent to neighbors in the next periodic routing update. Unfortunately, this means that many periodic updates must take place before all routers become aware of a change in network state. Until this occurs routers will have an inconsistent view of network state and routing loops can occur. This and other problems with distance vector algorithms has led to widespread adoption of an alternative class of algorithm called link state. The "open shortest path first" (OSPF; Moy, 1998) routing protocol is of this type.

In a link state algorithm each router measures the state of its local links; again, various measures of "distance" could be used. This information is then flooded to all other routers in the network. The result is that each router receives link state information from all other routers and from this information a routing table is calculated. Because all routers receive the same information, routing loops should not occur. Routing table calculation usually employs an efficient algorithm attributable to Dijkstra (1959).

Routing protocols such as RIP and OSPF are used within an AS and are referred to generically as "interior gateway protocols." Another class of protocol, "exterior gateway protocols," serves to exchange routing information between ASs [e.g., border gateway protocol (BGP); Rekhter & Li, 1995]. These protocols carry "reachability" information—lists of networks known to an AS and for whom it is prepared to carry traffic. Many issues, including commercial and security issues, have an impact on what is included in such lists.

The Physical Structure of the Internet

The Internet has a loose structure. Its topology is mainly a consequence of perceived commercial need being satisfied by a network service. The result is a broadly hierarchical structure; however, with some operators concentrating on providing "core" networks, others concentrating on connecting private users, and still others providing transit between users and the core. Figure 10 illustrates a possible configuration.

The core networks [called national service providers (NSP) in the United States] compete with each other to

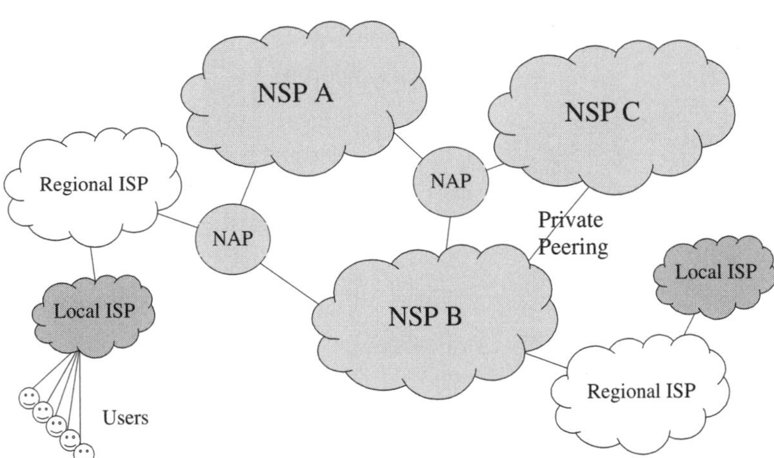

Figure 10: High-level Internet structure. The networks shown may have complex structure internally. Each is run by a separate administration and is an "autonomous system" in Internet terminology.

carry Internet traffic. They include internetMCI, Sprint-Link, PSINet, and UUNet Technologies. They have high-capacity links between their routers—capable of operating at gigabits per second and more. NSPs connect with each other in two ways:

1. Through independent "Network Access Points" (NAP). These are commercial operations and provide high bandwidth switching between networks. They are generally confined to a small geographical area (e.g., a single building) and consist of high-speed networks such as gigabit Ethernet that host routers belonging to the NSPs. NAPs are sometimes called metropolitan area exchanges (MAEs).
2. Through private "peering" arrangements. These are direct connections between routers belonging to the NSPs.

Regional Internet service providers (ISPs) are next in the hierarchy. As the name suggests, they cover a smaller geographical area than an NSP. To provide a service, they must connect to an NSP. This may be either direct or through an NAP. Local ISPs connect end users to the Internet. This may be via dial-up, ADSL, and so on (for many private users) or leased line (for corporate users).

Naturally all this must be paid for, and the ultimate source of revenue are the customers of the ISPs. It is not easy to discover precisely how money flows between the providers because such information is commercially sensitive. In principle anyone could construct an NSP or ISP and negotiate with existing operators to obtain interconnections. Existing operators may or may not welcome the newcomer—it is all a matter of commercial policy.

Peering arrangements vary. Two operators may simply agree to carry each other's traffic on a quid pro quo basis, or there may be payments in one direction or the other. Possibly an operator may agree to carry only certain traffic, based on source or destination for example. DIFFSERV (discussed in a subsequent section) will make all this more complex because it allows packets to be marked for special treatment. Operators will need to establish service-level agreements and accounting procedures to deal with this.

Continual improvements have been made in access technology that carries traffic between the customers' premises and the ISP. Much of this exploits the existing telecommunications infrastructure. The public switched telephone network (PSTN), in conjunction with MODEMs and ISDN, provides the ubiquitous dial-up service. This service provides ISPs with a convenient charging model based on "connect time" but takes no account of the volume of datagrams sent and received (and hence the real load imposed on the network). The point-to-point protocol (PPP; Simpson, 1994) is used over these connections; it provides access control and delimits datagrams on the wire. Faster access can be provided by asymmetric digital subscriber loop (ADSL) and cable modems that exploit telephone wiring and television cable, respectively. With these technologies, the full path from the customer's equipment to the ISP often involves other technologies such as Ethernet and ATM. Standards exist that specify how PPP may be used over these technologies, and this is evidently desirable because of PPP's access control and, not least, its familiarity (this does result in somewhat baroque architectures, however).

Variations on the Theme—Firewalls, Tunnels, Virtual Private Networks, Network Address Translation, and Proxies

The Internet architecture developed in an environment in which maximum openness and wide connectivity were principal objectives. Furthermore, the network was small, and there seemed to be few architectural limits to expansion. The situation has now changed; wide connectivity is frequently seen as a security threat, and the recent vast expansion has seen the depletion of the IPv4 address space. In this section, I discuss some adaptations (some would say distortions) of the architecture in response to this changing situation.

It is common to deploy a firewall router, which selectively discards datagrams. Such routers are placed so as to control access between a site and the wider Internet, usually with the aim of improving security. Control can vary in complexity. A simple control is to specify which ports can and cannot be used. For example, allowing only destination port 80 on outgoing datagrams effectively restricts outgoing traffic to World Wide Web requests. Controls may also operate on IP addresses and protocols. Firewalls may be operated by ISPs as well as end users. The aim then is either to protect end users from attack or to promote the ISP's commercial interests by restricting the activities available to some classes of user.

A way of exploiting the Internet while preserving independence from it is to build a virtual private network (VPN) from IP-in-IP tunnels. Figure 11 shows such an arrangement in which an organization has three widely spaced sites each with its own network of computers and

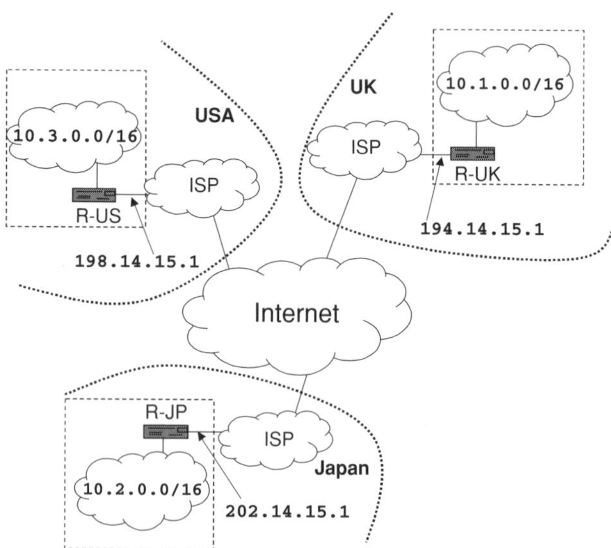

Figure 11: A virtual private network built on the Internet. An organization with three sites finds the Internet to be a cost-effective way of providing connectivity between them. The arrangement allows traffic to flow between the sites but excludes traffic to or from the wider Internet.

a connection via a router to a local ISP. Hosts on the organization's networks are allocated addresses from a network specifically designated to be private (such addresses should never appear on the "real" Internet). A datagram sent by a host on the U.S. site to one in the United Kingdom will be routed to the router *R-US*. This router, like the other two, has a real IP address allocated by the local ISP. Its routing table tells it that the datagram must be sent to the router *R-UK*. To achieve this datagram, complete with its header, becomes the data part of a new datagram with destination address 194.14.15.1. When the datagram reaches *R-UK* it is "unwrapped," and the original datagram is forwarded on to the United Kingdom network. If desired, the three external routers can be configured to disallow all traffic to or from the rest of the Internet. A further refinement is to use "secure tunnels" by exploiting the IPSec standards (Atkinson & Kent, 1998; discussed under IP security) and encrypting the tunneled datagrams.

The private address space can also help a site that has insufficient addresses for local hosts; for example, many consumer ISP contracts allocate just one IP address per customer even though the customer may have more than one host requiring an IP address. This problem can be solved in part by network address translation (NAT).

Figure 12 shows one way of using NAT as specified in RFC1631 (Egevang & Francis, 1994). It shows a single "real" IP address being shared by several hosts on a local network, each of which has a "private" IP address. As packets leave the site, the NAT gateway changes their source addresses in the IP header to the real IP address that has been assigned. The reverse transformation must be applied to the destination addresses of incoming packets; the problem is to know which private IP address should be selected. This is achieved by including the transport protocol ports in the mapping. The mapping ensures that all source ports currently in use are distinct. These source ports will be the destination ports of incoming IP datagrams and can be used to select the correct mapping. Thus an incoming datagram with destination port 5095 will have its destination IP address and port set to 192.168.1.1 and 5042, respectively.

NAT is a rather ugly fix and breaks an architectural rule that IP addresses should identify the end points of a communication. Some applications, notably FTP, make use of this rule, and NAT gateways have to treat FTP specially as a consequence. The number of such special cases seems likely to increase in the future.

The NAT operation described is fine provided the applications act as clients, but suppose a user wanted to run a Web server on the machine with address 192.168.1.1. The NAT gateway would map this address so that the outside world sees the server running at address 126.16.5.2, which is fine. The user, however, would like the server to appear to listen on the "standard" WWW port, port 80. This means a permanent mapping in the NAT gateway is necessary so that 198.168.1.1 port 80 always maps to 126.16.5.2 port 80. This demonstrates that NAT gateways have a natural firewall capability; if the NAT gateway does not have a mapping for port 80, no incoming Web request can succeed.

It is in no one's interest to generate unnecessary Internet traffic. World Wide Web proxy servers situated on a customer or ISP network aim to confine a sizable portion of Web traffic to the local area. Proxy servers maintain a cache of popular, recently accessed Web pages. Browsers are configured so that Web requests are sent not to the true destination server but to the proxy. If the requested page has been cached, the proxy will respond; otherwise it will forward the request to the true destination. Mechanisms exist to ensure that any cached copy is adequately up-to-date, but problems still arise. A variation on this theme is the so-called transparent proxy. Here Web requests are intercepted and redirected to a proxy server even though the user has not requested it and the browser has not been configured to permit it. This unwarranted interference with traffic has been justified on grounds of efficiency but is a clear breach of the Internet end-to-end principle. Problems, when they arise, are likely to be mysterious and intractable.

Multicast IP

Several modern applications require data to be delivered to multiple destinations, including multiway conferencing and video distribution. A network service that does this efficiently is called a multicast service. Many of the networks on the edges of the Internet are LANs, and these have inherent support for multicast. The aim of multicast IP is to route multicast datagrams across the Internet in a way which ensures they reach all the LANs where there are destination hosts. Efficient multicast should never send more than one copy of an IP datagram between two routers. It should be the job of routers to replicate an IP datagram and forward copies down multiple paths as necessary. The mechanisms for achieving this were developed mainly by Deering (1998). From a user's point of view,

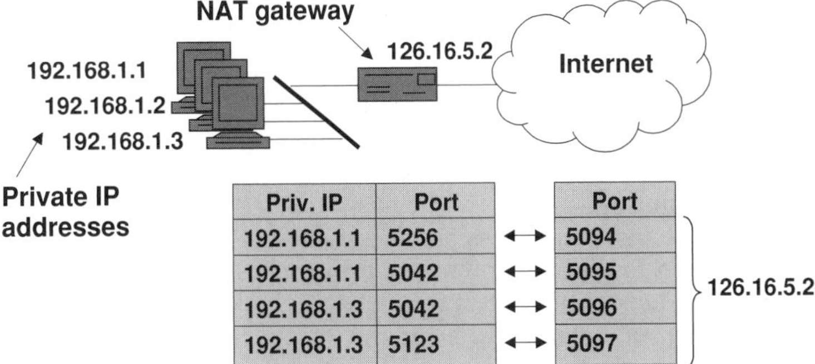

Priv. IP	Port		Port
192.168.1.1	5256	↔	5094
192.168.1.1	5042	↔	5095
192.168.1.3	5042	↔	5096
192.168.1.3	5123	↔	5097

Figure 12: Network address translation. The private IP addresses and ports used locally are mapped to/from real IP addresses and ports as they pass through the NAT router.

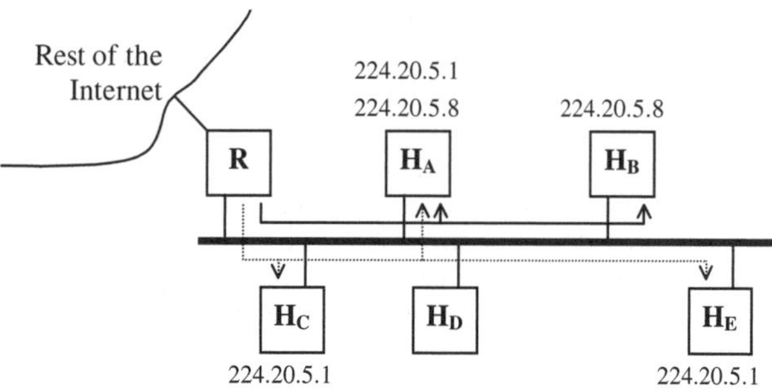

Figure 13: Multicast delivery to local area network hosts.

the model resembles that of a radio transmission where, to receive, one must "tune in" to a frequency. The Internet analog for a frequency is a multicast group address. Hosts wishing to receive multicasts to a particular multicast group address have to inform the network that they wish to do so. This "user to network signaling" is handled by the Internet group management protocol (IGMP; Fenner, 1997). Multicast addresses look like ordinary IP addresses, which means there is no problem with carrying them in the source and destination fields of IP datagrams. They are class D addresses with the following format:

Class D 1110XXXX XXXXXXXX XXXXXXXX XXXXXXXX

If a router on a LAN receives an incoming datagram with a multicast address (e.g., 224.20.5.1), it has to decide whether to multicast the datagram on the LAN. If there is at least one member of the 224.20.5.1 group on the LAN, the datagram must be multicast; otherwise, it should be dropped. For example, Figure 13 shows hosts on a LAN belonging to two multicast groups (224.20.5.1 and 224.20.5.8). Any datagram to either of these addresses must be multicast on the LAN. The router discovers group memberships on the LAN through IGMP.

Multicast Address Resolution

For transmission on a LAN to take place, the IP multicast address must be resolved to a LAN multicast address. In the case of Ethernet, for example, an algorithmic procedure is used that forms a MAC address as

<$00000001000000000010111100_2$> + <low-order 23 bits of the IP multicast address>

This is not a one-to-one mapping, and it is possible to end up with two IP multicast groups on a LAN mapped to the same MAC multicast address. This is unfortunate but not disastrous. It means that a host that has joined the group with address 224.20.5.1 will also receive datagrams intended for (e.g.) 224.148.5.1 and will have to filter these out with software.

Multicast Routing

A routing mechanism is necessary to ensure that all transmissions to a multicast address reach the correct set of routers and hence the correct set of LANs. In common with the normal Internet strategy, this mechanism has to be robust in the face of network failures. This can be achieved by minimizing the state information retained by routers and allowing this information to be continually refreshed, which requires an efficient dynamic multicast routing protocol. This turns out to be a difficult problem to crack and is still the subject of much research.

Several multicast routing protocols make use of information held by routers as a result of their normal unicast (host-to-host) operation. For example, a router employing a link-state routing protocol has enough information to be able to calculate a shortest path route from any source to any destination. By calculating shortest paths from a multicast source to all known destinations, a reasonably efficient multicast tree can be constructed. All routers involved should calculate the same tree so that no problems with loops result from inconsistencies. As it stands, this technique will deliver multicast datagrams to all destinations, including those that have no group members. This is solved by allowing routers to send "prune" messages saying, "do not forward datagrams for this address to me." The multicast extensions to open shortest path first protocol (MOSPF; Moy, 1994) is of this type. The distance vector multicast routing protocol (DVMRP; Waitzman, Partridge, & Deering, 1998) uses similar ideas but is based on a distance vector unicast routing protocol. Another protocol, protocol independent multicast (PIM; Estrin et al., 1997), uses similar techniques when many group members are concentrated in an area (dense mode) but a different technique when members are widely distributed (sparse mode).

IP Security

Many applications, especially in e-commerce, require security. In particular, they require strong authentication of the participants in a transaction and, possibly, traffic confidentiality. The basic Internet architecture and infrastructure is far from secure, for example:

1. In the normal mode of operation users have no control over the route taken by their datagrams. Thus their traffic may pass through insecure networks where it is subject to eavesdropping or modification.
2. No guarantees are given about the origin of data arriving at a host. The source IP address in the datagram header cannot be relied on because it is trivially easy to spoof.

Figure 14 shows some possibilities for adding security within the Internet architecture; each has its advantages and disadvantages:

1. Applications themselves can be provided with security extensions. This is exemplified by the secure hypertext transfer protocol (S-HTTP; RFC 2660), which extends the HTTP protocol used on the WWW and Pretty Good Privacy (PGP; RFC 2440), which may be used to secure e-mail. This approach benefits from being "end-to-end" and independent of the lower layers that are not required to provide any security assistance. Further, the specific security mechanisms used can be carefully tailored to the requirements of the application. The disadvantage is that each application must be treated

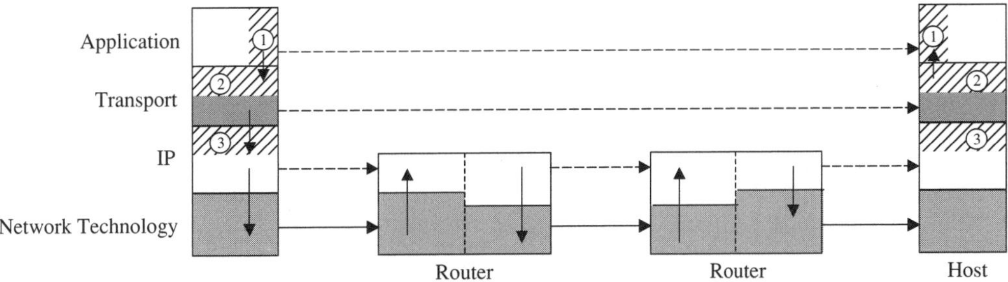

Figure 14: The basic Internet architecture (cf. Figure 6) showing some options for introducing security facilities: (1) as an extension to an application protocol; (2) as a sublayer in the transport layer; (3) as a sublayer in the Internet layer.

separately, both in terms of specifying the security extensions and implementing them.

2. A security sublayer may be provided to the transport layer. This is the approach used in the secure sockets layer (SSL), developed by Netscape, which was the basis for the transport layer security standard (TLS; RFC 2246). This is likely to be provided within the operating system and, once installed, is available for use by all applications. Applications may still need some modification so that they correctly invoke TLS features but this is likely to involve much less work than in 1. "End-to-end" benefits still accrue because no modification is required to the underlying IP layer. However, the facilities provided may not meet the requirements of all applications. Thus, for example, the general facilities provided by TLS do not meet all the requirements for e-commerce and this has resulted in the definition of a further transport sublayer secure electronic transaction (SET; SET 1997) by Visa and MasterCard. Further, different sublayers may be needed for different transport protocols. Thus TLS works with TCP but not with UDP.
3. A security sublayer may be provided to the IP layer. The great benefit of this approach is that security facilities become available to all Internet applications and transport protocols. There are also major management benefits in that traffic may be forced to conform to a locally defined security policy. For example, one could configure a system so that all Internet traffic must be encrypted or that all traffic for a particular application must be authenticated. The enforcement of such a policy is entirely the responsibility of the security sublayer and requires neither cooperation from nor modifications to applications. This is the approach of the IPsec standards (RFC 2401) that are discussed briefly below and more fully in Part 3 of this volume.

IPSec

A fundamental concept in the Internet security architecture (IPSec; Kent & Atkinson 1998) is the security association (SA). The granularity of a SA may vary; at one extreme a SA may be one-to-one with a particular user-level session and at the other an SA may cover all traffic between two sites. There is an initial handshaking phase between source and destination during which the parameters of the SA are negotiated. These parameters include details of the precise security mechanisms and options to be used (in fact, IPsec SAs are simplex, so, in general, a pair must be set up.)

IP datagrams carrying IPsec traffic have an extra header immediately following the IP header. Two types of headers are possible:

1. An authentication header (AH) is used when just authentication is required. This header includes a digital signature for the source of the datagram.
2. An encryption security payload (ESP) header is used when authentication and confidentiality is required. It includes parameters relevant to the encryption algorithm. The header is followed by the encrypted payload and an authentication trailer that has a function similar to that of the AH.

Figure 14 shows an IP security sublayer implemented solely in the hosts. This corresponds to the case of IPSec operating in transport mode. In this mode it is only the payload of the IP datagram that can be protected by encryption; the IP header fields, including the source and destination addresses, are sent in plain text. Clearly this must be the case because routers along the path to the destination must not be required to do any special IPsec processing—it is not practical to demand that all routers in the Internet change to accommodate security. Consequently, in transport mode, an eavesdropper may still identify source and destination hosts and so carry out traffic analysis. (Note that this deficiency is also present when confidentiality is provided by application extensions or transport sublayers.) However, in the case of IPsec transport mode, the source and destination IP addresses *are* authenticated so that IP address spoofing attacks are defeated.

IPsec can also operate in tunnel mode. This finds particular application in conjunction with VPNs built from IP-in-IP tunnels as described earlier. In tunnel mode, security is applied in a "security gateway" that might be implemented in a firewall router. A VPN might deploy security gateways at each site and would establish SAs between them. A datagram passing out through such a gateway forms the payload of a new, secured datagram whose destination IP address is that of the appropriate destination security gateway. In this case whole of the "inner" datagram, including its source and destination addresses, can be protected by encryption so that host identities are concealed. Tunnel mode may be attractive from a management point of view because it allows the security policy for a site to be implemented all in one place.

It should be noted that the various architectural approaches to implementing network security outlined above are not mutually exclusive. For example, IPsec does not meet the particular requirements addressed by SET. Conversely, SET does not conceal IP addresses. Therefore, in certain circumstances, the two may be employed together.

Mobile IP

There is a difference between wireless and mobile. A host on a wireless LAN may move physically around a building, but, as long as it remains on the same LAN, it has not moved as far as the Internet is concerned—it can still be reached by the same route. For the Internet, mobility occurs when a host moves to a location served by a new router. When this happens, the mobile host's IP address is wrong because its network prefix remains that of its "home" IP network. Unless this is tackled, the host will not receive IP datagrams because these will be routed to the home network. The problem is solved by means of two agent processes (see Perkins, 1996). The newly arrived host registers itself with the "foreign agent" (FA). If it is willing to accept the newcomer, the FA contacts the "home agent" (HA), which resides on the home network. From this point forward, all incoming packets are intercepted by the HA and forwarded to the FA; this uses IP-in-IP tunneling similar to that used in a VPN. The resulting route (source ⇒ HA ⇒ FA ⇒ mobile host) may be inefficient. The scheme is effective, however, because it requires no changes to be made to fixed hosts and routers.

Management in the IP Layer

ICMP

ICMP is the Internet control message protocol (Postel, 1981c). ICMP messages are used mainly to convey information about errors or conditions that require attention. There are many message types including the following:

- Echo request and response, used to probe hosts and routers to check whether they are alive and responding; The "ping" program, available on most systems, employs these messages
- Time exceeded, used to indicate that an IP datagram has been discarded by a router because its TTL field has reached zero
- Destination unreachable and host unreachable, used by routers to indicate discard for a variety of reasons.

The weakness of the ICMP mechanism is that its messages suffer the same problems as do other IP datagrams, thus one can never be sure they will be delivered. They can be regarded as providing useful hints about the nature of problems but cannot be relied on.

Host Configuration

To operate, an IP host needs several pieces of information, including its IP address, the address mask for the local network, the IP address of the local DNS server, and the IP address of at least one router. Configuring all this information by hand on a network with thousands of hosts would be an administrative nightmare. The dynamic host configuration protocol (DHCP; Droms, 1997) provides a solution. When a host starts up, it broadcasts an IP datagram requesting a DHCP server. Assuming such a server is present, it will reply with the relevant information. In many cases, the IP address allocation will be dynamic. This allows a pool of IP addresses to be shared among a larger number of hosts. Only those currently connecting to the Internet need be allocated addresses, which goes some way to tackling the shortfall of addresses in IPv4.

The IPv6

A major motivation for a new version of IP was the shortage of IPv4 addresses. IPv6 (Deering & Hinden, 1998) addresses are four times as long, which should give enough addresses for the foreseeable future. (If one IPv6 address is allocated each microsecond, the addresses will last for 10^{25} years). Other major driving factors were mobility, which requires multiple address allocations as a host moves through the Internet; ease of configuration so that simple devices can be plugged in and work without human intervention; security; and better support for different qualities of service.

The IPv6 header is shown in Figure 15. Despite the fourfold increase in address length, the header is just 40 bytes. This is something of an illusion, however, because some functions (e.g., security) require an additional "extension header."

The traffic class and flow label fields relate to QoS issues. Traffic class is used within the DIFFSERV scheme to indicate one of several predefined traffic classes. IPv6 routers should understand these classes and prioritize datagrams appropriately. The flow label relates to the finer grained INTSERV scheme. It is used by a host to mark a

4-bits	8-bits	4-bits	8-bits	8-bits
Version	Traffic Class	Flow Label		
Payload length			Next header	Hop limit
Source Address				
Destination Address				

Figure 15: Internet protocol version 6 header.

stream of related IP datagrams, which should be accorded a previously negotiated priority. These schemes are explained in the next section.

IPv6 wraps up several add-ons to IPv4 and makes these formally part of the protocol. These include ICMP, IGMP, DHCP, and IPsec. It has a much richer address structure that allows much greater scope for address aggregation; whereas IPv4 simply allows a collection of hosts to be aggregated into an IP network, IPv6 allows a hierarchy of aggregations. For example, one scheme has a "top-level" identifier followed by a "next level" identifier (probably denoting a particular site), a site identifier (like an IPv4 subnet), and an interface identifier (like an IPv4 host part).

The service provided by IPv6 is essentially unchanged, and the overall architecture remains as before; IPv6 provides simple datagram delivery, and the end-to-end layers (transport and application) build on this. To date IPv6 deployment has not been widespread. The two protocol versions can and do coexist, however; and pockets of IPv6 are beginning to emerge. It seems possible that the emergence of more powerful wireless devices such an "third-generation" mobile phones may see a ballooning of demand for IP addresses and a consequential rapid deployment of IPv6.

TRAFFIC MANAGEMENT IN THE INTERNET

For some time it has become clear that the basic "best efforts" IP service was not suitable for all applications. This is particularly so for applications with tight constraints on delay. These applications require some stronger guarantees on the maximum end-to-end delivery times for their IP datagrams (i.e., they require specialized QoS). This translates into a requirement for priority treatment by the routers through which their traffic passes. Several problems need to be addressed:

- How can applications tell the routers their requirements? We need some form of "signaling" between applications and the routers.
- How can routers identify which IP datagrams require which treatments?
- Can we build routers that can give different priorities to different applications so that their QoS requirements are met?

INTSERV

The Integrated Services (INTSERV) initiative (Braden, Clark, & Shenker, 1994) was the first attempt to address these problems. It introduced the concept of a "flow"—a sequence of IP datagrams all headed to the same destination(s) and all requiring the same QoS. An application which requires special QoS for a flow engages in an explicit negotiation with the network routers it will use. The resource reservation protocol (RSVP) (Braden, Zhang, Berson, Herzog, & Jamin, 1997) is employed for this signaling. The source sends an RSVP message describing the flow in terms of its peak and mean rates. The receiver then calculates the capacity that routers should reserve to meet the delay requirements. It then sends a reservation message asking all the routers along the path to reserve the required capacity. Of course the capacity might not be available, in which case an error message will be sent back to the receiver. In a CO network, this negotiation would be done only once, when the connection is set up. In the CL Internet, it must be repeated at intervals to cope with changing traffic patterns, changing routes, and so on.

During negotiation the source indicates how the flow is to be identified. This can be a combination of source and destination IP addresses, protocol identifiers, and ports. This means that routers have to look at multiple header fields (and know something about transport protocols) to determine to which flow an IP datagram belongs, which will certainly slow things down. IPv6 includes a 20-bit flow label field into which a (hopefully) unique value can be placed. This may enable routers to classify incoming IP datagrams by examining only one field.

DIFFSERV

It is now recognized that the INTSERV approach, used alone, is appropriate only for small networks. The problem is that hundreds of thousands of flows are likely to pass through routers on core networks, and managing all these is impossible. What is needed is something much more coarse grained that allows routers to implement a few "behaviors" suited to broad classes of traffic. This is the approach used in the differentiated services (DIFFSERV; Blake et al., 1998) scheme. The "type of service" field in the IP header, now renamed the DIFFSERV field, is used to indicate the class to which an IP datagram belongs. A router has only to look at this field to know which behavior should be applied.

Effectively DIFFSERV allows the Internet to offer several classes of service to its users. The basic class offers the familiar "best efforts" service and would be relatively cheap. Traffic with tight delay constraints would use a class guaranteeing very high priority—and would pay accordingly. For this to work, ISPs must have mechanisms in place to count packets belonging to each class so that appropriate charges can be made. They must also negotiate service level agreements with neighboring networks to ensure there is an onward commitment to treat high-priority traffic appropriately. Furthermore, the guarantees offered with respect to a particular traffic class cannot be completely open ended; sources will have to agree to keep the rate at which traffic is generated within prenegotiated bounds. Traffic will have to be "policed" to ensure that these bounds are respected. Despite these complications, there now seems to be momentum behind DIFFSERV that should lead to wide deployment.

Although DIFFSERV was originally seen as an alternative and more scalable approach to INTSERV and RSVP, the two can be seen as complementary. For example, RSVP may be used to request reservation of resources for a DIFFSERV service class. RSVP also has a role in traffic engineering in conjunction with MPLS.

Performance Issues

Traffic volumes continue to increase as do the capacity of networks and links; new applications require tighter bounds on delay. This has a number of implications for the engineering of Internet components:

- Host operating systems need better real-time performance. Some popular operating systems are poor in this regard and contribute a major proportion of end-to-end delay.
- Routers, especially core routers, must handle increased traffic volumes. At the same time, they are expected to classify IP datagrams on the basis of the DIFFSERV field and process accordingly. Coping with this increased rate and volume of per-datagram processing is challenging for router manufacturers. One approach, multiprotocol label switching (MPLS; Rosen, Viswanathan, & Callon, 2001), attempts to exploit the fact that a whole stream of IP datagrams is likely to require the same processing. MPLS labels such streams through the use of an additional field. Once a stream has been labeled, routers have only to look at the label to determine the route, the priority, and so forth.
- Generally, transmission rates increase while end-to-end delays remain constant. Thus ARQ protocols such as TCP must operate in an environment in which many more segments may be sent before an acknowledgment can be expected. This can lead to inefficient operation; some enhancements have been made to TCP to combat these.

CONCLUSION

The Internet is built through the implementation of a common service—the IP service—on its constituent networks. This is a minimalist service providing little more than basic connectivity. Keeping the IP service simple leaves maximum flexibility to the applications that may choose transport protocols suited to their needs. Many applications require reliable, sequenced delivery of data. These applications may employ the TCP protocol that satisfies these requirements and, additionally, assists with the management of congestion.

The IP service itself is based on the use of routers that relay traffic between networks. The routes followed are not normally predetermined and may vary with network load. IP addresses identify hosts and the IP networks to which these belong. Correct assignment of IP addresses is essential to Internet operation. Internet expansion has put pressure on the original addressing scheme. This has led to work-arounds such as NAT and, ultimately, to a much more flexible scheme within IPv6.

The management of congestion remains an issue and has an impact on newer, delay-sensitive applications. Initiatives such as DIFFSERV address the needs of such applications and are intended to lead to an Internet capable of carrying multiservice traffic having a variety of QoS requirements.

The early history of the Internet was characterized by the following philosophy: keep the network simple, and put the complexity in the hosts. More recently, commercial pressures have encouraged providers to add complexity to the network so as to offer "enhanced" services to their customers; firewalls, NAT gateways, tunnels, and proxies all reflect this strategy (and all bring awkward problems in their wake). At the same time, it is proving difficult to persuade providers and customers to support ostensibly more elegant enhancements such as IPv6, IP multicast, and IPSec. Thus we see a tension between Internet architects who wish to defend and build on the elegance of the original design and commercial interests who have customers to serve and need solutions that can be deployed straight away. One must hope that this tension will continue to be creative.

GLOSSARY

Autonomous System (AS) A collection of hosts, networks, and routers operated by a single administration. Routing within an AS is the sole responsibility of the AS administration. Routing between ASs uses a standardized exterior gateway protocol such as BGP.

Border Gateway Protocol (BGP) A protocol used to exchange routing information between autonomous systems at their edges (AS). The information indicates which ASs are reachable from the sending AS.

DIFFSERV An initiative aimed at providing quality of service control on the Internet by classifying traffic into a few broad categories. Each category is then given appropriate treatment by routers.

Dynamic Host Configuration Protocol (DHCP) A protocol that allows a host to obtain Internet configuration information from a server. DHCP is especially applicable when a host is first switched on and needs to obtain its IP configuration.

Domain Name (DN) A unique name that is used to name an object in the context of the Internet, for example, www.bluffco.com.

Domain Name System (DNS) A hierarchical system of servers that provides a directory service for the Internet. Each server manages part of the domain name space and communicates with other domain name servers to look up names in "foreign" domains.

File Transfer Protocol (FTP) The standard protocol on the Internet for transferring files between hosts. Its role has, to some extent, been usurped by HTTP.

Gateway In the context of the Internet, a gateway is an alternative name for a router.

Host A computer attached to a network on which applications run.

Hypertext Transfer Protocol (HTTP) The protocol used by a Web browser to retrieve information from a Web server.

Internet Control Message Protocol (ICMP) A protocol that provides simple management capabilities alongside the Internet Protocol. ICMP is used mainly for reporting problems and errors.

Internet Group Management Protocol (IGMP) The protocol used by hosts to manage their membership of IP multicast groups.

Internet Protocol (IP) The protocol that governs basic data delivery on the Internet. It defines the format of the IP datagram complete with its source and destination addresses. IP will attempt to deliver the datagram to the intended destination but will not attempt to recover any errors that may occur.

INTSERV An initiative aimed at providing quality of service control on the Internet through explicit reservation of resources.

IP Datagram A packet formatted according to the rules of the Internet protocol.

IPsec A protocol that can add confidentiality, integrity, and authentication to the Internet protocol.

IPv4 Version 4 of the Internet protocol. The version employed in the overwhelming majority of today's Internet traffic.

IPv6 Version 6 of the Internet protocol; A new standard that incorporates greatly expanded addressing and solutions to mobility, multicast, security, management, and configuration problems.

Network Address Translation (NAT) A scheme that allows several hosts to share a single "real" IP address.

Packet A combination of data plus control information that is treated as a unit by a data communication network.

Port A number that identifies a particular application or service available on a host.

Resource Reservation Protocol (RSVP) A signaling protocol that allows hosts to reserve Internet resources to obtain a desired level of quality of service.

Router A device that relays IP datagrams among networks. It determines where to send the datagram by referring its destination address to a routing table.

Transmission Control Protocol (TCP) A protocol that provides reliable, sequenced, flow-controlled data exchange between hosts. Common applications such as file transfer and the Web use TCP to provide the reliability they need.

User Datagram Protocol (UDP) A simple protocol that allows an IP datagram to be sent to a particular port on a particular host. UDP does not enhance the IP service in any way.

CROSS REFERENCES

See *Internet Security Standards; Routers and Switches; TCP/IP Suite.*

REFERENCES

Atkinson, R., & Kent, S. (1998). Security architecture for the Internet protocol. Internet RFC 2401.

Berners-Lee, T., Fielding, R., & Masinter, L. (1998). Uniform resource identifiers (URI): Generic syntax. Internet RFC 2396.

Blake, S., Black, D., Carlson, M., Davies, E., Wang, Z., & Weiss, W. (1998). An architecture for differentiated service. Internet RFC 2475.

Braden, R., Clark, D., & Shenker, S. (1994). Integrated services in the Internet architecture: An overview. Internet RFC 1633.

Braden, R., Zhang, L., Berson, S., Herzog, S., & Jamin, S. (1997). Resource ReSerVation Protocol (RSVP)—Version 1. Functional Specification. Internet RFC 2205.

Deering, S. E. (1998). Multicast routing in internetworks and extended LANs. *Proceedings of SIGCOMM ACM Special Interest Group on Data Communication '88,* 55–64. New York: ACM Press.

Deering, S. E., & Hinden, R. (1998). Internet Protocol, version 6 (IPv6) specification. Internet RFC 2460.

Dierks, T., & Allen, C. (1999). The TLS Protocol, version 1.0. Internet RFC 2246.

Dijkstra, E. W. (1959). A note on two problems in connection with graphs. *Numerische Mathematik, 1,* 269–271.

Droms, R. (1997). Dynamic host configuration protocol. Internet RFC 2131.

Egevang, K., & Francis, P. (1994). The IP network address translator (NAT). Internet RFC 1631.

Estrin, D., Farinacci, D., Helmy, A., Thaler, D., Deering, S., Handley, M., Jacobson, V., Liu, C., Sharma, P., & Wei, L. (1997). Protocol Independent Multicast-Sparse Mode (PIM-SM): Protocol specification. Internet RFC 2117.

Fenner, W. (1997). Internet Group Management Protocol, version 2. Internet RFC 2236.

Fielding, R., Gettys, J., Mogul, J., Frystyk, H., Masinter, L., Leach, P., & Berners-Lee, T. (1999). Hypertext Transfer Protocol—HTTP/1.1. Internet RFC 2616.

Fuller, V., Li, T., Yu, J., & Varadhan, K. (1993). Classless inter-domain routing (CIDR): An address assignment and aggregation strategy. Internet RFC 1519.

Jacobsen, V. (1988). Congestion avoidance and control. *Proceedings of Association of Computing Machinery SIGCOM ACM Special Interest Group on Data Communication '88,* pp. 314–329. New York: ACM Press.

Kent S., & Atkinson, R. (1998). Security architecture for the Internet protocol. Internet RFC 2401.

Klensin, J. (Ed). (2001). Simple mail transfer protocol. Internet RFC 2821.

Malkin, G. (1998). RIP version 2. Internet RFC 2453.

Metcalfe, R. M., & Boggs, D. R. (1976). Ethernet: Distributed packet switching for local computer networks. *Communications of the ACM, 19,* 395–404.

Mockapetris, P. (1987a). Domain names—concepts and facilities. Internet RFC 1034.

Mockapetris, P. (1987b). Domain names—Implementation and specification. Internet RFC 1035.

Moy, J. (1994). Multicast extensions to OSPF. Internet RFC 1584.

Moy, J. (1998). OSPF version 2. Internet RFC 2328.

Perkins, C. (Ed.). (1996). IP mobility support. Internet RFC 2002.

Plummer, D. C. (1982). An Ethernet address resolution protocol. Internet RFC 826.

Postel, J. (Ed.). (1980). User datagram protocol. Internet RFC 768.

Postel, J. (Ed.). (1981a). Internet protocol—DARPA Internet program protocol specification. Internet RFC 791.

Postel, J. (Ed.). (1981b). Transmission control protocol—DARPA Internet program protocol specification. Internet RFC 793.

Postel, J. (1981c). Internet Control Message Protocol—DARPA Internet program protocol specification. Internet RFC 792.

Postel, J., & Reynolds, J. K. (1985). File transfer protocol (FTP). Internet RFC 959.

Rekhter, Y., & Li, T. (1995). A border gateway protocol 4 (BGP-4). Internet RFC 1771.

Rescorla, E., & Schiffman A. (1999). The secure hypertext transfer protocol. Internet RFC 2660.

Rosen, E., Viswanathan, A., & Callon R. (2001). Multiprotocol label switching architecture. Internet RFC 3031.

Saltzer, J. H., Reed, D. P., & Clark, D. D. (1984). End-to-end arguments in system design. *ACM Transactions on Computer Systems, 2,* 277–288.

Schulzrinne, H., Casner S., Frederick R., & Jacobson V. (1996). RTP: A transport protocol for real-time applications. Internet RFC 1889.

SET Secure Electronic Transaction LLC (1997). SET Secure Electronic Transaction (TM), version 1.0, May 31, 1997—Book 1: Business description.

Simpson, W. (Ed). (1994). The point-to-point protocol (PPP). Internet RFC 1661.

Vetter, R. J. (1995). ATM concepts, architectures, and protocols. *Communications of the ACM, 38,* 30–38.

Waitzman, D., Partridge, C., & Deering, S. (1998). Distance vector multicast routing protocol. Internet RFC 1075.

Note: The Requests for Comment (RFCs) cited in this chapter are from the Internet Engineering Task Force and are available online on its Web site: http://www.ietf.org/rfc.html

TCP/IP Suite

Prabhaker Mateti, *Wright State University*

INTRODUCTION

It is difficult to imagine modern living without the Internet. It connects all kinds of computers systems from supercomputers, costing millions of dollars, to personal computers, worth no more than a couple of hundred. The networks that connect them are varied, from wireless to wired, from copper to fiber. All of this is enabled by protocols and software collectively known as the *TCP/IP Internet protocol suite* or simply TCP/IP.

TCP/IP is an open system. Its protocol specifications are public documents freely downloadable. Many of the implementations of the protocols are also open source. TCP/IP details constitute one or more college courses on computer networks. Entire textbooks have been written on the topic that this chapter is attempting to cover. Our goal is to present the practical TCP/IP landscape as it is today. This chapter describes the core protocols known as IP; TCP; essential protocols named UDP, ARP, ICMP, and DNS; and a few application protocols based on these. This chapter also highlights the security issues.

LAYERS

A computer system communicates with another system by sending a stream of bytes. The communication is actually between a process running on one system and one running on the other system. The two processes communicate information in a preagreed form known as a protocol. Computer protocols are is easier to understand as a stack of layers, each layer providing the functionality needed by the layer above it. In each layer, there are one or more protocols. There are three models of layers: the OSI, the DoD, and the "hourglass" models.

The OSI Model

The OSI model is officially recognized by the ISO (International Standards Organization). The OSI (open systems interconnection) model of computer networks has seven layers.

1. The bottom-most layer provides the physical means of carrying the stream of bits. Ethernet, Fast Ethernet, Wireless 802.11, T-carrier, DSL (digital subscriber line), and ATM are examples of this layer. All media are considered functionally equivalent. The differences are in speed, convenience, and cost. Converters from one media to another exist and make it possible to have different physical layers in a computer network.
2. The data link layer takes the raw stream of bits of the physical layer and, using its encoding functionality, sends and receives a meaningful message unit called a frame and provides error detection functions. A frame includes checksum, source and destination addresses, and data. The frame boundaries are special patterns of bits. Software of this layer will retransmit a frame if it is damaged, say because of a burst of noise on the physical layer. The data link layer is divided into the media access control (MAC) sublayer, which controls how a computer on the network gains access to the data and permission to transmit it, and the logical link control (LLC) sublayer, which controls frame synchronization,

flow control, and error checking. The data link layer describes the specification of interface cards to specific types of networks (e.g., Ethernet, and token ring). Example protocols from the TCP/IP suite that occupy this layer are SLIP and PPP.
3. The network layer accepts messages from the source host, converts them into packets of bytes, and sends them through the data link. This layer deals with how a route from the source to the destination is determined. This layer also deals with congestion control. The IP, address resolution protocol (ARP), reverse ARP (RARP), Internet control message protocol (ICMP), and IGMP belong to this layer.
4. The transport layer transfers data and is responsible for host-to-host error recovery and flow control. The TCP and UDP belong to this layer. UDP provides "connectionless service" and TCP provides "connection-oriented service."
5. The session layer establishes, manages, and terminates connections between the programs on the two hosts that are communicating. The concepts of ports and connections belong to this layer.
6. The presentation layer provides independence from possibly different data representations of the host machines. The HTTP (hypertext transfer protocol), FTP (file transfer protocol), telnet, DNS, SNMP (simple network management protocol), NFS (network file system), and so on belong to this layer.
7. The application layer supports the end-user invoked programs. FTP, HTTP, IMAP (Internet Message Access Protocol), NTP (Network Time Protocol), POP (Post Office Protocol), rlogin (Remote Login), SMTP (Simple Mail Transfer Protocol), SNMP, SOCKS, telnet, X-Window, Web services, and so on are part of this layer.

The DoD Model

The practical world of TCP/IP networking was in full use by the time the OSI model was formulated. Its unofficial model is referred to as the TCP/IP model, the DoD (U.S. Department of Defense) model, or even more simply the Internet model. The DoD model organizes the networks into four layers.

1. The link (or network access) layer deals with delivery over physical media. This layer maps to the data link and physical layers of the OSI model.
2. The network (or Internet) layer deals with delivery across different physical networks that connect source and destination machines. IP, ICMP, and IGMP are in this layer.
3. The transport (or host-to-host) layer deals with connections, flow control, retransmission of lost data, and so on. TCP, UDP are in this layer.
4. The application (or process) layer deals with user-level services, such as SMTP, FTP, rlogin, SSH, SSL, POP, and HTTP. This layer corresponds to the session, presentation and application layers of the OSI model.

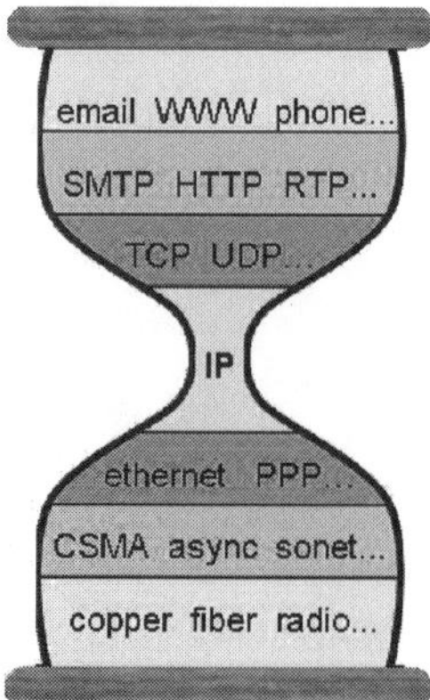

Figure 1: The hourglass model.

The Hourglass Model

Internet protocols can be described as following an hourglass model (Figure 1) with IP at the neck of the hourglass. The hourglass illustrates dependencies among the underlying networks, IP, and the applications.

Protocol Stack

The computer network literature talks of protocol stacks. Each item in the stack is a layer of software that implements a collection of protocols. In Figure 2, the relative heights indicate the level of functionality and the dependency of the layers. Except for the layer marked "physical" all others are software layers. The protocol stack is an integral component in a modern operating system.

In each protocol, there is a stream of bytes known as a frame, a datagram, a packet, or a segment depending on the "level." The data unit of each layer is encapsulated by the layer below it, similarly to how sheets of paper are enclosed in an envelope. Each layer adds control information typically prefixed to the data before passing on to the lower layer. An application data unit (AP) is encapsulated by the TCP layer, which prefixes a TCP header TCPH as (TCPH (AP)). The IP layer encapsulates it as (IPH (TCPH (AP))), where IPH is the IP header. Assuming Ethernet, it encapsulates it as (EH (IPH (TCPH (AP))) FSC), where EH is the Ethernet header and FSC is a frame check sequence generated by the Ethernet hardware.

Lower Layers

The OSI physical, data link, and network layers are collectively called the lower layers. In this section, we describe a few prominent entries from the lower layers.

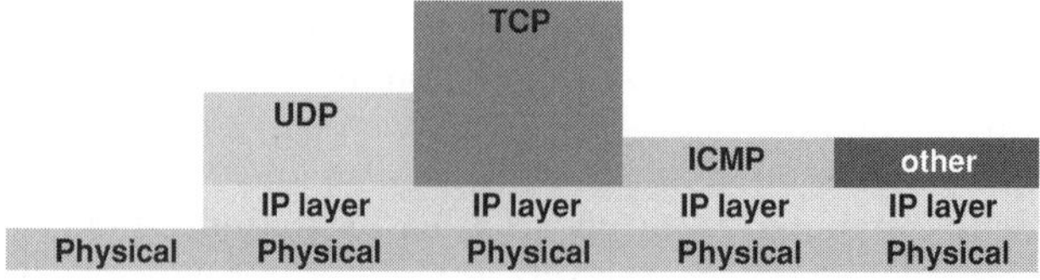

Figure 2: Protocol stack.

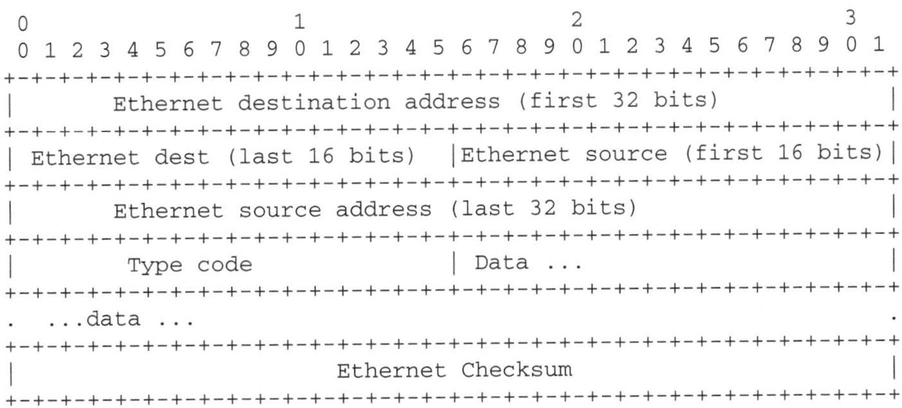

```
0                   1                   2                   3
0 1 2 3 4 5 6 7 8 9 0 1 2 3 4 5 6 7 8 9 0 1 2 3 4 5 6 7 8 9 0 1
+-+-+-+-+-+-+-+-+-+-+-+-+-+-+-+-+-+-+-+-+-+-+-+-+-+-+-+-+-+-+-+-+
|       Ethernet destination address (first 32 bits)            |
+-+-+-+-+-+-+-+-+-+-+-+-+-+-+-+-+-+-+-+-+-+-+-+-+-+-+-+-+-+-+-+-+
| Ethernet dest (last 16 bits)  |Ethernet source (first 16 bits)|
+-+-+-+-+-+-+-+-+-+-+-+-+-+-+-+-+-+-+-+-+-+-+-+-+-+-+-+-+-+-+-+-+
|       Ethernet source address (last 32 bits)                  |
+-+-+-+-+-+-+-+-+-+-+-+-+-+-+-+-+-+-+-+-+-+-+-+-+-+-+-+-+-+-+-+-+
|        Type code              | Data ...                      |
+-+-+-+-+-+-+-+-+-+-+-+-+-+-+-+-+-+-+-+-+-+-+-+-+-+-+-+-+-+-+-+-+
.  ...data ...                                                  .
+-+-+-+-+-+-+-+-+-+-+-+-+-+-+-+-+-+-+-+-+-+-+-+-+-+-+-+-+-+-+-+-+
|                    Ethernet Checksum                          |
+-+-+-+-+-+-+-+-+-+-+-+-+-+-+-+-+-+-+-+-+-+-+-+-+-+-+-+-+-+-+-+-+
```

Figure 3: Ethernet frame.

Ethernet

Ethernet can support IP and other protocols simultaneously. There are variations of Ethernet, and the plain Ethernet now refers to 10-megabits-per-second (Mbps) transmission speed, Fast Ethernet refers to 100 Mbps, and Gigabit Ethernet refers to 1000 Mbps. The media varieties include the current twisted pair (100Base-T, with RJ45 connectors), the original thick coaxial system (10base5), thin coaxial (10base2), and fiber optic systems (10basesF). Ethernet has been standardized by the Institute of Electrical and Electronics Engineers as IEEE 802.3.

Ethernet Frames. We describe the content of data units as a rectangular diagram such as the one shown in Figure 3. The width of such a diagram is always 32 bits, numbered from 00 to 31. The unit's digits of these bit indices are shown in the second row and the tens digits are shown in the first row.

An Ethernet controller is assigned a 48-bit MAC address by the factory. For communication among humans, the MAC address is written with each byte in hexadecimal, separating bytes with either a hyphen or a colon, as in 00-0A-E6-9B-27-AE. Every Ethernet frame has a 14-byte header that includes the MAC addresses of the source and destination and a 2-byte type code (see Figure 3). The type code identifies the protocol family (such as IP, ARP, and NetBEUI). The data field is from 46 to 1500 bytes in length. Following the data, there is a checksum computed by the Ethernet controller for the entire frame. Every device is expected to listen for Ethernet frames containing their destination address. All devices also listen for Ethernet frames with a wild-card destination address of FF-FF-FF-FF-FF-FF, called a broadcast address. When these packets are received by the Ethernet network interface card (NIC), it computes the checksum and throws the packet away if an error is detected by the checksum. If the type code is IP, the Ethernet device driver passes the data portion of the frame up to the IP layer of the OS. Under OS control, the NIC can be put into a so-called promiscuous state wherein the NIC listens to all frames regardless of their destinations.

Unswitched (Shared) Networks. All hosts attached to an Ethernet are connected to a shared signaling medium. Ethernet signals are transmitted serially, one bit at a time, over the shared medium that every attached host can observe. When a frame is sent out on the Ethernet, every controller on the local unswitched network can see the frame. Thus, Ethernet is a broadcast medium. To send data, a host waits for the channel to become idle and then transmits its frame. All hosts on the network contend equally for the transmission opportunity. Access to the shared medium is governed by the MAC mechanism based on the carrier sense multiple access with collision detection (CSMA/CD) system. This ensures that access to the network channel is fair and that no single host can lock out other hosts. If two or more devices try to transmit at the same instant, a transmit collision is detected, and the devices wait a random (but short) period before trying to transmit again.

Switched Networks. Today a typical end user connects to a full duplex switched Ethernet that uses switches instead of hubs to connect individual hosts or segments. A hub is an OSI physical layer device. It transmits the frames received from one port to all other ports it has. A switch is an OSI data link layer or network layer device. It builds ("learns") a table of ports and the MAC address it is connected to, reads the destination address of each frame, and forwards a frame it receives to only the port connected to the destination MAC address. Switched Ethernets extend the bandwidth by replacing the shared medium of legacy Ethernet with a dedicated segment for each station. Switched networks use either twisted pair or fiber optic cabling, with separate conductors for sending and receiving data. Collision detection is not necessary because the station and the switch are the only devices that can access the medium. End stations and the switch can transmit at will achieving a collision-free environment. Switched Ethernets also mitigate sniffing. However, many commercial switches can be "overwhelmed" into behaving as though they are hubs.

IEEE 802.11 a/b/g Wireless Networks

This section briefly describes wireless networks known as the IEEE 802.11 family (http://www.ieee802.org/11/). For a detailed treatment, read chapter 44: Wireless Local Area Networks. The 802.11a operates at a theoretical maximum

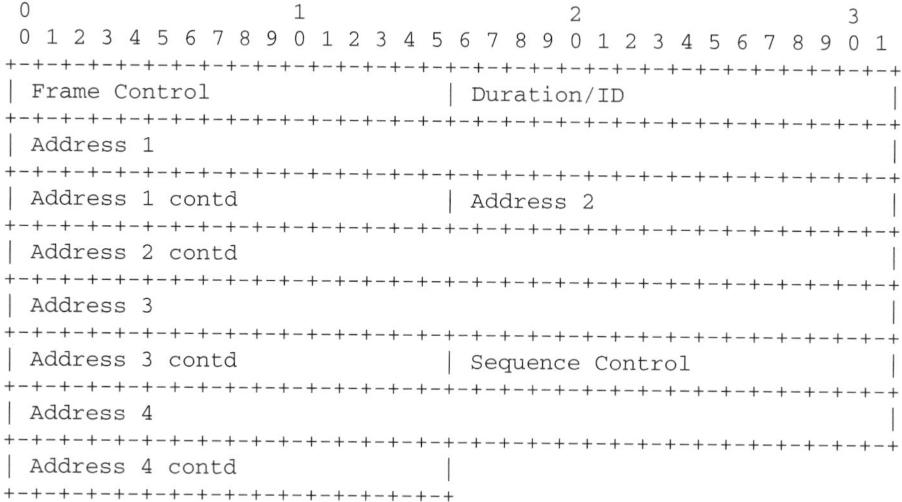

Figure 4: An IEEE 802.11 MAC header.

speed of 54 Mbps, 802.11b at 11 Mbps, and 802.11g at 54 Mbps.

Stations and Access Points. A wireless network station provides a radio link to another station. The station has a MAC address, a world-wide-unique 48-bit number, assigned to it at the time of manufacture, just as wired network cards do. An *access point* (AP) is a station that provides frame distribution service to stations associated with it. Each AP has a 0- to 32-byte-long service set identifier (SSID) that is used to segment the airwaves for usage. The AP itself is typically connected by wire to a LAN.

Frames. A dot-11 frame consists of a MAC header (see Figure 4) followed by a frame body of 0 to 2312 bytes and an FCS. There are three classes of frames. The *management* frames establish and maintain communications. The *control* frames help in the delivery of data. The *data* frames encapsulate the OSI network layer packets. These contain the source and destination MAC address, the BSSID, and the TCP/IP datagram.

Authentication and Association. Data can be exchanged between the station and AP only after a station is authenticated and associated with an AP. The association is a two-step process. A station that is currently unauthenticated and unassociated listens for management frames known as Beacon frames. The station and the AP mutually authenticate themselves by exchanging authentication management frames. In the second step, the station sends an association request frame, to which the AP responds with an association response frame that includes an association ID to the station. A station can be authenticated with several APs at the same time but associated with at most one AP at any time.

WEP and IEEE 802.11i. Wired equivalent privacy (WEP) is a shared-secret key system encrypting the payload part of the frames transmitted between a station and an AP. The WEP is intended to protect wireless communication from eavesdropping and to prevent unauthorized access to a wireless network. Unfortunately, WEP is insecure. The IEEE 802.11i was ratified in 2004. It provides robust encryption and authentication.

Asynchronous Transfer Mode

Asynchronous transfer mode (ATM) is widely deployed as a backbone technology. ATM uses 53-byte fixed-length packets called cells for transport. A 48-byte payload divides the data into different types. The ATM layer contains 5 bytes of additional information, referred to as overhead. Information is divided among these cells, transmitted, and then reassembled at their final destination. ATM is connection oriented. ATM itself consists of a series of layers. Its physical layer is based on various transmission media that range in speed from kilobits per second to gigabits per second. The layer known as the adaptation layer holds the bulk of the transmission.

Serial Line Internet Protocol

A serial network is a link between two computers over a serial line, which can be a dial-up connection over telephone lines or a direct connection between the serial ports of two computers. Serial line Internet protocol (SLIP; RFC 1055) defines the encapsulation protocol, just as an Ethernet frame envelopes an IP packet. Unlike Ethernet, SLIP supports only the IP and not multiple protocols across a single link. The serial link is manually connected and configured, including the specification of the IP address. SLIP provides no mechanisms for address negotiation, error correction, or compression. However, many SLIP implementations record the states of TCP connections at each end of the link, and use header compression that reduces the size of the combined IP and TCP headers from 40 to 8 bytes.

Point-to-Point Protocol

Point-to-point protocol (PPP; RFC 1661, RFC 2153) replaces the older SLIP, and is an encapsulating protocol for IP and other protocol datagrams over serial links. The encapsulation and framing adds 2, 4, or 8 bytes depending on the options chosen. PPP includes a link control protocol

(LCP) that negotiates the encapsulation format, sizes of packets, authentication methods, and other configuration options. The CCP (compression control protocol) used by PPP negotiates encryption. The IP control protocol (IPCP) included in the PPP configures the IP address and enables the IP protocol on both ends of the point-to-point link.

Point-to-Point Tunneling Protocol

Point-to-point tunneling protocol (PPTP) encapsulates PPP packets into IP datagrams. Its use is in providing virtual private networks (VPN). After the initial PPP connection to a PPTP server, a PPTP tunnel and a PPTP control connection are created. Tunneling is the process of sending packets of a certain protocol embedded in the packets of another protocol. PPTP uses an enhanced generic routing encapsulation (GRE) mechanism to provide a flow- and congestion-controlled encapsulated datagram service for carrying PPP packets.

INTERNET PROTOCOL

The details of IP and TCP are not directly experienced by the ordinary user unless a network sniffer is used. Nevertheless, it is crucial to understand these before attempting to understand the application protocols.

IP [RFC 791] delivers a sequence of bytes from a source host S to a destination host D, even when the hosts are on different networks, geographically vastly separated. The byte sequence and the destination are given to the IP layer by the upper layer. The IP layer forms an IP datagram from the sequence. An IP datagram consists of an IP header followed by a transport layer data. The IP layer software discovers routes that the packet can take from S to various intermediate nodes, known as routers, ultimately arriving at D. Thus, IP is routable. Each datagram travels independently even when the host S wishes to send several datagrams to D; each datagram delivery is made independently of the previous ones. The route that each packet takes may change. The sender, the receiver, and intermediary routers treat a datagram independently of others. Thus, IP is connectionless. The IP layer is designed deliberately not to concern itself with guaranteed delivery (i.e., packets may be lost or duplicated), but instead it is a "best effort" system. The ICMP described later aids in this effort.

IP Addresses

An operating system during boot-up assigns a unique 32-bit number known as its IP address to each NIC located in the host system. There is no rigid relationship between the Ethernet MAC address and the IP address. The IP address is obtained either by looking it up in a configuration file or via dynamic host configuration protocol (DHCP). The IP addresses are carefully controlled worldwide. The IANA, Internet Assigned Numbers Authority (www.iana.org), assigns the so-called public IP addresses to organizations and individuals upon application.

Dotted Quads and Octets

IP addresses are typically written in a dotted-quad notation, such as a.b.c.d, where a is the first byte, b the second, c the third, and d the fourth byte. Each of a to d is an octet, a number in the range 0 to 255.

Three address ranges known as class A, class B, and class C are of importance. In a class A address, the 0-th bit is always a 0, bits 1 through 7 identify the network, and bits 8 through 31 identify the host, permitting 2^{24} hosts on the network. In a class B address, the bit 0 is always a 1, bit 1 is always a 0, bits 2 through 15 identify the network, and bits 16 through 31 identify the host, permitting 2^{16} hosts on the network. In a class C address, bits 0 and 1 are both 1 always, bit 2 is a 0 always, bits 3 through 23 identify the network, and bits 24 through 31 identify the host, permitting 2^8 hosts on the network.

CIDR Nomenclature /24

Note that in each range of IP addresses assigned to a LAN segment, we use the smallest IP address to refer to the network itself, and the highest address as the broadcast address for the segment.

The classless interdomain routing (CIDR) model, first published in 1993, solves the problems of efficient utilization of IP address space (RFC 1520). Class C, with a maximum of 254 host addresses, is too small, whereas class B is too large to be densely populated, and making routing tables more compact.

A subnet is a collection of hosts whose IP addresses match in several bits indicated by the ones in a sequence of 32 bits known as a subnet mask, also written in the dotted-decimal notation. Thus, 255.255.255.0 is a mask of 24 ones followed by 8 zeroes. Because of this structure, the mask is also written as /24. Nodes and routers use the mask to identify the address of the network on which the specific host resides. The address of the network is the bitwise AND of the IP address and the mask. The host ID is the bitwise AND of the IP address and the complement of the mask. Occasionally, a network node X needs to discover certain information from other nodes, but the node X does not know the addresses of these others. In such situations, X broadcasts using special destination IP addresses. The direct broadcast address of X is the address whose host ID is all ones and whose network address equals that of X. The limited broadcast address is 255.255.255.255.

Public and Private Address Ranges

The following three blocks of the IP address space is intended for private internets: 10.0.0.0 to 10.255.255.255 (10/8 prefix, class A) 172.16.0.0 to 172.31.255.255 (172.16/12 prefix), and 192.168.0.0 to 192.168.255.255 (192.168/16 prefix, class C). That is, on the Internet at large, there must never be IP packets whose source or destination addresses are from the above ranges.

Most operating systems are internally structured to depend on the presence of a network layer. To facilitate this, the address 127.0.0.1 is assigned as the so-called address of the localhost (spelled as one word) and 127.0.0.0 as the localnetwork (spelled as one word). Packets sent to this address do not actually travel onto the external network. They simply appear as received on the local (artificial) device. When a machine is physically moved from one network to another, we must reassign an IP address that belongs to the new network. This is one of the problems that mobile IP solves.

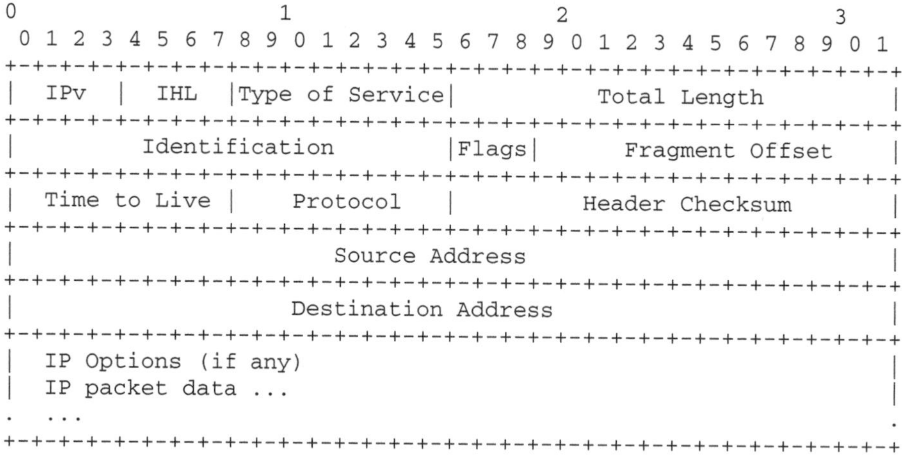

Figure 5: IP header.

IP Header

An IP header is a sequence of bytes that the IP layer software prefixes to the data it receives from the higher layers. The resulting IP header plus the data is given to the lower layer (e.g., the Ethernet card device driver). The byte layout of IP headers is shown in Figure 5. The header may or may not have the IP Options filed. Except for this field, all other fields are fixed in length as shown. Minimally (i.e., without the options), the IP header is 20 bytes in length. With IP options, an IP header can be as long as 60 bytes. IPv is the version number of the protocol; currently it is 4. IP version 6 is discussed later. The value of IHL multiplied by 4 is the length of the IP header in bytes. The type of service field specifies the "relative urgency" or importance of the packet. Total length is a 2-byte field giving the length, in bytes, of the entire packet including the header, options (if any), and the packet data.

Thus, the maximum length of an IP datagram is 65535 bytes. (IP over Ethernet limits this to 1500.) The identification field, flags, and fragment offset are used to keep track of the pieces when a datagram must be split up as it travels from one router to the next. IP fragmentation is discussed further below. The time to live (TTL) is a number that is decremented by 1 whenever the datagram passes through a router node. When it goes to 0, the datagram is discarded, and an error message is sent back to the source of this packet. The protocol field identifies the protocol of the data area. The header checksum field is a one's complement arithmetic sum of the entire header viewed as a sequence of 16-bit integers. The source address is the datagram's sender IP address, and destination address is the IP address of the intended recipient. The IP options may or may not be present. When present, its size can be one or more bytes.

Routing Protocols

When the source S and the destination D are on the same network, we have a direct delivery of the packet that does not involve routers. When the two hosts are not on the same network, in general, there can be multiple paths between the source and destination. Because of failures, maintenance, and other reasons, the intermediate nodes known as routers may come on or off during the delivery of packets. Thus, consecutive packets sent by a host S to a destination D may (have to) travel entirely disjoint routes depending on how the network is connected. The typical network host has only one NIC and hence is on only one network, and sending and receiving of network traffic is secondary to its main functionality.

Routers are specialized computer systems whose primary function (often their sole function) is to route network traffic. Routers must have multiple NICs, each on a separate network. A router examines the destination IP address of a packet and consults its routing tables that record information regarding where to deliver a packet next so that definite progress is made in moving the packet closer to its final destination. Routers are layer 3 devices.

Every network host (including routers) has a routing table, which can be visualized as a table of two columns: To send the packet to a final destination given in column 1, send the packet to the next hop whose IP address is given in column 2. The size of such a table can be greatly reduced by parametrizing the column 1 by its network address and also by including a default row in the table that acts as a catch-all. The default row indicates the next hop IP address for any packet whose destination network address does not match that of any other row. Once the next hop IP address is determined, the router uses the lower layer address (such as the Ethernet MAC) to deliver the packet to the next hop.

The routing table of an ordinary host rarely changes from boot-up to shut down. The tables of routers, however, must be dynamic and adjust to changing conditions, perhaps by the millisecond, of the Internet. Routing protocols keep the routing tables up-to-date. The Internet is a network of autonomous networks. Interior gateway protocols (IGPs) maintain the routing tables within an autonomous network. Routing information protocol (RIP) and open shortest path first (OSPF) are examples of IGPs. Border gateway protocol (BGP) is the most common protocol in use for routing among autonomous networks.

IP Fragments

When datagrams are too large to be sent in a single IP packet, because of interface hardware limitations, for example, they can be split up by an intermediate router unless prohibited by the Don't Fragment flag. IP fragmentation occurs when a router receives a packet larger than the maximum transmission unit (MTU) of the next network segment. All such fragments will have the same identification field value, and the fragment offset indicates the position of the current fragment in the context of the pre-split-up packet. Intermediate routers are not expected to reassemble the fragments. The final destination will reassemble all the fragments of an IP packet and pass it to higher protocol layers (such as TCP or UDP).

Mobile IP

As the mobile network host moves, its point of attachment may change, and yet to maintain existing transport-layer connections, it must keep its IP address the same.

The mobile node uses two IP addresses. The home address is static and is used to identify TCP connections. The care-of address changes at each new point of attachment. Whenever the mobile node moves, it registers its new care-of address with its home agent. The home agent redirects the packets to the current care-of address by constructing a new IP header that contains the care-of address as the destination IP address. This new header encapsulates the original packet, causing the home address to have no effect on the routing of the encapsulated packet until it arrives at the care-of address. When the packet arrives at the care-of address, the effect of this "tunneling" is reversed so that the packet once again appears to have the home address as the destination IP address. Mobile IP discovery of the care-of address uses an existing standard protocol called *router advertisement* (RFC 1256). A router advertisement carries information about default routers, and in addition carries further information about one or more care-of addresses. Home agents and care-of agents typically broadcast these advertisements at regular intervals (say, once every few seconds). A mobile node that needs a care-of address will multicast a router solicitation. An advertisement also informs the mobile node whether the agent is a home agent, a care-of agent, or both and therefore whether it is on its home network or a care-of network and about special features provided by care-of agents (for example, alternative encapsulation techniques).

The registration of the new care-of address begins when the mobile node, possibly with the assistance of the care-of agent, sends a registration request to the home address. The home agent typically updates its routing table. Registration requests contain parameters and flags that characterize the tunnel through which the home agent will deliver packets to the care-of address. The triplet of the home address, care-of address, and registration lifetime is called a binding for the mobile node. The home agent authenticates that registration was originated by the mobile node.

Each mobile node and home agent compute an unforgeable digital signature using one-way hash algorithm MD5 [Message Digest 5 (RFC 1321)] with 128-bit keys on the registration message, which includes either a time stamp or a random number carefully generated. Occasionally a mobile node cannot contact its home agent. The mobile node tries to register with another home agent by using a directed broadcast IP address instead of the home agent's IP address as the target for the registration request.

TRANSMISSION CONTROL PROTOCOL

TCP (RFC 793, RFC 3168) offers a client process a connection to a server process. This connection needs to be established, as needed. Once this connection is established, the TCP protocol guarantees the correct (both in content and in order) delivery of the data. TCP sends its message content over the IP layer and can detect and recover from errors. TCP, however, does not guarantee any speed of delivery, even though it offers congestion control.

Ports and Connections

Port numbers are used by the transport layer for multiplex communication between several pairs of processes. To each message, this layer adds addresses, called port numbers. The port numbers would have been assigned by the OS to certain processes. Thus, a connection is uniquely identified by a quadruple: source and destination IP addresses and source and destination port numbers. In this context, we often say quintuple, including the specific protocol (TCP/UDP/etc.) in use as the fifth element to make it clear that the port namespaces for UDP and TCP are separate. The IP addresses are supplied by the IP layer.

The ports 0-1023 are reserved for specific well-known services provided by privileged processes. For example, HTTP officially uses port 80, telnet officially uses port 23, and DNS officially uses port 53. The *dynamic* or *private* ports range from 1024 to 65535. Client processes and non-standard services are assigned port numbers by the operating system at run time. On most computer systems, there is a list of these port numbers and service names in a file named etc/services.

Reliable Transmission

TCP requires that every segment include an acknowledgment of the last data segment received in the other direction. TCP is a *sliding window* protocol with time-out and retransmits. If the sender does not receive an acknowledgment within the time-out period, it retransmits the segment. Acknowledgments are piggybacked on reply data. The window size specifies the number of bytes the receiver has as buffer space. The sender continues to send and slides the window ahead as long as acknowledgments are being received for bytes within the window.

TCP messages, called *segments*, are sent as one or more IP datagrams. A TCP header follows the IP header, supplying information specific to the TCP protocol. Figure 4 contains the details of the TCP segment. The letters |U|A|P|R|S|F| in the fourth row of the segment are abbreviated names for control bit flags: URG, urgent pointer field significant, ACK, acknowledgment field significant; PSH, push function; RST, reset the connection; SYN, synchronize sequence numbers; and FIN, sender is finished with this connection. These are further explained below.

The sequence number, together with the acknowledgment number, serves as a ruler for the sliding window protocol. While establishing the connection, the SYN flag is set to 1, and the client and the server exchange their initial sequence numbers.

The acknowledgment number is valid only when the ACK bit is set. This field contains the value of the next sequence number the sender of the segment is expecting to receive. Once a connection is established, this is always included. The DataX number multiplied by 4 is the number of bytes in the TCP header. This indicates where the data begin. Window size is described under Congestion Control. Urgent pointer is valid when URG is 1. Its value is a positive offset from the sequence number in this segment. Options, if any, are given at the end of the TCP header and are always a multiple of 8 bits in length. All options are included in the checksum. An option can be just a single byte, or it can be a byte of option-kind, followed by a byte of option-length and the actual option-data bytes. The option-length counts the two bytes of option-kind and option-length as well as the option-data bytes.

State Diagram

A TCP server process starts its life by passively opening a port and starts to listen to connection attempts from clients. This process causes a number of changes in the information maintained by the TCP layer software. These transitions are described by the state diagram shown in Figure 5. Below we describe two handshakes that establish a connection and close a connection.

Three-Way Handshake

This establishes connection between the initiating node (say A, the client) and the receiving node (say B, the server) of packets as follows:

1. A: "I would like to talk to you, B." A sends a packet with SYN = 1, and the initial sequence number (ISN) chosen by A to B.
2. B: "OK, let's talk." B replies with a SYN+ACK packet (i.e., SYN = 1, ACK = 1, acknowledgment number = sequence number received +1, and SYN =1 with sequence number set to the ISN of the server). If B was unwilling, it responds with a RST = 1 packet refusing the request for service. At this point, the state of the connection is known as *half-open*.
3. A: "Thanks for agreeing!" A sends a packet with ACK = 1, acknowledgment number = ISN of B + 1, SYN = 0, sequence number = previous sequence number + 1. The sequence number for SYN = 1 can be a zero, but that is not secure, so the sequence number is randomly chosen.

Here is an example where the client is on port 1037 establishing a connection with a service on port 80 (typically HTTP).

SYN	ACK	src	dst	sequence-number	acknowledgement-number
1	0	1037	80	102723769	0
1	1	80	1037	1527857206	102723770
0	1	1037	80	102723770	1527857207

Four-Way Handshake

This terminates a previously established connection, between A and B, as follows:

1. A sends to B a packet with FIN = 1, which indicates "no more data from A." This flag is used when closing a connection down the normal way. The receiving host B enters the CLOSE WAIT state and starts the process of gracefully closing the connection. Each end of the connection sends a packet with the FIN = 1. The receiver is expected to acknowledge a received FIN packet by sending a FIN = 1 packet.
2. B sends to A a packet with ACK = 1, acknowledging the FIN packet received.
3. B sends to A another packet, but now with FIN = 1.
4. A sends to B a packet with ACK = 1. No further packets are exchanged.

So, four packets are used to close a TCP connection in the normal situation. This is a teardown of two *half-closes*.

Closing a connection can also be done by using the RST flag set to 1, which indicates to the receiver that a reset should occur. The receiving host accepts the RST packet provided the sequence number is correct, and enters the CLOSED state and frees any resource associated with this instance of the connection. The RST packet is not acknowledged. A host H sends a connection resetting RST packet if host X requested a connection to a nonexistent port p on host H, or for whatever reason (idle for a long time, or an abnormal condition, etc.), the host H (client or the sever) wishes to close the connection. Resetting is unilateral. Any new incoming packets for that connection will be dropped.

Timers

TCP depends on many timers that the host must maintain per (attempted) connection as it follows the state diagram (see Figure 7).

The connection establishment timer is started on receiving the first packet of the three-way handshake. A typical value of this timer is 75 s. If a time-out occurs, the connection is aborted.

A FIN-WAIT timer is started when there is a transition from the FIN-WAIT 1 state to the FIN-WAIT 2 state. The initial value of this timer is 10 min. If a packet with FIN = 1 is received, the timer is canceled. On expiration of the 10 min, the timer is restarted with a value of 75 s. The connection is dropped if no FIN packet arrives within this period.

TIMED-WAIT timer is started when the connection enters the TIMED-WAIT state. This is to allow all the segments in transit to be removed from the network. The value of the timer is usually set to 2 min. On expiration of the timer, the connection is terminated.

A retransmission timer is started when a segment is sent. Its value, known as RTO retransmission timeout, is dynamically computed (RFC 2988). If the timer expires before an ACK is received, the segment is resent, and the timer is restarted.

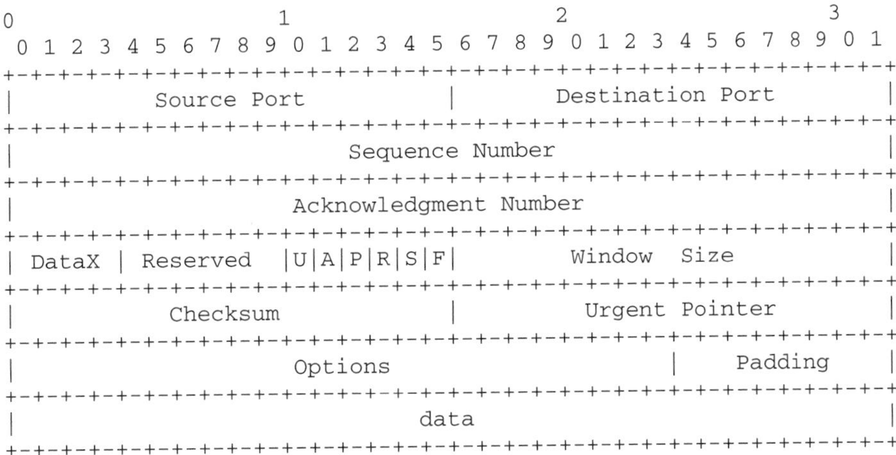

Figure 6: TCP header.

A persistence timer is used to detect if any window size updates were lost.

The KEEP-ALIVE timer lets us distinguish between the silences caused because there is no data to send from that caused by a broken connection. Setting a KEEP ALIVE timer allows TCP to periodically probe the other end. The default value of this timer is 2 hr. After the expiration of the timer, probes are sent to the remote end. The connection is dropped if the remote does not respond.

Flow and Congestion Control

The size of the sliding window is dynamically adjusted because of flow or congestion issues. Flow control prevents the sending process from overwhelming the receiving process. Each acknowledgment segment from a receiver advertises the buffer size it has available. If this size is larger than the current sliding window size, the sender can increase it. If it is smaller, the sender should decrease.

When a router begins to accumulate too many packets, it can send ICMP source quench messages to the senders of these packets. These messages should cause the rate of packet transmission to be slowed.

Congestion is a condition of significant delay caused by overload of datagrams at one or more routers. A congestion window size is dynamically computed by the sender based on network congestion. The TCP sliding window size is the minimum of the receiver window advertisement, and the congestion window. When a segment loss is detected, we assume that the loss is due to congestion, and the congestion window size is reduced by half. On observing that segments are not getting lost, the congestion window size is doubled. TCP congestion control has undergone major improvements resulting in TCP variants known as TCP Vegas, FastTCP, and so on that are soon to be adopted in actual implementations.

UDP, ICMP, DNS, ARP, AND RARP

User Datagram Protocol

UDP (RFC 768, 1980) is a connectionless transport protocol. It is a thin protocol on top of IP, providing high speed but low functionality. Delivery of UDP datagrams is not guaranteed. Nor can it detect duplicate datagrams. The UDP protocol is used mostly by application services where squeezing the best performance out of existing IP network is necessary, such as Trivial File Transfer (TFTP) and NFS and by the DNS.

The port numbers appearing in the UDP header (Figure 8) are similar to the TCP port numbers (see Figure 6), but the OS support required by UDP ports is much simpler and less resource consuming than that of TCP ports. The source port is the port of the sending process. When not meaningful, this field is set to 0. The destination port is the UDP port on the receiving machine, whose IP address is supplied by the IP layer. Length is the number of bytes in the datagram, including the UDP header and the data. Checksum is the 16-bit one's complement of the one's complement sum of the UDP header, the source and destination IP addresses obtained from the IP header, and the data, padded with zero bytes at the end (if necessary) to make a multiple of 2 bytes.

Internet Control Message Protocol

ICMP (RFC 792, 1981) manages and controls the IP layer, as in reporting network errors, such as a host or entire portion of the network being unreachable or a packet being directed at a closed port, reporting network congestion, assisting in trouble shooting, reporting time-outs, or forcing routing options. In general, much of the best effort in delivering IP datagrams is associated with ICMP. The purpose of the ICMP messages is to provide feedback and suggestions about problems, for example, when a datagram cannot reach its destination, when the gateway does not have the buffering capacity to forward a datagram, or when the gateway can direct the host to send traffic on a shorter route. To avoid the infinite regress, no ICMP messages are sent about ICMP messages. Also ICMP messages are sent only about errors in handling fragment zero of fragmented datagrams.

An ICMP message is sent as the data portion of an IP datagram. These IP datagrams are treated like all other IP datagrams. Each ICMP message begins with a 1-byte ICMP type field, which determines the format of the remaining data, a one-byte code field, and a 2-byte checksum. If the ICMP message is reporting an error, these 4 bytes are followed by the first 8 bytes of the IP datagram causing the error.

The popular network utilities ping and traceroute use ICMP. The ping command sends several echo requests, captures their echo replies, and displays statistics about speed and datagram loss. The traceroute utility constructs IP datagrams with well-chosen TTL values and collects the time-exceeded ICMP messages to map a route from the source to a destination IP address. ICMP helps improve the performance of the network. For example, ICMP redirect messages from a router inform a host that a different router is more optimal than it is for certain destinations.

Domain Name Service

Because of the mnemonic value, humans prefer to work with host names such as gamma.cs.wright.edu, where *gamma* is the name of the host, and *cs.wright.edu* is the name of the domain the host is in.

The DNS name space is a tree hierarchy (RFC 1035). The top-most subtrees are the top level domains such as .com, .edu, .net, and .org, and the country code domains such as .in, and .us. Subtrees of these are known as subdomains. The leaves are the individual hosts. A *fully qualified domain name* is the sequence of labels, separated by a dot, on the path from a node to the root of the tree.

A *domain name server* maintains the name space as a database. It can delegate the maintenance of any subdomain to another server. A delegated subdomain in the DNS is called a *zone*. The parent server keeps track of such delegations. There are 13 *root servers* (in 2004; visit http://www.root-servers.org) located in the United States and other countries. Each name server has authoritative information about one or more zones but may also have cached, but nonauthoritative, data about other parts of the database. A name server marks its responses to queries as authoritative or not.

The database is a collection of *resource records*, each of which contains a domain name and four attributes. The time-to-live (TTL) value indicates how long a nonauthoritative name server can cache the record. The class attribute of the record is "IN" for Internet. The third attribute, the record type A, AAAA, MX, and PTR, identifies what is stored as the fourth attribute, known as data value. The data of an A record is an IP address, of an AAAA record is an IPv6 address, and so on. The primary function is to answer a query to translate a fully qualified domain name into its IP address. This is done by retrieving the A record. A reverse look-up (also called an inverse query) is to find the host name given the IP address. This is done by retrieving the PTR record. Some network services use this to verify the identity of the client host. The mapping of names to addresses is not one-to-one. It is possible to associate a name with multiple IP addresses thus providing load distribution. A single IP address can be associated with multiple names, one being a *canonical* name and others perhaps more mnemonic thus providing host aliasing. The MX records map a host name to the canonical host name of the mail server and its IP address.

The DNS *resolver* is a piece of software. Every host is configured with at least one local name server N if it is to find hosts not listed in the etc/hosts file. Each host maintains a short cache table of fully qualified domain names to IP addresses. When a name is not found in either this file or this cache, the host enquires with N via the DNS protocol using the resolver. Either TCP or UDP can be used for DNS, connecting to server port 53. Ordinary DNS requests can be made with TCP, although UDP is used for normal operation. The protocol is stateless—all the information needed is contained in a single message.

An *iterative* DNS query to a name server D receives a reply with either the answer or the IP address of the next name server. If the name is in the local zone, the local name server N can respond to a query directly. Otherwise, N queries one of the root servers. The root server gives a *referral* with a list of name servers for the top-level domain of the query. N now queries a name server on this list and receives a list of name servers for the second-level domain name. The process repeats until N receives the address for the domain name. N then caches the record and returns the address or other DNS data to the querying host.

A *recursive* DNS query to D will make D obtain the requested mapping on behalf of the querying host. If D does not have the answer, it forwards the query to the next name server in the chain, and so on until either an answer is found or all servers are queried and hence returns an error code. Because recursive look-ups take longer and need to store many records, it is more efficient to provide a recursive DNS server for LAN users and an iterative server for Internet users.

Address Resolution Protocol

ARP (RFC 826, 1982) is typically used to determine the Ethernet MAC address of a device whose IP address is known (see Figure 9). This needs to be done only for outgoing IP packets, because IP datagrams must be Ethernet framed with the destination hardware address. The translation is performed with a table look-up.

Reverse ARP (RARP) (RFC 903) allows a host wishing to discover its own IP address to broadcast its Ethernet address and expect a server to reply with its IP address. The ARP cache accumulates as the host continues to network (see Table 1). If the ARP cache does not have an entry for an IP address, the outgoing IP packet is queued, and an ARP request packet that effectively requests "If your IP address matches this target IP address, then please let me know what your Ethernet address is" is broadcast. Once the table is updated because of receiving a response, all the queued IP packets can now be sent.

Table 1 A Small Portion of an ARP Cache

IP Address	Ethernet Address
130.108.2.23	08-00-69-05-28-99
130.108.2.1	00-10-2f-fe-c4-00
130.108.2.27	08-00-69-0d-99-12
130.108.2.20	08-00-69-11-cf-b9
130.108.2.10	00-60-cf-21-2c-4b
192.168.17.221	00-50-ba-5f-85-56
192.168.17.112	00-A0-C5-E5-7C-6E

The entries in the table expire after a set time period to account for possible hardware address changes for the same IP address. This change may have happened (e.g., because of the NIC being replaced).

ARP is an OSI layer-3 protocol, but it does not use an IP header. It has its own packet format as shown in Figure 7. The ARP request packet has zeroes in the target hardware address fields. It is broadcast on the local LAN without needing to be routed. The destination host sends back an ARP reply with its hardware address so that the IP datagram can now be forwarded to it by the router. An ARP response packet has the sender/target field contents swapped as compared to the request.

APPLICATIONS

Nearly all network applications are based on a client/server architecture where one process, the client, requests services from a second process, the server. Typically, the client and server processes are on different machines, but they need not be.

File Transfer Protocol, Telnet, and rlogin

The three application protocols described in this section are all based on TCP. They send authentication information and data in the clear (i.e., unencrypted) and hence are easily compromised by network sniffers. In addition, their authentication of host is simply the IP address. Consequently, utilities based on these protocols should not be used in situations where security is a concern. The SSH described later provides near equivalent functionality at a higher level of security.

File Transfer Protocol

FTP (RFC 959, 1985) uses two TCP connections, one called the control connection and the other the data connection. The client can issue a number of commands on the control connection that change various settings of the FTP session. All content transfer occurs on the data connection. The FTP client opens a control connection to port 21 of the FTP server machine. This connection persists the entire session. The format of data passed over the control connection is the same as that of telnet NVT. The GET command requests for the transfer of the contents that the server has (popularly known as downloading), and the PUT command requests the server to receive and store the contents that the client is about to send (popularly known as uploading). FTP is an insecure protocol. User name, password, and all data are transmitted in the unencrypted form.

Passive and Active modes of FTP

The data connection can be opened in two modes. In the active mode FTP, the server initiates a data connection as needed from its port 20 to a port whose number is supplied by the client via the PORT command. In the passive mode FTP, the server informs the client a port number higher than 1024 that the server has chosen, to which the

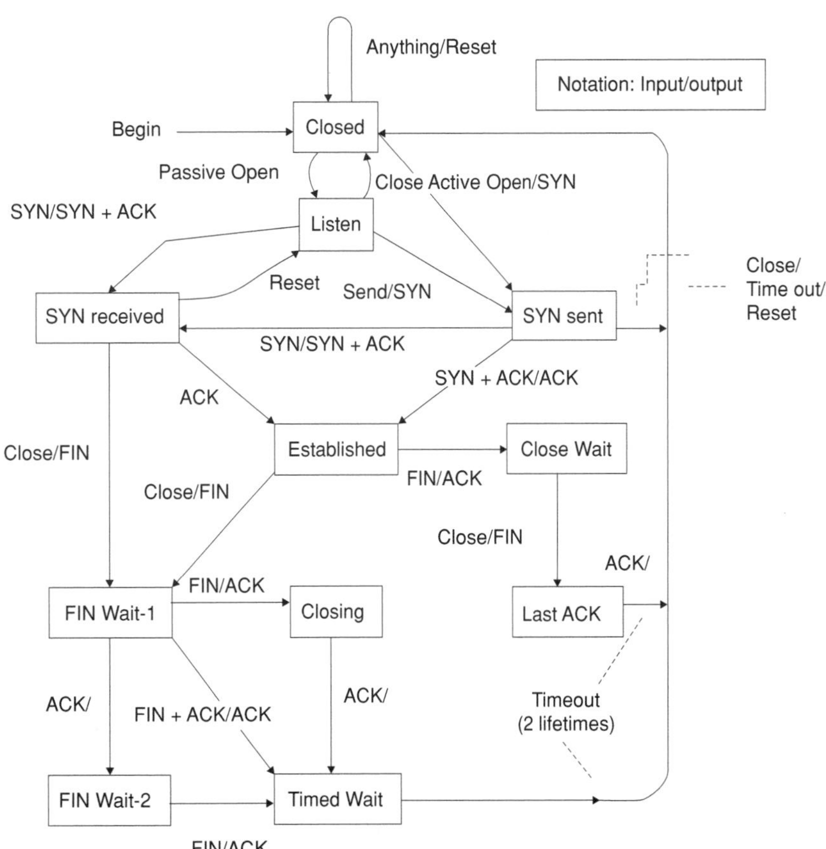

Figure 7: TCP state diagram.

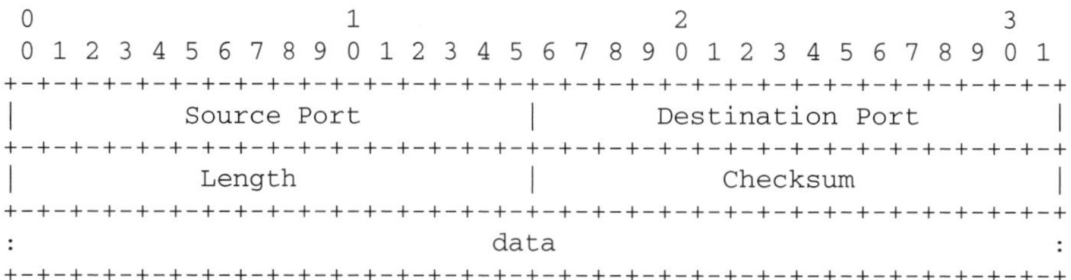

Figure 8: UDP header.

client initiates a data connection. Passive FTP is relevant in firewall setups that forbid initiation of a connection from an external host to the internal network.

Telnet

Telnet (RFC 854) establishes a TCP connection with a telnet server on the reserved port 23 and passes the keystrokes of the telnet client to the server and accepts the output of the server as characters to be displayed on the client. The server presents these keystrokes as input received from a pseudoterminal to the OS hosting the telnet server. Telnet defines a network virtual terminal (NVT) format as that which permits interoperability with machines that use different characters for common operations such as terminating a line and interrupting a run-away process. The telnet client typically maps the signal-generating keys of the keyboard to invoke the corresponding control functions of the NVT. The control functions are encoded as escape sequences of 2 bytes, the IAC (255), followed by the 1-byte code of the control function. Telnet uses the URGENT DATA mechanism of TCP to send control functions so that the telnet server can respond appropriately. Telnet is an insecure protocol. User name, password, and all data are transmitted in the unencrypted form.

rlogin

The rlogin protocol (RFC 1282) is similar in functionality to telnet and also operates by opening a TCP connection on the rlogin server machine at port 513. It is widely used between UNIX hosts because it provides transport of more of the UNIX terminal environment semantics than does the telnet protocol and because on many UNIX hosts it can be configured not to require user entry of passwords when connections originate from trusted hosts. Rlogin is an insecure protocol. User name, password, and all data are transmitted in the unencrypted form.

Secure Shell

SSH provides the functionality of telnet and rlogin but with greater security. There are three primary advantages in using ssh. (1) Telnet and rlogin do not authenticate the remote machine; SSH does. The SSH client maintains a database of server names and their authentication keys that the server offers the first time an SSH session is opened to the server. Subsequent SSH sessions compare the authentication key offered by the server with that stored in the client database. (2) The password that the user types as part of the login ritual is sent as clear text by telnet and rlogin; SSH sends it encrypted. (3) The data being sent and received by telnet and rlogin is also sent as clear text; SSH sends and receives it in encrypted form. The main disadvantages are the following. (1) Encryption and decryption consumes computing and elapsed time. (2) If the remote system has been legitimately reinstalled, and the installer was not careful to use the same authentication keys for the host, a false alarm may be raised. (3) SSH is susceptible to man-in-the-middle attack.

Dynamic Host Configuration Protocol

DHCP [RFC 2131, 1997] consists of a protocol for delivering host-specific configuration parameters from a DHCP server to a host and a mechanism for allocation of IP addresses to hosts. The IP configuration parameters that DHCP can supply include subnet mask, a list of default routers, TTL, and MTU. A typical host will use DHCP soon after booting into the OS to configure its network. DHCP assumes that the IP layer software will pass the packets delivered to the NIC of the host even though the IP address has not been assigned yet. DHCP has three mechanisms for IP address allocation. In automatic allocation, DHCP assigns a permanent IP address to a client. In dynamic allocation, DHCP leases an IP address to a client for a limited period (or until the client explicitly relinquishes the address). In manual allocation, the IP address is assigned manually but is conveyed to the client via DHCP. Dynamic allocation is the only one of the three mechanisms that allows automatic reuse of an address that is no longer needed by the client to which it was assigned.

Hypertext Transfer Protocol

HTTP (RFC 2616, 1999) is at the core of the World Wide Web. The Web browser on a user's machine and the Web server on a machine somewhere on the Internet communicate via HTTP using TCP usually at port 80. HTTPS (RFC 2660, 1999) is a secure version of HTTP. A Web browser displays a file of marked-up text with embedded commands following the syntactic requirements of the hypertext markup language (HTML). There are several ways of invoking these commands, the most common one being the mouse click. Most of the clickable links displayed by a Web browser are the so-called links that associate a URL (universal resource locators) with a visible piece of text or graphic. URLs have the following syntax:

scheme://[userName[:password@]]serverMachineName
[:port]/[path][/resource][?parm1=parma&parm2=
parmb].

```
0                   1                   2                   3
0 1 2 3 4 5 6 7 8 9 0 1 2 3 4 5 6 7 8 9 0 1 2 3 4 5 6 7 8 9 0 1
+-+-+-+-+-+-+-+-+-+-+-+-+-+-+-+-+-+-+-+-+-+-+-+-+-+-+-+-+-+-+-+-+
| Hardware Type                 | Protocol Type                 |
+-+-+-+-+-+-+-+-+-+-+-+-+-+-+-+-+-+-+-+-+-+-+-+-+-+-+-+-+-+-+-+-+
| HdwrAddr Len  | ProtoAddr Len | Operation Code                |
+-+-+-+-+-+-+-+-+-+-+-+-+-+-+-+-+-+-+-+-+-+-+-+-+-+-+-+-+-+-+-+-+
| Sender HdwrAddress (bytes 0,1,2,3)                            |
+-+-+-+-+-+-+-+-+-+-+-+-+-+-+-+-+-+-+-+-+-+-+-+-+-+-+-+-+-+-+-+-+
| Sender HdwrAddress (bytes 4,5)| Sender IP Address (bytes 0,1) |
+-+-+-+-+-+-+-+-+-+-+-+-+-+-+-+-+-+-+-+-+-+-+-+-+-+-+-+-+-+-+-+-+
| Sender IP Address (bytes 2,3) | Target HdwrAddress (bytes 0,1)|
+-+-+-+-+-+-+-+-+-+-+-+-+-+-+-+-+-+-+-+-+-+-+-+-+-+-+-+-+-+-+-+-+
| Target HdwrAddress (bytes 2,3,4,5)                            |
+-+-+-+-+-+-+-+-+-+-+-+-+-+-+-+-+-+-+-+-+-+-+-+-+-+-+-+-+-+-+-+-+
| Target IP Address (bytes 0,1,2,3)                             |
+-+-+-+-+-+-+-+-+-+-+-+-+-+-+-+-+-+-+-+-+-+-+-+-+-+-+-+-+-+-+-+-+
```

Figure 9: An ARP request/response packet.

A simple example of the above is http://www.cs.wright.edu/~pmateti/InternetSecurity, where the scheme was chosen to be http, the port defaults to 80, and the path given is ~pmateti/InternetSecurity. A click on such a link generates a request message from the browser process to the Web server process running on the remote machine www.cs.wright.edu, whose name is obtained from the link clicked. The browser then displays the page it receives from the server.

HTTP Message Format

The request and response are created according to the HTTP message format, which happens to be a sequence of human-readable lines of text. The first line identifies the message as a request or response. The subsequent lines are known as header lines until an empty line is reached. Following the empty line are lines that constitute the "entity body." Each header line can be divided into two parts, a left- and right-hand side, separated by a colon. The left-hand side names various parameters. The right-hand side provides their values. The request line has three components: a method (one of GET, POST, or HEAD), a URL, and the version number of HTTP (either 1.0 or 1.1) that the client understands. GET is the most common one among the methods. The POST method is used when the client sends data obtained from a user-filled HTML form. The HEAD method is used in program development. The response line also contains three components: HTTP/version-number, a status code (such as the infamous 404), and a phrase (such as Not Found, OK, or Bad Request). The entity body in a response message is the data, such as the content of a Web page or an image, that the server sends.

Authentication and Cookies

Web servers requiring user authentication send a `WWWAuthenticate:` header. The Web client prompts the user for a username and password, and sends this information in each of the subsequent request messages to the server. HTTP is stateless in that the HTTP server does not act differently to request based on previous requests. Occasionally, a Web service wishes to maintain a minor amount of historical record of previous requests. Cookies (RFC 29650 create a stateful session with HTTP requests and responses. The response from a server can contain a header line such as "Set-cookie: value." The client then creates a cookie stored on the client's storage. In subsequent requests sent to the same server, the client includes the header line "Cookie: value."

SECURITY

The TCP/IP suite has many design weaknesses so far as security and privacy are concerned, all perhaps because of the era (1980s) when the development took place; network attacks were unknown. For example, the ICMP redirect message, intended to improve routing performance, has often been used maliciously. In this section, we summarize some of these issues from a practical perspective. Some of these are protocol design weaknesses per se, whereas the rest are defects in the software that implements the protocols. All major OS have made improvements in their implementations of the protocol stack that mitigate or disable many of the attacks described below. Of course, the attack tools also improve.

Security Exploits

This section is an overview of security attacks in the core protocols. Space and scope considerations prevent us from discussing such attacks as the recent (2004) TCP reset attack leading to severe concerns in the routing protocol BGP used in large routers, and the Shrew denial of service attack exploiting the congestion control algorithms. Numerous chapters of this volume are devoted to a discussion of different subtopics of security. See, for example, chapters 137 (Hacking Techniques in Wired Networks), 138 (Hacking Techniques in Wireless Networks), and 150 (Network Attacks).

Sniffing

Sniffing is eavesdropping on the network. A (packet) sniffer is a wire-tap program. Sniffing is the act by machine S of making copies of a network packet sent by machine A intended to be received by machine B. Such sniffing, strictly speaking, is not a TCP/IP problem, but it is enabled by the near-universal choice of Ethernet, a broadcast media, as the physical and data link layers. Sniffing can be used for monitoring the health of a network as well as capturing the passwords used in telnet, rlogin, and FTP connections. Attackers sniff the data necessary in the exploits described below.

Depending on the equipment used in a LAN, a sniffer needs to be run either on the victim machine whose traffic is of interest or on some other host in the same subnet as the victim. In the normal mode, an NIC captures only those frames that match its own MAC address. In the so-called promiscuous mode, an NIC captures all frames that pass by it. The volume of such frames makes it a real challenge for an attacker to either immediately process all such frames fast or clandestinely store them for later processing.

An attacker at large on the Internet has other techniques that make it possible to install remotely a sniffer on the victim machine.

Illegal Packets

Packets containing "unexpected" values in some of the fields are illegal in the sense that a legitimate sender would not have constructed them. Software in the receiver ought to check for such illegal packets, but legacy software was not cautious. Attackers have written special programs that construct illegal packets and cause the receiving network hosts to crash or hang. The so-called Ping of Death attack of 1996 sent an ICMP echo request (ping) packet that was larger than the maximum permissible length (2^16-1).

TCP segments have a number of flags that have, collectively, a strong influence on how the segment is processed. However, not all the flags can be independently set or reset. For example, SYN FIN, SYN FIN PSH, SYN FIN RST, and SYN FIN RST PSH are all illegal combinations. Past implementations have accounted only for valid combinations, ignoring the invalid combinations as "will not happen."

An IP packet should not have source address and port equaling the destination address and port. The 1997 attack tool called *land* exploited this vulnerability.

IP Fragment Attacks

A well-behaving set of IP fragments is nonoverlapping. Malicious fragmentation involves fragments that have illegal fragment offsets. A fragment-offset value gives the index position of this fragment's data in a reassembled packet. For example, the fragments may be so crafted that the receiving host in its attempts to reassemble calculates a negative length for the second fragment. This value is passed to a function [such as memcpy()] that copies from/to memory, which takes the a negative number to be an enormous unsigned (positive) number. A pair of carefully crafted but malformed IP packets thus causes a server to "panic" and crash. The 1997 attack tool called *teardrop* exploited this vulnerability.

The RFCs require no intermediate router to reassemble fragmented packets. Obviously the destination must reassemble. Many firewalls do not perform packet reassembly in the interest of efficiency. These only consider the fields of individual fragments. Attackers create artificially fragmented packets to fool such firewalls. In a so-called tiny fragment attack, two fragments are created where the first one is so small that it does not even include the destination port number. The second fragment contains the remainder of the TCP header, including the port number. A variation of this is to construct the second fragment packet with an offset value less than the length of the data in the first fragment so that upon packet reassembly it overrides several bytes of the first fragment (e.g., if the first fragment was 24 bytes long, the second fragment may claim to have an offset of 20). Upon reassembly, the data in the second fragment overwrites the last 4 bytes of the data from the first fragment. If these were fragments of a TCP segment, the first fragment would contain the TCP destination port number, which is overwritten by the second fragment. Such techniques do not cause a crash or hang of a targeted system but can be used to bypass simple filtering done by some firewalls.

Fragmentation attacks are preventable. Unfortunately, in the IP layer implementations of nearly all OS, there are bugs and naïve assumptions in the reassembly code.

IP Address Spoofing

The IP layer of the typical OS simply trusts that the source address, as it appears in an IP packet is valid. It assumes that the packet it received indeed was sent by the host officially assigned that source address.

Replacing the true IP address of the sender (or, in rare cases, the destination) with a different address is known as IP spoofing. Because the IP layer of the OS normally adds these IP addresses to a data packet, a spoofer must circumvent the IP layer and talk directly to the raw network device. IP spoofing is used as a technique aiding an exploit on the target machine. Note that the attacker's machine cannot simply be assigned the IP address of another host T using ifconfig or a similar configuration tool. Other hosts, as well as T, will discover (through ARP, for example) that there are two machines with the same IP address.

IP spoofing is an integral part of many attacks. For example, an attacker can silence a host A from sending further packets to B by sending a spoofed packet announcing a window size of zero to A as though it originated from B.

TCP Sequence Number Prediction

TCP exploits are typically based on IP spoofing and sequence number prediction. In establishing a TCP connection, both the server and the client generate an initial sequence number (ISN) from which they will start counting the packets transmitted. Host Y accepts the packets from X only when correct SEQ/ACK numbers are used.

The ISN is (should be) generated at random and should be hard to predict. However, some implementations of the TCP/IP protocol make it rather easy to predict this sequence number. The attacker either sniffs the current SEQ+ACK of the connection or can algorithmically predict them.

Closing a Connection by FIN

The attacker constructs a spoofed FIN packet. It will have the correct SEQ numbers so that it is accepted by the targeted host. This host would believe the (spoofed) sender had no data left. Any packets that may follow from the legitimate sender would be ignored as bogus. The rest of the four-way handshake is also supplied by the attacker. A similar connection killing attack using RST is also well known.

Connection Hijacking

Suppose X and Y have a TCP connection. An attacker Z can send packets to Y spoofing the source address as X, at a time when X was silent. Y would accept these data and update ACK numbers. X may subsequently continue to send its segments using old SEQ numbers, as it is unaware of the intervention of Z. As a result, subsequent packets from X are discarded by Y. The attacker Z is now effectively impersonating X, using "correct" SEQ/ACK numbers from the perspective of Y. This results in Z hijacking the connection: host X is confused, whereas Y thinks nothing is wrong as Z sends "correctly synchronized" packets to Y. If the hijacked connection was running an interactive shell, Z can execute any arbitrary command that X could. Having accomplished his deed, a clever hijacker would bow out gracefully by monitoring the true X. He would cause the SEQ numbers of X to match the ACK numbers of Y by sending to the true X a segment that it generates of appropriate length, spoofing the sender as Y, using the ACK numbers that X would accept.

The SYN Flood

The SYN flood attack occurred in 1996. In the TCP protocol as designed, there is no limit set on the time to wait after receiving the SYN in the three-way handshake. An attacker initiates many connection requests with spoofed source addresses to the victim machine. The victim machine maintains data related to the connection being attempted in its memory. The SYN+ACK packets that the victim host sends are not replied to. Once the limit of such half-open connections is reached, the victim host will refuse further connection establishment attempts from any host until a partially opened connection in the queue is completed or times out. This effectively removes a host from the network for several seconds, making it useful at least as a stepping tool to other attacks, such as IP spoofing.

Storm Creation

There have been several attacks that generate enormous numbers of packets rendering (portions of) a network ineffective. The attackers send source spoofed packets to intermediary machines. These amplify the numbers of packets into a "storm."

ACK storms are generated in the hijack technique described above. A host Y, when it receives packets from X after a hijack has ended, will find the packets of X to be out of order. TCP requires that Y must send an immediate reply with an ACK number that it expects. The same behavior is expected of X. So, X and Y send each other ACK messages that may never end.

The attack tool of 1997, called *smurf* sends ICMP ping messages. There are three machines in smurfing: the attacker, the intermediary router, and the victim. The attacker sends to an intermediary an ICMP echo request packet with the IP broadcast address of the intermediary's network as the destination. The source address is spoofed by the attacker to be that of the intended victim. The intermediary puts it out on that network. Each machine on that network will send an ICMP echo reply packet to the source address. The victim is subjected to network congestion that could potentially make it unusable.

Legitimate applications or OS services can generate a storm of packets. On many systems, the standard services known as *chargen* that listens typically at port 19 and *echo* that listens typically at port 7 are enabled. *Chargen* sends an unending stream of characters intended to be used as test data for terminals. The *echo* service just echoes what it receives. It is intended to be used for testing reachability, identifying routing problems, and so on. An attacker sends a UDP packet to the port 19 with the source address spoofed to a broadcast address, and the source port spoofed to 7. The *chargen* stream is sent to the broadcast address and hence reaching many machines on port 7. Each of these machine will echo back to the victim's port 19. This ping-pong action generates a storm of packets.

A related attack called *fraggle* uses packets of UDP *echo* service in the same fashion as the ICMP echo packets.

ARP Poisoning

ARP poisoning is an attack technique that corrupts the ARP cache that the OS maintains with wrong Ethernet addresses for some IP addresses. An attacker accomplishes this by sending an ARP response packet that is deliberately constructed with a "wrong" MAC address. The ARP is a stateless protocol. Thus, a machine receiving an ARP response cannot determine if the response is because of a request it sent or not.

ARP poisoning enables the so-called man-in-the-middle attack that can defeat cryptographic communications such as SSH, SSL [see chapter 65: SSL/TLS (Secure Sockets Layer/Transport Layer Security)], and IPSec. An attacker on machine M inserts him- or herself between two hosts A and B by (1) poisoning A so that B's IP address is associated with M's MAC address, (2) poisoning B so that A's address is associated with M's MAC address, and (3) relaying the packets M receives A from/to B.

ARP packets are not routed, and this makes it very rewarding to the attacker if a router can be ARP poisoned.

Route Spoofing

An attacker can spoof routing information by three main mechanisms.

In the first mechanim, an attacker sends an ICMP redirect packet with the source address set to the regular router. The packet also contains the "new" router to use. An ICMP route redirect is normally sent by the default router to indicate that there is a shorter route to a specific destination. A host adds a host-route entry to its routing table after some checking all of which ineffective. Unlike ARP cache entries, host route entries do not expire. Name servers are obvious targets for this attack.

In a second way, RIP-based attacks work by broadcasting illegitimate routing information to passive RIP hosts and routers via UDP port 520. In both of the above cases, the redirection can be made to any host chosen by the attacker.

Third, source routing allows the sending host to choose a route that a packet must travel to get to its destination. Traffic coming back to that host will take the reverse route. The attacker designs a route so that the packets go through his site.

DNS Spoofing

The DNS answers that a host receives may have come from an attacker who sniffs a query and answers it with misleading data faster than the legitimate name server answers. The attacked host may in fact be a DNS server. Such DNS spoofing results in DNS cache poisoning, and all the clients of this server will receive false answers. During the reconnaissance stage of an attack, DNS zone transfers help map the targeted network. Some of these issues are specific to a software package called BIND that implements the DNS service. The DNS protocol is improved in the DNSSEC, which is expected to be deployed widely by adding authentication.

Covert Channels

Covert channels are the principle enablers in a distributed denial of service (DDoS) attack. A DDoS attacker covertly distributes (portions of) his attack tools over many machines spread across the Internet and later triggers these intermediary machines into beginning the attack and remotely coordinates the attack.

Covert channels are possible in nearly all the protocols of the TCP/IP suite. For example, ICMP echo request packets should have an 8-byte header and a 56-byte payload. ICMP echo requests should not be carrying any data. However, significantly larger ICMP packets can be generated carrying covert data in their payloads. Covert channels can be setup using the ID field of IP packets, IP checksums, TCP initial sequence numbers, or TCP timestamps.

ICMP Exploits

The ICMP protocol is a simple protocol with one message per packet. ICMP is also one of the easiest to exploit. In addition to the exploits described above, namely smurfing, route redirection, and covert channels, it has enabled several other exploits via reconnaissance and scanning.

Finger Printing a System

An attacker wants to identify the exact version of an OS running on a targeted victim. Nuances in the TCP/IP stacks implemented in the various OS, and versions of the same OS, make it possible to remotely probe the victim host and identify the OS. Such probing deliberately constructs illegal packets, and attempts to connect to each port and observes the responses it gets. The tool called *nmap* is comprehensive in this regard.

Buffer Overflows in Servers

A large number of TCP/IP server programs suffer from a class of programming errors known as buffer overflows. Many of these server programs run with the privileges of a super user. Among the many servers that suffer from such bugs are several implementations of FTP servers, the ubiquitous DNS server program called *bind*, the popular mail server called *sendmail*, and the Web server IIS, to name a few. An attacker supplies cleverly constructed inputs to such programs causing them to transfer control to executable code he or she has supplied. A typical code he supplies produces a shell that he can interact with from a remote machine with all the privileges of the super user.

Security Enhancements

A number of enhancements for TCP/IP have been made that are not yet in common use. Several of them (e.g., VPN and IP6) involve heavy use of encryption and require more computing power. As computing power in end-user hosts increases, we expect to see these universally deployed.

Several chapters of this volume are devoted to security enhancements. Virtual private networks (VPN) enable secure communication through public networks using cryptographic channels. See chapters 184 (Virtual Private Networks Basics) and 185 (VPN Architecture).

Authentication

Authentication is the process of verifying the credentials of a user, a node, or a service. Authentication protocols enable such procedures. Authentication protocols send or receive messages in encrypted form. Without encryption, it is like having a paper-thin door to a house. Some well-known authentication protocols are Kerberos, RADIUS, PAP and CHAP.

PAP [Password Authentication Protocol, (RFC 1334)] is a two-way handshake protocol designed for use with PPP. It sends the user name and password in plain text, obviously vulnerable to sniffing. CHAP [Challenge Handshake Authentication Protocol (RFC 1944)] is a three-way handshake protocol. The CHAP server sends the user client a challenge, which is a randomly generated sequence of bytes unique to this authentication session. The client encrypts the challenge using a previously issued secret key that is shared by both the client and CHAP server. The result, called a response, is then returned to the CHAP server. The CHAP server performs the same operation on the challenge it sent with the shared secret key and compares its results, the expected response, with the response received from the client. If they are the same, the client is assumed authentic.

IP6 and IPsec

The IP version 4 that currently dominates the Internet sends all its payload and headers in clear text. A determined attacker can install remote sniffers along every path that a communication from host B to host C and assemble full messages being sent at the application level. The IPsec protocol adds authentication and encryption. The IP version 6 includes IPsec and other enhancements to IP4. See chapters 63 (IPsec: Authentication Header and Encapsulating Security Payload) and 64 (IPsec: Internet Key Exchange).

TCP/IP Traffic Scrubbing

Scrubbing refers to forcing the TCP/IP traffic to obey all the rules of the RFCs. Reserved fields can be set to a random value; illegal combinations of flags are checked, and so on. Scrubbing is expected to be done not only at the originating hosts but also on the routers and especially in firewalls. Scrubbing adds to the computational burden of the hosts. Because of hidden assumptions made by programs beyond the specifications of the RFCs, scrubbing may disrupt interoperability.

CONCLUSION

The Internet and the World Wide Web are based on a suite of protocols and software collectively known as TCP/IP. It includes not only the transmission control protocol and Internet protocol but also other protocols such as UDP, ARP, DNS, and ICMP, and applications such as telnet, FTP, Secure Shell, and Web browsers and servers. We surveyed these topics starting from the seven-layer OSI model to recent improvements in the implementations of the protocol stack and security.

GLOSSARY

Big Endian A 32-bit integer is stored in four consecutively addressed bytes $a, a+1, a+2$, and $a+3$. In a big-endian system, the most significant byte of the integer is stored at a. In a little-endian system, the least significant byte is stored at a.

Byte A byte is a sequence of 8 bits. Viewed as an unsigned number, it is in the range of 0 to 255.

Checksum A checksum is a function of the sequence of bytes in a packet. It is used to detect errors that may have altered some of the numbers in the sequence. The IP checksum field is computed as the 16-bit one's complement of the one's complement sum of all 16-bit words in the header. For purposes of computing the checksum, the value of the checksum field is zero.

Client The process that establishes connections for the purpose of sending requests.

Connections In the connectionless communication, one process sends data to another without prior negotiation. The recipient does not acknowledge the receipt of the message, and the sender has no guarantee that the message is indeed delivered. In the connection oriented communication, there are three well-defined phases: connection establishment, data transfer, and connection release.

Datagram A sequence of bytes that constitutes the unit of transmission in the network layer (such as IP).

Frame The unit of transmission at the data link layer, which may include a header and/or a trailer, along with some number of units of data.

Host A device capable of sending and receiving data over a network. Often, it is a computer system with an NIC, but it can be a much simpler device.

Network A collection of links in which the hosts are connected either directly or indirectly.

Network Applications Programs that operate over a network.

Network Operating Systems These systems have network software built in and are aware of byte order issues.

Node A synonym for host.

Octet An 8-bit quantity on older computer architectures where the smallest addressable unit of memory was a word and not a byte.

Packet A generic term used to designate any unit of data passed between communicating entities and is usually mapped to a frame.

Process The dynamic entity that can be summarized as a "program during its execution on a computer system."

Program A file of binary data in a certain rigid format that is specific to each platform, capable of being both a client and a server. Our use of these terms refers only to the role being performed by the program for a particular connection rather than to the program's capabilities in general.

Protocol A formal and preagreed set of rules that govern the communications between two or more entities. The protocol determines the meaning of specific values occurring in specific positions in the stream, the type of error checking to be used, the data compression method, how the sender will indicate that it has finished sending a message, and how the receiver will indicate that it has received a message.

RFC Request for Comments documents are Internet standards, proposed designs, and solutions published by researchers from universities and corporations soliciting feedback and archived at http://www.rfc-editor.org/.

Server A process that accepts connections to service requests by sending back responses. It is also called a daemon.

Spoofing In IP spoofing, either the source or the destination address is fake. In DNS spoofing, a query receives fake response.

Tunneling The process of sending packets of a certain protocol embedded in the packets of another protocol.

CROSS REFERENCES

See *Internet Security Standards; IP-Based VPN; Security in Circuit, Message, and Packet Switching; VPN Architecture; VPN Basics.*

REFERENCES

Arkin, O. (2001). ICMP usage in scanning: the complete know-how. Retrieved December 2003, from http://www.sys-security.com/html/projects/icmp.html

Comer, D. (2000a). *Internetworking with TCP/IP: Vol. 1. Principles, protocols, and architecture* (4th ed.). Englewood Cliffs, NJ: Prentice Hall.

Comer, D. (2000b). *The Internet book: Everything you need to know about computer networking and how the Internet works* (3rd ed.). Englewood Cliffs, NJ: Prentice Hall.

Denning, D. E., & Denning, P. J. (1998). *Internet besieged: Countering cyberspace scofflaws*. Reading, MA: Addison Wesley.

Garfinkel, S., Spafford, G., & Schwartz, A. (2003). *Practical UNIX and Internet security* (3rd ed.). Sebastapol, CA: O'Reilly.

Gourley, D., & Totty, B. (2002). *HTTP: The definitive guide*. Sebastapol, CA: O'Reilly.

Halabi, B. (2000). *Internet routing architectures*. Indianapolis, IN: Cisco Press.

Hunt, C. (2002). *TCP/IP network administration* (3rd ed.). Sebastopol, CA: O'Reilly.

Iren, S., Amer, P. D., & Conrad, P. T. (1999). *The transport layer: Tutorial and survey*. ACM Computing Surveys, 31, 360¨C404.

Krishnamurthy, B., & Rexford, J. (2001). *Web protocols and practice: HTTP/1.1, networking protocols, caching, and traffic measurement*. Reading, MA: Addison Wesley.

Kurose, J. F., & Ross, K. W. (2003). *Computer networking: A top-down approach featuring the Internet* (2nd ed.). Reading, MA: Addison Wesley.

Mateti, P. (2002). Internet security class notes. Retrieved October 2002, from www.cs.wright.edu/!≪pmateti/InternetSecurity

Rowland, C. H. (1997). Covert channels in the TCP/IP protocol suite. *First Monday*. Retrieved December 2003 from http://www.firstmonday.dk/

Stallings, W. (2003). *Cryptography and network security: Principles and practice* (3rd ed.). Englewood Cliffs, NJ: Prentice Hall.

Stevens, W. R. (1993). *TCP/IP illustrated: Vol. 1. The protocols*. Reading, MA: Addison Wesley.

Stewart, J. W., III. (1999). *BGP4: Inter-domain routing in the Internet*. Reading, MA: Addison Wesley.

Tanenbaum, A. S. (2003). *Computer networks* (4th ed.). Englewood Cliffs, NJ: Prentice Hall.

NOTE: RFCs are archived at http://www.rfc-editor.org/

FURTHER READING

TCP/IP details are part of many college courses on computer networks. There are several textbooks. Of these, the three authoritative volumes of Comer's Internetworking with TCP/IP are classic technical references in the field aimed at the computer professional and the degree student. Volume I surveys TCP/IP and covers details of ARP, RARP, IP, TCP, UDP, RIP, DHCP, OSPF, and others. There are errata at http://www.cs.purdue.edu/homes/dec/tcpip1.errata.html *The Internet Book: Everything You Need to Know about Computer Networking and How the Internet Works* is a gentler introduction. The books listed above by Tanenbaum and Kurose and Ross are also popular textbooks. The book by Stevens discusses from a programming point of view.

Routing protocols are discussed briefly in the above books. The books by Halabi and Kurose and Ross cover this topic very extensively.

The HTTP protocol and related issues are thoroughly discussed in the books of Krishnamurthy and Rexford and Gourley and Totty.

The book by Denning and Denning is a high-level discussion of how the vulnerabilities in computer networks are affecting society. Mateti has an extensive Web site (http://www.cs.wright.edu/~pmateti/InternetSecurity) that has lab experiments and readings online. The book by Garfinkel and Spafford explores security from a practical UNIX systems view.

All the RFCs are archived at http://www.rfc-editor.org/. The Usenet newsgroup comp.protocols.tcp-ip is an active group and maintains a frequently asked questions (FAQ) document that is worth reading. The Technical Committee on Computer Communications of the IEEE Web site (http://www.comsoc.org/) maintains an extensive collection of conference listings. The *IEEE/ACM Transactions on Networking* is a peer-reviewed archival journal that publishes research articles.

The Web site www.cert.org issues timely and authoritative alerts regarding computer exploits and has a comprehensive collection of guides on security. The Web site http://www.phrack.org publishes detailed descriptions, often with ready-to-compile source code of vulnerabilities and tutorials.

Voice-over Internet Protocol (VoIP)

Roy Morris, *Capitol College*

INTRODUCTION

As with any advanced communications protocol, voice-over-Internet protocol (VoIP) brings with it many benefits along with offsetting negatives, including potential security risks and management issues. Whether provided over wire or wireless transmission, VoIP security poses unique risks and complexity. Its successful implementation requires compliance and compatibility with conventional telecommunications standards—whose basic designs date back to the early twentieth century—while it must "ride on" data transmission technologies of the Internet protocol (IP), whose basic designs were developed initially for time insensitive data during the very late 20th century. Complicating this is the increased wireless transmission with IP services, thus introducing some additional challenges. This chapter begins by explaining communications theory and conventional telephony, which predate the popularized Internet. They serve as a foundation for the VoIP, because almost all voice communications systems rely on those underlying theories. The chapter concludes with specifics of VoIP design and deployment, including addressing security concerns.

COMMUNICATIONS THEORY: BITS OF TRANSMITTED INFORMATION

Basic communications theory concepts form the building block of all communications applications and their understanding. VoIP is no exception. Communication is simply the transmission of information from one place (or device or person) to another, over a transmission network. Voice communications refers to transmitting the information contained in a voice signal. The distance traveled by a transmitted signal can be as short as from one chip to another chip on a circuit board to across the street to around the world or even to the most distant galaxies in outer space. The basic principles are the same, whether the transmission medium is wires or wireless.

Bits: The Most Basic Form of Information

In digital parlance, a bit is the smallest measure of information (Newton, 1998). It is the amount of information required to distinguish between two equally likely possibilities or choices. A bit, shortened from the term *binary digit*, can be used as a building block for all information or messages and/or as a measure of information. A bit is typically given one of two arbitrary logical values (e.g., 1 or 0). By stringing together bits, complex messages can be formed representing familiar message forms, such as letters, sentences, text documents, voice signals, pictures, and movies.

The key to the successful binary transmission of any type of information is that the transmitter and receiver of the binary transmission must understand the same standardized vocabulary used to digitally encode the information. Without some context (i.e., knowledge of how the original information was encoded), all binary strings look the same—like strings of 1s and 0s. What differentiates one kind of transmitted binary string from another is a common understanding between the encoder (at the transmitter) and decoder (at the receiver) of what that bit string represents (e.g., text vs. voice) and how it was encoded (e.g., did it use ASCII, if it was text? Did it use a particular voice coder/decoder, if it is voice?)

The encoding vocabulary used for encoding text is primarily ASCII (Truxal, 1990). ASCII has 128 standardized combinations of seven bits to represent 128 characters, including upper- and lowercase letters, numbers,

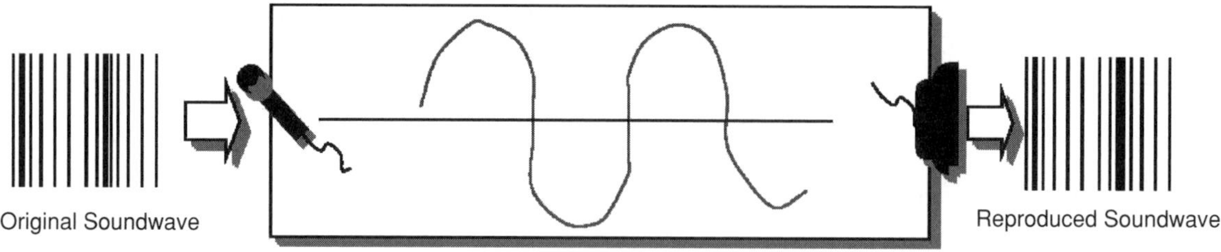

Figure 1: Transmission of a sound wave and its reconstruction.

and symbols. With such a universally understood binary text encoding scheme, we can transmit letters strung together to form large text documents that can be transmitted over digital transmission facilities, received, and ultimately displayed in distant locations.

Similarly, there are standardized voice communication encoding schemes that allow voice communication signals to be encoded as strings of 1s and 0s and then transmitted over data networks, received, and ultimately decoded and heard in distant locations. VoIP capitalizes on this ability, transmitting those strings of bits over a data network using the Internet protocol (IP).

Transmission of Voice Signals

Almost all voice communications signals begin as analog sound signals. An analog signal is one that is typically continuous in shape (i.e., no instantaneous changes in value) and analogous in shape to the original signal or physical phenomenon that created it (Newton, 1998). The physical signals that our bodies generate (e.g., sound and visual) and receive (i.e., sense) are analog (Truxal, 1990). This is very important in understanding the design of telephony systems, because almost all information transmitted in telephony is ultimately either originated and/or received by a human being.

When we speak or play an instrument, combinations of one or more waves of alternating compression and expansion of air are generated at the sound's source (e.g., the vocal chords in our throats or the reeds of instruments). Because sound energy in air does not travel well over long distances, long-distance communications requires that these sound waves be converted to alternate forms of energy by a transducer and then that signal energy be conveyed over a compatible transmission medium, such as an electronic transmission channel, which can maintain the signal's information integrity for transmission over long distances. For voice communications, the microphone of a telephone device is typically used to transform analog sound wave energy into analog electrical wave energy for transmission over a caller's local telephone wires.

To transform the electrical signal back to a sound wave at the receiving end of the transmission link so that the human ear can detect it, the analog electrical signal is applied to a "reverse microphone" transducer (such as the an earpiece of a telephone). The "reverse microphone," or speaker, outputs physical patterns of compressed air corresponding to the original sound wave. The entire transformation from analog sound wave to analog electrical signal and back to analog sound wave is illustrated in Figure 1.

The Characteristics of an Analog Voice Signal

Communications networks and their elements are designed to cost-effectively accommodate the signals they are intended to carry, with the least detectible degradation (e.g., distortion and delay). Telephony networks were optimized to carry analog voice signals over long distances using the most cost-effective technology available. However, the original designs were done from the late 1800s through the early 1900s and were influenced by the technology that was available at the time. Those voice-centric designs continue to influence telephony network design today so as to allow interoperation with established telephony networks, and the need for those established networks to be backwards compatible with older equipment (which sometimes dates back to the early 1900s).

A human voice signal is made up of alternating signal components of various frequencies, with most of its signal power within the range from 100 to 3400 alternating cycles per second. Although this range may vary somewhat from person to person, analog telephony networks were designed based on this assumption. Virtually all of the components of the telephone networks have been built to limit the frequencies transmitted to those in this voiceband. Any signal power carried on frequencies outside this voiceband is filtered out by the network equipment and, in turn, not transmitted.

This voiceband range is broad enough to allow a telephone listener both to recognize the person who is speaking and to understand what he or she is saying. High-fidelity devices, such as CDs and FM radio, transmit signal power over a wider range of frequencies (up to 10,000 cycles per second or more). With conventional telephony, any attempt to transmit sound from such devices would be filtered to include only the signal power in the voiceband frequency band. However, with the flexibility of VoIP, it is at least theoretically possible to cost-effectively deploy a customized high-fidelity telephony service that could co-exist with voiceband VoIP services because the underlying IP network will transmit for a particular IP connection as much data (and therefore as much voice signal information) as the transmission bandwidth will allow (Skype).

Digitizing an Analog Voice Signal

Most long-distance transmission systems in use today (including those using VoIP) transmit voice signals digitally.

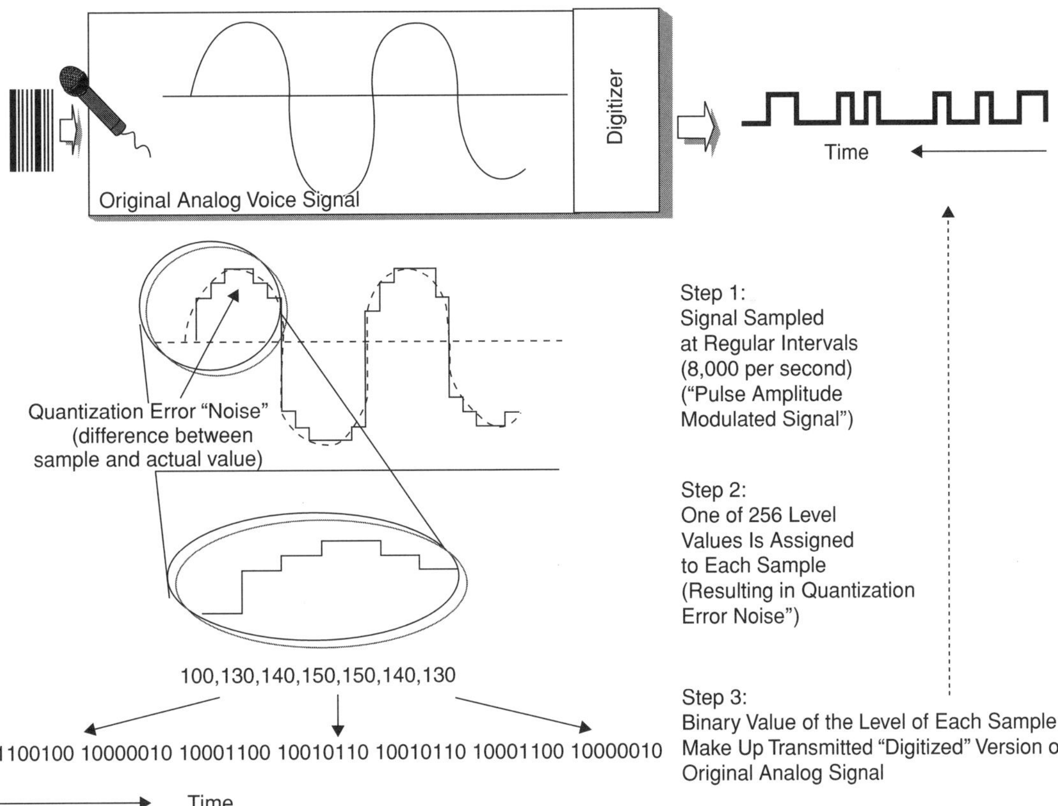

Figure 2: Digitization of a voice signal.

As mentioned, to transmit an analog signal digitally, its analog version must be transformed from its electrical analog form to a digital form, thus changing its representation from a varying electrical voltage to an equivalent string of discrete 0s and 1s. This transformation is done by a digitizer, sometimes referred to as an *analog-to-digital converter*, *A/D converter*, or *codec* (coder–decoder) (Newton, 1998; Truxal, 1990). A digitizer takes samples of the height (i.e., amplitude) of the incoming analog signal at regular time intervals (e.g., 8000 times per second). For each of these regularly timed signal measurements, the digitizer outputs a fixed-length digital number (expressed in terms of logical 0s and 1s) that corresponds to the size of the signal height measured for each sample (see, for example, Figure 2).

Depending on the digitizer, the number of bits that are used to represent each level of signal amplitude can vary. If eight bits are used to represent the measurements of each sample's height, then 256 height levels can be represented. The use of eight bits to represent each sample of a voice signal is fairly typical. The rounding error or difference between the height of each sample and the true height of the original signal at the sampled point is called *quantization error*.

If more than eight bits were used to represent each sample's amplitude, a larger number of discrete levels could be used to digitize a signal and, in turn, reduce the amount of quantization (or rounding error) noise. However, the additional bits for each sample would require additional transmission capacity with little offsetting benefit. Experience has shown that the human ear cannot easily detect the noise created by quantization error with eight-bit sample encoding.

Generally, the minimum rate at which a codec must sample a voice signal is the Nyquist rate. Nyquist determined that for a sampled representation of a signal to accurately capture the entire range of frequencies in the original signal, the samples must be taken at a rate that is more than two times the highest frequency component of the original signal. Thus, to transmit a voice signal digitally and achieve the same performance as conventional analog telephony networks, the transmitted voiceband signal, with its highest frequency assumed to be 3400 cycles per second, must be sampled at more than 6800 samples per second. It is common to oversample a voice signal using a sample rate of 8000 samples per second.

With 8-bit encoding per sample, the digital equivalent of a voiceband signal that is sampled 8000 times per second requires 64,000 bits per second to be transmitted (8000 samples per second times 8 bits per sample). This is known as the G.711 standard. Codecs often incorporate techniques for reducing the transmitted bit rate from the base amount of 64,000 bits per second. Some of those techniques include (1) using nonlinear (logarithmic) sampling levels, (2) transmitting only changes in signal levels, and, (3) removing redundant information while maintaining signal quality and minimizing processing delay, (Castelli, 2002). Companding uses nonlinear sampling levels. Companding has the effect of decreasing the number of sample levels required by using a disproportionate greater number of sample levels in the most relevant amplitude range for the signal. Companding also has the

Table 1 Summary of Compression Algorithm Performance

Compression	Bandwidth (kb/s)	MOS score	Delay (ms)
PCM (G.711)	64	4.4	0.75
ADPCM (G.726)	32	4.2	1
G.728	16	4.2	3.5
G.729	8	4.2	10
G.723.1	6.3	3.9	30
G.7231.1	5.3	3.5	30

Note: Packet headers add an additional demand of about 2 to 20 kbps depending on codec, packet size, transmission protocol, and compression. Thus, for example, a 64-kbps sample signal may require 84 kps to transmit because of packet header overhead. ALCATEL (2003).
Source: Cisco, Understanding Codecs: Complexity, Hardware, Support, MOS, and Negotiation (2002) and Sanford (1999).

secondary effect of reducing the quantization noise in the amplitude range with the highest concentration of sample levels, compared to that in noncompanded digitized signals, for a given number of bits per sample. Differential pulse code modulation (DPCM) is another method used to reduce the number of bits transmitted without compromising quality. DPCM transmits only the changes in sample levels rather than absolute levels. Another variation on DPCM is adaptive pulse code modulation, which can halve the bit transmission requirements. The trade-off of using these algorithms is increased processing, along with commensurate increased delay associated with that processing time. Current compression algorithms can reduce the 64,000-bit-per-second transmission requirement for a voice signal to as low as 8000 bits per second without incurring a substantial increase in delay.

Table 1 summarizes some of the most popular voice compression algorithms used in Internet telephony. The frame of reference is the G.711 standard. Note that its MOS (mean opinion score, an objective measurement of the perceived quality of the received voice, which ranges from 0 to 5) is 4.4. Processing delay is negligible. All other compression systems are more efficient (less than 64 kb/s of bandwidth consumption per voice conversation) but exhibit additional processing delays, which may cause additional problems in long, echo-prone circuits. For wide area networks (WAN), the G.729 standard is one of the most popular, because it represents a reasonable compromise between efficiency and delay performance, at a modest 10 ms. The G.711 is most popular around the campus, where bandwidth cost is generally not an issue. An alternate codec to G.711 is G.722, which provides 7-kHz quality (i.e., twice baseband voice) in the same 64-kbps transmission requirement (Audin, 2004).

THE TELEPHONY NETWORK

The Communications Network Topology

From a user's perspective, a telephone network is a big cloud that connects the originating points for transmitted information with terminating points for transmitting information. A network is actually made up of nodes interconnecting transmission links to form transmission paths for the transmitted information to move along. The transmission links in a typical network may use different transmission modalities (e.g., wire, wireless, and fiber). The nodes may contain electronic devices, such as switches, which establish a temporary or permanent path to be taken by the communicated information so as to enable the information to move from one link onto another link. Those nodes may also contain conversion devices that change the modality of the transmitted signal to allow it to pass between links using different modalities (e.g., connecting a wired link to a wireless link, an analog link to a digital link, or a fiber link to a copper wire link). See Figure 3.

Transmission Links

Transmission links, whether digital or analog, are typically carried over wire, fiber, or wireless medium (i.e., the atmosphere). Each physical medium has its own physical characteristics that limit the ability of the transmitted signal (whether analog or digitally encoded) to accurately and timely propagate.

Wire transmission medium includes wire pairs, coaxial cable, and even single wires (where the "return path" is the physical common ground). With wire transmission, a transducer varies the electrical pressure, or voltage, applied at the transmitting end of the transmission link in proportion to the signal to be transmitted. This varying voltage, in effect, pushes electrons on one wire and pulls electrons on the other wire. The electrons flow through a closed wire loop path to the node at the far end of the transmission link. At the far end of the transmission link, a transducer senses this electron movement, and pressures driving them, to recreate the transmitted signal or something corresponding to it.

Fiber links involve the transmission of communications using a light signal through a very high-quality, thin wirelike glass fiber. The signal is transmitted using a light transducer source [typically, a laser or light-emitting diode (LED)], located at the information source end of the transmission medium, that is turned on and then off or in varying intensities. Those variations are some function of the variations in the transmitted information signal. A "reverse" transducer at the far end node connected to the fiber link senses these variations in light intensity and ultimately deciphers the transmitted information.

Finally, wireless transmission links generate electromagnetic waves (such as radio and light waves) at the transmitting end that are propagated through the open

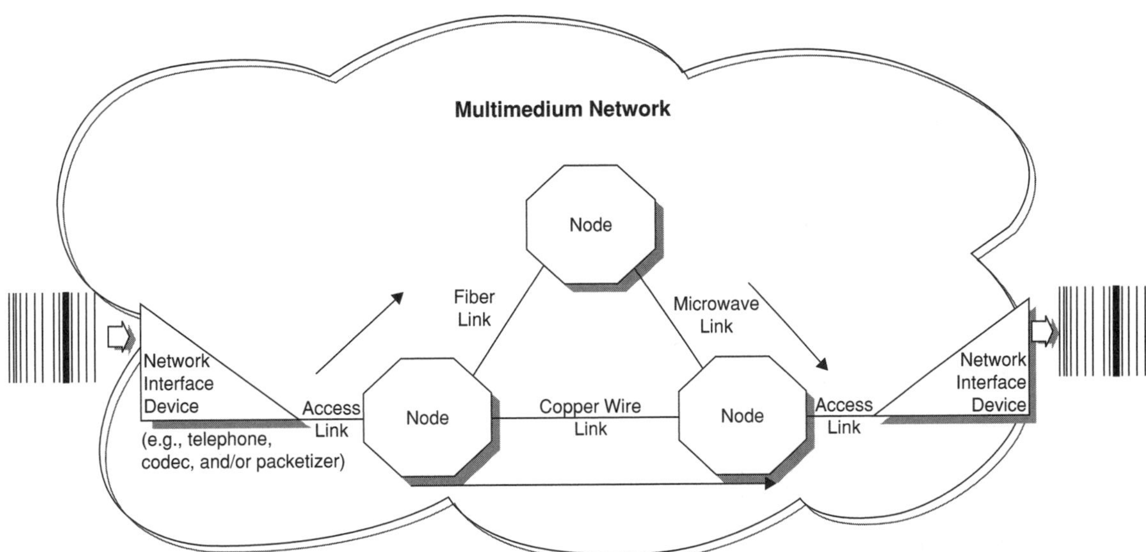

Figure 3: Multimedium network.

atmosphere. Some physical characteristic of the transmitted electromagnetic signal is varied as a function of the information transmitted. A receiver-type transducer at the receiving end of the open-atmosphere medium detects these variations in radio or light waves and, in turn, can recreate the original signal and the information transmitted.

Transmission System Imperfections: Noise, Loss, and Delay

Each transmission link in a network, and each node connecting those links, introduces some amount of noise, loss, and delay into the transmitted signal. These physical transmission imperfections affect both digitally and nondigitally encoded signals that are transmitted over them. However, depending on whether the signals transmitted are in the analog or digital form, the transmission channel's physical limitations manifest themselves somewhat differently—as described later in this chapter.

Transmission noise that invevitably mixes into the transmitted signal during transmission causes the signal received at the far end of a transmission link to differ from the originally transmitted source signal. Transmission noise is typically uncorrelated with the original transmission signal. Where substantial noise is present, detection and, therefore, reconstruction of the original transmitted signal at the receiving end is more difficult or impossible. Transmission noise, when corrupting a digitally encoded signal, can result in a receiver falsely identifying some of the 1s as 0s and some 0s as 1s.

The ability of a receiver to accurately detect the characteristics of the original transmitted signal, and therefore to accurately reproduce it, is directly a function of the signal-to-noise ratio (or S/N ratio) of the received signal. As the noise added by the transmission link becomes very large in comparison to the power of the transmitted signal, more errors in detection will occur. Boosting the power of the original signal at the transmitting end of the link can increase the signal-to-noise ratio, but this is not always possible because of concerns about such problems as crosstalk between adjacent channels and interference with other devices and systems. Special encoding schemes can be used to allow the receiver to check and/or correct for errors caused by random noise. The particular schemes for doing this error detection and correction are not important here, except to note that they all require the "overhead" of transmitting additional redundant information (and therefore additional bits) along with the digitally encoded version of the original signal.

There is one exception to the idea that noise is a bad thing. Specifically, a limited amount of noise may sometimes be intentionally *added* to a digitally transmitted voice signal during quiet periods, when neither party is speaking; otherwise the lack of noise could lead callers to perceive that the line has been disconnected.

Transmission loss refers to the loss of signal power as the original signal traverses a transmission link. Amplifying all or selected frequencies of the received signal at the receiving end of the link cannot always compensate for signal loss. For example, in the presence of noise, if there is significant overlap in the spectral power of the noise signal and the original signal, receiver amplification will tend to amplify the unwanted noise along with the original transmitted signal. The result would be little improvement in the receiver's ability to discriminate between the now amplified original transmission signal and amplified unwanted noise and thus accurately detect the signal. The frequency range over which the loss is relatively flat is known as the bandwidth.

Transmission delay (or latency) is a measure of how much later a signal is received compared to when it was transmitted. Delay can create two types of problems. The end-to-end transmitted signal delays can vary over the range of the signal spectrum. Spectral signal components of different frequencies can travel at different speeds, thus reaching the receivers at different times. For transmitted digital pulses, these differences in travel times can result in very distorted-looking versions of the pulses arriving at the receiving end as compared to the original signal. In turn, such delay distortion can make accurate detection of the binary signal very difficult. If the delay distortion characteristics of a channel can be determined in advance, they can be somewhat compensated for at the signal detector. The second type of delay is a delay in the time it takes for the information transmitted (assuming it is accurately reproduced) to arrive at its ultimate destination. For voice conversations, this delay, if long enough, can make voice communications almost impossible. When the round trip delay in a transmitted voice signal reaches on the order of a half second, the receiving and transmitting parties begin to notice this delay in two ways. First, the parties at both ends begin to speak before the other finishes speaking (because each party doesn't accurately know when the other has finished speaking). Second, and more importantly, without special echo cancellation circuitry in place, the parties at both ends begin to hear their own voices echoed back to their ears. This occurs because the electronics of a typical telephone network cause the far end of almost every call connection to echo back a weakened version of the transmitted signal to the originating end. Without echo cancellation circuitry, this echo is always present, but it is not noticeable until the round-trip delay becomes long enough.

All of these deficiencies of a "raw" transmission channel can have the effect of reducing the channel capacity, or throughput, of a transmission link. Channel capacity refers to the theoretical upper limit on how much information, in terms of bits per second, can be transmitted through a channel (Wozencraft & Jacobs, 1965).

Circuit-Switched Connections of a Call in a Conventional Telephony Network

VoIP networks must interoperate with conventional circuit-switched networks, in particular the ubiquitous public switched telephone network or PSTN. A VoIP network that cannot interoperate with, and therefore exchange calls with, the PSTN would be of little value to most telephone users. A network's value increases as it can be used to reach more users. Like other networks, the PSTN uses a hub-and-spoke architecture of transmission links and switches (Bell Laboratories, 1977/1983). Each user's telephone is typically connected by an individual circuit (usually referred to as a local loop) to a central office switching hub. In a small town, there may be only one central office, whereas in a large major metropolitan area, there could be several dozen central offices. In each central office hub, there is usually at least one switch. The switches used in traditional telephony are called circuit switches. A circuit switch will route a call over a dedicated path from one transmission link to another for the duration of the call (see, Figure 4). As described more fully below, this contrasts with the packet switching used in the Internet, which does not maintain a dedicated path connecting network links but instead passes information along shared "logical" paths on a packet-by-packet demand basis.

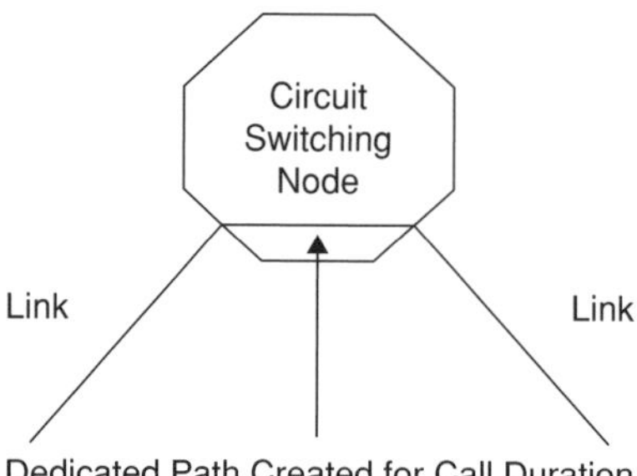

Figure 4: Circuit-switched connection between two links.

Originating the Call

As Figure 5 shows, when a caller picks up a telephone to make a call, the local switch in the caller's local central office (Node A) provides a dial tone that the caller

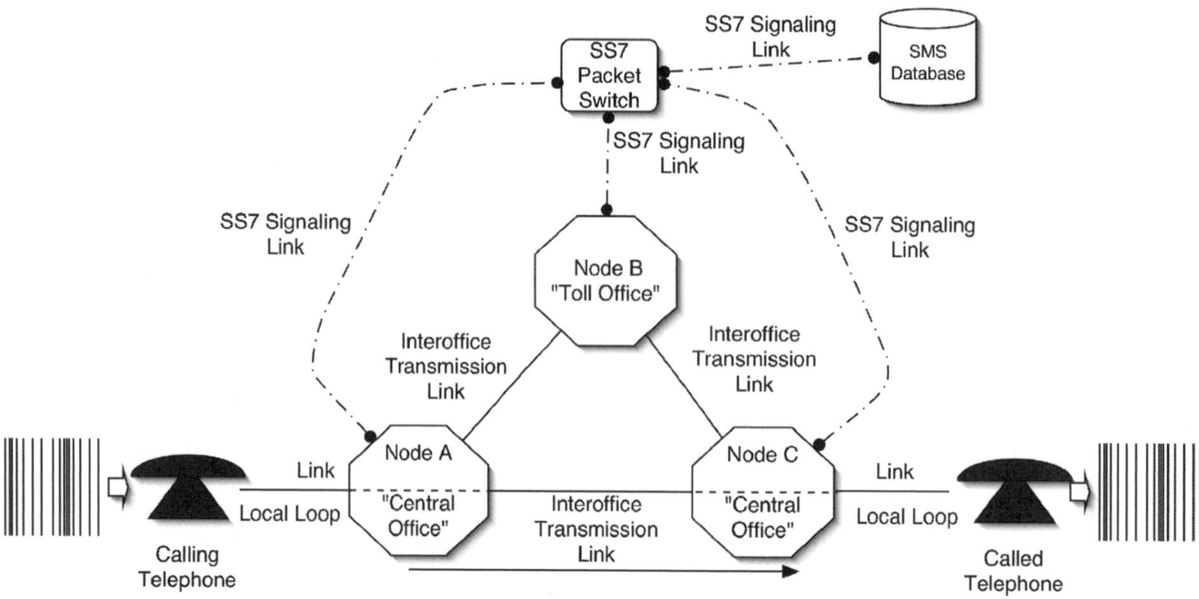

Figure 5: Conventional circuit-switched telephony network.

hears through the telephone. That dial tone indicates to the caller that the local telephone switch has seized his or her local telephone line and is ready to receive the digits of the telephone number that he or she wishes to dial. The processes of seizing the telephone line and returning dial tone are types of supervisory signaling.

The caller then enters, or dials, the telephone number of the called telephone. If the calling telephone is enabled with Touch-Tone signaling, the calling telephone signals to the local switch the digits dialed by using different combination of two Touch-Tones for each digit dialed. The routing information transmitted is called address signaling. The caller's local switch Node A detects these tone combinations and, in turn, determines the telephone number the caller is trying to call.

Circuit Switching to the Call's Destination

Each circuit switch has a routing look-up table for determining how to handle a call based on some or all of the calling and called numbers. If the local switch does not have adequate information in its routing tables to make a routing decision, most modern switches will hold the call and launch a packet data message to an external database (called a service management system or SMS). That message is routed from the switch to the SMS over a parallel data network called a Signaling System 7 (or SS7) packet network. The SMS returns routing instructions, via the SS7 packet network, to the switch that originated the routing query. The SS7 signaling standard came out of the conventional telephony industry.

If the local switch determines that the call needs to be connected to a local loop attached directly to that local switch, the switch will ring the local loop of the called telephone. At the same time, the switch returns a ringing sound signal to the calling party. Conversely, if the local switch determines that the called party's telephone is busy, the local switch returns a slow busy signal to the calling party.

As soon as the called party picks up its phone, the local switch creates a circuit-switched dedicated audio communications path between the calling party's local loop and the called party's local loop, thus completing a dedicated audio transmission path between the calling telephone and the called telephone. For the call's duration, that dedicated audio path is available for the transmission of voice signals, in both directions, between the calling and called party's telephones. If one or more of the links used to construct that path are digital, a codec in the connecting switch or other connecting device will make the necessary analog-to-digital conversion so that the voice signal may seamlessly traverse the boundaries between the analog and digital links.

If the called telephone's local loop is not directly connected to the calling telephone's local switch, the local switch must establish a connection to the called telephone through another switch or switches. For most modern PSTN switches, this requires that the originating switch launch an SS7 message, over the SS7 network, to reserve a path through other switches in the network for completing the desired communications path to the call's destination. If the far-end switch where the called party is located determines that the called party's line is busy, no circuit connections will be made, the path reservation for the connecting links is dropped, and the originating switch will return a slow busy signal to the calling party. However, if the reason the call cannot be completed is network congestion, the originating switch will return a fast busy to the calling party.

If the called party's line is not busy and a complete path to the called party's line can be established, the called party's local switch rings the called party's telephone. While the called party's phone is ringing, the calling party's local switch is returning an audible ringing signal to the calling party. When and if the called party answers, the switches instantly circuit-switch together the links along the reserved path to complete a dedicated path between the calling and called telephones.

Finally, it should be noted that some switches communicate interoffice signaling information using non-SS7 interoffice signaling arrangements, such as in-band signaling. Regardless of the supervisory and address signaling arrangement used, the net result of establishing a communications path between the calling and called telephone will be the same.

VOICE-OVER-INTERNET PROTOCOL

VoIP literally refers to the transmission of a digitized voice signal using digital packets, routed using the Internet protocol or IP. The driving forces for using VoIP are beliefs in its cost savings, flexibility, and the growing desire to combine voice and data transmission on one network. See, for example, Morris (1998), Cisco, VoIP Primer (2003), and Matthew (2002).

How Voice-over-Internet Protocol Transmission Works

Because a VoIP call is transmitted digitally, it begins with a digitization process similar to that used in conventional telephony. First, the voice signal is sampled at a rate greater than the Nyquist sampling rate, and those samples are digitized. Whereas conventional circuit-switched telephony transmits the digitized samples in a constant stream of synchronized (i.e., equally spaced in time) digital samples, VoIP transmits the digitized voice communications samples in asynchronous (i.e., unequally spaced in time), sequentially numbered packets of data. Each packet (which may contain many voice samples) contains its own IP formatted address information, which allows it to be routed over an IP network. Unlike conventional telephony, where each sample follows the path of the sample before it, each of the IP packets containing several samples of voice data may take an independent path (which path is shared with other data packets) to its destination. With each packet potentially taking a different route, particularly under network congestion situations, the packets may arrive at their destination out of order (or sometimes not at all). At the far end, the IP and other routing information is stripped from the packet, the voice samples are temporarily collected in a buffer and reordered as required, and then, if all goes well, the original voice signal is reconstructed, albeit, slightly delayed. For VoIP technology to have the functionality and flexibility of conventional

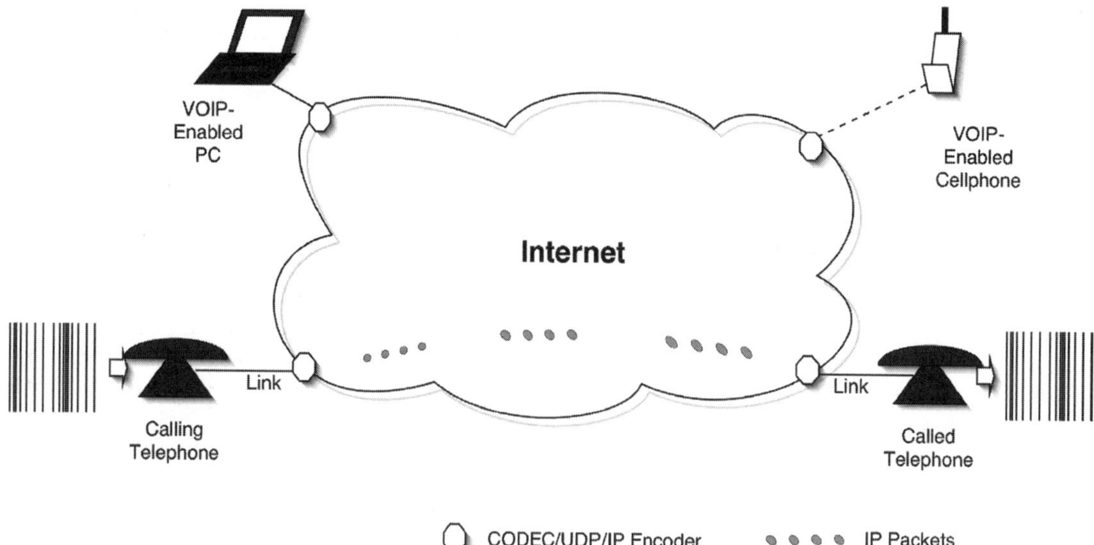

Figure 6: VoIP network.

telecommunications, some form of call control, in the form of supervisory and address signaling, is required. Figure 6 shows the basic VoIP transmission scheme.

Voice-over-Internet Protocol Signaling

VoIP signaling refers to signaling that can be used over an IP network to establish a VoIP call. It provides the needed functionality of supervisory and address signaling. VoIP call signaling comes in two predominant competing schemes: H.323 and Session Initiation Protocol (SIP). Each satisfies the generic needs of telephonic calling; specifically, each provides for the following:

- The calling phone to address and signal to the called telephone
- The called telephone to be able to signal its availability for receiving calls
- Establishing a transmission path between the calling and called telephone
- The called or calling telephone to be able to signal to the other phone that it has hung up and the tearing down of the transmission path once the call is over.

Figure 7 shows a generic signaling progression for establishing a VoIP call that might occur using H.323-type centralized call control arrangement. First, the calling telephone dials the called telephone's number (1). The calling phone forwards the dialed telephone number (address signaling) to a VoIP call controller—which is a special purpose server. That call controller does a lookup

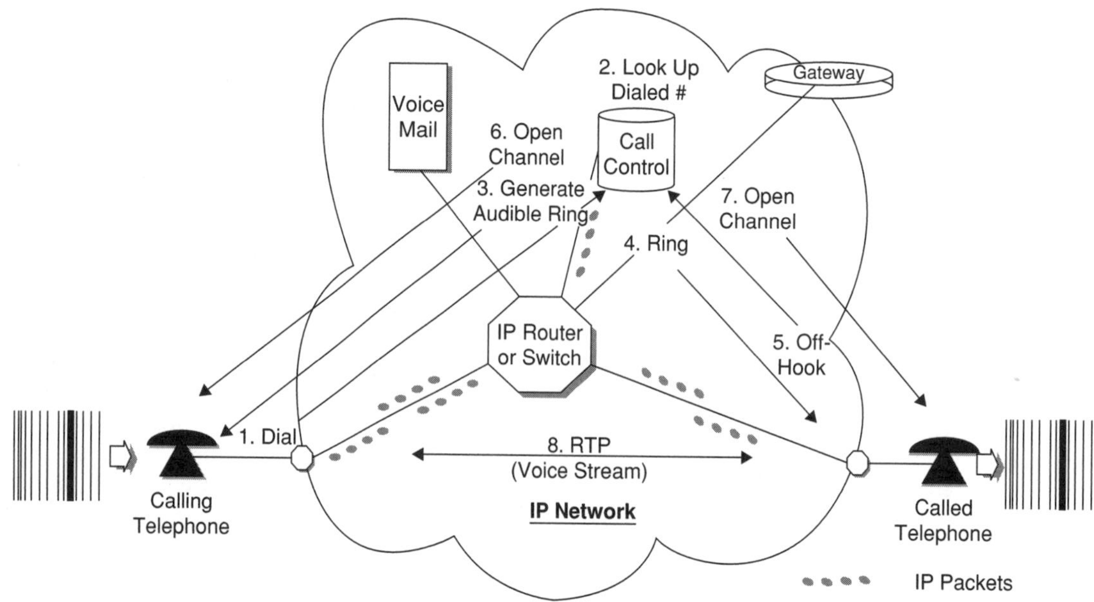

Figure 7: VoIP H.323-type signaling system using central call control.

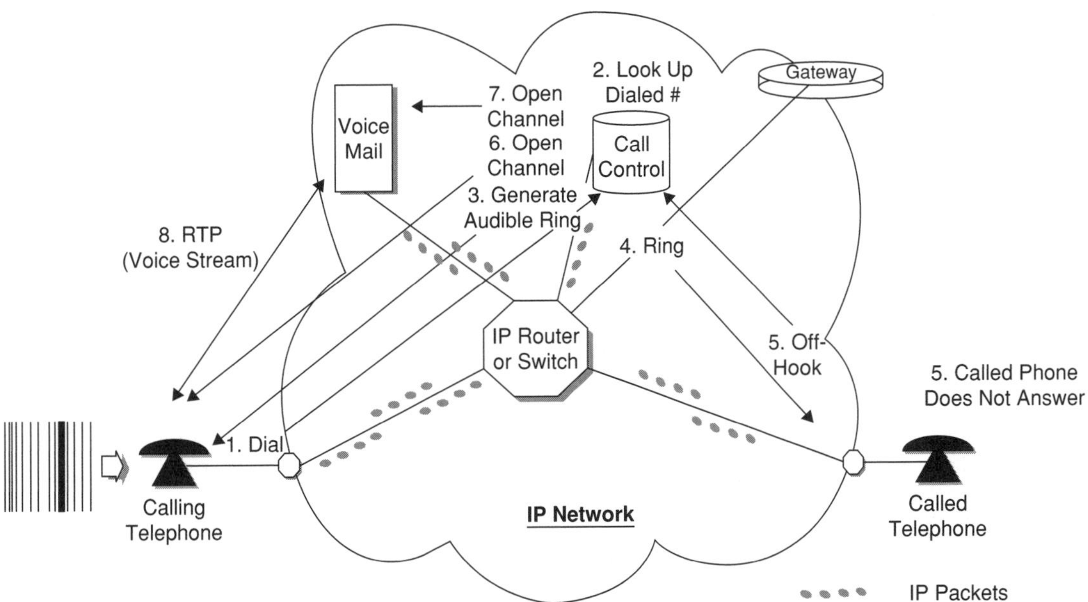

Figure 8: Called telephone unavailable with reroute to voice mail with H.323-type signaling.

(2) in a database for determining the IP address to reach the called telephone. If the called telephone is on the IP network, a call setup signal is routed to the called telephone to ring the called telephone (4). While the called telephone is ringing, a ringing signal is sent back to the calling telephone (3), which, in turn, generates a ringing sound in the caller's earpiece. When and if the called party answers the telephone, a series of signals to set up the channel path are returned to the calling and called telephones (5, 6, and 7).

A UDP/IP communications path is then set up between the calling and called telephone (8). The digitized voice is transported using the user datagram protocol (UDP) in the transport layer, with two protocols, RTP (real-time protocol) and RTCP (real-time control protocol), rather than TCP—which is often used by nonvoice data. UDP is connectionless and can transport data packets without acknowledging their receipt. UDP is nonstop with less address information overhead. The trade-off of using a UDP path is lower reliability than TCP. UDP packets may be dropped or arrive out of order, but if they do arrive they are more likely to arrive with less delay. This is a good trade-off for voice communications, which is reasonably tolerant to dropped packets (greater than 2 to 10%, with the lower tolerance where voice compression is used), but relatively intolerant to delay.

RTP over UDP provides packet sequence numbering, so out-of-order and/or missing packets are detectable at the far end. RTCP provides a separate signaling channel between the end devices (e.g., telephones) to allow exchange of information about packet loss, packet jitter, and packet delays, as well as additional information, such as the source's name, e-mail, phone, and identification [Real-Time Transport Protocol (RTP), 2001, August; Streaming Video Over the Internet, 2002].

Additional requirements for a commercial VoIP system include being able to produce information for billing and/or accounting for calls. Similarly, today's users demand that it provide other features, such as Caller ID and voicemail. These capabilities may reside in the call controller, IP telephones, and/or other devices in the IP network. Figure 8 shows how voicemail can be provided with H.323.

H.323 vs. SIP

In addition to H.323, SIP is the major competing standard for VoIP signaling. They have both evolved to offer very similar feature capabilities.

H.323 takes a more telecommunications-oriented approach than SIP. SIP takes an Internet-oriented approach. H.323 is the older of the two (Doron, 2001; Paketizer, 2003). It was developed under the International Telecommunications Union (ITU), a telecommunications standards group, and has gone through various revisions. (ITU-T, Recommendation H.323, 2000). One of the latest versions of H.323 standard (H.323 v3) is very robust in that it covers many possible implementations. However, H.323 is considered more difficult to implement than SIP due to its use of binary encoded signaling commands.

H.323 v.3 can be implemented with or without a call control server. Thus, an H.323 v.3 end device (e.g., a telephone) can be designed to set up a call either through a call control server or directly with another end device without using an intervening call control server. An H.323 v.3 call control server can be set up to relay the communications stream during the call, or the end devices can directly establish the communications RTP streaming channel between themselves. The call control server can be either stateless (i.e., not track a transaction or a session state) or stateful (i.e., track each transaction and/or call session state). The significance of this is that in the stateful configuration, H.323 v.3 is not as scalable. Finally, H.323 v.3 employs signaling protocols that can easily be mapped through a gateway for routing calls between the VoIP network and the public switched network.

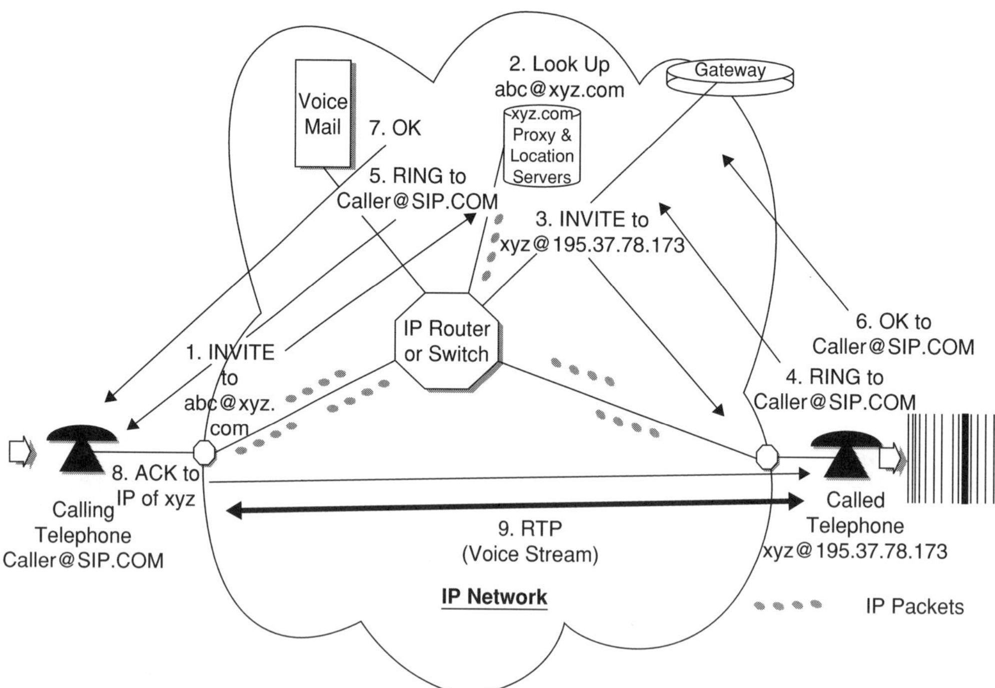

Figure 9: VoIP call routed using SIP signaling.

SIP is a Web-based architecture that was developed under the Internet Engineering Task Force (IETF). Like URLs and Web e-mail, SIP's messages are in ASCII text format that follow the HTTP programming model (i.e., using a grammar similar to that used to create basic Web pages), resulting in slightly lower efficiency in transmitting signaling information, as compared to the more efficiently encoded binary H.323 signaling messages. Also, SIP is very extensible, leading many vendors to implement variations that may be somewhat incompatible [IETF, SIP, 2004; IETF, SIP RFC2543bis (J. Rosenberg et al.), 2002].

An address used for routing a SIP messages is of the form SIPAddress@xyz.com. As shown in Figure 9, when a phone wishes to originate a call, it transmits an ASCII SIP INVITE message (1) addressed to the SIP address of the called phone (e.g., sales@xyz.com., where xyz.com is the domain name of the SIP proxy server for the called phone). Using conventional domain name server (DNS) look-up, the Internet routes this e-mail-type message to the SIP call control server, which may act as either a proxy server or a redirect server for the domain of the dialed called telephone address (here, xyz.com). To determine where the telephone is located, the proxy server or redirect server will query a location server (2), which will return the routing directions. What happens next depends on whether the call controller is acting as a proxy server or a redirect server for the called telephone.

For a proxy server, the location server will return the IP address for the called telephone. Using that IP address, the SIP INVITE message will be directed to the called telephone (3) along with the calling telephone's IP address. The called telephone will then return a RING message to the proxy server (4), which then forwards that RING message to the originating telephone (5). When the called phone answers, an OK message is returned (6 and 7), which includes the called telephone's IP address. Finally, the originating telephone (which now knows the IP address of the destination phone from the INVITE/OK message exchange) sends an ACK message to the IP address of the called telephone (8). The originating telephone then establishes an RTP communications link with the called telephone (9).

For a redirect server, the location server will return the redirected (i.e., forwarding) e-mail-style SIP address of the called telephone (e.g., sales@home.com or joe@home.com). The redirect server will then forward the INVITE request to the proxy or redirect server associated with that redirected address, and then the steps enumerated above will take place.

Each location server must track the IP address of each of the telephones in its SIP domain. Thus, each SIP telephone must register with its domain's location server via a registration server of its telephone service provider. An individual telephone can be registered with any registration server with which the user has a service arrangement. Registration binds each SIP telephone's IP address to its SIP address in its service provider's domain.

Note that a SIP call control server's primary purpose is to handle the routing of initial supervisory and address signaling information. Also note that, after the initial exchange of supervisory and address information, SIP end devices establish and maintain the communications channel without involvement of the SIP call control server. Like H.323 v.3, the SIP packets that carry the signaling messages almost always follow a different path from the path taken by the communications data. Finally, with SIP most of the intelligence resides in the end devices, as compared to being in the network, as is the case with conventional telephone networks and with H.323.

Because SIP proxy and redirect servers typically do not track a call's status after the call is set up, SIP is often viewed as being more scalable than H.323. When a call control server is configured to track call status, its resources must bear the added burden of such monitoring.

SIP's ASCII encoding is considered more extensible and open than the binary encoded signaling of H.323 v.3. SIP uses a very generic syntax for messages, which can be customized to fit the needs of different applications resident on end devices. For analysis of the various (and somewhat controversial) comparisons of SIP and H.323, see Dalgic and Fang (1999).

Integrating Voice-over-Internet Protocol into Conventional Circuit-Switched Telephony Networks

As previously noted, the value of a telephony network is a direct function of how many telephones are directly or indirectly connected to it; thus a VoIP network must be able to exchange calls (i.e., internetwork) with the PSTN such that a VoIP user can originate telephone calls to and receive telephone calls from a telephone user who is connected to the PSTN. In addition, for conventional telephone providers to deploy VoIP technology inside their networks, VoIP technology's presence must be imperceptible to their existing base of telephone users.

Figure 10 illustrates how a VoIP call can make a connection from a phone connected to an IP network to a phone on a PSTN network. A device, called a gateway, is used to translate signaling messages across the VoIP/PSTN network boundary and to transform the jittery voice packets on the IP side of the gateway into a synchronous stream of voice data information (if there is a digital voice circuit on the other PSTN side of the gateway) or an analog voice signal (if there is an analog voice circuit on the PSTN side of the gateway).

On the IP side, the VoIP signaling to the gateway looks much the same as the signaling that would be done to another end device on the IP network.

ENUM, the Fully Interoperable Numbering Plan

ENUM is a new standard for numbering plans that would allow seamless telephone number addressing between conventional and VoIP telephony (see, e.g., Neustar, 2003; IETF, Telephone Number Mapping (ENUM), 2004). It unifies Internet and conventional telephone addressing schemes by mapping E.164 (i.e., conventional telephone) numbers to a URL Internet- (and SIP) friendly format. With ENUM, a single global digital identifier system can serve equally subscribers attached to the PSTN or the Internet. The same identifier can be used to identify multiple devices, such as plain telephones, fax, voicemail, and data services, regardless of whether they are on the PSTN or public Internet, thus conserving scarce E.164 numbers and domain name resources.

As an example, a telephone number 1-305-599-1234 would map onto the URL 4.3.2.1.9.9.5.5.0.3.1.E164.arpa, with some of its components mirroring the conventional telephone number (in reverse order). A DNS query on this domain name would return a number of records, each listing a specific service registered to the owner of the E.164 number. Devices and services attached anywhere on the

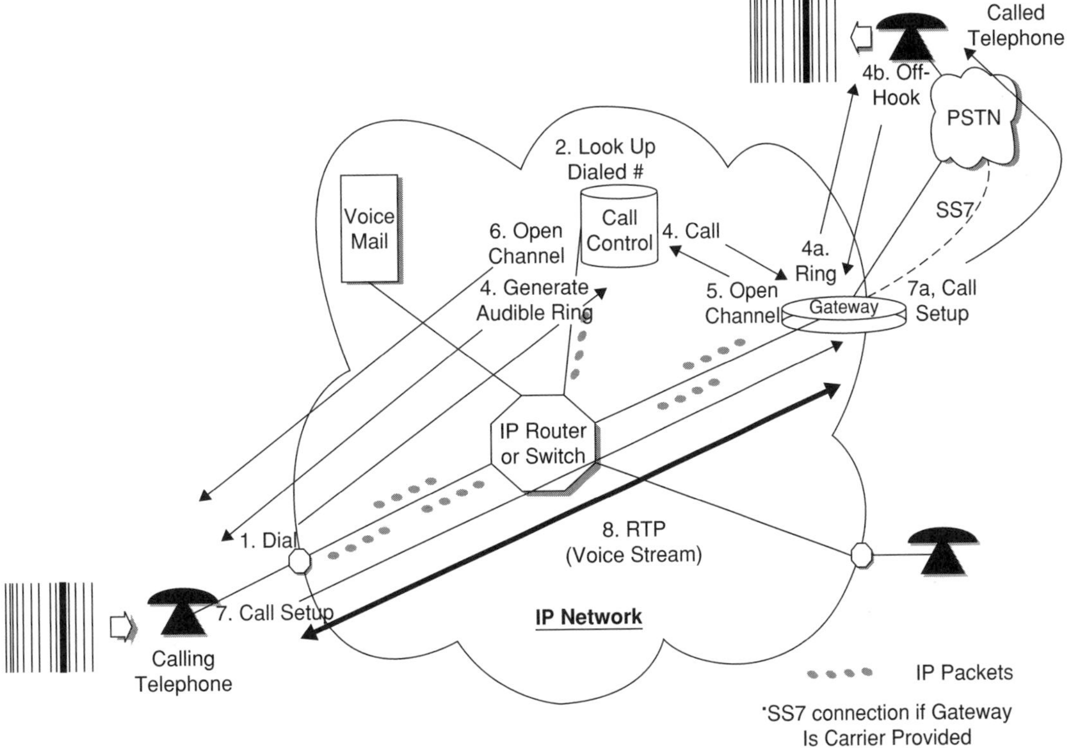

Figure 10: VoIP signaling internetworking with public switched network (PSTN).

public Internet or PSTN could be registered to this universal, fully portable, single-number identifier of their registered owner, allowing mobility around both the PSTN and the public Internet.

The flexibility of the ENUM standards raise new issues of privacy (e.g., disclosure of services registered to the owner), security [e.g., relative ease of ability of unauthorized telephone devices to "impersonate" the true owner of a number and receive and/or originate calls with their identity (identity spoofing and IP spoofing)], and administration (see below for more on security issues). Also, final agreement between Internet and traditional telecom industry represented by the ITU is still pending.

Quality-of-Service Issues

Transmission and routing can introduce effects that degrade the quality of VoIP. VoIP signals are not immune to the deficiencies of the facilities that transport and route them. These deficiencies can cause packet loss, jitter, and delay,

Packet loss refers to the loss of packets containing some of the voice samples during transmission. The loss might be caused by high bit error rates in the UDP transmission channel, misrouted packets, and/or congestion causing intermediate routing devices to drop packets. Because voice transmission is very sensitive to delay, the reassembly of the voice signal at the receiving end of the call cannot typically wait for the retransmission of erroneous or misrouted packets. However, voice transmission has a high tolerance for packet loss—mainly because the ultimate receiver of the signal (the human ear and/or intervening codec) does a good job of interpolating (i.e., filling in the gap) where a packet has been lost. There is a limit to how much packet loss can be tolerated. That limit depends on several factors, including (1) the nature of the sound being transmitted, (2) the correlation in time between the packets lost (i.e., are they bunched together or widely dispersed in time), and (3) the randomness of the losses. Because they do such an efficient job of squeezing out redundancy, some codecs that use data compression algorithms are not able to recover from the loss of as few as two packets in a row.

Jitter can also contribute to lower quality. With IP traffic often taking multiple routes during high congestion periods and/or mixed in with bursty IP packet traffic, the interarrival times of the packets at the receiving end may be irregular and/or the packets arrive out of order. Jitter can be overcome by buffering the packets—that is, temporarily storing them long enough to reorder them before forwarding them to the decoder. However, buffering has the negative consequence of adding more delay.

Delay in the transmission of voice packets can be minimized in several ways. One is overbuilding the IP network (i.e., ensuring that there is always excess capacity in the IP network for all traffic, including during peak traffic periods). Alternatively, priority routing can be afforded to voice traffic, at the expense of lower priority data traffic—which is more tolerant of delays. Separate treatment of voice from data can be done by virtual segregation or physical segregation from lower priority traffic. The former can be done at either the network or data link layer. For example, segregation can be done at the data link layer by using separate ATM channels for voice and data traffic and then assigning ATM-based priority treatment to the ATM channels carrying voice traffic. Where voice and data are mixed on the IP network, identifiers can be used to indicate to the intermediate network components (such as routers) that designated traffic (such as voice traffic) should be given priority.

An example of this last method is RSVP, the Resource Reservation Protocol. RSVP allows a VoIP application to request end-to-end QoS guarantee from a network. (Cisco, VoIP Call Admission Control Using RSVP, 2003.) If the guarantee cannot be provided, the call will not be allowed to go through. Where the guarantee cannot be secured, the traffic might be redirected to an alternate network or blocked (resulting in VoIP users receiving an "equipment busy" signal). At the current time, priority schemes such as RSVP typically do not work over the public Internet. This is because, among other reasons, the economic incentives are not there for intermediate Internet providers to honor any type of prioritization routing scheme, given that their reimbursement is the same for all traffic—regardless of its priority designation. Therefore the current market structure for public Internet backbone routing prevents the realization of a higher quality of service for VoIP traffic over the public Internet.

To differentiate themselves, some Internet backbone providers are introducing prioritization schemes such as MPLS-based networks, which are ATM-like in their attributes but operate at a mixture of layers 2 and 3 protocols in pure IP environments. As competition intensifies, public networks are expected to become friendlier to real-time services such as VoIP. Quality of service is discussed in detail elsewhere.

The Costs and Savings of Using the Voice-over-Internet Protocol

One source of VoIP's cost savings over conventional telephony is its ability to employ transmission more efficiently because of both the extensive use of compression algorithms and the statistical nature of its information transmission. However, such efficiencies will tend to be most significant to private networks and/or network providers whose transmission networks are capacity constrained.

A second source of VoIP's cost savings is lower capital cost per call using lower cost switching devices (i.e., Internet routers and switches). Again, networks with sunk investments in conventional technology with excess capacity would derive little benefit from such savings.

A third source of VoIP's savings is lower costs of administration, particularly in enterprise environments. A good deal of administrative cost is incurred in enterprises to accommodate the movement of telephone users within the enterprise. Each time a user moves to another office or enters or leaves the firm, the routing tables and directory of a conventional telephone system must be updated, often manually. VoIP's self-registration feature eliminates these administrative costs.

A fourth source of VoIP's savings comes from the "economies of scope" that VoIP can achieve by its ability to intermingle with other traffic on data networks, eliminating the need to segregate voice and data traffic, as is often done with conventional telephony. These savings are most easily exploited in the LAN and WAN enterprise environment or by data-centric carriers who wish to combine their voice and data traffic. Administrative savings also come from eliminating the conventional regime of separate administrative staffs for voice and data.

Finally, VoIP traffic on a data network looks like any other data on that network. This allows some carriers and enterprise users to avoid some of the economically distorting taxes that local, federal, and foreign regulatory regimes place on pure voice traffic, but not on data traffic. It is important to remember that the realization of these savings are application specific and may not be realized in every situation (see, e.g., Morris, 1998; "Cisco Seeks Bigger Role in Phone Networks," 2003).

One thing to keep in mind is how shifting from conventional telephony to VOIP changes how telephony is managed. Specifically, conventional telephony involves the management of transmission facilities dedicated to telephony services. Thus, the telephony management personnel must not only be concerned with managing the terminal devices that provide telephony services, they must also be concerned with the management and installation of the transmission and intermediate switching facilities (i.e, the OSI Layer 1 and higher) that are dedicated to telephony services. With VoIP, telephony service management is simplified because it is treated as simply another application riding on an existing data network. VoIP involves only OSI levels 5 through 7. Thus, VOIP telephony management does not have to deal with installation and maintenance of the underlying physical transmission and switching layer. However, voice services require higher transmission reliability (e.g., 99.99% availability) and, in turn, the lower OSI layers (levels 1 through 4) must be designed and managed to assure that the voice-grade reliability goal for the VoIP application is maintained. In other words, when properly engineered, there are indirect costs imposed on the lower OSI layers that carry VoIP because of the presence of the higher demands of VOIP.

Security Issues for the Voice-over-Internet Protocol

Security is a concern with VoIP, particularly because of the distributed nature of the call control, much of which is handled between end devices (see U.K Advisory, 2004; CERT Advisory, 2004). Some of the things that make certain configurations of VoIP attractive (e.g., self-registration of end devices, mixing voice with data traffic over an IP network, and software-controlled PCs acting as end devices) are also the sources of VoIP's vulnerability. Security issues, listed in Table 2, include the following: (1) eavesdropping, (2) toll fraud, (3) caller identity spoofing (4) IP spoofing, (5) replay, (6) message integrity, (7) viruses and (8) denial of service attacks (Cisco, SAFE: IP Telephony Security in Depth, 2003; Cisco, Security in SIP-Based Networks, 2003).

Eavesdropping refers to an unauthorized party "listening" to the packets and, in turn, being able to listen to the voice conversation. This problem exists with both VoIP and conventional analog/digital voice communications. In both cases, the simplest method of preventing this problem is to encrypt the digital signal at its source, the originating telephone. The problem encryption brings is overhead and computational load, which can introduce

Table 2 Network Security Issues and Their Solutions

Issues	Possible Solutions
Eavesdropping: Unauthorized interception of voice packets or Real-Time Transport Protocol (RTP) media stream and decoding of signaling messages (one particular attack is known as "Voice Over Misconfigured Internet Telephones" or "vomit").	Encrypt transmitted data using encryption mechanisms like Secure RTP.
Toll fraud.	Caller authentication and security codes.
Caller identity/packet spoofing: Impersonation of a legitimate user transmitting data.	Send address authentication (for example, endpoint IP and/or MAC addresses) between call participants.
IP Spoofing.	Use spoof mitigation filters at Level 3 switches and ISP edge, and stateful firewall.
Replay: The retransmission of a genuine message so that the device receiving the message reprocesses it.	Encrypt and sequence messages; in SIP this is offered at the application-protocol level by using CSeq and Call-ID headers.
Message integrity: Ensuring that the message received is the same as the message that was sent.	Authenticate messages by using HTTP Digest, an option supported on SIP-enabled phones and the SIP Proxy Server.
Viruses, Trojan Horses that Cause Network Overload, Unintended actions by devices, or Crashing of Devices.	Segregate voice from data segments, and don't use PC's as telephone devices.
Denial-of-service (DoS) attacks: Prevention of access to a network service by bombarding proxy servers or voice-gateway devices on the Internet with inauthentic packets.	Configure devices to prevent such attacks.

Sources: Cisco, SAFE: IP Telephony Security in Depth 2003; Cisco, Security in SIP-Based Networks 2003.

delay. Also, encryption can create problems for law enforcement agencies where they have a warrant to wiretap a telephone conversation.

Toll fraud is the problem of unauthorized persons making telephone calls over the network. This can be caused by unauthorized users originating calls on the IP network either on legitimate phones or over illegitimate phones. As with conventional telephony, this can be combated with security codes and other authentication methods.

Identity spoofing refers to a hacker tricking a remote user into believing he or she is talking to the person he or she dialed on the IP network, when, in fact, he or she is talking to the hacker. Again, security codes and other authorization methods are helpful here.

IP spoofing refers to theft of IP identity, where one end device is able to convince the IP network that its IP address is the same as a legitimate device's "trusted" IP address. This allows the device with the fraudulent IP address to intercept calls and/or perform toll fraud using that IP address, as well as launch attacks on the network. Spoofing the IP address of a gateway allows eavesdropping on telephone calls.

Infrastructure threats that are security threats to the data on an IP network are also threats to VoIP traffic. These include the following: denial of service attacks and viruses (which can crash or tie up critical network terminals and equipment) and message integrity (i.e., the alteration of the messages between transmission and receiving) (Cisco, Security in SIP-Based Networks, 2003; Steinklauber, 2003).

Some generally accepted recommendations for minimizing many of these security problems are to disable self-registration of VoIP end devices after initial network installation, to segregate voice from data traffic at level 2 or 3 using some form of secure "tunneling" (such as a VPN) where possible when traversing "external" infrastructure such as the public Internet, and to use a stateful firewall at the PSTN gateway. As noted, segregating data from voice services also provides the added benefit of maintaining different quality of service for data and voice.

CONCLUSION

VoIP holds great promise where the convergence of data and voice can occur. Internetworking and overcoming QOS issues remain some of the biggest challenges.

GLOSSARY

Analog Signal A continuous signal that, at any point in time, can have an infinite number of possible values and that is typically analogous in some characteristic to another signal or physical phenomenon.

Asynchronous Transfer Mode (ATM) A network transfer method, employed at the data link layer (level 2), for high-speed switched packet routing, which can establish virtual channels with a specified QoS.

Channel Capacity The theoretical upper rate limit, in bits per second, at which information can be transmitted over a transmission channel.

Circuit Switch A switch that makes a temporary or permanent dedicated transmission path between two transmission links that are attached to that switch, based on signaling information received prior to establishing the dedicated path.

Digital Encoding Encoding a signal in the form of a string of 1s and 0s.

Digital Transmission Transmission of information encoded as 1s and 0s.

Internet A global public network based on the Internet protocol, connecting millions of hosts worldwide and for which users often pay a fiat fee to access, with little or no charge for transmitting each packet of information. (Outside the United States, Internet access is often measured and charged on a usage basis, e.g., minutes or units of data.)

Internet Protocol (IP) A packet-switching protocol used for routing packets over and between and private networks that is "connectionless" (i.e., each packet making up the same message may take a different route to reach the ultimate destination).

Node A point of connection between transmission links, which may contain switches and/or converters to interconnect transmission links with differing modalities (e.g., for connecting wire links to wireless links, nondigitally encoded links to digitally encoded links, or fiber links to copper wire links).

Packet Router A type of packet-switching device that typically routes based on level 3 network address information (such as an IP address) and typically has the ability to choose optimal routing based on dynamically changing criteria and routing tables.

Packet Switch A type of packet-switching device that routes packets of data between links based on address information associated with each packet. A level 3 switch uses network addresses, such as IP addresses, to route packets of data. Level 2 switches uses data link layer addresses (which are typically local and/or hard-coded) for routing.

Public Switched Telephone Network (PSTN) A circuit-switched network that is provided by regulated common carriers who offer their voice telephone services to the general public.

Quality of Service (QoS) A set of performance parameters or criteria, such a bandwidth, jitter, packet loss, and delay, prespecified for a service.

Transducer A device actuated by signal power from one system and supplying signal power in another form to a second system; for example, a telephone receiver earpiece actuated by electric power of a received transmission signal and supplying acoustic signal power to the surrounding air, which the telephone user can hear, or a telephone microphone that has a quartz crystal that produces electrical signal power for transmission over wires from the mechanical acoustic power originating from the telephone user's voice.

Transmission The movement of information (whether or not digitally encoded) from one point to another via a signal carried over a physical medium, such as wires, fiber, radio, or light.

Transmission Link A transmission path connecting two nodes.

Voice Communication The transmission of information contained in a voice signal.

CROSS REFERENCES

See *Digital Communication; Internet Basics; Public Network Technologies and Security; Security and Web Quality of Service; Security in Circuit, Message, and Packet Switching; TCP/IP Suite; Wide Area and Metropolitan Area Networks.*

REFERENCES

ALCATEL Guide to VOIP Internet Telephony (April 2003). Retrieved March 28, 2005, from http://www.ind.alcatel.com/library/whitepapers/wp_IPT_Design-Guide.pdf

ASCII Table. Retrieved March 28, 2005, from http://web.cs.mun.ca/~michael/c/ascii-table.html

Audin, G. *VoIP? A Questions of Perspective*. Business Communications Review, April 2001, revised February 2004.

Bell Laboratories (1977, revised 1983). *Engineering and Operations in the Bell System*. Murray Hill, NJ: Bell Laboratories.

Castelli, M. (2002). *Network Consultants Handbook*. Indianapolis, IN: Cisco Press.

CERT® Advisory CA-2004-01 Multiple H.323 Message Vulnerabilities. (2004). Retrieved March 28, 2005, from http://www.cert.org/advisories/CA-2004-01.html

Cisco, Security in SIP-Based Networks. (2003). Retrieved March 28, 2005, from http://www.cisco.com/en/US/tech/tk652/tk701/technologies_white_paper09186a00800ae41c.shtml

Cisco seeks bigger role in phone networks. (2003, March 3). *New York Times*. Retrieved March 28, 2005, from http://www.nytimes.com/2003/03/03/technology/03CISC.html?ex=1075611600&en=8239a78ed028c9bb&ei=5070

Cisco, SAFE: IP Telephony Security in Depth. (2003). Retrieved January 30, 2004, from http://www.cisco.com/en/US/netsol/ns340/ns394/ns171/ns128/networking_solutions_white_paper09186a00801b7a50.shtml

Cisco, Understanding Codecs: Complexity, Hardware Support, MOS, and Negotiation. (2002). Retrieved January 30, 2004, from http://www.cisco.com/en/US/tech/tk652/tk701/technologies_tech_note09186a00800b6710. shtml

Cisco, VoIP Call Admission Control Using RSVP. (2003). Retrieved March 28, 2005, from http://www.cisco.com/univercd/cc/td/doc/product/software/ios121/121newft/121t/121t5/dt4trsvp.htm

Cisco, VoIP Primer. (2003). Retrieved March 28, 2005, from http://www.cisco.com/en/US/products/hw/switches/ps669/products_configuration_guide_chapter09186a008007f1fb.html

Dalgic, I., & Fang, H. (1999). Comparison of H.323 and SIP for IP telephony signaling. Retrieved March 2, 2005, from http://www.cs.columbia.edu/~hgs/papers/others/1999/Dalg9909_Comparison.pdf

Doron, E. (2001). SIP and H.323 for voice/video over IP—Complement, don't compete! *Internet Telephony*. Retrieved March 28, 2005, from http://www.tmcnet.com/it/0801/0801radv.htm

Hackers discovering new frontier: Internet telephony (2004, August 2). *New York Times*. March 28, 2005, from http://www.nytimes.com

Internet Engineering Task Force (IETF) SIP. (2004). March 28, 2005, from http://www.ietf.org/html.charters/sip-charter.html

Internet Engineering Task Force (IETF) Telephone Number Mapping (ENUM). (2004). Retrieved January 30, 2004, from http://www.ietf.org/html.charters/enum-charter.html

Internet Engineering Task Force (IETF), SIP RFC2543bis (J. Rosenberg et al.). (2002). SIP: Session Initiation Protocol, SIP WG Internet Draft. Retrieved March 28, 2005, from http://www.softarmor.com/wgdb/docs/draft-ietf-sip-rfc2543bis-08.txt

IPTEL, SIP v. H323. (2004). Retrieved March 28, 2005, from http://www.iptel.org/info/trends/sip.html

ITU-T, Recommendation H.323. (2003). Retrieved March 28, 2005, from http://www.itu.int/rec/recommendation.asp?type=folders&lang=e&parent=T-REC-H.323

ITU-T, ENUM Activities (2004). Retrieved March 28, 2005, from http://www.itu.int/osg/spu/enum/index.html

Morris, R. L. (1998). Voice over IP telephony: Sizzle or steak? Retrieved March 28, 2005, from http://members.aol.com/_ht_a/roym11/LoopCo/VOIP.html

Neustar. (2003). Retrieved March 28, 2005, from http://www.enum.org

Newton, H. (1998). *Newton's telecom dictionary* (14th expanded ed.). New York: Flatiron.

Packetizer, T. M. (2003). Comparisons between H.323 and SIP. Retrieved March 28, 2005, from http://www.packetizer.com/iptel/h323_vs_sip

Real-Time Transport Protocol (RTP). (2001, August). Retrieved March 28, 2005, from http://www.cs.columbia.edu/~hgs/teaching/ais/slides/rtp.pdf

Sanford. (1999). Packet voice technology: Cheap talk? Retrieved March 28, 2005, from http://www.applied-research.com/articles/99/ARTicle10Sanford.htm

Skype, Retrieved March 28, 2005, http://www.skype.com/products

Steinklauber, K. (May 15, 2003). *VoIP security in small businesses, Version 1.4b Option 1,* SANS Institute. Retrieved March 28, 2005, http://cnscenter.future.co.kr/resource/hot-topic/voip/Klaus_Steinklauber_GSEC.pdf

Truxal, J. G. (1990). *The Age of Electronic Messages*. Cambridge, MA: MIT Press.

U.K.'s National Infrastructure Coordination Centre (NICC) Advisory. January, revised October 2004). Retrieved March 28, 2005, http://www.niscc.gov.uk/niscc/docs/re-20040113-00387.pdf

Vijayan, J. (October 7, 2002). VoIP: Don't overlook security. *Computerworld*. Retrieved March 28, 2005, http://www.computerworld.com/securitytopics/security/story/0,10801,74840,00.html

Wozencraft, R., & Jacobs, M. (1965). *Principles of communications theory*. New York: John Wiley & Sons.

Security and Web Quality of Service

Tarek F. Abdelzhaer and Chengdu Huang, *University of Virginia*

INTRODUCTION TO SECURITY AND WEB QoS

The Web has become the preferred interface for a growing number of distributed applications with various demands for reliability, availability, security, privacy, timeliness, and network bandwidth, as shown in Figure 1. These properties are often called Web *quality of service* (Web QoS) dimensions. The new demands call for both network and end-system architectures for performance guarantees to satisfy quality of service. Deployment of QoS architectures has been much more successful at the application layer than at the network layer. The failure of network layer architectures such as int-serv, RSVP, and diff-serv is attributed in part to the lack of a good pricing model for network QoS, the lack of appropriate enforcement, and the lack of an end-to-end solution that spans multiple administrative domains and is upheld by all Internet service provides (ISPs) on the path of a client's packet. In the absence of an agreed-upon end-to-end solution, incremental deployment of QoS mechanisms by a subset of ISPs is not enough to guarantee QoS and does not encourage client buy-in. In contrast, end-system solutions can be implemented and priced entirely within a single administrative domain, which explains their recent success. In this chapter, we first review the main components of the Web architecture and describe the protocols that govern their interaction. We then discuss how this architecture and these protocols are affected by QoS considerations, and explore the different security considerations that emerge specifically in QoS-aware end systems.

WEB QoS ARCHITECTURE AND SECURITY IMPLICATIONS

The questions this chapter addresses are why did Web QoS emerge as a new challenge area, what makes this challenge important, and what implications does QoS have on security. Today, the World Wide Web is by far the largest source of Internet flows. The great majority of Internet connections use hypertext transfer protocol (HTTP), which is the protocol that governs Web access. Improving its performance, therefore, has dramatic global effects. Efforts to improve performance come in two flavors. First, infrastructure improvements, such as realizing higher bandwidth, faster servers, and better last-mile technologies, are pursued. This is largely a cost and capacity provisioning problem that motivates development of lower cost facilities and higher capacity switches and routers. Concurrently, a substantial amount of research is done to make Web performance more *predictable*. Performance is said to be predictable when its quality can be *guaranteed* in advance. Many societal and commercial forces contribute to this need. In particular, the commercialization of the Internet and the pricing of many Internet services play a significant role in elevating the idea of performance guarantees from a value-added option to a primary concern driven by contractual obligations. The need for guarantees gives rise to new concerns on balancing performance and additional processing needed for security. In particular, a new class of security breaches in which a malicious user or set of users attempts to cause the system to violate its guaranteed performance to others emerges. We call this class *denial-of-QoS attacks*. The simplest form of such an attack is one that attempts to overload the server.

Mechanisms for thwarting denial-of-QoS attacks are of growing importance. In traditional commercial products, commercial users of the Internet have grown to take quality guarantees for granted. Vendors have contractual obligations to accept returns of defective products or products that do not perform as advertised. Similarly, paying consumers of Internet-based services expect a performance guarantee or a money-back statement. Much as with other services, it will be important that clients and service providers be able to negotiate mutually acceptable quality levels in the service contract for a corresponding price. Denial-of-QoS attacks can therefore result in monetary losses to online business.

This relation between performance guarantees and revenue is manifested today in several domains. For example, ISPs often sign mutual service level agreements (SLAs), which among other things describe the performance that the traffic of one ISP should receive in the network of the other and the corresponding fee. Closer to the end user,

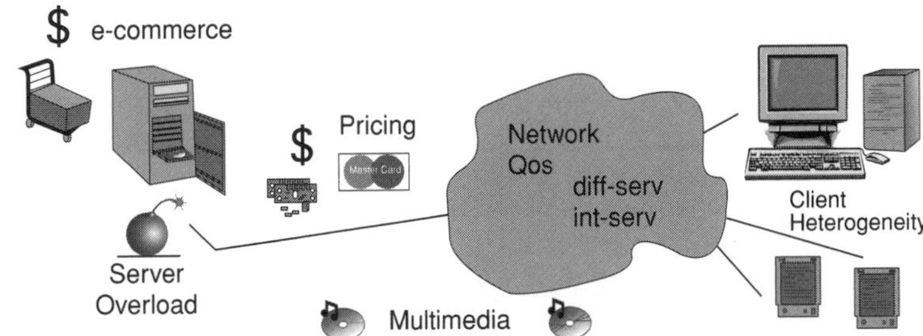

Figure 1: Web architectures and application.

online trading services sometimes tie their commission fees to performance in executing the trades. The fee is waived for trades delayed by more than a certain amount of time. In view of this emphasis on performance as a contractual obligation, a significant amount of research has been spent on architectures that enforce quality of service guarantees on the Web, even in the presence of malicious users. In the rest of this chapter, mechanisms and policies for QoS provisioning, QoS negotiation, and utility optimization, as well as means for protection against the corresponding denial-of-QoS attacks, will be discussed.

THE CHALLENGE OF QoS GUARANTEES

The most popular QoS attributes of importance in the Web infrastructure revolve around some notion of time. For example, guarantees may be needed on delay, or on the number of requests served per unit of time. We call such metrics *temporal*. A significant body of literature has addressed the issue of guaranteeing temporal QoS attributes in the absence of adequate prior knowledge of operating service conditions such as load and resource capacity. Until recently, the current state of the art in providing acceptable temporal performance to the users has been overdesign. Throwing money and hardware at a performance problem eventually ensures that there are enough resources to service incoming requests sufficiently fast. This approach, however, is inadequate for several reasons. First, it is rather expensive, because more resources are expended than is strictly necessary. Second, it provides the same service to all clients. In many cases, however, a service provider might want to use performance differentiation as a tool to entice clients to subscribe to a "better" (and more expensive) service. Third, the server provides only a best-effort service in that there are no bounds on worst-case performance. It is sometimes advantageous to be able to quantitatively state a performance guarantee for which users can be commensurately charged.

In the following sections, we describe several approaches for QoS guarantees in more detail. We then describe related security concerns and approaches for mitigating them. We begin by a brief review of the current Web architecture and the underlying principles of Web server operation (Figure 1). We then survey the modifications suggested to this architecture to provide security and performance guarantees to Web clients.

CURRENT WEB ARCHITECTURE

From an architectural standpoint, the World Wide Web is a distributed client–server system glued together by the hypertext transfer protocol (HTTP), which is simply a request–reply interface that allows clients (browsers) to download files from servers by (URL) name and allows one page to reference another, creating a logical mesh of links. The architecture is completely decentralized. By creating links from existing content, new content is seamlessly integrated with the rest of the Web.

HTTP

The main exchange between clients and servers occurs using HTTP. When a client requests a page from a server, only the text (hypertext markup language, HTML) portion is initially downloaded. If the page contains images or other embedded objects, the browser downloads them separately. At present, two important versions of HTTP are popular, namely HTTP/1.0 and HTTP/1.1. The most quoted difference of HTTP/1.1, and the primary motivation for its existence (Mogul, 1995), is its support for persistent connections. In HTTP/1.0, each browser request creates a new TCP connection. Because most Web pages are short, these connections are short-lived and are closed once the requested page is downloaded. Unfortunately, TCP is optimized for long data transfers. Each new TCP connection begins its life cycle with a connection setup phase, followed by a slow-start phase in which connection bandwidth gradually ramps up from a low initial value to the maximum bandwidth the network can support. Unfortunately, short-lived connections, such as those of HTTP/1.0, are closed before reaching the maximum bandwidth. Hence, transfers are slower than they need to be.

Persistent connections in HTTP/1.1 avoid the above problem by sending all browser requests on the same TCP connection. The connection is reused as long as the browser is downloading additional objects from the same server. This allows TCP to reach a higher connection bandwidth. Additionally, the cost of setting up and tearing down the TCP connection is amortized across multiple transfers. The debate over which protocol is actually better is still going on. For example, a disadvantage of HTTP/1.1 is its reduced concurrency, because only one TCP connection is used for all objects downloaded from the same server, instead of multiple concurrent ones. Another problem with HTTP/1.1 is that the server, having received and served a request from a client, does not know when to terminate the underlying TCP connection. Ideally, the connection must be kept alive in anticipation of subsequent future requests. However, if the client does not intend to send more requests, keeping the connection open only wastes server resources. The present default is to wait for a short period of time (around 30 s)

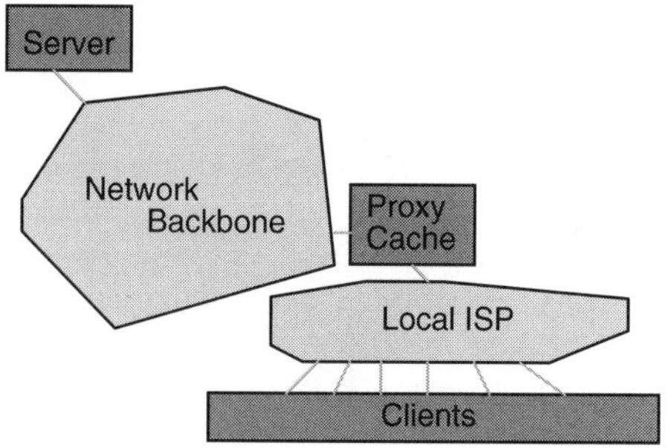

Figure 2: Web proxy caching.

after serving the last request on a connection. If no additional requests arrive during that period, the connection is closed. The problem with this policy is that significant server resources can be blocked waiting for future requests that may never arrive. It is therefore not obvious that the bandwidth increase of HTTP/1.1 outweighs its limitations.

Caching and Content Distribution

To improve Web access delays and reduce backbone Web traffic, caching and Web content distribution services have gradually emerged. These services attempt to redistribute content around the network backbone so that it is closer to the clients who access it. The difference between caching and content distribution lies in a data-pull versus a data-push model. Whereas caches store content locally in response to user requests, content distribution proxies proactively get copies of the content in advance.

There are generally three types of caches, namely proxy caches, client caches, and server caches. Proxy caches, shown in Figure 2, are typically installed by the ISPs at the interface to the network backbone. They intercept all Web requests originating from the ISP's clients and save copies of the requested pages when replies are received from the contacted servers. This process is called page caching. A request to a page already cached can be served directly from the proxy, thereby improving client-side latency, reducing server load, and minimizing backbone traffic for which the ISP is responsible to the backbone provider. An important question is what to do when the cache becomes full. To optimize its impact, a full cache retains only the most recently requested URLs, replacing those that have not been used the longest. This is known as the least recently used replacement policy. Several variations and generalizations of this policy have been proposed, e.g., to account for page size, cost of a page miss, and the importance of the client.

To improve performance further, client browsers locally cache the most recently requested pages. This cache is consulted when the page is revisited (e.g., when the client pushes the "back" button), hence obviating an extra access to the server. Finally, some server installations use server-side caches (also known as reverse proxies) to reduce the load on the server. The caching infrastructure significantly affects the user-perceived performance of the Web. Arlitt, Friedrich, and Jin (2000) compare the effects of different replacement policies on cache performance. Recent research efforts have addressed developing caches that provide some form of performance differentiation or QoS guarantees. A proxy cache, for example, can offer preferential treatment to content requested by a certain subset of clients or content belonging to a certain subset of providers. This mechanism will be described in later sections.

Recently, content distribution networks (CDN) have emerged as a technology that enables scalable content delivery from content providers to clients. Compared to Web caches, CDNs have the advantage that content can be prepopulated to their proxies based on the business relationships between CDN providers and content providers. CDNs also improved the ability of hosting content not cacheable by regular Web caches such as secure content and dynamic content.

PERFORMANCE GUARANTEES AND DENIAL-OF-QoS IN WEB SERVERS

In this section, we describe performance guarantee mechanisms for Web server end systems with an emphasis on enforcement considerations that prevent QoS violations in the presence of malicious clients and security attacks. As a running application example, consider a Web server farm that hosts multiple Web sites on behalf of different content providers. Web hosting is a growing business in which major investments are made by companies such as Intel, IBM, and Hewlett–Packard. We discuss the type of performance guarantees required, the parties to whom the guarantees are made, and the mechanisms used to enforce these guarantees in the face of denial-of-QoS attacks. The server farm example provides a context for describing the general classes of server performance challenges and helps illustrate solutions needed when resources are shared among multiple parties with different QoS requirements.

A Web hosting service interacts with at least three different parties:

(i) End users who access the hosted content;
(ii) Content providers who own the Web sites exported for hosting; and
(iii) Network providers who provide Internet connectivity to the Web hosting farm.

End users are typically interested in a fast response time; content providers care more about throughput, which translates into total capacity dedicated to their Web sites; and network providers care primarily about network bandwidth consumed by the hosting installation.

In general, the mechanisms to provide these guarantees lie either on servers (i.e., on the end system) or inside the network. Many QoS mechanisms inside networks such as int-serv and diff-serv have been proposed over the past 15 years. These technologies usually involve network users to make "reservations" so that different types of network service (traffic) will receive different qualities in terms of delay, packet drop ratio, and so forth. Although these QoS mechanisms on the network layer are vital for successful end-to-end QoS guarantees, their widespead deployment has yet to be realized. Because of their status quo of limited deployment, network layer QoS mechanisms have not suffered significant security attack yet. On the other hand, QoS guarantee mechanisms on the end system have been widely adopted by various operating system kernels and commercial application server products. Therefore, most malicious attacks are trying to exploit security holes or vulnerabilities of operating systems. In the following, we focus on mechanisms on the end system.

Performance Isolation

The most basic guarantee needed among multiple traffic classes is that of performance isolation. Informally, the guarantee states that the performance seen by any particular class of clients should be independent of the load imposed by any other class. For example, consider a Web server that hosts two Web sites, A and B. Unless proper action is taken, an attack on B may overload the entire server, preventing the clients of A from accessing the server as well. Performance isolation contains the problem by imposing limits that prevent any one site such as B from monopolizing the server. Hence, performance isolation localizes the effects of denial-of-QoS attacks. It acts as a fault-containment mechanism in fault-tolerant architectures. There are several different ways performance isolation may be implemented. They typically rely on some form of resource allocation and admission control. In the following subsections, we discuss some of the most important mechanisms for performance isolation in the operating system, middleware, and application layer.

Operating System Solutions

The core mechanism for performance isolation is resource reservation. Each Web site must be allocated its own resource quota on the Web server. Requests for that Web site are allowed to consume only those computing resources within the site's quota. Excess load on one site should not be allowed to divert resources dedicated to other sites. Traditionally, resource allocation and management is the responsibility of operating systems. Hence, the most fundamental solutions to performance isolation are operating system solutions.

Generally speaking, in a shared computing system, such as a server farm shared by multiple cohosted Web sites, common resources can be categorized into two different types: those shared in time and those shared in space. Space-shared resources include, for example, memory and disk space. Different processes may own different subsets of the resource concurrently and be denied access to resources owned by others. Space-sharing implies that the resource can be partitioned. Some resources, however, are indivisible. The prime example is the CPU. Indivisible resources can only be time-shared. In other words, they can only be allocated in their entirety to one process at a time. Clients are queued up on the time-shared resource. The queuing order and duration of resource access allowed by each client decide how the resource is shared.

Traditional operating systems such as UNIX implement a time-sharing scheduling policy, which allocates the processor one quantum at a time in a round-robin fashion among the waiting processes. This policy is inadequate for performance isolation in that it does not prevent any one class of clients from monopolizing the CPU. Consider our server farm example, where it is desired to isolate requests for different sites cohosted on the same platform. The CPU capacity available to one site under the UNIX time-sharing scheduling policy is roughly proportional to the number of processes serving that site at a given time. This number is in turn proportional to the client request rate. A Web site under attack with a large (malicious) request rate generates a large number of processes to serve these requests. It can therefore monopolize the CPU.

To ensure performance isolation, many researchers have addressed the problem of reservation of time-shared resources. The first effort on this subject came from the Real-Time Mach project at Carnegie–Mellon University and is called *processor capacity reserves*. The idea of processor capacity reserves is to implement separate accounting entities (the reserves), which keep track of the processing budgets allocated to abstract CPU activities. For example, a programmer can associate a budget with each separate Web site on the hosting server. The budget specifies the percentage of time that the CPU is allowed to spend on the corresponding site (e.g., 4 ms every 30 ms). The budget is replenished periodically. To enforce performance isolation, when a Web server reads a request, the request is classified and the corresponding budget is charged for the time it takes to serve the request. If the reserve is exhausted before the end of the period, the budget is said to have expired. When a budget expires, processes charged to that budget are blocked until the next replenishment period. Hence, these processes cannot jointly exceed the CPU allocation specified for their Web site.

One limitation of the aforementioned technique is the way accounting is done in the operating system. The party that the CPU is working for at any given time is identified in the operating system as either the kernel or a particular user process. Hence, only total kernel execution time and the total execution time of any single process can be measured. In particular, kernel execution time is not properly broken into independent activities. For example, the kernel-processing time of incoming requests is not properly attributed to the site for which the requests are destined and is thus not charged properly to the correct reserve. The problem is exacerbated by the inability to differentiate connections until they have been processed by the TCP/IP stack. To address the aforementioned accounting problem, resource containers (Banga, Druschel, & Mogul, 1999) have been proposed as a new operating system abstraction for resource reservation and performance isolation in monolithic kernels running server end systems. The authors of this approach make the observation that the accounting problem arises from the fact that in traditional operating systems the resource principal (i.e., the system entity capable of owning resources) is generally associated with a protection domain (such as a process). In server end systems, this association is not appropriate. The logical resource principal could be a user or a content provider. Depending on the server architecture, multiple processes can serve the same principal, or a single process can serve multiple principals. The resource principals should be charged for processing that occurs both on the kernel level and in user space. Banga et al. (1999) propose the abstraction of resource containers to resolve the dichotomy. In this approach, packet filters are placed at the lowest level of the protocol stack. These filters demultiplex incoming traffic into distinct categories (e.g., by IP address). All kernel and user-level processing of traffic in each category is charged to the corresponding resource container. As before, when the container is exhausted, the operating system stops processing the corresponding traffic type until the container is replenished. The approach has been shown to provide excellent isolation. In particular, it is very efficient in isolating denial-of-QoS attacks. For example, if the identity of the attackers is known, all traffic from them can be isolated and associated with a separate resource container of zero capacity. This traffic will thus be dropped, causing no negative effects on the rest of the system.

The need for early demultiplexing presents several challenges of its own. Such demultiplexing is typically performed based on fields in the TCP or IP header. Unfortunately, in many Web applications, client classification is a little more complex (Menasce, Almeida, Fonseca, & Mendes, 2000). Designing general purpose mechanisms to express such classification constraints at the operating system level is a challenging task, unless one is willing to sacrifice the application-independent nature of general purpose operating systems.

Another complication is that packets arriving at the bottom of the protocol stack (e.g., IP fragments) may not always have an application-layer header, which contains the information necessary for classification. These headers would be reconstructed higher in the communication protocol stack, which makes early classification more challenging. Construction of efficient packet filters for early classification based on application-specific information is therefore an important research challenge.

Middleware Approaches

When client classes are defined in an application-specific manner, a different solution to performance isolation is to develop middleware that augments generic operating system support with application-specific middleware policies. The operating system approach, described in the previous section, is perhaps the most efficient approach for fine-grained performance isolation. However, it suffers from the lack of generality and the lack of portability. The former refers to the difficulty of incorporating application-specific classification policies into the kernel. The latter (i.e., portability) stems from the fact that support for time-multiplexed resource reservation described earlier is still far from being a standard operating system feature. Thus, performance isolation solutions that do not *require* this support in the operating system are often preferred. These considerations lead to middleware solutions.

Middleware refers to any software layer that runs below the application and above the operating system. Generally, there are two types of middleware; that which is transparent to the application and that which requires application modification to adhere to a new interface. The former is more general in that it does not require access to application source code. Hence, a hosting service, for example, can develop in-house middleware components even when the source code for the Web server and the operating system is not available. Similarly, a middleware vendor can develop its software independently to interoperate with multiple Web server and operating system products without the need to modify their code.

An important challenge in designing transparent middleware services is to architect their (transparent) interaction with the server software. Such interaction is usually implemented by instrumenting standard dynamic shared libraries used by the server. Dynamic shared libraries are those loaded by the server at run time, as opposed to being precompiled together with server code. This feature is made possible because of late binding, supported by most operating systems today. In late binding, references to called library functions are not resolved until the call is made at run time and the corresponding library is dynamically loaded into the server's memory. It is therefore possible to make changes to the shared library without having to recompile or relink the server software. Once the server makes the standard library call, the new (modified) library gets invoked. In the case of middleware for performance isolation, the modified shared library may implement accounting functions that approximate resource containers.

One of the most obvious libraries to instrument is the socket library. Hewlett–Packard Labs researchers (Bhatti & Friedrich, 1999) were the first to suggest architectures where the socket library is replaced with a QoS-sensitive version, which implements performance isolation. In the context of regular socket calls, the QoS-sensitive library dequeues service requests from the server's well-known port and classifies them into per-class queues. The accept() or read() socket calls are modified so that no connections are accepted from a given per-class queue unless the budget of the corresponding class (maintained by the modified library) is nonzero. The scheme, shown in Figure 3, implements approximate performance isolation. It has been successfully integrated into a server platform sold by Hewlett–Packard, called Web QoS.

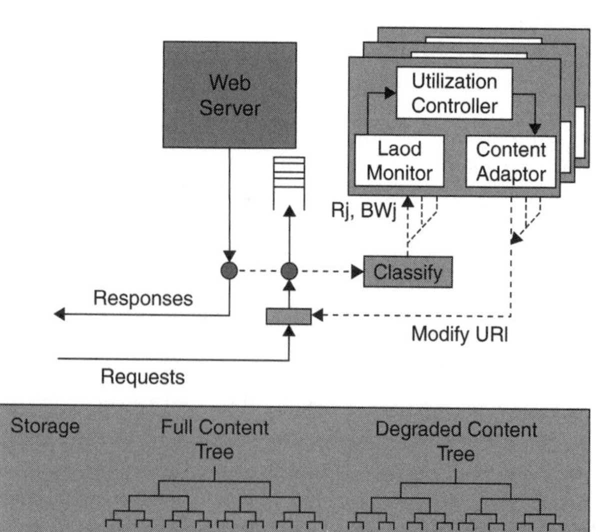

Figure 3: A middleware architecture for Web QoS.

A general problem with middleware approaches to performance isolation is their larger overhead. All requests (including malicious ones) must be processed by the operating system before reaching the middleware layer where they are classified and handled in accordance with their class. Hence, an attacker can overload the server by sending a large number of requests such that their operating system processing overhead alone is sufficient to saturate server resources. In view of this, middleware approaches for performance isolation can only elevate the threshold of overload, but not eliminate it completely. These mechanisms simply make it harder for an attacker to achieve denial of QoS. They do not address the operating system overhead spent on malicious requests.

Application-Layer Mechanisms

Current state-of-the-art Web servers, such as Apache (the most widespread Web server today), maintain a single process pool for all incoming requests. The single-pool architecture significantly complicates QoS provisioning because all requests are treated alike in the server. Hence, a group of attackers can send a large number of requests to the server until the entire process pool is consumed thereby denying QoS guarantees to other clients. In a multiclass server, attainment of performance isolation can be significantly simplified if the server is designed with QoS guarantees in mind. The single main feature that provides the most impact is to maintain a separate pool of processes for each traffic class. Once the server identifies an incoming request as belonging to a particular class, it is queued up for the corresponding process pool. Hence, attacker requests can be queued up in a separate queue from the rest of the clients, making it possible for these clients to continue to use their quota of server processes while an attack is underway. Several examples of this architecture have been proposed in the literature. QoS provisioning reduces to controlling the resource allocation of each separate pool.

Service Differentiation

An important second category of QoS guarantees is service differentiation. The goal of performance isolation, discussed previously, is to logically *partition* the resource so that each class of clients would get its own independent portion. Competition among classes is *eliminated* by giving each exclusive ownership over a subset of resources. Faults (such as overload due to an ongoing attack) are localized to individual resource partitions and hence are conveniently contained. In contrast, service differentiation policies do not attempt to partition the resource. The resource is *shared*. When the resource is in demand by multiple classes, the differentiation policy *resolves* the competition in a way that favors some class over others. Service differentiation policies are classified depending on what it means to "favor" a particular class. Regardless of the nature of differentiation, the system becomes susceptible to a different type of denial-of-QoS attack. Namely, an attacker can impersonate an important client and send enough requests to degrade service to others. Hence, *authentication* becomes important. Authentication refers to the act of verifying client identity to prevent identity theft. A server should not treat a client preferentially until the server has determined that this client is entitled to the preferential service. Authentication itself requires some processing time. Hence, an attacker can overload the server by continuously sending bogus requests that fail the authentication test but consume enough resources in the process such that the server becomes overloaded. One method to alleviate this attack is to delegate the authentication function to a separate dedicated machine. In the following, we describe the most common examples of service differentiation and their enforcement mechanisms.

Prioritization

The simplest method for providing differentiation is prioritization. Consider a situation where a Web service is accessed by two classes of clients: paying customers and nonmembers. The server offers two types of service: premium and basic. Assume that a dedicated authentication server that ensures that only authorized (i.e., paying) clients can get premium service exists. In contemporary Web services, paying customers are usually allowed access to protected parts of the Web site inaccessible to nonpaying users. This type of differentiation, however, fails to achieve its goal when the Web site is overloaded. In such a situation, a large group of nonpaying malicious users can increase load on the server to the extent that all users (including the paying ones) have difficulty accessing the site content. Performance isolation can be applied between paying and nonpaying users, but it suffers the problem of having to decide on the relative sizes of the respective resource partitions, which typically depend on the current load. One approach to circumventing this problem is to serve clients in absolute priority order. In this scheme all client requests are queued up in a single priority queue for server access. Under overload, the queue overflows. Clients at the tail of the queue are dropped. These clients, by construction of the queuing policy, are the lower priority ones. The mechanism ensures that denial-of-QoS attackers (who are presumably unauthenticated clients—hence are given a low priority) cannot degrade the performance of paying clients.

The problem with prioritization alone is that it fails to provide meaningful performance guarantees to the low-priority clients. The top priority class receives the best service, but very little can be predicted about the performance received by other classes. Prioritization, however, becomes an extremely useful analyzable tool once combined with admission control techniques discussed in the following.

Absolute Delay Guarantees

Prioritization, in conjunction with admission control, allows customizable absolute delay guarantees to an arbitrary number of client classes. Consider a case where there are N classes of paying clients. To recover a fee, the server is contractually obligated to serve each class within a maximum time delay specified in the corresponding QoS contract signed with that class. For example, in an online trading server, first-class clients may be guaranteed a maximum response time of 2 s, whereas economy clients are guaranteed a maximum response time of 10 s.

Failure to execute the trade within the guaranteed response time results in a commission waiver. Alternatively, in a Web hosting service, the content provider of each hosted site might have a QoS contract with the host that specifies a target service time and a fee paid to the host per request served within the agreed-upon delay. Hence, an overloaded hosting server, which consistently fails to meet the delay constraints, will recover no revenue from the content providers.

Because, in these examples, a host does not derive revenue from requests that miss their deadlines, admission control may be used against clients who are unlikely to meet their timing constraints. The rationale for such admission control is that scarce server capacity should not be wasted on clients who are unable to make revenue. Although theoretically admission control refers to a choice between acceptance and rejection, it is more realistic to choose between acceptance and *background service*. In other words, for the purposes of the following discussion, a rejected client is put in a separate lowest-priority queue to be served if resources permit.

Admission control has received much attention in Web QoS literature. Admission control algorithms may be classified into optimistic and pessimistic. The former type may admit clients optimistically even when they may miss their deadlines. The latter may reject them unnecessarily. Note that absence of admission control can be thought of as the extreme of optimistic admission control tests. Recent results (Abdelzaher & Lu, 2001) have shown that in a server with randomly arriving requests it is possible to use a constant-time admission control test to distinguish clients who will meet their deadlines from those who may not. The test is based on a running counter, which maintains a utilization-like metric. The counter is updated by a constant-time operation upon request arrivals and departures. If a request arrives while the counter is below a certain high-water mark, it is guaranteed to meet its deadline. Otherwise, the deadline may be missed and the request is served at the lowest priority level. Recent evaluation results of this admission control algorithm show that it rarely errs in the sense of unnecessarily rejecting requests. The test is shown to improve revenue at overload not only by eliminating resource consumption wasted on requests that miss their deadlines but also by favoring smaller requests (all other factors being equal) and hence improving server throughput. The derivation of the high-water mark representing the client admission threshold assumes that clients are served in a priority order such that more urgent requests are served first. A generalization of this test has later been proposed for first-in-first-out (FIFO) scheduling.

When priority-driven scheduling is used to meet deadlines, priority should be set proportional to urgency. There are two ways urgency can be defined. In the first, clients with shorter per-class response times are considered more urgent. The resulting priority assignment is called deadline-monotonic. In the second, urgency is defined by absolute deadline. The resulting priority assignment is called earliest-deadline-first (EDF). For example, consider a request arriving at time 0 with a maximum response time constraint of 10 s. At time $t = 9$, a second request of a different class with a maximum response time constraints of 2 s arrives. According to the deadline-monotonic priority assignment, the second request should receive higher priority because its maximum response time constraint, 2, is tighter than 10. According to EDF the first request should receive higher priority because its absolute deadline is $0 + 10 = 10$, which is before the absolute deadline of the second request, $9 + 2 = 11$.

EDF has been proved to be the optimal priority-driven scheduling policy. Deadline-monotonic scheduling is optimal among time-independent scheduling policies, i.e., those where priorities are assigned independent of absolute request arrival times. Optimality, here, is defined in terms of the ability to meet a larger number of deadlines. EDF can meet deadlines when deadline-monotonic scheduling fails because it takes arrival times into account. For instance, in the above example, if the first request has an execution time of 9.5 s, and the second request has an execution time of 1.5 s, both requests meet their deadlines under EDF, but not under deadline-monotonic scheduling. A problem with EDF is that it is less commonly implemented on standard operating systems, with the exception of embedded real-time operating systems where application timing is of prime importance. Deadline-monotonic scheduling is therefore a good compromise.

As previously, a separate authentication server would typically be required to determine the class of the incoming request. In this model, authorized paying clients can be served at a priority higher than that of nonpaying clients to mitigate denial-of-QoS attacks by the latter.

Statistical Delay Guarantees

An entirely different line of reasoning is to provide statistical guarantees on delays and deadline misses. Statistical guarantees require queuing analysis of the Web server. This analysis makes two types of assumptions. First, it must make assumptions regarding the queuing structure of the Web server. Second, it must make assumptions regarding the request arrival process. In the following, we outline the most important challenges underlying the statistical approach to QoS guarantees.

Consider the first challenge, namely, deriving the queuing structure of the Web server. This queuing structure depends on the protocol used. We describe HTTP 1.0 for illustration. Consider a typical multithreaded (or multiprocess) Web server. Packets arrive from the network, causing hardware and software interrupts that, respectively, read the packets from network interface cards and deposit them into a kernel-level input queue called the *IP queue*. In between interrupts, packets in the IP queue are processed by the kernel and queued for the particular application ports for which they are destined. These ports are often called sockets. Each socket is associated with an input queue, called the *listen queue*, where incoming connection requests are queued. Independently schedulable entities in the Web server, called *worker threads*, are blocked for data to be deposited at the listen queue. These threads are unblocked by request arrivals to execute the arriving requests. Each thread implements a loop that processes each incoming request and generates a response. Worker threads that have been unblocked by request arrival become runnable.

Multiple runnable threads may exist at a given time. The order in which such threads get the CPU to execute a request is determined by the CPU scheduling policy. This policy maintains a priority queue called the *ready queue*. The thread at the top of this queue executes for a particular time quantum or until it is blocked. Request processing by a worker thread typically entails access to one or more auxiliary server resources, the most notable being disk I/O. For example, in a Web server, disk I/O is usually needed to read the requested Web page from disk. Access to auxiliary resources blocks the calling thread, at which time it is queued for I/O until the awaited resource becomes available. Each resource usually has a queue, which determines the order in which accesses are served. We call it the *I/O queue*. The resource is made available to the thread at the top of the queue, at which time the corresponding thread becomes runnable again and re-enters the CPU ready queue. When request processing is done, the worker thread sends a response back to the client. Sending the response entails queuing data into the *outgoing packet queue* for transmission on the network.

The above discussion identifies five different queues involved in the Web server's queuing structure: namely the IP queue, the listen queue, the ready queue, the I/O queue (assuming a single I/O resource, e.g., disk), and the outgoing packet queue. The interconnection of these queues creates a queuing network with loops and other dependencies. For example, threads that repeatedly read and process disk data essentially loop between the ready queue and the I/O queue. Moreover, when the number of threads is fixed, dequeuing from the listen queue is synchronized with progress in the ready queue in that new requests are dequeued from the former only when some runnable thread has finished serving a request or has blocked. These factors make accurate analysis of the server's queuing structure difficult. Instead, many approximations are possible. For example, it is possible to consider only the queue for the bottleneck resource. The general idea is that a Web request is likely to spend most of its time waiting in the bottleneck queue.

The second challenge in providing statistical guarantees in Web servers is to identify the stochastic nature of the arrival process. Many queuing theory results assume a continuous Poisson arrival process. This process is characterized by an exponential distribution of interarrival times. This assumption does not hold for Web traffic. Research on Web characterization has identified that arrival of Web requests is generally modeled by a heavy-tailed distribution (Crovella & Bestavros, 1997). One distribution commonly used to model request interarrival times and request execution times is the Pareto distribution. Breslau, Cao, Fan, Phillips, and Shenker (1999) also determined that URL popularity follows a Zipf-like distribution. This information is important for studies of Web performance because it helps quantify the effects of caching. To experiment with Web performance in laboratory testbeds, Barford and Crovella (1998) developed a synthetic Web workload generator that faithfully reproduces the characteristics of realistic Web traffic, including its heavy-tailed distribution, URL popularity, and reference locality characteristics. The problem of providing queuing-theoretic performance predictions for such Web traffic arriving at a server modeled by the queuing structure outlined earlier is still an open research topic.

Statistical delay guarantees should only be provided to authenticated clients. Other QoS management mechanisms such as prioritizations or performance isolation should be used to defend against attacks launched by nonauthorized users.

Relative Guarantees

From queuing theory we know that delay experienced by a request is a function of server load. Ultimately, the only way one can reduce delay to meet deadline guarantees is to keep the load low enough. This implies denying service to some requests under high load to improve performance. In many cases, however, it is preferred that *all* clients receive service when capacity permits. One QoS-provisioning paradigm that subscribes to this model is *proportional relative differentiated services*.

Proportional relative differentiation was first proposed in the networking community in the context of delay differentiation in routers. It has since been extended to server end systems. In the relative differentiated services model, it is desired that the ratio between the performance levels of different classes of traffic be fixed; e.g., it may be that the delays of two traffic classes in a network router should be fixed at a ratio of 3:1. In general, if there are multiple traffic classes in the system, and if H_i is the measured performance of class i, the relative guarantee specifies that $H_1\colon H_2\colon\ldots\colon H_n = C_1\colon C_2\colon\ldots\colon C_n$, where C_i is the weight of class i. Hence, only relative delay between any pair of classes is specified. The absolute delay can take any value. When the system approaches overload, the delay of all classes increases, although some classes see a larger delay increase than others do in accordance with the relative delay guarantee. At present, mechanisms for providing relative delay differentiation are well understood, but not yet deployed.

Relative delay guarantees make the most sense under moderate server load. When the load is light, all classes see identically good service (no delay). When the load is very high, all classes suffer unacceptable delays and timeouts. In particular, in the presence of a denial-of-QoS attack, all classes will be affected, which is undesirable. Hence, from a security standpoint, it is useful to combine relative delay guarantees with absolute delay guarantees in a single framework. The combined architecture bounds the maximum delay of authenticated classes in addition to providing the correct delay ratio when the bound has not been reached. The architecture allows specifying a partial order on absolute and relative time constraints that determines which constraints should be relaxed first when network conditions make the combination unrealizable. Typically, in the presence of an attack, the relative constraints should be relaxed first, hence breaking the performance dependency among authenticated and unauthenticated lasses. The performance of authenticated classes (bound by absolute delay constraints) is then enforced.

Convergence Guarantees

In an environment where unpredictable traffic conditions make it impossible to satisfy absolute constraints, an alternative type of performance guarantee has recently been defined. This guarantee views QoS provisioning as a convergence problem and employs control theory to ensure stability and timeliness of convergence of system performance to the right specification (Abdelzaher, Shin, & Bhatti, 2002). The statement of the guarantee is that a performance metric, R, will converge within a specified exponentially decaying envelope to a fixed value, called the *set point*, and that the maximum deviation from the set point will be bounded at all times.

The absolute convergence guarantee is translated into a control loop such as those used in industrial control plants. The loop samples the measured performance metric (e.g., delay), compares it to the set point, and uses the difference to induce changes in resource allocation and load. Typically, it performs admission control to reduce load, and reallocates resources to alleviate the bottlenecks.

The use of control theory to control the performance of software processes has gained much popularity in recent years. Traditionally, control theory was used to model and control industrial processes described by difference equations. The intuitive reason that such a theory would be applicable to server performance control is that input load on a server resembles input flow into a water tank. The fill level of the server queue resembles the tank fill level. Admission control resembles a valve on the input flow pipe. Hence, the delay dynamics of a Web server are similar to flow and level control dynamics in a physical plant. The latter are well understood and can be described by difference equations. The second reason that control theory is becoming popular for server control is that feedback control loops are very robust to modeling errors. Hence, accurate models of software dynamics are not needed.

In the context of time-related performance metrics, it is interesting to classify the convergence guarantee loops, depending on the performance variable being controlled. As is the case with physical plants, the controlled output of interest affects the model of the system and whether the control loop is linear. Because most of control theory was developed for linear processes, the ability to satisfy the convergence guarantee is often contingent on the ability to approximate the server well by a linear model.

To a first approximation, rate metrics and queue length are easiest to control because they result in linear feedback loops. Rate can be controlled in much the same way physical flow is controlled in pipes. Queue length is simply the integral of rate, and therefore is also linear. Delay guarantees are more difficult to provide. This is because delay is inversely proportional to flow. If a request arrives at a queue of length Q, with a constant dequeueing rate of r, the queuing delay, d, of the request is $d = Q/r$. The inverse relation between the manipulated variable (rate) and the delay makes the control loop nonlinear. At present, providing convergence guarantees on delay remains an active research topic.

The effect of denial-of-QoS attacks on systems that provide convergence guarantees has not yet been investigated. In particular, it may be possible for an attacker to destabilize the system with sufficient knowledge of the feedback control loop, causing violations of convergence guarantees.

Challenges

In the previous section we outlined the semantics of the most important types of performance guarantees and corresponding security concerns. Next we summarize the challenges common to achieving these guarantees in Web servers in the presence of denial-of-QoS attacks.

Admission Control

A common enforcement mechanism of many QoS guarantee types in Web servers is client admission control. An important decision in the design of an admission controller is to choose the entity being admitted or rejected. In a Web server, admission control can operate on individual requests, individual TCP connections, or individual client sessions.

Per-request admission control is the simplest to implement, but has serious limitations. Consider an overloaded server operating at 300% capacity. Statistically, this means that two out of three requests must be rejected on average. For simplicity assume that all clients belong to the same class. Because client browsers typically issue multiple requests over the duration of the client's interaction with the server (even when downloading a single page), per-request admission control will uniformly cause each client to encounter failures in two-thirds of the accesses. Such service is virtually unusable. Per-request admission control discriminates against longer sessions. This has very negative implications, especially from an e-commerce perspective. For example, it has been shown in many studies that those e-shoppers who eventually complete a purchase from an online server typically have longer sessions with the server than occasional visitors who do not buy. Hence, discriminating against longer sessions gives a lower QoS precisely to those users who are more likely to generate revenue.

A better admission control scheme is to select a consistent subset of clients to admit. Those clients are admitted as long as they continue to send requests to the server within a specified time interval. The rest are consistently rejected. This scheme succeeds in making the service usable by at least some consistent subset of clients. It is also more meaningful in the context of addressing attacks on the server, as malicious clients may be tagged for rejection. This scheme is commonly called *session-based admission control*. It was first analyzed at length for Web servers by Cherkasova and Phaal (1999) and continues to be an important research topic (Chen & Mohapatra, 2002). Session-based admission control is more difficult than per-request admission control because at the time a session is admitted the server has no knowledge of the future load that it may impose, and whether the client is indeed malicious. Hence, it is difficult to decide how many and which sessions can be admitted. Different clients can impose substantially different load demands. For example, if the admitted client is a Web crawler, it may impose a much larger load than a human user. A mechanism for identifying malicious clients is needed. The admission controller must continuously refine the subset of clients to be admitted based on measurements of resulting load and outcomes of authentication.

Rejection Cost

Another issue tightly related to admission control is the cost of rejecting an incoming request. If admission control is based on the client identity obtained from browser-supplied cookies, a connection cannot be classified early inside the kernel. Instead, all requests must reach the application layer, where the server process can interpret the cookies and identify them as belonging to a particular class. Now imagine an overloaded server, which decides to admit all requests of class A and reject all requests of class B. Because the kernel cannot tell the two classes apart, all requests are forwarded to the application layer after being processed in the kernel. Kernel processing, as mentioned earlier, takes a nonnegligible overhead. This overhead is incurred whether the request is accepted or not. In particular, it is incurred for each rejected request. It is therefore called *rejection cost*. The rejection cost of a request can be more than half the cost of processing the request successfully. Hence, at overload, a significant portion of server capacity is wasted on request rejection. Rejection cost is therefore one of the primary challenges in mitigating denial-of-QoS attacks.

Consistent Prioritization

Many guarantee types, such as absolute delay guarantees, usually rely on priority-driven scheduling. Prioritization imposes a significant challenge in most mainstream operating systems. To be effective, all resource queues should be *identically* prioritized. Unfortunately, CPU priorities, which can be set explicitly in many operating systems, control only the order of the ready queue. It has been shown in recent studies that this queue is often not the bottleneck. In a previous section, we have identified at least five resource queues involved in a Web server. In many cases, the largest queue in the server is the listen queue on the server's well-known port. This queue is maintained in the TCP layer and is handled in FIFO order. Correct prioritization would imply prioritizing the socket listen queues as well. In I/O-intensive servers, such as those serving dynamically generated content, the I/O queue may be the bottleneck. Hence, disk access should be prioritized. Moreover, in a server implementing data structures protected by semaphores, it must be ensured that processes queued on a semaphore are awakened in consistent priority order. Unless all queues are consistently prioritized, an attacker can generate workload that overloads a nonprioritized resource, making that resource the performance bottleneck. Such an attack will circumvent any priority differentiation mechanisms employed by other resources to protect high-priority clients, because prioritizing access to nonbottleneck resources has only a marginal effect on performance. For example, if access to disk is not prioritized, an attacker can generate a disk-intensive workload, causing high-priority threads to block on disk I/O in a FIFO manner behind a large number of malicious low-priority ones.

Communicating priority information among multiple resources is a nontrivial undertaking. Proper operating system support must exist for priority inheritance across different resources. This support is complicated by the fact that blocking over nonpreemptive resources may cause involuntary priority inversion. The classical example of that is the case of two requests, A and B, where A is of higher priority. Let request B arrive first at some server and be blocked on a nonpreemptive resource such as a shared data structure protected by a semaphore. Request A arrives later and is blocked waiting for B to release the lock. Meanwhile, the progress of B may be interrupted by an arbitrary number of requests of intermediate priority. In this scenario, A is forced to wait for an arbitrary number of lower priority requests, even when all resource queues (including the semaphore queue) are correctly prioritized. The problem may be solved by the *priority ceiling protocol* developed at CMU, which bounds priority inversion. Unfortunately, current mainstream operating systems neither enforce resource priorities nor implement mechanisms for bounding priority inversion, such as the priority ceiling protocol. Thus, the current state of deployment is far from adequate for the purposes of implementing priority-based QoS support on Web server platforms that protects against denial-of-QoS attacks.

QoS Adaptation

The forgoing discussion focused on controlling load to provide time-related guarantees. The underlying assumption is that service must be provided by the deadline. There are no intermediate compromises. In the following, we present a case for QoS adaptation algorithms, which can negotiate intermediate performance levels within a predefined range deemed acceptable by the user. We describe mechanisms that implement adaptation in Web servers.

The Case for QoS Adaptation

Most QoS-sensitive applications have a certain degree of flexibility in terms of resource requirements. For example, JPEG images can be adapted to bandwidth limitations by lossy compression or resolution reduction. Dynamically generated pages can be replaced by approximate static versions to save execution time. Thus, when the server is overloaded, an alternative to rejection of further requests would be to adapt a quality of responses such that the load on the server is reduced. Many leading news and sports Web sites adopt this policy. For example, the appearance of the Cable News Network Web site (http://www.cnn.com) is often significantly simplified upon important breaking news to absorb the higher request rate. An instance of that was the great reduction in CNN site content during the first hours after the attack on the World Trade Center on September 11, 2001.

Content degradation is preferred to service outage for obvious reasons. One is that it maintains service to all clients, albeit at a degraded quality, which is preferred to interruption of service. Another is that it does not incur rejection cost because service is not denied. As mentioned previously, rejection cost can be considerable when user-level admission control is used.

To express the flexibility of adaptive Web applications, an expanded QoS-contract model is proposed. It assumes that the service exports multiple QoS levels with different resource requirements and utility to the user. The lowest level, by default, corresponds to request rejection. Its resource requirements are equal to the rejection cost, and it has no utility to the user. The objective is to choose a QoS level delivered to each user class such that utility is maximized under resource constraints. QoS adaptation should be used with great care as malicious clients can take advantage of it to artificially degrade server performance to a lower QoS level. Several content adaptation architectures have been proposed in Web QoS literature. They can be roughly classified into two general types, depending on the reason for adaptation, namely adaptation to network/client limitations and adaptation to server load. These two types are described in the following.

Adaptation to Network and Client Limitations

In the first type, adaptation is performed online and is sometimes called dynamic distillation or online transcoding. For example, see the work of Chandra, Ellis, and Vahdat (2000). The reason for such adaptation is to cope with reduced network bandwidth, or client-side limitations. Note that the dynamic distillation algorithm itself will in fact increase the load on the server. In effect, the algorithm implements a trade-off where extra computing capacity on the server is used to compress content on the fly to conform to reduced network bandwidth. Alternatively, transcoding or distillation proxies may be introduced into the network. For example, a transcoding proxy can identify a client as a wireless personal digital assistant device and convert a requested HTML page into wireless markup language for display on the client's limited screen. In the absence of additional protection mechanisms, an attacker can launch a denial-of-QoS attack on the transcoding proxy by requesting large volumes of content that require high-overhead transcoding operations. This is an inherent problem with all transcoding schemes.

Adaptation to client-side limitations can also be done using layered services. In this paradigm, content delivery is broken into multiple layers. The first has very limited bandwidth requirements and produces a rough version of the content. Subsequent layers refine the content iteratively, each requiring progressively more resources. JPEG images, for example, can be delivered in this manner. An adaptive service could control the number of layers delivered to a client, depending on the client's available bandwidth. A client with a limited bandwidth may receive a fraction of the layers only. The determination of the number of layers to send to the client can be done either by the server or by the client itself. For example, consider an online video presentation being multicast to the participants of a conference call. The server encodes the transmitted video into multiple layers and creates a multicast group for each layer. Each client then subscribes to receive a fraction of the layers as permitted by its resource capacity and network connectivity. Such adaptation architectures have initially been proposed in the context of streaming media. This technique has better security properties since slow clients cannot impose a large overhead on the server (unlike the case with transcoding).

Adaptation to Server Load

In the second type of adaptation, content is adapted to reduce server load. In this case, dynamic distillation or compression cannot be used because the server itself is the bottleneck. Instead, content must be preprocessed a priori. At run time, the server merely chooses which version to send out to which client. The server in such an architecture has multiple content trees, each of a different quality. For example, it can have a full content tree, a reduced content tree where some decorative icons, backgrounds, and long images have been stripped, and a low-quality text-only tree. A transparent middleware solution that features a software layer interposed between the server processes and the communication subsystem has been described. The layer has access to the HTTP requests received by the server and the responses sent. It intercepts each request and prepends the requested URL name with the name of the "right" content tree from which it should be served in accordance with load conditions. To decide on the "right" content tree for each client the interposed content adaptation layer measures the current degree of server utilization and decides on the extent of adaptation that will prevent underutilization or overload. This type of adaptation should be used with care. Otherwise, malicious clients may cause the server to downgrade its service to others.

An interesting question is whether load can be adapted in a continuous range when only a finite small number of different content versions (trees) are available. Such continuous adaptation is possible when the number of clients is large. To illustrate this point, consider a server with M discrete service levels (e.g., content trees), where M is a small integer. These levels are numbered $1, \ldots, M$ from lowest to highest quality. The level 0 is added to denote the special case of request rejection. The admission control algorithm is generalized, so that instead of making a binary decision, it determines a continuous value m, in the range $[0, M]$, which we call the degree of degradation. This value modulates server load in a continuous range. In this case, $m = 0$ means rejecting all requests (minimum load), and $m = M$ means serving all requests at the highest quality (maximum load). In general, when m happens to be an integer, it uniquely determines the service level (i.e., tree) to be offered to all clients. If m is a fractional number, composed of an integral part I and a fraction F (such that $m = I + F$), the two integers nearest to m (namely, I and $I + 1$) determine the two most appropriate service levels at which clients must be served. The fractional part F determines the fraction of clients served at each of the two levels. In effect, m is interpreted to mean that a fraction 1-F of clients must be served at level I, and a fraction F at level $I + 1$. The policy can be accurately implemented when the number of clients is large. It ensures that load can be controlled in a continuous range by fractional degradation and offers fine-grained control of delay and server utilization. Figure 4 shows an example of content (an image) with two service levels; regular (Figure 4a) and degraded (Figure 4b). In this example, the storage requirements of the degraded image are roughly an order of magnitude less than the requirements of the regular image.

Figure 4: Example of content degradation: (a) regular and (b) degraded content.

PERFORMANCE AND SECURITY CONSIDERATIONS IN WEB PROXY SERVERS

Before this chapter concludes, a word on performance and security considerations in proxy servers is in order. Proxy servers are intermediaries between the clients and the accessed Web servers. They are the main performance acceleration mechanism on the Web, which makes their study very important. QoS architectures should consider the effects proxy servers have on user-perceived Web performance and make use of them to satisfy client QoS requirements. Proxies may be used for caching, transcoding, or content distribution. A proxy intercepts incoming requests and attempts to serve them locally. If the requested content is not locally available the proxy may forward the request to another server (e.g., content distribution proxies), contact the origin server and save the response (Web proxy caches), or contact the origin server, transcode the response, and forward it to the client (transcoding proxy). Although current proxy servers typically treat all clients alike, there has been much talk on making them QoS-aware. For example, the server may offer preferential treatment to some classes of clients or classes of content.

Several research efforts have looked at biased replacement policies in proxy caches (Kelly, Chan, Jamin, & Mackie-Mason, 1999). Such policies attempt to maximize a weighted hit ratio, where weights are set in accordance with content importance. For example, content fetched from the preferred providers can have a higher weight and therefore a lower likelihood of being replaced. Another research direction is to determine dynamically the disk space allocation of a cache or a content distribution proxy such that content of preferred providers receives a higher hit ratio. In this approach, the "performance distance" between different content types can be controlled (Lu, Saxena, & Abdelzaher, 2001). For example, one can specify that preferred content is to receive twice the hit ratio of regular content. The underlying adaptive disk allocation policy uses feedback control to translate this specification into a dynamic disk space allocation that satisfies the specified requirement in the presence of dynamically changing load patterns.

Content distribution networks composed of multiple proxy servers situated around the Internet backbone bring another degree of freedom in Web QoS provisioning. The distribution provider may make agreements with content providers to distribute their content preferentially for a corresponding fee. Alternatively, the distribution provider may make agreements with certain ISPs to improve the quality of service to their clients by virtue of the content distribution network. An example of such a network is that introduced by Akamai. When a content provider authorizes a CDN provider to host its content, the CDN could create more than one replica of the content provider's Web objects on the CDN's servers. Obviously, the more replicas there are, the better average client access latency can be achieved because chances are clients' requests can be redirected to a replica closer than the origin server. The actual number of CDN servers hosting a Web content object is decided by its popularity, workload conditions of the CDN, and the QoS SLA between the CDN provider and the content provider. Supporting secure content distribution is an attractive feature of CDNs. It is envisioned that in the near future not only content but also "computation" of content providers will be distributed to CDNs. Security concerns must be carefully addressed before content providers are willing to authorize CDN providers to distribute their sensitive information, such as private data and Web applications.

Different from the scenario of clients directly communicating with servers, adding CDNs to the Web infrastructure makes each request from a client be intercepted by CDN servers. Hence, for those secure content requests, both the connection between clients and CDN servers and the connection between CDN servers and origin servers must be on top of secure channels. The level of protection used by the CDN servers should match those of the origin servers because stronger security protection means higher performance overhead and yet security is always as weak as the weakest link. For example, if the origin server uses 1024-bit keys for its content objects, then the CDN servers should also use 1024-bit keys to communicate with clients; if the origin server uses 128-bit keys, then there is no point incurring more overhead by using 1024-bits keys.

A security-related performance issue in CDNs is brought by the redirection mechanisms. CDNs use request redirection mechanisms such as DNS-based redirection and URL rewriting to offload content providers' origin servers and achieve a load balance. Note that redirection mechanisms do not necessarily guarantee that requests for some server's content from a client will always be directed to the same CDN server. Establishing SSL sessions has a very high overhead. If multiple requests of a single session happen to be redirected to different CDN servers, the overhead of initiating SSL sessions is amplified. Consider a scenario where a client established a SSL session with a CDN server and requested a Web page, which contains n embedded objects. The requests to download these objects, however, are redirected to n different CDN servers. This will incur n SSL sessions in total. This brings much higher workload to both the client and the CDN system. This problem requires the redirection mechanisms of CDN providers to be more intelligent. For example, if URL rewriting is used for request redirection, then the rewriting rule should make sure Web objects that are likely to be accessed together within a secure session will be rewritten to reside on the same CDN server. For DNS-based redirection, the DNS servers must maintain state information such that future queries from the same client are resolved to the same CDN server.

OTHER SECURITY ISSUES

The discussion on Web QoS so far has focused on denial-of-QoS attacks, raising the need for other security mechanisms such as authentication, secure sockets, and low-cost solutions to client request filtering. These issues are discussed next.

Client Authentication

As mentioned earlier, one fundamental problem of QoS performance isolation and differentiation is client identification. Different classes of clients need to be securely authenticated by robust and efficient methods. The simplest scheme is to identify the clients by their IP addresses. For example, the library of a university can configure its Web server to serve only those requests that originate from IP addresses within a certain range. This identification, however, is not accurate. In several cases, the IP address of the client is unavailable to the server. For example, it is possible that the client is behind a firewall or a proxy. In this case, it is the proxy's IP address that is seen by the server, not the client's. Besides, the granularity of authentication based on IP address can only be very coarse. Just because two different users used the same IP address does not mean they necessary should be granted the same permissions or receive the same level of QoS. Moreover, the ease of IP address masquerading makes this mechanism inherently vulnerable.

To identify clients, Web servers may use "cookies," which work similarly to passwords. The server sends a cookie, which basically is a piece of state information, to a client upon the first access. The client's browser automatically presents the server with this cookie when subsequent accesses are made. The server is therefore able to identify accesses that belong to the same client and separate them from those of another. Usually an expiration time is associated with a cookie. This capability may be used to implement session-based admission control. In general, cookies have several security flaws. For example, it is possible for cookies to be copied, allowing a third party to impersonate the client. Moreover, cookies are sent in plaintext.

The HTTP specifications (RFC 2617) provide two Web-specific authentication mechanisms, namely basic access authentication and digest access authentication. In basic authentication, clients are required to send a username/password pair to the server, in clear text, as part of their HTTP requests. The advantage of basic authentication is its simplicity. It requires no additional software support on the client side. However, basic access authentication is vulnerable to eavesdroppers. To avoid transmitting clear text, digest access authentication is added to HTTP/1.1. A server using the digest authentication mechanism first challenges the client using a nonce value. The client is then supposed to send the hash checksum of the username, the password, the given nonce value provided by the server, the HTTP request method, and the requested URI using some one-way hash function (e.g., MD5, SHA-1). This mechanism is more robust to eavesdropping because the most important feature of one-way functions is that it is *extremely* hard to figure out the original message from its hashed digest. Even if a sniffer gains access to the traffic between a client and the server, it is virtually impossible for him or her to decipher the client's username and password. Although it is supported by the Apache Web server, HTTP digest authentication still enjoys very little client support, causing it to remain in obscurity after having been proposed a few years ago.

It is worth mentioning that stronger authentication protocols generally cost more computation on both server and client sides. High computation overhead can be a depolyability hurdle for authentication schemes.

Performance Implications of SSL/TLS

In recent years, the secure sockets layer has been widely accepted on the Web as a very strong authentication system that can provide server/client mutual authentication (assuming both parties have a public key) and encrypted communication. Originally designed by Netscape, SSL has been standardized by IETF and called transport layer security (TLS). HTTP over SSL/TLS, also known as HTTPS, has received support from popular Web server systems such as Apache and Microsoft ISS and is now playing a very important role in e-commerce. SSL/TLS authentication is based on the public key infrastructure (PKI) and is typically used to authenticate the server to the client. In contrast, client authentication is usually done by supplying a password (shared secret). When an SSL-capable client communicates with a Web server, the identity of the server is first confirmed using digital certificates, which are issued by a trusted third party called the certificate authority (CA). When the initial authentication is complete, the client sends the server a "master secret" encrypted with the server's public key. The Web server then decrypts the "master secret" with its own private key. After that, a symmetric key is generated, which will be used to encrypt data sent between the client and the server during the session.

Secure communication over SSL/TLS, however, imposes significant performance penalties on Web systems. A previous study (Coarfa, Druschel, & Wallach, 2002) has shown that a standard Web server can handle only 10 to 30% of its normal load when processing secure SSL sessions. It is known that the largest performance cost of SSL is the handshake process of an SSL session, specifically the RSA operations to generate session keys. It is also shown that SSL/TLS is purely CPU intensive. Measures like reducing network traffic have very little effect on server performance.

The performance overhead of SSL/TLS has important implications on Web QoS service provisioning. Since an individual Web request/session is usually small, the overhead of establishing an SSL/TLS session can dominate the total cost of processing the Web request. This could diminish the effect of QoS differentiation mechanisms we discussed because the SSL/TLS overhead is equal for different client QoS classes. Imagine that establishing a SSL/TLS session takes 20 ms and that a QoS adaptation service makes the processing time for the requests in a session for two different client classes 5 and 10 ms, respectively, targeting for a QoS contract specifying a 1:2 service differentiation. The real response times experienced by the two classes of clients are actually 25 and 30 ms. This ratio is far from the 1:2 target.

Many solutions for alleviating the SSL/TLS performance penalty have been proposed. Since the task of SSL/TLS is purely CPU bound, one natural idea is using some dedicated components to offload this CPU workload. Today, hardware accelerators that perform operations of RSA are available from industrial vendors such as iVea, nCipher, and ArrayNetworks. These accelerates reduce load on the server CPU. Another approach that proved to be very effective in reducing SSL/TLS overhead is caching SSL session keys. The idea is that establishing an SSL session first attempts to reuse a cached session key, which was generated previously. Since session key generation is where the highest cost lies, reusing a session key greatly saves overhead. Only if the reuse attempt fails will a new session key generated. Experimental studies (Coarfa et al., 2002) showed that session key caching improves server throughput by two- to three-fold.

DoS/DDoS Attack

Denial of service (DoS) is known to be "an explicit attempt by attackers to prevent legitimate users of a service from using that service" (CERT, 1999). For example, attackers may send a huge volume of requests to saturate a server's operating system resources such as bandwidth and CPU capacity. Consequently, the server may no longer serve requests from legitimate users. All denial-of-QoS attacks discussed in this chapter are special cases of this category. DoS and its variant distributed DoS (DDoS) are becoming more and more frequent in today's Internet. In a recent measurement study (Moore, Voelker, & Savage, 2001), more than 12,000 attacks against more than 5,000 distinct targets were observed during a 3-week period. The target servers include famous e-commerce Web sites and small ISPs. DoS/DDoS attacks have a very significant impact on server's performance and sometimes cause service downtime, let alone QoS violations.

Although efficient means for preventing DoS attacks are still an open question, there are many defense mechanisms. One common practice for counteracting a DoS attack that is underway is to identify sources of the attackers and set up filters to drop packets from them. This kind of filters should be placed at the very early stage of packet processing (e.g., kernel TCP/IP stack or even border routers) so that the cost of dropping the packet is minimized. The drawback of this simple strategy is that oftentimes it is difficult to distinguish attackers from real requests because attackers can forge their source IP addresses since they do not expect meaningful responses from the target server. Besides, if the attacker identifying process gives false positives, packets from legitimate users will be dropped by mistake.

Many more intelligent solutions for defending specific DoS attacks have been devised. Take synchronization packet (SYN) flooding, the most common DoS/DDoS attack, for example. SYN flooding happens when attackers send a large number of TCP SYN packets but discard the SYN/ACK packets from the servers. Hence, the resources allocated for initiating the connections will not be released for a long time until TCP times out. A trivial solution for SYN flooding is for the operating system to randomly drop some SYN packets when a server detects that there are too many incomplete TCP connections lingering in the system. However, this is obviously not a desirable strategy because it may affect legitimate users. To alleviate the problem, we need mechanisms for reducing or even eliminating the resources consumed upon receiving a SYN packet. Two known approaches are SYN caching and SYN cookies. A SYN cache simply reduces the resource demand by allocating a much smaller structure to hold the initiation of TCP connection request. More resources will be taken on when the TCP handshake is completed. However, when there are too many incomplete connections in the system, the queue to hold SYN packets can overflow, causing packets to be indiscriminately dropped.

The SYN cookie goes one step further. It stores absolutely no state information. When a SYN is received, the server takes the hashing digest of the incoming information (IP address, port number, and sequence number) along with a secret key and makes the sequence number of the SYN/ACK sent back the digest. When the final handshake packet comes back from the client, the server uses the same hash function to get the digest of the incoming information of this packet. Note that the IP address and port number of this packet should be the same as those of the SYN packet and the sequence number of the SYN packet can be inferred from that of this packet. Also note that the digest the server just sent to the client will be included in this final handshake packet replied from the client. The server can compare the two digests. If they match, the state information structure will be allocated and the connection will be established. Otherwise, the packet will simply be discarded. Since SYN flooding attackers use forged IP addresses to send SYN packets, they will not be able to reply with a valid handshake packet.

Hence, the resource consumed on these packets is virtually zero. Actually, a server using a SYN cookie does not have to drop SYN packets even if the queue to hold SYN packet is full. The server simply sends back the SYN/ACK to the client, as if it has a queue of infinite length. The SYN cookie method is now included in FreeBSD kernel.

CONCLUSIONS AND FUTURE TRENDS

In this chapter, we briefly introduced the most important issues and mechanisms for providing quality of service in the modern Web architecture, as well as the implications of these mechanisms on security. The topic of providing secure quality of service guarantees is becoming increasingly important with the pricing of Internet services, and with the tendency to include performance requirements within the contractual obligations of service providers. The need for performance guarantees makes computing systems more vulnerable to attack, since impairing a system's ability to meet its performance requirements now constitutes a violation of its "proper" functionality. This performance-requirement-induced vulnerability gives rise to a multitude of denial-of-QoS attacks. In this chapter, the authors reviewed some of the most common attack methods, as well as mechanisms that can be used to mitigate their impact. The chapter also touched on security and performance considerations that arise in content distribution networks, as well as mechanisms for improving the performance of some essential components of any secure infrastructure. A particularly good reference for further readings on Web architecture, performance, QoS, and security issues is the recent book by Krishnamurthy and Rexford (2001).

GLOSSARY

Authentication The act of verifying client identity.

Backbone Provider A party that owns the communication fabric of an Internet backbone. Examples of backbone providers include AT&T, Sprint, MCI, and UUNET.

Cache Server A network server that acts as a cache of popular Web content and is able to serve it on behalf of the original servers.

Content Distribution Network A network of server platforms whose sole purpose is efficient content dissemination around the Internet backbone.

Cookies Small text files that servers put on the client's hard drive to save client and session information needed for future access.

Data-Pull Model A data communication model in which the client explicitly asks the server for data each time the data are needed.

Data-Push Model A data communication model in which servers unilaterally push data to the client without being asked. The model is a good optimization when future client requests can be accurately predicted.

Demultiplexing The separation of an incoming packet flow into multiple segregated flows. For example, demultiplexing must occur upon the arrival of a packet at a server, in order to queue the packet for the right recipient.

Differentiated Services A framework for classifying network traffic and defining different policies for handling each traffic class, such that some classes receive better service than others.

EDF (Earliest-Deadline-First) A scheduling policy that schedules the task with the earliest deadline first.

HTML (Hypertext Markup Language) A language for defining the content and appearance of Web pages.

HTTP (Hypertext Transfer Protocol) The protocol used for Web access in the current Internet; there are currently two popular versions, HTTP 1.0 and HTTP 1.1.

IP (Internet Protocol) The glue that connects the computer subnetworks of which the Internet is composed and is responsible for packet addressing and routing between Internet senders and receivers.

IP Fragment Part of an IP-layer message after fragmentation.

Kernel The core part of the operating system, typically responsible for scheduling and basic interprocess communication.

Microkernel An operating system architecture where most operating system functions are delegated to user-level processes, keeping the kernel small.

Packet A unit of data transfer across a network.

Persistent Connections Communication abstraction implemented by HTTP 1.1. It allows the same TCP connection to be reused by multiple Web requests to the same server. This is a main departure from the traditional "one request per connection" model of HTTP 1.0.

Proxy Server A specialized server that performs an auxiliary Web content management function such as content replication, caching, or transcoding.

QoS (Quality of Service) The quantifying of different performance aspects of Web access such as timeliness and throughput.

Semaphore An operating system construct used for synchronization.

Sockets The main interprocess communication abstraction, originally introduced in UNIX. A socket represents a connection endpoint. The connection is between two processes on the same or different machines.

TCP (Transmission Control Protocol) The transport protocol used for reliable data communication on the Internet.

Threads The smallest schedulable entities in multithreaded operating systems.

Transcoding The process of converting content on the fly from the server's format to a format more suitable to the client, or more appropriate for network load conditions.

Web hosting The business of providing resources (servers, disk space, etc.) to serving customers' Web pages. Typically, Web-hosting companies build large server installations of hundreds of machines for serving the Web sites. These installations are called server farms.

CROSS REFERENCES

See *Quality of Security Service: Adaptive Security; Security in Circuit, Message, and Packet Switching; Security Middleware; TCP/IP Suite; Web Hosting.*

REFERENCES

Abdelzaher, T. F., & Lu, C. (2001). Schedulability analysis and utilization bounds for highly scalable real-time services. In *IEEE Real-Time Technology and Applications Symposium*, Taipei, Taiwan.

Abdelzaher, T. F., Shin, K.G., & Bhatti, N. (2002). Performance guarantees for Web server end-systems: A control-theoretical approach. *IEEE Transactions on Parallel and Distributed Systems, 13*(1), 80–96.

Arlitt, M., Friedrich, R., & Jin, T. (2000). Performance evaluation of Web proxy cache replacement policies. *Performance Evaluation, 39*(1–4), 149–164.

Banga, G., Druschel, P., & Mogul, J. C. (1999). Resource containers: A new facility for resource management in server systems. In *Symposium on Operating Systems Design and Implementation* (pp. 45–58). New Orleans, LA.

Barford, P., & Crovella, M. (1998). Generating representative Web workloads for network and server performance rvaluation. In *Proceedings of the ACM SIGMETRICS '98 Conference*.

Bhatti, N., & Friedrich, R. (1999). Web server support for tiered services. *IEEE Network*, September/October.

Breslau, L., Cao, P., Fan, L., Phillips, G., & Shenker, S. (1999). Web caching and Zipf-like distributions: Evidence and implications. In *Proceedings of the IEEE Infocom '99 Conference* (pp. 126–134), New York. Piscataway, NJ: IEEE.

CERT. (1999). *Denial of service attacks*. Retrieved June, 1999 from http://www.cert.org/tech_tips/denial_of_service.html

Chandra, S., Ellis, C. S., & Vahdat, A. (2000). Application-level differentiated multimedia Web services using quality aware transcoding. *IEEE Journal on Selected Areas in Communication, 18*(12), 2444–2465.

Chen, H., & Mohapatra, P. (2002). Session-based overload control in QoS-aware Web servers. In *Proceedings of the IEEE Infocom 2002 Conference* (pp. 516–524), New York. Piscataway, NJ: IEEE.

Cherkasova, L., & Phaal, P. (1999). Session based admission control—A mechanism for improving performance of commercial Web sites. In *Proceedings of the International Workshop on Quality of Service* (pp. 226–235), London. Piscataway, NJ: IEEE.

Coarfa, C., Druschel, P., & Wallach, D. (2002). Performance analysis of TLS Web servers. In *Proceedings of Network and Distributed System Security Symposium (NDSS) '02*.

Crovella, M., & Bestavros, A. (1997). Self-similarity in World Wide Web traffic: Evidence and possible causes. *IEEE/ACM Transactions on Networking, 5*(6), 835–846.

Franks, J., Hallam-Baker, P., Hostetler, J., Lawrence, S., Leach, P., Luotonen, A., & Stewart, L. *HTTP authentication: Basic and digest access authentication* (RFC 2617).

Kelly, T., Chan, Y., Jamin, S., & Mackie-Mason, J. (1999). Biased replacement policies for Web caches: Differential quality-of-service and aggregate user value. In *Proceedings of the 4th International Web Caching Workshop*, San Diego.

Krishnamurthy, B., & Rexford, J. (2001). *Web protocols and practice: HTTP/1.1, networking protocols, caching, and traffic measurement.* Reading, MA: Addison–Wesley.

Lu, Y., Saxena, A., & Abdelzaher, T. (2001). Differentiated caching services: A control-theoretical approach. In *Proceedings of the 21st International Conference on Distributed Computing Systems* (pp. 615–622), Phoenix. Los Alamitos, CA: IEEE.

Menasce, D. A., Almeida, V., Fonseca, R., & Mendes, M. A. (2000). Business-oriented resource management policies for e-commerce servers. *Performance Evaluation, 42*(2–3), 223–239.

Mogul, J. C. (1995). The case for persistent-connection HTTP. *ACM Computer Communications Review, 25*(4), 299–313.

Moore, D., Voelker, G. M., & Savage, S. (2001). Inferring internet denial-of-service activity. In *Proceedings of the 10th USENIX Security Symposium*.

Mobile Devices and Protocols

Min Song, *Old Dominion University*

INTRODUCTION

Mobile devices are used for information generation, delivery, storage, and management; they can be carried and moved with ease. The mobile device market has extremely heterogeneous brands. They range from simple cellular phones to powerful laptop PCs. Generally speaking, however, they share similar physical characteristics, such as small screen size, short battery lifetime, limited input/output capability, limited computing power, and low network bandwidth. Nevertheless, mobile devices have become one of the fastest growing segments of the computer industry and will become the predominant medium for Internet access. There are two primary reasons for this trend. First, people want to communicate anytime and anywhere; and second, the rapid growth of wireless local area networks (WLAN) and new wireless transmission technologies have enabled higher connectivity.

This chapter provides an overview of two mobile device families. Each family is introduced from the following perspectives:

- Main functionality
- System resources (e.g., memory, computing power, and networking bandwidth)
- Input and output facilities
- Potential applications
- Embedded components (e.g., digital cameras, modems, and keyboards)
- Operating systems and software support

To better understand these devices, this chapter also outlines mobile communication protocols, security issues and measures, and mobile device management. In summation, we provide a conclusion and future trends. It should be noted that this chapter intends to present an overall picture of mobile devices and protocols as well as mobile device management. Many technologies and protocols cited in this chapter can be easily found elsewhere in this encyclopedia.

MOBILE DEVICE FAMILIES

Based on the main functionalities and the form factors, we classify mobile devices into two families as listed in Table 1. The first family includes mobile handsets, such as Web-enabled phones, personal digital assistants (PDAs), pagers, and portable storage devices. The second family includes mobile PCs, such as laptop PCs and tablet PCs. For a quick comparison among these mobile devices, Table 1 also provides the distinguished features of each device. It should be noted, however, that this list is not exhaustive: there are many other mobile devices available on the market. Next, we describe each family in detail.

Mobile Handsets

Web-Enabled Phone

For many years, the primary function of cellular phones was voice communication. However, starting in the year 2000, cellular phones have begun to incorporate basic data services, such as messaging and Web access. A Web-enabled phone is a cellular phone with features including Web access, messaging, e-mail, entertainment, address book, and customized applications. To access the Web or the Internet, a wireless application protocol (WAP) microbrowser is installed on each Web phone. The microbrowser allows users to access simplified versions of Web sites and to retrieve information such as stock quotes, weather forecasts, or news briefs. Messaging allows Web-enabled phones to send and receive short messages, which could include text, audio, and video. Most Web-enabled phones let users send and receive a short e-mail by running Microsoft Outlook or Web-based e-mail programs. The majority of Web-enabled phones also allow users to play games, listen to music, and take pictures. Most Web-enabled phones employ various digital transmision technologies, such as time division multiple access (TDMA) and code division multiple access (CDMA).

Web-enabled phones form a broad category, including Smartphones, WAP, i-Mode, Internet, Java, and GPS phones. Although the functionalities and features of these

Table 1 Mobile Devices Families

Mobile handsets	Web-enabled phone		Voice communication Web access Messaging E-mail Entertainment
	Personal digital assistant		Personal Information Management Word processing Web access Touch screen interface Handwriting recognition
	Pager		One- and two-way paging Address book E-mail Messaging
	Portable storage device		Large storage capacity Digital audio player Digital photo display Address book
Mobile PCs	Laptop PC		Most powerful mobile device High-speed networking connection Office applications Standard keyboard
	Tablet PC		Office applications Web access Digital ink input Handwriting recognition

mobile phones vary, essentially they share the same characteristics: small screen size, simple input and output facility, limited computing power, and low network bandwidth. A Web-enabled phone typically provides a small screen with between 6 and 12 lines of text, a standard 12-button keypad, and a few special keys (such as joysticks) for data entry. The typical phone battery life is from 3 days to a week depending on how often it is used.

Traditionally, Web-enabled phones create the wireless networking connection through a built-in wireless modem. Once connected, the user can perform voice calls or data communications or both at the same time. The rapid growth of wireless local area networks (WLANs) in the recent past provides an opportunity for large-scale WLAN integration into public phone networks. With the newly produced WLAN enabled handsets, users have immediate and convenient access to a wide variety of cost-effective high-bandwidth WLAN applications and services. One example is Nokia's 9500 Communicator. It provides extensive network access flexibility through WLAN, EDGE (enhanced data GSM environment), and Bluetooth.

Spurred by the ever-growing demands of business professionals, Web-enabled phones are expected to have more features in data processing and communications. Recently developed Web-enabled phones incorporate PDA features and have a larger screen to allow execution of data based tasks. One such phone is Samsung's SGH-D415. It can be easily converted into a full-size phone by sliding up the cover, exposing a wide display and large keypad. The 262,144-color display offers higher quality and richer images than conventional PDA displays. Users can receive and send multimedia messages of 100 kB each and store up to 1 MB of data. They may also download Java applets to broaden their mobile phone usage. When these phones also incorporated a global positioning system (GPS) receiver, the users can tell their exact location and send their position to a map on a friend's cell phone. The phone can even suggest a route to a user's friends.

Personal Digital Assistant

A PDA is a handheld mobile computer that assists users with its information management capabilities. The main operating systems used on PDAs are Windows CE, Palm OS, and Linux. Data are entered through either a small keyboard or a touchscreen with handwriting recognition. The output is a medium-sized color screen. Originally, PDAs were designed for personal information management (PIM). These tasks include, for example, address books, calendars, schedulers, calculators, to-do lists, and notes. More advanced PDAs have a preinstalled microbrowser for Web viewing, a built-in camera for video capture, still imaging and multimedia messaging. Some of them run word processing applications, spreadsheets, e-mail programs, and electronic book reading programs. Certain PDA models can even play music and record voice memos. Most PDAs can exchange information with a desktop or laptop PC by using synchronization utilities, such as Microsoft ActiveSync. Just like Web-enabled phones, the wireless networking connection is made through a built-in wireless modem, WLAN, EDGE, or Bluetooth.

PDAs are usually palm sized and typically have a touch screen and a stylus. The user must tap on an on-screen keyboard or enter data by writing on the screen with built-in character recognition support. Because PDAs are typically designed for handling basic PIM tasks, they generally have less memory (usually 2 MB), slower processors, and gray scale displays. Advanced PDAs usually have up to 256 MB RAM, processors at clock speeds of up to 1 GHz, and color displays. Therefore, they are able to handle other applications, including short message service (SMS), e-mail, and Web browsing.

Although PDAs are basically data-centric mobile devices, the convergence of voice and data functionalities in one device has added new features to PDAs. Recently developed PDAs, such as the RIM's BlackBerry 7780, the Nokia's 9210 Communicator, and the Ericsson's R380, are effectively PDA equipped phones. They integrate phone functionality, e-mail, SMS, Web browser, customized applications, and the Java development platform into a single wireless handheld device. Larger screens and easier data input make them more appealing devices for browsing wireless data than Web-enabled phones. More intelligent PDAs, such as Garmin's iQue 3200/3600, are designed for business users who want a device that can manage their personal information and deliver personal navigation in a single unit. They offer a fully integrated GPS that lets a user see an electronic map and get turn-by-turn directions.

Pagers

A pager is a small wireless device that uses a paging network to send and receive text messages (Beaulieu, 2002). To page someone, a person dials the service number, enters the number of the person to be paged, and sends out a short message. Immediately after a short transmission delay, the paged person will receive the message. For this reason, pagers are considered alerting devices. Originally, pagers were designed for one-way paging: the pager beeps and displays a short text message, and the paged person can take action accordingly. But the two-way pager enables the *paged* pager to automatically respond upon receiving a message. More recent paging devices, such as Motorola's Talkabout T900 2-Way, offer more features in addition to the basic paging services. These include the following:

- Wireless e-mail
- Calendar, address book, and memo pad
- Short message service (SMS)
- Information services (e.g., weather)
- Custom applications (e.g., Java)
- Preprogrammed reply capability
- Confirmed message delivery
- Automatic signature capability

These paging devices are essentially an e-mail pager with built-in Web phone functions. This indicates the convergence between two-way paging devices and Web phones. Pagers, however, have the unique features of low-cost and time sensitive messaging capability. A Web phone may act as a pager in terms of messaging and e-mail. The main difference is the network connection. Web-enabled phone users need to establish a dedicated network connection for messaging and sending e-mail, whereas in paging systems, the network connection is always there. Pager devices are specifically targeted at mobile professionals who depend on e-mail as a mission critical business tool.

Portable Storage Devices

Portable storage devices are the devices that are portable, lightweight, and durable and that allow users to permanently store their information. These devices include DVDs, CDs, memory sticks, Zip disks, SuperDisks, USB flash drives, hard drive MP3 players, and iPods. As an example, iPod will be detailed as follows.

iPod (http://www.apple.com/ipod/) features a combination of huge hard drive capacity and a digital audio player. The hard drives range from 20 GB to 80 GB, letting you easily slip up to 10,000 songs or 25,000 digital photos in your pocket and enjoy them wherever you go. With the click wheel, users can select playlists and scroll through a long list of albums or artists to choose their favorite song. The digital audio player is platform dependent. For Windows, it is called Musicmatch Jukebox Plus, whereas for Mac, it is called iTunes.

Popular iPod features include a calendar, address book, to-do list, alarm clock, games, and text reader. The iPod's Notes Reader lets users take text-based information such as news downloaded off the Web, stock tips, restaurant reviews, directions, and shopping lists anywhere. The iPod has a LCD display for viewing 6 to 10 lines of text at a time. Its battery life could be as long as 15 h. The newest member of the iPod family, the iPod Photo, displays 25 full-color thumbnails at a time. You can scroll through them the same way you scroll through song titles.

The iPod can be connected to a computer through either a FireWire (Mac or Windows) or USB (Windows only) port. Simply plug the iPod into the Mac or Windows computer to transfer music libraries and playlists. It is possible to load an entire CD onto an iPod in as little as 5 s. Users may also use the iPod to capture voice memos. The 40 GB iPod allows up to 28 days of continuous recording. The files automatically synchronize with the music library when it is connected to the computer.

Mobile PCs

Laptop PC

A laptop PC is a portable desktop PC. Like other mobile devices, laptop PCs can be carried and moved with ease. The main operating systems used on laptop PCs are Windows XP, Linux, and Mac OS X. A laptop PC typically has all the functions that a desktop PC has. These include the following:

- Office applications (e.g., word processing and spreadsheet processing)
- Web access
- E-mail
- Information services (e.g., weather and quotes)

- Multimedia (e.g., digital video and audio)
- Custom application (e.g., Java)
- Publishing
- Games

Laptop PCs are considered a special type of mobile device because of the following unique features:

- Powerful computing resource—most laptop PCs have the equivalent capabilities as desktop PCs. One configuration of a laptop would be as follows: Pentium Mobile Processor, Microsoft Windows XP Professional or Home Edition, video card with 64 MB or more of DDR video memory, 1 GB DDR SDRAM, and 40 GB internal hard drive. Thus laptop PCs can run the same operating systems and applications customized for desktop PCs.
- High-speed networking connection—most laptop PCs support both wired network connection (Ethernet 10/100/1000) and wireless network connection (802.11x and Bluetooth).
- Convenient input and output format—laptop PCs have screen sizes of up to 17 in. and the same keyboard as for desktop PCs. All laptop PCs also provide an embedded mouse as well as an external mouse.

Despite all these attractive features, the size and weight of laptop PCs limit their mobility. Because they run comprehensive operating systems and have complex hardware, it may take a few minutes to boot up the system; instead of a few seconds for other mobile devices. Laptop PCs that were produced prior to 2000 do not support wireless communications. These laptop PCs have to rely on the wired network connection, which is not convenient if a user is traveling.

Tablet PC

A tablet PC is a general purpose mobile computer with a large, integrated, interactive screen (Lee, Schnider, & Schell, 2004). Tablet PCs include many innovations, including handwriting recognition, longer battery life, a low-heat processor and an operating system that is a specialized version of Windows XP Professional. Users may write with a *digital pen* directly on the screen of the tablet PC, create handwritten documents, store, search, and review handwritten notes, and convert handwritten notes into text to use in other applications. A tablet PC typically has all the functions that a laptop PC has. However, a tablet PC is a perfect choice if you often need to be away from your desk or in an area where a laptop PC is not practical. Some tablet PCs, such as Acer's TravelMate 100, are able to morph between laptop and tablet layouts.

Tablet PCs are very similar to PDAs in terms of handwriting-enabled features. However, a tablet PC runs a more powerful and fully featured operating system. It also has a hard disk drive. Unfortunately, these features also mean that you cannot boot up a tablet PC nearly as rapidly as a PDA. Nevertheless, the tablet PC's large touch screen, digital pen, QWERTY keyboard, and sophisticated handwriting recognition and drawing capability have raised hopes that it might become the mobile device of choice for enterprise workers. These workers not only have to be mobile but also have to read, write, and type a great deal.

MOBILE PROTOCOLS

While there are two families of mobile devices, they generally employ the same communication protocols for messaging, e-mail, and Web access. Mobile protocols can be generally classified as peer-to-peer protocols and client-server protocols based on the communications model. In the peer-to-peer communication model, two mobile users send and receive messages instantly or by a store-and-forward manner. In the client/server communication model, a mobile user typically requests services or retrieve information from a more powerful server, which is typically a stand-alone unit. Next we introduce protocols deployed in each communication model.

Peer-to-Peer Protocols

Peer-to-peer protocols refer to protocols that enable one mobile user to send and receive messages to and from another mobile user. The operation can proceed instantly or in the store-and-forward manner. In the instant mode, the sender and receiver need to be well synchronized. The communication happens only if both peers are ready. Three well-known protocols are short message service (SMS), multimedia message service (MMS), and instant messaging (IM). In the store-and-forward mode, the sender starts the communication without synchronization with the receiver. Messages are temporarily stored on a server and retrieved later by the receiver. Whether or not the receiver is ready does not affect the operation of the sender. E-mail protocols work in the store-and-forward mode.

Short Message Service

This is a globally accepted wireless service protocol that provides a connectionless transfer of short text messages to and from mobile devices. It was first introduced in 1991 in Europe as part of the GSM standard. In North America, SMS was made available initially on digital wireless networks based on GSM, CDMA, and TDMA standards.

Figure 1 demonstrates the message delivery processes using the SMS protocol. Once a message is constructed at the source mobile device, it is sent over a wireless connection to the SMS center (SMSC) for that particular wireless carrier network. The SMSC then gets the message to the destination mobile device through the wireless carrier. To do this, the SMSC sends a SMS *request* to the home location register (HLR) to find the destination mobile device. Once the HLR receives the request, it responds to the SMSC with the destination mobile's status, which includes (1) inactive or active and (2) where the mobile is

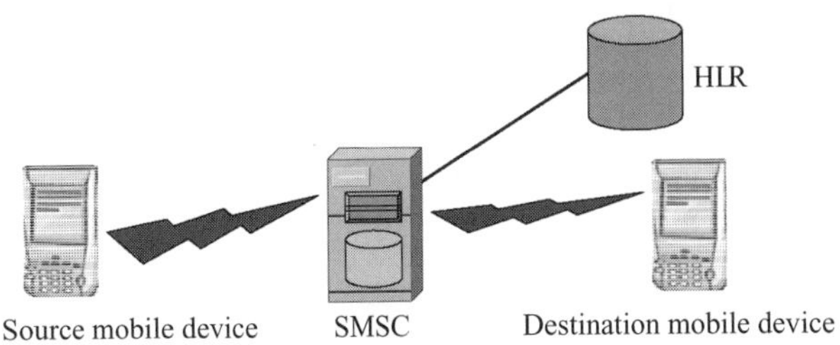

Figure 1: SMS architecture.

roaming. If the response is *inactive*, then the SMSC will act as a store-and-forward system and hold the message for a period of time. When the destination mobile device becomes active, the HLR sends a SMS *notification* to the SMSC, and the SMSC will attempt delivery. The SMSC transfers the message in a short message delivery point-to-point format to the serving system. The system pages the destination mobile, and if it responds, the message gets delivered. The SMSC receives verification that the message was received by the end user and then categorizes the message as *sent* and will not attempt to send again.

A distinguishing characteristic of SMS is that an active mobile handset is able to receive or submit a short message anytime and anywhere, independent of whether a voice or data call is in progress. SMS also guarantees delivery of the short message by the network. Temporary failures because of unavailable receiving mobiles are identified, and the short message is stored in the SMSC until the destination mobile becomes available. Initial applications of SMS focused on eliminating alphanumeric pagers by permitting two-way general purpose messaging and notification services, primarily for voice mail. As technology and networks evolved, a variety of services have been introduced, including e-mail, fax, and paging integration, interactive banking, information services, and integration with Internet-based applications.

With the advent of more mobile applications, some significant limitations of SMS have become apparent. The most serious of these is that messages must be no longer than 160 alphanumeric characters and contain no images or graphics. Another one is the lack of interoperability between network operators (Mallick, 2003). For these reasons, enhanced message service (EMS) was introduced to enable mobile devices to send and receive messages that have special text formatting (such as bold or italic), animations, pictures, icons, sound effects, and special ring tones. To help overcome the message size limitation, EMS allows for message concatenation. Because EMS is based on SMS, it can use SMSC the same way that SMS does. EMS messages that are sent to devices that do not support it will be displayed as SMS transmissions. The standard is considered an intermediate technology between SMS and multimedia message service (MMS), with more capabilities than SMS but fewer than MMS.

Multimedia Message Service

Multimedia message service (MMS) is a new standard in mobile messaging. Like SMS, MMS is a way to send a message from one mobile to another. The difference is that MMS can include not just text, but also images (JPEG, GIF format), audio (MP3, MIDI), and video (MPEG), or any combinations of the above. In addition, MMS also allows users to send MMS messages from a mobile phone to an e-mail address. This feature dramatically increases the scope of mobile communications. In addition, users can create, edit, preview, and send MMS multimedia messages, either via mobile handsets or via the Web. Each multimedia message contains a number of *pages*; each page may include content in different files associated with different media types. These files are incorporated into the slide show using the synchronized multimedia integration language (SMIL) (Bulterman & Rutledge, 2004). SMIL is an XML-based language specified by the World Wide Web Consortium (W3C) that is used to control the presentation of multimedia elements. Within the SMIL specification is a set of tags that can be used for defining the layout of each page and the time that each page is displayed.

MMS is an important emerging service that allows sending multiple media in a single message and sending a message to multiple recipients. The originator can easily create a multimedia message, using either a built-in or accessory camera, or can use images and sounds stored previously in the mobile. The message is first sent to the MMS Center (MMSC)—a similar concept to SMSC for SMS messages. Once the receiving mobile is located and is ready to receive messages, the MMSC immediately forwards the message to the receiving mobile and deletes the message from its memory. On a compatible mobile, the MMS message will appear with a new message alert. The picture message will open on the screen; the text will appear below the image and the sound will begin to play automatically. If the message is sent to a non-compatible MMS mobile the user will receive a SMS message. The user may then be given a Web site address to view the message. One of the main practical differences between MMS and SMS is that although SMS messages are limited to 160 bytes, an MMS message has no size limit and could be hundreds of kilobytes in size. MMS requires a 3G network to enable such large messages to be delivered, although smaller messages can be sent even with 2G networks using general packet radio services (GPRS).

Instant Messaging

Instant messaging is a type of real-time communications service that enables you to create a kind of private chat room with another individual over the Internet. IM allows you to maintain a list of people that you wish to contact, often called a contact list. You can send messages to any of the people on the contact list as long as that person is online. Typically, the IM system alerts you whenever somebody on your contact list is online. You can then initiate a chat session with that particular individual by opening up a small window where you and your contact can type in messages that both of you can see. Indeed, IM provides similar capabilities to other two-way messaging technologies, such as SMS, paging, and e-mail, with an addition of one significant feature: *presence* (Mallick, 2003). Presence lets you know the current status of the people with whom you are communicating.

Most of the popular IM programs provide a variety of features allowing your contacts to share your favorite Web links, music, images, and files stored on your device. ICQ is an example of IM program. The ICQ client that resides on your computer connects to an ICQ server and through the server communicates to your contacts, provided they are also ICQ members. AOL Instant Messenger (AIM), another IM program, supersedes ICQ by allowing AOL members to communicate with nonmembers.

Although AIM and ICQ are the leaders in the IM race, there are several other worthy entrants. Microsoft's MSN Messenger, like other IM programs, allows users to talk with other MSN Messenger users just like they would talk over the telephone. Another IM utility is Yahoo

Messenger. The interesting thing about Yahoo Messenger is how well it integrates with other Yahoo content and services. There are several utilities, such as Odigo and Omni, that combine various services. Odigo allows users to combine AIM, ICQ, and Yahoo Messenger contact lists. Omni lets users combine the functionality of AIM, ICQ, MSN Messenger and Yahoo Messenger, plus file-sharing utilities, all in one program.

E-mail Protocols

Three widely used e-mail protocols for mobile users are simple mail transfer protocol (SMTP), post office protocol version 3 (POP3), and Internet message access protocol (IMAP). SMTP is a protocol for sending e-mail messages from the e-mail client to e-mail server. When a mobile user wants to send an e-mail, his client application first establishes a TCP connection to port 25 of his e-mail server. The e-mail server will then look at the address to which this message is being sent and set up another TCP connection to the e-mail server at the destination address domain. When the destination e-mail server receives the message, it puts the message into the recipient's mailbox if such a recipient exists. Otherwise, an error report is returned to the message originator. Either case, the TCP connection will be released after the transmission is finished.

POP3 is a protocol used by e-mail client to retrieve the e-mail messages from the destination mail server. When mobile users check their e-mail, the client application establishes a TCP connection to port 110 of their e-mail server. Once the connection is set up, the POP3 protocol authorizes the user by checking the user's name and password. Once authorized, the user is allowed to access his stored messages and download the messages onto his local machine. Once the messages are delivered to the client they are deleted from the e-mail server.

IMAP is a protocol that allows e-mail clients *online* to process their e-mail. In this design, e-mail is still delivered to an e-mail server and the remote client reads the messages from the server using IMAP e-mail software. The messages are not all downloaded to the client machine. The client can ask for specific messages or search the server for messages meeting certain criteria. The user also has the option to save the messages locally. The mobile user receives the biggest advantage of the IMAP protocol because he or she simply needs a machine that is connected to the Internet to read his or her messages.

Client/Server Protocols

Client/server protocols refer to protocols that enable a mobile client to access a Web server or receive information from a Web server at anytime and anywhere. In this section, we outline hypertext transfer protocol (HTTP), handheld device markup language (HDML) notifications, wireless application protocol (WAP), WAP push protocol, and Web services.

HTTP

HTTP is a transfer protocol employed by mobile clients to access Web servers. It specifies what information mobile clients may send to servers and what responses they receive from servers. The original language to specify the information is hypertext markup language (HTML). HTML is a set of markup symbols or tags inserted in a file to tell a browser how to present output on a screen. HTML 4.1 is the latest version preceding the introduction of the extensible markup language (XML). Both HTML and XML contain markup symbols to describe the contents of a page or file. XML, however, describes content without style. More specifically, XML describes the content in terms of *what* data are being described. One of the most powerful features of XML is that it allows a user to construct other languages, including new markup symbols and attributes. However, both HTML and XML were designed for stand-alone Web servers and desktop PCs with a default window width of about 80 characters. This makes it unsuitable for handheld mobile devices. Three widely used markup languages for mobile devices are HDML, wireless markup language (WML), and compatible HTML (cHTML) (Lu, 2002).

A microbrowser on a mobile client typically connects to a Web server by establishing a TCP connection to port 80 on the server. After the connection is established, the mobile client sends request *methods* to the server. After the server receives the request, it retrieves the specified content and responds to the mobile client by sending the requested information in HDML, WML, or cHTML format. The microbrowser on a mobile client then interprets the information and displays it on the mobile device. With the current HTTP 1.1, it is possible to have multiple requests and responses take place under one TCP connection. The connection will be released on demand or after a given amount of time.

HDML Notifications

HDML notifications are the first form of push messaging available to mobile users (Mallick, 2003). They allow the server to send information to clients in a timely fashion—a process similar to SMS text messaging. But they differ from SMS in that they interact with the mobile device's microbrowser through the HDML gateway. One way to interact is to send an alert message, which typically contains a uniform resource locator (URL), to the device's microbrowser that will beep or display a visual signal to notify the user that new information is available. Another interaction method is to send notifications to mobile devices instructing them to remove certain URLs from the microbrowser's cache or preload contents into the microbrowser's cache. These kinds of operations are transparent to the users.

HDML notifications provide a powerful way to push contents to mobile users. However, because HDML notifications are a proprietary messaging technology developed by Openwave, they are only supported in Openwave microbrowsers.

WAP and WAP Push

WAP is a communication protocol between server applications and mobile clients (WAP 2.0, 2002). When a mobile client with a WAP browser accesses a Web server, it generates an encoded request in WML format and sends the request to a WAP gateway. The WAP gateway then forwards the request to the Web server. The Web server parses the request and responds to the WAP gateway with either

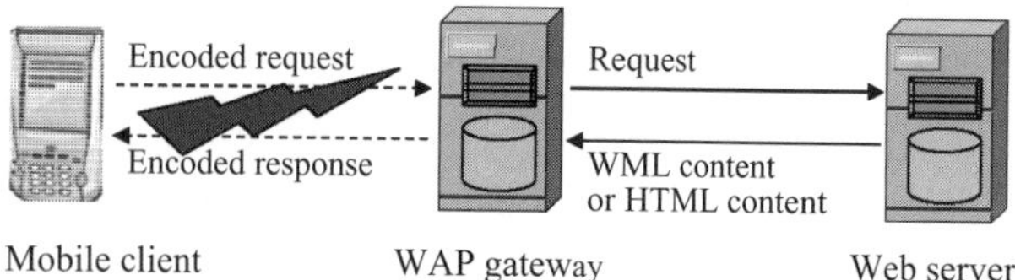

Figure 2: WAP communication model.

WML or HTML content (depending on whether the Web server provides WML content). If the server does not provide WML content, the Web server responds to the WAP gateway with HTML content. The WAP gateway needs to encode the HTTP response and return it to the WAP browser on the mobile client in WML format. Figure 2 illustrates this process, where mobile client could either retrieve a static document from the Web server or request the Web server to launch an application and return the results. In either case, the content is sent back to the mobile client for viewing or further processing. More information about WAP can be found in Chapter 68 (which is dedicated to WAP).

In the WAP communication model described above, a mobile client requests a service or information from a Web server, which then responds by transmitting information to the mobile client. This is known as *pull* technology. In contrast to this, there is a *push* technology, in which there is no explicit request from the client before the server transmits its content. WAP Push, first introduced in the WAP 1.2 specification, is the successor to HDML notifications. It is the delivery of content to the mobile device without previous user interaction (Openwave, 2002). Figure 3 depicts the WAP push structure. The push initiator (PI) is an application that pushes content and delivery instructions to the push proxy gateway (PPG) using the push access protocol (PAP). The PPG uses the push over-the-air (OTA) protocol to actually push the content to the WAP client over a wireless network. The PPG may also store the content temporarily if it cannot deliver the content immediately. It also maintains the status of each message, allowing the PI to cancel, replace, and request the current status of a message. The WAP client is a mobile device equipped with a WAP microbrowser to view the pushed content.

Web Service

"A Web service is a software system identified by a URI, whose public interfaces and bindings are defined and described using XML. Its definition can be discovered by other software systems. These systems may then interact with the Web service in a manner prescribed by its definition, using XML based messages conveyed by Internet protocols (W3C Web service, 2004)." Based on this definition, a Web service application is built from three major components:

1. A Web service registry, which stores information about Web service providers and Web services.
2. A Web service client, which makes use of a service offered on the Web. Web service clients can discover available Web services and get detailed information by searching the registry.
3. A Web service, which offers a service and is accessible via a standard messaging and transport protocol. Web services publish information about themselves in a Web service registry.

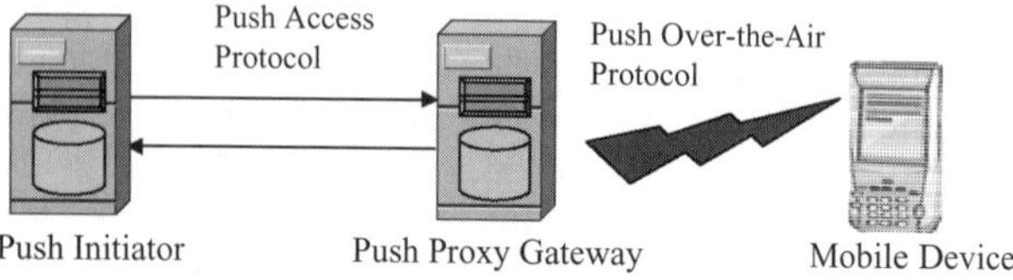

Figure 3: WAP push structure.

Accordingly, the following three technologies are the forefront for implementing a Web service:

1. Universal discovery, description and integration (UDDI) is a standard for Web service registries (UDDI Version 3.0.1, 2003). UDDI defines a set of services supporting the description and discovery of Web service providers, the available Web services, and the technical interfaces that may be used to access those services. Based on a common set of industry standards, including SOAP and XML, UDDI provides an interoperable, foundational infrastructure for a Web services-based software environment.
2. Simple object access protocol (SOAP) is a protocol for a program on client to call a Web service on server by sending XML data over HTTP (SOAP Version 1.2, 2003). It also specifies how the called program can return a response. Unlike other similar technologies (CORBA, Java RMI, and DCOM), SOAP is an open standards protocol; this provides interoperability among machines running different operating systems.
3. Web services description language (WSDL) is an XML-based specification that provides a standard format for describing Web services (WSDL Version 2.0, 2004). It contains the information about how to invoke the service and what, if any, response to expect. WSDL enables one to separate the description of the abstract functionality offered by a service from concrete details of a service description such as *how* and *where* that functionality is offered.

To deploy the Web services technology for mobile devices, mobile Web services were designed to enable mobile users to take advantage of wireless applications, such as mobile messaging and location-based services, and delivering integrated services across wired and wireless networks. Microsoft and Vodafone achieve this by using an XML-based Web services architecture, allowing developers to build new, innovative services across both fixed and wireless networks. IBM provides the Web services tool kit for mobile devices (WSTKMD) and the run-time environments that allow development of applications that use Web services on small mobile devices, gateway devices, and intelligent controllers. The Mobile SOAP server uses the WSTKMD run-time environment in conjunction with a mobile gateway server to receive SOAP requests from any SOAP client and to return a response. Other mobile

Web service initiatives include Sun's Javafirst project, Symbian's Action Engine mobile Web services platform, QUALCOMM's Binary Runtime Environment for Wireless (BREW), and GSM Association's M-Services.

MOBILE DEVICES SECURITY AND MEASURES

We start this section by first introducing the common security issues in computer networks. Then we clarify how these issues apply specifically to mobile devices and protocols. Network security issues can be divided into six closely interrelated areas:

1. Authentication: This deals with determining the identity of the communication partner.
2. Authorization: This determines whether an authenticated user has the permission to access the system resource or to receive services.
3. Confidentiality: This keeps the data encrypted so that the data are out of the hands of the third party.
4. Integrity: This ensures that the data has not been altered or corrupted in any way during the transmission or storage.
5. Availability: This prevents malicious users from blocking legitimate access to network resources or services.
6. Nonrepudiation: This guarantees that no communicating party can deny the fact that it once sent a message and deny the contents included in the message.

Many security issues in mobile networks are essentially the same as those described above. However, security protocols developed for desktop PCs do not work well on mobile devices. The mobility and wireless natures of mobile networks make the security more challenging. Indeed, special design attention is needed to provide an acceptable security level for mobile devices. In this section, we first introduce security attacks on mobile devices; then we examine mobile security measures at three levels: (1) the mobile-user level, (2) the mobile data and applications level, and (3) the network communications level.

Security Attacks on Mobile Devices

Security attacks on mobile devices can be in either passive mode or active mode. A passive attack does not attempt to damage the target mobile system. It performs the attack mainly by spoofing, eavesdropping, and installing malicious code. Information collected can be used to analyze the target mobile system and thus steal the confidential information. An active attack tries to damage the target mobile system completely and instantly. The main approaches for active attacks include, for example, denial of service (DOS), man-in-the-middle, and theft. Because of their natures, passive attacks are more difficult to detect and active attacks are more detrimental. Following are the typical attacks on mobile devices:

- Spoofing: This is an attempt to obtain unauthorized access to a mobile system by pretending to be a legitimate user. If the attacker succeeds, he or she can then create fake responses to the mobile system in an attempt to acquire further knowledge and access to the associated wireless network. It is possible to prevent spoofing by a strong combination of user authentication and authorization.
- Eavesdropping: This is a technique to monitor data flow on a mobile network. By listening to network data, unauthorized parties can obtain sensitive information that allows them to further damage mobile users. It is possible to prevent eavesdropping by deploying a strong confidentiality mechanism.
- Malicious code: This is a technique to install a small piece of code on mobile devices to perform damaging activities by stealing private information, modifying data, deleting data, and blacking screens. These codes could be in the format of spyware or viruses and can be triggered by certain events, such as network transmissions or event time. Even worse, they can easily be spread to other mobile devices or networks by a simple call. It is possible to combat this attack by embedding a strong authorization algorithm and to install on-device built-in security checks to ensure that only authorized code is allowed to execute.
- Denial of service: This is a technique to block legitimate access to the mobile devices. A wireless network is even more vulnerable to DOS attacks, because the attacker is not tied to a wired connection. In the case of mobile phones an attack can be mounted from anywhere in the world. Even worse, an authorized device could also become infected and consequently be used to mount a DOS attack. It is possible to reduce DOS attacks by limiting the devices authorized to connect to a mobile thus ensuring the availability.
- Man-in-the-middle (Zhang & Chen, 2004): In this technique an attacker intercepts the messages transmitted between the communicating parties. The intercepted messages can then be modified, delayed, relayed to another party, and replayed to the legitimate communicating party. Under this attack, an attacker could pretend to be an authorized user, to access a network or information, even when the captured information was strongly encrypted. It is possible to alleviate this attack by implementing a strong integrity system.
- Theft: Modern mobile devices are increasingly lightweight in design. Because of this, mobile devices tend to be easily lost or stolen and thus the data stored on devices and the network resources accessible through the devices are exposed to serious attack.

Except the theft attack, whose prevention depends primarily on device owners, other attacks occur at different communications levels, which are detailed next.

User-Mobile Level Security Measures

The main security issue at this level is user authentication (i.e., verifying that a person attempting to access a mobile device is a legitimate user). Security measures at this level help mitigate the attacks of spoofing, man-in-the-middle, and theft.

There are several mechanisms to perform authentication. The most common one is a strong username/password combination. Many mobile devices have built-in username/password functionality. This requires the user to authenticate before they are granted access to the device. When a user attempts to access the device with an incorrect username/password combination, the system imposes a time delay before allowing access again—a delay that increases exponentially with each attempt. A failure after a limited number of tries indicates an unauthorized usage. More rigorous authentication methods include (Dedo, 2004)

- Signature authentication
- Picture-based passwords
- Fingerprint authentication
- Smart card security
- Secure ID card authentication
- Certificate authentication on a storage card

By doing one or more of the aforementioned authentication processes, a user is required to authenticate every time he or she accesses the device and the associated network. Although this might be considered a usability drawback, it is an essential measure to combat attacks such as spoofing, man-in-the-middle, and theft.

Mobile Data and Applications Level Security Measures

The main security issue at this level is user authorization (i.e., verifying the person has the appropriate authority to access the data and run the applications stored on the device and the associated network). Security measures at this level help mitigate spoofing and theft attacks.

Mobile users often store important documents on the mobile device itself—either in the memory or a storage card that can store hundreds of megabytes to tens of gigabytes. To protect these documents as well as other sensitive data such as username/password and personal information, effective encryption algorithms are designed and implemented on the device itself and on external storage cards. There are a number of ways to encrypt the stored data to protect it from unauthorized access. For mobile PCs, Microsoft offers a mechanism for storing encrypted data in a relational database, protected with both 128-bit encryption and a password.

Recently, as more computing power and local storage become available on mobile devices, many more applications can be implemented on mobile devices. Such applications are also called smart client applications. In this case, the application may have a login page that authenticates against a local database. A user must log in to use a particular application regardless of whether the mobile device is connected to a network.

Network Communications Level Security Measures

The main security issues at this level are confidentiality, integrity, and nonrepudiation. Security measures at this level help mitigate the attacks of eavesdropping, DOS, and man-in-the-middle.

To protect data transmitted over the Internet and wireless networks, there are three steps needed before a user can transmit data (Brown, 1995; Zhang & Chen, 2004):

- Security provisioning: This is to generate and distribute credentials to both users and the network.
- Local registration: With the provisioned security information, a user can perform registration with the network to gain permission to use the network.
- Authentication and key agreement (AKA): The AKA provides a methodology to authenticate a user and to generate two keys, an encryption key and an integrity check key. In addition, there is also a secret key shared by the user and the network that is available only to the authentication center. Thus, the mobile and network mutual authentication allows mobile users and networks to authenticate each other (3GPP, 2002).

A broad range of security algorithms have been developed and deployed in the above three steps. The main measures are data encryption, digital certificates, Internet protocol security (IPSec), transport layer security (TLS), and WAP security.

Encryption algorithms (more details can be found in Chapters 108–117 of Volume II) encode information in such a manner that only the persons or applications with the correct key can decode it. Digital certificates (more details can be found in Chapter 56) provide a way to guarantee that a public key belongs to the party it represents (Mallick, 2003). For this to be successful, the certificate itself also has to be verified to ensure that it represents the claimed party. This is accomplished using a trusted third party called a *certificate authority*. IPSec (more details can be found in Chapters 64 and 65) is a set of protocols in the network layer to provide cryptographic security services that will flexibly support combinations of authentication, authorization, confidentiality, and integrity. TLS (more details can be found in Chapter 66) is a protocol in the transport layer to ensure confidentiality between communicating applications and their users on the Internet. When a server and client communicate, TLS ensures that no third party may eavesdrop any message.

WAP (more details can be found in Chapter 69) is a standardized protocol that allows a mobile device to retrieve information from a server. There are several components used by the WAP specifications to provide security. A WAP identity module (WIM) stores certificates and is used by the wireless transport layer security (WTLS) to provide a TLS-like secure connection between the mobile device and a WAP gateway. There are also functions defined that allow data to be signed. Earlier versions of the WAP specifications defined a WAP gateway that mapped the WAP protocols onto Internet protocols to allow WAP devices to connect to servers on an IP network. This allowed the transmission to become vulnerable at the WAP gateway. WAP 2.0 addresses the lack of end-to-end security by introducing support and services for Internet protocols into the WAP environment. Internet protocols can, therefore, be used directly between the client and wireless network and this eliminates the need for protocol translation at the WAP gateway. This provides secure end-to-end communications.

MOBILE DEVICE MOBILITY MANAGEMENT

Mobility is the ability for mobile devices to remain connected to the network continuously when they move. Mobility management consists of three components: (1) handoff management, (2) location management, and (3) roaming management. Handoff is a process in which a mobile device changes its network attachment point within the same administration domain. Location management is a process in which an association between the mobile device and its home network as the mobile device moves from one network to another. Roaming is a process where a mobile device changes its network attachment point between different administration domains.

Handoff Management

In an attempt to increase the system capacity, modern mobile networks are organized as a set of radio cells. Users tend to move in and out of cells frequently without notice. The system therefore needs to maintain the continuity of an ongoing connection whenever a user crosses the cell boundary. A typical example is that a mobile device moves from one cell to another and thus its radio channels will be changed from one base station to another base station. Because of the dynamic nature of the mobile networks, a changing of one radio channel to another within the same base station is also considered handoff. It should be noticed that handoff management is one of fundamental features of mobile networks. Essentially, all connections are established after a successful admission process. That means once the system admits a connection request, it is totally the network's responsibility to maintain the connection until the user tears it down. In an effort to reduce the handoff overhead, a cluster of neighboring cells can be grouped together and controlled by a mobile switching center (MSC). The MSC has much more computing power and functionalities than base stations. When a mobile device moves among cells within the same cluster, the handoff is mainly handled by the serving MSC. This is called *intraswitch handoff*. When a mobile device moves crossing the cluster boundary, the handoff must be handled at least by the two MSCs involved. This is called *interswitch handoff*. Because of the state information exchange between two MSCs, interswitch handoff takes longer than intraswitch handoff.

There are three methods for initiating handoffs. They are (1) mobile controlled handoff (MCHO), (2) network controlled handoff (NCHO), and (3) mobile assisted handoff (MAHO). In MCHO, the mobile device continuously monitors the quality of signals received from nearby base stations. When the signal level from a new base station exceeds that from the current base station, the mobile device realizes that it is leaving the current cell and entering a new cell. Thus the mobile device initiates the handoff and requests a new radio channel from the new base station. Because the mobile device controls the entire handoff process, a fast handoff is expected. However, this increases the complexity of the mobile devices.

In NCHO, the base stations continuously monitor the signal quality from individual mobile devices and report the measurements to the MSC. The MSC, which has a whole picture of the entire system, chooses the new base station and starts the handoff process. The mobile device operates in passive mode and thus a simple design is needed. However, this increases the burden of the network. A more desirable method is MAHO, in which the mobile device continuously measures the signal quality from nearby base stations and feeds this information back to the MSC via the current base station. The current base station also provides the distance information to the MSC. The MSC then makes a decision for handoff. MAHO achieves the balance between mobile device complexity and network burden; therefore it is widely used in today's mobile networks.

The handoff process can be in one of the four modes: hard, soft, backward, or forward handoff (Mark & Zhuang, 2004). During a hard handoff, a mobile device can receive user data from only one base station at any time. Thus, the old connection is terminated before a new connection is established. This mode of operation is called *break-before-make*. In the soft handoff, a mobile device receives copies of the same user data from two or more base stations simultaneously. The mobile is supposed to have the capability to recognize that the multiple copies actually represent the same data. Then the mobile uses signal processing techniques to determine the most likely correct value of the data from its multiple copies. Thus, soft handoff provides better reliability. This mode of operation is called *make-before-break*.

In backward handoff, the handoff is predicted ahead of time and initiated through the existing radio link. A sudden loss or rapid deterioration of the old link imposes a major problem in backward handoff. In forward handoff, the handoff is initiated via the new radio link associated with the new base station. Because of a late availability of the new radio link, forward handoff may cause a long delay. The general requirements when designing a handoff algorithm are low handoff delay and cell loss, scalable with network size, and reliability of recovering from link failures.

Handoff management is handled differently in mobile IP and cellular IP networks. In mobile IP, a mobile terminal needs to change its IP address when it moves into a new IP subnet and registers the new IP address with its home agent. This could lead to long handoff delay when the mobile is far away from its home agent. Cellular IP is designed to support fast handoff in a wireless network of limited size, for example, a network within the same administrative domain. Cellular IP reduces handoff latency by eliminating the need for a mobile to change its IP address while moving inside a Cellular IP network, hence reducing the delays caused by acquiring and registering new IP addresses.

Location Management

The term location in the context of mobile networks means which network the mobile is visiting, more specifically, which network attachment the mobile is using.

Location management typically includes the following three steps:

- Location discovery—a process to determine the mobile's current location
- Location update—a process to notify the mobile's home network of its current location
- Packet delivery—a process to deliver packets to the destination mobile

Location Discovery

To provide a wide geographical coverage and to support more users, a wireless mobile network is normally configured as an interconnection of many regional subnetworks. Each subnetwork may consist of multiple cells. These subnetworks are interconnected via intelligent routers such as MSCs or a backbone network such as the Internet or a satellite network. For message delivery purposes, a mobile device is identified with a home network where the mobile subscribes. Messages sent from other mobiles or fixed terminals are always delivered to its home network first. The association between the mobile and its home network is made through a registration process. The location register that belongs to the mobile's home network is called the home location register (HLR). When the mobile moves into a new subnetwork, it has to register its current location with a visitor location register (VLR) in the visiting network. The registration request sent by the mobile device should include its mobile identification number (MIN) among others. The base station in each subnetwork periodically broadcast beacon signals. A mobile listens to the pilot signals from the base stations in the subnetwork and uses these to identify its current subnetwork.

Location discovery can be initiated by either the mobile's home network or the mobile itself. In the former case, the home network does not maintain mobiles' precise locations at all times. It only needs to locate the mobile when there are messages destined to the mobile. Typically, the home network sends a message to the VLR through its association with the HLR. The VLR then locates the called mobile by broadcasting a polling message that contains the MIN of the called mobile. Upon receiving the polling message, the called mobile responds to the VLR through its current serving base station. The called MSC then knows where to forward the call. A communication channel between the message originator and the mobile can be established thereafter. If the location discovery is initiated by the mobile itself, the home network must know the current location of the mobile at all times. Therefore, the mobile must inform its home network whenever it enters a new subnetwork.

Location Update

A location update strategy determines when a mobile should perform location updates and what location-related information the mobile should send to its home network. One strategy is to update the mobile's precise location whenever it leaves its home network. This strategy makes the location discovery unnecessary. However, this strategy is not desirable if mobiles change their network attachment points frequently and there are no traffic destined to them. A number of strategies are designed to save scarce network and mobile resources. They can be classified into the following categories:

- Traffic-on-demand update: the home network does not maintain mobiles' precise locations at all times. The network only requests the mobile to update its location when it needs to deliver user traffic to it.
- Location-area-based update: A network can group a set of network attachments points into one location area. When the mobile and network have no traffic to send to each other, the network only needs to keep track of which location area a mobile is likely to be in.
- Movement-based update (Dutta et al., 2001; Noy, Kessler, & Sisi, 1995): A mobile performs a location update whenever it traverses a predetermined number of location areas.
- Distance-based update (Noy, Kessler, & Sisi, 1995; Wong & Leung, 2000): A mobile performs a location update whenever it has traversed a predetermined distance since its last update. Here the distance could be measured in many ways, such as physical distance or cell distance.

Each location update strategy has unique advantages and limitations. A potential drawback of the traffic-on-demand strategy is an unacceptable long end-to-end message delay. For location-area-based, movement-based, and distance-based strategies, location discovery is required to locate the precise location of a mobile when the network needs to deliver user traffic to it. Therefore, a proper trade-off is needed to achieve reduced overhead, high performance, and low complexity.

Packet Delivery

Packet delivery to mobiles is the process whereby a packet originator and the network use location information to deliver packets to a mobile. Packet delivery strategies can be classified into two basic categories:

1. Direct delivery: a packet originator first obtains the destination mobile's current location and then sends the packets directly to the current location of the destination mobile. In this case, the packet originator needs to maintain the mobile's location by itself or obtain location information from a location server.
2. Relayed delivery: a packet will be first sent to a mobility anchor point, which then relays the packet toward its final destination. In this case, the packet originator does not need to know the precise location of the destination mobile. What the originator needs to know is the address of the mobility anchor point, which typically is fixed.

Direct delivery could reduce the packet end-to-end delay by using the most direct path to the destination. However, the originator needs to have the ability to find the proper location server for the destination mobile. Relay delivery has fewer requirements on the packet originator. However, the packet end-to-end may be longer in relay delivery than that in direct delivery, because the mobility anchor point could become the performance bottleneck.

Roaming Management

Roaming is a process whereby a mobile user moves into a visited domain. Before proceeding to the discussion of roaming, we first define *home domains* and *visited domains* for a mobile user. A user's home domain is the domain where the mobile maintains a service subscription account, which contains information regarding the subscriber's identity, billing address, service plan, and security information needed to authenticate the user. Among other information, the service plan includes which networks the user is allowed to use (i.e., which networks the user can roam into and communicate with). When a mobile moves into a domain with which it does not have an account, this domain is called the mobile's visited domain.

Roaming is similar to handoff in the sense that a mobile changes its network attachment point in both cases. However, supporting roaming requires more network capabilities, such as roaming agreement between the mobile's home domain and the visited domains. A roaming agreement contains enough information for a visited domain to authenticate, authorize, and bill the roaming user. When a user enters a visited domain, the visited domain needs to determine if this user is allowed to use its networks. To make this decision, the visited domain needs to know who this user is, who the user's home domain is, and if there is an agreement between them.

CONCLUSIONS AND FUTURE TRENDS

We have introduced the basic concepts and general features of mobile devices. Particularly, we presented the specific features of Web-enabled phones, personal digital assistants, pagers, portable storage devices, laptop PCs, and tablet PCs. To better understand these mobile devices, we also outlined the protocols widely deployed by mobile devices and several mobile security issues and measures. It should be noted that this chapter provided only a framework of the mobile protocols and security. Readers are suggested to refer other chapters in volumes I and II that contain the details of individual topics, such as WAP, SMTP, HTTP, Mobile IP, 802.11x, Bluetooth, and the foundations of network security. Finally, this chapter reviewed mobile device management, which includes handoff management, location management, and roaming management.

We make two predictions for the next generation mobile devices. The first prediction regards the mobile domain itself. Specifically, various mobile devices within each family will converge to one unit. For example, we expect that a single mobile device will combine all the functions of Web-enabled phones, PDAs, pagers, and iPods. The second prediction pertains to both mobile and wireless domains. New mobile devices must be able to access any public wireless local area network services and connect to the wireless Internet through any available Internet connection services. However, there are a number of barriers preventing this. First, for the new mobile devices to run intensive computing applications, new technologies for processors, hard disks, and memories must be available. Second, for them to be truly portable, the size and weight must be significantly reduced. Third, new technologies to increase the network bandwidth for mobile devices must be developed. And finally, the battery lifetime must allow days of continuous usage.

GLOSSARY

Code Division Multiple Access A spread spectrum approach for the digital transmission of data/voice over radio frequencies.

Enhanced Data GSM Environment A faster version of the GSM wireless service.

Enhanced Message Service Enables mobile devices to exchange messages with formatted text, animations, pictures, icons, sound effects, and special ring tones.

Global System for Mobile Communications A digital cellular phone technology based on TDMA.

Handheld Devices Markup Language Specifications that allow Internet access from wireless devices such as handheld personal computers and smart phones.

Home location register A database containing subscriber information files about the subscriber and the current location of a subscriber's mobile station.

Hypertext transfer protocol It is the protocol used for Web access in the current Internet. Currently, it has two popular versions, HTTP 1.0 and HTTP 1.1.

Internet Message Access Protocol A protocol for e-mail clients to retrieve e-mail messages from a mail server while the mailboxes are on.

Internet Protocol Security A security protocol from the Internet Engineering Task Force (IETF) that provides authentication and encryption over the Internet.

Multimedia Message Service A messaging service for the mobile environment very similar to SMS or text messaging.

Simple Mail Transfer Protocol A protocol used to send e-mail on the Internet.

Simple Object Access Protocol A lightweight protocol for exchange of information in a decentralized, distributed environment.

Synchronized Media Integration Language A markup language designed to present multiple media files together.

Time Division Multiple Access A digital wireless telephony transmission technique

Uniform Resource Identifier The most common form of URI is the Web page address.

Universal Discovery Description and Integration An XML- and SOAP-based lookup service for Web service consumers to locate Web services and programmable resources available on a network.

Visitor Location Register A local database function that maintains temporary records associated with individual subscribers.

Voice eXtensible Markup Language A proposed specification for accessing voice recognition software via the Internet.

Wireless Identity Module It identifies and authenticates a wireless device on a wireless network.

Wireless Markup Language It allows the display of Web pages on mobile phones and PDAs.

CROSS REFERENCES

See *Bluetooth Security; Bluetooth Technology; Mobile Commerce; Security and the Wireless Application Protocol (WAP); Wireless Internet: A Cellular Perspective.*

REFERENCES

3GPP. (2002). *Technical specification group services and system aspects, 3G security, network domain security, IP network layer security*. Release 5, 3GPP TS 33.102, version 5.0.0. Retrieved November 15, 2004, from http://www.3gpp.org/ftp/tsg_sa/WG3_Security/_Specs/Old_Vsns/33210-500.pdf

Amotz, B.-N., Kessler, I., & Moshe, S. (1995). Mobile users: To update or not to update? *ACM/Balzer Journal of Wireless Networks, 1*, 175–185.

Beaulieu, M. (2002). *Wireless Internet, applications and architecture*. Boston: Addison-Wesley.

Bulterman, D. C. A., & Rutledge, L. (2004). *SMIL 2.0, interactive multimedia for Web and mobile devices*. New York: Springer-Verlag.

Brown, D. (1995). Techniques for privacy and authentication in personal communications. *IEEE Personal Communications, August* 6–10.

Dedo, D. (2004). *Windows mobile-based devices and security: Protecting sensitive business information*. Retrieved November 15, 2004, from www.microsoft.com/windowsmobile/

Dutta, A., Vakil, F., Chen, J. C., Tauil, M., Baba, S., Nakajima, N., & Schulzrinne, H. (2001). Application layer mobility management scheme for wireless Internet. *IEEE 3G Wireless 2001, May*.

Lee, V., Schnider, H., & Schell, R. (2004). *Mobile applications: Architecture, design, and development*. Upper Saddle River, NJ: Prentice Hall.

Lin, Y.-B., & Chlamtac, I. (2001). Wireless and mobile network architectures. New York: John Wiley & Sons.

Lu, W. W. (2002). *Broadband wireless mobile, 3G and beyond*. New York: John Wiley & Sons.

Mallick, M. (2003). *Mobile and wireless design essentials*. New York: John Wiley & Sons.

Mark, J. W., & Zhuang, W. (2004). *Wireless communications and networking*. Upper Saddle River, NJ: Prentice Hall.

Openwave. (2002). *WAP push technology overview*. Retrieved November 15, 2004 http://developer.openwave.com/docs/wappush_tech_overview.pdf

SOAP Version 1.2. (2003). *SOAP version 1.2. Part 1: Messaging framework*. Retrieved November 15, 2004, from http://www.w3.org/TR/soap12-part1/

UDDI Version 3.0.1. (2003). *UDDI Spec Technical Committee Specification*. Retrieved November 15, 2004, from http://uddi.org/pubs/uddi_v3.htm

W3C Web Service. (2004). *Web services architecture requirements*. Retrieved November 15, 2004, from http://www.w3.org/TR/wsa-reqs/#id2604831

WAP 2.0. (2002). *Wireless Application Protocol Technical White Paper*. Retrieved November 15, 2004, from http://www.wapforum.org/what/WAPWhite_Paper1.pdf

Wong, V. W.-S., & Leung, V. C. M. (2000). Location management for next generation personal communication networks. *IEEE Network, Sep./Oct.*, 18–24.

WSDL Version 2.0. (2004). *Web services description language (WSDL) version 2.0. Part 1: Core language*. Retrieved November 15, 2004, from http://www.w3.org/TR/2004/WD-wsdl20-20040803/

Zhang, T., & Chen, J.-C. (2004). *IP-based next-generation wireless networks*. New York: Wiley Interscience.

Bluetooth Technology

Brent A. Miller, *IBM Corporation*

INTRODUCTION

Launched in May 1998, Bluetooth wireless technology rapidly has become one of the most well-known means of communication in the information technology industry. The unusual name *Bluetooth* itself has garnered much attention (I discuss the origins of this name later), but the main reason for the focus that the technology receives from so many companies and individuals is the new capabilities that it brings to mobile computing and communication.

This chapter discusses many facets of Bluetooth wireless technology—its origins; the associated Bluetooth Special Interest Group; its applications, especially in personal area networks; how it works; and how it addresses security issues. I also present numerous references where more information can be found about this exciting new way to form wireless personal area networks (WPANs) that allow mobile devices to communicate with each other.

BLUETOOTH WIRELESS TECHNOLOGY

Bluetooth wireless technology uses radio frequency (RF) to accomplish wireless communication. It operates in the 2.4-GHz frequency spectrum; the use of this frequency range allows Bluetooth devices to be used virtually worldwide without requiring a license for operation. Bluetooth communication is intended to operate over short distances (up to approximately 100 m, although the nominal range used by most Bluetooth devices is about 10 m). Restricting communication to short ranges allows for low-power operation, so Bluetooth technology is particularly well suited for use with battery-powered personal devices that can be used to form a WPAN. Both voice and data can be carried over Bluetooth communication links, making the technology suitable for connecting both computing and communication devices, such as mobile phones, personal digital assistants (PDAs), pagers, and notebook computers. Table 1 summarizes these key attributes of Bluetooth wireless technology.

Bluetooth wireless technology originally was designed for cable replacement applications, intended to remove the need for a cable between any two devices to allow them to communicate. For example, a cable might be used to connect two computers to transfer files, to connect a PDA cradle to a computer to synchronize data, or to connect a headset to a telephone for hands-free voice calls. This sort of wired operation can often be cumbersome, because the cables used are frequently special-purpose wires intended to connect two specific devices; hence, they are likely to have special connectors that make them unsuitable for general-purpose use. This can lead to "cable clutter"—the need for many cables to interconnect various devices. Mobile users may find this especially burdensome because they need to carry their device cables with them to connect the devices when they are away from home, and even with a large collection of cables, it is unlikely that all of the devices can be plugged together. Nonmobile environments, too, can suffer from cable clutter. In a home or office, wires used to connect, say, computer peripherals or stereo speakers limit the placement of these items, and the cables themselves become obstacles.

Bluetooth technology attempts to solve the problem of cable clutter by defining a standard communication mechanism that can allow many devices to communicate with each other without wires. The next section explores the genesis and evolution of Bluetooth wireless communication.

Origins

The genesis of Bluetooth wireless technology generally is credited to Ericsson, where engineers were searching for a method to enable wireless headsets for mobile telephones. Realizing that such a short-range RF technology could have wider applications, and further realizing that its likelihood for success would be greater as an industry standard rather than a proprietary technology, Ericsson approached other major telephone, mobile computer, and electronics companies about forming an industry group to specify and standardize a general-purpose, short-range, low-power form of wireless communication. This small group became the Bluetooth Special Interest Group (SIG), discussed later.

Of special interest to many is the name "Bluetooth." Such a name for an industry initiative is unusual. A two-part newsletter article (Kardach, 2001) offers a full explanation of the name's origin; the salient points follow here. Some of the first technologists involved in early discussions about a short-range wireless technology were

Table 1 Key Bluetooth Technology Characteristics

Characteristic	Bluetooth Technology Attributes
Medium	Radio frequency (RF) in the 2.4-GHz globally unlicensed spectrum
Range	Nominally 10 m; optionally up to 100 m
Power	Low-power operation, suitable for battery-powered portable devices
Packet types	Voice and data
Types of applications	Cable replacement, wireless personal area networks
Example applications	Network access, wireless headsets, wireless data transfer, cordless telephony, retail and m-commerce, travel and mobility, and many other applications

history buffs, and the discussion at some point turned to Scandinavian history. A key figure in Scandinavian history is 10th-century Danish king Harald Blåtand, who is credited with uniting parts of Scandinavia. It is said that a loose translation of his surname to English produces "blue tooth." Those involved in early discussions of this technology recognized that it could unite the telecommunications and information technology (IT) industries, and hence they referred to it as "Bluetooth," after King Harald. At that time, Bluetooth was considered a temporary "code name" for the project. When the time came to develop an official name for the technology and its associated special interest group, the name Bluetooth was chosen after considering several alternatives. Today, this is the trademarked name of the technology and the incorporated entity (the Bluetooth SIG, discussed next) that manages it. In fact, the SIG publishes rules and guidelines (Bluetooth SIG, 2005a) for using the term.

The Bluetooth Special Interest Group

Formed in early 1998 and announced in May of that year, the Bluetooth SIG originally was a rather loosely knit group of five companies: Ericsson, Intel, IBM, Nokia, and Toshiba. These companies established themselves as Bluetooth SIG promoter members and formed the core of the SIG. Other companies were invited to join as adopter members, and the SIG's membership grew rapidly. The promoter companies, along with a few invited experts, developed the original versions of the Bluetooth specification (detailed later).

In December 1999, four additional companies—3Com, Lucent, Microsoft, and Motorola—were invited to join the group of promoter companies (later Lucent's promoter membership was transferred to its spin-off company, Agere Systems). By this time, the SIG's membership had grown to more than 2,000 companies. In addition to promoters and adopters, a third membership tier, called associate member, also was defined. Companies may apply to become associate members and must pay membership fees. Adopter membership is free and open to anyone. In general, promoter and associate members develop and maintain the Bluetooth specification; adopter members may review specification updates before their public availability.

The SIG's original purpose was to develop the Bluetooth specification, but it has taken on additional responsibilities over time. In 2001, the SIG incorporated and instituted a more formal structure for the organization, including a board of directors that oversees all operations, a technical organization led by the Bluetooth Architecture Review Board (BARB), a marketing arm, and a legal group. The SIG continues to develop and maintain the specification and promote the technology, including sponsoring developers' conferences and other events. One important function of the SIG is to manage the Bluetooth qualification program, in which products are tested for conformance to the specification. All Bluetooth products must undergo qualification testing. The SIG's official Web site (Bluetooth SIG, 2005b) offers more details about the organization and the qualification program.

Wireless Personal Area Networks

A *personal area network* (PAN) generally is considered to be a set of communicating devices that someone carries with him or her. A wireless PAN (WPAN), of course, is such a set of devices that communicate without cables, such as through the use of Bluetooth technology. One can imagine a "sphere" of connectivity that surrounds a person and moves with her or him, so that all of the devices in the WPAN remain in communication with one another.

WPANs need only short-range communication capability to cover the personal area, in contrast with local area (LAN) or wide area networks (WAN), which need to communicate across greater distances using established infrastructure. One source (Miller, 2001) contrasts PANs, LANs, and WANs, particularly Bluetooth technology, as a WPAN solution versus Institute of Electrical and Electronics Engineers (IEEE; 1999) 802.11 WLAN technology.

The usefulness of a WPAN derives primarily from the ability of individual devices to communicate with each other in an ad hoc manner. Each device still can specialize in certain capabilities but can "borrow" the capabilities of other devices to accomplish certain tasks. For example, a PDA is useful for quickly accessing personal information, such as appointments and contacts. A mobile telephone can be used to contact people whose information is stored in the PDA. Hence, a user might look up the telephone number of an associate and then dial that number on the mobile phone. With a WPAN, however, this process can be automated: once the telephone number is accessed, the PDA software could include an option to dial the specified phone number automatically on the mobile telephone within the WPAN, using wireless communication links to transmit the dialing instructions to the phone. When combined with a wireless headset in the same WPAN, this could enable a more convenient device usage model for the user, who might never need to handle the mobile telephone at all (it could remain stored in a briefcase). Moreover, the user interface of the PDA is likely to be easier to use than a telephone keypad for retrieving contact information. This allows each of the devices (PDA, mobile phone, and wireless headset in this example) to

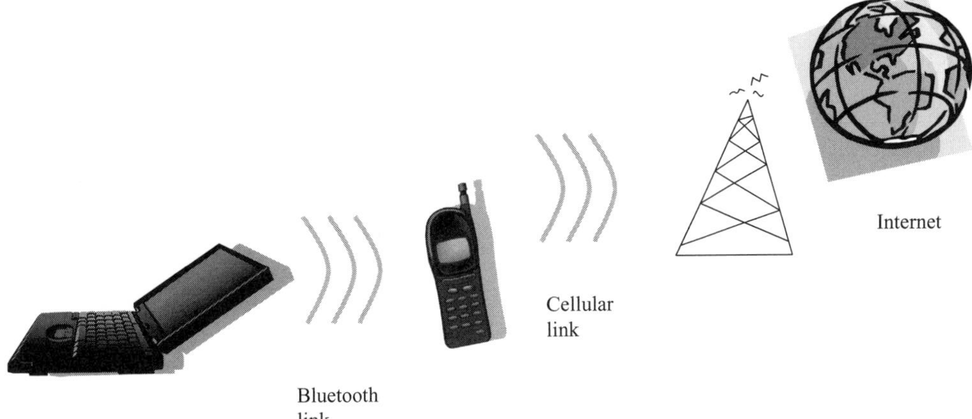

Figure 1: Dial-up networking illustration.

be optimized to perform the specific tasks that they do best. The capabilities of each device are accessed from other devices via the WPAN. This often is preferred over an alternative usage model, the "all-in-one" device (imagine a PDA that also functions as a mobile telephone). Such multifunction devices might tend to be cumbersome and are more difficult to optimize for specific functions.

Because it was developed primarily to replace cables that connect mobile devices, Bluetooth wireless communication is an ideal WPAN technology. Indeed, most of the popular usage scenarios for Bluetooth technology originate in a WPAN of some sort, connecting personal devices to each other or to other networks in proximity. The use of Bluetooth communication links in WPANs is illustrated next, in an examination of various Bluetooth applications.

Bluetooth Applications

Because Bluetooth technology primarily is about replacing cables, many of its applications involve well-known usage scenarios. The value that Bluetooth communication adds to these types of applications derives from the ability to accomplish them without wires, enhancing mobility and convenience. For example, dial-up networking is a task commonly performed by many individuals, especially mobile professionals. One of the original usage scenarios used to illustrate the value of Bluetooth technology involves performing dial-up networking wirelessly—with the use of a mobile computer and a mobile phone, both equipped with Bluetooth communication, dial-up networking no longer is constrained by cables. This application and others are detailed next.

Basic Cable Replacement Applications

These applications comprise the original set of usage models envisioned for Bluetooth wireless technology. When the SIG was formed and the technology began to be popularized, these applications were touted as the most common ways in which Bluetooth wireless communication would be used. Although many other, perhaps more sophisticated, applications for Bluetooth technology have been discovered and envisioned, these original usage models remain as the primary application set. Nearly all of these early applications involve a mobile computer or a mobile telephone and, for the most part, they involve performing typical existing tasks wirelessly.

One such application, already mentioned, is dial-up networking. In this application, a Bluetooth communication link replaces the wire (typically a serial cable) between a computer and a telephone. When the telephone is also a mobile device, the network connection can be entirely wireless; a Bluetooth wireless link exists between the computer and the telephone and a wide-area communications link (using typical cellular technology, such as the global system for mobile communication [GSM], time division/demand multiple access [TDMA], or others) carries the network traffic, using the mobile telephone as a wireless modem. Figure 1 depicts this usage model.

A variant of this application uses direct (rather than dial-up) connection to a network such as the Internet. In this case, the Bluetooth link allows a computer to connect to a network such as a LAN without using a cable. Together, these two applications (wireless dial-up networking and wireless LAN access) form a usage model that the SIG calls the *Internet bridge.* Both applications involve access to a network, using existing protocols, with the main benefit being the ability to access the network without the cables that typically are required to connect the network client computer.

Another type of cable replacement application involves data transfer from one device to another. One of the most common such usage models is transferring files from one computer to another. This can be accomplished with removable media (diskettes, CDs), with cables (via a network or a direct connection) or wirelessly (using infrared or Bluetooth communication, to name two ways). Infrared file transfer is not uncommon, but it requires the two devices to have a line of sight between them. Bluetooth file transfer operates similarly to that of IrDA infrared file transfer (in fact, the Bluetooth protocol stack, discussed later, is designed such that the same application can be used over either transport medium). Bluetooth communication, being RF-based, does not require a line of sight between the two devices, however. Moreover, through the use of standard data formats, such as *vCard* (Internet Mail Consortium, 1996a), *vCal* (Internet Mail Consortium, 1996b), and others, objects other than files can be exchanged between devices using Bluetooth links in a manner similar to that used with IrDA. So, for example, electronic business cards, calendar appointments, and contact information can be shared wirelessly among devices.

Building on this capability to exchange data objects is the application that allows these same objects to be synchronized. This means that data sets on two devices reflect the same information at the point in time when they are synchronized. Hence, in addition to simply sending a copy of contact information or a calendar appointment from one device to another, the full address book or calendar can be synchronized between the two devices so that they have the same set of contacts or appointments. This allows a user to enter information on any convenient device and then have that information reflected on other devices by synchronizing with those devices. In addition to the benefit of performing these tasks wirelessly, by using standard protocols and data formats, information can be exchanged easily among many kinds of devices. Specialized cables to connect two computers, or custom cradles to connect a PDA to a computer, are not needed once Bluetooth technology enters the picture. Instead, the same data can be exchanged and synchronized to and from notebook computers, PDAs, mobile phones, pagers, and other devices. This illustrates a hallmark of the value of Bluetooth technology: a single standard wireless link can replace many cables of various types, allowing devices that otherwise might not be able to be connected to communicate easily.

Another data transfer application is related to those just described, but it has a distinguished usage model because of the kind of data it transfers, namely, image data. The SIG calls this usage model the *instant postcard,* and it involves transferring pictures from one device to another. One reason that this application is separately described is because it involves the use of a digital camera. Today, when a camera captures new images, they typically are loaded onto a computer of some sort (or perhaps a television or similar video device) to be displayed. Through the use of Bluetooth wireless technology, this image transfer can be accomplished more easily, but once again, this standard form of wireless link enables the same data to be transferred to other types of devices. For example, rather than uploading photos to a computer, the photos might be transferred to a mobile phone. Even if the phone's display is not suitable for viewing the photo, it still could be e-mailed to someone who could view it on his computer or other e-mail device.

Until now, this chapter has focused on applications involving data, but Bluetooth wireless technology is also designed to transport voice traffic (audio packets), and some of the cable replacement applications take advantage of this fact. The most notable of these is the wireless headset. Cabled headsets that connect to a mobile phone are widely used today to allow hands-free conversations. Bluetooth technology removes the cable from the headset to the telephone handset, enabling wireless operation that can allow the phone to be stowed away in a briefcase, pocket, or purse. In fact, as noted earlier, this particular application was the basis for the invention of Bluetooth technology. As with the previously discussed applications, however, once a standard wireless link is established, additional ways to connect other kinds of devices present themselves. For example, the same Bluetooth headset used with a mobile phone might also be used with a stationary telephone (again to allow hands-free operation and increased mobility) and a computer (to carry audio traffic to and from the computer). Furthermore, although Bluetooth wireless communication was not originally designed to carry more complex audio traffic (such as digital music), advances are being made that will allow it to do so. With this capability, the same wireless headset also could be used with home entertainment systems, car audio systems, and personal music players. Hence, the Bluetooth SIG dubs this usage model the *ultimate headset.*

A variation on the wireless headset usage model is what the SIG calls the *speaking laptop.* In this application, Bluetooth links carry audio data in the same manner as for the headset application, but in this case the audio data is routed between a telephone and a notebook computer's speaker and microphone, rather than to a headset. One usage scenario enabled with this application is that of using the notebook computer as a speakerphone: A call made to or from a mobile telephone can be transformed into a conference call ("put on the speaker") by using the speaker and microphone built into nearly all portable (and desktop) computers.

Cordless telephony is another application for Bluetooth technology. With a Bluetooth voice access point, or cordless telephone base station, a standard cellular mobile telephone also can be used as a cordless phone in a home or office. The Bluetooth link carries the voice traffic from the handset to the base station, with the call then being carried over the normal wired telephone network. This allows mobile calls to be made without incurring cellular usage charges. In addition, two handsets can function as "walkie-talkies" or an intercom system, using direct Bluetooth links between them, allowing two parties to carry on voice conversations in a home, office, or public space without any telephone network at all. Because a single mobile telephone can be used as a standard cellular phone, a cordless phone, and an intercom, the SIG calls this cordless telephony application the *three-in-one phone* usage model.

Additional Applications

Although Bluetooth wireless technology was developed especially for cable-replacement applications such as those just cited, many observers quickly realized that Bluetooth communication could be used in other ways, too. Here I describe a few of the many potential applications of Bluetooth technology, beginning with those that the SIG already is in the process of specifying.

The Bluetooth SIG focused primarily on the cable-replacement applications already discussed in the version 1.x specifications that it released. The SIG is also developing additional profiles (detailed later) for other types of Bluetooth applications. Among these are more robust personal area proximity networking, human interface devices, printing, local positioning, multimedia, and automotive applications.

Bluetooth personal area networking takes advantage of the ability of Bluetooth devices to establish communication with each other based on their proximity to each other, so that ad hoc networks can be formed. The

Bluetooth network encapsulation protocol (BNEP) allows Ethernet packets to be transported via Bluetooth links, thus enabling many classic networking applications to operate in Bluetooth piconets (piconets are discussed at length in the section Bluetooth Operation). This capability extends the Bluetooth WPAN to encompass other devices. An example is the formation of an ad hoc Bluetooth network in a conference room with multiple meeting participants. Such a network could facilitate collaborative applications such as white-boarding, instant messaging, and group scheduling. Such applications could allow group editing of documents and scheduling of follow-up meetings, all in real time. Nonetheless, it should be noted that although this scenario resembles classic intranet- or Internet-style networking in some respects, Bluetooth personal area networking is not as robust a solution for true networking solutions as is a WLAN technology, such as IEEE 802.11.

Replacing desktop computer cables with Bluetooth communication links fundamentally is a cable-replacement application (dubbed the *cordless computer* by the SIG), and this was one of the originally envisioned Bluetooth usage scenarios, but the original specifications did not fully address it. The new *human interface device* (HID) specification describes how Bluetooth technology can be used in wireless computer peripherals such as keyboards, mice, joysticks, and so on. The Bluetooth printing profiles specify methods for wireless printing using Bluetooth communication, including "walk up and print" scenarios that allow immediate printing from any device, including mobile telephones and PDAs, as well as notebook computers, to any usable printer in the vicinity. This application of Bluetooth technology can obviate the need for specialized network print servers and their associated configuration and administration tasks.

Another application that can be realized with Bluetooth wireless technology is *local positioning.* Bluetooth technology can be used to augment other technologies, such as global positioning systems (GPS), especially inside buildings, where other technologies might not work well. Using two or more Bluetooth radios, local position information can be obtained in several ways. If one Bluetooth device is stationary (say, a kiosk), it could supply its position information to other devices within range. Any device that knows its own position can provide this information to other Bluetooth devices so that they can learn their current position. Sophisticated applications might even use signal strength information to derive more granular position information. Once position information is known, it could be used with other applications, such as maps of the area, directions to target locations, or perhaps even locating lost devices. *The Bluetooth local positioning profile* specifies standard data formats and interchange methods for local positioning information.

Multimedia applications have become standard on most desktop and notebook computers, and the Bluetooth SIG is pursuing ways by which streamed multimedia data, such as sound and motion video, could be used in Bluetooth environments. The 1 Mbps raw data rate of version 1 Bluetooth radios is not sufficient for many sorts of multimedia traffic, but the SIG is investigating methods for faster Bluetooth radios that could handle multimedia applications. The SIG is also developing profiles for multimedia data via Bluetooth links.

Another emerging application area is that of automotive Bluetooth applications. Using Bluetooth communication, wireless networks could be formed in cars. Devices from the WPAN could join the automobile's built-in Bluetooth network to accomplish scenarios such as the following:

- obtaining e-mail and other messages, using a mobile phone as a WAN access device, and transferring those messages to the car's Bluetooth network, where they might be read over the car's audio system using text-to-speech technology (and perhaps even composing responses using voice recognition technology);
- obtaining vehicle information remotely, perhaps for informational purposes (for example, querying the car's current mileage from the office or home) or for diagnostic purposes (for example, a wireless engine diagnostic system for automobile mechanics that does not require probes and cables to be connected to the engine); and
- sending alerts and reminders from the car to a WPAN when service or maintenance is required (for example, e-mail reminders that an oil change is due or in-vehicle or remote alerts when tire pressure is low or other problems are diagnosed by the vehicle's diagnostic systems).

The SIG, in conjunction with automotive industry representatives, is developing profiles for Bluetooth automotive applications. This area is likely to prove to be an exciting and rapidly growing domain for the use of Bluetooth wireless technology.

These new applications are only some of the potential uses for Bluetooth wireless technology. Many other domains are being explored or will be invented in the future. Other noteworthy applications for Bluetooth wireless communications include mobile e-commerce, medical, and travel technologies. Bluetooth devices such as mobile phones or PDAs might be used to purchase items in stores or from vending machines; wireless biometrics and even Bluetooth drug dispensers might appear in the future (the 2.4-GHz band in which Bluetooth operates is called the industrial, scientific, and medical band); and travelers could experience enhanced convenience by using Bluetooth devices for anytime, anywhere personal data access and airline and hotel automated check-in. In fact, this latter scenario, including the use of a Bluetooth PDA to unlock a hotel room door, has already been demonstrated (InnTechnology, 2000).

The Bluetooth Protocol Stack

A complete discussion of the Bluetooth protocol stack is outside the scope of this chapter. Numerous books, including Miller and Bisdikian (2000) and Bray and Sturman (2000) offer more in-depth discussions of Bluetooth protocols. Here, we present an overview of Bluetooth operation and how the various protocols may be used to accomplish the applications already discussed. A typical Bluetooth stack is illustrated in Figure 2. Each layer of the stack is detailed next.

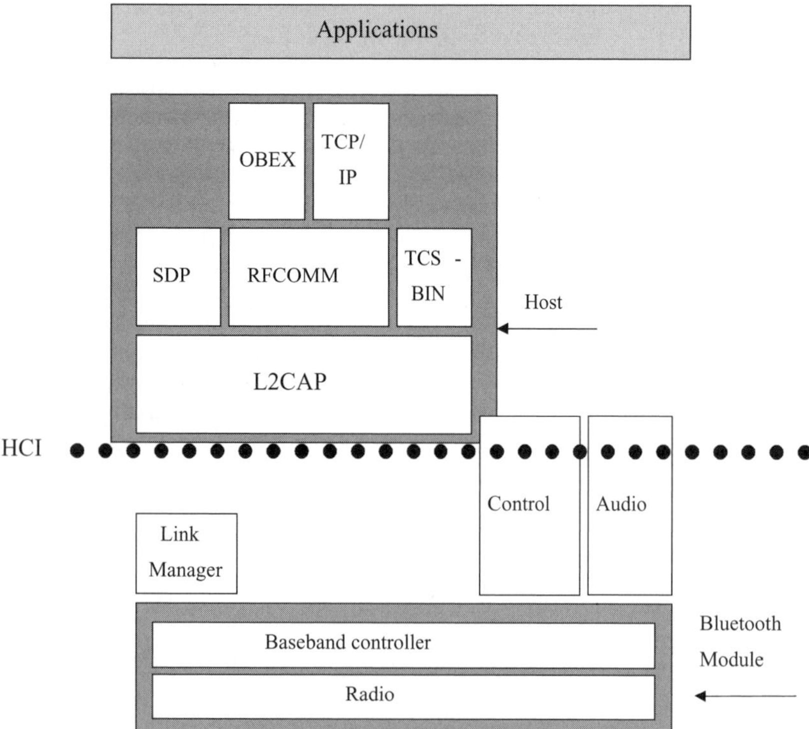

Figure 2: Bluetooth protocol stack.

Radio, Baseband, and Link Manager

These three protocol layers constitute the *Bluetooth module.* Typically, this module is an electronics package containing hardware and firmware. Today, many manufacturers supply Bluetooth modules.

The *radio* consists of the signal-processing electronics for a transmitter and receiver (transceiver) to allow RF communication via an *air interface* between two Bluetooth devices. As noted earlier, the radio operates in the 2.4-GHz spectrum, specifically in the frequency range 2.400–2.4835 GHz. This frequency range is divided into 79 channels (along with upper and lower guard bands), with each channel having a 1-MHz separation from its neighbors. *Frequency hopping* is employed in Bluetooth wireless communication; each packet is transmitted on a different channel, with the channels being selected pseudorandomly, based on the clock of the master device (master and slave devices are described in more detail later). The receiving device knows the frequency-hopping pattern and follows the pattern of the transmitting device, hopping to the next channel in the pattern to receive the transmitted packets.

The Bluetooth specification defines three classes of radios, based on their maximum power output:

1 mW (0 dBm),
2.5 mW (4 dBm), and
100 mW (20 dBm).

Increased transmission power offers a corresponding increase in radio range; the nominal range for the 0-dBm radio is 10 m, whereas the nominal range for the 20-dBm radio is 100 m. Of course, increased transmission power also requires a corresponding increase in the energy necessary to power the system, so higher power radios will draw more battery power. The basic cable replacement applications (indeed, most Bluetooth usage scenarios described here) envision the 0-dBm radio, which is considered the standard Bluetooth radio and is the most prevalent in devices. The 0-dBm radio is sufficient for most applications, and its low power consumption makes it suitable for use on small, portable devices.

Transmitter and receiver characteristics such as interference, tolerance, sensitivity, modulation, and spurious emissions are outside the scope of this chapter but are detailed in the Bluetooth specification (Bluetooth SIG, 2003).

The *baseband controller* controls the radio and typically is implemented as firmware in the Bluetooth module. The controller is responsible for all of the various timing and raw data handling aspects associated with RF communication, including the frequency hopping just mentioned, management of the time slots used for transmitting and receiving packets, generating air-interface packets (and causing the radio to transmit them), and parsing air-interface packets (when they are received by the radio). Packet generation and reception involves many considerations, including the following:

generating and receiving packet payload,
generating and receiving packet headers and trailers,
dealing with the several packet formats defined for Bluetooth communication,
error detection and correction,
address generation and detection,
data whitening (a process by which the actual data bits are rearranged so that the occurrence of zero and one bits

in a data stream is randomized, helping to overcome DC bias), and

data encryption and decryption.

Not all of these operations are necessarily performed on every packet; there are various options available for whether a particular transformation is applied to the data, and in some cases (such as error detection and correction), there are several alternatives that may be employed by the baseband firmware.

The *link manager,* as its name implies, manages the link layer between two Bluetooth devices. Link managers in two devices communicate using the *link manager protocol* (LMP). LMP consists of a set of commands and responses to set up and manage a baseband link between two devices. A link manager on one device communicates with a link manager on another device. (Indeed, this is generally the case for all the Bluetooth protocols described here; a particular protocol layer communicates with its corresponding layer in the other device, using its own defined protocol. Each protocol is passed to the next successively lower layer, where it is transformed to that layer's protocol, until it reaches the baseband, where the baseband packets that encapsulate the higher layer packets are transmitted and received via the air interface.) LMP setup commands include those for authenticating the link with the other device; setting up encryption, if desired, between the two devices; retrieving information about the device at the other end of the link, such as its name and timing parameters; and swapping the master and slave roles (detailed later) of the two devices. LMP management commands include those for controlling the transmission power; setting special power-saving modes, called hold, park, and sniff; and managing quality-of-service (QoS) parameters for the link. Because LMP messages deal with fundamental characteristics of the communication link between devices, they are handled in an expedited manner, at a higher priority than the normal data that is transmitted and received.

Control and Audio

The *control* and *audio* blocks in Figure 2 are not actual protocols. Instead, they represent means by which the upper layers of the stack can access lower layers. The control functions can be characterized as methods for inter-protocol-layer communication. These could include requests and notifications from applications, end users, or protocol layers that require action by another protocol layer, such as setting desired QoS parameters, requests to enter or terminate power-saving modes, or requests to search for other Bluetooth devices or change the discoverability of the local device. Often, these take the form of a user-initiated action, via an application, that requires the link manager (and perhaps other layers) to take some action.

The audio block in Figure 2 represents the typical path for audio (voice) traffic. Recall that Bluetooth wireless technology supports both data and voice. Data packets traverse through the L2CAP layer (described later), but voice packets typically are routed directly to the baseband, because audio traffic is isochronous and hence time critical. Audio traffic usually is associated with telephony applications, for which data traffic is used to set up and control the call and voice traffic serves as the content of the call. Audio data can be carried over Bluetooth links in two formats:

pulse code modulation (PCM), with either a-law or μ-law logarithmic compression, and

continuous variable slope delta (CVSD) modulation, which works well for audio data with relatively smooth continuity, usually the case for typical voice conversations.

Host–Controller Interface (HCI)

The HCI is an optional interface between the two major components of the Bluetooth stack: the *host* and the *controller*. As shown in Figure 2 and described earlier, the radio, baseband controller, and link manager constitute the module, which is often, but not necessarily, implemented in a single electronics package. Such a module can be integrated easily into many devices, with the remaining layers of the stack residing on the main processor of the device (such as a notebook computer, mobile phone, or PDA). These remaining layers (described next) are referred to as the host portion of the stack.

Figure 2 illustrates a typical "two-chip" solution in which the first "chip" is the Bluetooth module and the second "chip" is the processor in the device on which the host software executes. (The module itself might have multiple chips or electronic subsystems for the radio, the firmware processor, and other external logic.) In such a system, the HCI allows different Bluetooth modules to be interchanged in a device, because it defines a standard method for the host software to communicate with the controller firmware that resides on the module. So, at least in theory, one vendor's Bluetooth module could be substituted for another, so long as both faithfully implement the HCI. Although this is not the only type of partitioning that can be used when implementing a Bluetooth system, the SIG felt it was common enough that a standard interface should be defined between the two major components of the system. A Bluetooth system could be implemented in an "all-in-one" single module, where the host and controller reside together in the same physical package (often called a "single-chip" solution), although in this case, the HCI might still be used as an internal interface. When the two-chip solution is used, the physical layer for the HCI (that is, the physical connection between the host and the controller) could be one of several types. The Bluetooth specification defines three particular physical layers for the HCI:

universal serial bus (USB),

universal asynchronous receiver/transmitter (UART), and

RS-232 serial port.

Other HCI transports could be implemented; the Bluetooth specification currently contains details and considerations for these three.

Logical Link Control and Adaptation Protocol (L2CAP)

The logical link control and adaptation protocol (L2CAP) layer serves as a "funnel" through which all data traffic flows. As discussed earlier, voice packets typically are routed directly to the baseband, whereas data packets flow to and from higher layers, such as applications, to the baseband via the L2CAP layer.

The L2CAP layer offers an abstraction of lower layers to higher layer protocols. This allows the higher layers to operate using more natural data packet formats and protocols, without being concerned about how their data is transferred over the air interface. For example, the Service Discovery Protocol layer (discussed next) defines its own data formats and protocol data units. At the SDP layer, only the service discovery protocol needs to be handled; the fact that SDP data must be separated into baseband packets for transmission and aggregated from baseband packets for reception is not a concern at the SDP layer, nor are any of the other operations that occur at the baseband (such as encryption, whitening, and so on). This is accomplished because the L2CAP layer performs operations on data packets. Among these operations are segmentation and reassembly, whereby the L2CAP layer breaks higher layer protocol data units into L2CAP packets, which in turn can be transformed into baseband packets; the L2CAP layer conversely can reassemble baseband packets into L2CAP packets that in turn can be transformed into the natural format of higher layers of the stack.

An L2CAP layer in one Bluetooth stack communicates with another, corresponding L2CAP layer in another Bluetooth stack. Each L2CAP layer can have many channels. L2CAP channels identify data streams between the L2CAP layers in two Bluetooth devices. (L2CAP channels should not be confused with baseband channels used for frequency hopping. L2CAP channels are logical identifiers between two L2CAP layers.) An L2CAP channel often is associated with a particular upper layer of the stack, handling data traffic for that layer, although there need not be a one-to-one correspondence between channels and upper-layer protocols. An L2CAP layer might use the same protocol on multiple L2CAP channels. This illustrates another data operation of the L2CAP layer: protocol multiplexing. Through the use of multiple channels and a protocol identifier (called a *protocol-specific multiplexer*, or PSM), L2CAP allows various protocols to be multiplexed (flow simultaneously) over the air interface. The L2CAP layer sorts out which packets are destined for which upper layers of the stack.

Service Discovery Protocol (SDP)

The SDP layer provides a means by which Bluetooth devices can learn, in an ad hoc manner, which services are offered by each device. Once a connection has been established, devices use the SDP to exchange information about services. An SDP client queries an SDP server to inquire about services that are available; the SDP server responds with information about services that it offers. Any Bluetooth device can be either an SDP client or an SDP server, acting in one role or the other at different times.

SDP allows a device to inquire about specific services in which it is interested (called *service searching*) or to perform a general inquiry about any services that happen to be available (called *service browsing*). A device can perform an SDP service search to look for, say, printing services in the vicinity. Any devices that offer a printing service that matches the query can respond with a "handle" for the service; the client then uses that handle to perform additional queries to obtain more details about the service. Once a service is discovered using SDP, other protocols are used to access and invoke the service; one of the items that can be discovered using SDP is the set of protocols that are necessary to access and invoke the service.

SDP is designed to be a lightweight discovery protocol that is optimized for the dynamic nature of Bluetooth piconets. SDP can coexist with other discovery and control protocols; for example, the Bluetooth SIG has published a specification for using the UPnPdiscovery and control technology over Bluetooth links.

RFCOMM

As its name suggests, the RFCOMM layer defines a standard communications protocol, specifically one that emulates serial port communication (the "RF" designates radio frequency wireless communication; the "COMM" portion suggests a serial port, commonly called a COM port in the personal computer realm). RFCOMM emulates a serial cable connection and provides the abstraction of a serial port to higher layers in the stack. This is particularly valuable for Bluetooth cable-replacement applications, because so many cable connections—modems, infrared ports, camera and mobile phone ports, printers, and others—use some form of a serial port to communicate.

RFCOMM is based on the European Telecommunications Standards Institute (ETSI) TS07.10 protocol (ETSI, 1999), which defines a multiplexed serial communications channel. The Bluetooth specification adopts much of the TS07.10 protocol and adds some Bluetooth adaptation features. The presence of RFCOMM in the Bluetooth protocol stack is intended to facilitate the migration of existing wired serial communication applications to wireless Bluetooth links. By presenting higher layers of the stack with a virtual serial port, many existing applications that already use a serial port can be used in Bluetooth environments without any changes. Indeed, many of the cable-replacement applications cited earlier, including dial-up networking, LAN access, headset, and file and object exchange, use RFCOMM to communicate. Because RFCOMM is a multiplexed serial channel, many serial data streams can flow over it simultaneously; each separate serial data stream is identified with a *server channel*, in a manner somewhat analogous to the channels used with L2CAP.

Telephony Control Specification-Binary (TCS-BIN)

The TCS-BIN is a protocol used for advanced telephony operations. Many of the Bluetooth usage scenarios involve a mobile telephone, and some of these use the TCS-BIN protocol. TCS-BIN is adopted from the ITU-T Q.931 standard (International Telecommunication Union,

1998), and it includes functions for call control and managing wireless user groups. Typically, TCS-BIN is used to set up and manage voice calls; the voice traffic that is the content of the call is carried as audio packets as described earlier. Applications such as the three-in-one phone usage model use TCS-BIN to enable functions such as using a mobile phone as a cordless phone or an intercom. In these cases, TCS-BIN is used to recognize the mobile phone so that it can be added to a wireless user group that consists of all the cordless telephone handsets used with a cordless telephone base station. TCS-BIN is also used to set up and control calls between the handset and the base station (cordless telephony) or between two handsets (intercom).

TCS-BIN offers several advanced telephony functions; devices that support TCS-BIN can obtain knowledge of and directly communicate with any other devices in the TCS-BIN wireless user group, essentially overcoming the master–slave relationship of the underlying Bluetooth piconet (detailed later). It should be noted that not all Bluetooth telephony applications require TCS-BIN; an alternative method for call control is the use of AT commands via the RFCOMM serial interface. This latter method is used for the headset, dial-up networking, and fax profiles.

Adopted Protocols

Although several layers of the Bluetooth protocol stack were developed specifically to support Bluetooth wireless communication, other layers are adopted from existing industry standards. I already have noted that RFCOMM and TCS-BIN are based on existing specifications. In addition to these, protocols for file and object exchange and synchronization are adopted from the Infrared Data Association (IrDA), and Internet networking protocols are used in some applications.

The IrDA's *object exchange* (OBEX) protocol is used for the file and object transfer, object push, and synchronization usage models. OBEX originally was developed for infrared wireless communication, and it maps well to Bluetooth wireless communication. OBEX is a relatively lightweight protocol for data exchange, and several well-defined data types—including electronic business cards, e-mail, short messages, and calendar items—can be carried within the protocol. Hence, the Bluetooth SIG adopted OBEX for use in its data exchange scenarios; by doing so, existing infrared applications can be used via Bluetooth links, often with no application changes. In addition, the *infrared mobile communications* (IrMC) protocol is used for the synchronization usage model. Typically, infrared communication occurs via a serial port, so the adopted IrDA protocols operate via RFCOMM in the Bluetooth protocol stack.

Networking applications such as dial-up networking and LAN access use standard Internet protocols, including point-to-point protocol (PPP), Internet protocol (IP), user datagram protocol (UDP), and transmission control protocol (TCP). As shown in Figure 2, these protocols operate via the RFCOMM protocol. Once a Bluetooth RFCOMM connection is established between two devices, PPP can be used as a basis for UDP–IP and TCP–IP networking packets. This enables typical networking applications, such as network dialers, e-mail programs, and browsers, to operate via Bluetooth links, often with no changes to the applications.

Bluetooth Profiles

I have presented an overview of the Bluetooth protocols, which are described in (Bluetooth SIG 2003), the Bluetooth master specification. The Bluetooth SIG publishes multiple volumes of the specification, some of which define the Bluetooth *profiles*. Profiles offer additional guidance to developers beyond the specification of the protocols. Essentially, a profile is a formalized usage case that describes how to use the protocols (including which protocols to use, which options are available, and so on) for a given application. Profiles were developed to foster interoperability; they provide a standard basis for all implementations to increase the likelihood that implementations from different vendors will work together, so that end users can have confidence that Bluetooth devices will interoperate with each other. In addition to the profile specifications, the SIG offers other mechanisms intended to promote interoperability; among these are the *Bluetooth Qualification Program* (a definition of testing that a Bluetooth device must undergo) and *unplugfests* (informal sessions where many vendors can test their products with each other); detailed discussions of these programs are outside the scope of this chapter, but more information is available on the Bluetooth Web site (Bluetooth SIG, 2005b).

Our earlier discussion of Bluetooth applications presented several usage models for Bluetooth wireless communication. Many of these applications have associated profiles. For example, the dial-up networking profile defines implementation considerations for the dial-up networking application. Most of the applications cited here have associated profiles, and many new profiles are being developed and published by the SIG; the official Bluetooth Web site (Bluetooth SIG, 2005) has a current list of available specifications. In addition, there are some fundamental profiles that describe basic Bluetooth operations that are necessary for most any application. The version 1.1 profiles are illustrated in Figure 3. This figure shows the relationship among the various profiles, illustrating how certain profiles are derived from (and build upon) others.

The leaf nodes of the diagram consist of profiles that describe particular applications—file and object transfer, object push, synchronization, dial-up networking, fax, headset, LAN access, cordless telephony, and intercom. The telephony (TCS-BIN) profile includes elements that are common to cordless telephony and intercom applications; similarly, the generic object exchange profile describes the common elements for its children, and the serial port profile defines operations used by all applications that use the RFCOMM serial cable–replacement protocol. Note that the generic object exchange profile derives from the serial port profile; this is because OBEX operates via RFCOMM in the Bluetooth protocol stack.

The two remaining profiles describe fundamental operations for Bluetooth communication. The service discovery application profile describes how a service discovery application uses the service discovery protocol (described

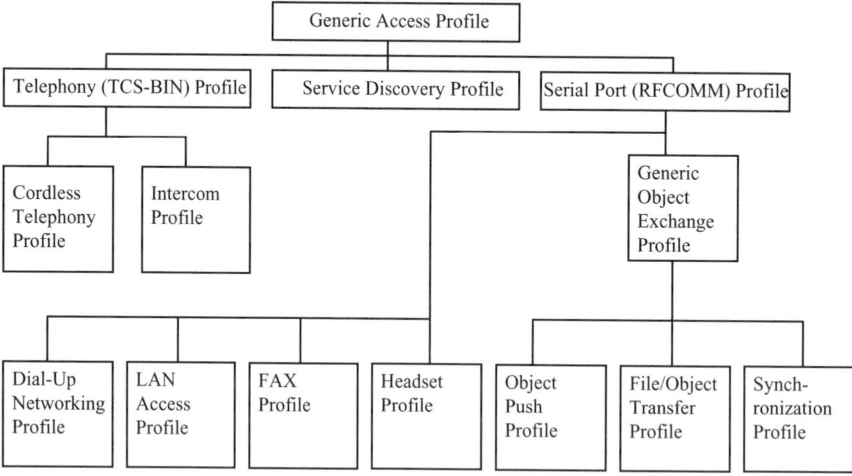

Figure 3: Bluetooth profiles.

earlier). The generic access profile is common to all applications; it defines the basic operations that Bluetooth devices use to establish connections, including how devices become discoverable and connectable, security considerations for connections, and so on. The generic access profile also includes a common set of terminology used in other profiles; this is intended to reduce ambiguity in the specification. The generic access and service discovery application profiles are mandatory for all Bluetooth devices to implement, because they form the basis for interoperable devices. Other works, including Miller and Bisdikian (2000), delve more deeply into the Bluetooth profiles.

Bluetooth Operation

Having discussed WPANs, Bluetooth applications, protocols, and profiles, I now turn our attention to some of the fundamental concepts of Bluetooth operation, illustrating an example flow for a Bluetooth connection.

At the baseband layer, Bluetooth operates on a master–slave model. In general, the *master* device is the one that initiates communication with one or more other devices. *Slaves* are the devices that respond to the master's queries. In general, any Bluetooth device can operate as either a master or a slave at any given time. The master and slave roles are meaningful only at the baseband layer; upper layers are not concerned with these roles. The master device establishes the frequency-hopping pattern for communication with its slaves, using its internal clock values to generate the frequency-hopping pattern. Slaves follow the frequency-hopping pattern of the master(s) with which they communicate.

When a master establishes a connection with one or more slaves, a *piconet* is formed. To establish the connection, a master uses processes called *inquiry* and *paging*. A master can perform an inquiry operation, which transmits a well-defined data sequence across the full spectrum of frequency-hopping channels. An inquiry effectively asks, "Are there any devices listening?" Devices that are in *inquiry scan* mode (a mode in which the device periodically listens to all of the channels for inquiries) can respond to the master's inquiry with enough information for the master device to address the responding device directly. The inquiring (master) device may then choose to page the responding (slave) device. The page is also transmitted across the full spectrum of frequency-hopping channels; the device that originally responded to the inquiry can enter a *page scan* state (a state in which it periodically listens to all of the channels for pages), and it can respond to the page with additional information that can be used to establish a baseband connection between the master and the slave. The master can repeat this process and establish connections with as many as seven slaves at a time. Hence, a piconet consists of one master and up to seven active slaves; additional slaves can be part of the piconet, but only seven slaves can be active at one time. Slaves can be "parked" (made inactive) so that other slaves can be activated. Figure 4 illustrates a typical Bluetooth piconet. Note that a device could be a slave in more than one piconet at a time, or it could be a master of one piconet and a slave in a second piconet. In these cases,

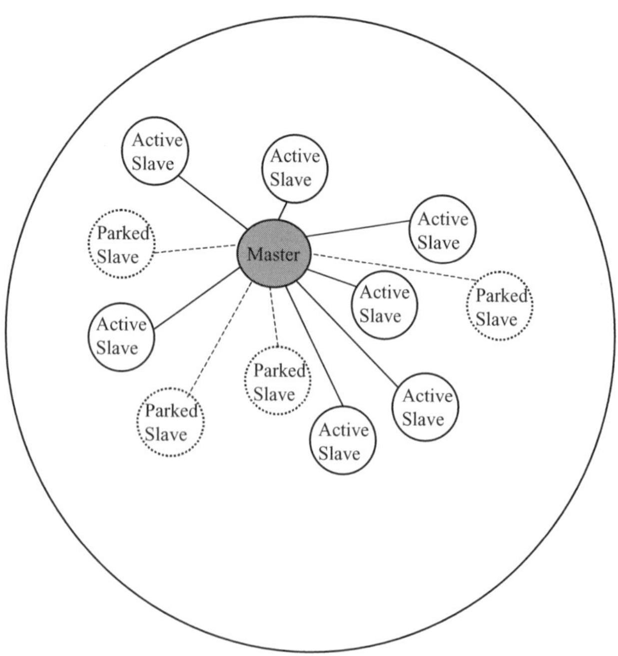

Figure 4: Example of a Bluetooth piconet.

the device participating in multiple piconets must use the appropriate frequency-hopping pattern in each piconet, so it effectively must split its time among all the piconets in which it participates. The Bluetooth specification calls such interconnected piconets *scatternets*.

Once a piconet is formed (a baseband connection exists between a master and one or more slave devices), higher layer connections can be formed, and link manager commands and responses may be used to manage the link. At some point, it is likely that an L2CAP connection will be formed for data packets (even if the main content for a link is voice traffic, an L2CAP data connection will be needed to set up and manage the voice links). A Bluetooth device can have one data (L2CAP) connection and up to three voice connections with any other Bluetooth device at a given time (recall, however, that L2CAP connections can be multiplexed, so many different data streams can flow over the single L2CAP connection). Once an L2CAP connection is established, additional higher layer connections can be established. If the devices are not familiar to each other already, it is likely that an SDP connection will be used to perform service discovery. RFCOMM and TCS-BIN connections also might be made, depending on the application. From here, applications can manage voice and data packets to accomplish their usage scenarios, which might be those defined by Bluetooth profiles or other ways to use Bluetooth wireless communication to accomplish a given task. Additional details about fundamental Bluetooth operations and connection establishment, including the various types of packets, master–slave communication protocols, and timing considerations, are outside the scope of this chapter but are detailed in works such as Miller and Bisdikian (2000) and Bray and Sturman (2000).

Bluetooth Security

A noteworthy aspect of Bluetooth operation is security. In the wireless world, security justifiably is a key concern for device manufacturers, device deployers, and end users. The Bluetooth specification includes security measures such as authentication and encryption, and the Bluetooth profiles discuss which security measures should be employed in various circumstances.

At the time that a link is established, Bluetooth devices may be required to authenticate themselves to each other. This is done using a shared-secret method (other methods such as those using public keys typically require some sort of central registry, which is not appropriate for WPANs that use ad hoc networking). The first device sends a randomly generated number to the second device, which performs some computation using a *link key* value and returns the result to the first device. If that value is the one expected by the first device, then it considers the second device authenticated. The second device might then, in turn, authenticate the first device so that the two devices are mutually authenticated with each other. Link keys are maintained by each device; a process called *pairing* can be used to generate a link key from an initialization key the very first time two devices are introduced to each other.

Once a link has been established, the data traffic over that link may be encrypted. The encryption key is derived from the link key, so devices that exchange encrypted traffic must have been already authenticated with each other. Bluetooth links support up to 128-bit encryption; the devices mutually agree on the encryption key size.

The Bluetooth profiles provide guidance about how and when to use authentication and encryption in Bluetooth wireless communication. The Generic Access Profile (described earlier) defines three different security modes (non-secure, service-level enforced security, and link-level enforced security) and the procedures to follow to achieve those levels of security in Bluetooth communications. Other profiles specify the security measures that should be used for various applications or scenarios. For example, the file transfer profile requires that both authentication and encryption be supported, and it recommends that they be used; the dial-up networking profile requires that all data be encrypted, in addition to device authentication.

Applications are free to impose additional security restrictions beyond those that are provided in the specification. For example, applications might choose to expose data or services only to authorized users or to implement more robust user authentication schemes. Certain applications might include other security mechanisms beyond those built into the Bluetooth devices, such as the use of public key infrastructure, certificates, or other methods. More details about the operation of Bluetooth security features are included in works such as Miller and Bisdikian (2000) and Bray and Sturman (2000).

CONCLUSION

This introduction to Bluetooth wireless technology has touched on what can be done with the technology (Bluetooth applications), how it began, how it now is managed (the Bluetooth SIG), and how it works (Bluetooth protocols, profiles, and operation, including security). The chapter focused on the application of Bluetooth wireless communication as a WPAN technology for connecting personal portable devices. I have presented several references where this topic is explored in greater detail.

With tremendous industry backing, a design to work with both voice and data, the ability to replace cumbersome cables, and many new products being deployed on a regular basis, Bluetooth wireless technology is poised to become an important way for people to communicate for the foreseeable future. From its genesis as a method to provide a wireless headset for mobile phones, this technology named for a Danish king continues to spread across the planet.

GLOSSARY

Bluetooth SIG The Bluetooth Special Interest Group, an industry consortium that develops, promotes, and manages Bluetooth wireless technology, including the Bluetooth qualification program and the Bluetooth brand.

Bluetooth Wireless Technology Name given to a wireless communications technology used for short-range voice and data communication, especially for cable-replacement applications.

Frequency-Hopping Spread Spectrum A method of dividing packetized information across multiple channels of a frequency spectrum that is used in Bluetooth wireless communication.

IEEE 802.11 A wireless local area network standard developed by the Institute for Electrical and Electronics Engineers that is considered complementary to Bluetooth wireless technology.

IEEE 802.15.1 A wireless personal area network standard developed by the Institute for Electrical and Electronics Engineers that is based on Bluetooth wireless technology.

Infrared Data Association (IrDA) An industry consortium that specifies the IrDA infrared communication protocols, some of which are used in the Bluetooth protocol stack.

Piconet A Bluetooth wireless technology term for a set of interconnected devices with one master and up to seven active slave devices.

Profile In Bluetooth wireless technology, a specification for standard methods to use when implementing a particular application, with a goal of fostering interoperability among applications and devices.

Radio Frequency (RF) Used in the Bluetooth specification to describe the use of radio waves for physical layer communication.

Wireless Personal Area Network (WPAN) A small set of interconnected devices used by one person.

CROSS REFERENCES

See *Bluetooth Security; Mobile Commerce; Mobile Devices and Protocols; Radio Frequency and Wireless Communications Security; Security and the Wireless Application Protocol (WAP); Wireless Channels; Wireless Internet: A Cellular Perspective.*

REFERENCES

Bluetooth Special Interest Group. (2003). *Specification of the Bluetooth system, master table of contents & compliance requirements.* Retrieved April 13, 2005, from https://www. bluetooth.org/spec/

Bluetooth Special Interest Group. (2005a). *Trademark info.* Retrieved April 13, 2005, from http://www.bluetooth.com/util/trademark.asp

Bluetooth Special Interest Group. (2005b). *The official Bluetooth Web site.* Retrieved April 13, 2005, from https://www.bluetooth.org/ (see also http://www.bluetooth.com).

Bray, J., & Sturman, C. (2000). *Bluetooth: Connect without cables.* New York: Prentice Hall PTR (2nd ed., 2001).

European Telecommunications Standards Institute. (1999). *Technical specification: Digital cellular telecommunications system (Phase 2+); Terminal equipment to mobile station (TE-MS) multiplexer protocol* (GSM 07.10). Retrieved April 13, 2005, from http://www.etsi.org

InnTechnology. (2000). *The Venetian Resort-Hotel-Casino and InnTechnology showcase Bluetooth hospitality services.* Retrieved March 28, 2003, from http://www.inntechnology.com/bluetooth/bluetooth_press_release.html

Institute of Electrical and Electronics Engineers. (1999). *Wireless standards package (802.11).* Retrieved April 13, 2005, from http://standards.ieee.org/getieee802

International Telecommunication Union. (1998). *Recommendation Q.931—ISDN user-network interface layer 3 specification for basic call control.* Retrieved April 13, 2005, from http://www.itu.org.

Internet Mail Consortium. (1996a). *vCard—The electronic business card exchange format.* Retrieved April 13, 2005, from http://www.imc.org/pdi

Internet Mail Consortium. (1996b). *vCalendar—The electronic calendaring and scheduling exchange format.* Retrieved April 13, 2005, from http://www.imc.org/pdi

Kardach, J. (2001). The naming of a technology. *Incisor, 34, pp. 10–12 and 37.* pp. 13–15, Surrey, UK: Click I.T.

Miller, B. (2001). *The phony conflict: IEEE 802.11 and Bluetooth wireless technology.* IBM DeveloperWorks. Retrieved March 28, 2003, from http://www-106.ibm.com/developerworks/library/wi-phone/?dwzone=wireless

Miller, B., & Bisdikian, C. (2000). *Bluetooth revealed: The insider's guide to an open specification for global wireless communication.* New York: Prentice Hall PTR (2nd ed., 2001).

FURTHER READING

Infrared Data Association. (2002). *IrDA SIR data specification* (and related documents). Retrieved April 13, 2005, from http://www.irda.org/displaycommon.cfm?an=1&subarticlenbr=7

Institute of Electrical and Electronics Engineers. (2001). *IEEE 802.15 Working Group for WPANs.* Retrieved April 13, 2005, from http://standards.ieee.org/getieee802

Suvak, D. (1999). *IrDA and Bluetooth: A complementary comparison.* Walnut Creek, CA: Infrared Data Association. Retrieved March 28, 2003, from http://www.irda.org/design/ESIIrDA_Bluetoothpaper.doc

Wireless Local Area Networks

M. S. Obaidat, *Monmouth University*
G. I. Papadimitriou, *Aristotle University, Greece*
S. Obeidat, *Arizona State University*

INTRODUCTION

Overview

In the past few years, we have seen wireless technology permeate every aspect of our lives. The fob on your key-chain (to open the car remotely), wireless mice and keyboards, and personal digital assistants (PDAs) that synchronize with your workstation are just a few examples. This proliferation of wireless devices was the result of the Federal Communications Commission (FCC) decision to open the ISM (industrial, scientific, and medical) band to the public. Wireless local area networks (WLANs) were among the domains that benefited from this release. This release from licensing motivated many companies and research laboratories to develop and implement wireless LAN solutions.

This disorganized and parallel effort resulted in the emergence of proprietary solutions that do not interoperate with each other. Lack of interoperability results in limited scope of acceptance because buyers of the technology from one vendor will either have to stick to that vendor or go through the pains of trying to work out a solution among different technologies. The IEEE 802.11 working group was formed to create a universal standard that can be followed by different vendors.

The first standard was released in 1997 and supported data rates up to 2 Mbps (IEEE, 1997). The specification defined both the physical and the media access control (MAC) layers. Other standards followed that addressed different requirements and provided higher data rates. These included the 802.11b, 802.11a, and 802.11g, which had higher data rates; the 802.11e, which had QoS support; the 802.11i, which had security; and others.

In parallel to the 802.11 effort, the European Telecommunications Standards Institute (ETSI) was working on the high-performance radio LAN (HIPERLAN) project. Unlike the 802.11 project, which tried to use available technology, the HIPERLAN was built from scratch; the development of HIPERLAN was not driven by existing technologies and regulations. Instead, it was designed to meet a defined set of goals. The HIPERLAN Type 1 supports data rates of up to 25 Mbps. HIPERLAN Types 2, 3 and 4 specify standards for wireless asynchronous transfer mode (ATM)-supporting data and quality of service (QoS) applications.

Applications of WLANs

Similar to their wired counterparts, wireless LANs can be used to provide connectivity within a limited geographic area. Mobility, the ability to move around while still connected to a network, is a great feature of wireless LANs. In a working environment where staff members need to be mobile yet constantly connected to the network, WLANs are inevitable. Doctors and nurses accessing patients' data instantly, work coordination among members at different locations, and students' access to their accounts and class information around the campus are just a few examples of how easy and convenient life can be with support for mobility. An implication of mobility is outdoors connectivity. A wired network stops where your sockets and phone lines stop. A wireless LAN can provide you with connectivity while sipping a cup of coffee while sitting at a street corner.

A less obvious advantage of WLANs is has to do with the feasibility of running wires. Wireless LANs can be used to connect two wired LANs in different buildings. This might be the only way to provide connectivity, because accessing a public property (e.g., to cross a street) is not always possible. In this scenario, two bridges or switches can

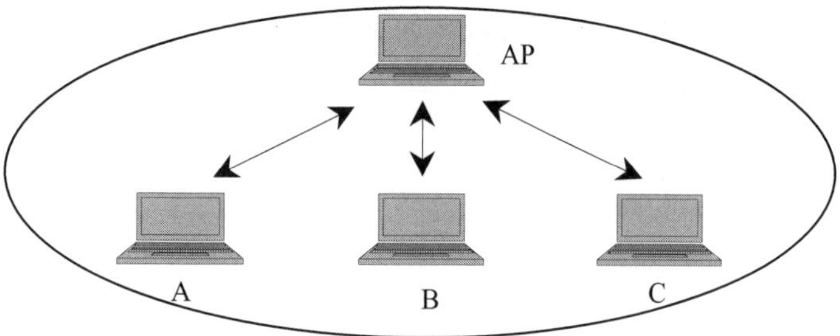

Figure 1: BSS organization of a wireless LAN.

communicate wirelessly with each other to connect the two LAN segments. Even within the same building, a wired network may be unfeasible or impossible. Examples include museums and historical buildings. In addition, the lack of infrastructure and ad hoc topology of WLANs can be used in places where fast deployment is needed, such as relief-and-recovery teams in disaster areas. Ad hoc networks allow a group of nodes to communicate with each other in a distributed, peer-to-peer manner, without prior arrangement. They can also be used for settings where temporary connectivity is needed. A meeting where people need to exchange files and presentations is an example.

Yet another advantage of wireless LANs is their cost-effectiveness. It is known that a major part of a traditional wired LAN's installation is cabling and its implications of running conduits. Getting rid of cabling allows seamless additions, deletions, and modifications of the topology with no cost whatsoever. Also, the costs needed to run and maintain wires are all eliminated in a WLAN.

Chapter Organization

The remainder of this chapter is organized as follows: the second section discusses the possible topologies of 802.11 MAC and the MAC protocol description. The possible physical layers and the necessary background information are provided in the third section. The fourth section discusses HIPERLAN Types 1 and 2. Security and QoS support in 802.11 are described in the next two sections. We conclude the chapter by briefly describing some advanced topics in wireless networks.

802.11 MAC

Possible Topologies

Wireless LANs can be either infrastructure based or ad hoc. The latter LANs have no preexisting infrastructure or centralized management to support the mobile nodes. They consist of wireless nodes that can freely and dynamically self-organize into arbitrary and temporary network topologies. On the other hand, an infrastructure WLAN is based on central control, for example, by using an access point. In this section we discuss both schemes. The following classification of the different organizations of a wireless LAN is based on the concept of a service set. A service set is nothing more than a logical grouping of nodes. A node belongs to only one service set. By "belong," we mean it listens to transmissions from only one particular service set.

Basic Service Set (BSS)

The basic service set (BSS) resembles the basic building block in the 802.11 architecture. Nodes in a BSS communicate with each other through an access point (AP). An AP is responsible for coordinating communication among the nodes by receiving a node's transmission and forwarding it to the respective receiver. It is analogous to a base station in a cellular network. A BSS is analogous to a cell in a cellular network. The coverage area of a BSS is called a basic service area (BSA). Figure 1 illustrates the concept of a BSS (Crow, Widjaja, Kim, & Sakai, 1997a).

Extended Service Set (ESS)

Figure 2 shows how multiple BSSs can be connected to each other by connecting their APs to a distribution system (DS) and forming what is called an extended service set (ESS). Even though the APs can connect to the DS via either wired or wireless connections, usually the connection is wired. The DS resembles the backbone of the ESS and is responsible for communicating MAC segments from one BSS to another or from one BSS to an external wired network (Crow, Widjaja, Kim, & Sakai, 1997a).

Independent Basic Service Set (IBSS)

The BSS and its extension (through an ESS) both resemble an infrastructure-based organization. The independent basic service set (IBSS), on the other hand, resembles

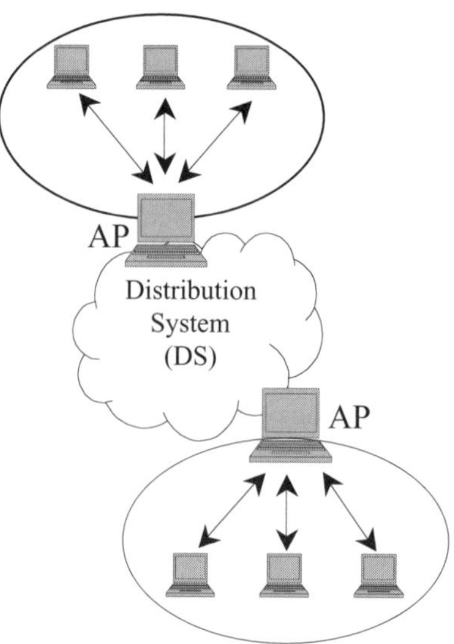

Figure 2: ESS organization of a wireless LAN.

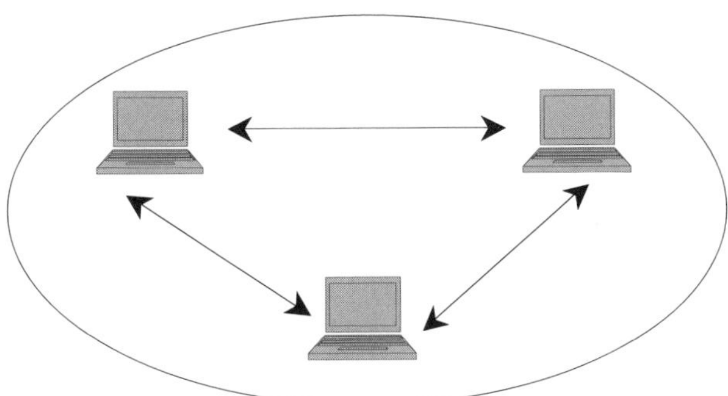

Figure 3: IBSS (ad hoc) organization of a wireless LAN.

the infrastructureless ad hoc arrangement; see Figure 3. In an IBSS, stations communicate in a peer-to-peer fashion in which no AP or any other intermediary is needed. At least two stations are needed to form an IBSS.

Access Modes: DCF

The distributed coordination function (DCF) is the basic access mode of the 802.11 standard. It is based on the carrier sense multiple access with collision avoidance (CSMA/CA) scheme. The DCF is a contention-based protocol. Stations have to compete every time they want to access the channel. Before delving into the details of the protocol, an important question that comes to mind is why a specialized MAC is need: why can't we simply adopt a wired MAC protocol? We start this section by answering this question and pointing out the issues that arise in a wireless communication context.

Why Wired Network Types of Channel Access Do Not Work

In the IEEE 802.3 Ethernet standard, carrier sense multiple access with collision detection (CSMA/CD) is used. The basic idea is that the sender senses the medium (a cable to which all the nodes in the Ethernet segment are attached) and if the medium is busy, the sender tries again later. If the channel is idle, on the other hand, the sender sends and keeps listening to the channel. If at any point during its transmission it hears a collision, it stops transmitting and sends a jamming signal.

The basic assumption in the CSMA/CD protocol is that a collision that takes place at the receiver can be detected at the sender. This is true because the signal strength is basically more or less the same throughout the medium. This assumption is not true for the wireless medium because the signal strength decreases as the distance from the transmitter increases. Thus, an event may take place and not detected by the transmitter. The hidden and exposed terminal problems discussed next stem from this fact. In addition, a wireless node does not have the ability to transmit and receive at the same time because its own transmission would swamp any other signal in the vicinity (Nicopolitidis, Obaidat, Papadimitriou, & Pomportsis, 2003; Schiller, 2000).

Figure 4 shows three stations: A, B, and C. The transmission range of A reaches B but not C. Similarly, the transmission range of C reaches B but not A. A's detection range (the range within which A can sense the medium) does not include C. C's detection range does not include A either.

Willing to transmit to B, A senses the channel and finds it idle. As a result, it starts transmitting. Meanwhile, C becomes interested in sending some data to B. C senses the channel but does not detect the ongoing transmission between A and B because it is out of its range. C also starts transmitting to B, which results in a collision at B that is not detected by either A or C. This problem, where two nodes are out of reach of each other but within the reach of a third node, is called the hidden terminal problem (or hidden node problem).

Another problem associated with the inability to detect collisions is the exposed terminal problem, which is illustrated in Figure 5. In this case, B is transmitting to A. C, willing to send to D, senses the channel and finds it busy. If C transmits, its transmission would not interfere with the ongoing transmission between B and A, because A is outside its range. C's transmission, even though it would collide with B, would not collide with A because the signal would be too weak to cause collision. Thus, C mistakenly postpones its transmission, even though it should not. In this case, we say that C is exposed to B.

Consider the situation where node A is closer to node C than node B, as shown in Figure 6. In this case even though both A and B can reach C, the signal power of A's transmission is much higher than that of B's transmission. As a result, C cannot hear B's transmission. To go around this problem, B has to compensate for the difference in distance by transmitting at a higher signal strength. This

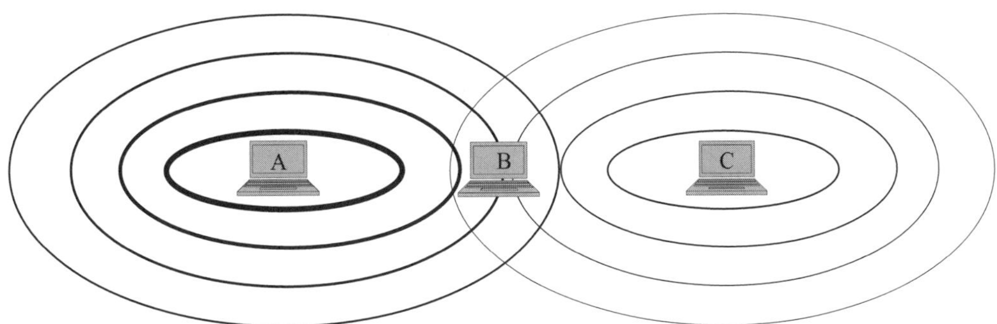

Figure 4: The hidden terminal problem: C is outside the transmission and detection range of A. Similarly, A is outside the transmission and detection range of C.

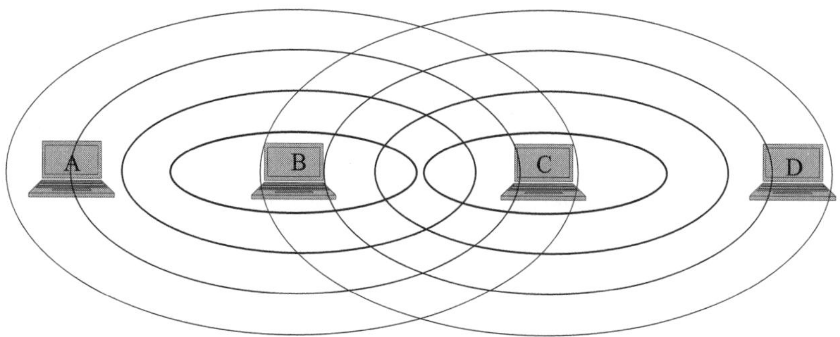

Figure 5: The exposed terminal problem: C, even though is out of A's range, is within B's range. Hence, it postpones transmitting to D even though it should not, because its transmission would not collide with A, even though it would collide with B.

is the near–far effect, and it contrasts to wired networks, where nodes receive more or less the same signal strength.

CSMA/CA

As discussed in the previous section, the wireless medium imposes its own requirements on a MAC protocol. The main issue to be dealt with is the inability of nodes to detect collisions, and therefore the necessity to eliminate or minimize collisions. That is exactly why CSMA/CA was proposed. In CSMA/CA, nodes perform two types of carrier sensing: physical carrier sensing and virtual carrier sensing, which refer to sensing at the physical and the MAC layers, respectively. A channel is considered busy if either the physical or the virtual carrier senses a busy channel indication. The physical carrier monitors the medium for any ongoing transmissions by looking at the strength of any received signal. Let us examine the case of the hidden terminal problem.

Figure 7 shows the same scenario as that in Figure 4. When node A decides to send to node B, it first sends a request-to-send (RTS) control packet. All nodes within the range of A overhear the RTS packet and postpone their attempt to transmit. When B receives the RTS packet, it sends back a clear-to-send (CTS) packet. All nodes in the range of B will defer any attempt to transmit. As we can see, C now is not going to transmit to B because it heard the CTS packet. This procedure is also known as the four-way handshake.

Although the RTS–CTS exchange mitigates the hidden terminal problem, it does not solve it entirely. For example, A and C may both transmit an RTS packet at the same time. Another possibility is that B sends a CTS at the same time as C sends an RTS, which results in a collision of both control packets at C. Node C does not hear the CTS sent to A nor a CTS for its own RTS and thus retransmits the RTS, which would collide with A's packet.

Collisions involving the RTS and CTS control packets carry a small penalty when compared with collisions of data packets. This is readily apparent from the sizes of the RTC and CTS packets (20 bytes and 16 bytes, respectively), in contrast to the maximum data packet size, which is 2346 bytes. Thus, the RTS–CTS exchange gives better overall performance.

The basic idea of virtual carrier sensing involves an announcement of the amount of time a node will be occupying the channel, so that all nodes hearing the announcement will defer their transmissions. To achieve this, every packet (be it a data packet, an RTS, or a CTS) carries a duration field, which indicates the amount of time the channel will be needed after the current packet transmission is done. This period includes the time to transmit the RTS, CTS, the data packet, and the returning ACK (acknowledgment). Every node maintains what is called a network allocation vector (NAV). Nodes adjust the values of their vectors as they overhear packet transmissions. A node attempts to check the channel status (whether idle or not) only when the duration in the NAV elapses.

Access priority to the wireless channel is provided through the use of inter-frame spacing (IFS), which is the duration of time that has to pass before trying to access the channel. Three IFSs are defined in the protocol; these are, in increasing order of importance, distributed coordination function IFS (DIFS), point coordination function IFS (PIFS), and short IFS (SIFS). The SIFS is the shortest

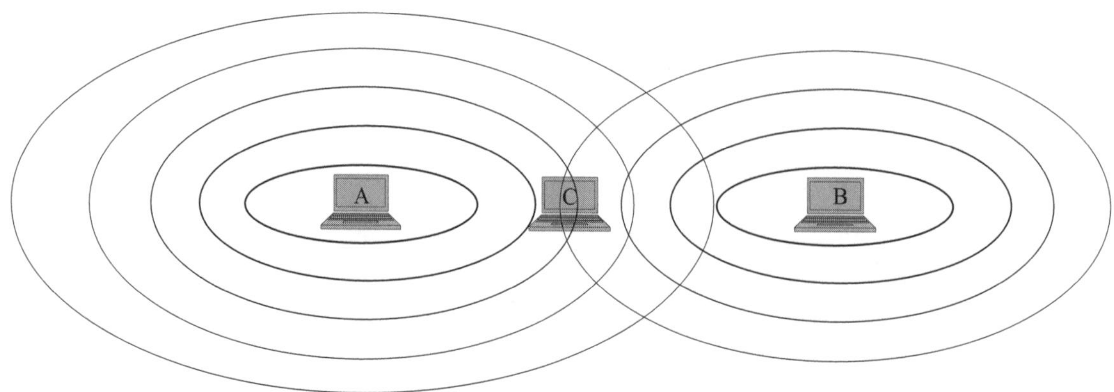

Figure 6: Near–far effect.

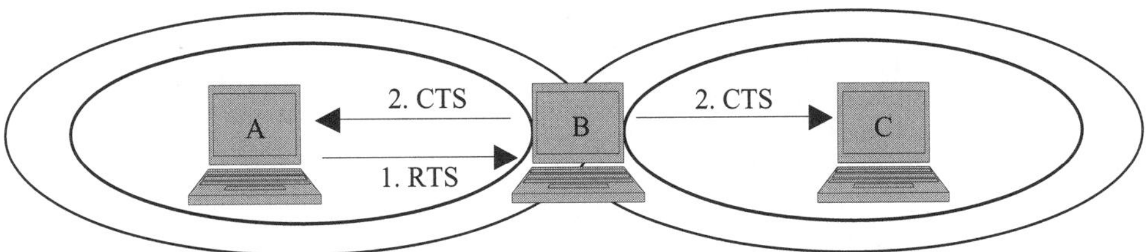

Figure 7: RTS–CTS control packet exchange.

amount of time and hence the highest priority, followed by the PIFS used by the PCF, and the DIFS, which is the time delay used by DCF frames.

Figure 8 shows how a frame transmission takes place along with the NAV table's adjustments at other nodes (those that are not involved in the current transmission). Prior to sensing the channel, a node has to wait the duration of a DIFS. After that, if the channel is idle, the node sends an RTS. The duration field is set to include the time for the CTS, the data packet, the ACK, and the SIFS durations that separate each one of these. When the receiver gets the RTS, it waits the duration of a SIFS and sends back a CTS. Upon receiving the CTS, the sender waits another SIFS and transmits the data packet, which is followed by another SIFS and an ACK. The success of these steps marks a successful packet transmission. Nodes wait the duration of a DIFS and contend for the channel again.

After a channel has been busy, the probability of more than one node trying to access the channel is large. The idle period following a DIFS interval is referred to as the contention window. To prevent collisions and enhance performance, nodes enter into a back-off period so that channel access demands are spread over time. Nodes calculate a random back-off interval. A station calculates the amount of back-off to be between 0 and the minimum size of the contention window (CWmin). A station transmits only when its back-off reaches 0 and the channel is idle. In case the transmission results in a collision, the station calculates a new contention window size equal to $2^{2+i} - 1$ time slots, where i is the number of consecutive collisions the station experienced. For every transmission failure, the station calculates a contention window until it reaches a maximum window size (CWmax). When the retry counter, i, exceeds a specific (user-defined) value, the packet is dropped. It must be mentioned that the countdown timer freezes when the channel is sensed to be busy and it is resumed once the wireless medium is detected to be subsequently idle for the DIFS time.

Access Modes: PCF

Unlike the DCF, which is a contention-based protocol used for data traffic, the point coordination function provides a contention-free protocol that can be used for connection-oriented real-time traffic such as voice. This is done by polling the stations one at a time. PCF needs an element called the point coordinator (PC), which decides when and which node can transmit according to a polling list (normally in round-robin fashion). We recommend the PC to be integrated with the AP. Given the centralized

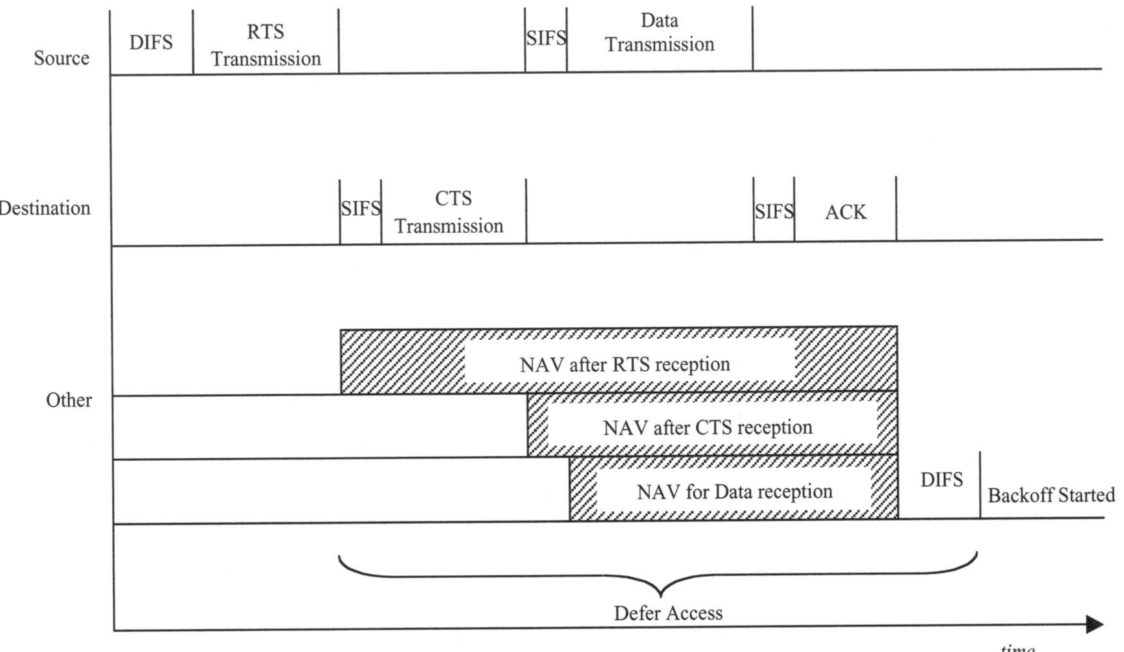

Figure 8: Frame transmission along with the changes in the NAV as time progresses.

approach of PCF, which depends on the AP for polling, PCF works only for the infrastructure-based topology and not for the ad hoc topology. It must be mentioned that PCF has not yet been implemented and of course is not available in any WLAN card. The protocol works by dividing time into contention-free periods (CFPs). The length of the CFP is manageable and determines how often the PCF runs. Each CFP consists of a contention-free portion followed by contention-based period (i.e., for DCF traffic). Each CFP must allow at least one DCF packet to be transmitted (so that DCF traffic does not starve). The portion allotted to PCF traffic is dynamic and the AP can change it as the traffic requirements change. For example, if a small number of nodes are interested in the PCF service, more time is allotted to the DCF function. The AP announces the beginning of a CFP by sending a beacon frame. Stations update their NAV to the maximum length of CFP, which is a defined parameter, *CFP_Max_Duration*. Periodically, the AP sends a beacon frame, which contains the remaining time of the CFP, *CFPDurationRemaining*.

To initiate the beginning of a CFP, the AP waits a PCF inter-frame space (PIFS), which is shorter than a DIFS. Thus, the AP gains access to the channel before any DCF station. It then sends a beacon frame, which is used for synchronization and a parameter-information announcement. At this point, all stations have updated their NAV, and no one will access the channel unless requested by the AP. The AP can send a poll frame, a data frame (i.e., forwarding from one station to another), a combination of data and poll, or a CFP end frame.

802.11 PHYSICAL LAYER

In this section, we discuss basic concepts related to the physical layer, followed by a discussion of the main problems associated with wireless channels. Afterward, we explain the different radio layers of the 802.11 standard. Finally, we close with a discussion of some of the physical-layer standards.

Concepts

Channel Coding and Modulation

Modulation is the process of changing the data stream to a form suitable for transmission via a physical medium. Two categories of modulation exist: analog modulation and digital modulation. Analog modulation works by impressing the analog signal containing the data onto a carrier wave, thereby changing a property of the carrier wave. Digital modulation refers to the mapping of one or more bits to a symbol where a symbol is the basic unit communicated between a transmitter and a receiver. This works by converting a bit string (digital data) to a suitable continuous time waveform. This conversion involves modifying one of the signal characteristics, such as the amplitude, frequency, or the phase, which gives rise to amplitude modulation, frequency modulation, or phase modulation; see Figure 9. Amplitude refers to the signal strength, frequency refers to the number of times per second the signal repeats its pattern (measured in Hz or cycles/sec), and phase refers to the relative position in time.

In digital modulation, the higher the number of bits mapped to a symbol, the denser the modulation scheme is said to be. The denser the modulation scheme, the more spectrally efficient it is. The number of bits per symbol depends on the modulation scheme used. For example, if the channel bandwidth is 1 MHz, the wave frequency is fixed and equal to the frequency of the carrier wave, and if every bit is mapped into a symbol, then the channel capacity is 1 Mbps. This holds because 1 million wave transitions per second are supported. On the other hand, if every two bits are mapped into one symbol, the channel capacity will be doubled to become 2 Mbps. Nonetheless, the increase in the number of bits per symbol is not arbitrary. The higher the number of bits per symbol, the higher the chances of error in recovering the bits at the receiving end.

Coding maximizing the benefit of transmission over noisy wireless channels by introducing redundancies in the bits transmitted, so that the receiver can still recover a reasonably distorted packet. To be able to recover more

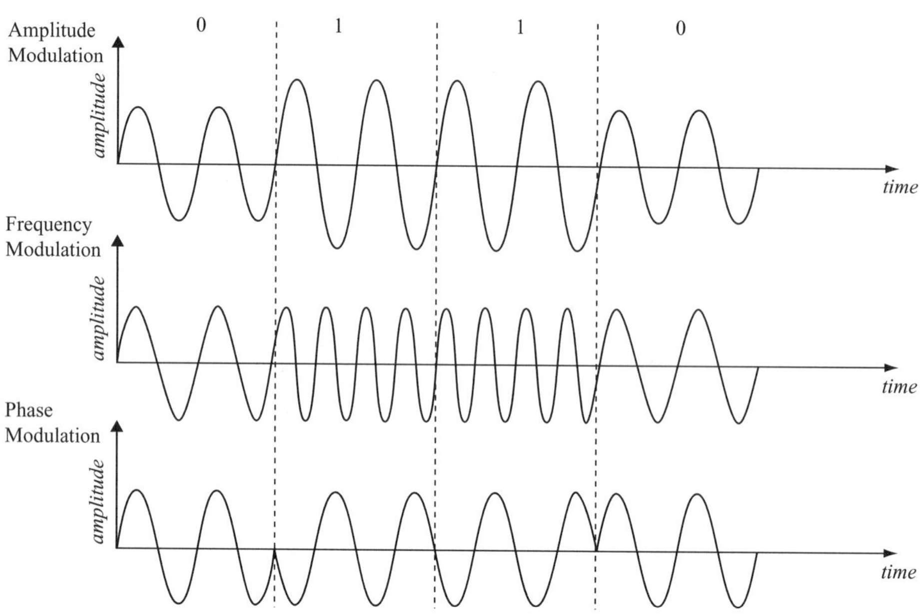

Figure 9: Illustration of amplitude, frequency, and phase modulations (bit sequence: 0110).

errors, more overhead bits have to be sent. Coding efficiency refers to the ratio between data and total bits in the stream. For example, a coding efficiency of 1/2 means that for every bit in the data stream, two bits have to be sent. One important issue in coding schemes is the computational complexity in implementing the code. This is especially important for portable wireless devices, which try to use their energy efficiently.

Antennas

An antenna is a device responsible for emitting or collecting electromagnetic waves for the purposes of transmission and reception. In other words, it is the interface between the transmitter or receiver and the air. In a nutshell, an antenna takes electrical signals from the transmitter and converts them into radio (i.e., electromagnetic) signals sent on the air, and captures radio signals from the air and converts them into electrical signals at the receiver. Antennas are characterized by many parameters including directivity or gain, polarity, and efficiency, among others (www.gigaant.com, 2004).

Before explaining directivity, let's define isotropic antennas. An isotropic antenna is an ideal antenna that radiates the same power in all directions. In other words, if we create a sphere around it and measure the power intensity at any point on the surface, we get the same value. Realistic antennas radiate more in some directions than others. Gain is amount of power "gained" in one direction at the expense of other directions.

Electromagnetic waves consist of coupled electric and magnetic fields. Polarization refers to the position and direction of the electric field with reference to the Earth's surface. An antenna can be horizontally or vertically polarized. The transmitting and receiving antennas have to have the same polarization; otherwise, a great amount of loss will occur. Efficiency of an antenna is defined as the ratio between the radiated power and the input power. An isotropic antenna has a gain of 1.

There are omnidirectional antennas (which provide a 360-degree radiation pattern), directional antennas (which focus radiation in one direction to provide greater coverage distance), and diversity antennas (which actually use more than one antenna for signal reception and transmit through the antenna with the best received signal).

Wireless Problems

Unlike wired transmissions, the wireless channel is impaired, which, along with the scarce spectral bandwidth, makes achieving medium wired quality extremely difficult. In this subsection, we briefly touch on the problems faced in wireless communications.

Path Loss. As a signal propagates from the transmitter to the receiver, it attenuates (i.e., losses its energy) with distance. Thus, the longer the distance, the weaker the signal received. The free space model refers to the signal strength when the path between the transmitter and the receiver is clear of obstacles and resembles a line of sight. In the free space model, the signal attenuates with the square of the distance (i.e., d^2 where d is the distance) (Nicopolitidis, Obaidat, Papadimitriou, & Pomportsis, 2003). Realistic modeling of path loss, however, depends

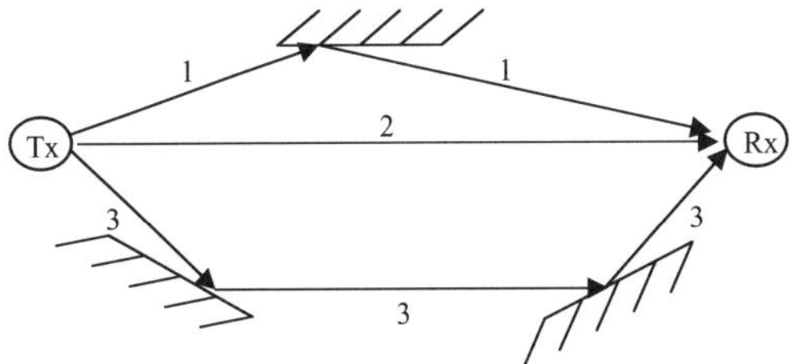

Figure 10: Illustration of a multipath propagation (numbers on the rays refer to the path number).

on many other factors including the reflecting objects and big obstructions in the path between the transmitter and the receiver. Depending on the model at hand, the signal strength decreases with distance and has an exponent ranging from 3 to 6.

Multipath Fading and Shadowing. When a signal is transmitted, multiple versions of the same signal take different paths to the receiver (see Figure 10). The first to arrive at the receiver is the one going through the line of sight (LOS), which is the path that does not have any obstacles between the transmitter and the receiver (Path 2 in Figure 10). Others, delayed versions, follow other paths resulting from obstacles in the path. These delayed copies, when arriving at the receiver, either add constructively or destructively. Notice that the obstacles in the path are not fixed in either number or in position. Mobility of the transmitter, receiver, or the objects in between changes the paths between the transmitter and the receiver. Thus, the signal quality varies with time. This phenomenon, where the signal quality depends on the multipath propagation, is referred to as multipath fading. Another type of fading is shadow fading. When the signal encounters a large obstacle in its way, such as a building, it is attenuated severely. The amount of absorption depends on the characteristics and size of the obstacle.

Interference. Interference refers to extraneous, unwanted signals that affect the proper system operation. Not only does interference affect the quality of the signal communicated from the transmitter to the receiver, it can also affect the functionality of the protocol. For example, the existence of another 802.11 network in the vicinity could make sources sense the channel as busy even though it is not.

Because wireless LANs work in the ISM band, which does not require any licensing, they are especially susceptible to interference. Microwave ovens, photocopying machines, medical equipment, Bluetooth-enabled devices (e.g., PDAs or laptops), and wireless phones are examples of possible sources of interferences. Obviously, the existence of another WLAN segment cannot be ruled out, especially as WLANs gain greater acceptance in the marketplace.

Many things can be done to deal with interference: survey the site to understand the geographic area in which the WLAN will work, transmit high power signals, and shut down other devices that can interfere, for example. Wireless LANs go around this problem by using spread spectrum techniques (http://www.wi-fiplanet.com; Geier).

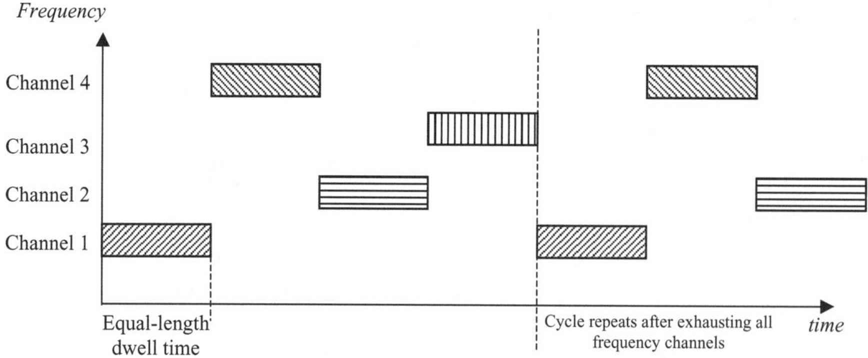

Figure 11: Four-channel FHSS system.

Radio Link

The IEEE 802.11 WLANs use either radio or infrared (IR) electromagnetic waves for transmitting data. In this section and the next we discuss both of these interfaces. Radio-based WLANs, which are more common than IR-based WLANs, operate on the ISM band because this band does not require any licensing from the FCC. The standard defines two physical-layer methods, frequency hopping spread spectrum (FHSS) and direct sequence spread spectrum (DSSS). The basic idea of spread spectrum (whether FHSS or DSSS) involves using a very wide bandwidth to communicate the data. By increasing the bandwidth, communication is more resilient to interference and fading because only a small portion of the bandwidth will be affected.

FHSS

In FHSS, the signal is spread by sending one frequency for a short period of time and then switching (hopping) to another frequency in a seemingly random fashion (see Figure 11). The hopping sequence and hopping rate are predefined and known to both the sender and the receiver. Two types of FHSS systems exist with different hopping rates. If multiple bits are transmitted over the same frequency channel, the system is called slow frequency hopping. On the other hand, if the hopping rate is greater than or equal to the bit rate, that is, if one bit or less is transmitted over a channel, the system is called fast frequency hopping. Because WLANs operate on the ISM band, many sources of interference may exist. If a source of interference happens to be in the vicinity of a slow-frequency-hopping transmission and is operating at a frequency that is also used by the slow-frequency-hopping system, it will corrupt all packets sent at that frequency channel. In a fast-frequency-hopping system, on the other hand, very few noise spikes will take place and the receiver will still be able to recover the data. Thus, fast hopping systems have better interference resilience (Bing, 2000).

The time spent in each frequency, known as the dwell time, is limited by the FCC to a maximum of 400 ms. This means it hops at least 2.5 times per second. In addition, the number of frequency channels used in the hopping sequence cannot go below six channels (i.e., 6 MHz) (Roshan & Leary, 2004). The 802.11 standard splits the available bandwidth into 79 channels, each 1 MHz wide.

The 802.11 physical layer supports two data rates: 1 Mbps and 2 Mbps. It consists of two sublayers: the physical-layer convergence protocol (PLCP) and the physical medium dependent (PMD). PLCP is responsible for adding necessary headers for synchronization, timing, and error control. The PMD is responsible for raw transmission of bits over the air; it mainly performs modulation of the data stream.

The PLCP adds a 128-bit header to frames arriving from the MAC layer (called PLCP service data units, PSDU). The header contains the following fields:

- A preamble, which has two subfields (96 bits).
  - Synch, an 80-bit sequence of alternating 0s and 1s starting with a 0. It is used at the receiver for time synchronization. In addition, if the receiver is using any antenna-diversity technique, it uses these bits to choose the best antenna. The transmitter and the receiver must be synchronized so that they switch from one frequency to another at the same time.
  - SFD (start of frame delimiter), a specific bit string (0000 1100 1011 1101) used at the receiver for frame timing.
- PSDU length word (PLW), a 12-bit field that indicates the size of the MAC frame.
- PLCP signaling field (PSF), a 4-bit field used to specify the data rate at which the frame was transmitted. Data rates range from 1 Mbps to 4.5 Mbps in increments of 0.5 Mbps. Table 1 shows the possible values along with the data rates they indicate (Nicopolitidis, Obaidat, Papadimitriou, & Pomportsis, 2003).
- HEC (header error control), an ITU-T cyclic redundancy check, CRC16, used for error detection.

Table 1 PSF Field Value and Supported Data Rate

Field value	Data rate
000	1 Mbps
001	1.5 Mbps
010	2 Mbps
011	2.5 Mbps
100	3 Mbps
101	3.5 Mbps
110	4 Mbps
111	4.5 Mbps

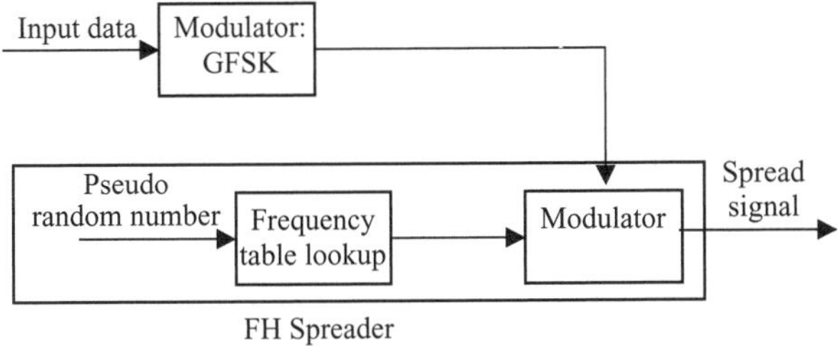

Figure 12: FHSS transmitter.

After receiving a bit stream from the PLCP sublayer, the PMD modulates it using Gaussian frequency shift keying (GFSK). Depending on the data rate supported (whether 1 Mbps or 2 Mbps), GFSK or 4 GFSK is used. 4GFSK translates every two bits into one signal element, which allows for doubling the rate. Frequency shift keying schemes, in general, convey the information by changing the frequency of the signal. Thus, the amplitude of the signal does not carry any information. This gives the flexibility of changing the transmission power as needed. In addition, the design of the transmitter and the receiver is simple. An important drawback of FSK-based schemes is that they are not spectrally efficient. That is, the amount of information conveyed per signal element is small when compared with other modulation schemes.

Figure 12 shows a block diagram of a FHSS transmitter. The input bits are fed into a GFSK modulator, which produces an analog signal from the data. A spreader that takes a pseudorandom number as an index for table lookup uses the table entry's frequency as the carrier frequency to be modulated by the output of the GFSK modulator. The resultant signal is the one transmitted in the air. The opposite process takes place at the receiving end to demodulate the received signal (Roshan & Leary, 2004).

DSSS

The main idea of DSSS is to spread the signal energy over a large bandwidth. To other unintended receivers, the signal can be treated as noise that can be easily rejected. As a result, the same frequency band can be used by multiple DSSS signals, which better uses the bandwidth and minimizes interference effects.

To achieve this spreading, DSSS systems map every bit in the data stream to an m-bit pattern called the pseudonoise code or chipping code. The number of bits in the code determines the spreading factor. The higher the spreading factor is, the more resilient the signal is to interference. However, this would be at the expense of bandwidth, which increases dramatically. The FCC specifies a minimum spreading factor of 10. That is, a maximum data rate of 10% of the available channel bandwidth can be provided. IEEE 802.11 uses an 11-chip spreading factor. That is, every bit in the data stream is replaced by 11 bits (chip sequence) to be transmitted via the channel. Even though this may seem very expensive, the fact that it minimizes interference effects results in enhancing channel quality, which translates into fewer corrupted packets, a better overall throughput performance, and a decrease in transmission delay because the need for retransmissions is reduced.

The receiver of a DSSS signal has to know the chipping-code mappings and has to be synchronized to the correct phase of the code. That is why every packet is prefixed with a preamble for synchronization purposes.

An important difference between code division multiple access (CDMA) systems and the DSSS system used by the 802.11 is that CDMA is based on code multiplexing. That is, multiple transmissions can take place at the same time as long as different communication pairs are tuned to different codes. This requires the availability of a code pool to choose from, the logic to choose a code, and complex receivers synchronized for a specific code. In contrast, DSSS wireless LANs use the one code, which allows for broadcast communication (Bing, 2000).

The 802.11 DSSS physical supports two rates: 1 Mbps and 2 Mbps. A subsequent standard, the 802.11b, supports data rates of 5.5 Mbps and 11 Mbps. Similar to the FHSS physical layer, the DSSS physical layer also consists of two sublayers: the PLCP and the PMD. The PLCP of DSSS is very similar to that of FHSS and serves the same purpose. The PMD modulates the data stream for transmission via the channel. The channel bandwidth supported by the 802.11 standard is 11 MHz, and given that the spreading factor is 11, the data rate that can be supported is 1 Mbps or 2 Mbps. The rate depends on the modulation scheme used. The DSSS physical layer uses differential binary phase shift keying (DBPSK), where every symbol carries one bit, which allows for a data rate of 1 Mbps. To support the 2 Mbps rate, differential quadrature phase shift keying (DQPSK) is used, where every symbol carries two bits from the data stream. Thus, in both cases, 1 mega symbols are being communicated. The difference is the number of bits to which a symbol is mapped.

Infrared (IR)

So far, we have discussed the radio-based flavor of wireless LANs. Unlike radio-based WLANs, infrared is not regulated; hence, plenty of bandwidth is available. In addition, it does not suffer from electromagnetic interference, which is a limiting factor for radio-based WLANs. However, IR-based WLANs have their own sources of interference (e.g., sunlight, fluorescent light), which can substantially degrade the network performance. Like visible light, infrared does not penetrate opaque objects (e.g., walls), which entails the need for an access point in every room. Even though this may seem a disadvantage, especially because in radio LANs and AP can provide large coverage, this has great advantages. First, it promises secure communication because eavesdropping or any security attack for that matter (e.g., denial of service) is very difficult from outside. Furthermore, it provides interference immunity by allowing each room to have a separate deployment, and thus large IR LANs can be built (Stallings, 2002).

IR wireless LANs are simpler to implement and hence are less expensive. This is attributed to their use of intensity modulation for data transmission, which only involves detecting the signal's amplitude, unlike radio systems in which the frequency and/or the phase need to be detected.

One main issue with IR LANs is the absence of products in conformance with the standard. This makes deploying

IR LANs limited to small-scale usage under one management domain. Two main flavors exist of IR LANs: directed and omnidirectional. A directed IR LAN is used to create point-to-point connections. The transmitter and the receiver must have a line of sight between them. Depending on the transmission power used, directed transmissions produce high performance in terms of transmission distance, bandwidth, and throughput achieved. Data rates ranging from 1 to 155 Mbps over a distance of 1–5 km can be provided (Bing, 2000).

Directed IR can be used in a campus-sized network where different segments need to be connected to each other. To do that, directed links across buildings are created to connect bridges or routers. Indoors, directed IR can also be used to connect different segments in any suitable arrangement (e.g., to connect Ethernet or token ring segments; Stallings, 2002).

Omnidirectional IR can be used in scenarios similar to radio LANs. A ceiling-mounted transceiver broadcasts to all nodes within line of sight (e.g., in a room). They can be used only in an indoor environment because they rely on reflections off objects (walls, ceilings, desks, etc.) to propagate in all directions. Even though these reflected copies allow for freedom of alignment for the transmitter and receiver, a substantial amount of the energy is lost, which limits the data rate and range of communication. Indoor omnidirectional IR LANs operate at a rate limited to 4 Mbps within a range of 10 to 20 m (Bing, 2000).

Physical-Layer Standards

New standards have been approved that achieve higher data rates. In this section, we briefly discuss the main differences among the 802.11 standards a, b, and g and how these higher rates are achieved.

IEEE 802.11b

802.11b defines the high rate DSSS (HR-DSSS) that allows data rates as high as 5.5 Mbps and 11 Mbps. The PLCP of the HR-DSSS defines two types of frames: long and short. The long-frame format is basically the same as in the case of DSSS. Few fields have been added, mainly to define the data rate communicated (whether 5.5 or 11 Mbps) and the modulation scheme used. The preamble and header are always communicated at a rate of 1 Mbps to ensure backward compatibility with DSSS. The short frame has the same format as the long one, with the exception that the number of bits used for a field is less, to minimize overhead. For example, as opposed to 128 bits for synchronization in the long frame, only 56 are used in the short one. The other difference is that the short frame's preamble and header are communicated at a rate of 2 Mbps (as opposed to 1 Mbps in the case of the long frame). Like before, the PMD basically is responsible for modulating the bit stream that it receives from the PLCP (Roshan & Leary, 2004).

Two modulation schemes are used: complimentary code keying (CCK) and packet binary convolutional coding (PBCC). Higher data rates are achieved in this way: like before, an 11-MHz bandwidth is used. However, the spreading code is 8 chips long rather than 11 chips, as in the 1-Mbps and 2-Mbps cases. In addition, the number of bits coded in an 8-chip code is different. Using the CCK modulation, every 4 bits from the data stream are encoded in an 8-chip code, thus allowing for a data rate equal to

$$11 \times 10^6 \times \frac{4\,bits}{8\,chips} = 5.5\ Mbps.$$

Similarly, the PBCC modulation scheme codes 8 bits in an 8-chip code, allowing for a data rate of 11 Mbps.

IEEE 802.11a

Unlike the 802.11b, which works in the 2.4-GHz ISM band, the 802.11a works in the unlicensed national information infrastructure (UNII) 5-GHz band. It supports data rates up to 24 Mbps and optionally up to 54 Mbps. In 802.11a, 300 MHz is used, which is divided into three 100-MHz bands, each with different maximum power output. The three bands used are 5.15–5.25 GHz, 5.25–5.35 GHz, and 5.725–5.825 GHz. Devices operating at these bands produce a power equal to 50 mW, 250mW, and 1W, respectively. The high power output allowed in the high band makes it more suitable for building-to-building devices (e.g., bridges connecting two LAN segments). The other two bands are suitable for indoor environments. Data is modulated using the orthogonal frequency division multiplexing (OFDM) scheme. The basic idea of OFDM is to minimize the inter-symbol interference (ISI) problem. ISI results when a symbol takes longer to reach the receiver. This delay, called delay spread, results from the multipath propagation discussed earlier. As a result of this delay, a symbol may arrive at the same time as another subsequent symbol. This can be dealt with by decreasing the number of symbols per second and thus ensuring that a symbol has an ample amount of time to reach before a subsequent symbol is sent. Obviously, this decreases the data rate achieved. Hence, what OFDM does is to break the channel bandwidth into subchannels. Each subchannel has a low symbol rate and thus low ISI. The subchannels are chosen to be orthogonal and thus low cochannel interference occurs. Hence, a receiver tuned at a given frequency sees all other signals as zero. Table 2 shows the data rates supported by the 802.11a standard along with the modulation scheme used.

IEEE 802.11g

The 802.11g standard is very recent. It was approved in 2003 and supports data rates up to 54 Mbps. Unlike

Table 2 Supported Data Rates and Modulation Schemes

Data rate (Mbps)	Modulation scheme
6	BPSK
9	BPSK
12	QPSK
18	QPSK
24	16-QAM
36	16-QAM
48	64-QAM
54	64-QAM

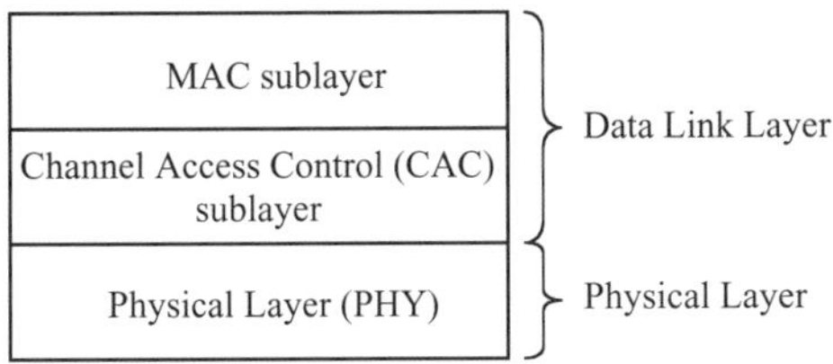

Figure 13: HIPERLAN/1 reference model.

802.11a, 802.11g operates in the ISM 2.4-GHz band and has backward compatibility with 802.11b. If all the devices in the network use 802.11g, the high data rates of 802.11g can be used. However, if any of the devices in the network uses 802.11b, all other devices have to switch to the low data rates supported by the 802.11b. The mandatory data rates are 6, 12, and 24 Mbps. The rest are optional. To ensure backward compatibility, the packet header and preamble are sent using CCK modulation, which is also used by the 802.11b, and the payload is sent using OFDM.

HIPERLANs

HIPERLAN Type 1

The high-performance radio LAN (HIPERLAN) Type 1 is the European counterpart of IEEE 802.11. It was developed by the European Telecommunications Standards Institute (ETSI). The protocol provides data rates of up 23.5 Mbps and supports low mobility conditions (1.4 m/s). Similar to its counterpart, its reference model, shown in Figure 13, covers both the physical (PHY) and the MAC layers. The physical layer is responsible for transmission and reception of raw data via the wireless channel. The channel access control (CAC) sublayer determines how nodes will access the channel and which nodes have the right to access by allowing access priority to be specified. The MAC defines the different protocols responsible for power conservation, multihop forwarding, security, and data transfer to upper layers (BRAN, 1998; Jain, 2004; Papadimitriou, Lagkas, Obaidat, & S. Pomportsis, 2003).

Unlike 802.11, HIPERLAN/1 has a single physical layer that is not based on spread spectrum techniques. It uses a narrowband modulation in the 5.15–5.30-GHz range. It is important to notice that HIPERLAN does not provide an IR physical interface. Two data rates are supported: a lower rate, 1.47 Mbps, which uses FSK modulation, and a high rate, 23.5 Mbps, which employs GMSK as a modulation scheme. Thus, every packet contains a low-rate header (sent at 1.47 Mbps) followed by a high-rate header and payload (sent at 23.5 Mbps); see Figure 14. By merely looking at the low-rate header, a node can decide whether it needs to listen to the rest of the packet. This way, if a packet is not meant for a node, it can save power by turning off its error correction, equalization, and other functionalities. The next paragraph contains more information about Figure 14 (Bing, 2000).

As the rate of data transmitted via a wireless channel increases, the effect of ISI increases. This is because symbol duration becomes smaller, and hence the delay spread effect becomes higher. To go around this problem, decision feedback equalization is employed. An equalizer eliminates the effect of ISI without enhancing the noise. Equalization involves a training sequence, which is known to the receiver to be transmitted by the sender. Upon receiving this sequence, the receiver compares it with the known sequence and adjusts its filter coefficients. At this moment, the receiver is ready to receive user data. Periodically, the receiver will need retraining to ensure effective ISI cancellation. The HIPERLAN standard does not specify what equalization technique to be used and leaves it to protocol implementers. GMSK has excellent power efficiency and spectral efficiency. It is a constant envelope scheme, which means the amplitude of the signal is constant. Hence, highly efficient power amplifiers can be used (no information loss will occur from nonlinear amplification because the signal amplitude is not carrying any information; Rappaport, 1996). In addition, forward error control (FEC) is used to increase the throughput by minimizing the need for retransmissions of bad packets. BCH is used where every 26 bits are coded into 31 bits (Nicopolitidis, Obaidat, Papadimitriou, & Pomportsis, 2003).

The MAC protocol of HIPERLAN/1 supports both asynchronous (data) as well as isochronous (audio and video) applications. The protocol does not reserve bandwidth for different users or application classes. However, it provides some kind of quality of service (QoS) by means of the supported priority scheduling scheme, which favors higher priority packets and takes into account their lifetime. HIPERLAN/1 MAC protocol is distributed, allowing for both infrastructure as well as ad hoc, multihop topologies. A node that senses the channel idle for 1700-bit times (in the high data rate) can transmit its packet with no overhead. However, the chances of the channel being idle for 1700-bit times are extremely low even for moderate load conditions. Thus, another mechanism can also grant channel access, which involves the use of the elimination yield—nonpreemptive multiple access (EY-NPMA). A station that senses a busy channel waits until the channel becomes idle, waits for 256-bit times (called the synchronization slot), and then runs EY-NPMA. In the

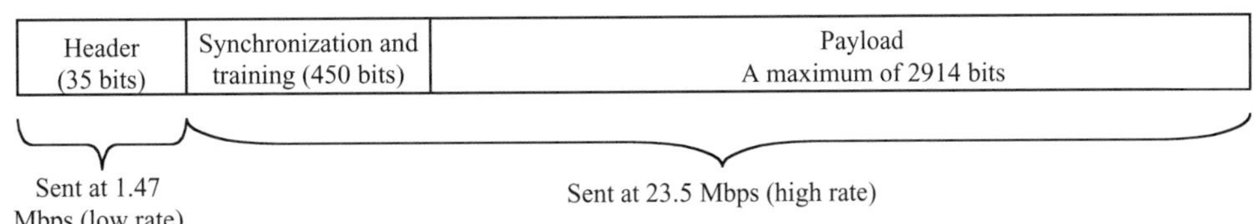

Figure 14: HIPERLAN/1 packet format. Source: Bing, 2000.

EY-NPMA scheme, channel access involves going through three phases, each of which can be thought of as a screening phase. In every phase, some nodes will drop from the competition, and the rest will move on to contend in the next phase. The third phase, however, does not guarantee a single winner, and thus collisions, even though unlikely, are still possible.

1. The prioritization phase consists of five slots, which allows for five priority levels. A station with priority r transmits a burst in slot $r + 1$, indicating a busy channel if and only if it does not sense a higher priority burst. The higher the node's priority, the faster it can get hold of the channel. At the end of this phase, one or more nodes (all with the same priority) will move on to the next phase. All others will have to wait until the next synchronization slot.
2. The elimination phase is 13 slots long. In this phase, stations that survived the previous phase transmit a burst for a number of slots geometrically distributed with a parameter $P = 0.5$. Thus, the burst length is one slot with probability 1/2, two slots with probability 0.25, and so on. Each station, at the end of its burst, senses the channel to see if a longer burst has been transmitted by others. If yes, the station quits contending for the channel. If not, however, it goes to the next phase. Obviously, the chances of more than one winner in this phase increases with the increase in the number of nodes that made it from the previous phase.
3. The yield phase: 15-slots long, all stations that made it to this phase back off for s slots, where s is also geometrically distributed with a parameter $P = 0.1$. A station sensing an idle channel at the end of its back-off interval can transmit its packet.

An overview of the EY-NPMA protocol is shown in Figure 15.

As we mentioned earlier, HIPERLAN/1 supports ad hoc topologies. This is achieved using a process called interforwarding. In simple terms, nodes can communicate with nodes out of their reach by transmitting to their neighbors, who forward the packet to their neighbors, and so on until it reaches its destination. For this to work properly, nonforwarding nodes need to know their direct neighbors, and forwarding nodes need to know routing information, that is, the next hop to get to a particular destination and the path length. The forwarding function is optional; a node may choose not to forward traffic. A node can forward packets in two modes: point to point and broadcast. In broadcast mode, the forwarding node, called a multipoint relay, forwards the packet to all neighbors. Nonmultipoint relays do not forward packets. The set of multipoint relays is chosen as the minimum set that covers all nodes within two hops from the node, thus minimizing the number of forwarding nodes.

Similar to other ad hoc networks, the multihop mode of HIPERLAN suffers from many problems. The dynamic nature of the network where nodes come and go makes maintaining correct information about the topology very difficult. In addition, the overhead involved in maintaining this information is very costly, especially in terms of energy, because mobile nodes are battery operated. Another problem that is aggravated in multihop networks is the wireless channel conditions. Dual Doppler effect (because both sender and receiver are both mobile), interference caused by parallel transmissions, and fading all make the chances of a packet reaching its destination successfully very small.

HIPERLAN Type 2

Upon completion of the HIPERLAN/1 standard, the ETSI decided to merge WLANs and wireless local loops, the communication between the end user and the service provider, into one protocol that is called broadband radio access networks (BRAN). The BRAN project standardizes wireless ATM protocols. This includes HIPERLAN Types 2, 3, and 4.

HIPERLAN/2 is very different from HIPERLAN/1 and has many salient advantages including these (Johnsson, 1999; Nicopolitidis, Obaidat, Papadimitriou, & Pomportsis, 2003):

- High data rates: HIPERLAN/2 supports data rates up to 54 Mbps.
- Connection-oriented: Communication between stations and the AP is connection oriented. A connection is established prior to any data transmission.

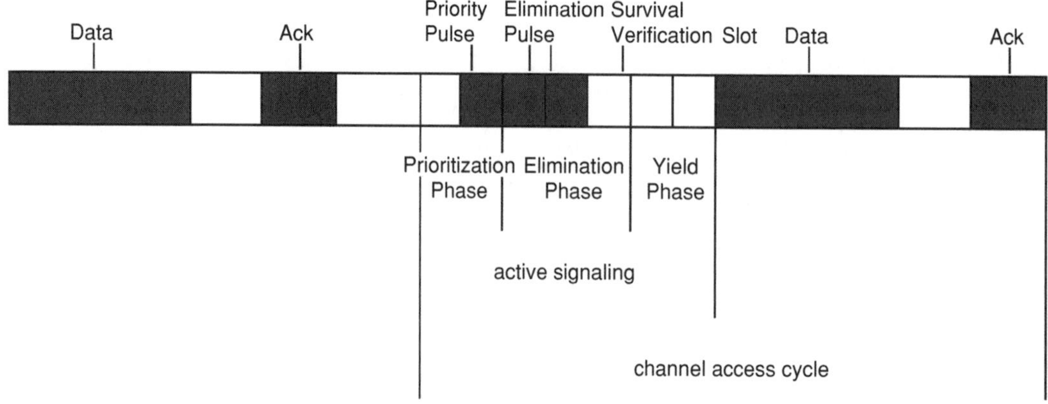

Figure 15: EY-NPMA protocol.

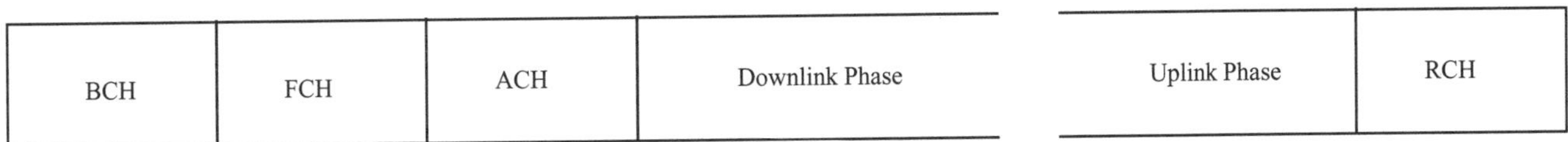

Figure 16: Format of the MAC frame in HIPERLAN/2.

- QoS support: HIPERLAN/2 provides QoS support because it is connection oriented and provides high data rates.
- Automatic frequency allocation: Unlike cellular networks where static radio-frequency planning is performed, the AP in HIPERLAN/2 performs dynamic frequency channel selection that is not in use by other APs, and that minimizes cochannel interference.
- Power saving: A mobile station can communicate to the AP its desire to schedule sleep periods to minimize power consumption. At the end of every sleep period, the station wakes up to see if the AP has sent any wake-up indication. If not, the station can go back to sleep for another period.

The physical layer of HIPERLAN/2 is very similar to that of 802.11a. They both operate in the 5-GHz band and use OFDM. In addition, they both offer data rates as high as 54 Mbps. To a great extent, the same modulation and coding schemes are used. However, synchronization and training sequences used are different.

Differences between the two protocols appear in the MAC layer. 802.11 is based on the CSMA/CA protocol. One problem is CSMA/CA that is probabilistic. A station does not have any guarantee that within a given time period it will be granted the channel to transmit. These delays would render supporting any real-time application very difficult even under moderate load conditions. HIPERLAN/2 is based on dynamic time division multiple access (TDMA) with time division duplexing (TDD). In a TDMA scheme, stations are dynamically assigned time slots according to their needs. Time slots are dynamically allocated depending on transmission needs. TDD means that part of the frame is used for the uplink (communication between the stations and the AP) and part for the downlink (from the AP to the stations). Once assigned a time slot, a station can transmit at regular basis during its slot. The AP notifies the stations when it is their time to transmit (Doufexi, Armour, Karlsson, Nix, & Bull, 2002; Papadimitriou, Lagkas, & Pomportsis, 2003).

A MAC frame has a duration of 2 ms and consists of different channels as shown in Figure 16. The broadcast channel (BCH) is a downlink channel through which the AP sends control information to all nodes in the network. This includes transmission power level, wake-up indicator, and identifier of the AP and the network, among other things. The frame control channel (FCH) is also a downlink channel that is used to announce how the rest of the current MAC frame has been allocated, that is, how much is allotted for the uplink, for the downlink, and for contention. The access feedback channel (ACH), also a downlink channel, conveys information regarding previous random access attempts that took place in the RCH. The downlink and uplink phases consist of a number of packets to be communicated from and to the AP, respectively. The number of slots and how much per station is based on the AP announcements during the FCH channel. The random access channel (RCH) is an uplink channel used to compete for slots in subsequent MAC frames. Results of contention are reported back to stations in subsequent frames' ACH channel (Johnsson, 1999).

WLAN SECURITY

Wireless networks are more vulnerable to security threats than wired networks. This is because of the broadcast nature of the wireless channel. Any node within the transmission range of a WLAN can access it. Thus, enforcing security measures is of high importance in a WLAN. Two mechanisms are usually used to minimize security threats: authentication and encryption. Authentication ensures that only authorized nodes can access the network and encryption ensures that confidentiality is maintained.

Encryption in 802.11

Encryption is the process of transforming human-readable data (called plain text) into an unreadable form (called cipher text). Encryption and decryption typically involve the use of a common secret between the sender and the receiver (called the encryption key). Figure 17 illustrates the idea of encryption. Two types of encryption exist: block cipher and stream cipher. They both involve generating a key (called a stream key) from a basic secret key. In block cipher, the plain text is divided into blocks, and each block is encrypted using a fixed-size stream key. In a stream cipher, on the other hand, the data stream is processed continuously (e.g., taking one byte at a time). In addition, the stream key size is not fixed. Block ciphers provide a higher level of security than stream ciphers. This, however, comes at the cost of being more computationally demanding.

The 802.11 standard uses the wired-equivalent privacy (WEP) protocol, which is based on the RC4 encryption algorithm. RC4 is a stream cipher that uses symmetric keys. That is, if the sender uses a key K_1 to encrypt the

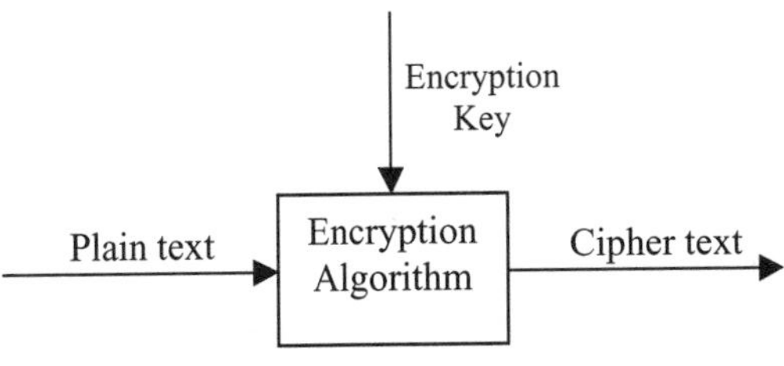

Figure 17: Block diagram of the encryption process.

data, the receiver uses the same key (i.e., K_1) to decrypt it. Symmetric key encryption is simple and requires a very trivial amount of computation. As we can see, the protocol tries to minimize the computation penalty introduced by encryption by using a stream, symmetric algorithm. The protocol does not provide any key distribution mechanism and thus assumes the keys to be manually configured in the client stations and the access point. Two key lengths are supported: 40 and 104 bits. The longer the key, the more difficult it is for an attacker to do a brute force attack in which all possible keys are tried.

If every time an encryption algorithm is that fed plain text P generates the same cipher text C, the algorithm is described as electronic code book (ECD). An attacker can do cryptanalysis to find patterns in the cipher text that can help him break the encryption. To provide more security, WEP goes around this problem by using a concept called initialization vectors (IVs). The goal is to change the encryption algorithm's output even if fed the same plain text. Thus, the encryption of a string P would result in a cipher text C_1, and if the algorithm is run again, using the same string P, it would produce a cipher text C_2, and so on.

An IV is nothing but a number to be added to the key that results in a new key. To ensure high randomness in the cipher text, it is good to change the IV for every frame sent. For the receiver to be able to decrypt the message, it needs access to the IV value used at the sender, and that is why every frame sent carries with it the IV used. The encryption process involves the following steps (Roshan & Leary, 2004):

1. For every arriving frame, generate a 24-bit IV and append it to the secret key K_1, resulting in a stream key K_2.
2. Calculate the integrity check value (ICV) of the arriving frame. The ICV is a CRC-32 that is used to ensure that the frame has not been tampered with and has not been corrupted in transmission.
3. Encrypt both the frame payload and the ICV using K_2.
4. Create a frame that contains the encrypted payload, the encrypted ICV, and the IV used for the encryption.

The opposite process takes place at the receiving end. Receiver extracts the IV value, constructs the stream key, uses it to decrypt the payload and the ICV, and finally compares the decrypted ICV with an ICV it calculates for the arriving payload. If both match, the frame is good.

Authentication in 802.11

802.11 supports two authentication mechanisms: open system authentication and shared key authentication. Open system authentication is a two-way authentication that is used when a high security level is not required. A station requesting authentication sends a request to the access point. The access point responds back with a frame indicating either approval or disapproval. The shared key algorithm is based on WEP and requires both the station and the access point to have a shared key. A four-way authentication process takes place, which can be described as follows:

1. Client sends authentication request to the AP.
2. AP sends back a challenge.
3. Client sends back the challenge encrypted.
4. The AP decrypts what is received and compares it with the challenge. A match results in successful authentication.

Another authentication method that is not part of the 802.11 standard, yet implemented by many vendors, is the MAC address authentication. Here the client's MAC address is compared against a list of MAC address considered to be authorized to access the network. This is vulnerable to device theft. Thus, it is better to be used in combination with the other two approaches to allow for more security. The MAC address list is stored in a separate server called the RADIUS server. During the authentication process, the AP communicates with the RADIUS server to see if the latter has the MAC address in question.

Vulnerabilities

It is well known that the 802.11 security mechanisms are vulnerable to all sorts of attacks. As an example, consider the shared key authentication process. The AP sends the challenge in clear text format, which makes the authentication procedure exposed to clear text attacks. An eavesdropper can get the challenge and the response, and, from these two, extract the stream key. This is easy because the encryption is a simple XOR operation between the plain text and the stream key. XORing the cipher text and the clear text gives the stream key. Using the stream key, the hacker can now be authenticated easily because he can encrypt any challenge the AP sends. Listening to the channel and obtaining all the information sent back and forth is very simple. All a hacker needs is a sniffing software tool, which can log all the communications taking place on the channel.

An easier way to get the key is to make an educated guess. Remember that the keys have to be manually set up. In many cases, users do not change the key as it comes from the manufacturer, which makes guessing a matter of knowing the default key/keys that come from different vendors.

The IV length (24 bits) is another security threat. Given a highly loaded network or a patient hacker, the AP will exhaust all IVs and start reusing them. The hacker can thus collect enough frames with the same IV, and can extract the common parts between them. This would therefore expose the secret key and expose the whole wireless LAN.

Yet another vulnerability is the lack of AP authentication, that is, having the AP authenticating itself to the station. A hacker passively listening on the channel for an ample amount of time can collect useful information that enables him to set up an AP. Nodes closer to this (rogue) AP will connect to it. This way, the attacker will collect valid users' information and use it in accessing the network. This would not have been possible if the AP needed to authenticate itself to the stations (http://www.wi-fiplanet.com/, Geier). Many other vulnerabilities have been pointed out by the research community and this reference contains a good list of such sources.

QoS SUPPORT: IEEE 802.11E

As users are getting used to wireless LANs, their expectations are becoming higher. Users want WLANs to provide the same functionality as that of a wired counterpart. In addition, the new applications of WLANs, including home-office networking and wireless local loop, that require delay- and loss-sensitive multimedia communication makes QoS support an inevitable extension. Corporate wireless networks are expected to provide voice over IP (VoIP) services that can reduce or even replace the need to use cell phones in the work environment. Home networks, where a wireless network can eliminate all the wires and connect different devices together, are another foreseeable use. Service providers would appreciate a wireless local loop to provide their services. This would provide be cost-effective and give them a competitive edge.

Challenges in Providing QoS Support over Wireless

The wireless channel is highly dynamic. The signal strength and quality are affected by fading, self-interference, and cochannel interference and noise, among others. In addition, nodes move in random patterns and change their access point as they move around. At the same time, energy consumption has to be minimized because the devices (laptops, PDAs, etc.) are battery operated. All these and other issues make supporting QoS over wireless a very challenging task.

As we have seen, the hidden terminal problem imposes difficulties in sensing channels and thus is a limiting factor of the performance of the MAC protocol used. The DCF of 802.11 uses a CSMA-based protocol, which involves back-off periods of random length. Therefore, by definition the DCF is not suitable for QoS support. The PCF, even though was proposed to address delay-sensitive applications, was found to provide poor performance for even a small number of voice communications. This is readily apparent because an increase in the number of PCF nodes results in an increase in the polling list. Hence, nodes wait for longer periods to get their chance to transmit. Another problem with PCF is its lack of different priority levels. One last thing: PCF works only in the infrastructure mode and not the ad hoc mode. Because of these reasons, 802.11e is being developed.

QoS Mechanisms

Before discussing IEEE 802.11e, it is important to note that it is still a draft and has not yet reached the standardization level. The 802.11e draft provides QoS support using two coordination functions: the hybrid coordination function (HCF) with contention avoidance and the HCF with polled access operation. The first is more commonly referred to as the enhanced DCF (EDCF).

Enhanced DCF (EDCF)

802.11e (i.e., both EDCF and HCF) supports four traffic classes known as access categories (AC) in the 802.11e terminology. Table 3 shows the different ACs and what applications they address. The protocol assumes the existence of a mechanism to classify the traffic. In other words, the protocol works with packets already marked with one of the four ACs.

Table 3 ACs and Applications Addressed

AC	Applications targeted
0	Low priority/best-effort traffic
1	Video probe
2	High-rate real-time (e.g., video)
3	Low-rate real-time (e.g., voice)

To put it in a nutshell, the protocol supports the different priorities mainly by changing two parameters: the interframe spacing and the limits of the contention window. Traditional DCF supports priority to gain the channel by introducing different IFSs for ACKs, PCF, and DCF. Similarly, EDCF uses different IFSs for different ACs (called arbitration IFSs, AIFSs). Thus, higher priority packets can acquire the channel before others. In addition, the size of the contention window is smaller for higher priority packets. The smaller the contention window size, the faster a node can gain the channel. The smaller the CW_{min} is, the smaller the back-off time. Furthermore, the faster a station reaches the CW_{max}, the faster it increments its retry counter, which results in faster channel gain.

In traditional DCF, a station has to contend for the channel for every packet it needs to transmit. EDCF, in contrast, allows transmission of more than one packet. The transmit opportunity (TXOP) is a parameter that defines the duration of time a station can seize the channel once it has gained access.

If you have ever been trying to make a phone call and heard the "all circuits are busy" message, then you are familiar with admission control. Given the limited amount of resources available, a network can support a defined volume of traffic for every AC. If the input traffic of a particular AC exceeds its defined limit, all sources belonging to that AC will suffer. To prevent such behavior, admission control is applied. The goal of admission control is to deny access to any source attempting to use the channel once the predefined limit has been reached. The distributed admission control (DAC) scheme of the EDCF monitors channel utilization and announces that information to all stations in its beacon message. When the available resources approach 0, sources stop initiating new stream sessions.

HCF with Polled Access Operation

The HCF operation is very similar to the PCF function. It relies on polling to meet different nodes' requirements. A logical entity called the hybrid coordinator (HC) that runs in the AP is responsible for scheduling and other processing related to the polling operation. Unlike the EDCF where the TXOP is predefined, the HCF provides a mechanism for stations to request a TXOP with specific characteristics. The HCF can operate in one of two modes: contention-free HCF and coexistence with the EDCF.

In the contention-free HCF, the AP polls the stations. In its poll message, the AP specifies the TXOP. A station that has some traffic to send replies back to the poll within an SIFS period. If the station does not have traffic or if the length of the TXOP is not enough, it replies with a null frame.

The HCF function can operate with both the EDCF and the DCF at the same time. To poll the stations, the AP waits a PIFS time, which is shorter than what a DCF or EDCF station would need to wait. Thus, the AP can gain the channel. Similarly, a polled station has to wait only an SIFS time to respond to a poll. Therefore, the HCF function can work smoothly during the contention period of EDCF or DCF.

The EDCF, even though it has the logic to indicate whether new traffic should be initiated, does not enforce any type of behavior on the nodes. The AP simply announces the available capacity. Whether to honor this information is totally up to the stations. HCF, on the other hand, has a strict admission-control mechanism. A station willing to initiate a stream has to consult with the AP, which determines whether the stream can be supported without affecting other streams. Stations communicate to the AP the QoS parameters they desire using the transmission specification (TSPEC). In the TSPEC, a station specifies the priority, data rate, delay, and frame size, among other parameters. The AP checks these requirements against the current network conditions and decides accordingly whether to honor the request, reject it, or provide the station with TSPEC that it can afford to support (i.e., renegotiate the requirements). The station may accept the offer or turn it back. A station is removed from the pollable list either when it explicitly deletes the TSPEC or when the TSPEC timer expires. The timer expires when the station sends a null-frame for a number of poll requests within a time interval defined by the TSPEC timer.

ADVANCED TOPICS

Bluetooth

Bluetooth is a low-power (1-mW), short-range (within 10 m) technology. It was initially proposed by Ericsson as a way for users to use their laptops for making phone calls via cell phones. Since then, the technology was adopted by many companies and for different applications, mainly for cable replacement and ad hoc networking (intercommunication among Bluetooth-enabled devices). Similar to WLANs, it works in the ISM band, and that is the reason why it uses high-rate frequency-hopping scheme.

A Bluetooth network is organized in piconets and scatternets. A piconet is a small network consisting of a master node and between one and seven slaves. The master node is responsible for choosing the communication channel, including frequencies and the hopping sequence used. Nodes in a piconet communicate through the master node and not directly. A node may belong to one or more piconets. This overlapping creates what is called a scatternet. This allows for multihop communication where overlapping nodes serve as forwarders from one piconet to another.

The protocol consists of the following five layers, which are responsible for link establishment and maintenance, security and error control, service discovery, and communication with higher layer protocols (Stallings, 2002; Nicopolitidis, Obaidat, Papadimitriou, & Pomportsis, 2003):

1. Radio layer: This layer deals with the specifications of the air interface. Frequency bandwidth, modulation, transmission power, and channel access are specified. The standard specifies the use of GFSK for modulation. It also specifies the use of FHSS operating in a 78-MHz bandwidth with each channel occupying 1 MHz. The hopping rate is equal to 1600 hops/sec and a maximum data rate of 1 Mbps.
2. Baseband layer: It specifies how FHSS with TDD/TDMA is to be used for communication between nodes in a piconet. To prevent interference, nodes in different piconets use code division multiple access (CDMA). That is, different piconets use different hopping sequences. Two types of communication can be used. The synchronous connection oriented (SCO) method is used for communication between a slave and a master and involves the allocation of fixed bandwidth. The other, asynchronous connectionless (ACL) method, is a point-to-multipoint communication between the master and all the slaves in a piconet.
3. Link manager protocol (LMP): As its name implies, this protocol specifies link setup and management between two Bluetooth devices, including issues of clock synchronization, authentication and key distribution for security purposes, the protocol version used, and the nodes' mode (master, slave), and so forth.
4. Logical link control and adaptation protocol (L2CAP): This protocol defines connectionless as well as connection-oriented services. It also allows for QoS support by letting a transmitter and a receiver negotiate QoS flow parameters such as delay and delay variation.
5. Service discovery protocol (SDP): It specifies how Bluetooth devices search for other Bluetooth devices and establish communication with them.

One domain where Bluetooth is envisaged to serve greatly is in home networking. Connectivity among different devices at home that provides both coordination and freedom from cables will be user-friendly technology.

Voice over 802.11

Even though wireless LANs were initially thought of as wireless versions of wired LANs, which implied they are solely for data communications, the fact that they are wireless introduces higher expectations. Voice over WLANs is one such example. A common network for both voice and data has a lower cost than operating two separate networks.

As we have seen, 802.11 DCF is the fundamental access method of the 802.11 and is used for data communications. It uses CSMA/CA for channel access with a backoff algorithm to reduce the possibility of collisions. Even though DCF was meant for data communications, studies have shown that it can be used for voice. However, the performance is relatively low (Prasad, 1999). Because it is a random assignment scheme, DCF provides unbounded delays under high loads. Randomness means that the network cannot provide deterministic guarantees regarding delay. It is important to mention that delay and delay variation (jitter) are the key impairments for voice communications (Obaidat & Obeidat, 2002; McDysan & Spohn, 1999).

The inability of CSMA protocols to support real-time traffic has been studied in the context of voice and data integration via Ethernet. It has been shown that Ethernet can provide good performance at low loads. Moreover, it is argued that the need for priority in WLANs is more pressing than in Ethernet for the following reasons:

1. WLANs provide lower rates than Ethernet, which result in high queuing and transmission delays.
2. CSMA/CA has throughput/delay characteristics that are worse than those of CSMA/CD.

It has been also shown that CSMA/CA "is not robust with respect to the network topology and the choice of routing protocol." This is with respect to non-real-time traffic, which means that the protocol performs worse with real-time traffic.

The PCF is used for real-time traffic that has delay bounds. However, it can operate only under the centralized scheme where there is a base station. This is because PCF uses polling to grant stations channel access. Many researches addressed the performance of voice and data over the PCF function of the IEEE 802.11. The performance of voice and data over the PCF function was studied with the assumption that voice communication takes place between stations that are in different BSSs. The conclusion is that the performance of the PCF function is poor and that only a few voice conversations can be supported. No echo cancellation was used; therefore, a small superframe size of 20 ms, which limits how many conversations can be in the polling list, is considered.

Crow, Widjaja, Kim, & Sakai (1997b) propose the use of echo cancellation for voice communication. However, they use a 420-ms superframe size that consumes most of the delay budget of voice. This implies that if voice has to go though an IEEE 802.11 link, it has to be the only link. In other words, you cannot have the wireless link as the last hop in the path between the source and the destination of the call. The authors suggest that when a voice station does not have any data to transmit or receive, it should be dropped from the polling list immediately. This way, the remaining bandwidth can be used by other stations. Nonetheless, leaving the list every time a station's silence period starts (i.e., the voice source is in the OFF state) will result in more delay at the beginning of every talk spurt, which will not be acceptable.

The performance of uncompressed voice (64 kbps) and data over IEEE 802.11 has been studied using an analytic approach. The conclusion is that the performance is low and, with the introduction of echo cancellation, more voice conversations can be achieved, but this will affect the bandwidth available to the data stations. A recommendation made to deal with voice traffic is not to drop a voice station from the polling list, even when it is silent. The point is that even though this will limit the number of voice communications, it controls delays and delay variations that result in a "reasonable" number of voice conversations.

All of the aforementioned studies use the same PCF parameters and trade one thing for another. The key parameters here are the super-frame size and the packet size. However, they all reach the same conclusion: that voice performance via PCF is poor. Choi, Prado, Shankar, and Mangold (2003) compare the performance of DCF and EDCF for voice, video, and data. They show that EDCF provides better performance in terms of frame loss and delay for voice. However, PCF is not considered in the comparison.

GLOSSARY

AC Access categories supported by the IEEE 802.11e standard to provide quality of service.

ACH Access feedback channel is a time channel used in the MAC protocol of the HIPERLAN/2 standard. It is a downlink channel used by the AP to inform the stations of previous random access attempts.

ACK Acknowledgement packet transmitted by the destination node to the source node to acknowledge the successful reception of a data packet.

ACL In a Bluetooth network, the asynchronous connectionless (ACL) is a point-to-multipoint communication between the master and all the slaves in a piconet.

Ad Hoc Network A network topology where there is no central control (base station or access point) and the stations are able to communicate directly.

AP Access point is a station that provides central control in a network cell

ATM Asynchronous transfer mode, a network technology based on transferring data in cells or packets of a fixed size.

Authentication The process of identifying an individual, usually based on a username and password.

Band A contiguous range of frequencies.

BCH Broadcast channel is a downlink channel through which the AP sends control information to all nodes in a HIPERLAN/2 network.

Block Ciphers An encryption type where the plain text is divided into blocks and each block is encrypted using a fixed-size stream key.

Bluetooth A low-power (1-mW), short-range (within 10-m) wireless network technology.

BRAN Broadband radio access networks is an ETSI project that standardizes the wireless ATM protocols, including HIPERLAN Types 2, 3, and 4.

BSA Basic service area is the coverage area of a BSS.

BSS The basic service set resembles the basic building block in the 802.11 architecture. It is analogous to a cell in a cellular network.

Carrier A wave form in a communications channel modulated to carry analog or digital signal information.

CCK Complimentary code keying is a modulation technique used in the IEEE 802.11b standard. Using CCK modulation, every four bits from the data stream are encoded in an eight-chip code, thus allowing for a data rate equal to 5.5 Mbps.

CDMA The code division multiple access technique is used to prevent interference among different nodes, which transmit simultaneously at the same frequency band.

CFP The contention-free period is a time interval defined by the PCF access mode.

Chip A chip sequence is used to replace a data bit in the IEEE 802.11 standard.

Coding Techniques Coding techniques maximize the benefit of transmission over noisy wireless channels by introducing redundancies in the bits transmitted so that the receiver can still recover a reasonably distorted packet.

Collision The situation that occurs when two or more nodes attempt to send a signal along the same channel at the same time. The result of a collision is generally a garbled message. All computer networks require some sort of mechanism to either prevent collisions altogether or to recover from collisions when they do occur.

Contention-Based Protocol A MAC protocol type, usually used in ad-hoc network topology, in which the nodes contend for medium access and there is no central control.

Contention-Free Protocol A MAC protocol type, usually used in infrastructure network topology, in which the nodes do not contend for medium access, but there is a central control that decides which node can transmit.

CSMA/CA Carrier sense multiple access with collision avoidance is a MAC protocol used by the IEEE 802.11 standard.

CSMA/CD Carrier sense multiple access with collision detection is a MAC protocol used by the IEEE 802.3 (Ethernet) networks.

CTS A clear-to-send packet is transmitted to the source node by the destination node in a IEEE 802.11 WLAN to show that it ready to receive data.

CW The contention window is a time interval that defines the range of the back-off time in a IEEE 802.11 WLAN.

DBPSK In a IEEE 802.11 WLAN, the DSSS physical layer uses a differential binary phase shift keying (DBPSK) modulation technique, where every symbol carries one bit, which allows for a data rate of 1 Mbps.

DCF The distributed coordination function is a contention-based protocol, which resembles the basic access mode of the 802.11 standard. It is based on the CSMA/CA scheme and assumes an ad hoc network topology.

DIFS The distributed coordination function IFS is the time delay used by the DCF frames.

Directional Antennas Directional antennas focus their radiation in one direction to provide greater coverage distance.

Diversity Antennas Diversity antennas receive on more than one element, and when transmitting, they send through the element with the best received signal.

DQPSK In a IEEE 802.11 WLAN, the differential quadrate phase shift keying (DQPSK) modulation technique is used to support a data rate of 2 Mbps, in which every symbol carries two bits from the data stream.

DSSS The direct sequence spread spectrum is a physical-layer protocol used by IEEE 802.11. The main idea of DSSS is to spread the signal energy over a large bandwidth so that to other unintended receivers the signal can be treated as noise that can be easily rejected.

ECD Electronic code book is any encryption algorithm that generates the same cipher text every time it is fed the same plain text.

EDCF The enhanced DCF protocol is used by the IEEE 802.11e standard. It uses traffic categories to support QoS.

ESS Multiple BSSs can be connected to each other by connecting their APs to a distribution system, forming what is called an extended service set (ESS).

ETSI The European Telecommunications Standards Institute.

Exposed terminal: The exposed terminal problem can appear in an ad hoc WLAN topology. Specifically, a node postpones its transmission because it wrongly estimates that its data would collide with another node's.

EY-NPMA The elimination yield—nonpreemptive multiple access protocol is a contention-based MAC protocol used by the HIPERLAN/1 standard.

FCC The main duty of the Federal Communications Commission is to regulate public airwaves in the United States.

FCH The frame control channel is a downlink channel that is used by the AP to announce how the rest of the current MAC frame has been allocated. It is used by the HIPERLAN/2 WLAN standard.

FEC Forward error control increases the throughput by minimizing the need for retransmissions of bad packets (used by HIPERLAN).

FHSS In frequency hopping spread spectrum (FHSS), the signal is spread by sending at one frequency for a short period of time and then switching (hopping) to another frequency in a seemingly random fashion. It is a physical layer protocol used by the IEEE 802.11 standard.

GFSK According to the IEEE 802.11 standard, the PMD sublayer modulates the data using the Gaussian frequency shift keying technique. Depending on the data rate supported (whether 1 Mbps or 2 Mbps), GFSK or 4GFSK is used. 4GFSK translates every two bits into one signal element, which allows the rate to be doubled.

GMSK The Gaussian minimum shift keying modulation scheme is used by the HIPERLAN/1 standard.

HCF The hybrid coordination function is a QoS supportive protocol used by the IEEE 802.11e standard.

HEC The header error control is an ITU-T cyclic redundancy check, CRC16, used for error detection by the IEEE 802.11 standard.

Hidden Terminal The hidden terminal problem can appear in an ad hoc WLAN topology using carrier sense. Specifically, a node's transmission collides with another node's because it is not able to detect the transmission of another node.

HIPERLAN High performance local area network is a WLAN standard defined by ETSI.

HR-DSSS The 802.11b defines the high-rate DSSS (HR-DSSS), which allows data rates as high as 5.5 Mbps and 11 Mbps.

IBSS The independent BSS resembles the infrastructureless ad hoc arrangement. In an IBSS, stations communicate in a peer-to-peer fashion where no AP or any other intermediary is needed. At least two stations are needed to form an IBSS.

IFS In a IEEE 802.11 WLAN, access priority to the wireless channel is provided through the use of interframe spacing (IFS), which is the duration of time that has to pass before a node can try to access the channel.

Infrastructure Topology A network topology where the medium access is controlled centrally (using a base station or access point).

Interference Interference refers to the extraneous, unwanted signals that affect the proper system operation. Not only does interference affect the quality of the signal communicated from the transmitter to the receiver, it can also affect the functionality of the protocol.

IR Infrared.

ISI The intersymbol interference problem results when a symbol takes a long time to reach the receiver. This delay, called delay spread, results from multipath propagation. As a result of this delay, a symbol may arrive at the same time as another subsequent symbol.

ISM The industrial, scientific, and medical band is a frequency band that does not require any licensing, so it is used by many wireless applications.

L2CAP The logical link control and adaptation protocol (L2CAP) is used by the Bluetooth standard and defines connection-less and connection-oriented services. It also allows for QoS support by letting a transmitter and a receiver negotiate QoS flow parameters such as delay and delay variation, among other things.

LMP The link manager protocol specifies link setup and management between two Bluetooth devices, including issues of clock synchronization, authentication, and key distribution for security purposes, the protocol version used, and the nodes' mode (master, slave).

MAC Medium access control.

Modulation Techniques Techniques used to modulate the data stream into a form suitable for physical transmission.

Multipath Fading and Shadowing When a signal is transmitted, multiple versions of the same signal take different paths to arrive at the receiver. The first to arrive at the receiver is the one going through the line of sight (LOS), which is the path that does not have any obstacles between the transmitter and the receiver. Other, delayed versions, follow other paths resulting from impinges on obstacles in the path. These delayed copies, when they arrive at the receiver, either add constructively or destructively. This phenomenon, where the signal quality depends on the multipath propagation, is referred to as multipath fading.

NAV In an IEEE 802.11 network, every node maintains what is called a network allocation vector (NAV). Nodes adjust the values of their vectors as they overhear packet transmissions. A node attempts to check the channel status (whether idle or not) only when the duration in the NAV elapses.

OFDM According to the IEEE 802.11a standard, the data is modulated using the orthogonal frequency division multiplexing (OFDM) scheme. OFDM breaks the channel bandwidth into subchannels. Each subchannel has a low symbol rate and thus low ISI. The subchannels are chosen to be orthogonal and thus low cochannel interference occurs.

Omnidirectional Antennas Omnidirectional antennas provide a 360-degree radiation pattern.

Path Loss As a signal propagates from the transmitter to the receiver, it attenuates (i.e., losses its energy) with distance. This phenomenon is called path loss. It depends on many other factors including the reflecting objects and big obstructions in the path between the transmitter and the receiver.

PBCC The packet binary convolutional coding is a modulation technique used in the IEEE 802.11b standard. Using the PBCC modulation, every eight bits from the data stream are encoded in an eight-chip code, thus allowing for a data rate equal to 11 Mbps.

PCF The point coordination function provides a contention-free protocol that can be used for connection-oriented real-time traffic such as voice in an IEEE 802.11 network. This is done by polling the stations one at a time. This polling is done by the AP.

PIFS In a IEEE 802.11 network, PCF interframe space (PIFS) is the short time interval that the AP has to wait to gain access to the channel before any other node.

PLCP The physical layer convergence protocol is a 802.11 sublayer protocol responsible for adding necessary headers for the purposes of synchronization, timing, and error control.

PLW A PSDU length word (PLW) is a 12-bit field that indicates the size of the MAC frame used by the physical layer of the IEEE 802.11 standard.

PMD The physical medium dependent sublayer is responsible for raw transmission of bits over the air; mainly performs modulation of the data stream. It is defined by the IEEE 802.11 standard.

PSF The PLCP signaling field (PSF) is a four-bit field used to specify the data rate at which the frame was transmitted. Data rates range from 1 Mbps to 4.5 Mbps in increments of 0.5 Mbps. It is defined by the IEEE 802.11 standard.

QoS Quality of service.

RC4 A stream cipher encryption algorithm that uses symmetric keys.

RCH The random access channel is an uplink channel used by the nodes to compete for slots in subsequent MAC frames. It is used by the HIPERLAN/2 MAC protocol.

RTS In an IEEE 802.11 WLAN, a request-to-send (RTS) control packet is initially transmitted by the source node to the destination node to get permission to transmit data.

SCO In a Bluetooth network, the synchronous connection oriented (SCO) method is a communication between a slave and a master and involves the allocation of fixed bandwidth.

SDP The service discovery protocol specifies how Bluetooth devices search for other Bluetooth devices and establish communication with them.

SIFS According to the IEEE 802.11 MAC protocol, the short IFS (SIFS) is the shortest amount of time and hence the highest priority followed by the PIFS and the DIFS.

Stream Ciphers In a stream-cipher encryption algorithm, the data stream is processed continuously (e.g., taking one byte at a time).

TDD The main idea of a time-division duplexing (TDD) protocol is that part of the frame is used for the uplink and part for the downlink.

TDMA In a time-division multiple access scheme, stations are dynamically assigned time slots according to their needs. Time slots are dynamically allocated depending on transmission needs.

TSPEC In an IEEE 802.11e network, stations communicate to the AP the QoS parameters they desire using the transmission specification (TSPEC). In the TSPEC, a station specifies the priority, data rate, delay, and frame size, among other things.

UNII The unlicensed national information infrastructure (UNII) band is a 5-GHz frequency band used by IEEE 802.11a and the HIPERLAN networks.

WEP The 802.11 standard uses the wired-equivalent privacy (WEP) protocol, which is based on the RC4 encryption algorithm. A better and more secure protocol called wi-fi protected access (WPA) has been released recently.

WLAN Wireless local area network.

CROSS REFERENCES

See *Bluetooth Security; Bluetooth Technology; Local Area Networks; Mobile Devices and Protocols; Security and the Wireless Application Protocol (WAP); Wireless Network Standards and Protocol (802.11).*

REFERENCES

Bing, B. (2000). *High speed wireless ATM and LANs*. Norwood, MA: Artech House.

Broadband Radio Access Networks (BRAN). (1998). *High performance radio local area network (HIPERLAN), type* 1 (Functional Specification V1.2.1).

Choi, S., DelPrado, J., Shankar, S., & Mangold, S. (2003). IEEE 802.11e contention-based channel access (EDCF) performance evaluation. In *Proceedings of the ICC 2003* (Vol. 2, pp. 1151–1156). IEEE: Anchorage, AK.

Crow, B. P., Widjaja, I., Kim, J. G., & Sakai, P. (1997a). Investigation of the IEEE 802.11 medium access control (MAC) sublayer functions. In *Proceedings of Infocom '97* (Vol. 1, pp. 126–133).

Crow, B. P., Widjaja, I., Kim, J. G., & Sakai, P. (1997b). IEEE 802.11 wireless local area networks. *IEEE Communications Magazine, 35(9),* 116–126.

Doufexi, A., Armour, S., Karlsson, P., Nix, A., & Bull, D. (2002). A comparison of HIPERLAN/2 and IEEE 802.11a. *IEEE Communication Magazine.*

Geier, J. (n.d.a). Retrieved April, 2004, from http://www.wi-fiplanet.com/tutorials/article.php/953511

Geier, J. (n.d.b). Retrieved April, 2004, from http://www.wi-fiplanet.com/tutorials/article.php/1457211

IEEE. (1997). Wireless LAN medium access control (MAC) and physical layer (PHY) specification (IEEE Std 802.11–1997). New York: Author.

Jain, R. (2004). Retrieved 2004 from http://www.cse.ohio-state.edu/~jain/cis788-99/ftp/wireless_lans/

Johnsson, M. (1999). *HiperLAN/2—The broadband radio transmission technology operating in the 5 GHz frequency band.* HiperLAN/2 Global Forum. Retrieved [date] from http://www.hiperlan2.com/

McDysan, D. E., & Spohn, D. (1999). *ATM theory and applications.* New York: McGraw-Hill.

Nicopolitidis, P., Obaidat, M. S., Papadimitriou, G. I., & Pomportsis, A. S. (2003). *Wireless networks.* Hoboken, NJ: John Wiley & Sons.

Obaidat, M., & Obeidat, S. (2002). Modeling and simulation of adaptive ABR voice over ATM networks. In Simulation: Transactions of the Society for Modeling and Simulation International (Vol. 78, No. 3, pp. 139–149). San Diego, CA: SCS.

Papadimitriou, G., Lagkas, T., Obaidat, M. S., & Pomportsis, A. S. (2003). A new approach to the simulation of HIPERLAN wireless networks. In *Proceedings of the 2003 European Simulation Symposium* (pp. 459–468). San Diego, CA: SCS.

Papadimitriou, G., Lagkas, T. D., & Pomportsis, A. S. (2003). HIPERSIM: A sense range distinctive simulation environment for HiperLAN systems. *Journal of Simulation, 79*(8), 462–481.

Prasad, A. R. (1999). Performance comparison of voice over IEEE 802.11 schemes. In *IEEE Vehicular Technology Conference* (pp. 2636–2640).

Rappaport, T. S. (1996). *Wireless communications* (1st Ed.). Upper Saddle River, NJ: Prentice Hall.

Roshan, P., & Leary, J. (2004). *802.11 wireless LAN fundamentals.* Indianapolis, IN: Cisco Press.

Schiller, J. (2002). *Mobile communications.* Boston, MA: Addison Wesley.

Stallings, W. (2002). *Wireless communications and networks.* Upper Saddle River, NJ: Prentice Hall.

Security in Wireless Sensor Networks

Mohamed Eltoweissy, *Virginia Tech*
Stephan Olariu and Ashraf Wadaa, *Old Dominion University*

INTRODUCTION

Recent technological breakthroughs in ultrahigh integration and low-power electronics have enabled the development of miniaturized battery-operated sensor nodes (sensors, for short) that integrate sensing, signal processing, and wireless communications capabilities (Akyildiz, Su, Sankarasubramaniam, & Cayirci, 2002; Estrin, Govindan, Heidemann, & Kumar, 1999; Pottie & Kaiser, 2000; Sohrabi et al., 2000; Min et al., 2001; Rabaey et al., 2000; National Research Council 2001). Together with innovative and focused network design techniques that will make possible massive deployment and sustained low-power operation, the small size and cost of individual sensors are key enabling factors for a large number of applications. Aggregating sensors into sophisticated computation and communication structures (the wireless sensor networks) will have a significant impact on the way people interact with their environment. Indeed, a large number of networked sensors will enable collecting, sharing, and processing enormous amounts of spatial and temporally dense data over, possibly, large geographical regions.

An example application of WSNs would be to enable the elderly and the disabled to live more independent lives. Sensors record and store a variety of information about individuals and their activities. Such information can be shared with other people or with a "smart" environment to offer needed services. Clearly, one of the issues involved here is *privacy*—the information is of sensitive nature and must be protected. At the same time, quick access to it may be necessary in the event of an emergency medical situation. Another example is effective monitoring and management of public infrastructure systems in a metropolitan area using an integrated information grid. The grid includes, among other components, WSNs that will capture, transport, and store a variety of information to be used to discover patterns in infrastructure state information, which can be presented to decision makers. Again, integrity and privacy of such information as well as timely access to it could be critical, especially in emergency situations.

The range of applications for WSNs continues to expand with continued research and development. In addition to these applications, many other applications, such as battlefield command and control, hazardous material detection, and emergency response, will use WSNs as mission-critical components. Consequently, this requires WSNs to provide timely, high-quality information with commensurate security protection in the face of adverse deployment conditions. This is complicated, however, by a number of limiting factors including the following:

(1) Characteristics of sensors: small size; modest computing, communication, and energy capabilities; and anonymity of sensors resulting from lack of fabrication-time identifiers.
(2) Features of current sensor and WSN technology: lack of security features at the physical level, structural weakness of WSNs, protocol-specific virtual infrastructures, and sporadic connectivity.
(3) WSN deployment: massive and dense deployment covering large geographical areas, unattended operation in hostile environments, and multihop ad hoc communications.

Another complicating factor is the WSN operation, which requires the collaboration of dynamic groups of sensors to accomplish their mission. Moreover, the staggering amounts of data that can be collected by WSNs further exacerbate the security problem. These factors greatly increase the number of possible points of failure and make sensors and WSNs increasingly vulnerable to a multitude of security threats including physical tampering, spoofing, denial of service, and impersonation, among many others. If an adversary can thwart the work of the network by altering the information produced, stopping production, or pilfering information, then the perceived usefulness of WSNs would be drastically curtailed.

A recent report by the National Research Council (2001) on embedded networks (including WSNs) states that "defining and then protecting system boundaries where physical boundaries are likely to be nonexistent and where nodes can automatically move in and out of the system will be a serious challenge. Further, managing the scale and complexity of EmNets, while at the same time handling the security challenges of mobile code and the vulnerability to denial-of-service attacks, will require significant attention from the research community." It follows that security is a fundamental issue that must be resolved for the potential of WSNs to be fully exploited.

The main goal of this chapter is to survey recent results in the area of WSN security and countermeasures. Further, to mitigate security threats, especially in massive deployment of networked sensors, a security solution is presented that provides managed network mission and tasks, communication anonymity and confidentiality, continuity of (secure) operation, and protection against physical tampering, impersonation, and denial of service. In general, salient characteristics of WSN security solutions include the following:

- lightweight, with minimal communication, storage, and computation overhead;
- scalable to massive deployment;
- minimal management at both sensor and network levels;
- high resiliency to dynamic configuration of the network and the task workgroups;
- dynamic adaptation to deployment context (e.g., hostile versus friendly environments);
- graceful degradation when the network becomes sparse over time; and
- high resiliency to node capture.

The remainder of this chapter is organized as follows: the second section provides a model for WSNs, The third section discusses security issues in WSNs; the fourth section presents countermeasures and reports on contemporary WSN security research. The fifth section describes a fresh approach to securing WSNs. The sixth section presents a proposal to securing sensors and WSNs based on the new approach. Finally, the seventh section concludes the chapter and outlines directions for future research.

WIRELESS SENSOR NETWORKS

Securing WSNs presents formidable scientific and engineering challenges to sensor and WSN researchers and designers. Numerous factors are at play. The capabilities and constraints of sensor hardware influence the type of security mechanisms that can be hosted on a sensor node platform. Also, the constraints on WSN communications and deployment greatly affect the selection of security mechanisms. In light of these constraints, it is necessary to describe the basic components of WSNs and to discuss security goals, threats models and attacks, and security countermeasures. After describing the components of sensors and WSNs in this section, the next sections discuss the main design issues, security issues, and related work. Our analyses reveal that although previous security solutions for WSNs are appropriate for networks of limited size, they are not applicable to large-scale WSNs.

From a purely architectural perspective, a WSN is a collection of individual sensors connected and dynamically configured in ad hoc wireless network topologies to provide support for detection and monitoring applications.

The Sensor Node

A sensor is an electronic device that is capable of detecting environmental conditions such as temperature, sound, or the presence of certain objects. Sensors are generally equipped with data processing and communication capabilities. The sensing circuitry measures parameters from the environment surrounding the sensor and transforms them into electric signals. Processing such signals reveals some properties about objects located and/or events happening in the vicinity of the sensor. The sensor sends such sensed data, usually via radio transmitter, to a command center either directly or through a data collection station (a base station or sink). The base station can perform fusion of the data to filter out erroneous data and anomalies and to draw conclusions from the data over a period of time. For example, in a reconnaissance-oriented WSN, sensor data indicates detection of a target and fusion of multiple sensor reports can be used for tracking and identifying the detected target.

A block diagram design of a typical sensor is depicted in Figure 1. The functionality of the sensing circuitry depends on the sensor capabilities. In general, the sensing circuitry generates analog signals whose properties reflect the surrounding environments. These signals are sampled using an A/D converter and stored in the on-board memory as a sequence of digital values. The sensed data can be further processed using a data processor (microprocessor

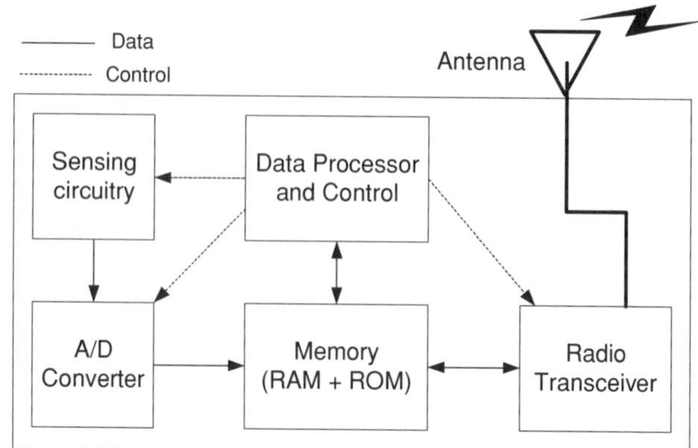

Figure 1: Block diagram of a typical sensor.

or DSP) prior to sending them over to the base station using the radio transceiver. The capabilities of the data processor are subject to a trade-off. A powerful DSP can be advantageous because it will allow the sensor to transmit only important findings rather than excessive raw readings. Reducing the sensor's traffic generation rate can save the energy consumed by the radio transmitter and can decrease radio signal interference and collisions among the deployed sensors. On the other hand, sophisticated data processing can consume significant energy and can be a cost and a design burden by increasing the complexity of the sensor design. In terms of WSNs, however, it may be better to have sensors where there is more processing at the processor rather than transmit all the values. This is because the energy expended in the execution of 800–1000 instructions is approximately equivalent to the energy expended in one transmission. In all cases, the sensor has to include some control logic to coordinate the interactions among the different functional blocks. Such control functions are also performed by the data processor.

Wireless sensors are not all created equal—they may have varied roles and capabilities depending on their intended application. Some sensors may be part of a mobile robot where commands can be given regarding location and mobility as well as regarding power supplied by a power generator. Others might be nanotechnology-based with no fabrication-time identifiers and nonrenewable power sources. Some may be incorporated into swarm devices that have considerable processing power. The vast majority of sensors, however, are small in size, with limited capabilities and low cost. The small form factor prohibits the use of long-lasting batteries and constrains sensors to low-power processors and small radios with limited bandwidth and transmission ranges. Likewise, deployment in massive numbers, combined with remote operations, preclude recharging or replacing batteries. Thus, sensors have to operate with the initial power budget: once the batteries are depleted, the sensor expires.

Recently, a number of advanced sensor devices have started to emerge. Most notable among these sensors is the MICA Mote developed by the University of California at Berkeley (Horton et al., 2002; Warneke, Last, Leibowitz, & Pister, 2001). A typical Mote node has 128 KB of flash memory, 4 KB of RAM, a low-power Atmel ATmega 128 processor (8-bit, 4 MHz), and runs with 2 AA batteries. Figure 2 hints at the size of one of the available configurations of Mote nodes. Motes are managed by the TinyOS operating system, also developed at the University of California Berkley. The TinyOS has a very small footprint and support self-configuration and power-down modes. A single-chip implementation of a Mote node is expected to be commercialized soon and to bring the cost of Motes to a very low level when mass produced.

Network Components

Typically, wireless sensors can be deployed either by strategically placing them at specific locations or by airdropping them in a remote area. Oftentimes, these sensors are deployed in a hostile environment where human oversight is very difficult, if not impossible. Such deployment

Figure 2: A picture of a Mote node, courtesy Univ. of California Berkley.

of sensors implies that the nodes are expected to perform sensing and communication with no continual maintenance or battery replenishment. Hence, they are built to be as self-sufficient as possible. Other forms of WSNs exist, for example, a WSN established among mobile robots. However, a detailed discussion of such networks is beyond the scope of this chapter.

Wireless communications may use protocols to implement multidrop topologies by emulating wired connections with radio frequency (RF) links using standards such as IEEE 802.11 to bring Ethernet connectivity to wireless networks. Alternatively, they may use lightweight communications protocols, such as the one described by Wadaa, Olariu, Wilson, Eltoweissy, and Jones (2005). Figure 3 illustrates the basic elements of a typical WSN, including sensors producing sensor information distributed in sensor patch(es), a sink or base station or gateway, and a route for sensor information. From a conceptual perspective, the sensors can be distributed in a patch (or field) to carry out some monitoring or detection function. As they detect an event or phenomenon, the relevant information is transmitted from sensor to sensor to local sink nodes (aggregation sensor nodes) to base station and on to user or command center and the outside world.

Because sensors are battery operated and their batteries typically cannot be recharged, keeping the sensor active all the time will limit the duration that the battery can last. Therefore, optimal organization and management of the WSN is very crucial to perform the desired function with an acceptable level of quality and to maintain sufficient sensor energy to last for the duration of the required mission. Mission-oriented organization of a WSN enables the appropriate selection of only a subset of the sensors to be turned on and thus avoids wasting the energy of sensors that do not have to be involved. Examples of energy-conscious network management techniques include multihop routing, data aggregation, and clever medium access control (Akyildiz, Su, Sankarasubramaniam, & Cayirci, 2002; Shah & Rabaey, 2002; Akkaya & Younis, 2005; Chandrakasan & Balakrishnan, 2000; Intanagonwiwat, Govindan, & Estrin, 2000; Younis, Youssef, & Arisha, 2003; Woo & Culler, 2001; Shih et al., 2001; Singh & Raghavendra, 1998; Jolly & Younis, 2005).

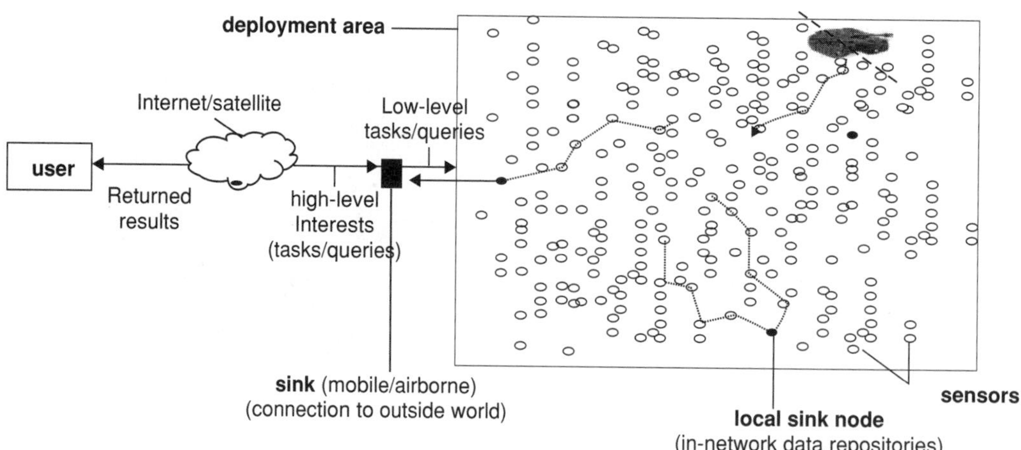

Figure 3: Illustrating a wireless sensor network and its interface.

SECURITY ISSUES IN SENSORS AND WIRELESS SENSOR NETWORKS

The main goal of this section is to discuss security goals, challenges to securing WSN, a classification of possible attackers, and a taxonomy of possible forms of attack and countermeasures.

Security Goals

Security goals for WSN are determined by the nature of the WSN applications. A general set of goals that may be representative of the requirements of a broad spectrum of WSN applications include confidentiality, authenticity, integrity, and availability. Related goals include authorized access, adaptive multilevel security, and interoperability.

- *Confidentiality* requires that the sender of data should be able to determine the set of receivers that have a right to read the data content. In WSN communications, because of changes in network membership, two types of confidentiality exist: backward (before joining) and forward (after departure) confidentiality.
- *Authenticity* means that the communicating partners should be able to unambiguously identify each other.
- *Integrity* of data means that data content remains unchanged inside the sensor and during transmission.
- *Availability* ensures that eligible participants with appropriate privileges will receive services as authorized. In WSNs, it is important to ensure the availability and continuity of secure services given an environment characterized by intermittent connectivity and autonomous sensor behavior.

In addition to the security goals mentioned, there are also extra requirements in terms of location confidentiality, cooperation fairness, and the absence of traffic diversion, according to Buchegger & Le Boudec (2002). Furthermore, for routing protocols to achieve availability and security, (Lundbey, 2000) addresses additional security objectives, such as certainty of discovery, isolation, lightweight computations, location privacy, self-stabilization, and byzantine robustness.

- *Cooperation and fairness:* There is a trade-off between cooperation and resource consumption. Nodes have to economize on their resources. Simultaneously, if the nodes do not forward messages, others might not forward either, thereby denying service.
- *Confidentiality of location:* In some situations, for example, in a military application, routing information can be equally or even more vital than the message content itself (Buchegger & Le Boudec, 2002). According to (Lundbey, 2000), the location of nodes should not be available to a malicious user.
- *No traffic diversion:* Routers (routing nodes) should be advertised and operated based on the selected routing protocol and should honestly reflect the knowledge of the network topology. By diverting the network traffic, nodes can work against that requirement.
- *Certainty of discovery:* This requires that if a route between two nodes exists, the route should be identified and correct.
- *Isolation:* Routing protocols should identify and can isolate misbehaving nodes. As an alternative, the routing protocol should be resistant to malicious nodes.
- *Lightweight computations:* Lengthy and demanding computations should be avoided if possible. Otherwise, the computations should have an effect on as few nodes as possible. The preferable case is that only the peer nodes should be required to be involved in the computations.
- *Self-stabilization:* If an attacker injects forged information into the routing path, the routing protocol should be able to recover in a limited amount of time.
- *Byzantine robustness:* This property is even more stringent than the self-stabilization property in that the routing protocol should be able to recover from attack as well as function properly during an attack.

Challenges for Securing WSNs

Whereas contemporary security mechanisms have tackled many identified attacks in general wire-based and wireless networks, numerous constraints and attributes make developing security solutions for sensors and WSNs both unconventional and challenging. For example, sensors are typically at the low end of computational and storage capabilities and do not have the capacity for performing hefty cryptographic transformations. In addition, the limited energy supply and available bandwidth, the deployment of large number of sensors, and the high error rate do not favor elaborate security protocols with frequent message exchange. Other factors that affect the security approach include the following:

(1) unattended operation, weak tamper protection, and hostile environment, which increase the likelihood of compromising stored security material;
(2) intermittent and ad hoc connectivity, which may result in failure to maintain synchronized security material that could isolate a sensor(s) from communicating with the rest of the network;
(3) limited preconfiguration resulting from the ad hoc nature, which limits the amount and type of security-enabling material necessary to deploy a secure WSN; and
(4) possibility of untrustworthiness of data paths resulting from unknown nodes in multihop communications.

An example of a major challenge to most contemporary security solutions for WSNs, especially those espousing flat structures (Perrig et al., 2002; Du, Deng, Han, & Varshney, 2003, is the (implicit) assumption of synchronized time. Assume that each packet is 240 bits long with transmission rate of 10 kbps; the required accuracy is 0.048 sec. This accuracy of the time synchronization is not really a problem; such granularity is easily achievable with most time synchronization protocols. The real problem is the feasibility of implementing contemporary energy-consuming time synchronization protocols in large-scale WSNs. Some approaches have suggested using broadcast communications to transfer time synchronization information in a more efficient manner. To secure the time synchronization information, however, the broadcast information must be authenticated. But the purpose of the time synchronization mechanism was to implement a broadcast authentication! In conclusion, we argue that most contemporary solutions are more suited for smaller-scale WSNs.

Classification of Attackers

Attackers may mount software as well as physical attacks on WSNs. Attackers may physically tamper wih sensor nodes, damaging part of the network. For example, the WSN introduced by Buczak & Jamalabad (1998) is subject to enemy attacks that could destroy a subset of nodes. On the other hand, referring to software attackers, Karlof and Wagner have classified security attackers, based on their capabilities, into *mote-class* attackers and *laptop-class* attackers. The mote-class attacker may have access only to a few nodes with the same level of capabilities of the deployed sensors, whereas the laptop-class attacker may have access to more powerful devices. In the latter case, malicious nodes have significant advantages over legitimate sensors through greater battery power, a more capable CPU, a high-power RF transmitter, or a highly sensitive antenna. A laptop-class attacker may jam or eavesdrop on an entire network and can launch a more damaging coordinated attack. Another distinction can be made between outsider attacks, such as the ones discussed so far, and insider attacks. In the latter case, an authorized participant in the WSN acts abnormally. Insider attacks can be conducted either through compromised sensors that are injected with the malicious code or by stealing secret material and then using laptop-class devices to clone native sensors' behavior to mount attacks.

Attacks on WSNs

In this chapter, attacks are classified according to their violation of the main security goals of confidentiality, integrity, authenticity, and availability.

Confidentiality attacks attempt to expose the data being stored or sent. Four types of attacks appear to be commonplace: traffic analysis, eavesdropping, man in the middle, and tampering. *Traffic analysis* allows an attacker to determine that there is activity on the network, the location of base stations, and the type of protocol being used in the transmission. *Eavesdropping* can be passive or active. An attacker who passively monitors traffic can read the data transmitted in the stream and also can gather information indirectly by examining the source of a packet, its destination, size, number, and time of transmission. Active eavesdropping extends the passive method to inject the attackers' packets into the data stream. The goal is to help the attacker decipher the data payload of the stream. Address spoofing is a typical example of active eavesdropping. A *man-in-the-middle* attack establishes a rogue intermediary that, for example, pretends to be a base station, and acts as a proxy to the actual network (impersonation). *Tampering* involves an attacker compromising data content stored in sensors' memory, usually by node capturing. The potential for tamper attacks is significant in a WSN with unattended deployment.

Attacks against integrity and authenticity generally require successful system intrusion and the use of one or more of the confidentiality-type attacks. Three primary classes of integrity and authenticity attacks can be identified: session hijacking, replay, and man in the middle. The objective in session hijacking is to break into an authenticated and authorized session that is underway and take it away from the owner. One of the attacker advantages here is that, if successful, the victim might not even realize that they are under attack. If the attacker can gain access to the session, the attacker can use it for any previously authorized purposes. The session can also (if unchecked by the host) be extended for long periods and be used multiple times. An identifying characteristic of the replay attack is that, for example, while a hijack attack will occur in real-time, replay attacks occur only after the fact. The object is to gain access by convincing the host that a valid client wants to associate. Information that has been previously gained through any means can be used for this purpose. Usually, the session that is the source of any information used in the replay is not altered or interfered with in any way, which can make detecting this kind of attack very difficult.

Availability or denial of service (DoS) attacks (Chan, Perrig, & Song, 2003; Wood & Stankovic, 2002) can be grouped into three categories, namely disabling service (e.g., sinkhole, HELLO flood [Karlof & Wagner, 2005]), exhaustion (e.g., inducing false positives), and service degradation (e.g., selective forwarding attack).

Karlof and Wagner (2005) describe some of the major network layer attacks on routing protocols used in WSNs. These attacks are described below:

- *Spoofed, altered, or replayed routing information*—these are grouped together because they achieve a similar goal for the attacker.
- *Selective forwarding*—the attacker inserts a compromised node in the data flow and may refuse to forward some but not all of the packets.
- *Sinkhole attacks*—the attacker tries to lure nearly all the traffic from a particular area through a compromised node, creating a metaphorical sinkhole with the adversary at the center.
- *Sybil attacks*—the attacker uses a single node that presents multiple identities to other nodes in the network (Douceur, 2002).
- *Wormholes*—the attacker, possibly more than one, creates a tunnel that appears to transfer data faster than routes in the original network. The attacker can then direct traffic to the tunnel or wormhole using selective forwarding (Hu, Perrig, & Johnson, 2002).
- *HELLO flood attacks*—the attacker broadcasts routing or other information with large enough transmission power in an attempt to convince every node in the network that the adversary is its neighbor.
- *Acknowledgement spoofing*—the attacker spoofs link layer acknowledgments for "overheard" packets addressed to neighboring nodes, thus convincing the sender that a weak link is strong or that a dead or disabled node is alive.

In addition to these general attacks, attackers can also exploit vulnerabilities within specific routing protocols. For more details on attacks on specific routing protocols, please refer to Karlof and Wagner (2005).

Attack Countermeasures

As stated in Karlof and Wagner (2005), the majority of outsider attacks against sensor network routing protocols can be prevented by simple link layer encryption and authentication using a globally shared key. The Sybil attack can be prevented with this countermeasure because strong authentication techniques will not allow nodes to accept multiple identities from the same node. The majority of selective forwarding and sinkhole attacks can be avoided because the adversary is prevented from joining the topology. Link layer acknowledgements can also be authenticated.

Major classes of attacks not countered by link layer encryption and authentication mechanisms are wormhole attacks and HELLO flood attacks (Karlof and Wagner 2005). Although an adversary is prevented from joining the network, nothing prevents him or her from using a wormhole to tunnel packets sent by legitimate nodes in one part of the network to legitimate nodes in another part to convince them they are neighbors or by amplifying an overheard broadcast packet with sufficient power to be received by every node in the network.

Link layer security mechanisms using a globally shared key are completely ineffective in the presence of insider attacks or compromised nodes (Karlof and Wagner 2005). Insiders can attack the network by spoofing or injecting bogus routing information, creating sinkholes, selectively forwarding packets, using the Sybil attack, and broadcasting HELLO floods. More sophisticated defense mechanisms are needed to provide reasonable protection against wormholes and insider attacks. The rest of this subsection concentrates on insider attacks. *The Sybil attack:* An insider cannot be prevented from participating in the network, but she should only be able to do so using the identities of the nodes she has compromised. Using a globally shared key allows an insider to masquerade as *any* (possibly even nonexistent) node. Identities must be verified. In the traditional setting, this might be done using public key cryptography, but generating and verifying digital signatures is beyond the capabilities of sensor nodes. One solution is to have every node share a unique symmetric key with a trusted base station. Two nodes can then use a Needham–Schroeder–like protocol to verify each other's identity and establish a shared key. A pair of neighboring nodes can use the resulting key to implement an authenticated, encrypted link between them. To prevent an insider from wandering around a stationary network and establishing shared keys with every node in the network, the base station can reasonably limit the number of neighbors a node is allowed to have and send an error message when a node exceeds it. Thus, when a node is compromised, it is restricted to (meaningfully) communicating only with its verified neighbors. This is not to say that nodes are forbidden from sending messages to base stations or aggregation points multiple hops away, but they are restricted from using any node except their verified neighbors to do so. In addition, an adversary can still use a wormhole to create an artificial link between two nodes to convince them they are neighbors, but the adversary will not be able to eavesdrop on or modify any future communications between them (Douceur, 2002).

HELLO *flood attacks:* The simplest defense against HELLO flood attacks is to verify the bidirectionality of a link before taking meaningful action based on a message received via that link. However, this countermeasure is less effective when an adversary has a highly sensitive receiver as well as a powerful transmitter. Such an adversary can effectively create a wormhole to every node within range of its transmitter/receiver. Because the links between these nodes and the adversary are bidirectional, this approach will unlikely be able to locally detect or prevent a HELLO flood.One possible solution to this problem is for every node to authenticate each of its neighbors with an identity verification protocol using a trusted base station. If the protocol sends messages in both directions via the link between the nodes, HELLO floods are prevented when the adversary only has a powerful transmitter because the protocol verifies the bidirectionality of the link. Although this does not prevent a compromised node with a sensitive receiver and a powerful transmitter from authenticating itself to a large number of nodes in the network, an observant base station may be able to detect a HELLO flood is imminent. Because such an adversary is required to authenticate itself to every victim before it can mount an attack, an adversary claiming to be a neighbor of an unusually large number of the nodes will raise an alarm.

Wormhole and sinkhole attacks: Wormhole and sinkhole attacks are very difficult to defend against, especially when the two are used in combination. Wormholes are hard to detect because they use a private, out-of-band channel invisible to the underlying sensor network. Sinkholes are difficult to defend against in protocols that use advertised information such as remaining energy or an estimate of end-to-end reliability to construct a routing topology because this information is hard to verify. Routes that minimize the hop-count to a base station are easier to verify, however hop-count can be completely misrepresented through a wormhole. When routes are established simply based on the reception of a packet, sinkholes are easy to create because there is no information for a defender to verify. A technique for detecting wormhole attacks is presented in Hu, Perrig, and Johnson (2002), but it requires extremely tight time synchronization and is thus infeasible for most sensor networks. Because it is extremely difficult to fit existing protocols with defenses against these attacks, the best solution is to carefully design routing protocols in which wormholes and sinkholes are meaningless (Karlof & Wagner, 2005). For example, one class of protocols resistant to these attacks is geographic routing protocols. Protocols that construct a topology initiated by a base station are most susceptible to wormhole and sinkhole attacks. Geographic protocols construct a topology on demand using only localized interactions and information and without initiation from the base station. Because traffic is naturally routed toward the physical location of a base station, it is difficult to attract it elsewhere to create a sinkhole. A wormhole is most effective when used to create sinkholes or artificial links that attract traffic. Artificial links are easily detected in geographic routing protocols because the "neighboring" nodes will notice the distance between them is well beyond normal radio range (Karlof & Wagner, 2005).

Selective forwarding: Even in protocols completely resistant to sinkholes, wormholes, and the Sybil attack, a compromised node has a significant probability of including itself in a data flow to launch a selective forwarding attack if it is strategically located near the source or a base station. Multipath routing can be used to counter these types of selective forwarding attacks. Messages routed via n paths whose nodes are completely disjointed are completely protected against selective forwarding attacks involving at most $n - 1$ compromised nodes and still offer some probabilistic protection when n or more nodes are compromised. However, completely disjointed paths may be difficult to create. Braided paths (Ganesan, Govindan, Shenker, & Estrin, 2001) may have nodes in common, but have no links in common (i.e., no two consecutive nodes in common). The use of multiple braided paths may provide probabilistic protection against selective forwarding and use only localized information. Allowing nodes to dynamically choose a packet's next hop probabilistically from a set of possible candidates can further reduce the chances of an adversary gaining complete control of a data flow.

Authenticated broadcast and flooding: Because base stations are trustworthy, adversaries must not be able to spoof broadcast or flooded messages from any base station. This requires some level of asymmetry: because every node in the network can potentially be compromised, no node should be able to spoof messages from a base station, yet every node should be able to verify them. Authenticated broadcast is also useful for localized node interactions. Many protocols require nodes to broadcast HELLO messages to their neighbors. These messages should be authenticated and impossible to spoof. Proposals for authenticated broadcast intended for use in a more conventional setting either use digital signatures and/or have packet overhead that well exceed the length of typical sensor network packet. μTESLA is a protocol for efficient, authenticated broadcast and flooding that uses only symmetric key cryptography and requires minimal packet overhead (Perrig et al., 2002). μTESLA achieves the asymmetry necessary for authenticated broadcast and flooding by using delayed key disclosure and one-way key chains constructed with a publicly computable, cryptographically secure hash function. Replay is prevented because messages authenticated with previously disclosed keys are ignored.

Prevention of denial-of-service attacks: Layered network architecture can improve robustness by circumscribing layer interactions and interfaces. A clean division of layers may be sacrificed for performance in sensor networks, however, reducing robustness. Each layer is vulnerable to different DoS attacks and has different options available for its defense. Some attacks crosscut multiple layers or exploit interactions between them. Wood and Stankovic, (2002) list the layers of a typical sensor network and describe each layer's vulnerabilities and defenses.

Resilience to physical node capture: One of the most challenging issues facing sensor networks is resiliency against node capture attacks. In traditional computing, physical security is often taken for granted: attackers can be denied physical access to our computers. Sensor networks disrupt that paradigm. In most applications, sensor nodes are likely to be placed in locations accessible to an attacker. This raises the possibility that an attacker could capture sensor nodes, extract cryptographic secrets, modify their programming, or replace them with malicious nodes under the attacker's control. Tamper-resistant packaging might be one defense, but this is expensive. Also, current tamper-resistance technology does not provide a very high level of security. Therefore, algorithmic solutions to the problem of node capture are preferable.

WIRELESS SENSOR NETWORK SECURITY RESEARCH

Alhough the problem of securing ad hoc networks has received a great deal of well-deserved attention in the literature (Chan, Perrig, & Song, 2003; Marti et al., 2000; Canetti & Pinkas, 1998; Wong, Gouda, & Lam, 1998;

Chang et al., 1999; Moharum, Mukkamala, & Eltoweissy, 2004). WSN are sufficiently different in their characteristics that security solutions designed specifically for ad hoc networks do not apply to them. In general, wireless sensor networks need to work unattended. In addition, the level of security in a WSN versus scalability and the efficiency with respect to energy, computation, and memory constitute the main design trade-offs. Recently, researchers focusing on WSN security have proposed a number of solutions (Perrig et al., 2002; Du, Deng, Han, & Varshney, 2003; Chang et al., 1999; Wang, Velayutham, & Guan, 2003; Kong et al., 2001; Zhu, Setia, & Jajodia, 2003; Wadaa, Olariu, Wilson, & Eltoweissy, 2004). These solutions address security goals to varying degrees. Although some solutions implement security at the link layer (e.g., SPINS; Chan, Perrig, & Song, 2003), most solutions use cryptographic key agreement/management schemes at higher layers (e.g., LEAP). Contemporary solutions overwhelmingly either assume or provide probabilistic tamper proofing. All key-based schemes, at least those known to us (except our own) assume nodes with unique identifiers and therefore do not address the case of anonymous nodes. Also, these solutions, in general, do not address "freshness" of keying material to support secure dynamic reconfiguration of the WSN and do not provide adaptive security at different levels of granularity.

Link Level Security Solutions

The pursuit of link layer mechanisms for tackling security concerns has been the choice for some research efforts. For example, enhancements were proposed to the IEEE 802.11 link layer protocols to ensure authenticated access and to detect denial of service attacks (Kyasanur & Vaidya, 2002). Although traffic authentication is applied per packet in Binkley and Trost (2001) to filter out bogus traffic, a per-session approach is proposed in Wang, Velayutham, and Guan (2003) to minimize overhead. In addition, using encryption keys to maintain data confidentiality and integrity at the link layer has been proposed in Perrig, et al. (2002) and http://www.bluetooth.com/upload/24Security_Chapter.PDF. We propose an approach that relies on frequency hopping and the sensor's genetic material to provide a simple and comprehensive solution to ensure authentication, confidentiality, and integrity. In addition, our approach is lightweight in terms of energy consumption. Cryptographic and encoded schemes extend the effective number of bits per packet transmitted, leading to increased energy consumption. In contrast, our approach can be very energy efficient because of the frequency hopping that limits traffic collision and the avoidance of the incorporation of data keys.

Cryptographic Key-Based Solutions

Solutions to securing sensors and WSNs mostly use cryptographic techniques (Perrig et al., 2002; Zhu, Setia, & Jajodia, 2003; Jolly, Kuşçu, & Kokate, 2002; http://www.bluetooth.com/upload/24Security_Chapter.PDF; Eschenauer & Gligor, 2002). Key agreement to bootstrap trust between communicating nodes is at the heart of these solutions (for a comprehensive survey, refer to (Kongial, 2000). There are three general types of key agreement schemes: predistribution, trusted server-based, and self-enforcing schemes. Predistribution keying protocols attempt to defray the high sensor transmission costs through a more intensive initial preconfiguration (Perrig et al., 2002; Du, Deng, Han, & Varshney, 2003). Some preconfiguration is always necessary but can reduce flexibility and impact security. Other techniques require less initial configuration. Trusted server-based keying protocols employ a centralized key distribution point to establish and maintain keys for a WSN. The central point can be a single centralized entity or distributed among trusted sensors (e.g., cluster or region heads; http://www.bluetooth.com/upload/24Security_Chapter.PDF). Energy consumption for centralized key distribution is typically localized with the center performing most of the work; however, the use of asymmetric cryptographic schemes can possibly lessen this cost by distributing the computational energy away from the center. Self-enforcing keying schemes, in general, depend on asymmetric cryptography, for example, public key certificates to distribute the establishment of keys throughout the group, sometime in a pair-wise fashion.

Carman, Kruus, and Matt (2000) studied energy consumption of a wide array of protocols for key agreement supporting confidentiality and authentication services in WSNs. Both symmetric key and asymmetric key protocols were included. The study concluded that although symmetric key–based protocols consume less energy, some of these protocols are not sufficiently flexible for use in dynamically reconfigurable networks, because they cannot efficiently handle unanticipated additions of sensors to the network. Public key–based establishment protocols offer more flexibility and scalability. The public key algorithms used in these protocols consume a great deal of computational and communications energy, however.

In the remainder of this section, some of the major research efforts in WSN security are discussed. The focus is primarily on broadcast authentication and key management.

Broadcast Authentication

Communications energy consumption has a great effect on the battery life of the sensor nodes. Communications energy can be conserved significantly by using broadcast transmissions in tasks such as distribution of initial keying material or transmission of sensor-reading data. These tasks could also be done using unicast transmissions but that would incur greater energy consumption.

In many cases, the broadcasted messages need to be *authenticated*. Authenticating a message means that the sender corroborates the origin and the content of the information using cryptographic tools. Note that message authentication implicitly provides data integrity (for if a message is modified, then the source has changed).

In the past few years, several broadcast authentication schemes for WSNs have been proposed (e.g., Perrig et al., 2002; Liu & Ning, 2003). Most schemes are variations of the μTESLA protocol (Perrig et al., 2002), which is designed to provide authenticated streaming broadcast for severely resource-constrained environments. In μTESLA, time is divided into uniform time intervals, and a unique secret key is associated with each time interval. These secret keys are generated using a one-way key chain. In time interval i, the sender uses the key of the current interval, Ki, to compute the message authentication code (MAC) of the packets in that interval. The key Ki is revealed after a certain time delay. The received packets are guaranteed to be authentic as long as they were received before the corresponding key was disclosed and the key has the one-way property (i.e., future keys cannot be predicted given the present and past keys).

μTESLA and its variations only rely on symmetric-key cryptosystems. Because of its efficiency and tolerance to packet loss, it is well suited for WSNs. However, this scheme is not an ideal solution for all WSN applications and is not suitable for large sensor networks. μTESLA is not appropriate for large WSNs because of the following reasons:

- To "bootstrap" μTESLA, each receiver needs to have at least one key from the one-way key chain generated by the sender. This key, along with other initial parameters, are sent to each receiver individually. In a large network, where the number of receivers is correspondingly large, this requires the sender to exhaust a great amount of energy in transmitting the initial parameters.
- In μTESLA, the sender and the receivers need to be time synchronized. The validity of the MAC keys (and therefore the authenticity of the packets) is directly dependent on the correct time synchronization of the sender and the receivers. To synchronize a large WSN, broadcast synchronization schemes are preferred over pair-wise synchronization schemes because of their small communication overhead. However, for security reasons, μTESLA cannot be used in conjunction with broadcast synchronization schemes.

Recent efforts to address the first problem have been somewhat successful (e.g., Liu & Ning, 2003). However, the solution to the second problem remains open.

Key Management

Recent key predistribution proposals (Wood & Stankovic, 2002; Du, Deng, Han, & Varshney, 2003; Zhu, Setia, & Jajodia, 2003; Wadaa, Olariu, Wilson, & Eltoweissy, 2004; Jolly, Kuşçu, & Kokate, 2002; Eschenauer & Gligor, 2002; Liu & Ning, 2003) provide techniques to securely set up pair-wise keys post-deployment while attempting to balance efficiency and tamper resistance. Eschenauer and Gligor (2002) proposed a distributed key establishment mechanism that relies on probabilistic key sharing among the nodes of a random graph and uses a shared-key discovery protocol for key establishment. Chan, Perrig, and Song (2003) presented several extensions to the mechanism and provided solutions for node authentication and key revocation. Jolly, Kuşçu, and Kokate (2002) proposed a hierarchical key management scheme for sensor networks. In this scheme, nodes only communicate with their gateway and each node shares a key with its corresponding gateway. Based on probabilistic key sharing and threshold secret sharing, Zhu, Setia, and Jajodia (2003) proposed a scheme for enabling two nodes in a network to establish a pair-wise secret key exclusively known to these nodes with overwhelming probability. In this scheme, a node only needs to know another node's id to be able to determine the keys it shares with that node. Under the scheme, all nodes are assumed to be trusted. Any node can generate the preloaded keys that any other node possesses. Thus, in principle a malicious node t, knowing the set of keys that a neighbor node x possess, need only receive and decrypt all messages destined to x to collect all shares for a pair-wise secret key that some other node y is establishing with x, and thus compromise the secret key that is being established, without any collusion. Du et al. (2003) and Liu and Ning (2003) proposed random key predistribution schemes that exploit deployment knowledge to avoid unnecessary key assignments. They have shown that the performance of WSNs can be substantially improved with the use of these schemes. However, the assumption of prior knowledge about deployment may not be applicable in many cases.

With the exception of LEAP in Zhu, Setia, and Jajodia (2003), in-network processing by a group of nodes has not been addressed. LEAP (localized encryption and authentication protocol) is a hybrid key agreement protocol implementing a suite of key agreement solutions using keys at four levels, namely network, neighborhood, node pair, and individual node levels, that are stored at the sensor node to accommodate the various communication models in WSNs. LEAP uses only the base station and the individual sensor nodes for all computation and communications. It also uses key translation from one hop to the next to ensure freshness of a network-level key.

Most existing solutions in security management in WSNs assume unique node identifiers and therefore do not address the case of anonymous nodes. Also, most schemes preload sensor nodes with individual (or small group) state information. Furthermore, most solutions do not address node rekeying or security at different levels of granularity. Quite recently, Wadaa, Olariu, Wilson, and Eltoweissy (2004) proposed a key management solution that assumes anonymous nodes and is applicable to members that are individual nodes or geographically affiliated subgroups of nodes. Also, their scheme preloads all nodes with identical states and supports both forward and backward secrecy as nodes are added or removed. The key management solution in Wadaa, Olariu, Wilson, and Eltoweissy (2004) is based on a combinatorial formulation of the key management problem and uses no communication to initialize nodes with their set of keys. The key management functions, however, are centralized in the base station.

NEW APPROACH TO SECURING SENSORS AND WSNs

WSN security research is in its infancy. There still is a need to provide new simple, energy-efficient solutions to securing sensors and WSNs. This section discusses an approach to satisfying the security goals subject to the myriad constraints imposed on sensors and WSNs. This chapter promotes a holistic security solution integrated within and encompassing the different network layers. This may result in more effective solutions to mitigate security threats, especially in massive deployment of WSNs with anonymous nodes. The approach should enable managed network mission and tasks, communication anonymity and confidentiality, and protection against physical tampering, impersonation, and denial of service. The solution components of the new approach include the following:

- innovative use of "sensor's genetic material" to affect randomized time and frequency hopping that limits traffic collision and avoids incorporating data keys;
- leveraging a location-based, color-coded virtual infrastructure as a common infrastructure supporting multitasking with reduced collision and lightweight WSN protocols including traffic anonymity, routing, authentication, and tamper proofing;
- a task-based operation model; and
- a lightweight, task-based synchronization protocol.

The result is a holistic lightweight adaptive security solution for large-scale WSNs that can securely operate unattended in hostile environment for an extended period of time. Subsequent sections describe the building blocks of the approach, and the final section discusses how these building blocks can be used to develop secure sensors and WSNs solutions.

Genetic Material

Sensors in our proposal are equipped with frequency-hopping communications capabilities. Also, sensors may have more than one sensing capability. The basic idea is to inject individual sensors prior to deployment with randomization capabilities that we refer to as *genetic material*. The genetic material of individual sensors enables behavioral parameters that can be tailored for group communication and cooperation, as well as for supporting a sophisticated task-based management scheme. In addition, the genetic material supports

- short-lived, group-oriented, and task-driven sensor synchronization;
- the use of a time-varying, parameterized frequency-hopping scheme;
- decentralized operation and management; and
- traffic anonymity.

Just prior to deployment (perhaps onboard the aircraft that drops them in the terrain), it is assumed that the sensors are injected with *genetic material* that includes

- a standard public domain, pseudorandom number generator;
- a set of tuples $(c_i, k(c_i))$, $(1 \leq i \leq p)$, where c_i is a color, and $k(c_i)$ is a *secret* associated with color c_i;
- a perfect hash function ϕ; and
- an initial time. At this point all the clocks are synchronous; later because of clock drift synchronization is lost.

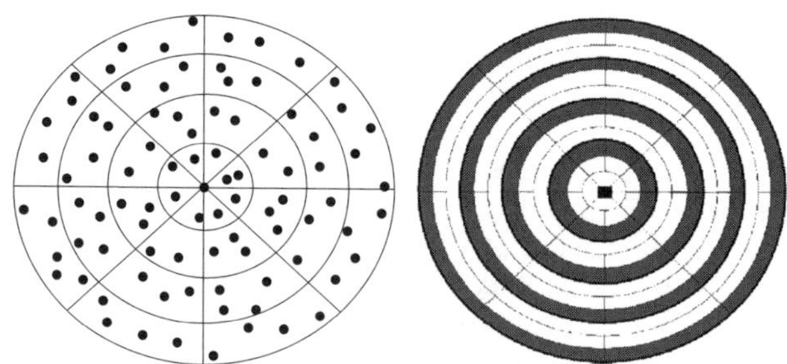

Figure 4: (a) Illustrating the dynamic coordinate system; (b) Illustrating color sets.

The Virtual Infrastructure

Because flat architectures do not scale and present a problem for large-scale synchronization, it is important to endow the WSN with a virtual infrastructure that can be leveraged for efficient protocol design. The virtual infrastructure that is proposed in Wadaa et al. (2004) 0 consists of

- a dynamic coordinate system,
- a cluster structure, and
- a communications structure that is described in some detail shortly.

To help with organizing the virtual infrastructure, it is assumed that a centrally placed training agent (TA) exists, equipped with a long-range radio that can communicate with both the base station and the sensors in the deployment area. More than one TA can coexist in a sensor field. For simplicity, only one TA is being considered in this chapter. The TA is assumed to have a steady power supply. Its precise role will become clear later. The dynamic coordinate system divides the deployment area into coronas and wedges (Figure 4) defined as follows:

Coronas. Using differential transmission power, the area is ruled into coronas determined by concentric circles of increasing radii centered at the TA. All coronas have the same width, slightly less than the sensor transmission range (the case for equal-width coronas was made in Wadaa et al., 2004).

Wedges. These are equiangular wedges centered at the TA obtained by using directional transmission.

The resulting coordinate system is dynamic because it can be reestablished in response to changing network conditions. By using signal strength readings obtained during the establishment of the coordinate system, each sensor selects one of the p colors, say `ci`, and remembers the associated secret `k(ci)`. All the other tuples in its memory are deleted at this point. The effect of this autonomous choice of colors by individual sensor nodes is that coronas are further subdivided into p color sets in an efficient way. In each corona, the color sets are numbered, in the same order, from `1` to `p` as shown in Figure 4b. As a result, the WSN is partitioned into p color graphs, where a color graph is the communication graph that has the

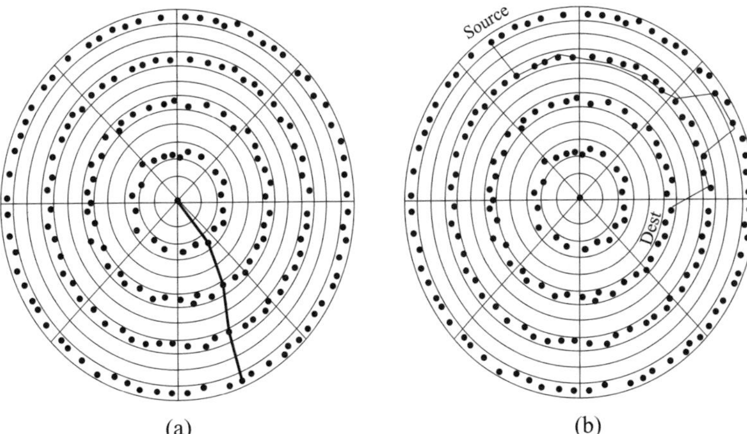

Figure 5: (a) Centralized communication structure; (b) Distributed communication structure.

sensors of the same color as vertices with two sensors connected by an edge whenever they are within transmission range of each other. This, in effect, establishes multiple networks, each with its own color code. It is worth noting that the assumed width of coronas combined with a massive deployment guarantee that the color graphs are (initially) connected with high probability. The optimum number of colors and dynamic merging/splitting of colors resulting from changing network dynamics are issues to be investigated.

The dynamic coordinate system suggests a simple clustering scheme, where a cluster is the locus of all sensors that have the same coordinates. It is important to note that clustering is obtained for free once the coordinate system is established. Also, our clustering scheme does not assume synchronization and accommodates sensor anonymity: sensors need not know the identity of the other sensors in their cluster. Depending on the way the information is collected in the WSN, two communication structures are contemplated. In the centralized structure illustrated in Figure 5 sensing data collected in a source cluster are routed, within the same wedge, along a virtual path to the TA, where the data are uploaded to the sink.

In the distributed structure illustrated in Figure 5 data collected in a source cluster are routed to a destination cluster from where the data are uploaded to the sink. Note that the routing illustrated in Figure 5 involves only sensors in the same color graph.

Task-Based Operation and Management

We take the view that the WSN performs tasks mandated by a remote end user. The task-based operation for WSN leverages the virtual infrastructure previously discussed. The task-based management system involves an *application layer* (high-level consumer of information produced by the WSN) and *middleware* (the interface between the WSN and the application layer).

To illustrate, the application issues A tasks, defined in terms of application-level abstractions, to be performed by the WSN. An A task takes the form of a tuple consisting of a high-level action and a desired level of QoS. As an example, the A task (Fire, q) requires that the occurrence of fire in the area of interest be correctly detected with probability of at least q, where q specifies the requested QoS.

The middleware, running at the base station, provides the interface between the application layer and the WSN. It parses the A tasks from the application layer, considers the current capabilities of the WSN including the remaining energy budget, and negotiates a contract with the application layer before committing the network. After a contract had been agreed upon, the middleware translates the corresponding A task into primitive tasks (P tasks) assigned to individual clusters. The clusters must then perform these P tasks at the QoS level required and send the data back to the sink for consolidation. The suitably consolidated information is then passed on to the application layer. A P task is a tuple T(A,c,S,D,π,Q), where

- `A` describes the action to be performed, say detecting the presence of smoke;
- `c` specifies the color graph to be used;
- `S` specifies the identity of the cluster tasked with data collection (sensing);
- `D` specifies the identity of the cluster tasked with storing the resulting information;
- π specifies the sequence of clusters along which the data is to be sent from `S` to `D`; and
- `Q` specifies the desired QoS.

In addition to the sensors in cluster `S`, a number of sensors are selected to act as routers, relaying the data collected to `D`. Collectively these sensors are the workforce `W(T)` associated with `T`. Note that the path π is either explicitly stated by the base station, along with `S` and `D`, or else is determined in a distributed way by the sensors in `W(T)`. The process by which `W(T)` is selected follows. During a time interval of length, the base station issues a call for work containing the parameters of T. The sensors that happen to wake up during the interval (and that satisfy the conditions specified (color, energy level, membership in S, D, or () stay awake and constitute W(T). It is intuitively clear that by knowing the number of sensors, the density of deployment, and the expected value of sleep periods, one can finetune (in such a way that W(T) is commensurate with the desired QoS. It is extremely important to note that a by-product of the call for work is that all the sensors in W(T) are synchronized for the duration of the task.

Sensor Synchronization

It is clear that to leverage the virtual infrastructure and the task-based view, the sensors participating in a task must be synchronized. Because large-scale synchronization in a WSN is impossible (Moharum, Mukkamala, and Eltoweissy 2004) proposed a synchronization scheme that is both group-based and short-lived. The discussion begins with a generic protocol that will be later specialized to suit the stated needs.

Using the genetic material, each sensor can generate (pointers into) three sequences of random numbers as follows:

- a sequence $t_1, t_2, \ldots, t_i$, of time epoch lengths;
- a sequence $n_1, n_2, \ldots, n_i, \ldots$ of frequency sets drawn from a huge universe, for example, the ISM band;
- for every i, $(i \geq 1)$, a permutation $f_{1i}, f_{2i}, \ldots$ of frequencies from the set n_i.

The interpretation of these sequences is as follows. Time is ruled into epochs: during the ith time epoch, of length ti, frequency set ni is used, subject to the hopping sequence $f_{1i}, f_{2i}, \ldots$ Thus, as long as a sensor is synchronous to the TA, it knows the current time epoch, the offset into the epoch, and the frequencies and the hopping pattern for that epoch. Suppose that the TA dwells τ microseconds on each frequency in the hopping sequence. For every i, $(i \geq 1)$, let l_i stand for t_i/τ. Thus, epoch t_i involves a hopping sequence of length l_i. Think of epoch t_i as being partitioned into l_i slots, with each slot using its own frequency selected by the hopping pattern from the set n_i. It is clear that determining the epoch and the offset of the TA in the epoch is sufficient for synchronization.

Our synchronization protocol is predicated on the assumption that sensor clock drift is bounded. Specifically, assume that whenever a sensor wakes up and its local clock shows epoch ti, the master clock at the TA is in one of the time epochs t_{i-1}, t_i, or t_{i+1}. Using its genetic information, the sensor knows the last frequencies λ_{i-1}, λ_i and λ_{i+1} on which the TA will dwell in the three times epochs t_{i-1}, t_i, and t_{i+1}, respectively. Its strategy, therefore, is to tune in, cyclically, to these frequencies, spending $\tau/3$ time units on each of them. It is clear that, eventually, the sensor meets the TA on one of these frequencies. Assume, without loss of generality, that the sensor meets the TA on frequency λ in some (unknown) slots of one of the epochs t_{i-1}, t_i, or t_{i+1}. To verify the synchronization, the sensor will attempt to meet the TA in slots $s+1$, $s+2$, and $s+3$ at the start of the next epoch. If a match is found, the sensor declares itself synchronized. Otherwise, the sensor will repeat this process. It is important to understand that the synchronization protocol outlined is probabilistic: even if a sensor declares itself synchronized, there is a slight chance that it is not. However, a missynchronization will be discovered quickly and the sensor will reattempt synchronization.

The generic synchronization protocol can be used as a building block for a more sophisticated task-based synchronization protocol. The motivation is that, because several color sets are present in a cluster, it is possible for a cluster to perform several tasks in parallel. However, any attempt at synchronization using the generic synchronization protocol will result in all the concurrent tasks using exactly the same frequency set and the same hopping sequence, creating frequent collisions and the need for subsequent retransmission. Suppose that one wishes to synchronize the workforce W(T) of a task T that uses some color graph c and that the generic synchronization protocol would show that the actual time epoch is t_i. The idea is to use the perfect hash function ϕ to compute a *virtual* time epoch t_j with $j = \phi(I, c, k(c))$ to be used by W(T). Therefore, the sensors in W(T) will act as if the real time were t_j, using the frequency set n_j and the frequency hopping sequence $f_{1j}, f_{2j}, \ldots$. Thus different concurrent tasks will employ different frequency sets and hopping sequences, minimizing the occurrence of collisions.

Note that this task-based synchronization is, in fact, a very powerful and lightweight physical layer encryption device. Indeed, to an outside observer, successive epoch lengths, hopping sets, and hopping patterns appear as the product of an unknown random process. Given that techniques are known to discover a hopping sequence by monitoring transmissions, security can only be provided if the design modifies the hopping sequence in less time than is required to discover the sequence. The choice of frequency-hopping parameters determines the time required to discover the sequence (the magnitude of the challenge to an adversary).

Security Proposal for Sensors and WSNs: Applying the New Approach

Ways in which the previously mentioned building blocks can be leveraged to address several important issues are described. These include making sensors tamper resistant, helping authentication, and providing traffic anonymity in WSNs. The following analogy with biology inspires our approach for securing individual sensors and WSNs. At birth, a crab is vulnerable because its shell is soft. In time, the shell hardens, affording appropriate protection. Because sensors are anonymous, they rely on received power levels from their neighbors to establish a unique signature of their neighborhood that is difficult to forge. The "hardening shell" paradigm applies in our context in the following way: immediately after deployment, individual sensors have no information about their neighborhood. In time, they overhear the transmissions of other sensors. Every time a new power level is detected, a new entry is recorded in the Neighborhood Signature Array (NSA) that individual sensors maintain. It is important to recall that the NSA is the only data available to the sensor node. This array establishes, in the obvious way, a signature of the neighborhood of the node. As discussed in the following sections, the NSA confers tamper resistance to individual sensors and can also be used for authentication purposes. In fact, the hardening shell paradigm refers to the fact that the protection afforded by the NSA increases with the number of neighbors recorded and, therefore, with time. Consequently, the vulnerability of individual sensors decreases with time.

Securing Individual Sensors

Because sensors must function unattended, the potential for physical tampering is significant. It is worth noting that although predeployment tamper detection may be worthwhile, post-deployment tamper detection is of little use because, in the vast majority of applications, inspecting individual sensors is impossible or impractical.

The most obvious tamper resistance strategies are hardware-based and involve special hardware circuits within the sensor to protect sensitive data, special coatings, or tamper seals. However, these solutions require extra circuitry that increases the cost and hardware complexity of sensors. Thus, not surprisingly, tamper resistance or tamper protection for sensors is not found in present-day sensors (Carman, Kruus, & Matt, 2000). Probabilistic tamper resistance for WSNs has been proposed in Chan, Perrig, and Song (2003) using cryptographic keys that incur noticeable overhead. Our solution to endowing sensors with tamper resistance does not require additional or more sophisticated hardware. The tampering threat model assumes that the adversary is either trying to force open an individual sensor in situ or is attempting to physically remove the sensor from the deployment area. The assumption is that once removed, the genetic material can be learned and the sensor compromised. The proposal is to guard against the first threat by blanking out the memory, triggered by a simple switch. The remainder of this section shows how the NSA can be used to endow sensors with tamper resistance. If a sensor is removed from the deployment area, it will notice changes in the signals received when compared to its NSA and erase its own memory. Note also that tampering attempts that involve the removal of several sensor nodes simultaneously will also be defeated because some node in the set of removed nodes will notice changes in its NSA and can alert the others.

Yet another possible solution to the tampering problem solution is as follows: The TA sends out periodically a control signal covering the entire deployment area that allows individual sensors to reconfirm their distance to the TA. If the sensor is removed from the area of deployment, it will notice changes in the signal strength received (and thus, color) from the TA and will erase its own memory, preventing the tampering agent from gaining access to information secret to the WSN.

Sensor authentication is one of the key problems in securing WSNs (Akyildiz, Su, Sankarasubramaniam, & Cayirci, 2002; Chan, Perrig, & Song, 2003; Wood & Stankovic, 2002). Frequency hopping and the tamper proofing scheme may prevent sensors from being compromised. The security threat for the purpose of authentication is an external sensor attempting to masquerade as a legitimate one. In particular, it is conceivable, although extremely unlikely, that the intruder is able to guess the set of frequencies and the hopping sequence in the current epoch and is requesting information from one of its neighbors. However, neighboring sensors exchange color information, which is orthogonal to frequency hopping, adding yet another barrier for the intruder.

The sensor authentication problem can also be tackled using the NSA signature array. Here, using the frequency-hopping scheme, neighboring sensors exchange and update periodically their NSA information (as well as color information). When sensor A wants to send data to B, the authentication procedure is to have A produce the proper NSA information. In fact, the NSA information is likely to change slowly over time as sensors deplete their energy. In this case, the authentication procedure may request, "Give me your next-to-last NSA reading."

Securing WSNs

Denial of service attacks that target key nodes in the communication network or compromise communications in some other way could undermine the functionality as well as the performance delivered by the WSN (Chan, Perrig, & Song, 2003; Wood & Stankovic, 2002). Particularly vulnerable are the components of the virtual infrastructure. Because knowledge of the virtual infrastructure can be instrumental for successfully compromising network security, maintaining the anonymity of the virtual infrastructure is a primary security concern. Somewhat surprisingly, in spite of its importance, the anonymity problem has not been addressed by prior work in WSNs. The aforementioned virtual infrastructure, developed by the authors, can be leveraged to provide traffic anonymity in WSNs. Solutions, leveraging the virtual infrastructure, define schemes for randomizing communications such that the cluster structure and coordinate system used remain undetectable and invisible to an observer of network traffic during both the setup and operation phases of the network. It is worth noting that traffic anonymity in wired networks is achieved by injecting spurious traffic into the network, essentially hiding the actual traffic. The associated cost in terms of energy makes this strategy impractical in WSNs. Two possible solutions can be contemplated. The *centralized* solution is by far the simplest and involves relying on traffic randomization specified by an entity external to the WSN. Consider a sequence T_1, $T_2, \ldots, T_n$ of P tasks to be performed by the WSN. Although the source cluster Si of task T_i may be dictated by specific interests of the end user, the choice of the destination cluster D_i and the specific path π_i along with the information is sent to D_i can be chosen externally in such a way that the overall traffic is randomized.

The *distributed* solution is more complex and it relies on the genetic material available at individual sensors. To understand the idea behind the distributed solution to the traffic anonymity problem, imagine that in time epoch t_i a cut through the coordinate system of Figure 4a is performed as illustrated in Figure 6. Consider a task $T = (A,c,D,\pi,Q)$ issued during time epoch t_i. The idea is that both D and π are determined by individual sensors (using their genetic material) as a function of the location of S and need not be specified explicitly. In Figure 6, the dark circles denote destination clusters and data is routed along a predetermined path. Because the cut is different from epoch to epoch, the net effect of this approach is to randomize the traffic in the WSN, making it look chaotic to an external observer.

In time, as individual sensors deplete their energy, the functionality of the WSN is bound to decrease. One of the main goals of our research is to address not only the ideal

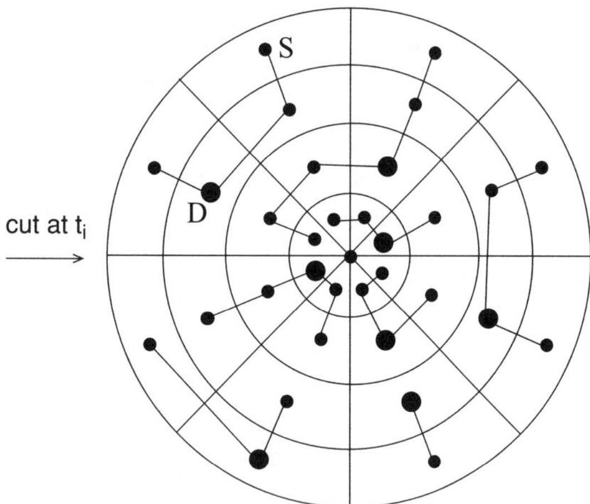

Figure 6: Illustrating the distributed solution.

case where all the sensors deployed function at their peak performance level, but, indeed, the point at which system performance decreases to a point where graceful degradation must be contemplated. One such situation, depicted in Figure 7, arises in the course of exploiting the WSN. Indeed, as the sensors exhaust their power budget more and more *gaps* will be formed in the communication structure. One proposal is to model the communication structure as a *circular arc graph* (Golumbic, 1980) and tap into known algorithmic resources that can help with the design of secure protocols for sparse WSNs.

CONCLUSION AND DIRECTIONS FOR FUTURE RESEARCH

It is anticipated that in the near future wireless sensor networks will be employed in a wide variety of applications, establishing ubiquitous networks that will pervade society. It is widely recognized that sensor network research is in its infancy (Akyildiz, Su, Sankarasubramaniam, & Cayirci, 2002). In particular, there is precious little known about how WSNs self-organize in a way that maximizes the effectiveness and operational longevity of the network and that guarantees a high level of availability in the face of potential security attacks. Given the characteristics of WSNs, security protocols developed for wired, cellular, or ad hoc networks do not apply. Also, cryptographic key–based solutions generally are too expensive for the tiny sensors. This chapter presented a survey of key conceptual and technological security issues in WSN environments. It also reported on some research efforts and solution to the problem of securing WSNs.

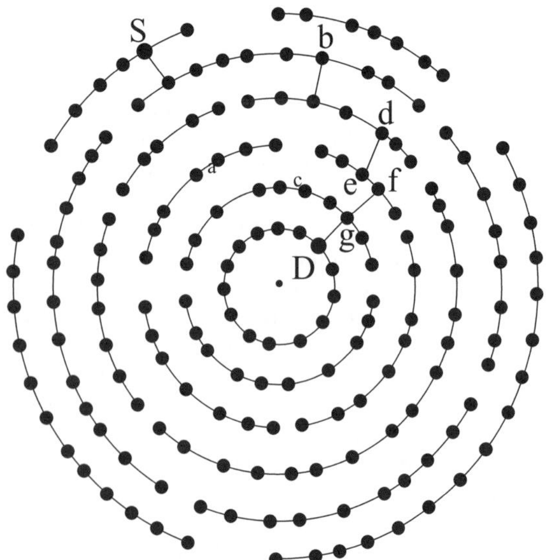

Figure 7: Illustrating sparsity in wireless sensor networks.

An aim of this chapter is to motivate the development of a holistic solution for securing WSNs. It has been shown that a suitable enhancement to the classic frequency-hopping strategy may provide a lightweight and scalable mechanism for securing sensors and WSNs. At the network level, a generic virtual infrastructure and lightweight communications and tasking protocols can be used to ensure sensor collaboration in a coherent and authentic way while hiding the details of the network topology and the information flowing among nodes. Tamper proofing and authentication of (initially) anonymous nodes are provided through the concept of neighborhood context.

Issues currently (at the time of writing) under investigation in our research include (a) sensor circuitry, storage, types, attributes, and behavior of the genetic material; (b) The placement of the TA, having multiple TAs, and the distribution of the TA's functions; and (c) The granularity of synchronization and adaptation to varying network conditions. Finally, modifications to the UCB motes are needed to achieve security objectives addressed in this chapter without demanding a boost in the sensor's capabilities that is inconsistent with the small cost and size requirements.

A major open research direction is securing multitier WSNs. As far as we know, comprehensive security solutions covering the different tiers of WSNs (sensor nodes to sinks including subsink layers) do not exist. Multitier architectures where different tiers may employ different security solutions is an area that warrants investigation. Although asymmetric cryptography is generally dismissed for WSNs, a multitier WSN may employ powerful nodes at higher tiers that may be capable of performing asymmetric cryptography. We envision the emergence of solutions that employ frequency hopping, symmetric cryptography, and asymmetric cryptography in a common framework.

Another area of research is context-aware privacy and security in WSNs. Because WSNs will present an essential component of the emerging pervasive computing environments and because these new environments must be sensitive to users' resources and environmental contexts, it is imperative that privacy and security solutions for WSNs are devised, taking into account context semantics and dynamics. For example, higher levels of security may be needed in an unfriendly context, whereas security may be relatively relaxed in friendlier contexts. Context definition and representation; agile security, services, and protocols; and privacy preservation in a changing environment are some of the open research problems.

ACKNOWLEDGMENTS

This work was supported in part by a grant from the Commonwealth of Virginia Technology Research Fund (SE 2001-01) .

GLOSSARY

Administrative Keys Cryptographic keys used to distribute session keys and other administrative keys.

Frequency Hopping A scheme where communications hop from one channel frequency to another in a pseudorandom fashion.

Key Management This refers to session and administrative key assignment, generation, and distribution.

Sensor Network A network where sensor nodes communicate with each other and with one or more base stations.

Sensor Node A device with computing, communication, and sensing capabilities.

Session Keys Cryptographic keys used in secure data communications.

Sink (or Base Station) A computing node charged with tasking sensor nodes and collecting data from them.

Training Agent A base station, or subbase station node, tasked to do WSN training.

Wireless Sensor Networks (WSNs) A sensor network with wireless links and no physical communications infrastructure.

WSN Security This refers to the protection of confidentiality, availability, integrity, and authenticity of data in WSNs.

WSN Training The process of bootstrapping a WSN and endowing it with a virtual infrastructure.

WSN Virtual Infrastructure A logical infrastructure that is built to help render the WSN functional by providing means for sensor node identification and communications.

CROSS REFERENCES

See *Computer and Network Authentication; Encryption Basics; Key Management; Radio Frequency and Wireless Communications Security; Wireless Channels.*

REFERENCES

http://www.bluetooth.com/upload/24Security_Chapter.PDF

Akkaya, K., & Younis, M. (2005). A survey on routing protocols for wireless sensor networks. *Journal of Ad Hoc Networks* (to appear).

Akyildiz, I. F., Su, W., Sankarasubramaniam, Y., & Cayirci, E. (2002). Wireless sensor networks: A survey. *Computer Networks, 38*, 393–422.

Binkley, J., & Trost, W. M. (2001). Authenticated ad hoc routing at the link layer for mobile systems. *Wireless Networks, 7*(2), 139–145.

Buchegger, S., & Le Boudec, J.-Y. (2002). Nodes bearing grudges: Towards routing security, fairness, and robustness in mobile ad hoc networks. In *Proceedings of the Tenth Euromicro Workshop on Parallel, Distributed and Network-based Processing* (pp. 403–410). [location]: IEEE Computer Society.

Buczak, A., & Jamalabad, V. (1998). Self-organization of a heterogeneous sensor network by genetic algorithms. In C. H. Dagli (Ed.), *Intelligent engineering systems through artificial neural networks* (Vol. 8). New York: ASME Press.

Canetti, R., & Pinkas, B. (1998, May). A taxonomy of multicast security issues (Internet draft).

Carman, D., Kruus, P., & Matt, B. (2000, September). *Constraints and approaches for distributed sensor networks security* (Technical Report 00–010). NAI Labs.

Chan, H., Perrig, A., & Song, D. (2003, May). Random key pre-distribution schemes for sensor networks. In *Proceedings of IEEE 2003 Symposium on Security and Privacy*, Berkeley, CA.

Chang, I., et al. (1999, March). Key management for secure Internet multicast using Boolean function minimization techniques. In *Proceedings of IEEE Infocom'99*.

Crossbow Technology. (n.d.). Retrieved from www.xbow.com

Douceur, J. R. (2002, March). The Sybil attack. In *1st International Workshop on Peer-to-Peer Systems (IPTPS '02)*.

Du, W., Deng, J., Han, Y. S., & Varshney, P. K. (2003, October). A pairwise key pre-distribution scheme for wireless sensor networks. In *Proceedings of the 10th ACM Conference on Computer and Communications Security (CCS '03)*, Washington, DC.

Eschenauer, L., & Gligor, V. (2002, November). A key management scheme for distributed sensor networks. In *Proceedings of the 9th ACM Conference on Computing and Communication Security*.

Estrin, D., Govindan, R., Heidemann, J., & Kumar, S. (1999, August). Next century challenges: Scalable coordination in sensor networks. In *Proceedings of the Fifth Annual International Conference on Mobile Computing and Networks (MobiCOM '99)*, Seattle, WA.

Ganesan, D., Govindan, R., Shenker, S., & Estrin, D. (2001, October). Highly resilient, energy-efficient multipath routing in wireless sensor networks. *Mobile Computing and Communications Review, 4*(5).

Golumbic, M. (1980). *Algorithmic graph theory and perfect graphs*. New York: Academic Press.

Horton, M., et al. (2002, April). Mica: The commercialization of microsensor motes. *Sensors Online Magazine*. Retrieved from http://www.sensorsmag.com/articles/0402/40/main.shtml

Hu, Y. C., Perrig, A., & Johnson, D. B. (2002, June). Wormhole detection in wireless ad hoc networks (Technical Report TR01-384). Houston, Texas: Department of Computer Science, Rice University.

Intanagonwiwat, C., Govindan, R., & Estrin, D. (2000, August). Directed diffusion: A scalable and robust communication paradigm for sensor networks. In *Proceedings of the 6th IEEE/ACM Annual Conference on Mobile Computing and Networks (MobiCOM'00)*.

Jolly, G., Kuşçu, M., & Kokate, P. (2002, November). A hierarchical key management method for low-energy wireless sensor networks (UMBC Online Document).

Jolly, G., & Younis, M. (2005) An energy efficient, scalable and collisionless MAC layer protocol for wireless sensor networks. *Journal of Wireless Networks and Mobile Computing* (to appear).

Karlof, C., & Wagner, D. (2005). Secure routing in sensor networks: Attacks and countermeasures. *AdHoc Networks*, Special Issue on Sensor Network Applications and Protocols (to appear).

Kong, J., et al. (2001). Providing robust and ubiquitous security support for mobile ad-hoc networks, In *Proceedings of the 9th International Conference on Network Protocols* (pp. 251–260). Los Alamitos, CA: IEEE CS Press.

Kyasanur, P., & Vaidya, N. (2002, August). Detection and handling of MAC layer misbehavior in wireless networks (Technical Report). Department of Computer Science, University of Illinois at Urbana–Champaign.

Liu, D., & Ning, P. (2003). Establishing pairwise keys in distributed sensor networks. In Proceedings of the ACM Conference on Computer and Communications Security (CCS '03) (pp. 52–61).

Lundberg, J. (2000). Routing security in ad hoc networks (Technical Report). Finland: Helsinki University of Technology.

Marti, S., et al. (2000, August). Mitigating routing misbehavior in mobile ad-hoc networks. In *Proceedings of MOBICOM '2000*, Boston.

Min, R., et al. (2001, January). Low power wireless sensor networks. In *Proceedings of Internation Conference on VLSI Design*, Bangalore, India.

Moharum, M., Mukkamala, R., & Eltoweissy, M. (2004). CKDS: An efficient combinatorial key distribution scheme for wireless ad hoc networks. In *IEEE Workshop on Energy-Efficient Wireless Computing and Networking (EWCN 2004)*.

National Research Council. (2001). Embedded everywhere. Washington, DC: National Academy Press.

Perrig, A., et al. (2002). SPINS: Security protocols for sensor networks. *Wireless Networks, 8*(5), 521–534.

Pottie, G. J., & Kaiser, W. J. (2000, May). Wireless integrated network sensors. *Communications of the ACM, 43*(5), 51–58. Rabaey, J. M., et al. (2000, July). PicoRadio supports ad hoc ultra low power wireless networking. *IEEE Computer, 33*, 42–48.

Shah, R., & Rabaey, J. (2002, March). Energy aware routing for low energy ad hoc sensor networks. In *Proceedings of the IEEE Wireless Communications and Networking Conference (WCNC)*, Orlando, FL.

Shih, E., et al. (2001, July). Physical layer driven algorithm and protocol design for energy-efficient wireless sensor networks. In *Proceedings of the 7th ACM Mobile Computing and Communication (MobiCom 2001)*, Rome, Italy.

Singh, S., & Raghavendra, C. S. (1998, July). PAMAS: Power aware multi-access protocol with signaling for ad hoc networks. *ACM Computer Communications Review*.

Sohrabi, K., et al. (2000). Protocols for self-organization of a wireless sensor network. *IEEE Personal Communications*, 7(5), 16–27. Spec takes the next step. (n.d.). Retrieved [date] from http://www.jlhlabs.com/jhill_cs/spec/index.htm

Wadaa, A., Olariu, S., Wilson, L., & Eltoweissy, M. (2004). Scalable key management for secure communications in wireless sensor networks. In *Proceedings of the International Workshop on Wireless Ad-hoc Networking*, Tokyo, Japan, March 23–26.

Wadaa, A., Olariu, S., Wilson, L., Eltoweissy, M., & Jones, K. (2004). Training a wireless sensor network. *Mobile Networks and Applications*.

Wadaa, A., Olariu, S., Wilson, L., Eltoweissy, M., & Jones, K. (2005, February). Training a sensor network. *MONET*, to appear.

Wang, H., Velayutham, A., & Guan, Y. (2003, December). A lightweight authentication protocol for access control in IEEE 802.11. In *Proceedings of IEEE Globecom 2003*, San Francisco, CA.

Wong, C. K., Gouda, M., & Lam, S. (1998, September). Secure group communications using key graphs. In *Proceedings of ACM SIGCOMM*, Vancouver, BC.

Woo, A., & Culler, D. (2001, July). A transmission control scheme for medium access in sensor networks. In *Proceedings of the 7th ACM Mobile Computing and Communication (MobiCom 2001)*, Rome, Italy.

Wood, A. D., & Stankovic, J. A. (2002). Denial of service in sensor networks, *IEEE Computer, 35*(10), 54–62.

Younis, M., Youssef, M., & Arisha, K. (2003). Energy-aware management in cluster-based sensor networks. *International Journal on Computer Networks, 43*(5), 649–668.

Zhu, S., Setia, S., & Jajodia, S. (2003, October). LEAP: Efficient security mechanisms for large-scale distributed sensor networks. In *Proceedings of the 10th ACM Conference on Computer and Communications Security (CCS '03)*, Washington, DC.

FURTHER READING

Burne, R., Kadar, I., Whitson, J., & Buczak, A. (2003). Self-organizing cooperative sensor network for remote surveillance: Improved target tracking results. In *Proceedings of the SPIE Conference on Unattended Ground Sensor Technologies and Applications*.

Chan, H., & Perrig, A. (2003, October). Security and privacy in sensor networks. *IEEE Computer, 36*(10): 103–105.

Eick, S. G., & Fyock, D. E. (1996). Visualizing corporate data. *IEEE Potentials, 15*(5), 6–11.

Gracanin, D., Eltoweissy, M., Olariu, S., & Wadaa, A. (2004, April). On modeling wireless sensor networks. *IEEE Workshop on Mobile Ad Hoc and Sensor Networks* (WMAN'04), to appear.

Heinzelman, W. (2000). Application specific protocol architectures for wireless networks. Unpublished doctoral dissertation, Department of Electrical Engineering, MIT.

Heinzelman, W., Chandrakasan, A., & Balakrishnan, H. (2000, January). Energy-efficient communication protocols for wireless microsensor networks. In *Proceedings of the Hawaii International Conference on System Sciences (HICSS)*.

Hill, J., Szewczyk, R., Woo, A., Hollar, S., Culler, D., & Pister, K. (2000, November). System architecture directions for networked sensors. In *Proceedings of 9th International Conference on Architectural Support for Programming Languages and Operating Systems (ASPLOS 2000)*, Cambridge, MA.

Jones, K., Wadaa, A., Olariu, A., Wilson, L., & Eltoweissy, M. (2003, August). Towards a new paradigm for securing wireless sensor networks. Paper presented at New Security Paradigms Workshop (NSPW 2003).

Krishnamachari, B., Estrin, D., & Wicker, S. (2002, June). Modeling data centric routing in wireless sensor networks. In *Proceedings of IEEE INFOCOM '02*. New York.

Levis, P., Lee, N., Welsh, M., & Culler, D. (2003, November). TOSSIM: Accurate and scalable simulation of entire tinyOS applications. In *Proceedings of the First International Conference on Embedded Networked Sensor Systems*, Los Angeles, CA.

Subramanian, L., & Katz, R. H. (2000, August). An architecture for building self configurable systems. In *Proceedings of IEEE/ACM Workshop on Mobile Ad Hoc Networking and Computing*, Boston, MA.

Tilak, S., Abu-Ghazaleh, N. B., & Heinzelman, W. (2002). A taxonomy of wireless microsensor network models. *ACM Mobile Computing and Communication Review (MC2R)*, 6(2), 1–8.

Wadaa, A. (2004, May). Unpublished doctoral dissertation, Department of Computer Science, Old Dominion University.

Warneke, B., Last, M., Leibowitz, B., & Pister, K. (2001). SmartDust: Communicating with a SmartDust: Communicating with a cubic-millimeter computer *IEEE Computer, 34*(1), 44–15.

Yao, Y., & Gehrke, J. (2002). The cougar approach to in-network query processing in sensor networks. *SIGMOD Record, 31*(3), 9–18.

Ye, F., Luo, H., Cheng, J., Lu, S., & Zhang, L. (2002, September). A two-tier data dissemination model for large-scale wireless sensor networks. In *Proceedings of the 8th IEEE/ACM Annual Conference on Mobile Computing and Networks (MobiCOM '02)*, Atlanta, GA.

Cellular Networks

Jingyuan Zhang, *University of Alabama*
Ivan Stojmenovic, *University of Ottawa, Canada*

INTRODUCTION

Cellular communications has experienced explosive growth in the past two decades. Today millions of people around the world use cellular phones. Cellular phones allow a person to make or receive a call from almost anywhere. Likewise, a person is allowed to continue the phone conversation while on the move. Cellular communications is supported by an infrastructure called a cellular network, which integrates cellular phones into the public switched telephone network.

The cellular network has gone through three generations. The first generation of cellular networks is analog in nature. To accommodate more cellular phone subscribers, digital TDMA (time division multiple access) and CDMA (code division multiple access) technologies are used in the second generation (2G) to increase the network capacity. With digital technologies, digitized voice can be coded and encrypted. Therefore, the 2G cellular network is also more secure. The third generation (3G) integrates cellular phones into the Internet world by providing high-speed packet-switching data transmission in addition to circuit-switching voice transmission. The 3G cellular networks have been deployed in some parts of Asia, Europe, and the United States since 2002 and will be widely deployed in the coming years.

This chapter gives an introduction to cellular networks. The rest of this chapter is organized as follows: the second section introduces basic cellular concepts, and the third section describes how the air interface is shared by multiple users. The fourth and fifth sections discuss how to track mobile users and how to assign channels to hand-off calls and new calls, respectively. The sixth section discusses the relevant security issues. The seventh section describes the evolution of cellular networks. The eighth section presents alternatives to cellular networks. The final section gives a summary.

BASIC CONCEPTS

A cellular network provides cell phones or mobile stations (MSs), to use a more general term, with wireless access to the public switched telephone network (PSTN). The service coverage area of a cellular network is divided into many smaller areas, referred to as cells, each of which is served by a base station (BS). The BS is fixed, and it is connected to the mobile telephone switching office (MTSO), also known as the mobile switching center. An MTSO is in charge of a cluster of BSs and it is, in turn, connected to the PSTN. With the wireless link between the BS and MS, MSs such as cell phones are able to communicate with wireline phones in the PSTN. Both BSs and MSs are equipped with a transceiver. Figure 1 illustrates a typical cellular network, in which a cell is represented by a hexagon and a BS is represented by a triangle.

The frequency spectrum allocated for cellular communications is very limited. The success of today's cellular network is mainly due to the frequency reuse concept. This is why the coverage area is divided into cells, each of which is served by a BS. Each BS (or cell) is assigned a group of frequency bands or channels. To avoid radio co-channel interference, the group of channels assigned to one cell must be different from the group of channels assigned to its neighboring cells. However, the same group of channels can be assigned to the two cells that are far enough apart such that the radio co-channel interference between them is within a tolerable limit. Typically, seven neighboring cells are grouped together to form a cluster, as shown in Figure 2. The total available channels are divided into seven groups, each of which is assigned to a cell. In Figure 2, the cells marked with the same number have the same group of channels assigned to them. Furthermore, the cells marked with different numbers must be assigned different groups of channels.

If there are a total of M channels allocated for cellular communications and if the coverage area consists of N cells, there are a total of $MN/7$ channels available in the coverage area for concurrent use based on the seven-cell reuse pattern. That is the network capacity of this coverage area. Because of explosive growth of mobile phone subscribers, the current network capacity may not be enough. Cell splitting is one technique that used to increase the network capacity without new frequency spectrum allocation (Black, 1996; Rappaport, 2002). In this technique, the cell size is reduced by lowering antenna

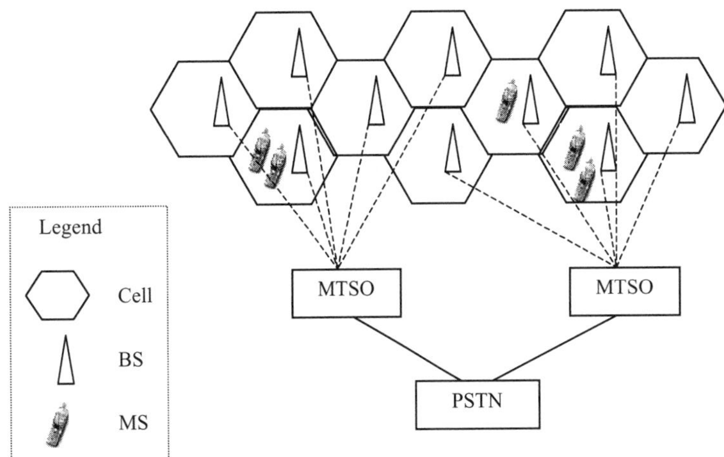

Figure 1: Typical cellular network.

height and transmitter power. Specifically, an original cell is divided into four smaller cells. After cell-splitting, the coverage area with *N* cells originally will be covered by 4*N* smaller cells. Therefore, the new network capacity is *4MN/7*, which is four times the original network capacity. In reality, bigger cells are not completely replaced by smaller cells. Therefore, cells of different sizes (e.g., pico, micro, and macro cells) may coexist in one area. This allows high-speed subscribers to use bigger cells, which reduces the number of hand-offs (to be explained later).

Sectoring is another technique to increase the network capacity (Black, 1996; Rappaport, 2002). In sectoring, the cell size remains the same, but a cell is divided into several sectors by using several directional antennas at the BS instead of a single omnidirectional antenna. Typically, a cell is divided into three 120° sectors or six 60° sectors. The radio co-channel interference will be reduced by dividing a cell into sectors, which reduces the number of cells in a cluster. Therefore, the network capacity is increased.

Digital technology can also be used to increase the network capacity. Transmission of digitized voice goes through three steps before the actual transmission: speech coding, channel coding, and modulation. Speech coding is to compress voice. For example, a short voice segment can be analyzed and represented by a few parameter values. These values cannot be transmitted directly because wireless transmission is error prone, and a small change in these values may translate into a big change in voice. Therefore, data representing compressed voice should be arranged carefully, and redundancy should be introduced such that a transmission error can be corrected or at least detected. This process is called channel coding. Finally, the output data from channel coding are modulated for transmission. The detailed information on speech coding, channel coding, and modulation can be found in three corresponding chapters in Rappaport (2002). A good speech-coding scheme combined with a good channel-coding scheme will greatly reduce the amount of bandwidth needed by each phone user and therefore increase the network capacity while keeping the quality of voice unchanged.

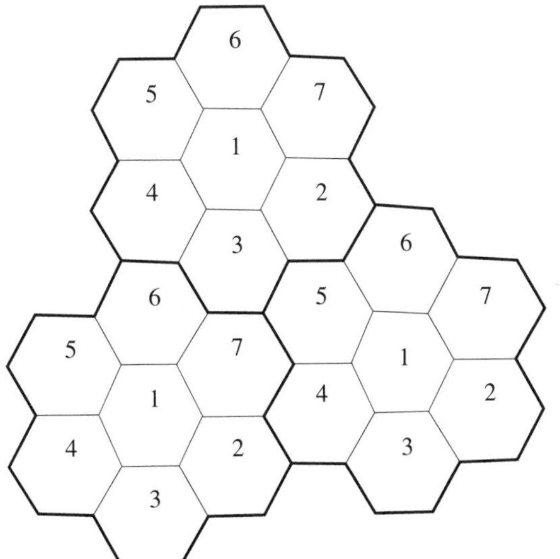

Figure 2: Frequency reuse.

The channels assigned to a cell are used either for voice or for control. A voice channel is used for an actual conversation, whereas a control channel is used to help set up conversations. Both voice and control channels are further divided into forward (or downlink) and reverse (or uplink). A forward channel is used to carry traffic from the BS to the MS, and a reverse channel is used to carry traffic from the MS to the BS. The channels assigned to a cell are shared by MSs located in the cell. Multiple access methods are used to share the channels in a cell.

Each MS has a home MTSO, which is the MTSO where the mobile user originally subscribed for wireless services. If an MS moves out of the home MTSO area, it is roaming. A roaming MS needs to register in the visited MTSO. An MS needs to be authenticated against the information kept in its home MTSO before any service can be rendered by the network. The services include making a call, receiving a call, registering the location, and so forth. These services are possible because of a widely used global, common channel-signaling standard named SS7 (Signaling System No. 7) (Modarressi & Skoog, 1992; Rappaport, 2002).

To make a call from an MS, the MS first needs to make a request using a reverse control channel in the current cell.

If the request is granted by MTSO, a pair of voice channels (one for transmitting and the other for receiving) is assigned for the call. Making a call to an MS is more complicated. The call is first routed to its home MTSO or its visited MTSO if it is roaming. The MTSO needs to know the cell in which the MS is currently located. Finding the residing cell of an MS is the subject of location management. Once the MTSO knows the residing cell of the MS, a pair of voice channels is assigned in the cell for the call.

If a call is in progress when the MS moves into a neighboring cell, the MS needs to get a new pair of voice channels from the BS of the neighboring cell so the call can continue. This process is called hand-off. A BS usually adopts a channel assignment strategy that prioritizes hand-off calls from neighboring cells over the new calls initiated in the current cell.

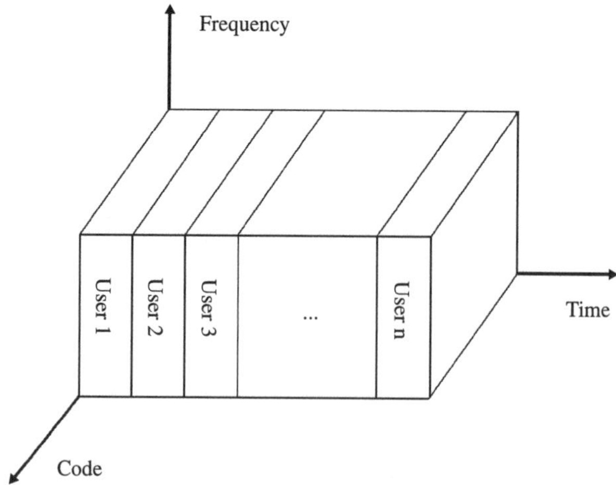

Figure 4: TDMA (time division multiple access).

MULTIPLE ACCESS METHODS

Within a cell covered by a BS, there are multiple MSs that need to communicate with the BS. Those mobile stations must share the air interface in an orderly manner so that no MSs within the cell interfere with each other. The methods for MSs to share the air interface in an orderly manner are referred to as multiple access methods. The popular multiple access methods include (frequency division multiple access) FDMA, TDMA, and CDMA.

FDMA divides the frequency spectrum assigned to the BS into several frequency bands, also known as channels, as shown in Figure 3. These channels are well separated and do not interfere with each other. An MS can use the assigned channel(s) exclusively. FDMA is used in the Advanced Mobile Phone System (AMPS) (Black, 1996, 1999). AMPS uses a total of 40 MHz in the 800-MHz spectrum, 825–845 MHz and 870–890 MHz, to be exact. (For ease of clarification, the additional 10 MHz added later is not considered here.) In AMPS, each channel has a bandwidth of 30 kHz, and the 40-MHz bandwidth translates into about 1332 channels. In the United States, it is required that two cellular communication providers be present in every market to encourage competition.

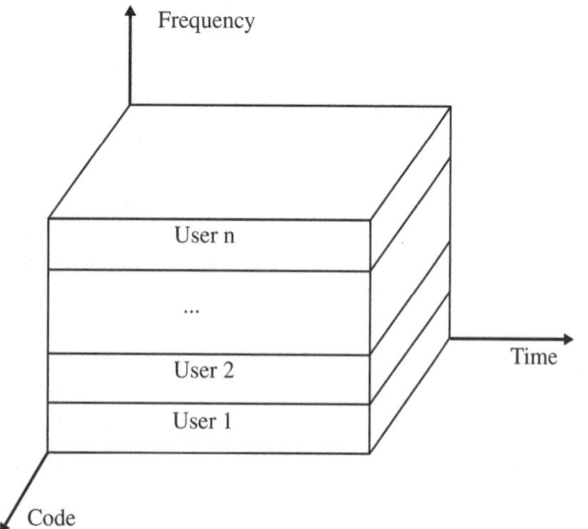

Figure 3: FDMA (frequency division multiple access).

Therefore, each cellular communication provider has 666 channels. AMPS uses FDD (frequency division multiplexing). That is, 333 channels are for communication from the BS to MSs and the other 333 channels are for communication from MSs to the BS. Among these 333 channels, only 312 channels are for voice traffic because 21 of them need to be used for control. Based on the seven-cell reuse pattern, only about 45 MSs within a cell can communicate with the BS simultaneously.

TDMA usually builds on FDMA and allows multiple MSs to share the same channel. In TDMA, time is slotted. In each time slot, only one MS is allowed to use the shared channel to transmit or receive. MSs take their turn transmitting or receiving in their allocated slots in a round-robin fashion. Although the channel is shared, no interference can arise among those sharing MSs because only one MS can use the channel at one time. Figure 4 illustrates the concept of TDMA.

Because an MS is not able to use the channel all the time, it is challenging to deliver voice, which is supposed to be continuous. Fortunately, an ordinary human can tolerate a delay of 20 milliseconds (ms). In D-AMPS (D for digital), a speech segment consists of 20-ms durations of speech. The speech segment is first digitized and then compared with the VSELP (vector sum excited linear predictive) Cookbook (Black, 1999). The index to the entry in the VSELP Cookbook that is closest to the digitized voice is transmitted instead of the digitized voice. The index is 159 bits long. At the receiving end, the digitized voice that is very close to the original voice can be retrieved based on the 159-bit index. In D-AMPS, which uses the same 30-kHz channel as AMPS, 159 bits (along with overhead bits for a total of 260 bits) can be transmitted in two of six time slots in a frame. At 25 frames per second, D-AMPS has three times the capacity of AMPS using the same number of channels. TDMA can operate in either the 800-MHz cellular spectrum (IS-54/D-AMPS; EIA/TIA, 1990) or the 1900-MHz PCS spectrum (IS-136; EIA/TIA, 1995).

CDMA takes an entirely different approach from TDMA. In CDMA, multiple MSs share the same wideband of spectrum. Instead of being assigned to time slots as in TDMA, each MS is assigned a unique sequence code. Each

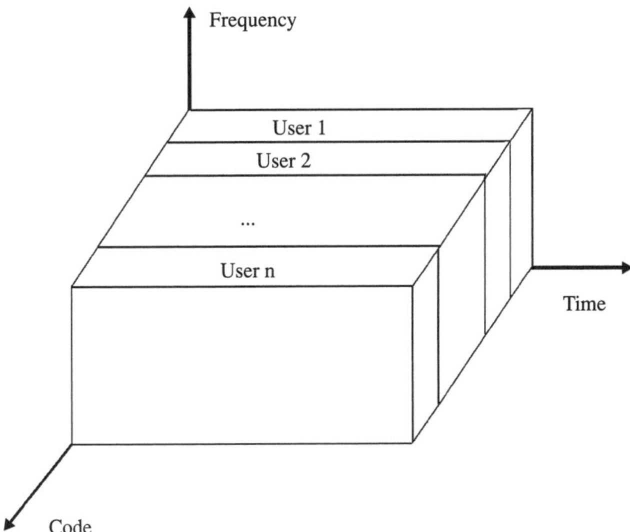

Figure 5: CDMA (code division multiple access).

MS's signal is spread over the entire bandwidth by the unique sequence code. At the receiver, that same unique code is used to recover the signal. Although the radio spectrum is shared, no interference can arise because the sequence codes used by the sharing MSs are basically orthogonal. Figure 5 illustrates the concept of CDMA. An excellent illustration of how CDMA encodes and decodes can be found in Stallings' text (2002). In principle, for CDMA to work, the signals received by the BS from different MSs must be at the same power level. To achieve this, a few bits in the forward control channel are set aside for power control. Specifically, the BS uses these bits to instruct each MS to increase or decrease its output power level such that all signals received at the BS have the same strength.

LOCATION MANAGEMENT

This section describes how to track an MS. How to keep track of an MS is the subject of location management in cellular networks. Because the exact location of an MS must be known to the cellular network when a call is in progress, location management tracks an active MS that is not in a call. (An MS is active when it is powered on.) Specifically, the cellular network needs to find out the exact cell in which an MS is located when an incoming call arrives for the MS.

An extreme case, known as "Never-Update" in Bar-Noy, Kessler, and Sidi (1995), is that an MS never tells the cellular network its location when it moves around. When an incoming phone call arrives for the MS, the cellular network needs to page all cells in the service area to find out the cell in which the MS is currently located so the incoming call can be routed to the BS of that cell. It will cost a great deal to page all cells in the service area. The other extreme case is known as "Always-Update," in which an MS needs to update its location whenever it moves into a new cell. When an incoming phone call arrives for the MS, the cellular network can just route the incoming call to the cell that is last reported by the MS. Obviously, there is no paging cost involved. However, the MS needs to tell the cellular network its location when it moves from cell to cell, which can also be very expensive.

There are two basic operations involved with location management: location update and paging. The paging operation is performed by the cellular network. When an incoming call arrives for an MS, the cellular network will page the MS in all possible cells to find out the cell in which the MS is located so the incoming call can be routed to the corresponding BS. The number of all possible cells to be paged is dependent on how frequent the location update operation is performed. The location update operation is performed by an MS. Both operations consume wireless bandwidth: location update uses reverse control channels, whereas paging utilizes forward control channels. Although the cost of location management involves both the wireline portion and the wireless portion of the cellular network, only the wireless portion is usually considered. This is mainly because the radio-frequency bandwidth is limited, whereas the bandwidth of the wireline network is easily expandable. Therefore, the location management cost is measured by the total wireless bandwidth consumed by both location update and paging operations, that is, the location update cost and the paging cost. There is a trade-off between the location update cost and the paging cost. For example, if an MS updates its location more frequently, the network knows the location of the MS better. It incurs a higher location update cost, but the paging cost will be lower when an incoming call arrives for the MS.

The location-areas scheme is used in current cellular networks. In the location-areas scheme, the whole service coverage area is partitioned into location areas, each of which consists of several contiguous cells. The BS of each cell broadcasts the ID of the location area to which the cell belongs. An MS knows the location area it is in by listening to the broadcasting from the BS. An MS updates its location (i.e., location area) whenever it moves into a cell that belongs to a new location area. When an incoming call arrives for an MS, the cellular network pages all the cells of the location area that was last reported by the MS. Figure 6 illustrates a coverage area with three location

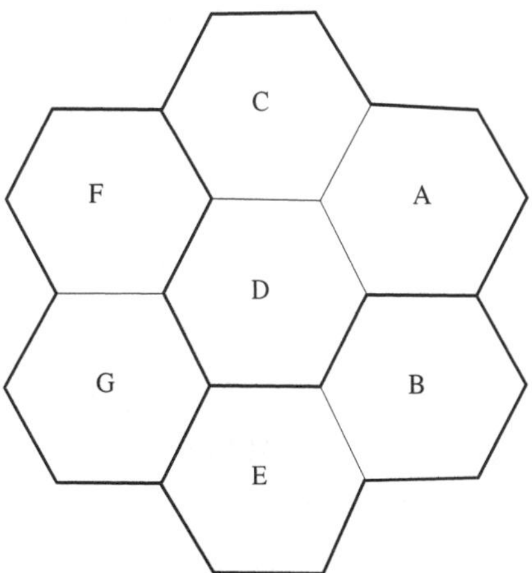

Figure 6: A service area with three location areas.

areas separated by wide lines. When an MS moves from cell A to cell B in the figure, it will report its new location area because cell A and cell B are in different location areas. No location update is necessary if the MS moves from cell A to cell C because cell A and cell C are in the same location area.

The location-areas scheme is a generalization of both Never-Update and Always-Update extreme cases. In Never-Update, all the cells in the coverage area belong to the same location area, and in Always-Update, each cell forms a location area. How to divide the whole coverage area into location areas greatly affects the location management cost. In reality, a location area consists of all the cells under the control of an MTSO. Each MTSO consists of two main databases: HLR (Home Location Register) and VLR (Visitor Location Register). HLR contains information for each MS that considers the location area covered by the MTSO as its home. Each MS can subscribe to one MTSO as its home. VLR records a list of the MSs that are currently located in the location area covered by the MTSO but do not consider the MTSO as their home. When an MS moves out of its home MTSO and visits another MTSO, the MS needs to register with the visited MTSO. The visited MTSO contacts the home MTSO about the MS. The home MTSO records the visited MTSO of the MS in its HLR. The visited MTSO updates its VLR about the MS. When a call is made to the MS, it is first addressed to the home MTSO of the MS. By checking the information stored in HLR about the MS, the call can eventually be routed to the visited MTSO. Finally, the visited MTSO pages the MS in the cells of its covered location area.

The location-areas scheme is global in the sense that all MSs transmit their location updates in the same set of cells, and it is static in the sense that the location areas are fixed. A location-update scheme can be classified as either global or local (Bar-Noy, Kessler, & Sidi, 1995; Ramanathan & Steenstrup, 1996). A location-update scheme is global if all MSs update their locations at the same set of cells, and a scheme is local (or individualized) if an individual MS is allowed to decide where to perform location update. From another point of view, a location-update scheme can be classified as either static or dynamic (Bar-Noy, Kessler, & Sidi, 1995; Ramanathan & Steenstrup, 1996). A location-update scheme is static if there is a predetermined set of cells at which location updates must be generated by an MS regardless of its mobility. A scheme is dynamic if a location update can be generated by an MS in any cell depending on its mobility. Recently there was a swarm of research on location management, especially how to reduce the cost of location management. For detailed information on recent research on location management, please refer to the survey in Zhang (2002).

HAND-OFF STRATEGIES AND CHANNEL ASSIGNMENT

The previous section described how to track the movement of an MS when it is not in a call. This section deals with the movement of an MS when it is in a call. When an MS is in a call, it has acquired two channels (one for transmitting and the other for receiving) from the current cell for communication with the BS. When the MS moves out of the current cell and enters a neighboring cell, the MS needs to acquire two channels from the neighboring cell in order for the call to continue. The process of transferring a call from the current cell to a neighboring cell is called hand-off. To a cell, a hand-off call is a call that is in progress in a neighboring cell and needs to be continued in the cell because of the movement of an MS. In contrast, a new call is a call that is started in the cell. As mentioned earlier, the number of channels assigned to each cell is limited. Channel assignment deals with how to assign available channels to new calls as well as hand-off calls.

The simplest channel assignment scheme is the fully shared scheme (FSS), in which all available channels are shared by hand-off calls and new calls. No distinction is made between a hand-off call and a new call. FSS is widely used in the current cellular networks because of its simplicity. In addition, FSS has the advantage of maximizing the utilization of wireless channels. The disadvantage is the increased dropping rate of hand-off calls. In general, it is less desirable to drop a hand-off call than to block a new call. The dropping probability of hand-off calls is considered as one of major metrics that measure the quality of service of calls.

Recently intensive research on channel-assignment schemes has been conducted to decrease the dropping probability of hand-off calls. One such scheme is the hand-off queuing scheme (HQS; Tekinay & Jabbari, 1991). When an MS detects that the received signal strength from the current BS is below a certain level, called the hand-off threshold, a hand-off operation is initiated. The hand-off operation first identifies the new BS into which the call is moving. If the new BS has unused channels, the call will be transferred to the new BS. If there is no unused channel available, the hand-off call will be queued until a channel is released by another call. The HQS scheme is feasible because there is a difference between the signal strength at the hand-off threshold and the minimum acceptable signal strength for voice communication. This gives an MS some time to wait for a channel at the new BS to become available. A new call will be blocked in the new cell until all the hand-off calls in the queue are served. Therefore, the HQS scheme decreases the dropping probability of hand-off calls while increasing the blocking probability of new calls because the scheme gives higher priority to hand-off calls.

The scheme proposed by Li, Shroff, and Chong (1999) goes one step further. When a hand-off call is not able to acquire the necessary channels in the new cell, the call is allowed to carry the channels in the current cell to the new cell, a concept the authors called channel carrying. However, carrying the channels from the current cell to the new cell may reduce the reuse distance of the channels and violate the minimum reuse distance requirement. To ensure the minimum reuse distance requirement is not violated, an $(r + 1)$-channel assignment scheme is used. That is, the same channels are reused exactly $(r + 1)$ cells apart. Here r is the minimum reuse distance. In this scheme, a channel can only be carried from the assigned cell to a neighboring cell, and the carried channel will be returned as soon as a local channel is available. By using channel carrying, a hand-off call can continue, even if there is no channel available in the new cell. Therefore, the dropping probability of hand-off calls will be reduced. However, the capacity of the cellular network is reduced because the $(r + 1)$-channel assignment scheme is used instead of r-channel assignment.

Another channel assignment scheme that prioritizes the hand-off call is referred to as the guard channel scheme (GCS; Tekinay & Jabbari, 1991). In GCS, each BS reserves a fraction of wireless channels exclusively for hand-off calls, and the remaining channels, called normal channels, are shared between hand-off calls and new calls. Both hand-off calls and new calls use the normal channels first. When the normal channels are used up, a new call will be blocked, but a hand-off call can still use the reserved channels. In this way, the dropping probability of hand-off calls will be reduced. The improvement in the dropping probability of hand-off calls is dependent on the number of channels reserved. However, a new call is blocked if there are only reserved channels left even though no hand-off calls exist. Therefore, the total utilization of wireless channels is decreased. There is a tradeoff between decreasing the blocking probability of hand-off calls and increasing the total channel utilization. The number of channels that should be set aside for hand-off calls depends on a lot of factors such as the mobility of MSs, the call duration, and so forth.

Kim et al. (1999) propose a dynamic channel reservation scheme (DCRS) based on mobility. Their goal is to guarantee the required dropping probability of hand-off calls while minimizing the blocking probability of new calls. As in GCS, the normal channels of DCRS are shared by both hand-off calls and new calls, and the guard channels are reserved for hand-off calls. However, the guard channels can also be used by new calls whose request probability is a function of the mobility of calls. The mobility of calls in a cell is defined as the ratio of the hand-off call arrival rate to the new call arrival rate. If there is no arrival of hand-off calls, the request probability will be one, and the guard channels will be used by new calls. If there is no arrival of new calls, the request probability will be zero, and the guard channels will be used by hand-off calls. When the arrival rate of hand-off calls is larger than that of new calls, the request probability is decreased quickly so the hand-off calls can use the guard channels. In this way, the dropping probability of hand-off calls is guaranteed. When the arrival rate of hand-off calls is lower than that of new calls, the request probability is decreased slowly so new calls have a chance to use available guard channels. This decreases the blocking rate of new calls without sacrificing the dropping probability of hand-off calls, which increases the total channel utilization.

AUTHENTICATION AND ENCRYPTION

Because cellular communication is carried out over the air interface, it is more vulnerable to fraud and eavesdropping. It is essential to have cell phone users authenticated and voice or data traffic encrypted. Authentication verifies whether a user is who he or she claims to be. Encryption is to use a key to scramble a message such that the message cannot be read by anyone but the holder of the correct key. There are two popular encryption methods, private key encryption and public key encryption. Both encryption methods can also be used for authentication. For more information on how these two encryption methods work and how they can be used for authentication, the reader is referred to Stallings' text (2003) or the corresponding chapters in this book. This section discusses how authentication and encryption are performed in cellular networks, including global system for mobile communications (GSM) and IS-41.

Every GSM mobile subscriber has an SIM (subscriber identity module) card that can be inserted into a mobile phone (Black, 1999; Mouly & Pautet, 1992). A phone with an SIM card inserted can be activated by entering the four-digit PIN (personal identification number) correctly. The SIM stores identity- and security-related information such as the IMSI (international mobile subscriber identity), the authentication key (K_i), the A_3 authentication algorithm, and the A_8 ciphering key generating algorithm. The authentication in GSM checks if the SIM is genuine, and it is based on a challenge-and-response method. A 128-bit random number is sent by the network to the MS as the challenge. The MS inputs the challenge and the authentication key (K_i) to the A_3 algorithm to generate the signed response (SRES), which is sent back to the network. The network compares the received SRES with the SRES provided by the authentication center. If they match, the mobile user is authenticated; otherwise, the user is not. Once the mobile user is authenticated, the A_8 algorithm uses the random number and the authentication key (K_i) to generate a ciphering key (K_c) at both ends of the air interface. The ciphering key (K_c) is used by the A_5 ciphering algorithm of the MS to encrypt and decrypt data.

To make GSM secure, all security specifications such as the A_3 and A_8 algorithms are kept secret. However, it is claimed a secret encryption algorithm prevents the brightest minds in the world from identifying flaws in them. Recently a group of researchers discovered that the method used for authentication in GSM was not strong enough to resist attack (GSM Cloning, n.d.). An attacker can repeatedly send the challenges and collect the responses. By analyzing the responses, the secret key can be determined. However, despite its security vulnerability, GSM is still the most secure public wireless system in the world.

For the cellular systems in North America including IS-54, IS-136, and IS-95, IS-41 is used for security (Black, 1999; EIA/TIA, 1993; Mohan, 1996). There are five authentication and privacy operations defined in IS-41: authentication of mobile station registration, authentication of mobile station originating a call, authentication of a call to a terminating mobile station, unique challenge–response procedure, and updating the shared secret data. The idea used for authentication in IS-41 is similar to that used in GSM. Both the authentication center and the MS share a secret key, referred to as SSD (shared secret data). SSD consists of two parts: SSD-A and SSD-B, each of 64 bits. SSD-A is used for authentication, and SSD-B is used for encryption. A BS periodically broadcasts a 32-bit random number, that is, the authentication challenge. At request of the network, an MS inputs the received authentication challenge, SSD-A, its ESN (electronic serial number), and its last six digits of the phone number to the CAVE (cellular authentication and voice encryption) algorithm to obtain the 18-bit response to the authentication challenge, which is sent back to the network. If the response matches the one calculated by the authentication center, the MS is authenticated. Once authenticated, the MS will receive two values, the signaling message encryption key for message encryption and the voice privacy mask for voice encryption.

EVOLUTION OF CELLULAR NETWORKS

Cellular systems became popular because of radio-frequency reuse, which allows more cell phone users to be supported. The cellular concept was first used in the AMPS in the United States. As a first generation of cellular systems, AMPS is a FDMA-based analog system. The 2G of cellular systems uses digital technologies. Two interim standards, IS-95 (CDMA-based) and IS-136 (TDMA-based), are used in the United States, and TDMA-based GSM is used in European countries. It is clear that the 3G of cellular systems will be CDMA-based. However, the GSM community is developing WCDMA to be backward compatible with GSM while the CDMA community tries to evolve CDMA into CDMA2000. Currently researchers are studying technologies for Beyond 3G (B3G) or fourth-generation (4G) networks.

In the late 1970s and early 1980s, AT & T Bell Laboratories developed the AMPS, which was the first-generation cellular system used in the United States (Rappaport, 2002; Young, 1979). It was first deployed in Chicago and Washington, DC, then in all the major U.S. cities. Currently it is still used in many rural areas. The Federal Communications Commission (FCC) initially allocated a 40-MHz spectrum in the 800-MHz band for the AMPS in 1983, and later in 1989 added an additional 10 MHz to accommodate the increasing demand for cellular phone services. AMPS is FDMA-based, with each channel occupying a narrow band of 30 kHz. AMPS is an analog system. It transmits 3-kHz voice signal over the 30-kHz channel using frequency modulation. IS-41 was originally developed to support the operations with AMPS. However, as an analog system, AMPS does not support voice encryption.

To overcome the limited capacity of AMPS, especially in large cities, D-AMPS (IS-54) was developed in the early 1990s (EIA/TIA, 1990). D-AMPS inherited a lot of features from AMPS. Specifically, in D-AMPS, the same AMPS allocation of frequency spectrum is used, and each channel is still 30 kHz wide. However, in D-AMPS, a 30-kHz channel can be shared by three users through the 2G TDMA digital technology. In a typical D-AMPS cell, some of the 30-kHz channels are assigned for analog AMPS traffic, whereas the others are for digital TDMA traffic. It means that D-AMPS allows a service provider to migrate from the first-generation analog technology to the 2G digital technology on a gradual basis. In a less densely populated area, all the channels can be assigned for AMPS traffic. When the demand increases, some channels will be converted from analog to digital. In a densely populated area, all the channels need to be assigned for TDMA traffic to meet the demand. IS-136, another prominent TDMA-based cellular system in the United States, is built on D-AMPS. Whereas D-AMPS provides dual-mode operations (both analog and digital), IS-136 provide pure digital operations. All the 30-kHz channels are shared by three users via TDMA digital technology. In addition, unlike D-AMPS, IS-136 also uses the digital control channels. IS-136 was initially developed on the 800-MHz cellular spectrum. It can be adopted onto the 1900-MHz PCS spectrum.

GSM is a 2G system developed to solve the incompatibility problem of different first-generation systems in Europe (Black, 1999; Mouly & Pautet, 1992; Rahnema, 1993). It is now widely deployed around the world including in the United States. GSM was first developed for Europe in the 900-MHz band (GSM 900), then expanded to the 1800-MHz band (1710–1880 MHz), which is named DCS 1800, and later renamed to GSM 1800. The North America version of GSM is called PCS 1900 because of its use of the 1900-MHz PCS spectrum. GSM uses the TDMA digital technology. The allocated spectrum is divided into multiple channels of 200 kHz using FDMA, and each 200-kHz channel is shared by as many as eight users using TDMA. One feature of GSM worth mentioning is the SIM card that can be inserted into a cellular phone to provide the owner's identity information. A cell phone without a SIM card inserted does not work. A SIM card can be inserted into any cell phone to make the phone usable.

Whereas IS-54, IS-136, and GSM are all TDMA-based, IS-95 is CDMA-based (EIA/TIA, 1995). As mentioned earlier, each user in CDMA is assigned a unique code to encode the data to be transmitted. Knowing the code of the transmitter, the receiver is able to recover the original data from the received data. CDMA is a very new 2G digital technology. Since its first launch in 1995, CDMA quickly became one of the world's fastest-growing wireless technologies. CDMA uses channels that are 1.25 MHz wide, and it is able to support up to 64 users with orthogonal codes. With CDMA, the same channel can be reused in a neighboring cell. CDMA is superior to FDMA and TDMA. In fact, CDMA provides roughly 10 times more capacity than analog systems, whereas TDMA provides 3 to 4 times more capacity than analog systems. In 1999, CDMA was selected by the International Telecommunications Union as the industry standard for new 3G cellular systems.

The goal of a 3G cellular system is to provide all kinds of services: voice, high-speed data, audio/video, and so forth. The high-speed data transmission is the main development focus. The CDMA and GSM communities are two major players in this effort. The 3G path adopted by the GSM community is first to GPRS, then to EDGE, and ultimately to WCDMA (Qualcomm CDMA Technologies, n.d.). Currently GSM provides data services of 9.6 Kbps using a single TDMA channel. Although multiple TDMA channels can be combined to provide high-speed data service, it is circuit switched. A service called general packet radio service (GPRS) is first developed to allow users to connect to packet-switched data networks via a different connection from the voice network. With GPRS, the raw data rate increases to approximately 170 Kbps. The next step is enhanced data rates for global evolution (EDGE). EDGE provides practical raw data rates of up to 384 Kbps using a new high-speed physical layer. Finally, WCDMA is used for the 3G version of the GSM community. In WCDMA, CDMA is used instead of TDMA, and the carrier bandwidth jumps from 200 kHz to 5 MHz to provide data rates of up to 2 Mbps. However, new frequency allocations, BSs, and MSs are required because of the change from TDMA to WCDMA.

The 3G path adopted by the CDMA community is first to CDMA2000 1x, then to 1xEV, and ultimately to 3x (Qualcomm CDMA Technologies, n.d.). The first step is to use one 1.25-MHz carrier to support packet data. In fact, CDMA phones and networks are already capable of handling packet data. The CDMA2000 1xEV consists of two phases. In Phase 1, one carrier (1.25 MHz) is dedicated to high-speed packet data, and one or more additional carriers are used for voice. In Phase 2, packet data and voice can be combined in the same carrier. Finally, CDMA2000 3x can use up to three 1.25-MHz carriers. When CDMA2000 uses three 1.25-MHz carriers, its total bandwidth approaches that of WCDMA. However, 3x is more flexible because three channels can be used independently or together as a single 3.75-MHz channel. The main advantage of the 3x approach is that it can be implemented in existing frequency allocations in CDMA, which also uses 1.25-MHz carriers.

Now researchers are developing technologies for B3G or 4G networks (Technologies Beyond 3G, n.d.). It is expected all the 4G network elements are digital and the entire network is packet-switched. 4G networks will integrate wireless local area networks (LANS) such as IEEE 802.11 and Bluetooth with wide area cellular networks. The data transmission rate of 4G communications will be much higher than 3G, at 20 to 100 Mbps in mobile mode.

ALTERNATIVES TO CELLULAR NETWORKS

This section describes alternatives to cellular networks. Although cellular networks use either the 800-MHz cellular spectrum or the 1900-MHz PCS spectrum, most of the alternatives use the license-free 2.4-GHz industrial, scientific, and medical (ISM) band. The alternatives introduced here include IEEE 802.11 wireless LAN, IEEE 802.16 wireless MAN (metropolitan area network), mobile ad hoc networks, and multihop cellular networks.

IEEE 802.11 wireless LAN is an infrastructure wireless network, similar to a cellular network (Crow, Widjaja, Kim, & Sakai, 1997; IEEE P802.11, n.d.). (IEEE 802.11 also supports peer-to-peer communication that is not frequently used.) Access points (APs) that are analogous to BSs in cellular networks are established to provide an extension to the wired network. The area covered by an AP is called the basic service area, which is analogous to a cell in cellular networks. The nodes in a basic service area form the basic service set. Any node in the basic service set can communicate with the AP directly. Their radio communication uses the license-free ISM band with direct sequence spread spectrum. Under 802.11b (a variation of the IEEE 802.11), the communication is kept at a maximum speed of 11 Mbps whenever possible. It drops back to 5.5 Mbps, then 2 Mbps, and finally down to 1 Mbps if signal strength or interference is corrupting data. New IEEE 802.11g extends the data rate to 54 Mbps from 11 Mbps of IEEE 802.11b. With IEEE 802.11 wireless LAN, a node is connected to the Internet world, and it is able to get any service the Internet provides.

IEEE 802.11 works well for wireless access in a local area. To use it for wireless access in a metropolitan area, its bandwidth is often insufficient, and it can experience interference from competitors because they use the same license-free ISM band. IEEE 802.16 standards are for broadband wireless access in a metropolitan area, and they use licensed bands (IEEE 802.16 Task Group e, n.d.). IEEE 802.16a is just for fixed broadband wireless access. IEEE 802.16e supports both fixed and mobile broadband wireless access. Therefore, hand-off between two towers is allowed in IEEE 802.16e.

Unlike cellular networks, mobile ad hoc networks (MANET for short) are infrastructureless. All nodes within the network can be mobile, and there is no fixed BS or centralized control (Macker & Corson, 1998). A mobile node can communicate with another one directly if one is within the transmission range of the other. Because the network topology for a MANET can dynamically change as a result of node mobility, a MANET is usually modeled by a dynamically changing graph. A MANET finds its applications in an environment where it may not be economically practical or physically possible to provide the necessary infrastructure, or the expediency of the situation may not permit its installation. For example, in a battlefield, it is not possible to install an infrastructure wireless network in the enemy's territory. In such a situation, a MANET is a good solution. Unlike in the cellular network, the route for communication between two nodes is not fixed in MANET. To send a message from one mobile node (the source) to another mobile node (the destination), a route between the source and the destination must be found. Designing a good routing protocol in a dynamically changing network is very challenging. For more information on routing protocols, please refer to routing surveys in Royer and Toh (1999) and Stojmenovic (2002).

The traditional cellular network is called a single-hop cellular network (SCN) because an MS in a cell can reach the corresponding BS with a single wireless hop, and a MANET is considered a multihop wireless network because intermediate nodes are required for communication between two nodes that are not within the transmission range of each other. Lin and Hsu (2000) proposed a new architecture, referred to as multihop cellular network (MCN), which combines the features of SCN and MANETs. MCN has many advantages over SCN. In SCN, two MSs communicate only via a BS even though they are in the same cell and mutually reachable. In MCN, these two MSs can communicate directly. In MCN, if a MS is not reachable from a BS in one hop, the BS will seek intermediate nodes to forward, which is not feasible in SCN.

SUMMARY

Cellular networks are based on the frequency reuse concept. In a cellular network, a service coverage area is divided into cells, each of which is served by a BS. Each BS is assigned a group of channels. The same set of channels can be assigned to the two cells that are far apart such that the radio co-channel interference between them is within a tolerable limit. Within a cell covered by a BS, multiple MSs want to communicate with the BS. Multiple access methods deal with how to share the channels assigned to a BS by the MSs located within the cell. FDMA, TDMA, and CDMA are three popular multiple access methods.

When an incoming call arrives for a MS, the cellular network needs to find out the exact cell in which a MS is located. How to track the movement of a MS is the subject of location management. Location management for cellular networks was discussed in this chapter. When a MS is in a call and moves from the current cell to a neighboring cell, the cellular network needs to transfer the call from the current cell to the neighboring cell. This process is called hand-off. A hand-off call is usually prioritized over a new call. Several channel assignment schemes that deal with new calls and hand-off calls were presented in this chapter.

Because wireless communication is carried out over the air interface, it is more vulnerable to fraud and eavesdropping. Therefore, authentication and encryption are two important issues in cellular networks. This chapter discussed authentication and encryption in GSM and IS-41. A cellular network integrates cell phones into the public switched telephone network. Whereas the first generation of cellular networks was analog, the 2G is digital. The 3G integrates cell phones into the Internet world by providing high-speed packet-switching data transmission. The evolution of cellular networks from the first generation to the 3G was presented. Technologies for B3G or 4G networks are being studied currently. Finally, this chapter discussed alternatives to cellular networks, including IEEE 802.11 wireless LAN, IEEE 802.16 wireless MAN, MANETs and MCNs. For further reading on cellular networks, please refer to these three excellent books: Agrawal and Zeng (2002), Black (1999), and Rappaport (2002).

ACKNOWLEDGMENTS

The authors thank Professor Hossein Bidgoli and five anonymous referees for their constructive comments and suggestions that greatly improved the quality of this chapter. The authors also thank Professor Phillip Bradford for many helpful discussions and his time to proofread the manuscript, and Mr. Zhijun Wang for drawing the figures in this chapter.

GLOSSARY

AMPS (Advanced Mobile Phone System) The first-generation analog cellular network developed in the United States.

BS (Base Station) A fixed station in the cellular network that connects mobile stations to the land telephone network by communicating with mobile stations via radio.

CDMA (Code Division Multiple Access) A digital cellular technology that allows multiple users to share a channel using different orthogonal codes.

Cell The area covered by a base station.

Cell Splitting A technique that divides a cell into multiple smaller cells to increase the capacity of a cellular network.

Cellular Network A network that divides a geographic area into cells such that the same radio frequency can be reused in two cells that are a certain distance apart.

FDMA (Frequency Division Multiple Access) An analog cellular technology that divides a wide band into multiple narrow bands to be used by multiple users.

GSM (Global System for Mobile Communications) A second-generation TDMA cellular network developed in Europe to achieve compatibility among European countries.

Hand-Off Channel switching for a call to continue when the mobile station involved in the call moves from one cell to another.

HLR (Home Location Register) An MSC database that stores information about the users who consider the area covered by the MSC as their home.

IS-54 A second-generation TDMA cellular network in the United States that uses the same cellular spectrum (800 MHz) as AMPS. It is also known as Digital-AMPS.

IS-95 A second-generation CDMA cellular network in the United States for both the cellular and PCS spectrums.

IS-136 A second-generation TDMA cellular network in the United States for both the cellular (800 MHz) and PCS (1900 MHz) spectrums.

Location Management A subject that deals with how to track an active mobile station.

MS (Mobile Station) A station in the cellular network that can communicate with base stations via radio even when it is in motion. Examples include cellular phones and wireless-capable laptops.

MTSO (Mobile Telephone Switching Office) The switching center that interconnects cellular phones with the land telephone network. It is also known as MSC (mobile switching center).

Multiple Access Method A method that allows multiple users in a cell to share the air interface in an orderly manner. Multiple access methods include FDMA, TDMA, and CDMA.

PSTN (Public Switched Telephone Network) The regular wireline telephone network.

TDMA (Time Division Multiple Access) A digital cellular technology that allows multiple users to share a channel using different time slots.

VLR (Visitor Location Register) An MSC database to temporarily store information about the users who are visiting the area covered by the MSC.

CROSS REFERENCES

See *Computer and Network Authentication; Encryption Basics; Radio Frequency and Wireless Communications Security; Wireless Channels.*

REFERENCES

Agrawal, D. P., & Zeng, Q.-A. (2002). *Introduction to wireless and mobile systems*. United States: Brooks/Cole.

Bar-Noy, A., Kessler, I., & Sidi, M. (1995). Mobile users: To update or not to update? *Wireless Networks, 1*(2), 175–185.

Black, U. (1996). *Mobile and wireless networks.* Upper Saddle River, NJ: Prentice Hall.

Black, U. (1999). *Second generation mobile and wireless networks.* Upper Saddle River, NJ: Prentice Hall.

Crow, B. P., Widjaja, I., Kim, J. G., & Sakai, P. T. (1997). IEEE 802.11 wireless local area networks. *IEEE Communications Magazine, 35*(9), 116–126.

EIA/TIA. (1990, May). Cellular system dual-mode mobile station–base station compatibility standard (IS-54). United States: EIA/TIA.

EIA/TIA. (1993, May). Cellular radio telecommunications intersystem operations: Authentication, signaling message encryption and voice privacy (TSB-51). United States: EIA/TIA.

EIA/TIA. (1995, May). Mobile station–base station compatibility standard for dual-mode wideband spread spectrum cellular system (IS-95). United States: EIA/TIA.

GSM cloning. (n.d.). Retrieved April 17, 2005, from http://www.isaac.cs.berkeley.edu/isaac/gsm-faq.html

IEEE 802.16 task group e (mobile wireless MAN). (n.d.). Retrieved April 17, 2005, from http://www.ieee802.org/16/tge/

IEEE P802.11, the working group for wireless LANs. (n.d.). Retrieved April 17, 2005, from http://grouper.ieee.org/groups/802/11/

Kim, Y. C., Lee, D. E., Lee, B. J., Kim, Y. S., & Mukherjee, B. (1999). Dynamic channel reservation based on mobility in wireless ATM networks. *IEEE Communications Magazine, 37*(11), 47–51.

Li, J., Shroff, N. B., & Chong, E. K. P. (1999). Channel carrying: A novel handoff scheme for mobile cellular networks. *IEEE/ACM Transactions on Networking, 7*(1), 38–50.

Lin, Y.-D., & Hsu, Y.-C. (2000). Multihop cellular: A new architecture for wireless communications. *Proceedings of IEEE INFOCOM.*

Macker, J. P., & Corson, M. S. (1998). Mobile ad hoc networking and the IETF. *Mobile Computing and Communications Review, 2*(1), 9–14.

Modarressi, A. R., & Skoog, R. A. (1992). An overview of signaling system no. 7. *Proceedings of the IEEE*, 80(4), 590–606.

Mohan, S. (1996). Privacy and authentication protocols for PCS. *IEEE Personal Communications, 3*(5), 34–38.

Mouly, M., & Pautet, M. B. (1992). *The GSM system for mobile communications.* [location not available]: Telecom.

Qualcomm CDMA Technologies. (n.d.). Retrieved April 17, 2005, from http://www.cdmatech.com/resources/glossary_full.jsp

Rahnema, M. (1993). Overview of the GSM system and protocol architecture. *IEEE Communications Magazine, 31*(4) 92–100.

Ramanathan, S., & Steenstrup, M. (1996). A survey of routing techniques for mobile communication networks. *Mobile Networks and Applications, 1*(2), 89–104.

Rappaport, T. S. (2002). *Wireless communications—Principles and practice*. Upper Saddle River, NJ: Prentice Hall.

Royer, E. M., & Toh, C. K. (1999). A review of current routing protocols for ad hoc mobile wireless networks. *IEEE Personal Communications, 6*(2), 46–55.

Stallings, W. (2002). *Wireless communications and networks*. Upper Saddle River, NJ: Prentice Hall.

Stallings, W. (2003). *Cryptography and network security* (3rd ed.). Upper Saddle River, NJ: Prentice Hall.

Stojmenovic, I. (2002). Position-based routing in ad hoc networks. *IEEE Communications Magazine, 40*(7), 128–134.

Technologies beyond 3G—4G vision, concepts & efforts. (n.d.). Retrieved April 17, 2005, from http://www.mobileinfo.com/3G/4GVision&Technologies. htm

Tekinay, S., & Jabbari, B. (1991). Handover and channel assignment in mobile cellular networks. *IEEE Communications Magazine, 29*(11), 42–46.

Young, W. R. (1979). Advanced mobile phone service: Introduction, background, and objectives. *Bell Systems Technical Journal, 58,* 1–14.

Zhang, J. (2002). Location management in cellular networks. In I. Stojmenovic (Ed.), *Handbook of wireless networks and mobile computing* (pp. 24–49). New York: John Wiley & Sons.

Mobile IP

M. Farooque Mesiya, *Rensselaer Polytechnic Institute*

INTRODUCTION

Mobile networking is becoming increasingly important as portable devices such as personal digital assistants (PDAs) and laptops become more powerful and less expensive, and as users need to be connected whenever and wherever they are. Mobile Internet protocol (IP) allows portable devices called *mobile nodes* to roam from one IP subnet to another while maintaining the communication sessions.

An IP address identifies a node (end point) as well as the subnet to which it is connected. The dual usage of IP addresses thus causes problems when a mobile node changes its point of attachment (indicated by a different *subnet prefix*) to the Internet. Packets destined to the mobile node would not be able to reach it while it is away from its home IP subnet because routing is based on the network prefix in a packet's destination IP address. To continue communication in spite of its mobility, a mobile node could change its IP address each time it moves to a new IP subnet. However, both ends of a TCP session need to keep the same IP address for the life of the session. Otherwise, existing sessions stop working and new sessions need to be started when a mobile node moves to another subnet.

Mobile IP allows the mobile node to use two IP addresses. Each mobile node is assigned a (permanent) IP address in the same way as any other node, and this IP address is known as the mobile node's *home address*. A mobile node's home address remains unchanged regardless of where the node is attached to the Internet. The IP subnet indicated by this home address is the mobile node's *home network*, and standard IP routing mechanisms will deliver packets destined to a mobile node's home address only to its home network. When away from its home network, a *care-of address* is associated with the mobile node and reflects the mobile node's current point of attachment to the *foreign network* that it is visiting.

The outline of this chapter is as follows: It begins with an overview of mobile IP in Internet protocol version 4 (Ipv4) environment (mobile Ipv4). The protocol mechanisms enabling operation of mobile Ipv4 are discussed next. Internet protocol version 6 (Ipv6), with its many advantages, provides a more integrated and efficient implementation in the form of mobile Ipv6. After a review of security threats in mobile IP environment, security design of mobile Ipv4 is covered. This is followed with an extensive discussion of protocol mechanisms designed to make mobile Ipv6 as secure as Ipv4.

OVERVIEW OF MOBILE Ipv4

The design of mobile IP has been guided by the need to provide mobility support on the top of existing IP infrastructure, *without requiring* any modifications to the routers, the applications, or the stationary end hosts (called *correspondent nodes*). This requirement implies that a mobile node must continuously use its permanent IP address even as it roams to another area. The mobile node basically works like any other node in its home network when it is at home. The packets destined to it are routed using traditional IP routing protocols. To provide support for mobility, Mobile IP requires the existence of two types of agents: one on the mobile node's home network, known as its *home agent*, and the other on the foreign network, known as its *foreign agent*. Typically, one or more routers on a network will implement the roles of both the home and foreign agents. Figure 1 shows mobile Ipv4 operational environment.

The home and foreign agents make themselves known by sending agent advertisement messages. After receiving an agent advertisement, the mobile node determines whether it is in its home network or in a foreign network. Whenever the mobile node moves to a foreign network, it obtains a care-of address from the foreign agent and then *registers* this new care-of address with its home agent, by way of the foreign agent. The association between a mobile node's home address and its care-of address, along

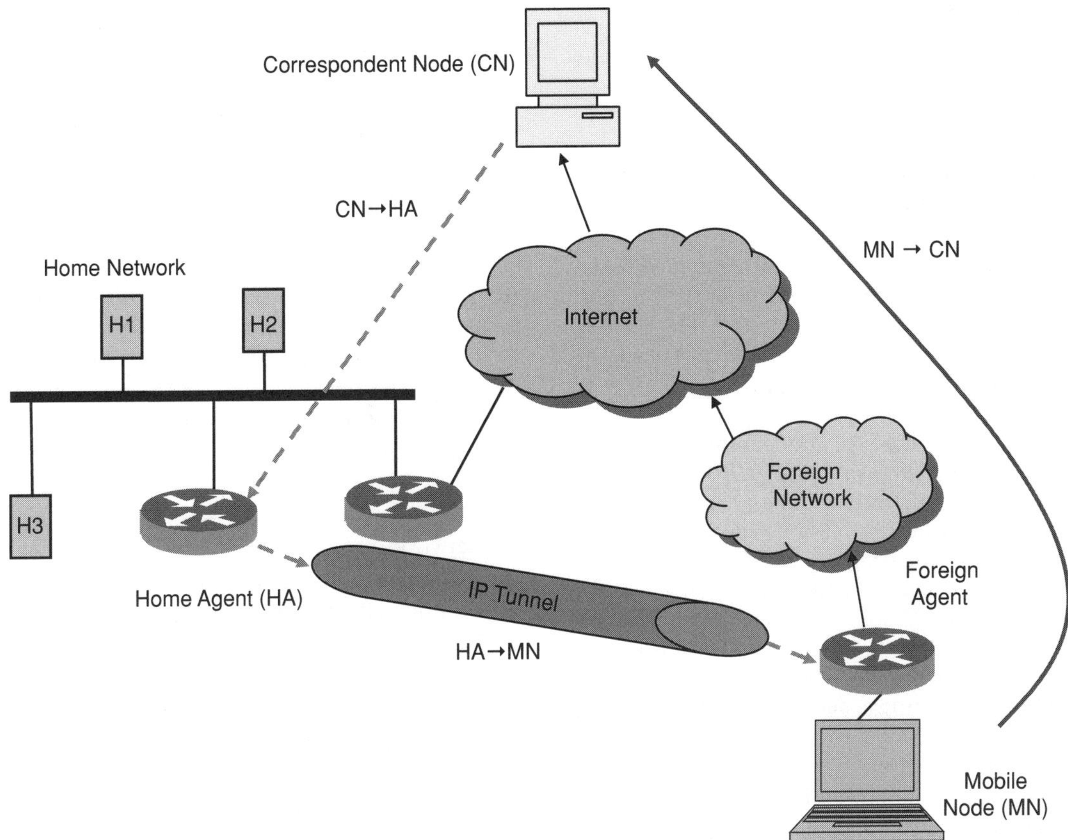

Figure 1: Mobile IP operation.

with the remaining lifetime of that association, is known as *binding*. While away from its home subnet, the mobile node's home agent maintains a record of the current binding of the mobile node. The home agent intercepts any packets on the home subnet addressed to the mobile node's home address using the proxy (Postel, 1984) and gratuitous (Stevens, 1994) *address resolution protocol* (*ARP*) mechanisms and tunnels them to the mobile node at its current care-of address. This tunneling uses Ipv4 encapsulation and the path followed by a packet while it is encapsulated is called a *tunnel*. Thus, the mobile node is reachable at any location in the Internet using its care-of address and its movement is transparent to the higher-layer applications that use the home address.

Mobile Ipv4 allows another kind of care-of address, called *collocated care-of address*, which is an IP address temporarily assigned to an interface of the mobile node itself. The subnet prefix of a collocated care-of address must equal the subnet prefix that has been assigned to the foreign link being visited by the mobile node. The collocated care-of address, acquired by an IP address-assignment procedure, such as *dynamic host configuration protocol* (*DHCP*; Stevens, 1994), might be used by the mobile node in situations where no foreign agents are available on a foreign link. A collocated care-of address can be used by only one mobile node at a time.

Packets transmitted by the mobile node (MN) to the correspondent (CN) node use normal IP packet format with the mobile node's address as the source IP address and the correspondent node's address as the destination IP address. These packets follow the default route

$$\text{MN} \rightarrow \text{CN}.$$

Note that *all* packets sent to a mobile node from a correspondent node must be routed first to the mobile node's home network and then forwarded to the mobile node at its current location by its home agent (HA), leading to this *triangle routing*:

$$\text{CN} \rightarrow \text{HA},$$
$$\text{HA} \rightarrow \text{MN}.$$

Mobile Ipv4 protocol with triangle routing is not optimal, especially in cases when the correspondent node is very close to the mobile node. It is, however, simple, because the number of control messages to be exchanged is limited and the address bindings are highly consistent, because they are kept at one single point (the home agent) for a given mobile node. One of the drawbacks of triangle routing is that the home agent is a fixed redirection point for the exchange of every IP packet, even if a shorter route is available between the correspondent and mobile nodes. This can lead to unnecessarily large end-to-end packet delay. The other drawback is that the network links connecting a home agent to the network can easily be overloaded.

MOBILE Ipv4 PROTOCOL OVERVIEW

Mobile Ipv4 includes the following extensions to support mobility in the Ipv4 environment (Perkins, 1997; 1998; 2002):

Agent discovery. A mobile node uses a discovery procedure to identify prospective home agents and foreign agents.

Registration. A mobile node uses an authenticated registration procedure to inform its home agent of its care-of address.

Tunneling. Tunneling is used to forward IP datagrams from a home address to a care-of address.

The registration protocol is an application-layer protocol that uses the *user datagram protocol* (*UDP*) as transport protocol to exchange registration request-reply messages at the well-known port number 434. For agent discovery, mobile IP modifies the existing *router advertisement* and *router solicitation* messages defined by the *Internet control message protocol* (*ICMP*; Stevens, 1994) by adding the appropriate extensions to the ICMP header. ICMP is a connectionless protocol well suited for the agent discovery operation. Finally, tunneling is performed at the IP level.

Agent Discovery

Agent discovery is a process by which a mobile node detects its change of location and identifies whether it is currently connected to its home network or a foreign network. The mobile node determines whether it is connected to the home or foreign link from agent advertisements sent periodically by agents (home, foreign, or both) as multicasts or broadcasts to the link. In case a mobile node does not receive any agent advertisement, or it does not have the patience to wait for the next agent advertisement, the mobile node can send an agent solicitation to request an agent advertisement from the agent to which it is attached. When a mobile node detects that it has moved by comparing the network prefix portions of the router IP address with its home IP address, it acquires a care-of address by reading it directly from the agent advertisement or by contacting a DHCP server.

The *agent advertisement extension* (Perkins, 2002) follows the ICMP router advertisement message fields and consists of the following fields as shown in Figure 2.

Type: 16 indicates that this is an agent advertisement extension.

Length: $(6 + 4N)$, where N is the number of care-of addresses advertised.

Sequence number: The count of agent advertisement messages sent since the agent was initialized.

Lifetime: The longest lifetime, in seconds, that this agent is willing to accept in any registration request from a mobile node.

The flags (R, B, H, F, M, G, r, and T) inform mobile nodes of special features of the advertisement:

R: Registration required. Registration with this foreign agent (or another foreign agent on this link) is required even when using a collocated care-of address.

B: Busy. The foreign agent will not accept registrations from additional mobile nodes.

H: This agent offers services as a home agent on this network.

F: This agent offers services as a foreign agent on this network.

M: This agent can receive tunneled IP datagrams that use minimal encapsulation (Perkins, 1996b).

G: This agent can receive tunneled IP datagrams that use *generic routing encapsulation* (*GRE*) (Perkins, 1996a).

r: Sent as zero; ignored on reception.

T: Foreign agent supports reverse tunneling (Montenegro, 2001).

Care-of address: The care-of address or addresses supported by this agent on this network. There must be at least one such address if the F bit is set. There may be multiple care-of addresses.

Registration

When a mobile node recognizes that it is on a foreign network and has acquired a care-of address, it needs to alert a home agent on its home network and request that the home agent forward its IP traffic. The registration process involves four steps as shown in Figure 3.

If the mobile node is using a collocated care-of address, then it registers directly with its home agent, rather than going through a foreign agent. The registration process uses two types of messages, carried in UDP segments.

The *registration request message* format is shown in Figure 4.

An explanation of the fields follows:

Type: 1 indicates that this is a registration request.

Lifetime: The number of seconds remaining before the registration is considered expired. A value of zero is a request for deregistration.

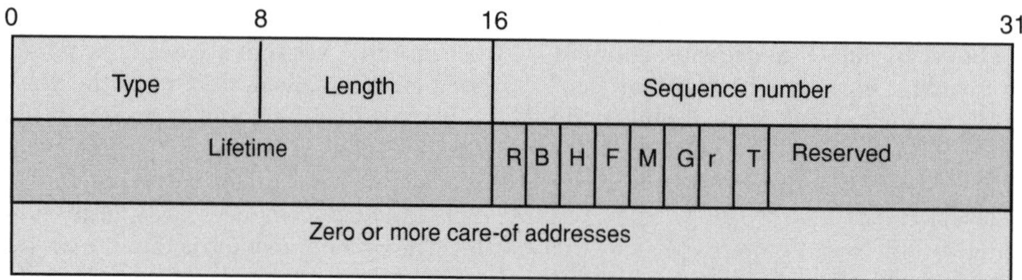

Figure 2: Agent advertisement extension format.

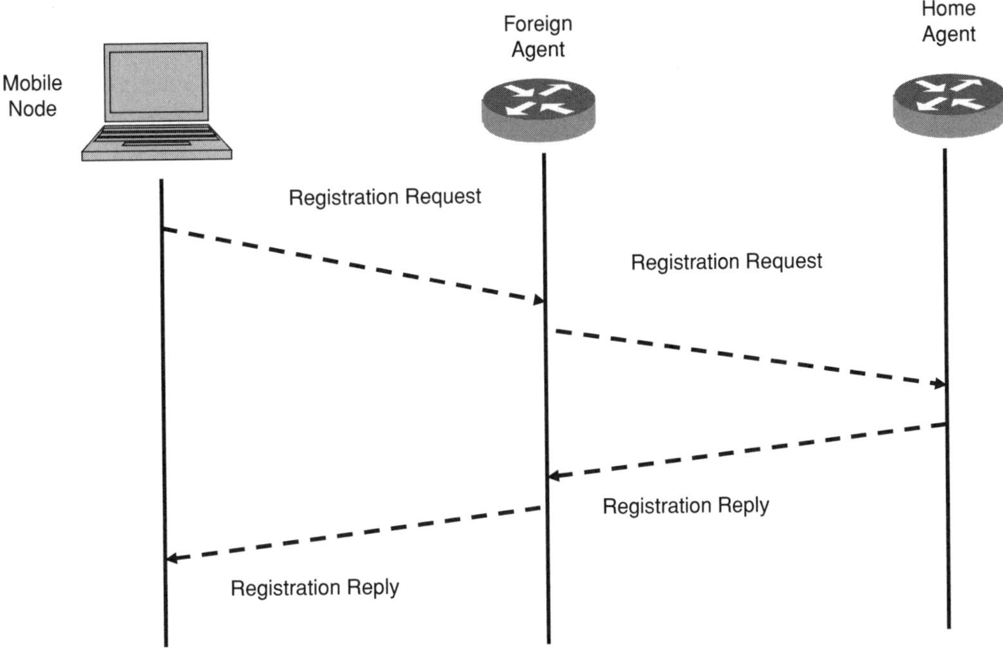

Figure 3: Registration procedure.

S: Simultaneous bindings. The mobile node is requesting that the home agent retain its prior mobility bindings. When simultaneous bindings are in effect, the home agent will forward multiple copies of the IP datagram, one to each care-of address currently registered for this mobile node. Multiple simultaneous bindings can be useful in wireless handoff situations to improve reliability.

B: Broadcast datagrams. This indicates that the mobile node would like to receive copies of broadcast datagrams that it would have received if it were attached to its home network.

D: Decapsulation by mobile node. The mobile node is using a collocated care-of address and will decapsulate its own tunneled IP datagrams.

x: Sent as zero; ignored on reception.

Care-of address: The IP address at this end of the tunnel. The home agent should forward IP datagrams that it receives with the mobile node home address to this destination address.

Identification: A 64-bit number generated by the mobile node, used for matching registration requests to registration replies and for security purposes.

Extensions: The only extension so far defined is the authentication extension (discussed later).

The *registration reply message* format is shown in Figure 5.

An explanation of the fields follows:

Type: 3 indicates that this is a registration reply.

Code: Indicates result of the registration request.

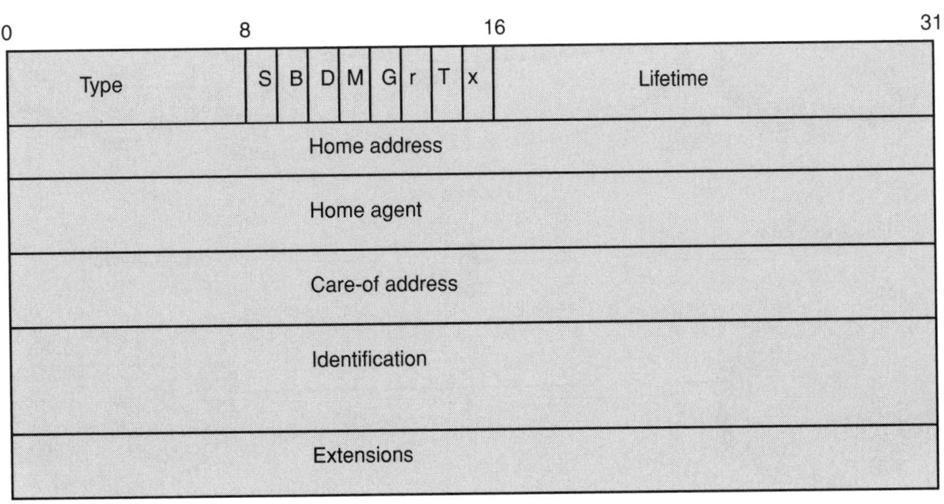

Figure 4: Registration request format.

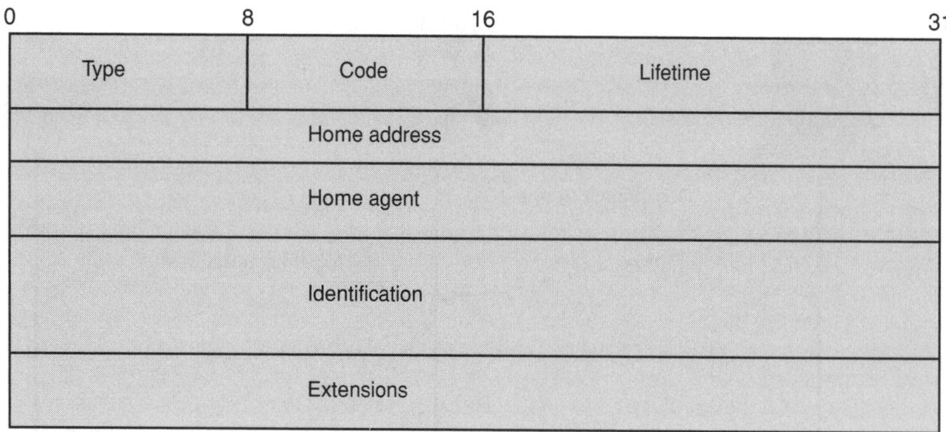

Figure 5: Registration reply format.

Lifetime: If the Code field indicates that the registration was accepted, the Lifetime field is set to the number of seconds remaining before the registration is considered expired. A value of zero indicates that the mobile node has been deregistered.

Identification: A 64-bit number used for matching registration replies to registration requests.

Tunneling

Tunneling is defined as the encapsulation of a certain data packet (the original or *inner* packet) into another data packet (the encapsulating or *outer* packet) so that the inner packet is opaque to the network via which the packet is routed (Leon-Garcia & Widjaja, 2004; Yuan & Strayer, 2001). The tunnel between two nodes across the network (e.g., global Internet), as shown in Figure 6, appears as a *single* link. The need for tunneling arises when it is not appropriate for the inner IP packet (in our case with the destination address as the original home IP address of the mobile node) to be handled directly by intermediate routers while traveling across the network. Mobile IP solves the problem by providing a *tunnel* between the home and the foreign agents. Two components uniquely determine a network tunnel: the end points of the tunnel and the encapsulation protocol used to transport the original data packet within the tunnel. In most cases, a tunnel has two end points: one where the tunnel starts (encapsulation) and one where the tunnel ends (decapsulation).

Two options for encapsulation are supported in mobile IP:

IP-in-IP encapsulation (Perkins, 1996a). This is implemented, as shown in Figure 7, by encapsulating each IP

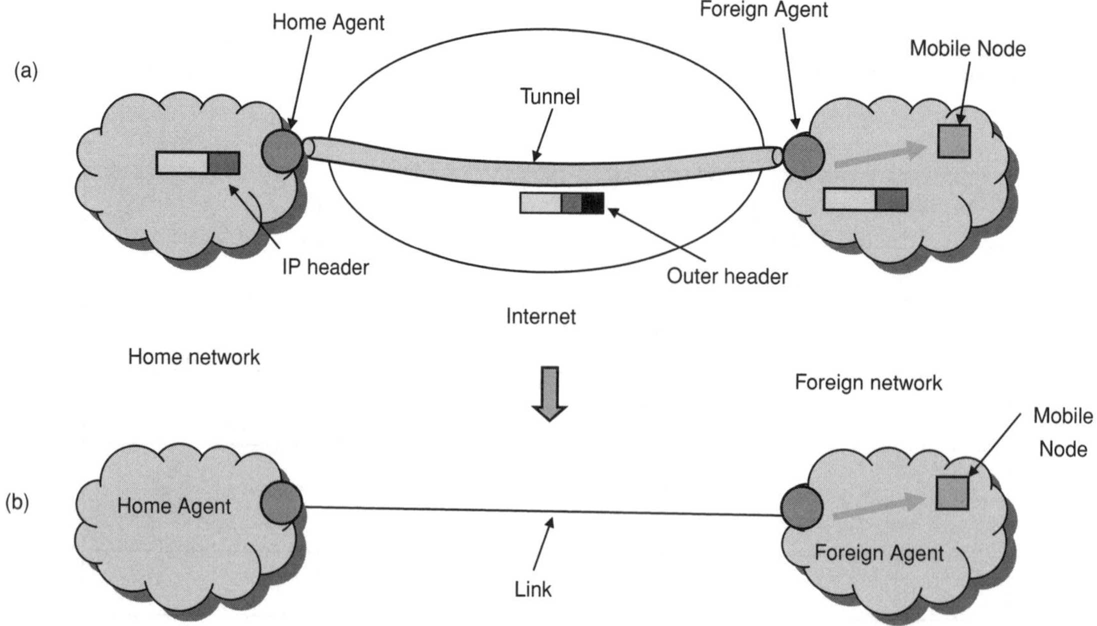

Figure 6: (a) Tunneling from Home Agent to Foreign Agent; (b) Virtual link between them.

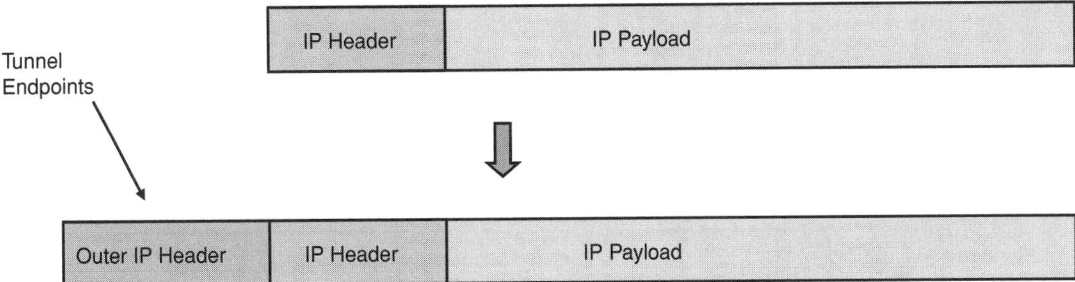

Figure 7: IP-in-IP encapsulation.

packet at the home agent with an outer IP header containing the home agent's address as the source IP address and the care-of address as the destination IP address. When the foreign agent receives the packet, it decapsulates the original IP packet with the correspondent node's address as the source IP address and the mobile node's home address as the destination IP address. The foreign agent now examines the header of the original inner IP packet and determines that the mobile node is connected to the same IP subnet. It can thus deliver the packet directly to the mobile node.

The original IP header is unchanged, as shown in Figure 8, except to decrement *time to live* (TTL) by 1. The outer header is a full IP header. The presence of the encapsulated IP packet is indicated by using protocol number 4 in the outer IP header. In the original IP header, the source address refers to the correspondent node that is sending the original datagram, and the destination address is the home address of the mobile node. In the outer IP header, the source and destination addresses refer to the entry and exit points of the tunnel. Thus, the source address typically is the IP address of the home agent, and the destination address is the care-of address for the intended destination.

Minimal encapsulation (Perkins, 1996b). This approach can be used if the mobile node, home agent, and foreign agent all agree to do so. With minimal encapsulation, the new header is inserted between the original IP header and the original IP payload as shown in Figure 9a. The presence of the minimal encapsulation is indicated by using protocol number 55 in the original IP header. The source and destination IP address fields are replaced by IP addresses of the tunnel end points. The home agent prepares the encapsulated datagram in the format of Figure 9a. This datagram is now suitable for tunneling and is delivered across the Internet to the care-of address. Figure 9b shows the fields of the minimal encapsulation header. At the care-of address, the fields in the minimal encapsulation header are restored to the original IP header and the former is removed from the datagram. The original IP datagram is now delivered to the mobile node using link-layer mechanisms.

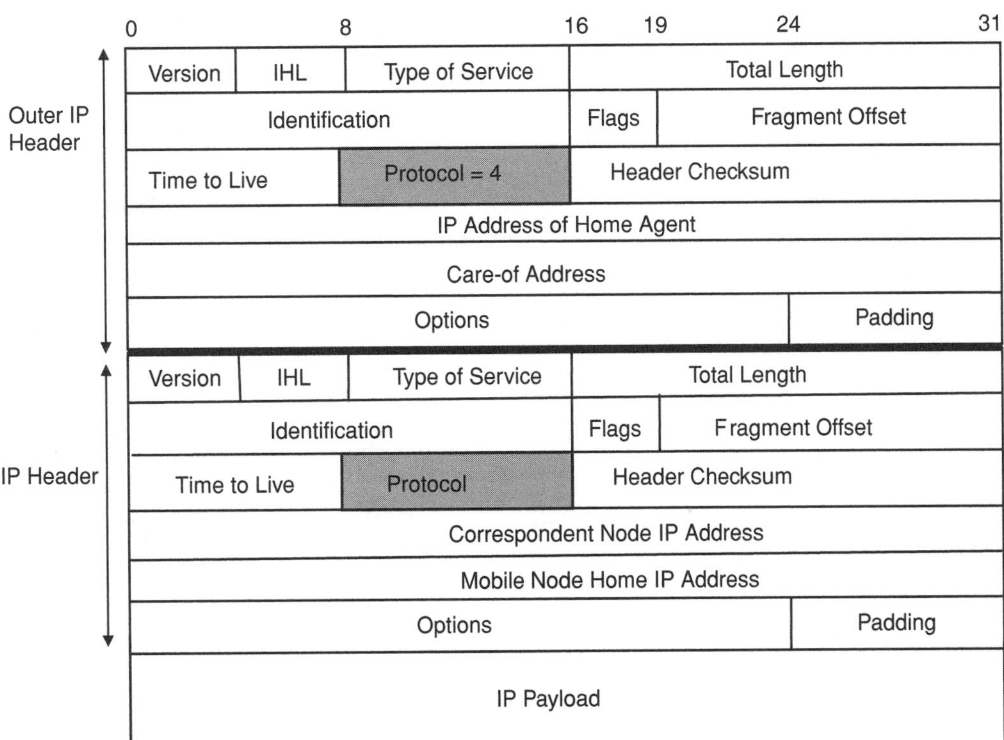

Figure 8: IPv4-in-IPv4 Encapsulation: Contents of outer IP header and IP header.

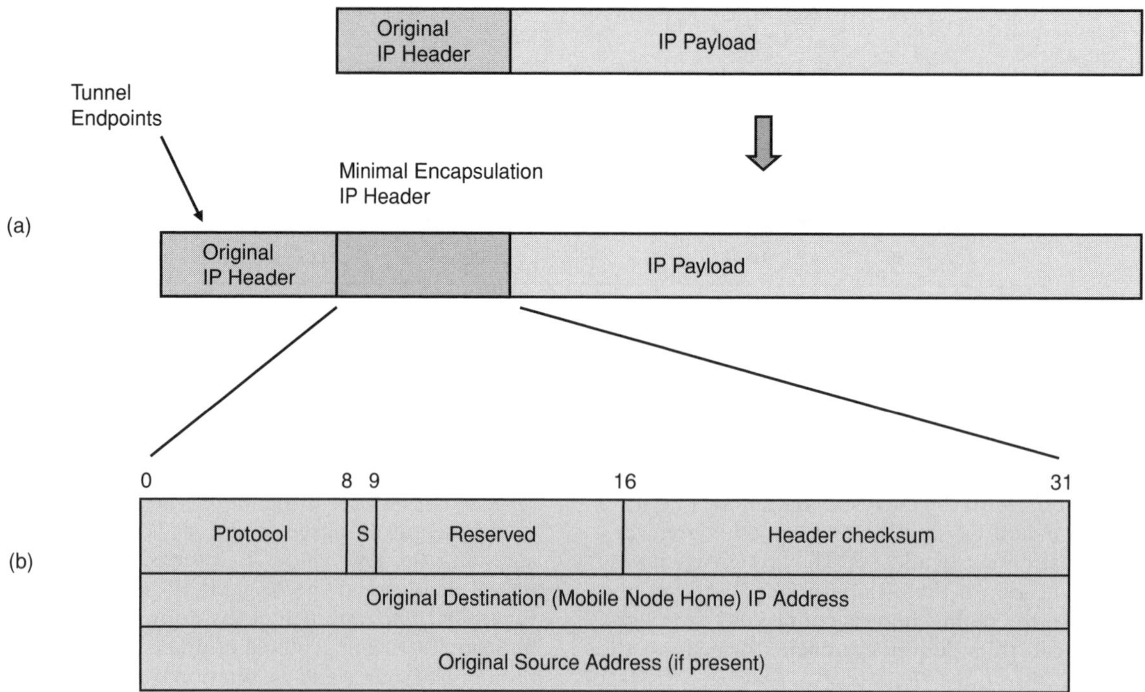

Figure 9: Minimal encapsulation.

ADVANTAGES OF Ipv6 FOR MOBILE IP

The design of mobile IP support in Ipv6 (mobile Ipv6) benefits both from the experiences gained from the development of mobile Ipv4 and from the opportunities provided by Ipv6. Mobile Ipv6 thus shares many features with mobileIpv4 but is integrated into Ipv6 and offers many other improvements. The important features of base Ipv6 protocol (Huitema, 1998) that facilitate mobility to be built into the protocol include the following:

Enough addresses. Ipv6 allows for about 2^{128} (340 undecillion) addresses needed for billions of IP-addressable wireless devices that are forecasted for the next two decades.

Address autoconfiguration for getting care-of addresses. In Ipv6, unlike Ipv4, multiple IP addresses are allocated to each network interface of a node. An Ipv6 node can automatically obtain a valid global Ipv6 address by either using either *stateless* or *stateful* autoconfiguration (explained later).

Advanced network management support. *Internet control message protocol for Ipv6* (*ICMPv6*) is an integral part of Ipv6 and supports advanced network management functions. ICMPv6 (Conta & Deering, 1998b) not only comprises three Ipv4 support protocols (ICMP, ARP, and *Internet group management protocol* [*IGMP*]), but also provides support for address autoconfiguration and mobility in Ipv6. ICMPv6 messages used for *neighbor discovery* (*ND*), which implements address autoconfiguration and address resolution functions, include router solicitation, router advertisement, *neighbor solicitation*, and *neighbor advertisement*.

Embedded security. *Internet security protocol suite* (*IPSec*) (Kent & Atkinson, 1998c; Stallings, 2002; Yuan & Strayer, 2001) is a specification of mechanisms at the network (IP) layer that provide a set of security services. These services are enabled through the use of two security protocols—the *authentication header* (*AH*) (Kent & Atkinson, 1998a) and the *encapsulating security payload* (*ESP*; Kent & Atkinson, 1998b) protocols—and through the use of cryptographic key management procedures and protocols, including Internet security association and key management protocol (ISAKMP; Maughan, Schertler, & Turner, 1998) and the Internet key exchange (IKE) protocol (Harkins & Carrel, 1998). Although the use of IPsec is optional in Ipv4, IPSec is mandatory in Ipv6 and is part of the Ipv6 protocol suite.

Address Autoconfiguration in Ipv6

Stateless address autoconfiguration (Thomson & Narten, 1998) allows an Ipv6 node to obtain a valid global Ipv6 address on every link by discovering the subnet prefix of the link through router solicitations and combining it with its own *interface ID*. The steps involved include the following:

1. The node builds up a *link local address* by concatenating the well-known *link local prefix* (FE80::/64) with its own interface ID as shown in Figure 10a. The interface ID is unique to each network interface of the node and is a EUI-64 number, which can be derived from an 8-byte Ethernet media access control (MAC) address. Link local addresses can only be used on the local link and are not routable.
2. The mobile node listens to router advertisements, which are transmitted periodically. Alternatively, the mobile node sends a router solicitation message on the network to request router advertisement using the link local address. The node can now construct the global

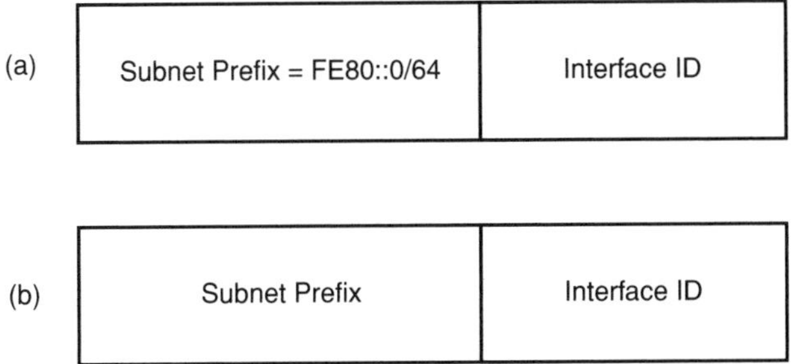

Figure 10: Stateless address autoconfiguration.

Ipv6 address by changing link local prefix to subnet prefix received via a router advertisement as shown in Figure 10b.

In **stateful address autoconfiguration** mode, the mobile node can obtain a new Ipv6 address by using the service of a protocol such as DHCPv6 (Droms et al., 2003). It is called stateful because a server manages which address is allocated to whom and maintains that state. This is the most widely used method in Ipv4.

By using either stateless or stateful address autoconfiguration mode, a mobile node can obtain a new care-of address on every link that it attaches to in the Internet. Therefore, *there are no foreign agents in mobile Ipv6.*

MOBILE Ipv6 OVERVIEW

Mobile Ipv6 optimizes the mobility support of the Ipv6 protocol by providing the following extensions (Johnson, Perkins, & Arkko, 2004):

1. A new extension header, called the *mobility header*, is used by mobile nodes, correspondent nodes, and home agents in all datagrams related to the creation and management of bindings.
2. A new option in the Ipv6 destination options extension header, the *home address destination option*, is used for route optimization.
3. A new type of Ipv6 routing header (*type 2 routing header*) is used for route optimization.
4. New Ipv6 ICMP messages are used to detect movement, to receive network prefixes, and in the dynamic home agent address discovery mechanism.

The basic operation of mobile Ipv6 is similar to mobile Ipv4 as shown in Figure 11. While a mobile node is attached to some foreign link away from home, it is addressable at one or more care-of addresses. The mobile node can acquire its care-of address through conventional Ipv6 mechanisms, and as such as there are no foreign agents in mobile Ipv6. As long as the mobile node stays in this location, packets addressed to this care-of address will be routed to the mobile node. The mobile node may also accept packets from several care-of addresses, such as when it is moving but still reachable at the previous link.

While away from home, a mobile node registers its primary care-of address with a home agent in its home network. The mobile node performs this binding registration by sending a *binding update* (*BU*) message to the home agent (Perkins & Johnson, 1996; Johnson, Perkins, & Arkko, 2004). The home agent replies to the mobile node

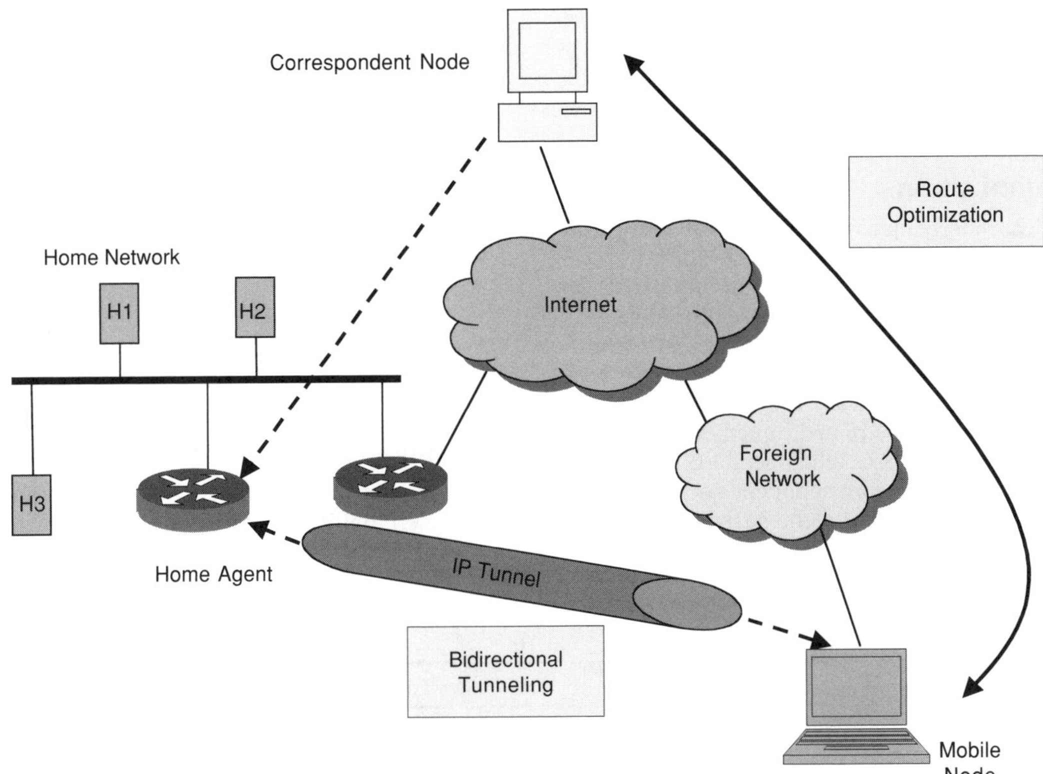

Figure 11: Mobile IPv6 operation.

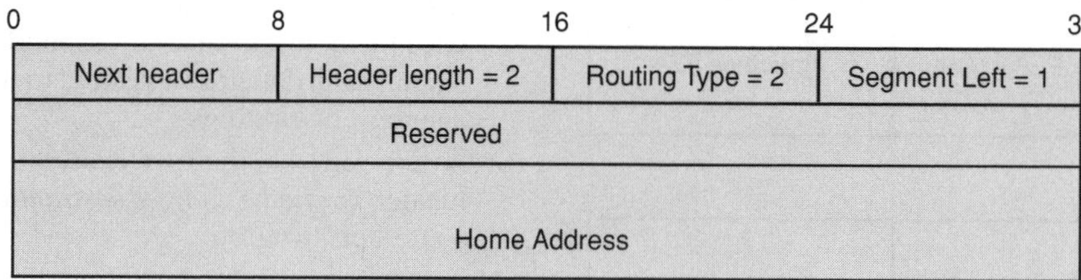

Figure 12: Type 2 Routing header.

by returning a *binding acknowledgement* (*BA*) message. Mobile nodes can provide information about their current location to correspondent nodes. This happens through the correspondent registration. As a part of this procedure, a *return routability test* (Nikander et al., 2003; Johnson, Perkins, & Arkko, 2004) is performed to authorize the establishment of the binding.

There are two possible modes for communications between the mobile node and a correspondent node. The first mode, *bidirectional tunneling*, does not require mobile Ipv6 support from the correspondent node and is available even if the mobile node has not registered its current binding with the correspondent node. Packets from the correspondent node are routed to the home agent and then tunneled to the mobile node as in mobile Ipv4. In this mode, the home agent uses *proxy neighbor discovery* (Narten, Nordmark, & Simpson, 1998) to intercept any Ipv6 packets addressed to the mobile node's home address on the home link. Each intercepted packet is tunneled to the mobile node's primary care-of address. Packets from the mobile node to the correspondent node are tunneled to the home agent (*reverse tunneled*) and then routed normally from the home network to the correspondent node. This tunneling is performed using Ipv6 encapsulation (Conta & Deering, 1998a). The second mode, *route optimization*, requires the mobile node to register its current binding at the correspondent node.

Route Optimization

The basic idea underlying route optimization (Perkins & Johnson, 1996; Johnson, Perkins, & Arkko, 2004) involves providing the correspondent node an up-to-date BU for the mobile node to eliminate the inefficient triangle routing. Ipv6 allows other Ipv6 nodes to receive BUs from a mobile node so that they will know how to deliver datagrams directly to the mobile node. Packets from the correspondent node can thus be routed directly to the care-of address of the mobile node. When sending a packet to any Ipv6 destination, the correspondent node checks its cached bindings for an entry for the packet's destination address. If a cached binding for this destination address is found, the correspondent node sets the destination IP address in the Ipv6 header to the care-of address of the mobile node. The type 2 routing header, as shown in Figure 12, is also added to the packet to carry the desired home address. Once the packet arrives at the care-of address, the mobile node retrieves its home address from the new routing header, and this is used as the final destination address for the packet (to allow transparency at higher layers for ongoing sessions).

Similarly, the mobile node sets the source address in the packet's Ipv6 header to its current care-of address. The mobile node adds its permanent Ipv6 home address in the home address option carried by the destination options extension header in Ipv6 as shown in Figure 13. The inclusion of home addresses in these packets makes the use of the care-of address transparent above the network layer (e.g., at the transport layer).

Routing packets directly to the mobile node's care-of address allows the shortest communications path to be used. It also eliminates congestion at the mobile node's home agent and home link. In addition, the effect of any possible failure of the home agent or networks on the path to or from it is reduced.

Mobile Ipv6 also provides support for multiple home agents and a limited support for the reconfiguration of the home network. In these cases, the mobile node may not know the IP address of its own home agent, and even the home subnet prefixes may change over time. A mechanism, known as *dynamic home agent address discovery* (Johnson, Perkins, & Arkko, 2004), allows a mobile node to dynamically discover the IP address of a home agent on its home link, even when the mobile node is away from home. Mobile nodes can also learn new information about home subnet prefixes through the *mobile prefix discovery* mechanism (Johnson, Perkins, & Arkko, 2004).

Binding Management Messages

Mobile nodes, correspondent nodes, and home agents use the new mobility header in all messages related to the creation and management of bindings. The format of the

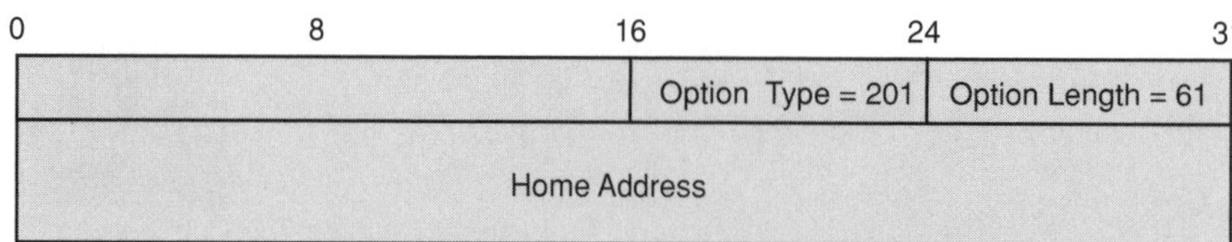

Figure 13: Destination options extension header: Home address option.

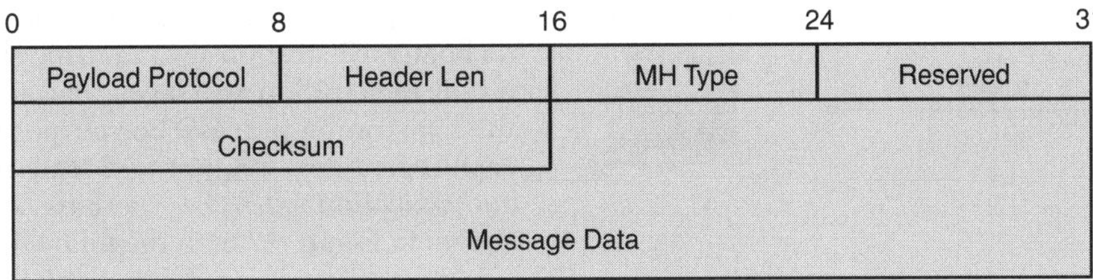

Figure 14: Mobility header format.

mobility header is shown in Figure 14. An explanation of the fields follows:

Payload protocol: Identifies the type of header immediately following the mobility header. Uses the same values as the Ipv6 next header field (Huitema, 1998).

Header len: Represents the length of the mobility header in units of eight octets, excluding the first eight octets.

MH type: Identifies the particular mobile Ipv6 binding management message type.

Message data: A variable-length field containing the data relevant to the indicated binding management message type.

A description of different binding management messages follows:

Binding update (BU): Used by a mobile node to notify other nodes of a new care-of address for itself. The BU uses the MH type value 5 in the mobility header.

Binding acknowledgement (BA): Used to acknowledge receipt of a BU. The BA has the MH type value 6 in the mobility header.

Binding refresh request: Used by correspondent nodes to request a mobile node to update its mobility binding. This message is typically used when the cached binding is in active use but the binding's lifetime is close to expiration. The correspondent node may use, for instance, recent traffic and open transport layer connections as an indication of active use. The binding refresh request message uses the MH type value 0 in the mobility header.

Binding error: Used by the correspondent node to signal an error related to mobility, such as an inappropriate attempt to use the home address destination option without an existing binding. The binding error message uses the MH type value 7 in the mobility header.

SECURITY THREATS IN MOBILE IP

Any mobility solution must protect itself against misuses of the mobility features and mechanisms. Unauthenticated or malicious BUs (registration messages) in mobile Ipv6 (mobile Ipv4) open the door for many types of attacks, a few of which are discussed here (Nikander et al., 2003; Johnson, Perkins, & Arkko, 2004).

Theft of Address

The most obvious danger in mobile Ipv6 is theft of address, that is, an attacker illegitimately claiming to be a given node at a given address and then trying to "steal" traffic destined to that address. Some basic forms of this attack include the following:

Hijacking. By means of false BUs, an attacker can redirect traffic to itself or another node and prevent the original node from receiving traffic destined to it. For instance, let us say node A and node B in Figure 15 have been communicating with each other. Then, an attacker, node C, sends a spoofed BU packet to node A, claiming to be node B with a care-of address of node C. This would cause node A to create a binding for node B's care-of address and subsequently send further traffic to node C, believing it to be node B's new care-of address. Node B would not receive the data it was intended to receive, and, if the data in the packets is not protected cryptographically, node C will be able to see all of the sensitive information from node A to node B.

Man-in-the-middle attack. The attacker sends spoofed BUs to both nodes A and B and inserts itself in the middle as shown in Figure 16. Consequently, the attacker would be able to see and modify the packets sent between node A and node B.

Replay Attacks

An attacker might also attempt to disrupt a mobile node's communications by *replaying* a BU that the node had sent earlier. If the old BU was accepted, packets destined for the mobile node would be sent to its old location and not its current location.

Denial of Service Attacks

As the name suggests, a denial of service attack renders a network, host, or other piece of network infrastructure unusable by legitimate users. Typically, a denial of service

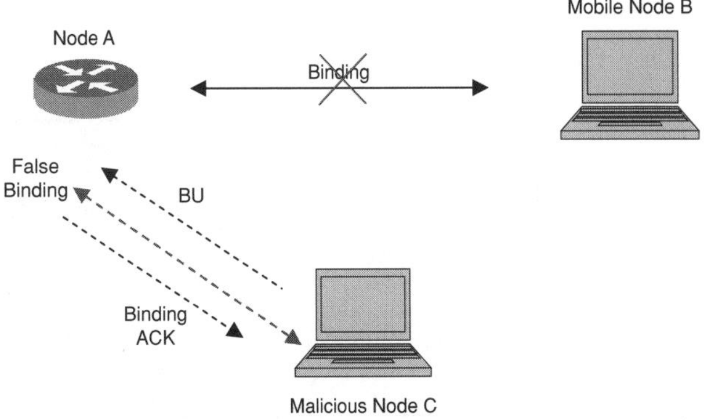

Figure 15: Theft of address: Hijacking.

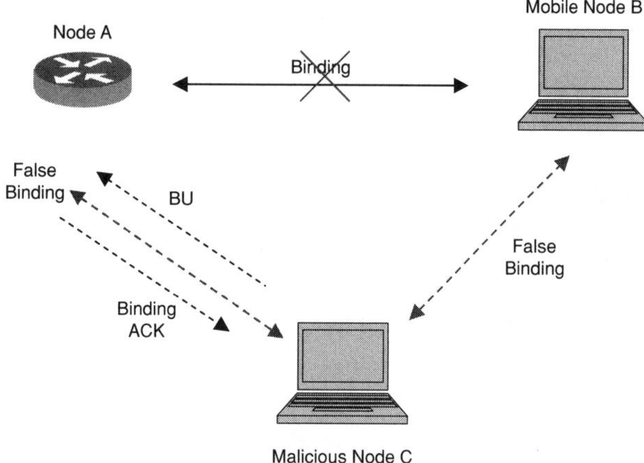

Figure 16: Theft of Address: Man-in-the-middle attack.

attack works by creating so much unnecessary work for the network node or server that legitimate work can not be performed. In mobile IP, a denial of service attack occurs when a malicious (mobile) node sends BUs in which the care-of address is set to the address of a victim node. If such BUs were accepted, the malicious node could lure the correspondent node (e.g., a server) into sending potentially large amounts of data to the victim; the correspondent node's replies to messages sent by the malicious mobile node will be sent to the victim host or network. For example, the correspondent node might be a video stream server that will send a high-bandwidth stream of video to anyone who asks for it. Note that the use of flow-control protocols such as *transmission control protocol* (*TCP*) does not necessarily defend against this type of attack, because the attacker can fake the acknowledgments. Even keeping TCP *initial sequence numbers* (ISN) secret does not help, because the attacker can receive the first few segments (including the ISN) at its own address and then redirect the stream to the victim's address. These types of attacks may also be directed to networks instead of nodes (e.g., TCP SYN flooding attack).

MOBILE Ipv4 SECURITY MECHANISMS

In mobile Ipv4, most of the potential threats are concerned with false registrations sent to home agents. Mobile Ipv4 prevents malicious nodes from being able to do bogus registrations by requiring strong authentication on all registration messages that are exchanged during the registration process. For purposes of authentication, each registration request and reply message contains an *authentication extension* (Perkins, 1997; 1998; 2002) as shown in Figure 17 with the following fields:

Type: Used to designate the type of this authentication extension.

Length: 4 plus the number of bytes in the authenticator field.

Security parameter index (SPI): Unique ID for security association.

Authenticator (authentication data): Contains 128-bit message digest of the registration message computed by using the keyed HMAC-MD5 (Krawczyk, Bellare, & Canetti, 1997; Stallings, 2002) authentication algorithm. The authenticator protects the entire registration request or reply message (UDP payload), any extensions prior to this extension, and the type, length, and SPI fields of this extension.

Three types of authentication extensions are defined:

Mobile-home: This extension must be present and provides for authentication of the registration messages between the mobile node and the home agent.

Mobile-foreign: The extension may be present when a security association exists between the mobile node and the foreign agent. The agent will strip this extension off before relaying a request message to the home agent and add this extension to a reply message coming from a home agent.

Foreign-home: The extension may be present when a security association exists between the foreign agent and the home agent.

The SPI within any of the authentication extensions defines the security context, which is used to compute the authenticator value and which must be used by the receiver to check that value. In particular, the SPI selects the authentication algorithm and mode and a secret (a shared key or appropriate public–private key pair) used in computing the authenticator.

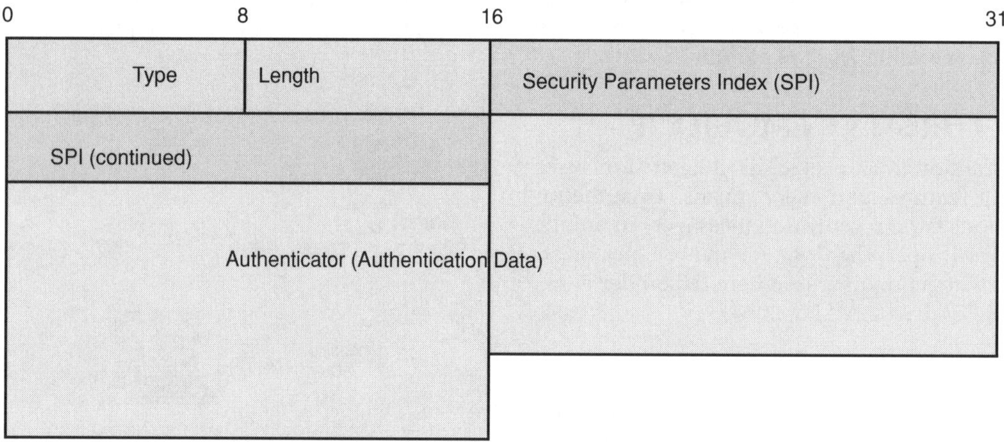

Figure 17: Authentication extension.

Note that the authenticator protects the identification field in the request and reply messages. As a result, the identification value can be used to thwart replay types of attacks. The identification value enables the mobile node to match a reply to a request. Furthermore, if the mobile node and the home agent maintain synchronization so that the home agent can distinguish a reasonable identification value from a suspicious one, then the home agent can reject suspicious messages. One way to do this is to use a time stamp value. As long as the mobile node and home agent have reasonably synchronized values of time, the time stamp will serve the purpose. Alternatively, the mobile node could generate values using a pseudorandom number generator. If the home agent knows the algorithm, then it knows what identification value to expect next.

MOBILE Ipv6 SECURITY MECHANISMS

Mobile Ipv6 introduces several additional security vulnerabilities into Ipv6. In mobile Ipv6, most of the potential threats are concerned with false bindings sent to home agents and correspondent nodes. As discussed earlier, mobile Ipv6's route optimization is built into the Ipv6 protocol rather than added as an extension to the protocol as with mobile Ipv4 and it greatly improves the efficiency of routing by eliminating triangle routing. However, route optimization also greatly increases the number of BUs sent by a mobile node to its correspondent nodes, and in doing so, it also greatly increases the security risk of mobile Ipv6. Mobile Ipv6 provides a number of security features that provide protection against many of the threats posed to mobile Ipv6 as a result of its new features.

Protection of Binding Updates to the Home Agent

The mobile node and the home agent use an IPsec *security association* (*SA*; Kent & Atkinson, 1998; Stallings, 2002; Yuan & Strayer, 2001) to protect the integrity and authenticity of the BUs and BAs. An SA creates a network-layer logical simplex connection to enable transfer of secure datagrams from source to destination hosts. That is, two SAs are needed to protect bidirectional traffic between two nodes, one for each direction. It is uniquely defined by the following three parameters:

Security parameter index (SPI): A 32-bit connection identifier, usually chosen by the destination end point of the SA, uniquely identifies the logical connection (SA).

Destination IP address: This is the address of the destination end point of the SA.

Security protocol identifier: This indicates whether the association is an AH (51) or ESP (50) security association.

SAs between the mobile nodes and the home agents use the ESP protocol in transport mode and use a non-null payload authentication algorithm (Arkko, Devarapalli, & Dupont, 2004) to provide data origin authentication, connectionless integrity, and optional antireplay protection. The formats of BU and BA messages between the mobile node and the home agent are shown in Figure 18.

To prevent the mobile node from sending a BU for another mobile node, the home agent checks that the given home address has been used with the right SA. Such a check is provided in the IPsec processing by having the security policy database entries unequivocally identify a single SA for protecting BUs between any given home address and home agent. To make this possible, it is necessary that the home address of the mobile node is visible in the BUs and BAs. The home address used in these packets is contained in either the source IP address field of the packet or in the home address destination option (in the destination options extension header) or the type 2 routing header.

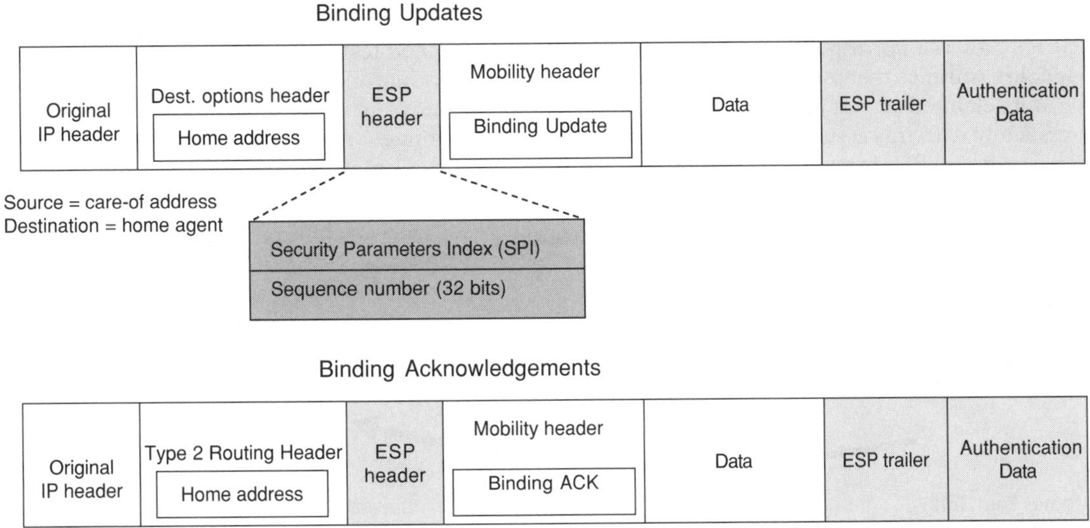

Figure 18: Security mechanisms for exchange of mobility messages between mobile nodes and home agents.

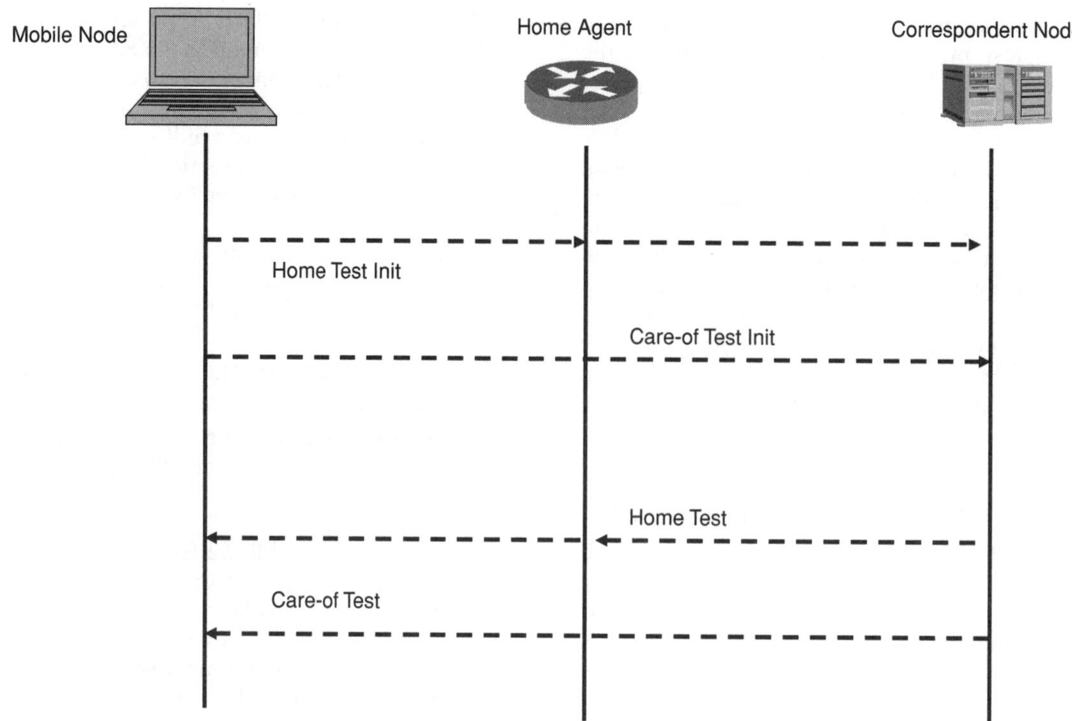

Figure 19: Return Routability Procedure (RRP): Message flow.

IPsec can provide antireplay protection only if dynamic keying is used (which may not always be the case).

Protection of Binding Updates to Correspondent Nodes

The protection of BUs sent to correspondent nodes does not require the configuration of security associations or the existence of an authentication infrastructure between the mobile nodes and correspondent nodes. Instead, a method called the *return routability procedure (RRP)* (Nikander et al., 2003; Johnson, Perkins, & Arkko, 2004) is used to assure that the right mobile node is sending the message.

The RRP enables the correspondent node to obtain some reasonable assurance that the mobile node is in fact addressable at its claimed care-of address as well as at its home address. Only with this assurance is the correspondent node able to accept BUs from the mobile node, which would then instruct the correspondent node to direct that mobile node's data traffic to its claimed care-of address. This is done by testing whether packets addressed to the two claimed addresses are routed to the mobile node. The mobile node can pass the test only if it is able to supply proof that it received certain data (the *keygen tokens*) that the correspondent node sends to those addresses. These data are combined by the mobile node into a binding management key, denoted Kbm. Figure 19 shows the message flow for the RRP.

The RRP consists of two tests, a *home (address) test* and a *care-of (address) test*. These tests are triggered by sending *home test init* and *care-of test init* packets. The RRP uses cookies and keygen tokens as opaque values within the test init and test messages, respectively.

The home and care-of test init messages, shown in Figure 20, are sent at the same time by the mobile node to the correspondent node, and they verify that the mobile node is reachable at its home and care-of addresses and request

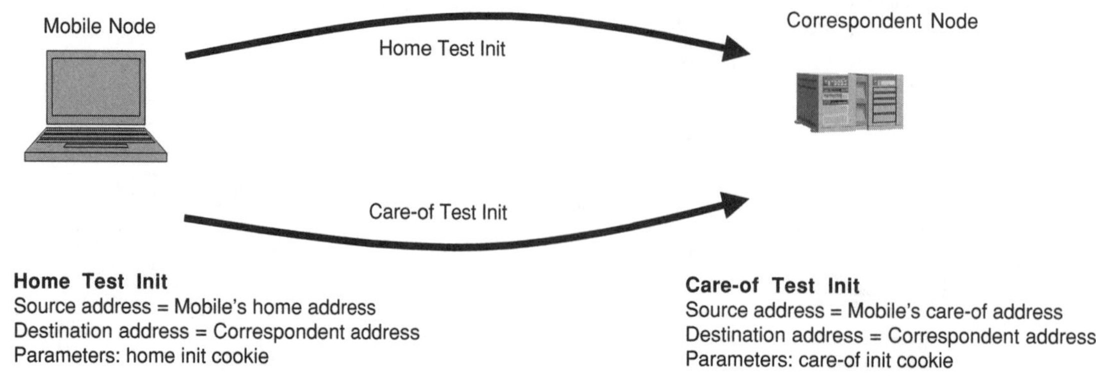

Figure 20: RRP: Test init messages from the mobile to correspondent node.

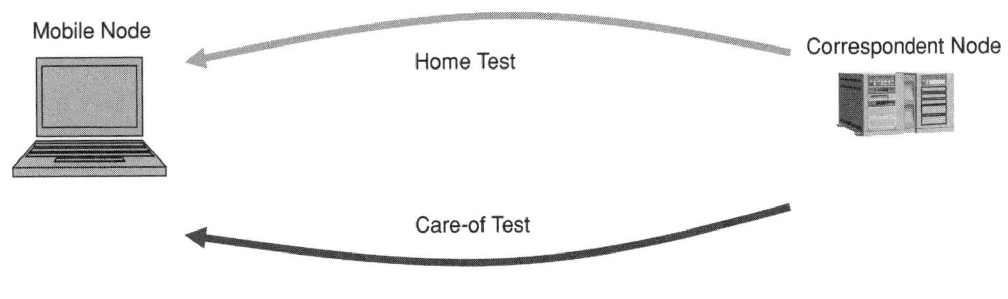

Home Test
Source address = Correspondent address
Destination address = Mobile's home address
Parameters:
- home init cookie
- home keygen token
- home nonce index

Care-of Test
Source address = Correspondent address
Destination address = Mobile's care-of address
Parameters:
- care-of init cookie
- care-of keygen token
- care-of nonce index

Figure 21: RRP: Test messages from the correspondent to mobile node.

keygen tokens to be sent from the correspondent node. The home test init message is reverse tunneled through the home agent. Each message also contains an *init cookie*, a 64-bit random value, which must be returned by the correspondent in the next step to verify the identity of the correspondent node. The mobile node remembers these cookie values to obtain some assurance that its protocol messages are being processed by the desired correspondent node.

The correspondent node, upon receiving the home test init message from the mobile node, generates a *home keygen token* from a hash function using the first 64 bits of the message authentication code (MAC) (Johnson, Perkins, & Arkko, 2004):

home keygen token = First (64, HMAC_SHA1 (Kcn, (home address | nonce | 0)))

where | denotes concatenation and HMAC_SHA1 (Kcn,m) denotes a MAC computed on message m with key Kcn using HMAC_SHA1 (Krawczyk, Bellare, & Canetti, 1997; Stallings, 2002) function. The final "0" inside the HMAC_SHA1 function is a single zero octet, used to distinguish home and care-of cookies from each other. Each correspondent node generates nonces at regular intervals. The home keygen token tests that the mobile node can receive messages sent to its home address.

Next the correspondent node, upon receiving the care-of test init message from the mobile node, generates a *care-of keygen token* from a hash function using the first 64 bits of the message authentication code (MAC) (Johnson, Perkins, & Arkko, 2004):

care-of keygen token = First (64, HMAC_SHA1 (Kcn, (care-of address | nonce | 1)))

Here, the final "1" inside the HMAC_SHA1 function is a single octet containing the hex value 01 and is used to distinguish home and care-of cookies from each other. The care-of keygen token tests that the mobile node can receive messages sent to its care-of address.

Next, the home and care-of test messages containing keygen tokens are sent simultaneously, as shown in Figure 21, from the correspondent node to the mobile node, in response to the mobile node's test init messages. Included in both messages are the init cookies, which verify for the mobile node that the test messages are being received from the correspondent node, or at least by a node in the path to the correspondent node. The home test message is sent to the mobile node via the home network, where it is presumed that the home agent will send the message to the mobile node inside the IPSec tunnel. This means that the mobile node needs to already have sent a BU to the home agent, so that the home agent will have received and authorized the new care-of address for the mobile node before the RRP.

When the mobile node has received both the home and care-of test messages, the RRP is complete. The mobile node now hashes the keygen tokens together to form a 20-octet binding management key Kbm (Johnson, Perkins, & Arkko, 2004):

Kbm = SHA1 (home keygen token | care-of keygen token)

The integrity and authenticity of the BU's messages to correspondent nodes is protected by using the Kbm to key the hash algorithm for this purpose. As a result of the procedure, the mobile node now has the security mechanism in place to send a verifiable BU to the correspondent node as shown in Figure 22.

When sending the BU, the mobile node includes its home address, the nonce indexes, sequence number, and the MAC. This new value of the MAC is calculated by hashing the Kbm with a concatenation of the care-of address, the correspondent node address, and the entire BU message itself. Once the correspondent node has verified the MAC, it can create a binding cache entry for the mobile. A BA is optionally sent by the correspondent node if the mobile node requests it. The BA contains the same sequence number as in the BU and also contains a MAC, which is calculated similar to the BU, by hashing the Kbm with a concatenation of the care-of address, correspondent node address, and the entire BA message itself.

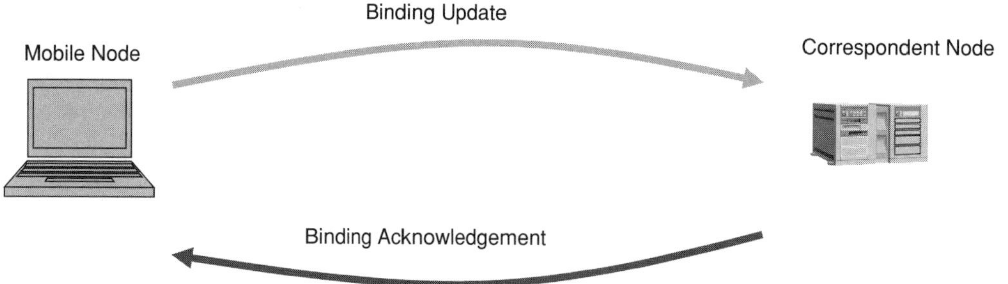

Binding Update (BU)
Source address = Mobile's care-of address
Destination address = Correspondent address
Parameters:
- home address (within Home address destination option)
- sequence number (within the Mobility header)
- home nonce index (within the Nonce indices option)
- care-of nonce index (within the Nonce indices option)
- MAC=First (96, HMAC_SHA1 (Kbm, (care-of address | correspondent address| BU)))

Binding Acknowledgement (BA)
Source address = Correspondent address
Destination address = Mobile's care-of address
Parameters:
- sequence number (within the Mobility header)
- MAC = First (96, HMAC_SHA1 (Kbm, (care-of address | correspondent address | BA)))

Figure 22: Binding update and acknowledgement messages.

CONCLUSION

Mobile Ipv4 provides protocol enhancements required for mobility support in networks based on current Ipv4. Much of the interest in mobile IP has shifted to Ipv6 in recent years, driven by the proposals to make the new IP protocol a mandatory part of the next generation of wireless networks. Mobile Ipv6 uses the same basic network entities as mobile Ipv4, except that there is no need for the foreign agent. Route optimization, which greatly improves the routing efficiency in mobile Ipv6, also enhances its security vulnerabilities by increasing the likelihood of false binding updates. The security design of mobile Ipv6 deals with this threat and provides the necessary mechanisms to make mobile Ipv6 as secure as Ipv4.

GLOSSARY

Agent Solicitation The message sent by a mobile node to request agent advertisement.

Binding The association of the home address of a mobile node with a care-of address for that mobile node, along with the remaining lifetime of that association.

Binding Management Key (Kbm) A key used for authorizing a binding cache management message (e.g., BU or BA). The return routability procedure provides a way to create a binding management key.

Care-Of Address The address associated with a mobile node while visiting a foreign link; the subnet prefix of this IP address is a foreign subnet prefix.

Collocated Care-Of Address An externally obtained local IP address temporarily assigned to an interface of the mobile node.

Cookie A random number used by a mobile node to prevent spoofing by a bogus correspondent node in the return routability procedure.

Correspondent Node A peer host with which a mobile node communicates. The correspondent node may be either mobile or stationary.

Foreign Agent A router with an interface on a mobile node's visiting network, which assists the mobile node in informing its home agent of its current care-of address.

Foreign Network A network other than a mobile node's home network to which the mobile node is currently connected.

Gratuitous ARP An ARP packet sent by a node to spontaneously cause other nodes to update an entry in their ARP cache.

Home Address An IP address that is assigned for an extended period of time to a mobile node. It remains unchanged regardless of where the node resides in the Internet. Standard IP routing mechanisms will deliver packets destined for a mobile node's home address to its home link.

Home Agent A router with an interface on the mobile node's home network link, which the mobile node keeps informing of its current location, the care-of address, as the mobile node moves from link to link. While the mobile node is away from home, the home agent intercepts packets on the home link destined to the mobile node's home address, encapsulates them, and tunnels them to the mobile node's registered care-of address.

Home Network A network having a network prefix matching that of a mobile node's home address.

IPSec Security Association A cooperative relationship formed by the sharing of cryptographic keying material and associated context. Security associations are simplex.

Keygen Token A number supplied by a correspondent node in the return routability procedure to enable the mobile node to compute the necessary binding management key for authorizing a BU.

Link A facility or medium via which nodes can communicate at the link layer.

Link-Layer Address An address that identifies the physical end point of a link. Usually, the link-layer address is the interface's medium access control (MAC) address.

Mobile Node A host or a router that can change its point of attachment from one link to another, while still being reachable via its home address.

Mobile Node's Foreign Link The link that the mobile node is visiting, which has been assigned the same subnet prefix as the subnet prefix of the mobile node's care-of address.

Mobile Node's Home Link The link that has been assigned the same subnet prefix as the subnet prefix of the mobile node's home address.

Nonce A random number used internally by the correspondent node in the creation of keygen tokens related to the return routability procedure. The nonces are not specific to a mobile node and are kept secret within the correspondent node. They are updated at regular intervals.

Nonce Index An index associated with each nonce to help the correspondent node identify which nonce, the current one or one of a previous few, was used with a particular message.

Subnet Prefix Specifies routing information to an IP subnet (link). In Ipv6, it is followed by an *interface identifier*, which specifies a node (host) attached to the link.

Tunnel The path followed by a datagram while it is encapsulated.

CROSS REFERENCES

See *Internet Architecture; IP-Based VPN; Mobile Devices and Protocols; TCP/IP Suite; VPN Basics.*

REFERENCES

Arkko, J., Devarapalli, V., & Dupont, F. (2004, June). *Using IPsec to protect mobile Ipv6 signaling between mobile nodes and home agents* (RFC 3776). Retrieved June 18, 2004, from http://www.rfc-editor.org/rfc/rfc3776.txt

Conta, A., & Deering, S. (1998a, December). *Generic packet tunneling in Ipv6 specification* (RFC 2473). Retrieved June 18, 2004, from http://www.rfc-editor.org/rfc/rfc2473.txt

Conta, A., & Deering, S. (1998b, December). *Internet control message protocol (ICMPv6) for the Internet protocol version 6 (Ipv6) specification* (RFC 2463). Retrieved June 18, 2004, from http://www.rfc-editor.org/rfc/rfc2463.txt

Droms, R., Ed. J, Bound, J., Volz, B., Lemon, T., Perkins, C., & Carney, M. (2003, July). *Dynamic host configuration protocol for Ipv6 (DHCPv6)* (RFC 3315). Retrieved June 18, 2004, from http://www.rfc-editor.org/rfc/rfc3315.txt

Harkins, D., & Carrel, D. (1998, November). *The Internet key exchange (IKE)* (RFC 2409). Retrieved June 18, 2004, from http://www.rfc-editor.org/rfc/rfc2409.txt

Huitema, C. (1998). *Ipv6: The new Internet protocol* (2nd Ed.). Upper Saddle River, NJ: Prentice Hall PTR.

Johnson, D., Perkins, C., & Arkko, J. (2004, June). *Mobility support in Ipv6* (RFC 3775). Retrieved June 21, 2004, from http://www.rfc-editor.org/rfc/rfc3775.txt

Kent, S., & Atkinson, R. (1998a, November). *IP authentication header* (RFC 2402). Retrieved June 18, 2004, from http://www.rfc-editor.org/rfc/rfc2402.txt

Kent, S., & Atkinson, R. (1998b, November). *IP encapsulating security payload (ESP)* (RFC 2406). Retrieved June 18, 2004, from http://www.rfc-editor.org/rfc/rfc2406.txt

Kent, S., & Atkinson, R. (1998c, November). *Security architecture for the Internet protocol* (RFC 2401). Retrieved June 18, 2004, from http://www.rfc-editor.org/rfc/rfc2401.txt

Krawczyk, H., Bellare, M., & Canetti, R. (1997, February). *HMAC: Keyed-hashing for message authentication* (RFC 2104). Retrieved June 18, 2004, from http://www.rfc-editor.org/rfc/rfc2104.txt

Leon-Garcia, A., & Widjaja, I. (2004). *Communication networks* (2nd Ed.). New York: McGraw–Hill.

Maughan, D., Schertler, M., & Turner, J. (1998, November). *Internet security association and key management protocol (ISAKMP)* (RFC 2408). Retrieved June 18, 2004, from http://www.rfc-editor.org/rfc/rfc2408.txt

Montenegro, G. (2001, January). *Reverse tunneling for mobile IP (revised)* (RFC 3024). Retrieved June 18, 2004, from http://www.rfc-editor.org/rfc/rfc3024.txt

Narten, T., Nordmark, E., & Simpson, W. (1998, December). *Neighbor discovery for IP version 6 (Ipv6)* (RFC 2461). Retrieved June 18, 2004, from http://www.rfc-editor.org/rfc/rfc2461.txt

Nikander, P., Aura, T., Arkko, J., Montenegro, G., & Nordmark, E. (2003, June). *Mobile IP version 6 route optimization security design background*. Retrieved June 21, 2004, from http://www.join.uni-muenster.de/Dokumente/drafts/draft-nikander-mobileip-v6-ro-sec-01.txt

Perkins, C. (1997, May). Mobile IP. *IEEE Communications Magazine, 35*(5), 84–99.

Perkins, C. (1998, January–February). Mobile networking through mobile IP. *IEEE Internet Computing, 2*(1), 58–69.

Perkins, C. (2002, August). *IP mobility support* (RFC 3344). Retrieved June 18, 2004, from http://www.rfc-editor.org/rfc/rfc3344.txt

Perkins, C., & Johnson, D. (1996, November). Mobility support in Ipv6. In *Proceedings of Mobicom '96* (pp. 27–37). New York: ACM.

Postel, J. (1984, October). *Multi-LAN address resolution* (RFC 925). Retrieved June 18, 2004, from http://www.rfc-editor.org/rfc/rfc925.txt

Stallings, W. (2002). *Cryptography and network security: Principles and practice*. (3rd Ed.). Upper Saddle River, NJ: Prentice-Hall.

Stevens, W. (1994). *TCP/IP illustrated. Vol. 1: The protocols.* Boston, MA: Addison-Wesley.

Thomson, S., & Narten, T. (1998, December). *Ipv6 stateless address autoconfiguration* (RFC 2462). Retrieved June 18, 2004, from http://www.rfc-editor.org/rfc/rfc2462.txt

Yuan, R., & Strayer, W. T. (2001). *Virtual private networks: Technologies and solutions* (1st Ed.). Boston, MA: Addison-Wesley.

IP Multicast and Its Security

Emilia Rosti, *Università degli Studi di Milano, Italy*

INTRODUCTION

IP multicast is an internetwork service that provides efficient delivery of data from one or more sources to a set of recipients, commonly known as a group (Deering, 1989). Examples of services that could take great advantage of multicast communication are live video/audio distribution (for example, videoconferencing and collaborative groupware), periodic data distribution (for example, software updates, newspaper/magazine distribution, and sport or stock quotes), Web server updates, pay-per-view services (for example, video on demand), and distributed videogames.

The goal of multicast is to reduce sender transmission overhead, network bandwidth usage, and the latency observed by receivers. If only one IP multicast datagram, or packet as we interchangeably call it, containing, for example, video information, can be sent to multiple teleconference sites instead of one packet per site, network bandwidth is saved and time synchronization is closer to optimal. For this to be possible, special addresses and routing schemes must be devised. Group management protocols that define how a host may join or leave a multicast group are also necessary.

The first experiments with multicast were performed in the early 1990s on the MBone research network (Almeroth & Ammar, 1997), a virtual network obtained by encapsulating multicast traffic in traditional unicast datagrams. General-purpose UNIX machines executing user-space ad hoc daemons were in charge of routing. Moving from MBone through a variety of protocols proposed by the networking community, multicast communication is now available by default in the TCP/IP stack. Research and standardization efforts are still ongoing, however, because some areas have not reached a final development stage or still can be improved (see, e.g., IETF, n.d.a; n.d.b; n.d.c; n.d.d). Group-based services may require secure communication, that is, that data traffic be protected from disclosure to unauthorized receivers or from unauthorized modifications and that group members be authenticated. Further restrictions on the receiver and/or sender group may be in place, for example, keeping their identity private while guaranteeing their membership. In general, it is implicitly assumed that the multicast primitive satisfies some basic security requirements, such as the confidentiality and the integrity of the information transmitted and the authenticity of the group members. Yet, IP multicast was not designed with integrated security services: data is sent in the clear and groups are open, and thus are vulnerable to a variety of threats (Ballardie & Crowcroft, 1995; Pinkas & Canetti, 1999; Canetti et al., 1999). This has sparked a wealth of research to propose efficient protocols to add security features to multicast primitives. An Internet Research Task Force (IRTF) on group security at large, GSEC, originally part of the initial secure multicast research group (SMug), was formed "to discuss issues related to multicast security." GSEC is actively working on various areas such as group policy management, group key management, and security technologies for open and closed groups (IETF, n.d.d). In parallel, a working group of the IETF on multicast security (MSEC) is active with the goal of "standardizing protocols for securing group communication over internets, and in particular over the global Internet" (IETF, n.d.d).

A secure multicast protocol must ensure that only authorized group members access, and possibly distribute, the information circulating in the group and that members join and leave the group in a controlled fashion. Cryptographic systems for traffic encryption and party authentication can be designed to satisfy such requirements. This requires, in turn, protocols for managing cryptographic key distribution and updates. Therefore, key management is the critical issue characterizing the problem of secure IP multicast and has been the subject of extensive research efforts in the past 15 years (see, for example, (Banerjee & Bhattacharjee, 2002; Balenson, McGrew, & Sherman, 2000; Ballardie, 1996; Ballardie & Crowcroft, 1995; Briscoe, 1999; Burmester & Desmedt, 1996; Canetti et al., 2000; Canetti et al., 1999; Caronni, Lubich, Aziz, Markson, & Skrenta, 1996; Chang, Engel, Kandlur, Pendarakis, & Saha, 1999; Chiou & Chen, 1989; Chu, Qiao, & Nahrstedt, 2002; Fiat & Naor, 1993; Hardjono & Cain, 2000; Harney & Harder, 1999; Harney & Muckenhirn, 1997a; Harney & Muckenhirn, 1997b; Huang & Mishra,

2003; Judge & Ammar, 2002; Matsumoto & Imai, 1988; Maugham, Schertler, Schneider, & Turner, 1998; Mittra, 1997; Molva & Pannerat, 2000; Moyer, Rao, & Rohatgi, 1999; Perrig, Song, & Tygar, 2001; Pinkas & Canetti,1999; Setia, Koussih, & Jajodia, 2000; Setia, Zhu, & Jajodia, 2002; Steiner, Tsudik, & Waidner, 2000; Waldvogel, Caronni, Sun, Weiler, & Plattner, 1999; Wallner, Harder, & Agee, 1999; Wong, Gouda, & Lam, 1998; Yang, Li, Zhang, & Lam, 2001; Zhang, Lam, Lee, & Yang, 2001; Zhu, Setia, & Jajodia, 2003). Because groups are likely to become larger and highly dynamic as multicast usage becomes widespread, membership changes will occur frequently. Therefore, the design of efficient and scalable key management protocols is crucial for the deployment of secure multicast services in real scenarios.

In this chapter, we review the basic concepts of IP multicast for Ipv4 with particular attention to addressing, routing, group management, and reliability. We discuss the security issues of such a communication service and present the main features of the most relevant key management schemes proposed in the literature to secure IP multicast communication.

This chapter is organized as follows: the second section reviews IP multicast, the third section illustrates the security issues in IP multicast and the requirements of a secure multicast protocol, the fourth section describes a selection of key management protocols, and the fifth section summarizes our contributions and concludes the paper.

IP MULTICAST

In this section, we illustrate the basic concepts of IP multicast within the Ipv4 context. IP multicasting is the ability to send IP datagrams to multiple nodes in a logical group, in such a way as to minimize the number of packets. An addressing scheme to efficiently identify the nodes in the group, a protocol to distribute the datagrams and thereby minimize their replication, and a protocol to manage nodes joining and leaving are the components of IP multicasting.

In the original service model (Deering, 1989), groups are open and public. Any node can send traffic to any multicast group, even if it is not a member of the destination group. Any node can be a receiver, that is, a group member. Routers ignore members' and sources' identities. As we discuss, such a general service model makes the design of efficient protocols for routing traffic, managing groups, and assigning addresses quite challenging.

In what follows, we review the addressing scheme and multicast routing protocols. We then describe how group management is performed and discuss the issues of reliable multicast communication.

Addressing

A multicast group is identified by a particular address, which allows a source to send a message simultaneously to all the hosts in the group without listing their individual IP addresses. Special addresses are necessary to distinguish groups from unicast addresses so that routers can handle multicast packets more efficiently. For this purpose, in Ipv4 the Internet Assigned Number Authority (IANA) reserved class D address space, that is, addresses with the four high-order bits equal to 1110, covering the range 224.0.0.0–239.255.255.255 (Reynolds & Postel, 1994). The remaining 28 bits of the address identify the group, for a total of about 268 million groups.

Table 1 Current Statically Reserved Multicast Addresses

Address Range	Usage
224.0.0.0–224.0.0.225	Local network control
224.0.1.0–224.0.1.255	Internetwork control
224.1.0.0–224.1.255.255	ST multicast groups
232.0.0.0–232.255.255.255	Source-specific multicast
233.0.0.0–233.255.255.255	GLOP
239.0.0.0–239.255.255.255	Administrative scoping

Some of the addresses of the class range are reserved for particular uses and may be assigned statically, whereas the rest are assigned dynamically to different multicast groups on a per-session basis and reclaimed when the session is terminated. Examples of statically assigned addresses are the 224.0.0.0–224.255.255.255 range, used for routing protocols, and the 233.0.0.0–233.255.255.255 range, known as the GLOP range, which is reserved for organizations that already have a reserved autonomous systems number (Meyer & Lotheberg, 2001). Among the set of dynamically assigned addresses, the range 232.0.0.0–232.255.255.255 is reserved for source-specific multicast (SSM) (Bhattacharya, 2003), that is, one-to-many groups. This service model has been gaining popularity because it is simpler than the many-to-many or any-source multicast (ASM) of the original proposal and the majority of commercially viable applications are one-to-many, for example, video on demand, news casting, and Web updates. To support ASM, the network must discover all sources for a given group and deliver the traffic to the group members, which accounts for the greater complexity of this model. With SSM, it is the user that typically specifies the source. When the receiver contacts its router to join a group, it specifies both the group and the sender, thus lifting the burden of source discovery from the network and simplifying multicast delivery. Table 1 reports a summary of the current address assignment (Albanna, Almeroth, Meyer, & Schipper, 2001).

To limit address space consumption and to allow routers to confine packets within an administrative domain, the higher end of the address space is reserved for administratively scoped applications (Meyer, 1998). Because such applications are not Internet-wide, they have no need for uniquely assigned addresses and the routers do not have to propagate the packets outside the network boundaries. Scope limitation used to be achieved by using specific values in the time-to-live (TTL) field of the IP header. This is an inheritance of MBone but is now deprecated because overloading the TTL with both packet lifetime and scope limitation semantic may result in ambiguity and cause difficulty when reconfiguring a distribution tree.

In IP multicast, no central authority exists that allocates addresses upon request. Because addresses are allocated in a distributed uncoordinated fashion, clashes are possible. Another issue is the exhaustion of the limited address space, as multicast becomes more popular, which calls for address reuse when sessions terminate. The multicast address allocation architecture proposed by the Malloc working group of the IETF copes with these issues by defining a three-layer hierarchical approach to address allocation (IETF, n.d.b; Thaler, Handley, & Estrin, 2000). A host dynamically requests an address to a multicast address allocation server (MAAS) using MADCAP, multicast address dynamic client allocation protocol (Hanna, Patel, & Shah, 1999). The server provides an address that is unique within its allocation domain, but not necessarily globally unique. Because there is no central authority enforcing address uniqueness, such an approach provides for scalability and locality of group members and low probability of address duplication across the Internet. To minimize clashes, routers claim sets of addresses at interdomain level for the MAASs in their domain using the multicast address-set claim (MASC) protocol (Kumar et al., 1998; Radoslavov et al., 2000), although domains do not have to allocate an address set for hosts in the domain to be able to allocate group addresses. A module for managing multicast address allocation in a protocol-independent manner, as well as for managing specific protocols used in allocating multicast addresses, has also been defined (Thaler, 2003). The module provides the ability to configure and monitor the status of multicast address allocation within the local domain, answering questions regarding how full a given scope is and who filled it up, who allocated a given address, and whether requests are being met.

Routing

Routing multicast traffic requires ad hoc protocols in order to deliver packets in a more efficient way than simply broadcasting them to the entire network or individually sending them as unicast messages to each receiver. The source sends only a single datagram and the routers replicate the datagram along the branches of a distribution tree. When the final router is reached, it delivers the packet to its local network. Because groups are open and sources do not have to be part of the group, routers do not necessarily know where the sender is or who the receivers are. How the distribution tree is built and what information a router stores and/or computes distinguishes the various routing protocols. This determines the "density" or "sparseness" of the routing protocols, that is, whether they are more efficient with densely or sparsely populated groups, respectively. Finally, multicast routing protocols may be suitable for intradomain or interdomain routing.

The simplest approach consists in building the spanning tree rooted at the source that connects all the group member networks, by using the "broadcast and prune" strategy. A packet is initially broadcast to the entire network. Each router that receives a packet performs a reverse path-forwarding check to identify the interface on the most efficient path to the source. All packets received on the other interfaces will be discarded. Routers that have group members in their domain forward the packets on the subnet. Otherwise, they return a "prune" message on the interface to the source. When a router receives prune messages on all interfaces but the one to the source, it sends a prune message back to the source. Otherwise, only the interfaces that have received a prune message are pruned. Protocols that adopt this paradigm are usually called "dense mode" protocols. The distance vector multicast routing protocol (DVMRP; Waitzman, Partridge, & Deering, 1988) and the protocol-independent multicast dense mode (PIM-DM; see Adams, Nicholas, & Siadak, 2003 for the latest specification) follow this approach. The former builds and maintains its own unicast routing table whereas the latter uses the existing one, independent of the protocol used to build it. With both protocols, a new tree rooted at the source must be built for each source in the group and state information is kept for each source at every router in the network, regardless of whether there are group members downstream.

An alternative to dense mode protocols, "sparse mode" protocols aim at optimizing multicast routing when members are widely distributed. They are also known as explicit join protocols, because group members send explicit join messages to a designated router acting as a rendezvous point (RP), or core. This allows for a better network bandwidth usage, because multicast traffic only flows through links that have been explicitly added to the tree. Sources and receivers in a group share a single tree rooted at the RP. Only routers along the distribution tree need to maintain state for each group, thus providing for better scalability with respect to dense mode protocols. Sources send packets to the RP, which forwards them to the registered members. As it is easy to understand, this is the critical aspect of sparse mode protocols. The RP can be a single point of failure and can easily become a performance bottleneck. Furthermore, it may force the use of less-than-optimal routes between the source and the receivers. The two popular sparse mode protocols, namely core based tree (CBT; Ballardie, 1997) and PIM sparse mode (PIM-SM; Estrin et al., 1998), address these issues differently. Robustness is achieved via the bootstrap router protocol that performs RP discovery and selects a backup RP if the primary one fails. CBT uses bidirectional trees to limit the hot spot effect on the RP, whereas PIM-SM allows the RP to switch forwarding from the shared tree to the shortest path tree to a given leaf router whenever traffic exceeds a given threshold.

A different type of protocol is MOSPF, multicast extensions to OSPF (Moy, 1994), which relies on the link-state routing paradigm of the OSPF unicast routing protocol to deliver multicast packets. Each MOSPF router floods its domain with information about the receivers in each group so that all routers can have the same view of group membership and build the correct tree. However, data is sent only to receivers that explicitly requested it, thus reducing the protocol overhead. Thus, while MOSPF is considered a dense protocol with respect to control information, it is a sparse one with respect to data.

The routing protocols presented so far are typically employed at intradomain level. Features such as the RP router of sparse mode protocols or the waste of resources to maintain state in routers not on the multicast distribution tree make them unsuitable for global deployment. Hierarchical interdomain routing has been proposed to address such an issue. The multiprotocol extensions to BGP (MBGP; Bates, Rekhter, Chandra, & Katz, 2000) and the border gateway multicast protocol (BGMP; Kumar et al., 1998; IETF, n.d.a; Thaler, 2004) are examples of interdomain protocols. MBGP was the initial response to the need for interdomain routing. It extends BGP-4 with the ability to provide next-hop information between domains, to provide reachability and policy control for multicast routing, and to route various types of network traffic. BGMP was proposed as the long-term solution to wide-scale interdomain routing, in association with the multicast address-set claim (MASC) protocol for hierarchical address space allocation. It strongly relies on the existence of a domain-oriented address allocation scheme to avoid collisions. BGMP is independent of the intradomain multicast routing protocol. It builds a bidirectional, shared tree of domains using a domain as global root for the distribution tree. Unlike the intradomain case, choosing the root domain is a delicate operation in the interdomain case because of administrative issues regarding the ownership of the root domain and the effect on performance that the location of the root may have. BGMP selects the domain of the group initiator as the root domain, hoping that this domain will be the source of most of the traffic.

The complexity of the general nature of the ASM model, that is, any source sending traffic to any group of receivers without any previous notification, the inadequacy of the unicast financial charging scheme, the lack of access control, and its limited scalability are behind the proposal of the source-specific multicast model. As mentioned in a previous section, SSM captures the single-source nature of most commercially viable applications, such as file distribution and Internet TV. It simplifies routing significantly because sources are unique and well known, and allows for a new addressing scheme. With the EXPRESS multicast protocol (Holbrook & Cheriton, 1999) groups are replaced by "channels," or <source, express destination address> pairs. This solves the problem of address collisions and address space scarcity. Nodes explicitly subscribe to channels, possibly also in an authenticated manner. This allows service providers to guarantee the channel owner exclusive use of the channel and subscribers to receive traffic only from a given channel. A single protocol supports both channel subscription and efficient collection of channel information such as subscriber count. Another proposal in this direction is represented by the simple multicast protocol (Perlman et al., 1999). SM builds on the bidimensional address space proposed by EXPRESS and the shared bidirectional trees of CBT. It identifies groups with <core, multicast address> pairs, which are sent by an end node to the router, thus eliminating the need for core router advertisements. Thanks to its simplicity and scalability, SM is suitable both for intra-and interdomain routing.

Group Management

In Deering (1989), multicast groups are public and open. Any node can be a source for any group, regardless of its being a member of the group. Any node can join any group. Group members do not know each other. Routers filter the traffic for a given group and then forward it on their LAN. How nodes join, leave, and interact with their local multicast router was first defined in the Internet Group Management Protocol (IGMPv1; Deering, 1989).

According to IGMPv1, routers periodically query their attached networks to determine which groups have members on them. They send an IGMP message to the reserved address 224.0.0.1, which identifies the "all hosts" group. Hosts reply with a membership report only if they are interested in any of the advertised groups, with a separate reply for each group in which they are interested. When no reports are received, the query times out and is discarded. A host that wants to join a group sends a membership report without waiting for the router query message. The router then adds the group to the membership list for the interface that received the report, unless it is already present. After joining, the router begins forwarding the multicast traffic onto the network segment. Note that sources do not have to join the group to be able to send traffic. If a host wants to leave a group, it simply does not reply to the router membership query and lets it time out. This makes the latency to leave a group longer than the one to join it, as a time-out must expire before the router detects the leave. Leave messages were added in the second version of the protocol.

The service model envisioned in the first two versions of the protocol has some drawbacks. Because there is no control on sources nor is their location known, flooding multicast groups is easy but establishing a distribution tree is hard. Furthermore, address uniqueness is not guaranteed, as we saw in the previous section. IGMPv3 (Cain, Deering, Kouvelas, Fenner, & Thyagarajan, 2002) addresses these issues by allowing hosts to specify the list of sources from which they are willing to receive traffic and the list of sources from which they do not want any traffic. This way unwanted traffic can be discarded at the network level, rather than blocked by the application, which wastes system resources. The service model converges toward a source-specific paradigm, making distribution tree establishment, source identification, and address collision avoidance easier.

Reliable Multicast

IP multicast is an unreliable service, as it is based on the IP protocol. Because multicast applications typically use UDP as a transport protocol, which is also unreliable, either the applications themselves implement the necessary services to add reliability or ad hoc reliable multicast protocols are adopted. To make multicast reliable, functionalities that implement error control and possibly congestion control must be added. Error control provides a solution to packet loss, whereas congestion control allows the system to maintain a smooth traffic flow. Error control can be performed reactively, that is, by retransmitting packets when a packet loss is detected, or proactively, that is, by sending redundant data as part of the normal traffic flow. Although the former is more efficient when packets are lost, the latter is better suited for slightly lossy links, that is, links where packets are corrupted rather than lost. Because in this case parity checks and other error correcting codes are adopted, proactive or forward error correction has been considered as an add-on to reliable multicast protocol of the reactive type. Various reliable multicast protocols, such as the scalable reliable multicast (SRM; Floyd, Jacobson, Liu, McCanne, & Zhang, 1995), the reliable multicast transport protocol (RMTP; Lin & Paul, 1996), the pragmatic general multicast (PGM; Speakman et al., 2001), or the light-weight multicast service (LMS; Papadopoulos, Parulkar, & Varghese, 1998), have been proposed that follow the retransmission approach. Error detection and recovery distinguish the various protocols. The nature of the applications that use them determines which one is more suitable.

An error is detected when the source receives a negative acknowledgement, or NACK, meaning that at least one node lost a packet, or when the source does not receive all of the expected ACKs confirming the reception of traffic from the receivers. SRM, PGM, and LMS are NACK-based protocols, whereas RMTP is ACK based. Protocols differ on how control messages are propagated from a receiver to the source, regardless of their type. This affects the amount of state the source or the multicast routers may have to maintain, hence the protocol scalability, and the amount of bandwidth consumed. Suppression mechanisms are usually in place that eliminate redundant control messages in entire subtrees, to avoid flooding the sender (implosion).

Once errors have been detected, retransmission is required. The issues to be considered in this case are which nodes resend the lost packet and how they resend it. In particular, it can be the source that unicasts the lost packet to the requesting receivers, or nodes in the distribution tree, whether routers or end hosts, that multicast the lost packet to an entire subtree. The goal is to minimize traffic retransmission to nodes that did not request it (exposure). The error detection and recovery strategies affect the recovery latency, that is, the average amount of time it takes to receive a reply after detecting a loss, and the adaptability of the protocol to dynamic membership changes.

Whereas in SRM the source waits for the NACKs and every member may perform retransmission with retransmission suppression in place to minimize traffic duplication, RMTP channels ACKs through a hierarchy of statically designated "ACK processor" nodes. Such nodes merge ACKs from their subtrees and unicast a single ACK up to their parents. They are also in charge of retransmission, using unicast or multicast depending on the percentage of nodes requesting it. In PGM, each router along the distribution tree forwards only one NACK for every packet loss up to the source, thus reducing the NACK traffic at the source. Routers also selectively retransmit traffic only to the nodes that sent NACKs. In LMS, routers select a receiver in their subtree as their substitute and forward all the control messages to it and redistribute messages from it to the subtree. Thus, the burden that in PGM was on the router in LMS has been shifted to a receiver, thus maintaining the router load light.

SECURE MULTICAST

Given the type of applications where multicast can be most useful, it would be beneficial from a security point of view if traffic were accessible only to a restricted set of users, and hosts joined and left a group in a controlled fashion. Based on these simple requirements, the main security issues in multicast communication can be divided into traffic-related and group-related issues. They are discussed in what follows and the requirements of a secure multicast protocol are derived.

Traffic Security

Limiting traffic access to a set of nodes means being able to control which nodes generate, read, and modify traffic. That is, confidentiality, integrity, and authenticity are the properties a secure multicast service should satisfy.

Confidentiality, that is, the requirement that all the traffic within a group may be read only by group members, may be satisfied in a soft way or in a strong, or long term, way. A soft requirement on confidentiality means that it is sufficient to delay access to traffic to nonmembers for a limited amount of time. This applies to cases where the value of the transmitted information depends on its timely and private distribution, because the information is bound to become public access anyway, for example, stock quotes or news feeds. Long-term secrecy implies that the traffic may not be accessible to nonmembers for long periods of time, thus requiring backward and forward secrecy. The former means that new members should not be able to read past traffic and the latter that former members should not be able to read present and future traffic. Long-term secrecy may be too strong for multicast, but cases such as corporate videoconferencing could still require it. Integrity guarantees that only authorized members may modify the traffic whereas authenticity allows the receiver to verify that a message was sent by a group member (group authenticity) or by a particular sender (source authenticity).

Cryptography is the mechanism to guarantee these three properties. Efficient schemes must be adopted to deal with large volumes of traffic, constraints on latency, bursty traffic, or a combination thereof. By combining cryptography with traffic padding, reordering, and delaying, protection from traffic analysis may also be achieved.

Group Security

Group security issues regard group member authentication and authorization, group control, member dynamics, damage containment, member collusion, and possibly anonymity. Group member authentication may take the weaker form where a host is only able to prove it belongs to the group, that is, membership authentication, or the stronger one where each host can prove both that it is a member and its declared identity. The latter could contrast with the possible requirement of anonymity, that is, keeping the identity of group members secret to nonmembers or to other members or keeping the identity of message senders secret. Anonymity could also conflict with the possible requirement of nonrepudiation, that is, the impossibility of denying to a third party that an action was performed, for example, sending or receiving a message. Such a requirement could be present in commercial systems to prevent disputes or frauds.

Group member authorization defines what a member is allowed to do, for example, receive only or receive and send, and possibly for how long, for example, whether the permitted activities can change during the lifetime of the group. Furthermore, a group may be open to receiving messages from nonmembers but may not be allowed to forward internal traffic outside.

Group control refers to the information the system maintains about group members, who has access to such information, and how. This implies, for instance, that group authentication could be mediated by a group controller or be distributed among all members. The same would apply to member subscription or revocation.

Member dynamics refers to whether the group is static, that is, members are defined at group creation time, or dynamic, that is, members can join at any time and possibly leave as they please. It also specifies how subscriptions and voluntary cancellations and/or revocations are dealt with. Membership changes should be secure, that is, they should not affect the security of the traffic before or after the change.

In case of restricted group access, making sure that the compromise of a subgroup or a single member would not jeopardize the privacy of the rest of the group or of other subgroups becomes an important factor. Damage containment indicates that a breach in a subgroup has limited effects on the rest of the group. Similarly, resisting member collusion, that is, members that cooperate to gain additional privileges, provides containment of the damage such malicious members can do.

A factor that should not be overlooked when designing a secure multicast service is group size. The cryptographic systems that guarantee traffic security may also provide for group security. Because large groups are expected to become prevalent in the future, scalability is a critical aspect of any acceptable solution. Additionally, the heterogeneous nature of the member of such large groups in terms of computational power, connectivity, and mobility, imposes further constraints and calls for ad hoc protocols, which are beyond the scope of this chapter.

Security Requirements

A solution for secure multicast should provide

- data confidentiality, integrity, and authenticity;
- group control, authentication, and authorization;
- secure leave and join;
- collusion resistance;
- compromise containment; and
- scalability.

The use of cryptographic techniques is the way to satisfy these requirements. Traffic is encrypted and digitally signed or MACed for confidentiality, integrity, and authentication. Membership is granted upon adequate electronic credentials, usually based on key certificates or analogous cryptographic identification tools. Joins and leaves trigger encryption key changes. Therefore, the core of secure multicast is the generation, distribution, updating, and revocation of cryptographic keys or the key management protocol. As we discuss in the next section, keys are used to encrypt/decrypt data traffic, the so-called traffic encryption keys (TEK), and to encrypt/decrypt the TEKs for their distribution, the so-called key encryption keys (KEK).

KEY MANAGEMENT FOR SECURE MULTICAST

Key management schemes define the key agreement mechanism at the beginning of a multicast session and the successive key exchanges during a session without rebuilding the group, that is, rekeying. The rekeying operation characterizes a key management protocol. Rekeying is required upon membership changes, that is, whenever a new member joins the group or a current member leaves it or is evicted, and to refresh the TEK to protect it from cryptanalytic attacks. Key refresh can be performed efficiently and in a totally distributed fashion. The GM multicasts an "update" message for the target key, possibly encrypted with the current TEK, which triggers the computation of a commonly agreed-upon one-way hash function applied to the current target key at each node. Keeping the nodes synchronized on the current version is critical for nodes to be able to access traffic. This form of key update is possible regardless of the specific key management scheme adopted.

Therefore, the focus is on the rekeying operation upon membership changes. Its efficiency in terms of the number of nodes affected by the key change, the number and size of messages exchanged, and the time required to the group members to compute the new key is critical for the actual deployment of the protocol. It depends upon the way keys are organized from a logical point of view and the potential dependency on each other. Scalability requires that the amount of processing be independent of the group size and the number of affected nodes be small. The amount of storage required for storing the keys each group member handles is also important for protocol scalability and applicability to environments with heterogeneous nodes, where some may have limited resources. Furthermore, security breaches in a subgroup should not expose the rest of the group.

Two main classifications have been proposed for key management protocols. In one case, protocols are classified based on the logical organization of the key set, that is, as a flat set, a collection of subgroups, or a tree-based hierarchy. In the other case, protocols are classified based on the relation between the keys in consecutive distribution rounds, namely as stateful or stateless protocols. Stateful protocols tie the keys distributed in a round to those distributed in the previous ones, so not receiving one key prevents a member from decrypting the traffic multicast afterward. With stateless protocols, keys in successive rounds are independent, so missing one key only introduces a temporary glitch in a member service. Independent keys also provide for containment in case of security breaches.

In the following sections, we present the most significant contributions, grouped according to the logical organization of the key set. We use GM to refer to the group manager that controls group membership and key distribution. Data distribution and key management are kept separate from a logical point of view, although the same node might perform them both.

Flat Schemes

In the simplest solution, each of the n group members shares a personal secret key with the GM, set up when the group is created either via the Diffie–Hellman key establishment algorithm or via the GM sending it to the member encrypted with its public key, if a public key cryptosystem is in place. Such key is used as the KEK for that member for the entire duration of its subscription.

When a member leaves the group or is evicted, the GM computes a new TEK and sends it to each member encrypted with its own personal key in a unicast message. As a performance improvement, the content of the n unicast messages can be combined in a single multicast message, n times the size of each unicast message. Assuming n members are left, the GM sends to the entire group G:

$$GM \Rightarrow G : [E_{K1}(TEK'), E_{K2}(TEK'), \ldots, E_{Kn}(TEK')]$$

where $\Rightarrow$ indicates the multicast communication primitive, Ki is the personal secret key the GM shares with member i, and $E_{Ki}(TEK')$ is the new group key TEK′ encrypted with key Ki. Each member retrieves its key based on the id (i) the GM assigned to it at join time. When a new member joins, either the GM distributes a new key as just described or the old members update the current TEK as if in a refresh and the new member receives the new TEK in a unicast message from the GM. In the first case, TEKs are independent of each other, containing the damages of key compromise between successive rounds. In the other case, key dependency is the price paid for a more efficient key update, but the use of one-way hash functions protects the sequence from cryptanalysis. Note that, if backward secrecy is not an issue, there is no need to "forward" the current key before sending it to a new member, thus reducing the amount of computation at each node for key update.

The group key management protocol (GKMP; Harney & Muckenhirn, 1997a; 1997b) and the scalable multicast key distribution scheme (Ballardie, 1996), which is an improvement of GKMP in terms of scalability, have been designed along this approach. Chu, Qiao, and Nahrstedt (2002) add copyright protection and the ability to identify possible infringers. Data with different watermarks is distributed to the members, thus allowing the system to single out the leaker(s) with a certain error probability.

The communication complexity of flat schemes is $O(n)$ if unicast messages are sent, but it is $O(1)$ if the key updates are multicast to the group. In this case, however, the message size may become prohibitively large in case of large groups, as it is proportional to the group size. On the other hand, only one cryptographic operation is required to compute the new key, either to decrypt the key extracted from the message or to compute a one-way hash function. In both cases, it does not depend on any group feature. Similarly, member storage occupation is very efficient, because two keys only must be stored: the one shared with the GM and the current TEK. On the contrary, GM storage is proportional to the group size. All the overhead of group management is on the GM, and minimum effort is required from the group members.

Although attractive for their simplicity, flat schemes are not scalable, because they quickly lead to the GM saturation. As the group size increases, the number of messages for key update, or the size of the single multicast message, becomes quickly excessive, especially with highly dynamic groups. Another limitation of such protocols is the central group manager, which might jeopardize the security of the entire group and become a performance bottleneck. Furthermore, because a common TEK is used for all the nodes, the compromise of a single node may lead to the compromise of the entire group. On the other hand, because in case of eviction successive TEKs are independent from each other, it is easy to isolate a compromised node by not sending it the new TEK.

Clustered Schemes

Clustered schemes were introduced to overcome the scalability limitations inherent in the flat schemes. According to Iolus (Mittra, 1997), the first clustered scheme, a group is partitioned into independent subgroups along the distribution tree. Each subgroup operates as a multicast group with its own address and is assigned to a subgroup controller, a trusted intermediary that operates locally on behalf of the GM. Subgroup controllers relay data to and from their subgroup and are the manager of the local secure multicast group. They establish a local TEK for their subgroup for each session and share a secret key with each member of their subgroup, established at member join and used for unicast communication. Subgroup controllers are organized into a virtual secure multicast group, possibly following a different protocol from the subgroups, with a group key and individual secret keys each subgroup controller shares with the GM. Figure 1 illustrates a multicast group organized in four subgroups, SG0, SG1, SG2, and SG3, with subgroup controllers SGC0, which happens to coincide with GM, SGC1, SGC2, and SGC3, forming the virtual secure multicast group.

The sender, which does not necessarily coincide with the GM or the local subgroup controller, multicasts traffic encrypted with a session key. The session key is piggybacked on traffic, encrypted with the local TEK of the subgroup. The subgroup controller remulticasts the encrypted traffic after decrypting and reencrypting the session key with the virtual group key. This provides for better performance than using the local TEK or the sender private key to encrypt traffic, as in both cases the subgroup

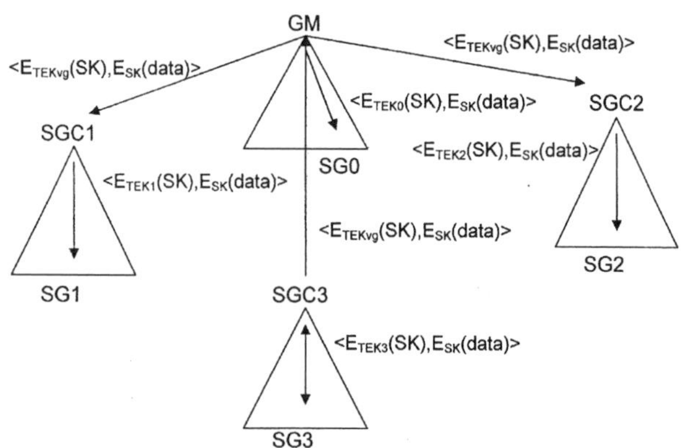

Figure 1: A simple multicast group organized in four subgroups, SG0, SG1, SG2, and SG3, with respective subgroup controllers GM, SGC1, SGC2, and SGC3. Arrows represent multicast communication and are labeled with the data multicast in the subnetwork.

controller would have to decrypt and encrypt the data packets rather than the few bytes of the session key. The process is illustrated in Figure 1. TEKi is the local TEK of subgroup SGi and TEKvg is the TEK of the subgroup controllers virtual secure multicast group. S, a node in subgroup SG3, generates traffic and multicasts packets to its subgroup comprising the encrypted data and the encrypted session key, that is, <E_{TEK3}(SK), E_{SK}(data)>. The local subgroup SGC3 decrypts the session key and reencrypts it with TEKvg, thus multicasting <E_{TEKvg}(SK), E_{SK}(data)> to the secure virtual group. When a subgroup controller SGi receives a packet, it transforms it into <E_{TEKi}(SK), E_{SK}(data)> by decrypting the session key and reencrypting it with its local TEK, and multicasts it to its local subgroup.

As the example shows, in clustered schemes multicasting is computation intensive, because of the cryptographic operations required at the subgroup controllers. This is the price paid for the group management locality the two-level node organization provides. Group membership changes are handled at subgroup level and do not affect any other subgroup. A new member sends its join request to the local subgroup controller, and if the request is accepted, a private key is established between the two. This key will then be used for all the unicast communications, such as the first local TEK distribution to the new member. When a member leaves, only the TEK of its subgroup must be updated. A rekeying on TEKvg is triggered also at the subgroup controller level only if the leaving member leaves behind an empty group. Containment of security breaches is a direct consequence of subgroup organization, because damages resulting from key compromise are limited to the victim subgroup.

Within each subgroup, the subgroup controller may adopt a flat scheme to distribute the local TEK, or any other scheme among those described in the next sections, based on the size of the subgroup and the nature of the members; see, for example, Huang and Mishra (2003). The same applies to the virtual secure multicast group comprising the subgroup controllers. Scalability is achieved by creating new subgroups when the size of the existing ones exceeds a given threshold. There is, however, a trade-off between the number of subgroups and their size. Few large subgroups improve the communication complexity in the virtual group whereas several small subgroups improve performance at subgroup level. In the worst case scenario, each subgroup comprises a single element, hence the virtual group comprises n nodes, and the communication complexity is $O(n)$. At the other extreme, only one group exists that contains all of the nodes and the clustered scheme reduces to whatever scheme is used at local level. In general, the number of subgroups is smaller than the size of each subgroup.

Similar considerations apply to the amount of storage each node uses. Because the GM multicasts traffic and keys to the subgroup controllers only, it stores an encryption key for each subgroup controller and the TEKvg. Subgroup controllers perform most of the work for traffic relay and key updates upon joins and leaves. They store keys for the group to which they belong, that is, the shared key with the GM, the TEKvg, and any control key the protocol at this level may require. They also store keys for the group they manage, that is, the local TEK, the individual keys shared with each member, and any control key the protocol they adopt may require. Members only store the local TEK, the key they share with their subgroup controller, and the possible control keys. The total number of keys in the system depends upon the actual protocols.

Clustered schemes strongly rely on the trust in dedicated nodes, that is, the subgroup controllers, because they access the data traffic to relay it. This could result in a serious weakness of the system in case of subgroup controller compromise. In this case, the damages affect the entire system.

The most famous clustered solution is Iolus (Mittra, 1997). Several other solutions were proposed that adopt the same divide-and-conquer approach, for example, IGKMP (Hardjono, Cain, & Monga, 1998), Kronos (Setia, Koussih, & Jajodia, 2000), and Molva and Pannerat (2000), Zhang, Lam, Lee, and Yang (2001), and Yang, Li, Zhang, and Lam (2001). In particular, Yang, Li, Zhang, and Lam (2001) focus on the reliability of aspect of secure key distribution, which is also addressed by some of the tree-based protocols. They are the first to make the case for batch rekeying as an effective and efficient way to deal with large dynamic groups. In this case, security is traded for performance, because former members might be able to access traffic until the next rekeying is performed after they left, and new members might be able to access all the traffic distributed with the current TEK at the moment they subscribed. Kronos introduces periodic rekeying in an IGKMP-like scheme, where subgroup controllers periodically generate the same key in an independent fashion, rather than receiving it from the GM. Because key generation does not depend upon the frequency of joins and leaves in the group, and it is performed locally rather than centrally at the GM, such a scheme provides excellent scalability. It also resists network partitioning, like all clustered schemes, as long as there is a sender in each of the partitions.

Tree-Based Schemes

Tree-based schemes, also generically referred to as LKH (logical key hierarchy) or keygraphs, were suggested in Wallner, Harder, and Agee (1999) and independently in Wong, Gouda, and Lam (1998). They address the problem of minimizing the communication complexity of the rekeying operation, without relying on secure third parties, such as the subgroup controllers. They introduce a hierarchy of control keys that allows the GM to efficiently multicast group key updates.

All the keying material is organized in a balanced tree of degree d maintained at the GM. Recent work has shown that unbalanced trees might be beneficial as they may lead to a considerable performance improvement in the rekeying process (Banerjee & Bhattacharjee, 2002; Zhu, Setia, & Jajodia, 2003). The key hierarchy is independent of the distribution tree. Keys in a subtree may, however, be assigned to members in a distribution subtree to keep into account their relative physical position, the expected duration of their membership, link loss probability, for the purpose of exploiting locality and/or different rekeying rates. The leaves are the keys established at join time, which each group member shares with the GM. The key at the root of the tree is the TEK. The keys along the

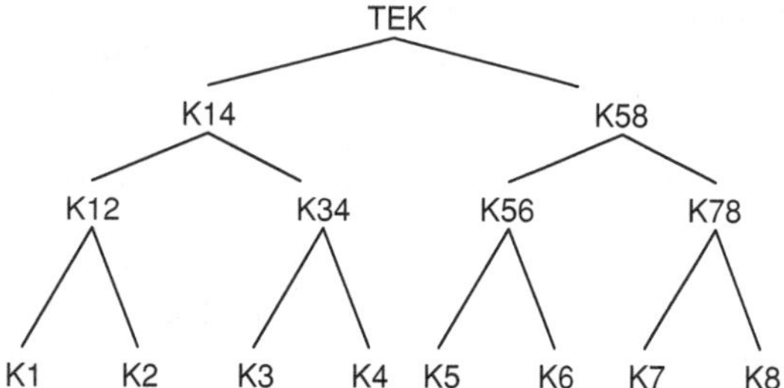

Figure 2: A balanced binary key tree for an eight-node multicast group. Keys K1 through K8 are the private keys each member shares with the GM for unicast communications. The keys along the path from the root to a leaf are the control keys.

internal nodes are the control keys used to distribute the TEK. Each group member stores all the keys along the path from its leaf node to the root. Figure 2 depicts a balanced binary key tree for a simple group comprising eight nodes. Keys K1 through K8 are the individual keys each node shares with the GM for unicast communication. K12, K34, K56, K78, K14, and K58 are the control keys.

During a rekeying operation, the group manager uses the hierarchy of KEKs to distribute the new TEK. Thus, as an example, the new TEK can be distributed to all nodes in Figure 2 by multicasting it separately encrypted with keys K14 and K58. Note that all the members in a subtree can decrypt any data encrypted with the key at the root of their subtree. The closer to a leaf the key used to encrypt data is, the fewer members can decrypt that data. Thus, by encrypting the TEK with a subset of keys in a subtree, it is possible to exclude a single participant or a group of participants from receiving the next TEK.

If node 7 in Figure 2 were evicted, or left voluntarily, all the keys node 7 has must be changed, that is, the TEK, K58, and K78. The new TEK can be distributed to the rest of the group by separately encrypting it with K14, K56, and K8. Note that none of the KEKs node 7 has is used to distribute the new TEK. Then $E_{K56}(K58')$ and $E_{K8}(K58', K78')$ are distributed. All the compromised KEKs and the TEK are replaced during a rekeying operation.

In case of a member joining, a new leaf is added to the tree, the KEKs between the new leaf and the root are recomputed to guarantee backward secrecy, and in case the tree requires adjustments for balancing purposes. The GM then distributes the KEKs between the leaf and the root to the new member using the shared key (K1 in Figure 2). The intermediate keys that were changed because of the addition of the new member are also transmitted to the members in the subtree where the new leaf was added. A new version of the TEK is then distributed or derived by each member by applying a one-way hash function to the current one. In case of a member leaving, the TEK must be updated and the KEKs along the path to the leaving member must be updated.

Because there is a single common key used to encrypt traffic, tree-based protocols do not provide containment. The compromise of a node exposes data traffic to unauthorized access along the entire multicast tree. Furthermore, although the key tree is significantly more efficient than flat key distribution, the key update requested upon each leave affects the entire group, thus affecting scalability when the group is highly dynamic.

When this scheme is applied to a group of n users, it requires each group member to store $O(\log_d n)$ keys, that is, all the keys along the path from the node to the root, whereas the GM must store $O(n)$ keys, because it also stores the individual keys shared with each member (K1 in Figure 2). The number of messages is on the order of $O(\log_d n)$. Later work improved the original scheme with respect to various aspects (Canetti et al., 1999; Banerjee & Bhattacharjee, 2002; Waldvogel, Caronni, Sun, Weiler, & Plattner, 1999; Chang, Engel, Kandlur, Pendarakis, & Saha, 1999; Balenson, McGrew, & Sherman, 2000; Burmester & Desmedt, 1996; Harney & Harder, 1999; Perrig, Song, & Tygar, 2001; Moyer, Rao, & Rohatgi, 1999; Zhu, Setia, & Jajodia, 2003). In some cases, attention is placed on the unreliable nature of IP multicast and provisions are made to guarantee keys will be received even in case of unreliable transmission (Setia, Zhu, & Jajodia, 2002; Perrig, Song, & Tygar, 2001). By organizing the key tree so as to concentrate members with high loss probability in one subtree and retransmitting key distribution messages to such subtree, reliable secure multicast is achieved.

Table 2 summarizes the main characteristics of the flat, clustered, and tree-based schemes, assuming a group of size n. In the case of clustered schemes, the group is organized in g subgroups, which we assume to have n/g members each, for the sake of simplicity. In the case of tree-based schemes, the keys are organized in a balanced tree of degree d and height $\log_d n$. The parameters considered for the comparison are the type of TEK, whether it is global for the entire group or not, the number of keys stored at the GM and at each member, the number of keys to be changed upon a join or a leave, and the number of cryptographic operations required when a multicast packet is transmitted. Note that for clustered

Table 2 A comparison of key management schemes with respect to type of TEK, number of keys stored at the GM and at each member, number of new keys to be distributed upon a join and a leave, number of cryptographic operations required by a multicast transmission, for a group of size n and organized in g subgroups in the case of the clustered scheme. For the clustered scheme, ranges are reported for some of the parameters because they depend upon the scheme adopted within each subgroup

Approach	TEK	No. Keys GM	No. Keys Member	Join	Leave	Crypto-Op
Flat	global	$N+1$	2	1	1	1
Clustered	local	$[g+1, \log_d g+1]$	$[2, \log_d n/g+1]$	$[1, \log_d n/g+1]$	$[1, \log_d n/g+1]$	$2g+1$
Tree-based	global	Σd^i $i=0,h$	$\log_d n+1$	$\log_d n+1$	$\log_d n+1$	1

schemes some of the parameters are given as ranges, because they depend upon the specific key management scheme adopted at each subgroup. So, for instance, the number of keys at a member can be as small as two in case of a flat scheme or as large as $\log_d n/g + 1$, in case of a tree-based solution.

As the table shows, the TEK is local only in clustered schemes. Although this provides for containment in case of compromise of the subgroup TEKs, it does not help if the group key of the virtual group, TEKvg, is compromised. Another aspect that should not be forgotten is that the apparent simplicity of the join and leave operations in the case of the flat scheme is paid in terms of the size of the message required to distribute the single key that must be changed, namely the TEK (see the fourth section). Note that in all cases, the join operation can be performed in a more efficient way by simply multicasting an "update" message to all the old members, which will generate a new local version of the current TEK by applying the same one-way function. When a tree-based scheme is adopted, such an update must be applied also to the KEKs along the path from the new node to the root, for a total of $\log_d n + 1$ key changes involving the n/d nodes in the subtree where the new node is added.

Other Schemes

In the approaches outlined, the goal is to improve the protocol communication complexity by balancing the distribution of keying material to the members and possible intermediate nodes so as to avoid sending the new key to each group member individually. Different approaches have been taken by Chiou and Chen (1989), Steiner, Tsudik, and Waidner (2000), Briscoe (1999), and Judge and Ammar (2002).

Chiou and Chen (1989) propose a solution based on the Chinese remainder theorem and that uses public key technology, thus trading communication complexity for computation. Securelock has communication complexity $O(1)$ but it requires that each group member perform $O(n)$ exponentiations to "unlock" the message, thus becoming prohibitively expensive for large groups.

Cliques, the solution proposed by Steiner, Tsudik, and Waidner (2000), generalize the Diffie–Hellman key agreement algorithm to a group of n users. In the so-called up-flow, each member raises the value it receives from another member to its own secret number and forwards the result to the next member. The last member starts the down-flow by multicasting the value it computed in the up-flow phase. Each member can calculate the key. Because the control messages and the number of exponentiations are linear in the group size, this solution does not scale.

In MARKS (Briscoe, 1999), a multicast session is divided in sets of time slices. During each one of such sets, different keys are distributed and used to encrypt data traffic. Binary hash trees are used to generate the encryption keys, which are the leaves of such trees. Intermediate nodes are the seeds needed to generate the keys. A new member admitted to the group for a certain subset of time slices receives the seeds necessary to generate the keys for the specific time range. Leaves are permitted only at join times, because they would otherwise require change the key tree.

In Gothic (Judge & Ammar, 2002), it is observed that, unlike what happens on the Internet with open multicast groups, with group access control in place, a host cannot receive the encrypted traffic of a multicast group before being a member. Therefore, there is no need to rekey the group either at joins or at leaves, except in the case where new (former) members belong to the same broadcast link as current group members. An architecture implementing a group policy management system and a group authorization system that control access to the group is proposed. It is shown that existing key management protocols may benefit dramatically from deployment in a system implementing group access control.

CONCLUSION

IP multicast is a fundamental tool for efficient communication of one-to-many and many-to-many services, such as videoconferencing, collaborative work, and periodic data distribution. Address allocation, routing, and group management are the key components of the multicast service. The original service model focusing on many-to-many communication makes address allocation and routing complex and heavy for the underlying network. The current trend is to shift the service paradigm toward easier-to-manage source-specific multicast, as one-to-many communication better suits commercially viable applications, such as video on demand or file distribution. Group management is also being adjusted to fit the less-general service model.

The open nature of IP multicast groups makes it impossible to provide added value services, for example, services based on fee payment or that require guarantees of the party identity. Secure multicast protocols provide for restricted access to traffic, group member authentication, and secure membership changes by employing cryptographic systems. At their core are key management schemes that provide the necessary keying material. The efficiency of such schemes, their ability to resist collusion of malicious members and to contain security breaches resulting from member compromise, the level of trust required in the participating nodes, their scalability to large group sizes, and their ability to deal with groups where members may join and leave at any time during a multicast session are critical parameters for secure multicast protocols evaluation.

GLOSSARY

Access Control The collection of policies and mechanisms used to restrict access to and usage of system resources to authorized users only.

Authentication The process by which a user verifies the declared identity of the other party in a communication.

Confidentiality Ensuring that information is accessible only to those authorized to have access.

Diffie–Hellman A cryptographic protocol that allows two communication parties to establish a shared key over an insecure channel.

Group Management The practice of managing multicast group membership.

Hash Function A function that maps values from a large domain into a smaller codomain.

Integrity Ensuring that information is modifiable only by authorized users.

Key Management The generation, distribution, and updating of cryptographic keying material.

MAC (Message Authentication Code) A one-way hash function that accepts a cryptographic key, used to generate a message digest for integrity check and authentication purposes.

Multicast Delivery of information to multiple destinations simultaneously.

One-Way Function A function that is easy to compute but difficult, that is, computationally hard, to reverse.

Routing The means of forwarding logically addressed packets from their local subnetwork toward their final destination.

Scalability The ability of a system to maintain quality performance or service under an increased system load.

Spanning Tree In graph theory, the tree that includes all the vertices of the graph.

CROSS REFERENCES

See *Access Control: Principles and Solutions; Computer and Network Authentication; Key Management; TCP/IP Suite.*

REFERENCES

Adams, A., Nicholas, J., & Siadak, W. (2005). *Protocol independent multicast—dense mode (PIM-DM): Protocol specification* (RFC 3973). Retrieved 2005 from http://www.ietf.org/rfc/rfc3973.txt

Albanna, A., Almeroth, K., Meyer, D., & Schipper, M. (2001). Guidelines for Ipv4 multicast address assignments (RFC 3171). Retrieved 2004 from http://www.ietf.org/rfc/rfc3171.txt

Almeroth, K., & Ammar, M. (1997). Multicast group behavior in the Internet's multicast backbone (MBone). *IEEE Communications Magazine, 35*(6), 124–129.

Banerjee, S., & Bhattacharjee, B. (2002). Scalable secure group communication over IP multicast. *IEEE Journal on Selected Areas in Communications, 20*(8), 1511–1527.

Balenson, D., McGrew, D., & Sherman, A. (2000). *Key management for large dynamic groups: One-way function trees and amortized initialization* (IETF Internet draft). Retrieved 2004 from http://www.securemulticast.org/draft-balenson-groupkeymgmt-oft-00.txt

Ballardie, A. (1996). *Scalable multicast key distribution* (RFC 1949). Retrieved 2004 from http://www.ietf.org/rfc/rfc1949.txt

Ballardie, A. (1997). *Core based tree (CRT version 2) multicast routing—protocol specification* (RFC 2189). Retrieved 2004 from http://www.ietf.org/rfc/rfc2189.txt

Ballardie, A., & Crowcroft, J. (1995). Multicast-specific security threats and counter-measures. In *Proceedings of the Network and Distributed System Security Symposium* (pp. 2–16). Washington, DC, USA: IEEE Computer Society.

Bates, T., Rekhter, Y., Chandra, R., & Katz, D. (2000). *Multiprotocol extensions for BGP-4* (RFC 2858). Retrieved 2004 from http://www.ietf.org/rfc/rfc2858.txt

Bhattacharya, S. (2003). An overview of source-specific multicast (SSM) (RFC 3569). Retrieved 2004 from http://www.ietf.org/rfc/rfc3569.txt

Briscoe, B. (1999). MARKS: Zero side-effect multicast key management using arbitrarily revealed key sequences. In *Proceedings of the First International Workshop on Networked Group Communication* (LNCS 1736, pp. 301–320). London, UK: Springer-Verlag.

Burmester, M., & Desmedt, Y. G. (1996). Efficient and secure conference key distribution. In *Proceedings of the Security Protocol Workshop* (pp. 119–129). London, UK: Springer-Verlag.

Cain, B., Deering, S., Kouvelas, I., Fenner, B., & Thyagarajan, A. (2002). *Internet group management protocol, version 3* (RFC 3376). Retrieved 2004 from http://www. ietf.org/rfc/rfc3376.txt

Canetti, R., Cheng, P., Giraud, F., Pendarakis, D., Rao, J., Rohatgi, P., & Saha, D. (2000). An IPSec-based host architecture for secure Internet multicast. In *Proceedings of the Network and Distributed System Security Symposium* (pp. 49–65). Reston, VA, USA: Internet Society.

Canetti, R., Garay, J., Itkis, G., Minciaccio, D., Naor, M., & Pinkas, B. (1999). Multicast security: A taxonomy and some efficient constructions. In *Proceedings of the IEEE INFOCOM '99* (Vol. 2, pp. 708–716). Los Alamitos, CA, USA: IEEE Press.

Caronni, G., Lubich, H., Aziz, A., Markson, T., & Skrenta, R. (1996). SKIP: Securing the Internet. In *Proceedings of the Fifth Workshop on Enabling Technologies* (pp. 62–67). Los Alamitos, CA, USA: IEEE Press.

Chang, I., Engel, R., Kandlur, D., Pendarakis, D., & Saha, D. (1999). Key management for secure Internet multicast using boolean function minimization techniques. In *Proceedings of the IEEE INFOCOM '99* (Vol. 2, pp. 689–698). Los Alamitos, CA, USA: IEEE Press.

Chiou, G. H., & Chen, W. T. (1989). Secure broadcasting using the secure lock. *IEEE Transactions on Software Engineering, 15*(8), 929–934.

Chu, H., Qiao, L., & Nahrstedt, K. (2002). A secure multicast protocol with copyright protection. *ACM SIGCOMM Computer Communication Review, 32*(2), pp. 42–60.

Deering, S. E. (1989). *Host extensions for IP multicast* (RFC 1112). Retrieved 2004 from http://www.ietf.org/rfc/rfc1112.txt

Estrin, D., Farinacci, D., Helmy, A., Thaler, D., Deering, S., Handley, M., et al. (1998). *Protocol independent multicast-sparse mode (PIM-SM): Protocol specification* (RFC 2362). Retrieved 2004 from http://www.ietf.org/rfc/rfc2362.txt

Fiat, A., & Naor, M. (1993). Broadcast encryption. In *Proceedings of CRYPTO '93* (LNCS 773, pp. 480–491). London, UK: Springer-Verlag.

Floyd, S., Jacobson, V., Liu, C.-C., McCanne, S., & Zhang, L. (1995). A reliable multicast framework for lightweight sessions and application level framing. In

Proceedings of ACM SIGCOMM '95 (pp. 342–356). New York, NY, USA: ACM Press.

Hanna, S., Patel, B., & Shah, M. (1999). *Multicast address dynamic client allocation protocol (MADCAP)* (RFC 2730). Retrieved 2004 from http://www.ietf.org/rfc/rfc2730.txt

Hardjono, T., & Cain, B. (2000). Key establishment for IGMP authentication in IP multicast. In *Proceedings of IEEE First European Conference on Universal Multiservice Networks* (pp. 247–252). Los Alamitos, CA, USA: IEEE Press.

Hardjono, T., Cain, B., & Monga, I. (1998). *Intradomain group key management protocol* (IETF Internet Draft). Retrieved 2004 from http://www.ietf.org/proceedings/98dec/I-D/draft-ietf-ipsec-intragkm-00.txt

Harney, H., & Harder, E. (1999). *Logical key hierarchy protocol* (IETF Internet Draft). Retrieved 2004 from http://www.securemulticast.org/draft-harney-sparta-lkhp-sec-00.txt

Harney, H., & Muckenhirn, C. (1997a). *Group key management protocol (GKMP) specification* (RFC 2093). Retrieved 2004 from http://www.ietf.org/rfc/rfc2093.txt

Harney, H., & Muckenhirn, C. (1997b). *Group key management protocol (GKMP) architecture* (RFC 2094). Retrieved 2004 from http://www.ietf.org/rfc/rfc2094.txt

Holbrook, H. W., & Cheriton, D. R. (1999). IP multicast channels: EXPRESS support for large-scale single-source applications. In *Proceedings of ACM SIGCOMM '99* (pp. 65–78). New York, NY, USA: ACM Press.

Huang, J., & Mishra, S. (2003). Mykil: A highly scalable key distribution protocol for large group multicast. In *Proceedings of IEEE Global Telecommunications Conference, GLOBECOM '03* (pp. 1476–1480). Los Alamitos, CA, USA: IEEE Press.

IETF. (n.d.a). *Border gateway multicast protocol working group*. Retreived 2004 from http://www.ietf.org/html.charters/bgmp-charter.html

IETF. (n.d.b). *Multicast-address allocation (malloc) working group*. Retrieved 2004 from http://www.ietf.org/html.charters/malloc-charter.html

IETF. (n.d.c). *Protocol independent multicast working group*. Retrieved 2004 from http://www.ietf.org/html.charters/pim-charter.html

IETF. (n.d.d). *GSEC and MSEC*. Retrieved 2004 from http://www.securemulticast.org

Judge, P., & Ammar, M. (2002). Gothic: A group access control architecture for secure multicast and anycast. In *Proceedings of IEEE INFOCOM 2002* (Vol. 3, pp. 1547–1556). Los Alamitos, CA, USA: IEEE Press.

Kumar, A., Radoslavov, P., Thaler, E., Alaettinoglu, C., Estrin, E., & Handley, M. (1998). The MASC/BGMP architecture for inter-domain muticast routing. In *Proceedings of ACM SIGCOMM '98* (pp. 93–104). New York, NY, USA: ACM Press.

Lin, J. C., & Paul, S. (1996). RMTP: A reliable multicast transport protocol. In *Proceedings of IEEE INFOCOM '96* (Vol. 3, pp. 1414–1424). Los Alamitos, CA, USA: IEEE Press.

Matsumoto, T., & Imai, H. (1988). On the key predistribution system—A practical solution to the key distribution problem. In *Proceedings of CRYPTO '87* (LNCS 293, pp. 185–193). London, UK: Springer-Verlag.

Maugham, D., Schertler, M., Schneider, M., & Turner, J. (1998). *Internet security association and key management protocol* (ISAKMP) (RFC 2408). Retrieved 2004 from http://www.ietf.org/rfc/rfc2408.txt

Meyer, M. (1998). *Administratively scoped IP multicast* (RFC 2365). Retrieved 2004 from http://www.ietf.org/rfc/rfc2365.txt

Meyer, D., & Lotheberg, P. (2001). *GLOP addressing in 233/8* (RFC 3180). Retrieved 2004 from http://www.ietf.org/rfc/rfc3180.txt

Mittra, S. (1997). Iolus: A framework for scalable secure multicasting. In *Proceedings of ACM SIGCOMM '97* (pp. 277–288). New York, NY, USA: ACM Press.

Molva, R., & Pannerat, A. (2000). Scalable multicast security with dynamic recipient groups. *ACM Transactions on Information and System Security, 3*(3), 136–160.

Moy, J. (1994). *Multicast extensions to OSPF* (RFC 1584). Retrieved 2004 from http://www.ietf.org/rfc/rfc1584.txt

Moyer, M., Rao, J., & Rohatgi, P. (1999). *Maintaining balanced key trees for secure multicast* (IETF Internet Draft). Retrieved 2004 from http://www.securemulticast.org/draft-irtf-smug-key-tree-balance-00.txt

Papadopoulos, C., Parulkar, G. M., & Varghese, G. (1998). An error control scheme for large-scale multicast applications. In *Proceedings of IEEE INFOCOM '98* (Vol. 3, pp. 1188–1196) Los Alamitos, CA, USA: IEEE Press.

Perlman, R., Lee, C-Y., Ballardie, A., Crowcroft, J., Wang, Z., Maufer, T., et al. (1999). *Simple multicast: A design for simple, low-overhead multicast* (IETF Internet Draft). Retrieved 2004 from http://www.cs.ucl.ac.uk/research/rama/draft-perlman-simple-multicast-03.txt

Perrig, A., Song, D., & Tygar, D. (2001). ELK, a new protocol for efficient large-group key distribution. In *Proceedings of IEEE Symposium on Security and Privacy* (pp. 247–262). Los Alamitos, CA, USA: IEEE Press.

Pinkas, B., & Canetti, R. (1999). A taxonomy of multicast security issues (IRTF Internet Draft). Retrieved 2004 from http://archive.dante.net/mbone/refs/draft-irtf-smug-taxonomy-01.txt

Reynolds, J., & Postel, J. (1994). *Assigned numbers* (RFC 1700). Retrieved 2004 from http://www.ietf.org/rfc/rfc1700.txt

Radoslavov, P., Estrin, E., Govindan, R., Handley, M., Kumar, S., & Thaler, D. (2000). *The multicast address-set claim (MASC) protocol* (RFC 2909). Retrieved 2004 from http://www.ietf.org/rfc/rfc2909.txt

Setia, S., Koussih, S., & Jajodia, S. (2000). Kronos: A scalable group re-keying approach for secure multicast. In *Proceedings of IEEE Symposium on Security and Privacy* (pp. 215–228). Los Alamitos, CA, USA: IEEE Press.

Setia, S., Zhu, S., & Jajodia, S. (2002). A comparative performance analysis of reliable group rekey transport protocols for secure multicast. *Performance Evaluation, 49*(1–4), 21–41.

Speakman, T., Crowcroft, J., Gemmell, J., Farinacci, D., Lin, S., Leshchiner, D., et al. (2001). *PGM reliable transport protocol specification* (RFC 3208). Retrieved 2004 from http://www.ietf.org/rfc/rfc3208.txt

Steiner, M., Tsudik, G., & Waidner, M. (2000). Key agreement in dynamic peer groups. *IEEE Transactions on Parallel and Distributed Systems, 11*(8), 769–780.

Thaler, D., Handley, M., & Estrin, D. (2000). *The Internet multicast address allocation architecture* (RFC 2908). Retrieved 2004 from http://www.ietf.org/rfc/rfc2908.txt

Thaler, D. (2003). *Multicast address allocation MIB* (RFC 3559). Retrieved 2004 from http://www.ietf.org/rfc/rfc3559.txt

Thaler, D. (2004). *Border gateway multicast protocol (BGMP): Protocol specification* (RFC 3913). Retrieved 2004 from http://www.ietf.org/rfc/rfc3913.txt

Waitzman, D., Partridge, C., & Deering, S. (1988). *Distance vector multicast routing protocol* (RFC 1075). Retrieved 2004 from http://www.ietf.org/rfc/rfc1075.txt

Waldvogel, M., Caronni, G., Sun, D., Weiler, N., & Plattner, B. (1999). The VersaKey framework: Versatile group key management. *IEEE Journal on Selected Areas in Communications, 17*(9), 1614–1631.

Wallner, D. M., Harder, E. J., & Agee, R. C. (1999). *Key management for multicast: Issues and architectures* (RFC 2627). Retrieved 2004 from http://www.ietf.org/rfc/rfc2627.txt

Wong, C. K., Gouda, M., & Lam, S. S. (1998). Secure group communications using key graphs. In *Proceedings of ACM SIGGOMM '98* (pp. 68–79). New York, NY, USA: ACM Press.

Yang, Y., Li, X., Zhang, X., & Lam, S. (2001). Reliable group rekeying: A performance analysis. In *Proceedings of ACM SIGCOMM 2001* (pp. 27–38). New York, NY, USA: ACM Press.

Zhang, X., Lam, S. S., Lee, D.-Y., & Yang, Y. R. (2001). Protocol design for scalable and reliable group rekeying. In *Proceedings of the SPIE Conference on Scalability and Traffic Control in IP Networks* (pp. 87–108). Bellingham, WA, USA: SPIE Press.

Zhu, S., Setia, S., & Jajodia, S. (2003). Performance optimization for group key management schemes for secure multicast. In *Proceedings of the 23rd IEEE International Conference on Distributed Computing Systems* (pp. 163–171). Los Alamitos, CA, USA: IEEE Press.

FURTHER READING

Fenner, B., & Meyer, D. (2003). *Multicast source discovery protocol (MSD)* (RFC 3618). Retrieved 2004 from http://www.ietf.org/rfc/rfc3618.txt

Hardjono, T., & Weis, B. (2004). *The multicast group security architecture* (RFC 3740). Retrieved 2004 from http://www.ietf.org/rfc/rfc3740.txt

Harkins, D., & Carel, D. (1998). *The Internet key exchange (IKE)* (RFC 2409). Retrieved 2004 from http://www.ietf.org/rfc/rfc2409.txt

McCloghrie, K., Farinacci, D., & Thaler, D. (2000). *Ipv4 multicast routing MIB* (RFC 2932). Retrieved 2004 from http://www.ietf.org/rfc/rfc2932.txt

TCP over Wireless Links

Mohsen Guizani and Anupama Raju, *Western Michigan University*

INTRODUCTION

The transport layer is the basic end-to-end building block of the Internet (TCP/IP) architecture and communications. Protocols above the transport layer concentrate on distributed applications processing, and protocols below the transport layer concentrate on the transmission, routing, and forwarding of application data. The transmission control protocol is a connection-oriented, reliable, byte stream service that provides data transfer that is reliable, ordered, fully duplex, robust, and flow controlled (Network Sorcery, n.d.; Rey, 1981)

Each TCP segment (shown in Figure 1) contains the source and destination *port number* to identify the sending and receiving application. A socket is a pair (IP address and port number); the ends of a connection are each sockets. The *socket pair* (client IP address, client port number, server IP address, and server port number) specifies the two end points that uniquely identify each TCP connection in an Internet and the port number.

There are six flag bits in the TCP header. One or more of them can be turned on at the same time:

U (URG) Urgent pointer field significant (the urgent flag is set).
A (ACK) Acknowledgment field significant.
P (PSH) Push function.
R (RST) Reset the connection.
S (SYN) Synchronize sequence numbers.
F (FIN) No more data from sender.

Because TCP is a connection-oriented protocol, before sending and receiving data, a connection must be established between the sender and receiver. TCP connection establishment is a three-way handshake procedure as shown in Figure 2. The initiating end (client) sends a SYN segment (a segment in which the SYN bit is set) specifying the port number of the server to which that the client wants to connect and the client's initial sequence number (198990 in this example). The server responds with its own SYN segment containing the server's initial sequence number (segment 2). The server also acknowledges the client's SYN by ACKing (acknowledging) the client's initial sequence number (ISN) plus one. The client must now acknowledge this SYN from the server by sending an ACK with the server's ISN plus one (segment 3).

The host that sends the first SYN is said to perform an *active open*. The other host, which receives this SYN and sends the next SYN, performs a *passive open*. When each end sends its SYN to establish the connection, it chooses an initial sequence number for that connection. The ISN should change over time, so that each connection has a different ISN. The purpose of these sequence numbers is to prevent packets that get delayed in the network from being delivered later and then misinterpreted as part of an existing connection.

Once the TCP connection is established, the data transfer can begin. Data are transferred over a TCP connection in TCP segments; however, TCP views the data as streams of octets. When the application has sent all its data and wishes to close the connection, it sends a CLOSE primitive to TCP, which sends a segment with the FIN flag set. Because a TCP connection is full duplex, each direction must be shut down independently when it is done sending data. When a TCP receives a FIN, the application is not notified explicitly (but the next read returns 0) that the other end has terminated that direction of data flow. The receipt of a FIN means there will be no more data flowing in that direction. However, the user can still send data after receiving a FIN. This is called a half-close.

Figure 3 shows TCP connection termination procedure. The end that first issues the close (sends the first

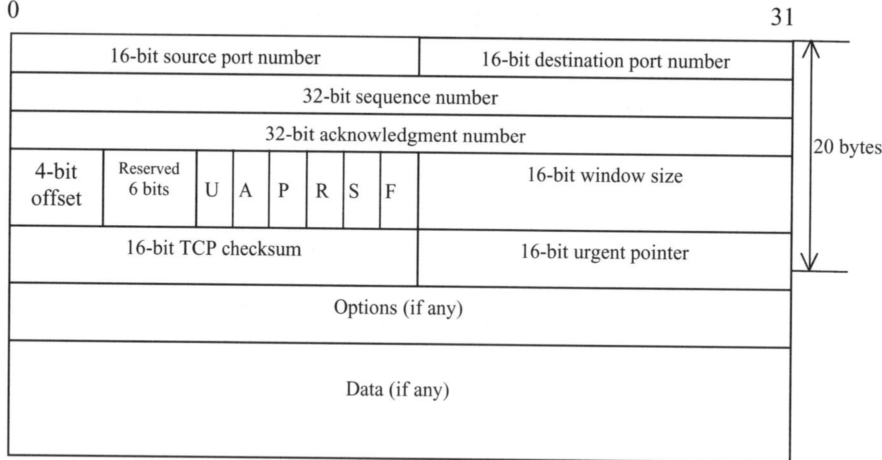

Figure 1: TCP segment format.

FIN) performs the *active close*, and the other end performs the *passive close*. The connection termination requires four TCP segments and is called a four-way handshake.

CONGESTION AVOIDANCE AND CONTROL

Modern implementations of TCP contain four intertwined algorithms: slow start, congestion avoidance, fast retransmit, and fast recovery (Stevens, 1997).

Slow Start

The slow start algorithm is used to control the transmission rate injected into the network. It operates by observing that the rate at which new packets should be injected into the network is the rate at which the acknowledgments are returned by the other end. Slow start adds another window called the congestion window (`cwnd`). When a new connection is established with a host on another network, the congestion window is initialized to one segment (current standard allows 1–4 segments). Each time an ACK is received, the congestion window is increased by one segment. The sender can transmit up to the minimum of the congestion window and the advertised window. The congestion window is based on the sender's assessment of perceived network congestion. The advertised window is related to the amount of available buffer space at the receiver for this connection.

Figure 4 illustrates the working of slow start algorithm. The horizontal direction is time. The continuous time line has been chopped into *round-trip time* (RTT) pieces stacked vertically with increasing time going down the page. The white, numbered boxes represent segments. The shadowed, numbered boxes represent the corresponding ACKs. The sender starts by transmitting one segment and waiting for its ACK. When the ACK is received, the congestion window is incremented from one to two, and two segments are sent. When both of those two segments are acknowledged, the congestion window is increased to four. This provides exponential growth in the size of the congestion window. From Figure 4, we see that the window size doubles in every RTT. This implies that the time to reach a window size of W is $\text{RTT} \times \log_2 W$.

However, this growth can be moderated by sending one ACK for every two segments received. At some point, the capacity of the connection can be reached, and an intermediate router will start discarding packets. This informs the sender that its congestion window has become too large and induces to reduce the size of the window.

Congestion Avoidance

Congestion avoidance is also used to control the data injected into the network. The algorithm works based on the assumption that packet loss is mainly due to congestion

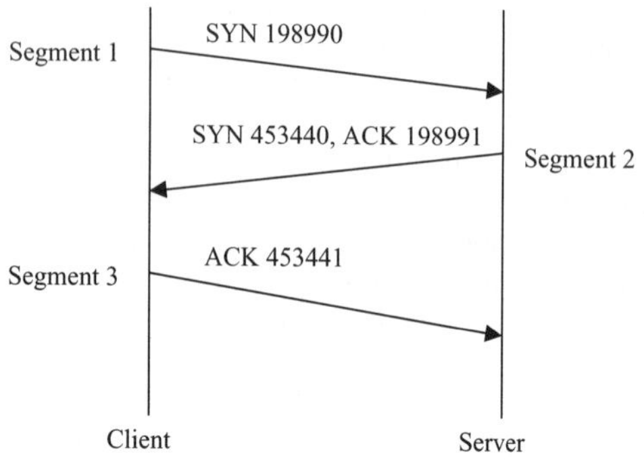

Figure 2: TCP connection establishment.

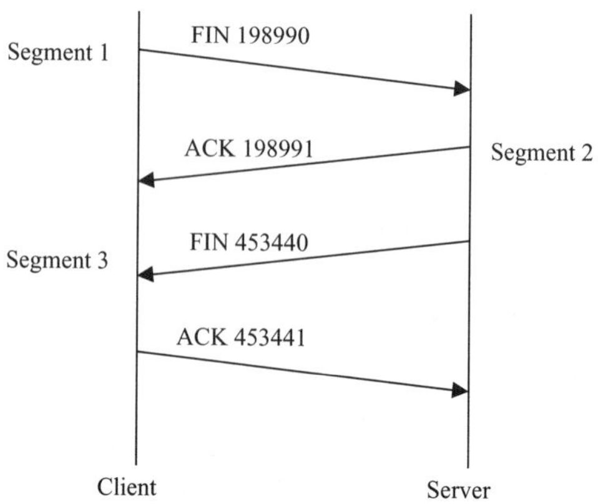

Figure 3: TCP connection termination.

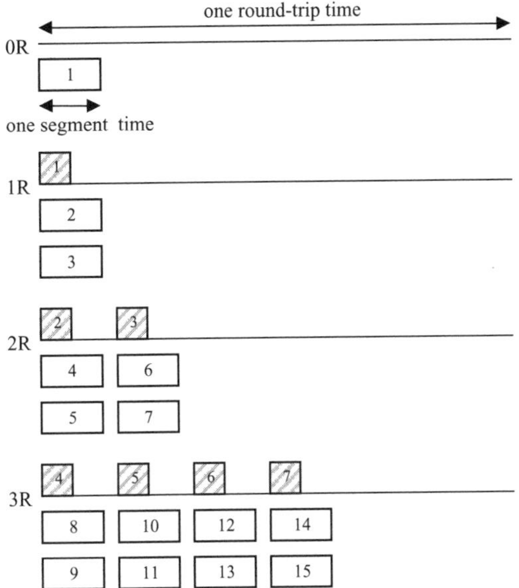

Figure 4: Slow start example.

in the network, somewhere between the source and destination. In congestion avoidance, on receipt of an ACK the cwnd is increased by 1/cwnd and if congestion occurs (`cwnd` = W) then `cwnd` is set to 0.5W. This avoids the exponential queue build-up. The packet loss is indicated by a time-out or by the receipt of duplicate ACKs.

Congestion avoidance and slow start are independent algorithms with different objectives. In practice, they are implemented together. Congestion avoidance and slow start require two variables to be maintained for each connection: a `cwnd` and a slow start threshold size (`ssthresh`). The combined algorithm operates as follows:

1. Initially set `cwnd` to one segment and `ssthresh` to infinity.
2. The TCP output routine never sends more than the minimum of cwnd and the receiver's advertised window.
3. When congestion occurs, one half of the current window size (W) is saved in `ssthresh`. Additionally, if the congestion is indicated by a time-out, `cwnd` is set to one segment (i.e., slow start).
4. When new data are acknowledged by the other end, increase `cwnd`, but the way it increases depends on whether TCP is performing slow start or congestion avoidance.

If `cwnd` is less than or equal to `ssthresh`, TCP is in slow start; otherwise, TCP is performing congestion avoidance. Slow start continues until TCP is halfway to where it was when congestion occurred, and then congestion avoidance takes over.

Congestion avoidance allows a linear growth of `cwnd`, compared to slow start's exponential growth. In congestion avoidance, the increase in `cwnd` should be at most one segment each RTT, whereas in slow start the increase in `cwnd` is equal to the number of ACKs received in each RTT.

Fast Retransmit

Fast retransmit detects lost segments (resulting from congestion) based on the duplicate ACKs received and retransmits them as quickly as possible. However, TCP cannot identify whether a received duplicate ACK is due to a lost segment or due to a reordering of segments. In fast retransmit, it is assumed that three or more *duplicate ACKs* (dupack) received in a row is a strong indication of a lost segment. TCP then performs a retransmission of the missing segment, without waiting for a retransmission timer to expire. During the retransmission, TCP enters slow start.

In Figure 5, segment 6 is lost during transmission. After receiving three dupacks `ssthresh` is set to 8/2 = 4 (i.e., W/2), `cwnd` is set to 1, and the segment 6 is retransmitted. Because the receiver cached the received segments (7–14), an ACK is sent for segment 14. As in slow start, for every ACK received, the `cwnd` is incremented by 1.

Fast Recovery

The fast recovery algorithm is an improvement of fast retransmit that allows high throughput under moderate

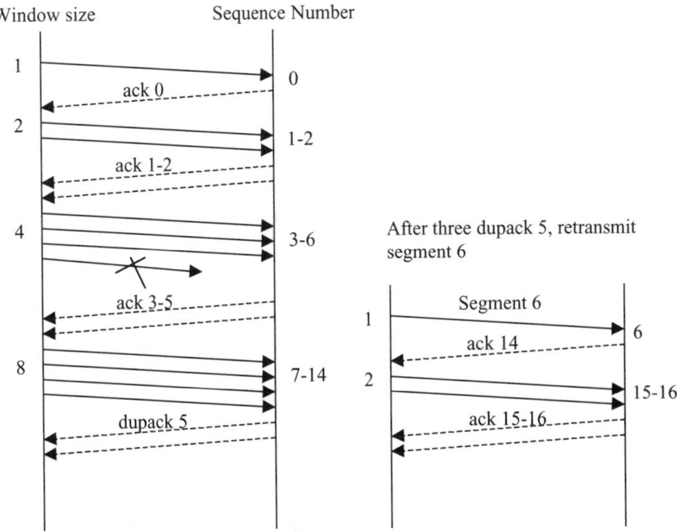

Figure 5: Fast retransmit example.

congestion, especially for large windows. Here, after fast retransmit sends the missing segment, congestion avoidance is performed. The reason for not performing slow start in this case is that the receipt of the duplicate ACKs tells TCP that more than one packet has been lost. There are still data flowing between the two ends, and TCP does not want to reduce the flow abruptly by going into slow start. The fast retransmit and fast recovery algorithms are usually implemented together.

TCP *SACK* (selective acknowledgment) is an extension to the normal TCP that allows the sender to recover from multiple packet losses in a window without resorting to coarse time-out (Mathis, Mahdavi, Floyd, & Romanow, 1996). Multiple packet losses from a window of data can have a catastrophic effect on TCP throughput. TCP uses a cumulative acknowledgment scheme in which received segments that are not at the left edge of the receive window are not acknowledged. This forces the sender to either wait an RTT to find out about each lost packet or to unnecessarily retransmit segments that have been correctly received. With a cumulative acknowledgment scheme, multiple dropped segments generally cause TCP to lose its ACK-based clock, reducing overall throughput. SACK is a strategy that corrects this behavior in the face of multiple dropped segments. With selective acknowledgments, the data receiver can inform the sender about all the segments that have arrived successively, so that the sender retransmits only the segments that have actually been lost.

Allman, Balakrishnan, and Floyd (2001) propose a new TCP mechanism that can be used to more effectively recover lost segments when a connection's congestion window is small or when a large number of segments are lost in a single transmission window. The "limited transmit" algorithm calls for sending a new data segment in response to each of the first two duplicate acknowledgments that arrive at the sender. Transmitting these segments increases the probability that TCP can recover from a single lost segment using the fast retransmit algorithm, rather than using a costly retransmission time-out.

The `cwnd` must not be changed when the new segments are transmitted. Assuming that these new segments and the corresponding ACKs are not dropped, this procedure allows the sender to infer loss using the standard fast retransmit threshold of three duplicate ACKs. This is more robust to reordered packets than if an old packet were retransmitted on the first or second duplicate ACK. Limited transmit can be used both in conjunction with, and in the absence of, the TCP SACK mechanism.

According to Mathis et al. (1996), Padhye and Floyd (2001), and Dobrota (2003), the popular TCP implementations are *Tahoe without fast retransmit* (includes slow start and congestion avoidance), *Tahoe* (includes also fast retransmit), *Reno* (Tahoe TCP with fast recovery), *New-Reno* (enhanced Reno TCP using a modified version of fast recovery), *Reno Plus* (on some Solaris systems), and *SACK*.

TCP OVER WIRELESS

TCP was originally designed for wired networks; however, with the advent of wireless technology, handheld devices, cell phones, and laptops have become popular as networked devices. Most of these devices interconnect using wireless links, and some of these devices require reliable data transfer. Because TCP is the most widely used transport-level protocol that provides reliable data transfer, it is important to improve its performance in wireless networks without any modification to the application interface provided by TCP on fixed hosts.

The current strong drive toward Internet access via wireless links includes wireless systems such as *cellular communications* (CC) and *wireless local area networks* (WLANs). Unlike conventional wired networks, wireless systems provide freedom of mobility to wireless hosts. Mobile networks can be classified as cellular networks and ad hoc networks.

A cellular network consists of mobile hosts served by a central coordinator (base station). The mobile hosts communicate directly only with the base station. If the hosts belong to the same cell, then the base station behaves as a one-hop relay. If the hosts belong to different cells, then a backbone network is used. In contrast, in an ad hoc network, mobile hosts establish a network without a backbone or base station. In such an environment, it may be necessary for one mobile host to enlist the aid of other hosts in forwarding a packet to its destination, because of the limited range of each mobile host's wireless transmissions. Figure 6 illustrates the communication pattern in cellular and ad hoc networks. CC, WLAN, and ad hoc

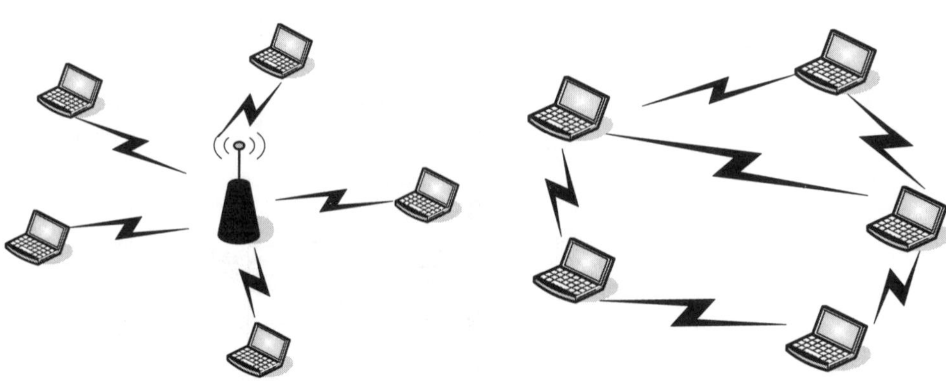

Figure 6: Cellular (left) and ad hoc (right) communication.

systems raise many performance issues, which in turn affect the performance of TCP.

Limitations in a Wireless Network

As discussed in the previous section, TCP adapts to changing end-to-end delay conditions and assumes that packet loss and delay are mainly due to network congestion. The source responds by reducing its window size and thereby reducing the transmission rate. In a network with wireless links and mobile hosts, the potentially high bit-error rate in the wireless channel can cause false alarms, which trigger congestion control. Consequently, end-to-end throughput and latency of detecting packet loss are severely degraded. Some of the limitations of a wireless network include these (Pentikousis, 2000):

- High bit-error rate: Wireless media are more prone to transmission losses, for example, because of fading channels, shadowing, and so forth. TCP was designed with a wired medium in mind, which has *bit-error rates* (BER) on the order of 10^{-6} to 10^{-8}. This translates into a segment loss rate of about 1.2% to 0.012% for 1500-byte segments. BER are much higher in the wireless domain, usually on the order of 10^{-3} and sometimes as high as 10^{-1}. With BER on the order of 10^{-3}, the packet loss rate is an order of magnitude more in a wireless environment (approximately 12%).
- Limited bandwidth: Wireless links offer less bandwidth as compared with the wired links. Wired Ethernet connections can offer 10 Mbps to 100 Mbps (theoretical maximum for Fast Ethernet). In contrast, wireless LANs using 802.11b support a maximum theoretical bandwidth of 11 Mbps. Therefore, optimum use of available bandwidth is essential.
- Longer RTT: The limited bandwidth in wireless media leads to longer latencies than wired media. This affects the overall throughput and increases interactive delays.
- Mobility: The frequent mobility of wireless devices contributes to data loss.
- Power consumption: Wireless devices have limited power and processing capacity, which require more efficient energy utilization techniques.

It is thus necessary to modify TCP such that it adapts to a wireless network without degrading the network performance.

TCP Performance in a Wireless Network

In this section, we discuss the TCP performance issues raised by the high transmission error rate and mobility in WLAN, CC, and ad hoc networks.

Impact of High Bit-Error Rate

The high bit-error rate in a wireless network is the primary source of performance degradation for TCP applications. Although some errors may be corrected by low-level *forward error correction* (FEC; Lin & Costello, 1983) codes, most errors may lead to packet corruption. Corrupted packets are discarded without being handed over to TCP, which assumes that these packets were lost. Because packet loss is considered a sign of network congestion, TCP reacts to these losses by reducing its congestion window. However, in most cases wireless transmission errors are not related to network congestion. Thus, these inappropriate reductions of the congestion window lead to unnecessary throughput reduction for TCP applications. The resulting throughput degradation can be very severe, depending on factors such as the distance between the sender and receiver and the bandwidth of the communication path.

Impact of High Bit-Error Rate in WLAN

In a typical WLAN infrastructure configuration (IEEE, 2005), there are two basic components (IEEE Standards Board, 1997): *access point* (AP) and *wireless client*. An access point/base station connects to a LAN by means of a wire, most often an Ethernet. Access points receive, buffer, and transmit data between the WLAN and the wired network infrastructure. A WLAN client may also be a desktop, laptop, or handheld device that is wireless enabled. Wireless-enabled devices use wireless *network interface cards* to connect to access points in the network.

A characteristic example of WLAN is the Lucent WaveLAN (Hassan & Jain, 2004). The WaveLAN suffers from a *frame-error rate* (FER) of 1.55% when transmitting 1400-byte frames over an 85-foot distance, with *clustered* losses. File transfer tests over a WaveLAN with a nominal bandwidth of 1.6 Mbps achieved a throughput of only 1.25 Mbps. This 22% throughput reduction resulting from a FER of only 1.55% is caused by the frequent invocations of congestion control mechanisms, which repeatedly reduce TCP's transmission rate. If errors were uniformly distributed rather than clustered, throughput would increase to 1.51 Mbps (Nguyen, Katz, Noble, & Satyanarayanan, 1996). This is consistent with other experiments showing that TCP performs worse with clustered losses (Fall & Floyd, 1996).

Table 1 shows the TCP throughput over a LAN path, consisting of a single WLAN, versus a WAN path, consisting of a single WLAN plus 15 wired links (Balakrishnan, Padmanabhan, Seshan, & Katz, 1996). It shows the throughput in the absence of any losses, the actual throughput achieved (with a FER of 2.3% for 1400-byte frames), and the percentage of the nominal bandwidth

Table 1 TCP Throughput

	Nominal bandwidth	Actual TCP throughput	% Achieved
LAN	1.5 Mbps	0.70 Mbps	46.66%
WAN	1.35 Mbps	0.31 Mbps	22.96%
IEEE 802.11	2 Mbps	0.98 Mbps	49%
IEEE 802.11b	11 Mbps	4.3 Mbps	39.1%

that was achieved. In WAN, this percentage is half of that in the LAN. Because TCP recovers from errors via end-to-end retransmissions, recovery is slower in high delay paths.

The success of the original WaveLAN and other similar, but incompatible, systems prompted the IEEE to create the 802.11 standard for WLANs (Ramani & Karandikar, 2000). The standard offers various enhancements over the original WaveLAN. Table 1 shows the nominal bandwidth and actual TCP throughput measured over a single link path, using either an IEEE 802.11 or an IEEE 802.11b WLAN. The percentages here show that the high-speed link (802.11b) is affected more by losses. Because TCP drastically reduces its throughput after each loss, it takes longer to reach the peak throughput supported by higher speed links.

Impact of High Bit-Error Rate in Cellular Networks

Unlike first-generation CC systems (analog), second-generation CC systems are digital. They are characterized by modest bit rates and circuit mode operation, using either TDMA (GSM and IS-54; Cellular Networking Perspectives, 2004; Ludwig & Rathonyi, 1999) or CDMA (IS-95; Hendry, n.d.; Karn, 1993) to share the medium. Digital CC links carry small frames, which may contain either encoded voice or data. Compared to WLANs, CC systems exhibit higher transmission and propagation delays because of the lower bit rates and longer distances involved. Because of the real-time requirements of voice telephony, FEC information is added to each frame, allowing damaged frames to be recovered without retransmissions. The traditional Internet approach is to delegate error control to higher layers of the network. This is adequate for wired links where losses resulting from errors are very rare. For error-prone wireless links, however, local (link-layer) error recovery can be faster and more adaptable to link characteristics. Voice-oriented CC systems offer a *nontransparent mode* that incorporates link layer-error recovery in addition to their native *transparent mode*.

Digital CC systems are interconnected to other networks using an *interworking function* (IWF; Alanko et al., 1994) located at the boundary of the CC system. A *radio link protocol* (RLP) is used between the wireless host and the IWF, offering IP datagram segmentation and reassembly (Karn, 1993). As a result, the wireless host may exchange IP datagrams with any host on the Internet, using the IWF for routing purposes. The RLP may also provide error recovery to hide wireless losses from the Internet (Nanda, Ejzak, & Doshi, 1994).

CC networks are divided up into cells where each cell is serviced by one or more radio transceivers (transmitter/receiver). The cellular topology of a network helps in frequency reuse. Cells, a certain distance apart, can reuse the same frequency, which ensures the efficient usage of limited radio resources.

CC links in transparent mode (for voice) suffer from a FER of 1% to 2%, after low-level error recovery, despite their short frames (Karn, 1993). Frame errors are less bursty than bit errors, because multiple frames are bit interleaved before transmission. Although this process reduces the loss rate and randomizes frame errors, thus avoiding audible speech degradation, it considerably increases processing delay because of interleaving before transmission and deinterleaving after reception. If we reduce the size of IP datagrams to reduce the packet loss probability, user data throughput also decreases because of the higher TCP/IP header overhead. TCP/IP header compression may be used over slow CC links, shrinking TCP/IP headers to 3 to 5 bytes (Jacobson, 1990). Header compression may, however, adversely interact with RTT(s), TCP error recovery, and link layer resets, leading to a loss of synchronization between the *compressor* and *decompressor*, thus causing entire windows of TCP data to be dropped (Ludwig, Rathonyi, Konrad, Oden, & Joseph, 1999).

Although the RLP used in the nontransparent mode of GSM (global system mobile communication) usually manages to recover from wireless losses before TCP timers expire (Ludwig, Rathonyi, et al., 1999), it exhibits high and widely varying RTT values. Measurements using ping over a GSM network in San Francisco showed that 95% of the RTT values were around 600 ms with a standard deviation equivalent to 20 ms (Ludwig & Rathonyi, 1999). Large file transfer experiments, however, reveal that RTT can be occasionally much higher with real applications over operational networks, reaching values of up to 12 s. The conclusion is that the high latency is due to interleaving, rate adaptation, buffering, and interfacing between GSM network elements (Ludwig & Rathonyi, 1999) .

Increasing the size of the TCP *maximum segment size* (MSS) reduces TCP/IP header overhead, thus improving bulk transfer throughput, but also increases the response time of interactive applications. Measurements over operational GSM networks show that TCP throughput is optimized for an MSS size of approximately 700 (Hassan & Jain, 2004). Although small fixed-size frames simplify RLP operation and make it more robust in worst-case conditions, choosing a frame size appropriate for prevailing conditions can provide throughput improvements of 18% to 23%, depending on the radio environment (Ludwig, Konrad, & Joseph, 1999).

When the end-to-end path includes multiple wireless links, the losses accumulate, leading to more frequent invocations of TCP congestion control mechanisms. This reduces throughput and also causes wireless links to remain idle for prolonged periods of time. Furthermore, when a TCP packet is lost after crossing some wireless links in the path, its retransmission has to cross them again, risking new losses and wasting wireless bandwidth. Losses have more pronounced effects on paths with higher end-to-end delay, which require TCP to maintain large transmission windows to keep data flowing. On such paths, TCP also suffers from *spurious time-outs*, that is, time-outs that would be avoided if the sender waited longer for acknowledgments. In addition to the high and unpredictable delays caused by RLP error recovery, CC systems explicitly allow prolonged disconnections during handoffs, causing numerous spurious time-outs (Hassan & Jain, 2004).

Impact of Mobility in Cellular Networks

To understand the impact of mobility in a network, we provide a brief introduction to the mobile Internet protocol (mobile IP; IEEE Computer Society, n.d.) and its operation. Mobile IP is an extension to the Internet protocol proposed by the Internet Engineering Task Force (IETF) to support user mobility. It enables mobile computers to stay connected to the Internet regardless of their location and without changing their IP address (Perkins, 1996). Because mobile IP is the most widely used standard to support mobility of Internet users, it has a direct impact on the performance of TCP connections.

IP routes packets from a source end point to a destination by allowing routers to forward packets from incoming network interfaces to outbound interfaces according to routing tables. The routing tables typically maintain the next-hop (outbound interface) information for each destination IP address, according to the number of networks to which that IP address is connected. The network number is derived from the IP address by masking off some of the low-order bits. Thus, the IP address typically carries with it information that specifies the IP node's point of attachment.

To maintain existing transport-layer connections as the mobile node moves from place to place, it must keep its IP address the same. In TCP, connections are indexed by a quadruplet that contains the IP addresses and port numbers of both connection end points. Changing any of these four numbers will cause the connection to be disrupted and lost. In contrast, correct delivery of packets to the mobile node's current point of attachment depends on the network number contained within the mobile node's IP address, which changes at new points of attachment. To change the routing requires a new IP address associated with the new point of attachment.

Mobile IP has been designed to solve this problem by allowing the *mobile node* to use two IP addresses. In mobile IP, the *home address* is static and is used, for instance, to identify TCP connections. The *care-of address* changes at each new point of attachment and can be thought of as the mobile node's topologically significant address; it indicates the network number and thus identifies the mobile node's point of attachment with respect to the network topology. The home address makes it appear that the mobile node is continually able to receive data on its *home network*, where mobile IP requires the existence of a network node known as the *home agent* (HA). Whenever the mobile node is not attached to its home network (and is therefore attached to what is termed a *foreign network*), the HA gets all the packets destined for the mobile node and arranges to deliver them to the mobile node's current point of attachment.

The basic entities of mobile IP operations are the *mobile host* (MH), the home network or the network to which the mobile host is connected, the foreign network or the network to which the mobile host has moved, and the *static corresponding host* (SH) with which the MH communicates. It also includes an HA in the home network and a *foreign agent* (FA) in the foreign network. The HA and FA are stationary.

When the mobile node is on its home subnet (the one specified by its IP address) the mobile node informs the HA of its presence. Once the mobile node has registered with the HA and is on the FA's network, IP traffic addressed to the mobile node is received by the HA, encapsulated in another IP datagram, and then *tunneled* to the FA. The FA

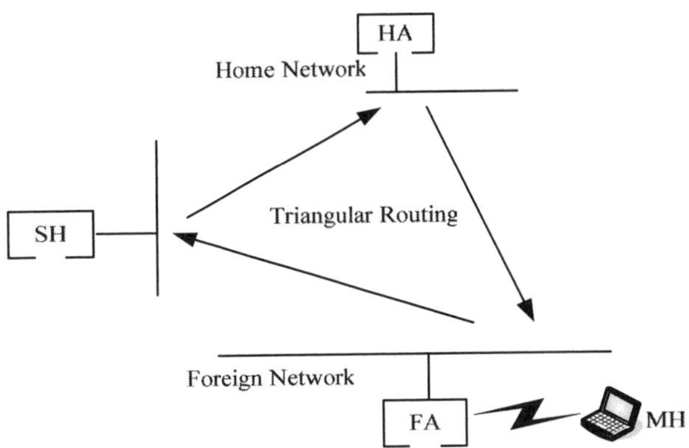

Figure 7: Mobile IP operation.

forwards the datagrams to the MH. In the reverse direction, the mobile node can bypass the HA and send datagrams directly to the SH. This result in a triangular routing of traffic (refer to Figure 7), which is not necessarily efficient but is effective. In addition, when a mobile node changes its location, it can register with a new FA, although traffic directed by the HA to the old FA will be lost until the new mobile node has registered its location.

Although mobile IP supports user mobility in the Internet, it suffers from several drawbacks. This is especially true for TCP connections because of the following reasons (Hassan & Jain, 2004):

1. *Blackouts*: Sinha, Monks, and Bhargavan (200), through field experiments, show that MH can experience periods of blackouts during mobility. Blackouts are periods during which the MH is not connected to the base station. It could be due to the specific location that the user is passing through, or fading, and can last for a few seconds. During a blackout, the TCP retransmission timer expires and is misinterpreted as network congestion. Hence, the congestion window is reset to one, and the TCP enters into the slow start mode. Thus, frequent blackouts will severely degrade TCP performance.
2. *Handoff latency*: When a MH moves from one cell to another, it takes some amount of time for mobile IP to react to the handoff (reroute packets to the new cell). In the meantime, the old base station drops the packets sent to the old cell. During these types of bursty losses, TCP retransmission timer expires, reset, its congestion windows and enters slow start mode. Thus, frequent handoffs degrade TCP throughput.
3. *Triangular routing and larger RTT*: When triangular routing of mobile IP is performed, the path from the SH to the MH is artificially long because of the two stage tunneling from the host to the HA and then from the HA to the MH. This results in increased RTT for the connection. Because TCP's throughput is inversely proportional to the RTT, increased RTT results in less throughput. In addition, some security mechanisms in the current Internet require even the reverse path from the MH to the static host to go through the HA, resulting in larger RTT.

Impact of Mobility in Ad Hoc Networks

Unlike conventional networks, in ad hoc networks, routing is a basic function of every node. The mobility of the nodes affects the performance of the routing protocol and TCP. This is due to these factors:

1. *Route failures*: An ad hoc network experiences frequent route failures because of mobility of the nodes. When there is a route failure, a TCP connection that is using the route potentially loses packets. Because TCP cannot distinguish between losses resulting from route failure and those resulting from congestion, it resets the congestion window and enters into the slow start mode. Because every route failure resets the congestion window and takes a few RTTs to resume to its available capacity, it experiences severe throughput degradation. In addition, ad hoc networks experience high RTT variations, resulting in a high mean deviation of the RTT because the retransmission time-out value is initially set to average RTT plus four times the mean deviation. This further exacerbates the problem, resulting in severe throughput degradation.
2. *Route recomputations*: When route failures occur, the routing protocol sends route error messages to the source. The TCP connection at the source will not be able to send any more packets until the route is recomputed. TCP perceives the route recomputation time as increased RTT, resulting in a more inflated retransmission time-out. The problem worsens when the network is heavily loaded because the recomputation time further increases.
3. *Network partitions*: Ad hoc networks communicate through multihop paths, where every node performs the routing functions. A partition in the network implies that the source and destination of a TCP connection belong to two different partitioned components of the network and cannot communicate (as long as the partition exists). During a partitioning, TCP resets the connection if the partition lasts for more than some predetermined amount of time (100 s). Even if the partitioned network gets connected again, TCP will enter the slow start phase. This behavior severely degrades the network performance.

Classification of Proposed Schemes

There are two fundamentally different approaches to improve TCP performance in wireless systems (Balakrishnan, Padmanabhan, Seshan, & Katz, 1996). The first approach hides any noncongestion-related losses from the TCP sender and therefore requires no changes to existing sender implementations. The rationale is that because the problem is local (to the wireless link), it should be solved locally, and that the transport layer need not be aware of the characteristics of the individual links. The second class of techniques attempts to make the sender aware of the existence of wireless hops and realize that some packet losses are not due to congestion. The sender can then avoid invoking congestion control algorithms when noncongestion-related losses occur.

We can classify the many schemes into three basic groups, based on their fundamental philosophy: end-to-end proposals, split-connection proposals, and link-layer proposals (Balakrishnan et al., 1996). The end-to-end protocols attempt to make the TCP sender handle losses through the use of two techniques: SACK and explicit loss notification (ELN). Split-connection approaches completely hide the wireless link from the sender by terminating the TCP connection at the base station. Such schemes use a separate reliable connection between the base station and the destination host. The second connection can use techniques such as negative or selective acknowledgments, rather than just regular TCP, to perform well over the wireless link. The link-layer solutions are between the other two classes. These protocols attempt to hide link-related losses from the TCP sender by using local retransmissions and perhaps FEC over the wireless link. Figure 8 illustrates a more detailed classification as in Ludwig (1999). Note that the fully shaded areas indicate whether a transport protocol or its implementation must be changed, or whether transport protocol dependent state has to be maintained in the network. The partially shaded areas indicate changes required at the link layer.

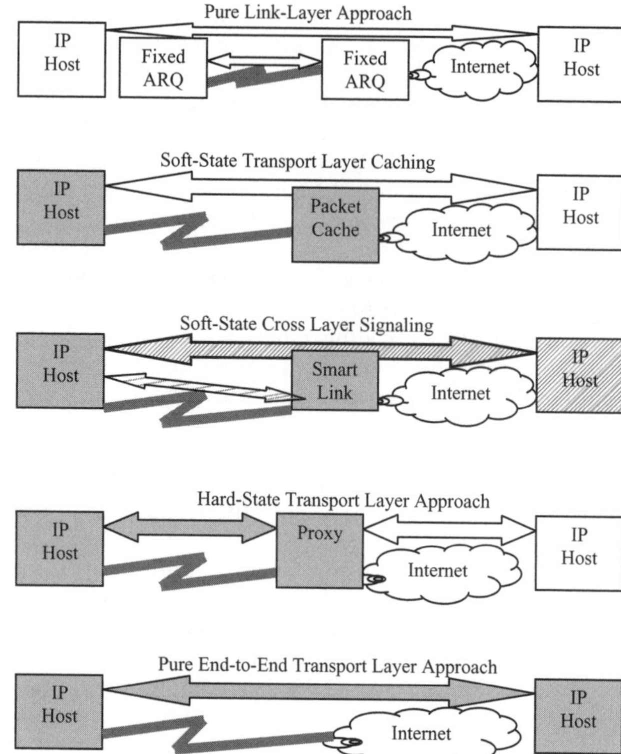

Figure 8: Classification of TCP over wireless approaches.

Pure Link-Level Approach: This approach hides the unwanted characteristics of the wireless links from the higher layers. A critical factor here is the link-level time-out value. An example is the AIRMAIL protocol, which is a link-layer protocol for indoor and outdoor wireless networks (Ayanoglu, 1995). However, pure link-level approaches alone will not be sufficient, because they cannot completely prevent the sender from timing out and invoking the congestion control mechanisms. To preserve the end-to-end semantics, other promising solutions propose to correct errors at the wireless link level by using a combination of FEC and ARQ (automatic repeat request; Balakrishnan et al., 1996).

Soft-State Transport-Layer Caching Approach: This approach maintains a soft state of the network. In other words, the state is not crucial and preserves the end-to-end semantics. The approach is aware of the transport layer and uses caching to prevent the sender from unnecessary invocation of the congestion control mechanism. The disadvantage is that it requires changes at the intermediate node (base station) and optionally at the mobile host. They also fail in the presence of encryption as intermediate nodes try to interpret the transport header.

Soft-State Cross-Layer Signaling Approach: In this approach, the transport-layer sender is aware of the wireless link. This can be achieved by having the link or the network layer send a signal to the transport-layer sender about specific events so that it can adapt accordingly. The advantage here is that it helps distinguish congestion losses from the error losses but this may not be possible if the network is extremely congested, in which case it is not possible for the network to inform the sender through any kind of signaling. They also involve changes at some or all of the intermediate nodes and at the transport layer of the sender's protocol stack in order to appropriate actions in response to the signals received from the network.

Hard-State Transport-Layer Approach: This approach encompasses all forms of splitting in that the end-to-end semantics may be sacrificed. The advantage here is that the wireless link is completely shielded from damage or loss. However, there is a high cost associated with the maintaining of the state information crucial to the end-to-end connection.

Pure End-to-End Transport-Level Approach: The advantage of an end-to-end approach is that a sender can quickly recover from multiple lost packets in a single RTT and that such an event is treated as one congestion signal instead of one signal for each lost packet.

PROPOSED SCHEMES FOR WIRELESS TCP

There are several proposed solutions to extend TCP in a wireless or heterogeneous network. In this section, some of proposed schemes are discussed.

Pure Link-Level Approaches

The techniques used here include adaptive FEC, interleaving, adaptive power control, and fully reliable and semireliable link-layer ARQ protocols. Pure link-layer solutions can yield excellent TCP bulk data throughput without interfering with end-to-end error recovery. Interactions between link-layer and end-to-end error recovery have been studied (Balakrishnan et al., 1996; Bhagwat, Bhattacharya, Krishna, & Tripathi, 1997). A key advantage is that local knowledge about the link's error characteristics, which can vary largely over short time scales, can be exploited to optimize error control efficiency. The second advantage is that it does not require any changes to the IP-based protocol stacks. The drawback is that the error control schemes are applied irrespective of the *quality of service* (QoS) requirements of individual flows sharing the link. A flow that requires link-layer ARQ cannot share the link with a delay-sensitive flow introduced by link-layer retransmissions. In contrast, an adaptive application might be able to tolerate higher loss rates in return for higher available bit rates than the link's channel coding scheme provides.

Soft-State Transport-Layer Caching Approaches

Snoop Protocol

Snoop (Balakrishnan et al., 1996; Balakrishnan, Seshan, & Katz, 1995) is classified as a TCP-aware link-level protocol. It involves modification of the network layer (IP) software at the *base station* by adding a module called `snoop`. The `snoop` module looks at every packet on the connection in either direction. It maintains a cache of TCP packets sent from the *fixed host* (FH) that have not been acknowledged by the MH. When a new packet arrives from the FH, `snoop` adds it to its cache and passes the packet on to the routing code that performs normal routing function. The `snoop` module also keeps track of all the acknowledgments sent from the mobile host. When a packet loss is detected (either by the arrival of a duplicate acknowledgments or by a local time-out), it retransmits the lost packet to MH if it has the packet cached. In this way, the base station hides the packet loss from the FH by not propagating duplicate acknowledgments, thereby preventing unnecessary invocations of the congestion control mechanisms at the sender (FH). It does not completely shield the sender from wireless losses as the sender may time-out because of repeated losses or bit errors caused by the wireless link. Because the protocol is TCP aware, it would fail if the packets were encrypted.

Soft-State Cross-Layer Signaling Approaches

Explicit Congestion Notification (ECN)

(ECN Ludwig & Rathonyi, 1999) is an extension proposed to *random early detection* (RED; Floyd & Jacobson, 1993). RED is an active queue management mechanism in routers that detects congestion before a queue overflows and provides an indication of this congestion to the end nodes. Routers using RED operate by maintaining two levels of threshold, minimum (min) and maximum (max). RED drops packets probabilistically if and only if the average queue size lies between the min and max. ECN, in contrast, marks a packet instead of dropping it when the average queue size is between min and max. Upon receipt of a congestion-marked packet, the TCP receiver informs the sender (in the subsequent acknowledgment) about incipient congestion, which in turn will trigger the congestion avoidance algorithm at the sender. ECN requires support from both the router as well as the end hosts, that is, the end-host TCP stack needs to be modified. Although it provides a simple solution, it cannot handle high bit-error rates.

Explicit Loss Notification (ELN)

ELN (Balakrishnan et al., 1996) adds an ELN option to TCP ACKs. When a packet is dropped in the wireless network, future cumulative acknowledgments corresponding to the lost packet are marked to identify that a noncongestion-related loss has occurred. Upon receiving this information along with duplicate acknowledgments, the sender may perform retransmissions without invoking congestion control procedures. ELN also cannot handle high bit-error rate.

Explicit Bad State Notification (EBSN)

ESBN (Bakshi, Vaidya, & Pradhan, 1997) proposes to update the TCP timer at the source to prevent the source from decreasing its congestion window, provided there is no congestion. EBSN's are sent to the source after every unsuccessful attempt by the base station to transmit packets over the wireless link. EBSN would cause the previous time-outs to be cancelled and new time-outs put in place, based on existing estimate of RTT and variance. The EBSN approach does not interfere with actual RTT or variance estimates, and at the same time prevents unnecessary time-outs from occurring. This, in turn, prevents time-outs for packets that had already been put on the network before the wireless link encountered the bad state. ESBN also cannot handle high bit-error rates.

Mobility Awareness Incorporated as a TCP Enhancement (MAITE)

MAITE uses link-layer messages to inform TCP of high BER and host disconnection resulting from mobility (Karn & Partridge, 1987). A high BER can be detected when the cyclic redundancy check on received frames continuously fails. Similarly, the MH disconnection can be detected by sensing the lack of the beacon that is periodically sent by the access point in WLAN standard implementations.

When the link layer detects a high BER it sends a HighBER notification message to the transport layer. During a HighBER period, the MH will freeze its TCP timers and will not attempt any transmissions until it receives a HighBEROver message from the link layer. Similarly, a disconnection notification message is used when a MH disconnects and the TCP timers freeze during this period.

Now that high BER and disconnections conditions are distinguished, any time-out that occurs at the transport level is only due to intermediate congestion and the regular congestion control mechanisms are followed.

Multiple Acknowledgments

The multiple acknowledgments method distinguishes the losses (congestion or other errors) on the wired link and those on the wireless link (Biaz, Mehta, West, & Vaidya, 1997). It uses two types of ACKs to isolate the wireless host and fixed network, such as *partial acknowledgment* (ACKp) and *complete acknowledgment* (ACKc). The sender strictly follows regular TCP when sending packets with slow start, congestion avoidance, fast retransmit, and fast recovery. RTO is the maximum time that can elapse between the reception of a packet at the base station and its acknowledgment by the MH.

When a sender gets ACKp with sequence number *Na* from the base station, the sender understands that the base station has received packets up to *Na* – 1 but is having difficulty sending these packets to the wireless host; that is, it has not received the acknowledgment from the wireless host after waiting for RTO time. So, the sender updates RTO to give more time to the base station to accomplish the retransmission. This will avoid end-to-end retransmissions, thus avoiding triggering the slow start and congestion avoidance mechanisms. On receipt of ACKp, the sender marks the corresponding packets. On time-out, the sender checks if the packets are marked; if they are not marked, then it acts as normal TCP would. If they are marked, then it will not retransmit and will not initiate any congestion control methods except backing off the timer.

ACKc is a complete acknowledgment of the received packet. When the sender receives ACKc, it takes the same steps as in normal TCP. Corrupted TCP segments are often detected at the data-link layer and discarded by the link-level drivers.

Hard-State Transport Layer Approaches

Indirect TCP (I-TCP)

The indirect protocol model for mobile hosts suggests that any interaction from a MH to a machine on the fixed network should be split into two separate interactions—one between the MH and its *mobile support router* (MSR) over the wireless medium and another between the MSR and the fixed host (FH) over the fixed network (Bakre & Badrinath, 1995). At the transport layer, use of indirection separates the flow control and congestion control functionality on the wireless link from that on the fixed network. It allows a separate transport protocol for the wireless link, which can support notification of events such as disconnections, relocation, and other features of the wireless link. This includes the available bandwidth to the higher layers that can be used by link-aware and location-aware mobile applications. Indirection also allows the base station to manage much of the communication overhead for a MH. Thus, a MH that runs a very simple wireless protocol to communicate with the MSR can still access fixed network services that may otherwise require a full TCP/IP stack running on the MH.

When a MH wishes to communicate with some FH using I-TCP, a request is sent to the current base station (which is also attached to the fixed network) to open a TCP connection with the FH on behalf of the MH. The MH communicates with its MSR on a separate connection using a variation of TCP that is tuned for wireless links and is also aware of mobility. The FH only sees an image of its peer MH that in fact resides on the MSR. It is this image that is handed over to the new MSR when the MH moves to another cell.

One consequence of using I-TCP is that the TCP acknowledgments are not end to end; instead, we have separate acknowledgments for the wireless and the wired parts of the connection. However, I-TCP does not yield weaker end-to-end semantics in comparison with regular TCP, provided that there are no base station failures and that the MH does not stay disconnected from the fixed network for too long.

Pure End-to-End Transport-Level Approaches

Freeze-TCP

Freeze-TCP is a true end-to-end mechanism and does not require any intermediaries (Goff, Moronski, Phatak, & Gupta, 2000). No change in TCP code is required on the sender side or the intermediate routers. Freeze-TCP can be classified as a proactive mechanism because it is a congestion-avoidance technique whereby the client takes care that the TCP on the sender side that does not invoke congestion control mechanism unnecessarily.

A MH can monitor the strength of its wireless signal and detect an impending handoff or a temporary disconnection (if the signal strength is fading, for instance). If a MH detects such a situation, it will advertise a zero window size, freeze all retransmit timers, and enter a persist mode. This includes sending *zero window probes* (ZWPs) until the receiver's window opens up. This prevents the sender from dropping its congestion window. Because these probes are not delivered reliably, the sender does not drop its congestion window if a ZWP itself gets lost.

If a receiver senses an impending disconnection, it will try to send out a few acknowledgments wherein its window size is advertised as zero. The issue here is how much in advance of the disconnection should the receiver start advertising a window size of zero. This period is called the warning period prior to disconnection and a reasonable warning period is the RTT (Goff et al., 2000). If the receiver shrinks its window to zero, all outstanding packets will be lost without affecting the sender's congestion window, and the sender will enter the persist mode described previously.

Wireless TCP (W-TCP)

W-TCP (Sinha, Venkitaraman, Sivakumar, & Bharghavan, 1999) was designed for wireless wide area networks and uses purely end-to-end semantics. It tries to distinguish random losses from congestion losses by measuring the packet interarrival time with the packet interdeparture time. It uses rate-based, rather than window-based, transmission control. It shapes its data traffic, never allows a burst of packet transmissions, and is fair when competing connections have different RTTs.

The basic idea here is that TCP should not reduce its transmission rate for just a packet loss as this happens very frequently in wireless networks. The sender does not decide if packets have to be transmitted because some of the ACKs have failed but probes the receiver to find out if a packet has to be resent. The transmission rates at the sender are controlled by the feedback of the receiver. W-TCP uses the ratio of the interpacket separation at the receiver and the interpacket separation at the sender as the primary metric for rate control rather than using packet losses and retransmit timeouts. W-TCP uses the standard TCP mechanism for flow control and connection management. The key aspect of congestion control is that it uses interpacket delay as a metric and performs the rate adaptation computation at the receiver's end. It thus distinguishes the cause of packet loss and behaves accordingly.

TCP- Santa Cruz (TCP-SC)

TCP-Santa Cruz (Parsa & Garcia-Luna-Aceves, 1999) uses a similar idea as in W-TCP. RTT is not considered as a metric for retransmission time-outs (Parsa & Garcia-Luna-Aceves, 1999). Instead, the sender depends on intermessage delay and explicit notifications (selective acknowledgments) for retransmissions. TCP-SC monitors the queue developing over a bottleneck link, and this determines whether congestion is increasing in the network. It can then distinguish losses as congestion-related or random and respond appropriately. Congestion is determined by calculating the relative delay that one packet experiences with respect to another as it traverses the network.

The losses resulting from congestion are usually preceded by an increase in the network bottleneck queue. A wireless loss, in contrast, can be identified as a random loss that is not preceded by a build-up in the bottleneck queue. TCP-SC monitors the changes in the bottleneck queue. Once losses are discovered, it retransmits without reducing the transmission window. This can also be implemented as a TCP option by utilizing the extra 40 bytes available in the options field of the TCP header.

Mobile-TCP (M-TCP)

M-TCP is designed to work well in the presence of frequent disconnections and low bit-rate wireless links and maintains end-to-end semantics (Brown & Singh, 1997). The implementation of M-TCP is based on a three-level hierarchy (refer to Figure 9). At the lowest level are the MH that communicate with *mobile support station* (MS) nodes in each cell. Several MSs are controlled by a machine called the *supervisor host* (SHH). The SHH is connected to the wired network, and it handles most of the routing and other protocol details for the mobile users.

The SHH uses the split connection approach for implementing M-TCP because it allows modifications in TCP on the mobile network. Thus, every TCP connection is split into two at the SHH. The TCP sender on the FH uses unmodified TCP to send data to the SHH, whereas the SHH uses M-TCP for delivering data to the MH. The FH sends TCP segments to the SHH. SHH passes them to the MH, which acknowledges the packets that it received. SHH, on receipt of ACKs, sends ACKs back to the FH. Unlike other

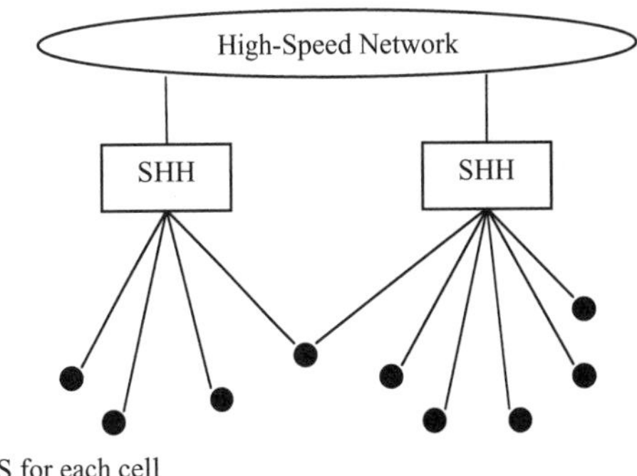

Figure 9: Three-level hierarchy of the network.

split connection techniques, it saves the ACK of the last byte to prevent loss of outstanding packets.

If the MH is disconnected, then the SHH will stop receiving ACKs and assumes that MH has been temporarily disconnected and sends the ACK of the last byte that it saved previously. This ACK will contain the advertised window of the MH as having size zero. The sender, upon getting the advertised window as zero, enters the persist mode and freezes all the timers related to the session, and starts sending the exponentially backed-off persist packets to the SHH. The SHH responds with the zero window size at the receiver to each persist packet, until it receives some nonzero window size indication from the MH. Upon receiving it, the SHH immediately replies to the persist packet as the appropriate window size and resumes all its freezed timers. Thus, the sender can resume transmitting at full speed. The FH resumes transmitting from the next byte that was unacknowledged.

TCP Westwood (TCPW)

TCPW is a sender-side modification of the TCP congestion window algorithm that improves upon the performance of TCP Reno implementation in wired as well as wireless networks (Mascolo et al., 2000). The general idea is to use the bandwidth estimate, BWE, to set the congestion window (`cwin`) and slow start threshold (`ssthresh`) after a congestion episode. The important distinguishing feature of TCPW with respect to TCP Reno is TCP Reno halves the congestion window after three duplicate acknowledgments or after a time-out, whereas TCPW attempts to select a slow start threshold and a congestion window consistent with the effective bandwidth used at the time congestion is experienced.

The source performs an end-to-end estimate of the bandwidth available along a TCP connection by measuring and averaging the rate of returning ACKs. Whenever a sender perceives a packet loss (i.e., a time-out occurs or three duplicate ACKs are received), the sender uses the bandwidth estimate to properly set the congestion window (`cwin`) and the low start threshold (`ssthresh`). In this way, TCPW avoids overly conservative reduction of `cwin` and `ssthresh` and thus it ensures faster recovery.

TCPW does not require inspection and/or interception of TCP packets at intermediate (proxy) nodes and complies with the end-to-end TCP design principles. It is very effective in mixed wired and wireless networks. When coexisting with TCP Reno, better throughput, delay performance, fairness, and friendliness (coexistence with connections from TCP variants) were observed in experimental studies (Mascolo et al., 2000). However, it performs poorly when random-packet-loss rate exceeds a few percent.

TCP Delayed Congestion Response (TCP-DCR)

TCP-DCR is based on the simple idea of allowing the link-level mechanism to recover the packets lost as a result of channel errors, thereby limiting the response of the transport protocol to mostly congestion losses (Bhandarkar & Reddy, 2004). TCP-DCR works in conjunction with a simple link-level protocol to provide the benefits of standard TCP implementations without the associated degradation in performance resulting from channel errors in wireless networks. In TCP-DCR, the response to the receipt of dupacks is delayed by a short bounded period τ. If the packet is recovered by link-level retransmission before the end of the delay period τ, TCP-DCR proceeds as if the packet loss never occurred. However, if the packet is not recovered by link-level retransmission by the end of the delay period, TCP-DCR protocol triggers the congestion recovery algorithms of fast retransmission and recovery. By doing this, we effectively change the paradigm of TCP that all losses are due to congestion to the paradigm that all losses are due to channel errors for a period of τ. It may be noted here that no changes need to be made for the TCP at the receiver, and base stations are not required to maintain any TCP-related state information.

Eifel

Retransmission ambiguity is defined as the TCP sender's inability to distinguish between an ACK for the original transmission from that of an ACK for its retransmission. The Eifel algorithm (Ludwig & Meyer, 2003) eliminates the retransmission ambiguity, thereby solving the problems caused by the *spurious time-outs* and *spurious fast retransmits*. Spurious time-outs are defined as time-outs that would not have occurred if the sender had waited "long enough." Spurious fast retransmits are defined as fast retransmissions that occur because of the reordering of packets beyond the dupack threshold (normally set to three). Experiments have shown that in fact a large number of time-outs and fast retransmissions that occur are really spurious. Spurious time-outs affect the TCP performance in two ways: TCP sender unnecessarily reduces its load and TCP sender is forced into the go-back-N retransmission mode.

The Eifel detection algorithm (Ludwig & Meyer, 2003) uses the TCP time stamps option to eliminate the retransmission ambiguity. It thereby allows a TCP sender to detect a posteriori whether it has entered loss recovery unnecessarily. This added capability of a TCP sender is useful in environments where TCP's loss recovery and congestion control algorithms may often get falsely triggered. This can be caused by packet reordering, packet duplication, or a sudden delay increase in the data or the ACK path that results in a spurious time-out.

Based on an appropriate detection algorithm, the Eifel response algorithm (Ludwig & Gurtov, 2004) provides a way for a TCP sender to respond to a detected spurious time-out. It adapts the retransmission timer to avoid further spurious time-outs and can avoid—depending on the detection algorithm—the often unnecessary go-back-N retransmits that would otherwise be sent. In addition, the Eifel response algorithm restores the congestion control state in such a way that packet bursts are avoided.

SECURITY

Security Issues

To provide security in a network, it is essential to understand the requirements of a secure communication. The basic requirements for a secure system are these:

Confidentiality: The data transmitted over a network should be able to accessible only to the intended receiver.

Cryptographic algorithms can be used to ensure confidentiality. It is a process of encrypting messages such that only the intended receiver can decrypt and use the message. Currently, there are two types of cryptosystems used, namely symmetric encryption and public key encryption. In symmetric encryption, a single key is used for both encryption and decryption. In public key encryption, in contrast, two different but mathematically related keys are used.

Integrity: The data received should be identical to the data sent. If not, any accidental or malicious changes should be detectable.

Availability: A service should be available for use to an authorized user at any time and without unreasonable delay.

Authentication: The identity of a user or service can be verified.

Accountability: It refers to the keeping and protecting of audit information so that the party responsible for any action affecting security can be tracked.

Nonrepudiation: It must not be possible for a user to deny sending or receiving a message. This requirement demands integrity and authentication.

Possible Attacks

This section discusses common attacks in a network and the possible countermeasures that can be used to minimize the risk of these attacks.

Sniffing/Eavesdropping

A packet sniffer is a software application that uses a network adapter card in promiscuous mode to capture all network packets that are sent across a LAN. Because specifications for network protocols, such as TCP/IP, are widely published, it is possible to sniff and interpret these packets. It can be used as an administrative tool as well as a hacking tool.

Given the radio-based nature of wireless networks, sniffing is always a possibility because communication is through open air, facilitating confidentiality and integrity attacks. Even if the data streams are successfully sniffed off the air, if the data are encrypted, then it will be of no use. In 802.11b, the *wired equivalent privacy* (WEP) can be used to encrypt data.

IP Spoofing

IP spoofing is a technique used to gain unauthorized access to computers whereby the intruder pretends to be a trusted computer either by using an IP address that is within the range of the network or by using an authorized external IP address. The intruder must first determine the IP address of a trusted host and then modify the packet headers so that it appears that his or her packets are coming from that trusted host. IP spoofing is mostly limited to providing anonymity for an attacker launching attacks against the IP layer, for example, SYN flooding, TCP session hijacking, and so forth.

Firewall arrangements can offer protection against IP spoofing. A firewall is a system designed to prevent unauthorized access to or from a private network. It examines all the messages that pass through the network and filters the messages that do not meet the specified security criteria.

Denial of Service Attacks

A denial of service (DoS) attack focuses on making a service unavailable for normal use, which is typically accomplished by exhausting some resource limitation on the network or within an operating system or application. It can be implemented using common Internet protocols, such as TCP and Internet control message protocol (ICMP). The attack exploits the weakness of the system being attacked rather than a software bug or security hole. DoS attacks can lead to severe degradation of network performance.

Application-Layer Attacks

Application-layer attacks can be implemented using several different methods. One of the most common methods is exploiting well-known weaknesses in software that is commonly found on servers, such as sendmail, PostScript, file transfer protocol (FTP), and so forth. For instance, if an organization that runs a public FTP service does not separate its sensitive organizational data, then with today's network speeds it may be possible to download all the sensitive data in a matter of minutes. In this way, by exploiting the weakness in the software, the attackers can gain access to a computer with the privileged access.

Man-in-the-Middle Attacks

A man-in-the-middle (MITM) attack is an attack where the attacker is able to read and modify messages between two parties without letting either party know that their communication has been compromised. The attacker must be able to observe and intercept messages going between the two victims. Using public key encryption, an attack might look as follows:

Adam wishes to communicate with Beth. Ed is an intruder who wants to eavesdrop on the conversation, or deliver a false message to Beth. Initially, before Adam and Beth communicate, Adam will ask Beth for her public key. Beth will send her public key to Adam, but Ed will intercept it and send Adam his own public key instead. Adam then encrypts his message with Ed's key (which he believes is Beth's) and sends it back to Beth. Ed again intercepts, decrypts the message, and reads the contents. He then encrypts the message (possibly altered) with Beth's key and sends it to Beth, who believes she has received it directly from Adam. Figure 10 illustrates this attack.

Standards in Wireless Networks

In this section, we discuss briefly the security standards available in WLANs. WLANs are implemented as an extension to wired LANs within a building and can provide the final few meters of connectivity between a wired network and the mobile user. WLANs are based on the IEEE 802.11 standard. In IEEE 802.11, the security services are provided by the WEP protocol. WEP does not provide end-to-end security but only security for the wireless portion of the connection. The three basic security services defined by IEEE for the WLAN environment are authentication, confidentiality, and integrity. Unfortunately,

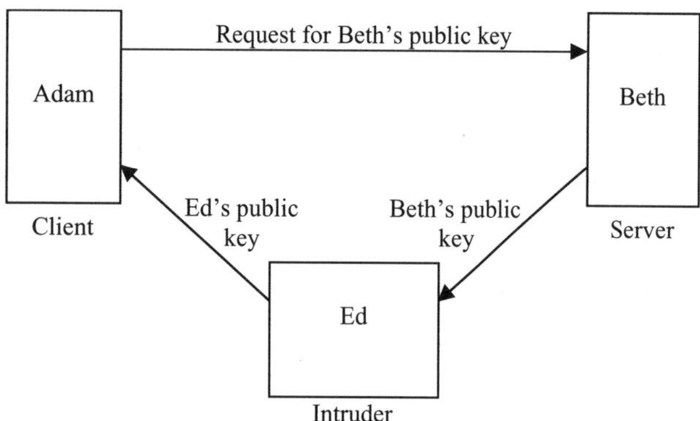

Figure 10: Man-in-the-middle attack.

several security flaws were identified in WEP. Although the application of WEP may stop casual sniffers, experienced hackers can crack the WEP keys in a busy network within 15 minutes. The standard also does not address other security services such as audit, authorization, and nonrepudiation.

To help address the security issues in WLANs, the IEEE 802.11 Working Group instituted Task Group "I" to develop 802.11i standard with enhanced security features. The 802.11i standard includes two main developments: *wi-fi protected access* (WPA) and *robust security network* (RSN; Cohen & O'Hara, 2003).

WPA uses *temporal key integrity protocol* (TKIP) to improve security of keys used with WEP. It changes the way keys are derived and rotates keys more often for security. It also adds a message-integrity-check function to prevent packet forgeries. Although WPA goes a long way toward addressing the shortcomings of WEP, not all users will be able to take advantage of it because WPA might not be backward-compatible with some legacy devices and operating systems. Moreover, not all users share the same security infrastructure. For instance, some users will have a PDA and lack the processing resources of a PC. TKIP/WPA may also degrade performance unless a WLAN system has hardware that will run and accelerate the WPA protocol. For most WLANs, there's currently a trade-off between security and performance without the presence of hardware acceleration in the access point.

RSN uses dynamic negotiation of authentication and encryption algorithms between access points and mobile devices. The authentication schemes proposed in the draft standard are based on 802.1X and extensible authentication protocol (EAP). The encryption algorithm is *advanced encryption standard* (AES). Using dynamic negotiation, EAP, and AES, RSN is significantly stronger than WEP and WPA. However, RSN will run very poorly on legacy devices. Only the latest devices have the hardware required to accelerate the algorithms in clients and access points, providing the performance expected of today's WLAN products.

THREATS TO TCP

This section describes a number of common attacks that exploit the limitations and inherent vulnerabilities in TCP (Morris, 1985).

SYN Flooding

SYN flooding is a DoS attack that occurs when a server receives several connection requests. The basis of this attack is the resource investment made by the target to support a TCP connection. The attack obliges the target to maintain, for some period of time, the invested resources. Eventually, because of the dwindling target's resources, the target becomes unable to respond to further legitimate requests. The attack exploits the three-way handshake procedure used in connection establishment over a TCP connection.

In SYN flooding, an attacking source initiates a TCP connection request to the server. The server responds to the request using a SYN ACK and waits for the source to respond. However, because the attacker does not wish to establish a TCP connection, it does not reply and so fails to complete the handshake. This leaves a half-open TCP connection. Because TCP can simultaneously support several half-open connections, the source may initiate several such requests and block the server from responding to other valid requests. This results in DoS. The situation lasts until a time-out occurs. When TCP reaches its maximum limit for half-open connection, all other pending requests will be queued in its backlog queue. Once the backlog queue is also full, all further requests to the TCP port will be ignored until the original requests begin to time-out and reset. After each time-out, the server port sends a RST to the unreachable client. At this point the attacker must repeat the process to continue the DoS attack.

The attacking host must ensure that the source IP address is spoofed (a routable but unreachable host), as the target host will be sending its response to this address. If the source address is reachable, then it will receive the SYN/ACKs sent by the server, as this would elicit an RST from that host and defeat the attack.

An analogy to understand SYN flooding: say there is a single telephone connection with 10 parallel lines, that is, the same number has 10 lines. If you use 10 telephones and dial this particular number 10 times, once from each telephone, then all the 10 parallel lines of the target telephone would be busy answering the 10 calls. Any additional calls to this number would not be able to go through. Thus as a result, we can say that the services of the target telephone have been rendered unavailable. SYN flooding is even worse than this scenario, as in the former the connection requests are from spoofed source addresses, thus making it difficult for the target system to trace the source of the attack.

Countermeasures

There is no single countermeasure to protect your system against SYN flood attacks. However, there are certain sets of steps, which can be followed to minimize the risk of damage caused by such attacks:

1. Reduce the duration of time required for a time-out of a connection to take place. This will ensure that if a large number of connection requests is sent to the target system, the spoofed requests would be discarded sooner, thus minimizing the hogging of memory.

2. Increasing the queue of connection requests. This means to increase the number of connection requests that can be accepted by a particular host at one time. However, one disadvantage is that it will result in hogging of more memory and resources of the host.
3. Installing vendor-specific updates and patches or by employing a firewall, which will detect SYN attacks and effectively respond with fake responses and try to trace back the spoofed source address to the actual attacker.

Sequence Number Attack

TCP segments are encapsulated within IP datagrams, and as a result there is no guarantee that the datagrams will follow the same route and therefore arrive in the order they were sent. Also, network errors may require datagrams to be resent. The TCP protocol uses sequence numbers to ensure that the application layer receives data in the same order that it was sent. Although this is a simple and effective method of ensuring a sequenced data stream, it unfortunately introduces vulnerability. If attackers can guess the correct sequence number, they can then generate their own TCP segments that will be accepted by the target host's TCP layer.

Despite the specification of ISN calculation in Rey (1981), the majority of TCP implementations simplify ISN allocation by incrementing using a constant value, a scheme originally introduced in Berkeley UNIX kernels. The Berkeley implementation of TCP increments the ISN clock by 128,000 each second and by a further 64,000 for each new connection. This practice is so widespread that it can be viewed as a standard, but it unfortunately introduces vulnerability into applications using security mechanisms.

An attacking host can forge a connection request to a server such that it appears to come from a host the server trusts. The server will then follow the connection establishment procedure described previously and send a segment back to the apparent client (that is, not the attacker), setting the SYN and ACK header bits. On receipt of this segment, the apparent client finds no record of a connection request and will respond by sending a RST segment, closing the connection request.

However, if the attacker ensures that the apparent client does not respond, then the attacker could forge the connection request, wait a suitable period of time to allow the server to respond with the SYN and ACK segments and then the attacker could forge another segment, this time containing the final ACK required for the three-way handshake. From the server's perspective, it has successfully completed the connection initiation phase and has an active connection with a trusted client.

The only requirement for this attack to be successful is the ISN. If the attacker chooses a quiet time, from the point of view of the server, then it can open a legitimate connection to the server to some public service, discover the ISN used on this connection, and then immediately begin the attack predicting the next ISN issued by the server to be 64,000 higher. Although nontrivial, this attack is usually successful within a few attempts. It is also popularly called the blind spoofing attack.

Countermeasures

- Increase the change rate of the initial sequence number variable. The TCP specification requires that this variable be incremented 250,000 times per second.
- Randomizing the ISN increment. This can be achieved by using a cryptographic algorithm for ISN generation.

TCP Session Hijacking

TCP session hijacking is also called nonblind TCP/IP spoofing. This attack can be viewed as impersonating a connection from another machine but not using prediction to find the sequence numbers. By sniffing packets between the server and the apparent client, the NSN (next sequence number) can become available to the attacker.

An intruder initiates a three-way handshake between a spoofed client and server. A spoofed TCP packet with the SYN flag set is sent to server, which responds to the client with a SYN and an ACK. At this point, the attacker sniffs the traffic off the wire to find what sequence number the server is expecting and then crafts an ACK packet using that information. The server, however, will think that the responses are arriving from the client. It has the same effect as blind IP spoofing (sequence number prediction), but can be used for a number of different purposes. It is used when the attacker is on the same network segment as the victim (spoofed client) host.

Countermeasures

- Prevent IP datagrams with source addresses outside their network from reaching the Internet. Unfortunately, there are many organizations that provide unregulated Internet access.
- A firewall can be used to block all IP datagrams from the Internet that are source routed or that have source addresses originating from the internal network.
- Trust relationships between hosts communicating across the Internet should never be permitted, unless they are used in conjunction with strong authentication and encryption.

TCP FIN and RST Bit Attacks

TCP packets have control flags, which indicate the status of a segment. The RST and FIN flags can be used for DoS attacks. Under normal circumstances the RST flag is used to reset a connection, whereas the FIN flag indicates that no more data will be sent and initiates shutdown of the connection. As with TCP session hijacking, the only requirement for this attack is the TCP sequence number. The attacker must have access to the IP datagrams sent between the server and spoofed hosts to predict the next possible TCP sequence numbers.

For a RST or FIN to be accepted, the TCP segment needs the correct sequence number, as there is no ACK involved. Therefore, the attacker simply analyzes the IP datagrams in the connection between the target and spoofed hosts and calculates the sequence number that the target host would expect the next TCP segment from the spoofed host to contain. The attacker then generates a TCP segment with the RST flag set and sends it in a spoofed IP datagram to the server. On receipt of the RST, the target host will prematurely terminate the connection with the spoofed host. A very similar attack can be launched with the FIN flag, thereby initiating an invalid TCP connection close request. The advantage of a FIN-based attack, from a hacker's point of view, is that TCP mandates that on receiving a segment with the FIN flag set, the host must reply with one of its own. It makes this attack more successful than the RST attack.

Countermeasure

Because TCP sequence number plays a vital role in this attack, the countermeasures described in the previous section are applicable here.

Land Attack

The land attack involves sending spoofed packet(s) with the SYN flag set to the victim's machine on any open port that is listening. If the packet(s) contain the same destination and source IP address as the host, the victim's machine can hang or reboot. In addition, most systems experience a total freeze up, where the mouse and keyboard become unoperational and the only solution is to reboot via a reset button on the system or by turning the machine off (Morris, 1985).

Countermeasure

Using a firewall to prevent spoofed packets can help reduce the effects of this attack.

SECURITY PROTOCOLS

In the previous section, we discussed the possible attacks on TCP and their countermeasures. In general, these attacks can be minimized by preventing unauthorized/malicious users from gaining access to the network. This is achieved using firewalls and proxies. In addition, cryptographic protocols such SSH, SSL, and IPSec can also be used to control access to the network. Cryptographic protocols are security protocols that use encryption to encode data to ensure privacy.

Secure shell (SSH; Lonvick, 2004) is a protocol for secure remote login and other secure network services over an insecure network. The *SSH transport layer protocol* (SSH-TRANS) typically runs on top of TCP/IP. It provides a single, full-duplex, byte-oriented connection between client and server, with privacy, integrity, server authentication, and MITM protection. It may also provide compression.

Secure sockets layer (SSL; Dierks & Rescorla, 2004) is the leading security protocol on the Internet. One advantage of SSL is that it is application-protocol independent. A higher-level protocol can layer on top of the SSL protocol transparently. Developed by Netscape, SSL has been merged with other protocols and authentication methods by the IETF into a new protocol known as *transport layer security* (TLS). TLS has goals and features similar to those of the SSH transport and user authentication protocols. It provides a single, full-duplex byte stream to clients, with cryptographically assured privacy and integrity and optional authentication. However, it differs from SSH in the following principal ways:

- TLS server authentication is optional: the protocol supports fully anonymous operation, in which neither side is authenticated. Such connections are inherently vulnerable to MITM attacks. In SSH-TRANS, server authentication is mandatory, which protects against such attacks.
- Both client and server authentication are done with X.509 public key certificates. This makes TLS a bit more cumbersome to use than SSH in practice, because it requires a functioning *public key infrastructure* (PKI) to be in place, and certificates are more complicated things to generate and manage than SSH keys. However, a PKI system provides scalable key management for your trouble, which SSH currently lacks.
- TLS does not provide the range of client authentication options that SSH does; public key is the only option.
- TLS does not have the extra features provided by the SSH component: the *SSH connection protocol* (SSH-CONN). SSH-CONN uses the underlying SSH-TRANS connection to provide multiple logical data channels to the application, as well as support for remote program execution, terminal management, tunneled TCP connections, flow control, and so forth.

SSH and SSL can protect TCP from session hijacking and injected data. However they cannot protect TCP from DoS attacks caused by spoofed packets.

IP security protocol (IPSec; Kent, 2004a; 2004b) is the security protocol developed by IETF as a part of Ipv6. It was designed to address security problems in Ipv4 such as session hijacking, spoofing, and snooping. As an encryption protocol, IPSec provides for secure encrypted data transmission at the network layer across the Internet. IPSec consists of two subprotocols:

- *Encapsulated security payload (ESP)* protects the IP packet data from third-party interference by encrypting the contents using symmetric cryptography algorithms (such as Blowfish, 3DES).
- *Authentication header (AH)* protects the IP packet header from third-party interference and spoofing by computing a cryptographic checksum and hashing the IP packet header fields with a secure hashing function. This is then followed by an additional header that contains the hash to allow the information in the packet to be authenticated.

ESP and AH can either be used together or separately, depending on the environment.

The IPSec headers (AH and ESP) can be used in transport mode or tunnel mode. In transport mode, IPSec can be used to directly encrypt the traffic between two hosts. In tunnel mode, IPSec can be used to build *virtual tunnels* between two subnets, which could be used for secure communication between two corporate networks. The latter is more commonly known as a *virtual private network (VPN)*.

Because IPSec supports several modes of operation, both sides must first decide on the security policy and mode to use, with which encryption algorithms they wish to communicate, and what type of authentication method to use. Once an IPSec tunnel is created, all protocols—such as TCP, UDP, and HTTP—are encrypted between the two communicating parties regardless of whether they have built in security and encryption. IPSec can protect TCP from session hijacking, spoofing, and DoS attacks. Other chapters discuss IPSec, SSH, and SSL in detail.

CONCLUSION

TCP is a connection-oriented, reliable, byte-stream, transport-layer protocol. It is the most commonly used transport-layer protocol in the Internet. The recent demand for wireless communication indicates that wireless communication links will be an integral part of the future internetworks. Hence, it is essential to study how TCP can be extended for use over wireless links. In this chapter, we provide an overview of the challenges and the proposed schemes to extend TCP over wireless links. Communication in a network is prone to security threats; hence, the requirements of a secure network and common threats in a network are discussed. Some security threats exploit the vulnerabilities in a protocol to attack a network. A summary of security threats that exploit the vulnerabilities in TCP and the services provided by TCP is provided. Although security threats are much greater in a wireless network than in a wired network, some general precautions are suggested that can minimize the risk of those threats.

GLOSSARY

Access Point In a WLAN, the access point receives, buffers, and transmits data between the WLAN and the wired network infrastructure.

Active Open The host that initiates a TCP connection request performs an active open.

Blackout A period during which the mobile host is not connected to a base station.

Congestion Window The sender's perception of network congestion.

Connection Oriented Connection oriented implies that the path between two communicating parties is fixed for the duration of their communication, and this necessitates a set-up phase (connection) and a tear-down (disconnect) phase.

Fast Recovery Congestion control algorithm: a sender invokes the fast recovery after fast retransmit. This algorithm allows the sender to transmit at half its previous rate (regulating the growth of its window based on congestion avoidance), rather than having to begin a slow start.

Fast Retransmit Congestion control algorithm: when a TCP sender receives several duplicate ACKs, fast retransmit allows it to infer that a segment was lost. The sender retransmits what it considers to be this lost segment without waiting for the full time-out.

Forward Error Correction (FEC) By adding redundant FEC information to each frame, damaged frames can be recovered without retransmissions.

Handoff Latency The time for mobile IP to react to a mobile host moving from one cell to another.

Hard-State Transport-Layer Approach An approach for extending TCP to wireless links that encompasses all forms of splitting such that the end-to-end semantics may be sacrificed.

Land Attack An attack involving the sending of spoofed packet(s) with the SYN flag set to the victim's machine on any open port that is listening.

Man-in-the-Middle (MITM) Attack An attack where the attacker is able to read (and modify) messages between two parties without either party knowing that their communication has been compromised.

Mobile IP An extension to the Internet protocol proposed by the Internet Engineering Task Force (IETF) to support user mobility.

Passive Open The host that responds to a TCP connection request performs a passive open.

Pure Link-Level Approach An approach for extending TCP to wireless links that hides the unwanted characteristics of the wireless links from the higher layers.

Retransmission Ambiguity Denotes the TCP sender's inability to distinguish between an ACK for the original transmission from that of an ACK for its retransmission.

Sequence Number In TCP the sequence number denotes the number assigned to the first byte of data in the current TCP segment.

Sequence Number Attack An attack in which the attacker guesses the correct sequence number and can then generate his or her own TCP segments that will be accepted by the target host's TCP layer. It is also called blind IP spoofing.

Slow Start Congestion control algorithm used to gradually increase the size of the TCP congestion window. It operates by observing that the rate at which new packets should be injected into the network is the rate at which the acknowledgments are returned by the other end.

Soft-State Cross-Layer Signaling Approach An approach for extending TCP to wireless links in which the transport layer sender is aware of the wireless link.

Soft-State Transport-Layer Caching Approach An approach for extending TCP to wireless links that maintains a soft state of the network that is aware of the transport layer and uses caching to prevent the sender from unnecessary invocation of the congestion control mechanism in response to packet loss.

Spurious Fast Retransmits The fast retransmissions that occur as a result of the reordering of packets beyond the dupack threshold.

Spurious Time-Outs The time-outs that would not have occurred if the sender had waited "long enough."

SYN Flooding A denial of service attack that occurs when a server receives several incomplete connection requests.

TCP FIN and RST Bit Attacks The RST and FIN flag are used to perform a DoS attack.

TCP Session Hijacking This has the same effect as blind IP spoofing (sequence number prediction), but can be used for a number of different purposes. It is also called nonblind TCP/IP spoofing.

Window Size This specifies the size of the sender's receive window, that is, the buffer space available in bytes for incoming data.

CROSS REFERENCES

See *Ad hoc Network Security; Cellular Networks; TCP/IP Suite; Wireless Local Area Networks*.

REFERENCES

Alanko, T., Kojo, M., Laamanen, H., Liljeberg, M., Moilanen, M., & Raatikainen, K. (1994). Measured performance of data transmission over cellular telephone networks. *Computer Communications Review, 24*(5), 24–44.

Allman, M., Balakrishnan, H., & Floyd, S. (2001, January). *Enhancing TCP's loss recovery using limited transmit* (RFC 3042). Retrieved May 2004, from http://www.faqs.org/rfcs/rfc3042.html

Ayanoglu, E., Paul, S., LaPorta, T. F., Sabnani, K. K., & Gitlin, R. D. (1995). AIRMAIL: A link-layer protocol for wireless networks. *Wireless Networks, 1*(1), 47–60.

Bakre, A., & Badrinath, B. (1995, May). I-TCP: Indirect TCP for mobile hosts. In *Proceedings of 15th International Conference on Distributed Computing Systems* (ICDCS, pp. 136–143). Vancouver, British Columbia, Canada: IEEE Computer Society Press.

Bakshi, B. S., Vaidya, N., & Pradhan, D. K. (1997). Improving the performance of TCP over wireless networks. In *Proceedings of 17th international conference on DCS* (pp. 365–373). Washington, DC: IEEE Computer Society Press.

Balakrishnan, H., Padmanabhan, V. N., Seshan, S., & Katz, R. H. (1996). A comparison of mechanisms for improving TCP performance over wireless links. In *Proceedings of ACM SIGCOMM '96* (pp. 256–269). Stanford, CA: Addison-Wesley and ACM Press.

Balakrishnan, H., Seshan, S., Katz, R. H. (1995). Improving reliable transport and handoff performance in cellular wireless networks. *Wireless Networks Journal, 1*(4), 469–481.

Bhagwat, P., Bhattacharya, P., Krishna, A., & Tripathi, S. K. (1997). Using channel state dependent packet scheduling to improve TCP throughput over wireless LANs. *Wireless Networks, 3*(1), 91–102.

Bhandarkar, S., & Reddy, A. L. N. (2004, August). *Improving the robustness of TCP to non-congestion events* (Internet Draft). Internet Engineering Task Force. Retrieved June 2004, from http://www1.ietf.org/proceedings_new/04nov/IDs/draft-ietf-tcpm-tcp-dcr-01.txt

Biaz, S., Mehta, M., West, S., & Vaidya, N. H. (1997, January 30). *TCP over wireless networks using multiple acknowledgements* (Tech. Rep. 97-001). College Station, TX: Texas A&M University.

Brown, K., & Singh, S. (1997). M-TCP: TCP for mobile cellular networks. *ACM Computer Communication Review, 27*(5), 19–43.

Cellular Networking Perspectives. (2004). *TDMA*. Retrieved January 2005, from http://www.cnp-wireless.com/tdma.html

Cohen, A., & O'Hara, B. (2003). *802.11i shores up wireless security*. Network World Fusion. Retrieved January 2005, from http://www.nwfusion.com/news/tech/2003/0526techupdate.html

Dierks, T., & Rescorla, E. (2004, June). *The TLS protocol version 1.1* (Internet Draft). Retrieved November 2004, from http://www.ietf.org/proceedings/04aug/I-D/draft-ietf-netconf-beep-01.txt

Dobrota, V. (2003). *Digital networks in telecommunications, Vol. 3. OSI and TCP/IP* (2nd ed.). Cluj-Napoca, Romania: Mediamira Science.

Fall, K., & Floyd, S. (1996). Simulation based comparisons of Tahoe, Reno and SACK TCP. *Computer Communications Review, 26*(3), 5–21.

Floyd, S., & Jacobson, V. (1993). Random early detection gateways for congestion avoidance. *IEEE/ACM Transactions on Networking, 1*(4), 397–413.

Goff, T., Moronski, J., Phatak, D. S., & Gupta, V. (2000). Freeze-TCP: A true end-to-end TCP enhancement mechanism for mobile environments. In *Proceedings of IEEE Conference on Computer Communications* (IEEE INFOCOM, pp. 1537–1545). Tel Aviv, Israel: IEEE Computer Society Press.

Hassan, M., & Jain, R. (2004). *High performance TCP/IP networking, concepts, issues and solutions* (pp. 153–205). Upper Saddle River, NJ: Prentice Hall.

Hendry, M. (n.d.). *CDMA*. Retrieved May 2004, from http://www.bee.net/mhendry/vrml/library/cdma/cdma.htm

IEEE. (2005). *Wireless local area network—IEEE 802.11 standard*. Retrieved January 2005, from http://www.ieee802.org

IEEE Computer Society. (2004). *Mobile Internet protocol web resources*. Retrieved May 2004, from http://www.computer.org/internet/v2n1/mobile.htm

IEEE Standards Board. (1997). *802 Part 11: Wireless LAN medium access control (MAC) and physical layer (PHY) specifications*. Retrieved from http://grouper.ieee.org/groups/802/11/main.html

Jacobson, V. (1990, February). *Compressing TCP/IP headers for low-speed serial links* (RFC 1144). Retrieved June 2004, from http://www.rfc-archive.org/getrfc.php?rfc=1144

Karn, P. (1993). The Qualcomm CDMA digital cellular system. In *Proceedings of the USENIX Mobile and Location-Independent Computing Symposium* (pp. 35–39). Cambridge, MA: USENIX Association.

Karn, P., & Partridge, C. (1987). Improving round-trip time estimates in reliable transport protocols. In *Proceedings of ACM SIGCOMM* (pp. 2–7). New York: ACM Press.

Kent, S. (2004a, September). *IP encapsulating security payload* (Internet Draft). Retrieved June 2004, from http://www.ietf.org/proceedings/04aug/I-D/draft-ietf-ipsec-esp-v3-08.txt

Kent, S. (2004b, December). *IP authentication header* (Internet Draft). Retrieved June 2004, from http://www.ietf.org/internet-drafts/draft-ietf-msec-ipsec-signatures-04.txt

Lin, S., & Costello, D. J., Jr. (1983). *Error control coding: Fundamentals and applications*. Englewood Cliffs, NJ: Prentice Hall.

Lonvick, C. (2004, December). *SSH transport layer protocol* (Internet Draft). Retrieved January 2005, from http://www.snailbook.com/docs/transport.txt

Ludwig, L., & Gurtov, A. (2004, September). *The Eifel response algorithm for TCP* (Internet Draft). Retrieved January 2005, from http://www1.ietf.org/proceedings_new/04nov/IDs/draft-ietf-tsvwg-tcp-eifel-response-06.txt

Ludwig, R. (1999, May). A *case for flow-adaptive wireless links* (Tech. Rep. UCB CSD-99-1053). Berkeley: University of California at Berkeley.

Ludwig, R., Konrad, A., & Joseph, A. D. (1999). Optimizing the end-to-end performance of reliable flows over wireless links. In *Proceedings of the ACM/IEEE MOBICOM '99* (pp. 113–119). Hingham, MA: Kluwer Academic.

Ludwig, R., & Meyer, M. (2003, April). *The Eifel detection algorithm for TCP* (RFC 3522). Retrieved January 2005, from http://rfc3522.x42.com/

Ludwig, R., & Rathonyi, B. (1999). Link layer enhancements for TCP/IP over GSM. In *Proceedings of the IEEE INFOCOM '99* (pp. 415–422). New York, NY: IEEE.

Ludwig, R., Rathonyi, B., Konrad, A., Oden, K., & Joseph, A. D. (1999). Multi-layer tracing of TCP over a reliable wireless link. In *Proceedings of the ACM SIGMETRICS '99* (pp. 144–154). New York: ACM Press.

Mascolo, S., Casetti, C., Gerla, M., Lee, S. S., & Sanadini, M. (2000). *TCP Westwood: Congestion control with faster recovery* (UCLA CS Tech. Rep. 200017). Los Angeles: University of California at Los Angeles.

Mathis, M., Mahdavi, J., Floyd, S., & Romanow, A. (1996, April). *TCP selective acknowledgement options* (RFC 2018). Retrieved May 2004, from http://www.faqs.org/rfcs/rfc2018.html

Morris, R. T. (1985, February). *A weakness in the 4.2BSD UNIX TCP/IP software* (Computing Science Tech. Rep. 117). Murray Hill, NJ: AT&T Bell Laboratories.

Nanda, S., Ejzak, R., & Doshi, B. T. (1994). A retransmission scheme for circuit-mode data on wireless links. *IEEE Journal on Selected Areas in Communications, 12*(8), 1338–1352.

Network Sorcery. (n.d.). *Transmission control protocol.* Retrieved May 2004, from http://www.networksorcery.com/enp/protocol/tcp.htm

Nguyen, G. T., Katz, R. H., Noble, B., & Satyanarayanan, M. (1996). A trace-based approach for modeling wireless channel behavior. In *Proceedings of the winter simulation conference* (pp. 597–604). New York: ACM Press.

Padhye, J., & Floyd, S. (2001). On inferring TCP behavior. In *Proceedings of the 2001 conference on applications, technologies, architectures, and protocols for computer communications* (pp. 287–298). New York: ACM Press.

Parsa, C., & Garcia-Luna-Aceves, J. J. (1999). Improving TCP congestion control over Internets with heterogeneous transmission media. In *Proceedings of the 7th IEEE International Conference on Network Protocols (ICNP)* (pp. 213–221). Riverside, CA: IEEE Computer Society Press.

Pentikousis, K. (2000). TCP in wired-cum-wireless environments. In *IEEE Communications Surveys & Tutorials, 3*(16), 2–14.

Perkins, C. (1996, October). *IP mobility support* (RFC 2002). Retrieved May 2004, from http://www.faqs.org/rfcs/rfc2002.html

Ramani, R., & Karandikar, A. (2000, December). Explicit congestion notification in TCP over wireless networks. In *Proceedings of IEEE International Conference on Personal Wireless Communications* (ICPWC, pp. 495–499). Hyderabad, India: IEEE Computer Society Press.

Rey, M. D. (1981, September). *Transmission control protocol* (RFC 793). Retrieved May 2004, from http://www.elook.org/computing/rfc/rfc793.html

Sinha, P., Monks, J., & Bhargavan, V. (2000). Limitations of TCP-ELFN for ad hoc networks. In *Proceedings of IEEE International Workshop on Mobile Multimedia Communications*. Tokyo, Japan: IEEE Computer Society Press.

Sinha, P., Venkitaraman, N., Sivakumar, R., & Bharghavan, V. (1999, August). W-TCP: A reliable transport protocol for wireless wide-area networks. In *Proceedings of ACM international conference in mobile computing and Networking* (MobiCom, pp. 301–316). Hingham, MA: Kluwer Academic.

Stevens, W. (1997, January). *TCP slow start, congestion avoidance, fast retransmit, and fast recovery algorithms* (RFC 2001). Retrieved June 2004, from http://www.faqs.org/rfcs/rfc2001.html

Air Interface Requirements for Mobile Data Services

Harald Haas, *International University Bremen*

INTRODUCTION

Current interest in wireless and cellular communications is aimed at high-speed data transmission. The fundamental system enhancements being developed will lead to many new mobile data services. Many different standards and systems have already appeared for cellular networks, wireless metropolitan area networks (MANs), wireless local area networks (WLANs), and personal area networks (PANs). Typical representatives, in the same order, are UMTS (universal mobile telecommunication system; http://www.umtsforum.org); WiMAX (http://www.wimaxforum.org, worldwide Interoperability for Microwave Access) standard, based on IEEE 802.16; and Wi-Fi (wireless fidelity) standard, based on IEEE 802.11 and Bluetooth. Although MANs, WLANs, PANs, and so forth are gaining significant momentum, cellular systems still offer the highest degree of mobility. Although cellular systems are the main carriers for mobile data services, mobile data services impose heavy demands on cellular systems, in particular with respect to security. For instance, if international roaming, such as in global standard for mobile communication (GSM), is to be implemented, the same security standard must be adopted by different operators in different countries. Because of the difficulty in such challenges, in the following we concentrate on cellular systems.

Some important facts and implications can be seen when looking at the history of cellular networks. To develop that thought, we analyze different generations of cellular systems using typical representatives from a European perspective. The list of systems mentioned in this review is incomplete, because our intention is to show the driving forces for cellular systems and the implications for future systems, with particular focus on mobile data services. The developments in cellular communications can be categorized into four major generations as illustrated in Figure 1.

The first significant shift was the transition from an analog system (first generation, 1G) to a digital system (second generation, 2G) both of which primarily supported a single service: voice. The second generation cellular systems also supported data services to a limited extent—the maximum data rate being approximately 10 kbps. The enhanced data rates for global evolution (EDGE) standard is considered a 2.5-generation system because it allows data rates up to 384 kbps. However, the spectrum efficiency and flexibility of second-generation systems are only moderate, and the deployment costs for the operators are high [e.g., one radio frequency (RF) unit in GSM can only handle eight voice users, whereas an RF unit in UMTS is able to serve about 70 voice users]. Data rates, spectrum efficiency, flexibility, and deployment costs were the main drivers for entering into the specification of third generation cellular systems. It was obvious that the new paradigm, wireless multimedia traffic, would have a significant effect on the air interface technology. Three factors are essential in this context: (a) high data transmission, (b) data rate scalability, and (c) adaptability to channel asymmetry with respect to UL and DL traffic. High data-rate transmission is necessary for services such as video transmission. Data rate scalability is required for the numerous supported multimedia services, each of which can demand a different transmission rate (Welzl, Franzens, & Mülhäuser, 2003), and adaptability to traffic asymmetry is required because, unlike voice, many data services impose different loads on the UL and DL channel. (For example, file downloads from the Internet require high capacity in DL direction and hardly any capacity in UL direction; Mohr, 1999; *Book of Visions,* 2001.) The air interface must be tailored to maximize efficient use of the radio spectrum.

With the advent of third-generation cellular systems it was possible for the first time to substantially increase the transmission rate on the air interface. The original goal was that third-generation (3G) cellular systems should achieve a maximum data rate per user of 2 Mbps. Data-rate scalability in 3G cellular systems is accomplished by use of CDMA (code division multiple access) technology. CDMA avoids splitting the radio resource into frequency sub-bands and time slots. All users transmit continuously using the entire channel bandwidth. The user data-rate is adjusted by a user-specific spreading code. The length of

1st Generation	2nd Generation	2.5 Generation	3rd Generation	4th Generation
NMT	GSM	EDGE	UMTS	?
analog, voice	digital, voice	digital, voice + packet data	digital, voice + high speed packet data	digital, voice + high speed packet data + ultra high data rates?

Figure 1: Generations and paradigm shifts in cellular communications.

the spreading code is inversely proportional to the data-rate. As a consequence, the flexibility of assigning variable data-rates is significantly improved when using CDMA. In UMTS, transmission rate enhancements and adaptability to channel asymmetry is supported by technology upgrades such as HSDPA (high speed downlink packet access). Currently fourth generation (4G) wireless system concepts are being discussed that should enable data rates up to 1 Gbps while at the same time maintaining data-rate scalability and support of channel asymmetry. This will primarily be achieved by multicarrier transmission techniques, network hierarchies and hybrid *ad hoc* and cellular networks.

In the past a new generation of cellular systems was launched about every 10 years. It is interesting to note that the development of the target data rate of each generation over the past 20 years is approximately equivalent to doubling the data rate every 18 months. This complies with Moore's law from microelectronics, which is not surprising because with increased signal processing capabilities, techniques that help to increase spectrum efficiency can be supported, such as antenna-array signal processing. Furthermore, the higher the spectrum efficiency, the higher the possible data rate for a fixed bandwidth.

In the near future, numerous mobile data-based services will be supported that will revolutionize the ways in which businesses, individuals, and machines operate. Wireless Internet, teleworking, wireless and interactive television, car-to-car communication, telemedicine and telediagnostics, mobile offices, and wireless home networking are only a few examples. So far, wireless services have been limited primarily to humans. Now the objective is to allow communication with and between everything and anything (ubiquitous services). If everything that moves becomes an object for mobile communication, the number of mobile terminals will increase dramatically and lead to much greater traffic.

In Japan, the leading country for mobile data services, the mobile Web browsing service is already widely used. The number of subscribers for this type of data service was 48.5 million (72% of mobile subscribers) at the end of 2001 and is still growing. Market analyses (Mohr, 1999) have predicted that in Europe more than 90 million mobile subscribers will use mobile multimedia services in the year 2010 generating about 60% of the traffic in terms of transmitted bits. This can be attributed to the effect that the majority of electronic and communications devices and digital communication systems [e.g., cellular, broadcast, fixed wireless access, wireless LANs, Bluetooth, xDSL (digital subscriber line), satellite, etc.] are either already digital or in the process of being transformed into digital systems.

In the private sector, personalization of information, such as leisure and entertainment preferences, stock portfolio management, and multimedia messaging services, are key drivers for mobile data services. In the business sector, WLAN infrastructures, in combination with wireless MAN infrastructures such as WiMAX, offer a cost-efficient alternative to wired networks. Because of such uses, current and future mobile data services might carry very sensitive information. An important quality criterion in mobile communication is global availability. This, in fact, was a key prerequisite that guaranteed GSM (http://www.gsmworld.com) its global success. Service availability "everywhere" and for "everyone," however, leads to great challenges for security, because general availability is clearly in contradiction with security. Personalized information and sensitive company data should not be accessible by "anyone" just because the information is available "everywhere." As a consequence, the more mobile data services become an integral part of our everyday life, the more important security issues will become. Therefore, in enhanced 2G systems, and in 3G systems, an entirely different approach was taken to overcome the security weaknesses of past generations.

A new set of cryptographic functions, globally designated as *Milenage*, were defined. The functions are transparent, as opposed to being secret such as the A3 and A5 algorithms in GSM (Gindraux, 2002; 3rd Generation Partnership, 2003b). The evolution from voice to data-based services results in another important issue involving global roaming. The huge variety of services and the possibility for operators to differentiate based on services makes it impossible to test all roaming partners' networks and to establish a common security standard (Roos, Hartmann, & Dutnall, 2003). Advanced and flexible security mechanisms will be necessary to reduce risk and enable private communication, commercial transactions, and m-business. Fortunately, many security mechanisms can be adopted from current wired Internet technology, because the underlying protocol, transmission control protocol/Internet protocol (TCP/IP), will be the same for both fixed and mobile data services. Therefore, in this chapter we concentrate on a different aspect. Mobile data services all rely on electromagnetic waves to carry information, and this is the key property that distinguishes them from existing Internet-based fixed line services. We therefore discuss particular air interface technologies and specific algorithms that lead to efficient spectral usage by mobile data services. Specifically, we stress the physical layer, the data link layer, and radio resource management. (We do not consider the ISO OSI model, because it is generally realized that this model is not entirely suitable for wireless communications; Lin, Zhou, & Giannakis, 2004.) For the higher-layer protocols and algorithms, the interested reader is referred to other chapters in this *Handbook*. Security-enabling functions, in the sense of mechanisms against fraud and misuse, such as ciphering and authentication, primarily reside in those higher-layer functions. Therefore, our main purpose in this chapter is to provide necessary background information on the underlying air interface technologies that serve as key enablers for mobile data services and to highlight how those technologies can support security protocols.

Reliable high data-rate transmission requires techniques that enhance the bandwidth efficiency of a cellular system because bandwidth is scarce and expensive. As a consequence, particular attention has to be paid to the physical limitations of the wireless channel. Therefore, we discuss spectral efficiency and interference problems.

In the past, including the third generation, air interfaces were predominantly designed based on link-level, that is, physical channel, requirements. The requirements of the actual mobile services were clearly neglected—primarily because it was unclear which mobile data services would be used ("killer applications"). However, the initial problems that systems such UMTS were facing showed that it is essential to include the mobile service requirements when designing an air interface. Therefore, in this chapter the air interface requirements are predominately derived from service properties. These requirements are discussed in the third section. Because of QoS and security requirements, the assignment of resources is an important issue, which is covered in the fourth section.

SPECTRAL EFFICIENCY AND INTERFERENCE

In some countries, such as the United Kingdom and Germany, the spectrum for the third-generation cellular system was auctioned. In Germany, for example, the operators paid approximately US $ 50 billion for 2×60 MHz + 20 MHz of frequency spectrum. About the same amount of money is assumed to be required to build the network infrastructure.

Current wireless-access technology for cellular operation allows the transmission of about 0.5 bits per Hz bandwidth, per cell. With new technological enhancements such as multiple-input multiple-output (MIMO) transmission, it is possible to improve this factor by an order of magnitude, which directly translates into an order of magnitude increase in revenue per bit, given constant service costs for the subscriber. In addition, because usually more than one user requests a particular service at any given time, a mobile communication system has to support several simultaneous high-data-rate transmissions. As a consequence, the bandwidth required would soon exceed physical limits. With 100 Mbps per user, 10 simultaneously active users per cell, and 0.5 bits/Hz/cell , the bandwidth required is 2 GHz per operator. Assuming, on average, four operators, this amounts to 8 GHz of radio frequency spectrum [neglecting guard bands and duplex distance in the case of the FDD (frequency division duplexing) technique], compared with 140 MHz in 3G systems.

In summary, the bit-per-Hertz cost factor and the requirement to transmit with very high data rates are the two main driving forces for increasing bandwidth efficiency. The efficiency of bandwidth usage in a cellular system is known as its spectral efficiency and is defined as

$$\kappa = \frac{\text{total traffic}}{\text{total bandwidth} \cdot \text{total area}}. \quad (1)$$

It can be seen that the spectral efficiency of a particular system is not determined by the traffic carried within a particular isolated cell, but rather by the traffic carried within some given area covered by several cells. In that way, cochannel interference (CCI) can be accounted for. The modified normalized Shannon channel capacity is introduced in the following to point toward potential techniques that might be used to increase spectral efficiency:

$$C \propto \min(R, T)\log_2\left(1 + \frac{SINR}{T}\right) \quad [\text{bits/(s}\cdot\text{Hz)}]. \quad (2)$$

Here R and T are respectively the number of antennas at the receiver and at the transmitter, and $SINR$ is the signal-to-interference-plus-noise ratio. This effectively takes account of both CCI and adjacent channel interference (ACI), and it assumes that interference is Gaussian. Equation (2) holds under the conditions of non-line-of-sight rich scattering channels. Moreover, it assumes ideal modulation and perfect channel coding. Therefore, Eq. (2) can be considered as an upper bound of spectral efficiency. Because in Eq. (2) multiple antennas at the receiver and at the transmitter are considered, we have a MIMO system. The $SINR$ is assumed to be the same at each receiving antenna. First, it can be observed that in a MIMO system the supportable traffic per cell increases linearly with the minimum number of antennas at either the transmitter or the receiver. This is intuitively clear because with multiple antennas, simultaneous transmissions can be realized. If cross-interference is then cancelled, R or T times, the number of bits can be transmitted per unit time. (This is analogous to having R or T pairs of wires in a cable.) Second, the supportable traffic per cell increases logarithmically with increasing $SINR$. The $SINR$ can be improved either by augmenting the transmitted power, provided that the interference doesn't rise proportionally, or by reducing the noise and interference power in the system. To sum up, Eq. (2) shows that there are three basic means that can be used to improve the spectral efficiency of a wireless system:

- using multiple antennas at the transmitter and/or at the receiver,
- increasing the received signal power level, and
- eliminating interference and noise.

Each of these is linked to specific technical concepts that are being intensively studied. For example, in combination with appropriate interference cancellation techniques, MIMO will increase the number of transmitted bits per unit time because of parallel data transmissions. Further, ad hoc communication will on average result in increased received power because of short hops, multiuser detection will reduce multiuser interference, and dynamic channel assignment will help to avoid CCI and thereby allow frequency reuse factors of about one in a cellular system.

SYSTEM REQUIREMENTS

Data services impose entirely different requirements on the air interface than voice. These requirements affect the physical layer as well as the data link layer and the entire radio resource management. (The latter two are referred to as the system level.) For instance, the particular modulation scheme (physical layer) affects the effective bit rate, and the packet scheduling (radio resource management) will have an impact on the delay. In turn, delay and throughput will jointly determine the QoS. Modulation and data scheduling are usually independent of each other because they are located at different levels of the protocols stack. This has proven to be a drawback, and therefore the key to solving these issues lies in joint layer considerations. Joint layer optimization requires new approaches and system solutions. Those high-level system functions that are affected most by joint layer considerations are discussed in this section.

Multiuser Access

The first three generations of mobile radio were based on a model of multiple access in which the radio resource was divided into discrete channels. These have variously made use of FDMA (frequency division multiple access), TDMA (time division multiple access), and CDMA. These are all well matched to systems supporting real-time, delay-constrained services such as voice. This was logical for services in which all users had the same bandwidth requirements and in which this represented a small fraction of the total bandwidth. Moreover, such were the delay constraints that a rigid structuring of the multiple access scheme was necessary.

Arguably, the existing (or soon-to-be-existing) generations already support these services, so that any new air interface for high-speed mobile data services will usefully be optimized for non-real-time, or packet, services. However, the requirements for these air interfaces will be such as to still allow limited delay performance as might be required, for example, for video. This poses great challenges on the air interface design. Moreover, in conventional cellular systems the available spectrum is subdivided into several partitions. Different operators obtain some fraction of the spectrum (either by a beauty contest in which a government controls the licensing of spectrum or by spectrum auction). With this spectrum partitioning, it is unavoidable that some adjacent carriers belong to different operators. Because in principal two operators do not coordinate their cellular network planning, adjacent channel interference is a severe issue unless large guard bands are introduced between adjacent carriers. Needless to say, these guard bands cause a loss in spectrum efficiency. As a consequence, bandwidth per channel has to increase in current and future high-speed mobile data services. Because of the particular filters required, the guard bands between adjacent carriers increase proportionally to the channel bandwidth. This clearly results in unwanted loss of spectrum efficiency—in particular, if one operator requires several channels because of the use of frequency reuse distances greater than one.

By the same reasoning, the duplex distance increases when using the FDD method. This means that the separation between UL and DL transmission is in the GHz range for a data rate up to 1 Gbps. It is obvious that finding paired frequency spectrums for such systems is very difficult, if not impossible. Therefore, it seems more advantageous, or even necessary, to avoid spectrum partitioning and to allow all operators to share common, very large, single-frequency resources. Intelligent DCA algorithms, scheduling algorithms, and medium access control (MAC) protocols, that is, intelligent radio resource management algorithms, are necessary to allow for fair management of the limited frequency resource.

In the case that only a short message has to be sent, for example an ARQ (automatic repeat request) in the UL, the message might either be spread across the entire bandwidth, thereby enabling a number of parallel transmissions (single-carrier transmission), or the transmitter might use a subset of subcarriers in the case of multicarrier transmission, such as OFDM (orthogonal frequency division multiplexing). With either approach it is possible to retain high bit granularity, which allows for high spectral efficiency.

In such a packet system the optimum approach for delay-constrained services would be to transmit the packets to the users in a single queue, with each user occupying the whole bandwidth for a short period. The more conventional approach of dividing the available bandwidth into parts and using these for packet data dilutes the statistical multiplexing advantage. Furthermore, the conventional approach causes multiuser access interference (MAI), which reduces spectral efficiency. Another reason why multiple access was needed in earlier systems was to make the bandwidth of the transmitted signal significantly exceed that of the source data. This was desirable to obtain multipath diversity in the radio channel. In future systems the source bandwidth will be large enough for many radio environments to provide the multipath diversity inherently. A suitable form of modulation could be OFDM, for example.

For these reasons, a wireless communication system for mobile data services should be based on pure queued packet transmission. In this case, random medium access is provided by using the CSMA (carrier sensing multiple access) protocol with random back-off strategies. New spectrum efficient medium access strategies exploiting the channel reciprocity provided by a TDD-based air interface are discussed in a later section. In the queued transmission scheme the BSs (base Stations), or MSs (mobile Stations) respectively, transmit the packetized data in succession on a single common channel. The packets will be output from a prioritized queue generated from the available traffic. A packet scheduler will be deployed to ensure that all QoS constraints are met.

Duplexing

With an ever-increasing demand for packet data services such as Web browsing and media streaming, data traffic on the air interface will soon exceed the amount of voice traffic. Although voice traffic puts symmetric loads on the UL and DL, this clearly does not hold true for packet data traffic. In the latter case, the traffic load in the two directions might differ significantly. For example, short ARQ messages might be sent in the UL direction, with large packets sent in a file download session. In general, data services require significant channel asymmetry with respect to UL and DL traffic—at least on an instantaneous basis. For IMT (International Mobile Telecommunications) 2000 systems the ITU (International Telecommunication Union) has predicted that, in 2010, on average the spectrum demand for the DL will be 300 MHz and for the UL 140 MHz. Estimates of the UMTS Forum differ even more, with 380 MHz for the DL and 160 MHz for the UL (*Book of Visions*, 2001). A further important observation in that study is that, with the availability of increased data rates for multimedia services, the asymmetry is continuing to grow. These numbers are average figures and do not provide a picture of the instantaneous traffic asymmetry. It is clear that for services such as video upload, the traffic imbalance is in favor of the UL; that is, significantly more resources are required in the UL direction.

In view of this, methods such as HSDPA used in UMTS only partially solve the problem of increasing traffic asymmetry because this method, for example, does not support fast file uploads. From this example it can easily be seen that the duplexing technique for mobile data services plays an important role. Therefore, in this section the different duplexing techniques are discussed and their relevance for data services are pointed out. In this context and based on the previous discussion, it should be emphasized that the duplexing technique is of much greater importance in such a system than any particular multiple access method.

1) Frequency Division Duplexing (FDD): The FDD technique is primarily used in first, second and third generation cellular systems. This can be attributed to the fact that voice was the predominate service in those systems. Voice has the following basic properties. First, it is a symmetric service. Second, it is a real-time service that does not tolerate large delays. Both properties make the FDD technique an ideal choice. The reasons are that the transmission on both links is continuous and that the bandwidths required for the UL and DL channels of a full-duplex link are identical. This property of FDD, however, results in a significient limitation for asymmetric services because in this case the duplex distanse for each channel would have to be different.

Figure 2 highlights this effect. If the bandwidth of channel $f_1^{(dl)}$ is different from the bandwidth of $f_2^{(dl)}$, the duplex distance for the channel, $f_1 = f_1^{(dl)} + f_1^{(ul)}$, would be different from the duplex distance of channel, $f_2 = f_2^{(dl)} + f_2^{(ul)}$.

Moreover, the dynamic adaptation of UL and DL bandwidth would require adjustable filters for the UL and DL channels. Both these requirements would result in very complex transmitters and receivers.

In addition, the fact that two separate frequency carriers are used for UL and DL traffic results in different channel characteristics for both links. As a consequence, the BS and MS need to estimate the channel properties. This creates overhead, which reduces the spectral efficiency and causes battery drain in the MS.

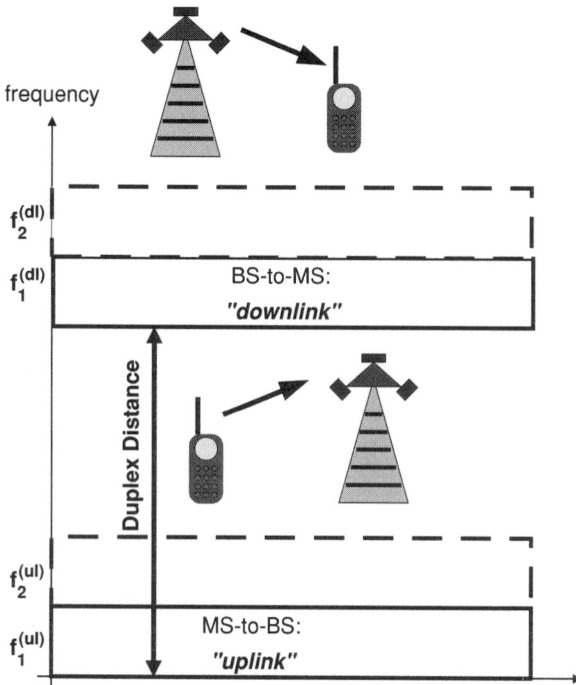

Figure 2: The FDD principle—different frequencies are used for uplink and downlink traffic. A fixed duplex distance between uplink channel and downlink channel is required. This renders the support of channel asymmetry difficult.

2) Time Division Duplexing (TDD): The TDD mode has primarily been used in hot-spot wireless data systems such as Bluetooth and WLAN. Recent developments such as the Chinese 3G standard TD-SCDMA (time division–synchronous code division multiple access) demonstrate that the TDD technology can also be used in cellular systems. The main advantage of TDD is its inherent flexibility in supporting traffic asymmetry. This can be explained with the aid of Figure 3. The UL and DL are arranged at the same frequency carrier and the two links are separated in time. The data rate on each link is proportional to the time duration, given a fixed channel bandwidth. Therefore, the level of asymmetry can be adjusted dynamically by changing the "switching point." This means that the time duration for each link can be changed without affecting the channel bandwidth. This is a very important property for mobile data services with different data-rate requirements.

In addition to its flexible support of traffic asymmetry, only the TDD mode offers an efficient and flexible support for ad hoc, multihop, or relaying communication. When a MS is in the ad hoc, multihop, or relaying mode it uses both BS functionality as well as MS functionality. This means it receives UL information from a neighboring MS and sends information in the DL direction to another neighboring MS. As a consequence, an MS needs to transmit and receive at the same carrier frequency, which can only be done using the TDD mode, as described earlier. Ad hoc, multihop, or relaying functionality will become a key property of future wireless systems that carry mobile data services. Therefore, a hybrid form of cellular and ad hoc mode operation may offer the most promising solution

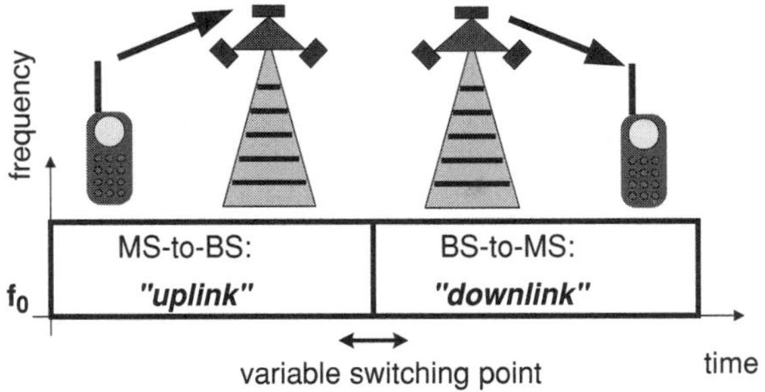

Figure 3: The TDD principle—uplink and downlink is at the same carrier frequency, but separated in time. Therefore, channel asymmetry can be easily supported by varying the *switching point*. In addition, if uplink and downlink transmission is within the coherence time of the channel, the channel is said to be reciprocal. This property is utilized to develop simplified receivers, for example, as used in prerake or joint transmission (Baier, Meurer, Weber, & Tröger, 2000).

to meet the requirements for high data-rates, highly unbalanced UL and DL traffic, and heterogeneous user distribution in future wireless systems. This stems from the fact that in cellular systems with high data-rate transmission, the cell radius shrinks significantly, which, in turn, would require a large number of BSs to avoid coverage "dead zones." This problem already exists in UMTS, and it will become more important with the envisaged high data rates of next generation wireless systems.

Because in TDD, the UL and DL use the same radio frequency channel, both directions experience the same propagation conditions. This results in channel reciprocity, provided that the TDD frame length is shorter than the coherence time of the channel (Ojanpera & Prasad, 1998).

Channel reciprocity has several implications for the system design. First, channel reciprocity can be exploited in the design of receiver structures. A notable example is the prerake architecture, first described by Esmailzadeh and Nakagawa (1993) and depicted in Figure 4. By using the prerake technique it is possible to retain the advantages of the rake combining, and at the same time use a simple single-path receiver at the mobile unit. The channel will only be estimated once, at the BS. With the knowledge of the channel impulse response, the BS performs the rake combining function *before* transmission (hence prerake). Thus, the output signal of the prerake combiner is the result of the convolution of the spread spectrum signal and the time-reversed channel impulse response. Because it is assumed that the channel does not vary between the reception and transmission periods, a simple receiver structure can be used at the mobile unit, ideally consisting only of a matched filter. Therefore, the signal processing and signaling effort is reduced as compared with single link transmission in a system that uses FDD.

In the previous paragraphs a number of advantages were mentioned that demonstrate that the TDD technology is ideally suitable for mobile data services. The most important disadvantage is described in the following. If the TDD interface is used in a multiple cell environment, severe interference problems can occur (Povey, Holma, & Toskala, 1997). These problems arise primarily because TDD is exposed to additional interference mechanisms (in comparison to FDD). These mechanisms are illustrated in Figure 5. This figure shows a simple cellular structure consisting of two adjacent cells.

In each cell a different level of asymmetry is used. This causes asynchronous TS overlaps, which has a significant impact on the total interference. In this context, the BSs not only interfere with the neighboring MSs, and vice versa (FDD equivalent interference scenario), but also with other BSs. Similarly, MSs interfere with adjacent MSs. The latter interference scenarios are depicted in Figure 5 (BS → MS and MS → BS interference is left out for clarity).

In particular, the interference between MSs can be severe given that the distance between two MSs at the cell boundary can be very small. To avoid BS ↔ BS and MS ↔ MS interference, the frames must be synchronized and both cells need to use the same level of asymmetry, that is, in all neighboring cells a BS or MS must transmit and receive at the same time. This clearly results in a significant limitation, which penalizes the most

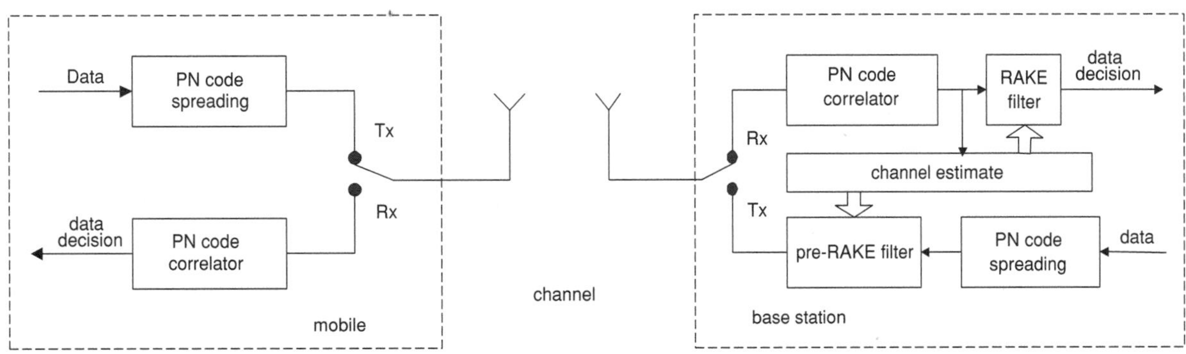

Figure 4: Block diagram of a prerake receiver. The signal to be transmitted in the downlink is convolved with the impulse response of the channel obtained from uplink transmission. As a consequence, the receiver at the mobile unit can be very simple (e.g., a matched filter). This particular prefiltering requires almost perfect correlation of the uplink and the downlink channel, which, for example, is provided by a TDD based air interface because uplink and downlink transmission is at the same radio frequency.

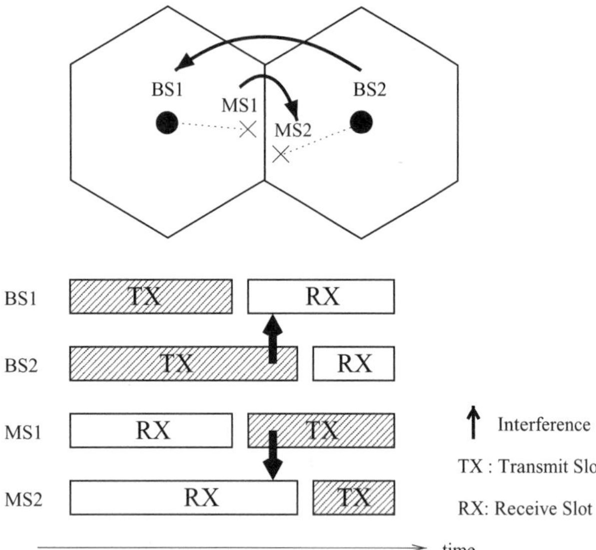

Figure 5: TDD specific interference scenarios in cellular TDD systems with cell-independent channel asymmetry. A mobile station can interfere with another mobile station. Similarly, a base station can interfere with neighboring base stations.

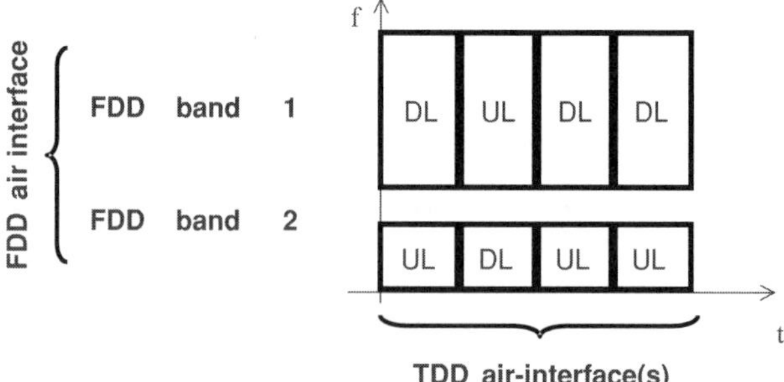

Figure 6: An example of hybrid duplexing in which one FDD radio frequency band has three times the bandwidth of the second FDD frequency band. It accounts for traffic asymmetry imposed by future mobile data services. Each frequency band can either be used for UL or DL. This finally results in two radio frequency bands of different bandwidth operated in the TDD mode.

important advantage of TDD in adapting to cell-specific traffic asymmetries. It has been shown that dynamic channel assignment algorithms are an effective means to solving this interference issue in a cellular TDD system (Punt, Sparreboon, Brouwer, & Prasad, 1998; Chen, Yoshida, Murata, & Hirose, 1998).

3) Hybrid Duplexing: The basic duplexing techniques, FDD and TDD, can be combined to generate hybrid duplexing solutions. An example of hybrid duplexing is depicted in Figure 6. In this example, the FDD radio frequency bands have different bandwidths, motivated by the fact that the usage of an air interface that primarily supports mobile packet services is highly unbalanced with respect to UL and DL. To be able to flexibly assign this asymmetry to either the UL or the DL, the link direction is not assigned to a particular radio frequency band. Therefore, TSs are introduced and FDD link directions may vary from TS to TS. For example, at the second TS, the UL and DL assignments are interchanged in Figure 6, that is, the channel asymmetry is now in favor of the UL as opposed to the DL in the first TS. Consequently, each FDD frequency band resembles a TDD air interface with each having a different bandwidth. A hybrid duplexing solution was used in the TDD underlay (Haas & Povey, 1999) concept that was proposed for UMTS.

4) Summary: An air interface that efficiently supports mobile data services is expected to use the TDD mode. In fact, WLAN systems have successfully demonstrated the deployment of TDD in a hot-spot environment for packet data transmission. However, if the TDD mode is used in a cellular environment, some TDD-specific issues have to be addressed. Because UL and DL transmissions use the same frequency band, additional interference scenarios might exist, namely MS-to-MS and BS-to-BS interference. The extent of these depends on cell-specific channel asymmetry and synchronization. These additional interference sources may cause severe capacity losses. But simple DCA algorithms might be found that avoid capacity losses. In fact, it has been demonstrated that in some cases capacity in a cellular TDD system can even be higher than in an equivalent FDD system (Haas, McLaughlin, & Povey, 2000).

Hybrid duplexing techniques can be considered as multiple TDD air interfaces.

Link Adaptation

Wireless and cellular system engineering is dominated by the challenging demands set by the communication medium. In particular, multipath propagation and Doppler effects cause frequency and time dispersion respectively. Hence, the amplitude of the received signal changes with location and with time. The variation can be several tens of decibels. Clearly, this affects the transmission performance significantly. Several trade-offs determine the performance of the communication link. The most important of these is spectral efficiency versus bit error performance. In the past, transmitters and receivers were sized for average channel characteristics. However, channel variation can be significant as indicated. Therefore, for most of the time the transmission technology is oversized (in favor of low bit-error performance), resulting in poor spectral efficiency.

The challenge is to find adaptive transmitters and receivers that adjust themselves to the varying nature of the channel. Modulation, coding, and power control are the key system functions that are affected by link adaptation. Adaptive modulation (Wong, Yeap, & Hanzo, 2000) changes the modulation order dependent on the channel state information (waterfilling). Incremental redundancy, or hybrid ARQ type II protocol (Sesia, Caire, & Vivier, 2004; 3rd Generation Partnership, 2004), changes the code rate, that is, the redundancy, depending on the channel state information, and power control adjusts the transmit power depending on the channel state information. All these techniques aim at flexible and robust spectrally efficient cellular systems. They all require feedback information. Hence, the feedback must be obtained in a timely manner; otherwise, the efficiency will suffer.

Because the overall system performance does not depend just on a single link or a single cell scenario, additional effects such as CCI, ACI, and MAI need to be considered. In this context, link adaptation can be particularly problematic for a packet system, because the transmitter needs feedback of the path loss and the interference environment, and possibly also the bit error performance at the peer entity, to set the power, the modulation order, or the channel coding. In addition, power control and adaptive modulation are mutually dependent because a change in transmitter power would alter the overall interference scenario. However, adaptive modulation with constant transmitter power maintains a fixed interference environment. Each transmitter can regularly transmit a signature that will allow its received power to be measured in the presence of interference from the other transmitters at each respective receiver. The mobile terminal can thus measure its available *SINR* and deduce an available bit rate for that particular link. In doing this the receiving terminal can use many criteria, including the history of *SINR* fluctuations, the required QoS, and the resources available at the terminal (e.g., the number of antennas or the processing capability). This approach is advocated in (Chawla & Quia, 1998), where it is shown that adaptive modulation without power control provides close to the optimum achievable performance.

Thus, for example, the mobile terminals will signal the available DL bit rate to the BS on the UL on a regular and frequent basis. This signaling need not necessarily be related to any specific expectation of data being received on the DL. Rather, it allows the BS to send data to that mobile unit at the correct rate whenever it has some to send. If a mobile terminal has not received data from the BS for awhile, the signaling rate can be reduced. Reliability can be preserved by underestimating the available bit rate. Whenever a packet is received from the BS at that MS, it then increases its bit transmission rate until a timeout period after the last packet is received. Additionally, bit rate change requests could be event driven, so that a static terminal would not inform the BS of the current available bit rate if this had not changed significantly. This, again, reduces the signaling traffic.

Alternatively, the modulation order can be fixed, and then to ensure the required *SINR*, the transmitter power has to be adjusted. The disadvantage to this is that increasing the transmitter power at one location results in greater interference at all nearby locations. As a consequence, the transmitter power for those mobiles has to be increased, which might result in a ping pong effect. This problem would be avoided by using adaptive modulation as described.

RADIO RESOURCE MANAGEMENT

The growth of wireless Internet access, and wireless text, picture, and video messaging services, suggest that fourth generation cellular mobile communications must adequately support a plurality of packet data services, with very high data rates, bursty traffic characteristics, heterogeneous QoS requirements, and traffic load asymmetry between cells and between the UL and DL in each cell. All the emerging mobile data services will have different QoS constraints. These need to be mapped onto a given radio frequency resource. Therefore, radio resource management is a key technique for efficient packet radio transmission in a wireless system. In addition, radio resource management has to deal with the particular constraints of radio transmissions, such as interference, which is discussed in the next section.

Moreover, ad hoc communication between mobile nodes requires decentralized radio resource management algorithms as opposed to centralized algorithms in conventional systems. Radio resource management can be subdivided into three main tasks: (a) DCA, (b) MAC protocols, and (c) packet scheduling. DCA algorithms for mobile data services, MAC algorithms, and packet scheduling techniques are discussed later.

Interference Considerations

From the definition of spectral efficiency it is clear that cochannel interference affects the spectral efficiency of a system, and is, therefore, an important parameter for MAC protocols and DCA algorithms. Furthermore, mobile data services require a transmission technology that caters for potentially very high data-rate transmission, variable UL/DL asymmetry, and so forth. Thus, the aim is to identify a technology that is resistant to interference, and which at the same time fulfills the requirements of mobile data services.

OFDM is viewed as a promising air interface technique in combination with TDMA to provide very high data rates for mobile data services, whereas TDD is considered the most efficient way to support UL/DL load asymmetry in a cellular mobile network. The potential disadvantage is that the TDD technology might result in additional interference in a cellular system that has 100% frequency reuse. In that case, the same radio frequency spectrum is used in all cells, and thus, no frequency planning is required. The reasons for a 100% frequency reuse are twofold: (a) It permits high spectral efficiency and (b) it permits high trunking efficiency for support of bursty packet data services.

Additional interference scenarios in TDD occur if neighboring cells have different UL/DL asymmetries. This can cause very high MS-to-MS and BS-to-BS intercellular interference in addition to the BS-to-MS and MS-to-BS intercellular interference scenarios known from conventional cellular systems (see Figure 7, for example). This situation is exacerbated in OFDM/TDMA-based systems, which have no processing gain from spreading but rely on powerful channel coding. Both BS-to-BS and MS-to-MS interference can be referred to as same-entity interference, whereas BS-to-MS and MS-to-BS interference is other-entity interference. In a TDD-based system with different UL/DL ratios in neighboring cells, both types of interference occur. In addition, both types of interference occur if slots in neighboring cells are not synchronized.

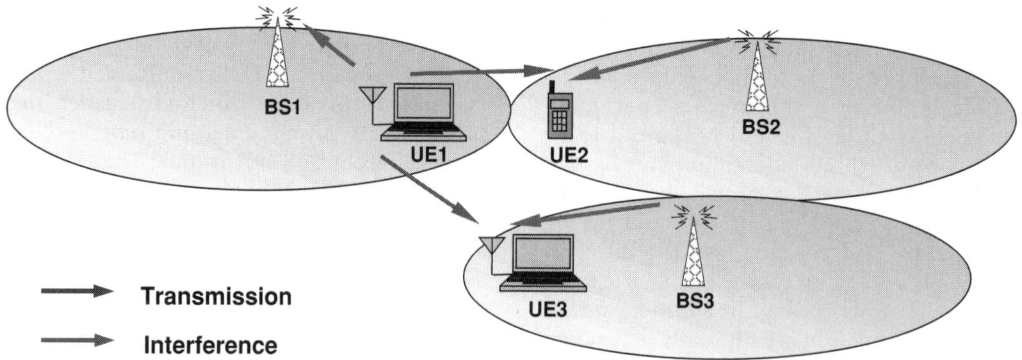

Figure 7: In a TDD-based cellular system with a frequency reuse of one, interference can potentially be significant because of the existence of mobile-to-mobile interference.

In general, slot synchronization in a TDD system affects the amount of same-entity and other-entity interference as is illustrated in Figure 8. This figure shows a possible TS arrangement between two cells. The model is composed of four entities: BSa, MSa, BSb, and MSb, where BSa and MSa, and BSb and MSb, respectively, form a communication link. That is, if BSa transmits, then MSa receives and vice versa. Lack of slot synchronization is modeled by an arbitrary time offset, t_{off}. This time offset is normalized by the TS duration t_{slot}, yielding the synchronization factor,

$$\alpha = \frac{t_{off}}{t_{slot}}. \quad (3)$$

Because of the frame misalignment, BSa and BSb interfere with each other, thereby creating I_{bb}. Similarly MSa and MSb interfere with each other and generate I_{mm}. Both types of interference have previously been categorized as same-entity interference. It can be found that same-entity interference is proportional to α. Similar properties can be found for other-entity interference, except that

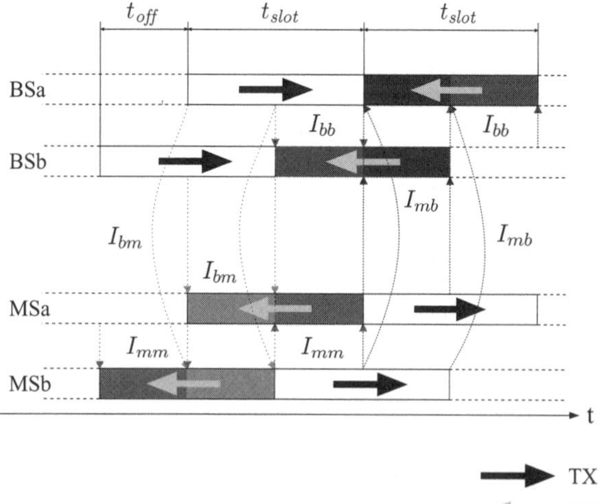

Figure 8: Interference in a TDD system dependents on slot synchronization. If the TSs in neighboring cells are time synchronized, that is, $t_{off} = 0$, the interference sets $\{I_{bb}, I_{mm}\}$ and $\{I_{bm}, I_{mb}\}$ will be disjointed.

it is proportional to $1 - \alpha$. Hence, as the synchronization factor α increases, other-entity interference diminishes, but same-entity interference increases, and vice versa. If $\alpha = 1$, only same-entity interference exists and similarly, if $\alpha = 0$, only other-entity interference exists. The consequence is that interference is present during the entire receive period. Because other-entity and same-entity interference can be considered as independent (because of different interference sources), the magnitude of each type of interference can vary greatly. Therefore, it is interesting to see whether it is possible to exploit the fact that same-entity interference and other-entity interference are different to minimize interference by altering frame synchronization. This particular property of TDD-based systems is exploited in DCA algorithms and MAC protocols, which are explained further in the following sections.

DCA Algorithms

In a cellular network a limited number of resources have to be managed in a way so as to enable a given user population to be served satisfactorily. This includes radio resource allocation methods that mitigate the detrimental impact of MAI, CCI, and ACI. Two main techniques can be distinguished (Ahlin & Zander, 1998; Cox & Reudink, 1974):

- static or fixed channel assignment (FCA) techniques and
- DCA techniques.

In the case of FCA, a fixed proportion of the available bandwidth is allocated to one cell. The same fractional bandwidth is only used in cells that are separated by a minimum distance. The frequency reuse distance ensures that CCI does not deteriorate the system performance greatly. However, it is well known that FCA techniques do not result in the most efficient use of the radio frequency spectrum. In contrast, DCA techniques enable a cellular system to adapt flexibly to different load situations, thereby increasing the throughput and decreasing the call blocking (Cox & Reudink, 1974). In addition, frequency planning can be avoided. An important issue, however, is to ensure that the DCA algorithm does not cause the system to become unstable. In this context, it is reported that under high-load conditions DCA algorithms can perform

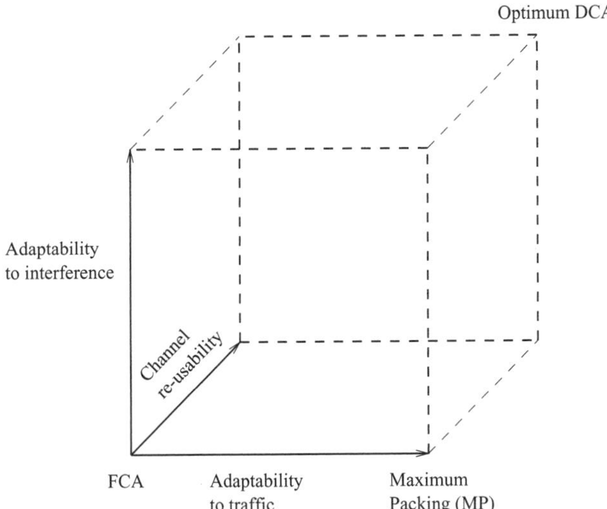

Figure 9: Three-dimensional classification of DCA algorithms.

worse than FCA techniques, because of continuous channel reassignments (Beck & Panzer, 1989). Consequently, systems have been designed in which FCA and DCA techniques are combined (Kunz, 1999; Tan, Soh, Gunawan, & Soong, 1989). As a result, for example, a subset of channels is assigned in a fixed way and the remaining channels are allocated to a common pool. A DCA algorithm uses the common pool from which it "borrows" channels to allocate them to cells where heavy traffic occurs. This way, the number of channels of a cell can be increased dynamically, but there is still a fixed number of channels, which ensure a certain QoS in situations where the entire network is heavily loaded.

A classification of different DCA approaches was made by Beck and Panzer (1989), which is repeated here for convenience (Figure 9). In the illustration, different DCA strategies are represented by points in the space, except the origin, which represents the FCA scheme. The three axes represent different optimization criteria.

A DCA algorithm can be designed to optimize the number of simultaneously active MSs in every cell (adaptability to traffic), resulting in maximum packing (MP). This requires knowledge about the load in every cell. A second criterion is the adaptability to interference variations, which is particularly important for interference-limited systems such as CDMA. This requires the DCA to have information on the instantaneous interference. A third criterion is to optimize the channel reuse distance, which would eventually mean that each channel can be used in every cell. An ideal DCA algorithm tries to optimize each of the three parameters, which would yield the optimum solution at the far upper corner of the cube. The ideal DCA algorithm would require information beyond the scope of a single cell. From this requirement it inherently follows that the respective DCA algorithm would ideally be operated at a central site. Consequently, two basic DCA schemes are distinguished:

- centralized DCA schemes and
- decentralized DCA schemes.

A centralized DCA algorithm collects the required information for channel assignment decisions from the associated BSs and MSs. This type of DCA algorithm is located at a higher hierarchical level of the mobile network architecture. A centralized DCA algorithm can, for example, be located at the radio network controller (RNC; Mihailescu, Lagrange, & Godlewski, 1999), which connects several BSs. The basic disadvantage is that a great amount of signaling is necessary to supply the vital information about the load, interference and channel status.

When using a decentralized DCA algorithm, the channel assignment decision is made by a local entity (Cimini, Foschini, Chin-Lin, & Milijanic, 1994; Das, Sen, & Jayaram, 1997a; Prakash, Shivaratri, & Singhal, 1999). Hence, the complexity is reduced considerably when using this type of DCA algorithm. The Digital European Cordless Telecommunications (DECT) standard uses such a decentralized DCA algorithm (Punt et al., 1998). Given that a decentralized DCA algorithm has only limited knowledge of the entire system, a global optimum is very difficult to achieve.

As a result of the DCA characterization in Figure 9, three types of strategies can be formulated:

1) *Traffic-adaptive channel allocation:* Instead of splitting the available frequency spectrum into subbands, which are then assigned to cells, traffic-adaptive channel allocation techniques try to assign the required bandwidth to cells dynamically (Haas, Winters, & Johnson, 1997). Compatibility matrices are set up to avoid use of the same frequency resource in a neighboring cell. Because the interference level from neighboring cells can vary significantly, the compatibility matrices have to be designed such that reliable connection under severe interference conditions is ensured. This results in capacity losses when using static compatibility matrices, because in low interference situations more channels per unit could be accommodated. The complexity of traffic-adaptive channel allocation algorithms increases exponentially with the number of cells. Because of this, graph theory is often used to solve these issues (Haas, Winters, & Johnson, 1997). The optimum traffic adaptive DCA algorithms result in the MP solution. This requires intracell handovers (channel reassignments). As a consequence, users may be reshuffled (although the QoS is still fulfilled) to optimize the total number of simultaneously active users. Hence, the complexity of MP strategies increases further, which makes this type of DCA algorithm difficult to analyze. Yeung and Yum (1995) proposed the cell group decoupling method to calculate upper bounds on blocking performance. However, the MP problem is easier to solve if the cells are placed along a line. In this scenario, the complexity only increases linearly with the number of cells. The optimum solution is found using the Greedy algorithm (Ahlin & Zander, 1998). In other studies, a different approach was taken to achieve the dynamic adaptation to traffic variations: channels were "borrowed" from a common pool and assigned to cells which experienced heavy traffic (Das, Sen, & Jayaram, 1997a; 1997b; Chang, Kim, Yin, &

Kim, 1998; Ortigoza-Guerrero & Lara-Rodriguez, 1996). This technique resembles the previously described combination of DCA and FCA methods.

2) *Reuse Partitioning:* The entire set of channels is divided into subsets, similar to the FCA strategy. But, in the case of reuse partitioning, every group of frequencies is associated with a different reuse distance (Zarder & Frodigh, 1992). A DCA algorithm always tries to use a channel with the lowest reuse distance, thereby increasing the capacity per unit area. It is reported that reuse partitioning algorithms can double the capacity of FCA schemes (Lucatti, Pattavina, & Trecordi, 1997).
3) *Interference-based DCA schemes:* Channels are assigned based purely on the interference power observed (no use of compatibility matrices). If the signal-to-noise ratio drops below a certain threshold, a new channel is acquired. This requires steady and reliable measurements of the interference power and power control to minimize interference. Because of its simplicity (easy to implement as distributed DCA algorithm) this type of DCA is widely used. Furthermore, interference-based DCA algorithms play an important role in CDMA systems, because they are interference limited (Shin, Cho, & Sung, 1999).

In TDD-based systems, which are ideally suitable for mobile data services, different sources of CCI exist. Moreover, an additional degree of freedom exists, namely, which TS to use for UL traffic and which to use for DL traffic. Both issues are addressed in interference-based DCA algorithms for TDD systems. In such systems, same-entity interference is, generally, viewed as most detrimental, and, therefore, it has been proposed to have the same TDMA frame structure in all cells with the same UL/DL slot allocation (Jeon & Jeong, 1999). This is referred to as common-slot-allocation (CSA), that is, an UL TS in one cell is also an UL TS in all other cells with the same being true for DL TSs. However, as demonstrated by Jeon and Jeong (2000), this is inefficient when the UL/DL load varies dynamically and independently in different cells. Therefore, more flexible slot allocation strategies, such as in Wieand Cho (2001), Lindstrom (2001), and Nasreddine and Lagrange (2003), have been proposed that permit same-entity interference provided the path gain estimates between same entities are sufficiently small. Also, it has been shown in Haas, McLaughlin, and Povey (2000) that occasionally same-entity interference is less than other-entity interference, and this diversity can be exploited to reduce overall intercellular interference. This has led to the development of various so-called time-slot-opposing (TSO) schemes (Haas & McLaughlin, 2001; Haas, Wegmann, & Flanz, 2002). Of all the proposed TSO strategies, random TSO (RTSO; Haas, Wegmann, & Flanz, 2002) is the most practical, as it requires no overhead in mitigating intercellular interference, as opposed to the centralized TSO technique proposed by Haas and McLaughlin (2001), which requires signaling to every node the path gains between every communicating node. The RTSO algorithm applies strategies similar to those known from frequency-hopping systems. It changes the TS configuration randomly, periodically, and independently within each cell (see Figure 10). Hence, instead

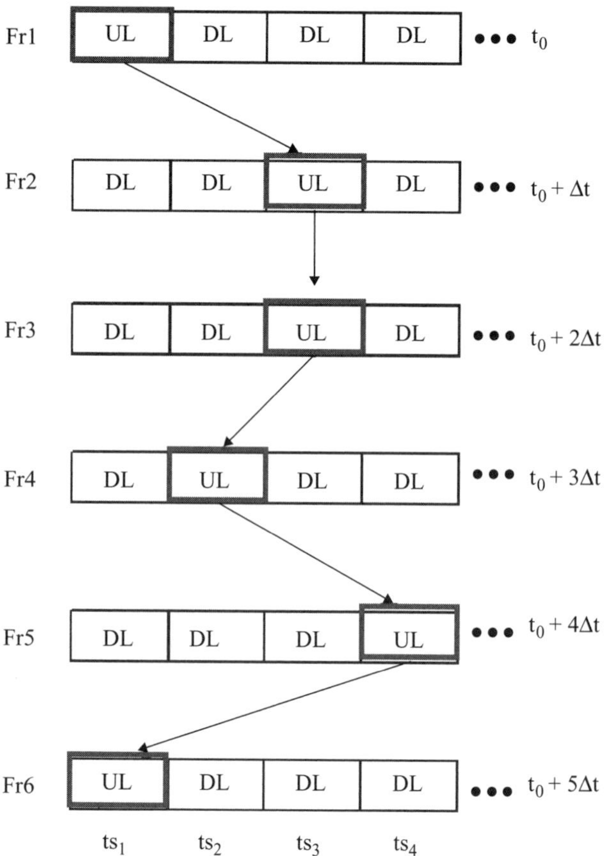

Figure 10: The RTSO algorithm randomly changes the alloted TS on a frame-by-frame basis. This means that during every frame period, each TS is exposed to a different level of interference. Therefore, analogies between this new TS-hopping approach and frequency-hopping systems can be drawn.

of changing the frequency, the TSs are changed according to a random sequence, which is reported to the MS during call establishment. Therefore, a user in a cell may experience other-entity interference within its allocated slot in one frame and same-entity interference in the next frame; that is, there is no bias shown against same- or other-entity interference. In this way RTSO exploits this inherent intercellular interference diversity to reduce the average intercellular interference. The RTSO algorithm has an important property: it does not require additional signaling during the duration of a call or session. These features make the RTSO algorithm suitable when cell-independent switching points are required. In addition, because the particular TS used for an arbitrary link randomly hops through the frame, a secure connection can be maintained if the hopping pattern is kept secret. If this is not sufficient, in addition to the TS hopping mechanism, frequency hopping can be applied. This results in a two-dimensional hopping process that increases transmission security significantly.

The RTSO is a "passive" slot allocation strategy and does not act to avoid high intercellular interference scenarios or act to mitigate high interference when it does occur. The strategies in Wie and Cho (2001), Lindstrom (2001), and Nasreddine and Lagrange (2003) are innovative and "active" in avoiding high intercellular interference, but at the expense of some signaling overhead. In Nasreddine and Lagrange (2003) a novel slot allocation strategy was presented, referred to as path gain division (PGD). PGD is an enhancement of the strategies presented in Wie and Cho (2001) and Lindstrom (2001) and showed performance improvement over the latter schemes. In PGD, the path gain between an MS requesting a slot allocation and an MS in a neighboring cell is estimated as the path gain between the former MS and the BS serving the latter. If the MS requests an UL slot allocation, the slot allocation is not permitted if there is at least one MS in a neighboring cell receiving data on the DL in the same TS where the path gain estimate between these two MSs is greater than a specified threshold, thus limiting same-entity interference. However, if the MS requests a DL slot allocation, the PGD scheme does not apply this restriction on same-entity interference, under the assumption that same-entity interference and average other-entity interference will be comparable in this case. Clearly, PGD implicitly gives preference to other-entity interference over same-entity interference, regardless of which is higher at the time. The performance of PGD is also expected to be compromised by the potentially high margin of error in its inter-MS path gain estimates, especially for large cell sizes.

MAC Protocols

Omiyi and Haas (2004) describe active and reactive strategy for mitigating high intercellular interference in a cellular mobile communications network for mobile data services with 100% frequency reuse. This strategy is denoted as channel-sensing TDMA TDD (CSTDMA TDD), and it uses a modified busy-tone broadcast/channel-sensing mechanism to avoid or mitigate high intercellular interference scenarios. CSTDMA TDD is a distributed medium access control (MAC) protocol, which is being applied in a novel way; that is, to mitigate intercellular interference, as opposed to mitigating intracellular interference as is typically the case. Therefore, CSTDMA TDD is applied in addition to an intracellular centralized MAC protocol and does not replace the latter. In this section, we evaluate the performance of CSTDMA TDD in minimizing intercellular interference and maximizing capacity and spectral efficiency, and compare it to the state-of-the-art, namely CSA, RTSO, and PGD.

CSTDMA TDD is a "busy-tone" broadcast protocol, which uses TDD to support the additional signaling and which is compatible with the air interface. A BS or MS receiver that is currently receiving data broadcasts a busy tone, which prevents potential interferers from transmitting. The busy tone is broadcast in minislots that occupy a portion of the time frame structure, with one minislot for every slot. Therefore, every BS or MS transmitter must listen to the minislots to determine if it can transmit as scheduled without causing significant interference to other users. Clearly, the inherent channel reciprocity of TDD is the enabling factor in this process—it would not work with an FDD-based air interface. The busy tone broadcast approach has the advantage, over pure carrier sensing, of avoiding both the hidden and exposed node problems, which are characteristic of the latter in the wireless environment. The fact that CSTDMA TDD resolves the exposed node problem is also an advantage over the RTS/CTS handshaking mechanism in 802.11 wireless LANs, which only combats the hidden node problem. In addition, the MAC signaling and information channels of the busy tone broadcast approach are physically orthogonal, and so they do not mutually interfere, unlike in RTS/CTS handshaking. Also, the busy tone broadcast approach requires less overhead than RTS/CTS handshaking and less stringent turnaround time constraints, which is especially critical in high-speed wireless networks. Finally, unlike traditional carrier-sensing/busy tone protocols, it seamlessly interoperates with the local centralized MAC protocol that coordinates cellular mobile communications. To support CSTDMA TDD, every BS (and cell) must be time synchronized. However, this is a typical requirement for TDMA TDD systems. In CSTDMA TDD, timeslots are organized into frames and a slot is either in contention or in reservation. A user is in contention mode if it attempts to transmit in a contention slot, and in reservation mode when it transmits in a reserved slot. There is no intracellular contention for cellular communication because the BS is in control locally at the cell level and schedules transmissions to avoid collisions among users in the same cell. However, there will be intercellular contention. Figure 11 shows the CSTDMA TDD flow chart. In CSTDMA TDD, when a user has data to transmit and is in contention mode, the transmission is scheduled for some random, future TDMA frame. The random time is determined as a function of congestion and real-time delivery requirements, and is based on the deadline-driven backoff strategy proposed by Omiyi (2000).

Within this frame, the transmitter selects an available contention slot, which is determined by not detecting a busy tone in the slot's conflict-signaling minislot in the preceding frame. The intended receiver does not broadcast a busy tone in the slot's minislot in the current frame if the transmission is received with unacceptable interference, that is, in outage, or if the transmission is received without outage but the transmitter indicates that it was not. However, if the transmission is received without outage and the transmitter indicates that it intends to continue its transmission in the subsequent TDMA frame, a busy tone is broadcast by the receiver in the slot's minislot in the current frame. Thus, the user effectively reserves the timeslot at the intended receiver in the next frame, and all other users that can detect the busy signal will not transmit in this slot in the next frame. The transmitter enters reservation mode and continues transmission in the same slot in the subsequent frame.

Figure 12 illustrates the principle of CSTDMA TDD. This figure shows three adjacent BSs, namely BS1, BS2, and BS3, with the user equipment (UE) associated with each BS, namely UE1, UE2, and UE3. This figure also shows an example timeslot structure for CSTDMA TDD, consisting of three timeslots per frame with a minislot between consecutive timeslots. In this example, BS1 begins transmitting on the DL to UE1 in the third timeslot in the first frame. Because there is no collision, the receiver UE1 broadcasts a busy tone in the next minislot and thus reserves the third timeslot in the next frame. This process

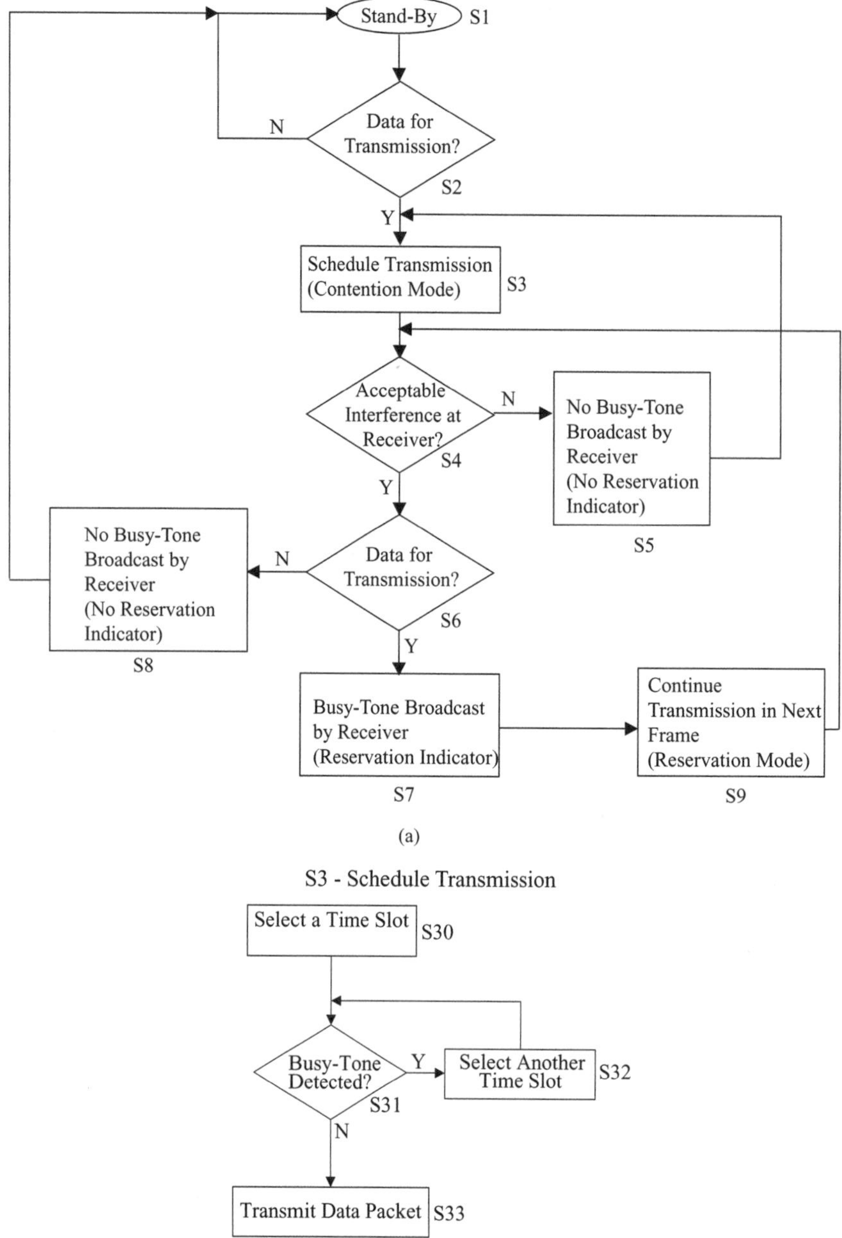

Figure 11: CSTDMA TDD flow chart: Every entity that wants to transmit a packet first checks whether the selected TS can be used by trying to detect an associated busy tone (S3). If a busy tone is detected a new potential TS will be selected for transmission, and the same procedure is carried out until either a free TS is found or the packet has to be buffered because of a lack of a free TS. If a TS is found, the packet will be transmitted. If interference at the receiver permits an error-free reception, a busy tone will be broadcast by the receiver indicating that the respective TS is now reserved (S4). If the interference at the receiver is too high, no busy tone is sent by the receiver which implicitly tells the transmitter to use a different TS (S5). The busy tone will be broadcast in the associated minislot until no further data is to be transmitted (S6). The important feature of this protocol is the implicit signaling using the reciprocity in TDD. If a transmitter does not hear a busy tone, this does not necessarily mean that there is no busy tone; it indicates that the received power at the minislot is too low, i.e., if that transmitter starts sending some data, it immediately follows that no significant interference at the other entity that has transmitted a busy tone can be expected.

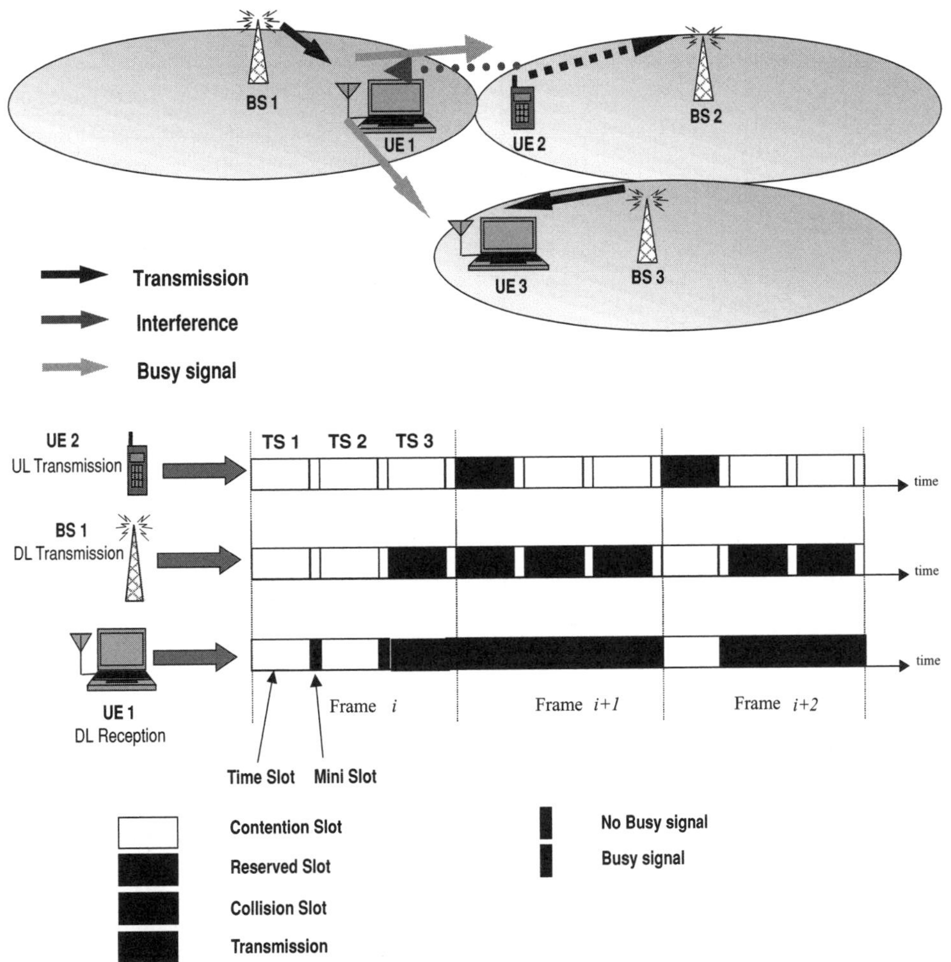

Figure 12: Illustration of the CSTDMA TDD principle: UE2 postpones its transmission on TS1 as long it detects a busy tone. Consequently, significant interference to UE1 can be avoided. UE2 transmits on TS2. BS3 can simultaneously transmit in TS1 because it does not hear the busy signal from UE1. Thereby an optimum, self-organizing reuse of radio resources is achieved.

is repeated in subsequent frames, where UE1 broadcasts a busy tone after each successful reception of data in the third timeslot. However, UE1 experiences a collision in the first TS of the second frame from a UL transmission of UE2 in the neighboring cell. Therefore, UE1 does not broadcast a busy tone in the minislot following this timeslot, with the result that it is unreserved by UE1 and BS1 discontinues transmission in it in subsequent frames. On the other hand, UE2 is allowed to continue its transmission in this timeslot in subsequent frames, because its receiver BS2 experienced no collision. Now a busy tone is only detected when the condition in Eq. (4) is satisfied, where P_{TB} is the fixed, known busy tone transmit power; P_{RB} is the received busy tone power, P_{TD} is the intended data transmit power of the user listening to the busy tone; and I_{thresh} is the interference threshold, that is, the maximum acceptable value of interference from a transmitting user to another user.

$$P_{RB} \leq P_{TB} \frac{I_{thresh}}{P_{TD}} \tag{4}$$

This MAC protocol is designed particularly for mobile data services with mixed QoS, mixed data rate, and mixed UL/DL asymmetry requirements. Dynamic system level simulations were carried out to evaluate the performance of the MAC protocol. The key system parameters can be found in Table 1.

Table 2 shows spectral efficiency results obtained from that simulation for 5% blocking, 5% outage, and QPSK modulation. It can be seen that the spectral efficiency of the TDD CSTDMA protocol is about an order of magnitude better than can be achieved using the CSA protocol. Similarly, the performance is improved by a factor of three as compared to the PGD technique.

Packet Scheduling

The packet-scheduling function in wireless systems is especially important for mobile data services in which many different services with specific QoS requirements exist. The four main physical-layer criteria with respect to QoS are (1) delay, (2) throughout, (3) outage, and (4) blocking. The first two are relevant for packet data services, whereas the latter two are relevant for circuit-switched services. Therefore, in the following we concentrate on delay and throughput. Formally the QoS requirement of some user, i, with respect to delay is defined as follows:

$$Pr\{W_i > T_i\} \leq \delta_i, \tag{5}$$

Table 1 Simulation Parameters

Parameter	Value
Number of cells	19
Number of slots per frame	7
Services	Mixed: voice and data
Data rate, voice	8 kbps
Data rate, data	128 kbps
Total DL/UL asymmetry	9.2:1
System bandwidth	20 MHz
Mobile speeds	36 km/h (50%), 3.6 km/h (50%)
BS separation	2000 m
C/I target	4.8 dB
Log-normal std. deviation	10 dB
Power control	C-based
Max. transmit power	30 dBm
Target received signal power	−100 dBm
CSTDMA TDD interference threshold	−103 dBm

where W_i is a packet delay for this user, and T_i and δ_i are the delay threshold and the maximum probability of exceeding it, respectively. A different notion of QoS is a requirement that the average throughput, R_i, provided to user i be not less than some predefined value r_i:

$$R_i \geq r_i. \tag{6}$$

All QoS criteria can be mapped onto different higher-layer service classes. In an initiative of the 3rd Generation Partnership Project (3GPP) four service classes are defined (2003a): (1) conversational class (e.g., voice), (2) streaming class (e.g., video streaming), (3) interactive class (e.g., Web browsing), and (4) background class (e.g., background download, e-mail). Voice, for example, is very sensitive to delay, blocking, and outage, but requires relatively low data rates, that is, throughput. These QoS properties are summarized in Table 3.

As opposed to a fixed line channel, the wireless channel changes with time and location. This corresponds to fast fading and slow fading respectively, caused by reflection, diffraction, and scattering. In a point-to-multipoint transmission scenario, for example, the signal amplitude at each receiver is significantly different and extremely difficult to predict. In addition, the interference level at any given location can vary significantly because the interference signal is subject to the same fading mechanism as the desired signal.

Table 2 Spectral Efficiency Comparison

Scheme	Spectral Efficiency, k (bits/s/Hz/cell)
TDD CSTDMA	1.334
TDD PGD	0.4
TDD CSA	0.13

Source: Omiyi and Haas (2004).

Table 3 Traffic Classes and Their QoS Requirements

Class	Attributes of Traffic
Conversational	Low delay and loss rate, low bandwidth
Streaming	Insensitive to delay, high bandwidth
Interactive	Bursty, moderate delay and loss rate, high peak bandwidth
Background	Highly tolerant of delay and loss rate, moderate bandwidth

Source: 3rd Generation Partnership Project (2003a).

The problem is even more complex: as opposed to optical or wire channels, the wireless channel results in a high number of erroneous detection of some bits or bit clusters. In data transmission, as opposed to voice transmission, bit errors are not tolerable. Therefore, strong error correction mechanisms must be used, such as turbo or Reed–Solomon error coding/decoding. The drawback of these techniques is that they result in increased delay. Other techniques, such as the slow start procedure in the TCP/IP protocol, cause significant reduction in the throughput. As a result, the QoS criteria can be traded off against each other, and selection of the appropriate processing of the individual incoming bit streams depends on the actual service. For this purpose, the channel state information (CSI) is of vital importance. As demonstrated in the example, physical layer functions (e.g. coding), and network functions (e.g. transmission protocols) all have an effect on QoS. As a consequence, and as stated in previous sections, joint optimization across all layers is necessary in mobile communications to improve the performance of cellular systems. (Straightforward implementation of the ISO OSI model is therefore not appropriate in the wireless context.)

A key role in the cross-layer optimization is placed on the data scheduler. The central task of the scheduler is to maximize the number of packets transmitted to multiple users in such a way that the QoS constraints of the respective services are sufficiently maintained. This is referred to as the *multiuser variable channel scheduling* problem (Andrews et al., 2001). An overview of a packet scheduler is depicted in Figure 13. Incoming data packets are first stored in a queue. The scheduler assigns some priority to a particular packet based on a metric that is ideally composed of the QoS parameters of that particular service to that the actual packet belongs: the CSI, the required signal-to-noise-ratio, the queue length, and previous feedback information (a packet may have to be rescheduled). The scheduler may trigger a particular error-correction mechanism at the physical layer. The selected and encoded packets are framed and sent on over the air interface. Higher-level feedback information such as ARQ is received and forms an input to the scheduler. From this description it can be seen that the scheduler has a nontrivial task to solve. Furthermore, it is also clear that link adaptation, scheduling, MAC, and DCA cannot be treated independently. For instance, link adaptation

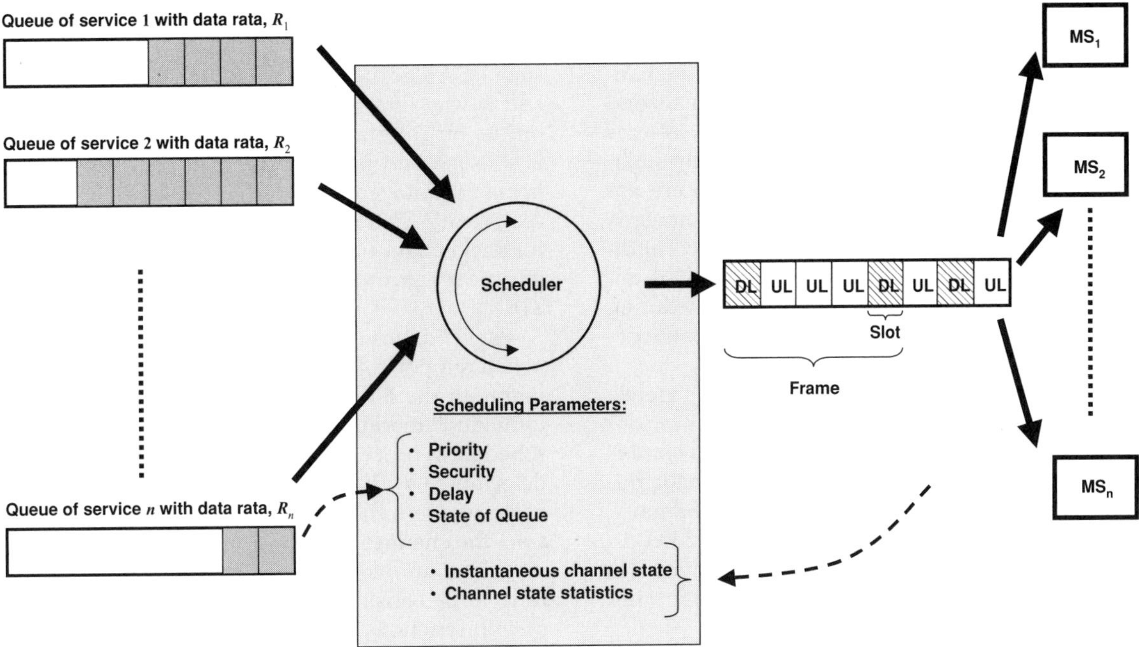

Figure 13: Different service classes and different users generate a number of data queues. The central task of the scheduler is to prioritize the packets in those queues based on service class parameters. As opposed to wired systems, the varying nature of the radio propagation channels of the spatially distributed users results in tremendously varying channel state characteristics. In addition, each of these users is exposed to interference resulting from radio resource reuse. Taking into account the prioritized service queues, the time-varying channel state characteristics and the interference at the respective receiver, the task of optimum scheduling (with regard to total throughput, delay, outage, and blocking) becomes nontrivial.

such as adaptive modulation may be used to favor data rate against bit-error performance. If, however, a packet of the conversational service class (especially delay sensitive, low bit-rate service) needs to be scheduled, the link adaptation strategy used is only suboptimum. The scheduler, which is informed of the particular service class—in this case the conversational class—might interact with the link adaptation algorithms to adjust the respective modulation technique.

In the following some state-of-the-art schedulers are introduced. The simplest and most straightforward scheduling scheme is round robin. Each queue, that is, each user, is served periodically regardless of priority, buffer length, channel state, and so forth. This is the most basic and most robust scheduling scheme. A round robin scheduler treats all users the same and is, therefore, not suitable for an environment that has to serve different QoS classes. More complex schemes introduce more or less sophisticated metrics. As different users (queues) fight for the same resource, the concept of "fairness" is vitally important. As a consequence, a whole family of so-called *weighted fair queuing* (WFQ) scheduling algorithms has been introduced; sometimes, they are also referred to as *generalized processor sharing* (GPS) algorithms (Nandita, Kuri, & Jamadagni, 2001). The key distinguishing feature of all these algorithms is the metric. For example, the buffer size can be used to control the scheduling of data packets. In this case, the metric is simply based on the buffer length. The buffer that stores the highest number of packets gets the highest priority for transmission. One possible metric of this type might be as follows: let n be the number of total packets in all queues. The weight for the jth queue is then simply $w_j = \frac{n_j}{n}$, where n_j are the number of packets in the jth queue. The main disadvantage is that this method is insensitive to delays. For example, a packet in the shortest queue will be considered with the lowest priority, but if this packet belongs to a delay sensitive service, WFQ results in a nonoptimum solution for this particular case. Therefore, an improvement is made such that each packet stored in a certain buffer is assigned a deadline, t_k, calculated as, $t_k = t_{class} - t$, where $k = 1, \ldots, n$, t_{class} is a parameter that depends on the service class of that particular packet and t is the queuing time in its own buffer. The first packet to be sent is the packet with the lowest deadline to expiration. It is important to emphasize that this algorithm is able to distinguish between different service classes with different QoS requirements. At the same time, it avoids long delays. The disadvantage of this algorithm is its increased complexity, because each packet in a single queue needs to be assigned a deadline. All these delay-based scheduling schemes have in common that they do not consider the CSI in the decision process. The main reason for this is that they originate from fixed line networks where the channel is known and time invariant. The consideration of the CSI for fair packet data scheduling in a mobile environment is vitally important. The mobile channel is subject to severe fluctuation because of multipath propagation. With respect to throughput it is, therefore, clearly not optimum to assign all users the same proportion of the available resources. To account for these channel effects, so-called *proportionally fair* scheduling schemes have been introduced (Andrews et al., 2001).

A typical algorithm of this type assigns those users who experience better channels proportionally more resources (time, frequency, power, etc.). If for example, the channel capacity of user A is 100 kbps and that of a second user B is 200 kbps, user A will obtain 1/3 of the resources and user B 2/3 of the resources. Thereby, the throughput is maximized, while at the same time all users are served (fairness component). Again, the disadvantage is that the user who is experiencing the worst channel conditions will get least attention, which might lead to long delays. In summary, the basic proportionally fair scheduling algorithm maximizes throughput but might violate the delay constraints for some users.

All basic schedulers described here use a single metric that yields a maximization of only a single QoS criterion. Further enhanced types of schedulers introduce a combination of different metrics (Nandita, Kuri, & Jamadagni, 2001; Yang, Tseng, & Cheng, 2003; Hossain & Bhargava, 2004; Xu, Shen & Mark, 2004; Borst & Whiting, 2003) to trade off the four basic QoS parameters (throughput, delay, outage, and blocking) as described at the beginning of this subsection.

SUMMARY AND CONCLUSION

In this chapter we have discussed the main prerequisites for the support of mobile data services from a system perspective. A brief review of the history of mobile communication systems revealed that state-of-the-art cellular systems are primarily designed for a single service—voice. In this context, our intention was to demonstrate that the variety of mobile data services required today and in the future imposes entirely different requirements on wireless systems to maximize the efficiency of use of the scarce radio spectrum. These requirements were discussed for the basic building functions of radio resource management: DCA algorithms, MAC protocols, and data scheduling, all of which have been introduced in previous chapters. In addition, specific solutions for these radio resource management functions for mobile data services have been proposed. With respect to the radio frequency spectrum, a number of arguments were provided that support the fact that the conventional approach of splitting the available spectrum into smaller pieces, which are then distributed to individual operators, will not be appropriate for high data-rate cellular systems. For the same reason, new wireless network architectures, such as ad hoc networking, will have to be introduced to enable the efficient support of mobile data services. Ad hoc communication could effectively support information security as the coverage range is very limited, that is, the spreading of information is inherently restricted.

The main finding with respect to the duplexing technique was that the TDD technology is the key enabler for mobile data services. All other relevant and enabling system functions, such as DCA algorithms, MAC protocols, and data packet scheduling, are optimized for TDD operation. Because the existing cellular systems almost exclusively use FDD technology (apart from the 3G standard in China termed TD-SCDMA), one can expect that next generation (4G and beyond) datacentric cellular systems will use TDD, given the anticipated growth of mobile data services. The additional interference scenarios in TDD will have to be arbitrated by intelligent DCA algorithms. One such DCA algorithm, referred to as RTSO, was introduced and it was shown that it also helps to increase security on the air interface if, for example, the hopping pattern is chosen appropriately. The TDD technology has a number of advantageous properties because it enables channel reciprocity. This property is exploited in MAC protocols for packet data-based wireless systems. Other issues such as time synchronization need to be dealt with when using TDD.

Packet data scheduling has an essential role in the efficient support of mobile data services because it has to maintain the different QoS constraints assigned to each individual mobile data service. However, an optimum scheduling process for wireless data services is not only determined by the QoS classes, but also by the actual state of the wireless channel. As opposed to fixed line transmission, the channel state in wireless systems is subject to severe fluctuations. This creates a number of trade-offs that have to be considered. These trade-offs also affect other system functions such as DCA algorithms and link adaptation methods (e.g., adaptive modulation). This makes clear the importance of optimizing a wireless system for packet transmission across different layers.

GLOSSARY

A3 The A3 algorithm is implemented in the subscriber identity module (SIM) cards and in GSM network authentication centers. It is used to authenticate the user. The authentication process is a challenge/response mechanism; when receiving a request to access its resources, the network sends a random number to the device (the challenge) and waits for a response. A function that takes the secret key stored in the SIM and the challenge as arguments is computed on the SIM and the result sent back to the network as a response. The network derives the same number using its own copy of the secret key and compares the result with the device's response. A match indicates that the device has been successfully authenticated.

A5 The A5 encryption algorithm scrambles the user's voice and data traffic between the handset and the base station to provide privacy. The A5 algorithm is implemented in both the handset and the base station subsystem (BSS). The effective key length is at most five bytes, which is its greatest weakness with respect to security.

Ad Hoc Information is directly sent from mobile to mobile or from device to device. Ad hoc communication does not require an infrastructure such as base stations in cellular communications.

CDMA CDMA multiple access technology using spread spectrum techniques. All users transmit and receive at the same time. Each user bit stream is multiplied by a unique, orthogonal (or pseudorandom) code that allows user separation at the receiver. The main advantage of CDMA is its inherent flexibility in assigning different data rates to different users.

Cellular The type of wireless communication that allows wide area coverage—in the ideal case, global coverage. The system uses many base stations to divide a service area into multiple cells. Cellular calls are transferred from base station to base station as a user travels from cell to cell.

FDD Uplink (reverse) link and DL (forward) link is separated in frequency domain.

FDMA Multiple access technique in which users share a common resource on a frequency basis. A given radio frequency band is divided into subbands. Each subband is used by a single user for a certain time period.

HSDPA HSDPA in UMTS enables peak data-rates on the *downlink* of up to 14.4 Mbps over a 5 MHz bandwidth, i.e., with HSDPA support of channel asymmetry with higher load requirements on the downlink is feasible. This is achieved by deploying adaptive modulation and coding (AMC), a technique used to compensate for variations in radio conditions. With this technique, a network node schedules the transmission of data packets to a user by matching the user's priority and estimated channel operating environment with the appropriate coding and modulation scheme, thus increasing throughput under favourable conditions.

IMT-2000 Global standard for third-generation (3G) wireless communications, defined by a set of interdependent ITU recommendations. IMT-2000 provides a framework for worldwide wireless access by linking the diverse systems of terrestrial and/or satellite-based networks.

MAN A collection of several LANs that are linked by faster backbone connections. A MAN is smaller than a WAN (wide area network), and an example is a college campus with several LANs linked on the same network.

Moore's Law More than 25 years ago, when Intel was developing the first microprocessor, company cofounder Gordon Moore predicted that the number of transistors on a microprocessor would double approximately every 18 months. To date, Moore's law has proven remarkably accurate.

OFDM A modulation technique with which information symbols are transmitted on spectrally overlapping adjacent subcarriers. Interference on adjacent subcarriers is avoided by an orthogonal transformation of the data symbols to be transmitted. Using this modulation method, low complex receivers for high data-rate transmissions can be realized—especially in a wireless context that is exposed to multipath propagation.

PAN Allows devices to work together and share information. Personal area networks can be created in public places, in the home, in the office, in a car. This network enables everyday devices to communicate wirelessly.

Rake A receiver architecture used in CDMA systems with which different time-delayed replicas of the transmitted symbol are collected and combined. Thereby, the received useful energy is maximized.

Roaming The ability to use the same service in different networks, usually in different countries, with the same terminal.

TDD Uplink (reverse) link and downlink (forward) link is separated in time domain.

TDMA Multiple access technique in which users share a common resource on a time basis. A transmission frame is divided into time slots (TSs). Each TS is used by a single user for a certain time period.

UMTS 3G system standardized by ETSI (European Telecommunications Standards Institute) under 3GPP along with other regional standards organizations.

Wi-Fi Wi-Fi is a nonprofit organization created to provide an interoperability certification for wireless LAN products based on the 802.11 standard.

WiMAX WiMAX is an industry trade organization formed by leading communications component and equipment companies to promote and certify compatibility and interoperability of broadband wireless access equipment that conforms to the IEEE 802.16 and ETSI HIPERMAN standards.

WLAN Wireless local area networks provide cable-free connection between notebooks, desktop PCs, printers, and office networks via wireless access points.

CROSS REFERENCES

See *Cellular Networks; Quality of Security Service: Adaptive Security; Radio Frequency and Wireless Communications Security; Security and Web Quality of Service; TCP over Wireless Links; Wireless Channels.*

REFERENCES

3rd Generation Partnership Project (3GPP), Technical Specification Group Services and System Aspects. (2003a). *Service and service capabilities* (3GPP TS 22.105 V6.2.0). Retrieved July 9, 2005, from http://www.3gpp.org/

3rd Generation Partnership Project (3GPP), Technical Specification Group Services and System Aspects, 3G Security. (2003b). *Specification of the A5/3 encryption algorithms for GSM and ECSD, and the GEA3 encryption algorithm for GPRS, document 1: A5/3 and GEA3 specifications (release 6)* (3GPP TS 55.216 V6.2.0).

3rd Generation Partnership Project (3GPP), Technical Specification Group Radio Access Network. (2004). *High speed downlink packet access (HSDPA)—Overall description, stage 2 (release 6)* (3GPP TS 25.308 V6.2.0). Retrieved July 9, 2005, from http://www.3gpp.org/

Ahlin, L., & Zander, J. (1998). *Principles of wireless communications*. Lund (Sweden), Studentlitteratur.

Andrews, M., Kumaran, K., Ramanan, K., Stolyar, A., & Whiting, P. (2001). Providing quality of service over a shared wireless link. *IEEE Communications Magazine, 39*(2), 150–154.

Baier, P. W., Meurer, M., Weber, T., & Tröger, H. (2000). Joint transmission (jt), an alternative rationale for the downlink of time division CDMA using multi-element transmit antennas. In *Proceedings of the IEEE Sixth International Symposium on Spread Spectrum Techniques and Applications, ISSSTA'00* (vol. 1, pp. 1–5).

Beck, R., & Panzer, H. (1989). Strategies for handover and dynamic channel allocation in micro-cellular mobile systems. In *Proceedings of the 1989 IEEE Vehicular Technology Conference* (vol. 1, pp. 178–185).

Borst, S., & Whiting, P. (2003). Dynamic channel-sensitive scheduling algorithms for wireless data throughput optimization. *IEEE Transactions on Vehicular Technology, 52*(3), 569–586. IEEE Piscataway, NJ, USA.

The book of visions 2001. Retrieved July 9, 2005, from http://www.wireless-world-research.org

Chang, K.-N., Kim, J.-T., Yim, C.-S., & Kim, S. (1998). An efficient borrowing channel assignment scheme for cellular mobile systems. *IEEE Transactions on Vehicular Technology, 47*(2), 602–608.

Chawla, K., & Quia, X. (1998). Throughput performance of adaptive modulation in cellular systems. In *Proceedings of the International Conference on Universal Personal Communications ICUPC '98* (pp. 945–950).

Chen, L., Yoshida, S., Murata, H., & Hirose, S. (1998). A dynamic timeslot assignment algorithm for asymmetric traffic in multimedia TDMA/TDD mobile radio. *IEICE Transactions: Fundamentals, E81–A*(7), 1358–1365.

Cimini, L. J., Foschini, G. J., Chih-Lin, I., & Miljanic, Z. (1994). Call blocking performance of distributed algorithms for dynamic channel allocation in microcells. *IEEE Transactions on Communications, 42*(8), 2600–2607.

Cox, D. C., & Reudink, D. O. (1974). Layout and control of high–capacity systems. In *Microwave mobile communications*. IEEE Press. IEEE Piscataway, NJ, USA.

Das, S. K., Sen, S. K., & Jayaram, R. (1997a). A distributed load balancing algorithm for the hot cell problem in cellular mobile networks. In *Proceedings of the 1997 Sixth IEEE International Symposium on High Performance Distributed Computing* (pp. 254–263). Portland, OR, USA.

Das, S. K., Sen, S. K., & Jayaram, R. (1997b). A dynamic load balancing strategy for channel assignment using selective borrowing in cellular mobile environment. *Wireless Networks, 3*(5), 333–347.

Esmailzadeh, R., & Nakagawa, E. M. (1993). Pre–RAKE diversity combining for direct sequence spread spectrum mobile communications systems. *IEICE Transactions: Communications, E76–B*(8), 1008–1015.

Gindraux, S. (2002). From 2G to 3G: A guide to mobile security. In *Third International Conference on 3G Mobile Communication Technologies* (Conf. Publ. No. 489, pp. 308–311).

Ghosh, A., Wolter, D. R., Andrews, J. G., & Chen, R. (2005). Broadband Wireless Access with WiMax/802.16: current performance benchmarks and future potential. *IEEE Communications Magazine, 43*(2), 129–136.

Haas, H., & McLaughlin, S. (2001). A dynamic channel assignment algorithm for a hybrid TDMA/CDMA–TDD interface using the novel TS—Opposing technique. *IEEE Journal on Selected Areas in Communication, 19*(10), 1831–1846.

Haas, H., McLaughlin, S., & Povey, G. J. R. (2000). A novel interference resolving algorithm for the TDD TD–CDMA mode in UMTS. In *Proceedings of the International Symposium on Personal, Indoor and Mobile Radio Communications PIMRC 2000* (pp. 1231–1335).

Haas, H., & Povey, G. J. R. (1999). A capacity investigation on UTRA–TDD utilising underused UTRA–FDD uplink resources. In *Proceedings of the 10th International Symposium on Personal, Indoor and Mobile Radio Communications PIMRC '99* (pp. A6–4).

Haas, H., Wegmann, B., & Flanz, S. (2002). Interference diversity through random time slot opposing (RTO) in a cellular TDD system. In *Proceedings of the IEEE Vehicular Technology Conference (VTC 2002-Fall)* (pp. 1384–1388).

Haas, Z., Winters, J. H., & Johnson, D. S. (1997). Simulation results of the capacity of cellular systems. *IEEE Transactions on Vehicular Technology, 46*(4), 805–817.

Holma, H., & Toskala, A. (2004). WCDMA for UMTS: Radio Access for Third Generation Mobile Communications. Hoboken, NJ: John Wiley & Sons.

Hossain, E., & Bhargava, V. K. (2004). Link-level traffic scheduling for providing predictive QoS in wireless multimedia networks. *IEEE Transactions on Multimedia, 6*(1), 199–217. IEEE Piscataway, NJ, USA.

Jeon, W. S., & Jeong, D. G. (1999). CDMA/TDD system for wireless multimedia services with traffic unbalance between uplink and downlink. *IEEE Journal on Selected Areas in Communication 17*, 939–946. IEEE Piscataway, NJ, USA.

Jeon, W. S., & Jeong, D. G. (2000). Comparison of time slot allocation strategies for CDMA/TDD systems. *IEEE Journal on Selected Areas in Communication, 18*(7), 1271–1278.

Kunz, D. (1999). Transitions from DCA to FCA behavior in a self–organizing cellular radio network. *IEEE Transactions on Vehicular Technology, 48*(6), 1850–1861.

Lin, Q., Zhou, S., & Giannakis, G. (2004). Cross–layer combining of adaptive modulation and coding with truncated ARQ over wireless links. *IEEE Transactions on Wireless Communications, 3*(5), 1746–1755.

Lindstrom, M. (2001). TDD resource allocation through inter-mobile interference avoidance. In *Proceedings of the 2001 IEEE 53rd Vehicular Technology Conference* (vol. 2, pp. 1027–1031).

Lucatti, D., Pattavina, A., & Trecordi, V. (1997). Bounds and performance of reuse partitioning in cellular networks. *International Journal of Wireless Information Networks, 4*(2), 125–134.

Mihailescu, C., Lagrange, X., & Godlewski, P. (1999). Dynamic resource allocation for packet transmission in TDD TD–CDMA systems. In *Proceedings of the 1999 IEEE Vehicular Technology Conference* (pp. 1737–1741).

Mohr, W. (1999). The UTRA concept: Europe's proposal for IMT 2000. In *Proceedings of the 1999 Global Communications Conference (GLOBECOM)* (vol. 5, pp. 2683–2688).

Mouly, M., & Pautet, M. B. (1992). The GSM System for Mobile Communications. Olympia, WA: Telecom Publishing.

Nandita, D., Kuri, J., & Jamadagni, H. S. (2001). Optimal call admission control in generalized processor sharing (GPS) schedulers. In *Proceedings of the Twentieth Annual Joint Conference of the IEEE Computer and Communications Societies (INFOCOM 2001)* (vol. 1, pp. 468–477). IEEE.

Nasreddine, J., & Lagrange, X. (2003). TDD resource allocation through inter-mobile interference avoidance. In *Proceedings of the IEEE Vehicular Technology Conference (VTC 2003-Spring)* (vol. 2, pp. 1410–1414).

Ojanpera, T., & Prasad, R. (1998). *Wideband CDMA for third generation mobile communications*. Artech House, Inc, Norwood, MA, USA.

Omiyi, P. (2000). *Medium access control for third generation cellular mobile systems*. Unpublished doctoral dissertation, University of Leeds.

Omiyi, P., & Haas, H. (2004a). Improving time-slot allocation in 4th generation OFDM/TDMA TDD radio access networks with innovative channel-sensing. In *Proceedings of the International Conference on Communications ICC'04* (vol. 6, pp. 3133–3137).

Omiyi, P., & Haas, H. (2004b). Maximising spectral efficiency in 4th generation OFDM/TDMA TDD hybrid cellular mobile/ad-hoc wireless communications. In *Proceedings of the IEEE Vehicular Technology Conference (VTC 2004-Spring)* (CD-Rom).

Ortigoza-Guerrero, L., & Lara-Rodriguez, D. (1996). Dynamic channel assignment strategy for mobile cellular networks based on compact patterns with maximised channel borrowing. *Electronics Letters, 32*(15), 1342–1343. IEE, Stevenage, UK.

Povey, G. J. R., Holma, H., & Toskala, A. (1997). TDD–CDMA extension to FDD–CDMA based third generation cellular system. In *Proceedings of the 1997 IEEE Sixth International Conference on Universal Personal Communications ICUPC '97* (ser. 2, vol. 2, pp. 813–817). San Diego, CA, USA.

Prakash, R., Shivaratri, N., & Singhal, M. (1999). Distributed dynamic fault–tolerant channel allocation for cellular networks. *IEEE Transactions on Vehicular Technology, 48*(6), 1874–1888. IEEE Piscataway, NJ, USA.

Punt, J. B., Sparreboom, D., Brouwer, F., & Prasad, R. (1998). Mathematical analysis of dynamic channel selection in indoor mobile wireless communication systems. *IEEE Transactions on Vehicular Technology, 47*(4), 1302–1313.

Roos, A., Hartmann, M., & Dutnall, S. (2003). Critical issues for roaming in 3G. *IEEE Communications Magazine, 10*(1), 29–35.

Sesia, S., Caire, G., & Vivier, G. (2004). Incremental redundancy hybrid ARQ scheme based on low-density parity check codes. *IEEE transactions on wireless communications, 52*(8), 1311–1321.

Shin, S. M., Cho, C.-H., & Sung, D. K. (1999). Interference–based channel assignment for DS–CDMA cellular systems. *IEEE Transactions on Vehicular Technology, 48*(1), 233–239.

Tan, P. T., Soh, C. B., Gunawan, E., & Soong, B. H. (1998). Dynamic flow model for borrowing channel assignment scheme in cellular mobile system. *Wireless Personal Communications, 6*(3), 249–264.

Welzl, M., Franzens. L., & Mülhäuser, M. (2003). Scalability and quality of service: A trade-off? *IEEE Communications Magazine, 41*(6), 32–36.

Wie, S.-H., & Cho, D.-H. (2001). Time slot allocation scheme based on a region division in CDMA/TDD systems. In *Proceedings of the 2001 IEEE 53rd Vehicular Technology Conference* (vol. 4, pp. 2445–2449).

Wong, C. H., Yeap, B. L., & Hanzo, L. (2000). Wideband burst-by-burst adaptive modulation with turbo equalization and iterative channel estimation. In *Proceedings of the 2000 IEEE 51st Vehicular Technology Conference* (pp. 2044–2048).

Xu, L., Shen, X., & Mark, J. W. (2004). Dynamic fair scheduling with QoS contraints in multimedia wideband DMA cellular networks. *IEEE Transactions on Wireless Communications, 3*(1), 60–73.

Yang, J.-S., Tseng, C.-C., & Cheng, R.-G. (2003). Dynamic scheduling framework on an RLC/MAC layer for general packet radio service. *IEEE Transactions on wireless communications, 2*(5), 1008–1016.

Yeung, K. L., & Yum, T.-S. P. (1995). Cell group decoupling analysis of a dynamic channel assignment strategy in linear microcellular radio systems. *IEEE Transactions on Communications, 43*(2–4), 1289–1292.

Zander, J., & Frodigh, M. (1992). Capacity allocation and channel assignment in cellular radio systems using reuse partitioning. *Electronics Letters, 28*(5), 438–440. IEE, Stevenage, UK.

Wireless Internet: A Cellular Perspective

Abbas Jamalipour, *University of Sydney, Australia*

INTRODUCTION

The wireless mobile Internet, which was a dream only a few years ago, is now progressing so fast that it could revolutionize the whole framework of the telecommunication industry. The wireless mobile Internet is not only an extension of the Internet into the mobile environment that gives users access to the Internet services while they are on the move, it is also about integrating the Internet and telecommunications technologies into a single system that covers all communications needs of human. With the extensive progress achieved during the past decade in wireless access technology, switching and routing in the Internet, and sophisticated hardware and software design, such a comprehensive Internet technology would no longer be a dream but a practical reality. Although the first cellular-based mobile Internet services provided users with a taste of an actual wireless mobile Internet system, there is still a need for more research to achieve the systematic goals of this network (Jamalipour, 2003).

Mobile and wireless Internet, as its name specifies, should provide a seamless transition from a geographically fixed domain into a mobile environment. By seamless transition, we mean that there should be no sensible change for a user who is connected to the Internet when moving from a fixed domain to a mobile domain. In a broad sense, this could be even the case when a user moves from one wireless network domain to another one. In technical terms, the Internet access for the user should be independent of the access technology used for the Internet services.

Changes in Network Protocol Stack

During the transition from the traditional wired Internet to the wireless Internet, network protocols and network architecture will be changed dramatically. In a mobile Internet system, the user should not feel a dramatic change in quality of service (QoS) for the user's current application. The quality measure most easily sensed is the connection speed or data bit rate, which affects the requirements for the maximum allowable delay. Changes to protocols affect all layers of the network protocol stack. The link layer (Layer 2) has to be modified to concurrently establish two or more connections via different access networks supported by the physical layer (Layer 1). This change in the link-layer protocol has to be incorporated into the computer operating system (OS) so that, for example, two Internet connections can be set up and maintained at the same time.

At the physical layer, mobile devices have to be equipped with multiple interfaces to different access networks (wired networks, such as Ethernet cables and dial-up modems, as well as wireless networks, such as wireless LANs and infrared and cellular modems). The physical layer has to include several interfaces to Layer 2 in order to manage the best connection to higher layers, and if one connection cannot meet the quality requirements of the application, a combination of two access networks can be granted. This would be the start of a heterogeneous systems era.

At the network layer (Layer 3), the Internet protocol (IP) needs major changes so that it can handle the routing and other tasks that would be required of the network layer in wired and wireless environments. Mobility of IP addresses should be accommodated in the future mobile Internet. Signaling requirements of the IP layer protocol have to be simplified to provide more spectrum efficiency in future wireless access networks. IP addressing and global address translation between heterogeneous networks must be performed in Layer 3.

The transport layer on top of the IP layer may be considered the main part that needs modifications for future mobile Internet networks. The legacy design of this layer for wired networks avoids efficient use of the radio-channel capacity, and thus major modifications and extensions are required at the transport layer to the transmission control protocol (TCP), which is predominantly used today, and the user datagram protocol (UDP).

In a mobile Internet, the mobile user does not see any difference between the currently available service providers at a given time and location, and it is assumed that a user may access the Internet regardless of his or her point of attachment to the network and the supporting access and core networks. Therefore, a system for authentication and authorization of users when they move across different networks must be established. Authentication provides the proof of the user's identity to the network that the user is going to access. This process is usually performed through an authentication procedure. Authorization determines what type of services may be provided to an authenticated user. Therefore, it is not sufficient that a user is in a capacity to connect to a network; the user must also be subscribed to a list of services that he or she is going to receive from the connecting network. Accounting, the third A in the network AAA (authentication, authorization, and accounting), provides a history of which services a user has utilized and at which times while connected to a network.

Mobile Internet will be only one of many different telecommunication technologies and hence needs to share limited resources. A sophisticated resource management strategy thus would be vitally necessary to share those resources among all coexisting technologies. Resource management schemes such as bandwidth management, admission control, congestion control, and so on will guarantee reliable performance of the network as well as a fair allocation of resources to all eligible users.

Next-Generation Networks and the Mobile Internet

The current network architectures used in either the wired Internet or the cellular networks would not be appropriate and efficient for a future wireless mobile Internet, even if we assume that the cellular networks will provide the major infrastructure of the mobile Internet. In recent years many people have discussed this issue and how it may be possible to change the existing network architectures to be utilized by a mobile Internet (Macker, Park, & Corson, 2001; McCann, & Hiller, 2000; MWIF, n.d.; Noerenberg, 2001; Oliphant, 1998; Ramjee, La Porta, Thuel, & Varadhan, 2000; Umehira, et al., 1999). One major issue is making the core network independent of the underlying access technology.

Currently several access networks exist, such as second- and third-generation (2G/3G) wireless cellular, wireless LAN (WLAN), and satellite networks, that offer a broad range of services. Access-specific end terminals are required for the subscribers to enjoy seamless services across these networks. At present there is no single system available that can effectively replace all these technologies and offer all these services with the same terminal. As a result research is underway to develop the next-generation network (4G or Beyond 3G—B3G) that will facilitate seamless mobility across heterogeneous technologies by means of a single handheld terminal. This envisaged network will be a fabric of internetworked existing and future access technologies (both wired and wireless) integrated together through an IPv6 transport protocol.

Several 4G/B3G network architectures have been proposed by researchers. Our review of these architectures has identified scope for improvement in the key areas of mobility and resource management. This has led us to develop a better common control and signaling mechanism to reduce battery power drain; to improve handover management across different networks for various degrees of mobility, resource reservation between peer end terminals to support real-time and non real-time applications; and end-to-end QoS management under varying network conditions; to design an adaptive handheld terminal to access heterogeneous services; and to create a reliable multicast protocol for signaling messages.

Chapter Outline

In this chapter, we propose a modular, open, hierarchical network architecture with cross-layer coordination for the future wireless Internet through well-defined message interfaces and distributed network functionalities. Our motivation for this research stems from the need to address the inherent limitations exhibited by contemporary 4G/B3G network architectures in the areas of mobility and resource management for the next-generation wireless Internet. We have aimed to improve on these network architectures by proposing suitable augmentations in the corresponding areas mentioned previously. Our novel augmentations in these areas enable seamless connectivity across different access networks. A software-defined, radio-based reconfigurable mobile terminal is used to access the proposed 4G/B3G network. In addition, a reliable multicast protocol is proposed over an incorporated common signaling system to support the signaling required for multicast services.

This chapter is organized as follows: after the general description of the mobile and wireless Internet provided in the first section, in the second section the heterogeneous network architecture of the future wireless mobile Internet is outlined. The third section summarizes some fundamentals of the wireless LAN, with emphasis on IEEE 802.11 standard. In this chapter, realization of wireless Internet by use of wireless LAN is also discussed. In the fourth section, we discuss the limitations of the key contemporary 4G architectures in terms of their essential components such as mobility and resource management techniques. Next we present the proposed internetworking architecture of the future wireless Internet. After that, we describe our proposal for the novel augmentations to the architecture, mobility management, resource management, and QoS techniques. The mobile terminal architecture of the future wireless networks is discussed in the seventh section. Reliable multicast signaling protocol is discussed in the eighth section and is followed by key conclusions for the chapter. These initiatives should pave

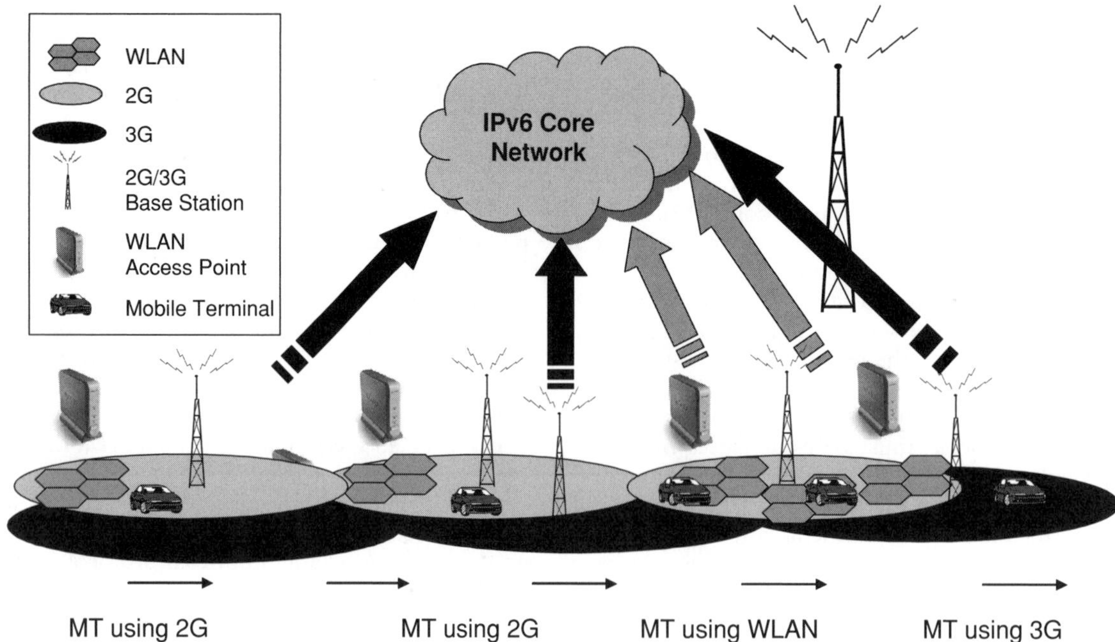

Figure 1: General view of the next-generation system showing overlapping heterogeneous access networks.

the way for the future mobile Internet infrastructure. The discussions provided in this chapter try to advance the knowledge of the network architecture necessary for the future mobile Internet and address fundamental issues related to the mobile Internet; thus, this chapter is considered as a comprehensive overview to the mobile and wireless Internet.

HETEROGENEOUS NEXT-GENERATION WIRELESS NETWORKS

The emergence of several access technologies has resulted in a multitude of heterogeneous systems targeting different service types, data rates, and users. Although the migration from first to 2G-generation cellular systems involved a transition from analog to digital technology, the evolution from 2G to 3G cellular system is driven by the popularity of the Internet and the need for data transmission availability on the move. The different available access technologies such as 2G GSM (Global System for Mobile communications) and IS-95 (cdmaOne); the enhanced data rate of the 3G packet-switched UMTS (Universal Mobile Telecommunication System) and CDMA2000; the high-capacity and high-bandwidth WLANs (IEEE 802.11, HIPERLAN, HIPERLAN2); and high-speed digital broadcast systems such as digital audio broadcast and digital video broadcast, with their own distinct characteristics, complement each other. However, the absence of a single architecture to integrate all existing and future systems prevents the subscribers from enjoying reliable and global end-to-end connectivity through a single subscription.

The main motivation for the research in next-generation network architecture is based on factors such as the following:

- Demand for better availability of services and applications.
- Global connectivity for any-type services at anytime, anywhere, and anyhow.
- Rapid increase in the number of wireless subscribers who want to make use of the same handheld terminal while roaming.
- Support for bandwidth-intensive applications such as real-time multimedia, online games, and videoconferencing as well as traditional voice service (VoIP).

The scalable and distributed next-generation (or 4G) network architecture is expected to offer any-type services over a diverse set of places such as indoor, outdoor, pedestrian, and vehicular locations. The services, as stated earlier, will be offered over a large range of overlapping access networks (e.g., WLAN, 2G, 3G, xDSL, DVB, DAB) that offer different data rates, coverage, bandwidth, delay and loss, QoS requirements, and so forth (Berezdivin et al., 2002; Frodigh et al., 2001; Gustafsson et al., 2003; Kellerer et al., 2002). Figure 1 shows a general view of such a next-generation system with overlapping heterogeneous access networks.

The key features visible to the user in such a network are the following:

- Mobile terminals will be able to autoconfigure to the specific access technology at the location of the terminal.
- Subscribers will have access to various services and enjoy a quality of service, cost, and security equivalent to wired LANs, even while running real-time applications.
- Ubiquitous and seamless connectivity will be provided through effective mobility, resource, and QoS management schemes.
- The investments made by the subscriber will be respected by limiting the changes required in the multi-access mobile terminal in terms of hardware or software.

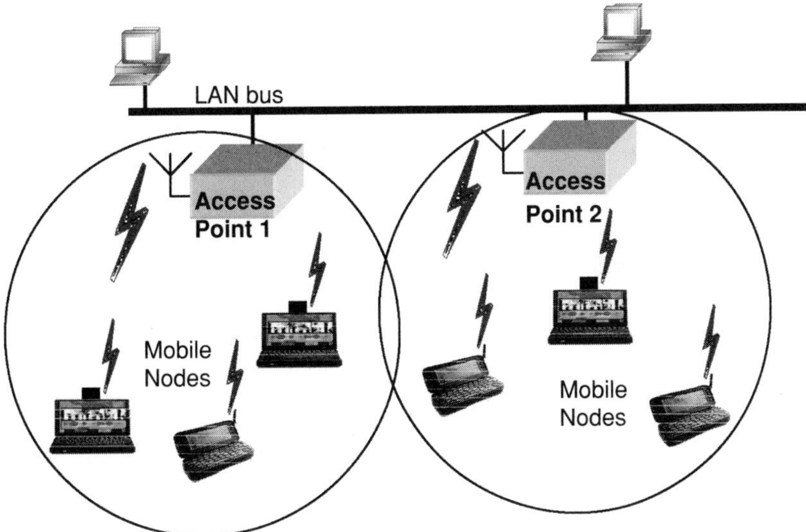

Figure 2: A basic illustration of a WLAN system.

The key research objectives for such a harmonized, heterogeneous 4G network architecture are these:

- Integration of all existing and future communication access systems through a common IPv6 (Internet protocol version 6) gluing mechanism.
- Development of a modular and scalable architecture with well-defined distributed network functionalities.
- Development of effective mobility, resource, and QoS management schemes to offer seamless connectivity and end-to-end QoS between peer end terminals.
- Development of the physical architecture of a QoS-enabled mobile terminal capable of accessing the Internet and real-time services via a multitude of access technologies.
- Offering similar services (subject to network capacity and service policy) in both home and visited networks based on preferences and the service agreement in the user's subscription.

WIRELESS LOCAL AREA NETWORKS

One of the extensions to the wired Ethernet is the WLAN, defined in the IEEE 802.11 standards (Crow et al., 1997; Forouzan, 2003; IEEE 802.11, n.d.). WLAN is becoming very popular by providing mobile Internet access in offices and campus buildings because of the ease in movement of users while connected to the Internet. IEEE 802.11 standards define a set of medium access protocols to extend the wired Ethernet into the wireless domain. The FCC (Federal Communications Commission) in 1985 modified the radio spectrum regulations for unlicensed devices, so that WLAN could operate within the ISM (industrial, scientific, and medical) bands, if the equipment operates with less than 1 Watt of power. The 902-MHz and 5.725-GHz bands can be used only in the United States, whereas the 2.4-GHz band is available globally (Forouzan, 2003). The usage of unlicensed ISM frequency spectrums simplifies deployment of a new WLAN with very few and low-cost equipments. Nomadic Internet access, portable computing, and multihopping, including ad hoc networking, are some of the applications of WLAN technology. Depending on the standard, WLANs can achieve speeds of 2 (IEEE 802.11), 11 (IEEE 802.11b), or 56 (IEEE 802.11a) Mbps in an ideal situation and good wireless channel conditions.

In principle, a WLAN domain can be provided easily through an access point (AP) cabled to the usual wired Ethernet in a LAN system. Therefore, the access point could be considered a router or a hub connecting several end hosts to the LAN system. The only difference here would be that the end host will access the AP through wireless channels rather than cables. Because each AP will give access to several end machines, some type of multiple access control has to be established by the AP to share the wireless channel among all end users. Spread spectrum technology, both direct sequence and frequency hopping, are used for this purpose in the standard.

Each AP in a WLAN system can provide coverage to mobile Internet users in an area of a maximum of 500 meters in radius. Therefore, by having several APs it is possible to establish a cellular-like WLAN. In such a case, cellular-type issues, such as handoff and maximum capacity, will become apparent. Figure 2 shows an illustration of a WLAN with two APs and several end machines. The users of a WLAN system can obtain an IP address through DHCP (dynamic host configuration protocol) similar to a dialup connection or by a fixed IP address provided by their network administrator similar to a desktop user.

Ad Hoc Networking Using Wireless LANs

The technology provided by IEEE 802.11 allows users also to dynamically form a private network without the need for an access point (Toh, 2002). Therefore, it is possible to make a temporary network of computers, for example, during a meeting, where no computer is a server. All users will have the same level of the network hierarchy. The computers in this network can exchange their data files through the WLAN network, which could be isolated from the local wired (wireless network). This is a very basic implementation of a mobile ad hoc network, which

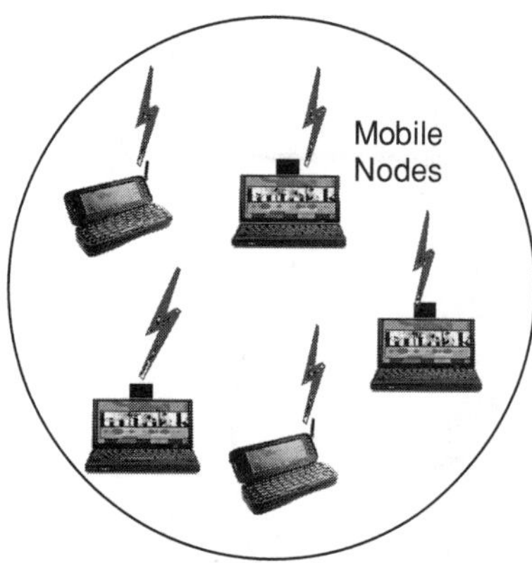

Figure 3: A basic illustration of an ad hoc network.

clearly does not have any infrastructure behind it. The Internet Engineering Task Force (IETF) has a working group called MANET (mobile ad hoc network) that develops the RFCs and standards for this emerging technology. Figure 3 shows an ad hoc network with four mobile computers, which can be compared to the configuration previously given in Figure 2.

IEEE 802.11 Specifications

The IEEE 802.11 standard defines two types of services for the WLAN: basic service set (BSS) and extended service set (ESS). In the BSS, a network of computers is established either with a central base station (or an AP) that can connect the users of the WLAN network to the other parts of the wired network with or without a central base station, which provides an ad hoc network among several users without any access to other parts of the network.

Two or more WLANs that are using the BSS can be connected through any of the IEEE LAN standards, such as Ethernet or token ring, to make an infrastructure of wireless LANs so that the system covers a larger geographical area, similar to the concept of cellular networks. This configuration is the ESS for the IEEE 802.11 standard. The WLAN illustration shown in Figure 2 is this ESS.

Two types of medium access control (MAC) are defined by IEEE 802.11: distributed configuration function (DCF) and point coordination function (PCF). DCF is the basic MAC protocol for WLAN and it is the only access for the ad hoc networking configuration. DCF is a contention access technique, which means that the WLAN users need to compete to get a channel for data transmission. DCF is based on the fundamental Internet MAC protocol CSMA (carrier sense multiple access) with additional collision avoidance (CA), which makes it CSMA/CA (Comer, 1999; Stallings, 2000). One reason for using CSMA/CA in WLAN and not the usual CSMA/CD (CSMA with collision detection) used in wired LANs is that detecting a collision is not as easy for wireless media as it is for wired systems. Also, for wireless channels there is always a chance of getting involved in the *hidden-terminal* problem.

On the wired network, another signal from a user can be detected by measuring the current signal power on the wire. However, in a wireless environment, it is possible that a user is in range of the base station and thus visible by it, but outside the range of another user, who is also seen by the base station. This phenomenon is called the hidden-terminal problem. Therefore, when a user wants to transmit his or her packet over the radio channel, detecting the radio signal power would show only other users presence in his range and not the hidden terminals. If the user transmits a packet and at the same time another hidden-terminal transmits his or her packet, both packets will be lost. The hidden-terminal problem is illustrated in Figure 4.

To avoid the hidden-terminal effect, the wireless MAC needs to add an extra packet exchange before a transmission to make sure that no one else is transmitting at the same time. Therefore, the base station in the WLAN acts as a server that allows a user to transmit or not after a request proposal.

The point coordination function is implemented on top of DCF for time-sensitive transmissions in an infrastructure WLAN architecture. PCF uses centralized, contentionless polling access by utilizing a software package called point coordinator (PC; Oliphant, 1998). PC software

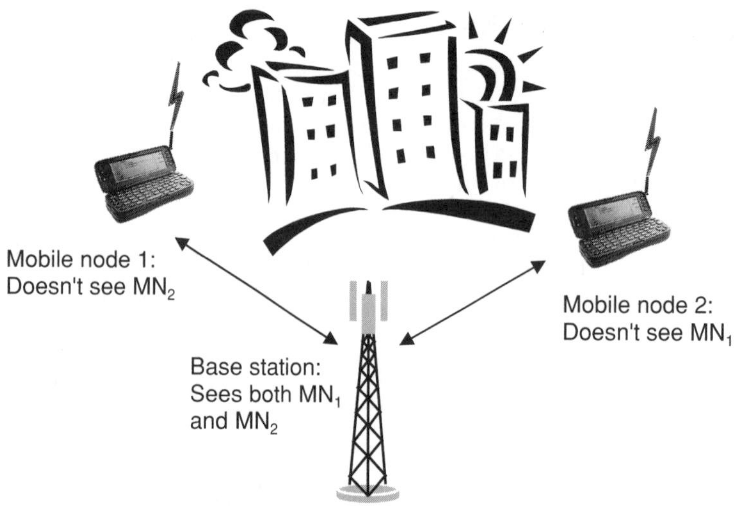

Figure 4: The hidden-terminal effect.

is located at the base station and polls users one after another to avoid any contention for their transmissions. As the PCF runs over the DCF, the sensing process of DCF is performed at the beginning of the PCF polling cycle only once.

IEEE 802.11 defines three types of specifications for the physical layer, based on frequency-hopping spread spectrum (FH-SS), direct sequence spread spectrum (DS-SS), and infrared communications. BPSK (binary phase shift keying) and QPSK (quadrature phase shift keying) were used as the modulation schemes in the DS-SS specifications of WLAN for its early standard, with a bit rate of 1 and 2 Mbps, respectively. Other modulation schemes have been added later in the IEEE 802.11b and IEEE 802.11a standards to allow higher bit rates of 5.5 and 11 Mbps, respectively. In the new standard IEEE 802.11b, the MAC and logical link control (LLC) layer protocols are kept the same as in original IEEE 802.11 and only the physical layer has been modified. For IEEE 802.11b, again DS-SS is utilized. Dynamic rate shifting is also allowed in IEEE 802.11b so that in a noisy environment bit rate could be decreased from 11 Mbps dynamically to 5.5, 2, or 1 Mbps.

WLAN for the Mobile Internet

WLAN is becoming increasingly popular, which makes it an appropriate solution to the future wireless Internet infrastructure. The mobile users' typical demand for information access is characterized by heavy data files and applications, and the WLAN can provide mobility and speed at the same time. Although the mobility feature of the WLAN is usually limited to a few hundred meters for a single AP, as it was discussed in the previous section, it is possible to increase this mobility coverage by deploying a cellular-type ESS wireless LAN.

The use of the wireless LAN as part of a future mobile Internet infrastructure comes for several reasons. In major structured hot spots such as airports and rail stations, the mobile radio infrastructure support of data communications seems to be inadequate and expensive. On one hand, for office users, mobility, simple and low-cost network scalability, and high-speed access are advantages. On the other hand, for home users, advantages of mobility without new wiring and, at the same time, high-speed access are the key issues. WLANs can also provide network flexibility: no infrastructure (ad hoc), a single-cell network (BSS), and a cellular topology (ESS). It also uses the unlicensed spectrum that reduces the end user's cost.

Simple structure and cost-efficient equipment involved in the WLAN can easily extend the fixed Internet into a mobile environment. On the negative side, in WLANs, mobility is supported on only a limited scale and is neither logically feasible nor economically efficient. Also, data integrity, user and network security, and billing methods are not sufficiently supported by the current standards. It is notable that however this can be done (as is ongoing) but this will add the complexity and cost of the network, which will result in negating some of the original advantages of the WLAN.

In a WLAN, traffic is loosely controlled through multiple access schemes, and more traffic requires better traffic management and licensed spectrum, adding the cost and network complexity. Also, it is important to mention that co-located WLANs could interferer with each other easily because they all use the same unlicensed frequency spectrum.

In recent years, it has become clear that although 2.5G/3G cellular systems can provide some infrastructure for mobile Internet service, they are not necessarily sufficient. Some reasons for this statement are that the cellular deployment timetable was not fast enough and their data-rate growth has not followed the rapid increase in new applications' bandwidth demands. In addition, the cellular tariffs are not easily reducible. Cellular radio access will remain the limiting factor in competing speed with wired networks. Moreover, the compatibility and roaming issues between IP networks and cellular systems are not necessarily resolved within cellular-only implementations. This will create a need for hybrid integrated networks.

Hybrid integrated networks imply horizontal communication among existing access technology including cellular, cordless, WLANs, short-range connectivity devices (such as Bluetooth technology), and wired networks. These need to be on a common platform to complement the services of each other and to be connected through a common, flexible, seamless IP-based core network. An advanced media access technology that connects the core network to different access technologies will be also required. The hybrid integrated network will provide global roaming and interworking among different access technologies, both horizontal (intrasystem) and vertical (intersystem) handover. This will also provide a seamless, transparent service negotiation including mobility, security, and quality (data rate, delay, dropping probability, etc.) among heterogeneous networks.

There are both long-term and short-term solutions to the mobile Internet realizations. In the long term, merging IP and cellular networks at core and access sides, reducing dissimilarities in the management of the two systems, and improving radio access technology and global interconnection of cellular and IP networks would be necessary. In the short term, however, other solutions, such as the use of available infrastructures, trying to accommodate simple systems within individual cellular networks, pushing IP-oriented applications into cellular services, gradual decreasing in traffic load from non-IP services, and blending all traffic data into one mixed type, are available. The short-term solutions would be used in order to be prepared for longer-term solutions.

WLAN is currently considered the most accessible network to start with for the short-term solutions. It provides a much higher speed than 3G systems: 11–54 Mbps and greater as compared with 300 Kbps–2 Mbps for the cellular 3G networks. It already has close relations with the legacy wired IP networks (basically it is an extension) and use of unlicensed spectrum and low-cost equipment that may enable low end-user tariffs; it is already deployed in major hot spots and is rapidly expanding and easily deployable anywhere. It has potential to integrate elements in its architecture with cellular 3G systems and the advantage of huge ongoing research toward its standardization, regulation, access control, and security. All these factors make WLAN a real potential starting point for the mobile Internet.

3GPP has already started the initiative for cellular WLAN internetworking architecture, which will be included in the 3GPP release 6 specifications. It is, however, important to mention that some issues still need to be considered:

- How to integrate a highly standardized system such as UMTS with a loosely standardized network, that is, the WLAN.
- How to standardize the WLAN network architecture or its radio interface.
- How to integrate a multiservice network such as UMTS with a mainly IP service network of WLANs.
- Whether the WLAN should be administrated by the UMTS operator or treated just as a foreign network.
- How to ensure user data routing and access to available services.
- Whether to use the UMTS core network or the IP backbone.

3GPP has investigated several integration options in cellular and WLAN networks (3GPP, 2002; 2003). The three main options are to use the WLAN as a peer network, with tight coupling or loose coupling. The peer network is really a kind of inclusion and not integration. In this method, WLAN and cellular systems are independently connected to the IP core network. In tight coupling, the WLAN is accommodated "tightly" inside the cellular core network, which will achieve virtual high speed at the end-user level. In the loose coupling scenario, we take advantage of both IP core network and cellular core network without getting virtual high speed. This would be a better option to get the two network, truly integrated. The loose coupling, however, will obviously have more overall complexity compared with the tight coupling, because signaling and data links are separated from each other and are handled by different networks. Ahmavaara, Haverinen, and Pichna (2003) and Salkintzis, Fors, and Pazhyannur (2002) provide detailed explanations of the three integration techniques and therefore these techniques are not discussed here because of limited space.

TECHNICAL REQUIREMENTS OF MOBILE INTERNET ARCHITECTURE

It is possible to identify several limitations in the contemporary 4G/B3G network proposals available in the literature. These are mainly in the areas of mobility and resource management. A brief discussion of these limitations is categorically given as follows.

Mobility Management

From the several 4G architectures proposed in the literature, we believe that the IST project, mobility and differentiated services in a future IP network (Mobydick; Mobydick, n.d.), and multimedia integrated network by radio access innovation (MIRAI; Inoue et al., 2002) are the few that have dealt with the mobility management issue. We categorize the mobility management limitations of both MIRAI and Mobydick in the following.

Binding Update. Mobydick adopts fast handovers for mobile IPv6 (FMIPv6), which increases the frequency of a BU to a distant HA and a CN after every migration to a new AP. This results in a considerable increase of signaling overhead, especially with a large subscriber base in urban areas. Although MIRAI uses a hierarchical structure, it does not offer faster connectivity or a data transfer path across adjacent domains.

Common Control Signaling. There is no common signaling mechanism that the end terminal can use to perform wireless system discovery and paging in Mobydick. As a result, the end terminal scans all access networks, which imposes significant drain on battery power. On the other hand, MIRAI's overlaid basic access network (BAN) architecture experiences different network conditions such as deep fades and co-channel interference, similar to the radio links within the corresponding access systems. Although BAN is a step toward offering a common control/signaling mechanism, such dynamic link characteristics limit its ability to provide a reliable, bidirectional, low data rate signaling channel.

Address Assignment. The stateless IPv6 autoconfiguration adopted in MIRAI is unreliable without duplicate address detection (DAD). However, DAD itself is not easily feasible in a wireless environment because of the absence of centralized infrastructure to detect terminals with duplicate addresses. Furthermore, it contributes toward increasing signaling load and handover latency.

Location Management. Mobydick is equipped with interfaces for wideband CDMA (UMTS–TDD), WLAN (802.11b), and Ethernet. As such, new technologies cannot be introduced without hardware changes. MIRAI on the other hand has a reconfigurable software-defined radio (SDR)-based end terminal that uses a global positioning system (GPS) receiver for location management. However, GPS cannot operate effectively in indoor environments of steel or concrete and also under thick foliage, such as in parks.

Resource Management

Resource management requires allocation/deallocation of resources to sustain a communication session. The allocation/deallocation is carried out within the serving domain and along the communication path between peer end terminals, before and during a session. Many resource management schemes have been proposed in literature that do not offer a truly global end-to-end scheme. For example, Nanda and Simmonds (2001) propose a centralized bandwidth broker (BB) for each domain that considers the profile of each piece of traffic encountered in the network and that supports dynamic allocations. However, this centralized approach suffers from a single point of failure, the BB. In addition, it is not stated how the ingress routers, egress routers, and BBs of the intradomain and interdomain are identified. Other schemes such as the

Mobydick project (Marques et al., 2003) propose a QoS broker, based on a hierarchical architecture. Their architecture, however, considers centralized QoS brokers shared across different domains, which increases the processing load on the QoS broker and also makes it a single point of failure.

The SMART/MIRAI (Havinga, Smit, Wu, & Vognild, 2001) project suggests that differentiated flows should use heterogeneous networks based on the QoS requirements, but does not propose any resource management scheme in this regard.

QoS Management During Handover

The QoS management schemes proposed in the literature either waste valuable resources by overprovisioning bandwidth or unfairly differentiating between real-time and non–real-time services. For example, the preemptive priority handover scheme of reserving bandwidth a priori to handover gives precedence to real-time traffic over non–real-time traffic (Lo & Lin, 1998). If enough resources are not available, then the non–real-time traffic may be slowed in comparison with the real-time traffic. Also, the handover requests get queued if all the reserved handoff channels are in use. MRSVP (a reservation protocol for an integrated services packet network with mobile hosts), proposed by Talukdar, Badrinath, and Acharaya (2001) is not scalable and wastes scarce resources by reserving bandwidth on different base stations even though the mobile host uses only one of the base stations.

The literature review has shown that algorithms can be devised to reduce the call-dropping probability but these do not ensure maintenance of QoS during handover, that is, if the mobile terminal (MT) moves from one cell area to another (Dingankar et al., n.d.). Ramnathan et al. (1999) have devised schemes that ensure some sort of reservation of bandwidth a priori to handover. These schemes are based on providing priority to handover calls rather than to local connections. The different strategies possible are the following:

1. ***Fixed strategy:*** Reserving a certain percentage of the bandwidth for handover requests.
2. ***Steady strategy:*** The base station is assumed to be aware of the steady fraction of connection requests for each traffic class. This fraction may be determined from historic traffic information available to the base station.
3. ***Dynamic strategy:*** In this strategy, each base station periodically queries neighboring base stations and computes an estimate of the rate at which handover connection requests are expected to arrive in the next update period. This estimate is derived from known stochastic of the connection duration times, cell residence times, and mobility patterns.

These strategies could be augmented with a preemptive priority handover scheme (Lo & Lin, 1998). In this scheme the real-time traffic is given precedence over non–real-time traffic. First, according to this scheme the handover requests get queued if all the reserved handoff channels are in use. Second, if enough resources are not available, then the non–real-time traffic may be slowed in comparison with the real-time traffic.

An approach taken by the MIND project (Mobile IP-based Network Developments; http://www.ist-mind.org) is to focus on the mobile nodes' architecture to ensure some QoS during the handover process (Ruiz et al., n.d.).

The overall aim of the MIND project is to facilitate the rapid creation of broadband multimedia services and applications that are fully supported when accessed by future mobile users from a wide range of wireless access technologies. MIND is a follow-up to the BRAIN (Broadband Radio Access for IP-based Networks) project. This project is partially funded by the European Commission in the framework of the IST Program.

Talukdar et al. (2001) developed a resource reservation protocol for an integrated services network with mobile hosts termed mobile RSVP (MRSVP). The idea behind MRSVP is to carry out advanced reservation of resources in the network to the most likely base stations with which the mobile host is likely to have handover sessions. Stochastic predictive algorithms predict these base stations. The advanced reservations are carried out via a proxy node that receives the reservation requests from all the mobile nodes in a subnet. The reservation requests are then channeled via the proxy nodes to the base stations in the subnet.

The main drawback of the MRSVP scheme is that bandwidth will be reserved for the same mobile host on different base stations, although the mobile host will be using only one of the base stations. This scheme thus locks up the resource required by a mobile host on multiple base stations.

Just like RSVP, MRSVP is also not scalable, and the scalability would be limited based on the number of mobile hosts that require signaling for resource reservation and also on the number of available channels and network topology.

INTERNETWORKING OF THE HETEROGENEOUS WIRELESS INTERNET

Internetworking Through IPv6

It is widely accepted that the next-generation heterogeneous network, as shown in Figure 5, will be all IP-based (see, for example, Berezdivin et al., 2002). IP version 6 (IPv6) is the promising candidate for the next-generation networks (Deering et al., 1998). The IPv6-based underlying transport mechanism will glue the heterogeneous networks together. The reasons for using IPv6 are enumerated:

- The address space of IPv4 is getting scarce and will not be able to cope with the expected number of mobile devices (such as cars, home appliances, and embedded electronics) in the future. IPv6 with its 128-bit address size will thus be required.
- IPv6 offers enhanced mobility support because of hierarchical addressing.
- IPv6 provides authentication and encryption that is enabled by IPsec and introduced through the extension headers.

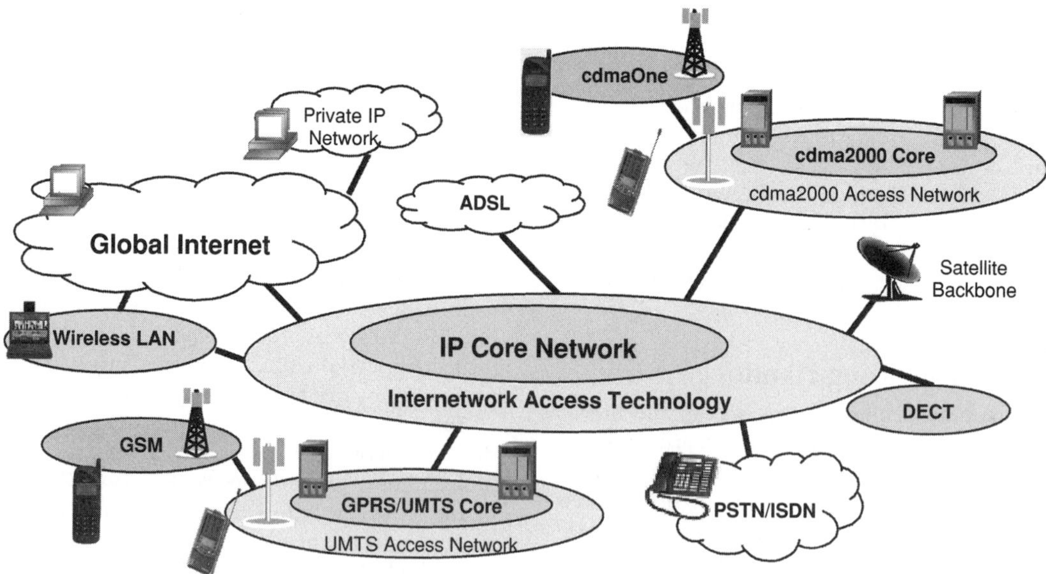

Figure 5: Overview of the next-generation heterogeneous network.

- IPv6 offers efficient packet processing in the routers because of fixed header size.
- IPv6 alleviates the ease in introducing existing Internet applications.

Therefore, the modular architecture of a 4G network is expected to have IPv6 as the dominant interworking layer. Unlike the TCP/IP protocol stack, where the adjacent layers solve particular problems, abide by stringent independent rules, and provide services to the upper layer, there will be cross-layer coordination (Carneiro et al., 2004) among different layers within the next-generation architecture. Such coordination will facilitate the network configuration by taking into consideration the access-specific information, available resources, and subscriber profile. For example, a video application, with a priori knowledge of the radio access network and user preferences, may adaptively vary the video rate as link quality deteriorates. Similarly, in the case of a highly mobile subscriber, the network may ascertain, by considering the service policy in the subscriber profile, whether the current resources available can support the ongoing session or whether a QoS renegotiation is required.

Technical Issues with Internetworking

Specification of an internetworking open architecture that enables seamless integration of mobile telephony and Internet services, independent of access technologies, requires implementation of novel mobility, resource, and QoS management schemes. Smooth interaction among these three schemes is essential for maintaining seamless connectivity and end-to-end QoS between peer end terminals. The key attributes of these schemes are given here:

1. Mobility management involves managing two forms of mobility.
   A) Terminal mobility, where the MT moves within and across network domains while continuing to receive access to telecommunication services without any data packet loss and with minimum handover delay (the time required to undergo successful handover).
   B) Personal mobility, where the subscriber obtains services in a transparent manner within any network and on any terminal, on the basis of subscriber identification and the network's ability to provide the requested services.
2. Resource management is the provision of adequate resources (allocation and deallocation) within both access and core network to support communication sessions. It involves
   A) The capability to offer services to roaming subscribers similar to their home network environments (subject to visited network capability and services) upon subscriber authentication.
   B) The management of local resources independent of roaming subscribers' home networks.
   C) The allocation of adequate resources required by end terminal applications before the commencement of a communication session and possible renegotiation during the session.
3. QoS management, which ensures QoS support to a wide range of services over dynamic link conditions. It involves these elements:
   A) The capability to set up a data path and negotiate QoS between peer end terminals at the commencement of a session and dynamic renegotiation to sustain data transfer during the session. Some of the QoS parameters that influence the negotiation include available bandwidth, data rate, user preferences, end terminal capacity, and application requirements.
   B) Distributed architecture that supports differentiated services, as per the user's service policy and type of subscription.

Because such schemes are imperative to the successful development and implementation of a modular 4G network

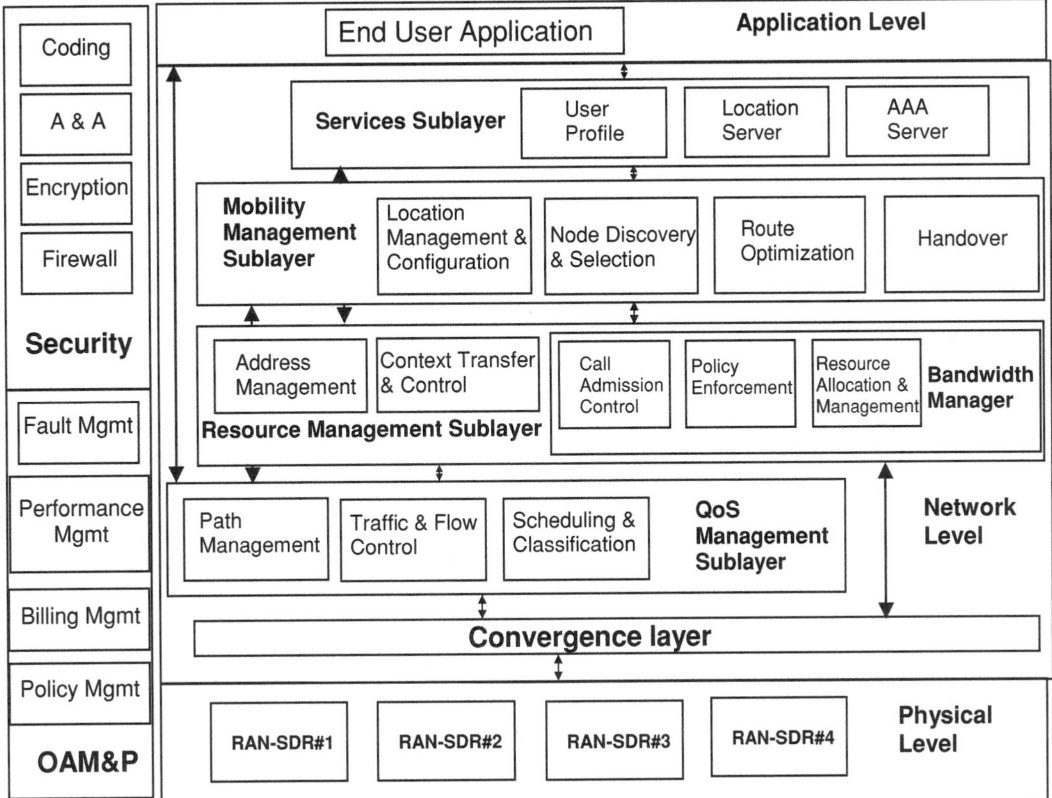

Figure 6: Proposed layered and modular 4G/B3G network architecture.

architecture, key issues considered in designing these schemes are the following:

1. Mobility management:
   - How to address both fast- and slow-moving subscribers?
   - How to handle intra-access router, interaccess router, and interdomain handovers that encompass both horizontal and vertical handovers?
   - How to solve the need for the mobile terminal to scan all possible access technologies for wireless system discovery with limited battery power?
   - How to reduce the signaling load when the mobile terminal experiences frequent handover across smaller cells?
2. Resource management:
   - How to ensure that resources, as required by the end terminal application, can be offered between peer end terminals?
   - How to make sure that resource allocation takes into consideration current network conditions?
   - How to provide a secure communication path between neighboring resource management entities, independent of the actual data communication path?
3. QoS management:
   - How to ensure end-to-end QoS between peer end terminals?
   - How to maintain QoS for an ongoing application session with degradation of link quality?
   - How to offer differentiated services across access and core networks based on subscriber profiles and service policies?

Layer Functionalities

Figure 6 depicts the proposed layered/level approach for the 4G/B3G network architecture shown in Figure 5. The functionalities provided by each layer and its modules are briefly described here.

Application. This layer comprises the third-party applications provided to the subscribers. Third party refers to applications provided by someone independent of the network operator. To enhance the service quality, value-added services can also be introduced with or without the subscriber's knowledge (a single subscription), as shown in the business model (MWIF, 2001) of Figure 7.

Network. This layer/level provides service control and mechanisms essential for the smooth operation of the

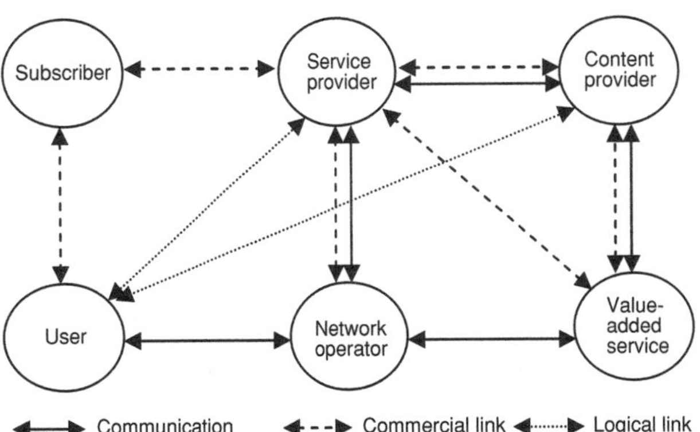

Figure 7: The business model.

network architecture. Acting as the linchpin, this layer provides management of services and dynamic cross-layer coordination between different layers to facilitate enhanced operation. Different sublayers comprising the network-layer functionality are listed:

- *Services sublayer.* The user profile, location server, and AAA server within this sublayer provide the repository for user preferences, dynamic information associated with the subscribers, terminal and service mobility, subscriber identity authentication, and charging information associated with the resource usage during user activity and so forth. The repositories are located both in the home network and the visited network.
- *Mobility management sublayer.* This sublayer consists of functions to enable subscribers with the ability to move among IP subnetworks, that is, to support roaming and handover control. This entity supports location update of a dormant or roaming subscriber, wireless system discovery and selection to initiate and sustain a communication session, optimization of the routing path between peer end terminals, seamless mobility with no packet loss, and minimum handover latency. This sublayer is primarily located within the serving domain to reduce signaling overhead during the handover period.
- *Resource management sublayer.* This sublayer manages IP addresses of roaming and home subscribers, initiates fast context transfer (e.g., user profile and QoS parameters) between access networks as the subscriber changes its point of attachment, and controls the resources within the domain through the bandwidth manager. Distributed throughout the serving domain, the bandwidth manager offers functionality regarding new call admission and support of existing sessions, session and service enforcement policy (e.g., expected QoS, valid times, routes), and allocation and deallocation of resources before and after a session between peer end terminals. This sublayer is located in home, visited, and all intermediate networks.
- *QoS management sublayer.* This sublayer offers end-to-end QoS service between peer end terminals through optimal path establishment before the commencement of a session and possible rerouting owing to link quality degradation. This can also be realized through effective traffic and flow control to eliminate bottlenecks, especially in access networks, and to offer differentiated services for different types of subscription and network policies. This sublayer is located in home, visited, and all intermediate networks.

Physical. This layer consists of core network and heterogeneous access networks. Reconfigurable SDR-based end terminals are required to support multimode services across a wide range of radio access networks (RANs).

The convergence layer allows access-independent network functionalities in the underlying network to communicate via different access technologies in a transparent manner, hiding access-specific signaling requirements within the layered architecture.

Finally, the security and OAM&P layer, spanning the entire layered architecture, involves the following functionalities:

- Assurance of authorized use of network resources and services by subscribers, and confidentiality and nonrepudiation of services and resources.
- Maintenance of all three layers (e.g., application, network, physical) during the life span of a communication session.
- Fault management when experiencing sudden breakdown of a link or a functional entity.
- Performance management to ensure user-requested QoS can be supported.
- Billing management in accordance with the real-time and non–real-time resource utilization during subscriber activity.
- Policy management to enforce functionality conforming to service policy and subscriber preferences.

Message Interfaces Between Layers

In next-generation mobile networks there must be cross-layer coordination among different entities within the architecture. Given here is a list of message interfaces among the functional entities to facilitate such cross-layer coordination:

- Wireless system discovery within the mobility management scheme requires BAN to provide a list of access networks and their associated QoS parameters capable of supporting end-terminal applications. Such a list is available through the interaction of application layer, QoS management sublayer, resource management sublayer, and mobility management sublayer.
- To support QoS-enabled application, direct communication between application layer and QoS sublayer are essential, such as adaptively varying the application rate to compensate for the link quality degradation.
- Mobility management involves location update, wireless system discovery, and so forth. Because services offered by the visited network depend on service policy and subscriber profiles, and because subscriber profiles are usually located at the serving domain repositories, signaling between the mobility management sublayer and the services sublayer is essential. For similar reasons, signaling between the services sublayer with resource management and the QoS management sublayer is necessary.
- Mobility management further requires a list of access technologies capable of supporting the end-terminal application. Such a list, along with the available resources, is available only from the resource management sublayer. Therefore, interaction between the mobility management sublayer and the resource management sublayer is essential.
- Furthermore, with vertical handover, it is possible that the requested application QoS cannot be supported by the underlying network. Therefore, interaction between mobility management and QoS management sublayers must take place to support QoS renegotiation between peer end terminals.

- Accounting information gathered from resources used, QoS provided, and time and duration of provision of network resources will be provided to the service management functions (OAM&P).
- Because the technology-specific RANs reside within the physical layer, the distributed functional elements within the network layer require a convergence layer to hide the underlying network from access-specific signaling and to communicate via diverse RANs.

Novel augmentations in mobility and resource management schemes incorporated in our layered 4G/B3G architecture aim to provide superior services as compared to other network architectures. A brief description of these augmentations is given in the following section.

AUGMENTATED MOBILITY, RESOURCE, AND QoS MANAGEMENT

Mobility Management

Two forms of mobility are encountered during seamless connectivity across heterogeneous networks, namely macromobility and micromobility. Macromobility is defined as mobility across different subnetworks (between the home network and the visited network), whereas micromobility refers to mobility across different APs within the same subnetwork (within the home network or the visited network). Although there is no exact solution to the mobility problem in a heterogeneous environment, well-established solutions for the wired Internet may be taken as guidelines.

Mobile IP (Johnson et al., 2003; Perkins, 1996) is a solution proposed in the wired Internet to resolve the macromobility problem. With Mobile IP, roaming subscribers enjoy Internet connectivity in a transparent manner without any manual configuration. In a visited network, a roaming host is required to register with its HA to access the Internet. While attaching to the foreign network to support a call, the host acquires a local care-of address (CoA) through either stateless or stateful autoconfiguration and performs a triangular route optimization (Johnson et al., 1998) to the CN. Packets addressed to the mobile host are delivered using regular IP routing to the CoA, thereby offering a transparent, simple, and scalable global mobility scheme.

Even though network support for seamless mobility was not considered when Mobile IP was originally developed, it finds applicability in the wireless environment through the endeavors of the Mobile IP Working Group (WG). In a wireless environment an MT frequently changes its point of attachment, that is, performs handovers to initiate or continue communication sessions with other nodes in the network (known as micromobility). Because a local CoA must be obtained and communicated to the HA and the CN after every migration, the significant latency introduced by Mobile IP causes considerable packet loss during the handover period (especially if the home and foreign network are far apart), rendering real-time data transfer useless until the CN is notified of the new CoA. The micromobility handover scenario is further aggravated with varying link conditions, higher subscriber mobility, and scarcity of resources.

With future networks composed of overlapping heterogeneous access networks glued together by a common IP core and nonproprietary protocols, the issues of both macromobility and micromobility need to be addressed. With hundreds of millions of wireless subscribers accessing the network in the future, service providers will have to resolve these issues in order to deliver quality service, minimize signaling, and scale to support the huge subscriber base. Hence, an effective mobility management scheme and reconfigurable MTs will be required to allow the 4G network architecture to provide real-time multimedia services with as little disruption as possible to the ongoing sessions.

We first discuss the mobility management in the two significant 4G architectures—Mobydick and MIRAI—and then we discuss our proposed mobility management scheme. We then summarize the key differentiators between our mobility management scheme and that of Mobydick and MIRAI.

Mobydick Mobility Management

The IST Mobydick proposed architecture offers an end-to-end QoS and seamless mobility across heterogeneous networks. Mobile end terminals, equipped with interfaces of W-CDMA (UMTS–TDD), WLAN (802.11b), and Ethernet, access the Internet through access routers (ARs) that provide interfaces between wireless access network and the wired core network. The network management entities such as QoS brokers, AAAC servers, and paging agents are located in the fixed core network.

Access to services across various administrative domains and different access technologies is provided according to the subscriber preferences stored in the subscriber profile at the home network. Seamless mobility and fast handover are provided through FMIPv6. However, FMIPv6 fails to eliminate handover latency completely. In addition, after every successful handover and after attaching to the new AR, the MT is required to send BU to both the HA and the CN. With highly mobile subscribers roaming across smaller cells that offer greater bandwidth and faster links, such BU results in considerable signaling load, especially with large subscriber bases in urban areas.

Because future networks will consist of overlapping heterogeneous networks, the MT is required to scan all terminal interfaces to find out available resources, determine whether a handover is imminent, select the target AR, and initiate a handover request to the current serving AR. The processing power required to listen to all broadcasts over different access technologies and select target AR after gathering required Layer 2 information imposes a considerable drain on the battery power. With small handheld terminals available in the market and drive toward increasingly miniaturized handsets, already limited battery power will be further compromised. It will be beneficial to have an energy-saving flexible system that offers minimal changes to the existing technologies through a common mechanism. However, such a common mechanism to provide Layer 2 information regarding all available access technologies within the radio coverage area is presently

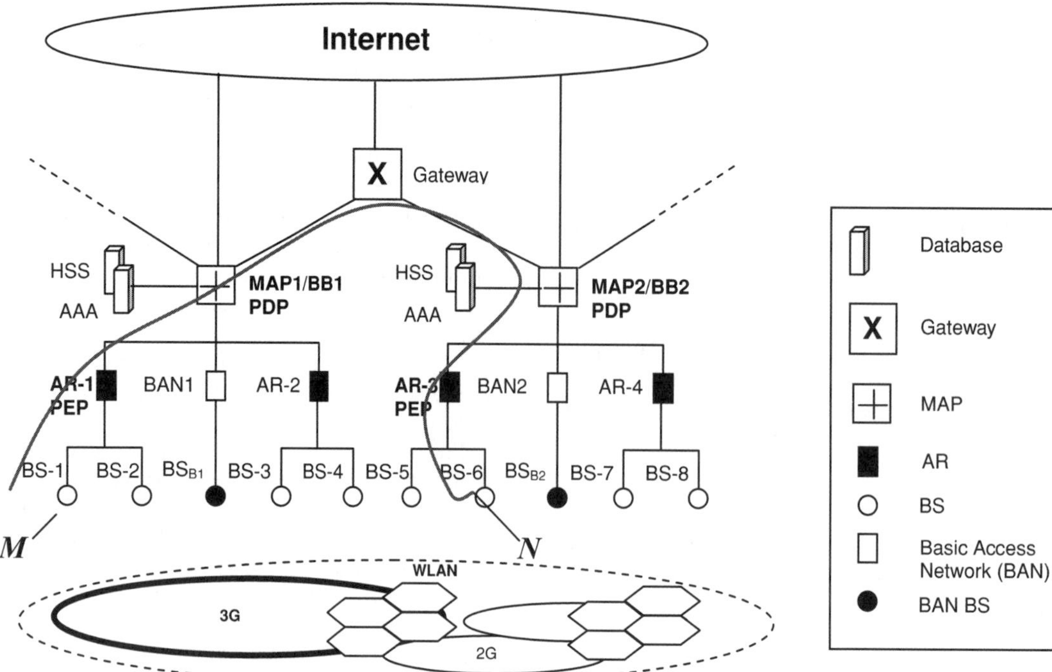

Figure 8: Hierarchical mobility management architecture.

absent in the Mobydick architecture. This common signaling mechanism will be essentially a low-bandwidth, low-cost dedicated network that provides paging, wireless system discovery, and assistance with mobility management. Currently these services are carried out inside the core and the access network in Mobydick architecture, thereby imposing additions to the already scarce radio resources of the access networks.

MIRAI Mobility Management

The MIRAI uses a hierarchical structure composed of base stations (BSs), ARs within the common core network (CCN), and a gateway router (GR) connected directly to the Internet. The signaling agent (SA), the key element in the architecture, is located on the same level as the ARs and maintains two databases, namely the location database (LDB) and resource database (RDB), for controlling the data transmission process within the domain. The BAN provides paging, wireless system discovery, and mobility management for the multiservice user terminal (MUT) through a common control and signaling channel.

The necessity of a common mechanism enveloping all access technologies to support such services is missing in the Mobydick project, whereas it has been addressed in the MIRAI architecture. This dedicated signaling network overlays the existing 2G cellular system, 3G cellular system, and WLANs to minimize the change to these systems. BSs belonging to this dedicated network and managed by the signaling gateway (SG) cover the whole geographical region of a domain. The entire MIRAI architecture is built around the BAN structure and the availability of a bidirectional, low-data-rate, reliable common control and signaling channel. However, with overlay BAN architecture, this low-data-rate channel will experience similar dynamic characteristics (e.g., deep fades, co-channel interference, and small SNR) as the radio links within these systems, rendering control data transmission unreliable.

During initial registration, a roaming MUT determines its exact location using a GPS receiver embedded in the terminal and sends the information (e.g., latitude, longitude, altitude) to the network via the BAN to facilitate location management and service optimization. However, GPS signaling is severely undermined within indoor environments or by the presence of thick foliage. Moreover, the MUT generates local CoA through stateless IPv6 autoconfiguration (from the domain subnet prefix broadcast over the BAN system). Usually the generation of a local CoA by stateless IPv6 autoconfiguration from subnet prefix ID is accompanied by DAD to determine the uniqueness of the CoA. It is extremely difficult to run DAD in a wireless environment, and without DAD the generated CoA runs the risk of being a duplicate within the domain, causing service disruption. Lastly MIRAI suffers from the absence of a definitive QoS-enabled MUT terminal with cross-layer coordination and an effective QoS and resource management scheme.

Proposed Mobility Management Scheme

An underlying hierarchical structure, as shown in Figure 8, is proposed to facilitate seamless mobility across heterogeneous networks. Fast handover for hierarchical mobile IPv6 (F-HMIPv6; Jung et al., 2004) is incorporated as the micromobility scheme within the hierarchical system, unlike Mobydick, which uses FMIPv6. Jung et al. (2004) state that F-HMIPv6 considerably reduces the handover latency even more than FMIPv6.

Within the hierarchical architecture, the lowermost tier is formed by BSs that are controlled by ARs. Unlike the overlaid BAN architecture in MIRAI, our mobility management scheme utilizes a *dedicated control and signaling* BAN system, independent from the existing heterogeneous access networks. This system provides (a) wireless system discovery and paging services, (b) location management, (c) support for vertical handover, and (d) simplicity and energy-reserving capability. All overlapping heterogeneous networks within the domain access the Internet through the mobility anchor point (MAP). The gateway (GW) connects multiple MAPs to offer faster connectivity and data transfer during interdomain handovers. Every domain is maintained by an administrative body and a service agreement exists among different access technology providers.

A roaming MT is identified by three IP addresses: (a) MT's home address, (b) MAP's IP address or regional care-of-address (RCoA), and (c) local CoA (LCoA) assigned by DHCPv6-enabled AR (every AR is allocated a pool of IPv6 addresses). The MAP, ARs, and BAN communicate among themselves through several Layer 2 signaling protocols, for example, PPP and L2TP, to formulate a list of resources offered by these heterogeneous access networks. The BAN periodically broadcasts this list of available access technologies within the coverage area on its reliable low-data-rate channel. This list includes Layer 2 ID of BSs, their associated AR IP addresses, and a limited number of QoS parameters, for example, supported data rate and video coding rate. If the list is too long to be accommodated in a single packet, it may be fragmented across smaller packets.

Similar to MIRAI, our proposed architecture utilizes micromobility protocols such as cellular IP (Campbell et al., 1999, 2000) and HAWAII (Ramjee et al., 2002) to support passive connectivity and paging. The home subscriber server (HSS) stores user profiles and service policy as repositories, whereas the AAA server stores authentication and accounting information. Both of these servers are located at MAP.

During the registration process, every node en route to the MAP caches (a) soft-state information of the LCoA of the MT and (b) interface ID over which the registration request packet is received. After initial registration, every subsequent data packet to and from the MT refreshes the routing path to the MAP and reduces the need for paging an MT with a recent data session history within a certain time-out period. The MT configured with LCoA listens to periodic broadcast of AR identification after the registration process, even in the sleep mode. This allows the MT to roam greater distances without initiating data sessions. Because the LCoA is valid only within the coverage area of a serving AR, if the MT roams into the coverage area of another AR then it must be configured with a new LCoA.

During inter-AR handover, in addition to context transfer (e.g., current session QoS parameters and video coding rate) between old and new ARs, the MAP bicasts data packets to both of these ARs. This consequently makes the change of LCoA and local handover process transparent from the distant HA and CN. During interdomain handover, the GW bicasts data packets to both the old MAP and the new MAP. As such, the GW allows faster connectivity across domains and hides the frequent interdomain handovers experienced by subscribers in fast-moving vehicles. A new BU to the HA and the CN is required only when there is an interdomain handover or a dormant MT roams into a new domain.

In our mobility architecture three types of handovers are possible: inter-BS, inter-AR, and inter-MAP. Inter-AR and inter-MAP handovers are the most challenging of the three. Figure 9 summarizes the signaling process required during the inter-MAP handover as part of the mobility management scheme in Figure 8. Let us assume that a roaming terminal "M" linked to AR2 has an ongoing session with a terminal "N" linked to AR3 in a different domain. As the MT leaves its serving domain, it initiates an inter-MAP handover. The complete inter-MAP handover process includes (a) RAN list broadcast and reply to ascertain availability, (b) handover trigger and request by MT, (c) resource negotiation by GW with MAP2, AR3 pair in the target domain, (d) bicasting of data packets to both MAP1 and MAP2 by GW, and (e) MT registration with AR3 to reestablish the data session. GW then sends a request to MAP1 to release the connection. In the absence of such a request, a time-out period applies. The trace of this inter-MAP handover is shown by the solid line in Figure 8.

Resource Management

A distributed BB architecture is proposed inside the domain where each router is capable of becoming a BB (although MAP seems to be the prime candidate to take on the role of a BB). Elected through an election process, for example, based on time online or edge routers, the primary BB is shadowed by a backup BB in case the primary BB were to fail. The functional elements of the BB include service level agreement (SLA) and service level specifications (SLS), neighboring BB database, admission control service (ACS), authentication and authorization, policy decision point (PDP), and so forth. The routers at the edge of the domain identify/deduce themselves to be the edge routers based on the hierarchical source address obtained from their neighboring routers during an OSPF link-state database build-up. Interdomain BB identification for end-to-end QoS admission control is carried out through interactions among edge routers. RSVP is used at the network edges with DiffServ used in the core network for fixed network connections. Furthermore, a subnetwork bandwidth manager (SBM) will be used at the AR so as to provide admission control for wireless connections.

Figure 8 also shows our resource management procedure during the setup of an interdomain communication session. The domains are DiffServ enabled and traffic is classified at the edge routers, in this case AR1 to AR4, and assigned to different behavior aggregates. Each behavior aggregate is identified by DSCP bits. Let us assume that a mobile unit "M" linked to BS4 needs to communicate with a peer mobile unit "N" linked to BS6. The BB1 will first verify with an AAA server if the mobile user "M" has permission to access the resources in its domain and if the request is for an intradomain or interdomain destination. In case of an interdomain request, the BB1 will develop a map of neighboring BBs that control different networks by constructing forwarding tables as in OSPF. The BB will

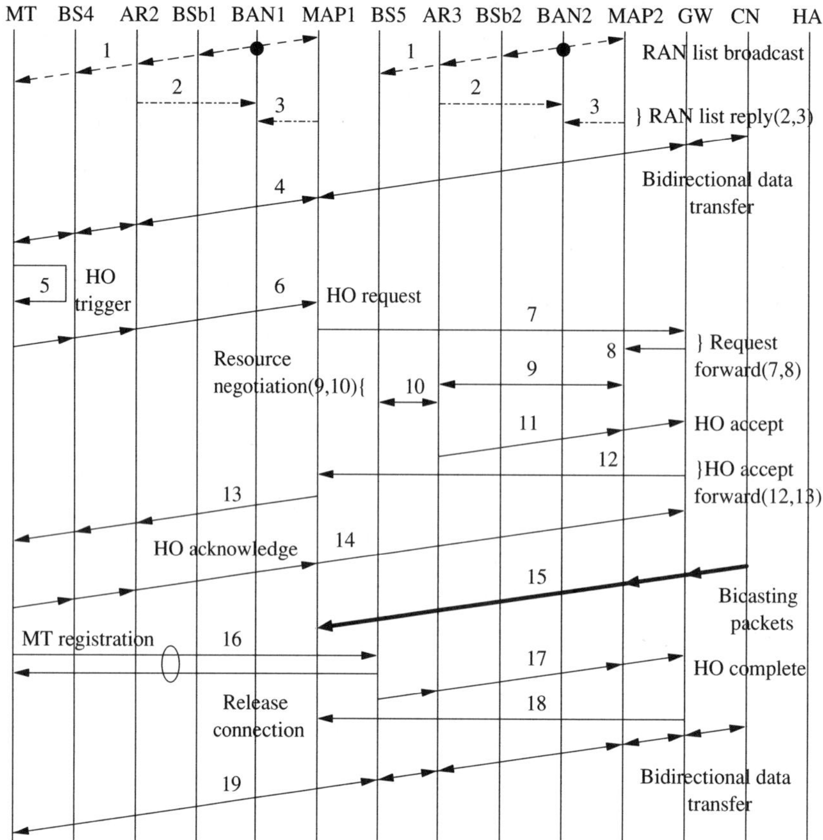

Figure 9: Bounce diagram for handover of MT "M" from BS4 to BS5 between different MAP domains (MAP1 to MAP2).

also incorporate a PDP to carry out admission control in its domain, based on prior administrative/dynamic policies. In a simple case, this will involve checking for the resource availability at the edge routers, that is, AR1–AR2 for the domain of MAP1. The BB1 will coordinate with the BB2 to determine (a) if the destination exists within BB2's domain and (b) if resources are available in its domain to support the traffic from "M" to "N." If not, BB2 will be able to negotiate with BB1 regarding "N's requirements." In case there are several BBs in between the source and destination, then coordination for resources will have to be carried out with each of the intermittent BBs. If the request for resources from BB2 is successful, then policy enforcement point (PEP) implemented in the AR will police the user "M" and verify "M" does not exceed the amount of resources it is paying for. The AR2 may also inform the AAA server of usage by the user "M," which is especially important in the case of prepaid subscribers. For this discussion, the trace of BB operation is shown by the broken line in Figure 8.

Quality of Service

QoS means the ability of the network to support an application irrespective of network conditions. This means that the application works satisfactorily irrespective of the changes that may occur on the network. A good tutorial on QoS can be found in Chalmers and Sloman (1999). The QoS is generally characterized by performance parameters:

- Delay (latency) of packet transfer
- Delay variation or jitter (time differences among the arrivals of packets on the same path)
- Throughput (rate at which the packets transit through a network)
- Packet loss (percentage of packets dropped or lost while transiting through a network)

The legacy IP infrastructure of the Internet was designed to offer best-effort service; that is, all network traffic is created equal and the service is based on availability rather than guarantees.

A common way by which network providers try to offer QoS is by bandwidth overprovisioning. However, such a method cannot cope with the rapidly increasing growth of the Internet as it requires too much of bandwidth reservation of the scarce communications resources. As such, initiatives have been taken by the IETF to offer degrees of IP-based QoS. Two popular methods proposed by WGs within the IETF to offer QoS are integrated services (IntServ) and differentiated services (DiffServ). RSVP protocol (Braden et al., 1997) is proposed by the IntServ WG, which essentially is a receiver-oriented reservation protocol. The receiver-oriented nature of the protocol allows support of diverse machine types on the Internet.

RSVP relies on the fact each router carrying the flow between the source and destination will maintain the state information of the reservation request. However, because there are several flows in a large network, the RSVP protocol results in a state explosion in the routers. As such, RSVP is not sufficiently scalable.

In contrast, the DiffServ protocol proposed by IETF is scalable because differentiation of service is offered for different traffic types by setting appropriate bits in the type of service (TOS) field of each packet. The TOS field is formed of a six-bit DiffServ code point (DSCP) field and two currently unused bits of each packet. The six bits of the DSCP subfield offer 64 unique service levels, which offer a very high level of traffic granularity. The IPv6 header has native support for DiffServ classification in the DSCP.

The DSCP corresponds to a per-hop behavior (PHB) that defines the relative priority and QoS parameters that a packet should be given by each node in a DiffServ domain. The PHBs have been standardized by the DiffServ WG based on the service type required. These are listed here:

- Best-effort PHB: For best-effort service.
- Expedited forwarding (EF-PHB): This is also referred to as premium service and is used to deliver guaranteed amount of bandwidth, while minimizing delay and packet loss. In effect it offers a virtual leased-line ToS.
- Assured forwarding (AF-PHB): This defines a class of service that is better than best effort but lower than that of EF. Within AF there are four different subclasses based on the drop precedence of the packet. IETF RFC 2597 describes the method for implementing the Olympic service model of AF—bronze, silver, and gold classes. Packets in gold class are forwarded ahead of the silver and bronze class. Silver class packets are forwarded ahead of the bronze class.

An important aspect of managing different traffic classes is traffic conditioning. The traffic conditioning in the DiffServ architecture offers

- Enforcement of SLAs among different domains.
- Classification of the traffic based on DSCP.
- Policing and modification of the traffic distribution characteristics in the network elements if required.
- A scheduling mechanism to manage the different class-type traffic in the routers. This is mainly done through queue management techniques such as weighted fair queuing and random early detection.

As such, no state information needs to be maintained at each router between the source and destination. Furthermore, faster processing can be achieved by aggregating the similar traffic-type flows and representing the aggregated flow by unique DSCP bits.

QoS-Enabled Handover

QoS-enabled handover can be enhanced by the use of an umbrella cell. Instead of making prior reservations by means of MRSVP, the MT could establish a link with the more-resourced umbrella cell. The MT may use the umbrella cell until either resource can be reserved with a new base station or until a set timer value expires. If the handoff timer value expires, the MT may be denied service from the new BS, or the new BS may use the tariff paid by the MT as a criteria to degrade some other MTs service in the local cell and provide the resulting resources to this new MT that wants to handoff.

Alternatively, during handover an Internet2-based mechanism known as alternative best-effort (ABE) service (Teitelbaum, n.d.) can be adopted to differentiate the best-effort service class into multiple "different but equal" BES classes that trade for delay or loss. In cases where a moderately loaded network is required to support applications with stringent real-time constraints such as interactive audio, ABE service will allow applications to choose between receiving lower end-to-end delay or receiving more overall throughput. A MT may use the ABE service during the handover period until resources are found and reserved in the new cell. This means that when a MT performs the handover algorithm it will consider all services to be best effort. It then will use the ABE-based algorithm to provide low latency or low throughput to services based on service requirements.

MOBILE TERMINAL ARCHITECTURE

The mobile terminal market is inundated with access-specific handheld terminals over a wide range of brands from various manufacturers. With a multitude of heterogeneous access networks glued together through a common mechanism, terminals built for specific systems (e.g., cellular, wired, and WLAN) will prove inadequate to support seamless mobility. Furthermore, constant evolution of link-layer standards and incompatibility of access technologies in different countries prohibit

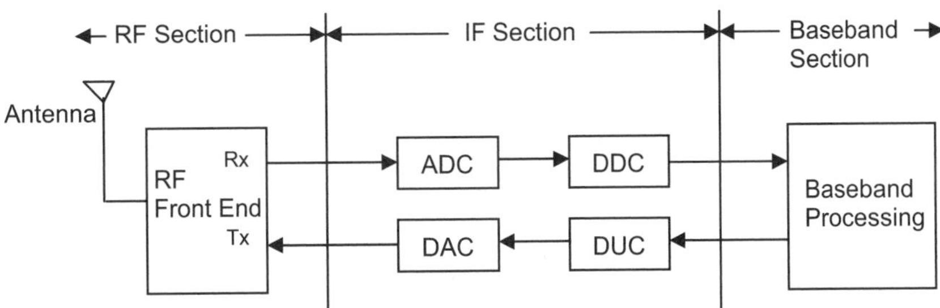

Figure 10: Block diagram of a traditional digital transceiver.

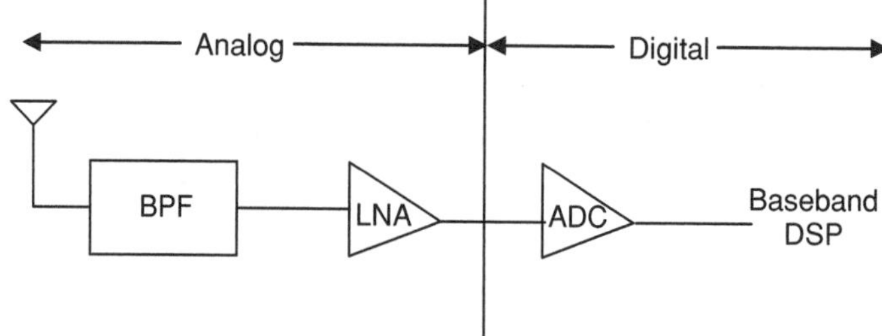

Figure 11: An ideal software radio receiver.

deployment of global roaming facilities. The limited services resulting from the presence of large-scale legacy (e.g., 2G) subscriber handsets complicate the impending problem.

Because the current digital transceivers shown in Figure 10 can support only one access technology, a unique standard is required to dynamically adapt to the radio environment in which the terminal is located. This will enable end-to-end connectivity over a wide range of frequency spectra in a highly diverse system with signaling requirements. SDR (Buracchini et al., 2000; WIPRO Technologies, 2002) promises to offer such a standard in a multiservice environment without being constrained by any specific standards. In SDR-based terminals, radio functionality for different access technology is implemented through software modules running on a generic hardware platform. Figure 11 shows the block diagram of an ideal software radio receiver.

The received analog signal is digitized by the analog-to-digital converter (ADC) and then processed by the reprogrammable baseband digital signal processor in accordance with the wireless environment in which the terminal is located. Because current conventional software radio technology utilizes only one antenna and one LNA (low noise amplifier), configuring the terminal over a wide range of frequencies pertaining to different access technologies will require parallel processing across multiple software modules, which will lead to further terminal design complexity and high power consumption and dissipation. Moreover, current ADCs are not fast enough to offer adequate service benefits. Even though development of such terminals is still in their infancy, with advancement in processing power and digital technology, it will be possible to offer SDR-based MT to provide global connectivity in the near future.

MIRAI (Mahmud et al., 2002) has proposed the physical architecture of an SDR-based MUT. However, because of the use of a single antenna, the MUT fails to provide multiaccess service (multiple streams over different access networks from the same application; Laine et al., 2000) for the purpose of load sharing and better utilization of the available resources. The only downside to the multiaccess service is that it may not be feasible in rural areas with sparse radio coverage and an absence of overlapping access networks. Also the use of a GPS receiver to determine the exact location of the MUT prohibits usage within indoor environments and in areas with thick foliage.

Figure 12 shows the physical architecture of the proposed reconfigurable SDR-based MT. Although somewhat similar to the MUT design in MIRAI, the MT does not have a GPS receiver and is equipped with multiple interfaces to meet the multiaccess service criteria.

The reconfigurable terminal communicates through the basic access component with the BAN to initiate a data session, respond to paging, or discover available resources to optimize service parameters. Different software modules can communicate over multiple interfaces to alleviate load sharing and spectrum usage.

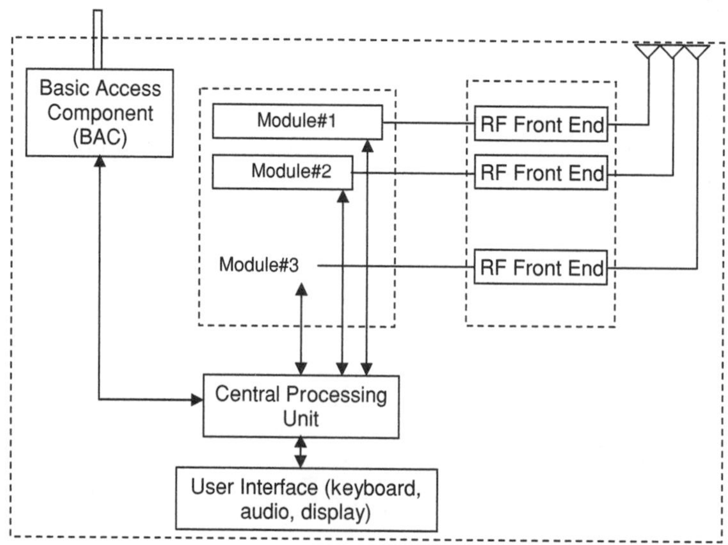

Figure 12: Physical architecture of SDR-based reconfigurable MT.

It is desired that the end-terminal architecture is modular (existing and future applications can be supported without any service disruptions), flexible (new signaling mechanism can be easily introduced), and open (relevant protocols developed later by bodies such as IETF can be supported). The proposed multiaccess, multiantenna, reconfigurable terminal meets all these criteria. In the envisioned 4G network environment, every proprietary handset (i.e., hardware platforms not compatible with each other) from different manufacturers is equipped with a SIM (subscriber identity module) or smart card. The software required to configure the terminal to the technology-specific access network at its geographical location is embedded in the card. The compiler residing within the central processing unit generates a hardware-specific executable code from the software/source code in the card. The source code will be written in a universal standard format, irrespective of the underlying hardware.

It is believed that instead of acquiring software through over-the-air downloading, which presents issues such as slow downloading rate, considerable downloading time, unreliable channel characteristics, and so forth, it will be beneficial to download the software from the SIM/smart card within the terminal. Such a mechanism not only ensures faster processing and error-free download, but also allows for larger memory to be supported. With numerous recharging outlets located at supermarkets, gas stations, hotels, airports, train stations, and so forth across the country, it becomes just a matter of recharging the SIM/smart card at a reasonable price to ensure that the terminal supports the most advanced and recent technologies. Across countries where operators support a different signaling and download scheme, such a process will save subscribers the cost of purchasing a new SIM/smart card.

Another feature absent in the MIRAI MUT is the capacity to support multicasting to various interest groups. In our opinion, multicasting will turn out to be highly desirable service criteria in future networks as online games and video on demand rise in popularity. With increasing subscriptions of divergent preferences, the network will experience a sharp increase in signaling load. Aggregation of signals and data streams, according to the predefined differentiated service agreement and QoS parameters, will be necessary to keep the signaling load within an acceptable level. Buffering, along with a timing mechanism, will have to be introduced for the aggregation of multiple streams. For example, in the event of sudden degradation of link quality, the access network will be able to buffer the data stream until the terminal is able to receive the data packets under favorable network conditions. Also, an aggregated reply on behalf of the multicast group will be sent to the peer source terminal following a time-out period.

Although the SDR-based reconfigurable terminal must be able to adapt itself to a wide range of access technologies already standardized or to be developed in the future, it is equally desirable that the terminal adapts to unpredictable events such as sudden degradation of link quality/handover by possibly having a prenegotiated set of countermeasures. This requires the capability to renegotiate QoS parameters based on a predefined set of QoS contracts without running a full end-to-end QoS negotiation between peer terminals.

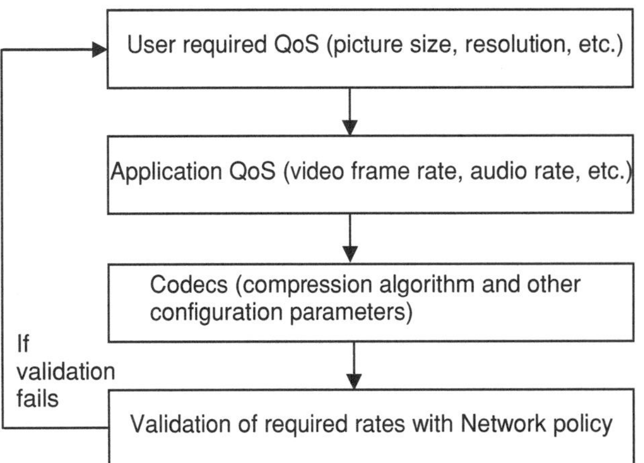

Figure 13: Mapping of QoS requirements between different entities in the end terminal.

As the link condition deteriorates, the MT may continue the ongoing session at a predefined QoS agreement, for example, a lower video rate, smaller frame size, or better coding scheme, to compensate for the degradation of the link quality. A signaling protocol such as piggybacking with low bandwidth requirements may be adopted to inform the peer end terminals of the required change. Apart from such capability, the terminal will have an operating system to support QoS functionality and will be QoS enabled through middleware. Currently it is assumed that all applications running on the terminal are somehow QoS enabled. However, in reality, not all applications running on the terminal are QoS enabled; therefore, middleware is required to QoS enable an application. Figure 13 shows the mapping of QoS-enabled application requirements in the proposed MT.

RELIABLE MULTICASTING

A multicast session involves sending control/signaling messages to multiple MTs in different domains by MAP in our architecture. To ensure reliable transfer of signaling information over bandwidth-limited BAN, we have proposed a reliable multicast protocol. Because establishing a TCP session or each signaling message would prove inefficient, this protocol is based on an underlying UDP transport protocol. Each receiver agent (RA) in the MT affiliates itself with a set of other receivers and a local AR (in our architecture) to form a multicast session. Messages to be delivered to all the receivers in the session are transmitted using one of the IP multicast addresses associated with that session. Our reliable multicast protocol promotes efficient bandwidth use by the aggregation of acknowledgment messages from individual receivers into a larger, hierarchical acknowledgment messages (HACKs). The net effect is that for each message sent via the BAN links to a potentially large number of receivers, only one acknowledgment (HACK) goes in the opposite direction to the sender. This allows explicit acknowledgment of messages to take place without requiring a flood of acknowledgment messages over the low-speed BAN links.

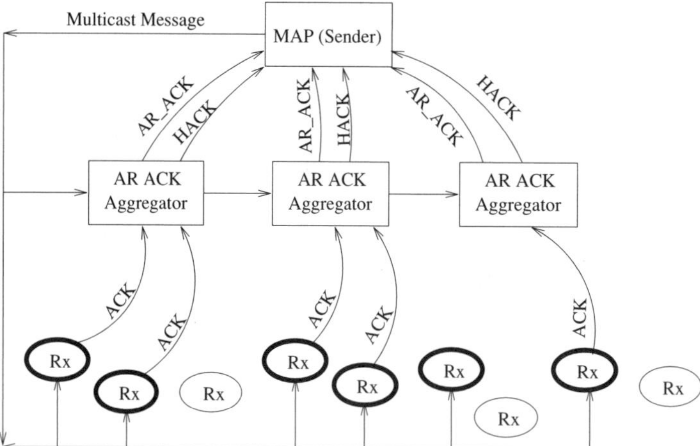

Figure 14: Reliable multicast operation.

As shown in Figure 14, all RAs and ACK aggregator agents (ARs in our architecture) associated with the multicast address receive the message sent by the MAP. Each message has an ID that is used in any acknowledgments limited to a particular multicast session and to detect and ignore duplicate transmissions. The ACK aggregators (ARs) associated with the multicast session on each AR zone will quickly and explicitly acknowledge reception of the message by sending an AR site acknowledgment message (AR_ACK) back to the sender. The AR_ACK is intended to allow timely retransmission by the sender in the event of packet loss on the BAN link. The ARs then collect the explicit ACKs from the receiver and produce a HACK, which will indicate the set of receivers that did not explicitly acknowledge the message. If all receivers successfully acknowledge the message, the HACK will contain "ALL_OK" and not an explicit list of successful receivers. It is possible for AR_ACK messages to be piggybacked onto a HACK as an optimization, reducing the number of packets required. When a receiver fails to acknowledge the message, the AR_ACK will be sent separately as indicated in Figure 14. This decouples the AR_ACK from the HACK and gives the MAP or other sender(s) the maximum amount of time to retransmit. The aggregators will wait for some specific time for an ACK from a RA before giving up and assuming it dead. During this time, the aggregator (AR) must retransmit a copy of the message on the local MT network in case it was dropped.

CONCLUSION

There is a gradual evolution occurring in the access network technology to offer more and more improved mobile services. Common mobile subscribers, with their mindset largely influenced by the Internet technology, expect the same level of service and application from mobile technology. Unfortunately the widespread proliferation of heterogeneous access technologies does not enable the consumer to use the same mobile terminal and enjoy a uniform level of service and applications globally. In this regard, a layered and modular architecture for 4G/B3G network was presented in this chapter to integrate the current access networks as well as those that would be developed in the future to support wireless Internet applications. We further described our novel augmentations in mobility, resource, and QoS management schemes adopted in the architecture. We then compared these augmented areas with the corresponding areas in contemporary architectures. We believe that these augmentations will consolidate the 4G/B3G network architectures proposed in the literature. Furthermore, a multiantenna and multiaccess mobile terminal architecture was proposed to facilitate seamless service. A reliable multicast signaling protocol over the BAN system was also described to support multicast services. The use of standards, specified by bodies such as IETF and MWIF (Mobile Wireless Internet Forum), in our proposed architecture makes our work viable for implementation and useful for the wider research community. Overall we believe that this proposal should make the next-generation network architecture flexible, make the handover process faster, allow the mobile terminal to support real-time applications anytime and anywhere, and make users transparent to different access networks that may exist. This will be the way toward real wireless Internet in the future.

ACKNOWLEDGMENTS

This work is partly supported by the International Science Linkages program established under the Australian government's innovation statement, Backing Australia's Ability. The author thanks his colleagues at the University of Sydney, Vinod Mirchandani and M. Rubaiyat Kibria, for their input to this chapter.

GLOSSARY

2G Second-generation wireless mobile cellular systems, mainly consisting of the global system for mobile communications (GSM) and cdmaOne.

3G Third-generation wireless mobile cellular systems, mainly consisting of the universal mobile telecommunications system (UMTS) and cdma2000.

Access Point (AP) The base station of a wireless LAN or other types of networks.

B3G The temporarily system name for those under development for Beyond 3G wireless mobile cellular systems, sometimes referred to as 4G.

Basic Service Set (BSS) The usual form of a WLAN network with just one access point and several mobile devices.

Carrier Sense Multiple Access with Collision Avoidance (CSMA/CA) The medium access control protocol used in WLANs to avoid too many packet collisions.

Digital Audio Broadcasting (DAB) A technique to digitally transmit high-quality audio signals such as radio, usually by the satellite.

Digital Video Broadcasting (DVB) A technique to digitally transmit high-quality video signals such as television, usually by the satellite.

Extended Service Set (ESS) The cellular topology network of a WLAN with more than one access point.

Handover Change of receiving of service from one base station to another one for a mobile user who is moving; sometimes referred to as a handoff.

Heterogeneous Networks A network that consists of different types of systems such as cellular and WLANs.

IEEE 802.11 The main WLAN standard, developed by IEEE. It has several versions including the popular 802.11b and is usually referred to as Wi-Fi.

IP Internet protocol, the main protocol used in the Internet at the network layer (Layer 3). Currently it is in version 4 (IPv4), but IPv6 will soon be implemented.

Medium Access Control (MAC) The protocol at Layer 2 of the network that controls and governs network access by multiple users.

Mobile Ad Hoc Networks (MANET) Networks that are prepared and maintained temporarily for a particular purpose such as the establishment of a network among the computers of people attending a meeting or among mobile terminals in a battlefield.

Mobility Management Set of techniques that control the movement of a mobile device within a network and is usually composed of two elements: location management and handoff management techniques.

Quality of Service (QoS) Maintaining the required service conditions for a user in a network, such as providing a minimum data-transfer speed.

Resource Management A set of management techniques in a network that ensures that available resources, as required by the end-terminal application, can be offered between peer end terminals. These techniques ensure that resource allocation takes into consideration the current network conditions.

Resource Reservation Protocol (RSVP) A reservation control mechanism that provides quality of service (QoS) to users by reserving resources beforehand; usually used in the Internet QoS establishment.

Transmission Control Protocol (TCP) The vastly used transport protocol in the Internet that provides reliable data transfer among Internet terminals.

User Datagram Protocol (UDP) The unreliable transport protocol for the Internet that provides a smaller delay as compared with TCP, at the expense of lower reliability, and is used for short message transfers or delay-sensitive applications.

Voice over IP (VoIP) A technique to deliver delay-sensitive voice packets via the Internet, which can provide lower costs to users.

Wireless Local Area Network (WLAN) An extension of the traditional LAN systems in which the physical layer is changed from cable or twisted pair into GHz radio frequency for easier scalability and mobility within a building or a campus.

CROSS REFERENCES

See *Ad hoc Network Security; Cellular Networks; IP Multicast and Its Security; Security and Web Quality of Service; Wireless Local Area Networks.*

REFERENCES

3GPP. (2002, December). *Feasibility study on 3GPP system to wireless local area network (WLAN) interworking* (Tech. Rep. 3GPP TR 22.934 v6.1.0). Retrieved from http://www.3gpp.org

3GPP. (2003, May). *3GPP system to wireless local area network (WLAN) interworking: System description* (Tech. Rep. 3GPP TS 23.234 v1.10.0). Retrieved from http://www.3gpp.org

Ahmavaara, K., Haverinen, H., & Pichna, R. (2003). Interworking architecture between 3GPP and WLAN systems. *IEEE Communications Magazine, 41*(11), 74–81.

Berezdivin, R., Breinig, R., & Topp, R. (2002). Next-generation wireless communications concepts and technologies. *IEEE Communications Magazine, 40*(3), 108–116.

Braden, R., Zhang, L., Berson, S., Herzog, S., & Jamin, S. (1997, September). *Resource reservation protocol (RSVP) version 1—Fundamental specifications* (RFC 2205). Retrieved 1 April 2005, from http://www.ietf.org/

Buracchini, E., (2000). The software radio concept. *IEEE Communications Magazine, 38*(9), 138–143.

Campbell, A. T., Gomez, J., Kim, S., Valkó, A. G., Wan, C.-Y., & Turányi, Z. R. (2000). Design, implementation and evaluation of cellular IP. *IEEE Personal Communications, 7*(4), 42–49.

Campbell, A. T., Gomez, J., & Valkó, A. G. (1999). An overview of cellular IP. In *IEEE Wireless Communications and Networking Conference (WCNC)* (Vol. 2, pp. 606–610). New Orleans, LA: IEEE Communications Society.

Carneiro, G., Ruela, J., & Ricardo M. (2004). Cross-layer design in 4G wireless terminals. *IEEE Wireless Communications, 11*(2), 7–13.

Chalmers, D., & Sloman, M. (1999). A survey of quality of service in mobile computing environments. *IEEE Communications Surveys, 2*(2), 2–10.

Comer, D. E. (1999). *Computer networks and Internets* (2nd ed.). Upper Saddle River, NJ: Prentice Hall.

Crow, B., Widjaja, I., Kim, J. G., & Sakai, P. T. (1997). IEEE 802.11 wireless local area networks. *IEEE Communications Magazine, 35*(9), 116–126.

Deering, S. (1998, December). *Internet protocol version 6 (IPv6) specification* (RFC 2460). Retrieved 1 April 2005, from http://www.ietf.org/

Dingankar, A. *QoS in Wireless LANs*. Retrieved 1 April 2005, from http://www.ee.vt.edu/~ldasilva/6504/final_report.doc

Forouzan, B. (2003). *Local area networks*. Boston, MA: McGraw-Hill Higher Education.

Frodigh, M., Parkvall, S., Roobol, C., Johansson, P., & Larsson, P. (2001). Future-generation wireless networks. *IEEE Personal Communications, 8*(5), 10–17.

Gustafsson, E., & Jonsson, A. (2003). Always best connected. *IEEE Wireless Communications, 10*(1), 49–55.

Havinga, P. J. M., Smit, G. J. M., Wu, G., & Vognild, L. (2001, June). The SMART project: Exploiting the heterogeneous mobile world. *Second International Conference on Internet Computing* (IC2001), Las Vegas.

IEEE 802.11. (n.d.). Retrieved 1 April 2005, from http://www.ieee802.org/11

Inoue, M., Wu, G., Mahmud, K., Murakami, H., & Hasegawa, M. (2002). Development of MIRAI system for heterogeneous wireless networks. In *13th IEEE International Symposium on Personal, Indoor and Mobile Radio Communications (PIMRC2002)* (Vol. 1, pp. 69–73). New York, NY: IEEE Communications Society.

Jamalipour, A. (2003). *The wireless mobile Internet—Architecture, protocols and services*. Chichester, England: Wiley.

Johnson, D. B. (2003, June). *Mobility support in IPv6* (IETF Draft). Retrieved 1 April 2005, from http://draft-ietf-mobileip-ipv6-24.txt

Johnson, D. B., et al. (1998, November). *Route optimization in mobile IP* (IETF Draft). Retrieved 1 April 2005, from http://draft-ietf-mobileip-optim-07.txt

Jung, H. Y. (2004, February). *Fast handover for hierarchical MIPv6 (F-HMIPv6)* (IETF Draft). Retrieved 1 April 2005, from http://draft-jung-mobileip-fastho-hmipv6-03.txt

Kellerer, W., Vögel, H.-J., & Steinberg, K.-E. (2002). A communication gateway for infrastructure-independent 4G wireless access. *IEEE Communications Magazine, 40*(3), 126–131.

Laine, J., Saaristo, S., Lemponen, J., & Harju, J. (2000). Implementation and measurements of simple integrated media access (SIMA) network nodes. In *IEEE International Conference on Communications (ICC)* (Vol. 2, pp. 796–800). New York, NY: IEEE Communications Society.

Lo, C., & Lin, M. (1998). QoS provisioning in handoff algorithms for wireless LANs. *Proceedings of the International Zurich Seminar on Broadband Communications, Accessing, Transmission, and Networking*. Zurich, Switzerland: IEEE Publications.

Macker, J. P., Park, V. D., & Corson, M. S. (2001). Mobile and wireless Internet services: Putting the pieces together. *IEEE Communications Magazine, 39*(6), 148–155.

Mahmud, K., et al. (2002). Mobility management by basic access network in MIRAI architecture for heterogeneous wireless systems. In *IEEE Global Telecommunications Conference (GLOBECOM)* (Vol. 2, pp. 1708–1712). Taipei, Taiwan: IEEE Communications Society.

Marques, V., Casado, A. C., Moreno, J. I., Aguiar, R. L., & Chaher, N. (2003). A simple QoS service provision framework for beyond 3rd generation scenarios. In *10th International Conference on Telecommunications (ICT2003)* (Vol. 2, pp. 1475–1481). Taiti, Papeete, French Polynesia: IEEE.

McCann, P. J., & Hiller, T. (2000). An Internet infrastructure for cellular CDMA networks using mobile IP. *IEEE Personal Communications Magazine, 7*(4), 6–12.

Mobile Wireless Internet Forum (MWIF). (n.d.). Retrieved 1 April 2003, from http://www.mwif.org

Mobile Wireless Internet Forum (MWIF). (2001, February). *Architecture requirements* (Tech. Rep. MTR-002). Retrieved 1 April 2003, from http://www.mwif.org

Mobydick. (n.d.). *Mobydick: Mobility and differentiated services in a future IP network—Final report.* Retrieved 1 September 2004, from http://www.ist-mobydick.org

Nanda, P., & Simmonds, A. J. (2001). Providing end-to-end guaranteed quality of service over the Internet: A survey on bandwidth broker architecture for differentiated services network. *Proceedings of the 4th International Conference on Information Technology (CIT-2001)* (pp. 211–216). Gopalpur-on-Sea, India: IEEE and local organizers.

Noerenberg, J. W., II. (2001). Bridging wireless protocols. *IEEE Communications Magazine, 39*(11), 90–97.

Oliphant, M. W. (1998). The mobile phone meets the Internet. *IEEE Spectrum, 8*, 20–28.

Perkins, C. (1996, October). *IP mobility support* (RFC 2002). Retrieved 1 September 2004, from http://www.ietf.org

Ramjee, R., La Porta, T. F., Thuel, S., & Varadhan, K. (2000). IP-based access network architecture for next-generation wireless data networks. *IEEE Personal Communications Magazine, 7*(4), 34–41.

Ramjee, R., Varadhan, K., Salgarelli, L., Thuel, S. R., Wang, S.-Y., & La Porta, T. (2002). HAWAII: A domain-based approach for supporting mobility in wide-area wireless networks. *IEEE/ACM Transactions on Networking, 10*(3), 396–410.

Ramnathan, P., Sivalingam, K. M., Agrawal, P., & Kishore, S. (1999). Dynamic resource allocation schemes handoff for mobile multimedia wireless networks. *IEEE Journal on Selected Areas in Communications, 17*(7), 1270–1283.

Ruiz, P., et al. (n.d.). *Advanced services over future wireless and mobile networks in the framework of the MIND project.* Retrieved 1 August 2004, from http://www.terena.nl/conferences/tnc2002/Papers/p3cl ruiz.pdf

Salkintzis, A. K., Fors, C., & Pazhyannur, R. (2002). WLAN–GPRS integration for next-generation mobile data networks. *IEEE Wireless Communications, 9*(5), 112–124.

Stallings, W. (2000). *Data and computer communications* (6th ed.). Upper Saddle River, NJ: Prentice Hall.

Talukdar, A. K., Badrinath, B. R., & Acharaya, A. (2001). MRSVP: A resource reservation protocol for an integrated services network with mobile hosts. *ACM Wireless Networks, 7*(1).

Teitelbaum, B. (n.d.). *Future priorities for Internet2 QoS.* Retrieved 1 August 2004, from http://www.internet2.edu/qos/wg/documents-informational/20011002-teitel baum-qos-futures.pdf

Toh, C.-K. (2002). *Ad hoc mobile wireless networks: Protocols and systems*. Upper Saddle River, NJ: Prentice Hall PTR.

Umehira, M., Nakura, M., Umeuchi, M., Murayama, J., Murai, T., & Hara, H. (1999). Wireless and IP integrated system architectures for broadband mobile multimedia services. *Proceedings of IEEE Wireless Communications and Networking Conference* (WCNC '99), New Orleans, 593–597.

WIPRO Technologies. (2002, August). *Software-defined radio—A technology overview* (White Paper). Retrieved 1 June 2004, from http://www.wipro.com/insights/softwareradio.htm

Security of Satellite Networks

Michele Luglio, *University of Rome Tor Vergata*
Antonio Saitto, *Telespazio*

INTRODUCTION

The use of man-made satellites for telecommunication purposes started in the second half of the past century, with the requirement to greatly enlarge the visibility range between two earth stations utilizing the radio spectrum as propagation means and to overcome the limitations imposed by the Earth's spherical nature. For many years, satellite systems have been conceived as an alternative to terrestrial (both cabled and radio) systems and even as competitor of those systems, from commercial and market points of view. In addition to the negative effect on market penetration, the view of satellites as competitor sometimes caused invalid comparisons in the efforts to perform tradeoff analyses. In fact, satellites actually represent an excellent, sometimes unique, means to complement terrestrial facilities in order to complete the global information infrastructure (GII), in which every component (terrestrial cabled, terrestrial wireless, and satellite) must play the most suitable role to provide telecommunication services to every individual or machine everywhere at any time as efficiently as possible.

In this scenario, as long as the telecommunication systems assume an ever more important role in daily life (both personal and professional), the security of information represents a very critical issue. Security must be ensured at different levels, each requiring different implications. A first level of security concerns the possibility of establishing a physical link between two or several remote users. A second level of security concerns protection of information from undesired reception or manipulation. As a component of the GII (global information infrastructure), for both aspects, satellites can provide an adequate level of security, as is stressed in the present chapter. As one of the most significant pieces of evidence, satellites are largely used by military. In addition, it is shown that satellites can even be utilized to provide security to other telecommunication systems.

In particular, a short history of satellite communications is presented; the main scenarios to utilize satellites are highlighted; the main characteristics of satellite systems are described; a reference scenario for security with satellite systems is introduced; communication, transmission, and information security issues are addressed; some examples of satellite systems actually implemented and operational that provide security communications are described; some elements on military satellite systems are provided; and finally, conclusions are drawn.

SHORT HISTORY OF SATELLITE COMMUNICATIONS

The satellite age can be assumed to have begun in 1687 when Newton theorized his law of gravitational force. In fact, the well-known equation

$$F = \frac{GMm}{r^2} \quad (1)$$

(where F is the force, G the gravitational constant, and M and m the two masses at distance r), which rules how two masses in space can be kept in equilibrium, represents the physical law that needs to be met to put a mass into an orbit around the Earth.

The satellite telecommunication age started when a body, in an orbit at relevant altitude (outside the atmosphere), was utilized as a mirror in space to connect two users located on the ground and so overcome the curvature of the earth's surface, if no other terrestrial infrastructures could efficiently provide telecommunication service. As a matter of fact, satellites in space can be used to achieve the same result Guglielmo Marconi achieved by working in the HF (high frequency) band, but can be extended to other frequency bands and therefore can obtain much better performance, but at the cost of increased complexity.

In this sense, after several science fiction papers and books, the paper "Extraterrestrial Relay" by Arthur Clarke, published by *Wireless World* in October 1945, represents the first real milestone of satellite telecommunications. In that paper, Clarke designed the orbital configuration of a satellite constellation utilizing an orbit located at 35,800 km over the Earth surface at the equator, coplanar with the equatorial plane, where the equilibrium between the gravitational force and the centrifugal force let a satellite appear fixed with respect to a point on the Earth surface. Clarke's constellation, called geostationary for this reason, was composed of three manned satellites angularly equally spaced 120° apart to get global coverage. Despite some limitations of this concept that are discussed in a later section, it represents the reference configuration for most of the satellite systems actually implemented. After Clarke's paper, another paper by John Pierce in 1954 titled "Telecommunication Satellites" suggests the use of unmanned satellites either in geostationary (GEO) or low Earth orbit (LEO).

Finally, in 1957, the Sputnik satellite launched by the former U.S.S.R. represented the first space mission. Even though not designed for telecommunication, the Sputnik mission validated the mechanical possibility of putting and keeping a body in orbit around the Earth.

After that, formal acts that actually set in motion the telecommunication satellite age include the Policy Statement on Communications Satellites signed by U.S. President John F. Kennedy in 1961; the U.S. Communications Satellite Act issued in 1962 with the birth of Comsat; the intergovernmental agreement Interim Arrangements for a Global Commercial Communications Satellite System, issued in 1964 with the birth of ICSC (Interim Communications Satellite Committee); and the formation of Intelsat (International Telecommunication Satellite, with headquarters in Washington D.C.), an intergovernmental organization.

For sake of conciseness, it will not be possible to mention and describe all the satellite systems (probably hundreds) implemented both for experimental and commercial missions. Nonetheless, a brief overview of the most important milestones is provided.

After some experimental missions using LEO, MEO, HEO (highly elliptical orbit), or GEO constellations (Score in December 1958, Courier in October 1960, ECHO I in August 1960, TELSTAR I in July 1962, RELAY I in December 1962, TELSTAR II in May 1963, SYNCOM II in July 1963, ECHO II in January 1964, RELAY II in January 1964, SYNCOM III in August 1964, and MOLNIYA I in April 1965), the first commercial satellite (Early Bird) was launched in April 1965 by Intelsat, which aimed to provide intercontinental fixed services utilizing a constellation in geostationary orbit. In 1976, Marisat was the first system composed of three satellites in GEO orbit to provide mobile services. It preceded the foundation of INMARSAT (International Maritime Satellite, with headquarters in London), another intergovernmental organization that aimed to provide mobile satellite services and which, in 1982, launched the first fully operational system targeted to maritime users. In the following years, INMARSAT provided service even on land masses and for aeronautical users.

In 1988, Omnitracs, the first system for land mobile services, was launched. In 1991, the Italian Italsat satellite represented the first satellite to work in the Ka band using a regenerative payload and multibeam antennas. In 1993, ACTS (Advanced Communication Technology Satellite), funded by the U.S. Congress, was launched as an experimental mission to further validate Ka-band technology, on-board processing, multibeam antennas, hopping beams, and on-board switching. In 1998, Iridium was the first satellite system designed for personal communications; it was followed a few years later by Globalstar. Both systems utilize LEO constellations. Despite limited commercial penetration, the two systems demonstrated the technical feasibility of implementing a network in the space and they are currently operational.

WHY AND WHEN TO USE SATELLITES

As mentioned in the previous sections, satellites must be considered a component of a global system and as such it is extremely important to carefully identify which kind of requirements can be satisfied by satellites and which market niches can be addressed. To this aim, satellites' main characteristics are listed and briefly discussed.

- *Costs independent of distance (within one satellite coverage):*

The cost of a satellite link is independent of distance, in contrast to terrestrial networks. In fact, because of the broadcast nature of the signal transmitted by the satellite, it can be received in all the coverage area. For this reason, trade-offs may be studied to find the distance threshold above which it would be cheaper to use satellites instead of terrestrial systems.

- *Efficient and cost effective for collecting, broadcasting, and multicasting:*

Satellites are very suitable for efficiently distributing and collecting signals for a very large population. In fact, because of their capability to cover very large areas, one repeater in space is able with just one carrier to reach theoretically infinite users. In the case of terrestrial fixed networks, as many connections as the number of users are required.

• *Unique in areas with scarce or no infrastructures:*
In scenarios involving developing countries or countries with unfriendly environments or low traffic requirements where the installation of terrestrial infrastructures is not economically feasible, the use of satellites, especially if they have already been deployed, is the only possibility.

• *Unique in case of disaster:*
In cases of natural disaster (earthquakes, storms) or war, when terrestrial infrastructures can be seriously damaged or even destroyed, the satellite facilities usually keep working. Even if a gateway earth station were damaged, other stations will continue to provide service.

• *Suitable for large coverage areas and long-range mobility:*
Because of their capability to cover very large areas (up to one third of the world), the satellite is particularly suitable to ensure long-range mobile services, such as in the aeronautical or maritime fields.

• *Relatively short deployment time:*
For large coverage areas, a satellite system can reach its target in a very short time as compared to a terrestrial infrastructure. For standard commercial satellites, even about 18 months can be sufficient to design, build, and launch the system. For more innovative solutions, more time may be needed. Moreover, to set up a network of satellite terminals using existing satellites can even take just a few weeks.

• *Flexible architecture:*
The satellite on-board architecture allows an extremely flexible use of resources. In fact, in cases of multibeam coverage, capacity to the different beams can be allocated unevenly in time according to actual requirements.

• *Bypass very crowded terrestrial networks:*
It is estimated that a typical Internet connection needs to pass through 17–20 routers on average. With satellites, very distant servers can be reached with only one link.

• *With the same terrestrial infrastructure, both fixed and mobile services:*
As with any radio system, the same infrastructure is able to provide both fixed and mobile services.

• *Extremely suitable for localization services worldwide:*
Last, because it is not telecommunication in strict sense, but not least in terms of commercial, strategic and social importance, the satellite solution is largely the most efficient for localization and navigation services. In fact, both the present global positioning system (GPS) and the forthcoming Galileo adopt this kind of architecture based on a limited number of satellites (24 and 30, respectively).

SATELLITE SYSTEM CHARACTERISTICS

Security can be provided to operate at any layer of the protocol stack (link, network, transport, or application). For this reason, assuming the Internet protocol stack as a reference, a brief description of the main characteristics for each layer will be presented.

Orbits

The satellite, by definition, describes an orbit around the Earth that has equilibrium between the centrifugal and the gravitational forces. The orbits can be classified according to eccentricity (circular or elliptical, where the Earth is located in one of the two focuses) or according to inclination with respect to the equatorial plane (equatorial, polar, or inclined; Maral & Bousquet, 2003; Lutz, Werner, & Jahn, 2000). Furthermore, they can be classified according to altitude: LEO (low Earth orbit), between 500 and 1,700 km; MEO (medium Earth orbit), between 5,000 km and 10,000 km and at more than 20,000 km; GEO (geosynchronous Earth orbit), at 35,800 km. The elliptical orbits can have the apogee between 39,000 km and 54,000 km. The altitudes below 500 km are not used to avoid atmospheric drag, whereas altitudes in-between LEO and MEO are not used to avoid the Van Allen belts.

The main geometrical parameters, as shown in Figure 1, are strictly correlated. In fact, once the altitude is defined, given an average Earth radius, the other parameters are calculated as a consequence. In particular, we highlight the two most important parameters: α_m (minimum elevation angle) and D_M (maximum user to satellite distance). The former assumes importance on the propagation channel, for both tropospheric effects and mobility, and the latter affects performance in terms of both free space losses and propagation delay, which represents the only really unavoidable impairments of satellite communications. Furthermore, the delay implies subjective disturbance in the case of real-time interactive services (e.g., videoconference) and objective disturbance in the case of delay sensitive protocols (e.g., TCP).

The geostationary orbit theoretically allows a satellite to be in a fixed position with respect to the Earth's surface. Actually, the presence of many forces in addition to the gravitational one induces a precession movement that may require a tracking system for the ground terminals.

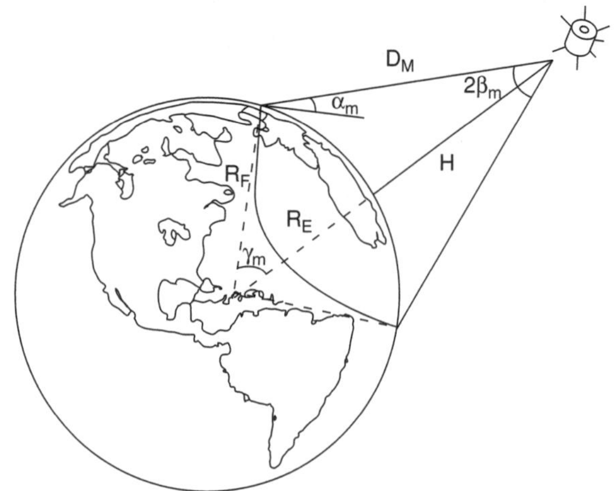

Figure 1: Geometrical parameter of a satellite link.

Satellite systems positioned in the GEO orbit are characterized by high delay (120–135 ms one-way) and high free space losses. The elevation angle α_m decreases as the latitude increases. On the other hand, the Earth can be covered with the simplest architecture, composed of just three satellites. In this respect, the limitations of the Clarke's conceptions concern the geometrical impossibility to cover the polar regions (above 70° latitude N and below −70° latitude S), the position of the satellites on the arc (not spaced 120° apart, but according to the requirements of the user distribution), and the number of satellites that, for capacity requirements, in some orbital positions can be more than one. If aiming at global coverage, two strategies are applicable: (a) the satellites positioned over the three ocean regions (Atlantic, Pacific, and Indian), which is the largely preferred configuration although it maximizes delay and free space losses (FSL), or (b) the satellites positioned over land masses (Europe/Africa, Asia/Australia, and America), which minimizes delay and FSL but must be interconnected through inter-satellite link (ISL) to achieve full connectivity.

Satellite systems utilizing LEO orbits perform better than those in GEO in terms of free space losses and propagation delay (20–40 ms), but a large number of satellites is necessary to provide full coverage and real time interactive services. The continuous movement of the satellites causes Doppler effects and frequent handovers between spots and between satellites. Moreover, an efficient tracking system is necessary on the ground station. The elevation angle can be very high at any latitude (even high latitude) and in general is time dependent.

Satellite systems utilizing MEO orbits show performance in-between the two previously presented. They are actually not utilized for telecommunication systems (just planned for ICO system) but are used for localization and navigation systems such as GPS (global positioning system) and the forthcoming Galileo.

Satellites in HEO orbits travel over an ellipse, inclined 63.4° with respect to the equatorial plane, in which the Earth is located in one of the two focuses. With respect to Keplero's law, satellites on this kind of orbits span equal areas in equal time intervals. As a consequence, they go very slowly around the apogee and appear almost fixed for users located at very high latitudes. Satellite handover, Doppler effect, and zoom effect represent the main drawbacks but these are not so critical. Delay and FSL are comparable to GEO.

The different orbital configurations need not be used alone but can be combined to create a hybrid constellation. For example, a constellation can be composed of one or more satellites in GEO orbit and one or more satellites in LEO orbits. The two components can either be interconnected to reciprocally extend coverage or be alternative points of access to improve availability.

Space Segment

The space segment consists of the spacecraft, which contains a number of pieces of equipment. In particular, it contains a power section (batteries and solar panels), a stabilization and propulsion section (including propellant), a TT&C (telemetry telecommand and control) section to remotely control the spacecraft's on-board motors, and, finally, a payload section, the communication component. The payload exploits communication between two Earth stations. The payload architecture can be transparent if it acts as a bent pipe (just change the frequency and amplify signals) or it can be regenerative if it implements some on-board processing (OBP) features, which means that it must at least demodulate and remodulate signals and separate the uplink from the downlink. In a transparent configuration, it is in charge of providing radio relay for links between earth stations, which involves capturing the carriers transmitted by the earth stations, amplifying the received carriers, changing carrier frequency, and radiating the carriers back. In a regenerative configuration, it can also regenerate signals, change polarization (if required), interconnect any beam to any beam, route packets, and switch messages. On-board switching can be implemented at either base band or microwave frequencies.

Terrestrial Segment

The Earth segment functionality includes the gateway to interconnect terrestrial networks and the NCC (network control center), which is in charge of configuration management, capacity/bandwidth management, acquisition/synchronization control, performance management, alarm management, security management, billing, and accounting. The NCC links all traffic terminals of the network through the master station (MS), which must reside at the same site as the network control center. Moreover, the network management system (NMS) is the graphical user interface (GUI) for network configuration management. The Earth terminals can be of two types: gateway and user terminals. The gateway, usually a big station, is in charge of connecting the satellite systems and the terrestrial networks. The user terminals represent the physical devices through which the users can access the satellite resources. They can be classified as fixed (very small aperture terminal, VSAT), transportable (VSAT-like, mounted on a vehicle but working in stationary conditions), or mobile (handheld, cellular-like). Each terminal is equipped with a base-band section and a radio frequency (RF) section. VSAT terminals can be connected in full mesh topology or in star topology. The former minimizes the use of the bandwidth and the delay (one hop), whereas the latter requires the presence of a hub to connect the terminals, thus needing a double hop, which increases delay and use of the bandwidth. Terminals suitable to the mesh topology are more complex and expensive than those utilized for star networks. Hybrid configuration is another possibility, which has trade-offs in performance.

Moreover, the TT&C Earth segment exchanges information with the TT&C section on-board.

Physical Layer

Physical layer concerns the capability to establish, to ensure, and to keep physical connectivity, taking into account propagation channel characteristics, and the capability to produce power on-board. In fact, the propagation channel is characterized by meaningful nonlinearity that strongly affects technical choices.

With regard to modulation, phase modulation schemes are usually adopted. The most used scheme is QPSK (Quadrature Phase Shift Keying), but in particular cases even higher order modulations are utilized. In particular, the recently approved DVB-S2 (digital video broadcasting—satellite 2) standard adopts adaptive modulation ranging from BPSK (Binary Phase Shift Keying) up to 32 APSK (Amplitude Phase Shift Keying).

Channel encoding introduces redundancy to protect signals against errors. In satellite communications, concatenated coding is often adopted to counteract both burst errors and random errors. For example, the present DVB-S (ETSI, 1997) standard adopts Reed Solomon block coding (204,188) to combat burst errors and convolutional coding (adaptive rate from 1/2 up to 7/8) to combat random errors. Also, turbo codes are actually used in recently launched systems (Giancristofaro, Piloni, Novello, Giubilei, & Tousch, 2000).

Interleaving, used to combat channel fluctuations resulting from multipath, aims at randomizing bit errors to change burst errors in random errors. It consists of rearranging the order of a sequence in deterministic way and then rebuilding the original sequence (Luglio, Bellini, Marinelli, Tartara, & Vatalaro, 1997). The bits can be arranged in a rows, of a matrix and transmitted in columns. Either block or convolutional interleaving can be implemented.

The coverage strategy can significantly affect the physical layer. In fact, multibeam coverage improves spatial selectivity (allowing frequency reuse) and gain, which allows less critical user terminal design and uneven power distribution at the price of increasing complexity and costs (Loreti, Luglio, & Palombini, 2000).

Another impairment, mainly resulting from multibeam coverage, is the intrasystem co-channel interference (Vatalaro, Corazza, Caini, & Ferrarelli, 1995; Caini, Carazza, Falciasecca, Ruggieri, & Vatalaro, 1992; Loreti & Luglio, 2002). It arises from the overlapping of several side lobes of the interfering beams with the main lobe of the interfered beam. In the case where every beam utilizes the same frequency (code division multiple access, CDMA), the overlapping of two main lobes can cause serious interference. In satellite systems, co-channel interference is more critical than in terrestrial cellular networks. In fact, for terrestrial systems morphology and man-made buildings sometimes isolate adjacent cells and zones, allowing a more significant use of frequency reuse.

Finally, OBP capabilities can greatly improve the link design because isolating uplink and downlink avoids direct transfer of noise accumulated on the uplink to the downlink. Furthermore, it achieves better performance in terms of the E_b/N_0 required, the reduced power needed on both links, and the reduced intermodulation.

MAC Layer

The same multiple access techniques developed and implemented on terrestrial systems are adopted. In particular, the classical orthogonal techniques are utilized: FDMA (frequency division multiple access), TDMA (time division multiple access), and CDMA or hybrid schemes such as MF-TDMA (multifrequency time division multiple access). FDMA can be implemented in different schemes: SCPL (single carrier per link), SCPS (single carrier per station), SCPC (single carrier per channel). Each scheme shows different performance in terms of efficiency and intermodulation products generation. The use of TDMA, more flexible than FDMA, requires a critical synchronization system that takes into account the variance of the propagation delay, which must be carefully considered also in the design of the guard time slots. CDMA (De Gaudenzi & Giannetti, 1998) allows full frequency reuse, satellite soft handover, satellite path diversity exploitation, and application of interference mitigation techniques such as multiuser detection (MUD).

Also, nonorthogonal random access techniques (Aloha or Slotted Aloha) or those based on the PRMA (packet reservation multiple access) concept are applicable. The latter, requiring a framelength longer than RTT (round trip time) to achieve significant efficiency, seems to be more suitable for systems in LEO orbit (Del Re, Fantacci, Giambene, & Walter, 1997).

Network Layer

Network issues for satellite systems are applicable whenever the satellite link is not considered just a branch in the network but routing operations are foreseen. In the latter case, two approaches can be adopted: connection-oriented, where the system performs routing at call setup, as in the "big-LEO" architectures, or a connectionless network, which performs routing hop-by-hop, as is used by the Internet. The latter approach is preferred because IP (Internet protocol) is connectionless, and thus by using IP a homogenous network protocol may be simpler and have lower overhead. Moreover, the use of IP protocol well suits multicast management, and, as in a terrestrial network, connectionless networks offer some degree of fault tolerance for data delivery. Against this approach, satellite networks (such as LEO systems) may be too dynamic for standard IP routing and Internet-style routers may require too much memory (maybe not compatible with the limited space on-board). Among the other problems with using IP, the TTL (time-to-live) and IP packet fragmentation are emphasized because of the huge delay when IP is applied to satellite systems (Partridge & Shepard, 1997).

Present satellite networks that provide multimedia wideband services offer an IP interface, although they use transparent payloads. For this kind of services, it is hoped that the use of regenerative payloads able to perform network-layer functionality in space will be a reality in a short time, offering the opportunity to more efficiently manage satellite networks.

Transport Layer

The transport-layer performance suffers a lot from satellite systems features. In fact, the most widely used transport-layer protocol, TCP (transmission control protocol), on which most of the Internet applications are based, is strongly delay sensitive and delay is the only impairment we cannot rid of, because it depends only on the speed of light in space. Nonetheless, if satellite systems aim to be perfectly integrated in the global network and to be really part of it, the utilization of the most used network protocol standard must be pursued. In this sense, a huge amount of research has been and is currently being done to try to mitigate the impairments resulting from delay on performance of TCP via satellite links (Allman, Glover, & Sanchez, 1999; Border, Kojo, Griner, Montenegro, & Shelby, 2001; Loreti, Luglio, Kapoor, Stepanek, Gerla, Vatalaro, et al., 2001; Luglio, Yahya Sanadidi, Stepanek, & Gerla, 2001). In particular, some of the proposed solutions are specifically designed for satellites whereas others are for more general environments. Many proposals are based on modification of the flow control (e.g., enlarging the dimension of the initial window, reducing the number of acknowledgments) and of the recovery mechanism (dynamic estimation of the available bandwidth, etc.); others are based on the modification of the architecture (e.g., splitting the path, terminating the connection at each step, and acknowledging packet reception). Among the latter type of solutions, some adopt standard algorithms or modified versions, and there are solutions typically known as accelerators, which are implemented in real systems and based on proprietary standards.

Application Layer

There is not a real limitation to provide any service through a satellite network. Every kind of service and relative application can be implemented by taking into account specific performance. In fact, the propagation delay affects performance of real-time interactive service (e.g., voice, videoconference) but, on the other hand, the suitability to multicast operation makes satellite systems more efficient and cost effective. In particular, both real-time and store and forward services, both fixed and mobile services, both narrow band and wideband services, unicast, multicast, and broadcast services are currently provided.

Standards

One of the most important factors affecting market penetration is the availability of common standards. In fact, it is well known that the availability of open standards has greatly favored the large diffusion of systems such as GSM (Global System Mobile). Actually, in the satellite arena, the DVB (digital video broadcasting) standard was issued in 1997 for broadcasting services (ETSI, 1997). It includes standards for terrestrial, cabled, and satellite systems. The DVB-S (DVB satellite) standard regulates the broadcasting of signals in digital format and how they must be processed before being transmitted. Two basic operations are regulated: base-band processing and satellite channel adaptation.

The base-band processing concerns the adoption of MPEG-2 (Moving Picture Expert Group—2) as the source coding technique on different source signals (video, audio, and data), the following (not mandatory) packetization of data of a single program into packetized elementary stream (PES), and the final multiplexing of a number of PES into the MPEG-2 transport stream (TS). The different data elements can carry independent timing information. In this way, audio information can be synchronized with video information in the receiver, even if they do not arrive aligned at the receiver, which allows the transmission of conventional television programs.

The satellite channel adaptation concerns the types of modulation and coding schemes to be adopted to meet the target quality of the signal (Bit Error Rate around 10^{-11}). This level of quality, called "quasi error free" (QEF), ensured at the MPEG-2 decoder input, allows the system to correctly rebuild audio and video information.

The processes involved in this adaptation are transport multiplex adaptation and randomization for energy dispersal, outer coding (i.e., Reed-Solomon), convolutional interleaving, inner coding (i.e., punctured convolutional code), base-band shaping, and modulation. The randomization is applied to make the RF spectrum similar white noise process. It is implemented over sequential groups of eight bytes by adding a pseudo-random binary sequence (PRBS) to the transport stream data. The channel coding is applied through three steps: outer code Reed-Solomon (204, 188, T = 8), convolutional interleaving with the aim to randomize errors occurring in bursts, and convolutional coding with a variable code rate (1/2, 2/3, 3/4, 5/6, and 7/8). Gray-coded QPSK modulation with absolute mapping (no differential coding) is adopted. Prior to modulation, the base-band signal is square-root-raised-cosine-filtered with a roll-off factor of 0.35.

The DVB approach offers a good degree of flexibility. A 38 Mbit/s data flux could contain eight standard definition television (SDTV) programs, four enhanced definition television programs (EDTV), or one high definition television (HDTV) program, all with associated multichannel audio and ancillary data services. In satellite applications, the maximum data rate for a data stream is typically about 38 Mbit/s. It can be accommodated in a 33-MHz satellite transponder and provides sufficient capacity to deliver, for example, four to eight standard definition television programs, 150 radio channels, 550 ISDN (integrated service digital network) channels, or any combination of these services.

Recently, the DVB-S standard was updated in the DVB-S2 version. In the new scheme, which modifies the satellite channel adaptation block only, adaptive modulation and coding (ACM) have been introduced. In particular, low density parity check codes (LDPC) have been selected with Bose–Chaudhuri–Hochquenghem (BCH) block code length 64,800-bit (or 16,200-bit) periodic structures that facilitate parallel decoding with about 50 decoding iterations. Available coding rates are 1/2, 3/5, 2/3, 3/4, 4/5, 5/6, 8/9, and 9/10. Moreover, five modulation formats, all optimized to operate over nonlinear transponders, have been selected: BPSK (1 bit/s/Hz), QPSK (2 bit/s/Hz), 8PSK (3 bit/s/Hz), 16APSK (4 bit/s/Hz), and 32APSK (5 bit/s/Hz). Then, three roll-off factors are allowed: 0.35, 0.25, and 0.20 (DVB-S: only 0.35). With the new standard, an optimization of spectral resources in

Table 1 Spectrum Allocation for Satellite Services

	Band	Uplink	Downlink
Fixed services	C	5,925–6,425 MHz 7,900–8,400 MHz	3,700–4,200 MHz 7,250–7,750 MHz 10.95–11.2 GHz
	Ku	13.75–14.5 GHz	11.45–11.7 GHz 12.5–12.75 GHz
	Ka	27.5–30 GHz 30–31 GHz	17.7–20.2 GHz 20.2–21.2 GHz
Mobile services	UHF	148–150.05 MHz	137–138 MHz
	L	1,626.5–1,660.5 MHz 1,610–1,626.5 MHz	1,525–1,559 MHz 2,483.5–2,500 MHz
	S	2,170–2,200 MHz 2,655–2,690 MHz 7,900–8,025 MHz	1,980–2,010 MHz 2,500–2,535 MHz 7,250–7,375 MHz
	Ka	29.9–30 GHz 30–31 GHz	20.1–20.2 GHz 20.2–21.2 GHz

the order of 30–40% is estimated. If confirmed, the satellite may compete in terms of costs with terrestrial services such as ADSL (asymmetric digital subscriber line).

The success of the DVB standard because of its capability to transmit a huge quantity of data in a very flexible way, with consequent availability of technology at low cost, extends its field of applicability beyond the transmission of only data information. In addition, the compatibility with IP protocol allows the processing of the IP packet in the DVB stream. As a consequence, first the use of DVB for one-way systems (DVB IP with return channel on terrestrial networks) has been introduced. The data are received through the same equipment (antenna and receiver) utilized for digital TV but the equipment is connected to a PC with a suitable decoder. Then, a two-way standard based on DVB was recently introduced with return channel on satellite (DVB RCS), which allows bidirectional communications up to 2 Mbit/s in the return link and shares the bandwidth on a MF-TDMA discipline. The user terminal is very similar to the receiving equipment but with a RF front-end working at 1–4 W. The great success and market penetration of this technology is leading researchers and standardization bodies to extend the use of DVB RCS for mobile services.

Another standard that has been evaluated by ETSI and that may be implemented in the near future concerns the satellite component of the UMTS (universal mobile telecommunication system; Caire, Corazza, De Gaudenzi, Gallinaro, Luglio, Lyons, et al., 2002). To ensure the maximum degree of compatibility with the W-CDMA (wideband CDMA) of the terrestrial component, the developed standard SW-CDMA (satellite wideband CDMA) is still based on CDMA.

It is very similar to the ETSI UTRA proposal and is suited to the specific satellite environment. To reach this aim, the main features have been identified: wide range of bearer services (from 2.4 kbit/s up to 144 kbit/s), power and spectral efficiency achieved through path diversity exploitation, coherent demodulation on the return link, multi-user detection scheme, overhead reduction using common pilot/beam approach, and compatibility with adaptive antenna systems. Moreover, user localization capabilities are implemented. Two bit-rate options are supported: 4.096 Mbit/s (frame duration = 10 ms) and 2.048 Mbit/s (frame duration = 20 ms). QPSK and dual-BPSK (for low data rate) modulations are adopted. The use of scrambling code is optional.

Spectrum Allocation

Spectrum allocation is performed by ITU-R and in particular by the World Radiocommunication Conference. Table 1 shows the allocated bandwidth for ITU region 2.

SATELLITE AND SECURITY: REFERENCE SCENARIO

The security scenario drastically changed at the beginning of the new century. On one side, there is the traditional need of protecting transmission from disturbances and communications from interception, but on the other side, there is the new need of protecting the physical integrity of the infrastructures, among which the telecom network is one of the most critical, and the even more important need to add intelligence to the network, which allows the capability of using the available information at the right time and at the right network node. These new system requirements are often synthesized using two acronyms: NCI (national critical infrastructure; White House, 2003) protection and NCC (network-centric communications).

In this new scenario, it is even more evident that there is no privileged telecommunications subsystem to ensure security, but the opportune utilization of each component and the right cooperation among all kinds of communication infrastructures (terrestrial cabled, terrestrial wireless, satellite, and HAPS/UAV) can provide the required level of security at the communication level and, as a consequence, when applicable, at human life protection. In this scenario, the key concepts are

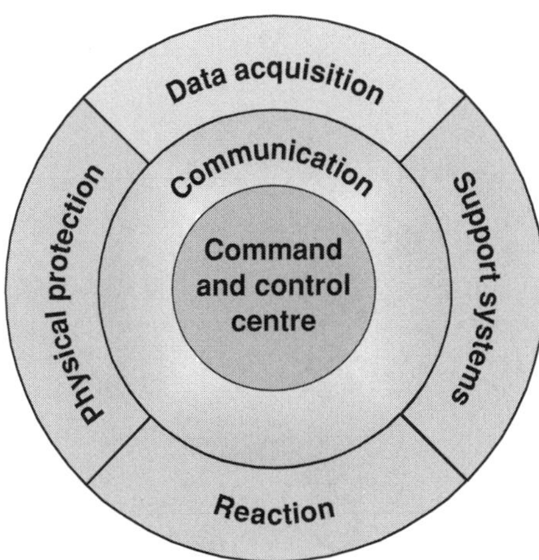

Figure 2: The communications system as the central ring of security architecture.

robustness, vulnerability, threat, attack (passive or active), reliability, availability, survivability, and countermeasure.

Security and Communications in the New Century

The telecommunication network is one of the most important and critical networks, which shall survive to any hostile activity with the highest probability. This concept has always been assumed for defense networks, but its extension to all the civilian uses is not trivial.

Information protection and redundancy are not sufficient to face the new threats of the century and it is not viable to change all the existing network architectures, even if security is nowadays a socially accepted expense. Security is therefore a complex process; potential threats shall be continuously analyzed and protection and security added where it is needed, using flexibility, modularity, and implementation velocity.

A communication system can be seen as the central ring of this complex architecture (Figure 2). The performance of the network shall be guaranteed against voluntary attacks and intrusions.

Telecommunication networks used by civilian entities must satisfy requirements on security, availability, and robustness that are more challenging than a few years ago, and satellites can be the key element without boosting prices and inflating deployment times to deliver performance such as the following:

1) *On the architecture:* High level of configurability: the capability of supporting different network connectivity and topology configurations (full mesh, hierarchical, star, polygonal, etc.). High level of robustness against unwanted failures and deliberated attacks: sensitive site protections, autonomous power supply, local redundancy, and alternate communication routes. High level of redundancy to face major failures: full duplication of the network hubs and control centers. Gracefully degradation of the network performance: no type of attack can cause a total outage of the network.

2) *On the services:* Voice services, IP services, multimedia services, data transfer services.

3) *On the users:* Fixed communications, hand-held terminal communications, mobile vehicular communications, naval communications, airborne communications.

Secure transmission capability: the capability of optimizing the transmission parameters (power, modulation type, number of users, coding rate, etc.).

Secure communication capability: the capability of protecting the information content against intruders using end-to-end encryption devices.

4) *On the evolution:* High level of scalability: the capability of growing with the customer's needs without change of key technologies. High level of modularity: the capability of endorsing additional services and technologies, without major architectural impacts.

5) *On the operations:* Full monitor and control of the network at the remote control center, easy commissioning capability, easy configuration capability, high level of maintainability, easy configuration upgrading, built-in training, redundant database synchronization, network statistics and metrics availability.

Effectiveness of Satellite on Security for Public and Private Users

Satellite networks are a key element to add flexibility, extend the coverage, and increase the resilience and the robustness of terrestrial networks. The satellite networks have the ability to overcome the network hierarchy and to connect a couple of points present in different network layers; in addition they allow to cover the territory without any physical infrastructure apart from the access point to the satellite. As a consequence, zero deployment time at the start-up of the system is needed, which adds security against volunteer attacks and safety against natural disasters.

A unique, well-known characteristic of satellite communications is the multicast capability, which allows distribution of information to all the connected sites in parallel using the same physical satellite channel.

The broadband solutions are typically based on multimedia satellite networks, which are composed of a hub connected with the control center and a large number of micro stations (with a diameter of less than 90 cm), capable of two-way transmission up to a few hundreds kbit/s and a receiving capability up to a few tenths Mbit/s (as in DVB RCS like systems previously introduced). An example of this architecture is shown in Figure 3, operating in the 11–14 GHz frequency band, where a typical bidirectional connectivity is represented: the forward link is a DVB standard flux whereas the return link works on a MF-TDMA discipline.

With respect to a traditional satellite link, the secure link shall manage the security procedure at the various agreed levels. It is very important to optimize the security session with respect to the overall optimization, considering that the satellite link for each security package exchange adds an additional 0.5-s delay. On the other hand, the satellite solution is very flexible and can operate at the user, back haul, and core network levels, which breaks the network hierarchy. Very often, this delay is strongly

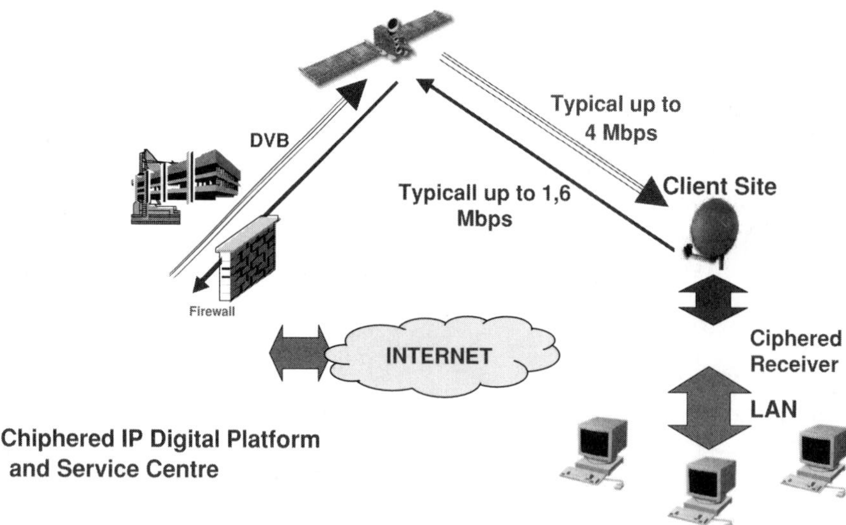

Figure 3: Typical fixed satellite service network used for security.

compensated by the hopping of a few routers in the terrestrial network. Indeed, the satellite network can directly connect the remote router with the control center, bypassing all the network layers. In a few cases, the application layer may require multiple hops between the access point and the server at the hub; this can imply some unwished additional latency time.

Satellite networks have an intrinsic security level supplied by the need to synchronize the access (TDMA technique), which is a function managed by the complex hub. In addition to this built-in security level, satellite networks can include cryptography devices for public and private keys. It is important to briefly analyze the effect of encryption on satellite transmissions: cryptography is based on the application of an algorithm to the transmission, which is based on the knowledge of the activation keys. This knowledge is limited to the end nodes of the encryption process. The strength of the encryption algorithm is a function of its complexity and is evaluated on the basis of the number of operations necessary to break it and on the not yet discovered set of rules necessary to break it.

Complexity plays a negative role for real-time encryption of high data rate stream. The encryption key can be private and public. In the former case, the key is distributed between the authorized correspondents. The key information is changed from time to time, and this is a very delicate phase of the overall encryption process. In the latter one, from the generation of two random numbers, a public modulus is generated and a procedure is available to the correspondents so that they have access to the clear information (NIST, n.d.). The network system security should be guaranteed at both information and communication levels. The encryption can be introduced as a service at three different levels:

- Link by link,
- Node by node, and
- End to end.

In the first case, security is managed from the user to the control center at each level of the network. In the second case, routers and switches are included in the protection level. Secure communications are managed at the routing level. In the third case, the encryption protection is solved out only at the final user destination, which offers the maximum level of protection. In the most general case, satellite communications (in a way similar to other subnetworks) can guarantee node-to-node protection more easily than end-to-end protection. When end-to-end is not viable, the critical network nodes, where encryption algorithms are applied, shall be adequately protected from potential intrusions.

A very special satellite encryption process applies to the point-to-multipoint transmission, very popular for TV broadcasting applications but also usable for videoconference services.

A list of encryption processes for TV satellites includes the following (*European satellite TV frequently asked questions*, n.d.):

- Videocrypt, originally English, works on PAL (**P**hase **A**lternating **L**ine) channels. There are two variants, the original Videocrypt, which should basically be used inside England, and Videocrypt II, which is meant for Europe outside the UK.
- Eurocrypt was developed with MAC (multiplexed analog component), and almost all MAC receivers have an integrated Eurocrypt decoder.
- Nagravision, also known as Syster, is mainly used in France, thus SECAM (**S**ysteme **E**lectronique pour **C**ouleur **a**vec **M**emoire) channels, but is also used with PAL in Germany and Spain, primarily by channels owned by France's Canal+ network.

Another system may be mentioned, Luxcrypt, used by the Dutch RTL4/V network; it does not need a smart card. Some other, less used systems also exist.

It is important to outline that studies and investigations are ongoing to allow the combined use of low orbiting

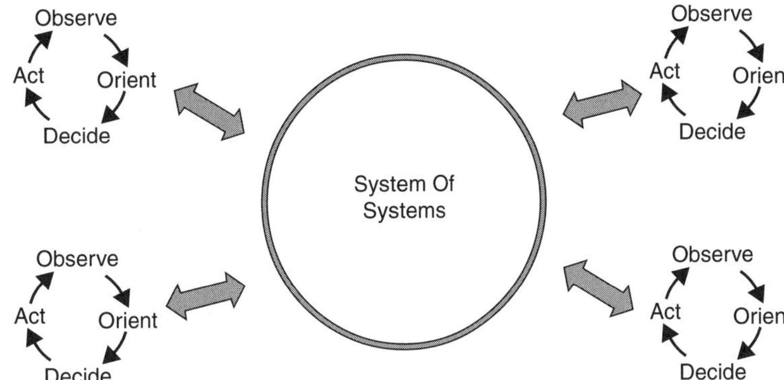

Figure 4: Multilevel OODA loop capability of a system of systems.

satellites (such as Globalstar and Iridium) with GEO stationary satellite, which would create an additional service channel, have virtually no latency time, and improve the overall performance of encrypted satellite channels (Carducci, 2004).

Importance of Satellite Systems in the Process of O^2DA

A system capable of fulfilling the main high level objective is very complex, has to be distributed over a wide territory, and is structured (from the operational point of view) in "functional cells" capable of performing on a local basis some specific (though sometimes more elementary) OODA loops (closed-loop observe-orient-decide-act chains of operational functions), which from a conceptual point of view are the "elementary modules" of a modern surveillance-awareness-decision-action system/process.

OODA is used for synthesizing a complex process necessary for supporting security in a very wide sense:

- The first phase (observe) consists in monitoring potential threats, monitoring the critical aspects of the system to be protected (including telecommunications and transmission), and reporting to the competent entities.
- The second one (orient) is probably the most delicate and is dedicated to prepare all the information needed for a correct counter measurement.
- The third one (decide) consists in implementing the strategy to face the threat.
- The last one (act) is dedicated to the countermeasurement application.

In addition to this "local OODA loop" capability (which may be rather independent from the presence of a national coordination system), these functional cells must also be capable to operate as part of the nationwide state border integrated management system (SBIMS), which is fully integrated with other (often more complex) decisional loops so as to permit the national coordination authorities:

- to have knowledge of the overall situation (observe and orient),
- to take in a minimum time the right decisions in face of a certain situation (decide), and
- to command specific appropriate counteractions, having then the possibility to be immediately informed of the results of such actions.

The system able to provide this multilevel OODA loop capability is a "system of systems" (see Figure 4). This is a well-consolidated approach for military operations, already in use in several parts of the world and highly appreciated for its ability to transform a large quantity of sparse "information" into a consolidated "knowledge" of the overall situation in a very short time. The idea of reporting to the central authorities a large quantity of information from remote sites and to centralize the decisional power is not new; what is now made possible by the progress in the "information technologies" is to close the OODA loops in real time, while a traditional, noncomputerized approach would take much longer.

The possibility of making different existing networks interoperable and making information available where it is needed at the correct time is based on the concept of network-centric communications, which is basically service independent. Network-centric communications will help to prevent cost explosion by increasing overall performance through the networking of existing systems.

The concept of network-centric communication supports the trend toward smaller and interoperable forces with the capability to dynamically connect and share sensors (regardless of platform), decision makers (regardless of location), and effectors (regardless of kind and location). With the concept of network-centric communications, it will be possible to designate reconnaissance data (targets) to each system, the best countereffect. Individual systems lose importance and a system of systems arises that shows their full performance only in the network. The network-centric communications operational architecture will closely couple the following capabilities:

- sensors,
- decision makers (command and control), and
- security enforcement/engagement unit.

Information superiority and the fast, secure, and appropriate knowledge on all levels are decisive according to the model of observe, orient (understand), decide, and act as fast as possible.

The additional elements of this new architecture are the sensor grid, which consists of the software applications associated with specific sensor peripherals and the software applications that enable multimode sensor tasking and data fusion; the information grid, which consists of a network of networks (communications paths, computational nodes, operating systems, and information management applications) that enables network-centric computing and communications across the security space domains; the engagement grid, which effectively exploits security space domain awareness to enable new operational capabilities for security enforcement/engagement unit employment.

The importance of the satellite systems as the key element for creating the overlay network among the existing networks, thereby minimizing the investment and optimizing the overall performance, is evident. Satellite links can easily interconnect the network nodes, supply the needed band when and where it is needed, complement the existing network coverage in a short time, and create real alternative paths to the existing terrestrial links without any terrestrial infrastructure but the access points.

COMMUNICATION, TRANSMISSION, AND INFORMATION SECURITY

In a typical communication scenario, with particular reference to wireless systems, we identify three levels of security: communication security, which refers to the capability to create a network with restricted access; transmission security, which refers to the capability to transmit and receive signals at physical level; and information security, which refers to information content and traffic flow protection.

Effectiveness of Satellite System Characteristics on Security Provision

Among the several aspects briefly overviewed previously, some are particularly relevant to security provision performance and affect the degree of security that is possible to ensure. In particular, we highlight the role that three characteristics (type and extension of the coverage area, broadcast nature of the signal from satellites, and accurate pointing and propagation delay) assume in the security scenario.

The coverage area is typically quite extended. This characteristic allows the network to serve a large number of users even in remote, isolated, and even impervious locations, where usually terrestrial infrastructures are not deployable (either for economic or feasibility reasons) and where typically some office that requires isolation for confidentiality can be located.

The broadcast peculiarity of the satellite signal, apparently a disadvantage from the security point of view, can be actually considered an advantage if the same key or set of keys must be distributed to a large set of users. Furthermore, the broadcast nature does not imply the capability to receive the signal for everybody. In fact, a highly directional antenna is mostly necessary and as a consequence accurate pointing must be implemented to receive just the electromagnetic signal from just one satellite; that does not imply the ability to decode the information, as will be stressed in the next section. In case an omnidirectional antenna is foreseen, no pointing is necessary but the latter aspect still applies.

The propagation delay, which is as previously mentioned the only unavoidable impairment, actually limits security implementation performance. In fact, in case frequent key distribution updating is required, as for example in the multicast scenario (Howarth, Iyengar, Sun, & Cruickshank, 2004), the huge delay introduces significant inefficiency.

Intrinsic Security

Despite the broadcast nature of transmission from satellite over a large area, some peculiarities of satellite equipments and their deployment make the system be intrinsically secure.

First of all, facilities and equipment are well localized and not spread over the territory and thus extremely easy to be garrisoned. As a consequence, the unauthorized access to telecommunication resources is practically impossible. On the contrary, it is well known that in the case of terrestrial public networks, based on the deployment over the territory of kilometers of cables, routers, and switches, the accessibility is much easier. In fact, it is sufficient to access one of the switches, which, being large in number and spread over the service area, are not easily monitored and continuously overseen.

Furthermore, the absence of an open, diffused standard, which actually represents a weakness from the market penetration point of view, represents an additional factor of security. In fact, to be able to not only receive the electromagnetic signal but to decode information, it is necessary to be authenticated by the NCC. The authentication process cannot be performed if the utilized standard is not known. The following two subsections will present two study cases that refer to two different access techniques. Of course, in case open SCPC is used, the procedures are simpler and the intrinsic security does not entirely apply.

Last but not least, a further peculiar characteristic ensuring security is represented by the extremely high level of reliability of both the space segment and terrestrial segment equipment. The former is necessary considering the practical impossibility to fix the devices once they are orbiting. It is achieved by utilizing the best performing materials to build circuits and mechanical components, through the implementation of the most accurate tests to check the resistance to mechanical vibrations to sudden and conspicuous thermal variations, and through the redundancy of all the critical devices (in some case, even 1:1). The terrestrial segment, even though not as reliable as the space segment for the obvious reason that it is easier to fix or replace in case of failure, shows a degree of reliability much higher than that of the terrestrial equivalent equipment. Nevertheless, the concept of redundancy is rigorously applied to the gateway stations. Definitively, such a degree of reliability increases the confidence of the satellite user that the service, once set up, will be provided with continuity and without interruption. This feature encourages the use of satellites for secure services that, in most of the cases dealing with, for example, human safety and disaster relief, need also the highest degree of survivability.

Security Management

As outlined previously, a cryptographic mechanism is one of the strongest ways to provide security services. NBS (now NIST) started in 1977 publishing DES (Data Encryption Standard) a suite of approved algorithms for unclassified but sensitive applications, based on an IBM effort.

New classes of algorithms have been added, such as secure hash algorithms and asymmetric algorithms for digital signatures. The suite of algorithms now provides different levels of cryptographic strength through a variety of key sizes, and the algorithms may be combined in many ways to increase the complexity of the protocols and applications.

When the satellite element is introduced, the network management of the keys shall take this into account operating via simulation, tests, and management procedures. The satellite has an effect on the key management lifecycle, which establishes a framework for the lifecycle of the cryptographic key (use, lifetime, validation, recovery issues) and on general key management, which encompasses the key management policy, the cryptography algorithm, the key size selection, and schemes.

The experience for point-to-point cryptographic connection is that the satellite system works reasonably well in a very wide area of applications, but a specific validation activity should be envisaged.

Communication Security Implementation

Commercial systems implement security mechanisms to allow only a restricted number of authorized users to access information or to establish connection. These mechanisms can be part of the standard or of a proprietary solution.

Conditional Access in DVB-S

Conditional access is based on encrypting signals to allow only a restricted number of users to view certain programs. The first level of restriction allows the view only to subscribers, whereas further levels can restrict the view to particular subsets of users (for example, users who view adult movies, have partial subscriptions, or are in particular geographic areas). Moreover, with conditional access, pay-per-view and video on demand can be implemented.

In DVB, conditional access is performed through three functions: scrambling/descrambling, entitlement checking, and entitlement management. The first aims at modifying the information sequence so that only users who know a secret password can recognize the original information. The second function broadcasts the encrypted secret codes to enable proper descrambling, utilizing a specific message (entitlement checking message). The third function is to manage this process.

The weakness of this technique is due to the broadcast's one-way transmission. In fact, because there is no return channel, it is not possible to realize eventual cloning of smart cards.

Security in DVB RCS Systems

In DVB RCS systems, security provision in the forward link is based on the previously mentioned DVB scrambling/descrambling mechanism. A similar mechanism can be applied to the return link, as well as authentication algorithms implemented at MAC layer (as that described in a previous section). Finally, because the communication is based on the IP interface, a further degree of security is provided through proper IP addressing. Additional IP security mechanisms (such as IPSec) can be applied, taking into account the constraints presented previously.

Security in the MF TDMA Case

Most of satellite networks operating on a MF-TDMA discipline are based on the use of proprietary standards, which represent an intrinsic level of security, with the drawback that they slow down market penetration. In fact, very robust authentication mechanisms are usually adopted. A terminal willing to either receive or transmit data within a certain network must continuously perform acquisition and synchronization procedures, which are impossible without the express authorization and cooperation of the network operator. As an example, the Viasat Linkway network case is described.

The network architecture is based on the presence of an NCC, a master reference terminal (MRT), and many traffic terminals (TT). The MRT acquires and keeps an univocal reference of each TT in its database, so that, before starting a traffic exchange, the MRT can send the reference burst (RB) to every TT to provide timing information and outbound signaling. The TTs send to NCC a signaling burst (SB) for inbound signaling to require bandwidth allocation, using the proper time slot in the frame, sometimes according to Aloha discipline. The TTs send a control burst (CB) to MRT that provides frequency, timing, and delay information, which can be used by the NCC to determine if any correction is needed. In fact, NCC knows the position of each TT, and thus the expected delay, even in case of terminals mounted on mobile vehicles (trucks or ships) when the position is continuously updated. Thus, TTs transmit the acquisition burst (AB) to the MRT. The arrival time is measured and compared with the expected time. If it arrives within a certain interval, the TT is accepted, otherwise not. All the TTs use a single AB timeslot in the frame. After acquisition, synchronization is kept with CBs. In addition, the commissioning of a new terminal requires a number of operations to be performed by the NCC: new site configuration with latitude, longitude, and RF information; new terminal definition; definition of appropriate service interface; definition of IP interface; and creation of a boot file for the new traffic terminal by loading it onto a floppy disk to be installed when commissioning the traffic terminal. (Boot files contain the information required for a terminal to acquire, transmit, and receive synchronization.)

Security in the CDMA Case

CDMA offers an inherent degree of security because discrimination among users is achieved by assigning a different code to each user, which modifies the spectral pattern of the signal. To decode information from the signal, the proper code must be known. For these reasons, military environments (where it was first developed in the 1970s) have a lot of interest in this kind of technology.

In addition to inherent security, CDMA networks can provide an additional degree of security by implementing a proper authentication mechanism. An example of such CDMA network is represented by the Globalstar system.

The CDMA scheme utilized by Globalstar system is based on Qualcomm CDMA standard, namely IS-41, derived from terrestrial IS-95. Security is provided as an authentication mechanism and as voice/data encryption applicability. The former is exploited by the SIM Card, similar to the terrestrial cellular systems; the latter can be implemented using end-to-end devices such as DCS-1800. In addition, the IS-41 user terminal (UT) utilizes a security module (SM), which stores long-term cryptographic keys as well as stores and executes cryptographic algorithms. The SM is associated to an UT HW identity through a unique electronic serial number (ESN). This association is stored in the HLR (home location register) to hamper the working of any SM into any other UT.

Transmission Security

As introduced previously, interference represents one of the main impairments that can either cause overall capacity limitation or even hamper transmission capability, should the interference level significantly degrade the SINR (signal to interference + noise ratio).

By taking advantage of this vulnerability of transmission capability, signals can be produced in the direction of the satellite antenna just aiming to degrade SINR to a level that hampers proper communication. Moreover, the extension of the coverage area makes it difficult to locate the eventual unwanted source. Such a phenomenon, named jamming, is typical of military operations, and is produced to disturb the other party's communication.

The protection from this kind of "aware" interference, derived from military technology, is typically a task of the on-board antenna capability of creating a variable number of nulls in the direction of the various interferers. The antenna design and manufacturing is based on the possibility of using sophisticated phased arrays, driven by a local intelligence. Because of the price reduction of the phase components and the microprocessing capability up to the highest frequency bands (in the antenna Rx mode), it is well within the next satellite generation to consider this antijamming technique for a governmental satellite system for security uses (National Bureau of Standards, 1977; Multimidea.net, n.d.).

Network Security

At present, most satellite networks for wideband services provide such an interface. To ensure security for IP via satellite, a number of service requirements are identified (Noubir & von Allmen, 1999): confidentiality (protection from passive attacks, unauthorized release of message content, and traffic flow analysis), authentication (the message sender is really who he claims to be), integrity (the message content is not modified), nonrepudiation (sender or receiver does not deny a transmitted message), access control (limit access), and key management and exchange (negotiate security keys between communication entities). Moreover, as concerns protection of the information content at network level, security can be ensured implementing the IPSec mechanism, which is a protocol operating between the IP layer and the TCP layer, as reported in Kent and Atkinson (1998c). In this way security is independent on upper layer protocols, traffic rerouting and network configuration modifications are preserved, and both real-time and non-real-time applications are protected. In particular, two protocols are proposed: authentication header (AH; Kent & Atkinson, 1998a) for integrity without confidentiality, and encapsulating security payload (ESP; Kent & Atkinson, 1998b) for confidentiality with optional integrity and authentication. In addition, two modes of operating are defined: transport mode (to protect upper-layer protocols) and tunnel mode (to protect the whole datagram). The former applies to host-to-host authentication, the latter to gateway-to-gateway and host-to-gateway, which is useful in case the same entity owns two or more private networks connected through the public Internet. As far as IPSec is concerned, the IP datagram is composed of three parts: IP header, TCP header, and user data. In transport mode, an IPSec header (AH or ESP) is inserted between the IP header and the TCP header. In tunnel mode, the whole IP packet is encapsulated in a new IPSec packet (a new IP header followed by an AH or ESP header). In both cases, the IP payload, composed of TCP header and user data, results in one indivisible protected unit. The keys used to encrypt and authenticate must be known only at the two end users. The intermediate nodes (routers) are only allowed to forward packets based on routing tables.

Definitively, all these mechanisms require keeping the end-to-end semantic. Thus, as long as the adopted upper-layer protocol does not introduce a violation of this concept, no particular problem arises in implementing IPSec in satellite networks, excluding the delay in key distribution. Nevertheless, to speed up the TCP process, modification to the standard mechanism must be introduced, as mentioned previously. When such modifications concerning the flow control mechanism, involve only the two end hosts, or involve the intermediate routers but do not require access to TCP data encapsulated in the IP packet, no particular incompatibility arises. In contrast, if splitting or some PEP or network address translator (NAT) options are implemented, as in most of the commercial systems for wideband services, the end-to-end semantic is violated. Thus, compatibility with standard IPSec implementation drops. In fact, relevant information to perform PEP mechanisms is present in the TCP header. In particular, the flow identification number (identifying source and destination port numbers) and the sequence numbers (used to match acknowledgements with the data segments) are necessary to be accessed for PEP operations. Both ESP protocol (encrypting TCP header inside the ESP header) and AH protocol (not allowing modification to ACK stream) are incompatible with PEP implementation.

To overcome these problems, a number of approaches can be adopted (Zhang & Singh, 2000), such as replacing

IPSec with a transport-layer security mechanism, tunneling one security protocol within another, using transport-friendly ESP format, and splitting IPSec into as many segments as the whole path is splinted, but each has its own limitations.

Another approach named multilayer IPSec (ML-IPSec) has been proposed. It is based on partitioning the IP packet into different parts and applying a different kind of protection to each. For example, two zones can be identified: TCP header and TCP data. The former can use a protection scheme with key shared among the source, the destination and a certain number of intermediate nodes, where PEP is implemented. The latter can use classical end-to-end protection with keys shared only between the source and destination hosts. This approach, other than showing full compatibility with standard IPSec, adds not too much complexity and performs very promisingly. Definitively, it looks the right solution to provide security; in fact, we can exploit TCP enhancement mechanisms (for example accelerators), largely utilized in commercial systems, and ensuring security applying standard algorithms, such as IPSec, as well. In addition, when multicast connectivity is exploited, which takes advantage of the already underlined suitability of satellite communications, additional problems arise and must be resolved (Howarth, Iyengar, Sun, & Chuickshank, 2004). As a matter of fact, multicast security is in general more complex than unicast security, and even more costly and performs less well if applied to satellite. In fact, the rekeying procedure must be performed for a number of reasons: regularly (every few seconds or minutes) to avoid cryptanalysis of traffic, on demand if the key may be compromised, when a new user join the group to avoid the possibility that previous traffic may be decrypted, and when a member leaves the group to avoid the possibility that future traffic may be decrypted. Because the key distribution is performed through the satellite, the cost of the operation can be high because the bandwidth is expensive and the delay is meaningful, especially if the multicast group membership updates frequently. To limit costs, efficient algorithm must be implemented.

Transport-Layer Security

It is also possible to provide security at the transport layer. In this case, the IP header (addresses) is not protected and therefore traffic analysis is possible, but key management is simplified. Two solutions are applicable: TLS (transport layer security) and SRTP (secure real-time transport protocol).

TLS is designed to provide privacy and is composed of two layers: TLS record protocol and TLS handshake protocol. The former works on top of TCP (and therefore is not useful for UDP connections, largely used for multicast and real-time traffic), which ensures privacy and reliability. Symmetric cryptography is used (DES or AES). The latter provides connection security at the authentication level before starting transmission of application data.

SRTP is a profile of real-time transport protocol (RTP). It provides confidentiality, message authentication, and replay protection.

Security Provision to Other Networks

To guarantee proper working conditions for several kind of terrestrial telecommunication networks, the ability to get localization information (especially for mobile services and search and rescue applications) and synchronization information is particularly relevant.

Satellites are actually used as a means to provide synchronization signals to terrestrial telecommunication networks (for example, cellular that is based on the IS-95 standard) and to support security by supplying the localization information of the network users. GPS Constellation and the forthcoming Galileo make this information available.

The GPS is a worldwide radio-navigation system utilizing a constellation of 24 satellites and their ground stations (Dana, 1994; European Space Agency, 2004). GPS uses these "man-made stars" as reference points to calculate accurate positions on the order of meters. In fact, with advanced forms of GPS, it is possible to get measurements accurate to a few centimeters.

GPS and, in a short while, Galileo work in five logical steps.

- "Triangulation" from satellites is the basic principle.
- To triangulate, a GPS receiver measures distance (called pseudo-range) using the travel time of radio signals;
- To measure travel time, GPS needs, on one side, a reasonably accurate internal clock and, on the other side, one additional unknown (the satellite time), which it achieves by solving the equation system;
- Along with distance, the satellite positions, which are communicated to the receiver in space, are used;
- Finally, a correction is needed for any delays the signal experiences as it travels through the atmosphere.

The possible use of GPS and Galileo for supporting the authentication procedure of the correspondent, delivering the relative position with a high degree of accuracy to the security authority, has the potential to increase the security level of the overall system.

SECURE SYSTEMS AND APPLICATIONS IMPLEMENTED USING SATELLITES

It is worth briefly presenting and describing some not exhaustive example of commercial secure services provided via satellite.

Euteltracs is the first European commercial mobile satellite service. Based on the Omnitracs project in United States, it provides message service, bidirectional two-way service, and localization. The system architecture is composed of five elements:

- user terminal, which exchanges messages with the service provider's network management center (SNMC) that is receiving the position;
- the SNMC connected to the hub station;
- the hub station, which consists of two front-end antennas and HTF (hub terminal facilities) to monitor, to process, and to control traffic between SNMC and the mobile terminals;

Table 2 Satellite Use Summary for Military Applications

Satellite Systems	Mission
Defense support program	Missile warning
Global positioning system (GPS) Galileo	Navigation
Nuclear detonation detection system	Nuclear detonation detection
Meteorological satellites	Weather and environmental monitoring
Defense satellite communications system:	Communications:
EHF band	Army fixed and mobile communications (EHF, SHF, UHF)
SHF band	Maritime communications (EHF, SHF, UHF)
UHF band	Air communications (SHF, UHF)

- the space segment; and
- the MCT (mobile communication terminal) mounted on the vehicle.

Euteltracs is at present used to provide secure services to several private police companies by remotely authorizing the opening of doors of vans used to carry money and jewels, thereby preventing and discouraging robberies.

Satellite Security Systems (S3) provides a number of secure services through the use of satellites (Satellite Securtiy Systems, n.d.). More specifically, they combine the use of telecommunication infrastructures (ReFlex by Motorola) and positioning systems (GPS).

In particular, S3 offers these products:

- First Responder Alert and Monitoring System (FRAMSM), which provides an end-to-end solution for monitoring, control, and decision support;
- FleetGuard™, aiming at fleet management and localization;
- GlobalGuard™ for fixed-point monitoring and control;
- GlobalGuard LE Systems™ for law enforcement, which are used in a variety of applications to track and monitor activities of suspect vehicles, cargo trailers, or any other asset that could be utilized in criminal activities; and
- IONIT School Transportation to enable school bus tracking and monitoring (based on GlobalGuard).

ELEMENTS ON MILITARY SATELLITES

Communications is vital to the modern military establishment. In particular, space systems are an integral part of the overall military forces. In fact, military satellites on the geostationary orbit have been launched by many nations (United States; France; United Kingdom; former U.S.S.R., now Russia; and Italy) and international organizations such as NATO (North Atlantic Treaty Organization).

Satellites permit direct communications with units on the battlefield. Lightweight mobile terminals can be erected in a matter of hours, thereby keeping advancing troops in constant contact with higher authorities. Today, the soldier in the field can use satellite links to establish direct and instantaneous communication with the national command authorities.

Satellites help confer a decisive advantage in terms of combat timing, battle space awareness, operating tempo, synchronization, maneuverability, and the application of firepower. In Table 2 a summary of possible use of satellites for military forces is presented.

The growth of the presence of military forces worldwide for peace keeping and peace enforcement missions has increased the use of commercial satellites for military applications. Most of civilian fleets have been used, such as Intelsat, Eutelsat, Inmarsat, Globalstar, Iridium, and others (see Figure 5).

The satellite systems have become the typical demonstration of dual-use systems. Technically, as is frequently noted, there is no clear difference between civil and military satellite systems. Orbital imagers and communications satellites are prime examples of dual-use technologies. For example, communication satellites can carry either military or civilian traffic, and navigation satellites are used both by the military and civilian communities. From a service point of view, military communications satellites are including a bunch of applications (see Figure 6). This approach tends to maximize the availability of new services and the use of all the available space bandwidth capability.

Figure 5: Milsat transportable station operating with commercial satellite. (Courtesy of Telespazio, Italy.)

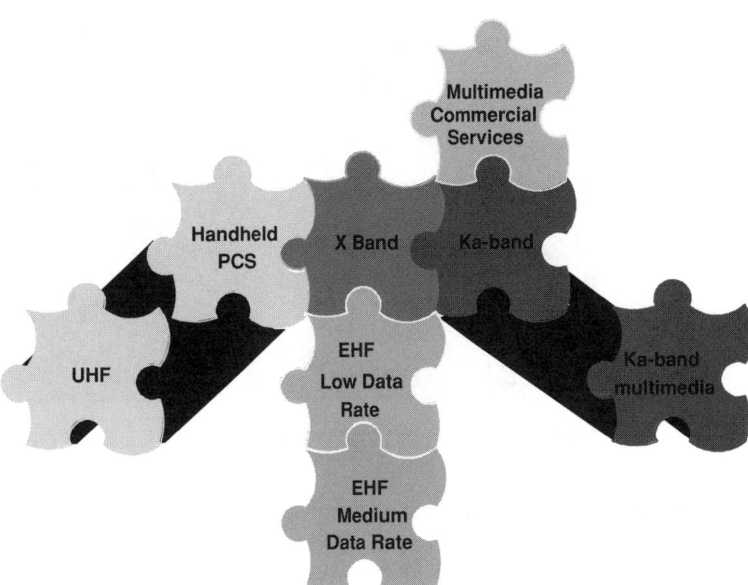

Figure 6: Milsat new service scenario.

Traditionally, military satellite systems have dedicated frequency bands and present better performance in terms of communications security, robustness, and availability performance.

Communications and Transmission Security

Military communication systems present the capability of providing secure, encrypted, and antijam-protected communications to prevent an external enemy from intercepting and interrupting vital communications in time of crisis. Encryption is based on private key schemes; the link protection is obtained with a number of techniques:

- direct sequence CDMA (code division multiple access);
- frequency-hopping CDMA;
- power control, forward correcting codes, and user bandwidth optimization; and
- antenna beam nulling antijam capability.

As introduced previously, antenna nulling capability is probably the most powerful technique to counteract one or multiple jammers and minimize the antenna gain in the directions of the jammer sources. This nulling capability is obtained via a phased array system capable of minimizing a number of jammers according to its freedom degree number (based on the number of elements of the phased array).

Navigation and Remote Sensing Satellites

In addition to communications, satellites are used for navigation and remote sensing. These applications are a fundamental complement to communications and they are typical dual-use services.

The best known navigation system is the GPS (briefly introduced previously), which supplies localization information with two different accuracies (the n code and the p code, reserved to military applications). The constellation is formed by 24 satellites orbiting at 20,000 km from the Earth surface on four different orbits (six satellites per orbit), inclined 55° on the equatorial plane. Localization is obtained using at least four satellites for triangulation. Navigation systems integrated with communications (typically via satellites) are essential for security, safety, and rescue in the following scenarios:

- airborne navigation systems,
- personal computers and other portable devices,
- vehicle and asset tracking systems,
- secure timing and synchronization systems, and
- smart munitions.

Remote sensing satellites are low orbiting (typical sun synchronous) and are capable of collecting images of the Earth surface either via passive sensors (optical, infrared, panchromatic) or active microwave sensors (SAR, scatterometers, radar altimeters).

These satellites produce images at low, medium, and high resolution (from a few meters to some tenths of centimeters), which are essential for battlefield analysis, early warning applications, border control, international agreement monitoring, disaster forecast, mapping, etc. Figure 7 shows the newest SAR system announced for early 2006: Cosmo skymed and its three observation modes.

CONCLUSIONS

Security represents a very critical and real important issue from the different points of view, spanning from information protection to human life security. To achieve the needed level of security, telecommunication systems surely play a crucial role and the satellite component can increase the capability thanks to its features. In fact, we believe that only through a strong connection among all the components of the GII an adequate level of security can be provided. In this chapter, the main contributions that the satellite can provide to overall security have been highlighted along with the main limitations. The use of

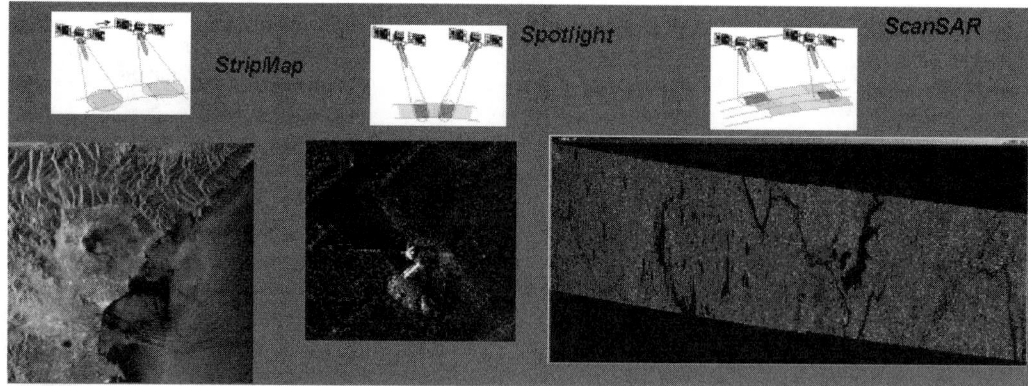

Figure 7: Active remote sensing (SAR) image acquisition modes. (Courtesy of Telespazio, Italy.)

satellites for civilian telecommunications and for military purposes has been mainly addressed. Also the use for localization and navigation and for Earth observation has been briefly highlighted.

GLOSSARY

Broadcast A connection allowing information transfer from one to everybody.

Conditional access A procedure to allow only a restricted subset of users to access information.

Coverage Area The area on the Earth's surface over which the signal-to-noise ratio in both up- and downlink for a user located inside is greater than the required ratio.

Forward Link The link from the hub station to the user terminal.

Gateway The earth station of a satellite system that ensures connection to terrestrial networks.

Global Information Infrastructure The concept of a unique telecommunication infrastructure at planetary level to provide services everywhere to everyone.

Multicast A connection allowing information transfer from one to many.

Multiple Access A regulated exploitation of a common resource by different users distributed at different locations.

Omnidirectional The characteristic of an antenna capable of transmiting and receiving electromagnetic power to and from any direction with the same gain.

Reliability The capability for equipment and systems to provide service without interruption from failure.

Return Link The link from the user terminal to the hub station.

Unicast A connection allowing information transfer from one to one.

CROSS REFERENCES

See *Cellular Networks; IP Multicast and Its Security; Radio Frequency and Wireless Communications Security; Wireless Channels.*

REFERENCES

Allman, M., Glover, D., & Sanchez, L. (1999, January). *Enhancing TCP over satellite channels using standard mechanism* (RFC 2488, http://www.rfc-editor.org/, January, 1999).

Blake-Wilson, S., Nystrom, M., Hopwood, D., Mikkelsen, J., & Wright, T. (2003, June). Transport layer security (TLS) extensions (RFC 3546, http://www.rfc-editor.org/, June 2003).

Border, J., Kojo, M., Griner, J., Montenegro, G., & Shelby, Z. (2001, June). Performance enhancing proxies intended to mitigate link-related degradations (RFC 3135, http://www.rfc-editor.org/, June 2001).

Caini, C., Corazza, G. E., Falciasecca, G., Ruggieri, M., & Vatalaro, F. (1992, October). A spectrum- and power-efficient EHF mobile satellite system to be integrated with terrestrial cellular systems. *IEEE Journal on Selected Areas in Communications, 10*, 1315–1325.

Caire, G., Corazza, G. E., De Gaudenzi, R., Gallinaro, G., Luglio, M., Lyons, R., Romero-Garcia, J., Vernucci, A., & Widmer, H. (2002, March). Wideband-CDMA for the satellite component of UMTS/IMT-2000. *IEEE Transactions on Vehicular Technology, 51*(2), 306–331.

Carducci, F. (2004). Satellite endowed encryption routing system—Diffie Hellman key agreement protocol (Internal Report). Marconi Selenia Communications, Rome.

Colcy, J. N., & Steinhäuser, R. (1993, June 16–18). *EUTELTRACS—The European experience on mobile satellite service*. Paper presented at the 3rd International Mobile Satellite Conference (IMSC '93) Pasadena, California.

Dana, P. H. (1994). *The global positioning overview*. Retrieved [date April 2004,] from http://www.colorado.edu/geography/gcraft/notes/gps/gps_f.html

De Gaudenzi, R., & Giannetti, F. (1998, May). DS-CDMA satellite diversity reception for personal satellite communication: Satellite-to-mobile link performance analysis. *IEEE Transactions on Vehicular Technology, 47*(2), 658–672.

Del Re, E., Fantacci, R., Giambene, G., & Walter, S. (1997). Performance evaluation of an improved PRMA protocol for low Earth orbit mobile communication systems. *International Journal of Satellite Communications, 15*, 281–291.

Elbert, B. (2000, November). *The satellite communications ground segment and Earth station handbook*. Norwood, MA: Artech House.

EMS Technologies. (n.d.) *Antennas: F-22 Intra-flight data link antenna system*. Retrieved [date April 30, 2004,] from http://www.emsstg.com/ defense/ant_data_link.asp

European satellite TV frequently asked questions. (n.d.) Retrieved [date, April 30, 2004] from http://www.funet.fi/index/esi/Satellite-TV-Europe-FAQ.html

European Space Agency. (2004, October 11). *How to build a constellation of 30 navigation satellites*. Retrieved April 6, 2005, from http://www.esa.int/export/esaSA/ESAV577708D_navigation_0.html

European Telecommunication Standard Institute. (1997, August). *Digital video broadcasting (DVB); Framing structure, channel coding and modulation for 11/12 GHz satellite services* (EN 300 421 V1.1.2, Sophia-Antipolis Cedex FRANCE).

European Telecommunication Standard Institute. (2000, January 21). *Digital video broadcasting (DVB); Interaction channel for satellite distribution systems* (TM2267r2 DVB-RCS001rev11, Sophia-Antipolis Cedex FRANCE).

Giancristofaro, D., Piloni, V., Novello, R., Giubilei, R., & Tousch, J. (2000, September 17–21). *Performances of novel DVB-RCS standard turbo code and its applications in on-board processing satellites*. Paper presented at IEEE European Mobile Personal Satcoms- Personal, Indoor and Mobile Radio Communications 2000, London.

Howarth, M. P., Iyengar, S., Sun, Z., & Cruickshank, H. (2004, February). Dynamics of key management in secure satellite multicast. *IEEE Journal on Selected Areas in Communications, 22*(2), 308–318.

Kent, S., & Atkinson, R. (1998a, November). *IP authentication header, IETF* (RFC 2402), http://www.rfc-editor.org/, November 1998.

Kent, S., & Atkinson, R. (1998b, November). *IP encapsulating security payload (ESP), IETF* (RFC2406, http://www.rfc-editor.org/, November 1998).

Kent, S., & Atkinson, R. (1998c, November). *Security architecture for the Internet protocol, IETF* (RFC 2401, http://www.rfc-editor.org/, November 1998).

Leo, M., & Luglio, M. (2003, February). Identification and performance evaluation of intersegment handover procedures for hybrid constellation satellite systems. *Wireless Communications and Mobile Computing, 3*(1), 87–97.

Loreti, P., & Luglio, M. (2002, July–August). Interference evaluations and simulations for multisatellite multispot systems. *International Journal of Satellite Communications, 20*(4), 261–281.

Loreti, P., Luglio, M., Kapoor, R., Stepanek, J., Gerla, M., Vatalaro, F., & Vazquez-Castro, M. A. (2001). LEO satellite systems' performance with TCP-IP applications. *Proceedings of Milcom 2001, Vol. 2* (pp. 811–815).

Loreti, P., Luglio, M., & Palombini, L. (2000, September). *Impact of multibeam antenna design on interference for LEO constellations*. Paper presented at the 11th IEEE International Symposium on Personal, Indoor and Mobile Radio Communications (PIRMC 2000), London.

Luglio, M., Bellini, S., Marinelli, M., Tartara, G., & Vatalaro, F. (1997, October). *Link design and fade countermeasures for multimedia satellite services in the frame of the SECOMS project*. Proceedings of ACTS Mobile Communication Summit '97, Aalborg, Denmark, Oct. 7–10, 1997, vol 1, pp. 37–42.

Luglio, M., & Pietroni, W. (2002). Optimisation of double link transmission in case of hybrid orbit satellite constellations. *AIAA Journal on Spacecrafts and Rockets, 39*(5).

Luglio, M., Yahya Sanadidi, M., Stepanek, J., & Gerla, M. (2004, February). On-board satellite "split TCP" proxy. *IEEE Journal on Selected Areas in Communications, 22*(2), 362–370.

Lutz, E., Werner, M., & Jahn, A. *Satellite systems for personal and broadband communications*. Springer, Berlin, 2000.

Maral, G., & Bousquet, M., 2003, *Satellite communications systems: Systems techniques and technology* (4th ed. Chichester). Wiley.

Maral, G., De Ridder, J., Evans, B. G., & Richharia, M. (1991). Low Earth orbit satellite systems for communications. *International Journal of Satellite Communications, 9*(2), 209–225.

National Bureau of Standards. (1977, January). *Data encryption, federal information processing standards* (Publ. 46).

NIST. (n.d.) *Key management guideline*. Retrieved [April 2004] from http://csrc.ncsl.nist.gov/CryptoToolkit/kms/key-management-guideline-(workshop).pdf

Noubir, G., & von Allmen, L. (1999). Security issues in Internet protocols over satellite links. In *Proceedings of the 50th Vehicular Technology Conference* (pp. 2726–2730).

Partridge, C., & Shepard, T. J. (1997, September–October). TCP/IP performance over satellite links. *IEEE Network*, 44–49.

Satellite security systems. (n.d.) Retrieved [date, April 30, 2004] from http://www.satsecurity.com

Vatalaro, F., Corazza, G. E., Caini, C., & Ferrarelli, C. (1995, February). Analysis of LEO, MEO, and GEO global mobile satellite systems in the presence of interference and fading. *IEEE Journal on Selected Areas in Communications, 13*(2), 291–300.

White House. (2003, February). *The physical protection of critical infrastructures and key assets*. Washington, DC: Author.

Y. Zhang, A multilayer IP security protocol for TCP performance enhancement in wireless networks IEEE Journal on Selected Areas in Communications, Vol 22, Issue 4, May 2004, pp. 767–776.

Security of Broadband Access Networks

Peter L. Heinzmann, *University of Applied Sciences Eastern Switzerland Rapperswil* and *cnlab Information Technology Research AG*

INTRODUCTION

"Broadband" Internet Access: Definition and Technologies

There is no generally accepted broadband definition. The U.S. Federal Communications Commission (FCC) defines "first-generation broadband" to mean "advanced telecommunications capability" and "advanced service" that differs from dial-up Internet access in several important ways (Powell et al., 2004):

- First, broadband Internet access provides high-speed connection with more than 200 Kb/s customer-to-provider (upstream) and provider-to-customer (downstream) transmission speeds.
- Second, unlike dial-up access, broadband provides always-on connections so that users can receive as well as send data without having to reconnect to the network.
- Third, broadband provides low latency.

Today, most broadband providers are offering services with download rates well in excess of 200 Kb/s and, given the asymmetric use of most residential subscribers, somewhat slower upload rates. Note that the International Telecommunication Union (ITU) uses the term broadband for "services with rates of more than 2,048 Kb/s" (ITU Internet Reports, 2003).

Broadband Internet access for residential users (i.e., subscribers or customers) is provided by a variety of "last mile" technologies. Depending on population density, geographic situation, or techno-political issues, one or several from the following technologies are used:

- **Cable technologies** give access to high-speed data services over coaxial cables that are part of community antenna television (CATV) operators' hybrid fiber–coaxial (HFC) infrastructures. The so-called data-over-cable (DOC) systems cover the whole CATV network area and offer typical download and upload speeds of up to 6 Mb/s and up to several hundred Kb/s, respectively (Dutta, 2001).
- **Copper technologies** provide for high-speed data services on the telephone operators' twisted-pair cable infrastructures. There are multiple variants of these so-called digital subscriber line (DSL) technologies. The most common variant of DSL is asymmetric digital subscriber line (ADSL), which has approximately 5.5 km maximum cable length and download and upload speeds of up to 3 Mb/s and up to 768 Kb/s, respectively (Starr, 2003; Bascher et al., 2004).
- **Fiber technologies** ensure ultra-high-speed services on specially installed fiber optic cable infrastructures. Fiber-to-the-home (FTTH) installations deliver up to 500 Mb/s data services and up to 870 MHz high-definition television services via fiber cables that terminate at the subscriber homes. Fiber-to-the-curb (FTTC) facilities terminate in the vicinity of the homes.
- **Unlicensed wireless technologies** provide up to 3 Mb/s for non-line-of-sight applications in the 902–928 MHz band and up to 54 Mb/s wireless fidelity (Wi-Fi), that is, wireless LAN (WLAN) in the 2.4 GHz and 5 GHz industrial, scientific, and medical (ISM) bands. Wi-Fi using the Institute of Electrical and Electronics Engineers (IEEE) 802.11 series standards became very common for Internet access via commercial and noncommercial hotspots. Another unlicensed wireless technology in line-of-sight areas is the worldwide interoperability for microwave access (WiMax), based on IEEE 802.16 series standards with up to 75 Mb/s speeds and covering up to 20 km in distance.
- **Licensed wireless technologies** allow for Internet access with broadband mobile services that are also referred to as third-generation (3G) mobile services.

Table 1 Broadband Transmission Speeds and Number of Homes per Distribution Point

Cable Infrastructure, Technology	Downstream Rate	Upstream Rate	Maximum Distance	Homes per Distribution Point
Existing coaxial CATV cables with fiber backbone (HFC), shared cable (bus), DOC	45 Mb/s	1.5 Mb/s	Up to several 10 km	1,000–2,000
One existing twisted pair (star), ADSL	6 Mb/s	640 Kb/s	5.5 km	1,000–3,000
Two (existing) twisted pairs (star), HDSL	2 Mb/s	2 Mb/s	7 km	NA
One existing twisted pair for the last 100 to 300 m (star), VDSL	50 Mb/s	20 Mb/s	300 m	100
	25 Mb/s	5 Mb/s	1 km	100
	12 Mb/s	1.5 Mb/s	1.5 km	100
Existing power lines, PLC	27 Mb/s	18 Mb/s	NA	1,000
New fiber installation and existing twisted pair for the last up to 100 m, FTTC/VDSL	25–50 Mb/s	25–50 Mb/s	100 m	10–50
New fiber installation to the home, FTTH	155 Mb/s	155 Mb/s	10 km	10–200

The commercially available technologies are wideband CDMA (WCDMA) and Universal Mobile Telecommunications System (UMTS), which allow for maximum downstream data rates of up to 2 Mb/s. The upstream speeds are typically around 300 Kb/s and it should be noted that the experienced delays may be significant (more than 100 ms round-trip).

- **Power line communication** (power line Internet) uses existing electrical power lines for symmetric Internet access at up to 45 Mb/s (Abe (2004). In the United States, it is called broadband over power lines (BPL); the Europeans use the term power line communication (PLC). The industrial "HomePlug" alliance was formed to standardize data networking via electrical wiring inside the premises (i.e., on the low voltage [230 V] level) at up to 14 Mb/s. HomePlug has now expanded its scope to include power line communication (Jones, 2004).

Currently, the most widely used technologies for broadband Internet access are ADSL and DOC. The ADSL connection generally transports voice and data services, and the DOC connection focuses on video and data services. Both ADSL ISPs and DOC ISPs are now moving towards "triple-play" service: delivering voice, data, and video. See Table 1 for comparisons of transmission speeds.

Broadband Market Situation

Broadband Internet access with upload data rates between 64 Kb/s and 800 Kb/s and download data rates between 128 Kb/s and 3 Mb/s has become affordable for many residential users. However, there are still many more private Internet-capable personal computers (PCs) connected to narrowband dial-up networks than to broadband networks (in 2003, only 14% of the U.S., 4% of the European, and 6.4% of the Swiss home PCs had a broadband connection). Nevertheless, there are around 100 million worldwide broadband subscribers today. The largest broadband markets are United States with 28 million, Europe with 23 million, Japan with 14 million, China with 12 million, and Korea with 11 million broadband subscribers (data from 2003; ITU Internet Reports, 2003).

DSL and DOC are by far the most important broadband technologies. The market share of the broadband technologies in a region or country is influenced by geographical, historical, and techno-political issues. DSL is the dominant broadband access technology in Asia and in most European countries; DOC is more widely used in the United States, Switzerland, the Netherlands, and Austria. See Figure 1.

In South Korea, cheap DSL access is available in 85% of the homes and unlimited broadband access costs $25/month for 2 Mb/s and around $34 a month for 8 Mb/s (flat rate). Japan uses mainly DSL but there are also FTTH systems (Saito et al., 2003).

In Germany, Deutsche Telekom, one of Europe's largest DSL broadband operators, has prevented large-scale upgrades of cable networks. German DSL ISPs offer a variety of tariff models (volume-based, time/volume limit-based, and flat rate; Stuart & Bhalla, 2003).

The U.K. and Swiss DSL/DOC broadband market is already fairly competitive. In Switzerland, where CATV traditionally has a very high penetration and where DOC networks are not controlled by the telecom operators, roughly 40% of connections are DOC and 60% are DSL (OFCOM, 2003). The cost for the widely used 100 Kb/s upstream and 600 Kb/s downstream ADSL service is about $35 per month (flat rate; Paltridge & Matsui, 2004).

Broadband Threats and Vulnerabilities

All Internet service subscribers should be aware of threats and vulnerabilities. Today, most people understand that their data traffic could be read or modified, that is, there is no guarantee of confidentiality and/or integrity of transmitted data (see Figure 2) because of various forms of wiretapping, sniffing, or traffic rerouting. Not everybody is aware of source or destination spoofing threats, which compromise the authenticity of the sender or receiver (see Figure 2). Such attacks (e.g., man-in-the-middle and

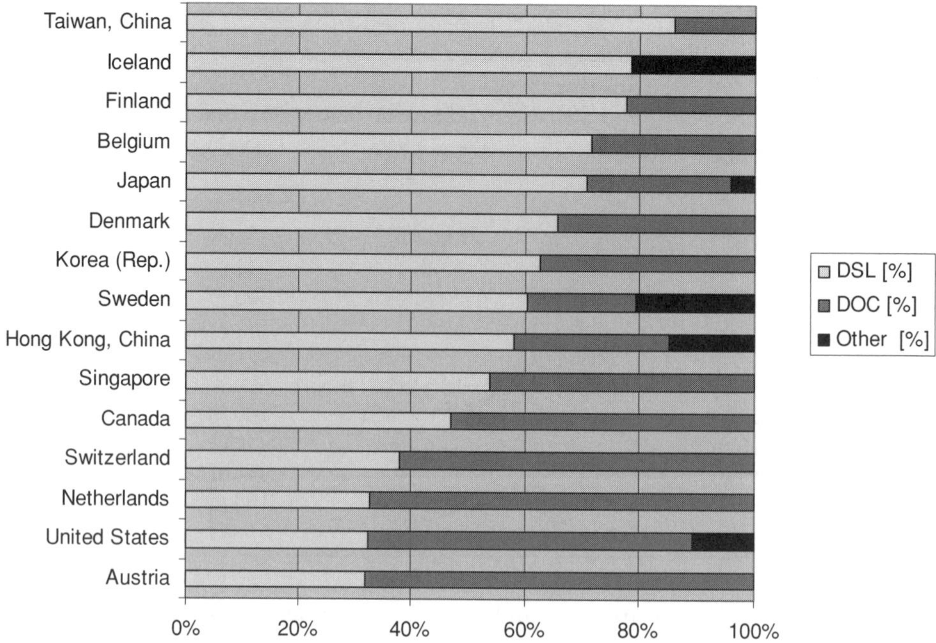

Figure 1: Broadband technology market share in various countries. Source: Powell et al., 2004.

phishing attacks) may result in identity theft and even financial loss. However, these attacks are similar in broadband and narrowband environments.

Computers from residential users with broadband connections are much more attractive for attackers than computers with narrowband connections because of the always-on connection and the high data rate. The always-on connection gives an attacker more opportunity to access a subscriber system and to test for vulnerabilities (see Figure 2). The high data rate makes broadband systems very attractive targets for the installation of all sorts of malicious mobile code. Most residential users are not aware of such threats and vulnerabilities. The exposure of their private data might be their own business. However, if their computer is hijacked by other people, this might also severely affect other Internet users. Today, the millions of vulnerable (unpatched) residential broadband computers are a dangerous source for distributed denial of service (DDOS) attacks (Shannon & Moore, 2003) and for worm and spam distribution (i.e., mass mailings). A mass mailer program self-replicates by sending itself out via e-mail. Typically, the program obtains e-mail addresses by searching in files on the system or responding to messages found in the e-mail client inbox. Mass mailers may be used to send spam mails. It is said that spam network services, which can be bought on the Internet underground, account for more than a third of all junk e-mails.

Many penetrated residential broadband computers have become a place for attackers to hide data and to anonymously distribute data, for example, copyright

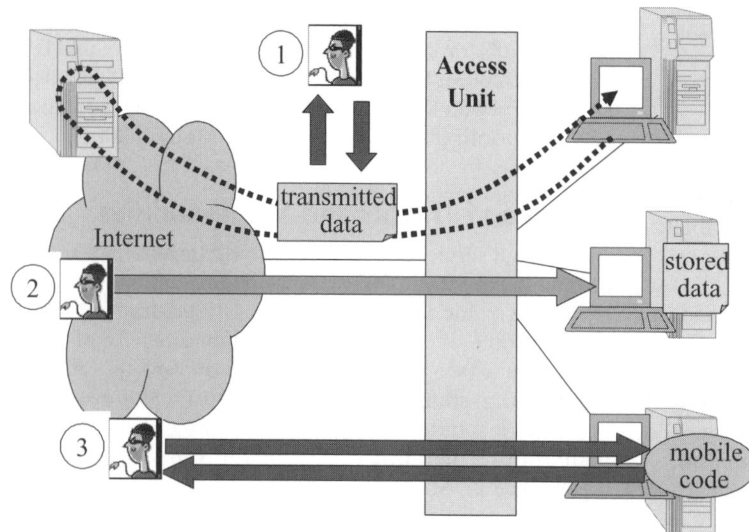

Figure 2: Basic threats and vulnerabilities: 1, attacking (read, modify) transmitted data; 2, accessing systems (scan for vulnerabilities), reading, modifying stored data; 3, using systems (install and execute programs).

protected material (Richmond (2004). (See also volume 3, part 1 of the *Handbook.*)

So-called blended threats exploit system vulnerabilities to distribute malicious mobile code, for example, viruses, worms, or Trojans (see Figure 2). The distribution takes place via e-mail and Web access as well as by programs that automatically scan for vulnerable computers and replicate themselves (worms). In 2003, blended threats accounted for 80% of attack activity. Examples of blended threats include Klez, Bugbear, SoBig, SQL Slammer, Nimda, and Code Red (McCarthy, 2003).

Some worms replicate themselves to designated IP network blocks of the compromised system's network or domain. If successful, the worm then uses the infected system as a platform from which to scan for new victims. The homogeneity and the high speed of the broadband network, the high number of vulnerable (unpatched) computers, and the high computing speed of target systems result in a dramatic rise of the speed of worm propagation. An unprotected PC can expect to become infected by a worm within minutes of being connected to an unprotected network. The actual survival time for a specific computer to be compromised will vary widely, depending on the filters applied by the ISP, the configuration of access units, and on the configuration of the subscriber's computer.

Once a system is compromised, there may be malicious code installed that allows the attacker to use the system remotely. A malicious code application that serves as an agent for another program or user is called a "bot" (short for robot). Many bots form a botnet, that is, an entire network of infected systems. The bots of a botnet can be controlled by issuing commands through Internet Relay Channel (IRC) (see volume 1, part 1, of the *Handbook*). There may be thousands of listening bots of a botnet that will execute any command issued by the controller of the botnet. Bots for denial-of-service attacks are called "zombies" (see volume 3, part 1 of the *Handbook*).

Some malicious code is now being installed with commercial interest. In 2004, growing evidence showed that underground companies exist that specialize in identity theft and spam (see volume 2, part 2 of the *Handbook*). Their malicious code will install spyware, which tracks Internet browser usage. Even more dangerous is their keystroke-logging software, which can compromise user passwords, credit card numbers, and other confidential information.

BROADBAND NETWORK SECURITY ISSUES

Broadband Network Architecture

Overview

Following the data path from an end-user device (i.e., customer premise's Equipment [CPE], or computer) to an Internet server, the main components and subsystems of a broadband Internet access system are identified (see Figure 3).

The subscriber's access unit (AU) is typically called a "modem" or "router" in an ADSL system and a "cable modem" (CM) in a DOC system. It provides an Ethernet

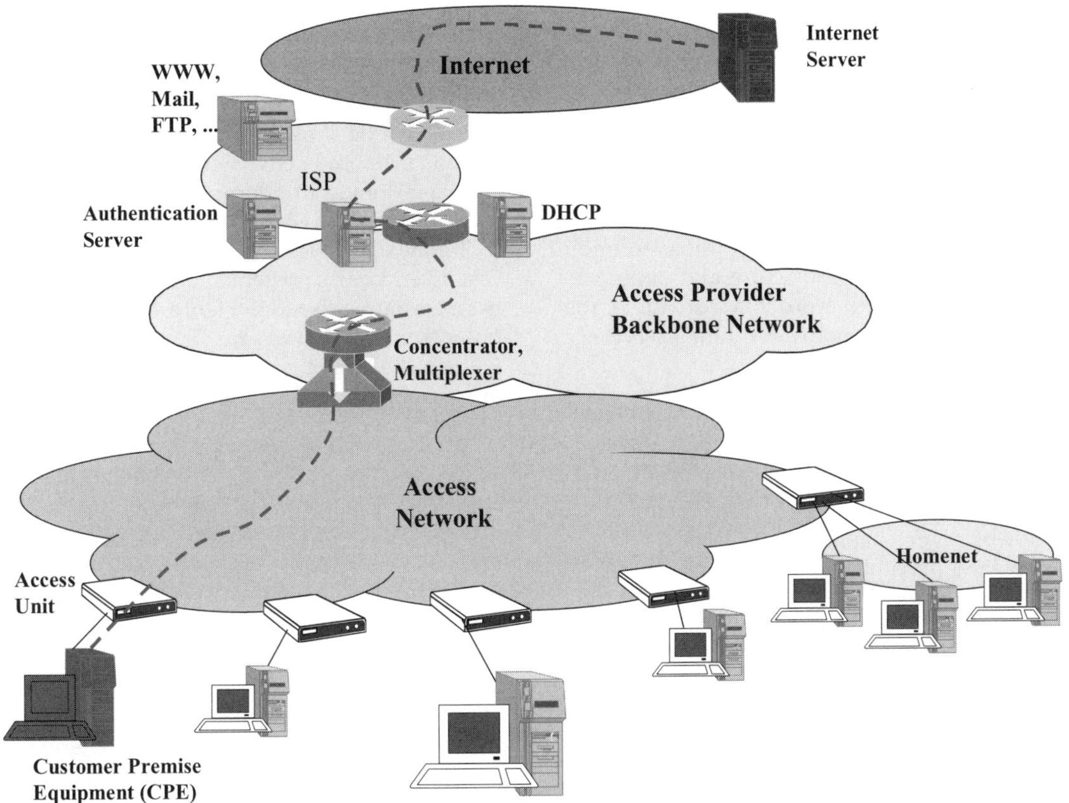

Figure 3: Architecture and components of broadband access systems.

or universal serial bus (USB) interface to attach the local subscriber's computer or communication equipment. Modems are owned by the subscriber or leased from the ISP; the latter is typically the case in DOC offerings. The access unit may act as a bridge or as a router. The bridge provides for transparent connectivity to the CPE. The router will typically incorporate network address translation (NAT) functions and therefore block connection attempts from the outside to the CPE.

The access network section consists of a telecom provider's telephone network wires or a cable television provider's coaxial cables, which connect the access modems with some concentration and multiplexing devices. This central device is called "digital subscriber line access multiplexer" (DSLAM) in an ADSL system or "cable modem termination system" (CMTS) in a DOC system. One CMTS typically controls one DOC cell with up to 2,000 cable modems. One DSLAM typically serves about 3,000 ADSL modems.

The access provider backbone network guarantees the connection of all multiplexers with the ISP authentication and gateway systems. The ISP assigns IP addresses with its dynamic host configuration protocol (DHCP) server. The ISP also takes care of the Internet peering contracts.

Data-Over-Cable (DOC)

Most cable network systems are based on the data-over-cable service interface specification (DOCSIS, Cable Television Laboratories, 2004). DOCSIS specifies how to operate a DOC system with cable modems (CM) and cable modem termination systems (CMTS). It defines the interaction between CM and CMTS on one side and between the CM and CPE on the other side. DOCSIS 1.0 describes how to deliver high-speed "best effort" services simultaneously with (analog) video services. DOCSIS 1.1 adds quality of service, which enables Internet protocol (IP) telephony, and DOCSIS 2.0 allows for higher upstream capacity (up to 30 Mb/s in both directions). The next generation network architecture (NGNA) shall lead to even higher capacity by using various compression technologies in an all-digital cable network. With NGNA, top North American cable operators are exploring options to unify their IP and MPEG video infrastructure and aiming to lower equipment costs, make more efficient use of the HFC spectrum, and promote high-value digital services.

Asymmetric Digital Subscriber Line (ADSL)

ADSL is the most common variant of DSL (Dutta-Roy, 1999). An ADSL subscriber access unit communicates with the DSLAM equipment at the other end of the (twisted-pair) telephone line, creating three channels: a high-speed downstream channel, a medium-speed upstream channel, and plain old telephone service (POTS). The POTS channel is split off from the digital modem by splitters, guaranteeing uninterrupted access for voice services. ADSL end users must be within 5.5 km of the local (central office) exchange.

There are variants of DSL with further restrictions on the maximum distance from the serving central office. Symmetric DSL (SDSL) delivers up to 2 Mb/s over a single line, whereas high-speed DSL (HDSL) uses two or three lines. The asymmetric very high-speed DSL (VDSL) supports downstream data rates of more than 50 Mb/s, but the subscribers must be within about 300 m from the local exchange switch. Rate-adaptive DSL (RADSL) extends the range from the central office (i.e., exchange switch) to up to 5.5 km but works with variable upstream speeds, depending on the quality and actual length of the telephone cable (TTC, 1998). Next-generation ADSL (ADSL2 and ADSL2+) are expected to offer higher bandwidth (12 Mb/s upstream and 25 Mb/s downstream), hence enabling service providers to offer triple play services (DSL Forum, 2003).

Basic Broadband Network Security Concerns

The basic security concerns in broadband networks (see Figure 4) are these:

1. Wiretapping and traffic rerouting to get access to transmitted data (passive [1a] and active wiretapping [1b]),
2. Direct access to subscriber systems to test for vulnerabilities,
3. Subscriber file and resource access to read and modify stored data, and to install and execute programs (mobile code),
4. Service parameter change to increase upload and download data rates.

Reading and/or changing another user's transmitted information by passive or active wiretapping has been heavily discussed in the context of DOC networks. Some authors claimed that passive wiretapping (see 1a in Figure 4) would be easy because of the broadcasting nature of the DOC downstream channel. There were also reports on successfully intercepting traffic via active wiretapping, that is, traffic rerouting or connection hijacking with address spoofing attacks (see 1b in Figure 4; Lindstrom, 2002). However, passive wiretapping is not really a problem as will be shown in following sections, and also the various proposed active wiretapping attacks are not possible any longer in appropriately configured broadband access systems (Cisco, 2002).

Today, the basic security concern should be about access to end users' systems (see 2 in Figure 4) and to end users' resources (see 3 in Figure 4). Access to another computer from within the same network or from the Internet is the basic aim of computer networking. However, there are a number of vulnerabilities that can be exploited if arbitrary packets can be sent to unpatched systems. Such attacks might lead to full control of the subscribers' system. The aim of such attacks could be the distribution and installation of malicious mobile code (e.g., worms) and the execution of distributed denial of service (DDOS) attacks. Massive DDOS attacks that are started from subscribers within broadband-attached systems have the potential to severely affect the network availability.

Most broadband ISPs see themselves as "data carriers" and do not offer special protection of transported data. Many ISPs are concerned about people using their service without permission or about users changing their service parameters to exceed their assigned service level (see 4 in Figure 4). This is known as "uncapping attacks" by which attackers try to overcome bandwidth limitations.

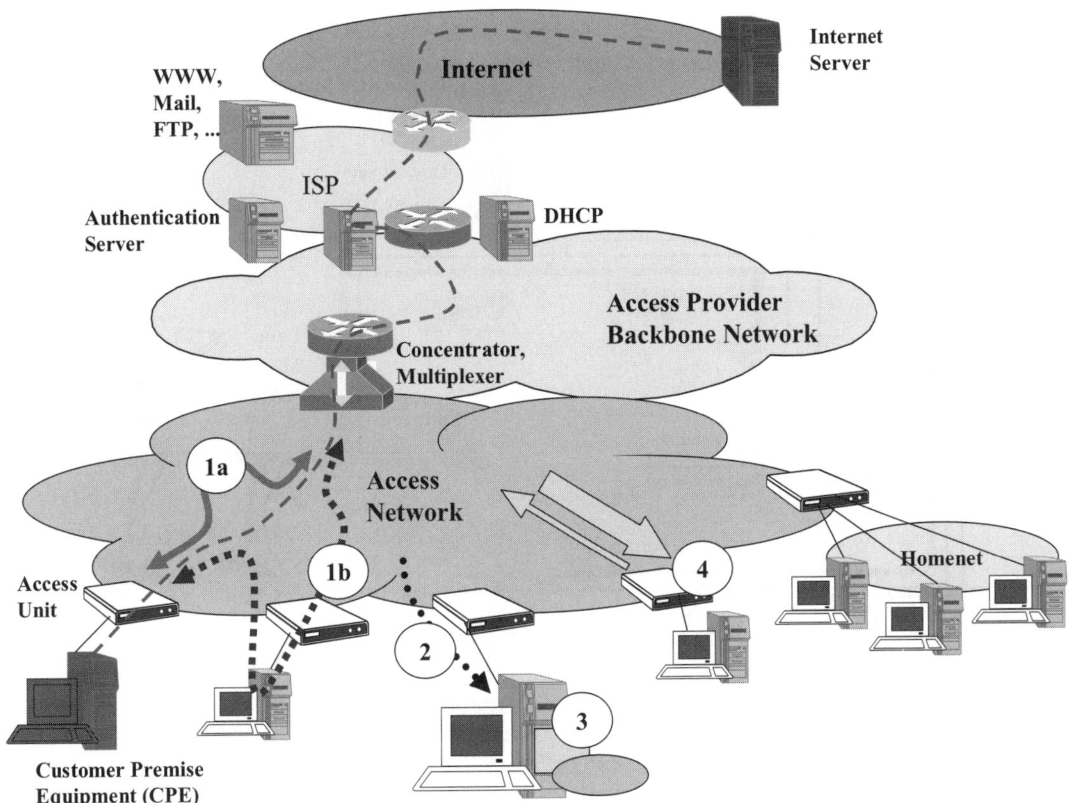

Figure 4: Security issues in broadband networks.

ISPs generally do not feel responsible for the security of their subscribers' systems. However, even just a few compromised user systems within an ISP's network may disable the correct function of the whole provider network. Performance may drop and hosts of the ISP's IP range may appear on spam-server blocking lists, which might lead to severe availability and reputation problems.

The following sections discuss the four basic types of attacks and outline differences with respect to DOC and ADSL networks. The focus is on Windows systems because they account for more than 95% of the home user systems (in August 2004; W3Schools, 2004).

Wiretapping

In ADSL systems, only data addressed to the connected subscriber is transmitted via the access cable from the DSLAM to the subscriber's site. Hence, there is no other subscribers' data on the cable that could be tapped at a specific subscriber's site.

In DOC systems, all data addressed to any of the subscribers in a given cell is sent in the 50–850 MHz frequency band from the CMTS to all subscribers. However, the cabling system, amplifiers, directional splitters, and couplers are designed such that upstream signals—sent in the 5–42 MHz frequency band toward the CMTS—do not reach all subscriber stations of the cell (see signals in Figure 5: transmitted signals from CM_b do not pass at CM_c, CM_d, and CM_e).

Because each cable modem is designed to receive/demodulate in the 50–850 MHz frequency band and to send or modulate in the 5–42 MHz frequency band, consumer brand cable modems cannot demodulate upstream signals. Only the CMTS is equipped to demodulate the upstream frequencies. For example, CM_a cannot demodulate the upstream signals from CM_b. In conclusion, using standard equipment, it is physically impossible to receive and demodulate upstream signals. Hence, the ideas that it would be easy to tap any data of other people at the subscriber's site is a false assumption.

As mentioned, all downstream signals reach all stations of a cell, and the signals are demodulated by all cable modems. However, the data packets are only forwarded to the CPE if the destination address of the packets (DA) matches the address of the modem. To forward all packets, a modem would have to be put in a sort of "promiscuous mode." For example, packets with DA = c (see Figure 5) are not forwarded to the CPE at CM_f unless this modem was set in promiscuous mode. Broadcast packets (DA = all) are received by all modems and forwarded to all CPE.

The DOCSIS 1.1 standard supports a baseline privacy interface (BPI+) that provides bidirectional encryption (Cable Television Laboratories, 2004). BPI+ prevents unauthorized access to data transport services by the CMTS and thereby enforces encryption of the traffic flows. The CMTS controls distribution of keying material to client CMs using an authenticated client/server key management protocol. DOCSIS 1.1 currently employs the cipher block chaining (CBC) mode of the U.S. Data Encryption Standard (DES) to encrypt a DOCSIS MAC frame's packet data. DOCSIS 2.0 also supports the

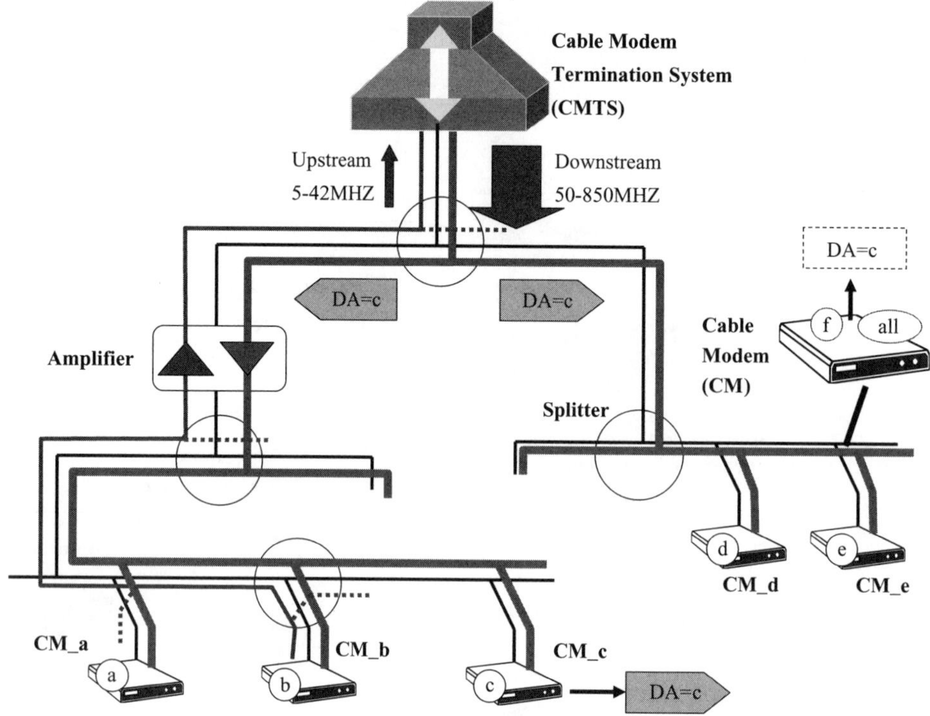

Figure 5: Signal propagation in DOC networks.

advanced encryption standard (AES; Woundy, 2001; Thornhill, 2001). (See volume 2, part 3 of the *Handbook*.)

Today, for example, all access units of the largest Swiss DOC provider use at least 40-bit DES encryption. Hence, even if somebody could demodulate all signals and have its modem in promiscuous mode, it would still not be possible to read the transmitted data unless the attacker was able to decrypt the data.

Direct Access to Subscriber Systems

Access Unit (NAT) Effects

Some broadband systems use routers to connect the CPE; others use bridge-type access units. The routers were mainly deployed with the intention of address reuse on the client's side. For this reason, such routers commonly provide network address translation (NAT) functionality. NAT routers became a key element in improving security because NAT routers in their default configuration do not allow connections from any Internet station to the CPE (Shieh et al., 2000). It is therefore impossible to exploit local computers' vulnerabilities or to access local resources (such as Windows shares).

To get an estimate on the percentage of directly—and therefore potentially vulnerable—broadband subscriber PCs, the company cnlab Internet Research AG, Rapperswil, Switzerland, carried out tests in Switzerland and Germany. In Switzerland, every month about 100,000 broadband subscribers use performance test applets, which are provided by cnlab (Cnlab, n.d.). Based on the data collected from these tests, the distribution of NAT and non-NAT access could be determined. The analysis of the distribution of NAT and non-NAT over time (see Figure 6) shows significant differences between ISPs. In February 2004, there were two Swiss providers with more than 40% of the CPEs directly reachable from the Internet (see Figure 6, providers Hi and Su). Among the five German DSL providers tested, there were between 37% and 45% directly reachable from the Internet.

The chart in Figure 6 indicates a general trend toward fewer CPEs being directly reachable from the Internet, that is, toward more NAT router and firewall installations.

The differences among the ISPs are mainly determined by the type of default installation and promotion of access system packages. Swiss provider Hi, for example, is a DOC provider with a default cable modem installation without NAT or firewall functionality. Provider Su ran several promotions with simple modems, that is, non-NAT ADSL access units.

Popup Messages

One of the obvious problems of direct access to always-on subscriber systems is Windows messenger service alerts popping up on the subscriber's computers (see Figure 7).

In their initial state, Microsoft Windows operating systems (98, ME, XP, 2000, NT) allowed anyone on the Internet to open Messenger windows on somebody else's screen. Unlike e-mail advertising, an individual that is online will instantly see the advertisement that pops up on the computer in front of all active windows, which forces the recipient to react to the ad. There are tools available for sending Windows Messenger service messages to ranges of IP addresses (Direct PopUp Advertiser, n.d.). Thanks to this instant message broadcasting to IP addresses, high-volume advertising across the Internet through instant pop-up windows is possible.

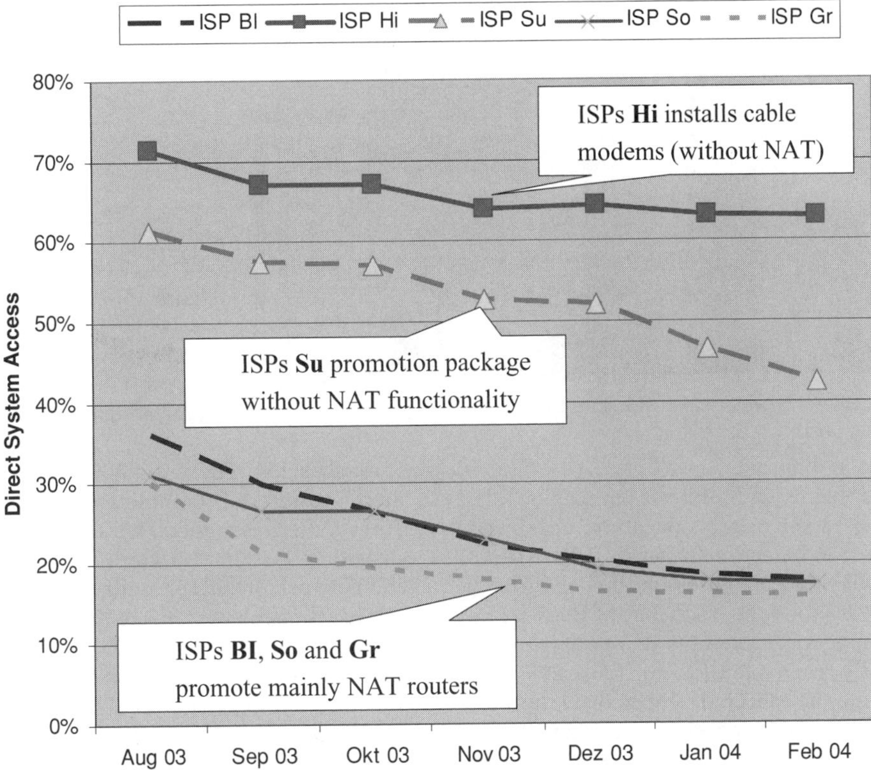

Figure 6: Percentage of subscribers of different ISPs with direct system access (evolution of the percentage of access units without NAT functionality).

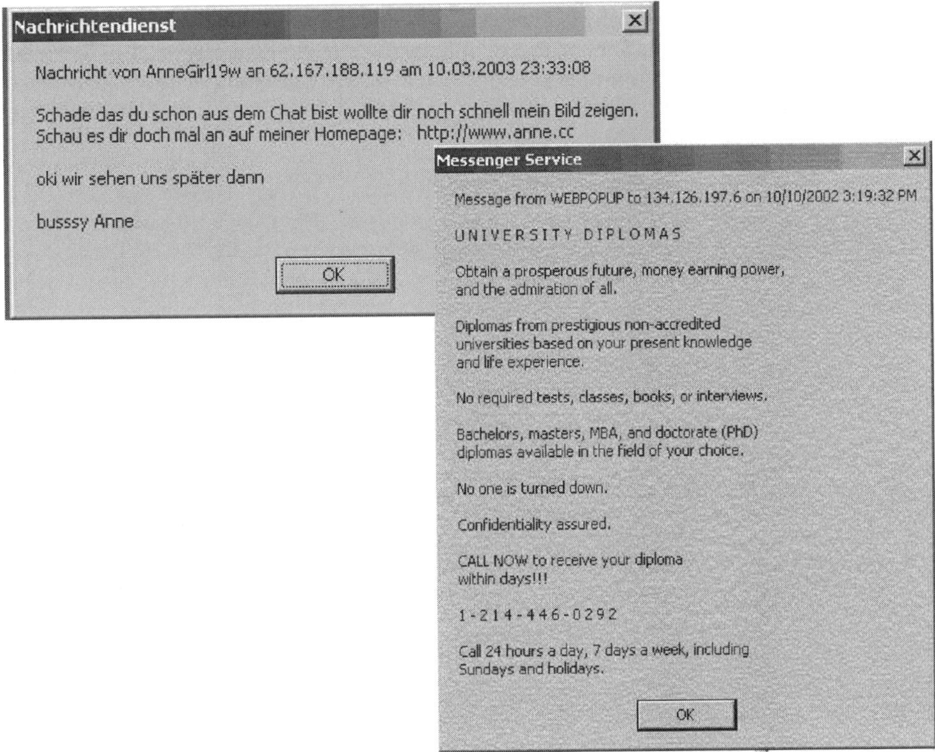

Figure 7: Pop-up windows sent to IP addresses.

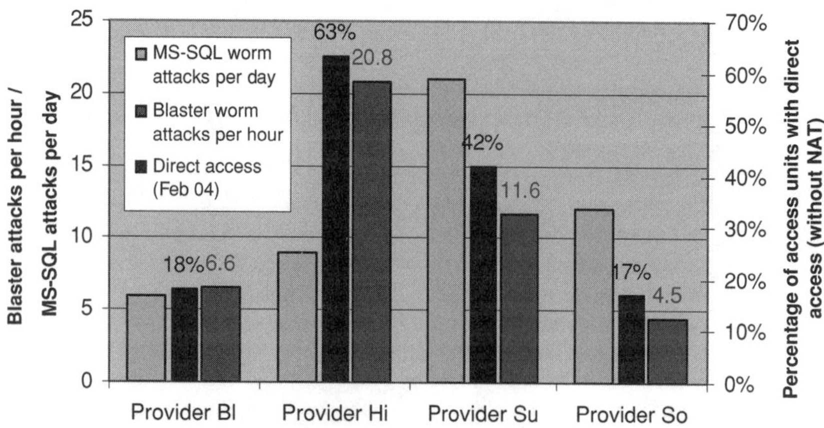

Figure 8: Blaster worm and MS-SQL attacks in relation to the percentage of directly accessible subscriber systems in different ISP networks (measurements date from February 2004).

Worm Propagation

One of the major problems with directly reachable CPEs in broadband networks is worm propagation. Cnlab has installed Snort Intrusion Detection Systems (IDS) to monitor "malicious mobile code activities" in the networks of various ISPs. Figure 8 shows the frequency of Blaster and MS-SQL worm propagation attempts in relation to the percentage of directly reachable CPEs for four ISPs.

The results indicate the expected strong correlation between the percentage of NAT access devices and Blaster worm activities: the more directly accessible CPEs in an ISP network, the higher the number of Blaster attacks per hour.

The Blaster worm (also known as Lovsan) exploits the DCOM RPC vulnerability on Windows 2000 and Windows XP installations via TCP port 135. If the worm has penetrated a system (let's say with IP address x.y.z.n), it tries to install itself on other systems in the same IP network by scanning other IP addresses in the x.y.z.n range. There is a 40% probability that the worm will increment the n part of the IP address by 1, in an attempt to find and exploit other computers based on the new IP address, until it reaches 254. There is a 60% probability that the generated IP address is completely random (Symantex, 2003). Hence, there is a good chance that the worm will mainly distribute within the same network. This explains why the network of the ISP with the highest percentage of directly accessible systems (63%) shows the highest number of Blaster attacks per hour. Those ISPs with small numbers of directly accessible systems have significantly fewer Blaster attacks per hour.

The MS-SQL worm (also known as SQL Slammer) targets systems running Microsoft SQL Server 2000, as well as Microsoft Desktop Engine (MSDE) 2000. It sends 376 bytes to the SQL server resolution service port (UDP port 1434). Because there are not many systems running Microsoft SQL Server or MSDE components, and because the worm sends itself to randomly selected IP addresses, there are fewer systems affected within the ISP network than with the Blaster worm.

The number of IDS alerts depends on the time of day and the ISP. Generally, a clear correlation between typical activity periods of the subscribers and the number of worm attacks can be observed (see Figure 9). The

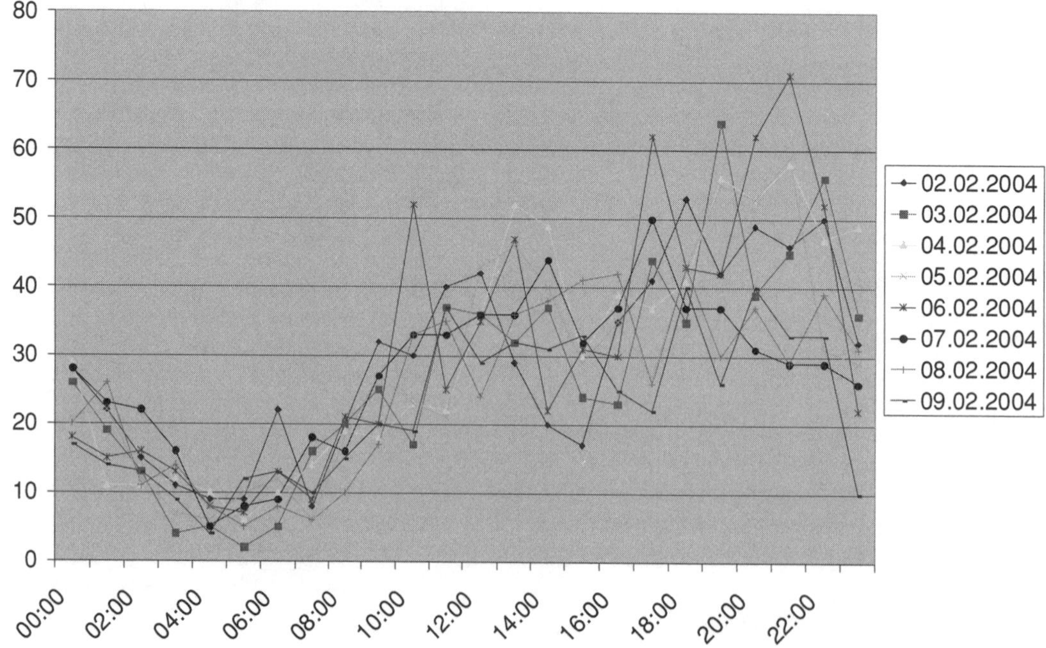

Figure 9: Number of Snort alerts per hour measured by time of day during eight days.

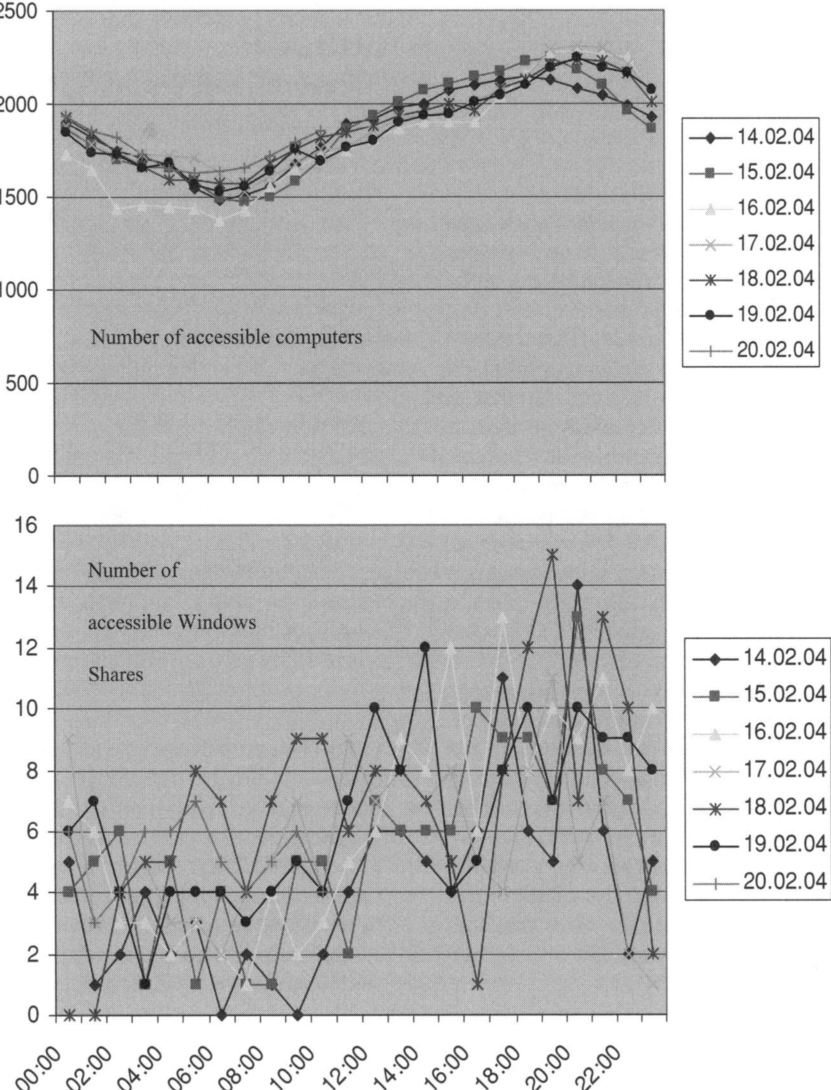

Figure 10: Number of accessible systems and Windows shares measured by time of day during seven days (of a total of 4,096 scanned addresses).

more active systems there are, the more attacks per hour there are.

Access to Subscriber Files and Resources

Open Windows Shares

The issue that has attracted the greatest attention in the public is access to subscriber files. Investigations in Switzerland show that in the first quarter of 2004, about 4% of the systems connected to broadband networks had accessible Windows shares that may or may not be password protected (see Figure 10).

Direct access from the Internet to a system with open Windows shares will give unauthorized access to the locally stored data files from anywhere in the Internet. Once Windows shares are activated, the computer is also exposed to other attacks because of the various opened services (e.g., NetBIOS name service at UDP port 137, NetBIOS datagram service at UDP port 138, NetBIOS session service at TCP port 139).

The number of accessible shares is clearly correlated with the typical activity periods of residential subscribers.

Installation of Mobile Code

The problem of open shares is not only relevant in connection with the exposure of private information. It can also be exploited for spreading malicious code. For example, the Biscuit worm, which attempts to copy itself to both the local host and reachable remote network shares, can propagate itself. Also, the Sobig worm attempts to copy itself to remote network shares. Finally, the Bugbear mass-mailing worm spreads via network shares. It has keystroke-logging and backdoor capabilities. This worm attempts to terminate the processes of various antivirus and firewall programs.

Having mass-mailing programs put on broadband subscribers' computers may create a problem or at least bad reputation for the ISP. Mass-mailing activity may result in the ISP's domain or some of ISP's IP addresses being published in spam databases. IP addresses of an ISP might, for example, be published on the antispam service SenderBase, which reports on the top senders (i.e., spammers) based on data provided from more than 9,000 organizations (SenderBase, n.d.).

Changing Service Parameters

An ISP's major security concern is to protect its own offerings. Broadband ISPs typically have different service offerings on their access units (e.g., 100–600 Kb/s, 400–2000 Kb/s upload and download data rates).

In DOC networks, the upload and download data rates are controlled in the CM. The service is defined upon TFTP download of the configuration parameters to the CM at modem boot up. The subscriber is identified by the CM physical address (MAC address) and optionally by certificate exchange with the CMTS. The subscriber might be able to change his CM configuration because he has physical access to the device. Such a "theft of service" attempts are known as "uncapping attacks" (How to Uncap DOCSIS Compliant Cable Modems, n.d.).

In ADSL networks, the upload and download data rates are defined by "hardware configuration" at the DSLAM. The subscriber is identified by username and password, which are sent to the ISP authentication system. "Uncapping" in ADSL seems rather unrealistic because the speed-limiting parameters would have to be changed at the DSLAM. However, working on a given ADSL connection with other users' accounts is simple. Hence, a subscriber who booked for a specific account can use the username and password of somebody else. This might be attractive when the other subscriber has some special services that the attacker would not get on his own account.

HOW TO IMPROVE BROADBAND SECURITY

Measures and Responsibilities

There are multiple possible ways to improve the security of broadband Internet access and there is not a single point or party responsible for security. All involved parties—ISPs, equipment manufacturers, software vendors, and subscribers—should take measures to fight all sorts of attacks. Figure 11 illustrates the situation and lists measures to improve the security in the broadband access environment.

The software vendors and equipment manufacturers should provide default installations that avoid unintended exposure of personal files and resources. Here are some examples of favorable default configurations:

- On the computer: Windows share access with transmission control protocol/Internet protocol (TCP/IP) is not enabled; personal firewall is activated.
- Communication equipment: access device has NAT or firewall functionality, default access unit configuration is not "always -on," that is, has inactivity timeout; access device cannot be configured via the Internet port.

Furthermore, software vendors and equipment manufacturers should provide simple, preferably automatic, reliable, and secure system patch and upgrade procedures. The introduction of Microsoft's Windows XP Service Pack 2 "Security Center" points in a good direction by adapting various default configurations and forcing the installation of personal firewall and antivirus software.

The subscribers (i.e., end users) should work with up-to-date antivirus software (see volume 3, part 2 of the

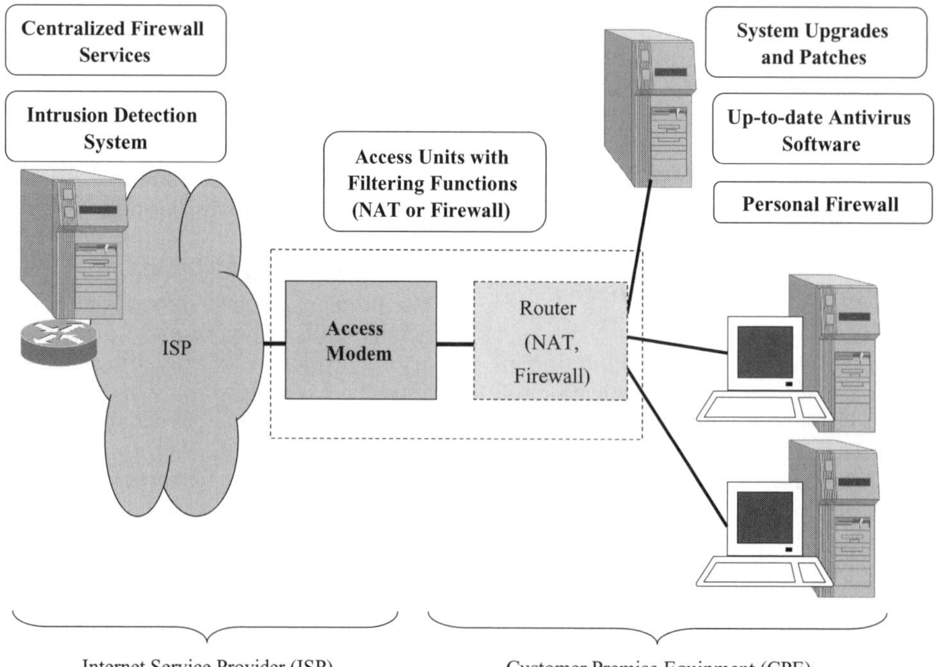

Figure 11: Measures to improve the security of broadband Internet access.

Table 2 Security Measures

Measures	Avoided Attack or Problem
NAT router or appropriate default installation or personal firewall	Access to Windows shares is not possible
NAT router or updated system software (patches installed) or updated antivirus software	Worms (e.g., Blaster) will not install themselves on the system and will not propagate

Handbook). They should update their operating system and install patches. Both antivirus software vendors as well as operating system vendors offer "automatic updates" to download the latest signature files and security updates. Before getting connected to the Internet, subscribers should block Windows file and print sharing over TCP/IP. The subscriber might also install a firewall (hardware and/or a software firewall; Kessler, 2000). However, as long as most users are not willing or not able to take at least the simplest security measures, they need support from the other involved parties (i.e., ISPs and software and equipment manufacturers; Meyer, 2003).

The ISPs should only promote access devices with NAT or firewall functionality (see volume 3, part 2, of the *Handbook*). Furthermore, they should take the opportunity and offer managed security services such as the following:

- centralized firewall services,
- subscriber security checking (offer tools and/or checks),
- identify problems (e.g., detect sources of attacks automatically) (see volume 3, part 3 of the *Handbook*).

Building Awareness

Many home users are not aware of the exposures when using the Internet. This became obvious after Swiss and German TV programs showed how simple it is to access Windows shares or subscriber systems in February and June 2004. The programs initiated a very heated debate with reports in newspapers and journals. Some ISPs reacted with immediate measures to improve security. Other ISPs denied any need to take security measures. At least the Swiss TV awareness-building exercise had a great effect. All ISPs added or improved the information about security problems on their Web sites and many people installed hardware firewalls or NAT routers, learned how to update their systems, and installed patches. Many subscribers installed personal firewalls and antivirus software (see volume III, part 3 of the *Handbook*).

Combination of Security Measures

One basic principle in security engineering is to combine multiple measures to protect exposed resources. This principle is also known as "layered security" or "in-depth defense" (see volume III, part 3 of the *Handbook*). Table 2 shows how the multiple measures protect against typical attacks or problems seen in broadband networks when at least one of them is implemented.

NAT routers do significantly improve security without requiring special skills of the subscribers. The default installation of NAT routers delivered to residential subscribers does not offer any port forwarding, and most residential users will not change the default configuration of the shipped access devices. Security could even be further improved if the access device would automatically terminate the Internet connection after a certain inactivity period (timeout).

Of course, the installation of a NAT device does not guarantee absolute protection: subscribers may change their access device default configuration to provide direct access to certain computers (e.g., local servers). There might be configuration problems or vulnerabilities of the access device itself. (A few years ago, a widely used NAT router was shipped with a default configuration that allowed telnet access via the Internet with the default password of "1234.")

Note that the NAT routers and firewalls do not protect against malicious code received by e-mail or Web pages. Here again the combination with other measures is recommended (e.g., user awareness education and virus scanning at e-mail servers and subscribers' computers).

CONCLUSION

The multitude of unprotected (residential) broadband network subscribers' computers offers high speed, always-on data sources that are a very attractive base for malicious code distribution. Therefore, broadband access requires better security measures of all involved parties: subscribers, software and equipment manufacturers, and ISPs. Without appropriate security measures there will be increasing problems with worms, DDOS attacks, and spam.

Many residential subscribers are not aware of security issues and are not capable of taking appropriate security measures. Measurements at Swiss and German ISP networks showed that up to 60% of the broadband subscriber systems can be accessed directly from the Internet and that a high percentage of those systems offer open Windows shares. Obviously, software vendors, equipment manufacturers, and ISPs must help the subscribers and offer tools and services to improve the security of the overall system.

There are little principle differences between ADSL and DOC broadband access security concerns. On one hand, ADSL has a minor advantage with regard to wiretapping at the subscriber's site because only those signals addressed to the specific subscriber get to the subscriber's site. DOC, on the other hand, offers encryption of all transmitted data packets.

For both ADSL and DOC, the access device should provide some filtering function (i.e., have a firewall or NAT function) to prevent direct access to customer premise equipment. The positive effect of NAT devices on broadband access network security was demonstrated based on measurements at Swiss and German ISP networks. There is a clear correlation between the number of NAT devices installed and the activity of certain worms (e.g., e-blaster): The more NAT and firewall devices installed, the fewer security problems are present.

GLOSSARY

Internet and security terms are defined at various places. The following list is based on definitions from Gartner (2003), SearchSecurity.com (n.d.), and SANS (n.d.).

ADSL Asymmetric digital subscriber line (ADSL) is a method for moving data via regular phone lines. A typical configuration of ADSL creates asymmetric transmission channels; for example, a subscriber can receive data (download) at 600 Kb/s and send (upload) data at 128 Kb/s.

AES The advanced encryption standard (AES) is a new Federal Information Processing Standard (FIPS) Publication that specifies a cryptographic algorithm for use by U.S. government organizations to protect sensitive (unclassified) information. AES is also widely used on a voluntary basis by organizations, institutions, and individuals outside of the United States.

BPI+ The baseline privacy interface (BPI) is defined as a set of extended services within the DOCSIS MAC sublayer. BPI gives subscribers data privacy across the CATV network by encrypting traffic flows between the CMTS and CM.

BPI of DOCSIS 1.0 uses RSA key management protocol and the electronic codebook (ECB) mode of DES to secure key exchanges between the CMTS and a CM. Privacy is in the form of 56-bit (the default) or 40-bit encryption.

BPI+ of DOCSIS 1.1 gives enhancements such as digital certificates to provide user authentication, key encryption with 168-bit triple DES (3DES), and1024-bit public key with Pkcs#1 version 2.0 encryption.

CM The cable modem (CM) is the client device for providing data via a cable TV network. It is an end-user CPE device with Ethernet or USB ports and network interface functions. An external cable modem device that incorporates some type of router functionality it is also called CPE cable router.

CMTS The cable modem's termination system (CMTS) is the central device for connecting the CATV network to the Internet. The CMTS is located in the head end of the CATV system. It creates a communication link (similar to a local area network) with the CMs at the subscribers' sites. CMTS is also known as cable broadband access platform (CBAP).

CPE The customer premise equipment (CPE) is located at the end user's home or business site and is connected to a PC that receives DOC- or DSL-based digital data communications service. Most CPE connect to PCs through a standard 10Base-T Ethernet card or USB connection.

DA Destination address (DA) is the address of a network device that is receiving data.

DDOS In a distributed denial-of-service (DDoS) attack, there are a multitude of compromised systems that attack a single target. The flood of incoming attacks to the target system denies the service to legitimate users.

DES Data encryption standard (DES) is an encryption block cipher developed in 1977 by IBM. It applies a 56-bit key to each 64-bit block of data, providing strong encryption based on symmetric cryptography. If DES is used with three keys, it is known as "triple DES" or 3DES. The standard was endorsed as an official standard by the U.S. government in 1977. In 2003, it was replaced by AES.

DOCSIS Data over cable service interface specification (DOCSIS) is the dominating cable modem standard. It defines the various interfaces between the radio frequency- (RF-) based cable network and the CM at the customer premises, as well as the associated CMTS at the head end. DOCSIS was accepted as a worldwide standard by the International Telecommunication Union (ITU) with technical variations for Europe and Japan.

DOS A denial-of-service (DoS) attack creates a situation in which users do not get the services they would normally get. Typically, the loss of service is the unavailability of a Web site, e-mail, or network connectivity. DOS can sometimes happen accidentally.

DSL The digital subscriber line (DSL) technologies provide remote access to the subscriber via the telephone companies' copper lines. There are various DSL technologies, for example, asymmetric DSL (ADSL), symmetric DSL (SDSL), ITU-standardized SDSL (G.SHDSL and SHDSL), ISDN-DSL (IDSL), and very high-speed DSL (VDSL).

DSLAM The digital subscriber line access multiplexer (DSLAM) is a traffic aggregation device that multiplexes upstream and downstream information in a DSL network. The DSLAM is usually located in a central office and connects to the central office switch to support voice service. On the network side, a DSLAM can interface with ATM, IP, or any other broadband service.

FTTL Fiber in the loop (FITL) means the provision and operation of fiber-optic media in the subscriber loop. FITL cable plants are of the "fiber to the curb" (FTTC) or "fiber to the home" (FTTH) type.

HDSL High bit-rate DSL systems (HDSL) enable full duplex transmission at up to 2 Mb/s via ordinary copper twisted pairs in unshielded cables. HDSL products can use up to three twisted copper pairs for transmission.

IDS An intrusion detection system (IDS) is a type of security management system for computers (host-based IDS) and networks (network-based IDS). It gathers and analyzes information from various areas within a computer or a network to identify possible security breaches.

ISP An Internet service provider (ISP) is a company that provides access to the Internet and other related services to its customers (subscribers). An ISP focusing on access is sometimes referred to as an Internet access provider (IAP). An ISP with focus on application services is also called application service provider (ASP).

MPLS Multiprotocol label switching (MPLS) is a technology for speeding up network traffic and for managing network quality of service (QoS). MPLS sets up a specific path for a given sequence of packets. The path is identified by a label put in each packet. This reduces the time needed for a router to look up the address to the next node to which to forward the packet.

NAT Network address translation (NAT) maps one or more global (outside) IP network addresses to local (inside) IP network addresses. NAT reduces the number of global IP addresses needed. The address mapping can be statically or dynamically defined.

Phishing Phishing is a type of attack (sometimes called carding or brand spoofing) where the attacker sends out legitimate-looking e-mails appearing to come from a Web site. This attack prepares for identity theft by faking a Web site that normally asks the target user for personal information, including credit card numbers, personal identification numbers, social security numbers, banking numbers, and passwords.

PLC Power line communication (PLC) uses existing electrical power lines for symmetric Internet access. In the United States, it is called broadband over power lines (BPL); the Europeans use the term power line communication (PLC). The industrial "HomePlug" alliance was formed to standardize data networking via electrical wiring inside the premises.

SNMP Simple network management protocol (SNMP) is the protocol governing network management and the monitoring of network devices and their functions. SNMP is described formally in the Internet Engineering Task Force (IETF) Request for Comment (RFC) 1157.

TCP/IP Transmission control protocol/Internet protocol (TCP/IP) is the transport/network layer protocol typically used for many Internet applications (e.g., http, mail, ftp). TCP provides for connection-oriented, reliable data transport and includes also flow and congestion control functions. Data flows are identified by port number/IP address quadruples.

TFTP Trivial file transfer protocol (TFTP) is a simple protocol to transport files via the Internet. It does not offer directory browsing and has no user authentication. TFTP uses the user datagram protocol (UDP) rather than the transmission control protocol (TCP). TFTP is described formally in Request for Comment (RFC) 1350.

UDP User datagram protocol (UDP) is the connectionless transport layer protocol widely used in the Internet (e.g., for applications such as DNS, TFTP, and SNMP). UDP provides port numbers to help distinguish different user requests.

USB Universal serial bus (USB) is a plug-and-play interface between a computer and add-on devices. USB supports 12 Mb/s data speed. Today, most new computers and peripheral devices are equipped with USB.

WLL Wireless local loop (WLL), also known as radio in the loop (RITL), is a point-to-multipoint radio-based transmission scheme. WLL systems can be based on a range of different technologies and standards, for example, local multipoint distribution service (LMDS).

xDSL x Digital subscriber line (xDSL) is a transmission scheme in the local loop of the plain old telephony service (POTS) network. The x signifies various standard types, for example, asymmetric DSL (ADSL), symmetric DSL (SDSL), high-speed DSL (HDSL), very high-speed DSL (VDSL), and rate-adaptive DSL (RADSL).

CROSS REFERENCES

See *Conducted Communications Media; Public Network Technologies and Security; Security in Circuit, Message, and Packet Switching; Wide Area and Metropolitan Area Networks.*

REFERENCES

Abe, J. (2004, June). Development of high speed power line communication modem. *SEI Technical Review, 58.*

Bascher, C., et al. (2004). Providing always-on broadband access to under-served areas. *Alcatel Telecommunications Review.*

Cable Television Laboratories. (2004, April 7). Data-over-cable service interface specifications DOCSIS 1.1, baseline privacy plus interface specification, SP-BPI+-I11-040407. Retrieved April 12, 2004, from http://www.cablemodem.com/downloads/specs/BPI+_I11-040407.pdf

Cisco. (2002, June 6). Cable source-verify and IP address security. *Cisco Report*. Retrieved April 20, 2004, from http://www.cisco.com/en/US/tech/tk86/tk803/technologies_tech_note09186a00800a7828.shtml

Cnlab Information Technology Research AG: Performance test applet. Retrieved April 20, 2004, from http://www.cnlab.ch

Direct popup advertiser. (n.d.) Retrieved April 20, 2004, from http://www.americaint.com/bulk-e-mail-software/Direct-Pop-Up-Advertiser/direct-popup-advertiser.htm

DSL Forum. (2003, March). ADSL2 and ADSL2plus—The new ADSL standards (White Paper). Retrieved October 11, 2004, from http://www.dslforum.org/aboutdsl/ADSL2_wp.pdf

Dutta, R. (2001, June). An overview of cable modem technology and market perspectives. *IEEE Communications Magazine.*

Dutta-Roy, M. (1999, September). A second wind for wiring—ADSL. *IEEE Spectrum.*

ITU Internet Reports. (2003, September). *Birth of broadband* (Fifth Report). ITU Internet Reports.

Gartner. (2003, August). Access systems definitions, 2003. *Gartner Dataquest Guide.*

How to uncap DOCSIS compliant cable modems. (n.d.) Retrieved July 11, 2005, from http://www.netwide.net/users/CableGuy/HowtoUncapDocsisCompliantCableModems.html

Jones, W. D. (2004, September). Amped up and ready to go—Broadband over power lines. *IEEE Spectrum.*

Kessler, G. C. (2000, July). Securing cable modems. *Information Security Magazine*. Retrieved April 12, 2004, from http://infosecuritymag.techtarget.com/articles/july00/features3.shtml

Lindstrom, D. (2002, March 5). Sniffing a cable modem network: Possible or myth? *SANS Report*. Retrieved April 20, 22004, from http://www.sans.org/rr/papers/26/623.pdf

McCarthy, I. (2003, September). Symantec Internet security threat report (Symantec White Paper).

Meyer, D. (2003, October/November). PC broadband security—Defensive measures you can take. *IEEE Potentials*.

OFCOM. (2003, April 16). *ADSL and TVcable modem connections in Switzerland*. (Federal Office of Communications Annual Report). Retrieved September 20, 2004, from http://www.bakom.ch/en/amt/aufgaben_visionen/geschaeftsberichte/jahresbericht_2003/index.html

Paltridge, S., & Matsui, M. (2004, June 15). *Benchmarking broadband prices in the OECD*. Paris France: Organization for Economic Co-operation and Development (OECD). Retrieved October 11, 1004, from http://www.oecd.org/dataoecd/58/17/32143101.pdf

Powell, M. K., et al. (2004, September 9). *Availability of advanced telecommunications capability in the United States* (Fourth Report to Congress, FCC 04-208, GN Docket No. 04-54). Federal Communications Commission.

Richmond, R. (2004, September 20). Money talks for hackers. Finance 24. Retrieved July 11, 2005, from http://www.finance24.co.za/Finance/Companies/0,1518-24_1592069,00.html

Saito, T., et al. (2003, December). Broadband FENICS. *Fujitsu Sci. Tech. Journal*.

SANS (SysAdmin, Audit, Network, Security) Institute glossary. (n.d.) Retrieved July 11, 2005, from http://www.sans.org/resources/glossary.php

SearchSecurity.com definitions. (n.d.) Retrieved July 11, 2005, from http://searchsecurity.techtarget.com

SenderBase e-mail reputation service. (n.d.) Retrieved July 11, 2005, from http://www.senderbase.org

Shannon, C., & Moore, D. (2003, December 10–11). SCO offline from denial-of-service attack. Retrieved July 11, 2005, from http://www.caida.org/analysis/security/sco-dos/

Shieh, S.-P., et al. (2000, November/December). Network address translators: Effects on security protocols and applications in the TCP/IP stack. *IEEE Internet Computing*.

Starr, T. (2003). Broadband DSL: A gateway to entertainment. *Alcatel Telecommunications Review*, 82–84.

Stuart, D. A., & Bhalla K. (2003, August). *DSL and cable modem services in Europe* (Operational Management Report). Gartner Group.

Symantec. (2003). *W32.Blaster.worm discovered on August 11, 2003*. Retrieved July 11, 2005, from http://securityresponse.symantec.com/avcenter/venc/data/w32.blaster.worm.html

Thornhill, C. (2001, November 1). Securing DOCSIS networks. *Cable Datacom News*. Retrieved April 20, 2004, from http://www.cabledatacomnews.com/nov01/nov01-6.html

TTC. (1998, May). ADSL basics (DMT) (Technical Notes). Retrieved October 11, 2004, from http://www.livingston.co.uk/fileadmin/downloads/uk/PDFs/ADSL_Basics.pdf

W3Schools: Operating systems statistics. (n.d.) Retrieved September 20, 2004, from http://www.w3schools.com/browsers/browsers_stats.asp

Woundy, R. (2001, March). Baseline privacy interface management information base for DOCSIS compliant cable modems and cable modem termination systems(RFC 3083). Network Working Group.

FURTHER READING

General Broadband Links

Analysys Research reports and online market intelligence information about broadband: http://www.analysys.com/telecoms/broadband/

Broadband system performance discussion, checks and tools: http://www.speedguide.net/

ITU New Initiatives Workshop on Promoting Broadband http://www.itu.int/osg/spu/ni/promotebroadband/index.html

Powerline Communication (PLC) Forum: http://www.plcforum.org, http://www.powerlinecommunications.net

Powerline home networking standardization HomePlug: http://www.homeplug.org/

ETSI Powerline Portal: http://portal.etsi.org/plt/Summary.asp

Cable Modem Organizations and Links

http://www.cable-modem.net/
http://www.cable-modems.org/
http://www.cablemodem.com/
http://www.tcomlabs.com/
http://www.cablelabs.com/
http://www.cabledatacomnews.com/

xDSL Organizations and Links

http://www.dslforum.org/
http://www.dslreports.com/

Security Links

CERT®Coordination Center http://www.cert.org/tech_tips/home_networks.html

The SANS Institute: http://www.sans.org/

SANS/FBI list of top 20 vulnerabilities http://www.sans.org/top20/

WormWatch: http://www.wormwatch.org/

Cooperative Association for Internet Data Analysis (CAIDA): http://www.caida.org/analysis/security/, http://www.caida.org/projects/cisco02security/, and http:// www.caida.org/projects/nsftrust/

Ad Hoc Network Security

Pietro Michiardi and Refik Molva, *Institut Eurecom, France*

INTRODUCTION

An ad hoc network consists of a set of wireless nodes that act both as data terminals and data transfer equipment to spontaneously form a temporary network without relying on any dedicated infrastructure. Security of ad hoc networks recently received much attention from the research community and a large number of solutions to protect ad hoc networks against various types of attacks have been published. Security in ad hoc networks is a severe problem because of the conjunction of several factors:

- Vulnerabilities resulting from radio communications: the lack of physical security and the ease of eavesdropping and spoofing call for strong security mechanisms in order to get security that is equivalent to standard wireline communications.
- Lack of a priori trust: most ad hoc networks consist of a set of nodes that are not part of any shared organization thus classical security paradigms based on preestablished trust among the parties are not applicable.
- Lack of infrastructure: security solutions based on dedicated components with predefined roles such as trusted third parties and key servers are not compatible with the basic definition of ad hoc networks whereby no component has a preassigned role.
- Requirement for cooperation: because of the lack of dedicated components such as routers and servers that implement network services, basic networking functions have to be carried out in a distributed fashion by the collaboration of a set of ordinary nodes, thus the performance of basic network operations such as packet forwarding and routing can be strongly affected by malicious or accidental lack of cooperation.

Research on ad hoc network security initially focused on routing protocols because these were deemed the most critical part of network control. The Key Management section is an overview of prominent routing security solutions that are based on various versions of ad hoc routing protocols. A close analysis of routing security work reveals that the majority of the requirements needed for the solutions and the suggested mechanisms are not new or specific to ad hoc networks, apart from a fundamental problem that was often left aside by routing security solutions, that is, key management with no a priori trust and lack of infrastructure. The Cooperation Enforcement section presents research proposals that address the key management problem in the context of ad hoc networks with various original approaches that generally aim at setting security associations in a collaborative way without relying on existing trust relationships. The Conclusion section gives a detailed overview of cooperation enforcement mechanisms and their validation. Figure 1 provides a schematic view of security requirements for mobile ad hoc networks (MANETs).

ROUTING SECURITY

Security of ad hoc routing protocols has recently become an important topic in the research community: unlike wired networks where routing functions are performed by dedicated nodes or routers, in MANET routing functions are carried out by all available nodes. Common routing security mechanisms consist of node and message authentication that refer to an priori trust model in which legitimate routers are believed to perform correct operations. In contrast, authentication of a node or its messages does not guarantee the correct execution of routing functions in open environments with lack of a priori trust, such as MANET.

Security exposures of ad hoc routing protocols are due to two different types of attacks: *active attacks* through which the misbehaving node has to bear some energy costs to perform some harmful operation, and *passive attacks* that mainly consist of lack of cooperation with the purpose of saving energy. Furthermore, misbehaving nodes can be part of the network and perform attacks by exploiting compromised nodes or by disrupting the normal routing operation (*insider attacks*) or can be unauthorized nodes that aim to cause congestion, propagate incorrect routing information, prevent services from working properly, or shut down them completely (*external*

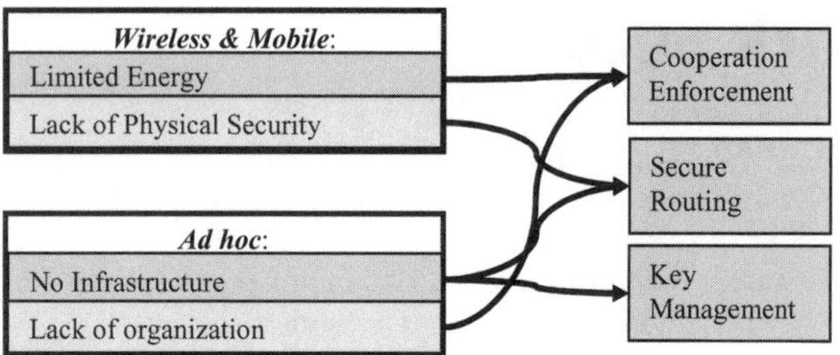

Figure 1: Security requirements for ad hoc network layer and corresponding solutions.

attacks). These threats exist because of the inherently limited physical security of mobile ad hoc networks. Indeed, it is easier to intercept communications and inject messages in the wireless communication medium than in an equivalent wired network.

Malicious nodes (i.e., active attackers) can disrupt the correct functioning of a routing protocol by modifying routing information, by fabricating false routing information, and by impersonating other nodes. Recent research studies (Perrig, Hu, & Johnson, n.d.) also brought up a new type of attack that goes under the name of *wormhole attack*. On the other side, selfish nodes can severely degrade network performances and eventually partition the network (Michiardi & Molva, 2002c) simply by not participating in the network operation.

In the existing ad hoc routing protocols, nodes are trusted in that they do not maliciously tamper with the content of protocol messages transferred among nodes. Malicious nodes can easily perpetrate integrity attacks by altering protocol fields to subvert traffic, deny communication to legitimate nodes (denial of service), and compromise the integrity of routing computations in general. As a result, the attacker can cause network traffic to be dropped, to be redirected to a different destination, or to take a longer route to the destination, thereby increasing communication delays. A special case of integrity attacks is spoofing, whereby a malicious node impersonates a legitimate node, which is possible because of the lack of authentication in the current ad hoc routing protocols. The main result of spoofing attacks is the misrepresentation of the network topology, which possibly causes network loops or partitioning. Lack of integrity and authentication in routing protocols can further be exploited through "fabrication," which refers to the generation of bogus routing messages. Fabrication attacks cannot be detected without strong authentication means and can cause severe problems, ranging from denial of service to route subversion.

A more subtle type of active attack is the creation of a tunnel (or wormhole) in the network between two colluding malicious nodes linked through a private connection bypassing the network. This allows a node to short-circuit the normal flow of routing messages, creating a virtual vertex cut in the network that is controlled by the two colluding attackers.

Another exposure of current ad hoc routing protocols is node selfishness that results in lack of cooperation among ad hoc nodes. A selfish node that wants to save battery life for its own communication can endanger the correct network operation by simply not participating in the routing protocol or by not forwarding packets. Current ad hoc routing protocols do not address the selfishness problem.

It has become obvious that security has to be taken into account at the early stages of the design of ad hoc routing protocols. However, if the design of secure routing protocols for MANET has not been a particularly demanding task, the provision of basic security services needed as building blocks for the secure routing protocol itself is still the greatest challenge that researchers are facing. To mitigate the complexity introduced by the pure ad hoc paradigm, the solutions proposed in the following sections rely on particular (and frequently limiting) assumptions that ease the task of bootstrapping security associations needed prior to the secure routing protocol execution. The attention of the research community is now focusing on the provision of self-organized key management services that can be used by secure routing protocols: this topic will be addressed in the Key Management section.

Secure Routing Proposals

Secure Routing Protocol (SRP)

The secure routing protocol (SRP; Papadimitratos & Haas, 2002) is designed as an extension compatible with a variety of existing reactive routing protocols. SRP combats attacks that disrupt the route discovery process and guarantees the acquisition of correct topological information: SRP allows the initiator of a route discovery to detect and discard bogus replies. SRP relies on the availability of a security association (SA) between the source node (S) and the destination node (T). The SA could be established using a hybrid key distribution based on the public keys of the communicating parties. S and T can exchange a secret symmetric key (KS,T) using the public keys of one another to establish a secure channel. S and T can then further proceed to mutual authentication of one another and the authentication of routing messages.

SRP copes with noncolluding malicious nodes that are able to modify (corrupt), replay, and fabricate routing packets. In the case of the dynamic source routing (DSR) protocol (Johnson & Maltz, 1996), SRP requires a six-word header containing unique identifiers that tag the discovery process and a message authentication code (MAC) computed using a keyed hash algorithm. To initiate a route request (RREQ), the source node has to generate the MAC of the entire IP header, the basic protocol RREQ packet, and the shared key KS,T.

The intermediate nodes that relay the RREQ toward the destination measure the frequencies of queries received from their neighbors to regulate the query propagation process: each node maintains a priority ranking that is inversely proportional to the query rate. A node that maliciously pollutes network traffic with unsolicited RREQ will be served last (or ignored) because of its low priority ranking.

Upon reception of a RREQ, the destination node verifies the integrity and authenticity of the RREQ by calculating the keyed hash of the request fields and comparing them with the MAC contained in the SRP header. If the RREQ is valid, the destination initiates a route reply (RREP) using the SRP header the same way the source did when initiating the request. The source node discards replays that do not match with pending query identifiers and checks the integrity using the MAC generated by the destination.

The basic version of SRP suffers from the route cache poisoning attack: routing information gathered by nodes that operate in promiscuous mode to improve the efficiency of the DSR protocol could be invalid, because of potential fabrication by malicious nodes. The authors propose two alternative designs of SRP that use an intermediate node reply token (INRT). INRT allows intermediate nodes that belong to the same group that share a common key (KG) to validate RREQ and provide valid RREP messages.

SRP suffers also from the lack of a validation mechanism for route maintenance messages: route error packets are not verified. However, to minimize the effects of fabricated error messages, SRP source-routes error packets along the prefix of the route reported as broken: the source node can thus verify that each route error feedback refers to the actual route and that it was originated at a node that is part of the route. A malicious node can harm only routes to which it actually belongs.

Assuming that the neighbor discovery mechanism maintains information on the binding of the medium access control and the IP addresses of nodes, SRP is proven to be essentially immune to IP spoofing (Papadimitratos & Haas, 2002).

SRP is, however, not immune to the wormhole attack: two colluding malicious nodes can misroute the routing packets on a private network connection and alter the perception of the network topology by legitimate nodes.

ARIADNE

Hu, Perrig, and Johnson (2002) present an on-demand, secure, ad hoc routing protocol based on DSR that withstands node compromise and relies only on highly efficient symmetric cryptography. ARIADNE guarantees that the target node of a route discovery process can authenticate the initiator, that the initiator can authenticate each intermediate node on the path to the destination present in the RREP message, and that no intermediate node can remove a previous node in the node list in the RREQ or RREP messages.

As for the SRP protocol, ARIADNE needs some mechanism to bootstrap authentic keys required by the protocol. In particular, each node needs a shared secret key (KS,D is the shared key between a source S and a destination D) with each node with which it communicates at a higher layer, an authentic TESLA (Perrig, Canetti, Song, & Tygar, 2001; 2000) key for each node in the network, and an authentic "route discovery chain" element for each node for which this node will forward RREQ messages.

ARIADNE provides point-to-point authentication of a routing message using a message authentication code (MAC) and a shared key between the two parties. However, for authentication of a broadcast packet such as RREQ, ARIADNE uses the TESLA broadcast authentication protocol. ARIADNE copes with attacks performed by malicious nodes that modify and fabricate routing information, with attacks using impersonation, and, in an advanced version, with the wormhole attack. Selfish nodes are not taken into account.

In ARIADNE, the basic RREQ mechanism is enhanced by eight additional fields used to provide authentication and integrity to the routing protocol as follows:

<ROUTE REQUEST, initiator, target, id, time interval, hash chain, node list, MAC list>

The initiator and target are set to the address of the initiator and target nodes, respectively. As in DSR, the initiator sets the id (identifier) to an identifier that it has not recently used in initiating a route discovery. The time interval is the TESLA time interval at the pessimistic expected arrival time of the request at the target, accounting for clock skew. The initiator of the request then initializes the hash chain to $MAC_{KS,D}$ (initiator, target, id, time interval) and the node list and MAC list to empty lists.

When any node A receives a RREQ for which it is not the target, the node checks its local table of <initiator, id> values from recent requests it has received to determine if it has already seen a request from this same route discovery. If it has, the node discards the packet, as in DSR. The node also checks whether the time interval in the request is valid: that time interval must not be too far in the future, and the key corresponding to it must not have been disclosed yet. If the time interval is not valid, the node discards the packet. Otherwise, the node modifies the request by appending its own address (A) to the node list in the request, replacing the hash chain field with H [A, *hash chain*], and appending a MAC of the entire REQUEST to the MAC list. The node uses the TESLA key K_{Ai} to compute the MAC, where i is the index for the time interval specified in the request. Finally, the node rebroadcasts the modified RREQ, as in DSR.

When the target node receives the RREQ, it checks the validity of the request by determining that the keys from the time interval specified have not been disclosed yet, and that the hash chain field is equal to

$$H[\eta n, H[\eta_{n-1}, H[\ldots, H[\eta_1, MAC_{KSD}(\text{initiator}, \text{target}, \text{id}, \text{time interval})]\ldots]]]$$

where η_i is the node address at position i of the node list in the request and where n is the number of nodes in the node list. If the target node determines that the request is valid, it returns a RREP to the initiator, containing eight fields:

<ROUTE REPLY, target, initiator, time interval, node list, MAC list, target MAC, key list>

The target, initiator, time interval, node list, and MAC list fields are set to the corresponding values from the RREQ, the target MAC is set to a MAC computed on the preceding fields in the reply with the key KDS, and the key list is initialized to the empty list. The RREP is then returned to the initiator of the request along the source route obtained by reversing the sequence of hops in the node list of the request.

A node forwarding a RREP waits until it is able to disclose its key from the time interval specified; then, it appends its key from that time interval to the key list field in the reply and forwards the packet according to the source route indicated in the packet. Waiting delays the return of the RREP but does not consume extra computational power.

When the initiator receives a RREP, it verifies that each key in the key list is valid, that the target MAC is valid, and that each MAC in the MAC list is valid. If all of these tests succeed, the node accepts the RREP; otherwise, it discards it.

To prevent the injection of invalid route errors into the network fabricated by any node other than the one on the sending end of the link specified in the error message, each node that encounters a broken link adds TESLA authentication information to the route error message, such that all nodes on the return path can authenticate the error. However, TESLA authentication is delayed, so all the nodes on the return path buffer the error but do not consider it until it is authenticated. Later, the node that encountered the broken link discloses the key and sends it over the return path, which enables nodes on that path to authenticate the buffered error messages.

ARIADNE is protected also from a flood of RREQ packets that could lead to the cache poisoning attack. Benign nodes can filter out forged or excessive RREQ packets using route discovery chains, a mechanism for authenticating route discovery, which allow each node to rate-limit discoveries initiated by any other node. The authors present two different approaches that can be found in Hu, Perrig, and Johnson (2002).

ARIADNE is immune to the wormhole attack only in its advanced version: by using an extension called TIK (TESLA with Instant Key disclosure) that requires tight clock synchronization between the nodes, it is possible to detect timing discrepancies caused by a wormhole.

ARAN

The ARAN secure routing protocol proposed by Dahill, Levine, Royer, and Shields (2002) is conceived as an on-demand routing protocol that detects and protects against malicious actions carried out by third parties and peers in the ad hoc environment. ARAN introduces *authentication*, message *integrity,* and *nonrepudiation* as part of a minimal security policy for the ad hoc environment and consists of a preliminary certification process, a mandatory end-to-end authentication stage, and an optional second stage that provides secure shortest paths.

ARAN requires the use of a trusted certificate server (T): before entering in the ad hoc network, each node has to request a certificate signed by T. The certificate contains the IP address of the node, its public key, a time stamp of when the certificate was created, and a time at which the certificate expires along with the signature by T. All nodes are supposed to maintain fresh certificates with the trusted server and must know T's public key.

The goal of the first stage of the ARAN protocol is for the source to verify that the intended destination was reached. In this stage, the source trusts the destination to choose the return path. A source node, *A*, initiates the route discovery process to reach the destination *X* by broadcasting to its neighbors a route discovery packet called RDP:

$$[\mathrm{RDP};\mathrm{IP_X};cert_A;\mathrm{N_A};\mathrm{t}]\mathrm{K_{A-}}$$

The RDP includes a packet type identifier ("RDP"), the IP address of the destination ($\mathrm{IP_X}$), *A*'s certificate ($cert_A$), a nonce $\mathrm{N_A}$, and the current time t, all signed with A's private key. Each time A performs route discovery, it monotonically increases the nonce.

Each node records the neighbor from which it received the message. It then forwards the message to each of its neighbors, signing the contents of the message. This signature prevents spoofing attacks that may alter the route or form loops. Let *A*'s neighbor be *B*. It will broadcast the following message:

$$[[\mathrm{RDP};\mathrm{IP_X};cert_A;\ \mathrm{N_A};\mathrm{t}]\mathrm{K_{A-}}]\mathrm{K_{B-}};cert_B$$

Nodes do not forward messages for which they have already seen the ($\mathrm{N_A}$; $\mathrm{IP_A}$) tuple. The IP address of A is contained in the certificate, and the monotonically increasing nonce facilitates easy storage of recently received nonces.

Upon receiving the broadcast, *B*'s neighbor *C* validates the signature with the given certificate. *C* then rebroadcasts the RDP to its neighbors, first removing B's signature:

$$[[\mathrm{RDP};\mathrm{IP_X};cert_A;\mathrm{N_A};\ \mathrm{t}]\mathrm{K_{A-}}]\mathrm{K_{C-}};cert_C$$

Eventually, the message is received by the destination, *X*, who replies to the first RDP that it receives for a source and a given nonce. There is no guarantee that the first RDP received traveled along the shortest path from the source. The destination unicasts a reply (REP) packet back along the reverse path to the source. Let the first node that receives the RDP sent by X be node *D*. *X* will send to *D* the following message:

$$[\mathrm{REP};\mathrm{IP_A};cert_X;\mathrm{N_A};\ \mathrm{t}]\mathrm{K_{X-}}$$

The REP includes a packet type identifier ("REP"), the IP address of A, the certificate belonging to *X*, the nonce and associated time stamp sent by *A*. Nodes that receive the REP forward the packet back to the predecessor from which they received the original RDP. All REPs are signed by the sender. Let *D*'s next hop to the source be node *C*. *D* will send to *C* the following message:

$$[[\mathrm{REP};\mathrm{IP_A};cert_X;\mathrm{N_A};\ \mathrm{t}]\mathrm{K_{X-}}]\mathrm{K_{D-}};cert_D$$

C validates *D*'s signature, removes the signature, and then signs the contents of the message before unicasting the following RDP message to *B*:

$$[[\mathrm{REP};\mathrm{IP_A};cert_X;\mathrm{N_A};\ \mathrm{t}]\mathrm{K_{X-}}]\mathrm{K_{C-}};cert_C$$

A node checks the signature of the previous hop as the REP is returned to the source. This avoids attacks where malicious nodes instantiate routes by impersonation and re-play of X's message. When the source receives the REP, it verifies that the correct nonce was returned by the destination as well as the destination's signature. Only the destination can answer an RDP packet. Other nodes that already have paths to the destination cannot reply for the destination. Whereas other protocols allow this networking optimization, by disabling this option ARAN removes several possible exploits and cuts down on the reply traffic received by the source.

The second stage of the ARAN protocol guarantees in a secure way that the path received by a source initiating a route discovery process is the shortest. Similar to the first stage of the protocol, the source broadcasts a *shortest path confirmation* (SPC) message to its neighbors: the SPC message is different from the RDP message only in two additional fields that provide the destination X certificate and the encryption of the entire message with X's public key (which is a costly operation). The onion-like signing of messages combined with the encryption of the data prevents nodes in the middle from changing the path length because doing so would break the integrity of SPC the packet.

Also, the route maintenance phase of the ARAN protocol is secured by digitally signing the route error packets. However, it is extremely difficult to detect when error messages are *fabricated* for links that are truly active and not broken. Nevertheless, because messages are signed, malicious nodes cannot generate error messages for other nodes. The nonrepudiation provided by the signed error message allows a node to be verified as the source of each error message that it sends.

As with any secure system based on cryptographic certificates, the key revocation issue has to be addressed to make sure that expired or revoked certificates do not allow the holder to access the network. In ARAN, when a certificate needs to be revoked, the trusted certificate server T sends a broadcast message to the ad hoc group that announces the revocation. Any node receiving this message rebroadcasts it to its neighbors. Revocation notices need to be stored until the revoked certificate would have expired normally. Any neighbor of the node with the revoked certificate needs to reform routing as necessary to avoid transmission through the now distrusted node. This method is not failsafe. In some cases, the distrusted node that is having its certificate revoked may be the sole connection between two parts of the ad hoc network. In this case, the distrusted node may not forward the notice of revocation for its certificate, which results in a partition of the network, because nodes that have received the revocation notice will no longer forward messages through the distrusted node, while all other nodes depend on it to reach the rest of the network. This only lasts as long as the distrusted node's certificate would have otherwise been valid, or until the distrusted node is no longer the sole connection between the two partitions. At the time that the revoked certificate should have expired, the distrusted node is unable to renew the certificate and routing across that node ceases. Additionally, to detect this situation and to hasten the propagation of revocation notices, when a node meets a new neighbor, it can exchange a summary of its revocation notices with that neighbor; if these summaries do not match, the actual signed notices can be forwarded and rebroadcasted to restart propagation of the notice.

The ARAN protocol protects against exploits using *modification*, *fabrication*, and *impersonation* but the use of asymmetric cryptography makes it a very costly protocol to use in terms of central processing unit (CPU) and energy usage. Furthermore, ARAN is not immune to the *wormhole* attack.

SEAD

Hu, Perrig, and Johnson (2002) present a *proactive* secure routing protocol based on the destination-sequenced distance vector protocol (DSDV). In a proactive (or periodic) routing protocol, nodes periodically exchange routing information with other nodes in attempt to have each node always know a current route to all destinations (Perkins & Bhagwat, 1994). Specifically, SEAD is inspired by the DSDV-SQ version of the DSDV protocol. The DSDV-SQ version of the DSDV protocol has been shown to outperform other DSDV versions in previous ad hoc networks simulations (Broch, Maltz, Johnson, Hu, & Jetcheva, 1998; Johansson, Larsson, Hedman, Mielczarek, & Degermark, 1999).

SEAD deals with attackers that *modify* routing information broadcasted during the update phase of the DSDV-SQ protocol: in particular, routing can be disrupted if the attacker modifies the sequence number and the metric field of a routing table update message. *Replay attacks* are also taken into account.

To secure the DSDV-SQ routing protocol, SEAD makes use of efficient *one-way hash chains* rather than relying on expensive asymmetric cryptography operations. However, like the other secure protocols presented in this chapter, SEAD assumes some mechanism for a node to distribute an authentic element of the hash chain that can be used to authenticate all the other elements of the chain. As a traditional approach, the authors suggest relying on a trusted entity that signs public key certificates for each node to ensure key distribution; each node can then use its public key to sign a hash chain element and distribute it.

The basic idea of SEAD is to authenticate the sequence number and metric of a routing table update message using hash chains elements. In addition, the receiver of SEAD routing information also authenticates the sender, ensuring that the routing information originates from the correct node.

To create a one-way hash chain, a node chooses a random initial value $x \in \{0, 1\}^{\rho}$, where ρ is the length in bits of the output of the hash function, and computes the list of values $h_0, h_1, h_2, h_3, \ldots, h_n$, where $h_0 = x$ and $h_i = \mathrm{H}(h_{i-1})$ for $0 < i \leq n$ for some n. As an example, given an authenticated h_i value, a node can authenticate h_{i-3} by computing $\mathrm{H}(\mathrm{H}(\mathrm{H}(h_{i-3})))$ and verifying that the resulting value equals hi.

Each node uses a specific authentic (i.e., signed) element from its hash chain in each routing update that it sends about itself (metric 0). Based on this initial element, the one-way hash chain provides authentication for the lower bound on the metric in other routing updates for that node. The use of a hash value corresponding to the sequence number and metric in a routing update entry prevents any node from advertising a route to some destination claiming a greater sequence number than that destination's own current sequence number. Likewise, a node cannot advertise a route better than those for which it has received an advertisement, because the metric in an existing route cannot be decreased because of the one-way nature of the hash chain.

When a node receives a routing update, it checks the authenticity of the information for each entry in the update using the destination address, the sequence number, and the metric of the received entry, together with the latest prior *authentic* hash value received from that destination's hash chain. Hashing the received elements the correct number of times (according to the prior authentic hash value) assures the authenticity of the received information if the calculated hash value and the authentic hash value match.

The source of each routing update message in SEAD must also be authenticated, because otherwise, an attacker may be able to create routing loops through the *impersonation* attack. The authors propose two different approaches to provide node authentication: the first is based on a broadcast authentication mechanism such as TESLA, the second is based on the use of message authentication codes, assuming a shared secret key between each couple of nodes in the network.

SEAD does not cope with *wormhole* attacks although the authors propose, as in the ARIADNE protocol, to use the TIK protocol to detect the threat.

Notes on the Wormhole Attack

The wormhole attack is a severe threat against ad hoc routing protocols that is particularly challenging to detect and prevent. In a wormhole attack, a malicious node can record packets (or bits) at one location in the network and tunnel them to another location through a private network shared with a colluding malicious node. Most existing ad hoc routing protocols, without some mechanism to defend them against the wormhole attack, would be unable to find consistent routes to any destination, severely disrupting communication.

A dangerous threat can be perpetrated if a wormhole attacker tunnels all packets through the wormhole honestly and reliably because no harm seems to be done: the attacker actually seems to provide a useful service in connecting the network more efficiently. However, when an attacker forwards only routing control messages and not data packets, communication may be severely damaged. As an example, when used against an on-demand routing protocol such as DSR, a powerful application of the wormhole attack can be mounted by tunneling each RREQ message directly to the destination target node of the request. This attack prevents routes more than two hops long from being discovered because RREP messages would arrive to the source faster than any other replies or, worse, RREQ messages arriving from other nodes next to the destination than the attacker would be discarded because they were already seen. Perrig, Hu, and Johnson propose an approach to detect a wormhole based on *packet leashes* (Perrig, Hu, & Johnson, n.d.). The key element is that by authenticating either an extremely precise time stamp or location information combined with a loose time stamp, a receiver can determine if the packet has traversed a distance that is unrealistic for the specific network technology used.

Temporal leashes rely on extremely precise time synchronization and extremely precise time stamps in each packet. The travel time of a packet can be approximated as the difference between the receive time and the time stamp. Given the precise time synchronization required by temporal leashes, the authors propose efficient broadcast authenticators based on symmetric primitives. In particular, they extend the TESLA broadcast authentication protocol to allow the disclosure of the authentication key within the packet that is authenticated.

Geographical leashes are based on location information and loosely synchronized clocks. If the clocks of the sender and the receiver are synchronized within a certain threshold and the velocity of any node is bounded, the receiver can compute an upper bound on the distance between the sender and itself and use it to detect anomalies in the traffic flow. In certain circumstances, however, bounding the distance between the sender and the receiver cannot prevent wormhole attacks: when obstacles prevent communication between two nodes that would otherwise be in transmission range, a distance-based scheme would still allow wormholes between the sender and the receiver. To overcome this problem, in a variation of the geographical leashes, the receiver verifies that every possible location of the sender can reach every possible location of the receiver based on a radio propagation model implemented in every node.

In some special cases, wormholes can also be detected through techniques that do not require precise time synchronization nor location information. As an example, it would be sufficient to modify the routing protocol used to discover the path to a destination so that it could handle multiple routes: a verification mechanism would then detect anomalies when comparing the metric (e.g., number of hops) associated to each route. Any node advertising a path to a destination with a metric considerably lower than all the others could raise the possibility of a wormhole.

Furthermore, if the wormhole attack is performed only on routing information while dropping data packets, other mechanisms can be used to detect this misbehavior. When a node does not correctly participate in the network operation by not executing a particular function (e.g., packet forwarding), a collaborative monitoring technique can detect and gradually isolate misbehaving nodes. Lack of cooperation and security mechanisms used to enforce node cooperation with the network operation is the subject of the next section.

KEY MANAGEMENT

Authentication of peer entities involved in ad hoc routing and the integrity verification of routing exchanges are the two essential building blocks of secure routing. Both entity authentication and message integrity call for a key management mechanism to provide parties involved in authentication and integrity verification with proper keying material. Key management approaches suggested by current secure routing proposals fall in two categories:

- Manual configuration of symmetric (secret) keys: the pair-wise secret keys can serve as key encryption keys in a point-to-point key exchange protocol to establish session keys used for authentication and message integrity between communicating nodes. If some dedicated infrastructure including a key server can be afforded, automatic distribution of session keys with a key distribution protocol like Kerberos can also be envisioned.

- Public key–based scheme: each node possesses a pair of public and private keys based on an asymmetric algorithm like RSA. Based on this key pair, each node can perform authentication and message integrity operations or further exchange pair-wise symmetric keys used for efficient authentication and encryption operations.

Secure routing proposals such as SRP assume manual configuration of secure associations based on shared secret keys. Most of other proposals such as ARIADNE rely on a public–key–based scheme whereby a well-known, trusted third party (TTP) issues public key certificates used for authentication. The requirement for such a public key infrastructure does not necessarily imply a managed ad hoc network environment and an open environment can be targeted as well. Indeed, it is not necessary for the mobile nodes that form the ad hoc network to be managed by the public key certification authority. However, the bootstrap phase requires an external infrastructure, which has to be available also during the lifetime of the ad hoc network to provide revocation services for certificates that have expired or that have been explicitly revoked.

Two interesting proposals presented in the next sections tackle the complexity of public key infrastructures in the ad hoc network environment through self-organization: public key management based on the concept of "web of trust," akin to pretty good privacy (PGP), and a public key certification mechanism based on polynomial secret sharing.

Recent solutions rely on ID-based cryptography and crypto-based ID: these two approaches try to improve public–key–based solutions by reducing the need for a centralized administration at the network bootstrap phase.

A symmetric shared key distribution protocol that allows any two nodes to share a common secret key for data confidentiality is also presented. Another interesting approach outlined in the following subsections is based on the distance-bouncing technique and provides a secure encounter tracking service to a MANET. Table 1 provides a summary of key distribution techniques available in the literature.

Public Key Management

ID, Public Key Binding with Certificates

Self-Organized Public Key Management Based on PGP

Capkun, Buttyan, and Hubaux (2002) propose a fully self-organized public key management system that can be used to support security of ad hoc network routing protocols. The suggested approach is similar to PGP (Zimmerman, 1995) in the sense that users issue certificates for each other based on their personal acquaintances. However, in the proposed system, certificates are stored and distributed by the users themselves, unlike in PGP, where this task is performed by online servers (called certificate directories). In the proposed self-organizing public key management system, each user maintains a local certificate repository. When two users want to verify the public keys of each other, they merge their local certificate repositories and try to find appropriate certificate chains within the merged repository.

The success of this approach very much depends on the construction of the local certificate repositories and on the characteristics of the certificate graphs. The vertices of a certificate graph represent public keys of the users and the edges represent public key certificates issued by the users. The authors investigate several repository construction algorithms and study their performance. The proposed algorithms take into account the characteristics of the certificate graphs in a sense that the choice of the certificates that are stored by each mobile node depends on the connectivity of the node and its neighbors in the certificate graph.

More precisely, each node stores in its local repository several directed and mutually disjoint paths of certificates. Each path begins at the node itself, and the certificates are added to the path such that a new certificate is chosen among the certificates connected to the last node on the path (initially the node that stores the certificates) and such that the new certificate leads to the node that has the highest number of certificates connected to it (i.e., the highest vertex degree). The authors call this algorithm the maximum degree algorithm, as the local repository construction criterion is the degree of the vertices in a certificate graph.

In a more sophisticated extension called the shortcut hunter algorithm, certificates are stored into the local repositories based on the number of the shortcut certificates connected to the users. The shortcut certificate is a certificate that, when removed from the graph, makes the shortest path between two users previously connected by this certificate strictly larger than two.

When verifying a certificate chain, the node must trust the issuer of the certificates in the chain for correctly checking that the public key in the certificate indeed belongs to the node identification (ID) named in the certificate. When certificates are issued by the mobile nodes of an ad hoc network instead of trusted authorities, this assumption becomes unrealistic. In addition, there may be malicious nodes that issue false certificates. To alleviate these problems, the authors propose the use of authentication metrics (Reiter & Stybblebine, 1999): it is not enough to verify a node ID key binding via a single chain of certificates. The authentication metric is a function that accepts two keys (the verifier and the verified node) and a certificate graph and returns a numeric value corresponding to the degree of authenticity of the key that has to be verified: one example of authentication metric is the number of disjoint chains of certificates between two nodes in a certificate graph.

The authors emphasize that before being able to perform key authentication, each node must first build its local certificate repository, which is a complex operation. However, this initialization phase must be performed rarely and once the certificate repositories have been built, then any node can perform key authentication using only local information and the information provided by the targeted node. It should also be noted that local repositories become obsolete if a large number of certificate are revoked, as then the certificate chains are no longer valid; the same comment applies in the case when the certificate graph changes significantly. Furthermore, PGP-like schemes are more suitable for small communities

Table 1 Summary of Key Distribution Approaches Available in the Literature

	Identity–Public Key Binding				No Identity	
	PGP Web of Trust	**Self-Organized CA Based on Secret Sharing**	**Identity-Based Cryptography**	**Crypto-Based Identity**	**Key Predistribution**	**Context-Aware**
Symmetric cryptography					X	X
Asymmetric cryptography	X	X	X	X		
Public key certificates	YES	YES	NO	NO	NO	YES
Bootstrap of security associations	PGP-like	Distribution of initial shares	Secure naming for unique identifiers	Self-generated keys	Get globally trusted key–pool	Self-generated hash chains
Drawbacks	Initialization, storage, transitivity of trust	Distribution of initial shares, peripheral nodes	ID spoofing, distribution of initial shares, KDC knows all secret keys	Bogus identity generation	Cover-free algorithms, only shared keys, no authentication	Viable only for small networks, reliance on tight timing
Advantages	Distributed approach	Distributed approach	No need for certificates, distributed approach	No need for certificates, no need for certification authority	No need for certificates, distributed approach	Self-organized, distributed approach

because that the authenticity of a key can be assured with a higher degree of trustiness. The authors propose the use of authentication metrics to alleviate this problem: this approach, however, provides only probabilistic guarantees and is dependent on the characteristics of the certificate graph on which it operates. The authors also carried out a simulation study showing that for the certificate graphs that are likely to emerge in self-organized systems, the proposed approach yields good performances both in terms of the size of the local repository stored in each node and scalability.

Authentication Based on Polynomial Secret Sharing. Luo and Lu (n.d.) present an authentication service whereby the public key certificate of each node is cooperatively generated by a set of neighbors based on the behavior of the node as monitored by the neighbors. Using a group signature mechanism based on polynomial secret sharing, the secret digital signature key used to generate public key certificates is distributed among several nodes. Certification services such as issuing, renewal, and revocation of certificates thus are distributed among the nodes: a single node holds just a share of the complete certificate signature key. The authors propose a *localized trust model* to characterize the localized nature of security concerns in large ad hoc wireless networks. When applying such trust model, an entity is trusted if any k trusted entities claim so: these k trusted entities are typically the neighboring nodes of the entity. A locally trusted entity is globally accepted and a locally distrusted entity is regarded untrustworthy all over the network.

In the suggested security architecture, each node carries a certificate signed by the shared certificate-signing key SK, whereas the corresponding public key PK is assumed to be well known by all the nodes of the network, thus certificates are globally verifiable. Nodes without valid certificates will be isolated, that is, their packets will not be forwarded by the network. Essentially, any node without a valid certificate is considered a potential intruder. When a mobile node moves to a new location, it exchanges certificates with its new neighbors and goes through mutual authentication process to build trust relationships. Neighboring nodes with such trust relationships help each other to forward and route packets. They also monitor each other to detect possible attacks and break-ins. Specific monitoring algorithms and mechanisms are left to each individual node's choice. When a node requests a signed certificate from a coalition of k nodes, each of the latter checks its records about the requesting node. If the requestor is recorded as a legitimate node, a partial certificate is computed by applying the local node's share of SK and returned to the requestor. Upon collecting k partial certificates, the requesting node combines them to generate the complete certificate of its public key as if issued by a centralized certification authority.

The multiple signature scheme used to build the certificate is based on a k-threshold polynomial secret-sharing mechanism. This technique requires a bootstrapping phase where a "dealer" has to privately send each node its share of the secret signature key SK. The authors propose a scalable initialization mechanism called "self-initialization" whereby the dealer only has to initialize the very first k nodes, regardless of the global network span. The initialized nodes collaboratively initialize other nodes: repeating this procedure, the network progressively self-initializes itself. The same mechanism is applied when new nodes join the network.

Certificate revocation is also handled by the proposed architecture and an original approach to handle roaming adversaries is presented to prevent a misbehaving node that moves to a new location from getting a valid certificate. Roaming nodes are defeated with the flooding of "accusation" messages that travel in the network and inform distant nodes about the behavior of a suspect node.

The main drawback of the proposed architecture is the requirement for a trusted dealer that initializes the very first k nodes of a coalition to the choice of the systemwide parameter k. To cope with the first problem, the authors propose to use a distributed RSA key pair generation (Shamir, 1979) for the very first k nodes. The other major limitation of the scheme is the strong assumption that every node of the network has at least k trusted neighbors. Moreover, the authors assume that any new node that joins the system already has an initial certificate issued by an offline authority or by a coalition of k neighbors.

Implicit ID, Public Key Binding without Certificates Toward Secure Key Distribution in Truly Ad Hoc Networks. The mechanism proposed by Khalili, Katz, & Arbaugh (2003) focuses on the problem of key generation and management for peer-to-peer communication in a truly ad hoc network, that is, a network in which both an infrastructure and a centralized authority are not available.

The proposal made by Kahlili et al. is based on the concept of ID-based cryptography and avoids the need for users to generate their own public keys and to distribute them throughout the network: the user's identity acts as their public key. This significantly reduces the computation necessary to join the network. Furthermore, as opposed to a CA-based solution (Zhou & Haas, 1999) where a user is required to propagate both his public key as well as a signature (by the CA) on his public key, in an ID-based system, users need only propagate their identity (which is typically included in every message anyway). This can lead to huge savings in bandwidth.

It is important to notice that the authors do not specify either the nature of the identity to be used or a means for authenticating users' identities before sending them (shares of) their secret key. Initial authentication of user's identities represents an important issue that is common to CA-based solutions: the entire security of the scheme is based on the initial validation of the data (identity) that will be certified for later use. The interested reader should refer to Boneh & Franklin (2001) to gather extensive information on ID-based cryptography.

Khalili, Katz, and Arbaugh (2003) suggest that at the time of network formation, the nodes willing to form the network decide on a mutually acceptable set of security parameters. Any node that is not satisfied by the choice of parameters can choose to refuse to participate in the network. The security parameters might include a threshold t of key service nodes, the number and identity of key service nodes, particular parameters of underlying schemes (e.g., key lengths), and a policy for key issuance. This initial negotiation is independent of the proposed scheme and the authors do not discuss it in any detail. It should be noted, though, that the initial policy negotiation is a potential target for active or byzantine adversaries, and the negotiation protocol should address this issue.

The initial set of nodes can then form a threshold key distribution center (KDC) for an ID-based scheme. These nodes will generate the master secret/public keys in a distributed manner such that fewer than t nodes cannot recover the master secret key. The master public key is given to all members of the network when they join, and the KDC can start issuing personal secret keys to nodes (including themselves) based on their identities and the key issuance policy. An identity can be something usually present in transmitted messages, like a MAC (or other network layer) address. To receive the private key corresponding to some identity, a node presents this identity and any extra material specified by the key issuance policy to t (or more) nodes forming the KDC and receives a share of their personal private key from each of them. With t correct shares, the node can then compute its personal private key within the network's ID-based system. It is important to notice that an efficient local mechanism to check the correctness of the individual shares and the computed private key has to be provided, but the authors do not provide any further information about which mechanism should be used.

Distributing the key generation and the KDC service prevents a single point of failure and resists compromise or insider attack (up to the threshold k). In addition, distributing the KDC in a t-out-of-n fashion makes the scheme flexible when some nodes are unreachable because of ad hoc conditions (mobility, link breaks, etc.) as long as at least k are still reachable.

The authors stress that the proposed scheme makes no assumption about the "security" of users' identities, for example, that they are set in hardware or cannot be spoofed. However, spoofing only needs to be prevented or detected by the nodes forming the KDC at the time of key issuance (and this can be done by requiring some "unspoofable" supporting material to be presented at the time of a key request). For completeness, the authors recommend a number of possibilities for user identities. One possibility is to use statistically unique cryptographically verifiable (SUCV) addresses (Montenegro & Castelluccia, 2002; applied to ad hoc networks by Bobba, Eschenauer, Gligor, & Arbaugh, 2002).

The solution presented by Khalili, Katz, & Arbaugh (2003) offers an interesting alternative to the classical certificate-based systems presented in this section and it should be noted that the authors target a fully independent ad hoc network where nodes act in a self-organized way. However, the initial establishment of a KDC using threshold cryptography *needs* the presence of an external authority or management that decides the threshold system parameters and that elects trusted nodes to participate to the initial set of nodes that form the KDC. This is obviously in contrast with the targeted self-organization characteristic of the network and a fully self-organized network setup is far from being achieved. It is important to remember that introducing new cryptographic techniques or an original combination of existing techniques could have the sole effect of moving the problem (self-organization) one step further and only giving the illusion of a security scheme adapted to a truly self-organized network.

Bootstrapping Security Associations for Routing in Mobile Ad Hoc Networks

Bobba et al. (2002) show how to bootstrap secure associations for the routing protocols of MANETs online, without assuming any trusted authorities or distributed trust-establishment services. The proposed scheme relies on the use of *statistically unique and cryptographically verifiable* (SUCV) identifiers (Montenegro & Castellucia, 2002) and public–secret key pairs generated by the nodes themselves, in much the same way that SUCVs are used in MobileIPv6 (MIPv6) to solve the address "ownership" problem (Montenegro & Castellucia, 2002). The authors present the bootstrapping solution in the context of the dynamic source routing (DSR) protocol and argue that the solution is applicable to other secure routing protocols, such as SEAD (Hu, Johnson, & Perrig, n.d.) and ARIADNE (Hu, Perrig, & Johnson, 2002).

Bobba et al. (2002) describe a method in which, to produce an IP address that is securely bound to a public key, a node generates a 64-bit pseudorandom value by applying a one-way, collision-resistant hash function to the public key of its (uncertified) public–private key pair. Then, the IP address is generated as the concatenation of a network-specific identifier (64 bits in MIP6) and the hash of the public key (64 bits). The binding between this IP address and the public key is secure because it is computationally unfeasible for an attacker (a) to create another <public, private> key pair whose hash generates the same IP address (because of the second preimage resistance of one-way, collision-resistant hash functions), and (b) to discover the secret key, or create a different one, for a given public key (by definition).

Because of the size of the resulting address space, this IP address is also statistically unique.

A source node can then use the secure binding to authenticate its IP address and the contents of its packets to an arbitrary destination node as follows. The node signs a packet with its private key and sends the signed packet to the destination address together with its public key (and IP address). The destination node verifies that the IP address is securely bound to the public key by computing the hash function of the received public key and comparing the result with the lower 64-bit field of the IP address. (Thus, the IP address "certifies" the validity of the public key, thereby preventing an attacker from spoofing the source address.) Then, the destination node authenticates the content of the packet by verifying the signature with the public key.

Bobba et al. (2002) propose the application of their ideas to the DSR route discovery phase, both in an asymmetric version and in a symmetric version, and analyze the performances and computational overhead of a MANET using cryptographically generated IP addresses.

It should be noted that other security solutions (Khalili, Katz, & Arbaugh, 2003) for MANET suggest relying on such a scheme to protect against spoofing attacks. However, the absence of a certification authority that validates the information locally generated by every node can have a drastic consequence on the overall security of the scheme. Indeed, there is nothing that prevents a malicious node from generating as many public–private key pairs as needed to produce bogus IP addresses for which it can securely prove possession. The only guarantee that the scheme proposed by Bobba et al. (2002) offers is that a legitimate node can be assured to be the only owner of an IP address. As another example, the scheme proposed in Montenegro & Castelluccia (2002) and in Bobba et al. (2002) could not be used to protect a MANET from identity spoofing using a cooperation enforcement mechanism based on reputation (see the Cooperation Enforcement section). Indeed, the scheme would only prevent a misbehaving node from using a legitimate node IP/ID to steal a positive reputation rating. It would allow, however, a misbehaving node to get rid of a bad reputation record simply by generating a new (verifiable) IP/ID and impersonating a new node joining the network.

Distribution of Symmetric Keys

Key Predistribution

Zhu, Xu, Setia, & Jajodia (2003) propose a symmetric pairwise secret key establishment protocol for ad hoc networks. Excluding a set-up phase where an offline key distribution center is needed, the main features of the proposed protocol are these:

- It is fully distributed—no online key server is required.
- It is computationally efficient—it relies only on symmetric cryptography.
- It is storage scalable—the storage requirements per node are independent of the size of the network.

The basic functioning of the protocol is the following: the pre–key distribution server deterministically selects a set of keys from a common key pool and delivers them to any node that wants to participate in the ad hoc network. The key selection is deterministic and based on the node identity, thus allowing any node to determine intersection/common keys with other nodes of the network.

When forming the network, any node that needs to establish a secret shared key with any other node in the network has to determine whether there is any *direct path* or *indirect path* to the desired recipient.

Consider as an example two nodes, u and v, that wish to communicate privately. Note that u and v may already share one or more keys from the pool of keys after the key predistribution phase. However, these keys are not known *exclusively* to u and v because every key of the key pool may be allocated to multiple nodes; hence, they cannot be used for encrypting any message that is private to u and v.

The goal of the proposed algorithm is to establish a key, sk, that is known exclusively to u and v. To establish sk, a sender node (say u) splits sk into multiple shares using a threshold secret-sharing scheme. It then transmits to the recipient (v) all these shares, using a separate secure *logical path* for each share. The recipient node then reconstructs sk after it receives all (or a certain number of) the shares and acknowledge the correct reception with a ciphered hello message using the common shared key.

There are *logical paths* between two nodes when (a) the two nodes share one or more keys (*direct path*) and (b) the two nodes do not share any keys, but through other intermediate nodes (called *proxies*) they can exchange messages securely (*indirect paths*). The protocol always uses any direct paths that exist between nodes in preference to indirect paths, because the use of an indirect path incurs additional computational and communication overhead.

Logical paths between two nodes can be easily found since the key predistribution algorithm is public and deterministic; a node u can independently compute the set of key IDs corresponding to a node v's key set. Therefore, without proactively exchanging the set of its key IDs with others, a node knowing the IDs of its neighbors can determine not only which neighbors share or do not share keys with it, but also which two neighbors share which keys. The latter knowledge is very valuable when node u does not share any keys with a node v, because node u can use a neighbor (say x) that shares keys with both of them as a *proxy*. For example, suppose node u shares a key k_{ux} with node x, node v shares a key k_{vx} with node x, but no shared key exists between node u and node v.

To transmit a message M to node v securely, node u executes the following steps:

$$u \rightarrow x : \{M\}_{k_{ux}}$$
$$x \rightarrow v : \{M\}_{k_{xv}}$$

The node x in the above example is called node u's *one-hop proxy* to v. More generally, node x is said to be node u's *i-hop proxy* if x is i hops away from u and x shares a key with both u and v respectively. If u and v do not have any direct paths or one-hop proxies to each other, they can resort to a proxy node of multiple hops away. Note that it is also possible to establish a logical path with multiple proxies involved. For example, if there is a shared key between u and x, between x and y, between y and v respectively, u and v can establish a logical path as well.

The idea proposed by Zhu, Xu, Setia, and Jajodia (2003) represents a distributed and efficient way of establishing a shared secret key between two nodes in a MANET but relies on the presence of an external authority and/or centralized management to compute and distribute the large amount of initial preshared keys. Furthermore, this limitation is accentuated by the need of undeniable and unspoofable node identities. The overall system security relies on the fact that every node is able to compute a pool of preshared keys with its neighbors to initiate a logical-path discovery to reach the desired recipient. As an example, by generating fake identities, a node could contact the pre–key distribution center and gather enough keying material to decrypt all the shares of a shared secret key and compromise the confidentiality of communication.

Context-Aware Key Management

SECTOR: Secure Tracking of Node Encounters in Multihop Wireless Networks

Chapkun, Buttyan, and Hubaux (2003) present a set of mechanisms for the secure verification of the time of encounters between nodes in multihop wireless networks with the aim of enabling any node to prove to any other node (or base station) its encounters with other nodes before or at some specific time. SECTOR can be used as a basic mechanism to prevent the wormhole attack (see the previous discussion on wormholes), to help securing routing protocols based on history of encounters (Dubois-Ferriere, Grossglauser, & Vetterli, 2003), or to provide topology monitoring both in pure ad hoc systems and in cellular networks.

The system model and the basic assumptions made by the authors require *loose time synchronization* between all the nodes forming the network and that nodes can measure time locally with nanosecond precision. Furthermore, the authors also assume that each node is equipped with a *special hardware module* that can temporarily take over the control of the radio transceiver unit of the node from the CPU. A node can be put in a special state where it is capable of responding to a one-bit challenge with a one-bit response essentially immediately, without the delay imposed by the usual way of processing messages. Lastly, the authors assume that the bits are correctly transmitted, meaning that there are no collisions and no jamming.

Security associations are provided prior to the network formation so that each node shares a symmetric, secret key with any other node and a central authority controls the network membership and assigns a unique identity to each node.

To provide a basis for secure and authenticated proofs of encounters, the MAD (mutual authentication with distance-bounding) protocol is introduced. Based on the Brands–Chaum technique (Brands & Chaum, 1993), the MAD protocol enables any two nodes to determine their mutual distance at the time of encounter and enhances the basic scheme by avoiding the use of a digital signature in favor of a more efficient symmetric scheme. Furthermore, the commitments bits that are used in the distance-bounding technique are firstly sent in the initialization phase of the protocol and then gradually revealed when the distance evaluation takes part: this ensures that the parties cannot send bits too early, and thus cannot cheat the other party by appearing to be closer than they really are.

The MAD protocol has to be used in conjunction with the GTE (guaranteed time of encounter) mechanism that consists in the construction of a particular type of Merkle hash tree (Merkle, 1980) in which leaves also contain time information about the disclosure of the hash-chain element. The root of the tree is then distributed in an authentic way to every other node of the network.

Any two nodes willing to exchange secure proof of the time of their encounter, verifiable by any other node of the network, will have to run first the MAD protocol to mutually authenticate themselves. Then they will disclose the element of the Merkle tree that corresponds to the actual time (every node is loosely synchronized): after authentication of the disclosed proof, the nodes have to store the released tree element to subsequently prove their encounter. The authors provide a detailed study that focuses on possible enhancements of the SECTOR protocol suite to meet specific requirements resulting from the presence of an infrastructure or a limited storage capacity of the devices. The interested reader should refer to Capkun,

Buttyan, & Hubaux (2003) to understand the different applications of SECTOR.

Although SECTOR provides a first tentative step to cope with secure tracking of node encounters in MANET, its application could be narrowed by the limiting requirements imposed by the design. The need for a deployed security infrastructure, preestablished security associations between nodes, or, in its advanced version, the use of TESLA keys for broadcasting authentic roots of the Merkle hash trees render SECTOR not adaptable to a short-lived, highly mobile, and dynamic network. In addition, the security of SECTOR relies on the presence of an external trusted authority that provides unique identities (and certificates) to the nodes of the network. If such an authority were not available, SECTOR would be vulnerable to attacks such as the forgery of proof of encounters.

Furthermore, as the authors suggest, storage requirements can be very demanding depending on the size of the network: this can be a serious limitation when considering heterogeneous MANETs formed by portable devices.

COOPERATION ENFORCEMENT

Selfishness is a new type of misbehavior that is inherent to ad hoc networks and cooperation enforcement is the countermeasure against selfishness. A selfish node does not directly intend to damage other nodes with active attacks (mainly because performing active attacks can be very expensive in terms of energy consumption), but instead it simply does not contribute to the network operation and saves battery life for its own communications. Selfishness can cause serious damage in terms of global network throughput and delay as shown by a simulation study of the effect of selfish behavior on the DSR routing protocol (Michiardi & Molva, 2002).

Current cooperation enforcement proposals for MANET can be classified as follows:

- Approaches based on threshold cryptography.
- Approaches based on micropayment.
- Approaches based on reputation.

The most significant proposals in each category are outlined in the following section. See Table 2 for a summary.

Cooperation Enforcement Mechanisms Based on Threshold Cryptography

Self-Organized Network-Layer Security in Mobile Ad Hoc Networks

Yang, Meng, & Lu (2002) suggest a mechanism whereby each node of the ad hoc network is required to hold a token to participate in the network operations. Tokens are granted to a node collaboratively by its neighbors based on the monitoring of the node's contribution to packet forwarding and routing operations. Upon expiration of the token, each node renews its token through a token-renewal exchange with its neighbors: the duration of a token's validity is based on the duration of the node's correct behavior as monitored by the neighbors granting/renewing the token. This mechanism typically allows a well-behaved node to accumulate credit and to renew its token less frequently as time evolves.

The token-based cooperation enforcement mechanism includes four interacting components: neighbor verification through which the local node verifies whether neighboring nodes are legitimate, neighbor monitoring that allows the local node to monitor the behavior of each node in the network and to detect attacks from malicious nodes, intrusion reaction that assures the generation of network alerts and the isolation of attackers, and security-enhanced routing protocol that consists of the ad hoc routing protocol including security extensions.

A valid token is constructed using a group signature whereby a mechanism based on polynomial secret sharing (Shamir, 1979) assures that at least k neighbors agree to issue or renew the token. The key set-up complexity of polynomial secret sharing and the requirement for at least k nodes to sign each token both are incompatible with high mobility and call for a rather large and dense ad hoc network. Furthermore, the duration of a token's validity increases proportionally with the duration of the node's correct behavior as monitored by its neighbors; this feature again calls for low mobility. The token-based cooperation enforcement mechanism is thus suitable for ad hoc networks where node mobility is low. Spoofing attacks, through which a node can request more than one token by claiming a different identity, are not taken into account by the proposal even if the authors suggest that MAC addresses can be sufficient for node authentication purposes.

Cooperation Enforcement Mechanisms Based on Micropayment Schemes

Nuglets

Buttyan and Hubaux (2001) present two important issues targeted specifically at the ad hoc networking environment: first, end users must be given some incentive to contribute in the network operation (especially to relay packets belonging to other nodes) and second, end users must be discouraged from overloading the network. The solution consists of a virtual currency called nuglets, which is used in every transaction. Two different models are described: the packet purse model and the packet trade model. In the packet purse model, each packet is loaded with nuglets by the source and each forwarding host takes out nuglets for its forwarding service. The advantage of this approach is that it discourages users from flooding the network, but the drawback is that the source needs to know exactly how many nuglets it has to include in the packet it sends. In the packet trade model, each packet is traded for nuglets by the intermediate nodes: each intermediate node buys the packet from the previous node on the path. Thus, the destination has to pay for the packet. The direct advantage of this approach is that the source does not need to know how many nuglets need to be loaded into the packet. On the other hand, because the packet generation is not charged, malicious flooding of the network cannot be prevented. There are some further issues that have to be solved: in the packet purse model, the intermediate nodes are able to take out more nuglets than they are supposed to; in the packet trade model, the

Table 2 Summary of Cooperation Enforcement Techniques Available in the Literature

	Token Based	Nuglets	Sprite	I-Pass	CONFIDANT	CORE
Incentive	Participation Token	Virtual currency	Virtual currency	Auctions	Reputation	Reputation
Punishment	Impact on route selection	Network utilization prevented	Network utilization prevented	Low bandwith	Impact on route selection	Gradual exclusion from network utilization
Monitoring Technique	Watchdog	N/A	N/A	N/A	Watchdog	Watchdog
Reintegration	Not provided	N/A	N/A	N/A	Need for specific mechanism	Inherent
Need for Security Infrastructure	YES	YES Tamper proof hardware	YES Credit Clearance Service	YES Credit Clearance Service	NO	NO
Drawbacks	Need for security infrastructure	Need for security infrastructure Need for tamper proof hardware Credits per route evaluation	Need for security infrastructure Credit Service Low mobility required	Reliance on watchdog Credit Service Complexity of auction scheme	Need for a reintegration mechanism Reputation propagation can be a weakness	Reliance on watchdog No reputation propagation
Advantages	No need for watchdog	No need for a Credit Service	No need for tamper proof hardware	Integration in real business scenarios	Reputation propagation	Low storage and computational requirements Functional reputation evaluation

intermediate nodes are able to deny the forwarding service after taking out nuglets from a packet.

Sprite

As opposed to the Nuglets approach, the proposal presented by Zhong, Chen, & Yang (2003) does not require a tamper-proof hardware. At a high level, the basic scheme of sprite can be described as follows. When receiving a message, a node keeps a signed receipt of the message generated by the source node. Later, when the node has a fast connection to a credit clearance service (CCS), it reports to the CCS the messages that it has received and forwarded by uploading its receipts. The CCS then determines the charge and credit to each node involved in the transmission of the message, depending on the reported receipts.

The main objectives of sprite consist in stimulating nodes to cooperate and preventing cheating by making it unattractive. The overall system architecture can be described as follows. To identify each node, the authors assume that each node has a public key certificate issued by a scalable certificate authority such as those proposed by Zhou & Hass (1999) and Luo and Lu (n.d.). When a node sends its own messages, the node will lose credit (or virtual money) to the network because other nodes incur a cost to forward the messages. On the other hand, when a node forwards others' messages, it should gain credit and therefore be able to send its messages later. There are two ways for a node to get more credit. First, a node can pay its debit or buy more credit using real money, at a variable rate to the virtual money, based on the current performance of the system. However, the preferred and dominant way to get more credit is by forwarding others' messages. To get credit for forwarding others' messages, a node needs to report to the CCS which messages it has helped to forward by presenting a valid message receipt. The choice of charging only the source (and not the destination) of a message derives from the fact that it prevents nodes to flood the network with useless messages.

The authors provide a detailed study of the payment/charging scheme parameters to make cooperation attractive and cheating behavior unappealing based on game theory. However, it can be argued that the basic assumptions made when providing an analytical study of the solution of the game are somehow misleading: indeed, the authors assume that a node is following the truth-telling strategy when a node truly received a message and reports a valid receipt to the CCS. Unfortunately, the key feature of the sprite protocol, namely the receipt used as a proof of forwarding, could constitute a weak point of the system. A receipt is generated by the source of a message, signed with the source's secret key and appended to the message that needs to be forwarded. Subsequent nodes on the path just need that receipt that can be gathered both by receiving the message (but not necessarily forwarding it) and by colluding with other nodes. The authors took into account this possibility when modeling the problem in game theoretical terms: indeed, system parameters are designed and tuned such that collusion does not pay. However, if the nodes had other means of exchanging receipts other than using their radio interfaces, then collusion and cheating could become attractive.

iPass

In the following approach, the authors adopt the "pay for service" model of cooperation and propose an auction-based incentive scheme to enable cooperative packet forwarding behavior in MANET. In iPass, each router constitutes a "smart market," where an auction process runs continuously to determine who should obtain how much of the bandwidth and at what price. The bidders are the set of traffic flows currently passing that router. Each flow carries a bid indicating its willingness to pay for the forwarding service. Based on these bids, the router runs a "generalized Vickrey auction" to determine the bandwidth allocation for the flows. A remarkable property of this auction is that it is *incentive compatible* for the users to place a bid equal to their true utilities for bandwidth. A user's utility for bandwidth reflects the valuation (or satisfaction) of the user if she is given such bandwidth, which may depend on the application being used.

Incentive compatible means that a user has no incentive to deviate from this bidding strategy, because it leads to higher payoff for the user, defined as the user's utility of winning the goods less the price to pay. Therefore, the user's bidding strategy is greatly simplified, and the outcome of the auction is *efficient*, meaning that it gives bandwidth to those users who need them the most.

From an end-to-end point of view, a flow usually travels through multiple hops (or auction markets) where it is allocated different amounts of bandwidth. This information is carried with each data packet to the receiver and returned to the sender as feedback, part of a *signaling protocol*. The sender should then police its rate in compliance with the allocated bandwidth. Therefore, besides creating an incentive for packet forwarding, the iPass scheme also assumes the task of flow control and possesses certain "differentiated service" capabilities based on the bids of the flows.

The reader interested in details of the generalized Vickrey auction scheme is advised to refer to Chen and Nahrstadt (2004) and MacKie-Mason and Varian (1994, 1995). It is important to notice here that the design of the iPass mechanism is incomplete: the authors suggest referring to Zhong, Chem & Yang (2003) to find guidelines to complete it with a payment protocol that allows the router node to claim a reward for forwarding the packet, for example, by saving a "receipt" of the packet, similar to sprite. Detail integration of the iPass scheme with a secure payment and auditing system remains a future direction.

As opposed to other cooperation enforcement schemes presented in this chapter, iPass appears very interesting because its inherent features makes it easy to integrate in real business scenarios. However, the main drawback of iPass is the general complexity of the auction scheme. It is sometimes important to keep in mind that a cooperation enforcement scheme is designed to cope with node selfishness that derives mainly from a limited quantity of energy available to mobile nodes. The continuous execution of a heavy cooperation enforcement mechanism could have serious consequences on the energy consumption of a node, which in turn would have the tendency to behave selfishly.

Cooperation Enforcement Mechanisms Based on Reputation

CONFIDANT

Buchegger and Le Boudec (2002, n.d.) proposed a technique called CONFIDANT (cooperation of nodes, fairness in dynamic ad hoc networks) that aims to detect malicious nodes by combining monitoring and reporting and by establishing routes by avoiding misbehaving nodes. CONFIDANT is designed as an extension to a routing protocol such as DSR. CONFIDANT components in each node include a network monitor, reputation records for first-hand and trusted second-hand observations about routing and forwarding behavior of other nodes, trust records to control trust given to received warnings, and a path manager to adapt the behavior of the local node according to its reputation and to take action against malicious nodes. The term reputation is used to evaluate routing and forwarding behavior according to the network protocol, whereas the term trust is used to evaluate participation in the CONFIDANT metaprotocol.

The dynamic behavior of CONFIDANT is as follows. Nodes monitor their neighbors and change their reputation accordingly. If they have a reason to believe that a node misbehaves, they can take action in terms of their own routing and forwarding and they can decide to inform other nodes by sending an ALARM message. When a node receives such an ALARM either directly or by promiscuously listening to the network, it evaluates how trustworthy the ALARM is based on the source of the ALARM and the accumulated ALARM messages about the node in question. It can then decide whether to take action against the misbehaving node in the form of excluding routes containing the misbehaving node, reranking paths in the path cache, reciprocating by noncooperation, or forwarding an ALARM about the node.

The first version of CONFIDANT was, despite the filtering of ALARM messages in the trust manager, vulnerable to concerted efforts of spreading wrong accusations. In a recent enhancement of the protocol, this problem has been addressed by the use of Bayesian statistics for classification and the exclusion of liars.

Simulations with nodes that do not participate in the forwarding function have shown that CONFIDANT can cope well, even if half of the network population acts maliciously. Further simulations concerning the effect of second-hand information and slander have shown that slander can effectively be prevented while still retaining a significant increase in detection speed as compared with using merely first-hand information.

The limitations of CONFIDANT lie in the assumptions for detection-based reputation systems. Events have to be observable and classifiable for detection, and reputation can only be meaningful if the identity of each node is persistent; otherwise, it is vulnerable to spoofing attacks.

CORE

The security scheme proposed by Michiardi and Molva (2002a, 2002b) stimulates node cooperation by a collaborative monitoring technique and a reputation mechanism. Each node of the network monitors the behavior of its neighbors with respect to a requested function and collects observations about the execution of that function: as an example, when a node initiates a route request (e.g., using the DSR routing protocol), it monitors its neighbors' processing of the request, whether with a route reply or by relaying the route request. If the observed result and the expected result coincide, then the observation will take a positive value; otherwise, it will take a negative value.

Based on the collected observations, each node computes a reputation value for every neighbor using a sophisticated reputation mechanism that differentiates between subjective reputation (observations), indirect reputation (positive reports by others), and functional reputation (task-specific behavior), which are weighted for a combined reputation value. The formula used to evaluate the reputation value avoids false detections (caused for example by link breaks) by using an aging factor that gives more relevance to past observations: frequent variations on a node behavior are filtered. Furthermore, if the function that is being monitored provides an acknowledgement message (e.g., the route reply message of the DSR protocol), reputation information can also be gathered about nodes that are not within the radio range of the monitoring node. In this case, only positive ratings are assigned to the nodes that participated to the execution of the function in its totality.

The CORE mechanism resists attacks performed using the security mechanism itself: no negative ratings are spread between the nodes, so it is impossible for a node to maliciously decrease another node's reputation. The reputation mechanism allows the nodes of the MANET to gradually isolate selfish nodes: when the reputation assigned to a neighboring node decreases below a predefined threshold, service provision to the misbehaving node will be interrupted. Misbehaving nodes can, however, be reintegrated in the network if they increase their reputation by cooperating to the network operation.

As for the other security mechanism based on reputation, the CORE mechanism suffers from the spoofing attack: misbehaving nodes are not prevented from changing their network identity, which allows the attacker to elude the reputation system. Furthermore, no simulation results prove the robustness of the protocol even if the authors propose an original approach based on game theory to come up with a formal assessment of the security properties of CORE.

VALIDATION OF COOPERATION ENFORCEMENT MECHANISMS THROUGH GAME THEORY

The main issue encountered when validating cooperation enforcement mechanisms is that in general they cannot be analyzed with the common validation techniques used for conventional security protocols. The reason that makes cooperation enforcement mechanisms difficult to assess is that a large fraction of current proposals provide only a fuzzy discrimination between legitimate nodes and misbehaving nodes: in general, it is hard to obtain a formal description of a mechanism that does not offer a boolean output.

Furthermore, especially for those mechanisms based on virtual currency or on reputation, a natural way to model the basic functioning of cooperation schemes that emerged in the literature is based on principles that take inspiration from microeconomic theory.

In particular, game theory appeared to be a very useful tool to validate and analyze cooperation enforcement mechanisms because it can be used to model conflict situations in which two or more parties have to evaluate which strategy they should follow to reach higher degrees of satisfaction. Specifically, players of a game can be modeled as rational and selfish entities; this modeling aims to maximize a utility function that grasps the nature of the interaction between them. The similarities of game theoretical models with the node selfishness problem in MANET recently attracted many researchers, and a growing number of proposals are available in the literature.

Before giving the details of the most significant proposals, it is interesting to answer the following question. If game theory can be used to model the interactions between nodes in a MANET, even with a high accuracy, is it better to begin with the design of a cooperation enforcement mechanism and then analyze it using game theory, or use game theory to provide a general model of an ad hoc network and derive the guidelines to design a cooperation enforcement mechanism? Obviously, the answer is not simple and in the next section, both approaches will be presented. One straightforward observation is that game theoretical modeling also has some limitations and it appears from the current proposals that security-related problems cannot be fully captured by a general model. Specifically, it is hard to model the situation in which the cooperation enforcement mechanism itself can be used to perform attacks against legitimate nodes. A basic example to explain this situation and that has been highlighted in the previous section is related to identity spoofing: even if the cooperation enforcement mechanism promises to stimulate node cooperation, the absence of a security infrastructure that provides unique and provable identity can jeopardize the network operation. The direct consequence is that most of the proposals based on a general game theoretical framework rely on restricting assumptions that are not used by mechanisms designed with security-related problems in mind.

General Framework

Srinivasan, Nuggehalli, Chiasserini, & Rao (2003) provide an analytical approach to study cooperation in MANET. The authors use a game theoretical framework to model the node selfishness problem: selfish nodes aim to preserve their available energy for their own communications but do not intentionally want to damage other nodes in the network (malicious nodes are neglected). No collusion between selfish nodes is assumed. In their work, the authors consider a finite population of *N* nodes. Each node, depending on its type (e.g., laptop, PDA, cell phone), is associated with an average power constraint. This constraint can be derived by dividing the node's initial energy allocation by its lifetime expectation. It is also assumed that time is slotted, that each session lasts for one slot, and that the traffic model is connection oriented. At the beginning of each slot, a source, destination, and several relays are randomly chosen out of the *N* nodes to form an ad hoc network. The source requests the relay nodes in the route to forward its traffic to the destination. If any of the relay nodes rejects the request, the traffic connection is blocked.

For each node, the authors define the normalized acceptance rate (NAR) as the ratio of the number of successful relay requests generated by the node to the number of relay requests made by the node. This quantity is an indication of the throughput experienced by the node. Then, the authors study the optimal tradeoff between the lifetime and NARs of the nodes. In particular, given the energy constraints and the lifetime expectation of the nodes, a set of feasible NARs is identified.

Because users are self-interested and rational, there is no guarantee that they will follow a particular strategy unless they are convinced that they cannot do better by following some other strategy. In game theoretic terms, a set of strategies which constitute a Nash equilibrium has to be identified. Ideally, the authors would like the Nash equilibrium to result in the rational and Pareto optimal operating point, that is, values of NAR such that a node cannot improve its NAR without decreasing some other node's NAR.

To achieve the equilibrium, the authors propose a cooperation enforcement mechanism (which they define as a distributed and scalable acceptance algorithm) called generous tit-for-tat (GTFT). The authors then prove that GTFT is a Nash equilibrium that converges to the rational and Pareto optimal NARs. The interested reader should refer to Srinivasan et al. (2003) for details on the modeling of node interactions in ad hoc networks.

It is important here to notice that the authors started with a generic node model and came up with a cooperation enforcement mechanism in which nothing but a well-known strategy profile can be found in the literature.

The limitations of a generic game theoretical approach to design a mechanism to cope with node selfishness clearly emerge, because some basic assumptions about the operation setting of the network cannot be taken into account following such a method. Specifically, the authors do not specify the nature of the ad hoc network. It is well known in the literature that ad hoc networks can be classified (among the possible classifications) as "open/self-organized" or "managed." In the first case, which is the one that attracted recent studies on cooperation enforcement mechanisms, no a priori trust can be assumed among the nodes of the network. If the network is completely self-organized, it means also that no external authority or infrastructure can be used to set up trust relationships among the nodes. There is no security mechanism available in the literature that solves (in a fully self-organized way) the interesting problem of key distribution in this type of networks. This means that it would be impossible to securely provide the "energy class" information that is a necessary requisite for the system model presented by the authors: in the discussion session, they admit the need for such a secure mechanism.

This first important observation confirms that the basic functioning of a cooperation enforcement mechanism derived from a game theoretical modeling could be jeopardized in the realistic scenario in which nodes do not correctly advertise their energy class. It follows the need for a complementary security mechanism to cope with this new type of misbehavior introduced by the cooperation enforcement mechanism itself.

By studying the GTFT acceptance algorithm, it is possible to evince some other interesting observations. The GTFT has been proposed to promote cooperation in the classical iterated prisoner's dilemma (Myerson, 1991; Axelrod, 1984; Osborne & Rubinstein, 1994) and is based on the tit-for-tat (TFT) strategy. In the general TFT policy selection for an iterated prisoner's dilemma game, a player cooperates on the first move and then copies her opponent's last move for all subsequent moves. The information on the other players' moves is gathered by an acknowledgment mechanism introduced by the authors in the "system model" section of Srinivasan et al. (2003). However, the network load is increased with some "control" traffic with the aim of providing a feedback mechanism for the decision-making algorithm. Every extra packet that needs to be sent costs some additional energy that has to be spent by the nodes of the network. When considering selfish nodes that are inclined to save energy for their own communications, it is questionable to think that they would spend more energy to "execute" the cooperation algorithm. However, thanks to theorem 2 through theorem 4, it is proved that a selfish node is better off executing correctly the acceptance policy algorithm. What happens if the acknowledgement messages used to estimate the other players' strategies are lost? Which is the consequence on the policy guessed by the "observing" node? What happens if the feedback information is fabricated to cheat? Again, the answer to these basic questions has to be found in some additional security mechanisms that render the initial cooperation enforcement mechanism heavier and more complex.

Game Theoretical Analysis of CORE

Michiardi and Molva (2003, n.d.) propose a game theoretical analysis of CORE (Michiardi & Molva, 2002a), which is outlined in a previous section. As opposed to the analysis proposed in that section, the authors first design the cooperation enforcement mechanism and then propose an analysis based on both uncooperative and cooperative game theory to assess the features of CORE.

With the uncooperative game theory approach, the authors model the interaction between any pair of nodes that belong to a valid path from a source to a destination, focusing on the strategy selection phase (forwarding policy) when a node requests that the other node forward packets that belong to a traffic flow. In a first phase, only selfish nodes are taken into account, and the game theoretical model is based on a node-centric evaluation of the action (fraction of packets that will be forwarded) that has to be selected. In this particular scenario, the authors demonstrate that without the support of a cooperation enforcement mechanism, the best strategy for a selfish node that tries to maximize its utility function is to save energy by refraining to forward packets on behalf of the requesting nodes. In a second phase, two random neighboring nodes involved in forwarding packets from a source to a destination are considered, where one node is selfish and the other one uses CORE to stimulate and eventually enforce the cooperation of its selfish neighbor. The authors only provide numerical results that highlight the behavior of the selfish node when asked to forward different type of traffic flow (uniform and random). Results are then compared with the TFT strategy.

By using a cooperative game theory approach, the authors model the selfishness problem, both with a node-centric and network-centric perspective, by adopting the ERC theory. In this setting, the authors aim to find a lower bound to the size of a coalition of cooperating nodes and to assess the ability of CORE to stimulate nodes to join the coalition. Although the formalization of the CORE mechanism in the function that defines the strategy selection of nodes is somewhat vague, it is interesting to notice how cooperative game theory can be used to assess the features of a cooperation enforcement mechanism as a coalition formation algorithm. Furthermore, the authors demonstrate that under the hypothesis that CORE can be used to balance the weight that a selfish node gives to the network-centric metric, as compared with the node-centric metric, the minimum size of a coalition of cooperating nodes corresponds at least to half of the network population.

A first observation that can be derived from the work presented by Michiardi and Molva is that game theory can be used not only as a powerful tool to understand the functioning of a particular cooperation enforcement mechanism but also as an effective technique for the fine-tuning of the mechanism under study. The advantage of the approach proposed by Michiardi and Molva (2003, n.d.) as opposed to a generic game theoretical framework is that the cooperation enforcement mechanism can be tailored to meet the security and robustness requirements of the particular environment of operation. As an example, the CORE mechanism does not suffer from attacks exploiting messages exchanged by nodes as in the one derived by Srinivasan et al. (2003), and this is because the authors designed the system without having to deal with the limitations imposed by a prior simplification resulting from the game theoretical modeling.

However, the drawback of the approach proposed by Michiardi and Molva consists in the complexity of introducing an analytical representation of a cooperation enforcement mechanism that is not designed to fit in a game theoretical framework. Precisely, the main criticism directed to the approach in Michiardi and Molva (n.d.) is that the function describing the way nodes decide which is the strategy to be taken in a particular situation (the utility function) is not compliant with the desirable properties of the classical utility functions used in game theory. The implication is that the authors were able to obtain some interesting numerical results, but no analytical results were provided.

CONCLUSION

Despite the lack of maturity of ad hoc networks, the security thereof has gathered much attention from the research community because of the novelty of their requirements as compared with to classical networks. Research activities in ad hoc network security fall in one of three areas: routing security, key management, and cooperation enforcement. In spite of the large number of solutions, ad hoc routing does not seem to raise any new security requirements with respect to routing in classical networks, apart from key management problems that are addressed by a large class of original work in a specific category.

Key management approaches try to answer the hard question of how to establish security associations with no a priori knowledge, no a priori trust, and lack of infrastructure. Several original key management schemes based on advanced cryptographic constructs such as threshold cryptography and ID-based cryptography are suggested but they all fall short of meeting the ultimate goal of building a keying infrastructure "from scratch" because they all involve an initial key set-up phase. Cooperation enforcement is another original requirement raised by ad hoc networks. Several approaches are suggested to tackle this problem but solutions still are in their infancy with respect to real-life scenarios and integration with basic networking functions.

GLOSSARY

Ad Hoc Routing Routing is a core concept of the Internet and many other networks. Routing provides the means of forwarding logically addressed packets from their local subnetwork toward their ultimate destination. In large networks, packets may pass through many intermediary destinations before reaching their destination. Routing occurs at layer 3 of the OSI seven-layer model. Ad hoc network routing protocols appear in networks with no or little infrastructure.

Asymmetric In the context of encryption, a type of cryptographic system in which a participant publishes an encryption key and keeps private a separate decryption key. These keys are respectively referred to as public and private. RSA and D–H are examples of asymmetric systems. Asymmetric is synonymous with public key.

Digital Signature In cryptography, digital signatures are a method of authenticating digital information.

Game Theory Game theory is a branch of mathematics that uses models to study interactions with formalized incentive structures ("games"). It has applications in a variety of fields, including economics, evolutionary biology, political science, and military strategy. Game theorists study the predicted and actual behavior of individuals in games, as well as optimal strategies. Seemingly, different types of interactions can exhibit similar incentive structures, thus all exemplifying one particular game.

Hash Function A hash function is a function that converts an input from a (typically) large domain into an output in a (typically) smaller range (the hash value, often a subset of the integers). A good hash function is one that experiences few hash collisions in the expected domain of strings it will have to deal with; that is, it would be possible to uniquely identify most of these strings using this hash.

Key A short data string parameterizing the operations within a cipher or cryptosystem and whose distribution determines relationships of privacy and integrity among communicating parties.

Key Pair The combination of a public and private key.

MAC In cryptography, a message authentication code (MAC) algorithm (also keyed-hash function) is an algorithm for generating a short string of information used to authenticate a message.

PKI In computing, a PKI (public key infrastructure) is an arrangement, usually carried out by software at a central location and other coordinated software at distributed locations, which provides for third-party (often termed a "trusted third party") vetting and vouching for user identities and for binding of public keys to users and vice versa. The term is used to mean both the certificate authority and related arrangements as well as, more broadly and somewhat confusingly, to mean use of public key algorithms in electronic communications. The later sense is erroneous because PKI methods are not necessary to use public key algorithms.

Private Key In an asymmetric or public key cryptosystem, the key that a communicating party holds privately and uses for decryption or completion of a key exchange.

Public Key In an asymmetric or public key cryptosystem, the key that a communicating party disseminates publicly.

Public Key Certificate A public key certificate is a block of bits containing, in a specified format, the public half of an asymmetric key algorithm key pair (the "public key"), together with identity information, such as a person's name, e-mail address, title, phone number, etc., together with the digital signature of all the data of some person or entity. They are also called identity certificates. In a typical PKI scheme, the signature will be of a certificate authority (CA). In a web of trust scheme, the signature is of either the user (a self-signed certificate) or other users ("endorsements"). In either case, the signature(s) on a certificate attest that the identity information and the public key belong together.

Secret Sharing In cryptography, secret sharing is a technique to distribute trust among a group of participants, allowing access to the secret only by those who share some predetermined number of parts of a secret. Adi Shamir and George Blakley independently invented it in 1979.

Spoofing In computer networking, the term Internet protocol spoofing (IP spoofing) is the creation of IP packets with a forged (spoofed) source IP address.

Symmetric A symmetric key algorithm is an algorithm for cryptography that uses the same cryptographic key to encrypt and decrypt the message. Symmetric key algorithms are generally much faster to execute electronically than asymmetric key algorithms. The disadvantage of symmetric key algorithms is the requirement of a shared secret key, with one copy at each end. Because keys are subject to discovery by a cryptographic adversary, they need to be changed often and kept secure during distribution and in service.

Tamper-Proof Hardware A system is said to be tamper-resistant if it is difficult to modify or subvert, even for an assailant who has physical access to the system. A common form of tamper resistance is a device or subsystem that contains information that is difficult to extract even with direct physical access. Tamper resistance finds application in smart cards and set-top boxes.

Wormhole A wormhole is a hypothetical topological modification of the network that is essentially a "shortcut" from one point to another point in the network, which allows packets to travel between them faster than it would take through a normal route.

CROSS REFERENCES

See *Encryption Basics; Key Management; Routers and Switches; Wireless Channels.*

REFERENCES

Axelrod, R. (1984). *The evolution of cooperation*. New York: Basic Books.

Bobba, R. B., Eschenauer, L., Gligor, V., & Arbaugh, W. A. (2002). Bootstrapping security associations for routing in mobile ad-hoc networks (Tech. Rep. TR 2002–44). College Park, MD: Institute for Systems Research, University of Maryland.

Boneh, D., & Franklin, M. (2001). *Identity-based encryption from the Weil pairing*. In Lecture Notes of Computer Science.

Brands, S., & Chaum, D. (1993). Distance-bounding protocols. *Advances in Cryptology EUROCRYPT '93*, Springer-Verlag LNCS 765, pp. 344–359, May 1993. http://www.springeronline.com

Broch, J., Maltz, D. A. Johnson, D. B., Hu, Y.-C., & Jetcheva, J. G. (1998). A performance comparison of multi-hop wireless ad hoc network routing protocols. In *Proceedings of MOBICOM 1998.*

Buchegger, S., & Le Boudec, J.-Y. (n.d.). Nodes bearing grudges: Towards routing security, fairness, and robustness in mobile ad hoc networks. In *Proceedings of the 10th Euromicro Workshop on Parallel, Distributed and Network-Based Processing.*

Buchegger, S., & Le Boudec, J.-Y. (2002). Performance analysis of the CONFIDANT protocol. In *Proceedings of MobiHoc 2002.*

Buttyan, L., & Hubaux, J.-P. (2001). *Nuglets: A virtual currency to stimulate cooperation in self-organized ad hoc networks* (Tech. Rep. DSC/2001/001). Lausanne, Switzerland: Swiss Federal Institute of Technology.

Capkun, S., Buttyan, L., & Hubaux, J.-P. (2002). Self-organized public-key management for mobile ad hoc networks. In *ACM International Workshop on Wireless Security, WiSe 2002.*

Capkun, S., Buttyan, L., & Hubaux, J.-P. (2003). SECTOR: Secure tracking of node encounters in multi-hop wireless networks. In *Proceedings of SASN 2003.*

Chen, K., & Nahrstedt, K. (2004). iPass: An incentive compatible auction scheme to enable packet forwarding service in MANET. In *Proceeding of ICDCS 2004 Conference.*

Dahill, B., Levine, B. N., Royer, E., & Shields, C. (2002). *ARAN: A secure routing protocol for ad hoc networks* (Tech. Rep. 02-32). University of Massachusetts.

Dubois-Ferriere, H., Grossglauser, M., & Vetterli, M. (2003). Age matters: Efficient route discovery in mobile ad hoc networks using encounter ages. In *Proceedings of MobiHoc, 2003.*

Hu, Y.-C., Johnson, D. B., & Perrig, A. SEAD: Secure efficient distance vector routing for mobile wireless ad hoc networks. In *Fourth IEEE Workshop on Mobile Computing Systems and Applications.*

Hu, Y.-C., Perrig, A., & Johnson, D. B. (2002). Ariadne: A secure on-demand routing protocol for ad hoc networks. In *Proceedings of MOBICOM 2002.*

Johansson, P., Larsson, T., Hedman, N., Mielczarek, B., & Degermark, M. (1999). Scenario-based performance analysis of routing protocols for mobile ad hoc networks. In *Proceedings of MOBICOM 1999.*

Johnson, D. B., & Maltz, D. A. (1996). Dynamic source routing in ad hoc wireless networks. In *Mobile Computing*, edited by Tomasz Imielinski and Hank Korth, Chapter 5, pp. 153–181, Kluwer Academic Publishers, 1996. http://www.springeronline.com

Khalili, A., Katz, J., & Arbaugh, W. A. (2003). Toward secure key distribution in truly ad-hoc networks. In *Proceedings of SAINT 2003 workshop.*

Luo, H., & Lu, S. (n.d.). *Ubiquitous and robust authentication services for ad hoc wireless networks* (Tech. Rep. UCLA-CSD-TR-200030). Los Angeles, CA: University of California at Los Angeles.

MacKie-Mason, J., & Varian, H. (1994, July). *Generalized vickrey auctions* (Working Paper) http://www-personal.umich.edu/~jmm/papers.html#gva

MacKie-Mason, J., & Varian, H. (1995). Pricing the Internet. In B. Kahin & J. Keller (Eds), *Public Access to the Internet*. Englewood Cliffs, NJ: Prentice-Hall.

Merkle, R. C. (1980). Protocols for public key cryptosystems. In *Proceedings of the IEEE symposium on security and privacy, 1980.*

Michiardi, P., & Molva, R. (2003). *Game theoretic analysis of cooperation enforcement in mobile ad hoc networks* (Research Rep. RR-03-092). Institut Eurecom, Sophia-Antipolis: France.

Michiardi, P., & Molva, R. (2002a). Core: A Collaborative REputation mechanism to enforce node cooperation in mobile ad hoc networks. In *IFIP—Communication and Multimedia Security Conference 2002.*

Michiardi, P., & Molva, R. (2002b, April). *Game theoretic analysis of security in mobile ad hoc networks* (Research Rep. RR-02-070). Institut Eurecom, Sophia-Antipolis: France.

Michiardi, P., & Molva, R. (2002c). Simulation-based analysis of security exposures in mobile ad hoc networks. In *Proceedings of European Wireless Conference, 2002.*

Michiardi, P., & Molva, R. (2003). A game theoretical approach to evaluate cooperation enforcement mechanisms in mobile ad hoc networks. In *Proceeding of WiOpt 2003 Workshop.*

Montenegro, G., & Castelluccia, C. (2002, February). Statistically unique and cryptographically verifiable (SUCV) identifiers and addresses. In *Proceedings of the 2002 networks and distributed systems security conference.*

Myerson, R. B. (1991). *Game theory: Analysis of conflict*. Cambridge, MA: Harvard University Press.

Osborne, M. J., & Rubinstein, A. (1994). *A course in game theory*. Cambridge, MA: MIT Press.

Papadimitratos, P., & Haas, Z. (2002). Secure routing for mobile ad hoc networks. In *Proceedings of CNDS 2002.*

Perkins, C. E., & Bhagwat, P. (1994). Highly dynamic destination-sequenced distance-vector routing (DSDV) for mobile computers. In *Proceedings of SIGCOMM 1994.*

Perrig, A., Canetti, R., Tygar, J. D., & Song, D. (2000). Efficient authentication and signing of multicast streams over lossy channels. In *IEEE Symposium on Security and Privacy, 2000.*

Perrig, A., Canetti, R., Song, D., & Tygar, J. D. (2001). Efficient and secure source authentication for multicast. In *Proceedings of NDSS 2001.*

Perrig, A., Hu, Y.-C., & Johnson, D. B. (n.d.). Wormhole protection in wireless ad hoc networks (Tech. Rep. TR01-384). Dept. of Computer Science, Rice University.

Reiter, M., & Stybblebine, S. (1999). Authentication metric analysis and design. *ACM Transactions on Information and System Security.*

Shamir, A. (1979). How to share a secret. *Communications of ACM.*

Srinivasan, V., Nuggehalli, P., Chiasserini, C. F., Rao, R. R. (2003). Cooperation in wireless ad hoc networks. In *Proceeding of Infocom 2003 Conference.*

Yang, H., Meng, X., & Lu, S. (2002). Self-organized network-layer security in mobile ad hoc networks. In *Proceedings of WiSe 2002 Conference.*

Zhong, S., Chen, J., & Yang, R. (2003). Sprite: A simple, cheat-proof, credit-based system for mobile ad-hoc networks. In *Proceeding of IEEE Infocom 2003 Conference.*

Zhou, L., & Haas, Z. J. (1999, November–December). Securing ad hoc networks. *IEEE Networks.*

Zhu, S., Xu, S., Setia, S., & Jajodia, S. (2003). Establishing pair-wise keys for secure communication in ad hoc networks: A probabilistic approach. In *Proceedings of ICNP 2003 Conference.*

Zimmermann, P. (1995). *The official PGP user's guide*. MIT Press. Cambridge, MA 02142-1493, USA.

FURTHER READING

Marti, S., Giuli, T., Lai, K., & Baker, M. (2000). Mitigating routing misbehavior in mobile ad hoc networks. In *Proceedings of MOBICOM 2000.*

Perkins, C. (n.d.). Ad hoc on demand distance vector (AODV) routing (Internet draft).

Urpi, A., Bonuccelli, M., & Giordano, S. (2003). Modeling cooperation in mobile ad hoc networks: A formal description of selfishness. In *Proceedings of WiOpt 2003 Workshop.*

PART 3

Standards and Protocols for Secure Information Transfer

Standards for Product Security Assessment

István Zsolt Berta, Levente Buttyán, and István VAJDA, *Budapest University of Technology and Economics, Hungary*

INTRODUCTION

Defining the concept of a "security product" is a difficult issue. Certain products are designed with security as their primary purpose. For example, the existence of firewalls, smart cards, or intrusion detection systems can only be explained by security reasons. On the other hand, products such as operating systems, word processors, or e-mail clients have other functionalities they must fulfill; otherwise, they cannot be sold, regardless of their security. However, security is still a critical issue in this latter group, too. Security is often not a product by itself, but a requirement that all products should fulfill to a certain degree. In this sense, every IT product can be considered a security product.

It might be relatively easy to evaluate the usability of a product by testing some of the most frequent scenarios. However, the security of a product is a lot harder to assess. Although it can be easy to predict and examine scenarios users are most likely to come across, we often do not know in advance what strategy the future malicious attacker will follow (Anderson & Needham, 1996).

In this chapter, an overview of existing security standards is presented. Several approaches exist for the assessment of the security of a product or a system; the main points are summarized in the second section. In the third section, an overview of Common Criteria, the internationally accepted criteria for the technical evaluation of security products, is presented. We introduce the key definitions and give some insight into the Common Criteria approach to security evaluation. In the fourth section, some practical aspects of Common Criteria are presented. International treaties and schemes that allow the mutual acceptance of the criteria are introduced, and the trends in Common Criteria evaluations are also examined. Finally, criticism from literature on the Common Criteria approach is reviewed.

APPROACHES FOR ASSESSING SECURITY

Approaches

The evaluation of the security of an IT product is a complex issue. Even professionals who specialize in IT security require a significant amount of time and resources to perform such a task. Many customers have neither the knowledge nor the resources to perform an in-depth evaluation. Moreover, it is often up to investors or managers and not IT professionals to make the decisions of choosing among various competing IT products. Such people may seek guidance from security standards to determine which product is more secure. On the other hand, developers may also choose to develop their product in accordance with these standards to ensure that it will fulfill them, so that they can claim that their product is secure. Several standards offer tools for security evaluation. Although they may vary in scope and technological detail they all follow one or more of the following three main approaches:

1. Evaluation of the *security of a product* is the simplest approach. In the case of tangible products, customers are primarily interested in the results of this approach, because they may easily rely on such evaluations when choosing among various competing products. However, if the product is complex, such evaluation may not be feasible. Unfortunately, IT products are not only very complex, but their life cycle is very short, too. Even if an IT product is not evaluated as a black box which means evaluators gain insight into its internal mechanisms, its security evaluation may still be very complex. For example, evaluating the source code of software products is not only long and time-consuming but is unlikely to uncover all errors unless formal methods are used.

Thus, the task is often simplified and is performed on a higher level of abstraction, so not the product but its production is evaluated.

2. Evaluation of the *security of production* may prove that the product was designed with security in mind. In this case, the manufacturer has to prove that threats and security issues were considered at each step of production. Note that in this case, the target of evaluation is not the product that the customer may buy but rather a business process of the manufacturer. Although customers may still rely on the results of such an evaluation to choose among products with security based on indirect proofs, it is often more useful for the investor who invests capital into the production. This way the investor can be convinced that no fatal mistakes were made during design or production. Manufacturers may also rely in court on the results of such evaluation if customers complain that the product is insecure.

   In a case of intangible products (such as services), customers are more interested in such evaluations, because in this case the product and the production are highly interconnected. They may gain confidence that the manufacturer (or service provider) outputs products (or services) with a constant quality.

3. Evaluation of the *security of the producer* (the company) is a generalization of the previous approach that extends evaluation to all business processes of a company. Such evaluation gives confidence that the management of the company considers security a critical issue, and the company outputs products that were designed with quality and security in mind. Some companies choose suppliers that have undergone such an evaluation.

In the preceding paragraphs, the words *quality* and *security* were used in parallel. Although they are not synonyms of each other, they are strongly interconnected. Although quality is difficult to define, one thing seems to be obvious: an insecure product cannot have high quality. For example, one widespread definition of quality is "conformance to specifications" (Crosby, 1995). Another definition for quality is "conformance to customer expectations" (Oakland, 1992). Thus, if customers expect a product to be secure, and find it insecure, they perceive that it has bad quality. Because security is a vital component of quality, quality management methods are also going to be considered as methods to increase security.

How Can We Assess the Security of a Production?

Because most products are too complex to be assessed directly, many methods choose to assess the process of production (or all processes in the organization that perform the production) instead. When assessing a process, it is examined to determine if certain principles of security engineering were used when the product was designed and created.

The design of a secure product should involve some kind of risk analysis. It is hard to speak about the security of a product unless it is—at least informally—examined against which threats it is supposed to be secure. Usually, a risk analysis needs to be performed that involves the identification of threats, the estimation of the amount of damage they cause, and the probability that they are likely to occur. Based on these values, a certain degree of risk can be assigned to each threat. The designer of the product should implement countermeasures to reduce such risks.

When the security of the production is assessed, it should be determined if such a risk analysis has been performed. It should also be determined if the set of risks the designer chose to reduce is sound and if the selected countermeasures cost-effectively reduce the selected risks.

Today's systems are usually not monolithic: they consist of components. Certain countermeasures require dedicated components in a system with security as their main purpose. (For example, a dedicated component for user authentication or one for the management of the access rights of a user.)

Generally, it is very hard to make a product secure *after* its production is finished. It is also considered to be very hard to increase the security of the system simply by adding components to it. Most methods of assessing the security require that security was a main concern from the very beginning. Based on the risk analysis, certain principles have to be formulated at the first stages of design, and formulation of principles at further stages (of design and implementation) may not be sufficient. Introducing security to a product in the early stages of design not only makes it more secure, it also lowers the cost of creating a secure product.

When the security of the production is assessed, it should be determined if these principles were formulated at the beginning and consciously followed throughout the entire process of production.

Other countermeasures are not restricted to one component but can be best practices or principles applied in components that have other purposes in the system. Some vulnerabilities do not originate from bad design but merely from bad implementation. These vulnerabilities should be reduced in the whole system.

Buffer overflow attacks are typical examples for this phenomenon. A buffer overflow vulnerability originates from a local blunder in the implementation, and sometimes it compromises the security of a whole system. In well-designed systems, an attacker who exploits a buffer overflow vulnerability does not gain access to other components of a system. However, a buffer overflow vulnerability can be combatted locally too.

A developer may choose to use tools and environments that simply do not allow this kind of attack. For example, the Java language always checks if an index is outside the boundaries of an array and raises an exception if it is so. If for some reason it is not possible to use such tools to prevent the attack, the developer should introduce policies to reduce this vulnerability. For example, programmers should be made conscious of this attack, they should be trained how to write code that does not have such vulnerabilities, and they should be motivated to follow these instructions. Still, it is advised to check or inspect the code they write for buffer overflow vulnerabilities.

When the security of the production is assessed, it should be determined if known best practices and principles were applied during the production and how they were enforced and documented.

Several standards exist that give a wide range of tools and methods both for development and assessments.

Overview of Standards

Various standards exists to evaluate security. In the rest of this section, a brief overview of the most important security standards follows. For a more detailed comparison see Initi@tive D^{21} (2001).

Common Criteria

The Common Criteria (CC) are result of an international cooperation to formulate mutually recognized common criteria for standardized security evaluation. The CC were founded by the sponsoring organizations of the existing U.S. (TCSEC), European (ITSEC), and Canadian (CTCPEC) criteria in 1996 (CC, 2004). The Common Criteria are "a library of standard security requirements to aid the specification and evaluation of IT products and systems" (Towns, 2000). The CC can be applied to any kind of product (or system), regardless of its type. Unlike previous standards (e.g., TCSEC), CC differentiates between which security features a product has (functional requirements) and how much confidence we have in these features (assurance requirements). A Common Criteria evaluation examines to what extent the target of evaluation fulfills the appropriate security requirements. The CC define seven evaluation assurance levels, where lower levels require functional testing, middle levels require documentation of high-level design and development environment controls, and high assurance levels require mathematical proofs and the use of formal methods for product verification.

Another major aim of Common Criteria is that evaluations of different products of the same type (e.g., operating systems or firewalls) should be comparable. Thus, products or systems can be evaluated against *protection profiles* that contain general, product-independent security requirements for a certain product types.

The Common Criteria are internationally accepted; version 2.0 became the ISO/IEC standard 15408. The current version of Common Criteria is 2.1.

The official Web site of Common Criteria is http://csrc.nist.gov/cc (Unfortunately the popular information portal http://www.commoncriteria.org was closed at the end of 2003.) See the third section for more details on the Common Criteria.

CobiT

CobiT (Control Objectives for Information and Related Technology) provides principles to improve control over IT-oriented and accompanying processes at an organization. It is nontechnical and provides managerial guidelines and control objectives to manage IT-related organizations with security as a primary focus.

The first version of CobiT was released by the Information Systems Audit and Control Foundation (ISACF); the current edition is the third one, published by the IT Governance Institute (ITGI).

The official website of CobiT is http://www.isaca.org/cobit

ISO 9000

The ISO 9000 series is set of standards that define methods to improve quality management at an organization. Although it provides a framework for quality assurance, it does not focus on security. It is a very general standard, so it can be applied to any company or organization.

ISO 9000 provides assurance to customers that the product was produced in a way that it will meet their requirements. According to ISO 9000, the best way to do this is to define the procedures, standards, and characteristics of the quality control system. This way the quality is "built into" the product or service (Slack, Chambers, & Johnston, 2001).

ISO 9000 follows the paradigm (Peters, Waterman, & Peters, 1988; Oakland, 1992) that an organization cannot only gain competitive advantage by improving its quality, but is also able to reduce its costs this way (e.g., by the elimination of waste from the production or by the reduction of customer complaints). Thus, ISO 9000 claims to be beneficial for both the organization adopting it and its customers.

By today, most countries have adopted ISO 9000 as their own quality management standard. The current version of the standard is ISO 9000:2000.

BS 7799

BS 7799 (ISO/IEC 17799) was developed by British industry, government, and commerce stakeholders in 1995. The standard describes several security controls under 10 major headings and addresses information security management issues. It not only raises information security problems but offers solutions to them, too. The standard stresses the importance of risk management and underlines that there is no need to implement all security controls, only those that are relevant to the specific scenario.

BS 7799 consists of two documents: Part 1, "The Code of Practice" is a collection of advice. It provides guidance to organizations on implementing an information security management system (ISMS) based on "the best practices" of the industry. Part 2, "Specification for Information Security Management Systems" sets out a rigorous set of requirements, so that it is possible for a third-party auditor to verify if a company complies with BS 7799. Many evaluators prefer BS 7799 over other standards for security assessment, because, for example, of certain reasons listed in the fourth section. Unfortunately, BS 7799 is not available free of charge. BS 7799 has undergone several revisions; the current version is BS 7799:2002. Part 1 is now an international standard as ISO 17799:2000 (Larson, 1999).

BSI IT Baseline Protection Manual

The IT Baseline Protection Manual was published by BSI (German Information Security Agency) in 1994. The

Baseline Protection manual recommends various security measures for typical IT systems with medium-level protection requirements (Schultz, 2001). Although this manual is system-specific, it is more technical than BS 7799 and CC. The Baseline Protection manual considers typical threats and gives detailed safeguards for these. The current version (October 2003) can be downloaded from the Web site of BSI: http://www.bsi.bund.de/gshb/english/etc/titel.htm

FIPS 140

Federal Information Processing Standard 140-2 (FIPS 140-2) describes U.S. government requirements that cryptographic modules should meet. It was developed by the NIST and is currently recognized as a de facto international standard for cryptographic modules. The four security levels of FIPS 140 cover a wide range of potential applications and environments in which cryptographic modules may be deployed. The standard also addresses the secure design and implementation of a cryptographic module.

The original version, 140-1, was superseded by 140-2, which is the current version of the standard. The official Web site of FIPS 140 is http://csrc.nist.gov/cryptval

Two Groups of Standards

As is shown in Figure 1, there are basically two groups of security (and quality) standards. One group (standards such as Common Criteria and FIPS 140) provides methods for the *assessment of a security product*. These methods usually describe *technical security requirements* and assess the security of a *product* or its *production*. The other group (standards such as CobiT, ISO 9000, and BS 7799) describes methodologies for the *assessment* and evaluation *of a company or a system* and its IT infrastructure. These standards usually provide managerial guidelines and do not go into technical details. They provide tools to assess the company, the *producer*, and its methods of *production*. Thus, the aim of these standards is to describe how a security-oriented company should operate without going into the details of specific products. (The IT Baseline Protection Manual seems to be the exception; it is system-specific but still gives technical advice [Initi@tive D^{21}, 2001.])

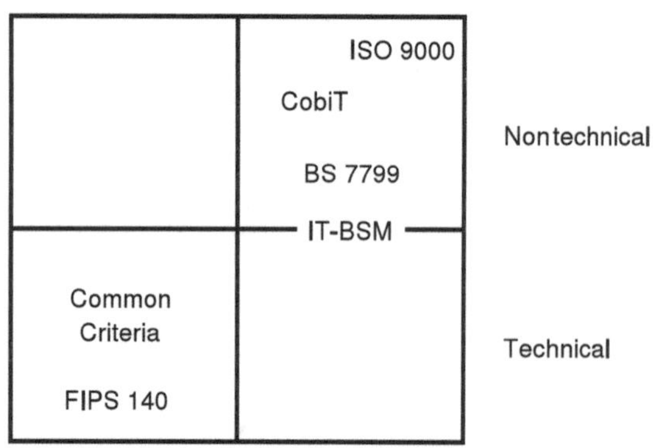

Figure 1: Two groups of security standards.

These two groups of standards should not be viewed as competing ones but rather as standards that should be used together. Evaluation against system-specific nontechnical standards (such as CobiT) may give confidence that an organization's managers consider security an important issue. However, these standards do not provide guidance on technical details. For example, a CobiT audit requires that an organization prepares certain important security policies (e.g., how to select or procure software, how to apply patches regularly, how to register users, how to select and train system administrators, and how to control that the system administrator keeps the regulations). However, the security of a system can be breached because of a single mistake even if the above policies are kept (e.g., because of the incompetence or mistakes of the system administrator or because of a critical bug in a purchased operating system, etc.). Naturally, standards describing an organization, a community of humans, can never give 100% assurance.

On the other hand, evaluation against a product-specific and technical standard (such as Common Criteria) provides confidence that a certain product (e.g., an operating system) is secure or secureable. However, no matter how secure a device is on its own, it does not necessarily make a system secure because no one can guarantee that it will be *used in a secure way*. Product-specific nontechnical standards give little or no guidance on how to train staff, how to formulate security policies, and so forth. For example, a security system of a company can be breached if the registration of users is inadequate, regardless of the security of the operating system. Nevertheless, these standards can give very strong confidence in the product itself. If formal methods are used (such as on high evaluation assurance levels of Common Criteria), mathematical proofs can be given that the product fulfills its specifications. On the other hand, whenever these standards describe the product's environment, they have to make assumptions about the organizational structure too. Although mathematical proofs can theoretically give 100% assurance, even formal verification has its own pitfalls.

The two groups of standards may be used together. For example, a company preparing for a CobiT audit may decide in its procurement policy to purchase only those products that have at least a certain Common Criteria evaluation assurance level.

Although the objectives of Common Criteria and FIPS 140 may seem similar in Figure 1, they are different in abstraction and focus of tests. Assessment against FIPS 140 means *conformance testing* against a cryptographic module, whereas assessment against Common Criteria means *evaluation* against a protection profile or security target (NIST, CSE, 1995). Moreover, FIPS 140 is only applicable in the case of cryptographic modules and requires evaluated (by TCSEC or by Common Criteria) operating systems.

Thus, Common Criteria are practically the only existing standards today that enable the assessment of any security product without placing restrictions on its type. In the rest of this chapter, a detailed introduction is presented on Common Criteria. In the third section, the scope and general approach of Common Criteria is introduced along with an overview of its main concepts. In the fourth section, some practical issues of Common Criteria are considered.

COMMON CRITERIA PARADIGM

The Common Criteria are the result of an international collaboration to develop a standard to evaluate the security of IT products and systems. After the Trusted Computer System Evaluation Criteria (TCSEC) was developed in the United States in the early 1980s, other nations started to elaborate their own evaluation criteria. Later, the Information Technology Security Evaluation Criteria (ITSEC) was published in Europe in 1991 as a joint effort of France, Germany, the Netherlands, and the United Kingdom. Canada published the Canadian Trusted Computer Product Evaluation Criteria (CTCPEC) in 1993, combining the merits of TCSEC and ITSEC. The United States published another criteria, the Federal Criteria for Information Technology Security (FC) in 1993, combining the European and North American concepts for evaluation criteria. Finally, the sponsoring organizations of TCSEC, ITSEC, CTCPEC, and FC decided to join their efforts and developed the internationally accepted Common Criteria. Their aim was to make CC an ISO standard. Version 1.0 of CC was published in 1996. The official name of CC in the ISO context is Evaluation Criteria for Information Technology Security. The current version of CC is 2.1.

Scope of Common Criteria

"The CC is a catalog of criteria and a framework for organizing a subset of the criteria into security specifications" (McEvilley, 2000). CC claim to aid consumers in the selection and comparison of IT products and systems. CC claim to aid developers and integrators in creating more secure and more valuable products and systems. CC also claim to aid evaluators by giving common evaluation criteria.

The value of information—and any other kind of good—is determined by the benefit a party can gain from receiving it (or the benefit a party can lose from not receiving it). This can be expressed as a monetary value by determining how much an external or internal (Slack, Chambers, & Johnston, 2001) customer would be willing to pay for the given good. (The work of Shapiro and Varian (1998) describes the economic mechanisms that drive economies of information goods.) Apart from its contents, three main attributes determine the value of information: confidentiality, integrity, and availability. CC address the protection of information for these three attributes.

- *Availability* means that the authorized users of an information system are able to access, deliver, or process the required data. The availability of information is breached when the authorized users cannot access the data needed for their work.
- *Confidentiality* means that only authorized users are able to access certain classified information. Confidentiality is violated if unauthorized people read or copy such classified information.
- *Integrity* means that information is unmodified, authentic, complete, and can be relied upon. Information can lose its integrity if it is modified by accident or by a malicious attack.

Thus, the more parties know a piece of information, the less valuable it is. The less reliable the information is, the less valuable it is. When a customer cannot access a piece of information, the customer is not willing to pay for it. Although availability is provided by the reliable operation of the system, confidentiality and integrity are limitations on the operations. These limitations are imposed to provide protection against attacks (either natural disasters or deliberate attacks of a malicious adversary).

Common Criteria do not deal with the following:

- CC do not deal with *administrative security measures* that are not directly related to IT security. However, administrative measures can be an important part of security implementation. Moreover, weak administrative measures can undermine an otherwise secure system. CC evaluations make assumptions about the *environment* but do not evaluate if the environment met fulfils these assumptions. Although it cannot be required from a product-specific security standard to *assess the environment* of the product, neglecting human-related aspects of security is a major weakness of CC.
- CC do not deal with administrative, legal, and procedural issues such as accredition, certification, and mutual recognition of CC evaluations in different countries.
- CC do not deal with *physical security implementations*, because it focuses on IT security, that is, the protection of information by means of logical security. However, in some cases physical features of a device can be used to attack logical security. For example, although the CC declare electromagnetic emanation control as out of scope, Agrawal et al. (2002) show methods to attack the logical security (uncover bits from a secret key) of a smart card based on its electromagnetic emanations. Such attacks against cryptographic devices, that based on their unintentional outputs (such as timing, power consumption, or electromagnetic emanations) are called side-channel attacks (Muir, 2001; Kelsey et al., 2000).
- *Evaluation methodology* is outside the scope of CC, because it is discussed in a separate document.
- *Definition of cryptographic algorithms*: Cryptography is one of the most important tools of IT security; thus, cryptography is not outside the scope of CC. However, CC relies on cryptographic algorithms as black boxes and assumes them to be secure. The evaluation of a cryptographic algorithm is a very hard problem, and no ultimate tool or method exists that can uncover all of the problems. Formal mathematical proofs exist for the security of only a few cryptographic algorithms. The confidence we have in their security originates from the guessed hardness of mathematical problems. The accepted evaluation method for a cryptographic algorithm is its publication, where it is evaluated by the broad academic (and industrial) community. Use of "home grown" cryptographic algorithms is usually strongly discouraged. Thus, declaring the evaluation of cryptographic algorithms to be outside the scope of CC is a reasonable assumption.

Approach

The Common Criteria address security as a degree of protection of certain assets. The assets belong to owners (e.g., consumers of a product), who value them. In the case of an information technology system, assets are information that should be protected for confidentiality, availability, and integrity. Unfortunately, these assets are subject to threats. Threats can be attacks or disasters or any undesired event that threaten these properties (confidentiality, availability, integrity) of the assets. They are raised by threat agents, who can range from abstract entities such as "forces of nature" to real attackers. They may raise threats maliciously, consciously, or just probabilistically. Owners would like to minimize the risk of these threats by successfully exploiting vulnerabilities in the protection of assets, so they impose countermeasures to reduce the vulnerabilities. This approach is illustrated in Figure 2.

One of the major aims of Common Criteria is to enable the comparison of evaluations of similar products. For such comparison, a common ground is required, and it should be expressed with CC terminology that the products are in fact similar. Thus, CC define the following concepts:

- A *target of evaluation* (ToE) is an IT product or system that is to be evaluated. Any associated documentation may also be considered as part of the ToE. Sometimes it is not the ToE itself that is evaluated, but the ToE description that the vendor has to prepare.
- A *protection profile* (PP) encapsulates the security requirements for a type of product at an abstract, vendor- and device-independent level. Protection profiles can be elaborated by a community of users or anyone else who would like to state security requirements for a type of product. Products evaluated under the same PP can be compared. Naturally, a single PP can be used for more than one evaluation.
- A *security target* (ST) is a representation of implementation-dependent requirements of a specific product. It is written by the product vendor. The ToE is always evaluated against an ST, and an ST may conform to a PP.

Thus, a community of users of a certain product can formulate a protection profile to state their security requirements for the product. For example, the Secure Signature Creation Device Protection Profile applies to smart cards, so different smart cards evaluated under this PP can be compared.

Naturally, it is not enough to evaluate that a ToE conforms to an ST; the ST (or PP) also has to be evaluated.

Thus, CC define the following three types of evaluation:

- *Evaluation of a PP* means assessing that the PP is complete, technically sound, and suitable for use as a statement of requirements for a ToE. CC define evaluation criteria for PPs in Part 3. After the evaluation, the PP is catalogued (in context of the applied evaluation scheme) so it can be used in the evaluation of ToEs.
- *Evaluation of a ST* is carried out against evaluation criteria for STs in CC Part 3. In such an evaluation, the ST is assessed if it is complete and technically sound. Moreover, if the evaluation is performed against a PP, then it also has to be assessed if the ST conforms to the specification of the PP. ST evaluation provides intermediate results only: the results of this evaluation are part of the documentation of the ToE evaluation. However, the vendor may reuse the ST when preparing the ST for the next version of the product.

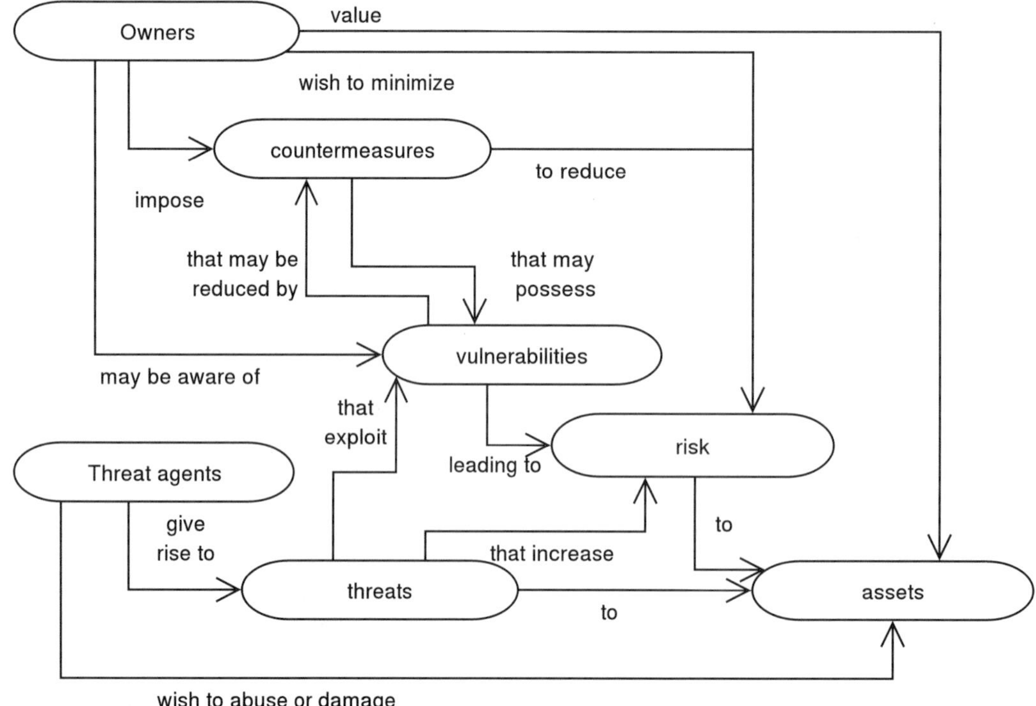

Figure 2: Security concepts and relationships.

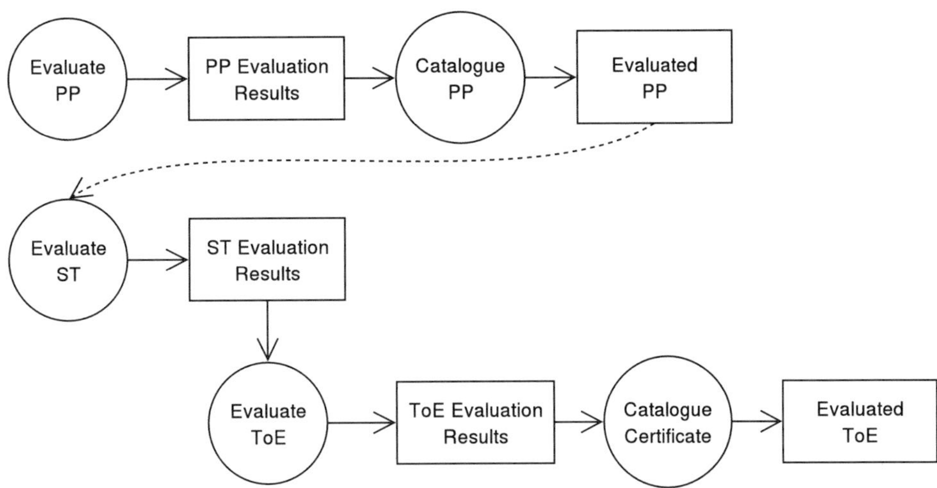

Figure 3: Evaluation results (source: CC, 2004).

- *Evaluation of a ToE* is the primary goal of Common Criteria. It is carried out against the evaluation criteria in CC Part 3. In such an evaluation, the ToE is always evaluated against an evaluated ST. Evaluated ToEs are catalogued in context of the applied evaluation scheme.

Figure 3 illustrates how the three types of evaluation are interconnected.

Security Requirements

Part 1 of Common Criteria gives an introduction and describes the general model. Parts 2 and 3 describe the security requirements in a catalogue format. Part 2 describes *functional* requirements that express what security features an IT product or system may have. Part 3 describes *assurance* requirements that express ways that could be used for gaining confidence that an IT product or system works according to the functional requirements.

Both functional and assurance requirements are organized into a hierarchical structure of *families* and *classes* (see Figure 4).

Each requirement has a unique CC name. The initial character of the name is "F" in case of functional and "A" in case of assurance requirements. This character

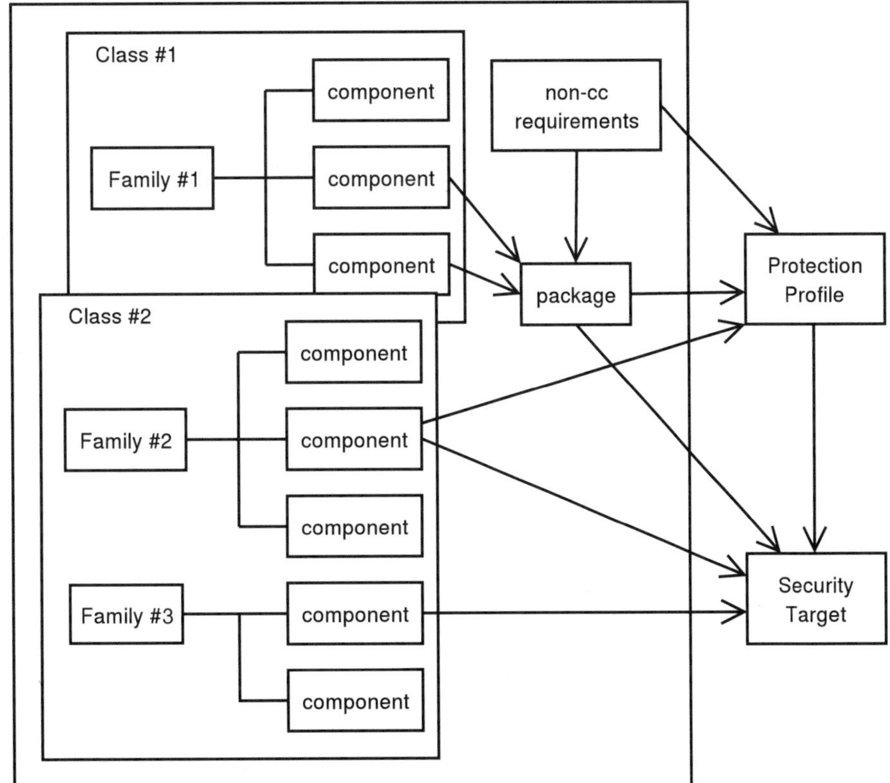

Figure 4: The security requirement components are organized into classes and families.

is followed by the two-character-long identifier of the class and the name of the family, separated by an underscore. The name of the requirement is terminated by the dot separated numbers of the component and the element.

For example, security requirement *FIA_UID.1.2* denotes element *2* from component *1*, family of *U*ser *I*dentification (*UID*) from the *f*unctional class of *I*dentification and *A*uthentication (*FIA*).

To define the security requirements, a subset of these requirements have to be selected and grouped into a PP or an ST. Requirements can also be organized into packages that can be reused in future evaluations.

Derivation of Requirements

In this section, a summary of an advised CC approach is presented that could be used to derive security requirements when developing a PP or ST (see Figure 5). This is the process that establishes the ToE specification as its final output.

Security Environment

Whenever a PP or ST is specified, a security environment has to be established in which the ToE is going to operate. Naturally, because PPs are generic and vendor- and product-independent, a specific ToE does not have to exist when this environment is specified.

The security environment includes all the relevant laws, organizational security policies, customs, expertise, and knowledge and thus defines the context in which the TOE is going to be used. The security environment also includes threats and attacks from the environment that have to be countered.

The following have to be taken into account when establishing the security environment:

- The CC are applicable when IT is used to guard certain *assets*. The protection of these assets is the goal of every security function in the ToE. Thus, a risk analysis should be performed about the threats that may arise to these assets.
- The *purpose of the ToE* is also a vital input to an evaluation, because its implications have to appear on every level of abstraction from high-level design to the implementation.
- The context, that is, the *physical environment*, of the ToE also has to be considered when establishing the security environment.

Three additional statements are prepared when the security environment is established:

- A statement of *assumptions*, which is a list of security aspects of the environment in which the ToE is going to be used. This statement contains assumptions of secure usage, assumptions on the scope and boundary of the ToE, and assumptions on its placement in the environment. These assumptions cover the relation of the ToE to humans. The assumptions are the circumstances in which the ToE will prove to be secure if it passes the evaluation.
- A list of *threats*, which is one of the outputs of the risk analysis. A threat is an ability of a so-called threat agent to exploit a vulnerability in the ToE intentionally or unintentionally. A threat can be any circumstance or event that may cause harm to the assets of the ToE in terms of confidentiality, integrity, or availability.
- *Organizational security policies*, which are the rules, practices, procedures, or guidelines imposed by the organization in which the ToE operates.

Security Objectives

The security environment could be used to define security objectives that could counter threats and address or rely on assumptions and policies when appropriate. Threats can be countered by the ToE or by its IT or non-IT environment. Certain countermeasures allow total elimination of certain threats, whereas others reduce the probability or magnitude of the damage a threat may cause. Some countermeasures only allow us to monitor (and thus better manage) the threat.

Only security objectives defined at this step are going to be addressed by security requirements.

Security Requirements

The security requirements are a refinement of the security objectives using the concepts of the CC. Thus, security requirements can be expressed using elements from the security classes in the CC. Functional requirements (CC Part 2) define the desired security behavior, such as identification or authentication, so they describe the security features a product has.

The assurance requirements can be used to specify a minimum strength level that should be consistent with the security objectives. Thus, the degree of assurance and rigor can be expressed with assurance requirements. CC Part 3 defines seven evaluation assurance levels (EALs) that provide a scale for security assurance.

Generally, two types of security requirements exist: requirements for the presence of desired behavior and requirements for the absence of undesired behavior. Normally, it is possible to prove that the former group of requirements is met to a certain level—for example, by testing. However, it can be very hard to demonstrate that requirements from the latter group are met, too. Although it is possible to prove or demonstrate that a product or system works properly, it might be very hard to prove that it does not have backdoors and hidden features.

ToE Summary Specification

The ToE Summary Specification in the ST defines the security requirements for the ToE. It also provides a high-level definition of security functions and assurance measures that are claimed to meet functional and assurance requirements.

ToE implementation

The implementation of the ToE is the realization of the ToE based on its security functional requirements and the ToE Summary Specification. The ToE meets its security objectives if it correctly implements all the security requirements of the ST (McEvilley, 2000).

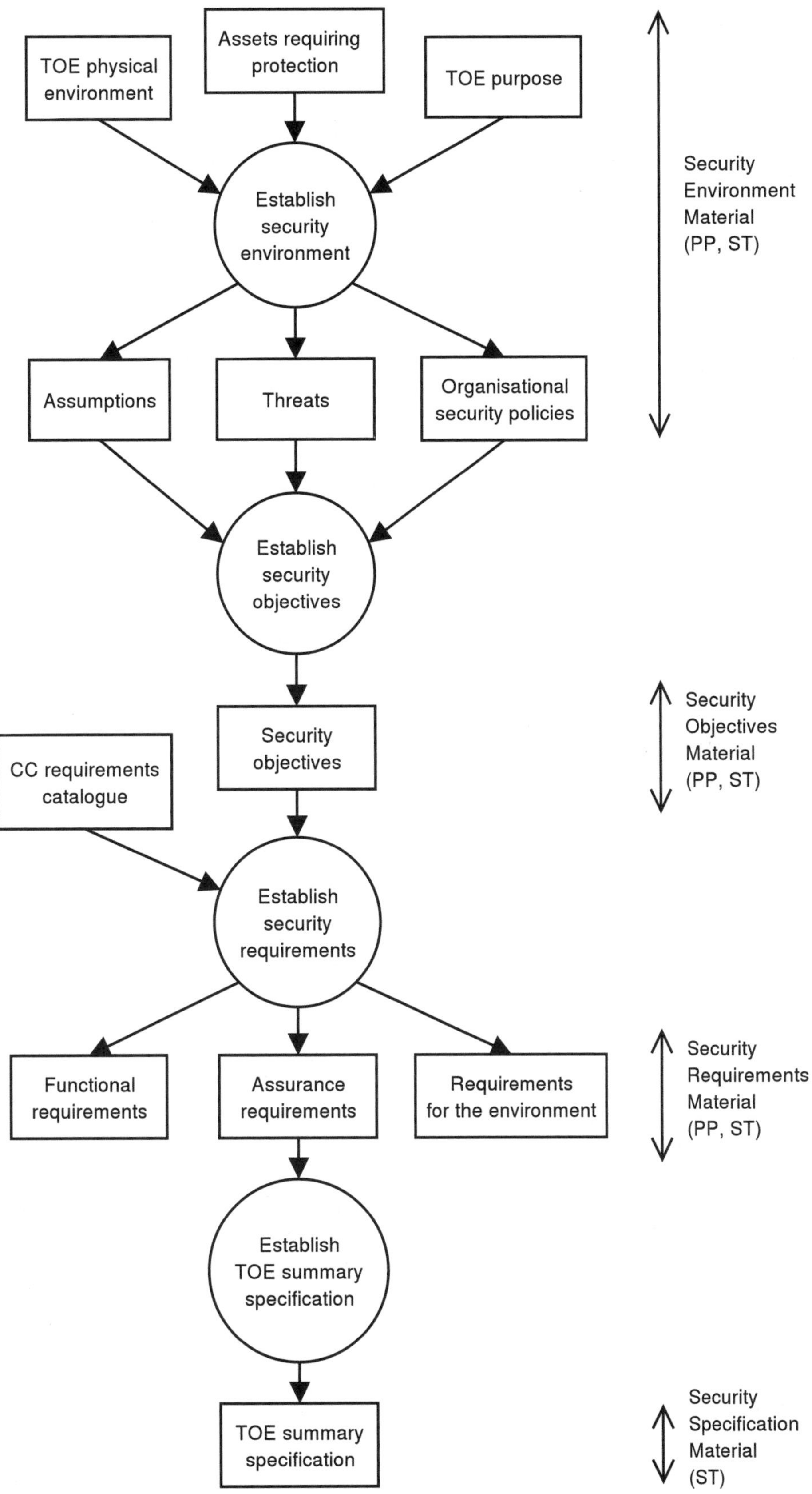

Figure 5: Derivation of security requirements.

Evaluation Assurance Levels

The result of an evaluation is a statement of to what extent a ToE can be trusted to conform to the requirements. CC define seven evaluation assurance levels. Basic levels such as EAL 1 and 2 require limited vendor involvement and functional testing. Medium levels such as EAL 3 and 4 require evidence that the vendor considered and minimized threats during the development. High levels such as EAL 5–7 require formal mathematical proofs that the ToE meets its security requirements.

EAL 1—functionally tested: The ToE is tested as it is available to the consumer. The evaluator tests if it works as described in its documentation. The testing is casual and can be performed without the aid of the vendor.

EAL 2—structurally tested: In addition to the testing of EAL 1, the vendor's development documentation is also examined. Although this requires cooperation from the vendor, it does not require any special investment.

EAL 3—methodically tested and checked: The vendor has to prove that it looked for vulnerabilities during the development phase. This EAL requires the vendor to have security engineering at the development phase but does not require changing the existing practices.

EAL 4—methodically tested, designed, and reviewed: This level requires rigorous testing and the thorough examination of the design control documentation. This is the last level that does not require specialist skills such as formal verification. A product can reach this level if its vendor consciously uses security engineering but did not specifically aim for a higher EAL (when the product was designed). According to CC (2004), "EAL 4 is the highest level at which it is likely to be economically feasible to retrofit an existing product line."

EAL 5—semiformally designed and tested: EAL 5 is the first level where it is not enough for the vendor to provide documentation and test results but has to (mathematically) *prove* statements about the security of the product. At this level, the statements are allowed to be semiformal.

EAL 6—semiformally verified design and tested: At this EAL the vendor has to prove that the product functions according to specifications. At this level, the statements are still allowed to be semiformal.

EAL 7—formally verified design and tested: This final EAL requires the vendor to provide *formal proofs on key parts of the ToE*. The complexity of the ToE has to be minimized. The evaluator is also required to repeat all tests the vendor has performed. Although EAL 7 is very rigorous, only this EAL could give 100% guarantee that the ToE is secureable if the assumptions about the security environment hold. (Note that EAL7 has its limitations, too.) Unfortunately, very few products qualify for EAL 7.

Although a product may receive EAL 1 certification without the help of the vendor, a product is unlikely to receive a certification higher than EAL 3 if it was designed before Common Criteria appeared. Today, most products receive EAL 4 certification. Levels above EAL 4 are highly infrequent.

COMMON CRITERIA IN PRACTICE

Common Evaluation Methodology (CEM)

The CC do not deal with evaluation methodology; it is discussed in a separate document, the Common Evaluation Methodology (CEM), which is a companion document to CC. The first part of CEM describes general principles about evaluation methodology, and the second part gives a detailed methodology for evaluations. It starts with PP and ST evaluation methodology and continues with methodology for EAL 1–4 evaluations. CEM is currently in version 1.0, but it is mandatory for the mutual recognition of certificates (CEM, 1999).

Common Criteria Recognition Arrangement (CCRA)

The international community has accepted CC through the Common Criteria Recognition Arrangement (CCRA), which is an international treaty about the mutual acceptance of CC certifications (CCRA, 2000). Countries can participate in CCRA as certificate *consumers* and certificate *authorizers*. Certificate-authorizer participant countries may elaborate a national CC evaluation scheme. This scheme should define the systematic organization for evaluation and certification. The Common Criteria, the scheme, and the methodology form the context of the evaluation (see Figure 6). Certificates issued in the context of such schemes are accepted by certificate-consuming participants. Typically, certificate authorizers are certificate consumers, too. Certificate-consuming participants cannot issue internationally accepted certificates. The list of CCRA participants can be found at http://niap.nist.gov/cc-scheme/ccra-participants.html. *International acceptance* is perhaps the greatest merit of CC. Thus, if a product received a certain level of CC evaluation in one CCRA participant country, there is no need to perform a reevaluation when introducing the product in another one. This treaty is beneficial for vendors, because it not only saves money but also provides shorter time-to-market intervals. Because several organizations (typically governments) follow the policy of procuring products with a certain EAL, having to reevaluate a product in each country also acts as a nontariff barrier of trade (Salvatore, 1995). This way, the international recognition of CC certificates also catalyzes the free flow of IT security goods.

Unfortunately, mutual recognition only works for EAL 4 and lower levels. One possible reason for this is that an evaluation is accepted via CCRA only if the methodology in the CEM companion document was used. However, CEM only describes methodologies for levels not higher than EAL 4. Perhaps it is due to the scarcity of products—and lack of experience—with high EALs that such methodology has not been elaborated for higher levels. The other possible reason is that countries wish to retain the right to certify products at high EALs because of the high value added by high-level certifications.

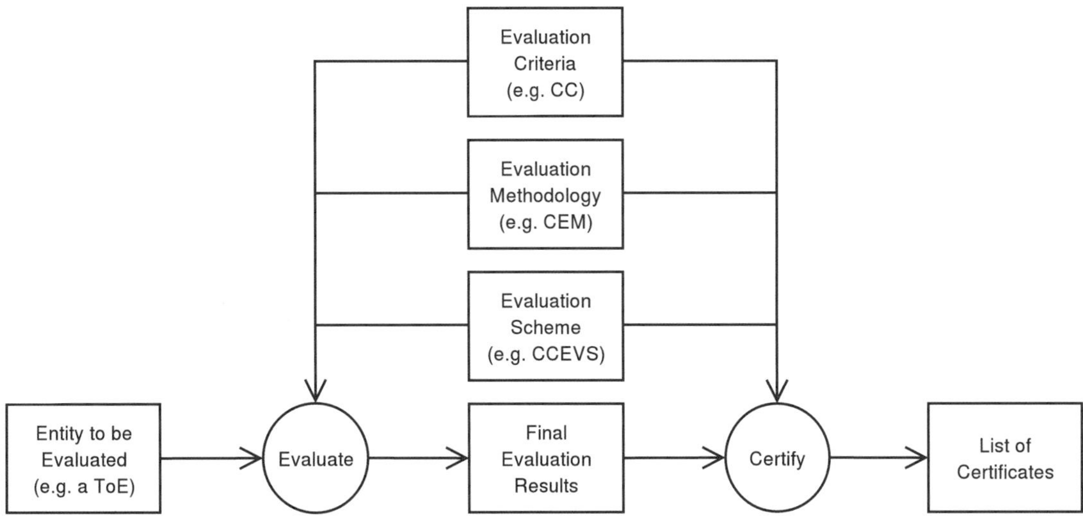

Figure 6: Evaluation context.

The home page of the Common Criteria evaluation and validation scheme (CCEVS), the U.S. CC evaluation scheme, is at http://niap.nist.gov/cc-scheme/.

Trends in Evaluations

Richard E. Smith, (2000a; 2000b) has collected data on government-endorsed security evaluations in the United States and in the United Kingdom from 1984 to 2000. Because his work embraced the early years too, when CC did not exist, his work was not limited to CC evaluations and therefore was based on previous standards such as TCSEC and ITSEC, too. Smith has come to the following key observations:

- Although several security products appear on the market, relatively *few products undergo security evaluation*. According to Smith, not more than one tenth of security products are evaluated.
- Despite the fact that the United States pioneered security evaluation, *most products are not evaluated in the United States*, and this trend is increasing. Often U.S. products are evaluated overseas. Smith argues that security evaluations are more expensive in the United States.
- The vast majority (more than 90%) of evaluations seek *EAL 3 or EAL 4* (or equivalent levels at other standards). Lower ratings are scarce, just as are higher ratings (which are mainly sought by military products).
- Although the main purpose of TCSEC was to establish security standards for operating systems and related access control products, Smith observed that *operating system evaluations no longer dominate*. Network security products (such as firewalls) and encryption devices account for most evaluations.

The four years that have passed since Smith performed his investigation have brought changes in this field. In the year 2000, CC were relatively young and the vast majority of evaluations were performed against ITSEC (in spite of the pioneering role of TCSEC in the field of security evaluation). Today, CC seem to be the most dominant set of evaluation criteria because of international acceptance. Many evaluators have even stopped performing evaluations against previous criteria.

Today, the proportion of evaluated products seems to have increased in the market (Rouchouze, 2002), perhaps because security evaluation starts to give a competitive advantage for products. More prestigious vendors have learned how to prepare their products for an evaluation, and enough time has passed to adopt development practices to the evaluation criteria. Some important consumers such as governments also tend to acknowledge security evaluation and prescribe it in policies and in laws. For example, in the European Union (EU, 1999) a digital signature can only become a "qualified signature" (accepted as fully equivalent with the traditional signature) if the signature creation device qualifies for a certain EAL against the SSCD (secure signature creation device) protection profile.

However, most evaluations still aim for EAL 4, even today. Perhaps the industry fails to achieve higher levels, or perhaps consumers do not require them. This question is examined in the next subsection.

Criticisms of CC

On one hand, CC have been used successfully since they were published. Year to year, more and more products are evaluated. On the other hand, despite CC evaluations, products in general do not tend to be more secure. Moreover, sometimes notoriously insecure products receive EAL 4 certification, practically the highest level a commercial product can receive.

EAL 4 is a level of assurance where the evaluator needs to perform little examination on the product itself but rather examines its documentation and the controls and business practices that were used during development. This means that if a vendor sacrifices enough funds and consciously focuses on producing CC-related documentation when developing the product, then it will pass a CC evaluation at EAL 4. (In contrast to this, no matter how secure a product is perceived to be, if the vendor did not lay emphasis on CC-related documentation in the development phase, because, for example, the product was developed before CC was published, the product cannot pass a CC evaluation at EAL 4.)

- *If a product has passed a security evaluation (e.g., against CC), it does not mean that it is secure; it means that it is secureable* (i.e., it is possible to configure it in a way to use it securely in a certain environment). The paradigm of product-based security evaluation (like that of CC and FIPS 140) can only consider a product in a certain environment. According to the CC, assumptions of secure usage are made when the security environment is established (see Figure 5), and any statement about the security of the ToE is only valid in context of these assumptions. For example, if an operating system is evaluated and certified against a protection profile, the evaluation is considered on a specific hardware of a specific vendor and is based on several assumptions about security measures and policies users are going to keep. Moreover, the evaluation is performed with a certain configuration of the OS, which might be significantly different from the default one. If any of these circumstances do not hold (the OS runs on a different hardware or in another configuration), the EAL the OS was certified at does not apply to the current situation.
- *If one product has a higher level of evaluation than another one, it does not mean it is more secure*. It means that the vendor was able to provide confidence about a higher level of security. Evaluation gives confidence that the manufacturer designed the product to be secure. However, only formal verification can guarantee that it works according to specifications. (Note that formal verification has its own pitfalls too. In the case of formal verification, an abstract mathematical model is constructed on the behavior of the product. Formal verification is able to prove that this abstract model conforms to the specifications. However, if the formal model does not describe the real product properly, the proof becomes irrelevant to the security of the product.)

  Because a security evaluation requires significant funds and paperwork, having a lower level of assurance only means that the manufacturer did not or could not aim for a higher level of assurance. For example, free open-source software is often developed and maintained by nonprofit organizations. Such organizations are unlikely to redesign and redevelop their product to be certified at a higher EAL. However, open source software has a very powerful security management system: volunteers from the open source community from all around the world continuously monitor the source code.
- It is not enough to check at which EAL a product was certified; the PP the product was evaluated against also has to be taken into account. For example, Shapiro (1996) reviews the evaluation of a well-known product and states that the PP it was evaluated against does not address the threats the community of users would like protection against. Results of evaluation against inappropriate criteria are useless for consumers, regardless of how high an EAL the product was certified against. Shapiro also questions the level of assurance an EAL 4 evaluation may provide and claims that because the vendor invested millions of dollars in this certification, it (or the fact that the vendor failed to achieve a higher level of certification or a certification against a better PP) proves the *insecurity* of the product. Naturally, a successful certification always gives confidence in security.

  The situation is even more critical if the evaluation is performed against an ST only. Because the ST was developed by the vendor, it often tends to be more consistent with marketing brochures than costumer requirements (Naaman, 2003).
- Another major weakness of the CC is that they do not address human-related security issues. Although these issues are included in the CC as assumption of secure usage, humans are far from being a stable and secure point of a system.

It is generally accepted that humans are a very weak link in the security chain. (For example, Anderson [1996] performed a survey on frauds against ATM machines and found that most attacks were performed by insiders or made use of human mistakes, ignorance, or implementation blunders.) CC can give extremely strong confidence about the security of a product, but only at higher EALs if formal methods are used. However, few products are able to reach these levels.

The CC can give assurance on the security of components of a system, but this does not say anything about humans—the link that connects these components. Perhaps a security standard that does not abstract out this weak link but tries to address it with control objectives and security policies might give more confidence in the security of a system.

Although in certain cases a CC certification may have little relevance to the security of a product, it surely means *added value*. Managers tend to buy products that have passed a CC evaluation even if they are more expensive and perceived to be less secure than their competitors. Thus, if the security of the system the manager is responsible for is breached, the manager is less likely to be held responsible for it, because the system relied on evaluated products.

Anderson also criticizes CC because the expenses of a CC evaluation (unlike those of a TCSEC evaluation) are paid by the vendor. He expresses distrust in the security of a system where security implementation and security evaluation are not paid by those parties who would suffer the consequences from inadequate security. Anderson (2001) argues that the IT market encourages vendors to sell insecure products, and he supports his statements with examples.

The CC provide internationally accepted criteria for performing security evaluations, and thus the CC are supposed to inhibit this trend by giving consumers more information on the quality and security of products. Unfortunately, the CC (and security evaluation in general) are used as a business method to add value to products, and thus perhaps might even catalyze this negative trend.

CONCLUSION

Security evaluation is an important concept because this is the only approach an individual consumer can rely on to gain confidence in the security of a product or system.

Today, the Common Criteria represent the only internationally accepted product-specific security standard that can be applied to any IT (security) product regardless of its type. It also enables the comparison of products of the same type from different vendors.

A Common Criteria evaluation is not only important as a mean of assessing the security of a product, but it is also a business method for gaining competitive advantage. The more confidence consumers gain in the security of a product, the more value is added to it. This is why the Common Criteria are not only accepted by users, but are also supported and sponsored by vendors and governments. Being the first internationally accepted criteria for security evaluation, the Common Criteria strongly determine the future of IT security.

GLOSSARY

Common Criteria (CC) A standard for security assessment.

Countermeasure Countermeasures are means to decrease vulnerabilities in a product or system.

Evaluation Assurance Level The degree of confidence that can be gained on how well a target of evaluation (TOE) meets the assurance requirements.

Protection Profile A product-independent statement of the security requirements of a certain class of products.

Security Evaluation The process of assessing if a product or service meets its security requirements.

Security Target A representation of implementation-dependent requirements of a specific product.

Target of Evaluation The product or service under evaluation.

Threat An undesired event that may reduce the value of certain assets.

Threat Agent A threat agent is an abstract entity that raises a threat. A threat agent may not only be a conscious human attacker, it can be a natural disaster, for example.

Vulnerability Threats exploit vulnerabilities to decrease the value of assets.

CROSS REFERENCES

See *Cryptographic Hardware Security Modules; Side-Channel Attacks; Software Development and Quality Assurance; The Common Criteria.*

REFERENCES

Agrawal, D., Archambeault, B., Rao, J., & Rohatgi, P. (2002, August). *The EM side-channel(s)*. Paper presented at the Workshop on Cryptographic Hardware and Embedded Systems 2002 (CHES 2002), Redwood City, CA.

Anderson, N. (1996). Why cryptosystems fail. In W. Stallings (Ed.), *Practical cryptography for data internetworks*, Los Alamitos, CA: IEEE Computer Society Press.

Anderson, R. (2001, December). *Why information security is hard—An economic perspective*. Paper presented at the 17th Annual Computer Security Applications Conference, New Orleans, LA.

Anderson, R., & Needham, R. (1996). Programming satan's computer: Lecture notes in computer science—*Computer Science Today*, Springer LNCS v 1000, pp. 426–441. Retrieved May 22, 2005, from http://citeseer.nj.nec.com/22376.html

CC. (2004). *Common Criteria 2.1*. Retrieved [dated] from http://csrc.nist.gov/cc

CCRA. (2000). *Arrangement on the recognition of Common Criteria certificates in the field of information technology security.* Retrieved May 22, 2005, from http://www.commoncriteriaportal.org/public/consumer/index.php?menu=3;http://niap.nist.gov/niap/library/cc-recarrange.pdf

CEM. (1999). *Common methodology for information technology security evaluation.* Retrieved May 22, 2005, from http://csrc. nist.gov/cc/CEM.html

Crosby, P. (1979). *Quality is free: The art of making quality certain*. New York, NY: McGraw-Hill Companies.

EU. (1999). *Directive 1999/93/EC of the European Parliament and of the council of 13 December 1999 on a community framework for electronic signatures.* Retrieved May 22, 2005, from http://europa.eu.int/eurlex/pri/en/oj/dat/2000/l_013/l_01320000119en00120020.pdf

Initi@tive D^{21}. (2001). *A comparative study of IT security criteria.* Retrieved May 22, 2005, from http://www.bsi.bund.de/gshb/

Kelsey, J., Schneier, B., Wagner, D., & Hall, C. (2000). Side channel cryptanalysis of product ciphers. *Journal of Computer Security, 8*(2–3), 141–158.

Larson, E. (1999). *European quality standards: A brief overview.* Retrieved May 22, 2005, from http://qualitydigest.com/mar99/html/body_standard.html

McEvilley, M. (2000, May). *Common Criteria tutorial—Introduction and general model.* Paper presented at the First International Common Criteria Conference, Baltimore, MD.

Muir, J. (2001). *Techniques of side channel cryptanalysis.* Unpublished masters thesis, University of Waterloo. Retrieved May 22, 2005, from http://www.math.uwaterloo.ca/~jamuir/papers/mmthesis-side-channel.pdf

Naaman, N. (2003, December). *A consumer's perspective on the application of the Common Criteria.* Paper presented at the 19th Annual Computer Security Applications Conference, Las Vegas, NV.

NIST, CSE. (1995). *Frequently asked questions for the cryptographic module validation program.* Retrieved May 22, 2005, from http://csrc.nist.gov/cryptval/140-1/CMVPFAQ.pdf

Oakland, J. (1992). *Total quality management.* Portsmouth, NH: Heinemann.

Peters, T., Waterman, R., & Peters, T. (1988). *In search of excellence—Lessons from America's best-run companies*. Lebanon, IN: Warner Books.

Rouchouze, B. (2002, May). *Why to use Common Criteria for IT-products or IT-systems.* Paper presented at the Third International Common Criteria Conference, Ottawa, Canada.

Salvatore, D. (1995). *International economics* (5th ed.). Harlow, England: Prentice–Hall.

Schultz, C. (2001). *BSI offers free IT baseline protection manual, solicits comments.* Retrieved May 22, 2005, from http://www.ieee-security.org/Cipher/Newsbriefs/1997/971004.bsiITmanual.html

Shapiro, C., & Varian, H. (1998). *Information rules: A strategic guide to the network economy.* Watertown, MA: Harvard Business School Press.

Shapiro, J. (1996). *Understanding the Windows EAL4 evaluation.* Retrieved May 22, 2005, from http://eros.cs.jhu.edu/~shap/NT-EAL4.html

Slack, N., Chambers, S., & Johnston, R. (2001). *Operations management* (3rd ed.). Harlow, England: Pearson Education Limited.

Smith, R. (2000a). *Historical trends in computer security evaluations.* Retrieved May 22, 2005, from http://www.smat.us/crypto/evalhist

Smith, R. (2000b, October). Trends in government endordsed security product evaluations. In *Proceedings of the National Information Systems Security Conference.* Gaithersburg, MD: National Institute of Standards and Technology, National Computer Security Center (pp. 279–287).

Towns, M. (2000, December). *Common Criteria paradigm.* Paper presented at the 16th Annual Computer Security Applications Conference, New Orleans, LA.

Digital Certificates

Albert Levi, *Sabanci University, Turkey*

INTRODUCTION

Public key cryptography has become popular in information and telecommunication security. Algorithms in this family use two different, but related, keys. One of them is kept private by the key owner, and the other is made public. The private key is used to decrypt messages as well as to sign digital information. The corresponding public key is used to encrypt messages and to verify digital signatures. Because these latter operations can be done by anyone, public keys need to be made public. Although public keys are widely known, it is not computationally feasible to obtain a private key using the corresponding public key.

Public key distribution is not an easy task. Public keys can be distributed through global directories or servers, but the key must be bound to the holder's identity. Without binding, the key holders could use any name they wanted. For example, suppose *Charlie* creates a key pair and publishes the public key as if he is *Bob*. Later *Alice* wants to obtain the *Bob's* correct public key. She queries the server and obtains the public key that seemingly belongs to *Bob*, but was actually uploaded by *Charlie*. In this way, *Charlie* can masquerade as *Bob*. This method of cheating is called *name spoofing*. The possible dangers of name spoofing are the following:

- Suppose *Charlie* has intercepted the encrypted messages from *Alice* to *Bob*. *Alice* has encrypted these messages using the fake public key of *Bob*, which actually belongs to *Charlie*. Because *Charlie* also knows the corresponding private key, he is now capable of decrypting these messages.
- Suppose *Bob* has digitally signed a message using his private key and sent it to *Alice*. Because the public key that *Alice* has for *Bob* is in fact incorrect, she cannot verify the signature on the message, even if it is legitimate.

There are some methods proposed in the literature to overcome the name-spoofing problem. When public key cryptography was first proposed by Diffie and Hellman (1976), the proposed method for public key distribution was a "public file" where the public keys and the corresponding owners were listed. The write access was limited to authorized users, but the read access was not limited. This idea would have been useful for small communities where there was no need to update the public file very often, but it was never realized because the demand was to provide for larger communities. Later, centralized online mechanisms were proposed to distribute public keys on demand (Popek & Kline, 1979), but such a service was never widely implemented mainly because of the dependency on online servers.

The concept of *certificate* was first proposed by Kohnfelder (1978) as a distributed public key distribution mechanism that did not need online servers. The idea was to employ trusted entities that would validate and endorse the *public-key-to-owner* binding with a digital signature.

A public key certificate (or identity certificate) is a digital binding between the identity and the public key of a user. Sometimes certificates are used to bind a credential or a permit to a public key without using the identity of the owner. This type of certificate is called an *attribute certificate* (or *authorization certificate*). The binding in a certificate is digitally signed by a trusted *certification authority* (*CA*). Anyone who wants to find a legitimate public key verifies the CA signature on the certificate. The verifier must trust that the CA has correctly bound the public key to the holder. The CA is responsible for verifying the holder's identity before issuing the certificate.

Obtaining legitimate public keys via certificate verification allows encrypted and authentic communication between two parties. Moreover, the signer cannot later deny sending a signed message, because his public key has been certified by a trusted CA. Nonrepudiation is very important in e-commerce and e-banking.

An example certificate issuance model is depicted in Figure 1. In this model, first, the user applies to a CA by providing his or her public key and some proof of identity. The CA verifies the identity and makes sure that the public key really belongs to the user. After that, the CA creates a certificate by digitally signing the necessary information. This certificate is stored in some public servers or databases.

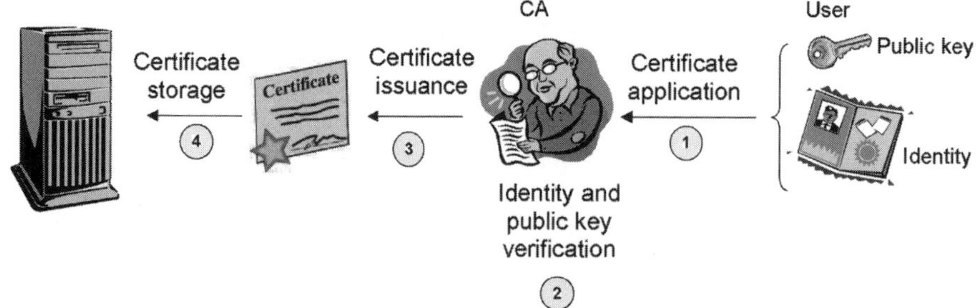

Figure 1: Example certificate issuance model.

A simple signed document verification scenario is depicted in Figure 2. Suppose the signer (not shown in the figure) previously signed a document using his or her private key. The verifier needs the correct public key of the signer for verification of this signature. To do so, first, the verifier obtains the signer's certificate from the public key server or database. Then, the signer verifies the signature of the CA on this certificate. This verification yields the correct public key of the signer. Using this public key and the signed document, the verifier verifies the signature on the document.

In this simple scenario, verification of the signer's certificate requires knowing the CA's public key and we assume that this public key is known to the verifier. However, in most cases, a series of certificates might be verified in a chain to reach the signer's certificate. This mechanism, called *certificate path*, is explained in a subsequent section.

As the public key cryptosystems and their applications become more widespread, the need for a secure public key distribution method became more and more important. At this point, the industry took up Kohnfelder's idea and practicalized the concept of certificates for commercial use. Since then, several standards have been issued and several secure applications have either adopted a standard or defined their own certification mechanism. Today digital certificates offer a promising market and are an enabler technology in Internet security for a wide range of applications from e-commerce to e-mail.

CERTIFICATE STRUCTURE

Attempts to standardize certificates were started in the late 1980s. The first standard was published by ITU-T (International Telecommunications Union) in 1988 as the X.509 recommendation (ITU-T, 1988). The same standard was also published by ISO/IEC (International Organization for Standardization/International Electrotechnical Commission) as International Standard 9495–8.

Other than X.509 certificates that bind an identity to a public key, there are other relatively less common certificate types. These are detailed in this section. First we start with classical X.509 identity certificates.

X.509v3 Certificate Characteristics and Structure

The X.509 recommendation was revised three times: in 1993, 1997, and 2000 (ITU-T, 1993, 1997, 2000). The certificate structure of the original 1988 recommendation is named version 1 (v1). Version 2 (v2) is the structure defined in the 1993 edition. X.509v2 is not so different than v1 (the details are given later in this subsection). The X.509 version 3 (v3) certificate structure is defined in the third edition of X.509 in 1997. The main distinguishing feature of the X.509v3 certificate structure is the extension fields, which are explained in the subsequent section in detail. The X.509 recommendation was revised once

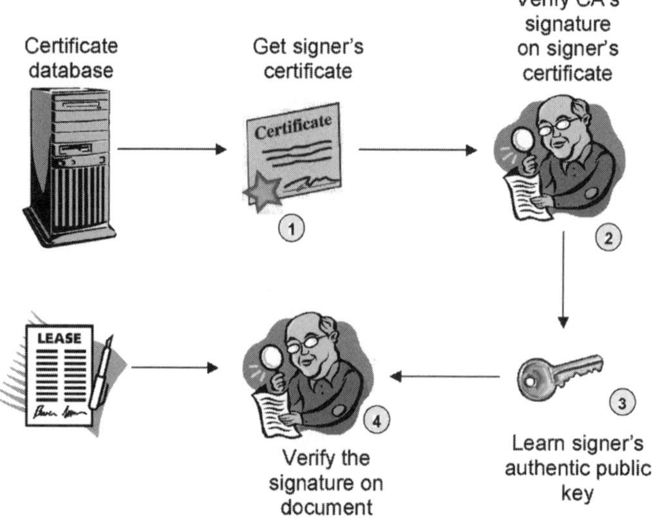

Figure 2: Simple signed document verification scenario.

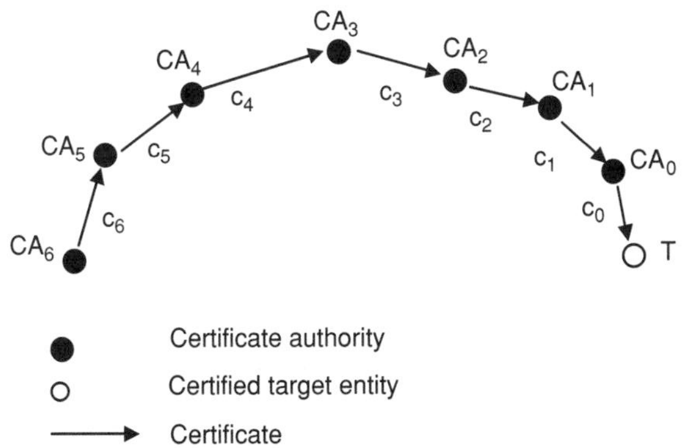

Figure 3: Example certificate path.

more in 2000, but the certificate structure was not updated in this revision.

The X.509v3 certificate structure includes identification and public key information for the *subject* (the entity for which the certificate has been issued) and identification for the *issuer* (authority who signed the certificate). In addition, the certificate structure includes some managerial fields such as serial number, version, and so forth.

A certificate is signed by a CA with a digital signature covering all applicable certificate fields. The signature algorithm and its parameters are included in a header to facilitate the verification process. The digital signature, which is a binary stream, is appended to the certificate.

Certificates are processed as a chain known as the *certificate path,* as exemplified in Figure 3. The last certificate of this path (c_0) is the certificate of the end user (T) whose public key is sought. Other certificates are CA certificates, that is, certificates issued by CAs to other CAs. The verifying agent starts the verification process with the first CA (CA_6) certificate (c_6). Generally, the first CA certificates are known as root CAs and their certificates are *self-signed* certificates, that is, both issuer and subject entities are the same. If such a self-signed certificate of a root CA is deemed trustworthy by the verifying agent, then the verification process can safely start with it. Such a root CA is called the *trust anchor* of the verification process. Verification of a self-signed certificate yields the verified public key of the root CA, which in turn is used to verify the next CA certificate. Verification of the next CA certificate yields its public key, and so on. Verifications continue until the last certificate on the path—which is for the end user—is verified and the end user's public key is found. In the example in Figure 3, once the verifier verifies c_6, he or she finds the public key of CA_5 and then, using this public key, verifies c_5. Verification of c_5 yields the public key of CA_4, and the chain goes on until c_0 is verified to find the public key of T.

In X.509, there is a clear distinction between CA certificates and end-user certificates. CA certificates, as the name suggests, are used for CAs, and CAs can issue certificates for other CAs. End-user certificates are issued for ordinary clients; end users can never issue certificates for other entities.

The certificates that are described in this subsection are identity certificates. Identity certificates are used to bind a public key to an owner who is explicitly identified in the certificate. The public key certificate framework defined in the X.509 specification mainly addresses identity certificates. This type of certificate is a critical component of a public key infrastructure (PKI). However, X.509 does not define a PKI in its entirety.

Names of the certificate issuer and subject are specified in X.509 using the X.500 family's distinguished name (DN) structure. A DN is simply a set of attribute and value pairs that uniquely identify a person or entity. It is a tree-based naming structure with a root at the top and a naming authority at every node. Assuming that each node ensures the uniqueness of the names that it assigns, the overall DN structure will yield globally unique entity names.

X.509 uses abstract syntax notation 1 (ASN.1) notation to describe certificates and related structures, and the ASN.1 *distinguished encoding rules* (DER) to encode these objects for sending.

The details of the X.509 certificate fields are given here and depicted in Figure 4. First we start with the fields included in the X.509v1 certificate structure and then continue with the additional fields of X.509v2 and v3.

Version: this determines the version of the certificate. Currently this value could be 1 (default value), 2, or 3.

Serial number: an integer value identifying the certificate. This value should be unique for each CA, but global uniqueness is not required. Thus, there is no need to have an authority for the distribution of certificate serial numbers.

Signature algorithm: the algorithm identifier for the algorithm and hash function used by the CA in signing the certificate.

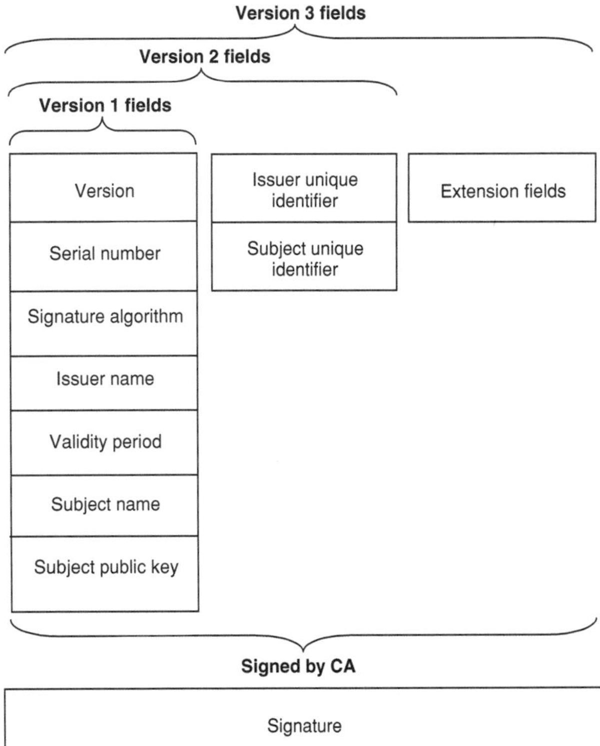

Figure 4: X.509 certificate fields.

Issuer name: DN of the CA that issued the certificate. This field identifies the CA but not necessarily in a unique way.

Validity: this specifies the time period during which the certificate is valid and the CA warrants that it will maintain information about the status of the certificate. This field contains two date and time values that determine the starting and the ending date and time.

Subject name: this identifies the owner of the certificate using the DN structure.

Subject public key information: the public key of the subject (owner of the certificate). Actually, the binding between this value and subject name fields are endorsed by the CA. This field also contains the algorithm corresponding to the key.

These fields exist in all three versions of X.509 and are the core fields of the certificates. In X.509v2 two more optional fields are added:

Issuer unique identifier and **subject unique identifier:** these fields are needed in case the subject and/or issuer DNs are assigned to two or more different users.

During the preparation of the third edition of X.509, it became apparent that more fields were needed. The X.509 committee put forward the concept of extension fields as a way to continue the expansion of the standard into the future. Because these extension fields were generic, it was possible to make use of them for different purposes without changing the certificate structure. Several extension fields were defined in the third edition of X.509 recommendation, where the extension fields were first included in the certificate structure (X.509v3). Later, some other extension fields were added in the fourth edition, but the certificate structure remained the same.

X.509v3 Extension Fields

An extension field consists of a unique extension identifier, a criticality flag, and the data part of the extension. Extensions are optional. The criticality flag determines how the verifier of the certificate reacts if it does not recognize the extension (this is possible when the particular extension is not implemented by the verification system). If the criticality flag is TRUE, then the certificate is treated as invalid. In contrast, if the flag is FALSE, then the extension is ignored.

In the third and fourth editions of the X.509 recommendation, several extensions were defined. These can be grouped in five categories, as listed:

1. Basic certificate revocation list (CRL) extensions
2. CRL distribution points and delta CRLs
3. Key and policy information
4. Subject and issuer attributes
5. Certification path constraints

The first two groups of extensions, which deal with CRLs, are discussed briefly in a subsequent section. The third and the fourth groups of extensions can be applied both to public key certificates and to CRLs. The last group is only for public key certificates. The latter three groups are briefly explained in the following sections.

Key and Policy Information

Additional information about the keys involved, including key identifiers for subject and issuer keys, indicators of intended or restricted key usage, and indicators of certificate policy, are contained in this group of extensions.

The **certificate policies** extension specifies the policies applied by the CA during the creation of the subject certificate. Each policy is identified by unique policy identifiers. In practice, policies map to certification practice statements (CPS) declared by the CAs. The verifying entity may put restrictions on certificate policies and, as a result, may not accept some certificates even if the signature is valid. This mechanism is a way to circumvent the blind trust that was inherent in the first two versions of the X.509 recommendation.

The **authority key identifier** extension is used to identify the public key of the CA that issued the certificate or CRL. One could argue that the issuer-unique-identifier field added to X.509v2 could solve the identification problem for the authority. However, because a CA could have more than one key pair, key-based identification was needed, and it was provided by this extension.

The **subject key identifier** extension is used to identify the public key of the subject to whom the certificate has been issued. This feature is useful when a subject has more than one public key and certificate.

The **key usage extension** limits the use of the public key to some certain cryptographic tasks such as digital signatures, key agreement, encipherment, and so forth.

The **extended key usage** extension is one of the visionary extensions. If the use of the key is not one of the basic usages described in the key usage extension field, this extension is used to specify a usage for the key. Such an extended usage is identified by an object identifier value that has to be formally registered according to ITU-T and ISO regulations.

The **private key usage period** extension is used to assign a different lifetime to the private key corresponding to the certified public key. Without this extension, the lifetimes of the public and private keys are the same. However, this is generally not the case in practice. Take, for example, the case of a digital signature application where the validity of the public key could be longer than the private key because the signed documents may have been verified after the private key expires. This extension is a mechanism that allows such flexibility. However, to utilize this extension, the signed documents should bear a time stamp that shows when the document was signed using the private key. Otherwise, it would be impossible for the verifier to check the expiration status of the private key used in the signature.

Subject and Issuer Attributes

The native naming mechanism of X.509 is the DN structure. The DN structure was specialized to the global distributed directory concept standardized by X.500 family of recommendations. This special structure did not meet the requirements of other applications that use X.509 certificates because each application needs a different naming mechanism. For example, a secure e-mail application needs e-mail addresses; a secure WWW application needs URLs as names. Because the requirements of these types of applications were so urgent, a temporary solution was found: the common name (CN) field of the DN structure was used to include such application-specific names. Although this temporary solution is still in use, a special extension field was added to X.509v3 to support alternative names for certificate issuer and subject. Alternative names can be in a variety of forms including an e-mail address, a URL, an IP address, and so forth. Moreover, a special form of name can also be defined via the *other name* option.

Certificate Path Constraints

These certificate extensions allow constraint specifications to be included in CA certificates (certificates for CAs issued by other CAs) to facilitate the automated processing of certificate paths. The constraints may restrict the types of certificates that can be issued by the subject CA or that may occur subsequently in a certification path. In this way, trust processing can be customized according to different needs. Although these extensions are included in CA certificates, processing and interpreting these extensions is mostly the task of the certificate path verification entity, that is, an end user. Four extensions are defined in this context: *basic constraints*, *name constraints*, *policy constraints*, and *inhibit any policy*.

The **basic constraints extension** indicates whether the subject may act as a CA or not. If so, a *certification path length* constraint may also be specified. If the length of the path exceeds the specified value, then the end-entity certificate is automatically disqualified.

The **name constraints extension** indicates a name space within which all subject names in subsequent certificates in a certification path are to be located. The idea behind this extension is to be able to implement policies based on trusted and distrusted CAs known by name.

The **policy constraints extension** specifies constraints that may require explicit certificate policy identification for the remainder of the certification path. If such policy identifiers are present in a certificate, then the forthcoming certificates on the path must bear the required or equivalent policy identifiers in order for the certificate path to be validated.

Normally, a CA may assert *any-policy* identifier in certificate policies extensions to trust a certificate for all possible policies. The **inhibit any-policy extension** specifies a constraint that indicates *any-policy* is not considered as an explicit match. This rule applies for all certificates in the certification path starting with the certificate that bears this extension. In this way, explicit identification for policies is enforced.

Other Types of Certificates

Other than X.509v3 identity certificates, there are some alternative certificate structures. One issue behind developing alternatives is to address the requirements of access control in certificates. Another issue is the unsuitability of lengthy formats for restricted applications such as WAP (wireless access protocol). Yet another issue is the belief that X.509 is not good at addressing the trust management requirements of liberal applications mainly because of the strict distinction between the concepts of CA and end users. Alternative certificate structures are discussed in this section.

Attribute Certificate Framework of X.509

Classical identity certificates (i.e., public key certificates) are used to assign a valid public key to an entity. The privileges of this entity are to be managed separately by the verifying system. This approach is criticized by the access control community, which believes that the two-step approach enforced by identity certificates is impractical. In the fourth edition of the X.509 recommendation, these concerns are addressed by the attribute certificate framework.

X.509 attribute certificates have a structure that is different than classical identity certificates. Although the identification of the certificate holder is still possible in attribute certificates, it is optional. The actual task of an attribute certificate is the binding of a privilege to an entity. After the verifying agent verifies the attribute certificate of an entity and authenticates it successfully, it gives access to the resources allowed within the certificate.

The certificate path concept is also valid for attribute certificates. However, there are some differences in terminology and roles as compared with identity certificates and PKI, because attribute certificates are used to implement PMI (privilege management infrastructure) rather than PKI. PMI defines the rules and the general concepts about using attribute certificates as a system for managing access control. Although the X.509 recommendation defines some critical components of a PMI, it does not define a PMI in its entirety.

In PMI, the root CA becomes the SOA (source of authority), which issues attribute certificates to AAs (attribute authorities). AAs, which are analogous to CAs in PKI, issue attribute certificates to end entities.

The fields of attribute certificates are briefly described as follows:

Version differentiates between the different versions of the attribute certificates.

Holder is an optional field that conveys the identity of the attribute certificate's holder.

Issuer conveys the identity of the AA that issued the certificate.

Signature identifies the cryptographic algorithm used to digitally sign the attribute certificate.

Serial number is the number that uniquely identifies the attribute certificate. The uniqueness is within the scope of the certificate issuer.

Validity period conveys the time period during which the attribute certificate is considered as valid.

Attributes contains a list of attributes (or privileges) associated with the certificate holder.

Issuer unique ID is an optional field that is used to uniquely identify the issuer of the attribute certificate when such an identification is necessary.

Similar to identity certificates, the structure of the attribute certificate allows some extension fields.

SPKI/SDSI Certificates

The simple public key infrastructure (SPKI; Ellison, 1999b; Ellison et al., 1999) was designed by an Internet Engineering Task Force (IETF) working group (Simple Public Key Infrastructure Charter, n.d.) led by Ellison (this working group is currently inactive). The SPKI certificates contain authorization information and bind the keys to that information. Thus, SPKI certificates are also called *authorization certificates*. The primary purpose of SPKI authorization certificates is to grant permissions. They also include the ability to delegate permissions to other entities. In that respect, it can be deduced that the basic aim of SPKI is quite similar to the X.509 attribute certificate framework, but the SPKI initiative started much earlier, in 1996.

Rivest and Lampson (1996) proposed simple distributed security infrastructure (SDSI). SDSI combines a simple PKI design with a means of defining groups and issuing group membership certificates. SDSI's groups provide simple, clear terminology for defining access control lists and security policies. The designs of SDSI and SPKI have merged in the SDSI 2.0 version.

Proponents of SPKI/SDSI have had two basic arguments against X.509 certificates:

- The X.509 certificate format is complicated and bulky.
- The concept of a globally unique identity (such as X.500's DN structure) will never be realized. Ellison (1999a) and Adams and Lloyd (1999) discuss some difficulties in dealing with globally unique names and DN. The main point here is the fact that globally unique names are not so meaningful without local significance. For example, "John Smith, from XYZ Co., NYC" may be unique, but does not help you to figure out that he is the person that you met on vacation unless you locally store the extra information "from the Canary Islands" in your address book.

SPKI certificates used public keys as the identities. Later, SPKI inherited the local name concept from SDSI. SDSI allows each user to define his or her own local name space and issue his or own certificates in that name space. SPKI associated SDSI local names with the keys. In this way, the SPKI/SDSI initiative avoided using global names in certificates.

The SPKI specifications developed by the IETF working group (Ellison, 1999b; Ellison et al., 1999) discuss concepts and provide detailed certificate formats, signature formats, and associated protocols. SPKI RFCs use S-expressions, a LISP-like parenthesized expression, as the standard format for certificates and define a canonical form for those S-expressions.

An SPKI authorization certificate has a number of fields similar to X.509 certificates, such as issuer, subject, and validity. However, the syntax and, most of the time, the semantics are different. Moreover, SPKI has a number of fields for access control and delegation. The structure of these fields is not strictly defined in the specifications. This is done deliberately to provide enough flexibility to applications that proliferate SPKI certificates.

The SPKI working group of the IETF (Simple Public Key Infrastructure Charter, n.d.) mentions "the key certificate format and associated protocols are to be simple to understand, implement, and use." However, according to Adams and Lloyd (1999), the sophisticated certificate structure of SPKI has diminished the intended simplicity.

The IETF work on SPKI was completed in 1999. Some libraries and prototype implementations have been developed (Ellison, n.d.). However, it is very hard to say that there is an important demand for SPKI certificates in the market (Adams & Lloyd, 1999).

WTLS Certificates

WAP (wireless access protocol; WAP Forum, 2001b) is a framework for developing applications to run over wireless networks. WAP, which was developed by an international industrywide organization called the WAP Forum, has a layered structure. WTLS (wireless transport layer security; WAP Forum, 2001a) is the security protocol of the WAP protocol suite. WTLS operates over the transport layer and provides end-to-end security, where one end is the mobile client and the other end is the WAP gateway. The WAP gateway acts as a proxy for the mobile client to access an application server, which is hosted somewhere on the Internet. The handicaps of the wireless environment are basically the limited processing power of mobile clients and the limited data transfer rate of the mobile communication environment. Thus, classical X.509 certificates are not so feasible for WTLS because of their lengthy format.

The WTLS standard (WAP Forum, 2001a) defines a special certificate structure, so-called WTLS certificates, that can be used in this restricted environment. In essence, a WTLS certificate is the light version of a X.509 certificate. The infrastructural rules of WTLS certificates are more or less the same as X.509, but some fields are either removed or simplified. WTLS certificate fields are explained in the following:

Certificate version determines the version of the certificate. Currently it is 1.

Signature algorithm describes the public key algorithm used for signing the WTLS certificate.

Issuer defines the CA who signed the certificate. Several name formats are available including the DN format employed by classical X.509 certificates.

Subject identifies the owner of the WTLS certificate. As with the issuer field, several name formats can be used.

Not valid before, not valid after: these fields determine the validity period of the WTLS certificate.

Public key type, parameters, public key: these three fields determine the public key to be certified along with its type and parameters.

WTLS certificates do not include any extension fields.

The use of elliptic curve cryptosystems (ECC; Menezes, 1993) is encouraged because of smaller key and signature sizes as compared to the RSA cryptosystem. Moreover, ECC implementations are known to be faster than those of its rivals.

PGP Key Signatures (Certificates)

Although PGP (Pretty Good Privacy) is known as an e-mail security software, its unique public key management offers a new certificate-like structure (although it is not 100% correct to name this structure *certificate*, we do so for the sake of consistency in terminology). The philosophy of PGP is to allow the utmost freedom to its users in selecting their trust anchors and trust policy. In such a system, there is no distinction between the CA and the end user. Indeed, in PGP, every end user can also be an authority resulting in a mesh-like certificate graph, known as a **web of trust**.

Actually, PGP's liberal approach has changed over time. Together with the commercialization of the software, commercial concerns have impaired the original liberal approach. This section highlights the original approach of version 2.6.

In PGP, every user, as verifier, determines his or her trusted entities and accepts certificates issued by them. A particular entity may be trusted by one user, but may not be trusted by another one. Moreover, this trust is not binary; the verifier may partially trust an entity as an authority. To deem a public key P belonging a user X as valid, the verifier should either (a) know X and issue the certificate for P or (b) obtain valid certificates for P issued by entities trusted by the verifier. In the latter case, the verifier should obtain one such certificate if the issuer is fully trusted or two such certificates if the issuers are partially trusted.

A PGP public key is stored together with all of the certificates issued for it. That is why obtaining a certificate is quite straightforward.

The structure is explained as follows:

Time stamp: the time stamp indicates the date and time that the key was generated. This is not lifetime. Original PGP does not grant lifetimes for keys and certificates. See the Certificate Revocation section for more details.

Key ID: key ID is an identifier for the key. This is actually the least significant 64 bits of the public key.

Public key: the public key of the owner together with necessary parameters.

User ID: this identifies the owner of the key. This field generally contains a textual name and an e-mail address.

Signatures: the digital signatures over this public key. These are issued by several people. Each signature entry also includes the identification of the signer.

Apart from these data that can be downloaded from public key servers, each user (verifier) adds some more information after storing a public key and its signatures into his or her local public key ring file. These are explained as follows:

Owner trust: this indicates how much the verifier trusts the owner of the public key as a certificate issuer for other people.

Signature trust: there is a signature trust field for each signature over a public key. This field indicates how much the verifier trusts the issuer of the signature. This field's value is copied from the owner trust value of the entry for the public key of the signature issuer.

Key legitimacy: this is a computed value that indicates whether the subject public key is deemed to be legitimate or not. It is computed by the PGP software using other fields of the public key entry in the key ring file and parameters set by the verifier.

ISSUES AND DISCUSSIONS

Apart from the structure and basic characteristics of certificates, there are several other issues that must be addressed. These issues are discussed in this section.

Certificate Revocation

X.509-based certificates have specific validity periods and a certificate is valid only within this period. However, various circumstances may cause a certificate to become invalid prior to the expiration of the validity period. Such circumstances might include change of name, change of association between the certificate owner and CA, and compromise or suspected compromise of the corresponding private key. Under such circumstances, the CA or the certificate owner needs to revoke the certificate.

The method for certificate revocation in X.509 is to employ the certificate revocation list (CRL) concept. A CRL is a signed list of unexpired but revoked certificates. The CRL structure includes serial numbers and the revocation dates of the revoked certificates. This list is signed by the corresponding CA. CRLs are issued periodically by the CAs. Each CRL invalidates the previous CRL. The certificate entries in a CRL are removed when the expiration dates of the revoked certificates are reached. A certificate, for which the validity period has not yet expired, should not appear in the most recent CRL of the issued CA to be verified successfully.

A supplementary approach to the CRL is the delta-CRL approach where the idea is to transfer incremental information when the revocation lists are updated and not to repeat the previously sent revocation information. This is done to save both time and bandwidth.

In addition to the base CRL message structure, two extension groups are dedicated for CRLs as well. These are *basic CRL extensions* and *CRL distribution points and delta-CRLs*.

Basic CRL extensions allow a CRL to

- Include indications of the reason for revocation.
- Include the date when the authority posted the revocation (for each revoked certificate).
- Provide flexibility for temporary suspension of a certificate.
- Include the scope of certificates covered by that list.
- Include CRL issue sequence numbers for each CRL issue to help certificate users to detect missing CRLs.

CRL distribution points and delta-CRLs extensions allow the complete set of revocation information from one CA to be partitioned into separate CRLs and allow revocation information from multiple CAs to be combined in one CRL. These extensions also support the use of delta CRLs described previously.

Online certificate status protocol (OCSP) is published as an RFC (Myers et al., 1999). It is a simple request/response protocol that requires online servers, so-called OCSP responders, to distribute the certificate status on demand. Each CA must run its own OCSP responder, unless several CAs collaborate on this issue. The main advantage of using OCSP is that the most up-to-date certificate status information, which is stored in the OCSP responder system, is returned because of the real-time response feature of the OCSP. However, in the CRL approach, there is latency between a particular revocation time and the next CRL or delta CRL issuance time. It should also be noted that the promptness of the response in the OCSP is only as good as the source of the revocation information. Here there might be some delays in storing the revocation data in the OCSP responder system, but this delay is not as large as in the CRL case.

Kocher (1998) has proposed certificate revocation trees (CRTs). CRTs are used to compile the revocation information on a single hash tree. CRTs provide an efficient and scalable mechanism to distribute revocation information. As Kocher mentions, CRTs are gaining increased use worldwide for several reasons. They can be used with existing protocols and certificates, and they enable the secure, reliable, scalable, and inexpensive validation of certificates (as well as digital signatures and other data). The main disadvantage of CRTs is that any change in the set of revoked certificates results in recomputation of the entire CRT.

PGP (Zimmermann, 1994) public keys and certificates may optionally have validity periods, but it is more common not to have them and to make them nonexpiring. Therefore, PGP public keys and certificates are valid until they are revoked. PGP public keys can be revoked only by the public key owner and by issuing a key revocation certificate. Similarly, certificates can be revoked by revocation certificates issued by the certificate signers. These revocation certificates invalidate the public keys/certificates; however, the revoked objects do not disappear. Moreover, there is no revocation list concept in PGP. Revocation certificates are distributed like the public keys and certificates. The most common approach is to use public key servers. The revocation certificates are kept in the public key servers together with the keys and certificates. If a key or certificate has a revocation certificate, then the verifier understands that this key or certificate is invalid.

Yet another and extreme approach to certificate revocation is not to have the revocation concept at all as in the SDSI (Rivest & Lampson, 1996) and SPKI (Ellison et al., 1999) systems. There is no CRL in these systems. Instead, each certificate is assigned an appropriate validity period. The certificate times out after this period and needs revalidation. Revalidations are performed either by the certificate issuers or by specific revalidation authorities. To revalidate a certificate, the certificate issuer re-signs the certificate content with a new time stamp. In contrast, revalidation authorities sign the whole certificate content and the original signature on it to revalidate a certificate.

A similar approach is also used for WTLS certificates. Because of the significant cost of existing revocation schemes in mobile environments, Verisign, Inc., a leading WTLS certificate provider, has chosen to issue short-lived certificates and reissue them within short intervals (say one day). In this way, the servers update their certificates every so often, but the mobile clients need not download anything for revocation control.

Certificate Distribution

The problem of certificate distribution is mostly addressed by the applications that use the certificates. In most cases, applications exchange necessary certificates at the beginning of the interaction or when needed; they do not rely on some other mechanism for the procurement of certificates. Some of these applications are discussed in the next section.

When the X.509 certificates were first proposed, the main idea was to make use of X.500 distributed directories for certificate distribution. The CAs would serve as directory servers, or they would publish the certificates that they issued to other directory servers. The verifier would query the directory to get the certificates on a certificate path to verify the public key of a specific end user. Although it is not exactly the same as the X.500 directories, DNSSEC (domain name system security extensions; Eastlake, 1999) also assumes a distributed approach. It may be too early to comment on the DNSSEC approach, but it is fairly clear that the X.500 directory approach is unlikely ever to come to fruition, as discussed by Ellison (n.d.). The main reason Ellison put forward is that collections of directory entries (such as employee lists, customer lists, contact lists, etc.) are considered valuable or even confidential by their owners and are not likely to be released to the world.

As described, PGP makes use of centralized databases (public key servers) for the distribution of keys and certificates. There are numerous PGP key servers all over the world. They are synchronized and keep the same information. Thus, it is sufficient to communicate with one of them for public key transfers. To see an example key server, readers may refer to http://www.keyserver.net, which currently holds more than 1.6 million PGP public keys. The main disadvantage of these key servers is that they keep the keys and certificates without any control and verification of authenticity; users should therefore verify the authenticity of these public keys on their own. As an alternative, PGP Corp. has recently announced a verified key service, called PGP Global Directory (PGP Corp., n.d.). The PGP Global Directory is a verified directory of PGP keys. Unlike previous servers that stored PGP keys indiscriminately, the PGP Global Directory allows users to upload and manage their keys in a verified manner. When uploading a key or performing other key management features, PGP Global Directory verifies a key by requiring a response to a verification e-mail sent to each e-mail address specified on the key. Because this is not a 100% secure authentication mechanism, there is always a risk that the verified key in the PGP Global Directory is not actually owned by the person who appears to own it. Thus, the PGP Global Directory should not be considered as a replacement for the PGP web of trust, but as an additional mechanism.

Peer-to-peer certificate transfer is another mechanism that should not be underestimated. Here the basic idea is the transfer of the certificate from one peer to another via an online/offline link such as an e-mail attachment or on a CD.

Certificates as Electronic IDs

One of the marketing strategies of certificates is to promote them as electronic versions of IDs. This analogy is intuitively appealing. There are, indeed, similarities between IDs and certificates: both are endorsed by authorities, both bear the name of the owner, both are small. However, a detailed analysis of certificates shows that there is a difference between certificates and IDs in terms of the participation of the holder in subsequent authentication and authorization transactions. The verification of an ID via the picture on it and the recognition of the authority's endorsement are sufficient for the owner to obtain privileges; the person holding the ID need not do anything extra. However, the verification of a certificate via the verification of the CA signature on it is not sufficient to make sure that the owner is really the person he or she claims to be. Certificate verification only helps the verifier confirm the public key of the certificate holder. The certificate holder should also show that he or she knows the private key corresponding to the public key in the certificate to prove his or her identity. This requires an extra protocol run embedded in applications, and the certificate holder should actively participate in this protocol.

Privacy Concerns

Identity certificates are not designed to provide privacy-enhanced transactions. An identity certificate contains personal information, such as name, addresses, date of birth, affiliation, and so forth, about its owner. Because certificates are stored in public registers, as explained previously, and certificates are in cleartext, the personal information stored in them may be obtained by anyone. This encourages identity theft. Moreover, whenever an identity certificate is used in an application, the privacy of the certificate owner can no longer be maintained. Most people would object to having to identify themselves in every transaction and interaction they undertake. Assuming that these applications use OCSP to check certificate validity, the activities of the certificate owner can be tracked using central OCSP logs. In this way, all of an individual's actions can be linked and traced automatically and instantaneously by various parties.

This discussion points to a significant privacy problem in using certificates. Attribute certificates may be considered as a primitive step to achieving privacy because they may not include the owner's identity. However, because these certificates are not issued in anonymously (at least the AA knows to whom it issued the certificate), we cannot say that attribute certificates address all of the concerns of privacy advocates.

In this regard, Stefan Brands' contributions to anonymity and privacy-enhancing techniques in certificates are worth mentioning. Brands (2000, 2002) proposed a different conception and implementation of digital certificates, called *digital credentials*, such that privacy is protected and anonymity is provided without sacrificing security. The validity of digital credentials and their contents can be checked, but the identity of the holder cannot be extracted, and different actions by the same person cannot be linked. Holders of digital credentials have control over the information to be disclosed to other parties.

Brands' book (2000) is a very good source of information on privacy-related discussions regarding certificates and other privacy-enhancing techniques.

PKIX and X.509

PKIX (X.509-based PKI) is a working group of the IETF established in 1995 (Public-Key Infrastructure, X.509, PKIX, n.d.). The initial role of this working group was to develop Internet standards needed to support an X.509-based PKI. The scope of PKIX has since expanded, and some new protocols have been developed that are related to the use of X.509-based PKIs on the Internet.

Although it seems that PKIX is only a user of X.509, the progress of X.509 has been extensively influenced by the PKIX working group because the X.509 standard was not sufficient to address the PKI issues of the Internet.

The PKIX working group has published several RFCs. A full list of these RFCs can be obtained at the charter Web site (Public-Key Infrastructure, X.509, PKIX, n.d.). Some of them that are directly related to certificate structure and processing are listed here:

- Algorithms and Identifiers for the Internet X.509 Public Key Infrastructure Certificate and CRI Profile (RFC 3279).
- An Internet Attribute Certificate Profile for Authorization (RFC 3281).
- Internet X.509 Certificate Request Message Format (RFC 2511).
- Internet X.509 Public Key Infrastructure Certificate and CRL Profile (RFC 3280).
- Internet X.509 Public Key Infrastructure Certificate Management Protocols (RFC 2510).
- Internet X.509 Public Key Infrastructure Certificate Policy and Certification Practices Framework (RFC 3647).
- Internet X.509 Public Key Infrastructure Data Validation and Certification Server Protocols (RFC 3029).
- Internet X.509 Public Key Infrastructure Proxy Certificate Profile (RFC 3820).
- Internet X.509 Public Key Infrastructure: Qualified Certificates Profile (RFC 3739).

APPLICATION PROTOCOLS BASED ON X.509 CERTIFICATES

The development of the PKIX standards and X.509 certificates encouraged several TCP/IP-based applications to provide security mechanisms featuring certificates. In this section, some of these applications are overviewed with some detail on how they utilize certificates.

PEM (privacy-enhanced mail) was one of the first protocols to utilize X.509. PEM provides encryption and authentication features to e-mails utilizing a variety of cryptographic primitives. RFCs 1421–1424 define PEM; RFC 1422 explains the certificate-based key management employed in PEM.

Because PEM was defined during the period when X.509v1 was the only certificate structure available, it was based on X.509v1. Consequently, it did not support any custom-defined policies and end-user-centric trust management. The PKI model of PEM was a strictly hierarchical one. The verifiers could not practice their own trust policies; thus, they had to blindly trust all authorities in this hierarchy in order to participate in the system. These strict regulations discouraged people from using PEM. Thus, PEM never reached a significant population. This experience showed that the certificate structure should be flexible to be able to implement different policies and user-centric trust management. This conclusion made the X.509 designers think about a flexible certificate structure that eventually yielded X.509v3.

SSL (secure sockets layer) is the most widely used certificate-based TCP/IP security mechanism. The aim is to create an upper-TCP security sublayer that can be used for several client–server applications such as HTTP (hypertext transfer protocol), FTP (file transfer protocol), POP3 (post office protocol version 3), SMTP (simple mail transfer protocol), IMAP (Internet mail access protocol), and so forth. SSL works in a session manner. Before the data connection, the end parties create a session key and forthcoming traffic is authenticated and encrypted using this session key. Session key generation requires some public key operations. Necessary public keys are distributed via X.509 certificates at the beginning of the protocol.

There is no enforced PKI model for SSL. Generally each CA generates a local hierarchy for the certificates issued by itself. Thus, there is no global PKI for SSL. Necessary root CA certificates are predistributed within client software such as MS Windows and Netscape.

The reason behind the success of SSL is mainly due to its flexibility in PKI topology and support given by key players in the industry. This industry support has come not only with root CA certificate predistributions, but also with integration of the protocol in key products such as operating systems, browsers, and other client applications. Thus, clients do not need to make any configurations to use SSL. Moreover, SSL is a protocol such that all necessary steps that are taken are transparent to the client. This is another reason behind the success of SSL.

S/MIME (secure/multipart Internet mail extensions) is the security enhancement on top of MIME, the Internet e-mail format standard. MIME describes content types for various types of attachments to e-mail messages. S/MIME defines secure content types for encrypted and signed e-mail messages that are to be sent peer to peer. The security functionality provided by S/MIME is not so different from its predecessor, PEM. The difference is in certificate and key management features: S/MIME uses X.509v3 certificates; a particular PKI is not assumed as in SSL; necessary root-CA certificates come with the e-mail client programs.

Although S/MIME follows the successful certificate and key management strategy of SSL, it has not achieved a significant user population. The main reason for this is that in e-mail applications, both end points are clients and they need to use certificates. Individuals generally refrain from spending time, money, and effort on such add-on utilities. This is exactly what has happened in the case of S/MIME, and the use of S/MIME has not been very significant. In contrast, the use of SSL is mostly in the form of server authentication where only the server uses certificate; clients rarely use certificates to authenticate themselves. It is quite reasonable for an organization to spend time, money, and effort to obtain certificates to secure its servers.

To improve the use of this important technology, e-mail vendors need to find a mechanism to make the system transparent to the clients so that they do not need certificates. One alternative, as in the DomainKeys proposal by Yahoo (Delany, n.d.), could be using S/MIME not end to end but between e-mail gateways (sender and receiver SMTP servers), and providing another solution (e.g., using SSL over POP3 or IMAP) in the local area. In this way, only e-mail gateways need to use certificates; clients do not. One disadvantage of this mechanism, however, is that end-to-end security is not provided.

Another e-mail security solution, which uses certificates among the servers but not for the clients, is proposed by Levi and Ozcan (2004). In this system, called PractiSES (practical and secure e-mail system), clients register to their domain servers free of cost. Once registered, they can send and accept signed/encrypted e-mails without dealing with the complexity of public key transfers. Domain servers arrange the necessary public key transfers in a collaborative way without putting an extra burden on the client side. Unlike DomainKeys, PractiSES provides end-to-end security.

SSH (secure shell) can also be considered as a secure version of telnet, that is, secure remote terminal application. In SSH, public key agreement techniques are utilized before the username/password transfer. When a common key is established, encryption is performed to ensure the confidentiality of the transferred data. In SSH, certificates may be used to facilitate public key transfers between the client and the server. When client certificates are used, authentication of the client can be performed using public key techniques rather than the classical username/password mechanism. In contrast, server certificates are used to initiate the initial key agreement and to establish server authentication to the client.

Although it may seem that at least a server certificate is necessary for an authenticated key agreement between the client and the server, this is not essential. SSH allows the transfer of the server public key to the client in cleartext form. The client checks the fingerprint of the key and accepts this public key as valid for all subsequent communications. To make sure that the key is correct, the client should double-check its fingerprint against a known source. This may not be feasible in a large distributed client–server system, but in the case of SSH this check may be performed because the number of servers is manageable.

IPSec (IP security) is the IP (Internet protocol) layer security architecture that has been standardized by an IETF working group (IP Security Protocol Charter, n.d.). IPSec architecture contains a set of concepts and protocols for authenticity, integrity, confidentiality, and key exchange/management at the IP layer. The IKE (Internet key exchange) protocol (Harkins & Carrel, 1998) of IPSec provides authenticated key exchange using a specific profile of X.509 certificates.

Use of Certificates in the Financial Services Industry

Certificates are being used by several applications operated by the financial services industry. Nowadays, e-banking applications targeted at individual customers are mostly SSL/TLS-based because such an approach requires minimal maintenance at the client end and, thus, makes the system scalable. However, financial institutions are keen to develop and/or obtain application-specific solutions for their corporate customers. Such applications use certificate-based solutions for key exchange and management.

With regard to e-payment, SET (SET Secure Electronic Transaction LLC; n.d.) defines protocols for certificate issuance and processing in the context of credit card payments via the Internet.

In 1998, NACHA (National Automated Clearing House Association) sponsored a successful pilot for CA interoperability for the Web shopping experience. Several banks and CAs participated in this pilot. Lessons learned from this pilot activity were published by NACHA (Prince & Foster, 1999).

The ANSI (American National Standards Institute) committee X9F (Accredited Standards Committee X9, n.d.) and ISO (International Organization for Standardization) Technical Committee 68 (TC68; ISO/TC68 Financial Services, n.d.) have developed some standards to profile X.509 certificates and CRL structures to provide for the particular needs of the financial services industry.

KEY PLAYERS IN THE INDUSTRY AND THEIR CERTIFICATION PRACTICES

The CAs that issue X.509v3 certificates for different applications follow a set of rules in their certification practices. These CAs, such as Verisign, Entrust, Baltimore, Globalsign, and so forth, follow slightly different approaches; however, the main idea is generally the same. The certification practice of each CA is declared on its Web site.

Certificate Classes

Certification practices propose different levels of identity verification in different classes of certificates. In this section, a general picture of these classes is given.

Class 1 certificates: The name of the subject entity is not checked. Only an e-mail address control is performed by sending an authentication string to the mailbox address that the subject entity provides in the certificate application. To complete the certificate issuance process, the subject entity should use this authentication string. That naively proves the ability of the subject entity's access to a mailbox. That mailbox address appears in the certificate. Some CAs also include the name of the subject entity in the certificate, specifying that the name is not validated. However, the appropriate action would be not to include a name in class 1 certificates, as some other CAs do. Class 1 certificate issuance is an online process. Class 1 certificates are mostly used for S/MIME.

Class 2 certificates: Name and some other information (such as address) of the subject entity are checked against a third-party database. Mailbox access control as in the class 1 certificates is also processed. The whole process is online.

Class 3 certificates: In addition to the mailbox access control, the subject entity should personally present an identity document to a registration authority. The level of assurance in identification is the highest of all the classes, but the process is offline and it may take several days to obtain the certificate. SSL server certificates are issued in this class. CAs also perform DNS control to make sure that the certified URL really belongs to the organization that claims to have it.

As can be seen, class 1 certificates provide the lowest degree of identity assurance but are the easiest to issue, whereas class 3 certificates provide the highest degree of identity assurance but are the most difficult to issue. Having said this, it should be mentioned that the certificate issuance process is not always fail-proof even for class 3 certificates because of the human factor involved in the certificate issuance process. An example of such an incident was reported by CERT® (Computer Emergency Response Team; CERT® Advisory CA-2001-04, 2001). The overview part of this report is quoted below with no comments.

> On January 29 and 30, 2001, VeriSign, Inc. issued two certificates to an individual fraudulently claiming to be an employee of Microsoft Corporation. Any code signed by these certificates will appear to be legitimately signed by Microsoft when, in fact, it is not. Although users who try to run code signed with these certificates will generally be presented with a warning dialog, there will not be any obvious reason to believe that the certificate is not authentic.

PKCS Standards Related to Certificates

The PKCS standards are specifications produced by RSA Laboratories in cooperation with secure systems developers worldwide for the purpose of accelerating the deployment of public key cryptography. Some of those standards, namely PKCS #6 (extended certificate syntax standard), PKCS #10 (certification request syntax standard), and PKCS #15 (cryptographic token information format standard), are related to certificates. These PKCS standards, except PKCS #6, mostly deal with implementation issues rather than defining new certificate types.

PKCS #6 standard, which was issued in 1993, describes the syntax for extended certificates. An extended certificate consists of an X.509v1 public key certificate and a set of attributes, collectively signed by the issuer of the X.509v1 public key certificate. These additional attributes were needed at that time because the X.509v1 certificate structure was rather limited. With the addition of extensions to X.509v3 certificates, PKCS #6 became redundant and RSA Laboratories started to withdraw their support for PKCS #6.

PKCS #10 is an important standard that describes syntax for certification requests. A certification request consists of a distinguished name, a public key, and optionally a set of attributes, collectively signed by the entity requesting certification. Certification requests are sent to a certification authority, which transforms the request into an X.509 public key certificate.

PKCS #15 is the cryptographic token information format standard. This standard aims at using cryptographic tokens as identification devices. To do so it defines different structures for the storage of different types of certificates, such as X.509, PGP, and WTLS certificates, in tokens.

SUMMARY AND CONCLUSION

This chapter has discussed different types of certificates together with some issues and standards associated with them. There is an important trend of certificate use in security applications. Classical client–server or peer-to-peer applications have been utilizing certificates for about a decade. Apart from these conventional applications, certificates have started to be included in smart cards as well. In this way, not only electronic and mobile commerce but also conventional card-based payment and identification schemes would utilize certificates. This wide range of applications makes certificates an important market where several companies are currently competing. These companies are mostly CA companies that issue certificates for end users and organizations.

Expiration of the RSA patent has created an opportunity for generating key pairs without paying royalties. However, CA companies have not reflected these savings in the cost of certificates. To improve the attractiveness of certificate-based solutions at the client end, CA companies need to revise their revenue models to attract more clients. Moreover, certificate-based solutions should be designed such that they provide flexibility and transparency for the clients.

GLOSSARY

Attribute Authority An authority that issues attribute certificates. In this way, the authority assigns privileges to certificate holders.

Attribute Certificates A data structure signed by an attribute authority for the binding of a privilege to an entity.

Certificate (or Digital Certificate) A data structure endorsed by an authority that binds an entity to an identity, attribute, characteristic, or privilege.

Certificate Path An ordered sequence of certificates, which is processed to obtain the public key of the last object on the path.

Certification Practice Statement (CPS) A document that describes (in detail) how a CA issues certificates and the policies observed by that CA.

Certificate Revocation List (CRL) A signed list indicating a set of certificates that are no longer considered valid by the certificate issuer.

Certificate Verification Verification of the signature on the certificate. In this way, the binding endorsed by the authority is assumed to be legitimate.

Certification Authority (CA) A well-known and trusted entity that issues public key certificates.

Delta CRL A partial certificate revocation list (CRL) that only contains entries for certificates that have had their revocation status changed since the issuance of the base CRL.

Digital Signature Digital information obtained by the application of a private key on a message.

Privilege Management Infrastructure (PMI) The infrastructure that is able to support the management of privileges in support of a comprehensive authorization service and in relationship with a public key infrastructure.

Public Key (Identity) Certificate A data structure signed by a certification authority for the binding of a public key to an entity whose identity is provided.

Public Key Infrastructure (PKI) The infrastructure for the management of public keys in support of authentication, encryption, integrity, or nonrepudiation services.

Root CA A top-level certification authority in hierarchical PKI.

S-Expression The data format chosen for SPKI/SDSI. This is a LISP-like parenthesized expression.

Self-Signed Certificate A certificate where the issuer and the subject are the same CA. Generally root CA certificates are of this type.

Subject The entity for which the certificate has been issued.

Trust Anchor An authority that is deemed trustworthy by a user.

CROSS REFERENCES

See *Digital Signatures and Electronic Signatures; IPsec: IKE (Internet Key Exchange); PGP (Pretty Good Privacy); PKCS (Public-Key Cryptography Standards); PKI (Public Key Infrastructure); Public Key Algorithms; S/MIME (Secure MIME); Public Key Standards: Secure Shell (SSH); Secure Sockets Layer (SSL); Security and the Wireless Application Protocol (WAP).*

REFERENCES

Accredited Standards Committee X9. (n.d.). *Financial industry standards*. Retrieved January 9, 2005, from http://www.x9.org/

Adams, C., & Lloyd, D. (1999). *Understanding public key infrastructures*. Indianapolis, IN: New Riders.

Brands, S. (2002). *A technical overview of digital credentials*. Retrieved December 16, 2004, from http://www.credentica.com/technology/overview.pdf

Brands, S. A. (2000). *Rethinking public key infrastructures and digital certificates: Building in privacy*. Cambridge, MA: MIT Press.

CERT. (2001). *Unauthentic "Microsoft Corporation" certificates* (Advisory CA-2001-04). Retrieved April 12, 2001, from http://www.cert.org/advisories/CA-2001-04.html

Delany, M. (n.d.). *Domain-based email authentication using public-keys advertised in the DNS (DomainKeys)* (Internet Draft). Retrieved December 27, 2004, from http://antispam.yahoo.com/domainkeys/draft-delany-domainkeys-base-01.txt

Diffie, W., & Hellman, M. E. (1976, November). New directions in cryptography. *IEEE Transactions on Information Theory*, *IT-22*(6), 644–654.

Eastlake, D. (1999). *Domain name system security extensions* (RFC 2535). Retrieved February 26, 2003, from http://www.ietf.org/rfc/rfc2535.txt

Ellison, C. (1999a, April). The nature of a usable PKI. *Computer Networks, 31*(9), 823–830.

Ellison, C. (1999b, September). *SPKI requirements* (RFC 2692). Retrieved December 23, 2004, from http://www.ietf.org/rfc/rfc2692.txt

Ellison, C. (n.d.). *SPKI/SDSI certificate documentation*. Retrieved December 23, 2004, from http://world.std.com/~cme/html/spki.html

Ellison, C., Frantz, B., Lampson, B., Rivest, R., Thomas, B., & Ylonen, T. (1999). *SPKI certificate theory* (RFC 2693). Retrieved December 23, 2004, from http://www.ietf.org/rfc/rfc2693.txt

Harkins, D., & Carrel, D. (1998). *The Internet key exchange (IKE)* (RFC 2409). Retrieved May 29, 1999 from http://www.ietf.org/rfc/rfc2409.txt

IP security protocol (IPsec) charter. (n.d.). Retrieved January 9, 2005, from http://www.ietf.org/html.charters/ipsec-charter.html

ISO/TC68 Financial Services. (n.d.). Retrieved January 9, 2005, from http://www.tc68.org/

ITU-T. (1988). *Information technology—Open systems interconnection—The directory: Authentication framework* (1st ed.). Recommendation X.509, ISO/IEC 9594-8. Geneva, Switzerland: Author.

ITU-T. (1993). *Information technology—Open systems interconnection—The directory: Authentication framework* (2nd ed.). Recommendation X.509, ISO/IEC 9594-8. Geneva, Switzerland: Author.

ITU-T. (1997). *Information technology—Open systems interconnection—The directory: Authentication framework* (3rd ed.). Recommendation X.509, ISO/IEC 9594-8. Geneva, Switzerland: Author.

ITU-T. (2000). *Information technology—Open systems interconnection—The directory: Public-key and attribute certificate frameworks* (4th ed.). Recommendation X.509, ISO/IEC 9594-8. Geneva, Switzerland: Author.

Kocher, P. (1998, February). On certificate revocation and validation. In *Proceedings of Financial Cryptography 98* (LNCS 1465; pp. 172–177). Berlin, Germany: Springer-Verlag.

Kohnfelder, L. M. (1978). *Towards a practical public-key cryptosystem*. Unpublished bachelor's thesis, Massachusetts Institute of Technology.

Levi, A., & Ozcan, M. (2004). Practical and secure e-mail system (PractiSES). *In Advances in Information Systems: ADVIS 2004—Third Biennial International Conference on Advances in Information Systems* (LNCS 3261; pp. 410–419). Berlin, Germany: Springer-Verlag.

Menezes, A. (1993). *Elliptic curve public key cryptosystems*. Norwell, MA: Kluwer Academic.

Myers, M., Ankney, R., Malpani, A., Galperin, S., & Adams, C. (1999). *X.509 Internet public key infrastructure on-line certificate status protocol—OCSP* (RFC 2560). Retrieved January 21, 2000, from http://www.ietf.org/rfc/rfc2560.txt

PGP Corp. (n.d.). *PGP global directory—Key verification policy*. Retrieved April 14, 2005, from https://keyserver-beta.pgp.com/vkd/VKDVerificationPGPCom.html

Popek, G., & Kline, C. (1979). Encryption and secure computer networks. *ACM Computing Surveys, 11*(4), 331–356.

Prince, N., & Foster, J. (1999). *Certification authority interoperability: From concept to reality*. Herndon, VA: NACHA.

Public-key infrastructure (X.509) (PKIX). (n.d.). Retrieved January 9, 2005, from http://www.ietf.org/html.charters/pkix-charter.html

Rivest, R., & Lampson, B. (1996). *SDSI—A simple distributed security infrastructure*. Retrieved December 23, 2004, from http://theory.lcs.mit.edu/~cis/sdsi.html

SET Secure Electronic Transaction LLC. (n.d.). Retrieved April 13, 2005, from http://web.archive.org/web/20020930024644/http://www.setco.org/

Simple public key infrastructure (SPKI) charter. (n.d.). Retrieved December 23, 2004, from http://www.ietf.org/html.charters/spki-charter.html

WAP Forum. (2001a, April 6). *Wireless transport layer security specification*. WAP-261-WTLS-20010406-a. Retrieved February 25, 2002, from http://www.wapforum.com

WAP Forum. (2001b, July 12). *Wireless application protocol architecture specification*. WAP-210-WAPArch-200100712-a. Retrieved April 4, 2002, from http://www.wapforum.com

Zimmermann, P. (1994). *PGP user's guide, Vol. 1: Essential topics; Vol. 2: Special topics*. Retrieved January 9, 2005, from http://www.pgpi.org/doc/guide/2.6.3i/en/

Internet E-Mail Architecture

Robert Gezelter, *Software Consultant*

INTRODUCTION

Electronic mail was the first mass application, now called a "killer app,"of the networked world. It dominated Internet traffic until the explosion of activity subsequent to the advent of the World Wide Web (WWW; a more complete description of the WWW is provided elsewhere in this *Handbook*). Many people incorrectly associate electronic mail with the Internet. Electronic mail predates the Internet, and even today there are electronic mail systems that use technologies other than those used on the Internet.

Today's electronic mail landscape is an ecosystem with many inhabitants.

The history of electronic mail is a complex tapestry of give and take among the research, business, academic, and other communities. It is a story of experiments in message content, transport, addressing, composition, and reception.

The original electronic mail concept was modest, providing for transmission of simple text messages. Today, electronic mail is used as a vehicle for all forms of media, from the original text messages envisioned on the first day to audio, video, and many forms of composite messages. It has, in effect if not in fact, become a lingua franca,the common language for the offline transmission of all forms of content across the global Internet.

STRUCTURE

Any electronic messaging system consists of several interrelated elements: addressing, transport, delivery, storage, message content, and message display.

Different electronic mail systems have different perspectives on these elements. In some architectures, which are specifications of message interchange rather than complete designs, there may be multiple, parallel implementations of functionality. The Internet Simple Mail Transfer Protocol architecture, known generally by its acronym, SMTP, is one such standard. Presently defined by the Internet Engineering Task Force's RFCs 2821 (Klensin, 2001) and 2822 (Resnick, 2001), SMTP speaks to the issues involving message addressing and transport, as well as baseline standards for message representation. However, SMTP does not cover the details of message delivery or storage and provides only the barest definition of message content beyond the mechanism for identifying the end of a message.

The delivery mechanism, the means by which a message is actually placed in an individual mailbox associated with a particular user, is a core component of any messaging system. Delivery is a completely separate matter from issues involved in the transport, addressing, or content of the messages.

TECHNOLOGY OF SYNTHESIS

The story of electronic mail does not begin with the circulation of RFC 772 (Sluizer & Postel, 1980), an antecedent to RFC 2821 and 2822, nor does it begin with the seminal decision formulating the *<user>*@*<system>* syntax, nor does it begin with the first intracomputer message sent between users, although each of these is certainly a familiar and important milepost on the evolutionary pathway of electronic mail.

The true story is a complex one, with interwoven contributions from many different sources, both within the computing community and from its predecessors, the civilian and military communications communities. In some cases, the chain of descent is clear. In other cases, the apparent connection is a case of convergent evolution; two evolutionary paths that independently produced similar designs. The products of these divergent experiences and communities have resulted in a message transport system that has transformed the world.

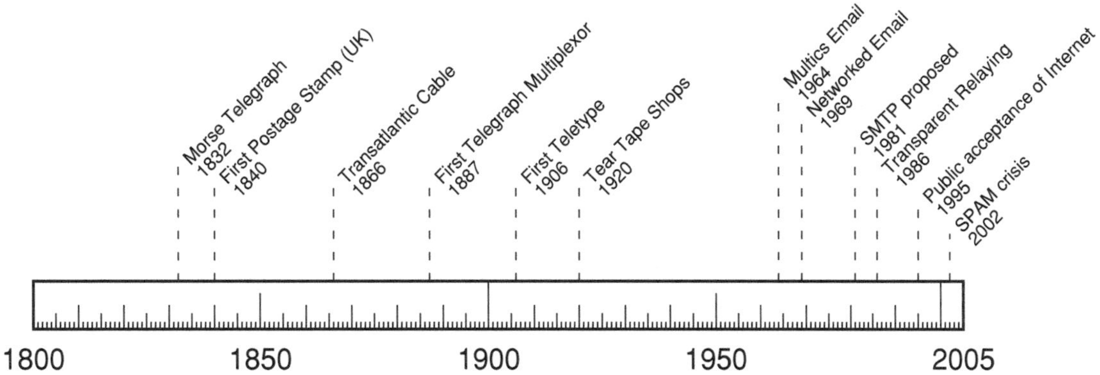

Figure 1: Messaging evolution, 1800–2005.

HISTORY

The original freestanding Internet electronic mail standard, RFC 772, authored by Suzanne Sluizer and Jon Postel, was published in September 1980. Although RFC 772 is an important milepost in the evolution of electronic mail, it did not spring forth fully formed from the void. It had, as its antecedents, a wealth of experience gained over the millennia in the management of message transmission, a body of knowledge that has been accumulating exponentially as communication has increased in volume and rate. See Figure 1 for a time line.

Pre-Internet

Reliable communication over distances has been a challenge since the beginning of time. Writing itself is a mechanism to allow knowledge to transcend distance and time by allowing it to be replayed at a later time without relying on an individual's memory.

The issues and approaches of Internet electronic mail have their most immediate roots in the postal and telegraphic systems of the past several centuries, particularly the 19th and 20th centuries.

Telegraphy

Samuel Morse invented the serial telegraph in 1832. Portending the data communications boom of the 1960s and 1970s, the United States was soon crisscrossed with telegraph wires, each coming and going to distinct points. Armies of telegraph operators worked these circuits, sending messages that quickly became the lifeblood of government and the financial, transportation, trading, and newspaper industries.

In a relatively short time, electronic communications went from spanning a single continent to connecting continents. The first commercially viable transoceanic telegraph cable across the Atlantic Ocean, from England to Newfoundland, became operational in 1866. It increased the usefulness of telegraphic communications. The time required for intercontinental communications changed from weeks or months to less than a day. Within less than half a century, the telegraphic network spanned the globe.

The second half of the 19th century also saw numerous inventions commercialized for the purpose of increasing the efficiency of telegraphy. Granville Woods invented the first multiplexers and repeaters in 1887. The invention of the Teletype by Charles Krum in 1906 further accelerated the volume and decreased the cost of messages.

The ever-increasing web of telegraph wires converging in important business centers led to what we would now refer to as message switching, albeit with humans doing most of the processing. The invention of the Teletype, and more important, the advent of punched paper tape, allowed the replacement of human telegraphers at what would now be called "intermediate nodes." Named after their primary activity, "tear-tape shops" functioned as message switches, with operators removing paper tape from output punches and readying it for reading on the complementary readers that represented the next leg of the journey to the tape's ultimate destination.

Although not generally understood as such, these semi-automated networks gave rise to what is identifiable as a progenitor of packet switching. The international tariffs governing these networks had limits on long messages. Long messages were broken into multiple parts, sent independently, and reassembled at the receiver. Perhaps the most famous such message is the belatedly delivered Japanese diplomatic message of December 7, 1941, that terminated negotiations with the United States and in effect declared war on the United States.

Postal Letter Routing Systems

Throughout the developed world, postal systems are taken for granted. The daily mail is dispatched and delivered. Letters traveling across the continent take a matter of days; small letters dispatched internationally are often at their destinations in less than a week. It seems so effortless that the postal system is seen as background. Reliable, relatively fast, postal service on a large scale is a fairly recent phenomenon.

The analogy between postal and electronic mail is deeper than just the name. Letters are deposited in a collection box, and by means generally not considered, arrive at their destination. The details of the means by which a letter dropped in the corner collection box travels to its destination across town, or across the country, is complex yet almost entirely imperceptible to most people. The details of the mechanism only become visible when problems occur.

Military Communications Systems

No history of electronic messaging can be complete without a discussion of military communications systems, particularly those of World War II and those subsequently developed for the U. S. military.

By the end of World War II in 1945, the military communications systems of the Allies were handling many thousands of messages per day.

Structured military communications were constructed on the basis of telegraphy, whether wired or wireless. In turn, telegraphic practices were no more than a codification of standard office practices, specifically those for memoranda. The procedures used in radio (wireless) telegraphy were adapted from those used in conventional telegraphy, with an increased emphasis on ensuring the identification of the recipient station and the ultimate destination of the message.

Memoranda have addressees, originators, and subjects, as well as bodies and attachments. They also have multiple classes of recipients, including those identified as receiving a copy (carbon copy—"cc:") and those who were sent, but not publicly acknowledged as having been sent, a copy (blind carbon copy–"bcc:"). Military communications systems codified these patterns of civilian business practice and added some elements of their own.

The military is a bastion of the practice of assigning multiple addresses to individuals. Messages may be addressed to individuals or to one of the individual's job titles or offices. For example, an officer will get some messages personally addressed to him as an individual and other messages addressed to him in each of his organizational roles. This is a very apt parallel for the business world, where an individual may have both a personal mail address, an individual mail address within the firm, a mail address associated with their place in the organizational chart (Vice President—Finance), and a mail address associated with each of their other responsibilities.

Corporate electronic mail systems involve many of the same issues as their military cousins. The best practices for commercial messaging systems are often the same as their military counterparts.

User Agents, Protocols, Implementations, and Architectures

When examining the history and evolution of electronic mail, it is also important to be conscious of four different components, or axes of variability. (See Figure 2)

Understanding electronic mail is enhanced by considering the different axes of variability. Some issues are clearly implementation decisions affecting a particular User Agent rather than limitations inherent in the protocol. Other issues are limits in the overall design and conception of the underlying protocols and affect every implementation that employs the protocol.

User Agent

A user's primary interface to the electronic mail system is referred to as a *User Agent*, to borrow the term used by the Internet RFCs. As such, they are the component of the electronic mail system most familiar to users. User Agents have a variety of implementation limitations, which are

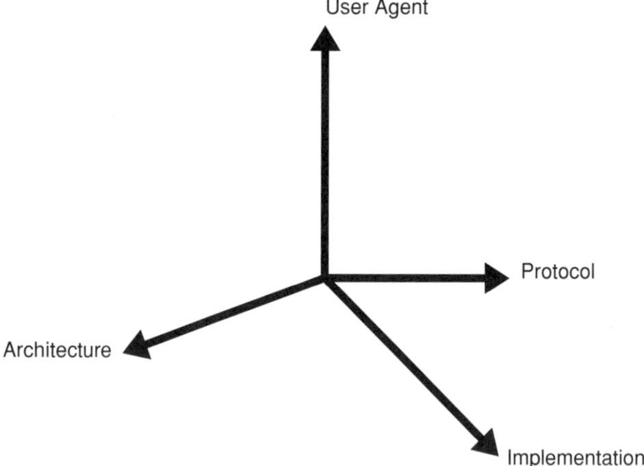

Figure 2: Axes of variability in electronic mail systems design.

the results of their specific implementation, not the requirements of the underlying protocols.

In the Internet-space, the necessary client/server aspects of Mail User Agents have resulted in the creation of dedicated purpose protocols such as POP3 (RFC 1939, Myers & Rose, 1996) and IMAP4 (RFC 1730, Crispin, 1994) for the connections between mail hosts and user clients.

Mail User Agents do not generally implement the core mail transport protocols. For the most part, they use dedicated protocols to access a user's message store on a mail host.

Protocol

An electronic mail protocol must address the fundamental issues of message content and addressing. There are many decisions possible. Some decisions are almost decorative, with many possibilities being different yet functionally equivalent. Other decisions impose presumptions about the content of electronic messages or the organizational philosophy of the senders and recipients.

In some cases, a multitude of protocols may be used when dealing with a particular message in its journey from sender to recipient. As an example, the simplest messages transmitted via the Internet make use of RFC 2821, a descendant of RFC 772, which governs the SMTP protocol itself, and RFC 2822, which governs the overall content and addressing. Messages involving more complex structures, such as attachments, will involve processing governed by additional specifications, such as the Multipurpose Internet Mail Extensions, known by its acronym, MIME (RFCs 2045–2049), which operate within the overall message structure specified by RFC 2822. Depending upon the nature of the specifications, the specifications may be only relevant to the source and destination mail user agents, or they may be relevant to intermediate nodes responsible for the transmission of the message. Another specification involved in en route processing of a message might be the CCITT's (now ITU–T's) X.400.

The systems providing interconnections and translations between one set of protocols and another are referred to as *gateways*. A message may go through any number of gateways during its journey from sender to recipient. Gateways may provide bridges between different electronic mail protocols or they may move electronic mail messages to/from other messaging systems, such as the Short Message Service, known by its acronym SMS, which is used to transmit text messages between mobile telephones.

Implementations

It is important to understand that the differences and restrictions imposed by particular implementations are separate from those that are inherently a fundamental part of the protocol itself. As an example, there have been implementations of SMTP that run over network protocols other than TCP/IP (Transmission Control Protocol/Internet Protocol). Such implementations may have minor restrictions beyond those relevant on a TCP/IP network layer.

Architectures

Some mail architectures are designed around the concept of a host or server central to the entire implementation that uses a common message store. In such architectures, electronic mail messages are comingled in a central database. Such a system has manageability advantages when considering issues such as electronic mail preservation and monitoring. The disadvantage of such a centralized system and unified message store is that a technical or operational problem affecting the database shuts down electronic messaging for everyone connected to that system.

At the other extreme, all user messages may be stored on individual user machines (or individual user accounts on intermediate-size systems). This approach yields the highest degree of operational independence, yet it also means that each individual electronic mail archive must be included within the backup regime. Increasingly, many industries (e.g., financial services in the United States) are subject to regulatory requirements to document the reception and transmission of electronic mail. Individual message stores in this context may pose compliance complications.

Another approach is for user messages to be stored on and forwarded through some smaller number of intermediate-sized systems, for example on a departmental or divisional basis. This forced routing provides an opportunity for compliance recording and monitoring, as well as the option to implement backup and retention policies.

Intrasystem Mail

Electronic mail does not become a recognizable computer application until the advent of time-sharing systems in the early 1960s. The first recorded civilian, intrasystem electronic mail was implemented by the CTSS team at MIT in 1964.

Two system facilities are required for electronic mail:

- Individual user logins
  Individual users must possess some form of distinguishable login. These logins must represent an individual or group.
- Interactive access
  All electronic mail systems are based upon some model of interactive computing. Although some systems, particularly commercial and military communications systems, make extensive use of computer technology, the source and destination documents are emphatically physical documents. Although it is common to produce printed copies of electronic mail, electronic mail is electronic-copy centric, not hardcopy-centric.

Networked Electronic Mail

The predecessor of today's Internet started its life as ARPAnet, a research project in packet switching technology for the Advanced Research Projects Agency of the United States Department of Defense. The first network nodes became operational in 1969, connecting the University of California at Los Angeles and SRI. The honor of the first application using the ARPAnet was the virtual terminal facility, the descendents of which are now known by the name of the virtual terminal protocol, RFC 854, *TELNET* (Postel & Reynolds, 1983). See Figure 3 for a time line of the past 40 years.

The ARPAnet expanded over the years, adding connections to additional universities and defense contractors. In the late 1970s, the advent of other networks and intrauniversity networks gave rise to a requirement to internetwork electronic mail (and other communications). This need to gateway, route, and deliver electronic mail among dramatically disparate networks was one of the evolutionary stimuli behind the sequence of Mail Transfer Protocol RFCs beginning with RFC 772 by Postel, et al. and the Domain Name System by Paul Mockapetris (RFC 882/883, Mockapetris, 1983).

Although the ARPAnet is an important part of the networking story, it should be viewed in context. Until the mid 1990s, the TCP/IP protocol stack, and its associated upper level protocols, were seen in the majority of organizations as an interesting research experiment. The majority of commercial organizations' internal electronic mail systems used networking technologies developed by computer manufacturers, such as Digital Equipment Corporation's DECnet and IBM's SNA.

Digital Equipment Corporation's VAX/VMS had peer-to-peer network connections at initial release in 1978, and electronic mail at its first major revision in 1980.

IBM announced a VM/370-based office automation system, the Professional Office System (generally referred to by its acronym, PROFS) in 1981. Digital Equipment's All-in-1™ office system, based on the VAX/VMS operating system, was announced in 1982.

There was also an active effort in messaging standardization by traditional international standards bodies, notably the Paris-based CCITT (Comité Consultatif International de Télégraphique et Téléphonique), culminating in Recommendation X.400, originally released in 1984.

Non-Internet Electronic Mail Systems

While Internet-based technologies were evolving from simple file transfer schemes, a variety of commercial systems had independently evolved from the original

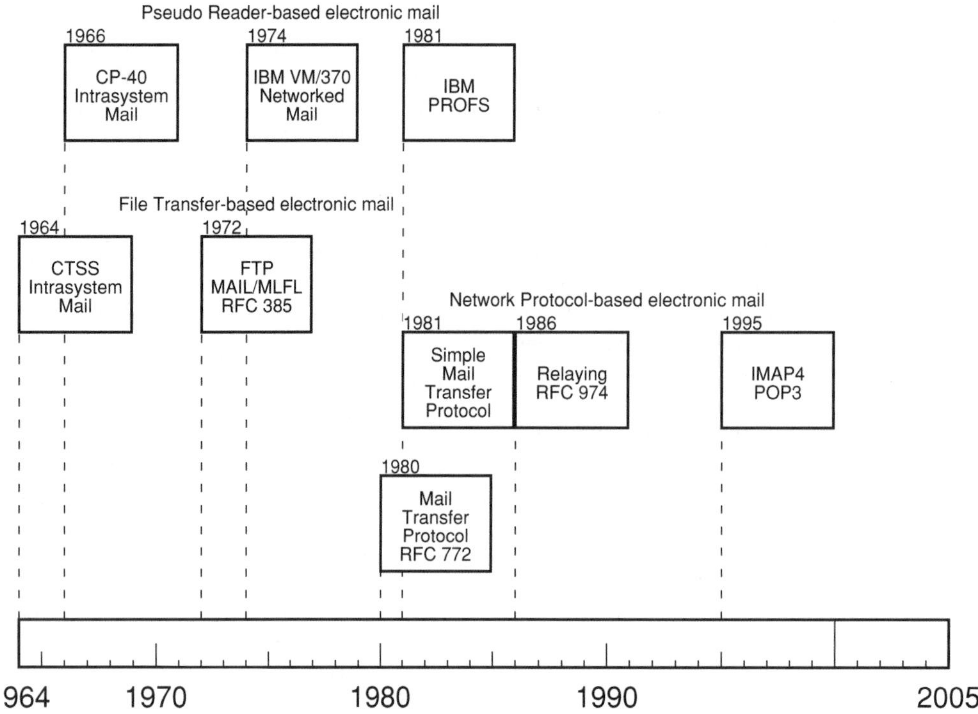

Figure 3: Four decades of evolution in electronic messaging.

electronic mail systems of CTSS and Multics. They developed many features, forms of which have been incorporated into other systems.

IBM's PROFS

IBM released PROFS in 1981 (Gardner, 1987). It was a commercialization of earlier internal work on mail systems, based upon VM/370 and its predecessors. PROFS is notable for its mail delivery mechanism, which differs from most other mail systems in that it does not require privileges or special mechanisms.

In the mid-1960s, IBM's Cambridge Scientific Center worked on a variety of projects related to time sharing that led to the development of VM/370. The antecedents of VM/370, CP-40 and its successor, CP-67, provided a virtual machine environment where each user was provided with the illusion of a dedicated mainframe. CMS (Conversational Monitor System) provided an interactive user environment that ran on a user's individual virtual machine. Shortly after its introduction, CP-67 was enhanced with a facility that allowed users to exchange files between different virtual machines. Shortly thereafter, this facility was used to implement an electronic mail system.

The VNET (VM Network) facility extended the existing file exchange facility to enable the store-and-forward exchange of files between different users on different physical machines (Hendricks & Hartmann, 1979). This delivery mechanism became generally available with the release of RSCS in 1974. RSCS provided VM/370 users with the ability to transfer files between different VM systems in a network. Files could be transferred between systems, even on routings that required storage of the file at the intermediate node. RSCS was thus a natural foundation for a store-and-forward electronic mail network. IBM, beginning in 1974, developed just such an application for internal use.

It is worth noting that for many years IBM maintained an internal, computerized implementation of a tear-tape messaging system, known as ITPS, within the company for the transmission of messages between IBM facilities. This system had a gateway that allowed electronic mail users to transmit messages to non–electronic mail users within the company, foreshadowing by at least a decade the day when Internet electronic mail under RFC 780 (Sluizer & Postel, 1980) would sprout gateways to systems not directly connected to the Internet.

Digital's Mail-11 Systems

The *Digital Network Architecture* is the set of specifications, developed by Digital for the DECnet series of networking products. Mail-11 is the unpublished specification that describes the handling of DECnet electronic mail.

Mail-11 was first released to users as part of RSTS/E for the PDP-11 in 1980. Mail-11 is designed to transmit text messages between nodes in a DECnet network. Mail-11 is not designed for the transmission of mail that contains attachments, although special provisions exist to transmit binary messages between cooperating nodes.

The Mail-11 implementation for the VAX/VMS (now OpenVMS) is actually implemented in two components: the mail receiver process, which does not require any system privileges for its operation, and a very limited mail-delivery component that has the privileges associated with the actual mail delivery into an individual user's mailbox.

An operational shortcoming is Mail-11's requirement that both the source and destination node be online at the time that the message is sent. There are no provisions for store-and-forward processing. In a small, local, or dedicated network, the requirement for simultaneous connectivity is an occasional annoyance. In larger networks, with greater numbers of machines and which require indirect connections, it becomes more of a limitation.

Digital's All-in-1™ Office Automation

Mail-11 was not the only electronic mail system sold by Digital Equipment Corporation. All-in-1 was marketed in the office automation market, as an all-encompassing product, a market niche similar to IBM's PROFS.

All-in-1 was a popular office automation and electronic mail system from its introduction in 1982 until the late 1990s. Originally implemented on Digital Equipment Corporation's VAX systems running VAX/VMS, All-in-1 provided a variety of office automation tools. With the advent of the 64-bit Alpha processor, All-in-1 became available on OpenVMS/Alpha.

All-in-1 mail could be connected to outside electronic mail systems including those based on SMTP and other mail systems using gateways. All-in-1 was a pioneer in the use of attachments to electronic mail messages, predating the widespread adoption of the MIME extensions to the SMTP standard.

uunet

uunet was originally a network of UNIX™systems running the standard UNIX uucp (unix-to-unix copy) utility to connect on a demand or scheduled basis between different systems. Mail routings in this network were explicitly enumerated. The inverse path was used for replies.

The primary users of uunet were machines that could not justify a full-time network connection, but needed a way to connect to the larger world. In some environments, such as university campuses and communities, uucp was used as a way to connect small systems to larger university systems on a regular basis for the exchange of electronic mail and news. The larger systems were often connected via leased lines to ARPAnet, CSNET, or NSFnet.

With time, uucp provided support for RFC 822-style addresses by the use of a so-called "smart host," a host defined to have better knowledge of the routing environment. In effect, this implements the same default routing options available when using the RFC 821/822 electronic mail infrastructure, which often uses a default mail route for systems unable to resolve addresses or connections to the outside world.

CSNET

Funded by the U.S. National Science Foundation in 1980, CSNET was a separate network from ARPAnet. CSNET was originally implemented using a Mail Transfer Agent known as MMDF (Multi-channel Message Distribution Facility) operating over dial-up circuits. Originally designed and implemented with uucp-style explicit routing in destination addresses, CSNET adopted RFC-822-compliant addressing in 1985.

CSNET as a separate network disappeared into the overall Internet for several reasons. Some of these reasons were technical, based upon the migration to IP. Other reasons were political and administrative. Originally, CSNET was conceived as a way to provide an electronic mail capability to computer science departments not connected to the ARPAnet. ARPAnet had a variety of restrictions originating from its status as a U.S. government–funded enterprise. Until 1995, connection to ARPAnet required an actively funded contract from the U.S. Department of Defense. CSNET, as originally conceived and implemented, was outside the ARPAnet restrictions.

The cessation of direct government funding for the ARPAnet, and the transition to a commercial carrier-owned infrastructure, removed the administrative reasons behind a separate CSNET.

FidoNet

FidoNet was implemented for motivations similar to those for uunet, but was personal system-centric rather than UNIX-centric. The structure of FidoNet is unashamedly hierarchical. By contrast, the structure of uunet was flat, with every node being theoretically equal and thus requiring explicitly enumerated routes.

FidoNet was designed as a minimal-structure messaging network, without an omnipresent name resolution mechanism. The FidoNet address unambiguously determined the routing for a message from its sender to its recipient. There is no need for external routing information.

In 1984, Tom Jennings originated FidoNet as a way of providing communications between microcomputer users via intermittent connection voice-grade telephone lines. The addresses are assigned in the form of <zone>:<net>/<node>.<point>.

In 1986, a gateway between FidoNet and the Internet was established. Several machines are listed in the Internet DNS as mail gateways for addresses in the fidonet.org zone. These gateways receive messages using RFC 821 on the Internet side and map addresses of the form p<*point*>.f<*node*>.n<*net*>.z<*zone*>.fidonet.org into their equivalent FidoNet addresses, and vice versa.

In many developed areas, the advent of relatively inexpensive broadband (digital subscriber line (DSL), or cable) connections has consigned Fidonet to history. However, in areas where broadband service is not available or not affordable, FidoNet and similar systems remain viable mechanisms for electronic messaging. In 2004, FidoNet still had more than 10,000 active members.

FidoNet contains a number of design elements intended to optimize the network for personal computers communicating on an irregular basis to exchange electronic mail and discussion group messages.

BITNET

In 1981, a number of university sites, led by the City University of New York, formed an electronic mail network called BITNET, based upon the RSCS facility in IBM's VM/370. BITNET also had a number of non-VM/370 nodes that implemented communications using RSCS-compatible protocols. Similar to PROFS, BITNET had, as its underlying structure, the virtual card readers and related components provided by IBM's RSCS on mainframes.

BITNET was primarily a mail transport network. Later, BITNET adopted the IP protocols developed for the ARPAnet and disappeared as a distinctive entity.

The Internet

A short review of the principles underlying the Internet is an important backdrop to the evolution of electronic mail (a full description of the evolution of the Internet can be found elsewhere in this *Handbook*).

- The Internet is a network of networks.
- Each network is composed of computer systems running a multitude of different operating systems on a wide variety of architectures.
- The computer systems are separately owned and managed. They are located over a widely diverse geographical area.
- The communications links constituting the network, or indeed the ones providing connectivity between two nodes on the network, cannot be presumed to be operational at any given moment in time.

Big Three

Internet RFCs number in the thousands. Even allowing for the convention that a revision of an RFC is assigned a new number, there are still literally hundreds of protocols. RFC stands for *Request for Comment*. This reflects the nature of the Internet Standards process, now organized by the Internet Engineering Task Force. Although the process has become more formal over the years, the fundamentals remain unchanged in concept. A proposal defining a particular function over the Internet will be written by an individual or small group, with some degree of input from the community. The draft will then be made available to the interested community, which will then comment on it, hence the name. RFCs may cover specifications, best current practices, or other matters.

Although there are thousands of extant RFCs, only a limited number are directly involved in the transmission and reception of electronic mail.

TELNET. Every network has to start somewhere, and the history of the global Internet is appropriately humble. The initial goal of ARPAnet was to provide resource sharing, primarily time sharing, for researchers throughout the ARPA-funded research community. In 1969, the global Internet's progenitor, ARPAnet, went online, with the initial connection established by way of network processors between two host computers, one each at UCLA and SRI. This first network session was referred to as a "virtual terminal session," the progenitor of the protocol now known as *TELNET*.

stelnet (a program implementing the TELNET protocol using SSL as an underlying technology to provide authentication and encryption) and *SSH* (secure shell) provide the secure implementations of a network terminal protocol. The exposure of unencrypted usernames and passwords has made *stelnet* and *ssh*, both of which have provisions for encryption, the protocols of choice for terminal communications.

TELNET itself still survives, for use in simple situations, and over otherwise encrypted network links.

FTP. For the first several years, electronic mail on the ARPAnet was dealt with as a special case of the File Transfer Protocol (FTP). Electronic mail was delivered to a special location on the destination system, and the destination system was responsible for its processing from that point. It is worthy of note that this design concept, effectively discarded with the advent of SMTP, a dedicated mail transfer protocol, resurfaced as a design pattern for implementations of higher integrity electronic mail systems.

A complete description of FTP can be found elsewhere in this *Handbook*.

SMTP. Originally referred to as MTP (Mail Transfer Protocol) and renamed as SMTP (Simple Mail Transfer Protocol) with the publication of RFC 788 (Postel, 1981) in November 1981, SMTP defines a dedicated protocol for the interchange of electronic mail on the Internet. The focus of MTP/SMTP is to provide for an interchange mechanism in internetting mail between different networks. It was not originally seen as the ultimate mail transport protocol.

A detailed description of SMTP is contained elsewhere in this *Handbook*.

Communications Infrastructure

Originally, both the FTP-based electronic mail provisions and the first few versions of the purpose-designed mail transfer protocol presumed connectivity between the originating host and the receiving host. However, the Internet community was far from unchanging. At the very moment that SMTP was being written, the underlying network was transitioning from a network composed of relatively few large hosts connected via a highly reliable network infrastructure to a more hierarchical structure. This structure embraced computing resources beyond the large-scale hosts that originally were part of ARPAnet. The changeover to IP allowed large numbers of smaller systems to connect through campus local area networks to ARPAnet.

The large-scale hosts that were already connected to ARPAnet became gateways and trusted intermediaries. SMTP was ideally positioned to adopt a new role within the Internet community, that of a protocol for "internetting" electronic mail from senders to recipients with provisions for intermediate relaying. This transitioned electronic mail from a point-to-point transfer mechanism to a store-and-forward message-switching architecture. In a store-and-forward architecture, messages travel from the originating system through an arbitrary number of intermediate nodes to the receiving system. This is an exact parallel to the tear-tape message-switching infrastructure used with punched paper tape. It is also analogous conceptually to the underlying structure of Internet packet switching, albeit using variable length packets over a vastly dilated time scale.

INTERNET ELECTRONIC MAIL GENERAL ARCHITECTURE

Today, most implementations of electronic mail adhere to the RFC 2821/2822 standards. Even where closed systems

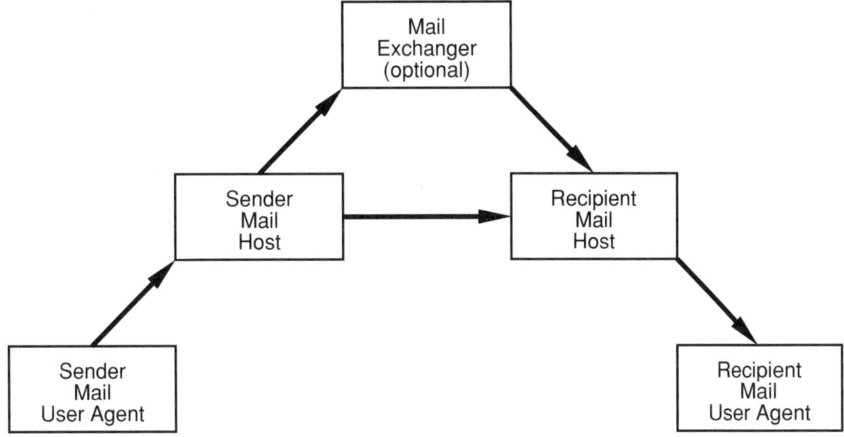

Figure 4: RFC 2821/2822, SMTP electronic mail architecture.

use different mechanisms, these RFCs establish the conventions by which mail is exchanged between systems. RFC 2821/2822, released in 2001, is a consolidation of all the enhancements and clarifications since the release of RFC 821/822 in 1982. The basic architecture of an RFC 2821 mail system is shown in Figure 4.

Conceptually, the RFC 2821 electronic mail system is an abstraction of the system by which a letter goes from the sender to the recipient, just as RFC 2822 defines the format and meaning of the address fields of the message.

Unlike the CCITT X.400 standard, which explicitly specified a model of how addresses related to organizations and how organizations were structured, RFC 2822 makes no such assumptions.

In principal, the address fields are composed of two elements separated by an @. The left-hand side identifies an entity to receive a particular message. The right-hand side corresponds to one or more systems, translatable to an IP address or addresses, either direct to one or more hosts (using a DNS A-record in the DNS) or to one or more mail exchangers (using a DNS MX-record). See Figure 5.

In actuality, the seeming black-and-white difference between a mail recipient on the left-hand side of an address and the host name on the right-hand side is blurred by the presence of gateways, forwarders, and aliases, any one (or all of which) can rewrite all or part of the addresses associated with a message.

Often, this rewriting can take place in several unconnected phases. The first hop of the journey may be covered within the sender's organization by an overall policy requiring all SMTP mail to be routed through one of several outgoing gateways. In some cases, this will be static. In other cases, the rewriting is done by intercepting the SMTP connection request of the sending system. This process may be repeated multiple times, depending upon the structure of the sending organization's or

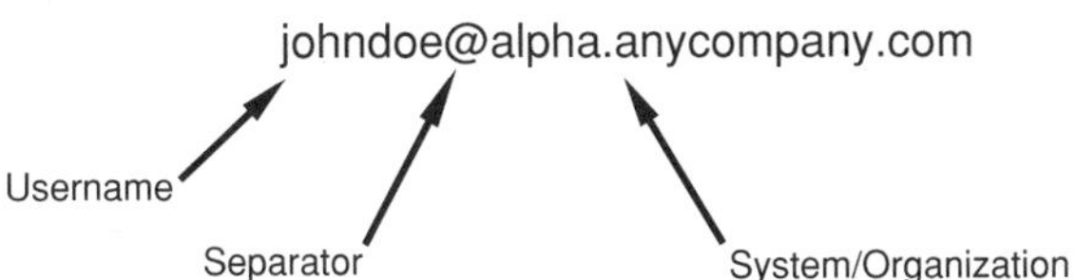

Figure 5: Electronic mail address components.

their Internet service provider's network, until the message reaches a mail exchanger that is permitted to establish outgoing SMTP connections to the recipient domain's mail exchangers. The message will then be received by one of the receiving organization's externally accessible mail exchangers. From this point, the process is inverted until the message reaches its recipient. At any stage in this process, on the sending or receiving side, either side of the address may be rewritten.

As an example, consider processing of electronic mail when many recipients in university communities had multiple aliases, one each for uunet, CSNET, ARPAnet, and BITNET. One reason for the different addresses might be message content. Until 1995, commercial content was not within the acceptable use policy of the ARPAnet. So, a user would, depending upon the message, address the mail to

- johnsmith@harvard.edu
- johnsmith@harvard.csnet
- johnsmith@harvard.bitnet
- johnsmith@harvard.uucp

Although each of these addresses would go from the same sender to the same recipient, the transport paths of the messages would differ. Many mail gateways had rewriting rules, mechanisms to syntactically rewrite addresses to explicitly route messages through specific gateways based upon the destination address.

Rewriting of electronic mail addresses occurs for many reasons. In some cases, such as a gateway, it is used to reformulate addresses from one convention's syntax to the differing syntax requirements of a different network or protocol. In other cases, it is used to convert addresses from an internal form to an external form. Rewriting may add or remove information for addresses, depending upon context. For example, as shown in Figure 6, a message may start with a sender address that contains an internal node name, which may be rewritten by a firewall/gateway to remove the internal node name. The recipient's firewall/gateway may similarly add internal information to the recipient address as the message is routed to its final destination.

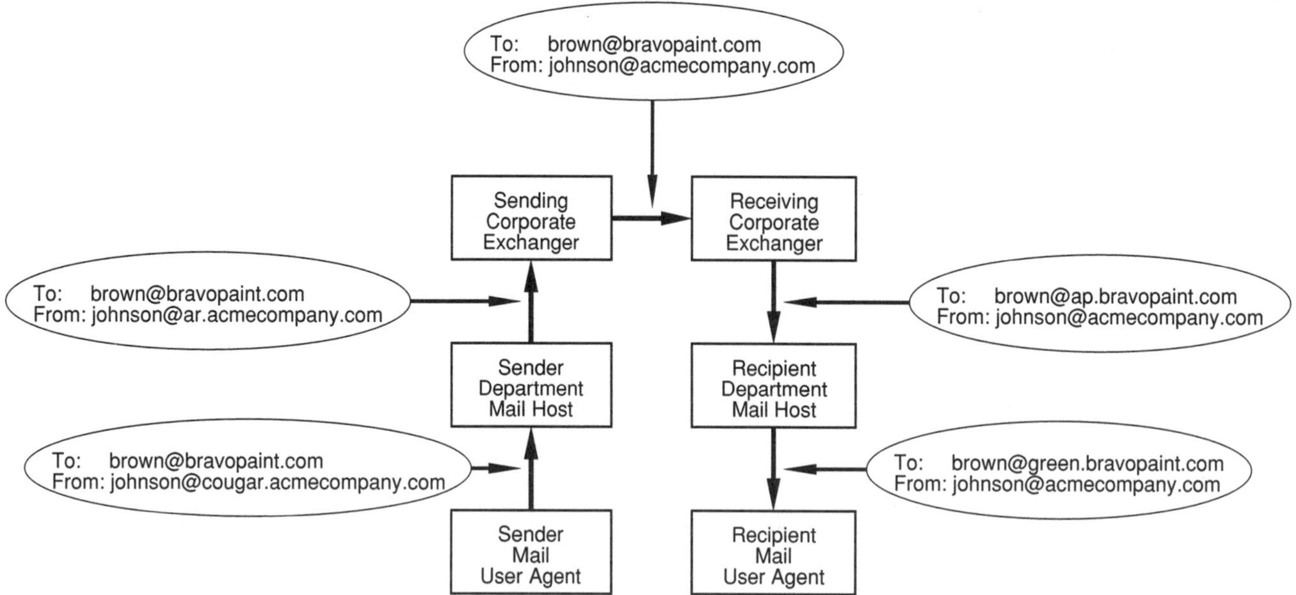

Figure 6: Rewriting of electronic mail addresses.

The actual routing of SMTP mail on ARPAnet and its descendant, the global Internet, is totally divorced from the addressing of the network and the hierarchy of carriers. There are hierarchies in some components, notably in the naming structure of DNS, but these are hierarchies of nomenclature, not structure. The IP address space is flat and featureless, without any inherent structural hierarchy.

In standard SMTP mail, there is a hierarchy of mail exchangers used to relay messages toward their ultimate destination, but it is a ranking of topology and capability, not a direct map of the network. For each different destination node, there is potentially a different set of mail relays; conversely, the same relay may occupy different relative positions in different relay paths specified in the DNS (Figure 7).

Applicable RFCs

A protocol, such as SMTP, may go through a long progression of RFC numbers as the specification is refined based upon implementation experience. A version of a program may (or may not) be compatible with another program written to an earlier RFC for the same protocol. Compatibility will depend upon the extent and character of the difference, as well as the degree to which the issue was foreseen by the developer.

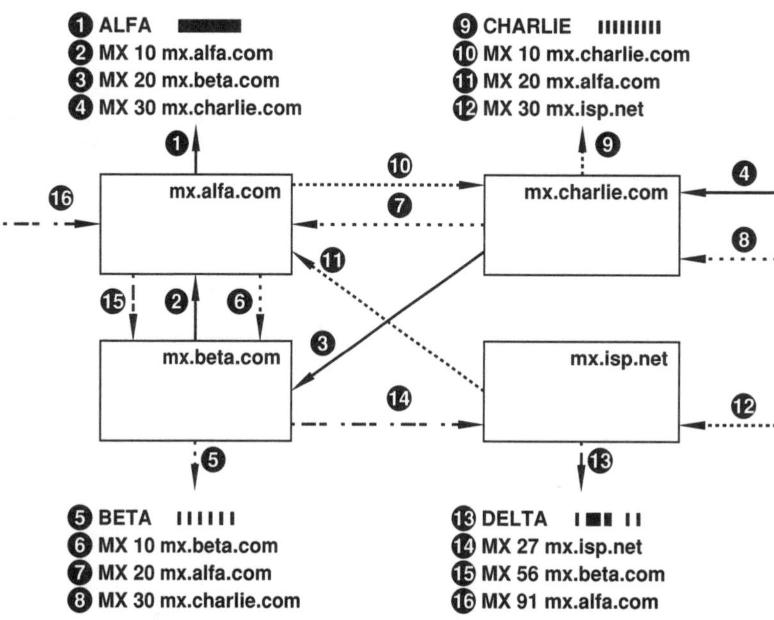

Figure 7: Mail exchangers may occupy different positions in the hierarchy.

Original

RFC 772, entitled "Mail Transfer Protocol" for ARPAnet electronic mail was purpose-designed and written by Suzanne Sluizer and Jon Postel in September 1980. From that origin, the Mail Transfer Protocol has been revised to deal with a number of issues, including hierarchical addresses and relaying.

Standards often piggyback on more fundamental standards by specifying the contents of an element within the bounds of the established definition. *MIME*, the "Multipurpose Internet Mail Extensions," which regulates the inclusion of attachments of various types within the bodies of electronic mail messages otherwise described by RFC 822 and its successors, is just one such example.

In an ideal world, the areas covered by related standards would be orthogonal, with no influences from one line of specifications to a related line. The real world, however, is far from perfect. Although many specifications take great pains to be upwardly compatible, this is far from a guarantee.

Present Day

SMTP is generally considered to be governed by RFCs 2821 and 2822, which describe the transport protocol for and the addressing of messages, respectively. Although RFC 2821 and 2822 govern the addressing and transport of electronic mail, they are not the only specifications that affect electronic mail. Other RFCs, for example, those for complex message types, referred to as MIME, and the User Agent specific protocols POP3 and IMAP4 are also part of the electronic mail infrastructure. See Table 1 for a summary.

SMTP makes limited presumptions about network services at or below the level of TCP. Therefore, there are implementations of SMTP with underlying protocols other than TCP/IP.

Dependencies

SMTP makes some presumptions about the underlying network environment. These assumptions ensure the correct operation of the protocol. On the level of the connection between the sender and recipient, the connections are presumed to be sequenced and error-free, 7-bit transparent connections.

It may seem to be an anachronism, but when the specifications were written, not all computers on the network used a consistent 8-bit version of ASCII. In the name of interchange, SMTP presumes that the connection between the two nodes is restricted to a subset of the 7-bit character set. The MIME extensions to SMTP define the means by which arbitrary 8-bit bytes can be encoded, which enables the handling of a wide range of data types beyond basic text mail.

Changes in the presumed network transport layer have limited effects. SMTP implementations are little affected by the difference in address sizes between IPv4 (32-bit addresses) and IPv6 (128-bit addresses). Outside of extremely limited issues, differences in the transport are irrelevant to an SMTP implementation.

DNS (Domain Name System)

Name resolution is the other component of the supporting infrastructure for mail transmission. Originally, each node on the ARPAnet used a local copy of what is still known as the "Hosts" file. By the early 1980s, the expansion and overall dynamic activity on ARPAnet made this approach problematical.

The original DNS specification (RFC 883, Mockapetris, 1983) was developed to provide a robust, flexible mechanism to resolve host names to IP addresses. The expansion of the ARPAnet to the wider community brought into question the presumption that electronic mail could always be directly sent from sending system to receiving system.

In an example of coevolution, a mail-relaying mechanism described in RFC 974 (Partridge, 1986) proposed changes to the DNS and to the processing of electronic mail governed by SMTP. These changes implemented a relay mechanism, through the creation of a new DNS record, the MX-record (Mail Exchanger). MX-records identify network nodes that act as a relay for a destination or group of destinations.

As a result, it became possible to describe internetwork gateways as a form of relay, obviating the need for special purpose code in every mailer to deal with the existence of other networks. For example, relaying mail to hosts connected to CSNET no longer required special provisions in mail systems, simply one or more MX-records identifying the CSNET gateways.

Nonhostile Environment

RFC 2821/2822 has a quaint presumption from an earlier time, that of an essentially benign operating environment. The underlying standard predates the modern Internet, to a time when the networked community was smaller, the message volumes were smaller, and moral suasion was a viable strategy to ensure adherence to network norms.

The most widely used implementation of RFC 821/822 (now RFC 2821/2822), a UNIX program known as *sendmail*, has been exploited to compromise many systems.

Table 1 Common RFCs Applicable to Internet Electronic Mail

RFCs	Category	Subject Area
2045–2049	Extended content	Multipurpose Internet Mail Extensions (MIME)
2821	Message transfer	Simple Mail Transfer Protocol
2822	Message contents	Internet message format
1939	User Agent protocol	Post Office Protocol, Version 3 (POP3)
1730	User Agent protocol	Internet Message Access Protocol (IMAP)

The 1988 Morris Worm exposed areas where sendmail did not take adequate measures to ensure its own integrity against malicious clients. Subsequently, sendmail has been found to be particularly vulnerable to such exploits and has generated a total of 36 warnings from the CERT (CERT.ORG) since 1990.

Mail Handlers

Electronic mail passes through many hands on the journey from sender to recipient. The end points of the system frequently are not part of the actual electronic mail infrastructure governed by RFC 2821/2822. Often, the first and last steps of the journey are provided by programs operating according to other protocols (e.g., POP3, IMAP4), whose roles are focused more on the end point origination and reception of messages than on the routing of messages through the network as a whole.

In today's Internet, where there are large volumes of spam, it is not unusual to see filters designed to eliminate such material at various stages in message routing. Often, the sheer economies of scale will mean there is at least some filtering at the firewall or gateway level to an internal network. There may also be additional levels of filtering at the Mail Host, or Mail User Agent level.

Mail User Agents

A Mail User Agent, to adopt the terminology used in various Internet RFCs, is a program that directly interacts with the user in the generation or reception of electronic mail. Mail User Agents often use the Post Office and Internet Message Access protocols to communicate with the message store located on the Mail Host.

Mail User Agents also represent a vulnerability. In the past few years, attacks targeting the display mechanism have increased in popularity. These attacks, which have often targeted personal computers, particularly systems running Microsoft's Outlook software, target Outlook's capabilities to execute code and HTML pages attached to documents.

IMAP4. IMAP4 (Internet Message Access Protocol, Version 4) is defined in RFC 1730 (Crispin, 1994). IMAP4 is a protocol designed for the communications between mail hosts and mail user agents.

POP3. POP3 (Post Office Protocol, Version 3) is defined by RFC 1939 (Myers & Rose, 1996). POP3 is a protocol for accessing a user's mail message store stored on a system other than the system that the user is using.

Toolkits/Utilities

Electronic messaging protocols, and SMTP in particular, are well suited for roles in applications more complex than straightforward electronic mail. In particular, SMTP's relaying and queuing make an excellent vehicle for conveying information through networks to remote locations, whether organizationally or geographically.

As an example, many file retrieval systems and information systems have been built upon a base consisting of a pseudouser and an application that processes messages received by that user.

Web browsers, such as Netscape and Internet Explorer, generally provide an electronic mail client, both to process mailto: URLs and as part of the integrated browsing experience.

An electronic mail client typically uses a mix of protocols, often using IMAP4 or POP3 for retrieving messages and manipulating the user's mailbox, and SMTP for sending outbound messages. Some implementations include both immediate and delayed transmission, which permits a mobile user the luxury of responding to electronic mail while not connected or connected via a low-bandwidth connection and sends all outgoing mail at a chosen point in the future.

Mail Transfer Agents

Often, at an ISP, there are a series of systems tasked to the management of in-transit electronic mail. These systems fall into two categories, relays and gateways.

Relays

An SMTP relay is a staging point for messages, analogous to the queue at a tear-tape shop. In most situations, the queue for an individual customer system at a relay will be of modest size. Often, there is more than a single layer of relays, providing geographic or organization depth to the resilience of the network for delivering electronic mail.

Consider a typical corporate environment for a company of medium size, for example 3,500 employees spread over several installations. To further illuminate the issues, suppose that a local or regional ISP serves some of the company's offices.

Structurally, the simplest electronic mail implementation would be a single large system to which every user connected to read their electronic mail. This approach does work, but ensuring accessibility and availability can be difficult and expensive. In that case, there would be a large system at a corporate-wide data center, and employees would use user agents or Web access via an intranet to access their mail. Between sites, a Virtual Private Network (VPN) using encrypted tunnels would provide the appearance of a single, company-wide network. One advantage of such an environment is the ease of dealing with a single system to manage in the context of records and archiving, a regulatory requirement in some organizations and industries.

A more distributed architecture would have multiple mail hosts, perhaps hierarchically organized along geographical or business unit lines. The implementation issue of user electronic mail addresses is independent of the routing of individual messages; after all, the addresses can be rewritten as well as routed.

Even a unified, company-wide mail host needs mail relays. Despite the best of intentions, network links will fail and usability of individual hosts will be disrupted. The simplest of electric devices fail; the humble plug or socket will, at some point, fail.

These failures can be within the company, in which case a mail relay at the corporate firewall can store mail for later forwarding, or at the ISP, where mail can be queued awaiting the repair of a damaged cable.

Thus, the best practices for an overall electronic mail architecture include the incorporation of multiple levels of relays to ensure robust queuing of messages in the event of the inevitable host and/or network interruptions.

Gateways

Gateways are responsible for providing connections for mail transmission between dissimilar networks. Generally, the networks employ different protocols, requiring a gateway to translate between the two protocols. Gateways are not directly involved with the queuing and storage of messages, acting merely as a translator between two networks.

In one sense, the corporate firewalls that separate an intranet from the Internet can be considered gateways. But in this sense, a gateway isolates two different and incompatible addressing schemes for the different networks. The addressing schemes could be any combination of network addresses, or mail addresses, or both.

Undefined Issues

Despite the volume of specifications that govern routing, content, and other interactions with electronic mail, there are many areas where issues are undefined.

This is not necessarily a design shortcoming. As in the case of the relationship between SMTP and MIME, the underlying specification (SMTP) has sufficient flexibility to allow the additional specification (MIME) to define the inclusion of nontext attachments in a compatible fashion.

Message Relay

Message relay is one of the most important facilities in the modern Internet. Without message relay, message transport would not be the robust mechanism we use everyday.

Message relay also means that a message may seem to come from a node that does not correspond to its sender address. The relaying node may belong to the sending organization, the receiving organization, an organization that is a correspondent of either (related organizations may mutually provide relays for each other for redundancy), or an ISP.

Address Content

The contents of message address lines may arbitrarily be within the specifications laid out in RFC 2822. An address could, at the receiving system, be an individual, a mailing list, a daemon, or some combination.

Other Networks

SMTP can and has been implemented using underlying infrastructure other than that provided by TCP/IP. So long as the alternative network transport is capable of providing the "reliable data stream channel" envisaged by SMTP, the implementation can be exact. In some cases, even protocols that do not completely conform to the model envisaged by SMTP can also be employed. For example, SMTP permits lines up to 998 characters in length. However, SMTP also acknowledges that many implementations have difficulties dealing with messages that contain lines longer than 78 characters. The MIME standards (RFC 2045–2049) specifically state that lines in encoded attachments should be 76 characters long, to deal with this particular concern.

Extendibility

Electronic mail has been, and continues to be, used as a carrier for a wide variety of content. The ability of electronic mail to transmit content between a sender and a recipient, without the need for both to be present, or indeed connected at the same time, is a powerful mechanism.

Foundation extensions such as MIME (RFC 2045–2049) provide a context that allows Internet electronic mail to become a transport for a wide variety of content.

In some cases, the content is binary, such as PEM (Privacy Enhanced Mail, RFC 1421–1423) or PGP (Pretty Good Privacy). In other cases, the content may be executable or multimedia files.

MIME

MIME (RFC 2045–2049) is a set of standards that provide for extending the simple text-message content presumption of SMTP into a vehicle for more complex data. The complexity may simply be a matter of longer lines, such as those generated by many word processing programs when word wrapping paragraphs, or extensive binary files.

PGP

Phil Zimmermann developed PGP in 1991. The idea behind PGP is to provide a mechanism to transmit secure messages between individuals without the need for a tree of digital certificates. As an example of the use of nested standards, as described earlier in this chapter, PGP messages are formatted or packaged using the MIME standard. PGP and PEM both provide technological solutions to confirm the authenticity of a message and to prevent a sender from disowning or repudiating a message.

PEM

Privacy Enhanced Mail is a set of standards for signed, private electronic mail, based upon a hierarchy of digital certificates. The problem with the deployment of PEM has been the difficulty of managing large numbers of digital certificates.

INFRASTRUCTURE SECURITY

Electronic mail has been both boon and bane. Electronic messaging has reduced the delays in business communication from days or weeks to seconds or minutes, while simultaneously reducing costs of transmission and delivery to mere fractions of a cent.

The Internet mail system makes presumptions about its operating environment. To be fair, RFC 2821 and its predecessors cannot be held responsible for all of the shortcomings, perceived or real in the overall Internet.

However, it is a fact that electronic mail, in the RFC 2821 model, does not have any form of inherently robust control over the integrity or authenticity of electronic mail. Individual mail server implementations are free to implement controls or limitations on mail relay, size, or content, but this is not standardized.

Some SMTP server implementations limit, or can be configured to limit, mail processing in a variety of ways, including

- size limits,
- limits on relaying (only within certain IP address ranges; typically the local network),
- requiring secure supplemental authentication (connecting with secure verifications of identity and encrypted connections, such as those provided by SSL),
- content checks,
- addressing limits, and
- refusing messages from machines listed on so-called "Black Hole" lists (a "Black Hole" list typically lists names and/or IP addresses of systems who have been associated with spam or open relays).

Unwanted Commercial Messages

In turn, this tremendous reduction in cost has given rise to a plague of unsolicited commercial electronic mail, generally referred to as spam. The volume of these unsolicited messages can be hundreds or thousands of messages per day per user, every day. The phenomenon of spam deserves far more extensive treatment than a section in a chapter, but some facts are worth noting:

- The scale of Internet connectivity is unprecedented. Never before in human history has it been possible for an individual to produce and send hundreds of thousands of messages per day to individual recipients at minimal cost. Even a relatively small Internet connection (tens of thousands of bits per second of bandwidth) is sufficient to send thousands of messages a day. Broadband connections only increase the scale of the problem.
- The low cost of Internet connectivity is unprecedented. Many users in the United States can obtain broadband connectivity for less than US$ 60.00/month. This means that even infinitesimal success rates for spam remain economically viable.
- The ready availability of inexpensive computing hardware makes it economical to produce large volumes of messages, including mass customized messages. Even the most inexpensive personal computer has the computational speed and mass storage to generate hundreds of thousands, if not millions, of messages per day.

Inevitably, spammers and antispammers are engaged in a technological arms race. The first wave of the spam epidemic was dealt with by simply filtering the originator addresses associated with unwanted commercial electronic mail.

A popular tactic for spam is to come through a relay, in the hope that message vetting will be less stringent from a known relay. Nothing should be further from the truth. Vetting provisions to detect and eliminate spam should not be based upon the node that relays the message.

Some commentators lump all solicited and semisolicited messages into one category. This practice is, in this author's opinion, not fair to all members of the network community. The large volume of barely, or totally, unsolicited electronic mail, typically relating to get-rich-quick schemes, dating, cut-rate pharmaceuticals, enhancement of various body parts, and the like, is one particularly offensive stratum. Almost invariably, the individuals sending these messages use forged addresses, misleading subject lines and, in many cases, other falsified headers. These combined measures make it increasingly difficult to separate legitimate messages from unsolicited messages of dubious legality.

External, semisolicited messages are another aspect of the problem. These messages are legitimate and appropriate, but from an individual's perspective, ill timed. Vendor newsletters, sales announcements, and electronic copies of statements are appropriate content, but the sheer volume can be overwhelming. Companies should provide mechanisms for customers to control the scale and frequency of such communications. Companies should also restrain the tendency to include large attachments with such files, instead using electronic mail to notify customers of the availability of information located on, for example, the Web site.

However, even if we were to magically eliminate this entire class of messages, problems remain. The ease of electronic messaging has spawned a tendency toward overuse. Even within organizations, the volume of legitimate messages can overwhelm recipients. This is particularly so when many individuals adopt the conservative measure of including large numbers of coworkers as addressees in messages of limited importance or relevance. This effect is not limited to larger organizations. It takes only a few individuals within an organization, each forwarding copies of messages to each of their coworkers, to bring productive work to a total standstill.

Regulatory requirements in some industries and countries also have an effect. Securities and Exchange Commission Rule 17a-4 in the United States, covering the financial and securities industry, requires the archiving of all electronic messages entering an organization, creating a mass of low-value material, all of which must be archived for years.

Archiving and compliance requirements may also be the determining factors in where messages are received. A centralized message store may be desirable from the compliance perspective.

Accountability

Ensuring that messages were sent or received remains a problem with Internet electronic mail. Many corporations have policies requiring that electronic mail go through certain gateways for vetting and archiving, both incoming and outgoing. The ability to send a message outside of the monitored channels, possibly with forged headers, is an ongoing problem.

Without resorting to PEM or PGP, and secure mechanisms for access to the systems generating electronic mail, it is not possible to prevent header forgery and the resulting lack of accountability.

Authenticity

Authenticity is a more serious problem. Since the use of the telegraph, authenticity has been an ongoing issue, with the reliability of a message hinging on the difficulty

Table 2 Currently Applicable Internet Requests for Comments (RFCs)

RFC 1421	Privacy Enhancement for Internet Electronic Mail: Part I: Message Encryption and Authentication Procedures
RFC 1422	Privacy Enhancement for Internet Electronic Mail: Part II: Certificate-Based Key Management
RFC 1423	Privacy Enhancement for Internet Electronic Mail: Part III: Algorithms, Modes, and Identifiers
RFC 1424	Privacy Enhancement for Internet Electronic Mail: Part IV: Key Certification and Related Services
RFC 1730	Internet Message Access Protocol—Version 4
RFC 1939	Post Office Protocol—Version 3
RFC 2045	Multipurpose Internet Mail Extensions (MIME) Part One: Format of Internet Message Bodies
RFC 2046	Multipurpose Internet Mail Extensions (MIME) Part Two: Media Types
RFC 2047	MIME (Multipurpose Internet Mail Extensions) Part Three: Message Header Extensions for Non-ASCII Text
RFC 2048	Multipurpose Internet Mail Extensions (MIME) Part Four: Registration Procedures
RFC 2049	Multipurpose Internet Mail Extensions (MIME) Part Five: Conformance Criteria and Examples
RFC 2821	Simple Mail Transfer Protocol
RFC 2822	Internet Message Format

of generating a false message and the costs or difficulties in sending it. However, there have been legal challenges to the authenticity of electronic messages since the beginning, hence the adoption of wire fraud statute, 18 USC §1343, in 1952.

The dramatic decrease in access costs and the resulting ubiquity of access have made forgery a straightforward activity well within the abilities of many adolescents. The present solution is often to use PGP with digital signatures. Unfortunately, the awkwardness of such solutions has prevented their adoption on a widespread basis.

It is to be hoped that the lowering costs of digital certificates, together with advances in managing certificate trees, will lead to increased ease of use.

SUMMARY

Electronic mail has dramatically changed from its beginnings in 1964 as a mechanism for communicating short messages between users of a single computer system. Today, electronic mail is used to move huge volumes of data over globe-spanning networks.

The mechanisms for processing electronic mail from its point of origin to its destination have evolved and continue to evolve. Far from being a tree of evolution, with each branch diverging from a common ancestor at MIT in 1964/1965, electronic mail evolution has been and continues to be a tapestry, with each thread interweaving and influencing the others.

Electronic mail will likely continue to evolve in the future, as requirements and needs change for the noninteractive transmission of files and documents. Security concerns, particularly the need to ensure privacy and authenticity while retaining ease of use, are the greatest issues for the future.

ACKNOWLEDGMENTS

I thank the numerous people who generously took the time to speak with me about their roles and recollections of events. I thank Susan Sluizer, Craig Partridge, Paul Mockapetris, Peter Capek, John Covert, and others. I also thank Fern Hertzberg for her assistance in organizing and copyediting this chapter.

GLOSSARY

All-in-1 Digital Equipment Corporation's integrated office automation and electronic mail system, originally released in 1982.

ARPAnet A research packet-switching network funded by the Advanced Research Projects Agency of the U.S. Department of Defense. ARPAnet's first link became operational in 1969. The ARPAnet was officially decommissioned in 1995 and transitioned into a commercially funded network.

CCITT (Comité Consultatif International de Télégraphique et Téléphonique) The Paris-based international standards body within the ITU (International Telecommunications Union) that develops international telegraphic and telecommunications standards. In March 1993, CCITT was reorganized as ITU Telecommunication Standardization Sector (ITU-T).

CTSS One of the first time sharing systems, the Compatible Time Sharing System was developed at the Massachusetts Institute of Technology in 1961–1963, based on a modified IBM 7094 system.

DECnet Digital Equipment Corporation's proprietary set of network protocols originally developed in the late 1970s for networking computer systems. DECnet was, from its initial origin, a peer-to-peer network, contrasted with IBM's SNA, which was hierarchical in philosophy.

DNS The domain name system is the Internet mechanism for resolving hierarchical node names to IP addresses. The protocol used by DNS is currently defined by RFCs 1034/1035.

IETF Established in 1986, the Internet Engineering Task Force is the branch of the Internet Architecture Board (IAB) responsible for coordinating the development of Internet standards.

Mail Exchanger A system that accepts mail in transit from one place to another in the SMTP (RFC 2821) architecture. This categorization is not exclusive; a mail exchanger may also play any or all of the other roles described in the RFC, in virtually any combination.

Mail Host A system that is hosting a message store.

Mail Transfer Agent A computer system that transfers mail from a user to its destination. This term was defined in the SMTP series of RFCs.

Mail User Agent The program that users utilize to access their mail. It may be an application running directly on a mail host with a local file, or it may be a client/server application accessing a remotely located message store using POP, IMAP, or other protocol.

Message Store A storage mechanism for electronic messages. Messages may be organized in a series of files in a directory structure, as part of a database, or some other mechanism. Other than the requirements for storage and retrieval, the SMTP specifications do not make statements about the internal organization of the message store.

MIME (Multipurpose Internet Mail Extensions) The set of IETF RFCs governing the encapsulation of non-text data types within standard RFC 2822 messages.

Node Name The fully qualified Internet Domain Name System (DNS) name of a system.

OpenVMS HP's operating system for VAX, Alpha, and Itanium processors, originally developed by Digital Equipment Corporation as VAX/VMS in conjunction with the VAX processors, released in 1978. OpenVMS is fully described elsewhere in the *Handbook*.

PROFS An IBM office automation and electronic mail system, originally released in 1981.

Protocol The contents and sequence of the information exchanged between two system components cooperating on a single task.

RFC A Request for Comment is a proposed or generally accepted Internet standard; see http://www.ietf.org/rfc for a repository of RFCs.

RFC 2821 The Internet Engineering Task Force RFC describing the Simple Mail Transfer Protocol.

RFC 2822 The Internet Engineering Task Force RFC governing the internal format of mail messages.

SMS (Short Message Service) A service for transmitting short text messages, often used for transmitting text messages to mobile devices such as mobile telephones.

SMTP (Simple Mail Transfer Protocol) The IETF specified protocol for the transmission of electronic mail, current defined by RFC 2821/2822; descended from the Mail Transfer Protocol originally defined by RFC 772.

SNA IBM's Systems Network Architecture is a proprietary set of network protocols for communications between mainframes and associated systems.

VAX/VMS See OpenVMS.

X.400 The CCITT (now ITU-T) standard for "message handling services."

CROSS REFERENCES

See *Internet Basics; PGP (Pretty Good Privacy); S/MIME (Secure MIME); SMTP (Simple Mail Transfer Protocol).*

REFERENCES

Balenson, D. (1993). Privacy Enhancement for Internet Electronic Mail: Part III: Algorithms, Modes, and Identifiers (RFC 1423). Retrieved May 7, 2005, from http://www.ietf.org/rfc/rfc1423.txt

Bhushan, A. (1972). Comments on the File Transfer Protocol (RFC 354) (RFC 385). Retrieved August 20, 2005, from http://www.faqs.org/rfcs/rfc385.html

Borenstein, N. & Freed, N. (1996). Multipurpose Internet Mail Extensions (MIME) Part Two: Media Types (RFC 2046). Retrieved May 7, 2005, from http://www.ietf.org/rfc/rfc2046.txt

Borenstein, N. & Freed, N. (1996). Multipurpose Internet Mail Extensions (MIME) Part Five: Conformance Criteria and Examples (RFC 2049). Retrieved May 7, 2005, from http://www.ietf.org/rfc/rfc2049.txt

Bush, R. (1993). FidoNet: Technology, use, tools, and history. *Communications of the ACM, 36*(8), 31–35.

Crispin, M. Internet Message Access Protocol, Version 4 (RFC 1730). Retrieved May 7, 2005, from http://www.ietf.org/rfc/rfc1730.txt

Crocker, D (1982). Standard for the format of ARPA Internet text messages (RFC 0822). Retrieved May 7, 2005, from http://www.ietf.org/rfc/rfc0822.txt

Freed, N., Klensin, J. & Postel. J. 2048 (1996). Multipurpose Internet Mail Extensions (MIME) Part Four: Registration Procedures (RFC 2048). Retrieved May 7, 2005, from http://www.ietf.org/rfc/rfc2048.txt

Gardner, P. C., Jr. (1987). A system for the automated office environment. *IBM Systems Journal, 20*(3), p. 321–345.

Hendricks, E. C., & Hartmann, T. C. (1979). Evolution of a virtual machine subsystem. *IBM Systems Journal, 18*(1) p. 111–143.

Kaliski, B. (1993). Privacy Enhancement for Internet Electronic Mail: Part IV: Key Certification and Related Services (RFC 1424). Retrieved May 7, 2005, from http://www.ietf.org/rfc/rfc1424.txt

Kent, S. (1993). 1422 Privacy Enhancement for Internet Electronic Mail: Part II: Certificate-Based Key Management (RFC 1422). Retrieved May 7, 2005, from http://www.ietf.org/rfc/rfc1422. txt

Klensin, J. (2001). Simple Mail Transfer Protocol (RFC 2821). Retrieved May 7, 2005, from http://www.ietf.org/rfc/rfc2821.txt

Linn, J. (1993). 1421 Privacy Enhancement for Internet Electronic Mail: Part I: Message Encryption and Authentication Procedures (RFC 1421). Retrieved May 7, 2005, from http://www.ietf.org/rfc/rfc1421.txt

Mockapetris, P. V. (1983). Domain names: Concepts and facilities (RFC 882). Retrieved May 7, 2005, from http://www.ietf.org/rfc/rfc0882.txt

Mockapetris, P. V. (1983). Domain names: Implementation specification (RFC 883). Retrieved May 7, 2005, from http://www.ietf.org/rfc/rfc0883.txt

Moore, K. (1996). MIME (Multipurpose Internet Mail Extensions). Part Three: Message Header Extensions for Non-ASCII Text (RFC 2047). Retrieved May 7, 2005, from http://www.ietf.org/rfc/rfc2047.txt

MMDF frequently asked questions list. (n.d.). Retrieved on May 7, 2005, from http://www.faqs.org/faqs/mail/mmdf-faq/part1/

Myers, J. & Rose, M. Post Office Protocol, Version 3 (RFC 1939). Retrieved May 7, 2005, from http://www.ietf.org/rfc/rfc1939.txt

Partridge, C. (1986). Mail routing and the domain system (RFC 974). Retrieved May 7, 2005, from http://www.ietf.org/rfc/rfc0974.txt

Postel, J. (1981). Simple Mail Transfer Protocol (RFC 788). Retrieved May 7, 2005, from http://www.ietf.org/rfc/rfc0788.txt

Postel, J. (1982). Simple Mail Transfer Protocol (RFC 821). Retrieved May 7, 2005, from http://www.ietf.org/rfc/rfc0821.txt

Postel, J. & Reynolds, J. K. (1983). Telnet Protocol Specification (RFC 854). Retrieved May 7, 2005, from http://www.ietf.org/rfc/rfc0854.txt

Resnick, R. (2001). Internet Message Format (RFC 2822). Retrieved May 7, 2005, from http://www.ietf.org/rfc/rfc2822.txt

Sluizer, S. & Postel, J. (1980). Mail Transfer Protocol (RFC 772), retrieved May 7, 2005, from http://www.ietf.org/rfc/rfc0772.txt

Sluizer, S. & Postel, J. (1981). Mail Transfer Protocol (RFC 780). Retrieved May 7, 2005, from http://www.ietf.org/rfc/rfc0780.txt

FURTHER READING

Albitz, P., & Liu, C. (2001). *DNS and BIND* (4th ed.). O'Reilly, Sebastopol, CA.

Bosworth, S., & Kabay, M. (2004). *Computer security handbook* (4th ed.). Wiley, New York, NY.

Deutsch, C. (2003, December 21). Planes, trucks, and 7.5 million packages: FedEx's big night. *The New York Times*, Section 3, p. 1.

Hafner, K., & Lyon, M. (1996). *Where wizards stay up late*. Simon & Schuster, New York, NY.

Hutt, A., Boswoth, S., & Hoyt, D. (1995). *Computer security handbook* (3rd ed.). Wiley, New York, NY.

Kahn, D. (1967). *Codebreakers* (1st ed.). Macmillan, New York, NY.

Layton, E. (1985). *And I was there*. William Morrow & Company, New York, NY.

McNamara, J. (1977). *Technical aspects of data communications (1st ed.)*. Digital Press, Boston, MA.

Quarterman, J. (1990). *The matrix*. Digital Press, Boston, MA.

Rusbridger, J., & Nave, E. (1991). *Betrayal at Pearl Harbor*. Summit Books, New York, NY.

Tannenbaum, A. (1981). *Computer networks*. Prentice-Hall, Englewood Cliffs, NJ.

PKI (Public Key Infrastructure)

Radia Perlman, *Sun Microsystems Laboratories*

INTRODUCTION

PKI is an acronym for "public key infrastructure." This chapter discusses what that means and the challenges associated with providing this functionality.

If Bob believes Alice's public key is pub_A, and Alice knows the private key associated with pub_A, then Bob can use pub_A to encrypt a message for Alice, or Alice can use the associated private key to prove to Bob that she is Alice (i.e., she can *authenticate* to Bob). The purpose of a PKI is to provide a convenient and secure method for obtaining the public key associated with some principal.

The basic idea is to have a trusted authority known as a CA (certification authority) digitally sign a message known as a *certificate*, thereby vouching that a particular key goes with a particular name. If Alice has been certified by the CA, Bob knows the CA's public key, Bob trusts that CA, and Bob receives Alice's certificate, then he can validate the CA's signature on that certificate and know Alice's public key. In the chapter about digital certificates in this volume, some examples of certificate formats that have been deployed are discussed. In this chapter, we concentrate on the concepts and ignore the formats.

There is not universal agreement on the definition of a PKI, the minimal functionality that one must provide to be credibly called a PKI, nor the limits of functions that might be provided by a PKI. Besides providing a secure mapping between a name and a key, other functions of a PKI are to provide timely revocation of certificates (such as if a private key were stolen), to enable users to obtain their own private key, and to provide certification of attributes or privileges.

Authentication

Authentication is generally assumed to mean proving one's identity, but like most words in the field, there is no universally agreed-upon definition. For instance, there might be a shared key for a group, and for purposes of access to some resource it might be enough to prove knowledge of the shared key. Some might consider this authentication, although this would definitely not be proving an identity, because proving knowledge of a key shared by a set of individuals does not distinguish between individuals. It just proves that you are one of the individuals in the set.

For most cases, however, the PKI will link an identity's name with a public key, and authentication will be done by proving knowledge of the associated private key.

Authorization

Authorization is the right to do something. A common method of specifying authorization is through an *access control list* associated with a resource, which specifies the identities authorized to access the resource, together with what access rights they have. For instance, for a file, some members might have read-only access, whereas others might have read and write access.

Usually authorization involves authentication because it is often convenient to specify authorization as a set of identity or rights pairs.

In contrast, another model of authorization is "credentials based," where possession of a credential implies authorization. In the real world, this might be a door key or the combination to a safe. In the network security world, sometimes knowledge of a key is thought of as a credential. The key might not be associated with any named identity, but it might be used to assure someone that two messages originated from the same source. In that case, one might claim that authentication has taken place and that the identity is "the holder of that private key."

We will discuss more issues associated with identity, authentication, and authorization later in this chapter.

Security without Public Key Cryptography

At first glance, security appears similar whether it is based on secret keys (symmetric keys) or public keys. Authentication, encryption, and integrity protection all

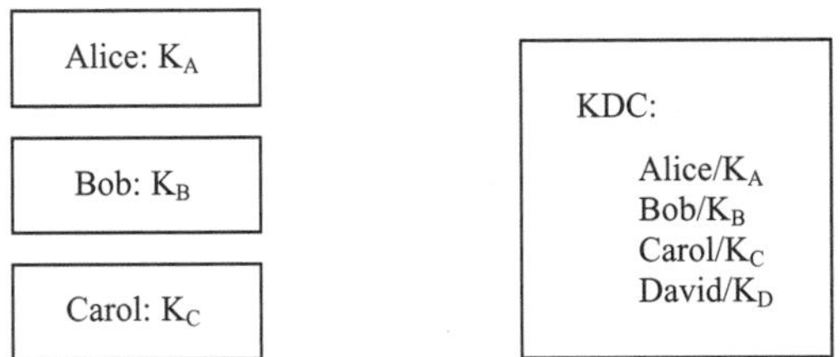

Figure 1: KDC knows one secret for each principal.

are possible. However, there are important functional differences.

One important aspect of public key cryptography is the ability to verify a signature without knowing the private value. In contrast, with secret key cryptography, the same secret that was used to generate the integrity check must be known by the verifier to verify the signature. This means that with secret keys, it is hard for Bob to prove to a third party that a message came from Alice. If only Bob and Alice know the secret, then if Alice sends a message to Bob using an integrity check based on their shared secret, Bob can know it came from Alice, but he cannot prove to anyone else that Alice generated the message because Bob could have created the same message. Also, with secret key cryptography, if Alice needs to send a message to multiple recipients and she has a different key she shares with each recipient, she has to generate an integrity check separately for each recipient, using the key she shares with that recipient. In contrast, with public key cryptography, Alice can sign the message using her private key and anyone can verify it using her public key.

Because it would be impractical to separately configure a key between every pair of entities that might want to communicate [an $O(n^2)$ solution], the usual solution is to use a key distribution center (KDC), as is done in Kerberos. The KDC stores a secret for each individual, and each individual only needs to store a single secret (the one the individual shares with the KDC). A diagram is shown in Figure 1.

If Alice wants to talk to Bob, she requests that the KDC introduce them. The KDC invents a new secret, K_{AB}, and prepares a message for Alice, encrypted with K_A (the secret the KDC shares with Alice), that tells her to use K_{AB} to talk to Bob. It also prepares a message for Bob, encrypted with K_B, that tells him to use K_{AB} to talk to Alice. See Figure 2 for an illustration.

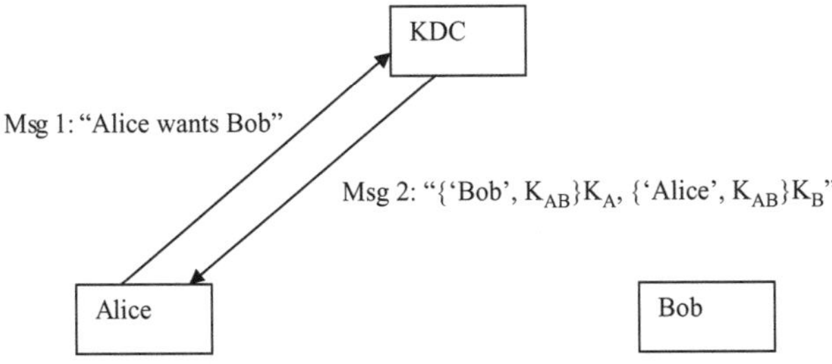

Figure 2: Message flow before Alice and Bob can talk, which uses secret keys.

FUNCTIONAL COMPARISON BETWEEN PUBLIC KEY- AND SECRET KEY-BASED SYSTEMS

If Alice and Bob each know their own private key, they each know the CA's public key, and they each have a certificate from the CA, then they can talk by exchanging certificates, without needing to talk to a third party. See Figure 3.

The functional differences between a PKI-based solution (one based on public keys) and a KDC-based solution (one based on secret keys) are described in the next few sections.

Security

The KDC-based solution will be less secure. The KDC has a highly sensitive database (secrets for all its clients). In contrast, a CA does not need to know anyone's private keys. It only certifies public keys and therefore does not have access to any secrets (other than its own private key).

A KDC must be online because it is needed to facilitate all conversations. This makes it an attractive target for network-based attacks. In contrast, the CA does not need to be online. It signs certificates once, and the certificate can be made accessible on the network, but the CA does not need to be accessible.

Because the KDC must be available to facilitate conversations, it must be replicated (because having it be down would be intolerable). Each replica needs to be physically secured. In contrast, it would not be a problem if the CA were down for some period of time. New users might not be able to be certified, but communication between existing clients would not be hindered (except possibly for revocation, although a revocation server could be different from the CA and have a different key—see the section on revocation in this chapter). Physically securing the CA is easy because it need not be accessible to the network.

The KDC needs to be a complicated system, capable of simultaneously communicating via the network to many clients simultaneously. This makes it likely that it will have security vulnerabilities. In contrast, the CA is a simple system. All it needs to do is sign certificates, a much simpler problem than communicating via a network. Plus, the CA need not be online, so if physical security is enforced, even if the CA had security vulnerabilities, they would not be exploitable. On the other hand, a real security flaw for any system is the involved humans, so if the CA operator can

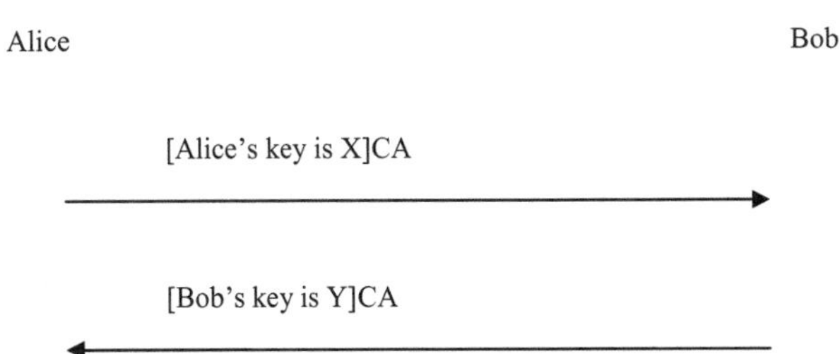

Figure 3: With certificates, Alice and Bob can immediately communicate.

be bribed or tricked or threatened, it would be possible to forge certificates.

Cost

The KDC solution will be more expensive, because the KDC is a complex, performance-sensitive, replicated system. A CA does not have these properties.

When Kerberos was designed, licensing of public key technology was prohibitively expensive, so the Kerberos designers needed to avoid public key technology. Once the RSA patent expired, a public key–based system became less expensive.

Performance

Public key cryptography is a lot slower than secret key cryptography. However, the performance of the mathematics is counteracted by the necessity, in KDC-based systems, of having additional round trips before connection setup in order to communicate with the KDC. Once a conversation is facilitated, whether with PKI or with KDC, a secret key is established between the parties, so performance is only an issue on conversation startup.

Interorganizational Communication

It is common for organizations to communicate with the outside world through a firewall. Because the KDC is the most security-sensitive box in the network, it is likely that the firewall administrator would want to block access to the KDC from outside the network. This would preclude setting up a conversation between parties in different organizations. In contrast, with a public key–based system, Alice and Bob can e-mail their certificates. Thus, a PKI-based system is more likely to work between organizations.

Issues with Public Key Infrastructure

Although on the surface a PKI-based system seems straightforward, there are many deeper issues, which we explore in the remainder of this chapter. If Alice knows her own private key, Bob knows the CA's public key, and Alice has a certificate signed by the CA that Bob trusts, then Bob can, for instance, send an encrypted message to Alice. However, how does Alice know her own private key? How does Bob know the CA's public key? How can Alice get securely certified? How can Bob obtain Alice's certificate?

PKI MODELS

In this section, we explore various ways of building the PKI. Who should be the initially trusted CAs? How does a principal obtain the CA's key? If Alice is not directly certified by a CA that Bob knows and trusts, how can Bob (or Alice) find a chain of certificates linking Alice's name with a CA that Bob trusts?

The public key(s) that Bob trusts a priori, and which are somehow securely known to Bob (e.g., by being installed on his system) are known as Bob's *trust anchors*.

Monopoly

In this model, the world chooses one organization, universally trusted by all countries, companies, organizations, and individuals, and configures that organization's public key into all software and all hardware. In other words, that key is everyone's trust anchor. Everyone obtains certificates from this one organization. This model is simple to understand and implement. However, there are problems:

- There is no such thing as a universally trusted organization.
- Even if everyone agreed to trust one organization, the entire security of the world would depend on that one organization never having an employee that could be tricked, bribed, or threatened into misusing the CA's private key.
- This model grants an eternal monopoly to one organization. Once widely deployed, it would be impractical to switch organizations if that organization started charging too much money or being careless about creating certificates, because it would mean reconfiguring everything and perhaps even changing hardware.
- The configured key can never be changed. If it ever was stolen, or if advances in cryptography warranted changing to a different algorithm or a different key size, it would be prohibitively expensive to change that key.

Oligarchy

In this model, instead of choosing a single organization, each piece of software (and perhaps hardware) comes preconfigured with several CA public keys. In some cases, users are allowed to edit that list. This eliminates the monopoly issue, but there are still problems:

- The default keys (the ones that come preconfigured) are those trusted by the software or hardware vendor, not necessarily the user.
- In the previous model, security depended on one organization never having a corruptible employee. Now there are more organizations, and a breach of an employee at any of those organizations will compromise the security of the world.
- Even if all the CAs in the default list are trustworthy, if the list is modifiable, a user can be tricked into using a platform with bad CA keys inserted. This can be because the user is using a platform in a public place (like at an Internet café) or because the user visited some site that presented a certificate signed by an unknown CA, the user was presented with a pop-up box with an obscure message about "unknown CA," and the user agreed to trust this CA forever.
- It would be impractical for even a sophisticated user to examine the list of configured CA keys to see if they are all legitimate. It is not enough to look at the organization names. It would be necessary to examine hashes of the keys.

Anarchy

In the previous models, there are no certificate chains. Alice must be directly certified by one of Bob's trust anchors. In this model, we allow chains of certificates.

In this model, users each configure their own trust anchors, based on who they have personally met, trust, and for whom they have securely received a public key. If Bob wants to find Alice's public key and Alice is not one of Bob's trust anchors, then Bob must somehow find an external source of certificates and search through them to try to find a path from one of his trust anchors to Alice's name.

This is the model used by PGP ("pretty good privacy"), a secure e-mail product. Often when there is a gathering of technical people, there is an event called a "PGP key signing party," in which people distribute their public keys and publicly announce their names and digests of their keys. Anyone who believes a person's identity and that the person has securely obtained his or her key can sign a certificate for that person. There are public databases of certificates to which anyone can contribute. Thus, if Bob wants Alice's key, and her key is not one of his trust anchors, he can search through a public database of certificates to see if he can find a path from one of his trust anchors to her name.

The problems with this model are these:

- This will not scale. If this was the model for Internet authentication, there are potentially billions of users, and if each signed, say, 10 certificates on average, the database of certificates would be on the order of 10s of billions. It would be unwieldy to search through such a database to try to find a mathematically valid sequence of certificates that would lead to Alice's name.
- Even if a path is found that mathematically works out (X1 is a trust anchor, X1 vouches for X2, X2 vouches for X3, X3 vouches for Alice), it does not mean that this path should be trusted. In a relatively small community of honest people, this scheme will seem to work, but once the community is infiltrated by people motivated to poison the database with incorrect information, there is no feasible way to securely find the key of someone several certificate hops away. Revocation is yet another issue. If someone's private key were stolen, how would they know everyone that needed to be notified?

Revocation is an interesting issue with this model. The designers of PGP suggest that to revoke your public key, you sign a revocation certificate (with the private key you want to revoke), stating "please stop using this public key for me because it has been compromised." If you knew all the certificate repositories in which anyone would be looking, you could then store the revocation certificate in each of them. That you would know all the repositories is a fairly major assumption. It also assumes that you can create such a revocation certificate (you need to know the compromised private key to create the certificate). In case the private key is on a smart card that got stolen, you would have needed to create the revocation certificate in advance, while you had control of the private key, and store it someplace for safekeeping so that it could be retrieved and distributed after the key was compromised.

As for all the users that might have your public key as one of their trust anchors, in order for revocation to work at all for them, they would have to periodically check the public certificate repositories to see if you have posted a revocation certificate.

Name-Based Trust

This is an important concept that says that instead of trust in a CA being a binary decision (the CA is either "trusted" or "not trusted"), a CA is trusted for certifying only certain name and key pairs. For this model, we assume a hierarchical name (such as a domain name server– style name). Each node in the namespace (say, "example.com") is represented by a CA, who is responsible for certifying names below it in the hierarchy. Thus, example.com might certify its child node "labs.example.com," which in turn might certify "alice.labs.example.com."

This trust policy is rather natural. The name by which an object is known implies who is trusted to certify its key. A person might be known by the name JohnDoe. Smalltown.Alaska.us, in which case it might be the town clerk of Smalltown, Alaska, USA, that would be trusted to certify their key. That person might also have an identity JD9975.RandomISP.com, in which case RandomISP would be trusted to certify the mapping between that identity and a key. Or, the person might be JohnD.Company.com, in which case Company would be trusted to certify the key of that identity. Or, the person might be agent99.freedomfighters.org, in which case freedomfighters.org would certify the mapping. It is in an organization's interest to take care to manage the key/name mappings of its members. These different identities may or may not use the same public key pair, and it is irrelevant that they might all map to the same human being. Each name is a different identity.

Top-Down, Name-Based

In this model, there is a root CA (representing the root of the namespace), each node in the namespace is represented by a CA, and each CA signs the key of each of its children. This model is scalable, and it is clear what path to take to lead to a node (follow the namespace). There are problems, however. The root must be configured to be everyone's trust anchor. If compromised, it can impersonate the world, because all certificate chains start with the root. It also gives the organization holding the root key a monopoly. We fix these problems in the next model.

Bottom-Up, Name-Based

We modify the previous model by also having each child in the namespace certify the parent. That way, the trust anchor need not be the root. With a tree, and links in both directions, one can start anywhere and navigate to anywhere else. The rule is that some principal in the namespace, probably a leaf node (say, AliceSmith.labs.Company.com) that wants the key of JohnD.Company.com, starts with its trust anchor (which could be anywhere, but the most elegant place is its own key). Starting at that place, the rule is that if you are already at an ancestor of the target name, then just follow the namespace down.

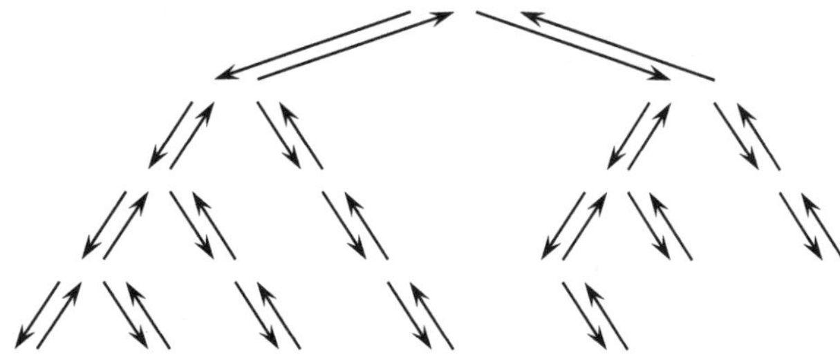

Figure 4: Name tree with bidirectional links.

Otherwise, go up as far as necessary to get to a least common ancestor (in this case it would be Company.com), and then go down from there. See Figure 4 for an example.

An additional important feature is the notion of a *cross link*. A cross link is where any node in the namespace can certify the key of any other node. Cross links are important for several reasons:

- They connect organizations before a global interconnected PKI exists.
- They bypass untrusted CAs higher in the hierarchy.

This might seem like it would lead to the anarchy model, but the rule is that only one cross link would be followed on any path. The rule is that one starts at the trust anchor, and if you are at an ancestor of the target, you go down. Otherwise, you look to see if there is a cross link from that point to an ancestor, in which case you follow it. If there is not, you go up a level and continue until you get either to the least common ancestor (in which case you go down) or to a cross link to an ancestor of the target (in which case you go down). See Figure 5 for an illustration.

The assumption is that PKIs would grow from the bottom. Each organization would grow its own PKI, and organizations would then link them together with cross links. Then, there would be a business case for providing root service. "We offer interorganizational certification. If you certify us, and let us certify you, you will have a path to the following *n* organizations that have already joined. This is how much we charge. This is how much liability we assume. This is how careful we are about checking before we certify keys."

There could be multiple roots in parallel, and different organizations might use a different subset of the roots. If there were many roots, it might be hard to find a common root, and there might be pairs of organizations that did not have a connected chain of certificates to each other.

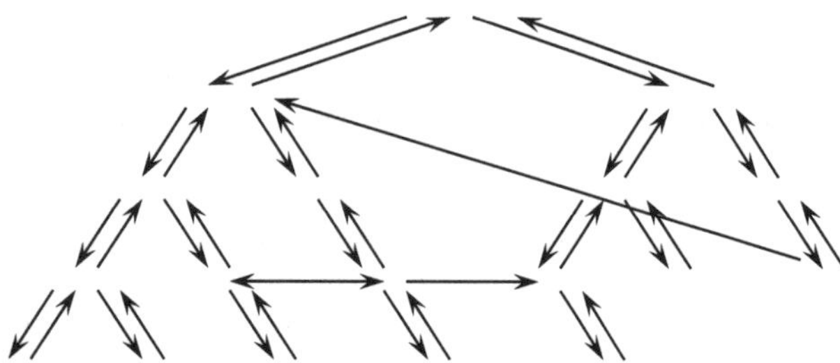

Figure 5: Name tree with bidirectional links and cross links.

The advantages of this model are these:

- To deploy public–key–based authentication and authorization within your organization, there is no need to get certificates from any outside organization.
- Certificate chain paths are easy to find.
- The policy is something that will make sense to people, without them needing to understand it, and be sufficiently flexible.
- Security of what are presumably the most security-sensitive operations, authentication between things in your own organization, is entirely in your hands. This is because chains of trust between two identities within your namespace never leave your namespace. Each of the certificates in the chain of certificates will have been issued by a CA within your organization.
- No single compromised key requires massive configuration.
- Configuration is minimal: a user's own private key can be her only trust anchor, and starting with one's own public key is the minimal configuration necessary.

Bridge Model

A model known as the bridge model had been adopted for the U.S. federal PKI. It is the same as the bottom-up model, except that the trust anchor is the root of the user's organization. This is practical in organizations in which all the workstations are centrally managed, so that in case the organization's root key changes, a central administrator can reconfigure all the machines.

To find a target's public key, start at the root of your own organization (say fbi.gov), and, if you are at an ancestor of the target, go down from there to the target's name. If not, then go up a level to what is called the "bridge CA," and then go down from there.

USING PKI

Regardless of what model is used for the trust anchors and certificate paths, there is also the problem of gathering the relevant certificates. Suppose Bob needs to know Alice's public key. There are various possibilities for gathering the chain:

- Alice could gather the chain and give them to Bob, for instance, in a real-time protocol, such as IPsec or SSL, or e-mail.
- Bob could gather the chain from some online certificate storage system.
- A helper node whose job it was to gather certificate chains could be queried, and it would gather the chain to be presented to Bob.
- The helper node might gather and verify the chain, and then sign an assertion that it has securely discovered that Alice's public key = P.

What does it mean to have a chain by which Bob will know Alice's public key? The chain must start with a trust anchor of Bob's and terminate with Alice's name. How could Alice or the helper node know what Bob's trust anchors are? The real-time protocols such as IPsec and SSL provide a method for Bob to inform Alice of his trust anchors. In PEM (privacy enhanced email, RFC 1422), the model is assumed to be the monopoly model, with the single root trust anchor configured into everything.

In the case of a helper node gathering and verifying the chain and asserting Alice's key to Bob, the helper node is completely trusted by Bob, and the trust anchor for the chain, and the legal chains, would be determined by the helper node.

In the case of Bob finding the certificate chain, it is clear what model the X.509 community had in mind because of the terminology. To them, building a chain from the target name to a trust anchor is known as building in the "forward direction," whereas building from a trust anchor to the target name is known as building in the "reverse direction." However, building from the target name is more suited to the monopoly model or perhaps the oligarchy model with very few roots.

Certificate Revocation

If a private key is stolen, it is important that the certificate vouching for the mapping between the compromised public key and the name no longer be honored. Certificates have expiration dates, but because it is expensive to issue certificates, the certificate is generally valid for a relatively long time (such as a year). It is unacceptable for someone who has stolen a private key to be able to impersonate a valid principal until the certificate expires. Therefore, there needs to be some method for more timely revocation.

There are two models in the real world for revoking credit cards when a card is reported stolen. One model is where a list of all the revoked but unexpired credit card numbers is distributed to all merchants, a model that was common several years ago. Today, instead, credit card revocation is done by having the merchant check, on each transaction, about the revocation status of a particular card.

In the PKI world, the first model is implemented through use of a CRL (certificate revocation list), periodically issued and signed by the CA or by a public key that the CA certifies as authorized to sign the CRL. The CRL contains a list of unexpired, revoked certificates. It must be issued periodically even if nothing changes, because otherwise there is no way to know whether an old CRL (before the relevant certificate was posted) was substituted for the most recent CRL. The period with which it needs to be posted must be no longer than the maximum amount of time it is acceptable for revocation to take effect.

It is possible for the CRL to get very large. In this case, it would be expensive for every principal that must verify certificates to download the latest CRL every period. In this case, an optimization to the CRL mechanism can be used that is known as a "delta CRL." A delta CRL contains a reference to the last full CRL, and it only states the changes that have occurred since that last full CRL. So, in many cases, the delta CRL will have no information (other than a pointer to the last full CRL). Only when the delta CRL starts to become large would it be necessary to issue a new full CRL, in which case the subsequent delta CRLs would be small again.

The other model for revocation is what is currently done in the credit card world. An online service accepts queries about specific certificates and responds with the revocation status of those certificates. Typically, this is done by the verifier.

CONCLUSION

PKI is very successfully deployed in the Web environment, but primarily in order for the server to authenticate to the client. Although some PKI-based email standards are in use, their wide adoption has been slow because of the difficulty in use of existing products. However, the basic concepts are sound, the advantages of having a widely deployed PKI are profound, and there is hope that sometime in the future PKI will be more widely deployed.

GLOSSARY

Authentication Showing proof of identity.

Authorization The right to access a resource or perform an action.

Certificate A signed assertion, usually the mapping between a name and a key.

Certification Authority A party that creates certificates.

KDC (Key Distribution Center) The server, in a secret key–based authentication system, that holds a key for every principal and allows secure introduction between principals.

PKI (Public Key Infrastructure) The databases, data structures, and protocols whereby public keys can be securely obtained.

Revocation Invalidation of a certificate.

CROSS REFERENCES

See *Computer and Network Authentication; Digital Certificates; Digital Signatures and Electronic Signatures; IPsec: IKE (Internet Key Exchange); PKCS (Public-Key Cryptography Standards); Public-Key Algorithms; S/MIME (Secure MIME); Secure Shell (SSH); Secure Sockets Layer (SSL).*

FURTHER READING

Adams, C., & Farrell, S. (1999). *Internet X.509 public key infrastructure certificate management protocols* (RFC 2510).

Boeyen, S., Howes, T., & Richard, P. (1999a). *Internet X.509 public key infrastructure LDAPv2 schema* (RFC 2587).

Boeyen, S., Howes, T., & Richard, P. (1999b). *Internet X.509 public key infrastructure operational protocols—LDAPv2* (RFC 2559).

Housley, R., Ford, W., Polk, W., & Solo, D. (1999). *Internet X.509 public key infrastructure certificate and CRL profile* (RFC 2459).

Housley, R., Polk, W., Ford, W., & Solo, D. (2002). *Internet X.509 public key infrastructure certificate and certificate revocation list (CRL) profile* (RFC 3280).

ISO/IEC 9594-8/ITU-T Recommendation X.509. (1997). *Information technology: Open systems interconnection: The directory: Authentication framework.*

Kaufman, C., Perlman, R., & Speciner, M. (2002). *Network security: Private communication in a public world* (2nd ed.). Englewood Cliffs, NJ: Prentice-Hall.

Myers, M., Adams, C., Solo, D., & Kemp, D. (1999). *Internet X.509 certificate request message format* (RFC 2511).

Myers, M., Ankney, R., Malpani, A., Galperin, S., & Adams, C. (1999). *X.509 Internet public key infrastructure online certificate status protocol—OCSP* (RFC 2560).

Pinchas, D., & Housley, R. (2002). *Delegated path validation and delegated path discovery protocol requirements* (RFC 3379).

S/MIME (Secure MIME)

Steven J. Greenwald, *Independent Information Security Consultant*

S/MIME (secure multipurpose Internet mail extensions) is a versatile standard designed to increase Internet e-mail security by providing authentication, message integrity, message origin nonrepudiation, and confidentiality. S/MIME is widely available because it is implemented in most modern e-mail user applications. Now in its third version, it can be considered fairly mature. S/MIME usually relies on X.509 certificates for key exchange. It assumes a threat environment in which adversaries can read and modify e-mail in transit and senders may wish to repudiate their messages. There are also some optional enhanced security services for S/MIME that provide signed receipts, security labels that can be used for MLS, RBAC, or other purposes, and signing of certificates to prevent certain vulnerabilities with X.509 certificate exchange. S/MIME may be a sensible choice for improving the security of e-mail systems on the Internet and is easy for users to employ.

S/MIME is short for secure MIME. MIME, a widely used Internet e-mail standard is an acronym for multipurpose Internet mail extensions. From this, we can immediately see that S/MIME is designed to be a way to make Internet e-mail more secure (this is sometimes referred to as "message security;" the terms "e-mail" and "message" will be intermixed in this chapter). S/MIME began with version 1 in 1995 (Galvin, Murphy, Crocker, & Freed, 1995), and is currently in its third version.

Caveat Lector: It is extremely important to view S/MIME as a way to achieve more (or better) security, and not as a security panacea. We usually cannot guarantee total e-mail security through the use of S/MIME alone (and frankly, probably not by any combination of means); as always, we should be concerned with the fundamental principle of *defense in depth* when it comes to implementing security mechanisms in particular threat environments. In this chapter, the term "security" is not meant to imply *total* security, but just *improved* security.

Version 3 of S/MIME, described in what is probably the most important S/MIME reference, RFC 2633 (RFC stands for Request for Comment), "S/MIME Version 3 Message Specification" (Ramsdell, 1999), provides a consistent way to send and receive S/MIME data via the ubiquitous Internet RFC 822 e-mail standard (Crocker, 1983). Standard Internet e-mail is often likened to sending a postcard through the mail: Anyone along the way can read the contents, the address is easily forged, and people along the way can alter the message on the postcard. The analogy is a good one, and S/MIME is an attempt to remedy these problems. It provides additional security services for e-mail in the areas of *authentication*, *message integrity*, and *nonrepudiation* (of the message's origin). S/MIME can also increase message *privacy* via confidentiality obtained through encryption.

The rest of this chapter features a brief history and overview of MIME, an examination of the objectives and threat environment of S/MIME, a look at S/MIME usage, an examination of the mechanisms used by S/MIME to achieve its security objectives, a look at how S/MIME messages are created and interpreted, a tour of the newer enhanced security services for S/MIME (RFC 2634), and a look at some alternatives to S/MIME.

A BRIEF HISTORY OF MIME

The most current version of MIME is available as a set of four Requests for Comments (RFCs 2045, 2046, 2047, and 2048), which are the default standard (Freed & Borenstein, 1996a, 1996b; Freed, Klensin, & Postel 1996; Moore, 1996). This section is a brief overview of the basic features and structure of MIME and is not intended to take the place of a detailed examination of MIME.

MIME is designed to enhance the venerable RFC 822 e-mail standard (Crocker, 1983). The problem with RFC 822 is that it addresses only textual e-mail. Before MIME, if nontext content (audio, video, image, non-ASCII (American Standard Code for Information Interchange) binary files, non-ASCII character sets, etc.) were required, ad hoc methods were used. A typical problem is that RFC 822 limits the message body to "printable" 7-bit ASCII characters. In today's world of rich character sets, many fonts, text sizes, and so forth, plain RFC 822 is often unsuitable. Before MIME, users would have to convert their data into 7-bit printable ASCII characters if they wanted to use the ubiquitous RFC 822 e-mail standard. For example, a program object file could be converted to printable hexadecimal characters (restricted to the characters 0 through 9 and A through F). This could be inefficient, and it certainly was not standardized because there were many schemes for doing such conversions.

MIME is a set of mechanisms designed to solve this problem. Basically, MIME consists of a set of predefined "Content-Types" that designate various types of data (e.g., audio, video, text, and image). A MIME encoded RFC 822 message has a message body that contains a special MIME header that gives a MIME version number and other data, and one or more "parts," in which each part is assigned a particular "Content-Type" header field. A message can contain parts of various content types via the "multipart" Content-Type. MIME is so flexible that even applications can be encoded as Content-Types (i.e., executable content such as programs or PDF files).

MIME also has a special Content-Transfer-Encoding header field that can be used to specify auxiliary encoding(s) that might be required for the various mail transport systems through which the message passes (and that requires special encoding[s]). There are two additional header fields named Content-ID and Content-Description that allow more descriptive power (if desired) for message parts.

MIME was designed from its beginnings in 1992 to be extensible, and it currently has a huge number of Content-Types. A typical modern example is the use of sending e-mail in both plain ASCII text and HTML. This is commonly done so that recipients who lack the ability to view HTML can read the plain ASCII text portion, and recipients who have HTML capability can view an HTML version of the text message, which might take advantage of HTML's variety of fonts, type size, colors, and so on.

Content types are further subdivided into subtypes. For example, a Content-Type of "image" is used for any one of the many available image formats. The specific image type is identified with a subtype. Suppose we are dealing with a JPEG image. We might see the following Content-Type and subtype: "image/jpeg." This system is flexible, because the high-level Content-Type part allows a mail agent to determine that the type is "image," even if the subtype is unknown to that agent. If types need to be mixed for some reason, then the "multipart" or "application" types can be used.

Parameters can also be added to content-subtypes and act as modifiers. An example might be the "charset" parameter that specifies a particular character set for text data. The names for all of these types and parameters are not case sensitive, and the system is flexible enough that the only thing implementers need worry about are two different types that have the same name or parameters. An example of this for text would be the following:

Content-Type: text/plain; charset=us-ascii; format=flowed
Content-Transfer-Encoding: 7-bit

This tells us that we are dealing with Content-Type "text" with content-subtype "plain" with two parameters: "charset" and "format" which have particular values assigned. The Content-Transfer-Encoding tells us that we are dealing with 7-bit words.

The following might be an example for an image:

Content-Type: image/jpeg; name="filename.jpg"
Content-Transfer-Encoding: base64

This example shows a Content-Type of "image" with a content-subtype of "jpeg" and has the parameter "name" with a particular value (in this case, the file name). The Content-Transfer-Encoding tells us that we are dealing with base64 encoding.

There is a lot more to MIME that this brief overview, and the interested reader or implementer should read the source documents cited earlier (RFCs 2045, 2046, 2047, and 2048) for more and definitive information.

S/MIME OBJECTIVES AND THREAT ENVIRONMENT

There are four major objectives for standard S/MIME: *authentication*, *message integrity*, *nonrepudiation*, and *message privacy*. In a real sense, these objectives also define the *threat environment* for which S/MIME was designed: an environment in which adversaries can read and modify messages. This threat environment is a fair assumption for the Internet and other systems that use RFC 822 type messaging.

Authentication

Authentication means that the recipient of a message can be assured that the message's identification of the sender is the actual identity of the sender, and not a spoofed, forged, or otherwise obscured version of the actual sender. This is an important and desirable property due to the ease with which RFC 822 e-mail headers can be forged. With good authentication, we can be reasonably assured that the sender is who or what it purports to be.

Message Integrity

Message integrity means that the recipient can be assured that the message received was not modified in transit. Messages can be modified by insertion of false information, deletion of information, or other trickery designed to cause security problems. This is an important property for anyone who wishes to be assured that e-mail is not tampered with in transit.

Nonrepudiation

Nonrepudiation means that the sender cannot deny sending a message (or the contents of a message). For example, if an unscrupulous person sent an order to their stockbroker via e-mail to sell 100 shares of stock and that stock later went up in price, it would be to the seller's advantage to repudiate the message to make more money. In other words, the seller would tell the broker that the message ordering the selling of the stock never occurred (or a message to sell less stock occurred, etc.). This is obviously an important property to have for financial systems, military systems, and other interests.

Message Privacy

Message privacy means that agents along the route from the sender to the receiver taken by the message cannot read the contents of the message. Going back to the postcard analogy, message privacy is, in a sense, an "envelope," (and in fact the term "enveloped-data" is used by S/MIME to refer to encrypted data along with its encrypted key). It is important to note that message privacy does not mean that the sender and receiver of the message cannot be identified but only that the contents of the message cannot be identified. This means that S/MIME offers no protection against traffic analysis.

Note that S/MIME is not specifically concerned with the high-level security property of *availability*. It makes no guarantee that a message will be delivered or that resources will be available for sending or receiving messages. Users of S/MIME should be cautioned that if there is a need for availability in a system, S/MIME is probably not a solution.

S/MIME provides authentication, message integrity, and nonrepudiation via digital signatures and provides message privacy through the use of encryption.

S/MIME USAGE

S/MIME is mainly used by *mail user agents* (MUAs)—in other words, standard RFC 822 Internet e-mail with MIME capable MUAs. S/MIME adds security services when sending messages and serves as an *interpretation* of the added cryptographic mechanisms for messages at the receiving end. Technically, S/MIME is not restricted to e-mail and any MIME transport mechanism (e.g., HTTP) can take advantage of S/MIME. RFC 2633 (Ramsdell, Ed. 1999) also mentions the following in section 1: "Further, S/MIME can be used in automated message transfer agents that use cryptographic security services that do not require any human intervention, such as the signing of software-generated documents and the encryption of FAX messages sent over the Internet." S/MIME takes advantage of the object-based features of MIME by creating MIME body types that serve S/MIME purposes. There are two basic body types: one used for digital signatures, and the other for encryption.

S/MIME allows secure messages to be exchanged in mixed transport systems (i.e., technically, *multi-level secure*, or MLS systems; in actuality, e-mail that has secure and nonsecure MIME parts). This means that (for example) a system that sends encrypted S/MIME messages might not be able to read (interpret) S/MIME messages it receives. Because of this, the various S/MIME RFCs make a distinction between *receiving* and *sending* agents (collectively known as *S/MIME agents*; note that a receiving agent can also be a sending agent, and vice versa). Another consideration is that heterogeneous MUAs might be used (in fact, for e-mail via the Internet, this is almost a certainty) and because of this the S/MIME standard recommends using a strategy of "be liberal in what you receive and conservative in what you send" (Ramsdell, 1999). For example, with the many cryptographic hash algorithms, encryption algorithms, and so forth, it is important that a MUA be able to handle on receipt as wide a variety of algorithms as possible, while retaining the ability to use a restricted set of algorithms for sending.

In practice, the average Internet e-mail user will use an X.509 public key infrastructure (PKI) to exchange certificates with other S/MIME e-mail users. Once valid certificates are exchanged (and the exchange can be done using S/MIME), the resultant S/MIME operations should be transparent to the users, who need only select the S/MIME options they want. For example, assuming a modern MUA, and once certificates are exchanged, if a user wished to send digitally signed or encrypted e-mail, the MUA would only require that those respective options be selected. For receipt of digitally signed mail, most modern MUAs will notify the user that the mail is digitally signed and automatically verify (or give a warning about) the digital signature. Encrypted mail will automatically be decrypted without any user intervention. Given that it is literally that simple, it is hard to understand why more users do not use S/MIME to digitally sign or encrypt important e-mail. One often-cited reason for not using S/MIME is that it is heavily reliant on PKI, and PKI has not become as widespread as its proponents have hoped.

S/MIME MECHANISMS

The two basic S/MIME mechanisms required are digital signatures and encryption. S/MIME uses the Public Key Cryptography Standard #7 (PKCS#7) cryptographic message syntax (CMS) for these purposes, and because every MIME body part must have a type, S/MIME uses the "application/pkcs7-mime" MIME type.

When digital signatures are used by S/MIME, multipart MIME is usually used (although another option is covered later). There are two options: the "multipart/signed" and the "application/pkcs7-signature" MIME types. This is more fully described in RFC 1847 (Galvin, Murphy, Crocker, & Freed, 1995).

Cryptographic Message Syntax Support

CMS offers a wide range of options and flexibility. As described in RFC 3369 (Housley, 2002), it is designed "to digitally sign, digest, authenticate, or encrypt arbitrary message content." It is a derivation of version 1.5 of PKCS #7 described in RFC 2315 (Kaliski, 1998), which was designed for privacy enhanced mail (described in RFCs 1421, 1422, and 1423).

CMS was designed to provide support for various types of content. Protocols and applications using CMS are expected to negotiate a set of common algorithms that are appropriate for their threat environment. This gives great flexibility, because new algorithms can be added more easily to CMS as they become available and as the state-of-the-art evolves.

In theory, there are five CMS content types that S/MIME can use: signed-data, enveloped-data, digested-data, encrypted-data, and authenticated-data. A brief description of each type follows. For more detailed information, see Housley (2002).

- **signed-data:** This type of content contains zero or more instances of digital signatures. It is a fairly standard digital signature method whereby a message digest (cryptographic hash) of the content is created, the message digest is then signed by encrypting it using the signer's private key, the signature information is collected into one "value" (object), and then a "SignedData" value is created that contains the message digest algorithm information (identification and parameters) as well as the content. The recipient independently computes a message digest in the same way that the sender did, and then uses the sender's public key to decrypt the signature and verify that the two message digests match.
- **enveloped-data:** This is simply encrypted content, as well as an encryption key. It is constructed by randomly generating a content encryption key (i.e., a session key) and encrypting the content encryption key for each recipient (there are various techniques, but one method is to encrypt using the recipient's public key, in which case only the recipient's private key can decrypt the content key). These data are collected together into a "RecipientInfo" value, the content is then encrypted using the content encryption key, and all of these are collected together to form an EnvelopedData value that can be considered an "envelope." A recipient opens the "envelope" by decrypting the content key and then decrypting the content.
- **digested-data:** This is simply a message digest (cryptographic hash) of the content. The digest is added to the content to create a "DigestedData" value. The recipient verifies the message digest by independently computing the message digest and comparing the two.
- **encrypted-data:** This is simply encrypted content but differs from enveloped data in that it does not contain a content key. Key management must be done by some other, unspecified, method (X.509 certificates are typical for S/MIME).
- **authenticated-data:** This is a method to verify content integrity. This type consists of any other type of content, a message authentication code (MAC; a digest or cryptographic hash), and an encrypted authentication key (more than one is key is allowed if there is more than one recipient). The idea is that the MAC and encrypted authentication key are enough to verify the integrity of the content.

Because CMS offers much flexibility, it is an obvious choice for S/MIME. The last three CMS content types are mentioned only for completeness, since S/MIME only uses the SignedData and EnvelopedData content types.

Backward Compatibility

There are many backward compatibility issues because S/MIME is in its third version. For a few examples, S/MIME Version 3 must support the SHA-1 cryptographic hash algorithm for backward compatibility. The MD5 message digest algorithm is recommended for backward compatibility but is not mandatory. S/MIME Version 3 should support the RSA public key system (PKCS-1) for compatibility with Version 2 digital signatures. For a complete list of all of the backward compatibility issues for Version 3 of S/MIME, see RFC 2633 (Ramsdell, 1999), section 2.

Diffie–Hellman Key Exchange

S/MIME must also support Diffie–Hellman (DH) key exchange. Because symmetric cryptography is always based on a shared secret between the sender and recipient of a message and because in some cases such a shared secret does not exist *ab initio*, DH is used for dynamically and securely constructing a shared secret key in the S/MIME threat environment. Of course, other methods exist and can be used, such as RSA. It is important to note that for algorithms such as DH and other cryptographic protocols, when the RFCs specify *random* numbers, truly random numbers must be used, and not pseudorandoms.

There are known problems with DH and S/MIME version 3, and these are addressed in RFC 2785 (Zuccherato, 2000). Basically, DH as used with S/MIME version 3 is vulnerable to the "small subgroup" attack. For a description of the attack, as well as potential remedies, see Zuccherato (2000).

X.509 Certificates

These play a major part in S/MIME. A full discussion of X.509 is beyond the scope of this chapter and is discussed elsewhere in this handbook. This chapter is restricted to discussing the role of X.509 with S/MIME.

For most use of S/MIME, X.509 certificates play a major role. For example, the typical Internet e-mail user will make use of the X.509 PKI to take advantage of the security features of S/MIME. In particular, X.509 works to disseminate the public keys used for both digital signatures and the exchange of symmetric keys for bulk encryption of message data. (Symmetric key encryption algorithms such as the Data Encryption Standard (DES) and its variants or the Advanced Encryption Standard (AES) are typically used for "bulk" encryption instead of using public key algorithms, because the latter are too inefficient for bulk encryption; however, public key systems are necessary for digital signatures and for encrypting symmetric algorithm "session keys," which are both small in size.)

Briefly, an X.509 certificate contains a public key along with some other data (such as a certificate expiration date and identification information about the certificate authority and user). Certificate authorities (CAs) are trusted third parties (TTPs) that create the certificates and sign them by encrypting them with the TTP's private key. MUAs typically come preloaded with certificates for CAs, but if they do not, there are X.509 methods for obtaining (or not, as the case may be) a certificate for a CA.

Because this chapter is not about X.509, the simplifying assumption is that both the sender and receiver MUAs use the same CA, and both have that CA's certificate (this is a reasonable assumption given that popular CA certificates come preloaded into most modern MUAs).

There are basically two X.509 certificate exchange cases to consider. Either the sender of an S/MIME message does not have the recipient's X.509 certificate or the recipient does not have the sender's X.509 certificate.

The sender lacks the recipient's certificate: This is a common situation when users first try to use S/MIME with one another. If the sender lacks the recipient's certificate, it probably means the sender lacks the recipient's public key. This means the sender cannot use encryption because that requires the recipient's public key to encrypt a content key. The sender can remedy this situation by sending an e-mail with the sender's certificate attached. This can be done with a special certificate transfer mechanism (covered later) or by simply sending a signed message (which, with most modern MUAs will cause the sender's certificate to be attached to the e-mail). When the recipient gets the e-mail, the certificate will be available and, with most modern MUAs, will automatically be entered into the recipient's certificate database (it is important to realize that some organizational-specific MUAs and also Web-based MUAs do not have S/MIME support at the time of writing). The recipient can then verify the signature by decrypting the certificate using the CA's public key, thus obtaining the sender's public key. At this point, the recipient only needs to reply to the e-mail with either a signed or encrypted message, which will contain the recipient's certificate (with most modern MUAs), and then the sender will then be able to decrypt that certificate to obtain the recipient's public key. Because of the lack of standardization among MUAs though, it is important that S/MIME compliance be tested before one relies on it.

The recipient lacks the sender's certificate: This is also a common situation, but it is not a particular problem with S/MIME. If the sender has the recipient's certificate (and thus public key), the sender can send digitally signed or encrypted mail to the recipient on request, which will automatically include the sender's certificate. If the sender does not have the recipient's certificate, a special certificate only message can be sent to the recipient to provide the sender's certificate. Of course, there are other methods to exchange certificates, such as sending diskettes through the regular mail or hand delivering them.

Once the sender and recipient have each other's public key, it becomes possible for each to digitally sign messages (so that the other can authenticate them) or to encrypt messages using a symmetric cryptographic algorithm session key (content key) that is exchanged by encrypting it with the recipient's public key so that it can only be decrypted with the recipient's private key. This is generally all transparent to the user.

Other Options

S/MIME has many options that are negotiable between sender and recipient. Some examples are the choice of symmetric algorithm, the choice of message digest (cryptographic hash function), key size, and so forth. The way the negotiation is done is fairly simple. Capability lists for each entity are created from information in previous communications. In addition, it is possible to use other methods (such as out-of-band communication). All options for a client need not be listed, and in general, options are listed in preference order. For example, a particular client might wish to use RC5 as a block cipher, specify a particular key length, the number of rounds, and the block size. RFC 2633 (Ramsdell, 1999), section 2.7.1 (for example), gives the rules for deciding how to negotiate the capabilities for the receiver. This flexibility is a major feature of S/MIME, especially with the rapidity with which cryptographic technology changes.

Multiple Recipients

Multiple recipients are allowed with S/MIME. The utility and convenience of sending one message to multiple recipients should be obvious, but in practice it poses an interesting security problem. RFC 2633 (Ramsdell, 1999) 2.7.3 warns about the following cryptographic vulnerability when using this capability:

> If a sending agent is composing an encrypted message to a group of recipients where the encryption capabilities of some of the recipients do not overlap, the sending agent is forced to send more than one message. It should be noted that if the sending agent chooses to send a message encrypted with a strong algorithm and then send the same message encrypted with a weak algorithm, someone watching the communications channel may be able to learn the contents of the strongly-encrypted message simply by decrypting the weakly-encrypted message.

An attack based on this potential vulnerability is fairly straightforward. The attacker simply cracks the message with the weakest encryption (presumably this is feasible). At this point, the attacker has the plaintext of the message and can perform a known-plaintext attack on the other recipients and perhaps derive the symmetric session (content) keys used. Even so, this type of known-plaintext attack is not a particularly worrisome threat because content keys should be changed often (in fact, once for each S/MIME transmission). However, assuming it can be done (a big assumption!), it allows the attacker to see the text of the most "highly" encrypted message. In effect, this is a "weak link in the chain" problem. If this problem is a serious consideration, why bother to use strong encryption when a weak algorithm will allow an attacker to feasibly decrypt the message in the first place? This is also a concern for "secure mailing lists," which are covered later.

CREATION AND INTERPRETATION OF S/MIME MESSAGES

All or any subparts of a MIME message may be secured with S/MIME, but it is important to note that the RFC 822 headers are not part of MIME and therefore are not necessarily secured by S/MIME in any way. This means that it is not possible to use S/MIME to hide the sender or recipient IDs. In any event, the parts that are to be secured are done so by making them *canonical MIME entities*. This allows the CMS to produce a *CMS object* that is then "wrapped" in MIME with the appropriate transfer encoding. It is that simple.

On receipt, the reverse happens: the security services for the appropriate S/MIME type are invoked which results in a MIME entity that is presumably passed on to a MIME capable user agent for further processing (such as decoding and presentation to the user).

The purpose of converting each MIME entity into a canonical form is so that it can be unambiguously (and uniquely) interpreted by the MUA that receives it (and the MUA's environment). Therefore, canonicalization is mandatory for enveloping (encrypting) and signing. Canonicalization details depend on the specific MIME type. This is more of a MIME issue than an S/MIME issue.

The "application/pkcs7-mime type" is used for CMS EnvelopedData and SignedData types. There are several types of application/pkcs7-mime objects, which gives great flexibility (and the potential for confusion if the MUAs are not in agreement).

Filename Extensions

When agents use S/MIME types, they should use specific filename extensions for particular types of S/MIME objects. Treating S/MIME objects as files is useful for several reasons. The objects can be handled as files and stored on disk. Also, for gateways that do not recognize S/MIME entities, treating an S/MIME object as a file causes the gateway to operate in a default manner (i.e., treat the entities as a generic attachment) that allows it to transition smoothly through the gateway. It also allows certain receivers to decide on the specific mechanism to use to handle that file (S/MIME) type, but note that this practice is *not* how standard S/MIME should work (the MIME types should be the determining criteria). Three filename extensions are used.

1. *Application/pkcs7-mime* This type is used for SignedData and EnvelopedData and uses the ".p7m" file extension.
2. *Application/pkcs7-mime* This type is used for "degenerate" SignedData "certs-only" messages (messages whose only function is to exchange an X.509 certificate) and uses the ".p7c" file extension.
3. *Application/pkcs7-signature* This type is used for digital signatures and uses the ".p7s" file extension.

Enveloped-Only Messages

An enveloped-only message is one that is encrypted along with its content (session) key but is not signed and is used for confidentiality and privacy. RFC 2633 warns (in section 3.2.2) that such messages do not guarantee message integrity because they are not signed (it is possible for an adversary to replace the encrypted data in such a way that it appears authentic).

The MIME entity is processed into a CMS object of type EnvelopedData. A copy of the content-encryption key (i.e., the session key) is also encrypted. The object is then turned into an application/pkcs7-mime entity. The "enveloped-data" parameter is used along with the ".p7m" file extension. RFC 2633 gives the following sample message.

```
Content-Type: application/pkcs7-mime; smime-type=
   enveloped-data; name=smime.p7m
Content-Transfer-Encoding: base64
Content-Disposition: attachment; filename=smime.p7m
rfvbnj756tbBghyHhHUujhJhjH77n8HHGT9HG4VQpfy
   F467GhIGfHfYT6
7n8HHGghyHhHUujhJh4VQpfyF467GhIGfHfYGTrfvbnj
   T6jH7756tbB9H
f8HHGTrfvhJhjH776tbB9HG4VQbnj7567GhIGfHfYT6g
   hyHhHUujpfyF4
0GhIGfHfQbnj756YT64V
```

Signed-Only Messages

There are two types of signed-only messages: application/pkcs7-mime with SignedData, and multipart/signed. The latter is the preferred method because the receiver can always view the cleartext MIME data (e.g., ASCII text) of a multipart/signed message, even if they are not S/MIME capable (granted, the signature portion itself will probably look like gibberish).

application/pkcs7-mime with SignedData: The MIME entity is processed into a CMS object of type SignedData and is turned into an application/pkcs7-mime entity. It uses the signed-data parameter with a file extension of ".p7m". RFC 2633 gives the following sample message (note that the actual signed message is not understandable to an S/MIME incapable MUA):

```
Content-Type: application/pkcs7-mime; smime-type=
   signed-data; name=smime.p7m
Content-Transfer-Encoding: base64
Content-Disposition: attachment; filename=smime.p7m
567GhIGfHfYT6ghyHhHUujpfyF4f8HHGTrfvhJhjH776t
   bB9HG4VQbnj7
77n8HHGT9HG4VQpfyF467GhIGfHfYT6rfvbnj756tbBg
   hyHhHUujhJhjH
HUujhJh4VQpfyF467GhIGfHfYGTrfvbnjT6jH7756tbB9
   H7n8HHGghyHh
6YT64V0GhIGfHfQbnj75
```

Signing Using the Multipart/Signed Format: This is also know as "clear signing" because it will be viewable by recipients who have no S/MIME capability. It is broken down into two parts: the first contains the entity that is signed and the second contains the actual CMS "detached" signature SignedData object. The "application/pkcs7-signature" MIME type is used and the "micalg" parameter denotes the message digest algorithm used. RFC 2633 gives the following sample message (note that the signed message itself is understandable even to an S/MIME incapable MUA):

```
Content-Type: multipart/signed; protocol="application/
   pkcs7-signature"; micalg=sha1; boundary=boundary42
–boundary42
```

Content-Type: text/plain

This is a clear-signed message.

–boundary42

Content-Type: application/pkcs7-signature; name=smime.p7s

Content-Transfer-Encoding: base64

Content-Disposition: attachment; filename=smime.p7s

ghyHhHUujhJhjH77n8HHGTrfvbnj756tbB9HG4VQpfyF467GhIGfHfYT6

4VQpfyF467GhIGfHfYT6jH77n8HHGghyHhHUujhJh756tbB9HGTrfvbnj

n8HHGTrfvhJhjH776tbB9HG4VQbnj7567GhIGfHfYT6ghyHhHUujpfyF4

7GhIGfHfYT64VQbnj756

–boundary42–

Signing and Encrypting

Both signing and encrypting a message are straightforward: the signed-only and encrypted-only formats are nested. The message can be signed first and then encrypted, or the opposite can be done. When signing first, the signatories are hidden by the encryption. When encrypting first, the signatories are not obscured by the encryption and can be verified without decrypting the message (this may be useful in some environments). RFC 2633 mentions the following security ramifications for the various methods.

> A recipient of a message that is encrypted and then signed can validate that the encrypted block was unaltered, but cannot determine any relationship between the signer and the unencrypted contents of the message. A recipient of a message that is signed-then-encrypted can assume that the signed message itself has not been altered, but that a careful attacker may have changed the unauthenticated portions of the encrypted message.

Certificates-Only Message

Certificates-only messages exist to allow exchanging X.509 certificates or certificate revocation lists. The certificates are turned into a CMS SignedData object and enclosed in an application/pkcs7-mime MIME entity with the certs-only parameter and the ".p7c" file extension.

ENHANCED SECURITY SERVICES FOR S/MIME (RFC 2634)

RFC 2634, titled "Enhanced Security Services for S/MIME" (Hoffman, 1999) describes four optional security enhancements for S/MIME. The four services are signed receipts, security labels, secure mailing lists, and signing certificates. Signed receipts, security labels, and secure mailing lists are useful for business and finance applications (among others). Signing certificates are used when certificates are transmitted with signed messages. The section is a cursory look at the enhanced security services (for more details, see RFC 2634).

Triple Wrapping

A system called *triple wrapping* is used for the security enhancements and is worth noting. Triple wrapping means that a message is signed, then encrypted, and then signed again (not necessarily by the original signers). The "inside" (first) signature is used for integrity, origin nonrepudiation, and binding security attributes to the content. Security attributes can be used for things such as access control. The second wrapping, the encrypted body, provides confidentiality, including hiding the inside signature. The "outside" (last) signature is used for authentication and integrity for information processed "hop-by-hop" where each "hop" is an intermediate entity such as a mail list agent. The attributes of the outside signature can be used for access control and routing decisions.

Signed Receipts

Signed receipts are an attempt to emulate the same physical concept with normal mail. A receipt is bound to the original message though a digital signature, so it may be used only for signed messages. If a recipient returns a signed receipt, then it provides proof to the sender that the message was delivered and that the recipient could verify the digital signature.

Security Labels

A security label is a set of information that helps define the sensitivity of the content. This information can be used to check if a user is authorized to access the S/MIME content (protect by encryption). Security labels can also be used for routing, can be used for an MLS hierarchy (e.g., "unclassified," "confidential," "secret"), and can be used for role-based access control (RBAC) so that one or more roles can be bound to the content.

Secure Mailing Lists

Mailing lists are handy and well known. When using S/MIME, it can become difficult to use a mailing list because recipients may have different encryption requirements. For a large number of recipients this can be a time-consuming task. *Mail list agents* (MLAs) can take a single message and do all of the recipient specific encryption processing. The MLA appears to the originator as a single message recipient, but it redistributes the message to all of the mailing list members automatically, thus reducing the management burden on the list administrator.

Secure mailing lists also have a feature to prevent mail loops. A mail loop happens when a mailing list is a member of another mailing list, and vice versa. In such a case, a message will bounce back and forth between the lists and create a cascade of messages. MLAs prevent mail loops by using an attribute of the outer signature of a triple wrapped message. If the MLA encounters its own unique identifier, it knows that a loop exists and will not send the message again.

Note that with secure mailing lists, the "weak link in the chain" effect mentioned earlier can happen.

Signing Certificates

There are several attacks against the signature verification process in S/MIME that are done by replacing the certificate(s) that are used for signature verification. A SigningCertificate attribute is designed to help protect against these attacks.

Security Issues With the Enhancements

The enhancements open up a whole area of security issues. It is important that the user understand what these are, because improper or naïve use could cause some horrific security problems. A full explication of this is given in section 6 of RFC 2634 and should be required reading for anyone using the enhancements.

ALTERNATIVES TO S/MIME

There are alternatives to S/MIME. One criticism of S/MIME is that it is reliant on the X.509 architecture and therefore TTPs (to some, this is not a criticism but a feature). Because the alternatives are covered in other chapters, they will not be discussed in any detail here. Some of them are using the digital signature standard (DSS), PGP, IPSec, SSL, Kerberos, and SSH (alone or in combination). Many of these can be used in conjunction with S/MIME.

One more alternative should be mentioned. That is to use standard RFC 822 e-mail with a "grow your own" solution. Unless you are an information system security researcher or an experienced developer, this could be difficult, expensive, and have a particularly dangerous outcome. Some of the issues that have to be dealt with are the key exchange problem, digital signatures, encryption, cipher suite compatibility, management and infrastructure issues, public key infrastructure issues, random and pseudorandom number generation, implementation details, and so forth.

Of course, there is one other option: avoid using e-mail for all sensitive transmissions.

CONCLUSIONS

We have seen that S/MIME is designed to be a way to make e-mail more secure. It is important not to lose sight of the fact that "more secure" does not mean "perfectly secure"—it is probable that S/MIME contains some serious flaws that will be discovered in the future (this is typical of virtual every security protocol). For example, one criticism of S/MIME (really, a criticism of existing security services) is that encrypted S/MIME messages can interfere with virus scanners (the kind the operate at the mail gateway); clearly unless the virus scanner possesses the key used for an encrypted message, it cannot reliably scan a message for a virus or other malware.

However, S/MIME often can be used to improve security, especially considering that most e-mail traffic is neither signed nor encrypted. S/MIME offers a relatively easy solution for users to get these services. It is also standardized, consistent, and present in most modern MUAs. Considering that RFC 822 e-mail specifies no security at all, S/MIME is a viable choice for adding authentication, message integrity, nonrepudiation, and increasing privacy via providing confidentiality through encryption. In addition, the S/MIME enhanced security services offers signed receipts, security labels (particularly important for MLS and RBAC), secure mailing lists, and signing of certificates to prevent certificate vulnerabilities. Although there are alternatives to S/MIME, given that it is implemented in most modern MUAs and is a well-established standard (being in its third version at the time of writing), it is a sensible choice for those looking to improve the security of their e-mail systems.

GLOSSARY

Certificate Authority (CA) Usually for X.509. A trusted third party used for the exchange of public keys (among other things).

Cryptographic Message Syntax (CMS) For a more detailed explanation, see the section with the same name in this chapter.

Diffie-Hellman key exchange protocol A method of creating a shared secret (a key) between two communicating entities with the goal that an eavesdropper can not deduce the key.

Mail List Agent (MLA) Software that handles distribution of e-mail from senders to a list of multiple recipients.

Mail User Agent (MUA) Typically the software used to read and send mail by a user.

Message Authentication Code (MAC) A type of cryptographic hash, or message digest.

Multipurpose Internet Mail Extensions (MIME) For a more detailed explanation, please see the section with the same name in this chapter.

Multi-Level Security (MLS) Security that uses a lattice structure to partially order a hierarchy of security labels/levels.

Public Key Cryptography Standard (PKCS) Retrieved January 5, 2004, from http://www.rsasecurity.com/rsalabs/pkcs/

Public Key Infrastructure (PKI) A system based on one or more trusted third parties that is designed to manage, store, disseminate, and revoke public keys. Typically X.509 for S/MIME.

Role-Based Access Control (RBAC) A system of access control based on labeled "roles" that contain privileges, where users associated with particular roles may exercise those privileges. Control.

Secure/Multipurpose Internet Mail Extensions (S/MIME) See this chapter.

Trusted Third Party (TTP) A third-party entity that is trusted by its users. Useful in situations where users may not trust one another.

CROSS REFERENCES

See *Digital Certificates; Digital Signatures and Electronic Signatures; E-Mail and Instant Messaging; Multilevel Security.*

REFERENCES

Crocker, D. (1983). *Standard for the format of ARPA Internet text messages* (STD 11, RFC 822). Retrieved January 5, 2004, from http://www.faqs.org/rfcs/rfc822.html

Crocker, S., Freed, N., Galvin, J., & Murphy, S. (1995). *MIME object security services* (RFC 1848). Retrieved January 5, 2004, from http://www.faqs.org/rfcs/rfc1848.html

Freed, N., & Borenstein, N. (1996). *Multipurpose Internet mail extensions (MIME) part one: format of Internet message bodies* (RFC 2045). Retrieved January 5, 2004, from http://www.faqs.org/rfcs/rfc2045.html

Freed, N., & Borenstein, N. (1996). *Multipurpose Internet mail extensions (MIME) part two: media types* (RFC 2046). Retrieved January 5, 2004, from http://www.faqs.org/rfcs/rfc2046.html

Freed, N., Klensin, J., & Postel, J. (1996). *Multipurpose Internet mail extensions (MIME) part four: Registration procedures* (RFC 2048). Retrieved January 5, 2004, from http://www.faqs.org/rfcs/rfc2048.html

Galvin, J., Murphy, S., Crocker, S., & Freed, N. (1995). *Security multiparts for MIME: Multipart/signed and multipart/encrypted* (RFC 1847). Retrieved January 5, 2004, from http://www.faqs.org/rfcs/rfc1847.html

Hoffman, P. (Ed.). (1999). *Enhanced security services for S/MIME* (RFC 2634). Retrieved January 5, 2004, from http://www.faqs.org/rfcs/rfc2634.html

Housley, R. (2002). *Cryptographic message syntax (CMS)* (RFC 3369). Retrieved January 5, 2004, from http://www.faqs.org/rfcs/rfc3369.html

Kaliski, B. (1998). *PKCS #7: Cryptographic message syntax version 1.5* (RFC 2315). Retrieved January 5, 2004, from http://www.faqs.org/rfcs/rfc2315.html

Moore, K. (1996). *MIME (multipurpose internet mail extensions) part three: Message header extensions for non-ASCII text* (RFC 2047). Retrieved January 5, 2004, from http://www.faqs.org/rfcs/rfc2047.html

Ramsdell, B. (Ed.). (1999). S/MIME version 3 message specification (RFC 2633). Retrieved January 5, 2004, from http://www.faqs.org/rfcs/rfc2633.html

Zuccherato, R. (2000). Methods for avoiding the "small-subgroup" attacks on the Diffie–Hellman key agreement method for S/MIME (RFC 2785). Retrieved January 5, 2004, from http://www.faqs.org/rfcs/rfc2785.html

PGP (Pretty Good Privacy)

Stephen A. Weis, *MIT Computer Science and Artificial Intelligence Laboratory*

INTRODUCTION

A fascinating story from the early 1990s Internet boom is the development of PGP, or "Pretty Good Privacy." PGP is a program for encrypting and digitally signing data and is most frequently used for e-mail. In fact, PGP may be the most well-known e-mail encryption software in existence with over 8 million users worldwide (PGP Corporation, n.d.). PGP's notoriety is largely due to the legal issues surrounding its creation, rather than for its technical merits.

PGP is one of the few examples of software created in blatant disregard of patent and export laws to evolve into a legitimate commercial product. Illegal software of this nature is sometimes referred to as *guerillaware* and might include peer-to-peer file sharing networks like Kazaa or DVD copying software such as DeCSS. The legal battles faced by PGP's creator, Phil Zimmermann, illustrate several policy barriers to developing cryptographic products that existed in the 1990s—namely, patent and export restrictions. Technically, PGP offers lessons of how performance, usability, and compatibility can affect adoption of a cryptographic product.

This chapter introduces PGP's applications and underlying cryptographic components in the first section. The second section presents a short history of PGP. The third section describes several PGP implementations and alternative secure e-mail models, followed by a section that analyzes several problems of PGP and suggests lessons that might be learned. The final section speculates future directions of PGP and e-mail security in general.

Basics of PGP

E-mail is a common fixture in most U.S. households, despite having inherent privacy and authenticity issues. Broadly speaking, PGP is an e-mail encryption program that can address some e-mail security concerns. More accurately, PGP is a public-key cryptographic suite, providing encryption, digital signatures, key generation, and key management functionality. Although PGP may be used to encrypt and sign arbitrary data and is often used for disk encryption, it is primarily used for e-mail encryption. For convenience, this chapter specifically discusses e-mail and may use the phrase "unencrypted e-mail" in cases where "unencrypted data" or "disk" might apply.

Anyone who can tap the network may intercept and read unencrypted traffic. Although tapping wires or corrupting network routers are not simple tasks, unencrypted wireless access points that are vulnerable to eavesdropping are becoming common. Snoops may intercept traffic sent through insecure access points and archive it for later analysis. This lack of privacy is inherent in most e-mail and instant messaging applications.

E-mail also lacks secure mechanisms to ensure message authenticity and integrity. As most spam recipients know, it is a trivial matter to send a message with an arbitrary "From:" header. Without cryptographic protection, it is easy to forge both message origins and contents. The lack of e-mail authentication is becoming more of a problem as viruses and worms cull e-mail addresses from infected hosts' address books or as "phishing" attacks forge official-looking e-mail in an attempt to steal login details.

How can you ensure that your message wasn't intercepted or modified in transit? How can you tell if a coworker really sent you a message with an attachment? How can you tell if a message really originated from an online stock broker or an auction site? PGP address all of these problems using public-key cryptography.

PGP guarantees e-mail privacy by encrypting messages with the recipient's public key. This encrypted e-mail can only be read by the holder of the corresponding private key, namely the intended receiver. PGP provides e-mail authenticity and integrity through digital signatures. Users can sign message contents and headers prior to encryption. This allows users to verify that signatures on message contents and headers correspond to the received plaintext message.

This abstract view of encryption and signatures ignores the problem of key distribution. How does the sender acquire the receiver's public key to encrypt? How does the receiver acquire the sender's public key to verify signatures? Essentially, how does any user know that any public key is authentic?

Most cryptographic systems rely on a public key infrastructure (PKI) to store and distribute public keys. All users in the system will implicitly trust some part of the PKI, usually a certain certificate authority (CA). All trust in the system is implicitly derived from trust in the CA. In practice, most PKIs are hierarchical and have one centralized authority that all users implicitly trust. One innovation of PGP is that it may either use a centralized PKI or a "web of trust" model, which is discussed in the following section.

Technology Highlights

The previous section takes a high-level approach to cryptographic primitives and omits details about specific algorithms or practical constraints. Encryption and signature algorithms were only used abstractly, without any consideration of how they applied to PGP. This section discusses some of PGP's technological features.

One of PGP's most distinctive contributions is the "web of trust" PKI model. Rather than relying on a centralized hierarchy of Certificate Authorities, any user in a PGP web of trust may issue a certificate binding an identity to a public key. For example, a user Alice may issue a certificate stating, "I believe that Bob's key is k. Signed, Alice." This operation is often referred to as "signing a key," for example, "Alice signs Bob's key." Although technically inaccurate, this phrase is useful in describing links in the web of trust.

For example, suppose a third user, Carol, already trusts Alice and receives Bob's public key. With Alice's certificate, Carol may reason, "I trust Alice. This certificate says Alice trusts k is Bob's key. Therefore, I will trust that k is Bob's key." Thus, certificates are transitive. Each user may have a policy to decide how much trust to put in a particular certificate. This process is illustrated in Figure 1.

The transitive property of certificates allows users in a web of trust to "recommend" public keys to other users. PGP's web of trust model also allows users to assign varying degrees of trust to different certificates. This model offers more flexibility than traditional, hierarchical PKIs, where all certificates are issued by trusted certificate authorities (CAs). In a web of trust, all users in a web of trust can effectively act as their own CA but must then decide whom they trust and to what degree.

Modern social networking services such as Friendster or Orkut capture the spirit of a web of trust PKI. The idea is that a close-knit group of people would sign each other's keys. Eventually, connections between different groups would allow two strangers to establish trust in each other through a network of mutual friends. PGP users are not limited to a web of trust. In practice, centralized key servers, such as pgp.mit.edu, may store and distribute keys and coexist with a web of trust.

Another key feature of PGP is its standardized formats for encrypted messages, signatures, certificates, and public keys. A standardized message format allowed PGP be integrated into a variety of mail clients and allowed a flexible public key infrastructure. PGP's message formats have evolved through several RFCs (requests for information; Internet Engineering Task Force, 1996). Much of the same functionality is also available in S/MIME's (secure multipurpose Internet mail extension) cryptographic message formats (Kaliski, 2003).

Theoretically, all of PGP's operations could be carried out using solely public key algorithms. However, public key operations are still too computationally intensive for most applications. Standardized public key primitives also typically have a maximum block size, which complicates operations on variable length or streaming data. As a practical optimization, PGP uses both public key encryption and symmetric encryption algorithms.

To encrypt a message, PGP will first generate a random *session key* to be used by a symmetric algorithm. As the name suggests, session keys are used for a single communication session and stored for a long term. Session keys should be indistinguishable from randomness and so are typically generated using a cryptographic pseudo-random generator or dedicated random number generation hardware.

The plaintext message will be encrypted under the session key using a symmetric algorithm. The session key is then encrypted using a public key encryption algorithm. Note that the session key is being treated both as a key and as a message. The ciphertext output from both operations is sent to the message recipient, who is able to decrypt the session key and recover the message plaintext.

A second performance and implementation issue arises in creating message signatures. Most practical signature algorithms have a maximum block size and are relatively costly operations. Rather than signing each block of a message, PGP will sign a *message digest* of the entire message. A message digest is a short string that is easy to compute from an arbitrary length string, such that it is difficult to find two messages that collide to the same digest. In practice, a cryptographic hash function such as MD5 or SHA-1 is used as a digest function. (However, weaknesses recently discovered in both MD5 and SHA-1 may make SHA-256 the de facto standard cryptographic hash function.)

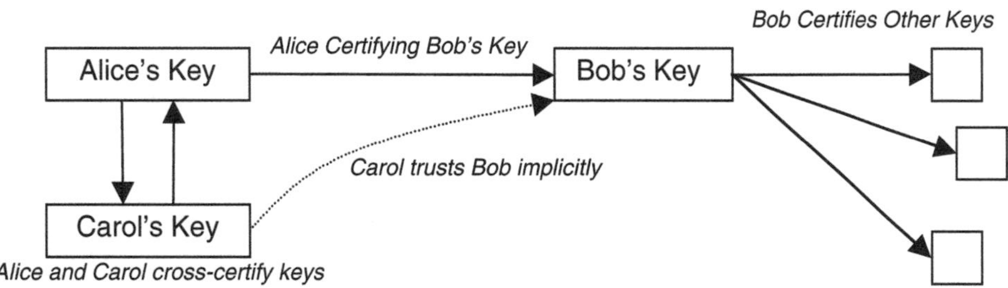

Figure 1: A "web of trust" between Alice, Bob, and Carol.

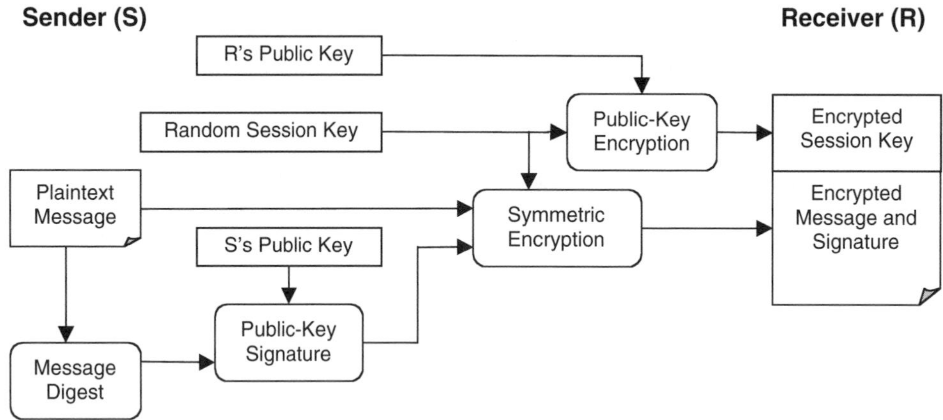

Figure 2: Dataflow diagram of PGP sign-and-encrypt process.

Typically, PGP users will first sign a message and encrypt both the message and the signature. This embeds an authentication and integrity check within the encrypted message that the recipient can verify. Figure 2 illustrates then entire sign-and-encrypt process.

Supported Algorithms and Key Recommendations

PGP supports the following public key encryption, signature, and key exchange algorithms:

- RSA
- El Gamal
- DSA
- Diffie–Hellman
- Elliptic curve public key algorithms.

PGP supports the following symmetric encryption algorithms:

- AES
- CAST
- Triple-DES
- IDEA
- Twofish.

PGP supports the following message digest algorithms:

- SHA-1
- MD5
- RIPEMD.

A common PGP configuration is to use RSA/IDEA/MD5 for public key, symmetric encryption, and message digest algorithms. Rather than for technical merits, this configuration was chosen specifically to avoid using the U.S. federal government's Data Encryption Standard (DES) and Secure Hash Algorithm (SHA-1) standards. Both of these standards, as well as DES's successor AES, are publicly available and patent-free (AES Homepage, n.d.).

RSA keys may be of various lengths, including 512, 1024, and 2048 bits. RSA keys of size 1024 are believed to be secure for all practical purposes. However, recent developments would allow a large organization to break a 1024-bit RSA public key in one year with $10–50 million dollars worth of hardware (Kaliski, 2003). RSA 2048-bit keys are still believed to be secure against powerful adversaries for the foreseeable future (Lenstra & Verheul, 2003). With these considerations, a patent-free, standardized PGP configuration with sufficient public key size is RSA-2048/AES/SHA-1, although there are no known breaks in RSA/IDEA/MD5 or any other supported configuration is insecure.

HISTORY OF PGP

Origins of PGP

The development of PGP may be traced to the convergence of three key technological threads starting in the late 1970s and continuing through the early 1990s. The first was the maturation of the field of public key cryptography. The second was the advent of personal computers, particularly among hobbyist enthusiasts. Third was the rise in network communications. For the first time, a sizable number of computer enthusiasts and college students were connecting to the Internet and bulletin board systems with personal computers powerful enough to support public key cryptography. Appropriately, public key cryptography seems to have both private and public origins. Some of the earliest pioneers were Ralph Merkle, Whitfield Diffie, and Martin Hellman, who laid the foundation of modern public key cryptography circa 1974 (Diffie & Hellman, 1976; Merkle, 1978). Of particular importance was the Diffie–Hellman key exchange protocol based on the hardness of the discrete logarithm problem. Their work was among the first "public" public key cryptography results.

These early developments inspired the creation of the RSA public key cryptosystem by Ronald Rivest, Adi Shamir, and Len Adleman (1978) around 1976–1977. RSA's security is based on the hardness of factoring large numbers, which is a famous outstanding mathematical problem.

It is likely that at least the intelligence communities in the United States and United Kingdom developed their own classified, "private" public key cryptographic primitives. In fact, documents declassified in the late 1990s reveal that in 1970, British researcher James Ellis outlined the possibilities for public key encryption (Ellis, 1970). Similar documents revealed that another British researcher, Clifford Cocks (1973), developed a classified RSA variant in 1973.

One of RSA's strongest advantages was the fact that the same public keys could both encrypt and sign documents. RSA could also be executed, albeit slowly, on the emerging personal computer market. In fact, RSA was practical enough to be a viable commercial product.

In 1983, the U.S. Patent Office granted a patent for RSA to the Massachusetts Institute of Technology (MIT; U.S. Patent No. 4,405,829, 1983). Although this patent expired in 2000, it would become an integral part of PGP's history. MIT granted full licensing rights of RSA to Rivest, Shamir, and Adleman, who founded a company to develop commercial cryptographic and security products called RSA Data Security. Today this company is a known as RSA Security.

In 1986, RSA Security released a program for encrypting e-mail with RSA called MailSafe. One problem with MailSafe was that its users could only send secure e-mail to other MailSafe users. As a result, MailSafe never developed a large user base and represented a small fraction of RSA Security's revenue.

One person who did acquire a copy of MailSafe was an independent computer scientist named Phil Zimmermann. At the time, Zimmermann had a strong interest in both cryptography and privacy rights. He had been considering developing his own implementation of RSA for the IBM PC. Although Zimmermann did and still does profit from the sale of PGP, he was also motivated by the idea that individual privacy is sacrosanct. In his own words, Zimmermann (2003, n.p.) comments on the reasons he wrote PGP: "PGP empowers people to take their own privacy into their own hands. There has been a growing social need for it. That's why I wrote it."

Zimmermann worked on RSA implementation until 1990. At this point, Zimmermann contacted RSA Security and requested a "free license" to use the patent-protected RSA algorithm. RSA Security denied his request, although they offered to sell Zimmermann a license. Zimmermann declined but nonetheless continued work on PGP. Because Zimmermann had no license to use RSA, releasing his software would violate U.S. patent laws.

A major catalyst in the eventual release of PGP was the U.S. Senate. The Comprehensive Counter-Terrorism Act of 1991 (S. 266 and H.R. 731, 1991), contained a clause in Section 2201 stating that electronic communication service operators and manufacturers of equipment were legally obligated to "ensure that communications systems permit the government to obtain the plain text contents of voice, data and other communications when appropriately authorized by law."

Broadly translated, an implementation of an encryption algorithm constituted "electronic communications service equipment." Essentially, S. 266 required that any software or hardware implementations of encryption algorithms contain "backdoors" allowing government to read any encrypted messages. Strong cryptography, unless approved by the government, would be illegal.

Rather, the government supported key escrow. Users would register their private keys with a government organization. Those keys would be available to law enforcement and intelligence organizations that obtained a subpoena. Although government support for cryptographic key escrow is essentially dead, security concerns could spur renewed interest in key escrow.

For example, the new U.S. Transport Security Agency (TSA) forbids the use of any non-TSA-approved luggage locks. Authorized TSA baggage screeners may unlock TSA-approved locks. Ironically, many people locked their luggage to protect against theft by the very same baggage handlers who now have a master key (Travel Sentry, n.d.).

Bill S. 266 spurred privacy rights organizations and software makers into action. This legislation came at a time when online communication was rapidly growing and when both individuals and corporations had legitimate interests in secure communications. The bill could have burdened software and hardware manufacturers with significant new costs. With strong lobbying from the Electronic Frontier Foundation (EFF) and RSA Security, the offending language that required government access to plaintext messages was quickly removed.

The appearance of S. 266 hastened Zimmermann's work on PGP until finally a stable version 1.0 was ready. PGP version 1.0 supported RSA and a weak symmetric algorithm called "Bass-O-Matic," which is discussed later in the chapter. In 1991, Zimmermann circulated the program to a few friends and colleagues. Someone eventually posted the PGP to Usenet. Internet sites around the globe promptly mirrored their own copies of PGP. The Pandora's Box of PGP was open.

Patent Infringement

PGP version 1.0 lacked one key component: a license to use the RSA algorithm. Although Phil Zimmermann requested a free license, RSA Security never offered nor granted one. PGP did offer some of the same functionality as RSA Security's MailSafe but represented little competitive threat. MailSafe accounted for a minute fraction of RSA Security's revenue. Most of their income came from licensing cryptographic patents.

RSA Security's failure to defend their RSA patent vigorously would set a dangerous precedent. Why would anyone pay a license fee when PGP was using RSA for free? Losing its RSA patent revenue stream represented the true threat to RSA Security's livelihood.

As a response, RSA Security conducted a campaign to eliminate the distribution of PGP. They threatened legal action against major online services, such as CompuServe and America Online, who did not remove copies of PGP from their systems. Universities and the EFF removed PGP from their own sites out of fear of litigation.

Although RSA Security successfully defended their RSA patent, their actions energized PGP enthusiasts. Every action to suppress the distribution of PGP inspired individual privacy advocates and cryptographic rights "cypherpunks" to mirror and distribute illegal copies of

PGP around the globe. A core group of users began to develop and PGP became a centerpiece in the debate over cryptographic rights and patent laws. As more people used PGP, technical problems emerged. Zimmermann never intended to release PGP 1.0 to the public. His code contained at least one fatal flaw. Not trusting the government's own DES encryption algorithm, Zimmermann cobbled together his own symmetric encryption algorithm called Bass-O-Matic (the name pays homage to a classic comedy sketch involving a fish blender). A cryptographer named Eli Biham quickly broke Bass-O-Matic and exposed severe security flaws. With more private individuals relying on PGP for secure communications, Zimmermann realized that he could not ignore patent issues and that PGP needed a thorough code review.

Phil Zimmermann and a group of international volunteers continued to develop PGP over the next 2 years, by adding features, fixing bugs, and making several major improvements. Notably, the International Data Encryption Algorithm (IDEA; Lai & Massey, 1990) replaced Bass-O-Matic as PGP's symmetric algorithm of choice. Volunteers also internationalized PGP by translating it into several languages and adding support for international character sets. By 1993, PGP version 2.3 had stabilized into a more or less robust product.

At this point, there was growing pressure from PGP users to settle its outstanding patent infringement issues. Particularly, potential business customers wanted to legitimize PGP. With its legality in question, corporate users could not risk using PGP without fear of litigation. PGP had few users outside a core following of privacy and cryptography buffs. Unless mainstream users could use it, PGP would remain relegated to the underground.

Rather than negotiate directly with RSA Security to obtain a license, Zimmermann decided to solicit companies that already held RSA licenses. Eventually, Zimmermann found a European suitor named ViaCrypt willing to sell PGP as a commercial product. ViaCrypt released ViaCrypt PGP version 2.4 in late 1993. This move may have hurt PGP's overall position. Zimmermann's "selling out" PGP to a company alienated some dedicated users and volunteer developers. Few users were willing to pay for a commercial product that they had always used for free. Worse, despite acquiring a license via ViaCrypt, corporate users remained skeptical about the legality of PGP.

Meanwhile, RSA Security had warmed to allowing free noncommercial RSA licenses. Granting noncommercial licenses encouraged research and peer review of RSA implementations. Following PGP's initial release, RSA Security released a reference implementation of RSA called RSAREF. Soon, products such as Mark Riordan's Internet Privacy Enhanced E-mail (RIPEM) were built on top of RSAREF and the new Privacy Enhanced E-Mail (PEM) standard (Internet Engineering Task Force, 1993). RIPEM was a free, patent-licensed and standardized alternative to PGP.

RSAREF contained two poison pills targeted at PGP. First, its programming interface did not allow access to functions specifically needed by PGP. Second, parties that previously violated RSA Security patents were denied a noncommercial RSAREF license. Regardless, RSA Security did offer a compromise to accommodate PGP. They would grant noncommercial licenses to a new version of PGP only if it were made intentionally incompatible with older "guerillaware" versions of PGP. Versions 2.3 and prior would not be able to communicate with later versions. This incompatibility was intended to avoid granting "amnesty" to users of patent-violating PGP versions. Zimmermann refused this offer.

During this time, a group of researchers at MIT had been building a legitimate version of PGP on top of RSAREF. They discovered that RSAREF version 2.0's new programming interface was sufficient to implement PGP. With the help of Zimmermann, MIT was prepared to release a PGP version 2.5 in early 1994. MIT PGP version 2.5 appeared to abide by the RSAREF license agreement. It would be difficult to argue that MIT was violating the very same patent it had originally granted RSA Security the rights to use.

RSA Security did object to PGP 2.5's backward compatibility, however, because it would allow illegal versions of PGP to communicate with legitimate versions. MIT and RSA Security reached a compromise. Rather than releasing version 2.5, MIT would release version 2.6 which had one new "feature": on September 1, 1994, version 2.6 would cease to be compatible with prior versions. This would offer an incentive for non-licensed users to upgrade, without immediate locking them out. Zimmermann agreed to this compromise because it gave prior users time to upgrade to a new version. For all intents and purposes, PGP's patent issues had finally been resolved. Yet Phil Zimmermann's legal troubles persisted.

Export Licenses

MIT PGP version 2.6 was the first version of PGP free of license issues. Although ViaCrypt PGP 2.4 appeared to be legal, version 2.6 was released with the express approval of RSA Security. Corporate customers could use PGP without fear of litigation.

Yet another legal issue loomed. Soon after its release, version 2.6 was quickly distributed to FTP (file transfer protocol) servers around the globe. This was strictly forbidden by U.S. export laws. In fact, all prior versions of PGP had also been illegally exported.

It was illegal to export encryption technology with key lengths greater than 40 bits without government approval; despite the fact that 40-bit keys were thought to be insecure. Typically, this led to having two versions of a product: a domestic version with 64- to 128-bit keys and an international version with weak, 40-bit keys. PGP's symmetric algorithm, IDEA, used 128-bit keys. Although IDEA was developed outside the United States, the export of PGP resulted in a federal investigation of Zimmermann.

At the time, U.S. export laws produced some complicated restrictions on cryptography. Encryption software was considered "munitions." Exporting code fell into the same legal class as exporting warheads or missile guidance systems. Although this categorization might seem severe, it does highlight the importance of cryptography with regard to national defense.

Because of freedom of speech guarantees, however, printed material did not fall under this restriction. A book was not considered an "encrypting device" like software source code. This idiosyncrasy in the law made it illegal to export encryption source code over a network or on a floppy disk but legal to print the identical source code in a book. Exporting a book containing the entire source code of PGP in machine-readable fonts was perfectly legal. This is exactly what Zimmermann (1995) did.

Foreign buyers quickly scanned Zimmermann's book and distributed the resulting source code. This exposed weaknesses in the government's case. How could someone be charged with exporting "munitions" that could be bought in a bookstore? Zimmermann's case also highlighted the outdated restriction on keys greater than 40 bits.

In early 1996, the federal case was dropped against Zimmermann with no charges being filed. Later that year, Zimmermann addressed the U.S. Congress on reforming cryptographic export laws. Over the next 4 years, the Electronic Frontier Foundation (n.d.), cryptographic researchers such as Ron Rivest, and several industry groups lobbied Congress for export law reform. In January 2000, cryptographic export laws were significantly loosened, allowing free export of cryptography except to state sponsors of terrorism.

PGP VARIANTS AND ALTERNATIVES

PGP Corporation and OpenPGP

Several versions of PGP are available today. PGP Corporation sells a variety of PGP products, namely, PGP Personal and PGP Universal, which are briefly discussed later in this section. Phil Zimmermann originally founded PGP Incorporated, which merged with ViaCrypt, in 1996. In 1997, Network Associates Incorporated acquired PGP Inc. In 2002, a newly formed PGP Corporation purchased all PGP products and intellectual property from Network Associates. Phil Zimmermann currently acts as a special advisor and consultant to PGP Corporation (n.d.).

Zimmermann also acts as the chairman for the OpenPGP alliance, which developed and advocates the OpenPGP standard (Internet Engineering Task Force, 1993). OpenPGP is a nonproprietary, secure e-mail standard. It defines formats for encrypted messages, signatures, and public key certificates. OpenPGP is similar in many respects to S/MIME, the Secure Multipurpose Internet Mail Extensions, developed by RSA Security (Internet Engineering Task Force, 1999). S/MIME is discussed briefly later in this section.

OpenPGP supports the RSA, Diffie–Hellman, DSA, and El Gamal public key algorithms. OpenPGP also supports the AES, CAST, 3DES, IDEA, and Twofish symmetric encryption algorithms and the SHA-1, MD5, RIPEMD-160, and MD2 hash algorithms. The standard has reserved fields for experimental and emerging cryptosystems, such as elliptic curve cryptography. Future developments in OpenPGP may add support for mobile devices or compatibility with S/MIME.

PGP Corporation's PGP Personal offers secure messaging and storage for home use. PGP Personal is a commercial product and offers full OpenPGP compatibility, although a freeware version is available for download. Version 9.0 Beta is the latest release as of early 2005. PGP Personal may be considered the legitimate heir of PGP and may even be purchased directly from Phil Zimmermann (2003).

MIT PGP Freeware and PGPi

An alternative OpenPGP-compliant implementation is MIT's PGP Freeware version 6.5.8 (MIT Distribution Center for PGP Freeware, n.d.). On September 20, 2000, the RSA patent expired and the algorithm became free for public use. Patents on Diffie–Hellman key exchange and other early work by Hellman, Merkle, and Pohlig have also subsequently expired.

The expiration of RSA's patent essentially grants amnesty for guerillaware versions of PGP. Most prominent of these PGP variants are internationalized versions developed by volunteers around the world, such as by the PGPi project (PGP International, n.d.). One unofficial international version of PGP, version 2.6.3i, has been translated into more than 25 languages and ported to several platforms. Currently, there are efforts to translate and port PGP freeware versions 6.0 and higher.

GnuPG

Another free, near-compliant OpenPGP alternative is the GNU Privacy Guard, or GPG. As with all software under the GNU Public License (GPL), GPG depends on no proprietary code. Because of the GPL, GPG cannot use any patented encryption algorithms, most notably the IDEA symmetric encryption algorithm.

An advantage to having several OpenPGP-compliant alternatives, such as GPG, is that attacks and software bugs affect smaller portions of the market. For example, a weakness discovered in the OpenPGP format that potentially leaked private keys did not affect GPG (Klima & Rosa, 2001).

S/MIME

An alternative secure messaging service similar to OpenPGP is S/MIME. S/MIME was originally developed by RSA Security and submitted to the Internet Engineering Task Force (1998, 1999) as a new standard. Most major e-mail clients, including Microsoft Outlook and Mozilla e-mail, have adopted S/MIME.

S/MIME and OpenPGP offer much of the same functionality. Unfortunately, the two standards are currently incompatible, although many commercial implementations do support both standards. Adding to the confusion is the existence of an OpenPGP precursor called PGP/MIME, which is also incompatible to S/MIME. The OpenPGP and S/MIME working groups have supposedly been meeting to discuss unifying the two standards. As of 2004, it is unclear whether the OpenPGP and S/MIME working groups will merge the two standards any time soon.

Server-Side and Web-Based Secure E-Mail

A facetious rule of thumb in designing security products is that every keystroke needed to use the product cuts the market in half. By this rule, the most successful products should be the ones that require the least user interaction, which appears to hold in practice. Millions of

Web browsers connect to Web sites securely using secure socket layer (SSL). This requires negligible interaction from the user. Many academic and corporate institutions have replaced Telnet, which communicated in plain text, with the Secure Shell, or SSH. For all intents and purposes, the user experience of SSH is identical to Telnet.

PGP Corporation has apparently adopted the strategy of transparent security. Their recent PGP Universal product moves the burden of signing and encrypting e-mail from the desktop to the server. Users compose and send e-mail as they would regularly and let a common e-mail server act as a security proxy.

Although this model caters to the corporate market, it could be adopted to Web-based e-mail clients. In fact, this is essentially the model used by Hushmail (http://www.hushmail.com), Ziplip (http:// www.ziplip.com), and other Web-based services. The Web-based approach addresses several of the usability issues discussed later.

Although implementation details may vary among services, they typically have similar models. Upon registering with a Web-based secure e-mail site, users will generate a public key pair that may either be stored by their browser or on the server side. Users may then connect to a Web site through an SSL connection and compose messages in their browser, similar to Hotmail or Yahoo Mail. The difference is that when sending messages, the user may sign and encrypt messages using the online service. Potentially, a Web-based service could also act as a portal to a PKI, allowing users to locate other recipients' public keys quickly.

Denial of service could be one effective attack against a centralized, server-side secure e-mail system. Because cryptographic operations are computationally expensive, flooding a server with many messages to encrypt, sign, or verify could create a performance bottleneck. Significantly degrading quality of service can frustrate users to the point where they fall back to plaintext e-mail. Of course, attackers could conduct this type of denial of service attack against servers in a centralized PKI. One advantage of PGP's web of trust model is that there is no single point of failure.

PGP PROBLEMS AND LESSONS

PGP is a useful case study in developing cryptographic software. It is an early example of the impact of laws and legislation on software development. In recent years, cases such as the Digital Millennium Copyright Act (DMCA) and conflicts over peer-to-peer file-sharing networks illustrate the interaction of laws and software. PGP is also an excellent example of the pitfall of forking in open source software development and of the effect of Metcalfe's law inherent in many security products. Finally, PGP brings to question the feasibility of developing widely used, user-level encryption software.

Changing Law for Changing Technology

PGP was an early example of how the existence of software can act as a catalyst for legal reform. At the time of its initial development, U.S. export laws were outdated and limited exported encryption to 40-bit keys. When the law was written, 40-bit keys offered a reasonable level of security. As technology progressed, the law did not keep up. Simply by existing, PGP exposed the need for new approaches in public policy dealing with technology. For example, the notion that it was illegal to export PGP on disk, but legal to export it as a book obviously satisfies no one (Zimmerman, 1995).

In 2004, we are seeing a similar phenomenon in peer-to-peer networks. Intellectual property laws are becoming more difficult to enforce as technology allows more simple and anonymous dissemination of copyrighted material. Similar to how PGP spurred export law reform, the widespread use of peer-to-peer networks may spur intellectual property law reform.

The Need for Industry Standards

Regardless of legality, a second obstacle to PGP's adoption was the proliferation of several incompatible variants. Part of the problem was the forced backward incompatibility of MIT PGP version 2.6, which was part of the compromise with RSA Security to acquire a noncommercial license. The effect of this incompatible fork in development was to fracture the market for PGP. Official versions, international versions, and guerillaware versions could not always communicate freely with each other. Although OpenPGP addresses this problem, the damage appears to have been done. Most major e-mail clients support S/MIME, notably Microsoft Outlook and Mozilla. These clients do not support OpenPGP by default. A lesson is that software creators need to assert control over their "brand." It would have been better for Phil Zimmermann to dissuade incompatible versions from calling themselves "PGP," although this would have been inimical to the free-wheeling spirit of PGP's creation.

When it was released in 1997, the OpenPGP brand and standard were already several years too late. Fragmenting the market was particularly bad for a secure e-mail product. Like telephones, instant messaging clients, or other network communication systems, the utility of PGP depended on the number of people using it. If few people used PGP, there was little incentive to install it.

Bob Metcalfe, who was one of the creators of Ethernet, first elucidated the notion that a network's utility is the square of the number of users. In fact, Metcalfe's law applies to all public key cryptographic systems. Only people with public keys registered in the PKI may communicate with each other. One exception is Identity-Based Encryption, discussed later.

"Why Johnny Can't Encrypt"

Obstacles to adopting PGP apply to most user level, public key cryptographic products. Learning to use public key encryption can be daunting. Users must start by understanding the privacy and authentication security threats in e-mail. They must also understand enough of the fundamentals of public key cryptography to generate public keys, locate other users' public keys, and register public keys with a PKI or sign keys in a web of trust.

The terminology used to describe public key operations is not intuitive for a layperson. In the real world, we do not have "public" and "private" physical keys, nor do we sign documents with keys. Perhaps a clever user interface could hide many of the technical details. Unfortunately, the PGP interface was developed for computer hobbyists and experts, which has fared poorly with nonexperts.

Two researchers at Carnegie Mellon University conducted a usability study on PGP 5.0's graphical user interface titled, "Why Johnny Can't Encrypt" (Whitten & Tygar, 1999). Several college students were given a brief tutorial in using PGP and provided technical assistance via e-mail. The students were then asked to perform several tasks, including creating a public key, signing a document and encrypting a message with someone else's public key. Some excerpts from the results are less than reassuring:

> Three of the twelve test participants accidentally emailed the secret to the team members without encryption . . . One participant forgot her pass phrase during the course of the test session and had to generate a new key pair . . . Among the eleven participants who figured out how to encrypt, failure to understand the public key model was widespread. Seven participants used only their own public keys to encrypt email to the team members.

In Ron Rivest's "Network and Computer Security" course at MIT, students are assigned to read "Why Johnny Can't Encrypt" and then send a PGP-signed and encrypted message to the course staff. Anecdotally, students take an average of 90 minutes to generate a public key pair, locate the course staff's public key, sign, and encrypt the message. If it takes a computer science student enrolled in a graduate network security course at MIT 90 minutes to use PGP, there is little hope for widespread adoption.

FUTURE DIRECTIONS AND CONCLUSION

The need for secure e-mail has increased dramatically in recent years. E-mail is the primary infection vector for worms and viruses. Malicious software and spammers frequently forge e-mail headers or hijack outgoing address books. Thieves frequently forge e-mail from online stockbrokers or auction sites to steal account information. These attacks all exploit the lack of e-mail authentication, which could be addressed using digital signatures.

E-mail privacy is another concern. Web sites frequently send confirmation passwords or sensitive information in plaintext through e-mail. Cellular telephones, personal digital assistants (PDAs) and laptops commonly send e-mail over wireless networks. All these technologies create more opportunities for attackers to spy on plaintext messages.

Regardless of these risks, there still has not been a large consumer demand for secure e-mail. Most users lack the concern, time, or savvy to use e-mail encryption, despite being supported by many e-mail clients such as Microsoft Outlook or Mozilla e-mail. Today, a small fraction of e-mail sent on the Internet is encrypted.

One public key cryptosystem that may lower the barrier to user adoption is identity-based encryption (IBE). Originally envisioned by Adi Shamir (1984), IBE is an alternative approach to generating public keys. Rather than requiring that receivers generate their public key first, senders can simply use the intended recipient's e-mail address as the public key. To clarify, the plaintext e-mail address *is* the public key. Upon receiving an identity-based encrypted message, the receiver will contact a trusted third-party server to fetch a decryption key. This third-party server need not be universally accessible and may reside behind a corporate firewall.

In 2001, researchers Dan Boneh and Matt Franklin (2001) designed a practical identity-based encryption scheme. A start-up called Voltage Security (2003) started selling IBE security products based on Boneh and Franklin's scheme. An advantage of IBE secure e-mail is that receivers do not have to be previously registered in the system. A sender may send a message to any e-mail address, giving impetus to the recipient to register with the system. Thus, an IBE system may not have the same network adoption problem as PGP or other security products.

Security concerns in mobile and pervasive computing devices such as cellular telephones, PDAs, or radio-frequency identification (RFID) tags, could be a major driver for widespread public key infrastructure deployment. In the cellular telephone market, the first generation of text messaging–based spam and viruses has already emerged. For example, in 2001 a virus struck Japanese cellular telephones, forcing them to dial the Japanese equivalent of 911 emergency services (Delio, 2001).

Because of these concerns, cell phones and mobile devices may be an emerging market for a standardized secure messaging format, such as OpenPGP. PGP Corporation already offers a lightweight product called PGP Mobile for Palm and Windows CE devices. There is also an effort within the OpenPGP alliance to accommodate smart cards and mobile and handheld devices.

A standardized PGP messaging format suitable for cellular telephones could be integrated into the Liberty Alliance's (2004) federated network identity management services. Liberty Alliance members include several large cellular phone manufacturers who could provide the critical mass of users necessary for a successful system. Cellular phone makers have a history of using proprietary encryption formats that have been broken (Goldberg & Briceno, 1998; Wagner, Schneier, & Kelsey, 1997). Open cryptographic standards would go far in bolstering the security reputation of cellular manufacturers.

In conclusion, PGP illustrates many of the problems involved in developing an abstract algorithm like RSA into a robust, practical product. Performance, legal issues, usability, and market conditions all influenced the course of PGP's development. The lessons from PGP may prove useful in developing other security or cryptographic applications in the future.

Despite its faults and the hurdles in its development, PGP is being used in critical applications and is literally saving lives. Patrick Ball, deputy director of the Science and Human Rights program at the American Association for the Advancement of Science, describes how human rights workers in Guatemala used PGP to securely report human rights violations (Ball, Kobrak, & Spirer, 1999).

Human rights workers encrypted database records with the public keys of nongovernmental organizations, such as the Amnesty International. Activists arrested and threatened with torture could not be forced to reveal private keys to large encrypted databases because they did not know them. Based on these experiences, the Crypto Rights Foundation (2003) is developing a secure human rights communication system based on PGP called High-Fire.

Perhaps the single biggest motivator for typical users to adopt PGP or other secure e-mail products is the deluge of unsolicited "spam" e-mail being sent on the Internet. By mid-2003, unsolicited advertisements accounted for more than 45% of e-mail traffic ("Stopping Spam," 2003). Legal remedies such as the recent CAN-SPAM Act passed in the United States may not stem the tide of unsolicited e-mail, because it is an international problem (Controlling the Assault of Non-Solicited Pornography and Marketing (CAN SPAM) Act, 2003).

A technological solution may be the best defense. Using PGP or other secure e-mail and rejecting all unsigned e-mail is one approach. Although spammers could create public keys and sign messages, this would increase their per-message cost. The high computational cost of signatures would be a benefit, because mass e-mailers would need orders of magnitude more processing power. Ironically, every unsolicited e-mail message sent hawking free prescription drugs, cheap home loans, or other once-in-a-lifetime opportunities may contribute to secure e-mail's eventual success.

GLOSSARY

Advanced Encryption Standard (AES) U.S. government-approved symmetric block cipher; designed as a replacement for Data Encryption Standard (DES).

Certificate Authority (CA) A public key infrastructure component that distributes public key certificates.

Guerillaware Software created in violation of patent, copyright, or export laws.

Identity-based encryption (IBE) A public-key cryptosystem where identities are used as public keys, making a public key infrastructures unnecessary.

Message Digest Computes a short "fingerprint" from a long input message that is highly unlikely to collide with other messages' fingerprints. Typically implemented with a cryptographic hash function.

Public Key Infrastructure (PKI) An entity that stores and distributes public key certificates.

RSA A Public key cryptosystem created by Rivest, Shamir, and Adleman in 1978.

Secure/multipurpose internet mail extensions (S/MIME) A secure messaging standard.

Secure Sockets Layer (SSL) A suite of protocols frequently used by Web browsers to encrypt transactions.

Session Key A random symmetric encryption key generated for a single session.

"Signing a Key" Issuing a digitally signed certificate that binds an identity to a public key.

Web of Trust A PKI model in which any user may issue certificates for any other user.

CROSS REFERENCES

See *Cryptographic Privacy Protection Techniques; Digital Signatures and Electronic Signatures; E-Mail and Instant Messaging; Encryption Basics; PKI (Public Key Infrastructure). IBE (Identity-Based Encryption), S/MIME (Secure MIME).*

REFERENCES

AES Homepage. (n.d.). Retrieved April 10, 2004, from http://csrc.nist.gov/

Ball, P., Kobrak, P., & Spirer, H. (1999). *State violence in Guatemala, 1960–1996: A quantitative reflection.* American Association for the Advancement of Science. Retrieved April 10, 2004, http://shr.aaas.org/guatemala/ciidh/qr/english/qrtitle.html

Boneh, D., & Franklin, M. (2001). Identity based encryption from the Weil Pairing. *Proceedings of Advanced in Cryptology—CRYPTO '01* (pp. 213–229). Springer-Verlag, New York.

Cocks, C. C. (1973). *A note on non-secret encryption.* United Kingdom: Communications-Electronics Security Group. Cheltenham.

Controlling the Assault of Non-Solicited Pornography and Marketing (CAN SPAM) Act, Pub. L. No. 108–187. (2003).

CryptoRights Foundation. (2003). Highfire: A human rights communication privacy system. Retrieved April 10, 2004, from http://www.cryptorights.org/research/highfire/

Delio, M. (2001). Hello 911, I've got a virus. *Wired News.* Retrieved April 10, 2004, http://www.wired.com/news/wireless/0,1382,44545,00.html

Diffie, W., & Hellman, M. (1976). New directions in cryptography. *IEEE Transactions on Information Theory, 22,* 644–654.

Electronic Frontier Foundation. (n.d.). Retrieved April 10, 2004, from http://www.eff.org

Ellis, J. H. (1970). *The possibility of secure non-secret digital encryption.* United Kingdom: Communications-Electronics Security Group. Cheltenham.

Garfinkel, S. (1995). PGP: Pretty Good Privacy. Cambridge, MA: O'Reilly and Associates.

Goldberg, I., & Briceno, M. (1998). GSM cloning. Retrieved April 10, 2004, http://www.isaac.cs.berkeley.edu/isaac/gsm-faq.html

Internet Engineering Task Force. (1993). Request for Comments 1421–1423. Retrieved April 10, 2004, from http://www.ietf.org

Internet Engineering Task Force. (1996). Request for Comments 1991. Retrieved April 10, 2004, from http://www.ietf.org

Internet Engineering Task Force. (1998). Request for Comments 2440. Retrieved April 10, 2004, from http://www.ietf.org

Internet Engineering Task Force. (1999). Request for Comments 2630–2634. Retrieved April 10, 2004, from http://www.ietf.org

Kaliski, B. (2003). *TWIRL and RSA key size* (Technical Report). RSA Laboratories. Bedford, MA.

Klima, V., & Rosa, T. (2001). *Attack on private signature keys of the OpenPGP format, PGP programs and other applications compatible with OpenPGP* (Technical Report). ICZ, Brno, Czech Republic.

Lai, X., & Massey, J. (1990). A proposal for a new block encryption standard. *Proceedings of Advanced in Cryptology—EUROCRYPT '90* (pp. 389–404). Springer-Verlag, Berlin.

Lenstra, A. K., & Verheul, E. R. (2001). Selecting cryptographic key sizes. *Journal of Cryptology, 14,* 255–293.

Liberty Alliance Project. (n.d.). Retrieved April 10, 2004, from http://www.projectliberty.org

Merkle, R. (1978). Secure communications over insecure channels. *Communications of the ACM, 21,* 294–299.

MIT Distribution Center for PGP Freeware. (n.d.). Retrieved April 10, 2004, from http://web.mit.edu/network/pgp.html

OpenPGP Alliance. (n.d.). Retrieved April 10, 2004, from http://www.openpgp.org

PGP Corporation. (n.d.). Retrieved April 10, 2004, from http://www.pgp.com

PGP International. (n.d.). Retrieved April 10, 2004, from http://www.pgpi.org

Rivest, R. L., Shamir, A., & Adleman, L. A. (1978). A method for obtaining digital signatures and public key cryptosystems. *Communications of the ACM, 21,* 120–126.

S. 266 and H.R. 731. (A bill to prevent and punish domestic and international terrorist acts, and for other purposes.) 102nd Congress of the United States Senate. (1991).

Shamir, A. (1984). Identity-based cryptosystems and signature schemes. *Proceedings of Advanced in Cryptology—CRYPTO '84* (pp. 47–53). Springer-Verlag, New York.

Stopping Spam. (2003, April 24). *Economist Magazine,* retrieved March 21, 2005 from http://www.economist.com/business/displayStory.cfm?story_id=1734216

Travel Sentry. (n.d.). Retrieved April 10, 2004, from http://www.travelsentry.org/

Wagner, D., Schneier, B., & Kelsey, J. (1997). Cryptanalysis of the cellular message encryption algorithm. *Proceedings of Advanced in Cryptology—CRYPTO '97* (pp. 526–538). Springer-Verlag, New York.

Whitten, A., & Tygar, J. D. (1999). *Why Johnny Can't Encrypt: A usability evaluation of PGP 5.0.* Presented at the 8th USENIX Security Symposium (pp. 12–13). Washington, D.C.

U.S. Patent No. 4,405,829. (1983). Washington, DC: United States Patent and Trademark Office.

Voltage Security. (2003). Homepage. Retrieved April 10, 2004, from http://www.voltage.com

Zimmermann, P. (1995). *PGP source code and internals.* Cambridge, MA: MIT Press.

Zimmermann, P. (2003). Homepage. Retrieved April 10, 2004, from http://www.philzimmermann.com

FURTHER READING

GNU Privacy Guard. (n.d.). Retrieved April 10, 2004, from http://www.gnupg.org

MIT PGP Key Server. (n.d.). Retrieved April 10, 2004, from http://pgp.mit.edu

Shamir, A., & Tromer, E. (2003). Factoring large numbers with the TWIRL device. *Proceedings of Advanced in Cryptology—CRYPTO '03,* pp. 1–26. Springer-Verlag, New York.

Wayner, P. (1997, December 24). British document outlines early encryption discovery. *New York Times,* pp. 1 (Technology Section).

SMTP (Simple Mail Transfer Protocol)

Vladimir V. Riabov, *Rivier College*

INTRODUCTION

Electronic mail (e-mail) is one of the most popular network services nowadays. Most e-mail systems that send mail over the Internet use simple mail transfer protocol (SMTP) to send messages from one server to another. The messages can then be retrieved with an e-mail client using either post office protocol (POP) or Internet message access protocol (IMAP). SMTP is also generally used to send messages from a mail client to a mail server in "host-based" (or Unix-based) mail systems, where a simple `mbox` utility might be on the same system [or via Network File System (NFS) provided by Novell] for access without POP or IMAP.

This chapter describes the fundamentals of SMTP, elements of its client–server architecture (user agent, mail transfer agent, ports), request–response mechanism, commands, mail transfer phases, SMTP messages, multipurpose internet mail extensions (MIME) for non-ASCII (American Standard Code for Information Interchange) data, e-mail delivery cases, mail access protocols (POP3 and IMAP4), SMTP software, vulnerability and security issues, standards, associations, and organizations.

SMTP FUNDAMENTALS

SMTP is used as the common mechanism for transporting electronic mail among different hosts within the transmission control protocol/Internet protocol (TCP/IP) suite. It is an application layer protocol. Under SMTP, a client SMTP process opens a TCP connection to a server SMTP process on a remote host and attempts to send mail across the connection. The server SMTP listens for a TCP connection on a specific port (25), and the client SMTP process initiates a connection on that port (Cisco SMTP, 2005). When the TCP connection is successful, the two processes execute a simple request–response dialogue, defined by the SMTP protocol (see RFC 821 for details), in which the client process transmits the mail addresses of the originator and the recipient(s) for a message. When the server process accepts these mail addresses, the client process transmits the e-mail instant message. The message must contain a message header and message text ("body") formatted in accordance with RFC 822.

Mail that arrives via SMTP is forwarded to a remote server, or it is delivered to mailboxes on the local server. POP3 or IMAP allow users download mail that is stored on the local server. Most mail programs such as Eudora allow the client to specify both an SMTP server and a POP server. On UNIX-based systems, Sendmail is the most widely used SMTP server for e-mail. Sendmail includes a POP3 server and also comes in a version for Windows NT ("What is SMTP?", 2005). The MIME protocol defines the way files are attached to SMTP messages. Microsoft Outlook and Netscape/Mozilla Communicator are the most popular mail-agent programs on Window-based systems.

The X.400 International Telecommunication Union standard (Tanenbaum, 2003) that defines transfer protocols for sending electronic mail between mail servers is used in Europe as an alternative to SMTP. Also, the message handling service (MHS) developed by Novell is used for electronic mail on Netware networks ("What is SMTP?", 2005).

SMTP MODEL AND PROTOCOL

The SMTP model (RFC 821) supports both end-to-end (no intermediate message transfer agents [MTAs]) and store-and-forward mail delivery methods. The end-to-end method is used between organizations, and the store-and-forward method is chosen for operating within organizations that have TCP/IP and SMTP-based networks.

A SMTP client will contact the destination host's SMTP server directly to deliver the mail. It will keep the mail item from being transmitted until it has been successfully copied to the recipient's SMTP. This is different from the store-and-forward principle that is common in many other electronic mailing systems, where the mail item may pass through a number of intermediate hosts in the same network on its way to the destination and where successful transmission from the sender only indicates that the mail item has reached the first intermediate hop ("Simple Mail Transfer Protocol" [SMTP], 2004).

The RFC 821 standard defines a client–server protocol. The client SMTP is the one, which initiates the session (that is, the sending SMTP) and the server is the one that responds (the receiving SMTP) to the session request. Because the client SMTP frequently acts as a server for a user-mailing program, however, it is often simpler to refer to the client as the sender-SMTP and to the server as the receiver-SMTP.

An SMTP-based process can transfer electronic mail to another process on the same network or to another network via a relay or gateway process accessible to both networks (Sheldon, 2001). An e-mail message may pass through a number of intermediate relay or gateway hosts on its path from a sender to a recipient. A simple model of the components of the SMTP system is shown in Figure 1.

Users deal with a user agent (UA). Popular user agents for UNIX include Berkeley Mail, Elm, MH, Pine, and Mutt. The user agents for Windows include Microsoft Outlook/Outlook Express and Netscape/Mozilla Communicator. The exchange of mail using TCP is performed by an MTA. The most common MTA for UNIX systems is Sendmail, and MTA for Windows is Microsoft Exchange 2000/2003. In addition to stable host-based e-mail servers, Microsoft Corporation has developed LDAP/Active-directory servers and B2B-servers that enhance mail-delivery practices. Users normally do not deal with the MTA. It is the responsibility of the system administrator to set up the local MTA. Users often have a choice, however, for their user agent (Stevens, 1993). The MTA maintains a mail queue so that it can schedule repeat delivery attempts in case a remote server is unable. Also the local MTA delivers mail to mailboxes, and the information can be downloaded by the UA (see Figure 1).

The RFC 821 standard specifies the SMTP protocol, which is a mechanism of communication between two MTAs across a single TCP connection. The RFC 822 standard specifies the format of the electronic mail message that is transmitted using the SMTP protocol (RFC 821) between the two MTAs. As a result of a user mail request, the sender-SMTP establishes a two-way connection with a receiver-SMTP. The receiver-SMTP can be either the ultimate destination or an intermediate one (known as a mail gateway). The sender-SMTP will generate commands, which are replied to by the receiver-SMTP (see Figure 1).

Both the SMTP client and server should have two basic components: UA and local MTA. There are few cases of sending electronic-mail messages across networks. In the

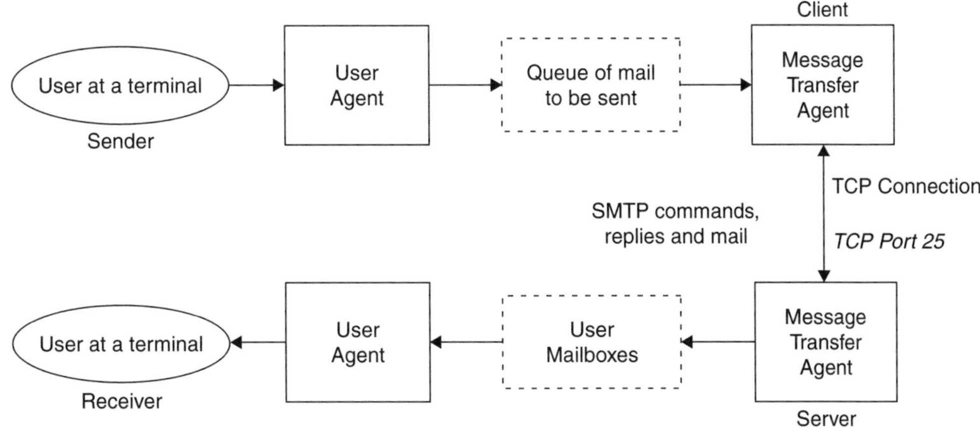

Figure 1: The basic simple mail transfer protocol (SMTP) model.

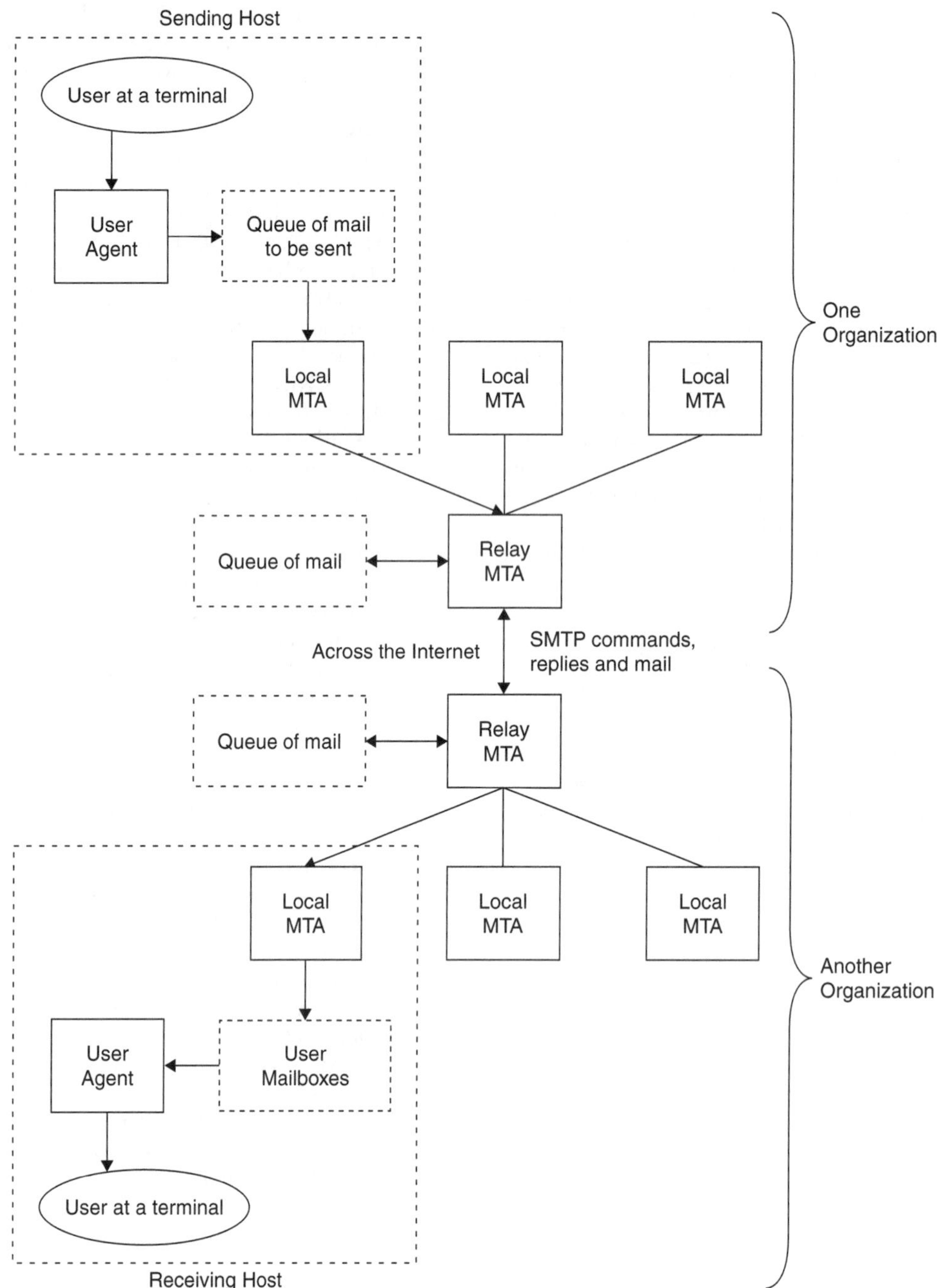

Figure 2: The simple mail transfer protocol (SMTP) model with relay mail transfer agents.

first case of communication between the sender and the receiver across the network (see Figure 1), the sender's UA prepares the message, creates the envelope, and puts message in the envelope. The MTA transfers the mail across the network to the TCP-port 25 of the receiver's MTA. In the second case of communication between the sending host (client) and the receiving host (server), *relaying* could be involved (see Figure 2). In addition to one MTA at the sender site and one at the receiving site, other MTAs, acting as client or server, can relay the electronic mail across the network.

The system of relays allows sites that do not use the TCP/IP protocol suite to send electronic mail to users on other sites that may or may not use the TCP/IP protocol suite. This third scenario of communication between the sender and the receiver can be accomplished through the use of an e-mail gateway, which is a relay MTA that can receive electronic mail prepared by a protocol other than SMTP and transform it to the SMTP format before sending it. The e-mail gateway can also receive electronic mail in the SMTP format, change it to another format, and then send it to the MTA of the client that does not use the TCP/IP protocol suite (Forouzan, 2003). In various implementations, there is the capability to exchange mail between the TCP/IP SMTP mailing system and the locally used mailing systems. These applications are called mail gateways or mail bridges. Sending mail through a mail gateway may alter the end-to-end delivery specification, because SMTP will only guarantee delivery to the mail-gateway host, not to the real destination host, which is located beyond the TCP/IP network. When a mail gateway is used, the SMTP end-to-end transmission is host-to-gateway, gateway-to-host, or gateway-to-gateway; the behavior beyond the gateway is not defined by SMTP.

USER AGENT

Introduced in RFC 821 and RFC 822, the SMTP defines user agent functionality, but not the implementation details. A survey of the SMTP implementations can be found in RFC 876. The UA is a program that is used to send and receive electronic mail. The most popular user agent programs for UNIX are Berkley Mail, Elm, MH, Mutt, Mush, and Zmail. Some UAs have an extra user interface (e.g., Eudora) that allows window-type interactions with the system. The user agents for Windows include Microsoft Outlook/Outlook Express and Netscape/Mozilla Communicator.

Sending e-Mail

Electronic mail is sent by a series of request–response transactions between a client and a server. An SMTP transaction consists of the envelope and message, which is composed of header (with `From:` and `To:` fields) and body (text after headers sent with the `DATA` command). The envelope is transmitted separately from the message itself using MAIL FROM and RCPT TO commands (see RFC 1123). A null line, that is, a line with nothing preceding the <CRLF> sequence, terminates the mail header. Some implementations (e.g., VM, which does not support zero-length records in files), however, may interpret this differently and accept a blank line as a terminator (SMTP, 2005). Everything after the null (or blank) line is the message body, which is a sequence of lines containing ASCII characters. The message body contains the actual information that can be read by the recipient.

Mail Header Format

The header includes a number of key words and values that define the sending date, sender's address, where replies should go, and some other information.

The header is a list of lines, of the form (SMTP, 2005):

```
field-name: field-value
```

Fields begin in column 1: Lines beginning with white space characters (SPACE or TAB) are continuation lines, which are unfolded to create a single line for each field in the canonical representation. Strings enclosed in ASCII quotation marks indicate single tokens within which special characters such as the colon are not significant. Many important field values (such as those for the "To" and "From" fields) are "mailboxes." The most common forms for these are the following:

- jsmith@mail.it.rivier.edu
- John Smith <jsmith@mail.it.rivier.edu>
- "John Smith" <jsmith@mail.it.rivier.edu>

The string "John Smith" is intended for human recipients and is the name of the mailbox owner. The string "jsmith@mail.it.rivier.edu" is the computer-readable address of the mailbox (the angle brackets are used to delimit the address but are not part of it). One can see that this form of addressing is closely related to the domain name system (DNS) concept (Internet Assigned Numbers Authority [IANA], 2005). In fact, the client SMTP uses the DNS to determine the IP address of the destination mailbox.

Some frequently used fields (key words) are the following:

- `to` Primary recipients of the message.
- `cc` Secondary ("carbon-copy") recipients of the message.
- `from` Identity of sender.
- `reply-to` The mailbox to which responses are to be sent. This field is added by the originator.
- `return-path` Address and route back to the originator. This field is added by the final transport system that delivers the mail.
- `Subject` Summary of the message. The user usually provides the summary.

Receiving e-Mail

The UA periodically checks the content of the mailboxes (see Figure 1). It informs the user about mail arrival by giving a special notice. When the user tries to read the mail, a list of arrived mail packages is displayed. Each line of the list contains a brief summary of the information about a particular package in the mailbox. The summary may include the sender mail address, the subject, and the time the mail was received or sent. By selecting any of the packages, the user can view its contents on the terminal display.

The SMTP Destination Address

The SMTP destination address (a mailbox address), in its general form *local-part@domain-name*, can take several forms (SMTP, 2005):

- user@host—For a direct destination on the same TCP/IP network.
- user%remote-host@gateway-host—For a user on a non-SMTP destination remote-host, via the mail gateway gateway-host.
- @host-a,@host-b:user@host-c—For a relayed message. This form contains explicit routing information. The message will first be delivered to host-a, who will resend (relay) the message to host-b. Host-b will then forward the message to the real destination host-c. Note that the message is stored on each of the intermediate hosts; therefore, there is no end-to-end delivery in this case. This address form is obsolete and should not be used (see RFC 1123).

Delayed Delivery

The SMTP protocol allows delayed delivery, and the message can be delayed at the sender site, the receiver site, or the intermediate servers (Forouzan, 2003).

In the case of delaying at the sender site, the client has to accommodate a spooling system, in which e-mail messages are stored before being sent. A message created by the user agent is delivered to the spool storage. The client mail transfer agent periodically (usually every 10 to 30 minutes) checks the spool to find the mail that can be sent. The mail will be sent only if the receiver is ready and the IP address of the server has been obtained though DNS. If a message cannot be delivered in the timeout period (usually about 3 to 5 days), the mail returns to the sender.

Upon receiving the message, the server-MTA stores it in the mailbox of the receiver (see Figure 1). In this case, the receiver can access the mailbox at any convenient time.

Finally, the SMTP standard procedures allow intermediate MTAs to serve as clients and servers. Both intermediate clients and servers can receive mail, store mail messages in their mailboxes and spools, and send them later to an appropriate destination.

Aliases

The SMTP mechanism allows one name, an alias, to represent several e-mail addresses (this feature is known as "one-to-many alias expansion"; Forouzan, 2003). Additionally, a single user can also be defined by several e-mail addresses (this is called "many-to-one alias expansion"). The system can handle these expansions by including an alias expansion facility (connected to the alias databases) at both the sender and receiver sites.

MAIL TRANSFER AGENT

MTAs transfer actual mail. The system must have the client MTA for sending e-mail and the server MTA for receiving mail (see Figure 1). The SMTP-related RFCs do not define a specific MTA. The UNIX-based MTA uses commonly the Sendmail utility. The most common MTA for Windows is Microsoft Exchange 2000/2003.

The "mta-name-type" and "address-type" parameters (e.g., `dnc` and `rfc822` for the Internet mail, respectively) are defined for use in the SMTP delivery status notification document (see RFC1891). An identification of other mail systems can also be used. One of the identification methods has been described in "The COSINE and Internet X.500 Schema" (section 9.3.18) in the RFC1274 document. The mail system names listed here are used as the legal values in that schema under the "otherMailbox" attribute "mailboxType" type, which must be a PrintableString. The "Mapping between X.400 (1988)/ISO 10021 and RFC 822" is described in the section 4.2.2 of the RFC1327 document. The names listed here are used as the legal values in that schema under the "std-or-address" attribute "registered-dd-type" type, which must be a "keystring" (for details, see Mail Parameters, 2002).

SMTP Mail Transaction Flow

The SMTP protocol (RFC 821) defines how commands and responses must be sent by the MTAs. The client sends commands to the server, and the server responds with numeric reply codes and optional human-readable strings. There are a small number of commands (less than a dozen) that the client can send to the server. An example of sending a simple one-line message and an interpretation of the SMTP connection can be found in Stevens (1993).

Although mail commands and replies are rigidly defined (see "Commands and Responses" later in this chapter), the exchange can easily be followed in Figure 3.

In this scenario (Comer, 1995; SMTP, 2005), the user `jsmith` at host `sun.it.rivier.edu` sends a note to users `darien`, `steve` and `bryan` at host mail.unh.edu. Here the lines sent by the server (receiver) are preceded by `S`, and the lines sent by the client (sender) preceded by `C`. Note that the message header is part of the data being transmitted. All exchanged messages (commands, replies, and data) are text lines, delimited by a <CRLF>. All replies have a numeric code at the beginning of the line.

The scenario includes the following steps (SMTP, 2005):

1. The client (sender-SMTP) establishes a TCP connection with the destination SMTP and then waits for the server to send a `220 Service ready` message or a `421 Service not available` message when the destination is temporarily unable to proceed.
2. The `HELO` command is sent, and the receiver is forced to identify himself by sending back its domain name. The client (sender-SMTP) can use this information to verify if it contacted the right destination SMTP. If the sender-SMTP supports SMTP service extensions as defined in the RFC 16511994, it may substitute an `EHLO` command in place of in RFC 1651. A receiver-SMTP, which does not support service extensions, will respond with a `500 Syntax error, command unrecognized` message. The client (sender-SMTP) should then retry with `HELO`, or if it cannot transmit the message without one or more service extensions, it should send a `QUIT` message. If a receiver-SMTP supports service extensions, it responds with a multiline `250 OK` messages that include a list of service extensions, which it supports.
3. The client (sender) now initiates the start of a mail transaction by sending a `MAIL` command to the receiver. This command contains the reverse-path, which can be used to report errors. Note that a path can be more than just the *user-mailbox@host-domain-name* pair. In addition, it can contain a list of routing hosts. Examples of this are when the mail passes a mail bridge or when the user provides explicit routing information in the destination address. If accepted, the server (receiver) replies with a `250 OK` message.
4. The second step of the actual mail exchange consists of providing the server SMTP with the destinations for the message (there can be more than one recipient). This is done by sending one or more `RCPT TO:<forward-path>` commands. Each of them will receive a `250 OK` reply if the destination is known to the server or a `550 No such user here` reply if it is not.
5. When all RCPT commands are sent, the client (sender) issues a `DATA` command to notify the server (receiver) that the message contents are following. The server replies with the `354 Start mail input, end with <CRLF>.<CRLF>` message.

```
S: 220 mail.unh.edu Simple Mail Transfer Service Ready
C: HELO it.rivier.edu
S: 250 mail.unh.edu

C: MAIL FROM:<jsmith@it.rivier.edu>
S: 250 OK

C: RCPT TO:<darien@mail.unh.edu>
S: 250 OK

C: RCPT TO:<steve@mail.unh.edu>
S: 250 OK

C: RCPT TO:<bryan@mail.unh.edu>
S: 550 No such user here

C: DATA
S: 354 Start mail input, end with <CRLF>.<CRLF>
C: Date: 26 Jan 2004  11:02:34 EST
C: From: John Smith <jsmith@it.rivier.edu>
C: Subject: Important meeting
C: To:  <darien@mail.unh.edu>
C: To:  <steve@mail.unh.edu>
C: cc:  <bryan@mail.unh.edu>
C:
C: Best wishes
C: See you soon...
C: .
S: 250 OK

C: QUIT
S: 221 mail.unh.edu Service closing transmission channel
```

Figure 3: An example of the interactive session between the client (C) and the server (S).

6. The client now sends the data line by line, ending with the sequence `<CRLF>.<CRLF>` line on which the receiver acknowledges with a `250 OK` or an appropriate error message if anything went wrong.
7. The following actions (SMTP, 2005) are possible after that:
   - The sender has no more messages to send; he will end the connection with a QUIT command, which will be answered with a `221 Service closing transmission channel` reply (see Figure 3).
   - The client (sender) has another message to send and simply goes back to Step 3 to send a new `MAIL` command.

In this description, only the most important commands that must be recognized in each SMTP implementation (see RFC821) have been mentioned. Other optional commands (the RFC 821 standard does not require them to be implemented everywhere) implement several important functions such as forwarding, relaying, mailing lists, and so on.

SMTP Commands

The commands formed with ASCII (text) are sent from the client to the server. The simple structure of the commands allows for building mail clients and servers on any platform. The list of commands and their description and formats are shown in Table 1. The command consists of a key word followed by zero or more arguments. Five commands (HELO, MAIL FROM, RCPT TO, DATA, and QUIT) are mandatory, and every implementation must support them. The other three commands (RSET, VRFY, and NOOP) are often used and highly recommended. The next six programs (TURN, EXPN, HELP, SEND FROM, SOML FROM, and SAML FROM) are seldom used.

For a full list of commands, see the RFC 821 "Simple Mail Transfer Protocol" and RFC 1123 "Requirements for Internet Hosts—Application and Support." For details of SMTP service extensions, see the RFC 1651 "SMTP Service Extensions," RFC 1652 "SMTP Service Extension for 8bit-MIMEtransport," RFC 1653 "SMTP Service Extension for Message Size Declaration," and RFC 2554 "SMTP Service Extension for Authentication."

The commands normally progress in a sequence (one at a time). The advanced pipelining feature introduced in the RFC 2920 document allows multiple commands to be sent to a server in a single operation of the TCP-send type.

Mail Service Types

The set of services desired from a mail server are sometimes characterized by the "hello" key word. The various mail service types are as follows (Mail Parameters, 2002):

- HELO for Simple Mail (see RFC821)
- EHLO for Mail Service Extensions (see RFC1869)
- LHLO for Local Mail (see RFC2033).

Table 1 Simple Mail Transfer Protocol (SMTP) Commands

Command	Description	Format	References
ATRN	Authenticated TURN		RFC2645
AUTH	Authentication		RFC2554
BDAT	Binary data		RFC3030
DATA	Data; used to send the actual message; all lines that follow the DATA command are treated as the e-mail message; the message is terminated by a line containing just a period	DATA Best wishes.	RFC821, RFC2821
EHLO	Extended Hello		RFC1869, RFC2821
ETRN	Extended TURN		RFC1985
EXPN	Expand; asks the receiving host to expand the mailing list sent as the arguments and to return the mailbox addresses of the recipients that comprise the list	EXPN: a b c	RFC821, RFC2821
HELO	Hello; used by the client to identify itself	HELO: sun.it.rivier.edu	RFC821, RFC2821
HELP	Help; requests the recipient to send information about the command sent as the argument	HELP: mail	RFC821, RFC2821
MAIL FROM	Mail; used by the client to identify the sender of the message; the argument is the e-mail address of the sender	MAIL FROM: jsmith@ sun.it.rivier.edu	RFC821, RFC2821
NOOP	No operation; used by the client to check the status of the recipient; requires an answer from the recipient	NOOP	RFC821, RFC2821
QUIT	Quit; terminates the message	QUIT	RFC821, RFC2821
RCPT	Recipient; used by the client to identify the intended recipient of the message; if there are multiple recipients, the command is repeated	RCPT TO: steve@unh.edu	RFC821, RFC2821
RSET	Reset; aborts the current e-mail transaction; the stored information about the sender and recipient is deleted; the connection will be reset	RSET	RFC821, RFC2821
SAML	Send to the mailbox or terminal; specifies that the mail have to be delivered to the terminal or the mailbox of the recipient; the argument is the address of the sender	SAML FROM: jsmith@ sun.it.rivier.edu	RFC821
SEND	Send; specifies that the mail is to be delivered to the terminal of the recipient and not the mailbox; if the recipient is not logged in, the mail is bounced back; the argument is the address of the sender	SEND FROM: jsmith@ sun.it.rivier.edu	RFC821
SOML	Send to the mailbox or terminal; it specifies that the mail is to be delivered to the terminal or the mailbox of the recipient; the argument is the address of the sender.	SOML FROM: jsmith@ sun.it.rivier.edu	RFC821
STARTTLS	Extended Hello with transport layer security		RFC3207
TURN	Turn; it lets the sender and the recipient switch positions whereby the sender becomes the recipient and vice versa (most SMTP implementations today do not support this feature; see RFC2821)	TURN	RFC821
VRFY	Verify; it verifies the address of the recipient, which is sent as the argument; the sender can request the receiver to confirm that a name identifies a valid recipient.	VRFY: steve@unh.edu	RFC821, RFC2821

Note: From "SMTP Specifications," 2005.

The EHLO key word has a numerical parameter SIZE for specifying the new format of e-mail messages (see RFC1870).

SMTP Service Extensions

SMTP (RFC821) specifies a set of commands or services for mail transfer. A general procedure for extending the set of services is defined in the STD11/RFC1869 document. The service extensions are identified by key words sent from the server to the client in response to the EHLO command (Mail Parameters, 2002). The set of service extensions are as follows:

- SEND—Send as mail (see RFC821)
- SOML—Send as mail or to terminal (see RFC821)
- SAML—Send as mail and to terminal (see RFC821)
- EXPN—Expand the mailing list (see RFC821)
- HELP—Supply helpful information (see RFC821)
- TURN—Turn the operation around (see RFC821)
- 8BITMIME—Use 8-bit data (see RFC1652)
- SIZE—Message size declaration (see RFC1870)
- CHUNKING—Chunking (see RFC3030)
- BINARYMIME—Binary MIME (see RFC3030)
- CHECKPOINT—Checkpoint/Restart (see RFC1845)
- PIPELINING—Command Pipelining (see RFC2920)
- DSN—Delivery Status Notification (see RFC1891)
- ETRN—Extended Turn (see RFC1985)
- ENHANCEDSTATUSCODES—Enhanced Status Codes (see RFC2034)
- STARTTLS—Start TLS (see RFC3207).

Some of these key words have parameters (for details, see Mail Parameters, 2002).

SMTP Responses

Responses are sent from the server to the client. A response is a three-digit code that may be followed by additional textual information. The meanings of the first digit are as follows:

- 2bc—positive completion reply; the requested command has been successfully completed and a new command can be started.
- 3bc—positive intermediate reply; the requested command has been accepted, but the server needs some more information before completion can occur.
- 4ab—transient negative completion reply; the requested command has been rejected, but the error condition is temporary, and the command can be sent again.
- 5ab—permanent negative completion reply; the requested command has been rejected, and the command cannot be sent again.

The second (b) and the third (c) digits provide further details about the responses. The list of typical reply codes and their description are shown in Table 2.

SMTP SERVER

The SMTP server sends and receives mail from other Internet hosts using the SMTP. The SMTP server processes all incoming and outgoing mail. Outgoing mail is spooled until the SMTP server can confirm it has arrived at its destination; incoming mail is spooled until users access it by using a POP3 or IMAP4 mail client. Spooling allows the transfer from client and server to occur in the background. The instructions on how to configure the SMTP server in the Windows NT environment and how to set options to provide security for the SMTP server are described in "How to Set SMTP Security Options" (2005).

ON-DEMAND MAIL RELAY

On-demand mail relay (ODMR), also known as authenticated TURN (ATRN), is an e-mail service that allows a user to connect to an Internet service provider (ISP), authenticate, and request e-mail using a dynamic IP address (instead of static IP addresses used in a "traditional" SMTP model) from any Internet connection (see RFC 2645). The initial client and server roles are short-lived, because the point is to allow the intermittently connected host to request mail held for it by a service provider. The customer initiates a connection to the provider, authenticates, and requests its mail. The roles of client and server then reverse, and the normal SMTP scenario proceeds. The provider has an ODMR process listening for connections on the ODMR port 366 (SMTP Specifications, 2005). On the server, this process implements the EHLO, AUTH, ATRN, and QUIT commands. Also, it has to be an SMTP client with access to the outgoing mail queues. An MTA normally has a mail client component, which processes the outgoing mail queues, attempting to send mail for particular domains, based on time or events, such as new mail being placed in the queue or receipt of an ETRN command by the SMTP server component. The ODMR service processes the outgoing queue on request. The ISP provider side has normal SMTP server responsibilities, including generation of delivery failure notices (SMTP Specifications, 2005).

MULTIPURPOSE INTERNET MAIL EXTENSIONS (MIME)

The RFC 821/ STD 10 standard specifies that data sent via SMTP is 7-bit ASCII data, with the high-order bit cleared to zero. This is adequate in most instances for the transmission of English text messages but is inadequate for non-English text or nontextual data.

There are two approaches to overcoming these limitations. In the first approach, the MIME were defined in RFC 1521 and RFC 1522, which specify a mechanism for encoding text and binary data as 7-bit ASCII within the mail envelope defined by the RFC 822 standard. MIME is also described in SMTP (2005).

In the second approach, the SMTP service extensions (RFC 1651, RFC 1652, and RFC 1653) define a mechanism to extend the capabilities of SMTP beyond the limitations imposed by the RFC 821 standard. The RFC 1651 document introduces a standard for a receiver-SMTP to

Table 2 Simple Mail Transfer Protocol (SMTP) Reply Codes

Code	Description
	Positive Completion Reply
211	System status or system help reply
214	Help message
220	*Domain* service ready; ready to start TLS
221	*Domain* service closing transmission channel
250	OK, queuing for node *node* started; requested command completed
251	OK, no messages waiting for node *node*; user not local, will forward to *forwardpath*
252	OK, pending messages for node *node* started; cannot VRFY user (e.g., information is not local) but will take message for this user and attempt delivery
253	OK, *messages* pending messages for node *node* started
	Positive Intermediate Reply
354	Start mail input; end with <CRLF>.<CRLF>
355	Octet-offset is the transaction offset
	Transient Negative Completion Reply
421	*Domain* service not available, closing transmission channel
432	A password transition is needed
450	Requested mail action not taken: mailbox unavailable; ATRN request refused
451	Requested action aborted: local error in processing; unable to process ATRN request now
452	Requested action not taken: insufficient system storage
453	You have no mail
454	TLS not available due to temporary reason; encryption required for requested authentication mechanism
458	Unable to queue messages for node *node*
459	Node *node* not allowed: *reason*
	Permanent Negative Completion Reply
500	Command not recognized: *command*; Syntax error
501	Syntax error in parameters or arguments; no parameters allowed
502	Command not implemented
503	Bad sequence of commands
504	Command parameter temporarily not implemented
521	*Machine* does not accept mail
530	Must issue a STARTTLS command first; encryption required for requested authentication mechanism
534	Authentication mechanism is too weak
538	Encryption required for requested authentication mechanism
550	Requested action not taken (command is not executed): mailbox unavailable
551	User not local; please try *forwardpath*
552	Requested mail action aborted: exceeded storage allocation
553	Requested action not taken: mailbox name not allowed
554	Transaction failed

Note: From "SMTP Specifications," 2005.

inform a sender-SMTP, which service extensions it supports. New procedures modify the RFC 821 standard to allow a client SMTP agent to request that the server responds with a list of the service extensions that it supports at the start of an SMTP session. If the server SMTP does not support the RFC 1651, it will respond with an error and the client may either terminate the session or attempt to start a session according to the rules of the RFC 821 standard. If the server does support the RFC 1651, it may also respond with a list of the service extensions that it supports. A registry of services is maintained by the Internet Assigned Numbers Authority (IANA, 2005); the initial list defined in the RFC 1651 document contains those commands listed in RFC 1123 as optional for SMTP servers.

Specific extensions are defined in RFC 1652 and RFC 1653. A protocol for 8-bit text transmission (RFC 1652) allows an SMTP server to indicate that it can accept data consisting of 8-bit bytes. A server, which reports that this extension is available to a client, must leave the high-order bit of bytes received in an SMTP message unchanged if requested to do so by the client.

The MIME and SMTP service extension approaches are complementary. Following their procedures (RFC 1652), nontraditional SMTP agents can transmit messages, which are declared as consisting of 8-bit data rather than 7-bit data, when both the client and the server conform to the RFC 1651 or RFC 1652 options (or both). Whenever a client SMTP attempts to send 8-bit data to a server, which does not support this extension, the client

Table 3 Data Types and Subtypes in a Multipurpose Internet Mail Extensions (MIME) `Content-Type` Header Declaration

Type	Subtype	Description
Text	Plain	Unformatted 7-bit ASCII text; no transformation by MIME is needed
Multipart	Mixed	Body contains ordered parts of different data types
	Parallel	Body contains no-ordered parts of different data types
	Digest	Body contains ordered parts of different data types, but the default is message/RFC822
	Alternative	Parts are different versions of the same message
Message	RFC822	Body is an encapsulated message
	Partial	Body is a fragment of a bigger message
	External-Body	Body is a reference to another message
Image	JPEG	Image is in JPEG format
	GIF	Image is in GIF format
Video	MPEG	Video is in MPEG format
Audio	Basic	String channel encoding of voice at 8 KHz
Application	PostScript	Adobe PostScript
	Octet-stream	General binary data (eight-bit bytes)

GIF = Graphics Interchange Format; JPEG = Joint Photographic Experts Group; MPEG = Motion Picture Experts Group.

SMTP must either encode the message contents into a 7-bit representation compliant with the MIME standard or return a permanent error to the user.

The SMTP service extension has the limitation on maximum length of a line (only up to 1,000 characters as required by the RFC 821 standard). The service extension also limits the use of non-ASCII characters to message headers, which are prohibited by the RFC 822 regulations.

The RFC 1653 document introduces the protocol for message size declaration that allows a server to inform a client of the maximum size message it can accept. If both server and client support the message size declaration extension, the client may declare an estimated size of the message to be transferred, and the server will return an error if the message is too large. Each of these SMTP service extensions is a draft standard protocol and each has a status of elective.

The MIME protocols define five header lines that can be added to the original header section to define the transformation parameters: MIME-version, content-type, content-transfer-encoding, content-id, and content-description. Each header line is described in detail in the following sections.

MIME-Version

The header line `MIME-Version: 1.1` declares that the message was composed using the (current) version 1.1 of the MIME protocol.

Content-Type

The header line `Content-Type:<type/subtype; parameters>` defines the type of data used in the body of the message. The identifiers of the content type and the content subtype are separated by a slash. Depending on the subtype, the header may contain other parameters. The MIME standard allows seven basic content types of data, the valid subtypes for each, and transfer encodings, which are listed in Table 3. Examples of the content-type headers can be found in Forouzan (2003).

Content-Transfer-Encoding

The `Content-Transfer-Encoding:<type>` header line defines the method to encode the messages into a bit-stream of 0s and 1s for transport. The five types of encoding are as follows:

- `7bit`—for NVT ASCII characters and short lines of less than 1,000 characters.
- `8bit`—for non-ASCII characters and short lines of less than 1,000 characters; the underlying SMTP protocol must be able to transfer 8-bit non-ASCII characters (this type is not recommended).
- `binary`—for non-ASCII characters with unlimited-length lines; this is 8-bit encoding. The underlying SMTP protocol must be able to transfer 8-bit non-ASCII characters (this type is not recommended).
- `base64`—for sending data made of bytes when the highest bit is not necessarily zero; 6-bit blocks of data are encoded into 8-bit printable ASCII characters (for details, see Forouzan, 2003; Stevens, 1993), which can then be sent as any type of character set supported by the underlying mail transfer mechanism.
- `quoted-printable`—for sending data that consist of mostly ASCII characters with a small non-ASCII portion; if a character is not ASCII, it is sent as three characters: the first character is the equal sign, and the next two are the hexadecimal representation of the byte.

Although the content type and encoding are independent, the RFC 1521 document recommends `quoted-printable` for text with non-ASCII data, and `base64` for image, audio, video, and octet-stream application data. This allows maximum interoperability with RFC 821 conformant MTAs (Stevens, 1993).

Content-Id

The header line `Content-Id: id=<content-id>` uniquely identifies the whole message in a multiple message environment.

Content-Description

The header line `Content-Description:<description>` defines whether the body is image, audio, or video.

Security Scheme for MIME

The S/MIME is a security scheme for the MIME protocol. It was developed by RSA Security and is an alternative to the pretty good privacy (PGP) encryption and digital signature scheme that uses public-key cryptography. The S/MIME scheme was standardized by IETF. According to "Report of the IAB Security Architecture Workshop" (RFC 2316), the designated security mechanism for adding secured sections to MIME-encapsulated e-mail is security/multipart, as described in "Security Multiparts for MIME: Multipart/Signed and Multipart/Encrypted" (RFC 1847).

The S/MIME is widely used by large companies that need to standardize e-mail security for both interorganization and intraorganization mail exchange (Internet Engineering Task Force [IETF] SMIME, 2005). It requires establishing a public-key infrastructure either in-house or by using any of the public certificate authorities (Sheldon, 2001).

MAIL TRANSMISSION TYPES

The SMTP (RFC821) and the Standard for the Format of Advanced Research Project Agency (ARPA) Internet Text Messages (RFC822) specify that a set of "Received" lines will be prepended to the headers of electronic mail messages as they are transported through the Internet (Mail Parameters, 2002). The received line may optionally include either or both a "`via`" phrase or a "`with`" phrase (or both). The legal value for the "`via`" phrase is intended to indicate the link or physical medium over which the message was transferred (e.g., the `UUCP` link type should be specified for the Unix-to-Unix Copy Program). The "`with`" phrase is intended to indicate the protocol or logical process that has been used to transfer the message (e.g., SMTP or ESMTP parameters are used respectively for SMTP [RFC821] or SMTP with service extensions [RFC1869] protocol types).

MAIL ACCESS MODES

To reach its final destination, an e-mail message should be handled by a mail server, the mail access protocol, and the mail client. A general concept of how these components work together is described in "Accessing Your Mail" (1997).

An Internet mail server (known as the mail transfer agent, described earlier) is the software responsible for transmitting and receiving e-mail across the Internet. The MTA software is run on a computer that has a connection to the Internet and is managed, monitored, and backed up by ISPs or a company's information services staff. Some mail servers store mail only until the user retrieves it, whereas others store user mail permanently. An e-mail user typically uses a mail client program to interact with the mail server (Rose, 1993).

A mail client (known as the mail user agent, described earlier) is the software that a user employs to read, send, file, and otherwise process the electronic mail. Usually running on a user's desktop computer, the mail client also manages related e-mail data (address books, spelling dictionaries, and stationery). The mail client connects to a mail server to retrieve new mail. Some mail clients also use the mail server to store all e-mail (Rose, 1993).

The communication between the mail client and mail server is regulated by the mail access protocol, a standardized set of transmitted commands and responses sent over many different types of network connections. The protocol commands (created for managing access to the Internet e-mail only) depend on a design approach that can significantly affect the manner, modes, characteristics, and capabilities of the interaction between the mail client and mail server ("Accessing Your Mail", 1997). The SMTP Protocol handles the task of the actual sending of e-mail on the Internet.

A mail access protocol operates in three common modes that differ in where and how a user stores and processes his or her mail ("Accessing Your Mail," 1997):

- **Offline mode**—e-mail is downloaded from a temporary storage on the mail server to the user's computer. After download, the mail is deleted from the server.
- **Online mode**—user's e-mail, his or her inbox, and all filed mail remains permanently on the mail server. By connecting to the server and establishing an e-mail session, the user can download a temporary copy of his or her e-mail and read it, or send e-mail. Once the connection is finished, the copy is erased from user's computer, and only the original remains on the server.
- **Disconnected/resynchronization mode**—combines both offline and online modes. A copy of the user's e-mail is downloaded to his or her computer(s), and the original message remains on the mail server. The user can change a local copy of his or her e-mail on any computer, then resynchronize all copies, including the original e-mail message on the server and copies on additional computers.

All three modes offer multiplatform support. This includes support for existing platforms such as UNIX, Microsoft Windows, and Apple Macintosh, and future platforms such as Java Mail Service–based network computers. All three modes, including their advantages and disadvantages, are discussed in detail in "Accessing Your Mail" (1997).

MAIL ACCESS PROTOCOLS

POP3

POP is used on the Internet to retrieve e-mail from a mail server. There are two versions of POP. The first, known as POP2 (RFC 937), became a standard in the mid-1980s and requires SMTP to send messages. Nowadays it has a status of "not recommended." The newer version, POP3 (RFC 1725), can be used with or without SMTP.

POP was designed primarily to support the offline access mode (RFC 1939). Typically, e-mail arrives from the network and is placed in the user's inbox on the server. POP is then used to transfer the mail from the user's inbox on the server to the user's computer. POP is designed so that mail client software can determine which messages have been previously downloaded from the server. The mail client can then download only new messages. POP also provides the ability to selectively delete messages from the server. It can be used by a mail client to perform basic resynchronization of the inbox on the server and on the user's computers. The client can leave the most recent messages on the server after they have been downloaded. These messages can then be downloaded a second time to a second computer. Additionally, some POP implementations provide optional features, such as allowing users to download only headers at one session, to review the topics, and then download selected bodies and attachments in a subsequent session to minimize connection times over slow links ("Accessing Your Mail," 1997).

POP servers are widely available both commercially and as freeware on a number of operating systems. Moreover, there are almost no interoperability issues between POP servers and mail clients, and users can use any POP mail client with any POP server. All ISPs support and use POP.

In the end-to-end application related to SMTP, the server must be available whenever a client (sender) transmits mail. If the SMTP server resides on an end-user PC or workstation, that computer must be running the server when the client is trying to send mail. For some operating systems (e.g., when a server program is activated on the VM SMTP service virtual machine or the MAIL program on DOS), the server becomes unavailable and unreachable by the SMTP client (SMTP, 2005). The mail-sending process will fail in these cases. Especially, it is important for single-user systems that the client has an accessible mailbox on various types of server (RFC 1725).

One of the simplest approaches to resolve this problem is to allow the end user to run a client program, which communicates with a server program on a host. This server program acts as both a sender and a receiver SMTP (SMTP, 2005). Here the end-user mailbox resides on the server, and the server system is capable of sending mail to other users.

In another approach, the SMTP server function has to be off-loaded from the end-user workstation, but not the SMTP client function. In this case, the user has a mailbox that resides on a server system, and he can send mail directly from the workstation. To collect mail from the mailbox, the user must connect to the mail server system.

The current post office protocol version 3 (RFC 1725) is a draft standard protocol, and its status is elective. POP3 extensions are described in RFC 2449. POP3 security options are introduced in RFC 2595. The RFC 1734 describes the optional AUTH command for indicating an authentication mechanism to the POP3 server, performing an authentication protocol exchange, and optionally negotiating a protection mechanism for subsequent protocol interactions (Sheldon, 2001).

IMAP4

IMAP is a protocol for retrieving e-mail messages (RFC 1064). The IMAP4 version is similar to POP3 but supports some additional features. For example, with IMAP4, the user can search through his or her e-mail messages for key words while the messages are still on the mail server. The user can then choose which messages to download to his or her machine.

IMAP uses SMTP as its transport mechanism. Following the simple analogy (Sheldon, 2001), IMAP servers are like post offices, whereas SMTP is like the postal carriers. IMAP uses TCP to take advantage of its reliable data delivery services, which are allocated on the TCP port 143. The latest IMAP version 4, revision 1 (IMAP4rev1) is defined in RFC 2060.

IMAP has many advanced features, such as the ability to address mail not by arrival number, but by using attributes (e.g., "Download the latest message from Smith"). This feature allows the mailbox to be structured more like a relational database system rather than a sequence of messages (Tanenbaum, 2003). Authentication mechanisms are described in RFC 1731. Security issues have been introduced in "IMAP4/POP Authorization for Simple Challenge/Response" (RFC 2195), "IMAP4 Login Referrals" (RFC 2221), and "IMAP4 Implementation and Best Practices" (RFC 2683).

SMTP SECURITY ISSUES

SMTP Vulnerabilities

The processes of retrieving e-mail from servers and managing data communication through the Internet are vulnerable to various attacks. A review of vulnerabilities can be found in "Vulnerability Tutorials" (2005) released by the Saint Corporation. The Common Vulnerabilities and Exposures (CVE) organization provides a list of standardized names for SMTP vulnerabilities and other information security exposures. All CVE references (CVE entries and CAN candidates) cited in this text can be found at the CVE Web site, provided in the references (CVE, 2005). Summaries of major SMTP vulnerability problems are given in Table 4.

A security audit of selected SMTP problems has been provided by the U.S. Computer Emergency Readiness Team (CERT) Coordination Center operated by Carnegie Mellon University, and E-Soft. Detailed information about vulnerability problems, possible actions of an attacker or spammer, recommendations for downloading updated versions of software, examples of code modification, and test results can be found on the CERT (2005) and Security Space ("SMTP Problems," 2005) Web sites.

The vulnerability problems can be grouped into several general high-risk categories: buffer overflow; redirection attacks through the firewall; bounced "piping" attacks; and host-shell-gaining attacks (see Table 4).

The medium-to-high risk category includes denial-of-service attacks. Low-to-medium-risk categories include mail relaying on the remote SMTP server, mail-queue manipulation attacks; debug-mode-leak category; and crashing antivirus-software attack ("SMTP Problems," 2005). Most SMTP-specific vulnerabilities occur from

Table 4 SMTP Vulnerability Problems *(CVE, 2005)*

CVE Name	Type of Vulnerability	Possible Attacker Intrusive Action
CVE-2004-309	Stack-based buffer overflow in the SMTP service support in vsmon.exe in Zone Labs ZoneAlarm before v. 4.5.538, ZoneLabs Integrity client v. 4.0.	It allows remote attackers to execute arbitrary code via a long RCPT TO argument.
CVE-2002-309	SMTP proxy in Symantec Enterprise Firewall v. 6.5.x includes the firewall's physical interface name and address in an SMTP exchange when NAT translation is made to an address other than the firewall.	It allows remote attackers to determine certain firewall configuration information.
CVE-2002-0055	SMTP service in Microsoft Windows 2000, Windows XP Professional, and Exchange 2000 to cause a DoS via a command with a malformed data transfer (BDAT) request.	An attacker may disrupt the SMTP service and, depending on the system configuration, potentially IIS and other Internet services as well. See also MS02-012.
CVE-2002-0054	SMTP service in Microsoft Windows 2000 and Internet Mail Connector (IMC) in Exchange Server 5.5 does not properly handle responses to NTLM authentication.	It allows remote attackers to perform mail relaying via an SMTP AUTH command using null session credentials.
CVE-2001-0894	Vulnerability in Postfix SMTP server that is configured to e-mail the postmaster: SMTP errors cause the session to terminate.	It allows remote attackers to cause a DoS (memory exhaustion) by generating a large number of SMTP errors, which forces the SMTP session log to grow too large.
CVE-2001-0692	Vulnerability in SMTP proxy in WatchGuard Firebox (2500 and 4500) v. 4.5-4.6.	A remote attacker may bypass firewall filtering via a base64 MIME encoded e-mail attachment whose boundary name ends in two dashes.
CVE-2001-0690	Format string vulnerability in Exim (v. 3.22-10 in Red Hat, v. 3.12 in Debian, and v. 3.16 in Conectiva) in batched SMTP mode.	It allows a remote attacker to execute arbitrary code via format strings in SMTP mail headers.
CVE-2001-0653	Local buffer overflow on Sendmail (v.8.11.x).	A local user may gain root privileges.
CVE-2001-0504	The authentication error on the remote SMTP server Microsoft Windows 2000. See also MS01-037.	An attacker may exploit this flaw to use the SMTP server as a spam relay.
CVE-2001-1203	Lotus Domino SMTP server (v. 4.63-5.08) is vulnerable to a DoS (central processing unit consumption) attack by forging an e-mail message with the sender as bounce@[127.0.0.1] (localhost).	It allows remote attackers to cause a DoS: the server enters a mail loop.
CVE-2000-1047	The Lotus Domino SMTP server (v.5.0.x) is vulnerable to buffer overflow when supplied a too long ENVID variable within a MAIL FROM command.	An attacker may use this flaw to prevent Domino services from working properly, or to execute arbitrary code on the host.
CVE-2000-1022	The mailguard feature in Cisco Secure PIX Firewall (v. 5.2(2) and earlier) does not properly restrict access to SMTP commands.	It allows remote attackers to execute restricted commands by sending a DATA command before sending the restricted commands.
CVE-2000-0507	The remote Imate SMTP server crashes when it is issued a HELO command with an argument longer than 1,200 characters.	vAn attacker may shut down the SMTP server.
CVE-2000-0488	Buffer overflow on the ITHouse mail server (v.1.04).	Remote attackers may execute arbitrary commands via a long RCPT TO mail command.
CVE-2000-0452	Buffer overflow in the remote Lotus SMTP server when the server is issued a too long argument to the MAIL FROM command.	An attacker may prevent the host from acting as a mail host and may execute arbitrary code on the system.
CVE-2000-0319	mail.local in the remote Sendmail server does not properly identify the .\n string, which indicates the message-text end.	A remote attacker may cause a DoS or corrupt mailboxes via a message line that is 2047 characters long and ends as .\n.

(*Continued*)

Table 4 *(continued)*

CVE Name	Type of Vulnerability	Possible Attacker Intrusive Action
CVE-2000-0075	Super Mail Transfer Package, later called MsgCore, has a memory leak.	Remote attackers may cause a DoS by repeating multiple HELO, MAIL FROM, RCPT TO, and DATA commands in the same session.
CVE-1999-0203	The remote Sendmail's SMTP server did not complain when issued the command (from piped program): MAIL FROM: |testing	An attacker may send mail that will be bounced to a program that allows him to execute arbitrary commands on the host.
CVE-1999-0096	The remote Sendmail SMTP server seems to pipe mail sent to the "decode" alias to a program.	An attacker can use this "decode" flaw to overwrite arbitrary files on the remote server.
CAN-2003-0818	Multiple integer overflows in Microsoft ASN.1 library (MSASN1.DLL). See also MS04-007.	An attacker may execute arbitrary code on this host by sending a specially crafted ASN.1 encoded packet with improper lengths.
CAN-2003-0743	Exim MTA (v. 4.21) heap overflow.	An attacker may gain a shell on this host.
CAN-2003-0714	Exchange remote buffer overflow: SMTP service is vulnerable to a flaw in the XEXCH50 extended verb (command).	An attacker may completely crash Exchange 5.5 and execute arbitrary code on Exchange 2000. See also MS03-046.
CAN-2003-0681	Remote Sendmail servers (v. 8.12.9 and earlier) have prescan() overflow on a remote buffer.	An attacker may gain root privileges.
CAN-2003-0540	Remote Postfix (v. 1.1.12) daemon multiple vulnerabilities.	An attacker may remotely disable it, or use it as a DoS agent against arbitrary hosts.
CAN-2003-0264	SLMail (v. 5.1) SMTP server experiences various overflows.	A cracker might execute arbitrary commands on this host or to disable it remotely.
CAN-2003-0161	Sendmail (v. 8.12.8 and earlier) servers have buffer overflow due to type conversion.	An attacker may gain remotely root privileges.
CAN-2002-1337	Remote header buffer overflow on Sendmail servers (v. 8.12.7 and earlier).	A remote attacker may gain root privileges.
CAN-2001-0713	A user may supply a custom configuration file to remote Sendmail servers.	A local attacker may regain the extra dropped privileges and run commands as root.

Note: The CAN number indicates a candidate for inclusion in the Common Vulnerabilities and Exposures (CVE) list of standard names for security problems. It must be reviewed by the CVE editorial board before it can be added to CVE (CVE, 2005).
DoS = denial of service; MIME = multipurpose internet mail extensions; NAT = network address translation; SMTP = Simple mail transfer protocol.

misapplied or unapplied patches related to Sendmail installations or misconfigured Sendmail daemons on the SMTP servers (Campbell, Calvert, & Boswell, 2003).

ISPs restrict access to their outgoing mail servers to provide better service to their customers and prevent spam from being sent through their mail servers. There are several methods for establishing restrictions that could result in denying users' access to their outgoing mail server.

Originally (see RFC 821), e-mail servers (configured for SMTP relay) did not verify the claimed sender identity and would simply pass the mail on with whatever return address was specified. Bulk mailers have taken advantage of this to send huge volumes of mail with bogus return addresses. This results in slowing down servers.

To fix the problem, the origin of a spam e-mail should be identified. An e-mail message typically transports through a set of SMTP servers (including the sender's and receiver's servers) before reaching the destination host. Along this pass, messages get "stamped" by the intermediate SMTP servers. The stamps release tracking information that can be identified in the mail headers. Mismatches between the IP addresses and the domain names in the header could unveil the real source of spam mail. The real domain names that correspond to the indicated IP addresses can be found out by executing a reverse DNS lookup. Modern mail programs have incorporated this functionality, which generates a `Received:` header line that includes the identity of the attacker (see examples in Campbell et al., 2003).

Antispoofing measures are under active development. Mail Abuse Prevention System (MAPS) and Open Relay Behavior-Modification System (ORBS) provide testing, reporting, and cataloging of e-mail servers configured for SMTP relay. These organizations maintain real-time blackhole lists (RBL) of mail servers with problematic histories. For protection and security purposes, companies may configure their SMTP servers and other e-mail service systems in such manner that any mail coming from RBL-blacklisted mail servers is automatically rejected (Campbell, 2003). Other initiatives for restricting the sender address spoofing include SPF, Hotmail domain cookies, and Microsoft's caller ID.

Also see "E-Mail Threats and Vulnerabilities".

SMTP Server Buffer Overflow Vulnerability

`Sendmail` contains a buffer overflow in code that parses e-mail addresses (CAN-2003-0161). When processing e-mail messages, `sendmail` creates tokens from address elements (user, host, domain). The code that performs this function (`prescan() in parseaddr.c`) contains logic to check that the tokens are not malformed or overly long. In certain cases, a variable in `prescan()` is set to the special control value –1, which may alter the program logic to skip the length checks. Using an e-mail message with a specially crafted address containing 0xFF, an attacker could cause the length checks to be skipped and overwrite the saved instruction pointer on the stack. A remote attacker could execute arbitrary code or cause a denial of service on a vulnerable system. Upgraded versions of `sendmail` should be used for protection.

Another remote buffer overflow in `sendmail` was reported (CAN-2002-1337). This vulnerability may allow remote attackers to gain root privileges of the `sendmail` daemon. A properly patched `sendmail` server (version 8.12.8) will drop invalid headers, thus preventing downstream servers from receiving them.

A buffer overflow in the mail server was identified as vulnerability in the Lotus Domino family of servers (Lotus, 2005) that includes an SMTP server (see Table 4, CVE-2000-0452). It supports extensions, which allow for the use of delivery status notifications that provide information about the delivery status of an e-mail message to the sender. An e-mail client specifying an identifier for an outgoing message optionally uses the `ENVID` key word. This identifier is included in any delivery status notifications regarding that message. By sending a long argument to the `ENVID` key word, it is possible to cause a buffer overflow in the mail server. A remote attacker could exploit this condition to cause a denial of service or to execute arbitrary code. The `ENVID` vulnerability was discussed in the S.A.F.E.R. Security Bulletin (S.A.F.E.R., 2000).

Another buffer overflow condition exists in the code that implements the policy feature that can be used to set relaying rules. With this feature, an e-mail administrator can specify rules to determine when the server may be used for relaying mail from one remote site to another. This vulnerability in Lotus Domino (S.A.F.E.R., 2001) could also be used to cause a denial of service or to execute arbitrary commands.

A third vulnerability posted to Security Focus (Bugtraq, 2005) could allow an attacker to cause a denial-of-service in Lotus Domino by sending a long argument to the `RCPT TO`, `SAML FROM`, or `SOML FROM` commands.

Also see "Server-Side Security".

Mail Relaying SMTP Vulnerability

The SMTP that is used by a mail server to send, receive, or route e-mail across a network requires the `MAIL FROM` (sender) address and the `RCPT TO` (recipient) address to be specified. Normally, either the sender or the recipient address is in the server's domain. Some SMTP servers accept any sender or recipient address without checking whether at least one of them is in the server's domain. On such servers, it is possible to supply a fake sender address and an arbitrary recipient address, which greatly facilitates the spread of spam. Even SMTP servers, which generally do not allow relaying, do allow it if the session originates from a host in the server's domain or from a host from which relaying is explicitly permitted. If the scan is performed from such a host, a false alarm may result. To resolve this issue, UNIX mail servers should be upgraded to the latest version of Sendmail, which does not allow relaying by default (Antirelay Parse, 2005).

Mail Relaying SMTP Vulnerability in Microsoft Windows 2000

A specific type of vulnerability in the default SMTP server running Microsoft Windows 2000 was discovered by Joao Gouveia ("Authentication Error," 2001). An SMTP implementation is provided with Microsoft Windows 2000, and it is installed by default. Microsoft Exchange Server also includes an SMTP service, but the component that performs SMTP authentication is different from the base SMTP Service in Windows 2000 and is not affected by the vulnerability. A flaw in the authentication process (CVE, 2001, No. 0504) used by the SMTP service that installs as part of Internet Information Services (IIS) could allow an unauthorized user to authenticate successfully to the service using incorrect credentials. An attacker can use this vulnerability to gain user-level privileges on the SMTP service, thereby enabling the attacker to use the service (e.g., to co-opt a server's resources for mass mailings) but not to administer it. The service can be used by an attacker to perform SMTP mail relaying. There have been cases in which threatening e-mails were relayed to prevent the recipient from being able to trace where they came from. This vulnerability affects only standalone machines (e.g., Web servers), not domain members or Microsoft Exchange mail servers running Windows 2000.

Customers who need SMTP services should apply the patch ("Patch Availability," 2005), which eliminates the vulnerability by ensuring that the SMTP service properly authenticates users before allowing them to levy requests on it. Also, proper firewalling could be used to prevent Internet users from exploiting the vulnerability. Recommendations for preventing the servers from relaying and spam can be found in Fugatt (2002, July 30).

Also see "Windows 2000 Security".

Encapsulated SMTP Address Vulnerability

The security vulnerability in Microsoft Exchange Server 5.5 (CVE, 2002, No. 0054) could allow an attacker to perform mail relaying via an Exchange server that is configured to act as a gateway for other Exchange sites, using the Internet Messaging Service.

The vulnerability lies in the way that site-to-site relaying is performed via SMTP. The SMTP service in Microsoft Windows 2000 and Internet Mail Connector in Exchange Server 5.5 does not properly handle responses to `NTLM` authentication, which allows remote attackers to perform mail relaying via an SMTP `AUTH` command using null session credentials. Encapsulated SMTP addresses could be used to send mail to any e-mail address. The method of configuring the Exchange Internet Mail Service (IMS) (called Internet Mail Connector in prior versions of

Exchange), is vulnerable to the attack. The IMS service provides encapsulated addresses, when used as a Site Connector, and uses a special form of addressing called "encapsulated SMTP," which is used to encapsulate various message types into SMTP addresses. The Exchange supports three kinds of Site Connectors: an X.400 connector, the Exchange Site Connector, and the Exchange Internet Mail Service. A malicious user could address e-mails using this format and route mail through an Exchange Server, even if mail relaying has been disabled.

Any customer who has configured an IMS on an Internet-connected Exchange Server should consider installing the patch ("Patch Availability," 2005) that eliminates the vulnerability.

Malformed Request Denial of Service

The SMTP service in Microsoft Windows 2000, Windows XP Professional, and Exchange 2000 is vulnerable to cause a denial of service via a command with a malformed data transfer (BDAT) request (CVE, 2002, No. 0055). By sending either a message with a corrupted time stamp or a malformed version of a particular SMTP command to the server, it is possible for a remote attacker to cause the mail service to crash and thus stop responding to legitimate requests.

Extended Verb Request Handling Flaw

IMS in Exchange Server 5.5 and Exchange 2000 do not require authentication before allowing a user to send a certain extended verb request. This vulnerability allows remote attackers to cause a denial of service (memory exhaustion) and to consume large amounts of memory by directly connecting to the SMTP service and possibly triggering a buffer overflow in Exchange 2000 (CVE, 2003, No. 0714). Command execution could be possible. The Microsoft Security Bulletin (2004, No. 03-046) recommends the patch to fix this vulnerability.

Reverse DNS Response Buffer Overflow

Microsoft Exchange does not check the length of the response from the DNS server before copying it into a fixed-length buffer (CVE, 2002, No. 0698). Therefore, a remote attacker who has control over a registered DNS server could cause a buffer overflow by creating a long, specially crafted reverse DNS entry and then issuing the `EHLO` command to Exchange. The overflow would crash the server or even allow the attacker to execute arbitrary commands. Microsoft Exchange 5.5 is affected by this vulnerability if the patch has not been installed. At the same time, Microsoft Exchange 2000 is not affected because it runs atop the native Windows 2000 SMTP service rather than the Internet Mail Connector. To fix the reverse DNS problem, the patch ("Patch Availability", 2005) should be applied.

Firewall SMTP Filtering Vulnerability

During expanded internal regression testing by Cisco, it was discovered that the Cisco Secure PIX Firewall feature "`mailguard`", which limits SMTP commands to a specified minimum set of commands, can be bypassed (CISCO, 2001). The filtering command `fixup protocol smtp[portnum]`, which is enabled by default on the Cisco Secure PIX Firewall, can fail. All users of Cisco Secure PIX Firewalls with software that provide access to SMTP Mail services are at risk. To exploit this vulnerability, attackers can make connections to an SMTP mail server (protected by the PIX Firewall) and can circumvent the expected filtering of the `mailguard` feature. If the mail server is not properly secured, an attacker may collect information about existing e-mail accounts and aliases or can execute arbitrary code on the mail server. Cisco has offered free software upgrades for all affected customers (CISCO, 2001).

Spoofing

On the Internet, mail is usually delivered directly from the sending host to the receiving host. This inherent "open" design of SMTP allows a host computer, which needs to deliver a message to another computer(s), to make a connection (or multiple connections) to some other SMTP server and ask that server to relay the message(s) on its behalf. Gateways can be used to bridge firewalls.

By denying access to a sending machine with a firewall, many companies and ISPs have been blocking the receipt of unwanted mail from known sources. The "blocked" senders of junk mail may attempt to deliver it through another computer by requesting the computer to route that mail for them. Senders of unsolicited e-mail can also use this method to hide their real identity by manipulating the headers in the message and then sending the message through client's system for delivery to its final destination. This "spoofing" action gives the appearance that the message originated from the relaying server. When a bulk mailer chooses a client's computer to deliver unsolicited mail to thousands of other people (known as "spamming"), the client's system immediately becomes busy delivering messages that did not originate with the client's users.

The SMTP server may protect the client's system against this type of abuse in two ways. First, the server allows administrators to configure the system to accept only mail originating from local users or destined for local users. Second, the server administrator can define systems from which the client never wants to receive mail. It blocks mail from known sources of spam mail ("Setting SMTP Security," 2005).

Also see "Networks Attacks."

Bounce Attack

In the case of anonymous file transfer protocol (FTP) services, the attacker can instruct the FTP server to send a file to the SMTP service being attacked on the victim's system (see "FTP Security Considerations, RFC 2577). Using the FTP server to connect to the service on the attacked computer makes it difficult to track down the attacker (Campbell et al., 2003). Particularly, a client -attacker can upload a file that contains SMTP commands to an FTP server. Then, using an appropriate PORT command, the client instructs the attacked server to open a connection to a third computer's SMTP port 25 and transfer the uploaded file containing SMTP commands to the third computer.

This action may allow the client-attacker to forge mail on the third computer without making a direct connection.

Restricting Access to an Outgoing Mail Server

The access to an outgoing mail server can be restricted by verifying that the computer is on the ISP's local network. When the user dials the modem and connects to the ISP, his computer is given an IP address that identifies him as being a part of that network. If the user has two ISPs and dials up to one and then connects to the other's mail server, it may prevent him or her from relaying mail because the computer is not identified as being on the local network for the provider. In this case, the user should try to use the SMTP server to dial up and connect to the Internet ("What Is SMTP Security?", 2005).

Another way to restrict access is to insist on a local domain return address. If users connect to the mail server for "domain.com," it may only allow them to send mail that is from "username@domain.com." Therefore, if they try to send mail from another account that has the return address of "username@anotherdomain.com," it may restrict them from relaying to another server ("What is SMTP Security?", 2005).

Mail Encryption

SMTP is not a secure protocol. Messages sent over the Internet are not secure unless some form of encryption is implemented. S/MIME is a widely used Internet e-mail standard. This and some other security topics (PGP, transport layer security [TSL], host-to-host encryption) are discussed in other chapters.

Also see "Encrypting E-Mail, PGP, S/MIME, TLS, and Virtual Private Networks (VPNs) Basics".

Bastille Hardening System

The Bastille Hardening System (Bastille Project, 2005) has been designed to "harden" or "tighten" UNIX-based operating systems. It currently supports the Red HatEnterprise 3, Debian, Mandrake, SuSE, and TurboLinux Linux distributions along with HP-UX and Mac OS X. The Bastille Linux Hardening software [Version 2.1.2 is available from the Source Forge Web site (Bastille Linux Project, 2005)] enhances the security of a Linux box by configuring daemons, system settings, and firewalling. Written in Perl, the Bastille Linux intends to improve Linux-based computer security. Among others, it has a revised `sendmail` module dedicated to secure holes that were discovered previously (see Table 4). A review of other service modules (Remote Access, Pluggable Authentification, DNS, Apache, FTP, SecureInetd, File Permission, Patch Download, and Firewall Configuration IPChains) can be found in Raynal (2000).

POP AND IMAP VULNERABILITIES

POP was designed to support offline mail processing (Rose, 1993). The mail is deleted from the server and is handled offline (locally) on the client machine. In the implementation of this protocol on a UNIX system, the server must run with root privileges; therefore, it can access mail folders and undertake some file manipulation on behalf of the user logging in. After login, these privileges are discarded. Vulnerability exists in the way the login transaction is handled in some implementations of these procedures (CERT, 2005). This vulnerability can be exploited to gain privileged access on the server. By preparing carefully crafted text to a system running a vulnerable version of the POP server, remote users may be able to cause a buffer overflow and execute arbitrary instructions with root privileges. They do not need access to an account on the system to do this. (Vulnerable POP versions are identified in CVE, 2001, No. 0443, and ("Vulnerability Tutorials," 2005).

POP servers allow non-UNIX users to access their mail on a machine without logging in. The servers give PC and Macintosh users a way to receive mail through another machine. When connecting to a POP server, the client transmits the users' `userid` and `password` in clear text. After authentication, users can access their mail. Each time the client reconnects to the POP server, the users' `userid` and `password` are transmitted. Some POP client programs check the server every few minutes to check for the arrival of new mail. These frequent checks increase the possibility of the machine, username, and password being discovered by a password sniffer "tuned" for POP mail systems.

This clear text password issue is resolved by using an optional command allowable for POP3 servers (RFC 1725). When the initial connection is made to a POP server, the server displays a time stamp in its banner. The client uses this time stamp to create an MD5 hash string that is shared between the server and client. The next time the client connects to the server (e.g., to check for new mail), it will issue the APOP command and the hash string. This method reduces the number of times that a user's `userid` and `password` are transmitted in clear text ("Vulnerability Tutorials," 2005). The current version of IMAP supports both online and offline operation, permitting manipulation of remote message folders. It provides access to multiple mailboxes (that can be allocated on multiple servers) and supports nested mailboxes as well as resynchronization with the server. The IMAP4 version also provides a user with the ability to create, delete, and rename mailboxes ("Vulnerability Tutorials," 2005).

The optional method, which is frequently used for IMAP4 (RFC 1734), provides another client's authentication mechanism (based on the AUTH command). This mechanism allows the client to specify authentication methods it knows about and to challenge the server to see whether it knows any of them as well ("Vulnerability Tutorials," 2005). If no authentication method can be agreed on, then the APOP command (RFC 1725) is used. Also, the latest Secure POP3 mail server (with APOP/IMAP4) can be installed.

Three other vulnerabilities have been discovered which affect different QPOP versions. The first is caused by the fact that the `euidl` command does not properly validate user input (CVE, 2000, No. 0442). This command could be used with a specially crafted e-mail message to gain shell access to the server with privileges of the mail group.

A valid account name and password would be required to exploit this vulnerability. The second vulnerability is a buffer overflow in the processing of the user's login name (CVE, 2001, No. 1046). By supplying a name longer than 63 characters, a remote attacker could crash the service or execute arbitrary commands. The third vulnerability (CVE, 2003, No. 0143) is in the `Qvsnprintf` function call, which is QPOP's own implementation of the `vsnprintf` function. A buffer overflow occurs as a result of a failure to add a terminating null byte, when creating long strings during subsequent calls to the `strcat` function, and allowing the execution of commands. Recommendations for resolving these issues can be found in ("Vulnerability Tutorials," 2005). Secure versions of POP3 (RFC 2449) and IMAP4 (RFC 2595) that use the public key encryption mechanism (Tanenbaum, 2003) are also available.

STANDARDS, ORGANIZATIONS, AND ASSOCIATIONS

Internet Assigned Numbers Authority

The IANA (2005) provides the central coordinating functions of the global Internet for the public needs. The IANA organization maintains a registry of the following services:

- Domain name services
- Database of indexes by Top-Level Domains code
- "Whois" service of domain name recognition
- IP address assignment services (for both IPv4 and IPv6)
- Protocol number assignment services

Internet Engineering Task Force Working Groups

Internet electronic mail was originally defined in the RFC821 standard as a part of the IETF project. Since August 1982, e-mail standards declared in this document were updated and revised by the IETF Detailed Revision/Update of Message Standards (DRUMS) Working Group. The group is also searching new directions in the electronic message communication through the Internet. The latest SMTP documents (including RFCs) can be found on the DRUMS Web site (IETF DRUMS, 2005).

The IETF Message Tracking Protocol (MSGTRK) Working Group is designing diagnostic protocols that a sender can use to request information from servers about the submission, transport, and delivery of a message, regardless of its status. The "Deliver by SMTP Service Extension" document (RFC 2852) specifies extensions to define message delivery time for making a decision to drop the message if it is not delivered within a specific time period. For diagnostic purposes, the "diagnostic-type" parameter (e.g., `smtp` for the Internet Mail) is defined for use in the SMTP delivery status notification (see RFC1891).

The IETF S/MIME Mail Security (SMIME) Working Group is developing S/MIME security standards. The latest S/MIME documents (including RFCs) can be found on the SMIME Web site (IETF SMIME, 2005).

Internet Mail Consortium

The Internet Mail Consortium Web site (IMC, 2005) publishes a complete list of electronic mail-related requests for comments documents (RFCs).

Mitre Corporation

The Mitre Corporation publishes a list of standardized names for all publicly known vulnerabilities and security exposures known as Common Vulnerabilities and Exposures (CVE, 2005).

CONCLUSION

SMTP is an application protocol from the TCP/IP protocol suite that enables the support of e-mail on the Internet. Mail is sent by a series of request–response transactions between a client and a server. The transactions pass the message, which is composed of header and body, and the envelope (SMTP source and destination addresses). The header contains the mail address(es), which consists of two parts: a local address (also known as a "user mailbox") and a domain name. Both SMTP client and SMTP server require a user agent (UA) and a mail transfer agent (MTA). The MTA function is transferring the mail across the Internet. The command–response mechanism is used by SMTP to transfer messages between an MTA client and an MTA server in three stages: connection establishment, mail transfer, and connection termination. The envelope is transmitted separately from the message itself using the `MAIL` and `RCPT` commands. MIME, which is an extension of SMTP, allows the transfer of non-ASCII (multimedia) messages. POP3 and the IMAP 4 together with SMTP are used to receive mail by a mail server and hold it for hosts. The SMTP's lack of security is a problem for businesses. The security in the SMTP transactions can be supported by S/MIME and other methods described in this chapter. Vulnerabilities of SMTP, POP, and IMAP servers (buffer overflow, mail relaying, spoofing, and other attacks) have been analyzed.

GLOSSARY

Body The text of an e-mail message. The body of a message follows the header information.

Bounce Attack An attack that uses a third party's FTP server to hide the true source of the attack from the victim.

Client Any application program used to retrieve information from a server. Internet clients include World Wide Web browsers, Usenet newsreaders, and e-mail programs.

Client–Server The relationship between two application programs. One program, the server, is responsible for servicing requests from the other program, the client.

Delivery Status Notification (DSN) An extended SMTP service that provides information about the delivery status of an e-mail message to the sender.

Disconnected–Resynchronization Mode A mail-access mode in which mail is synchronized between a server and a client computer. By synchronizing mail on the server, users can access their own mail from any computer that has access to the server where the mail is stored.

Domain Name System (DNS) A behind-the-scenes Internet service that translates Internet domain names to their corresponding IP addresses, and vice versa.

E-Mail Client An application that runs on a personal computer or workstation and enables the sender to send, receive, and organize e-mail. It is called a client because e-mail systems are based on a client–server architecture. Mail is sent from many clients to a central server, which reroutes the mail to its intended destination.

Encapsulated Address This address provides a way to send the e-mail to a site acting as a gateway for another site while indicating the server to which the message eventually needs to be sent. An encapsulated address consists of an address within an address; the outer address directs the mail to the gateway, which uses the inner address to determine where to send the e-mail. Because the Exchange Internet Mail Service (IMS) uses SMTP as its e-mail protocol, mails sent to an IMS will use encapsulated SMTP as their addressing scheme.

Gateway Software that translates data from the standards of one system to the standards of another. For example, a gateway might exchange and convert Internet e-mail to X.400 e-mail.

Header Part of an e-mail message that precedes the body of the message and provides the message originator, date, and time.

Internet Message Access Protocol (IMAP) An Internet protocol used by mail clients for retrieving e-mail messages stored on servers. The latest version, IMAP4, is similar to POP3 but supports some additional features; for example, a user can search through his e-mail messages for key words while the messages are still on mail server. The user can then choose which messages to download to his or her computer. While IMAP-based applications can operate in offline mode, they typically operate in online or disconnected–resynchronization mode.

Mail Access Protocol A standardized set of commands and responses responsible for communication between the mail client and mail server.

Mailbox A file where e-mail messages are stored.

Mail Client The software used to read, file, send, and otherwise process e-mail, typically running on a user's desktop computer.

Mail Relaying A legitimate practice in which e-mail is routed to an intermediate mail server, which then delivers it to the recipient's mail server. For example, a company can have several servers and one of them is designated as a mail gateway to the Internet. Any e-mail sent to the company would arrive at the gateway server and then be relayed to the appropriate server for delivery to the recipient. Malicious users sometimes try to perform unauthorized mail relaying.

Mail Server A computer typically managed by an ISP or information services department that handles receipt and delivery of e-mail messages. It also may store mail for the user on a temporary or permanent basis.

Mail Transfer Agent (MTA) The software that is running on a mail server that relays and delivers mail.

Multipurpose Internet Mail Extensions (MIME) An Internet standard that provides the transfer of nontext information, such as sounds and graphics, and non-U.S. English (such as Cyrillic, Chinese, or Japanese) via e-mail.

Mail User Agent (MUA) The software (also known as the mail client) used to read, file, send, and process e-mail, typically running on a desktop computer.

On-Demand Mail Relay (ODMR) A restricted profile of SMTP described in RFC 2645.

Port In a software device, a port is a specific memory address that is mapped to a virtual networking cable. Ports allow multiple types of traffic to be transmitted to a single IP address. SMTP traditionally uses port 25 for e-mail communication.

Post Office Protocol (POP) A protocol used to retrieve e-mail from a mail server in offline mode. An e-mail client that implements the POP protocol downloads all new mail from a mail server, terminates the network connection, and processes all mail offline at the client computer. The current version, POP3 can be used with or without SMTP.

Server A host computer that provides resources to client computers.

Simple Mail Transfer Protocol (SMTP) A protocol widely used to exchange e-mail between e-mail servers on the Internet.

Spam Undesired junk e-mail or junk postings offering dubious business deals.

User Agent (UA) An SMTP component that prepares the message, creates the envelope, and puts the message in the envelope.

CROSS REFERENCES

See *E-Mail and Instant Messaging; Internet E-Mail Architecture; Network Attacks; PGP (Pretty Good Privacy); S/MIME (Secure MIME).*

REFERENCES

Accessing your mail when and where you want on the Internet (1997, April 24). San Diego, CA: QUALCOMM, Eudora Division. Retrieved March 21, 2005, from http://www.eudora.com/pdf_docs/primer.pdf

Antirelay Parse. (2005). Sendmail organization, antirelay rules. Retrieved March 21, 2005, from http://www.sendmail.org/antirelay.Parse0.txt

Authentication error in SMTP service could allow mail relaying. (2001, July 5). Microsoft Security Bulletin, MS01-037. Retrieved March 21, 2005, from http://www.microsoft.com/technet/security/bulletin/MS01-037.mspx

Bastille Linux Project. (2005). Open Source Development Network. Retrieved March 21, 2005, from http://sourceforge.net/projects/bastille-linux/

Bastille Project. (2005). Retrieved March 21, 2005, from http://www.bastille-linux.org/

Bugtraq. (2005). Security Focus Archive, Vol. 1, No. 81696. Retrieved March 21, 2005, from http://www.securityfocus.com/archive/1/81696

Campbell, P., Calvert, B., & Boswell, S. (2003). *Security+ guide to network security fundamentals.* Boston: Cisco Learning Institute.

CA Vulnerability Information Center. (2000, March 8). @Work SmartServer3 SMTP vulnerability. Retrieved March 21, 2005, from http://www3.ca.com/securityadvisor/vulninfo/Vuln.aspx?ID=1972

CERT Computer Emergency Readiness Team. (2005). Vulnerability Database. Retrieved March 21, 2005, from http://www.cert.org/

Cisco Secure PIX Firewall SMTP Filtering Vulnerability, Version 1.1. (2001). Retrieved March 21, 2005, from http://www.cisco.com/warp/public/707/PIXfirewall SMTPfilter-regression-pub.shtml

Cisco SMTP. (2005). Retrieved March 21, 2005, from http://www.cisco.com/univercd/cc/td/doc/product/software/ioss390/ios390ug/ugsmtp.htm

Comer, D. F. (1995). *Internetworking with TCP/IP, Vol. 1: Principles, Protocols, and Architecture* (3rd ed.). Upper Saddle River, NJ: Prentice Hall.

CVE: Common Vulnerabilities and Exposures. (2005). Mitre Corporation. Retrieved March 21, 2005, from http://cve.mitre.org/

Forouzan, B. A. (2003). *TCP/IP Protocol Suite* (2nd ed.). New York: McGraw-Hill.

Fugatt, M. (2002, May 27). Blocking incoming mail using Microsoft Exchange 2000. Tutorials: Exchange 2000, Pentech Office Solutions. Retrieved March 21, 2005, from http://www.msexchange.org/tutorials/MF014.html

Fugatt, M. (2002, July 30). Understanding relaying and spam with Exchange 2000. Tutorials: Exchange 2000, Pentech Office Solutions. Retrieved March 21, 2005, from http://www.msexchange.org/tutorials/MF005.html

How to set SMTP security options in Windows 2000. (2005). Retrieved March 21, 2005, from http://support.microsoft.com/default.aspx?scid=http://support.microsoft.com:80/support/kb/articles/Q303/7/76.ASP&NoWebContent=1

The IMAP Connection. (2005). Retrieved March 21, 2005, from http://www.imap.org/

IMAP Information Center. (2005). Retrieved March 21, 2005, from http://www.washington.edu/imap/

Internet Assigned Numbers Authority. (2005). Retrieved March 21, 2005, from http://www.iana.org/

Internet Engineering Task Force Working Group: Detailed Revision/Update of Message Standards (DRUMS). (2005). Retrieved March 21, 2005 from http://www.ietf.org/html.chapters/OLD/drums-chapter.html

Internet Engineering Task Force Working Group. (2005). Message Tracking Protocol (MSGTRK). Retrieved March 21, 2005, from http://www.ietf.org/html.chapters/OLD/msgtrk-chapter.html

Internet Engineering Task Force Working Group. (2005). S/MIME Mail Security (SMIME). Retrieved March 21, 2005, from http://www.ietf.org/html.chapters/smime-chapter.html

Internet Mail Consortium. (2005). Retrieved March 21, 2005, from http://www.imc.org/rfcs.html

Lotus Domino SMTP Vulnerability. (2005). Retrieved March 21, 2005, from http://www.physnet.uni-hamburg.de/physnet/security/vulnerability/Lotus_Domino_SMTP_vulnerability.html

Mail Parameters. (2005). Retrieved March 21, 2005, from http://www.iana.org/assignments/mail-parameters

Microsoft Security Bulletins. (2005). Retrieved March 21, 2005, from http://www.microsoft.com/technet/security/bulletin/

Patch Availability, Microsoft Security Program. (2005). Retrieved March 21, 2005, from http://www.microsoft.com/technet/security/patchavail-ability.mspx

Raynal, F. (2000). Bastille Linux, MISC Magazine. Retrieved March 21, 2005, from http://www.security-labs.org/index.php3?page=103

RFC821 (STD 10): Simple mail transfer protocol, August 1982. Retrieved March 21, 2005, from ftp://ftp.rfc-editor.org/in-notes/rfc821.txt

RFC822 (STD 11): Standard for the format of ARPA—Internet Text Messages, August 1982. Retrieved March 21, 2005, from ftp://ftp.rfc-editor.org/in-notes/rfc822.txt

RFC876. Survey of SMTP implementations, September 1983. Retrieved March 21, 2005, from ftp://ftp.rfc-editor.org/in-notes/rfc876.txt

RFC937: Post office protocol—Version 2, February 1985. Retrieved March 21, 2005, from ftp://ftp.rfc-editor.org/in-notes/rfc937.txt

RFC1064: Interactive mail access protocol—Version 2, July 1988. Retrieved March 21, 2005, from ftp://ftp.rfc-editor.org/in-notes/rfc1064.txt

RFC1090: SMTP on X.25, February 1989. Retrieved March 21, 2005, from ftp://ftp.rfc-editor.org/in-notes/rfc1090.txt

RFC1123: Requirements for Internet hosts—application and support, October 1989. Retrieved March 21, 2005, from ftp://ftp.rfc-editor.org/in-notes/rfc1123.txt

RFC1274: The COSINE and Internet X.500 schema, November 1991. Retrieved March 21, 2005, from ftp://ftp.rfc-editor.org/in-notes/rfc1274.txt

RFC1327: Mapping between X.400 (1988)/ISO10021 and RFC 822, May 1992. Retrieved March 21, 2005, from ftp://ftp.rfc-editor.org/in-notes/rfc1327.txt

RFC1521: MIME (multipurpose internet mail extensions), part one: Mechanisms for specifying and describing the format of Internet message bodies, September 1993. Retrieved March 21, 2005, from ftp://ftp.rfc-editor.org/in-notes/rfc1521.txt

RFC1522: MIME (multipurpose internet mail extensions), part two: Message header extensions for non-ASCII Text, September 1993. Retrieved March 21, 2005, from ftp://ftp.rfc-editor.org/in-notes/rfc1522.txt

RFC1651: SMTP service extensions, July 1994. Retrieved March 21, 2005, from ftp://ftp.rfc-editor.org/in-notes/rfc1651.txt

RFC1652: SMTP Service Extension for 8bit-MIME transport, July 1994. Retrieved March 21, 2005, from ftp://ftp.rfc-editor.org/in-notes/rfc1652.txt

RFC1653: SMTP Service extension for message size declaration, July 1994. Retrieved March 21, 2005, from ftp://ftp.rfc-editor.org/in-notes/rfc1653.txt

RFC1725: Post office protocol—version 3, RFC1725, November 1994. Retrieved March 21, 2005, from ftp://ftp.rfc-editor.org/in-notes/rfc1725.txt

RFC1731: IMAP4 authentication mechanisms, December 1994. Retrieved March 21, 2005, from ftp://ftp.rfc-editor.org/in-notes/rfc1731.txt

RFC1734: POP3 AUTHentication command, December 1994. Retrieved March 21, 2005, from ftp://ftp.rfc-editor.org/in-notes/rfc1734.txt

RFC1845: SMTP service extension for Checkpoint/Restart, September 1995. Retrieved March 21, 2005, from ftp://ftp.rfc-editor.org/in-notes/rfc1845.txt

RFC1846: SMTP 521 reply code, September 1995. Retrieved March 21, 2005, from ftp://ftp.rfc-editor.org/in-notes/rfc1846.txt

RFC1847: Security Multiparts for MIME: Multipart/Signed and Multipart/Encrypted, October 1995. Retrieved March 21, 2005, from ftp://ftp.rfc-editor.org/in-notes/rfc1847.txt

RFC1869: SMTP service extensions, November 1995. Retrieved March 21, 2005, from ftp://ftp.rfc-editor.org/in-notes/rfc1869.txt

RFC1870: SMTP service extension for message size declaration, November 1995. Retrieved March 21, 2005, from ftp://ftp.rfc-editor.org/in-notes/rfc1870.txt

RFC1891: SMTP service extension for delivery status notification, January 1996. Retrieved March 21, 2005, from ftp://ftp.rfc-editor.org/in-notes/rfc1891.txt

RFC1939 (STD 53): Post office protocol, version 3, May 1996. Retrieved March 21, 2005, from ftp://ftp.rfc-editor.org/in-notes/rfc1939.txt

RFC1985: SMTP Service extension for remote message queue starting, August 1996. Retrieved March 21, 2005, from ftp://ftp.rfc-editor.org/in-notes/rfc1985.txt

RFC2033: Local mail transfer protocol, October 1996. Retrieved March 21, 2005, from ftp://ftp.rfc-editor.org/in-notes/rfc2033.txt

RFC2034: SMTP service extension for returning enhanced status codes, October 1996. Retrieved March 21, 2005, from ftp://ftp.rfc-editor.org/in-notes/rfc2034.txt

RFC2195: IMAP/POP authorization for simple challenge/response, September 1997. Retrieved March 21, 2005, from ftp://ftp.rfc-editor.org/in-notes/rfc2195.txt

RFC2221: IMAP4 login referrals, October 1997. Retrieved March 21, 2005, from ftp://ftp.rfc-editor.org/in-notes/rfc2221.txt

RFC2316: Report of the IAB Security Architecture Workshop, April 1998. Retrieved March 21, 2005, from ftp://ftp.rfc-editor.org/in-notes/rfc2316.txt

RFC2449: POP3 extension mechanism, November 1998. Retrieved March 21, 2005, from ftp://ftp.rfc-editor.org/in-notes/rfc2449.txt

RFC2554: SMTP service extension for authentication, March 1999. Retrieved March 21, 2005, from ftp://ftp.rfc-editor.org/in-notes/rfc2554.txt

RFC2577: FTP security considerations, May 1999. Retrieved March 21, 2005, from ftp://ftp.rfc-editor.org/in-notes/rfc2577.txt

RFC2595: Using TSL with IMAP, POP3 and ACAP, June 1999. Retrieved March 21, 2005, from ftp://ftp.rfc-editor.org/in-notes/rfc2595.txt

RFC2645: On-demand mail relay (ODMR) SMTP with dynamic IP addresses, August 1999. Retrieved March 21, 2005, from ftp://ftp.rfc-editor.org/in-notes/rfc2645.txt

RFC2683: IMAP4 implementation and best practices, September 1999. Retrieved March 21, 2005, from ftp://ftp.rfc-editor.org/in-notes/rfc2683.txt

RFC2846: GSTN address element extensions in e-mail services, June 2000. Retrieved March 21, 2005, from ftp://ftp.rfc-editor.org/in-notes/rfc2846.txt

RFC2852: Deliver by SMTP service extension, June 2000. Retrieved March 21, 2005, from ftp://ftp.rfc-editor.org/in-notes/rfc2852.txt

RFC2920: SMTP service extension for command pipelining, September 2000. Retrieved March 21, 2005, from ftp://ftp.rfc-editor.org/in-notes/rfc2920.txt

RFC3030: SMTP service extensions for transmission of large and binary MIME messages, December 2000. Retrieved March 21, 2005, from ftp://ftp.rfc-editor.org/in-notes/rfc3030.txt

RFC3191: minimal GSTN address format in Internet mail, October 2001. Retrieved March 21, 2005, from ftp://ftp.rfc-editor.org/in-notes/rfc3191.txt

RFC3192: Minimal FAX address format in Internet mail, October 2001. Retrieved March 21, 2005, from ftp://ftp.rfc-editor.org/in-notes/rfc3192.txt

RFC3207: SMTP service extension for secure SMTP over transport layer security, February 2002. Retrieved March 21, 2005, from ftp://ftp.rfc-editor.org/in-notes/rfc3207.txt

Rose, M. T. (1993). *The Internet Message, Closing the Book with Electronic Mail*, Upper Saddle River, NJ: Prentice Hall.

S.A.F.E.R. Security Bulletin. (2000), No. 001103.EXP.1.9. Retrieved March 21, 2005, from http://packetstorm.linuxsecurity.com/advisories/safer/safer.001103.EXP.1.9

S.A.F.E.R. Security Bulletin. (2001). No. 010123.EXP.1.10. Retrieved March 21, 2005, from http://archives.neohapsis.com/archives/win2ksecadvice/2001-q1/0034.html

Setting SMTP Security. (2005). Texoma, Inc. Retrieved March 21, 2005, from http://help.texoma.net/imail/user/setting_smtp_security.htm

Sheldon, T. (2001). *McGraw-Hill encyclopedia of networking & telecommunications*. New York: McGraw-Hill.

Simple Mail Transfer Protocol (SMTP). (2004). Retrieved September 24, 2004, from http://ulla.mcgill.ca/arts150/arts150bs.htm

SMTP problems. (2005). E-Soft, Inc. Retrieved March 21, 2005, from http://www.securityspace.com/smysecure/catdescr.html?cat=SMTP+problems

SMTP specifications. (2005). Retrieved March 21, 2005, from http://www.networksorcery.com/enp/protocol/smtp.htm

Stevens, W. R. (1993). *TCP/IP illustrated, volume I: the protocols*. Boston, MA: Addison-Wesley.

Tanenbaum, A. S. (2003). *Computer networks* (4th ed.). Upper Saddle River, NJ: Prentice Hall PTR.

Vulnerability Tutorials. (2005). Saint Corporation. Retrieved March 21, 2005, from http://www.saintcorporation.com/demo/saint/vulnerability_tutorials.html

What is SMTP? (2005). Retrieved March 21, 2005, from http://whatis.techtarget.com/definition/0,289893,sid9_gci214219,00.html

What is SMTP Security? (2005). Retrieved March 21, 2005, from http://help.westelcom.com/faq/what_is_smtp.htm

FURTHER READING

Microsoft Knowledge Base. (2005). Retrieved March 21, 2005, from http://support.microsoft.com/

Network World Fusion Encyclopedia. (2005). Retrieved March 21, 2005, from http://www.nwfusion.com/links/Encyclopedia/S/636.html

RFC1421: Privacy enhancement for Internet electronic mail, part I: Message encipherment and authentication procedures, February 1993. Retrieved March 21, 2005, from ftp://ftp.rfc-editor.org/in-notes/rfc1421.txt

RFC1422: Privacy enhancement for Internet electronic mail, part II: Certificate-based key management, February 1993. Retrieved March 21, 2005, from ftp://ftp.rfc-editor.org/in-notes/rfc1422.txt

RFC1423: Privacy enhancement for Internet electronic mail, part III: Algorithms, modes, and identifiers, February 1993. Retrieved March 21, 2005, from ftp://ftp.rfc-editor.org/in-notes/rfc1423.txt

RFC1505: Encoding header field for Internet messages, August 1993. Retrieved March 21, 2005, from ftp://ftp.rfc-editor.org/in-notes/rfc1505.txt

RFC1730: Internet message access protocol—Version 4, December 1994. Retrieved March 21, 2005, from ftp://ftp.rfc-editor.org/in-notes/rfc1730.txt

RFC1732: IMAP4 compatibility with IMAP2 and IMAP2BIS, December 1994. Retrieved March 21, 2005, from ftp://ftp.rfc-editor.org/in-notes/rfc1732.txt

RFC1733: Distributed electronic mail models in IMAP4, December 1994. Retrieved March 21, 2005, from ftp://ftp.rfc-editor.org/in-notes/rfc1733.txt

RFC1830: SMTP service extensions for transmission of large and binary MIME messages, August 1995. Retrieved March 21, 2005, from ftp://ftp.rfc-editor.org/in-notes/rfc1830.txt

RFC2045: MIME, part one: Format of Internet message bodies, November 1996. Retrieved March 21, 2005, from ftp://ftp.rfc-editor.org/in-notes/rfc2045.txt

RFC2046: MIME, part two: Media types, November 1996. Retrieved March 21, 2005, from ftp://ftp.rfc-editor.org/in-notes/rfc2046.txt

RFC2047: MIME, part three: Message header extensions for non-ASCII text, November 1996. Retrieved March 21, 2005, from ftp://ftp.rfc-editor.org/in-notes/rfc2047.txt

RFC2048: MIME, part four: Registration procedures, November 1996. Retrieved March 21, 2005, from ftp://ftp.rfc-editor.org/in-notes/rfc2048.txt

RFC2049: MIME, part five: Conformance criteria and examples, November 1996. Retrieved March 21, 2005, from ftp://ftp.rfc-editor.org/in-notes/rfc2049.txt

RFC2060: Internet message access protocol, Version 4rev1, December 1996. Retrieved March 21, 2005, from ftp://ftp.rfc-editor.org/in-notes/rfc2060.txt

RFC2061: IMAP4 compatibility with IMAP2BIS, December 1996. Retrieved March 21, 2005, from ftp://ftp.rfc-editor.org/in-notes/rfc2061.txt

RFC2062: Internet message access protocol—obsolete syntax, December 1996. Retrieved March 21, 2005, from ftp://ftp.rfc-editor.org/in-notes/rfc2062.txt

RFC2086: IMAP4 ACL extension, January 1997. Retrieved March 21, 2005, from ftp://ftp.rfc-editor.org/in-notes/rfc2086.txt

RFC2087: IMAP4 QUOTA extension, January 1997. Retrieved March 21, 2005, from ftp://ftp.rfc-editor.org/in-notes/rfc2087.txt

RFC2088: IMAP4 non-synchronizing literals, January 1997. Retrieved March 21, 2005, from ftp://ftp.rfc-editor.org/in-notes/rfc2088.txt

RFC2183: Communicating presentation information in Internet messages: The content-disposition header field, August 1997. Retrieved March 21, 2005, from ftp://ftp.rfc-editor.org/in-notes/rfc2183.txt

RFC2197: SMTP service extension for command pipelining, September 1997. Retrieved March 21, 2005, from ftp://ftp.rfc-editor.org/in-notes/rfc2197.txt

RFC2442: The batch SMTP media type, November 1998. Retrieved March 21, 2005, from ftp://ftp.rfc-editor.org/in-notes/rfc2442.txt

RFC2487: SMTP service extension for secure SMTP over TLS, January 1999. Retrieved March 21, 2005, from ftp://ftp.rfc-editor.org/in-notes/rfc2487.txt

RFC2505: Anti-spam recommendations for SMTP MTAs, February 1999. Retrieved March 21, 2005, from ftp://ftp.rfc-editor.org/in-notes/rfc2505.txt

RFC2821: Simple mail transfer protocol, April 2001. Retrieved March 21, 2005, from ftp://ftp.rfc-editor.org/in-notes/rfc2821.txt

RFC2854: The "text/html" media type, June 2000. Retrieved March 21, 2005, from ftp://ftp.rfc-editor.org/in-notes/rfc2854.txt

RFC3027: Protocol complications with the IP network address translator, January 2001. Retrieved March 21, 2005, from ftp://ftp.rfc-editor.org/in-notes/rfc3027.txt

RFC3348: The Internet message action protocol (IMAP4) child mailbox extension, July 2002. Retrieved March 21, 2005, from ftp://ftp.rfc-editor.org/in-notes/rfc3348.txt

RFC3461: Simple mail transfer protocol (SMTP) service extension for delivery status notifications (DSNs), January 2003. Retrieved March 21, 2005, from ftp://ftp.rfc-editor.org/in-notes/rfc3461.txt

RFC3463: Enhanced mail system status codes, January 2003. Retrieved March 21, 2005, from ftp://ftp.rfc-editor.org/in-notes/rfc3463.txt

RFC3464: An extensible message format for delivery status notifications, January 2003. Retrieved March 21, 2005, from ftp://ftp.rfc-editor.org/in-notes/rfc3464.txt

RFC Source Book (2003). Vol. 5, No. 4. Network Sorcery, Inc. Retrieved March 21, 2005, from http://www.networksorcery.com/enp/default0504.htm

Schmied, W. (2002, May 16) Product review: GFI software's mail essentials, tutorials: Exchange 2000. Retrieved March 21, 2005, from http://www.msexchange.org/tutorials/Product_Review_GFI_Softwares_Mail_essentials.htm

Set SMTP Security Options in Windows 2000 Download. (2005). Retrieved March 21, 2005, from http://www.securityconfig.com/software/alerts/set_smtp_security_options_in_windows_2000.html

SMTP protocol overview. (2005). Connected: An Internet Encyclopedia. Retrieved March 21, 2005, from http://freesoft.org/CIE/Topics/94.htm

SMTP Tutorial at RAD Data Communications. (1998). Retrieved March 21, 2005, from http://www.rad.com/networks/1998/smtp/smtp.htm

TrendMicro's InterScan VirusWall SMTP vulnerability (uuencode). (2000, April 5). Retrieved March 21, 2005, from http://www.securiteam.com/securitynews/5NP05151FW.html

Internet Security Standards

Raymond R. Panko, *University of Hawaii*

INTRODUCTION

When the Internet was created, security was left out of its TCP/IP standards. At the time, the crude state of security knowledge may have made this lack of security necessary, and the low frequency of attacks made this lack of security reasonable.

Today, however, security expertise is more mature. In addition, the broad presence of security threats on the Internet means that security today must be addressed deliberately and aggressively. In 2004, between 5% and 12% of all sampled traffic moving across ISP networks was malicious (Legard, 2004).

This article describes two ways to add standards-based security to the Internet.

- The first is for users to add standards-based security to individual dialogues, that is, to two-way conversations between pairs of communicating processes. Today, this can be done largely through the use of virtual private networks (VPNs) using the IPsec, SSL/TLS, and PPTP protocols. This "security overlay" approach is not as desirable as good general Internet security standards, but it solves many current user needs.
- The second approach is to add more security to central Internet standards. In addition to the "core three" standards (IP, TCP, and UDP), these central Internet standards include supervisory standards (such as ICMP, DNS, DHCP, SNMP, LDAP, and dynamic routing protocols), and application standards (such as SMTP, HTTP, and FTP). A major effort to retrofit existing Internet standards to add security is underway in the Internet Engineering Task Force under the "Danvers Doctrine," but this effort is far from complete.

In this article, we will look at these two broad approaches, in the order just presented.

This article will not look at security for single network standards, including Ethernet, wireless LANs, ATM, Frame Relay, and the Public Switched Telephone Network. These individual LANs and WANs operate at the physical and data link layers. As Figure 1 shows, the Internet is a collection of individual LANs and WANs connected by routers. Under normal circumstances, attackers can only send data link layer commands to hosts on their own LAN or WAN. Consequently, for attacks occurring over the Internet, only internet, transport, and application layer attacks are possible. This article focuses on Internet security standards, so it will not discuss attacks on individual LANs and WANs.

This article focuses more specifically on TCP/IP internetworking, which is used on the Internet, rather than on IPX/SPX, SNA, and other forms of internetworking, which cannot be used on the Internet. More formally, this article focuses on security in TCP/IP standards at the internet, transport, and application layers.

SECURITY THREATS

Before looking at security in Internet standards, we need to consider major security threats and defenses. We will begin with types of attacks, because IETF Internet security efforts have focused on one type of attack, namely attacks on dialogues.

Penetration Attacks

One set of threats against which networks, must guard is attackers attempting to penetrate into networks and hosts by sending probe and break-in messages. These include:

- Hacking (when humans intentionally access systems without authorization or in excess of authorization).

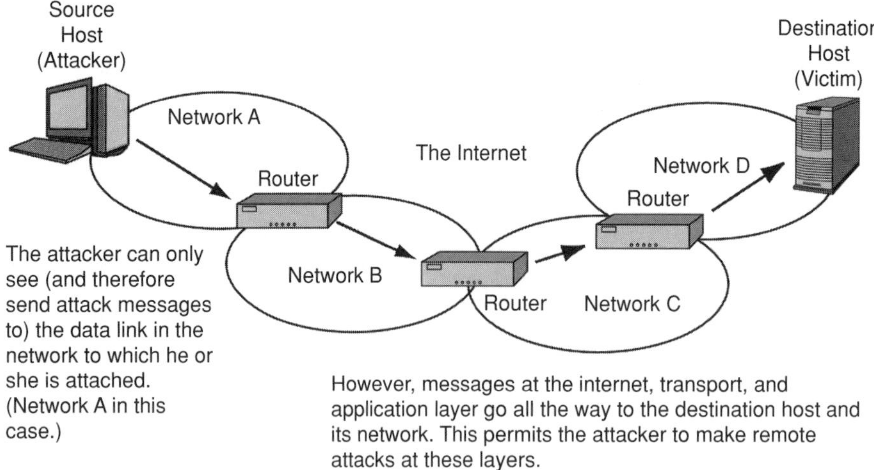

Figure 1: The reason for focusing on internet layer (and higher) security.

- Attempting to conduct denial-of-service attacks against networks or hosts by crashing them or overloading them to the point of being useless to their legitimate users.
- Automated malware attacks using viruses, worms, spam, and other undesirable content.

Attacks on Dialogues

Second, when two parties communicate, they normally engage in a dialogue, in which multiple messages are sent in both directions between two hosts. These dialogues must be secure against attackers who may wish to read, delete, alter, add, or replay messages.

An IETF Focus on Dialogue Security

In general, dialogue security has been the main focus of Internet Engineering Task Force efforts to add security to Internet (TCP/IP) standards. Hacking, denial-of-service attacks, and malware attacks are sometimes addressed, but this is comparatively uncommon. Consequently, we will focus on dialogue security in our discussion.

DIALOGUE SECURITY

In dialogue security, there are three major goals: confidentiality, authentication, and integrity. Confidentiality is relatively easy to provide, and integrity normally appears as a by-product of authentication. Authentication is the most difficult protection to apply, so we will focus the most attention on it.

Confidentiality

Confidentiality means that eavesdroppers who intercept messages en route over the Internet cannot read them. Encryption for confidentiality is the chief tool against unauthorized reading en route.

Encryption is relatively easy to do well if the security developer stays with strong and proven encryption algorithm. In the past, this meant DES and 3DES. Today, this means the Advanced Encryption Standard (AES), which is strong and places a comparatively light processing and memory burden on the communicating devices. AES has also been strongly tested and has survived many attempts to break it. If a security designer does not specify AES, it is incumbent on them to provide a very strong reason for this deviation from good practice.

Authentication and Integrity

Authentication means that the receiver of messages (called the verifier) can verify the identity of the sender (called the applicant or supplicant), in order to ensure that the sender is not an impostor. There are two forms of authentication.

- In *initial authentication*, one side proves its identity to the other side at or near the beginning of a dialogue.
- In *message-by-message authentication*, the sender continues to identify itself with every message, much as parties exchanging letters sign each letter. Message-by-message authentication is crucial to good security.

Integrity means that if a message has been captured and changed en route, then the receiver will be able to detect that a change has occurred. All forms of message-by-message authentication provide message integrity as a by-product. If a message is changed during transmission, either deliberately or through transmission errors, authentication will fail, and the receiver will discard the message.

Initial Authentication

As discussed later, when cryptographic protection systems begin to operate, they usually do initial mutual authentication. Virtual private network protocols, which add overlay protection on individual dialogues between hosts, tend to have well-developed initial authentication methods. All three major VPN standards—IPsec, SSL/TLS, and PPTP—have well-defined initial authentication stages.

However, when the IETF adds security to individual existing protocols, such as TCP, it usually implements message-by-message authentication but not initial authentication. Furthermore, it usually does this by providing HMAC authentication, which is discussed later. HMAC requires the two parties to have a shared secret key. Protocols that use HMACs usually are silent on how to distribute these secret keys. While these keys can be distributed manually, this approach will not scale to large and complex networks.

One possibility for the future is to require protocols to use the Extensible Authentication Protocol (EAP) (RFC 2284, 1998), which uses public key authentication with digital certificates for at least one of the two parties. This would work well in many cases in which a server needs to work with multiple clients. Clients can use weaker authentication mechanisms if appropriate.

Message-by-Message Authentication

Although initial authentication is important, the most complex authentication issues revolve around message-by-message authentication. Consequently, we will focus more specifically on message-by-message authentication. There are two common message-by-message authentication methods: HMACs and digital signatures. Both are described in more detail in the article on Electronic and Digital Signatures. However, we need to discuss them briefly here.

Digital Signatures and Digital Certificates

As discussed in the article on Electronic and Digital Signatures, when security uses digital signatures, a bit string called a digital signature is added to each outgoing message. More specifically, the sender creates a message digest by hashing the message and then encrypts this message digest with his or her own private key. Encrypting a message digest with the sender's private key is called signing the message digest. The sender transmits the digital signature along with the original message to the receiver.

As Figure 2 shows, to test the digital signature, the receiver (verifier) must know the public key of the *true party*—the party the sender claims to be. Normally, the receiver obtains the public key of the true party by obtaining the true party's digital certificate. The digital certificate, among other things, contains the name and public key of the true party. The receiver obtains the true party's digital certificate once and then uses the public key in the digital certificate to test the digital signature in each message.

The receiver must obtain the digital certificate from a trusted certificate authority (CA). One problem with digital certificates is that certificate authorities are not regulated in most countries, leading to questions about their trustworthiness. Although European countries are planning to create regulated CAs, the United States and most other countries are trusting market forces to self-regulate certificate authorities.

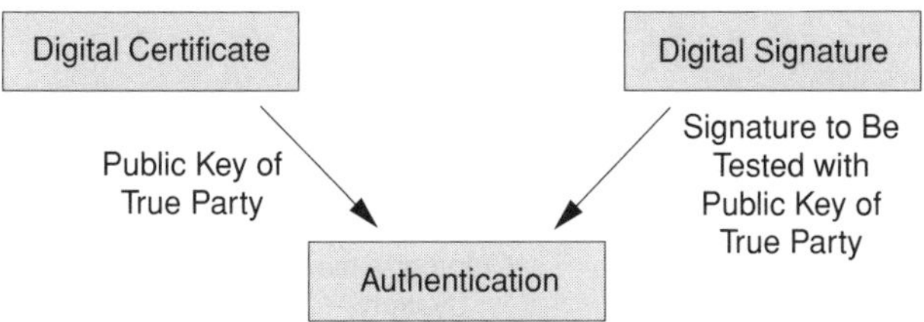

Figure 2: The need for digital certificates with digital signatures.
Source: Panko 2004.

Is it possible to obtain public keys without using certificate authorities? Pretty Good Privacy (PGP) offers one way to do so. Each user has a "key ring" of trusted public key/name pairs. If User A trusts User B, User A may trust User B's key ring, which may, of course, contain keys received through further distributed trust. If an impostor can dupe even one user, trust in the impostor can spread widely. This is not a good way to manage large public systems of routers, DNS hosts, and other sensitive devices.

Beyond these traditional approaches, efforts are now underway, as noted below in the section on Web service security, to develop federated authentication methods that allow one-to-one and one-to-few exchanges of digital certificates and other ways to share public keys.

It is also possible to distribute public keys manually. This works well in small systems, but it does not scale well to very large systems.

HMACs

Another tool for message-by-message authentication is the key-Hashed Message Authentication Code (HMAC). For HMAC authentication, two parties share a secret key. To send a message, one of the parties appends the key to the message, hashes the combination, and adds this hash (the HMAC) to the outgoing message. To test an arriving message, the receiver also adds the key to the message and hashes the combination. This creates another HMAC. If the received and computed HMACs are the same, the sender knows the secret key, which only the other party should use.

HMACs require less processing power than digital signatures because HMACs only involve hashing, which is a fast process. In contrast, public key encryption and decryption, which are used in digital signatures, are extremely processing intensive.

However, a secret key for HMAC authentication needs to be created and distributed securely for *each pair* of communicating parties. In large systems of routers and hosts, this can be highly problematic. One approach to reduce this problem is to use public key authentication for initial authentication, then use Diffie-Hellman key agreement or public key distribution (using either the RSA or DSA protocol) to send the secret keys between pairs of communicating parties. However, these approaches only work if there is good initial authentication.

Another "solution" to the key distribution problems is to use community keys, which are shared by all communicating parties in a community. The problem here, of course, is that if a single member of the community is compromised, attackers reading its community key will be able to authenticate themselves to all other members of the community. In addition, community keys are rarely changed because of the need to coordinate the change among many users. When there are many users communicating with a key that is rarely if ever changed, there is a large volume of communication encrypted with the same key. With a large volume of communication, cryptanalysts often can crack the key. Using community strings for security is a very bad idea.

Another problem with HMACs is repudiation. In repudiation, a party that sent a message denies that they sent it. With digital signatures, repudiation is technically impossible because only the true party should know the true party's private key, so only the true party could have sent the message. Digital signatures give nonrepudiation.

However, with HMACs, both sides know the shared secret key. So if the sender argues that the repudiated message was fabricated by the receiver, there is no possible technical counter-argument. HMACs do not give nonrepudiation.

ADDING OVERLAY SECURITY TO INDIVIDUAL DIALOGUES

As noted above, the first approach to creating standards-based security is for users to add security to individual existing dialogues. Effectively, this overlays security on the Internet for individual dialogues works without requiring the creation of completely new Internet standards.

Cryptographic Protection Systems (CPSs)

Secure dialogues require that confidentiality, authentication, and integrity be protected. This is a somewhat complex process involving several phases.

Cryptographic Protection System Phases

Establishing a secure dialogue with a CPS typically involves four sequential phases (although the specific operations and the order of operations can vary among cryptographic protection systems). Figure 3 illustrates these phases. The first three are quick handshaking phases at the beginning of the dialogue. After the secure dialogue is established, the two parties usually engage in a long ongoing secure conversation.

- First, the two parties must select security standard options within the range offered by a particular cryptographic protection system. For instance, in encryption for confidentiality, the system may offer the choice of a half dozen encryption methods. The communicating parties must select one to use in their subsequent exchanges. The chosen methodology may offer several options; these too must be negotiated.
- Second, the two parties must authenticate themselves to each other. Although initial authentication might seem like it should be the first step instead of the second, the two parties need the first phase to negotiate which authentication method they will use to authenticate themselves.
- Third, the two parties must exchange one or more secrets (keys are examples of secrets) securely. These secrets will be used in the ongoing dialogue phase that will take place after the initial three "hand-shaking" phases of the CPS are finished.
- Fourth, the security of the communication is now established. The two parties now engage in ongoing dialogue with message-by-message confidentiality, authentication, and integrity. Typically, nearly all communication takes place during this ongoing dialogue phase.

The User's Role

Few users have the training to select security options intelligently, much less handle authentication and other tasks. Consequently, cryptographic protection systems work automatically. The user selects a communication partner, and the systems of the two partners work through the four phases automatically.

At most, users may have to authenticate themselves to their own systems by typing a password, using an identification card, using biometrics, or using some other approach. This user authentication phase tends to be the weak link in CPSs because of poor security practices on the part of users, such as using weak passwords.

The Policy Role

Different security options have different implications for the strength of a cryptographic protection system's security. Users rarely are capable of selecting intelligently among options. Consequently, companies must be able to set policies for which methods and options will be acceptable under different circumstances, and they must be able to enforce these policies by promulgating them and enforcing their use.

Figure 4 shows how policy guides security in IPsec, which we will see later. In IPsec, security often is handled by IPsec gateways. When two IPsec gateways begin to communicate, they establish security associations, which are contracts for how security will be done. A policy server can tell the IPsec gateways what security association parameters they may select or not select. This ensures that the IPsec gateways do not select security associations that are too weak for the traffic they will carry. This approach works with host computers as well as with IPsec gateways.

PPP and PPTP VPNs

Dial-Up Security and PPP at the Data Link Layer

Early computer systems used dial-up security. As Figure 5 shows, the user dialed into a server, generally using the Point-to-Point Protocol (PPP) (RFC 1661, 1994) at the

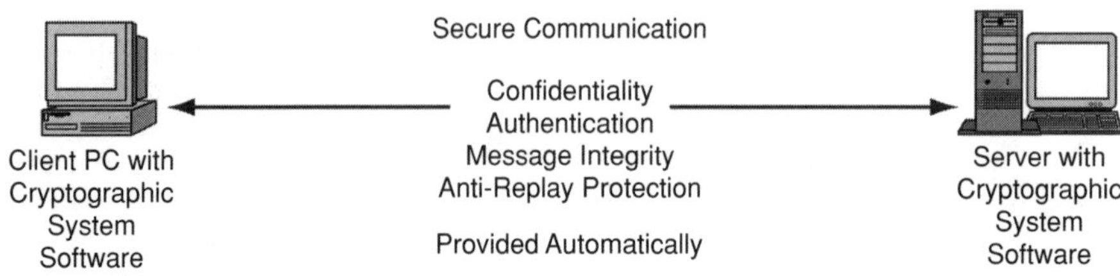

Figure 3: Cryptographic protection system (CPS).
Source: Panko 2004.

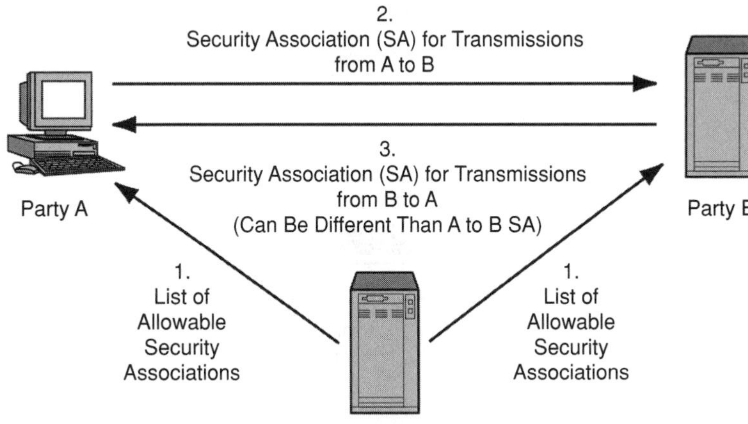

Figure 4: Policy-based security associations in IPsec.
Source: Panko 2004.

data link layer. Later, companies added security to this approach by creating remote access servers (RASs) for sites. The user dialed into the RAS, authenticated himself or herself (usually with a password), and then received access to all servers at a site or to selected servers.

If a company has several remote access servers, it normally uses a RADIUS server or some other authentication server to store authentication information remotely, as Figure 5 shows. This way, all RASs use the same authentication data. Otherwise, if a firm has several RASs, their authentication data may be inconsistent. An adversary may try different RASs until they find one that is configured incorrectly.

PPP can be used without security, but PPP offers moderately good encryption and several options for authentication ranging from nothing to very strong. Again, the dialogue partners must select the security options they wish to employ.

Tunneling

Although PPP is secure, it is limited to a single data link because it operates at the data link layer, as Figure 6 illustrates. However, when a connection is made over the Internet, each connection between a host and a router or between two routers is a separate data link. PPP cannot function over the Internet.

Consequently, Internet-based data link layer security approaches must use tunneling. In tunneling, a data link layer frame is placed within the data field of a packet—the opposite of the usual situation. Placing a message within another message is called tunneling.

The packet is sent from the user computer to the RAS, across multiple links. Finally, the RAS receives and reads the tunneled (encapsulated) frame. Although this effect seems needlessly complex, it allows us to use traditional PPP user-RAS security over the Internet.

Again, when a message is placed inside another message—especially within a packet—this is called tunneling. We will see later that IPsec also uses tunneling in one of its operating modes (tunneling mode, of course). Tunneling is a delivery technology, not a security technology (Panko, 2004). Many security articles and even textbooks confuse the two.

PPTP

The main tunneling protocol for PPP is the Point-to-Point Tunneling Protocol (PPTP) (RFC 2637, 1999). As its name suggests, PPTP does not have its own security. Rather, PPTP is a way to tunnel PPP frames over the Internet. PPTP uses PPP security methods (encryption and authentication), extending them over an entire Internet connection instead of over a single dial-up data link. PPTP has a number of moderate security weaknesses, but it is good for low-threat or medium-threat environments.

L2TP

Although PPTP works and is attractive, it is limited to transmission over an IP network such as the Internet.

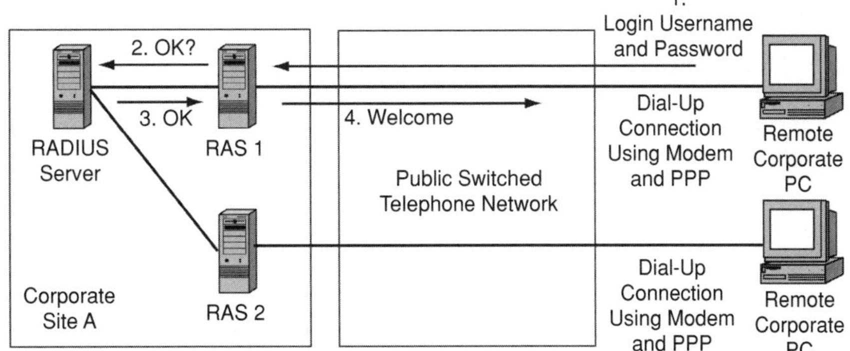

Figure 5: RADIUS authentication.
Source: Panko 2004.

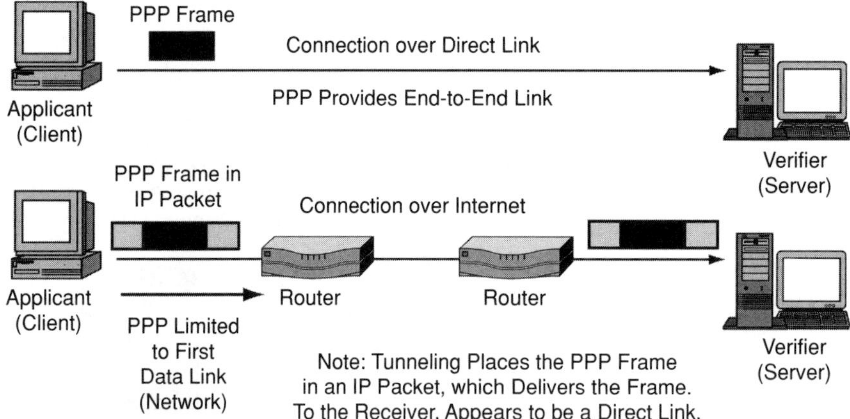

Figure 6: Tunneling PPP.
Source: Panko 2004.

The newer Layer 2 Tunneling Protocol (L2TP) (RFC 2661, 1999) can tunnel frames over a number of transmission mechanisms, including IP, Frame Relay, and ATM, to name just three (Tonsley, Valencia, Rubens, et al., 1999).

However, L2TP does not offer security by itself. It requires users to rely on the IPsec protocol discussed next to provide security at the Internet layer during transit. L2TP is a pure tunneling protocol, not a security protocol at all.

IPsec VPNs

The internet layer (the OSI Network layer) is the core layer in TCP/IP internetworking. The Internet Protocol (IP) is the main packet standard at this layer. IP comes in two versions—IP Version 4 (IPv4) and IP Version 6 (IPv6). IPv4 is the dominant version in use on the Internet today, but IPv6 is beginning to grow, especially in Asia, where relatively few IPv4 addresses were allocated when the Internet was first created.

The IPsec Effort

The Internet Engineering Task Force (IETF) has been working to retrofit IP to be more secure. Their effort has crystallized around a group of standards collectively called IPsec (IP security) (RFC 2411, 1998). Although IPsec was initially planned for IPv6, the IETF has developed it to work with IPv4 as well.

Encryption and Authentication

The dominant way to use IPsec is to employ the encapsulated security protocol (ESP) option, which offers both encryption and authentication. We will focus on ESP rather than on the authentication header (AH) option, which only provides authentication. AH is useful primarily when encryption is illegal; this is a rare situation.

Tunnel Mode

As Figure 7 shows, IPsec can operate in two modes: tunnel mode and transport mode. We will discuss tunnel mode first.

In tunnel mode, IPsec is handled by IPsec gateways at the two sites of the communicating parties, not by the computers of the communicating parties themselves. The packet to be delivered securely is tunneled by encapsulating it in another packet, encrypting the original packet, adding authentication, and sending the encapsulating packet from one IPsec gateway to the other. Although attackers can read the IP header of the encapsulating packet, they cannot read the secured packet; nor can they change the secured packet without the change being obvious.

Tunnel mode is attractive because it does not impose expensive installation and configuration burdens on each host. It does not require the individual hosts to have IPsec software on their computers or know how to configure the software. In fact, the users may not even be aware that IPsec is protecting their packets over the Internet. Even more importantly, it is not necessary to obtain a digital certificate for each host and install one on each host if tunnel mode is used; only the IPsec gateways need digital certificates.

The disadvantage of tunnel mode is that it does not provide any protection for the packet as it travels *within* the two sites. The focus is entirely on security during the Internet stage of transmission.

Transport Mode

In contrast, as Figure 7 also shows, IPsec's transport mode offers *end-to-end* encryption and authentication between the two computers in a dialogue. This approach provides security not only while packets travel through the Internet but also when the packets are passing through local site networks on their way to and from the Internet. Although the Internet exposes traffic to many attackers, there also are dangers within corporate networks. In fact, some of the worst attacks are made by corporate insiders working within corporate networks.

Although the end-to-end security of transport mode is attractive, it comes at a substantial price. Larger firms have thousands or even tens of thousands of PCs. Transport mode requires the configuration of IPsec software and a digital certificate on every PC to be protected. This is extremely expensive.

A more modest problem is that transport mode packets must have the IP address of the receiving computer in the destination address field of the packet header. If sniffers

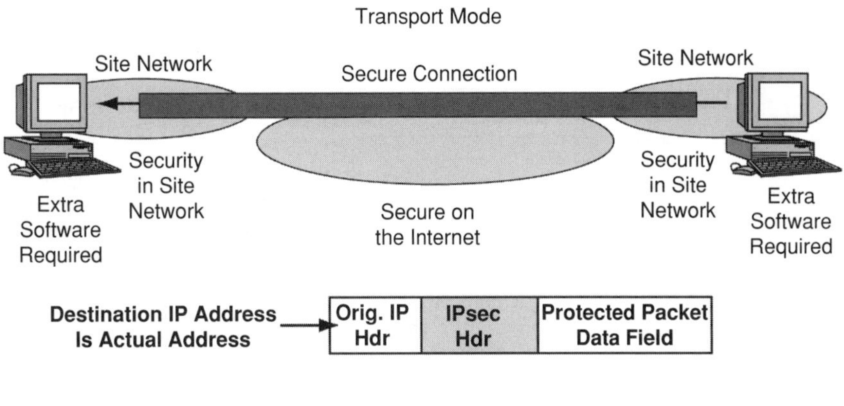

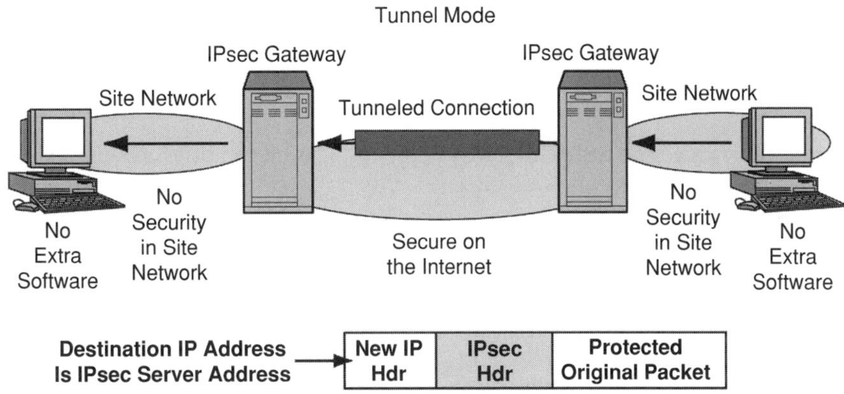

Figure 7: IPsec in tunnel mode and transport mode.
Source: Panko 2004.

can be placed along the route of these packets, attackers will be able to learn the IP addresses of many corporate hosts. This is a first step in most types of Internet-based attacks. In contrast, tunnel mode packets only have the IP addresses of the receiving IPsec gateway in their destination address fields. This only tells attackers about the IP address of a single machine that usually is well hardened against attacks.

Combining Tunnel Mode and Transfer Mode

One solution to the relative weaknesses of the two modes is to use both. The user can use transport mode to provide end-to-end security but also to use IPsec in tunnel mode between sites to hide IP addresses.

IPsec in IPv4 and IPv6

As noted at the beginning of this section, IPsec can be used with both IPv4 and IPv6. However, with IPv6, the use of IPsec is *mandatory* (Microsoft, 2004). With IPv4, however, IPsec is optional.

SSL/TLS VPNs

IPsec is a very complex security mechanism, but it has the advantage of transparency. This means that IPsec protects *all* higher-layer traffic at the transport and application layers automatically, without requiring higher-layer protocols to do any work or even be aware of this protection.

In some applications, dialogues are limited to World Wide Web or at most WWW and e-mail. Under these conditions, the costly burden of implementing IPsec is not justified, and many firms turn to a simpler protocol, Transport Layer Security (TLS), which was originally created by Netscape as Secure Sockets Layer (SSL) and was then renamed Transport Layer Security (TLS) by the Internet Engineering Task Force when the IETF took over the standard's development (RFC 2246, 1999). If your URL begins with "https", then you are using SSL/TLS.

While IPsec provides a blanket of protection at the internet layer, SSL/TLS creates a secure connection at the transport layer. This secure connection potentially can protect all application layer traffic. Unfortunately, SSL/TLS requires that applications be *SSL/TLS-compliant* to benefit from this protection. Although all browsers and WWW servers can use SSL/TLS, only some e-mail systems can use SSL/TLS, and few other applications can benefit from SSL/TLS protection at the transport layer.

SSL/TLS was created for electronic commerce, in which a residential client PC communicates with a merchant server. SSL/TLS requires the merchant to authenticate itself to the client using digital certificates and digital signatures. However, few residential client PC owners have digital certificates. So while SSL/TLS permits client authentication using a digital certificate, it makes client authentication optional. This lack of mandatory client authentication is a major security vulnerability that is intolerable in many situations. If SSL is used in dialogue security, client authentication should be required.

Vendors have begun to create semi-proprietary techniques to create remote access SSL/TLS VPNs for corporate use, and these techniques have become very popular.

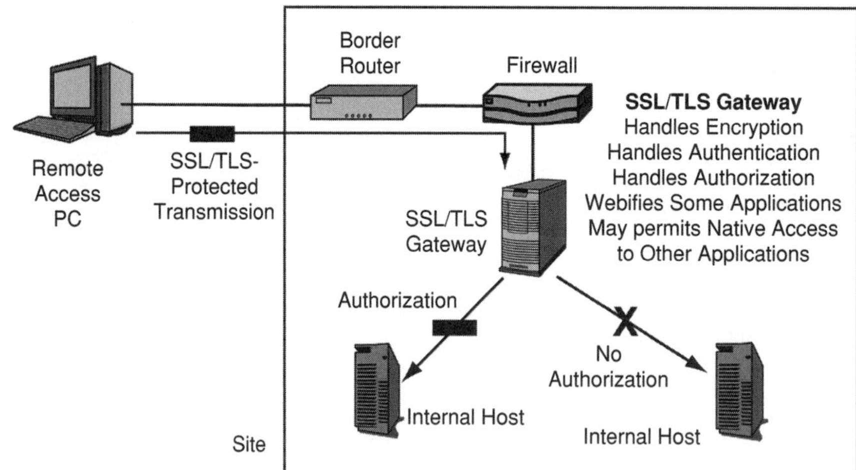

Figure 8: SSL/TLS using gateway operation.

As Figure 8 shows, the user firm places an SSL/TLS gateway server at each site, and users have an SSL/VPN connection to this gateway server. The gateway server provides initial client PC authentication using passwords or some other proprietary mechanism. The gateway server then connects the user to internal servers.

SSL/TLS gateway servers can even get around the limitations of SSL/TLS's HTTP focus. Of course, they can protect HTTP traffic easily because SSL/TLS does this automatically.

In addition, most SSL/TLS gateways can "webify" non-HTTP applications such as Microsoft Outlook—sending screen images over HTTP. If the browser will accept a downloaded add-in, many SSL/TLS gateways can even give the user protected access to traditional applications. However, both webification and application access via browser downloads requires proprietary techniques.

The main attraction of SSL/TLS is that the user can use any PC that has a browser, including those in Internet cafes. Unfortunately, trace information from the user's session continues to reside on the PC after the session. Plug-in browser software to remove these traces can be added to the browser, but this requires operating system privileges that users are not likely to have when they work on PCs in Internet cafes.

Multilayer Security

As Figure 9 shows, security can be applied at several standards layers. A major principle of security is defense in depth. Vulnerabilities are discovered in almost all security protections from time to time. Until they are fixed, the attacker has free access—unless the attacker must break through two or more lines of defense. With multiple protections in place, the company will still be protected while it repairs a broken security countermeasure.

Consequently, companies would be better protected if they added dialogue security to more than one layer, say by implementing both IPsec and application security. However, this is expensive, so it is not common.

Dialogue Security and Firewalls

Although adding security to dialogues passing through the Internet is attractive, it creates problems for firewalls. Firewalls need to examine arriving and leaving packets. However, almost all cryptographic protection systems encrypt packets for confidentiality.

Unless these packets are decrypted before passing through the firewall, the firewalls cannot scan their packets for attack signatures. Consequently, companies that buy added security by implementing cryptographic protection systems (CPSs) tend to lose some scanning security. This places a heavier burden on end stations to do scanning, and many end stations are client PCs whose owners lack the willingness, much less the knowledge, to do packet scanning.

One solution is to decrypt all incoming packets before they reach the border firewall, by placing a cryptographic gateway between the border firewall and the

Layer	Cryptographic Protection System
Application	Kerberos
Transport	SSL/TLS
Internet	IPsec
Data Link	PPP, PPTP
Physical	Not applicable. No messages are sent at this layer—only individual bits.

Figure 9: Multilayer security.

border router. However, this leaves the cryptographic gateway unprotected from Internet attacks. If the cryptographic gateway is taken over by attackers, the results can be disastrous.

ADDING SECURITY TO INDIVIDUAL INTERNET STANDARDS

Although adding dialogue security to individual dialogues works, it would be better for Internet standards themselves to offer high security. For instance, if DNS servers are disabled so that clients cannot find application servers, dialogue security will do little good.

When the Internet was first created, none of its standards offered any security. Today, several TCP/IP standards offer security. Unfortunately, the closer one examines their security features, the less adequate many appear. Fortunately, the IETF has a broad program to add security to a broad range of existing Internet standards individually.

A Broad IETF Commitment

The Danvers Doctrine

In 1995, a meeting of the IETF in Danvers, Massachusetts reached a consensus that the IETF should develop strong security for all of its protocols (Schiller, RFC 3365, 2002). Originally, the consensus was limited to a decision to use strong encryption keys rather than weak encryption keys that met existing export restrictions. Soon, however, this Danvers Doctrine expanded into a consensus to develop strong security for all TCP/IP protocols. As a first step, all RFCs are now required to include a section on security considerations. As we will now see, considerable progress has also been made in adding security to individual TCP/IP standards.

User Choice

Although all TCP/IP standards are to be given strong security, the IETF decided that it should be the option of individual organizations whether or not to implement security in individual protocols. In part, this decision reflects a desire not to force security on anyone. In part, it also reflects the fact that some networks are in protected environments that do not require security. However, an important consequence of the decision to leave security up to organizations is that organizations must decide which security options to use or not use.

There are five broad layers of functionality in networking—physical, data link, internet, transport, and applications. Implementing security at all layers would be horrendously expensive and generally unnecessary.

Consequently, many organizations will only wish to implement security at one layer. Although this would provide security, individual security technologies often are found to have vulnerabilities. To maintain protection during these periods of vulnerabilities, organizations probably will wish to implement security in the protocols at two layers at least, as noted earlier.

Security and Vulnerabilities

Security in Protocols

In discussing the security of Internet protocols, there are two issues. One is whether security has been built into the protocol at all and to what degree it has been placed in the protocol. This is the aspect of Internet protocol security we focus on in this article.

Protocol and Implementation Vulnerabilities

Another aspect of Internet protocol security is whether the protocol or its implementation has vulnerabilities that attackers can exploit. In some cases, the protocols themselves are exploitable because of design oversights. In more cases, vendor implementations cause problems. For instance both the BIND program, which is dominant for Domain Name System servers, and the Sendmail program, which is dominant on UNIX Simple Mail Transfer Protocol servers, both have had long and troubled histories of security vulnerabilities.

Implementation vulnerabilities are especially dangerous when the same flaw is discovered in multiple vendor code bases. (For example, in February 2001, two major vulnerabilities were found in the Simple Network Management Protocol Version 1 programs of multiple vendors.) This too can result in Internet-scale disruptions.

The worst case scenario is a serious vulnerability in a protocol itself because this will affect all products and may take some time to change. In 2003, for example, the TCP Reset vulnerability was discovered. It is difficult to insert messages into a TCP segment stream because TCP uses 32-bit sequence numbers. This gives over 4 billion possible sequence numbers. An attacker normally must guess the precise next sequence number that the receiver is expecting. However, TCP acknowledgements contain a Window size field. In an odd choice, the TCP standard specifies that if a TCP segment has its RST (reset) bit set, then the receiver will accept any sequence number within the Window size range. This greatly reduces the number of sequence numbers an attacker must try to cause the target to accept a RST message, which will break its connection with its communication partner. This is a denial-of-service attack. BGP, which has long sessions and uses large Window size values, is especially vulnerable to this attack. This is disturbing because BGP is critical for exchanging routing information between Internet core routers and between corporate border routers and Internet core routers. As discussed in the section on BGP later in this article, using TCP authentication can reduce the TCP Reset danger.

Lack of Code Diversity

For some protocols, a single code base is used by most or all vendor implementations. For instance, most DNS servers use BIND. In e-mail, use is dominated by SENDMAIL on Unix systems and Exchange on Microsoft mail servers. This means that if a vulnerability is found, an attack can produce Internet-scale disruptions. This is called the potato famine problem because the Irish Potato Famine was caused by a lack of genetic diversity in the Irish potato crop. The failure of many systems due to the same problem is also called a common mode failure.

Tardy Patching

In addition, when vendors release patches for vulnerabilities, many firms fail to install patches quickly or at all. This makes some vulnerabilities exploitable for weeks, months, or even years after they are discovered. All too often, firms only patch vulnerabilities in earnest when a virus or hackers create widespread damage.

Perspective

Although protocol and implementation vulnerabilities are important, they are situation-specific. This article focuses on security within Internet standards themselves.

The Core Three: IP, TCP, and UDP

There are three core standards at the heart of the Internet. These are IP, TCP, and UDP.

IP

The main job of the Internet Protocol (IP) (RFC 791, 1981) is to move packets from the source host to the destination host across the Internet, which consists of thousands of networks connected by routers. IP is a hop-by-hop protocol designed to govern how each router handles each IP packet it receives.

A packet may travel over one to two dozen routers as it passes from the source host to the destination host. Many core routers in the Internet backbone handle so much traffic that they can barely keep up with demand. To reduce the work done on each router, IP was designed as a simple, unreliable, and connectionless protocol. Although packet losses on the Internet are modest, IP is a "best effort" protocol that offers no guarantee that packets will arrive at all, much less arrive in order. Given this minimalist vision for IP, it is hardly surprising that security was completely left out of IP's core design. Given continuing router overload, it would be difficult to make IP secure throughout the Internet.

IPsec was created to add security to the Internet Protocol, making IPsec at least somewhat more than a security overlay method. However, IPsec cannot achieve its promise without a truly worldwide system of certificate authorities.

TCP

To compensate for IP's unreliability at the internet layer, TCP/IP was given a reliable sibling protocol, the Transmission Control Protocol (TCP) (RFC 793, 1981) at the transport layer. However, TCP was not created with security. When TCP was created, in the early 1980s, security technology was far too immature to be implemented. Today, there are no plans to add security to TCP given the IETF's focus on IPsec and IPsec's ability to provide security for higher-layer protocols. Later, however, we will see that TCP does have an authentication option, but it is only used in BGP.

UDP

When transport layer error correction is not required or is not practical, applications specify the User Datagram Protocol (UDP) (RFC 768, 1980) at the transport layer. Like TCP, UDP was created without security and is also not likely to receive security extensions because of the IETF's reliance on IPsec to protect UDP.

Administrative Standards

The "core three" Internet standards do most of the work of the Internet. However, several other administrative protocols are needed to keep the Internet functioning. We will look at security in the most important of these standards.

ICMP

IP merely delivers packets. It does not define any internet layer supervisory messages. To compensate for this lack, the IETF created the Internet Control Message Protocol (ICMP) (RFC 792, 1981) to carry supervisory information at the internet layer. ICMP messages are carried in the data fields of IP packets. ICMP messages allow hosts to determine if other hosts are active (by "pinging" them). ICMP also allow hosts to send error messages to other hosts and allows hosts to tell other hosts or routers to act differently than they have been acting. ICMP is a powerful tool for network managers.

Unfortunately, this power also makes ICMP a popular tool for hackers. Making ICMP less useful to hackers would also tend to make it less useful to network administrators, so the IETF has done nothing to implement ICMP security. For this reason, most corporate firewalls block all ICMP traffic except for outgoing pings (echo messages) and returning pongs (echo reply messages).

If ICMP were given good authentication, however, corporations might be more willing to allow it through firewalls. In addition, authenticated ICMP would protect against attacks generated within the firewalls at individual sites. However, there are no current IETF activities to add authentication and other security to ICMP. The reason may be that ICMP messages are carried in the data fields of IP packets, which can be protected by IPsec, including the authentication of the sending ICMP process.

Domain Name System (DNS)

Richard Clarke, former national coordinator for security, infrastructure protection, and counter-terrorism for the president of the United States, has characterized the domain name system (DNS) as one of the two greatest danger points on the Internet. (Later we will look at the second item on Clarke's list, BGP.)

In a sense, DNS is the telephone directory of the Internet. The domain name system (DNS) allows a source host to find the IP addresses of a target host if the source host only knows the target host's host name [RFC 1034, 1987].

The domain name system has multiple servers organized in a hierarchy. These are called DNS servers, or, sometimes, name servers.

There are two likely attacks on DNS servers. First, attackers may be able to "poison" the databases in DNS servers. When user computers send DNS request messages to poisoned servers, they will get incorrect IP addresses that send users to pornography sites, to sites containing Trojan horses, and to other undesirable sites. Companies can even poison their competitor's DNS listing so that all e-mail messages go first to the attacking company before being relayed to the victim's mail servers.

DNS poisoning is not just a theoretical concern. As long ago as 1997, users trying to reach InterNIC.com twice found themselves redirected to a competitor, alterNIC.com. The redirection episodes only stopped when a judge ordered alterNIC.com to stop the redirection. At the time, InterNIC.com was the only registrar for .com, .edu, .org, and .net. There have been many other instances of DNS poisoning since then. DNS poisoning is also known as DNS spoofing.

To address problems with DNS poisoning attacks, the IETF DNSSEC (DNS security extensions) Working Group is developing an authentication approach based on public key encryption with digital signatures (Rose, 2002). There are a (relatively) limited number of high-level DNS servers, so giving each a public key and a private key is not too daunting a challenge. As long as DNS servers do not get taken over so that their private keys can be stolen, authentication should be very good. Complicating matters somewhat, in mid-2004, the DSNSEC Working Group created *bis* versions of most of its RFCs to make DNSSEC somewhat weaker but easier to implement. Although DNSSEC is incomplete, a number of DNS servers now support its main elements. For more information, go to (http://www.dnssec.net).

Second, there is the possibility that attackers will use denial-of-service attacks to make DNS servers unavailable to users. Most client users only know the host names of the servers they use. Consequently, if the DNS were to fail for some period of time, clients could no longer reach servers.

As noted earlier, DNS is hierarchical, and if all DNS servers at the highest level are subjected to successful DoS attacks, clients would soon begin to lose the ability to access many servers. At the top level of the DNS server hierarchy, there are only 13 root DNS top-level domain (TLD) servers run by 10 different organizations; one of them periodically feeds changes to the others. Nearly all of these servers, furthermore, use the BIND DNS server program, which has a long history of vulnerability.

Although these root DNS hosts are geographically distributed, most use the same software, leaving them open to common mode attacks if vulnerabilities are found. Also, geographical distribution is not strong protection when there are only 13 targets to attack. In later 2002, a brief denial-of-service attack degraded the service given by nine of the 13 root DNS hosts. Had this attack been more intense, and had it continued over many hours or even some days, service disruption would have begun across the Internet.

The threat raised by such concentrated DNS resources is very real. The root DNS servers are well protected with both technical and human protections. However, below the root servers are top-level domain (TLD) DNS servers for the various generic (.com, .edu, etc.) and national (.jp, .ca, etc.) top-level domains. The degree to which the DNS servers of these top-level domains are distributed and have code diversity is unknown.

In addition, there are literally tens of thousands of corporate second-level domain DNS servers. Firms are required to have two and preferably three DNS servers. However, if these two or three servers are attacked, corporate communication will stop.

In traditional DNS, only the host names and IP addresses of servers are recorded. However, DNS has been extended by the IETF to dynamic DNS (DDNS). In this newer protocol, clients that receive temporary IP addresses from DNCP servers can register their temporary IP addresses with the firm's DNS server. This is very good because it extends the usefulness of DNS. However, it raises obvious poisoning security concerns that have not been addressed by the IETF.

Simple Network Management Protocol (SNMP)

The goal of the Simple Network Management Protocol (SNMP) is to allow a central administrative computer (the manager) to manage many individual managed devices. Figure 10 shows that the manager talks to an agent on each device. The manager does this by sending the managed devices Get messages (which ask for information on the device's status) or Set messages (which tell the managed device's configuration).

Obviously, SNMP is a powerful management tool. Unfortunately, it also is a golden opportunity for attackers. It potentially allows attackers to learn a great deal of information about target networks through Get commands. It

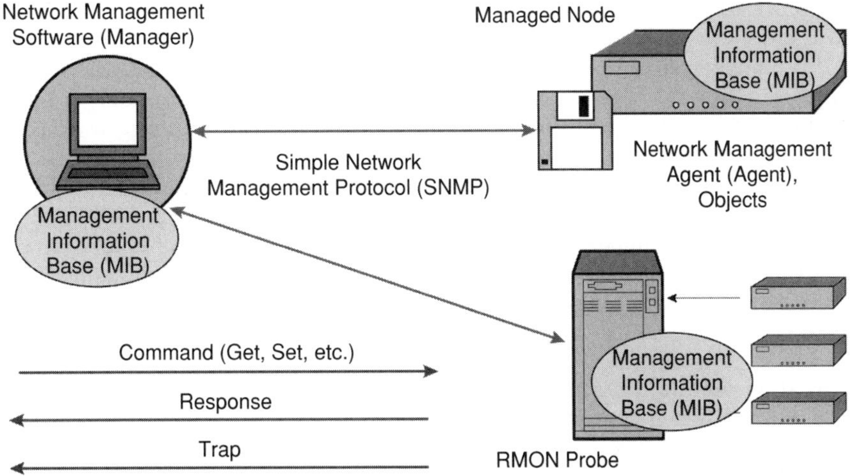

Figure 10: Simple network management protocol (SNMP).
Source: Panko 2004.

also allows them to inflict an endless amount of damage through the malicious use of the Set command to create misconfigurations on large numbers of devices. These misconfigurations can make the devices unusable or can even make the devices interfere with the operation of other devices.

SNMP Version 1 had no security at all, making the protocol extremely dangerous given its power. SNMP Version 2 was supposed to add security, but an inability to settle differences within the IETF prevented full security from being built into SNMP.

Version 2 did receive one authentication advance. To send SNMP messages to a Version 2 SNMP agent, a manager would have to know the agent's "community string," which is like a password. In practice, most firms have all of their agents use the same community string. In fact, many do not even change the vendor's default community string, which often is "public". In any case, SNMPv2 sends community strings in messages without encryption, so attackers with sniffers can quickly learn community strings.

There actually are four different possible community strings for manager-agent communication: read-only access to device agents, read/write access, read/write/all (which allows the modification of device settings), and trap (trap messages are warnings of problems sent by agents on managed devices) (Beckenhauer, 2002). Given the dangers inherent in writing and modification, many firms only set the read-only community string, and many products only set the read-only community string by default.

Only in Version 3 (http://www.snmplink.org/SNMPv3.html) did security get built into SNMP extensively. Version 3 offered confidentiality (optional), message-by-message authentication, message integrity, and time stamps to guard against replay attacks. It also offers the possibility of giving different devices different access to MIB data based on security restrictions.

Unfortunately, SNMP v3 authentication and message integrity is based on HMACs, which require the network administrator to know a secret bit string that is different for each managed device. This difficult situation could be alleviated if the standard specified the use of digital certificates for managers. Authentication and integrity would then only require that managed devices know the manager's public key, and there is no problem with shared public keys. In addition, public key encryption would allow the secure exchange of symmetric keys for bulk encryption for confidentiality. However, the large number of devices involved and the desire to keep processing loads on managed devices low (public key encryption is highly processing-intensive) has made public key authentication and integrity unattractive to standards makers.

For more information about SNMP security, read Blumenthal and Wijen (1998).

LDAP

Increasingly, companies store security information and other critical corporate information in central repositories called directory servers. To query data in a directory server, devices commonly use the Lightweight Directory Access Protocol (LDAP), which governs search request and responses.

The Internet Engineering Task Force has long understood the importance of creating good security for LDAP in light of the extreme importance of information contained in the directory. The core security focus of LDAP must be authentication because successful impostors could learn large amounts of damaging information about a firm if they could get wide access to this data by claiming to be a party with broad authorization to retrieve data. They could also do extensive damage by "poisoning" the directory with bad data.

The first version of the standard, LDAP v1, had no security and generally was rudimentary. LDAP v2 provided authentication options for the first time. It permitted initial anonymous, simple, and Kerberos 4 authentication.

- Anonymous authentication means that no authentication is needed for some users. These users would be given access to certain information on the server, much as anonymous FTP users are allowed to download information from selected parts of an FTP server. Generally speaking, anonymous authentication should be turned off on directory servers that contain any sensitive information.
- Simple authentication requires the user to transmit a username and password. This information is sent in the clear, without encryption. Anyone who reads the username and password will be able to authenticate themselves later as the party. This only provides protection against the accidental usage of LDAP.
- Kerberos 4 authentication uses a central authentication server separate from the directory server. Unfortunately, Kerberos 4 has known weaknesses. Most notably, Kerberos 4 uses a long-term pre-shared secret key to communicate with each device. If enough traffic uses this key, a cryptanalyst can determine the key and then impersonate the device. (Kerberos Version 5 only uses the long-term key for initial authentication and then uses a session key for remaining communication during a time-limited session.)

The latest version of the Lightweight Directory Access Protocol (LDAPv3) (RFC 2251, 1997) also supports anonymous and simple authentication. Again, anonymous authentication should not be turned on for sensitive servers. In addition, sites that use simple authentication should protect application-level LDAP traffic with lower-layer protection, most commonly SSL/TLS at the transport layer. This ensures that eavesdroppers will not be able to read the username and password.

LDAP v3 also supports the Simple Authentication Security Layer (SASL) (RFC 2222, 1997). This method allows the searcher and the directory server to authenticate each other in several ways, including Kerberos 5, HMACs, and external authentication. "External authentication" means that the parties can do authentication any way they wish, essentially taking authentication outside the LDAP process. For instance, if the searcher and directory server create a SSL/TLS connection at the transport layer, the authentication that takes place at that layer may be sufficient. SASL is extremely flexible, but companies using it must ensure that a sufficiently strong authentication option is selected.

Although LDAP v3 offers good authentication, it does not support public key authentication using digital signatures except through SASL or if the organization using it uses SSL/TLS and digital certificates for both parties to secure LDAP traffic.

LDAP v3 makes encryption for confidentiality optional. This may seem odd, but many firms use SSL/TLS at the transport layer to protect LDAP traffic. SSL/TLS does encryption for confidentiality, and many firms feel that also encrypting LDAP traffic at the application layer as well would be needlessly expensive.

A good source of information about LDAP security is Harrison (2002).

Address Resolution Protocol (ARP)

When a router receives a packet, it looks at the packet's destination IP address. Based on this destination IP address, the router sends the packet back out another interface (port), to the destination host or to a next-hop router (NHR) that will next handle the packet. We will use the term "target" for the destination host or next-hop router.

The destination IP address in the packet gives the target's IP address. However, to deliver the packet, the router must encapsulate the packet in a data link layer frame and deliver the frame to the target. This requires the router to know the data link layer address of the target, for instance, the target's Ethernet MAC address.

If the router does not know the target's data link layer address on an Ethernet network, the router must use the Address Resolution Protocol (ARP) (RFC 2251, 1997). The router first broadcasts an ARP request message to all hosts on the subnet connected to the port out which the packet is to be sent. In an Ethernet network, the broadcast MAC destination address is forty-eight ones. Switches on the subnet will deliver frames with this address to all hosts on the subnet. All hosts, on the subnet, furthermore, will accept frames with all-ones destination addresses.

Within a broadcast frame, the router sends an ARP request message. The ARP request message contains the IP address of the target. All hosts except the target ignore this message. The target, however, recognizes its IP address and sends an ARP reply message back to the router. This message tells the router the target's data link layer address.

Now that the router knows the target's data link layer address, the router takes the IP packet it has been holding and places it in a frame with the target's data link layer address in the destination address field. The router sends this frame to the target.

To handle future packets to the same destination IP address, the router also places the target's IP address and data link layer address in the router's ARP cache. When the next packet addressed to this IP address arrives, the router will not have to do ARP. It will simply look up the data link layer address in the ARP cache.

The Address Resolution Protocol assumes that all hosts are trustworthy. However, an attacker host can use this trust to make an attack. Specifically, an attacker's host can send ARP reply messages with the attacker's data link layer address and all possible IP addresses on its subnet. Due to the fact that ARP is stateless, routers should accept ARP response messages even if the router did not send an ARP request message. This approach will poison the ARP cache, causing the router to send all messages intended for most hosts on the subnet to be sent to the attacker.

In some cases, after reading frames, the attacker passes them on to the intended destination host. It may also be able to relay traffic going in the opposite direction. In this man-in-the-middle attack, the two sides are unaware that their traffic is being read and perhaps added to.

The widely available arpsniff program implements man-in-the-middle attack with extreme ease. However, the computer in the middle has to be on the same broadcast or ring subnet as the other two communicating partners for it to work. This makes arp spoofing difficult to implement. However, if a computer on a subnet is hacked remotely, the attacker does not have to be on the victims' subnet.

Currently, there are only preliminary efforts within the IETF to add authentication to the Address Resolution Protocol, under the ARPsec label.

ARP only works on Ethernet and other broadcast networks. Other protocols for finding host data link layer addresses associated with IP addresses are used for other types of non-broadcast network technologies. These generally suffer the same security exposures that ARP does.

Dynamic Host Communication Protocol (DHCP)

It is possible to manually configure a client PC by typing in its IP address and other configuration parameters needed to communicate over the Internet or a corporate internet. Servers typically are configured manually. However, client PCs normally are configured automatically by getting these configuration parameters from a Dynamic Host Configuration Protocol (DHCP) host (RFC 2131, 1997).

When a client PC boots up, it realizes that it has no IP address. It broadcasts a DHCPDISCOVER message to learn what DHCP servers are reachable. Each DHCP server that receives the discover message sends back a DHCPOFFER message that gives an offer specifying what IP address it will provide, a lease time (how long the client may keep the IP address), and other configuration information.

The client PC selects one offer and sends a DHCPREQUEST to the selected server. The DHCP server sends back a DHCPACK message acknowledging the acceptance and providing configuration parameters, including an IP address, subnet masks, DNS addresses, and other information. The client PC is now configured.

DHCP is built on connectionless UDP, which makes adding security difficult in general. More specifically, DHCP does not authenticate the client or the DHCP server, and this allows several possible attacks. For an example, an attacker posing as a client PC can repeatedly request DHCP service, each time accepting an IP address. Within a few seconds, the DHCP server will be drained of available IP addresses. If a legitimate client then requests configuration service, it will not be able to get an IP address and so will not be able to use the Internet or an internal corporate internet.

The attacker also can impersonate a DHCP server. The attacker will then respond to all DHCPDISCOVER messages with a very attractive offer (long lease duration, and so forth). If a client accepts this configuration information, this information may cause the client to send packets that cannot be delivered or to act in other ways that harm itself or other hosts.

The IETF is now working on DHCP authentication. RFC 3118 (2001) defines two authentication options for DHCP. The first involves a key that is shared by the client PC and by the DHCP server. This key, however, is transmitted in the clear. This easily-read transmission approach is only useful for protecting the client against a host that *accidentally* installed a DHCP server.

The second option requires each client to use a pair-shared secret key with each DHCP server. Only the DHCP server and the client will know this key. The client and server use this pair-shared secret to add a key-hashed message authentication code (HMAC) to each message. If companies adopt this option, they can have fairly strong authentication, although the authentication will not be as strong as it would be if digital signatures and digital certificates were used.

Dynamic Routing Protocols Operation. When a packet arrives at a router, the router compares the packet's destination IP address with the rows in its routing table. Each row represents a route to a subnet, network, or larger cluster of IP addresses that contains the destination IP address. The router finds all matches, selects the best match, and sends the packet back out according to instructions found in the best-match row.

How do routers get the information in their routing table? Quite simply, they talk to each other frequently, exchanging data on what they know, especially about recent changes. This communication is governed by dynamic routing protocols. These protocols specify both message exchanges and the types of information that will be exchanged.

Security Concerns. Dynamic routing protocols are dangerous because spoofed messages can serious poison routing tables and therefore can cause routers to black hole or mis-deliver most or all traffic. They can even cause a router to deliver all packets to a single target destination, creating an intense denial-of-service attack. Unfortunately, dynamic routing protocols traditionally have not used cryptographic authentication or other protections.

IETF Efforts. There are several routing protocols in common use, including OSPF, BGP, EIGRP, and IS-IS. Historically, each of these standards evolved separately, including security features. Today, however, the IETF has a working group on Routing Protocol Security Requirements (rpsec). As we will see, all current IETF routing protocols at least have HMAC authentication.

RIP. For communication within small firms, the IETF created a simple routing protocol called the Routing Information Protocol (RIP). Due to its simplicity, RIP has three main constraints (Panko, 2004).

First, RIP selects routes on the basis of the number of hops between routers to get to a destination network or subnet. Selecting the route with the least number of hops generally works well in simple networks but works poorly in large networks. Large networks usually have a mix of LAN and WAN links with widely different costs and speeds. Sending data over a WAN link is much more expensive than sending data over a LAN link, but RIP does not consider these costs or other factors.

Second, RIP only works in networks with a maximum of sixteen hops. In effect, it can only count to sixteen because its hop count field only has four bits. Again, this is not a problem in small networks.

Third, RIP does not scale well. Every minute or so, depending on configuration parameters, each router broadcasts its routing table to all routers on its subnet and also to all hosts on its subnet. With large routing tables, the disruptions caused by this intrusive broadcasting would create serious host and network performance problems. Again, however, RIP is for small networks.

Just as it has a simple general design, RIP initially had no security. RIP version 2 (RFC 2453, 1998), however, brought RIP security up to date. Most notably, RIPv2 has three authentication modes:

- Null authentication (RFC 1583) (no authentication at all)
- Simple password authentication (RFC 1583), in which the password is sent in the clear in every packet. This method is useful for systems that are accidentally set up as RIP routers.
- MD5 HMAC Authentication (RFC 2328). This method uses HMACs. RIP broadcasts to all other routers out of each interface, so all routers connected to a subnet must share the same subnet secret. Looked at another way, a router must have a different secret on each interface.

As in most other standards, there is no digital signature authentication. RIPv2 does have HMAC authentication, but this uses a community secret compared to a pair-shared secret.

The rpsec's publications discuss other problems with RIPv2's authentication and various ways to address them.

OSPF. For larger networks, most firms use the Open Shortest Path First (OSPF) dynamic routing protocol. This is a more sophisticated protocol for three reasons (Panko, 2004). First, it gives routers richer information about possible routes, so that routers can select best-match rows with greater effectiveness. Second, OSPF can serve large networks. Third, OSPF scales well because it only sends messages when there are changes and because selected area routers can centralize communication in a hub-and-spoke topology instead of sending messages in a dense mesh. OSPF should be used in all but the simplest networks.

OSPF Version 2 (RFC 2328, 1998) has the same authentication options as RIP. This includes the weakness of using group-shared HMAC secrets among all OSPF routers in an area. Jones and Le Moigne (2004) discuss other security vulnerabilities in OSPF. These vulnerabilities can lead to some attacks even if HMAC authentication is used. OSPF Version 3 is used with IP Version 3.

BGP. Both RIP and OSPF are interior dynamic routing protocols that are only used *within* the networks of individual corporations. However, firms need an exterior dynamic routing protocol to communicate with their Internet service provider's router. In addition, ISPs need an exterior dynamic routing protocol to communicate with one another.

On the Internet, a single exterior dynamic routing protocol is dominant: the Border Gateway Protocol (BGP). "Gateway" is the old term for "router," so BGP is a protocol for communication between border routers at the edges of their networks.

Richard Clarke, former national coordinator for security, infrastructure protection, and counter-terrorism for the president of the United States has labeled BGP as one of the two greatest dangers on the Internet. As noted earlier, Clarke's other nomination is DNS. DNS is dangerous because it potentially could be forced to redirect all Internet traffic in harmful ways. BGP is dangerous because if it is compromised, traffic over the Internet could be redirected in harmful ways by the routers that actually move traffic. The DNS danger is like vandals removing or switching around road signs. The BGP danger is like vandals blowing up bridges.

The most recent version of BGP, BGPv4 (see RFC 1771, 1995), has been in use for more than a decade and is used almost universally on the Internet. Despite its critical importance to the Internet, BGPv4 has no cryptographic security at all. However, BGP runs over TCP on Port 179, and a large number of BGP users employ an authentication mechanism in TCP (Stewart, 1999). This mechanism, described in RFC 2385 (1998), uses a pair-shared HMAC using MD5 (although the RFC calls it an MD5 digital signature). If a BGP messages is contained in a TCP segment with an improper HMAC, the transport layer discards the message before BGP even sees it.

Dialogues protected with MD5 HMACs are difficult to hijack. Attackers must not only guess TCP sequence numbers. They must also guess or learn the secret shared by the two routers being connected via TCP.

For stronger security, the two routers exchanging BGP messages can connect via IPsec with at least initial public key authentication. They could also connect via SSL/TLS. In either case, the two routers would need to have public and private keys. In addition, the routers would have to be fast enough to handle the large amount of additional work needed for IPsec or SSL/TLS. This approach does not work for other routing protocols, which use broadcasting (RIP) or multicasting (OSPF).

BGP routers have many options, which have varying levels of security and vulnerability. Windowsecurity.com (2002) has developed a template for securing BGP on the Cisco routers that dominate corporate and Internet use.

EIGRP and IS-IS. There are two other dynamic routing protocols to mention. For interior routing, many firms use Cisco's proprietary EIGRP interior dynamic routing protocol, which can handle the packets of multiple standards architectures in an integrated way. (RIP and OSPF are limited to IP packets.) In addition, OSI offers IS-IS, which would at least provide security by obscurity (not recommended). However, this article is about Internet security standards, and Internet transmission requires IP transmission.

Dynamic Routing Protocol Security: Perspective. To date, the focus on dynamic routing protocol security has been authentication. Unless IPsec or SSL/TLS are used to transmit BGP4 messages, the highest level of authentication for BGP4 is MD5 HMACs with pair-shared secrets. In addition, for interior routing, the highest level of security for RIP and OSPF is MD5 HMACs with group-shared secrets.

Another issue is that authentication assumes trust. If an attacker gets inside an organization managing a router or somehow compromises a router, they will be able to send poisoned routing information to other routers, and these other routers are likely to trust the information.

One way to reduce the danger of spurious trust is to block all incoming packets containing dynamic routing protocol information at the firm's border firewall—or at least, to limit incoming packets containing such information to one or two specific external routers.

Application Layer Standards

To users, the Internet is attractive because of its application standards for the World Wide Web, e-mail, and other popular services. While decent security is present for some application standards, many application standards continue to have only weak security—if they have any at all.

Hypertext Transfer Protocol (HTTP) over SSL/TLS

To communicate with a WWW server, a browser uses HTTP Version 1.1 (RFC 2616, 1999). HTTP is a simple protocol that offers no security by itself. However, all browser and WWW server programs support SSL/TLS security, and the use of SSL/TLS in e-commerce applications and other sensitive applications is overwhelming. HTTP over SSL/TLS uses Port 443 rather than HTTP's normal Port 80.

SSL/TLS allows both the browser and the webserver to authenticate each other using digital signatures and digital certificates. However, only the server is *required* to use a digital signature to authenticate itself. This is done because few PCs running browsers have digital certificates. Obviously, not requiring client authentication is a serious problem for protecting webservers against attack.

E-Mail Security

Security for e-mail is perhaps the great scandal in Internet Engineering Task Force history. Competing cliques within the IETF have consistently simply refused to cooperate in selecting security standards for e-mail. Consequently, companies that wish to implement e-mail security have to use a non-standard method to do so.

Not surprisingly, sending application layer e-mail traffic over a secure SSL/TLS transport connection is the most popular way to secure e-mail in organizations today. SSL/TLS is well understood, offers consumer-grade security, and has been widely used for HTTP security for several years. Another approach, S/MIME (RFC 2633 1999), is used by fewer organizations.

A third approach, Pretty Good Privacy (PGP) (RFC 1991, 1996), is used primarily by individuals. Organizations have tended to stay away from PGP because PGP uses user-based transitive trust. (If User A trusts User B, and if User B trusts User C, User A may trust User C). As noted earlier, this is not a good security policy. If a single user mistakenly trusts an impostor, others may unwittingly trust the impostor as well.

Also, PGP is now owned by a single vendor, making it a proprietary protocol. In addition, it has had a troubled development history. OpenPGP now offers a vendor-independent implementation of a near-PGP protocol, but there is no official reference standard for OpenPGP.

Remote Access Protocols: Telnet, Rlogin, Rsh, and SSH

The first ARPANET application was Telnet (RFC 854, 1983), which allows a user to log into a remote computer and execute commands there as if the user was a local user. This allows ordinary users to access remote services. It also allows system administrators to manage servers and routers remotely. This use of remote administration is attractive, but it must be done carefully or hackers will end up "managing" corporate servers and routers.

Unfortunately, Telnet has poor security. For example, Telnet does not encrypt host usernames and passwords. Sniffers can intercept usernames and passwords, allowing hackers to log in as these users with all of the privileges of these users.

Telnet should never be used for remote administration because hackers intercepting root passwords would be able to execute any commands on the compromised machine. Telnet is not alone in this respect. In the Unix world, rlogin and rsh do not even require passwords to gain access to a computer, although other conditions must apply.

For remote administration, some organizations turn to the Secure Shell (SSH) protocol, which offers good authentication, integrity, and authentication (Ylonen, Kivinen, Saarinen, *et al.*, 2002). Unfortunately, SSH Version 1 had security flaws, and although these have been fixed in SSH Version 2, many Version 2 implementations will also permit Version 1 connections, thus leaving the system open to attack. Another problem is that SSH is not an official TCP/IP protocol.

File Transfer Protocol (FTP) and Trivial File Transfer Protocol (TFTP)

Another early ARPANET service that continues to be popular on the Internet is File Transfer Protocol (FTP) (RFC 959, 1985), which allows a user to download files from a remote computer to his or her local computer and sometimes to upload files from his or her local computer to the remote computer. Unfortunately, FTP also sends usernames and passwords in the clear, making it very dangerous. In addition, while the use of Telnet has declined to the point where quite a few companies simply stop all Telnet traffic at their firewalls, FTP is still widely used. The FTPEXT Working Group is considering security for FTP. In addition, FTP can be protected by sending it over SSL/TLS if the FTP program allows this.

FTP has a simpler sibling, the Trivial File Transfer Protocol (TFTP) (RFC 1350, 1992). TFTP does not even require usernames and passwords, making it a darling of hackers who often use TFTP after taking over a computer to download their rootkits (collections of hacker programs) to automate their exploitation of the computer they now "own."

Web Services

An important emerging application class is Web services. Web service protocols allow programs on different computers to interact in a standardized way. Web services are creating a new level of interoperability between programs on different computers.

The figure shows that Web service interactions often are "chained," meaning that a single Web service message may initiate a series of other Web service messages.

Web services have only been operational since about 2000, and Web services standards are still rather embryonic. The three main Web service standards are SOAP, which governs the format of messages, UDDI, which is like a yellow pages and white pages for finding Web services relevant to a firm's need, and WSDL, which tells a firm exactly how to work with a specific Web service. However, many other standards need to be set before Web services can be used with confidence.

As in many other applications, security was an afterthought for Web services standardization. Consequently, Web service security standards are even more embryonic than Web service standards in general. Worse yet, Web service security standards have suffered from conflicts among vendors.

The initial security standards for Web services (SOAP, UDDI, and WSDL) were created by the World Wide Web Consortium (W3C). However, Microsoft, which had been a major driving force behind the first three standards, pulled its support from W3C. Rumor suggests that Microsoft did this because W3C only creates standards if the technology is not encumbered by patents (Koch, 2003). Microsoft, according to the rumor, wished to preserve its intellectual property rights.

Whatever its motivation, Microsoft and its main partners, IBM and VeriSign, moved their standards development efforts to OASIS (the Organization for the Advancement of Structured Information Standards). Their efforts were based on the Microsoft/IBM/VeriSign standards efforts called WS- (because all standards begin with WS and a dash).

Sun Microsystems and its allies initially supported a different family of standards, ebXML. In fact, it has been suggested that the IETF gave the WS- standards a cold reception at the 2000 IETF meeting because Sun had the chair role (Newcomer, 2003). However, when the ebXML effort fell apart, Sun threw its weight behind the WS- standards efforts at OASIS.

To confuse matters even further, Microsoft and its allies created a new standards organization, WS-I, where the I stands for interoperability. Initially, WS-I's purpose is to develop implementation profiles built from various Web services standards. Sun was excluded from WS-I but was eventually allowed to join as a board member.

In 2004, there was a major breakthrough when OASIS ratified the WS-Security standard submitted by Microsoft, IBM, and VeriSign in 2002. WS-Security, in a move toward openness, adopted several standards from W3C, including standards for encryption and digital signatures. In the near future, WS-Security should be extended to work with the OASIS SAML (Security Assertion Markup Language) standard, which specifies how organizations can exchange authentication information.

Unfortunately, WS-Security is only part of the framework created for Web service security by Microsoft, IBM, and VeriSign. To be effective, six more elements are needed: WS-Policy, WS-Trust, WS-Privacy, WS-Secure Conversation, WS-Federation, and WS-Authorization. Microsoft and its allies have not submitted these additional elements to OASIS, making the standardization of WS-Security a limited development.

Authentication is a complex issue for Web services standards. WS-Security does not have complete authentication, and Sun and its partners have developed a major authentication system under the auspices of the Sun-led Liberty Alliance. Although Sun has endorsed the Microsoft standards efforts, Microsoft has not done the same for the Liberty Alliance standards, probably because Microsoft has a competing authentication product, Passport.

Especially interesting aspects of the W3C standards are its XML Encryption and XML Signature standards, which are part of WS-Security. Obviously, these standards provide for encryption for confidentiality and digital signing. What makes them interesting is not their cryptographic methods but the fact that they can be applied to *parts* of a message as well as to the entire message. The capability to encrypt and sign parts of messages is important because some Web service messages go to more than one party, and only some parts of the message are relevant to (or should be read by) each party.

Web services security protocols have a long way to go before they are ready for use with confidence. In addition, the protocols that do exist still are subject to denial-of-service attacks and other dangers.

However, if a Web service interaction will only take place between two parties, it may be sufficient to protect and authenticate the communication using SSL/TLS. However, not having protection and authentication *within* messages via XML Encryption and XML Signature leaves Web services open to certain attacks.

Other Applications

There are many other Internet applications, and their standards vary widely in their degree of security. VoIP security is a particularly sensitive emerging standards application issue. In addition, database applications and many other applications are not even standards-based.

Unfortunately, many operating system installations automatically turn on quite a few applications without the knowledge of the systems administrators or users. For example, when SNMP vulnerabilities were found in 2002, it was discovered that many vulnerable machines should not have been running SNMP at all. An important rule in hardening clients and servers against attack is to turn off all applications that are not absolutely needed to run the computer.

THE STATE OF INTERNET SECURITY STANDARDS

Today, if two communication partners wish to communicate securely, they can do so by adding dialogue security on top of the nonsecure Internet transmission. For lightweight needs, they can turn to PPTP or SSL/TLS. For industrial-strength security, they can use IPsec.

General Insecurity

More generally, however, under the Danvers Doctrine, the standards that the Internet needs for message delivery (IP, TCP, and UDP), Internet supervisory standards (ICMP, DNS, SNMP, LDAP, etc.), and Internet application standards (WWW, e-mail, etc.) vary widely in security from none to semi-adequate. Consequently, the Internet today is rather fragile and open to seriously damaging attacks. Given the pace of security implementation in individual standards, the fragility of the Internet is not likely to change radically in the next two or three years. Even after more secure standards are developed, it will take several years for them to be widely adopted.

The Broad IETF Program

At the same time, there is an extremely broad concern with security across the IETF. Although some standards have better security than others, standards working groups appear to be playing leapfrog in their efforts to improve security across a broad spectrum of Internet standards.

The Authentication Problem

Digital Certificates

The most difficult problem in Internet security standards is authentication. Most Internet standards today from the IETF offer a maximum of HMAC message-by-message authentication.

However, unless authentication uses public key authentication (such as digital signatures) coupled with digital certificates managed by a reliable and well-regulated network of certificate authorities, authentication strength will only be moderate. However, creating large public key infrastructures will take years, and while European countries are moving to manage and regulate certificate authorities, the United States has adopted the let-the-market-do-it philosophy that has worked so well recently in the energy industry and in corporate financial reporting.

One option is to use public key authentication with digital certificates and then use HMACs for message-by-message authentication. Although this would lose nonrepudiation for individual messages, it would decrease the processing intensiveness of VPNs and other cryptographic protection systems. However, this still requires an infrastructure for managing public/private key pairs and digital certificates.

Distributed Authentication

Another problem is distributed authentication. There is unlikely to be a single global authentication authority. Consequently, multiple authentication authorities must be able to work together. Most importantly, there must be mechanisms for implementing transitive trust, in which an authentication authority trusts credentials provided by another authentication authority. In public key authentication, there has long been the concept of a hierarchy of certificate authorities, but no single CA tree is likely to emerge across the world.

More federated one-to-one and one-to-few horizontal trust systems are now under development, especially for Web services. These include the Liberty Alliance, IBM, and Microsoft (WS-* security) standards, and OASIS (the Organization for the Advancement of Structured Information Standards) standards.

The Primary Authentication Problem

One broad and deep problem in authentication is the primary authentication problem—proving the identity of a person or organization in the first place, say to give them a digital certificate or accept them as an employee. Identity theft has long allowed impostors to obtain fraudulent drivers' licenses and other authentication instruments. Even within closed systems, such as corporate networks, the prime authentication problem can be daunting. For consumer authentication and other large communities, the technical and operational problems for credible initial authentication are extremely daunting.

Protection from Denial-of-Service Attacks

One security threat that has barely been faced so far is the prospect of denial-of-service attacks. Although a few standards have taken some steps to reduce DoS attack risks, this is an area of little general development within the IETF.

Internet Forensics Standards

One area that we did not look at in this paper is standards to make the internet forensic, that is, able to collect and analyze traffic data in a way that would make the prosecution of attacks possible. Without forensics standards, it will continue to be nearly impossible to find and prosecute attackers.

The Internet Engineering Task Force to date has shown no interest in developing forensics standards. In fact, in 1999, the IETF polled its members about whether the IETF should develop protocols to support law enforcement requirements for wiretapping voice conversations carried over the Internet. There was a strong preponderance of comments against developing standards for implementing wiretapping (Macavinta, 1999).

GLOSSARY

Community Key, AKA Community Secret Secret shared by multiple devices within a network.

Cryptographic Protection System (CPS) Standards-based system for automatically providing multiple protections in a dialogue between two parties.

Danvers Doctrine An Internet Engineering Task Force decision to add security to all or nearly all TCP/IP protocols.

Denial-of-Service Attacks Attacks that attempt to render a computer or network useless to its user; not addressed in most Internet security efforts.

Dialogue The transmission of multiple messages in both directions between two hosts.

Dialogue Security Security applied to a dialogue (ongoing message exchange between two parties); often added on top of nonsecure Internet transmission.

Digital Signature Message-by-message authentication system based on public key encryption. To work very well, the parties should have digital certificates from trusted certificate authorities.

Dynamic Routing Protocol A protocol that routers use to communicate with one another to exchange information for their routing tables.

HMAC Key-Hashed Message Authentication Protocol. Message-by-message authentication system based on a secret key shared by two parties.

Internet Engineering Task Force (IETF) The body that creates TCP/IP standards for the Internet. Now engaged in a broad effort to add security to Internet standards.

In the clear When a message is transmitted without encryption for confidentiality or other cryptographic protections.

IPsec Family of standards for adding security to both IPv4 and IPv6 Internet Protocol transmission dialogues.

Kerberos Server Authentication system in which a central server gives out authentication and authorization information.

Multilayer Security Providing security at multiple standards layers in order to provide defense in depth.

Password Authentication Authentication in which the two sides know a password consisting of keyboard characters.

Policy Server In a security system, a server that tells devices how they must implement security

PPP Point-to-Point Protocol. Secure protocol for communicating over a point-to-point data link.

PPTP Point-to-Point Tunneling Protocol. Protocol that extends PPP transmissions over an internet; extends PPP security over the route.

RADIUS server A server that stores authentication data so that access servers can apply authentication criteria consistently. Name stands for Remote Authentication Dial-In User Service.

Remote Access Server (RAS) Security server at a site that terminates and manages a PPP connection or PPTP connection over the Internet

SSL/TLS Transport Layer Security (TLS). General standard for adding security at the transport layer. Formerly called Secure Sockets Layer (SSL) and still widely known by that name. Also called HTTPS because URLs beginning with "https" are requesting SSL/TLS security.

Virtual Private Network (VPN) Family of standards for adding security to a dialogue over an untrusted network, most commonly the Internet. Includes PPTP, IPsec, and SSL/TLS.

CROSS REFERENCES

See *Computer and Network Authentication; Digital Signatures and Electronic Signatures; Encryption Basics; Password Authentication; VPN Basics.*

REFERENCES

Note: In selecting RFCs, an attempt has been made to give the definitive base version of the standard.

(RFC 768) Postel, J., "User Datagram Protocol," August 1980.

(RFC 791) Postel, J., ed., "Internet Protocol—DARPA Internet Program Protocol Specification," September 1981.

(RFC 792) Postel, J., ed., "Internet Control Message Protocol DARPA Internet Program Protocol Specification, September 1981.

(RFC 793) Information Sciences Institute, "Transmission Control Protocol DARPA Internet Program Protocol Specification," September 1981.

(RFC 826). Plummer, D. C., "An Address Resolution Protocol," November 1982.

(RFC 854) Postel, J. & Reynolds, J., "Telnet Protocol Specification," May 1983. Actually, Telnet was developed in the early 1970s for the ARPANET; this RFC specifies the TCP/IP version Telnet.

(RFC 959) Postel, J. & Reynolds, J., "File Transfer Protocol (FTP)," October 1985. Actually, FTP was created in the 1970s for the ARPANET. This RFC is the specification for TCP/IP.

(RFC 1034) Mockapetris, P. "DOMAIN NAMES—CONCEPTS AND FACILITIES," November 1987.

(RFC 1350) Sollins, K., "The TFTP Protocol (Revision 2)," July 1992. The original version was RFC 783, which was published in 1981.

(RFC 1583) Moy, J., "OSPF Version 2," March 1994.

(RFC 1661) Simpson, W., "The Point-to-Point Protocol (PPP)," STD 51, July 1994.

(RFC 1771) Rekhter, Y. & Lo, T., "A Border Gateway Protocol 4 (BGP-4)," March 1995.

(RFC 1991) Atkins, D., Stallings, W., and Zimmerman, P., "PGP Message Exchange Formats," August 1996.

(RFC 2131) Droms, R., "Dynamic Host Configuration Protocol," March 1997.

(RFC 2222) Myers, J., "Simple Authentication and Security Layer (SASL)," October 1997.

(RFC 2246) Dierks, T. & Allen, C., *The TLS Protocol Version 1.0*, January 1999.

(RFC 2251) Wahl, M, Howes, T., and Kille, S., "Lightweight Directory Access Protocol (v3)," December 1997.

(RFC 2284) Blunk, L. & Vollbrecht, J., "PPP Extensible Authentication Protocol (EAP)," March 1998.

(RFC 2328) Moy, J., "OSPF Version 2," STD 54, April 1998.

(RFC 2385). Heffernan, J., "Protection of BGP Sessions via the TCP MD5 Signature Option," August 1998.

(RFC 2411) Thayer, R., Doraswamy, N. & Glenn R., "IP Security Document Roadmap," November 1998.

(RFC 2453) Malkin, G., "RIP Version 2," November 1998.

(RFC 2616) Fielding, R., Gettys, J., Mogul, J., Frystyk, H., Masinter, L., Leach, P., Berners-Lee, T., "Hypertext Transfer Protocol—HTTP 1/1," June 1999.

(RFC 2633) Ramsdell, B., "S/MIME Version 3 Message Specification," June 1999.

(RFC 2637) Hamzeh, K., Pall, G., Verthein, W., Taarud, J., Little, W., and Zorn, G. "Point-to-Point Tunneling Protocol (PPTP)," July 1999.

(RFC 2661) Tonsley, W., Valencia, A., Rubens, A., Pall, G., Zorn, G., & Palter, B., "Layer Two Tunneling Protocol 'L2TP,'" August 1999.

(RFC 2661) Townsley, W., Valencia, A., Rubens, A., Pall, G., Zorn, G., and Palter, B., "Layer Two Tunneling Protocol 'L2TP,'" August 1999.

(RFC 3118) Droms, R. & Arbaugh, W., "Authentication for DHCP Messages," June 2001.

(RFC 3365) Schiller, J., "Strong Security Recommendations for Internet Engineering Task Force Standard Protocols," August 2002.

Barabasi, A. L., "Scale-Free Networks," *Scientific American*, May 2003, pp. 50–59.

Beckenhauer, B., "SNMP Alert 2002: What is it all about?" February 21, 2002. http://www.sans.org/rr/protocols/SNMP_alert.php

Blumenthal, U. & Wijen, B., *User-Based Security Model (USM) for Version 3 of the Simple Network Management Protocol (SNMPv3)*, January 1998.

Harrison, R., *LDAP: Authentication Methods and Connection-Level Security Methods*, Internet Draft, November 2002.

Jones, E. & Le Moigne, O., "OSPF Security Vulnerabilities Analysis," draft-ietf-rpsec-ospf-vuln-00.txt, IETF, May 2004.

Koch, C., "The Battle for Web Services, CIO Magazine," October 1, 2003. http://www.cio.com/archive/100103/standards.html

Legard, D., "Analyst Digest: Worms Carry Heavy Cost," *Network World Fusion*, June 1, 2004.http://www.nwfusion. com/news/2004/0601analydiges.html

Macavinta, C., "Internet Protocol Proposal Raises Privacy Concerns," *CNET News.com*, October 14, 1999. http://news.com.com/2100-12-231403.html

Microsoft, "Introduction to IP Version 6," Updated March 31, 2004. http://www.microsoft.com/technet/itsolutions/network/security/ipvers6.mspx

Newcomer, E., "The Web Services Standards Mess," WebServices.org, December 2003. http://www.myweb services.org/index.php/article/articleview/1202/1/24

Panko, Raymond, *Business Computer and Network Security*, Upper Saddle River, NJ: Prentice-Hall, 2004.

Rose, S. "DNS Security Document Roadmap," draft-ietf-dnsext-dnssec-roadmap-06, IETF, September 5, 2002.

Stewart, J. W. III, *BGP4: Inter-Domain Routing on the Internet*, Addison-Wesley, 1999.

Thomas, Stephen A., *IP Switching and Routing Essentials*, New York: Wiley, 2002.

Wagner, M., "Increased Internet Centralization Threatens Reliability," *InternetWeek*, December 2, 2002. http://www.internetwk.com/story/INW20021202S0004

Windowsecurity.com, "Secure BGP Template Version 2.0, October 16, 2002. http://www.windowsecurity.com/whitepapers/Secure_BGP_Template_Version_20.html

Ylonen, T., Kivinen, T., Saarinen, M., Rinne, T., & Lehtinen, S., "SSH Authentication Protocol," Internet Draft, IETF, September 20, 2002.

Kerberos

William Stallings, *Independent Consultant*

INTRODUCTION

Kerberos is an authentication service developed as part of Project Athena at MIT. The problem that Kerberos addresses is this: Assume an open distributed environment in which users at workstations wish to access services on servers distributed throughout the network. We would like for servers to be able to restrict access to authorized users and to be able to authenticate requests for service. In this environment, a workstation cannot be trusted to identify its users correctly to network services. In particular, the following three threats exist:

- A user may gain access to a particular workstation and pretend to be another user operating from that workstation.
- A user may alter the network address of a workstation so that the requests sent from the altered workstation appear to come from the impersonated workstation.
- A user may eavesdrop on exchanges and use a replay attack to gain entrance to a server or to disrupt operations.

In any of these cases, an unauthorized user may be able to gain access to services and data that he or she is not authorized to access. Rather than building in elaborate authentication protocols at each server, Kerberos provides a centralized authentication server with the function of authenticating users to servers and servers to users. Unlike many authentication schemes, Kerberos relies exclusively on symmetric encryption, making no use of public key encryption.

Two versions of Kerberos are in common use. Version 4 (Miller, Neuman, Schiller, & Saltzer, 1988; Steiner, Neuman, & Schiller, 1988) is still widely used. Version 5 (Kohl, 1989) corrects some of the security deficiencies of version 4 and has been issued as a proposed Internet Standard (RFC 1510).

This discussion begins with a brief discussion of the motivation for the Kerberos approach. Then, because of the complexity of Kerberos, it is best to proceed to a description of the authentication protocol used in version 4. This enables us to see the essence of the Kerberos strategy without considering some of the details required to handle subtle security threats. Finally, we examine version 5.

MOTIVATION

If a set of users is provided with dedicated personal computers that have no network connections, then a user's resources and files can be protected by physically securing each personal computer. When these users instead are served by a centralized time-sharing system, the time-sharing operating system must provide the security. The operating system can enforce access control policies based on user identity and use the logon procedure to identify users.

Today, neither of these scenarios is typical. More common is a distributed architecture consisting of dedicated user workstations (clients) and distributed or centralized servers. In this environment, three approaches to security can be envisioned:

1. Rely on each individual client workstation to ensure the identity of its user or users and rely on each server to enforce a security policy based on user identification (ID)
2. Require that client systems authenticate themselves to servers, but trust the client system concerning the identity of its user
3. Require the user to prove identity for each service invoked; also require that servers prove their identity to clients

In a small, closed environment, in which all systems are owned and operated by a single organization, the first or perhaps second strategy may suffice. In a more open environment, however, in which network connections to other machines are supported, the third approach is needed to protect user information and resources housed at the server. This third approach is supported by Kerberos. Kerberos assumes a distributed client–server architecture and employs one or more Kerberos servers to provide an authentication service.

The first published report on Kerberos (Steiner et al., 1988) listed the following requirements for Kerberos:

- **Secure:** A network eavesdropper should not be able to obtain the necessary information to impersonate a user. More generally, Kerberos should be strong enough that a potential opponent does not find it to be the weak link.

- **Reliable:** For all services that rely on Kerberos for access control, lack of availability of the Kerberos service means lack of availability of the supported services. Hence, Kerberos should be highly reliable and should employ a distributed server architecture, with one system able to back up another.
- **Transparent:** Ideally, the user should not be aware that authentication is taking place, beyond the requirement to enter a password.
- **Scalable:** The system should be capable of supporting large numbers of clients and servers. This suggests a modular, distributed architecture.

To support these requirements, the overall scheme of Kerberos is that of a trusted third-party authentication service that uses a protocol based on that proposed by Needham and Schroeder (1978). It is trusted in the sense that clients and servers trust Kerberos to mediate their mutual authentication. Assuming the Kerberos protocol is well designed, the authentication service is secure if the Kerberos server itself is secure.

KERBEROS VERSION 4

Version 4 of Kerberos makes use of DES (Data Encryption Standard), in a rather elaborate protocol, to provide the authentication service. Viewing the protocol as a whole, it is difficult to see the need for the many elements contained therein. Therefore, we adopt a strategy used by Bill Bryant of Project Athena (Bryant, 1988) and build up to the full protocol by looking first at several hypothetical dialogues. Each successive dialogue adds additional complexity to counter security vulnerabilities revealed in the preceding dialogue.

After examining the protocol, this chapter considers other aspects of version 4.

A Simple Authentication Dialogue

In an unprotected network environment, any client can apply to any server for service. The obvious security risk is that of impersonation. An opponent can pretend to be another client and obtain unauthorized privileges on server machines. To counter this threat, servers must be able to confirm the identities of clients who request service. Each server can be required to undertake this task for each client–server interaction, but in an open environment, this places a substantial burden on each server.

An alternative is to use an authentication server (AS) that knows the passwords of all users and stores these in a centralized database. In addition, the AS shares a unique secret key with each server. These keys have been distributed physically or in some other secure manner. Consider the following hypothetical dialogue (the portion to the left of the colon indicates the sender and receiver, the portion to the right indicates the contents of the message, and the symbol || indicates concatenation):

$$\begin{aligned}&(\mathbf{1})\,\mathrm{C} \rightarrow \mathrm{AS}: && ID_C \,||\, P_C \,||\, ID_V\\ &(\mathbf{2})\,\mathrm{AS} \rightarrow \mathrm{C}: && Ticket\\ &(\mathbf{3})\,\mathrm{C} \rightarrow \mathrm{V}: && ID_C \,||\, Ticket,\\ &Ticket = E_{K_v}[ID_C \,||\, AD_C \,||\, ID_v]\end{aligned}$$

where

C = client
AS = authentication server
V = server
ID_C = identifier of user on C
ID_V = identifier of V
P_C = password of user on C
AD_C = network address of C
K_v = secret encryption key shared by AS and V
$||$ = concatenation.

In this scenario, the user logs on to a workstation and requests access to server V. The client module C in the user's workstation requests the user's password and then sends a message to the AS that includes the user's ID, the server's ID, and the user's password. The AS checks its database to see whether the user has supplied the proper password for this user ID and whether this user is permitted access to server V. If both tests are passed, the AS accepts the user as authentic and must now convince the server that this user is authentic. To do so, the AS creates a ticket that contains the user's ID and network address and the server's ID. This ticket is encrypted using the secret key shared by the AS and this server. This ticket is then sent back to C. Because the ticket is encrypted, it cannot be altered by C or by an opponent.

With this ticket, C can now apply to V for service. C sends a message to V containing C's ID and the ticket. V decrypts the ticket and verifies that the user ID in the ticket is the same as the unencrypted user ID in the message. If these two match, the server considers the user authenticated and grants the requested service.

Each of the ingredients of message (3) is significant. The ticket is encrypted to prevent alteration or forgery. The server's ID (ID_V) is included in the ticket so that the server can verify that it has decrypted the ticket properly. ID_C is included in the ticket to indicate that this ticket has been issued on behalf of C. Finally, AD_C serves to counter the following threat. An opponent could capture the ticket transmitted in message (2), then use the name ID_C and transmit a message of form (3) from another workstation. The server would receive a valid ticket that matches the user ID and grant access to the user on that other workstation. To prevent this attack, the AS includes in the ticket the network address from which the original request came. Now the ticket is valid only if it is transmitted from the same workstation that initially requested the ticket.

A More Secure Authentication Dialogue

Although the foregoing scenario solves some of the problems of authentication in an open network environment, problems remain. Two in particular stand out. First, we would like to minimize the number of times that a user has to enter a password. Suppose each ticket can be used only once. If user C logs on to a workstation in the morning and wishes to check his or her mail at a mail server, C must supply a password to get a ticket for the mail server. If C wishes to check the mail several times during the day, each attempt requires reentering the password. We can improve matters by saying that tickets are reusable. For a single logon session, the workstation can store the mail server ticket after it is received and use it on behalf of the user for multiple accesses to the mail server.

Under this scheme, however, it remains the case that a user would need a new ticket for every different service. If a user wished to access a print server, a mail server, a file server, and so on, the first instance of each access would require a new ticket and hence require the user to enter the password.

The second problem is that the earlier scenario involved a plaintext transmission of the password [message (1)]. An eavesdropper could capture the password and use any service accessible to the victim.

To solve these additional problems, we introduce a scheme for avoiding plaintext passwords and a new server, known as the ticket-granting server (TGS). The new but still hypothetical scenario is as follows:

Once per user logon session:

$$(1)\,\mathrm{C} \rightarrow \mathrm{AS}:\ \ ID_C \,||\, ID_{tgs}$$

$$(2)\,\mathrm{AS} \rightarrow \mathrm{C}:\ \ \mathrm{E}_{K_c}[Ticket_{tgs}]$$

Once per type of service :

$$(3)\,\mathrm{C} \rightarrow \mathrm{TGS}:\ \ ID_C \,||\, ID_V \,||\, Ticket_{tgs}$$

$$(4)\,\mathrm{TGS} \rightarrow \mathrm{C}:\ \ Ticket_v$$

Once per service session :

$$(5)\,\mathrm{C} \rightarrow \mathrm{V}:\ \ ID_C \,||\, Ticket_v$$

$$Ticket_{tgs} = E_{K_{tgs}}[ID_C \,||\, AD_C \,||\, ID_{tgs} \,||\, TS_1 \,||\, Lifetime_1]$$

$$Ticket_v = E_{K_v}\left[ID_C \,||\, AD_C \,||\, ID_v \,||\, TS_2 \,||\, Lifetime_2\right]$$

The new service, TGS, issues tickets to users who have been authenticated to AS. Thus, the user first requests a ticket-granting ticket ($Ticket_{tgs}$) from the AS. This ticket is saved by the client module in the user workstation. Each time the user requires access to a new service, the client applies to the TGS, using the ticket to authenticate itself. The TGS then grants a ticket for the particular service. The client saves each service-granting ticket and uses it to authenticate its user to a server each time a particular service is requested. Let us look at the details of this scheme:

1. The client requests a ticket-granting ticket on behalf of the user by sending its user's ID and password to the AS, together with the TGS ID, indicating a request to use the TGS service.
2. The AS responds with a ticket that is encrypted with a key that is derived from the user's password. When this response arrives at the client, the client prompts the user for his or her password, generates the key, and attempts to decrypt the incoming message. If the correct password is supplied, the ticket is successfully recovered.

Because only the correct user should know the password, only the correct user can recover the ticket. Thus, we have used the password to obtain credentials from Kerberos without having to transmit the password in plaintext. The ticket itself consists of the ID and network address of the user and the ID of the TGS. This corresponds to the first scenario. The idea is that this ticket can be used by the client to request multiple service-granting tickets. So the ticket-granting ticket is to be reusable. We do not wish an opponent to be able to capture the ticket and use it, however. Consider the following scenario: An opponent captures the login ticket and waits until the user has logged off his or her workstation. Then the opponent either gains access to that workstation or configures his workstation with the same network address as that of the victim. The opponent would be able to reuse the ticket to spoof the TGS. To counter this, the ticket includes a time stamp, indicating the date and time at which the ticket was issued, and a lifetime, indicating the length of time for which the ticket is valid (e.g., eight hours). Thus, the client has a reusable ticket and need not bother the user for a password for each new service request. Finally, note that the ticket-granting ticket is encrypted with a secret key known only to the AS and the TGS. This prevents alteration of the ticket. The ticket is reencrypted with a key based on the user's password. This ensures that the ticket can be recovered only by the correct user, providing the authentication.

Now that the client has a ticket-granting ticket, access to any server can be obtained with steps 3 and 4:

3. The client requests a service-granting ticket on behalf of the user. For this purpose, the client transmits a message to the TGS containing the user's ID, the ID of the desired service, and the ticket-granting ticket.
4. The TGS decrypts the incoming ticket and verifies the success of the decryption by the presence of its ID. It checks to make sure that the lifetime has not expired. Then it compares the user ID and network address with the incoming information to authenticate the user. If the user is permitted access to the server V, the TGS issues a ticket to grant access to the requested service.

The service-granting ticket has the same structure as the ticket-granting ticket. Indeed, because the TGS is a server, we would expect that the same elements are needed to authenticate a client to the TGS and to authenticate a client to an application server. Again, the ticket contains a time stamp and lifetime. If the user wants access to the same service at a later time, the client can simply use the previously acquired service-granting ticket and need not bother the user for a password. Note that the ticket is encrypted with a secret key (K_v) known only to the TGS and the server, preventing alteration.

Finally, with a particular service-granting ticket, the client can gain access to the corresponding service with step 5:

5. The client requests access to a service on behalf of the user. For this purpose, the client transmits a message to the server containing the user's ID and the service-granting ticket. The server authenticates by using the contents of the ticket.

This new scenario satisfies the two requirements of only one password query per user session and protection of the user password.

Table 1 Summary of Kerberos Version 4 Message Exchanges

(a) Authentication Service Exchange: To Obtain Ticket-Granting Ticket

(1) C → AS: $ID_c \| ID_{tgs} \| TS_1$

(2) AS → C: $E_{K_c}[K_{c,tgs} \| ID_{tgs} \| TS_2 \| Lifetime_2 \| Ticket_{tgs}]$

$Ticket_{tgs} = E_{K_{tgs}}[K_{c,tgs} \| ID_C \| AD_C \| ID_{tgs} \| TS_2 \| Lifetime_2]$

(b) Ticket-Granting Service Exchange: To Obtain Service-Granting Ticket

(3) C → TGS: $ID_v \| Ticket_{tgs} \| Authenticator_c$

(4) TGS → C: $E_{K_{c,tgs}}[K_{c,v} \| ID_v \| TS_4 \| Ticket_v]$

$Ticket_{tgs} = E_{K_{tgs}}[K_{c,tag} \| ID_C \| AD_C \| ID_{tgs} \| TS_2 \| Lifetime_2]$

$Ticket_v = E_{K_v}[K_{c,v} \| ID_C \| AD_C \| ID_v \| TS_4 \| Lifetime_4]$

$Authenticator_c = E_{K_{c,tgs}}[ID_C \| AD_C \| TS_3]$

(c) Client/Server Authentication Exchange: To Obtain Service

(5) C → V: $Ticket_v \| Authenticator_c$

(6) V → C: $E_{K_{c,v}}[TS_5 + 1]$ (for mutual authentication)

$Ticket_v = E_{K_v}[K_{c,v} \| ID_C \| AD_C \| ID_v \| TS_4 \| Lifetime_4]$

$Authenticator_c = E_{K_{c,v}}[ID_C \| AD_C \| TS_5]$

The Version 4 Authentication Dialogue

Although the foregoing scenario enhances security compared with the first attempt, two additional problems remain. The heart of the first problem is the lifetime associated with the ticket-granting ticket. If this lifetime is very short (e.g., minutes), the user will be repeatedly asked for a password. If the lifetime is long (e.g., hours), an opponent has a greater opportunity for replay. An opponent could eavesdrop on the network and capture a copy of the ticket-granting ticket and then wait for the legitimate user to log out. Then the opponent could forge the legitimate user's network address and send the message of step (3) to the TGS. This would give the opponent unlimited access to the resources and files available to the legitimate user. Similarly, if an opponent captures a service-granting ticket and uses it before it expires, the opponent has access to the corresponding service.

Thus, we arrive at an additional requirement. A network service (the TGS or an application service) must be able to prove that the person using a ticket is the same person to whom that ticket was issued.

The second problem is that there may be a requirement for servers to authenticate themselves to users. Without such authentication, an opponent could sabotage the configuration so that messages to a server were directed to another location. The false server would then be in a position to act as a real server and capture any information from the user and deny the true service to the user. These problems are now examined in turn (refer also to Table 1, which shows the actual Kerberos protocol).

First, consider the problem of captured ticket-granting tickets and the need to determine that the ticket presenter is the same as the client for whom the ticket was issued. The threat is that an opponent will steal the ticket and use it before it expires. To get around this problem, let us have the AS provide both the client and the TGS with a secret piece of information in a secure manner. Then the client can prove its identity to the TGS by revealing the secret information, again in a secure manner. An efficient way of accomplishing this is to use an encryption key as the secure information; this is referred to as a session key in Kerberos.

Table 1a shows the technique for distributing the session key. As before, the client sends a message to the AS requesting access to the TGS. The AS responds with a message, encrypted with a key derived from the user's password (K_c), that contains the ticket. The encrypted message also contains a copy of the session key, $K_{c,tgs}$, where the subscripts indicate that this is a session key for C and TGS. Because this session key is inside the message encrypted with K_c, only the user's client can read it. The same session key is included in the ticket, which can be read only by the TGS. Thus, the session key has been securely delivered to both C and the TGS.

Before proceeding, note that several additional pieces of information have been added to this first phase of the dialogue. Message (1) includes a time stamp, so that the AS knows that the message is timely. Message (2) includes several elements of the ticket in a form accessible to C. This enables C to confirm that this ticket is for the TGS and to learn its expiration time.

Armed with the ticket and the session key, C is ready to approach the TGS. As before, C sends the TGS a message that includes the ticket plus the ID of the requested service (message (3) in Table 1b). In addition, C transmits an authenticator, which includes the ID and address of C's user and a time stamp. Unlike the ticket, which is reusable, the authenticator is intended for use only once and has a very short lifetime. The TGS can decrypt the ticket with the key that it shares with the AS. This ticket indicates that user C has been provided with the session key $K_{c,tgs}$. In effect, the ticket says, "Anyone who uses $K_{c,tgs}$ must be C." The TGS uses the session key to decrypt the authenticator. The TGS can then check the name and address from the authenticator with that of the ticket and with the network address of the incoming message. If all match, then the TGS is assured that the sender of the ticket is indeed the ticket's real owner. In effect, the authenticator says, "At time TS_3, I hereby use $K_{c,tgs}$." Note that the ticket does not prove anyone's identity but is a way to distribute keys securely.

It is the authenticator that proves the client's identity. Because the authenticator can be used only once and has a short lifetime, the threat of an opponent stealing both the ticket and the authenticator for presentation later is countered.

The reply from the TGS, in message (4), follows the form of message (2). The message is encrypted with the session key shared by the TGS and C and includes a session key to be shared between C and the server V, the ID of V, and the time stamp of the ticket. The ticket itself includes the same session key.

C now has a reusable service-granting ticket for V. When C presents this ticket, as shown in message (5), it also sends an authenticator. The server can decrypt the ticket, recover the session key, and decrypt the authenticator.

If mutual authentication is required, the server can reply as shown in message (6) of Table 1. The server returns the value of the time stamp from the authenticator, incremented by 1, and encrypted in the session key. C can decrypt this message to recover the incremented time stamp. Because the message was encrypted by the session key, C is assured that it could have been created only by V. The content of the message assures C that this is not a replay of an old reply.

Finally, at the conclusion of this process, the client and server share a secret key. This key can be used to encrypt future messages between the two or to exchange a new random session key for that purpose.

Table 2 summarizes the justification for each of the elements in the Kerberos protocol, and Figure 1 provides a simplified overview of the action.

Kerberos Realms and Multiple Kerberi

A full-service Kerberos environment consisting of a Kerberos server, a number of clients, and a number of application servers requires the following:

1. The Kerberos server must have the user ID (UID) and hashed passwords of all participating users in its database. All users are registered with the Kerberos server.
2. The Kerberos server must share a secret key with each server. All servers are registered with the Kerberos server.

Such an environment is referred to as a **Kerberos realm**. The concept of *realm* can be explained as follows. A Kerberos realm is a set of managed nodes that share the same Kerberos database. The Kerberos database resides on the Kerberos master computer system, which should be kept in a physically secure room. A read-only copy of the Kerberos database might also reside on other Kerberos computer systems. All changes to the database must be made on the master computer system, however. Changing or accessing the contents of a Kerberos database requires the Kerberos master password. A related concept is that of a **Kerberos principal**, which is a service or user that is known to the Kerberos system. Each Kerberos principal is identified by its principal name. Principal names consist of three parts: a service or user name, an instance name, and a realm name

Networks of clients and servers under different administrative organizations typically constitute different realms. That is, it generally is not practical, or does not conform to administrative policy, to have users and servers in one administrative domain registered with a Kerberos server elsewhere. Users in one realm may, however, need access to servers in other realms, and some servers may be willing to provide service to users from other realms, provided that those users are authenticated.

Kerberos provides a mechanism for supporting such interrealm authentication. For two realms to support interrealm authentication, a third requirement is added:

3. The Kerberos server in each interoperating realm shares a secret key with the server in the other realm. The two Kerberos servers are registered with each other.

The scheme requires that the Kerberos server in one realm trust the Kerberos server in the other realm to authenticate its users. Furthermore, the participating servers in the second realm must also be willing to trust the Kerberos server in the first realm.

With these ground rules in place, we can describe the mechanism as follows (Figure 2): A user wishing service on a server in another realm needs a ticket for that server. The user's client follows the usual procedures to gain access to the local TGS and then requests a ticket-granting ticket for a remote TGS (TGS in another realm). The client can then apply to the remote TGS for a service-granting ticket for the desired server in the realm of the remote TGS.

The details of the exchanges illustrated in Figure 2 are as follows (compare Table 1):

(1) $\mathrm{C} \rightarrow \mathrm{AS}$: $ID_c \,||\, ID_{tgs} \,||\, TS_1$
(2) $\mathrm{AS} \rightarrow \mathrm{C}$: $E_{K_c}\left[K_{c,tgs} \,||\, ID_{tgs} \,||\, TS_2 \,||\, Lifetime_2 \,||\, Ticket_{tgs}\right]$
(3) $\mathrm{C} \rightarrow \mathrm{TGS}$: $ID_{tgsrem} \,||\, Ticket_{tgs} \,||\, Authenticator_c$
(4) $\mathrm{TGS} \rightarrow \mathrm{C}$: $E_{K_{c,tgs}}\left[K_{c,tgsrem} \,||\, ID_{tgsrem} \,||\, TS_4 \,||\, Ticket_{tgsrem}\right]$
(5) $\mathrm{C} \rightarrow \mathrm{TGS}_{rem}$: $ID_{vrem} \,||\, Ticket_{tgsrem} \,||\, Authenticator_c$
(6) $\mathrm{TGS}_{rem} \rightarrow \mathrm{C}$: $E_{K_{c,tgsrem}}\left[K_{c,vrem} \,||\, ID_{vrem} \,||\, TS_6 \,||\, Ticket_{vrem}\right]$
(7) $\mathrm{C} \rightarrow \mathrm{V}_{rem}$: $\mathrm{Ticket}_{vrem} \,||\, Authenticator_c$

The ticket presented to the remote server ($\mathrm{V}_{\mathrm{rem}}$) indicates the realm in which the user was originally authenticated. The server chooses whether to honor the remote request.

One problem presented by the foregoing approach is that it does not scale well to many realms. If there are N realms, then there must be $N(N-1)/2$ secure key exchanges so that each Kerberos realm can interoperate with all other Kerberos realms.

KERBEROS VERSION 5

Version 5 of Kerberos is specified in RFC 1510 and provides a number of improvements over version 4 (Kohl, Neuman, & Ts'o, 1994). This section begins with an overview of the changes from version 4 to version 5 and then looks at the version 5 protocol.

Differences Between Versions 4 and 5

Version 5 is intended to address the limitations of version 4 in two areas: environmental shortcomings and technical

Table 2 Rationale for the Elements of the Kerberos Version 4 Protocol (page 1 of 2)

	(a) Authentication Service Exchange
Message (1)	Client requests ticket-granting ticket
ID_C:	Tells AS identity of user from this client
ID_{tgs}:	Tells AS that user requests access to TGS
TS_1:	Allows AS to verify that client's clock is synchronized with that of AS
Message (2)	AS returns ticket-granting ticket
E_{K_c}:	Encryption is based on user's password, enabling AS and client to verify password, and protecting contents of message (2)
$K_{c,v}$:	Copy of session key accessible to client; created by AS to permit secure exchange between client and TGS without requiring them to share a permanent key
ID_{tgs}:	Confirms that this ticket is for the TGS
TS_2:	Informs client of time this ticket was issued
$Lifetime_2$:	Informs client of the lifetime of this ticket
$Ticket_{tgs}$:	Ticket to be used by client to access TGS
	(b) Ticket-Granting Service Exchange
Message (3)	Client requests service-granting ticket
ID_V:	Tells TGS that user requests access to server V
$Ticket_{tgs}$:	Assures TGS that this user has been authenticated by AS
$Authenticator_c$:	Generated by client to validate ticket
Message (4)	TGS returns service-granting ticket
$K_{c,tgs}$:	Key shared only by C and TGS; protects contents of message (4)
$K_{c,v}$:	Copy of session key accessible to client; created by TGS to permit secure exchange between client and server without requiring them to share a permanent key
ID_V:	Confirms that this ticket is for server V
TS_4:	Informs client of time this ticket was issued
$Ticket_V$:	Ticket to be used by client to access server V
$Ticket_{tgs}$:	Reusable so that user does not have to reenter password
$E_{K_{tgs}}$:	Ticket is encrypted with key known only to AS and TGS, to prevent tampering
$K_{c,tgs}$:	Copy of session key accessible to TGS; used to decrypt authenticator, thereby authenticating ticket
ID_C:	Indicates the rightful owner of this ticket
AD_C:	Prevents use of ticket from workstation other than one that initially requested the ticket
ID_{tgs}:	Assures server that it has decrypted ticket properly
TS_2:	Informs TGS of time this ticket was issued
$Lifetime_2$:	Prevents replay after ticket has expired
$Authenticator_c$:	Assures TGS that the ticket presenter is the same as the client for whom the ticket was issued; has very short lifetime to prevent replay
$E_{K_{c,tgs}}$:	Authenticator is encrypted with key known only to client and TGS, to prevent tampering
ID_C:	Must match ID in ticket to authenticate ticket
AD_C:	Must match address in ticket to authenticate ticket
TS_3:	Informs TGS of time this authenticator was generated
	(c) Client/Server Authentication Exchange
Message (5)	Client requests service
$Ticket_V$:	Assures server that this user has been authenticated by AS
$Authenticator_c$:	Generated by client to validate ticket
Message (6)	Optional authentication of server to client
$E_{K_{c,v}}$:	Assures C that this message is from V
$TS_5 + 1$:	Assures C that this is not a replay of an old reply
$Ticket_v$:	Reusable so that client does not need to request a new ticket from TGS for each access to the same server
E_{K_v}:	Ticket is encrypted with key known only to TGS and server, to prevent tampering
$K_{c,v}$:	Copy of session key accessible to client; used to decrypt authenticator, thereby authenticating ticket
ID_C:	Indicates the rightful owner of this ticket
AD_C:	Prevents use of ticket from workstation other than one that initially requested the ticket
ID_V:	Assures server that it has decrypted ticket properly
TS_4:	Informs server of time this ticket was issued
$Lifetime_4$:	Prevents replay after ticket has expired
$Authenticator_c$:	Assures server that the ticket presenter is the same as the client for whom the ticket was issued; has very short lifetime to prevent replay
$E_{K_{c,v}}$:	Authenticator is encrypted with key known only to client and server, to prevent tampering
ID_C:	Must match ID in ticket to authenticate ticket
AD_c:	Must match address in ticket to authenticate ticket
TS_5:	Informs server of time this authenticator was generated

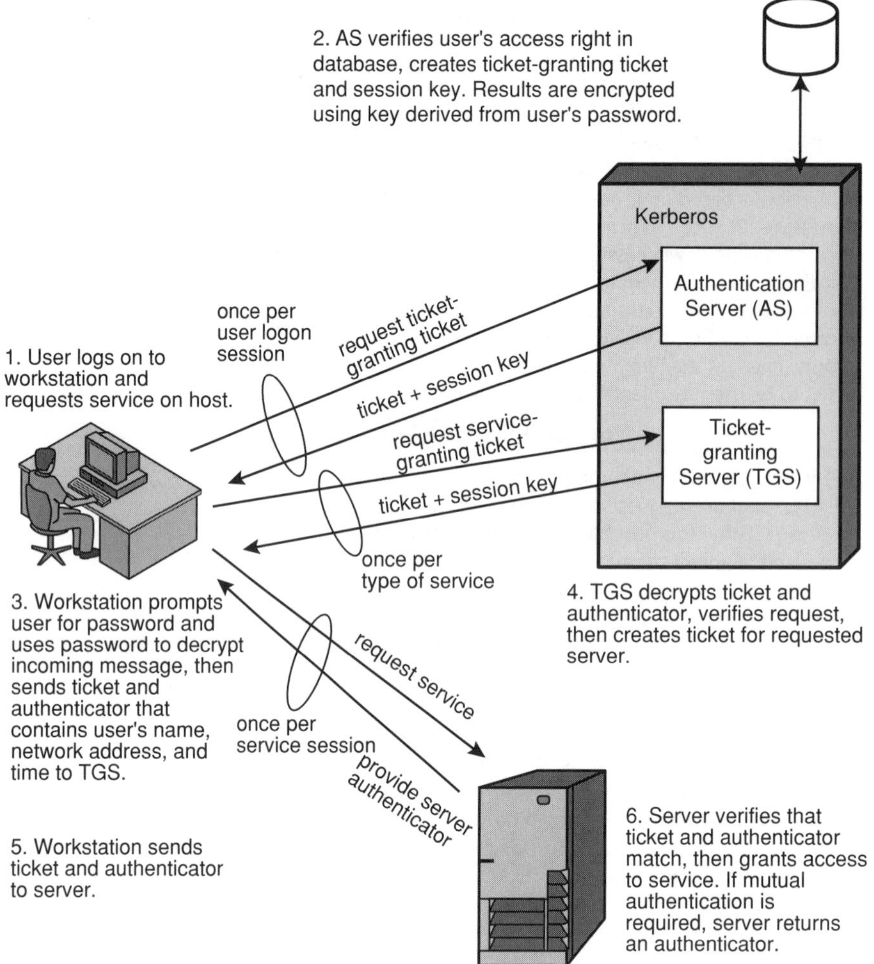

Figure 1: Overview of Kerberos.

deficiencies. Let us briefly summarize the improvements in each area (the following discussion follows the presentation in Kohl et al., 1994).

Version 4 of Kerberos was developed for use within the Project Athena environment and, accordingly, did not fully address the need to be of general purpose. This led to the following **environmental shortcomings:**

1. **Encryption system dependence:** Version 4 requires the use of DES. Export restriction on DES as well as doubts about its the strength are thus of concern. In version 5, ciphertext is tagged with an encryption type identifier so that any encryption technique may be used. Encryption keys are tagged with a type and a length, allowing the same key to be used in different algorithms and allowing the specification of variations on a given algorithm.
2. **Internet protocol dependence:** Version 4 requires the use of Internet protocol (IP) addresses. Other address types, such as the ISO (International Standards Organization) network address, are not accommodated. Version 5 network addresses are tagged with type and length, allowing any network address type to be used.
3. **Message byte ordering:** In version 4, the sender of a message employs a byte ordering of its own choosing and tags the message to indicate least significant byte in lowest address or most significant byte in lowest address. This technique works but does not follow established conventions. In version 5, all message structures are defined using Abstract Syntax Notation One (ASN.1) and Basic Encoding Rules (BER), which provide an unambiguous byte ordering.
4. **Ticket lifetime:** Lifetime values in version 4 are encoded in an 8-bit quantity in units of five minutes. Thus, the maximum lifetime that can be expressed is $2^8 \times 5 = 1280$ minutes, or a little over 21 hours. This may be inadequate for some applications (e.g., a long-running simulation that requires valid Kerberos credentials throughout execution). In version 5, tickets include explicit start and end times, allowing tickets with arbitrary lifetimes.
5. **Authentication forwarding:** Version 4 does not allow credentials issued to one client to be forwarded to some other host and used by some other client. This capability would enable a client to access a server and have that server access another server on behalf of the client. For example, a client issues a request to a print server that then accesses the client's file from a file server, using the client's credentials for access. Version 5 provides this capability.

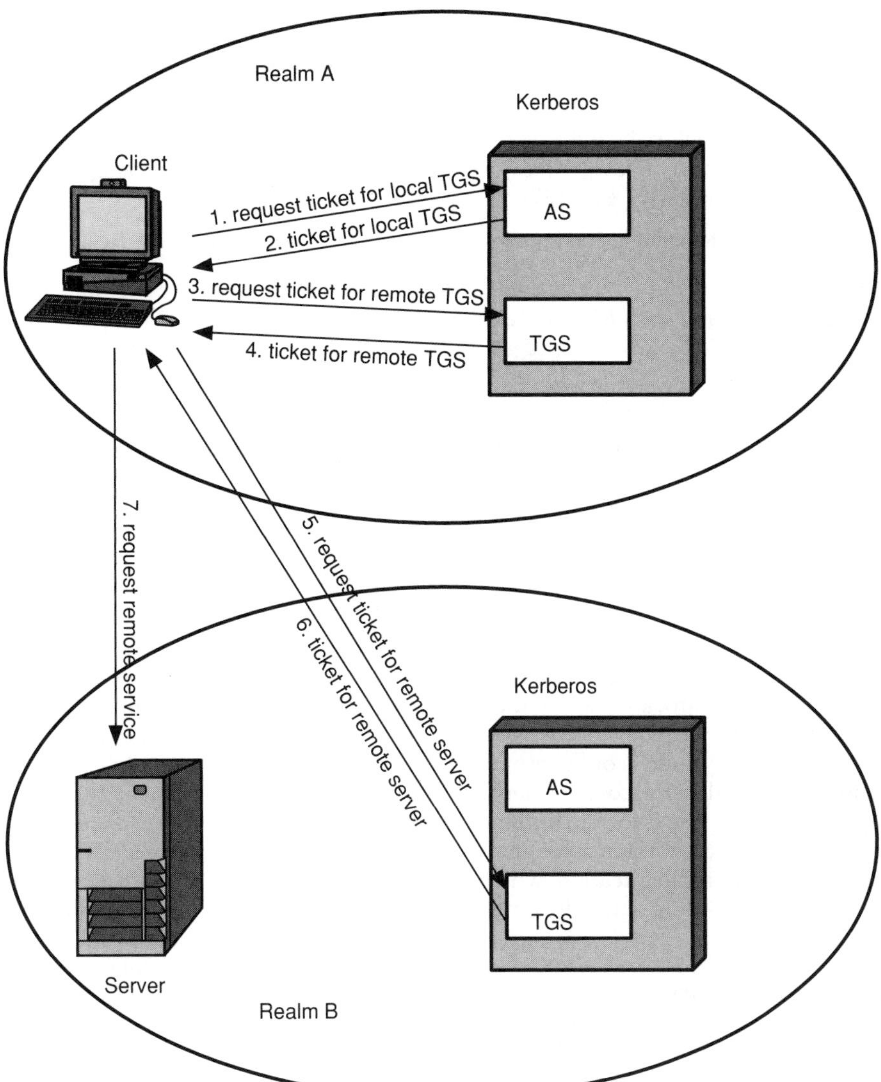

Figure 2: Request for service in another realm.

6. **Interrealm authentication:** In version 4, interoperability among N realms requires on the order of N^2 Kerberos-to-Kerberos relationships, as described earlier. Version 5 supports a method that requires fewer relationships, as described shortly.

Apart from these environmental limitations, there are *technical deficiencies* in the version 4 protocol. Most of these deficiencies were documented in (Bellovin & Merritt, 1990), and version 5 attempts to address these. The deficiencies are the following:

1. **Double encryption:** Note in Table 1 [messages (2) and (4)] that tickets provided to clients are encrypted twice, once with the secret key of the target server and then again with a secret key known to the client. The second encryption is not necessary and is computationally wasteful.
2. **PCBC encryption:** Encryption in version 4 makes use of a nonstandard mode of DES known as propagating block chaining (PCBC). It has been demonstrated that this mode is vulnerable to an attack involving the interchange of ciphertext blocks (Kohl, 1989). PCBC was intended to provide an integrity check as part of the encryption operation. Version 5 provides explicit integrity mechanisms, allowing the standard CBC mode to be used for encryption.
3. **Session keys:** Each ticket includes a session key that is used by the client to encrypt the authenticator sent to the service associated with that ticket. In addition, the session key may subsequently be used by the client and the server to protect messages passed during that session. However, because the same ticket may be used repeatedly to gain service from a particular server, there is the risk that an opponent will replay messages from an old session to the client or the server. In version 5, it is possible for a client and server to negotiate a subsession key, which is to be used only for that one connection. A new access by the client would result in the use of a new subsession key.
4. **Password attacks:** Both versions are vulnerable to a password attack. The message from the AS to the client

Table 3 Summary of Kerberos Version 5 Message Exchanges

(a) Authentication Service Exchange: To Obtain Ticket-Granting Ticket

(1) C → AS: Options $\|$ ID_c $\|$ $Realm_c$ $\|$ ID_{tgs} $\|$ $Times$ $\|$ $Nonce_1$

(2) AS → C: $Realm_c \| ID_c \| Ticket_{tgs} \| \mathrm{E}_{K_c}[K_{c,tgs} \| Times \| Nonce_1 \| Realm_{tgs} \| ID_{tgs}]$

$Ticket_{tgs} = E_{K\,tag}[Flag \| K_{c,tag} \| Realm_C \| ID_c \| AD_c \| Times]$

(b) Ticket-Granting Service Exchange: To Obtain Service-Granting Ticket

(3) C → TGS: Options $\| ID_v \| Times \| \| \| Nonce_2 \| Ticket_{tgs} \| Authenticator_c$

(4) C → TGS: $Realm_c \| ID_c \| Ticket_v \| \mathrm{E}_{K_{c,tgs}}[K_{c,v} \| Times \| Nonce_2 \| Realm_v \| ID_v]$

$Ticket_{tgs} = E_{K_{tgs}}[Flags \| k_{c,tgs} \| Realm_c \| ID_c \| AD_c \| Times]$

$Ticket_v = E_{K_v}[Flags \| \mathrm{K}_{c,v} \| Realm_c \| ID_c \| AD_c \| Times]$

$Authenticator_c = E_{K_{c,tgs}}[ID_c \| Realm_c \| TS_1]$

(c) Client/Server Authentication Exchange: To Obtain Service

(5) C → V: Options $\|$ Ticket_v $\|$ $\mathrm{Authenticator}_c$

(6) V → C: $\mathrm{E}_{K_{c,v}}[\mathrm{TS}_2 \| \mathrm{Subkey} \| \mathrm{Seq\#}]$

$Ticket_v = E_{K_v}[Flags \| k_{c,v} \| Realm_c \| ID_c \| AD_c \| Times]$

$Authenticator_c = E_{K_{c,v}}[ID_c \| Realm_c \| TS_2 \| Subkey \| Seq\#]$

includes material encrypted with a key based on the client's password. An opponent can capture this message and attempt to decrypt it by trying various passwords. If the result of a test decryption is of the proper form, then the opponent has discovered the client's password and may subsequently use it to gain authentication credentials from Kerberos. Version 5 does provide a mechanism known as preauthentication, which should make password attacks more difficult, but it does not prevent them.

The Version 5 Authentication Dialogue

Table 3 summarizes the basic version 5 dialogue. This is best explained by comparison with version 4 (Table 1). First, consider the *authentication service exchange*. Message (1) is a client request for a ticket-granting ticket. As before, it includes the ID of the user and the TGS. The following new elements are added:

- **Realm:** Indicates realm of user
- **Options:** Used to request that certain flags be set in the returned ticket
- **Times:** Used by the client to request the following time settings in the ticket:
  —from: the desired start time for the requested ticket
  —till: the requested expiration time for the requested ticket
  —rtime: requested renew-till time
- **Nonce:** A random value to be repeated in message (2) to ensure that the response is fresh and has not been replayed by an opponent

Message (2) returns a ticket-granting ticket, identifying information for the client, and a block encrypted using the encryption key based on the user's password. This block includes the session key to be used between the client and the TGS, times specified in message (1), the nonce from message (1), and TGS identifying information. The ticket itself includes the session key, identifying information for the client, the requested time values, and flags that reflect the status of this ticket and the requested options. These flags introduce significant new functionality to version 5. For now, we defer a discussion of these flags and concentrate on the overall structure of the version 5 protocol.

Let us now compare the *ticket-granting service exchange* for versions 4 and 5. We see that message (3) for both versions includes an authenticator, a ticket, and the name of the requested service. In addition, version 5 includes requested times and options for the ticket and a nonce, all with functions similar to those of message (1). The authenticator itself is essentially the same as the one used in version 4.

Message (4) has the same structure as message (2), returning a ticket plus information needed by the client, the latter encrypted with the session key now shared by the client and the TGS.

Finally, for the *client–server authentication exchange*, several new features appear in version 5. In message (5), the client may request as an option that mutual authentication is required. The authenticator includes several new fields as follows:

- **Subkey:** The client's choice for an encryption key to be used to protect this specific application session. If this field is omitted, the session key from the ticket ($K_{c,v}$) is used.
- **Sequence number:** An optional field that specifies the starting sequence number to be used by the server for messages sent to the client during this session. Messages may be sequence numbered to detect replays.

If mutual authentication is required, the server responds with message (6). This message includes the time stamp from the authenticator. Note that in version 4, the time stamp was incremented by one. This is not necessary in version 5 because the nature of the format of messages is such that it is not possible for an opponent to

Table 4 Kerberos Version 5 Flags

INITIAL	This ticket was issued using the AS protocol and not issued based on a ticket-granting ticket.
PRE-AUTHENT	During initial authentication, the client was authenticated by the KDC before a ticket was issued.
HW-AUTHENT	The protocol employed for initial authentication required the use of hardware expected to be possessed solely by the named client.
RENEWABLE	Tells TGS that this ticket can be used to obtain a replacement ticket that expires at a later date.
MAY-POSTDATE	Tells TGS that a postdated ticket may be issued based on this ticket-granting ticket.
POSTDATED	Indicates that this ticket has been postdated; the end server can check the authtime field to see when the original authentication occurred.
INVALID	This ticket is invalid and must be validated by the KDC before use.
PROXIABLE	Tells TGS that a new service-granting ticket with a different network address may be issued based on the presented ticket.
PROXY	Indicates that this ticket is a proxy.
FORWARDABLE	Tells TGS that a new ticket-granting ticket with a different network address may be issued based on this ticket-granting ticket.
FORWARDED	Indicates that this ticket has either been forwarded or was issued based on authentication involving a forwarded ticket-granting ticket.

create message (6) without knowledge of the appropriate encryption keys. The subkey field, if present, overrides the subkey field, if present, in message (5). The optional sequence number field specifies the starting sequence number to be used by the client.

Ticket Flags

The flags field included in tickets in version 5 supports expanded functionality compared with that available in version 4. Table 4 summarizes the flags that may be included in a ticket.

The INITIAL flag indicates that this ticket was issued by the AS, not by the TGS. When a client requests a service-granting ticket from the TGS, it presents a ticket-granting ticket obtained from the AS. In version 4, this was the only way to obtain a service-granting ticket. Version 5 provides the additional capability that the client can get a service-granting ticket directly from the AS. The utility of this is as follows: A server, such as a password-changing server, may wish to know that the client's password was recently tested.

The PRE-AUTHENT flag, if set, indicates that when the AS received the initial request [message (1)], it authenticated the client before issuing a ticket. The exact form of this preauthentication is left unspecified. As an example, the MIT implementation of version 5 has encrypted time stamp preauthentication, enabled by default. When a user wants to get a ticket, he or she has to send to the AS a preauthentication block containing a random confounder, a version number, and a time stamp, encrypted in the client's password-based key. The AS decrypts the block and will not send a ticket-granting ticket back unless the time stamp in the preauthentication block is within the allowable time skew (time interval to account for clock drift and network delays). Another possibility is the use of a smart card that generates continually changing passwords that are included in the preauthenticated messages. The passwords generated by the card can be based on a user's password but be transformed by the card so that, in effect, arbitrary passwords are used. This prevents an attack based on easily guessed passwords. If a smart card or similar device was used, this is indicated by the HW-AUTHENT flag.

When a ticket has a long lifetime, there is the potential for it to be stolen and used by an opponent for a considerable period. If a short lifetime is used to lessen the threat, then overhead is involved in acquiring new tickets. In the case of a ticket-granting ticket, the client would either have to store the user's secret key, which is clearly risky, or repeatedly ask the user for a password. A compromise scheme is the use of renewable tickets. A ticket with the RENEWABLE flag set includes two expiration times: one for this specific ticket and one that is the latest permissible value for an expiration time. A client can have the ticket renewed by presenting it to the TGS with a requested new expiration time. If the new time is within the limit of the latest permissible value, the TGS can issue a new ticket with a new session time and a later specific expiration time. The advantage of this mechanism is that the TGS may refuse to renew a ticket reported as stolen.

A client may request that the AS provide a ticket-granting ticket with the MAY-POSTDATE flag set. The client can then use this ticket to request a ticket that is flagged as POSTDATED and INVALID from the TGS. Subsequently, the client may submit the postdated ticket for validation. This scheme can be useful for running a long batch job on a server that requires a ticket periodically. The client can obtain a number of tickets for this session at once, with spread-out time values. All but the first ticket are initially invalid. When the execution reaches a point in time when a new ticket is required, the client can get the appropriate ticket validated. With this approach, the client does not have to use its ticket-granting ticket repeatedly to obtain a service-granting ticket.

In version 5, it is possible for a server to act as a proxy on behalf of a client, in effect adopting the credentials and privileges of the client to request a service from another server. If a client wishes to use this mechanism, it requests a ticket-granting ticket with the PROXIABLE flag set. When this ticket is presented to the TGS, the TGS is permitted to issue a service-granting ticket with a different network address; this latter ticket will have its PROXY flag set. An application receiving such a ticket may accept it or require additional authentication to provide an audit trail. For a discussion of some of the possible uses of the proxy capability, see Neuman (1993).

The proxy concept is a limited case of the more powerful forwarding procedure. If a ticket is set with the FORWARDABLE flag, a TGS can issue to the requestor a ticket-granting ticket with a different network address and the FORWARDED flag set. This ticket can then be presented to a remote TGS. This capability allows a client to gain access to a server on another realm without requiring that each Kerberos maintain a secret key with Kerberos servers in every other realm. For example, realms could be structured hierarchically. Then a client could walk up the tree to a common node and then back down to reach a target realm. Each step of the walk would involve forwarding a ticket-granting ticket to the next TGS in the path.

PERFORMANCE ISSUES

As client–server applications become more popular, larger and larger client–server installations are appearing. A case can be made that the larger the scale of the networking environment, the more important it is to have logon authentication. The question is, what impact does Kerberos have on performance in a large-scale environment?

Fortunately, the answer is that there is little performance impact if the system is properly configured. Keep in mind that tickets are reusable. Therefore, the amount of traffic needed for the granting ticket requests is modest. With respect to the transfer of a ticket for logon authentication, the logon exchange must take place anyway, so again the extra overhead is modest.

A related issue is whether the Kerberos server application requires a dedicated platform or can share a computer with other applications. It probably is not wise to run the Kerberos server on the same machine as a resource-intensive application such as a database server. Moreover, the security of Kerberos is best assured by placing the Kerberos server on a separate, isolated machine.

Finally, in a large system, is it necessary to go to multiple realms to maintain performance? Probably not. The 32,000-node application cited earlier is supported by a single Kerberos server. Rather, the motivation for multiple realms is administrative. If you have geographically separate clusters of machines, each with its own network administrator, then one realm per administrator may be convenient. This is not always the case, however.

CONCLUSION

Kerberos is an authentication protocol based on conventional encryption that has received widespread support and is used in a variety of systems. It is designed to provide strong authentication for client–server applications. The Kerberos protocol uses strong cryptography so that a client can prove its identity to a server (and vice versa) across an insecure network connection. After a client and server have used Kerberos to prove their identity, they can also encrypt all of their communications to ensure privacy and data integrity as they go about their business.

Kerberos does not solve all of the security problems facing a network manager, but it addresses many of the concerns raised in a client–server or similar networked environment. For the authentication application that Kerberos addresses, there are few other general-purpose alternatives. Most of the available solutions are limited to a single platform or single network operating system, whereas Kerberos is an Internet standard intended for use across all platforms and operating systems.

Kerberos is gaining increasing acceptance. For example, the Open Software Foundation's DCE (Distributed Computing Environment) uses version 5 of Kerberos for user authentication, and a number of vendors now offer Kerberos as part of their networking products. The public domain versions enjoy widespread use as well. As a tool for user authentication, Kerberos is likely to be one of the dominant approaches in the coming years.

GLOSSARY

Authentication A process used to verify the identity of a user involved in a data or message exchange.

Authentication Server A centralized Kerberos server with the function of authenticating users to servers and servers to users.

Kerberos An authentication protocol based on conventional encryption. In essence, Kerberos requires that a user prove his or her identity for each service invoked and, optionally, requires servers to prove their identity to clients.

Kerberos Realm An environment consisting of a Kerberos server, a number of clients, and a number of application servers.

Lifetime In Kerberos, the length of time for which a ticket is valid.

Nonce An identifier or number that is used only once.

Subkey A Kerberos client's choice for an encryption key to be used to protect this specific application session.

Ticket A package of information in a Kerberos exchange that includes identifiers and other parameters.

Ticket-Granting Server (TGS) A Kerberos server that creates tickets for use by Kerberos clients.

CROSS REFERENCES

See *Computer and Network Authentication; Encryption Basics; IBE (Identity-Based Encryption).*

REFERENCES

Bellovin, S., & Merritt, M. (1990, October). Limitations of the Kerberos authentication system. *Computer Communications Review*, pp. 119–132.

Bryant, W. (1988, February). *Designing an authentication system: A dialogue in four scenes*. Project Athena document. Retrieved from http://web.mit.edu/kerberos/www/dialogue.html

Kohl, J. (1989). The use of encryption in Kerberos for network authentication. *Proceedings of Crypto, 89*, pp. 35–43. Springer-Verlag.

Kohl, J., & Neuman, B. (1993, September). The Kerberos network authentication service. Internet Engineering Task Force, RFC 1510.

Kohl, J., Neuman, B., & Ts'o, T. (1994). The evolution of the kerberos authentication service. In Brazier, F., & Johansen, D. *Distributed Open Systems.* Los Alamitos, CA: IEEE Computer Society Press. Retrieved from http://web.mit.edu/kerberos/www/papers.html

Miller, S., Neuman, B., Schiller, J., & Saltzer, J. (1988, October 27). Kerberos authentication and authorization system. *Project Athena Technical Plan* (Section E.2.1). Cambridge, MA: Project Athena, Massachusetts Institute of Technology.

Needham, R., & Schroeder, M. (1978, December). Using encryption for authentication in large networks of computers. *Communications of the ACM,* pp. 993–999.

Neuman, B. (1993, May). Proxy-based authorization and accounting for distributed systems. *Proceedings of the 13th International Conference on Distributed Computing Systems*, pp. 283–291.

Steiner, J., Neuman, C., & Schiller, J. (1988, February). Kerberos: An authentication service for open networked systems. *Proceedings of the Winter 1988 USENIX Conference,* pp. 191–202, USENIX.

FURTHER READING

Garman, J. (2003). *Kerberos: The definitive guide.* Sebastopol, CA: O'Reilly.

IETF Kerberos Working Group. Retrieved from http://www.ietf.org/html.charters/krb-wg-charter.html

Information Sciences Institute Kerberos site. Retrieved from http://www.isi.edu/gost/info/kerberos

M.I.T. Kerberos Site. Retrieved from http://web.mit.edu/kerberos/www/

Rome, J. (n.d.). *How to Kerberize your site.* Retrieved from http://www.ornl.gov/~jar/HowToKerb.html

Tung, B. (1999). *Kerberos: A network authentication system.* Reading, MA: Addison-Wesley.

IPsec: AH and ESP

A. Meddeb, and N. Boudriga, *National Digital Certification Agency and University of Carthage, Tunisia*
Mohammad S. Obaidat*, *Monmouth University, NJ, USA*

TCP/IP LIMITATIONS AND IPsec RESPONSE

Nowadays, most of the Internet flows are left unprotected against cyber attacks. A packet that traverses the network can be intercepted by any host connected to the network (and lying along the transmission path). The packet can be replayed and its content can be modified or reproduced. Even the checksums, which are part of the Internet Packet format, if used as a security mechanism, cannot protect a packet from unauthorized alteration. The checksums were intended to protect against corruption caused by malfunctioning devices. If the data alteration is intentional, the attacker can recompute the checksum, and the packet will appear to be perfectly intact. This situation exists mainly because no real protection mechanism has been integrated into TCP/IP stack.

In order to provide security to their existing systems, many companies use firewalls. Such systems stand between LANs (which are considered as a trusted network) and the outside domain (which represents the untrusted world). Firewalls attempt to analyze the incoming packets of information and determine if they contain valid information. Integrating firewalls is considered a good security solution, however, this solution fails to provide various important security services such as origin authentication and anti-replay.

Recently, there has been an increasing demand to protect Internet flows while continuing to use the existing infrastructure. To achieve this goal, IPSec (IP security protocol) has been standardized by the IETF for IPv4. Because of the need for an IPv4 upgrade, it was reasonable that the new version of the Internet Protocol (IPv6) should provide IPSec as a predefined security system. Moreover, because the Internet is a large open network, the transition to the new version of the IP will not be immediate. Implementation should be compatible and adaptable to Ipv4 (AR series Router References Manual, 2003).

*Corresponding author

IPSec is a security protocol integrated to the IP layer, offering flexible cryptographic security services. These services are:

- **Data origin authentication/Connectionless data integrity:** This states that in a protected IP datagram, the source address, destination address, and datagram content cannot be maliciously modified in transit without detection by the receiver.
- **Replay protection:** This means that protected packets use a replay sequence number (provided from an increasing counter) to avoid replay attacks. Moreover, a replay sequence number window is defined, and only packets whose sequence number is in the window are accepted.
- **Confidentiality:** This means that an individual that is not taking part in a packet protection process (or security association) can not read the packet payload.

The above objectives are met through the use of traffic security protocols, which are the AH and the ESP. The IP AH protocol provides authentication for connectionless integrity and data origin authentication of IP packets. AH provides protection to an IP packet and to any further headers added by AH. The ESP protocol provides one or both of encryption for confidentiality and authentication for connectionless integrity and data origin authentication. ESP allows protection to an IP packet, but not to any further headers added by ESP. AH and ESP may be applied either alone or together to provide the desired set of security services for selected IP packets. They are designed to be algorithm-independent. This allows new algorithms to be added without affecting other parts of the implementation. The standards specify a set of default algorithms to ensure interoperability between IPSec implementations (Randall, Stephen, 1998). The use of these algorithms, with IPSec traffic protection and key management protocols, is intended to permit system and application developers to deploy high quality Internet layer and cryptographic security technologies (AR series Router References Manual, 2003).

IPSec sets up security associations (SAs), which refer to a set of attributes that provide security services to the traffic it carries. These services are afforded to an SA by the use of AH, or ESP, but not both. If both AH and ESP protection are needed by a traffic stream, then two or more SAs are created to provide protection to the traffic stream. To secure typical bi-directional communication between two hosts, or between two security gateways, two Security Associations (one for each direction) are required (AR series Router References Manual, 2003). SA can be nested, allowing different IPSec relationships to be active on the same link.

In order to establish a SA, IPSec relies on the Internet security association and key management protocol (ISAKMP, (Maughan, Schertler, Turner, 1998)), which defines protocol formats and procedures for security negotiation. An SA defines the used cryptographic algorithms and keys. It must be established between two peers before using IPSec and be defined for one of the two IPSec protocols (AH or ESP).

In addition to the SA concept, two other notions characterize the IPSec response. They are the security policy and the notion of mode. Security Policy constitutes a major feature of IPSec because it defines the rules used by the protocols to establish the behavior of the IPSec Policy over the traffic that flows to/from/via a node where IPSec is implemented. An IPSec rule consists of a series of data that determine a certain treatment to a specified traffic. As an example of policy to define these rules can contains: (a) a list of traffic flows, which can be defined by their source addresses, destination address, transport-level protocol, and the port; (b) a flow action, which specifies what treatment (e.g., allow, block, or negotiate security) to apply; (c) authentication methods, which defines the options for authentication during the initialization process, etc.

IPSec can operate in two modes: transport mode and tunnel mode. The transport mode is used between end-system hosts. It cannot be applied by an intermediate node (Router), because of the fragmentation and reassembly requirements. It is used by adding a new header to the IP and applying the cryptographic functions. With this method, the IP packet is totally protected without the protection of all the header fields.

With the tunnel mode, a new IP packet is created using an IP-in-IP tunneling construction. The secure functions are applied to the new packet as in transport mode. Therefore, the whole inner original packet is protected by IPSec (including header and payload), since this packet forms the payload of the outer packet. This mode provides better protection against traffic flow analysis. It is the unique mode between two security gateways. Another protocol used to negotiate the cryptographic keys is the IKE (Internet Key Exchange protocol). However, due to space limitation, we will not cover this aspect of the IPSec suite.

IPsec ARCHITECTURE

There are two major databases in the IPSec scheme: the Security Policy Database and the Security Association Database. The first database specifies the policies that determine the disposition of all IP inbound or outbound traffic from a host or security gateway in IPSec implementation. The security association database contains parameters that are associated with each security association. The main components of an IPSec architecture includes the A, the ESP, the Security Association Database (SAD), and the Security Policy Database (SPD).

Security Association Database

As defined below, a Security Association (SA) represents a contract between two peers and defines the security services that will be used between those two peers. The SA describes the cryptographic algorithms and the keys that will be used. The SAs are dynamic since they are expected to be regularly modified. The lifetime of an SA is limited by a maximum time duration or maximum number of protected bytes.

A security association is uniquely identified by a Security Parameter Index (SPI), an IP Destination Address, and a security protocol identifier (i.e., AH or ESP). By default, the Destination Address may be a Unicast address, an IP broadcast address, or a multicast group address. However, currently IPSec SA management mechanisms are defined only for Unicast address.

Two types of SA mode are defined: transport mode and tunnel mode SA. A transport mode SA defines a security association between two hosts. In IPv4, a transport mode security protocol header appears immediately after the IP header and any options, and before any higher layer protocols (e.g., TCP or UDP). In the same mode, in IPv6, the security protocol header appears after the base IP header and extensions, but it may appear before or after destination options, and before higher layer protocols (Kent, Atkinson, 1998).

A tunnel mode SA is essentially to be applied to a tunnel IP. Whenever the end of a security association is a security gateway, the SA should be in a tunnel mode. Therefore, a SA between two security gateways is always a tunnel mode SA since it is a SA between a host and a security gateway. We notice that for the case where traffic is destined to a security gateway (e.g., SNMP commands), which is acting as a host, a transport mode is allowed. Two hosts may establish a tunnel mode SA between them. The requirement for any transit traffic SA involving a security gateway to be a tunnel SA arises due to the need of avoiding potential problems with regard to fragmentation and reassembly of IPSec packets.

For a tunnel mode SA, there is an "outer" IP header that specifies the IPSec processing destination, and an "inner" IP header that specifies the final destination for the packet. The security protocol header appears after the outer IP header and before the inner IP header. If AH is employed in the tunnel mode, portions of the outer IP header afford protection, as well as all of the tunneled IP packet (i.e., all of the inner IP header is protected, as well as higher layer protocols). If ESP is employed in the same mode, the protection is afforded only to the tunneled packet, not to the outer header (Randall, Stephen, 1998).

As shown by Figure 1, data is normally processed at the network layer, where it is ultimately handed to the

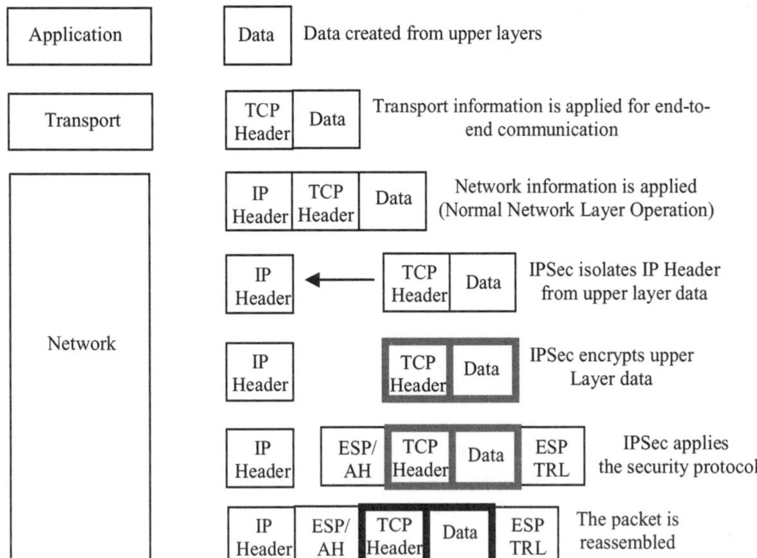

Figure 1: IPSec operations within transport mode (Tiller, 2001).

IPSec processing. In the transport mode, IPSec separates the original IP header from the remainig portions of the packet. The upper layer components are encrypted, and the AH header is calculated and inserted between the original IP header and the encrypted payloads of the original packet. By inserting an authentication protocol, the packet is afforded integrity of the data.

In the tunnel mode, IPSec encapsulates and encrypts the entire original packet and the AH protocol provides message integrity. After the creation of the authentication protocol header, a new IP header will be constructed to allow the remote client to send its data to the VPN gateway. Figure 2 presents the operation performed on the traffic of packets within a tunnel mode.

A SAD is designed by the IPSec response to contain all the SAs that are currently established with different IPSec peers. SAD is logically partitioned in two parts: the first part contains the SA protecting ingoing traffic, the second part contains the SA protecting outgoing traffic.

An SAD entry contains at least the following fields (Jourez, 2000):

- Destination IP address, IPSec protocol, and SPI: These are used to report on the packet destination, the IPSec protocol to be used (AH or ESP), and the Security Parameters Index (SPI), which is a 32 bit number, used to distinguish between the SA established to the same destination with the same IPSec protocol. These three values are a unique identifier for a specific SA.
- Sequence number counter: It is a 32 bit value used to generate a sequence number.
- Sequence counter overflow: This is a flag indicating whether a sequence number is exceeded. This value should prevent transmission of additional packets on the SA.
- Anti-replay window: This is a 32 bit counter and a bit-map or equivalent used to determine whether an inbound AH or ESP packet is a replay.

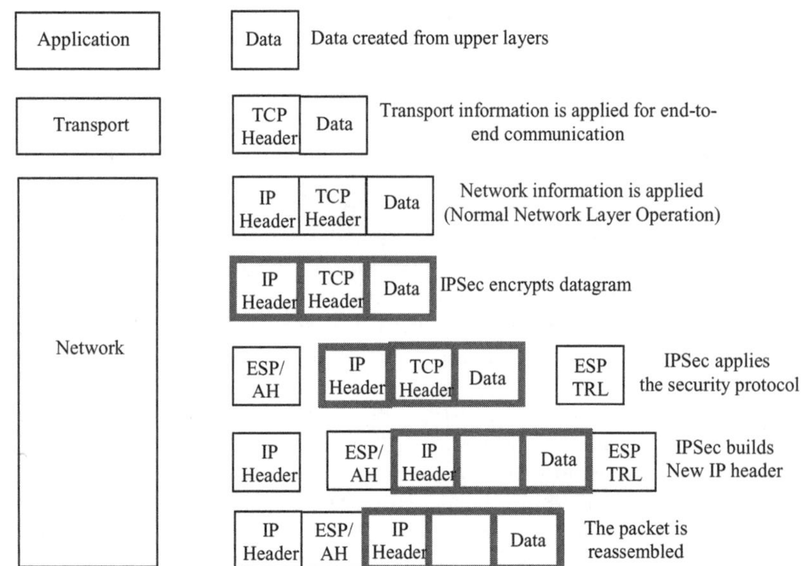

Figure 2: IPSec operations within tunnel mode (Tiller, 2001).

- AH parameters: This includes the authentication algorithm and the key to be used if AH is specified by the SA.
- ESP parameters for authentication: This includes the authentication algorithm and the key to be used if ESP is specified by the SA with authentication.
- ESP parameters for ciphering: This contains the encryption algorithm, the key and the initialization vector (IV) used if the SA specifies ESP.
- Mode: This field defines the mode used for the flow protection associated with the SA, i.e., tunnel or transport mode.
- Lifetime of the SA: This defines a time frame during which the SA will be used, or a maximum number of bytes protected by the SA.

A security policy may call for a combination of services for a particular traffic flow that is not achievable with a single SA. In such situations, it will be necessary to employ multiple SA to implement the required security policy. This is called "Security Association bundle" or "SA bundle." It is applied to a sequence of SA through which traffic must be processed to satisfy a security policy. The sequence order is defined by the policy. The SA that comprises a bundle may terminate at different endpoints. For example, one SA may extend between a mobile host and a security gateway and the next SA, may extend to a host behind the gateway.

Security Policy Database

A security policy database (SPD) contains the policies defined by the security system manager. As mentioned in the previous section, policies specify the security services that must be enforced. The SPD must be consulted during the processing of all traffic (incoming and outgoing), including non-IPSec traffic. When the traffic must be processed by IPSec, the SPD contains information about which IPSec protocol is used. In order to support this, the SPD requires distinct entries for inbound and outbound traffic. It is logically partitioned into two parts: one part considers the incoming traffic, while the other part considers the outgoing traffic.

The SPD must discriminate between traffic afforded by IPSec protection and traffic allowed to bypass IPSec. For any outbound or inbound datagram, three processing choices are possible: discard, bypass, or apply IPSec. The first choice refers to the traffic that is not allowed by the host to traverse the security gateway, or to be delivered to an application. The second choice refers to the traffic that is allowed to pass without additional IPSec protection. The third choice refers to the traffic afforded by IPSec protection. For such traffic, the SPD must specify the security services to be provided, protocols to be employed, and algorithms to be used. The SPD contains an ordered list of policy entries. Each policy entry is keyed by one or more selectors that define the IP traffic, encapsulated by this policy entry. These define the granularity of policies or SA. Each entry includes an indication of whether traffic matching this policy will be bypassed, discarded, or subject to IPSec processing. If IPSec processing is applied, the entry includes an SA (or SA bundle) specification, listing the IPSec protocols, modes, and algorithms to be employed, including any next requirements.

The selectors are defined by at least the following fields: destinations IP address, sources IP address, name (e.g., DNS user identifier, X.500 name, etc), data sensitivity level, transport layer protocol, and source and destination ports. A policy may specify whether a given SA must be negotiated for each different traffic flow matching the selector, or if a given SA may be used for those different flows. This is called the granularity of the policy. Finally, the policies in the SPD point to the SAs when they exist. This is a convenient way to retrieve a SA matching a specific policy.

Authentication Header

As mentioned above, AH ensures connectionless data integrity, data origin authentication, and optionally protection against replay for the entire packet. In fact, what is really authenticated is being in possession of shared secret, and not the IP address or the user having generated the packet. The authentication service offered by AH applies to the whole IP packet, payload as well as headers. Therefore, with AH, the data is readable, but remains protected from modification.

AH integrity and authentication are provided jointly, using an additional block added to protect the message. This block is called an Integrity Check Value (ICV). Thus, it is a generic term used to indicate either a Message Authentication Code (MAC) or a digital signature. Currently, all the proposed algorithms are obtained using a one-way hash function and a secret key. A generation of a digital signature is also possible to use a public key cryptography. Protection against replay is provided by a sequence number and its use can be selected by the recipient at the options negotiation moment.

The format of AH is depicted by Figure 3. It contains the following fields:

- Next header. This is an 8-bit value that gives the type of the payload that follows immediately the authenticator header (e.g., TCP, UDP).
- Payload length. This field contains an 8-bit value equal to the length of the AH, expressed as a number of 16-bit words contained in the header minus 1.
- Reserved field. This field is reserved for future use. Currently it is not used.

0 Next Header	Payload length	Reserved 31
Security Parameters Index (SPI)		
Sequence Number Field		
Authentication Data (variable)		

Figure 3: AH format (Doraswamy, Harkins, 1999).

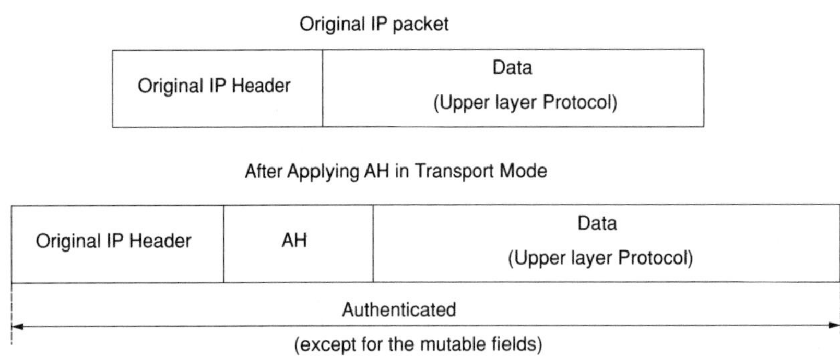

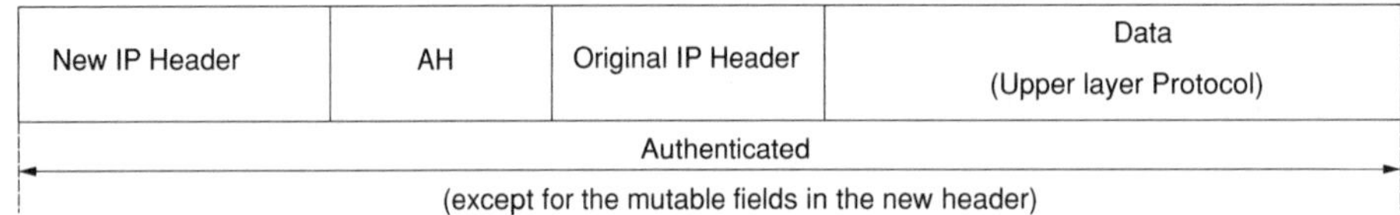

Figure 4: Position of AH in transport and Tunnel modes (IPv4) (Labouret, DAVIS, 2000, 2001).

- SPI field. This field is used to identify the appropriate SA.
- Sequence number. This field indicates the sequence number used for anti-replay. It is set by the source IPSec system and is monotonically increasing.
- Authentication data. This carries the authentication data using at least HMAC-MD5 and HMAC-SHA1 (Niels, Angelos, 2000). It is aligned to 32 bits by padding bits if necessary.

In the IPv6 context, AH is viewed as an end-to-end payload, and thus should appear after hop-by-hop, routing, and fragmentation extension headers. The destination extension header(s) options could appear either before or after the AH header depending on the semantics desired. In tunnel mode, the "inner" IP header carries the ultimate source and destination addresses, while an "outer" IP header may contain distinct IP addresses. Figure 4 indicates the position of AH and the service brought depending on the selected mode (transport or tunnel).

The authentication is computed over the whole IP packet in both tunnel and transport mode. This can lead to some problems since there are fields in the IP header (like TTL field) that may be modified while flowing through the network. To solve this problem, IPSec proposes to reset to 0, the fields included in the authentication computation.

Encapsulating Security Protocol (ESP)

ESP can ensure confidentiality, original authentication and data integrity, anti-replay service, and partial flow confidentiality (Kent, Atkinson, 1998). The different services may be selected separately. As in AH, authentication and integrity are two services that are often regrouped under the term "Authentication"; they are provided by the use of a Message Authentication Code (MAC). Protection against replay can be selected only if authentication was applied. It is provided by a sequence number, which is checked by the receiver of the packets (Labouret, 2000). In addition to the fields used in AH, the following fields of ESP are depicted in Figure 5:

- Initialization Vector (IV). This a vector used by the (current) ESP encryption algorithms.

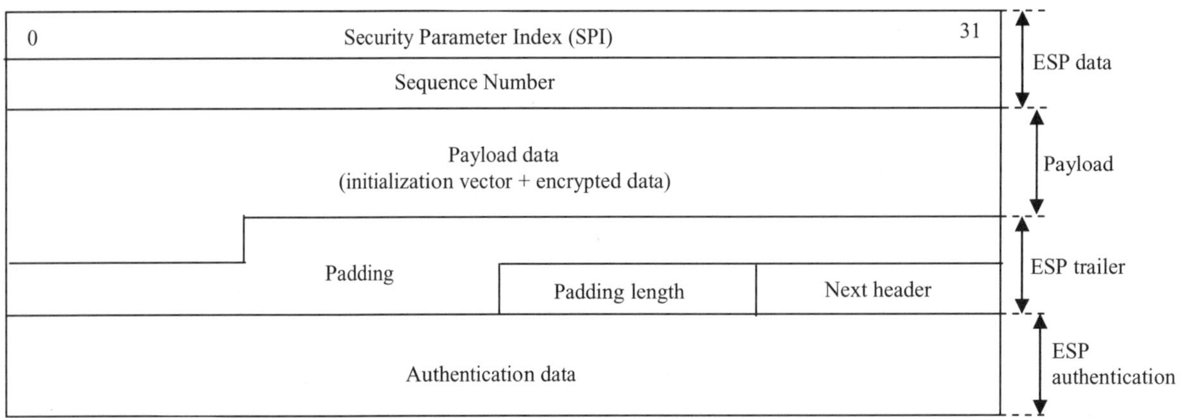

Figure 5: ESP format (Kent, Atkinson, 1998).

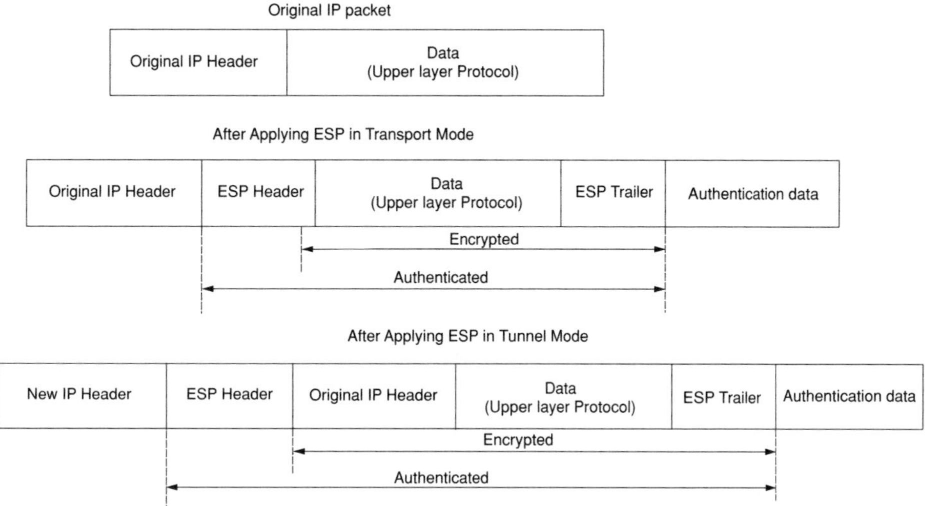

Figure 6: Position of ESP in transport and tunnel modes (IPv4) (Labouret, DAVIS, 2000, 2001).

- Padding. Padding bits are used to align the payload and the two following fields on a 32 bit boundary, as required by the encryption algorithm.
- Pad length. This is the size in bytes of the used padding.

If the confidentiality service is provided, then the Payload data, Padding, and Next header are encrypted. The initialization vector, which belongs logically to the Payload data is obviously never encrypted. In a minimal implementation, the selected encryption algorithm is DES. Other algorithms such as triple DES and AES may be used. In authentication service, ESP uses the same authentication algorithms as those used by AH. Figure 6 depicts the structure of an IPSec packets in its two modes of operation: transport and tunnel (Labouret, 2000).

IPsec PROCESSING

The IPSec processing is mainly classified into outbound versus inbound processing and AH versus ESP applications. Although the interface to various components of IPSec remains the same, packet processing is different between input and output. Protocol processing can be classified into SPD processing, SA processing, header processing, and transform processing. The SPD and SA processing are the same for both AH and ESP. The transform and header processing are differently realized with AH and ESP.

Outgoing Traffic Management

IPSec is applied to an outbound packet only after an IPSec implementation determines that there are associations between the packet and the SA. The first step in the IPSec processing is to query the SPD to find the applied policy on the outgoing packet. The selector is constructed from the traffic information found in the packet, such as, the source and destination IP address, the transport protocol, and the source and destination ports. The policy could specify the action to perform on the packet. If the packet must be discarded then, the action is performed and the IPSec processing ends. If the packet must be processed (i.e., IPSec applied), then either a SA exists for the given traffic, and so the SA is retrieved from the SAD, or the SA does not exist, and thus a new SA has to be created for the traffic.

If the SA is retrieved, the system gets the mode to be applied. If the tunnel mode is provided, then a new packet is created. The original packet becomes the payload of the new packet. In this case, the information of the original packet is left unmodified except for the TTL field of the IP header. Therefore, the checksum of the original packet must be recomputed. The header of the new IP packet is constructed from the original header by copying or computing parameters based on the SA content. Once the new packet is created, it may be processed by AH or ESP according to the SA. The next header field should be filled with the identifier of AH or ESP. After the AH or ESP processing, the packet could be reprocessed again by IPSec, if a bundle of SA is applied, or relayed to the lower communication layer.

Finally, we notice that fragmentation may occur after the IPSec processing. Fragmentation is needed because the IP datagram can become larger than the maximum transport unit supported by the underlying layer. This operation reduces the size of the IP packet by splitting it into parts with smaller size. Figure 7 describes the five steps of the IPSec processing. These steps summarize the above discussion: (a) receiving packet; (b) querying the SPD to discover the policy to apply; (c) querying SAD to retrieve the appropriate SA; (d) processing packet by applying AH or ESP using the SA; and (e) relaying the produced packet. Steps b, c, and d are looped until there are no more policies to apply.

AH Outbound Processing AH is applied to an outbound packet through the flowing steps:

1. Insertion of the AH header in the IP packet in processing.
2. Generation of the sequence number, which is set to 0 at the generation of the SA. This number is incremented and copied with each AH processing into the corresponding field of AH.

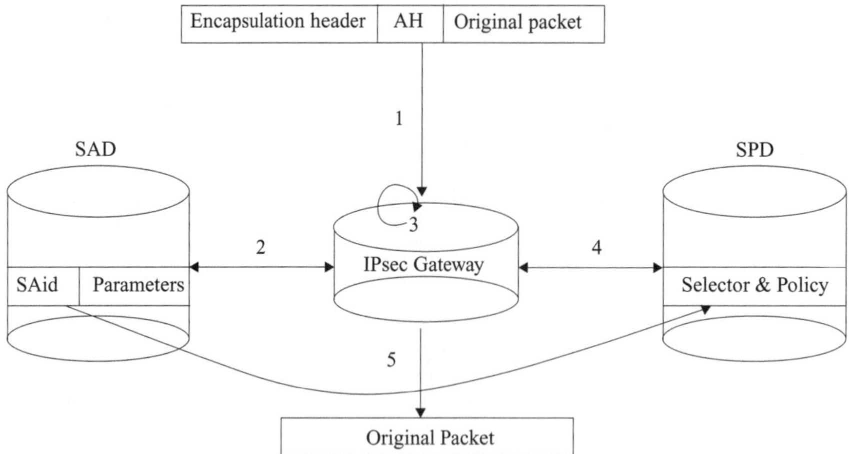

Figure 7: Outgoing traffic Processing (Jourez, 2000).

3. MAC computation. The algorithm of MAC computation defined by the SA is used to generate a message authentication code.
4. Padding. If required, the authentication data field is padded to align it to the IPv4 or IPv6 format
5. Fragmentation. The IP fragmentation can be applied to the packet after the AH processing

ESP Outbound Processing ESP is applied to an outbound packet only after an IPSec implementation determines that the packet is associated with an SA established for ESP processing. The steps for ESP outbound processing are (Jourez, Kent, & Atkinson, 2000, 1998):

1. Insertion of the ESP fields to the processed packet
2. Addition of the Padding if required. The fields Pad length and Next header are set to their values
3. Encryption. The ESP payload is encrypted using the algorithm and parameters specified by the SA. The application of the algorithm means that no ciphering is really applied
4. Generation of the sequence number. This is done in the same way as for AH processing
5. MAC computation. This is done if authentication is required. It is computed on the whole ESP packet with the exception of the last field containing the MAC. This step is skipped if authentication is not required
6. Fragmentation. If required, fragmentation is applied to the produced packet after the ESP processing.

Incoming Traffic Management

Before processing an incoming IP packet, the packet is reassembled. The IP packet that must be assembled is processed if its Next Protocol Field specifies AH or ESP. Otherwise, it is only checked using the SPD to verify if it matches the incoming policy. If the packet belongs to a traffic that does not have to be IPSec protected, then the packet is relayed; else, it is discarded.

For the other cases, the IPSec processing proceeds as follows: In the first step, the IP destination address, the IPSec protocol, and SPI are used to query the SAD in order to retrieve the SA used to protect the packet. In the second step, the destination checks the selectors to verify that they are defined by the SA, and if it is not the case, the packet is discarded. In the third step, an entry policy checks the packet selector to find out if this policy has been enforced. In the final step, the original packet is routed to the outgoing interface. During IPSec processing, AH or ESP may be applied.

AH Inbound Processing The different steps of the AH incoming traffic processing are described as follows:

1. **Sequence number validation.** If the retrieved SA specifies anti-replay protection, the sequence number is checked. If it is already encountered, the packet is discarded, else it is accepted.
2. **MAC validation.** The MAC value is verified by recomputing its value based on the SA parameters. If the received MAC value and the computed MAC value are equal, then the packet is accepted. Then in the next step, the AH is removed, the anti-replay is adjusted if necessary, and the AH processing is finished.

A sliding window is used to detect the duplication of the sequence number. It maintains the received sequence numbers between the lower and the upper bound of the window. When an incoming sequence number is lower than the lower bound of the window, then the packet is discarded. When the incoming number is greater than the higher bound, the window is slided upward and the sequence number is kept. A minimum window size of 32 bit must be supported. Another window size (larger than the minimum) may be chosen by the receiver.

If the received sequence number of the packet falls within the window, then the receiver will proceed to ICV verification. If the ICV validation fails, the receiver has to discard the received IP datagram as invalid. The audit log entry for this event should include the SPI value, date/time, Source Address, Destination Address, the Sequence Number, and the Flow ID (in the case of IPv6). Then, and only if the ICV verification succeeds, the received window is updated only if the ICV verification succeeds.

ESP Inbound Processing The following steps are included in the ESP processing:

1. **Sequence number validation.** This is done in the same way as in the AH case.
2. **MAC (Message Authentication Code) validation.** If authentication is required, the MAC value is recomputed and checked. If the two codes are not equal, the packet is discarded, else the processing continues.
3. **Original packet reconstruction.** This is done by: (a) decrypting the ESP Payload Data, Padding, Pad Length, and Next Header using the key, encryption, the algorithm mode, and the cryptographic synchronization data indicated by the SA; (b) adding any padding as specified in the encryption algorithm specification; and (c) reconstructing the original IP datagram from original IP header and the upper layer protocol information in the ESP Payload field for transport mode, or from tunnel IP header and the entire IP datagram in the ESP Payload field for the tunnel mode.

The reconstruction of the original datagram depends on the mode. At a minimum, in an IPv6 context, the receiver have to ensure that the decrypted data is an aligned 8-byte, to facilitate processing by the protocol identified in the Next Header field. If authentication has been selected, decryption and verification may be performed in serial or in parallel. If it is performed serially, then ICV verification should be performed first. If it is performed in parallel, verification must be completed before decryption. This order of processing facilitates the detection and the rejection of replayed packets by the receiver prior to decrypting the packet. This approach reduces the impact of denial of service attacks.

SECURITY POLICY MANAGEMENT

Security at the network layer can be used as a tool for at least two kinds of security architectures:

1. Security gateways: Security gateways use IPSec (Randall, Stephen, 1998) to enforce access control, protect the confidentiality and the authenticity of incoming and outcoming network, and to provide gateway services for virtual private networks (VPNs).
2. Secure end-to-end communication. Hosts use IPSec to implement host-level access control, to protect the confidentiality and the authenticity of network traffic exchanged between hosts, and to join virtual private networks.

As it has been stated, IPSec provides a reasonable basis for a wide range of protection schemes. This adds a large complexity to the SPD management, which becomes particularly critical where networks scale up and security policies get larger. When organizations deploy security gateways bridging heterogeneous regions that enforce different access controls and security policies, the wide range of choices of cryptographic parameters introduces the need for hosts and security gateways to identify and negotiate security parameters. Even more complexity arises as IPSec becomes the means through which various components enforce access control and VPN membership.

The level of protection offered by an IPSec is based on the requirements defined by the IPSec policies stored in the Security Policy Database. Policies should be established, maintained, and protected.

IPSec Policy Capabilities

IPSec Policy aims at providing a scalable and decentralized framework for managing, discovering and negotiating. It helps governing access, authorization, cryptographic mechanisms, confidentiality, data integrity, and other IPSec services. IPSec Policy is useful for a wide range of IPSec applications and modes of operation. In particular, we have the followings:

- IPSec Policy hosts may serve as IPSec endpoints, security gateways, network management hubs, or a combination of these devices. For this purpose, they can manage:
  - end-users computers, which may be fixed or mobile workstations offering remote access;
  - firewalls, which allow different levels of access to different classes of traffic and users classes;
  - VPN routers, which support links to other VPNs that can be controlled by a different organization's network policies; and
  - web and other servers, which might provide different services depending on the source of a client request.
- IPSec Policy administration can be inherently heterogeneous and decentralized. Two hosts can establish a security association without sharing a common security policy.
- The SA parameters, established between any pair of hosts, do not have to be specified in advance. An IPSec Policy will often have to negotiate and discover the mutually-acceptable SA parameters when two hosts attempt to create a new SA. Moreover, hosts can use policies that are not directly specified by an IPSec Policy language. For example, a host's IPSec Policy might be derived from a higher-layer security policy managed by some other systems.
- IPSec Policy must be scalable to support complex policy administration schemes. In small networks, the administrator should often control security policies (remotely, if needed) and must have the ability to change the policy on many different hosts at the same time. In larger networks, a host's policy might be governed by different authorities. Different parts of a policy might be "owned" by different entities and be organized in a complex hierarchy. Thus, IPSec Policy must provide a mechanism for delegating specific kinds of authority to different entities (Jourez, 2000).

IPSec Policy Configuration

In order to provide an efficient framework for the construction of coherent security policies and guarantee their interoperability, an IPSec Policy management should include the following components (Jourez, 2000):

- Policy Model. A Policy Model defines a well defined semantics that captures the relationship between IPSec SA and higher-level security policies. Policy specification, checking, and resolution should implement the semantics defined by the model. Moreover, the model should be independent of the specific policy mechanism.

- Security Gateway Discovery. The gateway discovery mechanism may be invoked by any host or gateway. Its goal is to determine if IPSec gateways exist between the initiator and the intended communication peer. The discovery mechanism may have to be invoked at any time, independent of existing security associations or other communication in order to detect topology changes.
- Policy Specification Language. In order to allow policy discovery, compliance checking, and resolution across a range of hosts, a common language is necessary to express the hosts' policies communicating with each other. Statements in this language are the output of policy discovery. They also provide the input to the policy resolution and compliance checking systems.
- Policy Discovery. A policy discovery mechanism must provide the essential information used by two IPSec endpoints to determine what kinds of SA are possible between the hosts. This is especially important for hosts that are not controlled by the same entity, and that might not initially share any common information about one another.
- Security Association Resolution. When two hosts have learned enough about each other's policies, it is possible to find an acceptable set of SA parameters that meets both hosts' requirements, and hence will lead to a successful creation of a new SA. Resolution aims to bridge heterogeneity between hosts' policies.
- Compliance Checking. When a host proposes the output of the SA resolution scheme, it must be checked for compliance with the local security policy. The created security of the SA should depend only on the correctness of the compliance checking stage. Even if the SA resolution scheme produces an incorrect result, it should not be possible to violate the specified policy of either host.

IPsec IMPLEMENTATIONS

IPSec can be implemented and deployed on end hosts and on gateways/routers depending on the security requirements of the users (Tiller, 2001). This section discusses the main features and implications of implementing IPSec on these network devices. There are merits of implementing IPSec in both routers and end hosts because they address different problems. The host implementation is most useful when security is implemented end to end. However, in cases where security is desired over a part of a network, router implementation is more useful.

Host Implementation

The host implementation has the following advantages. First, it provides an end to end security to implement all modes of IPSec. Second, it provides security to maintain the ability of user authentication in establishing IPSec connections. This kind of implementations can be classified into two classes: OS integrated implementation and Bump in the stack implementation.

OS Integrated In the host implementation, IPSec may be integrated within an OS. As IPSec is a network protocol, it may be implemented as part of the network layer (Doraswamy, Harkins, 1999). IPSec layer needs the use of the IP layer service to construct the IP header. There are various advantages of integrating IPSec with the OS. Among these are:

- This creates tight integration to the network layer as IPSec can benefit the network services such as fragmentation, and PMTU. In this case, implementation becomes very efficient.
- It is easier to provide security services
- All IPSec modes are supported

Bump in the Stack For companies providing solutions for VPNs and intranets, OS integrated solution has one serious disadvantage. On the end hosts, they have to work with the features provided by the OS vendors. This may limit their capabilities to provide advanced security solutions. To overcome this limitation, IPSec is implemented between the network and the data link layers. This is commonly referred to as a Bump in the Stack (BITS) implementation.

The major issue in this implementation is the duplication of effort. It requires implementing most of the features of the network layer such as fragmentation and route tables. Duplicating functionality leads to complications because it becomes more difficult to manage other issues such as fragmentation, PMTU, and routing.

An advantage of BITS implementation is its capability to provide a complete solution. This can be attractive to vendors providing integrated solutions such as firewalls. Vendors may prefer to have their own client when their OS may not have all the required features to provide a complete solution.

Router Implementation

The router implementation offers the ability to secure any packet between parts of a network. For example, an organization may want to secure only the packets destined to a distant branch as these packets traverse the Internet in order to build its VPN or Intranet. The IPSec implementation provides security using a tunnel mode (Doraswamy, Harkins, TILLER, 1999, 2001).

The following advantages are provided by router implementation:

- Ability to secure packets between two networks over a public network such as Internet.
- Ability to authenticate and authorize users, who enter the private network. This is the capability that many organizations use to permit their employees to telecommute their connections over the Internet to build VPN or Intranet.

There are two types of router implementation:

- Native implementation: This is similar to the OS integrated implementation on the hosts. In this case, IPSec is integrated with the router software.
- Bump in the Wire (BITW): This is similar to BITS implementation. In this case, IPSec is implemented in devices

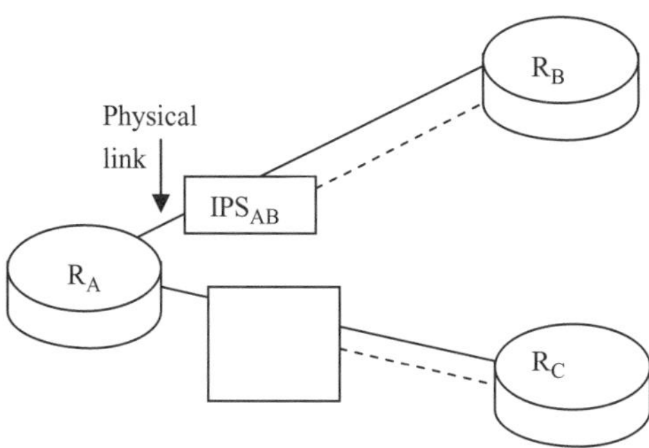

Figure 8: BITW deployment architecture (Doraswamy, Harkins, 1999).

attached to the physical interface of the router. These devices normally do not use any routing algorithm but the scheme is used only to secure packets. BITW is not a long-term solution as it is not possible to have a device attached to every interface of the router.

An example of the network architecture for the BITW implementation is shown in Figure 8.

In Figure 8, IPS_{AB} is a device that implements IPSec and R_A, R_B, R_C are routers. One of the secured links is between IPS_{AB} and R_B. The IPSec implementation has many implications on the packet-forwarding routers capabilities. They are expected to forward packets as fast as possible. Although, IPSec may not be used in the Internet core, the implementations should still be efficient. The packets that do not require security should not be affected because of the IPSec use. They should be forwarded at normal rates. Many implementations use some other hardware to perform signature operations, random number generation, encryption/decryption, and hashes calculation. There are special chipsets that assist the basic router hardware with security operations.

Another issue with router implementation is the IPSec contexts. Memory on the routers is still a scarce commodity, although this is changing as memory prices are falling. Since the router has to store huge routing tables and normally does not have very large storage for virtual memory support, maintaining too many IPSec contexts is a difficult issue.

LIMITATIONS, PERSPECTIVES AND ADVANCED ISSUES OF IPSEC

As described in the previous section, IPSec has the potential to add a useful layer of security to Internet traffic. The provided protections include source authentication, message integrity and confidentiality, anti-replay protection, and some sort of access control. Those protections qualify IPSec to be used efficiently in VPN gateways and remote hosts. The proliferation of Wireless LANs, 3G wireless networks, and mobile workers have made it highly desirable for remote hosts to be able to move among multiple networks (IP subnets) and even across different air interface technologies (Byoung-Jo, Srividhya, 2001). However, IPSec may risk two opposing types of failure. First, it may become so complex that it cannot be implemented in the hosts. Second, IPSec may fail to meet the needs of many components, which may be added with nonstandard (or proprietary) extensions (Frankel, 2001).

Advantages of IPSec

One of the main features of IPSec is that encrypted packets can be routed or switched on any network that supports IP traffic with no need to upgrade the network elements. This enables the packets to flow through LANs, Extranets and Intranets easily and transparently. It also means that there is no need for any modifications in the end hosts configurations. Unlike SSL, which only works with HTTP, IPSec can secure connections for all TCP/IP applications including a variety of protocols such as FTP, HTTP, SMTP, and TELNET. Moreover, due to its transparency, IPSec can also use other security layer protocols such as SSL and S/MIME. In addition, VPN solutions using IPSec as the basis for a common protocol can interoperate by opening up new services for securely sharing data.

Another advantage of IPSec comes from the fact that it is independent of network topologies. Since IPSec is adding security to the well-supported TCP/IP protocols, it interoperates with all network topologies including Ethernet, Token Ring, and PPP. Unlike other tunneling protocols like PPTP and its many variations like L2TP and STEP (none of them offers encryption), IPSec provides effective standards based on tunneling, authentication and encryption algorithms (Padmaraj, Nair, 2000).

The level at which IPSec protection is provided, the IP layer, constitutes also a major advantage. This means that all types of Internet traffic can be protected using IPSec, independently from the application conducting the communication. It also means that the granularity of protection can have a wide spectrum: A single SA can protect, for example, all communications between two hosts or two networks. The level and type of IPSec protection to be applied, as well as the keys to provide that protection, are both flexible and negotiable. Because specific applications do not have to be IPSec aware, users can be better protected. Moreover, a network administrator can determine and enforce either network or host policies.

Another important advantage of IPSec is that it can be deployed incrementally; unlike other network-related protocols or technologies. A business that leases private communication lines to link multiple sites can replace gradually one or more of those lines with an IPSec-protected VPN connecting the related sites. Moreover, IPSec is not limited to Enterprise wide use. A user who accesses remotely a PC can use IPSec to protect those communications (Frankel, 2001).

IPSec Limitations

Currently, the major operating systems and a growing number of devices are integrating standard compliant IPSec implementations. The current wide support to IPSec is significant. It will allow IPSec to be used as a universal security solution. However, IPSec is typically used only as an all or nothing protection for connecting two sites privately together or remote users to a central site and for end-to-end protection of application protocols. It is also rarely used for protecting the various control protocols of the Internet. This is unfortunate as the original goal of IPSec was to enable the protection of all types of communications between Internet nodes.

Other limitations of IPSec include (Arkko, Nikander, 2003):

- Lack of the power in policy specifications: The expressive power of the security policy entries needs to be increased in order to cover more information than the pair of addresses, the upper layer protocol identifier and the ports. Recent requirements have included description such as ICMP message types. Another shortcoming is the fact that IP addresses have not been extended by using semantic information. Given the example of the use of dynamic address assignment, and the growing use of mobility, privacy addressing, and multi-homing, an IP address does not identify this kind of hosts. A third lack is present because IPSec policies and security association parameters are tightly bound with IP addresses, this limits the freedom of the nodes when choosing the addresses used for communications. Given that not all protocols use static port numbers and that port numbers are not universally available in security gateways, decisions cannot always be made based on port numbers.
- Lack of application control over policies: Application control of policies is needed in various situations. First, it may be necessary to use IPSec in cases where there are no distinguishable selectors. Second, policies may need to be configured by applications for better quality assurance. Also, protocols can become widely deployed without the activation of the security. Third, end-host applications could set up the necessary entries since in many cases the expected policies are standardized. Some standard specifications require that the application is aware of the underlying security mechanisms, or at least when security mechanisms are activated.
- Lack of support for authorization and the inability to link authorization decisions with security processing: Not all peers have the same privileges. For example, the administrator of a host that is remotely connected has different privileges than an unknown peer connecting locally through IPSec. All peers whose identities are authenticated within a specific trust domain may still have different privileges. In order to use certificates for authorization, it is typically necessary to use either attribute certificates, create a separate certificate infrastructure for each different application, or introduce standardized extensions to the certificate formats to be able to express the authorization that the certificate represents. The traditional alternative, using local access control lists is not a viable option in a large network. More importantly, the security processing decisions require information from the application layer, or vice versa. In the current IPSec architecture all security processing is expected to be performed at the IPSec layer, and the application does not know if IPSec is being used. This makes it hard to accommodate finer decisions.

CONCLUDING REMARKS

According to the categories of IPSec limitations observed in the previous section, the following improvements appear necessary for the wider use of IPSec in securing applications (Arkko, Nikander, 2003):

- Make available a mechanism for applications to control policies. A specific application providing at least a default configuration for IPSec is recommended. This mechanism should help ensure that security is not accidentally turned off, and improve interoperability. It might help in dealing with the port number agility problem. The drawback of the approach is that it adds an additional problem to the applications. However, there is a trade-off between a one-time effort in software construction and manual configuration effort by all users, making the application based solution beneficial in the longer run. Unfortunately, such default configurations may not always suffice. For instance, the default configuration may not be compatible with specific requirements for protecting all traffic.
- Allow applications to make authorization decisions. One approach to allow applications to control authorization is to create an application programming interface (API) between IPSec and applications. The creation of this interface is particularly easy when the applications are parts of the IP stack such as in IPv6 control signaling. A standardized API would also make it possible for user space applications to rely on IPSec in order to provide meaningful security information to them. However, it is not enough to copy the IPSec security policy database functionality to the application layer; the application layer policy information has to be presented in semantic form. For instance, policies are based on application concepts rather than port numbers. In order to make use of the API, applications need tools to deal with authorization questions. Moreover, an application may have a need to perform certificate chain validation to a particular trusted root. Such needs can be satisfied either through the use of API or via specific libraries. The use of certificates for authorization purposes requires certificate mechanisms extensions to represent authorization information in an easy manner.
- Reduce the reliance on IP addresses in the policies. This reduction applies to IPSec security associations in policy entries and in application layer policies. An example of this approach is available in the form of the Host Identity Protocol (HIP) proposal. Reducing reliance on IP addresses is necessary to allow for address agility. While the enhancement of the expressive power of IPSec policies appears necessary, it seems hard to decide exactly how much more expressive policies should be used.
- Use IPSec in mobile environment: IPSec permits access to resources in protected corporate intranets while working remotely through an IPSec tunnel. Currently, IPSec does not support Mobile IP movements without breaking and re-establishing IPSec tunnels. Attempts have been made to solve this problem, including the establishment of IPSec tunnels over Mobile IP to enable mobility (Byoung-Jo, Srividhya, 2001).

GLOSSARY

Authentication Header (AH) provides authenticity guarantee for packets, by attaching strong crypto checksum to packets.

Encapsulating Security Payload (ESP) provides confidentiality guarantee for packets, by encrypting packets with encryption algorithms.

IPSec is a set of extensions to the IP protocol family providing cryptographic security services that provide for confidentiality and authentication of individual IP packets.

Security Association (SA) is a contract between two parties indicating what security parameters, such as keys, algorithms, and rules that were negotiated and agreed upon by two nodes.

Security Policy A set of rules that defines the network security parameters of an entity, including authentication, access control, content security, logging, network address translation, and other security components.

Transport mode IPSec mode of operation in which the data payload is encrypted, but the original IP header is left untouched.

Tunnel mode IPSec mode of operation in which the entire IP packet, including the header, is encrypted and authenticated and a new header is added, protecting the entire original packet.

CROSS REFERENCES

See *Computer and Network Authentication; IPsec; IKE (Internet Key Exchange); Security Policy Guidelines; TCP/IP Suite; VPN Basics.*

REFERENCES

Bell, D. E., & La Padula, L. J. (1976). *Secure computer systems: Unified exposition and Multics interpretation* (Tech. Rep. ESD-TR-75-306). Bedford, MA: MITRE Corporation.

Biba, K. J. (1977). *Integrity considerations for secure computer systems*. Technical Report MTR 3143, Bedford MA, MITRE Corporation.

British Standard Institute (BSI). (2000). *ISO 17799 toolkit: Policy templates.* Retrieved September 13, 2004, from http://www.iso17799software.com

Campbell, K., Gordon, L. A., Loeb, M. P., & Zhou, L. (2003). The economic cost of publicly announced information security breaches: Empirical evidence from the stock market. *Journal of Computer Security, 11*, 431–448.

Canavan, J. E. (2001). *Fundamentals of network security* (pp. 239–259). Norwood, MA: Artech House.

Canavan, J. E. (2003). *An information security policy: Development guides for large companies*. Bethesda, MD: SANS Institute.

Cholvy, L., & Cuppens, F. (1997, July). *Analyzing consistency of security policies*. Paper presented at the IEEE Symposium on Security and Privacy, Oakland, CA.

CSI/FBI. (2004). *Computer crime and security survey*. Retrieved January 24, 2005, from http://www.gocsi.com

Hare, C. (2000). Policy development. In H. F. Tipton & M. Krause (Eds.), *Handbook of information security* (Vol. 3, Chap. 20, pp. 353–389). New York, NY: Auerbach.

Internet Engineering Task Force (IETF). (1997). *Site security handbook* (RFC 2196). IETF Network Working Group. Retrieved August 24, 2004, from http://www.ietf.org/rfc/rfc2196.txt

Internet Security Systems (ISS). (2000). *Creating, implementing and managing the information security lifecycle.* Retrieved August 24, 2004, from http://documents.iss.net/whitepapers/securitycycle.pdf

Peltier, T. R. (2001). *Information security risk analysis*. New York, NY: Auerbach.

Purser, C. (2004). *A practical guide to managing information security*. Norwood, MA: Artech House.

Ryan, P. Y. A. (2000). *Mathematical models of computer security* (pp. 1–62). Lecture Notes in Computer Science, 2171. Berlin: Springer-Verlag.

Siewe, F., Cau, A., & Zedan, H. (2003, October). *A compositional framework for access control policies enforcement.* Paper presented at the ACM Conference on Computer Security, FMSE '03, Washington.

Swanson, M. (1998). *Guide for developing security plans for information technology systems* (NIST Special Publication 800-18). Retrieved September 4, 2004, from http://www.csrc.nist.gov/publications/nistpubs/800-18/Planguide.pdf

Tudor, J. K. (2001). Security policies, standards, and procedures. In *Information security architecture: An integrated approach to security in the organization* (pp. 79–100). New York, NY: Auerbach.

Wilson, M., & Hash, J. (2003). *Building an information technology security awareness and training program* (NIST Special Publication 800-50). Retrieved September 4, 2004, from http://www.csrc.nist.gov/publications/nistpubs/800-50/NIST-SP800-50.pdf

IPsec: IKE (Internet Key Exchange)

Charlie Kaufman, *Microsoft Corporation*

INTRODUCTION

The IPsec (Internet Protocol Security) protocol cryptographically protects messages sent over the Internet on a packet-by-packet basis, as opposed to other protocols such as secure sockets layer (SSL) or secure multipurpose Internet e-mail extension (S/MIME) that encrypt larger messages before breaking them into packets. The major advantage of the IPsec approach is that it can be done transparently to applications. It can be done by the underlying operating system—or even by an external networking device—without making any changes to applications. IPsec is commonly used to *tunnel* messages between two trusted networks over an untrusted network, where the ultimate sending and receiving machines are not aware of any cryptographic processing.

In order that the IPsec end points be able to protect messages cryptographically, they must agree on which cryptographic algorithms and keys to use. To detect and discard long delayed and replayed packets, they must also agree on sequence numbers and keep them in sync. This shared state is called a *security association,* or SA. Although all of this shared state could in theory be configured manually (and indeed, in some cases it is), it is more flexible and robust to have the end points initialize this shared state when needed using the *Internet key exchange* (IKE) protocol. Typically this is done when either end point starts up, and in some circumstances SAs will be forgotten and reinitialized if there are no packets to forward for an extended period. When IPsec is used to protect communication between a mobile end point (e.g., an employee's laptop computer) connecting through a public network to a protected corporate network, IKE is used to initialize an SA each time the mobile end point restarts or changes address.

Before IKE can be used to initialize an SA, the two end points need some information about one another. The initiator must know the address of the other end point, and if packets destined to multiple destinations are to be tunneled to this intermediate end point the initiator must know that. Both end points must know what sort of authentication they will require of the other end before being willing to establish the SA, and they must know what cryptographic algorithms they are willing to use. To allow the two end points to have their configurations updated independently, it is desirable to allow either or both end points to support multiple options and for them to find acceptable shared settings as part of the IKE negotiation. Otherwise, communications would fail in the interval between the updates of the two end points.

IKE is a protocol by which two parties (call them "Bob" and "Alice") establish an SA for the IPsec protocol. An SA is the shared state necessary to carry on a cryptographically protected conversation, including cryptographic keys, sequence numbers, identity of the other side, and policies for what traffic should be allowed. IKE negotiates cryptographic algorithms to use for the exchange, negotiates the types of traffic acceptable on the SA, performs mutual authentication, and establishes shared keys for the SA. There are two kinds of SA for carrying user data. The more commonly used is ESP (encapsulated security payload), which usually carries encrypted and integrity-protected data. The other is AH (authentication header), which carries data that is integrity protected but not encrypted. IKE version 1 is documented in RFCs (Requests for Comment) 2407 (Piper, 1998), 2408 (Maughhan, Schertler, Schneider, & Turner, 1998), and 2409 (Harkins & Carrel, 1998). The protocol underwent a major revision for fixing flaws, increasing efficiency, and simplification in IKE version 2, which is currently an Internet draft. IKE has some additional features such as denial of service protection, identity hiding, the ability to traverse NATs (network address translators), and the ability for a firewall to assign an internal address. This chapter discusses the operation of the basic protocol and the rationale for various options and extensions.

IKE USAGE SCENARIOS

There are three distinct scenarios in which IPsec and IKE are used. Rather than using three separate protocols to support them, IKE (and to a lesser degree IPsec) supports protocol variations for the three scenarios: gateway to

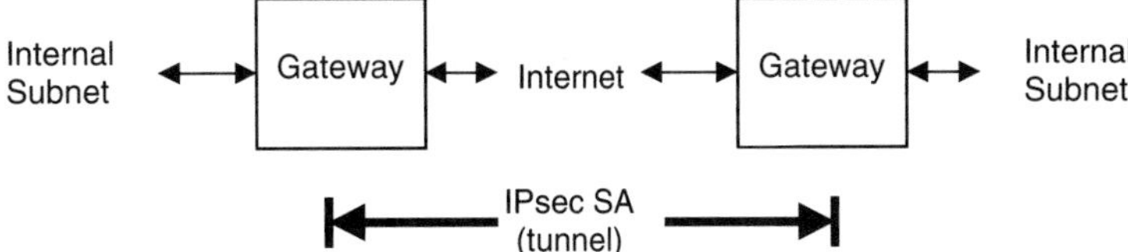

Figure 1: Internet Protocol Security (IPsec) used gateway to gateway.

gateway, end point to gateway, and end point to end point, each detailed in this section.

Gateway to Gateway

It is common for an organization to have an internal network (or intranet) connected to the Internet via a *firewall* or *gateway*. The systems deployed on the internal network often are not securely configured, so by filtering communications at the border, some degree of protection from external attacks can be applied en masse while still allowing the uses enabled by the insecure configurations to go on within the organization. If such an organization is geographically dispersed and its only means of communication between campuses is via the Internet, the filtering done by the firewall or gateway may prevent the internal applications from operating between campuses. Further, an organization may be concerned that sensitive e-mail traffic may be intercepted by eavesdroppers on the Internet. Although this could be addressed by deploying a secure e-mail solution such as S/MIME, an easier to deploy solution is to use IPsec to encrypt all "internal" traffic while it passes over the Internet. The protection is not as strong (because it is still exposed to internal eavesdroppers), but for many organizations it is considered adequate.

To address both of these problems, an organization can deploy IPsec-enabled gateways at its points of connection to the Internet. These gateways are configured with the set of addresses that are considered "internal" and for each such address the gateway through which packets to that address should be routed. The gateways set up pairwise IPsec SAs between one another. When a packet arrives destined for an internal address on another campus, that packet is wrapped in an IPsec packet, encrypted, and integrity protected. At the receiving gateway, the IPsec packet is decrypted, verified, and forwarded without having to pass the checks that would be done if the packet were coming in from the Internet. This allows insecure intranet applications to work between campuses and ensures that internal mail and other communications are encrypted when on public networks. Figure 1 illustrates the gateway-to-gateway IPsec scenario.

When IKE is setting up SAs between gateways, there are typically few enough gateways that manual configuration of addresses and cryptographic keys is feasible—and in fact easier than dealing with a public key infrastructure. There is no need to deal with revocation should a gateway be compromised; it would simply be removed from the configurations of the other gateways. Authentication and naming of individual gateways is similarly not an important issue. Gateways really need only know that they are talking to another gateway of the same organization. Once so assured, the gateways will allow unfiltered traffic to flow between the two parts of the internal subnet. This is the most straightforward use of IKE and IPsec.

End Point to Gateway

Another use of IPsec and IKE that is rapidly growing is the ability to connect a portable "roaming" end point into an organization's intranet using some public network (Figure 2). The growing popularity of wireless connectivity in public places makes it convenient for a traveler with a laptop computer to establish a high-speed connection to the Internet at some unpredictable address and use IPsec to securely tunnel to a corporate intranet. This scenario also occurs when people have cable modems or DSL (digital subscriber line) connectivity to the Internet from their homes and want to connect to their office networks.

There are a number of important differences in this scenario. The portable or home computer is not likely to be at a fixed address, so the gateway cannot be configured to know its address. In fact, the gateway will never initiate an SA. It will wait until remote computers request connections to the internal network. These remote computers are not likely to establish SAs to all of an organization's gateways. More likely, each will pick a single gateway and failover to another if the first one fails. Packets sent from within the internal subnet to the remote computer's address might end up at any gateway, however, and most will not know what to do with it. This problem is fixed by having the gateway own a pool of addresses on the internal subnet and assign one of those addresses to each remote computer connected. The remote computer then acts as though it were at that address but connected to the Internet through a gateway at its real address. Packets it sends have two headers—just like a packet that has been wrapped by a gateway. The outer header contains the address it got from its local Internet provider and the address of the gateway. The inner header contains the address the gateway assigned it and the address of the machine on the internal network that it wants to talk to. The gateway unwraps this packet, so the machine on the internal subnet sees an ordinary packet coming from one of the addresses belonging to the gateway. The network will automatically route return packets to the gateway, and the gateway will

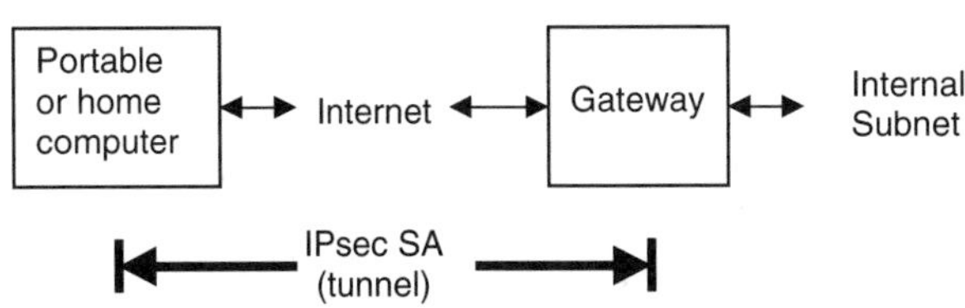

Figure 2: Internet Protocol Security (IPsec) used from an end point to a gateway.

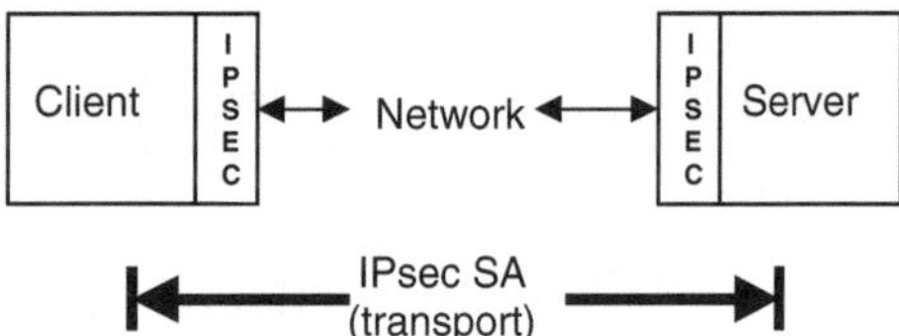

Figure 3: Internet Protocol Security (IPsec) used end-to-end SA = security association.

wrap them and send them on the SA currently associated with that address.

Unlike the gateway-to-gateway scenario, the portable computer is likely to not have its own IP address but rather be using a network address translator (or NAT) to allow multiple machines to share an IP address. These are commonly used, for example, to allow home users to connect multiple machines to a single cable modem or DSL line.

Typically, it is not the portable computer that is authenticated to the gateway but its human user. The expectation is that the computers might be stolen and should not be usable without the authorized person present, and it may be the case that the user is allowed to use any of a large pool of machines. Because an easy-to-use public key infrastructure for people remains to be deployed, authentication is most often by means of a password or some sort of physical authentication token (such as a smart card or challenge–response calculator). Gateways, in contrast, are more likely to have public keys and certificates.

One property this scenario shares with the gateway-to-gateway case is that authorization policy is fairly simple. The gateway does not care who the user is (except perhaps for auditing), and the user does not care to which gateway he connects. Once the user and gateway are satisfied they are talking to good peers, they pass traffic bypassing the filters the gateway imposes on Internet traffic.

End Point to End Point

A major intended use for IPsec, so far mostly unrealized, is to replace SSL as the preferred means to protect data cryptographically between computers on a network (Figure 3). This scenario is different from the others. First, there is no need for two sets of source and destination addresses because the end points of the IPsec SA and the end points of the communication are the same. IPsec optimizes this case by having IKE negotiate *transport mode*, in which the inner IP header is not included. When two sets of addresses are included, the IKE SA is said to use *tunnel mode*. In the IKE negotiation, the initiator can offer this optimization and the responder can (optionally) accept it. Doing so saves a few bytes in each packet, and the effort of encrypting and parsing them.

Perhaps more important, in this scenario, the identities authenticated as part of the IKE negotiation can be reused by applications running on the two systems for access control decisions (eliminating the need for some other authentication protocol to be used by applications). In the first two scenarios, the identities are only used to decide whether communication is to be allowed. Separate authentication protocols must be run on the tunneled connections. The configuration challenge in this scenario is for end points to know when IPsec protection should be used. If IPsec were universally deployed, running IKE would be part of the startup sequence when any end point tried to communicate with another. If a client node today tried to open an IPsec connection to a server, however, its request would most likely be rejected or ignored. Manually configuring clients with information about which servers support IPsec works well enough for demonstrations, but supporting this on a large scale will require deployment of some new Internet infrastructure. There is a proposal for storing this information in Domain Name System (DNS), but so far deployment is only experimental.

IKE PROTOCOL HANDSHAKE

Although the IKE protocol allows many variations, the following describes a simple and common execution of the IKEv2 protocol in four messages (the minimum). After these four messages have been processed, the two end points will have agreed on cryptographic algorithms and keys for both the IKE protocol itself and an IPsec SA for passing data (either ESP or AH). They will also have agreed on the kinds of data that will be passed over the SA and the starting sequence numbers.

In the basic exchange (Figure 4), the initiator (Alice) proposes one or more sets of cryptographic algorithms that are acceptable for the SA; Bob chooses among them and sends a single set back. Two such negotiations take place, one for the IKE SA (used to protect only messages used in the IKE protocol) and one for the ESP or AH SA (used to protect subsequent data).

The first two messages of the exchange perform a Diffie–Hellman exchange, in which Alice randomly chooses N_A and A and sends N_A and g^A mod p, Bob randomly chooses N_B and B and sends N_B and g^B mod p, and they both protect subsequent messages with keys generated as a function of N_A, N_B, and g^{AB} mod p.

In the second two messages, Alice and Bob identify themselves, authenticate themselves, and negotiate the cryptographic algorithms and kinds of data traffic to be passed over the ESP or AH SA. Because the second two messages are encrypted, an eavesdropper will not see even the names of the two participants (although in many cases these can be guessed from the IP addresses).

The *proof* provided in the second two messages must be based on some cryptographic authentication mechanism. For Alice to authenticate herself to Bob, she must prove knowledge of some secret that Bob knows is associated with Alice. The preferred types of keys are either a secret

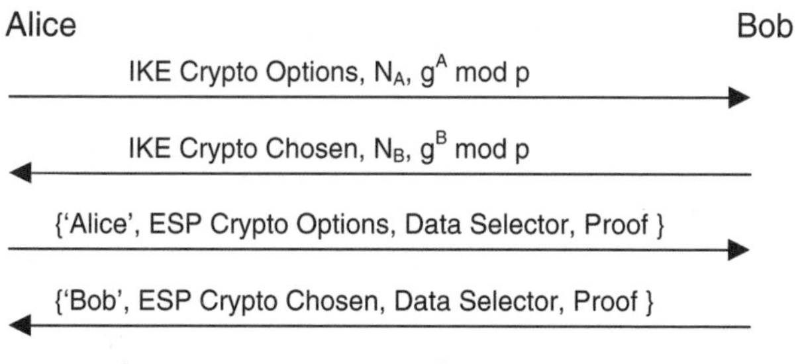

Figure 4: Basic Internet key exchange (IKF).

key known to both Alice and Bob, or a pair of private keys (where each party knows the corresponding public key of the other). In either case, the keys are used to protect the integrity of the IKE exchanges.

Authentication Keys

IKE was designed presuming that Alice and Bob would each have private keys and certificates, and be enrolled in a public key infrastructure. Unfortunately, public key infrastructure has been slow to roll out on the Internet, and many IPsec deployments still use secret keys to authenticate. There is nothing inherently less secure about secret key-based authentication, but it is much more difficult to administer securely. Some administrator must configure secrets into each pair of IPsec end points. To authenticate using secret keys, IKE assumes that there has been some sort of out-of-band mechanism whereby Alice and Bob are configured with a shared secret. In the case of public keys, IKE allows each side to transmit a certificate (or sequence of certificates), as well as an indication of preferred certificate issuers (in case several certificates are available). IKEv1 allowed the use of encryption with public keys as an alternative to signing for authentication, but this option was rarely used and was dropped from IKEv2.

Initial Diffie–Hellman Exchange

A real-time protocol is said to have *perfect forward secrecy* (PFS) if an attacker who records the entire session and then breaks into both communicating parties and learns all long-term secrets (or subpoenas them) after the session has ended, still cannot decrypt the session. There are two methods in use for achieving PFS, both using public key cryptography. One is by use of the Diffie–Hellman protocol. The other is for one party to create an ephemeral public key pair, certify the ephemeral public key with that party's long-term key, and have the other side communicate the session secret encrypted in the ephemeral public key. The former method is used in IKE. The latter is used in one of the variations of SSL designed for exportability.

Diffie–Hellman is a protocol that establishes a shared secret. It is based on the assumption that the discrete log problem is difficult to solve. The discrete log problem is stated as follows: given g, p, and g^X mod p, what is X? The protocol, between Alice and Bob, has each choose a private exponent (Alice chooses A, Bob chooses B), then raise g to that private exponent, mod p, transmit the result to the other, and then have each raise what is received from the other side to their own private exponent. The result will be that both calculate g^{AB} mod p. An eavesdropper who saw both messages would still have no way of calculating g^{AB} mod p.

The Diffie–Hellman exchange must be authenticated. Otherwise, an active attacker, Trudy, who is on the communication path between Alice and Bob could act as a man-in-the-middle, establishing a key between Alice and Trudy and a separate key between Trudy and Bob (Figure 5). Trudy can then act as go-between for the entire session, decrypting traffic received from Alice and reencrypting it for Bob, and doing the equivalent for traffic from Bob to Alice. She can also monitor, record, or even modify the messages as she processes them.

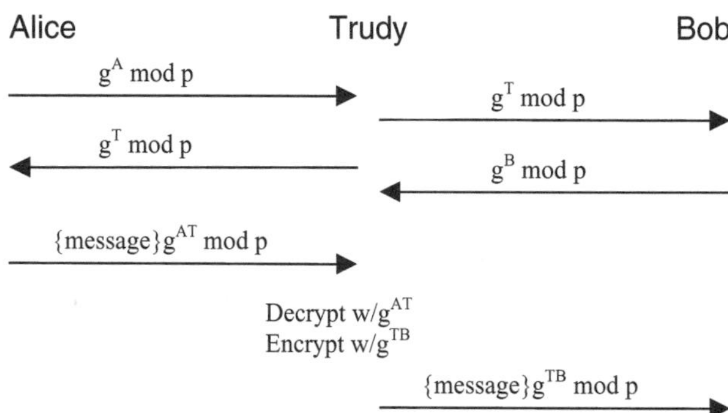

Figure 5: Man-in-the-middle attack.

Less-than-perfect forward secrecy can still be useful. In reality, it is unlikely that an attacker will manage to break into a system at the exact instant when a session ends. If the attacker were to break in a moment before the session ended, it would be able to steal the session key. It is reasonable to expect that some time will elapse before the communicating parties will be compromised. This means that some trade-off can be made between efficiency and "perfection." For a protocol such as IKE, based on Diffie–Hellman, the same g^A mod p can be used for many sessions (to save the work of computing g^A), provided that A and the session key are forgotten after any session using A is ended (thus this is only useful where multiple sessions are taking place in parallel). If A is remembered after sessions end, forward secrecy will be less than perfect.

In case both Alice and Bob are reusing their private Diffie–Hellman exponentials across sessions, the IKE exchange additionally has them exchange nonces (numbers that are randomly chosen from a large space) for each session. The session key is a function not only of the Diffie–Hellman key, but also the nonces. This ensures that even if the Diffie–Hellman keys are the same for two sessions, the session secrets will be different (provided the nonces are not also identical). It is important that the secret session keys be different for each session, because otherwise an attacker could take packets recorded from the first session and replay them as part of the second session.

Negotiation of Cryptographic Algorithms

It would undoubtedly yield a simpler protocol if the protocol specification gave fixed parameters for all the cryptography, but there are many reasons today's protocols generally include a negotiation to determine the cryptographic algorithms and their public parameters. One is to allow easy replacement of a protocol that is found to have weaknesses with one that is stronger. Another is to allow interoperability when, for instance, different countries have their own preferred algorithms. Similarly, export or import laws might preclude using the strongest cryptography.

Alice and Bob should negotiate to find the strongest set of algorithms that they are both capable of supporting. This negotiation must occur before the cryptographic part of the handhake because the cryptographic portion of the handshake cannot occur until there is agreement about what cryptographic algorithms to use. It is therefore important to avoid a "downgrade attack," in which an attacker removes the strong alternatives from the list of alternatives offered.

The way to detect a downgrade attack (and renegotiate as a result) is to protect the offered list of choices cryptographically. To do this, Alice and Bob can each certify their initially sent lists in a subsequent message after the cryptographic algorithms have been chosen. If the list as received is incorrectly certified or differs from what was initially transmitted, this can be detected at that point and the handshake can start over again. IKEv2 includes the entire contents of the first two messages of the exchange in the calculation of the proof that authenticates the two parties. IKEv1 was subject to this attack (see Zhou, 2000).

Identity Hiding

One of the goals of IKE was to enable hiding the identities (names) of the communicating parties from attackers. In IKEv2, identities are hidden from eavesdroppers because they are encrypted using the negotiated Diffie–Hellman key. Furthermore, the responder does not reveal its name until the initiator has authenticated, making it impossible to determine responder names through probing unless one is authorized to communicate with the responder. With IKEv1, the story is more complicated; which names were protected from which attacks varied according to the type of exchange and the type of authentication key being used. In the case of authentication using public encryption keys, if at least one of the parties knows the other's public encryption key in advance, identities can be hidden from both passive and active attackers because one party can send its identity encrypted in the other side's public key, together with whatever is necessary to authenticate, such as sending a certificate (also encrypted in the other side's public key).

IKEv1 attempted to provide similar protection in the case of a preshared secret key, but the scheme does not work in most scenarios. Because the responder has a different shared key with each potential correspondent, it would not know which key to use to decrypt the message containing the initiator name. The only way around this was for the responder to do a trial decryption with each potential initiator's key or somehow to determine the initiator's identity from its IP address. This variation was removed from IKEv2.

In the case of public signature keys, although identities can be hidden from passive attackers (attackers that only eavesdrop), the identity of each party must be revealed to the other. Whichever side reveals its identity first will be vulnerable to discovery (of his or her identity) if the other side is an attacker. Kaufman and Perlman (2000) argued that, under the circumstances, it would be preferable to preserve Alice's identity (the initiator) from active attack, because the initiator would most likely be a client, and the responder, Bob, would be a server at a fixed address. However, because IPsec is intended to be peer-to-peer, and the handshake can be initiated from either side, the argument was made in the initial version of IKEv2 that if Bob revealed his identity first, there would be the possibility of a polling attack in which anyone could initiate an IKE handshake and have Bob reveal his identity.

It is not clear how important this attack is in practice, but the IPsec working group decided in favor of avoiding the probing attack against Bob. This was somewhat controversial, with arguments within the IKEv2 working group ranging from "it's more important to protect the initiator's identity from active attack" to "identity hiding is an exotic and unimportant threat, and we've wasted too much time on it already."

When "legacy authentication" was added, it was decided to do it by adding the already designed EAP (extended authentication protocol [RFC2284; Blunk & Vollbrecht, 1998]) into the exchange (see the subsequent section, Extended Authentication Protocol). Many argued that in this exchange, in which the initiator was clearly a human, it was more important to hide the initiator's identity than the responder's. However, the consensus was that the initiator's identity was still hidden from passive attackers and that identity hiding from someone actively impersonating Bob's IP address was not sufficiently important to reopen the argument about whether it is more important to hide the initiator or responder identity from an active attacker.

Negotiation of Traffic Selectors

There is a policy database associated with IPsec that specifies what processing should be done for various types of traffic, based on sets of IP addresses for sources and destinations, and TCP and UDP port numbers (which sometimes reveal what application is communicating). When a data-passing SA is established, IKE negotiates the traffic that should be allowed on that SA. In IKEv1, one side proposes traffic parameters, and the other side can just accept or reject. IKEv2 allows a counterproposal of a subset of what was proposed. This allows the traffic parameters to be updated independently at the two IPsec end points with the lesser of the two values being negotiated while they disagree.

EXTENSIONS AND VARIATIONS

Denial of Service Protection

At the time when IKE version 1 was being designed, there were DoS (denial of service) attacks in which one node would initiate many connections to a server, using up all its state or computation resources (or both). Typically the attacker would send such packets with a forged IP source address to avoid prosecution for mounting the attack and to make it difficult to configure a rule into a firewall to drop packets from the attacker. (Subsequently, DDoS [distributed denial of service] attacks, for which the mechanism described here does not help, became more common. If the design were started today, this feature would probably not be included.)

One of the candidate proposals for IKE version 1 was known as Photuris (RFC2522 [Karn & Simpson, 1999]). The designers invented a mechanism, which has since been copied into a number of other protocols, known as a "stateless cookie." This is a mechanism whereby Bob can verify, before devoting significant computational resources or any state to Alice, that Alice can receive messages at the IP address she is putting into the source address of her packets. It is easy to put any address into the source address of an IP header, but it is more difficult to be able to receive packets sent to an address other than one's own IP address.

In Photuris, there was an initial exchange whereby Alice (an initiator) requests a cookie, Bob sends one, and then forgets about Alice. On her next message, she includes the cookie. The cookie has to be a value that is not predictable by anyone other than Bob, and is verifiable by Bob without Bob remembering what he sent. So the cookie is usually a value, which is a function of the initiator's IP address and a time-dependent secret known only to Bob.

In OAKLEY (RFC2412 [Orman, 1998]; another candidate protocol for IKE version 1), this design was extended to allow the initial exchange to be optional. If Bob is not under attack (as evidenced by not having an unusually high number of half-completed connections), Alice and Bob can skip the initial round trip. If Bob is under attack, he sends a cookie value and demands that Alice repeat her request, this time with a valid cookie.

PK2001 proposed a further enhancement whereby a cookie exchange could be included in the minimal four-message exchange (Perlman & Kaufman, 2001).

As finally specified, IKEv1 required a cookie exchange that did not protect from DoS attacks (because of some confusion within the standards committee). IKEv2 uses an OAKLEY-like mechanism that does protect against DoS attacks but sometimes extends the exchange to six messages. This was done in part to address the threats described in KPS2003 (Kaufman, Perlman, & Sommerfield, 2003).

Extended Authentication Protocol

In some cases, Alice is a human and does not have a cryptographic key. In this case, Alice might authenticate with a name or password or with a token card. A token card is a small object about the size of a small calculator with a display and sometimes a keyboard. There are several types. In one type, the token card displays the time of day (in units of minutes) encrypted with a key shared by that card and the server. In another type, the token card has a keyboard, Bob gives a challenge that the user must type into the keyboard, and the token card displays a function of the challenge and the token card's secret. Still another type is sequence based in which each time the token card is asked, it displays the next value, which is a function of the token card's secret and the sequence number.

IKE was initially designed with the assumption that there would be a cryptographic secret on each end, but support for what is called "legacy authentication" (use of passwords or token cards) was added. Because EAP can require a variable number of messages to complete, IKE was modified when using EAP to have a larger and variable number of messages before the exchange completes.

NAT Traversal

NAT (network address translation) is a technique by which nodes without global IP addresses can communicate to the greater Internet. A computer known as a NAT box has a pool of IP addresses, and when a node from inside is communicating outside, the NAT box assigns an IP address from its pool and remembers the mapping so as to be able to route return traffic to the correct internal node.

Often there are not enough addresses in the pool of global IP addresses to assign a unique one for each node communicating outside. In that case, a NAPT (network address and port translation) box is used. NAPT uses the ports in the TCP and UDP headers to differentiate among internal nodes.

With IPsec-encrypted packets, the NAPT box cannot see (much less change) the TCP and UDP ports. As a result, ESP and AH cannot generally be used through a NAPT box. To get around this, a UDP port (4500) was allocated for carrying encapsulated ESP traffic. The IKE handshake optionally contains information about the source and destination addresses and ports that each end "sees." If a NAT or NAPT box is detected, both the IKE SA and the ESP SA packets are encapsulated in UDP and sent using port 4500.

DIFFERENCES BETWEEN IKEV1 AND IKEV2

Two Phases

The IKEv1 protocol was designed with two phases. The first phase is a four- or six-message mutual authentication handshake that is potentially expensive because it likely uses public key cryptography. The second phase is a three-message exchange that completes the negotiation of cryptographic parameters for the ESP- or AH-encoded data to follow. The protocol was designed with two phases so that the second phase could be repeated multiple times within the context of the first phase to do periodic rekeying or to negotiate multiple sets of session parameters between a single pair of nodes. The first phase establishes an SA known as the IKE SA with a shared secret key between the two identities. The IKE SA's shared secret can then be used to cheaply establish more SAs. The idea of two phases was introduced in ISAKMP (Internet security association and key management protocol; RFC 2407 [Piper, 1998]), with the assumption that ISAKMP would be used to establish many SAs between the same pair of end points for different protocols. Indeed, protocol numbers were assigned for using ISAKMP to establish SAs for protocols such as the routing protocols OSPF and RIP. In fact, only IPsec used IKE. In PK2001, it was argued that IKE could be significantly simplified by removing the second phase, but the feedback from the working group was that experience from IKEv1 proved the phases useful for two reasons (Perlman & Kaufman, 2001):

- First, two firewalls might be providing virtual private network service across the Internet on behalf of multiple client networks. Although it is likely not to be any less secure to have traffic for all customers run over the same SA with the same key, it apparently makes some customers feel safer if their traffic is segregated using unique keys.
- If there are multiple quality of service classes that have very different delivery speeds, and if traffic for all of them went over a single SA, the resulting packet reordering

might make it difficult for the recipient to ensure that packets were not duplicated through use of sequence numbers. This might present a storage efficiency problem for the recipient because it would have to remember all the sequence numbers received. If all traffic were expected to be delivered approximately in order, it would be reasonable to only remember sequence numbers within a reasonably small window. If the probability of a packet being delayed is reasonably low so that packet $n + k$ is delivered before packet n, it is reasonable for the recipient to drop packet n if it arrives after packet $n + k$. However, if traffic is delivered with different qualities of service, there is no such window, and the recipient must remember all sequence numbers received in order to recognize replayed packets.

IKEv2 effectively includes support for the two phases, although in a different way than IKEv1. The initial exchange in IKEv2 initializes both the IKE SA and the first data SA with four messages. If the end points wish to establish additional data SAs, they can do so with only two additional messages per SA established. This provides the same functionality as IKEv1 with fewer messages and less variability in the messages. Support for establishment of additional SAs is optional in IKEv2, so a minimal implementation that does not require this functionality need not implement it.

IKEv1 Handshake

IKEv1 has two types of phase 1 handshakes: "main mode," which completes in six messages, and "aggressive mode," which completes in three messages. Both exchanges do mutual authentication and establish a session key, but main mode also hides identities, at least from passive attackers. For both main mode and aggressive mode, there are four exchanges, designed for different key types. The key types are public signature keys, preshared secret keys, and two types of exchanges based on public encryption keys (because the first set was inefficient, requiring multiple public key operations). That makes eight handshakes for the first phase. There is a ninth handshake with three messages for the second phase known as "quick mode."

Although all the handshakes are different, the basic structure of all the aggressive mode handshakes is that in message 1, Alice sends her Diffie–Hellman value, her nonce, and her identity, along with cryptographic proposals (Figure 6). In message 2, Bob sends his Diffie–Hellman value, his nonce, his identity, the chosen cryptographic protocols, and proof that he knows the key Alice associates with him. Then in message 3, Alice proves knowledge of the key Bob associates with her identity.

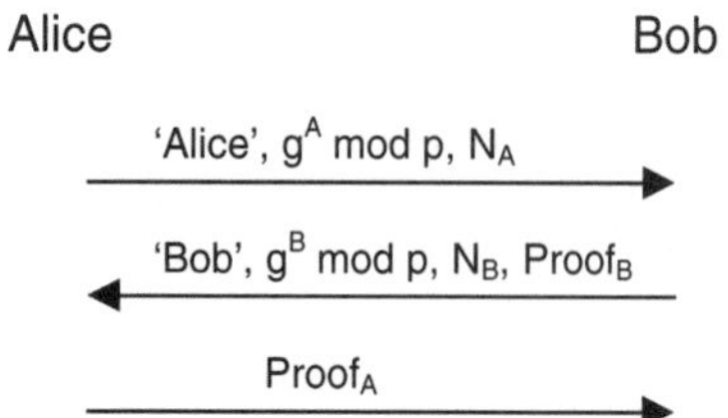

Figure 6: Internet Key exchange version 1 (IKEv1) aggressive mode exchange.

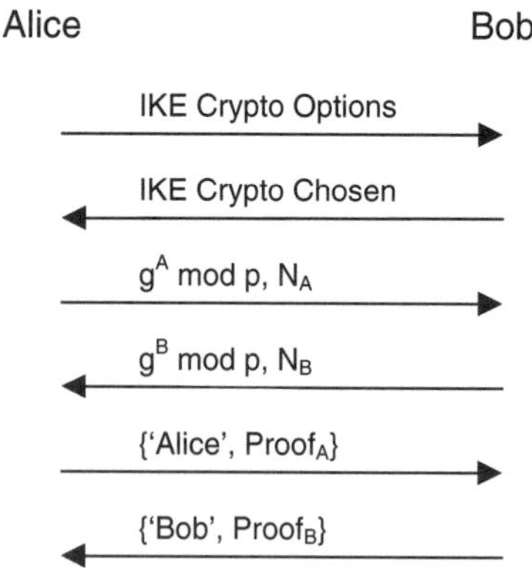

Figure 7: Internet Key exchange version 1 (IKEv1) main mode exchange.

Again, although all the handshakes are different, the basic structure of all the main mode handshakes (Figure 7) is that in messages 1 and 2, Alice proposes and then Bob chooses cryptographic algorithms. In message 3, Alice sends a Diffie–Hellman value and a nonce. In message 4, Bob does the same. In message 5, Alice sends her identity and proof of knowledge of her key. In message 6, Bob does the same. Messages 5 and 6 are encrypted in a key that is derived differently in each of the handshakes. In particular, in the one mandatory-to-implement method (main mode with preshared secret keys), Alice sends her identity encrypted in a key that is a function, among other things, of the key she shares with Bob. The problem is that Bob cannot decrypt the message unless he tries all possible keys of all possible correspondents. This, among other problems, was fixed in IKEv2.

Quick mode (phase 2; see Figure 8) starts with the shared key established in phase 1. It consists of three messages. In message 1, Alice sends her choice of SPI (security parameter index) for the IPsec packets (the value Bob should fill into the AH or ESP header so that Alice will know the context in which to interpret the packets), a nonce, proposals for IP addresses and TCP/UDP ports for traffic on the SA, and optionally initiates an additional Diffie–Hellman exchange. Bob responds with his SPI choice, nonce, chosen traffic selectors. Additionally, if Alice initiated a Diffie–Hellman exchange, Bob includes

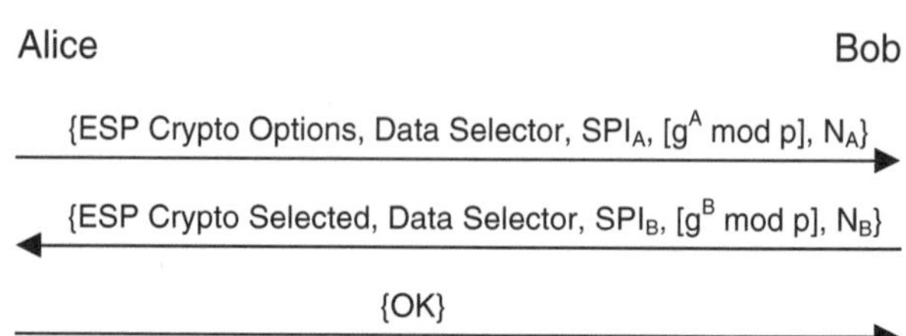

Figure 8: Internet Key exchange version 1 (iKEv1) quick mode (phase 2) exchange.

his own Diffie–Hellman response. Message 3 is just an acknowledgment by Alice that the handshake completed and traffic can now flow.

GLOSSARY

Active Attacker Someone trying to intercept or interfere with an encrypted communication who may eavesdrop on the conversation, attempt to impersonate one or the other end point, inject new or replayed messages, or modify messages in transit.

Advanced Encryption Standard (AES) A symmetric-key cipher also known as Rijndael, serving as successor to DES.

Denial of Service (DoS) A form of attack in which the goal is not to learn secret information or change any stored data, but simply to disrupt the functioning of a system—for example, overloading it to make it unresponsive.

Diffie–Hellman A public key cryptosystem used to agree on a secret (symmetric) key.

Distributed Denial of Service (DDoS) A form of denial of service attack in which the attack is not performed directly by the attacker but through a large number of compromised but otherwise innocent computers on the Internet (these computers are referred to as zombies).

Internet Key Exchange (IKE) The Internet Engineering Task Force standard protocol for initializing security associations for IPsec.

Passive Attacker An eavesdropper on an encrypted communication who does not initiate or modify any of the messages but tries to determine information about the encrypted content and/or encryption keys.

Perfect Forward Secrecy (PFS) A desirable property for a cryptographic protection mechanism. In a mechanism implementing perfect forward secrecy, an attacker who records a conversation and subsequently obtains all of the long term keys of the end points still cannot decrypt the recorded conversation.

Secure Internet Protocol (IPsec) The Internet Engineering Task Force standard protocol for cryptographically protecting IP packets.

Security Association (SA) The shared state in two IPsec end points, including cryptographic keys to be used to protect information, the kinds of information to be protected, addresses, sequence numbers, and names of correspondents.

Security Parameter Index (SPI) The field in the header of a message that indicates the connection context of the message (and hence the cryptographic keys and algorithms that should be used to process the message).

Transport Mode The technique used in an IPsec SA in which there is only a single pair of source and destination addresses, because the end points of the IPsec SA are the same as the end points of the communication.

Tunnel Mode The technique used in an IPsec SA in which there are two pairs of source and destination addresses. The outer addresses are used to route information between the IPsec end points, while the inner addresses route information between the communication end points.

CROSS REFERENCES

See *Computer and Network Authentication; Encryption Basics; IPsec: AH (Authentication Header) and ESP (Encapsulating Security Payload); VPN Basics*.

REFERENCES

Blunk, L., & Vollbrecht, J. (1998). *PPP extensible authentication protocol (EAP)*. RFC 2284. Retrieved May 2, 2005, from http://www.faqs.org/rfcs/rfc2284.html

Harkins, D., & Carrel, D. (1998). *The Internet key exchange (IKE)*. RFC 2409. Retrieved May 2, 2005, from http://www.ietf.org/rfc/rfc2409.txt

Karn, P., & Simpson, W. (1999). *Photuris: Session-key management protocol*. RFC 2522. Retrieved May 2, 2005, from http://rfc2522.x42.com/

Kaufman, C., & Perlman, R. (2000). Key exchange in IPsec: Analysis of IKE. *IEEE Journal of Internet Computing, 4*(6), 50–56.

Kaufman, C., Perlman, R., & Sommerfeld, B. (2003, October). DoS protection for UDP-based protocols. *Proceedings of the 10th ACM conference on computer and communications security*, Washington, DC.

Maughhan, D., Schertler, M., Schneider, M., & Turner, J. (1998). *Internet security association and key management protocol (ISAKMP)*. RFC 2408. Retrieved May 2, 2005, from http://dc.qut.edu.au/rfc/rfc2408.txt

Orman, H. (1998). *The Oakley key determination protocol*. RFC 2412. Retrieved May 2, 2005, from http://www.faqs.org/rfcs/rfc2412.html/

Perlman, R., & Kaufman, C. (2001). *Analysis of the IPsec key exchange standard*. WET-ICE security conference. Retrieved from May 2, 2005, http://sec.femto.org/wetice-2001/papers/radia-paper.pdf

Piper, D. (1998). *The Internet IP security domain of interpretation for ISAKMP*. RFC 2407.

Zhou, J. (2000). Further analysis of the Internet key exchange protocol. *Computer Communications, 23*, 1606–1612. Retrieved May 2, 2005, from http://www.i2r.a-star.edu.sg/icsd/publications/ZhouJianying_2000_ComCom00.pdf

FURTHER READING

Kaufman, C., Perlman, R., & Speciner, M. (2002). *Network security: Private communication in a public world* (2nd ed.). Englewood Cliffs, NJ: Prentice Hall.

Kent, S., & Atkinson, R. (1998). *Security architecture for the Internet protocol*. RFC 2401.

Secure Sockets Layer (SSL)

Robert J. Boncella, *Washburn University*

SECURE COMMUNICATION CHANNELS

Overview

This chapter provides an overview of how the SSL protocol and its variant the TLS protocol are used to establish and operate a secure communication channel. It is assumed that the readers of this chapter are nontechnical in their academic background. As a result some space will be spent in explaining the background concepts necessary for a full understanding of SSL and TLS. If the reader requires more technical detail (Boncella, 2000) is suggested.

This chapter has five major sections. First is a discussion of the need for and history of secure channels. Second is an overview of the internetworking concepts necessary to appreciate the details of SSL and TLS protocols. Third is a brief review of cryptographic concepts used in SSL and TLS. Fourth is a detailed exposition of SSL and TLS. The chapter concludes with a discussion of SSL and TLS protocol's status—its strengths and weakness and threats and possible alternatives to it.

The Internet can be used to provide a number of communication services. A user can take advantage of e-mail, news posting services, and information gathering services through Web browsing to name a few of its uses. Under certain conditions the user's expectation is that the service to be provided is legitimate, safe, and private—legitimate in the sense that the providers of the service are who they say they are, safe in the sense that the services or information being provided will not contain computer viruses or content that will allow the user's computer system to be used for malicious purposes, and finally, private in the sense that the provider of the requested information or services will not record or distribute any information the user may have sent to the provider in order to request information or services. The server's expectation is that the requestor of the information or service is legitimate and responsible—legitimate in the sense the user has been accurately identified, and responsible in that the user will not attempt to access restricted documents, crash the server, or use the server computing system as a means of gaining illegal access to another computer system. Both the server and the user have an expectation that their communications will be free from eavesdropping and reliable—meaning that their transmissions will not be modified by a third party. The purpose of Internet security is to meet the security expectations of users and providers. To that end, Internet security is concerned with client-side security, server-side security, and secure transmission of information.

Client-side security is concerned with the techniques and practices that protect a user's privacy and the integrity of the user's computing system. The purpose of client security is to prevent malicious destruction of a user's computer systems (e.g., by a virus that might format a user's fixed disk drive) and to prevent unauthorized use of a user's private information (e.g., use of a user's credit card number for fraudulent purposes).

Server-side security is concerned with the techniques and practices that protect the server software and its associated hardware from break-ins, server site vandalism, and denial-of-service attacks. The purpose of server-side security is to prevent modification of a site's contents; to prevent use of the server's hardware, software, or databases for malicious purposes; and to ensure reasonable access to a server's services (i.e., to avoid or minimize denial-of-service attacks).

Secure transmission is concerned with the techniques and practices that will guarantee protection from eavesdropping and intentional message modification. The purpose of these security measures is to maintain the confidentiality and integrity of user and server information as it is exchanged through the communication channel. This chapter focuses on a solution to the requirement for a secure channel.

Secure Channels

The Internet can be used for electronic communication. Those who use the Internet for this purpose, on occasion, have the need for that communication to be secure. Secure communication can be ensured by the use of a secure channel. A secure channel will provide three things for the user: authentication of those involved in the communication, confidentiality of the information exchanged in a communication, and integrity of the information exchanged in the communication.

SSL and its variant TLS are protocols that can be used to establish and use a secure communication channel between two applications exchanging information. For example, a secure channel may be required between a user's Web browser and the Web server the user has accessed. The paradigm example is the transfer of the user's credit card information to a Web site for payment of an online purchase. Another example would be an employee using the Web to send his or her check routing information to her employer for use in a direct deposit payroll request.

In addition to Web services, other services that might be in need of a secure channel would be e-mail, file transfer, and news posting. A discussion of how these services utilize a secure channel is presented at the end of the SSL Architecture section.

History of Secure Channels—SSLv1 to v3, PCT, TLS, STLP, and WTLS

SSL is a computer networking protocol that provides authentication of, confidentiality of, and integrity of information exchanged by means of a computer network. Netscape Communications designed SSL in 1994 when it realized that users of its browser needed secure communications. SSL version 1 was used internally by Netscape and proved unsatisfactory for use in its browsers. SSL version 2 was developed and incorporated into Netscape Navigator versions 1.0 through 2.X. This SSLv2 had weaknesses (Stein, 1998) that required a new version of SSL. During that time—1995—Microsoft was developing PCT (private communications technology) in response to the weaknesses of SSLv2. In response, Netscape developed SSL version 3, solving the weakness of SSLv2 and adding a number of features not found in PCT.

In May 1996, the Internet Engineering Task Force (IETF) authorized the TLS working group to standardize a SSL-type protocol. The strategy was to combine Netscape's and Microsoft's approaches to securing channels. At this time, Microsoft developed its secure transport layer protocol, which was a modification of SSLv3 and added support for UDP (datagrams) in addition to TCP support.

In 2002, the WAP Forum (wireless access protocol) adopted and adapted TLS for use in secure wireless communications with its release of WAP 2.0 Protocol Stack. This protocol provides for end-to-end security over wireless or combined wireless and wired connections (Boncella, 2002; WAP Forum, 2002).

An in-depth understanding of secure channels in general and SSL and TLS in particular requires familiarity with two sets of concepts. The first is how the client–server computing paradigm is implemented using the transmission control/Internet protocols (TCP/IP). The second set of concepts deals with cryptography. In particular, one needs to be familiar with the concepts of encryption, both symmetric and asymmetric (public key encryption), key sharing, message digests, and certification authorities.

The first set of concepts, clients and servers using TCP/IP, is discussed in the following section, and the cryptography concepts are reviewed following TCP/IP discussion.

INTERNETWORKING CONCEPTS

Clients and Servers

The Internet is implemented by means of interconnection of networks of computer systems. This interconnection provides information and services to users of the Internet. Computer systems in this interconnection of networks that provide services and information to users of computer systems are called servers. Services are provided by programs running on those computer systems. Computer systems that request services and information use software referred to as client software or simply clients. The communication channel between the client and server may be provided by an Internet service provider (ISP) that allows access to the communication channel for both the server and client. The communication of the client with a server follows a request–response paradigm. The client, via the communication channel, makes a request to a server and the server responds to that request via a communication channel.

The Web may be viewed as a two-way network composed of three components:

1. Clients
2. Servers
3. Communication path connecting the servers and clients

The devices that implement requests and services both are called hosts because these devices are "hosts" to the processes (computer programs) that implement the requests and services.

Communication Paths

The communication path between a server and a client can be classified in three ways:

1. An internet
2. An intranet
3. An extranet

An internet is an interconnection of networks of computers. However, the Internet (with an upper case I) refers to a specific set of interconnected computer networks that allows public access. An intranet is a set of interconnected computer networks belonging to an organization and is accessible only by the organization's employees or members. Access to an intranet is controlled. An extranet uses the Internet to connect private computer networks or intranets. The networks connected together may be owned by one organization or several. At some point, communication between hosts in an extranet will use a communication path that allows public access.

For a request or response message to travel through a communication path, an agreed-on method for message creation and transmission is used. This method is referred to as a protocol. The de facto protocol of the Internet is the TCP/IP protocol. An understanding of the client–server request–response paradigm requires an overview of the TCP/IP protocol. The TCP/IP protocol can best be understood in terms of the open system interconnection (OSI) model for data communication.

The OSI Model and TCP/IP

The open system interconnection model defined by the International Standards Organization (ISO) is a seven-layer model that specifies how a message is to be constructed for it to be delivered through a computer network communication channel. This model is idealized. In practice, few communication protocols follow this design. Figure 1 provides a general description of each layer of the model. The sender of the message, either a request or a response message, provides input to the application layer.

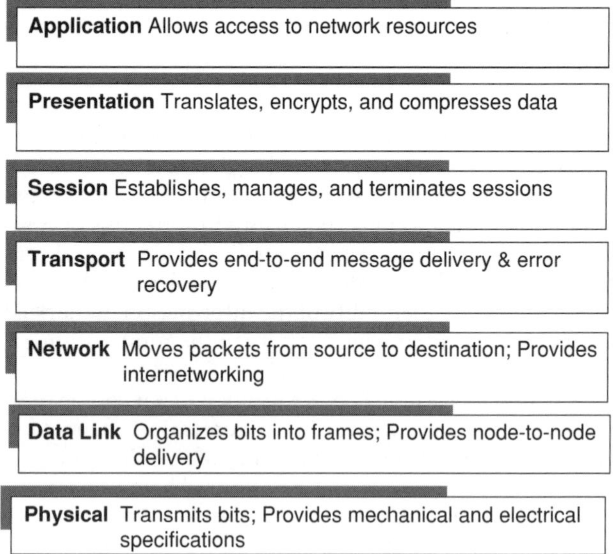

Figure 1: Open system interconnection (OSI) model.

The application layer processes sender input and converts it to output to be used as input for the presentation layer. The presentation layer, in turn, processes this input to provide output to the session layer, which uses that output as input, and so on, until what emerges from the physical layer is a signal that can be transmitted through the communication channel to the intended receiver of the message. The receiver's physical layer processes the signal to provide output to its data link layer, which uses that output as input and processes it to provide output to the receiver's network layer, and so on, until that message is accepted by the receiver.

This process is depicted in Figure 2. Figure 2 also illustrates the signal (message) being relayed through the communication channel by means of intermediate nodes. An intermediate node is a host that provides a specific service with the purpose of routing a signal (message) efficiently to its intended destination.

Figure 3 depicts the TCP/IP protocol on the OSI model. For our purposes the TCP/IP protocol is made up of four layers. What follows is a brief overview of the TCP/IP protocol. For an introduction to the details of TCP/IP, consult Forouzan (2000).

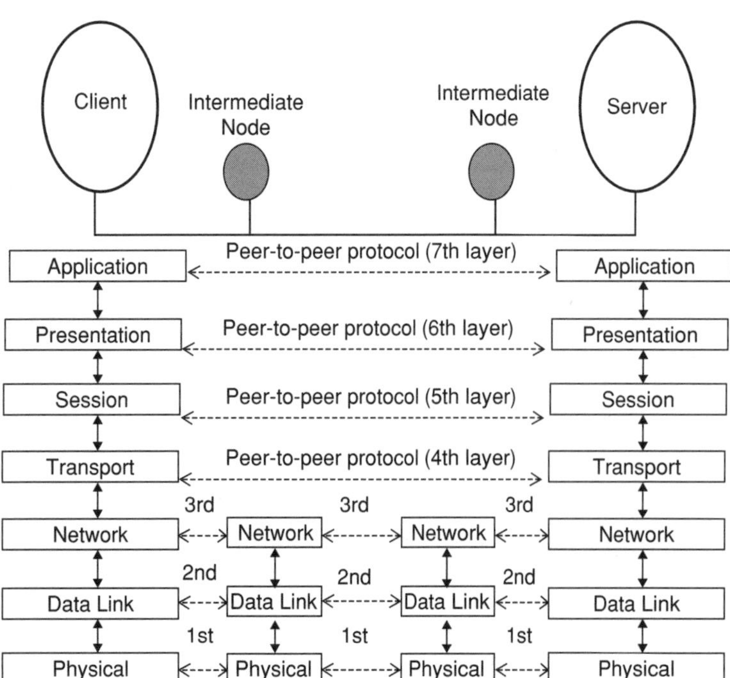

Figure 2: Messaging delivery using open system interconnection (OSI) model.

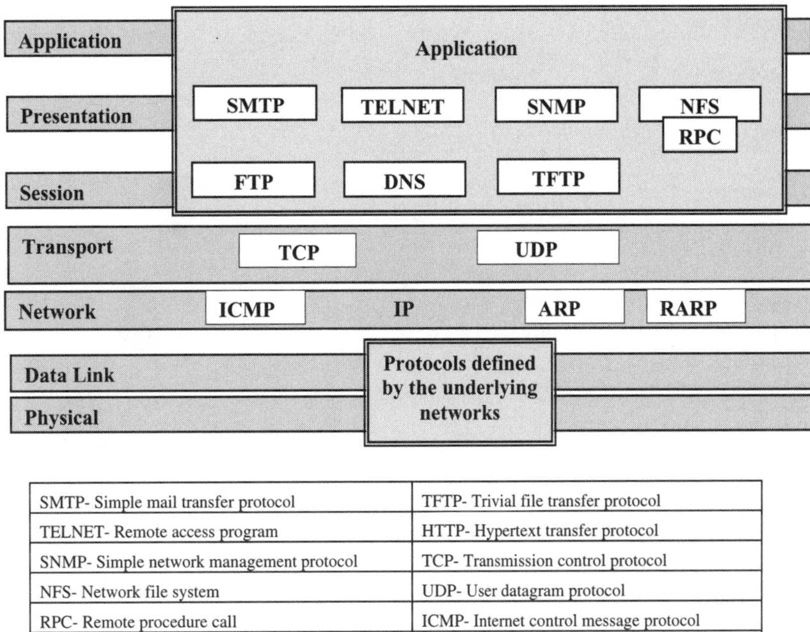

SMTP- Simple mail transfer protocol	TFTP- Trivial file transfer protocol
TELNET- Remote access program	HTTP- Hypertext transfer protocol
SNMP- Simple network management protocol	TCP- Transmission control protocol
NFS- Network file system	UDP- User datagram protocol
RPC- Remote procedure call	ICMP- Internet control message protocol
FTP- File transfer protocol	ARP - Address resolution

Figure 3: The open system interconnection (OSI) model and the transmission control/Internet protocol (TCP/IP).

The application layer contains a number of applications that a user may use as client processes to request a service from a host. The client processes are said to run on a local host. In most cases, the requested service will be provided by a remote host. In many cases, there will be a similarly named application on the remote host that will provide the service. For example, the user may open a Web browser and request HTTP (hyper text transfer protocol) service from a remote host to copy an HTML (hypertext markup language) formatted file into the user's Web browser. If the receiving host provides HTTP service, it will have a process running, often named HTTPD, that will provide a response to the client's request. Note that users need to specify the host by some naming method and the service they desire from that host. This is taken care of by the use of a universal resource locator (URL; e.g., http://www.washburn.edu). The application Layer produces a message that will be processed by the transport layer.

The client's request will pass through the local host's transport layer. The responsibility of the transport layer is to establish a connection with the process on the remote host that will provide the requested service. This client-process-to-server-process connection is implemented by means of port numbers. A port number is used to identify a process (program in execution) uniquely. Unique identification is necessary because local hosts and remote hosts may be involved in a number of simultaneous request–response transactions. The hosts' local operating systems, in concert with the TCP/IP protocol concept of port numbers, can keep track of which of several responses corresponds to the correct client process request on that local host and which request corresponds to the correct service on the remote host.

The transport layer will cut the message into units that are suitable for network transport. In addition to the port numbers, the transport layer adds information that will allow the message to be reconstructed in the receiver's transport layer. Other information is added to these units that allows flow control and error correction. The output from the transport layer is called a segment. The segment is composed of the data unit and a header containing the information described earlier. Figure 4 shows this process.

The output of the transportation layer, a segment, is sent to the network or IP layer. The responsibilities of the IP layer include providing the Internet or IP address of the source (requesting) host and destination (response) host of the segment. One important part of the IP address is a specification of the network to which the host is attached. Depending on the underlying physical network, the segments may need to be fragmented into smaller data units. The information from the segment header is duplicated in each of these fragments as well as the header information provided by the network or IP layer.

The output of the IP layer is called a datagram. The datagram is passed to the lowest layer, where the physical addresses associated with the source and destination hosts' IP addresses are added. The physical address of a host uniquely identifies the host on a network. It corresponds to a unique number of the network interface card (NIC) installed in the host. An example is the 48-bit-long Ethernet address provided by the manufacturer of an Ethernet card. When the TCP/IP protocol is installed on a host, that host's physical address is associated with an IP address. The physical address allows a particular host to be independent of an IP address.

To understand Internet security, we need to be aware of three concepts associated with the TCP/IP protocol:

1. Port address
2. IP addresses
3. Physical addresses

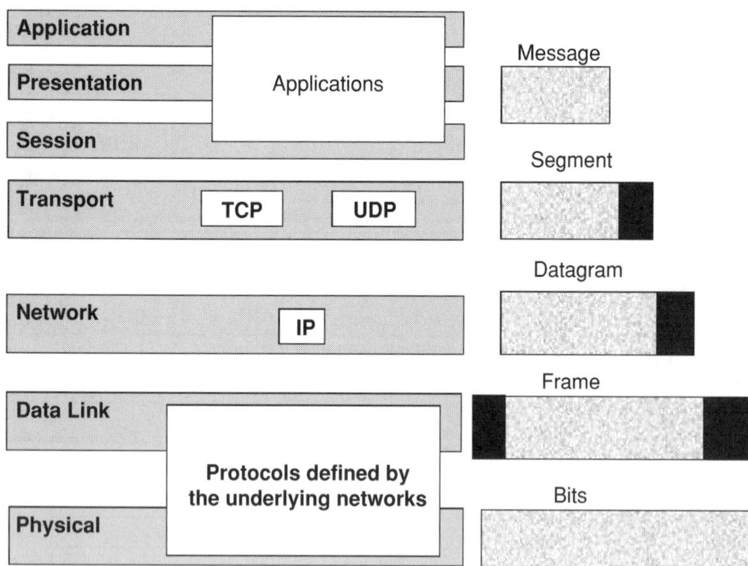

Figure 4: Transmission control/Internet protocol (TCP/IP) message delivery.

These concepts allow the request–response message to be exchanged by the intended processes (as specified by port numbers.). Those processes are running on hosts attached to the intended networks (as specified by the IP addresses) and, finally, running on the intended hosts (as specified by physical addresses). Figure 5 depicts these address assignments and the layers responsible for their assignments.

CRYPTOGRAPHIC CONCEPTS USED IN SSL AND TLS

The following is a brief review of these concepts. The details of each are provided elsewhere in the *Handbook of Information Security.* Volume 2, Part 3, will contain the details of most of these ideas.

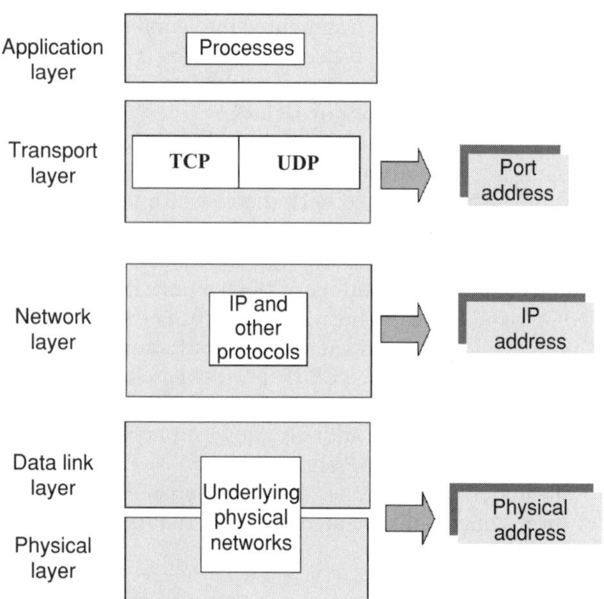

Figure 5: Address types and assignments in transmission control/Internet protocol (TCP/IP).

Encryption

Encryption is the process of converting plaintext (readable text) into ciphertext (unreadable text). Decryption is the process of converting ciphertext into plaintext. Usually this is done by means of a publicly known algorithm and a shared key. Encryption is vital in providing message confidentiality, client–server authentication, and message integrity. There are two methods of encryption: symmetric or secret key and asymmetric or public/private-key pair. Each method of encryption has its particular use. Symmetric encryption is used for encryption of the messages exchanged between a client and a server, whereas asymmetric encryption is used to exchange the common keys used by clients and servers in their symmetric encryption process. Asymmetric encryption may also be used for the encryption of messages.

Symmetric Encryption

There are two main types of symmetric encryption: stream ciphers and block ciphers. Stream ciphers combine 1 byte of the key with 1 byte of the plaintext to create the ciphertext in a byte-after-byte process. Block ciphers process plaintext in blocks of bytes, generally 8 or 16 bytes in length, into blocks of ciphertext.

RC4 is a widely used stream cipher. There are a number of block ciphers, including Data Encryption Standard (DES), Triple DES (3DES), and Rivest Cipher #2 (RC2). AES is another block cipher that is an improvement over DES in that it uses variable block sizes and has longer key lengths—128-, 192-, or 1256-bit keys. The specifics of these ciphers are discussed elsewhere in this volume.

Symmetric encryption requires the sender and receiver to share a secret key. This secret key exchange is a drawback of symmetric systems that is typically overcome by asymmetric or PKI systems.

Asymmetric Encryption

In asymmetric encryption a pair of keys, a public key and a private key, are used to carry out the encryption process. If the private key is used to create the ciphertext, then only the corresponding public key can be used to decrypt that ciphertext and vice versa. Asymmetric (or public/private-key) encryption can be used for key sharing, encryption, and digital signatures.

Key Sharing

There are two means to carry out key sharing. One is "key exchange" in which one side of the message exchange pair generates a symmetric key and encrypts it with the public key of the private–public key pair of the other side. The other technique of key sharing is "key agreement." In this technique each side of the message exchange pair cooperate to generate the same key that will be used for symmetric encryption. The RSA (named for its creators, Rivest, Shamir, Adelman) public key algorithm can be used for the key exchange technique. The Diffie–Hellman public key algorithm can be used for the key agreement technique. The details of these algorithms are discussed elsewhere in this text.

Message Digest Algorithms

Message digest algorithms are used to generate a "digest" of a message. A message digest algorithm computes a value based on the message content. The same algorithm and message content will generate the same value. If a shared secret key is included with the message before the digest is computed, then when the digest is computed the result is a message authentication code (MAC). If the client and server are sharing this secret key and know each other's message digest algorithms, they can verify the integrity of the message exchange.

Two commonly used message digest algorithms are Message Digest #5 (MD5), which computes a 16-byte value (128 bits), and Secure Hash Algorithm 1 (SHA-1), which computes a 20-byte value (160 bits).

Digital Signatures

Digital signatures are used for nonrepudiation. Public-key algorithms can be used for digital signatures. RSA is a means of providing a digital signature by the sender encrypting a known pass phrase with his or her private key. This pass phrase is generally a message digest of the message being sent. Only the corresponding public key will decrypt the ciphertext of the pass phrase to the correct plaintext. It should be noted that not all public–private key systems are "reversible" like RSA. The digital signature algorithm (DSS) is another algorithm that can be used for this purpose.

Certification Authorities

A certification authority (CA) is a trusted third party that is responsible for the distribution of the public key of a public–private key pair. The CA does this by issuing (and revoking) public key certificates. A standard for these certificates is X.509v3. This standard defines the fields contained in the certificate. This is a widely accepted standard and is used by most CAs.

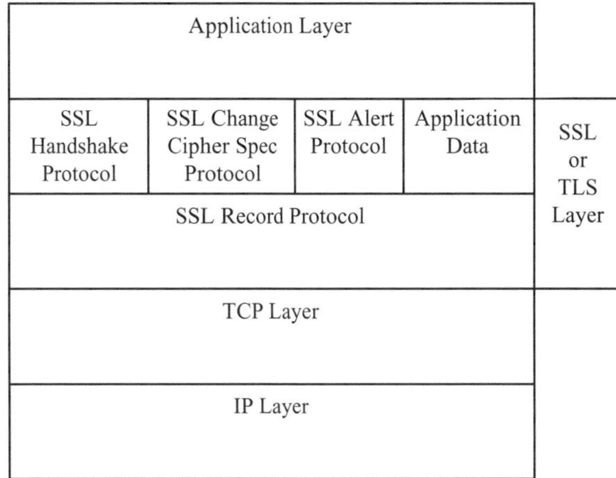

Figure 6: Secure socket layers (SSL) within transmission control/Internet protocol (TCP/IP).

SSL ARCHITECTURE

Overview

SSL is composed of four protocols. Three of the four, SSL handshake protocol, SSL change cipher spec protocol, and SSL alert protocol, are used to set up and manage secure communication channels. The remaining protocol, the SSL record protocol, provides the security service required by applications. The SSL lies between the application layer and the TCP layer of the TCP/IP protocols. This architecture is represented in Figure 6.

Once a secure channel has been established the SSL takes messages to be transmitted, fragments the message into manageable blocks, optionally compresses the data, applies a message authentication code (MAC), encrypts, prefixes the SSL record header, and sends the result to the TCP layer. Ultimately these data blocks are received and the data are decrypted, verified, decompressed, reassembled in the receiver's SSL layer, and then delivered to higher level clients. The technical details of these protocols are discussed in a number of places. The primary document is the Web page http://wp.netscape.com/eng/ssl3/ssl-toc.html.

A number of excellent secondary sources provide more background information as well as the specifications of the protocols. The interested reader is directed to Rescorla (2001) and Stallings (2003). The protocols used to establish a secure channel give SSL its flexibility for client–server communication.

SSL is flexible in the choice of which symmetric encryption, message digest, and authentication algorithms can be used. When an SSL client makes contact with an SSL server, they agree on the strongest encryption methods they have in common. Also, SSL provides built-in data compression. Data compression must be done before encryption.

For example, when an SSL connection is established for an SSL-protected HTTP connection, client-to-server and server-to-client communication is encrypted. Encryption includes the following:

URL of requested document
Contents of the document

Contents of browser forms
Cookies sent from browser to server
Cookies sent from server to browser
Contents of HTTP header, but not particular browser to particular server

In particular, socket addresses—IP address and port number—are not encrypted; however, a proxy server can be used if this type of privacy is required.

Connection Process Preview

The connection process is shown in Figure 7. Figure 7 and the following narrative serve as an overview of this process. To establish an SSL connection, the client (browser) opens a connection to a server port. The browser sends a "client hello" message—Step 1. A client hello message contains the version number of SSL that the browser uses, the ciphers and data compression methods it supports, and a random number to be used as input to the key generation process.

The server responds with a "server hello" message (Step 2). The server hello message contains a session ID and the chosen versions for ciphers and data compression methods the client and server have in common. The server sends its digital certificate (Step 3) which is used to authenticate the server to the client and contains the server's public key (Step 4). Optionally, the server may request a client to authenticate. If requested, the client will send a signed piece of data unique to this handshake and known to both the client and server as the client's means of authentication (Step 5). If the client cannot be authenticated, then connection failure results. Assuming a successful connection, the client sends a "ClientKey Exchange" message (Step 6). This message is a digital envelope created using the server's public key and contains the session key chosen by the client. Optionally, if client authentication is used, the client will send a certificate verify message (Step 7). The server and client send a "Change-CipherSpec" message (Step 8) indicating they are ready to begin encrypted transmission with the newly established parameters The client and server send finished messages to each other (Step 9). The finished messages are MACs of their entire conversation up to this point. (Recall: a MAC, message authentication code, is a key-dependent one-way hash function. It has the same properties as the one-way hash functions called message digests, but they have a key. Only someone with the identical key can verify the hash value derived from the message.) Accordingly, if the MACs match, then messages were exchanged without interference, and hence the connection is legitimate. Once the secure channel is established, application-level data

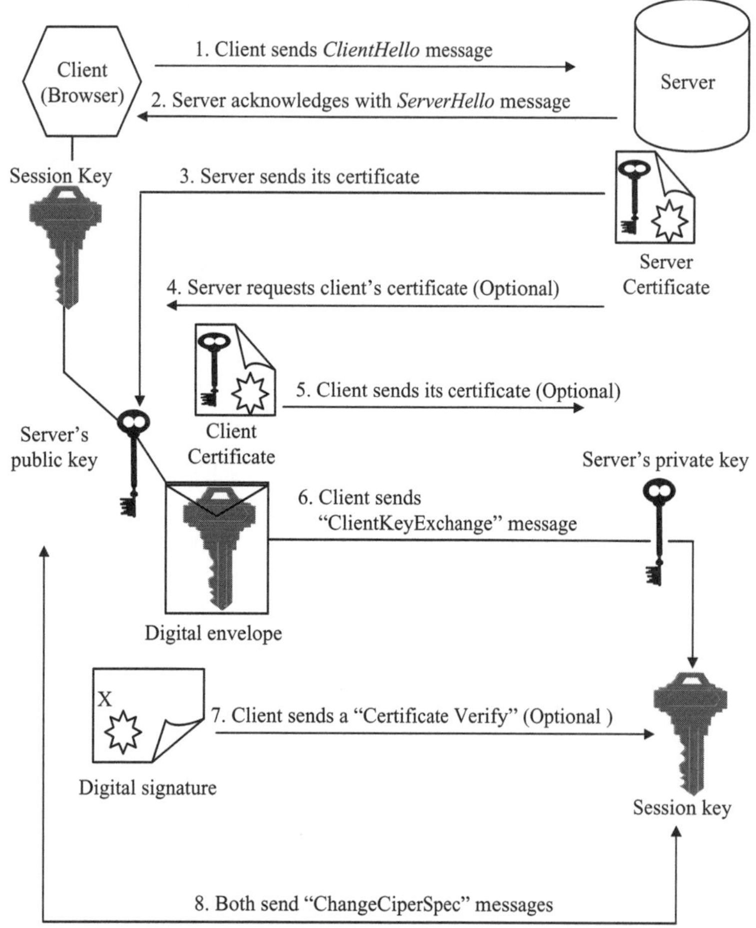

Figure 7: Secure socket layers (SSL) connection process.

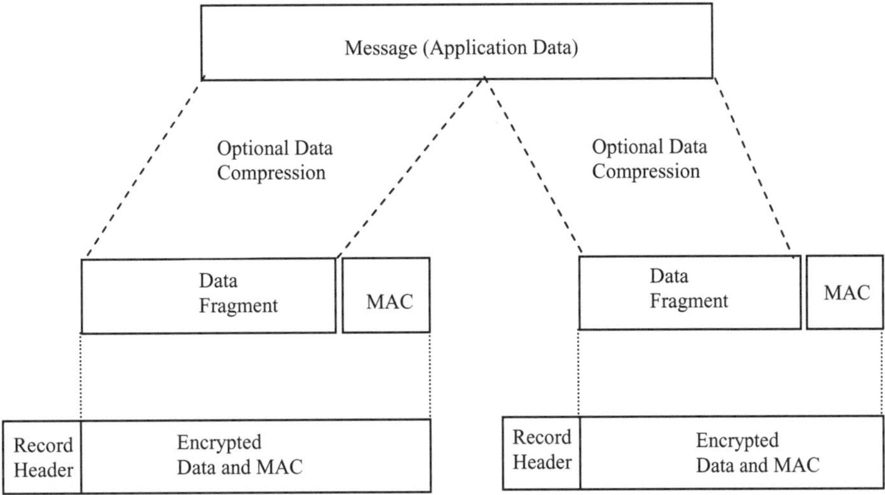

Figure 8: Secure socket layers (SSL) message protocol.

can be transmitted between the client and server using the SSL record protocol.

Record Protocol

The SSL record protocol provides two of the three essential requirements for secure transmission of data: confidentiality and message integrity. Confidentiality is provided by symmetric encryption that uses the shared session key exchanged between the client and server during the handshake protocol. This handshake protocol also defines a shared secret key that can be used to create a MAC, which can be used to ensure message integrity. The third requirement, authentication, is provided by the handshake protocol in its requirement of at least a server's certificate.

The record protocol processes a message by first breaking the message into fragments of equal fixed size, padding the last fragment as needed. The next step is optional compression of each fragment. Once the compression is completed, a MAC is computed for each fragment and appended to the fragment. The result is then encrypted using the key and algorithm agreed on by the client and server. An SSL record header is appended. Then this segment is passed to the TCP layer for processing. The received data are processed by the receiving protocol in the reverse process: data are decrypted, verified by means of the MAC, and decompressed if necessary, then the fragments are reassembled, and the result is passed on to the destination application. This process is depicted in Figure 8.

TLS—Transport Layer Security

TLS is an attempt by the IETF to specify an Internet standard version for SSL. The current proposed standard for TLS is defined in RFC 2246 (2002). The proposed TLS standard is very similar to SSLv3. The TLS record format is identical to the SSL record format. There are a few differences between SSL and TLS. Some of these are how MAC computations are carried out, how pseudorandom functions are used, including additional alert codes and client certificate types, and how certificate verification and finished message are carried out. The details of these differences are discussed in Stallings (2003).

SSL and TLS Protocols: Details

The preceding sections provide an overview of how a secure channel is set up and used. A better understanding of this process is obtained when a detailed examination of this process is presented. It is informative to work through each step of Figure 7 and detail how the protocols work to set up the secure channel. The following is an adaptation of information that may be found in specification documents for SSL (Netscape Communications, 1996, 1998).

Handshake Protocol

Of the four protocols that make up SSL and TLS, the handshake protocol is the most critical. This protocol is responsible for setting up the connection. It uses a sequence of messages that allows the client and server to authenticate each other and agree on encryption and MAC algorithms and their associated keys, as well as the key exchange algorithms to be used.

The format of the handshake protocol is simple, as depicted in Figure 9. The type field of the handshake protocol indicates 1 of 10 messages listed in Table 1. Length is the length of the message in bytes. Content is the parameters associated with the message type (cf. Table 1).

Step 1 of Figure 7 is the *ClientHello* message. Its parameters are as follows:

version The version of the SSL protocol by which the client wishes to communicate during this session. This should be the most recent version supported by the client.

random A client-generated random structure. This is a value 32 bytes long. The first four bytes are the time

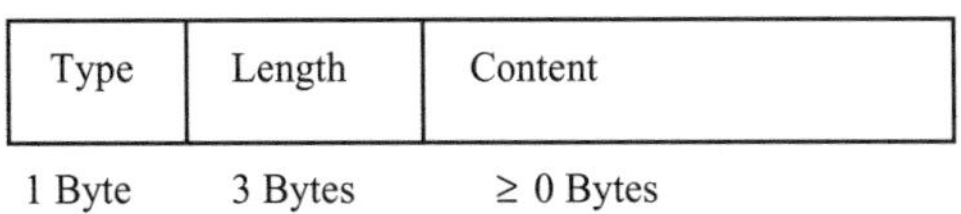

Figure 9: Handshake protocol layout.

Table 1 Handshake Protocol Messages

Message Type	Parameters
HelloRequest	Null
ClientHello	Version, random, session_id, cipher_suite, compression_method
Serverhello	Version, random, session_id, cipher_suite, compression_method
Certificate	Chain of X.509v3 certificates
ServerKeyExchange	Parameters, signatures
CertificateRequest	Type, authorities
ServerDone	Null
CertificateVerify	Signature
ClientKeyExchange	Parameters, signatures
Finished	Hash_value

of day the message was generated, and the remaining 28 bytes are created using a secure random number generator. This 32-byte value will be used as one of the inputs to the key generation procedure. The time stamp (first 4 bytes) prevents a possible "man in the middle" attack as well as protecting against reply attacks.

session_id The ID of a session the client wishes to use for this connection. This parameter will be *empty* if no session_id is available or the client wishes to generate new security parameters.

cipher_suites A list of the cryptographic options supported by the client, sorted descending preferences. If the session_id field is not *empty* (implying a session resumption request) this vector must include at least the cipher_suite from that session.

compression_methods A list of the compression methods supported by the client, sorted by client preference. If the session_id field is not *empty* (implying a session resumption request), this vector must include at least the compression method from that session. All implementations must support a null compression method (i.e., no data compression is used).

After sending the **client hello** message, the client waits for a **server hello** message. Any other handshake message returned by the server except for a **hello request** is treated as a fatal error.

Step 2 is the **server hello** message. The server processes the **client hello** message and responds with either a handshake_failure **alert** or a **server hello** message. The *ServerHello* message parameters are as follows:

server_version This field will contain the lower of that suggested by the client in the *ClientHello* message and the highest supported by the server.

random This structure is generated by the server and *must* be different from (and independent of) the *ClientHello* random structure.

session_id This is the identity of the session corresponding to this connection. If the *ClientHello* message session_id parameter was nonempty, the server will look in its session cache for a match. If a match is found and the server is willing to establish the new connection using the specified session state, the server will respond with the same value as was supplied by the client. This indicates a *resumed* session and dictates that the parties *must* proceed directly to the *finished* messages. Otherwise this field will contain a different value identifying the new session. The server may return an *empty* session_id to indicate that the session will not be cached and therefore cannot be resumed.

cipher_suite The single cipher suite selected by the server from the list in the *ClientHello* message cipher_suites parameter. For *resumed* sessions, this field is the value from the state of the session being resumed.

compression_method The single compression algorithm selected by the server from the list in the *ClientHello* message compression_methods parameter. For *resumed* sessions, this field is the value from the resumed session state.

Step 3 is the *Certificate* message. If the server is to be authenticated (which is generally the case), the server sends its certificate immediately following the *ServerHello* message. The certificate type must be appropriate for the selected cipher suite's key exchange algorithm and is generally an X.509.v3 certificate. The same message type is also used for the client's response to a server's *CertificateRequest* message.

If the server has no certificate or if a key exchange technique other than RSA or fixed Diffie–Hellman is used, the server will send *ServerKeyExchange* message. In this case, the parameters for this message will contain the values appropriate for the key exchange technique (see Stallings, 2003, for details).

In **Step 4** (optional), a nonanonymous server can optionally request a certificate from the client, if appropriate for the selected cipher suite. The *CertificateRequest* message has two parameters:

types A list of the types of certificates requested, sorted in order of the server's preference.

authorities A list of the distinguished names of acceptable certificate authorities.

After **Step 3** (or optional **Step 4**), the server will send a *ServerHelloDone* message to indicate that the server has sent all the handshake messages necessary for the server hello phase. After sending this message, the server will wait for a client response. When the client receives the *ServerHelloDone* message, the client will determine the validity of the server's certificate and the acceptability of the *ServerHello* message parameters. If the parameters and certificate are valid, the client will receive one or two messages.

Step 5 (optional) is the *Certificate* message. This is the first message the client can send after receiving a *ServerHelloDone* message. This message is only sent if the server requests a certificate. If no suitable certificate is available, the client should send a *NoCertificate* alert instead. This error is only a warning; however, the server may respond with a *FatalHandshakeFailure* alert if client authentication is required.

Step 6 is the *ClientKeyExchange* message. The content of the message will be based on the type of key exchange negotiated during the first phase of the handshaking process. The key exchange method is determined by the cipher suite selected and server certificate type. For example, if the client and server agree on the RSA key exchange method, the client generates a 48-byte *premaster_secret* and encrypts it with the public key from the server's certificate or uses the temporary public key from the server's *ServerKeyExchange* message.

If the server has requested a client certificate and it requires verification, the client will send a *CertificateVerify* message to provide explicit verification of its client certificate.

In **Step 8,** the client sends a *ChangeCipherSpec* message that indicates the client has switched to the negotiated cipher suit. All subsequent messages will be sent using those encryption algorithms and appropriate keys. It should be noted that the *ChangeCipherSpec* message is a separate protocol and not part of the handshake protocol. The purpose of this is to make SSL and TLS more efficient. The *ChangeCipherSpec* message consists of only 1 byte.

In **Step 9,** the client sends the handshake message *Finish*. The message is a concatenation of two message digest values. Each value is computed using a different message digest algorithm—MD5 and SHA—on the same data. The data are the master secret (described later) and the set of handshake messages sent up to this point.

In response to these two client messages, the server sends its version of the *ChangeCipherSpec* and a *Finished* message computer using that same data as the client. If this *Finished* message value differs from the *Finished* message value sent by the client then this indicates that the handshake has been modified and a secure channel may not be set up. When the client receives the *finish* message from the server, it does a comparison with its locally computed *finish* message value. If they match, then all is well; otherwise the secure channel may not be established.

Cipher Suites and Master Secrets

There are two more concepts that need to be presented to complete this discussion. In Step 1, the client sends a list of cipher suites to the server that the client is able to use. In Step 6, the client sends a pre_master_secret that will be used to compute the master secret. This master secret is then used to compute the key_block. This key_block is used to derive the keys that will be used with the algorithms specified in the cipher suites. The details of each of these need to presented.

Cipher Suites

The **cipher_suite** parameter of the *ClientHello* message provides a set of key exchange techniques, server authentication algorithms, bulk encryption algorithms, and message digest algorithms that the client can support. The client lists these sets in order of the client's preference. For example, one of the entries of this set may be

TLS_DHE_RSA_WITH_3DES_EDE_CBC_SHA

In this example, the key exchange technique is DHE, where DHE denotes ephemeral Diffie–Hellman. The Diffie–Hellman parameters are signed either by DSS or RSA. The signing algorithm used is specified after the DHE parameter. In this case, the signing algorithm is the RSA algorithm.

The bulk encryption and message digest algorithms follow the WITH delimiter, in which the bulk encryption is performed by 3DES_EDE_CBC, where 3DES_EDE_CBC denotes 3DES encryption using the encrypt–decrypt–encrypt mode in the cipher block chaining mode, and the message digest algorithm is SHA, where SHA denotes the secure hash algorithm.

Master Secret

The master secret creation is the vital component in setting up the secure channel. The master secret is used to compute the key_block. Once the key_block computed, it is partitioned into six keys that are used by the client and server in their communications. The computation of the key_block is as follows.

The *ClientKeyExchange* message provides the server with the pre_master_secret when using RSA. Otherwise this message contains the client's Diffie–Hellman parameters. The client and server use this 48-byte value along with the *ClientHello* random parameter value and *ServerHello* random parameter value (they both have copies of these) to create a hash value by using the MD5 and SHA algorithms in the same sequence on this common set of values. They will both compute the identical hash value. This value is the master secret that is shared (computed) by both. A similar process is used to compute the key_block, but instead of using the pre_master_secret in the computation, the master_secret is used. This results in a key_block that is "shared," computed independently but to the same value, by the client and server.

The size of the key_block is determined by the cipher specifications. These specifications give the number of bytes required for the bulk encryption keys (i.e., one for the client to use and one for the server to use), MAC keys, and, if necessary, initialization vector keys. Initialization vectors (IV) are necessary if a bulk encryption algorithm will be using the cipher block chaining mode.

This "shared" key_block is partitioned in the same sequence by the client and server. The first set of bytes is used in the client MAC secret. The second set is used for the server MAC secret. The third set is used for the client bulk encryption key. The fourth set is used for the server bulk encryption key. The fifth set of bytes is used for the

Table 2 Secure Internet Services and Their Associated Port Numbers

Keyword	Secure Port Number	Function
https	443/tcp	SSL/TLS Protected HTTP
ssmtp	465/tcp	SSL/TLS Protected SMTP mail sending
spop3	995/tcp	SSL/TLS Protected POP3 mail receiving
imaps	993/tcp	SSL/TLS Protected IMAP mail server
ftps-data	989/tcp	SSL/TLS Protected FTP data sending
ftps	990/tcp	SSL/TLS Protected FTP control
nntps (snews)	563/tcp	SSL/TLS Protected Usenet News
ssl-ldap	636/tcp	SSL/TLS Protected LDAP

client initialization vector. Finally, the last set of bytes is used as the server's initialization vector.

Secure Internet Services Implemented Using SSL

Many services using the Internet run over TCP. It is a simple task to convert these services to run over SSL. In particular, Web browsing services, e-mail services, and network news posting services have been converted to use SSL when appropriate. Table 2 contains the key word of each service and the ports they are assigned when using SSL.

STATUS OF SSL

SSLv3 and TLS 1.0 and Commercial Use

SSL and TLS primarily function to protect Web traffic using HTTP. For this to work, both the client and the server need to be SSL or TLS enabled. All major Web browsers, including Netscape Navigator and Microsoft Internet Explorer, support SSL and TLS. These browsers allow the user to configure how SSL or TLS will be used. In Netscape Navigator 6.0, the user may consult the Security Preferences panel and open the SSL option under the Privacy and Security selection. In Internet Explorer, the user may consult the Security entry in the Advanced Tab on the Internet Options selection in the drop down menu item for Tools. An interesting option in both browsers is the choice of whether to save the downloaded page to the local cache. The downloaded page is no longer encrypted and if it is saved to local storage it will be in plaintext. If the local machine is compromised or stolen (e.g., a laptop), that document is readable by any user.

When a secure channel has been established, these browsers will inform the user by means of a small padlock icon at the bottom of the browser. This indicates the page was downloaded using SSL or TLS. The URL of the Web page indicates if SSL is required on the part of the Web browser. A URL that begins with HTTPS indicates that SSL should be used by the browser. A number of Web servers support SSL and TLS. A sample of such programs is displayed in Table 3.

The details of what is required to install and set up an SSL/TLS Web server can be found in various of places. For a detailed overview, the reader is directed to Garfinkel and Spafford (2002) and to Stein (1998). For a technical discussion of what is required, the reader should consult Rescorla (2001).

Advantages, Disadvantages, Threats, and Alternatives to SSL/TLS

SSL and TLS provide server authentication, encryption of messages, and message integrity. This design has several advantages, disadvantages, threats, and alternatives.

Advantages

An important advantage of both SSL and TLS is they provide a generic solution to establishing and using a secure channel. This solution lies between the application and

Table 3 Web Servers That Support the SSL Protocol

Package	Creator	Obtain From
OpenSSL	OpenSSL Development Team	www.openssl.org
Apache mod_ssl (requires OpenSSL)	Apache Software Foundation	www.apache.org
Microsoft IIS	Microsoft Coporation	Bundled with WINNT, WIN2000 and WINXP
Netscape Enterprise and Suitspot	Netscape Communications	www.netscape.com
Covalent SSL (SSL Acclerator)	Covalent Technologies, Inc.	www.covalent.net
Apache Stronghold (commercial Apache)	C2Net	www.c2.net

TCP layers of the TCP/IP protocol suit. As illustrated in Table 2, this implies that any protocol that can be carried over TCP (e.g., ftp, nntp) can be guaranteed security using SSL or TLS.

Another advantage is that SSL's and TLS's designs are publicly available. Because of this, a large number of SSL and TLS implementations are available both as freeware and as commercial products. Furthermore, these implementations are designed as Application Programming Interfaces (APIs) that are similar to networking APIs. In a C/C++-based implementation, the SSL APIs emulate Berkeley sockets; in Java they emulate they Java socket class. As a result, it is a simple matter to convert a nonsecure application into a secure application using SSL or TLS.

Disadvantages

When using SSL/TLS for security, it must be remembered that the packets that make up the message are encrypted at the TCP layer. As a result, the IP information will be in clear text. Anyone monitoring the communication will be able to determine the source and destination address of the messages. This kind of traffic analysis could lead to information that ought to remain confidential.

In e-commerce, the application of SSL and TLS has several disadvantages. Both protocols are able to solve the problem of transmitting a credit card number securely, but they are not designed to help with other aspects of that type of transaction. In particular, they are not designed to verify the credit card number, communicate and request authorization for the transaction from the consumer's bank, and ultimately process the transaction. In addition, they are not designed to carry out additional credit card services (e.g., refunds, back order processing, debit card transactions).

An additional disadvantage of SSL/TLS is security of a credit card information on the server. In particular, if the credit card number is cached on the server, it will be stored in plaintext. If the server becomes compromised, that number would be available in plaintext.

Finally, SSL/TLS is not a global solution. In the United States, systems that use strong encryption cannot be exported.

Threats to SSL/TLS

SSL/TLS are vulnerable to the "man in the middle" attack. Such an attack takes place when a malicious host is able to intercept the transmission to and from a client requesting an Internet service and the server providing the Internet service. The malicious host carries out an SSL/TLS exchange with both the client and the server. The result is that the malicious host appears to be a server for the client and also appears to be the client to the server. In fact, the malicious host is really an intermediary between them and will have access to the information being exchanged between the client and server. In particular, the malicious host will set up session keys for use with the client and another set of session keys for use with the server. This threat can be dealt with by the client's use of server certificates issued by a trusted certification authority (CA). For additional details, see Ellison and Schneier (2000).

Alternatives to SSL/TLS

In the area of e-commerce, an alternative to SSL that does not have the disadvantages just cited is SET (secure electronic transaction). SET is a cryptographic protocol developed by Visa, Mastercard, Netscape, and Microsoft. It is used for credit card transactions on the Web and provides the following:

Authentication: All parties to a transaction are identified.

Confidentiality: A transaction is encrypted to foil eavesdroppers.

Message integrity: It is not possible to alter an account number or transaction amount.

Linkage: Attachments can only be read by a third party if necessary.

In addition, the SET protocol supports all features of a credit card system: cardholder registration, merchant registration, purchase requests, payment authorizations, funds transfer (payment capture), chargebacks (refunds), credits, credit reversals, and debit card transactions. Furthermore, SET can manage real-time and batch transactions and installment payments. In addition, because SET is used for financial transactions only, it can be exported and hence can be a global solution for e-commerce. The details of SET are discussed in another chapter.

In the area of providing a secure channel for messages, there are alternatives to SSL/TLS. One is IPSec (IP security), which is a set of open standards designed by IETF and specified in RFC 2401 (2002). IPSec provides for end-to-end encryption and authentication at the IP layer. IPSec is supported in Ipv4 and mandatory in Ipv6. Another alternative to SSL/TLS is SSH (secure shell). SSH is an application and protocol suite that allows a secure connection to be established between two computers that are using a public network. The SSH protocol architecture has three components:

1. Transport layer protocol, which provides server authentication, confidentiality, and data integrity
2. Authentication protocol, which provides user authentication
3. Connection protocol, which provides multiple data channels in a single encrypted tunnel

These protocols run on top of the TCP layer in the TCP/IP protocol suite, which is similar to SSL and TLS.

GLOSSARY

Advanced Encryption Standard (AES) A cipher that encrypts blocks of data of a variable size. In addition, it uses keys of 128, 192, or 256 bits.

Asymmetric Encryption A cryptographic algorithm that uses separate but related keys for encryption and decryption. If one key of the pair is used for encryption, the other key of the pair must be used for decryption. This is sometimes referred to as a public-key algorithm.

Authentication The process of verifying that a particular client or server is who it claims to be.

Block Cipher A cipher that encrypts blocks of data of a fixed size.

Certificate, Public Key A specified, formatted block of data that contains the name of the owner of a public key as well as the public key. In addition, the certificate contains the digital signature of a CA. This digital signature authenticates the CA.

Certification Authority (CA) A trusted entity that signs public key certificates.

Ciphertext The result of encrypting plaintext.

Confidentiality A condition in which information exchanged between a client and server is disclosed only to those intended to receive it.

Data Encryption Standard (DES) A widely commercially used block cipher.

Diffie–Hellman (DH) An asymmetric algorithm that generates a secret shared between a client and server on the basis of some shared, public, and randomly generated data.

Digital Envelope Used to send a symmetric key to recipient for use in future communications. It is created by the sender encrypting the symmetric key using the recipient's public key.

Digital Signature A data value computed using a public key algorithm. A data block is encrypted with the sender's private key. This ciphertext is not confidential but the message cannot be altered without using the sender's private key.

Digital Signature Standard (DSS) A digital signature algorithm developed by the National Security Agency (NSA) and endorsed by the National Institute of Standards and Technology.

Hash Function A function that maps a variable-length message into a value of a specified bit length. This value is the hash code. There is no known method that will produce the original message using the hash value of the message. There is no known way of creating two messages that hash to the same value.

Integrity Being able to ensure that data are transmitted from source to destination without unauthorized modification.

Internet Protocol A protocol that allows packets of data to be sent between hosts in a network or hosts in connected networks.

Message Digest #5 (MD5) A one-way hash algorithm.

Nonrepudiation Being able to ensure the receiver that the sender of a message did indeed send that message even if the sender denies sending it.

Rivest Cipher #2 (RC2) A block cipher sold by RSA data security. This is a 40-bit key cipher.

Rivest Cipher #4 (RC4) A stream cipher used in commercial products

Rivest, Shamir, Adelman (RSA) An asymmetric cipher (public-key cipher) that can encrypt and decrypt. It is also used to create digital signatures.

Secret Key A cryptographic key that is used with a symmetric algorithm.

Session Key A secret key that is used for a limited period of time. This time period covers the length of time there is communication between a client and a server.

Symmetric Algorithm A cipher that requires one shared key for both encryption and decryption. This shared key is a secret key, and the strength of the ciphertext depends on keeping the shared key secret.

Transmission Control Protocol (TCP) The Internet protocol that provides reliable communication between client and a server.

Triple DES (3DES) A cipher that uses DES three times with either two or three DES keys.

X.509 A public-key certificate standard.

CROSS REFERENCES

See *Digital Certificates; Digital Signatures and Electronic Signatures; Encryption Basics; Key Management; Secure Shell (SSH).*

REFERENCES

Boncella, R. J. (2000). Web security for e-commerce. *Communications of the AIS, 4,* Article 10. Retrieved October 1, 2002, from http://cais.isworld.org/

Boncella, R. J. (2002). Wireless security: An overview. *Communications of the AIS, 9,* Article 15. Retrieved March 5, 2003, from http://cais.isworld.org/

Ellison, C., & Schneier, B. (2000). Ten risks of PKI: What you're not being told about public key infrastructure. *Computer Security Journal, 16,* 1–7, Retrieved April 8, 2004, from http://www.schneier.com/paper-pki.html

Forouzan, B. A. (2000). *TCP/IP protocol suite*. Boston: McGraw-Hill.

Garfinkel, S., & Spafford, G. (2001). *Web security, privacy & commerce* (2nd ed.). Cambridge, MA: O'Reilly and Associates.

Netscape Communications. (1996). *SSL 3.0 specification*. Retrieved October 1, 2002, from http://wp.netscape.com/eng/ssl3/ssl-toc.html

Netscape Communications. (1998). Introduction to SSL. Retrieved October 1, 2002, from http://developer.netscape.com/docs/manuals/security/sslin/contents.htm

Rescorla, E. (2001). *SSL and TLS: Designing and building secure systems*. Boston: Addison-Wesley.

RFC 2246 (2002). *The TLS protocol version 1.0*. Retrieved October 1, 2002, from www.ietf.org/rfc/rfc2246.txt

RFC 2401 (2002). *Security architecture for the Internet protocol.* Retrieved October 1, 2002, from http://www.ietf.org/rfc/rfc2401.txt

Stallings, W. (2003). *Network security essentials: Applications and standards* (2nd ed.). Upper Saddle River, NJ: Prentice-Hall.

Stein, L. D. (1998). *Web security: A step-by-step reference guide*. Reading, MA: Addison-Wesley.

WAP Forum. (2002). *Wireless application protocol WAP 2.0*. WAP Forum Technical White Paper. Retrieved October 1, 2002, from http://www.wapforum.org/what /WAP-White_Paper1.pdf

FURTHER READING

Gast, M. (2002). *802.11 wireless networks: The definitive guide.* Cambridge, MA: O'Reilly and Associates.

National Institute of Standards and Technology. *Guidelines on securing public web Servers* (NIST Special

Publication 800-44). Retrieved April 8, 2004, from http:// csrc.nist.gov/publications/nistpubs/800-44/sp800-44.pdf. September 2002

Netscape Communications. (1999). How SSL works. Retrieved October 1, 2002, fromhttp://developer.netscape.com/tech/security/ssl/howitworks.html

Schneier, B. (1996). *Applied cryptography* (2nd ed.). New York: Wiley.

Schneier, B. (2000). *Secrets and lies: Digital security in a networked world*. New York: Wiley.

Smith, R. E. (1997). *Internet cryptography.* Reading, MA: Addison-Wesley.

Stallings, W. (2003). *Cryptography and network security: Principles and practice* (3rd ed.), Upper Saddle River, NJ: Prentice-Hall.

Thomas, S. (2001). *SSL and TLS essentials*. New York: Wiley.

Viega, J., Messier, M., and Chandra, P. (2000). *Network security with OpenSSL*. Cambridge, MA: O'Reilly and Associates.

PKCS (Public Key Cryptography Standards)

Yongge Wang, *University of North Carolina, Charlotte*

INTRODUCTION

Public key cryptography is based on asymmetric cryptographic algorithms that use two related keys, a public key and a private key. Given the public key, it is computationally infeasible to derive the private key. Users publish their public keys in a public directory, such as an lightweight directory access protocol (LDAP) directory and keep their private keys to themselves.

According to the purpose of the algorithm, there are public key encryption–decryption algorithms and signature algorithms. An encryption algorithm could be used to encrypt a data (for example, a symmetric key) using the public key so that only the recipient who has the corresponding private key could decrypt the data. Typical public key encryption algorithms are rivest-shamir-adleman (RSA) and (elliptic curve integrated encryption scheme; ECIES Standards for efficient cryptography group, 2000). A signature algorithm together with a message digest algorithm could be used to transform a message of any length using the private key to a *signature* in such a way that, without the knowledge of the private key, it is computationally infeasible to find two messages with the same signature, to find a message for a predetermined signature, or to find a signature for a given message. Anyone who has the corresponding public key could verify the validity of the signature. Typical public key digital signature algorithms are RSA, digital signature algorithm (DSA), and elliptic curve digital signature algorithm (ECDSA).

There have been extensive standardization efforts for public key cryptographic techniques. The major standards organizations that have been involved in public key cryptographic techniques are the following:

- **The International Organization for Standardization (ISO) and the International Electrotechnical Commission (IEC)** individually and jointly, have been developing a series of standards for application-independent cryptographic techniques. ISO has also been developing bank security standards under the ISO technical committee TC86–Banking and Related Financial Services.
- **The American National Standards Institute (ANSI)** has been developing public key cryptographic technique standards for financial services under Accredited Standards Committee (ASC) X9. For example, it has developed the standards ANSI X9.42 (key management using Diffie–Hellman), ANSI X9.44 (key establishment using factoring-based public key cryptography), and ANSI X9.63 (key agreement and key management using ECC).
- **The National Institute of Standards and Technology (NIST)** has been developing public key cryptography standards for use by U.S. federal government departments. These standards are released in Federal Information Processing Standards publications.
- **The Internet Engineering Task Force** has been developing public key cryptography standards for use by the Internet community. These standards are published in Requests for Comments (RFCs).
- **The (Institute of Electrical and Electronics Engineers)** IEEE 1363 working group has been publishing standards for public key cryptography, including IEEE 1363–2000, IEEE 1363a, IEEE P1363.1, and IEEE P1363.2.
- **Vendor-specific standards** This category includes PKCS standards described in this chapter, standards for efficient cryptography (SEC) standards, and others. SEC 1 and 2 are ECPK cryptography standards that have been developed by Certicom in cooperation with secure systems developers world-wide.

Table 1 Public Key Cryptography Standards (PKCS) Specifications

No.	PKCS Title	Comments
1	RSA Cryptography Standard	
2,4		Incorporated into PKCS 1
3	Diffie–Hellman Key Agreement Standard	Superseded by IEEE 1363a etc.
5	Password-Based Cryptography Standard	
6	Extended-Certificate Syntax Standard	Never adopted
7	Cryptographic Message Syntax Standard	Superseded by RFC 3369 (CMS)
8	Private-Key Information Syntax Standard	
9	Selected Object Classes and Attribute Types	
10	Certification Request Syntax Standard	
11	Cryptographic Token Interface Standard	Referred to as CRYPTOKI
12	Personal Information Exchange Syntax Standard	
13	*(reserved for ECC)*	Never published
14	*(reserved for pseudo random number generation)*	Never published
15	Cryptographic Token Information Syntax Standard	

IEEE = Institute of Electrical and Electronics Engineers; RFC = Request for Comment.

The PKCS standards, developed by RSA Laboratories (a Division of RSA Data Security) in cooperation with secure systems developers worldwide for the purpose of accelerating the deployment of public key cryptography, are widely implemented in practice and periodically updated. Contributions from the PKCS standards have become part of many formal and de facto standards, including ANSI X9 documents, IETF documents, and SSL/TLS (secure socket layer/transport layer security). The parts and status of PKCS standards are listed in Table 1 and are discussed in detail in the following sections. The descriptions are largely adapted from the PKCS documents. This chapter concludes with an example application that uses all these PKCS standards.

PKCS 1: RSA CRYPTOGRAPHY STANDARD

PKCS 1 v2.1, provides standards for implementing RSA algorithm-based public key cryptographic encryption schemes and digital signature schemes with appendix. It also defines corresponding ASN.1 syntax for representing keys and for identifying the schemes.

RSA is a public key algorithm invented by Rivest, Shamir, and Adleman (1978) that is based on the exponentiation modulo the product of two large prime numbers. The security of RSA algorithm is believed to be based on the hardness of factoring the product of large prime numbers. In PKCS 1 v2.1, the multiprime RSA scheme is introduced. Multiprime RSA means that the modulus isn't the product of two primes but of more than two primes. This is used to increase performance of RSA cryptographic primitives. In particular, in multiprocessor environments, one can exponentiate modulo each prime and then apply the Chinese remainder theorem to get the final results. However, one should be aware that the security strength of multiprime RSA is a different from the original RSA scheme. Assuming that the best way to attack multiprime RSA is to factorize the modulus and the best factorization algorithm is the number field sieve (NFS) algorithm, we can compute the approximate strength of some multiprime RSA schemes as listed in Table 2, where u is the number of primes. Similar tables for two primes RSA can be found in literature (e.g., Lenstra and Verheul, 2001).

RSA Keys

Let $n = r_1 \cdots r_u$ be the product of $u \geq 2$ distinct prime numbers of approximately the same size ($|n|/u$ bits each), where $|n|$ denotes the number of bits in n. For the case of $u = 2$, one normally uses p and q to denote the two prime numbers, that is, $n = pq$. A typical size for n is 1,024 bits, and $u = 2$. Let e, d be two integers satisfying $e \cdot d \equiv 1 \pmod{\chi(n)}$, where $\chi(n)$ is the least common multiple of $r_1 - 1, r_2 - 1, \ldots, r_u - 1$. We call n the RSA *modulus*, e the *encryption exponent*, and d the *decryption exponent*. The pair (n, e) is the *public key*, and the pair (n, d) is called the *secret key* or *private key*. The public key is public, and one can use it to encrypt messages or to verify digital signatures. The private key is known only to the owner of the private key and can be used to decrypt ciphertexts or to digitally sign messages.

To decrypt ciphertexts efficiently and generate digital signatures efficiently, the private key may include further information such as the first two prime factors and CRT exponents and CRT coefficients of each prime factor. For a prime factor r_i, its CRT exponent is a number d_i satisfying $e \cdot d_i \equiv 1 \pmod{(r_i - 1)}$, and its CRT coefficient t_i is a positive integer less than r_i satisfying $R_i \cdot t_i \equiv 1 \pmod{r_i}$, where $R_i = r_1 \cdot r_2 \cdots r_{i-1}$. PKCS 1 v2.1 specifies the format for such kind of enhanced private keys.

RSA Encryption Schemes

This section begins by describing a basic version of RSA encryption scheme. A message is an integer $m < n$. To encrypt m, one computes $c \equiv m^e \bmod n$. To decrypt the ciphertext c, the legitimate receiver computes $c^d \bmod n$.

Table 2 Security Strength of Multiprime RSA Schemes

Symmetric Key Size	RSA Modulus Size	u	Symmetric Key Size	RSA Modulus Size	u
80[a]	1,024	2	**192**[d]	7,680	4
73	1,024	3	175	7,680	5
112[b]	2,335	3	158	7,680	6
100	2,335	4	144	7,680	7
88	2,335	5	125	7,680	9
128[c]	3,072	3	**256**[e]	15,360	5
117	3,072	4	235	15,360	6
103	3,072	5	215	15,360	7
93	3,072	6	199	15,360	8

[a] Corresponding to the security level of symmetric key cipher Skipjack that is contained in the clipper chip, designed by National Security Agency (NSA)
[b] Corresponding to the security level of symmetric key cipher triple-DES, where DES is the Data Encryption Standards
[c] Corresponding to the security level of symmetric key cipher AES 128
[d] Corresponding to the security level of symmetric key cipher AES 192
[e] Corresponding to the security level of symmetric key cipher AES 256

Indeed,

$$c^d \equiv m^{ed} \equiv m \bmod n,$$

where the last equality follows by Euler's theorem.

For performance reasons, RSA is generally not used to encrypt long data messages directly. Typically, RSA is used to encrypt a secret key, and the data are encrypted with the secret key using a secret key cryptography scheme such as DES or AES. Thus, the actual data to be encrypted by RSA scheme are generally much smaller than the modulus, and the message (secret key) needs to be padded to the same length of the modulus before encryption. For example, if AES-128 is used, then an AES key is 128 bits. Another reason for a standardized padding before encryption using some randomness is that the basic version of RSA encryption scheme is not secure and is vulnerable to many attacks. PKCS 1 v2.1 provides two message padding methods: EME-PKCS1-v1_5 and EME-OAEP.

RSAES-PKCS1-v1_5 Padding

After EME-PKCS1-v1_5 padding to M, the padded message EM appears as follows:

$$EM = \boxed{0\times 00} \boxed{0\times 02} \boxed{\text{random octets}} \boxed{0\times 00} \boxed{M},$$

where "random octets" consists of pseudo-randomly generated nonzero octets and 0×00 octet is used to delimit the padding from the actual data. The length of "random octets" is at least eight octets. The top octet 0×00 guarantees that the padded message is smaller than the modulus n (PKCS 1 v2.1 specifies that the high-order octet of the modulus must be nonzero). If the padded message EM were larger than n, decryption would produce $EM \bmod n$ instead of EM. The next octet 0×02 is the format type. The value 0×02 is used to encryption and the value 0×01 is used for signature padding format RSASSA-PKCS1-v1_5 (RSASSA-PKCS1-v1_5 is no long recommended by RSA Lab). The resulting padded message EM is $|n|$ bits and is directly encrypted using the basic version of RSA.

Bleichenbacher (1998) pointed out that improper implementation of this padding method can lead to disastrous consequences. When the encrypted message arrives at the receiver's computer, an application decrypts it, checks the initial block, and strips off the random pad. However, some applications check for the two initial blocks 0×00 02, and if it is incorrect, they send the error message saying "invalid ciphertext." These error messages can help the attacker to decrypt ciphertext of his choice. PKCS 1 v2.1 recommends certain easily implemented countermeasures to thwart this attack. Typical examples include the addition of structure to the data to be encoded, rigorous checking of PKCS 1 v1.5 conformance in decrypted messages, and the consolidation of error messages in a client–server protocol based on PKCS 1 v1.5.

RSAES-OAEP Padding

EME-OAEP is based on Bellare and Rogaway's (1995) optimal asymmetric encryption scheme. Assuming that it is difficult to inverse the RSA function and the mask generation function in the OAEP padding has appropriate properties, RSAES-OAEP is proven to be secure in a stronger sense. The reader is referred to Bellare and Rogaway (1995) for details.

Let k be the length in octets of the recipient's RSA modulus, $k_0 < k$ be an integer, H be a hash function for which outputs are k_0-octets, and MGF be the mask generation function. For an input octet string x and an integer i, MGF(x, i) outputs a string of i octets. Let M be the k_1-octets message such that $k_1 < k - 2k_0 - 2$, and L be an optional label (could be an empty string) to be associated with the message. EME-OAEP first converts the message M to a $(k - k_0 - 1)$-octets data block DB that looks as follows:

$$DB = \boxed{H(L)} \boxed{\text{random octets}} \boxed{0\times 01} \boxed{M},$$

where "random octets" consists of pseudo-randomly generated octets. The length of "random octets" could be zero.

EME-OAEP then chooses a random k_0-octets string r, and generates the OAEP padded message EM as follows:

$$EM = \boxed{0 \times 00} \boxed{r \oplus \text{MGF}(DB \oplus \text{MGF}(r, k - k_0 - 1), k_0)} \boxed{DB \oplus \text{MGF}(r, k - k_0 - 1)}.$$

The resulting padded message EM is k-octets and is directly encrypted using the basic version of RSA. For decryption operations, EME-OAEP decoding method could be constructed directly.

RSA Signature Schemes With Appendix

We begin by describing a basic version of RSA signature scheme with appendix. A message is an integer $m < n$. To sign m, the owner of the private key (n, d) computes the signature $s \equiv m^d \bmod n$. To verify that s is a signature on m from the legitimate owner of the private key (n, d), one uses the corresponding public key (n, e) to compute $m' \equiv s^e \pmod n$. If $m' = m$, then the signature is valid; otherwise, the signature is invalid.

The basic version of RSA signature scheme can only generate signatures on messages less than $|n|$ bits. In addition, the basic version of RSA signature scheme is not secure. To address these issues, in practice, one first computes a message digest from a given message using a hash function such as message digest 5 (MD5) or secure hash algorithm 1 (SHA-1). The message digest is encoded using an encoding method and the resulting string is converted to an integer and is supplied to the basic RSA signature primitive.

PKCS 1 v2.1 provides two encoding methods for encoding message digests: EMSA-PKCS1-v1_5 encoding and EMSA-PSS encoding. Correspondingly, there are two signature schemes with appendix: RSASSA-PSS and RSASSA-PKCS1-v1_5. Although no attacks are known against RSASSA-PKCS1-v1_5, in the interest of increased robustness, RSASSA-PSS is recommended for eventual adoption in new applications. RSASSA-PKCS1-v1_5 is included in PKCS 1 v2.1 for compatibility with existing applications and is not discussed here. EMSA-PSS is based on the work of Bellare and Rogaway (1996). Assuming that computing eth roots modulo n is infeasible and the hash and mask generation functions in EMSA-PSS have appropriate properties, RSASSA-PSS provides secure signatures. This assurance is provable in the sense that the difficulty of forging signatures can be directly related to the difficulty of inverting the RSA function, provided that the hash and mask generation functions are viewed as black boxes or random oracles. The reader is referred to Bellare and Rogaway (1996) for more details.

Let k be the length in octets of the RSA modulus, H be a hash function for which outputs are k_0 octets ($k_0 < k$), and MGF be the mask generation function. For an input octet string x and an integer i, MGF(x, i) outputs a string of i octets. Let M be the message to be signed. EMSA-PSS first constructs octet strings M' and DB as follows:

$$M' = \boxed{0 \times 00\ 00\ 00\ 00\ 00\ 00\ 00\ 00} \boxed{H(M)} \boxed{\text{salt}}, \qquad DB = \boxed{\text{PS}} \boxed{0 \times 01} \boxed{\text{salt}},$$

where "salt" and "PS" consist of pseudo-randomly generated octets. The lengths of "salt" and "PS" could be zero, and the length of DB is $k - k_0 - 1$ octets.

EMSA-PSS then constructs the octet string EM' as follows:

$$EM' = \boxed{DB \oplus \text{MGF}(H(M'), k - k_0 - 1)} \boxed{H(M')} \boxed{0\times\text{bc}}.$$

Assume that the RSA modulus has $|n|$ bits, then the encoded string EM is obtained by setting the leftmost $8k - |n| + 1$ bits of the leftmost octet in EM' to zero. The resulting encoded string EM is k octets and is directly signed using the basic version of RSA signature scheme. The EMSA-PSS decoding process could to be constructed directly.

PKCS 3: DIFFIE–HELLMAN KEY AGREEMENT STANDARD (OUTDATED)

PKCS 3 v1.4 describes a method for implementing Diffie–Hellman key agreement, whereby two parties can agree on a secret key that is known only to them. PKCS 3 is superseded by modern treatment of key establishment schemes specified in IEEE 1363a (2003), ANSI 9.42, ANSI X9.44, ANSI X9.63, and so on. Basically, there are two types of key establishment schemes:

1. Key agreement scheme: a key establishment scheme in which the keying data established is a function of contributions provided by both entities in such a way that neither party can predetermine the value of the keying data. Diffie–Hellman key agreement scheme is an example of this category.
2. Key transport scheme: a key establishment scheme in which the keying data established is determined entirely by one entity. For example, one party chooses a random session key, encrypts it with the other party's public key, and sends the encrypted session key to the other party. The other party can then decrypt the session key. A special case of key transport scheme is the key wrap scheme in which the session key is encrypted with a preshared secret using a secret key cipher such as DES or AES.

PKCS 5: PASSWORD-BASED CRYPTOGRAPHY STANDARD

In many applications of public key cryptography, user security is ultimately dependent on one or more secret text values or passwords. For example, user's private key is usually encrypted with a password and the encrypted private key is kept in storage devices (see the section "Private Key Information Syntax Standard"). There are two essential problems with regard to password application, however: (a) A password is not directly applicable as a key to any conventional cryptosystem; (2) passwords are often chosen from a relatively small space.

Thus, special care is required to defend against search attacks. PKCS 5 provides a general mechanism to achieve an enhanced security for password-based cryptographic primitives, covering key derivation functions, encryption schemes, message-authentication schemes, and ASN.1 syntax identifying the techniques. It should be noted that other password-based cryptographic techniques are currently under standardization process in IEEE 1363.2.

Key Derivation Functions

A password-based key derivation function produces a key from a password, a random salt value, and an iteration count. The salt is not secret and serves the purpose of producing a large set of keys for one given password, among which one is selected at random according to the salt. An iteration count serves the purpose of increasing the cost of producing keys from a password, thereby also increasing the difficulty of attack. PKCS 5 v2.0 specifies two password-based key derivation functions PBKDF1 and PBKDF2. PBKDF1 is included in PKCS # 5 v2.0 only for compatibility with existing applications following PKCS 5 v1.5 and is not recommended for new applications.

PBKDF2 applies a pseudo-random function to derive keys. The length of the derived key is essentially unbounded. However, the maximum length for the derived key may be limited by the structure of the underlying pseudorandom function. Let H be a pseudo-random function with the outputs $hLen$ octets, $dkLen \leq (2^{32}-1) \times hLen$ the intended length in octets for the derived key, P the password (an octet string), S an eight-octet salt string, and c an iterating count. For each integer i, by repeatedly hashing the password, salts, and so on, one gets a sequence of $hLen$-octets strings:

$$U_1^i = H(P, S||\mathrm{INT}(i)),\ U_2^i = H\left(P, U_1^i\right),\ \ldots,\ U_c^i = H\left(P, U_{c-1}^i\right),$$

where INT(i) is a four-octet encoding of the integer i, most significant octet first. Then one computes the $hLen$-octet strings $T_i = U_1^i \oplus U_2^i \oplus \cdots \oplus U_c^i$ for each i. The derived key is the first $dkLen$-octet of the string $T_1||T_2||T_3||\cdots$. In other words, let $l = \lceil dkLen/hLen \rceil$ be the number of $hLen$-octet blocks in the derived key, rounding up, and $r = dkLen - (l-1) \times hLen$ be the number of octets in the last block. Then the $dkLen$-octet–derived key $DK =$ PBKDF2($P, S, c, dkLen$) appears as follows:

$$DK = \boxed{T_1 \mid T_2 \mid \cdots \mid T_l[0 \cdots r-1]}.$$

Encryption Schemes

PKCS 5 v2.0 specifies two encryption schemes password based encryption scheme 1 (PBES1) and PBES2. PBES1 is included in PKCS 5 v2.0 only for compatibility with PKCS 5 v1.5, and is not recommended for new applications. PBES2 combines the password-based key derivation function PBKDF2 with an underlying encryption scheme $\mathcal{E}$. Let M be the message to be encrypted, P be the password, k be the key length in octets for $\mathcal{E}$. For the PBES2 encryption, one first selects a salt S and an iteration count c, then one computes the derived k octets key $DK =$ PBKDF2(P, S, c, k). The ciphertext C for M is: $C = \mathcal{E}_{DK}(M)$. The decryption operation for PBES2 can be done similarly.

Message Authentication Schemes

In a *password-based message authentication scheme*, the message authentication code (MAC) generation operation produces a message authentication code from a message under a password, and the MAC verification operation verifies the message authentication code under the same password. PKCS 5 v2.0 defines the password-based message authentication scheme PBMAC1 that combines the password-based key derivation function PBKDF2 with an underlying message authentication scheme $\mathcal{A}$.

Let M be the message to be authenticated, P be the password, and k be the key length in octets for $\mathcal{A}$. For PBMAC1, one first selects a salt S and an iteration count c, and then computes the derived k octets key $DK =$ PBKDF2(P, S, c, k). The message authentication code T can be computed as $T = \mathcal{A}(M, DK)$. The MAC verification operation for PBMAC1 can be done similarly.

PKCS 6: EXTENDED-CERTIFICATE SYNTAX STANDARD (HISTORIC)

When PKCS 6 was drafted, X.509 was in version 1.0 and no `extensions` component was defined in the certificate. An X.509 v3 certificate can contain information about a given entity in the `extensions` component. Since the introduction of X.509 v3, the status of PKCS 6 is historic.

PKCS 7 AND RFC 3369: CRYPTOGRAPHIC MESSAGE SYNTAX (CMS)

PKCS 7 has been superseded by IETF RFC 3369 (Housley, 2002): cryptographic message syntax (CMS), which is the basis for the secure multipurpose internet mail extension (S/MIME) specification. CMS defines the syntax that is used to digitally sign, digest, authenticate, or encrypt arbitrary message content. In particular, CMS describes an encapsulation syntax for data protection. The syntax allows multiple encapsulations; one encapsulation envelope can be nested inside another. Likewise, one party can digitally sign previously encapsulated data. In the CMS syntax, arbitrary attributes, such as signing time, can be signed along with the message content, and other attributes, such as countersignatures, can be associated with a signature. A variety of architectures for certificate-based key management (e.g., the one defined by the IETF Public Key Infrastructure (PKIX) working group) are supported in CMS.

The CMS values are generated using ASN.1 with BER-encoding and are typically represented as octet strings. When transmitting CMS values in systems (e.g., e-mail systems) that do not support reliable octet strings transmission, one should use additional encoding mechanisms that are not addressed in CMS.

CMS defines one protection content type, ContentInfo, as the object syntax for documents exchanged between entities. ContentInfo encapsulates a single identified content

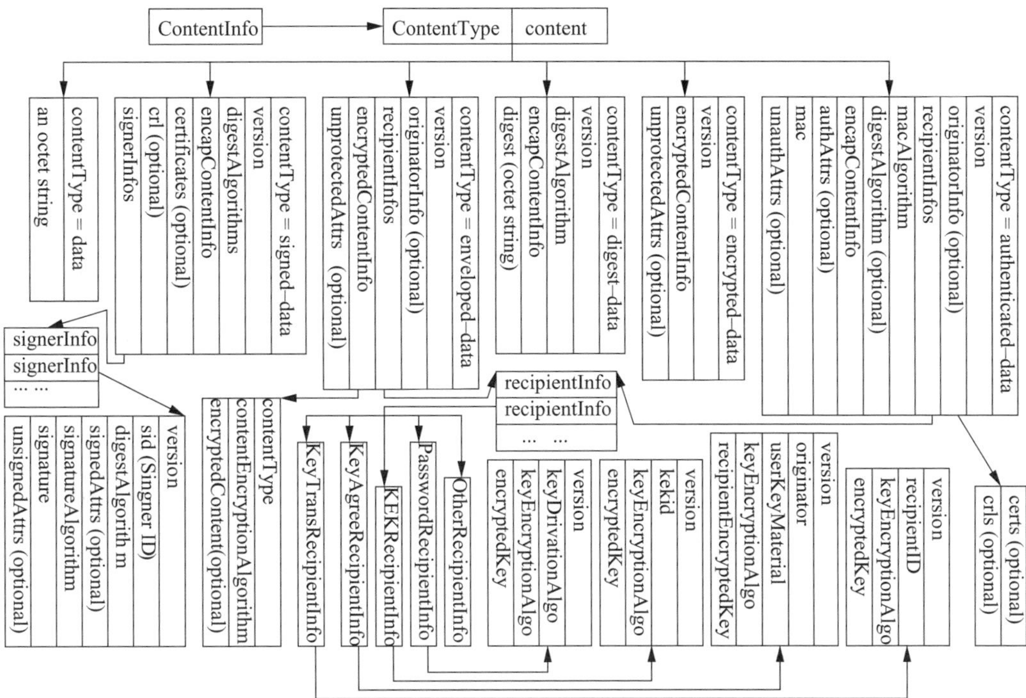

Figure 1: Cryptographic message syntax content types and their fields.

type and the identified type may provide further encapsulation. A ContentInfo object contains two fields: `contentType` (object identifier) and `content`. CMS defines six `contentTypes`: data, signed-data, enveloped-data, digested-data, encrypted-data, and authenticated-data. Additional content types can be defined outside the CMS document. The type of content can be determined uniquely by `contentType`. Figure 1 lists the value types in the `content` field for each CMS defined content type.

In Figure 1, digestAlgorithms is collection of message digest algorithm identifiers. encapContentInfo is the signed content, consisting of a content type identifier and the content itself. signedAttrs, unsignedAttrs, unprotectedAttrs, authAttrs, and unauthAttrs are sets of Attribute objects. An Attribute object is a sequence of two fields: attrType (object identifier) and attrValues (set of values).

PKCS 8: PRIVATE KEY INFORMATION SYNTAX STANDARD

The security of the public key cryptosystem is entirely dependent on the protection of the private keys. Generally, the private keys are encrypted with password and stored in some storage medium. It is important to have a standard to store private keys so that one can move private keys from one system to another system without any trouble. PKCS 8 v1.2 describes a syntax for private key information, which includes a private key for some public key algorithm and a set of attributes, and a syntax for encrypted private key information. A password-based encryption algorithm (e.g., one of those described in PKCS 5) could be used to encrypt the private key information.

Two objects, PrivateKeyInfo and EncryptedPrivate KeyInfo, are defined in this standard. A PrivateKeyInfo object contains the fields: version, privateKeyAlgorithm, privateKey, and attributes (optional), where privateKeyAlgorithm is the identifier of the private key algorithm, privateKey is the octet string representing the private key, and attributes is a collection of attributes that are encrypted along with the private key. An EncryptedPrivateKeyInfo object contains two fields: encryptionAlgorithm and encryptedData, where encryptionAlgorithm identifies the algorithm under which the private key information is encrypted, and encryptedData is the octet string representing the result of encrypting the private key information.

In practice, the PrivateKeyInfo object is BER encoded into an octet string, which is encrypted with the secret key to give the encryptedData field of the EncryptedPrivateKeyInfo object.

PKCS 9: SELECTED OBJECT CLASSES AND ATTRIBUTE TYPES

To support PKCS-defined attributes (e.g., to store PKCS attributes in a directory service) in directory systems based on lightweight directory access protocol (LDAP) and the X.500 family of protocols, PKCS 9 v2.0 defines two auxiliary object classes, pkcsEntity and naturalPerson. PKCS attributes could be packaged into these two object classes and be exported to other environments such as LDAP directory systems. PKCS 9 v2.0 also defines some new attribute types and matching rules that could be used in other PKCS standards. For example, it defines challengePassword and extensionRequest attribute types to be used in PKCS 10 attribute field, and it defines some attribute types to be used in PKCS 7 (CMS) signedAttrs, unsignedAttrs, unprotectedAttrs, authAttrs, and unauthAttrs fields, as noted earlier. All ASN.1 object classes, attributes,

Table 3 PKCS 9 Attribute Types for Use in Other Standards

Standard Name	Attribute Types
PKCS 7 and CMS	contentType, messageDigest, signingTime, sequenceNumber, randomNonce, and counterSignature (with syntax SignerInfo)
PKCS 10	challengePassword (with syntax DirectoryString) and extensionRequest (imported from ISO/IEC 9594-8 (1997))
PKCS 12 and 15	(user) friendlyName and localKeyId

CMS = Cryptographic message syntax.

matching rules, and types defined in PKCS 9 v2.0 are exported for use in other environments.

The pkcsEntity object class is a general-purpose auxiliary object class that is intended to hold attributes about PKCS-related entities. A pkcsEntity object class contains these fields:

pkcsEntity = | KIND (auxiliary type) | PKCSEntityAttributeSet (optional) | ID |.

The PKCSEntityAttributeSet may contain any of the following attributes: pKCS7PDU (with syntax ContentInfo), userPKCS12 (with syntax PFX), pKCS15Token (PKCS 15), encryptedPrivateKeyInfo (PKCS #8), and future extensions. These attributes should be used when the corresponding PKCS data (e.g., CMS signed or enveloped data; PKCS 12 personal identity information data; PKCS 8 encrypted private key data, etc.) are stored in a directory service.

The naturalPerson object class is a general-purpose auxiliary object class that is intended to hold attributes about human beings. A naturalPerson object class contains these fields:

naturalPerson = | KIND (auxiliary type) | NaturalPersonAttributeSet (optional) | ID |.

The NaturalPersonAttributeSet may contain any of the following (or future extensions) attributes:

emailAddress	countryOfCitizenship	countryOfResidence	pseudonym	placeOfBirth
serialNumber	unstructuredAddress	unstructuredName	gender	dateOfBirth

PKCS 9 also defines two matching rules, pkcs9-CaseIgnoreMatch and signingTimeMatch, which are used to determine whether two PKCS 9 attribute values are the same. Attribute types defined in PKCS 9 that are useful in other standards are listed in Table 3.

PKCS 10: CERTIFICATION REQUEST SYNTAX STANDARD

PKCS 10 v1.7 specifies syntax for certificate request. When one entity wants to get a public key certificate, the entity constructs a certificate request and sends it a certification authority, which transforms the request into an X.509 public key certificate. A certification authority fulfills the request by authenticating the requesting entity and verifying the entity's signature, and, if the request is valid, constructing an X.509 certificate from the distinguished name and public key, the issuer name, and the certification authority's choice of serial number, validity period, and signature algorithm. If the certification request contains any PKCS 9 attributes, the certification authority may also use the values in these attributes as well as other information known to the certification authority to construct X.509 certificate extensions. PKCS 10 does not specify the forms that the certification authority returns the new certificate. A certificate request is constructed with the following steps:

1. Construct a CertificationRequestInfo object containing fields "version," "subject," "subjectPKInfo," and "attributes," where "subject" contains the entity's distinguished name and "subjectPKInfo" contains the entity's public key. Some attribute types that might be useful here are defined in PKCS 9. An example is the challengePassword attribute, which specifies a password by which the entity may request certificate revocation. Another example is information to appear in X.509 certificate extensions.
2. Sign the CertificationRequestInfo object with the subject entity's private key.
3. Construct a CertificationRequest object containing fields "CertificationRequestInfo," "signatureAlgorithm," and "signature," where "signatureAlgorithm" contains the signature algorithm identifier, and "signature" contains the entity's signature.

PKCS 11: CRYPTOGRAPHIC TOKEN INTERFACE STANDARD

PKCS 11 v2.20 specifies an application programming interface (API), called "Cryptoki," to devices which hold cryptographic information and perform cryptographic functions. Cryptoki, pronounced "crypto-key" and short for "cryptographic token interface," follows a simple object-based approach, addressing the goals of technology independence (any kind of device) and resource sharing (multiple applications accessing multiple devices), presenting to applications a common, logical view of the device called a "cryptographic token." Cryptoki was intended from the beginning to be an interface between applications and all kinds of portable cryptographic devices, such as those based on smart cards, personal computer memory card international association (PCMCIA) cards, and smart diskettes. The primary goal of Cryptoki was a lower level programming interface that abstracts the details of the devices, and presents to the application a common model of the cryptographic device, called a "cryptographic token" (or simply "token").

PKCS 11 v2.20 specifies the data types and functions available to an application requiring cryptographic services using the ANSI C (1990) programming language. These data types and functions will typically be provided via C header files by the supplier of a Cryptoki library. Generic ANSI C header files for Cryptoki are available from the PKCS Web page.

Cryptoki isolates an application from the details of the cryptographic device. The application does not have to change to interface to a different type of device or to run in a different environment; thus, the application is portable.

Cryptoki is intended for cryptographic devices associated with a single user, so some features that might be included in a general-purpose interface are omitted. For example, Cryptoki does not have a means of distinguishing multiple users. The focus is on a single user's keys and perhaps a small number of certificates related to them. Moreover, the emphasis is on cryptography. Although the device can perform useful non-cryptographic functions, such functions are left to other interfaces.

Cryptoki is likely to be implemented as a library supporting the functions in the interface, and applications will be linked to the library. An application may be linked to Cryptoki directly; alternatively, Cryptoki can be a so-called shared library (or dynamic link library), in which case the application would link the library dynamically. The dynamic approach certainly has advantages as new libraries are made available, but from a security perspective, there are drawbacks. In particular, if a library is easily replaced, then there is the possibility that an attacker can substitute a rogue library that intercepts a user's personal identification number (PIN). From a security perspective, therefore, direct linking is preferable, although code-signing techniques can prevent many of the security risks of dynamic linking. In any case, whether the linking is direct or dynamic, the programming interface between the application and a Cryptoki library remains the same. Figure 2 describes the general cryptoki model.

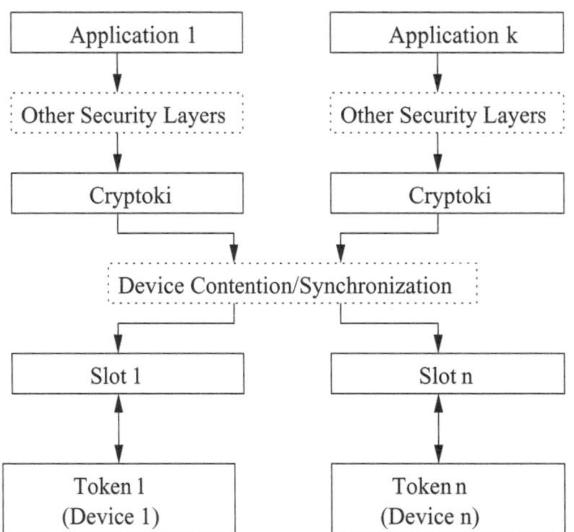

Figure 2: General Cryptoki model.

Cryptoki defines general data types, objects, and functions. The general data types include general information data types (e.g., CK_VERSION and CK_INFO), slot and token types (e.g., CK_SLOT_ID), session types (e.g., CK_SESSION_HANDLE), object types (e.g., CK_OBJECT_CLASS), data types for mechanisms (e.g., CK_MECHANISM_INFO), function types (e.g., CK_FUNCTION_LIST), and locking-related types (e.g., CK_CREATEMUTEX).

Cryptoki's logical view of a token is a device that stores objects and can perform cryptographic functions. Cryptoki recognizes three classes of objects, as defined in the CK_OBJECT_CLASS data type: data, certificates, and keys. An object consists of a set of attributes, each of which has a given value. A key object stores a cryptographic key. The key may be a public key, a private key, or a secret key; each of these types of keys has subtypes for use in specific mechanisms (cryptographic algorithms). For example, public key objects (object class CKO_PUBLIC_KEY) hold public keys and contains the following common attributes:

CKA_ID	CKA_KEY_TYPE	CKA_DERIVE	CKA_KEY_GEN_MECHANISM
CKA_WRAP	CKA_END_DATE	CKA_LOCAL	CKA_KEY_ALLOWED_MECHANISM
CKA_VERIFY	CKA_SUBJECT	CKA_TRUSTED	CKA_WRAP_TEMPLATE
CKA_ENCRYPT	CKA_START_DATE	CKA_CHECK_VALUE	CKA_VERIFY_RECOVER

According to their lifetime, objects are classified as "token objects" and "session objects." Further classification defines access requirements. "PIN" or token-dependent methods are required to access "private token" whereas no restriction is put on "public tokens."

In addition to the PIN protection to private objects on a token, protection to private keys and secret keys can be given by marking them as sensitive or unextractable. Sensitive keys cannot be revealed in plaintext off the token, and unextractable keys cannot be revealed off the token even when encrypted (although they can still be used as keys). It is expected that access to private, sensitive, or unextractable objects by means

Table 4 Session Events

Event	Occurs When
Log In SO	the SO is authenticated to the token.
Log In User	the normal user is authenticated to the token.
Log Out	the application logs out the current user (SO or normal user).
Close Session	the application closes the session or closes all sessions.
Device Removed	the device underlying the token has been removed from its slot.

other than Cryptoki (e.g., other programming interfaces or reverse engineering of the device) would be difficult. Cryptoki does not consider the security of the operating system by which the application interfaces to it. For example, because the PIN may be passed through the operating system, a rogue application on the operating system may be able to obtain the PIN.

Cryptoki provides functions for creating, destroying, and copying objects in general and for obtaining and modifying the values of their attributes. Objects are always well formed in Cryptoki. That is, an object always contains all required attributes, and the attributes are always consistent with the one from the time the object is created. This contrasts with some object-based paradigms in which an object has no attributes other than perhaps a class when it is created and is uninitialized for some time. In Cryptoki, objects are always initialized.

Cryptoki defines thirteen categories of functions: general-purpose functions (four functions including C_Initialize and C_Finalize), slot and token management functions (nine functions), session management functions (eight functions), object management functions (nine functions), encryption functions (four functions), decryption functions (four functions), message digesting functions (five functions), signing and MACing functions (six functions), functions for verifying signatures and MACs (six functions), dual-purpose cryptographic functions (four functions), key management functions (five functions), random number generation functions (two functions), and parallel function management functions (two functions). In addition to these functions, Cryptoki can use application-supplied callback functions to notify an application of certain events and can also use application-supplied functions to handle mutex objects for safe multithreaded library access.

Cryptoki has two user types: security officer (SO) and normal user. The function of SO is to initiate a token and to set the PIN for the normal user. Only the normal user has access to private objects in the token.

A mechanism specifies precisely how a certain cryptographic process is to be performed (e.g., a digital signature process or a hashing process). Cryptoki defines mechanisms for almost all available cryptographic operations that are currently used in the industry.

An application in a single address space becomes a "Cryptoki application" when one of its running threads calls the Cryptoki function C_Initialize and it ceases to be the "Cryptoki application" by calling the Cryptoki function C_Finalize. Cryptoki has support mechanisms for multithreading access.

Cryptoki requires that an application open one or more sessions with a token to gain access to the token's objects and functions. A session can be a read/write (R/W) session or a read-only (R/O) session. R/W and R/O refer to the access to token objects, not to session objects. In both session types, an application can create, read, write, and destroy session objects and read token objects. Table 4 lists session events.

Cryptoki header files define a large array of data types. Certain packing- and pointer-related aspects of these types are platform- and compiler-dependent; these aspects are therefore resolved on a platform-by-platform (or compiler-by-compiler) basis outside of the Cryptoki header files by means of preprocessor directives. These directives are described in the Cryptoki also.

PKCS 12: PERSONAL INFORMATION EXCHANGE SYNTAX STANDARD

PKCS 12 v1.0 describes a transfer syntax for personal identity information, including private keys, certificates, miscellaneous secrets, and extensions. Machines, applications, browsers, Internet kiosks, and so on that support this standard will allow a user to import, export, and exercise a single set of personal identity information. PKCS 12 can be viewed as building on PKCS 8 by including essential but ancillary identity information along with private keys and by instituting higher security through public key privacy and integrity modes.

There are four combinations of *privacy modes* and *integrity modes*. The privacy modes use encryption (public key–based or password-based) to protect personal information from exposure and the integrity modes (public key digital signature–based or password message authentication code–based) protect personal information from tampering. For example, in public key privacy mode, personal information on the source platform is enveloped using the trusted encryption public key of a known destination platform and the envelop is opened using the corresponding private key.

Although all combinations of privacy and integrity modes are permitted, certain practices should still be avoided. For example, it is unwise to transport private keys without physical protection when using password privacy mode. In general, it is preferred that the source and destination platforms have trusted public and private key pairs usable for digital signatures and encryption, respectively. When trusted public and private key pairs are not available, password modes for privacy and integrity could be used.

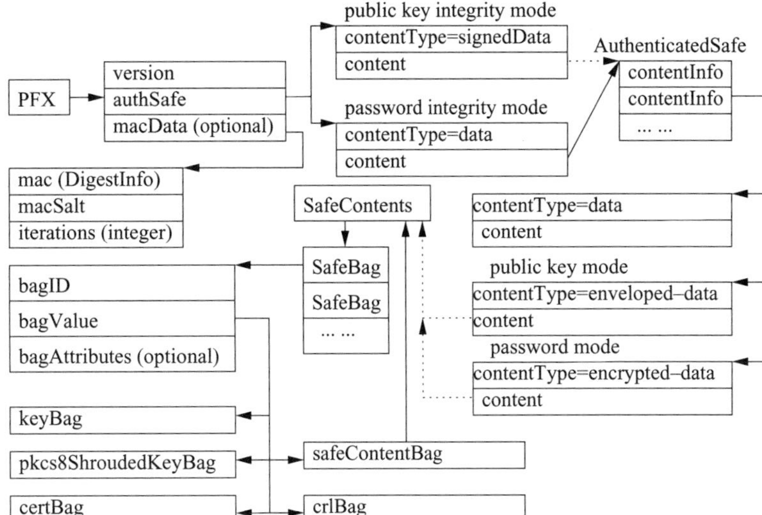

Figure 3: PFX object structure.

The top-level exchange PDU (protocol data unit) in PKCS 12 is called PFX. A PFX has three fields: version, authSafe, and macData (optional), where authSafe is a PKCS 7 ContentInfo. Figure 3 describes the structure of the PFX object.

It is straightforward to create PFX PDUs from the structure described in Figure 3. The data wrapped in the PFX could be imported by reversing the procedure for creating a PFX.

PKCS 15: CRYPTOGRAPHIC TOKEN INFORMATION SYNTAX STANDARD

Cryptographic tokens, such as Integrated Circuit Cards (or IC cards) are intrinsically secure computing platforms ideally suited to providing enhanced security and privacy functionality to applications. They can handle authentication information such as digital certificates and capabilities, authorizations, and cryptographic keys. Furthermore, they are capable of providing secure storage and computational facilities for sensitive information such as private keys and key fragments. At the same time, many of these tokens provide an isolated processing facility capable of using this information without exposing it within the host environment where it is at potential risk from hostile code (viruses, Trojan horses, and so on). Unfortunately, the use of these tokens for authentication and authorization purposes has been hampered by the lack of interoperability. First, the industry lacks standards for storing a common format of digital credentials (keys, certificates, etc.) on them. This has made it difficult to create applications that can work with credentials from a variety of technology providers. Second, mechanisms to allow multiple applications to share digital credentials effectively have not yet reached maturity.

PKCS 15 is a standard intended to enable interoperability among components running on various platforms (platform neutral), to enable applications to take advantage of products and components from multiple manufacturers (vendor neutral), to enable the use of advances in technology without rewriting application-level software (application neutral), and to maintain consistency with existing, related standards while expanding on them only where necessary and practical. As an example, the holder of an integrated circuit (IC) card containing a digital certificate should be able to present the card to any application running on any host and successfully use the card to present the contained certificate to the application. As a first step to achieve these objectives, PKCS 15 v1.1 specifies a file and directory format for storing security-related information on cryptographic tokens.

The PKCS 15 token information may be read when a token is presented and is used by a PKCS 15 interpreter which is part of the software environment (e.g., as shown in the Figure 4).

PKCS 15 v1.1 defines four general classes of objects: keys, certificates, authentication objects, and data objects. All these object classes have subclasses (e.g., private keys, secret keys, and public keys) for which instantiations become objects actually stored on cards. Objects can be private, meaning that they are protected against unauthorized access, or public. In the IC card case, access (read, write, etc.) to private objects is defined by authentication objects (which also includes authentication procedures). Conditional access (from a cardholder's perspective) is achieved with knowledge-based or biometric user information. In other cases, such as when PKCS 15 is implemented in software, private objects may be protected against unauthorized access by cryptographic means. Public objects are not protected from read-access.

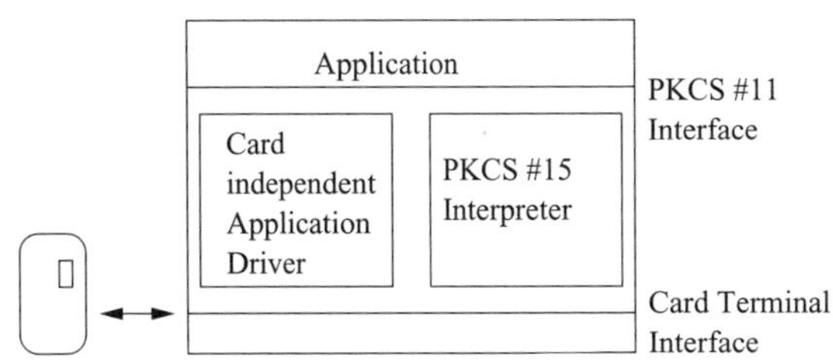

Figure 4: Embedding of a PKCS 15 interpreter (example).

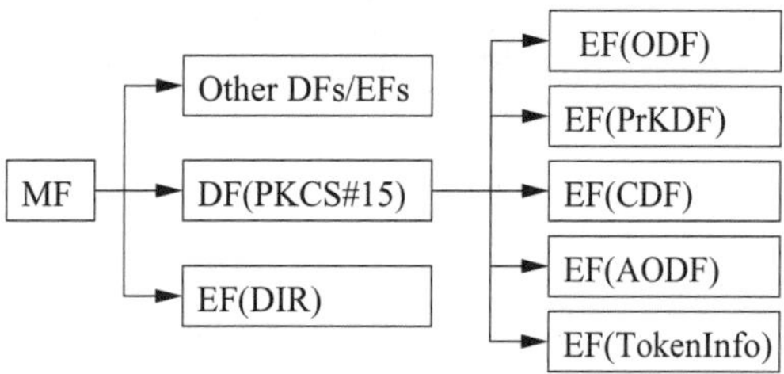

Figure 5: Typical PKCS 15 card layout and contents of DF(PKCS 15).

Whether or not they are protected against modifications depends on the particular implementation.

In general, an IC card file format specifies how certain abstract, higher level elements such as keys and certificates are to be represented in terms of more lower level elements such as IC card files and directory structures. A typical IC card supporting PKCS 15 has the file structure layout as in Figure 5, where the following abbreviations are used: MF (master file), DF(x) (dedicated file x), and EF(x) (elementary file x).

PKCS 15 defines syntax for application directory contents as in Table 5. PKCS 15–compliant IC cards should support direct application selection as defined in ISO/IEC 7816-4 Section 9 and ISO-IEC 7816-5 Section 6 (the full application identifier [AID] is to be used as parameter for a "SELECT FILE" command). The operating system of the card must keep track of the currently selected application and only allow the commands applicable to that particular application while it is selected. The AID data element consists of 12 bytes, and its contents are defined in PKCS 15.

Objects could be created, modified, and removed from the object directory file on a card. ASN.1 syntax for these objects have also been specified in PKCS 15.

AN EXAMPLE

This chapter concludes with an example application of different PKCS standards. Assume that we want to implement a smart card authentication system based on public key cryptography technology. Each user will be issued a smart card containing users' private key, public key certificate, and other personal information. Users can authenticate themselves to different computing systems (or banking systems) by inserting their smart cards into card readers attached to these computing systems and typing the password (or PIN).

RSA cryptographic primitives specified in PKCS 1 could be chosen as the underlying cryptographic mechanisms. First, user Alice needs to register herself to the system to get her smart card. In the registration process, the system first generates a public key/private key pair for Alice. Using PKCS 9, the system may create a naturalPerson object or a few attributes containing Alice's personal information. This information can then be used to generate a CertificateRequest object according to PKCS 10. The system can then send the CertificateRequest object to the certificate authorities (CAs) enveloped using CMS (PKCS 7). After the identity information verification, the CA signs Alice's public key to generate a certificate for Alice and sends it back to the system. After receiving Alice's certificate from the CA, the system can build a smart card for Alice. Using Alice's password (PIN) the system generates an EncryptedPrivateKeyInfo object for Alice according to PKCS 8 and PKCS 9 (PKCS 5 is also used in this procedure). PKCS 12 may then be used to transfer Alice's encrypted private key and personal information from one computer to another computer (e.g., from a server machine to the smart card making machine). Using the dedicated file format DF (PKCS 15), Alice's encrypted private key object EncryptedPrivateKeyInfo, certificate, and other personal information could be stored on the smart card. The card is now ready for Alice to use. At the same

Table 5 Application Directory Contents

EF(ODF)	An object directory file (ODF) contains pointers to other EFs (PrKDFs, PuKDFs, SKDFs, CDFs, DODFs, and AODFs)
EF(PrKDF)	A private key directory file (PrKDF) contains (references to) private keys
EF(PuKDF)	A public key directory file (PuKDF) contains (references to) public keys
EF(SKDF)	A secret key directory file (SKDF) contains (references to) secret keys
EF(CDF)	A certificate directory file (CDF) contains (references to) certificates
EF(DODF)	A data object directory file (DODF) is for data objects other than keys or certificate
EF(AODF)	An authentication object directory file (AODF) is for authentication objects such as personal identification numbers passwords, and biometric data
EF(TokenInfo)	A mandatory TokenInfo with transparent structure contains generic information about the card (e.g., card serial number, supported file types, algorithms implemented on the card) and its capabilities
EF(UnusedSpace)	An UnusedSpace file with transparent structure is used to keep track of unused space in already created elementary files
	Other EFs in the PKCS #15 directory contains the actual values of objects (such as private keys, public keys, secret keys, certificates and application specific data) referenced from within PrKDFs, SKDFs, PuKDFs, CDFs or DODFs

EF = Elementary file.

time, Alice may also get a copy of these private information on a universal serial bus (USB) memory stick. This personal information is stored on the memory stick according to PKCS 12.

Because all computing systems (e.g., different platforms from different vendors) support PKCS 11 API, when Alice inserts her card into an attached card reader, applications on these computing systems can communicate smoothly with Alice's smart card. In particular, after typing her password (PIN), Alice's smart card can digitally sign challenges from these computing systems and these computing systems can verify Alice's signature using the certificate presented by Alice's smart card. Thus, Alice can authenticate herself to these systems.

ACKNOWLEDGMENTS

The author thanks anonymous referees for the constructive comments on improving the presentation of this chapter. The author also thanks Dennis Hamilton (UoL KIT eLearning Division) for comments on PKCS 5 v2.0.

GLOSSARY

Abstract Syntax notation one (ASN.1) Defined in ISO/IEC 8824-1–4 (1995).

Advanced Encryption Algorithm (AES) A secret key cipher, as defined in FIPS PUB 197 (2001).

Attribute An ASN.1 type that identifies an attribute type (by an object identifier) and an associated attribute value.

Basic Encoding Rules (BER) Defined in X.690 (1994), is the set of rules for encoding ASN.1 defined data into a particular representation for transmitting to another system.

Cryptoki cryptographic token interface.

Data Encryption Standard (DES), Triple DES Secret key ciphers, as defined in FIPS PUB 46-3 (1999).

Key Derivation Function A function that produces a derived key from a base key and other parameters.

Lightweight directory access protocol (LDAP) Defined in Hodges and Morgan (2002).

MD5 A cryptographic hash function, as defined in Rivest (1992). MD5 reduces messages of any length to message digests of 128 bits.

Message Authentication Code (MAC) Scheme A cryptographic scheme consisting of a message tagging operation and a tag checking operation that is capable of providing data origin authentication and data integrity.

Octet An octet is a bit string of length 8. An octet is represented by a hexadecimal string of length 2. For example 0x9D represents the bit string 10011101.

Octet String An ordered sequence of octets.

Personal Identity Information Personal information such as private keys, certificates, and miscellaneous secrets.

PKCS 11 Token The logical view of a cryptographic device defined by Cryptoki.

PKCS 15 Elementary File Set of data units or records that share the same file identifier and that cannot be a parent of another file.

PKCS 15 Directory (DIR) File An elementary file containing a list of applications supported by the card and optional related data elements.

Protocol Data Unit (PDU) A sequence of bits in machine-independent format constituting a message in a protocol.

SHA-1, SHA-256, SHA-384, and SHA-512 Cryptographic hash function functions, as defined in FIPS PUB 180-2, (2002). SHA-1 (SHA-256, SHA-384, and SHA-512, respectively) reduces messages of any length to message digests of 160 bits (256 bits, 384 bits, and 512 bits, respectively).

CROSS REFERENCES

See *Digital Certificates; Digital Signatures and Electronic Signatures; Encryption Basics; Key Management; PKI (Public Key Infrastructure).*

REFERENCES

American National Standards Institute (1990). ANSI/ISO 9899: American National Standard for Programming Languages—C.

Bellare, M., & Rogaway, P. (1995). Optimal asymmetric encryption—how to Encrypt with RSA. In A. De Santis, (Ed.), *Advances in cryptology*, Eurocrypt '94, volume 950 of *Lecture Notes in Computer Science* (pp. 92–111). Springer Verlag.

Bellare, M., & Rogaway, P. (1996). The exact security of digital signatures—how to sign with RSA and Rabin. In U. Maurer (Ed.), *Advances in cryptology*, Eurocrypt '96, volume 1070 of *Lecture Notes in Computer Science* (pp. 399–416). Springer Verlag.

Bleichenbacher, D. (1998). Chosen ciphertext attacks against protocols based on the RSA encryption standard PKCS 1. In *Advances in Cryptology '98, Lecture Notes in Computer Science* 1462. Springer Verlag. Santa-Barbara, California.

FIPS PUB 46-3. (1999). Data encryption standard (DES). U.S. Department of Commerce/National Institute of Standards and Technology. http://csyc.nist.gov/publication/fips/fips46-3/fips46-3.pdf

FIPS PUB 180-2. (2002). Secure hash standard (SHS). U.S. Department of Commerce/National Institute of Standards and Technology. http://csrc.nist.gov/publication/fips/fips180-2/fips180-2.pdf

FIPS PUB 197. (2001). Specification for the advanced encryption standard (AES). U.S. Department of Commerce/National Institute of Standards and Technology.

Hodges, J., & Morgan, R. (2002). Lightweight directory access protocol (v3). IETF RFC 3377.

Housley R. (2002). Cryptographic message syntax (CMS). IETF RFC 3369.

ISO/IEC 8824-1–4 (1995). Information technology—abstract syntax notation one (ASN.1). Specification of basic notation.

Lenstra, A. K., & Verheul, E. R. (2001). Selecting cryptographic key sizes. *Journal of Cryptology, 14*, 255–293.

Rivest, R. (1992). The MD5 message-digest algorithm. IETF RFC 1321.

Rivest, R., Shamir, A., & Adleman L. (1978). A method for obtaining digital signatures and public-key cryptosystems. *Communications of the ACM, 21*, 120–126.

Standards for efficient cryptography group. (2000). Certicom Corp. Retrieved from http://www.secg.org/

X.690. (1994). ITU-T Recommendation X.690: Information technology—ASN.1 encoding rules: Specification of basic encoding rules (BER), canonical encoding rules (CER), and distinguished encoding rules (DER).

FURTHER READING

Adams, C., & Farrell, S. (1999). Internet X.509 public key infrastructure certificate management protocols. IETF RFC 2510. Retrieved from http://www.ietf.org/

Diffie W., & Hellman, M. E. (1976). New directions in cryptography. *IEEE Transactions on Information Theory*, IT-22:644–654.

IEEE 1363. (2000). Standards specification for public key cryptography. IEEE Press. http://grouper.ieee.org/groups/1363/

IEEE 1363a. (2003). Standards specification for public key cryptography: additional techniques. Draft.

ISO/IEC 9594-8. (1997). Information technology—open systems interconnection. The directory: Authentication framework.

Kaliski, B. S. (1993). An overview of the PKCS standards. RSA Laboratories, a Division of RSA Data Security. Retrieved from http://www.rsasecurity.com/rsalabs/pkcs/

Kaliski, B. S. (1993). A layman's guide to a subset of ASN.1, BER, and DER. RSA Laboratories, a Division of RSA Data Security. Retrieved from http://www.rsasecurity.com/rsalabs/pkcs/

Public-key cryptography standards #1, #3, #5, #6, #7, #8, #9, #10, #11, #12, #15. (2003). RSA Laboratories, a Division of RSA Data Security. Retrieved from http://www.rsasecurity.com/rsalabs/pkcs/

X.500. (1988). ITU-T Recommendation X.500: The directory—overview of concepts, models and services.

X.501. (1988). ITU-T Recommendation X.501: The directory—models.

X.509. (2000). ITU-T Recommendation X.509: The directory—public-key and attribute certificate frameworks.

Public Key Standards: Secure Shell

Xukai Zou, *Purdue University School of Science at Indianapolis*

SSH INTRODUCTION AND ITS HISTORY

The advent of the Internet and its rapid spread around the world have changed the way we look at communication. It is no longer restricted to telephones, couriers, or fax. Instead, in the present age of digital revolution, it is almost impossible to think of a world without the Internet. One of the often overlooked problems that arise with the use of the Internet for communication is security. Communication over the Internet often takes place in the form of a local workstation (client) making use of the services offered by a more powerful remote machine (server). Securing this transfer of data is one of the biggest challenges we face today.

This chapter is intended to give the reader an overview of a widely used security protocol called secure shell (SSH). It begins with a brief discussion about the history and the reason for the development of the protocol. The various services such as confidentiality, integrity and authentication and functionalities like secure command shell and secure file transfer are presented. The discussion then turns to the various data types and message formats used by SSH. The next section talks about the layered protocol architecture of SSH and details each of the layers. The discussion then moves to a protocol specifically developed for the purpose of secure file transfer, the secure file transfer protocol (SFTP). Next the focus is on SSH tunneling, TCP/IP port forwarding, and X forwarding. Key management in SSH is discussed thereafter, followed by consideration of the security aspects associated with SSH, such as the man-in-the-middle and denial of service attacks. The section also gives a comparison between the two versions of SSH. The chapter closes with discussion of SSH in the real world and takes a look at some practical implementations.

Conventional Ways of Remote Access and Problems

The traditional means of remote access are the following services under the UNIX environment:

- **rlogin:** a remote login program. It connects a user to the remote system and usually provides the user with a shell.
- **rsh (remote shell):** it executes a noninteractive command on the remote system.
- **rcp:** a remote copy program that can be used to transfer files to and from the remote machine.
- **telnet:** a terminal emulation program for TCP/IP networks. It is used to connect to servers on the Internet.

Unfortunately, these commands, often called the "r commands," are insecure. They make use of the concept of trusted hosts, which makes their use convenient, but the price that one has to pay for this convenience comes in the form of security risks. The concept used in these commands is that each remote machine has a file named /etc/hosts.equiv that contains the names of the trusted hosts. If any client is listed, the user is not asked for any password for authentication. This makes these commands insecure. While using the rlogin command, if the local host name is not found in the file on the remote machine, the client is prompted for a password. Similarly, telnet requires a user to log on first by providing user name and password, but even this does not make the communication secure because the password is transferred unencrypted over the network.

What Is the Secure Shell?

Secure shell is a protocol that provides secure network communication. It provides authentication, encryption, and data integrity. A more detailed definition for Secure Shell is the following (Van Dyke Software, 2003a): Secure Shell (SSH) provides an open protocol for securing network communications that is less complex and expensive than hardware-based VPN solutions. SSH secures the remote network connections by encrypting all the transmitted data, which include user names and passwords. This encryption saves the SSH session from vulnerabilities such as eavesdropping, hijacking, and IP spoofing.

History of SSH

SSH was developed with the view of making remote login and other remote network services secure. The main idea was to replace the existing, insecure commands such as rlogin and rsh and provide secure encrypted communications between untrusted hosts over an insecure network. The work on the first version, SSH1, began in the early 1990s. Secure Shell version 2 (SSH2) was submitted as an Internet Engineering Task Force (IETF) draft in 1997. The second version was developed to overcome some vulnerabilities which existed in SSH1.

SSH FUNCTIONALITY AND SERVICES

SSH was designed to replace telnet, FTP (file transfer protocol), and Berkeley Unix r commands. SSH attempts to offer a solution to the problem of securing data over insecure public networks.

Services

SSH addresses the three core security services that are important to maintain adequate security (Van Dyke Software, 2003a):

1. **Confidentiality:** This means that the transmitted data must be recognizable only to the authorized party. If someone steals the data during transmission, he or she should not be able to understand it. Confidentiality is achieved through encryption.
2. **Integrity:** This means that data should not be changed during transmission, and if it is changed, the authorized party receiving it should be able to notice that. Integrity is achieved by computing checksum or MAC (message authentication code) of the data being sent. This allows detecting any changes made during transmission.
3. **Authentication:** This means that both parties communicating should be able to identify each other. It is required to prevent identity spoofing by malicious people. Authentication is provided by using challenge passwords or public key cryptography and digital signatures.

Functionality

SSH is a protocol for secure remote logins and encrypted file transfer. It is now a de facto standard and can also tunnel arbitrary TCP/IP sessions over a single encrypted secure shell connection. Thus, the basic functionalities are as follows:

1. **Secure Command Shell:** Users of UNIX and DOS are familiar with the command shell known as a "command prompt" in the Windows environment. The SSH allows a user to run commands over a remote machine. It is also known as remote logon.

   SSH or remote logon allows the user to view and edit files and directories and access custom database applications. Administrators can start, view, or stop jobs remotely. They can view, create, or delete user profiles over the secure command shell. SSH command shell allows a user or administrator to do all the things remotely that he or she could do by logging on to a particular system.
2. **Secure File Transfer:** Conventional ways of data transfer include the RCP and FTP commands in UNIX and Windows. The problem with these commands is that they are not secure because the data are sent unencrypted and the passwords are sent in clear. Besides that, FTP uses two connections, one for control and one for data.

   Secure file transfer protocol (SFTP) is a separate protocol over the SSH protocol to handle file transfers. It encrypts user names, passwords, and data. Its advantage over FTP is that it uses the same port as the secure shell server. Another important function of SFTP is that it can be used to create a secure extranet (Van Dyke Software, 2003b). An extranet is a private network used by business firms to share securely part of their business information with vendors and perhaps other business partners. The term extranet arrives from the concept that it can also be viewed as an extension to the local intranet of any firm for some authorized users outside the company. This extranet can be used for uploading files and reports, making archives of data files, and remotely admistrating file oriented tasks.
3. **Data Tunneling for TCP/IP Applications:** Data tunneling, also known as port forwarding, allows securing data from normally insecure TCP/IP applications. Once it is set up, the SSH client sends data across an encrypted tunnel. The advantage of tunneling is that multiple applications can send data over a single encrypted tunnel. This eliminates the need to open additional vulnerable ports on a firewall or router.

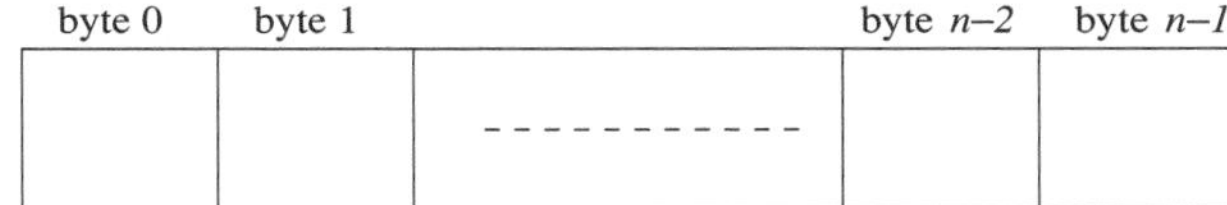

Figure 1: Representation of an array of *n* bytes -byte[*n*].

SSH DATA TYPES, MESSAGE FORMATS AND ALGORITHM NAMING

Data Types and Their Representation

The various data types that are used in the implementation of SSH are described in the following list.

1. **byte:** A byte represents 8 bits of data. Fixed length data can also be represented as an array of bytes. For example, an array consisting of *n* bytes is represented as byte[*n*] (Figure 1).
2. **Boolean:** A boolean value can either be true or false. A boolean value is stored as one byte. The value 0 represents false, and the value 1 represents true.
3. **uint32:** This represents a 32-bit unsigned integer and is stored as 4 bytes in order of decreasing significance (also known as the network byte order).
   Example: The number 699921578, in hex 0x29b7f 4aa, is stored as 29 b7 f4 aa.
4. **uint64:** This represents a 64-bit unsigned integer. It is stored as 8 bytes in the order of decreasing significance.
5. **String:** This is used to represent binary strings of arbitrary length. The binary strings can contain arbitrary binary data that include null characters. They are also used to store text in which case US-ASCII is used for internal names. The representation is shown in Figure 2.
   Example: The string *security* would be stored as 00 00 00 08 s e c u r i t y. The uint32 represents he length of the string, which is 8 in this case.
6. **mpint:** This format is used to represent multiple precision numbers in two's complement. It is stored as a string with 8 bits per byte with the *most significant bit* (MSB) first. A negative number has the value 1 as the most significant bit of the first byte of the data partition. The representation for number 0xab169fa637 is shown in Figure 3.
   Similarly, the representation for value -deadbeef (in hex) is 00 00 00 05 ff 21 52 41 11 (in hex).
7. **name-list:** This is used to represent a string containing a list of names separated by a comma. A list may be empty (containing zero names). However, a name must be non-zero length and contain no comma. According to the earlier string representation, name-list is represented as a unit32 followed by comma-separated names, as shown by the following examples:

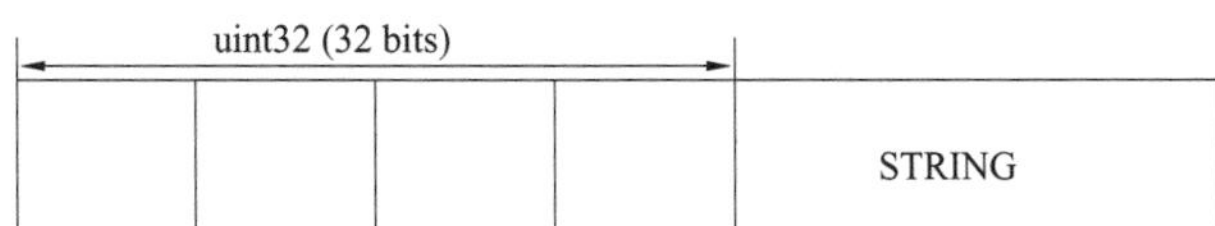

Figure 2: Internal representation of a string.

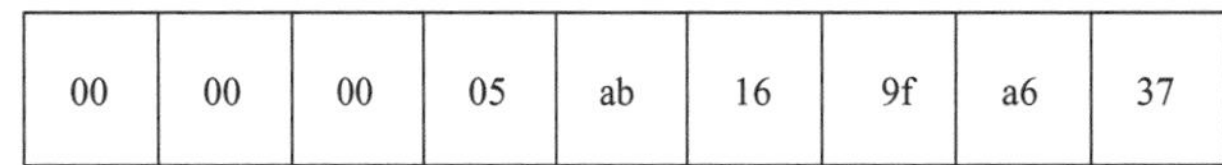

Figure 3: Internal Representation of 0xab169fa637.

Value	Representation (hex)
(), the empty list	00 00 00 00
("mlib")	00 00 00 04 6d 6c 69 62
("mlib", "zero")	00 00 00 09 6d 6c 69 62 2c 7a 65 72 6f

Message Numbers

SSH packets have message numbers attached that lie in the range of 1 to 255. The numbers have been allocated in the following manner.

Transport Layer Protocol:
1 to 19 Generic transport layer messages such as "connect," "disconnect," and "ignore"
20 to 29 Algorithm negotiation
30 to 49 Specific to the key exchange method used

User Authentication Protocol:
50 to 59 Generic authentication layer messages
60 to 79 Specific to the user authentication method used

Connection Protocol:
80 to 89 Generic connection layer protocol messages
90 to 127 Channel-related messages

Reserved for client protocols:
128 to 191 Reserved

Local Extensions:
192 to 255 Local extensions

Algorithm Naming

SSH uses names to refer to specific hash, encryption, and compression algorithms (e.g. sha-1 etc.). There are two formats in which these names can be associated with the algorithms:

1. There are certain names that have been reserved to be assigned by IETF. These names do not contain an at-sign (@). Examples include names like 3des-cbc, zlib etc.
2. There are additional names that can be defined by anyone. These names usually have the format yourciphername@yourcorporatename.com.

SSH PROTOCOL ARCHITECTURE

The SSH protocol runs on top of the TCP/IP protocol (Ylonen, Kivinen, Saarinen, Rinne, & Lehtinen, 2003b). It is composed of three layers (see Figure 4).

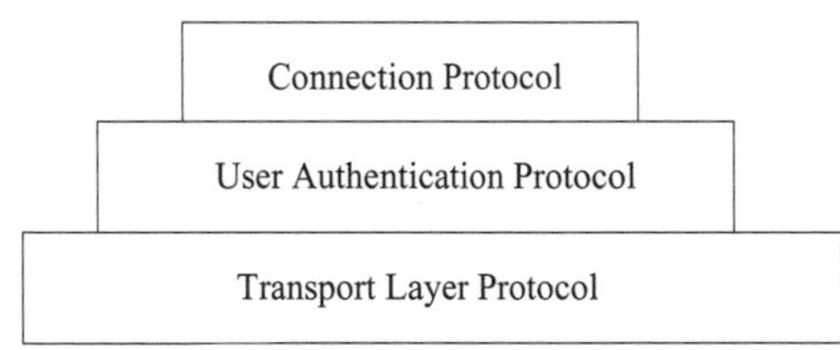

Figure 4: Protocol architecture.

1. Transport layer protocol (SSH-TRANS): Provides server authentication, confidentiality, and integrity. It runs on top of TCP/IP.
2. User authentication protocol (SSH-USERAUTH): Authenticates a client side user to the server. It runs on top of SSH-TRANS.
3. Connection protocol (SSH-CONNECT): Multiplexes an encrypted tunnel into several logical channels. It runs on top of SSH-USERAUTH.

The Transport Layer Protocol (SSH-TRANS)

The SSH Transport Layer is a low-level transport protocol that provides strong encryption, cryptographic host authentication, and integrity protection (Ylonen, Kivinen, Saarinen, Rinne, & Lehtinen, 2003c).

1. **Functions and position:** This protocol runs on top of TCP/IP and is at the bottom of the SSH protocol architecture. It has been designed to be simple and flexible to allow parameter negotiations and to minimize number of round trips. This protocol negotiates key exchange methods, public key algorithms, symmetric encryption algorithms, message authentication algorithms, and hash algorithms.
2. **Identification string exchange:** SSH works over any 8-bit clean, binary, transparent transport. When used over TCP/IP the server listens for connections over port 22. Once the connection is established, both parties must exchange the SSH protocol version number.

   The server may send other lines of data before the version string, but each should be ended by a carriage return and newline must be encoded in ISO-10646 UTF-8. The primary use of this feature is to allow TCP wrappers to display error messages before disconnecting.
3. **Host keys and fingerprints:** Every SSH server host should have a host key and may have multiple host keys. A *host key* is a private key and public key pair, but in general, it means the public key of a host. The SSH client will base on the host (public) key of a SSH server host to authenticate the host from the beginning. Thus ensuring the authenticity of a host key for a host is absolutely necessary to guarantee the security of SSH sessions and to prevent the man-in-the-middle attack.

   Nowadays, because of lack of public key infrastructure (PKI) and public key certificates, the verification of the host key for a SSH server host is left to the SSH users. Additional methods should be provided to verify the correctness of host keys. One of these methods is called a *fingerprint*, which in SSH is a hexadecimal value derived from the SHA-1 hash of a public key and is much shorter than the public key. The fingerprint of a host key should be made available for checking. The users of SSH client should verify the fingerprint of a host key by some means for which security does not rely on the integrity of the actual host key, such as by using a telephone or other external communication channel.
4. **Server authentication:** The authentication in this protocol is host based. There are two trust models that are widely employed for server authentication:
   - **Local Database:** Under this method, each client maintains a local database that stores the servers names and the corresponding host keys. The database gets filled in whenever the client connects to new servers. The first time the client connects to the server, the server sends its host key to the client and gives it an option of storing it in its local database. This method has an inherent flaw, which can lead to the man-in-the-middle attack, discussed in detail in the later section, "SSH Security."
   - **Employing a Certification Authority:** The other trust model employs a certification authority that stores the host key, and the authentication for the host is routed through this third party. This method has the advantage that the host key has to be stored securely only at one location, that is, the certification authority.
5. **Binary packet protocol:** All packets transmitted between the SSH client and the SSH server follow the binary packet protocol format, which is as follows:

uint32	packet_length
byte	padding_length
byte[n1]	payload; n1 = packet_length − padding_length−1
byte[n2]	random padding; n2 = padding_length
byte[m]	MAC (Message Authentication Code); m = MAC_length

   The length is measured in bytes. The packet_length does not include the MAC or the packet_length field itself. The random padding field is used for making the total length of (packet_length ‖ padding_length ‖ payload ‖ padding) a multiple of the cipher block size or 8, whichever is higher. The padding should be random bytes. The amount of padding is between 4 and 255 bytes. The client and the server may negotiate the MAC algorithm; however, it must be "none" initially. Once the MAC algorithm has been negotiated, the MAC field contains the MAC bytes and the length of the MAC depends on the MAC algorithm.
6. **Encryption algorithm:** An encryption algorithm and a key will be negotiated during the key exchange. When encryption is in effect, all the fields of the packet are encrypted by the algorithm chosen. The ciphers in each direction must run independently and implementations should allow choosing different ciphers in each direction.
7. **Data integrity:** Data integrity is protected by including a message authentication code in each packet. This MAC is computed from a shared secret packet sequence number and the contents of the packet.
8. **Key exchange:** Key exchange begins immediately after version string exchange by each side sending a list of supported algorithms. Each side may guess which algorithm the other side is using and may send an initial key exchange packet. The packet format is as follows:

byte	SSH_MSG_KEXINIT
byte[16]	cookie (random bytes)
string	kex_algorithms
string	server_host_key_algorithms
string	encryption_algorithms_client_to_server
string	encryption_algorithms_server_to_client
string	mac_algorithms_client_to_server
string	mac_algorithms_server_to_client
string	compression_algorithms_client_to_server
string	compression_algorithms_server_to_client
string	languages_client_to_server
string	languages_server_to_client
boolean	first_kex_packet_follows
uint32	0 (reserved for future extension)

Each algorithm list must be a comma separated list of algorithm names. The list must be sorted in order of preference with preferred (guessed) algorithm first.

The initial key exchange produces shared secret K and exchange hash H. The exchange hash H from the first key exchange is used as the unique session identifier (session_id). This session_id remains the same even if the keys are later exchanged again. K and H and the session_id are used by the client and the server to derive six keys as follows (three keys in each direction):

For client to server:
Initial IV = hash ($K\|H\|$"A"$\|$ session_id).
Encryption Key = hash ($K\|H\|$"B"$\|$ session_id).
Integrity Key = hash ($K\|H\|$"C"$\|$ session_id).

For server to client:
Initial IV = hash ($K\|H\|$"D"$\|$ session_id).
Encryption Key = hash ($K\|H\|$"E"$\|$ session_id).
Integrity Key = hash ($K\|H\|$"F"$\|$ session_id).

In these derivations, hash is the same hash algorithm that is used in initial key exchange methods. "A", "B"... are single characters ASCII 65, 66, ...

Keys with required length are derived from the above keys using the following process: If the above hash has more bits than the required key-length, key data are taken from the beginning of the hash. If the required key-length is longer than the output of the hash, the key is extended by computing hash of the concatenation of K, H, and the key so far, and appending the resulting bytes to the key. This can be summarized as follows:

$K_1 = \text{hash}(K\|H\|X\|$ session_id) //X can be "A", "B", etc.
$K_2 = \text{hash}(K\|H\|K_1)$
$K_3 = \text{hash}(K\|H\|K_2)$
...
KEY $= K_1\|K_2\|K_3\dots$

The basic steps in transport layer protocol are as follows (see also Figure 5):

- The SSH client initiates communication with the SSH server by connecting to the host and port number (22). If the server is up, a TCP connection between the server and client will be established by the underlying TCP/IP protocol.
- The server sends its version string to the client.
- The client sends its version string to the server.
- The server sends SSH_MSG_KEXINIT containing supported algorithms in the order of preference to the client.
- The client sends SSH_MSG_KEXINIT containing selected or supported algorithms in order of preference to the server.
- The server and client then will determine the same algorithms such as the host key algorithm, encryption algorithm, MAC algorithm, and compression algorithm. Then the server and client will begin the concrete key exchange based on the selected host key algorithm. The server host key will be sent to the client for authentication during the key exchange. Only one key exchange method is specified as required in the standard, that is, diffiehellman-group1-sha1. The key exchange for this method is discussed in detail in the section "Diffie–Hellman Key Exchange."

User Authentication Protocol (SSH-USERAUTH)

The SSH authentication protocol is a general purpose user authentication protocol that assumes the underlying protocols provide integrity and confidentiality, protection (Ylonen, Kivinen, Saarinen, Rinne, & Lehtinen, 2003a).

1. **Function and position:** This protocol runs on top of SSH-TRANS and provides a single authenticated tunnel for the SSH Connection Protocol.

   When this protocol starts, it receives a session identifier from SSH-TRANS. This identifier is the exchange hash in the first key exchange. It uniquely identifies a session and is used for signing to prove ownership of private key.
2. **Authentication protocol framework:** The server drives authentication at any given time by telling the client which authentication methods can continue the exchange. The client has the freedom to try the listed methods in any order, and thus the server has control over the authentication process, but the authentication process remains flexible for the client. It is recommended that the server has a timeout for authentication and should disconnect if the time period or the maximum number of attempts runs out.
3. **Authentication requests and message formats:** All the authentication requests must follow the following message format:

byte	SSH_MSG_USERAUTH_REQUEST
string	user name (in ISO-10646 UTF-8 encoding [RFC 2279])
string	service name (in US-ASCII)
string	method name (US-ASCII)

   The rest of the packet is method-specific. The server must ensure the user name specified in the request is valid. If not, it can send a false list of services to avoid disclosing user account information. If the server does not support the requested service, it should send a proper failure message.

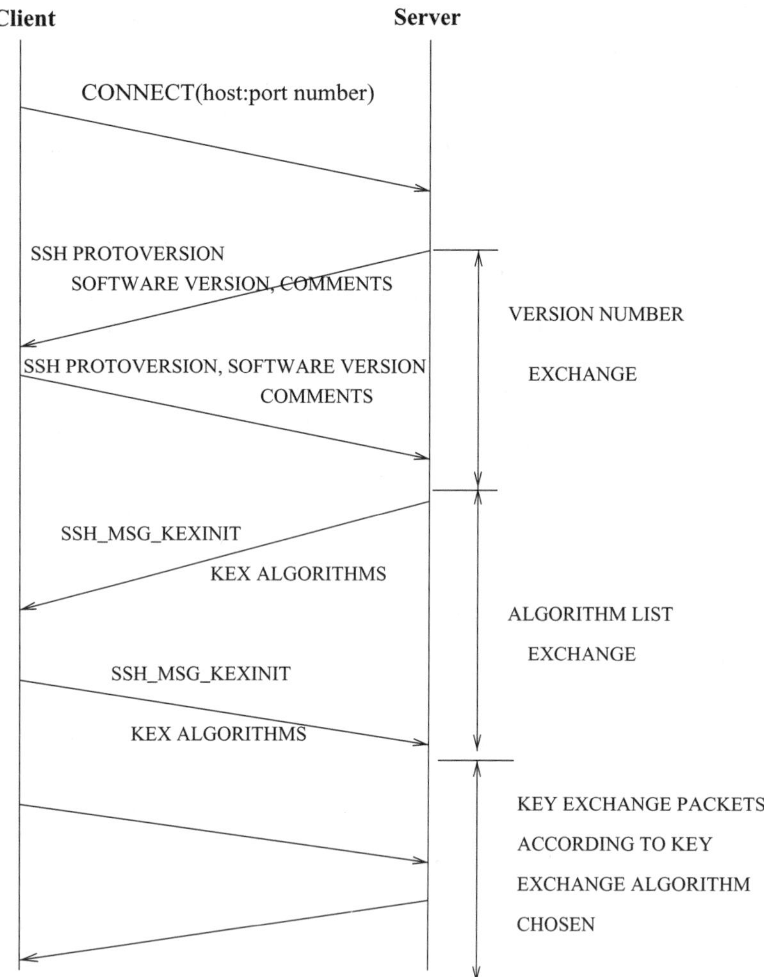

Figure 5: Transport layer protocol.

4. **Responses to authentication requests:** If the server rejects the authentication request for some reason, it should send the following message:

byte	SSH_MSG_USERAUTH_FAILURE
string	authentications that can continue
boolean	partial success

   Authentications that can continue is a comma-separated list of authentication method names that can be used to carry out the process. If partial success is true, it means that the last authentication method was successful, but still some more methods are required to complete authentication process. After it completes all the required authentication methods successfully, the server sends a success message as follows:

   byte SSH_MSG_USERAUTH_SUCCESS

5. **Authentication procedure:**
   - The client sends an authentication request with requested method as none.
   - Upon receiving this request, the server checks to determine whether the user name is valid.
   - If the user name is valid, it must reject the "none" request with a failure message. Otherwise, the server rejects the client.
   - The failure message contains a list of authentication methods the server supports.
   - Then the client fulfills all the required authentications in the order it finds suitable.
   - Upon completing all the authentication methods successfully, the server sends the success message.
   - Any authentication request after the success message is ignored.

   The authentication protocol message numbers range from 50 to 79.

6. **Authentication methods:** There are three basic authentication methods: public key based, password based, and host based. Out of the three only Public Key Method is REQUIRED and all implementations must support it.
   - **Public Key–Based Method:** This method works by sending a signature created with a private key of the user. The server checks that the key used indeed belongs to the user and the signature computed is correct. If both are valid, the request gets accepted. Otherwise (i.e., just one or neither of them is valid), the request is rejected.

     Private keys are generally stored in an encrypted form at the client machine. The user must supply a pass-phrase to generate a signature. To avoid unnecessary processing and user interaction the following message is provided:

```
byte      SSH_MSG_USERAUTH_REQUEST
string    user name
string    service
string    "publickey"
boolean   FALSE
string    public key algorithm name
string    public key blob
```

The algorithm name is from the list provided by transport layer protocol. The public key blob may contain certificates. The client can use this message to determine the algorithm or send a signature with the preferred algorithm. It is then the server's duty to check for validity of key and signature.

- **Password-Based Method:** All implementations should support password-based authentication. It uses the following packet format:

```
byte      SSH_MSG_USERAUTH_REQUEST
string    user name
string    service
string    "password"
boolean   FALSE
string    plaintext password (ISO-10646 UTF-8)
```

Note that even though a plaintext password is sent in the packet, the transport layer encrypts the entire packet. The implementations generally prompt the user to change a password on first logon and possibly again after some time when the password has expired.

- **Host-Based Method:** Some sites wish to allow authentication based on the host where the user is coming from. This form of authentication is optional and should be used carefully to prevent a regular user from obtaining the host's private key.

The Connection Protocol (SSH-CONNECT)

1. **Functions and Position:** This protocol has been designed to run on top of transport and user-authentication protocol. It provides interactive login sessions for the remote execution of commands, forwarded TCP/IP connections, and forwarded X11 connections (Ylonen, Kivinen, Rinne, & Lehtinen, 2003).
2. **Channel Mechanism:** All terminal sessions, forwarded connections, and other connection types are defined as channels. Multiple channels are multiplexed into a single connection. Channels are identified by numbers at each end of the connection. A request to open a channel contains the sender's channel number. Any other channel-related messages will contain the recipient's channel number for the channel. Channels are flow-controlled. Data may not be sent to a channel until a message is received to indicate that the window space is available.

Opening a Channel

If either side wishes to open a new channel, it can do so by sending the following message to the other side. It must include the local channel number and initial window size in the message.

```
byte      SSH_MSG_CHANNEL_OPEN
string    channel type (restricted to US-ASCII)
uint32    sender channel
uint32    initial window size
uint32    maximum packet size
channel type specific data follows
```

The remote side decides whether it wants to open the channel or not and sends a confirmation or failure message accordingly. The client may return some failure codes to indicate reasons.

Data Transfer

The window size specifies how many bytes the other party can send before it must wait for the window to be adjusted. Both parties use the following message to adjust the window:

```
byte      SSH_MSG_CHANNEL_WINDOW_ADJUST
uint32    recipient channel
uint32    bytes to add
```

After receiving this message, the recipient may send the given number of bytes more than it was previously allowed to send; the window size is incremented. Data transfer is done with messages of the following type:

```
byte      SSH_MSG_CHANNEL_DATA
uint32    recipient channel
string    data
```

The maximum amount of data allowed is the current window size. The window size is decremented by the amount of data sent. Both sides usually ignore all extra data sent after the allowed window is empty.

Closing a Channel

When either side no longer wishes to send more data to a channel, it sends the following message:

```
byte      SSH_MSG_CHANNEL_EOF
uint32    recipient_channel
```

No explicit response is sent to this message; however, the application may send end of the EOF to whatever is at the other end of the channel. Note that the channel remains open after this message, and more data may still be sent in the other direction. This message does not consume window space and can be sent even if no window space is available.

When either side wishes to terminate the channel, it sends

```
byte      SSH_MSG_CHANNEL_CLOSE
uint32    recipient_channel
```

Upon receiving this message, the party must send back a SSH_MSG_CHANNEL_CLOSE unless it has already sent this message for the channel. The channel is considered closed for a party when it has both sent and received SSH_MSG_CHANNEL_CLOSE, and the side may then reuse the channel number. Any side may send SSH_MSG_CHANNEL_CLOSE without having sent or received SSH_MSG_CHANNEL_EOF.

This message does not consume window space and can be sent even if no window space is available. The standard recommends that any data sent before this message be delivered to the actual destination, if possible.

Connection, (Interactive) Sessions, and Channels

In SSH specification, various terms are used to denote different concepts and operations. Once the SSH client and SSH server complete the transport layer protocol and user authentication protocol, there is a secure connection established between the client and the server. The connection is identified by a connection identifier, which is the *exchange hash H* from the first key exchange, also called *session identifier.* Then the connection protocol is executed to open one or multiple channels and multiplex them into the single connection. The channels may be in the form of a remote shell (i.e., an interactive session for remote execution of commands), a tunnel such as TCP/IP port forwarding and X11 forwarding, or a secure subsystem such as SFTP. In general, the first channel is automatically opened after successful user authentication and is an interactive session. The interactive session provides an interactive interface for the user of the SSH client to perform various tasks such as SFTP, X11 forwarding, and TCP/IP port forwarding by opening multiple channels. These channels are independent from the first channel (i.e., the initial interactive session) and from each other, and they all run on top of the secure connection.

A secure connection is associated with various parameters such as session keys, encryption algorithms, authentication algorithms, and compression algorithms, which are negotiated during the execution of the transport layer protocol and user authentication protocol. The connection provides necessary security support such as confidentiality and data integrity. The connection exists until either the client or server closes the connection or there is an abnormal termination at either end.

SECURE FILE TRANSFER PROTOCOL

Function and Position

The traditional methods for file transfer over the Internet do not provide adequate security to the data being transmitted. The trouble is that the user names, passwords, and the data are sent in plaintext, which can be easily intercepted.

SFTP is a secure file transfer protocol that makes use of the underlying SSH for authentication and encryption. Although it is a separate protocol by itself, SFTP is integrated with SSH to an extent that it is sometimes called a subsystem of SSH. SFTP is used from the SSH connection protocol when used with SSH (Galbraith, Ylonen, & Lehtinen, 2004).

The protocol follows a request–response model. The user, once authenticated by the SSH server via the user authentication protocol, sends requests to the server. There can be multiple requests pending at a time, and because each request and response transmitted contains a sequence number, the confusion as to which response is for which request is avoided.

General Packet Format

The format for the packets transmitted over the secure connection is as follows:

```
uint32          length
byte            type
byte[length-1]  data payload
```

The length field indicates the length of the type and data payload areas. The client generally determines the maximum packet size, which in turn depends on the maximum size of the read or write request it sends. Typically, a few more bytes are added to take care of the packet overheads.

Protocol Initialization

The file transfer protocol is initialized in a specific way, consisting of the following steps (see also Figure 6):

- The client does the first step in the initialization process. It sends an initialization packet (SSH_FXP_INIT, value = 1) to the server. It also includes its version number SFTP_PROTO_VERSION).

  The format of the SSH_FXP_INIT packet sent to the server by the client is

  ```
  unit32 version
  ```

- The server responds by sending a SSH_FXP_VERSION packet in which it supplies its lowest version and also the client version. Both sides should agree on a particular version of the protocol. The format of the SSH_FXP_VERSION packet sent to the client by the server is

  ```
  unit32 version
  < extension data >
  ```

  The extension data in these packets can be empty or can consist of details such as *packet length* or *maximum length of the packet.*

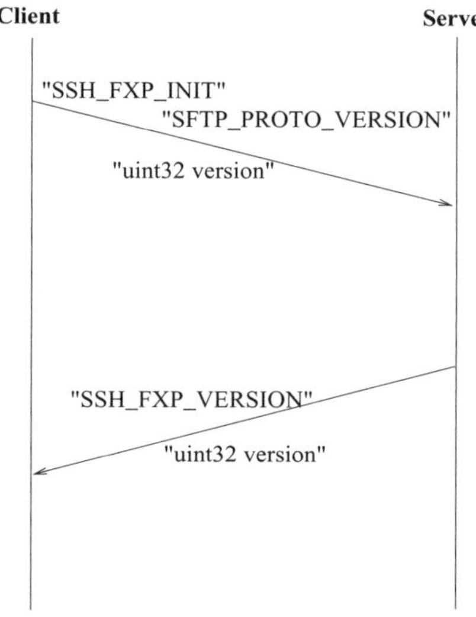

Figure 6: Protocol initialization in SFTP.

File Attributes

The protocol defines a new compound data type for defining file attributes. The data type is basically just a combination of certain flags that indicate the attributes. The encoding used by the server to send the file attributes is the same as used by the client. When the attributes are sent to the server, the flags field specifies which attributes are included and which are not. In the same way, while the attributes are received from the server, the flags specify which attributes are included. The flags specify which of the fields are present. Those fields for which the corresponding flag is not set are not present, that is, they are not included in the packet returned by the server.

A few examples are as follows:

unit32 flags
unit32 size present only if flag SSH_FILEXFER_ATTR_SIZE is set
unit32 uid present only if flag SSH_FILEXFER_ATTR_UIDGID is set
unit32 gid present only if flag SSH_FILEXFER_ATTR_UIDGID is set

The size field specifies the file size. The identifiers corresponding to the users and groups to which the file belongs to are represented by the uid and gid.

Requests From the Client to the Server

Once a user has been authenticated and is connected to the remote SSH server, the user can perform many functions. Normally the user connects to perform remote file manipulation on the server, which include opening a file, moving a file from one directory to another, or uploading a file to some remote location. There are many examples of this.

In SFTP, the requests from the client to the server represent the various file operations that a user can perform. Each request begins with an id field, which is a 32-bit identifier identifying the request made by the client. An example request is SSH_FXP_OPEN that is used to open a file. The server responds by sending the file handle, which can later be used to access the file.

Request Synchronization and Reordering

While implementing the file transfer protocol, the client may send multiple requests to the server. Ideally, the server should respond to the multiple requests in such a way that the client receives the results in the same way as if it had sent the requests one at a time and waited. If the multiple requests are nonoverlapping in nature, the server can process them in parallel or even reorder them. This cannot be done in cases where the requests for the same files overlap, however.

File Names

The file names are represented as strings and use the / delimiter as the directory separator. The concept is similar to that used in UNIX. File names that begin with the forward slash are relative to the root of the file system. These names are known as *absolute file names*. Other names that do not have a forward slash at the beginning of the file name refer to the user's home directory.

File Operations

There are a number of operations that can be performed on files using SFTP. Files can be opened and created by using the SSH_FXP_OPEN message. The data part of the message is as follows:

uint32 id
string filename
uint32 pflags
AATRS attrs

The file is opened in a binary mode. The id field is the request identifier as for all requests. The filename field specifies the file name. The attrs field specifies the initial attributes for the file. The pflags is a bitmask for which, we have the following bits defined:

SSH_FXF_READ: used to open a file for reading.

SSH_FXF_WRITE: used for writing to the file.

SSH_FXF_APPEND: used for appending to a file.

SSH_FXF_CREAT: used to creates a new file if the file does not exist

SSH_FXF_TRUNC: used to truncate a file with the same name to zero when creating a new file using SSH_FXF_CREAT

SSH_FXF_EXCL: used to fails the request if the file being created by SSH_FXF_CREAT already exists.

SECURE TUNNELING: TCP PORT FORWARDING AND X FORWARDING

TCP/IP Port Forwarding

SSH can be used for more than secure remote logins or secure file transfers. It can be used in a way to provide partial transparency so as to secure otherwise insecure TCP/IP applications and X window applications. SSH maintains the transparency by hiding the secure tunnel created using strong encryption and authentication and providing the user with a terminal session resembling that provided by telnet or rsh.

Port forwarding is a process by which SSH transparently encrypts (tunnels through a secure SSH link) the data stream from any TCP/IP connection that would otherwise be insecure (Barrett & Silverman, 2001). Following is a brief example of port forwarding.

Suppose a user uses his or her home machine, say "M," which runs any internet message access protocol (IMAP) or post office protocol (POP) e-mail client. The e-mail client would connect to a simple mail transfer protocol (SMTP) server running on another machine, say "S," to send his or her e-mails. Normally, this connection would be insecure and the user names and passwords would be transmitted in clear as plaintext over the network. But with the port forwarding service of SSH, the user can route the SMTP connection in such a way that it passes through SSH, which would securely encrypt the data over the connection.

Let us assume the SMTP server running on the server phoenix.cs.iupui.edu SMTP uses TCP port 25, and as such, the SMTP server would be listening to port 25 for incoming connection requests. If we wish to tunnel the SMTP connection through SSH, we would have to forward (i.e., map) the remote socket (phoenix.cs.iupui.edu, 25) to a local port on the home machine (the local host). We can select any port between 1024 and 65535, say 1098, for example.

Now the following command would create the tunnel:

$ssh – L1098 : localhost:25 phoenix.cs.iupui.edu

By this command, we not only login into phoenix.cs.iupui.edu but also forward the TCP port 1098 on M to port 25 on the server. The last step would be to make the e-mail reader program connect to the socket (localhost, 1098) instead of the socket (phoenix.cs.iupui.edu, 25) on the server to send e-mails. The connection path can be depicted by Figure 7.

The steps to forward the connection are as follows:

- The e-mail reader running on the home machine M sends data (the e-mail) to local port 1098.
- The SSH client running on M reads the data, encrypts it, and sends it through a secure SSH connection to the SSH server running on phoenix.cs.iupui.edu.
- The SSH server on phoenix decrypts the data and forwards it to the SMTP server listening on port 25.

This example assumes that both the SSH client and the e-mail reader application program are running on the same host machine (M). The same also applies with regard to the SSH server and the SMTP server. It is also possible, however, to have the SSH client and the e-mail reader (similarly, the SSH server and the SMTP server) running on two machines (suppose the two machines are in the same local area network (LAN) or there is no security threat between the two machines) and still use the TCP port forwarding service provided by SSH. The following example illustrates this.

Suppose that the e-mail reader application is running on the host machine M. The SSH client now runs on a different machine (68.1.1.4), and it listens to the interface 0.0.0.0 at port 1098. By listening to this interface, we make the SSH client accept any connection request irrespective of its origin, and the TCP application can reside in a physically different machine than the SSH client. The e-mail reader is configured to connect to the host running the SSH client at port 1098.

The SSH client encrypts the data as in the previous case and sends it through a secure SSH connection to the SSH server running on phoenix.cs.iupui.edu (134.68.140.4). The SSH server decrypts the data and forwards it to the SMTP server running on a different host. The SMTP server is configured to listen to the interface 0.0.0.0 at port 25. Again by making the SMTP server listen to 0.0.0.0, we make it accept any connection requests irrespective of the origin.

Note that the data is transmitted unencrypted between the SSH Server and the SMTP server. We assume that this is secure as they are part of the same LAN or inside the same corporate office. The entire process is shown in Figure 8.

X Forwarding

Having discussed how TCP port forwarding works, this section considers how forwarding can be applied to X

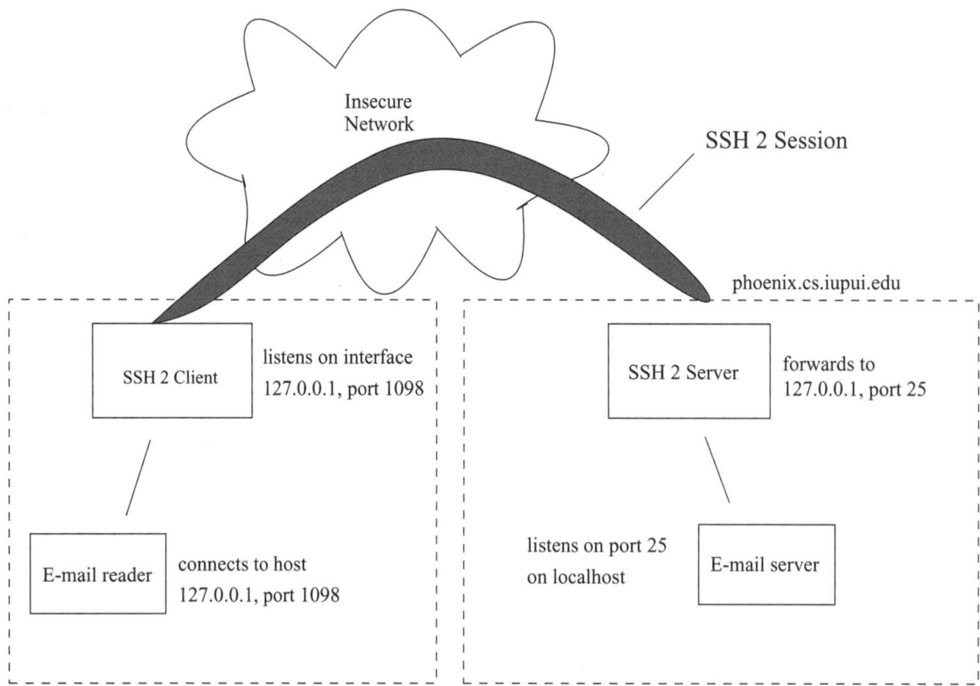

Figure 7: Port forwarding transmission control protocol/internet protocol connections locally. Figure was adapted with permission from Bitvise Software Ltd. (2002).

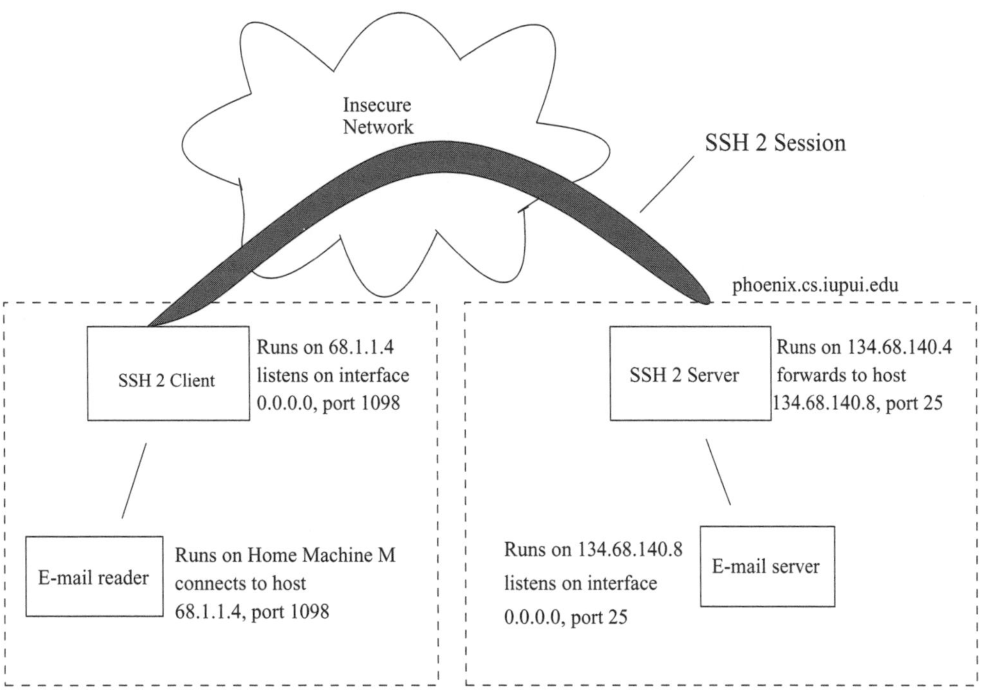

Figure 8: Remote Forwarding of TCP/IP Connections. Figure was adapted with permission from Bitvise Software (2002).

protocol connections. The X window system was developed at the Massachusetts Institute of Technology in the late 1980s, and it remains a popular window system for Unix workstations. It is freely available and completely transparent to the user. The user can run remote X applications that would open their windows on the user's local display (Barrett & Silverman, 2001).

The X Window System

The X window system, or X, is based on a client–server architecture and consists of two distinct parts—the X server and one or more X clients. X clients are windowing application programs such as paint programs or terminal emulators. The X server invariably runs on the machine to which the display is connected. The clients may run on the same machine, communicating directly with the server, or they might run on stand-alone workstations and communicate over the network using the X protocol.

A key part of X is the concept of display. When an X client is invoked, it needs to know which display to use. The DISPLAY environment variable indicates the location of the X server. Displays are named as strings of the form HOSTNAME:d, where HOSTNAME is the name (IP address) of the machine running the X server and controlling the display and d is the display number. It is an integer that allows a single server to control multiple displays.

Forwarding X Connections

The user is unlikely to be aware of X forwarding, but behind the scenes, the SSH client and server cooperate with each other to securely tunnel the X connection.

The process begins when the SSH client requests for X forwarding while connecting to the SSH server. If the server supports X forwarding, it creates a proxy X server running on the remote machine and allocates a "fake" display to it. In other words, it sets the DISPLAY environment variable in the user's remote shell to point to the proxy X display.

If the user runs an X client program, he or she is connected to the SSH server, which behaves just like a real X server. Once this connection has been established, the SSH client and server could then send X protocol data back and forth over this secure tunnel created and the whole process remains transparent to the user (Barrett & Silverman, 2001).

SSH KEY MANAGEMENT

Diffie–Hellman Key Exchange for the SSH Transport Layer

The SSH protocol performs the initial key exchange based on the Diffie–Hellman key exchange method. In technical terms, it is known as the diffie-hellman-group1-sha1 method (Friedl, Provos, & Simpson, 2003). The Diffie–Hellman key exchange method provides a mechanism for two parties to obtain a shared secret in such a way that either party alone cannot determine it. In SSH, to avoid a man-in-the-middle attack and provide host authentication, the key exchange is signed with the host key.

The key exchange that takes place is shown in Figure 9 and explained further in the following paragraphs.

The Setup

The server keeps a list of safe primes (a prime p is safe if $p = 2q + 1$, where q is also a prime) and the corresponding generators for the same. Here the client is "C" and the server is "S." p is a large safe prime and g is a generator for a subgroup of $GF(p)$. min is the minimal size of p (in bits) that the client is ready to accept. n is the size of the

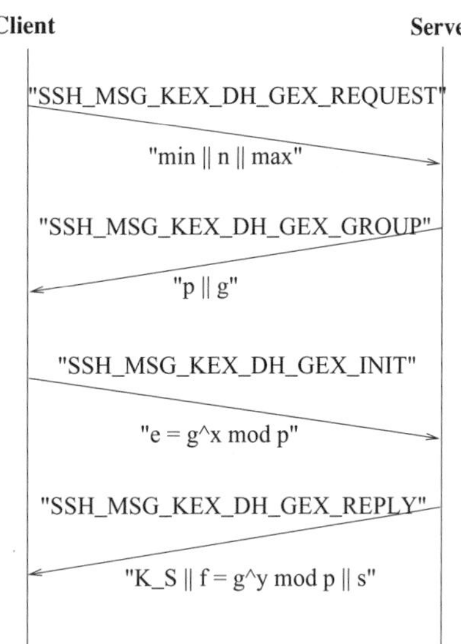

Figure 9: Diffie–Hellman key exchange for SSH transport layer.

modulus p in bits that the client would like to receive from the server. *max* is the maximum size of p that the client could accept. V_S is the version string of the server and V_C is the version string of the client. K_S is the public host key of the server. I_C is the KEXINIT message of the client and I_S is that of the server. The KEXINIT messages have been exchanged before this part begins. Note that the symbol || implies concatenation or being followed by.

The Working Process

Step 1: Client to Server
C sends "$min\|n\|max$" to S, indicating the minimal acceptable group size, the preferred size of the group, and the maximal group size in bits the client will accept.

Step 2: Server to Client
S finds a group that best matches the client's request, and sends "$p\|g$" to C.

Step 3: Client to Server
C generates a random number $x(1 < x < (p-1)/2)$. It computes $e = g^x mod\ p$, and sends "e" to S.

Step 4: Server to Client
S generates a random number $y(0 < y < (p-1)/2)$ and computes $f = g^y mod\ p$. It computes $K = e^y mod\ p$, $H = hash(V\_C \| V\_S \| I\_C \| I\_S \| K\_S \| min \| n \| max \| p \| g \| e \| f \| K)$ and signature s on H with its private host key. S sends "$K\_S\|f\|s$" to C.

Step 5: Client to Server
C verifies that K_S really is the host key for S (e.g., using one of the two trusted models described earlier, viz. certificates or a local database). C then computes $K = f^x mod\ p$, and $H = hash(V\_C \| V\_S \| I\_C \| I\_S \| K\_S \| min \| n \| max \| p \| g \| e \| f \| K)$ and verifies the signature s on H.

SSH Public Key File Format and Public Key Subsystem

It is important to exchange public keys to be able to use public key authentication. Public keys must follow a public key file format.

File Format: A key file is a text file, containing a sequence of lines. Each line in the file must not be longer than 72 bytes.

Line Termination Characters: To achieve the goal of exchanging public key files between servers, implementations are required to read files using any of the common line termination sequence, <CR>, <LF>, or <CR><LF>.

Begin and End Markers: The first line of a conforming key file must be a begin marker, which is the literal text:

— BEGIN SSH2 PUBLIC KEY —

The last line of a conforming key file MUST be a end marker, which is the literal text:

— END SSH2 PUBLIC KEY —

Key File Header: The key file header section consists of multiple RFC822-style header fields. Each field is a line of the following format:

Header-tag ':' ' '-Header-value

The Header-tag must not be more than 64 bytes. The header-value must not be more than 1,024 bytes. Each line in the header MUST NOT be more than 72 bytes.

A line is continued if the last character in the line is a \. If the last character of a line is a \, then the logical content of the line is formed by removing the \ and appending the contents of the next line.

The Header-tag must be US-ASCII. The header-value must be encoded in UTF-8 (Friedl et al., 2003).

A line that is not a continuation line and that has no ':' is assumed to be the first line of the base 64-encoded body. Compliant implementations must ignore unrecognized header fields. Implementations should preserve unrecognized header fields when manipulating the key file.

Existing implementations may not correctly handle unrecognized fields. During a transition period, implementations should generate key file headers that contain only a Subject field followed by a Comment field.

Subject Header: This field currently is used to store the login name that the key was generated under. For example:

Subject: user

Comment Header: This contains a user-specified comment that will be displayed when using the key. It is suggested that this field default to user@hostname for the user and machine used to generate the key. For example:

Comment: user@mycompany.com

Currently, common practice is to quote the Header-value of the Comment, and some existing implementations fail if these quotes are omitted.

Public Key File Body: The body of a public key file consists of the public key blob as described in the SSH transport draft.

"Public Key Algorithms,"-encoded in base 64 as specified in RFC-2045 "Base64 Content-Transfer-Encoding." As with all other lines, each line in the body must not be longer than 72 bytes. The following example shows a typical public key block.

—- BEGIN SSH2 PUBLIC KEY —-
Comment: "1024-bit RSA, converted from OpenSSH by galb@test1"
AAAAB3NzaC1yc2EAAAABIwAAAIEA1on8gxCGJJWSRT4uOrR13mUaUk0hRf4RzxSZ1
zRbYYFw8pfGesIFoEuVth4HKyF8k1y4mRUnYHP1XNMNMJl1JcEArC2asV8sHf6zSP
VffozZ5TT4SfsUu/iKy9lUcCfXzwre4WWZSXXcPff+EHtWshahu3WzBdnGxm5Xoi89zcE=
—- END SSH2 PUBLIC KEY —-

SECURITY

Comparison of SSH1 and SSH2

The work on secure shell has resulted in two versions of the protocol, which are quite different from but also somewhat incompatible with one another. The two versions are SSH1 and SSH2. SSH1 was developed as a replacement to the existing insecure UNIX commands such as rlogin, rcp, and rsh. SSH1 did not have a separate protocol for file transfer over the Internet, but soon certain vulnerabilities were found, and to overcome them, SSH1 was rewritten with improvements in security, performance, and portability.

The major improvement that was introduced by SSH2 over the first version was the introduction of a new protocol for transferring files (i.e., SFTP). SSH1 used separate TCP connections for control and data. A user could connect to the SSH1 server by sending a request at port 22 on the server (the port used by SSH). This connection was encrypted and hence secure, but FTP uses port 21 for communication. Therefore, the request would be forwarded to this port on the FTP server. Once the connection to the FTP server was established, the data transfer between the client and the server was done in clear, which was insecure. This was a serious vulnerability in SSH1, and FTP servers often became common targets for attacks.

SSH2 introduced the concept of a separate protocol for file transfer via the SFTP, which did not use the concept of port forwarding. Instead, SFTP was developed to work as a subsystem to be integrated with SSH2. Under the new scheme, a single secure connection to the SFTP server is made. The SFTP commands such as open, read, write, and so forth are tunneled through the existing SSH session making such data transmissions more secure. The key points of difference between the two versions are the following:

- SSH2 has a separate protocol for file transfer.
- The number of encryption algorithms supported by SSH2 is larger than SSH1.
- SSH2 is more secure compared with SSH1.
- SSH1 is subject to the man-in-the-middle attacks.
- SSH1 has more diverse authentication support.

The Man-in-the-Middle Attacks

The present implementations of SSH do not provide any mechanism for secure transmission of public keys of hosts. There is no method available for initial authentication of the host unless the client has already securely been given the public key of the host before, which it had stored in its database and which it can verify every time it needs to connect to the server.

The method followed is something like this. The client makes a request for a connection to a particular server. The server responds to the request by sending its public key. If the client is trying to connect to the host for the first time and does not have the host public key stored in its database, the user is prompted to store the same in its local database. This key is then later used for host authentication every time the client tries to connect to the same host. This method relies on the principle of initial trust, which eliminates the need to securely transmit the host keys prior to the communication between the client and the host. It makes the protocol vulnerable to what is known as the man-in-the-middle attack, however (Saito, Kito, Umesawa, & Mizoguchi, 2002).

In short, the man-in-the-middle attack is when attackers try to modify the transmission between the client and the server in such a way that they masquerade as the client for the server and the server for the client.

Three points of discussion for the man-in-the-middle attack are pertinent to SSH.

First, the attacker intercepts the authentic public key sent by the host and replaces it with its own. Here the attacker is able to mimic the server while communicating with the client. In certain cases, it can also do the same in the other directions (i.e., masquerade as the client to the server). When this happens, both the client and the server are fooled to accept the attacker as an authentic counterpart. This attack can be avoided to a certain extent if the client has been provided with the host key prior to the initial communication and the user decides not to continue with the new key received from the attacker, but instead decides to go with the key stored in the local database at its end.

The second case is similar to the first, although it is related to the secure transmission of the server host key to the client. If the public server keys are not securely distributed, the client cannot know whether it is talking with the intended server. If the attacker can modify this transmission, the client can be fooled into talking with the server. The attacker is able to establish client-attacker session and a corresponding attacker-server session. This can be avoided if the fingerprints of the server public keys are made available in such a way that the client can verify that once it gets the initial public key from the server.

In the third case, the attacker might be able to modify the packets in transit between peers once the connection has been established. This kind of attack is highly improbable under normal circumstances, thanks to the MAC algorithms used. It appears to be difficult, if not impossible, to construct inputs to a MAC algorithm to give a known output. If the MAC algorithm has a vulnerability or is weak enough, the attacker may be able to specify certain inputs to yield a known MAC output, and then the attacker might be able to alter the contents of the packets in transit.

Denial of Service Attacks

Denial of service (DoS) attacks are those in which the attacker bogs down the server by sending a large number of bogus requests, thereby rendering its services unavailable to the legitimate users. The SSH protocol is vulnerable to this type of attack in two ways (Ylonen et al., 2003b). First, because the protocol is designed to run over a reliable transport mechanism, the connection will be closed if there is any form of transmission error or message manipulation. Thus, an attacker can manipulate messages to cause the connection to be closed and the client to lose the services from the server.

The second type of DoS attack is when the connection setup and key exchange occur ahead of the user authentication phase. The attacker can force the server to conduct repeatedly the connection setup and key exchange, which are central processing unit and memory-intensive tasks, without authenticating. This will make the server unable to establish connections with the legitimate users.

SSH IN THE REAL WORLD

Operating Systems Support for SSH

Secure shell was initially introduced as a free open-source package under UNIX. Security firms have introduced various commercial implementations that are not open source. Implementations of SSH are available under UNIX as well as non-UNIX environments. The operating systems supported currently by one or the other implementation of SSH are Unix AIX, HP - UX, Linux, SUN Solaris, Windows 2000/NT/XP, Mac OS X, FreeBSD, and Cygwin.

Current Implementations

One of the leading vendors for the secure shell is SSH Communications, which provides a product called SSH Secure Shell (http://www.ssh.com). At present, it is the most widely used implementation of secure shell and has been deployed in many universities across the United States.

Van Dyke software (http://www.vandyke.com), another large security firm, offers products such as Secure CRT (terminal emulator) and Secure FX (for secure file transfer). Other vendors are F-Secure (offering F-Secure Tunnel and Terminal) and AppGate (offers AppGate client and server).

The implementations mentioned here are all commercial implementations, but some open-source implementations can be downloaded and used. These may not contain as many features as the commercial implementations, however. Two of the best known open-source projects that provide support for SSH and SFTP are OpenSSH and WinSCP.

OpenSSH (http://www.openssh.com) is a free open-source implementation of the secure shell and has support for SSH1 and SSH2 protocols. It provides the SSH program, used for remote logins; the sftp program, used for secure file transfer; and the scp program, used for secure copy of files. It also includes sshd, which is the server side of the package. OpenSSH is seeing increased use in the open-source world because it is simple and highly portable.

WinSCP (http://winscp.sourceforge.net/eng/) is an open-source SSH file transfer protocol and secure file copy client for Windows. The main objective behind the development of WinSCP was for safe copying of files between a local and a remote computer. It does provide some additional features to the user, including operations such as renaming files and folders, creating new folders, and changing folder properties.

Installation and Execution

Describing the procedure for downloading and executing SSH is beyond the scope of this chapter. This section briefly explains the compilation and installation details of OpenSSH, which remains one of the most widely used implementations in the open-source world.

Obtaining the Distribution

OpenSSH is a free implementation available at http:// www. openssh.com. Developed under the OpenBSD project, the main version of OpenSSH is specifically for the UNIX operating system.

Building and Installing the Distribution

The following steps are required to compile and install SSH. One must log on as the root user to execute the following commands:

- Change the directory to the root directory of the distribution and run the configure script in the distribution by:
  $ ./configure
- Then compile everything by:
  $ make
- Install everything by:
  $make install

Compile-Time Configuration

Building SSH does not appear to be difficult, but when building and installing a new security product, one should not blindly accept the default settings. In other words, system administrators should make sure that they know exactly what kind of settings the installed product will have.

Compile-time configuration can be performed by running the script configure before compiling the distribution. There are a set of configure flags that help change the default settings and configure SSH according to user needs. The complete set of configure flags can be seen with the following command:

$./configure—help

The most important compile-time flags associated with OpenSSH are as follows:

- —without-pam
  Pluggable authentication module (PAM) is an infrastructure developed by Sun Microsystems to support multiple authentication methods. PAM eliminates the hassles that are usually associated with a new authentication method. PAM helps programs perform authentication and authorization tasks using various authentication methods. It uses dynamically loaded libraries.
  By default, OpenSSH uses PAM for password authentication. By using the flag, the PAM support could be omitted.
- —with-md5-passwords
  Enables use of MD5 passwords
- —with-ssl-dir=PATH
  Sets the path to OpenSSL installation. It should be used only if OpenSSL is installed.
- —with-kerberos=PATH
  Enables Kerberos.
- —with-ipv4-default
  This makes OpenSSH use IPv4 unless we specify -6.
- —with-4in6
  OpenSSH supports IPv6 and this option is used to convert IPv4 addresses into IPv6.

Server-Side Configuration

The configuration decisions at the server end includes issues such as which authentication techniques should be used, the number of bits in the server key, and time out for idle connections. The following is an overview of the process.

Server Configuration

The SSH server in OpenSSH is named sshd. The SSH server is invoked automatically when the host computer is booted and if the server is running as a daemon. Alternately it could also be invoked manually. The server could be configured in the following ways:

- Using the server configuration file, usually found at /etc/sshd_config
- Using command-line options

Using the first method, one could change the configuration file and use that in place of the default configuration file by using the f option followed by the path for the alternate file:

$sshd f /usr/local/new_sshdconfig

Alternatively, we could use the command line options to configure the server. The advantage of this is that it can be used to debug the server. An example of the command line option would be using the -p option to specify the port number to be used by the server:

$ sshd p<port number>

Host Keys

Each SSH server has a host key that is persistent and uniquely identifies itself to the client. The two parts of the host key, the private key and the public key, are stored as two distinct files. For OpenSSH, the private key is stored in */etc/ssh_host_key*. The public key is stored at the same location and as a .pub appended to the name. For OpenSSH it is */etc/ssh_host_key.pub*.

Encryption Algorithms

The SSH server supports many encryption algorithms for secure transmission of data. The client selects a cipher from the list of algorithms that the corresponding server supports. The keyword Ciphers, which is either a comma-separated list of permissible algorithm names or a single string indicating a set of algorithms, serves the purpose.

CONCLUSION

The materials in the article are mainly based on the SSH standard specification from the Internet Society, that is, various IETF Internet Drafts on SSH. These drafts are available online (see the references), and readers are encouraged to refer to these documentation for detail. PuTTY (2004) helps greatly in the analysis of SSH mechanisms.

ACKNOWLEDGMENT

I thank Mr. Amandeep Thukral and Mr. Yogesh Karandikar for their help with the preparation of the chapter.

GLOSSARY

Channel An identified communication session created by SSH-CONNECT between the SSH client and the SSH server. Channels include interactive login sessions, remote execution of commands, forwarded TCP/IP connections, and forwarded X11 connections. All of these channels are multiplexed into a single encrypted tunnel established by SSH-TRANS and SSH-USERAUTH.

Connection Protocol (SSH-CONNECT) The top level of the three-level SSH architecture. SSH-CONNECT multiplexes the encrypted tunnel into several logical channels. It runs on top of SSH-USERAUTH.

Fingerprint A fingerprint in SSH is a hexadecimal value derived from the SHA-1 hash of a public key. It is much shorter (typically 128 bits) than the public key which makes it easy to memorize, store, and transfer. A fingerprint is used to verify the authenticity of a public key.

Hash Function A function that maps a string of random length to a value of fixed length. A hash function should satisfy the following three requirements: one-way, matching resistance, and collision resistance.

Host Key The public and private key pair generated by the SSH system for a host when the SSH system is installed on the host. Typically, the host key means the public key in the key pair. A host key is used to identify or authenticate the host.

Message Authentication Code (MAC) An authenticator that is a hash function of both the data to be authenticated and a secret key. In other words, MAC is a keyed hash function. It is also referred to as a cryptographic checksum.

Port Forwarding A process by which SSH transparently encrypts the data stream from any TCP/IP connection that would otherwise be insecure by means of tunneling through a secure SSH connection.

Public Key Certificate Binding of a public key with the identity of its owner, signed by a trusted certificate authority. It is used to obtain the authentic public key of a user or verify the authenticity of a claimed public key by a user.

(Digital) Signature A value computed for a message based on a user's private key such that a recipient of the message can verify, based on the public key of the user, that the message is really from the user.

Transport Layer Protocol (SSH-TRANS) The lowest level of the three-level SSH architecture. SSH-TRANS provides server authentication, confidentiality, and integrity. It runs on top of TCP/IP.

User Authentication Protocol (SSH-USERAUTH) The middle of the three-level SSH architecture. SSH-USERAUTH authenticates client side user to the server. It runs on top of SSH-TRANS.

CROSS REFERENCES

See *Computer and Network Authentication; Digital Certificates; Digital Signatures and Electronic Signatures; Encryption Basics; Hashes and Message Digests; VPN Basics.*

REFERENCES

Barrett, D. J., & Silverman, R. (2001). *SSH, the secure shell: The definitive guide*. O'Reilly and Associates.

Bitvise Software. (2002). WinSSHD: Secure remote access to your Windows machine. Retrieved from http://www.bitvise.com/port-forwarding.html

Friedl, M., Provos, N., & Simpson, W. (2003). Diffie Hellman group exchange for the SSH transport layer protocol (IETF Internet draft). Retrieved from http://www.ietf.org/internet-drafts/draft_ietf-secsh-dh-group-exchange-04.txt

Galbraith, J., Ylonen, T., & Lehtinen, S. (2004). SSH file transfer protocol (IETF Internet draft). Retrieved from http://www.ietf.org/internet-drafts/draft-ietf-secsh-filexfer-05.txt

PuTTY. A Free Telnet/SSH Client. http://www.chiark.greenend.org.uk/sgtatham/putty/, 2004.

Saito, T., Kito, T., Umesawa, K., & Mizoguchi, F. (2002). Architectural Defects of the Secure Shell. *Proceedings of 13th International Workshop on Database and Expert Systems Applications (DEXA'02), Aix-en-Provence, France, 2002.*

Van Dyke Software. (2003a). *An overview of the secure shell.* White Paper on Secure Shell.

Van Dyke Software. (2003b). Secure file transfer. White Paper on Secure File Transfer.

Ylonen, T., Kivinen, T., Rinne, T., & Lehtinen, S. (2003). SSH connection protocol (IETF Internet draft). Retrieved from http://www.ietf.org/internet-drafts/draft-ietf-secsh-connect-19.txt

Ylonen, T., Kivinen, T., Saarinen, M. J., Rinne, T., & Lehtinen, S. (2003a). SSH Authentication protocol (IETF Internet draft). Retrieved from http://www.ietf.org/internet-drafts/draft-ietf-secsh-userauth-21.txt

Ylonen, T., Kivinen, T., Saarinen, M. J., Rinne, T., & Lehtinen, S. (2003b). SSH protocol architecture (IETF Internet draft). Retrieved from http://www.ietf.org/internet-drafts/draft-ietf-secsh-architecture-16.txt

Ylonen, T., Kivinen, T., Saarinen, M. J., Rinne, T., & Lehtinen, S. (2003c). SSH transport layer protocol (IETF Internet draft). Retrieved from http://www.ietf.org/internet-drafts/draft-ietf-secsh-transport-18.txt

Security and the Wireless Application Protocol

Lillian N. Cassel and Cynthia Pandolfo, *Villanova University*

THE WIRELESS APPLICATION PROTOCOL

The wireless application protocol (WAP) is a collection of protocol standards whose purpose is to enable communication between handheld wireless devices and Internet-based service providers. Mobile devices vary greatly in capability. Some are compact, but fully powerful, computers. These are not the subjects of this chapter. WAP exists to accommodate the limitations of very small devices, generally mobile phones. Limited amounts of memory, both RAM and ROM, impact the performance characteristics of these devices. Applications and utilities, including security elements, must be optimized for the restricted environment. The service providers include Web servers providing content formatted especially for small wireless devices and other service providers who target the wireless devices exclusively.

This set of standards builds on existing standards, reusing or modifying where necessary to address the special needs of the handheld wireless community. The particular limitations of the wireless world include greatly restricted bandwidth, nonrobust connections, signal security limitations, the small screen on most devices, limited battery life, and restricted input options. Output from the handheld devices is generally limited to the small screen, although some devices can connect to other units, including projectors. Processor power and memory are other limitations for most target devices. Within these constraints, security is a particular challenge.

The Current Situation

The mobile telephone industry is currently suffering from disparity in standards that limit the usefulness of phones as they travel from one location to another. Currently, wireless system providers in the United States adhere to one of four different standards: IS-95 CDMA, TDMA, GSM, and iDEN. CDMA is Code Division Multiple Access and is the basis of the third-generation (3G) wireless transmission technologies WCDMA and CDMA2000. TDMA is Time Division Multiple Access in which each conversation has access to the carrier frequency only part of the time. There are a number of implementations of TDMA, including the Digital American Mobile System (D-AMPS), the Global System for Mobile communications (GSM), Personal Digital Cellular (PDC), and Integrated Digital Enhanced Network (iDEN). GSM is uniformly used throughout Europe allowing systems to roam and retain service over large areas. GSM is also the standard in use in most African nations (Digital mobile phone networks in Africa). PDC is the standard for cell phone access in Japan, where the widespread use makes it the second most used standard in the world. IDEN is a proprietary standard from Motorola. The lack of interoperability among the various standards is a serious limitation, restricting access as users move about.

An important characteristic of the communication mode is the basic model for connectivity. Connection can be either packet switched or circuit switched. Circuit switched means that a connected user consumes bandwidth for as long as the connection is maintained. Most systems charge by connection time, reflecting the consumption of bandwidth. Packet-switched connectivity means that the device consumes resources only when actually sending or receiving a transmission. There is no reason to disconnect the device from the network. This always-on feature has significant consequences for wireless service providers. As a result, the most actively used wireless services are those in Japan, where cell phone use is pervasive and services are always available, without the need for establishing a connection.

The mobile phone networks are moving toward advanced technologies, which will bring packet-based communication to the systems used outside Japan. Expectations are that the always-on characteristic will drive interest in and use of emerging applications available to the mobile phone users. If the experience in Japan translates into usage patterns in the rest of the world, the demand for applications will grow at a great rate in the near future. Developed to run over any and all of the mobile device transmission methods, the Wireless Application Protocol suite is the common set of standards that allows these applications to be available to all the wireless devices.

MOBILE ACCESS TO THE WORLD WIDE WEB AND OTHER DATA RESOURCES

The World Wide Web has become a utility, taken for granted as an information and communication resource. Similarly, the mobile communication device—whether phone or personal digital assistant—has become a part of the environment for many people. It is natural to look to combine these two. Access to existing Web pages is one goal of emerging standards and technologies for handheld, mobile, wireless devices. However, these devices offer opportunities to provide services and information feeds beyond what the Web provides. Web pages are dynamic, but they are not very responsive to the location of the visitor. Although there are location-specific services, such as yellow pages, most Web-based information is relatively static. A mobile user has different needs from a stationary browser. A mobile user might want to know what the traffic is just ahead or how to get from here to there. By combining the other features of the mobile device with a GPS system [or mobile positioning system (MPS) technologies], an application could address those questions. When a mobile user asks for information about nearby restaurants, the response needs to be organized for effective viewing on the small screen and must accommodate the limitations of imperfect connections. When a mobile user queries his or her bank balance before making a purchase, strong encryption must protect the data transferred without unduly impacting the amount of time required to get the answer.

One class of applications geared specifically to mobile users is localized data push. Assuming the user gives permission for such intrusion, a store may broadcast notice of a sale or even a special offer to a mobile device user who happens to be driving or walking nearby. Thus, the information obtained will be offered by a company or organization to attract the attention of a potential customer and entice with coupons or other offers. This type of communication depends on short-range data transfer using methods such as WLAN (wireless local area network) or Bluetooth. An example is the Flower framework for local wireless service (Hakkarainen, Lattunen, & Savikko, 2002). Such a service broadcasts to receivers that are in range and provide messages about special offers or just the existence of a business or service the device owner might patronize. Security in such an environment must depend on the ability of the device to reject dangerous files and to decline to submit user information in return.

Designing applications for the mobile device user requires different criteria from designing Web-based applications that will be accessed through large-screen devices with high-speed, reliable connections. When the information is requested by the user, income for the service provider is likely to be in the form of a charge for the amount of data delivered rather than advertising revenue. This means that the information presented to the user must be efficiently designed and delivered. The small screen size of most mobile devices requires consideration in designing the information presentation. Having to scroll both horizontally and vertically to see the content of a message is difficult with devices typically held and controlled by one hand. User responses must be obtained without the use of a full keyboard and often without an effective pointing device. The design challenges are significant.

Standards

WAP must deal with two sets of constraints: limitations of the wireless data networks and limitations of the handheld devices used to send and receive data. When compared to landline networks, the wireless data networks, regardless of the technology used, are characterized by the following:

- Less bandwidth
- More latency
- Less connection stability
- Nonconsistent availability

These characteristics are factors of the wireless environment independent of the type of device used. Bandwidth limitations and extra latency are characteristics of the wireless service currently available. Connection stability and consistency of service availability result from mobility and the need to move between bases.

The Wireless Application Protocol is motivated by the desire to bring the Internet to small, generally handheld devices (Wireless Application Protocol Specification, 2001). In addition to the limitations of wireless devices of all types, the handheld wireless devices are characterized by the following:

- Small screens
- Limited input options
- Less memory
- Less powerful CPUs

Although technology will improve the situation, some characteristics are inherent to the handheld device class: screen sizes will be small because an important feature of these devices is their small size and light weight. Battery life restrictions will limit CPUs and memory size. Input options include various implementations of a keyboard, none of which are ideal for significant typing. Output is limited to a small screen. Storage includes limited memory and some supplemental storage cards. WAP is a set of standards designed with these restrictions in mind. The WAP protocol stack is similar to the ISO OSI reference model (ISO/IEC, 1994) for the upper layers. Layers below the network layer are implied in the bearer protocols. Figure 1 shows the protocol stack with the WAP standards in place.

Wireless Application Environment

The wireless application environment (WAE) is a framework for the development of applications that can be accessed from many types of wireless devices from a variety of manufacturers. The goal is a structure in which operators and services providers can build their products

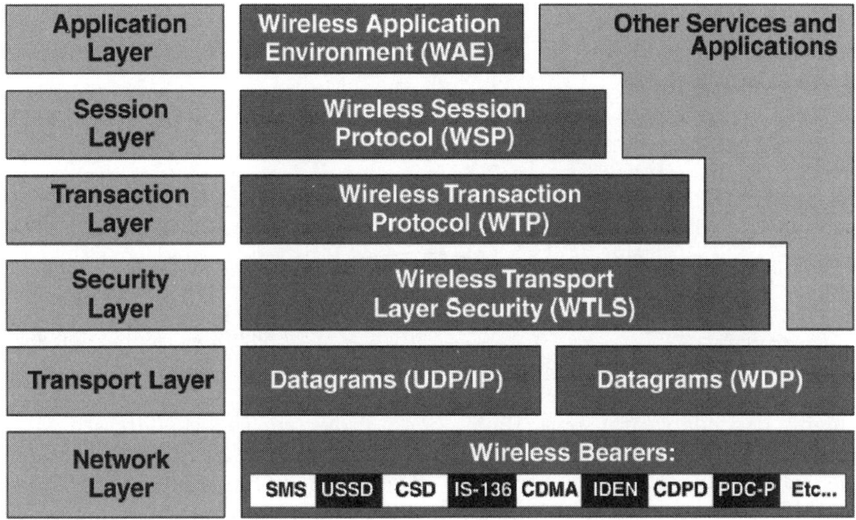

Figure 1: The WAP Stack (WAP Forum, 2002).

with confidence of interoperability with a wide variety of devices and applications. WAE includes XHTML Mobile Profile [HTMLMP], WML, WCSS, WMLScript, WBXML, vCARD, and vCalendar. Each of these is summarized briefly below:

- XHTML Mobile Profile. W3C is migrating HTML to XHTML, making it an XML application, and at the same time making it modular. Applications can be built using just the modules that are appropriate for the target devices. Starting with module XHTML Basic, XHTML Mobile Profile adds extensions suitable for the mobile devices.
- WML is the wireless markup language, an XML based markup language designed for use on devices characterized by low bandwidth connections, limited memory and restricted CPU capacity, a small screen, and limited user input interfaces.
- WCSS is the wireless cascading style sheet. Cascading style sheets are used in Web development to control display without sacrificing device independence. WCSS is specified for the special features of small mobile devices.
- WMLScript is a scripting language, roughly similar to JavaScript, designed to run on small mobile devices.
- WBXML is a compact, binary representation of XML documents intended to reduce the size of the files for transmission without losing semantic information.
- vCARD and vCalendar are industry standards for sharing address and calendar information.

Wireless Session Protocol

The wireless session protocol (WSP) offers the application layer consistent interfaces for session services. Two modes are offered. A connection mode runs over the wireless transaction protocol and a connectionless service runs directly over a datagram transport service. Initial versions of WSP offer browsing capabilities, including the equivalent of HTTP with implementation more suitable for wireless devices, plus facilities for long-lived sessions, session suspend/resume, data push, and capability negotiation.

Wireless Transaction Protocol

The wireless transaction protocol (WTP) provides services to allow browsing; specifically, WTP provides request response interaction between a client and a server. Unlike regular Web surfing with HTTP, WTP runs over a datagram service at the network layer. WTP enhances the service provided by unreliable datagrams to provide appropriate service levels to the higher layers, relieving the wireless device of the need to support all the services of TCP but providing a reliable service to the application. By using a datagram transport service, WTP eliminates the need for connection establishment and connection release activities. The protocol transmits a message as its basic unit, rather than a stream of bytes. WTP defines three classes of service:

1. Class 0: Unreliable invoke message with no result message.
2. Class 1: Reliable invoke message with no result message.
3. Class 2: Reliable invoke message with exactly one reliable result message.

Class 2 is the basic invoke/response service. Class 0 is available for an invoke message that will not be retransmitted if delivery fails and for which no response is expected. Class 1 is used for an invoke message that must be delivered or resent. The variations allow an application to function with a minimum of data transmission required.

Wireless Transport Layer Security

Wireless Transport Layer Security (WTLS) exists to provide privacy and security among communicating entities in a wireless environment. Security includes both data integrity and authentication services. The services of WTLS are optional and their use depends on the nature of the application and the vulnerability of the data it transmits.

Datagrams

Datagrams are transport protocol mechanisms that offer best effort delivery service without the high overhead

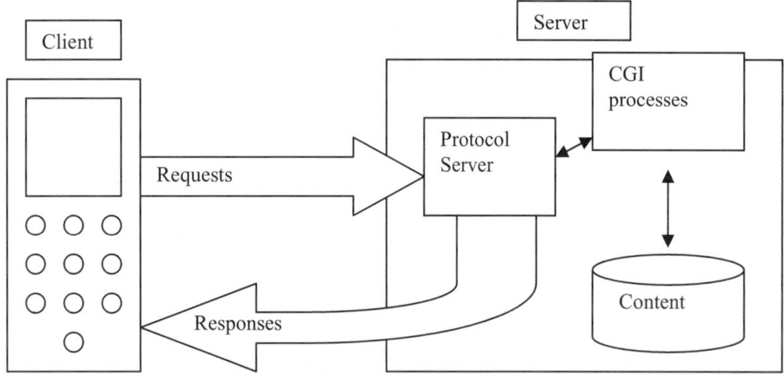

Figure 2: Direct Interaction Between the Wireless Client and Wireless Application Server.

required to provide highly dependable transport. Datagram transport protocols are lightweight, fast, and suitable for situations where the underlying network services are highly reliable or where the application will provide reliability and so services at the transport layer are redundant.

Access to wireless applications can be provided by direct connection to a WAP server that is also a content provider as illustrated in Figure 2. However, because most of the Internet content is present in Web sites designed to respond to HTTP requests and formatted in HTML that is often not suitable for the wireless device, standard access includes a gateway. The gateway receives requests using the WAP protocols and passes those requests to conventional web servers using HTTP. The gateway reformats responses for display on the limited device and encodes the response for transmission using the WAP protocol stack. Figure 3 shows wireless client interaction with a conventional Web server.

SECURITY

There are four aspects to security in general network communications:

1. Privacy. Content is visible only to the intended recipient and both parties have confidence that privacy is protected. This is addressed with various levels of encryption. The degree of confidence required will be weighed against processing costs to determine the appropriate level of encryption to use.
2. Integrity. Content is not modified between leaving the sender and arriving at the recipient's device. Digital signatures allow documents to be verified as being the same as was transmitted. A hash code is computed over the document and sent as part of the signature. If the hash code check on the recipient side does not produce the correct results, the document has been modified.
3. Authentication. The sender's identity can be verified with a very high degree of confidence. Passwords, authentication, and digital signatures identify the originator.
4. Nonrepudiation. The sender cannot later deny having sent the information. Digital signatures are the primary tools for binding the sender to the document or resource as sent.

The WAP protocol suite includes four standards related to security: (1) the WAP Identity Module (WIM) is a hardware chip used for client side authentication; (2) WML Script Crypto API (WMLSCrypt) provides access to the WML security function library; (3) wireless transport layer security (WTLS) sits above the transport layer

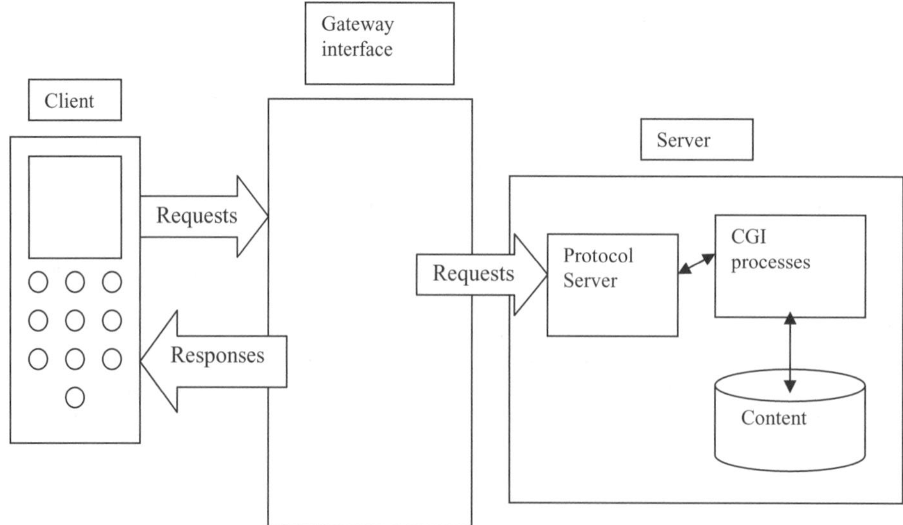

Figure 3: Wireless Application Client Interaction with a Conventional Web Server.

to provide basic security services; and (4) WAP Public Key Infrastructure (WPKI) is a wireless version of the Public Key Infrastructure (PKI). Thus, security in WAP consists of a hardware chip in the client device (WIM), a library of security-related objects and services and an application program interface to that library (WMSSCrypt), protocols for security services built on top of a standard transport layer (WTLS), and infrastructure and procedures for establishing trust relationships between a client and server (WPKI).

WAP Identity Modules

A WAP identity module or WIM, is a chip installed in the WAP-enabled device to facilitate client-side authentication. The chip implements WTLS Class 3 functionality, as described in the section on WTLS. WIMs can store key material such as the PKI root public key and the user's private key (Ashley, Hinton, & Vandenwauver, 2003). They are most commonly implemented using smart card chips. These chips have memory and storage for data and programs (Wireless public-key infrastructure, 2003). The basic requirement of WIMs is that they are tamper-resistant, meaning that certain physical hardware protection must be used. WIMs provide support for public key cryptography with RSA (see chapter 65) being mandatory and elliptic curve cryptography (ECC) (see chapter 113) optional. Each WIM comes configured by the manufacturer with two certificates and two sets of public-private keypairs. One keypair is used for signing and the other for authentication. The certificates bind the manufacturer's name with the public key side of the keypairs and allow for WTLS sessions to be established between the WIM and a WAP gateway before the user establishes an individual registered certificate (WAP Forum, 2001). The initial session is established with the built-in keys and may include a user-specific key.

The storage included in the smartcards used for most WIM implementations allow retention of certificates as well as programs and user data (Ashley et al., 2003). WIMs can store user certificates or user certificate references (e.g., URL-based references). The reference form is practical because of the substantial size of the actual certificates. However, storing the reference only imposes an additional communication requirement in using the certificate. It also requires confidence that the certificate is stored securely and remains valid for later use.

WML Script Crypto API

WML Script Crypto API (WMLSCrypt) is an application programming interface that allows WAP applications to access library items for security functions. The security objects and services are defined by other WAP security standards such as the PKI (see chapter 56). WML Script access the certificates, encryption keys, and other data stored in the embedded WIM chip. Specific functions supported by the WMLSCrypt include the following (Wireless public-key infrastructure, 2003):

- Generation of keypairs
- Store keys and other personal data
- Control access to stored keys and data
- Generate and verify digital signatures
- Encryption and decryption of data

An example WMLSCrypt function use is a call on Crypto.signText() to require a user to sign a string of text. The function is invoked by the WAP browser on the client device. The signature prevents the user from later denying having sent the text. This nonrepudiation function is essential to meaningful transactions conducted from easily portable (and easily lost) devices such as phones and PDAs. An application may implement the signText() function directly on the client device or invoke a call on a server. The signed text allows a server to validate the identity of the client and to retain the signed information for possible later use if the client denies the transaction (Ashley et al., 2003).

WAP Transport Layer Security

WTLS is based on the Transport Layer Security (TLS) protocol (see chapter 64) a derivative of the Secure Sockets Layer (SSL) protocol (Mikal, 2001). TLS is the de facto security implementation of the Internet. WTLS is used to authenticate communicating parties and encrypt and check the integrity of WML data when it is in transit. WTLS is a cryptography-based, PKI-enabled protocol that operates above the transport layer and addresses issues of authentication, privacy, integrity, and denial of service protection (Howell, 2003; Wireless public-key infrastructure, 2003).

- ***Authentication:*** WTLS uses digital signatures and public-key certificates to authenticate individuals, servers, or nodes prior to a session.
- ***Privacy:*** PKI-enabled, WTLS can encrypt data between communicating parties to provide privacy by preventing eavesdropping or unauthorized access. One-to-many communication is supported by using an authenticated and different encryption key for each communicating party.
- ***Data integrity:*** Hashing a document produces a data fingerprint allowing the detection of data modification.
- ***Denial of service attack protection:*** WTLS protects against denial of service attacks by detecting and rejecting data that has been replayed or has not been verified.

Unlike TLS, WTLS operates over user datagram protocol (UDP) rather than transmission control protocol (TCP) and also over wireless datagram protocol (WDP) in the absence of UDP [19]. In essence, WTLS takes TLS and tries to add datagram support, optimize the packet size, and select fast algorithms from the algorithm suite.

WTLS is a client/server protocol connecting the client and the WAP gateway. The session includes negotiation of security parameters, including the choice of encryption protocols, signature algorithms, public keys, and certificate exchanges. The choices depend on the capabilities of the cooperating client and server and the level of security needed for a particular application. After the encryption protocols have been selected during session established, communication is encrypted and should be safe from eavesdroppers. WTLS options include both a full handshake, with complete negotiation of security parameters, and a lightweight handshake in which security parameters of another session are reused.

WTLS also supports session suspend and resume. This allows sessions that last for extended periods, even for days at a time. This possibility represents a security risk in WTLS. A very long session represents a large number of messages exchanged with the same keys. This risk is managed by requiring keys to be renegotiated periodically during a session. Renegotiating keys is not as computationally expensive as establishing the keys in the first place, so renegotiation is more efficient than tearing down and reestablishing the session.

The WAP specification (Howell, 2003) defines three implementation classes. The first class provides support for anonymous key exchange with no authentication using Diffie–Hellman (Ashley et al., 2003) key exchange. The key exchange establishes an encrypted channel between the server and client (WAP Forum, 2001). The second class of WTLS provides support for certificate-based server authentication in which the server key is either anonymous or authenticated and the client key is anonymous. This class uses public key certificates with the WAP gateway using a WTLS certificate. The server provides a certificate mapping back to an entity trusted by the client. The third and final class uses certificate-based authentication of both client and server. Both the client and server keys are anonymous (using the manufacturer installed keys in the WIM) or authenticated. The client may possess a private key and public key certificate enabling it to identify itself to other entities in the network (WAP Forum, 2001). All classes of WTLS allow a username/password identification and authentication using WML forms sent between the server and the mobile devices (Ashley et al., 2003).

WTLS suffers from many security weaknesses. For instance, WTLS allows for weak encryption algorithms (Mikal, 2001). With some WAP clients, users can even disable WTLS encryption entirely. Markku-Juhani Saarinen (2003) introduced seven known security issues in his study, including a chosen plaintext data recovery attack, a datagram truncation attack, a message forgery attack, and a key-search shortcut for some exportable keys.

Certificates

WAP defines a WTLS certificate format, which is optimized for storage on mobile devices and for transmission over constrained networks (Howell, 2003). These certificates rely on the server to perform processing under some circumstances but provide all the functionality of other formats. Bandwidth savings also contribute to efficient operation in the wireless environment (Ashley et al., 2003).

Use of ECC, (see chapter 113) further reduces the size of certificates required. The keys for ECC are typically on the order of six times smaller than equivalent keys (Wireless public-key infrastructure, 2003). The general model is that server certificates will use the WTLS certificate format whereas client certificates will use X.509 format, but as far as possible will not be sent over the air or stored on the client (WAP Forum, 2001).

One security issue with these schemes comes from the very nature of the devices used. Because these devices are mobile, small, and easily mislaid, certificate loss is an issue. Where access to the certificate opens access to data or services that require strict control, the possibility of a lost phone becomes too great a risk. At the simplest level, this risk is addressed by placing a certificate on a certificate revocation list once it has been reported missing. Although that prevents further use of the certificate, it leaves too much vulnerable time for the protected data and services. An application also has options to validate the current user's identity ranging from a simple PIN through a SecureID token (Howell, 2003).

WAP Gateway

The WAP gateway is a form of proxy used to translate between WAP protocols and traditional Internet protocols. WAP gateways were defined in the WAP 1.2 protocol published by the WAP Forum in 2000 (WAP Forum, 2002).

The WAP gateway is a software application typically running on a computer in a building under the control of the mobile service provider (MSP) (Jørgensen & Juul, 2002). Many gateways include a "transcoding" function that will translate an HTML page into a WML page suited to a particular device. The WAP gateway has three main functions (Ashley et al., 2003): (1) DNS services such as resolving domain names used in URL's, (2) a control point for management of fraud and service utilization, and (3) a proxy, translating the WAP protocol stack to the Internet protocol stack.

Most WAP gateways are hosted on the network provider's own local network. If access is required to services hosted on another server somewhere across the network, the WAP gateway will act as a proxy for the client mobile device in establishing the required sessions with the remote host (Howell, 2003).

The WAP gateway has five layers: WDP, WTLS, WTP, WSP, and WAE as pictured in Figure 4 (Wireless Internet Provider, 2004). The WDP is the transport layer and provides adaptation to different types of bearer technologies. The WTLS is used for establishing a secure connection between the phone and the WAP gateway, as described in the previous section. The WTP is the transaction layer and handles the flow control. The WSP provides session management and converts WAP requests to HTTP requests and vice versa. The WAE works as a router between different applications.

The WAP gateway is responsible for providing four services to wireless applications (Jørgensen & Juul, 2002). The first is switching between transport protocols. The gateway in its communication with the mobile phone uses a transport protocol (WDP) that is connectionless and unreliable. In contrast, the transport protocol used by HTTP on the ordinary Internet is the connection-oriented and reliable protocol, TCP. In TCP, there is additional communication to ensure that all data actually gets through, and if not, it is retransmitted. At the risk of possible data loss, omitting the cost of TCP saves significantly on latency and bandwidth.

The second service provided by the gateway is compression. The gateway compresses the WML document

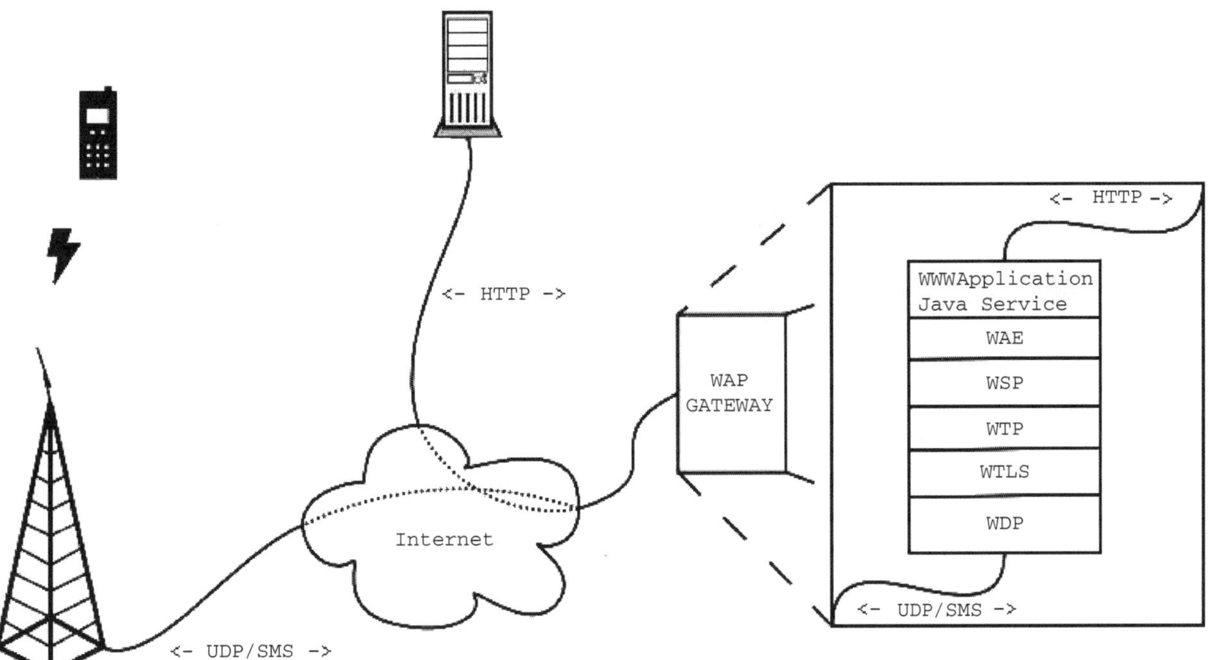

Figure 4: WAP Gateway (Wireless Internet Provider. Technical Description: WIP Mobilis Development Kit (MDK). http://www.wip.se/MDK/html/index.html).

before sending it to the mobile phone. The gateway applies lossless data compression so that the same information can be sent in a format that occupies fewer bytes. The compression relies on the predefined translation between the vocabulary of HTTP and WSP.

The third service is compilation. If a WML document contains embedded source code, the gateway compiles the code into a bytecode format, something that relieves the mobile phone of the task of parsing the code. WML documents may contain code written in the scripting language WML script, which is similar to the JavaScript language that may be embedded inside HTML documents. Such code is executed inside the browser.

The final service is decompression. The gateway reads and interprets the original WSP request, the compressed form of which is not understood by the Web server. The Web server expects the comparatively lengthy HTTP requests expressed as ordinary text rather than by greatly abbreviated numerical codes. Also, the gateway also invokes the services of a DNS (domain name server) to translate a symbolic Internet address into an IP number. In addition to reducing the processing that must be done in the restricted environment of the mobile device, these services also reduce the amount of data that must be sent from the mobile phone.

WAP Security Gap

As functional as the gateway is to WAP, it creates a major security gap in wireless applications. If the gateway is acting as a proxy, the mobile device's session is with the WAP gateway instead of the remote host's Web server. At the gateway, the secure session terminates and all encrypted material is decrypted (Howell, 2003). If there is a requirement for a secure session with the Web server, it will be established by the WAP gateway on behalf of the mobile device with the gateway using TLS to establish the secure session. Thus, the secure session established by the client is not between the mobile device and the Web server. Instead, there are two secure sessions; one between the mobile device and WAP gateway and one between the gateway and the Web server. Within the gateway, data are not encrypted during the translation processing, as illustrated in Figure 5. The Web service host has no control over the security that exists between the mobile device and the WAP gateway. Furthermore, the host has limited control over the TLS session between the gateway and the Web server and will be limited to providing security that does not exceed a level determined by the network operator.

Several solutions have been proposed to fix the gap at the WAP gateway ranging from ensuring that encryption and decryption happens in memory to putting a gateway at the host site (Howell, 2003), the only way to have complete control over security. However, these solutions are extreme and not easily implemented for most users. The WAP 2.0 specification seeks a more convenient solution to the gateway gap.

Transport Layer e2e

The WAP 2.0 specification replaces the WTLS security standard by TLS for secure end-to-end (e2e) data transport. This allows direct and secure connection between the phone-based client and the data serving site (Getgen, 2002). The TLS specification uses similar security mechanisms/algorithms to those of WTLS, including integrity confirmation, public key-based authentication of client and server either through use of certificates or anonymously, and message protection through secret key cryptography (Jeffs, 2001).

The process of communication in the e2e scheme is similar to the previous WAP gateway model as illustrated

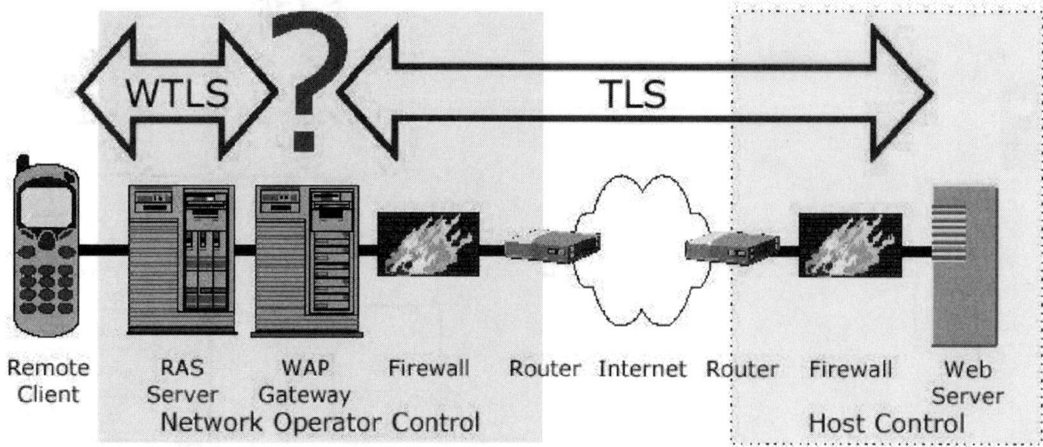

Figure 5: Gateway Problem[19]

in Figure 6. The WAP client tries to send a request through its default gateway to a secure domain (Ashley et al., 2003). The secure content server determines the need for security that requires use of its local WAP gateway. It responds to the initial client request with an HTTP redirect message. The redirect passes back to the client through the default gateway, which validates the redirect and sends it to the client. The client caches the new connection and uses the subordinate WAP gateway for further communication with the data server. After the connection is terminated the default gateway is reselected and used for subsequent communications.

e2e security changes the role of the WAP gateway to more of a smart router (Getgen, 2002). The gateway continues to be used for services such as performing server-initiated push of data, offering location-based services, and performing data compression to the message body (unencrypted text only) before it is transmitted over the air (Durham & Getgen, 2001). However, the gateway still has support for the previous architecture. Put simply, the role of the gateway changes from translator to an intelligent router reformatting data bits without reading the traffic.

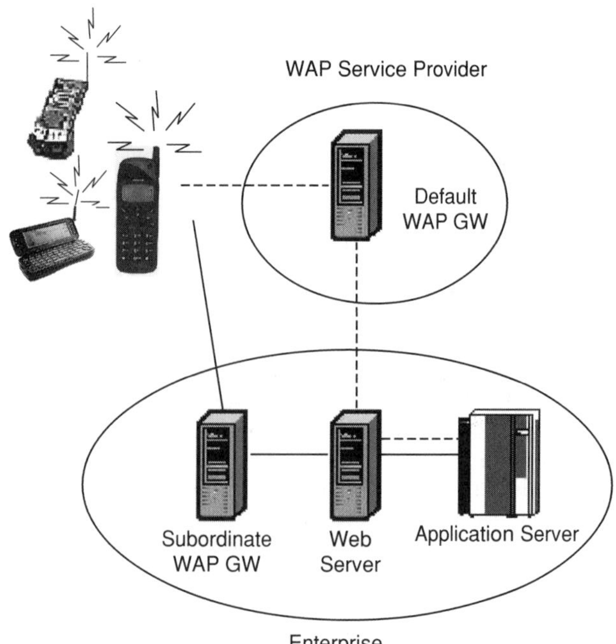

Figure 6: WAP e2e Security[16]

Although there is still a role for the gateway in the e2e scheme, some of its functionality is lost (Jørgensen & Juul, 2002). If code written in WML script is encrypted, it cannot be compiled, unless the gateway can first decrypt the script, thus breaking the end-to-end encryption. For the same reason, it would not be possible for the gateway to understand (decompress) the encrypted WSP requests, so the mobile phone has to use the much higher latency-incurring and more bandwidth-consuming HTTP requests. The gateways can no longer compress ordinary WML documents; because the gateway can no longer recognize WML tags, it cannot replace full tags with the shortened numeric representations.

The new e2e scheme is not without drawbacks. Some of the weaknesses in WTLS are also present in the current TLS/SSL used over the Internet, and will therefore also apply to the "profiled" TLS used by WAP 2.0 (Jeffs, 2001). Although opportunities for security enhancement are provided, there is no obligation to exchange certificates or to verify certificates and authenticate owners. If the application does not invoke these functions, no security enhancement is possible. Also, TLS allows anonymous Diffie–Hellman mode where exchanges are not supported by public key certificates. Finally, with TLS an active intruder is able to substitute a different public key for the requested public key and can then participate in the communication without the awareness of the client or server.

WAP PUBLIC KEY INFRASTRUCTURE

E-commerce depends on reliable communication between mobile devices and service providers. Reliability includes four basic components: Communication must be confidential. That means that no eavesdroppers can intercept and understand the communication. Communication must be authenticated. That means the user must be confident about the identity of the service provider.

Communication integrity must be provided. That means that the user must be able to sign the transaction and the server can know the identity of the user. Finally, the transaction must be safe from repudiation. Once the user has committed to the transaction, no later denial can occur.

These assurances are provided in the stationary, wired world through the Public Key Infrastructure. WPKI is an optimized extension of traditional PKI for the wireless environment (Wireless public-key infrastructure, 2003; Open Mobile Alliance, 2004). WPKIs manage relationships, keys, and certificates to enforce business policies. Current functionality in WPKI manages the security requirements of WAP 1.2. This includes CA Public Key Certificates for WTLS class 2 (client capability to authenticate the identity of a gateway), Client Public Key Certificates for WTLS class 3 (client private key is used to sign text) and Client Public Key Certificates used with WMLScript signText (Open Mobile Alliance, 2004). Future versions are intended to add security services, including application level end-to-end confidentiality and integrity.

WPKI uses the same four components as traditional PKI: an end-entity application (EE), the registration authority (RA), a certification authority (CA), and a PKI directory. An additional component, the PKI portal, interacts with the wireless device and the CA; it will include the functionality of the RA (Wireless public-key infrastructure, 2003). The CAs issue and revoke certificates; RAs confirm the validity of a public key with respect to a specific person or device. Certificates are issued to people, applications, and devices. The certificates are stored and used to sign digital documents or transactions.

WTLS Security Classses

There are three classes of WTLS security for wireless devices communicating with an application or information server. Class 1 provides no authentication. The wireless device uses WTLS to communicate with a WAP gateway. The WAP gateway communicates with the server with SSL. The encryption used to protect the communication must be undone within the gateway for the gateway to do the translation between the two security protocols. No authentication of the server or the user occurs (Nardone, 2004).

WTLS class 2 security allows the WAP device to authenticate the identity of the WAP gateway through which it communicates with the service provider. Both a two phase security and an end-to-end security model are defined. Both require an initial setup stage. In the two-phase model, the WAP device again uses WTLS to communicate with a WAP gateway and the WAP gateway uses SSL to communicate with the application or information server. Prior to this communication request, the WAP gateway generates a pair of keys, the public and private key. The WAP gateway requests a certificate through the WPKI portal. The WPKI portal confirms the identification of the gateway and forwards the certificate request to the certificate authority. The CA sends the gateway public certificate to the WAP gateway and stores the WAP gateway certificate in the online repository. With this phase complete, the WAP device establishes a WTLS session with the WAP gateway and the WAP gateway establishes a SSL/TLS session with the server. In future communications of this device through this gateway, the sessions can be established based on certificate information available between the WAP gateway and the device. This does not provide end-to-end security but does allow the device to authenticate the gateway that purports to provide a secure link to the desired server (Nordone, 2004).

End-to-end security eliminates the use of the WAP gateway and supports direct communication between the wireless device and the WAP server. The WAP server resembles a Web server but is able to communicate directly to wireless devices with WTLS. In this model, the initial setup consists of the same steps as before, but the WAP server takes the role of the gateway as well as the information or application server. The WAP server generates a pair of keys, a private key and a public key, and sends the certificate request to the WPKI portal. The WPKI portal confirms the identity of the WAP server and passes on the certificate request to the CA. The CA sends the Server Public Certificate to the WAP Server and stores the certificate in its on-line repository.

WTLS class 3 authentication extends the identity confirmation to include server authentication of the WAP Device. Cryptographic functionality for signing messages comes with the WMLScript Crypto Library. The function Crypto.sign.Text presents the user with a request to sign a body of text using an authenticated certificate. This facility adds to the basic authentication of SSL by providing persistence. The user connection to the text is stored for as long as that association is needed.

Class 3 authentication also requires an initial setup and then steps related to the authentication used in a session. The setup is similar to that in class 2 authentications but now is focused on the WAP Device. The WAP device requests a certificate through a WPKI portal. The request will travel through the WAP gateway unless the portal is acting as both portal and gateway (i.e., the portal is a WAP server offering certification). The WPKI portal confirms the identity of the WAP device, which is stored in its WIM, and forwards the request to the CA. The CA generates the user certificate and sends either the certificate or a certificate URL to the WAP device. The CA may store the certificate in its database. In future interactions between the gateway and this WAP device, the user signs the transaction and sends the transaction, the signature and the certificate (or certificate URL) to the application or information server. If the server receives a certificate URL, it retrieves the certificate from the CA database; that step is not needed if the user sends the actual certificate. The server verifies the signed transaction from the user and proceeds with the service. The user's certificates and keys are stored in the device's WAP identity module (WIM), which may be separate from or combined with the subscriber identity module (SIM). When these are combined, the card is called SWIM (subscriber WAP identity module). Implementation recommendations include minimization of the amount of user input from clients and of the persistent information about each PKI that any client should have to store.

The WTLS certificate format includes a validity period, which necessitates a provision of updates over the air before existing settings expire. Several different schemes

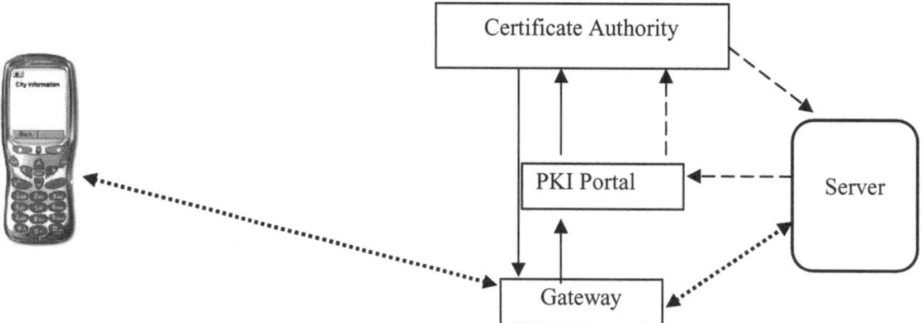

Figure 7: WTLS Class 2 Authentication.

were defined by the WAP Security Group (WSG) (Farrell, 2000):

- Out-of-band distribution: The user downloads the root CA information without regard to security in the channel but then must activate the CA by entering a 30-decimal digit value, which was received out of band. Although not attractive to the end user, this approach allows introduction of new CAs into the device without the user control.
- CA introduction: An existing CA digitally signs (validates) new CA information. Although much more attractive to the user, this scheme requires confidence on the part of one CA that the policies of the CA being introduced are appropriate. In some cases, liability issues may hinder this type of CA cooperation.
- Rollover: A variation on the CA introduction scheme allows the new CA to be identical to the old one.
- Other: The specification allows other mechanisms to be used when appropriately secure facilities are available.

Although WPKI can be looked at as an optimization of the traditional IETF PKIX standards for the wireless environment, a number of special features have been found necessary as a result of the wireless environment. Particularly WPKI optimizes the PKI protocols, certificate formats, and cryptographic algorithms and keys.

WPKI uses the ASN.1 Basic Encoding Rules (BER) and Distinguished Encoding Rules (DER) used to handle PKI services for WML and WMLSCrypt (Wireless public-key infrastructure, 2003). WML and the signText function in WMLSCrypt provide significant savings when encoding and submitting PKI service requests compared to traditional PKI methods.

Functioning of the WAP PKI

The capability established in WTLS class 2 establishes the authentic identity of the gateway with which a client is communicating. Early implementations allow communication between the phone and a gateway and between the gateway and a server. In this model the client (phone) depends on the gateway to establish the identity of the server. A later version of the protocol implementation allows the server to obtain its certificate directly from the certificate authority and the ensuing session with the user is between the phone and the server (Open Mobile Alliance, 2004). The gateway remains in use for routing, but the session is between the client and the server with no role for the gateway in authentication. Figure 7 illustrates both types of connection. First, the gateway communicates with CA through the PKI portal (solid lines in the figure). The CA provides the gateway public certificate to the gateway. Subsequently, the client communicates through the gateway to the server (dotted lines). Only the gateway has been authenticated. Later versions provide for end-to-end authentication: The gateway still obtains a certificate. However, the server also obtains a certificate from the CA (server public certificate) (dashed lines). The session proceeds between the client and the server with the gateway providing routing (dotted lines). The role of the gateway could be eliminated under this model.

LOOKING AHEAD

Expectations for Mobile Computing

It is hard not to think back to 1993 or 1994 when early Web pages were available and only a few people knew the basics of producing and deploying them. In the early years of the 2000s, the wireless Web is in a similar situation. Application development is necessary to drive demand which in turn will drive more development. E-commerce applications are core elements of the Web today and the security services that support them must be available on small handheld devices in addition to desktop and powerful portable computers. This is an area of active development with strong motivation for the service providers.

The Role of the Wireless Application Protocol

In June 2002, the WAP Forum became part of a larger collaboration of industries and standards bodies called the Open Mobile Alliance. They describe the formation as follows:

> The foundation of the Open Mobile Alliance was created by consolidating the efforts of the supporters of the Open Mobile Architecture initiative and the WAP Forum. In addition, the Location Interoperability Forum (LIF), SyncML, MMS Interoperability Group (MMS-IOP), and Wireless Village, each focusing on mobile service enabler specifications, announced that they have signed a Memorandum of Understanding of their intent to consolidate with the Open Mobile Alliance.

Thus, the work of the WAP Forum continues with a larger context and a much larger degree of commitment from the related industries. The role of these protocol efforts to join the industries that produce the client devices and those who produce the services and information sources will be crucial to the kind of open connectivity and roaming accessibility necessary to make the wireless Web as pervasive and important as the wired Web is today.

GLOSSARY

Code Division Multiple Access The basis of third-generation wireless transmission technologies.
Datagram A communication technique in which messages are broken into independent units that travel separately through network connections.
Data Push Access to the data is initiated by the provider, which pushes it toward the consumer.
D-AMPs Digital Advanced Mobile Phone Systems
Gateway An intermediate device that links incompatible communication systems.
GSM Global System for Mobile Communications
iDEN Integrated Dispatch Enhanced Network
PDC Personal Digital Cellular
Protocol Stack A layered view of the collection of protocols required to accomplish a large task.
TDMA Time Division Multiple Access
WAE Wireless Application Environment
WAP Wireless Application Protocol
WCSS Wireless Cascading Style Sheet
WML Wireless Markup Language
WBXML Compact binary representation of XML documents.
XHTML Extended hypertext metalanguage
WSP Wireless Session Protocol
WTP Wireless Transmission Protocol
WTLS Wireless Transport Layer Security

CROSS REFERENCES

See *Digital Certificates; Mobile Devices and Protocols; Wireless Internet: A Cellular Perspective.*

REFERENCES

Ashley, P., Hinton, H., & Vandenwauver, M. (2003). *Wired versus wireless security: The Internet, WAP and iMode for e-commerce*. Retrieved December 20, 2003, from http://www.acsac.org/2001/papers/61.pdf

Certicom. *Wireless public-key infrastructure*. Retrieved December, 20, 2003.

Digital mobile phone networks in Africa. http://www.cellular.co.za/gsm-africa.htm

Farrell, S. (2000). *Outlining wireless public key infrastructure*. Retrieved May 2, 2004, from www.baltimore.co.kr/downloads/pdf/baltimore_telepathy_wpkiwhitepaper.pdf

Getgen, K. (2002). *Securing the air: 2001—A security odyssey*. Retrieved December 20, 2003, from http://www-106.ibm.com/developerworks/library/wi-sec2.html?article=wir

Hakkarainen, T., Lattunen, A., & Savikko, V. (2002). *Flower—Framework for local wireless services. ERCIM News*, 50. Retrieved September 4, 2004, from http://www.ercim.org/publication/Ercim_News/enw50/hakkarainen.html

Howell, Ric. (2003). *WAP Security*. Retrieved December 20, 2003, from http://www.topxml.com/conference/wrox/wireless_2000/howell1text.pdf

Information technology - Open Systems Interconnection - Basic Reference Model: The Basic Model, ISO/IEC 7498–1:1994.

Jeffs, T. C. (2001). *Wireless application protocol 2.0 security*. Retrieved December 20, 2003, from http://www.sans.org/rr/papers/68/159.pdf

Jørgensen, N., & Juul, N. C. (2002). *Security issues in mobile commerce using WAP*. Retrieved December 20, 2003, from http://www.dat.ruc.dk/~ncjuul/papers/BledWAP3.pdf

Mikal, P. (2001). *WTLS: The good and bad of WAP security*. Retrieved December 20, 2003, from http://www.advisor.com/Articles.nsf/aid/MIKAP001

Nardone, M. (2004). *Wireless PKI model*. Retrieved September 6, 2004, from www.eurescom.de/~pub/seminars/past/2001/SecurityFraud/10-Nardone/10a Nardone/10nardone.pdf

Open Mobile Alliance. (2004). *WPKI*. Retrieved March 26, 2004, from OMA-SEC-WPKI-V1_0-20040326-C

Personal Communications Industry Association. Evolving network standards in the U.S. http://www.pcia.com/industryconnect/evolvingnetworks.htm

Saarinen, M.-J. (2005). *Attacks against the WAP WTLS protocol*. Retrieved July 29, 2005, from http://www.cc.jyu.fi/~mjos/wtls.pdf

WAP Forum. (2001a). Wireless application protocol specification. Retrieved July 2001.

WAP Forum. (2001b). *Wireless application protocol public key infrastructure definition*. Retrieved December 20, 2003.

WAP Forum. (2002). *Wireless application protocol WAP 2.0 technical white paper*. Retrieved January 2002, from http://www.wapforum.org

Wireless Independent Provider. (2005). *Technical description: WIP mobilis development kit (MDK)*. Retrieved July 29, 2005, from http://www.wip.se/MDK/html/index.html

FURTHER READING

Badrinath, B., Fox, A., Kleinrock, L., Popek, G., Reiher, P., & Satyanarayanan, M. (2000, December). A conceptual framework for network and client adaptation. *Mobile Networks and Applications*, 5(4).

Bisdikian, C., Boamah, I., Castro, P., Misra, A., Rubas, J., Villoutreix, N., Yeh, D., Rasin, V., Huang, H., & Simonds, C. (2002). Context and location: Intelligent pervasive middleware for context-based and localized telematics services. Proceedings of the Second International Workshop on Mobile Commerce.

Cohen, D., Herscovici, M., Petruschka, Y., Maarek, Y. S., & Soffer, A. (2002). Mobility and Wireless Access: Personalized pocket directories for mobile devices Proceedings of the eleventh international conference on World Wide Web.

Dornan, A. (2000). *GSM and TDMA cellular networks*. Retrieved July 29, 2005, from http://www.networkmagazine.com/article/NMG20000517S0169

Dornan, A. (2001). *WAP reaches the second generation*. Retrieved July 29, 2005, from http://www.networkmagazine.com/article/NMG20010823S0013

Elaarag, H. (2002, September). Improving TCP performance over mobile networks. *ACM Computing Surveys (CSUR), 34*(3).

Evans, H., & Ashworth, P (2001). *Getting started with WAP and WML*. Alameda, CA: Sybex.

Flynn, M., Pendlebury, D., Jones, C., Eldridge, M., & Lamming, M., (2000, December). The Satchel system architecture: Mobile access to documents and services. *Mobile Networks and Application, 5*(4).

Fraternali, P., & Paolini, P. (2000, October). Model-driven development of Web applications: The AutoWeb system. *ACM Transactions on Information Systems (TOIS), 18*(4).

Geng, X., Huang, Y., & Whinston, A. B. (2002, June). Defending wireless infrastructure against the challenge of DDoS attacks. *Mobile Networks and Applications, 7*(3).

Hadjiefthymiades, S., Matthaiou, V., & Merakos, L. (2002, August). Supporting the WWW in wireless communications through mobile agents. *Mobile Networks and Applications, 7*(4).

Jing, J., Sumi Helal, A., & Elmagarmid, A. (1999, June). Client–server computing in mobile environments. *ACM Computing Surveys (CSUR), 31*(2).

Jones, C. E., Sivalingam, K. M., Agrawal, P., & Chen, J. C. (2001, September). A survey of energy efficient network protocols for wireless networks. *Wireless Networks, 7*(4).

Joshi, A. (2000, December). On proxy agents, mobility, and web access. *Mobile Networks and Applications, 5*(4).

Marcus, A., & Chen, E. (2002, January). Designing the PDA of the future. *Interactions, 9*(1).

Munson, J. P., & Gupta, V. K. (2002, September). Context and location: Location-based notification as a general-purpose service. Proceedings of the Second International Workshop on Mobile Commerce.

Olsson, D., & Nilsson, A. (2002, June). MEP: A media event platform. *Mobile Networks and Applications, 7*(3).

Palen, L, & Salzman, M. (2002, June). Beyond the handset: Designing for wireless communications usability. *ACM Transactions on Computer-Human Interaction (TOCHI), 9*(2).

Perry, M., O'hara, K., Sellen, A., Brown, B., & Harper, R. (2001, December). Dealing with mobility: Understanding access anytime, anywhere. *ACM Transactions on Computer-Human Interaction (TOCHI), 8*(4).

Phan, T., Huang, L., & Dulan, C, (2002, September). Challenges: Integrating mobile wireless devices into the computational grid. Proceedings of the eighth annual international conference on Mobile computing and networking.

Samaras, G., & Panayiotou, C. (2002). Data and Content: Personalized portals for the wireless user based on mobile agents. Proceedings of the Second International Workshop on Mobile Commerce.

Shih, G., Simon S., & Shim, Y. (2002, June). A service management framework for M-commerce applications. *Mobile Networks and Applications, 7*(3).

Singhal, S., Bridgman, T., Suryanarayana, L., Mauney, D., Alvinen, J., Bevis, D., Chan, J., & Hild, S. (2001). The wireless application protocol. New York: ACM Press.

Steinberg, J., & Pasquale, J. (2002, May). Mobility and wireless access: A Web middleware architecture for dynamic customization of content for wireless clients. Proceedings of the Eleventh International Conference on World Wide Web.

Varshney, U., & Vetter, R. (2002, June). Mobile commerce: Framework, applications and networking support. *Mobile Networks and Applications, 7*(3).

WAP and iMode and microbrowsers. (2001). Retreived December 20, 2003, from http://www.it-director.com/article.php?articleid=2074

WAP Transport Layer End to End Security Approved Version 28-June-2001 http://www1.wapforum.org/tech/documents/WAP-187-TransportE2ESec-20010628-a.pdf

Wireless Application Environment Specification Version 9-Nov-2001

Wireless Application Protocol. Wireless Transaction Protocol Specification. Approved Version 19-February-2000. http://www1.wapforum.org/tech/documents/WAP-201-WTP-20000219-a.pdf

Wireless Application Protocol Wireless Session Protocol Specification. Version 5-November-1999 http://br.wmlclub.com/docs/especwap1.2/SPEC-WSP-19991105.pdf

Wireless Markup Language Version 2.0 Version 11-Sep-2001 http://www1.wapforum.org/tech/documents/WAP-238-WML-20010911-a.pdf

Yoshimura, T., Yonemoto, Y., Ohya, T., Etoh, M., & Wee, S. (2002, May). Mobility and wireless access: Mobile streaming media CDN enabled by dynamic SMIL. Proceedings of the Eleventh International Conference on World Wide Web.

Wireless Network Standards and Protocol 802.11

Prashant Krishnamurthy, *University of Pittsburgh*

INTRODUCTION

Wireless networks can be classified in many ways—based on mobility, topology, application, or coverage. For example, based on mobility, we may classify wireless networks as fixed, stationary, portable, or mobile. If we consider applications, we may look at wireless data networks and cellular voice networks. The topology of a wireless network may be based on a fixed infrastructure that enables mobile stations (MSs) to connect to the rest of the network or the topology may be ad hoc where MSs connect to one another in a peer-to-peer manner without assistance from a fixed infrastructure. The most popular classification is based on coverage—whether the wireless network provides service over a local area or a larger geographical region. *Wireless local area networks* (WLANs) typically cover areas ranging anywhere between parts of a building to a campus of an organization. *Wireless wide area networks* (WWANs) cover entire cities and even parts of a nation. Usually, WWANs provide lower data rates compared to WLANs and are more complex in architecture. The spectrum allocated to WWANs is typically licensed spectrum and there needs to be careful planning and deployment of WWANs. WLANs mostly form extensions to existing local area network (LAN) segments in organizations. They typically use unlicensed spectrum and as long as the interference is reasonable, they can be deployed by anyone, anywhere. Recently, WLANs are also being used to provide broadband Internet access in hotspots such as airports, cafes, and hotels.

There are several standards for WWANs and WLANs and they are primarily dependent on geography. The European Telecommunications Standards Institute (ETSI), based in France, is responsible for the standards activities in the European Union (EU) although these standards have been sometimes adopted in other parts of the world. In the United States, standards activities are less centralized. There are many organizations involved in standards activities such as the Institute for Electrical and Electronic Engineers (IEEE), American National Standards Institute (ANSI), the Telecommunications Industry Association (TIA), and so on. Typically, a standard is created based on input from several industry groups and once such standards are approved, the International Standards Organization (ISO) often adopts these standards (see list of URLs for standards bodies). Many of the details in this article are derived from the IEEE 802.11 standards and information available on the IEEE 802.11 Web site.

Standards for wireless technologies have to deal with a gamut of different issues starting from the spectrum that can be used by this technology going up to defining entities in the system and the detailed protocols between them. In this article, we briefly look at wireless network standards in general and focus on one particular WLAN standard—namely the IEEE 802.11 standard.

Wireless Wide Area Network Standards

Standards for WWANs focus on cellular telephone systems and wireless data services as overlays on top of the cellular systems. It is common to consider generations of wireless systems each spanning approximately a decade. The first generation of WWANs (spanning the 1980s) employed analog modulation schemes and a common example that is still deployed in the United States is the *Advanced Mobile Phone System* (AMPS) (Pahlavan, 2002). The capacity limitations of the first generation WWANs resulted in development of digital alternatives in the late 1980s. During the 1990s, digital cellular systems (called the second generation) were deployed based on standards developed by ETSI in Europe and TIA in the United States. The standards based on time division multiple access (TDMA) were the global system for mobile (GSM)

Table 1 Summary of Some WWAN Standards[1]

Standard	Standard Body	Spectrum (MHz)	Multiple Access	Primary Region
AMPS	TIA	824–849, Uplink 869–894, Downlink	FDMA	United States, Canada
IS-136	TIA	824–849, Uplink 869–894, Downlink	TDMA/FDMA	United States
IS-95	TIA	824–849, Uplink 869–894, Downlink	CDMA/FDMA	United States, Latin America, Asia
GSM	ETSI	890–915, Uplink 935–960, Downlink	TDMA/FDMA	Europe, Africa
CDPD	TIA	824–849, Uplink 869–894, Downlink	DSMA/TDMA	United States
GPRS	ETSI	890–915, Uplink 935–960, Downlink	Reservation/TDMA	Europe
cdma2000	3GPP2	824–849, Uplink 869–894, Downlink	CDMA	United States, Asia-Pacific
UMTS	3GPP	Varies	CDMA	Europe

[1]Spectra allocated to different standards are only representative and are different in different countries.

communications and the TIA interim standard 136 (IS-136). The former is widely deployed in Europe and other parts of the world. The latter, also called the North American TDMA or digital AMPS, is deployed primarily in North America. The standard based on code division multiple access (CDMA) was designed by Qualcomm and standardized later by TIA and ANSI. It is commonly called the IS-95 standard although there are several modifications that have followed. CDMA has better robustness under harsh wireless conditions and interference and has the potential to offer a larger capacity. The third generation of cellular telephone systems is thus based on CDMA. There are two competing paths—one that is a migration from IS-95, called cdma2000, and another that is a migration from GSM, called Universal Mobile Telecommunications System (UMTS). The former is being standardized by a consortium of standards bodies called 3GPP2 and the latter by a second consortium called 3GPP. 3GPP stands for Third Generation Partnership Project.

Wireless data services were typically overlaid on the cellular systems already in place during the 1990s. There are several proprietary wireless data services. Two open standardized common data overlays are the Cellular Digital Packet Data (CDPD) that is overlaid on AMPS and the General Packet Radio Service (GPRS) that is overlaid on GSM. The former was standardized by the CDPD forum in 1995 and the latter by ETSI. CDPD standardization is now handled by the TIA. Wireless data services use different multiple access mechanisms over the air compared to voice services that are circuit switched (Salkintzis, 1999). CDPD makes use of a technique called digital sense multiple access (DSMA) on the uplink and TDMA on the downlink. GPRS makes use of reservation of time slots for multiple access. In the third-generation, packet data services are integrated with the cellular telephone service in the standard. Table 1 summarizes some of these WWAN standards.

Wireless Local Area Network Standards

Like WWANs, standards activities for WLANs have also evolved geographically with the ETSI's Broadband Radio Access Network (BRAN) working on High Performance Radio LAN or HIPERLAN standards in Europe and the IEEE on the 802.11 series in the United States. In Japan, the Multimedia Mobile Access Communications (MMAC) working group under the Association of Radio Industries and Businesses (ARIB) works on WLAN standards. The spectrum used by WLANs is mostly unlicensed spectrum although some systems use licensed spectrum as well. Unlike WWANs, the only commercially successful WLAN standard has been the IEEE 802.11. HIPERLAN/1 was standardized in the mid-1990s and supported complex multihop ad hoc networking. The medium access mechanism in HIPERLAN/1 (Wilkinson, 1995) was based on a form of carrier sense multiple access called Elimination-Yield Non-Preemptive Multiple Access (EY-NPMA). HIPERLAN/2 has adopted a physical layer that is very similar to IEEE 802.11a and a medium access mechanism based on reservation and TDMA. However, both these standards have not been adopted successfully in commercial products. Recently, there have been efforts to harmonize the standards activities of ETSI, IEEE 802.11, and MMAC. Table 2 summarizes some of the 802.11, HIPERLAN, and MMAC standards.

In the rest of this article, we consider primarily the IEEE 802.11 standard in some detail and also look at some related protocols for security.

INTRODUCTION TO THE IEEE 802.11 STANDARD

Within the IEEE, there are several standards activities carried on by different groups. The IEEE 802 LAN/MAN Standards Committee is responsible for local

Table 2 Summary of Some WLAN Standards

Standard	Standard Body	Spectrum	Data Rate	Primary Medium Access	Primary Region
IEEE 802.11,b, g	IEEE	2.4-GHz ISM bands	1, 2, 5.5, 11, up to Mbps	CSMA/CA[1]	North America
IEEE 802.11a	IEEE	5-GHz U-NII and ISM bands	Up to 54 Mbps	CSMA/CA	North America
HIPERLAN/1	ETSI	5-GHz bands	23 Mbps	EY/NPMA[2]	Europe
HIPERLAN/2	ETSI	5-GHz bands	Up to 54 Mbps	TDMA Reservation	Europe
Wireless Access and WLAN	MMAC	5-GHz bands	20–25 Mbps	Wireless ATM	Japan

[1]CSMA/CA, Carrier Sense Multiple Access with Collision Avoidance.
[2]EY-NPMA, Elimination Yield Non-Preemptive Multiple Access.

area network (LAN) standards and metropolitan area network (MAN) standards. Individual working groups are in charge of a variety of LAN/MAN standards of which the 802.11 working group is responsible for *wireless local area networking* (WLAN) *standards.*

The 802.11 standard (Crow, 1997), like most LAN standards, is concerned only with the lower two layers of the OSI stack, namely the physical (PHY) and medium access control (MAC) layers. The MAC and PHY layers operate under the IEEE 802.2 logical link control (LLC) layer that supports many other LAN protocols. In the case of wired LAN standards such as 802.3, there are several physical layers that correspond to the same MAC specifications. A good example is IEEE 802.3, which was originally designed for thick coaxial cable but was subsequently revised to include thin coaxial cable, a variety of twisted pair cables, and even fiber optic links. In the same way, the IEEE 802.11 standard specifies a common MAC protocol that is used over many different PHY standards. The PHY standards are the "base" IEEE 802.11 standard, the 802.11b and g standards and the 802.11a standard. The MAC protocol is based on carrier sense multiple access with collision avoidance (CSMA/CA). An optional polling mechanism called point coordination function (PCF) is also specified. In addition to the MAC and PHY layers, the IEEE 802.11 standard also specifies a *management plane* that transmits management messages over the medium and can be used by an administrator to tune the MAC and PHY layers. The MAC layer management entity (MLME) deals with management issues such as roaming and power conservation. The PHY layer management entity (PLME) assists in channel selection and interacts with the MLME. A station management entity (SME) handles the interaction between these management layers. Figure 1 shows the protocol stack associated with IEEE 802.11.

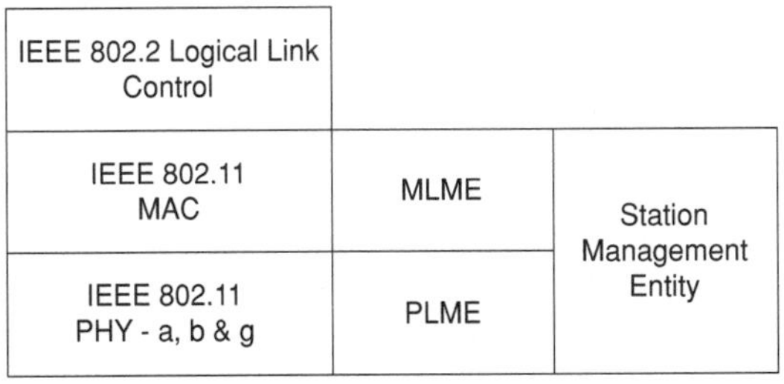 IEEE 802.2 Logical Link Control		
IEEE 802.11 MAC	MLME	Station Management Entity
IEEE 802.11 PHY - a, b & g	PLME	

Figure 1: Protocol stack of IEEE 802.11.

The base IEEE 802.11 standard specifies three different PHY layers—two using radio-frequency (RF) and one using infrared (IR) communications. The RF PHY layers are based on spread spectrum (SS), either direct sequence (DS) or frequency hopping (FH), whereas the IR PHY layer is based on pulse position modulation (PPM). Two different data rates are specified—1 and 2 Mbps for each of the three PHY layers. The RF physical layers are specified in the 2.4-GHz industrial, scientific, and medical (ISM) unlicensed frequency bands.

The IEEE 802.11b standard specifies the physical layer at 2.4 GHz for higher data rates—5.5 Mbps and 11 Mbps. The PHY layer makes use of a modulation scheme called complementary code keying (CCK). The transmission rate depends on the quality of the signal and it is backwards compatible with the DSSS based base-802.11 standard. Depending on the signal quality, the transmission rates could fall back to lower values. The 802.11g standard further increases the data rates to up to 54 Mbps in the 2.4-GHz ISM bands using orthogonal frequency division multiplexing (OFDM). The IEEE 802.11a standard (Kapp, 2002) deals with the PHY layer in the 5 GHz unlicensed national information infrastructure (U-NII) bands. Once again data rates up to 54 Mbps are specified in these bands with OFDM as the modulation technique. Depending on the PHY layer alternative, the frequency band is divided into several channels. Each channel supports the maximum data rate allowed by that PHY layer alternative.

In the next few sections, we discuss the IEEE 802.11 standard in a top-down manner. We first look at the topologies possible in IEEE 802.11 and also understand some of the management functions. We then take a detailed look at the MAC layer of 802.11 and discuss the different PHY layer alternatives. Once the basic operation of the 802.11 WLAN has been considered, it will be easier to delve into security issues in IEEE 802.11 and the recent ongoing activities to extend the standard further.

IEEE 802.11 WLAN OPERATIONS

The topology of an IEEE 802.11 WLAN can be one of two types—infrastructure or ad hoc (see Figure 2). In the infrastructure topology, an access point (AP) covers

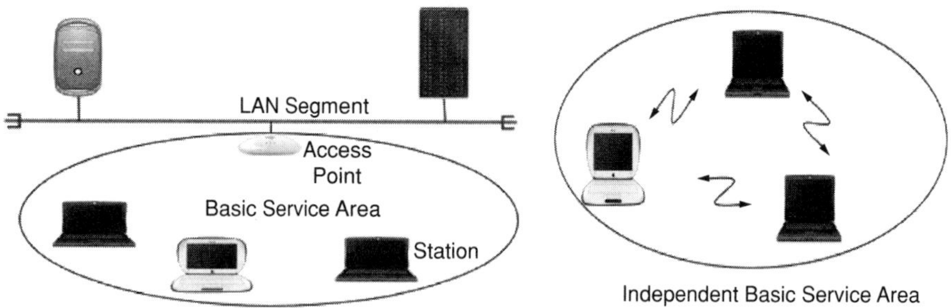

Figure 2: Topologies in IEEE 802.11

a particular area called the basic service area (BSA) and mobile stations (MSs) communicate with each other or with the Internet through the AP (Crow, 1997). The AP is connected to a LAN segment and forms the *point of access* to the network. All communications go through the AP. So a MS that wants to communicate with another MS first sends the message to the AP. The AP looks at the destination and sends it to the second MS. The AP along with all the MSs associated with it is called a basic service set (BSS). In the ad hoc topology (also called independent BSS or IBSS), MSs that are in range of each other can communicate directly with one another without a wired infrastructure. However, it is not possible for a MS to forward packets meant for another MS not in the range of the source MS. Figure 2 shows schematics of both topologies. MSs and APs are identified by a 48-bit MAC address that is similar to other MAC addresses at the link layer. In an infrastructure topology, the MAC address of the AP also forms the BSSID, a unique identifier of the BSS.

If we assume that the range of communication of any WLAN device, be it a MS or an AP is a region of radius R, we can look at the comparative advantages of the two topologies. A MS can communicate with another MS that is up to $2R$ away using an AP provided both MSs are within a distance R of the AP. The cost here is the additional transmission from the AP to the destination. In the ad hoc topology, a destination MS cannot be more than a distance R from the source MS. The advantage is that the information can be received in one hop.

Extending the Coverage in Infrastructure Topology

Depending on the environment in which it is deployed and the transmit powers that are used, an AP can cover a region with a radius anywhere between 30 and 250 feet. To cover a building or a campus, it often becomes necessary to deploy multiple APs that are connected to the same LAN. A group of such APs and the member mobile stations is called an *extended service set* (ESS). The coverage area is called the extended service area (ESA). The wired backbone that connects the different APs along with services that enable the ESS is called the *distribution system.* The distribution system, for example, supports roaming between APs so that MSs can access the network over a wider coverage area than before. This is similar to cellular telephone systems where multiple base stations provide coverage to a region, each base station covering only a cell.

Network Operations in an Infrastructure Topology

When a MS is powered up and configured to operate in an infrastructure topology, it can perform a passive scan or an active scan. In the case of a passive scan, the MS simply scans the different channels to detect the existence of a BSS. The existence of a BSS can be detected through *beacon* frames that are broadcast by APs pseudoperiodically. The reason why it is called pseudoperiodic is that the beacon is supposed to be transmitted regularly at certain intervals. However, the AP cannot preempt an ongoing transmission to transmit a beacon. When we discuss the MAC layer, we will see that any device has to wait for the medium to be free before transmitting a frame. If the medium is busy, the AP will transmit the beacon after the medium becomes free in which case, the beacon may not be precisely periodic. The beacon is a management frame that announces the existence of a network. It contains information about the network—the BSSID and the capabilities of the network (the PHY alternatives it supports, if security is mandatory, whether the MAC layer supports polling, the interval at which beacons are transmitted, timing parameters, and so on). The beacon is similar to certain control channels in cellular telephone systems (for instance, the Broadcast Control Channel—BCCH in GSM). The MS also performs signal strength measurements on the beacon frame. In the case of an active scan, the MS already knows the ID of the network that it wants to connect to. In this case, the MS sends a *probe request* frame on each channel. APs that hear the probe request respond with a *probe response* frame that is similar in nature to the beacon. In either case, the MS can create a scan report that provides it with information about the available BSSs, their capabilities, their channels, timing parameters, and other information. The MS makes use of this information to determine a compatible network that it can associate itself with.

To associate itself with an AP, the MS must authenticate itself if this is part of the capability of the network and we will look at this in a later section. Otherwise, as long as the MS satisfies the announced capabilities of the network, it can send an *association request* frame to the AP. The association request informs the AP of the intention of the MS to join the network and it also provides additional information about the MS such as its MAC address, how often it will listen to the beacon (called the *listen interval*), the supported data rates and so on. If the AP is satisfied with the capabilities of the MS, it will reply with an *association response* frame. In this message, the MS is given an association ID and this frame confirms that the MS is now able to access the network.

If a MS moves across BSSs or if it moves out of coverage and returns to the BSA of an AP, it will have to reassociate itself with the AP. For this purpose, it will use a *reassociation request* frame similar in form to the association request frame, except that the MAC address of the old AP will be included in the frame. The AP will respond with a *reassociation response* frame. A MS moving from one BSS to another will have to detect the drop in signal strength from the old AP and detect the beacon of the new AP before the reassociation request. It could also use a probe request message instead of detecting the beacon from the new AP.

Power management is an important component of network operations in an IEEE 802.11 WLAN. When MSs have no frames to send, they can enter a sleep mode to conserve power. If a MS is sleeping when frames arrive at an AP for it, the AP will buffer such frames. A sleeping MS wakes up periodically and listens to the beacon frames. How often it wakes up is specified by the listen interval mentioned earlier. The beacon frame also contains a field called the traffic indication map (TIM). This field contains information about whether packets are buffered in the AP for a given MS. If a MS detects that it has some frames waiting for it, it can wake up from the sleep mode and receive those frames before going back to sleep. The MS uses a *power-save poll* frame to indicate to the AP that it is ready to receive buffered frames.

If the MS chooses to leave the network or shutdown, it will send a *dissociation* frame to the AP. This frame will terminate the association between the MS and the network enabling the network to free resources that were previously reserved for the MS (such as the association ID, buffer space, etc.).

Network Operations in an Ad Hoc Topology

In an ad hoc topology, there is no fixed AP to coordinate transmissions and define the BSS. A MS that operates in ad hoc mode will power up and scan the channels to detect beacons from other MSs that may be in the vicinity and that may have set up an IBSS. If it does detects no beacons, it may declare its own network. If it detects a beacon, then the MS can join the IBSS in a manner similar to the process in the infrastructure topology. MSs in an IBSS may choose to rotate the responsibility of transmitting a beacon. Power management works in a similar way, except that the source MS itself has to send an announcement traffic indication map (ATIM) frame to the recipient MS.

THE IEEE 802.11 MAC LAYER

MSs in an IEEE 802.11 network have to share the transmission medium, which is air. If two MSs transmit at the same time and the transmissions are both in range of the destination, they may collide resulting in the frames being lost. The MAC layer is responsible for controlling access to the medium and ensuring that MSs can access the medium in a fair manner with minimal collisions. The medium access mechanism is based on carrier sense multiple access but there is no collision detection like the wired equivalent LAN standard (IEEE 802.3). Collisions are extremely hard to detect in RF because of the dynamic nature of the channel. Detecting collisions also incurs difficulties in hardware implementation because an MS has to be transmitting and receiving at the same time. Instead, the strategy adopted is to avoid collisions to the extent possible. In IEEE 802.11, there are two types of carrier sensing—physical sensing of energy in the medium and virtual sensing. Virtual sensing is implemented by decoding a duration field in the 802.11 frame that allows a MS to know the time for which a frame will last. This time is stored in a *network allocation vector* (NAV) that counts down to zero to indicate when the medium is free again. To illustrate the IEEE 802.11 MAC layer, we use the ad hoc topology as an example. However, the procedures are identical in an infrastructure topology as well.

The Distributed Coordination Function

We first describe the basic medium access process in IEEE 802.11 called the distributed coordination function (DCF). Consider Figure 3 that shows the basic method for accessing the medium in IEEE 802.11. A MS will initially sense the channel before transmission. If the medium is

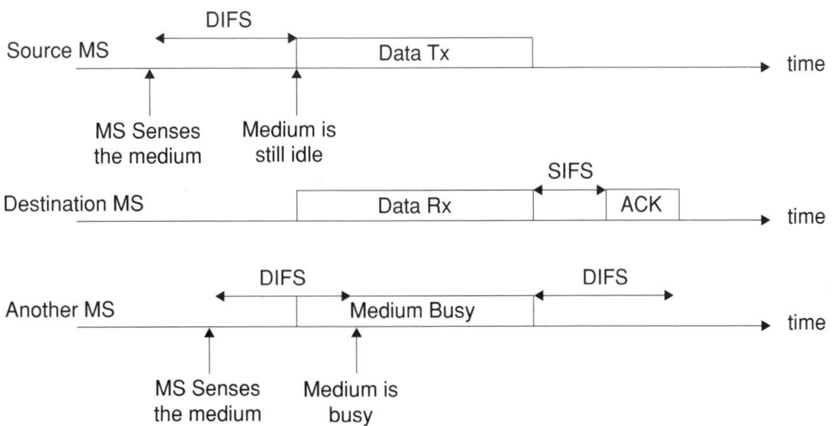

Figure 3: Basic medium access in IEEE 802.11.

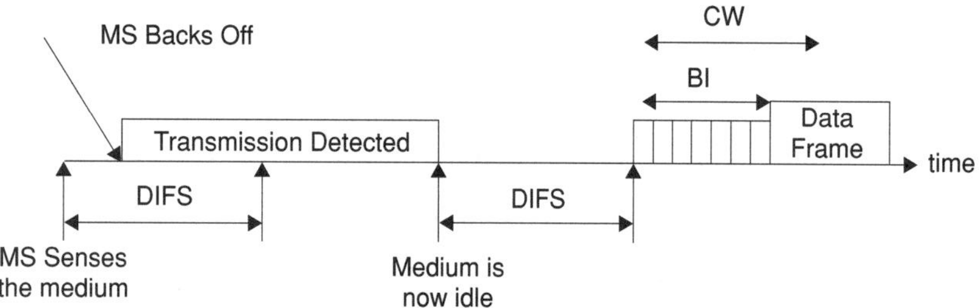

Figure 4: Backoff process in IEEE 802.11.

free, the MS will continuously monitor the medium for a period of time called the *distributed coordination function* (DCF) *interframe space* (IFS) or DIFS. If the medium is still idle after DIFS, then the MS can transmit its frame without waiting. Otherwise, the MS will enter a back off process. The rationale is that if another MS senses the medium after the first MS, it will also wait for DIFS. However, before a time DIFS expires, the first MS would have started its transmission. Upon hearing the transmission, the second MS will have to back off. The wireless medium is harsh and unreliable and hence all transmissions are acknowledged. The destination of the frame will send an acknowledgement (ACK) back to the source if the frame is successfully received as follows. It will wait for a time called the *short interframe space* (SIFS) and transmits the ACK. The SIFS value is smaller than the DIFS value. All IFS values depend on the physical layer alternative. Thus, any other MS that senses the channel as idle after the original frame was transmitted will still be waiting and ACK frames have priority over their transmissions. To maintain fairness and avoid collisions, the MS that senses the medium as free for a time DIFS and transmits a frame will have to enter the backoff process if it wants to transmit another frame immediately. The exception is when it is transmitting one frame in many fragments. In such a case, the MS can indicate the number of fragments in the first frame to be transmitted and occupy the channel till the frame is completely transmitted.

The backoff process works as follows. Once an MS enters the backoff process, it picks a value called the *backoff interval* (BI) that is a random value uniformly distributed between zero and a number called the *contention window* (CW). The MS will then monitor the medium. When the medium is free for at least a time DIFS, the MS will start counting down from the BI value as long as the medium is free. The counter is decremented every so often (called a slot). If the medium is sensed as occupied before the counter goes down to zero, the MS will freeze the counter and continue to monitor the medium. As soon the counter becomes zero, the MS can transmit its frame. This process is shown in Figure 4.

The IEEE 802.11 MAC supports *binary exponential backoff* as in IEEE 802.3. Initially, the CW is maintained at a value called CW_{min}, which is typically $2^5 - 1 = 31$ slots. So the BI will be uniformly distributed between 0 and 31 slots. If a packet is not successfully transmitted (this could be because of collisions or a channel error), the value of CW is essentially doubled. The MS will now pick a BI value that is uniformly distributed between 0 and $2^6 - 1 = 63$ slots. This process can be continued till CW reaches a value that is CW_{max} (usually 1023 slots). The rationale behind this approach is as follows. If there are many MSs contending for the medium, it is likely that one or more MSs may pick the same BI value. Their transmissions will then collide. By increasing the value of CW, it is likely that this probability will go down, thereby reducing collisions.

Frames may be lost because of channel errors or collisions. A positive ACK from the destination is necessary to ensure that the frame has been successfully received. In IEEE 802.11, each MS maintains retry counters that are incremented if no ACKs are received. After a retry threshold is reached, the frame is discarded as being undeliverable.

The Hidden Terminal Problem and Optional Mechanism

In wireless networks that use carrier sensing, there is a unique problem called the hidden terminal problem. Suppose all MSs are identical and have a transmission and reception range of R as shown in Figure 5.

The transmission from MS-A can be heard by MS-C but not MS-B. So when MS-A is transmitting a frame to MS-C, MS-B will not sense the channel as busy and MS-A is *hidden* from MS-B. If both MS-A and MS-B transmit frames to MS-C at the same time, the frames will collide. This problem is called the hidden terminal problem. There is a dual problem called the exposed terminal problem. In this case, MS-A is transmitting a frame to MS-D. This transmission is heard by MS-C, which then backs off. However, MS-C could have transmitted a frame to MS-B and the two transmissions would not interfere or collide. In this case, MS-A is called an *exposed terminal*. Both hidden and exposed terminals cause a loss of throughput.

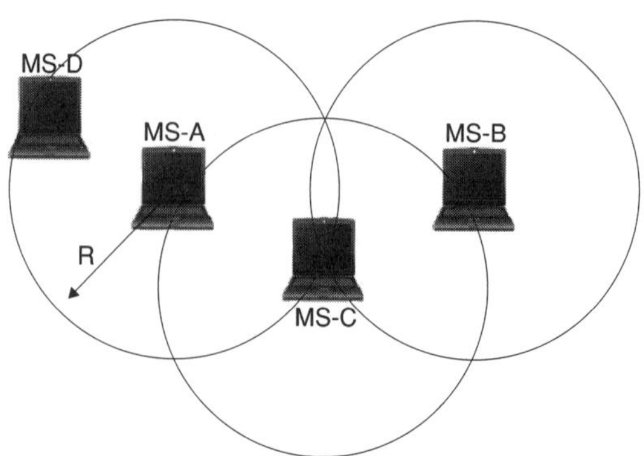

Figure 5: Illustrating the hidden and exposed terminal problems.

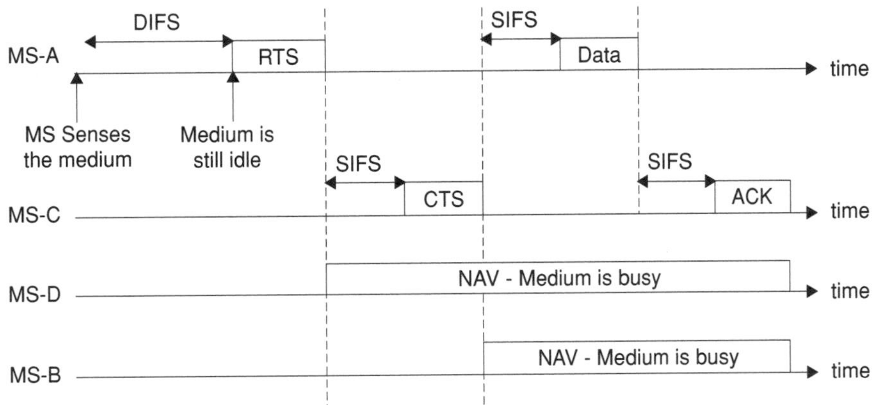

Figure 6: Operation of the RTS-CTS mechanism.

To reduce the possibility of collisions because of the hidden terminal problem, the IEEE 802.11 MAC has an optional mechanism at the MAC layer shown in Figure 6. Suppose MS-A wants to transmit a frame to MS-C. It will first transmit a short frame called the *Request-to-Send* (RTS) frame. The RTS frame is heard in the transmission range of MS-A and includes MS-C and MS-D but not MS-C. Both MS-C and MS-D are alerted to the fact that MS-A intends to transmit a frame and they will not attempt to simultaneously use the medium. This is achieved by the virtual carrier sensing process that sets the NAV to a value equal to the time it will take to successfully complete the exchange of frames. In response to the RTS frame, MS-C will send a *Clear-to-Send* (CTS) frame that will be heard by all MSs in its transmission range. This includes MS-B and MS-A but not MS-D. The CTS frame lets MS-A know that MS-C is ready to receive the data frame. It also alerts MS-B to the fact that there will be a transmission from some MS to MS-C. Consequently, MS-B will defer any frames that it wishes to transmit in anticipation of the completion of the communication to MS-C. This way, even though MS-B is outside the transmission range of MS-A, the CTS message can be used to *extend* the carrier sensing range thereby reducing the hidden terminal problem. Of course, it is quite possible that the RTS frame itself collided with a transmission from MS-B. In such a case, both MS-A and MS-B will have to enter the backoff process and retransmit their frames.

The RTS-CTS mechanism can be controlled in IEEE 802.11 by using an RTS threshold. All unicast and management frames larger than this threshold will always be transmitted using RTS-CTS. By setting this value to 0, all frames will use RTS-CTS. The default value that disables RTS-CTS for all packets is 2347. When RTS-CTS signals are used, the CTS frame is transmitted by the destination MS after waiting simply for a time equal to SIFS. This way, the CTS frame has priority compared to all other transmissions that have to wait for at least a time DIFS and perhaps an additional waiting time in backoff. Using the RTS-CTS signals reduces the throughput of a WLAN, but it may be essential to use this in dense environments.

The Point Coordination Function

One consequence of using CSMA/CA as described above with DCF is that it is impossible to have any bounds on the delay or jitter suffered by frames. Depending on the traffic load and the BI values that are picked, a frame may be transmitted instantaneously or it may have to be buffered until the medium becomes free. For real-time applications such as voice or multimedia, this can result in performance degradation especially when strict delay bounds are necessary. To provide some bounds on the delay, an optional MAC mechanism called the *point coordination function* (PCF) is part of the IEEE 802.11 standard (Crow, 1997). PCF provides contention-free access to frames using a polling mechanism described below.

The process starts when the AP captures the medium by sending a beacon frame after it is idle for a time called the *PCF interframe space* (PIFS). The PIFS is smaller than the DIFS and larger than SIFS. In the beacon frame, the AP, also called the point coordinator, announces a *contention-free period* (CFP), where the usual DCF operation will be preempted. All MSs that use only DCF will set a NAV to indicate that the medium will be busy for the duration of the CFP. The AP maintains a list of MSs that need to be polled during the CFP. MSs get onto the polling list when they first associate with the AP using the association request. The AP then polls each MS on the list for data. The polls are sent after a time SIFS and the ACKS to the poll and any associated data will be transmitted by the corresponding MS also after a time SIFS. If there is no response from a MS to a poll, the AP waits for a time PIFS before it sends the next poll frame or data. The AP can also send management frames whenever it chooses within the CFP. An example of PCF operations is shown in Figure 7.

The AP indicates the culmination of the CFP via a message called CFP-End. This is a broadcast frame to all MSs and frees the NAV in MSs that are only DCF based. Following the CFP, a contention period starts. In this period, it must be possible for a MS to transmit at least one maximum-length frame using DCF and receive an ACK. The CFP can be resumed after completion of the contention period. The PCF mechanism is optional in IEEE 802.11. Most commercial systems deployed today do not support PCF and real-time services do not have very good support in WLANs today. Note that polling has a lot of overhead especially if MSs do not have any frames to send when they are polled.

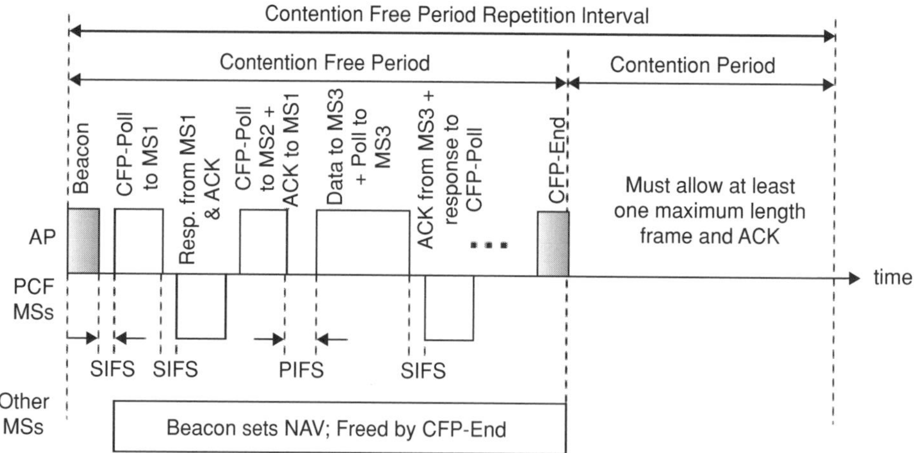

Figure 7: Operation of the PCF.

MAC Frame Formats

It is not the goal of this chapter to define the different frame formats of an IEEE 802.11 MAC frame and discuss the fields in great detail. However, some examples to illustrate the MAC frame formats are shown. Figure 8 shows the general format of a MAC frame. The most significant bit is last (right-most) and the bits are transmitted from left to right. The *frame control* field has two bytes and is composed of many fields. It carries information such as the protocol version, the type of frame [management (probe request, association, authentication, and so on), control (RTS, CTS, and so on), or data (pure data, CFP poll and data, null, and so on)], the number of retries, and whether the frame is encrypted (discussed later). The duration field is important to set the NAV during virtual carrier sensing.

There can be up to four address fields in the frame (Gast, 2002). The addresses can be different depending on the type of frame. Common addresses used are the source and destination addresses, the receiver address if the destination is different from the receiver (e.g., the receiver is the AP, but the destination is a wired node on the LAN segment), the transmitter address (once again, if the transmitter is different from the source, it is the AP), and the BSSID. The sequence control field is used in case there is fragmentation of frames. The frame body carries the payload from upper layers and the frame check sequence is a 32-bit cyclic redundancy check used to verify the integrity of the frame at the receiver. The frame format in Figure 8 is used in an infrastructure topology. In an IBSS, only three address fields are used.

The RTS and CTS frames are very short frames (20 and 14 bytes, respectively) and are shown in Figure 9. The ACK frames are very similar to the CTS frame.

Figure 10 illustrates the frame body of the beacon frame. The time stamp allows MSs to synchronize to a BSS. The beacon interval says how often the beacon can be expected to be heard. It is typically 100 ms but could be changed by an administrator. The capability information (2 bytes) provides information about the topology (whether infrastructure or ad hoc), whether encryption is mandatory, and whether additional features are supported. One such feature is *channel agility*, whereby the AP hops to different channels after a predetermined amount of time.

We have not yet discussed PHY layer alternatives. The parameter sets in the beacon provide information about the PHY layer parameters that are necessary to join the network. For instance, if frequency hopping (FH) is used, the FH parameter set will specify the hopping pattern. The traffic indication map (TIM) field is used to support MSs that may be sleeping as described earlier.

THE IEEE 802.11 PHYSICAL LAYER ALTERNATIVES

The IEEE 802.11 standards body has standardized several different PHY layer alternatives. When it was first

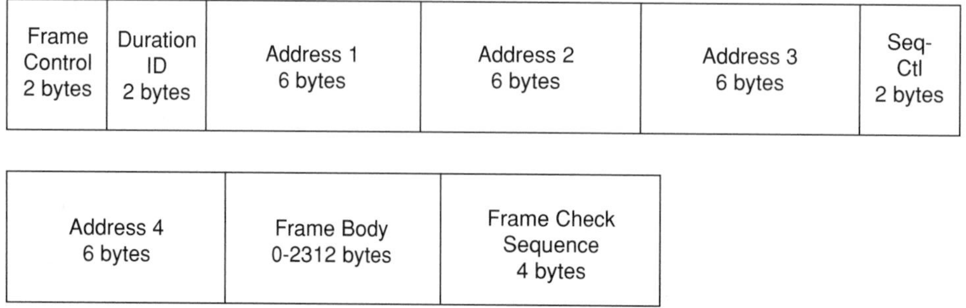

Figure 8: General format of a MAC frame.

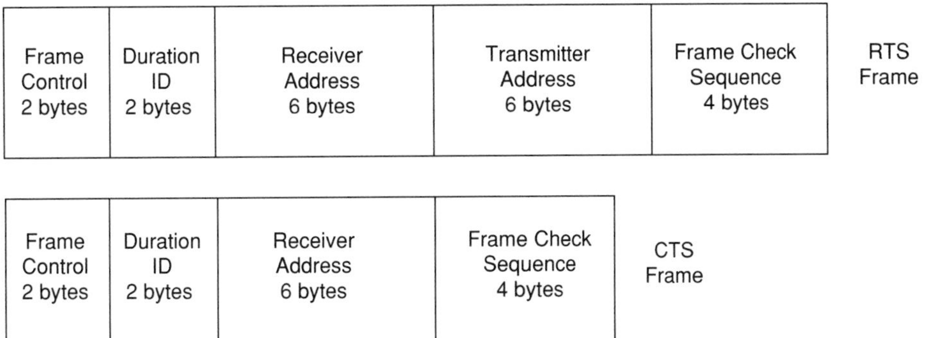

Figure 9: RTS and CTS frame formats.

standardized in 1997, there were three PHY layer options. We will call these options as the "base" IEEE 802.11 PHY layer alternatives. The IEEE 802.11b supports up to 11 Mbps in the 2.4-GHz ISM bands, the IEEE 802.11g standard supports up to 54 Mbps in the 2.4-GHz ISM bands and the IEEE 802.11a standard supports up to 54 Mbps in the 5-GHz U-NII bands. Before we discuss these alternatives, let us look at the PHY layer in IEEE 802.11.

The PHY layer in IEEE 802.11 is broken up into two sublayers—the *physical layer convergence protocol* (PLCP) and the *physical medium dependent* (PMD) layers. The PLCP includes a function that adapts the underlying medium dependent capabilities to the MAC level requirements. The PLCP would, for instance, add some additional fields to the frame to enable synchronization at the physical layer. The PMD actually determines how information bits are transmitted over the medium.

The Base IEEE 802.11 Standard

The base IEEE 802.11 standard specifies three different PHY layer alternatives. Two of these use RF transmissions in the 2.4-GHz ISM bands and one uses IR.

The FH Option

The first option for transmission in the 2.4-GHz ISM bands makes use of frequency hopping spread spectrum (FHSS) (Pahlavan, 2002). The entire band is divided into 1-MHz-wide channels and the specification makes it important to confine 99% of the energy to one such channel during transmission to reduce interference to the other channels. These restrictions are also because of the rules imposed by the Federal Communications Commission (FCC) in the United States. The standard specifies 95 such 1-MHz-wide channels and they are numbered accordingly. In the United States, only 79 of these channels are allowed. Devices that use the FH option hop between these channels when transmitting frames. The dwell time in each channel is approximately 0.4 s. The hop sequences (the channel hopping pattern) depends on mathematical functions. An example hopping pattern is {3, 26, 65, 11, 46, 19, 74, ...}. In the United States, each set of hopping patterns can have at most 26 different channels. This means that it is possible to create three *orthogonal* hopping sets (because there are 79 channels in the United States). If three APs use these three orthogonal hopping sets, there will be no interference between these networks. The modulation scheme used with FHSS is called *Gaussian frequency shift keying* (GFSK). This modulation scheme makes use of the frequency information to encode data. It is possible to use either two frequencies within the channel or four frequencies within the channel. In the former case, the data rate will be 1 Mbps and in the latter case, the data rate will be 2 Mbps. The advantage of the FHSS system is that the receivers are less complex to implement. The PLCP for the FHSS PMD introduces an 80-bit field for synchronization, a frame delimiter, and some fields to indicate the data rate. Depending on this field, the data rate can be modified in steps of 500 kbps from 1 to 4.5 Mbps. However, the standard supports only 1 and 2 Mbps. The values of SIFS and the slot for backoff in this option are 28 and 50 μs respectively.

The DS Option

The direct sequence spread spectrum (DSSS) modulation technique has been the most popular commercial implementation of IEEE 802.11. DSSS has some inherent advantages in multipath channels and can increase the coverage of an AP for this reason (Tuch, 1991). We briefly discuss the features of this PMD layer.

In a DSSS system, the data stream is "chipped" into several narrower pulses (chips), thereby increasing the occupied spectrum of the transmitted signal. One common way of doing this is to multiply the data stream (typically a series of positive and negative rectangular pulses) by a spreading signal (typically another series of positive and negative rectangular pulses, but with much narrower

Time Stamp 8 bytes	Beacon Interval 2 bytes	Capab. Info. 2 bytes	SSID Variable	FH Parameter Set 7 bytes	DS Param Set 2 bytes	CF Parameter Set 8 bytes	IBSS Parameter Set 4 bytes	TIM Var.

Figure 10: Frame body of the beacon frame.

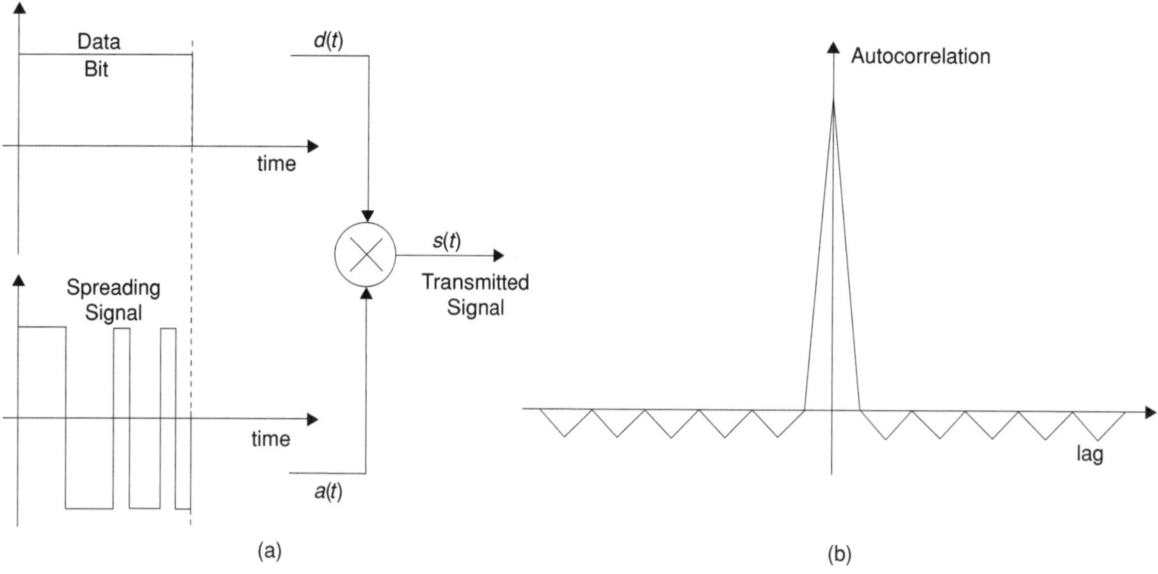

Figure 11: (a) Direct sequence spread spectrum; (b) autocorrelation of the Barker pulse.

pulses than the data stream). Whereas the data stream is random and depends on what needs to be transmitted, the spreading signal is deterministic. Figure 11(a) shows an example where the data stream $d(t)$ is multiplied by a spreading signal $a(t)$ to produce a signal $s(t)$ that is then modulated over an RF carrier. In this figure, 11 narrow pulses are contained within one broad data pulse. The pulses could have a positive (+) or negative (−) amplitude. This results in the bandwidth expanding by a factor of 11 and this is also called as the *processing gain*. The pattern of pulses in the spreading signal is $\{+, +, +, -, -, -, +, -, -, +, -\}$. This pattern is used in the IEEE 802.11 standard and it is called as a Barker sequence. The interesting property of the Barker sequence is that its autocorrelation has a very sharp peak and very narrow sidelobes as shown in Figure 11(b). Because of this property, it is possible for a receiver to reject interference from multipath signals and recover information robustly in a harsh wireless environment. The Barker sequence with differential binary phase shift keying (DBPSK) is used for data rates of 1 Mbps and the Barker sequence with differential quadrature phase shift keying (DQPSK) is used for data rates of 2 Mbps. In either case, the chip rate is 11 Mcps.

Unlike FHSS, a signal carrying 2 Mbps now occupies a bandwidth that is as large as 25 MHz. In the IEEE 802.11 standard, 14 channels are specified for the DSSS PMD. Channel 1 is at 2.412 GHz, channel 2 at 2.417 GHz, and so on. Only the first 11 channels are available for use in the United States. Figure 12 shows the channelization in the United States. Because each channel occupies roughly a 25-MHz bandwidth and the channel separation is only 5 MHz, there is significant overlap between channels. If two WLANs in the same vicinity were to use adjacent channels, there would be severe interference and throughput degradation. In the United States there are three *orthogonal* channels—channels 1, 6, and 11—that can be deployed without interference.

The PLCP sublayer once again introduces some fields for synchronization (128 bits), frame delimiting, and error checking. The PLCP header and preamble are always transmitted at 1 Mbps using DBPSK. The rest of the packet is transmitted using either DBPSK or DQPSK, depending on the data rate. The values of SIFS and the slot for backoff in this option are 10 and 20 μs respectively.

The IR Option

The third option in IEEE 802.11 is to use IR for transmission (Valadas, 1998). The spectrum occupied by the IR transmission is at wavelengths between 850 and 950 nm. The technique used for transmission is diffused infrared; that is, communications are omnidirectional. The range specified is around 20 m, but the transmissions cannot cross through physical obstacles. The modulation scheme used is pulse position modulation (PPM). A data rate of 1 Mbps is supported using 16-PPM and a data rate of 2 Mbps is supported using 4-PPM.

The IEEE 802.11b and 802.11g Standards

The DS option for IEEE 802.11, although successful, consumed a lot of bandwidth for the given data rate. The chip rate is 11 Mcps, but the maximum data rate is 2 Mbps. That is, one Barker sequence of 11 chips, transmitted every microsecond, can at most carry 2 bits of information. To increase the data rate, the IEEE 802.11b standard adopted a slightly different method. Instead of transmitting one 11-chip sequence every microsecond, with IEEE 802.11b, the device transmits one 8-chip codeword every 0.727 ms. Each 8-chip codeword can carry up to 8 bits of information for a maximum data rate of $8/(0.727 \times 10^{-6}) = 11$ Mbps. If the codeword carries only 4 bits of information, the data rate will be 5.5 Mbps. The codewords are derived from a technique called *complementary code keying* (CCK) (Halford, 1999).

CCK works as follows for the case when 8 bits are mapped into an 8-chip codeword. The incoming data

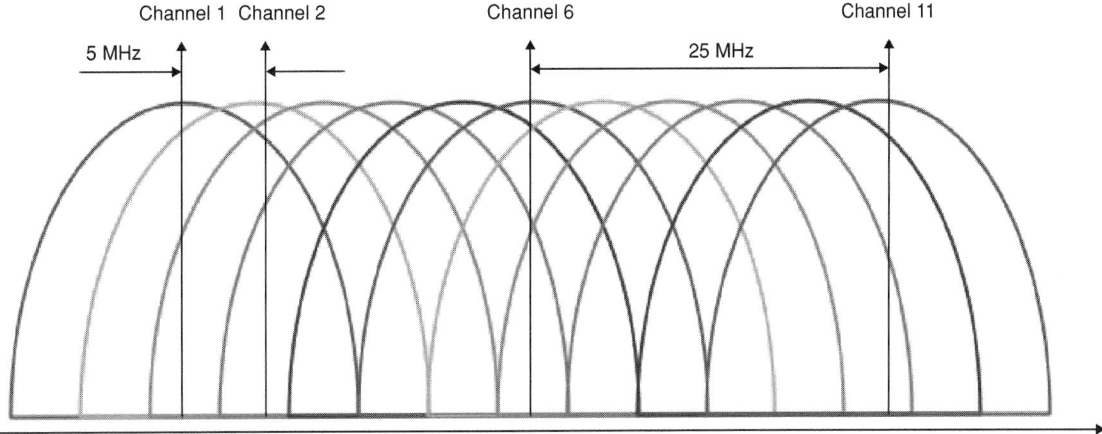

Figure 12: Channelization for IEEE 802.11 DS option.

stream is broken up into units of 8 bits. Suppose the least significant bit is d0 and the most significant bit is d7. Then, four phases are defined for each pair of bits as shown in the first two columns of Table 3. Depending on what the bits are, the phases then take on a value as shown in the third and fourth columns in Table 3. For example, if d5 = 0 and d4 = 1, then the phase $\varphi_3 = \pi$. Once the phases are determined, the 8-chip codeword is given by the following vector:

$$C = \left\{ \begin{matrix} e^{j(\varphi_1+\varphi_2+\varphi_3+\varphi_4)}, e^{j(\varphi_1+\varphi_3+\varphi_4)}, e^{j(\varphi_1+\varphi_2+\varphi_4)}, -e^{j(\varphi_1+\varphi_4)}, \\ e^{j(\varphi_1+\varphi_2+\varphi_3)}, e^{j(\varphi_1+\varphi_3)}, -e^{j(\varphi_1+\varphi_2)}, e^{j(\varphi_1)} \end{matrix} \right\}.$$

This vector has elements that belong to the set $\{+1, -1, +j, -j\}$, where j is the square root of -1. These four elements can be mapped in RF to the phase of the carrier and the receiver can decode this phase information to recover the data bits (Pahlavan, 2002).

The advantage of CCK is that it maintains the channelization of IEEE 802.11b while increasing the data rate by a factor of 5. CCK is also fairly robust to the degradations caused by multipath in the wireless environment. The values of SIFS and the slot for backoff in this option are 10 and 20 μs respectively. IEEE 802.11b also has an optional modulation method called packet binary convolutional coding (PBCC) that is not widely implemented.

The IEEE 802.11g standard maintains backwards compatibility with IEEE 802.11b and IEEE 802.11 DS options by including some mandatory and optional components. It specifies OFDM and CCK as the mandatory modulation schemes with a data rate of 24 Mbps as the maximum mandatory data rate. It also provides for optional higher data rates of 36, 48, and 54 Mbps. OFDM is the same

Table 3 Mapping for CCK

Dibit	Phase Parameter	Dibit (d_{i+1},d_i)	Phase
(d1, d0)	φ_1	(0,0)	0
(d3, d2)	φ_2	(0,1)	π
(d5, d4)	φ_3	(1,0)	$\pi/2$
(d7, d6)	φ_4	(1,1)	$-\pi/2$

modulation scheme that is used in IEEE 802.11a and we discuss it below.

The IEEE 802.11a Standard

One of the primary problems for huge data rates in wireless channels is what is called the coherence bandwidth of the wireless channel caused by multipath dispersion. The coherence bandwidth limits the maximum data rate of the channel to that which can be supported within this bandwidth. To overcome this limitation, we can send data in several subchannels so that many of them will get through correctly. Using several subchannels and reducing the data rate on each channel increases the symbol duration in each channel. If the symbol duration in each channel is larger than the multipath dispersion, errors will be smaller and it will be possible to support larger data rates. This principle can be exploited while maintaining bandwidth efficiency using a fairly old technique called OFDM. OFDM has been used in digital subscriber lines (DSL) as well to overcome the frequency variations over copper. OFDM enables spacing carriers (subchannels) as closely as possible and implementing the system completely in digital eliminating analog components to the extent possible. OFDM (Kapp, 2002) is used as the physical layer in IEEE 802.11a, HIPERLAN/2, and IEEE 802.11g.

IEEE 802.11a specifies eight 20-MHz channels (van Nee, 1999). As shown in Figure 13, several subchannels are created in OFDM using orthogonal carriers in each channel. Fifty-two subchannels are specified for each channel with a bandwidth of approximately 300 kHz each. Forty-eight subchannels are used for data transmission and four are used as pilot channels for synchronization. One OFDM symbol (consisting of the sum of the symbols on all carriers) lasts for 4 μs and carries anywhere between 48 and 288 coded bits. For example, at 54 Mbps, the OFDM symbol has 216 data symbols. With a code rate of 3/4, the number of coded bits per symbol will be $4 \times 216/3 = 288$. This is possible by using different modulation schemes—ranging from binary phase shift keying, where we have 1 bit per subchannel, to more complex modulation schemes, such as quadrature amplitude

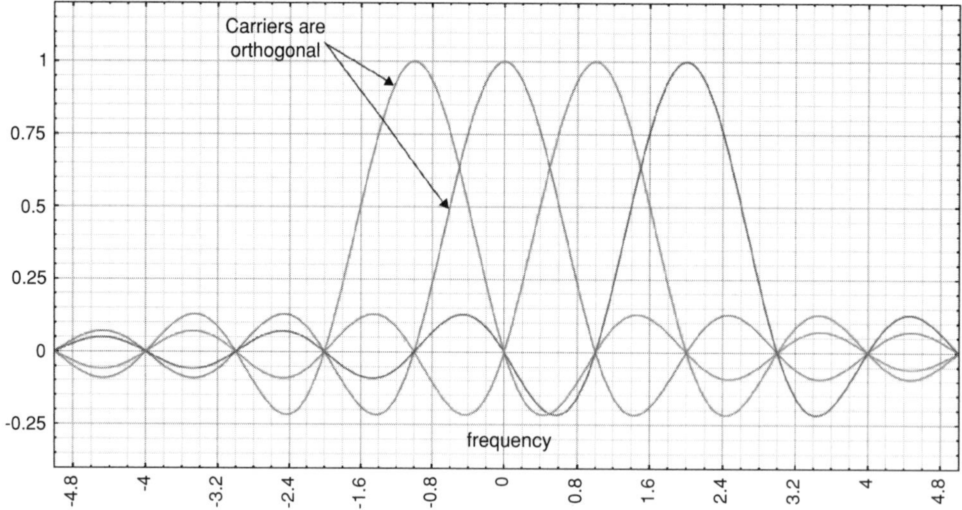

Figure 13: Orthogonal carriers in OFDM.

modulation (QAM). Error control coding also plays an important role in determining the data rate. Table 4 summarizes some features of the different supported data rates.

The PLCP in the case of 802.11a is a bit different in that there is no synchronization field. A rate field with 4 bits indicates the data rate that is being transmitted. This field is shown in Table 4 for different data rates. The preamble and header are always modulated using BPSK (lower data rates). The values of SIFS and the slot for backoff in this option are 16 and 9 μs respectively.

Summary of Physical Layer Alternatives

Table 5 summarizes the different PHY layer alternatives in IEEE 802.11.

SECURITY ISSUES AND IMPLEMENTATION IN IEEE 802.11

Security in wireless networks is an important problem, especially because it is extremely difficult to contain radio signals within a protected perimeter (Edney, 2004). Anyone can listen to radio signals and anyone can also potentially inject signals into the network. Typically, in any network wireless or wired, it is common to deploy security features or services such as confidentiality, entity authentication, data authentication and integrity and so on to protect against security threats (Stinson, 2002). The IEEE 802.11 standard has some mechanisms to provide confidentiality, integrity, and authentication at the link level. All data that leave the 802.11 link will not be protected. For instance, a MS communicating with an AP can have all its IEEE 802.11 frames that are on the air protected. Once the AP receives the frame, all protection is removed before it is transmitted on the distribution system. So additional security at the higher layers [such as IPSec or the Secure Sockets Layer (SSL)] may be required for some applications if the payload needs to be secure.

The original mechanism for providing confidentiality and authentication in IEEE 802.11 is called *wired equivalent privacy* (WEP) (Gast, 2002). Over the past few years, several attacks on WEP have been published in the literature. WEP makes use of the RC4 stream cipher with 40-bit keys (although there are options to use 128-bit keys in most commercial products today). Both the implementation of WEP and the RC4 algorithm itself have vulnerabilities that have rendered WEP nonsecure for today's applications. WEP was initially proposed in the standard as a self-synchronizing, exportable, efficient option. Although it does satisfy these three properties, its security has left much to be desired.

In what follows we discuss the original implementation of security in IEEE 802.11 and discuss enhancements that have been recently proposed.

Table 4 Data Rates and Associated Parameters in IEEE 802.11a

Data Rate (Mbps)	Modulation	Code Rate	Data Bits/Symbol	Coded Bits/Subchannel	PLCP Rate Field
6	BPSK	1/2	24	1	1101
9	BPSK	3/4	36	1	1111
12	QPSK	1/2	48	2	0101
18	QPSK	3/4	72	2	0111
24	16-QAM	1/2	96	4	1001
36	16-QAM	3/4	144	4	1011
48	64-QAM	2/3	192	6	0001
54	64-QAM	3/4	216	6	0011

Table 5 Summary of PHY Alternatives in IEEE 802.11

Standard	U.S. Spectrum (GHz)	Data Rates	Modulation Scheme
Base IEEE 802.11	2.402–2.479	1, 2 Mbps	GFSK, FHSS
	2.402–2.479	1, 2 Mbps	B/QPSK, DSSS
	850–950 nm	1, 2 Mbps	PPM, IR
802.11a	5.15–5.35, 5.725–5.825	6–54 Mbps	OFDM
802.11b	2.402–2.479	1, 2, 5.5, 11 Mbps	CCK
802.11g	2.402–2.479	1–54 Mbps	OFDM, CCK

Entity Authentication in IEEE 802.11

The mandatory entity authentication mechanism in IEEE 802.11 is called *open system authentication*. In this case, there is no real authentication. If one IEEE 802.11 device sends a frame to another, it is implicitly accepted. For example, a MS may simply send a frame to the AP choosing "open system" as the authentication algorithm (authentication algorithm = 0). The AP will simply accept it if open system access is allowed and send a response. From this transaction, the AP will obtain the MAC address of the MS for communication purposes.

A better authentication procedure is called *shared key authentication* where WEP is implemented (Gast, 2002). If the network is using WEP, shared key authentication is mandatory. The assumption is that all devices in the network share a secret key. A MS will send a frame for authentication with sequence number 0, the authentication algorithm set to 1 (to indicate shared key authentication). The AP will then send a challenge message (128 bits) in clear text to the MS along with its response. The MS will respond with an encrypted version of the challenge text. If the AP is able to verify the integrity of the reply, the MS is authenticated and it has the shared WEP key configured in it. Sometimes a MS will authenticate itself with several APs before associating itself with one of them. This process is called preauthentication. This authentication scheme is still not very secure, however, and also creates weaknesses in the protocol because of the way in which it is employed with a stream cipher.

Several commercial products also implement address filtering where only certain MAC addresses are allowed access to the network. This is not part of the standard and it is also possible for malicious users to spoof MAC addresses easily. However, address filtering is an additional security measure that is available for IEEE 802.11 networks.

Confidentiality and Integrity in IEEE 802.11

Confidentiality is simply provided in IEEE 802.11 by encrypting all packets using the RC4 stream cipher. Stream ciphers operate as follows. Using a secret key, a pseudorandom sequence of bits (called the key stream) is generated. If this sequence has a very long period and the algorithm is strong, it will be computationally impossible for someone to generate the sequence without knowing the secret key. The pseudorandom sequence thus generated will be XOR-ed with the MAC frame to make the contents of the frame secure from interception. RC-4 is one algorithm to generate the pseudorandom key stream. This algorithm makes use of a secret key and in the case of WEP an initialization vector (IV) that is 24 bits long. Because the key is constant for all transactions, the same pseudorandom key stream is generated if the IV is not changed. An attacker could capture two streams of encrypted frames, XOR them together, and eliminate the key stream. He would then have an XOR of two data frames. If by some chance he knows the contents of one data frame, he can get the other as well. Since the IV is only 24 bits long, it is possible for an attacker to break the encryption scheme. One well-publicized attack is the Fluhrer/Mantin/Shamir (FMS) attack on RC-4. In addition, there are several weak keys that could make the encryption scheme easier to break. It is also possible for an attacker to replay packets depending on the sequence numbers that are being used. To ensure that an attacker has not modified a message, the WEP protocol uses the in-built CRC to verify the integrity of the message. Checking the integrity of the message using the CRC has vulnerabilities that have been publicized in recent years.

Key Distribution in IEEE 802.11

The IEEE 802.11 standard does not specify how the shared keys must be distributed to devices (AP and MSs). It is usually a manual installation of keys where a user will type the key in the device driver software. This process is unfortunately not scalable and also has several human vulnerabilities. Users may write down the key on a piece of paper when they buy a new device and lose this paper. Some vendors have automated methods of key distribution. Cisco's Light Extensible Authentication Protocol makes use of the challenge/response mechanism to generate a key at the AP and an identical matching key locally in the MS that could then be used in a successful encrypted communication.

Ongoing and Proposed Security Features

A Task Group I of the IEEE 802.11 working group has prepared an enhanced security framework for IEEE 802.11 called 802.11i that was approved as a standard in June 2004. Several vendors have already implemented elements of this standard. This framework includes what is called a *robust security network* (RSN) that is similar to WEP but has several new capabilities in devices (Edney,

2004). It is possible for both WEP and RSN devices to coexist in a *transitional security network* (TSN).

A consortium of major WLAN manufacturers has set up the Wi-Fi Alliance that is looking at options to improve security in legacy devices while 802.11i is being standardized. The proposal from this alliance is called Wi-Fi Protected Access (WPA) that introduces enhancements to WEP called *Temporal Key Integrity Protocol* (TKIP). In this protocol, RC-4 is still used as the encryption algorithm. However, this protocol adds some features to overcome weakness of WEP. A message integrity code is used instead of the CRC check. It changes the way in which IVs are generated. It changes the encryption key for every frame, increases the size of the IV and also adds a mechanism to manage keys.

In 802.11i, RC-4 is replaced by the Advanced Encryption Standard (AES). In particular, the key stream and message integrity check will be generated by a counter mode cipher block chaining MAC protocol (CCMP). AES is a block cipher—it operates on fixed blocks of data unlike a stream cipher that generates a key stream. However, any block cipher can operate in different *modes* and cipher block chaining (CBC) is one such mode of operation. The counter mode is another mode of operation. It is expected that the counter mode will be used to generate the key stream and the CBC will be used to generate the message integrity check. Both these modes have been used in other systems with good security.

Both TKIP and AES-CCMP provide confidentiality and message integrity. To perform entity authentication, the IEEE 802.11 system has to still rely on challenge response protocols. Over the years, there have been several protocols developed for dial-up entity authentication and for port security in wired LANs. These include 802.1X, the extensible authentication protocol (EAP), and Remote Authentication Dial-In User Service (RADIUS). Note that all these protocols are not equivalent; for instance, both 802.1X and RADIUS could use EAP for entity authentication and key distribution. EAP itself would use some challenge/response protocol such as Challenge Handshake Authentication Protocol (CHAP) or SSL to authenticate the devices. Both WPA and RSN mandate 802.1X and EAP as part of the access control mechanism for 802.11 networks. Note that access control is increasingly becoming an important problem with the emergence of hot spot networks in airports, cafes and so on.

RECENT ACTIVITIES

Table 6 summarizes the status of the completed 802.11 group activities and lists some of the recent ongoing activities. There are some other amendments to the 802.11 standard that have been approved recently. They do not directly change the protocol on the air in the United States but provide extensions to the way 802.11 systems may operate. One of the important issues in wireless networks is roaming between different points of access to the wired network. This is possible only if equipment from different vendors supports the same set of protocols and is interoperable. Previously, there existed a task group F that had proposed an interaccess point protocol (IAPP) to achieve multivendor interoperability. For example, when a MS moves from one AP to another and sends a reassociation request, the new AP must be able to converse with the old AP over the distribution system to inform it of the handoff and to free the resources in the old AP. This is achieved using the IAPP now standardized as 802.11f in July 2003. The 802.11f standard specifies the information and format of the information to be exchanged between access points and includes the recommended practice for multivendor access point interoperability via the IAPP across distribution systems. The competing standard for wireless LANs in Europe is the HIPERLAN/2 standard that is specified for the U-NII bands. HIPERLAN/2 uses the same physical layer as IEEE 802.11a, although it accommodates a few different data rates. In this standard, there are mechanisms suggested for power measurement and control and radio resources management. Previously there existed a task group H that was enhancing the current 802.11 MAC and 802.11a PHY with network management and control extensions for spectrum and transmit power management in the U-NII bands with the possibility of dynamic channel selection capabilities. In this case, APs would be able to dynamically select channels based on information they can obtain about neighboring APs that may transmitting on the same channel. This way, a laborious network planning process could be simplified. The 802.11h standard completed in October 2003 considers such transmit power control (TPC) and dynamic frequency selection (DFS) to satisfy the regulatory aspects in Europe.

Outside of the standards that have been specified already, there are several ongoing activities in the IEEE 802.11 working group. There are several task groups that are engaged in enhancing aspects of the IEEE 802.11 standard. We discuss some of these ongoing activities in this chapter. In particular, we look at the following task groups.

Task Group E: The 802.11 DCF considers all traffic to be the same and provides only a best effort service. This task group is evaluating enhancements to the MAC layer so as to provide some mechanisms for supporting quality of service (QoS) in wireless LANs for real-time applications such as audio, video, and media stream distribution. One technique that is being actively considered is to have different IFS and CW values for different classes of traffic. For example, a traffic class with higher priority would have a smaller IFS and CW range so that it waits for a smaller time compared to a traffic class with lower priority. This way, time sensitive traffic could get access to the channel earlier. This technique is similar to service differentiation in wired networks.

Task Group J: This task group is considering enhancements to the current standard to provide operations in the frequency band between 4.9 and 5 GHz for use in Japan. The reason for this task group is to make changes in the 802.11 standard to accommodate the regulatory demands in this spectrum that exist in Japan. There will be expected changes to both the MAC and PHY layers to meet these regulations.

Task Group K: This task group is looking at enhanced radio resource management outside the purview of 802.11h. Once power measurements and reporting are possible in a standardized manner, they can be exploited to make better use of the spectrum, reduce interference and so on.

Task Group N: The current MAC and PHY layers of the IEEE 802.11 standard constrain the raw data rate to

Table 6 Summary of Task Groups and Status

Group	Group Activities	Status as of September 2004
A	5-GHz operation (High Data Rate Extension based on OFDM)	Completed
B	2.4-GHz operation (High Data Rate Extension up to 11 Mbps)	Completed
E	QoS enhancements to the MAC layer	Draft (not approved)
F	Interaccess Point Protocol	Completed (July 2003)
G	2.4-GHz operation (High Data Rate Extension up to 54 Mbps)	Completed
H	Spectrum and transmit power management in Europe	Completed (October 2003)
I	Security enhancements to 802.11	Completed (June 2004)
J	Operation in 4.9- to 5-GHz bands in Japan	In progress
K	Radio resource management	In progress
N	High throughputs greater than 100 Mbps	In progress
R	Fast roaming between access points	In progress
S	Mesh networking of access points	In progress (started in 2004)

54 Mbps and the throughput to a fraction of that depending on traffic load, channel conditions, and so on. A new task group is looking at an IEEE 802.11n standard that will look at both MAC and PHY enhancements to improve the throughput. Some of the ideas being floated to improve throughput are to use directional antennas, multiple-input/multiple-output (MIMO) with OFDM, throughput enhancements at the MAC layer, and so on.

Task Group R: In an authenticated system using 802.11i or even WEP, there is a substantial delay because of the reassociation and reauthentication procedures, when an 802.11 device hands off from one BSS to another within an ESS. Such delays can be as high as 15 s and are unacceptable for real-time traffic. As voice-over IP becomes more important and its use over wireless LANs increases, these delays must be reduced to acceptable levels without compromising security. Such enhancements to the current 802.11 standard to provide fast handoffs between different BSSs is the responsibility of Task Group R.

Task Group S: The idea of this task group is to develop enhancements to the current IEEE 802.11 standard to provide a method to configure the distribution system using the four MAC addresses thereby enabling some form of mesh networking between access points. This could be a wired or wireless mesh network that allows for automatic topology learning and dynamic path configuration over self-configuring multihop topologies. There are already proprietary protocols performing this task to extend coverage within homes, but the standard will allow for different scenarios with different requirements (e.g., quick set up and tear down and maximizing throughput). Table 6 provides a summary of the above activities.

Although not directly changing or adding to the standards, there are task groups that are involved in maintenance and other issues related to 802.11. Task group M is performing the maintenance of the 802.11 standard. Task group D is looking at regulatory domain updates. There are also some new proposed activities that are pending approval at various levels as of the time of the writing—an 802.11p effort on wireless access for the vehicular environment and an 802.11t that aims to recommend practices for wireless performance prediction. In addition, there are several study groups looking at harmonizing the 802.11 and the European ETSI standards and some investigating the possibility of improvements to the 802.11 standard to provide higher throughput.

Other IEEE Wireless Standards: The IEEE also has other wireless standards that it manages. The IEEE 802.15 standard looks at *personal area networks* (PANs) that are networks related to an operating space around one person. Examples of PANs are Bluetooth (Haartsen, 2000) networks. In fact 802.15 is based on Bluetooth. Like 802.11, in 802.15 there are many subcategories of standards. One of these subcategories called 802.15.4 is also commercially popular as the Zigbee standard. Another IEEE wireless standard is the 802.16 standard (WiMax) that looks at fixed wireless access. In this case, the goal is to provide fixed broadband wireless links to organizations and residences. These broadband links would replace the last hop copper or coaxial cable and provide Internet access, video, and telephone services to the customer.

GLOSSARY

Advanced Encryption Standard The encryption algorithm used in the latest security standard for 802.11.

Advanced Mobile Phone System The very first cellular telephone service in the United States.

Clear-to-Send Command used by an 802.11 mobile station to indicate to all other mobile stations in its receiving range about a pending transmission toward reducing the hidden terminal problem and to acknowledge an RTS packet.

Complementary Code Keying A modulation and encoding scheme used in the 802.11b standard to increase the data rate from 2 to 11 Mbps while maintaining the original chip rate of 11 Mcps.

Counter Mode with Cipher Block Chaining Message Authentication Code Protocol The method for ensuring confidentiality and authentication in 802.11i that uses the advanced encryption standard.

Direct Sequence Spread Spectrum A modulation technique used in the original 802.11 standard that spreads the spectrum providing robustness against multipath.

Distributed Coordination Function The basic medium access method in all 802.11 networks that uses carrier sense multiple access with collision avoidance.

Interframe Space The waiting time of 802.11 mobile stations to assist in collision avoidance. Different values are used for acknowledgements, regular frames, and polling frames.

Orthogonal Frequency Division Multiplexing The modulation scheme used in 802.11a and 802.11g standards. It splits the channel into many narrow subcarriers, thereby avoiding problems related to the coherence bandwidth of the radio channel.

Point Coordination Function An optional polling medium access mechanism that is not widely deployed in 802.11 systems.

Request-to-Send Frames used by an 802.11 mobile station to indicate to all other mobile stations in its receiving range about a pending transmission and reduce the hidden terminal problem.

Wired Equivalent Privacy The weak security protocol used in legacy 802.11 systems that made use of the RC-4 stream cipher to provide confidentiality and authentication in ways that did not make the system secure.

CROSS REFERENCES

See *Local Area Networks; Wireless Channels; Wireless Local Area Networks.*

REFERENCES

Crow, B. P., Widjaja, I., Kim, L.G., & Sakai, P.T. (1997a). IEEE 802.11 wireless local area networks. *IEEE Communications Magazine, 35*(9), 116–126.

Crow, B. P., Widjaja, I., Kim, L.G., & Sakai, P.T. (1997b). Investigation of the IEEE 802.11 medium access control (MAC) sublayer functions. *Proceedings of IEEE Infocom, 1*, 126–133.

Edney, J., & Arbaugh, W.A. (2004). *Real 802.11 security:Wi-Fi protected access and 802.11i*. Upper Saddle River, NJ: Pearson Education.

Garg, V. K. (2002). *Wireless network evolution: 2G to 3G*. Upper Saddle River, NJ: Prentice Hall.

Gast, M. S. (2002). *802.11 wireless networks: The definitive guide*. Sebastopol, CA: O'Reilly & Associates.

Haartsen, J.C., & Mattisson, S. (2000). Bluetooth—A new low-power radio interface providing short-range connectivity. *Proceedings of the IEEE, 88*(10), 1651–1661.

Halford, K., Halford, S., Webster, M., & Ander, C. (1999). Complementary code keying for RAKE-based indoor wireless communication. *IEEE International Symposium on Circuits and Systems, 4*, 427–430.

Kapp, S. (2002). 802.11a: More bandwidth without the wires. *IEEE Internet Computing, 6*(4), 75–79.

Pahlavan, K., & Krishnamurthy, P. (2002). *Principles of wireless networks: A unified approach*. Upper Saddle River, NJ: Prentice Hall.

Pattara-atikom, W., Krishnamurthy, P., & Banerjee, S. (2003). Distributed mechanisms for quality of service in wireless LANs. *IEEE Wireless Communications: Special Issue, 10*, 26–34.

Salkintzis, A. K. (1999). Packet data over cellular networks: The CDPD approach. *IEEE Communications Magazine, 37*(6), 152–159.

Stinson, D. (2002). *Cryptography: Theory and practice*. Boca Raton, FL: CRC Press.

Tuch, B. (1991). An ISM band spread spectrum local area network: WaveLAN. In *Proceedings of the 1st IEEE Workshop on WLANs* (pp. 103–111). Worcester, MA.

Valadas, R.T., Tavares, A. R., de O. Duarte, A. M., Moreira, A. C., & Lomba, C. T. (1998). The infrared physical layer of the IEEE 802.11 standard for wireless local area networks. *IEEE Communications Magazine, 36*(12), 107–112.

van Nee, R. et al. (1999). New high-rate wireless LAN standards. *IEEE Communications Magazine, 37*(12), 82–88.

Wilkinson, T. A., Phipps, T., & Barton, S. K. (1995). A report on HIPERLAN standardization. *International Journal on Wireless Information Networks, 2*, 99–120.

URLs of Standards Bodies

The American National Standards Institute—ANSI: http://www.ansi.org

The European Telecommunications Standards Institute—ETSI: http://www.etsi.org

The Institute of Electrical and Electronics Engineers—IEEE: http://grouper.ieee.org/groups/

The IEEE 802.11 Working Group: http://grouper.ieee.org/groups/802/11

The International Standards Organization—ISO: http://www.iso.org/

The Multimedia Mobile Access Communications—MMAC: http://www.arib.or.jp/mmac/e/index.htm

The Telecommunications Industry Association—TIA: http://www.tiaonline.com

The Third Generation Partnership Project—3GPP: http://www.3gpp.org

The Third Generation Partnership Project 2—3GPP2: http://www.3gpp2.org

P3P (Platform for Privacy Preferences Project)

Lorrie Faith Cranor, *Carnegie Mellon University*

INTRODUCTION

The Platform for Privacy Preferences (P3P 1.0) Specification defines a standard way for Web sites to encode their privacy policies in a computer-readable format and standard mechanisms for locating these policies and associating them with specific online content. Developed by the World Wide Web Consortium (W3C), P3P 1.0 was adopted as an official W3C Recommendation in April 2002 (Cranor, Langheinrich, Marchiori, Presler-Marshall, & Reagle, 2002a). P3P functionality has been built into popular Web browsers as well as browser add-ons and editing tools.

HOW P3P WORKS

Web sites that adopt P3P translate their privacy policies into a computer-readable format called XML (Bray, Paoli, Sperberg-McQueen, & Maler, 2000) and place the resulting P3P "policy" file on their Web sites. They also create an XML-encoded P3P "policy reference file" used to indicate the parts of a Web site to which a P3P policy applies.

Software tools that fetch and read P3P policies are referred to as "P3P user agents." P3P user agents may be stand-alone software tools or modules built into Web browsers or other software. To fetch a P3P policy, user agents use the HTTP protocol (Fielding, Gettys, Mogul, Frystyk, Masinter, Leach, & Berners-Lee, 1999) that Web browsers use to fetch Web content. Using this protocol, user agents send a request called a "GET" request to a Web site. If the site has the requested file, it responds by sending that file, along with some header information. If the site does not have the requested file, it responds with an appropriate error code.

To obtain a P3P policy, user agents first make a GET request for a site's P3P policy reference file. Most Web sites place their policy reference files at a standard "well-known location": /w3c/p3p.xml. Thus, P3P user agents can make a GET request for this file to learn the location of the P3P files on a Web site. After parsing this file, P3P user agents can make additional GET requests to obtain P3P policy files. As P3P policies generally apply to many (or all) URLs on a site, it is not necessary for user agents to fetch these files every time a user requests a new page on a site. By default, P3P files have a lifetime of 24 hr, meaning that if a user returns to a site within one day, no new P3P files need to be fetched. Optionally, P3P policies may be embedded in policy reference files to simplify site administration and reduce the number of round trips necessary to retrieve P3P files from a site.

P3P 1.0 also supports two additional mechanisms for locating policy reference files. Webmasters can place policy reference files at arbitrary locations on their sites and reference them through links embedded in HTML content or in special P3P HTTP headers. The HTML link method is provided primarily for the benefit of Web sites that are part of a larger site but are operated independently of the larger site. For example, many universities allow their students to create Web sites hosted on the university's Web server. Students may create their own P3P policies but do not have the ability to edit the policy reference file at the well-known location on the university server. The HTTP header method is provided primarily for use by sites that use more than one P3P policy reference file. Sites may wish to use more than one policy reference file if they have a very large number of P3P policies (for example, a site that hosts content for hundreds of other companies) or if they are concerned that a single policy reference file may reveal information about the structure of their site that they do not want to make public.

P3P 1.0 specifies a format for a P3P "compact policy" that can be transmitted in a P3P HTTP header sent in the same response in which a cookie is set (Kristol, 2001). P3P compact policies are short summaries of full P3P policies that describe a Web site's data practices for any cookies set during that HTTP response. Compact policies are optional for P3P-enabled Web sites; however, some P3P user agents rely on them heavily. Sites that use compact policies are also required to post full P3P policies and policy reference files.

P3P POLICIES

P3P policies are XML (Bray et al., 2000) documents that include standard information about a Web site's privacy practices. Much of this information is encoded in a multiple choice format and thus might not be as detailed as the information provided by a Web site in its human-readable privacy policy. However, the standardized format often results in clearer and more complete disclosures than Web sites typically make in their human-readable privacy policies.

Here is an example of a P3P policy for a Web site that does not collect very much information:

```
<POLICIES xmlns="http://www.w3.org/2002/01/P3Pv1">
<POLICY discuri="http://p3pbook.com/privacy.html" name="policy">
  <ENTITY>
    <DATA-GROUP>
      <DATA
       ref="#business.contact-info.online.email">privacy@p3pbook.com
      </DATA>
      <DATA
       ref="#business.contact-info.online.uri">http://p3pbook.com/
      </DATA>
      <DATA ref="#business.name">Web Privacy With P3P</DATA>
    </DATA-GROUP>
  </ENTITY>
  <ACCESS><nonident/></ACCESS>
  <STATEMENT>
    <CONSEQUENCE>Our Web server collects access logs containing
      this information.</CONSEQUENCE>
    <PURPOSE><admin/><current/><develop/></PURPOSE>
    <RECIPIENT><ours/></RECIPIENT>
    <RETENTION><indefinitely/></RETENTION>
    <DATA-GROUP>
      <DATA ref="#dynamic.clickstream"/>
      <DATA ref="#dynamic.http"/>
    </DATA-GROUP>
  </STATEMENT>
</POLICY>
</POLICIES>
```

This policy is encoded using the computer-readable language XML. An XML document contains a single XML element, which may contain other XML elements. Each element is composed of one or more XML tags. An XML tag begins with a left angle bracket (<) and ends with a right angle bracket (>). Some XML elements contain no other elements. These elements are represented by a single XML tag that ends with a slash character, for example `<nonident/>`. Elements that contain other elements are represented using a pair of XML tags that surround one or more other XML tags. In the above example, `<ACCESS><nonident/></ACCESS>` represents a nonident element, which is contained inside an ACCESS element. Some XML elements have attributes. In the above example the POLICY element has two attributes, discuri and name. The discuri attribute has the value *http://p3pbook.com/privacy.html* and the name attribute has the value *policy*.

The rest of this section provides an overview of the information included in a P3P policy in the order required by the P3P 1.0 specification. Not all elements of a P3P policy are detailed here.

POLICY attributes

The "discuri" and "opturi" attributes of the P3P POLICY element indicate the location of a site's human-readable privacy policy and human-readable description of opt-out mechanisms, respectively.

TEST

The TEST element indicates that a policy is for testing purposes only.

ENTITY

The ENTITY element identifies the legal entity making the representation of the privacy practices contained in the policy. It includes online or physical-world contact information for that entity.

ACCESS

The ACCESS element provides information about the ability of individuals to access information that a Web site has collected about them. Web sites choose one of six ACCESS choices that best describes their practices. Choices range from providing no access to providing access to all identified information.

DISPUTES

The DISPUTES element describes dispute resolution procedures that may be followed for disputes about a Web site's privacy practices. Sites may describe multiple dispute resolution procedures, including contacting a customer service representative, contacting an independent organization, filing a legal complaint, or relying on a particular law. Sites must provide a URL that references each dispute resolution procedure. They may also provide human-readable descriptions and images for each.

REMEDIES

The REMEDIES element describes remedies in case a privacy policy breach occurs. Sites may describe one type of remedy for each dispute resolution procedure, including correcting wrongful actions, monetary payments, and relying on a particular law.

STATEMENT

The STATEMENT element is used to indicate a set of data for which the same privacy practices apply. The STATEMENT element contains a number of other elements that represent types of data and data practices. Web sites typically create one or more statements in their P3P policies, each representing a bundle of data. For example, a site might create one statement for information collected in Web logs and another statement for information entered by users in an order form.

NONIDENTIFIABLE

The presence of the NONIDENTIFIABLE element in a P3P policy indicates that either a Web site does not collect identifiable information or the information it collects is anonymized.

CONSEQUENCE

The consequence element allows sites to provide a short human-readable explanation of their data practices.

PURPOSE

The PURPOSE element describes the ways that collected information may be used. Web sites must disclose as many of the 12 purpose choices as apply. Optionally, sites may use the "required" attribute of the PURPOSE element to indicate that a particular use of information is performed on an opt-in or opt-out basis.

RECIPIENT

The RECIPIENT element describes the extent to which information may be shared with other entities. Web sites must choose one or more of six possible types of recipients, including companies that use information only to help fulfill user requests, delivery companies, companies with similar privacy policies, companies with different privacy policies that are accountable to the entity collecting the data, any companies regardless of their privacy practices, and people who access information from a public area such as a bulletin board or chat room. Optionally, sites may use the "required" attribute of the PURPOSE element to indicate that sharing with a particular type of recipient is done on an opti-in or opt-out basis.

RETENTION

The RETENTION element describes how long a Web site may keep information. Rather than describe retention in terms of a number of days, weeks, or years, the retention element allows Web sites to select one of five possible types of retention policies, including retaining information only for the current online session, retaining information only long enough to perform the activity for which it was collected, retaining information only as long as needed for legal purposes, retaining information according to a policy described in the site's human-readable privacy practices, and retaining information indefinitely.

DATA

The DATA element describes the type of data a Web site may collect. Sites may describe specific pieces of information such as "first name" or "last name" or they may describe general categories of information. There are 17 categories of information defined in the P3P 1.0 specification.

A P3P PREFERENCE EXCHANGE LANGUAGE

A separate W3C specification called A P3P Preference Exchange Language (APPEL) provides syntax for encoding user preferences about privacy policies (Cranor, Langheinrich, & Marchiori, 2002b). APPEL is a rule-based language encoded in XML. P3P user agents can compare APPEL-encoded preferences with a P3P policy to determine whether a site's policy matches a user's preferences; however, P3P user agents are not required to use APPEL. Unlike the P3P 1.0 Specification, APPEL is not an official W3C Recommendation and is considered somewhat experimental. Nonetheless, it is used in several P3P software implementations.

Here is an example of an APPEL ruleset with four rules, including a default "otherwise" rule. Rules are evaluated in the order in which they appear in the ruleset. When the pattern in the body of a rule matches a P3P policy, the rule fires and the action described by the "behavior" attribute is carried out.

```
<appel:RULESET xmlns:appel="http://www.w3.org/2002/03/APPELv1"
            xmlns:p3p="http://www.w3.org/2002/01/P3Pv1">
<appel:RULE behavior="limited" description="Site does not allow you to
remove yourself from marketing/mailing list">
      <p3p:POLICY>
        <p3p:STATEMENT>
          <p3p:PURPOSE appel:connective="or">
            <p3p:contact required="always"/>
            <p3p:telemarketing required="always"/>
          </p3p:PURPOSE>
        </p3p:STATEMENT>
      </p3p:POLICY>
</appel:RULE>
<appel:RULE behavior="limited" description="This site collects data for
an unknown purpose">
```

```
      <p3p:POLICY>
        <p3p:STATEMENT>
          <p3p:PURPOSE>
            <p3p:other-purpose required="always"/>
          </p3p:PURPOSE>
        </p3p:STATEMENT>
      </p3p:POLICY>
</appel:RULE>
<appel:RULE behavior="limited" description="Unless you opt-out, this
site collects data for an unknown purpose">
      <p3p:POLICY>
        <p3p:STATEMENT>
          <p3p:PURPOSE>
            <p3p:other-purpose required="opt-out"/>
          </p3p:PURPOSE>
        </p3p:STATEMENT>
      </p3p:POLICY>
</appel:RULE>
<appel:RULE behavior="request">
      <appel:OTHERWISE/>
</appel:RULE>
</appel:RULESET>
```

P3P SOFTWARE

A variety of software tools and services have been developed that support P3P, including P3P user agents, P3P editors and validators, and services that help P3P-enabled Web sites.

Microsoft's Internet Explorer 6 (IE6) Web browser includes basic P3P functionality. IE6 checks the HTTP headers sent with cookies for P3P compact policies. Under IE6's default setting, cookies without compact policies may be blocked if they are set by a "third-party" Web site—that is, if they are associated with an advertisement or other content embedded in a Web page that is served from a different domain than the page in which it is embedded. Other cookies may be blocked or restricted depending on the substance of a compact policy and the user's cookie settings. A small icon featuring a picture of an eye with a Do Not Enter sign appears in the lower right corner of the browser window when a cookie is blocked or restricted. IE6 also offers a "privacy report" feature that users can select from the browser's View menu. Selecting this feature causes the browser to check for a site's full P3P policy. If the browser is able to fetch the policy, it parses the XML and displays a human-readable representation of the policy.

Netscape Navigator 7 has similar P3P features as IE6. It employs a slightly different cookie interface and default settings. Netscape can also generate a human-readable version of a site's P3P policy. The Netscape version of a P3P policy is shorter and uses sentence fragments and bulleted lists where IE6 uses complete sentences and paragraphs.

AT&T Privacy Bird is an IE5/6 add-on available as a free download (AT&T Privacy Bird, 2003). Once installed, a bird icon appears on the right side of the IE6 title bar. Privacy Bird checks for P3P policies at every site a user visits and compares them with the privacy preference settings the user has configured through a menu accessed by clicking on the bird. Privacy Bird checks for P3P policies for all content embedded in a page. At sites that match a user's privacy preferences, the bird icon turns green; at sites that do not match the icon turns red; and at sites that are not P3P enabled the icon turns yellow. Symbols in the bird's song "bubble" also help distinguish these three icons. In addition, users can optionally configure Privacy Bird to play distinctive sounds corresponding to the appearance of each icon. Privacy Bird can also generate and display a human-readable version of a site's P3P policy. Similar to the Netscape version, this version also uses short phrases and bulleted lists.

Future P3P user agents may be built into electronic wallets, search engines, and other tools. For example, a P3P-enabled search engine would allow users to sort their search results so that sites that match both their search criteria and their privacy preferences are listed first. Tools like this will allow users to more easily compare privacy policies at similar Web sites and identify sites with policies they find acceptable.

A number of companies have developed software and services to assist Web masters in P3P enabling their sites. One of the most popular P3P tools for Web sites is the P3P Policy Editor offered as a free download from the IBM Alphaworks Web site (Presler-Marshall, Gilmore, & Bleizeffer, 2004). This tool includes a graphical user interface that allows P3P policies to be visually constructed. The tool generates XML encoded P3P policies, as well as human-readable versions of each policy. It also generates policy reference files and compact policies and provides guidance on how IE6 will respond to a particular compact policy.

Some companies are exploring the use of P3P to assist in the maintenance of back-end customer information databases and to automate compliance with privacy policies. Database records can be annotated with information about the P3P policy in effect when the data were collected. In addition, IBM has proposed a language called Enterprise Authorization Language (EPAL) that is designed for writing detailed rules for data handling in an organization (Ashley, Hada, Karjoth, Powers, & Schunter, 2003). These very granular rules can then be mapped onto a less granular P3P policy for public dissemination.

W3C maintains an online P3P Validator (W3C P3P Validator, 2003). Users can type in the URL for a site and the Validator will check to see whether the site is properly P3P enabled. It checks to make sure P3P files are located in the proper locations on the site and use the correct syntax.

P3P ADOPTION

P3P will be most useful once it is widely adopted by Web sites. A number of surveys have been undertaken to assess P3P adoption. It is not feasible to check every Web site in existence for P3P compliance, nor is this a particularly useful metric. What is more interesting is to examine the fraction of P3P-enabled sites among the most popular sites on the Internet.

A July 2003 study found that 30% of the top 100 Web sites were P3P enabled and 23% of the top 500 sites were P3P enabled (Byers, Cranor, & Kormann, 2003). In general, the most popular sites are the ones most likely to be P3P enabled. Although these numbers demonstrate that there is a long way to go, these adoption levels are substantial for a specification that was published little over a year earlier.

Advertising networks and other Web sites that frequently set third-party cookies are among the early adopters of P3P, because of concerns that their cookies may be blocked by IE6. Many other companies adopted P3P early to demonstrate their commitment to privacy and to show corporate leadership on privacy issues.

CONCLUSION

The P3P 1.0 Specification represents the first standardized computer-readable encoding of privacy policies. Now that such an encoding exists, a variety of applications are possible that make use of it. P3P policies may be used to inform Web users about Web site privacy policies, compile statistics on Web site privacy policies, and assist companies in managing their data practices.

The P3P development process spanned over 5 years and involved dozens of individuals from around the world. Throughout this process, P3P has been somewhat controversial and has received much criticism. Many companies and industry groups voiced concerns about the extent to which P3P would require sites to make disclosures that they might not be required legally to make. They also expressed concerns that posting P3P policies might open companies up to additional liability. Conversely, some privacy advocates raised concerns that P3P would not serve to actually improve privacy protections for individuals (Hochheiser, 2002). Despite the international composition of the P3P working group, concerns were also raised that P3P was developing with too much of an American focus. Part of the reason the P3P development process took so long is that the working group attempted to address as many of these diverse concerns as possible (Cranor, 2002).

One of the major goals of P3P has been to provide an easy way for users to learn about Web site privacy policies without having to stop at every Web site and read a lengthy and difficult-to-understand privacy policy (Turow, 2003). As more sites adopt P3P and new P3P user agents emerge, this goal is beginning to be achieved. In addition, we are beginning to see some secondary effects of P3P. Because sites must choose between a number of "multiple choice" options when writing a P3P policy, they sometimes end up making clearer and more explicit statements in their P3P policies than they previously had in their human-readable privacy policies. Also, some sites have actually improved their privacy policies so that their P3P policies would not make them look bad or to avoid having their cookies blocked by IE6. Ideally, the increased transparency brought about by P3P will eventually result in more policy improvements and will facilitate more informed debate about the effectiveness of regulatory and self-regulatory privacy programs (Cranor & Wenning, 2002).

GLOSSARY

Identifiable Information Information that can be used to directly or indirectly identify a particular individual by reference to an identification number or to one or more factors specific to his or her physical, physiological, mental, economic, cultural, or social identity. In some cases information can be used by itself to identify a particular individual; in other cases it must be used in combination with other information to identify an individual.

Identified Information Information that can reasonably be used by a data collector to identify an individual. In some cases *identifiable* information may not be considered *identified* information because of the fact that the identifiable information identifies a particular individual only when combined with other information not readily available to the data collector.

Opt-In The ability of individuals to have a company or organization use or share their personal information on request. For example, an individual might ask to have her name put on a catalog mailing list. If individuals do not take explicit action to request that their information is used or shared for a particular purpose, they have not opted-in.

Opt-Out The ability of individuals to have a company or organization remove their names from marketing or mailing lists or refrain from sharing their personal information with other companies or organizations. Individuals must take explicit action to opt-out.

P3P Compact Policy A short summary of a Web site's P3P policy with respect to cookies. Compact policies are transmitted in P3P HTTP headers. Web sites that use compact policies must also post corresponding full P3P policies.

P3P Policy A computer-readable version of a Web site's privacy policy. P3P policies are encoded in XML and include information about the types of data a Web site collects and how it will be used.

P3P Policy Reference File An XML file that indicates the location of P3P policies on a Web site and the URLs to which each applies.

Privacy Policy A description of the privacy practices of a company or organization.

Third-Party Cookie A cookie associated with an image or other object embedded in a Web page that is served from a domain other than the domain from which that Web page is served.

URL Uniform resource locator; the address for a Web page. The P3P 1.0 specification also refers to uniform resource identifiers (URIs). URI is a more general term that includes URLs.

User Agent A software tool that can locate and fetch P3P policies and take actions on a user's behalf, such as displaying a human-readable version of a P3P policy or comparing the policy with a user's preferences.

Well-Known Location A standard location on a Web site where P3P policy reference files are posted. Although Web sites may post policy reference files at any location, posting them at the well-known location allows user agents to find them quickly. The well-known location for P3P policy reference files is /w3c/p3p.xml.

XML Extensible markup language; a computer-readable language used for representing information. P3P files are encoded using XML.

CROSS REFERENCES

See *Anonymity and Identity on the Internet; Cryptographic Privacy Protection Techniques; Privacy Law and the Internet*.

REFERENCES

Ashley, P., Hada, S., Karjoth, G., Powers, C., & Schunter, M. (2003). Enterprise Privacy Authorization Language (EPAL 1.2). W3C member submission. Retrieved November 10, 2003, from http://www.w3.org/Submission/2003/SUBM-EPAL-20031110/

AT&T Privacy Bird. (2003). Retrieved March 19, 2005, from http://privacybird.com/

Bray, T., Paoli, J., Sperberg-McQueen, C. M., & Maler, E. (2000). Extensible markup language (XML) 1.0 (2nd ed.). W3C Recommendation. Retrieved March 19, 2005, from http://www.w3.org/TR/REC-xml

Byers, S., Cranor, L., & Kormann, D. (2003). Automated analysis of P3P-enabled Web sites. In *Proceedings of the Fifth International Conference on Electronic Commerce (ICEC2003)*, October 1–3, 2003, Pittsburgh, PA. Retrieved March 19, 2005, from http://lorrie.cranor.org/pubs/icec03.html

Cranor, L. (2002). The role of privacy advocates and data protection authorities in the design and deployment of the platform for privacy preferences. *Proceedings of the Twelth Conference on Computers, Freedom and Privacy,* April 16–19, 2002, San Francisco, CA. Retrieved March 19, 2005, from http://doi.acm.org/10.1145/543482.543506

Cranor, L., Langheinrich, M., Marchiori, M., Presler-Marshall, M., & Reagle, J. (2002a). The platform for privacy preferences 1.0 (P3P1.0) specification. W3C recommendation. Retrieved March 19, 2005, from http://www.w3.org/TR/P3P/

Cranor, L., Langheinrich, M., & Marchiori, M. (2002b). A P3P preference exchange language 1.0 (APPEL1.0). W3C Working Draft. Retrieved March 19, 2005, from http://www.w3.org/TR/P3P-preferences/

Cranor, L., & Wenning, R. (2002). Why P3P is a good tool for consumers and companies. *GigaLaw.com*. Retrieved March 19, 2005, from http://www.gigalaw.com/articles/2002/cranor-2002-04.html

Fielding, R., Gettys, J., Mogul, J., Frystyk, H., Masinter, L., Leach, P., & Berners-Lee, T. (1999). Hypertext transfer protocol—HTTP/1.1. RFC 2616. Retrieved March 19, 2005, from http://www.ietf.org/rfc/rfc2616.txt

Hochheiser, H. (2002). The platform for privacy preference as a social protocol: An examination within the U.S. policy context. *ACM Transactions on Internet Technology, 2*(4), 276–306. Retrieved March 19, 2005, from http://doi.acm.org/10.1145/604596.604598

Kristol, D. (2001). HTTP cookies: Standards, privacy, and politics. *ACM Transactions on Internet Technology*, 1(2), 151–198. Retrieved March 19, 2005, from http://doi.acm.org/10.1145/502152.502153

Presler-Marshall, M., Gilmore, M., & Bleizeffer, T. (2004). P3P Policy Editor. IBM AlphaWorks. Retrieved March 19, 2005, from http://www.alphaworks.ibm.com/tech/p3peditor

Turow, J. (2003, June). Americans & online privacy: The system is broken. A report from the Annenberg Public Policy Center of the University of Pennsylvania. Retrieved March 19, 2005, from http://www.asc.upenn.edu/usr/jturow/internet-privacy-report/36-page-turow-version-9.pdf

W3C P3P Validator. (2003). Retrieved March 19, 2005, from http://www.w3.org/P3P/validator.html

FURTHER READING

Cranor, L. F. (2002). *Web Privacy with P3P.* Sebastopol, CA: O'Reilly.

Jamtgaard, L. (2002). The P3P implementation guide version 1.0. The Internet Education Foundation and the World Wide Web Consortium. Retrieved March 19, 2005, from http://p3ptoolbox.org/guide/

Presler-Marshall, M. (2002). The platform for privacy preferences 1.0 deployment guide. W3C Note. Retrieved March 19, 2005, from http://www.w3.org/TR/p3pdeployment

Reviewers List

Abdi, Ali New Jersey Institute of Technology
Abdu, Hasina University of Michigan, Dearborn
Aboelela, Emad University of Massachusetts, Dartmouth
Ackerman, Eric S. Nova Southeastern University
Ackermann, Ernest University of Mary Washington
Acquisti, Alessandro Carnegie Mellon University
Adigun, M. O. University of Zululand, South Africa
Aflaki, James Christian Brothers University
Agah, Afrand University of Texas, Arlington
Ahmad, Numan Deloitte & Touche (Middle East)
Aiman, Mark Purdue University
Akingbehin, Kiumi University of Michigan, Dearborn
Aksen, Deniz Koç University, Turkey
Albert, Raymond T. University of Maine
Ali, Sanwar Indiana University of Pennsylvania
Almgren, Magnus Chalmers University, Sweden
Aman, James R. Saint Xavier University
Anantharaju, Srinath North Carolina State University
Anjum, Forooq Telcordia
Antolovich, Michael Charles Sturt University
Apon, Amy University of Arkansas
Arbeláez, Harvey Monterey Institute of International Studies
Asadi, Mehran University of Texas, Arlington
Avoine, Gildas EPFL, Switzerland
Babad, Yair University of Illinois, Chicago
Backhouse, James London School of Economics and Political Science, UK
Baclawski, Kenneth Northeastern University
Bae, Benjamin B. Central Washington University
Bain, Jonathan Polytechnic University
Baker, Theodore P. Florida State University
Balfanz, Dirk Palo Alto Research Center
Balinsky, Alexander Cardiff University, UK
Ball, Nicholas L. University of Minnesota
Balthazard, Pierre A. Arizona State University West
Banks, William C. Syracuse University
Barlow, Judith Florida Institute of Technology
Baron, Jason R. University of Maryland
Barreto, Paulo LARC, Brazil
Barta, Dave University of Oregon
Bartos, Radim University of New Hampshire
Basham, Matthew J. St. Petersburg College
Baumgartner, Gerald Louisiana State University
Baxter, Steven R. Weber State University
Beck, James E. Carnegie Mellon University
Bell, Don R. Webster University
Benítez, Rubén Alvaro González Technical University of Catalonia, Spain
Bennette, Daniel University of Maryland, University College
Benyoucef, Morad University of Ottawa, Canada
Bergman, Clifford Iowa State University
Bergquist, Timothy M. Northwest Christian College
Bhatti, Arshad Saleem Institute of Information Technology, Pakistan
Bi, Xintong Mississippi State University
Biagioni, Edoardo S. University of Hawaii, Manoa
Bicakci, Kemal Vrije Universiteit Amsterdam, The Netherlands
Biham, Eli Technion, Israel
Birnhack, Michael University of Haifa, Israel
Bischof, H-P. Rochester Institute of Technology
Black, Sharon K. University of Colorado
Blanchette, Jean-François University of British Columbia, Canada
Blank, George New Jersey Institute of Technology
Blankenship, Jr. George C. The George Washington University
Blumer, Anselm Tufts University
Blustein, James Dalhousie University, Canada
Bockelman, Jay Oregon Institute of Technology
Bohner, Shawn Virginia Tech
Bohrer, Monty F. University of Sioux Falls
Boklan, Kent D. Queens College
Boldyreva, Alexandra Georgia Institute of Technology
Bollen, Johan Old Dominion University
Boncella, Robert J. Washburn University
Bonica, Ronald MCI, Inc.
Boostrom, Robert University of Southern Indiana
Booth, Lionel S. Tulane University
Borisov, Nikita University of California, Berkeley
Bortman, Eli C. Babson College
Boudriga, Noureddine University of Carthage, Tunisia
Bowie, Nolan A. Harvard University
Boyd, Kathy J. UMUC Europe
Boyd, Waldo T. CREATIVE WRITING (PTY)
Bradford, Phillip G. The University of Alabama
Braynov, Sviatoslav University of Illinois, Springfield
Brazel, Joseph F. North Carolina State University
Bremer, Oliver Nokia
Brenner, Susan W. University of Dayton
Bridges, Susan M. Mississippi State University
Britten, Jody S. Ball State University
Brown, Daniel Certicom Research
Brown, Eric Paul Department of Justice, BOP
Brown, Kevin F. Wright State University
Bruckman, Amy S. Georgia Institute of Technology
Brun, Todd A. University of Southern California
Bruß, Dagmar University of Hannover, Germany
Buchanan, Elizabeth A. University of Wisconsin, Milwaukee
Buell, Duncan A. University of South Carolina
Burns, Patrick C. Valdosta State University
Butler, Kevin AT&T Labs—Reserarch
Cai, Xiaomei University of Delaware
Caini, Carlo Università di Bologna, Italy
Calabresi, Leonello Advanced Systems S.r.l.
Callahan, Dale W. University of Alabama
Caloyannides, Michael Mitretek Systems
Canis, Randy L. Greensfelder, Hemker & Gale, P.C.
Cannady, James Nova Southeastern University
Cannistra, Robert M. Marist College
Cano, Jeimy J. Universidad de los Andes, COLOMBIA

Caronni, Germano Sun Microsystems Laboratories
Carver, Blake LISNews.com
Carvin, Andy EDC Center for Media & Community
Cavanaugh, Charles D. University of Louisiana, Lafayette
Cedeño, Walter Penn State, Great Valley
Cervesato, Iliano ITT Industries, Inc.
Chakrabarti, Alok New Jersey Institute of Technology
Chan, Tom S. Southern NH University
Chan, King-Sun Curtin University of Technology, Australia
Chan, Susy S. DePaul University
Chan, Charles Siu-cheung Queensland University, Australia
Chan, Philip Florida Institute of Technology
Chandra, Surendar University of Notre Dame
Chandramouli, Ramaswamy National Institute of Standards & Technology
Chapin, Steve J. Syracuse University
Chatterjee, Samir Claremont Graduate University
Chen, Yu-Che Iowa State University
Chen, Thomas M. Southern Methodist University
Cheng, Xiuzhen The George Washington University
Cheng, Qi University of Oklahoma
Chepkevich, Richard A. Hawaii Pacific University
Chepya, Peter Post University
Chess, David M. IBM Research
Chiasson, Theodore Dalhousie University, Canada
Chigan, Chunxiao (Tricia) Michigan Tech
Christensen, Chris Northern Kentucky University
Chu, Chao-Hsien Pennsylvania State University
Chung, Ping-Tsai Long Island University
Ci, Song The University of Michigan, Flint
Clements, John L. Titan Corporation
Climek, David State University of New York Institute of Technology
Cocco, Gregory T. Penn State University
Cochran, J. Wesley Texas Tech University
Compatangelo, Ernesto University of Aberdeen, UK
Connelly, Kay Indiana University
Constantiou, Ioanna Copenhagen Business School, Denmark
Corazza, Giovanni E. University of Bologna, Italy
Cornell, Lee D. Minnesota State University, Mankato
Cosar, Ahmet Middle East Technical University, Turkey
Costello, Steven R. McKendree College
Cotter, Robert E. University of Missouri, Kansas City
Craiger, J. Philip University of Central Florida
Crawford, Walt RLG
Crawford, George W. Penn State University
Crispo, Bruno Vrije Universiteit, Netherlands
Cronin, Eric University of Pennsylvania
Crouch, Mary Lou V. George Mason University
Cruickshank, Haitham S. University of Surrey, UK
Cukic, Bojan West Virginia University
Cukier, Michel University of Maryland
Cunningham, Chet Madisonville Community College
Curry, Ann The University of British Columbia, Canada
CustódioFederal, Ricardo Felipe University of Santa Catarina, Brazil
Damian, Mirela Villanova University
Dampier, David A. Mississippi State University
Daoud, Moh Las Positas College
Darabi, Houshang University of Illinois, Chicago
Davies, Todd Stanford University
Davis, Mark Charles University of Tulsa
Davis, Scott C. Old Dominion University
Davis, James P. University of South Carolina
Davis, Diane University of Texas, Austin
Davis, Lloyd M. University of Tennessee Space Institute
Dawson, Linda Monash University, Australia
De, George Richard T. University of Kansas
de, Lara Eyal University of Toronto, Canada
Dean, Susan T. UMUC, Europe
Deaton, Russell University of Arkansas
Deflem, Mathieu University of South Carolina
Deibert, Ronald J. University of Toronto, Canada
DeJoie, Tony Telcordia Technologies, Inc.
Delugach, Harry S. University of Alabama, Huntsville
Demir, Tamer Independent Consultant
Deng, Jing University of New Orleans
DeNoia, Lynn A. Rensselaer Polytechnic Institute
Dent, Alexander W. University of London, UK
Desai, Raj The University of Texas
DeVries, Delwyn D. The University of Tennessee
Dhamija, Rachna University of California, Berkeley
Dhar, Subhankar San Jose State University
Dickinson, Ron B. University of Maryland, European Division
Dietz, Steven Quintiles Transnational
Dinda, Peter A. Northwestern University
Dingledine, Roger Massachusetts Institute of Technology
Dingley, Kate University of Portsmouth, UK
Doeppner, Thomas W. Brown University
Dogdu, Erdogan Georgia State University
Domingo-Ferrer, Josep Rovira i Virgili University of Tarragona, Catalonia
Dommel, Hans-Peter Santa Clara University
Dong, Yingfei University of Hawaii
Dooley, John F. Knox College
Dorsz, Jeff Saddleback College
Doss, David L. Illinois State University
Durbano, James P. EM Photonics, Inc.
Eagle, Christopher S. Naval Postgraduate School
Edelman, Benjamin Harvard University
Edmead, Mark T. MTE Software, Inc.
Edoh, Kossi Delali Montclair State University
Ellison, Robert J. Carnegie Mellon University
El-Said, Mostafa M. The Pennsylvenia State University
Emam, Ahmed Western Kentucky University
Endicott-Popovsky, Barbara University of Idaho
En-Nouaary, Abdeslam Concordia University, Canada
Ensmenger, Nathan L. University of Pennsylvania
Erbacher, Robert F. Utah State University
Ercetin, Ozgur Sabanci University, Turkey
Erickson, Carl B. Atomic Object LLC.
Esichaikul, Vatcharaporn Asian Institute of Technology, Thailand
Esmailzadeh, Riaz Keio University, Japan
Esparza, Charles R. Glendale Community College
Esser, Randy Capitol College
Esterline, Albert C. North Carolina A&T State University
Evans, David University of Virginia
Evans, Barry G. University of Surrey, UK
Evers, Pamela S. University of North Carolina, Wilmington
Ewert, Craig C. UMUC-Europe
Fahd, Wissam Boulos Golden Gate University
Fan, Guangbin University of Mississippi
Farwell, William L. Deloitte & Touche LLP
Fausch, Scott Wright State University
Fawcett, Tom HP Laboratories

Fay, David International Planning & Research Corporation
Fernback, Jan Temple University
Field, Jr. Thomas G. Franklin Pierce Law Center
Figg, Bill Dakota State University
Filiol, Eric Army Signals School, France
Fischer, Susanna The Catholic University of America
Fischer, Michael M. J. Massachussets Institute of Technology
Fitzpatrick, Robert B. Robert B. Fitzpatrick PLLC
Fogg, Stephen L. Temple University
Fortin, David R. University of Canterbury, New Zealand
Fox, Richard Northern Kentucky University
Franchitti, Jean-Claude New York University
Frank, Michael P. FAMU-FSU College of Engineering
Frankel, Mark S. American Association for the Advancement of Science (AAAS)
Frankland, Erich Casper College
Franklin, Edward N., Jr. Golden Gate University
Frater, Michael University of New South Wales, Australia
Freberg, John D. Northwestern University
Fredenberger, William B. Valdosta State University
Freedman, Michael J. New York University
French, Geoffrey S. General Dynamics
Frincke, Deborah A. University of Idaho
Fu, Huirong North Dakota State University
Fuchsberger, Andreas University of London, UK
Gabrielson, Bruce Clayton Booz Allen Hamilton
Gad, Gerges A. University of Houston
Galbraith, Steven Royal Holloway, University of London,UK
Gannod, Barbara D. Arizona State University East
Garrett, Kelly University of Michigan
Garrett, Paul University of Minnesota
Gartin, Timothy J. KPMG
Gasaway, Laura N. University of North Carolina, Chapel Hill
Gassko, Irene Northeastern University
Gast, Jim University of Wisconsin, Platteville
Gates, Carrie Dalhousie University, Canada
Gauvin, Tony University of Maine, Fort Kent
Gearhart, Deb Dakota State University
Gehrmann, Christian Ericsson Mobile Platforms AB
Geiger, Jeffrey H. University of Richmond
Gemmill, Laurie Ohio Historical Society
Genetti, Jon D. University of Alaska, Fairbanks
Genosko, Gary Lakehead University, Canada
Gerdes, Michael D. RedSiren, Inc.
Gleason, B. J. University of Maryland, Asian Division-Korea
Goel, Sanjay University at Albany, SUNY
Goff, Don University of Maryland
Goldman, Eric Marquette University
Golle, Philippe Palo Alto Research Center
Gomulkiewicz, Robert W. University of Washington
Gonder, John S. Cisco Academy Manager
Good, V. Nathaniel S. University of California, Berkeley
Goodman, Seymour E. Georgia Institute of Technology
Gopalakrishnan, Suresh Tacit Networks Inc.
Gordon, Sarah Symantec Security Response
Goss, Kay C. Electronic Data Systems Corporation (EDS)
Gouda, Mohamed University of Texas, Austin
Govindavajhala, Sudhakar Princeton University
Grabosky, Peter Australian National University, Australia
Grabowski, Barbara T. Benedictine University
Greenstadt, Rachel Harvard University
Greenwald, Michael Lucent Technologies
Grimaila, Michael R. Air Force Institute of Technology
Grimaila, Michael Russell Texas A&M University, College Station
Groth, Jens University of Aarhus, Denmark
Guan, Yong Iowa State University
Guevin, Paul R., III Air University, United States Air Force
Guha, Arup Ratan University of Central Florida
Guild, Kenneth University of Essex, UK
Gunkel, David J. Northern Illinois University
Guo, Jinhua University of Michigan
Gupta, Zijiang Yang Ajay Western Michigan University
Gurtov, Andrei University of Helsinki, Finland
Gutmann, Peter University of Auckland, New Zealand
Haas, Matthew Corning Community College
Hać, Anna University of Hawaii, Manoa
Hafner, William Nova Southeastern University
Hafner, Carole D. Northeastern University
Haigh, Tom J. Adventium Labs Cyber Defense Agency
Hailes, Stephen University College, London, UK
Halavais, Alexander M. C. University at Buffalo
Hanchey, Cindy Meyer Oklahoma Baptist University
Harapnuik, Dwayne University of Alberta, Canada
Harn, Lein University of Missouri
Harrison, Robert Wilson Georgia State University
Hart, Richard University of New Hampshire
Hartpence, Bruce Rochester Institute of Technology
Hassanein, Khaled McMaster University, Canada
Hauri, S. Ronald Webster University
Hay, Brian University of Alaska, Fairbanks
Hayne, Stephen C. Colorado State University
He, Ling University of Florida
Heikes, Deborah K. University of Alabama, Huntsville
Heim, Michael R. Heim Seminars
Helmer, Guy G. Palisade Systems, Inc.
Helms, Susan University of Maryland, University College
Hennekey, Jos. F. Office of the Monroe County Sheriff
Herman, Joseph George Mason University
Herring, Susan Indiana University
Heydari, Hossain James Madison University
Higgs, Bryan J. Rivier College
Hinke, Thomas H. NASA Ames Research Center
Hmimy, Hossam H. Southern Methodist University
Hohenberger, Susan Massachusetts Institute of Technology
Holden, Stephen H. University of Maryland, Baltimore County
Hole, Kjell Jørgen University of Bergen, Norway
Holschuh, Douglas R. University of Georgia
Homayounmehr, Farid Stevens Institute of Technology
Hong, Xiaoyan University of Alabama
Hosseini, Jinoos (Jean) Northeastern University
Hottell, Matthew Indiana University
Houssaini, Sqalli Mohammed King Fahd University of Petroleum & Minerals, Saudi Arabia
Howland, Brian M. Boston University
Hsieh, Bin-Tsan National Cheng Kung University, Taiwan
Hsiung, Pao-Ann National Chung Cheng University, Taiwan
Hu, Qing Florida Atlantic University

Huang, Chin-Tser University of South Carolina
Hura, Gurdeep S. University of Idaho, Idaho Falls
Hurstell, Mark G. Tulane University
Hutchinson, William Edith Cowan University, Australia
Huth, Michael Imperial College, London, UK
Hwang, Jenq-Neng University of Washington
Ibrahim, Hassan University of Maryland, College Park
Ingle, Henry T. University of Texas, El Paso
Ippolito, John B. Allied Technology Group, Inc.
Isburgh, Nathan Austin Community College
Jackson, Bill Southern Oregon Unversity
Jackson, David Southern Oregon Unversity
Jacobs, Andrew T. SUNY Rockland
Jacoby, Betty Anne Montclair State University
Jaffe, Joshua M. A. Cryptography Research, Inc.
Jaglom, Andre R. Tannenbaum Helpern Syracuse & Hirschtritt LLP
Jakes, Penny University of Montana
Jamalipour, Abbas University of Sydney, Australia
Jewell, Ronnie D. Marshall University
Jiao, Changli University of Portland
Johnson, Eric N. Indiana University
Johnson, Chris W. University of Glasgow, UK
Jones, Greg University of North Texas
Jones, Paul The University of North Carolina, Chapel Hill
Jörgensen, Peter E. Florida State University
Jung, Eunjin The University of Texas, Austin
Jurik, Mads Independent Consultant
Jurinski, James John University of Portland
Kabara, Joseph University of Pittsburgh
Kabay, M. E. Norwich University
Kain, Mike Unisys Corporation and Drexel University
Kaliski, Burt RSA Laboratories
Kaplan, Marilyn R. University of Texas, Dallas
Karush, Gerald Southern New Hampshire University
Karygiannis, Tom National Institute of Standards and Technology (NIST)
Katz, Jonathan University of Maryland, University College
Katzenbeisser, Stefan Technische Universität München, Germany
Kaufman, Billie Jo American University
Kavanaugh, Andrea L. Virginia Tech
Kellep, Charles A. Capitol College
Kelley, George University of Cincinnati
Kelley, Michael S. Fidelity Information Services
Kent, M. Allen, Jr. Montana State University, Billings
Keromytis, Angelos D. Columbia University
Keys, Anthony C. University of Wisconsin, Eau Claire
Khalil, Ashraf Khalil Indiana University, Bloomington
Khan, Ahmed S. DeVry University
Kiddoo, Jim University of Alberta, Canada
Kieff, F. Scott Stanford University
Kilford, Lloyd J. California Institute of Technology
Kim, Jong Pohang University, Korea
King, Nancy J. Oregon State University
Klappenecker, Andreas Texas A&M University
Kleist, Virginia Franke West Virginia University
Koç, Çetin K. Oregon State University
Kochtanek, Thomas R. University of Missouri, Columbia
Kohel, David R. University of Sydney, Australia
Kong, Jiejun University of California, Los Angeles
Korba, Larry National Research Council, Canada
Korkmaz, Turgay The University of Texas, San Antonio
Korpeoglu, Ibrahim Bilkent University, Turkey
Kozma, John Powers Charleston County Public School System
Krishnamachari, Bhaskar University of Southern California
Krishnamurthy, Prashant University of Pittsburgh
Krizanc, Danny Wesleyan University
Krzyzanowski, Paul Rutgers University
Kukowski, Stuart H. Colorado School of Mines
Kurgan, Lukasz University of Alberta, Canada
Kurkovsky, Stan Columbus State University
Kwiat, Kevin A. Air Force Research Laboratory
Kwiatkowska, Mila University College of the Cariboo, Canada,
Kwok, Yu-Kwong The University of Hong Kong, Hong Kong
LaBar, Martin Southern Wesleyan University
Lally, Ann University of Washington Libraries
Lamb, Annette Purdue University
Langford, Barry R. Columbia College
Larson, James G. National University
Lau, Daniel L. University of Kentucky
Lazarevic, Aleksandar University of Minnesota
LeBlanc, Cathie Plymouth State University
Lee, Yeuan-Kuen Ming Chuan University, Taiwan
Lee, Joohan University of Central Florida
Lee, Ronald M. Florida International University
Lee, Steven B. San Jose State University
Leitner, Lee J. Drexel University
Lekkas, Panos C. Xstream Technologies LLC
Leme, Luis P. University of Maryland
Lerner, Michah Columbia University
Letterio, Pirrone EUTELSAT SA, France
Levesque, Allen H. Worcester Polytechnic Institute
Levi, Albert Sabanci University, Turkey
Levy, Irvin Gordon College
Lewis, James CSIS Technology
Li, Xiangyang University of Michigan
Li, Kang University of Georgia
Libert, Benoît UCL Crypto Group, Belgium
Lim, James City College of San Francisco
Lin, Xia Drexel University
Lin, Shieu-Hong Biola Univerity
Lincke-Salecker, Susan University of Wisconsin, Parkside
Lineman, Jeffrey P. Northwest Nazarene University
Linton, Ronald C. Columbus State University
Liotine, Matthew BLR Research
Liotta, Antonio University of Surrey, UK
Liu, Hongfang University of Maryland, Baltimore County
Liu, Mei-Ling L. California Polytechnic State University
Liu, Peng Penn State University
Lobo, Andrea Rowan University
Lok, Simon Columbia University
Long, Cherie Florida International University
Longstaff, Thomas A. Software Engineering Institute
Loper, D. Kall University of North Texas
Lorenz, Pascal University of Haute Alsace, France
Lou, Kenneth Z. Cerritos College
Louzecky, David University of Wisconsin
Loy, Stephen L. Eastern Kentucky University
Luglio, Michele University of Rome Tor Vergata, Italy
Lunce, Stephen E. Midwestern State University
Lupu, Emil C. Imperial College London, UK
Lynch, Thomas J., III Worcester Polytechnic Institute
Lynn, Benjamin Stanford University
Mabrouk, Adam S. Murray State University

Macchiavello, Chiara Università di Pavia, Italy
MacDonald, Ian M. The College of Saint Rose
Machunda, Zachary Boniface Minnesota State University,Moorhead
Maclay, Colin M. Harvard Law School
Madison, Michael J. University of Pittsburgh
Magill, Evan University of Stirling, Scotland
Mahoney, Matthew V. Florida Institute of Technology
Mahoney, Jim Marlboro College
Makedon, Fillia S. Dartmouth College
Maloof, Marcus A. Georgetown University
Mal-Sarkar, Sanchita Cleveland State University
Mangold, Stefan Swisscom Innovations, Switzerland
Mano, Chad D. University of Notre Dame
Mao, Wenbo Hewlett-Packard Laboratories
Marchany, Randy Virginia Tech
Markantonakis, Konstantinos Royal Holloway, University of London, UK
Marshall, Christopher S. Indianapolis-Marion County Public Library
Martel, Normand M. Medical Technology Research Corp.
Marton, Christine Global Health Informatics
Marty, Paul F. Florida State University
Mashburn, Ronald Gene West Texas A&M University
Mason, Sharon Rochester Institute of Technology
Massey, Dan Colorado State Universtiy
Matalgah, Mustafa M. The University of Mississippi
Mateti, Prabhaker Wright State University
Mattord, Herbert J. Kennesaw State University
Mayes, Keith Royal Holloway, University of London, UK
Mazzei, James A. University of Maryland
McCord, S. Alan Lawrence Technological University
McCoy, Mark R. University of Central Oklahoma
McFarland, Daniel J. Rowan University
McGinn, Mark L. St. Ambrose University
McGraw, Gary Cigital, Inc.
McIver, Jr. William J. State University of New York
McKeever, Susan Dublin Institute of Technology, Ireland
McKeown, Jim Dakota State University
McNeill, Kevin M. The University of Arizona
Mead, Nancy R. Carnegie Mellon University
Mehta, Chirag Santa Clara University
Menz, Mark J. Independendt Consultant
Metzler, Jim Ashton, Metzler & Associates
Meunier, Pascal Purdue University
Meyer, Linda Purdue University, Fort Wayne
Mikeal, Rosa Leslie University of Pennsylvania
Mikhailov, Mikhail GlovalSys Services (GSS)
Mikkilineni, Rao Golden Gate University
Millard, Bruce R. Arizona State University
Miller, Brent A. IBM Corporation
Miller, Benjamin Inside ID
Miller, Holmes E. Muhlenberg College
Min, John Northern Virginia Community College & Ruesch International
Minow, Mary LibraryLaw.com
Mirchandani, Vinod The University of Sydney, Australia
Mirkovic, Jelena University of Delaware
Mohammed, Shaheed N. Marist College
Montgomery, Todd L. West Virginia University
Moran, Douglas B. Tatzlwyrm Systems
Morel, Benoit Carnegie Mellon University
Morneau, Keith A. Northern Virginia Community College
Morse, Fitzgerald University of Evansville
Morton, Russell S. Winston-Salem State University
Morton, L. P. Northwood University
Moul, Dennis Carnegie Mellon University
Mucchi, Lorenzo University of Florence, Italy
Muermann, Alexander The Wharton School
Mukherjee, Sumitra Nova Southeastern University
Mukkamala, Ravi Old Dominion University
Muma, Kimberly S. Ferris State University
Murray, Jr. Ottis L. The University of North Carolina, Pembroke
Mussulman, James E. Southern Illinois University, Edwardsville
Muthukumaran, B. Sri Venkateswara College of Engineering, India
Myers, Robert A. Fairfield Resources International and Columbia University
Naccache, David Gemplus, France
Nadal, Jacob Craig Lab/Auxiliary Library Facility
Nagle, Luz E. Stetson University College
Naimi, Linda L. Purdue University
Nair, Suku Southern Methodist University
Naldurg, Prasad G. University of Illinois, Urbana-Champaign
Nance, Kara L. University of Alaska, Fairbanks
Napjus, Chris N. University of Maryland, University College
Nath, Ravi Creighton University
Neal, Lisa eLearn Magazine
Neary, Pat Central Michigan University
Neely, Michael J. University of Southern California
Nemec, Carol R. Southern Oregon University
Newby, Gregory B. Arctic Region Supercomputing Center
Newman, J. Richard Florida Institute of Technology
Ngo, Hung Q. SUNY, Buffalo
Nicolay, John Troy University
Nieporent, Richard Johns Hopkins University
Ning, Peng North Carolina State University
Noubir, Guevara Northeastern University
Nyberg, Kaisa Nokia Research Center, Finland
Nystedt, Magnus Francis Marion University
O'Boyle, Todd The MITRE Corporation
O'Donnell, Jon Clarion University of Pennsylvania
O'Neal, Charles W. Webster University
O'Connell, Ian J. University of Victoria, Canada
Odlyzko, Andrew The University of Minnesota
Olan, Michael Richard Stockton College
Opderbeck, David W. Seton Hall University
Oppenheimer, Priscilla Southern Oregon University
Osborne, Lawrence J. Lamar University
Oswald, Elisabeth Graz University of Technology, Austria
Ouyang, Jinsong California State University, Sacramento
Ozok, A. Ant University of Maryland, Baltimore County
Pallithekethil, Vijay Oommen Michigan Technological University
Palmeri, Anthony J. University of Wisconsin,Oshkosh
Palombo, James University of Maryland
Pan, Yin Rochester Institute of Technology
Pappu, Ravikanth ThingMagic LLC.
Paprzycki, Marcin Oklahoma State University
Parisi, Jr. Robert A. AIG eBusiness Risk Solutions

Parker, James Byron University of Maryland, Baltimore County
Parks, Lance M. Cosumnes River College
Pastore, Raymond S. Bloomsburg University
Patel, Nilesh University of Michigan, Dearborn
Paterson, Kenneth G. University of London, UK
Patterson, David A. The University of Tennessee
Paulo, Anthony Leo Aera Energy
Payne, Jr. Charles N. Adventium Labs
Pearce, Charles Gallaudet University
Peavy, Don E. Canyon College and University of Phoenix
Penzhom, W. T. University of Pretoria, South Africa
Pepin, Madeleine Our Lady of the Lake University
Pernul, Günther University of Regensburg, Germany
Peslak, Alan Penn State University
Peterson, Gilbert L. Air Force Institute of Technology
Peterson, Victoria L. Minnesota State University, Moorhead
Phelps, Daniel C. Florida State University
Phifer, Lisa Core Competence Inc.
Phillips, Ronnie J. Colorado State University
Phonphoem, Anan Kasetsart University, Thailand
Pickering, Andrew J. University of Maryland, University College
Pickett, Michael C. National University
Piotrowski, Victor University of Wisconsin, Superior
Platt, Richard G. University of West Florida
Plum, Terry Simmons Graduate School of Library and Information Science
Plumer, Danielle Cunniff The University of Texas, Austin
Podgorski, Andrew S. ASR Technologies Inc.
Powers, Dennis M. Southern Oregon University
Prescott, John E. University of Pittsburgh
Prestage, Andrew Kern County Superintendent of Schools
Preston, Jon A. Clayton College and State University
Prettyman, Steve Chattahoochee Technical College
Prevatte, Tenette Robeson Community College
Prince, Matthew John Marshall Law School
Probst, David K. Concordia University, Canada
Provos, Niels Google Inc.
Pruitt-Mentle, Davina University of Maryland
Pucella, Riccardo Cornell University
Putnam, Elizabeth Lucy Scribner Library
Pyun, Jae-Young Chosun University, Korea
Rafaeli, Sandro T&T, Brazil
Raghavan, Vijay V. Northern Kentucky University
Ramage, Michael L. Murray State University
Ramasastry, Anita University of Washington
Rao, H. R. SUNY, Buffalo
Rao, Shrisha Mount Mercy College
Rauch, Jesse Casper College
Rawat, Surendra Nortel Networks, Canada
Reavis, David R Texas A&M University, Texarkana
Recor, Jeff Olympus Security Group, Inc.
Reis, Leslie Ann The John Marshall Law School
Rejman-Greene, Marek British Telecommunications plc, UK
Ren, Jian Michigan State University
Rhodes, Anthony (Tony) Zayed University, Dubai
Rice, Doug Golden Gate University
Richardson, Sherry Clayton College & State University
Rijmen, Vincent Graz University, Austria
Riley, O'Connor Thomas North Carolina Wesleyan College
Ritter, Terry Independent Consultant
Robbin, Alice Indiana University
Roberts, G. Keith University of Redlands
Robila, Stefan A. Montclair State University
Robin, J. Scott Webster University
Robinson, Wendy Oakland University
Rogers, Marcus K. Purdue University
Rogers, William Biometric Digest
Rogerson, Kenneth Duke University
Rose, Gregory M. Washington State University
Roselli, Diane Marie Harrisburg Area Community College
Rosenbaum, Joseph I. Reed Smith LLP
Rosenthal, Arnon The MITRE Corporation
Rosti, Emilia Università degli Studi di Milano, Italy
Roth, Volker Fraunhofer IGD, Germany
Rowe, Mark R. Ohio University, Athens
Rowe, Neil C. U.S. Naval Postgraduate School
Rowe, Kenneth E. Purdue University
Rubin, Bradley S. University of St. Thomas
Rucinski, Andrzej University of New Hampshire
Ryan, Julie J. C. H. George Washington University
Ryan, Mark University of Birmingham, UK
Ryutov, Tatyana University of Sourthern California
Sahin, Haydar T. St. Philip's College & University of Texas, San Antonio
Salomonsen, Gorm Cryptomathic A/S, Denmark
Sanghera, Kamaljeet George Mason University
Santos, Andre Luiz Moura dos Georgia Institute of Technology
Saroiu, Stefan University of Washington
Sarolahti, Pasi Nokia Research Center, Finland
Sarosdy, Randall L. Akin Gump Strauss Hauer & Feld LLP
Sarwar, Badrul M. San Jose State University
Satterlee, Brian Liberty University
Saunders, John H. National Defense University
Savoie, Michael J. The University of Texas, Dallas
Scacchi, Walt University of California, Irvine
Schaefer, Marcus DePaul Unversity
Schaefer, Guenter Technische Universitaet, Berlin
Scharlau, Bruce A. University of Aberdeen, UK
Scheets, George Oklahoma State University
Schiano, William T. Bentley College
Schlesinger, Richard Kennesaw State University
Schneider, Ed Institute for Defense Analyses
Schneider, Ryan A. Troutman Sanders LLP
Schonfeld, Tibor George Washington University
Schuldes, Michael H. Dakota State University
Schwaig, Kathy Stewart Kennesaw State University
Schwartz, Daniel G. Florida State University
Schwartz, Ray The State University of New Jersey
Schwarz, S. J. Thomas Santa Clara University
Schweik, Charles M. University of Massachusetts, Amherst
Schwerm, Marie Marquette University
Schwiebert, Loren Wayne State University
Schwimmer, Brian University of Manitoba, Canada
Scott, Michael Dublin City University, Ireland
Scottberg, Brian P. COUNTRY Insurance and Financial ServicesSM
Segall, Richard S. Arkansas State University
Seleznyov, Alexandr University College, London
Selig, Gad J. University of Bridgeport & GPS Group, Inc.

Sengupta, Arijit Indiana University
Senie, Daniel Amaranth Networks Inc.
Servetti, Antonio Politecnico di Torino, Italy
Shah, Rahul Purdue University
Shakir, Ameer H. University of Maryland
Sharif, Hamid R University of Nebraska, Lincoln (Omaha Campus)
Sheriff, Mohamed Middlesex University, UK
Sherman, Richard C. Miami University
Sheu, Myron California State University, Dominguez Hills
Shimeall, Timothy J. Carnegie Mellon University
Shmatikov, Vitaly SRI International
Shoemaker, DC North Seattle Community College
Shumba, Rose Indiana University
Shumway, Russell M. Independent Consultant
Sicker, Douglas C. University of Colorado, Boulder
Siegel, Eric V. Prediction Impact
Silverberg, Alice Ohio State University
Simco, Greg Nova Southeastern University
Simmons, Ken Augusta Technical College
Sivalingam, Krishna University of Maryland, Baltimore County
Smit, Lodewijk T. University of Twente, The Netherlands
Smith, Richard E. University of St. Thomas
Smith, Anthony H. Purdue University
Snow, Charles George Mason University
Sobol, Stephen University of Leeds, UK
Somasundaram, Siva Stevens Institute of Technology
Song, Min Old Dominion University
Song, Hongjun The University of Memphis
Spitzner, Lance Honeynet Project
Squibb, Jeffery L. Southern Illinois University
Stachurski, Dale University of Maryland and Bowie State University
Stackpole, Bill Rochester Institute of Technology
Staddon, Jessica Palo Alto Research Center
Stahl, Bernd Carsten De Montfort University, UK
Stamp, Mark San Jose State University
Stanley, Richard A. Worcester Polytechnic Institute
Steichen, Dean J. Golden Gate University
Stein, Andreas University of Illinois, Urbana-Champaign
Stevens, Kenneth J. The University of New South Wales, Australia
Stevens, Mark North Carolina Wesleyan College
Stewart, John N. Independent Researcher
Stewart, William G. University of Maryland, University College
Stiller, Evelyn Plymouth State University
Stolfo, Salvatore J. Columbia University
Strickland, Susan Sam Houston State University
Striegel, Aaron University of Notre Dame
Stucke, Carl H. Georgia State University
Styer, Daniel F. Oberlin College
Subramanian, Mani Georgia Institute of Technology
Suleman, Hussein University of Cape Town, South Africa
Sullivan, David Oregon State University
Sullivan, Grant Dalhousie University, Canada
Sun, Zhili University of Surrey, UK
Sussan, Fiona Baruch College
Swedin, Eric G. Weber State University
Tabor, Sharon W. Boise State University
Tan, Pang-Ning Michigan State University
Tang, Yuan-Liang Chaoyang University of Technology, Taiwan, R.O.C.
Tang, Zaiyong Louisiana Tech University
Tanner, Rudolf UbiNetics, UK
Tate, Stephen R. University of North Texas
Taylor, Luck Ann The Pennsylvania State University
Teixeira, Marvi Polytechnic University of Puerto Rico
Teng, Wei-Guang National Taiwan University, Taiwan
Tesi, Raffaello University of Oulu, Finland
Thomadakis, Michael E. Texas A&M University,
Thomas, William H. Juniata College
Thomsen, Dan Tresys Technology
Thrasher, Ward Private Attorney
Tian, Jeff Southern Methodist University
Tibbs, Richard W. Radford University
Tien, Lee Electronic Frontier Foundation
Tirenin, Wladimir (Walt) Air Force Research Laboratory/Information Directorate (This is not an official endorsement by the U.S. Government.)
Todd, Byron Tallahassee Community College
Toshio, Okamoto Garret Santa Clara University
Toth, Mihaly Professor Emeritus
Toumpis, Stavros Telecommunications Research Center, Austria
Townsend, Anthony New York University
Toze, Sandra L. Dalhousie University, Canada
Tracy, Kim W. Lucent Technologies and North Central College
Traore, Issa University of Victoria, Canada
Trappenberg, Thomas P. Dalhousie University, Canada
Trimmer, Ken Idaho State University
Troell, Luther Rochester Institute of Technology
Trolin, Mårten Royal Institute of Technology, Stockholm
Trostmann, Manfred F. UMUC Maryland, Germany
Tsiounis, Yiannis InternetCash Corporation
Tu, Feili University of South Carolina
Tucker, Terrell Panama-Buena Vista Union School District
Tung, Brian USC Information Sciences Institute
Turk, Daniel Colorado State University
Turner, Stephen Walter The University of Michigan, Flint
Tyre, James S. Law Offices of James S. Tyre
Upadhyaya, Shambhu State University of New York, Buffalo
Uysal, Murat University of Waterloo, Canada
Van, Camp Julie C. California State University, Long Beach
van, Wyk Kenneth R. KRvW Associates, LLC
Varma, Umesh C. Campbell University
Vaughn, Jr. Rayford B. Mississippi State University
Venables, Phil Goldman Sachs
Venema, Wietse IBM T.J. Watson Research Center
Verheul, Eric PricewaterhouseCoopers Accountants N.V.
Verma, Arvind Indiana University
Vert, Gregory University of Nevada, Reno
Vesperman, Jennifer K. L. Author and Coordinator for LinuxChix
Viehland, Dennis W. Massey University, New Zealand
Villagrá, Víctor A. Technical University of Madrid, Spain
Vincze, Eva A. George Washington University
Vrbsky, Susan V. University of Alabama
Vrij, Aldert University of Portsmouth, UK
Wagner, Paul J. University of Wisconsin, Eau Claire
Walden, James W. The University of Toledo
Walker, Jesse R. Intel Corporation
Wallace, Jonathan D. Author and Attorney
Walls, Noretta University of South Alabama
Walsh, J. M. The University of North Carolina

Walter, Colin D. Comodo Research Lab, UK
Wang, Yongge University of North Carolina,Charlotte
Wang, Xunhua James Madison University
Ward, David O. Capitol College
Wareham, Jonathan D. Georgia State University
Warren, Matt Deakin University, Australia
Waters, Brent Princeton University
Watro, Ronald J. BBN Technologies
Watson, John W. Chipola College
Watson, Keith Purdue University
Wayman, James L. San Jose State University
Wechsler, Harry George Mason University
Weil, Steven Seitel Leeds & Associates
Weiler, Nathalie Swiss Federal Institute of Technolo, Switzerland
Weinberger, George M. Texas State University, San Marcos, Texas
Weindling, Mark L. Weindling Technology LLC
Weippl, Edgar R. University of Vienna, Austria
Weis, Stephen A. Massachusetts Institute of Technology
Weiss, Jill C. Florida International University
Wenning, Rigo W3C/ERCIM
Wespi, Andreas IBM Research Laboratory, Zurich
West, Robert C. U.S. Department of Homeland Security
West-Brown, Moira Independent Consultant
Westby, Jody R. American Bar Association
Wheeler, Deborah L. Oxford Internet Institute University of Washington, UK
Whelan, Claire Dublin City University, Ireland
Whitehead, Chris Columbus State University
Whitlock, Charles R. Experian
Whyte, Bill University of Leeds, UK
Wiegand, Nathan University of Alabama, Tuscaloos
Wilbert, Janet M. University of Tennessee, Martin
Willette, William W. University of Texas, Arlington
William, William Capitol College
Wines, William A. Miami University
Winston, Thomas G. Endicott College
Wojciechowski, Pawel EPFL, Switzerland
Wolcott, Peter University of Nebraska, Omaha
Wolff, Richard S. Montana State University
Wool, Avishai Tel Aviv University, Israel
Workman, Michael Florida State University
Worona, Steven L. EDUCAUSE
Wright, Rebecca N. Stevens Institute of Technology
Wu, Chwan-Hwa Auburn University
Wu, Hsin-Tai University of California, Los Angeles
Wu, Ningning University of Arkansas, Little Rock
Wu, Hongyi University of Louisiana, Lafayette
Xie, Geoffrey G. Naval Postgraduate School
Xu, Shouhuai University of Texas, San Antonio
Xu, Jun North Carolina State University
Xu, Shouhuai University of Texas, San Antonio
Xue, Guoliang Arizona State University
Yampolskiy, Aleksandr Yale University
Yan, Li Tie Institute for Infocomm Research, Singapore
Yang, Cheer-Sun West Chester University
Yang, Kun University of Essex, UK
Yang, Zijiang Western Michigan University
Yang, Mei University of Nevada, Las Vegas
Yao, Tim S. The University of Texas, El Paso
Yasinsac, Alec Florida State University
Yetnikoff, Arlene S. DePaul University
Yin, Yiqun Lisa RSA Laboratories
Youman, Charles E. Independent Consultant
Young, Adam L. Cigital, Inc.
Young, Stewart M. Stanford Law School
Youssef, Mahmoud Rutgers University
Yu, Ting North Carolina State University
Yu, Peter K. Michigan State University
Yuan, Yufei McMaster University, Canada
Yue, Wei T. University of Texas, Dallas
Zachary, John University of South Carolina
Zamboni, Diego IBM Zurich Research Laboratory, Switzerland
Zeadally, Sherali Wayne State University
Zhang, N. University of Manchester, UK
Zhang, Fangguo Sun Yat-sen University,China
Zhang, Zhi-Li University of Minnesota
Zhong, Sheng Stevens Institute of Technology
Zhou, Jianying Institute for Infocomm Research, Singapore
Zhu, Sencun George Mason University
Zhu, Feng Northeastern University
Ziegenfuss, Douglas E. Old Dominion University
Zielonka, Larry College of DuPage
Zilic, Zeljko McGill University, Canada
Zillner, Thomas University of Wisconsin
Zimmermann, Han-Dieter University of Muenster, Germany
Zomaya, Albert Y. The University of Sydney, Australia
Zou, Xukai Purdue University
Zuniga-Galindo, W. A. Barry University

Index